ANNOTATED TEACHER'S EDITION

The American Nation

Civil War to Present

Paul Boyer
Sterling Stuckey

HOLT, RINEHART AND WINSTON

A Harcourt Classroom Education Company

Austin • New York • Orlando • Atlanta • San Francisco • Boston • Dallas • Toronto • London

Cover: ***Fireworks over the Statue of Liberty celebrate the American spirit.***

Cover Photo: Rohan/Tony Stone Images; © CORBIS/Bill Ross (bkgd)

For acknowledgments, see page 1157, which is an extension of the copyright page.

Printed in the United States of America

ISBN 0-03-054602-2

1 2 3 4 5 6 7 8 9 032 04 03 02 01 00

ABOUT THE AUTHORS

Dr. Paul Boyer

Paul Boyer is the Merle Curti Professor of History at the University of Wisconsin, Madison, and director of the university's Institute for Research in the Humanities. He is also a member of the executive board of the Organization of American Historians, a member of the national advisory board of the PBS *American Experience* series, and is Editor-In-Chief of the forthcoming *Oxford Companion to United States History.* Awarded a Ph.D. from Harvard University in 1966, Dr. Boyer is the author of numerous articles and books. *Salem Possessed: The Social Origins of Witchcraft,* which he co-authored with Stephen Nissenbaum, won the John H. Dunning Prize of the American Historical Association.

Dr. Sterling Stuckey

Sterling Stuckey is Professor of History and holds the President's Chair at the University of California, Riverside, where he was presented the Distinguished Humanist Achievement Award. He is also a member of the editorial board of *The American Heritage Encyclopedia of American History.* Awarded a Ph.D. from Northwestern University in 1972, Dr. Stuckey is the author of numerous articles and the books *Slave Culture: Nationalist Theory and the Foundations of Black America* and *Going Through the Storm: The Influence of African American Art in History.* Dr. Stuckey is currently working under a Rockefeller Fellowship on a biography of Paul Robeson.

EDITORIAL REVIEW BOARD

DR. RONALD FOORE

Dr. Foore is the social studies department chair at Booker T. Washington Magnet High School in Tulsa, Oklahoma.

In addition to teaching American history, he also serves on the International Baccalaureate Faculty. He has served on the National Council for the Social Studies, was a vice president for the American Society for History Education, and is president-elect of the Oklahoma Council for the Social Studies. Dr. Foore is a recipient of the Tulsa Teacher of the Year award.

DR. YASUHIDE KAWASHIMA

Dr. Kawashima is a professor of history at the University of Texas at El Paso.

He received his Ph.D. from the University of California at Santa Barbara, as well as advanced legal degrees from Keio University in Japan. He specializes in American legal history. Dr. Kawashima is the author of numerous articles and three books, including *Puritan Justice and the American Indian.* He is a past winner of the Webb-Smith Essay Prize from the University of Texas at Arlington.

LUCINDA LUCERO SACHS

Ms. Sachs recently retired after teaching American history and other social studies courses for 29 years in the Albuquerque School District in New Mexico.

She holds Master's degrees in both Secondary Education and in History. She is a past recipient of the Crossing Boundaries writing contest from the *International Quarterly.* She has also been awarded numerous fellowships, including writing fellowships from the Provincetown Fine Arts Work Center in Massachusetts and from the Vermont Studio Center.

DR. NAN E. WOODRUFF

Dr. Woodruff is an associate professor of history at Penn State University.

She received her Ph.D. from the University of Tennessee. She specializes in 20th century southern history. Dr. Woodruff has published numerous articles as well as the book *Right as Rain: The Great Southern Drought, 1930–31.* She also served as an assistant editor for the *Booker T. Washington Papers.*

DR. ALFRED YOUNG

Dr. Young is a professor of history at Georgia Southern University.

He received his Ph.D. from Syracuse University. He specializes in African American history. Dr. Young has published numerous articles and is co-author of the book *Education and the Black Experience.* He is currently completing a biography of African American scholar John Hope Franklin. Dr. Young has served as an officer for the National Council for Black Studies and is a past recipient of the Black Student Union's Teaching Excellence Award.

CONTRIBUTORS

DR. PAUL HUTTON
Western History Association
University of New Mexico
Albuquerque, New Mexico

DR. RAYMOND HYSER
James Madison University
Harrisonburg, Virginia

DR. MARY CARROLL JOHANSEN
The Ranney School
Tinton Falls, New Jersey

DR. OTEY SCRUGGS
Syracuse University
Syracuse, New York

CONTENT REVIEWERS

DR. MARY C. BRENNAN
Southwest Texas State University
post–World War II, U.S. political

DR. MAUREEN FLANAGAN
Michigan State University
20th century, urban, political, women

DR. PAUL GILJE
University of Oklahoma
U.S., 1492–1865

DR. JULIE GREENE
University of Colorado at Boulder
U.S. labor, political

DR. MELVIN HOLLI
University of Illinois at Chicago
urban and ethnic

DR. RAYMOND HYSER
James Madison University
Gilded Age and Progressive Era

DR. F. DANIEL LARKIN
SUNY-Oneonta
late 19th, early 20th century

DR. CARL H. MONEYHON
University of Arkansas at Little Rock
southern, Civil War, Reconstruction

EDUCATIONAL REVIEWERS

PEGGY ALTOFF, SUPERVISOR
Carroll County Public Schools
Westminster, Maryland

DEAN BRINK
Roosevelt High School
Seattle, Washington

BARBARA HARBOUR
Lewis Cass Technical High School
Detroit, Michigan

DR. KAREN HOPPES
Lakeridge High School
Lake Oswego, Oregon

PAUL HORNE
A.C. Flora High School
Columbia, South Carolina

DOUG ODOM
El Dorado High School
El Dorado, Kansas

SUE REEDER
Winter Springs High School
Winter Springs, Florida

JACK ROUSSO
Roosevelt High School
Seattle, Washington

JENIFER ROWRAY
SE Polk High School
Runnells, Iowa

MADELEINE SCHMITT
St. Louis Public Schools
St. Louis, Missouri

DEANNA SPRING
Cincinnati Public Schools
Cincinnati, Ohio

ANDREW TURAY
Bronx High School
Bronx, New York

SUE WALLACE
Redlands East Valley High School
Redlands, California

GENNIE WESTBROOK
Calhoun High School
Port Lavaca, Texas

FIELD TEST TEACHERS

MATT BERGLES
Rangeview High School
Aurora, Colorado

VINCE CASTELLANO
Arvada Senior High
Arvada, Colorado

MARIAN HALEY
Aqua Fria Union High School
Avondale, Arizona

KEVIN MCNAMARA
Horizon High School
Thornton, Colorado

GREGORY K. MILLER
Douglas High School
Oklahoma City, Oklahoma

GARY MINOR
Canyon de Oro High School
Tucson, Arizona

ROBERTA MYRICKS
Clifford J. Scott High School
East Orange, New Jersey

ANNA PRONI
Miami Senior High School
Miami, Florida

TOM WORKMAN
Hobart High School
Hobart, Indiana

Success in Your Classroom Begins with

For Our Nation's Rich History

The American Nation grabs and holds your students' attention with a compelling narrative and stimulating in-text features—sparking their desire to learn.

Through Instructional Strategies that Work

The American Nation overflows with hundreds of teaching strategies that meet your objectives and help students with different learning styles and abilities master content.

To Use Technology in Meaningful Ways

The American Nation features a variety of fully integrated technology resources to capitalize on your students' interests in music, video, and multimedia.

Easy to Read, Easy to Understand

Successful Readers MUST HAVE:

- **(A)** **A format that provides opportunities to practice reading skills and strategies**
- **(B)** **Better ways to build their vocabulary**
- **(C)** **Comprehension strategies that help them understand what they've read**
- **(D)** **Definitions used in context**
- **(E)** **Engaging narrative that they want to read**

Before You Read—Activate Prior Knowledge

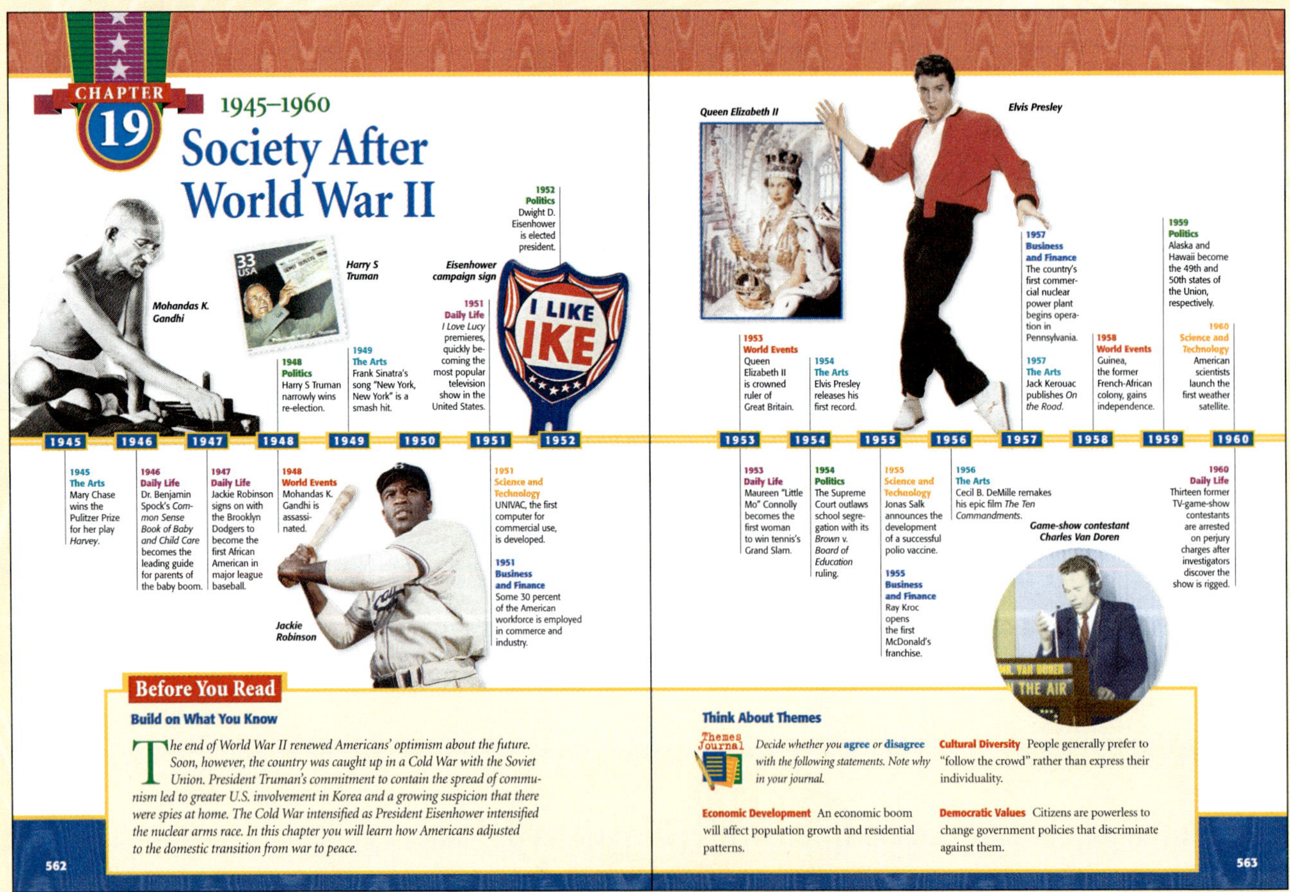

CHAPTER 19

1945–1960

Society After World War II

Mohandas K. Gandhi

Harry S Truman

Eisenhower campaign sign

Queen Elizabeth II

Elvis Presley

Jackie Robinson

Game-show contestant Charles Van Doren

1945 The Arts Mary Chase wins the Pulitzer Prize for her play *Harvey*.

1946 Daily Life Dr. Benjamin Spock's *Common Sense Book of Baby and Child Care* becomes the leading guide for parents of the baby boom.

1947 Daily Life Jackie Robinson signs on with the Brooklyn Dodgers to become the first African American in major league baseball.

1948 Politics Harry S Truman narrowly wins re-election.

1948 World Events Mohandas K. Gandhi is assassinated.

1949 The Arts Frank Sinatra's song "New York, New York" is a smash hit.

1951 Daily Life *I Love Lucy* premieres, quickly becoming the most popular television show in the United States.

1951 Science and Technology UNIVAC, the first computer for commercial use, is developed.

1951 Business and Finance Some 30 percent of the American workforce is employed in commerce and industry.

1952 Politics Dwight D. Eisenhower is elected president.

1953 World Events Queen Elizabeth II is crowned ruler of Great Britain.

1953 Daily Life Maureen "Little Mo" Connolly becomes the first woman to win tennis's Grand Slam.

1954 The Arts Elvis Presley releases his first record.

1954 Politics The Supreme Court outlaws school segregation with its *Brown* v. *Board of Education* ruling.

1955 Science and Technology Jonas Salk announces the development of a successful polio vaccine.

1955 Business and Finance Ray Kroc opens the first McDonald's franchise.

1956 The Arts Cecil B. DeMille remakes his epic film *The Ten Commandments*.

1957 Business and Finance The country's first commercial nuclear power plant begins operation in Pennsylvania.

1957 The Arts Jack Kerouac publishes *On the Road*.

1958 World Events Guinea, the former French-African colony, gains independence.

1959 Politics Alaska and Hawaii become the 49th and 50th states of the Union, respectively.

1960 Science and Technology American scientists launch the first weather satellite.

1960 Daily Life Thirteen former TV-game-show contestants are arrested on perjury charges after investigators discover the show is rigged.

Before You Read

Build on What You Know

The end of World War II renewed Americans' optimism about the future. Soon, however, the country was caught up in a Cold War with the Soviet Union. President Truman's commitment to contain the spread of communism led to greater U.S. involvement in Korea and a growing suspicion that there were spies at home. The Cold War intensified as President Eisenhower intensified the nuclear arms race. In this chapter you will learn how Americans adjusted to the domestic transition from war to peace.

562

Think About Themes

Themes Journal

Decide whether you **agree** *or* **disagree** *with the following statements. Note why in your journal.*

Economic Development An economic boom will affect population growth and residential patterns.

Cultural Diversity People generally prefer to "follow the crowd" rather than express their individuality.

Democratic Values Citizens are powerless to change government policies that discriminate against them.

563

A **time line** rich with period visuals begins each chapter and helps your students get the "big picture." **Before You Read** increases your students' reading comprehension by allowing them to build on prior knowledge and predict outcomes.

Build on What You Know bridges what your students have learned in previous chapters to what they'll learn in the upcoming chapter. **Think About Themes** allows your students to explore their conceptions about issues covered in the chapter.

Before You Read—Read for Understanding

Eyewitnesses to History rouses your students' interest at the beginning of a section with stirring anecdotes by the history-makers themselves.

Clearly defined **Objectives** establish a purpose for reading. **Key Terms** and **Key People** list the new vocabulary words and people important to each section.

SECTION 1 The Challenges of Peace

OBJECTIVES

Read to understand:

1. how the U.S. economy and American workers fared after World War II
2. what the most important issues of the 1948 election were
3. what the major goals of President Truman's Fair Deal were, and whether they were accomplished

KEY TERMS

GI Bill of Rights
Employment Act
Council of Economic Advisers
Taft-Hartley Act
Committee on Civil Rights
Dixiecrats
Fair Deal

KEY PEOPLE

J. Strom Thurmond
Henry Wallace
Thomas Dewey

EYEWITNESSES TO History

"When [the war] finally came to a conclusion, I think it set in motion [questions like] 'Here we are now. What are we going to do about life as we try to reestablish it in our community?'"

—Harold Toliver

The Homecoming *by Norman Rockwell*

Reverend Harold Toliver recalled how the end of World War II stirred both hopes and concerns for many Americans. Many New Deal supporters like Toliver looked to President Harry S Truman for guidance. They hoped that he would help the country recover from the war by continuing the reforms begun by President Roosevelt. "Franklin Roosevelt is not dead. His ideals live," declared New York mayor Fiorello La Guardia. President Truman tried to meet these expectations by promoting Roosevelt's ideals with his own reform programs.

The Problems of Demobilization

By mid-1946 more than 9 million men and women had been discharged from the military. The soldiers received a hero's welcome, but their return also sparked concern. How could the economy absorb all these new workers? Many Americans feared that the country would fall into an economic decline similar to the one that had followed World War I.

Postwar measures. Even before the war had ended, Congress began preparing for peace. Preventing an economic depression and helping war-weary veterans make the difficult transition to civilian life were top priorities. Congress passed the Servicemen's Readjustment Act of 1944, more commonly known as the **GI Bill of Rights**. The bill provided pensions and government loans to help veterans start businesses and buy homes or farms. Millions of veterans also received money through the GI Bill to attend college. Between 1944 and 1962 almost 8 million veterans attended college or technical schools on the GI Bill. This led to a dramatic increase in the number of American college graduates. Government worker Nelson Poynter described the impact of the GI Bill.

> "The GI Bill . . . had more to do with thrusting us into a new era than anything else. Millions of people whose parents or grandparents had never dreamed of going to college saw that they could go. . . . Essentially I think it made us a far more democratic people."

This recently issued stamp commemorates the passage of the GI Bill in 1944.

To ensure postwar economic growth, Congress passed the **Employment Act** of 1946. The act committed the government to promoting full employment and production. It also established the **Council of Economic Advisers** to confer with the president on economic policy.

564 CHAPTER 19

Key Terms are defined in context.

"All readers, even the best, sometimes struggle."

That's why *The American Nation* was designed to be an accessible text—one all your students will read and learn from. For starters, **outline-style headings** provide an easy-to-understand framework for the chapter. The narrative is "chunked" into **concise and meaningful blocks** of text—each with a main idea and a clear beginning and end. And **Reading Checks**—point-of-use comprehension questions—reinforce chapter objectives and give your students the opportunity to pause and reflect on what they've read, avoiding misconceptions and ensuring a thorough understanding.

While You Read—
Support Along the Way

Changing Ways Higher Education

Understanding Change Before the passage of the GI Bill, a college education was often something only the wealthy sought. Since then, obtaining a college education has become much more common. *What differences do you observe between the images of college students in the late 1940s and the late 1990s? What statistics in the chart surprise you the most? Why?*

	THEN	NOW
Number of Institutions of Higher Education	1,863	3,706
Annual Student Body Enrollment	2,281,000	14,715,000
Annual Number of Bachelor Degrees Conferred	496,874	1,191,000
Student Body (Female / Male)	32% / 68%	54% / 46%

Sources: *Historical Statistics of the United States; Statistical Abstract of the United States: 1998.* Data reflect 1950 and 1995.

THEN

NOW

Colorful **maps**, **charts**, and **graphs** communicate information in a concise and visually interesting way, and offer you an opportunity to assess your students' abilities to interpret statistical information.

Labor unrest. As inflation continued to rise, pec
hands. Freed from their wartime pledges not to str
off the job. They fought for wage increases and the
price controls. In 1946 almost 5 million workers w
President Truman generally supported labor un
strikes because he feared they would disrupt the ec
miners went on strike in
ordered the army to take co
of the United Mine Work
"You can't dig coal with bay
heavy fines on the union, L
work. Later, Truman threa
drafting the strikers int
spurred union leaders to n
In 1947 the Republica
bill designed to reduce the
bill was known as the **Taft**
power to end some strik
agreements. It also restricted unions' political contributions and required union officers to swear that they were not Communists. Truman vetoed the bill, but Congress overrode his veto.

The Taft-Hartley Act stirred angry debate. Conservative supporters of the bill argued that it corrected unfair advantages that had been given to labor by New Deal measures. Pro-labor supporters argued that it was a "slave labor law." Although the act limited the actions unions could take, organized labor continued to make some gains in the postwar years. For example, in 1948 General Motors and the United Automobile Workers (UAW) signed a contract that linked wage increases to increases in the cost of living. Union contracts also began to include such benefits as retirement pensions and health insurance.

INTERPRETING THE VISUAL RECORD

Labor unions. These workers marched in support of labor unions in 1946. ***What message do you think is conveyed by the signs the marchers are using?***

Interpreting the Visual Record questions turn photographs into valuable learning tools.

✔ **READING CHECK:** How did the U.S. economy and American workers fare after the war?

Reading Checks encourage your students to check their comprehension of chapter objectives as they read manageable portions of text.

The 1948 Election

By 1948 high inflation and labor unrest had decreased public support for President Truman. "To err is Truman," people joked. Despite his low standing in the polls, Truman continued to take a strong stand on controversial issues. His position on civil rights in particular became an important issue in the 1948 campaign.

The Committee on Civil Rights. In 1946 civil rights groups urged Truman to take action against the racism that stained American society. They pointed out that most African Americans throughout the nation faced segregation in schools and on buses and discrimination in housing and employment. Furthermore, in some areas African Americans continued to be lynched. Previous efforts to battle these conditions had met a wall of resistance.

566 CHAPTER 19

Additional Reading Support

Guided Reading Strategies covers content with hands-on activities that sharpen reading skills by focusing on each section's main ideas. These worksheets include vocabulary builders, review questions, outlines, and graphic organizers.

Graphic Organizer Activities provides innovative, imaginative ways of organizing chapter content. The clever graphics help your students grasp the material more readily.

Main Idea Activities for Reteaching and Sheltered English helps English-language learners and students having difficulty mastering content. Activities reexamine each section's core concepts using different formats, such as graphic organizers, visual cues, and extra vocabulary aids.

The **Audio Program** is a powerful tool for helping students learn or review chapter content with in-depth chapter summaries and self-check activity sheets. Great for Sheltered English students and those who respond to auditory learning. Available in English and Spanish.

After You Read—Check for Understanding

Section and **Chapter Reviews** reinforce reading comprehension with reviews of key terms and people, questions that check for content understanding and build critical-thinking skills, and activities involving graphic organizers.

SECTION 1 REVIEW

Define and explain the significance of the following terms:
GI Bill of Rights
Employment Act
Council of Economic Advisers
Taft-Hartley Act
Committee on Civil Rights
Dixiecrats
Fair Deal

Identify and explain the significance of the following individuals:
J. Strom Thurmond
Henry Wallace
Thomas Dewey

1. **Using Graphic Organizers** Copy the chart below. Use it to list the major successes of President Truman's Fair Deal program and changing public opinion of reform.

Successes	Public opinion
1.	1.
2.	2.
3.	3.
4.	4.

2. **Assessing Consequences** How did the end of World War II affect American workers?
3. **Synthesizing** What were the major issues of the 1948 presidential campaign?
4. **Taking a Stand** If you had been a voter in 1948, who would you have chosen for president? Why?

Critical Thinking

5. How did politics in the late 1940s reflect the ways that World War II had changed the United States?
Consider:
• what political steps were taken to ensure economic stability
• what political actions were taken to help veterans
• how political actions reflected desires to expand democracy

Review

Creating a Time Line

Copy the time line below onto a sheet of paper. Complete the time line by filling in the events and dates from the chapter that you think were most significant. Pick three events and explain why you think they were significant.

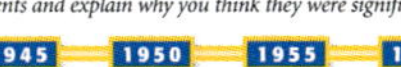

Writing a Summary

Using the Reading Checks as a guide, write an overview of the events in the chapter.

Identifying People and Ideas

Identify the following terms or individuals and explain their significance.

1. GI Bill of Rights
2. Dixiecrats
3. Fair Deal
4. automation
5. George Meany
6. baby boom
7. Elvis Presley
8. *Brown* v. *Board of Education*
9. Rosa Parks
10. beats

Understanding Main Ideas

SECTION 1

1. Why did the feared postwar economic depression never materialize?
2. How did civil rights issues affect the 1948 election?

SECTION 2

3. How did the economic prosperity of the 1950s affect the workforce?
4. What was suburban life like in the 1950s?

SECTION 3

5. What were some of the major successes and setbacks in ending segregation in the 1950s?
6. According to social critics, what were the weaknesses of American society in the 1950s?

Reviewing Themes

1. **Economic Development** How was the increase in population influenced by the economic boom of the 1950s?
2. **Cultural Diversity** How did some Americans rebel against the conformity of the 1950s?
3. **Democratic Values** How did members of minority groups fight discrimination during this decade?

Thinking Critically

1. **Comparing and Contrasting** What was the popular image of a mother's role in society in the 1950s? How did this image conflict with reality?
2. **Assessing Consequences** How did popular entertainment in the 1950s shape the economy?
3. **Identifying Values** What values came into conflict in the 1950s?
4. **Using Historical Imagination** Imagine that you are one of the Little Rock Nine. Are you willing to face constant harassment and threats of violence in order to go to a better school? Explain your answer.
5. **Problem Solving** What do you think was the greatest problem facing American society in the 1950s? If you had been president, what steps would you have taken to combat this problem?

Writing About History

Writing to Describe Write a brief paragraph describing the major concerns of workers in the late 1940s and how the government reacted to union efforts to address these problems. Use the following graphic to organize your thoughts.

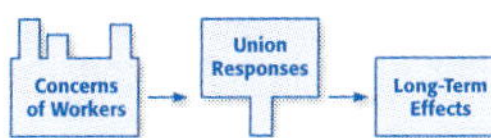

588 CHAPTER 19

Strategies for Success Review the **Strategies for Success** on *Conducting an Interview.* Then prepare for and conduct an oral history interview with one of the following:

a. a person who lived in an urban housing project during the 1950s
b. a person who grew up in the suburbs during the 1950s
c. a person who remembers following the Central High crisis or the Montgomery Bus Boycott as they took place
d. a person who listened to rock 'n' roll music during the 1950s

Linking History and Geography

School desegregation proceeded at different rates throughout the country. By 1964 which states were the slowest to achieve desegregation?

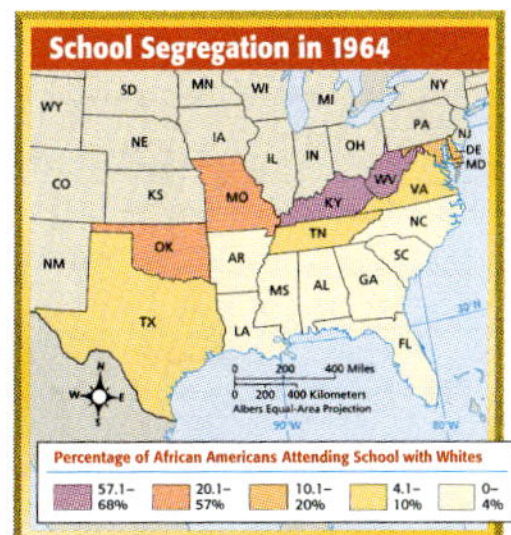

internetconnect

TOPIC: Popular Culture in the 1950s
GO TO: go.hrw.com
KEYWORD: SE1 Culture

Accessing the Internet through the HRW Web site, research the popular culture of the 1950s. Then create a poster or multimedia presentation that describes how the popular culture of the 1950s mirrored the social events of that decade.

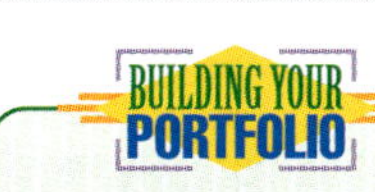

Complete one or all of the following projects independently or cooperatively.

1 Economic Development
Imagine that you are a staff member of the Department of Labor. ***Prepare an illustrated chart*** that shows how the U.S. government is assisting returning soldiers through various programs designed to help them find civilian jobs, attain college educations, or own their own homes.

2 Democratic Values
Imagine that you are a reporter assigned to cover civil rights issues. ***Develop an illustrated outline*** of the major civil rights events that occurred in the United States between 1945 and 1960.

3 Technology and Society
Imagine that you are the inventor of the electric guitar, an instrument made popular by rock 'n' roll musicians. ***Write an illustrated report*** describing how your invention has affected American culture.

SOCIETY AFTER WORLD WAR II 589

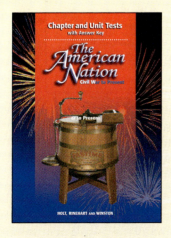

Chapter and Unit Tests
with Answer Key
The American Nation
Civil War to Present
HOLT, RINEHART AND WINSTON

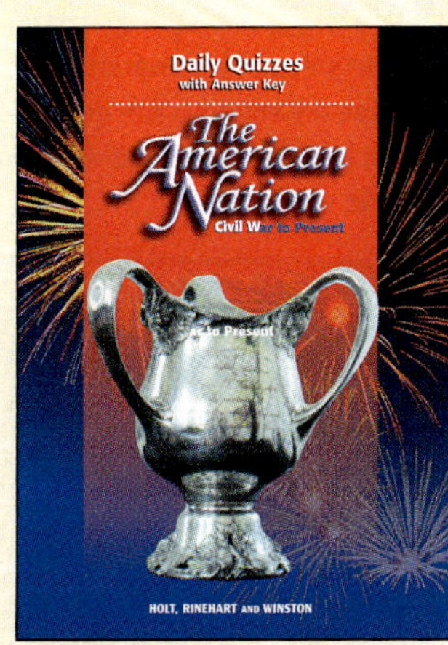

Chapter and Unit Tests, **Daily Quizzes**, and **Sheltered English Chapter and Unit Tests** are linked to chapter objectives and provide you with an accurate indication of your students' learning.

More assessment on page A22

Capturing the Emotions of History

History becomes meaningful through the voices of the past.

AMERICAN *Letters*

Voices of the Fifties

Many poets captured the spirit of the era in their verse. Beat poet Lawrence Ferlinghetti's "I am Waiting" challenged the confidence of postwar society. African American poet Naomi Long Madgett captured the feelings of many participants in the early civil rights movement in her poem "Midway."

from "I Am Waiting"
by Lawrence Ferlinghetti

I am waiting for my number to
be called
and I am waiting for the living
end
and I am waiting
for dad to come home
his pockets full
of irradiated [radioactive] silver
dollars
and I am waiting
for the atomic tests to end
and I am waiting happily
for things to get much worse
before they improve . . .
and I am waiting
for the human crowd
to wander off a cliff somewhere
clutching its atomic umbrella . . .
and I am waiting
for the meek to be blessed
and inherit the earth . . .
and I am waiting for forests and animals
to reclaim the earth as theirs
and I am waiting
for a way to be devised
to destroy all nationalisms
without killing anybody
and I am waiting
for linnets [birds] and planets to fall like rain
and I am waiting for lovers and weepers
to lie down together again
in a new rebirth of wonder.

Lawrence Ferlinghetti

"Midway"
by Naomi Long Madgett

I've come this far to freedom
and I won't turn back.
I'm climbing to the highway
from my old dirt track.
I'm coming and I'm going
And I'm stretching and I'm
growing
And I'll reap what I've been
sowing or my skin's not black.

Naomi Long Madgett

I've prayed and slaved and waited and I've sung
You've bled me and you've starved me but I've st
strong.
You've lashed me and you've treed me
And you've everything but freed me
But in time you'll know you need me and it won

I've seen the daylight breaking high above the bo
I've found my destination and I've made my vow
So whether you abhor me
Or deride me or ignore me,
Mighty mountains loom before me and I won't stop

UNDERSTANDING LITERATURE

1. Who is the "you" in Madgett's poem? Other t
the poet, who does the "I" in the poem repre
2. What image does Ferlinghetti present of life i
the 1950s?
3. How are Madgett's and Ferlinghetti's views o
1950s similar? How are they different?

586 CHAPTER 19

American Arts shows your students how history is reflected in period art, enriching their understanding. **American Letters** uses primary sources, such as literature, poetry, and songs, to give your students a rich view of the United States.

THROUGH OTHERS' EYES

Soviet View of the Cuban Missile Crisis

During the Cuban missile crisis, the world held its breath for several days as it teetered on the brink of nuclear war. In the end, the Soviets agreed to remove the missiles. Soviet premier Nikita Khrushchev related his memory of the crisis.

> **"It had been, to say the least, an interesting and challenging situation. The two most powerful nations of the world had squared off against each other, each with its finger on the button. You'd have thought that war was inevitable. But both sides showed that if the desire to avoid war is strong enough, even the most pressing dispute can be solved by compromise. . . . I'll always remember . . . President Kennedy with deep respect because, in the . . . alysis, he showed himself to be sober-minded and deter- . . . o avoid war."**

Through Others' Eyes brings a personal perspective to U.S. history as seen by individuals outside the United States.

★ HISTORICAL DOCUMENTS ★

PRESIDENT JOHN F. KENNEDY

Inaugural Address

John F. Kennedy delivered his inaugural address on January 20, 1961. It was a sunny but bitterly cold day in the nation's capital. The address contained the themes of challenge and sacrifice that had filled his speeches during the presidential campaign. His words that day inspired many Americans. This remains one of the most famous speeches in U.S. history.

In the long history of the world, only a few generations have been granted the role of defending freedom in its hour of maximum danger. I do not shrink from this responsibility—I welcome it. I do not believe that any of us would exchange

Historical Documents allows your students to hear the voices of history with excerpts from history-making speeches and writings.

Eye-catching **historical photographs**, **art**, and **illustrations** reinforce history content and heighten your students' understanding.

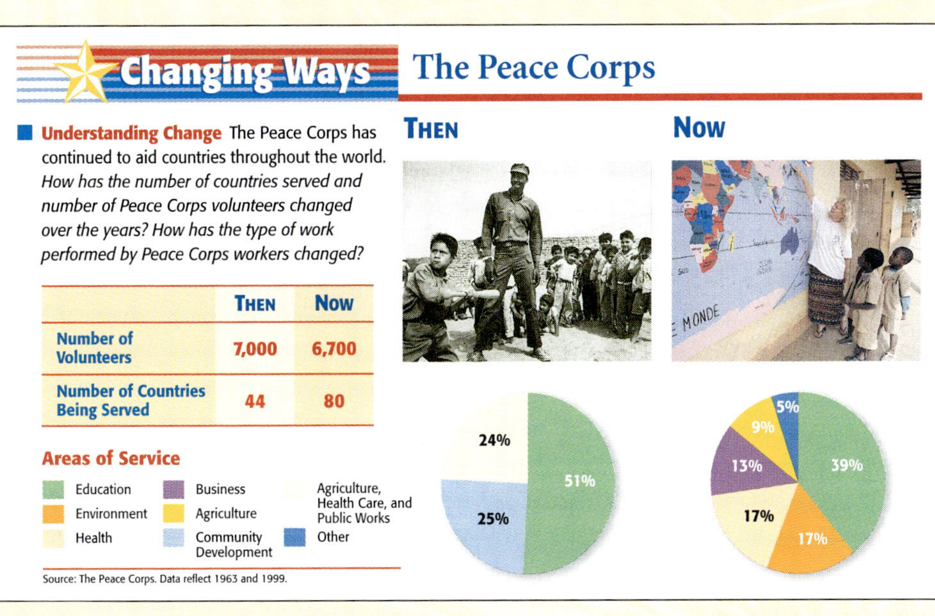

Changing Ways The Peace Corps

Understanding Change The Peace Corps has continued to aid countries throughout the world. *How has the number of countries served and number of Peace Corps volunteers changed over the years? How has the type of work performed by Peace Corps workers changed?*

	THEN	NOW
Number of Volunteers	7,000	6,700
Number of Countries Being Served	44	80

Areas of Service

Source: The Peace Corps. Data reflect 1963 and 1999.

Changing Ways gives your students a context for better understanding the links between past events and today.

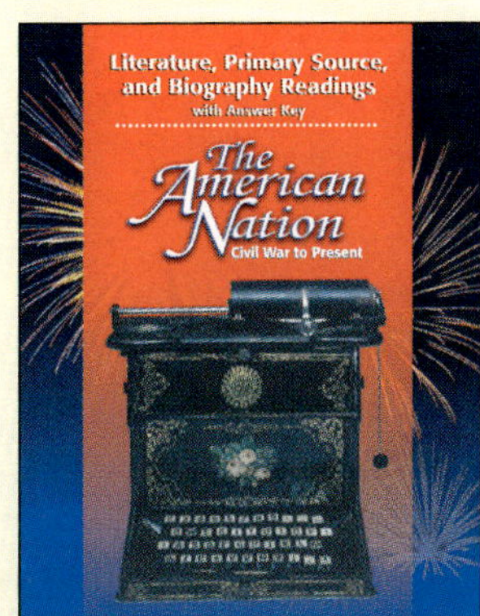

Literature, Primary Source, and Biography Readings exposes your students to important historical writings. This booklet contains literature, primary source, and biography readings, activities, and questions for each chapter.

Other features include:

- **Great Debates**
- **History in the Making**
- **Teen Life**
- **Biographies**
- **Presidential Lives**
- **Science and Technology**
- **The Religious Spirit**
- **Then and Now**

Linking Geography to History

Skill-building lessons and activities develop a geographic perspective.

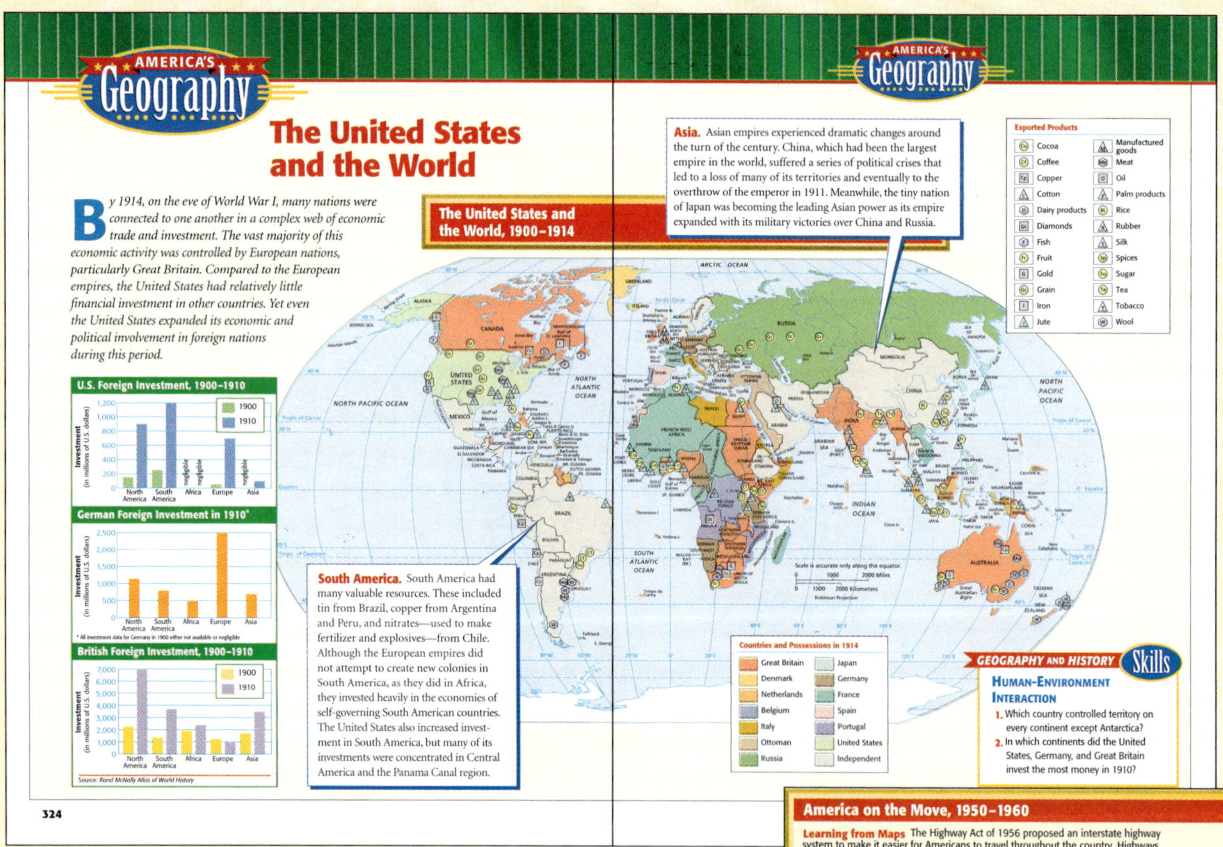
AMERICA'S Geography

The United States and the World

By 1914, on the eve of World War I, many nations were connected to one another in a complex web of economic trade and investment. The vast majority of this economic activity was controlled by European nations, particularly Great Britain. Compared to the European empires, the United States had relatively little financial investment in other countries. Yet even the United States expanded its economic and political involvement in foreign nations during this period.

South America. South America had many valuable resources. These included tin from Brazil, copper from Argentina and Peru, and nitrates—used to make fertilizer and explosives—from Chile. Although the European empires did not attempt to create new colonies in South America, as they did in Africa, they invested heavily in the economies of self-governing South American countries. The United States also increased investment in South America, but many of its investments were concentrated in Central America and the Panama Canal region.

Asia. Asian empires experienced dramatic changes around the turn of the century. China, which had been the largest empire in the world, suffered a series of political crises that led to a loss of many of its territories and eventually to the overthrow of the emperor in 1911. Meanwhile, the tiny nation of Japan was becoming the leading Asian power as its empire expanded with its military victories over China and Russia.

GEOGRAPHY AND HISTORY Skills

HUMAN-ENVIRONMENT INTERACTION

1. Which country controlled territory on every continent except Antarctica?
2. In which continents did the United States, Germany, and Great Britain invest the most money in 1910?

324

America's Geography explores a wide range of social studies themes, using maps and charts to show the influence of geography on American history.

America on the Move, 1950–1960

Learning from Maps The Highway Act of 1956 proposed an interstate highway system to make it easier for Americans to travel throughout the country. Highways helped spur the growth of suburbs.

LOCATION Which region had states that experienced a decline in population?

The generous use of **maps**, combined with informative captions and geography theme questions, helps build valuable map-reading skills.

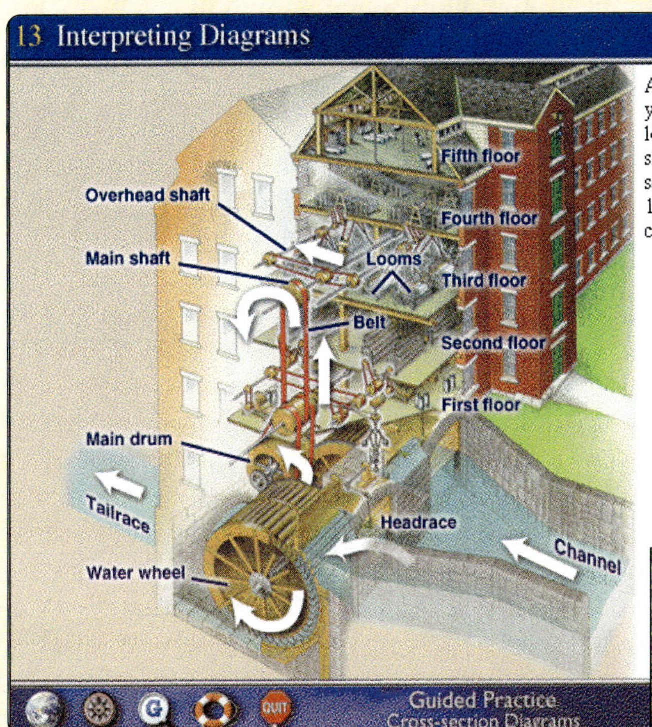

The Global Skill Builder CD-ROM is a comprehensive program containing interactive lessons that motivate your students to strengthen their map, graph, and computer skills.

Global Skill Builder
CD-ROM for Macintosh® and Windows®

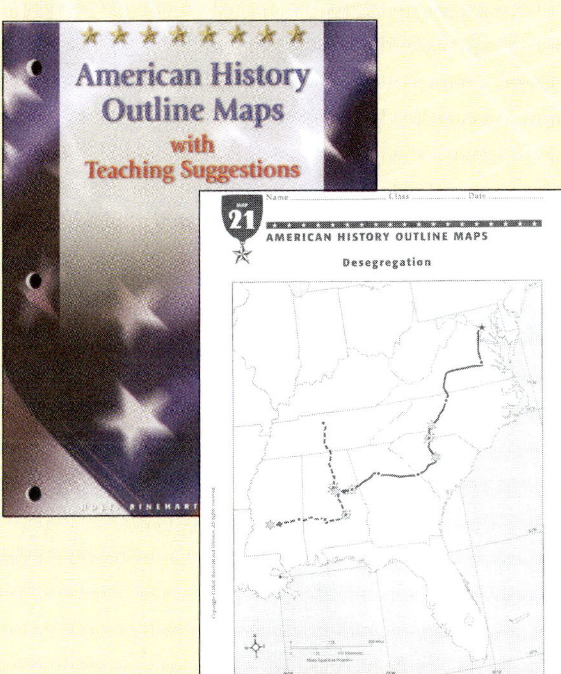

American History Outline Maps with Teaching Suggestions contains blackline masters of U.S. historical and contemporary maps. You can turn to the back of each blackline master for teaching suggestions for completing the map.

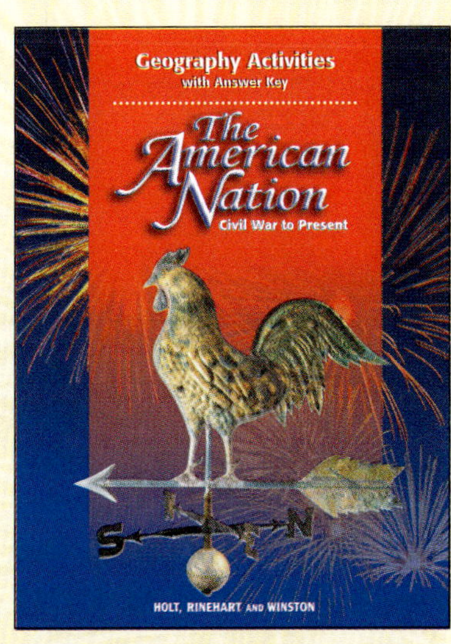

Geography Activities helps your students understand the role geography has played in our country's history through mapping and skills-related activities.

Annotated Teacher's Edition

Every tool you need to meet your instructional objectives is here.

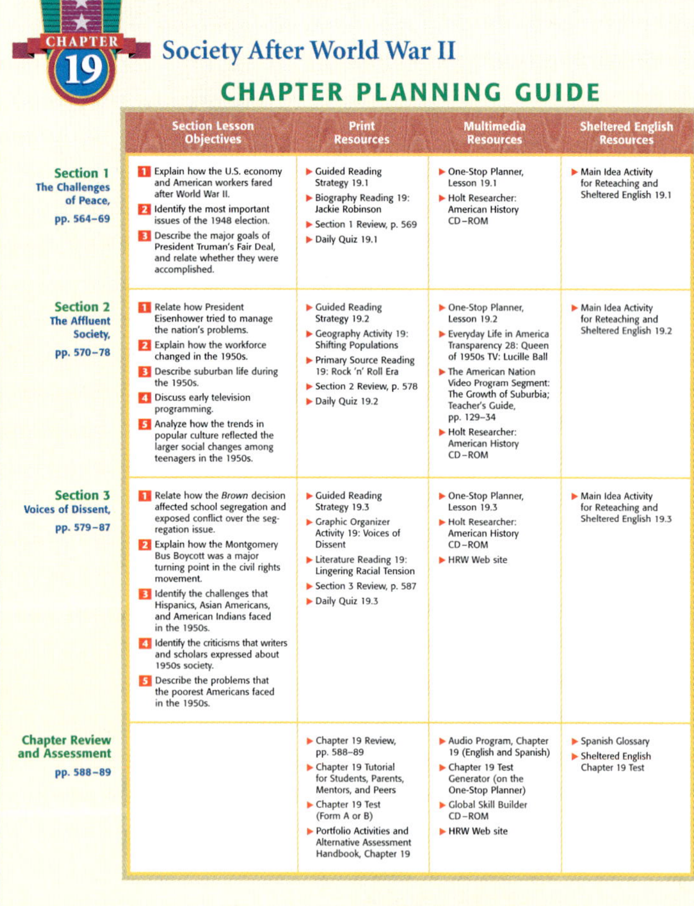

CHAPTER 19

Society After World War II

CHAPTER PLANNING GUIDE

	Section Lesson Objectives	Print Resources	Multimedia Resources	Sheltered English Resources
Section 1 The Challenges of Peace, pp. 564–69	1 Explain how the U.S. economy and American workers fared after World War II. 2 Identify the most important issues of the 1948 election. 3 Describe the major goals of President Truman's Fair Deal, and relate whether they were accomplished.	▶ Guided Reading Strategy 19.1 ▶ Biography Reading 19: Jackie Robinson ▶ Section 1 Review, p. 569 ▶ Daily Quiz 19.1	▶ One-Stop Planner, Lesson 19.1 ▶ Holt Researcher: American History CD–ROM	▶ Main Idea Activity for Reteaching and Sheltered English 19.1
Section 2 The Affluent Society, pp. 570–78	1 Relate how President Eisenhower tried to manage the nation's problems. 2 Explain how the workforce changed in the 1950s. 3 Describe suburban life during the 1950s. 4 Discuss early television programming. 5 Analyze how the trends in popular culture reflected the larger social changes among teenagers in the 1950s.	▶ Guided Reading Strategy 19.2 ▶ Geography Activity 19: Shifting Populations ▶ Primary Source Reading 19: Rock 'n' Roll Era ▶ Section 2 Review, p. 578 ▶ Daily Quiz 19.2	▶ One-Stop Planner, Lesson 19.2 ▶ Everyday Life in America Transparency 28: Queen of 1950s TV: Lucille Ball ▶ The American Nation Video Program Segment: The Growth of Suburbia; Teacher's Guide, pp. 129–34 ▶ Holt Researcher: American History CD–ROM	▶ Main Idea Activity for Reteaching and Sheltered English 19.2
Section 3 Voices of Dissent, pp. 579–87	1 Relate how the *Brown* decision affected school segregation and exposed conflict over the segregation issue. 2 Explain how the Montgomery Bus Boycott was a major turning point in the civil rights movement. 3 Identify the challenges that Hispanics, Asian Americans, and American Indians faced in the 1950s. 4 Identify the criticisms that writers and scholars expressed about 1950s society. 5 Describe the problems that the poorest Americans faced in the 1950s.	▶ Guided Reading Strategy 19.3 ▶ Graphic Organizer Activity 19: Voices of Dissent ▶ Literature Reading 19: Lingering Racial Tension ▶ Section 3 Review, p. 587 ▶ Daily Quiz 19.3	▶ One-Stop Planner, Lesson 19.3 ▶ Holt Researcher: American History CD–ROM ▶ HRW Web site	▶ Main Idea Activity for Reteaching and Sheltered English 19.3
Chapter Review and Assessment pp. 588–89		▶ Chapter 19 Review, pp. 588–89 ▶ Chapter 19 Tutorial for Students, Parents, Mentors, and Peers ▶ Chapter 19 Test (Form A or B) ▶ Portfolio Activities and Alternative Assessment Handbook, Chapter 19	▶ Audio Program, Chapter 19 (English and Spanish) ▶ Chapter 19 Test Generator (on the One-Stop Planner) ▶ Global Skill Builder CD–ROM ▶ HRW Web site	▶ Spanish Glossary ▶ Sheltered English Chapter 19 Test

CHAPTER OVERVIEW

When World War II ended, the United States faced multiple challenges created by the process of demobilization. Unemployment and inflation threatened to destroy the nation's hard-won economic equilibrium. A number of government initiatives, however, led the United States into a period of unprecedented prosperity.

The economic boom gave rise to a baby boom and new suburban developments. Suburban culture emphasized consumerism, conformity, and children. Some teenagers rebelled against this culture, idolizing fictional rebels and listening to rock 'n' roll. Television advertisements competed for teenagers' disposable income, as a growing number of Americans bought television sets.

Although many Americans viewed the postwar years as an era of peace and opportunity, others protested the continued presence of discrimination and society's emphasis on conformity. African Americans launched the modern civil rights movement in an attempt to integrate schools and transportation systems. Hispanics also organized to obtain equal rights.

TIME TAMERS

Block Scheduling

The teacher lesson plans for each section offer a variety of activity choices to help you present the material in a block scheduling format. For further suggestions on block scheduling, see the **Block Scheduling Handbook with Team Teaching Strategies**, pp. 109–14.

Smithsonian Institution

Internet Connections and Lesson 19
www.si.edu/hrw

Hands-On History Activities:

Classroom to Community The **Hands-On History Activities** help students make meaningful connections between events in American history and those in their own hometown. You may wish to use the Chapter 19 Activity, What Things Do You Really Need, to extend the chapter lessons, as alternative assessment, or as a block scheduling option.

Portfolio Projects

PORTFOLIO

The American Nation includes multiple portfolio projects in each Pupil's Edition chapter review, as well as each unit review. Chapter 19 Portfolio Project options on p. 589 include the following:

1. Students will **prepare an illustrated chart.**
2. Students will **develop an illustrated outline.**
3. Students will **write an illustrated report.**

The American Nation
INTERNET RESOURCE DIRECTORY

To access online materials for this chapter, go to **go.hrw.com** and type in the keywords listed below.

HRW ONLINE RESOURCES
GO TO: go.hrw.com

Online Maps
KEYWORD: SE1 Maps19
- Election of 1948

Online Charts
KEYWORD: SE1 Charts19
- Baby Boom
- Civil Rights in the Truman Era
- Homes with Television Sets

Online Reading Support
KEYWORD: SE1 Strategies19

Online Rubrics
KEYWORD: SE1 Rubrics

CHAPTER ENRICHMENT LINKS
Use these Web links to extend and enrich student learning for Chapter 19.
GO TO: go.hrw.com
KEYWORD: SE1 Ch19

CHAPTER INTERNET ACTIVITIES
GO TO: go.hrw.com
- Pupil's Edition Student Activity
  KEYWORD: SE1 Culture
  (Students analyze popular culture during the 1950s.)
- Teacher's Edition Student Activity
  KEYWORD: SE1 Gandhi
  (Students conduct research on Mohandas K. Gandhi.)
- Teacher's Edition Student Activity
  KEYWORD: SE1 LULAC
  (Students analyze the activities of Hispanic activist groups.)

ADDITIONAL
RESOURCES

Books for Teachers

Diggins, John Patrick. *The Proud Decades: America in War and Peace, 1941–1960.* W. W. Norton & Company, 1988. Offers a highly readable overview of the period.

Inglis, Fred. *The Cruel Peace.* Basic Books, 1993. Relates Cold War myths and realities.

Books for Students

Oakley, J. Ronald. *God's Country: America in the Fifties.* Barricade Books, 1990. Examines the decade and offers many entertaining and informative details.

Tames, Richard. *The 1950s: Picture History of the 20th Century.* Watts, 1990. and events of the decade. Particularly appropriate for students reading below grade level.

Primary Sources from the Period

Hansberry, Lorraine. *A Raisin in the Sun.* Random House, 1959. Profiles one African American family's search for a place to live.

Salinger, J. D. *The Catcher in the Rye.* Bantam Books, Holden Caulfield, a troubled teenager.

Multimedia Materials

The Age of Anxiety. Video, 24 min. AIMS Media. Reviews the Eisenhower years.

Postwar Hopes, Cold War Fears. Video, 58 min. PBS. Analyzes the effects of the Cold War on American life during the 1950s.

The **Chapter Planning Guide**, at the beginning of each chapter, organizes print and multimedia resources by section and highlights chapter review and assessment options in an easy-to-read table.

You can expand your students' horizons with fully integrated technology resources, such as **Smithsonian Institution** Internet connections.

For a quick introduction to the upcoming chapter, you can read the **Chapter Overview**, a summary of the chapter's main ideas and themes.

Books for Teacher, **Books for Students**, **Primary Sources from the Period**, and **Multimedia Materials** provide references to further explore chapter content.

Portfolio Projects introduces extended cooperative-learning activities at the beginning of the chapter to give your students plenty of planning time.

The **Internet Resource Directory** makes it easy to access online materials directly related to chapter topics by listing **go.hrw.com** resources and keywords.

The **Block Scheduling Handbook with Team Teaching Strategies** is more than a pacing guide. The daily lesson plans suggest practical ways to cover more than one textbook section in an extended class period. The handbook also suggests ways to link the study of social studies to other disciplines, such as language arts.

POINT-AND-CLICK PLANNING

with TestBuilder Software for Macintosh® and Windows®

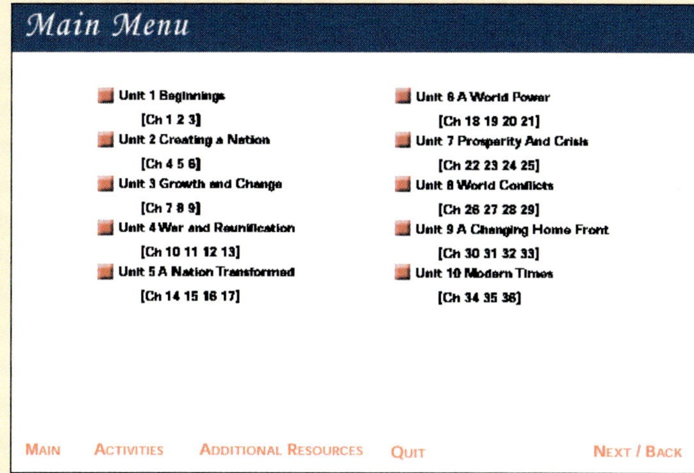

Everything you need is on disc! The *One-Stop Planner* makes planning and managing lessons a breeze. This time-saving planning software contains all print-based teaching resources and video segments for ***The American Nation,*** plus valuable assessment tools. The *One-Stop Planner* includes

- **editable** lesson plans in several word-processing formats
- a **powerful** test generator that allows you to create your own assessments
- **printable** program resources
- a direct launch to the **go.hrw.com** Internet site
- **video clips** from *The American Nation Video Program*

One-Stop Planner resources are presented in easy-to-understand, point-and-click menu formats. To preview or print out worksheets and tests, you simply make your selection and click. It's that easy.

Step-by-Step Lesson Cycle

You can find effective tips and techniques right where you need them.

After completing Section 2, students should be able to:

OBJECTIVE 1 *Relate how President Eisenhower tried to manage the nation's problems.*

OBJECTIVE 2 *Explain how the workforce changed in the 1950s.*

OBJECTIVE 3 *Describe suburban life during the 1950s.*

OBJECTIVE 4 *Discuss early television programming.*

OBJECTIVE 5 *Analyze how the trends in popular culture reflected the larger social changes among teenagers in the 1950s.*

LET'S GET STARTED!

As students enter the classroom, display Everyday Life in America Transparency 28, Queen of 1950s TV: Lucille Ball, from **American History Visual Resources**. Distribute the accompanying worksheet and ask students to answer the questions. Have volunteers share their answers. Then tell students that in Section 2 they will learn more about American society and popular culture during the 1950s.

Let's Get Started! activities are a great way to involve your students while you take roll.

TEACH OBJECTIVE 1

LEVEL 1: Pair students and ask them to write paragraphs describing how President Eisenhower tried to manage the nation's problems. *(Students should indicate that Eisenhower followed an approach known as Modern Republicanism. He cut some government programs while protecting and expanding others.)* Have volunteers read their paragraphs to the class. **Sheltered English, Cooperative Learning**

LEVEL 2: Tell students to imagine that they are President Eisenhower and that they have just retired from politics. Ask each student to write a short memoir explaining how Eisenhower attempted to manage the nation's problems. *(See the Level 1 lesson for the correct approaches.)* Have volunteers read their memoirs to the class.

LEVEL 3: Conduct a brief discussion on how President Eisenhower attempted to manage the nation's problems. *(See the Level 1 lesson for the correct approaches.)* Then ask each student to create a detailed graphic organizer that compares and contrasts Eisenhower's approaches with those of previous presidents during the 1900s. Suggest that students consult their textbooks if they do not remember specific details about earlier presidents. Have volunteers present their graphic organizers to the class. Then ask students to "grade" Eisenhower as a president. Conduct a debate between students with different opinions.

TEACH OBJECTIVE 2

ALL LEVELS: Ask students to share their preconceptions, if any, about the workforce in the 1950s. *(Answers will vary. Some students might suggest that many workers of the era were "men in gray flannel suits.")* Conduct a brief discussion of these preconceptions and stereotypes. To help students understand how the workforce changed in the 1950s, copy the graphic organizer on the chalkboard, omitting the italicized answers. Have each student complete it. **Sheltered English**

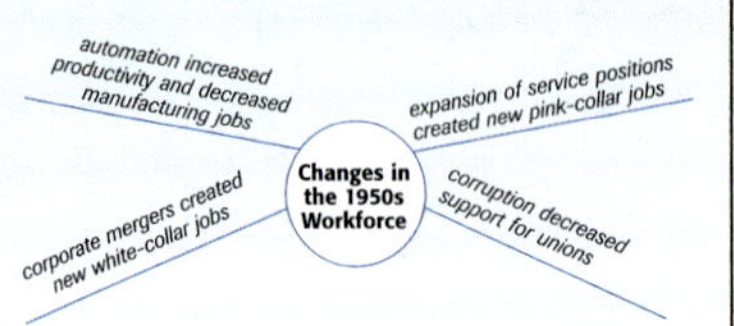

▶**ASSIGNMENT:** *Write the following terms on the chalkboard:* automation, white collar, pink collar, *and* Landrum-Griffin Act.

Graphic Organizer activities help your students classify information, identify cause-and-effect relationships, put events in sequence, and make comparisons.

TEACH OBJECTIVE 3

LEVEL 1: Conduct a discussion on suburban life during the 1950s. *(Suburban residents lived in nearly identical communities. Suburban life centered around the family. Consumption and conformity played important roles.)* Then ask students to identify some words that they associate with suburbs. *(Answers will vary. Students might list words such as* boring, pretty, *or* safe.*)* List the most common words on the chalkboard. Have each student use these words in a sentence describing suburban life during the 1950s. To conclude, ask students to express some of their own views on suburban life during the 1950s. Would they have wanted to live in a 1950s suburb? Why or why not? **Sheltered English**

LEVEL 2: Tell students to imagine that they are architects for a suburban-development firm during the 1950s. Have each student design and map a fictional suburb. Remind students to include items such as churches, community centers, and schools. Then ask students to write short reports to accompany their suburb plans. Students' reports should describe suburban life during the 1950s as well as discuss their own fictional suburbs. *(See the Level 1 lesson for the correct description.)* Have volunteers present their suburbs to the class. Students may wish to include their suburban maps and reports in their portfolios.

LEVEL 3: Ask a volunteer to read Lewis Mumford's statement on this page to the class. Then ask students to support or challenge Mumford's statement by describing suburban life during the 1950s. *(See the Level 1 lesson for the correct description.)* Note students' responses on the chalkboard. To extend the lesson, ask each student to outline or write a short story set in a suburb.

▶**ASSIGNMENT:** *Have students create cartoons that discuss suburban life during the 1950s. Have students write captions to accompany their cartoons.*

Teacher to Teacher

Karen Hoppes of Lake Oswego, Oregon, suggested the following activity: Organize students into small groups and tell them to imagine that they are members of a think tank in 1958. Have each group conduct research on American suburbs. Suggest that groups examine quality of life, juvenile delinquency, and so on. After groups have completed their research, tell them to prepare for committee meetings. Ask volunteers to conduct their meetings for the class.

Teach gives you **teaching suggestions** as well as **leveled suggestions** for each objective—enabling you to accommodate the different learners in your class.

Teacher to Teacher strategies offer you valuable classroom-tested ideas that have been developed and successfully applied by your peers.

TEACH OBJECTIVE 4

LEVEL 1: Pair students and ask them to list characteristics of early television programming. *(Pairs should note that major corporations sponsored many early television programs. These programs included dramas, quiz shows, situation comedies, sporting events, and variety shows.)* Have each pair write sentences describing each of the elements on its list. Ask volunteers to share their sentences. To conclude, have students create typical television listings from a newspaper as they might have appeared in the 195
Sheltered English, Cooperative Le

LEVEL 2: Conduct a brief discussion on early television programming. *(See the Level 1 lesson for the correct description.)* Then tell students to imagine that it is 1957 and they have been asked to rate the quality of television programming. Have each student create a television-viewing log describing all of the programs that he or she watched on a given day, noting which programs they liked best. *(Students should consider what types of programs would have appealed to them and why.)* Ask volunteers

Teach objectives offer strategies for students with varying learning styles and leveled activities for students with varying intelligence.

LEVEL 3: Conduct a brief discussion on early television programming. *(See the Level 1 lesson for the correct description.)* Then tell students to imagine that it is 1957 and that a major television studio has just announced a contest entitled Create the Show of the Year! Have each student write a proposal for a new television show. Students should also write brief analyses to accompany their proposals. Students' analyses should explain why their proposed shows would be popular in the 1950s national market. Students may wish to include their proposals and

SPOTLIGHT on the Game Show Scandal
Ask students to conduct research on the game-show scandal of the 1950s. Then tell students to imagine that they are modern-day historians. Have each student write a short article describing and analyzing the scandal, focusing on what it revealed about American culture during the 1950s. Alternately, tell students to imagine that they are Americans who watched game shows regularly and recently learned of the scandal. Have

TEACH OBJECTIVE 5

ALL LEVELS: Ask students to imagine that they have found a time capsule buried by teenagers in the 1950s. A note in the capsule explains that the items included represent trends in 1950s popular culture. As a class, have students brainstorm a list of items that might be in the capsule. Then have students create graphic organizers listing the contents of the capsule and how each item reflects social changes among teenagers in the 1950s. *(Students should note that fictional rebels and satirical magazines and comic books expressed teenagers' confusion and anger. Rock 'n' roll hinted at civil rights challenges to come.)* Have volunteers the class. **Sheltered English**

SPOTLIGHT on Rock Stars of the 1950s
Ask students to select one of the rock 'n' stars of the 1950s, such as Chuck Berry, Fats Domino, Buddy Holly, Elvis Presley, Little Richard, or Ritchie Valens. Ask students to conduct research on their chosen star. Then have each student write a short biography of his or her performer, discussing the person's background and music. Ask students to present information about their subject to the class. Then gather students' biographies and compile a rock 'n' roll encyclopedia.
Block Scheduling

Extend activities invite students to take their knowledge one step further.

REVIEW
Have students complete the **Section 2 Review** on p. 878.

ASSESS
Have students complete **Daily Quiz 29.2.** As **Alternative Assessment**, you may want to use the fictional suburb map or the television-viewing log in this section's lessons.

RETEACH
Have students complete **Main Idea Activity for Reteaching and Sheltered English 29.2.** Then assign each student a subsection of Section 2. Have students write five questions about the material in their assigned subsections. Collect the questions and use them to quiz the entire class. **Sheltered English**

EXTEND
Ask students to interview someone who lived in a suburb in the 1950s. Have students tape or transcribe the interviews. Then ask students to work together to create a collective oral history album of suburban residents of the 1950s. Students might want to illustrate the album with photographs of the people they interviewed. **Block Scheduling, Cooperative Learning**

Content-Rich Presentations

Energize your classroom presentations with compelling content support, accompanied by critical-thinking questions or activities.

ACROSS THE CURRICULUM
▸GOVERNMENT◂
Henry Wallace and Progressive Party. A president during Frankli Roosevelt's third term, H Wallace traveled to Chin Latin America, and Siber journeys strongly influen his political views. As th Progressive Party's pres tial candidate in 1948, h on a platform largely de to international issues. W who had been replaced Harry S Truman for Roos fourth term, believed tha Truman's firm stand tow the Soviet Union had th potential to result in wa also feared that it could to political persecution. commentators called W a "communist dupe" an "Stalinist stooge." Howe his views appealed to m Americans. He won mor 1 million popular votes i 1948 election.
CRITICAL THINKING Wh might Wallace have beli that Truman's approach t the Soviet Union could in war?
ANSWER: Students migh suggest that Wallace bel that Truman's approach too confrontational.

IN THE NEWS
The Continuing Fight Against Polio. Polio still exists in many nations. A World Health Organization (WHO) project to completely eradicate polio by the year 2000 began by targeting sp cific countries and launching massive inoculation campaig The WHO sponsored one such drive in India in 1996. India the virus strikes about 10,000 children per year, causing widespread physica disabilities. After the WHO shipped the polio vaccine, Indian officials at 500,000 health centers all over the country administered the sho If children refused to report f the shot, volunteers searche for them, and administered the vaccine. The effort was very successful—in just one day, some 120 million childr were vaccinated.
CRITICAL THINKING Why might polio still exist in some countries?
ANSWER: Students might suggest that polio and othe diseases tend to linger in nations with limited resources to fight them.

PEOPLE IN HISTORY
Oveta Culp Hobby. Be becoming secretary of the Department of Health, Education, and Welfare (H Oveta Culp Hobby played crucial role in World War 1942 Hobby became the f female colonel in U.S. hist when she accepted a pos as head of the newly crea Women's Army Auxiliary Corps—later known as the Women's Army Corps, or W Hobby believed that wom like men, had a responsib to help defend their count She once told WAC recrui "You have a debt and a d A debt to democracy, a d with destiny." Hobby even ally commanded more tha 100,000 WACs serving all the globe. She accepted t HEW position in 1953.
CRITICAL THINKING Do y think the federal governm should play a role in health education? Why or why n
ANSWER: Some students m suggest that the federal government has a special responsibility to protect citizens' health.

CULTURAL DIVERSITY
A Religious De Religion was an i social force during Church membersh grown dramaticall Catholic seminarie teries, and conver numerous applica popular culture re decade's interest A variety of books gious themes, suc Graham's *Peace w* and Dale Evans R *Angel Unaware*, be best-sellers. West Press began publi 26-volume *Library Classics* in the ear Hollywood made r oriented movies, p *Ben Hur*, *The Robe The Ten Command*
CRITICAL THINKIN factors might have for the increased religion in the 195
ANSWER: Answers Students might m influence of Cold or the desire to gi for peace and pro

HISTORY MAKERS SPEAK
Harriet Osborn i *Century*
Children in the Harriet Osborn, w into a suburb in described the rol played in the new "The suburbs wa place to raise chi children were ou focus. . . . There emphasis placed and bringing the their first year of Dr. Spock's guide and we would co all the time. . . . T few worries. We c the house, and w afford to clothe o everybody else c children. It was a was the America
ACTIVITY: Tell stu Osborn's husban World War II vete students to offer veterans and thei might have viewe life as "the Ameri

ECONOMIC DEVELOPMENT
A Reason to A month after W ended, the *CIO* that between th periods 1935 an 1940 and 1944, profits in the ste had risen 113 pe than $1 billion. of California stu in 1945 indicate workers earned week—totaling fa $2,700 per year t achieve a mode of living. Worke industries earne weekly wages.
CRITICAL THINK might the *CIO* the University of study, and other ments have affe
ANSWER: Studen cate that the art and other docu give rise to the launched after

TECHNOLOGY AND SOCIETY
Early Televisi television sets were nothing lik clearly focused displayed a fuz white picture. likened the exp "watching thro blinds"! In addi technological i vision sets were expensive—abo at a time when earned less tha In the early 195 the quality impr the price dropp Americans own 45 million telev
CRITICAL THINK might some fam so much mone sets during the
ANSWER: Stude suggest that th wanted the late

DEMOCRATIC VALUES
President Truman Civil Rights. Presid Truman appointed bot American and white to serve on the Comm on Civil Rights. In ad decrying racial violen committee's report c "the elimination of seg based on race, color, national origin, from life." Although Truma executive orders did achieve this goal, the expand opportunities African Americans.
CRITICAL THINKING might Truman's exec order on the military affected recruitment?
ANSWER: Students m suggest that it proba encouraged African American enlistment.

THEN AND NOW
American Fads. During the 1950s television advertising and teenagers' disposable incomes fueled many fads and crazes. The Hula Hoop was one of them. Introduced in 1958 by the Wham-O Manufacturing Company, the Hula Hoop became an immediate sensation. Frisbees and Wiffle balls were also popular during the 1950s.
CRITICAL THINKING Ask students to name three current fads. How might fads have changed since the 1950s?
ANSWER: Answers will vary. Students might suggest that current fads can be spread on the Internet, rather than through television advertising.

Getting Students Actively Involved

Dynamic ancillaries provide rich learning experiences.

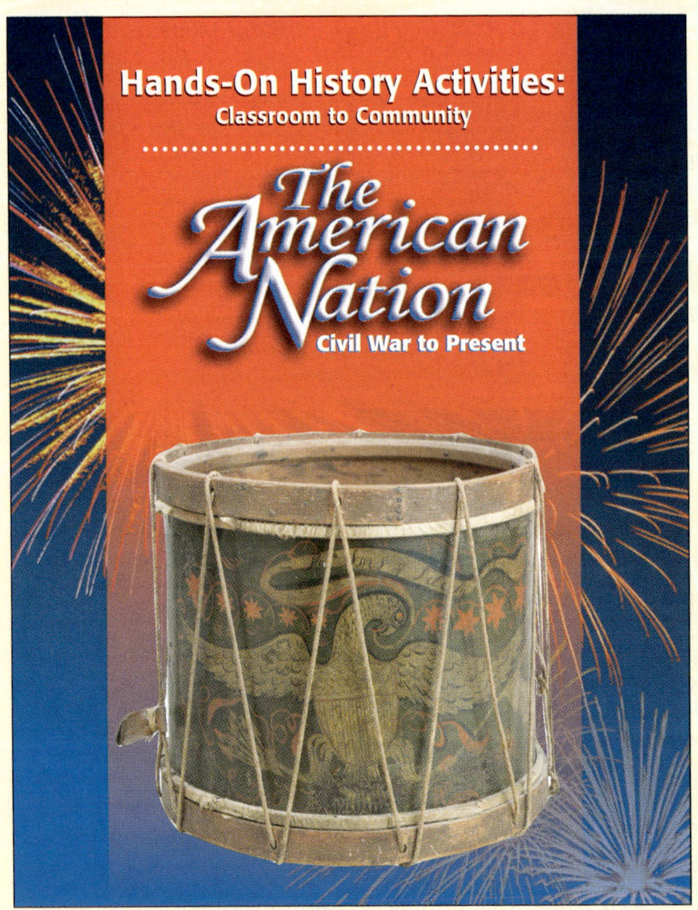

Hands-On History Activities: Classroom to Community is a great resource for group-oriented active-learning projects that combine chapter content, historical research, and students' creativity to focus on specific links between history and your students' local community.

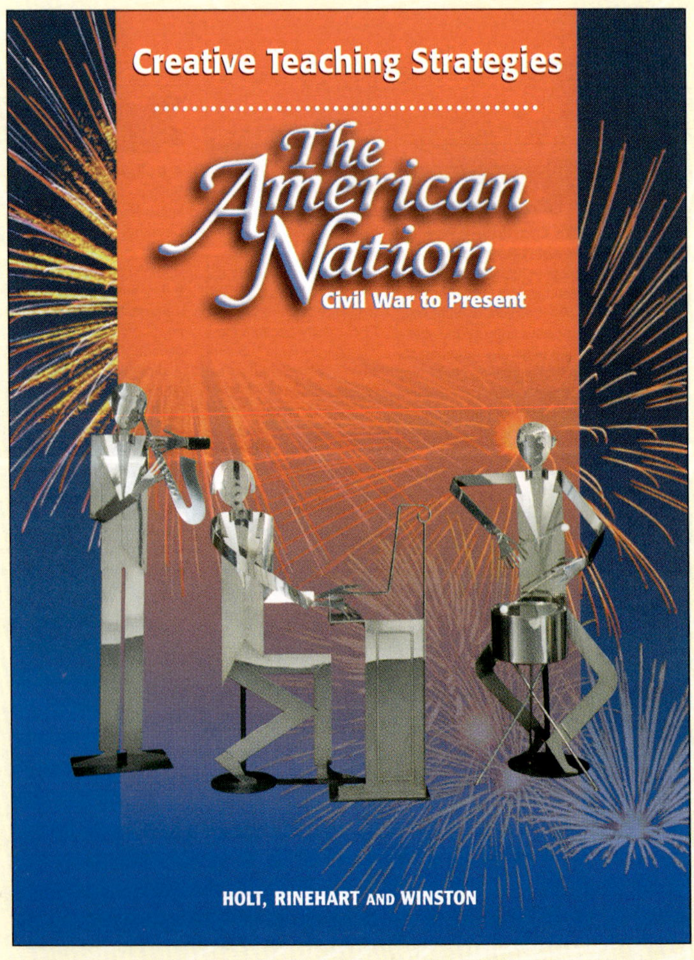

Creative Teaching Strategies contains innovative teaching strategies that can be customized to use at various points in your lesson. The wide range of cooperative-learning activities—including learning stations and simulations—motivates your students and helps them develop critical-thinking skills.

You can help the visual learners in your classroom gain a better understanding with **American History Visual Resources** and **Art in American History Transparencies**—full-color transparencies designed to maximize interest and comprehension.

Holt, Rinehart and Winston Social Studies

SR9 AH TOOLKIT

American History Teaching Toolkit

Student Projects

Analyzing a Written Source

Analyzing Current Events

Analyzing Political Cartoons

Cooperative Groupwork Skills

Preparing an Oral Report

The **American History Teaching Toolkit** provides an assortment of motivating online activities, such as organizing a dinner party with historical figures as guests.

American History Political Cartoons with Activities, Teaching Suggestions, and Answer Key

The Spread of Suburbia

American History Political Cartoons with Activities, Teaching Suggestions, and Answer Key offers a look into historical issues and helps your students strengthen their critical-thinking skills.

Online History

Here's how it works:

Groundbreaking online resources make history come alive!

New York Festivals Finalist

EDDIE Award for Educational Web Site

Now your students can safely and productively explore the Internet through **go.hrw.com**. This award-winning site links students to instructional activities, other sites, and additional resources directly related to chapter topics.

1 Simply type the address found in the textbook—**go.hrw.com**.

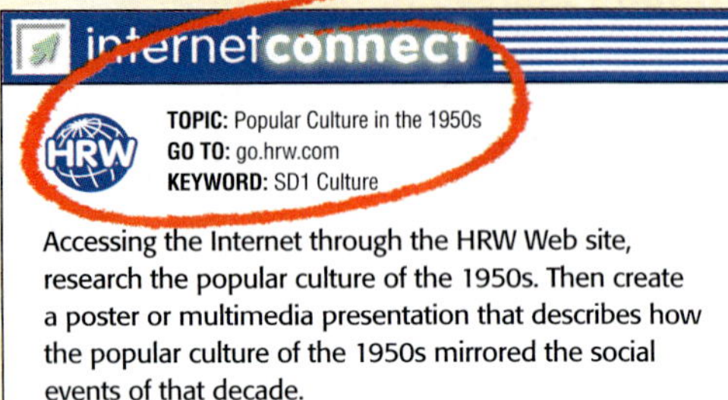

internet connect
HRW
TOPIC: Popular Culture in the 1950s
GO TO: go.hrw.com
KEYWORD: SD1 Culture
Accessing the Internet through the HRW Web site, research the popular culture of the 1950s. Then create a poster or multimedia presentation that describes how the popular culture of the 1950s mirrored the social events of that decade.

2 Enter the keyword—such as SD1 Ellis Island—that's provided in the textbook.

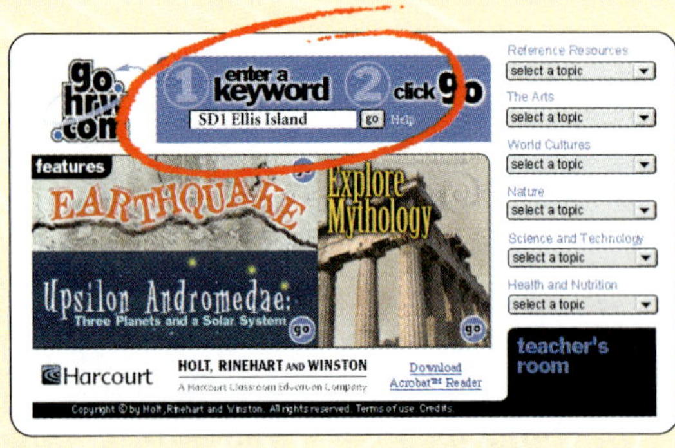

3 Read about each site's contents and follow navigation tips to complete the activity.

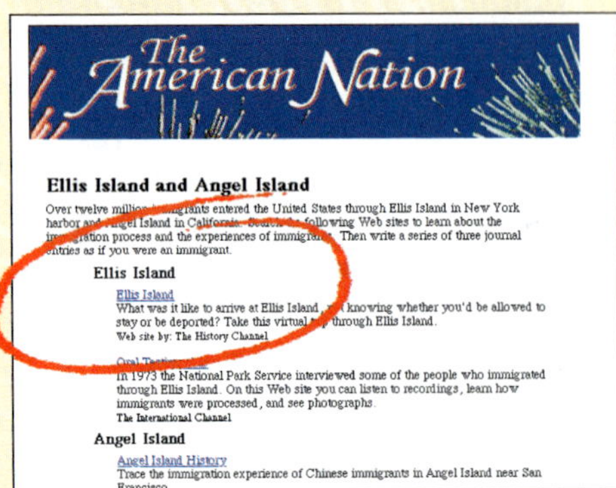

Smithsonian Institution®

The **Smithsonian Institution** is always open to your class! ***The American Nation*** now provides access to selected Smithsonian Web sites, giving you and your students unparalleled entry into a range of primary source materials, virtual tours, and online exhibits.

It's Easy!

1 Simply type the address found in the textbook—**www.si.edu/hrw**— and select Social Studies

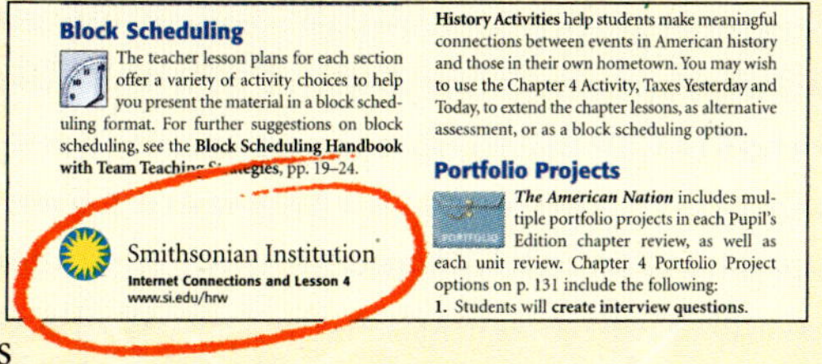

Block Scheduling

The teacher lesson plans for each section offer a variety of activity choices to help you present the material in a block scheduling format. For further suggestions on block scheduling, see the **Block Scheduling Handbook with Team Teaching Strategies**, pp. 19–24.

Smithsonian Institution
Internet Connections and Lesson 4
www.si.edu/hrw

History Activities help students make meaningful connections between events in American history and those in their own hometown. You may wish to use the Chapter 4 Activity, Taxes Yesterday and Today, to extend the chapter lessons, as alternative assessment, or as a block scheduling option.

Portfolio Projects

The American Nation includes multiple portfolio projects in each Pupil's Edition chapter review, as well as each unit review. Chapter 4 Portfolio Project options on p. 131 include the following:

1. Students will **create interview questions**.

2 Choose a time period

3 Select an exhibit

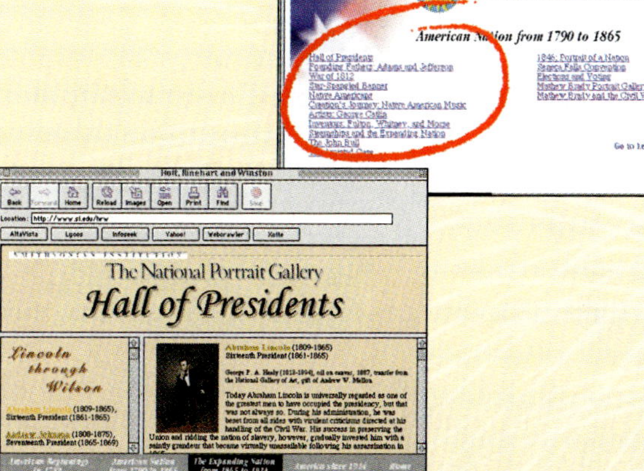

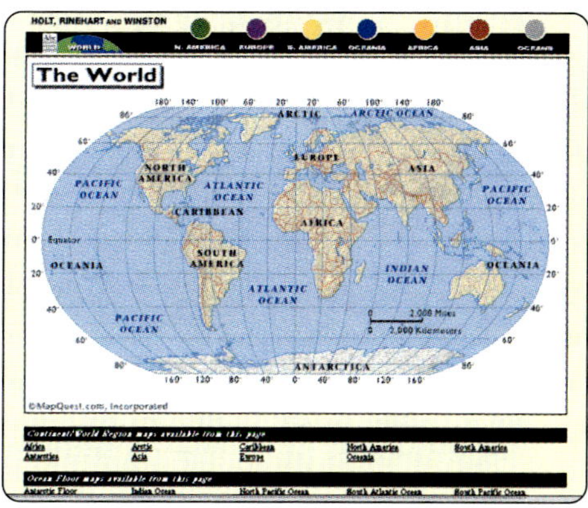

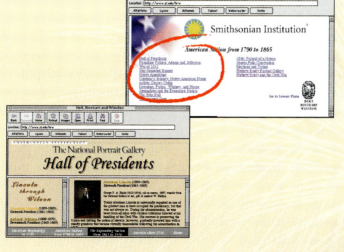

HRW Online Atlas, found on **www.hrw.com**, contains over 300 well-rendered and clearly labeled country and state maps, in English and Spanish, plus statistics. The Atlas's clean design and easy-to-use navigation tools make accessing information simple. What's more, these maps are continually updated so you can rest assured that you and your students have the latest and most accurate geographical content available. This is a must-have resource for your history classroom!

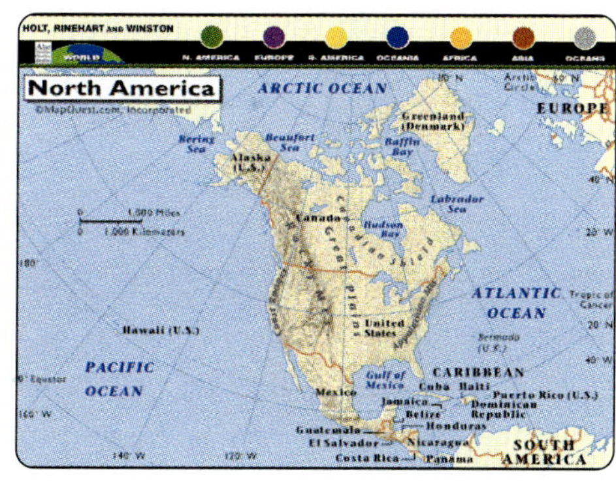

If You Can't Read, You Can't Learn with Text

RICHARD T. VACCA, Kent State University

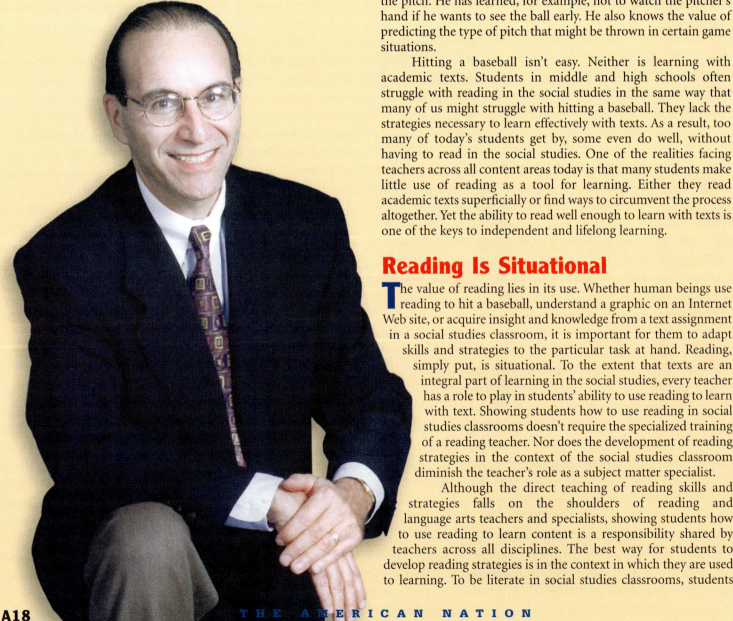

NOT TOO LONG AGO I was rummaging through a set of "preowned" *Sports Illustrated* magazines at a neighbor's yard sale. As I was browsing through an issue from 1978, I came across an excerpt from a book written by Reggie Jackson, then with the New York Yankees, on the art of hitting a baseball. The title of the excerpt caught my attention immediately because it asserted, "If you can't read, you can't hit." Although a baseball fan, I confess knowing little, other than the obvious, about hitting a baseball. However, as a literacy educator for more than 25 years, I profess knowing something about reading, having made the study of reading processes and reading to learn my life's work. And for this reason, I was intrigued by the connection between reading and hitting a baseball.

In the excerpt, Jackson explains how he must be able to "read" several kinds of information in a fraction of a second to be successful as a hitter. His brain almost instantly must anticipate and process the type of pitch, its speed, and the rotation on the ball so that he can time his stride and the swing of the bat. To do this with reasonable success, Jackson has developed a repertoire of strategies for "reading" the rotation on the ball and the speed of the pitch. He has learned, for example, not to watch the pitcher's hand if he wants to see the ball early. He also knows the value of predicting the type of pitch that might be thrown in certain game situations.

Hitting a baseball isn't easy. Neither is learning with academic texts. Students in middle and high schools often struggle with reading in the social studies in the same way that many of us might struggle with hitting a baseball. They lack the strategies necessary to learn effectively with texts. As a result, too many of today's students get by, some even do well, without having to read in the social studies. One of the realities facing teachers across all content areas today is that many students make little use of reading as a tool for learning. Either they read academic texts superficially or find ways to circumvent the process altogether. Yet the ability to read well enough to learn with texts is one of the keys to independent and lifelong learning.

Reading Is Situational

The value of reading lies in its use. Whether human beings use reading to hit a baseball, understand a graphic on an Internet Web site, or acquire insight and knowledge from a text assignment in a social studies classroom, it is important for them to adapt skills and strategies to the particular task at hand. Reading, simply put, is situational. To the extent that texts are an integral part of learning in the social studies, every teacher has a role to play in students' ability to use reading to learn with text. Showing students how to use reading in social studies classrooms doesn't require the specialized training of a reading teacher. Nor does the development of reading strategies in the context of the social studies classroom diminish the teacher's role as a subject matter specialist.

Although the direct teaching of reading skills and strategies falls on the shoulders of reading and language arts teachers and specialists, showing students how to use reading to learn content is a responsibility shared by teachers across all disciplines. The best way for students to develop reading strategies is in the context in which they are used to learning. To be literate in social studies classrooms, students must learn how to use language processes such as reading and writing to explore and construct meaning.

Because reading is situational, the potential for students of varying ability to struggle with academic texts is ever present. Sometimes there is the tendency to associate struggling readers solely with low-achieving students. But this might not always be the case. The dilemma facing most adolescents who struggle with reading is that few effectively learn how to learn with texts. They read words on a page, but often have little clue about how to construct meaning from what they read. Students who struggle with reading in social studies classrooms may go through the motions of reading but are likely to conceal some of their difficulties with materials assigned to them from their textbooks. Although they may have developed the ability to read print smoothly and accurately, students who struggle as readers usually don't know what to do with texts beyond just saying the words. They can handle the mechanics of reading but aren't *strategic* enough in their ability to handle the conceptual demands inherent in a social studies text.

National surveys of reading performance, such as the National Assessment of Educational Progress (NAEP), suggest that the majority of today's adolescents are capable of reading for literal understanding but have difficulty with more complex tasks. They struggle with the ability to think and learn with text. The most recent report, for example, NAEP 1998 Reading Report Card for the Nation and the States (Washington, D.C.: United States Department of Education), concludes that a majority of adolescents can read at *basic levels* of performance but have difficulty with more *advanced levels* of reading. What national assessments such as NAEP tell us is that middle and high school students, for the most part, develop the "basics" of reading but they don't know what to do with texts beyond recognizing bits and pieces of information that they encounter during reading.

Reading Is Strategic

Students who struggle with texts, regardless of ability level, often get lost in a maze of words as they attempt to read text assignments. Getting through text assignments to answer homework questions is often the only reason to read, if students read at all. The text doesn't make sense to them in ways that permit them to think deeply about ideas encountered during reading. One way to think about learning with text is that it is a conversation that takes place between the author and the reader. Author and reader engage in communication. But the talk usually is not the kind of loose, expressive discourse that might take place between two friends. The language of social studies texts is more formal than everyday discourse because the ideas that academic texts communicate often are complex and demanding. The author uses the language of an historian or a social scientist to communicate ideas. The reader uses *cognitive and metacognitive strategies* to engage in the conversation so that he or she can understand, respond to, and perhaps even question and challenge the author's ideas.

Scaffolding instruction is one of the best ways I know to help students become aware of and competent in the use of strategies they need to be successful. Used in construction, scaffolds serve as supports, lifting up workers so that they can achieve something that otherwise would not have been possible. The word *scaffold* is used as a metaphor in teaching and learning to suggest helping students to do what they cannot do at first. Instructional scaffolding simply means giving students a better chance to be successful with texts than if left on their own to use reading to learn. Scaffolding text learning involves the use of well-timed questions, explanations, demonstrations, and activities in well-planned lessons and provides instructional support for students in the application of reading strategies.

Throughout *The American Nation* there are numerous chapter suggestions and activities for reading to scaffold students' text learning experiences. Each chapter provides an *instructional framework* which allows you the flexibility to plan and use reading-related activities before, during, and after text assignments. For example, when faced with having to read an academic text, most students jump into the reading and plow through it as fast as they can just to get it finished. Plowing through what they read, without getting conceptually ready to explore ideas, isn't an effective strategy. It is similar to an athlete who fails to warm-up before the game or a musician who doesn't rehearse before going on stage to perform. Before students even begin to take on a text, there are beginning of chapter suggestions and activities to prepare them for the ideas that they will encounter when they begin reading.

In addition, the more skillful students become at using thinking strategies during reading, the more likely they will make sense of the topic by comprehending and interpreting what they read. Reading is all about making sense. During reading it is important that students keep their minds active. A successful reader monitors and keeps track of whether the author is making sense by asking: What is the author trying to say here? What does the author mean? Periodic "reading checks" within chapter sections help students to decide what's important and what's not important while reading. Strategic readers know how to tell the difference between main ideas and supporting ideas and how to extend thinking about the text after reading. Section review activities in each chapter help students to see the importance of analyzing, organizing, evaluating, and synthesizing information encountered during reading.

Internet-Supported Research and Collaboration: Curriculum-Based Learning Possibilities

JUDI HARRIS, University of Texas at Austin

Are you considering whether, or how, to use the Internet in your teaching? Booker T. Washington once wrote: *Nothing ever comes to one, that is worth having, except as a result of hard work.*

Up From Slavery: An Autobiography (1901) Chapter 12
http://xroads.virginia.edu/~hyper/WASHINGTON/cover.html

Such is the case with worthwhile, curriculum-based use of on-line tools and resources. The learning curve seems steep at first; sufficient Internet access for students can be difficult to arrange; there is information online that is inappropriate for in-school perusal; Internet-enriched projects take more time to prepare than textbook-based learning. Yet carefully-planned and assiduously-assessed online collaboration and online research activities can help students to explore and understand curriculum content and process in ways not possible or as powerful as those available using traditional tools and methods.

The ideas that follow can help you to ensure that any hard work that you do to integrate use of Internet tools and resources into your curriculum will be time and effort well spent; that your students' curriculum-related online activity will be "worth it."

Telecollaboration and Teleresearch

Internet-supported, curriculum-based learning can take many forms, but is essentially either *online collaboration,* also called "telecollaboration," or *online research,* also called "teleresearch." Telecollaborative learning activities are those in which students communicate electronically with others. Teleresearch learning activities are those in which students locate and use on-line information. Online collaboration and research are frequently combined in larger-scale educational projects. Both can be done using text, still images, animated images, and sound. Both are available in either synchronous (immediate) or asynchronous (delayed) modes. Both can reproduce what students already do when they collaborate and do research using earlier-vintage learning materials. Yet to make these new opportunities worth the time, effort, and other resources necessary to bring them into the classroom, it is important to use the new tools in new and powerful ways.

Collaborative online learning activities can offer many educational benefits to their participants. The nature of these benefits depends, in large part, upon the specifics of each activity's design, and how well what the activity makes possible educationally matches the needs and preferences of participating students. In general, curriculum-based telecollaboration is most appropriate when students can be well served by:

- Being exposed to multiple points of view, perspectives, beliefs, interpretations, and/or experiences.
- Comparing, contrasting, and/or combining similar information collected in dissimilar locations.
- Communicating with a real audience using written language.
- Expanding their global awareness.

Doing research online can offer an ever-expanding wealth and variety of current information to learners. Whether this abundance helps or hinders students' curriculum-based learning depends, like online collaboration, upon the activity's design, and also upon students' information-seeking and information-appraising skills. In general, curriculum-based teleresearch is most appropriate when students can be well served by:

- Accessing information not available locally.
- Viewing information in multiple formats (e.g., text, graphics, video).
- Comparing and contrasting differing information on the same topic.
- Considering emerging and very recent information (e.g., interim reports of research studies in progress).
- Delving deeply into a particular area of inquiry.

What is the range of Internet-supported telecollaboration and teleresearch appropriate for classroom use? Telecollaborative *activity structures* and teleresearch *activity purposes* can be used as "thinking tools" to classify different educational uses of the Internet.

Telecollaborative Activity Structures

Activity structures are flexible frameworks that describe curriculum-based telecollaboration. They help us to capture what is essential about the structure of a learning activity, and communicate that in such a way as to encourage the creation of context-appropriate environments for learning. There are 18 telecollaborative activity structures that have been identified to date (Harris, 1998). The structures are grouped into three genres of online activity:

- *Interpersonal Exchanges* are those activities in which individuals talk electronically with other individuals, individuals talk with groups or groups talk with other groups.
- *Information Collection and Analysis* activities are those which involve students collecting, compiling, and comparing different types of interesting information.
- *Problem-Solving* activities promote critical thinking, collaboration, and problem-based learning.

The activity structures are summarized in the table on the following page.

Teleresearch Activity Purposes

Surprisingly, a similar set of online *research* activity frameworks doesn't exist. Teleresearch is differentiated upon a distinct basis: the apparent learning *purposes* for locating and using online information. These six purposes include:

- Practicing information-seeking and information-evaluating skills.
- Exploring a topic of inquiry or finding answers to a particular question.
- Reviewing multiple perspectives upon a topic.
- Collecting data.
- Assisting in authentic problem solving.
- Publishing information syntheses or critiques for others to use in teleresearch.

One of the best ways to suggest that students do online research is to participate in a "WebQuest;" a structured, Web-based activity that helps students to use online information for higher-level thinking. The WebQuest Page (**http://edweb.sdsu.edu/webquest/webquest.html**) offers indexes of curriculum-based WebQuests developed and used by teachers all over the world. It also provides guidelines, templates, and training materials for those wanting to create and use these rich, inquiry-based explorations of K-12 curricular ideas.

More information about telecollaborative activity structures and teleresearch activity purposes is available in my book (see Reference below). Many examples of K-12 online collaboration and research are indexed at the book's Web site, located at: **http://ccwf.cc.utexas.edu/~jbharris/ Virtual-Architecture/.**

GENRE	ACTIVITY STRUCTURE	DESCRIPTION
INTERPERSONAL EXCHANGE	Keypals	Students communicate with others outside their classrooms via email about curriculum-related topics chosen by teachers and/or students. Communications are usually one-on-one.
	Global Classrooms	Groups of students and teachers in different locations study a curriculum-related topic together during the same time period. Projects are frequently interdisciplinary and thematically organized.
	Electronic Appearances	Students have opportunities to communicate with subject matter experts and/or famous people via email, videoconferencing, or chatrooms. These activities are typically short-term (often one-time) and correspond to curricular objectives.
	Telementoring	Students communicate with subject matter experts over extended periods of time to explore specific topics in depth and in an inquiry-based format.
	Question & Answer	Students communicate with subject matter experts on a short-term basis as questions arise during their study of a specific topic. This is used only when all other information resources have been exhausted.
	Impersonations	Impersonation projects are those in which some or all participants communicate in character, rather than as themselves. Impersonations of historical figures and literary protagonists are most common.
INFORMATION COLLECTION AND ANALYSIS	Information Exchanges	Students and teachers in different locations collect, share, compare, and discuss information related to specific topics or themes that are experienced or expressed differently at each participating site.
	Database Creation	Students and teachers organize information they have collected or created into databases which others can use and to which others can add or respond.
	Electronic Publishing	Students create electronic documents, such as Web pages or word-processed newsletters, collaboratively with others. Remotely-located students learn from and respond to these publishing projects.
	Telefieldtrips	Telefieldtrips allow students to virtually experience places or participate in activities that would otherwise be impossible for them, due to monetary or geographic constraints.
	Pooled Data Analysis	Students in different places collect data of a particular type on a specific topic and then combine the data across locations for analysis.
PROBLEM SOLVING	Information Searches	Students are asked to answer specific, fact-based questions related to curricular topics. Answers (and often searching strategies) are posted in electronic format for other students to see.
	Peer Feedback Activities	Students are encouraged to provide constructive responses to the ideas and forms of work done by students in other locations, often reviewing multiple drafts of documents over time. These activities can also take the form of electronic debates or forums.
	Parallel Problem Solving	Students in different locations work to solve similar problems separately and then compare, contrast, and discuss their multiple problem-solving strategies online.
	Sequential Creations	Students in different locations sequentially create a common story, poem, song, picture, or other product online. Each participating group adds their segment to the common product.
	Telepresent Problem Solving	Students simultaneously engage in communications-based realtime activities from different locations. Developing brainstormed solutions to real-world problems via teleconferencing is a popular application of this structure.
	Simulations	Students participate in authentic, but simulated, problem-based situations online, often while collaborating with other students in different locations.
	Social Action Projects	Students are encouraged to consider real and timely problems, then take action toward resolution with other students elsewhere. Although the problems explored are often global in scope, the action taken to address the problem is usually local.

NOTE: These definitions were co-written with Kara Dawson, University of Florida, and are based upon previously-published work by the author (Harris, 1998).

Activity Assessment

Before you and your students invest the time and energy necessary to transform an educational activity idea into a reality in your classroom, an important decision needs to be made. Stated succinctly, and in the form of a question, you must decide:

Is this potential educational use of the Internet "worth it" right now?

In other words,

- Will it enable us to do something worthwhile that was **not possible before**?

OR:

- Will it enable us to do something worthwhile **in a better way than before?**

Notice that the answers to these questions are temporary; they will change, over time, as we change, as our students change, and as the technical, informational, and interpersonal resources available to us change. Therefore, it is of vital importance to continue questioning ourselves in this manner, as new Internet-enriched collaboration and research opportunities emerge.

Reference

Harris, J. (1998). *Virtual architecture: Designing and directing curriculum-based telecomputing.* Eugene, OR: International Society for Technology in Education, http://www.iste.org/.

Program Components

Everyday Resources

Guided Reading Strategies

Graphic Organizer Activities

Main Idea Activities for Reteaching and Sheltered English

Audio Program in English and Spanish

Literature, Primary Source, and Biography Readings

Block Scheduling Handbook with Team Teaching Strategies

Hands-On History Activities: Classroom to Community

Creative Teaching Strategies

Citizenship Simulations and Case Studies

American History Political Cartoons with Activities and Teaching Suggestions

Geography Activities

American History Outline Maps with Teaching Suggestions

Writing About American History

Social Studies Skills Review

The Complete School Atlas

Technology Resources

One-Stop Planner CD–ROM with TestBuilder Software for Macintosh® and Windows®

Audio CD Program in English and Spanish

Holt Researcher: American History CD–ROM

Global Skill Builder CD–ROM

American History Simulations CD–ROM

American History Interactive Maps CD–ROM

International Cindy Award, Gold Medal

American Music Audio CD Program

The American Nation Video Program in English and Spanish

American History Visual Resources

Art in American History Transparencies

go.hrw.com Internet Activities

Smithsonian Institution Internet Connections and Lesson Plans

Assessment Resources

The **Standardized Test Practice Handbook** helps your students gear up for future standardized tests. Content-specific practice exposes them to a variety of question types commonly found on today's standardized assessments.

Chapter Tutorials for Students, Parents, Mentors, and Peers

Daily Quizzes

Chapter and Unit Tests

Sheltered English Chapter and Unit Tests

Portfolio Activities and Alternative Assessment Handbook

One-Stop Planner with Test Generator

Test Generator on the One-Stop Planner

Test-Item Listing

Contents

Civil War shoulder plate pierced by a bullet

American Beginnings

Program Pacing Guide can be found on the **One-Stop Planner** or online at **www.hrw.com/amnat**

A Nation Transformed

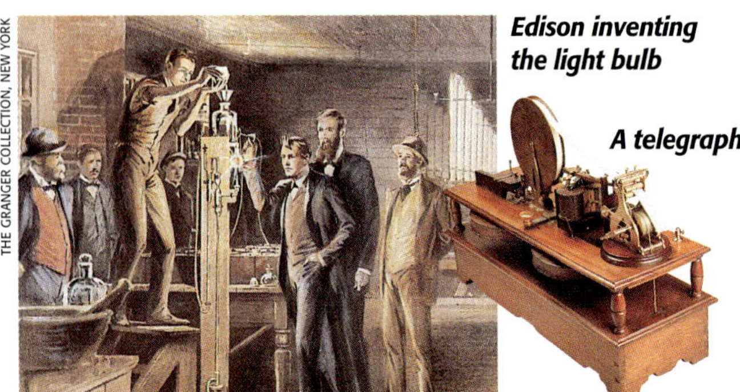

Edison inventing the light bulb

A telegraph

Fan from the 1800s

Program Pacing Guide can be found on the **One-Stop Planner** or online at **www.hrw.com/amnat**

Battle of Manila Bay in the Spanish-American War

A World Power

Program Pacing Guide can be found on the **One-Stop Planner** or online at **www.hrw.com/amnat**

Prosperity and Crisis

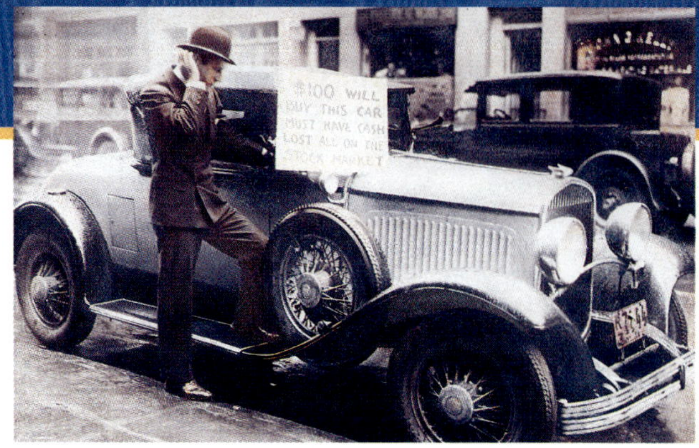

THE GRANGER COLLECTION, NEW YORK

Aftermath of 1929 stock market crash

King Oliver's Creole Jazz Band

Program Pacing Guide can be found on the **One-Stop Planner** or online at **www.hrw.com/amnat**

World Conflicts

Eisenhower campaign button

Program Pacing Guide can be found on the **One-Stop Planner** or online at **www.hrw.com/amnat**

A Changing Home Front

Women's rights march and civil rights button

Program Pacing Guide can be found on the **One-Stop Planner** or online at **www.hrw.com/amnat**

Modern Times

Ronald Reagan campaign button

John Glenn (waving) and fellow astronauts, 1998

Program Pacing Guide can be found on the **One-Stop Planner** or online at **www.hrw.com/amnat**

America in a Global Context

Boeing 747

South African civil rights leader Nelson Mandela

Program Pacing Guide can be found on the **One-Stop Planner** or online at **www.hrw.com/amnat**

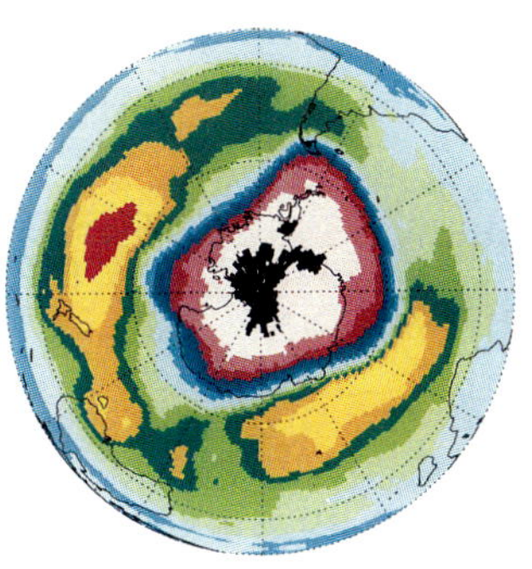

Image of Earth's ozone layer

Reference Section

Features

Norman Rockwell's Liberty Girl

BIOGRAPHIES AND PRESIDENTIAL *Lives*

Postage stamps of U.S. leaders

Changing Ways

Historical Documents

Science & Technology

Model T

Advertisement from the 1950s

Strategies for Success

Then and Now

Trucks transporting goods from American-owned factories in Mexico

Charts

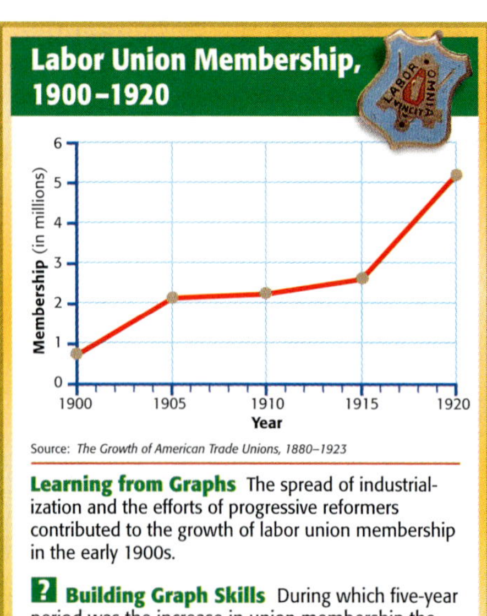

Source: *The Growth of American Trade Unions, 1880–1923*

Learning from Graphs The spread of industrialization and the efforts of progressive reformers contributed to the growth of labor union membership in the early 1900s.

? Building Graph Skills During which five-year period was the increase in union membership the smallest? During which period was it the largest?

Maps

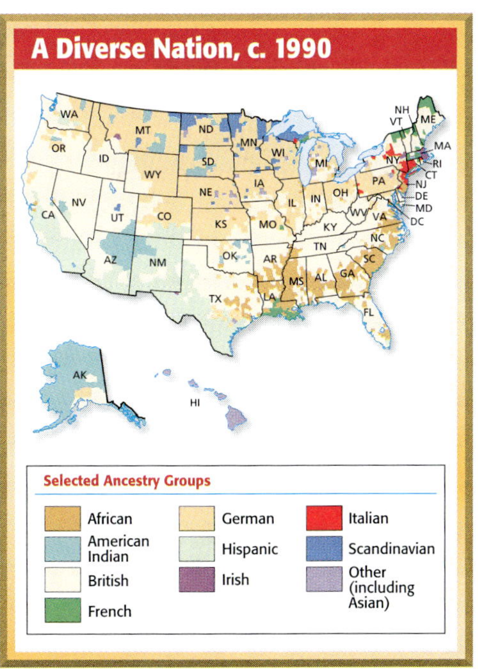
A Diverse Nation, c. 1990
WA
MT
ND
MN
OR
ID
SD
WI
MI
WY
NE
IA
NV
UT
CO
IL
IN
OH
PA
CA
KS
MO
KY
WV
VA
AZ
NM
OK
AR
TN
NC
SC
MS
AL
GA
TX
LA
FL
NH
VT
ME
MA
NY
RI
CT
NJ
DE
MD
DC
AK
HI
Selected Ancestry Groups
African
American Indian
British
French
German
Hispanic
Irish
Italian
Scandinavian
Other (including Asian)

Time Lines

Themes in American History

The American Nation Civil War to Present begins every chapter with a set of theme statements. These statements are drawn from seven broad themes central to American history: Global Relations, our Constitutional Heritage, Democratic Values, Technology and Society, Cultural Diversity, Geographic Diversity, and Economic Development. They provide a context for the historical events in each chapter. This context will help you understand the connections between historical events and see how past events are relevant to today's social, political, and economic concerns.

As you begin each chapter, examine the theme statements and agree or disagree with them based on your own experiences or prior knowledge. Keep a record of your answers in a themes journal. As you read the chapter, explore how the theme statements relate to its history. When you finish reading the chapter, look back at your answers to the theme statements and note whether you would now answer them differently. By using your themes journal to trace the themes through the book, you will be able to see how each theme has developed over time.

Global Relations

This theme asks you to explore the global context in which the United States exists. From its settlement by Asian immigrants tens of thousand of years ago to the first arrival of European, African, and later Asian immigrants to today, America has influenced and been influenced by other parts of the world. Your exploration of the Global Relations theme will help you understand how the relations the United States has maintained with other countries over time have affected our nation's political, social, and economic development. It will also help you appreciate the problems and possibilities of living in an interdependent world community.

U.S. gold dollar

Constitutional Heritage

The study of American history would not be complete without an exploration of the Constitution, the legal framework that structures our democratic government. The Constitutional Heritage theme asks you to think about the origin of the Constitution and the ways in which the Constitution has been interpreted and amended over time. You will explore how the laws and government institutions have evolved through amendments, Supreme Court rulings, and congressional actions. Your examination of this theme will encourage you to understand the part individuals play in promoting the goals—such as justice and democratic rights—enshrined in the Constitution's preamble.

Democratic Values

This theme concerns the continuing struggle to define and protect such democratic values as individual liberty, political representation, freedom of religion, and freedom of speech. The Democratic Values theme asks you to consider the impact of changing social, economic, and political conditions on these values. For example, in the years before the Civil War, enslavement of African Americans—a violation of the democratic value of individual liberty—was practiced in the South. Some slaveholders justified this practice by arguing that the democratic value of right to property should be the overriding concern. It took a bloody civil war to settle the issue. Conflicts over democratic values recur throughout American history, and this theme explores the attempts at resolution.

African American school, late 1800s

xviii

Technology and Society

From computers in your homes and classrooms to communications satellites orbiting the Earth, technology influences many aspects of society. The Technology and Society theme asks you to trace technological developments and explore their influence on the economy and our lives.

Cultural Diversity

Different ethnic, racial, and religious groups have all contributed to America's rich and unique culture. The Cultural Diversity theme asks you to explore how the United States has dealt with diversity from the days of the first encounters between American Indians and Spanish and English settlers to its status today as a haven for immigrants from all over the world.

Geographic Diversity

The majestic old-growth forests of the Pacific Northwest, the rich coal deposits of the Appalachian and Rocky Mountains, the oil fields of Texas and Alaska, and the tropical plantations on the volcanic islands of Hawaii have all enriched the U.S. economy. The Geographic Diversity theme asks you to consider how the development of the nation's diverse natural resources has shaped U.S. society, politics, and the economy. The theme also explores how government and public awareness of the effects of natural resource development has changed over time.

The Sojourner *rover on Mars*

Economic Development

The United States has developed one of the world's strongest economies. The Economic Development theme explores the influence of the nation's economy on domestic politics and social life and on international relations. The theme asks you to explore the implications of such economic issues as trade, depression and expansion, poverty, taxation, government regulation, and the status of workers.

Geography Themes

History and geography share many common elements. Geography describes how physical environments affect human events and how people influence the environment. Geographers have developed five themes:—location, place, region, movement, and human-environment interaction—to organize information.

Location describes a site's position. It is the spot on the earth where something is found, often expressed in terms of its position in relation to other places.

Place refers to the physical features and human influences that define a site and make it different from other sites. Physical features include landscape, climate, and vegetation. Human influences include land use, architecture, and population size.

Region is the common cultural or physical features of an area that distinguish it from other areas. One region may be different from another area because of physical characteristics, such as landforms or climate, or because of cultural features, such as dominant languages or religions.

Movement describes the way people interact as they travel, communicate, and trade goods and services. Movement includes human migration as well as the exchange of goods and ideas.

Human-Environment Interaction deals with the ways in which people interact with their natural environments, such as clearing forests, irrigating the land, and building cities. This theme is particularly important to the study of history in that it shows how people shape and are shaped by their surroundings.

Critical Thinking

and the Study of History

Throughout *The American Nation Civil War to Present,* you are asked to think critically about the events and issues that have shaped U.S. history. Critical thinking is the reasoned judgment of information and ideas. The development of critical thinking skills is essential to effective citizenship. Such skills empower you to exercise your civic rights and responsibilities. Helping you develop critical thinking skills is an important goal of *The American Nation.* The following 14 critical thinking skills appear in the sections reviews and chapter reviews.

1 Using Historical Imagination involves mentally stepping into the past to consider an event or situation as people at the time would have considered it. In putting yourself in their place, you might note whether they lived before or after historical turning points. Keep in mind what the people of the time knew and did not know. For example, to grasp the experience of a soldier wounded in the Civil War, you need to understand that little was known then about the causes of disease and infection.

2 Understanding Geography involves using the five themes of geography to analyze and understand the relationship between geography and historical events. In the United States, geography has greatly shaped the nation's economy, society, and political developments. The critical thinking skill allows students to explore how this has occurred.

An electric streetcar in New York City

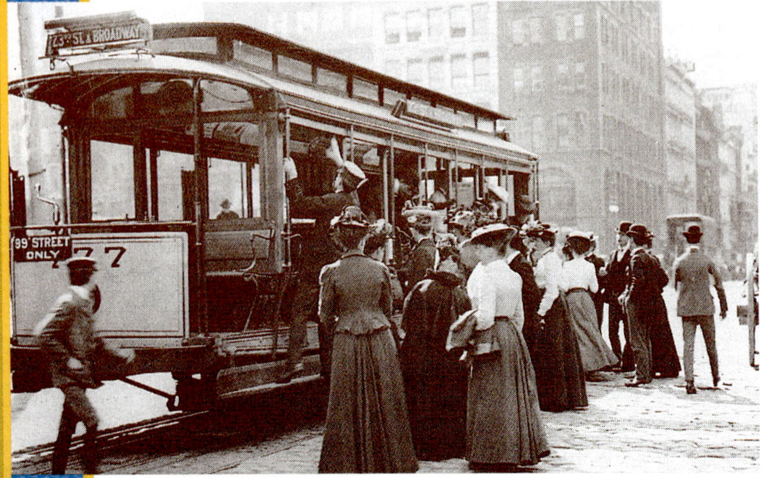

3 Recognizing Point of View means identifying the factors that influence the outlook of an individual or group. A person's point of view includes belief and attitudes that are shaped by factors such as age, gender, religion, race, and economic status. This critical thinking skill helps us examine why people see things as they do and reinforces the realization that people's views may change over time or with a change in circumstances.

4 Comparing and Contrasting examines events, situations, or points of view for their similarities and differences. *Comparing* focuses on both the similarities and the differences. *Contrasting* focuses only on the differences. For example, a comparison between the years immediately following World War I and II would note that both postwar economies had to adjust to decreased defense spending and the job requirements of returning veterans. In contrast, the United States was more involved in international politics after World War II.

5 Identifying Cause and Effect is part of interpreting the relationships between historical events. A cause is any action that leads to an event. The outcome of that action is an effect. To explain historical events, historians often point out multiple causes and effects. For example, economic and political differences between the North and South, as well as the issue of slavery, brought about the Civil War—which in turn had many far-reaching effects.

6 Analyzing is the process of breaking something down into its parts and examining the relationships between them. Analyzing enables you to better understand the whole. To analyze the outcome of the 1912 presidential election, for example, you might study the results state by state to show how

xx

The Homecoming ***by Norman Rockwell***

Woodrow Wilson won a majority in the electoral college without winning a majority of the popular vote.

7 Assessing Consequences means studying an action, an event, or a trend to predict its long-term effects—and to judge the desirability of those effects. *Consequences* often are effects that are indirect and unintended. They may appear long after the event that led to them.

8 Distinguishing Fact from Opinion means separating the facts about something from what people say about it. A fact can be proved or observed; an opinion, on the other hand, is a personal belief or conclusion. We often hear facts and opinions mixed in everyday conversation—as well as in advertising, in political debate, and in historical sources. Although some opinions can be supported by facts, in an argument, opinions do not carry as much weight as facts.

9 Identifying Values involves recognizing the core beliefs that a person or group holds. Values are more deeply held than opinions and are less likely to change. Values commonly concern matters of right and wrong and may be viewed as desirable in and of themselves. The values of freedom and justice, for example, motivated the struggle to abolish slavery, just as the value of equality has been a foundation of the civil rights and women's movements.

10 Hypothesizing means forming a possible explanation for an event, a situation, or a problem. A hypothesis is not a proven fact. Rather, it is a theory based on available evidence and tested against new evidence. A historian, for example, might hypothesize that the Civil War was primarily the result of a power struggle between the ruling classes of the North and South over control of the United States' western frontier. The historian would then organize the evidence to support this hypothesis and challenge other explanations of the war's causes.

11 Synthesizing is combining information and ideas from several sources or points in time to gain a new understanding of a topic or event. Much of the narrative writing in this book is a synthesis. It pulls together historical data from many sources and perspectives from many people into a chronological story of our nation.

12 Problem Solving is the process of reviewing a situation and then making decisions and recommendations for improving or correcting it. Before beginning, however, the problem must be identified and stated. For instance, in considering a solution to the nation's drug-abuse crisis, you might state the problem in terms of the relationship of drug addiction to violent crime. You would then propose and evaluate possible solutions or courses of action, selecting the one you think is best and giving reasons for your choice.

13 Evaluating assesses the significance or overall importance of something, such as the success of a reform movement or the legacy of a president. You should base your judgment on standards that others will understand and are likely to share. An evaluation of the early women's movement, for example, might assess the short- and long-term effects of its focus on women's suffrage.

ADA supporter

14 Taking a Stand is identifying an issue, deciding what you think about it, and persuasively expressing your position. Your stand should be based on specific information. In taking a stand, even on controversial or emotional issues, state your position clearly and give reasons to support it.

American Beginnings

Prologue: The New Nation

CHAPTER 1

As Paleo-Indians were populating North and South America, Asian and African kingdoms formed profitable trade networks. In the 1500s, competition for new trade routes led European countries to establish American colonies. In 1776 thirteen of Britain's North American colonies declared their independence. After winning the Revolutionary War, Americans created a new central government under the U.S. Constitution. The nation expanded to the Pacific Ocean, acquiring a large portion of its present-day territory in the Mexican War. Sectional tensions between the North and the South increased over time.

EXAMINING THE VISUAL RECORD

Ask students the questions below. Then use the annotations to expand class discussion.

1 ***Who might the woman holding the American flag have been? Why might she have been waving the flag?*** According to one of John Greenleaf Whittier's poems, Barbara Frietschie greeted Stonewall Jackson's attack on Frederick, Maryland, by heroically flying the American flag in the face of the invading army. However, Whittier commemorated the wrong woman. According to eyewitness accounts, Mary Quantrell waved her flag at the Confederates and got no response from Jackson. Frietschie, on the other hand, brought her flag out when the Union soldiers returned.

2 ***Why might the Confederate leader, Stonewall Jackson, appear to be heroically holding his men back?*** John Greenleaf Whittier claimed that when Stonewall Jackson saw Frietschie's brave gesture, "the noble nature within him stirred" and he told his troops, "Who touches a hair on yon gray head/Dies like a dog!"

ACTIVITY: Tell students to imagine that they are one of the people in the painting. Have each student write a short description of the scene.

UNIT 1

American Beginnings

Prehistory–1900

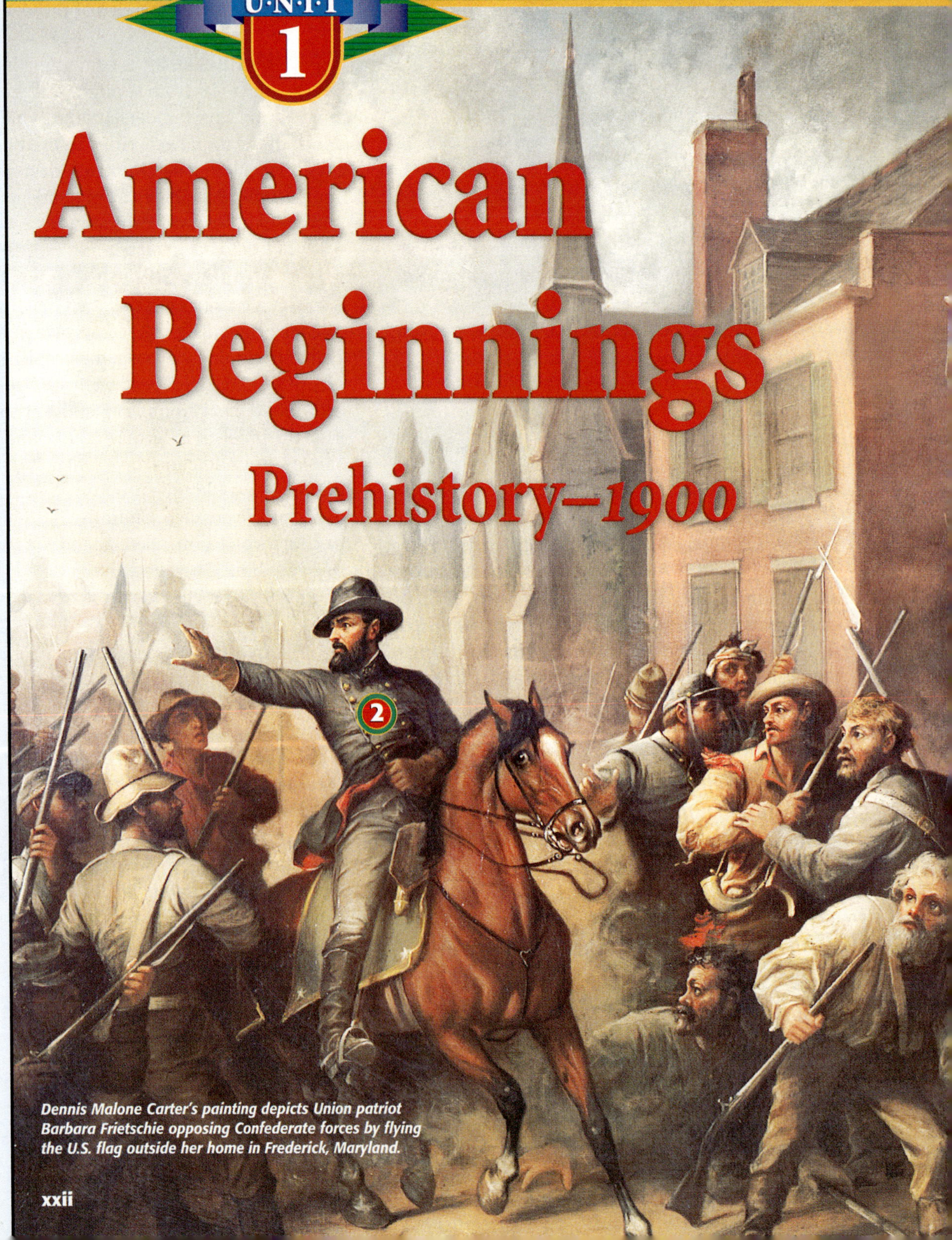

Dennis Malone Carter's painting depicts Union patriot Barbara Frietschie opposing Confederate forces by flying the U.S. flag outside her home in Frederick, Maryland.

Chapter 2 The Civil War

The Civil War began in April 1861, when Confederate forces attacked Fort Sumter in South Carolina. Southern forces were able to win the early battles of the war. Ultimately, however, the North's advantage in population and economic resources allowed Union forces to defeat the Confederacy. In April 1865 the Confederate Army surrendered to the Union Army. The Civil War devastated both sides. The Thirteenth Amendment, which was ratified in December 1865, formally abolished the institution of slavery.

Chapter 3 Reconstruction and the New South

After the Civil War, the United States had to rebuild its society and political system to assimilate many freed slaves. The Republican-led Congress passed legislation to help former slaves and to protect the rights of African Americans. African Americans eagerly participated in Reconstruction. However, many white people in the United States objected to African American rights and Reconstruction. In the 1870s, Reconstruction gradually slowed as a depression overtook the country. Jim Crow laws and the Supreme Court's decision in *Plessy* v. *Ferguson* helped to create two societies—black and white, separate and unequal—in the South.

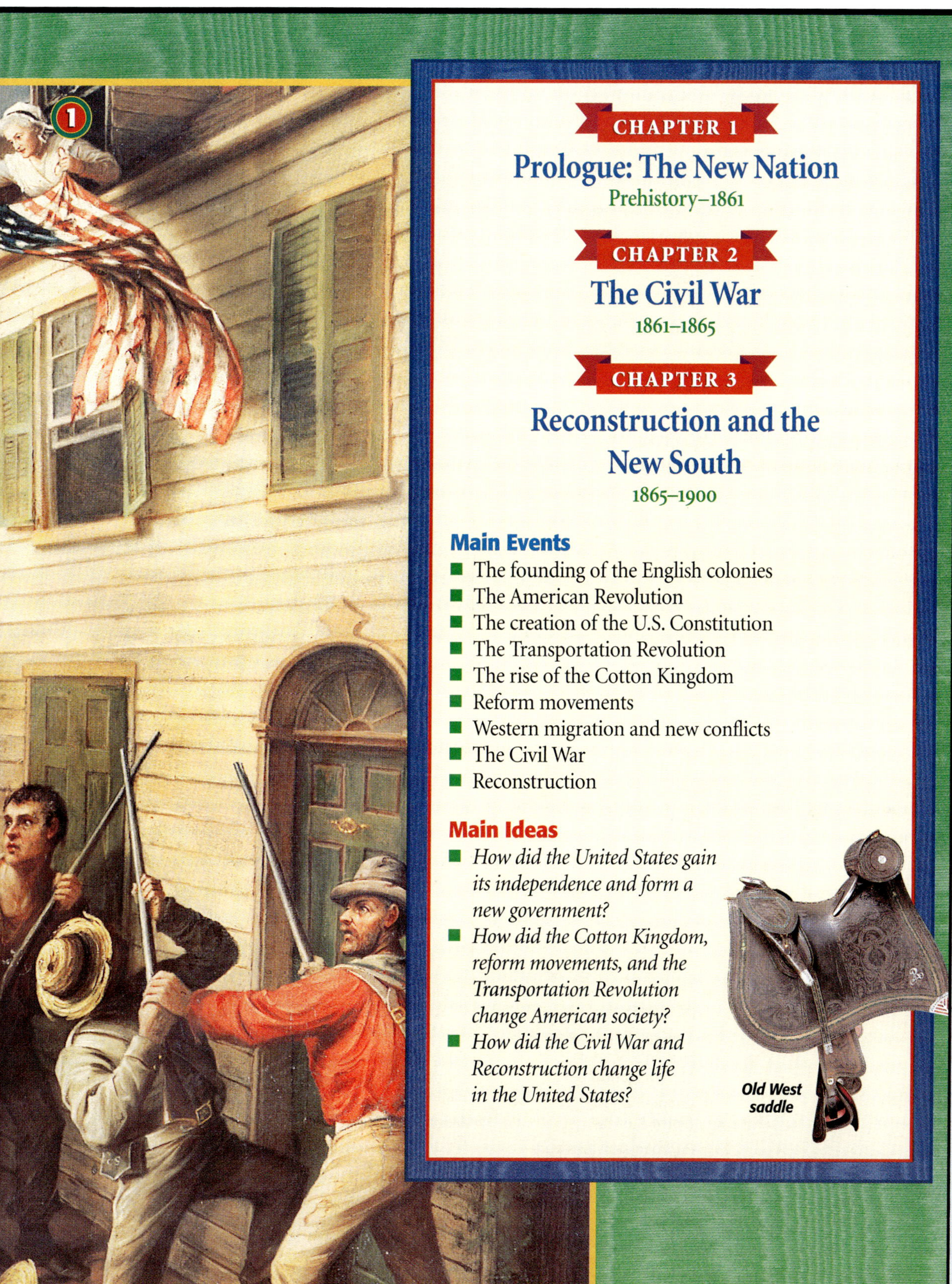

1

CHAPTER 1

Prologue: The New Nation

Prehistory–1861

CHAPTER 2

The Civil War

1861–1865

CHAPTER 3

Reconstruction and the New South

1865–1900

Main Events

- The founding of the English colonies
- The American Revolution
- The creation of the U.S. Constitution
- The Transportation Revolution
- The rise of the Cotton Kingdom
- Reform movements
- Western migration and new conflicts
- The Civil War
- Reconstruction

Main Ideas

- *How did the United States gain its independence and form a new government?*
- *How did the Cotton Kingdom, reform movements, and the Transportation Revolution change American society?*
- *How did the Civil War and Reconstruction change life in the United States?*

Old West saddle

INTRODUCE UNIT 1

Main Events

List the Main Events on the chalkboard. Ask students to select two and briefly describe what they know about the topics. Have volunteers share their descriptions. Later, when you have finished Unit 1, ask students to return to their original descriptions and revise them using the information they learned in the unit. Students should also create new descriptions for the other Main Events.

Main Ideas

Ask each student to read the Main Ideas and briefly answer the questions in writing. Share the ***Consider*** points with students as necessary. Later, when you have finished Unit 1, ask students to return to their original answers and revise them using the information they learned in the unit.

Colonization of the Americas

Consider:

- why European nations colonized the Americas
- why thirteen North American colonies sought independence

Reconstruction Outcomes

Consider:

- the response of many white southerners to African Americans' attempts to exercise their civil rights
- the effect of Jim Crow laws and *Plessy* v. *Ferguson*

Prologue: The New Nation

CHAPTER PLANNING GUIDE

	Section Lesson Objectives	Print Resources	Multimedia Resources	Sheltered English Resources
Section 1 The World by 1500, pp. 4–9	1 Identify the advances made by early Native American culture groups. 2 Describe how trade and exploration affected societies in Africa, Asia, and Europe. 3 Explain how the Spanish and English colonies in the Americas were settled. 4 Analyze the effect European settlement had on American Indians.	▶ Guided Reading Strategy 1.1 ▶ Literature Reading 1: American Indian Poetry ▶ Section 1 Review, p. 9 ▶ Daily Quiz 1.1	▶ One-Stop Planner, Lesson 1.1 ▶ Holt Researcher: American History CD–ROM	▶ Main Idea Activity for Reteaching and Sheltered English 1.1
Section 2 Creating a New Nation, pp. 10–16	1 Summarize how and why the colonies won their independence from Great Britain. 2 Explain how the Constitution formed the basis of a new government. 3 Identify domestic and foreign challenges that faced the new nation. 4 Discuss why the United States fought the War of 1812.	▶ Guided Reading Strategy 1.2 ▶ Geography Activity 1: The Native Americans ▶ Biography Reading 1: Pontiac ▶ Section 2 Review, p. 16 ▶ Daily Quiz 1.2	▶ One-Stop Planner, Lesson 1.2 ▶ The American Nation Video Program Segment: Designing a Nation; Teacher's Guide, pp. 27–32 ▶ Holt Researcher: American History CD–ROM	▶ Main Idea Activity for Reteaching and Sheltered English 1.2
Section 3 Growth and Change, pp. 21–27	1 Describe what changes took place in foreign and domestic policy in the early 1800s. 2 Discuss how industrialization and immigration affected northern society. 3 Explain how southern society and the slave system were organized. 4 Identify the social issues reformers addressed in the early to mid-1800s.	▶ Guided Reading Strategy 1.3 ▶ Primary Source Reading 1: Escape to Freedom ▶ Section 3 Review, p. 27 ▶ Daily Quiz 1.3	▶ One-Stop Planner, Lesson 1.3 ▶ American Music Selection 1: "The Erie Canal" ▶ Holt Researcher: American History CD–ROM ▶ HRW Web site	▶ Main Idea Activity for Reteaching and Sheltered English 1.3
Section 4 Westward Expansion and Sectional Conflict, pp. 28–33	1 Analyze the causes of the Texas Revolution and the Mexican War. 2 Explain why Americans began to settle the West. 3 Discuss how politicians addressed the expansion of slavery. 4 Identify what events led to the secession of the southern states.	▶ Guided Reading Strategy 1.4 ▶ Graphic Organizer Activity 1: Changes over Time ▶ American History Outline Map 9: Conflict over Slavery ▶ Section 4 Review, p. 33 ▶ Daily Quiz 1.4	▶ One-Stop Planner, Lesson 1.4 ▶ Holt Researcher: American History CD–ROM	▶ Main Idea Activity for Reteaching and Sheltered English 1.4
Chapter Review and Assessment pp. 34–35		▶ Chapter 1 Review, pp. 34–35 ▶ Chapter 1 Tutorial for Students, Parents, Mentors, and Peers ▶ Chapter 1 Test (Form A or B) ▶ Portfolio Activities and Alternative Assessment Handbook, Chapter 1	▶ Audio Program, Chapter 1 (English and Spanish) ▶ Chapter 1 Test Generator (on the One-Stop Planner) ▶ Global Skill Builder CD–ROM ▶ HRW Web site	▶ Spanish Glossary ▶ Sheltered English Chapter 1 Test

CHAPTER OVERVIEW

The first people arrived in the Americas as long as 12,000 to 40,000 years ago. Early Native American cultures in North and South America developed in relative isolation while trade networks connected kingdoms of Africa, Asia, and Europe. These networks soon led European explorers like Christopher Columbus to the Americas. Spain, England, France, and the Netherlands established colonies there, often with disastrous results for American Indians.

Thirteen American colonies declared their independence from British rule in 1776. After the Revolutionary War, the United States faced the challenge of forming an entirely new government. George Washington served as the nation's first president. The United States faced economic and political change and growth in its early years. As the North and the South developed separate economies—one relying on manufacturing, the other on slave-based agriculture—their interests in the Union came into conflict. The United States also expanded westward, which helped lead the country toward sectional conflict.

TIME TAMERS

Block Scheduling

The teacher lesson plans for each section offer a variety of activity choices to help you present the material in a block scheduling format. For further suggestions on block scheduling, see the **Block Scheduling Handbook with Team Teaching Strategies**, pp. 1–6.

Hands-On History Activities:

Classroom to Community The **Hands-On History Activities** help students make meaningful connections between events in American history and those in their own hometown. You may wish to use the Chapter 1 Activity, History of Transportation in Your Community, to extend the chapter lessons, as alternative assessment, or as a block scheduling option.

Portfolio Projects

The American Nation includes multiple portfolio projects in each Pupil's Edition chapter review, as well as each unit review. Chapter 1 Portfolio Project options on p. 35 include the following:

1. Students will **create a poster**.
2. Students will **conduct an interview**.
3. Students will **develop a series of drawings and captions**.

The American Nation
INTERNET RESOURCE DIRECTORY

To access online materials for this chapter, go to go.hrw.com and type in the keywords listed below.

HRW ONLINE RESOURCES
GO TO: go.hrw.com

Online Maps
KEYWORD: SE1 Maps1
- North America in 1754
- Federalist/Antifederalist

Online Charts
KEYWORD: SE1 Charts1
- War of 1812
- Slaveholding Families, 1850

Online Reading Support
KEYWORD: SE1 Strategies1

Online Rubrics
KEYWORD: SE1 Rubrics

CHAPTER ENRICHMENT LINKS
Use these Web links to extend and enrich student learning for Chapter 1.
GO TO: go.hrw.com
KEYWORD: SE1 Ch1

CHAPTER INTERNET ACTIVITIES
GO TO: go.hrw.com
- Pupil's Edition Student Activity
  KEYWORD: SE1 Columbus
  (Students explore Columbus's voyage and the later *encomienda* system.)
- Teacher's Edition Student Activity
  KEYWORD: SE1 Printing
  (Students examine the printing press.)
- Teacher's Edition Student Activity
  KEYWORD: SE1 Erie
  (Students investigate the Erie Canal.)

ADDITIONAL
RESOURCES

Books for Teachers

Gundersen, Joan R. *To Be Useful to the World: Women in Revolutionary America, 1740–1790.* Twayne, 1996. Focuses on gender roles during the Revolutionary period.

Potter, David M. *The Impending Crisis, 1848–1861.* Harper, 1976. Presents an overview of the pre–Civil War era; regarded as a classic by many historians.

Books for Students

Fleming, Thomas. *Liberty! The American Revolution.* Viking, 1997. Offers a readable overview of the Revolution. Particularly appropriate for students reading below grade level.

Wallace, Anthony F. C. *The Long, Bitter Trail: Andrew Jackson and the Indians.* Hill and Wang, 1993. Examines non-Indian perceptions of American Indians during the removal era.

Primary Sources from the Period

Patrick, John J., ed. *Founding the Republic: A Documentary History.* Greenwood Press, 1995. Includes letters and proclamations from both sides.

Stowe, Harriet Beecher. *Uncle Tom's Cabin.* Harper and Row, 1965. Offers an influential indictment of slavery.

Multimedia Materials

As It Was in Colonial America. Video, 59 min. January Productions. Details the lifestyles of colonial Americans.

The Dred Scott Decision. Video, 15 min. Afro-Am Distributing. Reviews the *Dred Scott* decision.

CHAPTER 1

Before You Read

Build on What You Know

Ask students to answer the following questions.

Why might the study of Asian, African, and European history be important to the study of American history?

Consider:

- the geographic origins of the first Americans
- the eventual connections between the different countries

What types of conflicts might have arisen between Great Britain and its colonies?

Consider:

- the issue of taxation
- the importance of political representation

exploring the time line

AMERICAN EVENTS

GEOGRAPHIC DIVERSITY

5000 B.C. ■ The Spread of Crops. The crops that Native Americans cultivated in present-day Mexico gradually spread to other locations in North America. Corn arrived in the eastern United States about A.D. 200, although it did not flourish for another 700 years. Beans arrived a century or two later. After the arrival of corn and beans in North America, many Native American tribes abandoned their local crops.

CRITICAL THINKING How might the crops cultivated in present-day Mexico have made their way to other locations in North America?

ANSWER: Answers will vary. Some students might suggest that traders and trade networks carried the seeds from Mexico to an area that is now part of the eastern United States.

CHAPTER 1

Prehistory–1861

Prologue: The New Nation

Stone tools used to grind corn

A navigator's astrolabe

5000 B.C.
Daily Life
Communities in Mexico cultivate corn.

A.D. 610
Daily Life
Muhammad receives a vision that directs him to establish the religion of Islam.

c. 850
Science and Technology
Arabs develop an improved astrolabe.

1521
Politics
Hernán Cortés captures the Aztec capital of Tenochtitlán.

5000 B.C. — A.D. 1 — 1500

2000 B.C.
Business and Finance
Trade routes begin to spread from the eastern Mediterranean throughout Europe.

A.D. 40
World Events
One of the earliest Christian churches is established in the Greek city of Corinth.

The printing press designed by Johannes Gutenberg

1452
Science and Technology
Johannes Gutenberg develops a printing press that uses movable type.

Before You Read

Build on What You Know

To understand America's diverse culture, it is necessary to know about the many different people and events that contributed to the development of the United States. In this chapter you will learn about how America came to be settled first by Native Americans and later by European colonists. You will also learn how colonists won their independence from Great Britain and founded the United States of America. Finally, you will examine how the new nation faced many challenges during its first 80 years of existence.

2

Think About Themes

*To help students create their Themes Journal entries, share the following examples of appropriate **agree/disagree** statements.*

Economic Development

Agree European explorers went in search of a direct trade route to the Indies.

Disagree Puritans came to North America to escape religious persecution.

Democratic Values

Agree The writers of the Constitution included several compromises in the document in order to satisfy as many Americans as possible.

Disagree The Spanish introduced the *encomienda* system in the Americas with little regard for the desires of American Indians.

Geographic Diversity

Agree The differing interests of the North and the South led to the Civil War.

Disagree The thirteen American colonies fought together for independence from Great Britain.

An early colonial tobacco plantation

Poster for a theatrical performance of Uncle Tom's Cabin

1627 Business and Finance Virginia exports 500,000 pounds of tobacco.

1640 The Arts The *Bay Psalm Book* is the first book published in the English colonies.

1721 Daily Life Regular postal service is established between London and New England.

1755 The Arts Mission Concepción is completed in San Antonio.

1775 Politics The Revolutionary War begins in Massachusetts at Lexington and Concord.

1789 World Events The French Revolution begins.

1803 The Arts Benjamin Latrobe takes over the construction of the U.S. Capitol.

1807 World Events Great Britain's Parliament abolishes the slave trade in the British Empire.

1846 Business and Finance Maine becomes the first state to prohibit the sale of alcohol.

1852 The Arts *Uncle Tom's Cabin* is published.

1861 Politics The Confederate States of America is formed.

1600 | 1700 | 1800 | 1861

The storming of the Bastille during the French Revolution

Think About Themes

*Decide whether you **agree** or **disagree** with the following statements. Note why in your journal.*

Economic Development The promise of wealth is the most important motivation for people to settle and explore new lands.

Democratic Values The desires of all people in a society must be met when making new laws and policies.

Geographic Diversity People in different geographic regions have deeply conflicting political interests.

exploring the time line

GLOBAL EVENTS

internet**connect**

TOPIC: Printing Press
GO TO: go.hrw.com
KEYWORD: SE1 Printing

Have students access the Internet through the HRW Web site to conduct research on the history of the printing press. Then have each student create an annotated time line displaying its transformation over time.

3

SECTION 1

After completing Section 1, students should be able to:

OBJECTIVE 1 *Identify the advances made by early Native American culture groups.*

OBJECTIVE 2 *Describe how trade and exploration affected societies in Africa, Asia, and Europe.*

OBJECTIVE 3 *Explain how the Spanish and English colonies in the Americas were settled.*

OBJECTIVE 4 *Analyze the effect European settlement had on American Indians.*

LET'S GET STARTED!

Write the following topics on the chalkboard: *early Native American culture groups, trade and exploration during the Middle Ages, the Spanish and English colonies in America, effect of European settlement on American Indians.* To begin the class, have students write as much as they can about one or more of these topics in five minutes. Emphasize that students must write for the entire time. Ask volunteers to read their summaries to the class. Tell students that in Section 1 they will learn about exploration and settlement in the Americas.

SECTION 1 RESOURCES

PRINT
- Guided Reading Strategy 1.1
- Literature Reading 1: American Indian Poetry
- Section 1 Review, p. 9
- Daily Quiz 1.1

MULTIMEDIA
- One-Stop Planner, Lesson 1.1
- Holt Researcher: American History CD–ROM

SHELTERED ENGLISH
- Main Idea Activity for Reteaching and Sheltered English 1.1

✓ READING TO UNDERSTAND
To help students master the section objectives, have them answer the **READING CHECKS** and complete **Guided Reading Strategy 1.1** as they read the section.

SECTION 1

The World by 1500

OBJECTIVES

Read to understand:
1. what advances were made by early Native American culture groups
2. how trade and exploration affected societies in Africa, Asia, and Europe
3. how the Spanish and English colonies in the Americas were settled
4. what effect European settlement had on American Indians

KEY TERMS

Paleo-Indians
Agricultural Revolution
Maya
Aztec
Inca
Middle Ages
feudalism
Crusades
Renaissance
Middle Passage
Puritans
Pilgrims

KEY PEOPLE

Christopher Columbus
Hernán Cortés

"[The islands were] full of trees of a thousand kinds, so lofty that they seem to reach the sky. . . . Some of them were in flower, some in fruit. . . . And the nightingale was singing, and other birds of a thousand sorts, in the month of November."

—Christopher Columbus

Colored woodcut from 1572 showing fruit trees on the island of Hispaniola

In October 1492 the daring explorer Christopher Columbus landed on an island in the Bahamas. The landscape and vegetation were like nothing Columbus had seen before. At once he decided to stake a claim for Spain. "[We] broke out the royal banner, and the captain's two flags with the green cross," he recalled. The Spanish and later European explorers believed that these beautiful lands were theirs for the taking. This European contact brought profound changes to the Americas, as well as to Europe and Africa. Columbus's voyage introduced the Americas to the rest of the world, thus beginning a new era of trade, colonization, and cultural exchange.

Native Americans

Although scientists disagree on the exact dates, they agree that the first people in the Americas came from Asia between 12,000 and 40,000 years ago. These people crossed over a land bridge that at the time connected Asia and present-day Alaska.

Early Americans. Called **Paleo-Indians**, the first Americans followed animal herds throughout North America. They hunted animals for food and clothing. They also gathered edible plants. Sometime between 10,000 and 5000 B.C. the climate in the Americas grew warmer. Scientists believe that during this period some Paleo-Indians moved south. Over thousands of years, different culture groups—each with its own language, laws, rituals and ways of gathering food—came to populate the Americas.

The lifestyle of the Paleo-Indians changed dramatically with the **Agricultural Revolution**. This shift occurred when people first began domesticating, or adapting and controlling, animals and plants to meet specific human needs. Communities in Mexico had begun growing crops by 5000 B.C. By 1500 B.C. farming had also become established in the Andes, Central America, and what is now the southwestern United States. Farming increased the quantity and reliability of food supplies. As a result, human populations increased, and people began to settle permanently in one place. Eventually, villages and then cities formed.

Native American cultures. By the A.D. 1400s more than 650 distinct groups lived in the Americas. Some of the earliest large civilizations arose in the region known as Mesoamerica—present-day southern Mexico and Central America.

TEACH OBJECTIVE 1

LEVEL 1: Have students make a collage of images that represent advances made by early Native American culture groups. *(Collages might include the development of agriculture, the domestication of animals, and the creation of a number system, a written language, a canal system, and large cities.)* Ask volunteers to present their collages to the class and explain the significance of various images. Display students' completed collages on the classroom wall. **Sheltered English**

LEVEL 2: Have students list some important advances of early Native American culture groups. *(See the Level 1 lesson for the correct advances.)* Write these on the chalkboard and tell students to select the one they think was the most important advance. Then have students write a paragraph explaining why they consider it the most important. Ask volunteers to read their paragraphs to the class.

LEVEL 3: Organize students into triads and assign each triad one culture group—Paleo-Indians, the Maya, the Aztec, or the Inca. Have each triad create a few pages of a children's book about the important advances of its early Native American culture group. Encourage students to assign jobs within their triads—such as artist, editor, and writer—to help them complete the assignment quickly and efficiently.
Cooperative Learning

The civilization of the **Maya** arose about A.D. 300, primarily in what is now southern Mexico and Guatemala. The Maya devised a number system and wrote with glyphs—symbols and images that represent ideas. During the 1100s the **Aztec** conquered central Mexico. The Aztec Empire ruled several million people. Aztec society was highly organized, with a strict class system.

Similar advances took place throughout the Americas. The **Inca**, a farming culture, rose to power in the Andes of South America. By the mid-1400s the Inca Empire included 12 million people and was the largest in the Americas. The Inca created a complex system of roads to connect their towns. The various culture groups of North America had smaller populations than their counterparts to the south. Native Americans developed societies in the Southwest, the Eastern Woodlands, and the Southeast.

✔ **READING CHECK:** What advances were made by early Native American culture groups?

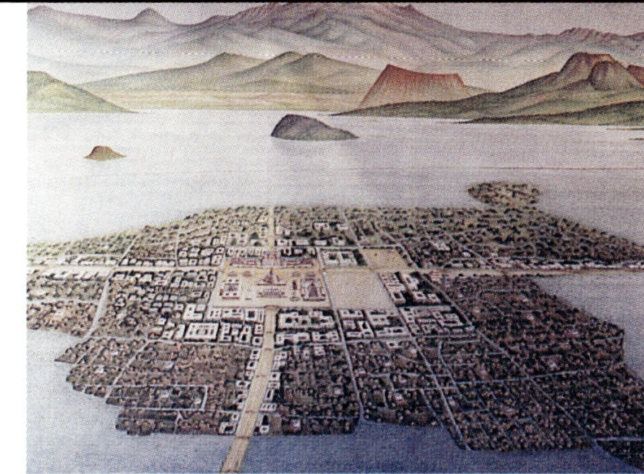

INTERPRETING THE VISUAL RECORD

Infrastructure. The capital of the Aztec Empire, Tenochtitlán, was built on an island. It used an advanced system of canals and had more than 300,000 residents. ***What does this image reveal about the organization of the Aztec Empire?***

Early World-Trading Kingdoms

While the cultures of North and South America developed in relative isolation from each other, trade networks already connected Africa, Asia, and Europe. These trade networks allowed for an exchange of cultural practices, goods, and ideas.

African and Asian trade. The Chinese Empire controlled much of ancient Asia. The Chinese made a variety of major technological advances, including the invention of paper and a system of printing. In the 1200s Mongol invaders from Central Asia overran China. The Mongols transformed China into the world's largest empire and opened China to trade with the West. After the Chinese regained control in the 1300s, China's leaders emphasized a policy of isolation.

Merchants continued to carry Chinese and other Asian goods to Africa. Many of these merchants were Muslims, who followed the religion of Islam. An Arab merchant named Muhammad had founded Islam in the early 600s. His teachings emphasized devotion to one God, whom he called Allah. By 750 vast areas of Africa, Asia, and Europe had become part of the Muslim Empire.

Trade helped many East African city-states grow powerful and wealthy. Prosperous kingdoms also arose in West Africa. In 772 Arab geographer al-Fazari described Ghana, the earliest of the West African kingdoms, as "the land of gold."

Europe during the Middle Ages. European trade with Africa and Asia had declined after the fall of the Roman Empire. From about A.D. 500 to 1500—a period called the **Middle Ages**—European society gradually recovered from the collapse of Roman authority. During the Middle Ages Europeans developed a system that historians call **feudalism**. In return for land and protection from invasion, feudal nobles pledged their loyalty and military assistance to more-powerful leaders. Feudal society operated under a rigid class system, with nobles at the top and serfs at the bottom. Daily life centered around villages and the influential Roman Catholic Church.

Copies of the Qur'an were carried by Muslim traders to introduce the Islamic faith to fellow travelers and merchants.

CULTURAL DIVERSITY

Aztec Warfare. The Aztec had a very pragmatic approach to warfare. They rarely destroyed enemies' cities and usually left the original rulers in power, requiring only that they pay tribute. This practice allowed the Aztec to receive payment without incurring the cost of rebuilding the conquered cities and ruling the conquered peoples. The Aztec then relied upon their tributaries to act as supply stations for Aztec armies. This strategy helped the Aztec build an enormous empire, but it had a dangerous weakness. If several defeated cities rebelled simultaneously, the Aztec would not have the means to end the uprisings.

CRITICAL THINKING Tell students that the Aztec did not have horses. How might the lack of horses have affected their military strategy?

ANSWER: Students might suggest that without horses the Aztec might have found it difficult to transport goods and to supply a far-flung army.

VISUAL RECORD ANSWER

Students might suggest that the Aztec had a highly organized empire.

TEACH OBJECTIVE 2

ALL LEVELS: To help students understand how trade and exploration affected the societies in Africa, Asia, and Europe, copy the following graphic organizer on the chalkboard, omitting the italicized answers. Have each student complete the graphic organizer. **Sheltered English**

Society	Effects of Trade and Exploration
Africa	*spread of Islam; brought wealth and power to city-states and kingdoms*
Asia	*China opened to West and became largest empire in the world; spread of Islam; spread of technology such as paper and printing*
Europe	*Crusades opened new trade routes; trade contributed to Renaissance, which spread new ideas and knowledge*

GLOBAL RELATIONS

The Children's Crusade. In 1212, thousands of children mounted their own crusade, hoping to win the Holy Land with love rather than force. In this Children's Crusade, a German boy named Nicholas traveled to Genoa, finally arriving with some 7,000 soldiers. Nicholas had told his troops that the waters of the Mediterranean Sea would part for them, but when the sea remained still, the crusade fell apart. Some participants returned home, while others traveled to Rome or Marseilles, where they were probably sold into slavery. Some historians argue that many of the soldiers on the Children's Crusade were not children at all, but rather people of all different ages. Other scholars argue that the story of the Children's Crusade in general has been manipulated and misrepresented throughout history.

CRITICAL THINKING Why might the story of the Children's Crusade have been misrepresented throughout history?

ANSWER: Students might suggest that the events have a romantic and tragic element that makes it an appealing story.

VISUAL RECORD ANSWER

Answers will vary. Students might suggest that the Europeans seem to be getting a better bargain.

INTERPRETING THE VISUAL RECORD

Exploration and trade. Europeans and Africans became increasingly involved in trade as European exploration continued. ***How is trade between Europeans and Africans depicted in this image?***

Feudal society began to change about 1100, partly as a result of the **Crusades**. The Crusades took place between 1096 and the late 1200s, when waves of Christian crusaders fought Muslims for control of Palestine in the eastern Mediterranean. The Crusades opened new trading routes for European merchants. Crusaders and traders returned home with classical Greek and Roman texts and new ideas in art, philosophy, and science. These ideas contributed to a rebirth of European learning and artistic creativity later known as the **Renaissance**. The Renaissance began in Italy in the 1300s and soon spread to the rest of Europe. The development of an improved printing press about 1450 greatly contributed to the spread of new ideas and knowledge.

The rise of nation-states took place near the end of the Middle Ages. National monarchies replaced feudal kingdoms throughout most of western Europe. England, France, and Spain were among the first to achieve national unity.

The Lure of Trade and Exploration

The new western European nations wanted direct access to Asian goods. Because Italian and Muslim merchants controlled the overland trade routes, explorers looked for a sea route to Asia. Advances such as astrolabes, compasses, and improved ship designs allowed Europeans to sail the stormy Atlantic Ocean.

Portugal led the way in exploration. By the 1430s Portuguese adventurers had explored and colonized islands off the northwest coast of Africa. In 1497 Vasco da Gama sailed around Africa and reached Asia the following year. Portugal's control of this sea route and its trading posts in Africa and Asia gave the Portuguese control of the East-West sea trade.

At first the Portuguese traded in spices and gold, but by the late 1500s the slave trade had become Portugal's major source of income. The slave trade devastated African society. Millions of Africans were taken from their homes and sold into slavery. Portuguese chronicler Gomes Eanes de Zurara described such scenes.

> **"Mothers would clasp their infants in their arms, and throw themselves on the ground to cover them with their bodies, . . . so that they could prevent their children from being separated from them."**

✔ **READING CHECK:** How did trade affect African, Asian, and European societies?

HOLT RESEARCHER — *Read More About It*

Free Find: Christopher Columbus

After reading about Christopher Columbus on the **Holt Researcher** CD–ROM, imagine that you are a reporter for a Spanish newspaper. Write a short article describing Columbus's adventures in America.

Christopher Columbus

Other European nations also desired a sea route to Asia. With Spain's financial support, explorer Christopher Columbus tried to reach Asia in 1492 by sailing west across the Atlantic Ocean.

Landing in the Americas. Columbus and his crew landed in the Bahamas, on an island he named San Salvador. The native people, whom Columbus called *Indios,* were mostly farmers, fishers, and traders.

TEACH OBJECTIVE 3

ALL LEVELS: Pair students and have one student create a time line of major events in the establishment of the Spanish colonies in the Americas while the other creates a time line of major events in the establishment of the English colonies. *(Spanish colonies' time lines should include: 1492—Columbus lands in the Americas; 1519—Cortés conquers the Aztec Empire; 1531—Pizarro attacks the Inca; 1780—Spanish America becomes one of the largest colonial empires. English colonies' time lines should include: 1607—first permanent settlement in Jamestown; 1620—Pilgrims found Plymouth; 1630s—Maryland is founded; 1663—Carolina is founded; 1664—English conquer Dutch colony of New Amsterdam; 1681—Pennsylvania is founded; 1732—Georgia founded as a buffer colony.)* Have students in all pairs combine their time lines to make one time line of the major events in the establishment of the Spanish and English colonies in the Americas. Have students write a paragraph comparing the colonies' development. Ask volunteers to read their essays to the class. Students may whish to include their time lines in their portfolios.

Sheltered English, Cooperative Learning

▶ASSIGNMENT *Have students write a poem that expresses the lure of the Americas for Spanish explorers and settlers. Ask volunteers to read their poems to the class.*

Columbus did not realize that he had not reached Asia. He ordered the construction of settlements and introduced the *encomienda* system to the Americas. Under this system Spanish colonists forced American Indians to work for them, often without pay. Some Spaniards, including Queen Isabella and the priest Bartolomé de Las Casas, protested this harsh treatment. Las Casas even praised American Indian culture.

> “Not only have [the Indians] shown themselves to be very wise peoples. . . . but they have equaled many diverse nations of the. . . past and present. . . and exceed by no small measure the wisest of all these.”

American Indians suffered from overwork and malnutrition under the *encomienda* system. Diseases introduced by the Europeans also proved deadly for American Indians, because they lacked resistance to these new sicknesses. In some areas the American Indian population was nearly wiped out by the mid-1500s. To replace native laborers, the Spanish imported African slaves.

The Spanish Empire. Spanish conquerors soon explored the Americas to claim land, gain riches, and spread Catholicism. Hernán Cortés arrived in Mexico in 1519. With the help of local American Indians, he conquered the wealthy Aztec Empire. Cortés built Mexico City on top of the ruins of the Aztec capital. He was soon appointed viceroy of the region and the Aztec were absorbed into the *encomienda* system. Another Spanish soldier, Francisco Pizarro, launched an attack on the Inca Empire in 1531. The Inca resisted for several years before the empire fell to the Spanish.

Spanish explorers spread out from both Central and South America. They established settlements in present-day Arizona, California, Florida, New Mexico, and Texas. By 1780 Spanish America comprised one of the largest colonial empires the world had ever known. Spanish settlers divided the land into farming communities and large ranching estates. They used American Indians as laborers.

One result of the Spanish conquests was the mixing of American Indian and European practices, creating a new culture. However, this cultural blending was sometimes limited by prejudice. For example, Spanish America developed a social structure in which individuals of full or mixed European heritage were given higher social status than Africans and American Indians.

The Catholic Church played a central role in the exploration and settlement of Spain's American colonies. Church-centered communities known as missions became a common form of Spanish settlement. Missionaries also attempted to convert American Indians to Catholicism. In their efforts to do so, however, they often criticized the traditional practices of Indian culture.

Then and Now

Sacred or Scientific Sites?

Over the years, many American Indian burial sites have been unearthed and destroyed when bones and artifacts have been removed from graves for research. This practice has led to a bitter conflict between some American Indians and the anthropologists and archaeologists doing the digging. Researchers argue that studying skeletal remains and the objects buried with them reveals much about American Indian cultures that might otherwise remain unknown. Skeletal remains also provide a physical record tracing the development and spread of many diseases. "Indians living today," argues one anthropologist, "stand to benefit from our conclusions."

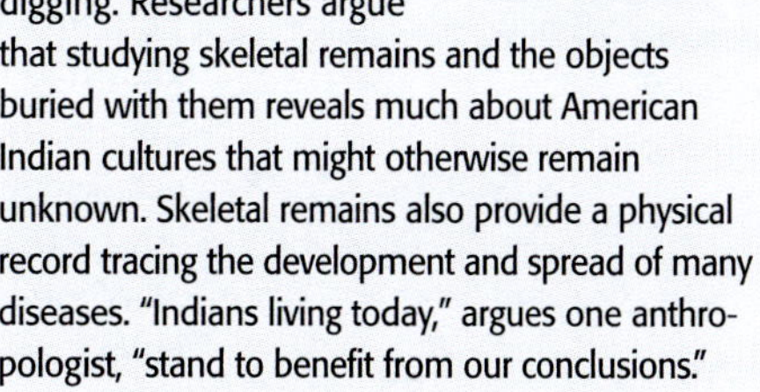

Pot found at an American Indian burial site

To many American Indians, however, the burial sites are sacred places that should not be disturbed. They believe that excavation of the sites shows a disregard for their cultural traditions. An attorney for a tribe in New Mexico recently asked: "Why single out Indians? Why not dig up everybody's ancestors?" Through recent lawsuits, some American Indians have succeeded in obtaining the return of their ancestors' remains for reburial. American Indians have been assisted in their efforts by the Native American Grave Protection and Repatriation Act, which Congress passed in 1990.

PEOPLE IN HISTORY

Hernán Cortés. As a young man, Hernán Cortés studied at the University of Salamanca. After two years, however, Cortés abandoned college and sailed to the Americas. His shrewd political sense served him well there. In 1511, for example, Cortés journeyed to Cuba and became close friends with the governor, who eventually asked Cortés to lead the expedition to Mexico. Later, however, the governor decided to dismiss him. Cortés found out and sailed to Mexico with his soldiers before the governor could find him.

CRITICAL THINKING How might Cortés's shrewd political sense have helped him conquer the Aztec Empire?

ANSWER: Students might note that once in Mexico, Cortés cleverly recruited Indian allies in his fight against the Aztec.

VISUAL RECORD ANSWER

(for p. 8)

Students might answer that life in Virginia is depicted as exciting and excellent.

TEACH OBJECTIVE 4

LEVEL 1: Have each student draw a series of pictures showing how European settlement affected American Indians. *(Students might draw scenes of Indians fighting each other for hunting grounds, Europeans clearing land, war between the two groups, or the devastation brought by disease.)* Display students' pictures around the classroom.
Sheltered English

LEVEL 2: Tell students to imagine that they are American Indians during the first big wave of European settlement. Have them write and present short monologues describing how European settlement has affected their tribe. *(See the Level 1 lesson for correct effects.)* Students may wish to include their monologues in their portfolios.

LEVEL 3: Organize students into groups of four or more. Have half of each group represent European settlers and the other act as American Indians. Tell students to imagine that they are representatives to a peace conference between European settlers and the American Indian tribe that once held the same land. Have them discuss their problems and brainstorm possible solutions before drafting a simple treaty that satisfies both groups. *(See the Level 1 lesson for correct issues.)*
Cooperative Learning

DEMOCRATIC VALUES

The Charter of 1606. Although the investors in the Plymouth and London Companies assumed the costs of colonization themselves, the approval of James I helped the companies attract other backers. James was involved in other ways as well. His highly detailed charter even specified that the London Company should consist of "certain Knights, Gentlemen, Merchants, and other Adventurers, of our city of London and elsewhere." It also stated that future colonists "shall have and enjoy all Liberties, Franchises, and Immunities . . . as if they had been abiding and born, within this our Realm of *England*."

CRITICAL THINKING Why might the Charter of 1606 have stated that future colonists would enjoy "all Liberties, Franchises, and Immunities" as those of people in England?

ANSWER: Students might suggest that King James was trying both to ensure that the companies could attract colonists and to establish the English legal tradition in the colonies.

VISUAL RECORD ANSWER

(for p. 9)

Students might suggest that they are exchanging animal furs.

NOVA BRITANNIA.
OFFERING MOST
Excellent fruites by Planting in
VIRGINIA.
Exciting all such as be well affected
to further the same.

LONDON
Printed for SAMVEL MACHAM, and are to be sold at
his Shop in Pauls Church-yard, at the
Signe of the Bul-head.
1609.

THE GRANGER COLLECTION, NEW YORK

INTERPRETING THE VISUAL RECORD

Recruiting. This pamphlet was published to attract settlers to Virginia. ***How does the pamphlet describe life in the Virginia colony?***

The English Colonies

By the 1600s the Dutch, English, and French had begun settling land in North America. England established 13 North American colonies during the 1600s and early 1700s. These colonies provided raw materials for England and served as a market for English goods. The different regions—the South, New England, and the Middle Atlantic—developed unique cultural traits.

The southern colonies. The first permanent English settlers arrived in Jamestown, Virginia, located near the Chesapeake Bay, in 1607. They survived with the help of local American Indians, but conflict grew increasingly common as the colonists expanded onto American Indian hunting grounds.

In the 1630s England established the colony of Maryland in the Chesapeake region. The economies of Virginia and Maryland relied heavily on tobacco. At first much of the farm labor was done by indentured servants—workers who were bound for a period of time to the person who paid for their passage to America. Eventually, however, tobacco farmers switched to slave labor. Enslaved Africans were brought across the Atlantic Ocean to the Americas on a horrible voyage known as the **Middle Passage**. Slave ships were packed so tightly that, wrote one captain, the captives "had not so much room *as a man in his coffin*." Although some people opposed slavery, it was practiced in all of the English colonies.

In 1663, English colonists founded Carolina, which was later divided into North and South Carolina. Slaves in South Carolina worked primarily on rice plantations and made up nearly two thirds of the population. Georgia was founded in 1732 as an attempt to provide a refuge for the poor and a buffer against attacks from Spanish Florida. The colony had few settlers in its first decades.

The New England colonies. In the early 1600s a group of Protestants known as **Puritans** emerged in England. The Puritans wished to reform, or "purify," the Anglican Church. Many Puritans were persecuted for their religious beliefs. In 1620 a group of Puritans known as the **Pilgrims** left England seeking religious freedom. They arrived in present-day Massachusetts and founded the colony of Plymouth.

Led by John Winthrop, another group of Puritans arrived in Massachusetts in 1630. Winthrop told his fellow settlers, "We must consider that we shall be as a city upon a hill. The eyes of all people are upon us." This colony was based on cooperation between church and state. Some people rebelled against this system and left Massachusetts to found new settlements. These settlements later became part of the colonies of Rhode Island and Connecticut.

The New England way of life stressed order and education to create a stable society. In addition to family farms, New Englanders developed prosperous fishing and trade.

The Pilgrims land at Plymouth Rock. Unlike other English colonists, the Pilgrims brought entire families along with them to help found a settlement.

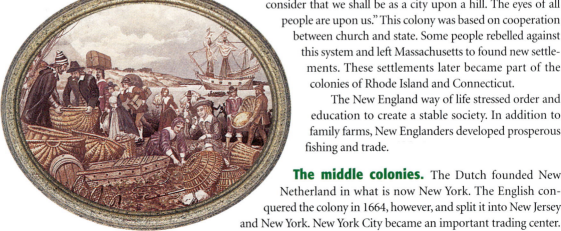

The middle colonies. The Dutch founded New Netherland in what is now New York. The English conquered the colony in 1664, however, and split it into New Jersey and New York. New York City became an important trading center.

REVIEW

Have students complete the **Section 1 Review** on p. 9.

ASSESS

Have students complete **Daily Quiz 1.1**. As **Alternative Assessment**, you may want to use the Spanish and English colonies time lines or the American Indian monologue in this section's lessons.

RETEACH

Have students complete **Main Idea Activity for Reteaching and Sheltered English 1.1**. Then organize students into groups and assign each group a subsection of Section 1. Have each group develop at least five questions and answers about the main ideas in its assigned material. Then have each group quiz another group. **Sheltered English, Cooperative Learning**

EXTEND

Have students write creative short stories set in one of the time periods and places covered in this section, such as the ancient Americas, Europe in the Middle Ages, the Spanish Empire in the Americas at its height, or the American colonial period. Tell them to make up believable characters and put them into interesting situations that reflect students' knowledge of the time period. Invite volunteers to read their stories to the class.
Block Scheduling

In 1681 Charles II repaid a debt to the Penn family by granting William Penn a large tract of land near New York. Penn wanted to make his colony, named Pennsylvania, a safe home for fellow Quakers—members of a radical and peaceful Protestant sect. He saw the colony as a "Holy Experiment" where people of different nationalities and religious beliefs could live together peacefully. Thousands of immigrants poured onto the colony's fertile farmlands. The colony of Delaware separated from Pennsylvania in 1704.

✔ **READING CHECK:** How were the Spanish and English colonies in the Americas settled?

THE GRANGER COLLECTION, NEW YORK

INTERPRETING THE VISUAL RECORD

Trade goods. Dutch colonists trade with American Indians. ***What type of goods are the two groups exchanging?***

Consequences for American Indians

The arrival of European settlers greatly altered the American Indian way of life. Europeans traded with American Indians, exchanging manufactured goods for animal pelts. The resulting fur trade led to fierce competition among American Indian tribes for hunting grounds and furs.

Europeans' desire for land had other disastrous consequences. Colonists cleared and settled what seemed to them wild or unused land. Such development threatened the American Indian way of life by destroying their food sources and damaging sites that were sacred to them. Disease and warfare with colonists also devastated the American Indian groups throughout North America. By the 1680s a Frenchman observed that American Indian tribes in New England had been greatly weakened. "The last Wars . . . have reduced them to a small Number," he reported.

✔ **READING CHECK:** What effect did European settlement have on American Indians?

SECTION  REVIEW

Define and explain the significance of the following terms:

Paleo-Indians
Agricultural Revolution
Maya
Aztec
Inca
Middle Ages
feudalism
Crusades
Renaissance
Middle Passage
Puritans
Pilgrims

Identify and explain the significance of the following individuals:

Christopher Columbus
Hernán Cortés

1. **Using Graphic Organizers** Copy the table below. Use it to list the key characteristics of the southern, New England, and middle colonies.

Southern Colonies
New England Colonies
Middle Colonies

2. **Analyzing** What were the key accomplishments of early Native American culture groups?
3. **Synthesizing** How did trade influence societies in Africa, the Americas, Asia, and Europe?
4. **Evaluating** What was the effect of European settlement on American Indians?

Critical Thinking

5. How did European trading goals change the history of the Americas?
Consider:
- how interest in trade led to the search for new trade routes
- how this search affected Christopher Columbus's journey
- how Columbus's landing in the Americas shaped their history

---

SECTION 1 REVIEW ANSWERS

Define and Identify

For significance, see the following pages:

- Paleo-Indians, p. 4
- Agricultural Revolution, p. 4
- Maya, p. 5
- Aztec, p. 5
- Inca, p. 5
- Middle Ages, p. 5
- feudalism, p. 5
- Crusades, p. 6
- Renaissance, p. 6
- Christopher Columbus, p. 6
- Hernán Cortés, p. 7
- Middle Passage, p. 8
- Puritans, p. 8
- Pilgrims, p. 8

1. southern colonies–relied heavily on tobacco farming, used indentured servants and slave labor; New England–settled by Puritans, stressed order and education, farmed, fished, and traded; Middle Colonies–the Dutch founded New Netherland, later taken by British and divided into New York and New Jersey; Pennsylvania founded as a "Holy Experiment" in tolerance
2. number systems, glyphs and agriculture
3. created an exchange of cultural practices, goods, and ideas
4. Europeans' desire for furs led to fierce competition among American Indians for hunting grounds and furs; European settlement destroyed Indian food sources; disease and warfare also devastated Indians
5. Europeans' search for direct access to Asian goods led to the discovery, exploration, and colonization of the Americas.

SECTION 2

After completing Section 2, students should be able to:

OBJECTIVE 1 *Summarize how and why the colonies won their independence from Great Britain.*

OBJECTIVE 2 *Explain how the Constitution formed the basis of a new government.*

OBJECTIVE 3 *Identify domestic and foreign challenges that faced the new nation.*

OBJECTIVE 4 *Discuss why the United States fought the War of 1812.*

LET'S GET STARTED!

To begin the class, have students preview Section 2 and recall all they can about American history from the mid-1700s through the early 1800s. Then tell them to write down several questions that they have about the material they are about to cover. Ask volunteers to read one or more of their questions to the class. Tell students to keep these questions in mind as they learn about the creation of a new nation in Section 2.

SECTION 2 RESOURCES

PRINT
- Guided Reading Strategy 1.2
- Geography Activity 1: The Native Americans
- Biography Reading 1: Pontiac
- Section 2 Review, p. 16
- Daily Quiz 1.2

MULTIMEDIA
- One-Stop Planner, Lesson 1.2
- The American Nation Video Program Segment: Designing a Nation; Teacher's Guide, pp. 27–32
- Holt Researcher: American History CD–ROM

SHELTERED ENGLISH
- Main Idea Activity for Reteaching and Sheltered English 1.2

✓ READING TO UNDERSTAND
To help students master the section objectives, have them answer the **READING CHECKS** and complete **Guided Reading Strategy 1.2** as they read the section.

Creating a New Nation

OBJECTIVES

Read to understand:
1. how and why the colonies won their independence from Great Britain
2. how the Constitution formed the basis of a new government
3. what domestic and foreign challenges faced the new nation
4. why the United States fought the War of 1812

KEY TERMS

Proclamation of 1763
Stamp Act
Boston Massacre
Boston Tea Party
Intolerable Acts
Declaration of Independence
Battle of Yorktown
Articles of Confederation
Constitutional Convention
federalism
Bill of Rights
Louisiana Purchase

KEY PEOPLE

George Washington
Thomas Jefferson
John Adams
Benjamin Franklin
Alexander Hamilton
John Marshall
Tecumseh

Tea package celebrating Boston Tea Party

“It seems we have troublesome times a coming, for there is great disturbance abroad in the earth and they say it is tea that caused it. So then if they will quarrel about such a trifling thing as that, what must we expect but war. I think or at least fear it will be so.”

—Jemima Condict Harrison

The Battle of Lexington

Jemima Condict Harrison was a young woman from New Jersey. She described the tension between Great Britain and the colonies in her diary in October 1774. During the early 1770s relations between Great Britain and the colonies worsened. Despite the growing crisis, some colonists still hoped for a peaceful resolution. Many, however, became convinced that war was inevitable.

Colonial Conflict

Conflict between Britain and France soon spilled over into their American colonies. The French and Indian War pitted British soldiers and colonial militia against the French and their American Indian allies. The British victory in the war led to the Treaty of Paris in 1763. This treaty granted Canada, Spanish Florida, and most French land east of the Mississippi River to Great Britain.

American Indians were soon angered by the large numbers of British settlers. Ottawa chief Pontiac called upon American Indian tribes to attack British forts on the frontier. Although Pontiac's Rebellion failed, it convinced British authorities to issue the **Proclamation of 1763**, which banned settlement west of the Appalachian Mountains. Land-hungry colonists ignored the law.

New taxes. Colonists also resented a series of new taxes passed to pay the war debts of the British government. British officials first passed a tax on sugar and molasses entering the American colonies. Parliament then passed the **Stamp Act** of 1765. This act levied a tax on printed matter of all kinds—including legal documents, newspapers, and even playing cards. In response, angry colonial merchants vowed not to buy or import British goods. Britain repealed the Stamp Act in 1766.

The following year Parliament placed import duties on basic items such as glass, lead, and tea. Once again the colonists opposed the tax. British troops known as Redcoats were sent to Boston to enforce the law. In 1770 an argument between colonists and Redcoats led the soldiers to open fire on the angry crowd, killing five people. The stunned colonists called this incident the **Boston Massacre**.

The Tea Act. Parliament repealed some of the new duties but reasserted its control in 1773 when it passed the Tea Act. This act angered colonists, who felt it gave Britain a monopoly on the tea trade. When the governor of Massachusetts allowed

TEACH OBJECTIVE 1

ALL LEVELS: To help students understand how and why the colonies won their independence from Great Britain, copy the following graphic organizer on the chalkboard, omitting the italicized answers. Have each student complete the graphic organizer. **Sheltered English**

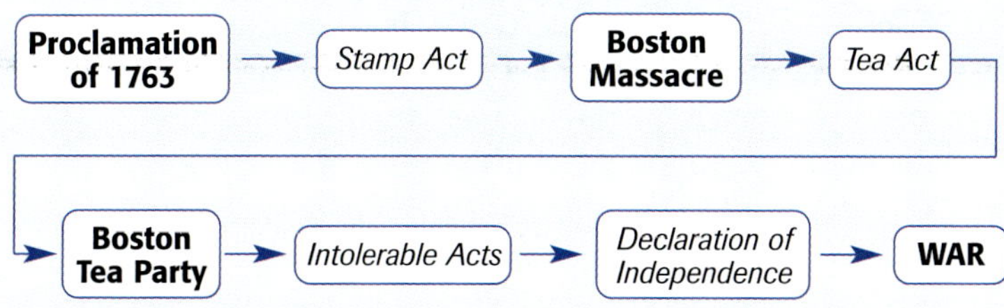

▸ASSIGNMENT: *Have students use the information in the graphic organizer to make a pamphlet that is meant to stir up dissatisfaction in the colonies by pointing out all the injustices committed by the British government.*

three shiploads of tea into Boston Harbor, colonists responded by boarding the ships at night. They threw more than 340 chests of tea into the water. News of the **Boston Tea Party** spread rapidly.

British officials were furious. Parliament responded by passing the Coercive Acts, which became known in the colonies as the **Intolerable Acts**. These laws closed the port of Boston, revoked the colony's charter, and ordered local officials to provide food and housing for British soldiers. The resentment toward the Intolerable Acts helped build colonial unity.

The Revolutionary War Begins

In the fall of 1774, colonial representatives met in Philadelphia at the First Continental Congress to discuss how to respond to British actions. They decided to remain loyal to the Crown but demanded their rights as British subjects. The meeting angered King George III, who considered the congressional delegates and colonists who agreed with them to be rebels. Parliament ordered General Thomas Gage to put a stop to the rebellion.

Early battles. General Gage's first act was to seize rebel military supplies stored in Concord, Massachusetts. In April 1775, British troops traveling to Concord were spotted by Patriots. Paul Revere and two other men galloped through the countryside to sound the alarm: "The British are coming!" On April 19 the Redcoats and Patriots clashed in Lexington, Massachusetts, where someone fired what became known as "the shot heard round the world."

News of these events had spread through the colonies by the time the Second Continental Congress opened in May. The congressional delegates agreed to establish the Continental Army "for the defense of American liberty." They placed George Washington of Virginia in command.

Declaring independence. Many colonists believed that the British government had violated their rights as British subjects. Patrick Henry expressed these views in a speech he delivered in Virginia. He declared, "Give me liberty, or give me death!"

Independence

Perhaps more than any other topic, the meaning of the American Revolution has provoked heated and ongoing debates among historians. The political fact of independence was one obvious consequence of the Revolution. Yet Thomas Jefferson's words "all men are created equal" have, from the time they were written, been a source of controversy.

Some historians have chosen to focus on the limitations of revolutionary ideas. Clearly, the Declaration of Independence did not create political liberty for everyone. American women continued to be excluded from political life after 1776. Many slaves fought for and gained their freedom during the Revolutionary War, but slavery as a system did not end. American Indians also failed to benefit from the Revolution. Many lost their lands and homes during the war, and few were recognized by either side for their service.

Other historians have viewed the Revolution as an event of great social consequence. Although America in the 1700s was full of inequalities, these scholars argue, the Revolution began to change Americans' ideas about how power should be distributed in society. No longer did people assume that a few "well-born" people should rule over everyone else. This fundamental change in attitude would eventually lead to the extension of democratic rights to all Americans, whatever their sex, race, or economic situation.

Recruitment posters like this one encouraged colonial men to join the Continental Army.

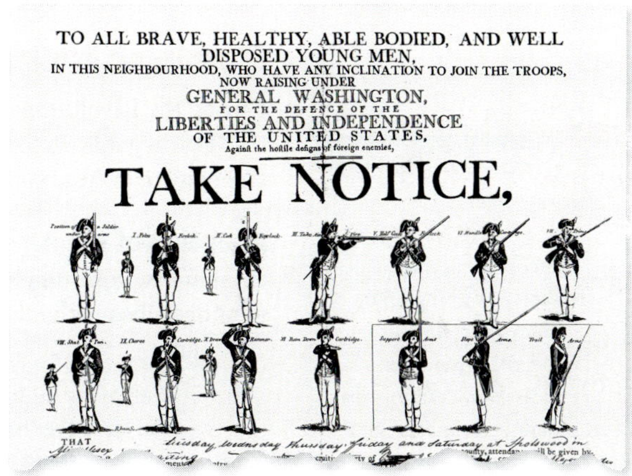

TO ALL BRAVE, HEALTHY, ABLE BODIED, AND WELL DISPOSED YOUNG MEN,
IN THIS NEIGHBOURHOOD, WHO HAVE ANY INCLINATION TO JOIN THE TROOPS,
NOW RAISING UNDER
GENERAL WASHINGTON,
FOR THE DEFENCE OF THE
LIBERTIES AND INDEPENDENCE
OF THE UNITED STATES,
TAKE NOTICE,

THEN AND NOW

Boycotts: An American Tradition. By refusing to buy British goods, colonists were using a method of protest that is still widespread—the boycott. Americans have boycotted goods for a wide variety of reasons. People have boycotted certain companies to protest high prices, disagreeable labor practices, or objectionable products. Many consumers boycotted food companies that caught and killed dolphins in the process of harvesting tuna. As a result, some companies changed their policies, and many tuna cans now bear the "dolphin-safe" label.

CRITICAL THINKING What can consumers hope to gain by boycotting a company's goods?

ANSWER: Students might indicate that if a company stands to lose a significant amount of business from a boycott, the company might be persuaded to change the practices that upset consumers.

THAT'S INTERESTING!

In 1836 American poet Ralph Waldo Emerson wrote a hymn for the dedication of a memorial at Concord. The hymn included the description of the first gunshot at Concord as "the shot heard round the world."

TEACH OBJECTIVE 2

LEVELS 1 AND 2: Organize students into groups of three or more and tell them to work together to create a triptych, or three-panel visual display, that explains how the Constitution formed the basis of a new government. *(Displays should note that the Constitution replaced the weak Articles of Confederation; that once 9 of 13 states had ratified it, the Constitution went into effect; and that the new government was based on federalism and had three separate branches.)* Tell students to include pictures, text, graphic organizers, and other elements to help convey their message. Encourage students to assign roles, such as artist, researcher, and writer, within their group to help them complete the assignment.
Sheltered English, Cooperative Learning

LEVEL 3: Have students write a ballad that recounts how the Constitution formed the basis of a new government. *(See the Levels 1 and 2 lesson for the correct steps.)* Ask volunteers to read or sing their ballads to the class.

HISTORY MAKERS SPEAK

Thayendanegea in *The World Turned Upside Down: Indian Voices from Early America*

Thayendanegea to the British. Many American Indians supported the British with the hope that they would protect Indian lands. After its defeat, however, Britain ceded many Indian lands to the United States. When Thayendanegea learned of the transfer, he sent the following message to the governor of Quebec: "Brother, listen with great attention to our words, we were greatly alarmed and cast down when we heard that news. . . . Brother, we, the Mohawks, were the first Indian Nation that took you by the hand like friends and brothers. . . . We continued your friends and allies . . . sacrificing numbers of our people and leaving their bones scattered in your enemies' country."

CRITICAL THINKING Why might Britain have ceded Indian lands to the United States?

ANSWER: Answers will vary. Some students might suggest that the British were unable to protect Indian lands, while others might suggest that Britain had never intended to.

MAP ANSWER
Spain

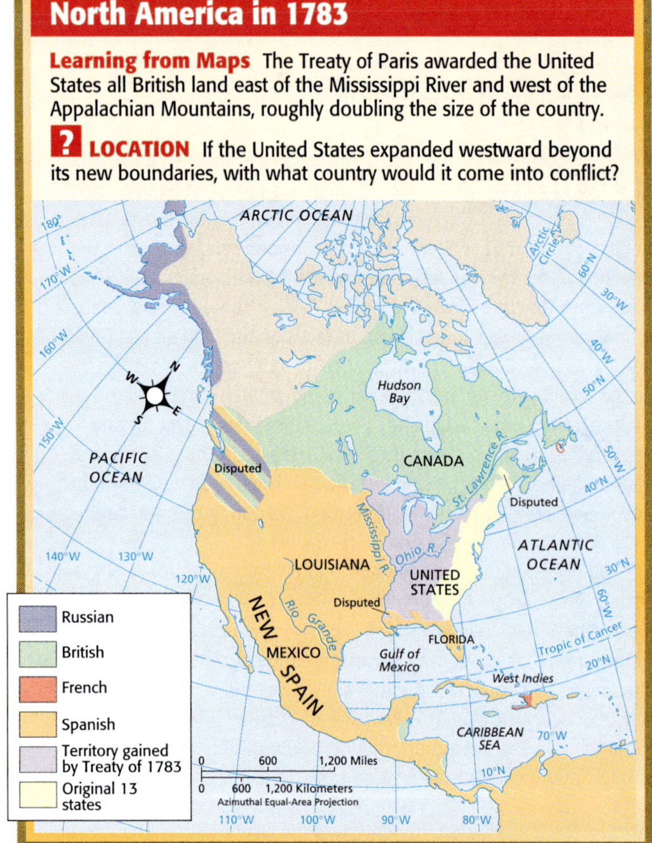

North America in 1783

Learning from Maps The Treaty of Paris awarded the United States all British land east of the Mississippi River and west of the Appalachian Mountains, roughly doubling the size of the country.

LOCATION If the United States expanded westward beyond its new boundaries, with what country would it come into conflict?

In June 1776 the Second Continental Congress appointed a committee to draft a formal **Declaration of Independence**. Thomas Jefferson of Virginia did most of the actual writing. The Congress adopted the Declaration on July 4, 1776.

War! The Continental Congress could not force states to support the war effort. As a result, George Washington faced troop shortages, widespread disease in army camps, and a lack of food and supplies. Furthermore, the Continental Army was small and poorly trained. Yet it had two key advantages over the British forces in the colonies. The Patriots often fought on familiar ground, and they believed strongly in their cause.

The British captured New York City in September 1776. They were close to winning the war until Washington's troops launched a Christmas night attack on soldiers based in Trenton, New Jersey. The victory greatly raised American morale. In October 1777 the Patriots defeated a large British army at Saratoga, New York. The victory persuaded France to ally with the Patriots and to provide military and economic support.

The war ended in autumn of 1781 when a combined American and French force trapped the outnumbered British near Chesapeake Bay. On October 19, 1781, General Charles Cornwallis surrendered after the **Battle of Yorktown**. The peace treaty between the former colonies and Britain was signed in September 1783. The treaty recognized the independence of the United States and granted it much of the land from the Atlantic Coast to the Mississippi River.

✔ **READING CHECK:** How and why did the colonies win their independence from Britain?

Forming a New Government

During the Revolutionary War years, many states had drafted constitutions that relied on republican theory. This theory states that political leaders receive their authority to make and enforce laws from the citizens.

Adoption of the Articles. The United States faced the challenge of forming an entirely new government. Delegate John Adams of the Second Continental Congress described his confidence in the future to a friend.

> **"You and I . . . have been sent into life at a time when the greatest lawgivers of antiquity [olden times] would have wished to live. How few of the human race have ever enjoyed an opportunity of making . . . government . . . for themselves and their children."**

Free Find:
George Washington
After reading about George Washington on the **Holt Researcher** CD–ROM, write a press release that describes his many accomplishments.

TEACH OBJECTIVE 3

LEVEL 1: Have students label one side of a sheet of paper "Domestic Challenges" and the other side "Foreign Challenges." Then tell students to list the domestic and foreign challenges the new nation faced. *(Students should include as domestic challenges: federal debt, farmers' protests, and conflicts with American Indians. Foreign challenges should include: inability to maintain neutrality in face of British aggression, Britain's supplying arms to American Indians, and conflicts between Americans siding with the British versus those siding with the French.)* **Sheltered English**

LEVELS 2 AND 3: Have students complete the Level 1 activity, leaving a few lines blank between items in each column. Tell them to fill in the blank spaces with how the federal government attempted to solve each problem. *(Students might answer that the government created a national bank and taxed whiskey to address the debt problem; called in state troops to deal with protest; signed a treaty with the Indians; signed a treaty on British aggression; did nothing to combat Britain's arming of Indians; and formed political parties to allow for British and French sympathies.)*

The states decided to join in a loose union under a plan called the **Articles of Confederation**. The plan went into effect in 1781. Under the Articles the government had the right to borrow and coin money, conduct foreign affairs, set policy toward American Indians, and settle disputes between the states.

The new government struggled to pay its war debts. It did not have the power to tax the people directly and had to appeal to the states for funds. Some states avoided paying their share of the national debt. As the nation's economic woes grew, indebted farmers rebelled in western Massachusetts. Although the rebellion was quickly defeated, it caused many people to believe the United States needed a more powerful government.

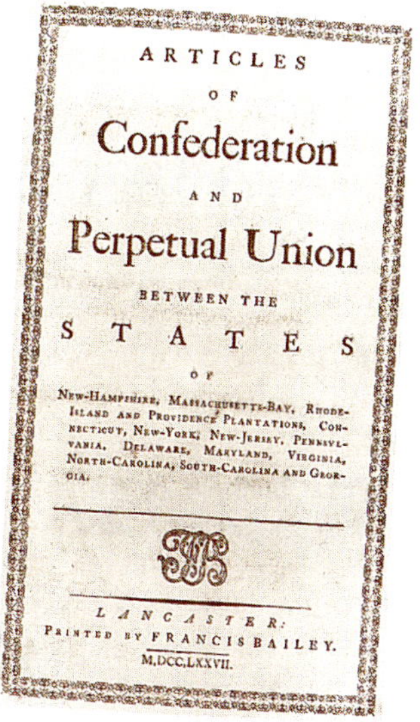

ARTICLES OF Confederation AND Perpetual Union BETWEEN THE STATES OF New-Hampshire, Massachusetts-Bay, Rhode-Island and Providence Plantations, Connecticut, New-York, New-Jersey, Pennsylvania, Delaware, Maryland, Virginia, North-Carolina, South-Carolina and Georgia.

LANCASTER: Printed by FRANCIS BAILEY. M.DCC.LXXVII.

Cover of the Articles of Confederation

The Constitutional Convention. These concerns led to the **Constitutional Convention,** held in Philadelphia in May 1787. George Washington, Benjamin Franklin, and 53 other state delegates debated how much power the central government should have. Some delegates supported **federalism**—the division of powers between a central government and the state governments.

After a series of debates and compromises, the delegates agreed on a two-house legislature. This model granted each state the same number of representatives in the upper house. Representation in the lower house was based on state population. The delegates also settled disputes between northern and southern colonies over how slaves would be counted to determine representation. The final compromise stated that each slave would be counted as three-fifths of a person. One group of delegates feared that a strong national government might violate personal liberties. These delegates insisted that a bill of rights be added to Constitution at a later date. When the Constitution was ready for ratification, there were heated debates in most states between its federalist supporters and antifederalist opponents. Finally, in 1788 the required 9 out of 13 states ratified the U.S. Constitution.

The Constitution. The framers of the Constitution created a federal government. The Constitution granted the federal government the authority to raise armed forces, coin money, and establish foreign policy. State governments retained local powers, such as establishing schools and conducting elections. Some powers, however, were shared by the central and state governments. These shared powers included the right to levy taxes and establish courts.

The framers of the Constitution wanted to prevent the central government from abusing its powers. As a result, they divided it into three branches. The legislative branch makes the laws. The executive branch sees that the laws are carried out. The judicial branch interprets and applies the laws. This separation of powers between the branches prevents any one branch from becoming too powerful. Using a system of checks and balances, each branch can restrict the actions of the other branches.

✔ **READING CHECK:** How did the Constitution form the basis of a new government?

INTERPRETING THE VISUAL RECORD

Constitutional Convention. George Washington accepts the signed Constitution. ***What does this image suggest about the delegates to the Constitutional Convention?***

CONSTITUTIONAL HERITAGE

The Constitution and Slavery. While the Constitution protected slavery in several of its provisions, it used curiously indirect wording to discuss that institution. For example, the provision that allowed slaveholders the right to pursue runaway slaves across state lines read, "No Person held to Service or Labour in one State . . . escaping into another, shall . . . be discharged from such Service or Labour." In fact, the word *slavery* did not appear in the Constitution until the Thirteenth Amendment abolished slavery in 1865.

ACTIVITY: Have students search the Constitution and its amendments for references to men or women. Then discuss what the references might suggest.

VISUAL RECORD ANSWER

Students might answer that all are white men.

The American Nation **VIDEO PROGRAM**

Designing a Nation; Teacher's Guide, pp. 27–32

Search 06322, Play to 14238
Videodisc 1, Side A

Play Pause

See *Teacher's Guide* for Spanish barcode.

TEACH OBJECTIVE 4

LEVEL 1: Have students design a recruiting poster for the War of 1812. To help inspire a sense of patriotism in possible recruits, posters should explain why the United States is fighting. *(Posters should include the practice of impressment, British attacks on American ships, and aiding American Indians who were attacking American settlers as they pushed westward.)* Ask volunteers to share their posters with the class. **Sheltered English**

LEVEL 2: Have students write an encyclopedia entry explaining why the United States fought the War of 1812. *(See the Level 1 lesson for correct reasons.)* Entries should also discuss the outcome of the war. *(Entries might mention that the war strengthened U.S. control over the Northwest Territory and improved relations somewhat with Great Britain).*

NOTE: For an additional teaching idea, see the Chapter 1 webbing lesson in the **Creative Teaching Strategies** handbook.

PEOPLE IN HISTORY

Alexander Hamilton. Despite Alexander Hamilton's political ambitions, he never ran for president. He wanted to be president but recognized that several factors—his birth outside of colonial America, his arrogant manner, and his unpopularity in the South—would prevent him from winning the presidency. Determined not to lose a national election, the practical Hamilton gave up his presidential dreams.

CRITICAL THINKING Why might Hamilton's arrogant manner have prevented him from winning the presidency?

ANSWER: Students might suggest that some Americans had a negative view of Hamilton's personal manner and connected it with his monarchist tendencies, which seemed to contradict the principles of the Revolution.

THAT'S INTERESTING!

In the United States, the French Revolution contributed to what some called Bastille fever, or an attempt to create social equality. For example, Boston residents renamed Royal Exchange Alley as Equality Lane. Some men abandoned the use of "Mr." and used "Citizen" instead.

SEPARATION OF CHURCH AND STATE

The principle of the separation of church and state, as set forth in the First Amendment, was uniquely American. The French and Spanish governments were influenced by the Catholic Church, and the British government was influenced by the Anglican Church, but the U.S. government was not directly tied to any one church.

New England church bell

Although colonial America was settled by people of various religious beliefs, most colonists were Christians. Despite the numerous religious groups in the colonies, most colonial governments used tax revenue to support specific churches. These included the Congregational Church in New England and the Anglican Church in the middle and southern colonies. To prevent the Anglican Church from influencing political matters, Thomas Jefferson wrote the Virginia Statute for Religious Freedom in 1779. This established a separation of church and state. To promote national unity, the framers of the U.S. Constitution followed the lead of the state constitutions and established a separation of church and state. This policy prevented a division among delegates holding different religious beliefs.

Even with this separation of church and state, American life remained deeply influenced by religious beliefs. Frenchman Alexis de Tocqueville visited the new nation in the 1830s. He observed, "In the United States religion exercises but little influence upon the laws and upon the details of public opinion, but it directs the manners of the community."

New Challenges

George Washington was the unanimous choice of the people for the first president of the United States. He knew that the actions of the new government would be a guide for future leaders.

Congress's first task was to create the **Bill of Rights**, which was ratified in 1791. These first 10 amendments to the Constitution include guarantees of freedom of speech, religion, and the press. They also established some rules for criminal and trial procedures. In addition, Congress created a federal court system as well as executive departments to assist the president.

Secretary of the Treasury Alexander Hamilton soon devised a system to repay the nation's war debts. To provide economic stability, Hamilton asked Congress to create a national bank. Secretary of State Thomas Jefferson objected, claiming that the Constitution did not give the central government the power to set up a bank. President Washington sided with Hamilton, and Congress chartered the bank in 1791.

To generate income, Congress passed a tax in 1794 on the production of whiskey. Pennsylvania farmers were hard hit by this measure, and they organized a militia to march on the city of Philadelphia. This militia quickly disbanded when President Washington called out some 13,000 state troops. Greater troubles brewed in the region between the Mississippi and Ohio Rivers known as the Northwest Territory. Settlers there continued to occupy land claimed by American Indians. Led by Miami chief Little Turtle, American Indian warriors defeated U.S. troops in 1791 but eventually surrendered in the summer of 1794. The following year more than 1,000 American Indian leaders signed a treaty with the U.S. government.

President Washington wanted the United States to remain neutral in foreign affairs. This goal proved difficult, however. After the French Revolution of 1789, France became a republic. France and Britain soon went to war. Both countries ignored the U.S. declaration of neutrality and seized American merchant vessels bound for enemy ports. Britain also angered U.S. officials by kidnapping American sailors and forcing them to serve in the British navy—a practice called impressment. The United States signed a treaty with Britain in 1794 to prevent a war over this issue.

The debate over foreign policy helped give rise to the first American political parties. By the mid-1790s there were two opposing parties. The Federalist Party was led by Alexander Hamilton and John Adams. The Federalists favored a strong national government and supported Britain. The Democratic-Republican Party was led by Thomas Jefferson and James Madison. Known as Republicans, this group wanted to limit the power of the federal government and tended to side with the French.

LEVEL 3: In a classroom discussion, have students list reasons the United States fought the War of 1812. *(See the Level 1 lesson for correct reasons.)* Then have students write an essay analyzing the outcome of the war and theorizing about the possible long-term impact if the United States had lost. Have volunteers read their paragraphs to the class and encourage the class to comment on each other's theories.

Teacher to Teacher

Jay Harmon of Baton Rouge, Louisiana, suggested the following activity: Have students research and discuss this "what if" question: What if Britain had won the Battle of New Orleans? Students should consider whether Britain would have ignored the Treaty of Ghent and kept the important port and how this might have affected U.S development.

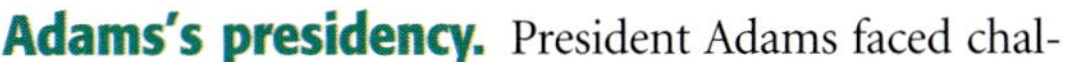

The Presidencies of Adams and Jefferson

President Washington decided not to seek a third term in 1796, leading to the first real contest for the presidency. According to the Constitution, the candidate with the most electoral votes became president, and the runner-up became vice president. Federalist John Adams was elected president, and Thomas Jefferson—Adams's Republican opponent—became vice president.

THE GRANGER COLLECTION, NEW YORK

INTERPRETING THE VISUAL RECORD

Political parties. In the presidential election of 1800 the Federalist and Democratic-Republican Parties used campaign banners like this one to build popular support for their candidates. ***How might a banner like this be used to gain support in an election?***

Adams's presidency. President Adams faced challenges both abroad and at home. French warships had begun seizing American ships bound for British ports. Soon France and the United States were fighting an undeclared war at sea. In 1798 the Federalist majority in Congress passed the Alien and Sedition Acts. These laws authorized the president to imprison or expel any foreigners deemed dangerous. The laws also targeted U.S. citizens, often Republicans, who wrote, said, or printed anything "false, scandalous, and malicious" about the government. Many Americans believed the new laws violated the freedoms guaranteed by the Bill of Rights.

Jefferson and the Supreme Court. Thomas Jefferson won the presidential election of 1800. President Adams rushed to appoint Federalist judges before Jefferson took office. However, not all of them received their commissions. Secretary of State James Madison refused to allow one of these judges, William Marbury, to take office. Marbury sued and took the case to the Supreme Court. Led by Chief Justice John Marshall, the Court ruled that it could hear the case only on appeal after it had gone through the lower courts. By denying that the case could go straight to the Supreme Court, Marshall declared part of an earlier judiciary act passed by Congress to be unconstitutional. With this decision, Marshall established the Supreme Court's most important role—that of final interpreter of the Constitution.

The Louisiana Purchase. Jefferson wanted to expand U.S. landholdings. In 1803 he sent James Monroe to France to try to purchase New Orleans and western Florida. Instead, French ruler Napoleon offered to sell the United States all of the huge western territory called Louisiana. For $15 million, or about 4 cents an acre, the United States completed the **Louisiana Purchase**. It doubled the size of the United States and added all or part of 13 future states to the nation. The purchase opened up the interior of the continent to American settlement.

Jefferson assigned two explorers, Meriwether Lewis and William Clark, to map the new territory. They left St. Louis in May 1804 and traveled west to the Pacific Ocean. The explorers were aided by American Indians such as Sacagawea, who acted as a guide and an interpreter. The expedition did not return to St. Louis for two and a half years. Meanwhile, explorer Zebulon Pike visited the upper Mississippi Valley in 1805, then traveled as far west as present-day Colorado. His journey helped spur expansion into Texas and the Southwest.

✔ **READING CHECK:** What domestic and foreign challenges faced the new nation?

As a guide and interpreter, Sacagawea greatly assisted Lewis and Clark during their exploration.

GEOGRAPHIC DIVERSITY

The Lewis and Clark Expedition. President Jefferson assigned Meriwether Lewis, who had been his private secretary, the task of observing and cataloging the plants and animals of the West. Along with other members of the expedition, Lewis recorded some 178 plants and 122 animals—all previously unknown in the United States. Among these were ponderosa pines, bighorn sheep, coyotes, prairie dogs, and grizzly bears. Lewis and Clark sent a prairie dog and a magpie back to the East. For a time, the animals lived in the White House.

ACTIVITY: Tell students to imagine that they are Meriwether Lewis. Have them create illustrated journals describing some of the plants and animals they saw on their expedition.

VISUAL RECORD ANSWER

Students might suggest that the portrait and symbols might appeal to voters.

SECTION 2 REVIEW ANSWERS

Define and Identify

For significance, see the following pages:

- Proclamation of 1763, p. 10
- Stamp Act, p. 10
- Boston Massacre, p. 10
- Boston Tea Party, p. 11
- Intolerable Acts, p. 11
- George Washington, p. 11

REVIEW

Have students complete the **Section 2 Review** on p. 16.

ASSESS

Have students complete **Daily Quiz 1.2.** As **Alternative Assessment**, you may want to use the Constitution triptych or the encyclopedia entries in this section's lessons.

RETEACH

Have students complete **Main Idea Activity for Reteaching and Sheltered English 1.2.** Then have each student create a detailed outline of the section. Pair students and have them exchange outlines. Tell them to use a different color ink to note any important information that is missing from each other's outlines. **Sheltered English, Cooperative Learning**

EXTEND

Organize students into four groups and assign each group one of the following topics: the American Revolution, the Constitution, challenges for the new nation, and the War of 1812. Then tell students to create a museum exhibit on their assigned topic. They may include reconstructed "artifacts" that pertain to the topic as well as models, drawings, maps, graphic organizers, and written or recorded explanations of the various items in the exhibit. Have students set up their exhibits in the classroom, the school library, or any other available display space. **Block Scheduling, Cooperative Learning**

- Declaration of Independence, p. 12
- Thomas Jefferson, p. 12
- Battle of Yorktown, p. 12
- John Adams, p. 12
- Articles of Confederation, p. 13
- Constitutional Convention, p. 13
- Benjamin Franklin, p. 13
- federalism, p. 13
- Bill of Rights, p. 14
- Alexander Hamilton, p. 14
- John Marshall, p. 15
- Louisiana Purchase, p. 15
- Tecumseh, p. 16

1. Articles of Confederation—powers: borrow and coin money, conduct foreign affairs, set American Indian policy, settle disputes between states; strengths: democratic, could make laws; weaknesses: could not tax people directly or pay its debts. Constitution—powers: raise armed forces, coin money, establish foreign policy, levy taxes and establish courts; strengths: shared power with states and balanced power in three branches; weaknesses: concentrated power at federal level, originally lacked a Bill of Rights.

2. The restriction of westward settlement and new taxes led to the declaration; their knowledge of the land and belief in their cause led to victory.

3. Impressment, seizure of ships, and an embargo reduced trade.

4. fighting between France and Britain and Tecumseh's uprising

5. Answers will vary but should reflect a knowledge of the early presidencies.

The Shawnee leader Tecumseh was both feared and respected by his opponents.

The War of 1812

By the early 1800s the United States was again drawn into the conflict between France and Britain. Britain continued its practice of impressment. In 1807 the British attacked an American ship, killing three American sailors and seizing four others. The incident outraged Americans. In response, President Jefferson urged Congress to pass the Embargo Act of 1807, which stopped shipments of American products to all foreign ports. This embargo backfired, hurting American merchants and farmers but having little effect on foreign markets.

Conflict also continued between American settlers pushing westward and the American Indians who occupied these lands. Tecumseh, a Shawnee leader, attempted to build a confederation of American Indian tribes to keep out the Americans. "Sell a country!" he cried. "Why not sell the air, the clouds, and the great sea?" Tecumseh's army was defeated in 1811 by U.S. soldiers under the command of General William Henry Harrison.

Many Americans believed that the British had aided Tecumseh's uprising. In 1812 Congress declared war on Britain. The U.S. Army failed to conquer Canada but did defeat the British and their American Indian allies in the Northwest Territory. The small U.S. Navy also won a series of battles, boosting morale. However, the United States suffered a major blow in 1814 when British troops burned much of Washington to the ground.

Neither side could gain a clear advantage. The United States finally won a decisive victory over the British in 1815 in New Orleans. By that time, however, the war was officially over. The treaty that ended the war strengthened U.S. control in the Northwest Territory but did not solve some key disputes. However, British and U.S. relations did improve in the years following the war.

✔ **READING CHECK:** Why did the United States fight the War of 1812?

SECTION  REVIEW

Define and explain the significance of the following terms:
Proclamation of 1763
Stamp Act
Boston Massacre
Boston Tea Party
Intolerable Acts
Declaration of Independence
Battle of Yorktown
Articles of Confederation
Constitutional Convention
federalism
Bill of Rights
Louisiana Purchase

Identify and explain the significance of the following individuals:
George Washington
Thomas Jefferson
John Adams
Benjamin Franklin
Alexander Hamilton
John Marshall
Tecumseh

1. **Using Graphic Organizers** Copy the following chart. Use it to compare the U.S. government under the Articles of Confederation and under the Constitution.

Articles of Confederation	Constitution
Government Powers:	Government Powers:
Strengths:	Strengths:
Weaknesses:	Weaknesses:

2. **Identifying Cause and Effect** What events led to the colonists' declaration of independence from Britain and to their victory in the Revolutionary War?
3. **Analyzing** How did fighting between France and Britain have a negative effect on American trade?
4. **Evaluating** What were the major causes of the War of 1812?

Critical Thinking

5. Which of the first three U.S. presidents do you think faced the most difficult problems? Explain your answer.
   Consider:
   - the establishment of the new government
   - domestic problems, such as conflict with American Indians
   - foreign problems, such as Britain's impressment of American sailors

HISTORICAL DOCUMENTS

The Declaration of Independence

In Congress, July 4, 1776
The unanimous Declaration of the thirteen united States of America,

When in the Course of human events, it becomes necessary for one people to dissolve the political bands which have connected them with another, and to assume among the Powers of the earth, the separate and equal station to which the Laws of Nature and of Nature's God entitle them, a decent respect to the opinions of mankind requires that they should declare the causes which impel them to the separation.

We hold these truths to be self-evident, that all men are created equal, that they are endowed by their Creator with certain unalienable Rights, that among these are Life, Liberty, and the pursuit of Happiness. That to secure these rights, Governments are instituted among Men, deriving their just powers from the consent of the governed, That whenever any Form of Government becomes destructive of these ends, it is the Right of the People to alter or to abolish it, and to institute new Government, laying its foundation on such principles and organizing its powers in such form, as to them shall seem most likely to effect their Safety and Happiness. Prudence, indeed, will dictate that Governments long established should not be changed for light and transient causes; and accordingly all experience hath shown, that mankind are more disposed to suffer, while evils are sufferable, than to right themselves by abolishing the forms to which they are accustomed. But when a long train of abuses and usurpations, pursuing invariably the same Object evinces a design to reduce them under absolute Despotism, it is their right, it is their duty, to throw off such Government, and to provide new Guards for their future security.—Such has been the patient sufferance of these Colonies; and such is now the necessity which constrains them to alter their former Systems of Government. The history

THE GRANGER COLLECTION, NEW YORK

The Declaration of Independence

Thomas Jefferson wrote the first draft of the Declaration in a little more than two weeks.

Democratic Values

According to the first paragraph, why is it important for the signers to justify their political break with Great Britain?

impel: force
endowed: provided

"Laws of Nature" and "Nature's God" refer to the belief common in the Scientific Revolution that certain patterns are constant and predictable and that they come from a supreme being. Natural or "unalienable" rights (the rights to life, liberty, and the pursuit of happiness) cannot be taken away.

usurpations: wrongful seizures of power
evinces: clearly displays
despotism: unlimited power

ACROSS THE CURRICULUM

▶LANGUAGE ARTS◀

The Words of the Declaration. The signers of the Declaration of Independence were not merely issuing a proclamation; they were trying to persuade colonists that King George had become a despot. In its original Greek form, despot meant "master" or "lord." Later, however, the word came to mean "absolute ruler" and referred to those who governed in a tyrannical, oppressive way.

ACTIVITY: Ask students to scan magazines and newspapers to find the word *despot.* Have each student select one example, bring it to class, and present it to the other students. Conduct a brief discussion on students' examples and the ways in which the term *despot* might have affected colonists who read it in the Declaration of Independence.

DEMOCRATIC VALUES ANSWER

The Declaration insists that "a decent respect to the opinions of mankind" requires the colonists to provide a justification for their break with Britain.

CONSTITUTIONAL HERITAGE

Tenure for Judges. The word *tenure* comes from the Latin verb *tenēre,* which means "to hold." In English, the word often refers to a term of office. In the United States, it also refers to a guaranteed position, such as those held by professors at many universities. The signers of the Declaration did not approve of the king's authority to determine the length of a judge's tenure. After the Revolutionary War, the framers of the Constitution determined that Supreme Court justices would have lifetime appointments.

CRITICAL THINKING Why might the framers of the Constitution have wanted judges to have lifetime tenures?

ANSWER: Students might suggest that the framers wanted judges to be impartial and independent.

DEMOCRATIC VALUES ANSWER

The Declaration states that the king refused to obey the law and to establish judicial powers, among other offenses. The Declaration states that the British Parliament passed acts to quarter troops, among other offenses.

tyranny: oppressive power exerted by a government or ruler
candid: fair

Beginning here the Declaration lists the charges that the colonists had against King George III.

relinquish: release, yield
inestimable: priceless
formidable: causing dread

annihilation: destruction

convulsions: violent disturbances

naturalization of foreigners: the process by which foreign-born persons become citizens
appropriations of land: setting aside land for settlement

tenure: term

a multitude of: many

Democratic Values

What wrongful acts stated in the Declaration have been committed by the king and the British Parliament?

quartering: lodging, housing

of the present King of Great Britain is a history of repeated injuries and usurpations, all having in direct object the establishment of an absolute Tyranny over these States. To prove this, let Facts be submitted to a candid world.

He has refused his Assent to Laws, the most wholesome and necessary for the public good.

He has forbidden his Governors to pass Laws of immediate and pressing importance, unless suspended in their operation till his Assent should be obtained; and when so suspended, he has utterly neglected to attend to them.

He has refused to pass other Laws for the accommodation of large districts of people, unless those people would relinquish the right of Representation in the Legislature, a right inestimable to them and formidable to tyrants only.

He has called together legislative bodies at places unusual, uncomfortable, and distant from the depository of their Public Records, for the sole purpose of fatiguing them into compliance with his measures.

He has dissolved Representative Houses repeatedly, for opposing with manly firmness his invasions on the rights of the people.

He has refused for a long time, after such dissolutions, to cause others to be elected; whereby the Legislative Powers, incapable of Annihilation, have returned to the People at large for their exercise; the State remaining in the mean time exposed to all the dangers of invasion from without, and convulsions within.

He has endeavored to prevent the population of these States; for that purpose obstructing the Laws of Naturalization of Foreigners; refusing to pass others to encourage their migration hither, and raising the conditions of new Appropriations of Lands.

He has obstructed the Administration of Justice, by refusing his Assent to Laws for establishing Judiciary Powers.

He has made Judges dependent on his Will alone, for the tenure of their offices, and the amount and payment of their salaries.

He has erected a multitude of New Offices, and sent hither swarms of Officers to harass our people, and eat out their substance.

He has kept among us, in times of peace, Standing Armies without the Consent of our legislature.

He has affected to render the Military independent of and superior to the Civil Power.

He has combined with others to subject us to a jurisdiction foreign to our constitution, and unacknowledged by our laws; giving his Assent to their Acts of pretended legislation:

For quartering large bodies of armed troops among us:

For protecting them, by a mock Trial, from Punishment for any Murders which they should commit on the Inhabitants of these States:

For cutting off our Trade with all parts of the world:

For imposing taxes on us without our Consent:

For depriving us in many cases, of the benefits of Trial by Jury:

For transporting us beyond Seas to be tried for pretended offences:

For abolishing the free System of English Laws in a neighboring Province, establishing therein an Arbitrary government, and enlarging its Boundaries so as to render it at once an example and fit instrument for introducing the same absolute rule into these Colonies:

For taking away our Charters, abolishing our most valuable Laws, and altering fundamentally the Forms of our Governments:

For suspending our own Legislature, and declaring themselves invested with Power to legislate for us in all cases whatsoever.

He has abdicated Government here, by declaring us out of his Protection and waging War against us.

He has plundered our seas, ravaged our Coasts, burnt our towns, and destroyed the lives of our people.

He is at this time transporting large armies of foreign mercenaries to complete the works of death, desolation and tyranny, already begun with circumstances of Cruelty & perfidy scarcely paralleled in the most barbarous ages, and totally unworthy the Head of a civilized nation.

He has constrained our fellow Citizens taken Captive on the high Seas to bear Arms against their Country, to become the executioners of their friends and Brethren, or to fall themselves by their Hands.

He has excited domestic insurrections amongst us, and has endeavored to bring on the inhabitants of our frontiers, the merciless Indian Savages, whose known rule of warfare, is an undistinguished destruction of all ages, sexes and conditions.

In every stage of these Oppressions We have Petitioned for Redress in the most humble terms: Our repeated Petitions have been answered only by repeated injury. A Prince, whose character is thus marked by every act which may define a Tyrant, is unfit to be the ruler of a free People.

Democratic Values

Why were the colonists protesting British tax policies?

The "neighboring Province" referred to here is Quebec.
arbitrary: not based on law
render: make

abdicated: given up

foreign mercenaries: soldiers hired to fight for a country not their own
perfidy: violation of trust

insurrections: rebellions

petitioned for redress: asked formally for a correction of wrongs

This painting by Robert Pine and Edward Savage depicts the Continental Congress voting for independence.

DEMOCRATIC VALUES

The Signers of the Declaration. The men who eventually signed the Declaration came from diverse backgrounds. Many, such as Arthur Middleton and Lewis Morris, grew up in wealthy families and received good educations. Others, such as Samuel Huntington and Roger Sherman, came from humble beginnings. One signer, George Taylor, had come to the colonies as an indentured servant. Taylor eventually received his freedom. He served the Continental Army during the Revolutionary War by producing munitions.

CRITICAL THINKING How might Taylor's life have reflected the ideals of the Declaration and the Revolution?

ANSWER: Students might suggest that Taylor's life reflected the importance of equal opportunity for all.

DEMOCRATIC VALUES ANSWER

The colonists protested the king's taxes because they were imposed without their consent.

DEMOCRATIC VALUES ANSWER

(for p. 20)

The colonists received their authority to declare independence from the colonial people themselves.

John Hancock. John Hancock had been at the forefront of the colonial drive for independence since the mid-1760s. Because of his leadership role in that movement, customs officers confiscated his ship, *Liberty*, in the late 1760s. A patriot mob attacked in response. The first man to sign the Declaration, Hancock signed his name in very large script in the middle of the page. According to legend, Hancock declared that the king would be able to read it without his spectacles. Today, asking for a person's "John Hancock" is synonymous with asking for his or her signature.

CRITICAL THINKING How might the confiscation of *Liberty* have further encouraged Hancock to support the independence movement?

ANSWER: Students might suggest that Hancock saw the confiscation as a prime example of British tyranny.

THAT'S INTERESTING!

After passing the Declaration of Independence, the members of the Continental Congress requested that copies be sent to the commanders of Patriot troops. When one reached George Washington, he read it to his soldiers, hoping to boost their morale.

unwarrantable jurisdiction: unjustified authority

magnanimity: generous spirit

conjured: urgently called upon

consanguinity: common ancestry

acquiesce: consent to

rectitude: rightness

Congress adopted the final draft of the Declaration of Independence on July 4, 1776. A formal copy, written on parchment paper, was signed on August 2, 1776.

Democratic Values

From whom did the signers of the Declaration receive their authority to declare independence?

The following is part of a passage that the Congress took out of Jefferson's original draft: "He has waged cruel war against human nature itself, violating its most sacred rights of life and liberty in the persons of a distant people who never offended him, captivating and carrying them into slavery in another hemisphere, or to incur miserable death in their transportation thither." ***Why do you think the Congress deleted this passage?***

Nor have We been wanting in attention to our British brethren. We have warned them from time to time of attempts by their legislature to extend an unwarrantable jurisdiction over us. We have reminded them of the circumstances of our emigration and settlement here. We have appealed to their native justice and magnanimity, and we have conjured them by the ties of our common kindred to disavow these usurpations, which, would inevitably interrupt our connections and correspondence. They too have been deaf to the voice of justice and of consanguinity. We must, therefore, acquiesce in the necessity, which denounces our Separation, and hold them, as we hold the rest of mankind, Enemies in War, in Peace Friends.

We, therefore, the Representatives of the united States of America, in General Congress, Assembled, appealing to the Supreme Judge of the world for the rectitude of our intentions, do, in the Name, and by Authority of the good People of these Colonies, solemnly publish and declare, That these United Colonies are, and of Right ought to be Free and Independent States; that they are Absolved from all Allegiance to the British Crown, and that all political connection between them and the State of Great Britain, is and ought to be totally dissolved; and that as Free and Independent States, they have full Power to levy War, conclude Peace, contract Alliances, establish Commerce, and to do all other Acts and Things which Independent States may of right do. And for the support of this Declaration, with a firm reliance on the Protection of Divine Providence, we mutually pledge to each other our Lives, our Fortunes and our sacred Honor.

John Hancock
Button Gwinnett
Lyman Hall
George Walton
William Hooper
Joseph Hewes
John Penn
Edward Rutledge
Thomas Heyward Jr.
Thomas Lynch Jr.
Arthur Middleton
Samuel Chase
William Paca
Thomas Stone
Charles Carroll of Carrollton
George Wythe
Richard Henry Lee
Thomas Jefferson
Benjamin Harrison
Thomas Nelson Jr.
Francis Lightfoot Lee
Carter Braxton
Robert Morris
Benjamin Rush
Benjamin Franklin
John Morton
George Clymer
James Smith
George Taylor
James Wilson
George Ross
Caesar Rodney
George Read
Thomas McKean
William Floyd
Phillip Livingston
Francis Lewis
Lewis Morris
Richard Stockton
John Witherspoon
Francis Hopkinson
John Hart
Abraham Clark
Josiah Bartlett
William Whipple
Samuel Adams
John Adams
Robert Treat Paine
Elbridge Gerry
Stephen Hopkins
William Ellery
Roger Sherman
Samuel Huntington
William Williams
Oliver Wolcott
Matthew Thornton

OBJECTIVE 4 *Identify the social issues reformers addressed in the early to mid-1800s.*

After completing Section 3, students should be able to:

OBJECTIVE 1 *Describe what changes took place in foreign and domestic policy in the early 1800s.*

OBJECTIVE 2 *Discuss how industrialization and immigration affected northern society.*

OBJECTIVE 3 *Explain how southern society and the slave system were organized.*

LET'S GET STARTED!

As students enter the room, play Selection 1, "The Erie Canal," from the **American Music Audio CD Program**. Pass out copies of the song's discussion guide and tell students to write a few sentences relating the song to what they can remember about the Transportation Revolution and westward expansion. Tell students that in Section 3 they will learn about changes in society, politics, and the economy during the 1800s.

Growth and Change

OBJECTIVES

Read to understand:

1. what changes took place in foreign and domestic policy in the early 1800s
2. how industrialization and immigration affected northern society
3. how southern society and the slave system were organized
4. what social issues reformers addressed in the early to mid-1800s

KEY TERMS

nationalism
Monroe Doctrine
American System
Missouri Compromise
Trail of Tears
strike
nativism
cotton gin
Underground Railroad
Second Great Awakening
Seneca Falls Convention

KEY PEOPLE

James Monroe
Henry Clay
Andrew Jackson
Harriet Tubman
Dorothea Dix
Frederick Douglass
Sojourner Truth
Elizabeth Cady Stanton
Susan B. Anthony

"[American pride] blazes out everywhere and on all occasions."
—Anonymous British observer

Frances Wright

Americans' patriotism was particularly strong after the War of 1812. They displayed this pride in their Independence Day celebrations. Parades, picnics, and joyous parties marked the occasion. Even some foreign citizens observed the holiday. In the 1820s Frances Wright of Scotland, a travel writer and sometime U.S. resident, gave a Fourth of July speech in New Harmony, Indiana. She praised the United States as the protector of "human liberty [and] the favored scene of human improvement." Soon, she predicted, "all mankind" would celebrate "the Jubilee of Independence."

Building a Young Nation

The War of 1812 filled many Americans with a sense of **nationalism**, or national pride. As Americans celebrated their independence, the young nation began a period of prosperity. Manufacturing in the United States had expanded during the war. In 1816 Congress tried to aid the economy by chartering the Second Bank of the United States and passing a protective tariff on imported goods.

Foreign policy. To ensure continued prosperity, President James Monroe worked to avoid conflict with other nations. In 1817 the United States and Britain agreed to limit their naval presence on the Great Lakes. In 1818 the two nations set the U.S.-Canada border at the 49th parallel. The United States also settled a border dispute with Spain over Florida, gaining East Florida in the process.

By 1819 most of Spain's Latin American colonies had declared independence. The United States decided to recognize these new republics. In 1823 President Monroe announced what came to be called the **Monroe Doctrine**. He vowed that the United States would oppose any European attempts to regain former Latin American colonies or to establish new ones in the Western Hemisphere.

A transportation revolution. In 1824 Representative Henry Clay of Kentucky drew the government's attention back to domestic issues. Clay proposed a plan known as the **American System** that would establish stronger protective tariffs to aid industrial development. The plan would also fund a national transportation system. Transportation was a major problem in the early 1800s. British actress Fanny Kemble described the experience of riding in a stagecoach in New York.

> "[Traveling] through bog and marsh, and ruts, . . . with the roots of trees protruding across our path, . . . and, more than once, a half-demolished tree or stump lying in the middle of the road."

SECTION 3 RESOURCES

PRINT

- Guided Reading Strategy 1.3
- Primary Source Reading 1: Escape to Freedom
- Section 3 Review, p. 27
- Daily Quiz 1.3

MULTIMEDIA

- One-Stop Planner, Lesson 1.3
- American Music Selection 1: "The Erie Canal"
- Holt Researcher: American History CD–ROM
- HRW Web site

SHELTERED ENGLISH

- Main Idea Activity for Reteaching and Sheltered English 1.3

✔ READING TO UNDERSTAND

To help students master the section objectives, have them answer the **READING CHECKS** and complete **Guided Reading Strategy 1.3** as they read the section.

Multimedia Resources

American Music Selection 1: "The Erie Canal"

TEACH OBJECTIVE 1

ALL LEVELS: To help students understand what changes took place in foreign and domestic policy in the early 1800s, copy the following graphic organizer on the chalkboard, omitting the italicized answers. Have each student complete the graphic organizer. **Sheltered English**

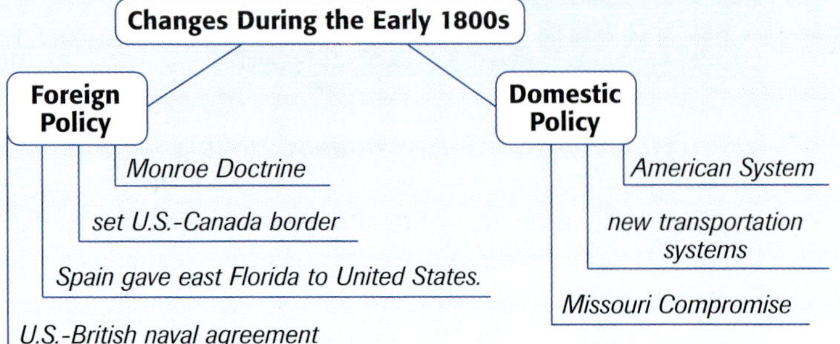

▸**ASSIGNMENT:** *Tell students to use the information in the graphic organizer to design commemorative stamps to celebrate one or more advancements in transportation during the early 1800s. Display stamps on the classroom wall.*

internet connect

TOPIC: Erie Canal
GO TO: go.hrw.com
KEYWORD: SE1 Erie

Have students access the Internet through the HRW Web site to conduct research on the history of the Erie Canal, the method of its construction, and the impact the canal had on transportation and the economy. Then create an illustrated guidebook that could be used in the visitor's center at the Erie Canal.

PRESIDENTIAL *Lives*

1758–1831
In Office 1817–1825

James Monroe

James Monroe was the last president to have fought in the Revolutionary War. He was also the last of the Founding Fathers to occupy the White House. Indeed, Monroe looked very much the colonial statesman. He wore a powdered wig and dressed in the fashion of an earlier age. He wore a cutaway coat, waistcoat, knee britches, long stockings, and buckled shoes.

Monroe's generally quiet personality matched his elegant appearance. Thomas Jefferson was a longtime friend of Monroe. Jefferson remarked that Monroe was "a man whose soul might be turned wrong side outward, without discovering a blemish to the world."

The federal government enacted much of the American System. In addition, some states began building their own canals and major roads. Newly developed steamboats combined with canals to provide faster and cheaper ways of shipping goods. By the 1830s steam-powered locomotives were also carrying passengers and cargo. These new transportation systems made possible the creation of national markets. For the first time, Americans could import needed goods and concentrate on producing only what was most profitable. Linking small communities to larger markets also increased the size of many towns.

The Missouri Compromise. The nation was also expanding westward. In 1819 the Missouri Territory applied for statehood as a slave state. The nation was then equally divided between 11 free states and 11 slave states. To prevent the admission of Missouri from upsetting this balance, Congress approved the **Missouri Compromise** in 1820. The agreement admitted Missouri as a slave state and Maine as a free state. It also banned slavery in the rest of the Louisiana Purchase north of Missouri's southern boundary.

The Rise of Jacksonian Democracy

Increasing westward expansion played an important role in the presidential elections of the 1820s. Voting rights were given to more adult white males, particularly in western states. Such voters helped elect Andrew Jackson to the presidency in 1828. A hero of the War of 1812, Jackson portrayed himself as "a man of the people."

Jackson changed the tone of politics in the United States. He replaced many existing government workers with his political supporters. He also appointed officeholders without regard to their social or economic class. Jackson's victory reflected a shift in America from an aristocratic society to one based on economic success.

Guests at a party for President Andrew Jackson cut into a giant wheel of cheese.

Jackson's American Indian policy. During the 1820s American Indians living in the East found themselves pressured to leave their lands. President Jackson suggested that they be moved westward, "where their white brothers will not trouble them." In 1830 Congress passed the Indian Removal Act. This act required American Indians living in the eastern United States to relocate to Indian Territory in present-day Oklahoma.

TEACH OBJECTIVE 2

LEVEL 1: Organize students into groups of four or five. Tell each group to imagine that they are a family of either laborers or recent immigrants living in the northern United States during the early 1800s. Have them work together to create a family scrapbook that explains how industrialization and immigration affected northern society. Students might include pictures, drawings, letters, newspaper clippings, and other items in their scrapbooks. *(Scrapbooks should include some of the following: increased use of machines in farming and manufacturing; increased poverty, worsening industrial conditions, more union and strike activity, new immigrant communities, and nativist protests.)* Call on a volunteer from each group to present its scrapbook to the class.
Sheltered English, Cooperative Learning

Most American Indians did not go willingly. Some wrote to Congress. Others chose to fight. In Florida the Seminole—aided by runaway slaves—fought the U.S. Army for seven years. Some Seminole managed to remain in Florida. The Cherokee used the U.S. court system to resist their removal. The Supreme Court ruled in their favor, limiting state power over them. However, Georgia officials—with the blessing of President Jackson—ignored the Court's order and continued their seizure of Cherokee lands. Without federal protection, the Cherokee were forced to move to Indian Territory. Some 4,000 Cherokee died on the march, which came to be known as the **Trail of Tears**. "Many fell . . . too faint with hunger or too weak to keep up with the rest," recalled one survivor.

INTERPRETING THE VISUAL RECORD

American Indian removal. Thousands of Cherokee from the southeastern United States were forced to move west on a journey known as the Trail of Tears. ***What does this image suggest about the conditions faced by the Cherokee on their journey?***

States' rights and economic woes. Most Americans were more concerned with the issue of states' rights than with the rights of American Indians. In 1828 Congress had passed a new tariff that doubled the rates on certain import items. Southerners, who relied heavily on imported goods, argued that the laws unfairly favored the industrial North. South Carolina threatened to secede and Congress agreed to lower the tariff rates.

Congress's rechartering of the Second Bank of the United States also caused great controversy. A few months before his re-election in 1832, Jackson vetoed the bank measure, sparking a fierce debate. By weakening federal control over the banking system, Jackson helped cause a financial crisis. Numerous banks were unable to meet people's demands to exchange their paper currency for gold and silver. As these banks failed, a full-scale depression began that lasted until 1843.

✔ **READING CHECK:** What changes in foreign and domestic policy took place in the early 1800s?

Northern and Southern Society

The cultural and economic differences between the North and the South grew during the 1800s. The North became less dependent upon agriculture, and slavery expanded in the South.

The industrial North. Manufacturing changed dramatically in the early 1800s. Mill owner Francis Cabot Lowell and others shifted from hand-powered weaving to machine production, which allowed cloth to be made more quickly. Young, single women flocked to work in industrial towns like Lowell, Massachusetts.

While the power looms transformed the factories, new tools transformed northern farms. Improvements to the plow and the development of the mechanized reaper made farm work easier and faster. Englishman Joseph Whitworth noted in 1854 that Americans "call in the aid of machinery in almost every department of industry."

ECONOMIC DEVELOPMENT

Southerners and the Tariff. Some southerners based their opposition to tariffs on the Forty Bale theory. According to this theory, a 40 percent tariff on imports made from cotton—items of clothing, for example—would raise prices by 40 percent, which in turn would reduce consumption of cotton goods by 40 percent. As a result, textile manufacturers would require less cotton and would thus reduce their demand for southern cotton by 40 percent. Southerners argued that they would therefore lose the profit on 40 out of every 100 bales of cotton they produced because of tariff increases. Although the Forty Bale theory was not economically sophisticated, it appealed to many southerners.

CRITICAL THINKING What might be the weakness in the Forty Bale theory?

ANSWER: Students might answer that it assumes that consumers will buy less when prices rise, which is not always the case with necessities such as clothing.

VISUAL RECORD ANSWER

Students might suggest that some Indians were forced to walk and to carry all their possessions.

LEVELS 2 AND 3: Pair students and tell them to imagine that they are consultants hired to ensure historical accuracy for a movie set in the northern United States during the early 1800s. Have students write a paragraph describing how industrialization and immigration affected northern society. *(See the Level 1 lesson for the correct effects.)* Encourage students to include drawings of what these people might have looked like. Ask volunteers to read their descriptions to the class. **Cooperative Learning**

TEACH OBJECTIVE 3

LEVELS 1 AND 2: Have students draw a series of pictures showing how southern society and the slave system were organized. *(Pictures should include plantation owners—leaders in society and politics; small farmers—the majority of southern whites; poor whites and free African Americans—the smallest group; slaves—most of whom were workers on plantations and farms.)* Drawings might be diagrams of plantations and farms, or they might be pictures of people in varying numbers to reflect relative population and political power, or any other reasonable imagery. **Sheltered English**

HISTORY MAKERS SPEAK

John Avery in *The Way We Lived: Essays and Documents in American Social History*, vol. 1

Mill Regulations. In 1848 John Avery, a mill agent, released rules regarding mill employees' conduct. "The [Hamilton Manufacturing] company will not employ any one who is habitually absent from public worship on the Sabbath, or known to be guilty of immorality. . . . These regulations are considered part of the contract, with which all persons entering into the employment of the Hamilton Manufacturing Company, engage to comply."

CRITICAL THINKING How might the rules that Avery established differ from typical workplace rules today?

ANSWER: Students might suggest that employers today cannot require that employees attend religious services.

THAT'S INTERESTING!

Slaves often resorted to ingenious means to gain their freedom. Some traveled north in disguise. Henry Box Brown mailed himself to freedom. In a journey lasting 26 hours, Brown was shipped from Richmond, Virginia, to Philadelphia, Pennsylvania.

Lowell Girls

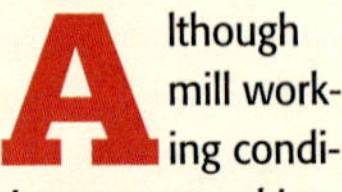

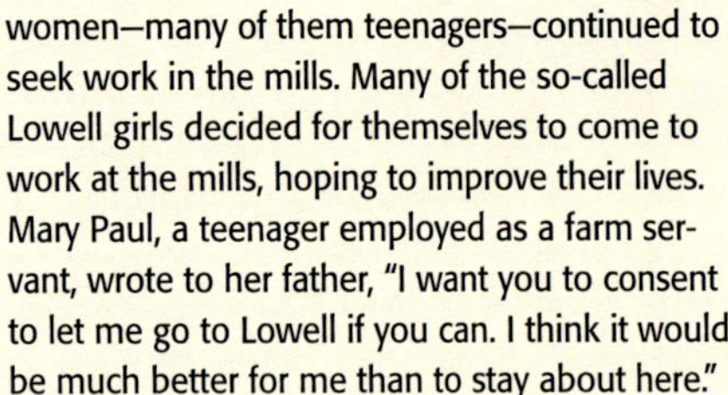

Although mill working conditions worsened in the 1830s, young women—many of them teenagers—continued to seek work in the mills. Many of the so-called Lowell girls decided for themselves to come to work at the mills, hoping to improve their lives. Mary Paul, a teenager employed as a farm servant, wrote to her father, "I want you to consent to let me go to Lowell if you can. I think it would be much better for me than to stay about here."

Life for the Lowell girls was difficult, and mill work was hard. However, many of the girls welcomed their independence and the opportunity to earn money. They used their salaries to help support their families, to get married, to purchase clothes and other personal items, and to pay for an education. Most girls saw mill work as a stepping-stone in their lives. This was a way of "bettering the condition of themselves and those they loved," wrote Lucy Larcom. She had come to Lowell at the age of 11 and went on to become a well-known poet.

Although labor in the mills was demanding, some teenagers coming from rural farms found that factory work opened up new paths and opportunities for them. Larcom wrote years later about her time at the mills. "I was every day making discoveries about life, and about myself. . . . I know that I was glad to be alive, and to be just where I was." Some Lowell girls took evening classes, formed literary societies, listened to lectures, attended plays and concerts, and even published a magazine, the *Lowell Offering*.

Industrial machinery provided new work opportunities for young women.

Despite the general prosperity, many workers lived in poverty. Entire families, including children, often worked long hours just to survive. Worsening industrial conditions prompted labor leaders to organize workers into unions. They sought such reforms as shorter workdays and higher wages. Unions used many methods to try to achieve their goals. These included the **strike**—the refusal to work until employers meet union demands. Union activity forced politicians to respond to the workers' complaints. By the 1840s several states had reduced the length of the workday.

The labor force grew larger in the 1830s as immigration to the United States soared. The largest group of immigrants came from Ireland. Irish immigrants faced prejudice and were often forced to settle in crowded city slums. The Irish were followed in the mid-1800s by a wave of German immigrants. Many settled in the rural Midwest. Smaller numbers of Dutch, Scandinavian, and Swiss immigrants also settled in the region. All of these immigrant groups formed tightly knit communities.

Some native-born Americans protested the immigrants' arrival. One wealthy New Yorker claimed that of the new immigrants "not one in twenty is competent [capable] to keep [provide for] himself." Such feelings gave rise to **nativism**—the favoring of native-born Americans over foreign-born residents.

✔ **READING CHECK:** How did industrialization and immigration affect northern society?

The Cotton Kingdom. The South had long relied on agriculture and slave labor. Industrialization developed much more slowly than in the North. Eli Whitney's invention of the **cotton gin**, a machine that made it easier to remove cotton seeds, led to the emergence of the South as the Cotton Kingdom. From 1815 to 1860, cotton represented more than half of all U.S. exports. Farmers in the Upper South grew mostly corn and tobacco.

Southern society reflected the importance of slavery to the region's economy. Just one in four southern white families owned slaves, but this group of slaveholders dominated society and politics. Most plantation owners held fewer than 20 slaves. Small farmers, who made up the majority of southern whites, were located beneath the planters on the social scale. They lived simply, grew their own food, and rarely owned slaves. Poorer white farmers made up a small percentage of the population.

By 1860 some 260,000 free African Americans lived in the South. White southerners greatly restricted the rights of free blacks. Laws prohibited them from voting, holding public meetings, and testifying in court against whites. An editorial in a newspaper for free African Americans stated, "Though we are not slaves, we are not free."

LEVEL 3: Tell students to create the table of contents and the book jacket summary for a book entitled Southern Society and the Slave System. *(See the Levels 1 and 2 lesson for correct organization.)* Inform students that the book discusses the organization and power structure of the South as well as the institution of slavery and those who rebelled against it.

SPOTLIGHT on the Underground Railroad

Pair students and ask them to create a brochure on the Underground Railroad. Brochures should include information on and quotations from conductor Harriet Tubman. Students should also include a map suggesting a possible route from the South to freedom.

Block Scheduling, Cooperative Learning

The Slave System

The increase in cotton cultivation resulted in an expansion of slavery. Some southerners criticized slavery, but planters argued that it was the only way to ensure an adequate supply of field workers. More than 75 percent of enslaved African Americans lived and worked on plantations and farms. Many worked from dawn to dusk. One former field hand explained, "The rule on the place was: Wake up the slaves at daylight, begin work when they can see, and quit work when they can't see." Slaveholders relied on various means, including physical punishment, to control their slaves. Rebellious slaves were sold away from family and community ties.

To endure these harsh circumstances, slaves devoted their rare free time to family and community. They developed a unique culture that drew on both African customs and their experiences in America. Slaves were forbidden to learn how to read. They told oral histories and folk tales to preserve and pass on their culture. They also expressed their spiritual beliefs through folk art, music, and religious services.

Slaves constantly protested their bondage, both through group and individual actions. Several small uprisings took place in the early 1800s. Then, in 1831 Nat Turner organized a violent revolt in Virginia. Turner and his followers killed some 60 whites before being captured. These uprisings led southern states to pass stricter slave codes that further limited slaves' activities.

Other methods of protest included disrupting the plantation routine through such tactics as faking illness or working slowly. Some slaves ran away and tried to gain their freedom in the North. Assistance came from the **Underground Railroad**, a network of white and African American people who helped escaped slaves reach the North. Escaped slave Harriet Tubman was the most famous and successful "conductor" on the Underground Railroad. She made at least 19 trips and escorted more than 300 slaves to freedom. "There was one of two things I had a right to," she stated. "Liberty or death: if I could not have one, I would have the other; for no man would take me alive."

✔ **READING CHECK:** How were southern society and the slave system organized?

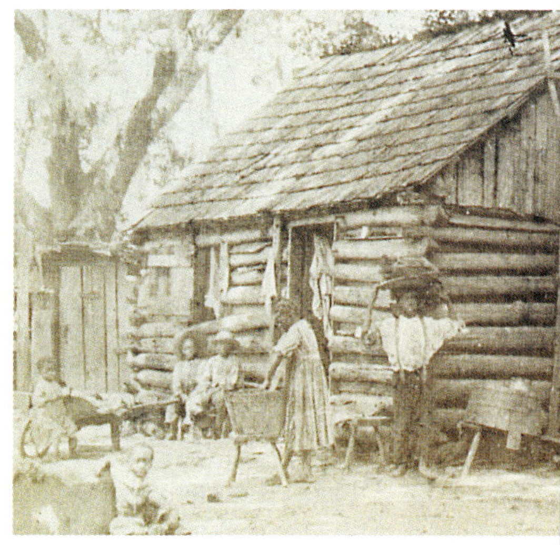

INTERPRETING THE VISUAL RECORD

Slave life. This 1860s image shows members of a slave family in front of their log cabin in the woods of Georgia. ***What does the image suggest about the living conditions of slaves?***

The Second Great Awakening and Social Reform

The social changes transforming American society led many people to turn to religion for direction. In the 1790s a renewed and powerful interest in religion—the **Second Great Awakening**—began spreading westward from New York. Huge crowds gathered to listen to sermons, sing hymns, and seek God's help in reforming their lives. Ministers expressed an optimistic belief that individuals could receive eternal salvation. Church membership soared, particularly drawing women and African Americans.

Many participants in the Second Great Awakening also worked to help solve social problems. Women took an active role in these efforts, particularly in the temperance movement. Many reformers believed that alcohol abuse led to criminal behavior, family violence, and poverty. Temperance groups succeeded in

Newspapers often published advertisements for the capture of runaway slaves.

ACROSS THE CURRICULUM

▶LITERATURE◀

Joel Chandler Harris and African American Folktales. Joel Chandler Harris, a white author, collected and presented African American folktales in his highly popular books. Harris grew up in Putnam County, Georgia, an area with a large African American population. As a boy, he worked on the *Countryman*, a weekly newspaper located on a local plantation. While there, he became acquainted with many slaves and spent much time listening to their stories. In the 1870s Harris began to work at the *Atlanta Constitution*, where he wrote articles about those tales. The articles were extremely successful, and Harris went on to write the books *Uncle Remus and His Friends*, *Mr. Rabbit at Home*, and *Uncle Remus and Br'er Rabbit*, which were also quite popular.

CRITICAL THINKING What might the success of Harris's books indicate about the nature of American culture?

ANSWER: Students might suggest that the success indicates that aspects of slave culture have been absorbed into American culture.

VISUAL RECORD ANSWER

Students might suggest that it reveals poor conditions.

TEACH OBJECTIVE 4

LEVEL 1: Ask students to list the social issues that reformers addressed in the early to mid-1800s. *(Students should mention temperance, education, poverty, care for people with mental illness, prison reform, abolition, and women's rights.)* Record students' responses on the chalkboard. Then call on volunteers to explain how reformers set about addressing one or more of the social issues listed. Allow students to refer to their textbooks. **Sheltered English**

LEVELS 2 AND 3: Have students list the social issues that reformers addressed in the early to mid-1800s. *(See the Level 1 lesson for the correct issues.)* Then pair students and have them choose one of these issues. Tell them to work together to write an article for a modern newsmagazine that is doing a retrospective on American reform movements from the 1800s to the present. Instruct students to write about how the movement began; how reformers in the 1800s worked to bring about change; and how their efforts or continuing efforts of present-day activists have affected modern American society. Encourage students to include pictures or diagrams to supplement their articles. **Cooperative Learning**

CULTURAL DIVERSITY

Dress Reform. Female reformers had to fight for what most women today consider a personal right: freedom to dress how one wants. During the mid-1800s, women were expected to wear long skirts that weighed about 20 pounds and corsets that put extreme pressure on the abdominal area. These corsets often broke ribs and damaged internal organs. When women tried to wear bloomers–baggy pantaloons under a short skirt–they were followed and jeered at. Despite the freedom of movement these clothes allowed, women's rights advocates had to forego their comfortable clothing because they distracted people too much from women's demands for suffrage.

CRITICAL THINKING Why might there have been resistance to a change in women's dress styles?

ANSWER: Students might suggest that some people feared that freedom of dress would encourage women to seek other freedoms.

VISUAL RECORD ANSWER

Students might cite books, desks, and a teacher.

Religious artwork illustrating the paths of good and evil

persuading many Americans to limit alcohol consumption. Some states even banned the sale of alcohol.

Reformers also worked to improve educational institutions. They argued for public, tax-supported elementary schools. They believed that schools were necessary to educate citizens about democratic values and to create a literate and disciplined workforce. Massachusetts established a model for free, public elementary education. Other states soon followed. Public high schools also opened, and college opportunities for women and African Americans expanded.

Many reformers wanted to create and improve facilities for disadvantaged people, such as mentally ill or poor Americans. Reformers established poorhouses where the able-bodied poor could work. Dorothea Dix began her crusade to help the mentally ill after seeing how badly they were treated in a Massachusetts prison. Her efforts resulted in the establishment of more than 100 hospitals across the nation where the mentally ill could receive professional treatment. Some reformers believed that criminals could be rehabilitated and then returned to the community as productive citizens. They sought to improve living conditions in prisons.

Not all reformers supported every cause or agreed with the reasons for reform. Some reformers were motivated by their religious beliefs to seek fair treatment for all people. Others argued that social reforms helped create good citizens for the republic. Regardless of their reasons, the reformers of the early 1800s helped improve the quality of life for many Americans.

The Fight to End Slavery

Most northern states had abolished slavery by the early 1800s. Reformers known as abolitionists believed that the institution of slavery should be outlawed in the entire United States. Some abolitionists established the African colony of Liberia for freed slaves. Many free African Americans rejected this plan, however. African American abolitionist Henry Highland Garnet explained his opposition.

> **"America is my home, my country, and I have no other. . . . I mourn because the accursed shade of slavery rests upon it. I love my country's flag, and I hope that soon it will be cleansed of its stains, and be hailed by all nations as the emblem of freedom and independence."**

In 1833 African American and white abolitionists formed the first national antislavery organization. The American Anti-Slavery Society called for abolition and racial equality. Frederick Douglass, an escaped slave, gave speeches about his life "suffered under the lash." He won the society many supporters.

The society excluded women from its membership. Nevertheless, women came to assume many important roles in its efforts. Sojourner Truth, also a fugitive slave, traveled through New England supporting abolition. The Grimké sisters, Sarah and Angelina, gave many antislavery speeches. Angelina Grimké published a pamphlet in which she urged southern women to join her cause. "I know you do not make the laws," she wrote, "but . . . if you really suppose you can do nothing to overthrow slavery, you are greatly mistaken."

INTERPRETING THE VISUAL RECORD

Education. Some reformers argued that all children deserved an education. ***What types of educational resources did this school have?***

REVIEW

Have students complete the **Section 3 Review** on p. 27.

ASSESS

Have students complete **Daily Quiz 1.3**. As **Alternative Assessment**, you may want to use the graphic organizer activity or the magazine article activity in this section's lessons.

RETEACH

Have students complete **Main Idea Activity for Reteaching and Sheltered English 1.3**. Organize students into four groups and assign one objective in this section to each group. Direct each group to write two questions and answers pertaining to its assigned objective. Collect the questions and answers and use them to review and quiz the entire class.

Sheltered English, Cooperative Learning

EXTEND

Organize students into four groups and assign each group one of the objectives in this section. Tell each group to invent a game to teach its assigned topic to students two years younger than themselves. Tell students to make their games fun and challenging. If possible, take the class to meet with a younger class and have them teach their games to the younger students.

Block Scheduling, Cooperative Learning

Southerners felt increasingly threatened by the growing movement. Opposition to abolition also rose in the North. Some northerners held prejudices against African Americans and feared that abolition would cause increased job competition. Violence against abolitionists increased in the 1830s.

A women's rights activist demands the right to vote.

The Fight for Women's Rights

In the late 1840s many female reformers began to struggle for their own rights. Sarah and Angelina Grimké and Sojourner Truth were among the first to combine the fight for abolition with the fight for women's rights.

Elizabeth Cady Stanton and Lucretia Mott organized the **Seneca Falls Convention** in New York in 1848. This gathering was the first national women's rights convention. Some 100 of the 300 participants signed a petition known as the Declaration of Sentiments. It called for legal reforms, particularly voting rights for women. Stanton argued that having the vote was crucial to winning full equality. She explained that "the power to choose rulers and make laws was the right by which all others could be secured."

Stanton and Susan B. Anthony campaigned for property rights for women in New York State. Responding to petitions, New York began permitting married women to own property, file lawsuits, and keep their earnings. Anthony also helped create a nationwide system of women's rights organizations. Achieving political and legal equality at the national level remained a struggle, however.

✔ **READING CHECK:** What societal issues did reformers address in the early to mid-1800s?

Read More About It

Free Find: Sojourner Truth's Narrative

After reading the selection by Sojourner Truth on the **Holt Researcher** CD-ROM, write a short essay explaining how you think her speech might have helped the antislavery and women's rights causes.

SECTION  REVIEW

Define and explain the significance of the following terms:

nationalism, Monroe Doctrine, American System, Missouri Compromise, Trail of Tears, strike, nativism, cotton gin, Underground Railroad, Second Great Awakening, Seneca Falls Convention

Identify and explain the significance of the following individuals:

James Monroe, Henry Clay, Andrew Jackson, Harriet Tubman, Dorothea Dix, Frederick Douglass, Sojourner Truth, Elizabeth Cady Stanton, Susan B. Anthony

1. **Using Graphic Organizers** Copy the organizer below. Use it to show the similarities and differences between the societies of the North and the South.

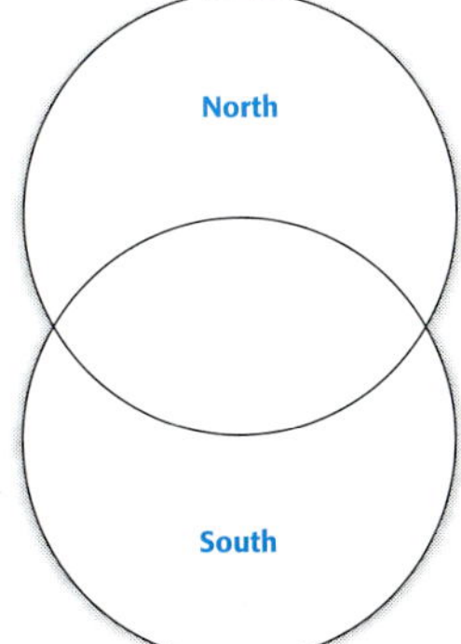

2. **Synthesizing** How did nationalism affect the development of the United States, in terms of the nation's foreign policy and its economy?
3. **Comparing and Contrasting** What were the similarities and differences among the reform movements of the early to mid-1800s?
4. **Using Historical Imagination** Imagine that you are an escaped slave living in the North. Write a brief speech describing your experiences as a plantation slave for an abolitionist meeting.

Critical Thinking

5. The Jacksonian era has been viewed as a period that contributed to the rise of American democracy. Do you agree with this assessment? Why or why not?

Consider:
- the process of American Indian removal
- the bank crisis and the tariff crisis
- how voting rights were expanded

SECTION 3 REVIEW ANSWERS

Define and Identify

For significance, see the following pages:

- nationalism, p. 21
- James Monroe, p. 21
- Monroe Doctrine, p. 21
- Henry Clay, p. 21
- American System, p. 21
- Missouri Compromise, p. 22
- Andrew Jackson, p. 22
- Trail of Tears, p. 23
- strike, p. 24
- nativism, p. 24
- cotton gin, p. 24
- Underground Railroad, p. 25
- Harriet Tubman, p. 25
- Second Great Awakening, p. 25
- Dorothea Dix, p. 26
- Frederick Douglass, p. 26
- Sojourner Truth, p. 26
- Elizabeth Cady Stanton, p. 27
- Seneca Falls Convention, p. 27
- Susan B. Anthony, p. 27

1. similarities—some agriculture, poor conditions for workers; differences—North: industrial, many immigrants; South: slavery

2. Nationalism led to the Monroe Doctrine, internal improvements, and westward expansion.

3. similarities—organized mostly by women, sought social change; differences—target of reform, reasons for reform

4. Answers will vary but should show an understanding of plantation slavery.

5. Answers will vary. Students should provide examples from the text to support their answers.

SECTION 4

After completing Section 4, students should be able to:

OBJECTIVE 1 *Analyze the causes of the Texas Revolution and the Mexican War.*

OBJECTIVE 2 *Explain why Americans began to settle the West.*

OBJECTIVE 3 *Discuss how politicians addressed the expansion of slavery.*

OBJECTIVE 4 *Identify what events led to the secession of the southern states.*

LET'S GET STARTED!

Write the following five dates on the chalkboard: *5000 B.C., 1492, 1776, 1812,* and *1861.* Have students write the major event of that year, as it relates to U.S. history. *(Students should answer Agricultural Revolution in the Americas, Columbus lands in the Americas, Declaration of Independence, war with Britain, and secession.)* Tell students that in Section 4 they will learn about the events that led up to the secession of the southern states and the formation of the Confederacy.

SECTION 4 RESOURCES

PRINT

- Guided Reading Strategy 1.4
- Graphic Organizer Activity 1: Changes over Time
- American History Outline Map 9: Conflict over Slavery
- Section 4 Review, p. 33
- Daily Quiz 1.4

MULTIMEDIA

- One-Stop Planner, Lesson 1.4
- Holt Researcher: American History CD–ROM

SHELTERED ENGLISH

- Main Idea Activity for Reteaching and Sheltered English 1.4

✔ READING TO UNDERSTAND
To help students master the section objectives, have them answer the **READING CHECKS** and complete **Guided Reading Strategy 1.4** as they read the section.

Westward Expansion and Sectional Conflict

OBJECTIVES

Read to understand:

1. what caused the Texas Revolution and the Mexican War
2. why Americans began to settle the West
3. how politicians addressed the expansion of slavery
4. what events led to the secession of the southern states

KEY TERMS

manifest destiny
Texas Revolution
Mexican War of 1846
Mexican Cession
popular sovereignty
Compromise of 1850
Kansas-Nebraska Act
Republican Party
Dred Scott decision
Confederate States of America

KEY PEOPLE

Juan Seguín
Harriet Beecher Stowe
Stephen Douglas
John Brown
Dred Scott
Abraham Lincoln

“Some of the women I saw on the road went through a great deal of suffering and trial. I remember distinctly one girl in particular about my own age that died and was buried on the road. Her mother had a great deal of trouble and suffering. It strikes me as I think of it now that Mothers on the road had to undergo more trial and suffering than anybody else.”

—Martha Ann Morrison

Conestoga wagon

Martha Ann Morrison traveled to Oregon Country at the age of 13. She recalled the extreme hardships many settlers endured during the westward journey. During the early 1800s American merchants and fur trappers had built trade links with residents of California, New Mexico, and Oregon Country. In the process, they established trails that brought a flood of new settlers like Morrison to the Far West in the 1840s and 1850s.

The Southwest

In 1845 magazine editor John L. O'Sullivan coined the term **manifest destiny**. This phrase expressed the belief held by many Americans that God intended the United States to expand westward to the Pacific Ocean. The idea of manifest destiny appealed to Americans who felt that a larger country would lessen population pressures, create new markets, and expand farmland.

Texas. Americans had begun settling in Texas with the permission of the Mexican government as early as 1821. In 1830, however, Mexico closed the Texas border to Americans. In 1833 General Antonio López de Santa Anna became Mexico's president and established himself as a dictator. These events angered many Texans. They started a rebellion known as the **Texas Revolution** in December 1835. Mexican troops arrived in February 1836 to recapture the city of San Antonio from the rebels. After suffering heavy losses the Mexican soldiers killed all the Texan troops occupying the Alamo, a Catholic mission. The revolution continued, and in April the Texans surprised Santa Anna's army near the San Jacinto River. Shouting “Remember the Alamo!” the Texans won a decisive victory. Mexico signed a treaty granting Texas its independence in the spring of 1836.

During the next few years, the government of the Republic of Texas encouraged European immigration in order to increase its population. European immigrants fared well in the new republic. Texans of Mexican descent, even those who had fought for Texas's independence, often found themselves the victims of violence and discrimination.

Robert Onerdonk's painting of the fall of the Alamo

TEACH OBJECTIVE 1

LEVEL 1: Have students work in pairs or triads to create illustrated time lines showing the sequence of events in the Texas Revolution and the Mexican War. *(Time lines should include: 1821—Americans begin settling in Texas; 1830—Mexico closes border to Americans; 1833—Santa Anna becomes Mexico's president; 1835—Texas Revolution begins; 1836—Texas independence; 1844—Polk elected president promising to annex Texas; 1846—United States declares war on Mexico.)* Students should include a sentence explaining how these events were causes of the Texas Revolution and the Mexican War. Ask volunteers to share their time lines with the class.
Sheltered English, Cooperative Learning

LEVELS 2 AND 3: Tell students to imagine that they are military leaders who fought in both the Texas Revolution and the Mexican War. Have them write an official report on one of these conflicts—including the causes, major events, and outcome—to file with their commanding officers at the end of the war. *(See the Level 1 lesson for the correct causes.)* Invite volunteers to read their reports to the class.

BIOGRAPHY *Juan Seguín*

Juan Seguín (se-GEEN) faced such discrimination. Born in 1806 into a prominent San Antonio family, Seguín developed a strong interest in politics. He harshly criticized Mexico's government during the 1830s, and he joined the rebels during the Texas Revolution. Seguín escaped the slaughter at the Alamo because he had left to find reinforcements for the besieged Texans. He later fought at San Jacinto. After the war Seguín served as the mayor of San Antonio.

In 1842 white settlers in San Antonio falsely accused Seguín of retaining his loyalties to Mexico. "The necessity to defend myself for the loyal patriotism with which I had always served Texas, wounded me deeply," he later recalled. Seguín fled to Mexico, where he lived out his final years. He died in 1890.

Read More About It

Free Find: Juan Seguín
After reading about Juan Seguín on the **Holt Researcher** CD–ROM, create a short story, song, or poem about Seguín's experiences in Texas.

The Mexican War of 1846. Tensions between the United States and Mexico remained high. In 1844 James K. Polk was elected president. Polk wanted to annex Texas to the United States. Congress voted to admit Texas into the Union despite opposition from Mexico. Conflict over the border between Texas and Mexico led the United States to declare war on Mexico in May 1846.

During the **Mexican War of 1846**, U.S. forces marched into central Mexico and seized control of New Mexico and California. U.S. troops were sometimes aided by American settlers in these regions. Despite these early successes, fierce fighting raged in Mexico. In September 1847 Mexico City finally fell to U.S. forces.

In February 1848 a treaty ended the war. Mexico gave up all its claims to Texas and surrendered a vast territory known as the **Mexican Cession**. This area included present-day California, Nevada, and Utah, and parts of Arizona, Colorado, New Mexico, and Wyoming. The United States agreed to pay Mexico $15 million for this land, which was occupied by some 80,000 Spanish-speaking citizens. Despite the treaty's guarantees, many of these people lost their lands.

✔ **READING CHECK:** What caused the Texas Revolution and the Mexican War?

The Lure of the West

When the United States took control of California, the area was lightly settled by Europeans. California changed dramatically with the discovery of gold in 1848, however. Thousands of people rushed to seek their fortune. By June 1849 more than 40,000 people had set off for California.

Mining camps soon sprang up to accommodate the migrants. These camps were often dirty, disorderly, and dangerous. Most of the miners did not find the great wealth they had hoped for. José Fernandez lived in northern California. He later recalled that "just as every day many [gold diggers] set out full of hope and confidence in the future, so every day many returned, disgusted with the mines."

By 1852 California's non–American Indian population had leaped from some 14,000 in 1848 to more than

INTERPRETING THE VISUAL RECORD
Miners. Miners at Auburn Ravine posed for this photograph in 1852. ***What does this image reveal about the variety of people who came to California in search of gold?***

GLOBAL RELATIONS

Los Niños Heroicos. At the time of the U.S. attack on Mexico City, Chapultepec served as Mexico's military academy. Although many Mexican soldiers fled as the U.S. Army approached, some teenage cadets refused to abandon their school. One boy was shot when he tried to save the Mexican flag. Another student was bayoneted when he tried to load his musket. In total, six teenage cadets died. After the war, Mexicans named these young soldiers *los niños heroicos*–the heroic children. Many Mexicans saw *los niños heroicos* as martyrs.

CRITICAL THINKING Ask students to name two or three American martyrs. What purpose might these martyrs have served in history?

ANSWER: Answers will vary. Students might name abolitionist Elijah Lovejoy or civil rights activist Martin Luther King Jr. Students might suggest that martyrs serve to inspire people to support a particular cause or remind them of the importance of the cause.

VISUAL RECORD ANSWER
Students might suggest that it shows great ethnic diversity.

TEACH OBJECTIVE 2

LEVELS 1 AND 2: Tell students to imagine that they are pioneers settling the West. Have them write a letter to a family member or friend who stayed in the East, telling him or her about why they moved to the West. *(Letters might include as reasons hunting and trapping, farm land, religious freedom, gold rush, adventure, and so on.)* **Sheltered English**

LEVEL 3: Have students write short stories set on a wagon train headed for the West. Students should mention in their stories why their characters are settling in the West. *(See the Levels 1 and 2 lesson for the correct reasons.)* Call on volunteers to read all or part of their stories to the class.

SPOTLIGHT on American Indians in the West

Tell students to imagine that they are American Indians living in California or Oregon in the mid-1800s. Have them create an oral history describing what is happening to their lives and population as American settlers arrive in the area. Students should conduct additional research as necessary to complete their oral histories. Ask volunteers to share their work with the class. **Block Scheduling**

DEMOCRATIC VALUES

Governing the Wagon Trains. Some pioneers created their own rules and regulations to keep order in the wagon trains. One group formed a Council of Ten to settle disputes and try offenders. The settlers allowed all men over the age of 16 to vote for the members of this council.

ACTIVITY: Organize students into groups of 8 or 10. Tell students to imagine that they are the members of a wagon train that will depart for Oregon Country tomorrow. Have each group create a list of at least five rules that will govern its group. Toward the end of class, have volunteers share their lists, justifying each rule.

STRATEGIES FOR SUCCESS

Applying the Strategy
Students should create a list of words with definitions.

Practicing the Strategy

1. a belief held by many Americans that God intended the United States to expand westward to the Pacific Ocean; text defines it
2. a practice allowing the citizens of a territory to vote whether to permit slavery; text defines it

220,000. These new immigrants were often intolerant. They frequently prevented original Spanish settlers, Chinese immigrants, and African Americans from mining for gold. Additionally, the gold rush led to disaster for many American Indians. Miners drove them off their gold-rich lands and even forced some of them to work in the mines. By 1860 California's American Indian population had decreased from some 300,000 to about 35,000.

The population of the Pacific Northwest also expanded in the mid-1800s. Thousands of families set out for Oregon Country along the Oregon Trail in the 1840s and 1850s, often in large groups of wagon trains. The settlement of Oregon Country led the United States and Britain to finalize the U.S.-Canada border.

American Indians often helped pioneers along the trail by serving as guides and selling them wild game for food. Yet eastern newspapers emphasized the attacks that did occur and reported massacres of pioneers. To ease settlers' fears, the U.S. government negotiated with American Indian tribes. In return for their not attacking pioneers, the United States promised to make annual payments to the American Indians and honor territorial boundaries. However, pioneers often introduced diseases that caused many American Indian deaths. Settlers also wiped out wildlife by clearing land and hunting. As a result, some American Indians tried unsuccessfully to drive the settlers out.

✔ **READING CHECK:** Why did Americans begin to settle the West?

Strategies for Success — Building Vocabulary

In your study of history, you will regularly come across new and unfamiliar words. Learning the meaning of these words will enlarge your vocabulary and help you understand new information and ideas.

How to Build Vocabulary

1. **Identify new words.** As you read your textbook or supplemental assignments, create a list of words that you cannot pronounce or define. When reading the text, make sure to review the key terms at the beginning of each section.
2. **Study the context of new words.** Study the paragraph and the sentence where you find a new word. This context, or setting, may provide clues to the word's meaning by giving examples or a definition using more familiar words.
3. **Use a dictionary.** Use a dictionary to learn the pronunciation and the precise meaning of each word on your list.
4. **Review new vocabulary words.** Look for ways to use new words—in homework assignments, classroom discussions, or even everyday conversation. The best way to master a new word is to use it.

Applying the Strategy

As you read Section 4, create a list of the new words that you encounter. Write down what you think each word means, then check your definitions against those in a dictionary.

Practicing the Strategy

Answer the following questions.

1. What does the phrase *manifest destiny* mean? How did its use in the section help you arrive at this definition?
2. What does the phrase *popular sovereignty* mean? How did its use in the section help you arrive at this definition?

TEACH OBJECTIVE 3

ALL LEVELS: To help students understand how politicians addressed the expansion of slavery, copy the following graphic organizer on the chalkboard, omitting the italicized answers. Have each student complete the graphic organizer. **Sheltered English**

CONFLICT OVER EXPANSION OF SLAVERY

Expansion	Congress's Efforts	Compromises and Acts
Texas and maintaining balance in Congress	*admitted Texas as slave state; extended Missouri Compromise*	
popular sovereignty versus prohibition of slavery in new territories	Compromise of 1850	*California admitted as free state; New Mexico divided and given popular sovereignty*
continued pressure from southern slaveholders	*Fugitive Slave Act*	made it a crime to assist runaway slaves and authorized arrest of escapees in free states
revived debate over slavery in new territories	*Kansas-Nebraska Act*	*granted popular sovereignty to new territories*

Slavery's Expansion

U.S. expansion westward reopened the debate over the spread of slavery. When the Republic of Texas petitioned for annexation to the United States in the 1840s, Congress had to decide whether Texas would be admitted as a slave or free state. In 1845 Congress settled on terms favorable to the South. It admitted Texas as a slave state and extended westward the dividing line that had been set by the Missouri Compromise.

Henry Clay urged Congress to compromise on the slavery issue.

The slavery debate in Congress. The addition of the Mexican Cession territories in 1848 caused further complications. Some senators proposed that any new territories rely on **popular sovereignty**. This practice would allow the citizens of each new territory to vote whether to permit slavery.

The presidential election of 1848 put Mexican War hero General Zachary Taylor in office. The recently formed Free-Soil Party also fared well. Its members demanded that Congress prohibit the expansion of slavery into the territories. When Congress assembled in December 1849, there was fierce debate over whether slavery would be allowed in California and New Mexico.

Representative Henry Clay presented a plan known as the **Compromise of 1850**. The plan tried to satisfy both northern and southern interests. California would be admitted as a free state. The New Mexico Territory would be divided into two territories, with the residents of each territory allowed to vote on whether to allow slavery. The plan also called for the abolition of the slave trade—but not slavery itself—in the District of Columbia. In addition, the plan proposed a new, stricter fugitive slave law, the Fugitive Slave Act. Congress passed Clay's compromise in September 1850 after a heated debate.

Reactions to the compromise. Although the Compromise of 1850 did not satisfy all Americans, most hoped that it had settled the slavery question. Politicians vowed to avoid further debate over slavery. Democrat Franklin Pierce won the presidency in 1852 after persuading both pro-slavery and antislavery supporters that he shared their views. Pierce's efforts to satisfy both groups contributed to his weakness as a leader, however. Abolitionists soon labeled him "a northern man with southern principles."

Abolitionists made appeals through antislavery literature that showed the inhumanity of slavery. Harriet Beecher Stowe's 1852 novel, *Uncle Tom's Cabin,* convinced many northern readers that slavery was morally wrong and should be abolished. By the end of the decade, the book had sold more than 2 million copies in the United States alone.

OPERATIONS OF THE FUGITIVE-SLAVE LAW.

INTERPRETING THE VISUAL RECORD

Fugitive Slave Act. Many antislavery northerners opposed the Compromise of 1850, which authorized the forcible capture of runaway slaves in free states. ***Does this engraving reflect a northern or southern perspective? Explain your answer.***

HISTORY MAKERS SPEAK

Abraham Lincoln in *Battle Cry of Freedom: The Civil War Era*

During the 1858 Illinois senatorial campaign, candidates Stephen Douglas and Abraham Lincoln participated in several debates. Douglas insisted that Lincoln supported full political and social equality for African Americans. Hoping to counteract Douglas's contentions—which were politically damaging at the time—Lincoln assured listeners, "I am not, nor ever have been in favor of bringing about in any way the social and political equality of the white and black races. . . . I am not nor ever have been in favor of making voters or jurors of negroes, nor of qualifying them to hold office."

CRITICAL THINKING How might modern-day historians characterize Lincoln's position?

ANSWER: Students might suggest that historians would probably characterize Lincoln's position in the context of the time.

VISUAL RECORD ANSWER

Answers will vary. Students might suggest a northern perspective because the slave is going unwillingly.

▶**ASSIGNMENT:** *Distribute copies of Map 9, Conflict over Slavery, from* ***American History Outline Maps****. Tell students to use the information in the graphic organizer from the Objective 3 activity to help them color the maps so that they show the changing balance of power between free states and territories and slave states and territories.*

TEACH OBJECTIVE 4

ALL LEVELS: Ask students to list events that led to the secession of the southern states. *(Students should list the growth of the Republican Party, the* Dred Scott *decision, and Lincoln's victory in the 1860 presidential election.)* Then have students write a paragraph explaining the action of the southern states immediately following Lincoln's election. *(Students should mention that days after the election several southern states seceded and that by early 1861 they had formed the Confederate States of America.)* Ask volunteers to share their paragraphs with the class. **Sheltered English**

MAP ANSWER

allowed Kansas and Nebraska territories to vote whether to allow slavery

SECTION 4 REVIEW ANSWERS

Define and Identify

For significance, see the following pages:

- manifest destiny, p. 28
- Texas Revolution, p. 28
- Juan Seguín, p. 29
- Mexican War of 1846, p. 29
- Mexican Cession, p. 29
- popular sovereignty, p. 31
- Compromise of 1850, p. 31
- Harriet Beecher Stowe, p. 31
- Stephen Douglas, p. 32
- Kansas-Nebraska Act, p. 32
- John Brown, p. 32
- Republican Party, p. 32
- Dred Scott, p. 32
- *Dred Scott* decision, p. 33
- Abraham Lincoln, p. 33
- Confederate States of America, p. 33

1. Charts will vary. Events include the Mexican War of 1846, the Mexican Cession, the discovery of gold in California, the Compromise of 1850, the Kansas-Nebraska Act, John Brown's raid, the *Dred Scott* decision, and Lincoln's election.

2. Mexico closed Texas to Americans; conflict over the border between Texas and Mexico

3. Answers should show a knowledge of the settlement of the Far West.

4. gold, available land, economic opportunity

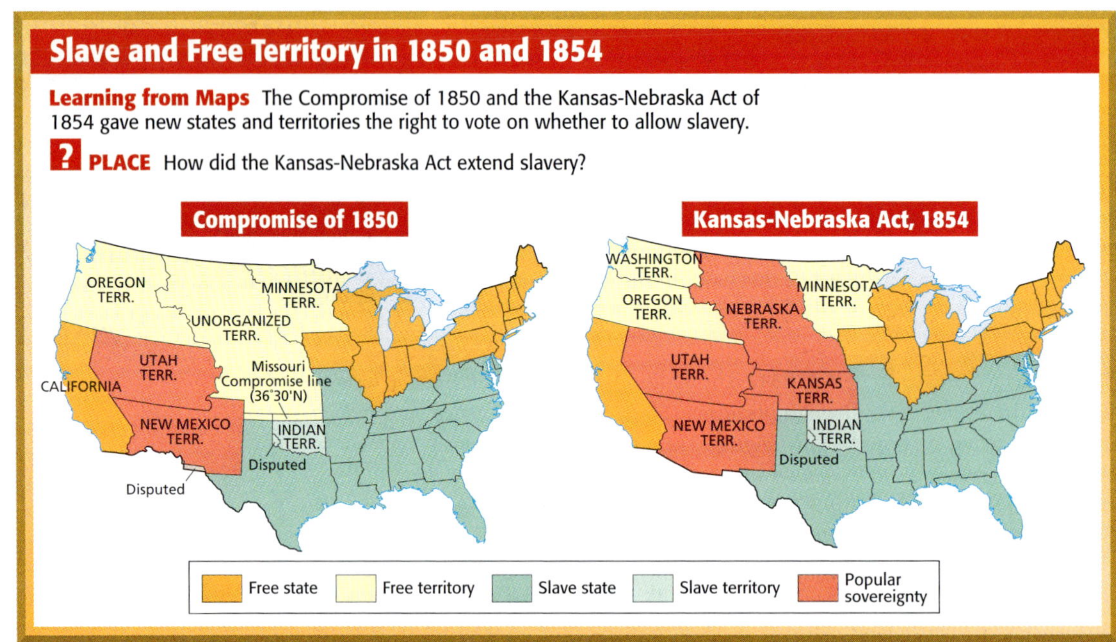

Trouble in Kansas. The slavery debate was revived in 1854. That year Illinois senator Stephen Douglas introduced the **Kansas-Nebraska Act**, which organized these new territories on the basis of popular sovereignty. By effectively repealing the Missouri Compromise, the act renewed southern hopes of expanding slavery. The Kansas-Nebraska Act also pitted antislavery and pro-slavery forces against one another for control of the new territories. As Kansas settlers prepared to elect their first territorial legislature in March 1855, some 5,000 pro-slavery Missouri residents crossed into the territory to cast ballots. These illegal votes helped elect a pro-slavery legislature that immediately passed laws supporting slavery. Antislavery settlers protested by electing their own legislature.

Soon violence erupted in Kansas. One well-known event was the Pottawatomie Massacre, ordered by abolitionist John Brown. He and his followers dragged five pro-slavery men from their beds and murdered them. This action enraged southerners, shocked northerners, and sparked additional violence in Kansas. The escalating slavery debate also led to violence in the halls of Congress, where a southern congressman attacked a northern senator.

Pro-slavery representative Preston Brooks attacks anti-slavery senator Charles Sumner on the floor of the Senate.

SOUTHERN CHIVALRY — ARGUMENT versus CLUB'S.

✔ **READING CHECK:** How did politicians address the expansion of slavery?

On the Brink of War

Antislavery voters flocked to a new political party gaining power in the North. The **Republican Party** included antislavery Democrats, Free-Soilers, and Whigs. Democratic candidate James Buchanan won the presidential election in 1856, however.

By the time Buchanan took office, another debate had begun over slavery. It was sparked by the slave Dred Scott's legal suit for his freedom. Scott argued that since he had lived with his owner in the free

REVIEW

Have students complete the **Section 4 Review** on p. 33.

ASSESS

Have students complete **Daily Quiz 1.4**. As **Alternative Assessment**, you may want to use the illustrated time lines or the pioneer letters activity in this section's lessons.

RETEACH

Have students complete **Main Idea Activity for Reteaching and Sheltered English 1.4**. Then assign groups of students to each objective in the section. Tell each group to create graphic organizers or other visual representations of the information pertaining to its assigned objective. Have students study each group's graphic organizer.
Sheltered English, Cooperative Learning

EXTEND

Organize students into four groups and assign each group one of the following topics: the Mexican War, settling the West, conflict over the expansion of slavery, or secession of the southern states. Have students work within their groups to create and present a short multimedia presentation about their topic. Encourage students to assign roles, such as artist, researcher, and writer, within their groups to help them accomplish the assignment. **Block Scheduling, Cooperative Learning**

state of Illinois, he should be free. The case eventually reached the U.S. Supreme Court. In the ***Dred Scott* decision**, the Court ruled that Scott was not a citizen and therefore could not bring suit in U.S. courts. The Court also declared the Missouri Compromise unconstitutional, stating that the federal government could not limit the spread of slavery.

The decision outraged abolitionists. African American leader Robert Purvis expressed the angry sentiments of the free African American community.

> “This atrocious [evil] decision furnishes final confirmation of the already well-known fact that, under the Constitution and government of the United States, the colored people are nothing and can be nothing but an alien, disenfranchised [deprived of rights] and degraded class.”

Republican Abraham Lincoln won the presidential election of 1860 with just some 40 percent of the popular vote. Despite his moderate stance on slavery, many southerners viewed his election as a victory for abolition. Within days of the election, several southern states voted to leave the Union. South Carolina was the first state to secede, followed by Mississippi, Florida, Alabama, Georgia, Louisiana, and Texas. Early in 1861, delegates from six of these states met and drafted a constitution for the **Confederate States of America**. Jefferson Davis of Mississippi became the provisional president of the Confederacy. Southerners justified their actions by asserting that because individual states had joined the Union voluntarily, they also had the right to withdraw from it. In a special session of Congress, President Lincoln said that the South must accept the election results. "When ballots have [been] fairly, and constitutionally decided," he said, "there can be no successful appeal back to bullets." Many southerners felt otherwise.

✔ **READING CHECK:** What events led to the secession of the southern states?

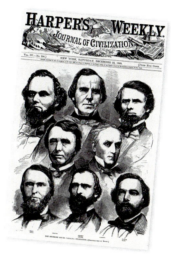

HARPER'S WEEKLY
JOURNAL OF CIVILIZATION

INTERPRETING THE VISUAL RECORD

Secession. Delegates from South Carolina were the first to vote to secede from the Union. ***Why do you think a publication like Harper's Weekly would put the delegates' portraits on its cover?***

SECTION  REVIEW

Define and explain the significance of the following terms:
manifest destiny
Texas Revolution
Mexican War of 1846
Mexican Cession
popular sovereignty
Compromise of 1850
Kansas-Nebraska Act
Republican Party
Dred Scott decision
Confederate States of America

Identify and explain the significance of the following individuals:
Juan Seguín
Harriet Beecher Stowe
Stephen Douglas
John Brown
Dred Scott
Abraham Lincoln

1. **Using Graphic Organizers** Create a flowchart using the boxes below as the first and last boxes of the chart. Fill in the events that led to the secession of the southern states.

The Republic of Texas petitions for annexation to the United States.
↓
Six southern states draft a constitution for the Confederate States of America.

2. **Analyzing** What were the causes of the Texas Revolution and the Mexican War of 1846?
3. **Hypothesizing** Would the Far West have been settled without the discovery of gold in California? Why or why not?
4. **Evaluating** What were the main reasons why Americans began to settle the west coast?

Critical Thinking

5. Why were attempts to resolve the slavery issue ineffective?
Consider:
• what northerners' reactions to the Fugitive Slave Act were
• why the popular sovereignty proposal failed
• what abolitionists' reactions to the *Dred Scott* decision were

5. Students might mention the importance of slavery to the southern economy and Americans' ideas of property rights.

Creating a Time Line

Each event should have an explanation and the correct date.

Writing a Summary

See the Reading Checks in each section for main ideas.

Identifying People and Ideas

1. Mesoamerican culture that arose about A.D. 300 in present-day southern Mexico and Guatemala
2. wars between 1096 and the late 1200s fought by Christians and Muslims for control of the Holy Land
3. voyage across the Atlantic Ocean endured by enslaved Africans
4. act of British Parliament that levied a tax on printed matter
5. final battle of the Revolutionary War
6. division of powers between a central government and state governments
7. machine that made it easier to remove seeds from cotton
8. fifth U.S. president, author of Monroe Doctrine
9. representative from Kentucky, proposed the American System

REVIEW AND ASSESSMENT RESOURCES

PRINT
- Chapter 1 Review, pp. 34–35
- Chapter 1 Tutorial for Students, Parents, Mentors, and Peers
- Chapter 1 Test (Form A or B)
- Portfolio Activities and Alternative Assessment Handbook, Chapter 1

MULTIMEDIA
- Audio Program, Chapter 1 (English and Spanish)
- Chapter 1 Test Generator (on the One-Stop Planner)
- Global Skill Builder CD–ROM
- HRW Web site

SHELTERED ENGLISH
- Spanish Glossary
- Sheltered English Chapter 1 Test

REVIEW

Have students complete the **Chapter 1 Review** on pp. 34–35.

ASSESS

Use one of the chapter tests to assess students' understanding of the content. For **Alternative Assessment**, see the **Portfolio Activities and Alternative Assessment Handbook.**

10. seventh U.S. president, forced American Indians in the eastern United States to move west

Understanding Main Ideas

1. The English government awarded charters to private companies that organized the settlements.

2. restriction of westward expansion and taxation without representation

3. repaying war debts, generating income, conflict with American Indians, war between Britain and France, westward expansion, and war with Britain

4. alcohol consumption, education, treatment of the disadvantaged and mentally ill, prison conditions

5. annexation of Texas, the Mexican Cession, gold in California

Reviewing Themes

1. the chance for wealth and fame

2. by applying to all citizens; by limiting citizenship to certain people

3. Differences in geography, climate, population, immigration, and religion led to regional differences.

CHAPTER 1 Review

Creating a Time Line

Copy the time line below onto a sheet of paper. Complete the time line by filling in the events and dates from the chapter that you think were most significant. Pick three events and explain why you think they were significant.

Writing a Summary

Using the Reading Checks as a guide, write an overview of the chapter.

Identifying People and Ideas

Identify the following terms or individuals and explain their significance.

1. Maya
2. Crusades
3. Middle Passage
4. Stamp Act
5. Battle of Yorktown
6. federalism
7. cotton gin
8. James Monroe
9. Henry Clay
10. Andrew Jackson

Understanding Main Ideas

SECTION 1

1. How were the English colonies in North America settled?

SECTION 2

2. Why did British colonists want independence from Great Britain?
3. What domestic and foreign problems did the first U.S. presidents face?

SECTION 3

4. What social problems did reformers hope to correct?

SECTION 4

5. What events led to the westward expansion of the United States in the mid-1800s?

Reviewing Themes

1. **Economic Development** What attracted explorers and traders to seek out distant lands?
2. **Democratic Values** How did the earliest U.S. laws and practices reflect the principles of a democratic society? How did they fail to reflect these principles?
3. **Geographic Diversity** Why did different regions of the United States develop different economies and political interests?

Thinking Critically

1. **Evaluating** How did Spain's American colonies develop differently from the English colonies?
2. **Identifying Values** What does the debate during the 1800s over slavery reveal about the differing morals of northern and southern society?
3. **Analyzing** How did the French and Indian War, the War of 1812, and the Mexican War of 1846 all affect the growth of the United States?
4. **Synthesizing** How were American Indians affected by European colonization and by the policies of the U.S. government?
5. **Using Historical Imagination** If you had been a European living in the 1600s, would you have wanted to immigrate to the Americas? Why or why not?

Writing About History

Writing to Create Copy the chart below and use it to list the major characteristics of life in the United States in the 1800s. Then choose one of the characteristics and write a poem about it.

The Economy	Key People/ Events	Foreign Policy	Domestic Changes/ Issues

RETEACH

Organize the class into four groups and assign each group one of the sections of this chapter. Have each group create and present a lesson that covers the important points of its assigned section. Tell students to be sure to cover all the sections' objectives when they present the material to the class. Also encourage them to give an oral quiz to the class after they present their lessons, to confirm that their students understood the information.
Sheltered English, Cooperative Learning

EXTEND

Organize students into pairs or triads. Tell them to create a graphic novel—a long story told with pictures and dialogue, as in comic books—that covers all the major objectives of the chapter. Students may create fictional characters to tell the story, or they may present the information as an illustrated history book. Help students to cover and bind their books, and display them in the classroom or elsewhere in the school.
Block Scheduling, Cooperative Learning

Strategies for Success Review the **Strategies for Success** on *Building Vocabulary.* Then create a list of at least 10 new words that you came across in this chapter. Write down a definition for each word, check it against the dictionary, and compose a sentence that uses the word in a different context.

Linking History and Geography

Study the map below. Which were New England colonies? middle colonies? southern colonies? Which region's colonies covered the most landmass?

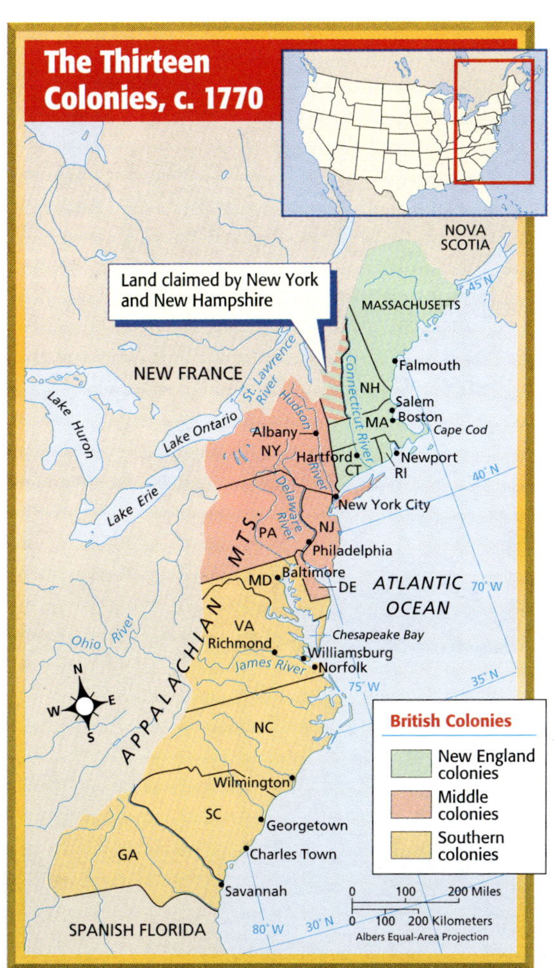

internetconnect

TOPIC: Columbus and the Spanish Empire
GO TO: go.hrw.com
KEYWORD: SE1 Columbus

Accessing the Internet through the HRW Web site, research and write a journal entry in which you assume the point of view of either Christopher Columbus or an American Indian in the *encomienda* system. Describe the impact of Columbus's journey on Europe and the Americas.

Complete one or all of the following projects independently or cooperatively.

1 Democratic Values

Imagine that you are a colonist protesting one of the new British taxes, such as the Stamp Act. ***Create a poster*** that demonstrates why you are opposed to the tax and that encourages other colonists to join your cause.

Colonial teapot

2 Geographic Diversity

Imagine that you are an American newspaper reporter in Texas in 1844. ***Conduct an interview*** of a native-born Texan, a Mexican government official, and a white settler to obtain their views about the possible U.S. annexation of Texas.

3 Cultural Diversity

Imagine that you are a colonial artist. ***Develop a series of drawings and captions*** that illustrates some of the ways in which contacts among European colonists, American Indians, and African slaves affected each culture.

Thinking Critically

1. Spain's colonies were run by the government, covered large areas, had small populations, and were meant to spread Catholicism and bring wealth to Spain. England's colonies were privately run, had larger populations in smaller areas, had various religions, provided raw materials for England, and served as a market for English goods.

2. The societies disagreed over the morality of slavery.

3. They led to the nation's expansion.

4. They were reduced in number and driven off their lands.

5. Answers will vary. Students may mention the risks of moving or the opportunities available in the Americas.

Writing About History

Students' poems will vary but should include some of the major people, events, and issues covered in the chapter.

Strategies for Success

Students' words will vary. Definitions should be correct, and sentences should use each word in an appropriate manner.

Linking History and Geography

New England colonies—Connecticut, Maine, Massachusetts, New Hampshire, and Rhode Island; middle colonies—Delaware, New Jersey, New York, and Pennsylvania; southern colonies—Georgia, Maryland, North Carolina, South Carolina, and Virginia; the southern colonies.

ACROSS THE CURRICULUM

▸ART◂

The Convention in Art. Howard Chandler Christy, the artist who painted the work to the right, was best known as an illustrator. He began work for *Scribners' Magazine* in 1898, illustrating current-events articles and stories. He also traveled to Cuba and Puerto Rico to provide the magazine with firsthand illustrations of the Spanish-American War. His illustrations eventually appeared on World War I recruitment posters. Christy began creating large oil paintings, mostly of historical scenes, late in his life. The painting to the right is huge—20 feet by 30 feet. It now hangs above the grand staircase in the Capitol in Washington, D.C.

CRITICAL THINKING In this painting, how does Christy show the importance of the Constitution?

ANSWER: Answers will vary. Some students might mention the men's serious expressions, George Washington's noble stance, the light on the document, or the grandeur of the room.

Delegates to the Constitutional Convention in 1787 signed the document that established the democratic government of the United States.

CONSTITUTION HANDBOOK

> *We the People of the United States, in Order to form a more perfect Union, establish Justice, insure domestic Tranquility, provide for the common defense, promote the general Welfare, and secure the Blessings of Liberty to ourselves and our Posterity, do ordain and establish this Constitution for the United States of America.*
>
> —Preamble to the Constitution

The delegates who met in the spring of 1787 to revise the Articles of Confederation included many of the ablest leaders of the United States. Convinced that the Confederation was not strong enough to bring order and prosperity to the nation, they abandoned all thought of revising the Articles. Instead, they proceeded to draw up a completely new Constitution. Patrick Henry called this action "a revolution as radical as that which separated us from Great Britain." Out of their long political experience, their keen intelligence, and their great learning, the framers of the Constitution fashioned a blueprint for a truly united nation—the United States of America.

Delegates met in Independence Hall in Philadelphia to draft the Constitution.

GLOBAL RELATIONS

The British Constitution. At the time of the American Revolution, Great Britain did not have a unified written constitution. Its constitution included the traditions of common law, royal decrees, important pieces of legislation such as Magna Carta, and commonly accepted practices. Parliament had full authority over this constitution. As Sir William Blackstone declared, "What Parliament doth, no power on earth can undo."

CRITICAL THINKING How was the U.S. Constitution different from the British constitution?

ANSWER: Students might answer that the U.S. Constitution was and is the supreme law of the land, while the British constitution was subject to the whims of Parliament.

PEOPLE IN HISTORY

Charles Pinckney. Some historians argue that Charles Pinckney of South Carolina played an important but forgotten role in the creation of the Constitution. During the convention, Pinckney submitted a plan to the Constitutional Convention. The later document incorporated some of his ideas. James Madison, who kept the only detailed notes at the convention, never mentioned the Pinckney plan, however. It became public only in 1818, when Pinckney sent a copy to John Quincy Adams. Historians have debated Pinckney's role ever since. Some claim that Madison, who hated Pinckney, attempted to squash evidence of his role. Others maintain that Pinckney faked the document he sent to Adams in order to inflate his role. The mystery remains.

CRITICAL THINKING What additional evidence might resolve the debate on Pinckney's role?

ANSWER: Answers will vary. Some students might suggest that an authenticated copy of the Pinckney plan from the Convention would resolve the dispute.

THE GRANGER COLLECTION, NEW YORK

The U.S. Constitution

An unknown observer once referred to the U.S. Constitution as "the most wonderful work ever struck off at a given time by the brain and purpose of man." Revised, modified, and amended, the Constitution has served the American people for more than 200 years, becoming a model for representative government around the world. The Constitution has successfully survived the years for two reasons. First, it lays down rules of procedure and guarantees of rights and liberties that must be observed even in times of crisis. Second, it is a "living" document, capable of being amended to meet changing times and circumstances.

To Form a More Perfect Union

The framers of the Constitution wished to establish a strong central government, one that could unite the country and help it meet the challenges of the future. At the same time, however, they feared a government that was too strong. The memories of the troubled years before the Revolution were still fresh. They knew that unchecked power in the hands of individuals, groups, or branches of government could lead to tyranny.

The framers' response was to devise a system of government in which power is divided between, in the words of James Madison, "two distinct governments"—the states and the federal government—and then within each government. In *Federalist Paper* "No. 51," Madison described the advantages of such a system.

> **"In the compound republic of America, the power surrendered by the people is first divided between two distinct governments, and then the portion allotted to each subdivided among distinct and separate departments. Hence a double security arises to the rights of the people. The different governments will control each other, at the same time that each will be controlled by itself."**

U.S. Constitution commemorative stamps

The seven Articles that make up the first part of the Constitution provide the blueprint for this system. To help guard against tyranny and to keep any one part of the federal government from becoming too strong, the framers divided the government into three branches—the legislative branch (Congress), the executive branch (the president and vice president), and the judicial branch (the federal courts)—each with specific powers. As a further safeguard, the framers wrote a system of checks and balances into the Constitution. Articles I, II, and III outline the powers of each branch of government and the checks and balances.

Article IV outlines the relations among the states and between the states and the federal government. Among the issues addressed are each state's recognition of other states' public records and citizens' rights, the admission of new states, and the rights and responsibilities of the federal government in relation to the states.

Article V specifies the process by which the Constitution can be amended. The framers purposely made the process slow and difficult. They feared that if the process was too easy, the Constitution—the fundamental law of the land—would soon carry no more weight than the most minor law passed by Congress.

Quill pen belonging to constitutional delegate James Madison

Article VI includes one provision that addressed the immediate concerns of the framers and two that have lasting significance. The short-term provision promises that the United States under the Constitution will honor all public debts entered into under the Confederation. The two long-term provisions declare the Constitution the supreme law of the land and prohibit religion being used as a qualification for holding public office.

Article VII is the framers' attempt to ensure ratification of the Constitution. The Constitutional Convention was summoned by the Congress to amend the Articles of Confederation. Under the Articles of Confederation, amendments had to be approved by all 13 states. Realizing that it would be difficult to get the approval of all the states—Rhode Island, for example, had not even sent delegates to Philadelphia—the framers specified that the Constitution would go into effect after ratification by only 9 states, not all 13. (This provision led some opponents of the Constitution to claim that it had been adopted by unfair means.)

Protecting Individual Liberty

Opposition to a strong central government was in part a concern over states' rights. But it was also rooted in the desire to protect individual liberties. American colonists had always insisted on the protection of their civil liberties—their rights as individuals against the power of the government. The Constitution contains many important guarantees of civil liberties. On a broad level, the separation of powers and the system of checks and balances help safeguard citizens against the abuse of government power. But the Constitution also contains provisions that speak directly to an individual's right to due process of law. For example, Section 9 of Article I prohibits both *ex post facto* laws and bills of attainder.

The Liberty Bell has become a symbol of the ideas of individual liberty protected in the Constitution.

An *ex post facto* law is a law passed "after the deed." Such a law sets a penalty for an act that was not illegal when it was committed. A bill of attainder is a law that punishes a person by fine, imprisonment, or seizure of property without a court

CULTURAL DIVERSITY

Religion and the Oath of Office. Article VI requires that many government officers, including some at the state level, take an oath in support of the Constitution. Some people, such as Quakers, cannot take oaths because of their religious beliefs, however. To accommodate this, Article VI allows for the option of affirming, or agreeing, to support the Constitution.

CRITICAL THINKING Why might the authors of the Constitution have required state officials to take an oath or to affirm support for the Constitution?

ANSWER: Students might suggest that the authors wanted to re-emphasize the supremacy of the Constitution. They may also have wanted to ensure that state officials understood their dual responsibility: to enforce the Constitution as well as the state laws.

trial. If Congress had the power to adopt bills of attainder, lawmakers could punish any American at will, and that person could do nothing to appeal the sentence. Instead, the Constitution provides that only the courts can impose punishment for unlawful acts, and then only by following the duly established law.

Section 9 of Article I also protects citizens by guaranteeing the privilege of the writ of *habeas corpus.* The writ of *habeas corpus* is a legal document that forces a jailer to release a person from prison unless the person has been formally charged with, or convicted of, a crime. The Constitution states that "the privilege of the writ of *habeas corpus* shall not be suspended, unless when in cases of rebellion or invasion the public safety may require it."

The Constitution also gives special protection to people accused of treason. The framers of the Constitution knew that the charge of treason was an old device used by tyrants to get rid of persons they did not like. Such rulers might bring the charge of treason against persons who merely criticized the government. To prevent such use of this charge, Section 3 of Article III carefully defines treason.

> **"Treason against the United States, shall consist only in levying War against them, or in adhering to their Enemies, giving them Aid and Comfort. No Person shall be convicted of Treason unless on the Testimony of two Witnesses to the same overt Act, or on Confession in open Court."**

Article III also protects the innocent relatives of a person accused of treason. Only the convicted person can be punished. No penalty can be imposed on the person's family.

The signing of the Constitution

CONSTITUTIONAL HERITAGE

Treason and the Supreme Court. The U.S. Supreme Court has heard only one case involving charges of treason. During World War II, German saboteurs entered the United States by submarine with the intent of destroying the U.S. war effort. Authorities accused Anthony Cramer, a U.S. citizen with German ties, of aiding these saboteurs. When Cramer was found guilty of treason, he appealed to the Supreme Court. In its 1945 decision in *Cramer* v. *United States*, the Court overturned his conviction. The Court determined that witnesses could testify only that Cramer had met with the saboteurs, not that he had provided them with any aid or assistance.

CRITICAL THINKING What provision in Article III led the Supreme Court to overturn Cramer's conviction for treason?

ANSWER: Students should indicate that his case did not meet the constitutional standard of providing "Aid and Comfort" to the enemy.

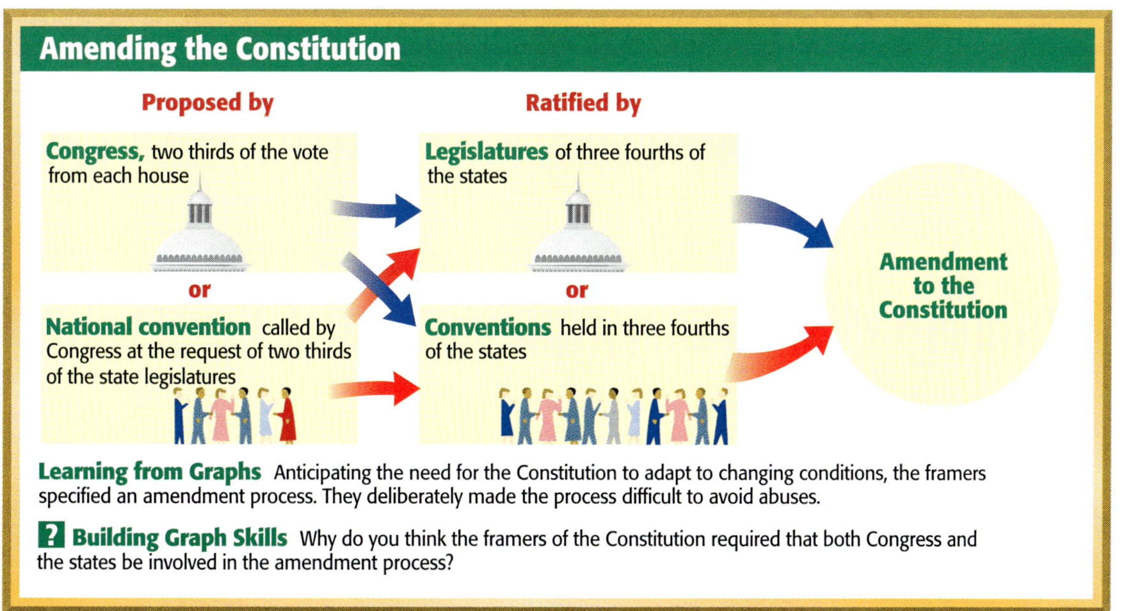

Learning from Graphs Anticipating the need for the Constitution to adapt to changing conditions, the framers specified an amendment process. They deliberately made the process difficult to avoid abuses.

? Building Graph Skills Why do you think the framers of the Constitution required that both Congress and the states be involved in the amendment process?

The Bill of Rights

Despite the safeguards written into the Articles of the Constitution, some states at first refused to ratify the framework because it did not offer greater protection to the rights of individuals. They finally agreed to ratification after they had been promised that a bill of rights would be added to the Constitution by amendment when Congress was called into session following ratification.

In 1789 the first Congress of the United States wrote some of the ideals of the Declaration of Independence into the Bill of Rights, the first 10 amendments to the Constitution. The Bill of Rights includes a protection for individuals against any action by the federal government that may deprive them of life, liberty, or property without "due process of law."

Among the guarantees of liberty in the Bill of Rights, several are especially important. The First Amendment guarantees freedom of religion, speech, press, assembly, and petition. The Fourth Amendment forbids unreasonable searches and seizures of any person's home. The Fifth, Sixth, and Eighth Amendments protect individuals from arbitrary arrest and punishment by the federal government.

The Bill of Rights was ratified by the states in 1791. It has remained one of the best-known features of the Constitution. The American people have turned to it for support whenever their rights as individuals have seemed to be in danger. No document in American history—except, perhaps, the Declaration of Independence—has been cherished more deeply.

HISTORY MAKERS SPEAK

Robert Whitehill in *The Bill of Rights: A Documentary History*

The Need for a Bill of Rights. Robert Whitehill, an Antifederalist who spoke at the Pennsylvania ratifying convention, explained the need for a Bill of Rights. "We know that it is the nature of power to seek its own augmentation [increase], and thus the loss of liberty is the necessary consequence of a loose or extravagant delegation of authority. . . . It is our duty to employ the present opportunity in stipulating [demanding] such restrictions as are best calculated to protect us from oppression and slavery."

CRITICAL THINKING

According to the excerpt, how did Whitehill view government entities?

ANSWER: Students should note that Whitehill believed that powerful bodies would always pose a threat to liberty, and that the people therefore needed protection against them.

GRAPH ANSWER

Students might suggest that the framers wanted to ensure that amendments would reflect the popular will instead of the desires of a small faction.

ACROSS THE CURRICULUM

▶GOVERNMENT◀

State Constitutions. Compared to certain state constitutions, the U.S. Constitution contains very few amendments. The California constitution has 493 amendments, while the South Carolina document contains 474 amendments. Alabama's constitution includes 618 amendments! The state requires that three fifths of the legislature approve proposed amendments.

CRITICAL THINKING Why might certain state constitutions have been amended so many times?

ANSWER: Answers will vary. Some students might suggest that it is relatively easy or simple to amend certain state constitutions.

THAT'S INTERESTING!

Several states have had more than one constitution. Louisiana has had 11 constitutions, and Georgia has had 10. Massachusetts, however, has had the same constitution since 1780.

Contents of the Constitution

Raising the new American flag, 1783

THE GRANGER COLLECTION, NEW YORK

President George Washington (left) and his advisers

State seals of North Carolina, Massachusetts, and New York

The bald eagle, a symbol of the United States

PEOPLE IN HISTORY

George W. Norris, Constitutional Advocate. During his long congressional career, George W. Norris not only wrote the Twentieth Amendment and worked for its passage but also supported the introduction of presidential primaries and the direct election of senators. Although he was a Republican, Norris rarely voted along party lines. In defense of his independence, he claimed he "would rather be right than regular."

ACTIVITY: Ask students to find examples of recent political reforms. Then have each student draft a bill or constitutional amendment that could be used to enact one of the reforms.

THAT'S INTERESTING!

The passage of the Fourteenth and Fifteenth Amendments dramatically increased African American political participation. Almost every institution of black life, particularly the church, worked to mobilize the African American vote. So many African American workers attended the Republican state convention in Virginia that Richmond's tobacco factories had to close during the convention.

HISTORY MAKERS SPEAK

John Marshall in *The American Testament*

The Preamble. Chief Justice John Marshall cited the Preamble in his decision in the 1819 case of *McCulloch* v. *Maryland.* "The government proceeds directly from the people; is 'ordained and established' in the name of the people; and is declared to be ordained 'in order to form a more perfect union, establish justice, ensure domestic tranquility and secure the blessings of liberty' to themselves and to their posterity. . . . The government of the Union, then . . . is emphatically and truly, a government of the people. In form and substance it emanates from them. Its powers are granted by them and are to be exercised directly on them and for their benefit."

CRITICAL THINKING Why might Marshall have cited the Preamble?

ANSWER: Students might suggest that Marshall believed that the Preamble summarized the purpose of the U.S. Constitution and government.

CONSTITUTIONAL HERITAGE ANSWER

a better union, justice, domestic peace, and liberty

The Constitution of the United States of America

Preamble
The short and dignified Preamble explains the goals of the new government under the Constitution.

Constitutional Heritage

According to the Preamble, what did the delegates hope the Constitution would provide for the nation?

PREAMBLE

*We the People of the United States, in Order to form a more perfect Union, establish Justice, insure domestic Tranquility, provide for the common defense, promote the general Welfare, and secure the Blessings of Liberty to ourselves and our Posterity, do ordain and establish this Constitution for the United States of America.**

Legislative Branch
Article I explains how the legislative branch, called Congress, is organized. The chief purpose of the legislative branch is to make the laws. Congress is made up of the Senate and the House of Representatives. The decision to have two bodies of government solved a difficult problem during the Constitutional Convention. The large states wanted membership in Congress to be based entirely on population. The small states wanted every state to have an equal vote. The solution to the problem of how the states were to be represented in Congress was known as the Great Compromise.

The number of members of the House is based on the population of the individual states. Each state has at least one representative. The current size of the House is 435 members, set by Congress in 1929.

ARTICLE I

Section 1. All legislative Powers herein granted shall be vested in a Congress of the United States, which shall consist of a Senate and House of Representatives.

Section 2. The House of Representatives shall be composed of Members chosen every second Year by the People of the several States, and the Electors in each State shall have the Qualifications requisite for Electors of the most numerous Branch of the State Legislature.

No Person shall be a Representative who shall not have attained to the Age of twenty-five Years, and been seven Years a Citizen of the United States, and who shall not, when elected, be an inhabitant of that State in which he shall be chosen.

Representatives and direct Taxes shall be apportioned among the several States which may be included within this Union, according to their respective Numbers~~, which shall be determined by adding to the whole Number of free Persons, including those bound to Service for a Term of Years, and excluding Indians not taxed, three fifths of all other Persons.~~ The actual Enumeration shall be made within three Years after the first Meeting of the Congress of the United States, and within every subsequent Term of ten Years, in such Manner as they shall by Law direct. The Number of Representatives shall not exceed one for every thirty Thousand, but

* Parts of the Constitution that have been ruled through are no longer in force or no longer apply.

each State shall have at Least one Representative; and until such enumeration shall be made, the State of New Hampshire shall be entitled to choose three; Massachusetts eight; Rhode Island and Providence Plantations one; Connecticut five; New-York six; New Jersey four; Pennsylvania eight; Delaware one; Maryland six; Virginia ten; North Carolina five; South Carolina five; and Georgia three.

When vacancies happen in the Representation from any State, the Executive Authority thereof shall issue Writs of Election to fill such Vacancies.

The House of Representatives shall choose their Speaker and other Officers; and shall have the sole Power of Impeachment.

Section 3. The Senate of the United States shall be composed of two Senators from each State, chosen by the Legislature thereof, for six Years; and each Senator shall have one Vote.

Immediately after they shall be assembled in Consequence of the first Election, they shall be divided as equally as may be into three Classes. The Seats of the Senators of the first Class shall be vacated at the Expiration of the second Year, of the second Class at the Expiration of the fourth Year, and of the third Class at the Expiration of the sixth Year, so that one third may be chosen every second Year; ~~and if Vacancies happen by Resignation, or otherwise, during the Recess of the Legislature of any State, the Executive thereof may make temporary Appointments until the next Meeting of the Legislature, which shall then fill such Vacancies.~~

No Person shall be a Senator who shall not have attained to the Age of thirty Years, and been nine Years a Citizen of the United States, and who shall not, when elected, be an Inhabitant of that State for which he shall be chosen.

The Vice President of the United States shall be President of the Senate, but shall have no Vote, unless they be equally divided.

The Senate shall choose their other Officers, and also a President pro tempore, in the Absence of the Vice President, or when he shall exercise the Office of President of the United States.

The Senate shall have the sole Power to try all Impeachments. When sitting for that Purpose, they shall be on Oath or Affirmation. When the President of the United States is tried, the Chief Justice shall preside: And no Person shall be convicted without the Concurrence of two thirds of the Members present.

Judgment in Cases of Impeachment shall not extend further than to removal from Office, and disqualification to hold and enjoy any Office of honor, Trust or Profit under the United States: but the Party convicted shall nevertheless be liable and subject to Indictment, Trial, Judgment and Punishment, according to Law.

Section 4. The Times, Places and Manner of holding Elections for Senators and Representatives, shall be prescribed in each State by the Legislature thereof; but the Congress may at any time by Law make or alter such Regulations, except as to the Places of choosing Senators.

Constitutional Heritage

According to the Constitution, who has the authority to fill a vacancy in the House of Representatives?

Every state has two senators. Senators serve a six-year term, but only one third of the senators reach the end of their terms every two years. In any election, at least two thirds of the senators stay in office. This system ensures that there are experienced senators in office at all times.

The only duty that the Constitution assigns to the vice president is to preside over meetings of the Senate. Modern presidents have given their vice presidents more and varied responsibilities.

In an impeachment, the House charges a government official of wrongdoing, and the Senate acts as a court to decide if the official is guilty.

Congress has decided that elections will be held on the Tuesday following the first Monday in November of even-numbered years. The Twentieth Amendment states that Congress shall meet in regular session on January 3 of each year. The president may call a special session of Congress whenever necessary.

IN THE NEWS

Impeachment. In December 1998 the House of Representatives impeached President Bill Clinton. The House brought two charges—perjury and obstruction of justice—against the president. In February 1999 the Senate voted on these charges. The body voted 45 guilty, and 55 not guilty on the perjury charge and 50-50 on the obstruction of justice charge. The votes did not reach the two-thirds majority required by the Constitution, and so the Senate acquitted Clinton of the impeachment charges.

CRITICAL THINKING Why might some observers have seen the Senate votes as a "humiliating defeat for the 13 House Republican 'managers' who had presented the case to the Senate"?

ANSWER: Students might suggest that neither charge garnered even a simple majority against Clinton, suggesting a weak initial case.

CONSTITUTIONAL HERITAGE ANSWER

the executive authority of the state

TECHNOLOGY AND SOCIETY

Tracking Congressional Votes. For many years, people learned about congressional proceedings in the *Congressional Record*, a bulky set of printed volumes. The Internet has allowed easier, faster access to the proceedings. The Library of Congress supports a Web site that covers every aspect of the government. In addition, independent organizations, such as Project Vote Smart, provide links to help track congressional votes.

CRITICAL THINKING Besides the *Congressional Record* and the Internet, how might citizens track votes or learn about congressional proceedings?

ANSWER: Answers will vary. Some students will suggest that citizens could call political offices, read newspapers, or watch television news programs.

CONSTITUTIONAL HERITAGE ANSWER

the House itself

Constitutional Heritage

According to the Constitution, who has the authority to judge elections, returns, and the behavior of congressmembers?

Congress makes most of its own rules of conduct. The Senate and the House each have a code of ethics that members must follow. It is the task of each house of Congress to discipline its own members. Each house keeps a journal, and a publication called the *Congressional Record* keeps records of what happens in congressional sessions. The general public can learn how their representatives voted on bills by reading the *Congressional Record.*

The framers of the Constitution wanted to protect members of Congress from being arrested on false charges by political enemies who did not want them to attend important meetings. The framers also wanted to protect members of Congress from being taken to court for something they said in a speech or in a debate.

The power to tax is the responsibility of the House of Representatives. Because members of the House are elected every two years, the framers felt that representatives would listen to the public and seek its approval before passing taxes.

The veto power of the president and the ability of Congress to override a presidential veto are two of the important checks and balances in the Constitution.

The Congress shall assemble at least once in every Year, and such Meeting shall be on the first Monday in December, unless they shall by Law appoint a different Day.

Section 5. Each House shall be the Judge of the Elections, Returns and Qualifications of its own Members, and a Majority of each shall constitute a Quorum to do Business; but a smaller Number may adjourn from day to day, and may be authorized to compel the Attendance of absent Members, in such Manner, and under such Penalties as each House may provide.

Each House may determine the Rules of its Proceedings, punish its Members for disorderly Behavior, and, with the Concurrence of two thirds, expel a Member.

Each House shall keep a Journal of its Proceedings, and from time to time publish the same, excepting such Parts as may in their Judgment require Secrecy; and the Yeas and Nays of the Members of either House on any question shall, at the Desire of one fifth of those Present, be entered on the Journal.

Neither House, during the Session of Congress, shall, without the Consent of the other, adjourn for more than three days, nor to any other Place than that in which the two Houses shall be sitting.

Section 6. The Senators and Representatives shall receive a Compensation for their Services, to be ascertained by Law, and paid out of the Treasury of the United States. They shall in all Cases, except Treason, Felony and Breach of the Peace, be privileged from Arrest during their Attendance at the Session of their respective Houses, and in going to and returning from the same; and for any Speech or Debate in either House, they shall not be questioned in any other Place.

No Senator or Representative shall, during the Time for which he was elected, be appointed to any civil Office under the Authority of the United States, which shall have been created, or the Emoluments whereof shall have been increased during such time; and no Person holding any Office under the United States, shall be a Member of either House during his Continuance in Office.

Section 7. All Bills for raising Revenue shall originate in the House of Representatives; but the Senate may propose or concur with Amendments as on other Bills.

Every Bill which shall have passed the House of Representatives and the Senate, shall, before it become a Law, be presented to the President of the United States; If he approve he shall sign it, but if not he shall return it, with his Objections to that House in which it shall have originated, who shall enter the Objections at large on their Journal, and proceed to reconsider it. If after such Reconsideration two thirds of that House shall agree to pass the Bill, it shall be sent, together with the Objections, to the other House, by which it shall likewise be reconsidered, and if approved by two thirds of that House, it shall become a Law. But in all such Cases the Votes of both Houses shall be determined by Yeas and Nays, and the Names of

the Persons voting for and against the Bill shall be entered on the Journal of each House respectively. If any Bill shall not be returned by the President within ten Days (Sundays excepted) after it shall have been presented to him, the Same shall be a Law, in like Manner as if he had signed it, unless the Congress by their Adjournment prevent its Return, in which Case it shall not be a Law.

Every Order, Resolution, or Vote to which the Concurrence of the Senate and House of Representatives may be necessary (except on a question of Adjournment) shall be presented to the President of the United States; and before the Same shall take Effect, shall be approved by him, or being disapproved by him, shall be repassed by two thirds of the Senate and House of Representatives, according to the Rules and Limitations prescribed in the Case of a Bill.

Section 8. The Congress shall have Power To lay and collect Taxes, Duties, Imposts and Excises, to pay the Debts and provide for the common Defense and general Welfare of the United States; but all Duties, Imposts and Excises shall be uniform throughout the United States;

To borrow Money on the credit of the United States;

To regulate Commerce with foreign Nations, and among the several States, and with the Indian Tribes;

To establish an uniform Rule of Naturalization, and uniform Laws on the subject of Bankruptcies throughout the United States;

To coin Money, regulate the Value thereof, and of foreign Coin, and fix the Standard of Weights and Measures;

To provide for the Punishment of counterfeiting the Securities and current Coin of the United States;

To establish Post Offices and post Roads;

To promote the Progress of Science and useful Arts, by securing for limited Times to Authors and Inventors the exclusive Right to their respective Writings and Discoveries;

To constitute Tribunals inferior to the supreme Court;

To define and punish Piracies and Felonies committed on the high Seas, and Offenses against the Law of Nations;

To declare War, grant Letters of Marque and Reprisal, and make Rules concerning Captures on Land and Water;

To raise and support Armies, but no Appropriation of Money to that Use shall be for a longer Term than two Years;

To provide and maintain a Navy;

To make Rules for the Government and Regulation of the land and naval Forces;

To provide for calling forth the Militia to execute the Laws of the Union, suppress Insurrections and repel Invasions;

To provide for organizing, arming, and disciplining, the Militia, and for governing such Part of them as may be employed in the Service of the United States, reserving to the States respectively, the Appointment of the

Constitutional Heritage

What must Congress do with a bill to make it a law once both houses have approved it?

The framers of the Constitution wanted a national government that was strong enough to be effective. Section 8 lists the powers given to Congress. The last sentence in the section contains the so-called elastic clause, which has been stretched—like elastic—to fit many different circumstances. The clause was first disputed when Alexander Hamilton proposed a national bank. Thomas Jefferson said that the Constitution did not give Congress the power to establish a bank. Hamilton argued that the bank was "necessary and proper" in order to carry out other powers of Congress, such as borrowing money and regulating currency. This argument was tested in the court system in 1819 in the case of *McCulloch* v. *Maryland,* when Chief Justice John Marshall ruled in favor of the federal government. Powers exercised by the government using the "elastic clause" are called implied powers.

DEMOCRATIC VALUES

American Indians.

American Indians are mentioned twice in the main body of the Constitution. Article I, Section 2, originally excluded Indians from population counts used to apportion congressional representation. Article I, Section 8, gives Congress the exclusive right to regulate commerce with Indian tribes. The Constitution also includes an indirect reference to American Indians. Article I, Section 10, prohibits the states from entering into compacts, or treaties, with foreign powers, which also includes Indian tribes.

CRITICAL THINKING What does the original Constitution reveal about attitudes toward American Indians in the late 1700s?

ANSWER: Students might suggest that the original Constitution reveals that the authors of the document did not consider American Indians—even those who lived within the borders of the United States—to be U.S. citizens.

CONSTITUTIONAL HERITAGE ANSWER

present it to the president

ACROSS THE CURRICULUM

▶GOVERNMENT◀

Suspending the Writ of *Habeas Corpus*. During the Civil War, President Abraham Lincoln suspended the writ of *habeas corpus*. Opposing his decision, Chief Justice Roger Taney argued that the authority to suspend the writ of *habeas corpus* belonged to Congress because that power was detailed in Article I, which is concerned with legislative matters. Lincoln, however, claimed that the Constitution was unclear on the matter. Congress resolved the dispute when it voted to approve the suspension. Presidents have suspended the writ of *habeas corpus* three times since the Civil War. Suspensions in 1871 and 1905 received congressional approval, but one instituted in 1941 did not. It was later ruled illegal by the Supreme Court.

CRITICAL THINKING Which branch of government has the authority to suspend the writ of *habeas corpus*?

ANSWER: Students might indicate that the history of suspensions indicates that presidents have the authority, with proper congressional approval.

CONSTITUTIONAL HERITAGE ANSWER

that no government officer could accept a title of nobility without consent of Congress

The delegates debated the articles of the Constitution in the Assembly Room of Independence Hall.

Officers, and the Authority of training the Militia according to the discipline prescribed by Congress.

To exercise exclusive Legislation in all Cases whatsoever, over such District (not exceeding ten Miles square) as may, by Cession of particular States, and the Acceptance of Congress, become the Seat of the Government of the United States, and to exercise like Authority over all Places purchased by the Consent of the Legislature of the State in which the Same shall be, for the Erection of Forts, Magazines, Arsenals, dock-Yards, and other needful Buildings;—And

To make all Laws which shall be necessary and proper for carrying into Execution the foregoing Powers, and all other Powers vested by this Constitution in the Government of the United States, or in any Department or Officer thereof.

If Congress has implied powers, then there also must be limits to its powers. Section 9 lists powers that are denied to the federal government. Several of the clauses protect the people of the United States from unjust treatment. For instance, Section 9 guarantees the right of the writ of *habeas corpus* and prohibits bills of attainder and *ex post facto* laws.

Section 9. ~~The Migration or Importation of such Persons as any of the States now existing shall think proper to admit, shall not be prohibited by the Congress prior to the Year one thousand eight hundred and eight, but a Tax or duty may be imposed on such Importation, not exceeding ten dollars for each Person.~~

The Privilege of the Writ of Habeas Corpus shall not be suspended, unless when in Cases of Rebellion or Invasion the public Safety may require it.

No Bill of Attainder or ex post facto Law shall be passed.

No Capitation, or other direct, Tax shall be laid, unless in Proportion to the Census or Enumeration herein before directed to be taken.

No Tax or Duty shall be laid on Articles exported from any State.

No Preference shall be given by any Regulation of Commerce or Revenue to the Ports of one State over those of another: nor shall Vessels bound to, or from, one State, be obliged to enter, clear, or pay Duties in another.

No Money shall be drawn from the Treasury, but in Consequence of Appropriations made by Law; and a regular Statement and Account of the Receipts and Expenditures of all public Money shall be published from time to time.

No Title of Nobility shall be granted by the United States: And no Person holding any Office of Profit or Trust under them, shall, without the Consent of the Congress, accept of any present, Emolument, Office, or Title, of any kind whatever, from any King, Prince, or foreign State.

Constitutional Heritage

What prohibitions does the Constitution make against nobility and titles from monarchies?

Section 10. No State shall enter into any Treaty, Alliance, or Confederation; grant Letters of Marque and Reprisal; coin Money; emit Bills of Credit; make any Thing but gold and silver Coin a Tender in Payment of Debts; pass any Bill of Attainder, ex post facto Law, or law impairing the Obligation of Contracts, or grant any Title of Nobility.

No State shall, without the Consent of the Congress, lay any Imposts or Duties on Imports or Exports, except what may be absolutely necessary for executing its inspection Laws: and the net Produce of all Duties and Imposts, laid by any State on Imports or Exports, shall be for the Use of the Treasury of the United States; and all such Laws shall be subject to the Revision and Control of the Congress.

No State shall, without the Consent of Congress, lay any Duty of Tonnage, keep Troops, or Ships of War in time of Peace, enter into any Agreement or Compact with another State, or with a foreign Power, or engage in War, unless actually invaded, or in such imminent Danger as will not admit of delay.

ARTICLE II

Section 1. The executive Power shall be vested in a President of the United States of America. He shall hold his Office during the Term of four Years, and, together with the Vice President, chosen for the same Term, be elected, as follows.

Each State shall appoint, in such Manner as the Legislature thereof may direct, a Number of Electors, equal to the whole Number of Senators and Representatives to which the State may be entitled in the Congress: but no Senator or Representative, or Person holding an Office of Trust or Profit under the United States, shall be appointed an Elector.

~~The Electors shall meet in their respective States, and vote by Ballot for two Persons, of whom one at least shall not be an Inhabitant of the same State with themselves. And they shall make a List of all the Persons voted for, and of the Number of Votes for each; which List they shall sign and certify, and transmit sealed to the Seat of the Government of the United States, directed to the President of the Senate. The President of the Senate shall, in the Presence of the Senate and House of Representatives, open all the Certificates, and the Votes shall then be counted. The Person having the greatest Number of Votes shall be the President, if such Number be a Majority of the whole Number of Electors appointed; and if there be more than one who have such majority, and have an equal Number of Votes, then the House of Representatives shall immediately choose by Ballot one of them for President; and if no Person have a Majority, then from the five highest on the List the said House shall in like Manner choose the President. But in choosing the President, the Votes shall be taken by States, the Representation from each State having one Vote; A quorum for this Purpose shall consist of a Member or Members from two thirds of the States, and a Majority of all the States shall be necessary to a Choice. In every Case, after~~

Section 10 lists the powers that are denied to the states. In our system of federalism, the state and federal governments have separate powers, share some powers, and are denied other powers. The states may not exercise any of the powers that belong solely to Congress.

Constitutional Heritage

According to the Constitution, under what circumstances could a state engage in war?

Executive Branch
The president is the chief of the executive branch. It is the job of the president to enforce the laws. The framers wanted the president and vice president's terms of office and manner of selection to be different from those of members of Congress. They decided on four-year terms, but they had a difficult time agreeing on how to select the president and vice president. The framers finally set up an electoral system, which varies greatly from our electoral process today. The Twelfth Amendment changed the process by requiring that separate ballots be cast for president and vice president. The rise of political parties has since changed the process even more.

HISTORY MAKERS SPEAK

Thomas Jefferson in *Encyclopedia of the American Presidency*

The Term of Office.
Toward the end of his second term in the White House, Thomas Jefferson received petitions from several state legislatures urging him to run for a third term. Jefferson explained his reasons for refusing to run again. "If some termination to the services of the Chief Magistrate be not fixed by the Constitution, or supplied by practice, his office, nominally four years, will in fact become for life, and history shows how easily that degenerates into inheritance."

CRITICAL THINKING Why might Jefferson have mentioned "inheritance"?

ANSWER: Students might suggest that Jefferson mentioned "inheritance" to emphasize his fears that without term limits, the presidency would be transformed into a monarchy.

CONSTITUTIONAL HERITAGE ANSWER

if it was invaded or in immediate danger

CONSTITUTIONAL HERITAGE

The Tyler Precedent. After President William Henry Harrison died only one month after taking office in 1841, Vice President John Tyler took the presidential oath of office. Some observers—and Tyler himself—believed that this was unnecessary. After all, the vice presidential oath had established him as the president's successor. At the same time, however, Tyler wanted to re-emphasize his claim on the presidency. He regarded himself as the rightful president, entitled to serve until the end of Harrison's term. Although some critics disagreed with his interpretation of the Constitution, Tyler established an important precedent—that when the president died or was seriously disabled, the vice president assumed the higher office with all its rightful powers.

CRITICAL THINKING On what grounds might Tyler's critics have objected to his position?

ANSWER: Students might note that they might have objected on constitutional grounds—Article II does not specify whether the vice president is an acting president or serves out the remaining term as president—and might have objected because of a personal dislike of Tyler.

CONSTITUTIONAL HERITAGE ANSWER

the president

~~the Choice of the President, the Person having the greatest Number of Votes of the Electors shall be the Vice President. But if there should remain two or more who have equal Votes, the Senate shall choose from them by Ballot the Vice President.~~

In 1845 Congress set the Tuesday following the first Monday in November of every fourth year as the general election date for selecting presidential electors.

The Congress may determine the Time of choosing the Electors, and the Day on which they shall give their Votes; which Day shall be the same throughout the United States.

No Person except a natural born Citizen~~, or a Citizen of the United States, at the time of the Adoption of this Constitution,~~ shall be eligible to the Office of President; neither shall any Person be eligible to that Office who shall not have attained to the Age of thirty-five Years, and been fourteen Years a Resident within the United States.

In Case of the Removal of the President from Office, or of his Death, Resignation, or Inability to discharge the Powers and Duties of the said Office, the Same shall devolve on the Vice President, and the Congress may by Law provide for the Case of Removal, Death, Resignation or Inability, both of the President and Vice President, declaring what Officer shall then act as President, and such Officer shall act accordingly, until the Disability be removed, or a President shall be elected.

Emolument means "salary, or payment." In 1999 Congress voted to set future presidents' salaries at $400,000 per year. The president also receives an annual expense account. The president must pay taxes only on the salary.

The President shall, at stated Times, receive for his Services, a Compensation, which shall neither be increased nor diminished during the Period for which he shall have been elected, and he shall not receive within that Period any other Emolument from the United States, or any of them.

The oath of office is administered to the president by the chief justice of the United States. George Washington added "So help me, God." All succeeding presidents have followed this practice.

Before he enter on the Execution of his Office, he shall take the following Oath or Affirmation:—"I do solemnly swear (or affirm) that I will faithfully execute the Office of President of the United States, and will to the best of my Ability, preserve, protect and defend the Constitution of the United States."

Constitutional Heritage

According to the Constitution, who is in charge of the nation's military forces?

Section 2. The President shall be Commander in Chief of the Army and Navy of the United States, and of the Militia of the several States, when called into the actual Service of the United States; he may require the Opinion, in writing, of the principal Officer in each of the executive Departments, upon any Subject relating to the Duties of their respective Offices, and he shall have Power to grant Reprieves and Pardons for Offenses against the United States, except in Cases of Impeachment.

According to this section the president can form a cabinet of advisers. Every president, starting with George Washington, has appointed a cabinet.

Most of the president's appointments to office must be approved by the Senate.

He shall have Power, by and with the Advice and Consent of the Senate, to make Treaties, provided two thirds of the Senators present concur; and he shall nominate, and by and with the Advice and Consent of the Senate, shall appoint Ambassadors, other public Ministers and Consuls, Judges of the supreme Court, and all other Officers of the United States, whose Appointments are not herein otherwise provided for, and which shall be established by Law: but the Congress may by Law vest the Appointment of such inferior Officers, as they think proper, in the President alone, in the Courts of Law, or in the Heads of Departments.

The President shall have Power to fill up all Vacancies that may happen during the Recess of the Senate, by granting Commissions which shall expire at the End of their next Session.

Section 3. He shall from time to time give to the Congress Information of the State of the Union, and recommend to their Consideration such Measures as he shall judge necessary and expedient; he may, on extraordinary Occasions, convene both Houses, or either of them, and in Case of Disagreement between them, with Respect to the Time of Adjournment, he may adjourn them to such Time as he shall think proper; he shall receive Ambassadors and other public Ministers; he shall take Care that the Laws be faithfully executed, and shall Commission all the Officers of the United States.

Section 4. The President, Vice President and all civil Officers of the United States, shall be removed from Office on Impeachment for, and Conviction of, Treason, Bribery, or other high Crimes and Misdemeanors.

ARTICLE III

Section 1. The judicial Power of the United States, shall be vested in one supreme Court, and in such inferior Courts as the Congress may from time to time ordain and establish. The Judges, both of the supreme and inferior Courts, shall hold their Offices during good Behavior, and shall, at stated Times, receive for their Services, a Compensation, which shall not be diminished during their Continuance in Office.

Section 2. The judicial Power shall extend to all Cases, in Law and Equity, arising under this Constitution, the Laws of the United States, and

The U.S. Supreme Court in the late 1990s

Every year the president presents to Congress a State of the Union message. In this message, the president explains the executive branch's legislative plans for the coming year.

This clause states that one of the president's duties is to enforce the laws.

 **Constitutional Heritage**

What actions might lead to the impeachment of a president, vice president, or other civil officer?

Judicial Branch

The Articles of Confederation did not make any provisions for a federal court system. One of the first things that the framers of the Constitution agreed upon was to set up a national judiciary. With all the laws that Congress would be enacting, there would be a great need for a branch of government to interpret the laws. In the Judiciary Act of 1789, Congress provided for the establishment of lower courts, such as district courts, circuit courts of appeals, and various other federal courts. The judicial system provides a check on the legislative branch; it can declare a law unconstitutional.

TECHNOLOGY AND SOCIETY

The State of the Union Message. Thomas Jefferson believed that personal appearances before Congress recalled the king's appearances before Parliament. So he sent written State of the Union messages. Some observers claim that television has transformed the annual message into the kind of pageant that Jefferson hoped to avoid. A national audience watches as the nation's political elite, including Congress and the Supreme Court, assemble to hear the president speak.

ACTIVITY: Ask students to consider Jefferson's beliefs. Then have each student write a half-page position paper either supporting or opposing televised State of the Union addresses.

THAT'S INTERESTING!

Woodrow Wilson appeared before Congress 26 times, more than any other president. Of the presidents since Wilson, Calvin Coolidge made the fewest appearances, addressing Congress just twice.

CONSTITUTIONAL HERITAGE ANSWER

treason, bribery, or other high crimes and misdemeanors

GLOBAL RELATIONS

Diplomatic Immunity. Many nations offer foreign diplomats such as ambassadors immunity from prosecution for civil and, in some cases, criminal charges. Known as diplomatic immunity, this practice is an agreement made under international law and is not required by the Constitution. In fact, Article III empowers the judiciary to prosecute charges against diplomats.

CRITICAL THINKING Why might nations offer foreign diplomats immunity from prosecution?

ANSWER: Students might suggest that nations want to protect diplomats against politically motivated lawsuits.

CONSTITUTIONAL HERITAGE ANSWER

that trials be by jury and that they be held in the state where the crimes were committed

Treaties made, or which shall be made, under their Authority;—to all Cases affecting Ambassadors, other public Ministers and Consuls;—to all Cases of admiralty and maritime Jurisdiction;—to Controversies to which the United States shall be a Party;—to Controversies between two or more States;~~—between a State and Citizens of another State;~~—between Citizens of different States;—between Citizens of the same State claiming Lands under Grants of different States, ~~and between a State, or the Citizens thereof, and foreign States, Citizens or Subjects.~~

In all Cases affecting Ambassadors, other public Ministers and Consuls, and those in which a State shall be Party, the supreme Court shall have original Jurisdiction. In all the other Cases before mentioned, the supreme Court shall have appellate Jurisdiction, both as to Law and fact, with such Exceptions, and under such Regulations as the Congress shall make.

Constitutional Heritage

What guidelines does the Constitution establish for criminal trials?

The Trial of all Crimes, except in Cases of Impeachment, shall be by Jury; and such Trial shall be held in the State where the said Crimes shall have been committed; but when not committed within any State, the Trial shall be at such Place or Places as the Congress may by Law have directed.

Congress has the power to decide the punishment for treason, but it can punish only the guilty person. Corruption of blood refers to punishing the family of a person who has committed treason. It is expressly forbidden by the Constitution.

Section 3. Treason against the United States, shall consist only in levying War against them, or in adhering to their Enemies, giving them Aid and Comfort. No Person shall be convicted of Treason unless on the Testimony of two Witnesses to the same overt Act, or on Confession in open Court.

The Congress shall have Power to declare the Punishment of Treason, but no Attainder of Treason shall work Corruption of Blood, or Forfeiture except during the Life of the Person attainted.

ARTICLE IV

The States

States must honor the laws, records, and court decisions of other states. A person cannot escape a legal obligation by moving from one state to another.

Section 1. Full Faith and Credit shall be given in each State to the public Acts, Records, and judicial Proceedings of every other State. And the Congress may by general Laws prescribe the Manner in which such Acts, Records and Proceedings shall be proved, and the Effect thereof.

Section 2. The Citizens of each State shall be entitled to all Privileges and Immunities of Citizens in the several States.

A Person charged in any State with Treason, Felony, or other Crime, who shall flee from Justice, and be found in another State, shall on Demand of the executive Authority of the State from which he fled, be delivered up, to be removed to the State having Jurisdiction of the Crime.

~~No Person held to Service of Labor in one State, under the Laws thereof, escaping into another, shall, in Consequence of any Law or Regulation therein, be discharged from such Service or Labor, but shall be delivered up on Claim of the Party to whom such Service or Labor may be due.~~

Section 3. New States may be admitted by the Congress into this Union; but no new State shall be formed or erected within the Jurisdiction of any other State; nor any State be formed by the Junction of two or more States, or Parts of States, without the Consent of the Legislatures of the States concerned as well as of the Congress.

The Congress shall have Power to dispose of and make all needful Rules and Regulations respecting the Territory or other Property belonging to the United States; and nothing in this Constitution shall be so construed as to Prejudice any Claims of the United States, or of any particular State.

Section 4. The United States shall guarantee to every State in this Union a Republican Form of Government, and shall protect each of them against Invasion; and on Application of the Legislature, or of the Executive (when the Legislature cannot be convened) against domestic Violence.

ARTICLE V

The Congress, whenever two thirds of both Houses shall deem it necessary, shall propose Amendments to this Constitution, or, on the Application of the Legislatures of two thirds of the several States, shall call a Convention for proposing Amendments, which, in either Case, shall be valid to all Intents and Purposes, as Part of this Constitution, when ratified by the Legislatures of three fourths of the several States, or by Conventions in three fourths thereof, as the one or the other Mode of Ratification may be proposed by the Congress; Provided that ~~no Amendment which may be made prior to the Year One thousand eight hundred and eight shall in any Manner affect the first and fourth Clauses in the Ninth Section of the first Article; and that~~ no State, without its Consent, shall be deprived of its equal Suffrage in the Senate.

ARTICLE VI

All Debts contracted and Engagements entered into, before the Adoption of this Constitution, shall be as valid against the United States under this Constitution, as under the Confederation.

This Constitution, and the Laws of the United States which shall be made in Pursuance thereof; and all Treaties made, or which shall be made, under the Authority of the United States, shall be the supreme Law of the Land; and the Judges in every State shall be bound thereby, any Thing in the Constitution or Laws of any State to the Contrary notwithstanding.

The Senators and Representatives before mentioned, and the Members of the several State Legislatures, and all executive and judicial Officers, both of the United States and of the several States, shall be bound by Oath or Affirmation, to support this Constitution; but no religious Test shall ever be required as a Qualification to any Office or public Trust under the United States.

Section 3 permits Congress to admit new states to the Union. When a group of people living in an area that is not part of an existing state wishes to form a new state, it asks Congress for permission to do so. The people then write a state constitution and offer it to Congress for approval. The state constitution must set up a representative form of government and must not in any way contradict the federal Constitution. If a majority of Congress approves the state constitution, the state is admitted as a member of the United States of America.

The Amendment Process
America's founders may not have realized just how enduring the Constitution would be, but they did make provisions for changing or adding to the Constitution. They did not want to make it easy to change the Constitution. There are two different ways in which changes can be proposed to the states and two different ways in which states can approve the changes and make them part of the Constitution.

National Supremacy
One of the biggest problems facing the delegates to the Constitutional Convention was the question of what would happen if a state law and a national law conflicted. Which law would be followed? Who decided? The second clause of Article VI answers those questions. When a national and state law are in conflict, the national law overrides the state law. The Constitution is the supreme law of the land. This clause is often called the "supremacy clause."

IN THE NEWS

Safeguarding the Flag.
In June 1999 the House of Representatives approved a proposed constitutional amendment allowing Congress to pass laws against desecrating the American flag. For the third time in four years the House had passed the proposed amendment, which had always failed to pass in the Senate. Supporters maintain that the flag is a national symbol that deserves protection, while opponents argue that such an amendment violates the right to free speech.

CRITICAL THINKING Would you support an amendment protecting the flag? Explain your answer.

ANSWER: Answers will vary. Some students might argue that the flag merits protection, while others might argue that flag-burning is a protected form of political expression and protest.

THAT'S INTERESTING!

One scholar estimates that a total of 10,431 amendments were proposed between 1789 and 1990!

HISTORY MAKERS SPEAK

William Short in *The Founders' Constitution*

Ratifying the Constitution. Article VII required nine states to ratify the Constitution before it took effect. William Short expressed concerns over this figure in a 1787 letter to James Madison. "I think the adoption by nine & refusal by four of the States is the worst possible situation to which the new plan can give birth; & it seems probable that that will be the situation. Would it not have been better to have fixed on the number eleven or twelve instead of nine? In that case the plan would have been either refused altogether or adopted by such a commanding majority as would almost necessarily have brought in the others in the end."

ACTIVITY: Tell students to imagine that they are James Madison. Have each student write a half-page letter responding to Short.

THAT'S INTERESTING!

Rhode Island initially refused to ratify the Constitution. In a popular vote just 237 people voted for it. 2,708 voted against ratification. The state finally ratified it in 1790, after the U.S. government created by the Constitution had already assumed control.

Ratification

The Articles of Confederation called for all 13 states to approve any revision to the Articles. The Constitution required that the vote of 9 out of the 13 states would be needed to ratify the Constitution. The first state to ratify was Delaware, on December 7, 1787. The last state to ratify the Constitution was Rhode Island, which finally did so on May 29, 1790, almost two and a half years later.

ARTICLE VII

The Ratification of the Conventions of nine States, shall be sufficient for the Establishment of this Constitution between the States so ratifying the Same.

Done in Convention by the Unanimous Consent of the States present the Seventeenth Day of September in the Year of our Lord one thousand seven hundred and Eighty seven and of the Independence of the United States of America the Twelfth. In witness whereof We have hereunto subscribed our Names.

George Washington—
President and deputy from Virginia

New Hampshire
John Langdon
Nicholas Gilman

Massachusetts
Nathaniel Gorham
Rufus King

Connecticut
William Samuel Johnson
Roger Sherman

New York
Alexander Hamilton

New Jersey
William Livingston
David Brearley
William Paterson
Jonathan Dayton

Pennsylvania
Benjamin Franklin
Thomas Mifflin
Robert Morris
George Clymer
Thomas FitzSimons
Jared Ingersoll
James Wilson
Gouverneur Morris

Delaware
George Read
Gunning Bedford Jr.
John Dickinson
Richard Bassett
Jacob Broom

Maryland
James McHenry
Daniel of St. Thomas Jenifer
Daniel Carroll

Virginia
John Blair
James Madison Jr.

North Carolina
William Blount
Richard Dobbs Spaight
Hugh Williamson

South Carolina
John Rutledge
Charles Cotesworth Pinckney
Charles Pinckney
Pierce Butler

Georgia
William Few
Abraham Baldwin

Attest: *William Jackson*, Secretary

THE AMENDMENTS

Articles in addition to, and Amendment of the Constitution of the United States of America, proposed by Congress, and ratified by the Legislatures of the several states, pursuant to the fifth Article of the original Constitution.

[The First through Tenth Amendments, now known as the Bill of Rights, were proposed on September 25, 1789, and declared in force on December 15, 1791.]

First Amendment

Congress shall make no law respecting an establishment of religion, or prohibiting the free exercise thereof; or abridging the freedom of speech, or of the press; or the right of the people peaceably to assemble, and to petition the Government for a redress of grievances.

Members of the Students Against Drunk Driving exercise their First Amendment right to expression by gathering in Washington, D.C., to speak out against drinking and driving.

Second Amendment

A well regulated Militia, being necessary to the security of a free State, the right of the people to keep and bear Arms, shall not be infringed.

The National Guard, which has replaced state militias, helps local citizens prevent a river from flooding.

Bill of Rights

One of the conditions set by several states for ratifying the Constitution was the inclusion of a bill of rights. Many people feared that a stronger central government might take away basic rights of the people that had been guaranteed in state constitutions. If the three words that begin the Preamble—"We the people"—were truly meant, then the rights of the people needed to be protected.

The First Amendment protects freedom of speech and expression, and forbids Congress to make any law "respecting an establishment of religion" or restraining the freedom to practice religion as one chooses.

Constitutional Heritage

What rights do the First and Second Amendments guarantee?

DEMOCRATIC VALUES

Children and Free Speech. Does the First Amendment protection of free speech extend to children in school? The Supreme Court responded to this question in its 1969 decision in *Tinker* v. *Des Moines Independent Community School District.* In December 1965 the school district had suspended five students for wearing black armbands as a symbol of protest against the Vietnam War. When lower courts upheld the suspension, attorneys asked the Supreme Court to consider the case. The Court determined that students in public schools had First Amendment rights. Schools could limit these expressions only if they could prove that such activities were disruptive to the educational process.

CRITICAL THINKING Do you agree with the Court's ruling? Explain your answer.

ANSWER: Answers will vary. Many students will probably agree with the ruling.

CONSTITUTIONAL HERITAGE ANSWER

the rights to a free press, free speech, free exercise of religion, and free assembly; the right to bear arms

HISTORY MAKERS SPEAK

Hugo Black in *Encyclopedia of the American Constitution*

Double Jeopardy. Justice Hugo Black explained the Fifth Amendment's ban on double jeopardy in a 1957 ruling. "The underlying idea . . . is that the state with all its resources and power should not be allowed to make repeated attempts to convict an individual for an alleged offense, thereby (1) subjecting him to embarrassment, expense and ordeal and (2) compelling him to live in a continuing state of anxiety and insecurity, as well as (3) enhancing the possibility that even though innocent he may be found guilty."

CRITICAL THINKING

According to the excerpt, what did Black perceive as the primary reason for the ban on double jeopardy?

ANSWER: Students should suggest that the state could use repeated prosecution to destroy individuals it regarded as enemies.

THAT'S INTERESTING!

The Third Amendment is one of the least controversial amendments to the Constitution. It provoked almost no debate in Congress and it has never been the subject of a Supreme Court decision.

A police officer may enter a person's home with a search warrant, which allows the law officer to look for evidence that could convict someone of committing a crime.

The Fifth, Sixth, and Seventh Amendments describe the procedures that courts must follow when trying people accused of crimes. The Fifth Amendment guarantees that no one can be put on trial for a serious crime unless a grand jury agrees that the evidence justifies doing so. It also says that a person cannot be tried twice for the same crime.

The Sixth Amendment makes several promises, including a prompt trial and a trial by a jury chosen from the state and district in which the crime was committed. The Sixth Amendment also states that an accused person must be told why he or she is being tried and promises that an accused person has the right to be defended by a lawyer.

Judges issue search warrants like this one to allow law enforcement officials to legally search a suspected criminal's property.

Third Amendment

No Soldier shall, in time of peace, be quartered in any house, without the consent of the Owner, nor in time of war, but in a manner to be prescribed by law.

Fourth Amendment

The right of the people to be secure in their persons, houses, papers, and effects, against unreasonable searches and seizures, shall not be violated, and no Warrants shall issue, but upon probable cause, supported by Oath or affirmation, and particularly describing the place to be searched, and the persons or things to be seized.

Fifth Amendment

No person shall be held to answer for a capital, or otherwise infamous crime, unless on a presentment or indictment of a Grand Jury, except in cases arising in the land or naval forces, or in the Militia, when in actual service in time of War or public danger; nor shall any person be subject for the same offense to be twice put in jeopardy of life or limb; nor shall be compelled in any criminal case to be a witness against himself, nor be deprived of life, liberty, or property, without due process of law; nor shall private property be taken for public use, without just compensation.

Sixth Amendment

In all criminal prosecutions, the accused shall enjoy the right to a speedy and public trial, by an impartial jury of the State and district wherein the crime shall have been committed, which district shall have been previously ascertained by law, and to be informed of the nature and

cause of the accusation; to be confronted with the witnesses against him; to have compulsory process for obtaining witnesses in his favor, and to have the Assistance of Counsel for his defense.

Seventh Amendment

In Suits at common law, where the value in controversy shall exceed twenty dollars, the right of trial by jury shall be preserved, and no fact tried by a jury shall be otherwise reexamined in any Court of the United States, than according to the rules of the common law.

The Seventh Amendment guarantees a trial by jury in cases that involve more than $20, but in modern times, usually much more money is at stake before a case is heard in federal court.

Eighth Amendment

Excessive bail shall not be required, nor excessive fines imposed, nor cruel and unusual punishments inflicted.

Ninth Amendment

The enumeration in the Constitution, of certain rights, shall not be construed to deny or disparage others retained by the people.

The Ninth and Tenth Amendments were added because not every right of the people or of the states could be listed in the Constitution.

Tenth Amendment

The powers not delegated to the United States by the Constitution, nor prohibited by it to the States, are reserved to the States respectively, or to the people.

How does the Tenth Amendment limit the powers of the federal government?

Eleventh Amendment

[Proposed March 4, 1794; declared ratified January 8, 1798]

The Judicial power of the United States shall not be construed to extend to any suit in law or equity, commenced or prosecuted against one of the United States by Citizens of another State, or by Citizens or Subjects of any Foreign State.

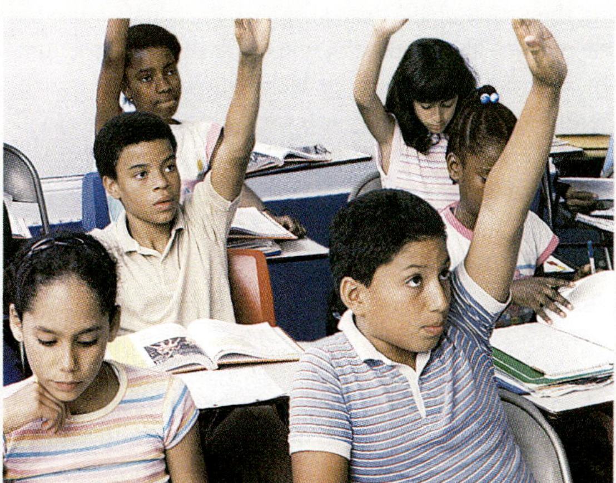

Many Americans consider attendance in free public schools a right of citizenship.

CONSTITUTIONAL HERITAGE

Cruel and Unusual Punishment. Do school disciplinary actions such as paddling constitute cruel and unusual punishment? After being roughly paddled, two Florida junior high students sued school officials on those grounds. In addition, they claimed that their right to due process had been violated because they had not received a hearing prior to being paddled. Their case eventually went to the Supreme Court. In *Ingraham* v. *Wright*, a 1977 ruling, the Supreme Court ruled that punishments such as paddling did not violate the students' Eighth Amendment rights. In a 5-4 decision, the Court determined that the Eighth Amendment applied to criminal punishments and not to disciplinary actions such as school paddlings. Moreover, the Court ruled that students who had been paddled could sue for damages; therefore hearings were not necessary.

ACTIVITY: Have students discuss *Ingraham* v. *Wright*. Then have each student write a one-page legal brief supporting or opposing the Court's decision.

CONSTITUTIONAL HERITAGE ANSWER

gives nondelegated powers to the states or to the people

DEMOCRATIC VALUES

Ending Slavery. In 1863 President Abraham Lincoln freed slaves in certain areas—namely those in rebellion against the United States. Some observers questioned the president's power to end slavery, however, and many doubted that his proclamation would remain in effect after the Civil War. In order to ensure that slavery was forever banned in the United States, these people called for a constitutional amendment prohibiting slavery.

CRITICAL THINKING Why might a constitutional amendment banning slavery have been necessary?

ANSWER: Students should suggest that observers believed that an amendment was necessary because of the legal questions surrounding Lincoln's actions. They might also have feared that white southerners would try to re-establish slavery after the war.

CONSTITUTIONAL HERITAGE ANSWER

the House of Representatives

The Twelfth Amendment changed the election procedure for president and vice president. Before this amendment, electors voted without distinguishing between president and vice president. Whoever received the most votes became president, and whoever received the next highest number of votes became vice president.

Constitutional Heritage

According to the Twelfth Amendment, who chooses the president if no candidate has received a majority of the electoral votes?

Twelfth Amendment

[Proposed December 9, 1803; declared ratified September 25, 1804]

The Electors shall meet in their respective states and vote by ballot for President and Vice President, one of whom, at least, shall not be an inhabitant of the same state with themselves; they shall name in their ballots the person voted for as President, and in distinct ballots the person voted for as Vice President, and they shall make distinct lists of all persons voted for as President, and of all persons voted for as Vice President, and of the number of votes for each, which lists they shall sign and certify, and transmit sealed to the seat of the government of the United States, directed to the President of the Senate;—The President of the Senate shall, in the presence of the Senate and House of Representatives, open all the certificates and the votes shall then be counted;—The person having the greatest number of votes for President, shall be the President, if such number be a majority of the whole number of Electors appointed; and if no person have such majority, then from the persons having the highest numbers not exceeding three on the list of those voted for as President, the House of Representatives shall choose immediately, by ballot, the President. But in choosing the President, the votes shall be taken by states, the representation from each state having one vote; a quorum for this purpose shall consist of a member or members from two thirds of the states, and a majority of all the states shall be necessary to a choice. ~~And if the House of Representatives shall not choose a President whenever the right of choice shall devolve upon them, before the fourth day of March next following, then the Vice-President shall act as President, as in the case of the death or other constitutional disability of the President;~~—The person having the greatest number of votes as Vice President, shall be the Vice President, if such number be a majority of the whole number of Electors appointed, and if no person have a majority, then from the two highest numbers on the list, the Senate shall choose the Vice President; a quorum for the purpose shall consist of two thirds of the whole number of Senators, and a majority of the whole number shall be necessary to a choice. But no person constitutionally ineligible to the office of President shall be eligible to that of Vice President of the United States.

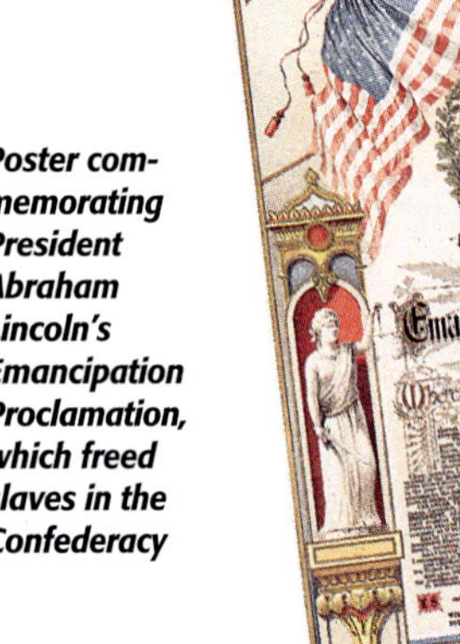

Poster commemorating President Abraham Lincoln's Emancipation Proclamation, which freed slaves in the Confederacy

Thirteenth Amendment

[Proposed January 31, 1865; declared ratified December 18, 1865]

Section 1. Neither slavery nor involuntary servitude, except as a punishment for crime whereof the party shall have been duly convicted, shall exist within the United States, or any place subject to their jurisdiction.

Section 2. Congress shall have power to enforce this article by appropriate legislation.

Fourteenth Amendment

[Proposed June 13, 1866; declared ratified July 28, 1868]

Section 1. All persons born or naturalized in the United States and subject to the jurisdiction thereof, are citizens of the United States and of the State wherein they reside. No State shall make or enforce any law which shall abridge the privileges or immunities of citizens of the United States; nor shall any State deprive any person of life, liberty, or property, without due process of law; nor deny to any person within its jurisdiction the equal protection of the laws.

Section 2. Representatives shall be apportioned among the several States according to their respective numbers, counting the whole number of persons in each State~~, excluding Indians not taxed.~~ But when the right to vote at any election for the choice of electors for President and Vice President of the United States, Representatives in Congress, the Executive and Judicial officers of a State, or the members of the Legislature thereof, is denied to any of the ~~male~~ inhabitants of such State~~, being twenty-one years of age, and~~ citizens of the United States, or in any way abridged, except for participation in rebellion, or other crime, the basis of representation therein shall be reduced in the proportion which the number of such male citizens shall bear to the whole number of ~~male~~ citizens ~~twenty-one years of age in such State.~~

Section 3. No person shall be a Senator or Representative in Congress, or elector of President and Vice President, or hold any office, civil or military, under the United States, or under any State, who, having previously taken an oath, as a member of Congress, or as an officer of the United States, or as a member of any State legislature, or as an executive or judicial officer of any State, to support the Constitution of the United States, shall have engaged in insurrection or rebellion against the same, or given aid or comfort to the enemies thereof. But Congress may by a vote of two thirds of each House, remove such disability.

Section 4. The validity of the public debt of the United States, authorized by law, including debts incurred for payment of pensions and bounties for services in suppressing insurrection or rebellion, shall not be questioned. But neither the United States nor any State shall assume or pay any debt or obligation incurred in aid of insurrection or rebellion against the United States~~, or any claim for the loss or emancipation of any slave~~; but all such debts, obligations and claims shall be held illegal and void.

Section 5. The Congress shall have power to enforce, by appropriate legislation, the provisions of this article.

Fifteenth Amendment

[Proposed February 26, 1869; declared ratified March 30, 1870]

Section 1. The right of citizens of the United States to vote shall not be denied or abridged by the United States or by any State on account of race, color, or previous condition of servitude.

Section 2. The Congress shall have power to enforce this article by appropriate legislation.

Constitutional Heritage

According to the Fourteenth Amendment, who is a citizen of the United States, and what rights do citizens have?

In 1833 Chief Justice John Marshall ruled that the Bill of Rights limited the national government but not the state governments. The later effect of this ruling was that states were able to keep African Americans from becoming state citizens. If African Americans were not citizens, they were not protected by the Bill of Rights. The Fourteenth Amendment defines citizenship and prevents states from interfering in the rights of citizens of the United States.

The Fifteenth Amendment extended the right to vote to African American men.

DEMOCRATIC VALUES

American Indian Citizenship. In its 1884 decision in *Elk* v. *Wilkins*, the Supreme Court ruled that American Indians were not automatically U.S. citizens. The case began when John Elk, an Omaha Indian, attempted to register to vote in Nebraska. The local official refused to accept his application, arguing that he was not a citizen. Elk's case eventually went to the Supreme Court, which ruled that American Indians could only become citizens by treaty provisions or acts of Congress. Thus, the Fourteenth Amendment did not apply to American Indians. It was not until 1924 that Congress passed an act granting citizenship to all American Indians.

CRITICAL THINKING What did *Elk* v. *Wilkins* indicate about attitudes toward American Indians in the 1880s?

ANSWER: Students should suggest that the case indicated that many Americans viewed American Indians as "foreigners" in their own lands.

CONSTITUTIONAL HERITAGE ANSWER

all persons born or naturalized in the United States; all the rights of citizens, including life, liberty, and the equal protection of laws

ACROSS THE CURRICULUM

▶GOVERNMENT◀

The Sixteenth Amendment. On the whole, Democrats tended to favor an income tax, while conservative Republicans generally opposed it. Ironically, Senator Nelson Aldrich of Rhode Island, a conservative millionaire Republican, introduced the constitutional amendment permitting an income tax. Aldrich assumed that his amendment would fail to gain adoption. He introduced the measure as a political move to forestall some Democrats from adding another income tax provision to a piece of tariff legislation. The Senate passed the Aldrich measure 77 to 0, however, and the House passed it 318 to 14. The necessary number of states approved it as well, and the amendment became part of the Constitution.

CRITICAL THINKING How might the history of the constitutional amendment process have made Aldrich confident that the income tax amendment would never be ratified?

ANSWER: Students should note that by 1913 the Constitution had been amended just five times.

CONSTITUTIONAL HERITAGE ANSWER

that they were to be elected by the people

Expanding on the federal government's right to levy taxes, outlined in Article I of the Constitution, the Sixteenth Amendment gave Congress the power to issue the income tax.

Constitutional Heritage

What new provisions does the Seventeenth Amendment establish for the election of senators?

Although many people believed that prohibition was good for the health and welfare of the American people, the Eighteenth Amendment was repealed 14 years later.

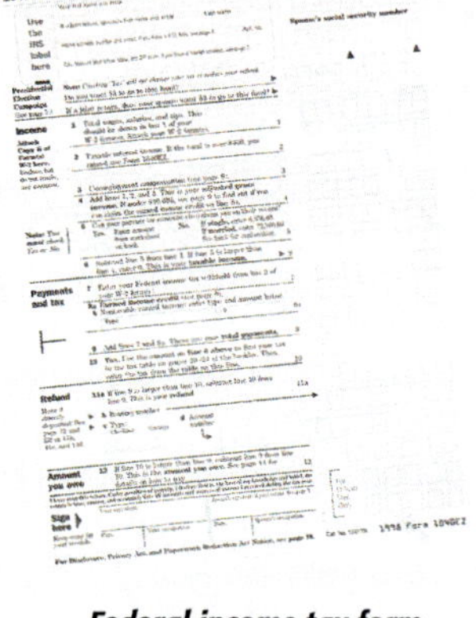

Federal income tax form

Sixteenth Amendment

[Proposed July 12, 1909; declared ratified February 25, 1913]

The Congress shall have power to lay and collect taxes on incomes, from whatever source derived, without apportionment among the several States, and without regard to any census or enumeration.

Seventeenth Amendment

[Proposed May 13, 1912; declared ratified May 31, 1913]

The Senate of the United States shall be composed of two Senators from each State, elected by the people thereof, for six years; and each Senator shall have one vote. The electors in each State shall have the qualifications requisite for electors of the most numerous branch of the State legislatures.

When vacancies happen in the representation of any State in the Senate, the executive authority of such State shall issue writs of election to fill such vacancies: Provided, That the legislature of any State may empower the executive thereof to make temporary appointments until the people fill the vacancies by election as the legislature may direct.

~~This amendment shall not be so construed as to affect the election or term of any Senator chosen before it becomes valid as part of the Constitution.~~

Eighteenth Amendment

[Proposed December 18, 1917; declared ratified January 29, 1919; repealed by the Twenty-first Amendment December 5, 1933]

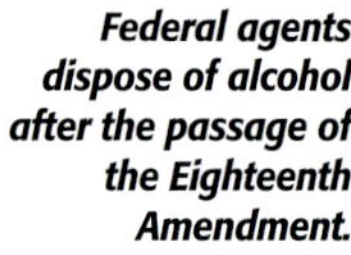

Federal agents dispose of alcohol after the passage of the Eighteenth Amendment.

~~**Section 1.** After one year from the ratification of this article the manufacture, sale, or transportation of intoxicating liquors within, the importation thereof into, or the exportation thereof from the United States and all territory subject to the jurisdiction thereof for beverage purposes is hereby prohibited.~~

~~**Section 2.** The Congress and the several States shall have concurrent power to enforce this article by appropriate legislation.~~

~~**Section 3.** This article shall be inoperative unless it shall have been ratified as an amendment to the Constitution by the legislatures of the several States, as provided in the Constitution, within seven years from the date of the submission hereof to the States by the Congress.~~

Nineteenth Amendment

[Proposed June 4, 1919; declared ratified August 26, 1920]

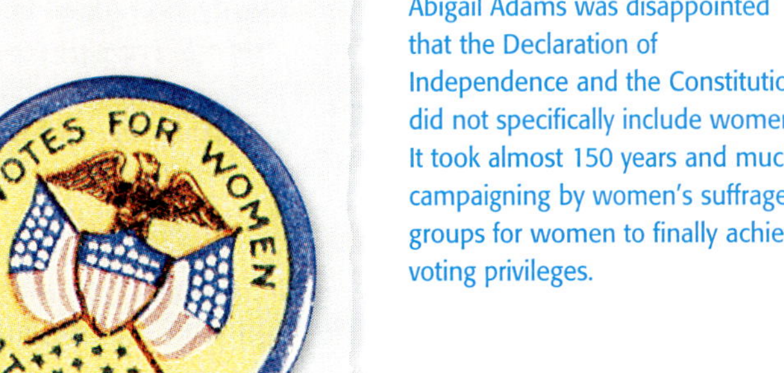

Women's suffrage button

The right of citizens of the United States to vote shall not be denied or abridged by the United States or by any State on account of sex.

Congress shall have power to enforce this article by appropriate legislation.

Abigail Adams was disappointed that the Declaration of Independence and the Constitution did not specifically include women. It took almost 150 years and much campaigning by women's suffrage groups for women to finally achieve voting privileges.

Twentieth Amendment

[Proposed March 2, 1932; declared ratified February 6, 1933]

Section 1. The terms of the President and Vice President shall end at noon on the 20th day of January, and the terms of Senators and Representatives at noon on the 3rd day of January, of the years in which such terms would have ended if this article had not been ratified; and the terms of their successors shall then begin.

Section 2. The Congress shall assemble at least once in every year, and such meeting shall begin at noon on the 3rd day of January, unless they shall by law appoint a different day.

Section 3. If, at the time fixed for the beginning of the term of the President, the President elect shall have died, the Vice President elect shall become President. If a President shall not have been chosen before the time fixed for the beginning of his term, or if the President elect shall have failed to qualify, then the Vice President elect shall act as President until a President shall have qualified; and the Congress may by law provide for the case wherein neither a President elect nor a Vice President elect shall have qualified, declaring who shall then act as President, or the manner in which one who is to act shall be selected, and such persons shall act accordingly until a President or Vice President shall have qualified.

Section 4. The Congress may by law provide for the case of the death of any of the persons from whom the House of Representatives may choose a President whenever the right of choice shall have devolved upon them, and for the case of the death of any of the persons from whom the Senate may choose a Vice President whenever the right of choice shall have devolved upon them.

~~**Section 5.** Sections 1 and 2 shall take effect on the 15th day of October following the ratification of this article.~~

~~**Section 6.** This article shall be inoperative unless it shall have been ratified as an amendment to the Constitution by the legislatures of three fourths of the several States within seven years from the date of its submission.~~

In the original Constitution, a newly elected president and Congress did not take office until March 4, which was four months after the November election. The officials who were leaving office were called "lame ducks" because they had little influence during those four months. The Twentieth Amendment changed the date that the new president and Congress take office. Members of Congress now take office on January 3, and the president takes office on January 20.

Constitutional Heritage

According to the Twentieth Amendment, who becomes president if a president-elect dies before taking office?

HISTORY MAKERS SPEAK

Abigail Adams in *The Way We Lived: Essays and Documents in American Social History*

Abigail Adams on Women's Rights. Women finally gained universal suffrage in 1920. Abigail Adams expressed her views on women's rights in a 1776 letter to her husband. "In the new Code of Laws which I will suppose it will be necessary for you to make I desire you would Remember the Ladies, and be more generous and favourable to them than your ancestors. Do not put such unlimited power into the hands of the Husbands. Remember all Men would be tyrants if they could. If particular care and attention is not paid to the Laidies we are determined to foment a Rebellion, and will not hold ourselves bound by any Laws in which we have no voice, or Representation. . . . Men of Sense in all Ages abhor those customs which treat us only as the vassals of your Sex."

CRITICAL THINKING Why did Adams believe that women must be included in the laws of the new government?

ANSWER: Students should note that she argued that women had the right to representation in the nation's laws.

CONSTITUTIONAL HERITAGE ANSWER

the vice president

CONSTITUTIONAL HERITAGE

The People and the Twenty-first Amendment. Because state conventions rather than state legislatures ratified the Twenty-first Amendment, voters could express their opinion of the proposed document when they cast ballots for the delegates to the conventions. Some 73 percent of Americans voted for antiprohibition delegates. Of the 38 states that held conventions on the amendment in a single year, 37 ratified it. Only one rejected it.

CRITICAL THINKING What might the reaction to the Twenty-first Amendment have indicated about reactions to the Eighteenth Amendment?

ANSWER: Students might indicate that the reaction to the Twenty-first Amendment indicated that the Eighteenth Amendment was highly unpopular.

THAT'S INTERESTING!

By rejecting the possibility of a third term in order to enjoy "the shade of retirement," President Washington set a two-term precedent that lasted until Franklin D. Roosevelt's presidency.

CONSTITUTIONAL HERITAGE ANSWER

indicates that no person can be elected to the office more than twice

The Twenty-first Amendment is the only amendment that has been ratified by state conventions rather than by state legislatures.

Twenty-first Amendment

[Proposed February 20, 1933; declared ratified December 5, 1933]

Section 1. The eighteenth article of amendment to the Constitution of the United States is hereby repealed.

Section 2. The transportation or importation into any State, Territory, or possession of the United States for delivery or use therein of intoxicating liquors, in violation of the laws thereof, is hereby prohibited.

~~**Section 3.** This article shall be inoperative unless it shall have been ratified as an amendment to the Constitution by conventions in the several States, as provided in the Constitution, within seven years from the date of the submission hereof to the States by the Congress.~~

From the time of President Washington's administration, it was a custom for presidents to serve no more than two terms of office. Franklin D. Roosevelt, however, was elected to four consecutive terms. The Twenty-second Amendment made into law the custom of a two-term limit for each president.

 **Constitutional Heritage**

How does the Twenty-second Amendment limit the years a president can remain in office?

Twenty-second Amendment

[Proposed March 24, 1947; declared ratified March 1, 1951]

Section 1. No person shall be elected to the office of the President more than twice, and no person who has held the office of President, or acted as President, for more than two years of a term to which some other person was elected President shall be elected to the office of the President more than once. ~~But this Article shall not apply to any person holding the office of President when this Article was proposed by the Congress, and shall not prevent any person who may be holding the office of President, or acting as President, during the term within which this Article becomes operative from holding the office of President or acting as President during the remainder of such term.~~

~~**Section 2.** This Article shall be inoperative unless it shall have been ratified as an amendment to the Constitution by the legislatures of three fourths of the several States within seven years from the date of its submission to the States by the Congress.~~

Until the Twenty-third Amendment, the residents of Washington, D.C., could not vote in presidential elections.

Aerial view of Washington, D.C.

Twenty-third Amendment

[Proposed June 16, 1960; declared ratified April 3, 1961]

Section 1. The District constituting the seat of Government of the United States shall appoint in such manner as the Congress may direct:

A number of electors of President and Vice President equal to the whole number of Senators and Representatives in Congress to which the District would be entitled if it were a State, but in no event more than the least populous State; they shall be in addition to those appointed by the States, but they shall be considered, for the purposes of the election of President and Vice President, to be electors appointed by a State; and they shall meet in the District and perform such duties as provided by the twelfth article of amendment.

Section 2. The Congress shall have power to enforce this article by appropriate legislation.

Twenty-fourth Amendment

[Proposed August 27, 1962; declared ratified February 4, 1964]

Section 1. The right of citizens of the United States to vote in any primary or other election for President or Vice President, for electors for President or Vice President, or for Senator or Representative in Congress, shall not be denied or abridged by the United States or any State by reason of failure to pay any poll tax or other tax.

Section 2. The Congress shall have power to enforce this article by appropriate legislation.

Constitutional Heritage

What practices does the Twenty-fourth Amendment outlaw?

Twenty-fifth Amendment

[Proposed July 6, 1965; declared ratified February 23, 1967]

Section 1. In case of removal of the President from office or of his death or resignation, the Vice President shall become President.

Section 2. Whenever there is a vacancy in the office of the Vice President, the President shall nominate a Vice President who shall take office upon confirmation by a majority vote of both Houses of Congress.

Vice President Lyndon Johnson was sworn in as president after John F. Kennedy's assassination.

Section 3. Whenever the President transmits to the President pro tempore of the Senate and the Speaker of the House of Representatives his written declaration that he is unable to discharge the powers and duties of his office, and until he transmits to them a written declaration to the contrary, such powers and duties shall be discharged by the Vice President as Acting President.

Section 4. Whenever the Vice President and a majority of either the principal officers of the executive departments or of such other body as Congress may by law provide, transmit to the President pro tempore of the Senate and the Speaker of the House of Representatives their written declaration that the President is unable to discharge the powers and duties of his office, the Vice President shall immediately assume the powers and duties of the office as Acting President.

Thereafter, when the President transmits to the President pro tempore of the Senate and the Speaker of the House of Representatives his written declaration that no inability exists, he shall resume the powers and duties of his office unless the Vice President and a majority of either the principal officers of the executive department or of such other body as Congress may by law provide, transmit within four days to the President pro tempore of

The illness of President Eisenhower in the 1950s and the assassination of President Kennedy in 1963 were the events behind the Twenty-fifth Amendment. The Constitution did not provide a clear-cut method for a vice president to take over for a disabled president or in the event of the death of a president. This amendment provides for filling the office of the vice president if a vacancy occurs. It also provides a way for the vice president to take over if the president is unable to perform the duties of that office.

CONSTITUTIONAL HERITAGE

Presidential Disability. President Ronald Reagan used the Twenty-fifth Amendment's provision regarding presidential disability in July 1985, when he underwent cancer surgery. Reagan wrote a letter informing Congress that Vice President George Bush would assume the powers of the presidency while Reagan was under anesthesia.

CRITICAL THINKING Why might Reagan have sent a letter to Congress informing them of his surgery?

ANSWER: Students might note that he sent the letter in order to comply with Section 3 of the Twenty-fifth Amendment.

THAT'S INTERESTING!

North Carolina did not ratify the Twenty-fourth Amendment. In response, a group of high school students started a ratification movement. The state ratified the amendment in 1989, the 200th anniversary of the Constitution.

CONSTITUTIONAL HERITAGE ANSWER

poll taxes and other voting taxes

PEOPLE IN HISTORY

Gregory Watson, Constitutional Advocate. In 1982 Gregory Watson was a student at the University of Texas at Austin. In a paper for a political science class he argued that a proposed amendment regarding congressional pay, once part of the Bill of Rights, could still be ratified. Only six states had ratified the proposed amendment, which had then been ignored for more than 200 years. Watson received a "C" on his paper, but he was determined to prove that he was correct. He spent more than $5,000 of his own money in an effort to convince state legislatures throughout the nation to ratify the amendment. Watson was successful, and in 1992 the proposal became the Twenty-seventh Amendment.

CRITICAL THINKING Do you think that the proposed amendment should have become part of the Constitution? Explain your answer.

ANSWER: Some students might argue that it was not necessary, since the states had ignored it for more than 200 years. Others might argue that state legislatures ratified the amendment, and so it met all necessary qualifications.

CONSTITUTIONAL HERITAGE ANSWER

until an election of representatives had convened

Constitutional Heritage

According to the Twenty-seventh Amendment, if senators or representatives were to vote for a pay raise for themselves, when would it take effect?

The Voting Act of 1970 tried to set the voting age at 18 years old. However, the Supreme Court ruled that the act set the voting age for national elections only, not state or local elections. This ruling would make necessary several different ballots at elections. The Twenty-sixth Amendment gave 18-year-old citizens the right to vote in all elections.

the Senate and the Speaker of the House of Representatives their written declaration that the President is unable to discharge the powers and duties of his office. Thereupon Congress shall decide the issue, assembling within forty-eight hours for that purpose if not in session. If the Congress, within twenty-one days after receipt of the latter written declaration, or, if Congress is not in session, within twenty-one days after Congress is required to assemble, determines by two-thirds vote of both Houses that the President is unable to discharge the powers and duties of his office, the Vice President shall continue to discharge the same as Acting President; otherwise, the President shall resume the powers and duties of his office.

Twenty-sixth Amendment

[Proposed March 23, 1971; declared ratified July 5, 1971]

Section 1. The right of citizens of the United States, who are eighteen years of age or older, to vote shall not be denied or abridged by the United States or by any State on account of age.

Section 2. The Congress shall have power to enforce this article by appropriate legislation.

Twenty-seventh Amendment

[Proposed September 25, 1789; declared ratified May 7, 1992]

No law, varying the compensation for the services of the Senators and Representatives, shall take effect, until an election of Representatives shall have intervened.

These students are helping a local candidate campaign for office.

Amendments to the Constitution

Amendment	Year Enacted	Subject
1st	1791	Personal and political freedoms
2nd	1791	Right to keep weapons
3rd	1791	Quartering of troops
4th	1791	Search and seizure; search warrants
5th	1791	Rights of accused persons
6th	1791	Speedy trial
7th	1791	Jury trial
8th	1791	Bails, fines, punishments
9th	1791	Rights of the people
10th	1791	Powers of the states
11th	1798	Suits against the states
12th	1804	Election of president and vice president
13th	1865	Abolition of slavery
14th	1868	Rights of citizens; privileges and immunities, due process, and equal protection
15th	1870	Extension of suffrage to African American men
16th	1913	Income tax
17th	1913	Direct election of senators
18th	1919	Prohibition of liquor
19th	1920	Women's suffrage
20th	1933	Change in dates for presidential and congressional terms of office
21st	1933	Repeal of prohibition
22nd	1951	Two-term limit on presidential tenure
23rd	1961	Right to vote in presidential elections for residents of the District of Columbia
24th	1964	Poll tax banned in federal elections
25th	1967	Presidential disability and succession
26th	1971	Lowering of voting age to 18
27th	1992	Legislative salaries

THE GRANGER COLLECTION, NEW YORK

The Bill of Rights

Slave chains

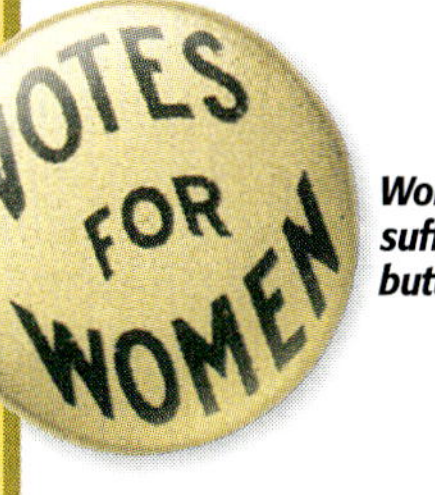

Women's suffrage button

Voter registration form

CONSTITUTIONAL HERITAGE

Failed Amendments. Only six proposed amendments that secured congressional approval failed to be ratified by the states. The first, a part of the original Bill of Rights, concerned congressional representation. Two amendments in the 1800s also failed. One regarded citizens who accepted titles of nobility from foreign governments and the other concerned slavery. During the 1900s amendments regarding child labor, equal rights, and congressional representation for the District of Columbia all failed. The Equal Rights Amendment and the District of Columbia amendment both contained deadlines, so they have no chance of being passed in the same manner as the Twenty-seventh Amendment.

CRITICAL THINKING Do you think that proposed amendments should include deadlines for ratification? Explain your answer.

ANSWER: Answers will vary. Some students might argue that deadlines place an unfair burden on the amendment's supporters.

The Civil War

CHAPTER PLANNING GUIDE

	Section Lesson Objectives	Print Resources	Multimedia Resources	Sheltered English Resources
Section 1 The Union Dissolves, pp. 68–74	1 Discuss the attempts made to compromise with the secessionists. 2 Analyze how the fall of Fort Sumter affected the relationship between the Union and the Confederacy. 3 Identify the advantages each side possessed at the beginning of the war. 4 Summarize the consequences of the First Battle of Bull Run.	▶ Guided Reading Strategy 2.1 ▶ American History Outline Map 13: Union and Confederacy ▶ Section 1 Review, p. 74 ▶ Daily Quiz 2.1	▶ One-Stop Planner, Lesson 2.1 ▶ American Music Selection 13: "All Quiet Along the Potomac" ▶ The American Nation Video Program Segment: Building an Army; Teacher's Guide, pp. 57–62 ▶ Holt Researcher: American History CD–ROM	▶ Main Idea Activity for Reteaching and Sheltered English 2.1
Section 2 The North and South Face Off, pp. 75–81	1 Contrast the military strategies of the North and South. 2 Describe the daily hardships soldiers faced. 3 Report on what life was like on the home front during the war. 4 Explain how civilians contributed to the war effort. 5 Discuss why some people opposed the war.	▶ Guided Reading Strategy 2.2 ▶ Literature Reading 2: The Reality of War ▶ Biography Reading 2: Clara Barton ▶ Section 2 Review, p. 81 ▶ Daily Quiz 12.2	▶ One-Stop Planner, Lesson 2.2 ▶ Everyday Life in America Transparency 12: Photograph of Civil War Casualties ▶ Holt Researcher: American History CD–ROM	▶ Main Idea Activity for Reteaching and Sheltered English 2.2
Section 3 Fighting the War, pp. 82–89	1 Explain how Union forces gained control of the Mississippi River. 2 Evaluate how the northern and southern forces fared in the eastern campaigns. 3 Analyze how the Union's victory at Antietam changed its war aims. 4 Recognize how African American soldiers aided the Union. 5 Assess the significance of the battles of Fredericksburg and Chancellorsville.	▶ Guided Reading Strategy 2.3 ▶ American History Political Cartoon 11: Changing Union Leadership ▶ Section 3 Review, p. 89 ▶ Daily Quiz 2.3	▶ One-Stop Planner, Lesson 2.3 ▶ Linking Geography and History Transparency 14: The War in the East and the West, 1861–1863 ▶ Holt Researcher: American History CD–ROM	▶ Main Idea Activity for Reteaching and Sheltered English 2.3
Section 4 The Final Phase, pp. 90–95	1 Explain the outcomes of the Battle of Gettysburg. 2 Assess the significance of the Union victory at Vicksburg. 3 Describe General Grant's strategy in the summer of 1864. 4 Describe General Sherman's strategies. 5 List the terms of surrender at Appomattox.	▶ Guided Reading Strategy 2.4 ▶ Primary Source Reading 2: The Gettysburg Address ▶ Geography Activity 2: The Siege of Vicksburg ▶ Graphic Organizer Activity 2: The Gettysburg Address ▶ Section 4 Review, p. 95 ▶ Daily Quiz 2.4	▶ One-Stop Planner, Lesson 2.4 ▶ Holt Researcher: American History CD–ROM ▶ HRW Web site	▶ Main Idea Activity for Reteaching and Sheltered English 2.4
Chapter Review and Assessment pp. 96–97		▶ Chapter 2 Review, pp. 96–97 ▶ Chapter 2 Tutorial for Students, Parents, Mentors, and Peers ▶ Chapter 2 Test (Form A or B) ▶ Portfolio Activities and Alternative Assessment Handbook, Chapter 2	▶ Audio Program, Chapter 2 (English and Spanish) ▶ Chapter 2 Test Generator (on the One-Stop Planner) ▶ Global Skill Builder CD–ROM ▶ HRW Web site	▶ Spanish Glossary ▶ Sheltered English Chapter 2 Test

CHAPTER OVERVIEW

Tensions between the North and South reached a crisis in 1861, when Confederate forces attacked Fort Sumter in South Carolina. When President Lincoln called for troops to put down the Confederate uprising, few people predicted that the American Civil War would last until 1865 and result in so many deaths.

The South's skilled military leaders, led by Robert E. Lee, were able to overcome the North's advantages in population and economic resources to win the early battles of the war. Ultimately, however, Union forces under Ulysses S. Grant were able to exploit the North's advantages to overcome Confederate forces. In 1865 the Confederate army surrendered to the Union army to end the war.

While the Civil War was significant for the devastation it caused, especially in the South, its significance extends also to the Emancipation Proclamation, which freed African Americans from slavery in the Confederate states and provided the final resolution of the issue of slavery in the United States.

TIME TAMERS

Block Scheduling

The teacher lesson plans for each section offer a variety of activity choices to help you present the material in a block scheduling format. For further suggestions on block scheduling, see the **Block Scheduling Handbook with Team Teaching Strategies**, pp. 7–12.

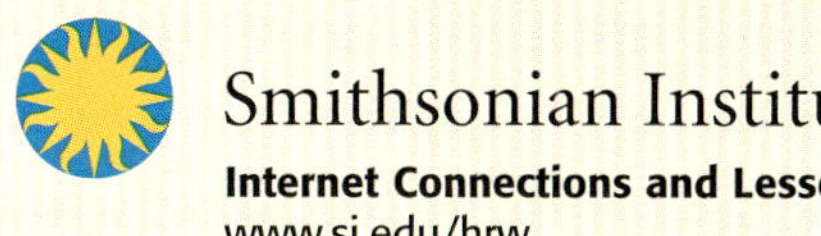

Smithsonian Institution®

Internet Connections and Lesson 2
www.si.edu/hrw

Hands-On History Activities:

Classroom to Community The **Hands-On History Activities** help students make meaningful connections between events in American history and those in their own hometown. You may wish to use the Chapter 2 Activity, Photography: Seeing Your Local History, to extend the chapter lessons, as alternative assessment, or as a block scheduling option.

Portfolio Projects

The American Nation includes multiple portfolio projects in each Pupil's Edition chapter review, as well as each unit review. Chapter 2 Portfolio Project options on p. 97 include the following:

1. Students will **write a letter.**
2. Students will **create a chart.**
3. Students will **write an editorial.**

The American Nation

INTERNET RESOURCE DIRECTORY

To access online materials for this chapter, go to go.hrw.com and type in the keywords listed below.

HRW ONLINE RESOURCES

GO TO: go.hrw.com

Online Maps

KEYWORD: SE1 Maps2

- Union and Confederacy, 1861
- Theaters of War, 1861–1865
- Southern Railroads, 1862–1865
- Far West Battles
- Emancipation
- Battle of Gettysburg

Online Charts

KEYWORD: SE1 Charts2

- Rating the North and South
- Soldiers' Occupations

Online Reading Support

KEYWORD: SE1 Strategies2

Online Rubrics

KEYWORD: SE1 Rubrics

CHAPTER ENRICHMENT LINKS

Use these Web links to extend and enrich student learning for Chapter 2.

GO TO: go.hrw.com
KEYWORD: SE1 Ch2

CHAPTER INTERNET ACTIVITIES

GO TO: go.hrw.com

- Pupil's Edition Student Activity
  KEYWORD: SE1 Photography
  (Students research the Civil War photography of Mathew Brady.)
- Teacher's Edition Student Activity
  KEYWORD: SE1 Red Cross
  (Students explore the history of the Red Cross.)
- Teacher's Edition Student Activity
  KEYWORD: SE1 Gettysburg
  (Students explore the geography of the Battle of Gettysburg.)

ADDITIONAL

RESOURCES

Books for Teachers

McPherson, James M. *Battle Cry of Freedom: The Civil War Era.* Ballantine, 1989. Provides a detailed account of the war in a lively narrative style.

Sutherland, Daniel E. *The Expansion of Everyday Life, 1860–1876.* HarperCollins, 1990. Describes everyday life in the North and the South during and after the Civil War.

Books for Students

McPherson, James M. *Marching Toward Freedom: Blacks in the Civil War, 1861–1865.* Facts on File, 1990. Discusses the role of African Americans in the war.

Meltzer, Milton. *Voices from the Civil War.* HarperCollins, 1990. Provides first-person accounts of the war experience. Particularly appropriate for students reading below grade level.

Primary Sources from the Period

Berlin, Ira, Joseph P. Reidy, and Leslie S. Rowland, eds. *Freedom's Soldiers.* Cambridge University Press, 1998. Provides first-person accounts of African American soldiers in the Union.

Davis, William C., ed. *Diary of a Confederate Soldier: John S. Jackman of the Orphan Brigade.* University of South Carolina Press, 1997. Provides the wartime impressions of a soldier from Tennessee.

Multimedia Materials

The Civil War. 9 videos, 11 hrs. PBS. Blends primary sources and commentary from historians in a comprehensive examination of the war and its consequences.

CHAPTER 2

Before You Read

Build on What You Know

Ask students to answer the following questions.

What tensions between the North and South might have led to the Civil War?

Consider:

- the issue of slavery
- the secession of southern states

What advantages might the North have used to win the Civil War?

Consider:

- the North's industrial resources
- the North's larger population

exploring the time line

AMERICAN EVENTS

ACROSS THE CURRICULUM

▶MUSIC◀

The "Battle Hymn of the Republic." Poet and abolitionist Julia Ward Howe wished to make a contribution to the Union cause in the Civil War. While she visited the Union encampment in Washington during the autumn of 1861, she was inspired by the tune to "John Brown's Body." At the urging of a friend, she decided to provide the tune with a better set of lyrics. Inspired in the middle of the night, she transformed, "John Brown's body lies a mouldering in the grave. . . ." into "Mine eyes have seen the glory of the coming of the Lord. . . ." *The Atlantic Monthly* paid her four dollars for her poem, the "Battle Hymn of the Republic," which was published in February 1862.

ACTIVITY: Ask students to provide examples of songs or works of art that are associated with a particular war.

CHAPTER 2

1861–1865

The Civil War

The bombardment of Fort Sumter

1864 camera

1861 Politics
Confederate forces open fire on Fort Sumter.

1861 World Events
Russian serfs gain their freedom.

1861 World Events
Great Britain and France purchase cotton from Egypt and India instead of from southern states.

1862 Politics
The Union captures New Orleans and wins the Battle of Antietam, while the Confederacy wins the Battle of Fredericksburg.

1862 The Arts
Mathew Brady presents "The Dead at Antietam," his first photographic exhibit of the Civil War.

1860 | 1861 | 1862

THE GRANGER COLLECTION, NEW YORK

Charles Dickens

1861 The Arts
British author Charles Dickens writes *Great Expectations.*

1861 Science and Technology
Archaeopteryx—a prehistoric skeleton that indicates a possible evolutionary link between birds and reptiles—is discovered in Europe.

Red Cross medal

1862 World Events
Jean-Henri Dunant of Switzerland proposes the founding of a voluntary relief organization—the International Red Cross.

1862 The Arts
Julia Ward Howe publishes a poem that becomes the "Battle Hymn of the Republic."

Sheet music for the "Battle Hymn of the Republic"

Before You Read

Build on What You Know

Tensions between the North and the South continued to grow throughout the 1850s. The crisis came to a head when a Republican, Abraham Lincoln, was elected president in 1860. In this chapter you will learn how the large population and industrial power of the North gave the Union better resources to fight the long and bloody Civil War that ensued. Although the South's defensive strategy and superior military leadership enabled it to win many of the war's early battles, the Confederacy was unable to overcome the Union forces.

Think About Themes

To help students create their Themes Journal entries, provide the following examples of appropriate **agree**/**disagree** *statements.*

Geographic Diversity

Agree During the Revolutionary War the Patriots successfully used guerrilla war tactics in forest regions.

Disagree During the Revolutionary War the Patriots lost their strategic advantage atop Bunker Hill.

Economic Development

Agree During the War of 1812 the British naval blockade hurt U.S. commerce.

Disagree U.S. domestic manufacturing increased as a result of the War of 1812.

Democratic Values

Agree Abolitionists and slaveholders disagreed sharply over the moral and political ramifications of slavery.

Disagree The vast majority of American citizens agree with the principles expressed in the Bill of Rights.

exploring the time line

GLOBAL EVENTS

TOPIC: Red Cross
GO TO: go.hrw.com
KEYWORD: SE1 Red Cross

Have students access the Internet through the HRW Web site to conduct research on the history of the Red Cross. Then have students create an annotated time line that presents the history of the International Red Cross, including information about the work performed by the Red Cross, notable achievements of the organization, and how the Red Cross is funded.

General Lee surrendering to General Grant

1863
Daily Life
Congress establishes free mail delivery to U.S. cities.

1863
Business and Finance
Tailor Ebenezer Butterick markets the first paper dress pattern.

1863
Politics
The Confederacy wins a victory at Chancellorsville; the Union wins at Gettysburg and Vicksburg.

1864
Business and Finance
"In God We Trust" first appears on U.S. coins.

1864
Science and Technology
Louis Pasteur invents the process of pasteurization.

1864 U.S. coin

1865
Politics
General Robert E. Lee formally surrenders his Confederate army to General Grant's Union forces at Appomattox.

1865
Science and Technology
Thaddeus Lowe invents a machine that makes ice.

1865
The Arts
Yale College opens the first Department of Fine Arts in the United States.

1864

1865

1863
Daily Life
Food riots break out in several southern states.

THE MUSEUM OF THE CONFEDERACY–RICHMOND, VIRGINIA

Southern women rioting for bread in 1863

1864
World Events
The French capture Mexico City and proclaim Archduke Maximilian of Austria emperor of Mexico.

1864
Politics
General Ulysses S. Grant becomes commander of all Union armies.

1865
Daily Life
John MacGregor pioneers canoeing as a sport.

1865
Science and Technology
The federal armory at Springfield, Massachusetts, has produced 1.6 million rifled muskets since 1861.

Think About Themes

Decide whether you **agree** *or* **disagree** *with the following statements. Note why in your journal.*

Geographic Diversity Geography has a significant impact on the way wars are fought.

Economic Development A nation's economy will be affected negatively by war.

Democratic Values Americans choose to interpret the meaning of individual liberty in different ways.

SECTION 1

After completing Section 1, students should be able to:

OBJECTIVE 1 *Discuss the attempts made to compromise with the secessionists.*

OBJECTIVE 2 *Analyze how the fall of Fort Sumter affected the relationship between the Union and the Confederacy.*

OBJECTIVE 3 *Identify the advantages each side possessed at the beginning of the war.*

OBJECTIVE 4 *Summarize the consequences of the First Battle of Bull Run.*

LET'S GET STARTED!

Play Selection 13, "All Quiet Along the Potomac," from the **American Music Audio CD Program** as students enter the classroom. Ask students to respond to "All Quiet Along the Potomac" in writing. After the song has ended, tell students that the song was written during the early part of the Civil War by a Confederate soldier. Tell students that in Section 1 they will learn about the beginning of the Civil War.

SECTION 1 RESOURCES

PRINT
- Guided Reading Strategy 2.1
- American History Outline Map 13: Union and Confederacy
- Section 1 Review, p. 74
- Daily Quiz 2.1

MULTIMEDIA
- One-Stop Planner, Lesson 2.1
- American Music Selection 13: "All Quiet Along the Potomac"
- The American Nation Video Program Segment: Building an Army; Teacher's Guide, pp. 57–62
- Holt Researcher: American History CD–ROM

SHELTERED ENGLISH
- Main Idea Activity for Reteaching and Sheltered English 2.1

✔ READING TO UNDERSTAND
To help students master the section objectives, have them answer the **READING CHECKS** and complete **Guided Reading Strategy 2.1** as they read the section.

The Union Dissolves

OBJECTIVES

Read to understand:
1. what attempts were made to compromise with the secessionists
2. how the fall of Fort Sumter affected the relationship between the Union and the Confederacy
3. what advantages each side possessed at the beginning of the war
4. what the consequences of the First Battle of Bull Run were

KEY TERMS

Crittenden Compromise
First Battle of Bull Run

KEY PEOPLE

Robert E. Lee
Joseph E. Johnston
Thomas "Stonewall" Jackson

KEY PLACES

Fort Sumter
Richmond
West Virginia

President Lincoln hoped to keep the Union together.

EYEWITNESSES TO History

"This proclamation was like the first peal of a surcharged thunder-cloud, clearing the murky air. The . . . whole North arose as one man. . . .

Hastily formed companies marched to camps of rendezvous. . . . Merchants and clerks rushed out from stores, bareheaded, saluting them as they passed. Windows were flung up; and women leaned out into the rain, waving flags and handkerchiefs.

I had never dreamed that New England . . . could be fired with so warlike a spirit."

—Mary Ashton Livermore

Mary Ashton Livermore

Mary Ashton Livermore wrote about the northern response to President Abraham Lincoln's call in April 1861 for volunteers to put down the southern rebellion. Such spirited enthusiasm swept the nation in early 1861. As war became inevitable, both sides prepared for what they believed would be a short conflict.

Last Attempts at Compromise

When President Abraham Lincoln took office in 1861, the nation stood on the brink of collapse. Seven southern states had already seceded from the Union—South Carolina, Mississippi, Florida, Alabama, Georgia, Louisiana, and Texas. Furthermore, the debate over secession continued to rage in the Upper South.

To preserve the Union, Senator John J. Crittenden of Kentucky had proposed the **Crittenden Compromise** in December 1860. Crittenden's plan called for the old Missouri Compromise line to be drawn west through the remaining territories. North of the line, slavery would be illegal; south of the line, slavery could expand. President-elect Lincoln quickly rejected the plan. Opposition to the spread of slavery united the Republican Party. Many Republicans might have turned against Lincoln if he had allowed slavery to expand. Lincoln did, however, support the part of Crittenden's plan that would protect slavery where it already existed.

Lincoln's willingness to allow slavery to continue hardly affected the secessionists, who were caught up in the excitement of creating a new nation. "It is a revolution . . . of the most intense character," wrote one southern senator. "It can no more be checked by human effort, for the time, than a prairie fire by a gardener's watering pot."

The new president was determined to preserve the Union. In his inaugural address, Lincoln insisted to southerners that secession was unconstitutional: "No State upon its own mere motion can lawfully get out of the Union." As president, he was bound to enforce the Constitution in every state.

✔ READING CHECK: What attempts were made to compromise with the secessionists?

TEACH OBJECTIVE 1

ALL LEVELS: Draw the following graphic organizer on the chalkboard. Tell students that it lists the positions of President Lincoln and secessionists regarding the issue of slavery and preservation of the Union and Senator Crittenden's attempts to find common ground with both sides. Discuss the organizer with students. Then organize students into groups of three and have each student in the triad play the role of either Abraham Lincoln, John J. Crittenden, or a secessionist leader. *(Students should use their completed organizers to assist in stating their positions in their roles.)* Have members of each group stage a discussion in which the secessionist should describe the government policy he or she would like to see in place; Crittenden should describe and offer his compromise; and Lincoln should summarize his beliefs and positions. **Cooperative Learning, Sheltered English**

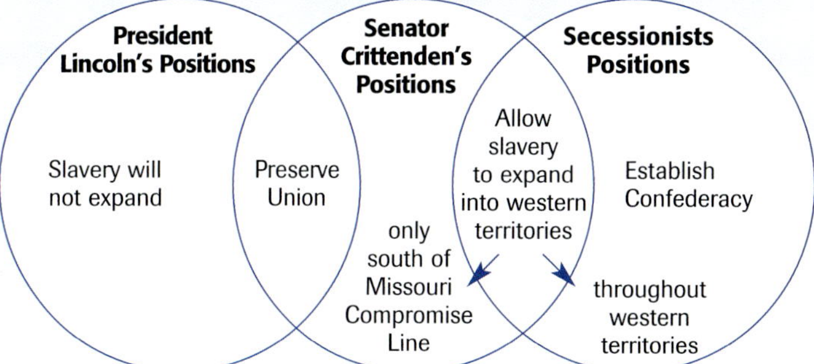

The Fall of Fort Sumter

The South did not respond to President Lincoln's pleas for unity. Instead, meeting little resistance, the Confederacy took over many federal forts, mints, and arsenals within its borders during the secession crisis. One fort that was very important to the South—Fort Sumter—remained under federal control.

Fort Sumter lay in a strategic location in the harbor of Charleston, South Carolina. The South needed the fort in order to control access to this major port city. In early March the fort's commander, Major Robert Anderson, sent word to Washington that he was nearly out of supplies. Without reinforcements, Sumter would soon fall to the Confederates.

The North did not want to lose the fort—it would be a sign that Lincoln would not protect federal property in the seceded states. The president hesitated, however, because the eight slave states that remained in the Union had threatened to secede if he used force against the Confederacy. Lincoln decided to resupply Fort Sumter, reasoning that if the Confederates fired on unarmed supply ships, then they, not the Union, would be the aggressors.

On April 6, 1861, Lincoln sent a messenger to alert South Carolina governor F. W. Pickens that supply ships were on their way, but that the ships carried only supplies, not troops or arms. Governor Pickens relayed the message to General P. G. T. Beauregard, the local Confederate military commander. Beauregard then ordered the federal troops to evacuate the fort. Major Anderson refused.

At 4:30 A.M. on April 12 the Confederate forces opened fire on Fort Sumter. Abner Doubleday, Anderson's second in command, described the scene within the fort.

> **"Showers of balls . . . and shells . . . poured into the fort. . . . When the immense mortar shells, after sailing high in the air, came down in a vertical direction and buried themselves in the parade ground, their explosion shook the fort like an earthquake."**

For 34 hours the Confederates bombarded Sumter. Finally, with much of the fort ablaze and their ammunition running low, Anderson and his men formally surrendered on April 13. Surprisingly, no one on either side was killed or seriously wounded during the fighting.

On April 15 Lincoln publicly announced the existence of a rebellion "too powerful to be suppressed by the ordinary course of judicial proceedings." He called

INTERPRETING THE VISUAL RECORD

Fortifications. The Confederate attack on Fort Sumter marked the beginning of the Civil War. ***What does the fort's location suggest about its importance?***

Abraham Lincoln

1809–1865
In Office 1861–1865

Superior leadership skills made Abraham Lincoln one of the nation's greatest presidents. The personal hardship of losing two children and the stresses of the Civil War took a toll, however. Lincoln endured periodic bouts of severe depression. He often used laughter to combat his depression. He believed laughter could "whistle down sadness," as a friend put it.

Throughout his life, Lincoln filled his everyday conversations with humor and homespun stories. "The Lord prefers common-looking people," he once said. "That is why he makes so many of them." On another occasion he commented about a book: "People who like this sort of thing will find this the sort of thing they like."

Even in personal defeat Lincoln put his famous dry wit to use. "I feel like the boy who stumped his toe," he said on losing the 1858 U.S. Senate race to Stephen Douglas. "I am too big to cry and too badly hurt to laugh."

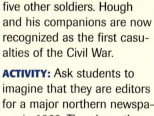

CONSTITUTIONAL HERITAGE

Fort Sumter and the Civil War's First Casualties. While no one on either side was killed or seriously wounded during the fighting at Fort Sumter, the conflict between the North and the South did not remain bloodless for long. Under the terms of his surrender, Major Anderson—who had been an instructor and friend of General Beauregard years earlier at West Point—was allowed to direct a 100-gun salute to the U.S. flag at Fort Sumter before evacuating the fort and returning to the North on a nearby steamship. During the salute, Private Daniel Hough's gun exploded, killing him instantly and wounding five other soldiers. Hough and his companions are now recognized as the first casualties of the Civil War.

ACTIVITY: Ask students to imagine that they are editors for a major northern newspaper in 1862. Then have them write a short editorial that discusses the importance of Fort Sumter's recent surrender.

VISUAL RECORD ANSWER

Students might mention that the fort is located in a harbor, which provides easy access to the city.

Multimedia Resources

American Music Selection 13: "All Quiet Along the Potomac"

TEACH OBJECTIVE 2

LEVEL 1: Have students study the map on this page. Pair students and have each pair use Outline Map 13, Union and Confederacy, from **American History Outline Maps** to create a map that represents the balance of power between the Union and Confederacy immediately before the fall of Fort Sumter. Tell students to use different colors to shade in Union states, Confederate states, and territories. Call on volunteers to use their maps, the map on this page, and the textbook to analyze how Fort Sumter's fall affected the relationship between the Union and the Confederacy. *(Students should mention that after the fort's fall, Lincoln considered the South to be in a state of rebellion.)* Write students' responses on the chalkboard. **Sheltered English, Cooperative Learning**

Teacher to Teacher

Doug Odom of El Dorado, Kansas, suggested the following activity: Tell students to imagine that Confederate forces have just captured Fort Sumter. Organize students into small groups. Have each group write a lead news story with a headline on the fall of Fort Sumter. Groups may assume the perspective of either a southern newspaper or a northern newspaper. Display students' articles around the classroom.

DEMOCRATIC VALUES

The Response to Lincoln's Call to Arms. President Lincoln's call for 75,000 three-month recruits on April 15, 1862, was met with considerable enthusiasm. More than 90,000 quickly volunteered, creating temporary food and housing shortages at many army recruitment centers. Such problems, however, did little to discourage most of the new soldiers. One observer described the prevailing attitude as "one . . . of patriotic exultation, when everyone seems willing to sacrifice everything for a common cause."

CRITICAL THINKING Why might Lincoln's call to arms have been met with enthusiasm?

ANSWER: Students might say that young men volunteered for the Union army because they believed in preserving the Union, disapproved of slavery, or craved adventure.

The American Nation **VIDEO PROGRAM**

Building an Army; Teacher's Guide, pp. 57–62

Search 00600, Play to 08592
Videodisc 1, Side B

Play Pause

See *Teacher's Guide* for Spanish barcode.

These women are filling cartridges at a federal arsenal in Watertown, Massachusetts.

for the states to provide 75,000 soldiers to put down the uprising. The recruits were to serve for just three months.

Choosing Sides

President Lincoln's fear of losing more states to the Confederacy quickly became a reality. Four more southern states—Arkansas, North Carolina, Tennessee, and Virginia—responded to the president's call for troops by seceding. The Confederates named Richmond, Virginia, as their capital.

Four other slave states—Delaware, Kentucky, Maryland, and Missouri—remained within the Union. Secession was never a serious threat in Delaware, where there were few slaves and most of the population sympathized more with the North than with the South. Kentucky, Maryland, and Missouri, on the other hand, were sharply divided over the issue of secession. The governors of both Missouri and Kentucky sympathized with the Confederacy, but neither state voted to secede. Lincoln kept Maryland in the Union by securing the state with federal troops. Maryland's secession would have meant losing the Union capital. Maryland surrounded Washington on three sides with already-seceded Virginia on the other side.

The mountainous counties of northwestern Virginia remained loyal to the Union as well. People living there held few slaves and had long resented the rich planter elite of the lowlands. They set up their own state government, and in 1863 the state was admitted to the Union as West Virginia. Although West Virginia had few slaves, slavery initially remained legal there.

The Upper South's white population remained divided over the issue of secession. Sections of several of these states raised Union regiments to fight the Confederacy. Some families were torn apart as members fought for opposing sides in the war.

One son of Kentucky senator John Crittenden became a Union general, and another became a Confederate general. President Lincoln's wife, Mary Todd, a southerner by birth, had four brothers and three brothers-in-law fighting in the Confederate army.

The Union and Confederacy in 1861

Learning from Maps Southerners argued that the Constitution, as a compact among sovereign states, gave the states the right to secede.

REGION What did the seceding southern states have in common with Missouri, Kentucky, Maryland, and Delaware?

Union states
Border states (part of the Union)
Confederate states
Territories
West Virginia (separated from Virginia in 1861 and joined the Union in 1863)

✔ **READING CHECK:** How did the fall of Fort Sumter affect the relationship between the Union and the Confederacy?

LEVELS 2 AND 3: Tell students to imagine that they are the captains of merchant ships that make frequent stops at Charleston, South Carolina, near Fort Sumter. In their roles as politically neutral traders, have them write three short letters to their ships' owners updating them on events and changes in South Carolina from 1860 to 1861. The first letter should cover rising tensions over Fort Sumter and its strategic importance; the second letter should describe the fall of Fort Sumter; and the third letter should evaluate the implications of its fall for the relationship between the Union and the Confederacy. *(See the Level 1 lesson for the correct strategic importance of Fort Sumter and the effect of the fort's fall on the relationship between the Union and the Confederacy.)* Students may wish to include their letters in their portfolios.

TEACH OBJECTIVE 3

LEVEL 1: Have students work in pairs to create a list of the Union's strengths. *(Students should mention larger population, greater industrial resources, more railroad lines, retained U.S. Navy.)* Have each pair also compile a list of the Confederacy's strengths. *(Students should mention that Confederates had to fight a defensive war and had excellent military leaders.)* After pairs have completed their lists, ask volunteers to write their list on the chalkboard. Have other students supply any missing information. Conclude by leading a classroom discussion of the advantages of each side.
Sheltered English, Cooperative Learning

Comparing North and South

The war that loomed after the fall of Fort Sumter appeared to be a mismatch. In many respects the North enjoyed military superiority over the South. The advantages held by the South were so important, however, that many objective observers expected a quick southern victory.

Northern advantages. With more than 22 million residents the North had a huge population advantage. The South's population totaled slightly more than 9 million, some 3.5 million of whom were slaves. As a result, the South had a much smaller pool of available soldiers.

The North also enjoyed an economic advantage. When the Civil War began, the North controlled more than 85 percent of the nation's industry and significant material resources. These advantages enabled the North to produce military supplies and replace lost or damaged equipment more rapidly than the Confederacy. Most southern wealth was in land and slaves.

Resources of the North and South in 1861

Resources	North	South
Total population	22,000,000	9,000,000*
Bank deposits	$189,000,000	$47,000,000
Railroad mileage	20,000 miles	9,000 miles
Number of factories	100,500	20,600

*Southern population includes 3,500,000 slaves
Sources: *American Heritage Picture History of the Civil War; Encyclopedia of American History*

Learning from Charts At the beginning of the Civil War, the North's abundant resources gave it a military advantage over the South.

? Building Chart Skills Which resource do you think had the greatest influence on the outcome of the Civil War?

In addition, since most of the nation's railroad lines were located in the Northeast and the Midwest, the Union could move troops and supplies with ease. Southern routes, in contrast, were short, with few connecting lines between major cities. Furthermore, because the North manufactured most of the nation's railroad equipment, the Confederacy found itself ill-prepared to replace broken or worn-out parts and equipment during the war.

Most of the U.S. Navy remained loyal to the Union, including such southern naval officers as David Farragut and Percival Drayton. With no ships and little naval expertise to draw upon, the South was forced to build its navy from scratch.

Southern advantages. The South had two important advantages over the North. The Confederacy had only to fight a defensive war, protecting its territory until the Union tired of the struggle. In contrast, the Union needed to conquer an area of about 750,000 square miles. This was twice the size of the original thirteen colonies. The South also had excellent military leadership. In fact, most southern victories would result from the battle strategies of skillful Confederate officers.

BIOGRAPHY *Robert E. Lee*

Among the ablest of southern military leaders was Robert E. Lee, who was born into a prominent Virginia family in 1807. His father was Henry "Light-Horse Harry" Lee, a Revolutionary War hero. Robert excelled as a student at the U.S. Military Academy at West Point. After graduating in 1829, he served first in the Army Corps of Engineers and then in the cavalry. In 1831 Lee married Mary Custis, great-granddaughter of Martha Washington and the heir to Arlington Plantation in northern Virginia.

Lee first tested his military abilities during the Mexican War of 1846. He took part in the capture of Veracruz, serving as a captain under General Winfield Scott.

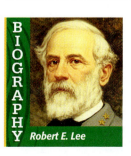

Read More About It

Free Find:
Robert E. Lee
After reading about Robert E. Lee on the **Holt Researcher** CD–ROM, write an obituary describing his accomplishments and his reasons for fighting for the Confederacy.

ECONOMIC DEVELOPMENT

The Industrial Superiority of the North. According to the 1860 U.S. census, northern factories turned out 97 percent of the country's firearms, 94 percent of its cloth, 93 percent of its pig iron, and more than 90 percent of its boots and shoes. While Confederate officials eventually managed to acquire guns from a variety of sources and to increase the South's production of iron and cloth, footwear remained a problem throughout the war. The meager supplies of boots and shoes that the Confederate army did obtain were smuggled from Massachusetts or removed from dead Union soldiers.

ACTIVITY: Have each student create a list of 10 material objects that a typical soldier needed to fight in the Civil War. Then have students debate whether the Union or the Confederate army had an easier time acquiring each of these necessities.

CHART ANSWER
Answers will vary. Students should clearly state and justify their answers.

MAP ANSWER
(for p. 70)
They were all slave states.

LEVELS 2 AND 3: Organize students into groups of four and instruct half of the groups to act as Union military strategists and the other half as Confederate military strategists. Have each group draw up a list of its own strengths and weaknesses. *(See the Level 1 answers for each side's strengths.)* Then have each group speculate on how it can (1) best utilize its strengths and compensate for its weaknesses and (2) how it can defend against its opponent's strengths and take advantage of any weaknesses. Have each group put its recommendations in a strategy position paper and choose a spokesperson to read it to the class. **Cooperative Learning, Block Scheduling**

▶ASSIGNMENT *Have each student write a song, poem, or journal entry about the beginning of the Civil War from the point of view of a person who has family members fighting on both sides of the conflict.*

HISTORY MAKERS SPEAK

A writer for the *Times* of London in *Battle Cry of Freedom*

A Daunting Military Challenge for the North. During the opening stages of the Civil War, many observers thought that the Union army would be unable to conquer the entire Confederacy. The remarks of a writer for the *Times* of London typified this opinion: "It is one thing to drive the rebels from the south bank of the Potomac, or even to occupy Richmond, but another to reduce and hold in permanent subjection a tract of country nearly as large as Russia in Europe. . . . No war of independence was ever terminated unsuccessfully except where the disparity of force was far greater than it is in this case."

CRITICAL THINKING How might the characterization of the Civil War as a "war of independence" have differed from Abraham Lincoln's view of the Civil War?

ANSWER: Students might suggest that Abraham Lincoln viewed the Civil War as a war to preserve the Union or a war to put down a rebellion.

This sword belonged to General Robert E. Lee.

Lee's skill and bravery impressed his commander and earned him a promotion. After working as superintendent of West Point from 1852 to 1855, Lee served briefly in Texas and eventually moved to Arlington, Virginia. In 1859 he led the federal troops that captured abolitionist John Brown at Harpers Ferry.

As southern states began to secede from the Union, General Scott advised President Lincoln to ask his old friend, Robert E. Lee, to command the Union forces. Faced with a difficult choice between country and state, Lee regretfully declined, resigning his commission. Scott told him sadly, "You have made the greatest mistake of your life, but I feared it would be so." Lee opposed slavery and secession, but he refused to fight against Virginia. Lee wrote a letter to his sister.

> **"With all my devotion to the Union and the feeling of loyalty and duty of an American citizen, I have not been able to make up my mind to raise my hand against my relatives, my children, my home. I have therefore resigned my commission in the Army, and save [except] in defense of my native State—with the sincere hope that my poor services may never be needed—I hope I may never be called on to draw my sword."**

The armies. Lee was called upon not only to draw his sword, but eventually to lead the South's army. Both sides quickly built up their military strength. By the end of 1861 the Union had more than 527,000 soldiers and the Confederacy slightly more than 258,000. Most of these soldiers were between the ages of 18 and 29, with drummer boys as young as 9 years old.

Estimates of how many men fought in the war vary because many men reenlisted after their initial commissions expired. The U.S. government placed the official wartime enlistment in the Union army at 2,672,341, with another 105,963 men enlisted in the navy or marines. According to U.S. government statistics, some 3,530 American Indians and some 180,000 African Americans served in the Union army. Noncommissioned African American officers numbered nearly 7,000. About 100 African Americans were commissioned.

Historians estimate that some 750,000 men enlisted in the Confederate army. This figure included some 5,500 Cherokee, Creek, Chickasaw, and Choctaw. These American Indians included many slaveholders lured by the promise of an all-Indian state following the war. Some Mexican Americans from New Mexico and Texas fought on both sides during the war.

✔ **READING CHECK:** What advantages did each side possess at the beginning of the war?

THROUGH OTHERS' EYES

European Views of the Civil War

The nations of Europe had their own aims and expectations with respect to the U.S. Civil War. Judging that a divided United States would be less threatening to Europe, some officials in France and Britain hoped that the South would win. Sir Edward Bulwer-Lytton, a member of the British Parliament, remarked that a Confederate victory would "be attended with happy results to the safety of Europe." Believing that it was already too late to save the Union, Bulwer-Lytton noted that a united America "would have hung over Europe like a . . . thunder-cloud. No single kingdom in Europe could have been strong enough to maintain itself against a nation that had once consolidated the gigantic resources of a quarter of the globe."

Russia, on the other hand, supported the Union. Russia wanted to keep the United States united and strong. This would help hold Britain and France in check and thereby maintain a balance of power in the world. Russian foreign minister Prince Gorchakov remarked to a U.S. diplomat: "You know the sentiments of Russia! We desire, above all things, the maintenance of the American Union as one indivisible nation."

TEACH OBJECTIVE 4

LEVEL 1: Organize the class into pairs. Have each pair create flash cards that identify significant people and events associated with the First Battle of Bull Run. *(Suggestions for side 1 and side 2 of the flash cards include: Union general—Irvin McDowell; Confederate general—Joseph E. Johnston; Confederate general—Thomas "Stonewall" Jackson; location of the battle—Manassas Junction (Virginia); result of the battle—Confederate victory; psychological consequences of battle—Union shock, Confederate overconfidence.)* When students have completed their flash cards, have them quiz each other using the flash cards.
Sheltered English, Cooperative Learning

LEVELS 2 AND 3: Have students explain why the First Battle of Bull Run represented a psychological victory as well as a military victory for the Confederacy. *(Students should mention that it gave the Confederacy great confidence while it shocked and demoralized the Union forces.)* Then ask each student to write a one-page scenario describing whether or not he or she thinks the course of the war might have been different if the Union had won the First Battle of Bull Run. Tell students to explain and justify their thoughts with examples and logical arguments. Ask volunteers to share their scenarios with the class.

Strategies for Success — Recognizing Fallacies in Reasoning

In order to evaluate historical arguments and ideas, students must be able to recognize fallacies in reasoning. A *fallacy* is a false or mistaken idea. When included in a sequence of reasoning, a fallacy may result in an unsound argument or unsupported conclusion.

Most fallacies in reasoning fall into several basic categories. *Single cause* means identifying one cause for an event while ignoring other causes. History is complex, and very few historical events resulted from just one cause. *Coincidence as cause* means attributing the cause of one event to another event simply because they occurred at or near the same time. *Irrelevant evidence* means an argument or assertion is based on information that it is not related to logically.

How to Recognize Fallacies in Reasoning

1. **Identify the main ideas.** As you read a historical source, identify its main ideas and supporting details. Each time you identify a main idea, make a preliminary judgment of its soundness.
2. **Identify cause and effect.** Take note of cause-and-effect relationships that are mentioned explicitly and that you can infer from the source. Make sure to check for complex connections such as multiple causes and long-term effects.
3. **Evaluate the reasoning.** After you finish reading the source, assess the quality of its historical reasoning. Ask yourself the following questions: Are the arguments in this source logical? Are the cause-and-effect relationships fully proven? Do the conclusions follow from the information provided?

Applying the Strategy

Examine the following statement and identify the fallacy in its reasoning.

> The Civil War was fought over the issue of a state's right to make its own laws. If northerners had not wanted to make slavery illegal in the South, the war would not have occurred.

Practicing the Strategy

Answer the following questions.

1. What type of fallacy in reasoning does the statement contain?
2. What additional information might help correct this reasoning error?

STRATEGIES FOR SUCCESS ANSWERS

Practicing the Strategy

1. single cause
2. Students might suggest that information about the controversy over the expansion of slavery, the secession process, and proposed compromises would help correct the reasoning error.

VISUAL RECORD ANSWER

(for p. 74)

Students might suggest that the troops had little training and were inexperienced in battle.

SECTION 1 REVIEW ANSWERS

Define and Identify

For significance, see the following pages:

- Crittenden Compromise, p. 68
- Robert E. Lee, p. 71
- Joseph E. Johnston, p. 73
- First Battle of Bull Run, p. 73
- Thomas "Stonewall" Jackson, p. 73

The First Battle of Bull Run

General Winfield Scott believed the new Union troops still needed several months of training. Likewise, a Confederate officer reported his men to be so lacking in "discipline and instruction" that it would be "difficult to use them in the field." Despite these reservations, President Lincoln ordered General Irvin McDowell and some 35,000 barely trained troops to Richmond, Virginia, in mid-July 1861.

This Union drum bears the eagle symbol of the federal government.

Fighting at Manassas. General McDowell's forces never reached Richmond. On July 21, 1861, some 35,000 Confederates met the Union troops near Manassas (muh-NAS-uhs) Junction, a railroad crossing about 30 miles outside Washington. Led by General Joseph E. Johnston, the Confederates dug in on high ground behind a creek called Bull Run. Northerners called the fighting that followed the **First Battle of Bull Run**. Southerners called it the Battle of Manassas.

At first the battle went in the Union's favor. The left flank of the Confederate line came close to cracking. Confederate general Thomas "Stonewall" Jackson and his men stopped the Union assault, however. Jackson's troops raced toward the Union line, filling the air with a terrifying scream: "Woh—who—ey! Who—ey!"

REVIEW

Have students complete the **Section 1 Review** on p. 74.

ASSESS

Have students complete **Daily Quiz 2.1**. As **Alternative Assessment**, you may want to use the flash cards or one-page scenarios for the Battle of Bull Run in this section's lessons.

RETEACH

Have students complete **Main Idea Activity for Reteaching and Sheltered English 2.1**. Have students work in pairs to write short summaries of each of the subsections of Section 1. Then group each pair with another pair, and ask the foursome to review each other's summaries, looking for key points that may have been missed. **Sheltered English**

EXTEND

Have each student create an illustrated time line of the events leading up to the first battle of the Civil War. Tell students to start their time lines in January 1861 with the inauguration of President Lincoln and end in July 1861 with the First Battle of Bull Run. Tell students to include 6 to 10 entries with an appropriate illustration for each one—they do not need exact dates for every entry. When students have finished their time lines, display them in the classroom. **Block Scheduling**

Locate

For locations, see the map on p. 70. For importance, see the following pages:

- Fort Sumter, p. 69
- Richmond, p. 70
- West Virginia, p. 70

1. northern advantages—larger population, more industry and material resources, extensive railroad lines, retention of U.S. Navy; southern advantages—defensive strategy, vast territory, excellent military leadership

2. It controlled access to the harbor of Charleston, South Carolina, and was a symbol of Union property in the seceded states. Its fall led Lincoln to declare the existence of a rebellion in the South and to call for soldiers to put down the rebellion; in turn, four more southern states seceded from the Union and joined the Confederacy.

3. Republicans rejected compromises allowing the spread of slavery to any western territories, and the secession process had progressed too far by the time compromises allowing the continuation of slavery in the South were proposed.

4. It contributed to the hasty and disorganized nature of the Union retreat.

5. Northerners who thought the Union would win the war quickly were frustrated by the defeat and the prospects of a longer war; southerners who hoped to defend their territory until the Union tired of the struggle were encouraged by the victory.

THE GRANGER COLLECTION, NEW YORK

INTERPRETING THE VISUAL RECORD

Bull Run. The fierce fighting and number of casualties at Bull Run surprised many Americans. ***What do you think made the First Battle of Bull Run such a bloody fight?***

The eerie sound, which came to be known as the Rebel Yell, sent chills through the northern troops.

The Union soldiers fell back and headed for Washington. Union colonel Andrew Porter wrote about the retreat.

> **"Soon the slopes . . . were swarming with our retreating and disorganized forces, while riderless horses and artillery teams ran furiously through the flying crowd. All further efforts were futile. The words, gestures, and threats of our officers were thrown away upon men who had lost all presence of mind, and only longed for absence of body."**

The aftermath of southern victory. The events at Bull Run caused most people to realize that the war would last longer than a few months. As a result, each side began to seriously train its forces for battle and to plan strategy. Confederate president Jefferson Davis named Joseph Johnston to command the Army of Northern Virginia and chose Robert E. Lee as his military adviser. President Lincoln named General George B. McClellan to head the Union forces.

The most important consequences of the First Battle of Bull Run may have been psychological. The defeat shamed and shocked the North. In the South, newspaper editorials proclaimed the superiority of the Confederacy. The victory lulled many Confederates into a false sense of security. Meanwhile, the Union army was becoming more determined.

✔ **READING CHECK:** What were the consequences of the First Battle of Bull Run?

SECTION  REVIEW

Define and explain the significance of the following terms:
Crittenden Compromise
First Battle of Bull Run

Identify and explain the significance of the following individuals:
Robert E. Lee
Joseph E. Johnston
Thomas "Stonewall" Jackson

Locate and explain the importance of the following places:
Fort Sumter
Richmond
West Virginia

1. **Using Graphic Organizers** Copy the graphic organizer below. Use it to list the military advantages of the North and the South at the beginning of the war.

Northern Advantages	Southern Advantages

2. **Identifying Cause and Effect** Why was Sumter an important fort, and how did its fall affect both the Union and the Confederacy?
3. **Analyzing** Why did efforts at compromise fail to prevent the Civil War?
4. **Assessing Consequences** How did soldiers' lack of training affect the First Battle of Bull Run?

Critical Thinking

5. How did northerners' and southerners' differing attitudes about the war affect reactions to the First Battle of Bull Run?
Consider:
- what northern and southern attitudes toward the war were before the battle
- what northern and southern reactions were after the battle
- how the attitudes and reactions related to one another

SECTION 2

After completing Section 2, students should be able to:

OBJECTIVE 1 *Contrast the military strategies of the North and South.*

OBJECTIVE 2 *Describe the daily hardships soldiers faced.*

OBJECTIVE 3 *Report on what life was like on the home front during the war.*

OBJECTIVE 4 *Explain how civilians contributed to the war effort.*

OBJECTIVE 5 *Discuss why some people opposed the war.*

LET'S GET STARTED!

Write the following scenario on the chalkboard and ask students to respond to it in writing as they enter the classroom. *You are a soldier in the Union army. The war has been going on now for more than three years, with no end in sight. How do you get through each day?* After students have completed their responses, tell them that in Section 2 they will learn about life during the Civil War.

The North and South Face Off

OBJECTIVES

Read to understand:

1. how the military strategies of the North and South differed
2. what daily hardships soldiers faced
3. what life was like on the home front during the war
4. how civilians contributed to the war effort
5. why some people opposed the war

KEY TERMS

Anaconda Plan
U.S. Sanitary Commission
conscription
Copperheads
habeas corpus

KEY PEOPLE

Mary Boykin Chesnut
Elizabeth Blackwell
Clara Barton
Sally Louisa Tompkins

"We are going to kill the last Yankee before [spring] if there is any fight in them still. I believe that J. D. Walker's Brigade can whip 25,000 Yankees."

—an Alabama soldier

This letter reveals the high spirits that marked the beginning of the war between the North and South. After joining the army, one volunteer from New York wrote his family, "I and the rest of the boys are in fine spirits . . . feeling like larks." People in both the North and the South had great confidence that their side would quickly win the war. In the North, author James Russell Lowell used a fictional character, Hosea Biglow, to describe this widespread optimism. Biglow recalled the days after Fort Sumter fell: "I hoped to see things settled 'fore this fall. The Rebbles licked, Jeff Davis hanged, an' all."

A Union soldier (top) and a Confederate soldier (bottom)

Strategies of War

From the beginning of the war, the North's primary goal was to restore the Union. To accomplish this goal, Lincoln and his military advisers adopted a three-part strategy. They sought first to capture Richmond, the Confederate capital; second, to gain control of the Mississippi River; and third, to institute a naval blockade of the South. The naval blockade was nicknamed the **Anaconda Plan** because it was designed to slowly squeeze the life out of the South like an anaconda snake. It was important because the South depended on foreign markets to sell its cotton and to buy supplies.

The North devised its battle strategy based on the region's geography. Since the Confederacy stretched from Virginia to Texas, the Appalachian Mountains divided most of the action in the Civil War into two arenas: the eastern theater and the western theater. The eastern theater lay east of the Appalachians. The western theater lay between these mountains and the Mississippi River. Control of the Mississippi River would enable the North to penetrate deep into the South. It would also prevent the Confederacy from using the waterway to resupply its forces.

While the North's strategy depended on dividing the South geographically, the South planned to capture Washington and invade the North. Southern leaders hoped for a successful offensive strike northward through the Shenandoah Valley into Maryland and Pennsylvania. They hoped this would shatter northern morale, disrupt Union communications, win European support, and bring the war to a speedy end.

Confederate leaders knew that winning the support of France or Great Britain was crucial to a victory for the South. Because the French and British economies depended heavily on cotton, the Confederacy had confidence that one of the nations would respond to the naval blockade by coming to the South's aid.

This cartoon illustrates General Scott's Anaconda Plan for a naval blockade of the Confederate states.

SECTION 2 RESOURCES

PRINT

- Guided Reading Strategy 2.2
- Literature Reading 2: The Reality of War
- Biography Reading 2: Clara Barton
- Section 2 Review, p. 81
- Daily Quiz 2.2

MULTIMEDIA

- One-Stop Planner, Lesson 2.2
- Everyday Life in America Transparency 12: Photograph of Civil War Casualties
- Holt Researcher: American History CD–ROM

SHELTERED ENGLISH

- Main Idea Activity for Reteaching and Sheltered English 2.2

✔ READING TO UNDERSTAND

To help students master the section objectives, have them answer the **READING CHECKS** and complete **Guided Reading Strategy 2.2** as they read the section.

TEACH OBJECTIVE 1

LEVEL 1: Pair students and tell them to imagine that they are high-level military advisers for the Union and the Confederacy. In each pair, one student should summarize one side's general battle strategies as a bulleted list of statements beginning with, "We will. . . ." The other student should summarize the other side's general battle strategies. *(Example: "We will capture Richmond, the Confederate capital.") (Students should mention that Union strategies included: capturing Richmond, gaining control of the Mississippi River, naval blockade of the South; Confederate strategies: capturing Washington, invading the North, and winning a foreign ally.)* Ask volunteers to share their list of statements with the class.
Sheltered English, Cooperative Learning

LEVELS 2 AND 3: Have students complete the Level 1 activity, and then have each student write a two-to-three-paragraph evaluation of each side's strategy. Tell students to ask themselves the following questions to help in writing their evaluations: *How strong is the strategy overall? Does it have any obvious weaknesses? How might leaders on each side work to ensure their plan's success? What could they use as a backup plan if their initial strategies fail?* Ask volunteers to read their evaluations to the class.

ECONOMIC DEVELOPMENT

Trading Across Enemy Lines. At times Union and Confederate troops alleviated shortages of vital provisions by trading with each other. Before the battle at Fredericksburg, for instance, groups of Union soldiers sent coffee, sugar, and overcoats across the Rappahannock River in exchange for southern tobacco. While commanding officers on both sides knew about this illicit bartering, most chose to ignore it.

CRITICAL THINKING Why might Union and Confederate officers have chosen to ignore illicit bartering between their troops?

ANSWER: Answers will vary. Students might surmise that officers ignored the bartering in order to keep the morale of their troops as high as possible.

VISUAL RECORD ANSWER

Students might describe camp life as uncomfortable, dirty, and companionable.

Multimedia Resources

Everyday Life in America Transparency 12: Photograph of Civil War Casualties

The South's strategy failed, however. Neither France nor Britain proved dependent on Confederate cotton. French and British mill owners had stockpiled cotton before Fort Sumter's fall. Once these reserves ran out, the mill owners turned to Egypt and India for new supplies. Additionally, French emperor Napoleon III's preoccupation with events in Mexico distracted him from the conflict between the Union and the Confederacy. With Napoleon's blessing, Mexico's ruling elite made the archduke of Austria, Maximilian, emperor in 1864. When widespread opposition to Maximilian broke out, Napoleon ordered French troops in Mexico to put down the resistance. In part because he did not want to fight two wars at the same time, Napoleon decided not to aid the Confederacy. The South's failure to secure French help meant that southerners had limited resources at their disposal.

✔ **READING CHECK:** How did the military strategies of the North and the South differ?

The Military Experience

While high-level leaders planned battle strategies, the officers under their command attempted to train troops to carry out these strategies. Young recruits in both the Union and Confederate ranks were generally enthusiastic when they first enlisted. Most of these newly recruited soldiers had little experience with military life, however.

Both sides faced shortages of clothing, food, and even rifles. At the beginning of the war, most troops did not even have standard uniforms. Some simply wore their own clothes from home. Eventually, each side adopted a distinguishing uniform. The Union chose blue and the Confederacy gray. However, many troops, particularly Confederates, lacked good shoes and warm coats throughout the war.

INTERPRETING THE VISUAL RECORD

Camp life. Union soldiers (top) and Confederate soldiers (bottom) relax in their camps. They used utensils like the folding knife and spoon shown to prepare their meals. ***Based on these images, how would you describe camp life?***

THE MUSEUM OF THE CONFEDERATE, RICH

This persistent lack of provisions, coupled with unsanitary conditions in most field camps, led to deadly problems of disease. What little food existed in the camps often was spoiled. Describing the old meat served to his company, one Confederate soldier wrote, "A decent dog would have turned up his nose at it, but a hungry man will eat almost anything."

Thousands of soldiers died from illnesses such as influenza, pneumonia, and typhoid. Doctors and nurses could do little to help, since most hospitals had little in the way of medical provisions. As a result, some soldiers had to endure surgery without pain-killing anesthetics. Many with seemingly minor injuries died from infected wounds. In fact, disease, infection, and malnutrition took the lives of more than 65 percent of the soldiers who died during the war.

Nowhere were conditions worse than in the filthy, overcrowded prisoner-of-war camps in the North and South. One nun who worked as a nurse during the war commented, "It is hard to be sick, but to be a sick prisoner of war is indeed a

TEACH OBJECTIVE 2

LEVEL 1: Pair students and tell them to imagine that it is 1870—five years after the end of the Civil War. Have one student in each pair play the role of a veteran Union soldier describing his experiences during the war, and have the other student interview the soldier to record an oral history by taking notes. Then have students switch roles, but this time the veteran will be a former Confederate soldier. *(Students should mention that common experiences included shortages of food, clothing, and rifles, and unsanitary conditions, and disease. Confederate soldiers often lacked good shoes and warm coats.)* Have students take turns sharing their interviews by summarizing their partners' oral histories for the class. **Sheltered English, Cooperative Learning**

LEVELS 2 AND 3: Tell students to imagine that they are historians who have been hired as consultants by a modern film production company that is making a movie about the Civil War. They have been asked to supply the filmmakers with detailed information about Union and Confederate soldiers' daily lives. Have each student prepare a short report covering clothing, food, sanitation, shelter, morale, pastimes, and so on. *(See the Level 1 lesson for the correct information.)* Ask volunteers to share their reports with the class.

heavy cross [burden]." Union prisoners held at Andersonville, a Confederate camp located in southwestern Georgia, endured the worst conditions, with no shelter and little food. At times, prisoners at Andersonville died at a rate of about 100 per day. In some camps more than 25 percent of the prisoners died before the end of the war.

In addition to their difficult living conditions, many soldiers suffered from extreme boredom, homesickness, and loneliness. Some men deserted, but most attempted to cope with their situation. Soldiers played cards, attended prayer meetings, sang, wrote letters home, or engaged in other recreational activities.

✔ **READING CHECK:** What were some of the daily hardships faced by soldiers?

AMERICAN ARTS

Mathew Brady's Photographs

The carving on Mathew Brady's tombstone reads "renowned photographer of the Civil War." Before the Civil War even began, Brady was already well known for his portraits of wealthy and famous Americans. When the war broke out in 1861, he set a goal of recording all the "prominent incidents of the conflict."

Because he had lost much of his eyesight, Brady took very few of the war photographs that were displayed in his galleries. Nonetheless, he was one of the first photographers to understand the dramatic impact that the art form could have on society. With this in mind, Brady financed, supervised, and organized groups of photographers to accompany Union troops. They created a pictorial history of the people and events of the war. Brady's photographers traveled to the battlefields in horse-drawn wagons that doubled as portable darkrooms, allowing photographs to be developed on location.

The long exposures required for these early photographs prevented photographers from recording any movement. While many photographers made portraits of soldiers and took pictures of equipment, fortifications, prisons, and hospitals, the most dramatic photographs are those of soldiers lying dead on battlefields. These images had a powerful effect on their audience. "If he has not brought bodies and laid them in our dooryards and along our streets, he has done something very like it," wrote the *New York Times* of one Brady exhibit.

Mathew Brady's Civil War photographs often shocked civilians by showing the horrors of the battlefield.

Understanding the Arts

1. What prevented Civil War photographers from recording movement in their photographs?
2. What is unusual about the bodies in the photograph above?

HISTORY MAKERS SPEAK

Sergeant James T. Wells in *Soldiers Blue and Gray*

Rations in a Union Prisoner-of-War Camp. Confederate soldier James T. Wells described the rations at the prisoner-of-war camp where he was held: "For breakfast, half-pint coffee, or, rather, slop water; for dinner; half-pint greasy water (called soup for etiquette), also a small piece of meat, perhaps three or four ounces. For bread . . . per day; this you could press together in your hand and take at a mouthful. . . . The writer has known large, stout men to lay in their tents at night and cry like little babies from hunger."

CRITICAL THINKING Why might the conditions at prisoner-of-war camps in the North and South have been so poor?

ANSWER: Answers will vary. Students might suggest that both sides were inexperienced at handling prisoners of war, preferred to use rations for their own troops, or simply were behaving cruelly.

AMERICAN ARTS ANSWERS

1. the long exposures required
2. They are lined up in a neat row.

TEACH OBJECTIVES 3 AND 4

LEVEL 1: Pair students and ask each pair to create at least two illustrations that show the roles and responsibilities of civilians on the home front or battlefield during the Civil War. *(Students might draw pictures of women working in factories, teaching former slaves, making uniforms for soldiers, nursing wounded soldiers, or of women and boys cultivating crops, civilians organizing patriotic events, and so on.)* After students have finished their illustrations, ask each pair to write captions for them. Display students' work in the classroom.
Sheltered English, Cooperative Learning

LEVEL 2: Tell students to imagine that they are civilians on the Union or Confederate home front or battlefield during the Civil War. Have each student write a series of five diary entries over the course of two or three years in which he or she talks about changing living conditions, activities in support of the war, and his or her emotions. *(Tell students to avoid mentioning their feelings about slavery; they should instead concentrate on their daily life, their contributions to the war effort, and their attitudes about the war itself.)* Ask volunteers to share one or two of their entries with the class.

GLOBAL RELATIONS

Immigration to the North During the Civil War. European immigrants—most of them arriving from Ireland, Germany, and Great Britain—filled factory jobs in the North, especially during the second half of the Civil War. While immigration to the United States fell below 100,000 in 1861 for the first time in almost 20 years, it rose sharply in 1863 and climbed to more than 250,000 in 1865. Many Europeans were encouraged to make the journey by organizations such as the American Emigrant Company, which was financed by northern industrialists who employed large numbers of immigrants in their factories.

CRITICAL THINKING Why might large numbers of Europeans have immigrated to the United States during the Civil War?

ANSWER: Answers will vary. Students might suggest that many immigrants sought job opportunities in the wartime economy of the North, with its expanded industrial production.

The Home Front

Mobilization for the war also had a profound effect on the Americans who stayed home during the conflict. Women and those men who were too young, too old, or physically unable to fight, fulfilled important responsibilities on the home front.

The North. In the North, women replaced the male factory workers and farmers who left for the battlefields. The Union's need for military supplies opened up more than 100,000 jobs for women in arsenals, factories, and sewing rooms. The nearly 450 women working as clerks in the Treasury Department served as the government's first female office workers. Other women worked as bankers, morticians, saloon keepers, and steamboat captains during the war. Women and boys took responsibility for growing food during the war, aided by new farm equipment such as the McCormick reaper that helped produce bumper crops. The Detroit *Free Press* reported in 1864 that women had grown much of the corn produced in Michigan that year.

Countless civilians also participated in volunteer groups that raised money for the Union cause or provided relief services for soldiers and their families. Ladies Aid Societies made bandages, bedclothes, and shirts for soldiers. The American Freedman's Aid Commission provided hundreds of female schoolteachers to educate former slaves. State and local governments established homes for injured soldiers and orphanages for the children of soldiers who died in the war.

HOLT RESEARCHER
Read More About It
Free Find:
Mary Boykin Chesnut
After reading about Mary Boykin Chesnut on the **Holt Researcher** CD–ROM, create several fictional journal entries describing some of the events of the Civil War.

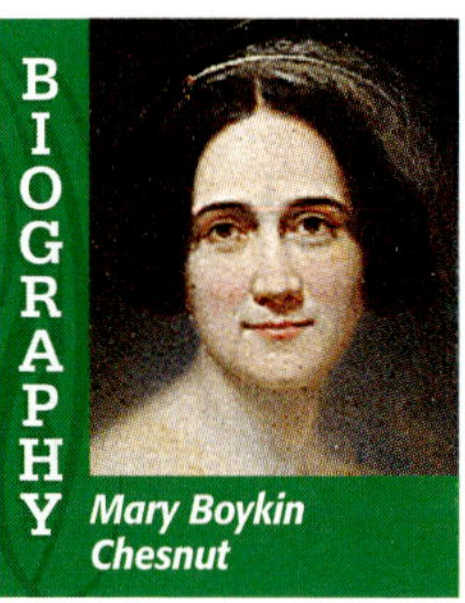

BIOGRAPHY
Mary Boykin Chesnut

The South. The diary of southerner Mary Boykin Chesnut provides a glimpse of life on the homefront during the war. The daughter of Mary and Stephen Miller, Mary Boykin was born in 1823 near Columbia, South Carolina. She grew up in a large and wealthy extended family that had lived in South Carolina since the 1750s. Mary followed her grandmother around like "her shadow." She learned how to manage the many different components of a plantation.

At the age of 17, after receiving a private education, Mary wed James Chesnut, heir to a nearby plantation. James Chesnut became an active politician. He served as a U.S. senator and later held several different positions in the Confederate and South Carolina governments. Mary Chesnut grew somewhat bored by plantation life. She found an outlet for her energetic personality in her passionate support of the Confederacy after war broke out. Living in Richmond, Virginia, during part of the war, she played an important role in political and military circles. She often wrote of her frustration, however, with what she saw as the incompetence of southern leaders. "Oh if I could put some of my reckless spirit into these . . . cautious lazy men!"

As the war progressed, Chesnut experienced pain and grief at the death of friends and family, as well as fear for the South's prospects. "With horror and amazement" she watched her world, "the only world we cared for, literally kicked to pieces." Chesnut eased the difficulty of her postwar life by preparing her diary for publication. Between 1881 and 1884 she rewrote her diary from the notes and entries she had made in the journal during the Civil War. Before the work was published, however, she died of heart failure in 1886 at the age of 63. Her diary was finally published in 1905.

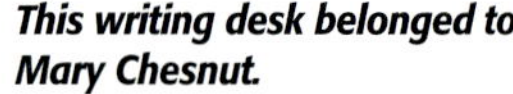

This writing desk belonged to Mary Chesnut.

LEVEL 3: Have each student write a fictional short story about life on the home front and civilian contributions to the war effort during the Civil War. *(See the Level 1 lesson for the correct contributions.)* Encourage students to come up with creative and interesting stories, but remind them to stay within the historical context covered in their textbooks. When students have completed rough drafts of their stories, have them exchange papers with a classmate to peer-edit each other's work. Give students time to write their final drafts and then ask volunteers to summarize their stories for the class. **Cooperative Learning**

▶**ASSIGNMENT** *Have each student make a broadside or sign protesting the continuation of the Civil War from a southern point of view.*

TEACH OBJECTIVE 5

LEVEL 1: Copy the following organizer located on the next page on the chalkboard. Tell students it relates to general and specific reasons why northerners and southerners opposed the Civil War. Have students copy the organizer into their notes. Discuss the graphic organizer with students. Then have each student use information from the completed graphic organizers to write six newspaper headlines—three about southern opposition and three about northern opposition to the war. Have volunteers share their headlines with the class. **Sheltered English**

Southerners like Chesnut supported the war effort with a series of patriotic events. At these parades and barbecues public figures urged young men to join the army, and wealthy members of society pledged money to buy arms and uniforms. Raffles and auctions raised much-needed funds for the Confederacy.

By 1862 the early romance with the war had faded, and the harsh effects of the blockade and providing for the war effort set in. The short supply of basic necessities such as shoes, clothing, and farm equipment caused inflation to skyrocket. In addition, the inability to obtain medicines caused untold suffering. City residents were hardest hit by the war. Many families lived in single rooms, using one fireplace for both heat and cooking. Food shortages forced people to live on beans, boiled potatoes, and corn fritters. Their social occasions became "starvation parties," with only water served for refreshment.

✔ **READING CHECK:** What was life like on the home front during the war?

Civilian Aid on the Battlefield

In addition to the vital roles they played on the homefront, many civilians, particularly women, actively aided the military. Some women even dressed like men so that they could fight. Cuban-born Loreta Janeta Velázquez (vay-LAHS-kays) disguised herself as a man and enlisted in the Confederate army. When she was found out and discharged, she became a spy for the South. Other women also served as spies. Rose O'Neal Greenhow was imprisoned for supplying information to the Confederacy. Mary Elizabeth Bowser, a maid who worked in Confederate president Jefferson Davis's home, and abolitionist Harriet Tubman both supplied information to the Union from behind enemy lines.

Many other women served the war effort in medical roles. Catholic nuns were among the most important female volunteers for medical duty. They sometimes transformed their convents into emergency hospitals throughout the North and the South. Many of these so-called nuns of the battlefield were Irish or German immigrants. They remained neutral and treated all victims of the war, becoming the only group allowed to move freely between Union and Confederate lines.

In the North, Elizabeth Blackwell, who was the first professionally licensed female doctor in the United States, helped run the **U.S. Sanitary Commission.** The commission worked to battle the diseases and infections that killed twice as many soldiers as bullets alone. Approximately 3,000 women served as nurses in the Union army. Some, like Clara Barton, ministered to the wounded on the battlefield. After the war, Barton founded the American Red Cross, which today serves disaster victims and others in need of assistance.

Growing Up During the Civil War

Children experienced the impact of the Civil War both at home and on the battlefield. Many older boys and girls took on increased responsibilities in their households and on their farms when their fathers and older brothers left to fight in the war. Younger children also suffered from hardships such as malnutrition and a lack of clothing, particularly in the South.

Somewhere between 250,000 and 500,000 boys fought in the Civil War. Elisha Stockwell Jr., a 15-year-old living in Wisconsin, explained how he joined: "I told the recruiting officer I didn't know just how old I was but thought I was eighteen." Many boys served as company musicians, particularly drummers or buglers.

Like the other soldiers, boys quickly learned that most of their time would be spent not in battle, but marching mile after mile and performing boring tasks in camp. When the time for combat did arrive, many boys, including Elisha Stockwell, regretted their decision to leave home. "As we lay there and the shells were flying over us," Stockwell recalled, "my thoughts went back to my home, and I thought what a foolish boy I was to run away and get into such a mess as I was in. I would have been glad to have seen my father coming after me."

The young boys in this Mathew Brady photograph are members of a Union drum corps.

DEMOCRATIC VALUES

African American Women and the Union Army. While such instances were rare, a few African American women played active roles in the Union army. Maria Lewis served as a soldier in a cavalry regiment from New York. Mary Dyson, a former slave, took part in several battles on the Union side while masquerading as a man. Susie King Taylor, whose husband volunteered for the Union army, accompanied his all-black regiment as it traveled through South Carolina, Georgia, and Florida. Taylor served as a nurse, did laundry, helped clean and maintain guns, and taught many of the men in the regiment to read.

ACTIVITY: Ask students how the military roles of women in the Civil War contrast with the roles of women who serve in the U.S. military today. Then call on volunteers for answers. Discuss students' responses.

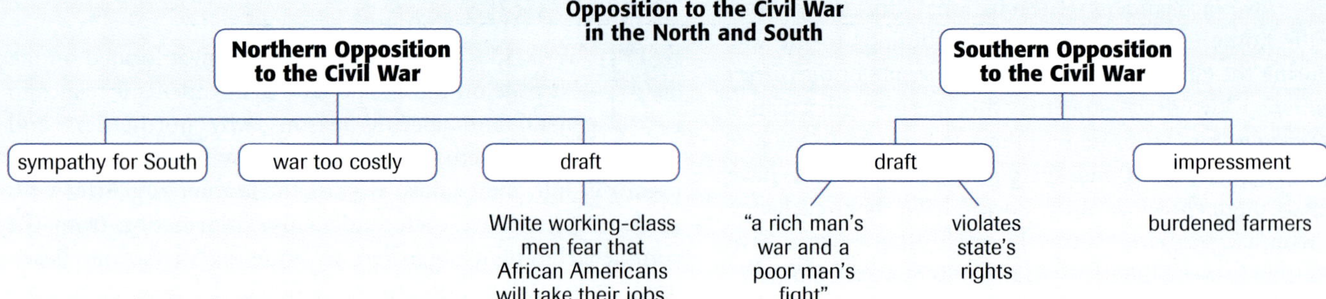

LEVELS 2 AND 3: Have each student create two political cartoons reflecting feelings of opposition toward the Civil War. One cartoon should express a southern point of view and the other a northern point of view. *(See the graphic organizer above for the correct feelings.)* Display students' cartoons around the classroom. Have volunteers present their cartoons to the class and explain the significance of symbols used in the cartoons.

THAT'S INTERESTING!

Union draft laws provided exemptions for the wealthy, who could pay a $300 fee to the government to avoid military service. Moreover, both the Confederate and the Union draft laws allowed conscripted men to hire substitutes.

VISUAL RECORD ANSWER

Students might suggest that wounded soldiers could receive medical attention quickly and that unsanitary conditions probably caused many soldiers to develop infections.

VISUAL RECORD ANSWER

(for p. 81)

Students might think not, as the cartoonist shows the "snakes" menacing liberty.

Define and Identify

For significance, see the following pages:

- Anaconda Plan, p. 75
- Mary Boykin Chesnut, p. 78
- Elizabeth Blackwell, p. 79
- U.S. Sanitary Commission, p. 79
- Clara Barton, p. 79
- Sally Louisa Tompkins, p. 80
- conscription, p. 80
- Copperheads, p. 81
- *habeas corpus*, p. 81

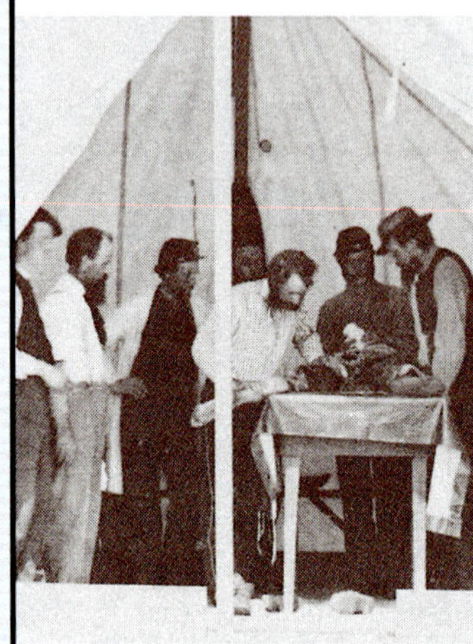

INTERPRETING THE VISUAL RECORD

Hospitals. Wartime conditions led to the need for battlefield hospitals like this one. ***What would be the advantages and disadvantages of such hospitals?***

Women in the South also provided medical aid to soldiers. Sally Louisa Tompkins was among the Confederate women who founded small hospitals and clinics. She was eventually commissioned as a captain in the Confederate army so that her Richmond, Virginia, hospital could qualify as a military hospital. This made Tompkins the only recognized female officer in the Confederate forces. Nurses experienced the horrors of war firsthand. Kate Cumming, a Confederate nurse from Alabama, wrote in her diary about her experiences at a makeshift hospital.

> **"The men are lying all over the house on their blankets, just as they were brought from the battlefield. . . . The foul air from this mass of human beings at first made me giddy and sick, but I soon got over it. We have to walk and, when we give the men anything, kneel in blood and water; but we think nothing of it at all."**

✔ **READING CHECK:** How did civilians contribute to the war effort?

Opposition to the War

Although many people on the home front worked to keep the war effort going and morale high, others voiced their displeasure with the war. Opposition grew as the bloody conflict dragged on longer than anyone had envisioned.

Southern opposition. Southern discontent intensified in the spring of 1862, when the Confederacy passed the first **conscription**, or draft, act in American history. Harsh living conditions in army camps as well as the difficulty of leaving families at home had caused a decrease in the number of southern volunteers. Southern military losses in the spring of 1862 convinced Jefferson Davis and southern generals of the draft's necessity.

The southern draft placed the major burden for fighting the war on poor farmers and working people. Draft exemptions for large plantation owners—who had led the Confederacy into war—created tension between wealthy southerners and nonslaveholding whites. Many white southerners openly criticized the policy. They claimed that it proved the conflict was a "rich man's war and a poor man's fight," as Confederate private Sam Watkins wrote in his memoirs. In response, plantation owners argued that some slaveholders had to remain at home to keep their slaves from running off. The Confederacy needed food and cloth, and few southerners believed that slaves would work without constant supervision.

Other southerners opposed the draft because they believed that it violated states' rights and freedom. These were the very principles that had led southern states to secede from the Union in the first place. Georgia governor Joseph E. Brown argued that "no act of the Government of the United States prior to the secession struck a blow at constitutional liberty so [fatal] as has been stricken by this conscription act."

Confederate soldiers carried this flag into battle.

As the war intensified, the Confederacy began to allow soldiers to pay farmers prices far below the market value for food, animals, and other property. This policy of impressment placed a heavy burden on food-producing families and led to serious food shortages. Many farmers called it robbery. Fear of starvation led to food riots in Alabama, Georgia, and North Carolina.

REVIEW

Have students complete the **Section 2 Review** on p. 81.

ASSESS

Have students complete **Daily Quiz 2.2.** As **Alternative Assessment**, you may want to use the oral history activity or the film company report on the daily life of soldiers in this section's lessons.

RETEACH

Have students complete **Main Idea Activity for Reteaching and Sheltered English 2.2.** Then organize students into groups of three. Have each group make an annotated outline of the section with brief summaries of each subsection.
Sheltered English

EXTEND

Tell students that the Civil War was the first major American conflict to be well documented by photographers. Organize students into groups of four or five and have them put together a visual presentation of 10 or more photographs from the Civil War. They may use an opaque projector or scan images into a computer for their presentations. If such equipment is not available, have students create a standing display of photocopied images with captions.
Block Scheduling, Cooperative Learning

Northern opposition. Discontent also surfaced in the North. Some northerners sympathized with the South and urged peace. Others believed that the war was proving too costly in terms of money and human life.

Republican sponsorship of a Union draft law in 1863 caused violence to break out in New York City. Democratic newspapers stirred the fears and passions of their readers. They claimed that the draft was designed to force white working-class men to fight for the freedom of African Americans who would then come north and steal their jobs. Angry whites raged through African American neighborhoods. They attacked and killed people and looted and burned buildings. They also destroyed the property of wealthy Republicans. By the time Union troops brought the rioting under control, more than 100 people had been killed.

Most northern Democrats who sympathized with the South did not actively interfere with the war effort. Known as **Copperheads**—a type of poisonous snake—most southern sympathizers limited their antiwar activities to speeches and newspaper articles. In an attempt to quiet the Copperheads, President Lincoln suspended some civil liberties, including the constitutional right of ***habeas corpus***—a protection against unlawful imprisonment. Thousands of Copperheads and other opponents of the war were arrested and held without trial.

THE GRANGER COLLECTION, NEW YORK

INTERPRETING THE VISUAL RECORD

Copperheads. This cartoon shows the United States fighting the threat of the Copperheads. ***Do you think the cartoonist had a favorable opinion of the Copperheads? Explain your answer.***

✔ **READING CHECK:** Why did some people oppose the war?

SECTION 2 REVIEW

Define and explain the significance of the following terms:
Anaconda Plan
U.S. Sanitary Commission
conscription
Copperheads
habeas corpus

Identify and explain the significance of the following individuals:
Mary Boykin Chesnut
Elizabeth Blackwell
Clara Barton
Sally Louisa Tompkins

1. **Using Graphic Organizers** Copy the graphic organizer below. Use it to explain how the North's military strategy differed from the South's at the beginning of the Civil War.

2. **Synthesizing** How were civilians on the home front affected by the war, and how did they aid the war efforts?
3. **Identifying Values** Why did some Americans on both sides, especially northern Democrats, oppose the war?
4. **Using Historical Imagination** Imagine that you are a young male soldier or a female civilian in either the North or the South during the Civil War. Write a diary entry describing your experiences during the war.

Critical Thinking

5. Was Sam Watkins correct in saying that the Civil War was "a rich man's war and a poor man's fight"? Explain your answer.
Consider:
   - what Watkins meant by "a rich man's war and a poor man's fight"
   - who fought in the war
   - how the war affected the rich and the poor differently

---

1. northern strategy, main goal–restore the Union; plan of action–capture Richmond, gain control of the Mississippi River, and set up a naval blockade of the South; southern strategy, main goal–defend territory and bring the war to a speedy end; plan of action–capture Washington, strike into Maryland and Pennsylvania, and win a foreign ally

2. Civilians on the home front lost family members to the war, filled vacated jobs, and dealt with wartime shortages and inflation. They aided the war efforts by producing food and supplies, participating in volunteer and relief groups, and raising money.

3. Some northern Democrats sympathized with the South or believed that the war was proving too costly. Others claimed that the Republican Party was forcing white working-class men to fight for the freedom of African Americans who would later take their jobs. Many southerners resented draft exemptions for the rich.

4. Diary entries will vary, but should describe clearly the responsibilities and hardships that the war placed on people.

5. Answers will vary. Students who agree might point out that poor people bore the majority of fighting responsibilities and wartime hardships. Those who disagree might contend that both the Union and Confederate causes were supported by people in all socioeconomic classes.

SECTION 3

After completing Section 3, students should be able to:

OBJECTIVE 1 *Explain how Union forces gained control of the Mississippi River.*

OBJECTIVE 2 *Evaluate how the northern and southern forces fared in the eastern campaigns.*

OBJECTIVE 3 *Analyze how the Union's victory at Antietam changed its war aims.*

OBJECTIVE 4 *Recognize how African American soldiers aided the Union.*

OBJECTIVE 5 *Assess the significance of the battles of Fredericksburg and Chancellorsville.*

LET'S GET STARTED!

Write this excerpt from the Emancipation Proclamation on the chalkboard: *"On the first day of January, a.d. 1863, all persons held as slaves within any state or designated part of a state, the people whereof shall then be in rebellion against the United States, shall be then, thenceforward, and forever free. . . ."* Tell students to respond to the excerpt. Tell students that in Section 3 they will learn about the Emancipation Proclamation.

SECTION 3 RESOURCES

PRINT

- Guided Reading Strategy 2.3
- American History Political Cartoon 11: Changing Union Leadership
- Section 3 Review, p. 89
- Daily Quiz 2.3

MULTIMEDIA

- One-Stop Planner, Lesson 2.3
- Linking Geography and History Transparency 14: The War in the East and the West, 1861–1863
- Holt Researcher: American History CD–ROM

SHELTERED ENGLISH

- Main Idea Activity for Reteaching and Sheltered English 2.3

✔ READING TO UNDERSTAND

To help students master the section objectives, have them answer the **READING CHECKS** and complete **Guided Reading Strategy 2.3** as they read the section.

SECTION 3 Fighting the War

OBJECTIVES

Read to understand:

1. how Union forces gained control of the Mississippi River
2. how the northern and southern forces fared in the eastern campaigns
3. how the Union victory at Antietam changed the Union's war aims
4. how African American soldiers aided the Union
5. what the significance of the battles at Fredericksburg and Chancellorsville was

KEY TERMS

Battle of Shiloh
Emancipation Proclamation
Battle of Antietam
54th Massachusetts Infantry

KEY PEOPLE

Ulysses S. Grant
David Farragut
George B. McClellan
James E. B. "Jeb" Stuart
Martin Delany
Ambrose E. Burnside

KEY PLACES

Fredericksburg
Chancellorsville

EYEWITNESSES TO History

"My heart kept getting higher and higher until it felt to me as though it were in my throat. I would have given anything then to have been back in Illinois, but I had not the moral courage to know what to do; I kept right on."
—Ulysses S. Grant

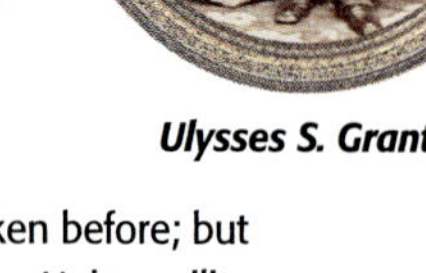

Ulysses S. Grant

Ulysses S. Grant began his service in the Civil War as a colonel of the 21st Illinois Regiment. Leading an attack on a Confederate camp in Missouri, he pressed forward despite his fear. When he learned that the Confederates had fled, Grant realized that the enemy colonel "had been as much afraid of me as I had been of him. This was a view of the question I had never taken before; but it was one I never forgot. . . . The lesson was valuable." Many other Union military leaders never grasped this important lesson.

The War in the West

During 1862 the Confederacy won most of the major battles in the East. President Lincoln had little luck finding a general able to defeat Confederate generals Stonewall Jackson, Joseph E. Johnston, and Robert E. Lee in the eastern theater. As a result, the Union's eastern forces had four different commanders in just one year. In the West, however, the Union forces led by Ulysses S. Grant achieved great success.

General Grant had won a reputation as a determined military leader. President Lincoln found him invaluable, exclaiming *"I can't spare this man. He fights."* In February 1862 Grant captured Fort Henry and Fort Donelson in Tennessee. Command of these two forts plus the city of Nashville—captured by other Union forces—gave the North control over Kentucky and much of Tennessee.

Shiloh. Marching toward Mississippi in the spring of 1862, Grant rested his troops near a small log church named Shiloh and waited for reinforcements. Grant knew that Confederate generals Albert Johnston and P. G. T. Beauregard were nearby in Corinth, Mississippi. He did not expect them to attack. On April 6, 1862, thousands of Confederate troops surprised Grant's soldiers, beginning the **Battle of Shiloh.** By day's end the Confederate forces had pushed Grant's men back to the Tennessee River.

Confederate commanders believed that they could finish off Grant's army the next morning. After their long day of fighting at a level of intensity not yet seen in the war, some of Grant's officers advised him to retreat before the Confederates could renew their attack in the morning. "Retreat?" Grant replied. "No. I propose to attack at daylight and whip them." Grant's plan received more support after fresh Union troops arrived during the night.

The fighting at the Battle of Shiloh was very bloody.

TEACH OBJECTIVE 1

LEVEL 1: Copy the graphic organizer on the following page on the chalkboard. Omit the italicized answers and ask volunteers to provide the results of the Union victories at Shiloh and New Orleans and write their responses on the chalkboard graphic organizer. Then have each student convert the information on the map on this page into a time line. Ask students to annotate the time line with information about critical battles in the fight for control of the Mississippi River. **Sheltered English**

LEVELS 2 AND 3: Have students complete the graphic organizer activity from the Level 1 lesson. Then ask each student to write one or two paragraphs to summarize the significance of the Union victories at Shiloh and New Orleans in the Union's quest to control the Mississippi River. Have volunteers read their paragraphs to the class.

▶**ASSIGNMENT** *Have students act as Union army communications officers to compose telegrams to Washington after the Battles of Shiloh and New Orleans reporting the outcome of each battle. Remind students that telegrams must be brief, descriptive, and to the point.*

Grant's April 7 surprise counterattack led to another day of fierce battle. By the middle of the afternoon, Grant's forces had subdued the Confederates. Southern general Beauregard gave the order to retreat. Both sides paid dearly, however. The Union suffered more than 13,000 casualties, and the Confederacy some 10,000—including General Johnston. Although Union forces were too badly hurt to pursue the Confederates, their victory at Shiloh gave the North a great advantage in the fight to control the Mississippi River valley.

Confederate forces fought desperately to stop the Union from controlling the Mississippi River.

New Orleans. Union control of the Mississippi River depended on its taking of New Orleans. It was the largest city in the South and a central port for supplying troops along and west of the river. Capturing New Orleans would allow the Union to cut off supplies to western Confederate forces and to move troops up the Mississippi River to join Grant's troops to the north. In late April 1862, Union ships commanded by David Farragut attacked the two forts guarding the approach to New Orleans from the Gulf of Mexico. After six days of unsuccessfully shelling the forts, Farragut decided to try to sail past them.

Seventeen Union warships advanced during the dark morning hours of April 24. The ensuing battle created a spectacular fireworks display. Confederate forces opened fire from gunboats, launched bombs from the shore, and pushed rafts set ablaze with towers of pine and pitch into the enemy ships. Despite the heavy pounding and nearly 200 casualties, all but four Union warships arrived in New Orleans. On April 29 the city was forced to surrender. Seventeen-year-old George Washington Cable witnessed the Union's capture of the city as "the crowds on the levee howled and screamed with rage."

By May 1862 the Union had achieved "a Deluge of Victories" in the West, as the New York *Tribune* reported. After the South's loss of 50,000 square miles of territory, 1,000 miles of navigable rivers, two state capitals, and its largest city, Confederate morale began to weaken. Mary Boykin Chesnut wrote after the capture of New Orleans, "Are we not cut in two? . . . I have nothing to chronicle but disasters. . . . The reality is hideous."

✔ **READING CHECK:** How did the Union win control of the Mississippi River?

The War in the West, 1862–1863

Learning from Maps The Union army and navy cooperated in gaining control of the Mississippi River.

? LOCATION Union victories at Fort Henry and Fort Donelson prevented the Confederates from moving into which Union state?

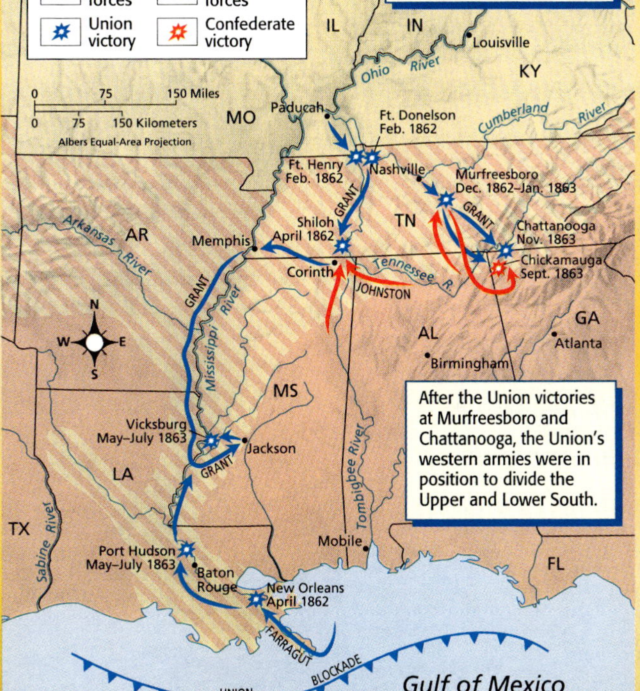

PEOPLE IN HISTORY

David Farragut. David Farragut was one of the Union's most effective and colorful military leaders. A southerner by birth, he had served in the U.S. Navy for 50 years and was a veteran of two wars when his home state of Virginia seceded in 1861. Farragut immediately moved to the North upon secession, where he offered his services to the Union cause. While leading a naval assault on Mobile Bay in August 1864, Farragut coined a phrase that because famous. When informed by a subordinate that his fleet would have to negotiate a harbor full of Confederate mines to capture the bay, Farragut shouted: "Damn the torpedoes! Full speed ahead!"

CRITICAL THINKING What two wars prior to the Civil War might David Farragut have served in as a member of the U.S. Navy?

ANSWER: Students should suggest that Farragut might have served in the War of 1812 and the Mexican War.

MAP ANSWER

Kentucky

Multimedia Resources

Linking Geography and History Transparency 14: The War in the East and the West, 1861–1863

outcome	results		results	outcome
Union victory at Shiloh	**1.** *Confederate general Albert Johnston was wounded.* **2.** *Victory gave the Union an advantage in their quest to control the Mississippi River valley from where they staged more offensives against southern cities along the Mississippi River.*	**Union Control of Mississippi River**	**1.** *Union gained control over mouth of the Mississippi River.* **2.** *South lost its largest city. Confederacy split in half.* **3.** *Confederate morale weakened.*	Union victory at New Orleans

ACROSS THE CURRICULUM

▶MILITARY SCIENCE◀

Officer Casualties During the Civil War. The severe wounds that General Joseph Johnston sustained at the Battle of Seven Pines were not unusual for a military officer during the Civil War. Because officers on both sides usually led their troops into battle, they were killed at a rate that was about 15 percent higher than that for enlisted men. Of all ranks, generals had the highest casualty rate–they were 50 percent more likely to be killed in battle than the soldiers they commanded.

CRITICAL THINKING Why might generals have had an even higher casualty rate than other officers during the Civil War?

ANSWER: Answers will vary. Students might suggest that both sides made a particular effort to kill opposing field generals in order to confuse and demoralize the enemy.

MAP ANSWER
Antietam and Gettysburg

84

Eastern Campaigns

While the Union racked up important victories in the West, President Lincoln remained committed to capturing Richmond. He ordered General George B. McClellan to return to Virginia in the spring of 1862.

The Peninsula Campaign. General McClellan trained his men well, teaching them both pride and discipline. His effectiveness as a military leader, however, suffered from his cautious nature. He often hesitated to commit his men to battle—much to the president's displeasure.

Lincoln reluctantly agreed to McClellan's strategy to take Richmond in what became known as the Peninsula Campaign. Rather than marching directly on the city, McClellan transported more than 100,000 men, 300 cannons, and 25,000 animals by water to the peninsula between the York and James Rivers. He planned to hit Richmond from the southeast, where the roads were better. This would put his army between Richmond and Confederate general Johnston's forces near Manassas, forcing the Confederates to move southward to defend Richmond. Once again, however, McClellan hesitated.

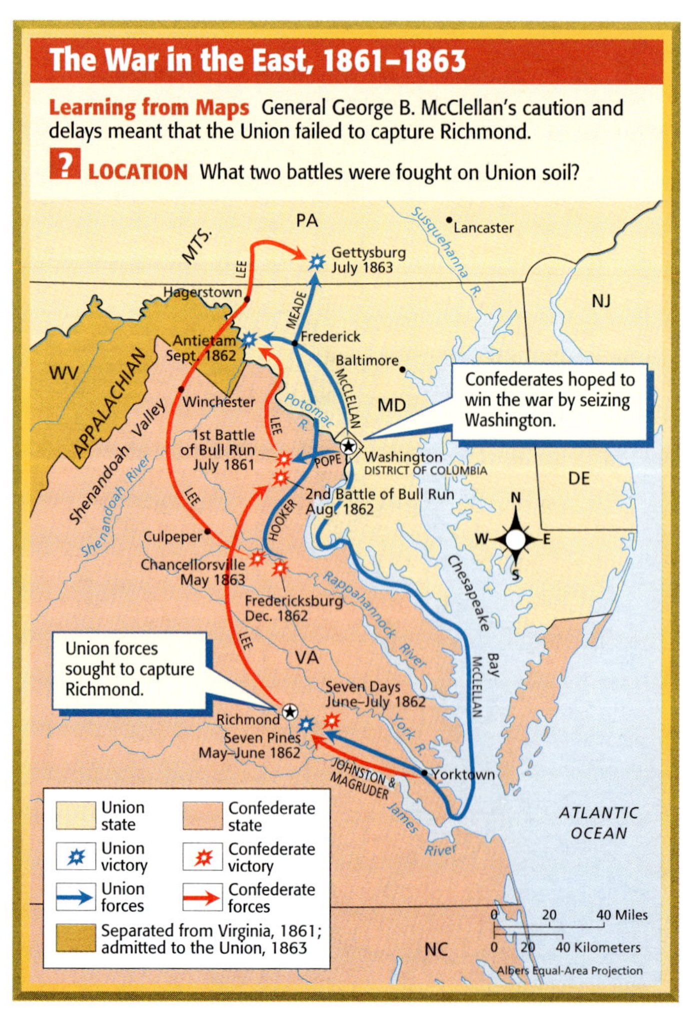

The War in the East, 1861–1863

Learning from Maps General George B. McClellan's caution and delays meant that the Union failed to capture Richmond.

LOCATION What two battles were fought on Union soil?

Yorktown and Seven Pines. In the first week of April 1862, General McClellan's forces met the Confederates at Yorktown, Virginia. Lincoln urged McClellan to attack but the general refused. He claimed that there were too many enemy troops. Actually, at first he faced only some 13,000 Confederates, led by General John B. Magruder. Lincoln sent a message warning that McClellan's "present hesitation . . . is but the story of Manassas repeated." He ordered, *"You must act."* Instead, McClellan decided to lay siege to Yorktown. He wrote to his wife that if Lincoln wanted to defeat the rebels "he had better come & do it himself." Meanwhile, Confederate general Johnston moved his troops to the peninsula.

Johnston's and Magruder's forces held Yorktown until the beginning of May. Just as McClellan was about to overrun the Confederate defenses, Johnston began a month-long retreat toward Richmond. McClellan followed, and on May 31, 1862, the two sides clashed just east of Richmond in the Battle of Seven Pines. The South fared badly. Confederate colonel John B. Gordon wrote:

TEACH OBJECTIVE 2

LEVEL 1: Pair students and have each pair write thumbnail summaries of each of the battles in the eastern campaigns. *(Pairs should mention that during the Peninsula Campaign, McClellan hesitated to attack Richmond. At Yorktown, McClellan refused to engage Confederate forces and instead laid siege to the city, which Confederate forces held. Confederate forces retreated toward Richmond, and Union and Confederate forces fought the Battle of Seven Pines, in which the South fared badly. The Seven Days Campaign was considered a victory for the South, even though they suffered more casualties, because McClellan retreated.)* Ask volunteers to read their summaries to the class. **Sheltered English, Cooperative Learning**

LEVELS 2 AND 3: Tell students to imagine that they are military historians writing an article for a historical journal. Have each student write an article that discusses the outcomes of each of the eastern campaigns as well as the strategies employed by both sides. *(See the Level 1 lesson for the outcomes; students should analyze the strategies of McClellan and the Confederate generals.)* Ask students to title their essays, and ask volunteers to read their articles to the class.

"I was left alone on horseback, with my men dropping rapidly around me. . . . My field officers . . . were all dead. Every horse ridden into the fight, my own among them, was dead. Fully one half of my line officers and half my men were dead or wounded."

General Johnston was among the seriously wounded. When Jefferson Davis placed Robert E. Lee in command of the Confederate forces in Johnston's place, Lee promptly halted the fighting.

Seven Days Campaign. Even though the Confederates were badly weakened, McClellan again sat and waited. Lee did not. In a daring maneuver, Lee sent a cavalry unit commanded by 29-year-old James E. B. "Jeb" Stuart to gather information on enemy positions. Using Stuart's information, the combined forces of Lee and Stonewall Jackson attacked the Union army in the Seven Days Campaign. This fierce battle lasted from June 25 to July 1. Union casualties numbered nearly 16,000. Confederate casualties were even higher—more than 20,000—but the battle was considered a victory for the South because McClellan retreated.

President Lincoln soon removed McClellan and gave General John Pope command of the army in the field. In late August, while marching to Richmond, Pope and his men were defeated by Lee's forces at the Second Battle of Bull Run. Soon after, McClellan was back in command of the eastern forces.

INTERPRETING THE VISUAL RECORD

Battles. Fighting in the Civil War was often fierce. ***Whose perspective is the artist trying to portray? Explain your answer.***

✔ **READING CHECK:** What were the results of the eastern campaigns?

A Shift in War Aims

As the months of warfare dragged on, many northerners began to question whether saving the Union without ending slavery was worth the price. Was it just or sensible, they asked, to sacrifice so much without the secessionist slaveholders who had caused the terrible bloodshed paying some price? "To fight against slaveholders, without fighting against slavery," charged abolitionist Frederick Douglass, "is but a half-hearted business."

Beginning to move against slavery. After fierce debate, Republicans pushed legislation through Congress in July 1862 that authorized African Americans to serve in the military. The legislation also freed slaves held by Confederate soldiers or by Confederate allies. President Lincoln signed the legislation. However, Horace Greeley, abolitionist editor of the New York *Tribune*, soon criticized Lincoln for not making slavery the central war issue. Lincoln replied by simply restating his original goal: "My paramount object in the struggle *is* to save the Union, and is *not* either to save or to destroy slavery."

Privately, however, the president had already concluded that slavery was too important to the southern war effort to be left alone. More slaves at work meant that more soldiers were available to fight against the Union. Lincoln hoped that if slaves learned that the North was fighting to free them, they would desert their masters, thereby weakening the South's economy.

This poster was made to commemorate Lincoln's decision to free southern slaves.

HISTORY MAKERS SPEAK

Abraham Lincoln in *Battle Cry of Freedom*

The Salvation of the Union and Abolition. In a carefully worded portion of his reply to Horace Greeley, the abolitionist editor of the *New York Tribune*, Abraham Lincoln explained: "If I could save the Union without freeing *any* slave I would do it, and if I could save it by freeing *all* the slaves I would do it; and if I could save it by freeing some and leaving others alone, I would also do that."

CRITICAL THINKING What might have been Lincoln's goal for freeing slaves?

ANSWER: Answers will vary. Students might suggest that Lincoln's ultimate goal was to save the Union.

VISUAL RECORD ANSWER

Students might suggest that the perspective of Union soldiers is being portrayed—Union soldiers are in the foreground, and the Union flag is shown.

TEACH OBJECTIVE 3

LEVEL 1: Have students read the excerpted text of the Emancipation Proclamation on this page. In a class discussion, ask students how this Proclamation represented a change in the Union's war aims. *(Students should mention that Lincoln originally set out simply to save the Union without undue regard for the issue of slavery.)* With the class, develop on the chalkboard a flowchart that begins with the Union's victory at Antietam and develops the change in the Union's war aims and the participation of African Americans in the Union cause. *(The Union victory gave Lincoln the political support to issue the Proclamation. African American soldiers enlisted on behalf of the Union side.)* Tell students to copy the flowchart into their notes. **Sheltered English**

LEVELS 2 AND 3: Have students read the excerpted text of the Emancipation Proclamation on this page. Then organize students into groups of three and have each group create a collage of images that represents the issuing and impact of the Emancipation Proclamation. Images might be symbolic or concrete reflections of events and emotions surrounding the Proclamation. Tell students that they should indicate the importance of Antietam to the change in Union war aims and characterize the Proclamation's reception in both the North and the South. *(See the Level 1 lesson for the correct importance of Antietam to the timing of the Emancipation Proclamation and the impact of the Proclamation.)* Display triads' collages around the classroom. **Cooperative Learning**

DEMOCRATIC VALUES

"Contrabands." In May 1861 three slaves escaped from a Confederate work camp in Virginia and fled to the Union outpost at Fortress Monroe. Similar to the strategy President Lincoln would use some two years later in characterizing the Emancipation Proclamation as part of the war effort, General Benjamin Butler, the commanding officer at Monroe, declared the slaves to be "contraband of war" and granted them sanctuary. Word of the incident spread quickly among local slaves, and by July almost 1,000 "contrabands" had escaped to the place they called "Freedom Fort."

CRITICAL THINKING Why might General Butler have declared that slaves who fled to Fortress Monroe were "contraband of war"?

ANSWER: Students might suggest that by referring to the slaves as "contraband of war," or property seized during war, Butler cut off any arguments from their former owners that they should be returned.

VISUAL RECORD ANSWER

(for p. 87)

Students might suggest that the flag symbolizes freedom and opportunity; the slaves symbolize oppression; the soldier symbolizes the mighty power of the Union.

★ HISTORICAL DOCUMENTS ★

PRESIDENT ABRAHAM LINCOLN

The Emancipation Proclamation

After the Union victory at Antietam, President Lincoln believed he could take action toward freeing slaves in the South. The excerpts below are from the final Emancipation Proclamation that took effect on January 1, 1863.

On the first day of January, A.D. 1863, all persons held as slaves within any state or designated part of a state, the people whereof shall then be in rebellion against the United States, shall be then, thenceforward, and forever free. . . .

Now, therefore, I, Abraham Lincoln, President of the United States . . . do order and declare that all persons held as slaves within said designated states . . . are, and henceforward shall be, free. . . .

And I further declare and make known that such persons of suitable condition will be received into the armed service of the United States to garrison [defend] forts, positions, stations, and other places, and to man vessels of all sorts in said service.

And upon this act, sincerely believed to be an act of justice, warranted by the Constitution upon military necessity, I invoke [call upon] the considerate judgment of mankind and the gracious favor of Almighty God.

The Emancipation Proclamation. President Lincoln lacked the constitutional authority to abolish slavery. As commander in chief of the armed forces, however, he did have the authority to institute military measures. Thus, in July 1862, Lincoln informed his cabinet that he planned to issue a new military order. As of a certain date, all slaves living in areas still rebelling against the United States would be free.

To quiet constitutional concerns about this order, Lincoln assured his cabinet that this **Emancipation Proclamation** would apply only to the Confederate states. This assurance also relieved concerns about the status of slaves in the border states.

President Lincoln decided to keep his plan secret until the Union won a major military victory. To issue the Proclamation when the war was going badly for the Union would look like an act of desperation. The needed victory came in September 1862.

Antietam

General Robert E. Lee went on the offensive in September 1862. Confederate diplomats still believed that Britain might offer support to the Confederacy. Most British government officials were ready to formally recognize the Confederacy as an independent nation. They were waiting, though, to see if Lee could win a major victory on Union soil. On September 4, 1862, Lee began crossing the Potomac River into Maryland with some 55,000 men. Over the next few days, however, Lee lost about 5,000 soldiers as exhausted, hungry, and sick troops fell by the wayside. Union forces lost track of the Confederate troops for four days. Then, surprisingly, two Union soldiers happened upon a copy of Lee's battle plans wrapped around a discarded pack of cigars.

These soldiers are but a few of the thousands who died at Antietam.

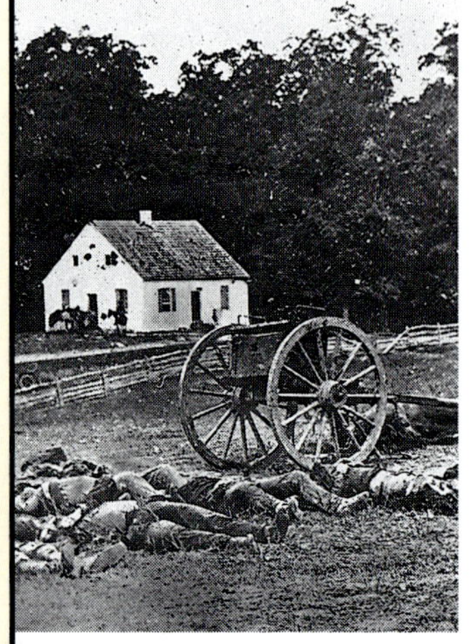

Armed with this information, General McClellan planned a counterattack. With some 75,000 troops, McClellan met Lee at Antietam (an-TEET-uhm) Creek in Maryland. The **Battle of Antietam** raged all day, becoming the bloodiest single-day battle in all of U.S. military history. The Confederates suffered more than 13,000 casualties; the Union more than 12,000.

Despite the Union army's good showing at Antietam, President Lincoln fired McClellan again after he allowed the Confederate troops to escape into Virginia. Although the Battle of Antietam was not a resounding Union victory, it raised confidence in the North. A major Confederate offensive had failed. This proved that General Lee could be defeated. Lee's loss also cost the South any hope of support from European countries.

TEACH OBJECTIVE 4

LEVEL 1: Pair students and have each pair gather five or more interesting quotations by and about African American soldiers who served during the Civil War, and then put them together with appropriate images and symbols in a small collage. In addition, have students write a one- or two-paragraph caption that summarizes the contributions of African American soldiers. *(Students' captions should mention the following: African American soldiers participated in the attack on Fort Wagner; nearly 180,000 African American men served in the Union army; 33,000 gave their lives; some African Americans served in the navy; more than 20 African American soldiers and sailors won the Congressional Medal of Honor.)* Display students' collages on the classroom wall. **Sheltered English, Cooperative Learning**

LEVELS 2 AND 3: Organize students into groups of five and have each group create a visual display that highlights African American soldiers' contributions to the Union's war efforts. *(See the Level 1 lesson for the correct contributions.)* Students' displays might include drawings, paintings, and photographs of African American soldiers; biographical information about African American heroes and leaders of the Civil War; graphic organizers to compare African Americans' wages to white soldiers' pay; and so on. Place students' displays around the classroom. **Cooperative Learning**

The Union victory at Antietam gave Lincoln the necessary political support to move forward with his plans to free the slaves in the South. On September 22, the president issued a preliminary draft of the Emancipation Proclamation that would go into effect the first of the year. When January 1, 1863, found the Confederacy still in rebellion, Lincoln's Proclamation brought a decisive change in the war.

✔ **READING CHECK:** How did the Union victory at Antietam help shift the Union's war aims?

African Americans Take Up Arms

Both the July 1862 act allowing African Americans to serve in the military and the Emancipation Proclamation encouraged African Americans to enlist in the Union army. The first official black regiments were organized in August 1862 in the Union-controlled Sea Islands of coastal South Carolina. Frederick Douglass viewed military service as a step toward citizenship for African Americans.

> **"Let the black man get upon his person the brass letters, U.S.; let him get an eagle on his button, and a musket on his shoulder and bullets in his pocket, and there is no power on earth which can deny that he has earned the right to citizenship."**

Many of the first African American soldiers recruited by the Union army served in the **54th Massachusetts Infantry**. This regiment earned an honored place in U.S. military history. In July 1863, Union forces began attacking Confederate-held forts near Charleston, South Carolina. The Union could not break the Confederates' hold. As a result, Brigadier General Truman Seymour decided to send some 6,000 Union troops in a desperate frontal attack against Fort Wagner—which guarded the entrance to Charleston Harbor. The 54th Infantry would lead the charge.

The attack on Fort Wagner represented the first time that African American troops had been assigned a key role in a military campaign. However, the Union commander knew that the 54th would suffer great losses in their frontal assault on the Confederate lines. African American troops also faced a danger that white Union soldiers did not. Black soldiers captured by the Confederates were treated as outlaws. They could face execution or be sold into slavery.

On the night of July 18, in the middle of a storm of gunfire, commanding officer Colonel Robert Gould Shaw and the 54th clawed their way to the top of Fort Wagner's sloping walls. Both armies suffered staggering losses in the prolonged fight. The siege finally ended September 6, when Confederate forces, unable to hold out, evacuated the fort.

Despite the courageous performance of African American volunteers, the Union army did not offer them full equality. For much of the war, black soldiers earned less than half the pay of white soldiers. After much criticism by black soldiers and their commanding officers, Congress finally equalized the pay scale in June 1864. In addition, white officers commanded each black regiment. Only about 100 African Americans were commissioned as junior officers. In 1865 Martin Delany became the first African American promoted to the rank of major.

THE LIBRARY COMPANY OF PHILADELPHIA

INTERPRETING THE VISUAL RECORD

Emancipation. This engraving celebrating the Emancipation Proclamation first appeared in 1863. ***What do you think the various elements in the image symbolize?***

HISTORY MAKERS SPEAK

Union soldiers in *Battle Cry of Freedom* and *Brother Against Brother*

Describing the Battle of Antietam. By many accounts, the fighting at the Battle of Antietam was the fiercest and most horrifying of the war. "In a second the air was full of the hiss of bullets and the hurtle of grape-shot," one Union soldier described. "The mental strain was so great that . . . the whole landscape for an instant turned slightly red." "No matter in what direction we turned," wrote another of the scene after the battle, "it was all the same shocking picture, awakening awe rather than pity, benumbing the senses rather than touching the heart, glazing the eye with horror rather than filling it with tears."

ACTIVITY: Have each student find a short description of another battle from the Civil War or a description of another war. Ask volunteers to read their descriptions to the class. To conclude, lead a discussion about what students' descriptions might reveal about the nature of each war.

SCIENCE & TECHNOLOGY ANSWERS

(for p. 88)

1. They caused bullets to spin as they left the gun.
2. Soldiers had to load bullets with a mallet.

TEACH OBJECTIVE 5

LEVEL 1: Tell students to imagine that they are newspaper reporters during the Civil War. Pair students and have each pair create a headline and topic sentence to assess the significance of the Battles of Fredericksburg and Chancellorsville. *(Pairs' headlines and topics sentences should mention that Confederate forces defeated Union forces, led by General Ambrose Burnside, at Fredericksburg; the Union army suffered more than 12,000 casualties. At Chancellorsville, Union forces, led by Joseph Hooker, were defeated by Confederate forces led by Robert E. Lee and Stonewall Jackson; however, the Confederates lost Stonewall Jackson, who was mistakenly shot by his own troops.)* Ask volunteers to read their headlines and topic sentences to the class.
Sheltered English, Cooperative Learning

LEVELS 2 AND 3: Have each student write a poem to assess the significance of the Battles of Fredericksburg and Chancellorsville. *(See the Level 1 lesson for the significance of the battles.)* Ask volunteers to recite their poems to the class.

SECTION 3 REVIEW ANSWERS

Define and Identify
For significance, see the following pages:

- Ulysses S. Grant, p. 82
- Battle of Shiloh, p. 82
- David Farragut, p. 83
- George B. McClellan, p. 84
- James E. B. "Jeb" Stuart, p. 85
- Emancipation Proclamation, p. 86
- Battle of Antietam, p. 86
- 54th Massachusetts Infantry, p. 87
- Martin Delany, p. 87
- Ambrose E. Burnside, p. 88

Locate
For locations, see the map on p. 84. For importance, see the following pages:

- Fredericksburg, p. 88
- Chancellorsville, p. 89

1. Shiloh–April 1862, Tennessee, surprise attacks staged by Confederate and then Union forces on two consecutive days, Union victory; New Orleans, April 1862, Louisiana, naval combat surrounding Union attempt to land warships in New Orleans, Union victory; Yorktown–April 1862, Virginia, Confederate retreat, Seven Pines–May–June 1862, Virginia; clash near Richmond following Union victory; Seven Days–June–July 1862, Virginia, daring Confederate offensive after recent defeat at Seven Pines, Confederate victory; Antietam–September 1862, Maryland, Union counterattack following Confederate offensive into Maryland, Union victory;

The Congressional Medal of Honor

Nearly 180,000 African American men served in the Union army, and more than 32,000 gave their lives. Some also served in the navy. More than 20 African American soldiers and sailors won the Congressional Medal of Honor.

✔ **READING CHECK:** How did African American soldiers help the Union cause?

New Union Commanders

The addition of African American soldiers came at a key time for the Union, which continued to suffer important defeats through the winter of 1862 and the spring of 1863. After Antietam, President Lincoln chose Ambrose E. Burnside to replace General McClellan.

Fredericksburg. On December 11 and 12, 1862, General Burnside sent some 114,000 Union soldiers across the Rappahannock (rap-uh-HAN-uhk) River near Fredericksburg, Virginia. General Lee and some 75,000 Confederate soldiers controlled the hills above the town. Reasoning that Lee would not expect a frontal attack, Burnside ordered his men across an open plain on the morning of December 13.

Lee took advantage of Burnside's positioning. From their high ground, the Confederates could easily pick off the Union soldiers as they crossed the open fields. The Union army suffered more than 12,000 casualties at Fredericksburg, and the

Science & Technology

Weapons and War

Technological developments changed the nature of warfare during the Civil War. Despite their great accuracy, rifles were seldom carried by the infantry before the 1850s. Rifles from this period had grooves carved inside the barrel that allowed a cone-shaped bullet to spin as it left the gun and travel four times farther than a bullet shot from a smoothbore barrel. Bullets large enough to spin, however, had to be rammed down the barrel with a mallet—which was awkward and time-consuming.

In 1848 a French army captain named Claude E. Minié developed a smaller bullet that could be easily rammed down a rifle's barrel. These bullets were extremely expensive, however. James H. Burton, an armorer at the Harpers Ferry Armory, created a less-expensive version of Minié's bullets. These "minié balls"—pronounced "minnie" by members of both armies—were used extensively during the Civil War.

Most soldiers on both sides of the conflict carried rifles by 1863. The primary effect of the change from smoothbores to rifles was an increase in the number of casualties.

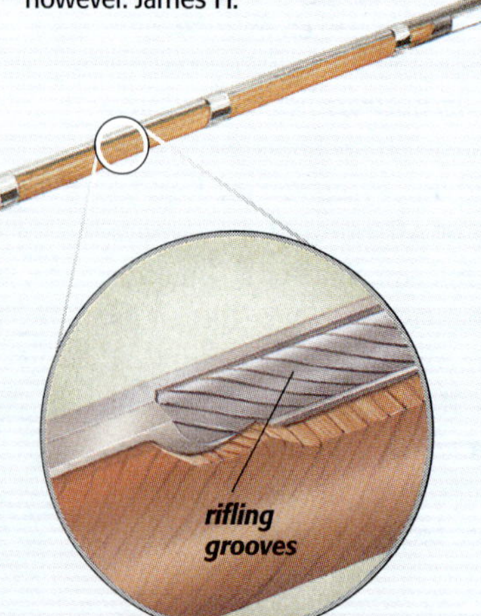

Understanding Science and History

1. What effect did the grooves in a rifle's barrel have?
2. What difficulties were involved in loading bullets that were large enough to spin inside a rifle barrel?

REVIEW

Have students complete the **Section 3 Review** on p. 89.

ASSESS

Have students complete **Daily Quiz 2.3**. As **Alternative Assessment**, you may want to use the collage and caption activity or the visual display activity in this section's lessons.

RETEACH

Have students complete **Main Idea Activity for Reteaching and Sheltered English 2.3**. Pair students and have each pair create a detailed, annotated time line for the years 1862 and 1863. Pairs should include a title for their time line as well as a one- or two-paragraph caption that summarizes the years' events and their significance for both sides.

Sheltered English, Cooperative Learning

EXTEND

Have students conduct research on recent civil war anywhere in the world and compare the causes, aims, tactics, and outcome of that conflict with the American Civil War. Tell students to present their conclusions in a three-to-five-page report.

Block Scheduling

Confederates some 5,000. One northerner bitterly referred to the battle as a "great slaughter pen."

Chancellorsville. President Lincoln transferred Burnside and gave command of the eastern forces to General Joseph "Fighting Joe" Hooker. The new commander offered a daring plan to crush Lee's forces. He proposed dividing his large army into three parts in order to cut off supply lines and attack them from both flanks. The strategy seemed workable, particularly since Hooker's 134,000 troops were more than double the Confederate troops.

By April 30, 1863, Hooker had positioned his men in a deep forest known as the Wilderness, near Chancellorsville, Virginia. Lee divided his troops, sending Stonewall Jackson and some 30,000 men through the Wilderness to outflank Hooker. When Hooker discovered the troop movements, he assumed that the Confederates were retreating. Instead, Lee and Jackson attacked the Union forces from two sides. After several days of fighting, Hooker withdrew in defeat.

General Stonewall Jackson is shot during the Battle of Chancellorsville.

The South paid dearly for its victory at Chancellorsville, however. Riding back to Confederate lines after dark, Stonewall Jackson was mistaken for a Union cavalryman and shot by his own troops. The two bullets that hit his left arm required it to be amputated. As with countless other soldiers, Jackson's battle wounds led to serious infection. Eight days later, Lee's most valued general died.

✔ **READING CHECK:** What was the significance of the Battles of Fredericksburg and Chancellorsville?

SECTION 3 REVIEW

Define and explain the significance of the following terms:
Battle of Shiloh
Emancipation Proclamation
Battle of Antietam
54th Massachusetts Infantry

Identify and explain the significance of the following individuals:
Ulysses S. Grant
David Farragut
George B. McClellan
James E. B. "Jeb" Stuart
Martin Delany
Ambrose E. Burnside

Locate and explain the importance of the following places:
Fredericksburg
Chancellorsville

1. **Using Graphic Organizers** Copy the graphic organizer below. Use it to list each major battle of 1862 and early 1863, including its date and location, a brief description of each battle, and the battle's outcome.

	Date	Location	Outcome
Shiloh			
New Orleans			
Yorktown			
Seven Pines			
Seven Days			
Antietam			
Fredericksburg			
Chancellorsville			

2. **Comparing and Contrasting** Why did the Battle of Antietam have a positive effect on northern morale while the battles at Fredericksburg and Chancellorsville had negative effects?
3. **Distinguishing Fact from Opinion** Some white leaders argued that African Americans would not make good soldiers. What evidence from the Civil War would contradict this claim?
4. **Hypothesizing** What might have happened if President Lincoln had issued the Emancipation Proclamation before the Battle of Antietam?

Critical Thinking

5. Why did the shift in the Union's war aims increase support for the war among some northerners?
Consider:
   - why some northerners had wanted a shift in goals
   - what the shift in war goals was
   - how Lincoln's stated goals in 1863 satisfied some previous critics of the war

Fredericksburg–December 1862, Virginia, Union advance across an open plain toward Confederate forces stationed in nearby hills, Confederate victory; Chancellorsville–May 1863, Virginia, multiple-flank fighting following complex troop movements through a dense forest, Confederate victory

2. Antietam foiled a major Confederate offensive, proved that General Lee was defeatable, cost the South any hope of support from European countries, and enabled President Lincoln to issue the Emancipation Proclamation. Fredericksburg and Chancellorsville demonstrated the continuing superiority of Lee's military leadership and resulted in heavy Union losses.

3. the performance of African American soldiers in the 54th Massachusetts Infantry during the Union assault on Fort Wagner in July 1863

4. Answers will vary. Some students might argue that issuing the Proclamation before Antietam would have looked like an act of desperation and thus would have raised Confederate morale.

5. Answers will vary. Most students should reason that including the end of slavery as a Union war aim brought greater support for the war from antislavery northerners.

SECTION 4

After completing Section 4, students should be able to:

OBJECTIVE 1 *Explain the outcomes of the Battle of Gettysburg.*

OBJECTIVE 2 *Assess the significance of the Union victory at Vicksburg.*

OBJECTIVE 3 *Describe General Grant's strategy in the summer of 1864.*

OBJECTIVE 4 *Describe General Sherman's strategies.*

OBJECTIVE 5 *List the terms of surrender at Appomattox.*

LET'S GET STARTED!

Write the following quotation on the chalkboard: "*Should I fall in the next fight killed or wounded I hope to fall with my face to the foe [enemy]. . . .*" Tell students that this quotation is from a letter by Lewis Douglass, an African American soldier. As students enter the classroom, have them respond in writing to it. What does Douglass mean by his comment? Tell students that they will learn about the final phase of the war in Section 4.

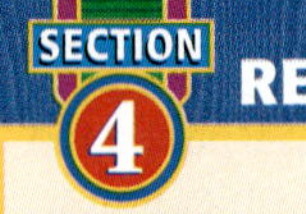

SECTION 4 RESOURCES

PRINT
- Guided Reading Strategy 2.4
- Primary Source Reading 2: The Gettysburg Address
- Geography Activity 2: The Siege of Vicksburg
- Graphic Organizer Activity 2: The Gettysburg Address
- Section 4 Review, p. 95
- Daily Quiz 2.4

MULTIMEDIA
- One-Stop Planner, Lesson 2.4
- Holt Researcher: American History CD–ROM
- HRW Web site

SHELTERED ENGLISH
- Main Idea Activity for Reteaching and Sheltered English 2.4

✔ READING TO UNDERSTAND
To help students master the section objectives, have them answer the **READING CHECKS** and complete **Guided Reading Strategy 2.4** as they read the section.

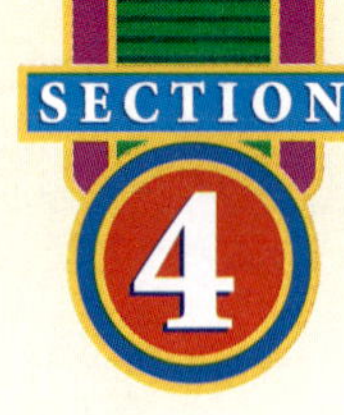

The Final Phase

OBJECTIVES

Read to understand:
1. what the outcomes were of the Battle of Gettysburg
2. why the Union victory at Vicksburg was significant
3. what General Grant's strategy was in the summer of 1864
4. what strategies General Sherman employed
5. what the terms were of the surrender at Appomattox

KEY TERMS

Battle of Gettysburg
Pickett's Charge
Gettysburg Address
Siege of Vicksburg
war of attrition
total war

KEY PEOPLE

George Meade
William Tecumseh Sherman

KEY PLACES

Gettysburg
Vicksburg
Atlanta
Savannah
Appomattox Courthouse

"There never were such men in an army before. They will go anywhere and do anything if properly led."
—Robert E. Lee

General Robert E. Lee

General Robert E. Lee praised his troops following their victory at Chancellorsville. The South received an enormous boost in confidence and morale from the victory, while northern morale plunged. When President Lincoln heard the news from the War Department on May 6, his face turned "ashen," a newspaper reporter recalled. "My God! my God! What will the country say?" Lincoln exclaimed. Republican Charles Sumner agreed. "Lost, lost, all is lost," he cried when he learned of the defeat. After achieving such an astounding victory with nearly half as many men as his enemy, Lee began to believe his men were invincible. Lee's confidence led him to devise his most ambitious plan to date—one that amazed and impressed other Confederate leaders.

Gettysburg

Following the victory at Chancellorsville, General Lee decided to invade the North again. This action would spare war-weary Virginia from further fighting. It also would allow Lee to resupply and feed his hungry troops by seizing provisions from the enemy.

In early June 1863 Lee crossed into Pennsylvania with some 75,000 troops. President Lincoln urged General Hooker to attack the Confederates before they could consolidate their troops. Hooker worried, however, that Lee's troops outnumbered his and hesitated to move. Fearing he had another General McClellan leading the army, Lincoln quickly replaced Hooker with General George Meade.

By the end of June, Confederate regiments had begun to assemble near the town of Gettysburg, Pennsylvania. When scouts reported a supply of shoes in the town, the Confederates organized a raiding party. The troops were unaware that two Union brigades had positioned themselves on high ground northwest of Gettysburg. As the Confederate raiding party approached the small town on July 1, it met a blaze of Union fire.

On the first day of the **Battle of Gettysburg**, the Confederates pushed the Union line back to Cemetery Hill and Cemetery Ridge. The Confederates held Seminary Ridge, a lower line of hills about a half mile away. Nevertheless, Lee knew that the danger to his forces would remain so long as the North held the higher ground. Expecting that Union reinforcements would

Thousands of Confederate and Union troops died in the Battle of Gettysburg.

TEACH OBJECTIVE 1

LEVEL 1: Pair students and have each pair create an annotated time line from June 1863 to November 1863 which includes the Battle of Gettysburg and related events. *(Time lines should include events beginning with Lee's move into Pennsylvania, gathering of Confederate troops near Gettysburg, first day of the Battle of Gettysburg, Pickett's Charge, Lee's retreat to Virginia, and ending with the Gettysburg Address.)* Have volunteers share their time lines with the class. Ask students to supply any information that may have been omitted from the time lines. Conclude by leading a class discussion about the outcomes of the battle.

Cooperative Learning, Sheltered English

LEVELS 2 AND 3: Have each student complete the time line activity from the Level 1 lesson. Students should incorporate a three-sentence summary of the outcome of the Battle of Gettysburg into their time lines. Then ask students to read the Gettysburg Address on this page. Have students paraphrase it using language more familiar to them. Encourage any student having trouble with the assignment to use a dictionary and a thesaurus to help them with difficult words. When students have finished paraphrasing Lincoln's speech, ask volunteers to read their summaries to the class.

NOTE: For an additional teaching idea, see the Chapter 2 resource speaker lesson in the **Creative Teaching Strategies** handbook.

soon be arriving, he decided to attack quickly. On July 2 General Lee charged the Union's left flank, trying without success to capture a dome-shaped hill called Little Round Top. The next day he ordered some 15,000 men commanded by George Pickett to rush the Union center on Cemetery Ridge. Only half of the Confederate soldiers survived **Pickett's Charge**. Confederate lieutenant G. W. Finley later wrote, "Men were falling all around us, and cannon and muskets were raining death upon us." With few men left, Pickett could not organize a second attack. Bad weather prevented Meade from pursuing the Confederates, however, and Lee retreated to Virginia.

A staggering number of young men lost their lives at Gettysburg. After three days of fighting, Union casualties numbered more than 23,000 and Confederate casualties more than 20,000. In November 1863 President Lincoln helped dedicate a cemetery at the Gettysburg battlefield. Lincoln spoke for only a few minutes, but his **Gettysburg Address** remains a classic statement of democratic ideals.

Although the Union army emerged victorious at Gettysburg, it once again narrowly failed to end the war. A disappointed President Lincoln complained, "Our Army held the war in the hollow of their hand and they would not close it." The battle, however, marked a critical turning point. The Union army had proved that the Confederacy could be beaten.

✔ **READING CHECK:** What were the outcomes of the Battle of Gettysburg?

★ HISTORICAL DOCUMENTS ★

PRESIDENT ABRAHAM LINCOLN

The Gettysburg Address

On November, 19, 1863, Abraham Lincoln dedicated a national cemetery at the Gettysburg battlefield. His short but powerful speech became a lasting reminder to all Americans of the democratic ideals for which the Union soldiers at Gettysburg had died.

Four score and seven years ago our fathers brought forth on this continent, a new nation, conceived [created] in Liberty, and dedicated to the proposition that all men are created equal.

Now we are engaged in a great civil war, testing whether that nation, or any nation so conceived and so dedicated, can long endure. We are met on a great battlefield of that war. We have come to dedicate a portion of that field, as a final resting place for those who here gave their lives that that nation might live. . . .

But, in a larger sense, we can not dedicate—we can not consecrate [make holy]—we cannot hallow—this ground. The brave men, living and dead, who struggled here, have consecrated it, far above our poor power to add or detract. The world will little note nor long remember what we say here, but it can never forget what they did here. It is for us the living, rather, to be dedicated here to the unfinished work which they who fought here have thus far so nobly advanced. It is rather for us to . . . highly resolve that these dead shall not have died in vain—that this nation, under God, shall have a new birth of freedom—and that government of the people, by the people, for the people, shall not perish from the earth.

internetconnect

TOPIC: Battle of Gettysburg
GO TO: go.hrw.com
KEYWORD: SE1 Gettysburg

Have students access the Internet through the HRW Web site to conduct research on the Battle of Gettysburg and its consequences for the North and South in the Civil War. Then have students write a summary of the battle and create a three-dimensional map of the battlefield that includes locations of famous engagements, indications of troop movements, and geographical features of the battlefield.

Lincoln Finds His General

The war continued in the West in 1863, with the Union attempting to control the Mississippi River valley. General Ulysses S. Grant won several significant victories for the North. President Lincoln soon recognized Grant's invaluable leadership.

Vicksburg. Grant knew that gaining full control of the Mississippi River required taking Vicksburg, Mississippi. Vicksburg's high river bluffs allowed the Confederate artillery to command an extensive area. In May 1863 Grant hatched a risky plan to take the city. Marching deep into enemy territory, he bottled up one Confederate force in nearby Jackson. Then he raced west to trap the other enemy force inside Vicksburg.

TEACH OBJECTIVE 2

LEVEL 1: Discuss with students why the Siege of Vicksburg represented a turning point in the Civil War. *(Students should mention that along with the fall of Port Hudson, Louisiana, Vicksburg gave the Union complete control of the Mississippi River and cut off Arkansas, Louisiana, and Texas from the rest of the Confederacy.)* Then ask students what probably would have happened if the Confederates had not surrendered at Vicksburg. *(Students might suggest that the people of Vicksburg would have starved to death because of the siege, or the city's Confederate defenders would have deserted out of hunger.)* Have volunteers compile on the chalkboard a list of reasons for Vicksburg's significance and alternative outcomes if the Confederates had not surrendered. **Sheltered English**

LEVELS 2 AND 3: Have each student complete the Level 1 activity and write a one-to-two-paragraph analysis of Grant's strategy at Vicksburg and the significance of the Union victory there. Why was Grant's strategy considered so brilliant and daring? What was the consequence of the Union victory? *(Students should mention that it was a risky maneuver to press so deeply into Confederate territory, but it was clever because it eliminated potential Confederate reinforcements from Jackson before the siege of Vicksburg began; see the Level 1 lesson for the battle's significance.)* When students have finished writing, have volunteers share their analysis with the class.

GEOGRAPHIC DIVERSITY

Surviving the Siege of Vicksburg. During the Siege of Vicksburg, Union artillery hurled as many as 2,800 shells into the city every day. The constant threat of death by explosion prompted many civilians to abandon their homes and move into caves that were dug into area hillsides. Some families even divided the caves into separate rooms and furnished them with carpets, chairs, and other household objects.

ACTIVITY: Ask students to imagine that they are elderly residents of Vicksburg during the Siege of Vicksburg. Then have them compose a short diary entry that explains how they are trying to survive the attack.

MAP ANSWER
(for p. 93)
almost 9 miles a day

VISUAL RECORD ANSWER
(for p. 94)
The railroad tracks and railcars have been destroyed, as has the railroad station.

GRAPH ANSWER
(for p. 94)
abut 250,000 Union deaths; about 170,000 Confederate deaths

Confederate cannons at Vicksburg fire at Union gunboats along the Mississippi River.

For six weeks General Grant and his men laid siege to the town, preventing any Confederate reinforcements from arriving. During the long **Siege of Vicksburg**, the city's defenders began eating mules and rats to keep from starving. One woman in the city wrote, "We are utterly cut off from the world, surrounded by a circle of fire." Finally, in late June the desperate Confederate soldiers sent a letter to their commander, urging him to surrender.

On July 3, 1863, General Grant and Confederate general John Pemberton met under an oak tree to discuss terms of surrender. The Confederates surrendered to Grant the next day. On July 8 the Confederate forces at Port Hudson, Louisiana, also fell. These victories gave the Union total control over the Mississippi River, thereby cutting off Arkansas, Louisiana, and Texas from the rest of the Confederacy.

✔ **READING CHECK:** Why was the Union victory at Vicksburg significant?

HOLT RESEARCHER — *Read More About It*

Free Find:
Southern Railroads
After reading about southern railroads on the Holt Researcher CD–ROM, create a map that shows how the railroads were vital to the Confederacy's war effort.

Summer of 1864. President Lincoln promoted General Grant to general in chief, commander of all Union forces, in the spring of 1864. Grant understood better than previous commanders how to take advantage of the North's soldiers and supplies. His strategy was to use these advantages against an enemy that was reeling from shortages. Grant informed Lincoln that he would march on Richmond, take his losses, and press on. He planned a **war of attrition**—that is, to continue fighting until the South ran out of men, supplies, and will.

In May 1864 Grant moved some 122,000 troops into the Wilderness near Chancellorsville, Virginia. For two days the northerners hurled themselves at some 66,000 Confederates, but the rebels held their ground. Grant's forces suffered nearly 18,000 casualties; the Confederates lost nearly 10,000.

Rather than rest, Grant pushed on, mile by bloody mile, just as he had promised Lincoln he would do. "I propose to fight it out on this line if it takes all summer," he wrote. Moving his forces a few miles to the south, Grant forced Lee to keep his weary men in the field. At Spotsylvania Court House, Virginia, Union and Confederate forces clashed several times between May 10 and May 19. Again, the Union forces suffered horrible losses. Shocked by the number of casualties, a southern soldier remarked of Grant: "We have met a man this time, who either does not know when he is whipped, or who cares not if he loses his whole army."

Ulysses S. Grant and his staff posed for this photograph at their headquarters in Cold Harbor, Virginia, in June 1864.

In mid-June Grant traveled south once more to attack Petersburg, Virginia. He hoped that capturing this railroad center would cut off Richmond's supplies. Lee held on, however. After three days even Grant was discouraged. Since May 12 his army had suffered some 60,000 casualties. He called off the direct assault and settled down to lay siege to Petersburg. Nevertheless, Grant's strategy was slowly succeeding. Lee's army steadily dwindled, and few reserves remained.

✔ **READING CHECK:** What was General Grant's strategy for winning the war in the summer of 1864?

▶**ASSIGNMENT** *Have students write a two-to-three-paragraph eulogy praising the Union soldiers who died while taking Vicksburg.*

TEACH OBJECTIVES 3 AND 4

LEVELS 1 AND 2: Draw on the chalkboard the following chart related to the strategies of Generals Grant and Sherman. Omit the italicized answers, and ask students to copy the organizer into their notebooks and complete it. Then have volunteers complete the organizer on the chalkboard. Conclude by leading a class discussion about the tactics employed by Grant and Sherman, and ask students if there are any recent or current wars to which they can apply one or both of these strategies. If yes, have them explain why the strategy applies; if no, have them contrast the tactics in recent wars to war of attrition and/or total war. **Sheltered English**

Grant's Strategy in 1864	*Sherman's* Strategy in 1864
war of attrition	total war
Reasoning:	**Reasoning:**
Use North's advantages in number of soldiers and industrial resources to fight until South runs out of men, supplies, and will	*Win war by destroying South's economic resources and demoralizing the populace*
Key Battles in Campaign:	**Key Battles in Campaign:**
Wilderness, Spotsylvania Court House, siege of Petersburg	*burning of Atlanta, capture of Savannah*

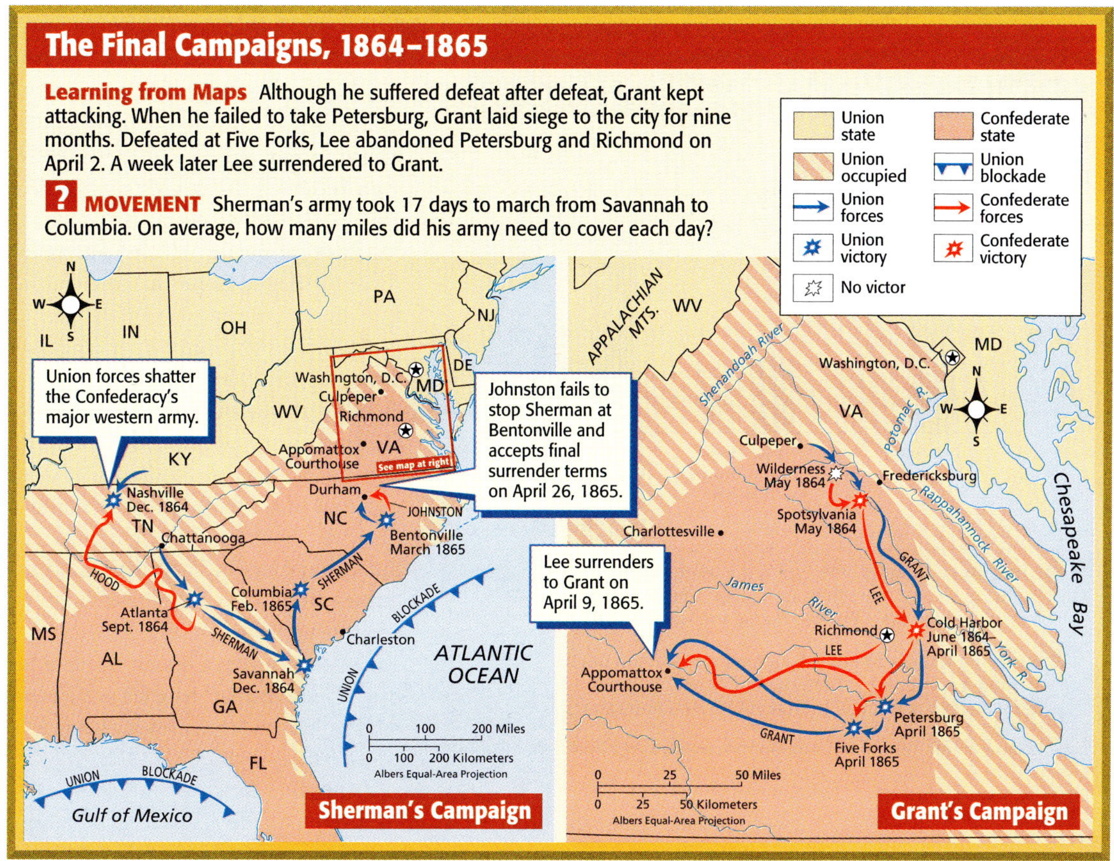

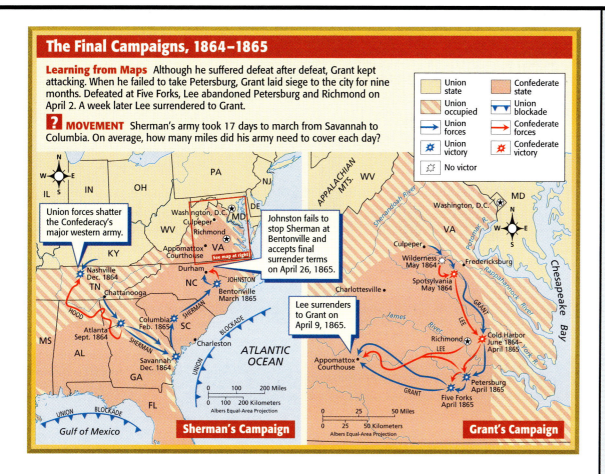

The Final Campaigns, 1864–1865

Learning from Maps Although he suffered defeat after defeat, Grant kept attacking. When he failed to take Petersburg, Grant laid siege to the city for nine months. Defeated at Five Forks, Lee abandoned Petersburg and Richmond on April 2. A week later Lee surrendered to Grant.

? MOVEMENT Sherman's army took 17 days to march from Savannah to Columbia. On average, how many miles did his army need to cover each day?

Sherman's March to the Sea

Union general William Tecumseh Sherman matched General Grant's determination. Moody, ambitious, and brilliant, Sherman had performed ably at Vicksburg and other battles. Grant rewarded Sherman by making him commander of the Tennessee army.

While Grant slowly pushed his way toward Richmond, Sherman undertook a campaign to destroy southern railroads and industries. In early May, he moved some 100,000 troops out of Tennessee toward Atlanta, Georgia. On his way, General Sherman repeatedly outmaneuvered Confederate general Johnston's forces. He then defeated General John Hood's attacks and pushed the Confederate forces back.

When Atlanta fell on September 2, 1864, the Confederates lost their last railroad link across the Appalachian Mountains. After ordering residents to evacuate, Sherman's men set fire to large portions of the city. Defending his tactics, he declared:

> **"If [southerners] raise a howl against my barbarity and cruelty, I will answer that war is war, and not popularity-seeking. If they want peace, they and their relatives must stop the war."**

General Sherman's troops burned much of Atlanta.

SECTION 4 **REVIEW ANSWERS**

Define and Identify

For significance, see the following pages:

- George Meade, p. 90
- Battle of Gettysburg, p. 90
- Pickett's Charge, p. 91
- Gettysburg Address, p. 91
- Siege of Vicksburg, p. 92
- war of attrition, p. 92
- William Tecumseh Sherman, p. 93
- total war, p. 94

Locate

For locations, see the map on p. 93. For importance, see the following pages:

- Gettysburg, p. 90
- Vicksburg, p. 91
- Atlanta, p. 93
- Savannah, p. 94
- Appomattox Courthouse, p. 95

1. 1. Grant is promoted to lead the Union Army.

2. Union forces under Grant and Confederate forces under Lee clash in the Wilderness and at Spotsylvania Court House in Virginia.

3. Union forces under Grant besiege Petersburg and then push their way toward Richmond, Virginia.

4. Union forces under Sherman capture Atlanta and march toward Savannah, Georgia.

5. President Lincoln wins re-election in 1864.

6. Union forces under Sherman capture Savannah.

7. Union forces under Grant capture Richmond.

8. Lee surrenders at Appomattox Courthouse.

LEVEL 3: Pair students to role-play Grant and Sherman. Have one student write a letter as Grant and the other student write a letter as Sherman explaining and justifying their military strategies. Then have each student exchange letters with his or her partner. When students have finished reading their partner's letter, ask volunteers to read their own letters to the class. Then lead the class in a discussion about how Grant's and Sherman's strategies differed from those of previous Union commanders. Ask students if they think the war would have ended any sooner or any differently if Grant and Sherman had been in charge from the beginning of the war.
Cooperative Learning

TEACH OBJECTIVE 5

ALL LEVELS: In a class discussion, have students list the terms of the Confederate surrender at Appomattox. *(Students should Confederate officers could keep their sidearms; all soldiers would be fed; they would be allowed to keep their horses and mules; and they would not be tried for treason.)* Ask students if they think that these terms were fair and reasonable. *(Answers will vary. Encourage students to justify their opinions.)* Then have students design postage stamps commemorating the surrender at Appomattox and the end of the Civil War. Have students make oversized, full-color mock-ups of their stamps to display in the classroom. **Sheltered English**

2. It proved that the Confederacy could ultimately be beaten.

3. Because the North needed to gain full control of the Mississippi River in order to win the war; this, in turn, required the capture of Vicksburg.

4. Grant planned a war of attrition, or one in which he would continue fighting until the South ran out of men, supplies, and will. Sherman waged a total war, or one in which he destroyed the South's economic resources. Answers about alternatives will vary but should address the idea of using less destructive tactics.

5. Answers will vary. Some students might suggest that the surrender terms promoted reconciliation by allowing Confederate soldiers to simply return home instead of holding them as prisoners.

CHAPTER 2 REVIEW ANSWERS

Creating a Time Line
Each event should have an explanation and the correct date.

Writing a Summary
See the Reading Checks in each section for main ideas.

Identifying People and Ideas

1. commanded the Confederate army

2. Confederate general accidentally shot after Chancellorsville

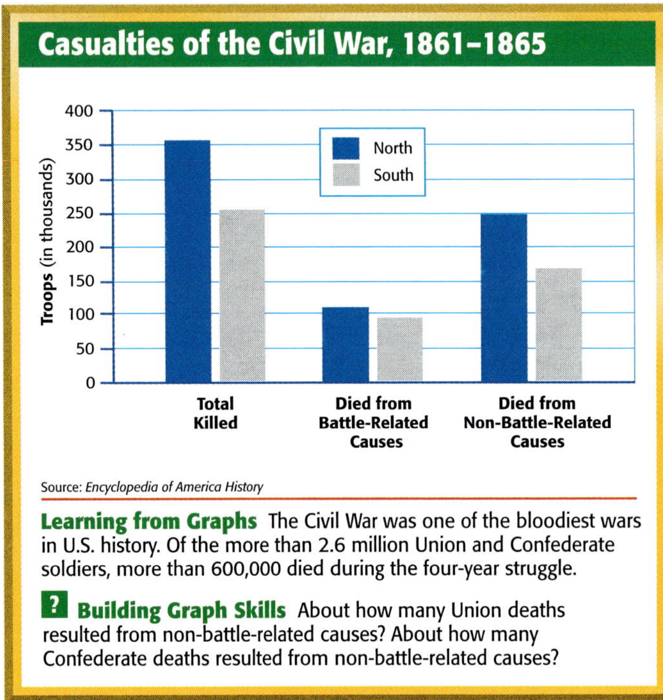

Source: *Encyclopedia of America History*

Learning from Graphs The Civil War was one of the bloodiest wars in U.S. history. Of the more than 2.6 million Union and Confederate soldiers, more than 600,000 died during the four-year struggle.

Building Graph Skills About how many Union deaths resulted from non-battle-related causes? About how many Confederate deaths resulted from non-battle-related causes?

The fall of Atlanta boosted President Lincoln's re-election campaign. The Union victory came at a critical moment when Lincoln appeared in danger of not even receiving his party's nomination. Many Republicans were upset that the war had dragged on for so long. Sherman's success renewed hope that the conflict would soon end. Lincoln won the election of 1864 against the Democratic candidate, General George McClellan.

After the burning of Atlanta, General Sherman's army raced rapidly toward the port city of Savannah, Georgia. Sherman's men took what supplies they could use and destroyed anything that might be helpful to the Confederates. They uprooted crops, burned farmhouses, slaughtered livestock, and tore up railroad tracks. In South Carolina, Mary Boykin Chesnut wrote in her diary, "Since Atlanta I have felt as if all were dead within me, forever. We are going to be wiped off the earth."

Although much of the destruction went beyond Sherman's orders, it stemmed from the general's strategy of fighting a **total war**. He believed that it was not enough to wage war against enemy troops. Rather, to win the war, the Union must strike at the enemy's economic resources. Sherman believed they "must make old and young, rich and poor, feel the hard hand of war. . . . We cannot change the hearts of those people of the South," he said, "but we can make war so terrible . . . that generations would pass away before they would again appeal to it." Although Sherman's tactics brought the Union's goals within reach, his actions left deep and bitter scars across the South.

In early December 1864, Sherman and his men reached Savannah, where they were resupplied by the Union navy. On December 22, the general sent President Lincoln a message: "I beg to present you, as a Christmas gift, the city of Savannah." One month later Sherman and his troops turned north in an effort to link up with General Grant's troops.

✔ **READING CHECK:** What strategies did General Sherman employ in his southern campaign?

INTERPRETING THE VISUAL RECORD
Total war. General William Tecumseh Sherman led his troops on a destructive march to the sea. ***What evidence of Sherman's total-war strategy can you identify in the photograph?***

Surrender at Appomattox

As General Sherman's army pushed northward through the Carolinas, General Grant's troops battered Richmond. On April 2, 1865, with Grant close on his heels, General Lee withdrew from Richmond. Within hours Union troops poured into the Confederate capital.

REVIEW

Have students complete the **Section 4 Review** on p. 95.

ASSESS

Have students complete **Daily Quiz 2.4**. As **Alternative Assessment**, you may want to use the role-playing exercise or Appomattox activity in this section's lessons.

RETEACH

Have students complete **Main Idea Activity for Reteaching and Sheltered English 2.4**. Then organize students into groups of five and have each group write 10 questions based on the information in the section (two questions per group member). Tell students to write the answers on a separate sheet of paper before exchanging questions with another group to answer. If time permits, have groups exchange questions again with different groups. **Sheltered English**

EXTEND

Have students study the time line at the beginning of this Chapter. Tell students to choose what they believe to be the two most important turning points in the Civil War. Have students identify and justify their choices in a two-to-three-paragraph essay. **Block Scheduling**

Lee's army was now only half the size of Grant's. Knowing his troops could not survive another summer like the one of 1864, Lee attempted to flee westward, hoping to join up with more troops. Grant cut off Lee's escape, however. With his once-proud army reduced to less than 30,000 men, many without food, Lee asked for terms of surrender.

On April 9, 1865, Grant and Lee met in a house in the tiny Virginia village of Appomattox Courthouse. Lee stood in full dress uniform with a jewel-studded sword at his side. Grant wore a private's shirt, unbuttoned at the neck. For a time the two men talked about their Mexican War days. Then they turned to the business at hand.

The terms of surrender were simple. Confederate officers could keep their side arms. All soldiers would be fed and allowed to keep their horses and mules. None would be tried for treason. "Let all the men who claim to own a horse or mule take the animals home with them to work their little farms," said Grant. "This will do much toward conciliating [uniting] our people," replied Lee.

As Lee rode off, Union troops started to celebrate the Union victory, but Grant silenced them. "The war is over," he said. "The rebels are our countrymen again." After the surrender, Lee returned to his men and quietly told them:

General Robert E. Lee signs the papers of surrender, ending the Civil War.

> **"I have done for you all that it was in my power to do. You have done all your duty. Leave the result to God. Go to your homes and resume your occupations. Obey the laws and become as good citizens as you were soldiers."**

The weary Confederates were then fed and allowed to depart for home. On April 26, 1865, General Joseph Johnston surrendered to General Sherman under similar terms at Durham Station, North Carolina. The war was over.

✔ **READING CHECK:** What were the terms of the surrender at Appomattox?

SECTION  REVIEW

Define and explain the significance of the following terms:
Battle of Gettysburg
Pickett's Charge
Gettysburg Address
Siege of Vicksburg
war of attrition
total war

Identify and explain the significance of the following individuals:
George Meade
William Tecumseh Sherman

Locate and explain the importance of the following places:
Gettysburg
Vicksburg
Atlanta
Savannah
Appomattox Courthouse

1. **Using Graphic Organizers** Copy the graphic organizer below. Use it to list the major events that occurred between General Grant's promotion and General Lee's surrender at Appomattox Courthouse.

   1. Grant is promoted to lead the Union army
   2. ____________
   3. ____________
   4. ____________
   5. ____________
   6. ____________
   7. ____________
   8. Lee surrenders at Appomattox Courthouse

2. **Assessing Consequences** How did the Battle of Gettysburg affect the course of the Civil War?
3. **Understanding Geography: Location** Why was the capture of Vicksburg necessary for the North to be in a position to win the war?
4. **Problem Solving** What were the strategies of Ulysses S. Grant and William Tecumseh Sherman? Was there another strategy that could have succeeded and led to less destruction in the South?

Critical Thinking

5. How did General Grant's terms of surrender promote reconciliation between the North and the South?
   Consider:
   - what the terms of the surrender were
   - how both sides reacted to the terms
   - what conditions he could have demanded

---

3. commanded Union forces; fired by Lincoln
4. first professionally licensed female doctor in U.S.; helped run the U.S. Sanitary Commission
5. became commander of the Union army in 1864; accepted Lee's surrender in 1865
6. northerners who sympathized with the South
7. Lincoln's military order freeing slaves in areas held by the Confederacy
8. first African American promoted to the rank of major
9. Grant's plan to continue fighting until the South ran out of men, supplies, and will
10. commanded the Union forces that captured Atlanta and Savannah

Understanding Main Ideas

1. Its fall led President Lincoln to declare the existence of a rebellion in the South and to call for soldiers to put down the rebellion.
2. They filled vacated jobs and aided the war efforts by producing food and supplies, participating in volunteer groups, and raising money.
3. The Union victory at Antietam provided Lincoln with the necessary political power to issue the Emancipation Proclamation.
4. Confederate officers could keep their side arms, and Confederate soldiers were fed, protected from trial for treason, and allowed to keep their animals and return home.

REVIEW AND ASSESSMENT RESOURCES

PRINT
- Chapter 2 Review, pp. 96–97
- Chapter 2 Tutorial for Students, Parents, Mentors, and Peers
- Chapter 2 Test (Form A or B)
- Portfolio Activities and Alternative Assessment Handbook, Chapter 2

MULTIMEDIA
- Audio Program, Chapter 2 (English and Spanish)
- Chapter 2 Test Generator (on the One-Stop Planner)
- Global Skill Builder CD–ROM
- HRW Web site

SHELTERED ENGLISH
- Spanish Glossary
- Sheltered English Chapter 2 Test

REVIEW
Have students complete the **Chapter 2 Review** on pp. 96–97.

ASSESS
Use one of the chapter tests to assess students' understanding of the content. For **Alternative Assessment**, see the **Portfolio Activities and Alternative Assessment Handbook**.

Reviewing Themes
1. Capture of the Mississippi River enabled the Union to divide the Confederacy geographically and thus weaken it considerably.

2. The North's industry, material resources, and railroads gave it a significant advantage over the South, which had an increasingly hard time provisioning its army over the course of the war because most of its wealth was in land and slaves.

3. It prompted some people to question whether it was a violation of an individual's liberty to force that individual to participate in the war.

Thinking Critically
1. Answers will vary. Some students might hypothesize that European aid to the South would have prompted the North to give up the struggle.

2. Such fears prompted President Lincoln to draft the Emancipation Proclamation in such a way that it only affected the status of slavery in the Confederacy.

3. It enjoyed superior military leadership and employed defensive tactics for much of the war; it also constituted a huge geographical area for Union forces to subdue.

4. Students who agree with draft opponents might argue that it placed the burden of fighting on the poor. Those who disagree might contend that the draft was necessary to sustain the war efforts of both sides.

Review

Creating a Time Line
Copy the time line below onto a sheet of paper. Complete the time line by filling in the events and dates from the chapter that you think were most significant. Pick three events and explain why you think they were significant.

Writing a Summary
Using the Reading Checks as a guide, write an overview of the events in the chapter.

Identifying People and Ideas
Identify the following terms or individuals and explain their significance.

1. Robert E. Lee
2. Thomas "Stonewall" Jackson
3. George B. McClellan
4. Elizabeth Blackwell
5. Ulysses S. Grant
6. Copperheads
7. Emancipation Proclamation
8. Martin Delany
9. war of attrition
10. William Tecumseh Sherman

Understanding Main Ideas
SECTION 1
1. What role did Fort Sumter play in the outbreak of the war?

SECTION 2
2. What contributions did civilians make during the war?

SECTION 3
3. What role did the Battle of Antietam play in the Emancipation Proclamation?

SECTION 4
4. What were the terms of Robert E. Lee's surrender at Appomattox Courthouse?

Reviewing Themes
1. **Geographic Diversity** What role did geography play in helping the North win the war?
2. **Economic Development** How did the economic resources of the North and the South affect the war?
3. **Democratic Values** How did the draft challenge ideas about individual liberty in the North and in the South?

Thinking Critically
1. **Hypothesizing** How might the outcome of the Civil War have been different if European powers had aided the South?
2. **Identifying Cause and Effect** How did fears of alienating the border states affect northern strategy during the war?
3. **Analyzing** How did the South, with fewer supplies and resources, manage to stall a northern victory for four years?
4. **Recognizing Point of View** Were those who opposed the draft correct in their assessment of its effects? Explain your answer.
5. **Comparing and Contrasting** How did people in the North and in the South experience the war in different ways?

Writing About History
Writing to Evaluate Write an essay evaluating whether total-war tactics were necessary for the Union to win the Civil War. Use the following chart to organize your thoughts.

RETEACH

Organize students into five groups and assign each group one of the following topics pertaining to the Civil War: the dissolution of the Union and the beginning of the war; daily life on the home front and on the battlefield; the early battles (through Antietam); the later battles; or war's end and impact of the war. Have each group prepare a magazine spread on its topic for a modern newsmagazine doing a special commemorative edition on the Civil War. They should focus on the events, people, and issues that most strongly affected their topic area. Tell groups to write a minimum of three articles and to include three or more images for their section of the magazine. When all the groups have finished their sections, have volunteers make a cover, a title page, and a table of contents for the completed magazine. Bind the magazine and put it on display in the classroom or school library.

Sheltered English, Cooperative Learning

EXTEND

Have students use the library to find examples of correspondence written during the Civil War. They might look for soldiers' letters home, generals' letters to their presidents, citizens' letters to editors of local newspapers, and so on. Have each student compile a mini-anthology of his or her 10 favorite letters, with a short explanation for why each one was selected.

Block Scheduling

Strategies for Success Review the **Strategies for Success** on *Recognizing Fallacies in Reasoning.* Then study the following statements and identify the reasoning error in each. Note additional information that would make each statement correct.

1. France and Britain did not support the Confederacy during the Civil War because it conscripted, or drafted, large numbers of young men into its army.
2. The Emancipation Proclamation was enacted on January 1, 1863, because the Confederacy had just scored a major victory at the Battle of Fredericksburg.
3. The North won the Civil War because it had a much more extensive railroad system than the South.
4. President Lincoln was dissatisfied with General McClellan because the military leader moved too quickly.
5. General Lee surrendered because Abraham Lincoln was elected for a second term as president.

Linking History and Geography

Study the map below and note how many slave and free states existed in 1860. Identify which slave states remained in the Union and explain why their location was significant.

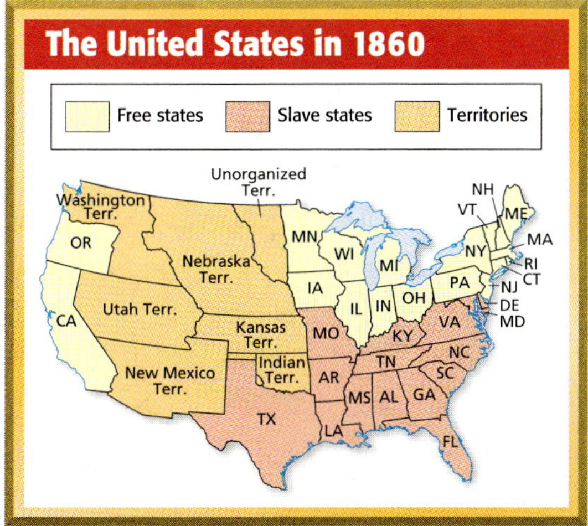

internetconnect

TOPIC: War Photography
GO TO: go.hrw.com
KEYWORD: SE1 Photography

Accessing the Internet through the HRW Web site, research the Civil War photography of Mathew Brady. Then create original poetry that reflects the content of the images in the photographs, the emotional mood of the photographs, and the context in which the photographs were taken.

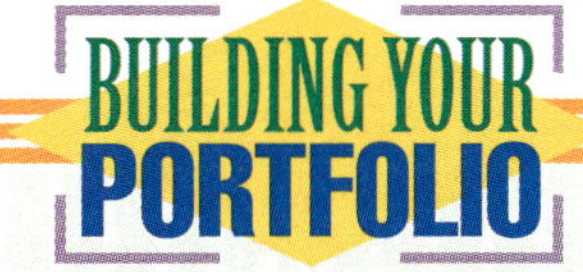

Complete one or all of the following projects independently or cooperatively.

1 Democratic Values

Imagine that you are an abolitionist in 1862. ***Write a letter*** to President Lincoln urging him to take a strong stand against slavery.

2 Geographic Diversity

Imagine that you are a member of a congressional committee attempting to formulate a compromise between the North and South to prevent a civil war. ***Create a chart*** that lists the economic, political, and social differences between the two sides that you think will be obstacles to an agreement and possible peaceful ways around these obstacles.

3 Cultural Diversity

Imagine that you are a reporter at Appomattox Courthouse. ***Write an editorial*** giving your impressions of General Lee's surrender and your evaluation of whether the war was worth the cost.

5. Answers will vary. Students might point out that many people in the South suffered economic deprivation while those in the North filled wartime industrial jobs.

Writing About History
Sherman's total war tactics: Sherman's objectives–destruction of the South's economic resources as well as its army. Sherman's reasoning–the war should be made so terrible that "those people of the South" are not tempted to engage in it again.

Strategies for Success
1. irrelevant evidence–the Confederacy's lack of European allies was not directly related to the issue of conscription
2. coincidence as cause–the Emancipation Proclamation was first drafted and issued several months earlier, shortly after the Union victory at Antietam
3. single cause–other factors contributed to the outcome
4. irrelevant evidence; Lincoln thought that McClellan moved too slowly
5. coincidence as cause; although Lincoln won re-election prior to Lee's surrender, his victory had no causal relationship to the surrender

Linking History and Geography
18 free states and 15 slave states; Missouri, Kentucky, Maryland, and Delaware remained in the Union. They were border states; Maryland nearly surrounds Washington, D.C.

LET'S GET STARTED!

Direct students' attention to the maps of the North before the Civil War and the South before the Civil War. Tell students to imagine that they are English journalists who traveled by rail through both regions. Have each student write a few sentences or paragraphs describing both regions. Ask volunteers to share their sentences or paragraphs with the class. Tell students that they will learn more about regionalism in the United States in the Unit 1 America's Geography.

TEACH AMERICA'S GEOGRAPHY—REGIONALISM

Tell students that maps and graphs can complement each other to provide a complete picture of a particular historical subject. Have students study the maps and the graph in the America's Geography feature. Then ask each student to write a few sentences or paragraphs summarizing the information presented there. **Sheltered English**

THEN AND NOW

The Expansion of Education. Although the South and the West had relatively few colleges and universities before the Civil War, both regions greatly expanded their educational institutions after the war. In 1850, for example, there were no colleges and universities in California. By 1995 the state had 348 such institutions.

ACTIVITY: Ask students to conduct research on the founding dates of local colleges and universities. Have each student create a detailed time line on the subject and present it to the class. Alternately, ask each student to write a short report tracing the growth of local colleges and universities.

THAT'S INTERESTING!

Willamette University in Salem, Oregon, was founded in 1842, making it one of the oldest universities in the West. Even so, Willamette University is some 200 years younger than Harvard, the first American university.

AMERICA'S Geography

Regionalism

By the mid-1800s the United States consisted of three distinct geographic regions, each with its own unique character and culture. Some people felt more loyalty to their region than to the nation as a whole. This concept of regionalism was particularly evident in the South. Unlike sectionalism, regionalism focuses more on cultural identity than political differences. Since regionalism primarily involves cultural identification, the regional identity of some states has shifted as the state's culture has changed. Many residents of Missouri, for instance, identified with the South before the Civil War. In the late 1800s, however, as industrialization, trade, and transportation increased in the state, its culture became closely identified with that of the Midwest.

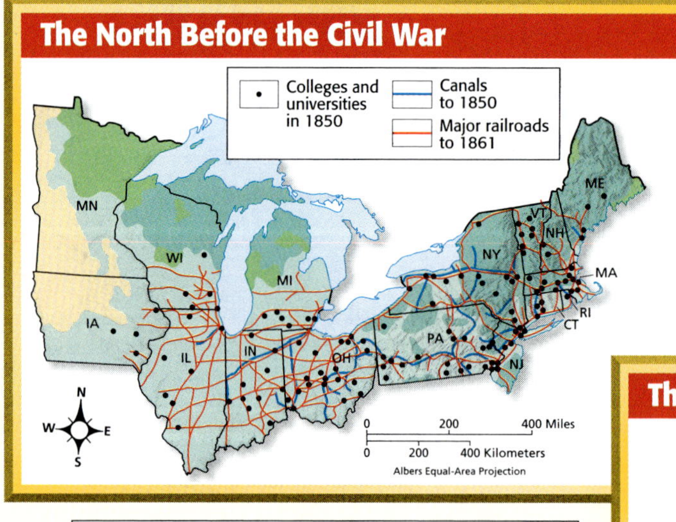

The North. The smallest region—the North—was the center of industrialization in the United States. It was also the center of higher education. In 1850 most of the country's colleges and universities—63 percent—were located in the North.

Evergreen forest	Tallgrass prairie	Shrub
Deciduous forest	Shortgrass prairie	Desert
Mixed forest		

The West. Although the West was the largest region of the country in 1850, it had the smallest population. The first centers of education in the West were located on the frontier. The Mormons of Utah and followers of the Oregon Trail established the region's first universities.

SPOTLIGHT on Oberlin College

Ask students to conduct research on Oberlin College, a leading northern college that played an important role in the abolition movement. Then tell students to imagine that they are modern-day historians. Have each student write a short paper explaining how Oberlin College typified the North and northern concerns in the era before the Civil War.

SPOTLIGHT on the Look of the West

Pair students and ask them to study the map on the West before the Civil War, paying close attention to the map legend. Have each pair consult a dictionary, science textbook, or encyclopedia in order to write definitions for the terms on the legend. Then ask each pair to use its definitions to write a few sentences describing a particular territory in the West.

Cooperative Learning

AMERICA'S Geography

The South Before the Civil War

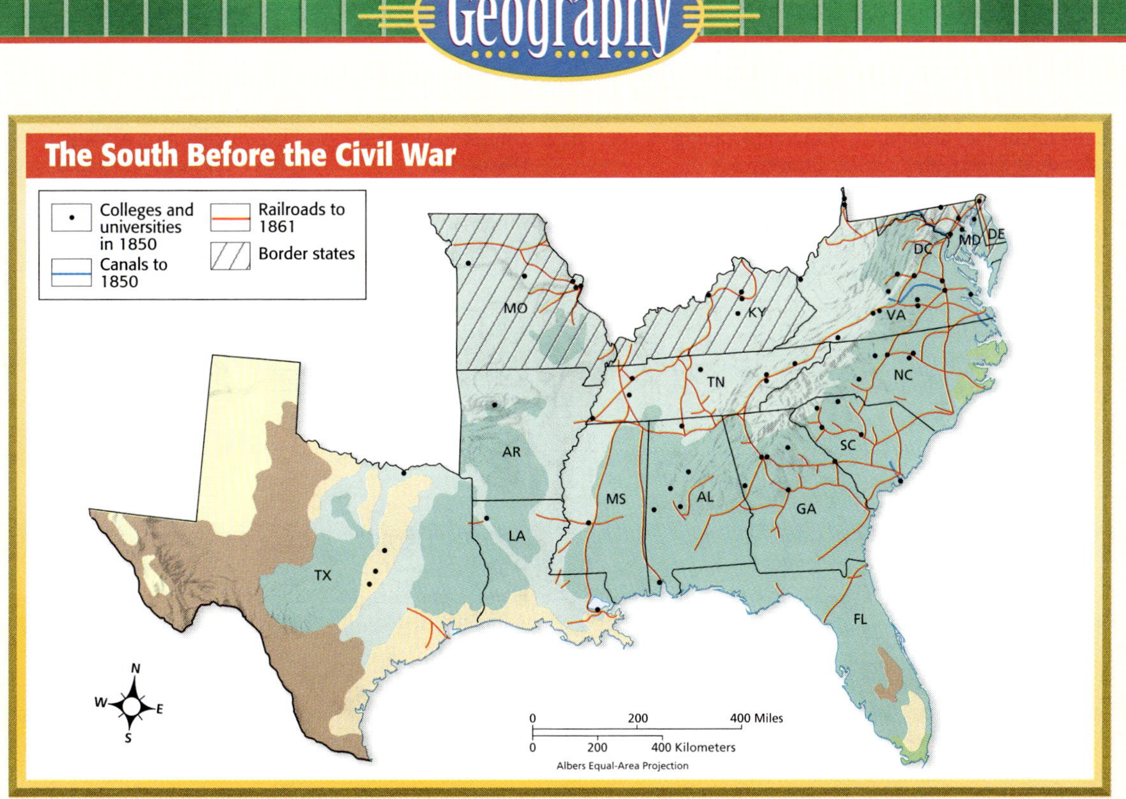

Diversity of Population, 1860

Population of the North, 1860

<1%, 2%, 98% | 26%, 74%

Population of the West, 1860

10%, 1%, 89% | 16%, 84%

Population of the South, 1860

<1%, 63%, 37% | 10%, 90%

White | Other Races | Rural | African American | Urban

Source: *Historical Statistics of the United States*

The South. Although the South had a larger population than the West, a smaller percentage of its population lived in urban areas. Many western settlers tended to move to booming cities such as San Francisco. Although the South had more colleges than the West, overall it lagged far behind the North in education. A majority of the country's residents who could not read lived in the South. Most were slaves who were not allowed to learn to read.

GEOGRAPHY AND HISTORY 

Region

1. How did the populations of the North, the South, and the West differ?
2. Which southern state had no colleges in 1850?

TECHNOLOGY AND SOCIETY

The Transportation Revolution and Regionalism. The Transportation Revolution helped reduce the regional and sectional differences between the North and the South, even though the South had far fewer railroads than the North. Railroads and canals linked the nation, allowing the exchange of ideas and goods.

CRITICAL THINKING Ask students to consider the issue of regionalism today. What factors or developments have helped reduce regionalism in the modern-day United States?

ANSWER: Answers will vary. Students might suggest that the Internet helps people overcome both regional and national differences.

AMERICA'S GEOGRAPHY ANSWERS

1. The North had the largest percentage of white residents and was the most urbanized region. The West had the largest percentage of non-white, non-African American residents. The South had the largest percentage of African American residents and was the most rural region.
2. Florida

Reconstruction and the New South

CHAPTER PLANNING GUIDE

	Section Lesson Objectives	Print Resources	Multimedia Resources	Sheltered English Resources
Section 1 Presidential Reconstruction, pp. 102–06	1 Describe the hopes and expectations that African Americans in the South had for their lives as freedpeople. 2 Relate how President Lincoln and Congress differed over plans for Reconstruction. 3 Explain how President Johnson's programs benefited former Confederates. 4 Evaluate how the Black Codes affected freedpeople.	▶ Guided Reading Strategy 3.1 ▶ Primary Source Reading 3: The Emancipation Proclamation ▶ Section 1 Review, p. 106 ▶ Daily Quiz 3.1	▶ One-Stop Planner, Lesson 3.1 ▶ American Music Selection 15: "When Johnny Comes Marching Home Again" ▶ Holt Researcher: American History CD–ROM	▶ Main Idea Activity for Reteaching and Sheltered English 3.1
Section 2 Congressional Reconstruction, pp. 107–14	1 Describe the issues that divided Republicans during the early Reconstruction era. 2 Explain why moderates and Radical Republicans joined forces and their actions. 3 Relate why President Johnson was impeached, and explain why the Senate acquitted him. 4 Explain why African Americans were crucial to the election of 1868 and how Republicans responded to their support.	▶ Guided Reading Strategy 3.2 ▶ American History Political Cartoon 3: Radical Reconstruction ▶ Section 2 Review, p. 114 ▶ Daily Quiz 3.2	▶ One-Stop Planner, Lesson 3.2 ▶ Holt Researcher: American History CD–ROM	▶ Main Idea Activity for Reteaching and Sheltered English 3.2
Section 3 Reconstruction in the South, pp. 115–19	1 Explain how African Americans attempted to improve their lives during the Reconstruction era. 2 Identify Republican reforms. 3 Relate how some African Americans responded to harassment by the Ku Klux Klan. 4 Describe why Reconstruction ended.	▶ Guided Reading Strategy 3.3 ▶ Graphic Organizer Activity 3: Evaluating Reconstruction ▶ Section 3 Review, p. 119 ▶ Daily Quiz 3.3	▶ One-Stop Planner, Lesson 3.3 ▶ Holt Researcher: American History CD–ROM ▶ HRW Web site	▶ Main Idea Activity for Reteaching and Sheltered English 3.3
Section 4 The New South, pp. 120–25	1 Analyze the drawbacks to the sharecropping system. 2 Assess how Jim Crow laws and the *Plessy* v. *Ferguson* decision changed life for southern African Americans. 3 Explain how African Americans attempted to improve their economic situation after Reconstruction. 4 Compare the views of Booker T. Washington and Ida B. Wells.	▶ Guided Reading Strategy 3.4 ▶ Geography Activity 3: Tenant Farming and Sharecropping ▶ Literature Reading 3: The Cruelty of Jim Crow Laws ▶ Biography Reading 3: Ida B. Wells-Barnett ▶ Section 4 Review, p. 125 ▶ Daily Quiz 3.4	▶ One-Stop Planner, Lesson 3.4 ▶ The American Nation Video Program Segment: The Tuskegee Institute; Teacher's Guide, pp. 63–68 ▶ Holt Researcher: American History CD–ROM	▶ Main Idea Activity for Reteaching and Sheltered English 3.4
Chapter Review and Assessment pp. 126–27		▶ Chapter 3 Review, pp. 126–27 ▶ Chapter 3 Tutorial for Students, Parents, Mentors, and Peers ▶ Chapter 3 Test (Form A or B) ▶ Portfolio Activities and Alternative Assessment Handbook, Chapter 3	▶ Audio Program, Chapter 3 (English and Spanish) ▶ Chapter 3 Test Generator (on the One-Stop Planner) ▶ Global Skill Builder CD–ROM ▶ HRW Web site	▶ Spanish Glossary ▶ Sheltered English Chapter 3 Test

CHAPTER OVERVIEW

The United States faced incredible challenges after the Civil War, including the need to assimilate many freed slaves. After President Lincoln's assassination, President Johnson issued a complete pardon to all rebels except former Confederate officeholders. Many Republicans in Congress wanted to reconstruct the South, creating a new region in which all men would enjoy equal rights. They created the Freedmen's Bureau to help former slaves and passed legislation to protect the rights of African Americans. African Americans eagerly participated in this Reconstruction.

Many in the United States objected to African American rights and Reconstruction. Some angry southerners joined the Ku Klux Klan to keep African Americans from exercising their rights. In the 1870s Reconstruction gradually slowed as a depression overtook the country. Jim Crow laws and the Supreme Court's decision in *Plessy* v. *Ferguson* soon helped to create two separate societies—black and white, separate and unequal—in the South.

TIME TAMERS

Block Scheduling

The teacher lesson plans for each section offer a variety of activity choices to help you present the material in a block scheduling format. For further suggestions on block scheduling, see the **Block Scheduling Handbook with Team Teaching Strategies**, pp. 13–18.

Internet Connections and Lesson 3
www.si.edu/hrw

Hands-On History Activities:

Classroom to Community The **Hands-On History Activities** help students make meaningful connections between events in American history and those in their own hometown. You may wish to use the Chapter 3 Activity, People Helping People, to extend the chapter lessons, as alternative assessment, or as a block scheduling option.

Portfolio Projects

The American Nation includes multiple portfolio projects in each Pupil's Edition chapter review, as well as each unit review. Chapter 3 Portfolio Project options on p. 127 include the following:

1. Students will **prepare a list of headlines, story ideas, and possible illustrations**.
2. Students will **create an outline**.
3. Students will **prepare a closing statement**.

The American Nation
INTERNET RESOURCE DIRECTORY

To access online materials for this chapter, go to **go.hrw.com** and type in the keywords listed below.

HRW ONLINE RESOURCES
GO TO: go.hrw.com

Online Maps
KEYWORD: SE1 Maps3
- African American Colleges

Online Charts
KEYWORD: SE1 Charts3
- Reconstruction Amendments
- Illiteracy in the South

Online Reading Support
KEYWORD: SE1 Strategies3

Online Rubrics
KEYWORD: SE1 Rubrics

CHAPTER ENRICHMENT LINKS
Use these Web links to extend and enrich student learning for Chapter 3.
GO TO: go.hrw.com
KEYWORD: SE1 Ch3

CHAPTER INTERNET ACTIVITIES
GO TO: go.hrw.com
- Pupil's Edition Student Activity
  KEYWORD: SE1 Johnson
  (Students examine Andrew Johnson's impeachment trial.)
- Teacher's Edition Student Activity
  KEYWORD: SE1 Fisk
  (Students conduct research on the history of the Fisk Jubilee Singers.)
- Teacher's Edition Student Activity
  KEYWORD: SE1 Reconstruction
  (Students conduct research on prominent African American Reconstruction politicians.)

ADDITIONAL RESOURCES

Books for Teachers

Foner, Eric. *Reconstruction: America's Unfinished Revolution, 1863–1877.* Harper & Row, 1988. Provides a thorough analysis of Reconstruction; considered a classic work of American history.

Simpson, Brooks D. *The Reconstruction Presidents.* University Press of Kansas, 1998. Discusses Reconstruction-era presidents.

Books for Students

Foner, Eric, and Olivia Mahoney. *America's Reconstruction: People and Politics After the Civil War.* HarperPerennial, 1995. Chronicles the Reconstruction era in an engaging manner. Particularly appropriate for students reading below grade level.

Thomas, Velma Maia. *Lest We Forget: The Passage from Africa to Slavery and Emancipation.* Crown Publishers, 1997. Offers an impressive array of photographs and documents.

Primary Sources from the Period

Fleming, Walter L., ed. *Documentary History of Reconstruction.* Peter Smith, 1950. Presents hard-to-find documents in one collection.

Multimedia Materials

The Background of the Reconstruction Period. Video, 20 min. BFA/SSSS. Discusses the historical and political issues of Reconstruction.

Reconstruction. Video, 35 min. EAV/SSSS. Examines the effects of Reconstruction on the North, the South, and African Americans.

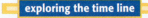

CHAPTER 3

Before You Read

Build on What You Know

Ask students to answer the following questions.

How might a society incorporate newly freed slaves?

Consider:

- the racial beliefs that contributed to the existence of slavery
- the economic and social needs of a disenfranchised population

How might a nation reunify after a bloody civil war?

Consider:

- the ideas and arguments that justified war
- the issue of lingering resentment

exploring the time line

AMERICAN EVENTS

internet connect

TOPIC: Fisk Jubilee Singers
GO TO: go.hrw.com
KEYWORD: SE1 Fisk

Have students access the Internet through the HRW Web site to conduct research on the Fisk Jubilee Singers and to listen to some of their music. Then tell students to imagine that they are music critics for a northern newspaper in the late 1800s. Have each student write a review that introduces the Fisk Jubilee Singers to readers and discusses the group's music.

CHAPTER 3

1865–1900

Reconstruction and the New South

Members of Congress cast votes on the impeachment of President Johnson

Harvesting cotton

THE GRANGER COLLECTION, NEW YORK

1865

1865 Politics
The passage of the Thirteenth Amendment abolishes slavery.

1866 Daily Life
Race riots erupt in Memphis and New Orleans.

1867 Business and Finance
Southern crops bring in just half their expected price, ruining many planters.

1867 Daily Life
Howard University is established for African American students.

1867 Politics
Congress passes the first Reconstruction Act.

1868 Politics
President Andrew Johnson is impeached.

1870

1871 The Arts
The Fisk Jubilee Singers tour the United States.

1875

1878 Business and Finance
Good land for growing cotton can be purchased in North Carolina for as low as $5 an acre.

1880

1881 The Arts
The Southern Art Union is organized.

1881 World Events
Alexander II, czar of Russia, is assassinated.

1881 Politics
The first Jim Crow law requires African Americans to ride in separate railway cars from whites.

The Fisk Jubilee Singers

Before You Read

Build on What You Know

Beginning with the framing of the Constitution and continuing through the Civil War, slavery caused political tension in the United States. Although many Americans agreed that slavery was incompatible with democratic ideals, it took a bloody civil war to finally bring an end to slavery. The war's end, however, raised a new challenge: how to bring emancipated slaves into a free society. In this chapter you will learn how the nation struggled to define the rights of freed African Americans, while also seeking to restore the southern states to the Union.

Think About Themes

*To help students create their Themes Journal entries, provide the following examples of appropriate **agree/disagree** statements.*

Constitutional Heritage

Agree Colonists rebelled against Great Britain after officials failed to accommodate political and economic demands.

Disagree The framers of the Constitution made it fairly difficult to amend the document.

Democratic Values

Agree The Federalists passed the Alien and Sedition Acts to protect the United States against treason.

Disagree The Constitution and the Bill of Rights established permanent and unalienable freedoms.

Economic Development

Agree In the antebellum South, planters' dependence on cotton limited the development of industry in the region.

Disagree The Market Revolution allowed different regions to specialize in different products, fostering economic growth.

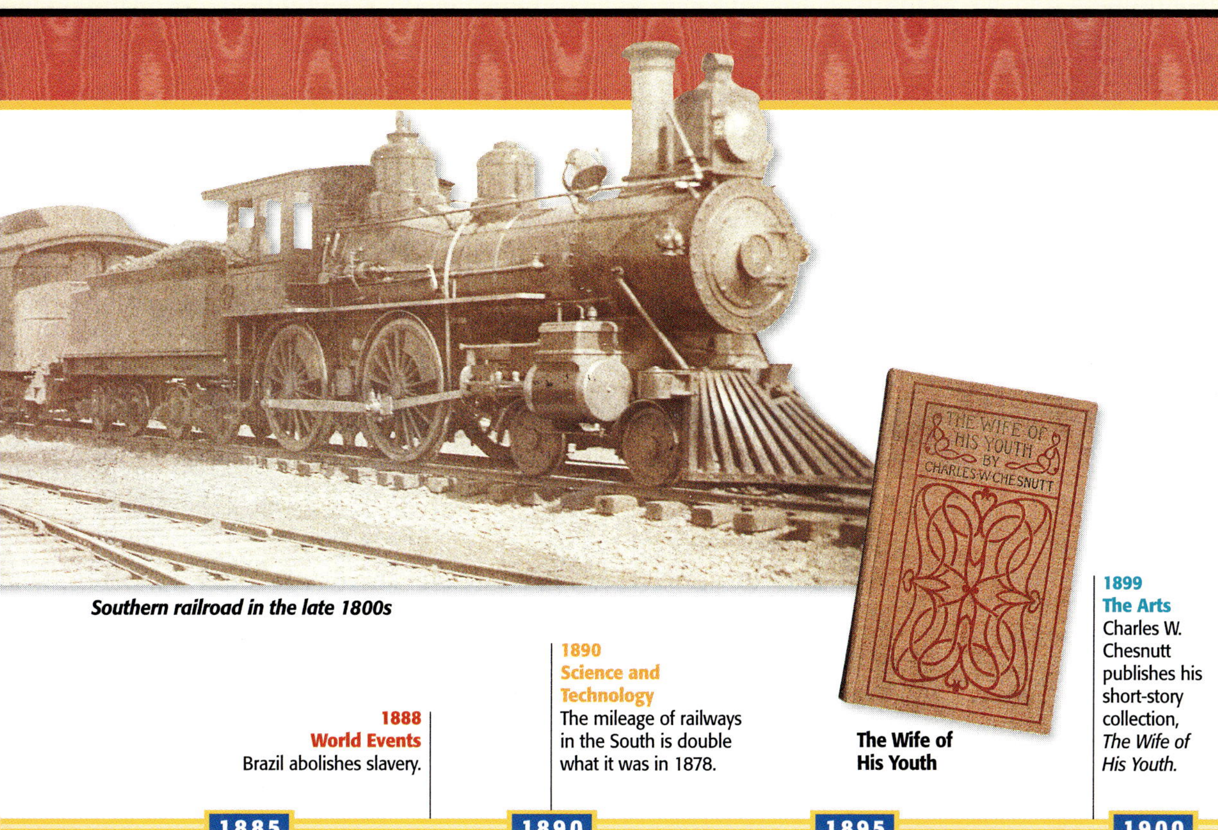

Southern railroad in the late 1800s

The Wife of His Youth

1885

1885 Daily Life Riots against Chinese immigrants break out in the Washington Territory.

1886 Politics The Georgia Supreme Court upholds the will of a former slaveholder who left much of his wealth to African American Amanda Eubanks, making her the wealthiest black woman in the United States.

1888 World Events Brazil abolishes slavery.

1890

1890 Science and Technology The mileage of railways in the South is double what it was in 1878.

1890 Business and Finance The value of tobacco products in Kentucky, North Carolina, and Virginia is almost $31 million.

1893 World Events New Zealand becomes the first country to give women the vote.

1895

1899 The Arts Charles W. Chesnutt publishes his short-story collection, *The Wife of His Youth.*

1900

Petition for voting rights by New Zealand women

Think About Themes

*Decide whether you **agree** or **disagree** with the following statements. Note why in your journal.*

Constitutional Heritage A government that cannot adapt to change poses a threat to the very society it has been created to govern.

Democratic Values A nation's definition of a democratic society changes over time in response to war and other significant events.

Economic Development A region's dependence on the sale of a single product ultimately serves to limit the region's economic development.

exploring the time line

GLOBAL EVENTS

GLOBAL RELATIONS

1888 ■ Brazil Abolishes Slavery. Slavery in Latin America was abolished gradually between 1823 and 1888. Many Latin American revolutionary leaders had realized the irony of using slaves to fight for freedom. Chile abolished slavery in 1823, and other nations soon followed until Brazil remained the only slaveholding country in Latin America. Many Brazilian slaves worked on *engenhos,* or sugar plantations; others worked on cattle ranches or in gold mines. The abolition of slavery in Brazil began with the 1871 Law of Free Birth, which stated that children born of slave mothers after that date were free. By the time Princess Isabel, daughter of Brazil's emperor, signed the "Golden Law" abolishing all slavery in 1888, only about 5 percent of Brazil's labor force was made up of slaves.

CRITICAL THINKING Why might Brazilians have called the law abolishing slavery the "Golden Law"?

ANSWER: Students might suggest that they might have wished to emphasize the law's goodness, beauty, and value to those whom it freed.

SECTION 1

After completing Section 1, students should be able to:

OBJECTIVE 1 *Describe the hopes and expectations that African Americans in the South had for their lives as freedpeople.*

OBJECTIVE 2 *Relate how President Lincoln and Congress differed over plans for Reconstruction.*

OBJECTIVE 3 *Explain how President Johnson's programs benefited former Confederates.*

OBJECTIVE 4 *Evaluate how the Black Codes affected freedpeople.*

LET'S GET STARTED!

As students enter the classroom, play Selection 15, "When Johnny Comes Marching Home Again," from the **American Music Audio CD Program**. Ask students to respond to the song in writing. Have volunteers share their responses. Tell students that composer Patrick Sarsfield Gilmore wrote "When Johnny Comes Marching Home Again" to celebrate peace. Then tell students that in Section 1 they will learn about the challenges of peace in the Reconstruction era.

SECTION 1 RESOURCES

PRINT
- Guided Reading Strategy 3.1
- Primary Source Reading 3: The Emancipation Proclamation
- Section 1 Review, p. 106
- Daily Quiz 3.1

MULTIMEDIA
- One-Stop Planner, Lesson 3.1
- American Music Selection 15: "When Johnny Comes Marching Home Again"
- Holt Researcher: American History CD–ROM

SHELTERED ENGLISH
- Main Idea Activity for Reteaching and Sheltered English 3.1

✔ READING TO UNDERSTAND

To help students master the section objectives, have them answer the **READING CHECKS** and complete **Guided Reading Strategy 3.1** as they read the section.

Multimedia Resources

American Music Selection 15: "When Johnny Comes Marching Home Again"

SECTION 1 Presidential Reconstruction

OBJECTIVES

Read to understand:

1. what hopes and expectations African Americans in the South had for their lives as freed people
2. how President Lincoln and Congress differed over plans for Reconstruction
3. how President Johnson's programs benefited former Confederates
4. how the Black Codes affected freedpeople

KEY TERMS

Reconstruction
amnesty
Thirteenth Amendment
Black Codes

KEY PEOPLE

John Wilkes Booth
Andrew Johnson

EYEWITNESSES TO History

> ***"Let a great earthquake swallow us up first! Let us leave our land and emigrate to any desert spot of the earth, rather than return to the Union."***
>
> **—Sarah Morgan**

Emancipation parade

Such feelings expressed by a white southern woman were common among many former Confederates after the Civil War. African Americans in the South reacted very differently. After Charleston, South Carolina, surrendered in February 1865, the city's African American residents hosted a parade they called a "jubilee of freedom." In April, after Union forces captured Richmond, Virginia, President Abraham Lincoln visited the city. African American T. Chester Morris wrote in the *Philadelphia Press,* "There is no describing the scene along the route. The colored population was wild with enthusiasm."

The Old South Destroyed

The Civil War inflicted mass devastation on the South, leaving many cities in ruins. A visitor to Columbia, South Carolina, described "a wilderness of crumbling walls, naked chimneys, and trees killed by flames." Illness swept the region, resulting in thousands of deaths in the South in the year after the war.

The Civil War also shattered the South's economy. Tens of thousands of Confederate veterans were left without jobs. Similarly, most of the approximately 4 million emancipated slaves found themselves homeless and penniless. "It came so sudden on 'em," recalled former slave Parke Johnston.

> **"Just think of whole droves of people, that had always been kept so close, and hardly ever left the plantation before, turned loose all at once, with nothing in the world, but what they had on their backs."**

Despite the obstacles, most freedpeople looked eagerly to the future. Like former slave Henry Turner, they yearned to enjoy their "rights in common with other men." They hoped to establish their own churches and schools and to legalize their marriages. Many freedpeople expected to choose their own livelihood. With freedom anything seemed possible, even finding family members who had been sold away. Former slave Hawkins Wilson sent a letter to his sister, address unknown, believing that it would somehow find its way to her. "Your little brother Hawkins is trying to find out where you are and where his poor old mother is," he wrote. "Let me know and I will come to see you."

INTERPRETING THE VISUAL RECORD

The South in ruins. Many southern cities lay in ruins after the Civil War. ***What problems do you think damage like this caused for southern residents?***

TEACH OBJECTIVE 1

LEVEL 1: Ask each student to create a graphic organizer displaying African Americans' hopes and expectations for their lives as freedpeople. *(Students' organizers should include the desire to establish churches and schools, legalize marriages, find family members who had been sold away, own land, and enjoy basic human rights.)* Ask volunteers to sketch their graphic organizers on the chalkboard. **Sheltered English**

LEVEL 2: Pair students and tell them to imagine that they are freedpeople living in Georgia. Have the members of each pair develop a short dialogue expressing their hopes and expectations for their lives as freedpeople *(See the Level 1 lesson for the correct hopes and expectations.)* Ask volunteers to perform their dialogues for the class. Then have each student write two or three paragraphs summarizing the material presented in the dialogues. **Cooperative Learning**

LEVEL 3: Tell students to imagine that they are freedpeople living in Georgia. Have each student write a short speech expressing his or her hopes and expectations for life as a freedperson to be delivered at a gathering of former slaves. *(See the Level 1 lesson for the correct hopes and expectations.)* Ask volunteers to deliver their speeches to the class.

Above all, African Americans hoped, like Garrison Frazier, "to have land . . . and till it by our own labor." Most wanted land to support themselves and to protect their independence. Many believed that it was their due. "Our wives, our children, our husbands, has been sold over and over again to purchase the lands we now locates upon," argued former slave Bayley Wyat. "We have a divine right to the land." General William T. Sherman had encouraged such hopes in January 1865, when he ordered part of South Carolina to be divided into 40-acre parcels and given to freedpeople. Rumors spread that the federal government would give each freedman "40 acres and a mule."

✔ **READING CHECK:** What hopes and expectations did African Americans in the South have for their lives as freedpeople?

President Lincoln and Reconstruction

President Abraham Lincoln wanted to bring the rebel states back into the Union quickly. He had not gone to war to destroy the South, but to preserve the Union. Even before the war's end, he had begun planning for **Reconstruction**—rebuilding the former Confederate states and reuniting the nation.

The beginning of Reconstruction.

To encourage southerners to abandon the Confederacy, Lincoln had issued the Proclamation of Amnesty and Reconstruction on December 8, 1863. The proclamation offered **amnesty**. This would give a full pardon to all southerners—except high-ranking Confederate leaders and a few others—who would swear allegiance to the U.S. Constitution and accept federal laws ending slavery. The proclamation also permitted a state to rejoin the Union when 10 percent of its residents who had voted in 1860 swore their loyalty to the nation.

Many members of Congress objected to this so-called Ten Percent Plan. They did not trust the Confederates to become loyal U.S. citizens or to protect the rights of former slaves. Congress laid out its own Reconstruction plan in the Wade-Davis Bill, passed in July 1864. The bill called for the Confederate states to abolish slavery and to delay Reconstruction until a majority of each state's white males took a loyalty oath. Lincoln vetoed the bill because he was not ready to "be inflexibly committed to any single plan of restoration," he said. In his second inaugural address, delivered on March 4, 1865, Lincoln clarified his goal for Reconstruction.

> **"With malice toward none, with charity for all, with firmness in the right as God gives us to see the right, let us strive on . . . to bind up the nation's wounds . . . to do all which may achieve . . . a just and lasting peace."**

✔ **READING CHECK:** How did President Lincoln and Congress disagree over the course Reconstruction should take?

Juneteenth

A recent Juneteenth parade in Texas

On June 19, 1865, Union soldiers arriving in Galveston, Texas, shared with the city's African Americans the contents of an important general order: "The people of Texas are informed that in accordance with a Proclamation from the Executive of the United States, all slaves are free." Since then, June 19 has been celebrated by African Americans in many areas of the South as Emancipation Day, or Juneteenth.

Complete with parades and marching bands, the earliest Juneteenth celebrations were usually held in rural areas. They often included rereadings of the proclamation, speeches, and songs. African Americans dressed up, cooked special food, danced, played baseball, and rejoiced in their freedom.

The celebration of Juneteenth declined in the early 1900s but regained its popularity in the 1960s. In 1980 Texas named Juneteenth an official state holiday. Today communities throughout the country still enthusiastically celebrate the holiday. Modern Juneteenth festivities include traditional elements, such as guest speakers, prayer services, and barbecues. Official Juneteenth festivals also offer a wide array of activities, such as pageants, lectures, art shows, and even a blues festival in Houston, Texas. Juneteenth celebrates African American freedom in addition to bringing people of all cultures together in harmony.

DEMOCRATIC VALUES

Wade-Davis Manifesto. After Lincoln vetoed the Wade-Davis Bill, Benjamin Franklin Wade and Henry Winter Davis, sponsors of the bill, attacked him in an editorial in the New York *Tribune.* Their attack, called the Wade-Davis Manifesto, accused Lincoln of "holding for naught the will of Congress" and declared that Lincoln's responsibility was "to obey and execute, not make the laws." The Manifesto was so bitter that it served to make Lincoln more popular and damaged the reputations of Wade and Davis.

ACTIVITY: Organize students into teams representing Congress and President Lincoln. Have teams debate the terms of the bill and Lincoln's right to override the popular congressional bill.

THAT'S INTERESTING!

During the Civil War, some freed slaves had formed their own towns. These towns were often established in areas where the Union Army had taken on the responsibility of supporting former slaves who had deserted the plantations.

VISUAL RECORD ANSWER

(for p. 102)

Students might mention housing and sanitation problems.

TEACH OBJECTIVE 2

LEVEL 1: Pair students and ask them to list the provisions of both President Lincoln's and Congress's Reconstruction plans. *(Pairs should list the following: Lincoln—wanted to abolish slavery, give amnesty to most southerners, and allow rebel states to rejoin the Union when 10 percent of the residents who had voted in 1860 pledged their loyalty to the Union. Congress—wanted to abolish slavery and delay Reconstruction until a majority of each state's white males took a loyalty oath.)* Create comprehensive lists on the chalkboard and ask students to evaluate the two plans.
Sheltered English, Cooperative Learning

LEVELS 2 AND 3: Organize students into two groups: President Lincoln and aides, and congresspeople and aides. Tell each group to prepare for a debate on the Reconstruction plans. Ask a spokesperson from each group to open the debate by summarizing the group's assigned Reconstruction plan. *(See the Level 1 lesson for the correct features of each plan.)* Then have students debate the advantages and disadvantages of each plan.
Cooperative Learning

▶**ASSIGNMENT** *Ask each student to write a one-page Reconstruction plan. Have students present their plans to the class. Then have students select the best plan. Ask students to justify their choices.*

THAT'S INTERESTING!

After news of Lincoln's assassination spread, many people worried that Confederates had plotted the whole affair. Mobs threatened imprisoned Confederate officers. Anyone resembling John Wilkes Booth was arrested, and even people who had once expressed antipathy to the North or toward Lincoln were thrown in jail by zealous law officers. Booth's brothers, also well-known actors, were threatened by a mob and arrested. In San Francisco, mobs destroyed newspaper offices that had shown Confederate sympathies.

STRATEGIES FOR SUCCESS

Practicing the Strategy

1. As a northerner, Greeley may have viewed the South with suspicion. As a southerner, Lee may have believed that the South was ready to rejoin the Union and obey its laws.
2. Greeley–the North should continue to control the South; based partly on his opinion that southerners were only waiting for a new chance to defeat the North. Lee–that it is time to restore harmony to the nation; based on the fact that the war had been won by the North.
3. Answers will vary. Students may answer that Greeley is more reliable because he bases his argument on the South's previous actions.

Strategies for Success: Comparing Points of View

Historians often encounter conflicting accounts of events because of differing points of view. Every person has a point of view, or personal frame of reference, from which he or she experiences and thinks about things. Factors such as age, sex, education, and family background, as well as social and historical circumstances, help to shape this point of view. Comparing points of view can lead to historical insights and a better understanding of the causes of historical conflicts.

How to Compare Points of View

1. **Identify the sources.** When you encounter conflicting historical accounts, verify the identity of each author or speaker. If possible, find out about the personal, social, and historical background of each source.
2. **Identify and compare the main ideas.** Identify the main idea expressed by each source. Then note the similarities and differences between these ideas.
3. **Examine the supporting details.** Determine whether each source supports its main idea with relevant facts, opinions, or a combination of both.
4. **Evaluate the points of view.** Use your analysis of the sources, main ideas, and supporting details, along with your knowledge of the historical period, to assess the reliability of each account and its accompanying point of view.

Applying the Strategy

Read and compare the following statements about how the Union should treat the South.

> These gentlemen of the South mean to win. They meant it in 1861 when they opened fire on Sumter. . . . They mean it now. The moment we remove the iron hand from the Rebels' throats they will rise and attempt the mastery.
>
> —*New York* Tribune *editor Horace Greeley*

> The war being at an end, the Southern states having laid down their arms and the questions at issue between them and the Northern states having been decided, I believe it to be the duty of everyone to unite in the restoration of the country and the reestablishment of peace and harmony.
>
> —*Confederate general Robert E. Lee*

Practicing the Strategy

Answer the following questions.

1. How do you think the background of each author affected his statement?
2. What is the main idea of each statement? Is this idea supported by facts, opinions, or both?
3. Whose point of view seems most reliable? Why?

After President Lincoln's assassination, the War Department offered a reward for the capture of John Wilkes Booth.

Lincoln's assassination. How Reconstruction might have developed under Lincoln's direction will never be known. On April 14, 1865, just days after General Robert E. Lee's surrender, Confederate sympathizer John Wilkes Booth shot the president as he and his wife watched a play at the Ford Theatre in Washington. Lincoln died early the following morning.

Across the country, Americans remembered Lincoln by displaying bits of black cloth outside their homes. Thousands filed through the rotunda of the nation's Capitol to pay their respects before he was laid to rest. Hundreds of thousands more stood beside railroad tracks as the funeral train made its way from Washington to Lincoln's burial site in Illinois.

Many ordinary Americans feared the impact that Lincoln's death might have on the country. Sidney George Fisher believed that his death might be harder on the South than the North. He noted, "Mr. Lincoln's humanity & kindness of heart stood between them [southerners] and the party of the North who urge measures of vengeance & severity." The assassination also increased the distrust between the North and the South. Many northerners believed that Booth was part of a conspiracy organized or encouraged by Confederate leaders.

TEACH OBJECTIVES 3 AND 4

ALL LEVELS: Discuss with students the effects of President Johnson's Reconstruction plan on former Confederates and the effects of the Black Codes on freedpeople. To help students fully understand the issues, copy the following graphic organizer on the chalkboard, omitting the italicized answers. Have each student complete it.
Sheltered English

President Johnson's Reconstruction Plan

↓

Benefits to Former Confederates
- *Blanket pardon for most rebels*
- *Easy terms of readmission to the Union: states had to nullify their acts of secession, abolish slavery, and refuse to pay war debts*

↓

Former Confederates Enact Black Codes

↓

Effects of Codes on African Americans
- *Tried to deprive freedpeople of equality*
- *Re-established white control over African American labor*

President Johnson and Reconstruction

After President Lincoln's death, Vice President Andrew Johnson assumed the presidency. Johnson was a Democrat, a one time slaveholder, and a former U.S. senator from Tennessee. He had been chosen as Lincoln's running mate in 1864 because of his pro-Union sympathies. Republican leaders had hoped he would appeal to northern Democrats and southern Unionists.

Despite his support for the Union and his wartime experience as Tennessee's military governor, Johnson proved ill-suited to the challenges of Reconstruction. Defining African Americans' new rights proved to be a challenge also. He favored a government controlled by white citizens. He also suffered, as one contemporary observer noted, from "almost unconquerable prejudices against the African race." Johnson also lacked Lincoln's political skill, often refusing to compromise.

In May 1865 Johnson issued a complete pardon to all rebels except former Confederate officeholders and the richest planters. These people he pardoned on an individual basis. Johnson's forgiveness extended to the rebel states as well. For readmission to the Union, his plan required only that they nullify their acts of secession, abolish slavery, and refuse to pay Confederate government debts. The last provision was intended to punish southerners who had financed the Confederacy.

Southerners, including General Robert E. Lee, enthusiastically supported President Johnson's plan. They liked it because it allowed Confederate leaders to take charge of Reconstruction. These men—some of whom continued to wear their army uniforms—dominated the new state legislatures. Even former Confederate vice president Alexander H. Stevens, who had been charged with treason, took office in the nation's capital as a representative.

These former Confederate lawmakers made sure that the new state constitutions did not grant voting rights to freedmen. When the lawmakers complained of the "painful humiliation" inflicted by the presence of African American soldiers in the South, President Johnson had the troops removed. By recognizing Mississippi's new government, Johnson even overlooked the state's refusal to ratify the **Thirteenth Amendment**—which Congress had passed in January 1865 to abolish slavery.

✔ **READING CHECK:** How did President Johnson's programs benefit former Confederates?

Read More About It

Free Find:
Andrew Johnson
After reading about Andrew Johnson on the **Holt Researcher** CD–ROM, imagine that you are in Washington at the time of Lincoln's assassination. Write a report on what plans for Reconstruction you expect Johnson to propose.

INTERPRETING THE VISUAL RECORD

Ex-Confederates. Many southern legislators like these continued to wear their Confederate uniforms when conducting political business. ***What message would the wearing of such uniforms convey?***

The Black Codes

President Johnson's actions encouraged former Confederates to adopt laws limiting the freedom of former slaves. These **Black Codes** closely resembled pre–Civil War slave codes. Mississippi, for example, simply recycled its old code, substituting the word "freedman" for "slave."

The Black Codes varied from state to state. However, they all aimed to prevent African Americans from achieving social, political, and economic equality with southern whites. African Americans could not hold meetings unless whites were present. The code also forbade them to travel without permits, own guns, attend schools with whites, or sit on juries. Most importantly the codes re-established white control over African American labor.

ACROSS THE CURRICULUM

▶GOVERNMENT◀

A Nation Still Divided. Southern newspapers praised Johnson, calling him "a statesman of God's creation." At the same time, many northerners could not overcome their distrust of the South. One Ohioan who traveled in the South after the war observed, "Since the war ended I've been a conservative; I've considered [Radical Republicans] dangerous men, who didn't understand the South, wanted to humble it . . . and were standing in the way of peace. . . . I came [to the South] with the kindest feelings for the people down here. . . . I thought the South wanted [peace]. But I was tremendously mistaken. They hate us and despise us and all belonging to us. They call us cut-throats, liars, thieves, vandals, cowards, and the very scum of the earth. . . . I tell you I'm going home to be a radical."

CRITICAL THINKING Why might southerners have had such distrust for northerners?

ANSWER: Students might suggest that southerners were still angry about losing the Civil War and their way of life.

VISUAL RECORD ANSWER

Some students might suggest that the former Confederates retained their power or that the wearing of such uniforms signified defiance of Reconstruction measures.

REVIEW

Have students complete the **Section 1 Review** on p. 106.

ASSESS

Have students complete **Daily Quiz 3.1**. As **Alternative Assessment**, you may want to use the dialogue or the Reconstruction plan debate in this section's lessons.

RETEACH

Have students complete **Main Idea Activity for Reteaching and Sheltered English 3.1**. Then organize the class into small groups and assign each group one of the section objectives. Have each group prepare two or three newspaper headlines capturing the main ideas of its assigned section. Ask each group to share its headlines with the class. Invite students to comment on the accuracy and insight of the headlines.

Sheltered English, Cooperative Learning

EXTEND

Ask students to conduct research on the Black Codes. Then organize students into triads and tell them to imagine that they are meeting to discuss the Codes. Have each triad develop a plan responding to the Black Codes. Triads should fully determine the costs of the chosen action. Have each triad present its response plans to the class and ask students to evaluate the efficacy and applicability of each.

Cooperative Learning, Block Scheduling

SECTION 1 REVIEW ANSWERS

Define and Identify

For significance, see the following pages:

- Reconstruction, p. 103
- amnesty, p. 103
- John Wilkes Booth, p. 104
- Andrew Johnson, p. 105
- Thirteenth Amendment, p. 105
- Black Codes, p. 105

1. Lincoln's Plan—offered amnesty to most southerners who would accept the new laws and permitted states to rejoin the Union with a 10 percent vote; Congress's Plan—required Confederate states to abolish slavery and required white males of the states to take a loyalty oath; Johnson's Plan—pardoned most rebels and required states to abolish slavery and nullify acts of secession

2. a time of hope and optimism about possible landownership and reunion of families

3. Johnson's plan allowed former Confederates to go unpunished and run their governments as they wanted, including limiting African Americans' rights by restricting their movement.

4. Black Codes attempted to prevent African Americans from achieving social, political, and economic equality with whites.

5. Lincoln's and Johnson's plans seemed to focus on the issue of secession, while Congress's plan showed more concern for the issue of abolition of slavery.

Many laws in the South were passed to maintain an African American labor force to work the fields of white-owned plantations.

Without slaves to do the work, "our fields everywhere lie untilled," one white southerner said. To force former slaves to return to the fields, some local codes prohibited African Americans from living in towns unless they were servants and from renting land outside of towns or cities. Several states required freedpeople to sign long-term labor contracts. Those who refused could be arrested and have their labor put up for auction. Other codes required African Americans to obtain a special license to work in a skilled profession.

The codes also allowed judges to decide whether African American parents could support their children. Children without "adequate" support could be bound, or hired, out against their will. The former owner usually was given the first opportunity to bid. Judges' decisions were often arbitrary. In North Carolina an African American man who worked and supported a wife and child was still considered an "orphan" to be bound out. Some courts hired out children without even informing their parents.

Many African Americans realized that emancipation had not greatly improved their daily lives. Of the Black Codes, one African American veteran demanded, "If you call this Freedom, what do you call Slavery?" Although African Americans immediately denounced these laws as "a disgrace to civilization," they had little political power. Many felt they had to accept the codes in order to survive.

Northerners criticized the Black Codes as an attempt to re-establish slavery. The Chicago *Tribune* reprinted the Mississippi code and proclaimed,

> **"The men of the North will convert the State of Mississippi into a frog pond before they will allow such laws to disgrace one foot of soil in which the bones of our soldiers sleep and over which the flag of freedom waves."**

✔ **READING CHECK:** How did the Black Codes affect the lives of freedpeople?

SECTION  1 REVIEW

Define and explain the significance of the following terms:
Reconstruction
amnesty
Thirteenth Amendment
Black Codes

Identify and explain the significance of the following individuals:
John Wilkes Booth
Andrew Johnson

1. **Using Graphic Organizers** Copy the chart below. Use it to compare the Reconstruction plans of President Lincoln, Congress, and President Johnson.

Lincoln's Plan	Congress's Plan	Johnson's Plan

2. **Synthesizing** What was life like for southern African Americans immediately after the Civil War?
3. **Recognizing Point of View** Why might President Johnson's plan for Reconstruction have been considered unfair by many Americans, particularly southern African Americans?
4. **Analyzing** How did the Black Codes attempt to limit opportunities for African Americans?

Critical Thinking

5. How did disagreements over Reconstruction policy reflect different views about what the lasting effects of the Civil War should be?
   Consider:
   - Congress's views
   - President Lincoln's views
   - President Johnson's views

SECTION 2

After completing Section 2, students should be able to:

OBJECTIVE 1 *Describe the issues that divided Republicans during the early Reconstruction era.*

OBJECTIVE 2 *Explain why moderates and Radical Republicans joined forces and their actions on behalf of African Americans.*

OBJECTIVE 3 *Relate why President Johnson was impeached, and explain why the Senate acquitted him.*

OBJECTIVE 4 *Explain why African Americans were crucial to the election of 1868 and how Republicans responded to their support.*

LET'S GET STARTED!

Write the following statement on the chalkboard: *It is 1867. In what circumstances—and for what offenses—is it right and proper to remove a president from office?* As students enter the classroom, ask them to answer the question. Have volunteers share their responses. Then tell students that in Section 2 they will learn more about the impeachment of President Johnson.

Congressional Reconstruction

OBJECTIVES

Read to understand:

1. what issues divided Republicans during the early Reconstruction era
2. why moderates and Radical Republicans joined forces, and what actions they took on behalf of African Americans
3. why President Johnson was impeached, and why the Senate did not remove him from office
4. why African Americans were crucial to the election of 1868, and how Republicans responded to their support

KEY TERMS

Freedmen's Bureau
Civil Rights Act of 1866
Fourteenth Amendment
Reconstruction Acts
Fifteenth Amendment

KEY PEOPLE

Thaddeus Stevens
Frederick Douglass
Ulysses S. Grant

"Reformation must be effected; the foundation of [southern] institutions, both political, municipal, and social must be broken up and relaid, or all our blood and treasure have been spent in vain. This can only be done by treating and holding them as a conquered people. . . . The whole fabric of southern society must be changed, and never can it be done if this opportunity is lost. Without this, this Government can never be, as it has never been, a true republic."

—Thaddeus Stevens

Thaddeus Stevens

Pennsylvania representative Thaddeus Stevens issued this challenge to Congress in 1865. Many southerners argued that such a harsh approach to Reconstruction would only lead to another civil war. "The day of reckoning cometh, and it will be terrible," warned one southern newspaper.

The Moderates Versus the Radicals

Even Republicans disagreed over the course Reconstruction should take. The issue of African American voting rights proved particularly divisive. Most Republicans were moderates who viewed Reconstruction as a practical matter of restoring the southern states to the Union. Their main concern was keeping former Confederates out of government. They favored giving African Americans some civil equality but not the vote.

Supporters of African American suffrage. In contrast, Radical Republicans like Thaddeus Stevens insisted that African Americans be given the right to vote. These Republicans believed that the proper aim of Reconstruction was to create a new South where all men would enjoy equal rights.

Few northerners, even abolitionists, supported giving African Americans in the South the right to vote. Some Republicans even supported giving the vote only to northern African American men. Although few Americans publicly supported voting rights for African Americans, Frederick Douglass did. Douglass demanded "the immediate, unconditional, and universal 'enfranchisement [right to vote] of the black man, in every State in the Union.'"

BIOGRAPHY *Frederick Douglass*

Frederick Douglass was born into slavery in 1817 on a tobacco plantation in eastern Maryland. His mother was hired out when he was still an infant. He later recalled that he did not see his mother "more than four or five times in my life." When Douglass was about six years old, he was sent to a nearby plantation where he ran errands and performed simple chores. Douglass learned in 1825 that he was to be sent away from the plantation to Baltimore. He received this news with

Read More About It

Free Find:
Frederick Douglass
After reading about Frederick Douglass on the **Holt Researcher** CD–ROM, imagine that you are a reporter during the 1840s. Write a short book review of Douglass's autobiography for a local paper.

SECTION 2 RESOURCES

PRINT

- Guided Reading Strategy 3.2
- American History Political Cartoon 3: Radical Reconstruction
- Section 2 Review, p. 114
- Daily Quiz 3.2

MULTIMEDIA

- One-Stop Planner, Lesson 3.2
- Holt Researcher: American History CD–ROM

SHELTERED ENGLISH

- Main Idea Activity for Reteaching and Sheltered English 3.2

✔ READING TO UNDERSTAND

To help students master the section objectives, have them answer the **READING CHECKS** and complete **Guided Reading Strategy 3.2** as they read the section.

TEACH OBJECTIVE 1

LEVELS 1 AND 2: Write the following statements on the chalkboard: *1) The main goal of Reconstruction is to create an entirely new South and give African Americans the right to vote. 2) The main goal of Reconstruction is to restore the southern states to the Union, keep former Confederates out of government, and give African Americans some civil equality.* Have students label the statements as representing the views of either moderate Republicans or Radical Republicans. *(The first statement represents the views of Radical Republicans, while the second represents the views of moderate Republicans.)* Then have each student write one or two paragraphs explaining how these political issues affected the Republican Party during the early Reconstruction era. **Sheltered English**

LEVEL 3: Tell students to imagine that they are either a moderate Republican or a Radical Republican. Have each student write a one-page position statement describing his or her position on Reconstruction and analyzing how it differs from that of other Republicans. *(See the Level 1 lesson for the correct issues and divisions.)* Ask volunteers to read their position papers to the class.

HISTORY MAKERS SPEAK

Reverend E. J. Adams in *Lift Every Voice*

A Stirring Public Speaker. African American reverend E. J. Adams spoke to a gathering of people celebrating the passage of the Reconstruction Acts. Adams reiterated the importance of universal manhood suffrage and ended his speech with an ironic twist on demands for social equality that received "great cheering": "Again, a perfect Union, justice, domestic tranquillity, the common defense, the general welfare, and the blessings of liberty cannot be secured without universal suffrage. It is the only means of defense for the illiterate and the poor. . . . I do not, however, wish to be understood that I advocate or wish for social equality. God forbid that. For some of my mean white drunken enemies may sneak into my house and marry my daughter."

CRITICAL THINKING Do you think that Adams supported women's voting rights? Why or why not?

ANSWER: Students might suggest that, based on the quotation above, Adams probably only supported manhood suffrage.

VISUAL RECORD ANSWER

Students might suggest that freedpeople aspired to achieve prosperity and a secure family life.

INTERPRETING THE VISUAL RECORD

Family records. After the Civil War, many former slaves tried to find lost relatives. ***What ideals does this family record registry suggest about prosperity and family life for African Americans after the Civil War?***

"joy" and "ecstasy." Douglass spent most of the next seven years in the household of Hugh and Sophia Auld, looking after their young son. Sophia Auld also taught him to read and write.

Douglass was sent to a farm some 40 miles from Baltimore when he was about 15 years old. Longing for freedom, Douglass began planning his escape. One of the other slaves involved, however, betrayed the plan. Douglass was spared the common punishment of being sold. Instead, his captors returned him to Baltimore where he worked in the shipyards for the next two years. In 1838 he again decided to run away. Using borrowed papers that stated he was a free African American sailor, Douglass traveled north. Douglass arrived in New York on September 4, 1838. He became a leader in the antislavery cause and wrote his life story, the *Narrative of the Life of Frederick Douglass,* which was published in 1845.

After the war, Douglass embraced the policies of Reconstruction and Radical Republicanism. He remained active, editing a newspaper in Washington and serving as president of the Freedmen's Bank. Along with several other African Americans, Douglass attempted to advise President Johnson on how to keep "peace between races," hoping to bring an end to the ongoing violence in the South. He served as a U.S. marshal, a recorder of deeds, and as the U.S. minister to Haiti. Douglass died of heart failure on February 20, 1895.

Land reform. Some political leaders emphasized African American suffrage and civil equality. Others, though, saw land reform as the key to changing southern society. Representative Thaddeus Stevens agreed with Senator Charles Sumner of Massachusetts, who insisted that "the great plantations . . . must be broken up, and the freedmen must have the pieces." According to Stevens, economic independence for the former slaves would ensure their freedom. Such independence would also destroy the political power of the "proud, bloated, and defiant rebels."

Despite the efforts of Stevens and Sumner, land reform—particularly government seizure of land—never won wide support. The *New York Times* accused land reformers of starting "a war on property . . . to succeed the war on Slavery." Even many Radical Republicans were skeptical of land reform. They believed that African Americans could achieve social and economic independence if they were granted civil equality, the right to vote, and the right to labor freely.

✔ **READING CHECK:** What issues divided the Republican Party during the early years of the Reconstruction era?

THROUGH OTHERS' EYES

Latin American Views of Reconstruction

Having experienced civil war in their own countries, some wealthy Latin Americans traveled to the United States in the 1860s and 1870s, where they witnessed Reconstruction firsthand. Some Latin Americans saw the Reconstruction of the South as the triumph of a strong, centralized government.

Other Latin Americans praised Reconstruction's economic programs. Several Brazilian visitors felt that the U.S. government's programs effectively aided former slaves to become skilled workers and farmers, which, in turn, helped promote industrialization and cotton production in the South. Still others complained that Reconstruction eroded the small-town life of the South by turning the region over to the hands of big business. Not everyone saw this as a negative, however. Many Mexicans, Brazilians, and Colombians hoped that the U.S. system of business would serve as a model for Latin America.

Still other Latin Americans saw Reconstruction as a blueprint for the day when their countries would end slavery. As Camacho Roldán of Colombia said, when Abraham Lincoln freed the American slaves, he "prepared the way for freedom for the three millions more in the Spanish colonies and Brazil."

TEACH OBJECTIVE 2

LEVEL 1: Working as a class, create a flowchart displaying why moderate and Radical Republicans joined forces and what actions they took on behalf of African Americans. *(Flowcharts should indicate that Republicans joined forces to protect African Americans from postwar violence. They overrode presidential vetoes to pass the Civil Rights Act of 1866 and extend the Freedmen's Bureau. They also passed the Fourteenth Amendment.)* Ask students to select the congressional action that they believe most helped southern African Americans. Conduct a debate on the issue. **Sheltered English**

LEVEL 2: Tell students to imagine that it is 1866 and that they are editorial writers for a Washington newspaper. Have each student write two editorials: one urging moderate and Radical Republicans to join forces to protect African Americans against postwar violence, and one urging Republican congressmembers to pass the Civil Rights Act, extend the Freedmen's Bureau, or pass the Fourteenth Amendment. Ask volunteers to read their editorials to the class. Students may wish to include their editorials in their portfolios.

Congress Versus Johnson

The split between the moderate Republicans and Radical Republicans did not last long, however. In early 1866 Congress began hearings on conditions in the South. Witness after witness testified before the Joint Committee on Reconstruction presenting evidence of postwar violence. African Americans recounted stories of murder and of homes, schools, and churches reduced to "ashes and cinders." Southern Unionists told of death threats. These reports and others like them convinced moderate Republicans to join forces with the Radical Republicans.

INTERPRETING THE VISUAL RECORD

Freedmen's Bureau. Established by Congress, the Freedmen's Bureau provided southerners with food, clothing, and other services. ***What does this drawing reveal about the role of the Freedmen's Bureau?***

The Freedmen's Bureau. One move made by the Republicans was to extend the life of the **Freedmen's Bureau**. Congress had created the bureau in March 1865 to aid the millions of southerners left homeless and hungry by the war. The bureau distributed food and clothing, served as an employment agency, set up hospitals, and operated schools.

The Freedmen's Bureau played a major role in providing education for African Americans, who had been denied this opportunity under slavery. By 1869 hundreds of schools for African Americans had been established in the South. Many of the teachers were women from the North. Northerners also helped establish colleges for black southerners, including Atlanta University in Georgia, Howard University in Washington, and Fisk University in Nashville, Tennessee. Union general Samuel Chapman Armstrong, who had led African American troops in the Civil War, founded the Hampton Institute in Virginia in 1868.

The Freedmen's Bureau also helped settle contract disputes between African American laborers and white planters. In most cases the bureau encouraged laborers to continue working on plantations, even under unfavorable conditions. Two freedmen who believed that their contracts were unfair sued Mary Jones, a plantation owner. The bureau agent forced the men to go back to work. Once they returned to the plantation, Jones expressed her feelings.

> **"that in . . . doubting my word they [the African American men] had offered me the greatest insult I ever received in my life; that I had considered them friends and treated them as such . . . ; but that now they were only laborers under contract, and only the law would rule between us."**

Congress had originally intended for the Freedmen's Bureau to remain in operation for one year. In light of the congressional hearings on postwar violence, however, most members of Congress supported legislation to extend the life of the agency. African Americans largely agreed. Many thought that the Freedmen's Bureau too often encouraged former slaves to remain on plantations and to sign labor contracts. However, they acknowledged that the bureau's presence forced white southerners to recognize the emancipation of slaves. One African American told a government official that "if the Freedman Bureau was removed, a colored man would have better sense than to speak a word in behalf of the colored man's rights, for fear of his life."

Southern African Americans struggled to improve their lives after the Civil War.

HISTORY MAKERS SPEAK

General Oliver O. Howard in *In Their Own Words*

The Freedmen's Bureau. General Oliver O. Howard faced opposition from all sides. Because he insisted that the freedmen find work immediately, Republicans accused him of exchanging one slavery for another. Because he supported the rights of freed slaves, Democrats believed he was their enemy. Howard, however, believed that the Freedmen's Bureau's work was very important. He wrote, "The work of my officers in obtaining recognition of the negro as a man instead of a chattel before the civil and criminal courts took the lead. . . . In land and labor matters the Bureau found existing conditions the settlement of which would brook no delay if we were to prevent race wars or starvation; but under the title of justice was the first active endeavor to put the colored man or woman on a permanent basis on a higher plane."

CRITICAL THINKING Why might Howard have wanted freed slaves to find work immediately?

ANSWER: Students might suggest that he wanted them to prove that they were men, not "chattel."

LEVEL 3: Tell students to imagine that it is 1867 and that they are Radical Republican senators preparing to retire from Congress. Have each student write a resumé of the actions that he or she took on behalf of African Americans during the previous year. Students should preface their resumés with a brief statement explaining that they joined forces with moderate Republicans to pursue these actions. *(See the Level 1 lesson for the correct factors and actions.)* Post students' resumés and statements around the classroom.

▶**ASSIGNMENT** *Have each student write a summary of the subsection entitled Congress Versus Johnson.*

SPOTLIGHT on the Civil Rights Act of 1866

Have students closely examine the political cartoon on this page. Then pair students and ask each pair to create a political cartoon commenting on the Civil Rights Act of 1866. Have each pair write a caption for its cartoon. Then ask students to present their cartoons to the class. To conclude, conduct a brief discussion on the Civil Rights Act of 1866.

Block Scheduling, Cooperative Learning

THAT'S INTERESTING!

Philanthropists Anson M. Sperry and John W. Alford decided that a bank for freed slaves would help teach them thrift. African Americans were to set up societies to collect and deposit money in one of the Freedmen's Savings Banks. Unfortunately, when the bank was passed into the hands of a new board of directors, the money deposited there was no longer safe, and the bank eventually closed. More than 61,000 depositors lost nearly $3 million in savings.

VISUAL RECORD ANSWER

(for p. 109)

Students might suggest that the drawing reveals that the group helped maintain peace between white and black southerners.

VISUAL RECORD ANSWER

Students might mention that the poster shows a blind Liberty and a white man whipping a black man at her feet.

VISUAL RECORD ANSWER

(for p. 111)

Students might mention that the illustration shows the violence and the dead.

INTERPRETING THE VISUAL RECORD

Civil Rights Act of 1866. Despite the passage of the Civil Rights Act of 1866, many African Americans continued to suffer much as they did under slavery. ***How does this poster mock the effectiveness of the civil rights legislation?***

In an attempt to weaken the bureau, President Johnson sent two generals to tour the South in 1866. Johnson hoped that the generals would uncover complaints about the organization. Instead, they encountered widespread support among African Americans for the agency. In February 1866 Congress passed the Freedmen's Bureau Bill to extend the life of the agency. To the surprise of many, Johnson vetoed the bill, citing constitutional and financial reasons. "It was never intended that the Freedmen should be fed, clothed, educated and sheltered by the United States," he said.

The Civil Rights Act of 1866. Furious with the president, Congress promptly passed the **Civil Rights Act of 1866**, the first civil rights law in the nation's history. Although the act declared that everyone born in the United States was a citizen with full civil rights, it did not guarantee voting rights. Legislators designed the act to overturn discriminatory laws and the Supreme Court's 1857 *Dred Scott* ruling that African Americans were not citizens. "If the President vetoes the Civil Rights Bill," wrote one Ohio senator, "we shall be obliged to draw our swords."

Johnson did not heed the warning, however. He vetoed the bill, arguing that it would centralize power in the federal government. Johnson's veto eroded his support in Congress and united both moderate and Radical Republicans against him. Congress overrode Johnson's veto of the Civil Rights Act. Returning to the matter of the Freedmen's Bureau, Congress passed a new bill to extend it, and overrode yet another presidential veto.

The Fourteenth Amendment. Congressional Republicans feared that a future Congress controlled by Democrats might repeal the Civil Rights Act. They therefore wrote the act's provisions into the **Fourteenth Amendment**, passed in June 1866. The amendment required states to extend equal citizenship to African Americans and all people "born or naturalized in the United States." It also denied states the right to deprive anyone of "life, liberty, or property without due process of law." Further, it promised all citizens the "equal protection of the laws." The amendment's ratification in July 1868 granted the nation's citizens rights—enjoyed equally by all—that could be enforced by the federal government.

The Fourteenth Amendment did not guarantee African American voting rights. It did, however, reduce the number of representatives a state could send to Congress based on how many of the state's male citizens were denied the right to vote. The more African American men who were not allowed to vote, the fewer representatives that state could send to Congress. Republicans hoped that southern states would give African Americans the right to vote rather than lose their representation in Congress.

✔ **READING CHECK:** Why did moderate and Radical Republican lawmakers join forces, and what actions did they take on behalf of African Americans?

SPOTLIGHT on Andrew Johnson

Ask students to conduct research on Andrew Johnson and his Reconstruction policies. Then tell students to imagine that they are modern-day historians. Have each student give Johnson a presidential "grade" and write a one-page essay justifying that grade. Ask students to share their grades with the class. Conduct a debate on students' different assessments of Johnson's presidency. **Block Scheduling**

SPOTLIGHT on Race Riots

Tell students to imagine that it is 1866 and that they are reporters in New Orleans, Louisiana. Have each student write a short article analyzing the causes of the race riot there. Have volunteers read their articles to the class. Then tell students to imagine that they are Radical Republicans. Ask students to think of and discuss three or four ways to prevent race riots and protect African American rights. **Block Scheduling**

The Radicals Come to Power

President Johnson tried to make the Fourteenth Amendment an issue in the 1866 congressional elections. Calling the Radical Republicans traitors, he campaigned throughout the Midwest in support of candidates who opposed the amendment. Most voters were not receptive, however. Many people felt deeply troubled by the ongoing violence against African Americans in the South.

Race riots. Race riots were becoming increasingly common in the South. On May 1, 1866, two carriages collided on the streets of Memphis. When police officers arrested the African American driver but not the white one, a group of African American veterans protested. A white mob soon gathered. The resulting conflict led to a three-day spree of violence in which white rioters—consisting mainly of police officers and firefighters—killed 46 African Americans and burned 12 schools and four churches. "If anything could reveal . . . the demoniac spirit . . . toward the freedmen," one reporter noted, this violence would.

In July 1866 the Louisiana legislature called for new elections, which placed a Confederate mayor in power in New Orleans. In response, Louisiana governor James Madison Wells, a planter and former slaveholder, supported the Radical Republicans. He attempted to give African Americans the vote, to bar former Confederates from voting, and to form a new state government. His actions led to a white uprising. More than 30 African Americans and three white Republicans were killed in the resulting riot. General Philip H. Sheridan, President Johnson's military commander in Texas and Louisiana, referred to the event as "an absolute massacre."

The elections of 1866 and the Reconstruction Acts. Such violence made President Johnson's call for leniency toward the southern rebels seem particularly absurd. Johnson's campaign called for a stronger union between the North and the South. However, his speeches filled with angry protest displeased voters. While speaking in St. Louis, he even blamed Congress for the New Orleans riot. Wisconsin senator James R. Doolittle estimated that the president's campaign tour cost his candidates about 1 million votes. Fearing they might lose the fruits of their Civil War victory, northerners overwhelmingly voted Republican in 1866. Firmly in command of Congress, the Republicans, with the Radicals at the helm, seized control of the Reconstruction process.

Although the issue had previously divided their party, Republicans quickly decided that African Americans must have the vote. In January 1867 a bill granting African Americans the vote in the District of Columbia passed over Johnson's veto. Congress next extended this right to the country's territories. Despite Johnson's

PRESIDENTIAL *Lives*

Andrew Johnson

1808–1875
In Office 1865–1869

Born in North Carolina, Andrew Johnson was a self-made man who never attended school. Johnson was very young when his father died, and his mother apprenticed him to a tailor when he was 14. One person commented that the young Johnson "was very industrious and quiet, talked but little, and always had a book by his side." Later, Johnson's wife taught him to write and to do simple arithmetic.

After moving to Tennessee in 1826, Johnson did well as a tailor. Although he bought property, Johnson never identified with the planter class. His loyalties were to farmers and artisans, and he always saw himself as a political outsider. Johnson never forgot his early poverty. He continued to make all his own clothes until he went to Washington. Even after he became president, Johnson often stopped by tailor shops to chat.

INTERPRETING THE VISUAL RECORD

Race riots. In 1866 southern whites in Louisiana attacked African Americans and white Republicans. ***How does this illustration reflect the event as "an absolute massacre?"***

ACROSS THE CURRICULUM

▶SOCIOLOGY◀

Race Riots and Lynchings. For decades after the Civil War, race riots continued to break out in areas of high racial tension. Ida B. Wells-Barnett, an ardent antilynching activist, chronicled the New Orleans riot of 1892, which began when a black man, Robert Charles, shot at police officers who had for no apparent reason drawn guns on him and his friend. One police officer was killed and one was wounded. Charles then fled through the city while hundreds of white men flooded the streets in search of him. Rioters beat, shot, and killed many African Americans who crossed their paths, finally finding Charles and shooting him to death. In addition to riots, some white southerners participated in lynch mobs. Some lynchings were secret actions in the middle of the night, while others were well-publicized affairs attended by thousands.

CRITICAL THINKING How might race riots and lynchings have represented one of the unmet challenges of Reconstruction?

ANSWER: Students might suggest that although Reconstruction granted legal equality to African Americans, many white southerners were determined to prevent African Americans from achieving social equality.

TEACH OBJECTIVE 3

ALL LEVELS: To help students understand why President Johnson was impeached and why the Senate acquitted him, copy the following graphic organizer on the chalkboard, omitting the italicized answers. Ask each student to complete it. After students have completed their graphic organizers, discuss President Johnson's impeachment with the class. **Sheltered English**

The Impeachment of President Johnson

Reasons Why the House Voted to Impeach	Reasons Why the Senate Voted to Acquit
• *General dislike of Johnson's lenient Reconstruction policies*	• *Weak case against Johnson*
• *Johnson's violation of the Tenure of Office Act*	• *Hypercritical attacks on Johnson*
• *Johnson's "scandalous" speeches and "disgraceful" acts*	• *Fear that impeachment would weaken future presidents and threaten checks and balances*

HISTORY MAKERS SPEAK

Shelby M. Cullom and John Sherman in *In Their Own Words*

Impeachment Trial. Shelby M. Cullom was a moderate Republican congressman. Cullom believed that President Johnson's public behavior contributed to the House's case against him: "[Johnson] denounced Congress. He threatened to 'kick people out of office,' in violation of the Tenure of Office Act. He was undignified in his actions and language. In the end, Cullom voted for the impeachment articles, "feeling at the same time a little doubtful of our course."

CRITICAL THINKING Why might Cullom have been doubtful about his decision, even when he knew that Johnson had declared his intention to violate the Tenure of Office Act?

ANSWER: Students might suggest that Cullom may have questioned the motives behind the impeachment proceedings or the constitutionality of the act.

VISUAL RECORD ANSWER

Students might suggest that the images' solemnity reflects the importance of the event.

declaration that "old southern leaders . . . must rule the South," Republicans passed the **Reconstruction Acts** of 1867. These acts divided the former Confederacy—with the exception of already-reconstructed Tennessee—into five military districts. Union army troops were stationed in each district to enforce order. To gain re-admission to the Union, states were required to ratify the Fourteenth Amendment as well as submit to Congress new constitutions guaranteeing all men the vote. The act further required that African Americans be allowed to vote for delegates to the state constitutional conventions as well as to serve as delegates.

Presidential Impeachment

The Radical Republicans knew that the success of the Reconstruction Acts depended on their enforcement. They were equally sure that President Johnson would not cooperate. To protect Reconstruction policies and Republican office-holders, Congress passed the Tenure of Office Act in 1867. This act required Senate approval of a replacement before the president could remove an appointed official who had been confirmed by the Senate.

Believing the law unconstitutional, Johnson put it to the test. In February 1868 he removed Secretary of War Edwin Stanton, an ally of the Radical Republicans. The House of Representatives responded by voting to impeach the president. The House charged Johnson with violating the Tenure of Office Act, making "scandalous" speeches, and bringing Congress "into disgrace."

Some senators argued that such flaws were not impeachable offenses. Senator Lyman Trumbull of Illinois, a Johnson critic, predicted, "No future President will be safe who happens to differ with a majority of the House and two-thirds of the Senate." Trumbull worried that an aggressive Congress threatened the checks and balances of the Constitution. Other senators shared his fear.

The case against Johnson was weak from the start. The impeachment articles did not really address the Radical Republicans' underlying grievances against Johnson: that he was unfair, governed poorly, and tried to halt Congress's plan for Reconstruction. Many members of Congress even feared that Johnson might lead the country into another civil war.

Johnson's Senate trial began in March 1868. Seven members of the House of Representatives stated the case for impeachment. These representatives were so critical in their attack, however, that public opinion began to turn against them. One representative even waved a blood-stained nightshirt that he asserted came from a white northerner who had been beaten by southerners. Within a month, some prominent people were calling for Johnson's acquittal. A writer for the *Nation* claimed that the House had made Johnson a villain without proving any charges.

The trial lasted eight weeks, unfolding in front of a gallery of eager spectators. On May 16, 1868, the Senate voted to acquit the president. The final tally fell one vote short of the two-thirds majority needed to convict Johnson and remove him

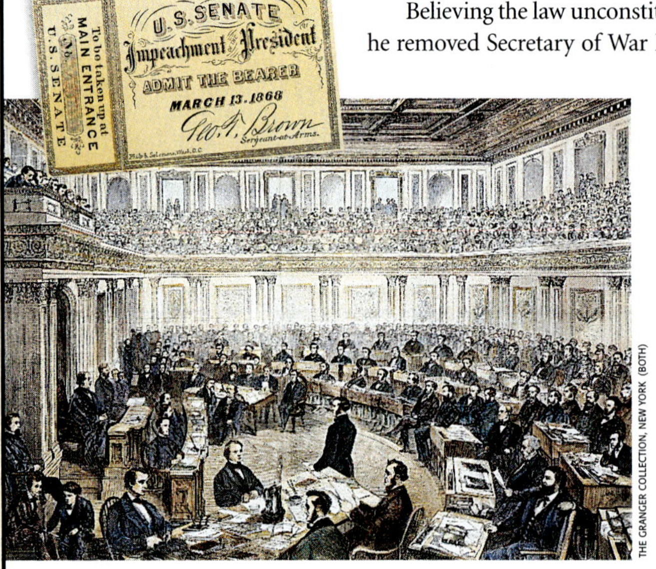

THE GRANGER COLLECTION, NEW YORK (BOTH)

INTERPRETING THE VISUAL RECORD

Impeachment. Admittance to President Johnson's impeachment was limited. Visitors and reporters were required to present a ticket to gain entry to the Senate gallery. ***How do these images reflect the importance and drama of the event?***

TEACH OBJECTIVE 4

LEVEL 1: Pair students and tell them to imagine that they are magazine editors preparing a special issue on the history of U.S. elections. Have each pair create an outline on the election of 1868 and its aftereffects. Students' outlines should explain why African Americans were crucial to this election and how Republicans responded to their support. *(African American votes helped Ulysses S. Grant win the presidency. The Republicans responded by passing the Fifteenth Amendment to extend the vote to African American men.)* Students may wish to include their outlines in their portfolios. **Sheltered English, Cooperative Learning**

LEVELS 2 AND 3: Ask students to reread the quotation on this page. Then tell students to imagine that it is the week before the election of 1868 and that they are Republicans. Have each student write a half-page speech persuading African Americans to vote for Republicans despite intimidation in the South. Then tell students to imagine that it is the week after the election. Have each student write a half-page speech informing African Americans how the Republican Party intends to respond to their support. *(See the Level 1 lesson for the correct responses.)* Ask volunteers to read their speeches to the class.

from office. Risking the disapproval of their party and their constituents, seven Republican senators had joined 12 Democratic senators to vote for acquittal. The entire proceedings, concluded Republican senator Joseph Smith Fowler of Tennessee, had become "mere politics." The ordeal, however, took a toll on many of the legislators. Iowa senator James W. Grimes suffered a stroke after his constituents denounced him as a traitor for supporting the president. More importantly, with 35 senators from his own party against him, Johnson's power was broken.

✔ **READING CHECK:** Why was President Johnson impeached, and why did the Senate fail to remove him from office?

PRESIDENTIAL *Lives*

Ulysses S. Grant

1822–1885
In Office 1869–1877

Born in Ohio, Ulysses S. Grant graduated from the U.S. Military Academy at West Point in 1843 but had no intentions of making a career of military service. "A military life had no charms for me, and I had not the faintest idea of staying in the army even if I should be graduated, which I did not expect." Contrary to his expectations, Grant stayed in the army until 1854.

Grant was plagued by failure after resigning his commission. He drifted through a series of jobs, including peddling firewood and collecting rents. He tried his hand at farming without much success. His financial problems were such that in 1857 Grant was forced to pawn his gold watch for $22. When the Civil War broke out in 1861, Grant was almost 39 years old and clerking at his family's leather-goods store in Galena, Illinois. He returned to the army as a colonel and at last found success. His presidency followed in 1869.

After leaving office, Grant and his wife toured the world for more than two years. Back in New York, he unsuccessfully tried to make his fortune in business. He had just completed writing his memoirs when he died in 1885.

Further Political Difficulties

The Radical Republicans' attempt to force President Johnson from office as well as their emphasis on African American suffrage cost them some popular support. Many voters had grown tired of the problems posed by Reconstruction. Some northern legislatures even joined the voices opposing African American voting rights.

The election of 1868. As the 1868 election neared, the Radical Republicans sensed trouble. To retain voters, they nominated General Ulysses S. Grant for president. General Grant lacked political experience but was a popular war hero.

The Democrats chose former New York governor Horatio Seymour to run against Grant. Seymour had sharply criticized the Lincoln administration during the Civil War. Secretary of State William Henry Seward noted that the Democrats "could have nominated no candidate who would have taken away fewer Republican votes." Seymour's running mate, Francis Preston Blair, further diminished Seymour's chances when he pursued a campaign strategy based on white supremacy.

Southern Democrats relied on economic threats against African Americans to keep them from voting for the Republicans. One white Democrat addressed African Americans.

> "We have the capital and give employment. We own the lands and require labor to make them productive. . . . You desire to be employed. . . . We know we can do without you. We think you will find it very difficult to do without us. . . . We have the wealth."

Despite such tactics, new African American voters supported the Republican ticket. Grant defeated Seymour in a very close race, and Republicans realized that African American voters had given them their narrow win.

Southern Democrat officials such as the election judge shown in this engraving often prevented African Americans from voting for Republican candidates.

ACROSS THE CURRICULUM

▶POLITICAL SCIENCE◀

Thomas Nast's Political Cartoons. For more than 20 years Thomas Nast sketched political cartoons for a popular magazine called *Harper's Weekly.* Nast's cutting cartoons showed his support for Radical Republicans and often made fun of Andrew Johnson and the Democrats. To make his points in the briefest way possible, Nast often created symbols to represent groups or ideas. For example, Nast invented the animal symbols that the major political parties still use today: the Republican elephant and the Democratic donkey.

ACTIVITY: Have each student draw an editorial cartoon depicting a Reconstruction-era issue.

VISUAL RECORD ANSWER

(for p. 114)

Students might suggest that they conveyed a sense of patriotism and signaled wider political inclusion.

SECTION 2 REVIEW ANSWERS

Define and Identify

For significance, see the following pages:

- Thaddeus Stevens, p. 107
- Frederick Douglass, p. 107
- Freedmen's Bureau, p. 109
- Civil Rights Act of 1866, p. 110

REVIEW

Have students complete the **Section 2 Review** on p. 114.

ASSESS

Have students complete **Daily Quiz 3.2**. As **Alternative Assessment**, you may want to use the Republican Party resumé or the election of 1868 outline in this section's lessons.

RETEACH

Have students complete **Main Idea Activity for Reteaching and Sheltered English 3.2**. Then assign each student one of the subsections in Section 2. Have students write four questions about the material in their subsections. Then distribute the questions to students, making sure that no one receives his or her own, and ask them to answer the questions. Have students return their questions to the author, who should check them and correct them, if necessary. **Sheltered English**

EXTEND

Have students conduct research on President Johnson's response to his impeachment trial. Then tell students to imagine that they are Johnson on the day after their vindication. Have each student write a speech responding to the trial and expressing his or her feelings about the acquittal. Have volunteers deliver their speeches to the class. **Block Scheduling**

- Fourteenth Amendment, p. 110
- Reconstruction Acts, p. 112
- Ulysses S. Grant, p. 113
- Fifteenth Amendment, p. 114

1. Freedman's Bureau Bill—supported operation of the Freedman's Bureau; Civil Rights Act of 1866—declared everyone born in the U.S. a citizen with full rights; Fourteenth Amendment—gave all citizens equal citizenship and equal protection; Reconstruction Acts—divided South into military districts and required states to give black men the right to vote; Tenure of Office Act of 1867—required president to obtain Senate approval before removing an official confirmed by the Senate; Fifteenth Amendment—gave African American men the right to vote

2. African American voting rights; Johnson's veto of the Freedman's Bureau Bill and the Civil Rights Act of 1866

3. Fourteenth Amendment—required states to extend equal citizenship to all people and promised equal protection under law—Fifteenth Amendment gave African American men the vote

4. Answers will vary. Some students might suggest that white men could more easily accept giving the vote to men than to all women.

5. Some students might say yes because Johnson was limiting attempts to improve conditions in the South.

INTERPRETING THE VISUAL RECORD

Celebration. This poster was created to celebrate the passage of the Fifteenth Amendment. ***What might be the significance of the flags at the top of the poster?***

The Fifteenth Amendment. Eager to protect their power in the North as well as in the South, the Republicans drafted the **Fifteenth Amendment**. It stated, "The right of citizens of the United States to vote shall not be denied or abridged by the United States or by any state on account of race, color, or previous condition of servitude."

The passage of the Fifteenth Amendment in February 1869 and its subsequent ratification in 1870 brought triumph to African Americans and Radical Republicans. Abolitionist William Lloyd Garrison rejoiced in "this wonderful, quiet, sudden transformation of four millions of human beings from . . . the auction-block to the ballot-box." The amendment failed to guarantee African Americans the right to hold office, however. It also did not prevent states from limiting the voting rights of African Americans through discriminatory requirements.

Significantly, the Fifteenth Amendment failed to extend the vote to women. Women's rights leaders, most of them former abolitionists, had split over the amendment. Arguing that "this hour belongs to the negro," one group had urged women to postpone the more controversial women's suffrage issue so as not to endanger passage of the amendment. Elizabeth Cady Stanton replied: "My question is this: Do you believe the African race is composed entirely of males?" Stanton and others opposed ratification of the Fifteenth Amendment until all women were also given the vote. The bitter debate over the amendment alienated many African American women from the women's movement.

✔ **READING CHECK:** Why were African Americans crucial to the presidential election of 1868, and how did Republicans respond to their support?

SECTION 2 REVIEW

Define and explain the significance of the following terms:
Freedmen's Bureau
Civil Rights Act of 1866
Fourteenth Amendment
Reconstruction Acts
Fifteenth Amendment

Identify and explain the significance of the following individuals:
Thaddeus Stevens
Frederick Douglass
Ulysses S. Grant

1. **Using Graphic Organizers** Copy the graphic organizer below. Use it to describe the major legislation that Congress passed to implement its plan for Reconstruction.

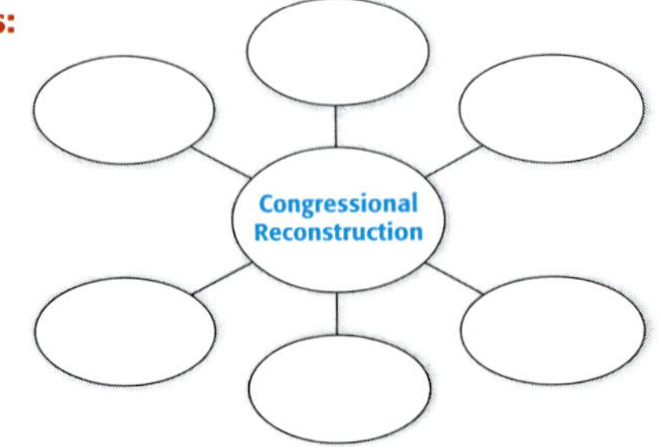

2. **Identifying Cause and Effect** What issues divided the Republican Party in the 1860s? What actions of President Johnson served to unite the party?
3. **Evaluating** What rights did the Fourteenth and Fifteenth Amendments guarantee for African Americans?
4. **Recognizing Point of View** In what way was the passage of the Fifteenth Amendment a reaction by the Republican Party to the results of the election of 1868?

Critical Thinking

5. Was Congress justified in its effort to remove President Johnson from office? Explain your answer.
Consider:
- why Congress impeached President Johnson
- what Johnson's defense was
- if the conflict could have been resolved any other way

SECTION 3

After completing Section 3, students should be able to:

OBJECTIVE 1 *Explain how African Americans attempted to improve their lives during the Reconstruction era.*

OBJECTIVE 2 *Identify Republican reforms.*

OBJECTIVE 3 *Relate how some African Americans responded to harassment by the Ku Klux Klan.*

OBJECTIVE 4 *Describe why Reconstruction ended.*

LET'S GET STARTED!

Write the following question on the chalkboard: *Some historians have described the effects of Reconstruction as "revolutionary." What political, economic, and social changes would you expect from a "revolutionary" era?* As students enter the classroom, ask them to respond to the question in writing. Have volunteers share their responses. Then tell students that in Section 3 they will learn about the effects of Reconstruction in the South.

Reconstruction in the South

OBJECTIVES

Read to understand:

1. how African Americans attempted to improve their lives during the Reconstruction era
2. what reforms the Republican governments enacted
3. how some African Americans responded to harassment by the Ku Klux Klan
4. what caused Reconstruction to end

KEY TERMS

carpetbaggers
scalawags
Ku Klux Klan
Enforcement Acts
Panic of 1873
Civil Rights Act of 1875
Redeemers
Compromise of 1877

KEY PEOPLE

Samuel J. Tilden
Rutherford B. Hayes

"The people of New Orleans witnessed last night one of the noblest scenes of which an American city can boast, . . . a phalanx [group] of freemen walking the streets with national colors flying and transparencies enunciating [spelling out] the principles of a free government."

—*New Orleans Tribune*

African Americans enjoying the right to vote

The African American newspaper the *New Orleans Tribune* described the festivities that took place in May 1867 after the passage of the Reconstruction Acts. The evening ended with skyrockets and dancing in the streets. "This marks a new and glorious era in our history," the newspaper proudly declared.

African American Activism

With the passage of the Reconstruction Acts, African Americans saw a new era begin. The rise of Congressional Reconstruction gave the former slaves further hope for equal citizenship. Many registered to vote and began lobbying for the equality promised by the Civil Rights Act and the Fourteenth Amendment. Even the churches found that "politics got in our midst" and overtook "our revival or religious work," according to one African American minister.

African Americans joined political groups such as the Union League. Begun in the North as a patriotic club, the league spread the views of the Republican Party to freed slaves as well as to poor whites. In addition to sponsoring political activity, the Union League built schools and churches for African Americans and helped care for the sick. African American education and literacy expanded greatly during Reconstruction. White northerners founded many schools, but African Americans launched educational institutions as well. The league also provided African Americans with a place to develop their political skills. After literate members read newspapers aloud, everyone present debated the issues of the day. "We just went there," explained one Union League member, "and we talked a little; made speeches on one question and another."

Desiring to create a better life for themselves, African Americans established schools and other institutions that served freed slaves.

As African Americans became more involved in politics, they served as delegates to all the state constitutional conventions. In Louisiana and South Carolina, African American delegates outnumbered whites. In other states they made up 10 to 40 percent of the delegates. Although many of these new delegates were black southerners, northern African Americans participated as well.

✔ **READING CHECK:** How did African Americans attempt to improve their lives during the Reconstruction era?

SECTION 3 RESOURCES

PRINT

- Guided Reading Strategy 3.3
- Graphic Organizer Activity 3: Evaluating Reconstruction
- Section 3 Review, p. 119
- Daily Quiz 3.3

MULTIMEDIA

- One-Stop Planner, Lesson 3.3
- Holt Researcher: American History CD–ROM
- HRW Web site

SHELTERED ENGLISH

- Main Idea Activity for Reteaching and Sheltered English 3.3

✔ READING TO UNDERSTAND

To help students master the section objectives, have them answer the **READING CHECKS** and complete **Guided Reading Strategy 3.3** as they read the section.

TEACH OBJECTIVES 1 AND 3

ALL LEVELS: Conduct a class discussion on the ways in which African Americans tried to improve their lives during Reconstruction and the ways in which some African Americans responded to harassment by the Ku Klux Klan. To help students understand these issues, copy the following graphic organizer on the chalkboard, omitting the italicized answers. Have each student complete it. **Sheltered English**

Efforts to Improve Lives
- *registered to vote*
- *joined and formed political organizations*
- *lobbied for political equality*
- *built churches and schools*
- *served as delegates to state constitutional conventions*

African American Life During Reconstruction

Responses to Ku Klux Klan
- *retaliated by burning barns*
- *lobbied for congressional protection*

PEOPLE IN HISTORY

Blanche K. Bruce. Blanche K. Bruce was one of the first African American U.S. senators, serving for Mississippi from 1875 to 1881. Before his election to the Senate, Bruce was an educator and entrepreneur and was well respected among his colleagues. A fellow politician wrote that Bruce and other black congressmen "were as a rule studious, earnest, ambitious men, whose public conduct . . . would be honorable to any race." Bruce was not re-elected to the Senate in 1881 because Democrats had regained control of the South. He continued working in government, however, becoming the first African American register of the treasury under President Garfield and briefly under President McKinley.

CRITICAL THINKING Why might the Democrats' "redemption" of the South have affected Bruce's election to the Senate?

ANSWER: Students might suggest that in "redeeming" the South, the Democrats displaced many black voters and officials.

VISUAL RECORD ANSWER

Students might mention that the cartoon shows carpetbaggers riding to power on the back of a woman who represents the South.

INTERPRETING THE VISUAL RECORD

Carpetbaggers. Many southerners believed that northerners had come to impose their ideas and way of life on the South. ***How is this belief expressed in this cartoon?***

Reconstruction Governments

The arrival of northern Republicans—both whites and African Americans—eager to participate in the state conventions increased resentment among many white southerners. They called these northern Republicans **carpetbaggers**. The newcomers, they joked, were "needy adventurers" of "the lowest class" who could carry everything they owned in a carpetbag—a type of cheap suitcase.

Former Confederates heaped even greater scorn on southern whites who had backed the Union cause and now supported Reconstruction. They called these whites **scalawags**, or scoundrels. They viewed them as "southern renegades, betrayers of their race and country."

Reconstruction supporters soon formed a Republican alliance. Although they disagreed on issues such as land reform, they saw themselves as the "party of progress, and civilization." They hoped to seize economic and political power from the planters and then rebuild the South, improving conditions for poor white farmers and African Americans alike.

The Republican alliance used its political leverage to draft new state constitutions. The Republican state governments abolished property qualifications for jurors and political candidates. They also guaranteed white and African American men the right to vote. Once Congress approved the new constitutions, state legislators raised taxes to finance new road, bridge, and railroad construction as well as to increase services, such as free public education.

✔ **READING CHECK:** What reforms did the Republican governments enact?

The Ku Klux Klan

The Reconstruction governments' reforms, the election of African Americans to office, and African Americans' growing political participation were soon met by a vicious response. Angry white southerners formed secret terrorist groups to prevent African Americans from voting. One such group, the **Ku Klux Klan**, was founded in 1866 by six former Confederates. The organization grew quickly, attracting planters, lawyers, and other professionals, as well as poor farmers and laborers.

Concealing their identity with hoods and robes, Klan members used threats and violence to prevent African Americans from voting.

Klan attacks. The head of the Klan—"Grand Wizard" Nathan Bedford Forrest, a former slave-trader and Confederate general—bluntly warned Republicans that he intended "to kill the radicals." This was no idle threat. The Klan and similar groups were determined to destroy the Republican Party, to keep African Americans from voting, and to frighten African American political leaders into submission. The Klan murdered or attacked many Republican legislators and leaders—both white and black. Klan members also attacked African Americans who voted for Republican candidates.

The Klan did not limit its attacks to politically active African American and white Republicans, however. Klansmen assaulted and killed thousands of African Americans whom they regarded as too successful. One North Carolina freedman recalled the words of the Klansmen who had beaten him:

TEACH OBJECTIVE 2

LEVEL 1: Pair students and tell them to imagine that they are Republican officials in the South. Have each pair create two or three banners with slogans that describe reforms enacted by Republican governments. *(Pairs' banners should mention two or three of the following: the creation of new state constitutions, the abolition of property qualifications for jurors and candidates, the creation of new services, and the establishment of new roads and bridges.)* Ask volunteers to present and discuss their banners with the class.
Sheltered English, Cooperative Learning

LEVELS 2 AND 3: Tell students to imagine that they are Republican officials in the South. Have each student write a short political platform describing Republican reforms in the region. *(See the Level 1 lesson for the correct reforms.)* Ask volunteers to read their platforms to the class.

TEACH OBJECTIVE 4

LEVEL 1: Pair students and tell them to imagine that it is 1878 and that they are southern African Americans. Have each pair develop a short dialogue describing the factors that ended the Reconstruction era. *(Pairs' dialogues should discuss general economic problems, the Panic of 1873, the reaction to rising immigration, the actions of the southern Redeemers, and the Compromise of 1877.)* Ask volunteers to perform their dialogues for the class.
Sheltered English, Cooperative Learning

> "[They] told me the law—their law, that whenever I met a white person, no matter who he was, whether he was poor or rich, I was to take off my hat."

Klansmen also burned homes, schools, and churches, and stole livestock in an effort to chase African Americans and pro-Reconstruction whites from the South.

Steps against the Klan. African Americans struck back at the Klan when possible. Often able to recognize their tormentors by voices and other physical characteristics—despite the members' hoods and long robes—some African Americans retaliated by burning barns of Klansmen. More often, African Americans gathered in defense of an intended victim. Residents of the African American town of Avery, Alabama, learned that Klan members planned to burn their schoolhouse. "Let them come," declared Miles Prior, who organized a group of armed men. "Fifty men couldn't burn that schoolhouse and let me live." The Klansmen backed down and left the schoolhouse intact.

As the violence mounted, African Americans demanded that Congress act to "enable us to exercise the rights of citizens." Congress responded to this call in 1870 and 1871 by passing legislation designed to stop violence against African Americans. Known as the **Enforcement Acts**, these three laws empowered the federal government to combat terrorism with military force and to prosecute guilty individuals. The Democrats called them the Force Acts and claimed that they threatened individual freedom.

✔ **READING CHECK:** How did some African Americans respond to harassment by the Ku Klux Klan?

Changes in Reconstruction

For a time the federal government's intervention brought a dramatic decline in Ku Klux Klan violence. However, the attention of Republicans increasingly turned toward national economic issues and political corruption in the North. Gradually the interest of Republicans in Reconstruction faded.

Shifting Republican interests. A particularly severe economic depression, known as the **Panic of 1873**, hit the nation. Republican leaders came under pressure as workers threatened strikes and farmers demanded relief. The partnership between antilabor, northern businesspeople—who formed the core of the Republican Party—and the freed slaves had never been a stable one. Soon it dissolved altogether.

Republicans also abandoned universal voting rights as thousands of immigrants joined the Democratic Party. Some Republicans claimed that universal suffrage "cheapened the ballot." Their calls to restrict the voting rights of immigrants and the urban poor weakened public support for African Americans' rights as well.

Interpretations of Reconstruction

BY OTEY SCRUGGS

For a century afterward, the standard interpretation of Reconstruction among historians was that northern "carpetbaggers," southern "scalawags," and uneducated African Americans combined to impose tyrannical rule over the defeated South. They forced southern whites to organize groups like the Ku Klux Klan in order to overturn corrupt Republican state governments. This view became permanently stamped on the popular mind through the 1915 film *Birth of a Nation.* African American historian W. E. B. Du Bois challenged this interpretation in his monumental 1935 study, *Black Reconstruction in America.* The civil rights movement of the 1950s and 1960s completely overturned the older historical view of Reconstruction.

More recent interpretations tend to analyze the intersection between economic forces—land, labor, and transportation—and the political process. Not only were the ex-slaves guaranteed political and civil rights, recent historians note, but some steps were also taken toward economic justice. Central in the new explanation is the assertive role played by African Americans themselves. Some historians argue that it was the fear that African Americans would leave their assigned place at the bottom of the sociopolitical structure that really ended Reconstruction.

TECHNOLOGY AND SOCIETY

Film and the Birth of a Myth. Southern Democrats, in their desire to return to the South's pre-Civil War social structure, helped to build myths about Reconstruction. These myths portrayed carpetbaggers as corrupt exploiters and freed slaves as either violent, lazy, or childlike. D. W. Griffith's 1915 film, *The Birth of a Nation,* contributed to this mythology and reinforced racist ideas of black inferiority and white supremacy. Based on Thomas Dixon's novel *The Clansman,* the movie portrayed black government officials as buffoons and most freedmen as lusting after white women. Griffith's heroes are members of the KKK who ride in on horses to restore the social order. *The Birth of a Nation* was the first movie to cost more than $100,000 to produce and the first ever to be shown at the White House.

CRITICAL THINKING How might *The Birth of a Nation* have affected people's ideas about Reconstruction?

ANSWER: Students might suggest that the movie blurred the distinction between myth and historical fact.

LEVELS 2 AND 3: Tell students to imagine that they are modern-day historians. Have each student write a one-page summary describing the factors that ended the Reconstruction era. *(See the Level 1 lesson for the correct factors.)* Have volunteers read their summaries to the class. Then have students select what they consider to be the most significant factor. If students' opinions differ, conduct a debate on the issue.

▶**ASSIGNMENT** *Distribute Activity 3, Evaluating Reconstruction, from* ***Graphic Organizer Activities****, and have each student complete it.*

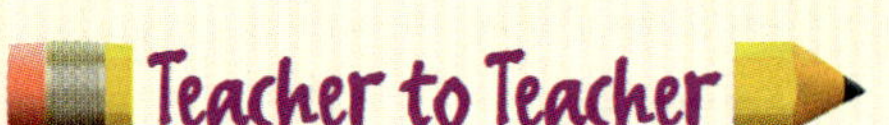

Barbara Harbour of Detroit, Michigan, suggested the following activity: Ask students to consider the effectiveness of the Reconstruction era by examining its social, political, and economic policies and implications. Have each student write a brief essay on the topic.

THAT'S INTERESTING!

James T. Rapier, an African American who had recently represented the United States at the World's Fair in Paris, urged the House of Representatives to pass the Civil Rights Act of 1875. "I submit that I am degraded as long as I am denied the public privileges common to other men, and the members of this House are correspondingly degraded by recognizing my political equality while I occupy such a humiliating position. . . . I feel this humiliation very keenly; it dwarfs my manhood, and certainly it impairs my usefulness as a citizen."

internetconnect

TOPIC: African American Reconstruction
GO TO: go.hrw.com
KEYWORD: SE1 Reconstruction

Have students access the Internet through the HRW Web site to conduct research on Reconstruction as well as notable African Americans of that period. Then have each student write an informative essay that explains the different phases of Reconstruction as well as African Americans' contributions to this period.

MAP ANSWER
Tennessee

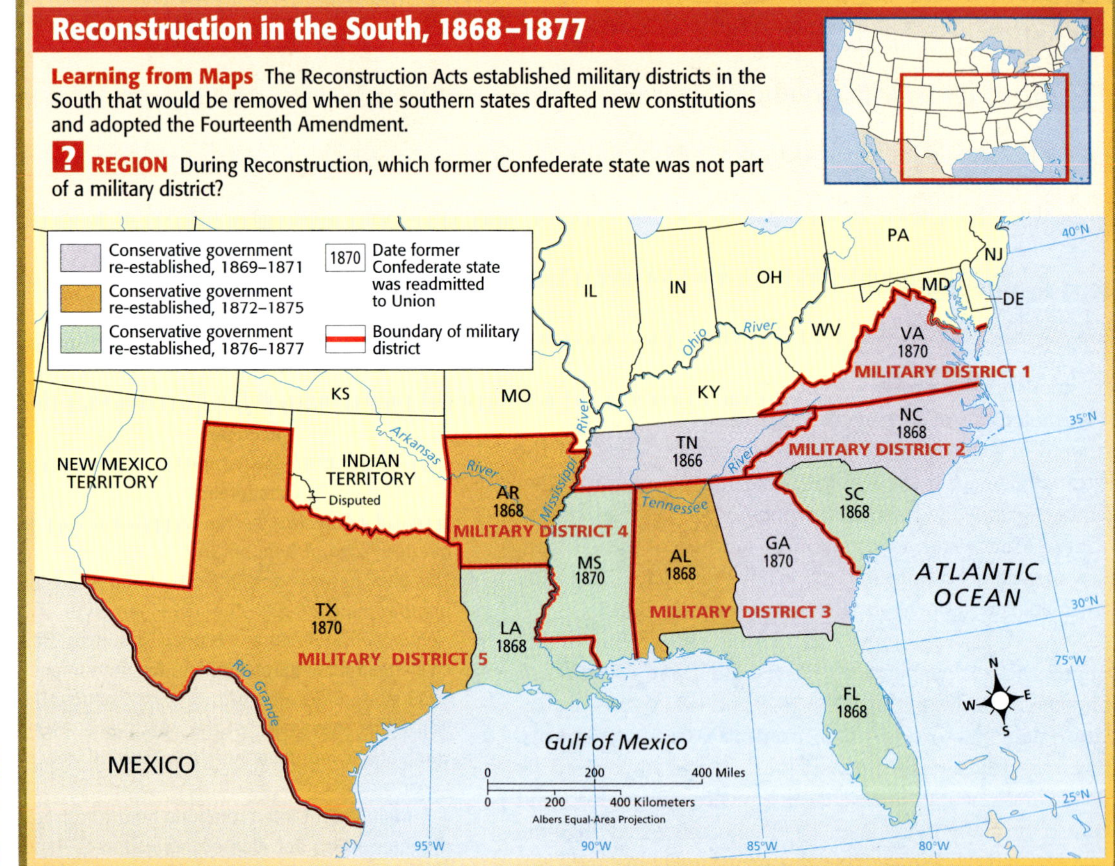

Reconstruction in the South, 1868–1877

Learning from Maps The Reconstruction Acts established military districts in the South that would be removed when the southern states drafted new constitutions and adopted the Fourteenth Amendment.

? REGION During Reconstruction, which former Confederate state was not part of a military district?

As Republican attention shifted away from Reconstruction, southern African Americans faced increasing violence.

The southern Redeemers. The discontent caused by the Panic of 1873 turned voters against the Republican-controlled Congress. In the 1874 congressional elections Democrats gained dozens of seats in the House, giving them a 60-seat majority. In the South the Democrats attracted white voters with promises of lower taxes and through appeals to white supremacy.

When Congress reconvened, Republicans made one final effort to enforce Reconstruction by enacting the **Civil Rights Act of 1875**. This bill prohibited businesses that served the public—such as hotels and transportation facilities—from discriminating against African Americans. However, white Republican supporters of the bill had begun to see Reconstruction as a political burden.

Many southern white Democrats reached the same conclusion. Convinced that the federal government would not stop them, Mississippi Democrats used terrorism to win the 1875 state elections. In Clay County, against a backdrop of Confederate flags, white Democrats shot and killed several African Americans who declared their intention of voting Republican. The next year Democrats in Louisiana and South Carolina adopted similar tactics to "redeem," or win back, their states from the Republicans. These supporters of white-controlled governments called themselves the **Redeemers**.

In 1876 the Redeemers focused on the presidential election, which pitted Democrat Samuel J. Tilden of New York against Republican Rutherford B. Hayes

REVIEW

Have students complete the **Section 3 Review** on p. 119.

ASSESS

Have students complete **Daily Quiz 3.3.** As **Alternative Assessment,** you may want to use the set of banners or the Reconstruction dialogue in this section's lessons.

RETEACH

Have students complete **Main Idea Activity for Reteaching and Sheltered English 3.3.** Then ask each student to outline Section 3. Ask volunteers to share their work and create a comprehensive outline on the chalkboard. Review the outline with students and ask them to determine likely short-answer and essay questions. **Sheltered English**

EXTEND

Have students conduct research on Reconstruction governments before "redemption." Ask students to pick one government. Then have each student write a two-to-three-page essay describing the actions of the selected government and evaluating its effectiveness. Students may wish to include their essays in their portfolios. **Block Scheduling**

---

of Ohio. Opponents of Reconstruction vowed to win the election even "if we have to wade in blood knee-deep." In the popular vote they succeeded: Tilden beat Hayes by some 250,000 votes. The electoral vote was another story.

The election results in four states were challenged by various parties. A commission set up to rule on the validity of the returns gave Hayes the presidency by one electoral vote. Democrats in the House protested. To defuse the crisis, leading Republicans and southern Democrats struck a deal—the **Compromise of 1877**. In return for the Democrats' acceptance of Hayes as president, the Republicans agreed to withdraw the remaining federal troops from the South.

Denied federal protection, the last of the Reconstruction governments fell. Once in power, the Redeemers rewrote state constitutions and overturned many of the Reconstruction governments' reforms. African American Charles Harris, a former legislator from Alabama, protested,

> **"We obey laws; others make them. We support state educational institutions, whose doors are virtually closed against us. . . . From these and many other oppressions . . . our people long to be free."**

✔ **READING CHECK:** What caused the Reconstruction era come to an end?

Great Debates

Reconstruction

The relative successes and failures of Reconstruction have long been debated by scholars. In many ways, Reconstruction did not accomplish its goals. The failure of land-reform efforts allowed white planters to maintain control over many southern institutions. Southern African Americans saw little economic improvement because the basic economic structure of the South remained intact. They also achieved few lasting civil and political rights.

The new state constitutions adopted in the South during the Reconstruction era, however, did help reform the states' judicial and legislative systems. African American leaders also created institutions—churches, schools, and strong family networks—that helped sustain black communities through the difficult post-Reconstruction years. The Reconstruction era also left a legal legacy. Although they were rarely enforced for almost a century, the Civil Rights Act of 1866 and the Fourteenth and Fifteenth Amendments provided an important legal framework that enabled later civil rights leaders to win back voting rights for African Americans and to end legal segregation.

SECTION 3 REVIEW

Define and explain the significance of the following terms:
carpetbaggers
scalawags
Ku Klux Klan
Enforcement Acts
Panic of 1873
Civil Rights Act of 1875
Redeemers
Compromise of 1877

Identify and explain the significance of the following individuals:
Samuel J. Tilden
Rutherford B. Hayes

1. **Using Graphic Organizers** Copy the graphic organizer below. Use it to describe the similarities and differences between the tactics of the Ku Klux Klan and the Redeemers, and how African Americans responded to the groups.

2. **Evaluating** What role did African Americans play in shaping Reconstruction?
3. **Assessing Consequences** How did the Republican governments change legislation in southern states?
4. **Hypothesizing** What special abilities and knowledge might African American legislators have been able to bring to the new southern governments?

Critical Thinking

5. How and why did Reconstruction fail to achieve its goals?
Consider:
- what the goals of Reconstruction were
- what events and issues ended Reconstruction
- what goals were left unmet

SECTION 3 REVIEW ANSWERS

Define and Identify
For significance, see the following pages:
- carpetbaggers, p. 116
- scalawags, p. 116
- Ku Klux Klan, p. 116
- Enforcement Acts, p. 117
- Panic of 1873, p. 117
- Civil Rights Act of 1875, p. 118
- Redeemers, p. 118
- Samuel J. Tilden, p. 118
- Rutherford B. Hayes, p. 118
- Compromise of 1877, p. 119

1. similarities—terrorized and killed people to achieve their ends; differences—unlike the Klan, the Redeemers operated in the open, often as government officials. African Americans responded by burning barns of Klansmen or gathering in defense of an intended victim.

2. joined political groups and tried to vote for candidates who supported their rights; opened churches and schools to educate black children

3. It helped extend voting rights, raised taxes for transportation and education, and abolished property qualifications for jurors and political candidates.

4. Answers will vary. Students might suggest that African Americans could pinpoint specific areas where their rights were violated to draft viable legislation.

5. Answers will vary. Students might indicate that the economic depression in 1873 refocused legislators' energy and allowed Democrats to gain control of Congress.

SECTION 4

After completing Section 4, students should be able to:

OBJECTIVE 1 *Analyze the drawbacks to the sharecropping system.*

OBJECTIVE 2 *Assess how Jim Crow laws and the* Plessy v. Ferguson *decision changed life for southern African Americans.*

OBJECTIVE 3 *Explain how African Americans attempted to improve their economic situation after Reconstruction.*

OBJECTIVE 4 *Compare the views of Booker T. Washington and Ida B. Wells.*

LET'S GET STARTED!

Write the following question on the chalkboard: *Is freedom without equality really freedom?* As students enter the classroom, ask them to respond to the question in writing. Have volunteers share their responses. Then tell students that in Section 4 they will learn about conditions in the post-Reconstruction South and how African Americans responded to those conditions.

SECTION 4 RESOURCES

PRINT

- Guided Reading Strategy 3.4
- Geography Activity 3: Tenant Farming and Sharecropping
- Literature Reading 3: The Cruelty of Jim Crow Laws
- Biography Reading 3: Ida B. Wells-Barnett
- Section 4 Review, p. 125
- Daily Quiz 3.4

MULTIMEDIA

- One-Stop Planner, Lesson 3.4
- The American Nation Video Program Segment: The Tuskegee Institute; Teacher's Guide, pp. 63–68
- Holt Researcher: American History CD–ROM

SHELTERED ENGLISH

- Main Idea Activity for Reteaching and Sheltered English 3.4

✔ READING TO UNDERSTAND

To help students master the section objectives, have them answer the **READING CHECKS** and complete **Guided Reading Strategy 3.4** as they read the section.

The New South

OBJECTIVES

Read to understand:

1. what the drawbacks were to the sharecropping system
2. how Jim Crow laws and the *Plessy* v. *Ferguson* decision changed life for southern African Americans
3. how African Americans attempted to improve their economic situation after Reconstruction
4. how Booker T. Washington and Ida B. Wells differed in their opinions of how African Americans should respond to Jim Crow laws

KEY TERMS

sharecropping
crop-lien system
poll taxes
literacy tests
segregation
Jim Crow laws
Plessy v. *Ferguson*

KEY PEOPLE

Madame C. J. Walker
Booker T. Washington
Ida B. Wells

“[Former slaves exhibit] a growing dislike to being controlled by or working for white men. They prefer to get a little patch where they can do as they choose.”

—Anonymous white farmer

Former slave tending to the family garden

This Tennessee planter noted the increasing desire among freedpeople to own their own land. Frances Leigh, another planter, remarked that as soon as her field hands were paid, many of them purchased small plots of land, usually in the pine woods “where the land was so poor they could not raise a peck of corn to the acre.” Although Leigh thought the field hands had been cheated in these land deals, she could not help but notice the enthusiasm the African American farmers brought to their new lives under freedom.

Changing Economies in the South

Some southern planters lost their lands after the Civil War because they could not pay their debts or their taxes. Most of their lands fell into the hands of other planters or northern investors.

Sharecropping. Whether planters were southerners or northerners, however, all were faced with labor shortages. Few whites or former slaves wanted to work for the low wages planters were willing—or, in many cases, able—to pay.

Some planters solved their labor problems with **sharecropping**. Under this system a farmer worked a parcel of land in return for a share of the crop, a cabin, seed, tools, and a mule. Sharecropping enabled planters to get their lands worked when they did not have enough cash to pay laborers. Sharecropping gave laborers a place to live and lands to work without close supervision. By the end of the 1870s many poor white southerners and the majority of African Americans in the South worked as sharecroppers.

The arrangement had a serious drawback, however. Sharecroppers had no income until harvest time. To obtain needed supplies each year, they had to promise their crops to local merchants who then sold them goods on credit. Any outstanding debts were added to their bills the following year. This arrangement was known as the **crop-lien system**. A lien is a creditor's legal claim on the debtor's property.

In effect, the system made it impossible for sharecroppers to work their way out of poverty or to gain independence. Former slave Thomas Hall judged the system to be “little better than slavery.” The crop-lien system kept the southern economy tied primarily to one-crop agriculture. Merchants gave credit only to farmers who grew certain crops, most often cotton. As a result, cotton displaced other crops to such an extent that the South had to import food and animal feed from the North.

✔ READING CHECK: What were the drawbacks of the sharecropping system?

African American families like this one suffered under the sharecropping and crop-lien systems.

TEACH OBJECTIVE 1

LEVEL 1: Pair students and tell them to imagine that they are African American sharecroppers who have decided to protest the system. Have each pair create two or three protest signs detailing the drawbacks to the sharecropping system. *(Pairs should note that sharecroppers had no income until harvest time, forcing them to participate in the crop-lien system. Pairs should also note that sharecropping required farmers to concentrate on one crop only, leaving them and the region dangerously dependent on outside suppliers for human and animal food.)* Have each pair present its protest signs to the class. Then display the signs around the classroom.
Sheltered English, Cooperative Learning

LEVEL 2: Tell students to imagine that they are African American sharecroppers talking with visiting northern relatives. Have each student write a brief monologue on the drawbacks to the sharecropping system. *(See the Level 1 lesson for the correct drawbacks.)* Ask volunteers to perform their monologues for the class.

Changing Ways The South

Understanding Change Much has changed in the South since the late 1800s, yet much remains the same. Although the average income in the South is nearly that of the national average, it still lags behind in wealth. *How has the South's population changed? How has the average per capita income changed as compared to the rest of the country?*

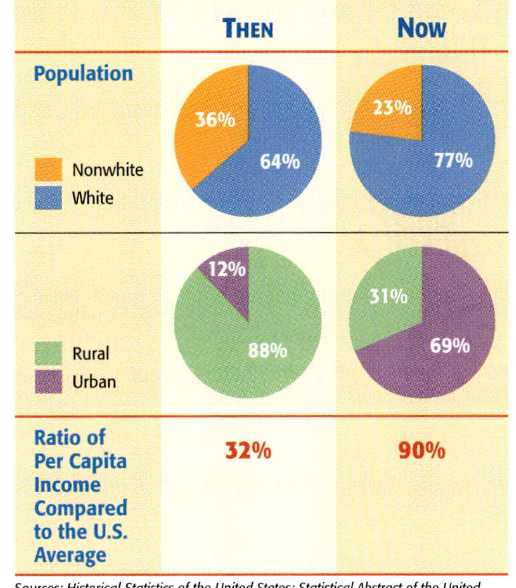

Sources: *Historical Statistics of the United States; Statistical Abstract of the United States: 1997.* Data reflects 1870 and 1990.

Industrial growth. Henry W. Grady, the editor of the Atlanta *Constitution*, believed that one-crop agriculture kept the South in poverty and economically dependent on the North. The New South, he argued, should manufacture its own goods. Supporters of this New South idea joined with northern and British investors to finance factories and ironworks, while southerners raised the capital to build textile mills and other enterprises. Southern railroads were rebuilt and integrated into northern rail systems.

Not everyone benefited equally from industrialization in the South, however. Factory owners and investors profited at the expense of poorly paid workers. White industrial workers in the South earned far lower wages than their northern counterparts. Most African Americans could not find any factory work at all. Many industrial workers were forced to buy goods on credit from the company store and to live in ramshackle company houses. Like sharecroppers, they soon found themselves locked in a cycle of debt.

THE GRANGER COLLECTION, NEW YORK

INTERPRETING THE VISUAL RECORD

The New South. Many southerners supported the building of new industries and railroad systems in the late 1800s. ***How does this painting express the goals of the New South movement?***

The Rise of Jim Crow

For African Americans, the so-called New South closely resembled the Old South. They were tied to the land through sharecropping and by their exclusion from most factory jobs. Moreover, Democrats had taken control of the southern state legislatures and stepped up their attempts to strip African Americans of their rights.

To deprive African Americans of the right to vote, southern legislatures instituted **poll taxes**—fixed taxes imposed on every voter—and **literacy tests**—tests that barred those who could not read from voting. Because most African American southerners were poor and had been denied an education, these legal barriers

GEOGRAPHIC DIVERSITY

Exodusters. After Reconstruction ended, many southern African Americans wanted to migrate to a safer region, that offered more opportunities. Several thousand black southerners moved to Kansas, where the Homestead Act of 1862 had made land available and affordable. Those migrants who sought a better life in the Midwest were known as *exodusters.*

CRITICAL THINKING Tell students that the word *exodus* has been used to describe the movement of an oppressed people. Why might migrating African Americans have been called *exodusters*?

ANSWER: Students might suggest that migrating African Americans were called *exodusters* because they had been oppressed in the South.

CHANGING WAYS ANSWERS

the proportion of whites has grown and the population has become more urban; it has grown from 32 percent to 90 percent of the U.S. average

VISUAL RECORD ANSWER

Students might suggest that it shows the emergence of a new, better South.

LEVEL 3: Ask students to list the drawbacks of the sharecropping system. *(See the Level 1 lesson for the correct drawbacks.)* Then organize students into small groups. Have each group develop a post-Reconstruction agricultural plan that would provide planters with labor while also providing African Americans with land and supplies. Have students share their plans with the class. Then ask students to realistically evaluate the plans, given conditions in the post-Reconstruction South. Would they have worked there, given the existence of Redeemers and people who believed in African American inferiority? **Cooperative Learning**

▶ASSIGNMENT *Have students read the Thomas Hall quotation on the section opener page, in which the former slave observed that the sharecropping system was "little better than slavery." Then tell students to write two or three paragraphs evaluating Hall's statement and determining if sharecropping offered African Americans a significant degree of independence or trapped them in a no-win economic situation.*

CONSTITUTIONAL HERITAGE

Separate and Equal?

In *Plessy* v. *Ferguson,* the Supreme Court upheld the rights of businesses to segregate people according to race. The justices wrote, "We consider the underlying fallacy of the plaintiff's argument to consist in the assumption that the enforced separation of the two races stamps the colored race with a badge of inferiority. . . . The argument assumes that social prejudice may be overcome by legislation. . . . Legislation is powerless to eradicate racial instincts or to abolish distinctions based upon physical differences." Justice Harlan, the only justice to vote against segregation, argued, "The law regards man as man, and takes no account of his surroundings or his color when his civil rights . . . are involved."

ACTIVITY: Organize students into small groups and have each group debate whether the Fourteenth Amendment supports or outlaws separate-but-equal facilities.

VISUAL RECORD ANSWER

Students might suggest that the church provided African Americans with a place where they could seek support from each other and build community solidarity.

Jim Crow laws prohibited African Americans from riding on "whites only" railroad cars.

effectively disfranchised African Americans. Even literate African Americans often "failed" the test, since white officials decided who passed. These rules, however, were often waived for poor or illiterate whites. Whites also used violence and intimidation to prevent African Americans from voting.

To further deprive African Americans of their rights, state legislatures initiated a series of laws designed to enforce **segregation**, or separation, of the races. These provisions were called **Jim Crow laws**, so-named after a minstrel song that contained the refrain "Jump—jump—jump Jim Crow." Passed in Tennessee in 1881, the first of these laws required separate railway cars for African Americans and whites. By the 1890s all southern states had legally segregated public transportation and schools. Segregation soon extended to cemeteries, parks, and other public places.

African Americans sued for equal treatment under the Civil Rights Act of 1875, but the Supreme Court refused to overturn the Jim Crow laws. In the *Civil Rights Cases* of 1883 the Court ruled that the Fourteenth Amendment prohibited only state governments, not individuals or businesses, from discriminating against African Americans. The Supreme Court upheld segregation again in ***Plessy* v. *Ferguson***, a lawsuit brought in 1896 after African American Homer Plessy was denied a seat in a first-class railway car. The Court ruled that "separate but equal" facilities did not violate the Fourteenth Amendment. Justice John Marshall Harlan disagreed, declaring, "Our Constitution is color-blind, and neither knows nor tolerates classes among citizens."

✔ **READING CHECK:** How did the enactment of Jim Crow laws and the *Plessy* v. *Ferguson* decision change life for southern African Americans?

INTERPRETING THE VISUAL RECORD

Segregation. African Americans established many institutions to serve their community. ***How does this image of an African American church service reflect the importance of community during the Jim Crow era?***

African American Life

Despite segregation, in some southern cities a growing African American middle class began to emerge, made up of doctors, government workers, teachers, and lawyers. African Americans formed mutual aid societies, started businesses, supported churches, and built schools. The African Methodist Episcopal (AME) Church, the AME Zion Church, and the African American Baptist Church grew rapidly.

Farmers and planters. Most African Americans had little opportunity to improve their economic status. Despite numerous obstacles, however, some did purchase farmland and in a few cases large plantations. According to writer Charles Nordhoff, African Americans in Georgia owned "nearly 400,000 acres of farming real estate, besides city property."

Some African Americans also formed cooperatives to buy farmland. In addition to producing crops and providing jobs, the cooperatives often provided for the care of sick members "if unable to care for themselves." Cooperatives sometimes imposed taxes "to provide for the education of the young and the comfortable maintenance of the aged and helpless."

TEACH OBJECTIVE 2

LEVEL 1: Have each student list the provisions of the Jim Crow laws and the *Plessy* v. *Ferguson* decision. *(Students should note that the Jim Crow laws introduced widespread segregation, and that the* Plessy *v.* Ferguson *decision codified that segregation.)* Then have students annotate their lists, describing how the laws and the decisions affected African Americans in the post-Reconstruction South. *(The laws limited African Americans' opportunities.)* Ask volunteers to share their annotations with the class. **Sheltered English**

LEVELS 2 AND 3: Tell students to imagine that it is 1896 and that they are southern African Americans. Have each student write a one-page letter to the editor of a northern African American newspaper describing how Jim Crow laws and the *Plessy* v. *Ferguson* decision has changed his or her lives. *(See the Level 1 lesson for the correct changes.)* Ask volunteers to read their letters to the class. Students may wish to place their letters in their portfolios.

NOTE: For an additional teaching idea, see the Chapter 3 open interviewing lesson in the **Creative Teaching Strategies** handbook.

Black Writers During the Late 1800s

Many African American writers of the post-Reconstruction period focused their attention on the difficulties faced by African Americans after their emancipation, as well as on the African American experience more generally. Charles W. Chesnutt's 1899 story "The Wife of His Youth" deals with the choice one man must make between the woman he married while still a slave and the young widow he is courting. Paul Laurence Dunbar's 1890s poem "Ode for Memorial Day" expresses the pain of the Civil War and its joyful outcome.

from "The Wife of His Youth"

by Charles W. Chesnutt

Suppose that this husband, soon after his escape, had learned that his wife had been sold away, and that such inquires as he could make brought no information of her whereabouts. Suppose that he was young, and she much older than he; that he was light, and she was black; that their marriage was a slave marriage, and legally binding only if they chose to make it so after the war. Suppose, too, that he made his way to the North, as some of us have done, and there, where he had larger opportunities, had improved them, and had in the course of all these years grown to be as different from the ignorant boy who ran away from fear of slavery as the day is from the night. Suppose, even, that he had qualified himself, by industry, by thrift, and by study, to win the friendship and be considered worthy. . . . And then suppose that accident should bring to his knowledge the fact that the wife of his youth, the wife he had left behind him, . . . was alive and seeking him, but that he was absolutely safe from recognition or discovery, unless he chose to reveal himself. My friends, what would the man do?"

Collection of poetry by Charles W. Chesnutt

from "Ode for Memorial Day"

by Paul Laurence Dunbar

Done are the toils and the
wearisome marches. . . .
Out of the blood of a conflict
fraternal,
Out of the dust and the
dimness of death,
Burst into blossoms of glory
eternal
Flowers that sweeten the world with their breath.
Flowers of charity, peace, and devotion
Bloom in the hearts that are empty of strife;
Love that is boundless and broad as the ocean
Leaps into beauty and fulness of life.
So, with the singing of paeans [praises] and chorals,
And with the flag flashing high in the sun,
Place on the graves of our heroes the laurels
Which their unfaltering valor has won!

Paul Laurence Dunbar

UNDERSTANDING LITERATURE

1. How does Chesnutt portray slave marriage in "The Wife of His Youth"?
2. How does Dunbar refer to the ideals behind the fighting of the Civil War?
3. What sentiments about life after the Civil War do these authors express?

AMERICAN LETTERS ANSWERS

1. as an informal contract that was not legally binding
2. heroic and valorous
3. Chesnutt shows that African Americans cannot escape their slave past; Dunbar envisions a peaceful world.

***The American Nation* VIDEO PROGRAM**

The Tuskegee Institute;
Teacher's Guide, pp. 63–68

Search 33609, Play to 40728
Videodisc 1, Side B

Play

Pause

See *Teacher's Guide* for Spanish barcode.

VISUAL RECORD ANSWER

(for p. 124)

Students might mention that the ad describes the products' virtues in great detail.

SECTION 4 REVIEW ANSWERS

Define and Identify

For significance, see the following pages:

- sharecropping, p. 120
- crop-lien system, p. 120
- poll taxes, p. 121
- literacy tests, p. 121
- segregation, p. 122
- Jim Crow laws, p. 122
- *Plessy* v. *Ferguson*, p. 122

TEACH OBJECTIVES 3 AND 4

ALL LEVELS: To help students understand the ways in which African Americans attempted to improve their economic situation after Reconstruction—and how Booker T. Washington and Ida B. Wells responded to Jim Crow laws— copy the following graphic organizer on the chalkboard, omitting the italicized answers. Ask each student to complete it. Discuss students' organizers as a class.
Sheltered English

The End of Reconstruction and Jim Crow Laws

African Americans' Attempts to Improve Their Economic Situation
- *Formed aid societies and cooperatives*
- *Supported churches and schools*
- *Supported businesses*

Booker T. Washington's Response to Jim Crow Laws
- *Wanted African Americans to achieve economic independence*
- *Discouraged African Americans from protesting discrimination*

Ida B. Wells's Response to Jim Crow Laws
- *Urged African Americans to protest discrimination*
- *Wanted African Americans to leave the South*

- Madame C. J. Walker, p. 124
- Booker T. Washington, p. 125
- Ida B. Wells, p. 125

1. advantages–allowed a small degree of personal freedom for African Americans and poor whites, allowed planters to maintain a cheap labor force; disadvantages–kept sharecroppers in permanent debt to planters and merchants, kept southern economy tied mostly to cotton crops

2. limited their access to public transportation, services, and education

3. Students' articles will vary. Students should mention mutual aid societies and cooperatives.

4. Students should mention that although both worked to better African Americans' lives, Washington emphasized economic independence and avoidance of conflict, while Wells focused on ending racist violence through activism.

5. Students might note that the two Souths were virtually the same, with African Americans in positions of servitude and whites in power both economically and politically.

CHAPTER 3 REVIEW ANSWERS

Creating a Time Line
Each event should have an explanation and a correct date.

Writing a Summary
See the Reading Checks in each section for main ideas.

Industry and business. African Americans also formed nonagricultural cooperatives. In cities such as Baltimore, Charleston, and Richmond, cooperatives bought large parcels of land. They then sold that land to members for building homes. After being excluded from dock work, African Americans in Baltimore organized the Chesapeake, Marine, and Dry Dock Company. This cooperative raised and borrowed thousands of dollars to buy a shipyard and a marine railway. It hired 1,000 African American caulkers and carpenters to do repair work, won a government contract, and paid off its entire debt within five years.

Some African Americans also owned small businesses such as barber shops, blacksmith shops, general stores, and restaurants. African American women could be found in open-air markets throughout southern cities, selling candy and vegetables. A leading African American entrepreneur, Madame C. J. Walker, became one of the first women in the United States to become a millionaire.

Madame C. J. Walker

Madame C. J. Walker was born Sarah Breedlove in 1867 in Louisiana. Her parents were poverty-stricken sharecroppers, and Walker worked in the cotton fields as a child. She married at age 14 and gave birth to her daughter, A'Leila, four years later. By the time Walker was 20, her first husband had died, apparently killed by a lynch mob. For the next 17 years she worked as a cook and laundress.

By 1905 Walker had developed a hair-conditioner treatment for African American women. With her life savings of $1.50, she opened a hair preparations company, which she operated out of the attic of her home. Six months later she married journalist C. J. Walker, who adopted her daughter. The couple traveled for the next year and a half to promote Walker's products, leaving A'Leila Walker behind to run the mail-order business.

After divorcing her husband, Walker and her daughter moved in 1908 to Pittsburgh, Pennsylvania, where they founded Leila College, a beauty school. Soon cosmetologists were practicing the Walker method for hair care. By 1910 Walker had established beauty parlors, production facilities, and laboratories throughout the country and in the Caribbean and South America. Within another nine years, 25,000 African American women were Walker "agents," selling her products.

By 1914 Walker's company was earning more than $1 million per year. Until her death in 1919, Walker was a generous contributor to African American causes, particularly schools and equal rights organizations. She relentlessly promoted the belief that African Americans could better themselves economically. During one public speech, Walker said:

> **"The girls and women of our race must not be afraid to take hold of business endeavor. . . . I want to say to every Negro woman present, don't sit down and wait for the opportunities to come. . . . Get up and make them!"**

✔ **READING CHECK:** How did African Americans attempt to improve their economic situation after Reconstruction?

INTERPRETING THE VISUAL RECORD

Entrepreneurship. Madame C. J. Walker built a factory for the production of beauty products in Indianapolis, Indiana, in 1910. ***How do you think this advertisement might have helped Walker sell her merchandise?***

REVIEW

Have students complete the **Section 4 Review** on p. 125.

ASSESS

Have students complete **Daily Quiz 3.4**. As **Alternative Assessment**, you may want to use the sharecropper monologue or the post-Reconstruction agricultural plan in this section's lessons.

RETEACH

Have students complete **Main Idea Activity for Reteaching and Sheltered English 3.4**. Then have students define the key terms in the section and use them all in two or three summary paragraphs. **Sheltered English**

EXTEND

Have students conduct research on *Plessy* v. *Ferguson.* Then tell students to imagine that they are modern-day television reporters preparing a segment on historic Supreme Court cases. Have each student prepare a three-to-five minute segment on this case. Students' segments should explain how the case wound up in Court, analyze the majority ruling, and assess the impact of the decision on race relations, especially in the South. Ask volunteers to perform their news segments for the class. **Block Scheduling**

Responses to the Jim Crow Era

Despite the success of some individuals, African Americans continued to encounter widespread discrimination in the late 1870s. Two influential African American leaders differed in their approaches to this discrimination.

Booker T. Washington believed that African Americans should concentrate on achieving economic independence, which he saw as the key to political and social equality. He urged African Americans to seek practical training in trades and professions. He discouraged them from protesting against discrimination, arguing that it merely increased whites' hostility. At the same time, however, Washington secretly provided support to groups fighting Jim Crow laws and racial violence.

Some African American leaders disagreed with Washington's public position calling for cooperation with southern whites. They argued instead that African Americans should protest unfair treatment. Civil rights activist, journalist, and teacher Ida B. Wells—later Wells-Barnett—focused her attention on stopping the lynching of African Americans. In fiery editorials she urged African Americans to leave the South. She herself moved from Memphis to Chicago. Wells uged others to follow her example.

> **"There is therefore only one thing left that we can do; save our money and leave a town which will neither protect our lives [nor] property."**

Although lynchings decreased only slightly in the early 1900s, Wells's tireless efforts kept the public's attention focused on the issue.

✔ **READING CHECK:** How did Booker T. Washington's and Ida B. Wells's beliefs represent differing approaches to how African Americans should have responded to Jim Crow laws?

Booker T. Washington founded the Tuskegee Institute in 1881.

Read More About It

Free Find: Ida B. Wells

After reading the biography on Ida B. Wells on the **Holt Researcher** CD–ROM, write a short biography that describes her political activities and accomplishments.

SECTION 4 REVIEW

Define and explain the significance of the following terms:
sharecropping
crop-lien system
poll taxes
literacy tests
segregation
Jim Crow laws
Plessy v. *Ferguson*

Identify and explain the significance of the following individuals:
Madame C. J. Walker
Booker T. Washington
Ida B. Wells

1. **Using Graphic Organizers** Copy the graphic organizer below. Use it to explain the advantages and disadvantages of the sharecropping system. Consider the effects of the sharecropping system on the landowner, the laborers, and the southern economy as a whole.

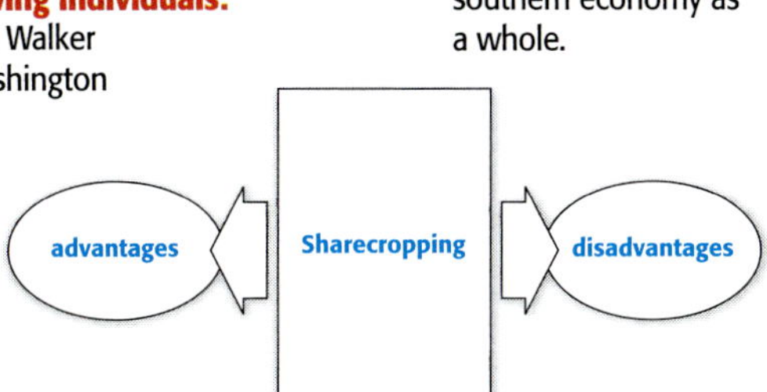

2. **Assessing Consequences** How did the Jim Crow laws affect African Americans?
3. **Using Historical Imagination** Imagine that you are a reporter for a national magazine after Reconstruction. Write a brief article summarizing how African Americans are working together to improve their social and economic situations.
4. **Comparing and Contrasting** Write a brief paragraph comparing and contrasting the views of Booker T. Washington and Ida B. Wells.

Critical Thinking

5. How did the New South compare to the antebellum South?

Consider:
- how the economy changed or stayed the same
- how racial attitudes changed or stayed the same
- how political power changed or stayed the same

Identifying People and Ideas

1. full pardon, proposed for southerners after the Civil War
2. succeeded Lincoln as president and disagreed with Republicans about Reconstruction
3. laws limiting the freedom of African Americans in the South
4. divided the former Confederacy into five military districts and gave African American men the right to vote for delegates to the state constitutional convention as well as serve as delegates
5. northerners who moved to the South after the war
6. agreement in which Democrats accept Hayes as president and Republicans agree to withdraw remaining federal troops from the South
7. system under which poor farmers worked lands owned by others in exchange for a share of the crop
8. laws enacted to enforce segregation
9. African American female entrepreneur who made beauty products for African Americans
10. African American leader and educator who advocated economic independence and political neutrality

Understanding Main Ideas

1. Lincoln's plan offered amnesty to most southerners who would accept the new laws and permitted states to rejoin the Union with a 10 percent vote. Johnson's plan

REVIEW AND ASSESSMENT RESOURCES

PRINT

- Chapter 3 Review, pp. 126–27
- Chapter 3 Tutorial for Students, Parents, Mentors, and Peers
- Chapter 3 Test (Form A or B)
- Portfolio Activities and Alternative Assessment Handbook, Chapter 3

MULTIMEDIA

- Audio Program, Chapter 3 (English and Spanish)
- Chapter 3 Test Generator (on the One-Stop Planner)
- Global Skill Builder CD–ROM
- HRW Web site

SHELTERED ENGLISH

- Spanish Glossary
- Sheltered English Chapter 3 Test

REVIEW

Have students complete the **Chapter 3 Review** on pp. 126–27.

ASSESS

Use one of the chapter tests to assess students' understanding of the content. For **Alternative Assessment**, see the **Portfolio Activities and Alternative Assessment Handbook.**

pardoned most rebels and required states to abolish slavery and nullify acts of secession.

2. Johnson's plan pardoned most rebels and required states to abolish slavery and nullify acts of secession. The Radical Republicans' plan required Confederate states to abolish slavery and required white males of the states to take a loyalty oath.

3. Freedman's Bureau Bill, Civil Rights Acts of 1866 and 1875, Fourteenth and Fifteenth Amendments, Reconstruction Acts, Enforcement Acts

4. The Panic of 1873 forced legislators to change focus and helped Democrats win more seats in Congress. The withdrawal of federal troops from the South in 1877 allowed southerners to change social practices.

5. Most poor farmers had to become sharecroppers. Southern industry increased, but the workers were paid much less than workers in northern factories.

6. segregated blacks and whites in all facets of life

Reviewing Themes

1. acknowledged that African Americans were citizens and that the federal government had taken back control of the South

2. By recognizing that African Americans were citizens, the United States was expanding its definition of democracy.

3. the southern economy was dependent on cotton, which displaced other crops as a result of the crop-lien system.

Review

Creating a Time Line

Copy the time line below onto a sheet of paper. Complete the time line by filling in the events and dates from the chapter that you think were most significant. Pick three events and explain why you think they were significant.

Writing a Summary

Using the Reading Checks as a guide, write an overview of the events of the chapter.

Identifying People and Ideas

Identify the following terms or individuals and explain their significance.

1. amnesty
2. Andrew Johnson
3. Black Codes
4. Reconstruction Acts
5. carpetbaggers
6. Compromise of 1877
7. sharecropping
8. Jim Crow laws
9. Madame C. J. Walker
10. Booker T. Washington

Understanding Main Ideas

SECTION 1

1. How did the Reconstruction plans of President Lincoln and President Johnson differ?

SECTION 2

2. How did President Johnson's plans for Reconstruction differ from Radical Republican plans?
3. What laws did Congress pass to protect the rights of African Americans?

SECTION 3

4. Why did Reconstruction come to an end?

SECTION 4

5. How did conditions for southern farmers and laborers change from 1865 to 1900?
6. How did Jim Crow laws affect African Americans?

Reviewing Themes

1. **Constitutional Heritage** How did the Thirteenth, Fourteenth, and Fifteenth Amendments change the U.S. Constitution to reflect changing conditions after the Civil War?
2. **Democratic Values** How was democracy in the United States expanded during Reconstruction?
3. **Economic Development** What role did cotton play in the New South?

Thinking Critically

1. **Hypothesizing** How might conditions in the New South have been different if land had been distributed to African Americans after the war?
2. **Evaluating** Why did many southern whites react so strongly to gains made by African Americans during Reconstruction?
3. **Identifying Cause and Effect** What political gains did African Americans make during Reconstruction?
4. **Using Historical Imagination** Imagine that you are a senator during the impeachment trial of President Johnson. How would you vote? Why?
5. **Taking a Stand** Do you agree or disagree with the Compromise of 1877? Why or why not?

Writing About History

Writing to Express Imagine that you are an African American sharecropper in the postwar South. Write a letter to a local newspaper explaining how Reconstruction policies have affected your economic and social status and why you oppose the Compromise of 1877. Use the following graphic organizer to help organize your thoughts.

Reconstruction Policies → 

→ Reasons for Supporting Compromise

RETEACH

Write the following statement from the textbook (see Section 4 for full context) on the chalkboard: *"For African Americans, the so-called New South closely resembled the Old South."* Organize the class into small groups. Have each group create a detailed outline of the events that created the reality of that statement. Compare groups' outlines and conduct a discussion on the failed promise of the Reconstruction era.

Sheltered English, Cooperative Learning

EXTEND

Ask students to conduct research on Booker T. Washington and Ida B. Wells. Then tell students to imagine that they are conducting a roundtable discussion with the two figures. Have each student write a transcript of the discussion. Students should include their questions and the figures' answers to those questions. Have students read portions of their transcripts to the class.

Block Scheduling

Strategies for Success Review the **Strategies for Success** on *Comparing Points of View.* Then reconsider the excerpt below from President Lincoln's second inaugural address. Compare the excerpt to the quotation included in the Strategies for Success, and answer the questions that follow.

> "With malice toward none, with charity for all, with firmness in the right as God gives us to see the right, let us strive on . . . to bind up the nation's wounds . . . to do all which may achieve and cherish a just and lasting peace."

1. How do you think President Lincoln's personal background and political circumstances influenced what he said in his second inaugural address?
2. What is the main idea of the excerpt? Is this idea supported by facts, opinions, or both?
3. Does Lincoln's point of view more closely resemble that of Horace Greeley or Robert E. Lee? Why?

Linking History and Geography

Study the map below. Where were most African American colleges that were founded before 1900 located? Explain why you think this pattern was the case.

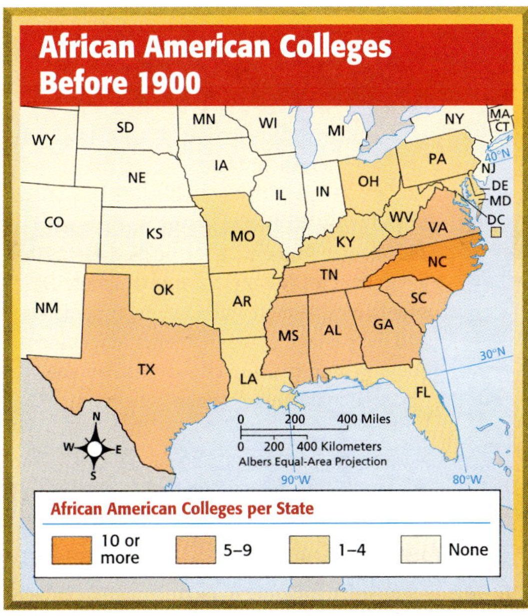

internet connect

TOPIC: Impeachment of Andrew Johnson
GO TO: go.hrw.com
KEYWORD: SE1 Johnson

Accessing the Internet through the HRW Web site, research the impeachment trial of Andrew Johnson. Concentrate on the circumstances that led to the trial, the trial proceedings, and the results of the trial. For a group activity, assume the roles of the principal figures and dramatize a part of the trial in front of the class. For an individual activity, write a statement that explains why you would have voted to convict or acquit the president.

BUILDING YOUR PORTFOLIO

Complete one or all of the following projects independently or cooperatively.

THE PRESIDENT IS DEAD!

WAR DEPARTMENT,
Washington, April 15, 1865.
To MAJ. GEN. DIX.
Abraham Lincoln died this morning at 22 minutes after Seven o'clock.
E. M. STANTON, Sec. of War.

1 Geographic Diversity

Imagine that you are a newspaper editor. ***Prepare a list of headlines, story ideas, and possible illustrations*** to explain how people in different parts of the nation feel about the assassination of President Abraham Lincoln.

2 Democratic Values

Imagine that you are a southern governor opposed to northern politicians' plans for the South during Reconstruction. ***Create an outline*** for a Reconstruction plan that would address the interests of planters, former soldiers, and African Americans in your state.

3 Constitutional Heritage

Imagine that you are an attorney representing Homer Plessy. ***Prepare a closing statement*** arguing that segregation, as practiced in "separate but equal" facilities for African Americans and whites, violates the Fourteenth Amendment.

Thinking Critically

1. Landownership would have given freedpeople more economic and political independence.
2. The gains threatened whites' economic and political dominance.
3. The Fourteenth and Fifteenth Amendments laid the groundwork for later enforcement of African American rights, and some African Americans served in state and national offices.
4. Answers will vary. Students should clearly identify the reasons for their positions.
5. Answers will vary. Students should clearly identify the reasons for their positions.

Writing About History

Answers will vary. Students should clearly identify the reasons for their positions.

Strategies for Success

1. Lincoln seemed to base his actions on religious and moral principles. As president of a divided nation, it was in his interest to encourage a quick resolution.
2. The passage is not based on facts but on a desire for peace.
3. His view more clearly resembles Lee's view that immediate reconciliation is possible.

Linking History and Geography

Most African American colleges were founded in the Southeast. This might have been because this was where a greater percentage of African Americans lived.

REVIEW AND ASSESSMENT RESOURCES

PRINT
- Unit 1 Review, pp. 128–29
- Unit 1 Test (Form A or B)
- Portfolio Activities and Alternative Assessment Handbook, Unit 1

MULTIMEDIA
- Global Skill Builder CD–ROM

SHELTERED ENGLISH
- Spanish Glossary
- Sheltered English Unit 1 Test

To review elements of Unit 1 in a single class period, assign one of the following activities or graphic organizers, omitting the italicized answers, to individuals or groups.

1 Cultural Diversity

Have each student write a poem expressing the ways in which people of different cultures interacted in the Americas. Students should describe the positive and negative aspects of these interactions. Ask volunteers to recite their poems to the class.

A Selection from Further Reading

The Forty-Niners. In *The World Rushed In: The California Gold Rush Experience*, J. S. Holliday uses a variety of primary sources to create a composite portrait of miners. In the following excerpt, Holliday evaluates the motives of the forty-niners. "Goldseekers were not settlers or pioneers in the tradition of America's westward migration. These people came as exploiters, transients, ready to take, not to build. Whether in the diggings or in San Francisco, Sacramento City, or Stockton, they found themselves surrounded by crowds of hurrying men concerned only with how to make the greatest amount of money in the shortest time. With that common motive, they also shared an indifference toward California and its future."

COMPREHENSION According to Holliday, what motivated the forty-niners?

ANSWER: Students might suggest that according to Holliday the miners were motivated by the prospect of making a quick profit without a long-term investment.

UNIT 1

Review

Outlined below are four projects. Independently or cooperatively, complete one and use the products to demonstrate your mastery of the historical concepts involved.

1 Cultural Diversity

People from many different cultures exchanged technology, food, religion, and ideas in the Americas. Imagine that you are an anthropologist who studies the way people of different cultures meet and interact. ***Create a journal entry*** recording how two different groups interact and chronicling their cultural differences. Describe what advantages and disadvantages each group experienced as a result of the contact. You may wish to use portfolio materials you designed in the unit chapters to help you.

The First Thanksgiving 1621 ***by J. L. G. Ferris***

Georgia cotton plantation

2 Democratic Values

Throughout the early- and mid-1800s abolitionists encouraged the extension of democratic values by working to end the institution of slavery. ***Create an illustrated time line*** of the political events that led to the Civil War and the end of slavery. Be sure to include the Emancipation Proclamation and the passage of the Thirteenth Amendment. You may wish to use portfolio materials you designed in the unit chapters to help you.

2 Constitutional Heritage

FEDERALISM

Federal Government	Both	State Governments
• authority to raise armed forces • power to coin money • authority to establish foreign policy	• right to levy taxes • right to establish courts	• right to establish schools • authority to conduct elections • other local powers

3 Geographic Diversity

RECONSTRUCTION

Benefits to the North
- provided new economic opportunities to many northerners
- provided an opportunity to extend "northern" ideals into the South

Benefits to the South
- provided new economic and social opportunities to many African Americans in the region
- resulted in the creation of new roads and schools

Which Region Reaped the Most Benefits? Why?

3 Geographic Diversity

Differences between the North and the South created a rift that led to the Civil War and left deep scars that Reconstruction failed to erase. ***Create an outline for an argument in a debate*** that discusses whether Reconstruction served the political, economic, and social interests of the North more than the South. You may wish to use portfolio materials you designed in the unit chapters to help you.

Carpetbag carried by northerners traveling south during Reconstruction

4 Constitutional Heritage

The Thirteenth Amendment ended the institution of slavery. It did not, however, end legal discrimination against African Americans. ***Create an outline and a visual aid for a press conference*** to discuss these issues. Your questions at the conference should focus on how the lives of African Americans have changed with the adoption of the new amendment. You may wish to use portfolio materials you designed in the unit chapters to help you.

Segregated classroom from the early 1900s

Further Reading

Faber, Doris and Harold. *The Birth of a Nation.* Scribner, 1989. Review of the significant events in the early development of the U.S. federal government.

Foner, Eric. *A Short History of Reconstruction, 1863–1877.* HarperCollins, 1990. An overview of Reconstruction.

Holliday, J. S. *The World Rushed In: The California Gold Rush Experience.* Simon and Schuster, 1983. Eyewitness accounts of the California Gold Rush.

Josephy, Alvin M. Jr., ed. *America in 1492: The World of the Indian Peoples Before the Arrival of Columbus.* Vintage, 1993. Panorama of North and South American life from prehistoric times to the early 1400s.

Mellon, James M. *Bullwhip Days: The Slaves Remember.* Avon Books, 1988. Interviews with former slaves.

Meltzer, Milton, ed. *Voices from the Civil War.* HarperCollins, 1989. Northern and southern views of the war and its effects from 1861 to 1865.

Wheeler, Richard. *Voices of 1776.* Meridian, 1991. Firsthand accounts of the American Revolution from both the British and American sides.

Internet Connect and Holt Researcher CD–ROM Review

In assigned groups, develop a multimedia presentation about America from prehistory to 1900. Choose information from the chapter Internet Connect activities and from the Holt Researcher CD–ROM that best reflect the major topics of the period. Write an outline and a script for your presentation.

A Selection from Further Reading

African Americans in the South. In *A Short History of Reconstruction*, Eric Foner provides a survey of American society and politics during Reconstruction. In the following excerpt, Foner explains how Reconstruction affected African Americans in the South.

"Although thwarted in their bid for land, blacks seized the opportunity created by the end of slavery to establish as much independence as possible in their working lives, consolidate their families and communities, and stake a claim to equal citizenship. Black participation in Southern public life after 1867 was the most radical development of the Reconstruction years."

COMPREHENSION According to Foner, how did the experience of African Americans in the South change during Reconstruction?

ANSWER: Students might note that during Reconstruction, southern African Americans were able to obtain some measure of economic independence, reinforce their families and communities, and begin to take part in politics.

UNIT 2

A Nation Transformed

CHAPTER 4 The Western Crossroads

Beginning in the 1840s, large numbers of white settlers began to migrate to lands west of the Mississippi River. These settlers were drawn by the prospect of land, railroad construction work, the cattle boom, and gold and silver. Their migration and encroachment of American Indian land led to violent conflicts. Ultimately, the government forced the outnumbered Indians onto reservations.

CHAPTER 5 The Second Industrial Revolution

During the Second Industrial Revolution, innovations in the steel and oil industries led to new advances in transportation. The invention of the telegraph and the telephone made it easier for people to communicate. Entrepreneurs established profitable new corporations. Workers often labored in unsafe factories for low wages, joined labor unions, and went on strike.

EXAMINING THE VISUAL RECORD

Ask students the questions below. Then use the annotations to expand class discussion.

1 *Why might this building be the only one to include decorative elements?* While it was cheaper and more efficient to leave industrial buildings undecorated, American business owners believed that it was important for some buildings–in this case, what seems to be the train station– to include decorative elements such as cupolas and fancy windows or lively paint colors.

2 *Why might this artist depict the factory in such a naturalistic scene?* During the 1800s, many Americans hoped that machines and industry would coexist with the natural world. Some people worried that the machine would destroy pastoral scenes such as this one. Thus prints like this one often showed reassuring images of nature and industry peacefully co-existing.

ACTIVITY: Ask students to imagine that it is 1875 and that they are British journalists visiting this rail car works. Have each student write an article describing the factory, its setting, and American beliefs about industry and nature.

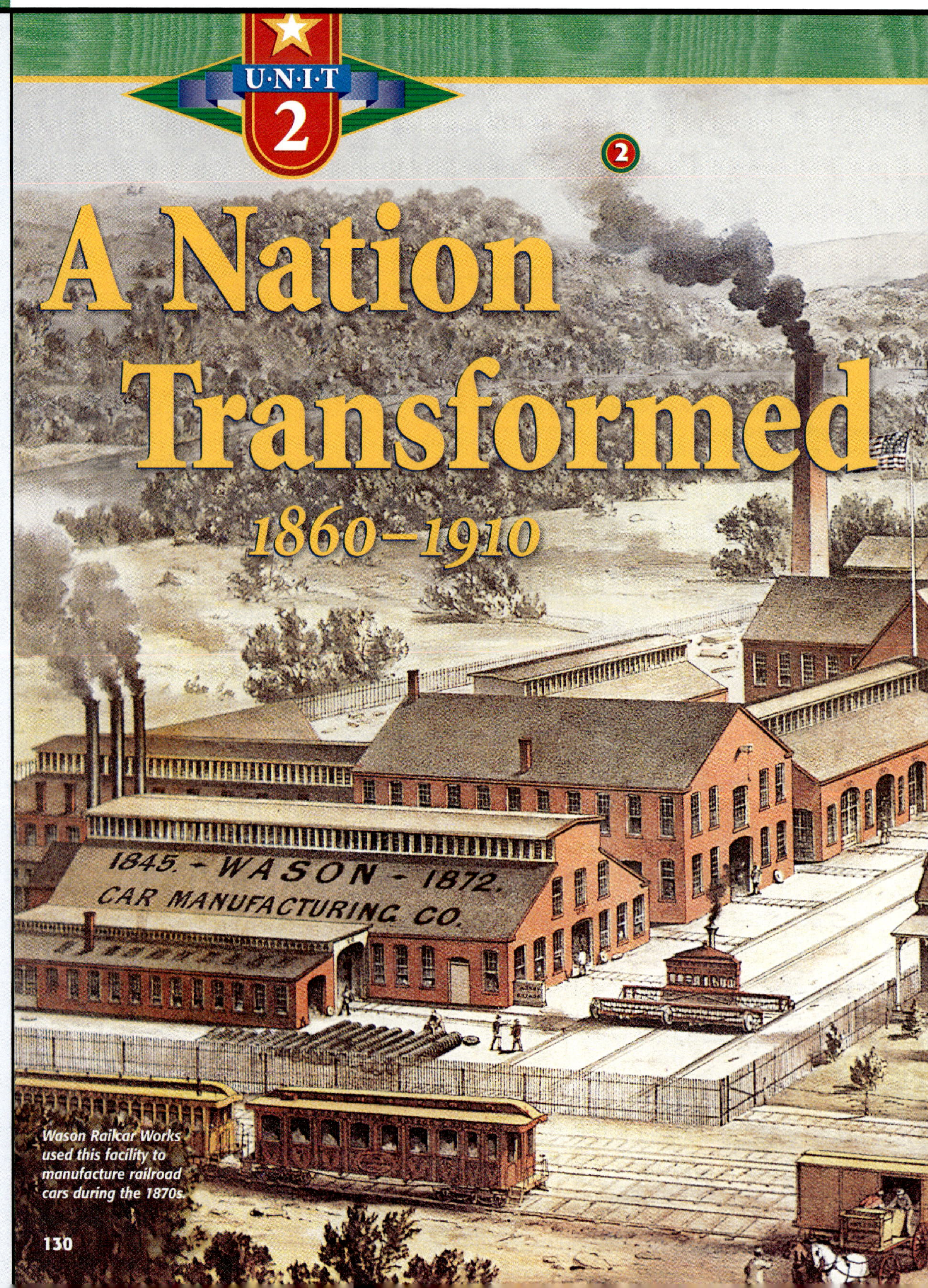

Wason Railcar Works used this facility to manufacture railroad cars during the 1870s.

130

CHAPTER 6 The Transformation of American Society

In the late 1800s and early 1900s, the United States became a more urbanized, ethnically diverse society. Millions of immigrants came to the United States from southern and eastern Europe. The majority of these immigrants lived in cities, where they often worked and lived in difficult conditions. Technological advances also helped to reshape American life during the period.

CHAPTER 7 Politics in the Gilded Age

Political machines and political bosses dominated politics in some cities during the late 1800s. These machines and bosses supplied jobs and services in return for votes. Corruption in national politics led to calls for political reform, including the abolition of the patronage system. The desire for reform also motivated farmers, who formed cooperatives and lobbies. Farmers also joined the new Populist Party.

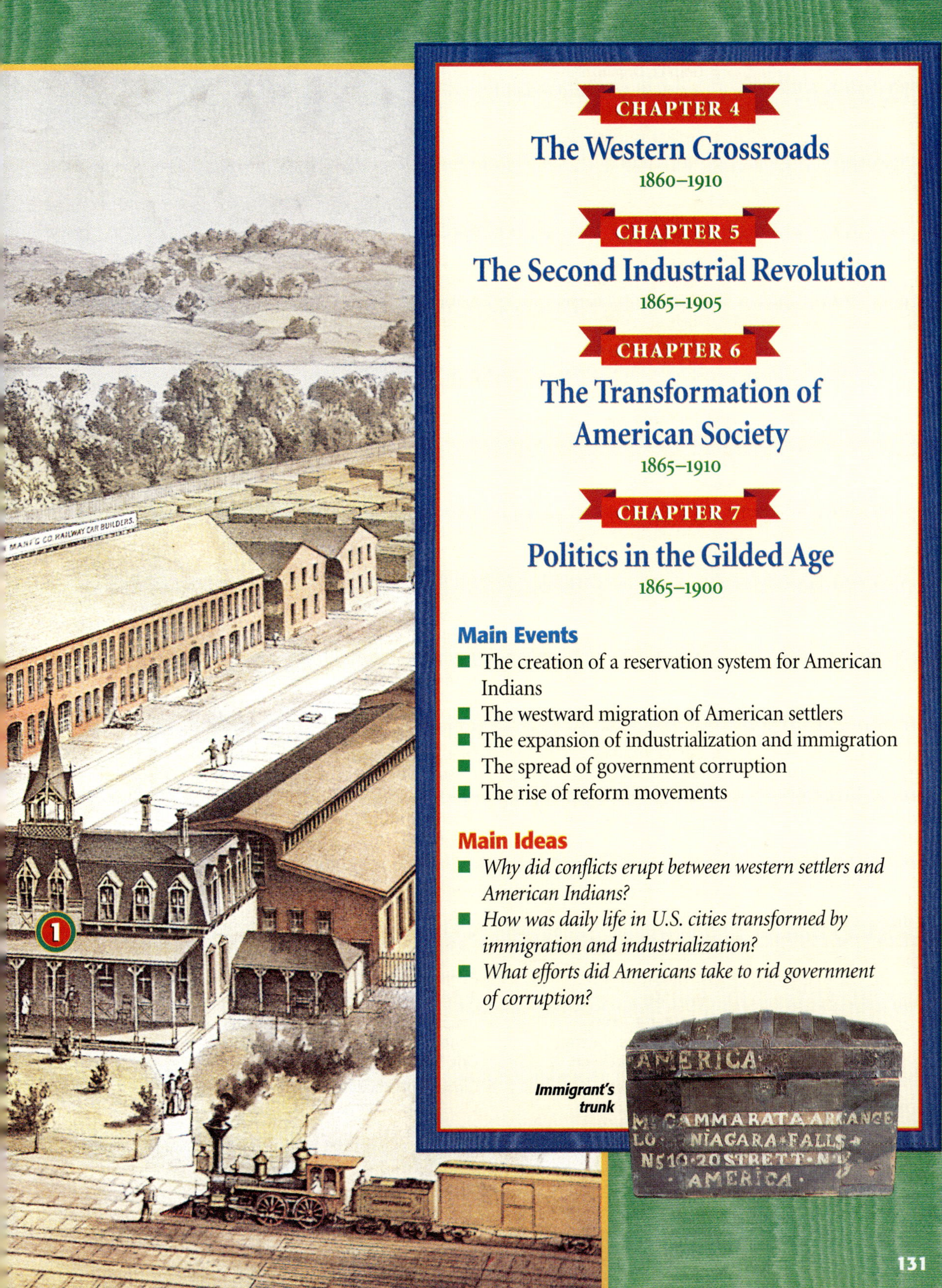

Immigrant's trunk

Main Events

- The creation of a reservation system for American Indians
- The westward migration of American settlers
- The expansion of industrialization and immigration
- The spread of government corruption
- The rise of reform movements

Main Ideas

- *Why did conflicts erupt between western settlers and American Indians?*
- *How was daily life in U.S. cities transformed by immigration and industrialization?*
- *What efforts did Americans take to rid government of corruption?*

INTRODUCE UNIT 2

Main Events

List the Main Events on the chalkboard. Ask students to select two and briefly describe what they know about the topics. Have volunteers share their descriptions. Later, when you have finished Unit 2, ask students to return to their original descriptions and revise them using the information they learned in the unit. Students should also create new descriptions for the other Main Events.

Main Ideas

Ask each student to read the Main Ideas and briefly answer the questions in writing. Share the ***Consider*** points with students as necessary. Later, when you have finished Unit 2, ask students to return to their original answers and revise them using the information they learned in the unit.

Conflicts Between Western Settlers and American Indians

Consider:

- land ownership
- desire to expand vs. desire to maintain historic ties to land

Immigration and Industrialization

Consider:

- the social and cultural backgrounds of immigrants
- the effects of technological advances on workers and the workplace

The Western Crossroads

CHAPTER PLANNING GUIDE

	Section Lesson Objectives	Print Resources	Multimedia Resources	Sheltered English Resources
Section 1 War in the West, pp. 134–41	1 Explain why the U.S. government created the American Indian reservation system. 2 Identify the sources of conflict between the Plains Indians and the U.S. government. 3 Describe how Chief Joseph, Geronimo, and Sarah Winnemucca responded to white treatment of American Indians. 4 Discuss how the U.S. government tried to assimilate American Indians.	▶ Guided Reading Strategy 4.1 ▶ Geography Activity 4: American Indian Lands in the West ▶ Primary Source Reading 4: "Massacre at Wounded Knee" ▶ Biography Reading 4: Geronimo ▶ Graphic Organizer Activity 4: American Indian Leaders ▶ Section 1 Review, p. 141 ▶ Daily Quiz 4.1	▶ One-Stop Planner, Lesson 4.1 ▶ Art in American History Transparency 15: Navajo Eye Dazzler Blanket ▶ Holt Researcher: American History CD–ROM ▶ HRW Web site	▶ Main Idea Activity for Reteaching and Sheltered English 4.1
Section 2 Western Farmers, pp. 142–48	1 Discuss how the U.S. government promoted economic development in the West. 2 Understand why people migrated west. 3 Explain how the environment influenced farming practices and daily life in the West. 4 Describe the difficulties that farm families faced on the Great Plains.	▶ Guided Reading Strategy 4.2 ▶ American History Outline Map 15: Western Railroads and Cattle Trails ▶ Literature Reading 4: Life on the Prairie ▶ Section 2 Review, p. 148 ▶ Daily Quiz 4.2	▶ One-Stop Planner, Lesson 4.2 ▶ The American Nation Video Program Segment: Linking the Nation; Teacher's Guide, pp. 69–74 ▶ Holt Researcher: American History CD–ROM	▶ Main Idea Activity for Reteaching and Sheltered English 4.2
Section 3 The Cattle Boom, pp. 149–54	1 Discuss how cattle and sheep ranching developed in the West. 2 Explain what life was like for cowboys and residents of cattle towns. 3 Describe what ranches were like. 4 Understand why the cattle boom on the open range ended.	▶ Guided Reading Strategy 4.3 ▶ Section 3 Review, p. 154 ▶ Daily Quiz 4.3	▶ One-Stop Planner, Lesson 4.3 ▶ American Music Selection 16: "O Bury Me Not" ▶ Art in American History Transparency 17: Prospecting for Cattle Range ▶ Holt Researcher: American History CD–ROM	▶ Main Idea Activity for Reteaching and Sheltered English 4.3
Section 4 The Mining Boom, pp. 155–59	1 Describe the role mining played in bringing more people west. 2 Explain how the arrival of families changed life in mining camps. 3 Discuss why large companies took over most mining operations, and explain how this changed the lives of miners.	▶ Guided Reading Strategy 4.4 ▶ Section 4 Review, p. 159 ▶ Daily Quiz 4.4	▶ One-Stop Planner, Lesson 4.4 ▶ Holt Researcher: American History CD–ROM	▶ Main Idea Activity for Reteaching and Sheltered English 4.4
Chapter Review and Assessment pp. 160–61		▶ Chapter 4 Review, pp. 160–61 ▶ Chapter 4 Tutorial for Students, Parents, Mentors, and Peers ▶ Chapter 4 Test (Form A or B) ▶ Portfolio Activities and Alternative Assessment Handbook, Chapter 4	▶ Audio Program, Chapter 4 (English and Spanish) ▶ Chapter 4 Test Generator (on the One-Stop Planner) ▶ Global Skill Builder CD–ROM ▶ HRW Web site	▶ Spanish Glossary ▶ Sheltered English Chapter 4 Test

CHAPTER OVERVIEW

In the mid-to late 1800s, many Americans moved westward. Some were drawn by the prospect of land, which was promised to settlers by the Homestead Act. Others helped to build the railroads that linked the East and West Coasts. Yet others were lured by the cattle boom or by the prospect of riches in gold and silver mines.

The encroachment of white settlers onto American Indian territories led to violent conflicts between Indians and the U.S. government. Indians were pushed, often unwillingly, into reservations. Many conflicts arose when the U.S. government—often in response to settlers' hunger for land or gold—violated the terms of its treaties with American Indian groups. While the Sioux won a victory at the Battle of the Little Bighorn, they were soon thereafter defeated at Wounded Knee in 1890, the last major conflict between American Indians and the government.

TIME TAMERS

Block Scheduling

The teacher lesson plans for each section offer a variety of activity choices to help you present the material in a block scheduling format. For further suggestions on block scheduling, see the **Block Scheduling Handbook with Team Teaching Strategies**, pp. 19–24.

Hands-On History Activities:

Classroom to Community The **Hands-On History Activities** help students make meaningful connections between events in American history and those in their own hometown. You may wish to use the Chapter 4 Activity, Agriculture and You, to extend the chapter lessons, as alternative assessment, or as a block scheduling option.

Portfolio Projects

The American Nation includes multiple portfolio projects in each Pupil's Edition chapter review, as well as each unit review. Chapter 4 Portfolio Project options on p. 161 include the following:

1. Students will **compose an oral account**.
2. Students will **prepare a pamphlet**.
3. Students will **prepare a government report**.

The American Nation
INTERNET RESOURCE DIRECTORY

To access online materials for this chapter, go to go.hrw.com and type in the keywords listed below.

HRW ONLINE RESOURCES
GO TO: go.hrw.com

Online Maps
KEYWORD: SE1 Maps4
- The Oklahoma Land Rush
- The Great Plains
- Mining Centers

Online Charts
KEYWORD: SE1 Charts4
- The Bison Population
- The U.S. Government and the West
- The Cost of Establishing a Farm

Online Reading Support
KEYWORD: SE1 Strategies4

Online Rubrics
KEYWORD: SE1 Rubrics

CHAPTER ENRICHMENT LINKS
Use these Web links to extend and enrich student learning for Chapter 4.
GO TO: go.hrw.com
KEYWORD: SE1 Ch4

CHAPTER INTERNET ACTIVITIES
GO TO: go.hrw.com
- Pupil's Edition Student Activity
  KEYWORD: SE1 Writers
  (Students explore the works of western writers.)
- Teacher's Edition Student Activity
  KEYWORD: SE1 Pony
  (Students conduct research on the history of the Pony Express.)
- Teacher's Edition Student Activity
  KEYWORD: SE1 Sioux
  (Students examine tribal pictographs.)

ADDITIONAL
RESOURCES

Books for Teachers

Nabakov, Peter, ed. *Native American Testimony.* Viking Penguin, 1992. Uses first-person accounts to relate the history of Indian-settler relations.

White, Richard. *"It's Your Misfortune and None of My Own": A New History of the American West.* University of Oklahoma Press, 1991. Offers an excellent scholarly history of the West.

Books for Students

Brown, Dee. Bury *My Heart at Wounded Knee.* Holt, Rinehart and Winston, 1971. Narrates the history of western settlement from the perspective of American Indians; considered a classic work.

Time-Life Books, *The Wild West.* Warner, 1993. Provides an illustrated history of western settlement. Particularly appropriate for students reading below grade level.

Primary Sources from the Period

Jackson, Helen Hunt. *A Century of Dishonor.* Indian Head Books, 1993. Examines dealings between the U.S. government and American Indians.

Twain, Mark. *Roughing It.* The Library of America, 1984. Recounts Mark Twain's adventures in western mining towns.

Multimedia Materials

The American West: Myth and Reality. Video, 52 min. EAV/SSSS. Debunks television and movie myths about the West.

Ghost Town Hunters. Video, 50 min. Provides a tour of mining camps and "boom and bust" towns in the West.

CHAPTER 4

Before You Read

Build on What You Know

Ask students to answer the following questions.

Why might Americans have settled in the West?

Consider:

- "push" and "pull" factors such as violence at home and better economic opportunities in another region
- political agreements that expanded U.S. territory in the West

How might American Indians have fared as a consequence of American settlement in the West?

Consider:

- the loss of Indian lands to settlers
- violent conflict with settlers and the U.S. government

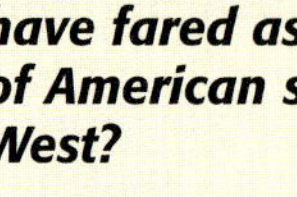

exploring the time line

AMERICAN EVENTS

internet connect

TOPIC: Pony Express
GO TO: go.hrw.com
KEYWORD: SE1 Pony

Have students access the Internet through the HRW Web site to conduct research on the history of the Pony Express. Then have each student write a brief essay that illustrates the differences between the actual history of the Pony Express and the myths that surrounds it.

CHAPTER 4

1860–1910

The Western Crossroads

Pony Express stamp

Signing of the Alaska treaty

Queen Victoria

1860
Daily Life
The Pony Express begins delivering mail between Missouri and San Francisco.

1867
Politics
Congress approves the purchase of Alaska from Russia.

1876
World Events
Queen Victoria of Great Britain becomes Empress of India.

1876
Politics
Colorado becomes the 38th state admitted to the Union.

1883
Business and Finance
Railroad companies create the time-zone system.

1860 — **1870** — **1880**

1861
World Events
The Italian parliament declares Italy a kingdom.

1860
Science and Technology
Oliver Winchester introduces the repeating rifle.

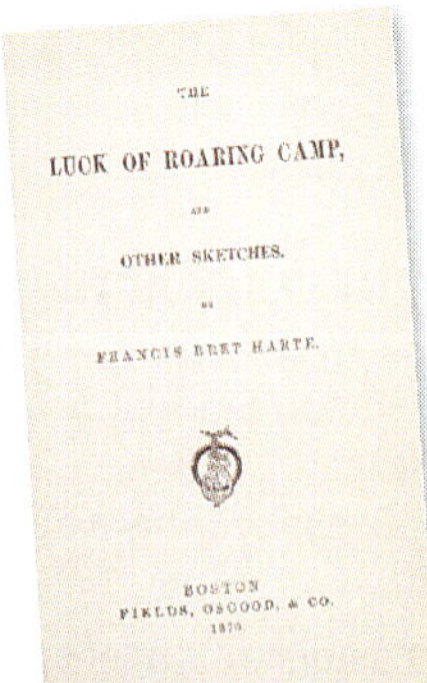

Bret Harte's The Luck of Roaring Camp

1870
The Arts
Bret Harte publishes *The Luck of Roaring Camp,* about life in California.

1873
Daily Life
Cable streetcars are introduced in San Francisco.

1873
Business and Finance
A severe economic depression slows the growth of railroad networks.

1879
Daily Life
Thousands of African Americans migrate from the South to Kansas.

1878
Politics
The Timber and Stone Act allows for the sale of western public land that cannot be used for farming.

Before You Read

Build on What You Know

The resolution of the Oregon boundary dispute in 1846 and the Treaty of Guadalupe Hidalgo in 1848 reshaped the United States. These treaties opened up more than 1 million square miles of western land for U.S. settlement. In this chapter you will learn that Americans who settled in the West came for many reasons. American Indians suffered the consequences of this settlement. They endured continued conflict and violence as non-Indians established farms and ranches in the lands of the American West.

132

Think About Themes

To help students create their Themes Journal entries, provide the following examples of appropriate **agree**/**disagree** *statements.*

Cultural Diversity

Agree Cultural differences between the Cayuse and white settlers in Oregon Territory led to violence.

Disagree Despite substantial cultural differences, the Wampanoag helped the English settlers in the Plymouth colony.

Economic Development

Agree The environmental impact of the fishing trade in colonial New England was not readily apparent.

Disagree Americans' desire to expand trade between states led to the building of the Erie Canal, railroads, and the National Road.

Technology and Society

Agree The development of new manufacturing technologies led some factory owners to employ children, who often worked under harsh conditions.

Disagree Cyrus McCormick's mechanical reaper allowed farmers to harvest grain more easily.

A Sioux child's doll

U.S. troops posing with Hotchkiss guns

1885
World Events
King Leopold II of Belgium assumes sovereignty over the African Congo.

1886–87
Daily Life
Devastating winter storms lash the Great Plains.

1889
Daily Life
President Harrison opens to settlers Oklahoma Territory lands that had been reserved for American Indians.

1890

1890
Politics
Troops of the U.S. 7th Cavalry attack Sioux camped at Wounded Knee Creek in South Dakota.

1890
Business and Finance
The Midwest is the center of the meatpacking industry.

1896
World Events
Italy recognizes Abyssinia—modern-day Ethiopia—as an independent nation.

1896
Daily Life
Americans living in rural areas receive mail delivery for free.

1898
The Arts
The Royal Italian Opera performs Puccini's *La Boheme* in San Francisco.

1900

1905
World Events
Czar Nicholas II of Russia institutes reforms after a series of strikes paralyzes the nation.

1906
Science and Technology
An astronomical observatory opens at Mt. Wilson, California.

1910

Settlers racing to claim land in Oklahoma

Think About Themes

Decide whether you **agree** *or* **disagree** *with the following statements. Note why in your journal.*

Cultural Diversity Cultural differences between groups can lead to misunderstandings and even violence.

Economic Development The impact that some economic activities have upon the environment is not readily apparent.

Technology and Society Improvements in technology may actually worsen conditions for some laborers.

exploring the time line

GLOBAL EVENTS

GLOBAL RELATIONS

1905 ■ Bloody Sunday in Russia. The series of strikes that prompted Czar Nicholas II to institute reforms in Russia were sparked by an event that occurred on January 9, 1905—a date that became known as "Bloody Sunday." Early that morning, thousands of workers gathered in St. Petersburg to present the czar with a list of economic and political grievances. When the demonstrators ignored orders to disperse, Russian troops opened fire on them. By the end of the day more than 130 people lay dead. Bloody Sunday outraged people across the nation, inspiring many strikes.

CRITICAL THINKING Tell students that a priest led the Bloody Sunday march and that many participants viewed it as a religious procession. Why might some observers have viewed it as a primarily political function rather than a religious one?

ANSWER: Some students might point to the workers' grievances, which were economic and political rather than religious.

SECTION 1

After completing Section 1, students should be able to:

OBJECTIVE 1 *Explain why the U.S. government created the American Indian reservation system.*

OBJECTIVE 2 *Identify the sources of conflict between the Plains Indians and the U.S. government.*

OBJECTIVE 3 *Describe how Chief Joseph, Geronimo, and Sarah Winnemucca responded to white treatment of American Indians.*

OBJECTIVE 4 *Discuss how the U.S. government tried to assimilate American Indians.*

LET'S GET STARTED!

Write the following quotation on the chalkboard: *"One of our hands holds the rifle and the other the peace-pipe, and we blaze away with both instruments at the same time. The chief consequence is a great smoke—and there it ends."* As students enter the classroom, ask them to respond to the statement in writing. *Who might be quoted on the chalkboard? What idea might the speaker be trying to convey?* Tell students that in Section 1 they will learn about American Indian resistance to U.S. government policies toward Indians.

SECTION 1 RESOURCES

PRINT

- Guided Reading Strategy 4.1
- Geography Activity 4: American Indian Lands in the West
- Primary Source Reading 4: "Massacre at Wounded Knee"
- Biography Reading 4: Geronimo
- Graphic Organizer Activity 4: American Indian Leaders
- Section 1 Review, p. 141
- Daily Quiz 4.1

MULTIMEDIA

- One-Stop Planner, Lesson 4.1
- Art in American History Transparency 15: Navajo Eye Dazzler Blanket
- Holt Researcher: American History CD–ROM
- HRW Web site

SHELTERED ENGLISH

- Main Idea Activity for Reteaching and Sheltered English 4.1

✓ READING TO UNDERSTAND

To help students master the section objectives, have them answer the **READING CHECKS** and complete **Guided Reading Strategy 4.1** as they read the section.

SECTION 1

War in the West

OBJECTIVES

Read to understand:

1. why the U.S. government created the American Indian reservation system
2. what the sources of conflict between the Plains Indians and the U.S. government were
3. how Chief Joseph, Geronimo, and Sarah Winnemucca responded to white treatment of American Indians
4. how the U.S. government tried to assimilate American Indians

KEY TERMS

Bureau of Indian Affairs
Sand Creek Massacre
Battle of the Little Bighorn
Massacre at Wounded Knee
Dawes General Allotment Act

KEY PEOPLE

Cochise
John M. Chivington
Sitting Bull
George Armstrong Custer
Wovoka
Chief Joseph
Geronimo
Sarah Winnemucca

KEY PLACES

Standing Rock Reservation
Bosque Redondo Reservation

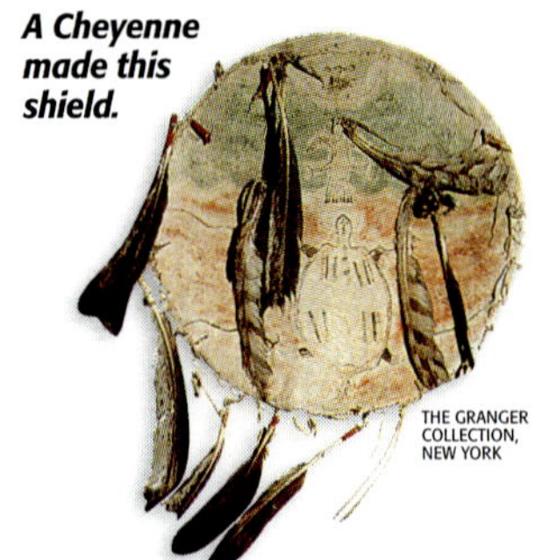
A Cheyenne made this shield.

THE GRANGER COLLECTION, NEW YORK

EYEWITNESSES TO History

"When I was young, I walked all over this country, east and west, and saw no other people than the Apaches. After many summers I walked again and found another race of people had come to take it."
—Cochise

Chiricahua Apache

Cochise, a Chiricahua (chir-uh-KAH-wuh) Apache leader, mourned over the crisis faced by American Indians as white settlers poured into their homelands. The Chiricahua Apache resisted, however. During the 1850s the Chiricahua had permitted settlers traveling to California to pass through Apache lands in present-day Arizona. In 1861, however, a rancher accused the Chiricahua of stealing a child and cattle from his ranch. U.S. Army officials attempted to hold Cochise and his relatives hostage until the child and cattle were returned. The incident led to years of deadly warfare between the Chiricahua and the United States.

Indian Country

By 1850 most American Indians—some 360,000—lived west of the Mississippi River. The 1851 Treaty of Fort Laramie had guaranteed American Indian land rights on the Great Plains. However, as non-Indians moved west in search of farmland and gold, government officials sought to acquire additional American Indian lands. They negotiated new treaties in which American Indians agreed to move to reservations. In return, Indians received some money and guarantees that the reservation lands would be theirs forever. These treaties also promised yearly supplies for 30 years.

In addition to opening new lands to settlement, some government officials hoped that keeping American Indians on the reservations would force them to become farmers. This would also force some American Indians to abandon their traditional ways of life. The **Bureau of Indian Affairs** (BIA) was the government agency responsible for managing American Indian issues. BIA chief Luke Lea supported the reservation system. He declared in 1850 that American Indians should "be placed in positions where they can be controlled, and finally compelled by stern necessity to resort to agricultural labor or starve." Other officials recognized the harm this would do to American Indians. Thomas Fitzpatrick was an Indian agent who had helped to negotiate several treaties. In 1853 Fitzpatrick condemned the notion of a reservation system as "expensive, vicious, [and] inhumane."

American Indians who went willingly to the reservations discovered that the U.S. government often failed to honor its treaties. In addition, the government reduced the size of many reservations as settlers demanded more land. To make matters worse, in many cases the promised supplies never arrived. Government agents often diverted elsewhere the supplies intended for American Indians.

TEACH OBJECTIVE 1

LEVEL 1: Pair students and tell them to imagine that they are newspaper reporters who have been assigned to cover American Indian issues in the mid-1800s. Have each pair write four newspaper headlines that express the U.S. government's reasons for creating the American Indian reservation system. *(Pairs' headlines should include the desire for farmland and gold, the desire for control, and the desire for assimilation.)* Ask volunteers to share their headlines with the class.
Sheltered English, Cooperative Learning

LEVEL 2: Tell students to imagine that it is 1885 and that they live in New Jersey but plan to move to Arizona. Have each student write a short editorial explaining and commenting on why the U.S. government created the American Indian reservation system. *(See the Level 1 lesson for answers. Students' editorials should tend to support the reservation system out of consideration for their impending move.)* Have volunteers read their editorials to the class. Then ask students to consider the issue of historical self-interest. Would their responses to the reservation system have been different if they were American Indians in the West? If they were neutral French observers? How? Conduct a discussion on students' responses.

Anger over inadequate supplies and broken treaties exploded into violence on the Santee Sioux reservation in 1862. When a government agent refused to release food supplies even though people were starving, the Sioux attacked the Indian agency and nearby farms and towns. Army troops soon ended the uprising and executed 38 Sioux for their actions. The tribe was relocated, first to the Dakota Territory and then to Nebraska.

✔ **READING CHECK:** Why did the U.S. government create the American Indian reservation system?

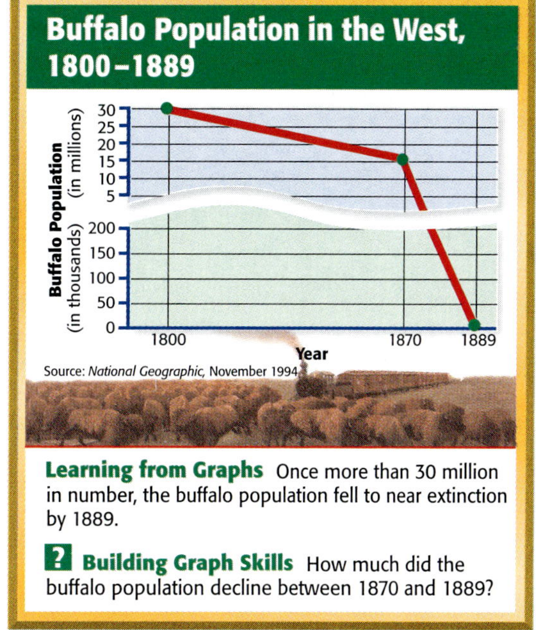

Learning from Graphs Once more than 30 million in number, the buffalo population fell to near extinction by 1889.

Building Graph Skills How much did the buffalo population decline between 1870 and 1889?

Years of Struggle

Many Plains Indians, including independent groups of Arapaho, Cheyenne, Comanche, and Sioux, refused to live on the reservations. The importance of following the roaming buffalo herds to their cultures caused them to reject the restrictions of settled life.

The Plains Indians faced strong opposition. Some 20,000 U.S. Army troops, many of them Civil War veterans, were assigned to confine the tribes to the reservations. The army also enlisted some American Indians as scouts or as soldiers. Struggling to confine or relocate American Indians, U.S. troops occasionally became involved in violent conflicts with groups of American Indians.

Sand Creek. One early confrontation in the West between the military and American Indians occurred in Colorado Territory. Eager to open more land to U.S. settlers, territorial governor John Evans pressured the Cheyenne and Arapaho to sell their hunting grounds and move to reservations. In 1861 some Cheyenne and Arapaho leaders agreed to move their groups to a reservation south of the Arkansas River. Others, however, refused to leave.

Cheyenne and Arapaho forces clashed with the local militia throughout the summer of 1864. By fall, Cheyenne chief Black Kettle had tired of the fighting. On the way to Fort Lyon to surrender, his group camped along Sand Creek. While most of the Cheyenne men were away hunting, U.S. Army colonel John M. Chivington and some 700 Colorado volunteers arrived at the camp. Having raised a U.S. flag above his lodge as a sign of peace, Black Kettle reassured his people that they were safe. One eyewitness later recalled, "Suddenly the troops opened fire on this mass of men, women, and children, and all began to scatter and run." Some 200 of Black Kettle's group, most of them women and children, died in the **Sand Creek Massacre**.

Chivington defended his actions, declaring, "It is right and honorable to use any means under God's heaven to kill Indians." However, the slaughter horrified most Americans. A congressional committee investigating the incident called Sand Creek a "scene of murder and barbarity." Shock over the massacre led some members of Congress to call for reform of the government's Indian policy.

INTERPRETING THE VISUAL RECORD

Buffalo. This painting by John Mix Stanley features a scene of the West. ***What does the painting reveal about the techniques American Indians used to hunt buffalo?***

CULTURAL DIVERSITY

African American Soldiers in the West. Many of the soldiers who served in the West after the Civil War were African Americans. In 1866 the U.S. Army organized four new units—the 9th and 10th Cavalries and the 24th and 25th Infantries—that were composed entirely of black enlisted men, most of whom were former slaves. Under the command of white officers, these soldiers took part in a number of bloody Indian battles throughout the West. By 1890 the government had awarded the Congressional Medal of Honor to 14 of the soldiers for bravery.

CRITICAL THINKING Why might some African Americans have enlisted in the U.S. Army after the Civil War?

ANSWER: Students might suggest that army service offered a unique career opportunity to African Americans during this period.

VISUAL RECORD ANSWER

Students might suggest that Indian techniques required skill with the spear.

GRAPH ANSWER

by about 15 million

LEVEL 3: Tell students to imagine that they are high-level government officials preparing to unveil the American Indian reservation system. Have each student write a short speech explaining why the U.S. government created the system. *(See the Level 1 lesson for the correct answers.)* Ask volunteers to present their speeches to the class. Then ask students to consider the reasons presented in those speeches. Do any of those reasons seem justified today? If not, why? *(Press students to consider modern-day advances in civil rights.)* Conduct a discussion on students' responses.

TEACH OBJECTIVE 2

LEVEL 1: Pair students and have each pair list the sources of conflict between the Plains Indians and the U.S. government. *(Pairs should list the conflicts over land and reservations, the conflicts over broken promises and treaties, and the conflicts over the Ghost Dance.)* Then ask each pair to synthesize the material on its list into a written paragraph. Have volunteers read their paragraphs to the class.

Sheltered English, Cooperative Learning

MORE ON THE MAP

The Black Hills. The Black Hills region received its name from the Sioux, who first migrated to the area during the 1700s. The called it "Paha Sapa," or the "hills that appear black in color." The Black Hills region contained an abundance of wildlife and plenty of wood and water. Over the years it became an important place for the tribe–one that held spiritual meaning.

ACTIVITY: Ask students to identify places that have strong meanings or values to a particular cultural or ethnic group. Have volunteers share their responses. Then ask each student to describe a given place in writing, explaining its cultural importance.

MAP ANSWER

Wounded Knee

VISUAL RECORD ANSWER

(for p. 137)

Students might suggest that he viewed it as chaotic and violent.

Multimedia Resources

Art in American History Transparency 15: Navajo Eye Dazzler Blanket

The Sand Creek Massacre shocked many Americans.

While government officials debated reform, news of the Sand Creek Massacre swept across the Plains, prompting raids by the Arapaho and Cheyenne. The Sioux also stepped up their attacks. Neither side emerged victorious, however. To end the fighting, the U.S. government created a peace commission to negotiate new treaties. Meeting with the southern Plains Indians in 1867, Senator John B. Henderson told them that the buffalo would soon be gone, so "the Indian must change the road his father trod." One Comanche replied, "I love the open prairie, and I wish you would not insist on putting us on a reservation." Despite such feelings, tribal leaders signed the Treaty of Medicine Lodge. Southern Plains Indians agreed to give up much of their lands in exchange for reservations in Indian Territory. The following year, in a second Treaty of Fort Laramie, the Sioux agreed to move to a reservation in the Black Hills region of South Dakota.

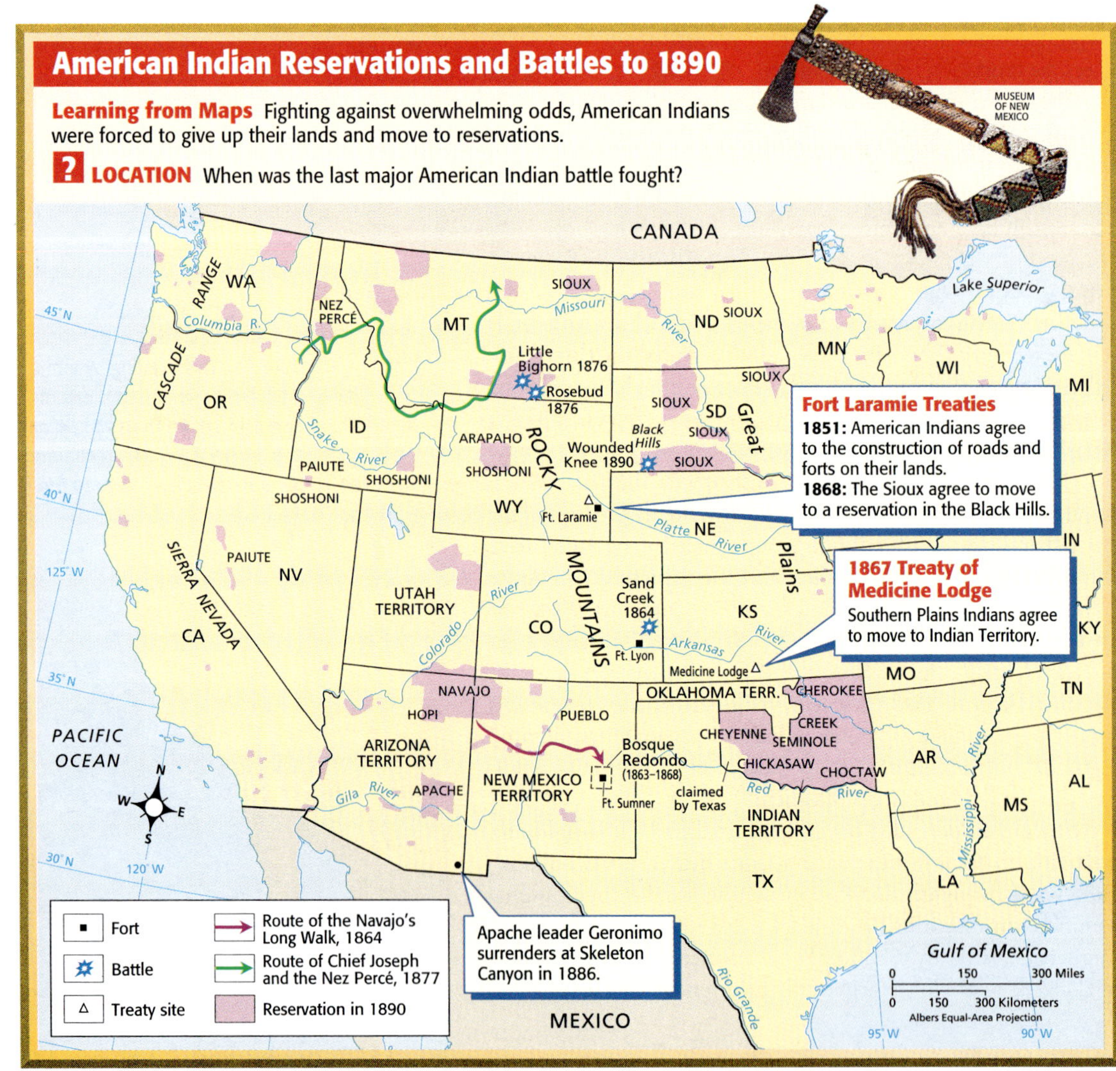

American Indian Reservations and Battles to 1890

Learning from Maps Fighting against overwhelming odds, American Indians were forced to give up their lands and move to reservations.

? LOCATION When was the last major American Indian battle fought?

LEVEL 2: Organize the class into groups of four, with two members of each group assuming the roles of U.S. government officials and two members assuming the roles of Plains Indians. Have the two sides within each group identify the sources of conflict between American Indians and the government. *(See the Level 1 lesson for the correct conflicts.)* Then ask groups to negotiate treaties with specific provisions to satisfy both sides. *(Groups' treaties should address the major sources of conflict identified in the Level 1 lesson.)* Ask a spokesperson from each group to share his or her group's treaty with the class, and have other students assess its recommendations, considering both fairness and practicality. **Cooperative Learning**

LEVEL 3: Tell students to imagine that they are investigative reporters for an 1890 edition of the St. Louis *Post-Dispatch.* Have each student write a short investigative report on the sources of conflict between American Indians and the U.S. government. *(See the Level 1 lesson for the correct conflicts.)* Have volunteers read their reports to the class.

▶**ASSIGNMENT** *Have each student create a crossword puzzle that utilizes all the key terms and key people in the subsection entitled Years of Struggle. Students should provide clues for the answers. Tell students to exchange their crossword puzzles and solve the puzzle they receive.*

Little Bighorn. The peace was short-lived, however. In 1874 the government violated the terms of the 1868 Treaty of Fort Laramie by sending an army expedition into the Black Hills to search for gold. Gold was discovered, and the government tried to negotiate a new treaty with the Sioux. The Sioux refused. War clouds again gathered over the Plains.

Sitting Bull

Tatanka Iyotake, a Lakota Sioux also called Sitting Bull, emerged as an important leader of Sioux resistance. Born about 1831 along the banks of the Missouri River, Sitting Bull was nicknamed "Slow" as a child. At age 14 he fought in his first battle, a small skirmish with the Crow Indians. As a result, he earned the right to wear an eagle feather, a symbol of bravery, and was given the name Sitting Bull.

Over time, Sitting Bull gained the respect of his people for his courage, wisdom, generosity, and ability to endure pain without complaint. He became known as a spiritual leader and medicine man. Committed to the traditional Sioux way of life, Sitting Bull strongly opposed the intrusion of non-Indians onto Sioux lands. He mocked American Indians who willingly moved to reservations. "You are fools," he argued, "to make yourselves slaves to a piece of fat bacon, some hard-tack [biscuits], and a little sugar and coffee." Many agreed, and by the spring of 1876 thousands of Sioux and their Cheyenne allies were camped on Rosebud Creek in southern Montana.

During the summer of 1876, Sitting Bull had a vision in which he saw soldiers attacking an American Indian village. However, the soldiers and their horses were upside down, which Sitting Bull understood to mean that they would all die. Inspired by this vision, several hundred American Indians rode off to fight U.S. troops. During the Battle of the Rosebud in June 1876, the Indians battled an army twice the size of their own. Although they did not achieve an outright victory, their performance at Rosebud gave them confidence in their ability to fight the U.S. soldiers.

After the battle, the Indians proceeded west to camp near a stream known by the army as Little Bighorn River. They were joined by hundreds of American Indians fleeing the BIA-sponsored encampments, where food was in short supply. By late June the camp contained some 2,500 men prepared to fight.

On the morning of June 25, 1876, General George Armstrong Custer and about 600 members of the U.S. Army 7th Cavalry reached the American Indian camp. Although his troops had ridden through most of the night, Custer ordered an immediate attack. After dividing his men so that they could attack from three sides, Custer led a battalion of more than 200 men into the camp. Cheyenne warrior Two Moons described the battle. "We circled all round . . . swirling like water around a stone. We shoot, we ride fast, we shoot again. Soldiers drop, and horses fall on them." After the final attack, which lasted less than an hour, Custer and every soldier in his battalion lay dead.

The **Battle of the Little Bighorn** proved to be the last victory for the Sioux. The shock of Custer's

Read More About It

Free Find: Sitting Bull

After reading about Sitting Bull on the **Holt Researcher** CD–ROM, imagine that you are an author preparing a biography of Sitting Bull. Create an outline that shows the reasons why you think he was a good or bad leader for his people.

INTERPRETING THE VISUAL RECORD

The Little Bighorn. Kicking Bear created this painting of the Battle of the Little Bighorn. ***What do you think Kicking Bear thought of the Battle of the Little Bighorn?***

CULTURAL DIVERSITY

Reservations and the Battle of the Little Bighorn. Like Sitting Bull, many American Indians despised reservations, a dislike that helped spark the Battle of the Little Bighorn. Several factors inspired this response. Many reservations were located on poor soil, unsuitable for farming. In addition, they rarely resembled traditional tribal grounds. Many American Indians regarded reservations as little more than concentration camps.

CRITICAL THINKING Why might many reservations have been located on poor soil?

ANSWER: Students might suggest that white settlers probably complained when reservations were sited on good land.

THAT'S INTERESTING!

Although a popular general, George Armstrong Custer had a slightly checkered military record. He graduated at the bottom of his class at West Point, and in 1867 he was court-martialed and temporarily suspended from command for a number of offenses, including overmarching his troops and leaving his post without permission.

SPOTLIGHT on Combatants in the West

Have students conduct research on one of the following people: Cochise, John M. Chivington, Sitting Bull, George Armstrong Custer, Wovoka, Chief Joseph, or Geronimo. Direct students to concentrate their research on the person's experiences in the West and in the conflict over the region. Then ask each student to write a biography on his or her chosen figure. Students' biographies should describe how the person was regarded in his day as well as how the person is remembered today. **Block Scheduling**

SPOTLIGHT on the Ghost Dance

Organize students into small groups and tell them to imagine that they are anthropologists in the West in the late 1800s. Have each group create a set of detailed field notes describing and analyzing the Ghost Dance. In their notes, students should discuss elements such as clothing and rituals as well as the larger political significance of the dance. Have students present their notes to the class.
Cooperative Learning, Block Scheduling

CULTURAL DIVERSITY

The Ghost Dance. Some government agents saw the Ghost Dance as a threatening social movement. Agent D. F. Royer described the dance by writing, "Indians are dancing in the snow and are wild and crazy. . . . [The] employees and Government property at this agency have no protection and are at the mercy of these dancers. . . . The leaders should be arrested and confined in some military post until the matter is quieted."

CRITICAL THINKING Why might government agents have found the Ghost Dance so threatening?

ANSWER: Students might suggest that the Ghost Dance seemed culturally alien and therefore particularly threatening to some agents.

internetconnect

TOPIC: Sioux Nation
GO TO: go.hrw.com
KEYWORD: SE1 Sioux

Have students access the Internet through the HRW Web site to conduct research on the Sioux and to learn about the pictographs, such as the story robe, that the Sioux used to depict important tribal events. Have each student design a "story robe" that portrays the tribe's history. Students should include a written explanation of their illustrations.

HISTORY *IN THE MAKING*

George Custer

BY PAUL F. HUTTON

Many Americans were shocked in 1876 to learn of George Armstrong Custer's death at the Battle of the Little Bighorn. A popular figure with the American people, Custer was the subject of magazine articles that celebrated his battles with Indians during the early 1870s. After his death, poets, novelists, and artists responded to the nation's sense of loss with works that portrayed Custer as a hero who gave his life to end the Indians' domination of the American West. The play *Custer's Last Charge* kept the image of the heroic Custer alive during the 1880s and 1890s. In the 1900s, filmmakers produced nearly 20 movies before 1941 that portrayed Custer as a defender of the settlers.

However, some people questioned Custer's reputation. Novels such as Frederic Van de Water's *Glory-Hunter* depicted Custer as a brutal man. Films such as *Sitting Bull* (1954) portrayed the American Indians as courageously defending their homelands against a cruel Custer. Histories that offered the Indian perspective of the wars on the Plains further eroded the Custer myth to such a degree that in 1991 Congress passed legislation removing Custer's name from the national monument at Little Bighorn.

defeat prompted the army to increase its efforts to move the American Indians onto reservations. Over the next several months the American Indian forces broke into smaller groups to evade army troops. Group by group, they surrendered and settled near the BIA encampments. Sitting Bull fled to Canada but eventually returned and settled on the Standing Rock Reservation in Dakota Territory.

The Ghost Dance. The final chapter of the Plains Indian–U.S. Army wars took place on the Pine Ridge Reservation in South Dakota. Unhappy with life on the reservation, many Sioux took heart when they heard the message of Wovoka (woh-VOH-kuh). A Paiute, Wovoka began a religious movement known as the Ghost Dance. He claimed that the Ghost Dance could cause white settlers to vanish, dead Indian ancestors to return to life, the buffalo to return, and traditional Indian ways of life to revive.

Wovoka's message brought hope to discouraged American Indians throughout the West. The Sioux living on reservations in the Dakotas wore "Ghost Shirts," believing that the shirts' special symbols could stop bullets.

James McLaughlin, the BIA agent at the Standing Rock Reservation, dismissed the Ghost Dance as an "absurd craze." However, some government officials feared that the religious movement would inspire rebellion. When the Ghost Dance spread to Standing Rock Reservation, the military ordered the arrest of Sitting Bull, who had joined the movement. When reservation police surrounded Sitting Bull's cabin on December 15, 1890, a skirmish broke out and 14 Indians—including Sitting Bull—were killed.

Wounded Knee. Frightened and angry after Sitting Bull's death, many Sioux joined the Ghost Dancers farther west. Some traveled with Big Foot, a Sioux leader who had initially supported the Ghost Dance but had gradually turned away from it. Government officials wanted to arrest Big Foot because they feared he might cause trouble. Hoping to avoid conflict with army troops, Big Foot decided to lead his group to the Pine Ridge Reservation. On December 28, 1890, army troops found Big Foot and some 350 members of his group. The Sioux made camp for the night along Wounded Knee Creek.

The next morning, Colonel James Forsyth of the 7th Cavalry ordered the removal of Indian rifles. Reinforced by four Hotchkiss guns that fired exploding shells, some 500 mounted soldiers surrounded the camp. When the Sioux surrendered only a few guns, soldiers began to search the tepees. Tensions ran high. Nerves snapped, and the Sioux and U.S. soldiers began shooting. The Hotchkiss guns ripped into the camp. By day's end some 300 Sioux and about 30 U.S. soldiers had been killed. Some people declared that Custer and the 7th Cavalry had been "avenged," but the **Massacre at Wounded Knee** shocked many Americans. The

Some Ghost Dancers believed that Ghost Shirts such as this one protected them from harm.

TEACH OBJECTIVE 3

ALL LEVELS: To help students understand how certain American Indians responded to white treatment, copy the graphic organizer to the right on the chalkboard, omitting the italicized answers. Have each student complete it. Then pair students and ask each pair to write one or two paragraphs assessing the effectiveness of American Indian responses in the late 1800s. *(Pairs' paragraphs should indicate that many of the responses were ineffective, given the enormous power of the U.S. government.)* Have volunteers read their paragraphs to the class. **Sheltered English, Cooperative Learning**

AMERICAN INDIAN RESPONSES TO WHITE TREATMENT

Chief Joseph	Geronimo	Sarah Winnemucca
agreed to move tribe to a reservation; fled from the U.S Army; eventually surrendered	*fled a reservation with his tribe; raided settlements; eventually surrendered*	*called attention to problems; made speeches; participated in political activities*

▸ASSIGNMENT: *Tell students to imagine that they are Chief Joseph, Geronimo, or Sarah Winnemucca. Have each student write a short speech responding to white treatment of American Indians.*

incident marked the end of the bloody conflict between soldiers and American Indians on the Great Plains.

✔ **READING CHECK:** What were the sources of conflict between the Plains Indians and the U.S. government?

The End of Resistance

American Indians west of the Great Plains were also forced to resettle. The Nez Percé tried to remain in their homelands in northeastern Oregon. They surrendered much of their land in an 1855 treaty and agreed to remain on a reservation. When settlers moved onto reservation land, the Nez Percé did not turn to violence. When the government ordered the Nez Percé to relocate to a reservation in Idaho, their leader Chief Joseph, reluctantly agreed. However, some young Nez Percé killed 11 white settlers. Fearing war, the Nez Percé fled, with the army in close pursuit.

The Nez Percé journeyed east and north through Idaho, Wyoming, and Montana, picking up additional followers along the way. The group eventually numbered from 700 to 800. They hoped to escape to Canada, but winter weather made travel difficult. Chief Joseph surrendered to the U.S. Army just 30 miles from the Canadian border. An interpreter wept as he relayed the leader's surrender statement.

> **"I am tired of fighting. Our chiefs are killed. . . . It is cold and we have no blankets. The little children are freezing to death. . . . My heart is sick and sad. From where the sun now stands, I will fight no more forever."**

The Nez Percé were first sent to prison in Kansas, then to a reservation in Indian Territory. In 1885 the U.S. government permitted some to return to the reservation in Oregon, but sent Chief Joseph and some 150 others to a reservation in Washington State.

In the mid-1870s, the government forced the seminomadic Apache in New Mexico and Arizona to settle on the San Carlos Reservation, along Arizona's Gila River. When army troops moved into the territory in 1881, the Apache leader Geronimo fled the reservation with about 75 followers. Geronimo's group raided settlements throughout Arizona and Mexico. After the women and children following Geronimo were captured in 1884, Geronimo surrendered and briefly accepted reservation life. By 1885, however, Geronimo and 134 followers escaped from the reservation and resumed raids on settlements. On September 4, 1886, with his followers outnumbered, Geronimo gave up. "Once I moved about like the wind," he told his captors. "Now I surrender to you and that is all." After his final surrender, Geronimo and his followers were sent to Florida as prisoners of war. His surrender marked the end of armed resistance to the reservation system in the Southwest.

THE GHOST DANCE

The Ghost Dance combined elements from American Indian religions and Christianity. The son of a medicine man, Wovoka lived for a time with a white family that regularly read Bible passages aloud. Kicking Bear, who brought Wovoka's message to the Sioux, told them they would be "led by the Messiah who came once to live on earth with the white man." This reference to Jesus Christ revealed Christianity's influence on Wovoka's thought.

A Ghost Dance

The Ghost Dance was similar to the Paiute round dance. Men and women formed a circle by holding hands and then stepped to the left. Dancers had their faces painted and wore Ghost Shirts—cotton garments decorated with pictures of animals and sacred symbols. The Sioux added features from their own Sun Dance, making the circle around a sacred pole and at times staring into the Sun as they performed the dance.

James Mooney was a social scientist who interviewed several Ghost Dancers in 1891. He interpreted the religion as the spiritual expression of a people whose societies had been devastated. "Hope becomes a faith and the faith becomes a creed [belief] of priests and prophets, until the hero is a god and the dream a religion, looking to some great miracle of nature for its culmination [climax] and accomplishment," he explained. The Ghost Dance movement faded away when the promised miracle never occurred.

PEOPLE IN HISTORY

Chief Joseph. Chief Joseph, whose Nez Percé name meant "thunder rolling down from the mountains," belonged to a family of prominent tribal leaders. His father, Joseph the Elder, was a respected buffalo hunter who helped negotiate the 1855 treaty that temporarily secured a reservation for the Nez Percé in their native homelands. His brother, Olikut, was a skilled warrior who helped plan the tribe's defense strategy during its unsuccessful flight to Canada. Chief Joseph himself had a reputation as both a brave fighter and a gifted diplomat, and by the time he was in his mid-30s he had been recognized by U.S. authorities as the most influential of the Nez Percé leaders.

CRITICAL THINKING Why might Chief Joseph have agreed to relocate the Nez Percé to a reservation in Idaho?

ANSWER: Students might suggest that Chief Joseph agreed to relocate the Nez Percé because he knew that a war against the U.S. Army would end in disaster for the tribe.

TEACH OBJECTIVE 4

ALL LEVELS: Ask volunteers to identify ways in which the federal government attempted to assimilate American Indians. Have volunteers list these ways on the chalkboard. *(Students should list the establishment of reservations, the creation of Indian schools, and the passage of the Dawes Act.)* Then ask students to assume the role of an army officer at Fort Sumner. Have each student write a short memo assessing the assimilation of the Navajo. Ask volunteers to read their memos to the class. Then lead a class discussion about how the government responded to the plan's failure and the resulting consequences for the Navajo. **Sheltered English**

SPOTLIGHT on the Carlisle Indian School

Have students conduct research on the Carlisle Indian School. Students should take note of the school's programs and operating period. Then have students consider the following questions: *Were American Indian students successfully assimilated into "white" culture? What was student life like at the school? Was the assimilation there designed to benefit American Indians?* Ask each student to respond to the questions in an essay. **Block Scheduling**

ACROSS THE CURRICULUM

▶LITERATURE◀

Helen Hunt Jackson. Before she became an Indian rights activist, Helen Hunt Jackson was a successful poet and journalist. Under pseudonyms such as "No Name," "Rip Van Winkel," and "Sax Holm," she wrote hundreds of poems and articles that appeared in a variety of publications. Ralph Waldo Emerson once referred to her as the "greatest American woman poet."

ACTIVITY: Ask each student to consult a literary anthology and select a poem written by a woman in the late 1800s. Have students read their poems to the class. Then conduct a discussion on common themes and styles.

VISUAL RECORD ANSWER

(for p. 141)

Students might point to the boys' hair and clothing.

SECTION 1 REVIEW ANSWERS

Define and Identify

For significance, see the following pages:

- Cochise, p. 134
- Bureau of Indian Affairs, p. 134
- John M. Chivington, p. 135
- Sand Creek Massacre, p. 135
- Sitting Bull, p. 137
- George Armstrong Custer, p. 137

Helen Hunt Jackson's 1881 book chronicled the mistreatment of American Indians.

Voices of Protest

By the 1880s, American Indians had surrendered more than half a billion acres to the U.S. government. In addition to military conflicts with the army, Indians suffered as settlers killed most of the buffalo herds. With the loss of the buffalo, American Indians had little hope of maintaining an independent existence on the Plains. "All our people now were settling down in square gray houses, scattered here and there across this hungry land," recalled Black Elk of the Teton Sioux.

Troubled by the treatment of American Indians, reformers organized groups such as the Indian Rights Association and the Women's National Indian Association. These groups urged the federal government to craft a more humane Indian policy. Helen Hunt Jackson of Massachusetts supported this cause. In 1881 she wrote an influential book, *A Century of Dishonor*, that criticized the government for its years of broken promises and mistreatment of American Indians.

Thoc-me-tony, a Paiute reformer also known as Sarah Winnemucca, called attention to the problems of American Indians. Winnemucca noted that although the government had authorized the building of two mills on the Paiute reservation, they were never constructed. She wondered:

> **"The [mills] were never seen or heard of by my people, though the printed report . . . says twenty-five thousand dollars was appropriated to build them. Where did [the money] go? . . . Is it that the government is cheated by its own agents who make these reports?"**

The forced removal of the Paiute to the Yakima Reservation in Washington Territory in 1878 so outraged Winnemucca that she began lecturing on the Paiute's behalf to non-Indian audiences. In 1880 she asked President Rutherford B. Hayes to allow the Paiute to return to their homelands. Hayes agreed, but the BIA's agents did not carry out the president's order.

✔ **READING CHECK:** How did Chief Joseph, Geronimo, and Sarah Winnemucca respond to white treatment of American Indians?

Sarah Winnemucca demanded fair treatment for American Indians.

Assimilating American Indians

Many government officials and most reformers viewed assimilation, or the cultural absorption of American Indians into "white America," as the only long-term way to ensure Indian survival. To speed the process of assimilation, the U.S. government established a system of American Indian schools. Some Indian children attended reservation schools, but others were forced to leave their families to attend boarding schools. At the schools, students were forced to speak only English, to wear "proper" clothes, and to change their names to "American" ones. The schools were places of misery for most students. Luther Standing Bear later recalled, "How lonesome I felt for my father and mother!"

Government officials had hoped that life on reservations would force American Indians to become farmers and adopt the lifestyles of non-Indian settlers. In 1887 Congress passed the **Dawes General Allotment Act**, which required that Indian lands be surveyed and that American Indian families receive an allotment of 160 acres of reservation land for farming. Any land that remained

REVIEW

Have students complete the **Section 1 Review** on p. 141.

ASSESS

Have students complete **Daily Quiz 4.1**. As **Alternative Assessment**, you may want to use the headlines or the investigative reports in this section's lessons.

RETEACH

Have students complete **Main Idea Activity for Reteaching and Sheltered English 4.1**. Then pair students and have each pair create an illustrated time line that covers the period from 1850 to 1890. For each entry on the time line, ask pairs to include a brief annotation describing its impact on American Indians. Have each pair work and discuss its time line with another pair. **Sheltered English, Cooperative Learning**

EXTEND

Tell students to conduct research on the life of one of the American Indian leaders discussed in Section 1. Have each student present his or her research to the class in the form of a question-and-answer interview. **Block Scheduling**

would be sold. The Indian Rights Association claimed that private ownership of land would lead to "the gradual breaking up of the reservations." This assessment proved correct. In less than 50 years, they lost two thirds of their land. Some of the land was sold to settlers and developers as surplus when allotments were made. In other cases, Indians sold or were cheated out of their allotments.

Despite the government's hopes, many American Indians rejected farming. Even before the Dawes Act, the government had tried to force the Navajo to abandon sheep raising and become settled farmers. To carry out this plan, the U.S. Army waged military campaigns against the Navajo in northwestern New Mexico and northeastern Arizona in 1863. Soldiers destroyed Navajo houses, herds of sheep, and corn crops. Without food or shelter, many Navajo surrendered in early 1864.

That same year, the U.S. Army led the Navajo on the Long Walk, a forced march to the Bosque Redondo Reservation in eastern New Mexico. Soldiers stationed at nearby Fort Sumner prevented the Navajo from leaving the reservation. The U.S. government gave the Navajo seeds and farming tools, but the land was not suitable for farming. Because the few trees were quickly cut down, the Navajo had to use roots for firewood. Many Navajo died from malnutrition and disease.

In 1868 the government admitted its failure and granted the Navajo a reservation in New Mexico and Arizona. They rebuilt their communities, concentrating on sheep raising, weaving, and silversmithing. By the 1880s their economy had stabilized and their population had begun to increase.

✔ **READING CHECK:** How did the U.S. government try to assimilate American Indians?

INTERPRETING THE VISUAL RECORD

Assimilation. These photographs show three American Indian boys before and after they attended an American Indian school. ***What evidence of their assimilation can you see?***

SECTION  REVIEW

Define and explain the significance of the following terms:
Bureau of Indian Affairs
Sand Creek Massacre
Battle of the Little Bighorn
Massacre at Wounded Knee
Dawes General Allotment Act

Identify and explain the significance of the following individuals:
Cochise
John M. Chivington
Sitting Bull
George Armstrong Custer
Wovoka
Chief Joseph
Geronimo
Sarah Winnemucca

Locate and explain the importance of the following places:
Standing Rock Reservation
Bosque Redondo Reservation

1. **Using Graphic Organizers** Copy the chart below. Use it to describe the conflicts between the United States and various American Indian tribes.

Tribe & Leader	Conflict	Outcome
Cheyenne		
Sioux		
Nez Percé		
Apache		

2. **Analyzing** Why did the U.S. government attempt to resettle American Indians on reservations?
3. **Taking a Stand** How would you have responded to protests made by Chief Joseph, Geronimo, and Sarah Winnemucca against the treatment of American Indians?
4. **Distinguishing Fact from Opinion** How did the experience of the Navajo weaken the argument of some government officials that the best solution for American Indians was to assimilate into white culture?

Critical Thinking

5. Could conflict between American Indians and the U.S. government have been avoided as white settlement increased? If so, how?
Consider:
• what the root causes were of the conflict
• how each side viewed the other
• what mistakes each side made in dealing with the other side

• Battle of the Little Bighorn, p. 137
• Wovoka, p. 138
• Massacre at Wounded Knee, p. 138
• Chief Joseph, p. 139
• Geronimo, p. 139
• Sarah Winnemucca, p. 140
• Dawes General Allotment Act, p. 140

Locate

For locations, see the map on p. 136. For importance, see the following pages:

• Standing Rock Reservation, p. 138
• Bosque Redondo Reservation, p. 141

1. Cheyenne–Black Kettle; dispute over hunting grounds and move to reservations; Sand Creek Massacre and resettlement on a reservation. Sioux–Sitting Bull; government intrusion on Sioux lands; Battle of the Little Bighorn, Massacre at Wounded Knee. Nez Percé–Chief Joseph; settler intrusions on Nez Percé land; pursuit, by U.S. Army, surrender and imprisonment and eventual settlement of tribe on reservations. Apache–Geronimo; army intrusion on Apache territory; flight of Geronimo and followers, surrender of Geronimo.

2. clear land for settlers and assimilate American Indians

3. Some students might suggest accommodation to demands.

4. the disastrous experience at Bosque Redondo and the subsequent success

5. Some students might argue that conflict was unavoidable; others might claim that conflict could have been avoided.

SECTION 2

After completing Section 2, students should be able to:

OBJECTIVE 1 *Discuss how the U.S. government promoted economic development in the West.*

OBJECTIVE 2 *Understand why people migrated west.*

OBJECTIVE 3 *Explain how the environment influenced farming practices and daily life in the West.*

OBJECTIVE 4 *Describe the difficulties that farm families faced on the Great Plains.*

LET'S GET STARTED!

Write the following scenario on the chalkboard: *You are a farmer in the Mississippi Valley, where land has grown expensive. The government will give you 160 acres of land in Oklahoma, but you are unfamiliar with the land and climate there, and you will be separated from most of your family. Will you move to Oklahoma anyway?* Have students respond to the scenario in writing. Have volunteers share their responses with the class. Tell students that in Section 2 they will learn more about opportunities in the West.

SECTION 2 RESOURCES

PRINT

- Guided Reading Strategy 4.2
- American History Outline Map 15: Western Railroads and Cattle Trails
- Literature Reading 4: Life on the Prairie
- Section 2 Review, p. 148
- Daily Quiz 4.2

MULTIMEDIA

- One-Stop Planner, Lesson 4.2
- The American Nation Video Program Segment: Linking the Nation; Teacher's Guide, pp. 69–74
- Holt Researcher: American History CD–ROM

SHELTERED ENGLISH

- Main Idea Activity for Reteaching and Sheltered English 4.2

✔ READING TO UNDERSTAND
To help students master the section objectives, have them answer the **READING CHECKS** and complete **Guided Reading Strategy 4.2** as they read the section.

Western Farmers

OBJECTIVES

Read to understand:

1. how the U.S. government promoted economic development in the West
2. why people migrated west
3. how the environment influenced farming practices and daily life in the West
4. what difficulties farm families faced on the Great Plains

KEY TERMS

Homestead Act
Pacific Railway Act
Morrill Act
Exodusters
sod houses
U.S. Department of Agriculture
bonanza farm

KEY PEOPLE

Benjamin Singleton
Willa Cather

EYEWITNESSES TO History

"To say that I was homesick, discouraged, and lonely, is but a faint [poor] description of my feelings. . . . Not a tree, plant nor shrub on which to rest my weary eye, to break the monotony of the sand beds and cactus of the Great American Desert."

—Annie Green

A pioneer woman in southern California receives the deed to her homestead.

Annie Green moved to Colorado in 1870. She and her husband were among the thousands of American families who headed west to the Great Plains in the years following the Civil War. Green felt like "a stranger in a strange land" in her new home. In order to reassure her husband she "resolved . . . to cultivate [encourage] a cheerful disposition." Like many settlers, Green and her family discovered that hard work, determination, and a little luck were necessary to prosper.

Economic Development of the West

During the Civil War, Republicans sought to manage western development to ensure that the new western states and territories would be free of slavery. They also wanted them to be populated by independent farmers who would improve the land. After the southern states seceded from the Union, Republicans took the opportunity to pass a series of acts in 1862 to put public lands to productive use.

Land acts. Three government land acts increased non-Indian settlement of the Great Plains. The **Homestead Act** permitted "any citizen or intended citizen to select any surveyed land up to 160 acres and to gain title to it after five years' residence" if the person cultivated the land. The Civil War slowed the initial response to the act. Eventually, however, some 400,000 families took advantage of the offer. The **Pacific Railway Act** gave lands to railroad companies to develop a railroad line linking the East and West Coasts. The **Morrill Act** granted more than 17 million acres of federal land to the states. The act ordered the sale of this land to finance the construction of agricultural and engineering colleges. The Morrill Act led to the eventual founding of more than 70 state universities.

Competition for land was fierce. In October 1889, for example, a flood of prospective settlers responded to a government offer of free homesteads in Oklahoma. The acreage came from former Creek and Seminole lands. In March, President Benjamin Harrison had announced that the land would be available to the first takers beginning at noon on April 22. By the appointed day, about 50,000 people had gathered to race one another for the land. Some rode horses or bicycles. Others pushed wheelbarrows filled with supplies. Subsequent "runs" took place in other parts of Oklahoma. This occurred at the expense of American Indians, who lost nearly 12 million acres in Oklahoma to non-Indian settlers.

COLLECTION OF THE NEW-YORK HISTORICAL SOCIETY

Posters like this one persuaded many people that a better life waited for them out west.

TEACH OBJECTIVE 1

ALL LEVELS: To help students understand how the U.S. government promoted economic development in the West, copy the chart on the chalkboard, omitting the italicized answers. Have each student complete it. Then organize the class into triads and tell students to imagine that they are writers and artists hired to create full-page newspaper ads to publicize government programs designed to attract settlers and railroad companies to western lands. Tell students that their ads should combine appealing images with lists of incentives to attract settlers to the Great Plains. Have each triad present its advertisement to the class.
Sheltered English, Cooperative Learning

GOVERNMENT ACTIONS TO AID ECONOMIC DEVELOPMENT IN THE WEST

Homestead Act	Pacific Railway Act	Morrill Act
permitted "any citizen or intended citizen" to have 160 acres of land	*gave lands to railroad companies to develop a transcontinental railroad linking the East and West Coasts*	*granted more than 17 million acres of land to be sold to finance the construction of agricultural and engineering colleges*

The railroads. Railroad companies also lured settlers to the West. Between 1869 and 1883, four rail lines were built across the West. Within 10 years of the passage of the Pacific Railway Act, the U.S. government had given railroad companies more than 125 million acres of public land. State and local governments donated nearly 100 million acres of additional land. These grants limited the amount of land available to settlers under the Homestead Act. Government officials believed that railroad companies would promote western settlement and economic growth. Railroad companies sold any surplus land to homesteaders in an effort to offset the high cost of laying tracks. The homesteaders benefited from the nearby railroad lines, using them to ship their crops to distant markets.

Eager to encourage settlement along their rail routes, railroad companies advertised in the East and in Europe. The companies offered to pay the fares of potential land buyers and sell them land on credit. Some railroad companies gave free trips to newspaper reporters, who then wrote glowing reports of the land and towns along the rail line. One Indiana editor wrote:

> "I never saw finer country in the world than that part of Kansas passed over by the Atchison, Topeka & Santa Fe [rail]road. Corn waist high, wheat in the shock [stacked], oats in fine condition, and vegetables in abundance."

✔ **READING CHECK:** How did the U.S. government promote the economic development of the West?

INTERPRETING THE VISUAL RECORD

The road west. With tickets like this one, many migrants rode the rails to their new homes in the West, sometimes riding on flatcars to get there. ***What do you think travel conditions were like for the migrants in this photograph?***

Moving West

The West lured migrants who hoped for a better life. Some sought economic opportunity. Others hoped to find racial tolerance. Three main groups traveled westward after the Civil War: white Americans from the East, African Americans from the South, and immigrants from foreign countries.

White newcomers came from more-settled areas of the eastern United States. Because of the high cost of transporting supplies, it was mainly middle-class farmers and businesspeople who could afford to move west. Some farmers came in search of more fertile soil. Civil War veterans, particularly those from the South, came to make a new start. The majority of white settlers moved from states in the Mississippi Valley, where land had grown expensive and difficult to obtain. A Nebraska settler explained simply, "I am well satisfied that I can do better here than I can in Illinois." Susan Lomax, who moved west with her family from Mississippi, offered a different reason: "We wanted to come to a new country so our children could grow up with the country."

For African Americans, moving west offered a chance to escape the violence and persecution they faced following the withdrawal of federal troops from the South in 1877. Kansas particularly appealed to African American settlers, as John Brown had fought against slavery there. The biggest rush of black settlers occurred during the so-called Kansas Fever Exodus of 1879. Some 20,000 to 40,000 African

This Schuttler Wagon Company advertisement offers a depiction of the migration of farmers to the West in search of fertile soil.

GEOGRAPHIC DIVERSITY

Railroad Workers. Railroad workers for both companies, many of whom were immigrants from Ireland and China, braved severe weather and the threat of attack by American Indians as they laid over 1,500 miles of track across rough terrain. Hundreds of these workers died in explosions and other industrial accidents along the way.

CRITICAL THINKING What other dangers might railroad workers have faced as they laid track?

ANSWER: Students might mention dangers such as animal attacks and snake bites.

***The American Nation* VIDEO PROGRAM**

Linking the Nation; Teacher's Guide, pp. 69–74

Search 29399, Play to 33608
Videodisc 1, Side B

Play Pause

See *Teacher's Guide* for Spanish barcode.

VISUAL RECORD ANSWER

Students might suggest that the travel conditions were uncomfortable and harsh.

TEACH OBJECTIVE 2

LEVEL 1: Pair students and assign each pair one of the following roles: white settlers from the East, African Americans from the South, Scandinavians, Chinese, Irish, Germans, or Russian Mennonites. Ask pairs to create advertising slogans urging people to move west. Remind students that their slogans should appeal to people like themselves. *(Pairs should indicate that white Americans sought cheaper lands or to make a new start, African Americans wanted to escape persecution in the South, Scandinavians had "America Fever," Irish moved to the Plains after building railroads, Germans moved from the Mississippi Valley, Russian Mennonites moved after they lost military service exemption, and many Chinese came during the Gold Rush and turned to farming.)* Have volunteers present their slogans to the class.
Cooperative Learning, Sheltered English

LEVELS 2 AND 3: Assign each student one of the roles mentioned in the Level 1 lesson. Have each student, in his or her assigned role, write a series of letters to a relative explaining his or her reasons for moving west. *(See Level 1 lesson for the correct reasons.)* Students should describe what they think might surprise or disappoint them about life in the West, and how they are faring in the West. Have volunteers share their letters with the class.

TECHNOLOGY AND SOCIETY

Windmills. Daniel Halladay, a mechanic from Connecticut, invented the first commercially successful American windmill. Halladay's windmill featured broad, paddle-shaped wooden blades to catch the wind and use its power to pump water or grind grain. Unlike traditional European models, Halladay's windmill pivoted automatically so that it always faced the wind. Western farmers found this design feature to be especially useful in the ever-shifting winds of the Great Plains. The windmill also controlled its own speed despite the strength of the wind—another feature that western farmers appreciated.

ACTIVITY: Tell students to imagine that they are Nebraska farmers who have just installed their first Halladay windmill. Have each student write a series of short diary entries describing the windmill and its effects.

VISUAL RECORD ANSWER

Students might point to the sod house and the prairie grass.

INTERPRETING THE VISUAL RECORD

Exodusters. Many African Americans escaped persecution in the South by moving west. ***What evidence can you see that this family is homesteading on the Great Plains?***

Americans fled the South, where violence had broken out during elections in 1878. Known as **Exodusters**, these African American settlers trekked west, following leaders such as Benjamin "Pap" Singleton, a 70-year-old former slave.

European immigrants also flocked to the western United States. "America Fever" infected thousands of Danes, Norwegians, and Swedes. In 1882 alone, more than 100,000 left their homes for the American West. In addition, many Irish who had helped build the railroads and a great number of Germans who had settled in the Mississippi Valley decided to move to the Plains.

Russian Mennonites, members of a Protestant sect, also migrated to the Great Plains. After the Russian czar ended the Mennonites' special privileges, including exemption from military service, American railroad companies urged them to move to the United States. The Mennonites brought with them experience in farming wheat on the Russian steppes, or grasslands, including a hardy wheat variety that thrived on the Great Plains. They may have also brought the Russian thistle, a plant that became well known throughout the West as the tumbleweed.

Many of the Chinese immigrants who had come to the United States during the California Gold Rush had also turned to farming by 1880. In California alone, some 3,200 Chinese farmers raised crops in 1880. Throughout the West, Chinese immigrants worked as farm laborers, produce vendors, or sharecroppers. Some owned large farms. In 1870 one Chinese farmer in Sacramento County, California, earned $9,500 from farming. This was an enormous amount for the time.

✔ **READING CHECK:** Why did various groups of people migrate to the West?

This Chinese worker is tending an irrigation ditch in a California orchard.

Western Environments and Farming

Although settlers homesteaded some 80 million acres of public land in the Great Plains between 1862 and 1900, the region did not immediately prosper. Even though the land was free, supplies and transportation were expensive. In addition, the environment posed problems for farmers.

Scarce resources. Water was in short supply throughout much of the West. In parts of the Southwest, Hispanic and American Indian farmers had developed effective irrigation systems that used canals, dams, and sloping fields to control water flow. They established farms that fanned out in thin strips from water sources so that all community members had access to water. New settlers adopted these methods to survive. The Great Plains also had few water sources. Many farmers had to travel several miles to a river or stream where they would fill large barrels and haul them back to the farm. Digging wells proved difficult and time-consuming. One Nebraska farmer spent two years digging with a pick and shovel before reaching water 300 feet below the surface. Many settlers hired professional drillers who used drilling equipment developed by petroleum companies. Farmers also used new models of windmills to draw the water from their wells. These were wind-powered water pumps designed to withstand the region's strong winds.

TEACH OBJECTIVE 3

LEVEL 1: Pair students and have each pair create a graphic organizer that contains the problems western farmers faced and the solutions to those problems. *(Pairs should indicate the following problems: lack of water, lack of trees, strong winds, and harsh winters. Pairs should indicate the following solutions: dry farming, buffalo manure for fuel and as a building material, and new varieties of wheat suitable for the Great Plains.)* When students have completed their organizers, ask volunteers to draw their organizers on the chalkboard and explain them to the class.
Sheltered English, Cooperative Learning

LEVEL 2: Pair students and ask one to assume the role of a newspaper reporter and the other to assume the role of a Plains farmer. Have each pair develop a newspaper interview about how farmers adapted their farming practices and daily lives to the environment in the Great Plains. *(See Level 1 lesson for the correct methods.)* Ask pairs to prepare transcripts of questions and answers. Ask volunteers to present their interviews to the class. **Cooperative Learning**

Trees were another scarce resource on the Great Plains. Settlers developed clever solutions to cope with the lack of wood for fuel or building materials. Some burned dried buffalo manure, an excellent source of fuel. Settlers built **sod houses**, buildings made from chunks cut from the heavy topsoil that were stacked like bricks. A layer of soil covered the roof, which was made of a few scarce pieces of wood. Building with sod was difficult, however. A Kansas settler wrote, "The sod is heavy and when you take 3 or 4 bricks on a litter or hand barrow, and carry it 50 to 150 feet, I tell you it is no easy work."

Created in 1862, the **U.S. Department of Agriculture** (USDA) helped farmers adapt to their new environment. USDA experts sought out and publicized new varieties of wheat suitable for the Great Plains, where the environment was too harsh for traditional winter wheat. These new wheat crops replaced the grasses that had once covered the Great Plains. USDA agents also began teaching dry farming—new planting and harvesting techniques that conserved moisture. For example, agents advised farmers to plow deep furrows to bring moisture to the surface and to break up the soil after a rainfall to prevent evaporation.

Windmills drew water from beneath the ground, allowing settlers to farm the Great Plains.

New farming equipment. The development of new farming equipment also helped the Plains farmers. James Oliver's plow factory in South Bend, Indiana, produced thousands of plows with sharp, durable blades that could slice through the tough sod of the Plains. "Self-binding" harvesters not only cut wheat but also tied it into bundles. The combine cut wheat, separated it from the plant, and cleaned the grain all in one operation. Many of the new farming devices used steam-powered engines. However, the new technology plunged many small farmers into debt when they bought the equipment necessary to compete with larger landholders.

Efficient new farm machinery and cheap, abundant land enabled some companies to create a new kind of large-scale operation, the **bonanza farm**. Most bonanza farms were owned by large companies and operated like factories, with machinery, professional managers, and specialized laborers for different tasks. These large farms required from 500 to 1,000 extra workers at planting and harvesting times. Most owners divided their vast enterprises into small units, with a foreman in charge of each. Migrant workers, who were often unemployed cowboys possessing "nothing but small bundles containing a clean shirt and a few socks," performed much of the seasonal labor.

The era of bonanza farming soon faded. When weather conditions were favorable, bonanza farms produced large profits because of lower production costs. Because bonanza farm owners bought seed and equipment in bulk, suppliers often gave them special deals. However, in times of severe drought or low wheat prices, bonanza farm profits fell. With fewer workers to pay and less money invested in equipment, family farmers could better handle boom-and-bust cycles. By the 1890s most bonanza farms had been broken up into smaller farms.

✔ **READING CHECK:** How did the environment influence farming practices and daily life in the West?

INTERPRETING THE VISUAL RECORD

Bonanza farms. As the Great Plains were opened to farming, some companies created large, factory-like farms. ***What suggests that this was a bonanza farm and not a family-owned farm?***

GLOBAL RELATIONS

The Global Grain Market. As well as plunging into debt to buy necessary equipment, farmers on the Great Plains confronted declining grain prices during most of the late 1800s. Much of this decline was due to the heightened availability of grain on the world market. Along with the yield improvements brought about by mechanization, the opening of new farmland in Argentina, Canada, and Russia helped lead to large increases in global supplies of wheat and corn. As a result, the price of wheat fell from $1.45 a bushel in 1866 to 80 cents in the mid-1880s and under 50 cents in the mid-1890s.

CRITICAL THINKING Besides supplies and equipment, what expenses might Great Plains farmers have had to meet in the course of raising and marketing their crops?

ANSWER: Students might suggest that farmers had to pay for the storage of their crops in grain elevators and the transport of their crops on railroads.

VISUAL RECORD ANSWER

Students might mention the many machines.

LEVEL 3: Tell students to assume the role of a member of a Plains farm family. Have each student write a short story that includes a description of the environmental hardships associated with living on the Great Plains and the ways in which farmers adapted to the environment. *(See the Level 1 lesson for the correct methods.)* Have volunteers read their stories to the class.

NOTE: For an additional teaching idea, see the Chapter 4 collage lesson in the **Creative Teaching Strategies** handbook.

Teacher to Teacher

Jack Rousso of Seattle, Washington, suggested the following activity: Organize the class into two groups, and write the following statement on the chalkboard: Government subsidies, not individual initiatives, were the main factor in the settlement of the American West. *Have one group support the statement and the other group oppose it. After each group has had time to prepare, conduct a debate on the statement.*

HISTORY MAKERS SPEAK

Washington Keller in *Far From Home: Families of the Westward Journey*

The Look of the West. Washington Keller recorded his own description of the West in a letter to his son-in-law: "You have no idea how this country impresses itself on one who has never seen a treeless, fenceless & in many instances houseless country. . . . There is a lack of everything except land. There is plenty of fine land & if any person will get a lot of this land & then go to work & put all the labor that is necessary to make a home for a human being on it in the course of 9 or 10 years he will have one of the finest most productive farms in America."

CRITICAL THINKING Why might Keller have been so euphoric in his description?

ANSWER: Students might suggest that Keller believed that the land and the region offered enormous opportunities.

AMERICAN LETTERS ANSWERS

1. Foote—"high" and "great;" Garland—"wide," and "sunny," "windy."
2. Garland describes the prairie, while Foote describes a wooded, hilly area with a river.
3. that it was wide, varied, and beautiful

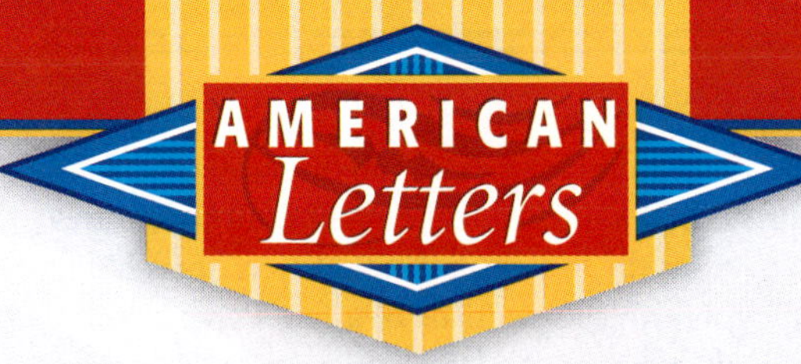

The Western Novel

Several writers recognized the great beauty of the American West. Hamlin Garland, who as a boy hated farm life in Wisconsin, described the Great Plains in his 1899 novel, Boy Life on the Prairie. *Mary Hallock Foote, an artist and writer who lived in California, described the western landscape in her 1894 short story, "A Cloud on the Mountain."*

from *Boy Life on the Prairie*
by Hamlin Garland

Hamlin Garland

For a few days Lincoln and Owen had nothing to do but to keep the cattle from straying, and they seized the chance to become acquainted with the country round about. It burned deep into Lincoln's brain, this wide, sunny, windy country,—the sky was so big and the horizon line so low and so far away. The grasses and flowers were nearly all new to him. On the uplands the herbage [grasses] was short and dry and the plants stiff and woody, but in the swales the wild oat shook its quivers of barbed and twisted arrows, and the crow's-foot, tall and willowy, bowed softly under the feet of the wind, while everywhere in the lowlands, as well as on the sedges, the bleaching white antlers of monstrous elk lay scattered to testify of the swarming millions of wild cattle which once fed there.

To the south the settlement thickened, for in that direction lay the country town, but to the north and west the unclaimed prairie rolled, the feeding ground of the cattle, but the boys had little opportunity to explore that far. One day his father said:—

"Well, Lincoln, I guess you'll have to run the plough team this fall. I've got so much to do around the house, and we can't afford to hire."

This seemed a very fine and manly commission [task], and the boy drove his team out into the field one morning with vast pride.

from "A Cloud on the Mountain"
by Mary Hallock Foote

Mary Hallock Foote

Ruth Mary . . . paused often in her work and looked towards the high pastures with the pale brown lights and purple shadows on them, rolling away and rising towards the great timbered ridges, and these lifting here and there along their profiles a treeless peak or bare divide into the regions above vegetation.

She had no misgivings about her home. Fences would not have improved her father's vast lawn, to her mind, or white paint the low-browed front of his dwelling; nor did she feel the want of a stair-carpet and a parlor-organ. She was sure that they, the strangers, had never seen anything more lovely than her beloved river dancing down between the hills, tripping over rapids, wrinkling over sand-bars of its own spreading, and letting out its speed down the long reaches where the channel was deep.

UNDERSTANDING LITERATURE

1. Identify some of the words that each author uses to describe the landscape.
2. How did the geography described in the two excerpts differ?
3. Based on these passages, how did the two authors feel about the western landscape?

TEACH OBJECTIVE 4

LEVEL 1: Have each pair create a list of the problems faced by farm families on the Plains. *(Pairs' lists should include poor housing, blizzards and bone-chilling cold weather, droughts, swarms of insects, prairie fires, and hard work.)* Then have pairs create graphic organizers that incorporate all of the problems mentioned above. Have volunteers draw their graphic organizers on the chalkboard and discuss them. **Sheltered English, Cooperative Learning**

LEVELS 2 AND 3: Tell students to imagine that they are travelers from New York stranded on the Nebraska plains. Have each student write a short memoir of the experience focusing on the problems that farm families faced in the region. *(See the Level 1 lesson for the correct problems.)* Have volunteers read their memoirs to the class. Students may wish to include their memoir in their portfolios.

▶**ASSIGNMENT** *Tell students to imagine that they are part of a Plains farm family. Have each student write a monologue describing his or her daily life. Encourage students to include their personal feelings about how the conditions are affecting their parents, siblings, neighbors, and themselves.*

Farm Life on the Plains

Farm families on the Plains faced many problems for which inventors, manufacturers, and agricultural experts had no ready answers. Sod houses were well insulated, windproof, and fireproof. However, they were also damp and dirty. Many families hung a canopy inside the house to prevent dirt falling from the ceiling from landing on the dinner table. The roofs leaked and sometimes even collapsed in rainy weather. One woman described her efforts to keep herself and her baby dry in their sod house during a spring rainstorm.

INTERPRETING THE VISUAL RECORD

Home on the plains. Sylvester Rawding and his family posed for this photograph outside their home in Custer County, Nebraska, in 1886. ***What does the Rawding family's house appear to be made of?***

> **"The house leaked so badly that we rolled the bedding up and tied it with a rope, and put the oil cloth from the table over it to keep it dry. I put the baby on top of the roll and put the parasol over it to keep her dry. Soon the rain ran off the ribs of the parasol and soaked around the baby so I fixed a place for her in the cupboard shelf–the only dry place in the house. I walked around with a slicker, a man's hat and overshoes to keep dry."**

Harsh weather and hard work. The climate of the Great Plains caused hardships for farming families. Winter on the Plains often brought blizzards and bone-chilling cold. The summer heat on the Plains could be just as fierce. Settlers described droughts during which "the earth opened in great cracks several inches across and two feet deep." There was no relief as "the leaves on the trees shriveled and dried up, and every living thing was seeking shelter from the hot rays of the sun."

Insects also created problems on the Great Plains. In the 1870s farmers faced swarms of grasshoppers that devoured everything in their path, even the wooden handles of farming tools. Farmers killed thousands of the greedy insects to little effect. Moaned one homesteader: "Two new grasshoppers arrived to attend each dead one's funeral."

Settlers dreaded the raging fires that sometimes swept across the prairies. Most families sent someone onto the roof at night to search the horizon for signs of fire in the distance. Farmers soon learned to plow firebreaks—cleared areas with nothing to burn—around their houses and fields.

Even in good times, Plains farming demanded hard work from everyone in the family. Men did most of the heavy labor of building houses, fencing the land, and farming. In addition to household and child-rearing tasks, women often spent hours in the field. In 1878 a Kansas newspaper praised a local woman who "does her own plowing. . . . This year she has one hundred acres of fine wheat and will cut and bind it herself." Another woman wrote home to her family in the East, explaining that she had been her husband's "sole help in getting up and stacking at least 25 tons of hay and oats." Many farm wives also cared for garden plots, preserved fruits and vegetables, and tended farm animals.

Children had to do their share, too. Their chores included fetching water, tending gardens, and churning butter. One farmer described his two-year-old son, Baz, who could "run all over, fetch up cows out of the stock fields, or oxen, carry in stove wood and climb in the corn crib and feed the hogs and go on errands down to his grandma's."

Harsh winter weather added to the difficulties of life on the Great Plains.

ACROSS THE CURRICULUM

▶BIOLOGY◀

Grasshopper Plagues on the Great Plains. The grasshopper plagues that swept through the Great Plains during the 1870s left a vivid impression on the people who lived through them. Years later, settlers recalled watching with horror as masses of the insects snapped off tree limbs and piled on the ground until they lay over four inches deep. Homesteader Mary Lyon recalled: "When they came down they struck the ground so hard it sounded almost like hail. There was a watermelon patch in our garden and the melons were quite large. . . . By the evening of the second day they were all gone."

CRITICAL THINKING Why might the grasshopper plagues of the 1870s have persuaded some settlers to abandon farming on the Great Plains?

ANSWER: Students might suggest that the plagues persuaded some settlers that farming on the Great Plains would always be a risky enterprise.

VISUAL RECORD ANSWER

Students might suggest that it was made of sod.

REVIEW

Have students complete the **Section 2 Review** on p. 148.

ASSESS

Have students complete **Daily Quiz 4.2.** As **Alternative Assessment,** you may want to use the advertising slogans or short story in this section's lessons.

RETEACH

Have students complete **Main Idea Activity for Reteaching and Sheltered English 4.2.** Then write the following statement on the chalkboard: "*On the Great Plains, nature was sometimes the farmer's friend but more often the farmer's foe.*" Have each student list evidence from the section to support the statement. Then have each student write a paragraph on the topic. **Sheltered English**

EXTEND

Have students conduct research on an invention or innovation that helped farmers on the Great Plains. Then have each student write a short report on his or her chosen invention or innovation. Have students present their work, including illustrations when possible, to the class. **Block Scheduling**

SECTION 2 REVIEW ANSWERS

Define and Identify

For significance, see the following pages:

- Homestead Act, p. 142
- Pacific Railway Act, p. 142
- Morrill Act, p. 142
- Exodusters, p. 144
- Benjamin Singleton, p. 144
- sod houses, p. 145
- U.S. Department of Agriculture, p. 145
- bonanza farm, p. 145
- Willa Cather, p. 148

1. problem–scarce water; solution–irrigation systems, wells, windmills, and dry farming; problem–few trees; solution–buffalo chips for fuel and sod houses; problem–difficult growing conditions; solution–new varieties of wheat and new farming equipment

2. passed the Homestead Act, Pacific Railway Act, Morrill Act, and established the U.S. Department of Agriculture

3. Bonanza farms were less equipped to handle boom-and-bust agricultural cycles than small farms.

4. Students' letters will vary. Students should discuss specific reasons for moving west and specific conditions in the West.

5. Answers will vary. Some students might argue that the hardships of living in the West prompted most settlers to regret their decision to move to the region.

Read More About It

Free Find: Willa Cather

After reading about Willa Cather on the **Holt Researcher** CD–ROM, draw a picture of what you think her home on the Great Plains looked like. Include captions explaining the various elements in your drawing.

BIOGRAPHY

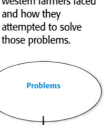

Willa Cather

Storytellers of the Plains. Western writers recorded stories about life on the Great Plains. Willa Cather, born in Virginia in 1873, was one such writer. As a young girl Cather traveled west with her family to a farm in Nebraska. Her grandparents had moved there eight years earlier.

Although she was homesick for Virginia, Cather soon found Nebraska fascinating. "I think the first thing that interested me after I got to the homestead was a heavy hickory cane . . . which my grandmother always carried with her when she went to the garden to kill rattlesnakes," Cather wrote. "She had killed a good many snakes with it, and that seemed to argue that life might not be so flat as it looked there."

The Cather family soon moved to the nearby town of Red Cloud, where Willa attended high school. After graduating from the University of Nebraska, she taught high school in Pittsburgh and then took a job as an associate editor for *McClure's* magazine in New York. She turned to writing full-time in 1912. Cather published her first novel about life on the Plains, *O Pioneers!,* in 1913. In a 1925 interview she explained, "I write only of the Mid-Western American life that I know thoroughly." Cather's other novels—including *My Ántonia,* published in 1918, and *Death Comes for the Archbishop,* published in 1927—also examined life in the American West.

My Antonia *portrays prairie life.*

Although some settlers such as Cather were inspired by the West, difficulties overwhelmed many Plains farmers. Many were forced to abandon their farms. However, thousands stayed. They formed communities with churches and schools, newspapers and clubs, and even theaters and concert halls. Although harvests might be poor one year, there was always hope for better luck to come.

✔ **READING CHECK:** What difficulties did families face as they farmed the Great Plains?

SECTION 2 REVIEW

Define and explain the significance of the following terms:

Homestead Act
Pacific Railway Act
Morrill Act
Exodusters
sod houses
U.S. Department of Agriculture
bonanza farm

Identify and explain the significance of the following individuals:

Benjamin Singleton
Willa Cather

1. **Using Graphic Organizers** Copy the flowchart below. Use it to describe environmental problems that western farmers faced and how they attempted to solve those problems.

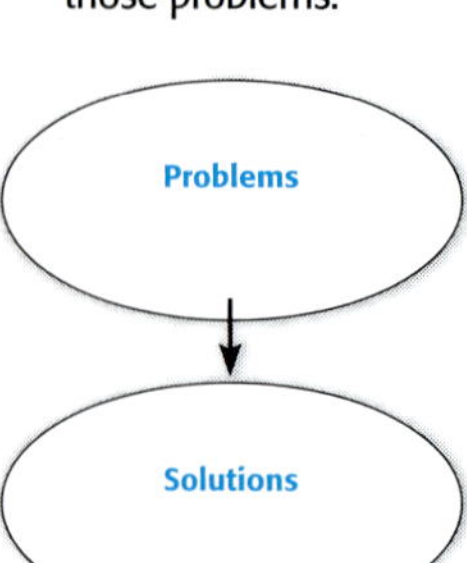

2. **Synthesizing** How did the U.S. government promote economic development and assist farmers in the West?
3. **Understanding Geography: Location** Why did large-scale farms fade more quickly than smaller farms during the late 1800s?
4. **Using Historical Imagination** Imagine that you are a migrant to the West in the late 1800s. Write a letter to relatives explaining why you came to the Great Plains and how your life has changed.

Critical Thinking

5. Do you think the hardships faced by settlers on the Plains caused most of them to regret their decision to move west? Why or why not?
Consider:
   - why most people moved west
   - what their experiences were in the West
   - what they gained and lost from the experience

SECTION 3

After completing Section 3, students should be able to:

OBJECTIVE 1 *Discuss how cattle and sheep ranching developed in the West.*

OBJECTIVE 2 *Explain what life was like for cowboys and residents of cattle towns.*

OBJECTIVE 3 *Describe what ranches were like.*

OBJECTIVE 4 *Understand why the cattle boom on the open range ended.*

LET'S GET STARTED!

As students enter the classroom, play Selection 16, "O Bury Me Not," from the **American Music Audio CD Program.** Ask students to respond to "O Bury Me Not" in writing. After the selection has ended, tell students that it is a classic cowboy song. Tell students that in Section 3 they will learn more about cattle drives and cowboys.

The Cattle Boom

OBJECTIVES

Read to understand:

1. how cattle and sheep ranching developed in the West
2. what life was like for cowboys and residents of cattle towns
3. what ranches were like
4. why the cattle boom on the open range ended

KEY TERMS

Texas longhorn
long drives
railhead
open range
barbed wire

KEY PEOPLE

Joseph Glidden

KEY PLACES

Abilene
Dodge City
Cheyenne
Ogallala

EYEWITNESSES TO History

"[Abilene was] a very small, dead place, consisting of about one dozen log huts, low, small, rude affairs, four-fifths of which were covered with dirt for roofing; indeed, but one shingle roof could be seen in the whole city."

—Joseph McCoy

Joseph McCoy

Joseph McCoy, a young cattleman from Illinois, described the bleak town of Abilene, Kansas, which he visited in 1867. Despite the town's outward appearance, McCoy recognized opportunity when he saw it. He noted that Abilene was "the farthest point east at which a good depot for cattle business could be made" because it had a railroad line. McCoy purchased property and had stockyards constructed. Meanwhile, he instructed a friend to go to Texas to convince cattle owners to bring their herds to Abilene. From there they could be shipped east to packing plants. McCoy's vision transformed the West, sparking an economic boom that entered both American history and myth.

Well suited to living on the Plains, Texas longhorns helped the cattle industry grow.

Ranching in the West

Spaniards who imported cattle from Spain in the 1500s were the earliest ranchers in the American West. By the 1850s, Texans had interbred English cattle with Spanish cattle to produce a new breed—the **Texas longhorn**. Although their meat was typically tough and stringy, longhorns were hardy, able to travel long distances on little water, and could live year-round on grass. Equally important, longhorns were immune to Texas fever, a cattle disease carried by ticks.

The growth of eastern cities ensured an increasing demand for beef. Texas cattle ranching grew rapidly after the Civil War, spreading across the Great Plains as the buffalo died out. In 1866 a steer that could bring about $4 in Texas could be sold for $40 or more in eastern markets.

Sheep ranching, also introduced by the Spanish, was an important economic activity in the West. American Indian groups, including the Pueblo and the Navajo, raised sheep in New Mexico and Arizona. During the California Gold Rush, thousands of sheep were herded to California to feed the hungry miners. Cowboys despised sheep, which they believed ate the roots of the grass and ruined it for cattle. Early environmentalist John Muir called them "hoofed locusts" for the damage they did to the prairie. Clashes between shepherds and cowboys at times became violent. Angry cowboys even drove herds of sheep off cliffs.

Despite such conflicts, sheep ranching remained a profitable enterprise. Basque shepherds, originally from a region in northern Spain, emigrated from South America and ranged their flocks of sheep in California. By 1900 some 10,000 Basques were living in the West.

✔ **READING CHECK:** How did cattle and sheep ranching develop in the West?

SECTION 3 RESOURCES

PRINT

- Guided Reading Strategy 4.3
- Section 3 Review, p. 154
- Daily Quiz 4.3

MULTIMEDIA

- One-Stop Planner, Lesson 4.3
- American Music Selection 16: "O Bury Me Not"
- Art in American History Transparency 17: Prospecting for Cattle Range
- Holt Researcher: American History CD–ROM

SHELTERED ENGLISH

- Main Idea Activity for Reteaching and Sheltered English 4.3

✔ READING TO UNDERSTAND

To help students master the section objectives, have them answer the **READING CHECKS** and complete **Guided Reading Strategy 4.3** as they read the section.

Multimedia Resources

American Music Selection 16: "O Bury Me Not"

TEACH OBJECTIVE 1

ALL LEVELS: To help students understand how both cattle and sheep ranching developed in the West, copy the graphic organizer tot he right on the chalkboard, omitting the italicized answers. Have each student complete it. Then have students create fill-in-the-blank sentences using key terms from the subsection entitled Ranching in the West. Ask students to exchange sentences and complete them.
Sheltered English

▶**ASSIGNMENT** *Write the following questions on the chalkboard:* How did cattle and sheep ranching develop in the West? What factors related to population and the economy led to the growth of the cattle and sheep industry following the Civil War? *Have each student write several questions in response to the questions.*

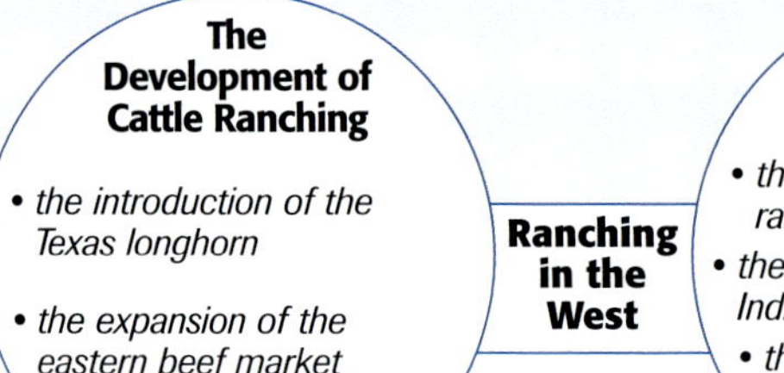

CULTURAL DIVERSITY

A Famous African American Cowboy. A number of African American cowboys became well known for their extraordinary skills at the trade. Bill Pickett, a son of former slaves, achieved nationwide fame for inventing bulldogging, a rodeo event in which a contestant subdues a steer by grabbing its horns and wrestling it to the ground. Pickett toured the United States and abroad giving "bulldogging" demonstrations during the early 1900s, but discrimination often prevented him from competing on the rodeo circuit. In 1972–40 years after his death in a ranching accident–Pickett became the first black honoree at the National Rodeo Hall of Fame.

ACTIVITY: Ask students to conduct research on a famous cowboy. Then have each student prepare a short oral report on his or her subject to present to the class.

VISUAL RECORD ANSWER

Students might suggest that the men's clothing indicates that they are Mexican or Mexican American.

Multimedia Resources

Art in American History Transparency 17: Prospecting for Cattle Range

INTERPRETING THE VISUAL RECORD

Ranching. In 1877 James Walker painted this scene, called *Vaqueros of California Roping Horses in a Corral. From their clothing, what can you tell about the men in the painting?*

The Cattle Industry

The workers who took care of a rancher's cattle were known as cowboys. Popular culture romanticized cowboy life, but it was difficult. Cowboys worked hard in all kinds of weather and made little money. Most worked the range for just seven years before settling down in towns or on farms.

The cowboys. Many of the cowboys were Confederate veterans of the Civil War. African American, Mexican, and Mexican American cowboys made up about one third of the some 35,000 cowboys in the West. African American cowboys managed to escape most of the discrimination of the postwar era. They worked, bunked, and ate alongside fellow cowboys. They also received the same wages.

Mexican ranch hands known as vaqueros had worked with cattle and horses since long before the days of the cattle boom. In the 1880s most Mexican and Mexican American cowboys worked on ranches in Texas. Mostly sons of ranchers or farmers, vaqueros sometimes owned their own ranches. Although they were paid higher wages and treated better than those who handled menial ranch jobs, Mexican cowboys often encountered discrimination.

Life on the trail. Moving the cattle from Texas to the rail lines in Missouri and Kansas posed a major problem for cattle ranchers. To reach the railroads, cowboys herded as many as 3,000 cattle on **long drives**. These overland treks covered hundreds of miles and lasted several months. The trail usually ended in Kansas because cattle herded to Missouri often contracted Texas fever. Over the years, cowboys drove some 4 million cattle from Texas to Kansas.

On a typical long drive, a trail boss managed a crew of about 10 cowboys. The cook rode in front of the herds in a chuck wagon that carried food and the cowboys' bedrolls. Managing the herd was a tough job. River crossings, where swift currents might drown hundreds of animals, proved particularly hazardous. George Duffield headed a long drive in 1866. He described one river crossing: "We worked all day in the river & at dusk got the last beefe over. . . . There was one of our party drowned today . . . & several narrow escapes."

The worst danger was a stampede. Almost any unexpected sound—a coyote's wail, a thunderclap, a sneeze—could panic the cattle. Cowboys learned to prevent stampedes by "circling around and around the terrified herd, singing loudly and steadily, . . . [with other cowboys] separating a bunch here and there."

Cattle drives were long journeys that required the supervision of an experienced trail boss.

Cattle Towns

Every long drive ended at a **railhead**, a town located along a railroad, where brokers bought cattle to ship east on railroad cars. The Kansas towns of Abilene, Dodge City, and Wichita were among the best-known railhead stops. They came to be known as cattle towns. Farther north and west, long drives ended in Cheyenne, Wyoming, and Ogallala, Nebraska.

TEACH OBJECTIVE 2

LEVEL 1: Pair students and have each pair write a series of sentences that describe what life was like for cowboys and residents of cattle towns. *(Pairs' sentences should mention demanding working conditions, isolation, and trail drives for cowboys. For residents of cattle towns, pairs' sentences should mention businesses, the end of drives, and the growth of towns.)* Ask volunteers to write their sentences on the chalkboard. **Sheltered English, Cooperative Learning**

LEVEL 2: Tell students to imagine that they are cowboys or residents of cattle towns. Have each student create a poem or song that describes his or her life. *(See the Level 1 lesson for the correct descriptions.)* Have volunteers recite or sing their compositions for the class.

Early cattle towns consisted of little more than a general store, a hotel or boardinghouse, a railroad depot, and a stockyard. Towns that attracted enough cattle business grew larger. They bustled with activity from spring to fall, when the long drives took place. Cowboys were paid at the end of the drive. They usually got a shave and a haircut upon arriving in town, then bought new clothes. After completing their purchases, many cowboys visited gambling halls and saloons, freely spending their hard-earned money.

Prosperous cattle towns attracted businesspeople, doctors, lawyers, and their families. Once families arrived, the cattle towns built schools, hired teachers, and established police forces to maintain order. Reformers, many of them women, set out to "civilize" the rough cowboy towns by organizing poor-relief and temperance societies. However, their calls to limit alcohol consumption met with little success so long as cattle town economies depended on saloons.

✔ **READING CHECK:** What was life like for cowboys and the residents of cattle towns?

THE GRANGER COLLECTION, NEW YORK

This engraving of Dodge City shows the arrival of cowboys driving a herd of cattle to market.

AMERICAN ARTS

Frontier Artists

The American West captured the imagination of artists. They were eager to portray its natural beauty and the lives of its inhabitants. Perhaps the most influential artist was Frederic Remington. This New Yorker painted and sculpted a wide variety of subjects including American Indians, cowboys, and mountain men. Remington's work celebrated western settlement, as did paintings by Charles Wimar. Wimar saw the story of the West as an epic of heroic conquest. Not all artists glorified western settlement, however. Charles Russell lived in Montana for most of his life and worked for over a decade as a cowboy. Russell was more sensitive to the settlers' impact on the land and on American Indians.

American Indians were often portrayed as either savages or noble people. In both cases, frontier art gave the general impression that they were doomed to vanish from the West. Art historians have also noted that frontier artists concentrated on images of men at work or play. They usually neglected the role that women played in the settlement of the West. Eliza Barchus became known for her depictions of life in Oregon. However, she was one of the few female artists in the West whose work received significant attention.

***Frederic Remington's* Defending the Waterhole**

Understanding the Arts

1. How did frontier art portray American Indians?
2. What elements of the West most interested frontier artists?
3. What image of the West does the painting by Remington above suggest?

ACROSS THE CURRICULUM

▶ART◀

Charles Russell. Charles Russell was born in Missouri but moved to Montana as a teenager. Although he once considered traveling to Europe to study painting in "the noted art schools of the old world," he stayed in the United States and concentrated on western themes. Unlike many artists who portrayed the settlement of the West, Russell mourned the impact that this settlement had on American Indians. In a letter to a friend, he once wrote: "The Red Man was the true American. The history of how they fought for their country is written in blood, a stain that time cannot grind out."

CRITICAL THINKING What did Russell mean when he called Indians the "true Americans"?

ANSWER: Students might suggest that Russell was referring to the fact that American Indians populated North America before European Americans.

AMERICAN ARTS ANSWERS

1. as savages or noble people
2. its natural beauty and inhabitants
3. that it was an arid, threatening, dangerous region

LEVEL 3: Organize students into groups of four. Have each group create a skit about cowboy or cattle town life. *(See the Level 1 lesson for the correct descriptions.)* Characters in the skit should be based on the people who might have lived in or passed through cattle towns in the mid- and late-1800s. Have volunteers perform their skits for the class.
Cooperative Learning

TEACH OBJECTIVE 3

ALL LEVELS: Have students work in pairs to create a "business opportunity" ad for ranchers and their families and a "help wanted" ad for cowboys. Pairs' ads should describe ranch life. *(Pairs' ads should mention cattle, cowboys, drives, assorted ranch chores, and more. A business opportunity ad might read: Ranch with 5,000 acres, 400 head of cattle available in Texas to hardworking family. Men's duties include rounding up cattle and maintenance of fences and range. Women's duties include housework, cooking, fence-mending, and herding.)* Have volunteers share their ads with the class.
Sheltered English, Cooperative Learning

CULTURAL DIVERSITY

Cowboy Clothing. While cowboys occasionally splurged on "fancy" attire at the end of a long drive, most pieces of cowboy clothing were quite utilitarian. Cowboy hats, for instance, were used to fan campfires, signal colleagues, and could hold feed horses, as well as protect their wearers from the sun and the rain. Bandannas, which cowboys wore over their faces to avoid choking on trail dust, also served as towels, slings, and bandages. Vests, which kept cowboys warm without hindering their arm movements, supplied multiple pockets for carrying matches, papers, and other personal items.

CRITICAL THINKING Why might many cowboys have called their hats "Stetsons"?

ANSWER: Students might suggest Stetson was the name of a popular brand of hats. Tell students that John Batterson Stetson, a hatmaker from New Jersey, created the brand.

Ranch Life — teen Life

Teenagers often shared the burden of the hard work of ranching. One of 14 children in a Colorado ranching family, Jake Goss started working with horses when he was 13. Two years later he found work on a neighboring ranch, cutting hay and branding cattle. By age 17, Goss owned 23 head of cattle. He knew the responsibilities that came with ownership. When he broke his arm so badly that "it was hangin' out my sleeve with splinters," he stayed with the calves until someone could take his place. A little over a year later, he bought his own ranch, which he worked for most of the rest of his life.

Raising cattle today

Young women also did their share of work on the ranches. Agnes Morley Cleveland grew up on the family ranch in New Mexico. Later she recalled, "Cattle became the circumference of our universe and their behavior absorbed our entire waking hours." Cleveland rode the range in search of lost calves, checked fences for damage, and branded cattle. Once she discovered that a sheriff had mistreated one of her favorite horses. When he refused to return it, Cleveland stampeded a herd of 50 to 60 horses through his camp.

Ranching

As the U.S. government converted more American Indian territory into public land, cattle ranching spread west into Colorado and New Mexico and north into the Dakotas, Kansas, Montana, Nebraska, and Wyoming. The government allowed cattle ranchers to use public land as **open range**, or free grazing land. This access to free pastureland helped make cattle ranching profitable. The introduction of higher-grade cattle breeds from the East Coast and from Europe led to even bigger profits.

Ranch profits. Although many families established ranches, mainly large investment companies took advantage of the government's offer of land. Financed by eastern and European investors, these companies created huge ranches. A group of Chicago investors owned the 3.5-million-acre XIT Ranch in the Texas Panhandle. A Scottish enterprise called the Prairie Cattle Company owned an even more impressive spread: 5.5 million acres in Colorado, New Mexico, and Texas, with 139,000 head of cattle.

Most ranches were smaller than these, but many still covered thousands of acres. Large ranches were necessary because cattle needed vast expanses of grazing land to get enough nourishment. Cattle also needed access to water. Streams, rivers, and lakes determined the size and location of ranches. "Wherever there is any water, there is a ranch," noted one Colorado cattleman.

Ranch life. Both cattle and sheep ranches demanded hard labor from ranch families. Everyone had to work to ensure that the ranch prospered. On most ranches, women did housework, cooked for all the hired cowboys, and helped out with fence-mending, herding, and other chores. Some women organized their own ranch-related businesses. Because ranches were far apart, loneliness took its toll. Susan Newcomb, a Texas ranch wife, described the isolation of ranch life.

> **"A man that is cowhunting with a lively crowd has no idea how long and lonesome the time passes with his wife at home. . . . A man can see his friends, hear the news and pass the time . . . while his wife is at home and sees and hears nothing until he returns from a long trip tired and worn out."**

The roundup. During the spring and fall, ranch life centered on the roundup. With help from the cowboys, ranchers drove their cattle from the open range to a central location. Here cowboys from each ranch "cut out," or separated, the cattle, which were identified by each ranch's distinctive brand. The cattle would then be rounded up for the long drive to a railhead.

Cowboys generally lived together in a bunkhouse, although they often slept outdoors during the summer months. When not working a roundup, cowboys

SPOTLIGHT on Cattle Ranches Have students conduct research on a well-known western cattle ranch in the late 1800s. Ask each student to write a report about the ranch. **Block Scheduling**

TEACH OBJECTIVE 4

LEVEL 1: Pair students and tell them to imagine that they are newspaper reporters. Have each pair write newspaper headlines announcing the decline of the cattle boom on the open range. Pairs' headlines should also explain this decline. *(Pairs' headlines should mention the cattle glut, barbed wire fencing, depletion of grass, and bad weather.)* Have volunteers read their headlines to the class. **Sheltered English, Cooperative Learning**

LEVELS 2 AND 3: Ask students to complete the Level 1 lesson. Then have each student select a headline and write an article to accompany it. Students' headlines and articles should explain the end of the cattle boom. *(See the Level 1 lesson for the correct answers.)* Ask volunteers to read their articles to the class. Students may wish to include their articles in their portfolios.

The Cattle Boom and Western Railroads, late 1800s

Learning from Maps The development of railroads and cattle trails allowed for the transportation of livestock and goods between eastern and western states.

? MOVEMENT What geographic feature made travel to the Pacific coast particularly difficult?

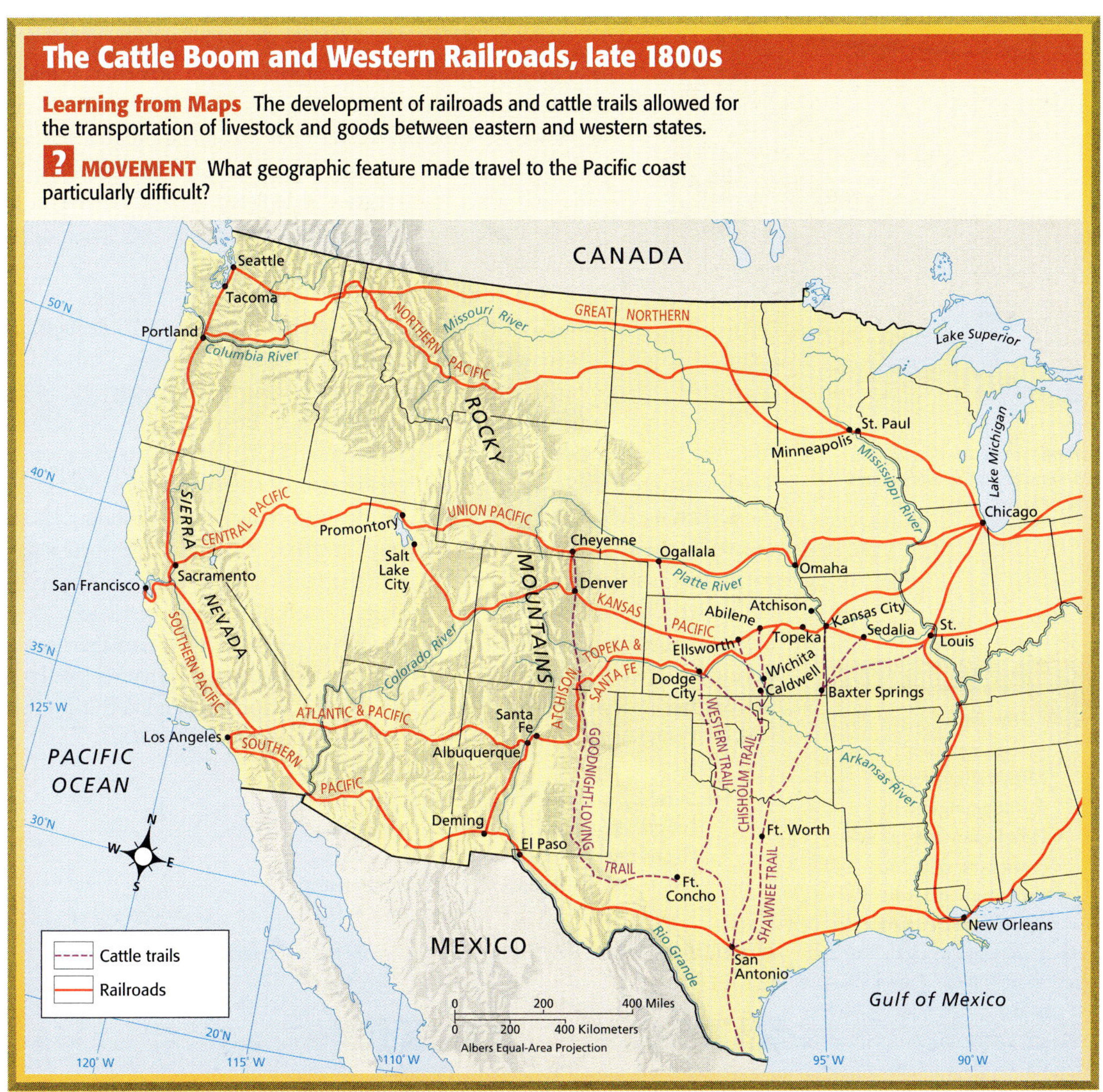

rode the range to check water sources and search for lost or injured cattle. As ranching became big business, ranch owners began to treat cowboys more like common laborers. In 1888 the XIT Ranch published a list of 23 rules for cowboys, including bans on pistols, card playing, and "intoxicating liquors."

✔ **READING CHECK:** What were ranches like?

A Colt revolver

The End of the Cattle Boom

The cattle boom lasted about 20 years. Several factors led to its early end. First, ranchers eager for large profits crowded the open range with too many cattle. Prices crashed in 1885, as supply far exceeded demand. In 1882 cattle had brought $35 a head in Chicago. They sold for only $8 in 1885. Second, open-range ranching declined after the invention of **barbed wire**. Illinois farmer Joseph Glidden

DEMOCRATIC VALUES

Cattle Rustling in the West. In addition to searching for lost cattle, cowboys on the range watched for rustlers, or cattle thieves. After the Civil War, high beef prices and the enormity of the open range encouraged the formation of a few large "rustler gangs," some of which consisted of American Indians. Most rustlers, however, were former cowboys who hoped to use the cattle to start their own ranches. The owners of large ranches hired special detectives to track down cattle thieves, but these efforts were usually fruitless. Juries rarely convicted accused rustlers, even with the presence of significant evidence against them.

CRITICAL THINKING Why might juries in the West have been reluctant to convict accused cattle rustlers?

ANSWER: Students might suggest that juries were often made up of cowboys or former cowboys who sympathized with the motives of the rustlers.

MAP ANSWER
the Rocky Mountains

REVIEW

Have students complete the **Section 3 Review** on p. 154.

ASSESS

Have students complete **Daily Quiz 4.3.** As **Alternative Assessment,** you may want to use the fill-in-the-blank sentences or the "business opportunity ad" in this section's lessons.

RETEACH

Have students complete **Main Idea Activity for Reteaching and Sheltered English 4.3.** Have students make a list of possible topics for an encyclopedia article titled Cowboys and the Cattle Boom. Have volunteers share their lists with the class, explaining why each topic should be included in an article.
Sheltered English

EXTEND

Ask students to conduct research on one of the prominent cattle towns of the West. Students should explore the town's economic and cultural activities. Then have each student write a report on the selected town. Students should provide illustrations and possibly maps to supplement their reports.
Block Scheduling

SECTION 3 REVIEW ANSWERS

Define and Identify
For significance, see the following pages:

- Texas longhorn, p. 149
- long drives, p. 150
- railhead, p. 150
- open range, p. 152
- barbed wire, p. 153
- Joseph Glidden, p. 153

Locate
For locations, see the map on p. 153. For importance, see the following page:

- Abilene, p. 150
- Dodge City, p. 150
- Cheyenne, p. 150
- Ogallala, p. 150

1. rise—new cattle breeds, the growth of eastern cities, and access to free grazing land; fall—declining prices for beef, barbed wire, bad weather, and the blizzard of 1887

2. workers who took care of cattle for ranchers; demanding and dangerous in comparison to isolating

3. Cattle drives caused many towns at railheads to grow larger and prosper.

4. Cowboys tended to drink and gamble; town officials wanted to organize their communities along traditional lines.

5. demanded long hours and dangerous work, imposed an isolated lifestyle, and resulted in relatively little pay

THE GRANGER COLLECTION, NEW YORK

Barbed wire made fencing economical on the wide-open Great Plains.

patented this cheap fencing material in 1874. Ranchers initially refused to use barbed wire, fearing that it would injure their cattle. However, by the 1880s cattle ranchers and farmers had erected miles of barbed wire across the open range to control access to land and water. As overgrazing depleted the grass cover, cattle needed more access to pasturelands to survive. Fencing limited the availability of open land.

Bad weather dealt the final blow to the open range. On the southern Plains a severe winter in 1885–86 and a drought in 1886 diminished many herds. The following year, terrible blizzards hammered the northern Plains. On January 15, 1887, temperatures reached 46 degrees below zero in some areas. After the worst was over, thousands of starved and frozen cattle were discovered. The losses were incredible. Some ranchers lost up to 90 percent of their herds.

Declining prices for beef, the end of the open range, and devastating losses caused by the 1887 blizzards ruined many ranchers. The end of the open range meant that ranchers had to buy their own rangeland. Some large ranching corporations went broke. However, other ranchers learned from their experiences. They invested more money in ranching operations and raised hay to feed their cattle during harsh winters. Because sheep could survive on the weeds that replaced the native grasses destroyed by overgrazing, sheep ranching expanded during this period. A song of the time described the end of the era of the cowboy.

> **"Good-by, old trail boss, I wish you no harm;
> I'm quittin' this business to go on the farm.
> I'll sell my old saddle and buy me a plow;
> And never, no, never, will I rope another cow."**

HOLT RESEARCHER — *Read More About It*
Free Find:
Cowboy Songs
After reading about cowboy songs on the Holt Researcher CD–ROM, create your own song about the work you or a family member performs.

✓ **READING CHECK:** Why did the cattle boom on the open range end?

SECTION 3 REVIEW

Define and explain the significance of the following terms:
Texas longhorn
long drives
railhead
open range
barbed wire

Identify and explain the significance of the following individual:
Joseph Glidden

Locate and explain the importance of the following places:
Abilene
Dodge City
Cheyenne
Ogallala

1. **Using Graphic Organizers** Copy the chart below. Use it to describe the factors that led to the growth of ranching and the factors that led to its decline.

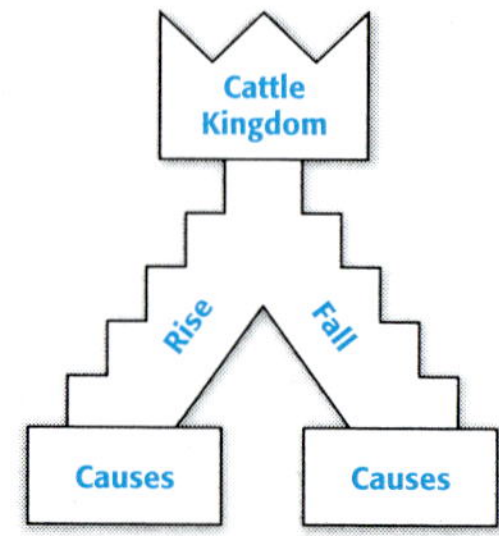

2. **Evaluating** Who were the cowboys? How did their lives on the long drives differ from their lives on the ranch?
3. **Assessing Consequences** How did the cattle drives affect the economy and growth of towns at railheads?
4. **Identifying Values** Why did officials in some towns want to banish cowboys? What values did these officials hold?

Critical Thinking

5. How did business needs shape the lives of those who lived on ranches?
   Consider:
   - what the business goals of the ranches were
   - how life was organized on the ranches
   - who lived and worked on ranches

After completing Section 4, students should be able to:

OBJECTIVE 1 *Describe the role mining played in bringing more people west.*

OBJECTIVE 2 *Explain how the arrival of families changed life in mining camps.*

OBJECTIVE 3 *Discuss why large companies took over most mining operations, and explain how this changed the lives of miners.*

LET'S GET STARTED!

As students enter the classroom, tell them to read the poem on this page and respond to it in writing. Conduct a brief discussion on students' responses, focusing on how the poem might have represented the sentiments of those who migrated west to seek their fortunes as miners. Tell students that in Section 4 they will learn more about mining and life in mining camps and towns.

The Mining Boom

OBJECTIVES

Read to understand:

1. what role mining played in bringing more people west
2. how the arrival of families changed life in mining camps
3. why large companies took over most mining operations, and how this changed the lives of miners

KEY TERMS

Comstock Lode
patio process
hydraulic mining
hard-rock mining

KEY PEOPLE

William H. Seward

"The men who worked in the mines . . . were [a] happy-go-easy set of fellows, fond of good living, and not particularly interested in religious affairs. . . .

Men quarreled at times and firearms were discharged with but slight provocation. Nevertheless they all had an acute instinct of right and wrong . . . [and] a high sense of honor."

—J. N. Flint

This silver bar was minted in San Francisco.

Virginia City, Nevada, enjoyed an economic boom that began in 1859 when prospectors discovered silver in the region. Thirty years later, J. N. Flint recalled life in a prosperous mining town. Flint recalled that while working in the mines he longed for "the companionship of forest trees, green fields and running brooks," all of which were missing in the arid regions surrounding Virginia City. Flint's recollections capture the atmosphere of the towns where people hoped to make their fortunes by digging for gold and silver.

Western Mining

The economic impact of mining changed the face of the West. Farmers and ranchers slowly expanded across the Great Plains, establishing homesteads and ranches. Meanwhile, miners raced across the continent, hoping to be the first to strike it rich. Mining opened many new regions in the West to settlement.

Gold and silver. The first promising mining discoveries after the California Gold Rush took place in Colorado. Prospectors found gold near Pikes Peak in late 1858. By early 1859, thousands of people had flocked to Colorado. A popular tune captured their enthusiasm.

> "The gold is there, 'most anywhere.
> You can take it out rich, with an iron crowbar,
> And where it is thick, with a shovel and pick,
> You can pick it out in lumps as big as a brick."

The song exaggerated the riches, however. Many prospectors left in disappointment by midsummer.

In 1859 the Carson River valley in present-day Nevada was another center of frantic activity. In addition to gold, the area contained the famous **Comstock Lode**, one of the world's richest silver veins. Over a period of 20 years its mines yielded more than $500 million worth of precious metals.

Some miners went south to Arizona, where Hispanics had been mining silver since the mid-1700s. Hispanic miners introduced mining methods that originated in Mexico and South America. These methods included a mill that separated gold

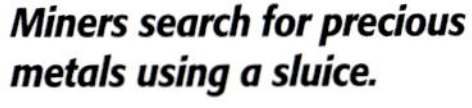

Miners search for precious metals using a sluice.

SECTION 4 RESOURCES

PRINT

- Guided Reading Strategy 4.4
- Section 4 Review, p. 159
- Daily Quiz 4.4

MULTIMEDIA

- One-Stop Planner, Lesson 4.4
- Holt Researcher: American History CD–ROM

SHELTERED ENGLISH

- Main Idea Activity for Reteaching and Sheltered English 4.4

✔ READING TO UNDERSTAND

To help students master the section objectives, have them answer the **READING CHECKS** and complete **Guided Reading Strategy 4.4** as they read the section.

TEACH OBJECTIVE 1

ALL LEVELS: Ask students what role mining played in bringing more people west. *(Students should indicate that mining lured people to the West by offering the possibility of enormous wealth.)* To help students understand where people migrated, copy the graphic organizer to the right on the chalkboard, omitting the italicized answers. Have each student complete it. **Sheltered English**

▶ASSIGNMENT: *Write the following scenario on the chalkboard:* You have just heard about the enormous mineral deposits at the Comstock Lode in Nevada. Will you travel there and try to strike it rich despite the immense risks, or will you stay at home and try to get ahead in your regular job? *Have each student write a few paragraphs in response to the scenario.*

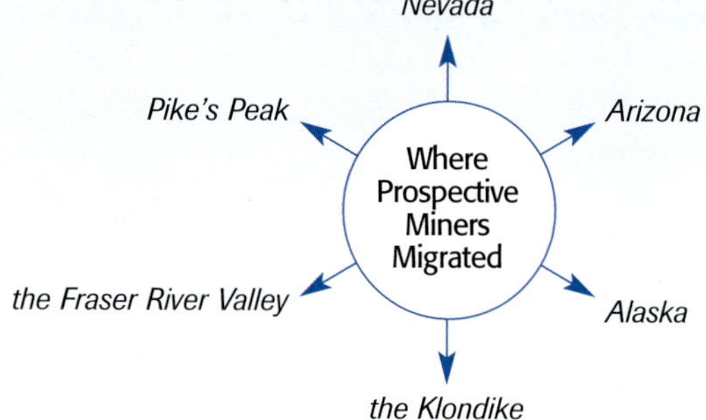

GEOGRAPHIC DIVERSITY

Travel to the Gold Fields. High boat fares forced the majority of prospectors to travel through Alaska to the Klondike on foot. The extreme conditions forced many gold seekers to give up their dreams of riches and return to the United States. Historians estimate that more than 50,000 people who embarked on the trip turned around and headed back before they reached the Klondike.

ACTIVITY: Tell students to imagine that they are prospectors traveling through Alaska to the Klondike. Have each student decide whether to continue and to explain that decision in writing.

STRATEGIES FOR SUCCESS ANSWERS

Practicing the Strategy

1. for most cattle ranches and mining operations—well-financed investment companies; some ranches—private families.
2. promoted both industries by acquiring land for ranches and mining companies
3. paid workers
4. promoted the rapid emergence of socially unstable communities
5. ranching—damaged the native grasses and resulted in overgrazing; mining—altered the physical landscape with mines and other operations

THE GRANGER COLLECTION, NEW YORK

Individual prospectors often made the first discovery of precious metals, but it took large companies to extract the valuable ore.

from quartz and the ***patio* process**—which used mercury to extract silver from ore. The newer arrivals used these methods to mine the Comstock Lode and the region around Tucson, in present-day Arizona. Other miners headed north.

Northern ventures. During the late 1850s some miners pushed as far north as the Fraser River valley of British Columbia. This movement into Canada had important consequences for Russia and the United States. Russia, which at that time owned Alaska, offered to sell it to the United States. U.S. Secretary of State William H. Seward negotiated the purchase of Alaska in 1867. Seward believed the price, which came out to less than 2 cents an acre, was a good deal.

Many Americans, however, considered Alaska worthless, ridiculing the purchase as "Seward's Folly" or "Seward's Ice Box." However, Seward's confidence that Alaska "possesses treasures . . . equal to those of any other region of the continent" proved correct. In 1896, prospectors discovered gold in the Klondike district of Canada's Yukon Territory, which bordered Alaska. This discovery launched the Klondike Gold Rush. By the summer of 1897, Yukon miners had extracted gold worth more than $1 million. For the next two years, almost 100,000 people traveled through Alaska to seek their fortunes. Gold discoveries in Alaska in 1898 and 1902 attracted even more settlers.

✔ **READING CHECK:** What role did mining play in bringing more people to the West?

Strategies for Success — Comparing and Contrasting

Comparing and contrasting are fundamental aspects of historical study. To *compare* is to examine the similarities and the differences between two or more events, ideas, people, situations, social groups, or things. To *contrast* is to explore only the differences between two or more subjects. Comparing and contrasting are particularly effective techniques for organizing historical information, tracking change over time, and understanding the origins of different points of view.

How to Compare and Contrast

1. **Identify the similarities.** When you encounter subjects that require comparison, observe the ways in which they are alike. Each time you identify a similarity, assess its importance. Record your findings.
2. **Identify the differences.** When you have noted as many similarities as possible, examine the ways in which your subjects are different. Each time you identify a difference, assess its importance. Record your findings.
3. **Put the comparison to use.** Use the results of your comparison, along with your knowledge of the historical period, to form generalizations and draw conclusions about your subjects.

Applying the Strategy

Review the material on cattle ranches in Section 3 and mining companies in this section. Then create a list of similarities and differences between the two industries.

Practicing the Strategy

Answer the following questions.

1. Who invested in cattle ranches and mining companies?
2. What role did the U.S. government play in the ranching and mining industries?
3. Who supplied the labor in each industry?
4. How did each industry affect community formation in the West?
5. How did each industry affect the western environment?

TEACH OBJECTIVE 2

LEVEL 1: Pair students and have each pair create a before-and-after chart of the ways in which mining towns changed with the arrival of families. *(Pairs should indicate the following relationships: before—mining towns were unstable, temporary residences; after—families brought stability, transformed towns into permanent towns; before—mining towns were violent, vigilante communities; after—arrival of families brought law and order, establishment of churches, newspapers, schools, and cultural establishments.)* Then tell students to imagine that they are miners who witnessed a camp transform into a town. Have each student write a before-and-after paragraph expressing his or her impressions of that time. **Sheltered English, Cooperative Learning**

LEVELS 2 AND 3: Conduct a discussion on how the arrival of families in mining towns went hand-in-hand with an increase in law and order, the establishment of churches, newspapers, schools, and cultural activities. Pair students and have each pair draw two comic strips with dialogue balloons that characterize mining-town life before and after families arrived. *(See the Level 1 lesson for the correct changes.)* Ask volunteers to present their comic strips to the class. **Cooperative Learning**

Life in Mining Communities

Mining camps sprang up overnight wherever news of possible wealth brought prospectors together. Unlike ranching and farming, prospecting was typically not a family enterprise. Most camps initially consisted almost entirely of male residents. A visitor to one Colorado mining camp estimated the population to be about 4,000, with just 12 female inhabitants.

The settlers. Mining camps drew a wide range of settlers. One newspaper reporter wrote, "Here were congregated the most varied elements of humanity . . . belonging to almost every nationality and every status of life." In the mining regions of Southern California, many Californios, Chileans, Mexicans, and Peruvians maintained their own separate settlements. In other mining areas the mix of prospectors included U.S. citizens, Irish and Chinese men who had come to work on the railroads, and miners from the Cornwall region of England.

At first, life in the mining camps was crude, and comforts were few. Moreover, the atmosphere in most camps was one of intense competition. Prospector William Parsons remembered.

> **"a mad, furious race for wealth, in which men lost their identity almost, and toiled and wrestled, and lived a fierce, riotous, wearing, fearfully excited life; forgetting home and kindred [family], abandoning old steady habits."**

Such brutal competition led to discrimination in the mining camps. Miners in the Cripple Creek camp in Colorado forcibly excluded eastern and southern Europeans as well as Hispanics. In 1882 a mob of masked men drove the Chinese inhabitants of Rico, Colorado, out of town. The local newspaper called the incident "one of the most shameful affairs that ever disgraced any so-called civilized country and would have met the hearty approval of the most barbarous savage." Most Chinese miners left the Rocky Mountain camps because of the hostile treatment they received from other miners.

Instability. Western mining camps were some of the most violent places in the United States during the late 1800s. Tensions between ethnic groups often led to fighting. Gamblers and swindlers swarmed in, and conflicts over claims set off brawls. Deadwood, South Dakota, gained a reputation as a particularly rough town. An outlaw's haven, Deadwood became the final resting place of lawman Wild Bill Hickok, shot dead as he played cards. Legend has it that Hickok was holding a pair of aces and a pair of eights, which thereafter became known as the dead man's hand.

The absence of law enforcement sometimes led people in mining camps to form vigilante committees to combat theft and violence. Montana newspaper editor Thomas Dimsdale claimed that it was "an absolute necessity that good, law-loving, order-sustaining men should unite for mutual protection and salvation of the community." However, vigilante committees often used violence to resolve the community's problems, hanging the accused after a quick trial.

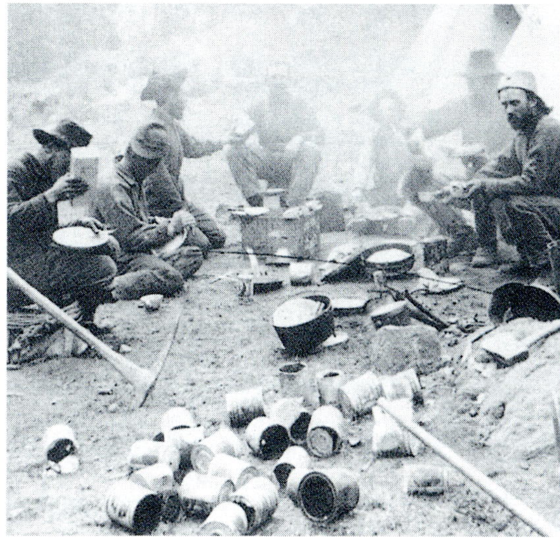

INTERPRETING THE VISUAL RECORD

Mining. Mining camps were often little more than a hastily constructed group of tents or shacks. ***What do you think miners ate while in camp?***

Read More About It

Free Find:
Mining Camps

After reading about mining camps on the **Holt Researcher** CD–ROM, imagine you are a reporter for an East Coast magazine. Write an article for your readers that describes a day in a mining town.

VISUAL RECORD ANSWER

Students might suggest that they ate canned food.

VISUAL RECORD ANSWER

(for p. 158)

Students might point to the permanent buildings in the background

VISUAL RECORD ANSWER

(for p. 159)

Students might suggest that it degraded the landscape and environment.

SECTION 4 REVIEW ANSWERS

Define and Identify

For significance, see the following pages:

- Comstock Lode, p. 155
- *patio* process, p. 156
- William H. Seward, p. 156
- hydraulic mining, p. 159
- hard-rock mining, p. 159

1. social effects–ethnic diversity, intense economic competition, violence, new growth of communities; political effects–formation of unions by miners; economic effects–establishment of prosperous businesses in mining towns, domination of large, well-financed companies in the mines; environmental effects–damage to rivers and flooding problems

2. offered new economic opportunities

3. Mining camps were violent places because they were the scene of intense economic

TEACH OBJECTIVE 3

LEVELS 1 AND 2: Pair students and ask each pair to compile a list of the reasons why corporations took over mining operations and the changes that resulted for individual miners. *(Pairs should note the following causes and effects: causes—easily accessible ore deposits had been removed and expensive technologies were required to remove deep deposits; technological knowledge rather than luck was required to locate deep deposits of ore; effects—miners became laborers for corporations rather than self-employed individuals; working conditions in mines were dangerous; some miners formed unions to obtain better wages and working conditions.)* Then have pairs create picket signs that striking miners might have created to protest their working conditions.
Sheltered English, Cooperative Learning

LEVEL 3: Ask students to imagine that they are miners who were previously self-employed but have since started working for a mining company. Have each student write a short story that chronicles the changes that took place when mining companies took over mining operations, and how those changes affected individual miners. *(See the Levels 1 and 2 lesson for the correct causes and effects.)* Students should use the facts from their textbooks in writing their stories.

competition between men of many different ethnic and social groups. They became more stable with the arrival of businesses and families.

4. early miners–hoped to attain individual success by "striking it rich" at an easily accessible claim; mining company owners–hoped to establish large, profitable enterprises that extracted minerals from deep within the ground

5. Answers will vary. Some students might claim that mining benefited the West because it promoted the establishment of multicultural communities.

Creating a Time Line
Each event should have an explanation and the correct date.

Writing a Summary
See the Reading Checks in each section for main ideas.

Identifying People and Ideas
1. leader of Sioux resistance
2. encounter between the U.S. Army and the Sioux in 1890
3. congressional act requiring the allotment and sale of Indian lands
4. provided settlers with 160 acres of land in return for settling and cultivating it for five years
5. African Americans who migrated from the South to Kansas during the late 1870s
6. writer who wrote about life on the Great Plains

The Old West

Conflicting images of life in the West reflect the continuing debate over the meaning of western settlement. Books, movies, and television programs offer one side of the debate. Most Americans are familiar with images such as a solitary miner panning for gold in a remote mountain stream; a cowboy riding off alone into the sunset; and a farm or ranch family carving out a living on the empty Plains. These legendary western figures represent the American ideal of rugged individuals conquering a barren and uninhabited land. Seen this way, the history of western settlement is a powerful and deeply meaningful symbol of the American Dream.

However, many historians choose to focus on other aspects of western development. They argue that most westerners, including cowboys and miners, labored for others–often large companies–rather than for themselves. In addition, western settlers relied upon assistance from the federal government. It sold lands at low rates, subsidized railroad development, and used the military to remove American Indians. These historians view the West as a land shaped by technology, big business, and the federal government–a portrayal radically different from the "Wild West" of outlaws, lone cowboys, and isolated pioneers.

Stability came to the mining camps as they grew into towns. The camps attracted a host of businesses eager to feed and clothe the miners. James Morley of Montana noted, "I shouldn't have the patience to count the business places" in an area that "only eighteen months ago . . . was a 'howling desert.'" Owners of saloons and stores had a better chance of striking it rich than miners. Cooking, cleaning, and providing lodging were especially profitable. One industrious woman boasted that she earned "nine hundred dollars in nine weeks, clear of all expenses, by washing!" Later known as the Cattle Queen of Montana, Elizabeth Collins was offered a job as cook at a Montana mining camp. She recalled, "Prompted by kindness and a desire to see these hardworking men as comfortable as possible—also craving for the $75 per month—I promptly accepted the offer."

The few children living in the camps had unique opportunities to earn money. They hunted for gold dust under the raised, wooden sidewalks or panned and scavenged for gold dust after the miners had finished for the day. Much more profitable, however, was selling fresh food to miners, who quickly grew tired of eating canned food. One brother and sister made $800 one summer selling butter and bacon to the miners.

With the arrival of more families, many camps turned into permanent communities. Prosperity brought law and order and the establishment of churches, newspapers, schools, and even theaters and music groups. Denver and Boulder, Colorado; Carson City, Nevada; and Helena, Montana, all began as mining camps before evolving into major urban centers.

✔ **READING CHECK:** How did the arrival of families change life in the mining camps?

INTERPRETING THE VISUAL RECORD
A new town. Helena, Montana, is one mining camp that developed into a prosperous city. ***What evidence indicates that Helena is no longer a temporary community?***

Mining as Big Business

Individual prospectors roaming the West with their packhorses and hand tools made the earliest strikes, or mining discoveries. However, the era of the lone miner did not last long. Within a few years after a strike, most of the easily accessible mineral deposits were "worked out." Mining ore deposits deep below Earth's surface required resources and technology far beyond the means of the average prospector. As a result, mining became dominated by large, well-financed companies.

REVIEW

Have students complete the **Section 4 Review** on p. 159.

ASSESS

Have students complete **Daily Quiz 4.4**. As **Alternative Assessment**, you may want to use the picket signs or short stories in this section's lessons.

RETEACH

Have students complete **Main Idea Activity for Reteaching and Sheltered English 4.4**. Organize students into small groups and assign each group a subsection. Tell each group to develop questions about the main ideas in its subsection. Then have each group exchange its questions with another group and work to answer the questions.

Sheltered English, Cooperative Learning

EXTEND

Have students conduct research on the antiviolence movements that sprang up in many western towns. Then pair students and have each pair create a graphic organizer or a visual display comparing and contrasting antiviolence movements in the late 1800s with modern-day antiviolence movements. Ask volunteers to share their work with the class.

Cooperative Learning, Block Scheduling

Mining companies relied on technological know-how rather than on guesswork or luck. Corps of college-educated geologists and engineers located the ore and instructed the companies on how best to extract the minerals—copper, iron, lead, and zinc—in demand by factories in the East.

To reach the ore, companies used one of two methods. In **hydraulic mining**, water shot at high pressure ripped away gravel and dirt to expose the minerals beneath. This process devastated the environment. The displaced soil choked rivers and caused flooding. **Hard-rock mining** involved sinking deep shafts to obtain ore locked in veins of rocks.

New technology changed the working conditions in the mines. Laborers sank the shafts, built the tunnels, drilled, and processed the ore. The work was dirty and dangerous. Temperatures deep in the mines sometimes rose as high as 150°F. Poor ventilation contributed to respiratory illnesses. Cave-ins, rockfalls, and the use of explosives such as dynamite sometimes caused injury or death. Injured miners had little hope of receiving compensation for their suffering. After William Kelley was blinded in a mining accident, the Montana Supreme Court ruled that it was "an unforeseen and unavoidable accident incident to [part of] the risk of mining." The mining company did not have to pay Kelley any damages.

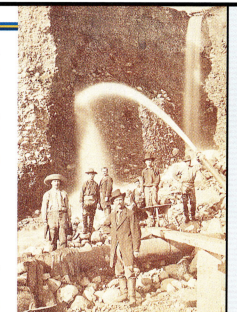

INTERPRETING THE VISUAL RECORD

Hydraulic mining. These Colorado miners are using a water hose to sift through dirt in search of gold. ***What impact did this type of mining have on the landscape and environment?***

As the hope of sudden riches faded, miners grew dissatisfied with wages and working conditions. In some communities miners formed unions. Dues paid to the unions helped injured miners and the families of miners who had been killed on the job. Unions also negotiated with or battled against owners who tried to cut wages. Many also opposed Chinese miners, who were willing to work for lower pay. During the early 1900s, mining increasingly became the task of large companies. Mining companies greatly affected the landscape and the environment of the West.

✔ **READING CHECK:** Why did large companies take over most mining operations? How did this change affect the lives of miners?

SECTION  4 REVIEW

Define and explain the significance of the following terms:
Comstock Lode
patio process
hydraulic mining
hard-rock mining

Identify and explain the significance of the following individual:
William H. Seward

1. **Using Graphic Organizers** Copy the graphic organizer below. Use it to explain the ways in which mining affected the United States during the late 1800s.

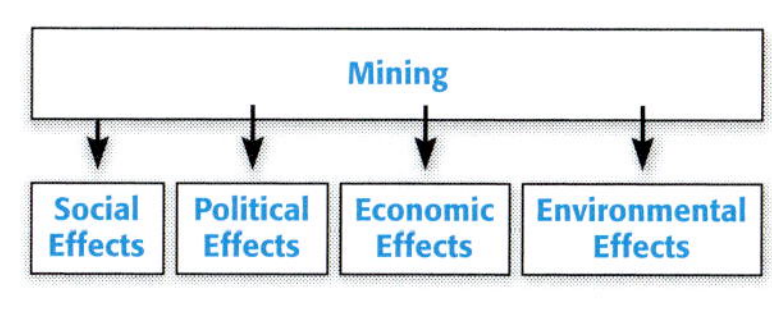

2. **Assessing Consequences** How did mining encourage the migration of people westward?
3. **Synthesizing** Why were the mining camps often violent places? How did they change over time?
4. **Comparing and Contrasting** How did the methods of the early miners and those of mining company owners differ?

Critical Thinking

5. Overall, do you think the mining era benefited or harmed the West?
Consider:
- how the mining boom benefited the West
- what harm the boom caused to the West
- how the boom could have been handled differently

7. cattle breed suited for life on the Great Plains
8. obtained a patent for barbed wire in 1874
9. rich silver vein that attracted miners to Nevada
10. mining method in which water ripped away gravel and dirt to expose minerals

Understanding Main Ideas

1. how—fled from and occasionally engaged in armed conflict with U.S. Army forces; why—did not want to give up their lands and traditional ways of life
2. By forcing American Indians to farm and assume private ownership of land, the government hoped to assimilate Indians into "white America." However, as a result of government actions, many American Indians lost their lands and others rejected farming; many Navajo died from disease and malnutrition.
3. find economic opportunities or an atmosphere of racial tolerance
4. rise—the introduction of new cattle breeds, the growth of eastern cities, and access to free grazing land; fall—declining prices for beef, the impact of barbed wire on the open range, and severe weather during the mid-1880s

CHAPTER 4 REVIEW AND ASSESSMENT RESOURCES

PRINT

- Chapter 4 Review, pp. 160–61
- Chapter 4 Tutorial for Students, Parents, Mentors, and Peers
- Chapter 4 Test (Form A or B)
- Portfolio Activities and Alternative Assessment Handbook, Chapter 4

MULTIMEDIA

- Audio Program, Chapter 4 (English and Spanish)
- Chapter 4 Test Generator (on the One-Stop Planner)
- Global Skill Builder CD–ROM
- HRW Web site

SHELTERED ENGLISH

- Spanish Glossary
- Sheltered English Chapter 4 Test

REVIEW

Have students complete the **Chapter 4 Review** on pp. 160–61.

ASSESS

Use one of the chapter tests to assess students' understanding of the content. For **Alternative Assessment,** see the **Portfolio Activities and Alternative Assessment Handbook.**

5. took over most of the mining business from individual prospectors and hired many miners to under dangerous and unhealthy conditions

Reviewing Themes

1. Disagreements between the Sioux and the U.S. government over the dispensation of Sioux lands helped lead to the massacre.

2. farming—destroyed wildlife habitats and caused erosion; mining—choked rivers and caused flooding; ranching—depleted grass cover

3. moved the work underground, making it more dangerous and unhealthy

Thinking Critically

1. Answers will vary. Students might suggest that fewer white settlers would have moved to the West.

2. Answers will vary. Students might suggest that some settlers attained economic independence, but that others were disappointed by the hard work and living conditions.

3. African Americans were able to establish some small farms and towns, but they continued to experience discrimination and limited economic prospects. Some Mexican Americans were paid higher wages, but they experienced discrimination.

4. similar—came from a variety of ethnic backgrounds, worked hard and dangerous jobs, and helped form communities that were initially unstable; different—wages and occupations

Review

Creating a Time Line

Copy the time line below onto a sheet of paper. Complete the time line by filling in the events and dates from this chapter that you think were most significant. Pick three events and explain why you think they were significant.

Writing a Summary

Using the Reading Checks as a guide, write an overview of the events in the chapter.

Identifying People and Ideas

Identify the following terms or individuals and explain their significance.

1. Sitting Bull
2. Massacre at Wounded Knee
3. Dawes General Allotment Act
4. Homestead Act
5. Exodusters
6. Willa Cather
7. Texas longhorn
8. Joseph Glidden
9. Comstock Lode
10. hydraulic mining

Understanding Main Ideas

SECTION 1

1. How and why did different American Indian tribes resist relocation to reservations?
2. How did the government fail to achieve its goal of assimilation?

SECTION 2

3. Why did many Americans choose to move to the West during the second half of the 1800s?

SECTION 3

4. What led to the rise and fall of the Cattle Kingdom?

SECTION 4

5. How did mining companies change the daily lives of miners in the West?

Reviewing Themes

1. **Cultural Diversity** How did differing views of white settlement in the West contribute to the Massacre at Wounded Knee?
2. **Economic Development** In what ways did farming, mining, and ranching alter the western landscape and environment?
3. **Technology and Society** How did new technology change the ways in which miners worked?

Thinking Critically

1. **Hypothesizing** How would western settlement have been different if the U.S. government had honored all the treaties it signed with American Indians?
2. **Evaluating** Did most settlers find what they were expecting in the West? Why or why not?
3. **Recognizing Point of View** In what ways did African Americans and Mexican Americans experience both expanded opportunities and limitations in the West?
4. **Comparing and Contrasting** How were the experiences of cowboys and miners similar and different?
5. **Analyzing** How does the history of the Old West differ from many images of it presented in popular culture?

Writing About History

Writing to Describe Copy the graphic organizer below. Use it to list the major aspects of life in Plains settlements, in cattle towns, and in mining towns. Then write an essay comparing and contrasting two of the types of communities.

Plains Settlements	Cattle Towns	Mining Towns

RETEACH

Pair students and tell them to imagine that they have been asked by a San Francisco newspaper to write a column discussing one of the four major issues discussed in the chapter—Indian policy, Western farmers, the cattle boom, or the mining boom. In their articles, students should present background information as well as the positive and negative aspects of the topic. Students should include an original illustration related to the topic in their articles.
Sheltered English, Cooperative Learning

EXTEND

Have students conduct research on a major discovery of gold or silver during the mining boom, such as Pikes Peak, Comstock Lode, Klondike Gold Rush, and the Alaskan gold discoveries. Ask students to concentrate on the pertinent facts associated with the find, such as the date and the value of the metals discovered there, and present those, along with any other interesting facts, in a paper. **Block Scheduling**

Strategies for Success Review the **Strategies for Success** on *Comparing and Contrasting*. Then reread the subsection entitled Moving West in Section 2 and answer the following questions.

1. What similar motivations did migrants from the East, African Americans from the South, and immigrants from Europe and Asia have for moving to the American West?
2. What different motivations did each of these groups have for moving to the West?
3. What conclusions does this comparison help you draw about the pursuit of opportunity in the West?

Linking History and Geography

The mining boom shaped many areas in the West. Study the map below and identify which states or territories had both silver- and gold-mining regions. Which states or territories had major lodes?

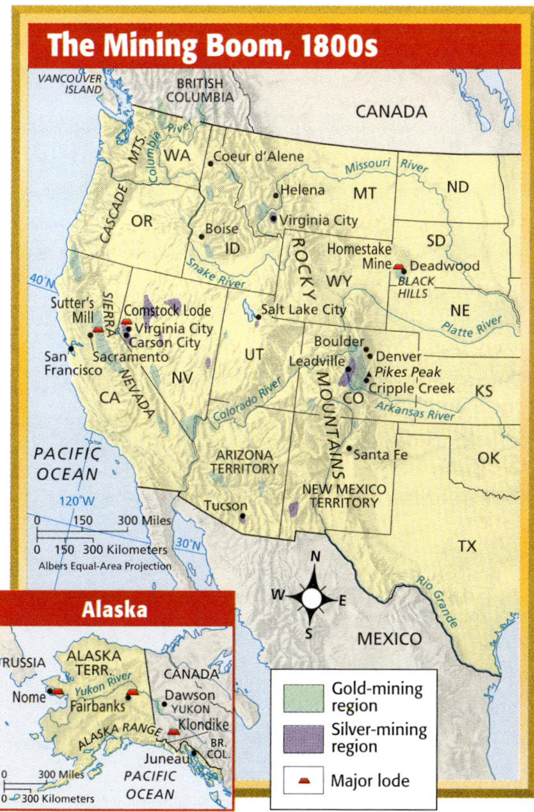

TOPIC: Western Writers
GO TO: go.hrw.com
KEYWORD: SE1 Writers

Accessing the Internet through the HRW Web site, research the work of Willa Cather, Bret Harte, and Laura Ingalls Wilder. Then create an annotated display that illustrates the differences among the writers as well as how their work helped shape the public's perception of the West.

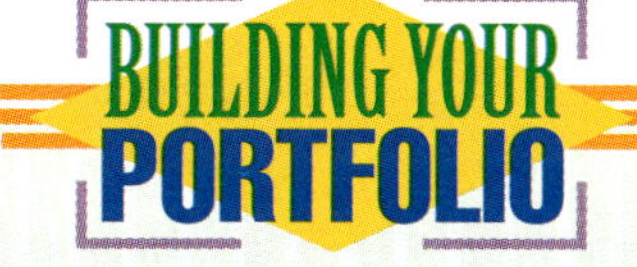

Complete one or all of the following projects individually or cooperatively.

1 Global Relations

Imagine that you are a Sioux living on the Pine Ridge Reservation in South Dakota in 1895. ***Compose an oral account*** for your grandchildren that describes how conflict between the Sioux and non-Indian settlers has affected your life and the lives of other Sioux. Be sure to include details of the conflict.

Ho for Kansas!
Brethren, Friends, & Fellow Citizens:
I feel thankful to inform you that the
REAL ESTATE
AND
Homestead Association,
Will Leave Here the
15th of April, 1878,
In pursuit of Homes in the Southwestern Lands of America, at Transportation Rates, cheaper than ever was known before.
Benj. Singleton, better known as old Pap,
NO. 5 NORTH FRONT STREET.

2 Geographic Diversity

Prepare a pamphlet that advertises one region of the West in order to attract settlers.

3 Economic Development

Prepare a government report that discusses the working conditions in mines. Conclude your report with recommendations for improving the lives of the miners.

5. Answers will vary. Students might suggest that life in the West was more difficult and less romantic than typically portrayed.

Writing About History
plains settlements—farm work, environmental difficulties, harsh climate and living conditions; cattle towns—economic activity and growth, drinking and gambling, establishment of schools, police forces, and reform societies; mining towns: economic activity and growth, large male majority, ethnic diversity, competition and violence, civic institutions

Strategies for Success
1. moved in search of economic opportunity
2. Some migrants from the East moved to find better soil or to start anew after the Civil War; many African Americans moved to escape racist violence in the South; some immigrants moved to escape poor living conditions in their native countries.
3. Answers will vary. Students might suggest that the comparison shows that settlers moved to the West for a wide variety of specific reasons, but that they all hoped to find a better life there.

Linking History and Geography
Alaska, South Dakota, California, Nevada

The Second Industrial Revolution

CHAPTER PLANNING GUIDE

	Section Lesson Objectives	Print Resources	Multimedia Resources	Sheltered English Resources
Section 1 The Age of Invention, pp. 164–72	**1** Describe how the development of steel and oil refining affected U.S. industry. **2** Recount the innovations that were made in transportation. **3** Explain how innovations in communications technology changed business practices and daily life in the United States. **4** Discuss why Thomas Edison wanted to open a research laboratory, and how it changed American life.	▶ Guided Reading Strategy 5.1 ▶ Literature Reading 5: To a Locomotive in Winter ▶ Section 1 Review, p. 172 ▶ Daily Quiz 5.1	▶ One-Stop Planner, Lesson 5.1 ▶ Holt Researcher: American History CD–ROM ▶ HRW Web site	▶ Main Idea Activity for Reteaching and Sheltered English 5.1
Section 2 The Rise of Big Business, pp. 173–80	**1** Describe the arguments business leaders and social critics made about government's role in business. **2** Recount how business strategies changed during the Second Industrial Revolution. **3** Discuss how entrepreneurs took advantage of changes in business organization. **4** Explain how new methods of marketing products changed American life.	▶ Guided Reading Strategy 5.2 ▶ American History Political Cartoon 17: The Power of Trusts ▶ Geography Activity 5: Pullman's Company Town ▶ Primary Source Reading 5: The First Department Store ▶ Biography Reading 5: Frank Woolworth ▶ Section 2 Review, p. 180 ▶ Daily Quiz 5.2	▶ One-Stop Planner, Lesson 5.2 ▶ The American Nation Video Program Segment: The Standard Oil Company; Teacher's Guide, pp. 81–86 ▶ Holt Researcher: American History CD–ROM	▶ Main Idea Activity for Reteaching and Sheltered English 5.2
Section 3 Labor Strives to Organize, pp. 181–87	**1** Understand why some Americans wanted trusts to be banned, and how the government responded. **2** Describe the working conditions that laborers faced in the new age of rapid industrialization. **3** Discuss how the Knights of Labor attempted to address the needs of many workers. **4** Explain how businesses reacted to strikes in the late 1800s, and how this affected unions.	▶ Guided Reading Strategy 5.3 ▶ Graphic Organizer Activity 5: Industrial Problems of the Late 1800s ▶ Section 3 Review, p. 187 ▶ Daily Quiz 5.3	▶ One-Stop Planner, Lesson 5.3 ▶ Holt Researcher: American History CD–ROM	▶ Main Idea Activity for Reteaching and Sheltered English 5.3
Chapter Review and Assessment pp. 188–89		▶ Chapter 5 Review, pp. 188–89 ▶ Chapter 5 Tutorial for Students, Parents, Mentors, and Peers ▶ Chapter 5 Test (Form A or B) ▶ Portfolio Activities and Alternative Assessment Handbook, Chapter 5	▶ Audio Program, Chapter 5 (English and Spanish) ▶ Chapter 5 Test Generator (on the One-Stop Planner) ▶ Global Skill Builder CD–ROM ▶ HRW Web site	▶ Spanish Glossary ▶ Sheltered English Chapter 5 Test

CHAPTER OVERVIEW

The Second Industrial Revolution changed the ways in which Americans lived and worked. Innovations in the steel and oil industries led to new advances in the transportation industry. The invention of the telegraph and the telephone made it easier for people to communicate with one another.

During the Second Industrial Revolution, entrepreneurs set out to gain economic wealth. Business leaders like Andrew Carnegie, John D. Rockefeller, and Cornelius Vanderbilt established corporations that made them millions of dollars. With the rapid growth of manufacturing, companies used advertising to persuade consumers to buy their products.

The demand for labor soared under the new industrial order. Many of these workers labored in unsafe factories. As conditions grew worse, some workers joined labor unions and went on strike.

TIME TAMERS

Block Scheduling

The teacher lesson plans for each section offer a variety of activity choices to help you present the material in a block scheduling format. For further suggestions on block scheduling, see the **Block Scheduling Handbook with Team Teaching Strategies**, pp. 25–30.

Hands-On History Activities:

Classroom to Community The **Hands-On History Activities** help students make meaningful connections between events in American history and those in their own hometown. You may wish to use the Chapter 5 Activity, Technology and You, to extend the chapter lessons, as alternative assessment, or as a block scheduling option.

Portfolio Projects

The American Nation includes multiple portfolio projects in each Pupil's Edition chapter review, as well as each unit review. Chapter 5 Portfolio Project options on p. 189 include the following:

1. Students will **create a list of grievances.**
2. Students will **outline a plan.**
3. Students will **make a visual chart.**

The American Nation

INTERNET RESOURCE DIRECTORY

To access online materials for this chapter, go to go.hrw.com and type in the keywords listed below.

HRW ONLINE RESOURCES

GO TO: go.hrw.com

Online Maps
KEYWORD: SE1 Maps5
- Labor Strikes, 1870–1900

Online Charts
KEYWORD: SE1 Charts5
- Inventions, 1850–1900

Online Reading Support
KEYWORD: SE1 Strategies5

Online Rubrics
KEYWORD: SE1 Rubrics

CHAPTER ENRICHMENT LINKS

Use these Web links to extend and enrich student learning for Chapter 5.
GO TO: go.hrw.com
KEYWORD: SE1 Ch5

CHAPTER INTERNET ACTIVITIES

GO TO: go.hrw.com
- Pupil's Edition Student Activity
  KEYWORD: SE1 Edison
  (Students examine Thomas Edison's life and work.)
- Teacher's Edition Student Activity
  KEYWORD: SE1 Dreyfus
  (Students conduct research on the Dreyfus Affair in France.)
- Teacher's Edition Student Activity
  KEYWORD: SE1 Wright
  (Students explore the technology of the early airplane.)

ADDITIONAL

RESOURCES

Books for Teachers

Sclereth, Thomas J. *Victorian America: Transformations of Everyday Life, 1876–1915.* HarperCollins, 1992. Surveys the social history of the late 1800s.

Smith, Page. *The Rise of Industrial America.* Penguin, 1990. Presents social history.

Books for Students

Hughes, Thomas P. *American Genesis.* Penguin, 1990. Focuses on technology and the nation's development.

James, Portia. *The Real McCoy.* Smithsonian Institution Press, 1990. Examines inventions of African Americans. Particularly appropriate for students reading below grade level.

Primary Sources from the Period

Bellamy, Edward. *Looking Backward.* Penguin, 1985. Serves as a classic meditation on technology and society.

Carnegie, Andrew. Joseph Frazier Wall, ed. *The Andrew Carnegie Reader.* University of Pittsburgh Press, 1992. Presents Carnegie's writings.

Multimedia Materials

Industrial Revolution in Pittsburgh. Video, 20 min. Agency for Industrial Technology. Explores the impact of the Industrial Revolution on the Pittsburgh steel industry.

The Pullman Strike. Video, 20 min. Multi-Media Productions/SSSS. Describes major events in this seminal labor conflict.

Women in American Life—1880–1920. Video, 17 min. National Women's History Project. Explores significant changes in women's lives.

CHAPTER 15

Before You Read

Build on What You Know

Ask students to answer the following questions.

How might inventions have begun to launch a new age of American industrialization?

Consider:

- the historical effects of single inventions such as the cotton gin
- the ways in which inventions can affect and transform the workplace and general productivity

Why might poor working conditions have led many American workers to organize unions?

Consider:

- the effects of dangerous working environments
- the effects of wide disparities in wealth

exploring the time line

AMERICAN EVENTS

PEOPLE IN HISTORY

1879 ■ Frank W. Woolworth. Frank Woolworth left his family farm to work as a sales clerk at Moore & Smith's Corner Store in Watertown, New York. After five years, Woolworth borrowed money from his employer to open his Great Five Cent Store, which closed down quickly because of its poor location. Woolworth then moved to Lancaster, Pennsylvania, where he opened the world's first five-and-ten cents store. In 1884 Woolworth opened a 25¢ store, but he closed it down quickly when it did not attract as much business as the five-and-tens. Until his death in 1919, Woolworth continued expanding his company, opening more stores every year, and building an international empire.

CRITICAL THINKING How does Woolworth's life story reflect American ideals about free enterprise and equal opportunity?

ANSWER: Students might suggest that Woolworth's life represents the American democratic ideal that it is possible for anyone to rise from poverty to wealth through hard work.

CHAPTER 5

1865–1905

The Second Industrial Revolution

Pullman Sleeping Car

1865
Business and Finance
George Pullman patents a railway sleeping car.

1869
Politics
Uriah S. Stephens establishes the Knights of Labor, the first major national union.

The first telephone

1876
Science and Technology
Alexander Graham Bell receives a patent for the telephone.

1879
Science and Technology
Thomas Edison uses bamboo fiber in his design for the first long-lasting incandescent lightbulb.

1879
Business and Finance
Frank W. Woolworth establishes the first of a chain of Woolworth dime stores.

Edison's lightbulb

1865 **1873** **1881**

1869
The Arts
Horatio Alger Jr. begins publishing the series *Luck and Pluck.*

1874
Daily Life
Mary Ewing Outerbridge establishes the first American tennis courts on Staten Island, New York.

1876
The Arts
American artist Winslow Homer paints *The Cotton Pickers.*

HORSMAN'S CELEBRATED LAWN TENNIS

Advertisement picturing a Staten Island sports club

The Cotton Pickers *by Winslow Homer*

Before You Read

Build on What You Know

During the first half of the 1800s, both the U.S. population and westward settlement expanded rapidly. This growth was fueled by immigration, industrialization, and the economic opportunities of the frontier. After the Civil War these trends accelerated even more. In this chapter you will learn about the many inventions that began a new age of industrialization in the United States. Poor working conditions in the new industries, however, led many American workers to organize unions to improve their daily lives.

Think About Themes

To help students create their Themes Journal entries, provide the following examples of appropriate **agree**/**disagree** *statements.*

Economic Development

Agree In the late 1700s, inventions such as the spinning jenny vastly increased American textile production, in turn leading to economic growth.

Disagree During the Spanish Golden Age, treasure from the Americas rather than technological innovations propelled Spain's economy.

Technology and Society

Agree Some women believed that their work in the Lowell mills gave them new economic and personal opportunities.

Disagree The invention of the cotton gin expanded slavery, leading to heightened misery for many African Americans.

Democratic Values

Agree In furthering economic growth, business leaders helped widen the middle class, leading to greater equality. In protesting dangerous workplace conditions, labor leaders utilized the right to free speech.

Disagree Some business leaders broke unions, depriving laborers of the right to express themselves in the workplace.

exploring the time line

GLOBAL EVENTS

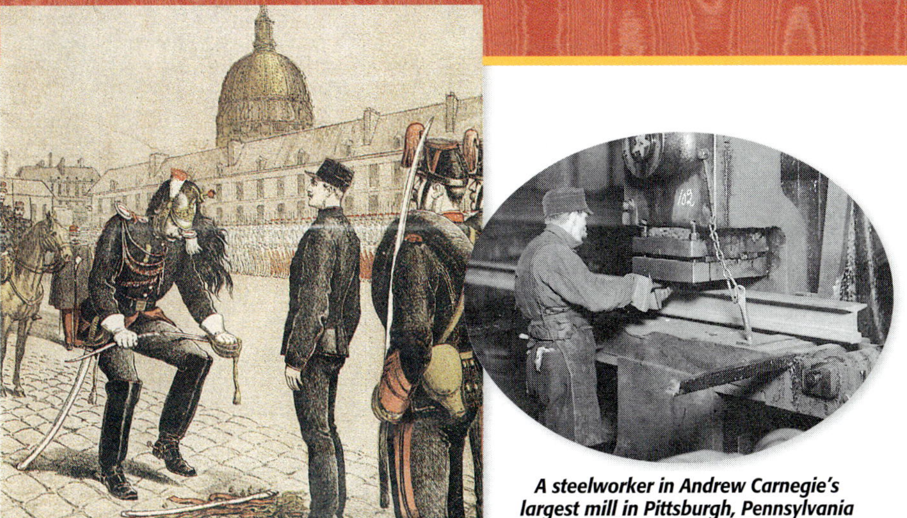

The public humiliation of French army captain Alfred Dreyfus

A steelworker in Andrew Carnegie's largest mill in Pittsburgh, Pennsylvania

TOPIC: Dreyfus Affair
GO TO: go.hrw.com
KEYWORD: SE1 Dreyfus

Have students access the Internet through the HRW Web site to conduct research on the Dreyfus affair. Then ask students to create one or two political cartoons about the incident. Have students write captions to accompany their political cartoons. Ask volunteers to present their cartoons and their captions to the class.

1884
The Arts
Mark Twain publishes *The Adventures of Huckleberry Finn.*

1886
Politics
1,500 U.S. labor strikes erupt.

1889

1890
Politics
The Sherman Antitrust Act is passed, outlawing monopolies and trusts that restrain trade.

1893
World Events
Europe sinks into a major economic depression.

1893
Daily Life
The first motorcar to be built in the United States is completed by the Duryea brothers.

1894
World Events
Alfred Dreyfus is arrested on questionable treason charges, leading to political upheaval in France.

1897

1901
Business and Finance
Andrew Carnegie sells his steel company to J. P. Morgan for nearly $500 million.

1903
Science and Technology
The Wright brothers test their airplane near Kitty Hawk, North Carolina.

1905

A strike turns violent in Chicago, Illinois.

The Duryea brothers ride in their horseless carriage.

Think About Themes

Decide whether you **agree** *or* **disagree** *with the following statements. Note why in your journal.*

Economic Development Technological innovations lead to economic growth by increasing production and industrialization.

Technology and Society Technology brings about social reform and improves people's daily lives.

Democratic Values The actions of both American business leaders and labor organizers lead to greater equality and an expansion of democracy.

163

SECTION 1

After completing Section 1, students should be able to:

OBJECTIVE 1 *Describe how the development of steel and oil refining affected U.S. industry.*

OBJECTIVE 2 *Recount the innovations that were made in transportation.*

OBJECTIVE 3 *Explain how innovations in communications technology changed business practices and daily life in the United States.*

OBJECTIVE 4 *Discuss why Thomas Edison wanted to open a research laboratory, and how it changed American life.*

LET'S GET STARTED!

Write the names of the following inventions and innovations on the chalkboard: *computers, the Internet, airbags, cell phones,* and *video games.* As students enter the classroom, ask them to pick one or two and write a paragraph describing their importance in Americans' daily lives. Ask volunteers to read their paragraphs aloud. Then tell students that in Section 1 they will learn about the inventions and innovations that transformed Americans' daily lives in the late 1800s.

SECTION 1 RESOURCES

PRINT

- Guided Reading Strategy 5.1
- Literature Reading 5: To a Locomotive in Winter
- Section 1 Review, p. 172
- Daily Quiz 5.1

MULTIMEDIA

- One-Stop Planner, Lesson 5.1
- Holt Researcher: American History CD–ROM
- HRW Web site

SHELTERED ENGLISH

- Main Idea Activity for Reteaching and Sheltered English 5.1

✔ READING TO UNDERSTAND

To help students master the section objectives, have them answer the **READING CHECKS** and complete **Guided Reading Strategy 5.1** as they read the section.

The Age of Invention

OBJECTIVES

Read to understand:

1. how the development of steel and oil refining affected U.S. industry
2. what innovations were made in transportation
3. how the innovations in communications technology changed business practices and daily life in the United States
4. why Thomas Edison wanted to open a research laboratory, and how it changed American life

KEY TERMS

Bessemer process
patent
transcontinental railroad
trunk lines
telegraph

KEY PEOPLE

Edwin L. Drake
Elijah McCoy
George Westinghouse
Alexander Graham Bell
Thomas Alva Edison
Lewis Latimer

EYEWITNESSES TO History

"The telephone is a curious device that might fairly find place in the magic of Arabian Tales. Of what use is such an invention? Well, there may be occasions of state when it is necessary for officials who are far apart to talk with each other."

—New York *Tribune* reporter

1876 Centennial Exposition

A reporter visiting the 1876 Centennial Exposition in Philadelphia discussed in the New York *Tribune* his amazement at the invention of the telephone. In the years following the Civil War, the United States experienced a wave of scientific discoveries and inventions. Americans celebrated this "age of invention" at the exposition in Philadelphia. Inventors presented new technologies such as the telephone to the public for the first time. The potential impact of these inventions on the future of American business and daily life was uncertain.

Industrial Innovations

From 1865 to 1900 the United States experienced a surge of industrial growth. These years marked the beginning of a Second Industrial Revolution. This new era of industrial transformation began with numerous discoveries and inventions that significantly altered manufacturing, transportation, and the everyday lives of Americans.

Coal and steam made possible the original Industrial Revolution in the United States. Coal-fed steam engines powered factories. These factories in turn produced the goods that generated economic growth. In the late 1800s an abundance of steel helped spur a second period of industrialization. Steel was used in the construction of heavy machinery that mass-produced goods. Steel was also used to build railroad tracks, bridges, and tall city buildings.

Steel. Metal workers and manufacturers had known of steel long before the Second Industrial Revolution. Until the mid-1800s, however, the process of converting iron ore into steel was too expensive to be used practically. In the 1850s, however, Henry Bessemer in Great Britain and William Kelly in the United States both developed a method of steelmaking that burned off the impurities in molten iron with a blast of hot air. Known as the **Bessemer process**, this method could produce more steel in a day than the older techniques could turn out in a week. American engineer Alexander Holley adapted and improved the Bessemer process. Largely because of this process, American steel production skyrocketed from about 15,000 tons in 1865 to more than 28 million tons by 1910.

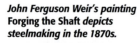

John Ferguson Weir's painting* Forging the Shaft *depicts steelmaking in the 1870s.

The production of steel required iron ore. Barges and steamers carried unprocessed iron ore from the Midwest

TEACH OBJECTIVE 1

ALL LEVELS: Ask students to define the words *refine* and *refinery*. *(Students might suggest that to refine something is to make it better.)* Ask students how improved refining processes might have affected industrial growth in the late 1800s. *(Students might suggest that improved processes would have fueled economic growth.)* To help students understand how the development of steel and oil refining affected U.S. industry, copy the following graphic organizer on the chalkboard, omitting the italicized answers. Have each student complete it. **Sheltered English**

Refining Processes in the United States

Steel

Effects on Industry
- *provided a strong, inexpensive source of building material*
- *allowed the expansion of the railroad industry*
- *allowed the construction of sophisticated machinery, bridges, tall buildings, and so on*

Oil

Effects on Industry
- *resulted in the production of kerosene for fuel or light*
- *allowed the manufacturing of other important industrial petroleum products*
- *helped machinery operate*

through the Great Lakes to the southern shores of Lake Michigan and Lake Erie. Cities such as Gary, Indiana; Cleveland, Ohio; and Pittsburgh, Pennsylvania, became major centers for steel manufacturing. Coal mined in Pennsylvania and West Virginia provided an inexpensive source of fuel for steel production.

The increased availability of steel in the late 1800s resulted in its widespread industrial use. A major consumer of steel was the railroad industry, which began replacing iron rails with stronger, longer-lasting steel ones. Recognizing its strength as a building material, builders began to use steel in the construction of bridges and buildings. Using steel to create a skeletal frame in buildings allowed architects to design larger, multistory buildings. Steel's resistance to rust also made it an ideal material for everyday items such as nails and wire.

Oil. Like the advances in steel production, the development of a process to refine oil also affected industrial practices. American Indians and settlers had known of the existence of crude oil for hundreds of years. Some Indians used this unprocessed dark thick ooze for medicinal purposes and to grease wagons and tools.

By the late 1850s, however, chemists and geologists from a number of countries had made significant progress in developing a process to refine crude oil. With this process, crude oil could be turned into kerosene, which could be burned in lamps to produce light or used as a fuel. Kerosene provided a cheap substitute for whale oil, which had become increasingly difficult to acquire.

Noting the growing demand for this inexpensive fuel, Edwin L. Drake used a steam engine to drill for oil near Titusville, Pennsylvania, in 1859. The venture seemed so impractical that curious onlookers questioned Drake's sanity, calling the project Drake's Folly. When the oil began to flow at a rate of some 20 barrels a day, however, other prospectors, or "wildcatters," hurried to dig their own wells. Like the California Gold Rush of 1849, the oil boom in western Pennsylvania created intense excitement and encouraged prospecting. Prospectors even referred to oil as "black gold." By the 1880s oil wells dotted Ohio, Pennsylvania, and West Virginia. Production topped 25 million barrels of oil in 1880 alone.

Although kerosene remained a primary product of oil refining, by 1880 refiners had developed other petroleum products that increased the industrial uses of oil. Refiners developed waxes and lubricating oil for use in new industrial machines. Elijah McCoy made a significant contribution to the industrial use of oil. The son of runaway slaves, McCoy invented a lubricating cup that fed oil to parts of a machine while it was running.

Like other inventors, McCoy received a **patent**—a guarantee to protect an inventor's rights to make, use, or sell the invention. McCoy's innovative breakthrough helped many kinds of machines operate more smoothly and quickly.

✔ **READING CHECK:** How did the development of steel and oil refining affect U.S. industry?

INTERPRETING THE VISUAL RECORD

Black gold. Edwin Drake, wearing a top hat, visits his oil well drilled in 1859 near Titusville, Pennsylvania. ***What materials did Drake use to construct his well?***

PEOPLE IN HISTORY

Elijah McCoy. Elijah McCoy's parents sent him to the University of Edinburgh in Scotland, where he studied to be an engineer. When he returned to the United States with his engineering certification, he could not find a job. Although many companies were looking for engineers, none would hire an African American. McCoy took a job shoveling coal and lubricating machines. Because the machines had to be stopped, lubricated by hand, and then restarted, companies lost production time. McCoy worked for two years, spending his own money and using scrap metal, to create an automatic lubricator. After patenting his invention, McCoy soon improved upon his creation and developed other lubricating devices. He also invented the ironing board, the rubber heel for shoes, and a lawn sprinkler. Others tried to sell their own versions of the automatic lubricator, but buyers knew that McCoy's was the most dependable. Before buying they would ask, "Is this the *real* McCoy?"

ACTIVITY: Have each student write a monologue about some aspect of McCoy's life.

VISUAL RECORD ANSWER

Students might mention wood and iron.

TEACH OBJECTIVE 2

LEVEL 1: Pair students and assign pairs one of the following transportation innovations: the railroad, the automobile, the airplane. Tell each pair to imagine that it is shortly after the introduction of its assigned innovation. Ask each pair to develop a two-to-three-minute dialogue describing the effect of its innovation on Americans' daily lives. *(Pairs should indicate that all three innovations made travel more efficient and brought Americans into closer contact with each other. Railroads promoted western settlement, urban growth, and economic prosperity. Automobiles were largely limited to wealthy Americans. Airplanes offered new transportation possibilities.)* Have at least three pairs—one representing each of the innovations—perform their dialogues for the class.
Sheltered English, Cooperative Learning

LEVEL 2: Assign students one of the following transportation innovations: the railroad, the automobile, the airplane. Tell students to imagine that it is shortly after the introduction of their assigned innovation. Have each student write two or three half-page diary entries discussing the effects of his or her assigned innovation on Americans' daily lives. *(See the Level 1 lesson for the correct effects.)* Ask volunteers to read their entries to the class. Students may wish to include their diary entries in their portfolios.

ACROSS THE CURRICULUM

▶BUSINESS◀

Race of the Railroads. The 1862 Railroad Act established that the transcontinental railroad would be built by two railroad companies: Union Pacific and Central Pacific. Union Pacific began building the railroad west from Omaha, Nebraska. It was to connect eventually with the Central Pacific, which was being constructed east from Sacramento, California. The two companies began a race to build the most rail, since they were paid and given land grants for each mile of track. In 1868, when completion was near, Charles Crocker of Central Pacific advised his partner Leland Stanford to "work on as though Heaven were before you and Hell behind you." Together, the two companies were granted more than 30 million acres of land.

CRITICAL THINKING How might the race to the last railroad spike be like other events in U.S. history?

ANSWER: Students might mention the Gold Rush, the settlers' competition for land grants after the Homestead Act, or any other instance of intense competition for economic gain.

VISUAL RECORD ANSWER

Students might mention that the men are celebrating the end of the construction.

Transportation

Innovations in the steel and oil industries led to a surge of new advances in the transportation industry. Many of the discoveries during this "age of invention" contributed to the development of new, more technologically advanced forms of transportation.

New technology in the late 1800s resulted in a massive expansion of the American railroad network. Entirely new discoveries laid the groundwork for air flight and the automobile. These developments in transportation made travel much more efficient. This brought Americans into closer contact with each other. Railroads linked isolated regions of the country to the rest of the United States.

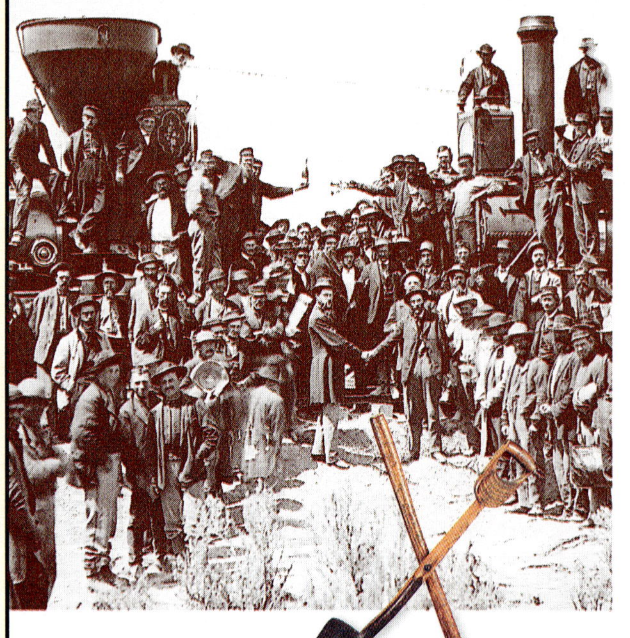

INTERPRETING THE VISUAL RECORD

Transcontinental railroad. The completion of the first transcontinental railroad in 1869 allowed trains to transport goods and people from coast to coast in a matter of days. ***How does this photograph reveal the importance of this moment to U.S. history?***

Railroads. The availability of cheap steel provided by the Bessemer process had a significant impact on railroad expansion. As steel production soared, prices dropped dramatically. Steel that had sold for $100 a ton in 1873 went for $12 a ton by the late 1890s. The availability of cheaper steel encouraged railroad companies to lay thousands of miles of new track.

The rapid increase of railroad lines led to a more efficient network of rail transportation. Prior to the Civil War, most railroads in the United States were short. They averaged some 100 miles in length and primarily served local transportation needs. In 1860, passengers and freight traveling between New York and Chicago, for example, had to change lines 17 times over a period of two days. By the next decade, however, the rapid expansion of rail lines allowed passengers and freight to make the same trip in less than 24 hours without changing trains.

The country's first **transcontinental railroad** was completed in 1869. The project was completed when the Central Pacific and Union Pacific Railroads were joined to create a single rail line from Omaha, Nebraska, to the Pacific Ocean. To celebrate its completion, railroad tycoon Leland Stanford hammered in the last spike at Promontory, Utah. By 1900 almost a half-dozen **trunk lines**, or major railroads, crossed the Great Plains to the Pacific coast. Feeder, or branch, lines connected the trunk lines to outlying areas. This huge railroad grid joined every state and linked remote towns to urban centers.

Additional innovations further improved rail transportation. Bigger, more efficient locomotives made it possible to pull larger loads at faster speeds. George Westinghouse's compressed-air brake increased railroad safety by enabling the locomotive and all its cars to stop at the same time. Granville T. Woods improved on Westinghouse's air brake. He also developed a communications system that enabled trains and stations to send and receive messages.

Changes in track design also improved rail service. Double sets of tracks allowed train traveling in opposite directions to pass each other. Equally important,

LEVEL 3: Organize students into small groups and tell them to imagine that they are modern-day magazine editors preparing a special issue on the effects of transportation innovations such as railroads, automobiles, and airplanes. Have each group develop a six-page insert for the magazine, devoting two pages to each transportation innovation. Groups' inserts should describe the innovations, discuss their effects, and possibly illustrate significant aspects. *(See the Level 1 lesson for the correct effects.)* Have spokespeople present the inserts.
Cooperative Learning

SPOTLIGHT on the Horseless Carriage

Pair students and ask them to conduct research on the horseless carriage and the early automobile. Then have each pair create a flowchart or another type of graphic organizer tracing the development and introduction of the horseless carriage and the early automobile. Ask volunteers to present their flowcharts or graphic organizers to the class. Then conduct a brief discussion on the ways in which the horseless carriage and the early automobile transformed American life.
Cooperative Learning, Block Scheduling

the adoption in the 1870s of a standard gauge, or width between the rails, made rail transportation faster and cheaper. Passengers and freight no longer had to be transferred from train to train each time they reached a different line.

The growth of railroads had far-reaching consequences. Railroads increased western settlement by making travel affordable and easy. They also stimulated urban growth. Wherever railroads were built, new towns sprang up, and existing towns grew into major cities.

The economic impact of the railroads was immeasurable. For much of the late 1800s railroad companies provided many of the country's jobs. They also spurred the growth of other industries. The railroad companies' demands for locomotives, rails, and railcars poured money into the steel and railroad-car construction industries. Innovations like refrigerated freight cars helped develop the meatpacking industry. In addition, the network of railroad lines allowed companies to sell their products nationally. A Pennsylvania steel foundry could obtain iron ore from the Great Lakes region, and a Philadelphia furniture company could sell its products in small midwestern towns.

Railroads also shaped American popular culture and folk music. One ballad immortalized Casey Jones, the Illinois Central engineer killed in a crash with a freight train in 1900. Other songs celebrated famous trains like the Wabash Cannonball.

INTERPRETING THE VISUAL RECORD
Railroads. The Illinois Central Railroad connected rural Americans with the rest of the world. ***What do the various images in this cartoon represent?***

The horseless carriage. The innovations in oil refining in the late 1800s led to advances in the development of motors and the creation of a new mode of transportation. The horseless carriage, a self-propelled vehicle and forerunner to the automobile, had originally been developed about 1770. A French artillery officer named Nicolas-Joseph Cugnot had mounted a steam engine to a three-wheeled carriage. The use of steam power for these early automobiles was expensive and inefficient for the small amount of power needed for these carriages.

Efforts to develop a gasoline-powered engine led to the creation of a more practical self-propelled vehicle. Innovations in oil refining led Nikolaus A. Otto to invent the first internal combustion engine powered by gasoline in 1876. In the 1880s ambitious designers in Europe and the United States attempted to use this gasoline engine to power horseless carriages. In 1893 Charles and J. Frank Duryea built the first practical motorcar in the United States.

The 1890s brought further innovations to the horseless carriage. By the turn of the century, more Americans had begun to use the carriages in their daily lives. The use of this new mode of transportation was limited, however, since only wealthy citizens could afford it. Nevertheless, automobile production rapidly became a substantial commercial industry.

Airplanes. The internal combustion engine also led to advances in flight. Using small gasoline engines, Orville and Wilbur Wright of Dayton, Ohio, developed one of the first working airplanes.

The Wright brothers had experimented with glider designs. They also experimented with engines based on European designs in the mid-1890s. On December

internet connect

TOPIC: Wright Brothers
GO TO: go.hrw.com
KEYWORD: SE1 Wright

Have students access the Internet through the HRW Web site to conduct research on the Wright brothers' first flight. Tell students to imagine that they are modern-day multimedia designers. Have each student create a two-to-four-minute computer slide show discussing the science of flight, the design and aerodynamics of the early airplane, and the procedures that the Wright brothers used to build and test their craft.

VISUAL RECORD ANSWER

Students might suggest that the train represents the Illinois Central Railroad, the map represents the United States, and the inset images represent regions of the United States.

VISUAL RECORD ANSWER

(for p. 168)

Students might mention training in Morse code.

CHANGING WAYS ANSWERS

(for p. 169)

Students should mention handwritten letters, live theater, hammer, fireplace, and livestock. Students might mention that it would take a longer time for people to get to their destinations, wash their clothes, or heat their food.

TEACH OBJECTIVE 3

LEVEL 1: Write the names of the following innovations on the chalkboard: *the telegraph, the telephone,* and *the typewriter.* Then pair students and ask each pair to write before-and-after scenarios for the three innovations. Scenarios should describe how the innovations changed both business practices and daily lives. *(Pairs should indicate that the telegraph allowed businesses to place long-distance orders very quickly, as did the telephone. The telegraph allowed the quick production of legible documents. All three innovations brought Americans closer together.)* Have volunteers present their scenarios to the class. Students may wish to include their scenarios in their portfolios. **Sheltered English, Cooperative Learning**

LEVEL 2: Tell students to imagine that it is 1884 and that they are businesspeople preparing to retire. Have each student write a one-to-two-page memoir describing the impact of the telegraph, the telephone, and the typewriter on his or her business and personal lives. *(See the Level 1 lesson for the correct effects.)* Students may wish to illustrate their memoirs. Have volunteers read their memoirs to the class.

TECHNOLOGY AND SOCIETY

Telegraph Monopolies. In the early days of the telegraph, the six major companies agreed to divide the national market into six regions. By 1866, however, Western Union had consolidated all of the other companies, thereby creating a monopoly. The consolidation allowed Western Union to standardize its rates, equipment, and language, leading to a reduction in telegraph costs. The Associated Press (AP), a group of allied newspapers that used telegraphs to communicate news stories, formed an association with Western Union. This alliance gave the AP control of virtually all the news in the country–a situation that angered owners of smaller newspapers.

CRITICAL THINKING Why might smaller newspapers have been at a disadvantage to the Associated Press?

ANSWER: Students might suggest that it would have been difficult for a small news service with few resources to compete with the vast network of AP newspapers.

With experience gained from operating a bicycle shop and experimenting with small engines and gliders, the Wright brothers developed a plane and made the first piloted flight in 1903.

17, 1903, near Kitty Hawk, North Carolina, Orville Wright made the first piloted flight—12 seconds and 120 feet—in a powered plane. Orville Wright made a statement summing up the significance of the achievement.

> **"This flight lasted only twelve seconds, but it was, nevertheless, the first in the history of the world in which a machine carrying a man had raised itself by its own power into the air in full flight, had sailed forward without reduction of speed, and had finally landed at a point as high as that from which it started."**

The Wright brothers' first flight received little public attention or press coverage. Some Americans even questioned its inappropriateness for human beings. However, as word of their achievement spread, a surge of related inventions and patents by other engineers dramatically demonstrated the importance of this new form of transportation.

✔ **READING CHECK:** What innovations were made in transportation in the late 1800s?

Communications

Just as developments in transportation made traveling easier and brought people into closer contact, innovations in communications technology also brought Americans closer together. These advances also furthered the growth of American industry.

Telegraph. One of the most significant advances in communications in the 1800s was the **telegraph**. The telegraph was developed by Samuel F. B. Morse as a means of communicating over wires with electricity. The telegraph attracted little attention when Morse filed for a patent on his version in 1837. In time, however, people recognized its business potential. Using Morse's dot-and-dash code, a telegraph operator could send a business order to a distant location in minutes.

By 1866 Western Union, the leading telegraph company, had more than 2,000 telegraph offices. The telegraph grew along with the railroad. Telegraph companies established offices in train stations and strung telegraph wire on poles alongside the railroad lines. Telegraphs sent information for businesses, the government, newspapers, and private citizens.

Gradually, Americans began to see the importance of the telegraph to the daily functioning of the nation and its businesses. A reporter for *Harper's Magazine* compared the telegraph to the nervous system of the human body.

> **"Every phase of the mental activity of the country is more or less represented in this great system. . . . Almost instantaneously . . . [information] reaches the nearest ganglion [nerve center] of our great artificial nervous system, and it spreads simultaneously in every direction throughout the land."**

INTERPRETING THE VISUAL RECORD

Telegraph. Developed by Samuel Morse, this telegraph and receiver allowed for communication over long distances with electricity. ***Based on these images, what type of training or skills do you think a telegraph operator would need?***

LEVEL 3: Have students pick one of the following innovations: the telegraph, the telephone, or the typewriter. Tell students to imagine that they are businesspeople shortly after the widespread introduction of their chosen innovation. Have each student prepare a three-to-four-minute speech encouraging his or her manager to adopt the innovation and describing its possible effect in business and personal terms. *(See the Level 1 lesson for the correct effects.)* Have at least three students—one for each innovation—deliver their speeches to the class. Students may wish to include the written version of their speeches in their portfolios.

▶**ASSIGNMENT** *Have each student create a flowchart representing the effects of the telegraph, the telephone, and the typewriter on business and daily life.*

SPOTLIGHT on Alexander Graham Bell

Pair students and tell them to imagine that it is December 1876 and that they are preparing to interview Alexander Graham Bell. Have each student write five interview questions. Then have each student exchange his or her list with their partner and answer the questions. Ask volunteers to draw upon their questions and answers to enact their interviews for the class. **Cooperative Learning, Block Scheduling**

Changing Ways Technology in Daily Life

Understanding Change The "age of invention" transformed American life. Much of the technology developed in the late 1800s remains important today. Examine the chart of items used for various purposes in the mid-1800s and today. *What items used in the mid-1800s are still in use by some people today? How has their use changed? How would life today be different without the items on the right?*

Technology	Then	Now
Energy	firewood	oil, natural gas, nuclear power
Transportation	horse and buggy	automobile
Communication	handwritten letters	Internet
Popular Entertainment	live theater	television, films
Household Appliances	washboard underground icehouse hammer fireplace livestock	washing machine refrigerator electric drill microwave oven lawnmower

Data reflects mid-1800s and 1999.

THEN

NOW

THE GRANGER COLLECTION, NEW YORK

Telephone. Patented by Alexander Graham Bell in March 1876, the "talking telegraph," or telephone, had an even greater impact. Bell demonstrated his invention at the Philadelphia Centennial Exposition in June 1876. Judges there pronounced it "perhaps the greatest marvel hitherto [thus far] achieved by the electric telegraph." Businesses quickly found the telephone indispensable. By the end of the 1800s more than a million telephones had been installed in American offices and homes.

Early telephones required operators to connect callers, and many women rushed to fill these newly created jobs. A former telephone operator described the fast-paced work.

> **"On the second floor where the switchboards were located there arose a dull roar like that of locusts on a sunburnt prairie, a sense of many voices without any one being distinguishable. . . . I could see their hands working swiftly, pulling cords out of the holes, jabbing others in. Serving the Thing that signaled them with little flashing lights, making them hurry, hurry."**

THE GRANGER COLLECTION, NEW YORK (BOTH)

INTERPRETING THE VISUAL RECORD

Telephone. Alexander Graham Bell's invention of the telephone created new employment opportunities for women. ***What does the photograph below of telephone operators during the late 1800s reveal about the positive and negative aspects of the job?***

PEOPLE IN HISTORY

Alexander Graham Bell. After receiving financial support, Alexander Graham Bell, along with a young man named Thomas Watson, began work on inventing the harmonic telegraph, later known as the telephone. By accident, Bell and Watson discovered how to make the telephone work. Bell's patent for the telephone—which many have called the most valuable single patent in history—was filed in February 1876. At first his device only transmitted rough sounds. Bell's first intelligible words were transmitted on March 10, 1876: "Mr. Watson, come here, I want to see you." Although Bell never became extremely rich from his invention of the telephone, he did become independently wealthy.

CRITICAL THINKING How might life be different if the telephone had not been invented?

ANSWER: Students might mention that it would take longer for information to be disseminated and the Internet could not have been invented.

VISUAL RECORD ANSWER

Students might suggest that positive aspects included employment opportunities and companionship and that negative aspects included boredom.

SPOTLIGHT on Electricity

Tell students to name emotions that they might have felt upon first seeing electric light. *(Students might list such emotions as shock, happiness, fear, wonder, and so on.)* Write students' responses on the chalkboard. Then ask students to study the image of Edison and the electric light on p. 171. Tell them to imagine that they are one of the observers in the image. Have each student write a one-page letter to a friend in Iowa describing the experience. Students should draw upon the emotions listed on the chalkboard in their letters. Students may wish to include their letters in their portfolios. **Block Scheduling**

SPOTLIGHT on the Typewriter

Have students conduct research on the effect of the typewriter on women's lives, focusing on employment opportunities and the workplace. Then tell students to imagine that they are women living in Chicago, Illinois, in the mid- to late-1800s. Have each student write a series of diary entries that discuss his or her life before and after the introduction of the typewriter. Ask volunteers to read their entries to the class. Students may wish to include their diary entries in their portfolios. **Block Scheduling**

THAT'S INTERESTING!

Author Mark Twain was excited when he learned about typewriters. He rushed out to buy one, writing letters in all capitals to his friends about its usefulness: "THE MACHINE HAS SEVERAL VIRTUES. . . . IT PILES AN AWFUL STACK OF WORDS ON ONE PAGE. IT DON'T MUSS THINGS OR SCATTER INK BLOTS AROUND. OF COURSE IT SAVES PAPER."

SCIENCE & TECHNOLOGY ANSWERS

1. They found a filament that would light up without burning up and discovered that carbonized bamboo fiber could last for an average of 600 hours of use.
2. It creates a vacuum, reducing the oxygen around the filament.

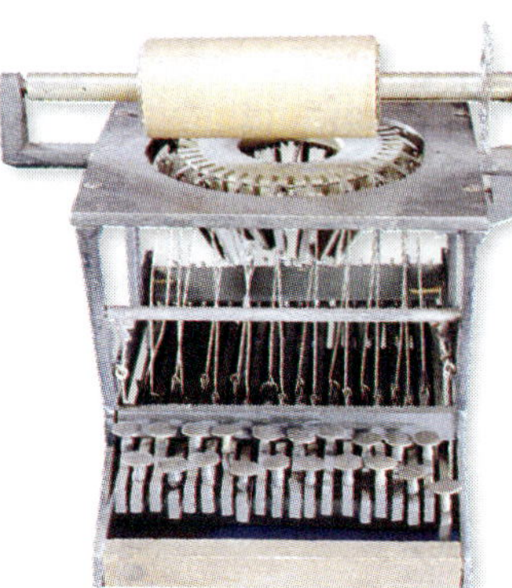

Christopher Sholes's typewriter revolutionized business communication.

Typewriter. Christopher Sholes developed the typewriter in 1867. By allowing users to quickly produce easily legible documents, the typewriter revolutionized communications. Sholes sold his typewriter patent in 1873 to E. Remington & Sons. Although other typewriter designs had preceded Sholes's design, his was the first to be marketed. Sholes's keyboard design, with only a few changes, is still used today in typewriters and computers. Carbon paper, also introduced during this period, allowed users of typewriters to produce multiple copies of a document at the same time.

The invention of the typewriter soon gave rise to the use of typing pools. These business departments were made up of many clerical workers whose main task was to type. Women made up the majority of workers in the typing pools. The pools offered many working-class women the opportunity to move into a skilled profession for the first time. Lillian Sholes, Christopher Sholes's daughter, was probably the first professional female typist. Christopher Sholes was aware of the impact of the typewriter on communications and on the expansion of job opportunities for women. He later wrote, "I feel that I have done something for the women who have always had to work so hard."

✔ **READING CHECK:** How did innovations in communications technology change business practices and the daily lives of Americans?

Science & Technology

Electricity

The late 1800s brought significant advances in the uses of electricity. One such advance was the lightbulb. In simple terms, the lightbulb produces light when electricity flows through a filament that resists that flow. This resistance gives off energy in the form of heat—so much heat that the filament glows, producing light. To prevent the filament from being consumed by the heat, inventors created a vacuum through the use of a glass bulb. This reduces the oxygen around the filament. The bulb was filled with inert gas.

While many inventors experimented with the incandescent lightbulb, Thomas Edison and his team at Menlo Park, New Jersey, made the most significant contributions by finding a filament that would light up without burning up. Edison and his associates discovered in 1880 that carbonized bamboo fiber could last an average of 600 hours. Eventually filaments made of the element tungsten were used.

Power plants soon arose to supply electricity for lightbulbs in homes and industries. However, electricity could not be transmitted over long distances with direct current (DC) because too much energy was lost in transportation over power lines. Inventor Nikola Tesla patented an alternating current (AC) generator that could produce electricity for transmission over longer distance with less loss of energy. With this advance, the use of electricity spread rapidly.

Understanding Science and History

1. What advances did Edison's team make with the lightbulb and electricity?
2. What purposes does the glass bulb serve?

TEACH OBJECTIVE 4

LEVEL 1: Tell students to imagine that it is 1876 and that Thomas Edison has just opened his research laboratory. Ask each student to write three headlines commemorating the event. Students' headlines should also explain why Edison wanted to open the laboratory. *(Students' headlines should note that Edison hoped to make important and profitable advances in science.)* Then tell students to imagine that it is 1880. Have each student write three headlines on Edison's various inventions and their effects on American life. *(Students should note that Edison's inventions included the lightbulb, the phonograph, and the early motion-picture camera. All transformed American life in various ways.)* Students may wish to include their headlines in their portfolios. **Sheltered English**

LEVELS 2 AND 3: Tell students to imagine that it is 1876 and that Thomas Edison has just opened his research laboratory. Ask each student to write a half-page newspaper article describing the event. Students' articles should also explain why Edison wanted to open the laboratory. *(See the Level 1 lesson for the correct reasons.)* Then tell students to imagine that it is 1880. Have each student write a half-page newspaper article on Edison's various inventions and their effects on American life. *(See the Level 1 lesson for the correct inventions and their effects.)* Students may wish to include their articles in their portfolios.

Edison and Menlo Park

Thomas Alva Edison was another pioneer of communications technology. His first major invention was a telegraph that could send up to four messages over the same wire simultaneously. Edison's early inventions had a significant impact on telegraphic communications. However, his influence on American life extends well beyond the history of the telegraph. An active innovator, Edison and his fellow researchers made significant discoveries and advances in electricity, lightbulbs, phonographs, and early motion-picture cameras.

Thomas Edison

Born in a small Ohio town in 1847, Edison received the majority of his schooling at home. He became a newsboy at age 12 and later worked as a telegraph operator. An eager amateur scientist, Edison conducted experiments and read widely in his spare time. In 1869 he patented an electric vote recorder. That year he also received his second patent, for a telegraphic stock ticker. Other inventions followed. In 1876 he went into the "invention business" full-time. He opened a workshop in Menlo Park, New Jersey, where he assembled a team of researchers. Excited about his new facility, Edison sent an invitation to a friend to come visit.

> **"Brand-new laboratory . . . at Menlo Park . . . the prettiest spot in New Jersey, on the [Pennsylvania] Railway, on a High Hill. Will show you around, go strawberrying."**

Edison promised that he and his fellow researchers would deliver "a minor invention every ten days and a big thing every six months or so." He kept his word. His researchers invented the phonograph in 1877 and the lightbulb in 1879. When he died in 1931, the "Wizard of Menlo Park" held more than 1,000 patents. Describing his process of invention to a colleague, Edison explained the secret to his success.

> **"I have the right principle and am on the right track, but time, hard work and some good luck are necessary too. It has been just so in all of my inventions. The first step is an intuition, and [it] comes with a burst, then difficulties arise. . . . Months of intense watching, study and labor are requisite [required] before commercial success or failure is certainly reached."**

Edison's work at Menlo Park was a team effort. Some of the most significant contributions to the development of the lightbulb were made not by Edison but by his assistant Lewis Latimer. Latimer was also a skilled draftsman. As an expert in patent law, Latimer testified in several court cases to support Edison's patents.

Read More About It (HOLT RESEARCHER)

Free Find:
Thomas Edison

After reading about Thomas Edison on the **Holt Researcher** CD–ROM, create a list of the most important of Edison's inventions and explain why each was significant.

INTERPRETING THE VISUAL RECORD

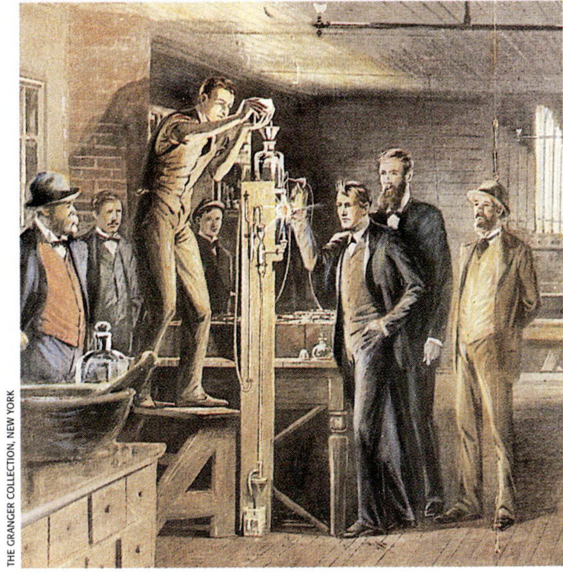

Menlo Park. Thomas Edison's team at Menlo Park developed more than 1,000 patented inventions. ***What conclusions can be drawn from this image about the working environment at Menlo Park?***

THAT'S INTERESTING!

Beginning in 1863, Thomas Edison worked at several different telegraph companies in Michigan, Ohio, Indiana, and Tennessee. The reason he worked at so many different companies was that he would get fired for experimenting with the office equipment without permission, and for sometimes being careless in attending to his telegraph responsibilities.

VISUAL RECORD ANSWER

Students might conclude that the working environment was one of teamwork and experimentation.

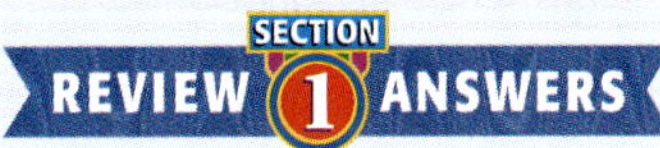

SECTION 1 REVIEW ANSWERS

Define and Identify

For significance, see the following pages:

- Bessemer process, p. 164
- Edwin L. Drake, p. 165
- Elijah McCoy, p. 165
- patent, p. 165
- transcontinental railroad, p. 166
- trunk lines, p. 166
- George Westinghouse, p. 166
- telegraph, p. 168
- Alexander Graham Bell, p. 169
- Thomas Alva Edison, p. 171
- Lewis Latimer, p. 171

REVIEW

Have students complete the **Section 1 Review** on p. 172.

ASSESS

Have students complete **Daily Quiz 5.1**. As **Alternative Assessment**, you may want to use the communication innovation speech or the Thomas Edison newspaper article in this section's lessons.

RETEACH

Have students complete **Main Idea Activity for Reteaching and Sheltered English 5.1**. Then have each student create a graphic organizer displaying the innovations introduced during the Second Industrial Revolution. Students' organizers should describe the innovations, identify their inventors, and explain their effects. Have students present their organizers to the class and then display them around the classroom.
Sheltered English

EXTEND

Have students conduct research on Nikola Tesla. Then tell students to imagine that they are producers of a popular television biography show. Have each student create a three-to-five-minute video presentation on Tesla's life and inventions. Ask volunteers to play their videos for the class. **Block Scheduling**

1. industry–Bessemer process, Henry Bessemer and William Kelly, helped railroad expansion; transportation–compressed-air brake, George Westinghouse, increased railroad safety; internal-combustion engine, Nikolaus A. Otto, helped develop automobiles; airplane, Orville and Wilbur Wright, encouraged development of air travel; communication–telegraph, Samuel F. B. Morse, provided communication across wide distances; telephone, Alexander Graham Bell, provided communication across wide distances and jobs for women; typewriter, Christopher Sholes, increased print production

2. Answers will vary. Students might mention increased ease of travel and communication and expanded job opportunities.

3. Answers will vary. Students might argue that people may not have recognized the wide range of possibilities or that they had gotten along fine without the advances before.

4. Answers will vary. Students might argue that the researchers could be more creative and efficient as a team. Their combined efforts produced important inventions like the lightbulb, which changed people's lifestyles.

5. Students might argue that working as a team and in a laboratory provides opportunities for funding and for sharing ideas. Or they might argue that working as a team inhibits individual creativity and personal recognition.

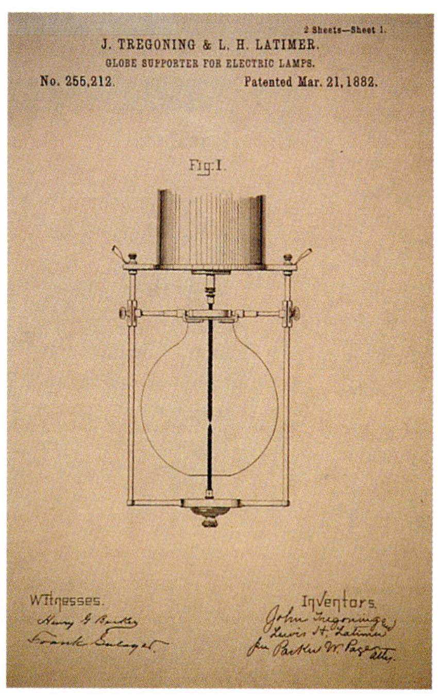

Lewis Latimer developed a globe supporter for the electric lightbulb in 1882.

In 1882 Edison opened one of the world's first electric power plants in New York City. Edison's New York plant served only a few buildings. Using direct current (DC) electricity the plant could only deliver electricity to the homes and offices in a very small area surrounding the plant. Despite the initial limitations, New Yorkers marveled at the new advances. One reporter from the *New York Times* explained that with electric lighting in the newspaper's offices, "it seemed almost like writing by daylight."

George Westinghouse and Nikola Tesla made additional advances beginning in the late 1880s. They developed a transformer that could transmit a high-voltage alternating current (AC) over long distances. The development of the alternating current allowed continued expansion of the use of electricity in urban households and industry.

At the 1893 World's Columbian Exposition in Chicago, Illinois, a Westinghouse-Tesla generator powered the twinkling lights outlining the major buildings at night. The electric lights enchanted visitors. They marveled at the "fairyland" and frequently referred to the illuminated exposition as the White City. To many witnesses, it symbolized a transformation of American life. Indeed, by the end of the century, electric lights had begun to replace gaslights. The availability of electrical power also made possible another major change. In many cities, horse-drawn vehicles gave way to electric streetcars.

✔ **READING CHECK:** Why did Thomas Edison open a research laboratory? How did it change American life?

SECTION 1 REVIEW

Define and explain the significance of the following terms:
Bessemer process
patent
transcontinental railroad
trunk lines
telegraph

Identify and explain the significance of the following individuals:
Edwin L. Drake
Elijah McCoy
George Westinghouse
Alexander Graham Bell
Thomas Alva Edison
Lewis Latimer

1. Using Graphic Organizers Copy the graphic organizer below. Use it to list and describe the various innovations that affected industry, transportation, and communications in the late 1800s.

Industry

Inventions	Inventors	Effects

Transportation

Inventions	Inventors	Effects

Communications

Inventions	Inventors	Effects

2. Evaluating How was American daily life transformed by the technological innovations of the late 1800s?

3. Hypothesizing Many technological advances such as the telegraph and the Wright brothers' flight attracted little public attention or respect at first. Why might these important breakthroughs not have been recognized at the time they occurred?

4. Identifying Cause and Effect Why did Thomas Edison establish a research laboratory, and how did it change society?

Critical Thinking

5. If you were an inventor, what would be the advantages and disadvantages of working in a laboratory like Edison's Menlo Park, rather than on your own?
Consider:
- aspects of working on your own
- aspects of working in a group
- the results that might come from both types of work

After completing Section 2, students should be able to:

OBJECTIVE 1 *Describe the arguments business leaders and social critics made about government's role in business.*

OBJECTIVE 2 *Recount how business strategies changed during the Second Industrial Revolution.*

OBJECTIVE 3 *Discuss how entrepreneurs took advantage of changes in business organization.*

OBJECTIVE 4 *Explain how new methods of marketing products changed American life.*

LET'S GET STARTED!

Write the following words on the chalkboard: *luck* and *pluck*. As students enter the classroom, ask them to define the terms. *(Students should define* luck *as good chance and* pluck *as being persistent.)* Have volunteers share their definitions. Then tell students that many business leaders of the late 1800s and early 1900s attributed their successes to a combination of luck and pluck. Tell students that in Section 2 they will learn more about these business leaders.

The Rise of Big Business

OBJECTIVES

Read to understand:

1. what various arguments business leaders and social critics made about the role of government in business
2. how business strategies changed during the Second Industrial Revolution
3. how entrepreneurs took advantage of changes in business organization
4. how new methods of marketing products changed American life

KEY TERMS

laissez-faire capitalism
free enterprise
communism
social Darwinism
corporation
trust
monopoly
vertical integration
horizontal integration

KEY PEOPLE

Horatio Alger Jr.
Andrew Carnegie
John D. Rockefeller
Cornelius Vanderbilt
George Pullman

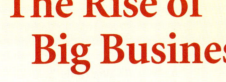

"Eureka! We have found it. Here was something new to all of us, for none of us had ever received anything but from toil."

—Andrew Carnegie

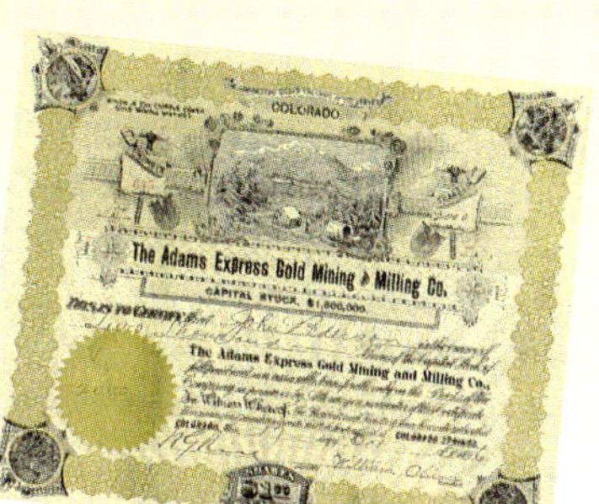

Certificate of business investment

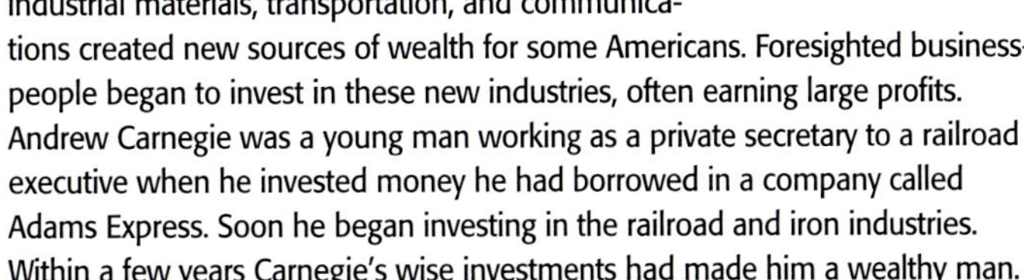

Young Andrew Carnegie recalled his excitement after receiving his first payment of profits from investments. The rapid technological advances in industrial materials, transportation, and communications created new sources of wealth for some Americans. Foresighted businesspeople began to invest in these new industries, often earning large profits. Andrew Carnegie was a young man working as a private secretary to a railroad executive when he invested money he had borrowed in a company called Adams Express. Soon he began investing in the railroad and iron industries. Within a few years Carnegie's wise investments had made him a wealthy man.

A New Capitalist Spirit

Entrepreneurs, or risk-taking businesspeople, set out to gain economic wealth by building industries that took advantage of the era's new technological advances. Many of these industries made enormous profits. With the rapid increase in business ventures and wealth, new ideas began to emerge that would transform traditional business practices.

Motivated to gain wealth and better their lives, business leaders shared an American ideal of self-reliant individualism. During the Second Industrial Revolution, Horatio Alger Jr. published a popular series of stories that reflected the increasing importance placed on individualism. These novels, such as those in the 1869 *Luck and Pluck* series, were typically based on a rags-to-riches theme. In these stories poor children improve their social and financial status through hard work and self-motivation. Like the characters in Alger's stories, many American business leaders attributed their successes to their work ethic. A high regard for individualism and self-reliance led many business leaders to champion the ideal of **laissez-faire capitalism.** *Laissez-faire* means "to let people do as they choose." The theory of laissez-faire capitalism calls for no government intervention in the economy. Most business leaders believed that the economy would prosper if businesses were left free from government regulation and allowed to compete in a free market. This idea is sometimes called **free enterprise.** These entrepreneurs argued that any government regulation would reduce individuals' prosperity and their self-reliance.

Critics respond. Business leaders hoped to keep industry free of government regulation. However, some critics argued that the rapid industrialization of factory life was harmful and unjust to the working class. This view of capitalism was most

Horatio Alger celebrated rugged individualism.

SECTION 2 RESOURCES

PRINT

- Guided Reading Strategy 5.2
- American History Political Cartoon 17: The Power of Trusts
- Geography Activity 5: Pullman's Company Town
- Primary Source Reading 5: The First Department Store
- Biography Reading 5: Frank Woolworth
- Section 2 Review, p. 180
- Daily Quiz 5.2

MULTIMEDIA

- One-Stop Planner, Lesson 5.2
- The American Nation Video Program Segment: The Standard Oil Company; Teacher's Guide, pp. 81–86
- Holt Researcher: American History CD–ROM

SHELTERED ENGLISH

- Main Idea Activity for Reteaching and Sheltered English 5.2

✔ READING TO UNDERSTAND

To help students master the section objectives, have them answer the **READING CHECKS** and complete **Guided Reading Strategy 5.2** as they read the section.

TEACH OBJECTIVE 1

ALL LEVELS: Ask students if, at present, the federal government has any role in business. *(Students should indicate that the federal government regulates businesses and, at times, assists them in various ways.)* Ask students if they approve of this involvement. *(Students' answers will vary.)* To help students understand how business leaders and social critics of the late 1800s and early 1900s regarded government involvement, copy the following graphic organizer on the chalkboard, omitting the italicized answers, and have each student complete it. After students have done so, ask them to re-evaluate their original answers based on information in their graphic organizers. **Sheltered English**

ARGUMENTS REGARDING GOVERNMENT'S ROLE IN BUSINESS

Business Leaders
- *argued that individuals should be self-reliant*
- *argued that businesses would prosper in the absence of government interference*
- *argued that government interference would reduce self-reliance*

Social Critics
- *argued that factory life and poor working conditions harmed workers*
- *argued that all citizens should own all means of production*
- *argued that government assistance would prevent the best businesses from rising to the top*

HISTORY MAKERS SPEAK

Lester Ward in *Social Darwinism in American Thought*

Critique of Social Darwinism. Although some businessmen and philosophers subscribed to theories of social Darwinism, others argued against it. Sociologist Lester Ward argued for a separation of natural law and social theory. Because Ward had grown up in poverty and observed the capabilities of those around him, he believed that poverty was not a clear indication of a person's inferiority. He argued that biological theories did not apply to the social world: "The fundamental principle of biology is natural selection, that of sociology is artificial selection. The survival of the fittest is simply the survival of the strong, which implies and would better be called the destruction of the weak. If nature progresses through the destruction of the weak, man progresses through protection of the weak."

CRITICAL THINKING In what two ways might Ward define "progresses" in the last sentence?

ANSWER: Students might indicate that for nature progress entails the survival of the strongest and most fit. For society, however, progress seems defined by humane actions rather than competitive success.

forcefully argued in the mid-1800s by Karl Marx, a German philosopher. Marx proposed a political system that would remove the inequalities of wealth. He developed a political theory, later called marxism, that called for the overthrow of the capitalist economic system.

Marx argued that capitalism allowed the bourgeoisie—the people who own the means of production—to take advantage of the proletariat—the workers. From this argument, Marx suggested that a new society could be formed on principles of **communism**. This theory proposes that individual ownership of property should not be allowed. In a communist state, property and the means of production are owned by everyone in the community. The community in turn ideally provides for the needs of all the people equally without regard to social rank.

Charles Darwin never expected his scientific theories of biology to be applied to social issues.

Social Darwinism. American businesspeople also responded to some of the same concerns about the working class raised by Marx. These business leaders began to embrace the newly emerging theory of **social Darwinism**. Originally proposed by English social philosopher Herbert Spencer, social Darwinism adopted the ideas of Charles Darwin's biological theory of natural selection and evolution. Social Darwinists argued that society progressed through natural competition. The "fittest" people, businesses, or nations should and would rise to positions of wealth and power. The "unfit" would fail. Following the law of the "survival of the fittest," social Darwinists believed that any attempts to help the poor or less capable actually slowed social progress. "Nature's cure for most social and political diseases is better than man's," wrote American educator and philosopher Nicholas Murray Butler.

Some religious leaders offered religious support for social Darwinism by suggesting that great wealth was a sign of Christian virtue. Baptist minister Russell H. Conwell declared, "You ought to get rich, and it is your duty to get rich. . . . To make money honestly is to preach the gospel."

✔ **READING CHECK:** What arguments did business leaders and social critics make about the role of government in business?

The Corporation

In the late 1800s a series of changes took place in the way businesses were organized. At the close of the Civil War, businesses typically consisted of small companies owned by individuals, families, or two or more people in a partnership. These traditional business organizations proved unable to manage some of the giant new industries such as oil, railroads, or steel. Nor could these organizations raise the money needed to fund such industries. Business leaders therefore turned to another form of business organization—the **corporation**. Corporations had existed in one form or another since colonial times. In a corporation, organizers raise money by selling shares of stock, or certificates of ownership, in the company. Stockholders—those who buy the shares—receive a percentage of the corporation's profits, known as dividends.

Read More About It

Free Find:
Andrew Carnegie
After reading about Andrew Carnegie on the Holt Researcher CD–ROM, write a short essay about Carnegie's values. Be sure to discuss his work ethic and philanthropy.

Giving advice to a group of young men, steel baron Andrew Carnegie urged them to invest in stocks as he had. He suggested, "If any of you have saved as much as $50 or $100 I do not know any branch of business into which you cannot plunge at once." Although stockholders could earn large profits from the companies, they played little or no part in the corporation's daily operations. One corporate

TEACH OBJECTIVES 2 AND 3

LEVEL 1: Pair students and ask pairs to list new forms of business strategies that emerged from the Second Industrial Revolution. *(Pairs should name the corporation, the trust, and the monopoly.)* Write responses on the chalkboard, along with the following entrepreneurs' names: *Andrew Carnegie, John D. Rockefeller, Cornelius Vanderbilt, George Westinghouse,* and *George M. Pullman.* Ask each pair to write topic sentences explaining how the entrepreneurs took advantage of changes in business organization. Pairs should write one sentence for each entrepreneur. *(Pairs should indicate that Carnegie created corporations and used vertical integration to dominate the steel industry. Rockefeller also created corporations and used horizontal integration to dominate the oil industry. Vanderbilt bought and consolidated many railroad lines. Westinghouse introduced and controlled a crucial railroad innovation, and Pullman controlled the passenger-railroad-car industry.)* Ask volunteers to read their sentences to the class. Students may wish to include their sentences in their portfolios. **Sheltered English, Cooperative Learning**

executive described owning shares of stock as simply representing "nothing more than good will and prospective [future] profits."

A corporation has several advantages over small businesses. First, a corporation's organizers can raise large sums of money by selling stock to many people. Second, unlike small-business owners, stockholders enjoy limited liability. In other words, they are not responsible for the corporation's debt. Finally, a corporation is a stable organization because it is not dependent on a specific owner or owners for its existence. A corporation continues to exist no matter who owns the stock. Moreover, the public ownership and trading of stock provides another source of income for entrepreneurs. For example, a former New York grocery clerk named Jay Gould later became a successful stock market manager. Gould earned an estimated $77 million just from trading railroad stock.

Corporations, however, needed more than organizational stability to deal with the economic climate of the late 1800s. Where competition was fierce, prices and profits tended to rise and fall wildly. Some corporations responded by forming trusts. In a **trust**, a group of companies turn control of their stock over to a common board of trustees. The trustees then run all of the companies as a single enterprise. This practice limits overproduction and other inefficient business practices by reducing competition in an industry. If a trust gains exclusive control of an industry, it holds a **monopoly**. With little or no competition, a company with a monopoly has almost complete control over the price and quality of a product.

✔ **READING CHECK:** How did business strategies change in the Second Industrial Revolution?

INTERPRETING THE VISUAL RECORD

Trusts. Many Americans grew tired of trusts and the control over the prices and quality of goods the companies could have. ***How are trusts represented in this cartoon? How does this reflect Americans' suspicions of trusts?***

Carnegie and Steel

Steel leader Andrew Carnegie was a master at utilizing these new business strategies. Carnegie began life in humble surroundings. He was born in 1835 in the attic of a small one-story house in Dunfermline, Scotland. His father was a weaver in the textile industry. In 1848, at the age of 12, Carnegie immigrated to the United States. That same year, Carnegie began his first job, working at a cotton mill, winding thread onto bobbins, or spools, for $1.20 a week.

BIOGRAPHY *Andrew Carnegie*

At age 17, Carnegie took a job as a private secretary to a railroad company superintendent. He quickly advanced to a management position. Saving money from his earnings and borrowing from others, Carnegie began to invest in stock in numerous ventures such as bridges, iron, oil, railroads, and telegraph lines. These early investments further inspired Carnegie's entrepreneurial interest and provided the capital that allowed him to invest in the steel industry.

HISTORY MAKERS SPEAK

Andrew Carnegie in "The Bugaboo of Trusts"

Carnegie Defends Trusts. In response to the growing public criticism of trusts, Andrew Carnegie wrote an article titled "The Bugaboo of Trusts." In this article he argued that trusts were not harmful and that the government need not attempt to regulate business to prevent trusts. He wrote, "There is not the slightest danger that serious injury can result to the sound principles of business from any or all of these movements. The only people who have reason to fear Trusts are those foolish enough to enter into them. The Consumer and the Transporter, not the Manufacturer and the Railway owner, are to reap the harvest."

CRITICAL THINKING How might one evaluate Carnegie's argument according to the success or failure of trusts as discussed in this section?

ANSWER: Students might suggest that trusts like Rockefeller's seem to have been extremely stable, and the benefits in his case certainly did fall to the owner.

VISUAL RECORD ANSWER

Students might mention that trusts are represented as heavyweights; it shows the fear of being "squeezed out."

LEVEL 2: Tell students to imagine that they are modern-day historians preparing to write entries for an encyclopedia on the Second Industrial Revolution. Have each student create a detailed outline describing how business strategies changed during the Second Industrial Relation and the ways in which entrepreneurs took advantage of those new strategies. *(See the Level 1 lesson for the correct strategies and methods.)* Ask two or three volunteers to copy their outlines onto the chalkboard. Then conduct a debate on the material presented in the outlines. Do students regard vertical and horizontal integration as fair? Trusts and monopolies?

LEVEL 3: Tell students to imagine that they are modern-day historians preparing to write entries for an encyclopedia on the Second Industrial Revolution. Have each student write a one-to-two-page entry describing the business strategies that arose during the Second Industrial Revolution and the ways in which entrepreneurs took advantage of those new strategies. *(See the Level 1 lesson for the correct strategies and methods.)* Ask two or three volunteers to read their entries to the class. Then conduct a debate on the material presented in the entries. Do students regard vertical and horizontal integration as fair? Trusts and monopolies?

▶**ASSIGNMENT** *Distribute Cartoon 17, The Power of Trusts, from **American History Political Cartoons**, and have each student complete the attached questions and activity.*

PEOPLE IN HISTORY

Andrew Carnegie. After the sale of his company, Carnegie turned his attention to philanthropy. His first task was to establish free public libraries. He provided funds for almost 3,000 buildings for libraries in English-speaking countries, some 1,900 of them in the United States alone. Carnegie gave money to establish pension funds for his former steelworkers and for college professors. He also created four foundations as a way to help bring about world peace: the Carnegie Endowment for International Peace, the Carnegie Hero Fund, the Church Peace Union, and the Simplified Spelling Board. The latter foundation was established because Carnegie believed that if English spellings were more phonetic, English could become the universal language "for the promotion of international understanding."

CRITICAL THINKING How might libraries have fit into Carnegie's philosophy of self-help?

ANSWER: Students might suggest that libraries are frequented by people who seek to improve their minds.

PHILANTHROPY AND THE GOSPEL OF WEALTH

During the late 1800s, many people began to see a relationship between religious values and earning great wealth. In fact, many supporters of free enterprise believed that accumulating great wealth was a sign of God's blessing, in spite of the sometimes ruthless business practices that might be used to gain that wealth. These supporters, nevertheless, were compelled by their religious values to believe that the power and wealth they accumulated must be used responsibly to better society. This philosophy became known as the Gospel of Wealth.

In his essay "The Gospel of Wealth," Andrew Carnegie insisted that the wealthy had a solemn obligation to use their riches for the advancement of society. In Carnegie's view the rich had been chosen to serve as "stewards of wealth."

"The man who dies . . . rich," Carnegie argued, "dies disgraced." He believed that the rich had a responsibility to give their wealth to society before their death. Like many social Darwinists, Carnegie believed that giving aid directly to the poor would increase the poor's dependency on others. The best way to help the poor, he said, was "to place within [their] reach the ladders upon which the aspiring can rise." Carnegie's "ladders" included universities and libraries.

Carnegie Library in Pittsburgh

Carnegie entered the iron and steel business in the early 1860s. He readily admitted that he understood little about making steel, but he did know how to run an iron business. Carnegie hired the best people in the steel industry and drove them relentlessly. He fitted his plants with the most modern machinery.

Carnegie's real success, however, lay in reducing production costs. Carnegie realized that by buying supplies in bulk and producing goods in large quantities he could lower production costs and increase profits. This principle is known as economies of scale. To control costs, Carnegie also used **vertical integration**—that is, he acquired companies that provided the materials and services upon which his enterprises depended. For example, Carnegie purchased iron and coal mines, which provided the raw materials necessary to run his steel mills. He also bought steamship lines and railroads to transport these materials. An admirer explained the great advantages of this approach.

> **"From the moment these crude stuffs were dug out of the earth until they flowed in a stream of liquid steel in the ladles, there was never a price, profit, or royalty paid to an outsider."**

Because Carnegie controlled businesses at each stage of production, he could sell steel at a much lower price than his competitors.

In 1899 Carnegie organized all of his companies into the Carnegie Steel Company. It dominated the steel industry. When Carnegie sold his company in 1901 to banker J. P. Morgan for nearly $500 million, he retired as the world's richest man. Although Carnegie gained great wealth, money was not his only motivation. Through hard work, simple living, and large philanthropic, or charitable, donations, Carnegie also sought to be viewed as a virtuous citizen. Describing his philosophy as "the Gospel of Wealth," Carnegie insisted that the rich were morally obligated to manage their wealth in a way that benefited their fellow citizens. He explained:

> **"This, then, is held to be the duty of the man of wealth: To set an example of modest, unostentatious [simple] living, shunning display or extravagance . . . the man of wealth thus becoming the mere trustee and agent for his poorer brethren. . . . In bestowing [giving] charity, the main consideration should be to help those who will help themselves; . . . to give those who desire to rise the aids by which they may rise."**

Carnegie donated more than $350 million to charity. Much of the funds were used to establish public libraries and other institutions that provide the tools for individuals to better their lives.

SPOTLIGHT on New Forms of Business Organization

Ask students to conduct research on Andrew Carnegie and vertical integration and on John D. Rockefeller and horizontal integration. Have each student create an annotated graphic organizer displaying the results of the research. Ask volunteers to present their graphic organizers to the class. Then display them around the classroom. **Block Scheduling**

NOTE: For an additional teaching idea, see the Chapter 5 issue strip lesson in the **Creative Teaching Strategies handbook**.

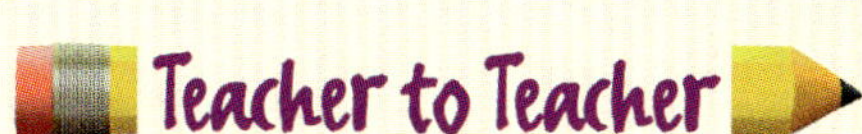

Sue Reeder of Winter Springs, Florida, suggested the following activity: Ask students to select a prominent entrepreneur, such as Andrew Carnegie, John D. Rockefeller, Cornelius Vanderbilt, George Westinghouse, or George Pullman. Then tell each student to write a short biographical "Who Am I?" monologue in the role of his or her chosen entrepreneur, omitting the person's name. Have volunteers deliver their monologues to the class and ask students to identify the entrepreneur.

Rockefeller and Oil

The business career of tycoon John D. Rockefeller, one of the founders of the Standard Oil Company, followed a course similar to Andrew Carnegie's. After earning a small fortune in the wholesale food business, Rockefeller entered the growing oil-refining industry in 1863. During its early years, the oil-refining industry was composed of numerous small, fiercely competitive companies. Arguing that such competition was inefficient, Rockefeller set out to gain control of the industry.

Like Carnegie, Rockefeller used vertical integration to make his company more competitive. He acquired barrel factories, oil fields, oil-storage facilities, pipelines, and railroad tanker cars. By owning companies that contributed to each stage of oil refining, Rockefeller was able to sell his oil for a cheaper price than his competitors. His main method of expansion was called **horizontal integration**—one company's control of other companies producing the same product. Standard Oil tried to control the oil refineries it could not buy, establishing one of the nation's first trusts in the early 1880s.

INTERPRETING THE VISUAL RECORD

Standard Oil. Oil towns like this one in Pennsylvania became more common as Standard Oil grew. ***How did the expansion of the oil industry alter the landscape in this photograph?***

To drive his competitors out of business, Rockefeller made deals with suppliers and transporters to receive cheaper supplies and freight rates. George Rice, a small oil refiner driven out of business by Rockefeller's practices, complained to the U.S. Industrial Commission in 1899.

> **"I have been driven from pillar to post, from one railway line to another, for twenty years, in the absolutely vain endeavor [wasted attempt] to get equal and just freight rates with the Standard Oil Trust, . . . but which I have been utterly unable to do. I have had to consequently shut down, with my business absolutely ruined."**

Rice was not alone. Rockefeller forced most of his rivals to sell out. By 1880 the Standard Oil Company controlled some 90 percent of the country's petroleum-refining capacity. Despite his competitive business practices, Rockefeller, like Carnegie, gave generously to various charities. He also established a fund to support the arts, created a medical institute, and gave more than $80 million to the University of Chicago. During his lifetime, Rockefeller donated approximately $550 million to philanthropic causes.

The Railroad Giants

Andrew Carnegie and John D. Rockefeller profited hugely from technological innovations in the steel and oil-refining industries, respectively. Other entrepreneurs built large fortunes by capitalizing on the booming railroad industry.

PEOPLE IN HISTORY

John D. Rockefeller. Many people believed that Rockefeller's business methods were both unfair and unethical. Beginning in the late 1870s, Rockefeller and his colleagues faced a series of court challenges and legislative inquiries. Although Rockefeller testified at some of the court proceedings, he refused to publicly respond to newspaper attacks. These attacks took a toll on his health, however, and in 1901 Rockefeller lost all of his hair. After essentially retiring from Standard Oil, Rockefeller began looking for "creative" ways to give away his money.

ACTIVITY: Tell students to imagine that they are as wealthy as Rockefeller. Ask students to list three "creative" ways to give away their money.

The American Nation **VIDEO PROGRAM**

The Standard Oil Company; Teacher's Guide, pp. 81–86

Search 21229, Play to 29398
Videodisc 1, Side B

Play Pause

See *Teacher's Guide* for Spanish barcode.

VISUAL RECORD ANSWER

Students might mention that the oil industry dominated the physical landscape.

TEACH OBJECTIVE 4

LEVEL 1: Write the following phrases on the chalkboard: *the creation of a consumer culture, department stores, catalogs,* and *chain stores.* Pair students and have each pair write a paragraph describing how these developments and items changed American life during the late 1800s and early 1900s. *(Pairs' paragraphs should indicate that the creation of a consumer culture strengthened economic growth during the period. Department stores and chain stores gave women a new place to work and shop, while catalogs gave rural residents access to a variety of goods.)* Ask volunteers to read their paragraphs to the class. **Sheltered English**

LEVEL 2: Tell students to imagine that it is 1885 and that they work at a young advertising agency that has just landed a new industry account. Have each student create two or three advertisements presenting new marketing methods or selling forms and describing the ways in which the methods or forms have changed American life. *(See the Level 1 lesson for the correct methods and changes.)* Students might create an advertisement for a national catalog, for example, or a national department store. Have volunteers present their advertisements to the class. Students may wish to include their advertisements in their portfolios. **Sheltered English**

THAT'S INTERESTING!

Wealthy families often showed off their riches at extravagant parties. At one Vanderbilt dinner party, guests found a trough filled with sand in the middle of the dining room table. Each guest received a sterling silver pail and shovel and were allowed to dig in the sand, where they found loose diamonds, emeralds, and rubies.

STRATEGIES FOR SUCCESS ANSWERS

Practicing the Strategy

1. Competition between various small companies was inefficient.
2. vertical and horizontal integration, deals for cheaper supplies
3. Most other oil refiners had to sell out, and Rockefeller controlled 90 percent of U.S. petroleum refining.
4. Students might argue that Rockefeller could have avoided putting all of his rivals out of business and maintained competition instead of working to be the only controller of oil.
5. Students might support Rockefeller's practices as successful competition, or they might argue that his practices were unfair and led to no competition at all.

VISUAL RECORD ANSWER

(for p. 179)

Students might mention the cow, the blue ribbon, and the product itself.

Strategies for Success: Evaluating Historical Actions

Evaluating the actions of individuals and groups is a practice that students of history do routinely. To *evaluate* is to make a judgment about the significance, worth, or desirability of something. An evaluation of a historical action should be based on the range of choices available to the historical actor as well as on the effects the action had on an individual or society.

How to Evaluate a Historical Action

1. **Establish the context.** When you encounter an action that requires evaluation, identify the historical setting and the specific steps through which the action was completed. Make sure that you understand the assumptions and the goals of the individual or group that took the action.
2. **Determine the outcome.** Once you have established the context of the action, determine its results. Make sure that you recognize any unintended consequences or long-term effects of the action.
3. **Consider alternative courses of action.** Identify other courses of action that the individual or group could have taken. Then assess the potential advantages and disadvantages of these alternatives.
4. **Evaluate the action.** Use your analysis of the action, along with your consideration of possible alternatives, to make a judgment about its value and significance.

Applying the Strategy

Review the material in this section on John D. Rockefeller and the oil industry. As you do so, evaluate the business practices that Rockefeller and his Standard Oil Company employed.

Practicing the Strategy

Answer the following questions.

1. What were Rockefeller's assumptions and goals concerning the oil industry?
2. What business practices did Rockefeller employ through Standard Oil?
3. What were the results of Rockefeller's business practices?
4. What other courses of action could Rockefeller have taken? What do you think the results of these actions would have been?
5. What is your evaluation of Rockefeller's business practices?

Cornelius Vanderbilt's railroad investments brought him power and wealth.

THE GRANGER COLLECTION, NEW YORK

Vanderbilt. Cornelius Vanderbilt was a pioneer of the railroad industry. Prior to the Civil War, Vanderbilt operated a profitable shipping business. When the use of water traffic slowed during the war, however, he invested more in railroads. By 1869, just four years after the war's end, Vanderbilt had gained control over the New York Central Railroad and two other lines that connected the Central with New York City. He continued to add to his railroad holdings. Soon he controlled lines between Chicago, Cleveland, New York, and Toledo.

Vanderbilt extended his railroad system by purchasing smaller lines. He then combined them to make direct routes between urban centers. By providing more efficient service, Vanderbilt took advantage of the growing demand for rail transportation. At the time of his death in 1877, Vanderbilt controlled more than 4,500 miles of railroad track. His personal fortune was estimated at $100 million.

Westinghouse. George Westinghouse also made a large fortune in the railroad industry. At the age of 23, Westinghouse established the Westinghouse Air Brake Company. He hoped to capitalize on his invention, the compressed-air brake. The air brake was an important safety feature for the railroad industry. The brakes made it possible for trains to haul more cars and to travel at greater speeds.

LEVEL 3: Tell students to imagine that they are modern-day historians studying the marketing methods and advertising in the late 1800s and early 1900s. Have each student create a design for an artifact from that period. Students might draw a detailed illustration of a catalog, for example, or a department store display window. Then have each student write three or four paragraphs describing how that artifact—and the method or form that it represented—changed American life. *(See the Level 1 lesson for the correct methods and changes.)* Students may wish to include their designs and their paragraphs in their portfolios.

SPOTLIGHT on George Pullman and Company Towns

Ask students to conduct research on George Pullman and his company town. Then have each student complete one of the following activities: write a short biography of Pullman, create an annotated map of Pullman's community, or write a script for a tour of the town. Have volunteers present their work to the class. Then conduct a debate on the concept of company towns. Do such towns represent corporate paternalism or corporate generosity? Would students themselves want to live in a company town? Would they feel differently if they had been alive in the 1880s? **Block Scheduling**

Railroad investors were initially skeptical of the air brake. Vanderbilt condemned the invention as trying to "stop a train with wind." After several dramatic public demonstrations, however, Westinghouse's business grew. Within five years of his invention, more than 7,000 passenger cars were equipped with the compressed-air brake.

Pullman. One of the most successful railroad giants was George Pullman. He designed and manufactured railroad cars that made long-distance rail travel more comfortable. Pullman created a massive passenger-railroad-car industry. His factories built sleeping cars, dining cars, and luxurious cars for wealthy passengers. With an increasing demand for his sleeping cars, Pullman decided to build a new factory south of Chicago in 1880.

The company town of Pullman, Illinois, contained everything the company thought workers should need.

Disturbed by the poor conditions of city life, Pullman set out to create a company town. He hoped that it would encourage educated, healthy, peaceful, and virtuous workers. Pullman built a planned community next to his factory. The town offered Pullman's employees and their families clean, well-built homes, shops, a church, a library, a theater, medical and legal offices, and an athletic field. Pullman strictly controlled daily life in the company town, causing dissatisfaction to grow among many of the workers. Expressing a common feeling of the residents, economist Richard Ely proclaimed in 1884 that Pullman's town represented a "benevolent [kindly], well-wishing feudalism, which desires the happiness of the people, but in such a way as shall please the authorities."

✔ **READING CHECK:** How did entrepreneurs take advantage of changes in business organization?

INTERPRETING THE VISUAL RECORD

Advertising. During the late 1800s manufacturers began to use advertisements like this one to entice customers to buy their products. ***What images in the advertisement relate to the product?***

Mass Marketing

Industrialists knew that using new inventions, cutting production costs, and reducing competition were not the only ways to increase profits. They also developed new methods of marketing to sell their products.

Marketing products. With the rapid growth of manufacturing, companies developed new ways of pursuading consumers to purchase their products. Brand names and packaging played important roles in promoting goods. For example, the name "Standard Oil" conveyed the idea that the company's product set the industry standard. Other companies used brightly colored packages or unique logos to set their products apart.

Companies also used advertising to promote their products. Magazines, newspapers, and roadside billboards carried advertisements urging people to buy "the Purest" soap or telephones "warranted to work *one mile,* unaffected by changes in the weather."

ECONOMIC DEVELOPMENT

Collectibles and Contests. Advertisers in the late 1800s adopted many methods still used in advertising. To improve brand loyalty, manufacturers began giving away trading cards emblazoned with their product's name and colorful pictures. These cards gave customers a sense of relationship with the manufacturer. To increase readership, many magazines offered cash prizes to readers who created the best advertisement for a product featured in the magazine. At the same time, the contest announcements encouraged readers to try the product. One contest announcement urged, "*Try* Ribbon Dental Cream, if you are not already using it. . . . Our advice is *not* to write [the ad] until you really *believe* every word that you write."

ACTIVITY: Have students create an advertisement to attract fans to the school's next sporting event.

VISUAL RECORD ANSWER

(for p. 180)

Students might mention the store's physical enormity.

SECTION 2 REVIEW ANSWERS

Define and Identify

For significance, see the following pages:

- Horatio Alger Jr., p. 173
- laissez-faire capitalism, p. 173

REVIEW

Have students complete the **Section 2 Review** on p. 180.

ASSESS

Have students complete **Daily Quiz 5.2**. As **Alternative Assessment**, you may want to use the Second Industrial Revolution outline or the marketing-method artifact in this section's lessons.

RETEACH

Have students complete **Main Idea Activity for Reteaching and Sheltered English 5.2**. Then assign students subsections of Section 2. Ask each student to summarize the assigned subsection and to write five questions and answers on the material. Collect students' questions and use them to quiz the class. **Sheltered English**

EXTEND

Have students conduct research on Cornelius Vanderbilt. Then ask students to study the political cartoon on p. 178, which portrays Vanderbilt and his business activities. Have each student write a half-page analysis of the cartoon, discussing the artist's probable intentions and effects. Then have students create their own political cartoons depicting Vanderbilt. Ask students to present their cartoons to the class. Then, as a class, choose the most effective cartoon. Have students explain and justify their selections. **Block Scheduling**

- free enterprise, p. 173
- communism, p. 174
- social Darwinism, p. 174
- corporation, p. 174
- trust, p. 175
- monopoly, p. 175
- Andrew Carnegie, p. 175
- vertical integration, p. 176
- John D. Rockefeller, p. 177
- horizontal integration, p. 177
- Cornelius Vanderbilt, p. 178
- George Pullman, p. 179

1. Carnegie–used vertical integration to revolutionize steel production; Rockefeller–used horizontal integration to expand his oil company; Vanderbilt–extended railroad system by buying small lines and making direct routes between cities; Westinghouse–revolutionized railroad industry with the air brake; Pullman–created comfortable passenger cars

2. Business leaders opposed government intervention in the economy, as did social Darwinists. Other social critics believed that government should correct social inequalities.

3. The theory may have encouraged Carnegie and Rockefeller to compete more intensely.

4. Rural dwellers were able to buy some products by catalog. Department stores provided a variety of goods at lower prices.

5. Students might argue that developments created jobs and wealth; others might assert that some business practices inhibited opportunities for others to become involved.

INTERPRETING THE VISUAL RECORD

Marketing. Mail-order companies offered goods such as clothing, farm equipment, furniture, and musical instruments. ***What ideas does this catalog convey?***

This increase in the use of advertising and brand names helped create a new, lively consumer culture in the United States. The expansion of manufacturing and mass marketing transformed the daily lives of many Americans, even those outside the large urban centers who gained access to new products.

Products such as Ruthstein steel-soled shoes and the Scotch Knocker horse collar were advertised to farmers through local newspapers, mail-order publications, and special catalogs that catered to the rural market. Mail-order companies like Montgomery Ward and Sears, Roebuck, and Co. offered a seemingly endless variety of goods. Customers selected goods from a catalog, then ordered, paid for, and received the merchandise by mail.

The department store. In cities, new types of stores that sold a variety of goods were created to cater to the demands of the urban market. Department stores carried a wide variety of products under one roof. Pioneered by business leaders such as John Wanamaker in Philadelphia, Marshall Field in Chicago, and R. H. Macy in New York City, department stores bought products in bulk and could therefore offer low prices to consumers.

Department stores became the special domain of women, both as places to work and as places to shop. Wanting to create a homelike and welcoming atmosphere in their stores, department-store owners hired young women to work as clerks. Department-store advertisements also targeted women as customers.

Like department stores, chain stores—stores with branches in many cities—bought goods in large quantities. They then passed on their savings to customers. Perhaps the most famous chain store was founded by Frank W. Woolworth in 1879. By 1900 Woolworth had a network of 59 stores.

✔ **READING CHECK:** How did new methods of marketing products change American life?

SECTION 2 REVIEW

Define and explain the significance of the following terms:
laissez-faire capitalism
free enterprise
communism
social Darwinism
corporation
trust
monopoly
vertical integration
horizontal integration

Identify and explain the significance of the following individuals:
Horatio Alger Jr.
Andrew Carnegie
John D. Rockefeller
Cornelius Vanderbilt
George Pullman

1. **Using Graphic Organizers** Copy the web below. Use it to describe the major entrepreneurs of the late 1800s, what business each pursued, and how they revolutionized their industries.

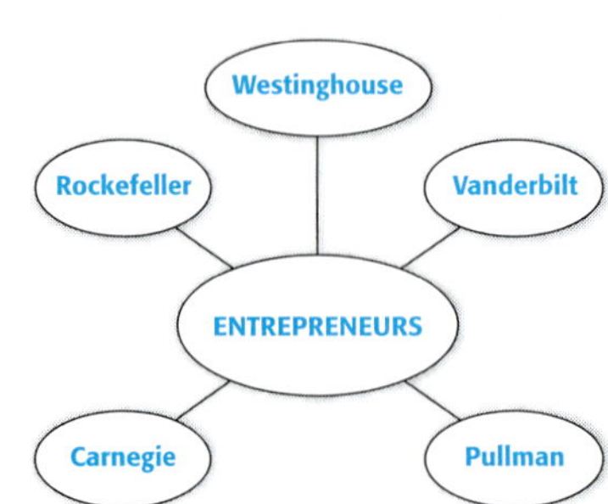

2. **Recognizing Point of View** How did business leaders and social critics view government's role in business differently?
3. **Hypothesizing** How do you think the theory of social Darwinism shaped the business practices of Andrew Carnegie and John D. Rockefeller?
4. **Assessing Consequences** In what ways did new marketing practices change life in the United States?

Critical Thinking

5. Did the business developments of the late 1800s create opportunities or limit them? Explain your answer.
Consider:
- how business opportunities were created
- how business opportunities were limited
- whether businesses more often created new opportunities or limited them

SECTION 3

After completing Section 3, students should be able to:

OBJECTIVE 1 *Understand why some Americans wanted trusts to be banned, and how the government responded.*

OBJECTIVE 2 *Describe the working conditions that laborers faced in the new age of rapid industrialization.*

OBJECTIVE 3 *Discuss how the Knights of Labor attempted to address the needs of many workers.*

OBJECTIVE 4 *Explain how businesses reacted to strikes in the late 1800s, and how this affected unions.*

LET'S GET STARTED!

Write the following scenario on the chalkboard: *It is 1890. You work in a factory. Last month, your little brother was hurt in a workplace accident, but the company refuses to fix the machine that hurt him. Do you join a union to protest unsafe working conditions, even though the stakes may be high?* As students enter the classroom, ask them to respond to the scenario in writing. Have volunteers share their responses. Then tell students that in Section 3 they will learn more about efforts to form unions.

Labor Strives to Organize

OBJECTIVES

Read to understand:

1. why some Americans wanted trusts to be banned, and how the government responded
2. what types of working conditions laborers faced in the new age of rapid industrialization
3. how the Knights of Labor attempted to address the needs of many workers
4. how businesses reacted to strikes in the late 1800s, and how this affected unions

KEY TERMS

Sherman Antitrust Act
Knights of Labor
Great Upheaval
Haymarket Riot
anarchists
American Federation of Labor

KEY PEOPLE

Terence V. Powderly
Mary Harris Jones
Eugene V. Debs

KEY PLACES

Haymarket Square
Homestead
Pullman

"It is true that wealth has been greatly increased . . . but these gains are not general. In them the lowest class do not share. . . . This association of poverty with progress is the great enigma [mystery] of our times."

—Henry George

American economist Henry George

Henry George offered this critical look at American life during the 1870s in his book *Progress and Poverty.* Although a few entrepreneurs earned huge profits from rapid industrialization, many more Americans experienced severe poverty and poor working conditions. Indeed, industrial life was often terribly harsh for the men, women, and children who worked in the factories. Describing her first impression of Kansas City in 1888, Kate Richards O'Hare later recalled, "The poverty, the misery, the want, the wan-faced [pale] women and hunger pinched children, . . . the sordid [dirty], grinding, pinching poverty of the workless workers . . . will always stay with me."

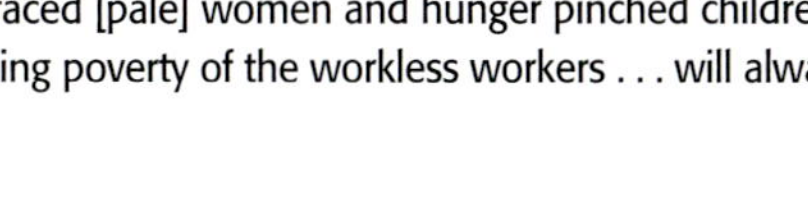

Government and Business

The U.S. government's policies concerning business practices most often benefited the industrialists, not the workers. Supporters of laissez-faire capitalism claimed to oppose government interference in business activities. However these same business leaders welcomed government assistance when it helped them. By placing high tariffs on imports, the U.S. government allowed American businesses to dominate the domestic market. In 1875, for example, Congress raised tariff rates to make imported steel considerably more expensive than domestic steel.

At the same time, the government did little to regulate business practices, despite growing pressure from the general public. As Carnegie Steel, Standard Oil, and other large corporations grew in power, many Americans demanded that trusts be outlawed. These critics reasoned that without competition, these large monopolies would have no incentive to maintain the quality of their goods or keep prices low. Congress responded in 1890 by passing the **Sherman Antitrust Act**, which outlawed all monopolies and trusts that restrained trade. However, the law failed to define what constituted a monopoly or trust and thus proved difficult to enforce.

While serving the interests of corporations, the U.S. government offered little assistance to American industrial workers. Government leaders were often distracted by issues of political corruption and paid little attention to the widening gulf between the wealthy and the poor. By 1890 just 10 percent of the population controlled close to 75 percent of the nation's wealth. At the same time, nearly 50 percent of unskilled industrial workers in the United States earned less than

Some Americans saw the monopoly as a giant octopus.

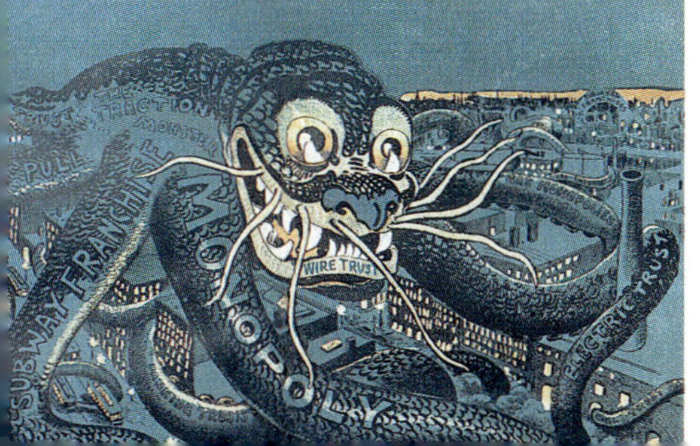

SECTION 3 RESOURCES

PRINT

- Guided Reading Strategy 5.3
- Graphic Organizer Activity 5: Industrial Problems of the Late 1800s
- Section 3 Review, p. 187
- Daily Quiz 5.3

MULTIMEDIA

- One-Stop Planner, Lesson 5.3
- Holt Researcher: American History CD–ROM

SHELTERED ENGLISH

- Main Idea Activity for Reteaching and Sheltered English 5.3

✓ READING TO UNDERSTAND

To help students master the section objectives, have them answer the **READING CHECKS** and complete **Guided Reading Strategy 5.3** as they read the section.

VISUAL RECORD ANSWER

(for p. 182)

Students might mention the manufacturing industry.

TEACH OBJECTIVE 1

ALL LEVELS: Discuss the definition of *trusts* with the class. Then ask students to share their personal feelings about trusts. Do students think that trusts are fair? Do they think that trusts pose quality or pricing issues? To help students understand why some Americans wanted trusts to be banned and how the government responded, copy the following graphic organizer on the chalkboard, omitting the italicized answers. Have each student complete it. **Sheltered English**

Americans' Arguments Against Trusts
- *argued that without competition, large monopolies would not maintain quality or keep prices low*

Government Response
- *passed the Sherman Antitrust Act*

Problems with Act
- *failed to define a monopoly or trust*
- *presented serious enforcement problems*

HISTORY MAKERS SPEAK

Carroll D. Wright in *Working Girls of Boston*

Working Girls of Boston. In the 1880s sociologist Carroll D. Wright sent investigators to interview working women in Boston. He recorded their observations in *The Working Girls of Boston.* According to Wright, the women made so little money that they often went without food. He wrote of one woman who often went "without her supper as well as other meals, because she did not have the money to pay for them." One woman whose husband had died had to support two children, working such long hours sewing that she damaged her eyesight. A doctor ordered her to stop working, but she had no other means of support, "and so she has kept on working. Her eyes weep constantly, she cannot see across the room and 'the air seems always in a whirl' before her."

ACTIVITY: Have students interview a family member or neighbor about the kind of work he or she does. Then have each student write an oral history of that person's story.

VISUAL RECORD ANSWER

(for p. 183)

Students might mention the machinery's moving parts and the child's age and height.

$500 per year. By providing a cheap source of labor, these workers were essential to the nation's industrialization.

✔ **READING CHECK:** Why did some Americans demand that trusts be made illegal? How did the federal government respond?

The New Working Class

The demand for labor soared under the new industrial order. These jobs were filled largely by the flood of immigrants who came to the United States during the late 1800s. A working-class newspaper, *Workingman's Advocate,* explained that immigrants "viewed a sojourn [temporary stay] in America as a means to acquire capital with which to purchase land, provide dowries for their daughters, and assist their sons to enter business." By 1900 about one third of the country's industrial workers were foreign-born.

African Americans. These immigrant workers were joined by hundreds of thousands of rural Americans who moved to the cities in search of jobs. Among this group were thousands of African Americans from the South who moved north to find work. In Chicago, for example, by 1900 more than 80 percent of the city's African American workers had been born in states south of Illinois.

Some northern and midwestern industries offered working opportunities to African Americans. The vast majority of southern industries, however, barred African Americans from holding factory jobs. Nearly all southern textile workers were native-born whites. Cigar factories did employ some African Americans—women cleaned and sorted tobacco leaves, men made the cigars—but their numbers were few. In 1891 just 7,400 black southerners held industrial jobs.

Many African Americans from the South hoped to find improved conditions in the North, but industrial employment remained out of reach for most. The best jobs still went to native-born white workers or to immigrants. Even skilled African American male laborers generally found themselves confined to the dirtiest or most dangerous work or to such service-related jobs as gardening.

INTERPRETING THE VISUAL RECORD

Workers. While southern industries often barred African Americans from holding factory jobs, African American workers occasionally found employment opportunities in northern and midwestern industries. ***In what type of industry do you think these African American women might be employed?***

Women and children. African American women in northern cities competed with poor immigrant women for domestic jobs and unskilled factory work. Most women worked because their families needed the income. As a state official in Massachusetts noted, "A family of workers can always live well, but the man with a family of small children to support, unless his wife works also, has a small chance of living properly." The number of female workers doubled between 1870 and 1890. By 1900 women accounted for about 18 percent of the labor force—with some 5 million workers.

The number of children in the workforce doubled during this period for the same reason. By 1890 close to 20 percent of American children between ages 10 and 15—some 1.5 million in all—worked for wages. In the textile mills of North Carolina, one

TEACH OBJECTIVE 2

LEVEL 1: Pair students and tell them to imagine that they work in a factory in Michigan. Have each pair develop a two-to-four-minute dialogue describing working conditions during the Second Industrial Revolution. *(Pairs' dialogues should reflect the following conditions: low pay, long hours, unsafe working environments, and the possibility of racial discrimination.)* Ask volunteers to perform their dialogues for the class. **Sheltered English, Cooperative Learning**

LEVEL 2: Tell students to imagine that they have just emigrated from Greece and that they work in a factory in Michigan. Have each student write a one-page letter to a friend in Greece describing working conditions in the United States. *(See the Level 1 lesson for the correct conditions.)* Have volunteers read their letters to the class. Students may wish to include their letters in their portfolios.

in every four workers was younger than 16 years old. The ratio was much lower in Massachusetts mills—1 in 20.

Across the nation, countless boys and girls worked in garment factories or at home, making clothing or other items by the piece. Others labored in the nation's canneries, mines, and shoe factories. Pauline Newman began working at a garment factory in New York in 1901 while still a child. Describing her experiences, she recalled, "It wasn't heavy work, but it was monotonous, because you did the same thing from seven-thirty in the morning till nine at night."

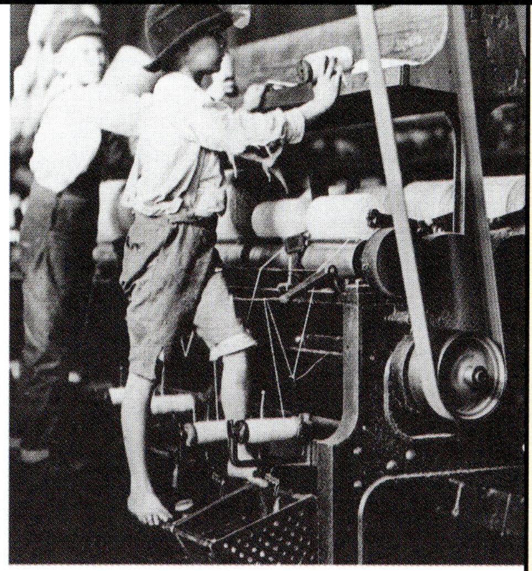

INTERPRETING THE VISUAL RECORD

Working conditions. Many children working in factories worked long hours in unsafe working conditions. ***What aspects of this child's working conditions might be dangerous?***

Working Conditions

Children in the labor force often faced terrible conditions. In some textile mills, for instance, children worked 12-hour shifts—often at night—for pennies a day. Low wages and long hours affected all industrial workers, however, regardless of their age, sex, or race. Conditions were particularly difficult for unskilled workers. Most unskilled white male laborers worked at least 10 hours a day, six days a week, for less than $10 a week. Many African American, Asian American, and Mexican American men worked the same number of hours for even lower wages. Furthermore, employers made few allowances for women and children, expecting them to work the same number of hours as men for sometimes as little as half the pay.

Such long hours left workers exhausted at the end of the day. This fatigue made already unsafe working conditions even more dangerous. In 1881 alone, some 30,000 railroad workers were killed or injured on the job. Most employers felt no responsibility for work-related deaths and injuries. They made little effort to improve workplace safety.

Many workers endured hardships that extended beyond the factory. Some employers sought to increase their control over their workers. They built company towns, where the company owned the workers' housing and the retail businesses they used. Residents of company towns usually received their wages in scrip. This was paper money that could be used only to pay rent to the company or to buy goods at company stores. Prices at company stores were usually much higher than at regular stores. Workers often spent whole paychecks on necessities like food and clothing.

✔ **READING CHECK:** What types of working conditions did laborers face in the new age of industrialization?

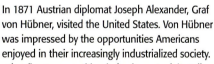

THROUGH OTHERS' EYES

Austrian View of U.S. Workers

In 1871 Austrian diplomat Joseph Alexander, Graf von Hübner, visited the United States. Von Hübner was impressed by the opportunities Americans enjoyed in their increasingly industrialized society. He noted, however, that fierce competition in business took its toll on working people.

"In the New World man is born to conquer. Life is a perpetual struggle, . . . a race in the open field across terrible obstacles, with the prospect of enormous rewards for reaching the goal. The American cannot keep his arms folded. He must embark on something, and once embarked he must go on and on forever; for if he stops, those who follow him would crush him under their feet. His life is one long campaign, a succession of never-ending fights, marches, and countermarches.

In such a militant existence, what place is left for the sweetness, the repose [rest], the intimacy of home or its joys? Is he happy? Judging by his tired, sad, exhausted, anxious, and often delicate and unhealthy appearance, one would be inclined to doubt it. Such an excess of uninterrupted labor cannot be good for any man."

HISTORY MAKERS SPEAK

Henry George in *Progress and Poverty*

The Price of Industrialization. Henry George formulated a theory explaining why poverty increased despite great progress in production. He argued that "all advantages gained by the march of progress go to the owners of land, and wages do not increase. . . . The mere laborer has thus no more interest in the general advance of productive power than the Cuban slave has in advance in the price of sugar. . . . [Thus] labor is exposed to certain effects of advancing civilization which, without the advantages that naturally accompany them, are positive evils, and of themselves tend to reduce the free laborer to the helpless and degraded condition of the slave."

CRITICAL THINKING How might the basis of George's argument differ from Carnegie or Rockefeller's beliefs about business practices?

ANSWER: Students might mention that George views the situation from the perspective of workers who barely make enough money to survive, while Carnegie and Rockefeller approach the situation from the perspective of someone who makes a great deal of money.

LEVEL 3: Tell students to imagine that they work in a factory in Michigan. Have each student develop a four-to-five-minute monologue describing working conditions during the Second Industrial Revolution. *(See the Level 1 lesson for the correct conditions.)* Ask volunteers to present their monologues to the class.

▶**ASSIGNMENT** *Tell students to imagine that they work in a factory in Michigan. Have each student write a poem or short story describing working conditions during the Second Industrial Revolution.*

TEACH OBJECTIVE 3

LEVEL 1: Organize students into five groups. Assign each group one of the following roles: skilled workers, unskilled workers, female workers, African American workers, and Chinese workers. Ask each group to write a topic sentence explaining how or whether the Knights of Labor has met its needs as workers. *(The Knights of Labor welcomed skilled and unskilled workers along with women. Although the Knights admitted African American workers after a certain point, many members did not accept them. The Knights actively discriminated against Chinese workers.)* Have each group read its topic sentence to the class. Then, in a classroom discussion, ask students to evaluate the Knights' approach. Was it fair? Was it justifiable,

DEMOCRATIC VALUES

Knights of Labor. When the Knights of Labor drafted the preamble to their constitution, they wrote that they were "calling upon all who believe in securing 'the greatest good to the greatest number' to aid and assist us." The preamble emphasizes the importance of workers' minds as well as the safety and financial value of their physical work. For example, item XIV asks for "the reduction of the hours of labor to eight per day, so that the laborers may have more time for social enjoyment and intellectual improvement."

ACTIVITY: Have students conduct research on present-day labor unions, focusing their research on the constitutions of these labor unions.

MAP ANSWER

(for p. 186)

Nevada

VISUAL RECORD ANSWER

(for p. 187)

the fire and the weapons

SECTION 3 REVIEW ANSWERS

Define and Identify

For significance, see the following pages:

- Sherman Antitrust Act, p. 181
- Knights of Labor, p. 184

The Knights of Labor

As conditions grew worse, workers called for change. Alone they could do little. If they banded together, they reasoned, the factory owners and politicians might listen to their demands.

Led by Uriah Stephens, nine Philadelphia garment workers founded the **Knights of Labor**, one of the earliest national unions, in 1869. It remained largely a white male organization until 1879, when Terence V. Powderly, an Irish Catholic machinist and the mayor of Scranton, Pennsylvania, became its leader. Under his leadership the Knights' membership expanded rapidly.

Powderly wanted the Knights of Labor to attract workers who were often excluded from other unions. He therefore opened the union to both skilled and unskilled laborers. Powderly also welcomed thousands of women into the union's ranks. A number of women, including Mary Harris Jones, played prominent roles in the Knights of Labor.

HOLT RESEARCHER

Read More About It

Free Find:

Mother Jones

After reading about Mary Harris Jones on the **Holt Researcher** CD–ROM, write a short speech that she might have given to workers that draws upon her life experiences.

BIOGRAPHY

Mary Harris Jones

Born in Cork, Ireland, in 1830, Mary Harris came to the United States as a young child. She married George Jones, a union supporter, in 1861. Six years later, after her husband and four children died in a yellow fever epidemic, she began to devote herself to the labor movement. At the invitation of striking workers, Jones became an organizer for the Knights of Labor in the 1870s. Declaring that her place was "wherever there is a fight," she organized strikes, marches, and demonstrations. In 1912 Jones explained to a reporter the reasons behind her activism.

> **"My life work has been to try to educate the worker to a sense of the wrongs he has had to suffer, and does suffer—and to stir up the oppressed to a point of getting off their knees and demanding that which I believe to be rightfully theirs."**

Frank J. Ferrell, a member of the Knights of Labor, introduces the union leader Terence V. Powderly at a rally.

THE GRANGER COLLECTION, NEW YORK

Jones's ambitious drive to educate and organize laborers was so effective that some opponents called her "the most dangerous woman in America." Because she viewed her actions as more motherly than radical, most people called her Mother Jones. Jones was sentenced to 20 years in jail for her part in a 1912 West Virginia strike, but a public outcry caused the governor of the state to free her. Mother Jones continued fighting for the rights of America's working people until her death in 1930. She was 100 years old.

Although the Knights of Labor offered membership to female workers, Powderly did not encourage African Americans to join the union until 1883. By the mid-1880s the Knights claimed some 60,000 black members. African American delegate Frank Ferrell spoke at the Knights' 1886 national convention in Richmond, Virginia. He told the crowd, "One of the objects of our Order is the abolition of these distinctions which are maintained by creed or color."

given the prejudices of the time? If students had formed a union during the Second Industrial Revolution, which workers would they have admitted?
Sheltered English, Cooperative Learning

LEVEL 2: Tell students to imagine that they are members of the Knights of Labor who want to reform the organization. Have each student write a three-to-four-minute speech describing the ways in which the Knights have succeeded and failed in their attempts to meet the needs of workers. *(See the Level 1 lesson for the correct successes and failures.)* Ask volunteers to deliver their speeches to the class.

LEVEL 3: Tell students to imagine that they are planning to start a new union, one that will rival the Knights of Labor. Have each student create a three-fold brochure advertising this new union. Remind students that in order to succeed, they will have to attract members from the Knights. In order to do so, their brochures should discuss the ways in which the Knights have both succeeded and failed in their attempts to meet workers' needs. Students' brochures should also outline the ways in which the new union will be better then the Knights. *(See the Level 1 lesson for the correct successes and failures.)* Ask students to present their brochures to the class. Have students select the best new union. Students should justify their choices.

Not all African American Knights, however, agreed with this assessment. "The white Knights of Labor prevent me from getting employment because I am a colored man," complained a North Carolina mason, "although I belong to the same organization." Still, the Knights did more than other early unions to try to meet the needs of African American workers. The Knights were not equality-minded when it came to everyone, however. Powderly, like many working-class Americans, actively opposed Chinese workers, claiming they stole jobs from white Americans.

Powderly led the Knights of Labor for 15 years. Under his leadership, the union fought for temperance, the eight-hour workday, equal pay for equal work, and an end to child labor. By 1886 the Knights boasted a membership of more than 700,000.

✔ **READING CHECK:** In what ways did the Knights of Labor attempt to address the needs of many workers?

The Great Upheaval

The Knights of Labor owed its phenomenal growth partly to the great railroad strike of 1877. The union also grew after a successful strike that the Knights had launched against railroad tycoon Jay Gould in 1884. Both strikes made workers more willing to press for the better working conditions being championed by the Knights. The union enjoyed immense popularity. However, in 1886 the nation experienced a year of intense strikes and violent labor confrontations that became known as the **Great Upheaval**.

By 1886, American workers were ready for action. An economic depression in the early 1880s had led to massive wage cuts. Workers demanded relief. When negotiations with management failed, many workers took direct action. By the end of 1886 some 1,500 strikes involving more than 400,000 workers had swept the nation. Many of these strikes turned violent, as angry strikers clashed head-on with aggressive employers and police officers. Perhaps the most notorious of these confrontations was the **Haymarket Riot**.

Then and Now

Labor Unions

Teamsters picketing during the UPS strike

Labor unions' membership and organization have changed over the years. Their goals today, however, are not so different from earlier groups. Despite a gradual decline in membership, unions are still involved in American life. They continue to have an impact on working conditions. Several strikes in recent years have attracted much media attention.

In 1997 about 185,000 members of the Teamsters' union struck against United Parcel Service (UPS) over pensions and the increasing use of part-time laborers. The 15-day strike caused delays in shipping for many businesses. However, during the strike, the union received a great deal of support. One Gallup Poll reported that 55 percent of the public approved of the strike. Many Americans shared the concerns of the strikers. As one labor expert suggested, "What's on the bargaining table gets discussed at the dinner table, too." The strikers' efforts resulted in additional full-time jobs. In 1998 the United Auto Workers (UAW) union also received public support. That year it launched a strike against General Motors to protest both the loss of jobs to foreign factories and unsafe working conditions. However, the UAW strikers' gains were not as decisive as those of the Teamsters in the UPS strike.

The Haymarket Riot. The seeds for the Haymarket Riot were sown when some 40,000 Chicago workers joined a strike against the McCormick Harvesting Machine Company. On May 1, 1886, they struck to demand an eight-hour workday. Although local craft unions launched the strike, it soon fell under the leadership of a group of political radicals and **anarchists**. These anarchists were people who oppose all forms of government. On May 3 a confrontation between the police and the strikers left two strikers dead.

In protest, strikers called a meeting for the next day in Chicago's Haymarket Square. Peaceful and small, the rally was about to break up when nearly 200 police officers arrived. Suddenly, a bomb exploded in the midst of the police, who responded with gunfire. When the smoke cleared, some 70 officers lay wounded. Seven police

- Terence V. Powderly, p. 184
- Mary Harris Jones, p. 184
- Great Upheaval, p. 185
- Haymarket Riot, p. 185
- anarchists, p. 185
- American Federation of Labor, p. 186
- Eugene V. Debs, p. 187

Locate

For locations, see the map on p. 186. For importance, see the following pages:

- Haymarket Square, p. 185
- Homestead, p. 187
- Pullman, p. 187

1. Haymarket Riot—eight-hour workday; left people dead and allowed employers to tighten labor controls. Homestead—protest a wage cut; several deaths; Pullman—protest a wage cut; government troops, deaths, property damage, and end of ARU

2. People feared that market-controlling trusts would raise prices or produce poor-quality goods; the government passed the Sherman Antitrust Act.

3. Students should mention long hours, low pay, and unsafe conditions.

4. encouraged women, African Americans, and unskilled workers to join unions

5. Answers will vary. Students might argue that workers believed that their strikes might be successful and win them better wages and working conditions.

TEACH OBJECTIVE 4

LEVEL 1: Ask students to list the ways in which businesses responded to strikes in the late 1800s. *(Students should list blacklists, yellow-dog contracts, lockouts, and violent attacks.)* Write students' responses on the chalkboard. Then ask students to list the effects of these strategies on unions. *(On the whole, these techniques hurt most unions. They also caused many skilled workers to break with unskilled workers and join the American Federation of Labor.)* Write students' responses on the chalkboard. Then ask each student to use the information on the chalkboard to write a paragraph explaining how businesses responded to strikes in the late 1800s and how those responses affected unions. **Sheltered English**

LEVELS 2 AND 3: Organize students into two groups, one representing business leaders and one representing union leaders. Ask the first group to discuss possible responses to strikes and the other group to discuss possible responses to business reprisals. Then have each group select several spokespeople. Have spokespeople make a three-to-five-minute speech describing their possible responses. *(See the Level 1 lesson for the correct responses.)* Then conduct a debate between business leaders and union leaders on resolving conflicts. After the debate, ask students to consider the conflicts between the two groups. Was consensus possible, given the time and their different issues? What might have been a fair, acceptable consensus? **Cooperative Learning**

Creating a Time Line

Each event should have an explanation and the correct date.

Writing a Summary

See the Reading Checks in each section for main ideas.

Identifying People and Ideas

1. method of producing steel cheaply and quickly
2. African American who invented a way to lubricate machine parts with oil while the machine was running
3. allowed people to communicate over distances using Morse code
4. inventor who advanced studies of electricity and communications
5. steel magnate who contributed much money to charities
6. belief that society progresses through natural competition
7. a group of companies that assign control of their stock to a common board of trustees
8. one company's control of all similar companies or industries
9. labor leader who organized strikes and demonstrations
10. name for the series of strikes that took place in 1886

Understanding Main Ideas

1. Railroads and communications aided the growth of many different kinds of businesses and allowed people

Attention Workingmen!
GREAT
MASS-MEETING
TO-NIGHT, at 7.30 o'clock,
AT THE
HAYMARKET, Randolph St, Bet. Desplaines and Halsted.
Good Speakers will be present to denounce the latest atrocious act of the police, the shooting of our fellow-workmen yesterday afternoon.
Workingmen Arm Yourselves and Appear in Full Force!
THE EXECUTIVE COMMITTEE
Achtung, Arbeiter!
Große
Massen-Versammlung
Heute Abend, 8 Uhr, auf dem
Heumarkt, Randolph-Straße, zwischen Desplaines- u. Halsted-Str.
Gute Redner werden den neuesten Schurkenstreich der Polizei, indem sie gestern Nachmittag unsere Brüder erschoß, geißeln.
Arbeiter, bewaffnet Euch und erscheint massenhaft!
Das Executiv-Comite.

This poster encouraged workers to rally at Haymarket Square.

officers and one civilian were dead. The police arrested eight well-known anarchists—only one of whom had been present—charging them with conspiracy. All eight were found guilty of incitement to murder. Four were hanged.

Worker activism declines. Despite the early wave of protests and strikes, worker activism actually decreased by the close of the year. Encouraged by the Haymarket convictions, employers struck back at the unions. Employers drew up blacklists—lists of union supporters—that they shared with one another. Blacklisted workers found it almost impossible to get jobs. Many employers also forced job applicants to sign agreements—called yellow-dog contracts by the workers—promising not to join unions. When these measures failed and workers struck anyway, many companies instituted lockouts. They barred workers from their plants, and brought in nonunion strikebreakers. Many of these strikebreakers were African Americans or others who felt abandoned by the unions. As labor suffered repeated defeats, the tide of public sentiment turned against workers. Union membership shrank.

Alarmed by the violence of the Great Upheaval and by the response of the employers, many skilled workers broke ranks with the unskilled laborers. They joined the **American Federation of Labor** (AFL), a new union founded by Samuel Gompers in 1886. The AFL organized independent craft unions into a group that worked to advance the interests of skilled workers.

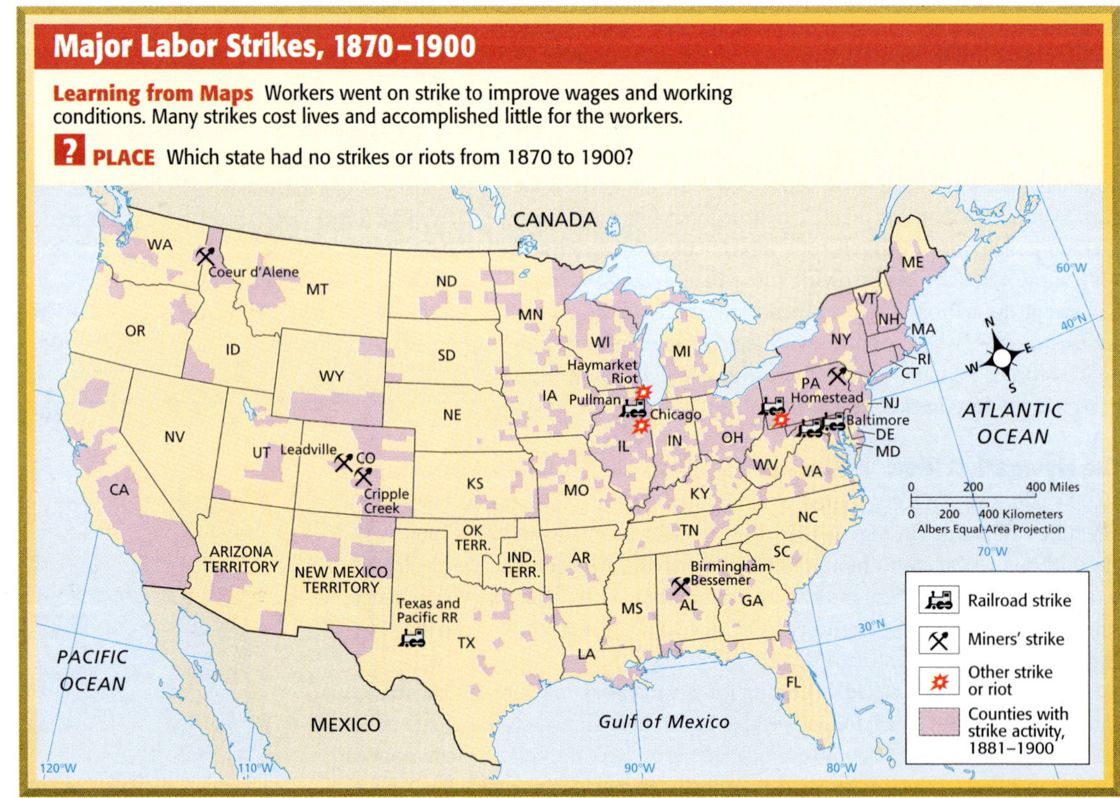

Major Labor Strikes, 1870–1900

Learning from Maps Workers went on strike to improve wages and working conditions. Many strikes cost lives and accomplished little for the workers.

? PLACE Which state had no strikes or riots from 1870 to 1900?

REVIEW

Have students complete the **Section 3 Review** on p. 187.

ASSESS

Have students complete **Daily Quiz 5.3.** As **Alternative Assessment**, you may want to use the Knights of Labor brochure or the business leaders–union leaders presentation and debate in this section's lessons.

RETEACH

Have students complete **Main Idea Activity for Reteaching and Sheltered English 5.3.** Then organize students into four groups. Assign each group one of the Section 3 objectives. Have each group create an outline of the material relating to its assigned objective. Then ask each group to copy its outline onto the chalkboard, omitting some of the information in its original outlines. Have groups compete to fill in the most blanks. **Sheltered English, Cooperative Learning**

EXTEND

Pair students and tell them that in the late 1800s union leaders used songs to help motivate members. Have students conduct research on labor songs. *(You might suggest that students start with Philip Sheldon Foner's* American Labor Songs of the Nineteenth Century.*)* Then ask each pair to write the lyrics to an original union song. Have students read their lyrics to the class. **Block Scheduling, Cooperative Learning**

The Homestead and Pullman Strikes

Industrial unrest broke out again in 1892 at Andrew Carnegie's Homestead Steel Works in Homestead, Pennsylvania. In June, workers went on strike to protest a wage cut. Managers responded by instituting a lockout and hiring some 300 guards to protect the plant. A violent clash between strikers and the guards in early July resulted in 16 deaths.

In June 1894, workers at the Pullman sleeping-car factory in Pullman, Illinois, went on strike. George Pullman had cut wages but refused to lower rents or prices at the stores in his company town. As head of the American Railway Union (ARU), Eugene V. Debs supported the Pullman strikers. They urged other union members to refuse to work or ride on all trains that included Pullman cars. Debs proclaimed:

> "The struggle . . . has developed into a contest between the producing classes and the money power of the country. . . . Workingmen are entitled to a just proportion of the proceeds of their labor."

In support of the strikers, railroad workers brought rail traffic to a halt throughout the Midwest. The railroad companies quickly turned to the federal government for help. The government ordered an end to the ARU strike, claiming that the strikers were committing a federal offense by preventing the delivery of U.S. mail. When ARU officials ignored the order, they were jailed.

Meanwhile, President Grover Cleveland ordered federal troops into Pullman in July. The troops helped to restore normal factory operations. In the process, the Pullman strike had been broken and the ARU destroyed.

✔ **READING CHECK:** How did businesses react to the strikes in the late 1800s? How did this affect unions?

THE GRANGER COLLECTION, NEW YORK

INTERPRETING THE VISUAL RECORD

Homestead Strike. After the violent confrontation between strikers and some 300 hired guards at the Homestead Steel Works, violence spread to other plants. ***How does this image convey the tension caused by these strikes?***

like Carnegie and Rockefeller to gain control of whole areas of production.

2. Laissez-faire capitalists welcomed government intervention that allowed them to eliminate competition, but they did not want government to interfere in their operations. Marxists believed that government should regulate business operations to ensure that workers are treated fairly.

3. Workers faced low wages, long hours, and unsafe surroundings. Children worked the same long hours as adults. Some companies paid workers in scrip, forcing them to spend their pay in company stores.

Reviewing Themes

1. Railroads and communications aided the growth of many different kinds of businesses and created jobs for millions of people.

2. Students might mention increased ease of travel and communication and expanded job opportunities.

3. Unions organized workers to fight for better conditions and were sometimes successful, but businesses and government began limiting union activity and public sentiment turned against unions.

Thinking Critically

1. The ability to produce more steel cheaply led to the rapid expansion of railroads. Cities like Philadelphia and Cleveland grew around the steel industry, and railroads connected these cities and allowed fast travel between cities all over the country. Telegraph companies followed railroads,

SECTION 3 REVIEW

Define and explain the significance of the following terms:
Sherman Antitrust Act
Knights of Labor
Great Upheaval
Haymarket Riot
anarchists
American Federation of Labor

Identify and explain the significance of the following individuals:
Terence V. Powderly
Mary Harris Jones
Eugene V. Debs

Locate and explain the importance of the following places:
Haymarket Square
Homestead
Pullman

1. **Using Graphic Organizers** Copy the graphic organizer below. Use it to explain what labor unions hoped to accomplish with strikes and what effects the strikes actually had.

Strikes → Intended Effects → Actual Effects

2. **Recognizing Point of View** Why did some Americans oppose trusts? How did the government respond to their concerns?
3. **Using Historical Imagination** Imagine that you are an industrial laborer in the United States during the late 1800s. Describe your working conditions.
4. **Analyzing** How did union organizers such as Terence Powderly attempt to represent diverse groups of workers?

Critical Thinking

5. Why did some union workers participate in strikes despite the potential of danger?
Consider:
- the violence that occurred during some strikes
- the grievances union workers had
- what they hoped to gain by striking

REVIEW AND ASSESSMENT RESOURCES

PRINT
- Chapter 5 Review, pp. 188–99
- Chapter 5 Tutorial for Students, Parents, Mentors, and Peers
- Chapter 5 Test (Form A or B)
- Portfolio Activities and Alternative Assessment Handbook, Chapter 5

MULTIMEDIA
- Audio Program, Chapter 5 (English and Spanish)
- Chapter 5 Test Generator (on the One-Stop Planner)
- Global Skill Builder CD–ROM
- HRW Web site

SHELTERED ENGLISH
- Spanish Glossary
- Sheltered English Chapter 5 Test

REVIEW
Have students complete the **Chapter 5 Review** on pp. 188–89.

ASSESS
Use one of the chapter tests to assess students' understanding of the content. For **Alternative Assessment**, see the **Portfolio Activities and Alternative Assessment Handbook.**

stringing lines and setting up offices along with the railroad construction.

2. Answers will vary. Students should support their choices with examples.

3. Industrialists like Rockefeller gave generously to charities but seemed not to care that their business practices forced people out of their livelihoods. Pullman tried to make people happy by building a company town, but his rigid control contributed to his workers' dissatisfaction.

4. Although the claim that the corset always does good may pass for a fact with some supporting evidence, none of the words represent true facts but are only opinions about how the corset looks and how it can make women look. The adjectives "vigorous" and "graceful" are open to interpretation.

5. Answers will vary. Some students might argue that union organization would have been more popular because some people were discouraged from joining unions by the violence associated with them. Other students might argue that unions would have been even less effective if companies and governments did not demonstrate their willingness to resort to violence against workers. This willingness may have encouraged some people to believe that workers really did need improvements.

Writing About History
The short story outlines should include the information presented in the graphic organizer.

Review

Creating a Time Line
Copy the time line below onto a sheet of paper. Complete the time line by filling in the events and dates from the chapter that you think were most significant. Pick three events and explain why you think they were significant.

Writing a Summary
Using the Reading Checks as a guide, write an overview of the events in the chapter.

Identifying People and Ideas
Identify the following terms or individuals and explain their significance.

1. Bessemer process
2. Elijah McCoy
3. telegraph
4. Thomas Edison
5. Andrew Carnegie
6. social Darwinism
7. trust
8. monopoly
9. Mary Harris Jones
10. Great Upheaval

Understanding Main Ideas
SECTION 1
1. How did innovations in the transportation and communications industries affect business practices?

SECTION 2
2. How did laissez-faire capitalism and marxism interpret the role of government in business differently?

SECTION 3
3. Describe the working conditions laborers faced during the late 1800s.

Reviewing Themes
1. **Economic Development** What impact did new technology have on the nation's economy?
2. **Technology and Society** How did technological developments change Americans' daily lives in the late 1800s?
3. **Democratic Values** Why did unions only partially succeed in ensuring the rights of working people?

Thinking Critically
1. **Synthesizing** Describe how the steel, railroad, and telegraph industries were interconnected.
2. **Taking a Stand** What do you think was the single most important invention of the late 1800s? Why?
3. **Identifying Values** How did the business practices of some industrialists contradict their philanthropic values?
4. **Distinguishing Fact from Opinion** Read the following statement from an 1882 advertisement for an "electric corset." Then identify which words or phrases represent opinions. "A wonderful invention for ladies who desire vigorous health and a graceful figure. They always do good, cannot harm."
5. **Hypothesizing** What might have happened to unions if violence involving strikers had not occurred in the late 1800s?

Writing About History
Writing to Create Using a business leader or an industrial factory worker as a main character, create an outline for a short story. Use the graphic organizer below to help you organize your story.

Setting:
Main Character:
Secondary Characters:
Conflict:
Plot:
Resolution:

RETEACH

Pair students and have each pair use at least three quarters of the key terms and key people in Chapter 5 to create a "hidden words" puzzle or a crossword puzzle. Ask each pair to exchange its puzzle with another pair and to solve them. Then conduct an overview discussion on the Second Industrial Revolution and ask students to fill in the gaps.
Sheltered English, Cooperative Learning

EXTEND

Organize students into groups of six and assign each member one of the following roles: factory owner, factory foreman, union leader, worker from Ireland, worker from Russia, and child worker from Italy. Tell students to imagine that it is 1895 and that the factory owner is touring the plant. During the tour, however, a large machine topples over and blocks an exit, leaving the six people above trapped in a small room for hours. Have each group create a 10-to-15-minute play on the events and conversations that follow in the small room. Groups' plays should focus on events related to the Second Industrial Revolution, such as working conditions, social beliefs, immigration, unions, and so on. Have each group perform its play for the class. **Block Scheduling, Cooperative Learning**

Strategies for Success Review the **Strategies for Success** on *Evaluating Historical Actions.* Then reread the material in Section 3 on the Pullman strike and answer the following questions.

1. Why did workers at the Pullman sleeping-car factory in Chicago go on strike? How did the strike spread to other unionized railroad workers?
2. How did the railroad companies and federal government respond to the strike?
3. What were the ultimate results of each group's actions?
4. What other courses of action could each group have taken during the strike? What do you think the results of these actions would have been?
5. What is your evaluation of the actions that each group took during the strike?
6. What conclusions can you draw concerning the justifications each group had for its actions?

Linking History and Geography

Study the map below. Considering the location of most industries in the late 1800s, what generalizations can be made about the relationship between geography and industrialization? Explain why these trends might have occurred.

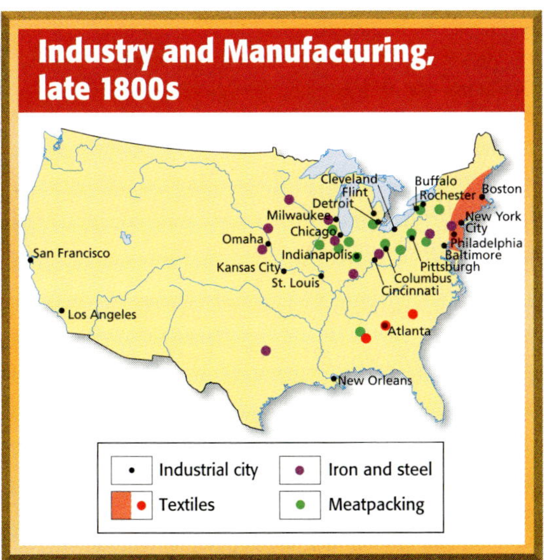

internetconnect

TOPIC: Thomas Edison
GO TO: go.hrw.com
KEYWORD: SE1 Edison

Accessing the Internet through the HRW Web site, research the life of Thomas Alva Edison and the inventions he and his research team developed at the Menlo Park laboratory. Then choose an invention and write a description of its function and its social impact.

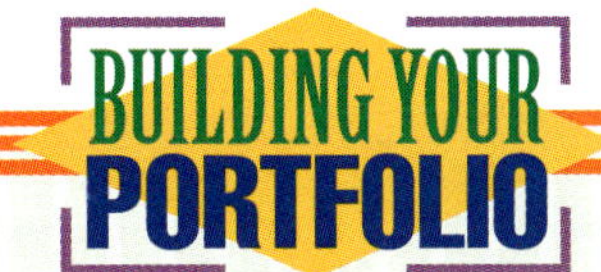

Complete one or all of the following projects independently or cooperatively.

1 Democratic Values

Imagine that you are an employee at Pullman's sleeping-car factory and live in his company town. ***Create a list of grievances*** that you and your fellow workers want addressed. In order to rally support for your cause, compose a slogan or song to encourage your fellow workers.

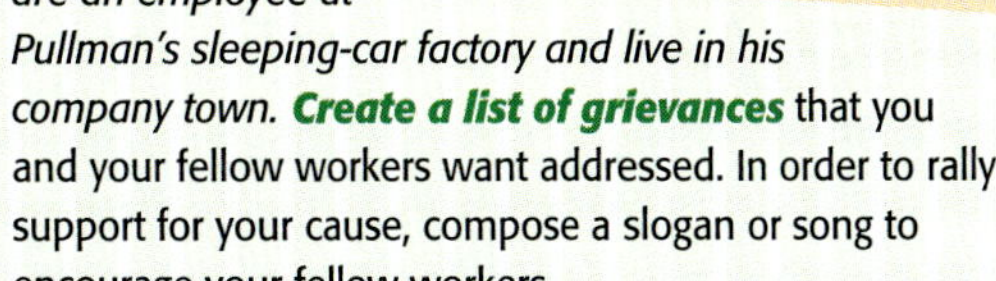

2 Technology and Society

Imagine that you are a land speculator attempting to develop a rural area. ***Outline a plan*** to use new technologies such as the telephone, electric lighting, and innovations in transportation to attract residents and businesses.

3 Economic Development

Imagine that you are the executive of a small but rapidly growing oil, steel, or railroad company. You are about to make a speech to your stockholders about the long-range plans of your company. ***Make a visual chart*** presenting your plans for helping the company grow. Include informative diagrams to illustrate your strategy.

Strategies for Success

1. Workers at the Pullman factory went on strike to protest a wage cut. Other rail workers went on strike after their companies threatened to fire them if they refused to handle Pullman cars. Debs influenced the additional strikes by arguing that workers should support other workers in the fight for fairness.
2. Railroad companies threatened their workers, and the government invented a reason to become involved by connecting mail cars to Pullman cars. The city of Cleveland ordered federal troops to stop the strike.
3. Violence erupted and caused many deaths and property damage. The strike was broken, and the ARU was destroyed.
4. Answers will vary. Students might argue that the government could have avoided sending armed troops to deal with strikers, thereby avoiding the massive destruction that resulted.
5. Answers will vary. Students should provide examples to support their arguments.
6. Answers will vary. Students should provide examples to support their arguments.

Linking History and Geography

Factories are mostly located on waterways or in major cities. Factories used the water for power, and the cities provided a sufficient number of workers.

The Transformation of American Society

CHAPTER PLANNING GUIDE

	Section Lesson Objectives	Print Resources	Multimedia Resources	Sheltered English Resources
Section 1 The New Immigrants, pp. 192–97	1 Explain how immigration changed during the late 1800s. 2 Describe the challenges immigrants faced as they settled in the United States. 3 Discuss where immigrants found assistance. 4 Relate why nativists opposed new immigration.	▶ Guided Reading Strategy 6.1 ▶ American History Political Cartoon 14: Attitudes Toward Immigration ▶ Geography Activity 6: Immigrant Groups in New York City ▶ Primary Source Reading 6: An Immigrant's Story ▶ Section 1 Review, p. 197 ▶ Daily Quiz 6.1	▶ One-Stop Planner, Lesson 6.1 ▶ The American Nation Video Program Segment: Community Ties: San Francisco's Chinatown; Teacher's Guide, pp. 75–80 ▶ Holt Researcher: American History CD–ROM	▶ Main Idea Activity for Reteaching and Sheltered English 6.1
Section 2 The Urban World, pp. 198–204	1 Analyze how technological innovations altered the urban landscape. 2 Discuss the social values that the new class of wealthy city-dwellers expressed. 3 Explain how life changed for middle-class Americans during the late 1800s. 4 Describe what urban life was like for the poorest city-dwellers. 5 Identify how social reformers used settlement houses and churches to improve the lives of the poor.	▶ Guided Reading Strategy 6.2 ▶ American History Political Cartoon 15: Urban Life ▶ Literature Reading 6: A New Social Class ▶ Graphic Organizer Activity 6: Daily LIfe in the Cities ▶ Section 2 Review, p. 204 ▶ Daily Quiz 6.2	▶ One-Stop Planner, Lesson 6.2 ▶ Holt Researcher: American History CD–ROM ▶ HRW Web site	▶ Main Idea Activity for Reteaching and Sheltered English 6.2
Section 3 Daily Life in the Cities, pp. 205–11	1 Understand how public education and colleges changed in the late 1800s. 2 Explain how publishers appealed to readers. 3 Discuss how outdoor activities and sports provided a source of leisure for Americans. 4 Describe the new forms of popular music and theater that developed in the late 1800s.	▶ Guided Reading Strategy 6.3 ▶ Biography Reading 6: Frederick Olmsted ▶ Section 3 Review, p. 211 ▶ Daily Quiz 6.3	▶ One-Stop Planner, Lesson 6.3 ▶ American Music Selection 18: "Twilight Rag" ▶ Holt Researcher: American History CD–ROM	▶ Main Idea Activity for Reteaching and Sheltered English 6.3
Chapter Review and Assessment pp. 212–13		▶ Chapter 6 Review, pp. 212–13 ▶ Chapter 6 Tutorial for Students, Parents, Mentors, and Peers ▶ Chapter 6 Test (Form A or B) ▶ Portfolio Activities and Alternative Assessment Handbook, Chapter 6	▶ Audio Program, Chapter 6 (English and Spanish) ▶ Chapter 6 Test Generator (on the One-Stop Planner) ▶ Global Skill Builder CD–ROM ▶ HRW Web site	▶ Spanish Glossary ▶ Sheltered English Chapter 6 Test

CHAPTER OVERVIEW

In the late 1800s and early 1900s, millions of immigrants—a large number from eastern and southern Europe—came to the United States. These immigrants, many of whom had fled persecution or poverty in their native countries, often faced a difficult adjustment to life in the United States. Immigrant communities helped new immigrants adjust to life in the United States, as did various religious institutions and settlement houses.

During the same period, technological advances helped reshape American life, especially in cities. These advances enabled architects to build skyscrapers and engineers to develop forms of mass transit, which led to the outward expansion of urban areas. Urban culture took on a new shape as well with new newspapers, books, parks, spectator sports, and music.

TIME TAMERS

Block Scheduling

The teacher lesson plans for each section offer a variety of activity choices to help you present the material in a block scheduling format. For further suggestions on block scheduling, see the **Block Scheduling Handbook with Team Teaching Strategies**, pp. 31–36.

Hands-On History Activities:

Classroom to Community The **Hands-On History Activities** help students make meaningful connections between events in American history and those in their own hometown. You may wish to use the Chapter 6 Activity, Leisure Time—Today and Yesterday, to extend the chapter lessons, as alternative assessment, or as a block scheduling option.

Portfolio Projects

The American Nation includes multiple portfolio projects in each Pupil's Edition chapter review, as well as each unit review. Chapter 6 Portfolio Project options on p. 213 include the following:

1. Students will **write a letter**.
2. Students will **create a comic strip**.
3. Students will **plan an itinerary**.

The American Nation
INTERNET RESOURCE DIRECTORY

To access online materials for this chapter, go to **go.hrw.com** and type in the keywords listed below.

HRW ONLINE RESOURCES
GO TO: go.hrw.com

Online Maps
KEYWORD: SE1 Maps6
- The Largest Cities, 1900

Online Reading Support
KEYWORD: SE1 Strategies6

Online Rubrics
KEYWORD: SE1 Rubrics

CHAPTER ENRICHMENT LINKS
Use these Web links to extend and enrich student learning for Chapter 6.
GO TO: go.hrw.com
KEYWORD: SE1 Ch6

CHAPTER INTERNET ACTIVITIES
GO TO: go.hrw.com
- Pupil's Edition Student Activity
  KEYWORD: SE1 Ellis Island
  (Students conduct research on Ellis Island or Angel Island.)
- Teacher's Edition Student Activity
  KEYWORD: SE1 Baseball
  (Students explore the history of baseball.)
- Teacher's Edition Student Activity
  KEYWORD: SE1 Sullivan
  (Students explore the architecture of Louis Sullivan.)

ADDITIONAL
RESOURCES

Books for Teachers

Reiss, Steven A. *Sport in Industrial America, 1850–1920.* Harlan Davidson, 1995. Studies the social functions of sports in the United States.

Schlereth, Thomas J. *Victorian America: Transformations of Everyday Life, 1876-1915.* HarperCollins, 1992. Surveys social history in the late 1800s.

Books for Students

Daniels, Roger. *Coming to America.* HarperCollins, 1990. Examines the experiences of several different immigrant groups.

Hoobler, Dorothy and Thomas Hoobler. *The Italian American Family Album.* Oxford, 1994. Discusses Italian immigrants; is part of a series on ethnic Americans.

Primary Sources from the Period

Addams, Jane. *Twenty Years at Hull-House.* Macmillan, 1910. Recounts Addams' settlement house experiences.

Riis, Jacob. *How the Other Half Lives: Studies among the Tenements of New York.* Belknap Press, 1970. Serves as the classic study of tenement life; includes many poignant photographs.

Multimedia Materials

The Chinese-American: Early Years. Video, 20 min. Handel Film. Illustrates the contributions of Chinese immigrants in the United States.

Ellis Island. Video, 150 min. A&E. Includes interviews with immigrants and rare film footage.

Before You Read

Build on What You Know

Ask students to answer the following questions.

How might new technologies lead to economic development?

Consider:

- how technology changes the ways in which goods are produced
- how demand for new goods generates economic growth

Why might many immigrants choose to live in urban areas?

Consider:

- the point of entry for most new immigrants
- the existence of immigrant communities

exploring the time line

AMERICAN EVENTS

internetconnect

TOPIC: Baseball
GO TO: go.hrw.com
KEYWORD: SE1 Baseball

Have students access the Internet through the HRW Web site to conduct research on the history of baseball. Then have each student create one or more commemorative baseball cards that portray milestones in the history of baseball. The front of each card should have an illustration, and the back should have a caption that discusses the milestone.

1865–1910

The Transformation of American Society

Edwin Booth

The World

The New York World

1868 Business and Finance The first professional training schools for pharmacy and architecture are established.

1869 The Arts *Romeo and Juliet* opens in New York, starring the popular actor Edwin Booth.

1876 The Arts Mark Twain publishes *The Adventures of Tom Sawyer.*

1883 Business and Finance Joseph Pulitzer purchases the *New York World,* a daily newspaper.

1865 1870  1875 1880 1885

1865 World Events The Salvation Army is founded in London by religious revivalist William Booth.

1869 Daily Life Aaron Champion organizes the first professional baseball team, the Cincinnati Red Stockings.

1876 Science and Technology British inventors introduce the first bicycle to the United States at the Centennial Exposition in Philadelphia.

1885 Science and Technology William Le Baron Jenney constructs the Home Insurance Co. Building in Chicago.

Cincinnati Red Stockings professional baseball team in 1869

Bicycle advertisement from the 1800s

Before You Read

Build on What You Know

During the late 1800s many innovative thinkers made significant scientific discoveries, inventions, and advances in technology. These breakthroughs, along with developments in American business practices, launched a new age of industrialization. In this chapter you will learn about the impact of new immigrants on these industries and on American life. Immigration and industrialization led to rapid growth in U.S. cities. This growth generated a series of broad transformations in the daily lives of nearly all Americans.

Think About Themes

To help students create their Themes Journal entries, provide the following examples of appropriate **agree/disagree** *statements.*

Cultural Diversity

Agree Beginning in the 1840s, Irish immigrants brought many new traditions to the United States.

Disagree Many German immigrants learned English and abandoned their native language, at least in the public sphere.

Technology and Society

Agree Innovations in steel production resulted in the expansion of some cities and the widespread use of steel to build tall buildings.

Disagree The development of the cotton gin expanded slavery, thus greatly worsening life for enslaved African Americans.

Democratic Values

Agree The expansion of democracy during Andrew Jackson's presidency allowed more Americans to participate in public institutions.

Disagree Many public institutions denied equal access or services to African Americans in the 1800s.

Ellis Island immigration station

Phoebus Theodore Levene

1909 Science and Technology Discoveries by Russian American chemist Phoebus Theodore Levene lead to the identification of RNA and eventually DNA.

1892 Politics The U.S. Bureau of Immigration opens a processing station on Ellis Island.

1899 Daily Life Dankmar Adler and Louis Sullivan design the Carson Pirie Scott & Co. store in Chicago.

1903 Daily Life The first World Series is played between the Pittsburgh Pirates and the Boston Red Sox.

1890 — 1895 — 1900 — 1905 — 1910

1891 Daily Life Dr. James Naismith invents the game of basketball.

1896 The Arts Charles M. Sheldon's best-selling novel, *In His Steps*, is published.

1897 Daily Life Steeplechase amusement park opens on Coney Island, New York.

1899 The Arts Scott Joplin's "Maple Leaf Rag" becomes an instant commercial success and a ragtime classic.

1905 The Arts Edith Wharton publishes *The House of Mirth*.

1905 Daily Life In one season of intercollegiate football, 18 student athletes die and 154 are seriously injured.

"Maple Leaf Rag" sheet music

Think About Themes

Decide whether you **agree** *or* **disagree** *with the following statements. Note why in your journal.*

Cultural Diversity Mass immigration introduces new cultural values and ways of life to society.

Technology and Society New technological developments revolutionize life for Americans of all social and economic backgrounds.

Democratic Values Public institutions such as schools attempt to better the lives of all Americans.

exploring the time line

GLOBAL EVENTS

THEN AND NOW

1865 ■ The Salvation Army. Apprenticed to a pawnbroker as a young boy, William Booth experienced a religious conversion as a teenager. This conversion led him to become a Methodist preacher and a revivalist. In 1865 Booth founded the religious and charitable organization that would eventually become the Salvation Army. Booth patterned his organization after the British Army, creating corps led by officers. He established himself as general for life. In the 1880s and beyond, the Salvation Army spread to the United States, Australia, and modern-day Sri Lanka. Today, the organization works in more than 80 countries, using some 112 languages to teach the gospel.

CRITICAL THINKING Why might Booth have established himself as general for life? How might this have affected his organization?

ANSWER: Students might suggest that Booth wanted to retain absolute control over the Salvation Army. Students might suggest that this absolute control could have led to dissension within the ranks.

191

SECTION 1

After completing Section 1, students should be able to

OBJECTIVE 1 *Explain how immigration changed during the late 1800s.*

OBJECTIVE 2 *Describe the challenges that immigrants faced as they settled in the United States.*

OBJECTIVE 3 *Discuss where immigrants found assistance.*

OBJECTIVE 4 *Relate why nativists opposed new immigration.*

LET'S GET STARTED!

Write the quotation from the following page on the chalkboard: *"Despite these harsh conditions, many immigrants clung to the hope for a better life."* Have students respond to the quotation in writing by creating a list of the "harsh conditions" to which the passage might refer. Then have students create a list of some characteristics of the "better life" that immigrants might have hoped to create for themselves. Tell students that in Section 1 they will learn more about the lives of immigrants who came to the United States in the late 1800s and early 1900s.

SECTION 1 RESOURCES

PRINT

- Guided Reading Strategy 6.1
- American History Political Cartoon 14: Attitudes Toward Immigration
- Geography Activity 6: Immigrant Groups in New York City
- Primary Source Reading 6: An Immigrant's Story
- Section 1 Review, p. 197
- Daily Quiz 6.1

MULTIMEDIA

- One-Stop Planner, Lesson 6.1
- The American Nation Video Program Segment: Community Ties: San Francisco's Chinatown; Teacher's Guide, pp. 75–80
- Holt Researcher: American History CD–ROM

SHELTERED ENGLISH

- Main Idea Activity for Reteaching and Sheltered English 6.1

✔ READING TO UNDERSTAND
To help students master the section objectives, have them answer the **READING CHECKS** and complete **Guided Reading Strategy 6.1** as they read the section.

SECTION 1 The New Immigrants

OBJECTIVES

Read to understand:

1. how immigration changed during the late 1800s
2. what challenges immigrants faced as they settled in the United States
3. where new immigrants found assistance
4. why nativists opposed new immigration

KEY TERMS

old immigrants
new immigrants
steerage
benevolent societies
Chinese Exclusion Act
Immigration Restriction League

KEY PEOPLE

Dennis Kearney
Grover Cleveland

EYEWITNESSES TO History

"All of a sudden, we heard a big commotion and we came to America and everybody started yelling—they see the Statue of Liberty. . . . I remember my father putting his arms around my mother and the two of them standing and crying and my father said to my mother, 'You're in America now. You have nothing to be afraid of.'"

—Esther Gidiwicz

Immigrant passport

Esther Gidiwicz and her mother immigrated to New York from Romania in 1905. Like many immigrants, Esther already had family members and friends in the United States, including her father. These friends provided a network of support for her. While urban life in New York for immigrants was frighteningly new and hectic, many immigrants settled in neighborhoods where residents often spoke their native language and provided a village-like community. Esther described her mother's first experience shopping in the United States. "The butcher was very nice to her, and she was so happy that they spoke to her. They spoke in her language."

This family of immigrants arrived in New York in 1905.

The Lure of America

Esther Gidiwicz was just one of the millions of immigrants who came to the United States in search of opportunity and a better life. These hopes brought a new wave of immigrants to the United States during the late 1800s.

A new wave of immigrants. From 1800 to 1880, more than 10 million immigrants came to the United States. Often called the **old immigrants**, many of them were Protestants from northwestern Europe. Then, a new wave of immigration swept over the United States. Between 1891 and 1910, some 12 million immigrants arrived on U.S. shores. The increase was so great that by the early 1900s, about 60 percent of the people living in the nation's 12 largest cities were either foreign-born or had foreign-born parents.

About 70 percent of these **new immigrants** were from southern or eastern Europe. Among the many nationalities were Czech, Greek, Hungarian, Italian, Polish, Russian, and Slovak. Most were Catholic, Greek Orthodox, or Jewish. Arabs, Armenians, Chinese, French Canadians, and Japanese also arrived by the thousands.

Like the old immigrants, many new immigrants came to the United States to escape poverty or persecution. Most of the Armenian and Jewish families fled their homelands to escape religious or political persecution. Most of the Italian and Slavic immigrants were men seeking economic opportunities in the United States that were scarce in their home countries. Many made enough money in the United States to return home and buy land. Others, however, put down roots and stayed.

TEACH OBJECTIVE 1

LEVEL 1: Discuss changes in immigration to the United States during the late 1800s. Compare the national origins, religious backgrounds, and reasons for immigration of new immigrants to those of old immigrant groups coming to the United States. Pair students and have each pair create a graphic organizer to list and characterize these changes in immigration. *(Pairs should indicate that the majority of new immigrants came from southern and eastern Europe—old immigrants were primarily from northwestern Europe; new immigrants tended to be Roman Catholic, Greek Orthodox, or Jewish—old immigrants were mostly Protestant; new immigrants and old immigrants alike came to seek economic opportunity and religious freedom.)* Ask volunteers to display their organizers and present them to the class.
Cooperative Learning, Sheltered English

LEVELS 2 AND 3: Tell students to imagine that they work for a U.S. government agency that compiles immigration data in the year 1910. Organize the class into pairs. Have each pair create an informational pamphlet about how immigration to the United States in the late 1800s changed from immigration in previous eras. Encourage members of each group to illustrate their pamphlets and to include pertinent facts and statistics. *(See the Level 1 lesson for answers.)* Call on volunteers to present their pamphlets to the class. **Cooperative Learning**

Carla Martinelli's father left a poor northern Italian village for the United States. "My *papà mia* was a barber. He went to America twice, back and forth," she recalled. "I was young. He went to get work. Make money." Carla's reasons for immigrating were more complicated. She explained:

> **"When I was sixteen, I was supposed to marry a man in Italy, but I didn't want him. My mama tell me, 'Either you marry this guy or you go to America.' But I told her, 'I don't like him.' She say, 'Then you go to America.' That's why I came to America. There was nothing in Italy, nothing in Italy. That's why we came. To find work, because Italy didn't have no work. Mama used to say, 'America is rich, America is rich.'"**

Read More About It

Free Find:
Immigrant Voices
After reading the selection of immigrant stories on the Holt Researcher CD–ROM, write your own story about what you might have experienced as an immigrant coming to the United States.

The journey. Many immigrants learned of the opportunities available in the United States from railroad and steamship company promoters. These companies painted a tempting—and often false—picture of the United States as a land of unlimited opportunity. Some railroad companies exaggerated the availability of employment opportunities. The steamship lines also charged low fares to attract passengers.

Most of the millions who yielded to these appeals found the journey difficult and dangerous. The ocean voyage was no pleasure trip for those traveling in the poorest accommodations, called **steerage**. Traveling in steerage, immigrants resided below deck on the ship's lower levels near the steering mechanisms. The quarters were cramped, with no privacy and little ventilation. Despite these harsh conditions, many immigrants clung to the hope for a better life in the United States.

✔ **READING CHECK:** How did immigration change during the late 1800s?

Arriving in America

Millions of newcomers in the late 1800s first set foot on U.S. soil on Ellis Island in New York Harbor or Angel Island in San Francisco Bay. Both islands served as immigration stations during this period.

Ellis Island opened in 1892 to receive record numbers of European immigrants. Upon their arrival, many immigrants caught their first glimpse of the Statue of Liberty, a symbol of hope for many. As one immigrant explained, "All of us [immigrants] . . . clustered on the foredeck . . . and looked with wonder on this miraculous land of our dreams."

All newcomers who passed through Ellis Island were subjected to a physical exam. Those with contagious diseases, mental disorders, or serious health problems like tuberculosis were deported. Those who passed the physicals entered a maze of crowded aisles where inspectors questioned them about their background, job skills, and relatives. Those with criminal records, or without the means to support themselves, were sent back. The vast majority were allowed to stay.

Total Immigration to the United States, 1860–1900

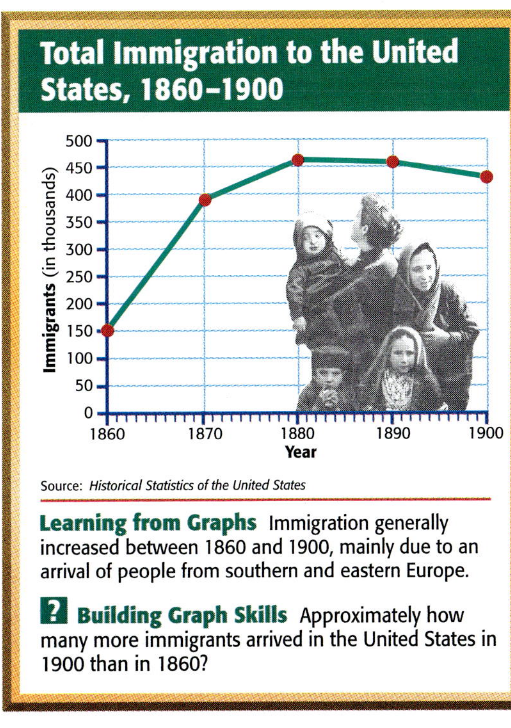

Source: *Historical Statistics of the United States*

Learning from Graphs Immigration generally increased between 1860 and 1900, mainly due to an arrival of people from southern and eastern Europe.

? Building Graph Skills Approximately how many more immigrants arrived in the United States in 1900 than in 1860?

IN THE NEWS

Ellis Island. In 1998 Ellis Island was the subject of a Supreme Court decision. Some years earlier, the state of New Jersey had sued the state of New York over control of the island. The Supreme Court ruled that the original portion of the island, some 3 acres, belonged to the state of New York, and the remaining portion of the island, some 24 acres, belonged to New Jersey. The 24 acres had been added to the island during the years that it served as an immigration center. In its ruling, the Supreme Court cited an 1834 agreement between the two states that the waters surrounding the island belonged to New Jersey–thus supporting New Jersey's claim to the added land. In a dissenting opinion, Justice John Paul Stevens noted that the identity cards issued to immigrants who arrived on Ellis Island noted that they had arrived in New York, not New Jersey.

CRITICAL THINKING Do you agree or disagree with the Court's ruling? Explain.

ANSWER: Some students might argue that the 1834 agreement between the two states was binding, while others might believe that the identity cards were compelling evidence.

GRAPH ANSWER
around 290,000

TEACH OBJECTIVE 2

LEVEL 1: Discuss the challenges faced by immigrants in their attempt to settle in the United States in the late 1800s. Then pair students, and provide them with the following list of answers: **1.** railroad and steamship companies, **2.** steerage, **3.** Ellis Island or Angel Island, **4.** physical exams, **5.** immigration inspectors, **6.** deportation, **7.** Chinese applicants. Ask pairs to create a crossword puzzle with clues for the answers provided. *(Pairs should provide the following clues:* ***1.*** *often advertised U.S. opportunities to immigrants;* ***2.*** *a ship's poorest accommodations;* ***3.*** *points of entry for European and Asian immigrants;* ***4.*** *immigrants had to undergo these to prove that they were healthy;* ***5.*** *questioned immigrants about their backgrounds, job skills, and relatives;* ***6.*** *fate for immigrants with serious diseases;* ***7.*** *faced strict immigration laws.)* Have students exchange and solve each others' puzzles.
Cooperative Learning, Sheltered English

LEVELS 2 AND 3: Tell students to imagine that they are new European or Asian immigrants to the United States in the late 1800s. Have each student write a letter to a family member or friend back home describing the challenges of his or her journey to the United States and experience passing through Ellis Island or Angel Island. *(See the Level 1 lesson for the correct challenges.)* Ask volunteers to read their letters to the class.

THEN AND NOW

Angel Island. In order to circumvent strict immigration laws, many Asian immigrants used false papers that claimed they were related to current residents. Immigration officials ruthlessly interrogated these "paper sons and daughters." The panel asked one 11-year-old boy 83 pages of questions, a process that took days. Immigrants who failed the Angel Island interrogations faced detainment and deportation. While detained, many carved poems in the walls of their cells. In the late 1970s, Victor "Trader Vic" Bergerson, a restaurant owner, donated a black granite monument to commemorate the immigrant experience on Angel Island. The inscription on the monument reads, "Leaving their homes and villages, they crossed the ocean/Only to endure confinement in these barracks/Conquering frontier and barriers, they pioneered/A new life by the Golden Gate."

ACTIVITY: Tell students to imagine that they are Asian immigrants detained at Angel Island. Have each student write a poem commemorating his or her experience.

CHANGING WAYS ANSWERS

other European countries; North and South America

Changing Ways Immigration

Understanding Change In the late 1800s, immigration patterns changed dramatically as more immigrants came to the United States from eastern Europe. In recent years, immigration patterns have shifted again, as more immigrants come from other parts of North and South America and from Asia. *Where did the most immigrants come from then? now?*

THEN

1% 1% 3% 8% 7% 4% 22% 20% 30% 4%

NOW

1% 1% 1% 1% 2% 12% 37% 38% 7% 2%

Immigration

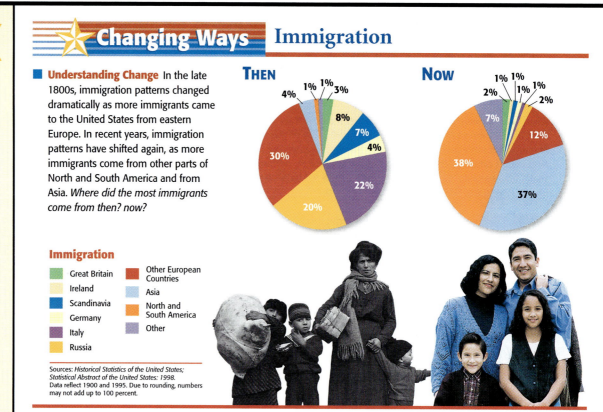

- Great Britain
- Ireland
- Scandinavia
- Germany
- Italy
- Russia
- Other European Countries
- Asia
- North and South America
- Other

Sources: *Historical Statistics of the United States; Statistical Abstract of the United States: 1998.*
Data reflect 1900 and 1995. Due to rounding, numbers may not add up to 100 percent.

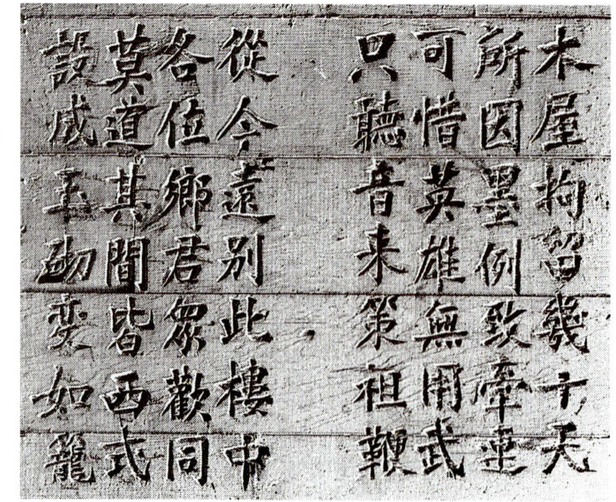

Imprisoned and waiting for rulings in their cases, Chinese immigrants often carved poems such as this one on their cell walls.

On Angel Island, thousands of Asian newcomers, mostly from China, underwent similar processing. Chinese applicants faced strict immigration laws. These laws limited entrance to certain skilled groups or to individuals who could show that their parents were born in the United States.

Some applicants who could not meet the restrictions were deported. Others were detained on the island as they awaited a ruling on their cases. For most immigrants, the anxiety they experienced during processing gave way to a renewed sense of hope once they finally set foot on their adopted homeland.

✔ **READING CHECK:** What challenges did immigrants face as they settled in the United States?

A New Life

Many immigrants found life in the United States an improvement on the conditions of their homeland. Nevertheless, the newcomers frequently endured hardships in their new home. Most immigrants settled in crowded cities where they could find only low-paying unskilled jobs. As a result, they were generally forced into poor housing located in crowded neighborhoods and slums.

TEACH OBJECTIVE 3

ALL LEVELS: To help students understand where new immigrants found assistance, copy the following graphic organizer on the chalkboard, omitting the italicized answers. Have each student complete it.
Cooperative Learning, Sheltered English

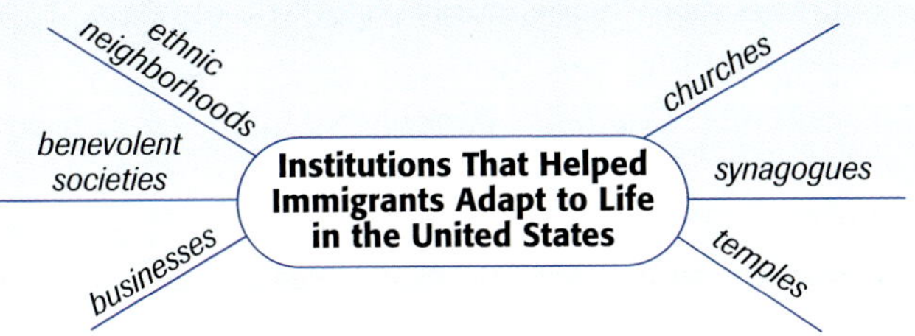

Teacher to Teacher

Ronald Foore of Tulsa, Oklahoma, suggested the following activity: Conduct a class discussion about the resources and institutions that help new immigrants adjust to life in the United States. Then organize students into triads. Have each triad create an immigration handbook that contains information for new immigrants. Ask volunteers to present their handbooks to the class.

Immigrant communities. Many industrial cities of the Northeast and Midwest became a patchwork of ethnic neighborhoods with numerous pockets of diverse immigrant communities. Social reformer Jacob Riis was himself a Danish immigrant. He noted that an 1890s map of New York City colored according to nationality, "would show . . . more colors than any rainbow." Settling in close-knit immigrant communities, newcomers found institutions and neighbors that made their transition more bearable both financially and culturally. In these neighborhoods, for example, residents often spoke the same languages and followed the customs of the old country.

Religious institutions. The neighborhood churches, synagogues, and temples provided community centers that helped immigrants maintain a sense of identity and belonging. In Chicago religious organizations such as the United Hebrew Relief Association, which served Jews, and the St. Vincent de Paul Society, which served mainly Irish Catholics, provided economic assistance to needy immigrants in their communities. Moreover, some churches, such as St. George's Episcopal Church in New York City and Russell H. Conwell's Baptist Temple in Philadelphia provided many services. They offered day care for children, gymnasiums, reading rooms, sewing classes, social clubs, and training courses for new immigrants.

Residents in many cities formed religious and non-religious aid organizations known as **benevolent societies** to help immigrants in cases of sickness, unemployment, and death. The size and number of charitable organizations grew rapidly along with the boom in immigration. They attempted to provide an important function by helping immigrants obtain education, health care, and jobs. Some benevolent societies offered loans to new immigrants to start businesses. Others set up insurance plans that provided money for families whose breadwinners were sick or had died. "We visit our sick and bury our dead" was one society's slogan.

Americanization. Immigrants were often urged by employers, public institutions, and sometimes even their own family members to join the American mainstream. Many older

ORTHODOX RELIGIONS

Greek Orthodox icon

Many new immigrants were members of orthodox religious communities. Orthodox religions generally follow traditional practices that strictly conform to the faith's religious doctrines. For example, Orthodox Judaism closely follows the Torah, the Jewish holy book, applying its principles to daily life. The Greek and Russian Orthodox faiths strictly follow ancient rites and teachings of the early Christian Church.

The Greek and Russian Orthodox Churches grew out of a split between the Roman Catholic Church and the Christian Church of the Byzantine Empire in 1054. The split resulted from the breakup of the Roman Empire and controversies including the use of icons, or sacred images, and the role of the pope. The Greek Orthodox Church is particularly known for its intricate mosaics and decorative icons. The Russian Orthodox Church has a long tradition of missionary work. Russian missionaries established Orthodox churches in Alaska during the late 1700s when Russians were settling in the region. In 1864 the first Orthodox church was established in the United States, in New Orleans. Orthodox churches, particularly in large cities, provided a community center and important services for immigrants.

MUSEUM OF THE CITY OF NEW YORK

INTERPRETING THE VISUAL RECORD

Americanization. For some immigrant children the process of Americanization began as soon as they arrived in the United States. ***How do the activities portrayed in this photo of immigrant children support this argument?***

CULTURAL DIVERSITY

Americanization. Americans conducted both public and private efforts to promote the Americanization of immigrants. The state of New Jersey provided civics and English language classes to newcomers. The North American Civic League conducted similar programs in many cities. The Immigrants Protective League offered such classes in Chicago, Illinois. Some businesses also provided English classes to immigrant workers.

CRITICAL THINKING Why might so many businesses and organizations have attempted to Americanize immigrants?

ANSWER: Some students might argue that businesses and organizations intended to assist immigrants. Others might claim that Americans feared or disliked the immigrants' native cultures.

VISUAL RECORD ANSWER

Students might mention that many of the children are holding American flags.

VISUAL RECORD ANSWER

(for p. 196)

Students might mention that he sells food.

TEACH OBJECTIVE 4

LEVEL 1: Have students work in pairs to identify and list the various cultural and economic reasons that nativists used to justify their opposition to immigration. *(Pairs should cite the following cultural reasons: immigrants had different religions, different languages, were held responsible for crime, poverty, violence, and radical politics; economic reasons: immigrants work cheaply to rob Americans of jobs and cause wages to be lowered.)* Ask students to share their lists with the class. Then lead a class discussion about the nativist response to immigration to the United States during the late 1800s. **Sheltered English, Cooperative Learning.**

LEVELS 2 AND 3: Tell students to imagine that they must create an editorial page for an urban newspaper during the late 1800s or early 1900s. Pair students and have each pair write an editorial that summarizes and points out potential problems with the nativist view of immigration. *(See the Level 1 lesson for the correct nativist views.)* Tell students to also draw a political cartoon that is critical of the nativist response to immigration. Have volunteers share their editorial pages with the class. **Cooperative Learning**

▶**ASSIGNMENT:** *Distribute Cartoon 14, Attitudes Toward Immigration, from* ***American History Political Cartoons.*** *Have each student study the cartoon and answer the accompanying questions.*

PEOPLE IN HISTORY

Dennis Kearney. Dennis Kearney was born in Ireland in 1847 and became a sailor as a boy. In 1872 he moved to San Francisco, became an American citizen, and opened a trucking business. Although he lacked a formal education, Kearney enjoyed reading and publicly debating social issues. He initially supported Chinese immigration, but later led the call for legislation excluding the Chinese from the United States. In his speeches, Kearney bitterly condemned journalists, businessmen, and lawyers as the enemies of the working class, and demanded an end to Chinese immigration.

CRITICAL THINKING Why might Kearney, himself an immigrant, have opposed Chinese immigration?

ANSWER: Students might point to his fear of economic competition from the Chinese.

The American Nation **VIDEO PROGRAM**

Community Ties: San Francisco's Chinatown; Teacher's Guide, pp. 75–80

Search 40729, Play to 48257
Videodisc 1, Side B

Play

Pause

See *Teacher's Guide* for Spanish barcode.

This seamstress is using a sewing machine in a New York City sweatshop.

immigrants cherished their ties to the old country. By contrast, their children often adopted American cultural practices and tended to view their parents' old-world language and customs as old-fashioned. A second-generation Polish immigrant expressed bittersweet feelings about his parents' way of life. It was, he noted, "a slowly decaying world of aged folks living largely in a dream. One day it would pass and then there would remain only Americans whose forebears had once been Poles."

The immigrant worker. Whether they adopted American habits or remained tied to the traditions of their homeland, most new immigrants shared a common work experience. Many did the country's "dirty work."

Whether in construction, mines, or sweatshops, most immigrants found their work to be difficult. The labor was physically exhausting. Hours were long, and wages were low. At the age of 15, Sadie Frowne began working in a garment factory in Brooklyn, New York. In 1902, Frowne recalled:

> **"The machines go like mad all day, because the faster you work the more money you get. Sometimes in my haste I get my finger caught and the needle goes right through it. . . . At the end of the day one feels so weak that there is a great temptation to lie right down and sleep."**

Some immigrants worked as many as 15 hours a day to earn a living wage. Even the best-paid workers made little more than the minimum necessary to support themselves and their families.

✔ **READING CHECK:** Where did new immigrants find assistance?

INTERPRETING THE VISUAL RECORD

Chinese immigrants. Barred from many occupations, Chinese immigrants often opened their own businesses. ***What services does this Chinese American merchant provide to his community?***

The Nativist Response

Immigrant workers played an important role in running the factories that contributed to a strong U.S. economy. Nevertheless, many native-born Americans saw immigration as a threat. They agreed with poet Thomas Bailey Aldrich, who warned against a "wild motley [ragged] throng [crowd]." He argued that immigrants brought "unknown gods and rites" and spoke "accents of menace." Many saw these newcomers as too different to fit into American society. Others went further, blaming immigrants for social problems such as crime, poverty, and violence as well as for spreading radical political ideas.

Nativists also opposed immigration for economic reasons. Many charged that the immigrants' willingness to work cheaply robbed native-born Americans of jobs and lowered wages for all. Supported by nativist workers, labor unions began demanding restrictions on immigration. Nativists achieved the greatest success in the West.

Chinese exclusion. For years Chinese laborers had been tolerated—and taken advantage of—on the West Coast, particularly in California. However, as unemployment mounted following the Panic of 1873 workers grew less tolerant. The new Workingmen's Party of California angrily cried, "The Chinese must go." The party leader, Dennis Kearney, was himself an Irish immigrant. He addressed crowds across the state, exciting them with his vicious speeches. Mobs attacked the Chinese, killing some and burning the property of others.

REVIEW

Have students complete the **Section 1 Review** on p. 197.

ASSESS

Have students complete **Daily Quiz 6.1**. As **Alternative Assessment**, you may want to use the crossword puzzle or letter to a friend or relative in this section's lessons.

RETEACH

Have students complete **Main Idea Activity for Reteaching and Sheltered English 6.1**. Then organize students into triads. Have each triad create an illustrated outline of Section 1. Display triads' outlines around the classroom. **Sheltered English, Cooperative Learning**

EXTEND

Have students conduct research on nativist activities in the late 1800s and early 1900s. In addition to examining the Immigration Restriction League, students might analyze the American Protective Association, the Chinese Exclusion Act, or conflicts between native-born and immigrant workers in industries such as coal mining. Have each student share his or her findings in a report or narrative. **Block Scheduling**

Leaders of California's Chinese community appealed to the authorities for protection. Help, however, was not forthcoming. In fact, the state's political leaders responded by amending the state constitution to forbid Chinese residents to own property or work at certain jobs.

In 1882 Congress passed the **Chinese Exclusion Act**, which denied citizenship to people born in China and prohibited the immigration of Chinese laborers. The act made conditions worse for Chinese Americans. In 1885 a mob in Rock Springs, Wyoming Territory, murdered 28 Chinese and drove out hundreds more. Neither the Chinese Exclusion Act nor the violence completely stopped Chinese immigrants from coming to the United States. Many Chinese immigrants still came to the United States only to be held for months at immigration stations.

INTERPRETING THE VISUAL RECORD

Nativist response. Nativists believed that immigration led to increasing social problems and robbed native-born workers of jobs. ***How does this 1870 cartoon satirize the nativist reaction to Chinese immigration?***

Immigration Restriction League. Immigrants endured additional discrimination as new organizations took up the anti-immigration cause. Founded in 1894 by wealthy Bostonians, the **Immigration Restriction League** sought to impose a literacy test on all immigrants. Congress passed such a measure, but President Grover Cleveland vetoed it, calling it "illiberal, narrow, and un-American." Over the next several years Congress tried several times—without success—to pass a similar measure. Despite efforts to impose restrictions, immigration continued. Contrary to nativists' arguments, the new immigrants made positive contributions to American society. The rapid industrialization of the United States in the late 1800s would have been impossible without immigrant workers. Their varied cultures also added new dimensions to American life.

✔ **READING CHECK:** Why did nativists oppose new immigration?

SECTION  REVIEW

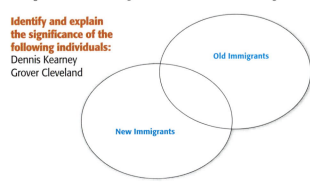

Define and explain the significance of the following terms:
old immigrants
new immigrants
steerage
benevolent societies
Chinese Exclusion Act
Immigration Restriction League

Identify and explain the significance of the following individuals:
Dennis Kearney
Grover Cleveland

1. **Using Graphic Organizers** Copy the graphic organizer below. Use it to describe the differences and similarities of the old immigrants and the new immigrants.

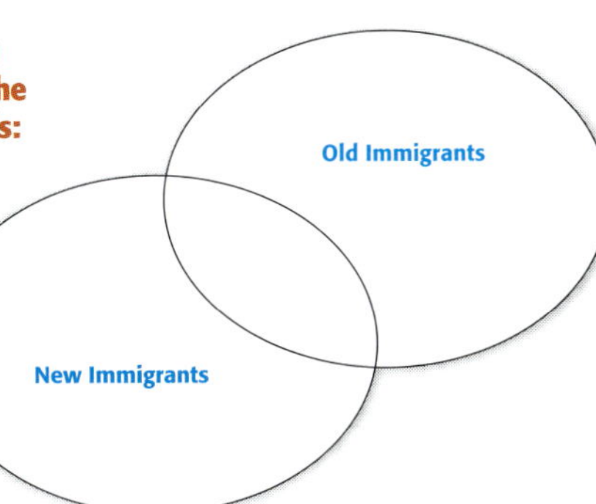

2. **Using Historical Imagination** Imagine that you are a recent immigrant to the United States in 1900. What aspects of the journey to the United States and the adjustment to American life do you think were most difficult?
3. **Analyzing** Where did immigrants find assistance in adjusting to American life?
4. **Assessing Consequences** How did the new immigrants contribute to making American society more diverse?

Critical Thinking

5. Imagine that you are a member of Congress arguing against nativist legislation like the Chinese Exclusion Act. What arguments could be made to support your cause?
Consider:
• how immigrants have contributed to U.S. history
• why the Chinese were singled out for exclusion
• how the Chinese contributed to American life

VISUAL RECORD ANSWER

Students might suggest that the cartoon shows the nativists barely escaping over the wall before they kick the ladder away from it.

Define and Identify
For significance, see the following pages:
- old immigrants, p. 192
- new immigrants, p. 192
- steerage, p. 193
- benevolent societies, p. 195
- Dennis Kearney, p. 196
- Chinese Exclusion Act, p. 197
- Immigration Restriction League, p. 197
- Grover Cleveland, p. 197

1. differences–countries of origin; similarities–reasons for immigrating to the United States
2. Answers will vary. Students might mention the experience of steerage, poor living conditions, or nativist attacks.
3. from religious institutions and benevolent societies
4. They brought cultural practices from their native countries.
5. Answers will vary. Arguments should include a discussion of the economic and cultural benefits that the Chinese contributed to the United States and should discuss racism aimed at the Chinese.

SECTION 2

After completing Section 2, students should be able to:

OBJECTIVE 1 *Analyze how technological innovations altered the urban landscape.*

OBJECTIVE 2 *Discuss the social values that the new class of wealthy city-dwellers expressed.*

OBJECTIVE 3 *Explain how life changed for middle-class Americans during the late 1800s.*

OBJECTIVE 4 *Describe what urban life was like for the poorest city-dwellers.*

OBJECTIVE 5 *Identify how social reformers used settlement houses and churches to improve the lives of the poor.*

LET'S GET STARTED!

Write the following phrase on the chalkboard: *urban life.* As students enter the classroom, ask them to respond to the phrase in writing, identifying the images and ideas that it evokes on a personal level. Ask volunteers to share their responses. Tell students that in Section 2 they will learn more about how urban developments in the late 1800s have affected modern-day cities.

SECTION 2 RESOURCES

PRINT
- Guided Reading Strategy 6.2
- American History Political Cartoon 15: Urban Life
- Literature Reading 6: A New Social Class
- Graphic Organizer Activity 6: Daily Life in the Cities
- Section 2 Review, p. 204
- Daily Quiz 6.2

MULTIMEDIA
- One-Stop Planner, Lesson 6.2
- Holt Researcher: American History CD–ROM
- HRW Web site

SHELTERED ENGLISH
- Main Idea Activity for Reteaching and Sheltered English 6.2

✔ READING TO UNDERSTAND
To help students master the section objectives, have them answer the **READING CHECKS** and complete **Guided Reading Strategy 6.2** as they read the section.

The Urban World

OBJECTIVES

Read to understand:
1. how technological innovations altered the urban landscape
2. what social values the new class of wealthy city-dwellers expressed
3. how life changed for middle-class Americans during the late 1800s
4. what urban life was like for the poorest city-dwellers
5. how social reformers used settlement houses and churches to improve the lives of the poor

KEY TERMS

skyscrapers
mass transit
suburbs
nouveau riche
conspicuous consumption
tenements
settlement houses
Social Gospel

KEY PEOPLE

Elisha Otis
Jane Addams
Janie Porter Barrett
Caroline Bartlett

"The rushing streams of commerce have worn many a deep and rugged chasm. Each of these canyons is closed in by a long frontage of towering cliffs, and these soaring walls of brick and limestone and granite rise higher and higher with each succeeding year."

—Henry Blake Fuller

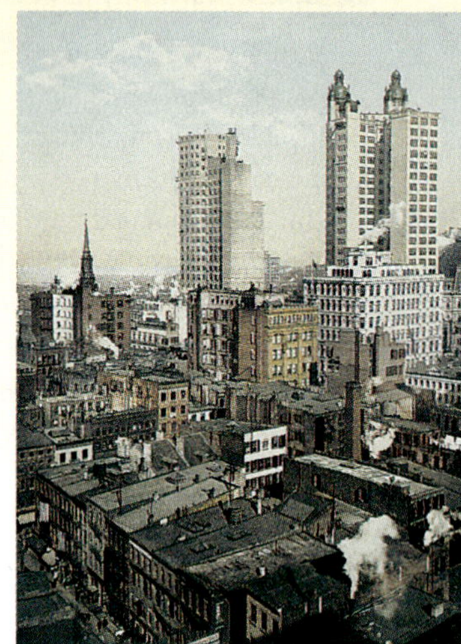

New York City in 1901

Henry Blake Fuller of Chicago described the emergence of the multistory buildings in his 1893 novel, *The Cliff-Dwellers.* During the late 1800s U.S. cities experienced "growing pains" as a result of a massive increase in population. Horace Greeley summed up the problem when he wrote, "We cannot all live in cities, yet nearly all seem determined to do so." New technological developments, such as multistory buildings, changed life for many residents in America's growing cities. The construction of tall buildings also greatly altered the urban landscape.

The Changing City

Before the Second Industrial Revolution, cities were compact. Few buildings were taller than three or four stories. Even in the largest cities, most people lived less than a 45-minute walk from the city center. By the late 1800s new technological innovations and a flood of immigrants began to transform the urban landscape. Between 1865 and 1900, the percentage of Americans living in cities doubled, from 20 percent to 40 percent. This population growth had a wide-ranging impact on urban life in the United States. Improvements in technology contributed to the increase of people living in cities.

In order for urban centers to accommodate the growing number of residents, architects needed to build **skyscrapers**, or large, multistory buildings. The height of buildings had previously been limited to some five stories, the number of flights of stairs that most people could comfortably climb. In 1853 Elisha Otis solved this problem with the development of the mechanized elevator. The elevator allowed architects to construct buildings well above the former five-story limit.

The use of masonry walls to support the entire weight of structures had also limited building height. Architects solved this problem by developing steel frames for buildings. The steel frame relieved the walls from the burden of carrying the weight of the building. It also allowed buildings to be built to new heights and with more windows and less wall space devoted to supporting the building. The introduction of the skyscraper transformed city life by accommodating a greater concentration of workers in the central business districts.

While skyscrapers extended cities upward, the development of **mass transit** extended U.S. cities outward. Mass transit included forms of public transportation such as electric commuter trains, subways, and trolley cars. Prior to the

The Flatiron Building's internal steel skeleton is visible.

TEACH OBJECTIVE 1

LEVEL 1: Pair students and tell them to imagine that they are newspaper reporters. Ask each pair to create three headlines to describe how technological innovations altered the urban landscape. *(Pairs' headlines should note that steel frames and the elevator allowed architects to construct taller buildings, and mass transit enabled cities to expand outward.)* Ask volunteers to read their headlines to the class.
Sheltered English, Cooperative Learning

LEVEL 2: Have students study the photographs of cities on this page and the previous page. Then have each student create a detailed sketch of a fictional city block in 1899. Ask students to annotate their drawings with captions explaining how technological innovations changed the urban landscape. *(See the Level 1 lesson for the correct innovations and their effects.)* Students may wish to include their annotated sketches in their portfolios.

LEVEL 3: Tell students to imagine that they are living in a busy city during the late 1800s. Have each student write a letter to a family member living in a rural area to describe technological innovations and their impact on the urban landscape. *(See the Level 1 lesson for the correct innovations and their effects.)* Ask volunteers to read their letters to the class.

development of mass transit, a typical city covered about three square miles. Such a city extended as far as a person could travel walking in a few hours. With the development of mass transit, workers no longer had to live within walking distance of jobs or markets. With the growth of mass transit systems, some urban areas expanded to cover as much as 20 square miles.

Frank J. Sprague, an electrical engineer who had worked with Thomas Edison, designed one of the first mass transit systems. Sprague's electric trolley, or streetcar, began serving Richmond, Virginia, in 1887. Other cities quickly adopted the invention. By 1895 the nation boasted over 10,000 miles of electric railways.

INTERPRETING THE VISUAL RECORD

Electric streetcars. Streetcars such as this one in New York City provided transportation to areas previously outside the city limits. ***What social background do you think the passengers of this streetcar were from?***

The expansion of transportation to areas beyond the urban center led to the growth of **suburbs**—residential neighborhoods on the outskirts of a city. Commuter railroads offered the first chance for wealthy residents to settle outside the built-up city core. The daily fares of 15 to 25 cents had effectively excluded the working classes and poor from suburban life. The expansion of streetcar transportation made commuting and, in turn, suburban life more affordable. The five-cent flat-rate fares charged by some transit companies allowed middle-class office workers and some skilled laborers the opportunity to leave the city. Mass transit altered urban life by helping create suburbs. One Philadelphia resident argued that the streetcar encouraged the "spread of the city over a vast space, with all the advantages of compactness and also the advantages of pure air, gardens, and rural pleasure."

✔ **READING CHECK:** How did technological innovations alter the urban landscape?

Growth of Cities, 1880–1900

Learning from Maps The population of urban centers grew significantly between 1880 and 1900.

REGION Which region had the greatest number of large cities in both 1880 and 1900?

Urban Population
- 50,000–100,000
- 100,000–300,000
- 300,000–1,000,000
- More than 1,000,000

1880

1900

TECHNOLOGY AND SOCIETY

City Traffic. From August to December 1906, the Minneapolis city engineer conducted traffic surveys. These surveys revealed that on an average day, 786 bicycles, 183 cars, and 2,722 horse-drawn vehicles traveled the city's streets.

ACTIVITY: Tell students to imagine that it is 1906 and that they are standing on a Minneapolis street corner. Have each student write a short description of the scene.

internet connect

TOPIC: Louis Sullivan
GO TO: go.hrw.com
KEYWORD: SE1 Sullivan

Have students access the Internet through the HRW Web site to conduct research on Louis Sullivan and his architecture. Then have each student create a scale drawing of the front of a hypothetical building based on Sullivan's architectural style. Ask students to write a short essay explaining how their buildings illustrate Sullivan's work principles.

VISUAL RECORD ANSWER

Students might suggest that based on clothing, the passengers are probably from the middle or upper-middle class.

MAP ANSWER

the East

TEACH OBJECTIVE 2

LEVEL 1: Tell students to imagine that they are editors of a school textbook. Pair students and have each pair create an outline for a section on the social values of the upper classes in the early 1900s. *(Outlines should show conspicuous consumption and imitation of British Victorian culture to be main topics; subtopics for conspicuous consumption include ostentatious homes, extravagant balls, and philanthropy; subtopics for British Victorian culture include obsession with maintain proper decorum, role of women as homemakers.)* Have volunteers read their outlines to the class.
Sheltered English, Cooperative Learning

LEVELS 2 AND 3: Have students work in groups of three or four to prepare an issue of a magazine designed to express the social values of wealthy city-dwellers during the early 1900s. *(See the Level 1 lesson for the correct upper-class values).* Have each group prepare interviews, pictures, and news stories on social events such as a debutante ball, and present etiquette advice. Have each group assemble its magazine, create a title for it, and prepare a cover. Have students display their magazines and present them to the class. **Cooperative Learning**

PEOPLE IN HISTORY

Thorstein Veblen.
Thorstein Veblen was born in Wisconsin in 1857, the son of very poor Norwegian immigrants. The family moved to Minnesota eight years later. Veblen's father insisted that his son receive an education, so Veblen attended Carleton College, where people viewed him as a strange and unpleasant young man. Unable to find a job after receiving a doctoral degree from Yale in 1884, Veblen returned to the Minnesota farm. The next years were extremely unhappy ones for him. In 1891, desperate to do something with his life, Veblen went to Cornell College. Once again, people saw him as an odd outsider—he arrived wearing a coonskin cap. However, he quickly achieved prominence, publishing his most famous work, *The Theory of the Leisure Class*, in 1899.

CRITICAL THINKING How might Veblen's background have shaped his thought?

ANSWER: Students might suggest that his rural upbringing and his status as an outsider made him a keen observer of American society.

VISUAL RECORD ANSWER

Students might mention that it shows the expensive and elegant furniture and accessories in the house.

INTERPRETING THE VISUAL RECORD

Nouveau riche. After earning vast fortunes in new industries such as railroads and steel manufacturing, wealthy urban residents built large, elaborately decorated homes. ***How does this photograph of Cornelius Vanderbilt's New York City home reflect his enormous wealth?***

Upper-Class Life

As the landscape of U.S. cities evolved, the social habits of city-dwellers were also changing. During the late 1800s a new class of wealthy city-dwellers emerged. Distinguished by their social values, these Americans became known as the **nouveau riche** (noo-voh REESH), a French term meaning "newly rich." There had been wealthy people in America since colonial times. However, the urban upper class of the late 1800s was a new breed. The nouveau riche—individuals like Andrew Carnegie, John D. Rockefeller, and Cornelius Vanderbilt—made their money in new industries, such as steel, mining, or railroads. Their quickly earned fortunes usually dwarfed those of the old upper-class bankers, landowners, and merchants.

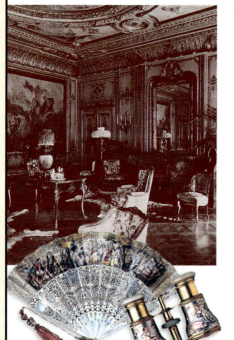

Some upper-class urban residents carried accessories such as this fan and pair of opera glasses when in public.

Conspicuous consumption.

Many members of this nouveau riche class of city-dwellers made an effort to publicly display their wealth. For the newly rich, author William Dean Howells noted sarcastically, "The dollar is the measure of every value, the stamp of every success." Many of the nouveau riche spent their great wealth freely so that everyone would know how successful they were. Social scientist Thorstein Veblen labeled this behavior **conspicuous consumption**.

Elegant residential streets such as New York City's Fifth Avenue served as showcases for the wealth of the nouveau riche. They built large houses whose design imitated Gothic castles or Italian Renaissance palaces. Andrew Carnegie even purchased an actual Scottish castle. In the summer the urban wealthy class left their city homes for equally magnificent country estates. The nouveau riche thought nothing of paying thousands of dollars to stage one night's amusement. Mr. and Mrs. Bradley Martin of New York, for example, once hosted a fancy ball at the Waldorf-Astoria Hotel in 1897 that was estimated to cost $370,000.

Many Americans criticized such extravagances. Ward McAllister, a lawyer and member of the "Four Hundred"—the wealthiest group of New York's upper class—came to their defense. "The mistake made by the world at large is [in thinking] that fashionable people are selfish, frivolous, and indifferent [do not care about] to the welfare of their fellow creatures." Indeed, some wealthy people did support social causes. They gave money to art galleries, libraries, and museums; endowed universities; and established new opera companies, symphony orchestras, and theater groups. As critics quickly pointed out, however, not all rich men and women saw philanthropy as a way to do good. Some simply used it as another opportunity to display their wealth.

Imitating British Victorian culture.

While nouveau riche Americans were occupied with parading their wealth, many were also concerned with maintaining a proper level of social behavior. Many American members of the new upper class imitated the strict standards of social behavior and etiquette of British Victorian culture, which developed under the reign of Queen Victoria.

During the late 1800s magazines like *Godey's Lady's Book, The Ladies' Home Journal,* and *The Modern Housewife* instructed upper class Americans on how to behave properly while visiting social peers and dining. These publications governed marriage and home life in addition to setting standards for social interaction.

TEACH OBJECTIVE 3

ALL LEVELS: Conduct a brief discussion on changes in middle-class life during the late 1800s. To help students understand these changes, copy the following chart on the chalkboard, omitting the italicized answers. Have each student complete it. **Sheltered English**

▸ASSIGNMENT: *Have each student create an outline of the subsection entitled Middle-Class Life. Then have students write a brief paper comparing and contrasting middle-class life in the late 1800s and the late 1900s.*

MIDDLE-CLASS LIFE DURING THE LATE 1800s	
Change: Professionalization	**Change: Women's Lives**
created a demand for workers educated in specialized fields	*received more opportunities to work outside the home*
led to the establishment of professional schools and organizations	*lightened their domestic chores with sewing machines, servants, and so on*
expanded the middle class	*increased participation in cultural and social activities*

Victorian literature and instructive guides held up an ideal of domestic life. This ideal glorified the role of the woman as a homemaker. According to this vision, the home was the sole domain of the Victorian woman. Her responsibilities included organizing and decorating the home as well as offering moral and social guidance to her family. Although the Victorian woman had a certain moral authority within the home, her influence was typically limited to private life.

✔ **READING CHECK:** What social values did the new class of wealthy city-dwellers express?

Middle-Class Life

During the late 1800s the growth of new industries brought about an increase in the number of middle-class city-dwellers. As with the upper class, a middle class of doctors, lawyers, small-business owners, and teachers had existed since colonial times. However, by the late 1800s the rise of modern corporations had swelled the ranks of the middle class with accountants, clerks, engineers, managers, and salespeople.

Professionalization. New industries and a growing urban population created a huge demand for educated workers with a mastery of specialized fields. These fields included education, engineering, law, and medicine. Prior to the late 1800s, however, few standards or organizations existed to certify the professional standing of doctors, lawyers, teachers, or technicians. City-dwellers had few means for choosing truly skilled professionals.

During the 1870s and 1880s professional schools and organizations were formed to set standards, issue licenses, and review practices within specialized occupations. The creation of these schools and professional organizations gave more respect to these professions and their middle-class practitioners.

Middle-class women. Despite the demand for middle-class professionals, few women were permitted in professional occupations. Nevertheless, rapid urban growth did increase the opportunities for women to work outside the home. The Victorian-era upper class and earlier generations of middle-class Americans had viewed work outside the home as a male activity. The rise of big business, however, created a variety of new jobs, such as salesclerks, secretaries, and stenographers. Business owners increasingly hired young, single women to fill these positions, paying them lower wages than men. By 1910 some 35 percent of the nearly 2 million clerical workers were women.

Most married middle-class women, however, worked in the home. Smaller families, increased reliance on purchased goods, and new household technologies such as running water changed middle-class women's domestic work. For example,

teen Life: The Debutante Ball

Prior to the age of 17 or 18, teenagers from wealthy families were not usually included in social functions in the late 1800s, although they were trained in proper etiquette. Some upper class schools required students to take classes in "ballroom deportment," to prepare them to participate in formal dances as adults. Debutante balls, also called coming-out parties, marked the time when young women of upper-class Victorian social circles were formally presented and accepted as members of high society.

Debutante ball

Before a young woman's debut into society, she would spend weeks training. She would practice gracefully climbing in and out of a carriage, walking elegantly, and acting according to proper etiquette when dining, greeting guests, and being courted. "There were so many of these little rules to remember," explained Katherine Chorley, reflecting upon her Victorian childhood, "but we were drilled (by Nanny) so that it was no effort to remember them."

One of the main functions of the debutante ball was for young women to meet prospective husbands. Most Victorian socialites viewed marriage as the most important event in a woman's life. Young women involved in high society during the Victorian Age usually married within two or three years after their coming-out parties.

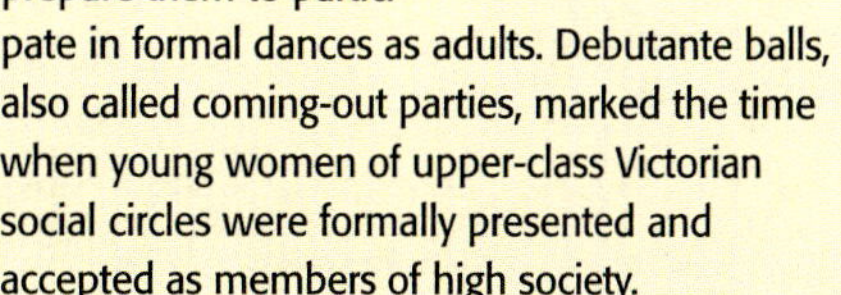

ECONOMIC DEVELOPMENT

Women and Work. In the early 1900s the entry of women into a given profession usually signaled the departure of men from that profession. Men did not want to compete with women because women usually received lower wages. In addition, the entry of women into a profession sometimes meant a decline in a job's status. Salesclerks, who were usually men, often had the authority to bargain with customers and purchase goods for the store. When department stores hired women to serve as clerks, however, the responsibilities of the position narrowed. Salesclerks were expected to do little more than display the merchandise and accept the customers' money.

CRITICAL THINKING What might the circumstances that women faced in the workplace have revealed about the status of women in American society during the early 1900s?

ANSWER: Students might suggest that many people still regarded women as second-class citizens who were not as capable as men.

TEACH OBJECTIVE 4

LEVEL 1: Have students work in pairs to list the conditions associated with the lives of the urban poor. *(Pairs' lists should include housing shortages, high rents, crowded tenements, raw sewage, garbage, and pollution from factories, spread of diseases, discrimination against African Americans.)* Then have each pair use its lists to create three or four protest signs that demand an improvement in the living conditions of the poor. Have volunteers present their protest signs to the class. **Sheltered English, Cooperative Learning**

LEVELS 2 AND 3: Tell students to imagine that they among the urban poor in the early 1900s. Have each student write a letter to his or her city alderman describing the conditions of life for the poor. *(See the Level 1 lesson for answers.)* The letter should conclude with a request that the alderman sponsor some program to improve the living conditions of the poor. Ask volunteers to read their letters to the class. Students may wish to include their letters in their portfolios.

ACROSS THE CURRICULUM

▶GEOGRAPHY◀

Housing and the Urban Poor. Not all poor Americans lived in tenements. In one area of Chicago, the urban poor lived in apartment blocks with less than three stories or even in small farm buildings. In one Philadelphia neighborhood, poor people lived in three- or four-story row houses; in a Boston neighborhood, they lived in two-story row houses in dirty alleys. In New York City, however, particularly the Lower East Side, tenements dominated the housing scene.

CRITICAL THINKING How might living in the Boston row houses have endangered residents' health?

ANSWER: Students might note that the Boston row houses were located in dirty alleys, thus creating sanitation problems that probably endangered residents' health.

VISUAL RECORD ANSWER

Students might suggest that the women are employed in clerical jobs.

VISUAL RECORD ANSWER

Students might suggest that the room looks crowded, and that family members are sitting on the bed.

INTERPRETING THE VISUAL RECORD

Middle-class women. The rapid growth of industry during the late 1800s created new opportunities for middle-class women to work outside the home. ***What type of work are these women employed in?***

the availability of ready-made clothing lightened the sewing loads of many middle-class women. The use of hot and cold running water meant that doing laundry no longer required pumping, hauling, and heating the water. Some middle-class families could afford to hire servants to handle many household chores. In such families, women had more free time to focus on their children and to take part in the growing number of cultural events in cities. Many women joined reading and social clubs. Others participated in and led reform movements.

✔ **READING CHECK:** How did life change for middle-class Americans during the late 1800s?

How the Poor Lived

Most city-dwellers lived worlds away from the comfort of the middle class or the luxury of the wealthy. Although industries and factories offered new opportunities to working-class men and women, the ever-growing population of laborers eager to work kept wages low. Living conditions for the working-class city-dwellers during the late 1800s were made worse by housing shortages and the rising cost of rent. To make ends meet, working-class families often had to rent out parts of their homes or apartments to boarders.

New York City served as a magnet for hundreds of thousands of immigrants and other migrants. Some 43,000 **tenements**—poorly built apartment buildings—housed more than 1.6 million poor New Yorkers in 1900—nearly half the city's population. These rundown buildings were usually clustered in poor neighborhoods. These neighborhoods were typically within walking distance of the factories, ports, and stockyards where many poor city-dwellers worked. The dark, airless tenements sometimes housed as many as 12 families per floor. Outside the crowded tenements, raw sewage and piles of garbage littered unpaved streets and alleys. Worse still, the slums usually adjoined industrial areas where factories belched pollution. "The stink is enough to knock you down," one New York resident complained. In such an environment, sickness and death were common.

INTERPRETING THE VISUAL RECORD

Tenements. In his study of the urban working class, Jacob Riis explained that an entire immigrant family would frequently live in a single room that served as the bedroom, parlor, and dining room. ***How does this photograph support Riis's description?***

Although all residents of poor neighborhoods faced grim conditions, African Americans typically experienced the greatest difficulties. Because of widespread discrimination, most could get only low-paying jobs. African Americans also had to pay outrageous rents for the most appalling apartments, and faced frequent police harassment. Yet many preferred living in the North to the South. As one African American journalist explained, "They sleep in peace at night; what they earn is paid them, if not they can appeal to the courts. They vote without fear of the shot-gun, and their children go to school."

✔ **READING CHECK:** What was urban life like for the poorest Americans?

TEACH OBJECTIVE 5

LEVEL 1: Have students work in pairs to create a graphic organizer that shows the similarities and differences between settlement houses and churches of the Social Gospel movement. *(Pairs' organizers should note the following: similarities—both offered various educational and cultural opportunities for adults and children, both were committed to improving living conditions of the poor; differences—churches of the Social Gospel movement based their activities on Christian principles, while settlement houses were nonreligious/secular).* Ask volunteers to present their organizers to the class. Then lead a class discussion about the work of social reformers in settlement houses and in churches during the Social Gospel movement. **Sheltered English, Cooperative Learning**

LEVELS 2 AND 3: Have students work in pairs to create separate pamphlets that describe and promote the activities and programs sponsored by settlement houses and churches of the Social Gospel movement. *(See the Level 1 lesson for answers.)* Have volunteers share their pamphlets with the class. **Cooperative Learning**

▶**ASSIGNMENT:** *Tell students to imagine that they are settlement house leaders or church officials who are preparing to retire after a long career that stretched from the late 1800s to the early 1900s. Have each student write a short memoir assessing his or her efforts to improve the lives of the poor.*

The Drive for Reform

In the late 1800s few government programs existed to help the poor. What assistance the poor received was limited to charitable handouts of food and clothing. Some idealistic young Americans were certain that more must be done to assist poor city-dwellers.

The settlement houses. To confront the problem of urban poverty head-on, some reformers established and lived in **settlement houses**—community service centers—in poor neighborhoods. Settlement houses offered educational opportunities, skills training, and cultural events to neighborhood residents. Jane Addams was at the forefront of the American settlement-house movement.

Jane Addams

Jane Addams was born in 1860 to a wealthy family in Cedarville, Illinois. There, she grew up in an atmosphere of politics and philanthropy. Her Quaker father was a strong abolitionist. As a state senator he had worked to pass social reform legislation. The young Addams set out to be a doctor. A back problem, however, ended her studies. She eventually decided to dedicate her life to helping the urban poor.

Addams began her settlement-house work in 1889. She and Ellen Gates Starr established Hull House, located in a run-down mansion in one of Chicago's immigrant neighborhoods. The early days of Hull House were busy. "Memory of the first years at Hull-House is more or less blurred with fatigue," Addams recalled.

Addams founded the settlement house with the ambition of providing social and cultural services to needy Americans. In her memoir, *Twenty Years at Hull-House,* she elaborated:

> **"The Settlement casts aside none of those things which cultivated men have come to consider reasonable and goodly, but it insists that those belong as well to that great body of people who, because of toilsome [hard-working] and underpaid labor, are unable to procure [obtain] them for themselves."**

Addams's central goals were to provide educational and cultural opportunities to the poor and to improve living conditions in the neighborhoods. She also hoped that Hull House would provide fulfilling careers for settlement-house volunteers, who were mostly young women. She expected that for "young women who had been given over too exclusively to study," Hull House "might restore a balance of activity" and help them "learn of life from life itself."

The volunteers who joined Addams were mostly young, college-educated women. They set up a day nursery and kindergarten for the children of working mothers and gave adult-education classes. The experience gained at settlement houses provided the women with the skills and knowledge to make important contributions to social reform and politics.

In time, Addams's work expanded to include other important causes. She tirelessly promoted women's suffrage and

Read More About It

Free Find:
Jane Addams

After reading about Jane Addams on the **Holt Researcher** CD–ROM, create a list of community services you would provide if you worked in a settlement house.

INTERPRETING THE VISUAL RECORD

Hull House. Jane Addams recorded in her memoir how she and other volunteers at Hull House provided important services such as day care and education for immigrants. ***How do you think these immigrant children benefited from the settlement house?***

HISTORY MAKERS SPEAK

Dorothea Moore in *Eighty Years at Hull-House*

Life at Hull House. Social worker Dorothea Moore described Hull House in an 1897 article. "Hull-House stands not so much for a solution as a place of exchange. . . . This is the heart of the movement. This is the reason for the settlement. . . . It must help that direct human touch of richer with poorer, wise with simple, learned with untaught, dynamic with static which has for its aim the realization by all the children of their kinship with the great family."

CRITICAL THINKING What did Moore regard as the true importance of Hull House?

ANSWER: Students might suggest that Moore regarded "exchange," or interaction, as the true significance of Hull House. It brings people of diverse backgrounds together in a positive environment.

VISUAL RECORD ANSWER

Students might suggest that they benefited by receiving the opportunity to interact with other children.

REVIEW

Have students complete the **Section 2 Review** on p. 204.

ASSESS

Have students complete **Daily Quiz 6.2**. As **Alternative Assessment**, you may want to use the protest signs or letter to the city alderman in this section's lessons.

RETEACH

Have students complete **Main Idea Activity for Reteaching and Sheltered English 6.2**. Tell students to reread the Section 2 objectives. Then have each student write a summary sentence or paragraph for each of the objectives. Students' summaries should clearly address the stated objectives and should synthesize information from the textbook. **Sheltered English**

EXTEND

Have students locate and read an article or book by an important figure associated with events and trends depicted in this section, such as Jane Addams, Thorstein Veblen, W.E.B. DuBois, Andrew Carnegie, or Charles Sheldon. Then ask each student to comment on his or her chosen figure and article or book in a written report. Have volunteers read their reports to the class. **Block Scheduling**

SECTION 2 REVIEW ANSWERS

Define and Identify

For significance, see the following pages:

- skyscrapers, p. 198
- Elisha Otis, p. 198
- mass transit, p. 198
- suburbs, p. 199
- nouveau riche, p. 200
- conspicuous consumption, p. 200
- tenements, p. 202
- settlement houses, p. 203
- Jane Addams, p. 203
- Janie Porter Barrett, p. 204
- Social Gospel, p. 204
- Caroline Bartlett, p. 204

1. upper class–conspicuous consumption; middle class–professionals with some interest in reform; poor–hard lives with few opportunities

2. grew tall with skyscrapers and outward with transportation such as streetcars

3. made possible the expansion of cities and the growth of suburbs

4. different–Addams had political interests, while Bartlett was motivated by religion; similar–offered aid and assistance to the poor

5. Answers will vary. Students should note that cities offered new jobs, but also harsh living conditions for the poor. Students might also mention that cities grew in size in the late 1800s, indicating that most people saw them as sources of opportunity.

INTERPRETING THE VISUAL RECORD

Kindergarten. Acting in accordance with the Social Gospel, Caroline Bartlett organized kindergarten classes and other public services out of her People's Church in Kalamazoo, Michigan. ***What public services does this kindergarten class provide to the community of Kalamazoo?***

served as president of the Women's International League for Peace and Freedom from 1919 until her death in 1935. Worldwide recognition for her efforts came in 1931, when she was awarded the Nobel Peace Prize.

Hull House served as a model for others hoping to aid the poor. In 1890 African American teacher Janie Porter Barrett founded one of the first African American settlement houses—the Locust Street Social Settlement—in Hampton, Virginia. Three years later, Lillian Wald started the Henry Street Settlement on New York's Lower East Side. By the end of the century, nearly 100 settlement houses had opened across the country.

The Social Gospel movement. At the same time that the settlement houses began their work, a number of Protestant ministers joined the battle against poverty. They developed the idea of the **Social Gospel**, which called for people to apply Christian principles to address social problems. Washington Gladden, a Congregational minister in Columbus, Ohio, was an early leader of the Social Gospel movement. Arguing that the church had a moral duty to confront social injustice, Gladden led crusades to improve conditions for industrial workers.

Many churches attempted to act according to the Social Gospel by providing classes, counseling, job training, libraries, and other social services. Caroline Bartlett's People's Church in Kalamazoo, Michigan, was one such church. Bartlett became a Unitarian minister in 1889, the same year she began her work at what became the People's Church. Drawing on Social Gospel ideals, Bartlett threw open the doors of her church seven days a week. She established a free public kindergarten and a gymnasium and offered classes in domestic and industrial skills. Bartlett also set up a meals program for workers and sponsored creative activities.

✔ **READING CHECK:** How did social reformers use settlement houses and churches to improve the lives of the urban poor?

SECTION 2 REVIEW

Define and explain the significance of the following terms:
skyscrapers
mass transit
suburbs
nouveau riche
conspicuous consumption
tenements
settlement houses
Social Gospel

Identify and explain the significance of the following individuals:
Elisha Otis
Jane Addams
Janie Porter Barrett
Caroline Bartlett

1. **Using Graphic Organizers** Copy the graphic organizer below. Use it to describe the class divisions that developed in the cities and what characteristics distinguished the different social groups.

2. **Understanding Geography: Human-Environment Interaction** In what ways did the physical landscape of U.S. cities change in the late 1800s?
3. **Assessing Consequences** How did new technological developments change city life?
4. **Comparing and Contrasting** How was the work of Jane Addams at Hull House and Caroline Bartlett at the People's Church similar? How was it different?

Critical Thinking

5. Did city life in the late 1800s offer more opportunities or more limitations for most residents? Explain your answer.
Consider:
- what opportunities the city offered
- what limitations the city imposed
- whether most city residents experienced more limits or more opportunities

SECTION 3

After completing Section 3, students should be able to:

OBJECTIVE 1 *Understand how public education and colleges changed in the late 1800s.*

OBJECTIVE 2 *Explain how publishers appealed to readers.*

OBJECTIVE 3 *Discuss how outdoor activities and sports provided a source of leisure for Americans.*

OBJECTIVE 4 *Describe the new forms of popular music and theater that developed in the late 1800s.*

LET'S GET STARTED!

As students enter the classroom, play Selection 18, "Twilight Rag," from the **American Music Audio CD Program.** Ask students to respond to the song in writing. Then tell students "Twilight Rag" is by Scott Joplin, an African American composer whose work had a great influence on American music. Tell students that in Section 3 they will learn about American culture, both popular and sophisticated, during the late 1800s and early 1900s.

Daily Life in the Cities

OBJECTIVES

Read to understand:

1. how public education and colleges changed in the late 1800s
2. how publishers appealed to readers
3. how outdoor activities and sports provided a source of leisure for Americans
4. what new forms of popular music and theater developed in the late 1800s

KEY TERMS

compulsory education laws
yellow journalism
City Beautiful movement
vaudeville
ragtime

KEY PEOPLE

John Dewey
Frederick Law Olmsted
Walter Camp
James Naismith
Edwin Booth
Scott Joplin

"It must be admitted unhesitatingly that we are only just learning how to play. We steal away for our holidays . . . determined to rest and take life at its easiest. We promise ourselves to forswear all thoughts of business and the outer world."

—Caspar W. Whitney

The Sail Boat Pond, Central Park, New York City.

Relaxing in a city park

Caspar W. Whitney thus described Americans' changing views of leisure in the late 1800s. The incredible pace of industrialization and urban growth greatly affected daily life in U.S. cities. The daily struggles of work and crowded living conditions prompted many city-dwellers to seek leisure activities. Many urban residents relaxed in new city parks. They enjoyed watching and playing sports, attended new musical and theater shows, and found leisure through reading daily newspapers and literature.

Education

U.S. cities grew rapidly during the late 1800s. Urban life became increasingly difficult for workers and those with little education. To aid the urban working class, social reformers worked to expand educational opportunities.

Few children had access to public education during the early 1800s. Noting the steady growth of U.S. cities, reformers urged the expansion of public schools to educate this new population of urban children. The movement gained momentum after 1860, as more and more states began to pass **compulsory education laws**—laws requiring parents to send children to school. From 1870 to 1900, the number of students in school grew from some 7 million to more than 15 million—from 57 percent of the school-age population to 72 percent. Expenditures for these schools rose from about $63 million in 1870 to some $215 million in 1900.

As enrollments grew, educational reformers proposed that schools do more than teach reading, writing, and arithmetic by rote memorization. One of the main reformers was philosopher John Dewey. His "Laboratory School" at the University of Chicago stressed cooperative "learning by doing." He also emphasized art, history, and science. Ella Flagg Young, superintendent of schools in Chicago, worked with Dewey to fulfill his ideas. Most urban schools, however, were slow to adopt the new teaching methods.

Other reformers like William Torrey Harris and Elwood Cubberley stressed different issues. They believed that one essential function of public education was to instruct students in matters beyond reading and writing. They hoped to instruct students—particularly immigrant children—in proper behavior, civic loyalty, and American cultural values. Reformers like Cubberley

The expansion of public education required the construction of new public schools such as this one.

SECTION 3 RESOURCES

PRINT

- Guided Reading Strategy 6.3
- Biography Reading 6: Frederick Olmstead
- Section 3 Review, p. 211
- Daily Quiz 6.3

MULTIMEDIA

- One-Stop Planner, Lesson 6.3
- American Music Selection 18: "Twilight Rag"
- Holt Researcher: American History CD–ROM

SHELTERED ENGLISH

- Main Idea Activity for Reteaching and Sheltered English 6.3

✔ READING TO UNDERSTAND

To help students master the section objectives, have them answer the **READING CHECKS** and complete **Guided Reading Strategy 6.3** as they read the section.

Multimedia Resources

American Music Selection 18: "Twilight Rag"

TEACH OBJECTIVE 1

LEVEL 1: Have students work in pairs to identify the major changes in the public education and colleges after 1860. Then have pairs write topic sentences that summarize the changes in the educational system and their benefits. *(Pairs' sentences should mention the passage of compulsory education laws, new methods of teaching, an expanded curriculum and a greater number of colleges. Benefits included more students attending school, new subjects, new opportunities for higher education.)* Ask volunteers to read their topic sentences to the class. **Cooperative Learning, Sheltered English**

LEVELS 2 AND 3: Ask students to identify the changes in public education and colleges in the late 1800s. Then tell students to imagine that they are educational reformers in 1860. Have each student write a letter to the state board of education that advocates the changes that he or she has identified and explains how those changes will benefit students. *(See the Level 1 lesson for the correct changes and benefits.)* Ask students to read their letters to the class.

▶**ASSIGNMENT** *Have each student write a poem about how the public education system changed in the late 1800s.*

HISTORY MAKERS SPEAK

John Dewey in *Schools of Tomorrow*

Dewey on Education. John Dewey expressed some of his thoughts on education in a book co-written with Evelyn Dewey. "We exaggerate school learning compared with what is learned in the ordinary course of living. We are, however, to correct this exaggeration, not by despising school learning, but by looking into that extensive and more efficient training given by the ordinary course of events."

CRITICAL THINKING Why might Dewey have praised "training given by the ordinary course of events"?

ANSWER: Students might suggest that Dewey appreciated the educational benefits of everyday life.

STRATEGIES FOR SUCCESS ANSWERS

Practicing the Strategy

1. compulsory school laws
2. increased from some 7 million to some 15 million
3. founded schools and developed new educational theories
4. enrolled and taught in schools
5. became more available and included some reforms
6. strengths–tried to improve learning and offered more access for women; weaknesses–discriminated against minorities

This teacher instructs her students in a Washington, D.C., public school classroom in the early 1900s.

and Harris feared the effects of mass immigration. They hoped that public education would help cities avoid social unrest by instilling a sense of order and discipline in the immigrant and working-class students.

Even with this drive to teach American values, children of many different cultures in most public schools during this era remained segregated by race. Most schools for African American, Asian American, and Hispanic students were poorly equipped. State and local governments spent little money on them. The expansion of public schools, however, did create more opportunities for young women. In 1900 about 60 percent of high school graduates were female.

The number of American colleges and their enrollments also rose during this period. At the close of the Civil War, the United States had approximately 500 colleges. By 1900 that number had grown to 1,000 institutions. Meanwhile, the enrollment in American colleges had expanded from 50,000 to 350,000 students. Although more students began to seek higher levels of education, colleges remained primarily accessible to wealthy and upper-middle-class students.

✔ **READING CHECK:** How did public education and colleges change in the late 1800s?

Strategies for Success Analyzing

Much like comparing and contrasting, analyzing is a basic skill used in historical study. To *analyze* is to break a topic or issue down into its essential parts and examine the relationships between those parts. Analyzing enables one to gain a more complete understanding of a subject, particularly when the subject can be interpreted in varying ways. As a result, analyzing helps one to draw conclusions about the subject.

How to Analyze

1. **Identify the subject.** Identify the topic or issue that you wish to analyze. You may want to rephrase the topic or issue as a question to be answered.
2. **Examine the facts.** Examine each piece of information that your source material provides about the subject. Make sure to study any statistics or graphic information carefully.
3. **Examine different points of view.** If the subject can be interpreted in varying ways, identify the main idea expressed by each side. Then determine whether each idea is supported by facts, opinions, or a combination of both.
4. **Draw conclusions.** Use your examination of facts and ideas to draw conclusions and evaluate any different points of view. If you rephrased the subject for analysis as a question, answer it.

Applying the Strategy

Formulate a question about U.S. public education during the late 1800s. Then analyze the material in the subsection above entitled Education and answer your question.

Practicing the Strategy

Answer the following questions.

1. What new education laws did some states begin to pass after 1860?
2. How did school attendance figures change between 1870 and 1900?
3. What activities did educational reformers engage in during the late 1800s?
4. How did women participate in the public education system during the late 1800s?

Use your responses to answer the following questions.

5. How did U.S. public education change during the late 1800s?
6. What were the strengths and weaknesses of the public education system during the late 1800s?

TEACH OBJECTIVE 2

LEVEL 1: Organize the class into pairs. Have each pair compile a list of the ways in which newspaper and book publishers appealed to readers in the late 1800s and early 1900s. *(Pairs' lists should mention that newspaper publishers printed sensational news stories/"yellow journalism"; lavish illustrations and photographs; comic strips, including "The Yellow Kid"; advice columns; women's sections; and sports sections. Book publishers printed adventure stories, "Elsie Dinsmore" stories, realistic books about city life, and novels that focused on Christian principles.)* Ask volunteers to present their lists to the class. Conclude by leading a class discussion about the newspapers and books that appealed to readers during the late 1800s, and why these newspapers and books held such appeal. **Sheltered English, Cooperative Learning**

LEVELS 2 AND 3: Tell students to imagine that they are market analysts for the publishing industry during the late 1800s. Have each student prepare a market analysis report for his or her industry that describes how newspaper and book publishers appealed to readers and analyzes the popularity of certain newspaper features and novels. *(See the Level 1 lesson for the correct methods.)* Have volunteers present their reports to the class.

Publishing

The expansion of public education made newspapers and literature more important in the daily lives of many Americans. The growing number of students meant that by 1900 some 90 percent of Americans could read. This rise in literacy launched an age of publishing. Print media became the primary source of information for urban populations.

Popular journalism. Along with an increase in literacy, new developments in printing technology spurred a dramatic rise in the number of newspapers published during the late 1800s. During the 1870s and 1880s printers developed an inexpensive new type of paper that was durable enough to withstand high-speed printing. Using this paper allowed publishers to print a huge volume of newspapers. Between 1865 and 1910 the number of daily newspaper publications in the United States increased from about 500 to approximately 2,600. Circulation grew as these papers sold for just pennies each.

Daily newspapers in the same city often battled each other for a larger number of readers. The wildest circulation wars took place in New York between Joseph Pulitzer's *New York World* and William Randolph Hearst's *New York Journal.* To attract readers, publishers developed new journalistic practices. The *World* tried to win readers by running sensational news stories. It also used fancy illustrations and photographs. The *Journal* competed with even more sensational stories. Both papers attempted to appeal to a broad readership by including comic strips, advice columns, special women's sections, and separate sports sections.

The World

CRISPI ARRAIGNS THE JUDGES OF DREYFUS

BLIZZARD PARALYZES ALL NEW ENGLAND: THIRTY-SIX LIVES LOST AND $7,000,000 IN PROPERTY.

THE EARLY BIRD CATCHES THE WORM—NIT.

INTERPRETING THE VISUAL RECORD

Yellow journalism. Earning the name yellow journalism, newspapers such as the *New York World* published sensational stories and color cartoons like this one featuring "The Yellow Kid" to attract readers. ***What aspects of this cartoon might attract readers to the newspaper?***

The newspapers also competed for readers by publishing the popular comic series "The Yellow Kid," one of the first cartoons published in color. The lead character was a young tenement dweller who was dressed in a yellow gown and reflected stereotypes many Americans had about immigrants. The hugely popular cartoon inspired many critics to refer to the *World* and the *Journal's* style of sensational reporting as **yellow journalism**.

Literature. The publication of popular literature also experienced significant growth as a result of the increase of literacy among Americans. Dime and half-dime novels promoted by publishers like Erastus Beadle attempted to entice readers with adventure stories. Beadle wrote frontier novels such as *Deadly Eye* and *Spitfire Saul, the King of the Rustlers.* Martha Finley's stories about virtuous character Elsie Dinsmore gained a huge following among young girls.

Older readers favored realistic books about city life. For example, Edith Wharton's 1905 novel, *The House of Mirth,* describes the conflicts between New York City's nouveau riche and old upper class. Published in 1885, William Dean Howells's *Rise of Silas Lapham* weaves a tale of greed and social ambition.

CULTURAL DIVERSITY

Public Libraries. Public libraries expanded access to newspapers and books in the late 1800s. Early libraries tended to be organized as private reading rooms. In the mid-1800s, however, cities began to establish tax-supported public libraries. Historians regard the founding of the Boston Public Library in 1852 as the beginning of a large-scale trend. Although open to the public, many of the early public libraries served the interests of middle- and upper-class citizens. Librarians regarded it as their responsibility to provide readers with quality literature, often refusing to order dime novels and other pulp books that were popular with the working classes.

CRITICAL THINKING Why might librarians in early public libraries have wanted to order and stock only "good" novels?

ANSWER: Students might suggest that the librarians wanted to "improve" their patrons with "good" books.

VISUAL RECORD ANSWER

Students might point to its color, its vibrancy, and possibly its prejudicial portrait of Asian Americans.

TEACH OBJECTIVE 3

LEVEL 1: Have pairs of students create charts that list the different outdoor activities and spectator sports that engaged city-dwelling Americans in the late 1800s and explain how these activities provided sources of leisure for urban residents. *(Pairs' lists should mention that park excursions offered refuge from crowded city life; bicycling provided an activity for people who visited city parks, croquet was an activity for people who visited city parks; baseball and football attracted participants and spectators.)* Ask volunteers to present their charts to the class. Conclude by leading a class discussion about the outdoor activities and spectator sports that Americans enjoyed in the 1890s. **Cooperative Learning, Sheltered English**

LEVELS 2 AND 3: Tell students to imagine that they work for a large city's chamber of commerce or tourist bureau in the 1890s. Pair students and have pairs create brochures that list the leisure activities participated in by the city's residents as well as reasons why city residents find these activities to be appealing. *(See the Level 1 lesson for the correct reasons.)* Ask students to present their brochures to the class. **Cooperative Learning**

NOTE: For an additional teaching idea, see the Chapter 6 brainstorming lesson in the **Creative Teaching Strategies** handbook.

GEOGRAPHIC DIVERSITY

Central Park. Frederick Law Olmsted envisioned Central Park as a place where urban dwellers could enjoy nature. In accordance with this vision, he opposed most recreational activities in the park. Park officials allowed only those recreational activities that did not affect the park environment, such as boating.

CRITICAL THINKING How might Olmsted's vision of the park as a place to enjoy nature have benefited visitors even while limiting them?

ANSWER: Students might suggest that Olmsted's vision allowed visitors to enjoy the natural world but deprived them of certain recreational activities, such as baseball.

THAT'S INTERESTING!

In many cities, park development benefited only middle- and upper-class citizens. In Chicago's suburbs, for example, there were 1,500 acres of world-renowned parks. In three of the city's largest and poorest urban neighborhoods, however, there were no parks at all.

Then and Now

Amusement Parks

Advertisement for an amusement park on Coney Island

The original amusement parks of the late 1800s provided places for middle- and working-class families to find inexpensive leisure activities just outside the city. Borrowing ideas from the hugely popular world fairs like the 1893 Chicago Exposition, parks like Dreamland, Luna, and Steeplechase on Coney Island offered grand architecture, mechanical rides, small replicas of exotic places and foreign villages, daily theatrical shows, and re-enactments of current events. One journalist described the amusement parks of Coney Island as an "enchanted, story book land of . . . domes, minarets [towers], lagoons, and lofty aerial flights. . . . It was a world removed—shut away from the sordid clatter and turmoil of the streets."

Today's theme parks offer a similarly fantastic escape. While the price has risen from the 10-cent admission to Coney Island to more than $35 for one day's admission to many amusement parks, parks continue to provide a way for many Americans to retreat from everyday life into a world of fantasy. Disneyland founder Walt Disney once explained, "I don't want the public to see the world they live in while they're in Disneyland, I want them to feel they're in another world."

Frederick Law Olmsted's design for Central Park created a rural setting in the heart of New York City.

THE GRANGER COLLECTION, NEW YORK

The most commercially successful novels during the late 1800s, however, were ones that focused on Christian principles. Charles M. Sheldon's 1896 novel, *In His Steps,* was the era's most popular book, selling millions of copies. Sheldon depicted characters who addressed their personal problems by asking the question, "What would Jesus do?"

✔ **READING CHECK:** How did publishers appeal to readers?

Leisure Time in Urban Parks

During the late 1800s Americans increasingly counted on leisure activities to provide relief from busy city life. City planners developed large urban parks to offer a natural refuge from the crowded, built-up city. Urban residents eagerly used these parks as a space for relaxation where they could participate in a variety of new leisure activities.

In 1857 landscape architect Frederick Law Olmsted designed Central Park in New York City. He sought to create a rural setting within New York's urban environment. The park included pedestrian paths, ponds, and trees. Olmsted designed the 2.5-mile-long park for people of all social classes to gather and enjoy the natural landscape. In 1871 more than 10 million people visited the park—roughly 30,000 visitors each day.

Olmsted's success helped spur an American planning movement known as the **City Beautiful movement**. The movement adopted a number of ideas from a British planning movement called Garden City. Supporters of the City Beautiful movement stressed the importance of including public parks and attractive boulevards in the design of cities. Those city planners claimed that such designs could be a civilizing influence for city-dwellers.

Americans took advantage of those new city parks to pursue a variety of outdoor activities during this period. Bicycling became immensely popular among both men and women during the late 1800s. By the turn of the century about 4 million Americans were riding bicycles. Playing croquet in city parks was also popular among Americans. In this simple game, a player uses a mallet to drive a ball through a series of wire wickets, or small arches. Played on lawns and park grounds, croquet was a sociable sport that became a fashionable pastime for many middle-class women.

Leisure and Sports

During the late 1800s many Americans spent their leisure time playing the era's new organized sports. Many urban residents found sports like baseball and football exciting to play as well as watch. Afternoon games and matches became a regular activity

SPOTLIGHT on Baseball, Football, and Basketball

Have students select one of the following sports: baseball, football, or basketball. Ask students to conduct research on the history of their chosen sport. Then have each student develop a project on the topic. Students might write a short story, essay, or report; create a visual display of some kind; develop a multimedia presentation; and so on. Ask students to complete their projects and then present their work to the class. **Block Scheduling**

TEACH OBJECTIVE 4

ALL LEVELS: Conduct a brief discussion on new forms of popular music and entertainment that developed in the late 1800s. Then copy the following graphic organizer to the right on the chalkboard, omitting the italicized answers. Have each student complete it. To conclude, pair students and ask each pair to write paragraphs comparing and contrasting popular entertainment in the late 1800s and the late 1900s. **Sheltered English, Cooperative Learning**

for many urban residents. During the late 1800s a number of spectator sports in the United States became increasingly more professional.

Baseball. Popular myth holds that Abner Doubleday invented the game of baseball. However, the basic organization and rules of the game actually evolved in the early and mid-1800s from the British game called rounders. Prior to the Civil War, young middle- and working-class city-dwellers organized neighborhood baseball teams. These teams like the New York Knickerbockers played teams in surrounding neighborhoods and cities. The outbreak of the Civil War interrupted the development of these clubs. However, the war greatly expanded the popularity of the sport. Troops from all over the United States grew familiar with the game.

In 1869 Aaron Champion organized the first professional baseball team, the Cincinnati Red Stockings. Talented players such as Harry Wright no longer had to balance a busy baseball schedule with work. The Red Stockings were a success, beating every team they played that year. Other clubs soon began to hire professional ball players as well.

Concerned about issues of gambling, players' contracts, and standardized rules, William Hulbert organized the National League in 1876. He created a governing body for the sport. Hulbert also established rules for play, strict guidelines for players' contracts, and rules limiting players' association with gamblers.

Baseball's popularity continued to rise. By 1890 professional teams were drawing an estimated 60,000 fans daily. A second professional league was founded in 1900. Three years later the first World Series was held between the Pittsburgh Pirates and the Boston Red Sox.

Baseball had become, in one sportswriter's words, "the national game of the United States." Not all Americans were allowed to play in the professional leagues, however. In 1887 team manager Adrian "Cap" Anson refused to let his team play against teams with African American players. Anson's action and the widespread discrimination in the baseball leagues resulted in African Americans being excluded from major league teams for 60 years. African Americans formed their own league, however, which produced many outstanding players.

INTERPRETING THE VISUAL RECORD

Baseball. Fans used scorecards such as this one to keep track of their favorite teams' records and statistics. ***How is the late-1800s baseball gear pictured here similar to the equipment used today?***

Football. Like baseball, many Americans enjoyed watching football during their leisure time. Similar to soccer and the British game of rugby, football developed during the late 1800s on the college campuses of upper class New England schools. Walter Camp played football for Yale during the late 1870s. He made considerable contributions to the structure of the sport, establishing many of the rules and principles of the game. Discussing the spirit of the game, Camp stated, "There is no substitute for hard work and effort beyond the call of mere duty. That is what strengthens the soul and ennobles one's character."

As football grew in popularity among college students in the late 1800s, many people objected to the violent nature of this sport. The *Chicago Tribune* documented the deaths of 18 college players and 46 high school players in the 1905 season. The sport's brutality led to discussions in Congress about outlawing it. Rule changes reduced the sport's danger. Football's popularity continued to grow.

Walter Camp poses in his Yale football uniform.

CULTURAL DIVERSITY

Baseball Fans. Historians have learned that most baseball fans were from the middle and upper classes. Many games were played in the mid-afternoon, when professionals such as bankers could leave work but laborers were still on the job. Moreover, some baseball clubs established high ticket prices, which kept working-class fans away from the game. Finally, many ballparks were some distance from the city, requiring fans to pay streetcar fares that were often too expensive for workers.

CRITICAL THINKING Why might many games have been played in the mid-afternoon?

ANSWER: Students might suggest that lighting at night was technically difficult or impossible during the late 1800s.

VISUAL RECORD ANSWER

Students might point to the leather mitt and the shape and size of the ball.

VISUAL RECORD ANSWER

(for p. 210)

Students might suggest that they engaged in physical activity and teamwork.

VISUAL RECORD ANSWER

(for p. 211)

Students might mention that it showed a couple dancing on the cover.

NEW FORMS OF ENTERTAINMENT IN THE LATE 1800S	
Form	**Characteristics**
Theater	*wide range of types; from Shakespearean to vaudeville*
Music	*ragtime music, which inspired lively dances*

LEVEL 1: Conduct a brief discussion on new forms of popular music and entertainment that developed in the late 1800s. *(See the graphic organizer on the following page for the correct forms and characteristics.)* Pair students and tell them to imagine that they work for a musical theater in the 1890s. Have each pair create theater handbills that advertise the new forms of musical entertainment that appeared in the late 1800s. In their handbills, students should describe the unique characteristics of these forms of entertainment and explain why these forms appealed to the public. Have volunteers present their handbills to the class.
Sheltered English, Cooperative Learning

SECTION 3 REVIEW ANSWERS

Define and Identify
For significance, see the following pages:

- compulsory education laws, p. 205
- John Dewey, p. 205
- yellow journalism, p. 207
- Frederick Law Olmsted, p. 208
- City Beautiful movement, p. 208
- Walter Camp, p. 209
- James Naismith, p. 210
- Edwin Booth, p. 210
- vaudeville, p. 210
- ragtime, p. 210
- Scott Joplin, p. 211

1. reading–popular journalism, novels; sports–baseball, football, basketball; entertainment–theater, vaudeville, ragtime music

2. supplied more readers and consumers–enlarged the audience

3. public education–taught civic virtues; yellow journalism–informed Americans

4. working class–vaudeville, baseball; the wealthy–theater, croquet, watching professional sports; income levels limited the activities of the poor

5. Answers will vary. Students might point to the benefits of having places to enjoy nature and to play games. Without such places, life in urban areas would be more stressful.

INTERPRETING THE VISUAL RECORD
Basketball. Basketball served as a popular recreational activity for college students during the winter months. ***How do these female college students benefit from playing basketball?***

Basketball. Like football, basketball was first played by students. James Naismith, a physical educator in Springfield, Massachusetts, invented the game of basketball in 1891. He was attempting to find a sport that could entertain a group of unruly students during the long, cold months of winter. Naismith claimed that basketball "demanded and fostered alert minds and supple [flexible] bodies. Decisions had to be made quickly. Play had to be neat and nimble [quick]." By the mid-1890s colleges in the East and Midwest had created both male and female teams. Basketball was one of the few sports during the late 1800s in which women's participation was encouraged.

✔ **READING CHECK:** How did outdoor activities and sports provide a source of leisure for Americans?

Entertainment

While sports like baseball provided entertainment for many city-dwellers, others sought different sources of amusement. During the late 1800s people of every income level spent leisure time enjoying music and the theater.

Theater. Rapid urban growth brought many new entertainment seekers into U.S. cities. Many of these city-dwellers turned to the stage for entertainment. Portraying William Shakespeare's tragic heroes, Edwin Booth proved to be one of the most popular attractions of the 1860s and 1870s. Booth was considered one of the premier actors of his day. Due to public demand one season, Booth acted in 100 consecutive performances of *Hamlet.* Tickets for his opening performance in *Romeo and Juliet* in 1869 sold for as much as $125.

While the classic Shakespearean plays attracted a sophisticated audience, many Americans preferred more melodramatic shows. Because of their easily identifiable character types, these shows attracted a broad working-class audience. Often the villain was cast as a wealthy aristocrat, while the hero and heroine represented honest working-class people.

Attracting a similar audience, **vaudeville**—the French word for "light play"—was a type of variety show that featured a wide selection of short performances. Vaudeville shows often included animal acts, comics, famous impersonations, jugglers, magicians, singers, and skits. Some promoters of vaudeville became highly successful and went on to open chains of theaters.

***Edwin Booth, the brother of President Lincoln's assassin, was one of the era's most popular actors. He drew critical praise for his performance in* Hamlet.**

Ragtime. Performed in vaudeville shows at the turn of the century, a new form of music known as **ragtime** proved popular with audiences. Created by African American musicians, ragtime emerged during the 1890s. It varied radically from the traditional Victorian waltzes and marches popular earlier that century. Copying the customary foot stomping of audiences listening to folk songs, ragtime pianists played a stomping or driving rhythm with the left hand and a syncopated or improvised melody with the right hand.

REVIEW

Have students complete the **Section 3 Review** on p. 211.

ASSESS

Have students complete **Daily Quiz 6.3.** As **Alternative Assessment**, you may want to use the charts or handbills in this section's lessons.

RETEACH

Have students complete **Main Idea Activity for Reteaching and Sheltered English 6.3.** Organize the class into small groups. Assign each group one of the following topics: education, publishing, leisure time in urban parks, leisure and sports, and entertainment. Have each group prepare a visual display illustrating the major events, trends, persons, and ideas associated with the assigned topic. Have groups show and explain their posters to the class.
Sheltered English, Cooperative Learning

EXTEND

Have students conduct research on the history of vaudeville in the United States, including the types of acts included in vaudeville shows and popular vaudeville performers. Then have each student present his or her findings in an essay. Alternately, ask each student to create a vaudeville show that would have been popular during the late 1800s. Have students create advertisements and programs for their shows. Ask volunteers to present their essays or show descriptions to the class. **Block Scheduling**

BIOGRAPHY

Scott Joplin

Known as the King of Ragtime, Scott Joplin was born into a family of musicians from East Texas in 1868. Joplin learned to play the piano before the age of seven. In his early teens, he began playing in bars and saloons throughout the Mississippi Valley. After playing briefly at the Chicago Exposition in 1893, Joplin settled in the St. Louis area and concentrated on composing new musical arrangements and experimenting with syncopated melodies.

As the ragtime craze spread across the United States, Joplin further refined his style. He found a growing audience for his music. Hearing Joplin play at the Maple Leaf Club in 1899, John Stillwell Stark immediately offered to publish Joplin's tune, the "Maple Leaf Rag." The tune became an instant hit. It sold hundreds of thousands of copies in the first decade of publication and made Joplin's name a household word.

After the success of the "Maple Leaf Rag" and several vaudeville tours, Joplin gave up playing for audiences. He began to concentrate on teaching music and composing. He spent much of the rest of his life working on an opera that had little success. Nevertheless, Joplin's ragtime songs remained popular among young city-dwellers even after his death in 1917.

Known as rags, ragtime songs inspired a host of new dances whose liveliness and self-expression contrasted sharply with the restraint of Victorian culture. Dances like the Cakewalk, the Grizzly Bear, and the Turkey Trot became popular in dance halls. Young middle- and working-class city-dwellers eagerly pursued these new forms of entertainment and leisure.

✔ **READING CHECK:** What new forms of popular music and theater developed in the late 1800s?

INTERPRETING THE VISUAL RECORD

Ragtime. The popularity of ragtime music grew with the emergence of lively dances. ***How did the publisher of this ragtime tune incorporate the dance craze into the marketing of the sheet music?***

SECTION  REVIEW

Define and explain the significance of the following terms:
compulsory education laws
yellow journalism
City Beautiful movement
vaudeville
ragtime

Identify and explain the significance of the following individuals:
John Dewey
Frederick Law Olmsted
Walter Camp
James Naismith
Edwin Booth
Scott Joplin

1. **Using Graphic Organizers** Copy the graphic organizer below. Use it to describe the different leisure activities that were popular in the late 1800s.

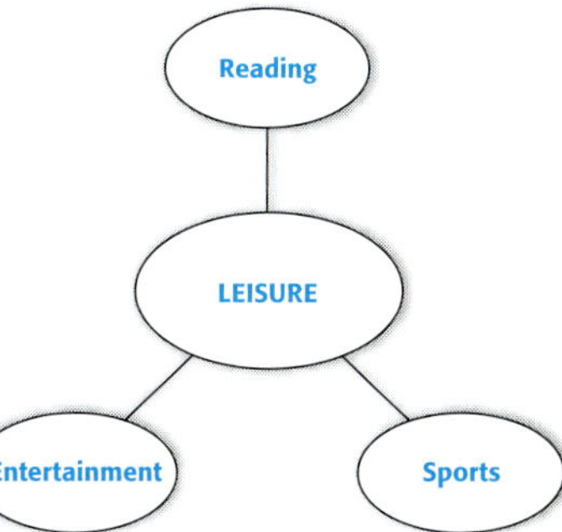

2. **Synthesizing** What impact do you think the expansion of public education had on the publishing industry of the late 1800s?
3. **Identifying Values** How did the development of public education and yellow journalism reflect democratic values?
4. **Evaluating** What leisure activities attracted working-class people? What did wealthy people do for leisure? What reasons can you give to explain why one economic class would take up different leisure practices than other classes?

Critical Thinking

5. Why is it important to set aside public "green space," such as parks, in cities?
Consider:
- what benefits green space offers to city-dwellers
- what might happen if green space were not set aside

CHAPTER 6 REVIEW ANSWERS

Creating a Time Line
Each event should have an explanation and the correct date.

Writing a Summary
See the Reading Checks in each section for main ideas.

Identifying People and Ideas
1. immigrants who arrived from 1891 to 1910
2. religious and secular aid organizations that helped immigrants
3. developed the mechanized elevator, making skyscrapers feasible
4. forms of public transportation that extended cities outward
5. spending designed to prove wealth and status
6. leader of the settlement house movement
7. laws requiring parents to send children to school
8. designer of Central Park whose ideas helped foster the City Beautiful movement
9. style of sensational reporting
10. musician known as the King of Ragtime

Understanding Main Ideas
1. More immigrants arrived from southern and eastern Europe.
2. They claimed that immigrants could not fit into American society and caused problems such as poverty and crime.

REVIEW AND ASSESSMENT RESOURCES

PRINT

- Chapter 6 Review, pp. 212–13
- Chapter 6 Tutorial for Students, Parents, Mentors, and Peers
- Chapter 6 Test (Form A or B)
- Portfolio Activities and Alternative Assessment Handbook, Chapter 6

MULTIMEDIA

- Audio Program, Chapter 6 (English and Spanish)
- Chapter 6 Test Generator (on the One-Stop Planner)
- Global Skill Builder CD–ROM
- HRW Web site

SHELTERED ENGLISH

- Spanish Glossary
- Sheltered English Chapter 6 Test

REVIEW

Have students complete the **Chapter 6 Review** on pp. 212–13.

ASSESS

Use one of the chapter tests to assess students' understanding of the content. For **Alternative Assessment**, see the **Portfolio Activities and Alternative Assessment Handbook.**

3. population—immigrants and other Americans came to cities in search of opportunities; size—mass transit allowed cities to grow outward
4. to give urban residents relief from the city environment
5. by offering popular, appealing entertainment to a wide variety of people

Reviewing Themes

1. native languages, cultures, and religious beliefs
2. Mass transit changed the size of cities; elevators made skyscrapers feasible; bicycles provided a new leisure activity.
3. They offered education and information to almost all Americans.

Thinking Critically

1. The literacy test was intended to discourage immigration, and almost all Americans are descendants of immigrants.
2. took classes in English and in American cultural values
3. affected the type and frequency of entertainment
4. the growth in leisure time and the desire for a way to escape crowded urban environments
5. Answers will vary. Students might mention overcrowding or nativism. Regardless of their choices, students should offer solutions and justify them.

Review

Creating a Time Line

Copy the time line below onto a sheet of paper. Complete the time line by filling in the events and dates from the chapter that you think were most significant. Pick three events and explain why you think they were significant.

Writing a Summary

Using the Reading Checks as a guide, write an overview of the events in the chapter.

Identifying People and Ideas

Identify the following terms or individuals and explain their significance.

1. new immigrants
2. benevolent societies
3. Elisha Otis
4. mass transit
5. conspicuous consumption
6. Jane Addams
7. compulsory school laws
8. Frederick Law Olmsted
9. yellow journalism
10. Scott Joplin

Understanding Main Ideas

SECTION 1

1. What changes occurred in the pattern of immigration during the late 1800s?
2. Why did nativists argue against immigration?

SECTION 2

3. Why did cities grow in terms of population and size during the late 1800s?

SECTION 3

4. For what purpose did urban planners design large city parks?
5. How did popular literature, journalism, and other types of entertainment cater to a broad audience?

Reviewing Themes

1. **Cultural Diversity** What cultural practices did immigrants bring to the United States in the late 1800s?
2. **Technology and Society** How did technological developments alter U.S. cities and change the daily lives of city-dwellers?
3. **Democratic Values** In what ways did settlement houses, public schools, and newspapers assist all Americans equally?

Thinking Critically

1. **Evaluating** Why do you think President Grover Cleveland called a bill that would require all immigrants to take a literacy test "un-American?"
2. **Synthesizing** In what ways were new immigrants Americanized?
3. **Drawing Conclusions** How did class differences influence the way urban Americans enjoyed their leisure time?
4. **Identifying Cause and Effect** What factors led to a growth in the popularity of playing and watching sports during the late 1800s?
5. **Problem Solving** What do you think was the biggest problem facing U.S. cities in the late 1800s? How would you have solved this problem?

Writing About History

Writing to Persuade Imagine that you run a settlement house. Write a letter to a wealthy family persuading them to donate money to your settlement house. Be sure to explain the purpose of the settlement house, the specific programs it offers, and its effects on the city. Use the following chart to help organize your thoughts.

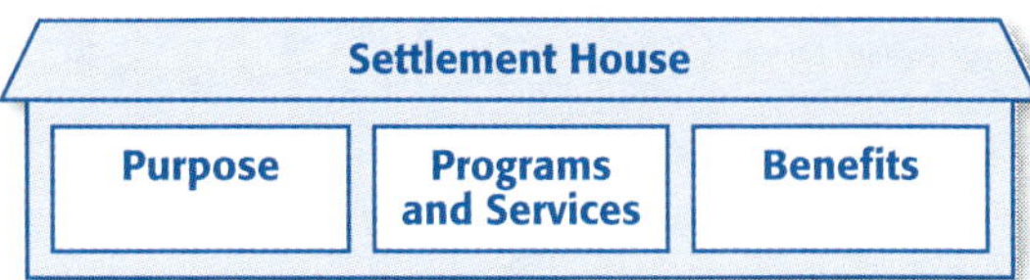

RETEACH

Organize the class into three groups. Assign each group one of the sections in this chapter. Have groups create outlines of the major topics and subtopics in their assigned sections. Then rotate the outlines to the next group and have that group add specific information. Rotate the detailed outlines to the next group to evaluate thoroughness and accuracy.
Sheltered English, Cooperative Learning

EXTEND

Have students locate and read excerpts of *Looking Backward* by Edward Bellamy. Have each student write an essay comparing the late 1800s with two other time periods: the late 1900s as described by Bellamy and the late 1900s as they actually were. You may wish to have each student concentrate on one theme in order to make the analysis more manageable.
Block Scheduling

Strategies for Success Review the **Strategies for Success** on *Analyzing*. Then reread the Section 1 subsection entitled The Nativist Response and answer the following questions.

1. What reasons did nativists have for opposing immigration to the United States?
2. How were economic concerns of working-class, native-born Americans a factor in the nativist response to immigration?
3. Explain the purpose of the Chinese Exclusion Act and the Immigration Restriction League.

Use your responses to answer the following questions.

4. Why and how did nativists respond to increased immigration during the late 1800s?
5. What political goals did the nativists hope to achieve? Were they successful?

Linking History and Geography

Settlement houses and benevolent societies often existed in cities with large immigrant populations. Study the map below. If the relationship between settlement houses, benevolent societies, and immigration holds true, what conclusions can you draw about patterns of immigrant population in the early 1900s?

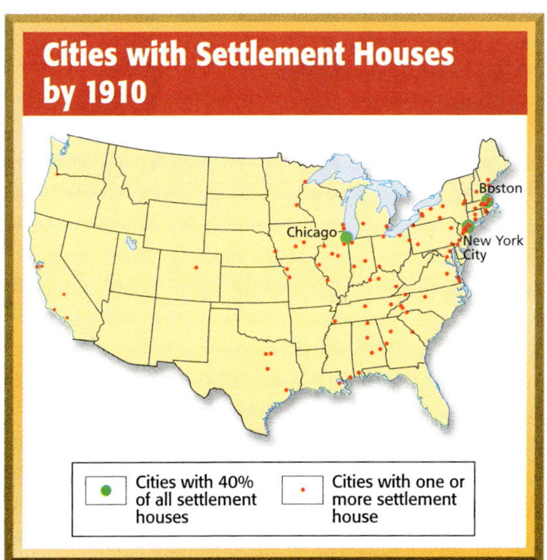

internetconnect

TOPIC: Ellis Island and Angel Island
GO TO: go.hrw.com
KEYWORD: SE1 Ellis Island

Accessing the Internet through the HRW Web site, research Ellis Island or Angel Island. In addition to general information about these places, look for specific information about the process by which immigrants were admitted to the United States and the conditions under which they waited for permission to enter. Then, imagining that you are an immigrant, write a journal entry that contains specific references to information found in your research.

BUILDING YOUR PORTFOLIO

Complete one or all of the following projects independently or cooperatively.

Woman bicycling in the late 1800s

1 Cultural Diversity

Imagine that you are a new immigrant in the United States during the late 1800s and that you have a family member who is planning to immigrate as well. ***Write a letter*** to your relative describing your experiences during the journey, what type of job you found, and who helped you adjust to American life.

2 Technology and Society

Imagine that it is 1900 and you are a middle-class city office worker who is about to retire. ***Create a comic strip*** to share with your grandchildren that describes the technological changes you have witnessed in the past 45 years and the impact of those changes on your daily life.

3 Economic Development

Imagine that you are a member of a working-class family living in a tenement during the late 1800s. Keeping your small budget in mind, ***plan an itinerary*** of leisure activities for an entire month.

Writing About History
purpose—to aid the impoverished in American society; programs and services—education, skills training, cultural events; benefits—helped immigrants become productive laborers and improved the quality of urban life

Strategies for Success

1. believed that immigrants could not fit into American society and that they brought poverty, crime, and radical politics to the United States
2. wanted to protect jobs and to save them for native-born Americans
3. Chinese Exclusion Act—to prevent the immigration of the Chinese; Immigration Restriction League—to limit the number of immigrants admitted to the country
4. Because nativists blamed immigrants for a number of social ills, they used both violence and political lobbying to prevent immigrants from entering the country.
5. to ban or decrease immigration; passed the Chinese Exclusion Act

Linking History and Geography
Most immigrants tended to settle in the East and Midwest.

LET'S GET STARTED!

Write the following statement on the chalkboard: *The West has always been a land of immigrants and migrants—those who emigrated from another country, and those who migrated from another region.* Ask each student to respond to the statement in writing. Have volunteers share their responses. Tell students that they will learn more about immigration and shrinking distances in the United States in the Unit 2 America's Geography.

TEACH AMERICA'S GEOGRAPHY—CONQUERING DISTANCE

Pair students and tell them to imagine that they are modern-day historians studying the theme of conquering distance in the mid- to late 1800s. Have each student write a paragraph summarizing the information presented in the America's Geography feature. Remind students they will need to choose their wording very carefully to create a full, useful summary. **Sheltered English**

GLOBAL RELATIONS

Immigration Rights. The U.S. government originally encouraged the increase in Chinese immigration. In part to provide cheap labor for the transcontinental railroad companies, in 1869 a U.S. treaty granted Chinese visitors and residents most-favored-nation treatment. Many Americans began to resent the growing Chinese population, however. In 1870 Congress banned Asian immigrants from naturalization. In 1882, under pressure from western states, Congress passed the Chinese Exclusion Act to completely bar the immigration of Chinese workers. Congress later expanded and extended the act.

CRITICAL THINKING How might Chinese officials have responded to the exclusion of their emigrants to the United States?

ANSWER: Students might suggest that Chinese officials disliked the ban and attempted to ban American visitors or emigrants to China.

AMERICA'S GEOGRAPHY ANSWERS

1. In 1900 a smaller percentage of Chinese Americans lived in California than in 1870. By 1900 some had settled in the North Atlantic region.
2. Germany

AMERICA'S Geography

Conquering Distance

Conquering Distance Overseas

The late 1800s saw massive population shifts in the United States. Between 1860 and 1910, some 23 million immigrants crossed the Atlantic and Pacific Oceans to reach America (see map at right). Many of these immigrants joined the millions of people making the cross-country trek to settle the American West. This westward migration was aided by railroad lines and improved systems of communication that linked numerous western cities together, forming the basis of a modern transcontinental economy.

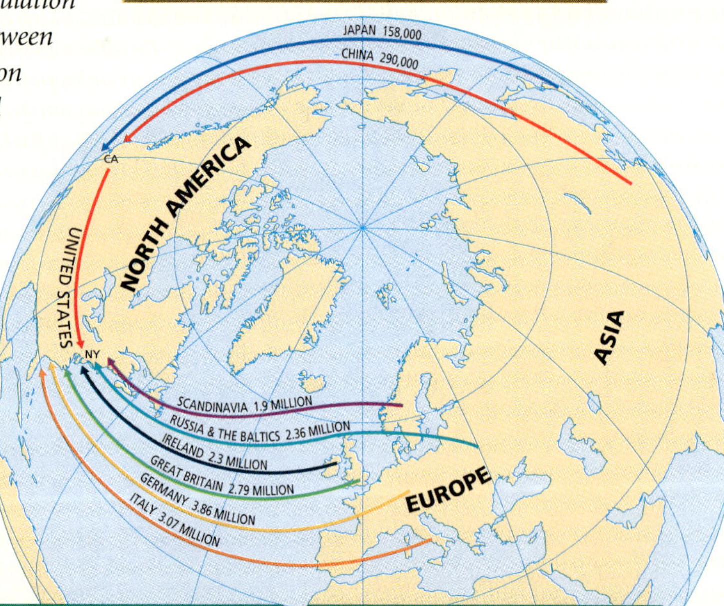

Asian immigration. Immigrants from Asia had to travel twice as far as European immigrants to reach the United States. Although most Chinese immigrants initially settled along the West Coast, some eventually journeyed across the United States. In 1870 a Massachusetts factory owner began recruiting Chinese laborers from California to take the place of striking workers. As this practice caught on, more Chinese laborers made the trip to the East Coast. This migration led to the development of thriving Chinatowns in Boston and New York.

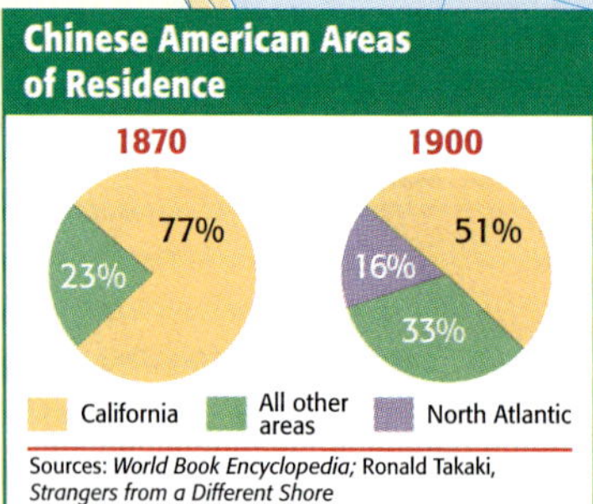

Sources: *World Book Encyclopedia;* Ronald Takaki, *Strangers from a Different Shore*

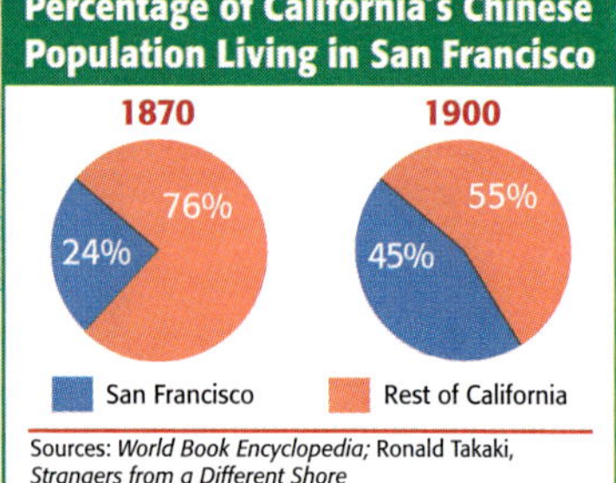

Sources: *World Book Encyclopedia;* Ronald Takaki, *Strangers from a Different Shore*

GEOGRAPHY AND HISTORY Skills

MOVEMENT

1. How did the location of Chinese American settlement shift between 1870 and 1900?
2. What country contributed the most immigrants to the United States between 1860 and 1910?

SPOTLIGHT
on Western Immigrants

Tell students to imagine that they are immigrants who just settled in the West. Students may choose to be Chinese immigrants in San Francisco, for example, or Finnish immigrants in Minneapolis. Have each student write a few sentences or paragraphs describing his or her experiences in the West. Remind students that they should discuss the theme of conquering distance in their sentences or paragraphs.

SPOTLIGHT
on Western Railroads

Ask students to study the map on conquering distance across the West. Have students pick a western railroad line or company and conduct research on its founding and influence in the West. Have each student write a short presentation on his or her topic. Ask volunteers to deliver their presentations to the class.

Conquering Distance across the West

Major railroad
Cattle trail
Other trail
Area settled by 1890
DUTCH Ethnic settlement area
SIOUX American Indian reservation

0 200 400 Miles
0 200 400 Kilometers
Albers Equal Area Projection

Western Population Growth, 1860–1910

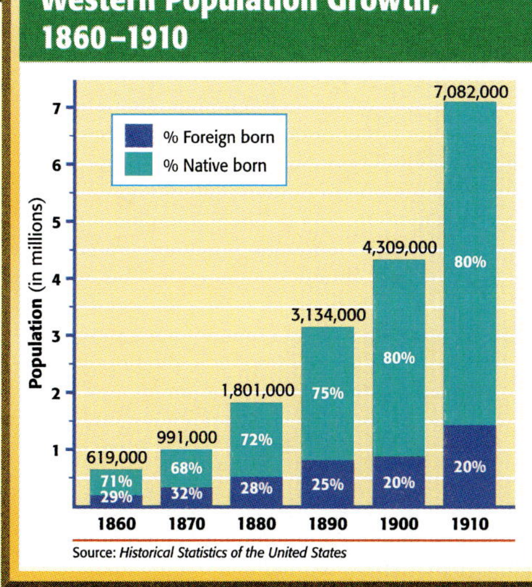

Source: *Historical Statistics of the United States*

Immigrant migration. As the network of railroads and western population increased, many immigrants began settling inland, rather than staying in cities on the East or West coast. This migration resulted in the presence of distinct ethnic traditions and cultures in many western cities.

GEOGRAPHY AND HISTORY

LOCATION

1. In what year was the percentage of foreign-born residents living in the West the highest?
2. Identify the ethnic groups that established western settlements.

MORE ON THE MAP

San Francisco. In the late 1700s the Spanish built a fort and a mission on the site of present-day San Francisco. In 1835, traders built a small village in the region. By 1848 San Francisco was a town of some 800 people. The California Gold Rush brought massive changes to the area. Miners and merchants arrived in droves. The population reached 50,000 in 1860.

CRITICAL THINKING What might San Francisco have been like in the absence of the California Gold Rush?

ANSWER: Some students might suggest that San Francisco would have remained a small town or that San Francisco would have boomed at a later date.

THAT'S INTERESTING!

Between 1890 and 1930, one out of every three Americans had either been born in a foreign country or had a parent who had been born in a foreign country.

AMERICA'S GEOGRAPHY ANSWERS

1. 1870
2. Chinese, Czech, Danish, Dutch, Finnish, German, Irish, Mexican, Norwegian, Polish, and Swedish

215

Politics in the Gilded Age

CHAPTER PLANNING GUIDE

	Section Lesson Objectives	Print Resources	Multimedia Resources	Sheltered English Resources
Section 1 Political Machines, pp. 218–23	1 Explain how political machines emerged in U.S. cities. 2 Analyze why immigrants were important to political machines. 3 Describe how corruption and illegal activities developed in many political machines. 4 Identify the events that led to the collapse of public support for the Tweed Ring.	▶ Guided Reading Strategy 7.1 ▶ American History Political Cartoon 16: Tammany Hall ▶ Geography Activity 7: The Growth of Urban Areas ▶ Biography Reading 7: Thomas Nast ▶ Section 1 Review, p. 223 ▶ Daily Quiz 7.1	▶ One-Stop Planner, Lesson 7.1 ▶ Holt Researcher: American History CD–ROM ▶ HRW Web site	▶ Main Idea Activity for Reteaching and Sheltered English 7.1
Section 2 Restoring Honest Government, pp. 224–30	1 Identify the scandals that plagued the Grant administration. 2 Explain why Americans wanted political reform, and analyze how this desire affected the Republican Party. 3 Describe President Arthur's changing positions on civil service reform, and analyze how this affected his political party. 4 Describe how President Harrison dealt with President Cleveland's reforms.	▶ Guided Reading Strategy 7.2 ▶ Graphic Organizer Activity 7: An Expanding Population ▶ Literature Reading 7: A New Kind of Politician ▶ Section 2 Review, p. 230 ▶ Daily Quiz 7.2	▶ One-Stop Planner, Lesson 7.2 ▶ The American Nation Video Program Segment: The American Red Cross; Teacher's Guide, pp. 201–02 ▶ Holt Researcher: American History CD–ROM	▶ Main Idea Activity for Reteaching and Sheltered English 7.2
Section 3 The Populist Movement, pp. 231–37	1 Describe the factors that led to economic hardships for farmers. 2 Explain what the farmers' movements hoped to achieve, and what weakened their efforts. 3 Discuss why farmers supported money backed by silver. 4 Identify the issues that the Populist Party supported. 5 Explain how silver affected the economy and the 1896 presidential election.	▶ Guided Reading Strategy 7.3 ▶ Primary Source Reading 7: A Call for Reform ▶ Section 3 Review, p. 237 ▶ Daily Quiz 7.3	▶ One-Stop Planner, Lesson 7.3 ▶ Everyday Life in America Transparency 16: Farming Technology, Late 1800s ▶ Holt Researcher: American History CD–ROM	▶ Main Idea Activity for Reteaching and Sheltered English 7.3
Chapter Review and Assessment pp. 238–39		▶ Chapter 17 Review, pp. 238–39 ▶ Chapter 7 Tutorial for Students, Parents, Mentors, and Peers ▶ Chapter 7 Test (Form A or B) ▶ Portfolio Activities and Alternative Assessment Handbook, Chapter 7	▶ Audio Program, Chapter 7 (English and Spanish) ▶ Chapter 7 Test Generator (on the One-Stop Planner) ▶ Global Skill Builder CD–ROM ▶ HRW Web site	▶ Spanish Glossary ▶ Sheltered English Chapter 7 Test

CHAPTER OVERVIEW

Political machines and political bosses came to dominate politics in some cities during the late 1800s. These machines and bosses relied on the support of immigrants, supplying jobs and services in return for immigrants' votes. On the whole, machines and bosses were corrupt. They used graft, bribes, and kickbacks to line their own pockets and promote their own agendas.

Corruption plagued national politics as well, particularly during the Grant administration. This corruption led some to call for political reform, including civil service reform. Supporters argued that many political appointments should be determined on the basis of merit, not patronage.

The desire for reform affected farmers' movements as well. Angered by high storage and freight rates, oversupply, and low prices, farmers organized cooperatives and lobbied for various kinds of assistance. Farmers also joined the new Populist Party. The movement could not command national attention, however, and withered toward the end of the 1800s.

TIME TAMERS

Block Scheduling

The teacher lesson plans for each section offer a variety of activity choices to help you present the material in a block scheduling format. For further suggestions on block scheduling, see the **Block Scheduling Handbook with Team Teaching Strategies**, pp. 37–42.

Internet Connections and Lesson 7
www.si.edu/hrw

Hands-On History Activities:

Classroom to Community The **Hands-On History Activities** help students make meaningful connections between events in American history and those in their own hometown. You may wish to use the Chapter 7 Activity, The Local Political Scene, to extend the chapter lessons, as alternative assessment, or as a block scheduling option.

Portfolio Projects

The American Nation includes multiple portfolio projects in each Pupil's Edition chapter review, as well as each unit review. Chapter 7 Portfolio Project options on p. 239 include the following:

1. Students will **write a short story**.
2. Students will **draft a letter**.
3. Students will **create a political cartoon**.

The American Nation INTERNET RESOURCE DIRECTORY

To access online materials for this chapter, go to go.hrw.com and type in the keywords listed below.

HRW ONLINE RESOURCES

GO TO: go.hrw.com

Online Maps
KEYWORD: SE1 Maps7
- Agricultural Regions, 1900

Online Reading Support
KEYWORD: SE1 Strategies7

Online Rubrics
KEYWORD: SE1 Rubrics

CHAPTER ENRICHMENT LINKS

Use these Web links to extend and enrich student learning for Chapter 7.

GO TO: go.hrw.com
KEYWORD: SE1 Ch7

CHAPTER INTERNET ACTIVITIES

GO TO: go.hrw.com

- Pupil's Edition Student Activity
  KEYWORD: SE1 Cartoons
  (Students create political cartoons.)
- Teacher's Edition Student Activity
  KEYWORD: SE1 Zulu
  (Students trace the rise and fall of the Zulu Nation.)
- Teacher's Edition Student Activity
  KEYWORD: SE1 Tammany
  (Students conduct research on the Tammany Hall machine.)

ADDITIONAL RESOURCES

Books for Teachers

McMath, Robert C. *American Populism: A Social History, 1877–1898.* Hill & Wang, 1993. Discusses the social history of the Populist movement.

Books for Students

Blassingame, Wyatt. *The Look-It-Up Book of Presidents.* Random House, 1996. Provides an entry for each U.S. president. Particularly appropriate for students reading below grade level.

Dictionary of Finance and Banking. Oxford University Press, 1997. Offers clear definitions of economic terms.

Primary Sources from the Period

Jones, Mother. Mary F. Parton, ed. *The Autobiography of Mother Jones.* C. H. Kerr, 1990. Presents Mother Jones's viewpoints. Particularly appropriate for students reading below grade level.

Mellon, Thomas. *Thomas Mellon and His Times.* University of Pittsburgh Press, 1994. Presents Mellon's autobiography and an insightful social history of the Gilded Age.

Multimedia Materials

The 1880s. Video, 32 min. Kaw Valley/SSSS. Describes politics and popular culture in the decade.

Populism: Where Historians Disagree. Two filmstrips, 33 min. Random House Media. Presents opposing viewpoints of the Populist Party.

CHAPTER 7

Before You Read

Build on What You Know

Ask students to answer the following questions.

How might Americans attempt to restore honest government?

Consider:

- the existence of bribes and "sweetheart" deals
- the issue of patronage versus merit in hiring civil servants

How might rural Americans attempt to become more politically active?

Consider:

- the importance of forming mutual-interest associations
- the possible power of unified economic actions

exploring the time line

AMERICAN EVENTS

PEOPLE IN HISTORY

1871 ■ Thomas Nast. Born in Germany, Thomas Nast moved to New York City with his family as a small boy. He studied with Theodore Kaufman, who painted mostly historical scenes. In 1855 Nast began work at *Frank Leslie's Illustrated Newspaper,* where he began to draw cartoons to accompany stories. A fervid Unionist, Nast made many sketches of the Civil War, often concentrating on soldiers and their daily routines. Ulysses S. Grant commented, "He did as much as any man to preserve the Union and bring the war to an end." Nast's Boss Tweed cartoons also had an enormous impact, helping to bring down the notorious political machine. William Marcy Tweed found them so effective that he attempted to bribe Nast with a luxurious European tour.

CRITICAL THINKING How might Nast's drawings have helped end the Civil War?

ANSWER: Students might indicate that Nast's Civil War drawings focused on soldiers, and thus showed the devastation of the conflict.

CHAPTER 7

1865–1900

Politics in the Gilded Age

Young Mother Sewing by Mary Cassatt

U.S. gold dollar

1865

1866 Politics
Political boss William Marcy Tweed takes over the Tammany Hall political machine.

1869 Business and Finance
Jay Gould's and Abel Rathbone Corbin's attempt to corner the gold market fails, causing a massive drop in the price of gold.

1870

1870 World Events
The kingdom of Italy is unified under the leadership of Victor Emmanuel II.

1871 The Arts
Thomas Nast begins his series of cartoons attacking the Tweed Ring.

1873 Business and Finance
The U.S. Congress votes to stop coining silver and to convert money to the gold standard.

1875

1877 Daily Life
Puck, a weekly periodical featuring double-page cartoons, is published.

1877 Politics
The Farmers' Alliance movement begins in Texas.

1879 World Events
The Zulu nation, founded in 1816, is dissolved by British forces after a violent military campaign.

1880

1880 The Arts
American impressionist artist Mary Cassatt paints *Young Mother Sewing.*

A Thomas Nast cartoon of the Tweed Ring

THE GRANGER COLLECTION, NEW YORK

A leader of the Zulu nation

Before You Read

Build on What You Know

Life for many Americans changed dramatically during the late 1800s. Rapid industrialization and new opportunities drew increasing numbers of people to U.S. cities. In this chapter you will learn that politics in the United States during the late 1800s was frequently corrupt. These episodes of corruption inspired new efforts to restore honest government. Meanwhile, rural Americans grew more politically active, attempting to improve the conditions of their daily lives.

Think About Themes

To help students create their Themes Journal entries, provide the following examples of appropriate ***agree/disagree*** *statements.*

Cultural Diversity

Agree The Republican Party stayed in power during Reconstruction because it had the support of Radical Republicans.

Disagree The Federalists rose to power despite their fairly limited group of supporters.

Democratic Values

Agree Hiring on the basis of test scores ensures the placement of qualified officials.

Disagree Elected officials have the right to fill posts with party supporters.

Geographic Diversity

Agree On the whole, the highly populated Northeast has not supported agricultural parties and has thus limited their national effectiveness and popularity.

Disagree Abraham Lincoln won the presidency in the election of 1860 despite his views on slavery, an issue of crucial concern to the South.

The first gasoline-powered tractor

William Jennings Bryan giving a speech

Eastman Kodak's Brownie box camera

1883 Politics The U.S. Congress establishes the Civil Service Commission.

1885 World Events The Indian National Congress is formed in British-controlled India.

1888 Science and Technology William S. Burroughs patents a machine that adds, subtracts, and prints.

1889 The Arts Mark Twain publishes the novel *A Connecticut Yankee in King Arthur's Court.*

1892 Science and Technology The first gasoline-powered tractor is built in Iowa.

1892 Politics The Populist Party is founded.

1895 Daily Life The Kellogg brothers patent peanut butter.

1896 Politics William Jennings Bryan delivers his "Cross of Gold" speech.

1897 Science and Technology The world's largest refracting telescope, with a 40-inch lens, is installed at the Yerkes Observatory in Wisconsin.

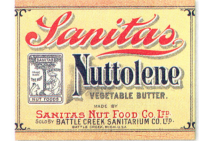

1900 Daily Life Eastman Kodak introduces a Brownie box camera that sells for $1, making photography accessible to nearly everyone.

1885 | 1890 | 1895 | 1900

An adding machine

Peanut butter advertisement

exploring the time line

internet connect

TOPIC: Zulu Nation
GO TO: go.hrw.com
KEYWORD: SE1 Zulu

Have students access the Internet through the HRW Web site to conduct research on the history of the Zulu Nation and its founder, Shaka Zulu. Then have each student write an informative essay that outlines the rise and fall of the Zulu Nation.

Think About Themes

Decide whether you **agree** *or* **disagree** *with the following statements. Note why in your journal.*

Cultural Diversity In order to gain power, political parties in large U.S. cities must attract supporters from diverse groups of residents.

Democratic Values Testing is the best way to determine who should be hired to fill government jobs.

Geographic Diversity New political parties cannot win national power if they focus only on issues of concern to one geographic region.

217

SECTION 1

After completing Section 1, students should be able to:

OBJECTIVE 1 *Explain how political machines emerged in U.S. cities.*

OBJECTIVE 2 *Analyze why immigrants were important to political machines.*

OBJECTIVE 3 *Describe how corruption and illegal activities developed in many political machines.*

OBJECTIVE 4 *Identify the events that led to the collapse of public support for the Tweed Ring.*

LET'S GET STARTED!

Write the following term on the chalkboard: *Political Machine.* As students enter the classroom, ask them to list words or phrases that they associate with the term. Have volunteers share their words or phrases with the class. *(Answers will vary. Some students might list words such as corruption, boss, or immigrant.)* Discuss the term with students, providing a definition and examples of its use in this section. Then tell students that in Section 1 they will learn about political machines in the late 1800s.

SECTION 1 RESOURCES

PRINT
- Guided Reading Strategy 7.1
- American History Political Cartoon 16: Tammany Hall
- Geography Activity 7: The Growth of Urban Areas
- Biography Reading 7: Thomas Nast
- Section 1 Review, p. 223
- Daily Quiz 7.1

MULTIMEDIA
- One-Stop Planner, Lesson 7.1
- Holt Researcher: American History CD–ROM
- HRW Web site

SHELTERED ENGLISH
- Main Idea Activity for Reteaching and Sheltered English 7.1

✔ READING TO UNDERSTAND
To help students master the section objectives, have them answer the **READING CHECKS** and complete **Guided Reading Strategy 7.1** as they read the section.

Political Machines

OBJECTIVES

Read to understand:
1. how political machines emerged in U.S. cities
2. why immigrants were important to political machines
3. how corruption and illegal activities developed in many political machines
4. what events led to the collapse of public support for the Tweed Ring

KEY TERMS

political machines
political bosses
graft
kickbacks

KEY PEOPLE

Alexander Shepherd
James Pendergast
George Washington Plunkitt
William Marcy Tweed
Thomas Nast

“I know what Parks is doing, but what do I care. He has raised my wages. Let him have his [illegal gains]!”

—Anonymous city worker

A New York official voting in the early 1900s

This city worker was responding to the charges of corruption of a New York politician. Despite the public awareness of corruption, local political leaders managed to gain broad support from their voters by offering favors and jobs. Many of these jobs came from public-works projects. The growth of urban centers during the late 1800s meant that cities required new streets, new sewer systems, and larger police and fire departments. Unfortunately, the need for these services also created an opportunity for political leaders to gain power and personal wealth.

The Rise of the Political Machine

The overwhelming growth of urban populations in the United States during the late 1800s created new challenges for city governments. New demands were placed on public services such as fire, police, and sanitation departments. Growing urban populations also required the expansion or new construction of bridges, parks, schools, streets, sewer systems, and utility systems. With the support of very well organized political parties, city council members and district representatives took charge of city governments. They oversaw new public services and, in many cases, pocketed money meant for the public good.

Political bosses. During the late 1800s well-organized political parties dominated city governments in the United States. Because of their success in getting their members elected to local political offices, these parties were called **political machines**. Powerful **political bosses** managed these machines. Bosses dictated party positions on city ordinances and made deals with business leaders. They also controlled the precinct captains, aldermen, and council members who kept the machine running smoothly.

Although bosses provided party leadership, the real strength of political machines lay in the relationship between precinct captains and potential voters living in the urban neighborhoods. By offering jobs, political favors, and services to local residents, precinct captains won support for the political machine. At election time, ward bosses and precinct captains instructed local residents to vote for their selected candidates. This practice ensured the continued power of the political machine.

Growing American cities struggled to meet increasing demands for public services such as sanitation services.

TEACH OBJECTIVE 1

LEVEL 1: Pair students and tell them to imagine that they live in a large U.S. city in the late 1800s. Have each pair develop a list of urban problems and needs. *(Students should list the need for fire, police, and sanitation services as well as the need for stable jobs.)* Briefly discuss the lists and ask pairs to write paragraphs explaining how these urban problems and needs led to the emergence of political machines in cities. *(Students should note that the machines provided services and jobs to loyal supporters.)* Then ask students to consider their lists and paragraphs. Would they have supported political machines, even if those machines were corrupt? Did the pressing need for services justify any political machine that supplied them successfully?
Sheltered English, Cooperative Learning

LEVELS 2 AND 3: Tell students to imagine that they are successful bosses welcoming a young new member to their political machine. Have each student develop a brief monologue describing how political machines emerged in U.S. cities. *(See the Level 1 lesson for the correct factors.)* Ask volunteers to perform their monologues for the class. Students may wish to include the scripts for their monologues in their portfolios.

Public services. During the late 1800s political machines attempted to provide the public services required by growing U.S. cities. Political bosses such as Alexander Shepherd of Washington financed expanded sewer and water systems, paved streets, and provided other public services. Between 1871 and 1873 Shepherd's board of public works spent $20 million, creating significant civic improvements and new jobs in the nation's capital. This boom of public-works projects meant that bosses could distribute many jobs among loyal supporters.

By providing jobs, political favors, and services to local residents, political machines were able to win support from many poor and working-class city-dwellers. Political bosses and local precinct representatives often formed close relationships with local voters.

✔ **READING CHECK:** How did political machines emerge in American cities?

This "Tammany Bank" was inspired by political corruption in the 1870s. Place a coin in the Tammany politician's hand and he deposits it in his pocket.

Immigrants and Political Machines

Because political machines helped the urban poor, new immigrants often became particularly loyal supporters of political machines. New immigrants in the largest cities commonly suffered from harsh living and working conditions.

Machine politicians often met immigrants as soon as they arrived in the United States. They helped the newcomers get settled in their new homeland. During the 1890s Tammany Hall, the powerful Democratic political machine in New York City, sent numerous party workers to Ellis Island to meet the new immigrants. The party workers assisted the immigrants by finding them temporary housing and jobs. Tammany Hall workers also helped immigrants become naturalized citizens and thus eligible to vote for Tammany Hall candidates. Tammany Hall gained considerable power during the 1860s and early 1870s. However, Tammany officials failed to offer any extensive programs to address poverty and poor housing conditions.

Political bosses ensured voter loyalty among immigrant groups by providing jobs in exchange for votes. James Pendergast was a particularly well-liked boss in Kansas City, Missouri. He began his political career while running a saloon in the industrial river-bottom district where many immigrants lived and worked. Pendergast gained considerable political support by providing jobs and special services to his African American, Irish American, and Italian American constituents. "There is no kinder hearted or more sympathetic man in Kansas City than Jim Pendergast," said one Kansas City resident. "He will go down in his pockets after his last cent to help a friend. No man is more easily moved to sympathy or good sense than Jim Pendergast." Another immigrant described the efforts of a local political boss.

> **"To this one he lends a dollar; for another he obtains a railroad ticket without payment; he has coal distributed in the depth of winter; . . . he sometimes sends poultry at Christmas time; he buys medicine for a sick person; he helps bury the dead."**

James Pendergast ran a political machine in Kansas City, Missouri.

ACROSS THE CURRICULUM

▶GOVERNMENT◀

Tammany Government. The founders of Tammany Hall formed the organization in 1789 and named it after Tammanend, a powerful Delaware chief. They created the group as a benevolent and fraternal organization to oppose what they saw as aristocratic dominance within the Federalist Party. Over time, the society became a political organization linked with the emerging Democratic Party.

CRITICAL THINKING Why might the founders of Tammany Hall have named the organization after Tammanend?

ANSWER: Students might suggest that the founders probably wanted to portray the organization as powerful, just like Tammanend.

internetconnect

TOPIC: Tammany Hall
GO TO: go.hrw.com
KEYWORD: SE1 Tammany

Have students access the Internet through the HRW Web site to conduct research on the Tammany Hall political machine in New York City. Then ask students to imagine that they work for a newspaper in New York City. Have each student write a newspaper editorial about an issue that was affected by Tammany Hall politics.

TEACH OBJECTIVE 2

ALL LEVELS: Tell students to imagine that it is 1880 and that they are recent immigrants. Ask students to describe the ways in which political machines might help them survive and prosper in the United States. *(Answers will vary. Some students might note that the machines provided services and jobs.)* To help students understand why immigrants were important to political machines, copy the following graphic organizer on the chalkboard, omitting the italicized answers. Have each student complete it. **Sheltered English**

Political Machines and Immigrants

Why Immigrants Were Important to Machines
- *represented a huge supply of supporters and voters*
- *tended to be particularly loyal to machines*

Ways in Which Machines Recruited and Rewarded Immigrants
- *welcomed immigrants upon arrival*
- *found immigrants tempora[ry] housing and jobs*
- *helped immigrants becom[e] naturalized citizens*
- *helped immigrants with finances, funerals, and so on*

HISTORY MAKERS SPEAK

George Washington Plunkitt in *Eyewitnesses and Others*

The Secret of a Successful Boss. Political bosses provided far more than jobs and services to new immigrants. They also provided a sense of human contact and concern—a fact that endeared them to many people adjusting to a new country and a new society. One political boss said, "To learn real human nature you have to go among the people, see them and be seen. I know every man, woman, and child in the Fifteenth District. . . . I know what they like and what they don't like, what they are strong at and what they are weak in, and I reach them by approachin' at the right side. Here's how I gather in the young men. I hear a young feller that's proud of his voice, thinks that he can sing fine. I ask him to come around to Washington Hall and join our Glee Club. He comes and sings, and he's a follower of Plunkitt for life."

ACTIVITY: Have students suggest how modern-day politicians use similar strategies to reach their constituents.

VISUAL RECORD ANSWER

Students might suggest that it reveals a system of mutual reward.

Most political machines maintained their political power with the support of immigrant voters. In some cities, however, immigrants became active members of political machines, serving as officeholders, organizers, and representatives. In Boston, for example, the Irish American population was highly influential in the local Democratic machine. During the mid-1800s Irish Americans in Boston accounted for more than one third of the city's voters.

Because Irish Americans spoke English as a first language, they had slightly easier access to American political processes than many other immigrant groups. Many Irish Americans who were loyal to the political machine in Boston were rewarded with jobs in the local police and fire departments. Ambitious Irish American politicians rose quickly through the ranks of Boston's political machine. Second-generation immigrants John F. Fitzgerald—President John F. Kennedy's grandfather—and James Michael Curley both rose from the ranks of local boss to become mayor of the city during the late 1800s.

✔ **READING CHECK:** Why were immigrants important to political machines?

INTERPRETING THE VISUAL RECORD

Corruption. Working for the Tammany Hall political machine, these men are rewarded with new shoes for voting illegally. ***What does this photograph reveal about the effectiveness of Tammany Hall's organization?***

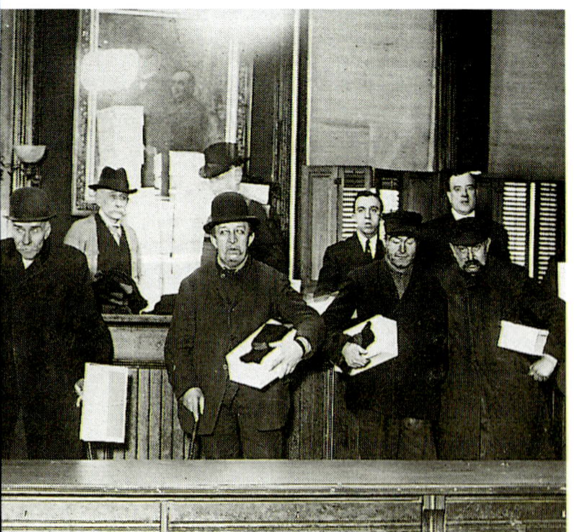

Graft and Corruption

Political machines often resorted to corruption in their attempt to take control of city governments. Although political machines successfully got party members reelected, machine corruption often interfered with the important functions of city government.

Election fraud. For political machines to maintain their power, their candidates had to win elections. When jobs and political favors were not enough to build popular support during elections, some political machines turned to fraud. A New York resident testified before the U.S. House of Representatives on election fraud.

> **"Gangs or bodies of men hired for the purpose, assembled at these headquarters where they were furnished with names and numbers, and under a leader or captain, they went out . . . in nearly every part of the city, registering many times each, and when the day of election came these repeaters, supplied abundantly with intoxicating drinks, and changing coats, hats, or caps, as occasion required to avoid recognition or detection, commenced the work of 'voting early and often.'"**

Voting fraud was widespread in many U.S. cities. For example, during one election in Philadelphia, a voting district with just 100 registered voters somehow returned 252 votes!

Graft. Once inside city government, political bosses often became even more corrupt. They looked for ways to increase their own political power and personal wealth. One way to get rich was to take advantage of the massive amounts of public funds involved in providing essential city services. Many city officials practiced

TEACH OBJECTIVE 3

LEVEL 1: Pair students and tell them to imagine that they are city officials attempting to end corruption in political machines. Have each pair create a dialogue describing how corruption and illegal activities developed in political machines. *(Students should note that machines hired men to "vote early and often" and that bosses took bribes, payoffs, and kickbacks.)* Ask volunteers to perform their dialogues for the class. **Sheltered English, Cooperative Learning**

LEVELS 2 AND 3: Briefly discuss political machines and corruption with students. Then organize students into small groups and tell them to imagine that they are investigative reporters. Have each group prepare an article describing how corruption developed in political machines. *(See the Level 1 lesson for the correct factors.)* Students should include examples of corruption, analyze its impact on city residents, and offer solutions. Ask volunteers to read their articles to the class.
Cooperative Learning

▶**ASSIGNMENT** *Distribute Cartoon 16, Tammany Hall, from* ***American History Political Cartoons****, and have each student complete it.*

graft—the acquisition of money or political power through illegal or dishonest methods. Graft was a common problem in almost every U.S. city with a powerful political machine.

Politicians often received bribes, payoffs, or **kickbacks**—payments of part of the earnings from a job or contract. Business leaders often paid kickbacks when lobbying for an opportunity to provide public services for a city. During the late 1890s a railway corporation paid Chicago aldermen as much as $25,000 to vote for local ordinances that would grant it special privileges. Also in Chicago, business leader Charles Tyson Yerkes built an empire of street railway lines by paying Alderman John Powers to support city ordinances favorable to his company. Yerkes was granted a virtual monopoly over Chicago's mass transit system. Explaining his loyalty to Yerkes, Powers once confessed, "You can't get elected to the [city] council unless Mr. Yerkes says so."

NEW-YORK HISTORICAL SOCIETY

This painting shows Tammany Hall.

Strategies for Success Synthesizing

Synthesizing is a key part of interpreting the past. To synthesize is to combine information and ideas from several different sources or points of view to obtain a new understanding of a topic or event. Most of the narrative writing in *The American Nation* is a synthesis. It pulls together data from a variety of sources to form an original account of our nation's history.

How to Synthesize

1. **Identify the subject and sources.** Identify the general topic or issue addressed by your sources. Then, if possible, find out about the personal, social, and historical background of the author of each source.
2. **Analyze the sources.** Examine carefully the information that each source provides about the subject. If your sources present different points of view, identify the main idea expressed by each source and determine whether it is supported by facts, opinions, or a combination of both.
3. **Compare and contrast the sources.** Examine the similarities and the differences between the information and ideas in your sources. As you do so, look for ways to link the sources together. Try to account for any different points of view.
4. **Form your own interpretation of the subject.** Use your analysis and comparison of the sources, along with your knowledge of the historical period, to form your own interpretation of the subject.

Applying the Strategy

Read George Washington Plunkitt's description of "honest graft" on the next page. Then synthesize this description with the following account of "honest graft" from a recent historical text.

> **"George Washington Plunkitt, a Tammany ward 'heeler' or boss, liked to call [the practice of profiting from one's office] 'honest graft,' a fair exchange of cash, influence, liquor, and above all jobs for working-class votes. Plunkitt and his fellow Tammany bosses lined their own pockets, stealing millions of dollars from the public treasury while allowing important decisions on issues such as public transportation to be made by those private entrepreneurs willing to pay large bribes."**

Practicing the Strategy

Answer the following questions.

1. Are the ideas expressed in each of these sources based on facts, opinions, or a combination of both?
2. How are these two accounts of "honest graft" similar? How are they different?
3. Based on these two sources and the knowledge you have gained from the text, what is your interpretation of "honest graft"?

ECONOMIC DEVELOPMENT

Graft in Action. Graft helped political machines make enormous profits. In order to claim these profits, machine-associated service providers padded their bills, charging cities up to 85 percent extra. This graft had an enormous impact on municipal funds. The New York City courthouse, for example, should have cost $3 million to construct. After widespread graft, however, it cost $11 million.

ACTIVITY: Tell students to imagine that they are investigative reporters who have found evidence of graft. Have them write the first few paragraphs of a newspaper article announcing the discovery.

STRATEGIES FOR SUCCESS ANSWERS

Applying the Strategy
Students should compare and contrast the sources and present their own interpretations of the material.

Practicing the Strategy

1. combination of both
2. Both acknowledge that honest graft resulted in some improvements for urban residents. Plunkitt sees honest graft as acceptable, however, while the historian views it as inherently corrupt.
3. Students should offer evidence to support their interpretations.

TEACH OBJECTIVE 4

LEVEL 1: Ask students to name the events that led to the collapse of public support for the Tweed Ring. *(Students should name the Thomas Nast cartoons and the* New York Times *articles.)* Then tell students to imagine that it is 1880 and that they are newspaper headline writers. Have each student write three headlines for editorials denouncing the Tweed Ring. Post the headlines around the classroom. **Sheltered English**

LEVEL 2: Ask students to name the events that led to the collapse of public support for the Tweed Ring. *(See the Level 1 lesson for the correct events.)* Then tell students to imagine that it is 1880 and that they are editorial writers. Have each student write a brief editorial denouncing the Tweed Ring. Have volunteers read their editorials to the class.

LEVEL 3: Ask students to name the events that led to the collapse of public support for the Tweed Ring. *(See the Level 1 lesson for the correct events.)* Then tell students to imagine that it is 1880 and that they are novelists. Have each student write a fable, or a story intended to prove a truth, denouncing the Tweed Ring. Remind students that fables often use animals to represent humans and human weaknesses. Ask volunteers to read their fables to the class. Students may wish to include their fables in their portfolios.

HISTORY MAKERS SPEAK

An unidentified writer in *The Nation*

Choosing a Candidate. When George Washington Plunkitt, a Tammany Hall boss, died in 1924, *The Nation,* one of the leading reform journals of the time, eulogized him as "one of the wisest men in American politics." According to *The Nation,* Plunkitt understood that to voters "honesty doesn't matter; efficiency doesn't matter; progressive vision doesn't matter. What matters is the chance of a better job, a better price for wheat, better business conditions."

CRITICAL THINKING Is *The Nation's* view of politics idealistic or pragmatic? Explain.

ANSWER: Students might answer pragmatic because the writer suggests that the help Plunkitt provides makes his corruption irrelevant.

AMERICAN ARTS ANSWERS

1. donkey–the Democratic Party; elephant–the Republican Party
2. caricature, analogy, use of recognizable images, literary allusion

VISUAL RECORD ANSWER

(for p. 223)

Students might suggest that the striped clothes look like prison garb.

When journalists and reformers began speaking out against the corruption of machine politics, some bosses attempted to defend their practices and personal economic gain. Political boss George Washington Plunkitt of Tammany Hall explained what he called "honest graft."

> **"My party's in power in the city, and it's goin' to undertake a lot of public improvements. Well, I'm tipped off, say, that they're going to lay out a new park at a certain place. . . . I go to that place and I buy up all the land I can in the neighborhood. Then the board of this or that makes its plan public, and there is a rush to get my land. . . . Ain't it perfectly honest to charge a good price and make a profit on my investment and foresight? . . . Well, that's honest graft."**

✔ **READING CHECK:** How did corruption and illegal activities develop in many political machines?

AMERICAN ARTS

Thomas Nast's Cartoons

One of the most influential political cartoonists of the late 1800s was Thomas Nast. Nast's cartoons increased the importance of cartoons in the American press. Nast drew cartoons with recognizable images and made creative use of standard cartoonist techniques such as caricatures—the portrayal of political figures with comically exaggerated features. Many of the common characters used in modern-day political cartoons, such as Uncle Sam, the Republican elephant, and the Democratic donkey, were first popularized by Nast. Editors for *Harper's Weekly* claimed that Nast's bold and witty cartoons increased the magazine's subscriptions by some 200,000.

The popularity of Nast's cartoons for *Harper's Weekly* inspired other journals to hire political cartoonists to boost circulation. Throughout the late 1800s publications such as *Puck, Judge,* and *Life* hired political cartoonists to offer witty and sharp commentary on political events. In doing so, political cartoonists perfected their use of analogies and literary allusions to refer to political events and characters. For example, many cartoonists portrayed politicians as Shakespearean characters such as Hamlet and Caesar, who engaged in political intrigue, to depict particular events of American political life. As in modern-day political cartoons, the cartoons of the late 1800s offered critical political commentary as well as humor.

Thomas Nast cartoon depicting U.S. political parties in the 1880s

Understanding the Arts

1. What do the donkey and the elephant represent in this cartoon?
2. What techniques do cartoonists use to depict political events?

REVIEW

Have students complete the **Section 1 Review** on p. 223.

ASSESS

Have students complete **Daily Quiz 7.1.** As **Alternative Assessment**, you may want to use the political boss monologue or the corruption dialogue in this section's lessons.

RETEACH

Have students complete **Main Idea Activity for Reteaching and Sheltered English 7.1.** Then assign students subsections of Section 1. Have each student create a crossword puzzle using important names and terms from the assigned subsection. Have students exchange puzzles, complete them, and then return them to their creators for grading. **Sheltered English**

EXTEND

Write the names of the following political bosses on the chalkboard: *Alexander Shepherd, James Pendergast, John Powers, George Washington Plunkitt,* and *William Marcy Tweed.* Have students research one of these bosses. Tell students to present their research in the form of a report. Students' reports should include basic biographical information about the boss, detail his rise in the given political machine, and describe his fall, if appropriate. Ask volunteers to present their reports to the class. **Block Scheduling**

The Tweed Ring. Plunkitt's bold admission of his own graft offers a clue as to the amount of corruption in Tammany Hall. Tammany Hall had a long history as a social and political organization dating back to 1789. However, it is best known for the period during the 1860s when William Marcy Tweed reigned as its boss.

Tweed had considerable control over the issuing of contracts for public projects and government jobs. Tweed and his ring of political supporters used this position of power to gain bribes and kickbacks. Historians have estimated that the Tweed Ring collected more than $200 million in graft between 1865 and 1871.

Tweed's political power and control over the Tammany machine collapsed abruptly when public opinion turned against him. The corruption of Tammany Hall and the Tweed Ring was mercilessly revealed in a series of political cartoons drawn by Thomas Nast. In 1871 Nast published some 50 cartoons in *Harper's Weekly* that sharply criticized Tweed and Tammany Hall. Aware of the power of Nast's cartoons to influence public opinion, Tweed demanded, "Stop them . . . pictures. I don't care so much what the papers write about me. My constituents can't read. But . . . they can see pictures."

Along with a series of articles published in the *New York Times,* Nast's cartoons exposed the corruption of Tammany Hall and contributed to Tweed's indictment for fraud and extortion in 1871. Tweed escaped from jail but was arrested in Spain. Officials there recognized him from one of Nast's drawings. While serving the remainder of his 12-year sentence, Tweed died in jail.

INTERPRETING THE VISUAL RECORD

Tweed Ring. Thomas Nast's cartoons helped expose Boss Tweed. ***What characteristics of this cartoon suggest corruption?***

✔ **READING CHECK:** What events led to the collapse of public support for the Tweed Ring?

SECTION  REVIEW

Define and explain the significance of the following terms:
political machines
political bosses
graft
kickbacks

Identify and explain the significance of the following individuals:
Alexander Shepherd
James Pendergast
George Washington Plunkitt
William Marcy Tweed
Thomas Nast

1. **Using Graphic Organizers** Copy the graphic organizer below. Use it to explain how political machines built support for their candidates.

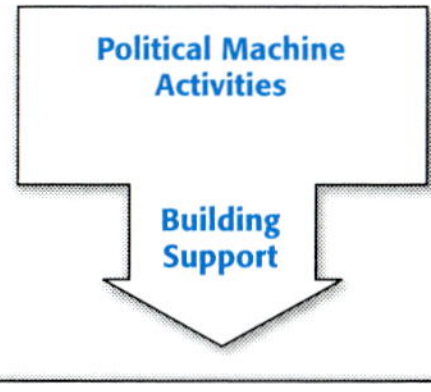

2. **Synthesizing** What kinds of corrupt activities did political bosses engage in once they gained power?
3. **Analyzing** How did political machines build support among immigrant groups?
4. **Hypothesizing** Despite the evidence of corruption, political machines retained strong public support. Why did people continue to support the machines?

Critical Thinking

5. Review the Thomas Nast cartoon at the top of this page. What effect did Nast's political cartoons have on public support for the Tweed Ring?
Consider:
- how William Marcy Tweed is portrayed in the cartoon
- what political statement a newspaper reader might be able to interpret from the drawing
- what the cartoon does that newspaper articles cannot do

SECTION 1 REVIEW ANSWERS

Define and Identify

For significance, see the following pages:

- political machines, p. 218
- political bosses, p. 218
- Alexander Shepherd, p. 219
- James Pendergast, p. 219
- graft, p. 221
- kickbacks, p. 221
- George Washington Plunkitt, p. 222
- William Marcy Tweed, p. 223
- Thomas Nast, p. 223

1. political machine activities—created hierarchical political organizations, provided new public services, offered favors, found jobs for voters, helped immigrants get settled, assisted in immigrant naturalization; response of loyal supporters—voted for the machine candidates, sometimes assisted in election fraud, ignored graft by leaders

2. Political bosses often participated in voter fraud, acquired money or political power through dishonest practices, and received bribes for awarding government contracts.

3. helped new arrivals find housing and jobs; helped them become citizens; improved neighborhood conditions

4. Students might mention that political machines often rewarded citizens by improving their living situations and giving them government jobs.

5. turned public opinion against it

SECTION 2

After completing Section 2, students should be able to:

OBJECTIVE 1 *Identify the scandals that plagued the Grant administration.*

OBJECTIVE 2 *Explain why Americans wanted political reform, and analyze how this desire affected the Republican Party.*

OBJECTIVE 3 *Describe President Arthur's changing positions on civil service reform, and analyze how this affected his political party.*

OBJECTIVE 4 *Describe how President Harrison dealt with President Cleveland's reforms.*

LET'S GET STARTED!

Write the following scenario on the chalkboard: *You are a leading member of Political Party X. You are extremely concerned about corruption in government. How do you attempt to reform the system? Do you make such attempts even though they might split your party and cause your own political demise?* As students enter the classroom, ask them to respond to the scenario in writing. Tell students that in Section 2 they will learn how Gilded Age officials attempted to reform politics—and how those reforms affected political parties.

SECTION 2 RESOURCES

PRINT

- Guided Reading Strategy 7.2
- Graphic Organizer Activity 7: An Expanding Population
- Literature Reading 7: A New Kind of Politician
- Section 2 Review, p. 230
- Daily Quiz 7.2

MULTIMEDIA

- One-Stop Planner, Lesson 7.2
- The American Nation Video Program Segment: The American Red Cross; Teacher's Guide, pp. 201–02
- Holt Researcher: American History CD–ROM

SHELTERED ENGLISH

- Main Idea Activity for Reteaching and Sheltered English 7.2

✔ READING TO UNDERSTAND

To help students master the section objectives, have them answer the **READING CHECKS** and complete **Guided Reading Strategy 7.2** as they read the section.

Restoring Honest Government

OBJECTIVES

Read to understand:

1. what scandals plagued the Grant administration
2. why Americans wanted political reform, and how this desire affected the Republican Party
3. why President Arthur's positions on civil service reform changed, and how this affected his political party
4. how President Harrison dealt with President Cleveland's reforms

KEY TERMS

Gilded Age
Stalwarts
Pendleton Civil Service Act
mugwumps

KEY PEOPLE

James A. Garfield
Chester A. Arthur
Grover Cleveland
Benjamin Harrison

"Mr. Lincoln . . . held that ours is a government of the people, by the people, for the people. I maintain, on the contrary, that it is a government of politicians, by politicians, for politicians."
—William McElroy

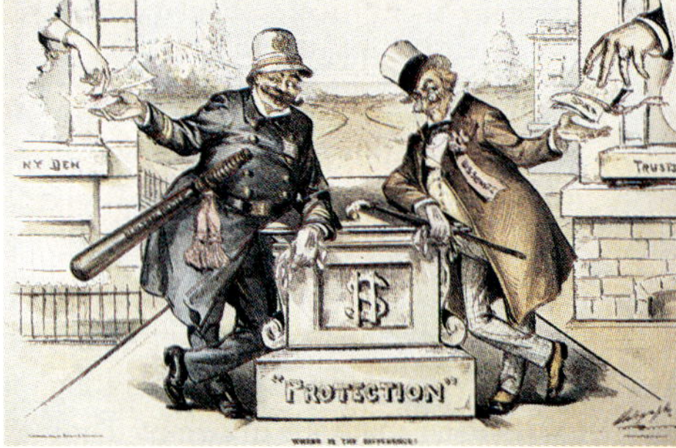

Political cartoon depicting corruption

William McElroy expressed a sentiment held by many Americans in this fictional letter of advice to a young politician that was printed in the *Atlantic Monthly* in 1880. Corruption and fraud affected politics at a national level as well as locally. During the late 1800s national scandals exposed illegal financial practices by high-ranking politicians. Many Americans began to question the character of some elected officials. Most observers of the time offered similar condemnations of national political life. "One might search the whole list of Congress, Judiciary, and Executive [branches] during the 25 years 1870 to 1895, and find little but damaged reputation," claimed historian Henry Adams. "The period was poor in purpose and barren in results."

Scandal in the White House

In 1869 political boss William Tweed and his gang looted the New York City treasury. That same year, Ulysses S. Grant began his service as president of the United States. Republican Party leaders seeking a moderate candidate had selected Grant to run for the presidency. His fame as a Union army general made him a popular candidate. With the slogan "Let us have peace," Grant won the election. He seemed to be the leader the country needed to get through the post–Civil War years.

These headlines report the economic troubles of 1869.

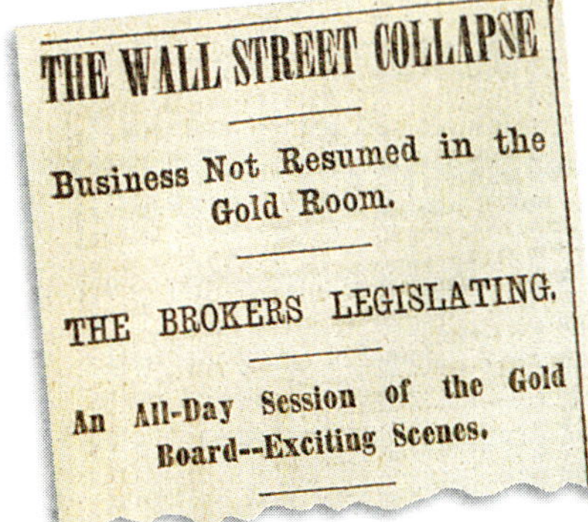

THE WALL STREET COLLAPSE

Business Not Resumed in the Gold Room.

THE BROKERS LEGISLATING.

An All-Day Session of the Gold Board--Exciting Scenes.

Grant's first term. Grant's first term in office, however, was marred by several scandals. Grant's troubles began on Black Friday—September 24, 1869. On that day financier Jay Gould and James Fisk—the president's brother-in-law—made an attempt to corner the gold market. Many Wall Street investors and speculators were ruined financially. A congressional investigation into the event revealed that Gould and Abel Rathbone Corbin had tried to influence the government's financial policies to their own benefit. The president refused to follow Gould and Corbin's advice, but the two spread rumors anyway that Grant had agreed with them. These rumors had led to widespread speculation in the gold market. There was even some evidence that the president's wife, Julia Grant, had invested $500,000 in the gold market.

In 1872 an even greater scandal surfaced. This time Grant's vice president, Schuyler Colfax, was involved. In 1867, directors of the

Teacher to Teacher

Sue Reeder of Wintersprings, Florida, suggested the following activity: Organize students into groups of two or three. Ask groups to carefully read the material on the scandals during Ulysses S. Grant's presidency. Have each group create a political cartoon on one or more of these scandals. Then ask groups to exchange cartoons. Ask groups to identify the main characters, actions, and themes of the cartoons.

TEACH OBJECTIVE 1

LEVEL 1: Ask students to name and describe the scandals that plagued the Grant administration. *(Students should mention the gold market scandal, the Crédit Mobilier scandal, and the Whiskey Ring scandal.)* Briefly discuss those scandals. Then tell students to imagine that it is 1875 and that they are planning to attend a town meeting on the scandals. Have each student prepare written notes describing how the scandals have affected his or her view of politics. *(Students should note that the scandals led people to be more skeptical of politics and politicians.)* Ask volunteers to use their notes to give a brief speech on the topic to the class. **Sheltered English**

Union Pacific Railroad had formed the Crédit Mobilier corporation. They then awarded the company contracts to build a section of the transcontinental railroad. Union Pacific Railroad stockholders gave or sold shares of stock in the construction of the transcontinental railroad to congressmembers. The stockholders hoped to gain influence and favorable legislation.

The Crédit Mobilier stock proved to be a profitable deal for the members of Congress. Congress issued federal subsidies for the cost of the railroad construction. The U.S. government paid little attention to Crédit Mobilier's operations and was unaware of costs of the construction it had subsidized. Crédit Mobilier was able to overcharge Union Pacific by more than $20 million. These excess profits went straight into the pockets of Crédit Mobilier's stockholders. These stockholders included members of Congress such as Schuyler Colfax, who was then Speaker of the House. Although the schemes took place before Grant became president, the subsequent scandal tarnished his administration's image because of Colfax's position as vice president.

Newspaper editor Horace Greeley ran against President Grant in the 1872 election.

The election of 1872. The multiplying scandals encouraged political opponents to challenge Grant in the presidential election of 1872. Many critics saw the corruption in Grant's administration as a by-product of the spoils system. Rather than award civil service jobs as rewards, they wanted ability to be the deciding factor. Reformers proposed that applicants who earned the highest grades on competitive examinations should receive the jobs.

Civil service reform was the battle cry of *New York Tribune* editor Horace Greeley, Grant's Liberal Republican opponent in the 1872 presidential race. The Liberal Republican Party was formed by Republicans shocked by the Grant scandals and tired of Reconstruction. Hoping to benefit from the split in the Republican Party, Democrats also threw their support behind Greeley.

Liberal Republicans saw the Crédit Mobilier scandal as a nail in Grant's political coffin. However, Grant played on his image as a war hero and easily won re-election. Disheartened and exhausted, Greeley died just 24 days after the election. His party did not last much longer. It seemed that civil service reform was finished too.

✔ **READING CHECK:** What scandals plagued the Grant administration?

Grant's second term. The episodes of corruption continued during Grant's second term in office. In 1874 a new scandal erupted over the taxation of whiskey. Some officials at the Treasury Department who had received their positions as a result of the spoils system were charged with accepting bribes from distillers and distributors of whiskey. In return, treasury officials reduced the amount of taxes that the whiskey distributors had to pay. Public exposure of the so-called Whiskey Ring further encouraged reformers. Hoping to end the fraud under the spoils system, reformers pushed to end the practice of granting jobs as political rewards. The scandals also increased many Americans' distrust of politicians.

INTERPRETING THE VISUAL RECORD

Grant's administration. Public exposure of corruption in Grant's administration led to increasing opposition to the spoils system. ***What does this cartoon suggest about Grant's administration?***

THE GRANGER COLLECTION, NEW YORK

ECONOMIC DEVELOPMENT

Scandals in the Grant Administration. The Crédit Mobilier scandal was only one of the scandals that plagued the Grant administration. In another example of corruption, Grant's secretary of war, William W. Belknap, collected yearly bribes from merchants who had the exclusive and very profitable rights to trade with American Indians on reservations and with frontier army posts.

CRITICAL THINKING How might Belknap's actions have harmed the economy?

ANSWER: Students might suggest that by exchanging exclusive trade rights for bribes, Belknap limited entrepreneurial opportunities.

THAT'S INTERESTING!

Scholar Ari Hoogenboom argues that historians of the Gilded Age have relied too heavily on sources by reformers, leading to a misguided portrait of the era. He believes that reformers exaggerated events and were "outsiders" who wanted to displace the "insiders" and take their places.

VISUAL RECORD ANSWER

Students might answer that the cartoon suggests that the Grant administration was a circus and allowed corruption to flourish.

LEVELS 2 AND 3: Ask students to name and describe the scandals that plagued the Grant administration. *(See the Level 1 lesson for the correct scandals.)* Briefly discuss those scandals. Then tell students to imagine that it is 1875 and that they have just read a magazine article devoted to the scandals. Have each student write a letter to the editor describing how the scandals have affected his or her view of politics. *(See the Level 1 lesson for the correct effects.)* Students' letters should also express their conception of "good government." Students may wish to include their letters in their portfolios.

▶**ASSIGNMENT** *Write the following quotation by Mark Twain (see this page for full context) on the chalkboard:* "In a free country like ours, where any man can run for Congress and anybody can vote for him, you can't expect immortal purity all the time—it ain't in nature." *Have each student write several paragraphs evaluating the quotation in light of what he or she has learned about politics in the Gilded Age.*

NOTE: For an additional teaching idea, see the Chapter 7 interrupted film lesson in the **Creative Teaching Strategies** handbook.

THAT'S INTERESTING!

Although some writers criticized corruption during the Gilded Age, others actively participated in it, accepting bribes from political bosses and business owners. This corruption led one editor to write, "All being corrupt together what is the use of investigating each other."

AMERICAN LETTERS ANSWERS

1. to appear to the public to be fighting corruption, without having to actually punish anyone
2. He is pragmatic and ruthless.
3. to show corrupt aspects of American politics

THAT'S INTERESTING!

(for p. 227)

James Bryce, a political observer, characterized Gilded Age politics by saying, "[The Democrats and the Republicans] were like two bottles. Each bore a label denoting the kind of liquor it contained, but each was empty."

Mark Twain's Political Writings

Throughout his literary career, Mark Twain had a rare ability to present compelling and often humorous stories that dealt with important issues in American society. Twain used satire, a form of writing that uses humor to point out human faults. In the 1873 novel The Gilded Age, *Twain and co-author Charles Dudley Warner present a satirical conversation about Congress's inability to weed out corrupt politicians. Twain's 1889 novel,* A Connecticut Yankee in King Arthur's Court, *offers a commentary on American political ambition. In the tale a Connecticut man finds himself transported back in time to medieval England. The excerpt describes the man's thoughts as he begins to discover that he is in the 500s, not the 1800s.*

from *The Gilded Age*

"I think Congress always tries to do as near right as it can, according to its lights. A man can't ask any fairer than that. The first preliminary it always starts out on, is to clean itself, so to speak. It will arraign [put on trial] two or three dozen of its members, or maybe four or five dozen, for taking bribes to vote for this and that and the other bill last winter."

Mark Twain

"It goes up into the dozens, does it?"

"Well, yes; in a free country like ours, where any man can run for Congress and anybody can vote for him, you can't expect immortal purity all the time—it ain't in nature. . . ."

"So Congress always lies helpless in quarantine ten weeks of a session. That's encouraging. Colonel, poor Laura will never get any benefit from our bill. Her trial will be over before Congress has half purified itself.—And doesn't it occur to you that by the time it has expelled all its impure members there may not be enough members left to do business legally?"

"Why I did not say Congress would expel anybody. . . . But good God we *try* them, don't we!"

from *A Connecticut Yankee in King Arthur's Court*

Wherefore, being a practical Connecticut man, . . . I made up my mind to two things: if it was still the nineteenth century and I was among lunatics and couldn't get away, I would presently boss that asylum or know the reason why; and if, on the other hand, it was really the sixth century, all right, I didn't want any softer thing: I would boss the whole country inside of three months; for I judged I would have the start of the best-educated man in the kingdom by a matter of thirteen hundred years and upward.

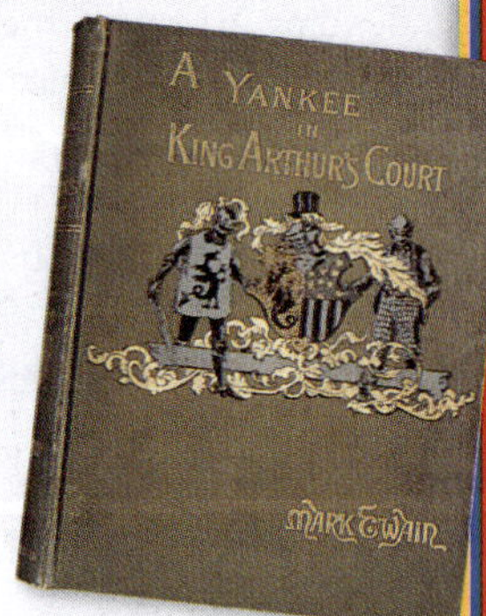

Cover of *A Connecticut Yankee in King Arthur's Court*

UNDERSTANDING LITERATURE

1. Why would Congress try its members for corruption but not expel them?
2. How does the Connecticut man resemble politicians in the late 1800s?
3. How does Twain use humor and exaggeration in these selections to portray American political life?

TEACH OBJECTIVE 2

LEVEL 1: Tell students to imagine that they are pro-reform Americans. Have each student design a poster in support of reform. Posters should clearly explain why Americans wanted reform during the Gilded Age. *(Students' posters should somehow note the existence of widespread corruption and the desire for honest officials.)* Have students present their posters to the class. Then have students write a topic sentence explaining how the desire for reform affected the Republicans. *(Different views on reform split the party into the Stalwarts and the Half-Breeds.)* Students may wish to include their posters and their sentences in their portfolios.
Sheltered English

LEVEL 2: Tell students to imagine that they are pro-reform Americans preparing to speak at a congressional meeting on political corruption. Have each student write a brief speech explaining why he or she wants political reform. *(See the Level 1 lesson for the correct reasons.)* Ask volunteers to deliver their speeches to the class. Then ask students how different attitudes toward reform affected the Republicans. *(See the Level 1 lesson for the correct effect.)* Ask students if this split was inevitable. Was there any way, given the realities of the time, that the Republicans could have maintained party unity?

Politics of the Gilded Age. The politics of scandal and corruption shocked and troubled many voters. Citizens began to cast a more skeptical eye on the behavior and ethical standards of their political leaders. In 1873 Mark Twain and Charles Dudley Warner published a satirical novel. The book examined the values of wealthy Americans and the nature of national politics after the Civil War. Twain and Warner titled their novel *The Gilded Age.* They believed that politics was like the base material that hides beneath the glittering gold surface of a gilded object. In politics corruption and greed lurked below the polite and prosperous luster of American society during the late 1800s. The image struck a chord, and the era became known as the **Gilded Age**.

The authors had ample evidence to support their view—particularly in the area of politics. Despite the upper and middle classes' adoption of British Victorian culture, Twain argued that Americans were actually driven by "money lust." Twain accused Americans of holding the motto "Get rich; dishonestly if we can, honestly if we must." Politicians of both parties—and at every level of government—made speeches about the great honor of holding public office. However, they often showed more interest in taking advantage of their positions to steal from the public treasury than in serving the public good. "Unless you can get . . . a Senator, or a Congressman, . . . to use his 'influence' in your behalf, you cannot get an employment of the most trivial nature in Washington," wrote Twain. "Mere merit, fitness and capability, are useless baggage to you without 'influence.'" Motivated by a distrust of political leaders, many Americans began to push for political reforms during the Gilded Age.

Mark Twain and Charles Dudley Warner's novel* The Gilded Age *described American political life as a gilded surface with corruption and greed lying underneath.

The Struggle for Reform

Reforming the spoils system again became a major issue in the 1876 presidential campaign. Democrats hoped to make the corruption of the Grant administration a campaign issue. They nominated New York governor Samuel J. Tilden as their presidential candidate. Tilden had won national attention by helping break up the corrupt Tweed Ring. The Republicans also nominated a reform candidate, Ohio governor Rutherford B. Hayes, who was a well-known supporter of civil service reform. Hayes narrowly won the election.

A split in the Republican Party. President Hayes's reform efforts soon angered his party. The Republicans had split into two groups—nicknamed the **Stalwarts** and the Half-Breeds—over the issue of patronage, or rewarding political supporters with government jobs. Led by Senator Roscoe Conkling of New York, the Stalwarts strongly opposed reform. Conkling referred to the proposed merit system for government jobs as "snivel service."

Led by James G. Blaine of Maine, who claimed to support reform, the Half-Breeds did not completely oppose patronage jobs. Julius Bing was an early supporter of civil service reform. While still a young congressional aide, Bing published an article in the journal *The North American Review.* He argued in favor of the use of civil service exams to grant jobs on merit rather than by patronage.

INTERPRETING THE VISUAL RECORD

Civil Service Reform. Examinations like this one, for railway mail clerks, helped ensure that government workers were qualified for the jobs they held. ***What categories were railway mail clerks tested in?***

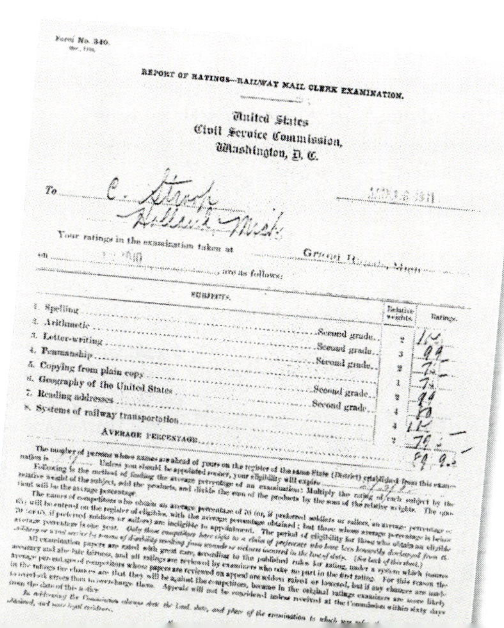

Form No. 340.

REPORT OF RATINGS—RAILWAY MAIL CLERK EXAMINATION.

United States
Civil Service Commission,
Washington, D. C.

To C. Stroh
Holland, Mich.

Your ratings in the examination taken at Grand Rapids, Mich. are as follows:

SUBJECTS.		Relative weights.	Ratings.
1. Spelling			
2. Arithmetic	Second grade.	2	[illegible]
3. Letter-writing	Second grade.	3	[illegible]
4. Penmanship	Second grade.	2	[illegible]
5. Copying from plain copy		1	[illegible]
6. Geography of the United States	Second grade.	2	[illegible]
7. Reading addresses	Second grade.	4	[illegible]
8. Systems of railway transportation		4	[illegible]
AVERAGE PERCENTAGE		2	[illegible]

HISTORY MAKERS SPEAK

James Bryce in *Voices of America: Readings in American History*

The Trouble with Politics. One English observer blamed the political chaos of the Gilded Age on the politicians themselves. Historian James Bryce wrote, "The hard commercial spirit which pervades the meetings of a joint-stock company is the spirit in which most politicians speak of public business, and are not blamed for speaking. . . . In no country is the ideal side of public life . . . so ignored by the mass and repudiated by the leaders. This affects not only the elevation but the independence and courage of public men; and the country suffers from the lack of what we call distinction in its conspicuous figures."

CRITICAL THINKING

According to Bryce, what caused "the lack of distinction" in American politicians?

ANSWER: Students might point out Bryce's comments about politicians' desire for profit and the public's casual attitude toward corruption.

VISUAL RECORD ANSWER

Students might cite spelling, arithmetic, letter-writing, penmanship, copying from plain copy, geography, reading addresses, and systems of railway transportation.

LEVEL 3: Tell students to imagine that they are modern-day historians working on a history of the Gilded Age. Have each student write a one-page essay explaining why Americans wanted political reform and how that desire affected the Republicans. *(See the Level 1 lesson for the correct reasons and effect.)* Ask volunteers to read their essays to the class. Students may wish to include their essays in their portfolios.

SPOTLIGHT on the Pendleton Civil Service Act

After students have read the entire section, ask them to conduct research on the Pendleton Civil Service Act. Then tell students to imagine that the following people attended a press conference on the act: Roscoe Conkling, Julius Bing, Chester Arthur, James Blaine, Grover Cleveland, Samuel Tilden, and Benjamin Harrison. Assign students to play these roles and ask other students to act as reporters, politicians, and interested citizens. Have each main participant present a short statement on his reaction to the Pendleton Civil Service Act. Then act as a moderator and conduct the press conference. Remind the reporters and citizens to question each participant about his position and his record.

Block Scheduling, Cooperative Learning

PEOPLE IN HISTORY

Chester A. Arthur. When Charles Guiteau shot President Garfield, many Americans were horrified at the thought of Chester A. Arthur becoming president. Many viewed Arthur as a corrupt spoilsman in thrall to Stalwart leader Senator Roscoe Conkling. Garfield lived for 80 days after the assassination attempt, however, and during that time Arthur rose in public opinion. Many people believed that he acted with dignity during the crisis and showed great concern for Garfield and his family. After Garfield died, Arthur participated in a national outpouring of grief.

CRITICAL THINKING Would Arthur's actions after the assassination attempt have convinced you to support him? Why or why not?

ANSWER: Some students might argue that the assassination attempt changed Arthur and made him a better person.

***The American Nation* VIDEO PROGRAM**

The American Red Cross; Teacher's Guide, pp. 201–02

Search 49210, Play to 50586
Videodisc 1, Side B

Play Pause

See *Teacher's Guide* for Spanish barcode.

Then and Now

Civil Service

Although the Pendleton Civil Service Act transferred just 10 percent of federal jobs to a merit-based system of hiring, the act did create the Civil Service Commission (CSC). The CSC established policies for examination and hiring based on merit rather than political patronage. At the time, many officials were concerned that geographical biases of the testing would cause most jobs to go to well-educated New Englanders. To avoid this bias in testing, the CSC specified that the examinations should be "practical in character." The exam should test applicants on skills and knowledge closely related to the actual tasks of the job.

Modern Americans taking a civil service exam

The use of civil service examinations has greatly expanded since 1883. The variety of government jobs requiring exams has also grown. The federal government disbanded the CSC in 1978 and assigned its tasks to other federal agencies. Many state and city civil service commissions still exist to oversee nonfederal government jobs. Today, examinations are given to applicants for positions in fields such as air-traffic control, foreign service, law enforcement, and postal service. Once employed, civil service employees have special protection against politically motivated dismissals. To ensure the strength of the merit system, civil service commissions review dismissals to verify that employees are dismissed only for reasons directly related to job performance.

> **"Argument against the reform of the present chaos is the fear of a permanent bureaucracy, and of the anti-republican tendencies of such permanent institutions. We entertain no such apprehensions [fears]. A permanent bureaucracy is only dangerous when it is *incompetent and practically irresponsible.*"**

Civil service reform remained controversial within both political parties throughout the Gilded Age.

Hayes chose not to run for re-election in 1880, noting the political conflict between the Stalwarts and the Half-Breeds within his own party. He explained to his wife, "I am heartily tired of this life of bondage, responsibility, and toil." At the Republican convention, the Stalwarts and the Half-Breeds battled to control the party ticket. The Half-Breeds won. They named the relatively unknown senator James A. Garfield as the Republican Party's presidential candidate. To satisfy the Stalwarts, they placed Conkling's political ally Chester A. Arthur on the ticket as the vice presidential nominee.

✔ **READING CHECK:** Why did Americans want political reform? How did this desire affect the Republican Party?

Garfield's assassination. Garfield edged out his Democratic rival, Civil War veteran General Winfield Scott Hancock, by fewer than 10,000 votes. His presidency was short-lived, however. On July 2, 1881, Garfield was shot, less than four months after his inauguration. The assassin was Charles Guiteau (guh-TOH), a mentally unstable man who had unsuccessfully sought a government job. Ironically, in the days before the incident Garfield had refused to increase the security around the White House. He commented, "Assassination can no more be guarded against than death by lightning; and it is not best to worry about either."

President James A. Garfield was shot by Charles Guiteau in a Washington train station.

TEACH OBJECTIVES 3 AND 4

ALL LEVELS: Write the following names on the chalkboard: *James A. Garfield, Chester A. Arthur, Grover Cleveland,* and *Benjamin Harrison.* Ask students to list what they know about these presidents. Have volunteers share their responses. *(Most students will probably not know much about the listed presidents.)* Tell students that this period can be confusing because of the quick shifts in political power. To help students understand how these presidents viewed political reform during the Gilded Age, copy the following graphic organizer on the chalkboard, omitting the italicized answers. Have each student complete it. **Sheltered English**

President Arthur and Reforms
- *supported reform after the assassination of President Garfield*
- *helped pass Pendleton Civil Service Act*

Effect on the Republicans and the Election of 1884
- *split the Republicans*
- *Stalwarts voted for James Blaine, the Half-Breed candidate; reform Republicans voted for Grover Cleveland, the Democratic candidate*

President Cleveland's Reforms
- *doubled the number of federal jobs requiring civil service exams*
- *promoted reform in general*

President Harrison's Response
- *returned to political patronage*
- *spent money on Republican pet projects*

Guiteau had believed that killing Garfield would further the Stalwart cause. The shooting had the opposite effect, however. After Garfield died in September, his successor, Arthur, responded sympathetically to the calls for reform and abandoned his opposition to it.

Reforms and reactions. In 1883 President Arthur helped secure passage of the **Pendleton Civil Service Act**. The bill established the Civil Service Commission to administer competitive examinations to those people seeking government jobs. The act proved to be an important step toward reform. It established as law the idea that federal jobs below the policy-making level should be filled based on merit. Critics charged, however, that the act was of limited value. They noted that it applied to only about 10 percent of all federal jobs.

PRESIDENTIAL *Lives*

Grover Cleveland

1837–1908
In Office 1885–1889 and 1893–1897

Grover Cleveland is the only U.S. president to serve two nonconsecutive terms. After completing his first term, Cleveland did not miss the busy life of the presidency. He wrote in 1889, "You cannot imagine the relief which has come to me with the termination of my official term." Enjoying his free time, Cleveland described his new interests, "I started the fishing branch of the firm business today. . . . I caught twenty-five fish with my own rod and line."

In 1892 the Democratic Party began searching for a candidate to run against Benjamin Harrison. They again called upon Cleveland. He was not eager to run again after his defeat four years earlier. "The office of President has not, to me personally, a single allurement [attraction]." Nevertheless, Cleveland felt compelled by a sense of duty to his party to run for the presidency.

Angered by Arthur's reform efforts, many Stalwarts refused to support his bid for the 1884 Republican presidential nomination. Instead, they cast their votes for James Blaine, the leader of the Half-Breeds. Blaine's nomination upset Republican reformers. They charged that the candidate "wallowed in spoils like a rhinoceros in an African pool." Called **mugwumps**—the Algonquian word for "big chiefs"—these reformers supported the Democratic candidate, Grover Cleveland. Like Samuel Tilden, Cleveland had gained national attention when he opposed Tammany Hall while governor of New York.

Instead of a discussion of the issues, mudslinging dominated the campaign. A bachelor, Cleveland was accused of fathering a child out of wedlock. He refused to participate in the mudslinging however, replying, "The other side can have a monopoly of all the dirt in this campaign." The New York *World* defended Cleveland, listing four reasons for supporting the candidate. "1. He is an honest man; 2. He is an honest man; 3. He is an honest man; 4. He is an honest man." Despite the charges against Cleveland's character and private life, he won the election.

✔ **READING CHECK:** How did Chester A. Arthur change his position on civil service reform after Garfield's assassination? How did this affect his political party?

James Blaine (left), leader of the Half-Breeds, won the Republican Party nomination for president in 1884. Grover Cleveland (right) received the Democratic nomination.

Advances and Setbacks

Proclaiming that "a public office is a public trust," President Cleveland entered the White House determined to promote political reform. Cleveland hoped to end the days when government jobs were handed out in reward for political favors. Toward this end, he doubled the number of federal jobs requiring civil service exams.

DEMOCRATIC VALUES

"Rum, Romanism, and Rebellion." New York governor Grover Cleveland should have been able to expect strong support from Democratic voters in New York City in the 1884 presidential election. Tammany Hall bosses were feuding with Cleveland, however, and it appeared that many of the organization's Democratic members would not vote. Shortly before the election, though, a Blaine supporter commented that the Democrats were the party of "Rum, Romanism, and Rebellion." Newspapers widely reported the comment, and many of Tammany's Irish American voters interpreted it as a nativist insult to their heritage and religion. They voted for Cleveland in large numbers. This support helped Cleveland win the close election.

CRITICAL THINKING Why might Irish Americans have objected to the term "Romanism"?

ANSWER: Students might suggest that "Romanism" referred to Catholicism because the Vatican is based in Rome.

REVIEW

Have students complete the **Section 2 Review** on p. 230.

ASSESS

Have students complete **Daily Quiz 7.2.** As **Alternative Assessment,** you may want to use the political reform poster or the political reform speech in this section's lessons.

RETEACH

Have students complete **Main Idea Activity for Reteaching and Sheltered English 7.2.** Then organize students into small groups. Ask groups to reread the objectives at the beginning of the section. Have each group discuss the objectives in round-robin style, with one student in each group recording the answers. Then have recorders read their groups' answers to the entire class. **Sheltered English, Cooperative Learning**

EXTEND

Ask students to conduct research on various historical interpretations of the Gilded Age. Ask each student to select one historian and to find one sentence from his or her work that comments on the age in an interesting, enlightening way. Have students present their sentences in class, offering relevant background information and explaining why the sentence accurately reflects the Gilded Age. **Block Scheduling**

SECTION 2 REVIEW ANSWERS

Define and Identify

For significance, see the following pages:

- Gilded Age, p. 227
- Stalwarts, p. 227
- James A. Garfield, p. 228
- Chester A. Arthur, p. 228–29
- Pendleton Civil Service Act, p. 229
- mugwumps, p. 229
- Grover Cleveland, p. 229
- Benjamin Harrison, p. 230

1. voters' reaction to the Grant administration—citizens become more skeptical about the behavior and ethical standards of their political leaders; types of reform desired—civil service reform; impact on the Republican Party—party splits into Stalwarts and Half-Breeds

2. because they might have believed that a merit system would favor those who could afford a good education

3. the assassination of Garfield; the Stalwarts nominated Blaine in 1884. The mugwumps threw their support to the Democrat, Cleveland, who won.

4. Cleveland—supported civil service reform; Harrison—believed in the spoils system

5. Students might mention that the corruption that came out of his office eventually led to civil service reform.

Read More About It

Free Find:
Grover Cleveland
After reading about Grover Cleveland on the Holt Researcher CD–ROM, write a short essay summarizing the role of Cleveland in the history of civil service reform in the United States.

Cleveland's support of reform efforts outraged many Stalwarts and Democratic legislators. One Democratic member of Congress defended the spoils system by arguing that civil service reform was inconsistent with the U.S. republican electoral process.

> **"Take the President. On this theory, Cleveland should have said to Arthur on March 4th [inauguration day], 'Mr. Arthur, it's true the people have chosen me to fill your place. But I believe that when a man is in office and is doing well, he should not be disturbed. Everyone says you are a good President, so I'll just go back to my law practice in Buffalo and leave you in the White House.'"**

Although Cleveland's stand on reform annoyed some party leaders, he won the Democratic presidential nomination in 1888. To oppose him, the Republicans chose Benjamin Harrison of Indiana, a grandson of the ninth president, William Henry Harrison. Cleveland won the popular election by some 100,000 votes. However, Harrison came out on top in electoral votes and won the race.

The new president and Congress quickly set out to reward their supporters, thereby weakening the reform efforts of Cleveland. The Republicans filled practically every job not on the civil service list with members of their own party. During 1890 Republican politicians controlled Congress and the presidency. They passed laws easily, spending considerable amounts of money on Civil War pensions for Union veterans—who mostly voted Republican—and other pet projects. Congress spent money so freely that it became known as the Billion Dollar Congress.

✔ **READING CHECK:** How did President Harrison deal with the reform efforts of President Cleveland?

SECTION  REVIEW

Define and explain the significance of the following terms:
Gilded Age
Stalwarts
Pendleton Civil Service Act
mugwumps

Identify and explain the significance of the following individuals:
James A. Garfield
Chester A. Arthur
Grover Cleveland
Benjamin Harrison

1. **Using Graphic Organizers** Copy the graphic organizer below. Use it to explain how the desire of voters for political reform influenced Republican Party politics.

Voters' reaction to the Grant administration
↓
Types of reform desired
↓
Impact on the Republican Party

2. **Identifying Values** Why do you think many Stalwarts argued that ending the spoils system was antirepublican and contrary to the democratic heritage of the United States?
3. **Identifying Cause and Effect** What caused President Arthur to change his position on civil service reform? What effect did this have on his party?
4. **Comparing and Contrasting** How did President Harrison's position on civil service reform differ from his predecessor?

Critical Thinking

5. What were the long-term effects of President Grant's administration on U.S. politics? Be sure to discuss the public reaction to Grant's administration.
Consider:
- the degree of national political corruption
- the public's opinion of politics and politicians
- the efforts made by national politicians to rid government of corruption

After completing Section 3, students should be able to:

OBJECTIVE 1 *Describe the factors that led to economic hardships for farmers.*

OBJECTIVE 2 *Explain what the farmers' movements hoped to achieve, and what weakened their efforts.*

OBJECTIVE 3 *Discuss why farmers supported money backed by silver.*

OBJECTIVE 4 *Identify the issues that the Populist Party supported.*

OBJECTIVE 5 *Explain how silver affected the economy and the 1896 presidential election.*

LET'S GET STARTED!

Display Everyday Life in America Transparency 16, Farming Technology, Late 1800s, from **American History Visual Resources**. As students enter the classroom, ask them to evaluate in writing the pictured machine. Then tell students that the pictured machine is a steam engine designed to drive a mechanical thresher. Tell students that in Section 3 they will learn more about farming in the late 1800s.

The Populist Movement

OBJECTIVES

Read to understand:

1. what factors led to economic hardships for farmers
2. what the farmers' movements hoped to achieve, and what weakened their efforts
3. why farmers supported money backed by silver
4. what issues the Populist Party supported
5. how silver affected the economy and the 1896 presidential election

KEY TERMS

National Grange
cooperatives
Interstate Commerce Act
graduated income tax
gold standard
Bland-Allison Act
Sherman Silver Purchase Act
Populist Party

KEY PEOPLE

Mary Elizabeth Lease
James B. Weaver
William McKinley
William Jennings Bryan

"The farmers of the United States are up in arms. . . . The American farmer is steadily losing ground. His burdens are heavier every year and his gains are more meager [small]."

—Washington Gladden

This Kansas family has been forced off their farm.

Washington Gladden, a Congregational minister in Columbus, Ohio, described the plight of the farmer during the late 1800s. Farmers had endured severe hardships and received little political support. Falling crop prices, rising railroad rates, and mounting expenses forced many farmers to default on their mortgages and loans. Foreclosures by banks forced many farmers off their land. Desperately attempting to preserve their way of life, many farmers began organizing, pressing for political solutions to their problems.

The Farmers' Plight

In addition to transforming urban life, the surge in industrialization during the late 1800s changed farmers' lives significantly. The rapidly growing population in the urban centers had to be fed. Farmers responded by raising more crops and animals each year. Unfortunately for Americans, farmers in other nations did the same. Prices soon tumbled as supply exceeded demand. At the same time, farm costs, such as railroad freight charges and the price of new machinery, continued to rise. As farm profits plunged, many farmers bought more land and increased production. This greater production pushed prices even lower.

To make matters worse, most farm families had borrowed money to pay for their land or to buy new equipment. They often put their farms up as security for loans. Those who could not repay the loans lost their farms. Many ended up as tenant farmers. Others were forced to become farm laborers. One Minnesota farmer expressed the bitterness felt by many farmers.

> "I settled on this land in good faith; built house and barn, broken up part of the land. Spent years of hard labor grubbing [digging], fencing, and improving. Are they going to drive us out like trespassers?"

To farmers, the situation seemed terribly unfair. The merchants who sold farm equipment were making money. Also prospering were the bankers who lent farmers money and the railroads that hauled the farmers' grain and livestock to market. All that the farmers had to show for their long days of backbreaking labor were rising debts. One farmer wrote, "The railroads have never been so prosperous. . . . The banks have never done a better . . . business. . . . And yet agriculture languishes [declines]."

✔ **READING CHECK:** What factors led to economic hardships for farmers?

This tractor was powered by kerosene.

SECTION 3 RESOURCES

PRINT

- Guided Reading Strategy 7.3
- Primary Source Reading 7: A Call for Reform
- Section 3 Review, p. 237
- Daily Quiz 7.3

MULTIMEDIA

- One-Stop Planner, Lesson 7.3
- Everyday Life in America Transparency 16: Farming Technology, Late 1800s
- Holt Researcher: American History CD–ROM

SHELTERED ENGLISH

- Main Idea Activity for Reteaching and Sheltered English 7.3

✔ **READING TO UNDERSTAND**

To help students master the section objectives, have them answer the **READING CHECKS** and complete **Guided Reading Strategy 7.3** as they read the section.

Multimedia Resources

Everyday Life in America Transparency 16: Farming Technology, Late 1800s

TEACH OBJECTIVE 1

LEVEL 1: Tell students to imagine that it is 1875 and that they are farmers in the Midwest. Have each student create a flier or handbill describing the factors that led to economic hardships for farmers. *(Students' fliers should include the following: heavy debts, high freight and machinery costs, and falling crop prices.)* Ask volunteers to present their work to the class. Students may wish to include their fliers or handbills in their portfolios. **Sheltered English**

LEVELS 2 AND 3: Tell students to imagine that it is 1875 and that they are farmers in the Midwest. Have each student write a letter to a friend describing the factors that led to economic hardships for farmers. *(See the Level 1 lesson for the correct factors.)* Students might also want to discuss the formation of a farmers' organization to combat some of those factors. Have volunteers read their letters to the class. Students may wish to include their letters in their portfolios.

ECONOMIC DEVELOPMENT

Farmers' Woes. The drop in crop prices during the late 1800s hurt many farm families. In 1870 wheat averaged $1.04 per bushel, corn $0.52 per bushel, and cotton about $15 per pound. By 1895 wheat averaged $0.51 per bushel, corn $0.25 per bushel, and cotton $7.62 per pound. As crop prices fell, western farmers faced higher prices for shipping their crops than eastern shippers did. In 1897 the price per ton per mile to ship goods on the Pennsylvania Railroad east of Chicago was $0.56; on the Burlington Railroad from Chicago to the Missouri River $0.78; and on the Burlington Railroad west of the Missouri River $1.28.

CRITICAL THINKING Why might railroads have charged western farmers higher rates for shipping their goods?

ANSWER: Answers will vary. Some students might mention that the western railroads ran through sparsely settled land where fewer goods were shipped.

VISUAL RECORD ANSWER

Students might answer that the poster shows farmers enjoying healthy, happy lives and depicts prosperous farms and communities.

Farmers Organize

Farmers began organizing in an attempt to improve their situation. Many farmers joined local organizations that were committed to assisting them in their day-to-day struggles. These organizations soon merged to form a nationwide movement. Hoping to better their lives by provoking reforms in railroad and banking practices, many farmers supported these rapidly growing national organizations.

The Grange movement. The first major farmers' organization, the National Grange of the Patrons of Husbandry, or the **National Grange**, was founded by Oliver Hudson Kelley in 1867. Kelley created the Grange primarily as a social organization. As membership increased and farmers' financial problems grew, the Grange began tackling economic and political issues.

To lower costs, some Grange members formed **cooperatives**, or organizations in which groups of farmers pooled their resources to buy and sell goods. Cooperative members sold their products directly to big-city markets. They bought farm equipment and other goods in large quantities at wholesale prices—thereby cutting costs. The Grange's main focus, however, was on forcing states to regulate railroad freight and grain-storage rates. In the early 1870s state legislatures began to respond to pressure from farmers. Illinois, Iowa, Minnesota, and Wisconsin passed "Granger laws" that created state commissions to standardize such rates.

Many railroad companies challenged the Granger laws in the courts. In a victory for farmers in 1877, the Supreme Court declared in the case of *Munn* v. *Illinois* that state legislatures had the right to regulate businesses such as railroads that involved the public interest. However, the Court modified its decision nine years later, in *Wabash* v. *Illinois*, ruling that state governments had no power to regulate traffic that moved across state boundaries. Only the federal government had that right, the justices ruled.

INTERPRETING THE VISUAL RECORD

The National Grange. The National Grange established cooperatives and pushed for legislation that would assist farmers. ***How does this poster celebrate the lives of American farmers?***

THE GRANGER COLLECTION, NEW YORK

The Court's decision led directly to the passage of the **Interstate Commerce Act** in 1887. The act prohibited railroads from giving secret rebates, or refunds, to large shippers or charging more for short hauls than for long hauls over the same line. It also stated that railroad rates had to be "reasonable and just." To monitor railroad activities, the act created the Interstate Commerce Commission (ICC). However, the ICC was given little power to enforce its rulings. When it charged railroads with violating the law, the courts almost always ruled in the railroads' favor.

The Alliance movement. While the National Grange lobbied on behalf of railroad regulation, a more powerful farm organization—the Farmers' Alliance—took shape. Beginning in Texas in the 1870s, the Alliance movement spread quickly. Debt-ridden farm families eagerly embraced the Alliance message of unity and hope. Like the Grange, the Alliance organized cooperatives to buy equipment and to market farm products. The Alliance offered farmers low-cost insurance. It also lobbied for tougher bank regulations, government ownership of the railroads, and a **graduated income tax** that taxed higher incomes at a higher rate.

TEACH OBJECTIVE 2

ALL LEVELS: To help students understand more about farmers' movements, copy the following graphic organizer on the chalkboard, omitting the italicized answers. Have each student complete it. Then ask students to consider the efforts that farmers' movements undertook to help farmers. Which effort would have been most helpful to farmers? Why? Make sure that students fully justify their selections. **Sheltered English**

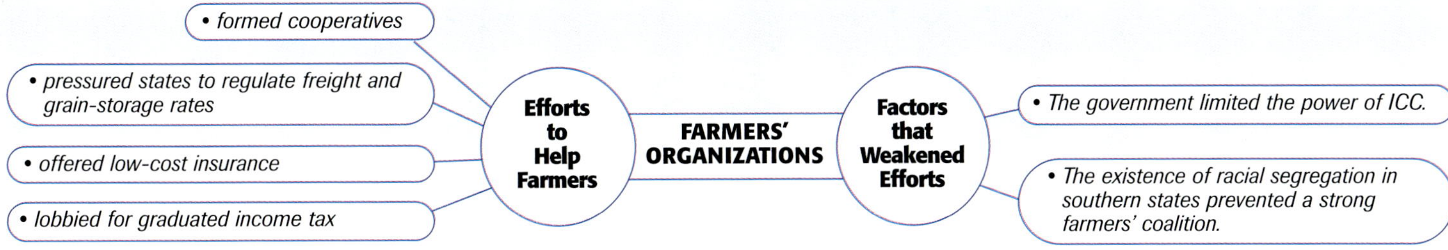

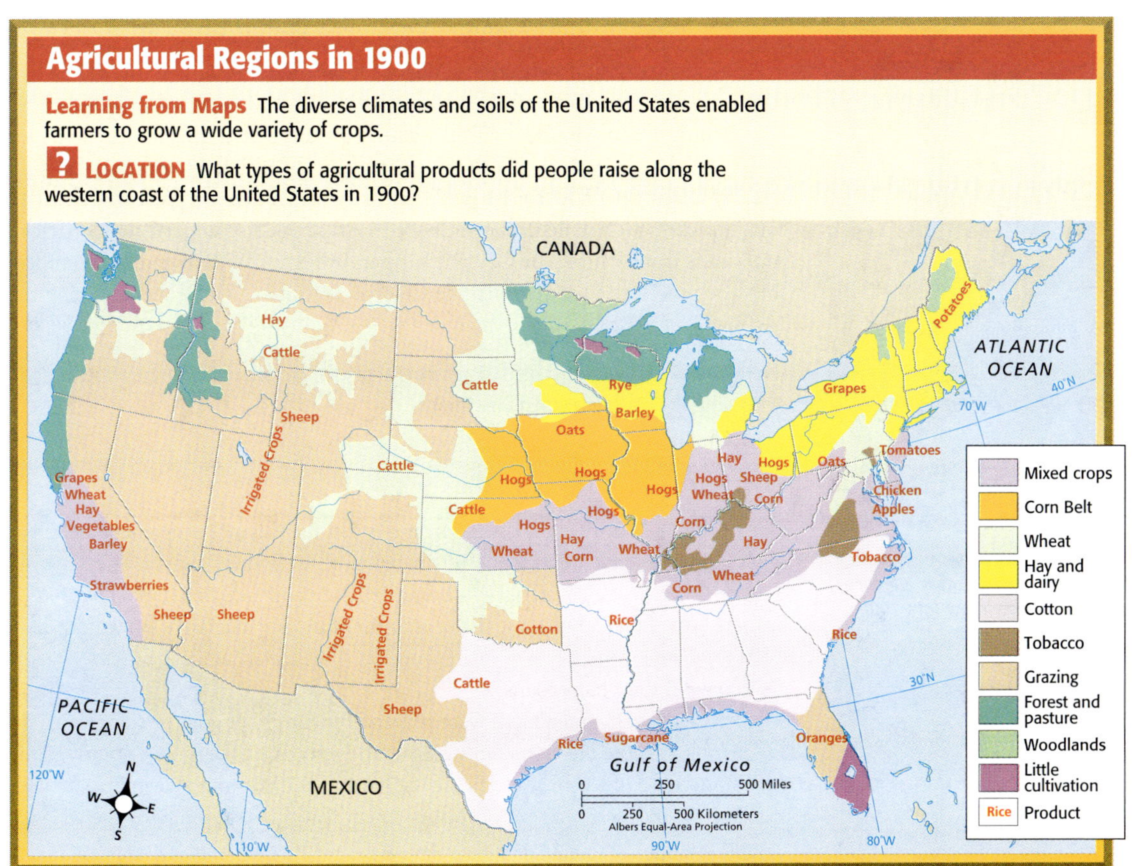

Agricultural Regions in 1900

Learning from Maps The diverse climates and soils of the United States enabled farmers to grow a wide variety of crops.

? LOCATION What types of agricultural products did people raise along the western coast of the United States in 1900?

By 1890 the Alliance movement claimed more than 1 million members. Alliance leaders traveled the country urging people to take action. Among the most effective speakers was Mary Elizabeth Lease from Kansas. She told her audiences:

> **"The great common people of this country are slaves, and monopoly is the master. . . . The politicians said we suffered from overproduction. Overproduction, when 10,000 little children, so statistics tell us, starve to death every year in the United States. . . . We will stand by our homes and stay by our fireside by force if necessary, and we will not pay our debts to the loan-shark companies until the government pays its debts to us."**

The Alliance movement consisted of three organizations: the National Farmers' Alliance, the all-white Southern Alliance, and the Colored Farmers' Alliance. Each organization pushed for the same legislative goals and helped their members in times of hardship. Nevertheless, a variety of reasons kept the Alliance organizations from consolidating their leadership into one single organization.

African American farmers. Despite the common goals of the Southern and Colored Farmers' Alliances, they remained separate, segregated institutions. Racial divisions in southern society prevented a tight coalition of farmers that crossed color lines.

Mary Elizabeth Lease spread the cause of the Alliance movement, speaking out against monopolies.

PEOPLE IN HISTORY

Mary Elizabeth Lease. Born in 1850, Mary Elizabeth Lease grew up on a farm in Pennsylvania and moved to Kansas in 1870 to teach at a Catholic girls' school. She married Charles Lease in 1873, and the two struggled at farming for 10 years. Lease, who found being a farmer's wife "dreary" and "lonely," formed the Hypatia Society, a group for women to discuss current issues. She also supported the growing spirit of revolt of debt-ridden Kansas farmers. In 1885 Lease spoke to the Union Labor Party, a group supported by farmers. Between 1890 and 1894, Lease reached the pinnacle of her speaking career working on behalf of the Farmers' Alliance and the Populist Party. Known for her fiery temper, Lease is sometimes credited with coining the phrase that Kansas farmers should "raise less corn and more hell" to improve their lot.

ACTIVITY: Have students write minutes from a meeting of a group such as the Hypatia Society. Remind students to include the date, a list of people attending, old business, and new business.

MAP ANSWER

grapes, wheat, hay, barley, vegetables, strawberries

TEACH OBJECTIVES 3 AND 5

LEVELS 1 AND 2: Conduct a brief discussion on farmers' support for money backed by silver. Then pair students and have each pair create some kind of graphic—such as a flowchart or a graph—representing and explaining farmers' support. *(Students should indicate that farmers wanted to increase the paper money supply, and that they saw silver-backed paper currency as a way to achieve their goal.)* Next, tell students to imagine that it is 1897 and that they are Populist farmers. Have each pair develop a brief dialogue on how the silver issue affected the 1896 presidential election. *(Students should note that silver was a central issue, that the Populists supported Bryan because of his stand on silver, and that William McKinley won the presidency with the support of business leaders who opposed free silver.)* Ask volunteers to perform their dialogues for the class. **Sheltered English, Cooperative Learning**

THAT'S INTERESTING!

The 1849 gold rush led to the decline in the value of gold in relation to silver. Realizing that their silver dollars were now worth more than their face value, owners melted them and then sold them commercially. This caused silver dollars to virtually disappear from the market.

CHANGING WAYS ANSWERS

declined 35 percent; risen 336.5 acres per farm *(from 147.5 to 484 acres per farm)*

VISUAL RECORD ANSWER

(for p. 235)

Students might answer paper money backed by silver as well as by gold because farmers hoped that free silver would increase the amount of money in circulation and lead to rising prices for farm products.

African American farmers looked to the Colored Farmers' Alliance for assistance in the late 1880s.

The racial divisions within the Alliance movement brought about the violent end of the Colored Farmers' Alliance. In 1891 Colored Farmers' Alliance leader R. M. Humphrey organized a strike of cotton pickers demanding to be paid $1 for every 100 pounds picked. The strike led to a series of violent confrontations in Arkansas between white farmers and African American cotton pickers. At least 15 cotton pickers were killed. The violence in Arkansas discouraged many African Americans from joining the Colored Farmers' Alliance. With dwindling membership, the power and influence of the Colored Farmers' Alliance faded during the 1890s.

✔ **READING CHECK:** What did farmers involved in the national farmers' movements hope to achieve? What weakened their efforts?

The Money Question

One of the most important issues for farmers in the Alliance movement as well as other agrarian movements was the expansion of the money supply. They favored the printing of more greenbacks—the paper money used during the Civil War. The farmers hoped that an increase in the amount of money in circulation would allow them to charge more for their farm products. This would make it easier for farmers to pay off their bank loans.

Before the war, greenbacks were redeemable for either gold or silver coins. In 1873 Congress voted to stop coining silver and to convert the money supply to the **gold standard**. Under this system, each dollar was equal to and redeemable for a set amount of gold. The amount of money in circulation was limited by the amount of gold held in the U.S. Treasury.

Changing Ways The American Farmer

■ **Understanding Change** Farming was once a primary occupation in the United States. *By how much has the percentage of workers engaged in farming changed? Calculate the average farm size then and now. How has it changed over time?*

	THEN	NOW
Population Employed in Farming (Farming / Nonfarming)	Farming 38%, Nonfarming 62%	Farming 3%, Nonfarming 97%
Number of farms	5.7 million	2 million
Total farmland	841 million acres	968 million acres

Sources: *Historical Statistics of the United States; Statistical Abstract of the United States: 1997.* Data reflect 1900 and 1996.

LEVEL 3: Tell students to imagine that is 1902 and that they are midwestern farmers preparing to retire. Have each student write at least four short memoir pieces about his or her career: two entries discussing why they supported paper currency backed by silver, and two entries on how silver affected the election of 1896. *(See the Level 1 lesson for the correct reasons and effects.)* Have volunteers read their memoir pieces to the class. Students may wish to include their memoirs in their portfolios.

▶**ASSIGNMENT** *Have each student write summaries of the following subsections: The Money Question and The Election of 1896. Ask two volunteers—one representing each subsection—to read their summaries to the class. Have these volunteers field questions from the other students about the content of their given subsection.*

TEACH OBJECTIVE 4

LEVEL 1: Tell students to imagine that they are Populist Party workers. Have each student design several pieces of political paraphernalia identifying the Populist position on various issues. *(Students' items should note that the Populists supported a graduated income tax, bank regulation, government ownership of railroad and telegraph companies, the free coinage of silver, immigration restrictions, a shorter workday, and voting reforms.)* Students might design campaign buttons, pens, shirts, dishtowels, and so on. Have students present their items to the class. Then have students select the most effective item, clearly justifying their choices.

Sheltered English

The conversion to the gold standard resulted in a decrease in the amount of money in circulation and a lowering of prices. Many farmers demanded that the government back the money supply with silver. This metal was plentiful in the West—as was gold. Bowing to pressure, Congress passed the **Bland-Allison Act** in 1878 and the **Sherman Silver Purchase Act** in 1890. Both acts required the government to buy silver each month and mint it into coins. Because the government bought so little silver, however, the money supply did not increase enough to satisfy silver supporters.

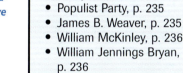

INTERPRETING THE VISUAL RECORD

The silver issue. Many American farmers supported the printing of paper money backed by silver. ***Which form of currency do you think most farmers would have preferred Americans to use? Why?***

Disappointed Alliance members threw themselves into the 1890 elections, supporting any candidate who backed their pro-farmer platform. The results of their efforts were remarkable. Alliance-backed candidates won more than 40 seats in Congress, four southern governorships, and numerous other political offices.

✔ **READING CHECK:** Why did farmers demand that paper money be backed by silver?

A Decade of Populist Politics

Pleased by their successes in the 1890 election, Alliance movement leaders sought to build on their popular support by forming a new political party. Throughout the 1890s Alliance leaders began a large grassroots campaign, gaining a considerable amount of influence on national politics.

The Populist Party. Between 1891 and 1892, Alliance members met with labor leaders and other reformers to draw up plans for a national political party. The People's Party was founded at a convention in St. Louis in February 1892. This coalition of Alliance members, farmers, labor leaders, and reformers became more commonly known as the **Populist Party**.

The party platform echoed National Grange and Alliance demands. It called for a graduated income tax, bank regulation, government ownership of railroad and telegraph companies, and the free, or unlimited, coinage of silver. The platform also called for restrictions on immigration, a shorter workday, and voting reforms.

The Populists nominated James B. Weaver to run in the 1892 presidential election against Republican incumbent Benjamin Harrison and Democrat Grover Cleveland. Cleveland was a former president who had lost to Harrison in the 1888 election. Although Cleveland won the 1892 election, the Populist Party elected more than 10 party members to Congress as well as numerous state leaders. Weaver pulled in a respectable 1 million popular votes, carrying four western states and 22 electoral votes.

This ticket entitled its holder to attend the Populist Party convention in 1892.

✔ **READING CHECK:** What issues did the Populist Party support?

Economic depression. In May 1893, just two months after Cleveland took office, one of the country's leading railroad companies failed. The failure triggered the Panic of 1893, a financial panic that sent stock prices plunging. The country quickly slid into an economic depression. By the end of 1893, some 3 million people

SECTION 3 REVIEW ANSWERS

Define and Identify

For significance, see the following pages:

- National Grange, p. 232
- cooperatives, p. 232
- Interstate Commerce Act, p. 232
- graduated income tax, p. 232
- Mary Elizabeth Lease, p. 233
- gold standard, p. 234
- Bland-Allison Act, p. 235
- Sherman Silver Purchase Act, p. 235
- Populist Party, p. 235
- James B. Weaver, p. 235
- William McKinley, p. 236
- William Jennings Bryan, p. 236

1. Grange—political issues: regulation of railroad freight and grain-storage rates; supporters: farmers in the Midwest; Alliance—political issues: tougher bank regulations, government ownership of the railroads, and graduated income tax; supporters: debt-ridden farmers; Populist—political issues: graduated income tax, bank regulation, government ownership of railroad and telegraph companies, and free coinage of silver; supporters: Alliance members, farmers, labor leaders, and reformers

2. regulation of railroad freight and grain-storage rates would cut back on their production expenses

3. racial divisions

LEVEL 2: Tell students to imagine that they are high-level Populist Party officials preparing to speak at the organization's annual conference. Have each student write a speech identifying the issues supported by the Populist Party. *(See the Level 1 lesson for the correct issues.)* Ask volunteers to deliver their speeches to the class. Then conduct a discussion about the Populist Party. If students had been farmers in the 1890s, would they have joined the party? If students had been industrialists, would they have opposed it? Students may wish to include the text of their speeches in their portfolios.

LEVEL 3: Pair students and tell them to imagine that they are high-level Populist Party officials preparing to open an office in rural Iowa. Have each pair write a party platform identifying the issues supported by the Populist Party. *(See the Level 1 lesson for the correct issues.)* Have volunteers read their platforms to the class. Then conduct a discussion about the Populist Party. If students had been farmers in the 1890s, would they have joined the party? If students had been industrialists, would they have opposed it? **Cooperative Learning**

4. Business leaders who were terrified of Bryan's populism contributed millions of dollars to the Republican campaign.

5. Students might mention that farmers who were continuing to have difficulty paying their mortgages hoped that an increase in the money supply would allow them to charge more for their crops and make it easier to pay off their bank loans.

Creating a Time Line
Each event should have an explanation and the correct date.

Writing a Summary
See the Reading Checks in each section for main ideas.

Identifying People and Ideas

1. well-organized political parties that dominated city governments in the United States in the late 1800s

2. the acquisition of money or political power through illegal or dishonest practices

3. Tammany Hall political boss in the 1860s who was indicted for fraud and extortion in 1871

4. Republican group that strongly opposed civil service reform

5. became president when Garfield was assassinated; supported civil service reform

Free Find: William Jennings Bryan
After reading about William Jennings Bryan on the **Holt Researcher** CD–ROM, explain how his political views were influenced by his family and his experiences growing up in the midwestern United States.

were unemployed—100,000 in Chicago alone. In New York City some 20,000 homeless people desperately sought shelter in jails. Strikes and protests swept the country.

The depression had many causes, including a worldwide financial panic. However, President Cleveland chose to focus only on one cause—the Sherman Silver Purchase Act. This law required the government to pay for silver purchases with Treasury notes redeemable in either gold or silver. New discoveries of silver decreased the metal's value, and people rushed to exchange their notes for gold. The situation put a terrible strain on the Treasury's gold reserves. To protect the gold standard and to restore confidence in the economy, Cleveland called for Congress to repeal the Sherman Silver Purchase Act. Congress did so in October 1893.

The Election of 1896

President Cleveland's actions saved the gold standard, but this did not end the debate on the money supply. Silver became a central issue in the 1896 election.

The Republicans chose Ohio governor William McKinley as their presidential candidate and adopted a conservative platform upholding the gold standard. A deeply split Democratic Party rejected President Cleveland. Instead, they nominated free-silver supporter William Jennings Bryan, a two-term representative from Nebraska. Because its free-silver platform had been adopted by the Democratic Party, the Populist Party threw its support behind Bryan.

BIOGRAPHY

William Jennings Bryan

Bryan. William Jennings Bryan was born in 1860 into a very religious and Democratic family. Bryan's father served in the Illinois state senate and on the Illinois circuit court, guided by his religious beliefs and his Democratic ideals.

Bryan was greatly influenced by his father. At the age of 21 he left his childhood home in Salem, Illinois, to attend law school in Chicago. After receiving his law degree, Bryan eventually moved to Lincoln, Nebraska. He established a law firm and ran for political office as a Democratic candidate in Nebraska, a predominantly Republican state. At the age of 31, Bryan was elected to the U.S. House of Representatives.

Bryan's youth, charisma, and strong support of silver-backed currency gained him broad support among populists within the Democratic Party in the 1890s. During the Democratic convention where he received the nomination to run for president, Bryan gave his now famous "Cross of Gold" speech. He stressed the importance of the silver issue to farmers and less-fortunate people all over the United States.

> **"If they [the Republicans] dare to come out in the open field and defend the gold standard as a good thing, we will fight them to the uttermost. Having behind us the producing masses of this nation and the world, supported by the commercial interests, the laboring interests, and the toilers everywhere, we will answer their demand for a gold standard by saying to them: You shall not press down upon the brow of labor this crown of thorns, you shall not crucify mankind upon a cross of gold."**

Judge ***magazine published this cartoon on its cover after William Jennings Bryan gave his "Cross of Gold" speech.***

REVIEW

Have students complete the **Section 3 Review** on p. 237.

ASSESS

Have students complete **Daily Quiz 7.3**. As **Alternative Assessment**, you may want to use the silver graphic or the Populist Party political paraphernalia in this section's lessons.

RETEACH

Have students complete **Main Idea Activity for Reteaching and Sheltered English 7.3**. Then pair students and have each pair create a detailed outline of Section 3. Ask volunteers to share their outlines and create a master outline on the chalkboard. Have students consult the outline and suggest five true-false questions, five matching questions, three short answer questions, and one essay question. Ask students to provide rough answers to their questions.

Sheltered English, Cooperative Learning

EXTEND

Have students conduct research on farmers' problems in the 1890s and 1990s. Then have each student create a Venn diagram displaying the similarities and differences in farmers' problems in the two decades. Ask volunteers to present their diagrams to the class. Students may wish to include their diagrams in their portfolios. **Block Scheduling**

Bryan remained politically active throughout his life. He published several papers on populism and ran for political office repeatedly during the early 1900s. He died in 1925.

The end of populism. Terrified of Bryan's populism, many business leaders contributed millions of dollars to the Republican campaign. When the popular votes were counted, McKinley had edged out Bryan by some 500,000 votes. The Populists were in shock. Free silver had proven too weak an issue for a national campaign, and urban workers and immigrants had found little that appealed to them in the Populists' agenda.

The election defeat and improvements in farmers' economic conditions brought an end to the power of the Populist Party. However, the party's platform laid the groundwork for future reform. As Populist leader Mary Elizabeth Lease noted in 1914, "The seeds we sowed out in Kansas did not fall on barren ground."

✔ **READING CHECK:** How did silver affect the economy and the 1896 presidential election?

PRESIDENTIAL *Lives*

1843–1901
In Office 1897–1901

William McKinley

William McKinley used presidential power so effectively that a Republican newspaper concluded: "No executive in the history of the country . . . has given a greater exhibition of his influence over Congress." Even his political enemies respected his tact and persuasiveness. Speaker of the House Tom Reed said of him with envy, "My opponents in Congress go at me tooth and nail, but they always apologize to William when they are going to call him names."

A courteous manner characterized McKinley in private life as well. He was devoted to protecting and caring for his wife, Ida. She suffered headaches and seizures that often kept her from fulfilling her role as first lady. He stayed close to her during state dinners and receptions. If she fainted, he would tend to her, continuing with conversation so as not to embarrass her.

SECTION 3 REVIEW

Define and explain the significance of the following terms:
National Grange
cooperatives
Interstate Commerce Act
graduated income tax
gold standard
Bland-Allison Act
Sherman Silver Purchase Act
Populist Party

Identify and explain the significance of the following individuals:
Mary Elizabeth Lease
James B. Weaver
William McKinley
William Jennings Bryan

1. **Using Graphic Organizers** Copy the chart below. List the political concerns and typical supporters of the National Grange, the Farmers' Alliance, and the Populist Party.

	Grange	Alliance	Populist
Political Issues			
Supporters			

2. **Hypothesizing** Considering the economic troubles that farmers faced, why do you think many of them supported the political agenda of the National Grange?
3. **Evaluating** What factors weakened the Alliance movement?
4. **Analyzing** Why did William Jennings Bryan lose the 1896 presidential election?

Critical Thinking

5. The currency issue was debated nationally for more than 40 years in the United States. Why do you think the debate over silver-backed currency lasted so long?
Consider:
- who wanted a gold standard and who wanted silver-backed money
- what reasons each group had for supporting its view
- how silver influenced the economy

6. elected president in 1884 and supported civil service reform
7. organization founded by Oliver Hudson Kelley in 1867 that tackled farmers' economic and political issues
8. speaker on behalf of the Alliance movement
9. system in which each dollar is equal to and redeemable for a set amount of gold, and the amount of money in circulation is limited by the amount of gold held in the U.S. Treasury
10. free-silver advocate who was the Democratic Party's candidate in the 1896 presidential campaign and who also received support from the Populist Party; lost the election to Republican William McKinley

Understanding Main Ideas

1. offered jobs, political favors, and services to local voters
2. Thomas Nast's political cartoons in *Harper's Weekly* and a series of articles in the *New York Times*
3. Stalwarts—strongly opposed civil service reform; Half-Breeds—favored the use of civil service exams to grant jobs on merit rather than by patronage
4. prompted reformers to call for the end of the spoils system
5. a graduated income tax, bank regulation, government ownership of railroad and telegraph companies, the free coinage of silver, immigration restrictions, a shorter workday, and voting reforms

REVIEW AND ASSESSMENT RESOURCES

PRINT

- Chapter 7 Review, pp. 238–39
- Chapter 7 Tutorial for Students, Parents, Mentors, and Peers
- Chapter 7 Test (Form A or B)
- Portfolio Activities and Alternative Assessment Handbook, Chapter 7

MULTIMEDIA

- Audio Program, Chapter 7 (English and Spanish)
- Chapter 7 Test Generator (on the One-Stop Planner)
- Global Skill Builder CD–ROM
- HRW Web site

SHELTERED ENGLISH

- Spanish Glossary
- Sheltered English Chapter 7 Test

REVIEW

Have students complete the **Chapter 7 Review** on pp. 238–39.

ASSESS

Use one of the chapter tests to assess students' understanding of the content. For **Alternative Assessment**, see the **Portfolio Activities and Alternative Assessment Handbook.**

6. Business leaders who were terrified of Bryan's populism contributed millions of dollars to McKinley's campaign.

Reviewing Themes

1. Political bosses provided jobs, political favors, and services to local residents in exchange for their vote.
2. Answers will vary. Students might suggest that Stalwarts felt that civil service reform would create a permanent bureaucracy with anti-republican tendencies.
3. Although farmers in the Midwest, West, and South supported Bryan's pro-farmer policies, urban workers and immigrants had found little that appealed to them in the Populists' agenda.

Thinking Critically

1. They received jobs or gained valuable city services in exchange for voting for particular candidates.
2. believed that killing Garfield would further the Stalwart cause; no, Arthur responded to the calls for civil service reform
3. Answers will vary. Students might mention that the Grange established cooperatives that allowed farmers to cut costs and were successful in getting Illinois, Iowa, Minnesota, and Wisconsin to pass "Granger laws."

Review

Creating a Time Line

Copy the time line below onto a sheet of paper. Complete the time line by filling in the events and dates from the chapter that you think were most significant. Pick three events and explain why you think they were significant.

Writing a Summary

Using the Reading Checks as a guide, write an overview of the events in the chapter.

Identifying People and Ideas

Identify the following terms or individuals and explain their significance.

1. political machines
2. graft
3. William Marcy Tweed
4. Stalwarts
5. Chester A. Arthur
6. Grover Cleveland
7. National Grange
8. Mary Elizabeth Lease
9. gold standard
10. William Jennings Bryan

Understanding Main Ideas

SECTION 1

1. What did political machines do to build and maintain support for their party?
2. What caused the decline in public support for the Tweed Ring?

SECTION 2

3. What did the Stalwarts want? What reforms did the Half-Breeds want?
4. What role did President Grant's administration play in the civil service reform movement?

SECTION 3

5. What issues did the Populist Party support?
6. Why did the Populists lose the 1896 election?

Reviewing Themes

1. **Cultural Diversity** How were political machines able to unite immigrant groups to support their candidates?
2. **Democratic Values** Why might many Stalwarts have considered civil service reform a violation of the democratic heritage of the United States?
3. **Geographic Diversity** Why did William Jennings Bryan win such strong support in some parts of the country but so little in other regions?

Thinking Critically

1. **Drawing Conclusions** Why do you think voters supported corrupt political machines?
2. **Identifying Cause and Effect** What motivated Charles Guiteau to assassinate President Garfield? Did he accomplish his political goal?
3. **Evaluating** Overall, were the National Grange and Farmers' Alliance movements a success or a failure? Explain your answer.
4. **Analyzing** Was "the Gilded Age" an appropriate nickname for the late 1800s? Why or why not?
5. **Hypothesizing** Would William Jennings Bryan have won the election of 1896 if he had not focused so much on the gold and silver issue? Why or why not?

Writing About History

Writing to Persuade Copy the following graphic organizer and use it to explain the give-and-take relationship between political machines and voters. Then write a letter to the editor of a newspaper to persuade the public to support civil service reform. Be sure to explain how civil service reform would change the relationship between political machines and voters.

RETEACH

Pair students and assign them one of the sections in Chapter 7. Have each pair write three questions about the material. Then have students present their questions to the entire class in the form of a "quiz game." The pair that answers the most questions correctly, excluding their own, will win the "quiz game." **Sheltered English, Cooperative Learning**

EXTEND

Have students conduct research on the Populist Party. Ask students to focus on a specific candidate—either national, regional, or local. Have each student write a brief biography on his or her chosen figure. Students' biographies should include basic biographical and political information. Students should also illustrate their biographies if possible. Have volunteers present their biographies to the class. Then compile the biographies into a Populist Party yearbook. **Block Scheduling**

Strategies for Success Review the **Strategies for Success** on *Synthesizing*. Then review the Eyewitnesses to History feature that opens Section 3. Synthesize its content with the description below about the Alliance movement, and answer the question that follows.

> [The Alliance movement] was, first and most centrally, a movement that imparted [passed on] a sense of self-worth to individuals and provided them with the instruments of self-education about the world they lived in. The movement taught them to believe that they could perform specific political acts of self-determination.
>
> —*Lawrence Goodwyn,* The Populist Moment, *1978*

Based on these two sources and the knowledge you have gained from the text, why do you think farmers supported the Alliance movement during the late 1800s?

Linking History and Geography

Study the map below. Which candidate won the most states? What regions of the United States gave the most support to William Jennings Bryan? to William McKinley? Why might that be so?

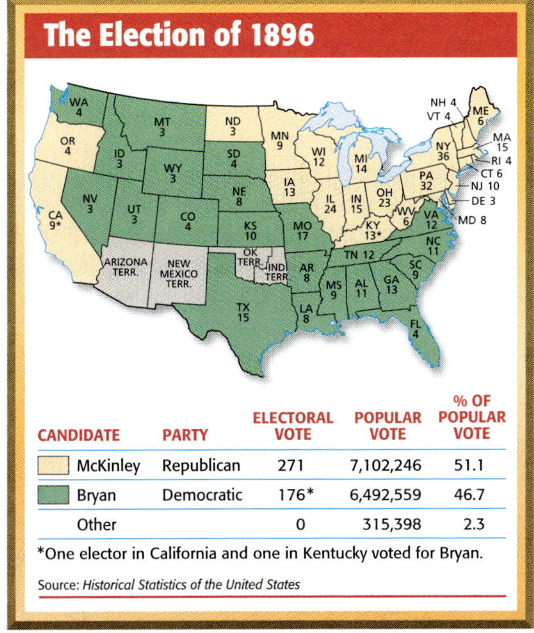

The Election of 1896

CANDIDATE	PARTY	ELECTORAL VOTE	POPULAR VOTE	% OF POPULAR VOTE
McKinley	Republican	271	7,102,246	51.1
Bryan	Democratic	176*	6,492,559	46.7
Other		0	315,398	2.3

*One elector in California and one in Kentucky voted for Bryan.

Source: *Historical Statistics of the United States*

internetconnect

TOPIC: Political Cartoons
GO TO: go.hrw.com
KEYWORD: SE1 Cartoons

Accessing the Internet through the HRW Web site, research the work of the political cartoonist Thomas Nast. Then create a political cartoon that addresses an issue of the Gilded Age.

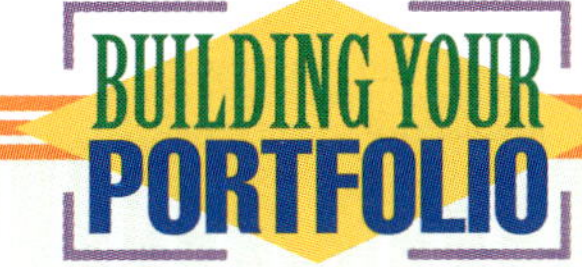

Complete one or all of the following projects independently or cooperatively.

1 Democratic Values

Imagine that you are a political satirist, like Mark Twain, living in the Gilded Age. ***Write a short story*** about an episode of corruption during the period.

2 Economic Development

Imagine that you are a farmer who has just joined the National Grange movement. ***Draft a letter*** to a neighboring farmer that explains the hardships you have experienced and why you think joining the Grange movement will help solve your problems.

3 Constitutional Heritage

Imagine that you are living in a large city during the late 1800s and want a government job. In this particular city, a political machine runs the local government but there is a strong possibility that a merit-based civil service system will soon be used to hire people. ***Create a political cartoon*** that explains what you need to do to get a job in either the patronage system or a merit-based hiring system.

4. Answers will vary. Students might note that the name is appropriate for the late 1800s, since the prevalence of political machines showed that many politicians were interested in taking advantage of their positions.

5. Answers will vary. Students might mention that he probably would not have won the election, since urban workers and immigrants found little that appealed to them in the Populists' agenda.

Writing About History
Letters should include the information presented in the graphic organizer.

Strategies for Success
Participation in the Alliance movement during the late 1800s gave many people a sense of pride and allowed them to fight for issues that specifically affected them and their livelihood.

Linking History and Geography
McKinley; the South and the West; the Northeast and much of the Midwest; the areas that supported McKinley were more urban and industrial

REVIEW AND ASSESSMENT RESOURCES

PRINT

- Unit 2 Review, pp. 240–41
- Unit 2 Test (Form A or B)
- Portfolio Activities and Alternative Assessment Handbook, Unit 2

MULTIMEDIA

- Global Skill Builder CD–ROM

SHELTERED ENGLISH

- Spanish Glossary
- Sheltered English Unit 2 Test

To review elements of Unit 2 in a single class period, assign one of the following activities or graphic organizers, omitting the italicized answers, to individuals or groups.

1 Cultural Diversity

CONFLICTS IN LATE 1800S AMERICA

- **Conflicts over Westward Expansion**
  - *conflict between settlers and American Indians*
  - *conflict between expansionists and opponents*
- **Conflicts over Immigration**
  - *conflict between nativists and immigrants*
- **Conflicts over Industrialization**
  - *conflict between workers and owners*
  - *conflict between reformers and owners*

A Selection from Further Reading

War on the Great Plains. In *The Long Death: The Last Days of the Plains Indians*, Ralph K. Andrist provides a vivid account of the struggles between the U.S. Army and American Indians on the Great Plains. In the following excerpt, he describes the harsh reality of these conflicts: "Let there be no mistake: the wars of the plains were not clean, crisp little tableaux [scenes] of cavalry . . . meeting thundering charges of Sioux and Cheyenne warriors. . . . They were not that kind of conflict at all. As in all wars, men died unpleasantly, and often in extreme agony. Women and children suffered along with the warrior and soldier, and the Army made it a part of strategy to destroy the enemy's food and possessions in order to leave him cold, hungry, and without the will to resist."

COMPREHENSION According to Andrist, how did the reality of war on the Great Plains differ from popular myth?

ANSWER: Students might suggest that war on the Great Plains was not made up of picturesque clashes between fearless combatants but rather involved widespread suffering and deprivation.

Review

BUILDING YOUR PORTFOLIO

Outlined below are four projects. Independently or cooperatively, complete one and use the products to demonstrate your mastery of the historical concepts involved.

American Indian refusing to let a wagon train pass

1 Cultural Diversity

Westward expansion, immigration, and industrialization often created conflicts between different groups in American society. ***Develop a series of dramatic sketches*** and monologues that address these conflicts and explore the positive consequences of cultural diversity for society. You may wish to use portfolio materials you designed in the unit chapters to help you.

Advertisement for union labels

2 Economic Development

In the late 1800s technological advances and the growth of industry dramatically changed the lifestyles and work habits of many Americans. Imagine that you own a factory. ***Prepare a presentation*** highlighting the technological developments being used in your factory. Be sure to describe how the changes in the factory affected the lives of workers and what problems you have encountered as workers have unionized. You may wish to use portfolio materials you designed in the unit chapters to help you.

3 Technology and Society

Write the following phrases on the chalkboard: population, size, new forms of transportation, the growth of the suburbs, and new immigrant neighborhoods. Have each student write one or two sentences describing how each item affected American cities during the late 1800s. Ask volunteers to read their sentences to the class.

4 Democratic Values

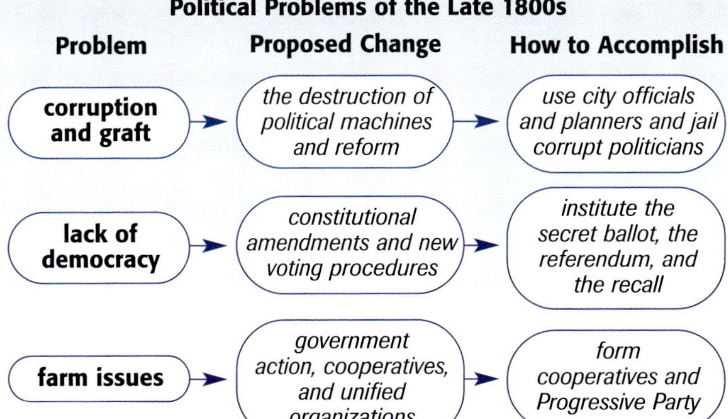

Political Problems of the Late 1800s
Problem
Proposed Change
How to Accomplish
corruption and graft
the destruction of political machines and reform
use city officials and planners and jail corrupt politicians
lack of democracy
constitutional amendments and new voting procedures
institute the secret ballot, the referendum, and the recall
farm issues
government action, cooperatives, and unified organizations
form cooperatives and Progressive Party

Washington, D.C., streetcar

THE GRANGER COLLECTION, NEW YORK

3 Technology and Society

With the increasing industrialization in the late 1800s, cities across the United States expanded in population and in size. **Create a map** of a major U.S. city in 1910 that illustrates the growth of the city. Be sure to include new forms of transportation, the growth of suburbs, and the development of immigrant neighborhoods. You may wish to use portfolio materials you designed in the unit chapters to help you.

4 Democratic Values

Corruption in various levels of government and problems in rural America led many citizens to work for political change. **Create a series of flip charts for a meeting** between politicians, farmers, and reform-minded citizens to discuss what political changes are needed and how these groups can work together to accomplish the reforms. You may wish to use portfolio materials you designed in the unit chapters to help you.

Cartoon depicting political corruption

THE GRANGER COLLECTION, NEW YORK

Further Reading

Andrist, Ralph K. *The Long Death: The Last Days of the Plains Indians.* Macmillan, 1993. History of the struggle of the Plains Indians.

Coan, Peter Morton. *Ellis Island Interviews: In Their Own Words.* Facts on File, 1997. A broad collection of accounts recalling immigration experiences.

Katz, William L. *The Black West.* Open Hand, 1987. History of the African American pioneers who helped develop the West.

Luchetti, Cathy, and Carol Olwell. *Women of the West.* Orion, 1982. Firsthand accounts of women's lives in the West taken from photographs and diaries.

Mohl, Raymond A. *The New City: Urban America in the Industrial Age, 1860–1920.* Harlan Davidson, 1985. A thorough history of the changes in urban life during the late 1800s.

Schlereth, Thomas J. *Victorian America: Transformations in Everyday Life, 1876–1915.* HarperCollins, 1991. Detailed historical overview of the impact of immigration, expansion, and industrialization on American society.

Internet Connect and Holt Researcher CD–ROM *Review*

In assigned groups, develop a multimedia presentation about America between 1860 and 1910. Choose information from the chapter Internet Connect activities and from the Holt Researcher CD–ROM that best reflect the major topics of the period. Write an outline and a script for your presentation, which may be shown to the class.

A Selection from Further Reading

Urban America During the Second Industrial Revolution. In *The New City: Urban America in the Industrial Age 1860–1920*, Raymond A. Mohl discusses how life in urban America changed during the Second Industrial Revolution. In the following excerpt, he argues that these changes were both positive and negative: "Industrial capitalism triggered economic and social change along a broad front of urban life—and not all of it was positive. Unbounded growth and almost unimaginable opportunity coexisted with deadly disease, grinding poverty, political corruption, and social disorder. Many of [these] economic, social, and political patterns . . . persisted well into the [1900s]."

COMPREHENSION According to Mohl, what positive and negative changes occurred in urban America during the Second Industrial Revolution?

ANSWER: Students might note positive changes such as rapid economic growth and new social and economic opportunities and negative changes such as disease, poverty, political corruption, and social disorder.

UNIT 3

A World Power

The Age of Reform

CHAPTER 8

Enormous disparities in wealth developed during the Gilded Age. Progressive reformers sought to focus attention on the social problems created by these disparities. Activists also hoped to bring about reform in business and politics. Labor unions attempted to organize workers and to obtain better working conditions and wages for industrial workers.

Progressive Politicians

CHAPTER 9

Progressive politicians hoped to improve the United States by making voting processes more democratic. President Theodore Roosevelt worked to regulate the food-and-drug industry and to preserve the environment. Roosevelt helped William Howard Taft win the 1908 election, but the two clashed soon after. Roosevelt re-entered politics, creating a split in the Republican Party and helping Democrat Woodrow Wilson win the 1912 presidential election.

EXAMINING THE VISUAL RECORD

Ask students the questions below. Then use the annotations to expand class discussion.

1 *Where might the armored cruiser depicted in the painting have been returning from?*
The armored cruiser Brooklyn sailed into New York Harbor with the rest of the victorious U.S. fleet that had been deployed to Cuba during the Spanish-American War. The U.S. fleet had defeated the Spanish squadron in July 1898. Shortly thereafter, the United States and Spain signed a peace protocol to end fighting in the Spanish-American War.

2 *What methods do you think the painter used to convey the power of the fleet and the celebratory mood of the fleet's return?*
The painter, Fred Pansing, placed the flagship Brooklyn in the foreground of the painting to emphasize the size and power of the 8,000-ton ship. The number of American flags in the painting, as well as the placement of the flag at the top of the painting, convey the American triumph.

ACTIVITY: Tell students to select a recent moment of triumph or celebration for the United States. Have each student create an image or a poem depicting that moment.

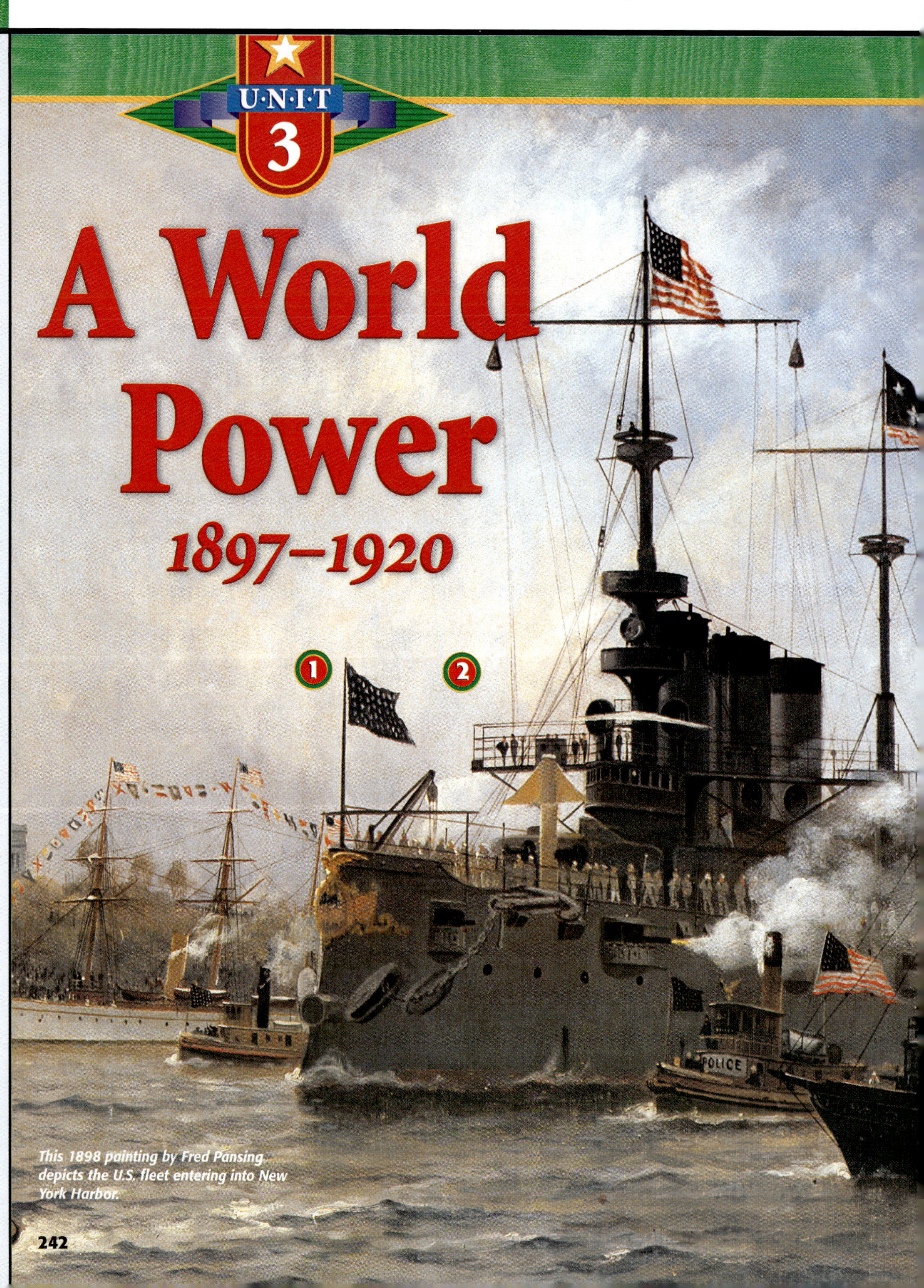

This 1898 painting by Fred Pansing depicts the U.S. fleet entering into New York Harbor.

CHAPTER 10 America and the World

After the Second Industrial Revolution, the United States took a new interest in world affairs and imperialist expansion, partly out of the quest for new markets. The United States acquired Hawaii and seized control of Cuba, Puerto Rico, and the Philippines. Theodore Roosevelt used his Roosevelt Corollary to the Monroe Doctrine to justify interventions in several Latin American countries.

CHAPTER 11 World War I

In 1914 war engulfed Europe, with the Central Powers battling the Allied Powers. The war soon settled into a stalemate. The United States attempted to stay neutral in the conflict, but eventually declared war. The infusion of U.S. troops helped the Allies win the war. President Wilson encouraged the United States to accept the Treaty of Versailles, but a faction of Republican senators rejected the treaty.

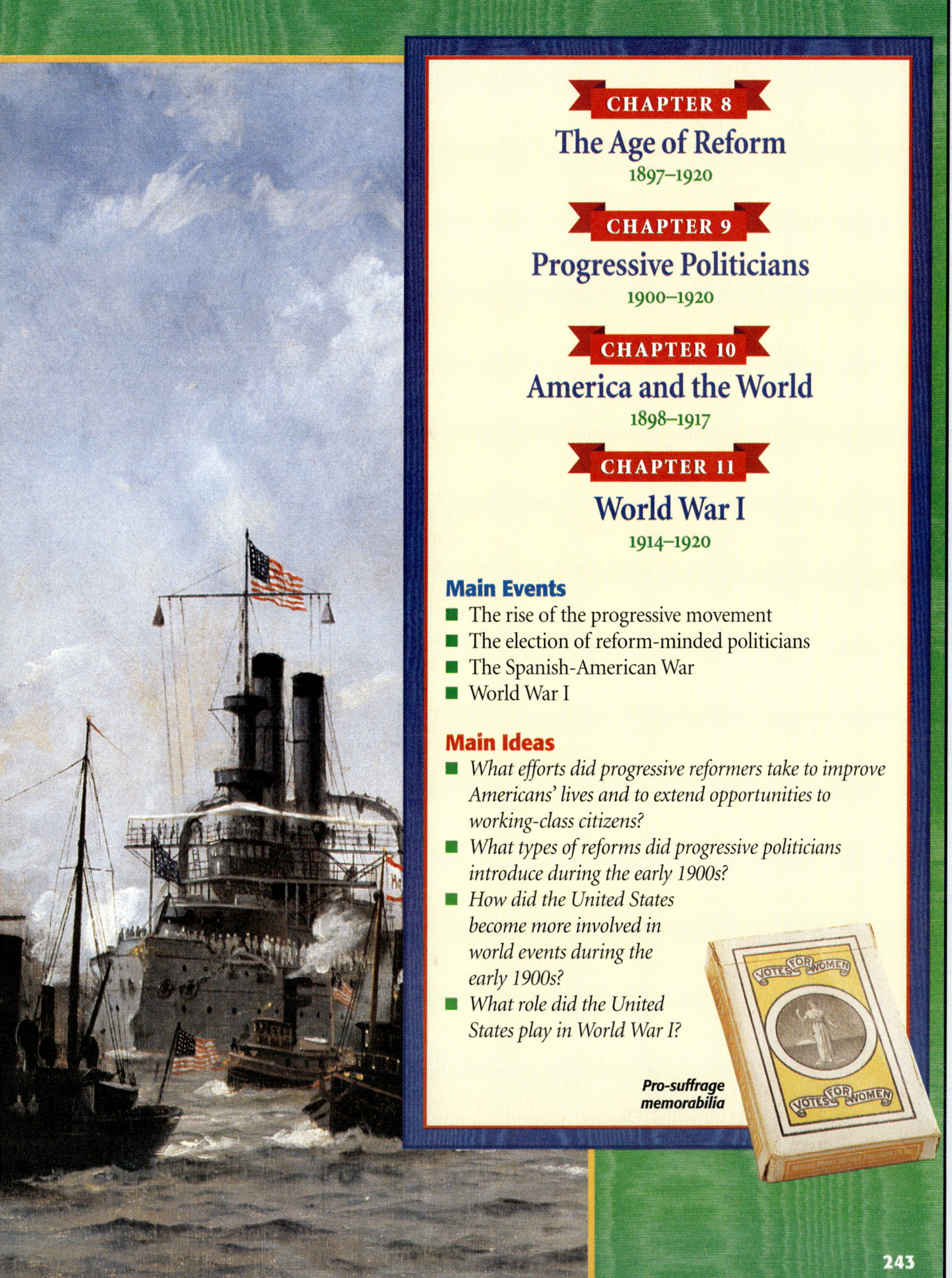

Main Events

- The rise of the progressive movement
- The election of reform-minded politicians
- The Spanish-American War
- World War I

Main Ideas

- *What efforts did progressive reformers take to improve Americans' lives and to extend opportunities to working-class citizens?*
- *What types of reforms did progressive politicians introduce during the early 1900s?*
- *How did the United States become more involved in world events during the early 1900s?*
- *What role did the United States play in World War I?*

Pro-suffrage memorabilia

INTRODUCE UNIT 3

Main Events

List the Main Events on the chalkboard. Ask students to select two and briefly describe what they know about the topics. Have volunteers share their descriptions. Later, when you have finished Unit 3, ask students to return to their original descriptions and revise them using the information they learned in the unit. Students should also create new descriptions for the other Main Events.

Main Ideas

Ask each student to read the Main Ideas and briefly answer the questions in writing. Share the ***Consider*** points with students as necessary. Later, when you have finished Unit 3, ask students to return to their original answers and revise them using the information they learned in the unit.

The Efforts of Progressive Reformers

Consider:

- the effects of high immigration, high population growth, and industrialization on cities
- issues such as workplace injuries and child labor

The American Role in World War I

Consider:

- the date that the United States entered the war
- the effect of a massive infusion of troops

The Age of Reform

CHAPTER PLANNING GUIDE

	Section Lesson Objectives	Print Resources	Multimedia Resources	Sheltered English Resources
Section 1 The Progressive Movement, pp. 246–51	1 Discuss the backgrounds of the reformers. 2 Identify issues that concerned progressives, and explain how they tried to make changes. 3 Specify issues that muckrakers addressed. 4 Summarize how progressive writers and thinkers viewed American society.	▶ Guided Reading Strategy 8.1 ▶ Literature Reading 8: A Muckraker's Report ▶ Section 1 Review, p. 251 ▶ Daily Quiz 8.1	▶ One-Stop Planner, Lesson 8.1 ▶ Everyday Life in America Transparency 18: Progressives and Children, Early 1900s ▶ Holt Researcher: American History CD–ROM	▶ Main Idea Activity for Reteaching and Sheltered English 8.1
Section 2 Reforming the New Industrial Order, pp. 252–57	1 Identify workplace problems that progressives targeted. 2 Explain what the results of the Triangle Shirtwaist Fire were. 3 List and describe the rulings that the Supreme Court made on labor laws. 4 Summarize union successes and failures.	▶ Guided Reading Strategy 8.2 ▶ Geography Activity 8: Limiting the Workday ▶ Graphic Organizer Activity 8: The Progressive Ideal ▶ Section 2 Review, p. 257 ▶ Daily Quiz 8.2	▶ One-Stop Planner, Lesson 8.2 ▶ Holt Researcher: American History CD–ROM	▶ Main Idea Activity for Reteaching and Sheltered English 8.2
Section 3 Reforming Society, pp. 258–65	1 Describe how reformers tried to improve life in U.S. cities. 2 Discuss how reformers hoped to improve moral standards. 3 Report on how African Americans and American Indians organized to improve their lives. 4 Explain why immigrants were left out of some progressive reforms, and recognize how they contributed to other reforms.	▶ Guided Reading Strategy 8.3 ▶ Primary Source Reading 8: A Call for Urban Reform ▶ Biography Reading 8: Carry Nation ▶ Section 3 Review, p. 265 ▶ Daily Quiz 8.3	▶ One-Stop Planner, Lesson 8.3 ▶ Art in American History Transparency 20: Thompson and Bleecker Streets ▶ Holt Researcher: American History CD–ROM ▶ HRW Web site	▶ Main Idea Activity for Reteaching and Sheltered English 8.3
Chapter Review and Assessment pp. 266–67		▶ Chapter 8 Review, pp. 266–67 ▶ Chapter 8 Tutorial for Students, Parents, Mentors, and Peers ▶ Chapter 8 Test (Form A or B) ▶ Portfolio Activities and Alternative Assessment Handbook, Chapter 8	▶ Audio Program, Chapter 8 (English and Spanish) ▶ Chapter 8 Test Generator (on the One-Stop Planner) ▶ Global Skill Builder CD–ROM ▶ HRW Web site	▶ Spanish Glossary ▶ Sheltered English Chapter 8 Test

CHAPTER OVERVIEW

The industrial development of the Gilded Age helped create great disparities in wealth and an underclass of the urban poor. Progressive reformers, including many college-educated women, sought to focus attention on the social problems that had resulted from industrial development. They concentrated their efforts on reforming big business and an often-corrupt political system.

The progressive movement and labor unions often excluded African Americans, American Indians, and immigrants. W. E. B Du Bois and other African American leaders worked to end racial discrimination and obtain civil rights for African Americans. American Indians also organized to solve the problems facing Indians. Ironically, the practical reforms sought by immigrants were often supported by the same political machines that progressives usually denounced.

TIME TAMERS

Block Scheduling

The teacher lesson plans for each section offer a variety of activity choices to help you present the material in a block scheduling format. For further suggestions on block scheduling, see the **Block Scheduling Handbook with Team Teaching Strategies**, pp. 43–48.

Smithsonian Institution®

Internet Connections and Lesson 8
www.si.edu/hrw

Hands-On History Activities:

Classroom to Community The **Hands-On History Activities** help students make meaningful connections between events in American history and those in their own hometown. You may wish to use the Chapter 8 Activity, Workplace Reform in the Past and Present, to extend the chapter lessons, as alternative assessment, or as a block scheduling option.

Portfolio Projects

The American Nation includes multiple portfolio projects in each Pupil's Edition chapter review, as well as each unit review. Chapter 8 Portfolio Project options on p. 267 include the following:

1. Students will **write an editorial.**
2. Students will **prepare a speech.**
3. Students will **sketch out designs.**

The American Nation
INTERNET RESOURCE DIRECTORY

To access online materials for this chapter, go to go.hrw.com and type in the keywords listed below.

HRW ONLINE RESOURCES
GO TO: go.hrw.com

Online Maps
KEYWORD: SE1 Maps8
- Dry States, 1890–1919
- Lynchings, 1890–1920

Online Charts
KEYWORD: SE1 Charts8
- Degrees Earned, 1890–1920
- Union Membership, 1864–1921

Online Reading Support
KEYWORD: SE1 Strategies8

Online Rubrics
KEYWORD: SE1 Rubrics

CHAPTER ENRICHMENT LINKS
Use these Web links to extend and enrich student learning for Chapter 8.
GO TO: go.hrw.com
KEYWORD: SE1 Ch8

CHAPTER INTERNET ACTIVITIES
GO TO: go.hrw.com
- Pupil's Edition Student Activity
  KEYWORD: SE1 Realism
  (Students research the work of photographers of the "social realism" school.)
- Teacher's Edition Student Activity
  KEYWORD: SE1 NAACP
  (Students research the history of the NAACP.)
- Teacher's Edition Student Activity
  KEYWORD: SE1 Motion
  (Students explore early cinema themes and styles.)

ADDITIONAL
RESOURCES

Books for Teachers

Brasch, Walter M. *Forerunners of Revolution: Muckrakers and the American Social Conscience.* University Press of America, 1990. Examines the role of muckrakers.

Diner, Steven J. *A Very Different Age: Americans of the Progressive Era.* Hill and Wang, 1998. Examines the goals and activities of different groups of progressives.

Books for Students

Schneider, Carl, and Dorothy Schneider. *American Women in the Progressive Era, 1900–1920.* Facts on File, 1992. Tells the history of women during the Progressive Era.

Tames, Richard. *Nineteen Hundred to Nineteen Nineteen.* Watts, 1991. Provides a photographic history of the 1900s and 1910s.

Primary Sources from the Period

Dreiser, Theodore. *Sister Carrie.* Bantam, 1992. Tells the story of a young woman's experience in a city.

Norris, Frank. *The Octopus.* Penguin, 1986. Details corporate greed during the Gilded Age.

Multimedia Materials

Muckrakers and Reformers. Sound filmstrip, 10 min. Multi-Media Productions/SSSS. Examines the goals of reformers.

The Progressive Era: Reform Works in America. Video, 23 min. Britannica. Examines the Progressive Era.

CHAPTER 8

Before You Read

Build on What You Know

Ask students to answer the following questions.

How might industrialization during the Gilded Age and the resulting inequalities of wealth have caused social problems?

Consider:

- the low wages paid to many workers
- the existence of dangerous working conditions

How might people have responded to various social ills resulting from industrialization?

Consider:

- the causes of those problems
- the impact of large-scale social reform movements

exploring the time line

AMERICAN EVENTS

internetconnect

TOPIC: NAACP
GO TO: go.hrw.com
KEYWORD: SE1 NAACP

Have students access the Internet through the HRW Web site to conduct research on the history of the National Association for the Advancement of Colored People (NAACP). Then ask each student to write a short essay that discusses the founding of the organization, its early leaders, and some of the issues that motivated the organization in its early years.

CHAPTER 8

1897–1920

The Age of Reform

British troops in Africa

Building the New York City subway

1900
The Arts
Theodore Dreiser publishes the novel *Sister Carrie.*

1902
World Events
The British defeat the Dutch Boers in Africa.

1904
Science and Technology
The first completed section of the New York City subway system opens to the public.

1898 | 1900 | 1902 | 1904 | 1906 | 1908

1900
Daily Life
The average laborer earns $1.50 a day for 10 hours of work.

Poster for The Great Train Robbery

1903
Daily Life
The Great Train Robbery, the first movie to tell a story, is produced.

1905
The Arts
H. Siddons Mowbray begins work on a mural for the J. P. Morgan Library in New York.

1905
World Events
The Russian czar's troops fire on unarmed protesters, beginning the Russian Revolution of 1905.

1907
Science and Technology
Engineers develop suspension insulators, which soon allow power lines to carry up to 150,000 volts of electricity.

Before You Read

Build on What You Know

Although industrial development during the Gilded Age generated great profits for some Americans, it also created many problems. Moreover, politics became increasingly corrupt as leaders sought financial gains. Populists, ministers, and reformers such as Jane Addams tried to bring the nation's attention to those Americans left out of economic prosperity. In this chapter you will learn about the large-scale reform movements that swept the United States at the beginning of the 1900s and the effects that these movements had on American society.

Think About Themes

To help students create their Themes Journal entries, provide the following examples of appropriate **agree/disagree** *statements.*

Economic Development

Agree The poor working conditions in the Lowell textile mills led the Massachusetts legislature to mandate a 10-hour limit on workdays.

Disagree In a capitalist economy, government regulation of business would interfere with the operation of the free market.

Democratic Values

Agree Abolitionists argued that the nation had a moral duty to put an end to the institution of slavery.

Disagree The constitutional guarantee of equal protection under the law does not provide for special assistance to the poor and weak.

Constitutional Heritage

Agree The abolitionist movement provided the impetus behind the passage of the Thirteenth Amendment, which abolished slavery.

Disagree The Bill of Rights was passed without the backing of a reform movement.

Busy New York City street

The Whitney Museum of American Art

The American Federation of Labor logo

1909 The Arts
Gertrude Vanderbilt Whitney opens a modern art gallery in New York.

1909 Politics
The National Association for the Advancement of Colored People is founded.

1910 Daily Life
About one third of American working men and women live in poverty.

1913 World Events
Norway grants women full political rights.

1913 Business and Finance
The United States is the world's leading producer of coal.

1914 Daily Life
Some 2 million skilled workers belong to the American Federation of Labor.

1914 Business and Finance
The total value of U.S. imports reaches nearly $2 billion.

1915 Science and Technology
Deaths from tuberculosis drop significantly thanks to the efforts of the National Tuberculosis Association.

1916 Business and Finance
Local canning companies merge to form California Packing, a nationwide organization to market their goods.

1917 Politics
Congress proposes the Eighteenth Amendment, which prohibits the manufacture, sale, and distribution of alcoholic beverages.

1920 Daily Life
More than half of all Americans live in urban areas.

1910 1912 1914 1916 1918 1920

A young boy working in a coal mine

Temperance leader Carry Nation

Think About Themes

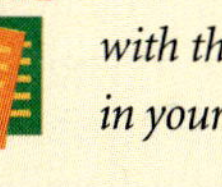

Decide whether you **agree** *or* **disagree** *with the following statements. Note why in your journal.*

Economic Development State governments have a responsibility to regulate how businesses treat workers.

Democratic Values A democracy has a duty to protect and assist the poorest and weakest of its citizens.

Constitutional Heritage Reform movements are necessary in order to lay the groundwork for constitutional change.

exploring the time line

GLOBAL EVENTS

GLOBAL RELATIONS

1905 ■ The Russian Revolution. On Sunday, January 9, 1905, Father George Gapon led a group of workers, their wives, and their children toward the czar's Winter Palace in St. Petersburg, Russia. The marchers, singing hymns and bearing no weapons, intended to petition the czar to end an ongoing war, to grant civil rights, and to reduce the workday to eight hours. When the marchers ignored an order to stop marching, the czar's troops fired on them, killing hundreds. This incident, called Bloody Sunday, angered the nation and encouraged hundreds of thousands of people to demand changes. The following strikes temporarily paralyzed Russia. Eventually, however, the revolution ended.

CRITICAL THINKING How might the 1905 revolution in Russia have compared to earlier events in the United States?

ANSWER: Answers will vary. Students might discuss the Boston Massacre or the Haymarket Riot.

245

SECTION 1

After completing Section 1, students should be able to:

OBJECTIVE 1 *Discuss the backgrounds of the reformers.*

OBJECTIVE 2 *Identify issues that concerned progressives, and explain how they tried to make changes.*

OBJECTIVE 3 *Specify issues that muckrakers addressed.*

OBJECTIVE 4 *Summarize how progressive writers and thinkers viewed American society.*

LET'S GET STARTED!

As students enter the classroom, have them write down at least three of the main goals of the Populist Party. *(Students might list graduated income tax, bank regulation, government ownership of railroad and telegraph companies, free coinage of silver, immigration restrictions, a shorter workday, and voting reforms.)* Have volunteers share their lists with the class. Then tell students that in Section 1 they will learn more about the progressives.

SECTION 1 RESOURCES

PRINT

- Guided Reading Strategy 8.1
- Literature Reading 8: A Muckraker's Report
- Section 1 Review, p. 251
- Daily Quiz 8.1

MULTIMEDIA

- One-Stop Planner, Lesson 8.1
- Everyday Life in America Transparency 18: Progressives and Children, Early 1900s
- Holt Researcher: American History CD–ROM

SHELTERED ENGLISH

- Main Idea Activity for Reteaching and Sheltered English 8.1

✔ READING TO UNDERSTAND

To help students master the section objectives, have them answer the **READING CHECKS** and complete **Guided Reading Strategy 8.1** as they read the section.

The Progressive Movement

OBJECTIVES

Read to understand:

1. what the backgrounds of the reformers were
2. what issues concerned progressives, and how they tried to make changes
3. what issues muckrakers addressed
4. how progressive writers and thinkers viewed American society

KEY TERMS

progressivism
McClure's Magazine
muckrakers

KEY PEOPLE

Lincoln Steffens
Ida Tarbell
Ray Stannard Baker
Theodore Dreiser
Edith Wharton
Herbert Croly

"The 'tramp' comes with the locomotive, and almshouses [poorhouses] and prisons are as surely the marks of 'material progress' as are costly dwellings, rich warehouses, and magnificent churches."

—Henry George

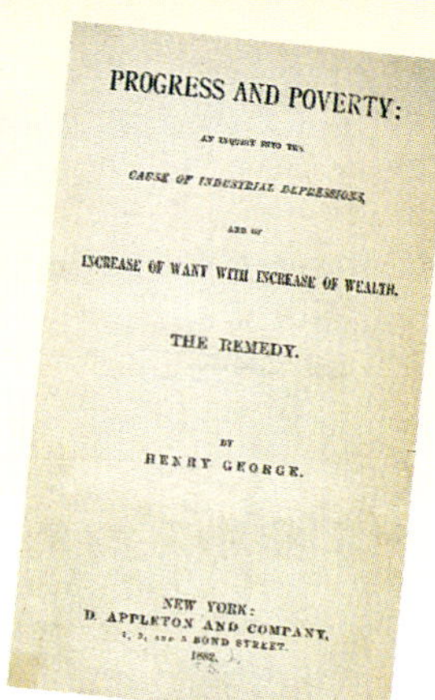

PROGRESS AND POVERTY:
AN INQUIRY INTO THE
CAUSE OF INDUSTRIAL DEPRESSIONS,
AND OF
INCREASE OF WANT WITH INCREASE OF WEALTH.
THE REMEDY.
BY
HENRY GEORGE.
NEW YORK:
D. APPLETON AND COMPANY,
1, 3, AND 5 BOND STREET.
1882.

***Henry George's* Progress and Poverty**

Henry George wrote these words in his 1879 book, *Progress and Poverty.* In the book he discussed the problems facing the United States as both the number of poor people and the nation's wealth increased. George hoped for a time when the country's progress might be measured by its movement "toward equality, not toward inequality." *Progress and Poverty* soon became a best-seller. One economist noted that it was read by tens of thousands of members of the working and lower classes "who never before looked between the covers of an economics book." By the early 1900s a drive for economic and social reform had begun. Many Americans sought to make the country's laws and institutions more responsive to the conditions of the nation's poorest and most disadvantaged citizens.

The Progressive Spirit

By the early 1900s industrialization had transformed the United States. Economic growth led to many new goods and services as well as an expanding middle class. However, growth also widened the gap between the rich and the poor and led to unsafe working conditions and crowded cities.

Such problems aroused a spirit of reform known as **progressivism.** In the late 1800s members of the Populist Party had protested what they saw as unfair business practices and had pressed for government action to stop them. Populism was mainly a rural movement. Progressivism, however, focused on urban problems, such as the plight of workers, poor sanitation, and corrupt political machines.

The progressives. People from all walks of life participated in reform efforts during the Progressive Era. However, most progressives were native born, middle or upper class, and college educated. Many Americans' first exposure to the social problems of the industrial United States came while taking college courses. "My life began at Johns Hopkins University," progressive Frederic Howe recalled. "I came alive. I felt a sense of responsibility. I wanted to change things."

Men and women of the urban middle class—doctors, engineers, ministers, small-business owners, social workers, teachers, and writers—found progressivism particularly attractive. This urban middle class had grown from some 750,000 in 1870 to about 10 million by 1910. Kansas editor William Allen White described this change. He said that by the 1900s populism had "shaved its whiskers, washed its shirt, put on a derby, and moved up into the middle class."

TEACH OBJECTIVE 1

LEVEL 1: Pair students and ask each pair to create a list of words that they associate with progressive reformers. *(Pairs might list words such as urban or involved.)* Have students share their lists with the class. To help students understand the backgrounds of reformers, copy the following graphic organizer on the chalkboard, omitting the italicized answers. Have pairs complete it.
Sheltered English, Cooperative Learning

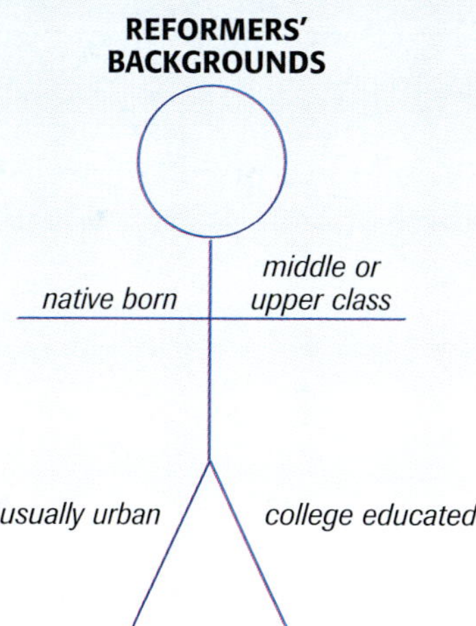

Women and progressivism. Previous generations of women had joined reform efforts because they were an acceptable way for women to influence politics and society. Many middle-class women were drawn to the progressive movement for the same reason. Women enrolled in colleges in increasing numbers during the early 1900s, but their career choices remained limited. Reform work offered college-educated women a way to use their knowledge of medicine, psychology, sociology, and other subjects.

In 1909 Ella Flagg Young became Chicago's superintendent of schools—the first woman to hold such a job in a major city. Young promoted public education by raising teachers' salaries. Published in 1910, Rheta Childe Dorr's widely read book *What Eight Million Women Want* noted the special role of women in the reform movement. "Women have ceased to exist as a subsidiary [lower] class in the community," she wrote. "The modern . . . educated woman came into a world which is losing faith in the commercial ideal and is endeavoring to substitute in its place a social ideal."

Some women made careers of reform work. Others volunteered their time through groups such as the General Federation of Women's Clubs and the National Association of Colored Women. Women also participated in the 1913 Progressive Party convention in Chicago. The party's platform supported women's suffrage and an end to child labor. Describing her experience as a delegate, Jane Addams wrote that it did not seem strange for women to take part. "It would have been much more unnatural if they had not been there, when such matters of social welfare were being considered."

✔ **READING CHECK:** What were the backgrounds of many of the reformers?

Bachelor's Degrees Awarded, 1900–1920

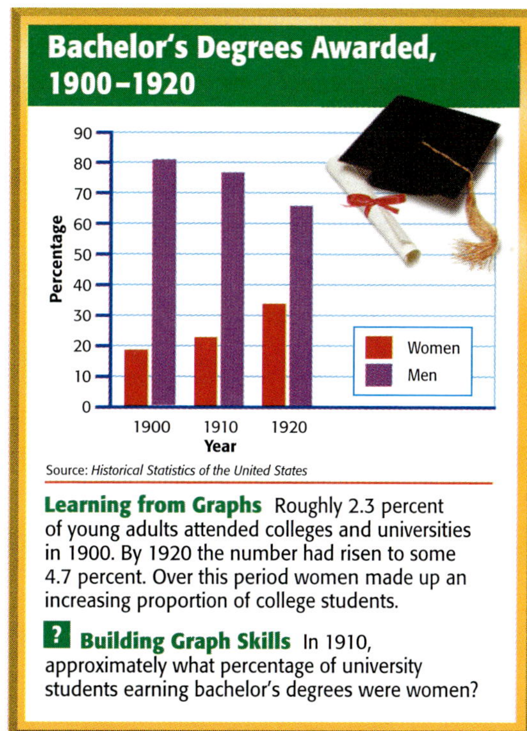

Source: *Historical Statistics of the United States*

Learning from Graphs Roughly 2.3 percent of young adults attended colleges and universities in 1900. By 1920 the number had risen to some 4.7 percent. Over this period women made up an increasing proportion of college students.

? Building Graph Skills In 1910, approximately what percentage of university students earning bachelor's degrees were women?

Progressive Issues

Progressives tried to reform American institutions while preserving ideals of the past, such as a sense of community. Progressive reformers took a leading role in promoting change in the United States.

A dangerous workplace. A major concern of the progressives was the way corporate America did business. Industrial workers often faced dangerous conditions and long hours. In 1910 some 70 percent of all American industrial laborers worked an average of 54 hours a week. As a result, American workers had higher accident rates than workers in other industrialized countries. In one Pittsburgh steel mill 3,723 laborers—25 percent of its workforce—were injured or killed on the job each year between 1907 and 1910.

INTERPRETING THE VISUAL RECORD

Education for women. These women attended Vassar College in the 1920s. ***What can you determine about their economic background?***

DEMOCRATIC VALUES

Women's Suffrage. Many female progressives worked for equal voting rights. Other female activists opposed women's suffrage. The National Association Opposed to Women's Suffrage (NAOWS), formed in 1911, was headed by Mrs. Arthur M. Dodge. The association distributed antisuffrage literature and coordinated state efforts. The women of NAOWS believed that suffrage and political involvement would cause women to lose their focus on being wives and mothers.

CRITICAL THINKING What arguments might pro-suffrage activists have advanced against antisuffragists?

ANSWER: Answers will vary. Students might suggest that pro-suffrage activists might have argued that female voters would be better able to care for their families if they had a voice in laws that affected them.

CHART ANSWER
just over 20 percent

VISUAL RECORD ANSWER
Students might suggest that the women appear to be from the middle or upper classes.

LEVEL 2: Tell students to imagine that they are modern-day screenwriters working on a screenplay about a progressive reformer. Have each student invent a main character for the screenplay. Ask students to describe their characters in writing, focusing on their backgrounds, interests, and motivations. *(See the Level 1 graphic organizer for the correct backgrounds.)* Ask volunteers to share their character descriptions with the class.

LEVEL 3: Ask students to complete the Level 2 lesson. Then have each student write a short scene featuring his or her progressive reformer. Remind students that their scenes should focus on their characters' backgrounds, interests, and motivations while also presenting a cohesive story or moment. Ask volunteers to read or enact their scenes for the class.

▶**ASSIGNMENT:** *Have each student create a detailed outline of the subsection entitled The Progressive Spirit.*

NOTE: For an additional teaching idea, see the Chapter 8 structured discussion lesson in the **Creative Teaching Strategies** handbook.

HISTORY MAKERS SPEAK

John Dewey in *Ethics*

John Dewey and Democracy. Progressive philosopher John Dewey emphasized the practical applications of philosophy. He wrote, "Philosophy is of account only if it affords guidance to action." Dewey favored public education that prepared students to participate fully in democracy. In *Ethics*, Dewey argued that "A just social order promotes in all its members habits of criticizing its attained goods and habits of projecting schemes of new goods. It does not aim at intellectual and moral subordination."

CRITICAL THINKING How might Dewey's argument have been used to justify women's suffrage?

ANSWER: Students might indicate that Dewey argued that all citizens should be able to criticize and change their society. Women could not do that effectively if they could not vote.

Multimedia Resources

Everyday Life in America Transparency 18: Progressives and Children, Early 1900s

THE SOCIAL GOSPEL AND PROGRESSIVISM

Charles M. Sheldon's 1896 Social Gospel novel, *In His Steps,* focused on characters in a typical midwestern city who based their behavior on the question, "What would Jesus do?" The results were remarkable. Manufacturers ran their businesses for the benefit of employees, and wealthy businesspeople bought slum property and improved it for the benefit of the tenants. While such dramatic results were not often seen in real life, Social Gospel thought had a profound effect on the progressive movement. Many progressives, including Jane Addams, were greatly influenced by the Social Gospel writers. Progressivism promoted the same goals as Social Gospel thinkers, including the abolition of child labor as well as the support of higher wages, industrial regulations, and shorter workweeks.

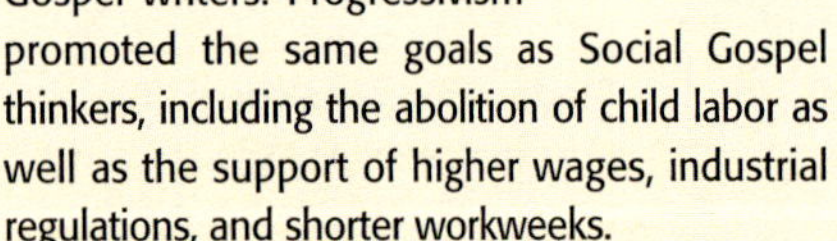

Walter Rauschenbusch

Walter Rauschenbusch, a professor at Rochester Theological Seminary in New York, was one of the leading writers and thinkers of both the Social Gospel movement and the progressive movement. In *For God and the People: Prayers of the Social Awakening* (1910), he called for "a new type of Christian." He wanted Christians to become involved in social issues as an extension of their love for God. Rauschenbusch wrote prayers for specific groups of workers, such as his "For Children Who Work," "For Workingmen," and "For Women Who Toil." He participated actively in the Social Gospel movement, helping to popularize it. He also moved it more concretely toward the progressive movement's goal of addressing the social consequences of industrialization and rapid urban growth.

These conditions led progressives to demand limits on corporate power. They promoted laws to prohibit monopolies and to help smaller businesses compete in the economy. Progressives also called for an eight-hour workday, a minimum wage, safer working conditions, and an end to child labor. Not surprisingly, most business owners opposed such legislation.

Social problems. Like the Populists, progressives wanted the people to have greater control of the government. They called for new election reforms and proposed political measures to make government more responsive to the desires of the voters. Reformer Benjamin Parke De Witt wanted to give "the people direct and continuous control over all the branches of government." Like Populists and Social Gospel ministers, progressives were inspired by the spirit of social justice. Progressive Theodore Roosevelt wrote, "If we wish to do good work for our country, we must be unselfish."

Progressives firmly believed in the power of science and technology to solve social problems. Progressive philosopher John Dewey believed that public education should prepare students to function well and efficiently in society, not simply give them factual knowledge. To this end, Dewey promoted a curriculum closely tied to real-life activities.

With the help of universities, progressives began many social-research projects. Some progressives, however, worried that the university might become too involved. Jane Addams warned against turning settlement houses "into one more laboratory; another place in which to . . . observe and record."

✔ **READING CHECK:** With what issues did progressives concern themselves, and how did they try to make changes?

Built for the 1893 World's Columbian Exposition in Chicago, the "White City" showed what many progressives thought modern cities should be like.

THE GRANGER COLLECTION, NEW YORK

TEACH OBJECTIVE 2

LEVEL 1: Conduct a brief discussion on the broad range of social issues that concerned progressive reformers, and tell students that progressives tried to reform business, government, and society. Pair students and then have each pair create a graphic organizer that depicts progressive goals and the institutions that progressives tried to reform. *(Pairs' graphic organizers should note that progressives wanted to reform industrial practices, end child labor, reform the electoral system, and work for social justice. In order to do so, progressives demanded limits on corporate power, proposed new political measures, and tried to harness the power of science and technology to solve social problems.)* Have volunteers present their graphic organizers to the class.
Sheltered English, Cooperative Learning

LEVELS 2 AND 3: Ask students to identify the issues that were important to progressives. *(See the Level 1 lesson for the correct progressive issues.)* Then tell students to imagine that they are newspaper reporters during the Progressive Era. Have each student choose an issue that concerned progressive reformers and write an article that is sympathetic to progressive goals. Articles should assume a firsthand perspective, describe the problem or issue, and propose a solution to the problem. Ask volunteers to read their articles to the class.

Inspiration for Reform

Progressive journalists helped spread the reform message. Popular magazines such as *Munsey's* and *Everybody's* published stories exploring corruption in politics and business as well as social problems such as slums and child labor. ***McClure's Magazine***, another national magazine, had been founded in 1893 by the reform-minded Scotch-Irish immigrant S. S. McClure.

Articles in* McClure's Magazine *informed the public about how corruption in business and politics affected their lives.

The muckraking press. In 1906 Theodore Roosevelt described in a speech a man with a muckrake who "fixes his eyes . . . only on that which is vile and debasing [harmful and corrupt]." The vivid image stuck, and investigative journalists became known as **muckrakers**—a name many accepted with much pride. Walter Lippmann, a young progressive, noted in 1914 that "muckraking was what the people wanted to hear."

McClure's publication in October 1902 of "Tweed Days in St. Louis," by journalists Lincoln Steffens and Claude Wetmore, marked the real beginning of this style of journalism. The article exposed the corrupt political machine in St. Louis, comparing it to Boss Tweed's control of New York City.

Ida Tarbell

Tarbell and Standard Oil. In November 1902 *McClure's* ran the first installment of Ida Tarbell's "History of the Standard Oil Company." Tarbell, the daughter of an independent oil producer, was born in western Pennsylvania in 1857. Tarbell was deeply angered when John D. Rockefeller's Standard Oil Company began swallowing up independent oil companies. Her father's company went bankrupt.

In 1876 Tarbell entered Allegheny College as the only female in an incoming class of 40 "hostile or indifferent" males, as she recalled. After graduation she began her career as a writer. By the 1890s she was writing a popular series for *McClure's*. In 1900 *McClure's* assigned her to investigate Standard Oil. Tarbell published her findings in a series of 19 articles on Standard Oil's business practices.

> **"One of the most depressing features . . . is that instead of such methods arousing contempt, they are more or less openly admired. . . . There is no gaming table in the world where loaded dice are tolerated, no athletic field where men must not start fair. Yet Mr. Rockefeller has systematically played with loaded dice. . . . Business played in this way loses all its sportsmanlike qualities. It is fit only for tricksters."**

McClure's readers hailed Tarbell as "the Terror of the Trusts." Unlike many other reporters, Tarbell was dismayed to find that she had been labeled a muckraker. Many of her readers continued to expect such exposés and seemed uninterested in more-balanced findings. "Was it not as much my business as a reporter to present this [the favorable] side of the picture as to present the other?" Tarbell wondered. Later in life she participated in numerous government conferences and committees dealing with such issues as defense, industry, and unemployment. Five years before her death in 1944, she wrote her autobiography, *All in the Day's Work*.

Read More About It

Free Find: Ida Tarbell
After reading about Ida Tarbell on the **Holt Researcher** CD–ROM, create a magazine cover for a muckraking story about a present-day issue that concerns you.

ACROSS THE CURRICULUM

▶LITERATURE◀

Naturalism. Many of the novelists who focused on social problems during the Progressive Era wrote in a style called "naturalism." Like literary realists, naturalists tried to portray "a direct impression of life," rather than a romantic, or unrealistic, impression. Naturalists went further, however, and chose to represent characters in situations completely beyond their control. Naturalist Jack London explained, "Man is not a free agent, and free will is a fallacy exploded by science long ago." Characters in naturalistic fiction usually have no chance to change their lives. They are controlled by their surroundings–such as the tenement and the factory. They are also controlled by inherited characteristics and unconscious, animalistic desires. Naturalistic fiction also often depicted scenes from impoverished and violent neighborhoods and followed characters as they descended into criminal activities.

CRITICAL THINKING Why might some reformers have found naturalistic fiction to be an impetus for reform?

ANSWER: Students might suggest that naturalistic fiction convinced some reformers that they could improve people's lives by improving their environments.

TEACH OBJECTIVES 3 AND 4

LEVEL 1: Pair students and ask each pair to list the issues explored by muckraking journalists and progressive writers. *(Pairs should note that muckrakers explored corruption in business and urban politics, social problems such as slums and child labor, and racism. Progressive writers explored exploitation of the weak by industrial society, the idea that government should use its powers to promote social welfare, and the social responsibility of private citizens.)* Then have pairs write topic sentences to describe how progressive writers and thinkers viewed American society. Have volunteers read their sentences to the class.
Sheltered English, Cooperative Learning

LEVELS 2 AND 3: Ask students to identify the issues explored by muckraking journalists and progressive writers. *(See the Level 1 lesson for the correct issues.)* Then have each student write a short essay on how progressive writers and thinkers viewed American society. *(See the Level 1 lesson for the correct perspective.)* Have students discuss their essays in small groups.
Cooperative Learning

▸**ASSIGNMENT** *Have each student write three slogans to generate public support for the progressive movement. Slogans should focus on one or more of the goals of the movement.*

ACROSS THE CURRICULUM

▸LITERATURE◂

The Railroad's Vast Influence. In *The Octopus,* Frank Norris depicts an epic struggle between California wheat farmers and the railroad. Norris based his novel on a real struggle between ranchers and a railroad corporation. The ranchers had leased land from the railroad and improved it with irrigation. The railroad had promised to sell them the land at a low price per acre, but at the time of the sale, the railroad raised the prices as much as eight times more than the original price. In his novel, Norris creates an image of the railroad as a tentacled beast that grabs up everything in its path—a "leviathan with tentacles of steel."

ACTIVITY: Have each student write a brief description of some aspect of industrialization using a metaphor from nature—such as an octopus—to enrich his or her description.

STRATEGIES FOR SUCCESS ANSWERS

Practicing the Strategy

1. the family's living conditions and the family itself
2. that the family is poor and struggling
3. Some students might point to evidence of poverty and suggest that the picture does accurately reflect conditions.

This cartoon shows Standard Oil as a giant octopus that crushes all opposition in its tentacles.

Muckraking books. Books by other muckraking writers poured off the presses. In 1904 Lincoln Steffens documented urban political corruption in *The Shame of the Cities.* Writer Ray Stannard Baker toured the nation in 1904 examining the plight of African Americans. Published in 1908, Baker's *Following the Color Line* described a lynching in Springfield, Ohio.

> "The worst feature of all in this Springfield lynching was the apathy of the public. No one really seemed to care. . . . If ever there was an example of good citizenship lying flat on its back . . . Springfield furnished an example of that condition."

✔ **READING CHECK:** What issues did muckrakers address?

Strategies for Success

Interpreting the Visual Record: Photographs

The visual record of an event, period, or place can help one understand its history in ways the written word sometimes cannot. Like other historical sources, however, photographs must be interpreted carefully. If a photograph includes people, their knowledge of the photographer's presence is important. Spontaneous snapshots usually look much different than ones that are posed. Furthermore, every photograph has a frame, or set of borders, that includes some details and excludes others. The manner in which a photographer selects this frame is another crucial issue. Finally, a photographer's choice of camera equipment, lighting, and developing technique all affect the appearance of a photograph. It is therefore important to analyze the manner in which a photograph is produced along with its actual content.

How to Interpret a Photograph

1. **Identify the subject.** Look at the photograph as a whole and identify its basic subject.
2. **Study the details.** Examine the details in the photograph for information about its historical context.
3. **Determine the photographer's point of view.** Look for information that suggests the photographer's purpose. Note how the photograph was framed and if anyone in the photograph knew it was being taken.

Applying the Strategy

The photograph below depicts an immigrant family in their New York City tenement. It was taken in 1910 by Jessie Tarbox Beals, a muckraking photographer who documented urban living conditions.

Practicing the Strategy

Study the photograph above to answer the following questions.

1. What information is provided by the photograph?
2. What message is Beals trying to communicate about the family in the photograph?
3. Does the photograph seem to represent accurately the urban living conditions of immigrant workers during the early 1900s? Explain your answer.

REVIEW

Have students complete the **Section 1 Review** on p. 251.

ASSESS

Have students complete **Daily Quiz 8.1**. As **Alternative Assessment**, you may want to use the progressive reforms graphic organizer or the scene from the screenplay in this section's lessons.

RETEACH

Have students complete **Main Idea Activity for Reteaching and Sheltered English 8.1**. Organize students into small groups. Assign one section objective to each group member. Direct students to write a few sentences or paragraphs addressing their assigned objectives. Have students share their paragraphs with the rest of their group.
Sheltered English, Cooperative Learning

EXTEND

Have students read Upton Sinclair's *The Jungle,* Lincoln Steffens's *The Shame of the Cities,* Ray Stannard Bakers's *Following the Color Line,* or another muckraking piece from the late 1800s or early 1900s. Have each student create a multimedia presentation on his or her work and present it to the class.
Block Scheduling

Writers and Social Problems

Novelists and intellectuals also explored the darker side of the new industrial society's effect on people's behavior and values. In their works, these writers presented stories of the harsh effects of industrial society on the poor.

In novels such as *Sister Carrie* (1900) and *The Financier* (1912), Theodore Dreiser depicted workers brutalized by greedy business owners. In Edith Wharton's 1905 work, *The House of Mirth,* the closed-mindedness of elite society leads the good-hearted heroine to social isolation and despair.

Progressive intellectuals proposed alternatives to the idea that fierce competition was the best formula for social progress. In *The Promise of American Life* (1909), political theorist Herbert Croly argued that the government should use its regulatory and tax powers to promote the welfare of all its citizens. He opposed the government's support of the interest of business owners over other Americans.

In 1902, in *Democracy and Social Ethics,* Jane Addams urged private citizens to show more social responsibility as well. "We are bound to move forward or [slip backward] together. None of us can stand aside; our feet are mired [stuck] in the same soil, and our lungs breathe the same air." Although progressives such as Addams and Croly wanted to transform U.S. society and its values, they remained committed to democracy. Most progressives sought reforms of local government, businesses, and city life to ensure that the full promise of democracy became available to all citizens.

These Progressive Era books explored the challenges of American life in the new industrial age.

✔ **READING CHECK:** How did progressive writers and thinkers view American society?

SECTION  REVIEW

Define and explain the significance of the following terms:
progressivism
McClure's Magazine
muckrakers

Identify and explain the significance of the following individuals:
Lincoln Steffens
Ida Tarbell
Ray Stannard Baker
Theodore Dreiser
Edith Wharton
Herbert Croly

1. **Using Graphic Organizers** Copy the graphic organizer below. Use it to explain what issues progressives addressed and how they hoped to bring about change.

Progressives		
Big Business	Political Rights	Social Justice

2. **Analyzing** What characteristics describe the background of many of the progressive reformers?
3. **Evaluating** What issues did muckraking journalists concentrate on during the first decades of the 1900s? What effects did their articles have on politics and the lives of poor Americans?
4. **Using Historical Imagination** Imagine that you are a progressive novelist in the early 1900s. Create an outline for an article or short story that reflects an issue of concern to you.

Critical Thinking

5. In what ways were the goals of Populists and progressives similar and different?
Consider
   - what the goals of the Populists were
   - what the goals of the progressives were

SECTION 1 REVIEW ANSWERS

Define and Identify
For significance, see the following pages:

- progressivism, p. 246
- *McClure's Magazine*, p. 249
- muckrakers, p. 249
- Lincoln Steffens, p. 249
- Ida Tarbell, p. 249
- Ray Stannard Baker, p. 250
- Theodore Dreiser, p. 251
- Edith Wharton, p. 251
- Herbert Croly, p. 251

1. big business—called for limiting monopolies, the eight-hour workday, a minimum wage, safer conditions, and child labor restrictions; political rights—election reforms; social justice—called for less poverty and the application of science and technology to solve social problems
2. Many of the reformers were native born, educated, and from the middle or upper classes.
3. corruption, urban living conditions, and child labor; captured public attention and helped create change
4. Students' outlines will vary. Students should incorporate progressive concerns such as big business, political rights, and social justice.
5. Both wanted greater public control of government and a graduated income tax, but Populists focused on rural concerns while progressives emphasized urban concerns.

SECTION 2

After completing Section 2, students should be able to:

OBJECTIVE 1 *Identify workplace problems that progressives targeted.*

OBJECTIVE 2 *Explain what the results of the Triangle Shirtwaist Fire were.*

OBJECTIVE 3 *List and describe the rulings that the Supreme Court made on labor laws.*

OBJECTIVE 4 *Summarize union successes and failures.*

LET'S GET STARTED!

Write the following statements on the chalkboard: *Progressives were mostly native-born, college-educated individuals. (True) Progressives wanted businesses to enact a 14-hour workday. (False.) Progressives wanted to limit or end child labor. (True)* As students enter the classroom, ask them to determine if each statement is true or false. Tell students to rewrite false statements to make them true. Then tell students that in Section 2 they will learn more about progressives' efforts to reform the workplace.

SECTION 2 RESOURCES

PRINT

- Guided Reading Strategy 8.2
- Geography Activity 8: Limiting the Workday
- Graphic Organizer Activity 8: The Progressive Ideal
- Section 2 Review, p. 257
- Daily Quiz 8.2

MULTIMEDIA

- One-Stop Planner, Lesson 8.2
- Holt Researcher: American History CD–ROM

SHELTERED ENGLISH

- Main Idea Activity for Reteaching and Sheltered English 8.2

✔ READING TO UNDERSTAND

To help students master the section objectives, have them answer the **READING CHECKS** and complete **Guided Reading Strategy 8.2** as they read the section.

Reforming the New Industrial Order

OBJECTIVES

Read to understand:

1. what workplace problems progressives targeted
2. what the results of the Triangle Shirtwaist Fire were
3. what rulings the Supreme Court made on labor laws
4. what successes and failures unions saw in the early 1900s

KEY TERMS

Triangle Shirtwaist Fire
freedom of contract
Muller v. *Oregon*
closed shop
socialism
International Ladies' Garment Workers Union
open shop
Industrial Workers of the World

KEY PEOPLE

Samuel Gompers
Florence Kelley
Rose Schneiderman
Louis D. Brandeis
William "Big Bill" Haywood

"Miners' families . . . had to make their purchases of all the necessaries of life, meager [few] as they were, from the company stores at double the prices for which they could be had elsewhere. . . . It was a common saying that children were brought into the world by the company doctor, lived in a company house . . . were buried in a company coffin, and laid away in the company graveyard."

—Samuel Gompers

Samuel Gompers

Union leader Samuel Gompers explained in his *Autobiography* how mining companies controlled the lives of their workers. As one union official stated, the company owned "every single thing there is" in the entire town, from the miners' homes to the buildings in the community—even school and church buildings. Some mining companies paid little attention to safety conditions underground. Mines owned by John D. Rockefeller, for example, experienced cave-ins and serious explosions that took the lives of miners almost every year.

Reforming the Workplace

In 1900 the average laborer worked nearly 10 hours a day, six days a week, for about $1.50 a day. Women and children earned even less.

Female and child laborers. In the early 1910s almost half of the women who worked in such jobs as factory workers, store clerks, and laundresses earned less than $6 a week. The Commission on Industrial Relations reported in 1916 that this salary "means that every penny must be counted, every normal desire stifled, and each basic necessity of life barely satisfied."

Women often faced significant barriers when they tried to increase their income. For instance, pieceworkers could be penalized for working too fast. Rebecca August, a buttonhole maker in Chicago, recalled that she was paid 3.5 cents per buttonhole. When her supervisor realized how many buttonholes she was able to make—and thus how much money she could earn—he cut her pay. The supervisor said, "It was an *outrage* for a *girl* to make $25 a week." When August tried to organize a protest, her employer fired her.

The commission's report also attacked child labor practices. It declared "The Nation is paying a heavy toll in ignorance, deformity of body or mind, and premature old age [among children]." In *The Bitter Cry of the Children* (1906), John Spargo charged the textile industries with the "enslavement of children." He reported that children were employed to do work that he "could not do . . . and live."

This political cartoon shows child workers as the slaves of big business.

TEACH OBJECTIVE 1

LEVEL 1: Conduct a discussion about the workplace reforms that progressives hoped to institute. Then have each student list progressives' goals for workplace reform in the early 1900s. *(Students should note that progressives wanted to limit or end child labor, increase women's wages, limit working hours, and establish minimum wages and workplace safety standards.)* Ask students to think about the jobs they might hold in a few years when they enter the working world. Write the following questions on the chalkboard: *What do you expect in terms of working conditions, wages, and hours? What conditions would you consider to be unacceptable? What would you do about unacceptable circumstances if you encountered them?* Have students take turns responding to these questions. Encourage students to make connections between their responses and the progressive agenda. **Sheltered English**

LEVELS 2 AND 3: Tell students to imagine that it is 1904 and that they are progressive reformers. Have each student write a letter to a state legislator demanding laws to improve the workplace. *(See the Level 1 lesson for the correct reforms.)* Tell students to identify specific workplace problems, to suggest specific changes they would like to see made, and to provide evidence of poor workplace conditions to back up their demands. Ask volunteers to read their letters to the class.

Spargo found that few child laborers had ever attended school or could read. Many mothers explained that they put their children to work in the mills because it was either that or starve. During an investigation of a miners' strike in 1903, a nine-year-old child reported that he was being forced to pay money that his father, who had died in the mine, owed to the company for rent.

INTERPRETING THE VISUAL RECORD

Labor reform. This poster calls for a national eight-hour workday. ***What symbols of work do you see in the picture?***

Labor laws. Progressives and labor union activists campaigned for new laws that would prohibit or limit child labor and improve conditions for female workers. Reformer Florence Kelley worked tirelessly for this cause. She helped persuade the Illinois legislature in 1893 to prohibit child labor as well as to limit the number of hours women could work.

Although most children worked in agriculture, children in the factories—more than 2 million by 1910—faced the worst conditions. Reformers heard stories of supervisors splashing cold water on children's faces to keep them awake and of young girls working 16 or more hours a day in canning factories. Orphans also were sent to work in factories. "Capital has neither morals nor ideals," cried one critic.

In 1904 Kelley helped organize the National Child Labor Committee to persuade state legislatures to pass laws against employing young children. By 1912, child-labor laws had been passed in 39 states. Some states even limited older children's employment to 8 or 10 hours a day and barred them from working at night or in dangerous occupations. Other states required that children be able to read and write before they were sent to work.

Enforcement of such laws was lax, however. Claiming that their business success depended on cheap child labor, many employers simply refused to obey the laws and continued to hire child workers. George Creel was a journalist and the author of *Children in Bondage* (1913). He estimated that "at least two million children were being fed annually into the steel hoppers of the modern industrial machine . . . all mangled in mind, body, and soul."

Progressives also campaigned for laws that would force factories to limit the long hours employers demanded of their adult workers. In 1903 Florence Kelley helped lobby the Oregon legislature to pass a law limiting female laundry workers to 10-hour days. Earlier, Utah had enacted a law limiting workdays in certain dangerous occupations to eight hours.

Progressive reformers also fought for higher wages. Some 30 million men and 7.5 million women were employed in 1910, and about one third of them lived in poverty. That year Catholic Church official Monsignor John Ryan called for "the establishment by law of minimum rates of wages that will equal or approximate the normal standards of living for the different groups of workers." Two years later Massachusetts responded to progressive lobbying by passing the nation's first minimum-wage law. This law set base wages for women and children. Other states gradually followed suit. Not until 1938, however, did Congress pass a national minimum-wage law.

✔ **READING CHECK:** What workplace problems did progressives target in the early 1900s?

Labor leaders encourage workers to attend a speech by Samuel Gompers on the fight for a shorter workday.

HISTORY MAKERS SPEAK

John Spargo in *The Bitter Cry of the Children*

Children at Work. John Spargo's *The Bitter Cry of the Children* exposed the scandal of child labor. Spargo described the work of young boys in coal mines by writing, "Crouched over the chutes, the boys sit hour after hour. . . . From the cramped position they have to assume, most of them become more or less deformed and bent-backed like old men. . . . Sometimes . . . a boy is mangled and torn in the machinery, or disappears in the chute to be picked out later smothered and dead." Spargo concluded, "This great nation in its commercial madness devours its babes." Although Spargo's details alerted many reformers of the need for rapid change, the Supreme Court often overturned reform successes.

CRITICAL THINKING Why might the Supreme Court have ruled against child labor reforms?

ANSWER: Some students might argue that the Supreme Court may not have accepted the progressive philosophy of an expanded role for the government in business affairs.

VISUAL RECORD ANSWER

Students might mention the beehive, the arm, and the hammer.

TEACH OBJECTIVE 2

LEVEL 1: Tell students about the workplace conditions that led to the deaths of so many women in the Triangle Shirtwaist Fire. Inform students that the New York legislature established the nation's strictest fire-safety code as a result of the fire. Then tell students to imagine that they are reporters for a New York City newspaper at the time of the fire. Have students work in pairs to create headlines about the fire and its aftermath. *(Pairs headlines might mention that fire doors were kept locked; that the company's workers had demanded—and not obtained—safer working conditions during a strike; the number of deaths caused by the fire; the public's outrage; and the subsequent passage of the fire-safety code.)* Have volunteers read their headlines to the class. **Sheltered English, Cooperative Learning**

LEVELS 2 AND 3: Ask students about the results of the Triangle Shirtwaist Fire. *(See the Level 1 lesson for the correct effects.)* Then tell students to imagine that they are New York state legislators at the time of the Triangle Shirtwaist Fire. Organize students into committees of four. Have each committee propose and discuss possible legislative solutions to the problem of workplace safety and then draft a public-safety law or series of laws to help protect workers in the future. Ask members of each group to read the provisions of their law or laws to the class. **Cooperative Learning**

PEOPLE IN HISTORY

Mary Elizabeth Drier. Mary Elizabeth Drier served on the commission that investigated the Triangle Shirtwaist Fire. At that point, Drier had a long career as a progressive. In her mid-twenties, she began working in a settlement house. Over the years, her interest in labor rights grew, and she later served as president of the New York chapter of the National Women's Trade Union League. She also participated in a 1909 shirtmakers strike. After the Triangle Shirtwaist Fire, she assumed an important role on the commission that helped work for important labor reforms. One fellow member called her the "soul" of the body. In the early and mid-1910s, Drier turned her efforts to the question of suffrage.

ACTIVITY: Tell students to imagine that they are Mary Elizabeth Drier. Have each student write a short editorial condemning the Triangle Shirtwaist Fire and calling for labor reforms.

VISUAL RECORD ANSWER

Students might suggest that the damage was horrible and that the public was outraged by it.

THROUGH OTHERS' EYES

Mexican View of Progressivism

Progressive reformers won shorter workdays, better working conditions, and other improvements for many U.S. workers. Such changes, however, were unknown to the immigrants who crossed the border from Mexico to work the fields, mines, and railroads of the southwestern United States. These immigrant workers experienced both harsh working conditions and bitter prejudice. In 1910 the Mexican newspaper *Diario del Hogar* wondered what drove "our workingmen, so attached to the land, to abandon the country [Mexico], even at the risk of the Yankee contempt with which they are treated on the other side of the Bravo [Rio Grande]." Some Mexican laborers were assaulted or lynched. Venustiano Carranza, Mexico's president from 1917 to 1920, claimed that 114 Mexicans had been murdered across the border.

The Triangle Shirtwaist Fire

Progressives also sought to improve workplace safety. A tragic event in 1911 catapulted the need for such reforms onto the front pages of the nation's newspapers. On Saturday, March 25, some 500 employees—most of them young Jewish or Italian immigrant women—were completing their six-day workweek at New York City's Triangle Shirtwaist Company. As they rose from their crowded work tables and started to leave, a fire erupted in a rag bin.

Within moments the entire eighth floor of the 10-story building was ablaze. Escape was impossible. There were only two stairways, and because managers were afraid workers would steal fabric, most of the fire doors were kept locked. Some women tried to take the freight elevators to safety, but the elevator jammed as women on higher floors jumped down the elevator shaft to flee the flames. Desperate for a way out, some 60 workers leaped from the windows to their death. "I looked upon the heap of dead bodies," wrote a journalist who witnessed the fire. "I remembered their great strike of last year in which these same girls demanded more sanitary conditions and more safety precautions in the shops. These dead bodies were the answer."

Through the night, weeping family members wandered among the crushed bodies on the sidewalk, looking for their loved ones. By the time firefighters gained control of the blaze, some 140 workers had perished in the **Triangle Shirtwaist Fire**. Rose Schneiderman, a Women's Trade Union League organizer, argued that only a strong working-class movement could bring real change to the workplace. She noted:

> **"This is not the first time girls have been burned alive in the city. Each week I must learn of the untimely death of one of my sister workers. Every year thousands of us are maimed. The life of men and women is so cheap and property is so sacred. There are so many of us for one job it matters little if 143 of us are burned to death."**

It did matter to the public, however. Popular outrage was so great that lawmakers soon passed protective legislation to help workers. As a result of the Triangle Shirtwaist Fire the New York legislature enacted the nation's strictest fire-safety code.

✔ **READING CHECK:** What were the results of the Triangle Shirtwaist Fire?

INTERPRETING THE VISUAL RECORD

Unsafe working conditions. The Triangle Shirtwaist Fire was a terrible tragedy that horrified many Americans. ***What can you determine about the extent of the damage caused by the fire and the tone of the public reaction to the fire?***

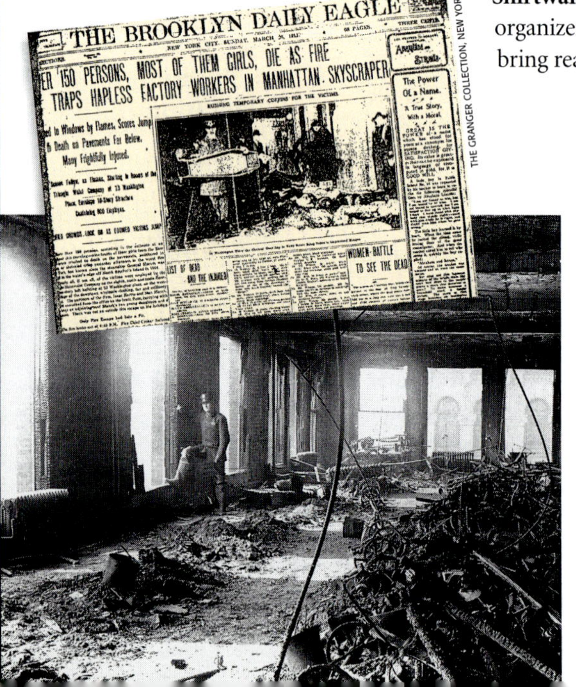

THE BROOKLYN DAILY EAGLE

NEW YORK CITY, SUNDAY, MARCH 26, 1911

…ER 150 PERSONS, MOST OF THEM GIRLS, DIE AS FIRE TRAPS HAPLESS FACTORY WORKERS IN MANHATTAN SKYSCRAPER

…ed to Windows by Flames, Scores Jump to Death on Pavements Far Below. Many Frightfully Injured.

The Power Of a Name. A True Story, With a Moral.

WOMEN BATTLE TO SEE THE DEAD

LIST OF DEAD AND THE INJURED

THE GRANGER COLLECTION, NEW YORK

TEACH OBJECTIVE 3

LEVEL 1: To help students understand how the Supreme Court ruled on labor laws, copy the following graphic organizer on the chalkboard, omitting the italicized answers. Ask each student to complete it.
Sheltered English

LEVELS 2 AND 3: Have students complete the Level 1 lesson. Then tell students to imagine that they are editors of a labor law encyclopedia. Have each student write entries for the cases *Lochner* v. *New York* and *Muller* v. *Oregon*. Students should summarize each case, the Supreme Court's ruling, and the Court's reasoning in each case.

SUPREME COURT RULINGS ON LABOR LAWS

Conflict or Case	Ruling
In response to social legislation, business owners claimed that laws regulating their businesses unfairly deprived them of property.	*The Court sided with business owners and overturned much early social legislation.*
***Lochner* v. *New York*—New York law limited bakers' workdays to 10 hours.**	*The Court overturned the 10-hour workday, citing freedom of contract—workers should be free to accept any working conditions.*
***Muller* v. *Oregon*—Employer challenged the 10-hour workday.**	*The Court upheld 10-hour workday law based on the "Brandeis Brief," which contained examples of the harm that long hours had on women's health.*

Progressivism and the Supreme Court

As more states passed protective legislation, business owners fought back through the courts. The Fourteenth Amendment to the Constitution prohibits states from depriving "any person of life, liberty, or property, without due process of law." Owners claimed that laws regulating their businesses deprived them of their property unfairly. The Supreme Court sided with business owners and declared much of the early social legislation unconstitutional.

The Court also ruled that some social legislation violated the Constitution by denying workers their **freedom of contract**, or the freedom to negotiate the terms of their employment. In the 1905 case *Lochner* v. *New York*, the Court overturned a New York law limiting bakers' workdays to 10 hours. Workers, the Court ruled, should be free to accept any conditions of employment that business owners required—even if that meant working 14 or 16 hours.

The Supreme Court did uphold some social legislation. In the 1908 case ***Muller* v. *Oregon***, an employer challenged the 10-hour-workday law that Florence Kelley had helped push through the Oregon legislature. Kelley and another woman, Josephine Goldmark, responded quickly. Goldmark gathered information for the brief, or legal argument, to defend the law. Kelley asked Goldmark's brother-in-law, a brilliant lawyer named Louis D. Brandeis, to argue the case.

The "Brandeis Brief" contained many examples of the harm that working long hours did to women's health and well-being. This research convinced the Court to uphold the Oregon law and became a model for the defense of other social legislation. Justice David Brewer noted that although the materials presented by Brandeis might not be authoritative, "they are significant of a widespread belief that woman's physical structure . . . [justifies] special legislation restricting or qualifying the conditions under which she should be permitted to toil."

INTERPRETING THE VISUAL RECORD

Factory work. These women are canning olives in a California factory. ***What does the picture reveal about the conditions of factory work?***

✔ **READING CHECK:** What rulings did the Supreme Court make on labor laws?

Labor Unions

Progressive reformers were not the only ones fighting for workers' rights. Labor unions continued to fight for better working conditions and for the **closed shop**—a workplace where all the employees must belong to a union. Most union members favored "working within the system." They wanted to change how workers were treated, but they did not want to threaten capitalism's very existence. Some, however, wanted to replace capitalism with an economic system controlled by workers. Many in this group favored **socialism**, or the system under which the government or worker cooperatives own most factories, utilities, and transportation and communications systems.

Labor Union Membership, 1900–1920

Membership (in millions): 0, 1, 2, 3, 4, 5, 6
Year: 1900, 1905, 1910, 1915, 1920

Source: *The Growth of American Trade Unions, 1880–1923*

Learning from Graphs The spread of industrialization and the efforts of progressive reformers contributed to the growth of labor union membership in the early 1900s.

? Building Graph Skills During which five-year period was the increase in union membership the smallest? During which period was it the largest?

PEOPLE IN HISTORY

Louis Brandeis. Louis Brandeis, known as the "People's Attorney," earned a reputation as a caring defender of moral causes. When Brandeis argued a case, he overwhelmed the opposition with a series of facts, statistics, and expert opinions; he based very few of his arguments on established legal precedents. Because Brandeis often argued cases against businesses and the government, many people labeled him a radical. Despite his reputation, however, Brandeis was a trusted adviser to President Woodrow Wilson, who nominated Brandeis to the Supreme Court in 1916.

ACTIVITY: Organize students into two groups. Have groups debate a progressive issue.

THAT'S INTERESTING!

Some activists focused on reforming the practices of food companies, demanding that producers label their products with the actual ingredients of the contents.

VISUAL RECORD ANSWER

Students might suggest that the picture reveals that the conditions were cramped and crowded.

GRAPH ANSWER

1905–1910; 1915–1920

TEACH OBJECTIVE 4

LEVEL 1: Write the following headers on the chalkboard: *Union Successes* and *Union Failures.* Then pair students and have each pair make a bulleted list of items that fit under each header. *(Pairs should note the following: successes—most unions increased membership; the ILGWU got wage increases and reduced working hours in some companies and got aid from progressive organizations; the IWW accepted women and minorities and won a major strike; failures—the AFL excluded many unskilled workers and promoted racist policies; the ILGWU did not get closed-shop status; the IWW failed in its goal to end capitalism and faded from power.)* After students have completed their lists, discuss unions' successes and failures as a class. **Sheltered English, Cooperative Learning**

LEVELS 2 AND 3: Have students complete the Level 1 lesson. Then have each student write two or three paragraphs comparing and contrasting the aims, strategies, and relative effectiveness of the AFL and the IWW. Ask volunteers to read their paragraphs to the class.

▶ASSIGNMENT *Write the following question on the chalkboard:* What industrial reform accomplished by the progressives or labor unions do you consider to be the most important? Why? *Have each student write a one-to-two-paragraph response to the question.*

DEMOCRATIC VALUES

The Boston Police Strike. After World War I, when prices were increasing but wages were not, the Boston police union joined the American Federation of Labor (AFL). Boston's police commissioner, who argued that a police-union affiliation was illegal, suspended several officers. In response, the police union went on strike, and some of Boston's citizens engaged in rioting and looting. The governor of Massachusetts and future president, Calvin Coolidge, sent the State Guard to Boston to keep order. The police commissioner began hiring new police officers to replace the strikers. Samuel Gompers, head of the AFL, asked for Governor Coolidge's help in discussing settlement terms with the commissioner, but Coolidge refused, saying, "There is no right to strike against the public safety by anybody, anywhere, anytime."

CRITICAL THINKING Why might Coolidge have considered a police strike a threat to the public safety?

ANSWER: Students might argue that Coolidge considered police officers a vital part in upholding public safety.

VISUAL RECORD ANSWER

(for p. 257)

Students might suggest that the picture reveals that the government was hostile toward the strikers.

The AFL. The major labor organization in these years remained the American Federation of Labor (AFL). The AFL favored working within the system. Led by Samuel Gompers, the AFL grew fourfold from 1900 to 1914. Gompers used the same organizational structure as trusts. "We welcome their organization," he said. "When they assume a right for themselves, they cannot deny that same right to us."

The AFL excluded unskilled workers—most of whom were eastern European immigrants or African Americans. AFL leaders believed that skilled workers had the greatest potential to cause change. However, this approach left most urban workers without organized support. By 1902 only about 3 percent of African American workers were union members.

The ILGWU. One AFL union that tried to organize unskilled workers was the **International Ladies' Garment Workers Union** (ILGWU). Established in 1900 in New York City, it sought to unionize workers—mainly Jewish and Italian immigrant women—employed in sewing shops. In 1909, workers at three different New York factories walked off their jobs. The workers then turned to the ILGWU to call a general strike. Union leaders hesitated, but the speech of Clara Lemlich, a young Jewish immigrant, changed their minds. "I am a working girl, one of those striking against intolerable conditions," she addressed a crowd of garment workers. "I am tired of listening to speakers who talk in generalities. What we are here for is to decide whether or not to strike. I offer a resolution that a general strike be declared—now." The frenzied crowd agreed with her.

This label identified clothes made by ILGWU members.

In November female garment workers staged the "Uprising of 20,000." Thousands of workers heeded the union's call and walked off their jobs to demand that their companies recognize the ILGWU as their union. The strike lasted through the bitter winter. Hard-pressed strikers received generous aid from progressive groups such as the Women's Trade Union League. This organization of wealthy women supported the efforts of working women to form unions. Many employers brought in African American women to take the place of their strikers, but several hundred of these workers went on strike also. One young African American woman wrote, "It's a good thing, this strike is. It makes you feel like a real grown-up person."

The strike's results were mixed. Most employers agreed to many of the ILGWU's demands, including wage increases and reduced working hours. However, they were determined to run an **open shop**, or nonunion workplace. Thus, they refused to recognize the union—the ILGWU's most basic demand. After this strike, ILGWU membership rose from 400 to 65,000.

Songbooks like this one for the IWW helped strengthen support for the union cause.

THE GRANGER COLLECTION, NEW YORK

The IWW. While Gompers and the AFL unions negotiated with business owners for worker gains, a new union emerged with a different agenda. Founded in Chicago in 1905, the **Industrial Workers of the World** (IWW) opposed capitalism. Referring to the Continental Congress that had declared U.S. independence, IWW leader William "Big Bill" Haywood asserted:

> **"Fellow workers, this is the continental congress of the working class. We are here to confederate the workers of this country into a working-class movement that shall have for its purpose the emancipation of the working class from the slave bondage of capitalism."**

REVIEW

Have students complete the **Section 2 Review** on p. 257.

ASSESS

Have students complete **Daily Quiz 8.2.** As **Alternative Assessment**, you may want to use the labor law encyclopedia entry or list of union successes and failures in this section's lessons.

RETEACH

Have students complete **Main Idea Activity for Reteaching and Sheltered English 8.2.** Then have students write the section's headings and subheadings on a sheet of paper, leaving a space between each. Ask students to list the main ideas of each heading and subheading in the appropriate space. Suggest that students find partners and compare main ideas.
Sheltered English, Cooperative Learning

EXTEND

Have students use the library or the Internet to conduct research on the growth and philosophical changes of the AFL (now the AFL–CIO) from the early 1900s to the present. Tell students to use the information they find to create an annotated time line on the subject. **Block Scheduling**

Haywood denounced the AFL's cooperation with business owners and its failure to include unskilled workers. He vowed to organize lumber workers, migrant farmworkers, miners, and textile workers to overthrow the capitalist system. The IWW enlisted African American, Asian American, and Hispanic American workers. An IWW-led union in Philadelphia succeeded in raising wages for its largely African American membership from $1.25 a day to $4 a day. The IWW also actively recruited female workers and the wives of male workers. An IWW newspaper expressed optimism that union women working "side by side with men in strikes will soon develop a fighting force that will end capitalism and its horrors in short order."

The Wobblies, as the members of the IWW came to be called, pursued their goals through boycotts, general strikes, and industrial sabotage. Their greatest hour came in 1912. That year, they led 20,000 workers in a strike against the textile mills of Lawrence, Massachusetts, to protest large cut in wages. After a bitter and much publicized two-month strike, the mill owners gave in.

Success was short-lived, however. Several later IWW-led strikes failed miserably. Most Americans grew fearful of the IWW's revolutionary aims and methods. As member Frederick C. Mills put it, the IWW "is trying to teach them [poor or unemployed workers] how to get their share of the goods of this world." The government cracked down on the union with increasing force. The government believed, perhaps, that IWW members, as described by Mills, were "living, eating and breathing agitation, agitation that is really anarchy." Disagreements among IWW leaders also weakened the union's power. Within a few years the IWW collapsed and eventually faded from power.

INTERPRETING THE VISUAL RECORD

IWW strike. The local militia was called in to break the IWW-led strike in Lawrence, Massachusetts. ***What does this picture reveal about the government's attitude toward strikers?***

✔ **READING CHECK:** What successes and failures did labor unions see in the early 1900s?

SECTION 2 REVIEW

Define and explain the significance of the following terms:
Triangle Shirtwaist Fire
freedom of contract
Muller v. *Oregon*
closed shop
socialism
International Ladies' Garment Workers Union
open shop
Industrial Workers of the World

Identify and explain the significance of the following individuals:
Samuel Gompers
Florence Kelley
Rose Schneiderman
Louis D. Brandeis
William "Big Bill" Haywood

1. **Using Graphic Organizers** Copy the chart below. Use it to describe the successes and failures unions experienced in the early 1900s.

Unions	
Successes	Failures

2. **Problem Solving** What solutions would you have proposed to improve working conditions for women and children?
3. **Assessing Consequences** How did the Triangle Shirtwaist Fire lead to improved workplace safety?
4. **Identifying Values** What concerns prompted the Supreme Court to strike down some progressive legislation?

Critical Thinking

5. Were the goals of employers and the goals of employees in the early 1900s really in conflict? Explain your answer.
Consider:
• what the goals of employers were
• what the goals of employees were
• how meeting the goals of one group might affect the other group

SECTION 2 REVIEW ANSWERS

Define and Identify
For significance, see the following pages:
- Florence Kelley, p. 253
- Triangle Shirtwaist Fire, p. 254
- Rose Schneiderman, p. 254
- freedom of contract, p. 255
- *Muller* v. *Oregon*, p. 255
- Louis D. Brandeis, p. 255
- closed shop, p. 255
- socialism, p. 255
- Samuel Gompers, p. 256
- International Ladies' Garment Workers Union, p. 256
- open shop, p. 256
- Industrial Workers of the World, p. 256
- William "Big Bill" Haywood, p. 256

1. successes–wage increases and fewer working hours; failures–the AFL excluded unskilled workers and the government cracked down on the IWW and contributed to its collapse

2. Answers will vary. Students might suggest higher wages and fewer hours.

3. called attention to serious and widespread safety violations

4. The Court worried that some legislation violated constitutional rights to property and freedom of contract.

5. Answers will vary. Students might argue that their goals were in conflict because workers wanted fair treatment, while employers wanted to realize as much profit as possible.

SECTION 3

After completing Section 3, students should be able to:

OBJECTIVE 1 *Describe how reformers tried to improve life in U.S. cities.*

OBJECTIVE 2 *Discuss how reformers hoped to improve moral standards.*

OBJECTIVE 3 *Report on how African Americans and American Indians organized to improve their lives.*

OBJECTIVE 4 *Explain why immigrants were left out of some progressive reforms, and recognize how they contributed to other reforms.*

LET'S GET STARTED!

Write the following categories on the chalkboard: *City Life, Morality, Racial Discrimination,* and *Immigrants' Lives.* As students enter the classroom, have them copy the list of headers, leaving a few lines between each. Tell students to write a sentence or two predicting how each topic will represent an issue for progressives in this section. Ask volunteers to read one or more of their predictions to the class. Tell students that in Section 3 they will learn more about progressive social reforms.

SECTION 3 RESOURCES

PRINT
- Guided Reading Strategy 8.3
- Primary Source Reading 8: A Call for Urban Reform
- Biography Reading 8: Carry Nation
- Section 3 Review, p. 265
- Daily Quiz 8.3

MULTIMEDIA
- One-Stop Planner, Lesson 8.3
- Art in American History Transparency 20: Thompson and Bleecker Streets
- Holt Researcher: American History CD–ROM
- HRW Web site

SHELTERED ENGLISH
- Main Idea Activity for Reteaching and Sheltered English 8.3

✔ READING TO UNDERSTAND
To help students master the section objectives, have them answer the **READING CHECKS** and complete **Guided Reading Strategy 8.3** as they read the section.

Reforming Society

OBJECTIVES

Read to understand:
1. how reformers tried to improve life in U.S. cities
2. how reformers hoped to improve moral standards
3. how African Americans and American Indians organized to improve their lives
4. why immigrants were left out of some progressive reforms, and how they contributed to other reforms

KEY TERMS

prohibition
Woman's Christian Temperance Union
Eighteenth Amendment
National Association for the Advancement of Colored People
National Urban League
Society of American Indians

KEY PEOPLE

Lawrence Veiller
Daniel Burnham
Billy Sunday
Frances Willard
W. E. B. Du Bois

This little girl is collecting firewood on the city streets.

EYEWITNESSES TO History

"The home is very unattractive for children and they are glad to get out to meet their friends. They want to supply a social need, and they go out and meet other friends and the home has no tie upon them. . . . The tenement house is not the only thing, but a very strong influence. I believe the entire economic conditions in this country are another influence."

—Henry Moscowitz

A subway porter

Tenement resident Henry Moscowitz described to a progressive journalist the negative effects on a family that accompanied the poverty and other ills of the cities. Reformers hoped that increasing wages would help bring many families out of poverty, but they knew that other factors affected the quality of people's lives. Progressives therefore set out to attack numerous ills that they believed weakened American society.

Reforming City Life

By 1920, for the first time in U.S. history, more than 50 percent of Americans lived in urban areas. As urban populations soared, cities struggled to provide garbage collection, safe and affordable housing, health care, police and fire protection, and adequate public education. "The challenge of the city," declared one progressive, "has become one of decent human existence."

Cleaning up the city. Some reformers called for a campaign to make the cities a more healthful and livable home for all residents. "The community is one great family," explained Louise DeKoven Bowen, the president of Chicago's Woman's City Club. "Each member of it is bound to help the other." Various women's clubs, men's clubs, and reform organizations enlisted the aid of local governments to clean up the cities. Some groups took the cleanup campaign literally, working to rid the cities of garbage. Other organizations worked for better housing or to improve public education.

Lawrence Veiller (VYL-uhr), a settlement-house worker, attacked irresponsible tenement owners "who for the sake of a large profit on their investments sacrifice the health and welfare of countless thousands." As the secretary to the New York State Tenement House Commission, Veiller campaigned tirelessly for improved housing. In 1900 he questioned Henry Moscowitz, who in 17 years had lived in 14 different tenements on New York's Lower East Side. Moscowitz described the stench, dirt, and noise, and the lack of light, fresh air, water, electricity, and bathing facilities.

The commission discovered that New York had "the most serious tenement house problem in the world." In 1901 Veiller succeeded in getting the New York

TEACH OBJECTIVE 1

LEVEL 1: Conduct a discussion about the steps that progressive reformers took to improve life in U.S. cities. Then pair students and tell them to imagine that they are progressive reformers who are going to lead a parade for urban reform. Ask each pair to create a series of parade banners that publicize the ways in which progressives tried to improve city life. *(Pairs should note that progressives tried to rid cities of garbage, provide better housing, improve public education and public health, build playgrounds, provide city planning, and redesign Chicago and other cities).* Ask volunteers to display and describe their banners to the class. **Sheltered English, Cooperative Learning**

LEVELS 2 AND 3: Tell students to imagine that they are muckraker journalists who have decided to target urban living conditions in their next exposé. Have each student write short articles describing urban life in any large city of the early 1900s. Tell them to conclude their articles with proposed solutions to the urban problems they have described. *(See the Level 1 lesson for the correct solutions.)* Students may wish to include their articles in their portfolios.

▸**ASSIGNMENT** *Have each student come up with a list of 10 ways to improve modern-day urban living conditions, using the strategies of the 1900s progressives as a model.*

State Tenement House Bill passed. The law required that any new tenements be built around open courtyards that would let in light and air. New buildings also had to contain one bathroom for each apartment or for every three rooms. Previously, bathrooms in apartment buildings had been limited to one or two for an entire floor. Housing reformers in other states used the New York law as a model for their own legislative proposals.

To further improve urban living conditions, a group of physicians and reform-minded citizens formed the National Tuberculosis Association. The group focused on education and on lobbying the government to fund special hospitals to treat victims of tuberculosis. Thanks in part to this effort, by 1915 the death rate from "the white plague" had dropped significantly.

Other reformers campaigned for the creation of safe places for children to play. A 1908 Massachusetts law required all cities with a population greater than 10,000 to hold a referendum on whether that city should build at least one playground. Within the year, 41 out of 42 cities had shown their support for such actions. By 1920 cities had spent millions of dollars building playgrounds.

Some middle- and upper-class Americans objected to spending tax dollars on recreational facilities for the poor. One journalist in Lawrence, Massachusetts, reported that "pandemonium [disorder] reigned" when "bands of foreigners and trouble makers" used public space to celebrate the Fourth of July. Cleveland city council member Frederic Howe was shunned by his upper-class friends for supporting recreational facilities for the poor. However, Howe and his allies succeeded. "On Saturday and Sunday the whole population played baseball in the hundreds of parks laid out for that purpose," Howe reported.

City planning. The city-planning movement grew out of progressives' belief that cleaned-up cities would produce better citizens. The first National Conference on City Planning was held in 1909. Its participants hoped that wise planning could halt the spread of slums and beautify cities. Beautiful cities and impressive public architecture, they argued, would instill patriotism among the immigrant population.

In 1909 Daniel Burnham, a leading architect and city planner, produced a magnificent plan for redesigning Chicago. It was the first comprehensive plan to redesign a U.S. city. The centerpiece of Burnham's vision for Chicago was a soaring city hall that would inspire all residents to be good citizens. "Make no little plans," said Burnham. "They have no magic to stir men's blood."

City-planning commissions in Cleveland, San Francisco, and Washington, D.C., also hired Burnham to develop grand schemes for their cities. His plans were never fully built, but some, such as those for Washington, D.C., were a success. Above all, his efforts helped people realize that city planning—developing parks, building codes, sanitation standards, and zoning—was a necessary function of municipal government.

✔ **READING CHECK:** How did reformers try to improve life in U.S. cities?

INTERPRETING THE VISUAL RECORD

City planning. Daniel Burnham (left) created the plan for redesigning Chicago. ***What are the unique characteristics shown in the design?***

TECHNOLOGY AND SOCIETY

Edith Abbott and Chicago Tenements. In 1936 Edith Abbott and her colleagues at the School of Social Service Administration at the University of Chicago published research on Chicago's tenements. Abbott's team found buildings that held 40 apartments whose windows were located no more than six inches from the building next door. Consequently, light and air could not circulate to most of the rooms.

CRITICAL THINKING How might the absence of air circulation have contributed to health problems and despair?

ANSWER: Students might suggest that air circulation is essential for the removal of stale, moldy air.

Multimedia Resources

Art in American History Transparency 20: Thompson and Bleecker Streets

VISUAL RECORD ANSWER

Students might note the soaring city hall.

 Teacher to Teacher

Peggy Altoff of Westminster, Maryland, suggested the following activity: Ask students to write an essay about a modern "muckraker," conducting additional research as necessary. Students should discuss whether or not the term muckraker *accurately describes this person's activities.*

SPOTLIGHT on Art

Tell students that the Ash Can School was a group of eight painters who painted realistic scenes of New York City during the Progressive Era. The term "ash can" refers to the often bleak nature of the painters' subjects, such as humble backyards, tenements, or garbage cans. Have students conduct research on one of the painters of the Ash Can School. Ask each student to write a report that includes biographical information about the artist as well as information about his or her artwork, subjects, and methods. **Block Scheduling**

GEOGRAPHIC DIVERSITY

The Role of Playgrounds. The Playground Association of America, formed in 1906, attempted to prepare urban street children for work and adulthood by teaching them organized games that emphasized rules, self-control, and group loyalty. One Playground Association motto was, "A boy without a playground is father to the man without a job."

CRITICAL THINKING What programs or institutions today might help prepare children for work and adulthood?

ANSWER: Students might mention programs or institutions such as kindergartens or after-school activities.

AMERICAN ARTS ANSWERS

1. the success of several fairs in which architects and designers had created urban centers with large open spaces
2. He moved it from the Mall to Capitol Hill.

VISUAL RECORD ANSWER

(for p. 261)

Students might suggest that there was greater demand for tickets in the afternoon and evening than in the morning.

AMERICAN ARTS

Shaping Public Space

The City Beautiful movement in the early 1900s rose out of the success of several fairs that led architects and designers to create large open spaces in urban centers. For instance, Frederick Law Olmsted, a landscape architect for the World's Columbian Exposition of 1893, had created a series of lagoons surrounding Chicago's tall and shapely buildings. These pools of water, along with electric lights, reflected off the monumental buildings and led people to call Chicago the "Magic City."

Soon Daniel Burnham and other architects set to work to improve other U.S. cities. In Washington, D.C., the Senate Parks Commission assigned the task of completing Pierre Charles L'Enfant's original plans for the city to a team of architects, artists, and planners. They looked to the colonial cities of the United States as well as the great capitals of Europe for inspiration.

One of Burnham's first actions was to move the railroad station from the Mall. He located it on Capitol Hill, where it served as a gateway to the city. The surrounding landscaping accented the station's monumental proportions. Although work halted during World War I, in the 1920s the lands around the Potomac River were transformed into level ground. Builders created the Lincoln Memorial and a decorative canal known as the Reflecting Pool, which connects the Lincoln Memorial to the Washington Monument. During the 1920s many public buildings made of white stone were built, and sculptures were erected, transforming Washington, D.C., into an impressive national capital.

The design of Washington, D.C., incorporates many of the ideas of city planning.

Understanding the Arts

1. What gave rise to the City Beautiful movement of the early 1900s?
2. What did Daniel Burnham do to the railroad station in Washington, D.C.?

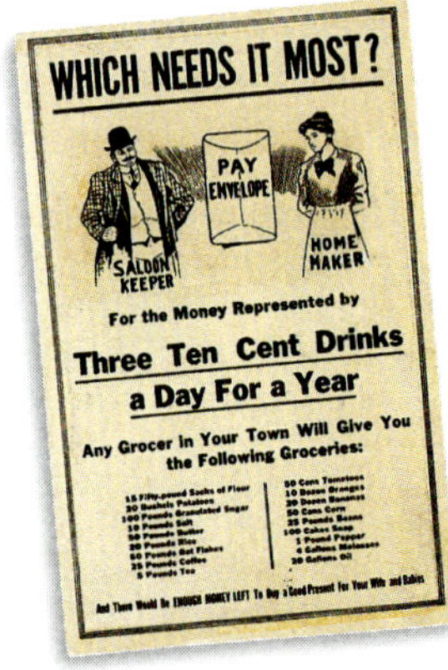

This poster encouraged support for prohibition.

Moral Reform

Progressives also wanted to "clean up" what they considered to be immoral behavior. They called for **prohibition**—a ban on the manufacture, sale, and transportation of alcoholic beverages—and the closing of the nation's saloons. Reformers believed that prohibition would reduce crime and the breakup of families.

Journalists described alcohol as "the arch enemy of progress." Magazines published articles such as "The Story of an Alcohol Slave, as Told by Himself." Muckraker George Kibbe Turner wrote in *McClure's Magazine* in 1909 that to truly reform the rapidly growing U.S. cities, the saloons must be closed.

The drive for prohibition took many forms. During the Progressive Era, many colleges did not allow student athletes to drink. Some industrialists initiated programs intended to convince their workers to not drink alcohol. School textbooks included information on the dangers of alcohol.

TEACH OBJECTIVE 2

ALL LEVELS: To help students understand how reformers hoped to improve moral standards, copy the following graphic organizer on the chalkboard, omitting the italicized answers. Have each student complete it. Then pair students and tell them to imagine that they are progressive activists during the early 1900s. Have each pair create a full-page newspaper ad to protest either the sale and use of alcohol or the content of movies. Ask volunteers to display and explain their advertisements to the class.

Sheltered English, Cooperative Learning

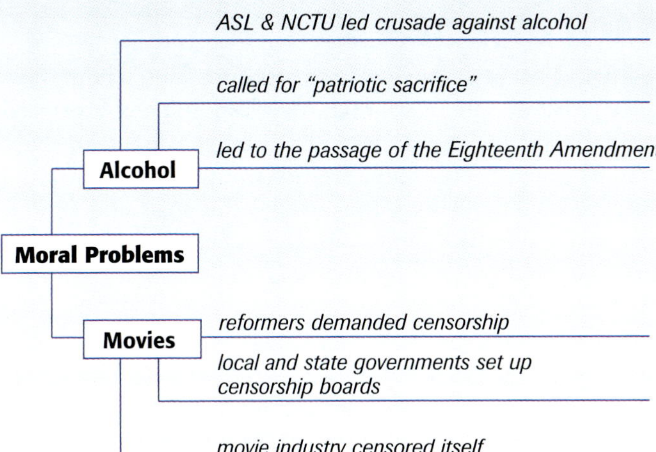

The passage of prohibition. The Anti-Saloon League (ASL) and the **Woman's Christian Temperance Union** (WCTU) led the crusade against alcohol. By 1902 the ASL had branches in 39 states with 200 paid staff members.

Thousands of volunteer speakers, many of them Protestant ministers, spread the antisaloon message in the nation's churches. Billy Sunday, an ex-ballplayer turned Presbyterian evangelist, preached that saloons were "the parent of crimes and the mother of sins." Frances Willard headed the WCTU from 1879 to 1898. Willard eventually made the WCTU a powerful national force for temperance, moral purity, and the rights of women.

During World War I, prohibitionists drew on Americans' spirit of patriotic sacrifice. The U.S. Navy banned the consumption of alcohol in 1914. During the vote on prohibition in Congress, Senator William Kenyon of Iowa drew on this fact. He asked, "If liquor is a bad thing for the boys in the trenches, why is it a good thing for those at home?"

In 1917 Congress proposed the **Eighteenth Amendment**, which barred the manufacture, sale, and distribution of alcoholic beverages. The states ratified it in 1919. However, the amendment proved unpopular and difficult to enforce. It was repealed in 1933.

The coming of prohibition inspired this sheet music. This fan shows WCTU leader Frances Willard.

Moviegoing. The growing popularity of the newly invented motion picture worried some urban reformers who believed that movies were a threat to morality. The first movie to tell a story, *The Great Train Robbery*, was made in 1903. By 1910, millions of Americans were going to the movies each week. In 1916 the *New York Times* reported that films were the fifth-largest U.S. industry.

To the urban poor, a 5- or 10-cent movie ticket—bought at movie houses called nickelodeons—offered cheap, readily available entertainment. Many middle-class Americans, however, believed that movies—particularly the steamy romances—and movie houses were immoral and sources of temptation. Writer William Dean Howells described the situation.

> **"The pictures thrown upon the luminous [lighted] curtain of the stage have been declared extremely corrupting to the idle young people lurking in the darkness before it. The darkness itself has been held a condition of inexpressible depravity [immorality] and a means of allurement [attraction] to evil."**

Declaring that moviegoing promoted immoral values, reformers demanded that movies be censored. Several states and cities set up censorship boards to ban movies they considered immoral. In 1909 the movie industry began to censor itself.

✓ **READING CHECK:** How did reformers hope to improve Americans' moral standards?

INTERPRETING THE VISUAL RECORD

Movie theaters. The popularity of motion pictures led to the building of fancy theaters. ***Why do you think the cost of admission varied by time of day?***

Progressivism and Racial Discrimination

For nonwhites the progressive movement had mixed results. Most progressives were concerned about the plight of the poor. However, few white progressives devoted very much energy to the

PEOPLE IN HISTORY

Frances Willard. Frances Willard was an energetic reformer who focused on the temperance movement but extended her work to other reform issues as well. She argued that "no one can adequately lead any movement who has not imagination enough to see that movement in its relations to others equally important." Eventually, she became a socialist and criticized the wealthy as wanting to keep people in poverty. "I charge upon the drink traffic (alcohol business)," she declared, "that it keeps people down, and capitalists and politicians know it."

CRITICAL THINKING Why might Willard have argued that alcohol "keeps people down?"

ANSWER: Students might suggest that she pointed to family violence or lost work or the potential for alcohol to limit people's energy for political or social action.

TOPIC: Early Motion Pictures
GO TO: go.hrw.com
KEYWORD: SE1 Motion

Have students access the Internet through the HRW Web site to conduct research on early movies. Then have each student write a script outline for a movie that incorporates both the techniques of early films and the concerns of Progressive Era urban activists.

TEACH OBJECTIVE 3

LEVEL 1: Conduct a brief discussion about how African Americans and American Indians organized during the Progressive Era. During the discussion, have students identify the organizations founded by African Americans and American Indians and the goals and actions taken by these organizations. *(Students should note that African Americans founded the NAACP and the Urban League; the NAACP worked through the courts to obtain civil rights for African Americans, and the Urban League fought for racial equality; American Indians founded the Society of American Indians to address problems facing Indians and publicize the accomplishments of famous American Indians).* Then pair students and have each pair design a billboard publicizing the mission and activities of one of these organizations.
Sheltered English, Cooperative Learning

LEVELS 2 AND 3: Organize students into small groups and tell them to imagine that they are African Americans or American Indians working to obtain equal rights during the early 1900s. Have half of the groups draft an organizational platform for an African American civil rights group, and have the other half of the groups draft a platform for an American Indian group. *(See the Level 1 activity for the correct goals.)* Both platforms should include specific wording related to improving the lives of African Americans and American Indians.
Cooperative Learning

DEMOCRATIC VALUES

The Niagara Movement. In 1905, before the founding of the National Association for the Advancement of Colored People, W. E. B. Du Bois and others met at Niagara Falls. The Niagara Movement, as this group was called, drafted a "Declaration of Principles," which protested discrimination against African Americans and asked for the support of others in ending that discrimination. "We believe that [African Americans] should protest emphatically and continually against the curtailment of their political rights. . . . We especially complain against the denial of equal opportunities to use in economic life. . . . We protest against the 'Jim Crow' car, since its effect is and must be, to make us pay first-class fare for third-class accommodations. . . . To ignore, overlook, or apologize for these wrongs is to prove ourselves unworthy of freedom." The Niagara Movement lasted only a few years before disbanding because of a lack of financial support.

CRITICAL THINKING Why might the declaration have argued overlooking wrongs proved African Americans unworthy of freedom?

ANSWER: Students might suggest that the declaration implied that overlooking wrongs constituted a failure to assert constitutional rights.

problems of discrimination and prejudice against African Americans and American Indians. Some progressives expressed open prejudice against these groups. Many African Americans and American Indians, however, drew on progressive ideas to develop programs appropriate to their communities.

BIOGRAPHY *W. E. B. Du Bois*

Views of Du Bois. One of the most influential African American leaders to emerge during this period was W. E. B. Du Bois (doo BOYS). Born in 1868 in Great Barrington, Massachusetts, Du Bois had a happy childhood. Du Bois attended Sunday school with African American and white children. Not until high school did he begin to realize that his skin color caused some people not to like him. He had many friends among the white students, however.

Read More About It

Free Find:
W. E. B. Du Bois
After learning about W. E. B. Du Bois on the **Holt Researcher** CD–ROM, write a poem that describes Du Bois's life.

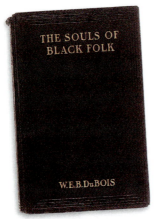

A bright student, Du Bois was encouraged by his school's principal to prepare for college. Great Barrington's residents and churches raised money to send Du Bois to Fisk University, an African American school in Nashville, Tennessee. After graduating, he studied history in Germany and at Harvard University. In 1895 he became the first African American to earn a doctorate from Harvard. Two years later he was appointed as a professor of history and economics at Atlanta University, a leading African American college, where he taught until 1910.

By the early 1900s Du Bois was recognized as a brilliant thinker and strong supporter of African American civil rights and culture. He believed that access to a college education and vocational training offered the best chance of progress for African Americans. He also believed that African Americans should be politically active in the struggle for racial equality. Du Bois's view contrasted sharply with that of African American leader Booker T. Washington. Washington argued that African Americans should not spend their time fighting discrimination. He urged African Americans to focus on improving their own education and economic prosperity. Du Bois believed that this focus would unfairly make African Americans responsible for correcting racial injustice.

Throughout his life Du Bois maintained a passionate interest in Africa, which he regarded as the spiritual homeland of all black people. In his influential 1903 book, *The Souls of Black Folk,* Du Bois eloquently expressed his dual identity as both African and American.

> **"One ever feels his two-ness—an American, a Negro; two souls, two thoughts, two un-reconciled strivings. He [the African American] simply wishes to make it possible for a man to be both a Negro and an American, without being cursed and spit upon by his fellows, without having the doors of Opportunity closed roughly in his face."**

***W. E. B. Du Bois's* The Souls of Black Folk**

In the 1920s Du Bois organized a series of Pan-African congresses that attracted black leaders from around the world. This was done to create greater unity among people of African descent. During the 1930s and 1940s Du Bois continued his career as a scholar and political activist. By the 1950s he, like many prominent American intellectuals, had embraced socialism for its promise of social justice. In 1961, at age 93, Du Bois joined the Communist Party and moved to Ghana. He died there two years later.

TEACH OBJECTIVE 4

LEVEL 1: Pair students and have each pair list the reasons why immigrants were excluded from some progressive reforms. *(Pairs should mention racism and a lack of respect for immigrants' cultures.)* Then ask pairs to list how immigrants contributed to other reforms. *(Pairs should note that immigrants worked through political machines to establish worker-protection and public-health programs, playgrounds, public baths and parks.)* Then have pairs create three political cartoons that comment on the situation of the immigrant poor and the contributions that immigrant communities made to reform efforts. Display pairs' cartoons around the classroom. **Cooperative Learning, Sheltered English**

LEVEL 2: Tell students to imagine that they are poor immigrant workers who are faced with the pressure to assimilate. Have each student write a series of diary entries describing the struggles of daily life and the reforms that he or she seeks to improve his or her life. *(See the Level 1 lesson for the correct struggles and contributions.)* Have volunteers read their diary entries to the class.

African Americans organize. In 1909 Du Bois and a group of African American and white progressives met in New York City. They discussed the lynching of two African American men in Springfield, Illinois, the previous year. Out of this meeting came the **National Association for the Advancement of Colored People** (NAACP), an organization dedicated to ending racial discrimination. Du Bois edited its monthly magazine, *The Crisis,* which publicized cases of racial inequality. The publication also called for social reforms that would ensure equal rights for African Americans. By 1918 the magazine's circulation had risen to 100,000.

The NAACP used the court system to fight restrictions on voting and on other civil rights. In 1915 it won its first major victory in *Guinn* v. *United States.* In this case the Supreme Court outlawed the "grandfather clause." Southern states had used the clause to ensure that suffrage requirements designed to keep African Americans from voting would not apply to whites. Two years later NAACP lawyers won *Buchanan* v. *Warley,* which overturned a Louisville, Kentucky, law requiring racially segregated housing. As a result, similar laws were struck down across the country.

The **National Urban League** also fought for racial equality. Founded in 1910 by concerned African Americans and white reformers, the league worked to improve job opportunities and housing for urban African Americans. One of its goals was to help African American migrants from the South adjust to their new lives in northern cities. The NAACP and the National Urban League made some important gains for African American citizens. Nevertheless, most African Americans still faced discrimination.

ANNUAL CONFERENCE NUMBER

THE CRISIS

A RECORD OF THE DARKER RACES

W. E. B. Du Bois wanted **The Crisis** *to honestly address important issues.*

Lynchings, 1889–1918

Learning from Maps Some 75 percent of lynching victims were African American men. Most of the other victims were white men. However, women, American Indians, Hispanics, and Asian Americans were also victims of lynch mobs.

? REGION In which region did most lynchings occur?

Lynchings of Whites and African Americans

Period	Whites	African Americans
1889–1893	261	571
1894–1898	223	549
1899–1903	77	465
1904–1908	25	342
1909–1913	32	308
1914–1918	27	253
TOTALS	645	2,488

Source: *Historical Statistics of the United States*

Number of Lynchings

None; 1–5; 6–20; 21–50; 51–100; 101–200; 201–300; 301–386

0 300 600 Miles
0 300 600 Kilometers
Albers Equal-Area Projection

DEMOCRATIC VALUES

American Indians and Progressivism. Historian Donald Parman wrote that the American Indian "was primarily a bystander, seldom a participant, often a victim, and rarely a beneficiary of progressive reforms." Much of the progressive attention toward American Indian concerns focused on how to assimilate American Indians into white culture and ignored the issue of land grants and land rights. Progressive president Teddy Roosevelt wrote to American Indian leader Chief No Shirt, "The earth is occupied by the white people and the red people. . . . If the red people would prosper, they must follow the mode of life which has made the white people so strong; and that it is only right that the white people should show the red people what to do and how to live right."

ACTIVITY: Tell students to imagine that they are Chief No Shirt. Then have each student write a response to Roosevelt's letter.

MAP ANSWER
in the South

VISUAL RECORD ANSWER
(for p. 265)
Answers will vary. Some students might argue that the title of the poster reflects respect for diversity.

LEVEL 3: Organize most of the students into two "face-off" panels. Ask one panel to assume the role of progressives in the early 1900s and the other panel to represent immigrants. Have the members of each panel discuss ways of helping the immigrant poor from that particular panel's point of view *(See the Level 1 lesson for the correct struggles and contributions.)* Ask the rest of the class to question and challenge panel members on their positions. Close the discussion by asking the progressive panel to list proposals for reforms to help immigrants on the chalkboard and the immigrant panel to support or reject each proposal and to explain why. **Cooperative Learning**

SPOTLIGHT on Immigrants and Political Machines

Have students conduct research on the relationship between immigrants and big-city political machines during the early 1900s. Then have each student write a report addressing the reasons why immigrants supported political machines despite the machines' reputation for corruption. Students' reports should also address the types of reforms that were supported by political machines. **Block Scheduling**

SECTION 3 REVIEW ANSWERS

Define and Identify

For significance, see the following pages:

- Lawrence Veiller, p. 258
- Daniel Burnham, p. 259
- prohibition, p. 260
- Woman's Christian Temperance Union, p. 261
- Billy Sunday, p. 261
- Frances Willard, p. 261
- Eighteenth Amendment, p. 261
- W. E. B. Du Bois, p. 262
- National Association for the Advancement of Colored People, p. 263
- National Urban League, p. 263
- Society of American Indians, p. 264

1. improving garbage collection, housing, and public health education; making safe and healthy public spaces; supporting prohibition

2. Some reformers wanted to force people to abstain from alcohol; others wanted to censor movies.

3. They both organized groups to call attention to discrimination, to emphasize the successes of members of their ethnic groups, and to work for governmental change. The NAACP succeeded in changing some laws; the SAI suffered from internal dissension and eventually lost influence.

4. Many believed that alcohol was responsible for the destruction of families and for crime.

5. Some students might indicate that they would not have supported the progressives

American Indians organize. Demands for equal rights and greater opportunities for American Indians also surfaced during this period. It had become clear that the Dawes Act of 1887 had caused many American Indians to lose their property to land speculators and fall deeper into poverty. Some progressives took up the American Indians' cause. They argued for a more gradual approach: slowing down land allotment and maintaining the reservation system for a time. In 1911 a group of 50 American Indians, most of them middle-class professionals, formed the **Society of American Indians** to address the problems facing Indians. One of its members, Seneca historian Arthur C. Parker, urged American Indians "to strike out into the duties of modern life and . . . find every right that had escaped them before."

Jim Thorpe was one of the greatest athletes in U.S. history.

Although some members supported strengthening tribal values, most favored complete assimilation. The organization publicized the accomplishments of famous American Indians such as Olympic gold medalist Jim Thorpe and lobbied against the use of insulting terms for Indians. Members also discussed ways to improve Indian civil rights, education, health, and local government. The organization's moderate positions on most issues, however, led to disputes with members who wanted more aggressive action. These disputes weakened the organization.

Dr. Carlos Montezuma, a Yavapai Apache member of the society, criticized the Bureau of Indian Affairs for mismanaging reservations. Other members refused to take such a strong antigovernment stand, and the group's influence declined. However, the Society of American Indians did provide a forum for American Indian leaders. It laid the groundwork for later attempts to improve conditions for American Indians.

✔ **READING CHECK:** How did African Americans and American Indians organize to improve their positions in American society during the Progressive Era?

Immigrants and Assimilation

The progressive movement had mixed results for immigrants as well. On one hand, many reformers sympathized with the plight of the newcomers who labored in factories and were crowded into slum tenements. These reformers lobbied for laws to improve immigrants' lives and to better conditions in the workplace and in city slums.

At the same time, however, progressives also criticized immigrants. They accused them of immoral behavior such as drinking and gambling and denounced immigrant support for big-city political machines. Some native-born Americans with progressive ideals favored restricting immigration. In 1916 a prominent New Yorker named Madison Grant published *The Passing of the Great Race*. In this book he expressed racist opinions about African Americans, Jews, and immigrants from southern and eastern Europe. Yet Grant was also a progressive who supported environmental protection, urban planning, and other reforms.

Many progressives believed that immigrants should be "Americanized" as quickly as possible. William Maxwell was a prominent New York educator. He declared that his goal was to make the public school "a melting pot which converts the children of the immigrants of all races and languages into sturdy, independent American citizens." Russian immigrant Eugene Lyons described the effects of this process on immigrants.

REVIEW

Have students complete the **Section 3 Review** on p. 265.

ASSESS

Have students complete **Daily Quiz 8.3**. As **Alternative Assessment**, you may want to use the graphic organizer or the civil rights platform in this section's lessons.

RETEACH

Have students complete **Main Idea Activity for Reteaching and Sheltered English 8.3**. Then ask students to write a question and answer that covers the main idea for each subsection in the section. Select students to read their questions to the class. Have the class try to answer each question. **Sheltered English**

EXTEND

Have students conduct research on reformers who are questioning the impact of television, movies, music, and video games on society today. Have each student write a short essay comparing and contrasting the present-day crusade with reformers' efforts in the Progressive Era. **Block Scheduling**

"We sensed a disrespect for the alien traditions in our homes and came unconsciously to resent and despise those traditions . . . because they seemed [impossible] barriers between ourselves and the adopted land."

Chinese immigrant Victor Wong recalled that in school, teachers tried to "dissuade us . . . from everything Chinese. Their view of the Chinese ways was that they were evil, heathen, non-Christian." The lack of respect for their cultural backgrounds led some immigrants to reject the assistance of social reformers.

Some progressives welcomed the diversity that immigrant groups brought to the United States. In his 1924 book, *Culture and Democracy in the United States*, philosopher Horace Kallen supported pluralism. He envisioned a nation that would be home to a number of distinctive cultures. Some immigrants also supported a course of Americanization that could be achieved without giving up their ethnic identities.

Poor immigrants and the political bosses who represented them supported middle-class progressives when they fought for practical reforms such as worker protection and public-health programs. For example, a New York state legislative committee set up to investigate factory conditions after the Triangle Shirtwaist Fire won strong backing from New York City's immigrant-based Democratic machine. In his autobiography, Frederic Howe asserted that New York City owed its playgrounds, public baths, and public parks, among other services, to Irish immigrants and their political machines. "Unconsciously aiming to shape the state to human ends," he declared, "the Irish have made New York what it is."

✔ **READING CHECK:** Why were immigrants left out of some progressive reforms, and how did immigrants contribute to other reforms?

INTERPRETING THE VISUAL RECORD

Americanizing immigrants. This poster was created to encourage immigrants to learn English. ***Do you think that the poster shows respect for immigrants' culture?***

SECTION  REVIEW

Define and explain the significance of the following terms:
prohibition
Woman's Christian Temperance Union
Eighteenth Amendment
National Association for the Advancement of Colored People
National Urban League
Society of American Indians

Identify and explain the significance of the following individuals:
Lawrence Veiller
Daniel Burnham
Billy Sunday
Frances Willard
W. E. B. Du Bois

1. **Using Graphic Organizers** Copy the organizational web below. Use it to explain the different approaches that progressives took in cleaning up cities.

2. **Synthesizing** How did some reformers attempt to influence the personal behavior of Americans?
3. **Comparing and Contrasting** What methods did African Americans and American Indians use to fight racism and discrimination, and how successful were they?
4. **Identifying Values** Why did progressives support prohibition and the elimination of saloons?

Critical Thinking

5. If you had been an immigrant in 1910, would you have supported the progressive movement? Explain your answer.
Consider:
- how some progressives treated immigrants
- how some immigrants contributed to reform
- how the progressive movement affected immigrants overall

because many of them wanted to limit immigrant rights. Others might argue that they would have supported the progressives because they were trying to improve the overall quality of American life.

CHAPTER 8 REVIEW ANSWERS

Creating a Time Line
Each event should have an explanation and a correct date.

Writing a Summary
See the Reading Checks in each section for main ideas.

Identifying People and Ideas

1. a reform movement focused on improving urban life
2. journalists who wrote about corruption in politics, business, and society
3. muckraker who wrote about lynchings
4. leader of the American Federation of Labor
5. activist who worked for child labor restrictions
6. the freedom of workers to negotiate their terms of employment
7. system under which cooperatives own the means of production and services
8. settlement-house worker who campaigned for improved housing
9. leader of the Woman's Christian Temperance Union
10. group formed to address injustices and problems faced by American Indians

REVIEW AND ASSESSMENT RESOURCES

PRINT
- Chapter 8 Review, pp. 266–67
- Chapter 8 Tutorial for Students, Parents, Mentors, and Peers
- Chapter 8 Test (Form A or B)
- Portfolio Activities and Alternative Assessment Handbook, Chapter 8

MULTIMEDIA
- Audio Program, Chapter 8 (English and Spanish)
- Chapter 8 Test Generator (on the One-Stop Planner)
- Global Skill Builder CD–ROM
- HRW Web site

SHELTERED ENGLISH
- Spanish Glossary
- Sheltered English Chapter 8 Test

REVIEW

Have students complete the **Chapter 8 Review** on pp. 266–67.

ASSESS

Use one of the chapter tests to assess students' understanding of the content. For **Alternative Assessment**, see the **Portfolio Activities and Alternative Assessment Handbook**.

Understanding Main Ideas

1. became activists and worked with volunteer organizations
2. published widely and publicized need for social reforms
3. limiting the length of the workday, raising wages, imposing restrictions on child labor, and ensuring that women and ethnic minorities received better wages
4. determined that laws could not limit employer's right to property or worker's freedom to contract; upheld laws limiting workday hours
5. They worked to improve garbage collection, housing, and public education. They also supported urban planning and prohibition.
6. They organized groups to call attention to discrimination, to emphasize the successes of members of their ethnic groups, and to work for governmental change. The NAACP brought cases of discrimination to court.

Reviewing Themes

1. in response to pressures from progressive reformers
2. supported education and child labor reforms; also worked to limit racial discrimination; their efforts were partially successful, but government and businesses were powerful enough to reverse some changes and block others
3. published stories and articles describing the evils of alcohol use and advocated prohibition in churches

CHAPTER 8 Review

Creating a Time Line

Copy the time line below onto a sheet of paper. Complete the time line by filling in the events and dates from the chapter that you think were most significant. Pick three events and explain why you think they were significant.

Writing a Summary

Using the Reading Checks as a guide, write an overview of the events in the chapter.

Identifying People and Ideas

Identify the following terms or individuals and explain their significance.

1. progressivism
2. muckrakers
3. Ray Stannard Baker
4. Samuel Gompers
5. Florence Kelley
6. freedom of contract
7. socialism
8. Lawrence Veiller
9. Frances Willard
10. Society of American Indians

Understanding Main Ideas

SECTION 1

1. How did women work for progressive goals?
2. What roles did intellectuals, muckrakers, and writers play in the progressive movement?

SECTION 2

3. Which labor issues did reformers hope to remedy through legislation?
4. How did the Supreme Court rule on labor issues?

SECTION 3

5. What actions did progressive reformers take to improve conditions in cities?
6. How did African Americans and American Indians address the problems facing their communities?

Reviewing Themes

1. **Economic Development** Why did states pass laws to protect workers' rights?
2. **Democratic Values** How did progressives propose to extend opportunities to all citizens? Were they successful in these efforts? Why or why not?
3. **Constitutional Heritage** How did progressives help win passage of the Eighteenth Amendment?

Thinking Critically

1. **Analyzing** How did industrialization influence progressive reform efforts?
2. **Hypothesizing** How might the course of reform have been different if the Supreme Court had been more supportive of early social legislation?
3. **Comparing and Contrasting** How did the American Federation of Labor and the Industrial Workers of the World differ in their views on the scope and nature of labor reform?
4. **Taking a Stand** Write a brief paragraph explaining your position on spending tax dollars on city improvements.
5. **Problem Solving** Imagine you are a progressive reformer. Outline a campaign to improve safety in the workplace.

Writing About History

Writing to Persuade Imagine that you are Louis D. Brandeis. Write a closing argument to convince the Supreme Court to uphold laws that guarantee workers' rights. Use the following graphic to organize your thoughts.

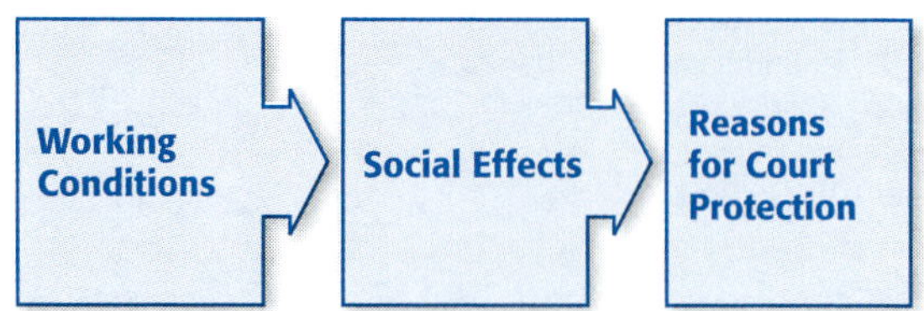

RETEACH

Organize students into groups of four or five. Assign each group one of the following topics: Reforming Big Business and the Workplace or Reforming Society. Have each group prepare a multimedia presentation on the assigned topic. Groups should focus on the people, events, and issues that were affected by the progressive movement during the late 1800s and early 1900s. Encourage groups to use a variety of audio and visual components in their presentations. Have members of each group make their presentations to the class. Tell students to take notes on each presentation.

Sheltered English, Cooperative Learning

EXTEND

Tell students the progressives placed great emphasis on the value of education. They believed that a free and equal public education for all would ensure better involvement in the democratic process and help downtrodden groups to get attention for the issues that affected their communities. Have students conduct research to locate a sample curriculum for a typical public school of the early 1900s. Tell each student to write a short essay comparing this curriculum to his or her own.

Block Scheduling

Strategies for Success

Review the **Strategies for Success** on *Interpreting the Visual Record: Photographs*. Then study Arnold Genthe's photograph of a Chinese immigrant family below and answer the following questions.

1. What information is provided by the details in this photograph?
2. What message is Genthe trying to convey about the family in the photograph?
3. How does the photograph contribute to your understanding of progressive attempts to "Americanize" immigrants to the United States?

THE GRANGER COLLECTION, NEW YORK

Linking History and Geography

Study the map below. Do any regional trends exist in the timing of different states' banning of alcohol? What might explain such differences?

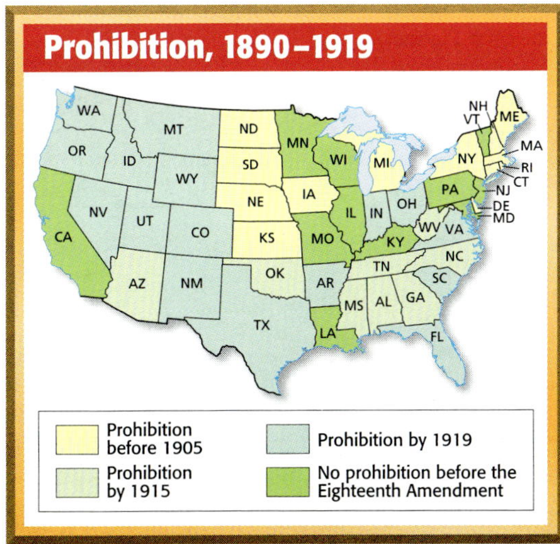

internet connect

TOPIC: "Social Realism" Photography
GO TO: go.hrw.com
KEYWORD: SE1 Realism

Accessing the Internet through the HRW Web site, research the issues that photographer Jacob Riis and other artists in the "social realism" school illustrated in their work. Then create an annotated photo essay in which you dramatize social issues within your own community or school. Include captions that contain information about the social problem dramatized in your photographs as well as how the photograph illustrates this information.

BUILDING YOUR PORTFOLIO

Complete one or all of the following projects independently or cooperatively.

1 Economic Development
Imagine that you are a progressive reformer in the early 1900s. ***Write an editorial*** for *McClure's* or another progressive magazine. Editorials might examine corporate abuses, poor working conditions, or public-health concerns. Be sure to suggest a possible solution to the problem.

2 Democratic Values
Imagine that you are a progressive reformer working to promote women's rights. ***Prepare a speech*** on women's rights to deliver at an Independence Day celebration. Be sure to outline the various problems and concerns faced by women in the early 1900s.

3 Technology and Society
Imagine that it is the early 1900s and you are an architect interested in redesigning your town in order to make it more accessible and pleasant. ***Sketch out your designs*** and write a paragraph describing how these changes will improve the quality of life in your town.

Thinking Critically

1. by contributing to poor working conditions and urban overcrowding
2. Students might note that working conditions might have improved more quickly.
3. The AFL wanted to work within the system for workers' rights and they excluded unskilled workers. The IWW wanted to abolish capitalism and invited all workers of all skills and ethnicities to join.
4. Students' paragraphs will vary. Students should support their arguments with examples.
5. Students' campaigns will vary. Students should mention specific improvements.

Writing About History

Students should include some of the following points: working conditions—safety hazards, low pay, and long work hours; social effects—death, injury, family disruption, and poverty; reasons for court protection—the need to protect children and other workers.

Strategies for Success Answers

1. The man is wearing American clothing while his family is wearing Chinese clothing.
2. the closeness of the family
3. Students might suggest that Americanization would involve the abandonment of traditional dress.

Linking History and Geography

Great Plains states and the New England states tended to ban alcohol before other states; reform efforts in those regions might explain such trends.

Progressive Politicians

CHAPTER PLANNING GUIDE

	Section Lesson Objectives	Print Resources	Multimedia Resources	Sheltered English Resources
Section 1 Reforming Government, pp. 270–74	1 Summarize the reforms that were enacted to make U.S. voting procedures more democratic. 2 Describe how reformers sought to improve city governments. 3 Discuss the goals of progressive state leaders.	▶ Guided Reading Strategy 9.1 ▶ Section 1 Review, p. 274 ▶ Daily Quiz 9.1	▶ One-Stop Planner, Lesson 9.1 ▶ Holt Researcher: American History CD–ROM	▶ Main Idea Activity for Reteaching and Sheltered English 9.1
Section 2 Roosevelt and the Square Deal, pp. 275–81	1 Discuss how the response to the miners' strike and Square Deal reflected President Roosevelt's governing style. 2 Summarize why the government tried to regulate trusts and the food and drug industry. 3 Explain the stand that Gifford Pinchot and Theodore Roosevelt took on the environment.	▶ Guided Reading Strategy 9.2 ▶ Geography Activity 9: Theodore Roosevelt—A Biographical Map ▶ Section 2 Review, p. 281 ▶ Daily Quiz 9.2	▶ One-Stop Planner, Lesson 9.2 ▶ The American Nation Video Program Segment: Yosemite National Park; Teacher's Guide, 87–92 ▶ Holt Researcher: American History CD–ROM ▶ HRW Web site	▶ Main Idea Activity for Reteaching and Sheltered English 9.2
Section 3 Reform Under Taft, pp. 282–86	1 Relate what progressive reforms were enacted during President Taft's administration. 2 Explain what divisions in the Republican Party led to the formation of the Progressive Party. 3 Describe how Woodrow Wilson won the 1912 presidential election.	▶ Guided Reading Strategy 9.3 ▶ Biography Reading 9: Eugene Debs ▶ Section 3 Review, p. 286 ▶ Daily Quiz 9.3	▶ One-Stop Planner, Lesson 9.3 ▶ Holt Researcher: American History CD–ROM	▶ Main Idea Activity for Reteaching and Sheltered English 9.3
Section 4 Wilson's "New Freedom," pp. 287–93	1 Describe how Woodrow Wilson's proposals affected big business and U.S. citizens. 2 Explain how President Wilson attempted to help farmers and laborers, and how successful his efforts were. 3 Discuss how American women gained the right to vote.	▶ Guided Reading Strategy 9.4 ▶ Literature Reading 9: Life as a Factory Worker ▶ Primary Source Reading 9: Child Labor Practices ▶ Graphic Organizer Activity 9: Women's Suffrage ▶ Section 4 Review, p. 293 ▶ Daily Quiz 9.4	▶ One-Stop Planner, Lesson 9.4 ▶ Holt Researcher: American History CD–ROM	▶ Main Idea Activity for Reteaching and Sheltered English 9.4
Chapter Review and Assessment pp. 294–95		▶ Chapter 9 Review, pp. 294–95 ▶ Chapter 9 Tutorial for Students, Parents, Mentors, and Peers ▶ Chapter 9 Test (Form A or B) ▶ Portfolio Activities and Alternative Assessment Handbook, Chapter 9	▶ Audio Program, Chapter 9 (English and Spanish) ▶ Chapter 9 Test Generator (on the One-Stop Planner) ▶ Global Skill Builder CD–ROM ▶ HRW Web site	▶ Spanish Glossary ▶ Sheltered English Chapter 9 Test

CHAPTER OVERVIEW

Like other social reformers, progressive politicians hoped to improve life in the United States. They attempted to make voting processes more democratic by instituting the initiative, the direct primary, the recall, the secret ballot, and more. Progressive politicians also tried to improve city life. The use of city planners and city managers began in full force in the early 1900s.

With Theodore Roosevelt's succession to the presidency in 1901, the progressives had an advocate in the nation's highest office. President Roosevelt attempted to balance the needs of average citizens and business leaders. He worked to regulate the food and drug industries and to preserve the environment. Roosevelt helped his secretary of war, William Howard Taft, win the election of 1908, but the two clashed soon after. Roosevelt re-entered politics and formed the Progressive Party, creating a split in the Republican Party. This split helped Democrat Woodrow Wilson win the presidential election of 1912. Like his predecessors, Wilson pursued a progressive agenda.

TIME TAMERS

Block Scheduling

The teacher lesson plans for each section offer a variety of activity choices to help you present the material in a block scheduling format. For further suggestions on block scheduling, see the **Block Scheduling Handbook with Team Teaching Strategies**, pp. 49–54.

Smithsonian Institution®

Internet Connections and Lesson 9
www.si.edu/hrw

Hands-On History Activities:

Classroom to Community The **Hands-On History Activities** help students make meaningful connections between events in American history and those in their own hometown. You may wish to use the Chapter 9 Activity, Equal Rights for Women, to extend the chapter lessons, as alternative assessment, or as a block scheduling option.

Portfolio Projects

The American Nation includes multiple portfolio projects in each Pupil's Edition chapter review, as well as each unit review. Chapter 9 Portfolio Project options on p. 295 include the following:

1. Students will **write a platform**.
2. Students will **write an editorial**.
3. Students will **create a campaign poster**.

The American Nation
INTERNET RESOURCE DIRECTORY

To access online materials for this chapter, go to **go.hrw.com** and type in the keywords listed below.

HRW ONLINE RESOURCES
GO TO: go.hrw.com

Online Maps
KEYWORD: SE1 Maps9
- National Parks
- Election of 1912

Online Reading Support
KEYWORD: SE1 Strategies9

Online Rubrics
KEYWORD: SE1 Rubrics

CHAPTER ENRICHMENT LINKS
Use these Web links to extend and enrich student learning for Chapter 9.
GO TO: go.hrw.com
KEYWORD: SE1 Ch9

CHAPTER INTERNET ACTIVITIES
GO TO: go.hrw.com
- Pupil's Edition Student Activity
  KEYWORD: SE1 Parks
  (Students explore aspects of the National Parks System.)
- Teacher's Edition Student Activity
  KEYWORD: SE1 Oil
  (Students conduct research on oil production.)
- Teacher's Edition Student Activity
  KEYWORD: SE1 Food
  (Students examine the issue of food safety in the early 1900s.)

ADDITIONAL
RESOURCES

Books for Teachers

Clements, Kendrick A. *The Presidency of Woodrow Wilson.* University Press of Kansas, 1993. Discusses Woodrow Wilson's presidency.

Gould, Lewis L. *The Presidency of Theodore Roosevelt.* University Press of Kansas, 1991. Evaluates Theodore Roosevelt's performance in the White House; another volume in this excellent series of presidential histories.

Books for Students

Miller, Nathan. *Theodore Roosevelt.* W. W. Morrow, 1992. Relates Theodore Roosevelt's life story. Particularly appropriate for students reading below grade level.

Whitelaw, Nancy. *Theodore Roosevelt Takes Charge.* Albert Whitman, 1992. Chronicles the life of Theodore Roosevelt.

Primary Sources from the Period

Norris, Frank. *The Octopus.* R. Bentley, 1971. Relates a fictional tale of political corruption.

Riordan, William L. *Plunkitt of Tammany Hall.* Bedford Books, 1994. Offers an insider's view of corruption.

Multimedia Materials

The Progressive Impulse. Video, 30 min. RMI Media. Examines the motives behind progressive reform.

Theodore Roosevelt: American. Video, 27 min. Educational Video Services. Uses photographs and political cartoons to help students understand Theodore Roosevelt's life.

CHAPTER 9

Before You Read

Build on What You Know

Ask students to answer the following questions.

Why might many Americans have become interested in reforming society?

Consider:

- the many social problems created by rapid industrialization and urbanization
- the effects of a widening split between the rich and the poor

How might Americans have attempted to conquer the negative effects of industrialization and urbanization?

Consider:

- the causes of such problems
- the possible constitutional remedies to such problems
- the importance of protest

exploring the time line

AMERICAN EVENTS

internet**connect**

TOPIC: Oil Production
GO TO: go.hrw.com
KEYWORD: SE1 Oil

Have students access the Internet through the HRW Web site to conduct research on the production of oil during the first 50 years of the 1900s. Then have each student create two graphs: one that shows the increase in oil production and one that shows the price of gasoline. Have students write summary statements that compare and contrast the two graphs.

CHAPTER 9

1900–1920

Progressive Politicians

Oil gusher in Spindletop oil field

African American farmers in the early 1900s

1900
Daily Life
A hurricane strikes Galveston, Texas, killing at least 6,000 people.

1901
Science and Technology
Oil production increases with new drilling practices that yield an estimated 100,000 barrels a day in a nine-day period in one Texas well.

1904
Business and Finance
The U.S. Supreme Court rules that the Northern Securities Company has violated antitrust laws and orders it dissolved.

1904
Daily Life
The winning vehicle in the Vanderbilt Challenge Cup automobile race averages 52.2 miles per hour.

1906
Politics
Congress passes the Meat Inspection Act.

1906
Science and Technology
Lee De Forest invents the three-element vacuum repeater for telephones, improving voice quality in long-distance calls.

1906
The Arts
Upton Sinclair publishes his novel *The Jungle.*

1908
Business and Finance
Thirty-five percent of American workers are employed in agriculture.

1908
Politics
A White House conference on conservation leads to the creation of a commission to study natural resource issues.

1900 | 1904 | 1908

Hurricane damage in Galveston, Texas, in 1900

Cover of Upton Sinclair's novel ***The Jungle***

Before You Read

Build on What You Know

During the early 1900s, many Americans took a new interest in reforming society. Now known as the Progressive Era, this time period was marked by great optimism and faith in scientific efficiency. Progressive reformers set out to conquer such negative effects of industrialization and rapid urbanization as unsafe working conditions, long hours, low wages, and slum housing. In this chapter you will learn about the successes and failures of progressive politicians, including Presidents Theodore Roosevelt, William Howard Taft, and Woodrow Wilson.

268

Think About Themes

To help students create their Themes Journal entries, provide the following examples of appropriate **agree**/**disagree** *statements.*

Democratic Values

Agree Some companies have developed sound, widely applicable management techniques.

Disagree Many leading entrepreneurs of the Second Industrial Revolution ran their companies as near dictatorships.

Economic Development

Agree Many entrepreneurs of the Second Industrial Revolution viewed laissez-faire economics as crucial to sound business operations.

Disagree Throughout American history, many reformers have argued that the federal government should regulate businesses in order to protect citizens and the environment.

Constitutional Heritage

Agree The Founding Fathers could not foresee the changes created by rapid industrialization and urbanization.

Disagree The Constitution contains timeless principles that are the foundation of American democracy.

THE GRANGER COLLECTION, NEW YORK

George Bellow's **Lone Tenement,** *completed in 1909*

1910 World Events A Chinese army tries to take direct control of Tibet's government by force.

1912 Politics Theodore Roosevelt and his supporters form the Progressive Party.

1913 Business and Finance The Federal Reserve Act reorganizes the national banking system.

1914 Politics The Clayton Antitrust Act is passed.

1914 Science and Technology The amount of electric power used in manufacturing industries reaches 3.8 million horsepower.

1917 The Arts The era of the American Renaissance in art draws to a close.

1917 Daily Life Americans spend $175 million on electrical appliances.

1917 World Events Mexico adopts a new constitution.

1919 Business and Finance Per capita income among southerners is 40 percent lower than the national average.

1920 Politics The Nineteenth Amendment gives American women the right to vote.

1912 — 1916 — 1920

PROGRESSIVE PARTY FOR PRESIDENT

Theodore Roosevelt campaign banner

MR. PRESIDENT
WHAT WILL YOU DO
FOR
WOMAN SUFFRAGE

Suffrage supporter

Think About Themes

Decide whether you **agree** *or* **disagree** *with the following statements. Note why in your journal.*

Democratic Values The management of a business corporation provides a good model for city government.

Economic Development Government regulation of business should never limit or restrict the free-enterprise system.

Constitutional Heritage Each new generation should reinterpret the Constitution for itself, as social and economic realities change.

exploring the time line

GLOBAL EVENTS

IN THE NEWS

1910 ■ China and Tibet. Conflict between China and Tibet continued throughout the 1900s. In 1951 China assumed control of Tibet, claiming that the region had always been a Chinese province. The Tibetans disagreed, arguing that they had long been an independent nation. The Tibetans later revolted, but the Chinese crushed the rebellion and the Dalai Lama, the spiritual leader of Tibet, went into exile. In November 1998 the Dalai Lama met with U.S. government officials, leading Chinese leaders to protest. Months later, Tibetans in India and Nepal held protests in remembrance of the rebellion. During the protests the Dalai Lama claimed that the Chinese continued to oppress the people of Tibet.

CRITICAL THINKING Why might Chinese leaders have protested the Dalai Lama's visit with top American officials?

ANSWER: Students might suggest that the meeting gave support to the Tibetan contention that the Chinese occupation of Tibet was illegal.

SECTION 1

After completing Section 1, students should be able to:

OBJECTIVE 1 *Summarize the reforms that were enacted to make U.S. voting procedures more democratic.*

OBJECTIVE 2 *Describe how reformers sought to improve city governments.*

OBJECTIVE 3 *Discuss the goals of progressive state leaders.*

LET'S GET STARTED!

As students enter the classroom, ask them to list two goals and two strategies of progressive reformers. *(Students might note that reformers wanted to improve cities, help immigrants, and end political corruption. They might also note that reformers attempted to lobby for new laws, pressure the federal government, and conduct protests.)* Have volunteers share their responses. Then tell students that in Section 1 they will learn how progressive reformers and politicians attempted to reform American politics in the early 1900s.

SECTION 1 RESOURCES

PRINT
- Guided Reading Strategy 9.1
- Section 1 Review, p. 274
- Daily Quiz 9.1

MULTIMEDIA
- One-Stop Planner, Lesson 9.1
- Holt Researcher: American History CD–ROM

SHELTERED ENGLISH
- Main Idea Activity for Reteaching and Sheltered English 9.1

✓ READING TO UNDERSTAND
To help students master the section objectives, have them answer the **READING CHECKS** and complete **Guided Reading Strategy 9.1** as they read the section.

SECTION 1 Reforming Government

OBJECTIVES

Read to understand:
1. what reforms were enacted to make U.S. voting procedures more democratic
2. how reformers sought to improve city governments
3. what the goals of progressive state leaders were

KEY TERMS

direct primary
Seventeenth Amendment
initiative
referendum
recall
Wisconsin Idea

KEY PEOPLE

Samuel M. Jones
Tom Johnson
Robert M. La Follette

EYEWITNESSES TO History

"*The American reformer's story is a modern tragedy of defeat, humiliation, martyrdom. . . . [There is evidence] to show the regular, outrageous grafting . . . in all public business.*"
—Oliver McClintock

Author Lincoln Steffens

Pittsburgh reformer Oliver McClintock "knew and could prove what was going on," progressive reformer Lincoln Steffens wrote. Steffens's eye-opening book *The Shame of the Cities* vividly depicted the workings of turn-of-the-century urban politics. In many cities, he said, a boss controlled municipal government. The boss had a strong opponent, however—the reformer.

Government Corruption

Progressive reformers such as Lincoln Steffens found corruption at all levels of government, from city hall to Washington, D.C. City political machines were often linked to the Democratic or Republican state machines. The state machines catered to special interests, making deals with railroads, lumber companies, or anyone else seeking tax breaks or other favors from state legislatures. In return, the machines expected generous gifts, often in the form of campaign contributions.

In the 1890s some people began referring to the U.S. Senate as the Millionaire's Club. Some said that Senator James McMillan of Michigan represented shipping and lumber interests instead of his constituents. Others argued that Senator Joseph Foraker of Ohio put Standard Oil's needs above all others. Often put into power by state machines, some U.S. senators accepted bribes to vote the way corporations wished. In 1906 progressive writer David Graham Phillips published "The Treason of the Senate," a series of articles documenting how special interests influenced U.S. politics.

This 1889 cartoon criticizes the influence of trusts on the U.S. Senate.

THE GRANGER COLLECTION, NEW YORK

"The greatest single hold of 'the interests' is the fact that they are the 'campaign contributors.' . . . Who pays the big election expenses of your congress man, of the men you send to the legislature to elect senators? Do you imagine those who foot those huge bills are fools? Don't you know that they make sure of getting their money back, with interest?"

Election Reforms

Reformers seeking a return to honest government rallied to the slogan, "Give the government back to the people!" Only when government listened to the public's voice, they believed, could the urgent problems facing Americans be fixed.

Progressives sought to break the power of the bosses by reforming the election process. First, they wanted to take the power of choosing political candidates away from political machines. Therefore, progressives pushed for the **direct primary**—

TEACH OBJECTIVE 1

ALL LEVELS: Ask students to characterize the state of voting practices in the United States before the advent of voting reforms in the early 1900s. *(Students should indicate that the practices were highly corrupt.)* Ask students how they would have attempted to reform such practices, had they been reformers or officials. *(Answers will vary. Some students will suggest measures to decrease corruption.)* To help students understand the actual reforms that took place during the period, copy the following graphic organizer on the chalkboard, omitting the italicized answers. Have each student complete it. **Sheltered English**

- **direct primary**—*voters pick the candidates to run in a general election*
- **Seventeenth Amendment**—*voters elect their senators directly*
- **secret ballot**—*candidates are selected from a single, uniform ballot*
- **initiative**—*gives voters the power to initiate legislation*
- **referendum**—*allows voters to approve or veto a recently passed law*
- **recall**—*enables voters to remove an elected official from office*

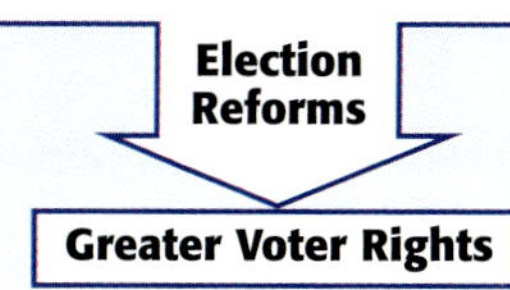

▶**ASSIGNMENT** *Ask each student to write one or two paragraphs explaining how the election reforms of the early 1900s made government more democratic and more responsive to the people rather than to special interests.*

---

a nominating election in which voters choose the candidates who later run in a general election. Mississippi adopted the direct primary in 1902. Wisconsin followed in 1903. By 1916 most others states had done the same.

Next, progressives proposed to change the method of electing U.S. senators. The U.S. Constitution gave the power to elect senators to state legislatures. Progressives believed that this procedure made it easy for the political bosses and machines with influence over state officials to control government. By 1912 the progressive tide had grown strong enough that Congress proposed the **Seventeenth Amendment**, which gave voters the power to elect their senators directly. The amendment was ratified the next year.

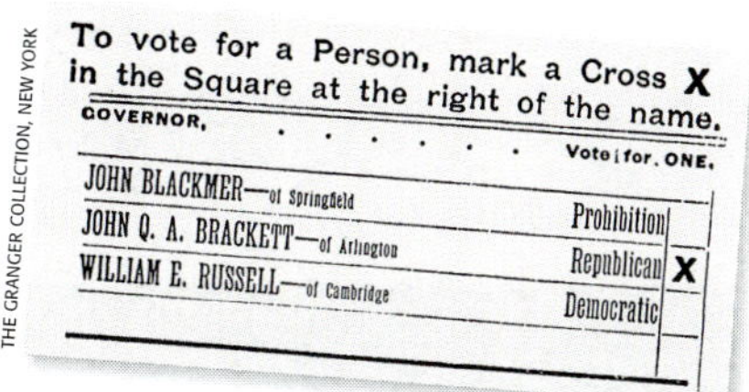
To vote for a Person, mark a Cross X in the Square at the right of the name.

GOVERNOR.	Vote for ONE.	
JOHN BLACKMER—of Springfield	Prohibition	
JOHN Q. A. BRACKETT—of Arlington	Republican	X
WILLIAM E. RUSSELL—of Cambridge	Democratic	

THE GRANGER COLLECTION, NEW YORK

The Australian ballot lists all candidates on a single, uniform sheet of paper.

Progressives also sought to reform the voting process itself. At the time, each political party printed its own ballot in a distinctive color. At polling places, the colored ballots made it easy to see how people voted. Without secrecy, voters could be pressured to support certain candidates. To lessen this threat, progressives proposed using the secret ballot. Developed in Australia, the secret ballot lists all candidates on a single, uniform sheet of paper. The ballot is also printed at public expense. By 1910 most states had switched to the secret ballot.

Finally, progressives urged states to adopt three additional election-reform measures: the initiative, the referendum, and the recall. The **initiative** gives voters the power to initiate, or introduce, legislation. If a certain percentage of voters in a state—usually 5 to 15 percent—sign a petition, a proposed policy must be put on the ballot for public approval. The **referendum** is a companion to the initiative. By securing a specified number of signatures on a petition, citizens can force the legislature to place a recently passed law on the ballot, allowing voters to approve or veto the measure. The **recall** enables voters to remove an elected official from office by calling for a special election.

Many reformers believed they were making major changes. William Allen White referred to voting reforms as "a big moral movement in democracy." In 1910 White claimed victory for reformers.

> **"Today in states having the primary under the state control the corporation [political machine] candidate for any public office is handicapped."**

In practice, however, the effects of the voting reforms were mixed and business continued to influence elections.

✔ **READING CHECK:** What reforms were enacted to make U.S. voting procedures more democratic?

THROUGH OTHERS' EYES
The Australian Ballot

In 1855 William Nicholson of Victoria proposed a motion in Australia's legislature that "in the opinion of this House any new Electoral Act should provide for electors recording their vote by secret ballot." The following year the act passed. By 1887 the use of an official secret ballot had been established throughout Australia in national and local elections. The new law required that voters be provided with private voting booths where they could strike out the names of the candidates they did not select on a preprinted ballot. The ballots were then deposited in a locked box in the presence of voting officials.

The success of the ballot system in Australia encouraged ballot reform in Great Britain. Francis S. Dutton, a member of South Australia's legislature, described the effects of Australia's secret ballot reform to a specially appointed British parliamentary committee. "The very notion of exercising coercion [force] and improper influence absolutely died out of the country," he announced. Robert Torrens, former premier of South Australia, also testified. He described the voting situation before the ballot reform. "We had . . . bribery, a great deal of rioting, and broken heads, and broken panes of glass, and of smashing windows; exactly the same thing that goes on in this country." In 1872 a law enacting the "Australian" ballot passed the British House of Commons.

DEMOCRATIC VALUES

Third Parties and Secret Ballots. After the adoption of the secret ballot, states printed and issued the tickets, as opposed to political parties doing so. Independent and third-party candidates sometimes face obstacles when they try to find a place on these ballots. In Florida, for example, independent party candidates must acquire signatures from 3 percent of the voters registered in the previous election before being placed on the ballot as a candidate for governor or U.S. senator. In 1992 third-party candidates needed 196,000 signatures.

CRITICAL THINKING Why might such requirements be imposed on third-party candidates?

ANSWER: Some students might argue such requirements are used to prevent frivolous candidates from running, while others might argue that the two leading parties want to prevent challenges to their power.

THAT'S INTERESTING!

Some people call the modern-day Congress a Millionaires' Club. In 1999 six members of Congress had fortunes valued at $40 million or more, including Senator John Kerry of Massachusetts, whose worth was estimated at $675 million.

TEACH OBJECTIVE 2

LEVEL 1: Pair students and tell them to imagine that it is 1905 and that they are reformer city officials in the Midwest. Have each pair develop a three-to-four-minute dialogue describing how it will seek to improve its city government. *(Pairs should mention attempts to improve the police force, improve municipal services, enact labor reforms, and hire city managers.)* Ask volunteers to perform their dialogues for the class. **Sheltered English, Cooperative Learning**

LEVEL 2: Tell students to imagine that it is 1905 and that they are reformer city officials in the Midwest. Have each student write a half-page letter to the editor of the local newspaper describing how he or she will seek to improve city governments. *(See the Level 1 lesson for the correct plans.)* Ask volunteers to read their letters to the class. Students may wish to include their letters in their portfolios.

LEVEL 3: Organize students into triads and tell them to imagine that it is 1905 and that they are reformist city officials in the Midwest. Have each triad discuss the ways in which it will seek to improve city governments. *(See the Level 1 lesson for the correct plans.)* Then have each triad write short public notice statements describing the need for such reforms and explaining the benefits of such reforms. Ask volunteers to present their public notice statements to the class. **Cooperative Learning**

PEOPLE IN HISTORY

Samuel M. Jones. Samuel M. Jones was born in Wales and moved to the United States with his family soon after his birth. As a young man he worked in the Pennsylvania oil fields. He later became extremely wealthy manufacturing oil-field equipment. Concerned about the lives of his factory workers, Jones approved an eight-hour workday and gave his employees paid vacations. His efforts made him well known and immensely popular. Some 55,000 mourners attended his funeral in 1904.

CRITICAL THINKING How might Jones have differed from many other American businesspeople of the period?

ANSWER: Students might suggest that Jones adopted many labor reforms before they were required by law.

VISUAL RECORD ANSWER

Students might suggest that kindergartens provided education, socialization, and a sense of community.

Reforming City Government

The drive to clean up city government typically owed its successes to enthusiastic local leaders and active reformers. Through such efforts, the "good-government" campaign put some reform mayors into office.

Two of the most successful reform mayors were elected in Ohio. Both Samuel M. Jones and Tom Johnson were self-made men who earned their fortunes early in life. Then in midlife they traded business for politics.

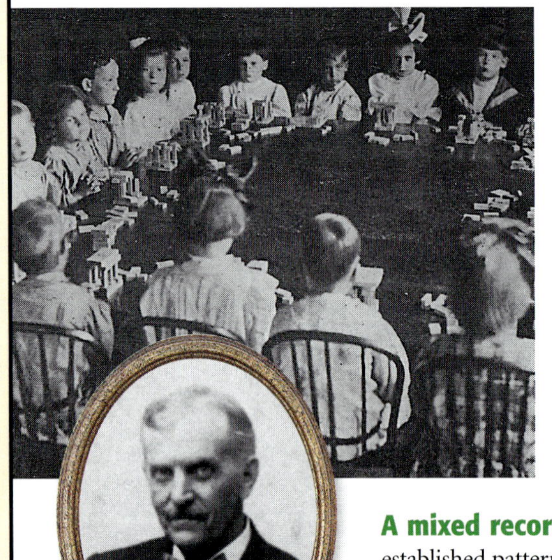

INTERPRETING THE VISUAL RECORD

Reforming city government. Samuel M. Jones enacted many reforms as mayor of Toledo, Ohio. ***How do you think kindergartens like this one benefited the residents of Toledo?***

The mayors. Samuel M. "Golden Rule" Jones's nickname came from his belief in the biblical Golden Rule—"Do unto others as you would have them do unto you." Seeking to apply this principle to government, Jones successfully ran for mayor of Toledo in 1897. During the next seven years he overhauled the police force, improved municipal services, set a minimum wage for city workers, and opened kindergartens for children.

During this same period, Tom Johnson served as Cleveland's mayor. Johnson created new, more humane rules for the treatment of prisoners by Cleveland's police department. He also strongly supported a new, fairer single tax system. Frederic Howe described Johnson's desire for such a system as "a passion for freedom, for a world of equal opportunity for all." Johnson's success led Lincoln Steffens to call him "the best mayor of the best governed city in the United States."

A mixed record. A few popular mayors alone, however, could not conquer established patterns of corruption in city government. The reformers' attempts to achieve basic governmental changes had mixed results. Lincoln Steffens concluded that voters did not necessarily prefer democratic governments because machine-run politics was more predictable. Reformers were also disappointed by some of the results of their direct government movement that encouraged voters' input in government decisions. For instance, voters rejected some measures favored by progressives such as municipal ownership of public utilities, tax reform, and pensions for city employees.

Electoral reform was further hindered by the fact that many middle-class progressives feared that the lower classes might gain too much power. They wanted to curb the power of big business, but feared that urban masses would gain too great a voice in political decision making. One reform leader, F. E. Chadwick of Newport, Rhode Island, maintained that a voter who paid higher taxes "should be assured a representation in the committee which . . . spends the money which he contributes." Chadwick believed that a "truly democratic" government would "give the property owner a fair show."

City commissions and managers. A devastating hurricane that struck Galveston, Texas, in 1900 produced an alternative to the political machine. A tidal wave created by the storm killed at least 6,000 people and destroyed the city. Galveston's government was unable to cope with the emergency. The state legislature therefore named a five-person city commission to rebuild the area. The commissioners were experts in their fields rather than party loyalists. Citizens

TEACH OBJECTIVE 3

LEVEL 1: Conduct a discussion on progressive state leaders and their goals. *(On the whole, progressive state leaders wanted to enact the direct primary, increase taxes on railroads and public utilities, pass laws that curbed lobbying, establish stricter controls on certain industries, and so on.)* List the main points of this discussion on the chalkboard. Ask each student to use the chalkboard list to write a paragraph on the goals of progressive state leaders. Students may wish to include their paragraphs in their portfolios. **Sheltered English**

LEVELS 2 AND 3: Tell students to imagine that they are Robert M. La Follette, Charles Evans Hughes, James Vardaman, or another progressive state leader. Have each student write a three-to-five-minute speech explaining and justifying his or her goals for progressive reforms. *(See the Level 1 lesson for the correct goals.)* Ask volunteers to deliver their speeches to the class. Students may wish to include their speeches in their portfolios.

▶**ASSIGNMENT** *Write the following statement on the chalkboard:* In cities, business was often the friend of government reform. At the state level, however, business was often its foe. *Have each student write two or three paragraphs assessing this statement, including evidence that supports his or her points.*

praised the commission as being more honest and efficient than the city's previous government. Galveston kept the system, and other cities in the United States soon established similar commissions.

The desire for increased government efficiency also gave rise to the hiring of city managers. These individuals are expert administrators employed to run cities as they might run a business.

✔ **READING CHECK:** How did reformers try to improve city government?

Strategies for Success — Interpreting the Visual Record: Political Cartoons

Much like photographs, political cartoons can serve as unique and valuable sources of historical information. A *political cartoon* is a humorous or satirical drawing that presents an opinion about a specific person, group, issue, idea, or event. Political cartoons usually appear in the editorial sections of newspapers and newsmagazines. While some express a positive outlook, the great majority are critical of their subjects.

Political cartoonists frequently use caricatures and symbolism to communicate their message. A *caricature* is a drawing that exaggerates or distorts a subject's physical features. *Symbolism* is the use of an image or thing to stand for something else. The image of "Uncle Sam," for instance, is often used to represent the United States in political cartoons. Along with caricatures and symbolism, many political cartoonists use labels, speech balloons, and other forms of text to clarify the meaning of their artistic work.

How to Interpret a Political Cartoon

1. **Identify the subject.** Look at the figures and objects in the cartoon and identify its basic subject. If the cartoon has a title, examine it for clues about the cartoonist's point of view.
2. **Examine the caricatures and symbols.** If the cartoon uses caricatures, note how each figure is distorted or exaggerated and determine the meaning of the distortion or exaggeration. If the cartoon employs symbolism, determine what each symbol represents.
3. **Study the labels.** Read any labels, speech balloons, captions, or other text that may help clarify the meaning of the cartoon.
4. **Determine the cartoonist's message.** Use your examination of the figures, objects, and text in the cartoon to determine the cartoonist's message.
5. **Put the information to use.** Compare the cartoonist's message with information about the historical period that you have gained through other sources. In turn, use the results of this comparison to form generalizations and draw conclusions.

Applying the Strategy

Study the political cartoon to the right, entitled "The Police Version of it." As you do so, note the cartoonist's use of symbolism and determine the cartoonist's message.

THE POLICE VERSION OF IT.
"Let no guilty man (or woman) escape—widout dey put up de stuff!"
THE GRANGER COLLECTION, NEW YORK

Practicing the Strategy

Answer the following questions.

1. What does the vise in this cartoon symbolize?
2. How do the labels on the human figures help clarify the meaning of the cartoon?
3. What message is the cartoonist trying to communicate with this cartoon?
4. Why is the cartoon entitled "The Police Version of it"?

ACROSS THE CURRICULUM

▶GEOGRAPHY◀

The Galveston Hurricane. Many scholars regard the 1900 Galveston hurricane as one of the worst natural disasters in American history. At one point during the hurricane, the entire city was underwater—in some places by as much as 15 feet. The hurricane and flood destroyed some 2,600 houses. Aided by progressive managers and planners, however, the city was able to recover and flourish. To protect against future storms, officials built an enormous seawall. In 1961 this seawall lessened the damage from a potentially devastating hurricane and flood.

CRITICAL THINKING Besides seawalls, how else might city officials try to protect urban areas against natural disasters?

ANSWER: Some students might mention dikes or earthquake safeguards.

STRATEGIES FOR SUCCESS ANSWERS

Practicing the Strategy

1. the effort to squeeze out bribes or kickbacks
2. The labels indicate the identities of the figures.
3. that police officers tried to get bribes or kickbacks
4. The title refers to police graft.

REVIEW

Have students complete the **Section 1 Review** on p. 274.

ASSESS

Have students complete **Daily Quiz 9.1**. As **Alternative Assessment**, you may want to use the city official dialogue or progressive state leader speech in this section's lessons.

RETEACH

Have students complete **Main Idea Activity for Reteaching and Sheltered English 9.1**. Then have each student write a summary sentence for each subsection in Section 1. Select students to read their statements to the class. Have the class choose the best summary sentence for each subsection, justifying its selections. **Sheltered English**

EXTEND

Have students conduct research on Robert M. La Follette. Then pair students. Ask one member to act as a radio interviewer and the other to act as La Follette. Have both members prepare written material for the interview. Then ask volunteers to conduct their interviews in front of the class. To conclude, ask the students to discuss the accuracy of both the questions and the responses. Did they reflect the governor's personality? Did they reflect the political issues of the time?
Cooperative Learning, Block Scheduling

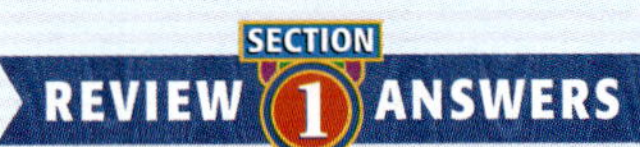

Define and Identify

For significance, see the following pages:

- direct primary, p. 270
- Seventeenth Amendment, p. 271
- initiative, p. 271
- referendum, p. 271
- recall, p. 271
- Samuel M. Jones, p. 272
- Tom Johnson, p. 272
- Robert M. La Follette, p. 274
- Wisconsin Idea, p. 274

1. state reforms–direct primary, secret ballot, initiative, referendum, recall; city reforms–better services, city managers; shared reforms–better treatment for prisoners
2. that Americans regarded corruption as inevitable and acceptable
3. used city commissions and city managers rather than elected politicians
4. the Seventeenth Amendment–allowed the direct election of senators; the secret ballot–allowed voters to choose candidates secretly and independently
5. The Wisconsin Idea reforms included the direct primary, regulation of public utilities, and limits on lobbying–all key elements in the progressive agenda.

As one of the progressive movement's most energetic leaders, Robert M. La Follette supported a reform program in Wisconsin that became a model for other states.

Reforming State Government

The spirit of reform also stirred many politicians at the state level. In Wisconsin, Robert M. "Fighting Bob" La Follette began his political career as a loyal Republican. However, he soon found himself at odds with Wisconsin's Republican political machine, which was dominated by railroad and lumber interests. La Follette served as a county district attorney and as a member of Congress in the late 1800s. He then signaled his break with the party machine by refusing a bribe from a party boss.

Elected governor in 1900, La Follette vigorously backed a reform program—soon known as the **Wisconsin Idea**—that became a model for other states. First, La Follette called for a direct primary. Although he was opposed by the Republican machine for two years, La Follette refused to accept a compromise. He declared that "in legislation *no bread* is often better than *half a loaf*." He then urged the state legislature to increase taxes on railroads and public utilities—electric, gas, and streetcar companies—and to create commissions to regulate these companies in the public interest. La Follette helped pass laws that curbed excessive lobbying. He also backed labor reforms and worked to conserve Wisconsin's natural resources. In 1905 the Wisconsin legislature elected La Follette to the U.S. Senate. La Follette remained committed to "the struggle between labor and those who would control, through slavery in one form or another, the laborers."

La Follette influenced other state leaders. New York governor Charles Evans Hughes established stricter controls of insurance companies and utilities. Progressive Democrat James Vardaman of Mississippi and Hoke Smith of Georgia led white farmers in a fight against corporate power. As governor, Vardaman abolished the use of convict labor. He also regulated corporations and improved social services for poor whites. However, these southern progressives often supported racial segregation and tried to keep African Americans from voting.

✔ **READING CHECK:** What goals did progressive state leaders have?

SECTION 1 REVIEW

Define and explain the significance of the following terms:
direct primary
Seventeenth Amendment
initiative
referendum
recall
Wisconsin Idea

Identify and explain the significance of the following individuals:
Samuel M. Jones
Tom Johnson
Robert M. La Follette

1. **Using Graphic Organizers** Copy the diagram below. Use it to explain what reforms progressives proposed at the city and state levels and where those reforms overlapped.

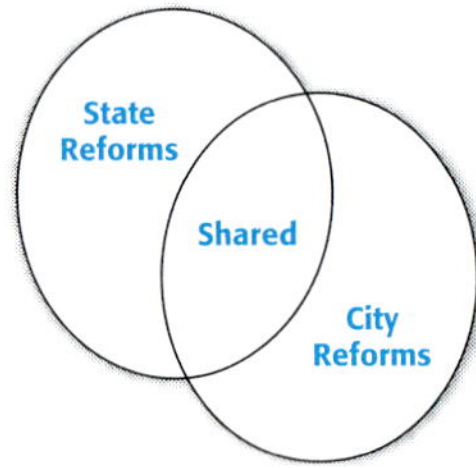

2. **Identifying Values** What did the widespread corruption in U.S. politics reveal about political values in the early 1900s?
3. **Evaluating** How did many U.S. cities try to increase government efficiency and lessen corruption?
4. **Assessing Consequences** How did changes in voting procedures enable government leaders to be elected more democratically?

Critical Thinking

5. Why can it be said that the Wisconsin Idea reforms were examples of the progressive spirit?
Consider:
   - the reforms that made up the Wisconsin Idea
   - your definition of the progressive spirit
   - how well the Wisconsin Idea lived up to the ideals of the Progressive Era

SECTION 2

After completing Section 2, students should be able to:

OBJECTIVE 1 *Discuss how the response to the miners' strike and Square Deal reflected President Roosevelt's governing style.*

OBJECTIVE 2 *Summarize why the government tried to regulate trusts and the food and drug industry.*

OBJECTIVE 3 *Explain the stand that Gifford Pinchot and Theodore Roosevelt took on the environment.*

LET'S GET STARTED

As students enter the classroom, have them examine the illustration of a drug advertisement in this section. Have them read the quotation by Samuel Hopkins Adams to the right of the illustration. Ask students to respond to the illustration and the quotation in writing, explaining what the pills were supposed to do and why Adams wrote what he did. Have volunteers share their responses. Tell students that in Section 2 they will learn how reformers attempted to protect consumers against unsubstantiated claims.

Roosevelt and the Square Deal

OBJECTIVES

Read to understand:

1. how the response to the miners' strike and Square Deal reflected President Roosevelt's governing style
2. why the government tried to regulate trusts and the food and drug industries
3. what stand Gifford Pinchot and Theodore Roosevelt took on the environment

KEY TERMS

arbitration
Square Deal
Elkins Act
Hepburn Act
Meat Inspection Act
Pure Food and Drug Act
reclamation

KEY PEOPLE

Theodore Roosevelt
Upton Sinclair
Gifford Pinchot

"[The tower] assumes a magical aspect, as if it had been summoned forth by the genius of our united people."
—Cosmopolitan Magazine

Pan-American Exposition button

A writer for *Cosmopolitan Magazine* described the Electric Tower at the Pan-American Exposition held in Buffalo, New York, in 1901. Standing 375 feet tall, the tower served as a powerful symbol of American success. Americans at the turn of the century saw this and the other exhibits at the Pan-American Exposition as commemorating their industrial progress, rising prosperity, and increasing world power. The visit of President William McKinley was intended to be the highlight of the exposition. He believed that such public festivities not only recorded American achievements and led to greater enthusiasm and energy for industrial pursuits, but also brought joy to the American people.

Roosevelt Becomes President

In 1900 President McKinley ran for re-election with Theodore Roosevelt as his running mate. The Democrats again nominated William Jennings Bryan and made free silver and the economy the focus of their campaign. However, in 1900 most Americans felt prosperous, and McKinley and Roosevelt sailed to victory.

As governor of New York, Roosevelt had worked to reform government and regulate big business. New York's conservative Republican Party leaders were angered by this progressive activism. They had tried to ease Roosevelt out of state office by persuading him to run as vice president. Senator Mark Hanna, a conservative from Ohio, was alarmed by this move. He warned that there would be "only one life between this madman and the Presidency."

Roosevelt takes office. The nation was shocked when, on September 6, 1901, anarchist Leon Czolgosz shot McKinley at the Pan-American Exposition. An unemployed laborer, Czolgosz claimed to act on behalf of the poor and the forgotten. A week later the president died, and Roosevelt became the nation's chief executive.

Roosevelt was just 42 years old when he took the presidential oath. He set about the task of reform with enthusiasm and energy. Roosevelt brought dynamic leadership to the progressive movement. He helped reshape the country as surely as he renamed the Executive Mansion the White House.

During the Gilded Age U.S. presidents generally took a hands-off approach to government. Roosevelt, however, believed that the president should use the office as a "bully pulpit" to speak out on vital issues. One of Roosevelt's goals as president was to fight against class distinctions. "No republic can permanently exist when it becomes a republic of classes," he warned.

Theodore Roosevelt served as vice president to President William McKinley. After the assassination of McKinley in 1901, Roosevelt became president.

SECTION 2 RESOURCES

PRINT

- Guided Reading Strategy 9.2
- Geography Activity 9: Theodore Roosevelt—A Biographical Map
- Section 2 Review, p. 281
- Daily Quiz 9.2

MULTIMEDIA

- One-Stop Planner, Lesson 9.2
- The American Nation Video Program Segment: Yosemite National Park; Teacher's Guide, 87–92
- Holt Researcher: American History CD–ROM
- HRW Web site

SHELTERED ENGLISH

- Main Idea Activity for Reteaching and Sheltered English 9.2

✔ READING TO UNDERSTAND

To help students master the section objectives, have them answer the **READING CHECKS** and complete **Guided Reading Strategy 9.2** as they read the section.

Teacher to Teacher

Lucinda Lucero Sachs of Albuquerque, New Mexico, suggested the following activity: Ask students to read the subsection entitled Roosevelt Becomes President. Ask them to consider his involvement in the United Mine Workers' Strike. Then write the following question on the chalkboard: Should government regulate business or keep its hands off? *Act as a moderator and conduct a debate on the topic.*

TEACH OBJECTIVE 1

LEVEL 1: Conduct a brief lecture on Theodore Roosevelt as a reform president. Then organize students into triads. Have each triad create four newspaper headlines on President Roosevelt's governing style—two on his handling of the miners' strike and two on his Square Deal. *(Students' headlines should indicate that Roosevelt encouraged both sides in the strike to accept arbitration, demonstrating his concern for both workers and businesses. This concern informed his Square Deal as well.)* Ask each triad to write topic sentences or lead-in sentences for each of its newspaper headlines. Have spokespeople read their triad's topic sentences to the class.
Sheltered English, Cooperative Learning

ECONOMIC DEVELOPMENT

The Importance of Coal. In the early 1900s, many Americans used coal to heat their homes. As the miners' strike continued into the cold autumn months, many Americans feared that they would be unable to heat their homes. The price of remaining coal supplies rose dramatically, from $5 to $20 per ton. Some people panicked at the prices and shortages. In one New York town residents chopped down telegraph poles to use as firewood.

CRITICAL THINKING Which energy supplies do Americans depend on today?

ANSWER: Students might suggest that many Americans now depend on electricity and gasoline.

THAT'S INTERESTING!

Coal miners purchased goods at mining company stores, which often took advantage of them. Andrew Chippie, a 12-year-old miner whose father had been killed in a mine accident, surrendered his wages—just 40 cents a day—to the Markle Coal Company in order to pay his dead father's store debt.

VISUAL RECORD ANSWER

Students might suggest that the miners look like they are pleased with President Roosevelt's efforts.

PRESIDENTIAL *Lives*

1858–1919
In Office 1901–1909

Theodore Roosevelt

Theodore Roosevelt enjoyed the limelight. As one of his children remarked, Roosevelt always wanted to be "the bride at every wedding, the corpse at every funeral." This hero of the Rough Riders became a legend in his own time. Roosevelt always lived life to the fullest. "No President has ever enjoyed himself as much as I have enjoyed myself," he claimed. An old friend explained Roosevelt's great love of life: "You must always remember that the President is about six [years old]."

Roosevelt was an all-around athlete whose energy was legendary. For example, when the French ambassador once visited the White House, he and the president played tennis, jogged, and then worked out with weights. Roosevelt turned to his guest and asked, "What would you like to do now?" "If it's just the same with you, Mr. President," said the ambassador, "I'd like to lie down and die."

The United Mine Workers strike. Soon after Roosevelt became president, a labor dispute helped define his approach to the office. In the spring of 1902 some 150,000 coal miners struck for higher wages and recognition of their United Mine Workers union. The mine owners—mostly railroad companies—refused to negotiate. As the strike dragged on, Washington Gladden, a reform minister, petitioned Roosevelt for help. Speaking on behalf of working-class laborers, Gladden wrote, "You can speak as no one else can speak for the plain people of this country. Every workingman knows you are his friend; no capitalist of common sense can imagine that you are his enemy." Thousands signed this petition, which was sent to the White House.

Conservatives urged Roosevelt to send in the U.S. Army to force the strikers to return to work, while some progressives wanted him to place the mines under federal control. Instead, Roosevelt encouraged the two sides to accept **arbitration**. Arbitration is the process by which two opposing sides allow a third party to settle the dispute. As winter approached, Roosevelt threatened to take over the mines. This convinced the mine owners to agree to his plan of appointing a commission of arbitrators.

After a five-week investigation, the arbitrators announced their decision. They gave both the miners and the mine owners part of what they had wanted. The workers won a shorter workday and higher pay, but the mining companies did not have to recognize the union or bargain with it. It was a landmark compromise. For the first time, the federal government had intervened in a strike to protect the interests of the workers and the public. Satisfied, Roosevelt pronounced the compromise a "square deal."

INTERPRETING THE VISUAL RECORD

Labor. President Theodore Roosevelt met with these coal miners during the 1902 United Mine Workers strike. ***What type of reaction do you think these strikers had to Roosevelt's efforts?***

The Square Deal. The **Square Deal** became Roosevelt's 1904 campaign slogan. He promised to "see to it that every man has a square deal, no less and no more." This pledge summed up Roosevelt's belief in balancing the interests of business, consumers, and labor. Roosevelt's Square Deal called for limiting the power of trusts, promoting public health and safety, and improving working conditions.

The president was so popular with voters that no Republican dared challenge him for the 1904 nomination. Even the *New York Sun,* a pro–big business, antireform newspaper, supported Roosevelt. The paper preferred "the impulsive candidate of the party of conservatism to the conservative candidate of the party which the business interests regard as permanently and dangerously impulsive." Roosevelt won the election, easily defeating his Democratic opponent, Judge Alton Parker of New York.

✔ **READING CHECK:** How did the response to the miners' strike and the Square Deal reflect President Roosevelt's governing style?

LEVELS 2 AND 3: Tell students to imagine that they are modern-day historians. Have each student write a one-page paper analyzing how the miners' strike and Square Deal reflected President Roosevelt's governing style. *(See the Level 1 lesson for the correct points.)* Ask volunteers to read their papers to the class. Then conduct a discussion on Roosevelt and his policies. Have students use information from their papers and their textbooks to assign Roosevelt a "grade" as a reform president. Encourage students to fully explain and justify their ratings.

TEACH OBJECTIVE 2

LEVEL 1: Conduct a brief lecture on the practices of trusts and the food and drug industry in the early 1900s. *(Trusts often competed unfairly, forced companies to give them rebates or discounts, sold inferior products, or corrupted public officials. Many companies sold inferior or dangerous products with little concern for consumers.)* Pair students and tell them to imagine that it is 1906, and that they are reformers concerned about trusts and food and drug industry practices. Tell each pair to imagine that it has just discovered major corporate violations. Have each pair create two wanted posters for fictional violators. The posters should include text and illustrations that describe the violations. Ask volunteers to present their wanted posters to the class. Then ask students to explain how the government responded to such violations. *(Students should note that the government passed the Elkins Act, the Hepburn Act, and two consumer-protection laws in 1906.)*
Sheltered English, Cooperative Learning

Regulating Business

President Roosevelt sought to regulate large corporations during both of his terms in office. Although he considered big business essential to the nation's growth, he also believed companies should be forced to behave responsibly. "We don't wish to destroy corporations," he said, "but we do wish to make them subserve [serve] the public good." The public agreed with him. As journalist Walter Lippmann wrote, "The trusts made enemies right and left. . . . Labor was no match for them, state legislatures were impotent [powerless] before them."

Trustbusting. In 1902 the president took action, directing the U.S. attorney general to sue the Northern Securities Company. Controlled by J. P. Morgan and railroad barons James J. Hill and E. H. Harriman, the company monopolized railroad shipping from Chicago to the Northwest. In 1904 the Supreme Court ruled that the monopoly violated the Sherman Antitrust Act and ordered the corporation dissolved. Justice John Marshall Harlan wrote, "It is manifest [obvious] that if the Anti-Trust Act is held not to embrace a case such as is now before us, the plain intention of the legislative branch of the Government will be defeated."

Encouraged by this victory, the Roosevelt administration launched a "trustbusting" campaign. It filed 44 suits against business combinations believed not to be in the public interest. It was not size that mattered, Roosevelt declared, but whether a particular trust was good or bad for the public as a whole. "Bad" trusts did such things as forcing companies to give them discounts or rebates, selling inferior products, competing unfairly, and corrupting public officials. As Roosevelt put it, "We draw the line against misconduct, not against wealth."

The Roosevelt administration also promoted railroad regulation. At the president's urging, Congress passed two laws that turned the Interstate Commerce Commission (ICC) into a significant regulatory agency. The first, the 1903 **Elkins Act**, forbade shipping companies from accepting rebates, or money given back in return for business. Politicians as well as railroad owners supported this new law. The second, the 1906 **Hepburn Act**, authorized the ICC to set railroad rates and to regulate other companies engaged in interstate commerce, such as pipelines and ferries.

INTERPRETING THE VISUAL RECORD

Trustbusting. Responding to public concerns, President Theodore Roosevelt made great efforts to break up trusts. ***What roles are Roosevelt and the trust assigned in this 1904 cartoon entitled "Jack the Giant-Killer"? Why?***

Practices of food and drug companies. Roosevelt also responded to growing public concern about practices of the food and drug industries. By the early 1900s clear evidence existed that some drug companies, food processors, and meat packers were selling dangerous products. Scientific developments had enabled industrial chemists to add substances to food to make it appear fresh. Chemists learned that churning spoiled butter with skim milk would make it look fresh. It was then sold as fresh butter. The chemical formaldehyde was added to old eggs to take away their odor. The eggs too were then sold as fresh. North Dakota's food commissioner Edward F. Ladd found that most foods he analyzed had chemical additives. "There was but one brand of catsup which was pure," he reported at a meeting in 1904. The other brands contained pulp and skins, unripe and overripe tomatoes, and preservatives.

HISTORY MAKERS SPEAK

Theodore Roosevelt in *For the Record: A Documentary History of America*, Vol. 2

Battling the Trusts. In a 1901 message to Congress President Roosevelt explained his battle against trusts. "When the Constitution was adopted, at the end of the eighteenth century, no human wisdom could foretell the sweeping changes, alike in industrial and political conditions, which were to take place by the beginning of the twentieth century. . . . The conditions are now wholly different. . . . I believe that a law can be framed which will enable the National Government to exercise control along the line above indicated."

CRITICAL THINKING Did Roosevelt argue that the Constitution is flawed?

ANSWER: Students should suggest that he argued that contemporary circumstances required the government to expand its ability to regulate the trusts.

VISUAL RECORD ANSWER

Students might observe that President Roosevelt is portrayed as a small figure—the "Jack" of the title—against many large, imposing figures—the "Giants" of the title.

LEVEL 2: Tell students to imagine that it is 1904, and that they are reformers concerned about the practices of trusts or the food and drug industry. Have each student write a half-page letter to the editor describing such practices and calling for government action. *(See the Level 1 lesson for the correct practices.)* Ask volunteers to read their letters to the class. Then conduct a brief discussion on government responses to trusts and food and drug industry practices. Ask students to explain how the government attempted to curb violations. *(See the Level 1 lesson for the correct responses.)* Next ask students to express their own opinions about these government actions. Were they enough, given the size of the problem? What more could the government have done?

LEVEL 3: Tell students to imagine that it is 1904, and that they are reformers concerned about the practices of trusts and food and drug industry. Have each student prepare a two-to-three-minute statement to the congressional committee investigating such practices. *(See the Level 1 lesson for the correct practices.)* Ask volunteers to read their letters to the class. Then ask students to explain how the government attempted to curb violations. *(See the Level 1 lesson for the correct responses.)* Next ask students to express their own opinions about these government actions. Were they enough, given the scope of the problem? What more could the government have done?

PEOPLE IN HISTORY

Alice Lakey. Alice Lakey pursued a career as a concert singer until poor health forced her to retire from the stage. The daughter of a man who was extremely picky about his food, she soon became interested in food issues. She helped found the American Pure Food League, chaired a committee on food issues for the National Consumer's League, and served on the New York Milk Committee.

CRITICAL THINKING What might Lakey's story have revealed about who participated in the progressive movement?

ANSWER: Students might suggest that Lakey's story indicates the important role that women played in the progressive movement.

VISUAL RECORD ANSWER

Students might mention that the advertisement claims that Carter's Little Liver Pills will prevent sick headaches.

INTERPRETING THE VISUAL RECORD

Protecting the consumer. The Pure Food and Drug Act established regulations to prevent drug companies from making false claims about their products. ***What claims does this drug advertisement make?***

Some drug companies sold worthless over-the-counter medicines that contained dangerous drugs such as alcohol, cocaine, or morphine. Journalist Samuel Hopkins Adams wrote about drug industry abuses.

> **"Gullible [easily fooled] America will spend this year some seventy-five millions of dollars in the purchase of patent [over-the-counter] medicines. . . . It will swallow huge quantities of alcohol, an appalling amount of opiates and narcotics."**

Adams charged that the drug companies' claims that their "health tonics" could cure everything from baldness to cancer amounted to fraud. Edward Bok, another journalist, compared the label for Mrs. Winslow's Soothing Syrup, used to bring pain relief to teething babies, with a British label for the same medicine. The British label marked the tonic "Poison."

Read More About It

Free Find:
Reform Journalist
After reading about muckraking journalists on the **Holt Researcher** CD–ROM, write a short essay that explains how these journalists were able to influence the politics of their era.

Protecting the consumer. Reformers worked to put pressure on the government to pass laws requiring manufacturers to use pure ingredients in their products. As the primary purchasers of foods and medicines, many women participated in this movement. For example, Alice Lakey set up a series of lectures to alert Americans to this danger. At the St. Louis Exposition of 1904 the groups working for food reform set up a booth where they displayed artificially colored foods. They extracted the dyes from the foods, and then demonstrated how that very dye could be used to color wool and silk fabric. The exhibit attracted attention from politicians, journalists, and consumers alike. Then, in 1906, Upton Sinclair published *The Jungle,* an explosive novel that depicted the wretched and unsanitary conditions at a meatpacking plant.

Responding to public pressures, Roosevelt ordered Secretary of Agriculture James Wilson to investigate the conditions in the packing houses. "We saw meat shovelled from filthy wooden floors, piled on tables rarely washed, pushed from room to room in rotten box carts," Wilson stated in his final report. "In all of which processes it [the meat] was in the way of gathering dirt, splinters, floor filth, and the expectoration [saliva] of tuberculous and other diseased workers." The report was so shocking that the *New York Post* composed a jingle based on it.

> **"Mary had a little lamb,**
> **And when she saw it sicken,**
> **She shipped it off to Packingtown,**
> **And now it's labelled chicken."**

Stamps like this one from the early 1900s were used to label unsafe foods.

In 1906 the U.S. Congress enacted two new consumer-protection laws. The **Meat Inspection Act** required federal government inspection of meat shipped across state lines. The **Pure Food and Drug Act** forbade the manufacture, sale, or transportation of food and patent medicine containing harmful ingredients. The law also required that containers of food and medicines carry ingredient labels.

✔ **READING CHECK:** Why did Roosevelt and other government officials want to regulate trusts and the food and drug industries?

▶ASSIGNMENT *Ask students to examine the illustration at the top of the previous page. Then write the following statement on the chalkboard:* Advertisements for "miracle" cures are a thing of the past. *Tell each student to write two or three paragraphs assessing the statement. Students may wish to include advertisements from modern-day magazines or newspapers with their paragraphs to prove or disprove the statement.*

SPOTLIGHT on Progressive Literature

Tell students to imagine that they are progressive writers. Have each student write a two-to-three-page short story about some aspect of life during the early 1900s, approaching the topic from a progressive viewpoint. Students might write about corruption in city or state government, for example, or unsafe food and drug practices. Students could also write about a natural disaster, such as the Galveston hurricane, and its aftereffects. Remind students that their short stories must have clearly identifiable characters and themes. Have volunteers read their short stories to the class.
Block Scheduling

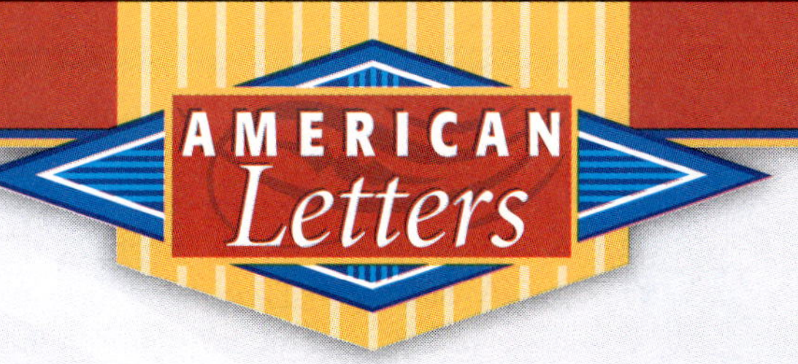

Progressive Literature

During the Progressive Era literature reflected the concerns and social ills of the time. It also influenced political reform. Frank Norris's 1901 novel The Octopus *portrays railroad financiers as villains in a story involving railroads and wheat growers in California. In the excerpt below, wheat farmers have formed a committee to try to secure the election of a commissioner who will crack down on the railroads. Upton Sinclair's* The Jungle *(1906) revealed to a horrified American public the conditions of Chicago's meatpacking industry. The excerpt below describes a typical scene at a meatpacking plant.*

from *The Octopus*
by Frank Norris

The campaign for Railroad Commissioner had been very interesting. At the very outset [beginning] Magnus's committee found itself involved in corrupt politics. The primaries had to be captured at all costs and by any means, and when the convention assembled it was found necessary to buy outright the votes of certain delegates. The campaign fund raised by contributions from Magnus, Annixter, Broderson, and Osterman was drawn upon to the extent of five thousand dollars.

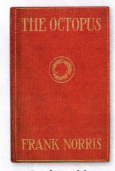

Only the committee knew of this corruption. The League, ignoring ways and means, supposed as a matter of course that the campaign was honourably conducted.

For a whole week after the consummation [completion] of this part of the deal, Magnus had kept to his house, refusing to be seen, alleging [complaining] that he was ill, which was not far from the truth. The shame of the business, the loathing [disgust] of what he had done, were to him things unspeakable. . . . He was hopelessly caught in the mesh. Wrong seemed indissolubly [permanently] knitted into the texture of Right. He was blinded, dizzied, overwhelmed, caught in the current of events, and hurried along he knew not where. He resigned himself.

Frank Norris's 1901 novel

from *The Jungle*
by Upton Sinclair

There were the wool-pluckers, whose hands went to pieces even sooner than the hands of the pickle-men; for the pelts of the sheep had to be painted with acid to loosen the wool, and then the pluckers had to pull out this wool with their bare hands, till the acid had eaten their fingers off. . . . Some worked at the stamping-machines, and it was very seldom that one could work long there at the pace that was set, and not give out and forget himself, and have a part of his hand chopped off. . . . Worst of any, however, were . . . those who served in the cooking-rooms. . . . Their peculiar trouble was that they fell into the vats; and when they were fished out, there was never enough of them left to be worth exhibiting,—sometimes they would be overlooked for days, till all but the bones of them had gone out to the world as Durham's Pure Leaf Lard!

Upton Sinclair's 1906 novel

UNDERSTANDING LITERATURE

1. How did Magnus win the election in *The Octopus?*
2. According to *The Jungle,* what were working conditions like in the meatpacking plant?
3. How is corruption depicted by both writers?

THAT'S INTERESTING!

A socialist interested in the plight of the working class, Upton Sinclair hoped that his novel would spark interest in labor reform. He included graphic details about meat processing in order to support his main idea—the exploitation of workers. "I aimed at the public's heart and by accident hit it in the stomach," he wrote. Sinclair invested his earnings from *The Jungle* in a socialist community in New Jersey.

AMERICAN LETTERS ANSWERS

1. by buying votes
2. hazardous and even fatal
3. Both writers depict corruption as an accepted part of political and business life in the United States.

internetconnect

TOPIC: Food Safety
GO TO: go.hrw.com
KEYWORD: SE1 Food

Have students access the Internet through the HRW Web site to conduct research on the issue of food safety during the early 1900s. Then tell students to assume one of the following roles: a worker in a slaughterhouse or a congressperson. Have each student write a journal entry about the need for passing food safety legislation in his or her chosen role.

TEACH OBJECTIVE 3

ALL LEVELS: Ask students to identify three or four ways of protecting the environment. *(Students might mention creating national parks, creating sanctuaries, restoring damaged areas, and following other conservation policies.)* Ask students who it was that first instituted some of these environmental policies. *(Some students might identify Theodore Roosevelt or Gifford Pinchot, but more students will not know.)* To help students understand Roosevelt's and Pinchot's role in environmental protection, copy the following graphic organizer on the chalkboard, omitting the italicized answers. Have each student complete it. **Sheltered English**

Theodore Roosevelt
- *recognized that natural resources were limited*
- *recognized that business usually took precedence, to the detriment of the environment*
- *created forest reserves*
- *started a reclamation policy*
- *worked to create national parks*

The Environment

Gifford Pinchot
- *was a dedicated forester*
- *coined the word* conservation
- *wanted to protect the environment*

▶**ASSIGNMENT** *Have each student create one or two editorial cartoons on Theodore Roosevelt and the environment.*

GEOGRAPHIC DIVERSITY

Conservation and Preservation. Advocates of conservation, such as Gifford Pinchot, viewed the environment as an important—although not inviolable—source of natural resources. Advocates of preservation, such as John Muir, opposed the commercial development of the environment. Pinchot and Muir had once been close friends, but their relationship ended when Pinchot promoted sheep grazing in forest areas. Ironically, magazine readers who lived in crowded urban areas proved to be the most ardent supporters of Muir and preservationist organizations such as the Sierra Club and the American Civil Association.

CRITICAL THINKING Why might urban residents have ardently supported preservation?

ANSWER: Students might mention that urban residents probably viewed natural areas as unsullied spaces.

***The American Nation* VIDEO PROGRAM**

Yosemite National Park; Teacher's Guide, pp. 87–92

Search 08593, Play to 15913
Videodisc 1, Side B

Play

Pause

See *Teacher's Guide* for Spanish barcode.

***Thomas Moran attempted to convey the beauty and grandeur of Yellowstone National Park in his painting* The Grand Canyon of the Yellowstone.**

Protecting the Environment

President Roosevelt's most enduring legacy may be his work in the conservation movement. He recognized that the natural resources of the United States were limited and that the needs of business had always taken priority over the environment. "In the past, we have admitted the right of the individual to injure the future of the Republic for his own present profit," he charged. "The time has come for a change."

At the end of the 1800s the country's public land was being lost to greed and mismanagement. Lumber companies acquired the rights to forestland and proceeded to cut down every tree. Ranchers grazed cattle and sheep in government-owned forests and left not even a blade of grass or a seedling behind. In 1891 fires destroyed 12 million acres of forests. Most had been started by cowhands, hunters, or sheepherders.

Gifford Pinchot (PIN-shoh) was a strong conservationist, forester, and a friend of Roosevelt. He first came up with the word *conservation* to describe the need to protect the country's natural environment. Pinchot wrote, "The conservation of

National Parks and Conservation, 1872–1984

Learning from Maps The National Park System includes parks, monuments, and historic parks. It protects the nation's cultural and historic sites as well as its natural wonders.

LOCATION Which state has the greatest land area set aside in national parks?

REVIEW

Have students complete the **Section 2 Review** on p. 281.

ASSESS

Have students complete **Daily Quiz 9.2**. As **Alternative Assessment**, you may want to use the President Roosevelt "grade" or the trust and food and drug industry wanted posters in this section's lessons.

RETEACH

Have students complete **Main Idea Activity for Reteaching and Sheltered English 9.2**. Then tell each student to create an annotated time line of domestic affairs during the Roosevelt presidency. Ask volunteers to present their time lines to the class. **Sheltered English**

EXTEND

Organize students into two groups, one focusing on Theodore Roosevelt and the other on Gifford Pinchot. Have students conduct research on the assigned figure. Then tell students to imagine that their figure has just died, and that they have been selected to deliver the eulogy at his funeral. Have each student write a three-to-five-minute eulogy on either Roosevelt or Pinchot and his attempts to protect the environment. Have two students—one eulogizing Roosevelt and one eulogizing Pinchot—deliver their speeches to the class. **Block Scheduling**

natural resources is the key to the future. It is the key to the safety and prosperity of the American people." The president proved receptive to Pinchot's ideas and made conservation a priority during his second term.

Roosevelt withdrew from sale millions of acres of public land and set aside nearly 150 million acres as forest reserves. At his urging, Congress created national parks and wildlife sanctuaries. In 1902 Congress passed the Newlands Reclamation Act. This law allowed money from the sale of public lands to be used for irrigation and **reclamation**—the process of making damaged land productive again. Roosevelt also organized a 1908 White House conference on conservation. This led to the creation of a National Conservation Commission to study natural resource issues. The conference also inspired the establishment of conservation agencies in 41 states.

Although conservation plans limited the amount of land in private hands, some businesspeople supported this new trend. Minnesota railroad business leader James J. Hill, for instance, listened to Pinchot's predictions. Hill acknowledged that using up all of the nation's mineral resources would endanger future generations—and future business. At times, the needs of the industrialists and the reformers were not so far apart. One of Pinchot's associates pointed out that conservation "was only a means to an end and the end was economic justice."

✔ **READING CHECK:** What stand did Gifford Pinchot and President Roosevelt take on the environment?

National Parks

Today, the National Park Service manages some 380 sites on more than 80 million acres of land. As in previous years, the Park Service is caught between those who wish to preserve and expand park land and those who want to make use of the natural resources. Conservationists charge that businesses are destroying wildlife habitats and old-growth forests. Business leaders counter that the demand for wood and mineral products—not to mention the protection of thousands of jobs—requires the use of wilderness resources.

Lawmakers and Park Service officials also face the problem of maintaining the parks while containing costs. More than 280 million people visit the national parks annually. To counteract the strain on park resources, officials have proposed that visitation be limited.

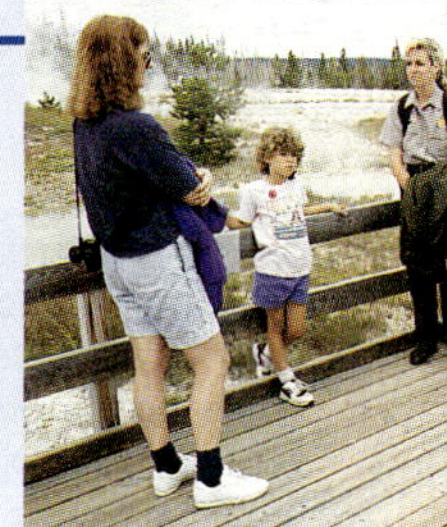

National park guide

MAP ANSWER

(for p. 280)

Idaho

SECTION 2 REVIEW ANSWERS

Define and Identify

For significance, see the following pages:

- Theodore Roosevelt, p. 275
- arbitration, p. 276
- Square Deal, p. 276
- Elkins Act, p. 277
- Hepburn Act, p. 277
- Upton Sinclair, p. 278
- Meat Inspection Act, p. 278
- Pure Food and Drug Act, p. 278
- Gifford Pinchot, p. 280
- reclamation, p. 281

1. labor—allowed workers to bargain with business owners; business—regulated businesses, limited their power; consumers—protected them from dangerous products

2. both reflected his desire to offer opportunities to all Americans

3. saw the acts as a way to protect consumers and to force companies to act in a responsible manner; protected consumers from substandard goods and dangerous additives

4. conservationists—supported Roosevelt and wanted to protect the environment; industrialists—some wanted free reign over the environment, while others recognized the need to preserve natural resources

5. His efforts ended the era of unquestioned government support for business interests.

SECTION 2 REVIEW

Define and explain the significance of the following terms:
arbitration
Square Deal
Elkins Act
Hepburn Act
Meat Inspection Act
Pure Food and Drug Act
reclamation

Identify and explain the significance of the following individuals:
Theodore Roosevelt
Upton Sinclair
Gifford Pinchot

1. **Using Graphic Organizers** President Roosevelt's Square Deal promised to balance the interests of business, labor, and consumers. Copy the graphic organizer below. Use it to describe Roosevelt's actions toward these groups.

Labor
Business
Consumers
Square Deal

2. **Identifying Values** How were President Roosevelt's values reflected in the Square Deal and in his handling of the miners' strike?
3. **Identifying Cause and Effect** Why did reformers support the Meat Inspection Act and the Pure Food and Drug Act? How did these acts help consumers?
4. **Taking a Stand** Take a stand on the side of either the conservationists or the industrialists and explain how that group might feel about Roosevelt's environmental policies.

Critical Thinking

5. How did Roosevelt's actions against trusts and railroads reflect a break with the past?
Consider:
- Roosevelt's policies against trusts and railroads
- previous policies against trusts and railroads
- how Roosevelt's policies compared to those of previous administrations

SECTION 3

After completing Section 3, students should be able to:

OBJECTIVE 1 *Relate what progressive reforms were enacted during President Taft's administration.*

OBJECTIVE 2 *Explain what divisions in the Republican Party led to the formation of the Progressive Party.*

OBJECTIVE 3 *Explain how Woodrow Wilson won the 1912 presidential election.*

LET'S GET STARTED!

Write the following question on the chalkboard: *Is true unity ever possible within a political party, or are all parties bound to be split by dissension at some point?* As students enter the classroom, ask them to respond to the question in writing. Have volunteers share their responses. Then tell students that in Section 3 they will learn why the Republican Party split over the issue of reform and how that split affected the presidential election of 1912.

SECTION 3 RESOURCES

PRINT

- Guided Reading Strategy 9.3
- Biography Reading 9: Eugene Debs
- Section 3 Review, p. 286
- Daily Quiz 9.3

MULTIMEDIA

- One-Stop Planner, Lesson 9.3
- Holt Researcher: American History CD–ROM

SHELTERED ENGLISH

- Main Idea Activity for Reteaching and Sheltered English 9.3

✔ READING TO UNDERSTAND

To help students master the section objectives, have them answer the **READING CHECKS** and complete **Guided Reading Strategy 9.3** as they read the section.

Reform Under Taft

OBJECTIVES

Read to understand:

1. what progressive reforms were enacted during President Taft's administration
2. what divisions in the Republican Party led to the formation of the Progressive Party
3. how Woodrow Wilson's won the 1912 presidential election

KEY TERMS

Mann-Elkins Act
Sixteenth Amendment
Payne-Aldrich Tariff
Ballinger-Pinchot affair
Progressive Party
New Freedom

KEY PEOPLE

William Howard Taft
Richard Ballinger
Joseph Cannon
George Norris
Woodrow Wilson
Eugene Debs

“He is not an American, you know, he is America.”
—John Morley

Theodore Roosevelt

Many people agreed with British diplomat John Morley's assessment of President Theodore Roosevelt. By the time Roosevelt neared the end of his second term in office, he was one of the most admired men in the world. Despite such international praise, Roosevelt decided not to run for president again. "The country needs a change," he declared. "We have had four years of uprooting and four years of crusading. The country has had enough of it and of me." To take himself out of the public eye, Roosevelt set out on a year-long safari to Africa as soon as the election of 1908 had ended.

Taft Takes Office

At the 1908 Republican convention President Roosevelt threw his support behind his secretary of war, William Howard Taft. Taft won the nomination on the first ballot. At the time, Roosevelt fully believed that Taft had the same reform tendencies as he did. He even told a friend that rarely had "two public men . . . ever been so much at one in all the essentials of their beliefs and practices." The Democrats again nominated William Jennings Bryan, whose pro-labor platform won the backing of the American Federation of Labor. However, the Democratic platform and Roosevelt's stances were actually quite similar. The Democrats lost the election by a wide margin in the electoral college, but by just 1.25 million popular votes.

It quickly became clear that Taft would be a different kind of president than Roosevelt. Roosevelt enjoyed being in the public eye. Taft did not. Although Taft had worked in government for years, most of his experience had come through appointed positions. He had avoided the often hostile realm of electoral politics. "I don't like politics," he once wrote. "I don't like the limelight."

William Howard Taft received the Republican Party nomination for president in 1908.

An intelligent but cautious man, Taft was fearful of overstepping the bounds of his presidential authority. Nevertheless, he chalked up a long list of accomplishments. His administration filed 90 antitrust suits, more than twice the number begun under Roosevelt.

At Taft's urging, Congress passed the **Mann-Elkins Act** in 1910, extending the regulatory powers of the Interstate Commerce Commission to telephone and telegraph companies. Taft also promoted environmental conservation by adding vast areas to the nation's forest reserves. He supported reforms to aid working people, particularly child laborers.

TEACH OBJECTIVE 1

LEVEL 1: Organize students into triads. Draw a four-column chart on the chalkboard and label the columns with the following headings: *Business Regulations, Conservation Policies, Labor Policies, Economic Policies.* Have each triad note President Taft's progressive reforms in the correct areas. *(Triads should note that Taft urged Congress to extend the power of the Interstate Commerce Commission, added land to the forest reserves, helped create a Department of Labor and passed labor-safety laws, and worked for the adoption of the Sixteenth Amendment.)* Then have triads write paragraphs summarizing Taft's achievements as a reformer.
Sheltered English, Cooperative Learning

LEVEL 2: Tell students to imagine that they are progressive Republicans during William Howard Taft's presidency. Have each student write a short political memoir discussing Taft's progressive reforms and describing his or her own reactions to those reforms. *(See the Level 1 lesson for the correct reforms.)* Ask volunteers to read their memoirs to the class. Students may wish to include their memoirs in their portfolios.

With his approval, Congress created the Department of Labor to enforce labor laws. Congress also passed mine-safety laws and established an eight-hour workday for employees of companies holding contracts with the federal government.

The Taft administration was partly responsible for the adoption of the **Sixteenth Amendment**. Proposed in 1909 and ratified in 1913, the amendment permitted Congress to levy taxes based on an individual's income. Progressives had long supported such a graduated income tax as a way to fund needed government programs in a fair manner.

✔ **READING CHECK:** What progressive reforms were enacted during President Taft's administration?

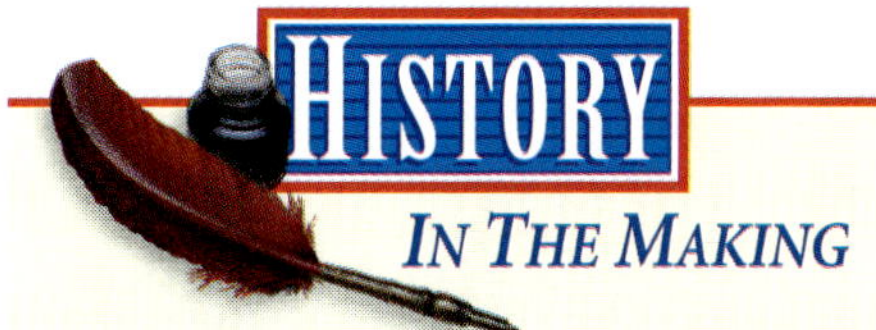

Views of Taft

BY RAYMOND HYSER

Many historians have compared William Howard Taft with Theodore Roosevelt. While Roosevelt expanded the power of the presidency and supported social-welfare legislation, Taft was reluctant to use the full powers of the presidency. He believed that judicial interpretation of the law was paramount. In a time when the American people demanded progressive change and presidential leadership, Taft moved slowly and narrowed presidential power.

Historians have offered critical assessments of Taft's presidency. Making the inevitable comparison with the Roosevelt presidency, they have emphasized Taft's political blunders and indecisiveness to explain his failings as president. One early biographer, however, argued that he was successful because he supported important legislation through a hostile Congress. In recent years, historians have provided a more balanced, objective view of Taft. Donald Anderson argues that Taft believed in the constitutional limits on the presidency and he held an almost religious commitment to the rule of law. This philosophy helps explain the conflict between Roosevelt's and Taft's leadership styles. Paola Coletta argues that Taft ranks as an "average" president who had a solid legislative record. He was a "constitutional conservator," whose term was bracketed by two powerful progressive presidents (Roosevelt and Wilson).

Taft Angers the Progressives

Despite these reforms, President Taft lost the support of progressive Republicans. This split began in April 1909 with the passage of a tariff bill.

The Payne-Aldrich Tariff. Both Taft and the progressives favored tariff reductions to lower the prices of consumer goods. Some conservative members of Congress, however, wanted high tariffs to protect American industries. They won out when the House sent a low-tariff bill to the Senate, and Senator Nelson Aldrich of Rhode Island turned it into a high-tariff measure.

Taft could have vetoed the bill or pressured Aldrich to change the tariff rates. However, Taft lacked the political skill to oppose conservative Republicans in Congress. Despite his misgivings, he signed the **Payne-Aldrich Tariff**, as the bill was called. To make matters worse, he called it "the best tariff bill that the Republican party ever passed." Outraged progressives accused Taft of betraying the reform cause.

The Ballinger-Pinchot affair. Progressives also attacked Taft for sabotaging former president Roosevelt's conservation program. The dispute revolved around Taft's secretary of the interior, Richard Ballinger, who believed that the Roosevelt administration had exceeded its authority when it stopped the sale of public land. Ballinger approved the sale of a vast tract of coal-rich Alaska timberland. As head of the U.S. Forest Service, Gifford Pinchot attacked Ballinger for favoring private interests over conservation. Taft warned Pinchot to stop criticizing Ballinger. When Pinchot ignored this warning, Taft fired him.

Taft's administration later restored the Alaskan land to the federal forest reserve. However, for progressives, the **Ballinger-Pinchot affair** signaled Taft's weakness on conservation. Taft also made one particularly dangerous enemy—Theodore Roosevelt. While Taft sent letters to Roosevelt, then on safari in Africa, defending the actions of his administration, Pinchot visited his old friend. After

CONSTITUTIONAL HERITAGE

The Sixteenth Amendment. The federal government enacted a personal income tax law in 1894. The next year, however, the Supreme Court determined that the tax was unconstitutional. In its ruling, the court noted that the Constitution bans direct taxes unless they are imposed equally upon the states according to their populations. Under the 1894 law, states with larger populations paid proportionally higher taxes. The Sixteenth Amendment eliminated this objection.

CRITICAL THINKING Why might some believe that the Sixteenth Amendment was necessary?

ANSWER: Students might respond that unless the Constitution was amended, all proposed income taxes would be declared unconstitutional.

THAT'S INTERESTING!

Theodore Roosevelt helped William Howard Taft devise a public relations strategy to win the presidency. Roosevelt advised his protégé to avoid being photographed while playing tennis or golf, both of which many Americans viewed as elitist sports.

LEVEL 3: Write the following statement on the chalkboard: *William Howard Taft—a true progressive.* Have each student write a one-to-two-page essay responding to the statement. Students' essays should discuss Taft's reforms and evaluate those reforms in light of Theodore Roosevelt's performance as president. *(See the Level 1 lesson for the correct reforms.)* Have volunteers read their essays to the class. Students may wish to include their essays in their portfolios. After students have read their essays to the class, ask them to reread the feature on the previous page. Then conduct a discussion on Taft and his presidency. How was Taft's performance as a president? Have historical views of Taft's presidency been irrevocably influenced by Theodore Roosevelt's strong personality and performance? Is it possible to have an "unbiased" view of Taft or any other president?

▸**ASSIGNMENT** *Tell students to imagine that they are progressive Republicans during William Howard Taft's presidency. Tell them to imagine that they are preparing to interview Taft. Have each student compile a list of five or more questions about his reforms. Tell students to answer their own questions as Taft might have answered them.*

PEOPLE IN HISTORY

Gifford Pinchot. After graduating from Yale University, Gifford Pinchot studied at forestry schools in Austria, France, Germany, and Switzerland. When he returned home, he began to practice forest management and conservation at Biltmore, the lavish North Carolina estate of industrialist Cornelius Vanderbilt. In 1898 Pinchot became the head of the agency that eventually became the U.S. Forest Service. Under Gifford Pinchot's leadership, the organization–and the natural resources under its control–expanded enormously. In 1898 it oversaw 19 national forests. By 1909 there were 149 national forests.

CRITICAL THINKING Why might Pinchot have reacted so strongly to Richard Ballinger's sale of the Alaskan timberland?

ANSWER: Students might respond that Pinchot had devoted his life to forestry preservation. He regarded Ballinger's act as extremely dangerous.

VISUAL RECORD ANSWER

Students might suggest that the cartoon shows the two taking totally different approaches to win the nomination.

Theodore Roosevelt's **The New Nationalism** *outlined his view of government's role in American society.*

speaking with Pinchot, Roosevelt confided in Senator Henry Cabot Lodge, "I don't think that under the Taft . . . regime there has been a real appreciation of the needs of the country." Roosevelt soon broke with Taft over the Pinchot controversy.

Roosevelt and the elections of 1910. In the congressional elections of 1910, Roosevelt campaigned on behalf of progressive Republicans who opposed Taft. Roosevelt proposed a program called New Nationalism—a series of tough laws to protect workers, ensure public health, and regulate business. He declared:

> "The true friend of property, the true conservative, is he who insists that property shall be the servant and not the master of the commonwealth. . . . The citizens of the United States must effectively control the mighty commercial forces which they have themselves called into being."

Government, Roosevelt said, must become the "steward [manager] of the public welfare." His call for a more activist federal government represented an even more progressive position than he had taken as president. Delighted, reformers hailed the New Nationalism as a revival of the progressive spirit.

Despite Roosevelt's help on the campaign trail, the Republicans lost control of the House of Representatives for the first time in 16 years. Nearly all the newly elected Democrats unseated conservative Republicans. Roosevelt, as well as Taft, was deeply disappointed by the election.

INTERPRETING THE VISUAL RECORD

Republican Party division. After the elections of 1910, president Taft and former president Theodore Roosevelt held increasingly opposing positions on progressive reforms. ***How does this cartoon depict the opposition between Taft and Roosevelt?***

THE GRANGER COLLECTION, NEW YORK

The Republican Party Divides

Not long before Theodore Roosevelt proposed New Nationalism, a bitter dispute in Congress had further deepened the gulf between President Taft and the progressives. In the spring of 1910, progressive Republicans in Congress launched a major attack on Speaker of the House Joseph "Uncle Joe" Cannon of Illinois, a conservative Republican. Cannon, a 73-year-old tobacco-chewing poker player, was one of Washington's most powerful politicians. He ruled the House with an iron hand, appointing all its committees and naming their chairpersons. As head of the powerful Rules Committee, which determined the order of business in the House, Cannon prevented bills he opposed from even reaching the House floor for debate.

The Cannon debate. Progressives charged that Cannon used his power to block reform legislation. "Not one cent for scenery," he had growled in dismissing a call for environmental protection. In March 1910 Representative George Norris, a progressive from Nebraska, began an effort to break Cannon's power. Norris proposed that House members elect the Rules Committee and that the Speaker be excluded from membership on it.

After a heated debate, Norris's motion passed. A year later, the representatives also stripped the Speaker of the House of the power to appoint members to other committees—a major progressive victory. However, Taft's refusal to take their side throughout this bitter debate angered many progressives.

TEACH OBJECTIVES 2 AND 3

ALL LEVELS: Ask students how and why Woodrow Wilson won the presidential election of 1912. *(Most students will not be able to answer the question.)* To help students understand how a split in the Republican Party and the creation of the Progressive Party helped ensure Wilson's election, copy the following graphic organizer on the chalkboard, omitting the italicized answers. Have each student complete it. After students have completed the graphic organizer, write the following saying on the chalkboard: *Don't cut off your nose to spite your face.* Ask each student to write a half-page essay discussing the statement in relation to the Republican Party and the election of 1912. **Sheltered English**

Divisions in the Republican Party
- *members differed over William Howard Taft's performance—some saw him as eroding Theodore Roosevelt's policies*
  - *the Ballinger-Pinchot affair*
  - *the attack on Joseph Cannon*

↓

The Formation of the Progressive Party

↓

Effect on the Presidential Election of 1912
- *split the Republican Party*
- *siphoned votes from Taft and gave votes to Woodrow Wilson*
  - *resulted in a Democratic victory and the election of Wilson*

Roosevelt returns to politics. Completely at odds with President Taft, Theodore Roosevelt decided to run again for the presidency. Borrowing a prize-fighting term, he declared, "My hat is in the ring." Roosevelt won almost every Republican state primary, including the one in Taft's home state, Ohio.

Nevertheless, Taft's allies firmly held control of the party machinery. At the Republican Convention, they refused to seat many of Roosevelt's delegates. "Don't you realize you're wrecking the Republican Party?" shouted one progressive senator. When Taft won the nomination, Roosevelt's supporters walked out. Their leaders organized their own convention, asking those in the Roosevelt camp to oppose this "crime which represents treason to the people." They adopted a platform based on the New Nationalism and nominated Roosevelt as their presidential candidate. Thus was born the **Progressive Party**, also called the Bull Moose Party after Roosevelt declared that he felt "fit as a bull moose" to run.

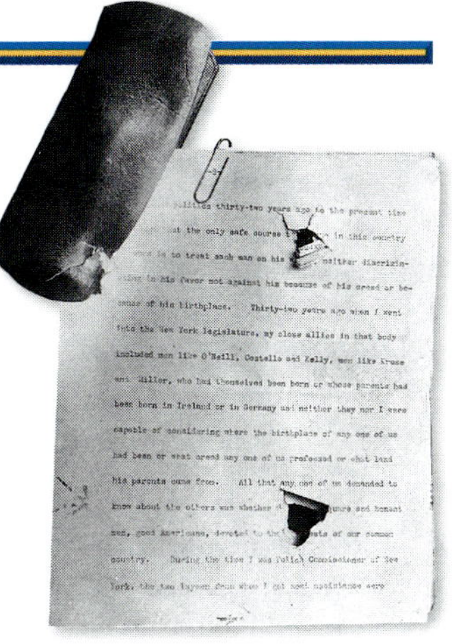

While giving a speech in 1912, Theodore Roosevelt was wounded in an assassination attempt. He finished the speech with a bullet lodged in his body.

✔ **READING CHECK:** What were the divisions within the Republican Party that led to the formation of the Progressive Party?

A Democratic Victory

The division in the Republican Party practically assured a Democratic victory. The Democrats united behind one candidate, Governor Woodrow Wilson of New Jersey. He ran on a platform calling for tariff reduction, banking reform, laws benefiting wage earners and farmers, and stronger antitrust legislation.

The Wilson program. A native of Virginia and a political newcomer, Wilson had long nurtured dreams of high office. He eventually became a professor of political science at Princeton University in New Jersey. Wilson later served as its president. He was elected governor in 1910. In his short time as governor, he fought the state's Democratic Party bosses and pushed through laws regulating business. Wilson's status as an outspoken reformer and eloquent speaker made him the presidential choice of progressives in the Democratic Party.

In the 1912 campaign, Wilson's **New Freedom** program made proposals to help small businesses. He also called for a return to an America where people were free from the heavy hand of big business and government. Wilson asserted:

The Election of 1912

Learning from Maps Although Wilson won the electoral vote by a landslide, the only states outside the former Confederacy where he won at least half the popular vote were Kentucky, Maryland, and Oklahoma.

? LOCATION Which state split its electoral vote?

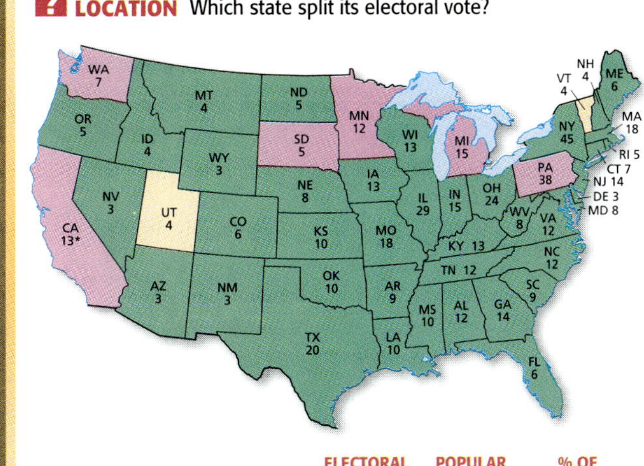

CANDIDATE	PARTY	ELECTORAL VOTE	POPULAR VOTE	% OF POPULAR VOTE
Wilson	Democratic	435*	6,296,547	41.9
T. Roosevelt	Progressive	88	4,118,571	27.4
Taft	Republican	8	3,486,720	23.2
Debs	Socialist		900,672	6.0
Other parties			235,025	1.6

*Two electors in California voted for Wilson.

Source: *Historical Statistics of the United States*

DEMOCRATIC VALUES

The Republican Nomination. On the whole, Republican voters favored Theodore Roosevelt over William Howard Taft. In the 13 states that held party primaries, Roosevelt received some 1.1 million votes, while Taft received only some 74,000. These results earned Roosevelt the votes of 278 delegates, while Taft earned the votes of only 48 delegates. However, Taft received most of the votes of the delegates from those states that used party conventions rather than primaries to select delegates, a fact that revealed his control of the party machinery.

CRITICAL THINKING Was the result of the nomination a democratic one?

ANSWER: Some students might argue that it did not represent the true preferences of the voters.

THAT'S INTERESTING!

Woodrow Wilson did not learn to read until he was nine years old, and for the rest of his life he read very slowly. Some historians believe that he may have suffered from a learning disability such as dyslexia. Nevertheless, Wilson graduated from Princeton and taught in many prestigious universities.

MAP ANSWER
California

REVIEW

Have students complete the **Section 3 Review** on p. 286.

ASSESS

Have students complete **Daily Quiz 9.3.** As **Alternative Assessment,** you may want to use the President Taft reforms graphic organizer or President Taft reforms essay in this section's lessons.

RETEACH

Have students complete **Main Idea Activity for Reteaching and Sheltered English 9.3.** Then organize students into small groups. Have each group create a detailed outline of Section 3. Ask groups to exchange their outlines and use them to write paragraphs summarizing the material in the section. **Sheltered English, Cooperative Learning**

EXTEND

Write the following statement on the chalkboard: *President Taft identified the right problems, but offered the wrong solutions.* Have each student write a short essay evaluating the statement and responding to it. **Block Scheduling**

SECTION 3 REVIEW ANSWERS

Define and Identify

For significance, see the following pages:

- William Howard Taft, p. 282
- Mann-Elkins Act, p. 282
- Sixteenth Amendment, p. 283
- Payne-Aldrich Tariff, p. 283
- Richard Ballinger, p. 283
- Ballinger-Pinchot affair, p. 283
- Joseph Cannon, p. 284
- George Norris, p. 284
- Progressive Party, p. 285
- Woodrow Wilson, p. 285
- New Freedom, p. 285
- Eugene Debs, p. 286

1. Taft deviates from Roosevelt's programs; Roosevelt breaks with Taft; Taft defeats Roosevelt for the 1912 Republican nomination; Roosevelt runs as the Progressive Party candidate

2. expanded the powers of the Interstate Commerce Commission, promoted conservation, filed antitrust suits, supported labor laws and the income tax

3. Taft might have retained Roosevelt's support, prevented a split within the Republican Party, and won the 1912 presidential election.

4. Answers will vary. Some students might argue that Taft compiled an impressive record as a reformer.

5. The candidates' platforms revealed that all the parties—from the Republicans to the socialists—wanted progressive reforms.

Read More About It

Free Find:
Woodrow Wilson

After reading about Woodrow Wilson on the Holt Researcher CD–ROM, imagine that you are a political journalist. Write a short summary of the outcome of the election and what it says about the desires of American voters.

Woodrow Wilson's moderate reform proposals attracted many voters during the 1912 election.

> **"The only way that government is kept pure is by keeping . . . channels open, so that . . . there will constantly be coming new blood into the veins of the body politic."**

Although Wilson shared the progressive belief that government should be an agent of reform, he believed that if government became too strong it could limit individual freedom. He believed that reform efforts should seek to remove barriers to free competition but not significantly alter the free-enterprise system.

Wilson sweeps the election. Wilson's reform goals differed from those of Roosevelt, who accepted the new corporate and industrial order even as he proposed to regulate and control it. Wilson's ideas also differed from another candidate for president, Eugene Debs of the Socialist Party. The Socialist Party had done very well in the 1910 elections. It supported a radically different economic order, including public ownership of all major industries. In Debs, Wilson, and Roosevelt, American voters had a choice of three strong, reform-minded candidates. Even Taft supported some reform programs, although he appeared to represent a more conservative viewpoint.

As expected, Wilson won the election. Some Republicans even voted for him, seeing it as a vote against Roosevelt. Wilson received 435 electoral votes to Roosevelt's 88 and Taft's 8. Debs won more than 900,000 popular votes but no electoral votes. Of the more than 15 million votes cast, the three reform-minded challengers received some 11 million. Although Wilson won just 6 million popular votes, he took office with a strong call for reform.

✔ **READING CHECK:** How did Woodrow Wilson win the 1912 presidential election?

SECTION 3 REVIEW

Define and explain the significance of the following terms:

Mann-Elkins Act
Sixteenth Amendment
Payne-Aldrich Tariff
Ballinger-Pinchot affair
Progressive Party
New Freedom

Identify and explain the significance of the following individuals:

William Howard Taft
Richard Ballinger
Joseph Cannon
George Norris
Woodrow Wilson
Eugene Debs

1. Using Graphic Organizers Copy the diagram below. Use it to explain the steps that led from Taft's victory in 1908 to Wilson's victory in 1912.

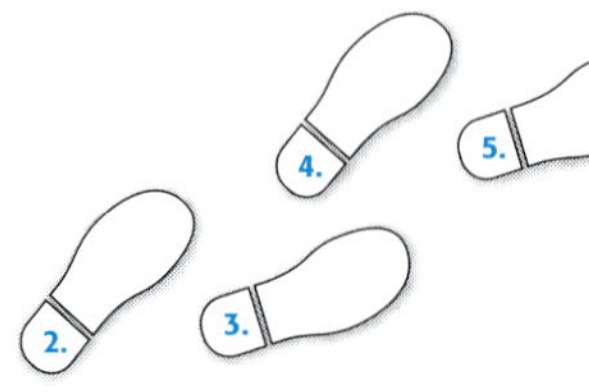

6. With the Republican Party divided, Wilson wins easily in 1912.
5.
4.
3.
2.
1. Taft wins in 1908 with Roosevelt's support.

2. Synthesizing What progressive reforms did President Taft institute?

3. Hypothesizing What might have happened if Taft had vetoed the Payne-Aldrich Tariff and not fired Gifford Pinchot?

4. Distinguishing Fact from Opinion Supporters of the Progressive Party believed that Taft betrayed the progressive ideals of the Roosevelt administration. Comparing Taft's reform record to Roosevelt's, was this a fair assessment? Why or why not?

Critical Thinking

5. What did the positions of the candidates in the 1912 election reveal about the range of progressive reform ideas?

Consider:

- what the positions of the candidates were in 1912
- how well those positions reflected progressive ideals

After completing Section 4, students should be able to:

OBJECTIVE 1 *Describe how Woodrow Wilson's proposals affected big business and U.S. citizens.*

OBJECTIVE 2 *Explain how President Wilson attempted to help farmers and laborers, and how successful his efforts were.*

OBJECTIVE 3 *Discuss how American women gained the right to vote.*

LET'S GET STARTED!

Write the following scenario on the chalkboard: *It is 1914. You are a woman. You do not have the right to vote. How do you go about winning that right? Do you work within the system for change, or do you stage protests? Do you use "any means necessary"—including illegal ones?* As students enter the classroom, ask them to respond to the scenario in writing. Have volunteers share their responses. Tell students that in Section 4 they will learn how American women gained the right to vote.

Wilson's "New Freedom"

OBJECTIVES

Read to understand:

1. how President Wilson's proposals affected big business and U.S. citizens
2. how Wilson attempted to help farmers and laborers, and how successful his efforts were
3. how American women gained the right to vote

KEY TERMS

Federal Reserve Act
Clayton Antitrust Act
Federal Trade Commission
Adamson Act
Keating-Owen Child Labor Act
National American Woman Suffrage Association
Nineteenth Amendment

KEY PEOPLE

Alice Paul
Carrie Chapman Catt

EYEWITNESSES TO History

"We have been proud of our industrial achievements, but we have not . . . stopped . . . to count the . . . fearful physical and spiritual cost to the men and women and children upon whom the . . . weight and burden of it all has fallen. . . . This is not a day of triumph; it is a day of dedication. Here muster [gather], not the forces of party, but the forces of humanity."

—Woodrow Wilson

President Wilson and friend Edward M. House

President Woodrow Wilson eloquently summed up the spirit of the progressive reform movement in his first inaugural address on March 4, 1913. In the months before his inauguration, Wilson prepared for the work ahead of him. Wilson turned to his friend, Edward M. House for help planning his cabinet and policies. Wilson considered House a man who "wants . . . to serve the common cause and to help me and others."

Reform on Many Fronts

President Wilson and Edward House settled on a cabinet that included the first-ever secretary of labor, a position that went to a labor leader. Its creation was in itself a progressive act. Wilson's appointments attempted to reflect and satisfy the divisions within the Democratic Party.

After settling on a cabinet, Wilson presented his legislative agenda. It included tariff and banking reforms and stronger antitrust laws. The program was opposed by business groups and lobbyists, but Wilson skillfully rallied support in Congress and among the American people.

Tariffs. Wilson's first priority was to lower tariffs. This had long been a goal of the Democratic Party's southern pro-agriculture wing. Wilson knew that supporters of big business had blocked tariff reduction during Taft's presidency. To plead his case, Wilson addressed both houses of Congress in person—something that had not been done since President John Adams's administration. The opponents of a lower tariff did not easily give way to presidential pressure. Describing the strength of the business lobby, Secretary of Agriculture David Houston wrote, "It was impossible to move around without bumping into [lobbyists]—at hotels, clubs, and even private houses." Wilson criticized the "money without limit" spent by the lobbyists and began a public campaign to combat their influence.

His strategy worked. Despite initial Senate opposition Congress passed the Underwood Tariff Act in 1913. It reduced tariffs to their lowest levels in more than 50 years. To make up for lost revenue, the bill introduced a graduated income tax. This would tax people with high incomes at a higher rate than those with low incomes. The new tax affected people earning $20,000 or more per year.

In his inaugural address on March 4, 1913, President Woodrow Wilson explained that reform legislation would be a top priority.

SECTION 4 RESOURCES

PRINT
- Guided Reading Strategy 9.4
- Literature Reading 9: Life as a Factory Worker
- Primary Source Reading 9: Child Labor Practices
- Graphic Organizer Activity 9: Women's Suffrage
- Section 4 Review, p. 293
- Daily Quiz 9.4

MULTIMEDIA
- One-Stop Planner, Lesson 9.4
- Holt Researcher: American History CD–ROM

SHELTERED ENGLISH
- Main Idea Activity for Reteaching and Sheltered English 9.4

✔ READING TO UNDERSTAND

To help students master the section objectives, have them answer the **READING CHECKS** and complete **Guided Reading Strategy 9.4** as they read the section.

TEACH OBJECTIVE 1

ALL LEVELS: To help students understand how President Wilson's proposals affected big business and U.S. citizens, copy the graphic organizer at the right on the chalkboard, omitting the italicized answers. Ask each student to complete it. After students have finished their graphic organizers, ask them to write paragraphs evaluating the overall success of Wilson's reforms. **Sheltered English**

▶**ASSIGNMENT** *Tell students to imagine that they are public relations advisers to President Wilson. Ask each student to develop a media campaign to "sell" Wilson's business reforms to the American public. Remind students that their campaigns must explain the reforms, as well as present supporting arguments.*

PRESIDENT WILSON AND BIG BUSINESS

TARIFF REFORM
reform: *Underwood Tariff Act*
effects: *allowed the government to investigate corporations; allowed the government to issue "cease and desist" orders*

BANKING REFORM
reform: *Federal Reserve Act*
effects: *created "bankers' banks" stabilized the banking system; helped small farmers gain access to lower interest rates*

GENERAL BUSINESS REFORM
reform: *Clayton Antitrust Act*
effects: *extended the 1890 Sherman Antitrust Act; helped the government regulate monopolies*

reform: *Federal Trade Commission*
effects: *allowed the government to investigate corporations; allowed the government to issue "cease and desist" orders*

HISTORY MAKERS SPEAK

Woodrow Wilson in *For the Record: A Documentary History of America*, Vol. 2

Wilson and the Trusts. Wilson explained his opposition to trusts in a campaign speech. "You know, of course, how the little man is crushed by the trusts. He gets a local market. The big concerns come in and undersell him in his local market, and that is the only market he has; if he cannot make a profit there, he is killed. They can make a profit through all the rest of the Union, while they are underselling him in his locality, and recouping themselves by what they can earn elsewhere. Thus their competitors can be put out of business, one by one, wherever they dare to show a head."

CRITICAL THINKING
According to Wilson, how did trusts eliminate competition?

ANSWER: Students should respond that Wilson indicated that trusts dropped their prices to drive local competitors out of markets. The trusts could do this because they made profits elsewhere.

VISUAL RECORD ANSWER
(for p. 289)
Students might suggest that she wanted to serve as an important presence in support of reform.

Woodrow Wilson

1856–1924
In Office 1913–1921

Woodrow Wilson had a reputation for being overly serious and inflexible. He often found it difficult to compromise. At times he opposed legislation that he himself had originally proposed if it had been amended by someone else. He once told a political associate, "I am sorry for those who disagree with me. . . . Because I know they are wrong."

Yet, despite his seriousness, Wilson was superstitious when it came to the number 13, which he believed was his lucky number. He pointed out that there were 13 letters in his name and often referred to the fact that the United States originally had 13 states. When he sailed to Europe for the Paris Peace Conference following World War I, he even instructed the captain to delay docking for one day. He wanted to arrive on the 13th of December.

The tax rate ranged from 1 percent for people earning $20,000 to 6 percent for those earning more than $50,000. By 1916, individuals who made as little as $3,000 annually also had to pay income tax. Supporters argued that the income tax created a fairer tax system.

Banking. Next on Wilson's agenda was banking reform. At the time, no central fund existed from which banks could borrow to prevent collapse during financial panics. As a result, banks commonly failed when many people withdrew their deposits at the same time. Reform was clearly necessary, but Americans disagreed on how to change the banking system. Conservative business groups wanted to give the nation's large private banks more control. In contrast, many Democrats and progressive Republicans wanted the government to run the system.

Wilson helped draft the **Federal Reserve Act** of 1913, which combined these two views. It created a three-tiered banking system. At the top was the Federal Reserve Board, a group appointed by the president and charged with running the system. At the second level were 12 Federal Reserve banks, under mixed public and private control. These "bankers' banks" served other banks rather than individuals. At the third level were private banks, which could borrow from the Federal Reserve banks at interest rates set by the Board. The bill particularly helped farmers by giving them access to lower interest rates. "It puts them on a footing with other business men and masters of enterprise, as it should," Wilson pointed out. "They will find themselves quit of many of the difficulties which now hamper them in the field of credit."

This 1913 cartoon depicts President Wilson's antitrust legislation as a fence protecting small businesses.

Big business. Having achieved important tariff and banking reforms, Wilson turned to business regulation. He wanted to limit the power of monopolies, which he viewed as a threat to small businesses. Toward this end, Wilson backed passage of the **Clayton Antitrust Act** in October 1914. This act clarified and extended the 1890 Sherman Antitrust Act by clearly stating what corporations could not do. For example, companies could not sell goods below cost to drive competitors out of business. Nor could they buy competing companies' stock to create a monopoly. The bill did not outlaw these actions in all cases. It was only illegal when the government could prove that a company was doing these things to intentionally create a monopoly. One senator concluded that the original Clayton bill "was a raging lion with a mouth full of teeth." The act as passed, however, had

TEACH OBJECTIVE 2

LEVEL 1: Ask students to identify how President Wilson attempted to help farmers and laborers. *(Students should note that Wilson urged Congress to pass the Federal Farm Loan Act and the Federal Workmen's Compensation Act.)* Ask students to assess the success of these efforts. *(Students should note that Wilson failed to settle the 1916 railroad strike or to end child labor.)* Tell students to imagine that they are either farmers or workers. Have each student write a 25-word telegram to President Wilson urging him to support pro-farmer or pro-worker legislation. Ask volunteers to read their telegrams to the class. Students may wish to include their telegrams in their portfolios. **Sheltered English**

LEVELS 2 AND 3: Tell students to imagine that they are modern-day historians attending a conference. Tell students to imagine that the keynote speaker has just made the following statement: *President Wilson accomplished so much on behalf of farmers and laborers that he deserves to be known as "the friend of the people."* Have each student prepare a two-to-three-minute response to the statement. *(See the Level 1 lesson for the correct points.)* Remind students that their responses must be grounded in fact and should draw on the material presented in the textbook. Ask volunteers to deliver their responses to the class.

"degenerated [been reduced] to a tabby cat with soft gums, a plaintive [sad] mew, and an anemic appearance." Despite its shortcomings, the American Federation of Labor (AFL) enthusiastically praised Wilson's support of the Clayton Act. AFL leader Samuel Gompers called it "the Magna Charter of American labor."

As part of the New Freedom program, the Wilson administration backed the creation of the **Federal Trade Commission** (FTC) by Congress in September 1914. The FTC was authorized to investigate corporations. It could issue "cease and desist orders" to corporations engaged in unfair or fraudulent practices and use the courts to enforce its rulings. The FTC targeted abuses such as mislabeled products and false claims. Progressives were displeased, however, when Wilson appointed a number of people who were sympathetic to big business to the commission.

Advertisements like this one made unsupported claims about a product's benefits.

✔ **READING CHECK:** How did Wilson's proposals affect big business and U.S. citizens?

Wilson and Workers

In 1914 Walter Lippmann assessed President Wilson's New Freedom program. He wrote, "The New Freedom means the effort of small business men and farmers to use the government against the larger collective organization of industry." Throughout his first term, Wilson supported legislation to aid working people.

Farm and labor acts. Congress passed the Federal Farm Loan Act in 1916. This act provided low-interest loans to farmers by setting up 12 federal farm-loan banks, each with $750,000 capital to distribute to needy farmers. Some politicians complained that the act used "public resources to do for some what is not done for others." However, the law won strong support in rural areas of the United States.

Also in 1916, a railroad strike threatened to paralyze the nation's rail lines. Wilson invited labor leaders and railroad managers to the White House to work out an agreement. He reminded both sides about the disastrous effects such a strike could have on the nation's economy and citizens. When these efforts failed, he addressed Congress in support of a law that would reduce the workday for railroad workers from 10 to 8 hours without a cut in pay. The ensuing **Adamson Act** not only won applause from reformers but prevented the strike.

Congress also passed the Federal Workmen's Compensation Act with Wilson's support to provide benefits to federal workers injured on the job. Other Wilson labor initiatives included a provision in the Clayton Antitrust Act that affirmed labor's right to strike so long as property was not permanently damaged.

Child labor. The Wilson administration was less successful in its campaign against child labor. For years progressives had wanted to keep young children from working in factories, mills, and mines. Labor organizer Mother Jones later recalled the impact of such work.

> **"Every day little children came into Union Headquarters, some with their hands off, some with the thumb missing, some with their fingers off at the knuckle. They were stooped little things, round shouldered and skinny. Many were not over ten years of age."**

INTERPRETING THE VISUAL RECORD

Mother Jones. Mary Harris Jones fought for better working conditions and child labor laws throughout her life. At the age of 70, she marched in this 1910 protest march. ***Why do you think Mother Jones continued to march in protests?***

ECONOMIC DEVELOPMENT

The Federal Trade Commission. President Wilson viewed the Federal Trade Commission as an organization to foster cooperation between government and business. He therefore appointed businessmen, such as industrialist Edward Hurley, to head the FTC. Many progressives, however, saw the FTC as an agency to observe and regulate industries. Wilson's appointments confused and angered them.

CRITICAL THINKING What might Wilson's appointments to the FTC have revealed about his attitudes toward industry?

ANSWER: Students may suggest that Wilson's appointments revealed that he wanted to work with business leaders, not oppose them.

THAT'S INTERESTING!

Among the reform measures passed during Wilson's presidency was the Seaman's Act, which set labor standards for sailors on U.S. ships and those on foreign ships visiting U.S. ports. One provision of the act stipulated that at least 75 percent of a vessel's crew understand the language spoken by the ship's officers.

SPOTLIGHT on the Armory Show

Ask students to conduct research on the Armory Show. Have students select one artist whose work appeared in the show, such as Vincent Van Gogh, Paul Cézanne, or Marcel Duchamp. Ask each student to create a five-minute multimedia presentation on his or her chosen artist. Students' presentations should offer general biographical information, discuss the person's entry into art, describe the artist's work, and possibly display selected pieces. Ask volunteers to display their multimedia presentations to the class. Students may wish to include tapes or scripts of their presentations in their portfolios.
Block Scheduling

SPOTLIGHT on Child Labor

Ask students to conduct research on modern-day efforts to eradicate child labor, especially those efforts led by teenagers. Have each student prepare a short oral presentation on the issue. Students should discuss specific efforts, describe their causes, and assess their effects. Ask volunteers to deliver their presentations to the class. Then have students select the most effective effort. To extend the lesson, ask students to somehow participate in the fight against child labor. Students might write letters to their representatives, for example, or collect signatures on petitions. **Block Scheduling**

ECONOMIC DEVELOPMENT

Child Labor. Children played an important role in the nation's economy during the early years of the 1900s. The 1900 census revealed that some 1.75 million children between the ages of 10 and 15 held jobs. Ten years later, the number had risen to some 1.99 million. Many parents forced their children to work. The average family needed at least $800 a year to survive, but the average unskilled job paid less than $500 a year, creating a dangerous shortfall.

ACTIVITY: Tell students to imagine that it is 1916 and that they are child workers. Have each student write a letter to President Wilson asking him to pass child labor laws.

THAT'S INTERESTING!

Children in Georgia's Columbus Manufacturing Mill worked from 5:30 A.M. to 5:30 P.M. without a lunch break. Mill owner Frederick Gordon opposed child labor laws because mill owners had made a "gentleman's agreement" to limit 10-year-olds to a 66-hour week.

AMERICAN ARTS ANSWERS

1. to introduce modern art to the American public
2. They argued that modern artists did not possess talent.

Rising protests against child labor from the National Consumers' League and other groups prompted Congress to pass the **Keating-Owen Child Labor Act** in 1916. Backed by Wilson, the act outlawed the interstate sale of products produced by child labor. In 1918, however, the Supreme Court declared the law unconstitutional because it restricted commerce instead of directly outlawing child labor. Another law, passed in 1919, met the same fate.

✔ **READING CHECK:** How did President Wilson attempt to help farmers and laborers? How successful were these efforts?

AMERICAN ARTS

The Armory Show

The progressive reform spirit influenced art as well as economic policies in the early 1900s. Just as reformers attacked business trusts, artists tackled the leading American museums' control over which paintings and sculptures the public saw. Determined to introduce the American public to modern art, a small group of artists formed the Association of American Painters and Sculptors (AAPS) in 1912. The group combed galleries and studios in Berlin, Munich, Paris, and The Hague in search of works to display. On February 17, 1913, the International Exhibition of Modern Art opened in the 69th Regiment Armory in New York City. The Armory Show, as it was called, presented some 1,600 works by both European and American artists.

Newspaper reporters raved about the show, calling it "an event not to be missed." Art critics were not so kind. They blasted Vincent Van Gogh as "unskilled" and Paul Cézanne as "absolutely without talent." As for Marcel Duchamp's *Nude Descending a Staircase,* one critic described it as "an explosion in a shingle factory." Ironically, the critics' hostility boosted attendance, which exceeded the organizers' wildest dreams.

Even if it failed to win over some critics to modern art, the Armory Show was a huge success in terms of attendance and publicity. Before the show moved to Chicago, the AAPS honored its "friends and enemies" in the press with a steak dinner. Speeches were made; diners sang and danced. One hostile critic offered grudging praise. "It was a good show," he said, "but don't do it again."

Marcel Duchamp's **Nude Descending a Staircase**

Understanding the Arts

1. What was the purpose of the Armory Show?
2. How did some critics react to modern art?

TEACH OBJECTIVE 3

LEVEL 1: Ask students to reread the subsection entitled Different approaches. Then organize students into two groups, one representing the National American Woman Suffrage Association's (NAWSA) approach to voting rights, and one representing the National Woman's Party's approach to voting rights. Act as the moderator and conduct a debate between the groups based on strategies. *(The NAWSA group should support a nonpartisan, local approach, while the National Woman's Party group should support a national, more radical approach.)* When the debate is finished, ask each student to write one or two paragraphs discussing the different strategies and explaining how American women gained the right to vote. *(Women pressed for a constitutional amendment, pressured appropriate senators, and finally gained the right to vote with the Nineteenth Amendment.)* Students may wish to include their paragraphs in their portfolios. **Sheltered English**

LEVEL 2: Tell students to imagine that it is 1930 and that they are suffragists preparing to speak at a 10th-anniversary celebration of the Nineteenth Amendment. Have each student write a three-to-four-minute speech describing how women gained the right to vote. *(See the Level 1 lesson for the correct factors.)* Ask volunteers to deliver their speeches to the class. Students may wish to include their speeches in their portfolios.

The Struggle for Women's Suffrage

Another part of the progressive agenda—the campaign for women's suffrage—faced strong opposition. Liquor interests feared that women would vote for prohibition. Businesses feared that the vote would empower women to demand better wages and working conditions. When one state senator expressed the belief that the vote would rob women of their beauty and charm, a suffragist reacted angrily.

> **"We have women working in the foundries. . . . Women in the laundries . . . stand for 13 or 14 hours in the terrible steam and heat with their hands in hot starch. Surely these women won't lose any more of their beauty and charm by putting a ballot in a ballot box once a year than they are likely to lose standing in foundries or laundries all year."**

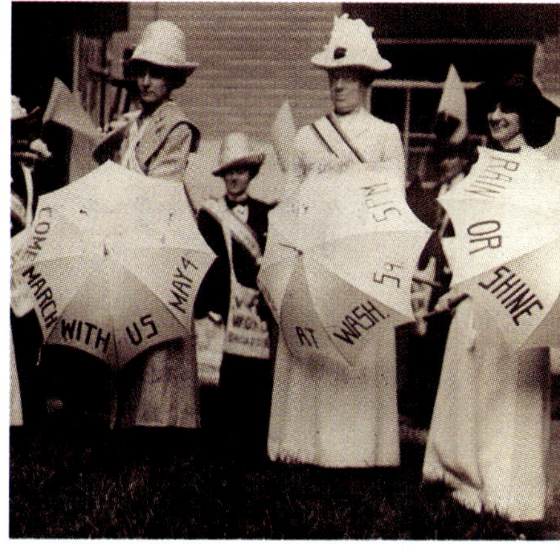

INTERPRETING THE VISUAL RECORD

Women's suffrage. Suffragists struggled to convince both men and women that politics was a proper activity for women. ***In what ways do you think these demonstrators were able to further the suffragist cause?***

Different approaches. One leading force in the suffrage movement was the **National American Woman Suffrage Association** (NAWSA), founded in 1890. Its first two presidents, Elizabeth Cady Stanton and Susan B. Anthony, distrusted party politics because of Republican leaders' failure after the Civil War to press for voting rights for women. As a result, they took a nonpartisan, local approach, trying to get state legislatures to grant women the vote. They achieved few successes in their first few years of lobbying, however. By 1901 just four states, all located in the western region of the country, had given women full voting rights.

In 1914 Alice Paul, a militant young Quaker suffragist, broke away from NAWSA. She formed a second organization, the Congressional Union for Woman Suffrage, which in 1916 became the National Woman's Party. The party adopted a national rather than a state-by-state strategy, focusing on passing a constitutional amendment guaranteeing women the right to vote.

Paul had studied in Britain and adopted the attention-getting protest tactics used by British suffragists. For example, in January 1917, after Wilson's re-election, the National Woman's Party began round-the-clock picketing of the White House in an effort to pressure Wilson to support a suffrage amendment. They held banners asking, "Mr. President, What Will You Do for Woman Suffrage?" and "How Long Must Women Wait for Liberty?" Some women chained themselves to railings. Many were arrested. Some went on hunger strikes in prison. Paul's efforts convinced thousands of women of the importance of the suffragists' cause.

Meanwhile, the suffrage movement picked up momentum. Massachusetts, New Jersey, New York, and Pennsylvania all held special referendums on women's suffrage in 1915. Although the motions were defeated in each state, support for women's suffrage ranged from 35 to 46 percent of the total votes. NAWSA saw its membership grow to nearly 2 million. Energized by the leadership of the highly skilled organizer Carrie Chapman Catt, the organization continued its use of traditional political strategies to attain voting rights.

Alice Paul gives a speech to members of the National Woman's Party.

GLOBAL RELATIONS

British Suffragists. Many American suffragists were inspired by their British counterparts, some of whom used radical protest methods. Emmeline Pankhurst of the Women's Social and Political Union, and her daughter, Christabel, were militant protesters. They invaded political meetings and demanded the right to participate. When barred entry to meetings, the protesters disguised themselves as boys, messengers, or cleaning ladies to gain admittance. In one instance, a radical suffragist climbed atop a roof and threw roof tiles through a skylight at a speaker. Initially, most American women rejected such extreme behavior, choosing instead to march in parades to draw attention to their cause.

CRITICAL THINKING Are radical protest methods–including violent or illegal methods–ever justified?

ANSWER: Answers will vary. Some students might argue that in extreme cases, such as those signaled by near-complete political disenfranchisement, radical methods are justified.

VISUAL RECORD ANSWER

Students might suggest that the women themselves look very proper.

LEVEL 3: Tell students to imagine that they are suffragists who have been asked to supply political advice to women in a country without universal suffrage. Have each student write a one-to-two-page paper summarizing how American women gained the right to vote. *(See the Level 1 lesson for the correct factors.)* Students may wish to conclude their papers with specific suggestions about how the women from the other country should go about winning the right to vote. Students may wish to include their papers in their portfolios.

▸**ASSIGNMENT** *Distribute Activity 9, Women's Suffrage, from* ***Graphic Organizer Activities****, and have each student complete it.*

NOTE: For an additional teaching idea, see the Chapter 9 collage lesson in the **Creative Teaching Strategies** handbook.

SECTION 4 REVIEW ANSWERS

Define and Identify

For significance, see the following pages:

- Federal Reserve Act, p. 288
- Clayton Antitrust Act, p. 288
- Federal Trade Commission, p. 289
- Adamson Act, p. 289
- Keating-Owen Child Labor Act, p. 290
- National American Woman Suffrage Association, p. 291
- Alice Paul, p. 291
- Carrie Chapman Catt, p. 291
- Nineteenth Amendment, p. 293

1. banking–created the Federal Reserve; big business–helped pass the Clayton Antitrust Act; child labor–attempted to limit, but failed; women's rights–ratification of the Nineteenth Amendment; farm and labor–passed loan and benefit acts; tariffs–reduced tariffs

2. continued progressive reforms, including antitrust and labor legislation

3. He did not support women's suffrage in the 1916 election.

4. failed to achieve goals such as banning child labor

5. child workers and railroad workers–failed to secure passage of protection laws; farmers–signed important aid legislation; federal workers–allocated benefits

Magazine covers from the 1920s celebrated the success of the suffrage movement.

BIOGRAPHY

Carrie Chapman Catt

A new NAWSA leader. Carrie Chapman Catt was born Carrie Clinton Lane in 1859 in Wisconsin. From childhood on, Catt was interested in women's rights. When she was 13, Catt was surprised that her mother was not going to vote in the presidential elections of 1872. "I think it's very unfair that women can't vote, don't you?" she asked a neighbor boy.

In 1877 Catt began attending Iowa State Agricultural College—now Iowa State University. While at school, Catt won for female students the right to speak at the school literary society. There she initiated a debate on women's suffrage. She argued: "How is it possible that a woman who is unfit to vote, should be the mother of, and bring up, a man who is?"

After graduating in 1880, Catt went to work as a teacher. She became superintendent of schools of Mason City, Iowa, in her second year. In 1885 she resigned her position after marrying Leo Chapman. Married women were not allowed to work in the schools. Catt began working as co-editor with her husband on the local newspaper. She also wrote a weekly feature called "Woman's World." After Chapman died of typhoid fever, Catt began a new career as a lecturer.

Catt soon became involved with the women's suffrage movement and served as a delegate at the NAWSA convention. About this time, she married George Catt, who enthusiastically supported her work. Over the next decade, Carrie Chapman Catt continued to travel and campaign on behalf of women's suffrage. In 1900 she became the president of NAWSA. She remained president until 1904, when she resigned to serve as president of the International Woman Suffrage Alliance (IWSA). As president of IWSA, Catt traveled around the world, seeking to win women to the cause of feminism. After returning to the United States, Catt again threw herself into the task of achieving women's suffrage. Catt remained a political and social activist until her death in 1947.

Success. Launching what came to be called Catt's Winning Plan in 1916, NAWSA won a string of successes for suffrage at the state level. After the United States entered World War I in 1917, leaders of the movement—along with millions of American women—lent strong support to the war effort. Their patriotism helped

Great Debates: The Progressive Legacy

Although progressivism made reforms in many areas, some of its reforms failed to bring about the anticipated changes. Although the government's ability to regulate the economy and pay for new programs improved, many business regulations fell short of remaking the capitalist system. Reforms such as the initiative, referendum, and recall were primarily used at the local level. Thus they had little impact on broad questions of national public policy.

One of progressivism's greatest successes, the settlement-house movement, improved opportunities for women, brought urban reform, and focused attention on the plight of immigrants. However, few of the settlement-house workers addressed the problems of African Americans. The progressive presidents showed little interest in racial issues. Some critics argued that President Theodore Roosevelt set back the African American cause in 1906. White residents in Brownsville, Texas, had started violent protests against black soldiers at a nearby fort. Despite little evidence that the soldiers were involved in any violence, Roosevelt issued dishonorable discharges to the entire company to pacify the white community. Presidents Taft and Wilson both supported racial segregation.

Despite these shortcomings, some scholars note that progressives took real strides toward making the new industrial society more just, orderly, and humane. Their efforts to end child labor, protect workers and consumers, and promote conservation profoundly influenced the nation. Supporters argue that their greatest legacy was the demonstration that the U.S. democratic system could respond and adapt to changes in American life.

REVIEW

Have students complete the **Section 4 Review** on p. 293.

ASSESS

Have students complete **Daily Quiz 9.4.** As **Alternative Assessment**, you may want to use the President Wilson telegram or the voting rights strategy debate in this section's lessons.

RETEACH

Have students complete **Main Idea Activity for Reteaching and Sheltered English 9.4.** Then organize students into pairs and assign them a subsection. Ask each pair to write three true-or-false statements about the material in its assigned subsection. Collect these statements and use them to quiz the class as a whole. Have students recast false statements to make them true. **Sheltered English, Cooperative Learning**

EXTEND

Have students conduct research on the women's rights movement during the 1910s and pick a significant figure. Have each student develop a three-to-four-minute monologue about the figure, explaining his or her background, approach to women's rights, and overall success or failure. Ask volunteers to deliver their monologues to the class. **Block Scheduling**

---

weaken opposition to women's suffrage. Even President Wilson came out in support of women's suffrage in a speech in 1918.

A 1918 Senate vote on a constitutional amendment to grant women the vote fell short by just two votes. Suffragists immediately targeted four senators up for election that November who had voted against women's suffrage. A strong message was sent to other politicians when three of the four lost their re-election bid. Finally, in 1919, Congress proposed the **Nineteenth Amendment**, granting women full voting rights. It was ratified in 1920.

Labor lawyer Crystal Eastman declared at the amendment's passage, "What we must do is to create conditions of outward freedom in which a free woman's soul can be born and grow." Carrie Chapman Catt declared, "Now that we have the vote let us remember we are . . . free and equal citizens. Let us do our part to keep it a true and triumphant democracy." She cautioned, however, that the vote was only an "entering wedge." Women still had to force their way through the "locked door" of political decision making.

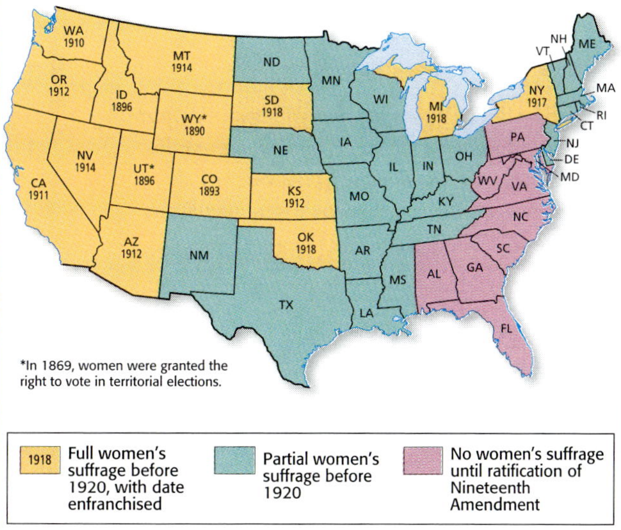

✔ **READING CHECK:** How did American women gain the right to vote?

Women's Suffrage, 1893–1920

Learning from Maps Before 1920 women's suffrage rights in the United States varied widely according to where they lived.

REGION Which section of the United States took the lead in granting the vote to women?

*In 1869, women were granted the right to vote in territorial elections.

1918 Full women's suffrage before 1920, with date enfranchised

Partial women's suffrage before 1920

No women's suffrage until ratification of Nineteenth Amendment

SECTION 4 REVIEW

Define and explain the significance of the following terms:
Federal Reserve Act
Clayton Antitrust Act
Federal Trade Commission
Adamson Act
Keating-Owen Child Labor Act
National American Woman Suffrage Association
Nineteenth Amendment

Identify and explain the significance of the following individuals:
Alice Paul
Carrie Chapman Catt

1. **Using Graphic Organizers** Copy the web below. Use it to describe the reforms passed during Woodrow Wilson's administration.

2. **Analyzing** How did the Wilson administration build on the work of previous presidents?
3. **Recognizing Point of View** Why did some suffragists argue that President Wilson was not doing enough for women's suffrage?
4. **Evaluating** How well did the progressive politicians accomplish the goals of progressive reformers?

Critical Thinking

5. How successful was Wilson in enlisting the "forces of humanity" to help child laborers, farmers, and railroad and federal workers?
Consider:
- what Wilson meant by "forces of humanity"
- Wilson's reforms for farmers, railroad and federal workers, and child laborers
- how these groups were helped by reforms

MAP ANSWER
the western section

CHAPTER 9 REVIEW ANSWERS

Creating a Time Line
Each event should have an explanation and the correct date.

Writing a Summary
See the Reading Checks in each section for main ideas.

Identifying People and Ideas
1. election reform that allowed voters to introduce legislation
2. Toledo, Ohio, mayor who enacted many reforms
3. permitted the federal government to set railroad rates and to regulate companies engaged in interstate commerce
4. process of making damaged land productive
5. Taft's interior secretary whose conflict with Gifford Pinchot was a political disaster for the president
6. Democrat elected to the presidency in 1912 and 1916
7. Wilson's reform platform
8. reorganized the banking system
9. reduced the hours of railroad workers without reducing pay
10. suffragist who advocated militant strategies

REVIEW AND ASSESSMENT RESOURCES

PRINT
- Chapter 9 Review, pp. 294–95
- Chapter 9 Tutorial for Students, Parents, Mentors, and Peers
- Chapter 9 Test (Form A or B)
- Portfolio Activities and Alternative Assessment Handbook, Chapter 9

MULTIMEDIA
- Audio Program, Chapter 9 (English and Spanish)
- Chapter 9 Test Generator (on the One-Stop Planner)
- Global Skill Builder CD–ROM
- HRW Web site

SHELTERED ENGLISH
- Spanish Glossary
- Sheltered English Chapter 9 Test

REVIEW

Have students complete the **Chapter 9 Review** on pp. 294–95.

ASSESS

Use one of the chapter tests to assess students' understanding of the content. For **Alternative Assessment**, see the **Portfolio Activities and Alternative Assessment Handbook.**

Understanding Main Ideas

1. allowed experts to manage cities and reduced corruption
2. influenced political leaders in other states
3. embodied Roosevelt's belief in balancing the needs of business, labor, and consumers
4. failures—engendered conflict; successes—limited trusts, passed labor and tax reforms
5. to help small businesses and to help Americans pursue their lives free of government interference

Reviewing Themes

1. by instituting reforms such as the secret ballot, the initiative, the recall, and the referendum
2. by balancing opposing needs and regulating industry to prevent unfair competition
3. Female voters often supported reform measures.

Thinking Critically

1. Taft's decision to support tariff increases angered many progressive voters.
2. business and liquor interests
3. Taft might have gained enough votes to win re-election.

Review

Creating a Time Line

Copy the time line below onto a sheet of paper. Complete the time line by filling in the events and dates from the chapter that you think were most significant. Pick three events and explain why you think they were significant.

Writing a Summary

Using the Reading Checks as a guide, write an overview of the events in the chapter.

Identifying People and Ideas

Identify the following terms or individuals and explain their significance.

1. initiative
2. Samuel M. Jones
3. Hepburn Act
4. reclamation
5. Richard Ballinger
6. Woodrow Wilson
7. New Freedom
8. Federal Reserve Act
9. Adamson Act
10. Alice Paul

Understanding Main Ideas

SECTION 1

1. What were the strengths of the city-commission and city-manager forms of government?
2. How did the Wisconsin Idea lay the foundation for further reforms?

SECTION 2

3. How did the Square Deal reflect President Theodore Roosevelt's approach to government?

SECTION 3

4. What failures and successes did President Taft experience during his term in office?

SECTION 4

5. What were the basic points of President Wilson's New Freedom program?

Reviewing Themes

1. **Democratic Values** How did reformers seek to limit the power of big business and make government more democratic in the early 1900s?
2. **Economic Development** How did President Roosevelt attempt to regulate business without discouraging free enterprise?
3. **Constitutional Heritage** Why did some reformers view the Nineteenth Amendment as a means of accomplishing reform in politics and business?

Thinking Critically

1. **Evaluating** How did the controversy over tariffs contribute to Taft's defeat in the 1912 election?
2. **Analyzing** What interests worked against the campaign for women's suffrage in the early 1900s?
3. **Hypothesizing** How might the presidential election of 1912 have been different if the Progressive Party had not been formed?
4. **Comparing and Contrasting** Compare the successes of Presidents Roosevelt, Taft, and Wilson in enacting reform legislation.
5. **Using Historical Imagination** Imagine that you are a voter considering the new legislation enacted to reform voting procedures. Do you think these reforms will influence your voting practices? Why or why not?

Writing About History

Writing to Evaluate Write an essay evaluating the progressives' record. Use the following graphic to organize your thoughts.

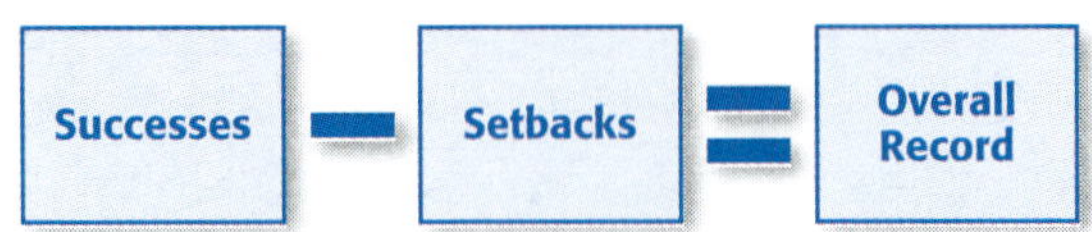

RETEACH

Pair students and randomly assign pairs one of the sections. Have each pair write three questions about the material, taking care to ensure the accuracy of the questions. Then have each pair present its questions to the entire class in the form of a quiz show. The pair that answers the most questions correctly, excluding its own, wins the quiz show.
Sheltered English, Cooperative Learning

EXTEND

Ask students to reconsider the basic problems caused by political machines. Then have students think about those problems in light of the local and state reforms initiated by the Progressive reformers. Ask students whether the reforms restored confidence or merely continued the status quo. To conclude, have students write a two-to-three-page report on how other reforms might have improved American life in the early 1900s, conducting additional research as necessary.
Block Scheduling

Strategies for Success Review the **Strategies for Success** on *Interpreting the Visual Record: Political Cartoons.* Then study the cartoon below and answer the questions that follow.

1. What do the characters and the setting in this cartoon represent?
2. How do the captions and labels help clarify the meaning of the cartoon?
3. What message is the cartoonist trying to communicate through this cartoon?
4. How does the cartoon contribute to your understanding of business trusts and progressive "trustbusting" in the early 1900s?

THE LION-TAMER

Linking History and Geography

One method that progressives used to fight child labor was increased use of laws to require children to be in school. Study the map below. Which section of the country was the last to adopt compulsory education laws?

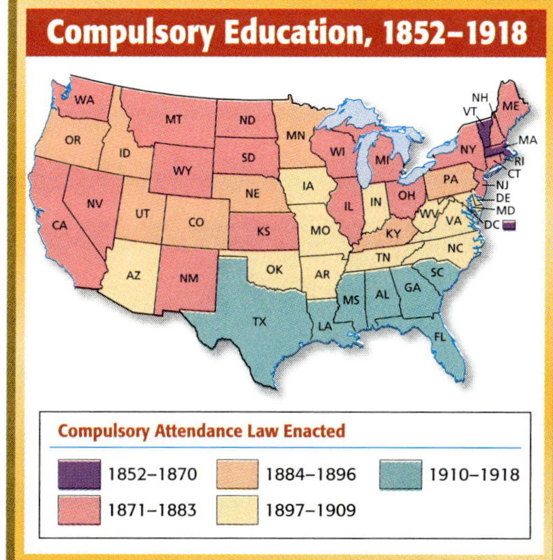

internet connect

TOPIC: National Parks
GO TO: go.hrw.com
KEYWORD: SE1 Parks

Accessing the Internet through the HRW Web site, research information about the National Parks System established by President Theodore Roosevelt. Look for information on the history of the parks, their geographical features, and their locations. Then create postcards for at least three of the parks with illustrations on the front and descriptive information on the back.

BUILDING YOUR PORTFOLIO

Complete one or all of the following projects independently or cooperatively.

1 Constitutional Heritage

Imagine that you are a delegate at the 1912 Progressive Party convention. **Write a platform** for the party that translates the problems of political machines, women's suffrage, business regulation, and worker protection into specific reforms your party hopes to institute.

2 Democratic Values

Imagine that you are a supporter of women's suffrage during the 1910s. **Write an editorial** indicating why you believe that progressives are not adequately addressing the needs of working-class women.

3 Economic Development

Imagine that you are a campaign worker for either Roosevelt, Taft, or Wilson. **Create a campaign poster** that shows the reforms your candidate enacted and the reforms the others failed to get passed.

4. All three presidents approved reform legislation. Roosevelt's efforts protected consumers and the environment; Taft's efforts regulated or broke trusts; Wilson's efforts enacted some labor reform laws.
5. Answers will vary. Students should discuss the secret ballot, the recall, the referendum, and the initiative.

Writing About History
Students' essays should include information about business regulation, consumer protection, and voting reform. Essays should discuss specific progressives and should evaluate setbacks such as the failure of child labor laws.

Strategies for Success
1. Roosevelt attempting to "tame" the trusts in a hostile business environment
2. indicate the identities of the "lions" and give details as to themes
3. that Roosevelt took on an enormous challenge when he attempted to control the trusts
4. gives a sense of the challenge and battle

Linking History and Geography
the South

America and the World

CHAPTER PLANNING GUIDE

	Section Lesson Objectives	Print Resources	Multimedia Resources	Sheltered English Resources
Section 1 Expansion in the Pacific, pp. 298–304	1 Identify the major factors that drove imperialism. 2 Explain how the United States acquired Hawaii. 3 Describe the U.S. role in China. 4 Discuss how Japan became a world power.	▶ Guided Reading Strategy 10.1 ▶ Geography Activity 10: Foreign Powers in China, 1911 ▶ Section 1 Review, p. 304 ▶ Daily Quiz 10.1	▶ One-Stop Planner, Lesson 10.1 ▶ Holt Researcher: American History CD–ROM	▶ Main Idea Activity for Reteaching and Sheltered English 10.1
Section 2 War with Spain, pp. 305–11	1 Recount how Spain responded to the revolt in Cuba. 2 Discuss the major causes of the Spanish-American War. 3 Describe the major battles of the Spanish-American War. 4 Explain what happened to the Philippines after the Spanish-American War.	▶ Guided Reading Strategy 10.2 ▶ Primary Source Reading 10: Teddy Roosevelt's Cavalry ▶ Literature Reading 10: Protesting Military Action ▶ Section 2 Review, p. 311 ▶ Daily Quiz 10.2	▶ One-Stop Planner, Lesson 10.2 ▶ Everyday Life in America Transparency 19: Photojournalism in the Spanish-American War ▶ Holt Researcher: American History CD–ROM ▶ HRW Web site	▶ Main Idea Activity for Reteaching and Sheltered English 10.2
Section 3 Expansion in Latin America, pp. 312–16	1 Explain how the United States governed Cuba and Puerto Rico. 2 Describe the major obstacles to building the Panama Canal. 3 Summarize U.S. policy toward Latin America during the late 1800s and early 1900s.	▶ Guided Reading Strategy 10.3 ▶ Graphic Organizer Activity 10: Changes in Cuba ▶ Biography Reading 10: William Gorgas ▶ Section 3 Review, p. 316 ▶ Daily Quiz 10.3	▶ One-Stop Planner, Lesson 10.3 ▶ The American Nation Video Program Segment: The Panama Canal; Teacher's Guide, pp. 93–98 ▶ Holt Researcher: American History CD–ROM	▶ Main Idea Activity for Reteaching and Sheltered English 10.3
Section 4 Conflict with Mexico, pp. 317–21	1 List the major events of the Mexican Revolution. 2 Explain why the United States intervened in Mexico. 3 Report on the outcomes of the Mexican Revolution.	▶ Guided Reading Strategy 10.4 ▶ Section 4 Review, p. 321 ▶ Daily Quiz 10.4	▶ One-Stop Planner, Lesson 10.4 ▶ Holt Researcher: American History CD–ROM	▶ Main Idea Activity for Reteaching and Sheltered English 10.4
Chapter Review and Assessment pp. 322–23		▶ Chapter 10 Review, pp. 322–23 ▶ Chapter 10 Tutorial for Students, Parents, Mentors, and Peers ▶ Chapter 10 Test (Form A or B) ▶ Portfolio Activities and Alternative Assessment Handbook, Chapter 10	▶ Audio Program, Chapter 10 (English and Spanish) ▶ Chapter 10 Test Generator (on the One-Stop Planner) ▶ Global Skill Builder CD–ROM ▶ HRW Web site	▶ Spanish Glossary ▶ Sheltered English Chapter 10 Test

CHAPTER OVERVIEW

After the Second Industrial Revolution, the United States began to play a greater role in world affairs. The quest for new markets partly fueled this new interest in world affairs as the United States, following the lead of several European nations, established trade with China. Like many European nations, the United States also indulged its imperialist ambitions, acquiring Hawaii and seizing control of Cuba, Puerto Rico, and the Philippines during the Spanish-American War.

In addition to acquiring new territories, the United States exercised its powers in the Western Hemisphere. Eager to build a canal in Panama and cut travel time between the Caribbean and the Pacific, the United States aided Panamanian rebels who declared independence from Colombia and acquired the right to build the canal from the new government. The Roosevelt Corollary asserted the right of the United States to act as a police power in enforcing the Monroe Doctrine. This corollary and other statements cloaking self-interest were used to justify interventions in several Latin American countries and in Mexico during the Mexican Revolution.

TIME TAMERS

Block Scheduling

The teacher lesson plans for each section offer a variety of activity choices to help you present the material in a block scheduling format. For further suggestions on block scheduling, see the **Block Scheduling Handbook with Team Teaching Strategies**, pp. 55–60.

Internet Connections and Lesson 10
www.si.edu/hrw

Hands-On History Activities:

Classroom to Community The **Hands-On History Activities** help students make meaningful connections between events in American history and those in their own hometown. You may wish to use the Chapter 10 Activity, Property Annexation in Your Community, to extend the chapter lessons, as alternative assessment, or as a block scheduling option.

Portfolio Projects

The American Nation includes multiple portfolio projects in each Pupil's Edition chapter review, as well as each unit review. Chapter 10 Portfolio Project options on p. 323 include the following:

1. Students will **write a memorandum.**
2. Students will **create a series of recruiting posters.**
3. Students will **plan a campaign.**

The American Nation
INTERNET RESOURCE DIRECTORY

To access online materials for this chapter, go to **go.hrw.com** and type in the keywords listed below.

HRW ONLINE RESOURCES
GO TO: go.hrw.com

Online Maps
KEYWORD: SE1 Maps10
- Panama Canal Zone
- U.S. Interests in Latin America

Online Charts
KEYWORD: SE1 Charts10
- U.S. Foreign Trade, 1865–1915

Online Reading Support
KEYWORD: SE1 Strategies10

Online Rubrics
KEYWORD: SE1 Rubrics

CHAPTER ENRICHMENT LINKS
Use these Web links to extend and enrich student learning for Chapter 10.
GO TO: go.hrw.com
KEYWORD: SE1 Ch10

CHAPTER INTERNET ACTIVITIES
GO TO: go.hrw.com
- Pupil's Edition Student Activity
KEYWORD: SE1 Panama
(Students conduct research on the construction of the Panama Canal.)
- Teacher's Edition Student Activity
KEYWORD: SE1 Nobel
(Students examine the accomplishments of American Nobel Laureates.)
- Teacher's Edition Student Activity
KEYWORD: SE1 Spanish
(Students conduct research on the Spanish-American War.)

ADDITIONAL
RESOURCES

Books for Teachers

LaFeber, Walter. *Panama Canal: The Crisis in Historical Perspective.* Oxford University Press, 1990. Discusses the history of the Panama Canal.

Musicant, Ivan. *Empire by Default: The Spanish-American War and the Dawn of the American Century.* Henry Holt, 1998. Offers a detailed account of the war.

Books for Students

Dolan, Edward F. *Panama & the United States: Their Canal, Their Stormy Years.* Watts, 1990. Describes the history of relations between Panama and the United States to 1990.

Marrin, Albert. *The Spanish-American War.* Atheneum, 1991. Explores the causes and consequences of the war; examines yellow journalism and also discusses President Roosevelt's role.

Primary Sources from the Period

Liliuokalani. *Hawaii's Story.* Charles E. Tuttle, 1971. Presents the autobiography of the last queen of Hawaii.

Roosevelt, Theodore. *The Rough Riders.* Corner House, 1971. Presents Theodore Roosevelt's account of his Spanish-American War experiences.

Multimedia Materials

The Spanish-American War. Video, 28 min. Dallas Community College. Examines the causes of the war.

United States History: U.S. and the World (1865–1917). Video, 30 min. Library Video Company. Includes a discussion of the Open Door Policy and dollar diplomacy.

Before You Read

Build on What You Know

Ask students to answer the following questions.

Why might Americans have looked to expand abroad in the late 1800s?

Consider:

- the results of westward expansion
- the need for markets for American goods

Why might the United States have become involved in events in Cuba, Mexico, China, and Japan?

Consider:

- the proximity of Cuba and Mexico to the United States
- the economic interests of the United States on the global scale

exploring the time line

AMERICAN EVENTS

internet**connect**

TOPIC: Nobel Prize Winners
GO TO: go.hrw.com
KEYWORD: SE1 Nobel

Have students access the Internet through the HRW Web site to conduct research on one of the American Nobel Prize winners. Then have each student write a commendation speech that outlines the winner's achievements and contributions.

CHAPTER 10

1898–1917 America and the World

Theodore Roosevelt as an international police officer

THE GRANGER COLLECTION, NEW YORK

A hamburger

1898 World Events The Spanish-American War is fought.

1898 Science and Technology Marie Curie discovers radium, the first known radioactive element.

1898 The Arts H. G. Wells's *War of the Worlds* is published.

1899 Politics The U.S. Senate votes to annex the Philippines.

1900 Daily Life The hamburger is introduced in New Haven, Connecticut.

1900 The Arts *The Wizard of Oz* by L. Frank Baum is published.

1901 Business and Finance J. P. Morgan creates the United States Steel Company, the world's first billion-dollar corporation.

1901 Science and Technology The Nobel Prizes are awarded for the first time.

1904 Politics Theodore Roosevelt states his corollary to the Monroe Doctrine.

1904 World Events The Russo-Japanese War begins.

1898 | 1900 | 1902 | 1904 | 1906

H. G. Wells

The Nobel Prize

Before You Read

Build on What You Know

After recovering from the Civil War, the United States resumed its economic growth and westward expansion. Creating tremendous wealth for some and jobs for many, the Industrial Revolution transformed the nation. In this chapter you will learn how the United States established itself as a world power. After more than a century of following George Washington's advice and avoiding foreign entanglements, the United States became deeply involved in events abroad, from nearby Cuba and Mexico to distant China and Japan.

Think About Themes

To help students create their Themes Journal entries, provide the following examples of appropriate **agree/disagree** *statements.*

Global Relations

Agree During the colonial era, the Spanish felt compelled to introduce their culture and religion to the New World, thus "civilizing" native inhabitants.

Disagree During the early national period, the United States tried to isolate itself from the world despite its relative strength.

Economic Development

Agree Investments can create new industries and jobs.

Disagree Spanish investment in the Americas tended to be more exploitative than constructive; the nation removed huge amounts of gold and silver without investing in the local economy.

Democratic Values

Agree Democratic principles require that people be allowed to create their own governments.

Disagree The United States was able to introduce its form of democracy and liberty to the states created from the Louisiana Purchase.

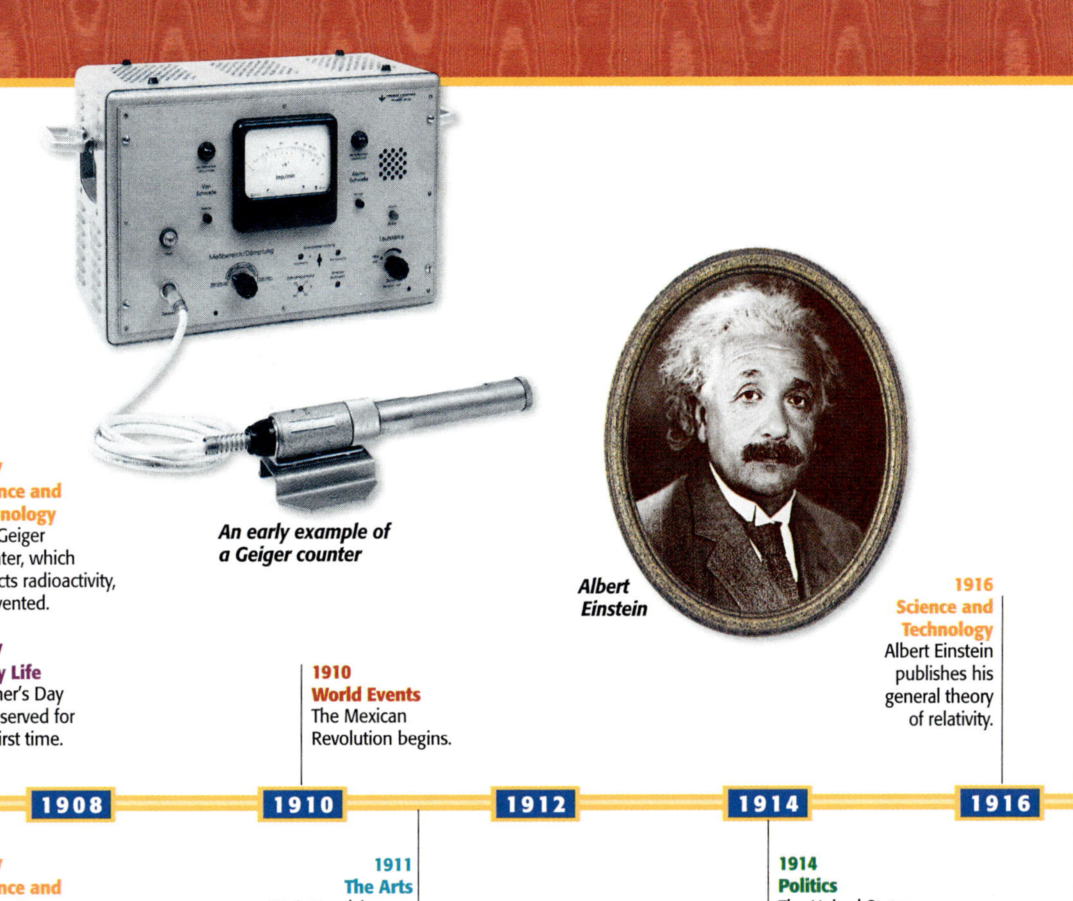

An early example of a Geiger counter

Albert Einstein

Sheet music of W. C. Handy's "Memphis Blues"

1907 Science and Technology The Geiger counter, which detects radioactivity, is invented.

1907 Daily Life Mother's Day is observed for the first time.

1907 Science and Technology Frenchman Paul Cornu constructs the first vertical flying helicopter that can hold a person.

1907 The Arts Pablo Picasso paints *Les Demoiselles d'Avignon,* a masterpiece in the cubist style of painting.

1910 World Events The Mexican Revolution begins.

1911 The Arts W. C. Handy's song "Memphis Blues" gains great popularity.

1914 Politics The United States occupies the city of Veracruz, Mexico.

1916 Science and Technology Albert Einstein publishes his general theory of relativity.

1908 | 1910 | 1912 | 1914 | 1916

exploring the time line

GLOBAL EVENTS

GLOBAL RELATIONS

1904 ■ The Russo-Japanese War. In 1895, at the end of a war between China and Japan, the Japanese sought the right to use the Chinese port called Port Arthur. European powers conspired to prevent Japanese access to the port, however. Just three years later Russia leased the port, which angered the Japanese. Soon after, Russia occupied the Chinese province of Manchuria, which the Japanese perceived as a threat. In February 1904, when Japanese forces invaded Port Arthur, the Russo-Japanese War began. The Japanese crushed Russia's Far Eastern fleet and defeated Russian forces in Manchuria. Russia's Baltic Fleet traveled for seven months to arrive at the scene of the fighting, only to be quickly destroyed by the Japanese navy.

CRITICAL THINKING What might the progress of the Russo-Japanese War have revealed about the Japanese navy?

ANSWER: Students might suggest that the war revealed that Japan possessed a formidable navy.

Think About Themes

Decide whether you **agree** *or* **disagree** *with the following statements. Note why in your journal.*

Global Relations Business interests often play a key role in the making of foreign policy.

Economic Development Investments by foreigners will greatly benefit a country's economy.

Democratic Values The acquisition of foreign colonies conflicts with democratic principles and the ideal of liberty.

297

SECTION 1

After completing Section 1, students should be able to:

OBJECTIVE 1 *Identify the major factors that drove imperialism.*

OBJECTIVE 2 *Explain how the United States acquired Hawaii.*

OBJECTIVE 3 *Describe the U.S. role in China.*

OBJECTIVE 4 *Discuss how Japan became a world power.*

LET'S GET STARTED!

Write the definition of "imperialism" on the chalkboard. *(Imperialism is the quest for colonial empires.)* As students enter the classroom, tell them to read the definition of imperialism on the chalkboard and to list three reasons why the United States might have pursued imperialist policies in the late 1800s and the early 1900s. *(Students might suggest that the United States wanted to gain territories or resources.)* Ask volunteers to share their responses with the class. Then tell students that in Section 1 they will learn more about U.S. imperialism in the Pacific.

SECTION 1 RESOURCES

PRINT

- Guided Reading Strategy 10.1
- Geography Activity 10: Foreign Powers in China, 1911
- Section 1 Review, p. 304
- Daily Quiz 10.1

MULTIMEDIA

- One-Stop Planner, Lesson 10.1
- Holt Researcher: American History CD–ROM

SHELTERED ENGLISH

- Main Idea Activity for Reteaching and Sheltered English 10.1

✔ READING TO UNDERSTAND

To help students master the section objectives, have them answer the **READING CHECKS** and complete **Guided Reading Strategy 10.1** as they read the section.

Expansion in the Pacific

OBJECTIVES

Read to understand:

1. what major factors drove imperialism
2. how the United States acquired Hawaii
3. what the U.S. role in China was
4. how Japan became a world power

KEY TERMS

imperialism
subsidy
spheres of influence
Open Door Policy
Boxer Rebellion
Russo-Japanese War

KEY PEOPLE

Henry Cabot Lodge
Alfred Thayer Mahan
Kalakaua
Liliuokalani
John Hay
Matthew Perry

EYEWITNESSES TO History

"A new consciousness seems to have come upon us—the consciousness of strength—and with it a new appetite, the yearning to show our strength. . . . Ambition, interest, land hunger, pride, the mere joy of fighting, whatever it may be, we are animated by a new sensation. We are face to face with a strange destiny. The taste of Empire is in the mouth of the people even as the taste of blood in the jungle. It means an Imperial policy, the Republic, renascent [reawakened], taking her place with the armed nations."

—Washington Post

This cartoon shows Uncle Sam gathering the fruits of imperialism.

This editorial appeared in a June 1896 edition of the *Washington Post*. It reflected the growing strength of the United States and Americans' willingness to use this strength. The United States was ready to join the other great powers of the world and compete in a global economy.

The Impulse for Imperialism

In March 1889 in the South Pacific harbor of Apia, in present-day Western Samoa, seven warships—one British, three German, and three U.S.—faced off. Before a shot could be fired, a typhoon struck, destroying all but the British ship and possibly preventing a war. **Imperialism**—the quest for colonial empires—had led these three nations to the brink of war. Between 1876 and 1915 a handful of industrialized nations seized control of vast areas of Africa, Asia, and Latin America.

Imperialism was driven by a need for markets and raw materials as well as the desire for power and prestige. Aided by efficient machines and abundant capital, workers in these industrial nations produced far more goods than could be consumed at home. In response, industrialists turned to Africa, Asia, and Latin America for new customers and new sources of raw materials. To protect these new markets from competition, industrialized nations tried to colonize these areas. Senator Henry Cabot Lodge of Massachusetts explained that the United States needed to join this competition to maintain its economic and military strength.

A modern navy helped the United States compete against other global powers.

"Small states are of the past and have no future. . . . The great nations are rapidly absorbing for their future expansion and their present defense all the waste places of the earth. It is a movement which makes for civilization and the advancement of the race. As one of the great nations of the world, the United States must not fall out of the line of march."

American enthusiasm for overseas expansion never matched that of the European powers, but support did grow during the late 1800s. One particularly influential supporter was Alfred Thayer

TEACH OBJECTIVE 1

ALL LEVELS: To help students understand the forces that motivated imperialism between 1876 and 1915, copy the graphic organizer at right on the chalkboard, omitting the italicized answers. Have each student complete it. Ask volunteers to read their answers to the class. Conclude by discussing with students the implications of the factors listed in the graphic organizer. **Sheltered English**

▶**ASSIGNMENT** *Tell students to imagine that they are editors who need to prepare jacket copy for a book on imperialism. Have each student write a paragraph on the major factors that drove imperialism.* (See the graphic organizer for the correct factors.) *Ask volunteers to read their book jacket summaries to the class.*

Factors That Drove Imperialism

1. *the need for markets*
2. *the need for raw materials*
3. *the desire for power*
4. *the desire for prestige*

Imperialism

Mahan of the U.S. Naval College. In his widely read book *The Influence of Sea Power upon History,* Mahan argued that the United States needed a strong navy to protect its economic interests in foreign markets. Mahan wrote that such a navy required overseas bases.

> **"Having . . . no foreign establishments, either colonial or military, the ships of war of the United States, in war, will be like land birds, unable to fly far from their own shores. To provide resting-places for them, where they can coal and repair, would be one of the first duties of a government proposing to itself the development of the power of the nation at sea."**

Other supporters of expansion claimed that the United States had a duty to spread its political system and the Christian religion throughout the world. Whatever the reason, many Americans supported expansion. The competition for territory and markets across the globe is what led the United States, Great Britain, and Germany to clash in Samoa in 1889. Ten years later, the United States won control over Eastern Samoa, and Germany gained control over Western Samoa. Today Western Samoa is independent, while Eastern (or American) Samoa remains a U.S. territory.

✔ **READING CHECK:** What major factors drove imperialism?

Acquiring Hawaii

Another Pacific island nation—Hawaii—also interested imperial powers. The Hawaiian Islands had a tropical climate and fertile, lava-enriched soil. In 1778 British explorer Captain James Cook visited the islands and renamed them the Sandwich Islands. About 1800 the Hawaiian chief Kamehameha united the eight major islands, creating a monarchy that held power until 1893.

The Hawaiian Islands lie some 2,000 miles west of California in the Pacific Ocean. They were the perfect place to build the naval bases and coaling stations that Alfred Thayer Mahan suggested the United States needed. To others the Hawaiians were an uncivilized people who needed to be introduced to modern industrial society and Christianity. One early visitor described Hawaiian culture.

> **"The ease with which the Hawaiians on their own land can secure their food supply has undoubtably interfered with their social and industrial advancement. . . . [It] relieves the native from any struggle and unfits him for sustained competition with men from other lands. The fact that food is supplied by nature takes from the native all desire for the acquisition of more land. Today's food can be had for the picking, and tomorrow's as well. Instead of grasping all he can get, he divides with his neighbor, and confidently expects his neighbor to divide with him."**

THE AMERICAN MISSIONARY MOVEMENT

During the early 1800s Christian missionary societies in the United States began sending missionaries to other parts of the world. The missionary movement grew steadily over the years and then expanded rapidly toward the end of the century. It grew from 16 American missionary societies in the 1860s to 90 in 1900. Tens of thousands of American Christians traveled abroad to spread their religious faith. Women played a major role in the missionary movement and made up many of the missionary groups in foreign countries.

Missionary Grace Roberts in Manchuria in 1903

Lottie Moon was one such woman. After teaching school in Kentucky and Georgia, she entered missionary service in 1873. For the next 40 years she worked at Southern Baptist stations in northeastern China. The missionary experience not only brought change to nations such as China, but also changed the missionaries themselves. As Lottie Moon wrote, her time in China changed her from "a timid self-distrustful girl into a brave self-reliant woman." In addition to teaching their religious beliefs, missionaries offered classes in mathematics, science, and English.

PEOPLE IN HISTORY

Alfred Thayer Mahan. Born in 1840, Alfred Thayer Mahan was the son of a professor at the U.S. Military Academy at West Point, New York. As a teenager, Mahan entered the U.S. Naval Academy. He served in the U.S. Navy during the Civil War, carrying out blockade duty and other jobs that did not require meritorious service. In 1884 he was invited to join the faculty of the U.S. Naval War College. His lecture notes from the classes he taught at the academy were published as *The Influence of Sea Power upon History.* Surprisingly, Mahan suffered from seasickness and an intense fear of the ocean, and he hated to be on board ships at sea.

CRITICAL THINKING How might Mahan have gained his insights regarding the importance of sea power?

ANSWER: Students might suggest that he formulated these insights by studying history rather than by serving extensively on ocean-bound ships, which he hated.

TEACH OBJECTIVE 2

LEVEL 1: Pair students and have each pair create an annotated time line from the 1820s to the 1890s that chronicles the events leading to the U.S. acquisition of Hawaii. *(Pairs' time lines should include the following events: the 1820s—American missionaries arrive in Hawaii; the 1870s—Americans control most of the land and trade; 1875—a treaty exempts Hawaiian sugar from U.S. tariffs; 1876—U.S. officials demand Pearl Harbor in exchange for tax-free status for Hawaiian sugar; 1887—the Hawaiian League forces King Kalakaua to sign the Bayonet Constitution; 1891—Liliuokalani becomes queen of Hawaii; 1893—in response to Liliuokalani's plan to publish a new constitution, supporters of annexation overthrow the monarchy, set up a provisional government, and proclaim Hawaii a U.S. protectorate; 1898— U.S. annexes Hawaii.)* Ask volunteers to present their time lines to the class. **Sheltered English, Cooperative Learning**

LEVEL 2: Tell students to imagine that they are editors for an encyclopedia of Pacific history. Have each student write an entry tracing the factors that led to the acquisition of Hawaii. *(See the Level 1 lesson for the correct events.)* Have volunteers read their entries to the class. Students may wish to include their entries in their portfolios.

TECHNOLOGY AND SOCIETY

Visiting Hawaii. Hawaii's location made it an excellent place to resupply ships and rest crews making the journey across the Pacific Ocean. The trading ship *Columbia,* which was on its way to China, was the first American ship to make such a stop. In 1789 the *Columbia* spent 24 days in Hawaii before departing. After that visit, American merchant ships regularly stopped in Hawaii.

CRITICAL THINKING What technological limitations might have made it necessary for ships to stop in Hawaii?

ANSWER: Students might mention that ships lacked refrigeration and needed new supplies, including fresh food.

THAT'S INTERESTING!

Between the 1820s and 1850s, some 85 percent of the world's whaling ships could be found in the Pacific Ocean. The Pacific whalers often visited Hawaii. Over the course of 19 years some 1,700 whaling ships, most of them American, stopped in Honolulu.

VISUAL RECORD ANSWER

Students might note that the harvesting appears extremely difficult and unpleasant.

INTERPRETING THE VISUAL RECORD

Sugar. These workers are harvesting sugarcane. American settlers built a profitable sugar industry in Hawaii. ***Does harvesting sugarcane appear to be difficult work? Explain your answer.***

During the 1800s ships began arriving in Hawaii more often. The ships brought missionaries, settlers, and traders. They also brought diseases that reduced the Hawaiian population from about 300,000 in 1778 to fewer than 150,000 by 1819.

American influence. The first U.S. contact with the Hawaiian Islands was made by Pacific trading and whaling ships that stopped at the islands for refreshments and supplies. In the 1820s Protestant missionaries from New England traveled to the islands to convert Hawaiians to Christianity. Missionaries and their families settled on the islands and began raising crops, particularly sugar.

American investors in the sugar industry gradually increased their control over the islands. As Hawaii's economy boomed, sugar planters grew rich. Hawaiian sugar production rose, and the influence of Americans increased. Expansion of the sugar industry meant that more laborers were needed. Since Hawaiians were dying off at a high rate, planters brought in thousands of Japanese and Chinese workers, who soon outnumbered Hawaiians. By the 1870s Americans controlled most of Hawaii's land and trade. They exercised growing influence over the Hawaiian king Kalakaua (kah-LAH-KAH-ooh-ah), who took the throne in 1874.

An 1875 treaty exempted Hawaiian sugar from U.S. tariffs. In exchange, Hawaii promised not to grant territory or special privileges in the islands to any other country. In 1886, U.S. officials demanded control of Pearl Harbor in exchange for renewing tax-free status for Hawaiian sugar. Kalakaua refused. Some 400 American businesspeople, planters, and traders in Hawaii then formed the secret Hawaiian League. Their goal was to overthrow the monarchy and persuade the United States to annex Hawaii.

In July 1887 the League forced Kalakaua at gunpoint to sign a new constitution that limited his role to that of a figurehead. It also limited native Hawaiians' right to hold office in their own country. Hawaiians resented what they called the Bayonet Constitution. Kalakaua had no choice but to renew the treaty and grant the United States exclusive rights to build a fortified naval base at Pearl Harbor.

In 1890 Congress enacted the McKinley Tariff, which created a crisis by ending Hawaii's favored position in the sugar trade. The law permitted all countries to ship sugar duty-free to the United States. It also gave sugar producers in the United States a **subsidy**—a government bonus payment—of two cents per pound. This caused sugar prices to drop, and the Hawaiian economy suffered.

Read More About It

Free Find: Liliuokalani

After reading about Liliuokalani on the Holt Researcher CD–ROM, write a song that honors her work on behalf of the Hawaiian people.

BIOGRAPHY *Liliuokalani*

A nationalist queen. In 1891 Kalakaua died and his sister Liliuokalani (li-lee-uh-woh-kuh-LAHN-ee) succeeded him. Liliuokalani was a champion of Hawaiian nationalism and pledged to regain "Hawaii for the Hawaiians." Liliuokalani was born into a Hawaiian ruling family in 1838. As a young girl she saw the monarchy reclaim Hawaiian independence after a brief British takeover. She never forgot the pride she felt as the Hawaiian flag was again raised over her native land.

LEVEL 3: Organize students into two groups and tell them to imagine that they are modern-day participants in a roundtable discussion entitled U.S. Imperialism in Hawaii: 1820–1898. Have one group act as historians and the other group act as facilitators and questioners. Have each group prepare notes to assist it in its specific role, and then conduct the roundtable discussion. *(See the Level 1 lesson for the correct events.)* After the discussion, ask students to express their personal opinions of the acquisition of Hawaii. **Cooperative Learning**

▶ASSIGNMENT *Tell students to imagine that it is the 1890s and that they are Hawaiians. Have each student create three or four protest signs in opposition to U.S. imperialist activities in Hawaii.*

SPOTLIGHT on the Hawaiian Sugar Industry

Have students conduct research on the history of the Hawaiian sugar industry through the early 1900s. Ask each student to write a report that includes information about the major figures in the sugar industry, the people who worked in the industry, and the connection between sugar barons and the push for U.S. annexation of the islands. Students may wish to include their reports in their portfolios. **Block Scheduling**

Early in her reign, Queen Liliuokalani began working to overturn the Bayonet Constitution and replace it with one that would return power to native Hawaiians. In 1893 she announced her plan to publish a new constitution. In response, the supporters of annexation forcibly occupied government buildings, declared the end of the monarchy, and set up a provisional government of their own. Without authorization, the U.S. minister to Hawaii, John L. Stevens, ordered marines ashore from the cruiser *Boston*, supposedly to protect American lives and property. With Gatling guns and cannons in place, the marines took up positions facing Iolani Palace and Liliuokalani.

No shots were fired, and the revolutionaries established a new government with Sanford B. Dole as president. Again acting without authority, Stevens recognized the new government and proclaimed Hawaii to be under U.S. protection on February 1, 1893. "The Hawaiian pear is now fully ripe," proclaimed Stevens, "and this is the golden hour for the United States to pluck it." Not wanting to see Hawaiians killed, a deeply saddened Queen Liliuokalani reluctantly surrendered her throne.

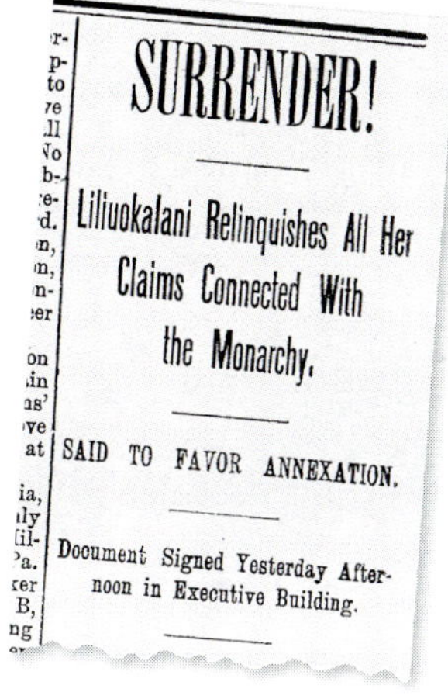

SURRENDER!

Liliuokalani Relinquishes All Her Claims Connected With the Monarchy.

SAID TO FAVOR ANNEXATION.

Document Signed Yesterday Afternoon in Executive Building.

The overthrow of the Hawaiian monarchy raised few criticisms in the American press.

> **"I, Liliuokalani, . . . protest against any and all acts done against myself and the constitutional government of the Hawaiian kingdom. . . . Now, to avoid any collision of armed forces and perhaps the loss of life, I do, under this protest, and impelled by said forces, yield my authority until such time as the government of the United States shall . . . undo the action of its representatives and reinstate me."**

The new government petitioned the United States for annexation, but anti-imperialists and Democratic senators blocked the proposed treaty. Newly elected president Grover Cleveland withdrew the treaty and ordered an investigation. The investigator's report condemned the revolt and the U.S. role in it. The report also proposed putting Liliuokalani back on the throne. Cleveland supported the report and asked the provisional government to resign. Dole, however, refused to step down.

Unwilling to use military force to restore Liliuokalani, Cleveland reluctantly recognized the Dole government but refused to approve annexation. From 1894 to 1898 the independent Republic of Hawaii waited for a friendly Washington administration. It came with the election of President William McKinley. The United States annexed Hawaii on July 7, 1898, despite the opposition of most of Hawaii's population.

This postcard shows the tropical beauty of Hawaii.

Liliuokalani lived out the rest of her life in Honolulu, serving as a proud reminder of Hawaii's past. She died in 1917 and was buried in the Royal Mausoleum. Hawaii became a U.S. territory in 1900 and the 50th state in 1959. In 1993 Congress apologized for the U.S. role in Liliuokalani's overthrow.

✔ **READING CHECK:** How did the United States acquire Hawaii?

ECONOMIC DEVELOPMENT

Hawaii and California. The California Gold Rush had a startling impact on the sugar industry in Hawaii. The miners desired sugar and other Hawaiian food products, sparking a new boom. The price of sugar rose from about 6 cents per pound to 15 cents, creating a profit for sugar producers. As a result, Hawaiian land that had sold at $1.00 per acre soon cost five times as much.

CRITICAL THINKING Why might Hawaiian land prices have increased after the boom?

ANSWER: Students might suggest that the land was more valuable because sugar was more profitable.

THAT'S INTERESTING!

In the 1850s sugarcane planted on one acre of land yielded one ton of sugar. Technical improvements later increased the yield to 2.5 tons per acre and then 4.5 tons per acre. Some land in Maui produced as much as 6.5 tons of sugar per acre.

TEACH OBJECTIVE 3

LEVEL 1: Ask students to describe the U.S. role in China. *(Students should indicate that the U.S. called for an Open Door Policy, which was designed to give all nations equal access to trade and investment in China and to maintain Chinese sovereignty.)* Tell students to imagine that they are newspaper reporters covering U.S.-China relations in the 1890s and early 1900s. Pair students and have each pair write three or four headlines that delineate the principles of the U.S. Open Door Policy in China. *(Pairs' headlines should include the following principles: all ports in foreign spheres of influence should be open to all nations; Chinese officials should be allowed to collect all tariffs and duties; foreign nations should guarantee equal harbor, railroad, and tariff rates to all nations trading in China; China should retain its sovereignty.)* Ask volunteers to read their headlines to the class.
Sheltered English, Cooperative Learning

LEVELS 2 AND 3: Pair students and tell them to imagine that they are State Department advisers to Secretary of State John Hay. Have each pair write a summary and justification of the U.S. role in China and the Open Door Policy for President McKinley. *(See the Level 1 lesson for the correct U.S. role and the correct points of the Open Door Policy.)* Have spokespeople read the summaries to the class. **Cooperative Learning**

DEMOCRATIC VALUES

The Hawaiian Revolt. Lorrin A. Thurston, an attorney who lived in Hawaii, explained why many Americans favored annexation. He noted that in 1892 foreigners owned some 80 percent of the land in Hawaii, but they made up less than 30 percent of qualified voters. In addition, Americans paid more than 25 percent of the taxes collected in Hawaii. The foreign landowners feared that native Hawaiians would use the political system to increase taxes on foreigners.

CRITICAL THINKING Do you think that Thurston's argument was valid? Explain.

ANSWER: Answers will vary. Some students might suggest that since foreigners controlled most of the land they were liable for most of the taxes.

THAT'S INTERESTING!

At the conclusion of the Boxer Rebellion, China was ordered to pay the United States $25 million, of which the United States returned $17 million. The Chinese used most of the money to fund the education of Chinese students in the United States.

VISUAL RECORD ANSWER

Students might identify the flags of the United States, Great Britain, France, Holland, and Spain.

INTERPRETING THE VISUAL RECORD

China trade. Merchant ships unloaded their goods at Whampoa Anchorage near Canton, China. ***How many flags of different nations can you identify?***

U.S. Involvement in China

Hawaii was valuable to the United States in part because it was a convenient stopping point for American trading ships sailing to China. Trade between China and the United States began in 1784 when the American ship *Empress of China* sailed for the port of Guangzhou.

Spheres of influence. In 1843 China officially opened five ports to trade with the United States and Europe. For the next 50 years China's rulers struggled to keep foreign interests from overrunning the country. In 1895, however, the Chinese government faced a threat from another direction. Japan attacked and defeated China, seizing China's Liaotung Peninsula, the large island of Taiwan, and Korea. European powers quickly took advantage of China's weakened position. Britain, France, Germany, and Russia carved out **spheres of influence**—regions where a particular country has exclusive rights over mines, railroads, and trade.

The Open Door Policy. The United States was in danger of being squeezed out of the China trade. Senator Henry Cabot Lodge declared, "We ask no favors; we only ask that we shall be admitted to that great market upon the same terms with the rest of the world." In 1899 Secretary of State John Hay called for an **Open Door Policy**, which would give all nations equal access to trade and investment in China.

That September Hay sent a series of Open Door notes to the European powers and Japan that asked them to agree to three principles. First, he asked that they keep all ports in their spheres open to all nations. Second, he asked that Chinese officials be allowed to collect all tariffs and duties. Finally, he requested that they guarantee equal harbor, railroad, and tariff rates in their spheres to all nations trading in China. Since the European nations and Japan neither rejected nor accepted the principles, Hay announced that the Open Door Policy had been accepted.

This Chinese print shows the Boxers attacking westerners.

The Boxer Rebellion. Chinese resentment of foreigners continued to grow. A secret society called the Fists of Righteous Harmony—known as the Boxers by westerners—circulated handbills blaming foreigners and missionaries for China's troubles. One handbill claimed that because "the Catholic and Protestant religions are insolent [disrespectful] to the gods, . . . the rain clouds no longer visit us. But 8 million Spirit Soldiers will descend from Heaven and sweep the Empire clean of all foreigners!"

In the spring of 1900 the Boxers attacked Western missionaries and traders in northern China, killing about 300. Known as the **Boxer Rebellion**, this uprising was supported by some Chinese government officials. The Boxers laid siege to the large, walled-in foreign settlement in Beijing, China's capital. Foreign countries responded by sending troops to China. In August, after an eight-week siege, the international force rescued the foreigners.

John Hay feared that Japan and other nations would use the Boxer Rebellion as an excuse to seize control of additional Chinese

TEACH OBJECTIVE 4

LEVEL 1: Pair students and ask pairs to list the steps that Japan took after 1854 to become a world power. *(Pairs should indicate the following steps: **1**—Japan agreed to Western demands for trade; **2**—Japan industrialized rapidly; **3**— Japan built up its army and navy; **4**—Japanese troops attacked Russian forces in 1904, starting the Russo-Japanese War; **5**—Japan negotiated a peace treaty with Russia.)* Ask volunteers to read their lists to the class. Have other students fill in any gaps in the lists.

Sheltered English, Cooperative Learning

LEVELS 2 AND 3: Tell students to imagine that they are advisers to the leaders of a developing country who are seeking historical examples of countries that developed rapidly. Have each student write a short analysis of the steps Japan took to become a world power. *(See the Level 1 lesson for the correct steps.)* Ask volunteers to read their analyses to the class.

▶ASSIGNMENT *Tell students to review George Washington's position on expansion and American involvement in foreign countries. Then have each student write a one-page speculative essay to assess what Washington's reactions might have been to the expansion of U.S. territory and influence discussed in this section. Students' essays should specify three actions taken by the United States, speculate on Washington's response to each action, and give the reasons why Washington would react in a particular way.*

territory. In a second series of Open Door notes, Hay pressured the foreign powers to observe open trade throughout China and to preserve China's right to rule its own territory. China retained its sovereignty as a nation but was forced to pay the European powers $333 million for damages.

✔ **READING CHECK:** What role did the United States play in China?

Strategies for Success — Interpreting Economic Data

The use of economic data can broaden one's understanding of many historical topics. Information about exports, imports, incomes, prices, and production rates, for instance, can provide one with valuable clues about everyday life in a nation or region or the interactions between different nations or regions.

Like other historical statistics, however, economic data must be interpreted carefully. The information in a given chart or graph serves as a snapshot that shows one specific part of an economy from one specific angle. When interpreting this information, it is important to consider what you already know about the historical period.

How to Interpret Economic Data

1. **Determine the nature of the data.** Read the title of the chart or graph to identify the type of economic data it presents. Then read all of its headings, subheadings, and labels to determine the categories, amounts, and time intervals in which it presents the data.
2. **Analyze the details.** Study the information in the chart or graph carefully and systematically. Take note of increases or decreases in quantities, and look for trends, relationships, and conflicts in the data.
3. **Put the data to use.** Use your analysis of the data, along with your knowledge of the historical period, to form generalizations and draw conclusions.

Applying the Strategy

Study the graph below, which shows the value of U.S. exports to China between 1898 and 1908.

Practicing the Strategy

Use the graph below to answer the following questions.

1. In which year was the value of U.S. exports to China at its lowest? In which year was it at its highest?
2. Why do you think the value of U.S. exports to China rose and fell several times between 1898 and 1908?

U.S. Exports to China, 1898–1908

Sources: *Historical Statistics of the United States*

GLOBAL RELATIONS

Protecting China. The Open Door Policy guaranteed Chinese sovereignty by preventing European nations from carving the country up into smaller colonies. However, Chinese sovereignty was the result and not the goal of the Open Door Policy. Officials in the U.S. government never conducted any negotiations or consultations with Chinese leaders. Nonetheless, the Chinese were pleased by the policy, which remained an important part of Sino-American relations for the first half of the 1900s.

CRITICAL THINKING Why might the United States have wanted China to remain an independent nation?

ANSWER: Students might suggest that an independent China provided the United States with important economic opportunities, such as trade.

STRATEGIES FOR SUCCESS ANSWERS

Practicing the Strategy

1. 1901; 1905
2. Students might suggest that events such as the Boxer Rebellion and Russo-Japanese War probably affected the volume of trade.

REVIEW

Have students complete the **Section 1 Review** on p. 304.

ASSESS

Have students complete **Daily Quiz 10.1**. As **Alternative Assessment**, you may want to use the annotated time line or the Japan list in this section's lessons.

RETEACH

Have students complete **Main Idea Activity for Reteaching and Sheltered English 10.1**. Organize the class into four groups and assign each group one of this section's objectives. Have groups rewrite their objectives into question form. Finally, tell groups to formulate answers to their questions using relevant items from the list of key terms, key people, and key places, and other information from the textbook. Call on each group to read its question and answer to the class. Invite other students to correct errors or to add missing information.
Sheltered English, Cooperative Learning

EXTEND

Have students conduct research on the views of Alfred Thayer Mahan, Henry Cabot Lodge, or Theodore Roosevelt on the expansion of U.S. territory and influence at the beginning of the 1900s. Have each student report his or her findings in an essay. **Block Scheduling**

Define and Identify

For significance, see the following pages:

- imperialism, p. 298
- Henry Cabot Lodge, p. 298
- Alfred Thayer Mahan, p. 298
- Kalakaua, p. 300
- subsidy, p. 300
- Liliuokalani, p. 300
- spheres of influence, p. 302
- John Hay, p. 302
- Open Door Policy, p. 302
- Boxer Rebellion, p. 302
- Matthew Perry, p. 304
- Russo-Japanese War, p. 304

1. The Hawaiian League forces Kalakaua to sign the Bayonet Constitution; the McKinley Tariff creates a crisis in the sugar industry; Liliuokalani announces her intent to write a new constitution; annexationists carry out a revolt.
2. They desired foreign resources and markets.
3. resulted in a second series of Open Door notes
4. Answers will vary. Some students might argue that setting up a sphere of influence in a foreign country violates that country's sovereignty.
5. Japan was a rising power, and Roosevelt sent the Great White Fleet as a message that the United States could respond with force in the event of a conflict between the two nations.

Collectively known as the Great White Fleet because of the way they were painted, U.S. warships made stops in ports around the world as a show of U.S. military strength.

An Emerging Japan

Japan's 1894 invasion of China marked its emergence as an imperial power. Just 41 years earlier Japan had ended its almost complete isolation from the rest of the world. President Millard Fillmore had sent Commodore Matthew Perry to persuade Japan to open its doors to trade with the West. In 1854 Perry's fleet of seven warships sailed into Edo—present-day Tokyo—and presented Japan's rulers with gifts that included a telegraph transmitter and a model train.

The Japanese leaders agreed to the Western demands for trade. They reasoned that if they did not, foreigners might seize control of their nation. Japan rapidly transformed itself into an industrial power and built up its army and navy. Japan and Russia had long been rivals for Chinese territories. In February 1904, Japanese troops attacked Russian forces in Manchuria, starting the **Russo-Japanese War**.

The war worried President Theodore Roosevelt. He feared that if Russia won it might cut off U.S. trade with Manchuria, and if Japan won, it might threaten free trade in Asia. By May 1905, after winning a series of crucial battles, the Japanese asked Roosevelt to negotiate peace with Russia. In Portsmouth, New Hampshire, Roosevelt and representatives of the two countries hammered out a treaty that granted neither side all it wanted. Roosevelt was awarded the Nobel Peace Prize for his efforts.

Japan had become a modern world power and a rival to the United States for influence in China and the Pacific. Concerned by Japan's growing power, Roosevelt decided to remind the Japanese of America's military might. In late 1907 he sent a fleet of four destroyers and 16 battleships, painted a dazzling white, on a 46,000-mile world cruise that included a stop in the Japanese port of Yokohama.

✔ **READING CHECK:** How did Japan become a world power?

SECTION 1 REVIEW

Define and explain the significance of the following terms:
imperialism
subsidy
spheres of influence
Open Door Policy
Boxer Rebellion
Russo-Japanese War

Identify and explain the significance of the following individuals:
Henry Cabot Lodge
Alfred Thayer Mahan
Kalakaua
Liliuokalani
John Hay
Matthew Perry

1. **Using Graphic Organizers** Copy the chart below. Use it to list the events that led to the U.S. annexation of Hawaii.

1. Kalakaua becomes king of Hawaii in 1874.
2.
3.
4.
5.
6. The United States annexes Hawaii on July 7, 1898.

2. **Analyzing** Why did the United States and European nations begin to follow a policy of imperialism in the 1800s?
3. **Assessing Consequences** How did foreign expansion in Asia and the Boxer Rebellion affect U.S. policy toward China?
4. **Taking a Stand** Do you think any nation is ever justified in setting up a sphere of influence in a foreign country? Explain your answer.

Critical Thinking

5. Why did President Roosevelt decide to send a fleet of U.S. ships to Japan?
Consider:
- what the relationship had been between the United States and Japan
- how Japan's power had grown
- why Roosevelt saw Japan as a threat to U.S. interests

SECTION 2

OBJECTIVE 4 *Explain what happened to the Philippines after the Spanish-American War.*

After completing Section 2, students should be able to:

OBJECTIVE 1 *Recount how Spain responded to the revolt in Cuba.*

OBJECTIVE 2 *Discuss the major causes of the Spanish-American War.*

OBJECTIVE 3 *Describe the major battles of the Spanish-American War.*

LET'S GET STARTED!

As students enter the classroom, tell them to imagine that they are the president of the United States. Ask each student to speculate, in writing, on the circumstances that justify U.S. intervention in the internal affairs of other countries. List students' responses on the chalkboard. Tell students that in Section 2 they will learn about U.S. involvement in disputes between Spain and its colonies in the Caribbean and in the Pacific during the 1890s.

War with Spain

OBJECTIVES

Read to understand:

1. how Spain responded to the revolt in Cuba
2. what the major causes of the Spanish-American War were
3. what the major battles of the Spanish-American War were
4. what happened to the Philippines after the Spanish-American War

KEY TERMS

USS *Maine*
Spanish-American War
Teller Amendment
Rough Riders
Philippine Government Act
Jones Act of 1916

KEY PEOPLE

José Martí
Valeriano Weyler
William Randolph Hearst
William McKinley
George Dewey
Emilio Aguinaldo

KEY PLACES

Cuba
Puerto Rico
Manila
Santiago
San Juan Hill

"We know that they have formed a government; that they have held two elections. . . . They have risen against oppression, compared to which the oppression which led us to rebel against England is as dust in the balance. . . . No useful end is being served by the bloody struggle that is now in progress in Cuba, and in the name of humanity it should be stopped. . . . The responsibility is on us; we cannot escape it. We should . . . put a stop to that war which is now raging in Cuba and give to that island once more peace, liberty, and independence."

—Henry Cabot Lodge

THE GRANGER COLLECTION, NEW YORK

The United States protects Cuba from Spain.

In a speech delivered to the Senate on February 20, 1896, Senator Henry Cabot Lodge called for the United States to intervene in a rebellion in Cuba. Many Americans were eager to flex the nation's military muscle and put an end to a war so near its shores. Other people also wanted the United States to assert more authority and drive Spain out of the Western Hemisphere.

Conflict in Cuba

Supporters of U.S. expansion had long been interested in the Caribbean island of Cuba, located just 90 miles from the Florida Keys. In the late 1800s Cuba simmered with unrest. Cuba and its Caribbean neighbor Puerto Rico were the last of the Spanish colonies in the Americas. Since 1868, Cubans had launched a series of unsuccessful revolts against Spanish rule. To put down the rebellion, the Spanish government exiled many leaders of the independence movement.

BIOGRAPHY *José Martí*

Foremost among these Cuban exiles was the poet José Martí. Born in Havana, Cuba, on January 28, 1853, Martí joined in a revolt against Cuba's Spanish rulers when he was just 15 years old. For his actions, Martí was banished to Spain, where he earned a university degree. He later worked in Mexico and in Guatemala. Martí returned to Cuba in 1878 but was banished again for his activism. He moved to New York City, where he worked for Cuban independence.

While in New York Martí wrote poems and newspaper articles promoting Cuban independence. He also urged Cuban exiles to mount an invasion of Cuba. "Let us rise up at once with a final burst of heartfelt energy . . . for the true republic, those of us who, with our passion for right and our habit of hard work, will know how to preserve it." When Cubans launched another revolt in February 1895, Martí and other exiles joined them. Martí became a martyr for Cuban independence when he was killed months later in a battle.

SECTION 2 RESOURCES

PRINT

- Guided Reading Strategy 10.2
- Primary Source Reading 10: Teddy Roosevelt's Cavalry
- Literature Reading 10: Protesting Military Action
- Section 2 Review, p. 311
- Daily Quiz 10.2

MULTIMEDIA

- One-Stop Planner, Lesson 10.2
- Everyday Life in America Transparency 19: Photojournalism in the Spanish-American War
- Holt Researcher: American History CD–ROM
- HRW Web site

SHELTERED ENGLISH

- Main Idea Activity for Reteaching and Sheltered English 10.2

✔ READING TO UNDERSTAND

To help students master the section objectives, have them answer the **READING CHECKS** and complete **Guided Reading Strategy 10.2** as they read the section.

TEACH OBJECTIVES 1 AND 2

LEVEL 1: Tell students that the revolt in Cuba against Spanish rule provided supporters of U.S. expansion with an opportunity to intervene in Spanish-Cuban affairs. Copy the graphic organizer at right on the chalkboard, omitting the italicized answers. Then pair students and have each pair fill in the answers. Ask volunteers to share their answers with the class. Conclude by leading a discussion about the Spanish response to events in Cuba and the causes of the Spanish-American War.
Sheltered English, Cooperative Learning

Spanish Response to the Revolt in Cuba
- *exiled many leaders of the independence movement*
- *sent soldiers to battle rebels*
- *sent General Valeriano Weyler to put down the revolt*

American Intervention in Spanish-Cuban Affairs

Major Causes of the Spanish-American War
- *imperialist ambition*
- *humanitarian sympathy for the rebels*
- *yellow journalism*
- *the destruction of the USS* Maine

GLOBAL RELATIONS

General Weyler and the War. General Weyler ordered all *pacificos,* or farmers who took no part in the conflict between Cuba and Spain, to move to fortified towns. They were allowed only eight days to leave their farms, which Spanish troops then destroyed. However, no preparations were made to feed and house the *pacificos,* who were forced to live in abandoned buildings and to beg for food.

ACTIVITY: Have students discuss Weyler's concentration camp policy and the issue of human rights in wartime. Then ask each student to write a statement from a U.S. government official protesting Weyler's policy.

THAT'S INTERESTING!

Spain attempted to defend General Weyler's concentration camp policy by comparing it to General William Sherman's March to the Sea during the Civil War. This comparison did not impress Secretary of State John Sherman, who by coincidence was the brother of the Civil War general.

VISUAL RECORD ANSWER

Answers will vary. Some students might suggest that the artist tried to rally public opinion against Spain.

In 1896 Spain sent General Valeriano Weyler to put down the revolt. He forced thousands of farmers into concentration camps to prevent them from aiding the rebels. Some 200,000 Cubans died from starvation and disease in the camps.

✔ **READING CHECK:** How did Spain respond to the revolt in Cuba?

The United States Reacts

Many Americans saw similarities between the Cubans' struggle and the American Revolution and were therefore sympathetic to the Cuban rebels. The American press encouraged war with Spain and branded Weyler "the Butcher." Two New York City newspapers, William Randolph Hearst's *New York Journal* and Joseph Pulitzer's *New York World*, used sensational tales of Spanish atrocities to attract readers and sell more papers.

HOLT RESEARCHER — Read More About It

Free Find: William Randolph Hearst
After reading about William Randolph Hearst on the Holt Researcher CD–ROM, create a newspaper front page about current news stories that reflects Hearst's style of journalism.

BIOGRAPHY
William Randolph Hearst

The influence of the media. Perhaps no American journalist was more interested in the Cuban situation than William Randolph Hearst. His father had made a fortune in the California gold fields and was a rich man when his only son was born in 1863. When Hearst was 10 he and his mother traveled to Europe.

Hearst was an undisciplined student prone to mischief—he was expelled from his high school and finished his studies at home with tutors. He then attended Harvard University where he displayed little interest in academics but great enthusiasm for business and publishing. Hearst left Harvard in his junior year and got a job in New York as a reporter for Pulitzer's *World*.

Hearst's father owned the *San Francisco Examiner.* In 1887 Hearst persuaded his father to let him run the newspaper. Using a sensational style of reporting, Hearst soon turned around the failing *Examiner*. After reviving that newspaper, he returned to New York in 1895 to run the *Journal* and challenge Pulitzer. Hearst explained his view of the role of newspapers.

> "The newspaper is the greatest force in civilization. . . . Newspapers form and express public opinion. They suggest and control legislation. They declare wars. They punish criminals, especially the powerful. They reward with approving publicity the good deeds of citizens everywhere. The newspapers control the nation because they REPRESENT THE PEOPLE."

INTERPRETING THE VISUAL RECORD

Remember the *Maine!* The explosion of the battleship *Maine* led to the Spanish-American War. *What do you think the artist's purpose was in painting this scene?*

Hearst's growing newspaper empire made him a wealthy man. He built a mansion in San Simeon, California, and filled it with art and rare artifacts from around the globe. His lavish lifestyle continued until his death in 1951.

The *Maine* incident. Believing that newspapers should shape public opinion and policy, Hearst pressed for U.S. intervention in Cuba. In 1897 he sent artist Frederic Remington to Cuba to create drawings showing Spanish cruelty, which Hearst could use to increase U.S. support for war with Spain. President William McKinley, however, was a veteran of the

LEVEL 2: Have each student write two or three paragraphs to summarize the Spanish response to the revolt in Cuba and the major causes of the Spanish-American War. *(See the Level 1 graphic organizer for the correct responses and causes.)* Ask volunteers to read their paragraphs to the class.

LEVEL 3: Tell students to imagine that they are historians who must write an article entitled The Expansionist Moment: Spain's Response to the Revolt in Cuba and the Causes of the Spanish-American War for a journal of history. Have each student write a one-page article on the topic. *(See the Level 1 graphic organizer for the correct responses and causes.)* Ask volunteers to read their articles to the class.

TEACH OBJECTIVE 3

LEVEL 1: Tell students that the battles of the Spanish-American War were fought in Cuba, the Philippines, and Puerto Rico. Pair students and have each pair write a multiple-choice test about the major battles of the Spanish-American War. *(Pairs should indicate that the major battles of the Spanish-American War were the U.S. naval bombardment of Manila Bay in the Philippines, the battle for Manila, the battle for El Caney, the battle for San Juan Hill in Cuba, the battle between the U.S. and Spanish navies off the coast of Cuba, and the battle between U.S. and Spanish forces in Puerto Rico.)* Ask students in each pair to exchange their tests with another pair and then complete them. **Sheltered English, Cooperative Learning**

Civil War and resisted the calls for war. "I have been through one war. I have seen the dead piled up, and I do not want to see another," he explained.

Events soon changed McKinley's stance. On February 9, 1898, the *Journal* published a letter written by Spain's minister to the United States, Enrique Dupuy de Lôme, that had been intercepted by a Cuban spy and sold to Hearst. In this letter de Lôme ridiculed McKinley as "weak, and a bidder for the admiration of the crowd." Americans were outraged at the remarks, which the *Journal* called "the worst insult to the United States in its history."

The nation teetered on the brink of war until a tragedy in Cuba pushed it over the edge. The battleship **USS *Maine*** had been sent to Havana to protect U.S. lives and property. On February 15 the *Maine* blew up, killing 260 sailors. "DESTRUCTION OF THE WAR SHIP MAINE WAS THE WORK OF AN ENEMY!" screamed the *Journal's* headline, although there was no proof of this. Some historians believe that a fire in a coal bin caused the explosion. At the time, however, many Americans blamed Spain. "Remember the *Maine!*" became the rallying cry of war supporters.

Spanish officials agreed to a U.S.-proposed peace plan, but it was too late. On April 11 McKinley asked Congress to intervene in Cuba "in the name of humanity, in the name of civilization, and in behalf of endangered American interests." On April 25 Congress declared war on Spain. The **Spanish-American War** had begun.

✔ **READING CHECK:** What were the major causes of the Spanish-American War?

$50,000 REWARD.—WHO DESTROYED THE MAINE?—$50,000 REWARD.

NEW YORK JOURNAL AND ADVERTISER

DESTRUCTION OF THE WAR SHIP MAINE WAS THE WORK OF AN ENEMY.

$50,000! $50,000 REWARD! For the Detection of the Perpetrator of the Maine Outrage!

Assistant Secretary Roosevelt Convinced the Explosion of the War Ship Was Not an Accident.

The Journal Offers $50,000 Reward for the Conviction of the Criminals Who Sent 258 American Sailors to Their Death. Naval Officers Unanimous That the Ship Was Destroyed on Purpose.

$50,000! $50,000 REWARD! For the Detection of the Perpetrator of the Maine Outrage!

NAVAL OFFICERS THINK THE MAINE WAS DESTROYED BY A SPANISH MINE.

INTERPRETING THE VISUAL RECORD

The media. The destruction of the *Maine* was front-page news throughout the United States. ***How does the* New York Journal *explain the sinking?***

War with Spain

On April 20, 1898, Congress recognized Cuba's independence and voted to use U.S. military force to help Cuba attain it. Congress also adopted the **Teller Amendment**. This stated that once Cuba won its independence from Spain, the United States would "leave the government and control of the Island to its people."

Fighting in the Philippines. The war's first battle was fought halfway around the world in the Spanish-held Philippine Islands. Weeks before war was declared, Assistant Secretary of the Navy Theodore Roosevelt had cabled secret orders to Commodore George Dewey in Hong Kong. In the event of war between the United States and Spain, Dewey was to attack the Philippines.

As dawn broke on May 1, 1898, Dewey's fleet steamed across Manila Bay, in the Philippines. Commodore Dewey stood on the bridge of his flagship, *Olympia.* He trained his eyes on the Spanish guns on the shore and the small Spanish fleet anchored in the harbor. The Spanish sighted the Americans and opened fire, but Dewey's ships were out of range. The U.S. ships slowly moved closer to shore. Shortly after 5:30 A.M., Dewey told the *Olympia*'s captain: "You may fire when you are ready, Gridley." The bay echoed with the roar of naval guns. As shells crashed into several Spanish vessels, they erupted into flames.

Led by George Dewey, U.S. forces destroyed the Spanish fleet in the Battle of Manila Bay.

THEN AND NOW

The *Maine*. Shortly after the *Maine* exploded, a U.S. court of inquiry declared that a mine had caused the damage to the ship, a ruling later supported by the U.S. Army Corps of Engineers. In the 1970s, however, an investigatory team studied photographs of the ship and announced that an internal explosion had caused the damage. The debate continued when a later group examined the photographs and said that the evidence was inconclusive—the *Maine* might have been sunk by a mine or by an internal explosion.

CRITICAL THINKING What might the differing interpretations indicate?

ANSWER: Students might suggest that the interpretations indicate that the photographic evidence currently available is not sufficient to solve the mystery.

internetconnect

TOPIC: Spanish-American War
GO TO: go.hrw.com
KEYWORD: SE1 Spanish

Have students access the Internet through the HRW Web site to conduct research on the Spanish-American War, including the sinking of the *Maine.* Then have each student create a radio script describing the sinking of the *Maine* and reporting on the war.

LEVELS 2 AND 3: Tell students to study the map of the Spanish-American War and to review the explanation of land and naval engagements during the war. Then have each student write an essay that discusses the major battles of the Spanish-American War. *(See the Level 1 lesson for the correct battles.)* In their essays, students should use the evidence provided in the textbook to support or reject the following premise: "The Spanish-American War was decided primarily at sea."

SPOTLIGHT on the Spanish View of the Spanish-American War

Have students conduct research on Spanish views of the Spanish-American War. Students should research how General Weyler's actions were regarded in Spain, the Spanish response to U.S. actions during the war, and whether the war had popular support from the Spanish public. Ask students to present their findings in a short essay. Have volunteers present their essays to the class. **Block Scheduling**

TECHNOLOGY AND SOCIETY

Balloons in Wartime. As the troops prepared to take the heights over Santiago, army officers launched a hot air balloon to make observations of the enemy soldiers. Unfortunately, the balloon revealed the position of the Americans to the Spanish soldiers, who fired in the direction of the balloon and caused numerous casualties among the American troops. Eventually, the balloon itself was shot down.

CRITICAL THINKING What modern-day technologies might have replaced observation balloons?

ANSWER: Students might mention satellites and high-altitude planes.

VISUAL RECORD ANSWER

Students might suggest that it is unusual for most of the soldiers to be on foot.

VISUAL RECORD ANSWER

(for p. 307)

The Journal *attributes the sinking to the work of an enemy. Some students might suggest that the newspaper did not have proof of its explanation.*

Multimedia Resources

Everyday Life in America Transparency 19: Photojournalism in the Spanish-American War

U.S. troops in Cuba were poorly prepared for the tropical conditions they faced.

Dewey's fleet easily defeated the small Spanish fleet guarding the Philippine city of Manila. To capture the city, Dewey obtained the support of a rebel army of Filipino patriots led by Emilio Aguinaldo (ahg-ee-NAHL-doh). Filipinos had been fighting for independence from Spain for two years. Cut off by Dewey's warships and surrounded by Aguinaldo's rebels, Spanish forces in the Philippines surrendered on August 14, 1898.

Fighting in Cuba. Victory in Cuba proved more difficult than in the Philippines. With a regular army of just some 28,000 soldiers, the U.S. War Department was unprepared for land battles. U.S. troops had received little training and were outfitted in heavy wool uniforms—the only ones that army storehouses could supply—when they sailed for tropical Cuba in mid-June 1898. A soldier described life once the troops arrived in Cuba.

> **"Heavy rains pouring down, no tents for cover, . . . standing in trenches in a foot of water and mud, day and night. . . . Ration issue consisting of a slice of sow belly, hardtack, and some grains of coffee. . . . Then came the issue of fleece-lined underwear in a 132 [degree] climate. . . . Then came on malaria."**

On July 1, U.S. troops attacked the Spanish fort at Santiago. Their aim was to capture the territory above Santiago. This included El Caney and San Juan Hill, which would let them aim their guns down on Spanish troops. One U.S. division overcame Spanish forces at El Caney.

Lieutenant Colonel Theodore Roosevelt had resigned his naval post. In the war's most famous battle, he led a cavalry unit of about 1,000 soldiers toward the garrison on San Juan Hill. Composed largely of college athletes, cowboys, American Indians, and ranchers, the unit was known as the **Rough Riders**.

Because their horses had not been shipped to Cuba, the Rough Riders had to charge on foot under intense Spanish fire. The African American 9th and 10th Cavalries cleared the way for the final surge. By nightfall, U.S. troops controlled the ridge above Santiago. Then, on July 3, the U.S. Navy sank the Spanish fleet off the coast of Cuba as it tried to escape from a U.S. naval blockade. The battle resulted in more than 400 Spanish casualties. Two weeks later, Spanish troops in Cuba surrendered. Meanwhile, U.S. troops defeated Spanish forces in Puerto Rico.

INTERPRETING THE VISUAL RECORD

San Juan Hill. Theodore Roosevelt led a cavalry unit known as the Rough Riders in the Spanish-American War. ***What is unusual about the cavalry soldiers shown in the painting?***

The war proved costly for Spain. By the terms of the peace treaty, Spain gave up all claim to Cuba and ceded Puerto Rico and the Pacific island of Guam to the United States. Spain also gave up control of the Philippines in return for a U.S. payment of $20 million. By gaining control of overseas territories, the United States moved into the ranks of the imperialist world powers. Expansionists expressed delight, but the quest for empire troubled many Americans. Furthermore, the United States paid a heavy human toll for the war. Some 5,400 soldiers died, nearly 400 in battle and the rest from disease or food poisoning.

✔ **READING CHECK:** What were the major battles of the Spanish-American War?

TEACH OBJECTIVE 4

LEVEL 1: Tell students to imagine that they are foreign correspondents who have been assigned to cover the Philippines for a newspaper. Pair students and have each pair write four headlines to describe events in the Philippines after the Spanish-American War. *(Pairs' headlines should note that Emilio Aguinaldo set up a provisional government in the Philippines, that the United States annexed the Philippines, Filipino independence fighters battled U.S. soldiers for control of the Philippines, that U.S. forces put down the rebellion in 1902, that the United States passed the Philippine Government Act to establish a government for the Philippines and that the Philippines gained its independence on July 4, 1946.)* Ask volunteers to read their headlines to the class. **Sheltered English, Cooperative Learning**

LEVEL 2: Pair students and ask each pair to write a two-paragraph summary of the fate of the Philippines after the Spanish-American War. *(See the Level 1 lesson for the correct events.)* Then ask pairs to draw a series of political cartoons with captions to illustrate the events in the Philippines. Display the cartoons around the classroom. **Cooperative Learning**

Literature of the Spanish-American War

At the time of the Spanish-American War, the United States was still deeply divided by sectional tensions. Some of the literature that was inspired by the war tried to encourage a sense of unity among all Americans. Other writers, particularly journalists, tried to portray an accurate picture of the fighting. The two excerpts below illustrate these themes. In the first, Stephen Crane reports for the New York World *on the real-life experiences of soldiers. In the second excerpt, from* Crittenden, *a novel by John Fox Jr., a former Confederate soldier is rewarded for his services in the Spanish-American War.*

from "Night Attacks on the Marines and a Brave Rescue"

by Stephen Crane

Stephen Crane

GUANTANAMO, July 4.—The night attacks were heart-breaking affairs, from which the men emerged in the morning exhausted to a final degree, like people who had been swimming for miles. From colonel to smallest trumpeter went a great thrill when the dawn broke slowly in the eastern sky, and the weary band quite cheerfully ate breakfast. . . . Afterward the men slept, sunk upon the ground in an abandon [physical exhaustion] that was almost a stupor [daze].

Lieut. Neville, with his picket [forward group] of about twenty men, was entirely cut off from camp one night, and another night Neville's picket and the picket of Lieut. Shaw were cut off, fighting hard in the thickets [forests] for their lives. At the break of day the beleaguered [surrounded] camp could hear still the rifles of their lost pickets.

The guerrillas were still lurking [hiding] in the near woods, and it was unsafe enough in camp without venturing into the bush.

Volunteers from Company C . . . went out under Lieut. Lucas. They arrived in Neville's vicinity just as he and his men, together with Shaw and his men, were being finally surrounded at close range. Lucas and his seventeen men broke through the guerrillas and saved the pickets, and the whole body then fell back to Crest Hill. That is all there is to it.

from *Crittenden: A Kentucky Story of Love and War*

by John Fox Jr.

"You're a Sergeant, Crittenden," said the Captain.

He, Crittenden, in blood and sympathy the spirit of secession—bearer now of the Stars and Stripes! How his heart thumped, and how his head reeled when he caught the staff and looked dumbly up to the folds; and in spite of all his self-control, the tears came.

Right at that moment there was a great bustle in camp . . . and the victorious Stars and Stripes rose up. . . . On the very stroke of twelve, there came thunder—the thunder of two-score and one salutes. And the cheers—the cheers! . . . And on a little knoll not far away stood Sergeant Crittenden, swaying on his feet—colour-sergeant to the folds of the ever-victorious, ever-beloved Old Glory waving over him, with a strange new wave of feeling surging through him. For then and there, Crittenden, Southerner, died straightaway and through a travail of wounds, suffering, sickness, devotion, and love for that flag—Crittenden, American, was born.

UNDERSTANDING LITERATURE

1. What adjectives does Stephen Crane use to describe the soldiers' experiences?
2. How does the excerpt from *Crittenden* address the divisions in American society?
3. What similarities and differences do you notice in the two excerpts?

PEOPLE IN HISTORY

Stephen Crane. Born the youngest of 14 children, Stephen Crane dropped out of college and moved to New York City to pursue his writing. He spent a great deal of time in the city's Bowery slum while researching his first novel, *Maggie: A Girl of the Streets.* The novel, which discusses a young girl's descent into dissipation, was so unconventional that Crane was forced to use a pseudonym and to publish it himself. He struggled through months of poverty until he made important literary contacts and published *The Red Badge of Courage*, a well-known novel about the Civil War.

ACTIVITY: Have students reread the excerpt by Crane on this page. Conduct a brief discussion on the excerpt's literary style. Then have each student write a short piece about a current event in the style of the excerpt.

AMERICAN LETTERS ANSWERS

1. "heart-breaking," "stupor," and "unsafe"
2. uses the symbol of the American flag to address regional divisions between northerners and southerners.
3. The excerpts differ in style—Crane was more journalistic and Fox was more literary—but share the Spanish-American War as a subject.

LEVEL 3: Tell students to imagine that they are Filipinos after the Spanish-American War. Have each student write a series of diary entries that chronicle major events in the history of the Philippines from the end of the Spanish-American War through the Philippines' independence. *(See the Level 1 lesson for the correct events.)* Ask students, in their roles as Filipinos, to include their emotions during these major events. Ask volunteers to read their entries to the class.

▶ASSIGNMENT *Have each student write a position paper on the question of whether the United States should have annexed the Philippines. To help students form a position, tell students to ask themselves when and under what circumstances, if any, annexation is proper or justified? Encourage students to examine the issue of annexation of the Philippines in its historical context.*

▶ASSIGNMENT *Have each student create a poster or a slogan to express his or her views on the U.S. decision to annex the Philippines. Call on volunteers to explain their views. Display students' posters around the classroom.*

NOTE: For an additional teaching idea, see the Chapter 10 analyzing political cartoons lesson in the **Creative Teaching Strategies** handbook.

CULTURAL DIVERSITY

Race and Annexation. Issues of race played a role on both sides of the debate regarding the annexation of the Philippines. Those who favored expansion declared that Americans had a responsibility to care for the nonwhite population of the islands. This group quoted the recently published poem, "The White Man's Burden," by British author Rudyard Kipling, in support of their claim. Opponents of annexation argued that Filipinos would demand entry into the United States. In order to calm these and other fears, the Senate approved a resolution that made it clear that Filipinos would not become U.S. citizens and the islands would never become a state.

ACTIVITY: Help students obtain a copy of Kipling's poem "The White Man's Burden." Conduct a discussion of the meaning of the poem and Kipling's justification of imperialism.

MAP ANSWER
Manila Bay

VISUAL RECORD ANSWER
(for p. 311)
Students might suggest that the cartoon justifies U.S. actions by portraying Emilio Aguinaldo as a dictator.

U.S. control brought modern developments like electricity, telephones, and streetcar service to the Philippines.

Uproar over the Philippines

In 1898 few Americans even knew where the Philippines were. Even President McKinley confessed that before he consulted a globe, he could not locate the islands "within two thousand miles." Now Americans faced an urgent question: Should Filipinos be forced to accept U.S. rule?

The debate over annexation. Some Americans questioned whether it was proper or wise for the United States to annex any foreign territory and rule its government and its people. Expansionists argued forcefully in favor of annexation. In addition to supporting annexation for commercial and security reasons, some believed that the United States would bring democracy to the Philippines. Others held that U.S. rule of the islands was necessary to keep out European powers. Charles Denby, a former U.S. minister to China, warned opponents of annexation that times had changed. "We have a great commerce to take care of. We have to compete with the commercial nations of the world in far-distant markets. Commerce, not politics, is king."

Opponents of annexation responded that by denying the Philippines independence, the United States would violate its own ideals expressed in the Declaration

Spanish-American War, 1898

Learning from Maps The Spanish-American War was primarily decided at sea. The U.S. Navy easily conquered the Spanish fleets protecting Cuba and the Philippines. Both Spanish fleets were destroyed, while the Americans suffered few casualties.

? LOCATION Where did Commodore George Dewey destroy the Spanish fleet?

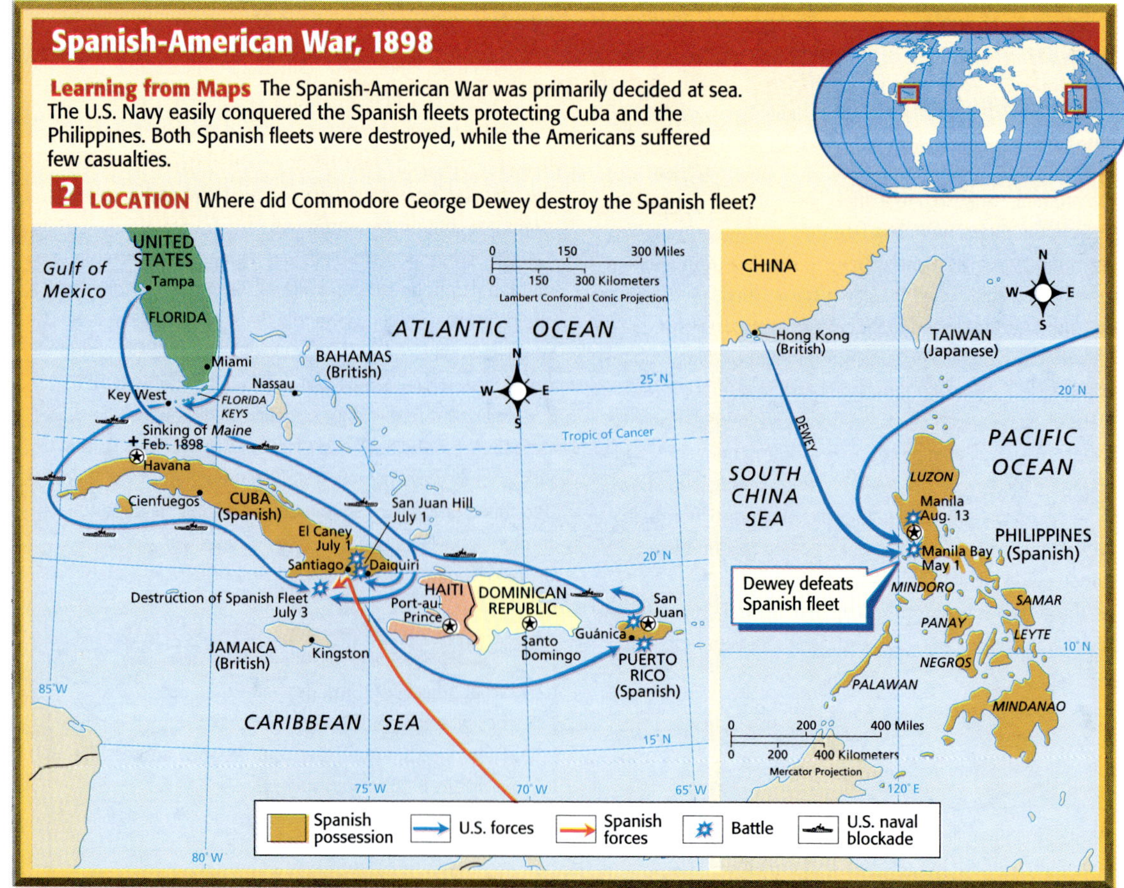

REVIEW

Have students complete the **Section 2 Review** on p. 311.

ASSESS

Have students complete **Daily Quiz 10.2.** As **Alternative Assessment**, you may want to use the war test or the Philippines headlines in this section's lessons.

RETEACH

Have students complete **Main Idea Activity for Reteaching and Sheltered English 10.2.** Then write each term in the Section Review on an index card. Give one to each student. On the back of the card, have the student write a brief paragraph explaining the term and its importance for the causes, the course, or the consequences of the Spanish-American War. Then pair students. Have one student read the "clue" on the back of the card and have his or her partner guess the term that it describes. Have students then form different pairs and repeat the process.
Sheltered English, Cooperative Learning

EXTEND

Have students conduct research on the Anti-Imperialist League. Then pair students and have each pair compose a dialogue based on its research to explain the reasons why members of the league opposed annexation.
Cooperative Learning, Block Scheduling

---

of Independence. In June 1898, opponents of U.S. imperialism formed the Anti-Imperialist League and announced their beliefs.

> **"We regret that it has become necessary . . . to reaffirm that all men, of whatever race or color, are entitled to life, liberty, and the pursuit of happiness. . . . The subjugation of any people is 'criminal aggression' and open disloyalty to the . . . principles of our Government."**

After a fierce debate, the Senate narrowly approved the treaty, annexing the Philippines on February 6, 1899.

Conquest and early rule. Emilio Aguinaldo had already set up a provisional government and proclaimed himself president of the new Philippine Republic. He warned that Filipinos would go to war if "American troops attempt to take forcible possession. Upon their heads will be all the blood which may be shed." For the next three years, Filipino independence fighters battled U.S. soldiers for control of the Philippines. By the time U.S. forces crushed the rebellion in 1902, hundreds of thousands of Filipinos and more than 4,000 U.S. soldiers had lost their lives.

In 1902 the U.S. Congress passed the **Philippine Government Act**, also known as the Organic Act, which established a governor and a two-house legislature to rule the Philippines. The United States would appoint the governor and the legislature's upper house, but Filipino voters would elect the lower house. The **Jones Act of 1916** granted Filipinos the right to elect both houses of their legislature. On July 4, 1946, the United States finally granted independence to the Philippines.

INTERPRETING THE VISUAL RECORD
Filipino opposition. This cartoon shows U.S. military power crushing Emilio Aguinaldo's government. ***How does the cartoon justify U.S. actions in the Philippines?***

✔ **READING CHECK:** What happened to the Philippines after the Spanish-American War?

SECTION 2 REVIEW

Define and explain the significance of the following terms:
USS *Maine*
Spanish-American War
Teller Amendment
Rough Riders
Philippine Government Act
Jones Act of 1916

Identify and explain the significance of the following individuals:
José Martí
Valeriano Weyler
William Randolph Hearst
William McKinley
George Dewey
Emilio Aguinaldo

Locate and explain the importance of the following places:
Cuba
Puerto Rico
Manila
Santiago
San Juan Hill

1. **Using Graphic Organizers** Copy the chart below. Use it to list the actions taken by the United States and Spain leading up to and during the Spanish-American War.

United States
Spain

2. **Identifying Cause and Effect** How did Spain's reaction to the revolt in Cuba lead the United States to declare war against Spain in 1898?
3. **Understanding Geography: Human-Environment Interaction** What territories did the United States gain as a result of the Spanish-American War?
4. **Evaluating** How did publisher William Randolph Hearst influence the U.S. government to declare war on Spain?

Critical Thinking

5. Why did Filipinos rebel against the United States after the Spanish-American War?
Consider:
- the reasons the United States became involved in the Philippines
- the role of Filipino rebels in the war against Spain
- why the United States did not initially grant independence to the Philippines

SECTION 2 REVIEW ANSWERS

Define and Identify
For significance, see the following pages:
- José Martí, p. 305
- Valeriano Weyler, p. 306
- William Randolph Hearst, p. 306
- William McKinley, p. 306
- USS *Maine,* p. 307
- Spanish-American War, p. 307
- Teller Amendment, p. 307
- George Dewey, p. 307
- Emilio Aguinaldo, p. 308
- Rough Riders, p. 308
- Philippine Government Act, p. 311
- Jones Act of 1916, p. 311

Locate
For locations, see the map on p. 310. For importance, see the following pages:
- Cuba, p. 305
- Manila, p. 308
- Puerto Rico, p. 308
- Santiago, p. 308
- San Juan Hill, p. 308

1. United States—bombarded Spanish fleet at Manila Bay, captured heights above Santiago, destroyed Spanish fleet in Cuba, defeated Spanish troops in Puerto Rico; Spain—defended Manila Bay, Santiago, and Puerto Rico
2. The United States was sympathetic to the Cuban rebels.
3. Puerto Rico, Guam, and the Philippines
4. built public support for the war in his newspapers
5. turned against the United States when it annexed the Philippines instead of supporting independence

SECTION 3

After completing Section 3, students should be able to:

OBJECTIVE 1 *Explain how the United States governed Cuba and Puerto Rico.*

OBJECTIVE 2 *Describe the major obstacles to building the Panama Canal.*

OBJECTIVE 3 *Summarize U.S. policy toward Latin America during the late 1800s and early 1900s.*

LET'S GET STARTED!

As students enter the classroom, tell them to read the quotation from Charles Elliot Norton on this page. Ask students to respond to the quotation in writing, recalling the information presented in Sections 1 and 2 of this chapter. Students should explain what Norton might have meant when he referred to the United States's "unique position as a potential leader in the progress of civilization." Tell students that in Section 3 they will learn about the expansionist activities of the United States in Latin America.

SECTION 3 RESOURCES

PRINT

- Guided Reading Strategy 10.3
- Graphic Organizer Activity 10: Changes in Cuba
- Biography Reading 10: William Gorgas
- Section 3 Review, p. 316
- Daily Quiz 10.3

MULTIMEDIA

- One-Stop Planner, Lesson 10.3
- The American Nation Video Program Segment: The Panama Canal; Teacher's Guide, pp. 93–98
- Holt Researcher: American History CD–ROM

SHELTERED ENGLISH

- Main Idea Activity for Reteaching and Sheltered English 10.3

✔ READING TO UNDERSTAND

To help students master the section objectives, have them answer the **READING CHECKS** and complete **Guided Reading Strategy 10.3** as they read the section.

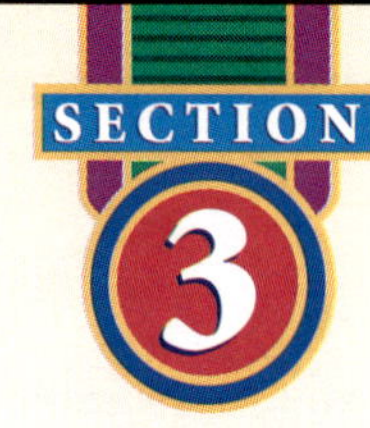

Expansion in Latin America

OBJECTIVES

Read to understand:

1. how the United States governed Cuba and Puerto Rico
2. what the major obstacles to building the Panama Canal were
3. what U.S. policy toward Latin America during the late 1800s and early 1900s was

KEY TERMS

Platt Amendment
protectorate
Foraker Act
Hay–Bunau-Varilla Treaty
Roosevelt Corollary
dollar diplomacy

KEY PEOPLE

Leonard Wood
Philippe Bunau-Varilla

KEY PLACES

Panama Canal

EYEWITNESSES TO History

"We believe that America had something better to offer to mankind than those aims she is now pursuing. . . . She has lost her unique position as a potential leader in the progress of civilization and has taken up her place simply as one of the grasping and selfish nations of the present day."

—Charles Elliot Norton

U.S. soldiers questioning Filipino women

In this 1899 letter, Charles Elliot Norton expressed his disappointment with the United States for seizing an empire by force and for annexing the Philippines. Many Americans shared Norton's concerns about the course the United States was following. Supporters of U.S. actions, however, argued that the territories would benefit from U.S. rule and protection.

Governing Cuba and Puerto Rico

As the power of the United States grew in the Pacific, its role in Latin America expanded as well. Wanting to restore order in Cuba and Puerto Rico quickly and protect U.S. investments, President McKinley set up military governments to rule the islands. McKinley appointed General Leonard Wood as governor of Cuba in 1899. Wood authorized the construction of schools and a sanitation system. U.S. Army doctors Walter Reed and William Gorgas led sanitation efforts to reduce the mosquito population. Carlos Finlay (feen-LY), a Cuban doctor, had theorized that mosquitoes spread yellow fever. He was right. The sanitation system drained pools of standing water where mosquitoes bred. It all but eliminated yellow fever.

Wood also oversaw the drafting of a new constitution that limited Cuba's independence. Congress agreed to remove U.S. troops from the island only if Cuba made the **Platt Amendment** part of its constitution. The amendment limited Cuba's freedom to make treaties with other countries and authorized the United States to intervene in Cuban affairs as it saw necessary. It also required Cuba to sell or lease land to the United States for naval and fueling stations. This last clause led to the establishment of a U.S. naval base at Guantánamo Bay. In effect, the Platt Amendment made Cuba a U.S. **protectorate**. This meant that the United States promised to protect Cuba from other nations but reserved the right to intervene in Cuba's affairs. In 1902, after Cuba reluctantly accepted the Platt Amendment, U.S. troops withdrew. Over the next three decades, the United States intervened in Cuba several times. The Platt Amendment remained in force until 1934, when the United States renounced its right to intervene in Cuba.

U.S. policy in Puerto Rico followed a different course. The United States ruled the island as a territory like Samoa or the Philippines in the Pacific. The **Foraker Act** of 1900 established that Puerto Rico's governor and upper house of the legislature would be appointed by the United States. It also established that a lower

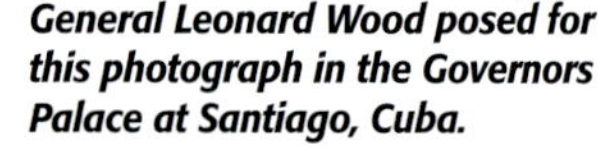

General Leonard Wood posed for this photograph in the Governors Palace at Santiago, Cuba.

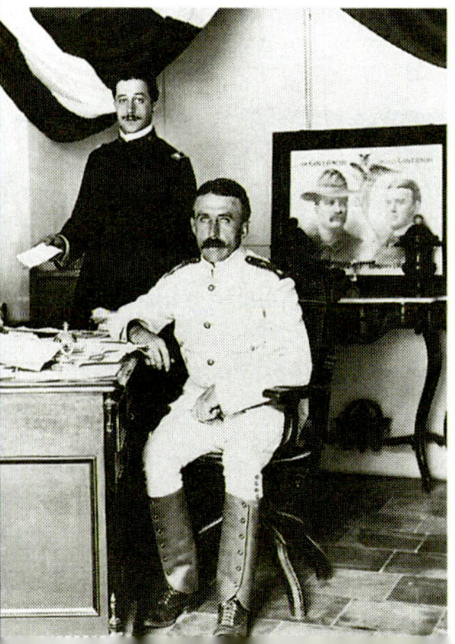

TEACH OBJECTIVE 1

ALL LEVELS: Conduct a brief discussion of how the United States governed Cuba and Puerto Rico. Then copy the following graphic organizer on the chalkboard, omitting the italicized answers. Have students complete it. Ask volunteers to share their answers with the class.
Sheltered English

▶ASSIGNMENT *Have each student outline the provisions of the Platt Amendment and draw a political cartoon that illustrates his or her position on the question of whether or not the Platt Amendment violated the Teller Amendment passed by Congress in 1898.*

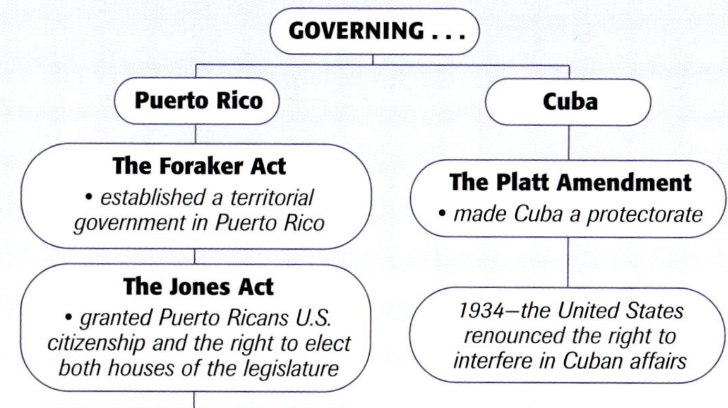

house would be elected by Puerto Ricans. The Jones Act of 1917 granted Puerto Ricans U.S. citizenship and gave them the right to elect both houses of their legislature. In 1952 Puerto Rico became a self-governing commonwealth of the United States, with continuing ties of citizenship and trade with the mainland.

✔ **READING CHECK:** How did the United States govern Cuba and Puerto Rico?

HOLT RESEARCHER *Read More About It*

Free Find: Foraker Act

After learning about the Foraker Act on the **Holt Researcher** CD–ROM, write an encyclopedia entry describing the act's historical importance.

The Panama Canal

Having interests in both the Caribbean and the Pacific, the United States wanted to cut the travel time between the seas. Traveling around South America took several weeks. The United States proposed digging a canal across Central America.

Early steps toward a canal. In the 1880s, led by the man who had built the Suez Canal in Egypt, a French company began building a canal across the 50-mile-wide Isthmus of Panama. After less than 10 years and the loss of some 20,000 lives and more than $280 million, the French abandoned the effort.

In 1901 Secretary of State John Hay began negotiations with the Republic of Colombia—of which Panama was then a part. In 1903 a treaty was drafted. In return for a 99-year lease on a six-mile strip of land across the isthmus, the United States agreed to pay Colombia $10 million and a yearly rental of $250,000. However, Colombia's senate held out for better terms and adjourned without ratifying the treaty. President Roosevelt was furious. He vowed that the Colombians would not be allowed "to bar one of the future highways of civilization."

Revolution in Panama. Events in Panama soon turned in Roosevelt's favor. Key Panamanian leaders who wanted the canal built began plotting revolution against the Colombian government. Helping them was Philippe Bunau-Varilla (boo-noh-vah-ree-yah), the former chief engineer for the French canal-building attempt.

Bunau-Varilla traveled to Washington, D.C., to get American support for the revolution. On October 9, 1903, he met privately with President Roosevelt. On November 2 the U.S. gunboat *Nashville* arrived in Panama. The following day, Panamanians began their rebellion. U.S. Marines prevented Colombian forces from reaching the rebels.

The victorious rebels quickly set up a new government and declared Panama an independent nation. The United States recognized the Republic of Panama two days later, and Hay began negotiating a new canal treaty with Panama's special envoy, Bunau-Varilla. The **Hay–Bunau-Varilla Treaty** gave the United States complete and unending sovereignty over a 10-mile-wide Canal Zone. President Roosevelt later boasted, "I took the Canal Zone and let Congress debate."

Panama Canal Zone

Learning from Maps After the Spanish-American War, pressure increased to build a U.S.-controlled canal through Central America.

? MOVEMENT If you enter the Panama Canal from the Caribbean Sea on the Atlantic side, which direction will you travel to exit to the Pacific Ocean?

ACROSS THE CURRICULUM

▶GEOGRAPHY◀

A Home for the Canal. Panama was not the only location considered for the construction of a canal between the Atlantic and Pacific Oceans. During the 1800s, most Americans assumed that it would be built in Nicaragua, while others hoped that it would be built across southern Mexico.

CRITICAL THINKING Why might many Americans have favored the construction of a canal in Mexico?

ANSWER: Answers will vary. Some students might suggest that Mexico's proximity to the United States made it a favored site.

MAP ANSWER
Southeast

***The American Nation* VIDEO PROGRAM**

The Panama Canal;
Teacher's Guide, pp. 93–98

Search 00598, Play to 07996
Videodisc 2, Side A

Play Pause

See *Teacher's Guide* for Spanish barcode.

TEACH OBJECTIVE 2

LEVEL 1: Pair students and tell them to imagine that it is 1905 and that they are American artists living in Panama. Have each pair create four or five postcards depicting the construction of the canal. On the back of each postcard, students should write a brief description of the obstacles that workers encountered. *(Pairs' postcards should note the following obstacles: harsh working conditions, shortages of labor and materials, and an outbreak of yellow fever.)* Have volunteers present and display their postcards around the classroom. **Sheltered English, Cooperative Learning**

LEVEL 2: Pair students and have each pair write a short poem describing the major obstacles to building the Panama Canal. *(See the Level 1 lesson for the correct obstacles.)* Have volunteers read their poems to the class. **Cooperative Learning**

LEVEL 3: Organize the class into groups of four. Have each group write a brief play about the major obstacles to building the Panama Canal. *(See the Level 1 lesson for the correct obstacles.)* Have volunteers perform their plays for the class. **Cooperative Learning**

▸ASSIGNMENT *Have each student write a one-page letter to a newspaper to support or oppose President Theodore Roosevelt's actions in securing for the United States the right to build a canal in Central America. Tell students to explain their positions.*

GLOBAL RELATIONS

The Colombian Government. Colombians faced many problems as they considered the canal treaty with the United States. Colombia had just gone through a civil war, and the country's leader did not have firm control over the government. Colombia was very poor, and the legislature, which saw the proposed canal as a source of revenue, delayed ratification of the treaty, hoping to obtain more favorable terms from the United States. Theodore Roosevelt, however, regarded Colombia's actions to be "blackmail."

CRITICAL THINKING How might Roosevelt's perceptions and his eagerness to build the canal have affected his response to Colombia's delay in ratifying the treaty?

ANSWER: Students might suggest he ignored the concerns and needs of the Colombian people as expressed by the legislature.

SCIENCE & TECHNOLOGY ANSWERS

1. blasting a path through the Continental Divide
2. some 6,000 lives; $375 million

314

This cartoon pokes fun at the many schemes that led to the building of the Panama Canal.

Building the canal. Work on the canal began in 1904. However, harsh working conditions and shortages of labor and materials hampered U.S. efforts. The situation grew worse when a serious outbreak of yellow fever hit. By early 1905 the project had reached a near standstill.

To put the project back on track, Roosevelt appointed John F. Stevens as chief engineer and architect. Stevens tackled the technical problems and army colonel Dr. William C. Gorgas worked on improving living conditions. Gorgas applied to Panama the lessons he had learned in Cuba. By 1906 yellow fever had almost been eliminated. Malaria was under control by 1913.

Canal construction soon resumed. More than 60 giant steam shovels bit into the land, digging out nearly 160 trainloads of earth each day. More than 43,000 workers, many recruited from the British West Indies, built the canal. On August 15, 1914, the SS *Ancon* completed the first passage through the Panama Canal.

✔ **READING CHECK:** What were the major obstacles to building the Panama Canal?

Science & Technology

The Panama Canal

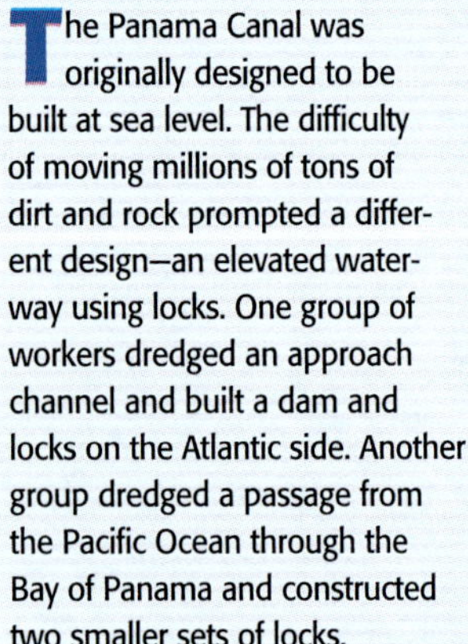

The Panama Canal was originally designed to be built at sea level. The difficulty of moving millions of tons of dirt and rock prompted a different design—an elevated waterway using locks. One group of workers dredged an approach channel and built a dam and locks on the Atlantic side. Another group dredged a passage from the Pacific Ocean through the Bay of Panama and constructed two smaller sets of locks.

The hardest task fell to another group, which had to blast an eight-mile-long channel through the mountainous Continental Divide. Geologic faults, heavy rains, and shifting earth caused frequent and often fatal avalanches. Finally, on October 10, 1913, President Woodrow Wilson signaled crews to dynamite the protective dike at the south end of the channel. In a dramatic finale, water from the two sides rushed together—85 feet above sea level.

The human and economic costs of building the canal were staggering: some 6,000 workers died, and about $375 million was spent. However, the seemingly impossible had become a reality. The United States—and the rest of the world—now had a "Path Between the Seas."

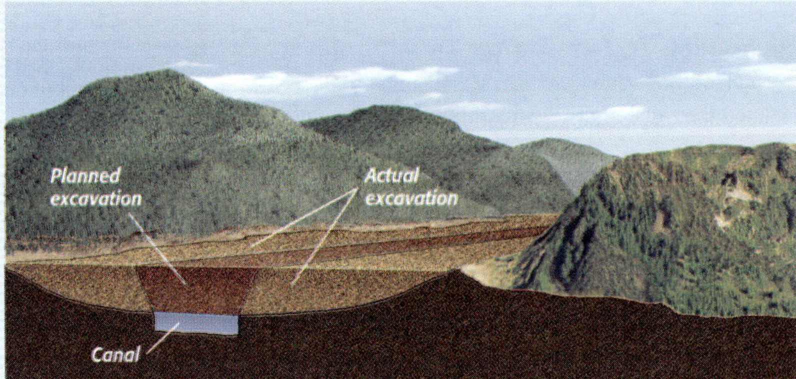

Understanding Science and History

1. What was the most difficult obstacle that the builders of the Panama Canal had to overcome?
2. What was the cost of the canal in dollars and in lives?

TEACH OBJECTIVE 3

LEVELS 1 AND 2: Organize students into triads. Have each triad develop a graphic organizer that outlines U.S. policy toward Latin America during the Roosevelt, Taft, and Wilson administrations. *(Triads should note that Roosevelt's policy was shaped by the Roosevelt Corollary, which claimed police powers for the United States in the Western Hemisphere; Taft favored dollar diplomacy, or the investment of U.S. capital in Latin America to supplant European investments; Wilson wanted to establish constitutional democracies in Latin America.)* Ask volunteers to present their graphic organizers to the class. **Sheltered English, Cooperative Learning**

LEVEL 3: Have each student compose an imaginary conversation among Roosevelt, Taft, and Wilson on U.S. policy toward Latin America. *(See the Levels 1 and 2 lesson for the correct policies.)* In the conversation, students should have each president argue in favor of his interpretation of the Monroe Doctrine and justify the application of U.S. power in support of his policy. Students may wish to include the text of their conversations in their portfolios.

Relations with Latin America

The United States has a long history of involvement in Latin America. Since the early 1800s it has sought to limit the influence of foreign nations there.

Applying the Monroe Doctrine. Beginning in 1823 the Monroe Doctrine cast the United States as protector of the Western Hemisphere. For much of the century the doctrine served as little more than an idle threat. This changed following the Spanish-American War. Presidents Theodore Roosevelt, William H. Taft, and Woodrow Wilson actively enforced the Monroe Doctrine as a way to protect U.S. interests in Latin America.

Latin America's wealth of raw materials and its many potential laborers and consumers attracted a flood of European and American capital during the late 1800s. Much of this capital was in the form of high-interest bank loans. Many Latin American countries welcomed the loans, but the high interest rates made them difficult to repay. Foreign powers often intervened to collect the loans.

The Roosevelt Corollary. President Roosevelt made it clear that he intended to enforce the Monroe Doctrine in 1904. The Dominican Republic was unable to repay its European lenders. Fearing that the Europeans would use force to collect the loans, he issued the **Roosevelt Corollary** to the Monroe Doctrine.

> **"If a nation . . . keeps order and pays its obligations, it need fear no interference from the United States. Chronic wrongdoing . . . in the Western Hemisphere . . . may force the United States, however reluctantly, . . . to the exercise of an international police power."**

Without seeking approval from any Latin American nation, Roosevelt had put into practice a West African proverb that he was fond of quoting. "Speak softly and carry a big stick; you will go far." The United States pledged to use armed forces to prevent any European country from seizing Dominican territory. To satisfy the Europeans' demand for repayment, the United States took control of collecting all Dominican customs duties. In 1916 civil unrest shook the Dominican Republic, and the U.S. government sent in marines. They remained until 1924. Some Latin American countries objected to Roosevelt's policy. Despite these protests, U.S. intervention in Latin America continued.

★ HISTORICAL DOCUMENTS ★

PRESIDENT THEODORE ROOSEVELT

The Roosevelt Corollary

Since it was first announced, the Monroe Doctrine had guided U.S. foreign policy in the Western Hemisphere. Events in the early 1900s led President Theodore Roosevelt to modify the Monroe Doctrine with the Roosevelt Corollary.

It must be understood that under no circumstances will the United States use the Monroe Doctrine as a cloak for territorial aggression. We desire peace with all the world, but perhaps most of all with the other peoples of the American Continent. There are, of course, limits to the wrongs which any self-respecting nation can endure. It is always possible that wrong actions toward this Nation, or toward citizens of this Nation, in some State unable to keep order among its own people, unable to secure justice from outsiders, and unwilling to do justice to those outsiders who treat it well, may result in our having to take action to protect our rights; but such action will not be taken with a view to territorial aggression, and it will be taken at all only with extreme reluctance and when it has become evident that every other resource has been exhausted.

HISTORY MAKERS SPEAK

Theodore Roosevelt in *Messages and Papers of the Presidents*

The Roosevelt Corollary. President Roosevelt explained the reasons behind his corollary. "Our interests and those of our southern neighbors are in reality identical. While they thus obey the primary laws of civilized society they may rest assured that they will be treated by us in a spirit of cordial and helpful sympathy. We would interfere with them only in the last resort, and then only if it became evident that their inability or unwillingness to do justice at home and abroad had violated the rights of the United States or had invited foreign aggression."

CRITICAL THINKING What might the phrase "primary laws of civilized society" mean?

ANSWER: Students might suggest that the phrase means the laws that are important to civilized societies. Other students might suggest that this phrase is vague and gave the United States wide latitude in Latin America.

VISUAL RECORD ANSWER

(for p. 316)

Students might suggest that the photograph indicated that the marines were engaged in jungle warfare.

REVIEW

Have students complete the **Section 3 Review** on p. 316.

ASSESS

Have students complete **Daily Quiz 10.3**. As **Alternative Assessment**, you may want to use the Panama Canal postcards or the Latin America graphic organizer in this section's lessons.

RETEACH

Have students complete **Main Idea Activity for Reteaching and Sheltered English 10.3**. Then organize students into pairs. Have each pair create a one-page outline of Section 3. Remind students that they will need to choose events and material very carefully to produce an inclusive outline in just one page. Have volunteers present their outlines to the class.
Sheltered English, Cooperative Learning

EXTEND

Write the following question on the chalkboard: *Does the Constitution follow the flag?* Have students investigate the Insular Cases in which the Supreme Court addressed this question to determine whether peoples in the nation's newly acquired colonial territories were entitled to the rights and privileges guaranteed by the Constitution. Have each student report his or her findings in an essay. **Block Scheduling**

SECTION 3 REVIEW ANSWERS

Define and Identify
For significance, see the following pages:
- Leonard Wood, p. 312
- Platt Amendment, p. 312
- protectorate, p. 312
- Foraker Act, p. 312
- Philippe Bunau-Varilla, p. 313
- Hay–Bunau-Varilla Treaty, p. 313
- Roosevelt Corollary, p. 315
- dollar diplomacy, p. 316

Locate
For location, see the map on p. 313. For importance, see the following page:
- Panama Canal, p. 313

1. Roosevelt–use military force to act as a police power; collected Dominican customs duties and sent marines to Dominican Republic; Taft–use U.S. economic influence to drive out European influence; made loans to Nicaragua and sent marines to crush revolt and protect investments; Wilson–establish democratic governments; sent marines to Haiti after revolution there
2. Cuba–became a U.S. protectorate and then independent; Puerto Rico–became a territory and then a commonwealth
3. promised great profit in light of a canal
4. harsh working conditions, shortages of labor and materials, and an outbreak of yellow fever; improved living conditions, technical expertise, and scientific knowledge
5. allowed the United States to bypass negotiations with Colombia and build the canal

INTERPRETING THE VISUAL RECORD
Intervention. These U.S. Marines were part of the force sent to Nicaragua by President Taft in 1912. ***What does the photograph suggest about the type of fighting the marines did while in Nicaragua?***

Dollar diplomacy. Roosevelt's successor as president, William H. Taft, expanded U.S. influence in Latin America. Taft favored "substituting dollars for bullets"—economic influence for military force—as a means of protecting U.S. interests in Latin America. This policy came to be called **dollar diplomacy**. Taft suggested replacing European loans with American ones. He argued that increasing U.S. economic power would reduce the chances of European intervention. By 1914 American capital in Latin America had grown to over $1.6 billion, invested mainly in mines, railroads, and banana and sugar plantations.

Taft put dollar diplomacy to the test in Nicaragua. At the invitation of the Nicaraguan president, American bankers made loans totaling $1.5 million to Nicaragua in 1911. The following year, Taft sent more than 2,000 marines to crush a revolt and to protect the American investments.

Taft's successor, President Woodrow Wilson, believed that democratic governments, not U.S. dollars, would keep European powers out of Latin America. To keep Germany from taking control of strategic Caribbean territory, Wilson sent marines to several countries to put down rebellions and establish constitutional governments. In 1915, when revolution shook Haiti, Wilson sent in marines. Haiti was forced to accept a treaty that gave the United States powers in running the Haitian government, and the marines stayed until 1934. Some 1,500 Haitians died resisting U.S. control.

✔ **READING CHECK:** What was U.S. policy toward Latin America during the late 1800s and early 1900s?

SECTION  3 REVIEW

Define and explain the significance of the following terms:
Platt Amendment
protectorate
Foraker Act
Hay–Bunau-Varilla Treaty
Roosevelt Corollary
dollar diplomacy

Identify and explain the significance of the following individuals:
Leonard Wood
Philippe Bunau-Varilla

Locate and explain the significance of the following place:
Panama Canal

1. **Using Graphic Organizers** Copy the chart below. Use it to describe how Presidents Roosevelt, Taft, and Wilson interpreted the Monroe Doctrine. Then give an example of how each president applied the Monroe Doctrine in Latin America.

	Description	Example
Roosevelt		
Taft		
Wilson		

2. **Evaluating** How did the U.S. relationship with Cuba and Puerto Rico change after the Spanish-American War?
3. **Assessing Consequences** How did the growth in trade with Asia affect American public support for building a canal in Panama?
4. **Understanding Geography: Human-Environment Interaction** What obstacles did the environment of Panama present to building a canal, and how were they overcome?

Critical Thinking

5. Why did the United States support the Panamanian rebels and recognize the Republic of Panama?
Consider:
- U.S. interest in building a canal
- the negotiations between the United States and Colombia
- President Roosevelt's foreign policy

SECTION 4

After completing Section 4, students should be able to:

OBJECTIVE 1 *List the major events of the Mexican Revolution.*

OBJECTIVE 2 *Explain why the United States intervened in Mexico.*

OBJECTIVE 3 *Report on the outcomes of the Mexican Revolution.*

LET'S GET STARTED!

As students enter the classroom, have them read the quotation by Francisco Madero on this page. Ask each student to list the grievances cited by Madero. Call on volunteers to share their lists with the class. Then tell students that in Section 4 they will learn about the major events of the Mexican Revolution, why the United States became involved, and how the revolution ended.

Conflict with Mexico

OBJECTIVES

Read to understand:

1. what the major events of the Mexican Revolution were
2. what the causes of U.S. intervention in Mexico were
3. what the outcomes of the Mexican Revolution were

KEY TERMS

Mexican Revolution

KEY PEOPLE

Porfirio Díaz
Emiliano Zapata
Francisco Madero
Victoriano Huerta
Venustiano Carranza
Francisco "Pancho" Villa
John J. Pershing

KEY PLACES

Veracruz
Columbus

"A force of tyranny . . . oppresses us in such a manner that it has become intolerable. . . . The Mexican people . . . are thirsty for liberty, and . . . they reject with energy the Government of General Díaz. . . . Therefore, and in echo of the national will, I declare the late election illegal. . . . The people . . . anxiously call me from all parts of the country, to compel General Díaz by force of arms, to respect the national will."

—Francisco Madero

Francisco Madero was a leader of the Mexican Revolution.

Francisco Madero ran for president of Mexico in the election of 1910. However, Porfirio Díaz—Mexico's longtime dictator—ordered Madero arrested and imprisoned. Madero fled to San Antonio, Texas, where on November 20, 1910, he issued the Plan of San Luis Potosi calling upon Mexicans to take up arms against the government. The war he began would last 10 years.

Mexico Under Díaz

Mexican president Porfirio Díaz had come to power in 1876 after Mexico had suffered almost 66 years of war and unrest. When Díaz took over, Mexico was in sad shape. The mines that had once been sources of great wealth were neglected or abandoned. Crime and violence was widespread. Díaz's first goal was to impose order, which he did by crushing or controlling his opponents.

Díaz's success in bringing order to Mexico attracted foreign investors. Confident that Díaz's government would protect their investments, foreigners poured millions of dollars into building Mexico's industries. Mexico had less than 500 miles of railroads when Díaz took office. By 1910 the country had 15,000 miles of railroads. Petroleum production began about the turn of the century and expanded rapidly. The mining industry, which had been largely inactive since colonial times, boomed again thanks to foreign capital. By 1908, American companies controlled three quarters of all Mexican mining operations.

By 1913 total foreign investments in Mexico amounted to some $2 billion, with more than half coming from the United States. However, although Díaz did improve Mexico's economy, foreign investors and Díaz's friends were the primary beneficiaries of this economic growth. Little trickled down to workers and peasants, and most Mexicans lived in poverty.

THE GRANGER COLLECTION, NEW YORK

Porfirio Díaz ruled Mexico for more than 25 years.

The Mexican Revolution

In 1910 Porfirio Díaz ran for re-election. Using force and fraud, he won his eighth term as president. However, opposition to Díaz's dictatorship had been growing. In the south, Emiliano Zapata led a rebel army that demanded land for the mostly American Indian peasant population. An American Indian himself, Zapata had

SECTION 4 RESOURCES

PRINT

- Guided Reading Strategy 10.4
- Section 4 Review, p. 321
- Daily Quiz 10.4

MULTIMEDIA

- One-Stop Planner, Lesson 10.4
- Holt Researcher: American History CD–ROM

SHELTERED ENGLISH

- Main Idea Activity for Reteaching and Sheltered English 10.4

✔ READING TO UNDERSTAND

To help students master the section objectives, have them answer the **READING CHECKS** and complete **Guided Reading Strategy 10.4** as they read the section.

TEACH OBJECTIVE 1

LEVEL 1: Have volunteers assume the role of one of the following people: Porfirio Díaz, Emiliano Zapata, Francisco Madero, and Victoriano Huerta. Then have volunteers line up in any order and explain why and how "he" participated in the Mexican Revolution. *(Volunteers should indicate the following: Porfirio Díaz—used force and fraud to win an 8th term as president of Mexico; Emiliano Zapata—led a rebel army demanding land for the mostly American Indian peasant population; Francisco Madero—unified the various opposition forces and won the presidency after Díaz's overthrow; Victoriano Huerta—seized control of the government and restored calm.)* As volunteers present their statements, have students guess the speaker's identity and write it on a sheet of paper with notes from his statement for review purposes. After all four speakers have made their statements, have students discuss who each speaker represented. **Sheltered English**

LEVELS 2 AND 3: Write the following statement on the chalkboard: *The Mexican Revolution was not really a revolution at all. Instead, it was a contest for power among military and political factions whose objective was control of government rather than implementation of a revolutionary program.* Have each student write an essay that supports or refutes the statement. Students should use the major events of the Mexican Revolution as evidence for their positions. *(See the Level 1 lesson for the correct events.)* Have volunteers read their essays to the class.

GLOBAL RELATIONS

Mexico and Texas. Texas served as a refuge for many Mexican revolutionaries and rebels. However, individuals such as Francisco Madero had to be certain that they did not violate American neutrality laws. While in San Antonio, Texas, he composed his *Plan de San Luis Potosí.* However, he backdated it by a month so that he could claim that he wrote it in Mexico rather than in the United States, thereby remaining in compliance with American neutrality laws.

CRITICAL THINKING Why might Mexican rebels have fled to Texas?

ANSWER: Students might mention its geographic proximity to Mexico.

VISUAL RECORD ANSWER

Students might suggest that the revolutionaries look poor.

CHANGING WAYS ANSWER

Today, the value of Mexican exports to the United States is greater than the value of U.S. exports to Mexico.

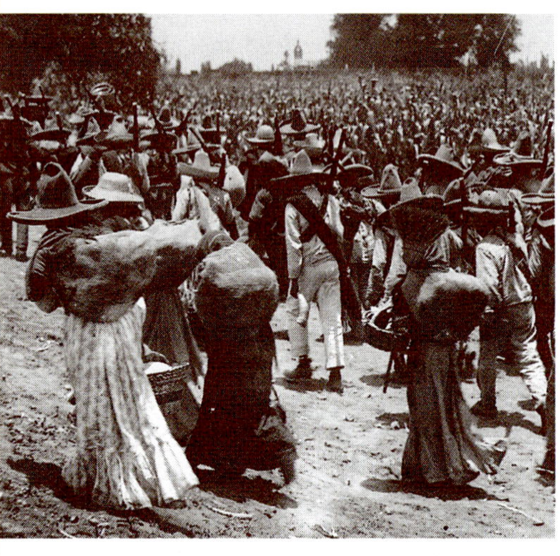

INTERPRETING THE VISUAL RECORD

The revolutionaries. Followers of Emiliano Zapata, known as *zapatistas,* march in August 1914. ***What does the photograph reveal about the forces that fought the Mexican Revolution?***

been a tenant farmer on a sugar plantation. He is said to have been inspired to revolt because his master's horses lived in tiled stables while he and his family lived in dirt-floored shacks. Mexican intellectuals also organized against the Díaz government, reaching a high point with the 1909 publication of a book by Andrés Molina Enríquez. In his book Enríquez called for land redistribution and predicted that "it will come, whether in peace . . . or by revolution."

A wealthy landowner from northern Mexico, Francisco Madero was an unlikely candidate to unify the various opposition forces. He was considered a dreamer and an idealist, but his ideas sparked the **Mexican Revolution** that toppled the Díaz dictatorship. Rebel forces defeated Díaz's troops in key cities in northern and central Mexico. In May 1911, with mobs roaming the streets of Mexico City, Díaz resigned. He went into exile in Paris, where he died in 1915.

In Mexico's first democratic elections in 30 years, Madero easily won the presidency. The United States recognized Madero's government and placed an embargo on arms sales to his opponents. Madero tried to establish a democratic government but was soon overwhelmed by the very forces that he had unleashed in toppling Díaz.

Led by Díaz's nephew, supporters of the former dictator rebelled against Madero. For 10 days in February 1913 the roar of cannons echoed through the streets of Mexico City as rebels fought for control of the country. Many people died in the violence before Madero's commanding general, Victoriano Huerta (WER-tah), seized control of the government and restored calm. Huerta imprisoned Madero, who was then murdered when he allegedly attempted to escape. Four major revolu-

Changing Ways: Mexico and the United States

Understanding Change The economies of the United States and Mexico have been linked for many years. The United States used to ship more goods to Mexico than it received in return. In recent years that has changed. Fewer trade restrictions have boosted trade between the two countries. Mexico now produces many items for export to the United States. *Based on the information provided, how do you think the economic relationship between the United States and Mexico has changed?*

	THEN	NOW
Value of U.S. Exports to Mexico	$208 million	$71.4 billion
Value of Mexican Exports to the United States	$179 million	$85.9 billion

Sources: *Historical Statistics of the United States; Statistical Abstract of the United States: 1998.* Data reflect 1920 and 1997.

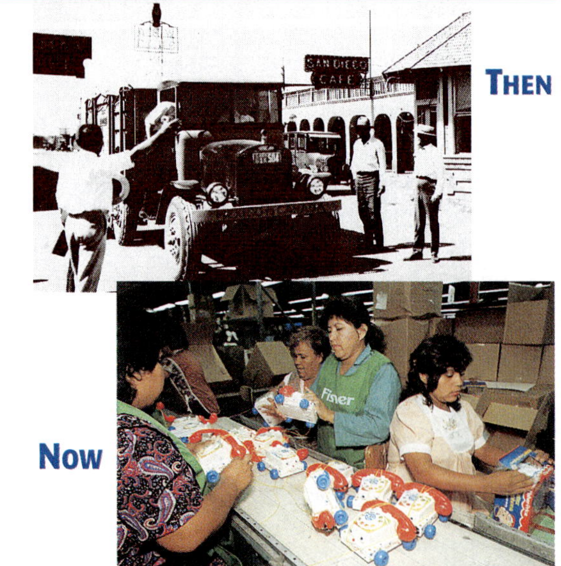

THEN

NOW

TEACH OBJECTIVE 2

LEVEL 1: Tell students to imagine that they are President Wilson. Have each student write a few sentences explaining why he intervened in Mexico in 1914. *(Students' responses might suggest that the outrage over Francisco Madero's murder and the arrest of crew members from the USS* Dolphin *by soldiers loyal to Huerta contributed to Wilson's decision to intervene.)* Have volunteers read their sentences to the class. **Sheltered English**

LEVELS 2 AND 3: Tell students to imagine that they are exchange students living in Mexico during the Mexican Revolution. Have each student write a one-page letter to a friend at home that explains why the United States intervened in Mexico. *(See the Level 1 lesson for the correct reasons.)* Call on volunteers to read their letters to the class.

TEACH OBJECTIVE 3

ALL LEVELS: To help students understand how the United States, Pancho Villa, and Venustiano Carranza contributed to the outcomes of the Mexican Revolution, copy the graphic organizer on the following page on the chalkboard, omitting the italicized answers. Have each student complete it. Discuss the completed graphic organizer with students. **Sheltered English**

tionary armies continued to fight Huerta. However, their leaders—Venustiano Carranza (bay-noos-TYAHN-oh kahr-RAHN-sah), Francisco "Pancho" Villa, Emiliano Zapata, and Álvaro Obregón (oh-bray-GAWN)—were not united.

✔ **READING CHECK:** What were the major events of the Mexican Revolution?

U.S. Intervention

Victoriano Huerta soon gained recognition from most European countries. However, Francisco Madero's murder outraged Woodrow Wilson, the new U.S. president, who angrily refused to recognize Huerta. Wilson called Huerta's government a "government of butchers." In February 1914 Wilson lifted the embargo on arms sales to the revolutionary armies and adopted a policy of "watchful waiting." Wilson was looking for an opportunity to drive Huerta from power.

The USS* Dolphin *was involved in an incident that gave President Wilson a reason to intervene in Mexico.

Tampico. On April 9, 1914, an incident occurred that gave Wilson his opportunity. The USS *Dolphin* had been stationed in Mexican waters near the port of Tampico, which was under Huerta's control. Several crew members from the *Dolphin* went ashore for supplies and were arrested by soldiers loyal to Huerta. The Americans were quickly released unharmed, and the Mexicans' superior officer apologized for the incident. However, the U.S. admiral demanded a

> **"formal . . . apology for the act, together with your assurance that the officer responsible for it will receive severe punishment. Also that you publicly hoist the American flag in a prominent position on shore and salute it with twenty-one guns."**

President Wilson supported this unusual demand, which placed the United States in the ironic position of requesting an official apology from a government it did not recognize. On April 20 the president appeared before Congress asking for approval for the use of armed forces against Mexico. Congress moved swiftly, approving the use of force on April 22, but events in Mexico moved even faster.

The occupation of Veracruz. Before Congress could act, Wilson learned that a German ship transporting arms to Huerta was heading for Veracruz. He ordered the U.S. Navy to seize the port of Veracruz. On April 21, U.S. forces stopped the German ship. Under the cover of a naval bombardment, marines then landed at Veracruz. Huerta's forces had already withdrawn from the city, and only civilians and local authorities remained. During the brief struggle for control of the city, 19 marines were killed. Some 300 Mexicans died during the bombardment.

At this critical stage, Argentina, Brazil, and Chile—sometimes called the ABC powers—organized a conference to resolve the crisis. In June the conference proposed a plan that called for Huerta's resignation and the creation of a provisional government. Huerta refused, but his enemies were closing in. That July Huerta resigned and fled to Spain.

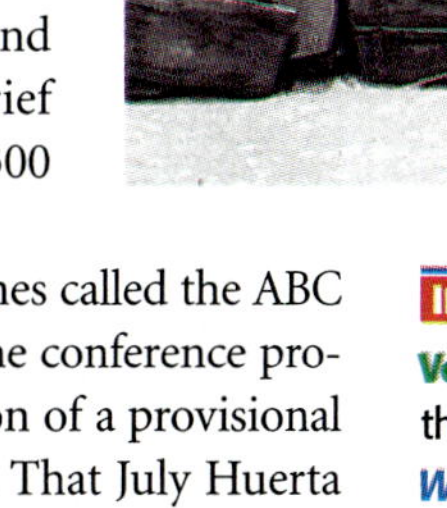

INTERPRETING THE VISUAL RECORD

Veracruz. U.S. sailors help secure the customhouse in Veracruz. ***What appears to be happening in the photograph?***

✔ **READING CHECK:** What factors caused the U.S. intervention in Mexico?

HISTORY MAKERS SPEAK

William Jennings Bryan in *Foreign Relations*

Opposing Huerta. In 1913 Secretary of State Bryan explained the American goal regarding Mexico. "The present policy [of the United States] . . . is to isolate General Huerta entirely; to cut him off from foreign sympathy and aid and from domestic credit, whether moral or material, and to force him out. It hopes and believes that isolation will accomplish this end and shall await the results without irritation and impatience." U.S. forces, however, proceeded to occupy Veracruz in April 1914.

CRITICAL THINKING Why might U.S. actions have contradicted the secretary of state's statement?

ANSWER: Answers will vary. Some students might suggest that Bryan had not been informed about actual U..S intentions.

MAP ANSWER

(for p. 320)

Cuba, the Dominican Republic, Haiti, Nicaragua, and Panama

VISUAL RECORD ANSWER

Students might suggest that the soldiers appear to be running away from gunfire.

OUTCOMES OF THE MEXICAN REVOLUTION

United States	Pancho Villa	Venustiano Carranza
• *President Wilson orders a military expedition into Mexico to capture Villa dead or alive* • *Gen. Pershing leads forces into Chihuahua* • *The United States stations National Guardsmen along the Mexican border*	• *controls nearly two thirds of Mexico with Emiliano Zapata* • *suffers defeat in 1915 by Alvaro Obregón, after which Villa disbands his army* • *raids Columbus, New Mexico* • *goes into hiding*	• *calls constitutional convention in December 1916* • *puts new constitution into effect in February 5, 1917* • *new constitution declares that Mexico owns all mineral, oil, and water rights*

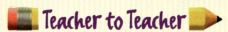

Teacher to Teacher

James Pyne of Flossmoor, Illinois, suggested the following activity: Tell students to imagine that they are President Wilson preparing to appear before Congress to ask for approval to use armed forces against Mexico. Have each student write a speech to Congress in support of intervention in Mexico.

SECTION 4 REVIEW ANSWERS

Define and Identify

For significance, see the following pages:

- Porfirio Díaz, p. 317
- Emiliano Zapata, p. 317
- Francisco Madero, p. 318
- Mexican Revolution, p. 318
- Victoriano Huerta, p. 318
- Venustiano Carranza, p. 319
- Francisco "Pancho" Villa, p. 319
- John J. Pershing, p. 321

Locate

For locations, see the map on p. 320. For importance, see the following pages:

- Veracruz, p. 319
- Columbus, p. 320

1. Diaz–resigned and went into exile; Madero–overthrown and assassinated; Huerta–resigned and fled to Spain; Carranza–oversaw new constitution

2. Many Americans regarded Mexico as unstable and a danger to U.S. security.

3. Answers will vary. Some students might argue that U.S. actions constituted a violation of Mexico's sovereignty.

4. U.S. intervention caused death and destruction but led to Huerta's removal from office.

5. Answers will vary. Some students might oppose the Veracruz occupation and U.S. demands in Tampico but support operations against Villa.

The Revolution Winds Down

Pancho Villa (second from right) inspects his troops' rifles.

By early 1915 Mexico was in chaos. Pancho Villa and Emiliano Zapata controlled nearly two thirds of the country. In March Venustiano Carranza re-entered Mexico City and assumed the title of "First Chief." He promised to protect American lives and property. The United States recognized his government in October 1915.

Pancho Villa's raid. In April 1915 Carranza's general, Álvaro Obregón, defeated Villa's troops in the central state of Guanajuato. After another major defeat, Villa disbanded his army. Villa was upset by the U.S. recognition of Carranza and decided to take revenge on the Americans. Villa explained his reasoning.

> **"We have decided not to fire a bullet more against Mexicans, our brothers, and to prepare and organize ourselves to attack the Americans in their own dens and make them know that Mexico is a land for the free and a tomb for thrones, crowns, and traitors."**

In March 1916 some of Villa's men crossed the border into New Mexico to raid Columbus, a small, isolated town. Striking at dawn, Villa's men burned and looted the town. In the battle 18 Americans—ten civilians and eight soldiers—and more than 100 of Villa's men were killed.

U.S. Interests in Latin America, Early 1900s

Learning from Maps U.S. policy in Latin America was aimed at protecting U.S. interests and keeping other European countries out of the area.

PLACE Which countries were U.S. protectorates?

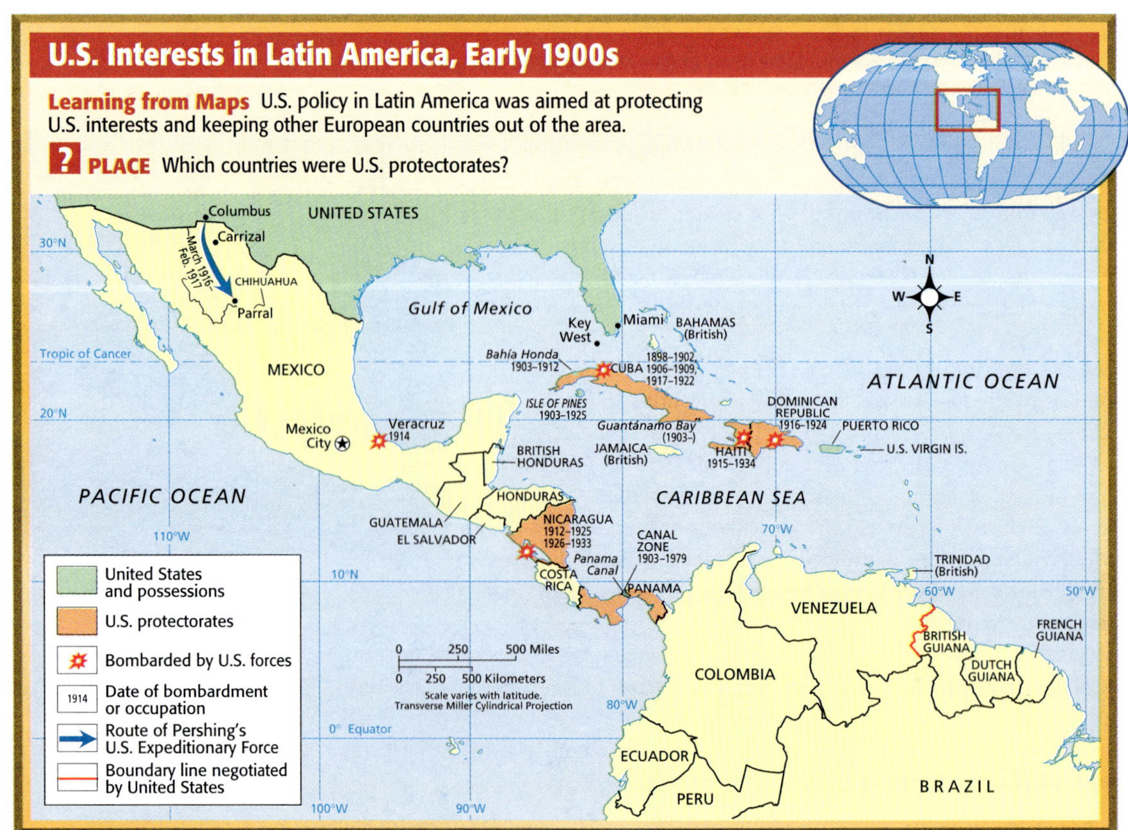

REVIEW

Have students complete the **Section 4 Review** on p. 321.

ASSESS

Have students complete **Daily Quiz 10.4**. As **Alternative Assessment**, you may want to use the intervention sentences or the Mexican Revolution letter in this section's lessons.

RETEACH

Have students complete **Main Idea Activity for Reteaching and Sheltered English 10.4**. Then organize students into triads. Have each triad create an annotated time line of the Mexican Revolution and its aftermath. Ask volunteers to present their time lines to the class. Then display the time lines around the classroom to help students review the material.
Sheltered English, Cooperative Learning

EXTEND

Ask students to conduct research on modern-day relations between the United States and Mexico. Have each student present his or her research in a short essay. Ask volunteers to read their essays to the class. Then conduct a discussion on the information presented in the essays. **Block Scheduling**

Pursuing Pancho Villa. Without requesting approval from the Carranza government, President Wilson ordered a military expedition into Mexico to capture Villa "dead or alive." A week after Villa's raid on Columbus, General John J. Pershing led his forces into Chihuahua, Villa's home state. Although Pershing later increased his troop size to more than 10,000 men, Villa still eluded capture. The deeper Pershing pushed into Mexican territory, the more the Mexicans resented the Americans.

When one of Pershing's cavalry units attempted to pass through the town of Carrizal, the commander of the Mexican garrison refused passage. Pershing chose to enter Carrizal rather than bypass the town, and a battle followed.

By early September 1916 nearly 150,000 U.S. National Guardsmen were stationed along the Mexican border. Wilson realized that the threat of war increased with each day U.S. troops remained in Mexico. The president finally ordered U.S. troops withdrawn in January 1917.

THE GRANGER COLLECTION, NEW YORK

General John Pershing (center) led the unsuccessful expedition to capture Pancho Villa.

Carranza in power. With Pancho Villa in hiding and Emiliano Zapata contained in the south, Venustiano Carranza called a constitutional convention in December 1916. After two months of negotiations, a new constitution was completed and put into effect on February 5, 1917. This new constitution contained several revolutionary ideas. It placed the interests of common welfare above individual rights and provided protection for workers. This protection included an eight-hour workday, an end to child labor, and the right to form unions and bargain collectively.

Most significant to the United States was the constitution's declaration that the nation owned all mineral, oil, and water rights. This part of the constitution would have important effects on American oil companies operating in Mexico in the 1930s.

✔ **READING CHECK:** What were the outcomes of the Mexican Revolution?

SECTION  4 REVIEW

Define and explain the significance of the following term:
Mexican Revolution

Identify and explain the significance of the following individuals:
Porfirio Díaz
Emiliano Zapata
Francisco Madero
Victoriano Huerta
Venustiano Carranza
Francisco "Pancho" Villa
John J. Pershing

Locate and explain the significance of the following places:
Veracruz
Columbus

1. **Using Graphic Organizers** Copy the chart below. Use it to list various leaders who fought for control of Mexico and what happened to them.

Leader		What Happened?
	→	
	→	
	→	
	→	
	→	

2. **Recognizing Point of View** How did the Mexican Revolution affect American views of Mexico?
3. **Taking a Stand** Did the United States have the right to stop a German ship from delivering its cargo to Mexico? Explain your answer.
4. **Synthesizing** How did U.S. intervention both help and hurt Mexico?

Critical Thinking

5. Do you think the Mexican Revolution resulted in a positive outcome for Mexico? Explain your answer.
Consider:
- the conditions under Porfirio Diaz
- the goals of the revolutionary leaders
- the government established by Venustiano Carranza

CHAPTER 10 REVIEW ANSWERS

Creating a Time Line
Each event should have an explanation and the correct date.

Writing a Summary
See the Reading Checks in each section for main ideas.

Identifying People and Ideas
1. the quest for colonial empires that marked the late 1800s and early 1900s
2. Hawaiian queen overthrown in a revolt led by Americans
3. areas where a particular country has exclusive rights to mines, railroads, and trade
4. U.S. secretary of state who created the Open Door Policy
5. Cuban poet and exile who died in the 1895 revolt against Spain
6. Filipino rebel leader who initially allied with the United States to defeat the Spanish but later fought against American troops
7. U.S. general who was appointed governor of Cuba in 1899
8. Taft's policy of using economic power to limit European influence in Latin America
9. Mexican dictator driven from office by rebels
10. Mexican leader whose government received U.S. recognition in 1915

REVIEW AND ASSESSMENT RESOURCES

PRINT

- Chapter 10 Review, pp. 322–23
- Chapter 10 Tutorial for Students, Parents, Mentors, and Peers
- Chapter 10 Test (Form A or B)
- Portfolio Activities and Alternative Assessment Handbook, Chapter 10

MULTIMEDIA

- Audio Program, Chapter 10 (English and Spanish)
- Chapter 10 Test Generator (on the One-Stop Planner)
- Global Skill Builder CD–ROM
- HRW Web site

SHELTERED ENGLISH

- Spanish Glossary
- Sheltered English Chapter 10 Test

REVIEW

Have students complete the **Chapter 10 Review** on pp. 322–23.

ASSESS

Use one of the chapter tests to assess students' understanding of the content. For **Alternative Assessment**, see the **Portfolio Activities and Alternative Assessment Handbook.**

Understanding Main Ideas

1. the desire for markets, raw materials, power, and prestige; the desire to spread democracy and Christianity

2. imperialist ambition, yellow journalism, humanitarian concerns, and the *Maine* incident

3. tried to negotiate a treaty with Colombia, supported Panamanian rebels, negotiated the Hay–Bunau-Varilla Treaty to gain control over Canal Zone, and started to build the canal

4. Francisco Madero, Emiliano Zapata, Victoriano Huerta, Francisco "Pancho" Villa, and Venustiano Carranza

5. President Wilson wanted Huerta, whom he regarded as a murderer, removed from office and ordered intervention.

Reviewing Themes

1. Americans wanted to protect their investments there.

2. fostered economic growth, but failed to distribute profits to the impoverished Mexican people

3. The United States imposed a government on the Filipinos against their will.

Thinking Critically

1. Americans wanted to control the Philippines but only wanted a stable government of some kind in Mexico.

2. Japan possessed the military might to resist European imperialists.

CHAPTER 10 Review

Creating a Time Line

Copy the time line below onto a sheet of paper. Complete the time line by filling in the events and dates from the chapter that you think were most significant. Pick three events and explain why you think they were significant.

1898 | 1907 | 1916

Writing a Summary

Using the Reading Checks as a guide, write an overview of the events in the chapter.

Identifying People and Ideas

Identify the following terms or individuals and explain their significance.

1. imperialism
2. Liliuokalani
3. spheres of influence
4. John Hay
5. José Martí
6. Emilio Aguinaldo
7. Leonard Wood
8. dollar diplomacy
9. Porfirio Díaz
10. Venustiano Carranza

Understanding Main Ideas

SECTION 1

1. What led industrialized nations to seek overseas colonies in the late 1800s and early 1900s?

SECTION 2

2. What were the major causes of the Spanish-American War?

SECTION 3

3. What steps did the United States take to build the Panama Canal?

SECTION 4

4. Who were the major leaders that participated in the Mexican Revolution?
5. How and why did the United States intervene in Mexico?

Reviewing Themes

1. **Global Relations** Why was the U.S. interested in controlling Cuba?
2. **Economic Development** How did foreign investors affect Mexico's economy?
3. **Democratic Values** Why might some people argue that U.S. actions in the Philippines conflicted with democratic principles?

Thinking Critically

1. **Evaluating** Why did the U.S. government oppose the revolution led by Emilio Aguinaldo in the Philippines but support the revolution led by Venustiano Carranza in Mexico?
2. **Analyzing** Why was Japan not divided into European spheres of influence like China?
3. **Hypothesizing** What might have been the effect on U.S. relations with Cuba, Puerto Rico, and the Philippines if the United States had adopted an Open Door Policy toward each of those countries?
4. **Using Historical Imagination** Imagine that President Cleveland had reinstated Liliuokalani as queen of Hawaii. Write a paragraph describing what might have happened to Hawaii.
5. **Assessing Consequences** How does the Spanish-American War continue to affect the United States today?

Writing About History

Writing to Explain Write an essay that traces the negotiations and events that helped the United States build and control the Panama Canal. Use the following graphic organizer to help you prepare your essay.

1. **A canal across Panama is proposed.**
2.
3.
4.
5. **United States builds Panama Canal.**

RETEACH

Organize students into small groups. Ask half of the members in each group to write headlines reflecting the events discussed in Sections 1, 2, 3, and 4. Then have the other members in each group write two- or three-paragraph news stories that explain one of the headlines. Have a representative from each group read the headline and news story to the class.
Sheltered English, Cooperative Learning

EXTEND

Have each student use the textbook, the library, and other sources to create a biographical dictionary of the Mexican Revolution. Entries should include biographical data on key figures of the revolution who were discussed in this chapter, including Americans Woodrow Wilson and John J. Pershing. Have students arrange their entries in alphabetical order and include pictures, maps, or other visuals where appropriate.
Block Scheduling

Strategies for Success Review the **Strategies for Success** on *Interpreting Economic Data.* Then study the graph below and answer the following questions.

1. What was the value of U.S. exports in 1885? in 1915?
2. By how much did U.S. imports increase between 1895 and 1915?

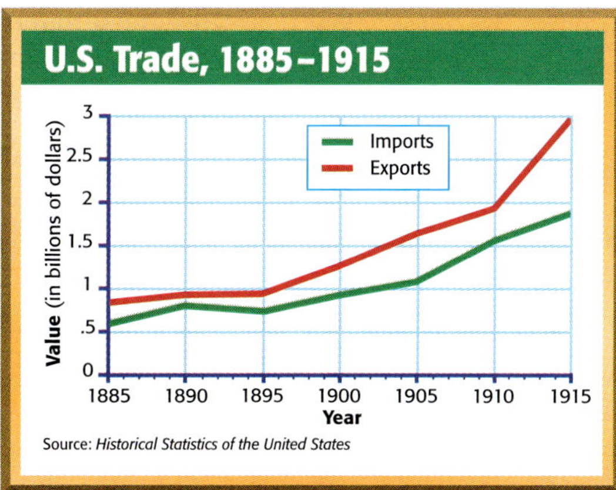

Linking History and Geography

Study the map below. How many islands in the Pacific were under U.S. control by 1900?

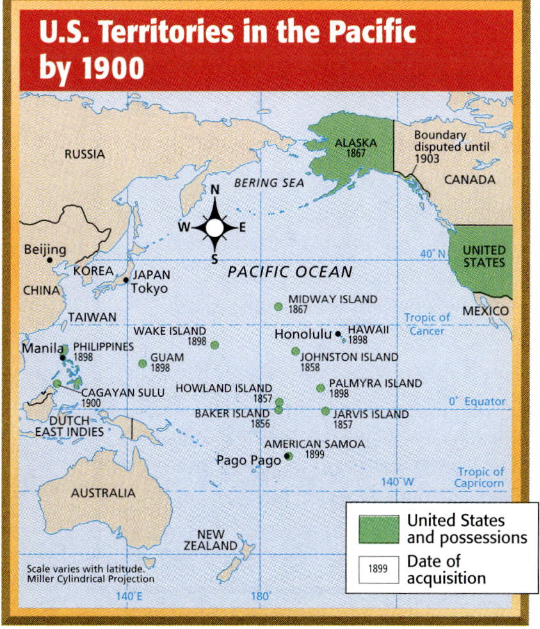

internetconnect

TOPIC: Panama Canal
GO TO: go.hrw.com
KEYWORD: SE1 Panama

Accessing the Internet through the HRW Web site, research the construction of the Panama Canal. Then create a poster in which you outline the steps in the canal's construction. Your display should include illustrations, graphics, and a table with at least 10 statistics about the canal.

Complete one or more of the following projects independently or cooperatively.

1 Global Relations

Imagine that you are a member of the State Department in the early 1900s. ***Write a memorandum*** to the president that addresses concerns about U.S. relations with China, Japan, South America, Mexico, or Spain. Your memorandum should mention specific issues dealing with each country or region.

2 Cultural Diversity

Imagine that you are a U.S. Army recruiting officer in 1898. ***Create a series of recruiting posters*** aimed at attracting a wide range of recruits—such as American Indians, college students, cowboys, and would-be adventurers—to serve in the Spanish-American War.

3 Democratic Values

Imagine that you are a descendant of Queen Liliuokalani living in Hawaii today. ***Plan a campaign to raise awareness*** about Hawaii's history as an independent nation.

3. Each nation would have remained independent and had its own form of government, although each would probably have been economically exploited.
4. Answers will vary. Some students might depict an independent Hawaii allied with the United States.
5. Answers will vary. Some students might discuss American relations with Cuba and Puerto Rico.

Writing About History
Students' essays will vary. However, students might refer to the following events: the French fail in their efforts to build a canal; Colombia refuses to ratify a treaty allowing the United States to build a canal; the United States supports the Panamanian revolution.

Strategies for Success Answers
1. about $600 million, about $1.9 billion
2. about $800 million

Linking History and Geography
12 island groups

LET'S GET STARTED!

Write the following question on the chalkboard: *Is it ever right for one country to become deeply involved in the affairs of another nation, whether due to economic or political interests?* As students enter the classroom, ask them to answer the question in writing. Have volunteers share their responses. Then tell students that they will learn more about how and why the United States took a larger role in the world in the Unit 3 America's Geography.

TEACH AMERICA'S GEOGRAPHY—THE UNITED STATES AND THE WORLD

Ask students to study the America's Geography feature, paying careful attention to the graphs on foreign investment and the map legend on exported products. Then write the following question on the chalkboard: What factors motivated imperialism in the early 1900s? Have each student answer the question in a few sentences. *(Students should note that the graphs and the legend indicates that economic interests helped fuel imperialism.)* Then ask students to create political cartoons and captions commenting on imperialism. **Sheltered English**

ECONOMIC DEVELOPMENT

Foreign Trade. The desire for foreign trade guided much of U.S. foreign policy in the early 1900s. Events such as the annexation of Hawaii, the construction of the Panama Canal, and even the Spanish-American War were all economically linked. Alfred Thayer Mahan, a well-known naval officer and author, argued that foreign trade was necessary for national growth. Mahan also advocated a strong merchant marine and overseas commercial outposts to help achieve this goal.

CRITICAL THINKING What else might Mahan have suggested to achieve national growth?

ANSWER: Students might suggest that Mahan probably would have supported a strong navy and possible overseas colonies.

THAT'S INTERESTING!

Henry Cabot Lodge expressed a common expansionist sentiment when he declared that "from the Rio Grande to the Arctic Ocean there should be but one flag and one country."

AMERICA'S Geography

The United States and the World

By 1914, on the eve of World War I, many nations were connected to one another in a complex web of economic trade and investment. The vast majority of this economic activity was controlled by European nations, particularly Great Britain. Compared to the European empires, the United States had relatively little financial investment in other countries. Yet even the United States expanded its economic and political involvement in foreign nations during this period.

U.S. Foreign Investment, 1900–1910

Investment (in millions of U.S. dollars): 0, 200, 400, 600, 800, 1,000, 1,200
Legend: 1900, 1910
North America; South America; Africa (negligible, negligible); Europe; Asia (negligible)

German Foreign Investment in 1910*

Investment (in millions of U.S. dollars): 0, 500, 1,000, 1,500, 2,000, 2,500
North America; South America; Africa; Europe; Asia

* All investment data for Germany in 1900 either not available or negligible

British Foreign Investment, 1900–1910

Investment (in millions of U.S. dollars): 0, 1,000, 2,000, 3,000, 4,000, 5,000, 6,000, 7,000
Legend: 1900, 1910
North America; South America; Africa; Europe; Asia

Source: *Rand McNally Atlas of World History*

The United States and the World, 1900–1914

South America. South America had many valuable resources. These included tin from Brazil, copper from Argentina and Peru, and nitrates—used to make fertilizer and explosives—from Chile. Although the European empires did not attempt to create new colonies in South America, as they did in Africa, they invested heavily in the economies of self-governing South American countries. The United States also increased investment in South America, but many of its investments were concentrated in Central America and the Panama Canal region.

SPOTLIGHT on the Imperialism Debate

Organize students into two large groups—one that supports American imperialism and one that opposes it. Then ask students to conduct research on the imperialism debate in the United States during the late 1800s and early 1900s. Remind students that their research should cover both their own position and that of their opponents. Give groups time to prepare their arguments. Then conduct a debate on American imperialism. **Cooperative Learning**

SPOTLIGHT on China

Pair students and ask each pair to conduct research on the overthrow of the Chinese emperor in 1911, focusing on how the event affected the country's domestic and international affairs. Tell students to create an annotated outline showing the rise and fall of Chinese imperialism.
Cooperative Learning

AMERICA'S Geography

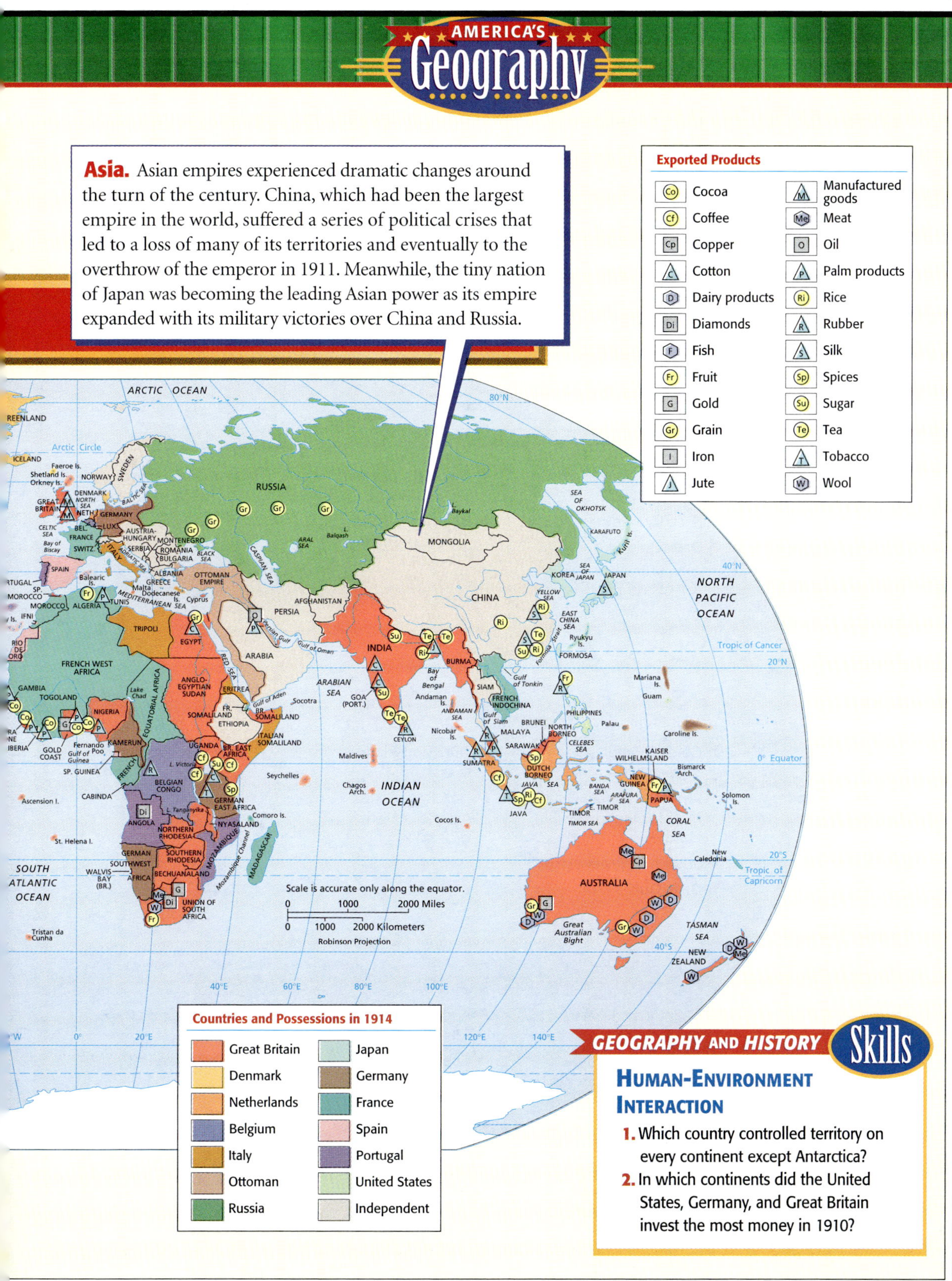

Asia. Asian empires experienced dramatic changes around the turn of the century. China, which had been the largest empire in the world, suffered a series of political crises that led to a loss of many of its territories and eventually to the overthrow of the emperor in 1911. Meanwhile, the tiny nation of Japan was becoming the leading Asian power as its empire expanded with its military victories over China and Russia.

GEOGRAPHY AND HISTORY Skills

HUMAN-ENVIRONMENT INTERACTION

1. Which country controlled territory on every continent except Antarctica?
2. In which continents did the United States, Germany, and Great Britain invest the most money in 1910?

ACROSS THE CURRICULUM

GEOGRAPHY

The British Empire. The phrase "the Sun never sets on the British Empire" was never more evident than in the early 1900s, when the British had interests in every continent, including Africa.

CRITICAL THINKING Why might the United States have not shown much of an interest in Africa?

ANSWER: Students might suggest that the great distance between North America and Africa might have dissuaded the United States from becoming involved there.

THAT'S INTERESTING!

Albert J. Beveridge, an Indiana politician, revealed the motives for imperialism when he said, "It is a noble land that God has given us; a land that can feed and clothe the world. . . . It is a mighty people that He has planted on this soil. . . . Have we no mission to perform, no duty to discharge to our fellow-men?"

AMERICA'S GEOGRAPHY ANSWERS

1. Great Britain
2. The United States invested the most in South America; Germany invested the most in Europe; Great Britain invested the most in North America.

World War I

CHAPTER PLANNING GUIDE

	Section Lesson Objectives	Print Resources	Multimedia Resources	Sheltered English Resources
Section 1 World War I Breaks Out, pp. 328–32	1 Identify the major causes of unrest in Europe. 2 Discuss the results of the strategy that was used during the early fighting in the war. 3 Explain why the war settled into a stalemate.	▶ Guided Reading Strategy 11.1 ▶ American History Political Cartoon 20: Conflict in the Balkans ▶ Geography Activity 11: World War I ▶ Section 1 Review, p. 332 ▶ Daily Quiz 11.1	▶ One-Stop Planner, Lesson 11.1 ▶ The American Nation Video Program Segment: Weaponry and Warfare; Teacher's Guide, pp. 99–104 ▶ Holt Researcher: American History CD–ROM	▶ Main Idea Activity for Reteaching and Sheltered English 11.1
Section 2 The United States Goes to War, pp. 333–39	1 Relate the challenges the United States faced while trying to remain neutral. 2 Identify the events that led to U.S. entry into the war. 3 Explain how the United States prepared its military for World War I. 4 Describe the types of experiences Americans had while serving in Europe.	▶ Guided Reading Strategy 11.2 ▶ Primary Source Reading 11: A Dark Moment in History ▶ Graphic Organizer Activity 11: Americans in World War I ▶ Literature Reading 11: Inside World War I ▶ Biography Reading 11: Jeannette Rankin ▶ Section 2 Review, p. 339 ▶ Daily Quiz 11.2	▶ One-Stop Planner, Lesson 11.2 ▶ Holt Researcher: American History CD–ROM ▶ HRW Web site	▶ Main Idea Activity for Reteaching and Sheltered English 11.2
Section 3 The War at Home, pp. 340–46	1 Describe how the U.S. government prepared the nation for war. 2 Discuss how organized labor and volunteers contributed to the war effort. 3 Explain why African Americans moved to the North. 4 Relate how the government created support for, and limited opposition to, the war.	▶ Guided Reading Strategy 11.3 ▶ Section 3 Review, p. 346 ▶ Daily Quiz 11.3	▶ One-Stop Planner, Lesson 11.3 ▶ Holt Researcher: American History CD–ROM	▶ Main Idea Activity for Reteaching and Sheltered English 11.3
Section 4 The War's End and Aftermath, pp. 347–53	1 List the final events of World War I. 2 Identify the goals of President Wilson's Fourteen Points. 3 Summarize the terms of the Treaty of Versailles. 4 Explain why the U.S. Senate rejected the Treaty of Versailles. 5 Discuss the global impact of World War I.	▶ Guided Reading Strategy 11.4 ▶ American History Outline Map 17: World War I in Europe ▶ Section 4 Review, p. 353 ▶ Daily Quiz 11.4	▶ One-Stop Planner, Lesson 11.4 ▶ Holt Researcher: American History CD–ROM	▶ Main Idea Activity for Reteaching and Sheltered English 11.4
Chapter Review and Assessment pp. 354–55		▶ Chapter 11 Review, pp. 354–55 ▶ Chapter 11 Tutorial for Students, Parents, Mentors, and Peers ▶ Chapter 11 Test (Form A or B) ▶ Portfolio Activities and Alternative Assessment Handbook, Chapter 11	▶ Audio Program, Chapter 11 (English and Spanish) ▶ Chapter 11 Test Generator (on the One-Stop Planner) ▶ Global Skill Builder CD–ROM ▶ HRW Web site	▶ Spanish Glossary ▶ Sheltered English Chapter 11 Test

CHAPTER OVERVIEW

In 1914 war engulfed Europe, with the Central Powers—Germany, Austria-Hungary, the Ottoman Empire, and Bulgaria—battling the Allied Powers—Britain, France, Russia, and eventually Italy. At the beginning of the war Germany tried to score a quick victory by invading France through Belgium. Unexpected resistance rebuffed the German attack, however, and the war soon settled into a stalemate. The United States attempted to stay neutral in the conflict, but German U-boat attacks and the revelation of Zimmerman Note pushed the Senate to declare war in April 1917. While the U.S. government attempted to redirect the economy and train thousands of soldiers, volunteers conserved precious materials and supported the war effort.

The massive infusion of U.S. troops helped the Allies win the war. In November 1918 Germany surrendered. The task of securing the postwar peace remained, however. President Wilson outlined his goals in the Fourteen Points and encouraged the United States to accept the Treaty of Versailles. A faction of Republican senators rejected the treaty.

TIME TAMERS

Block Scheduling

The teacher lesson plans for each section offer a variety of activity choices to help you present the material in a block scheduling format. For further suggestions on block scheduling, see the **Block Scheduling Handbook with Team Teaching Strategies**, pp. 61–66.

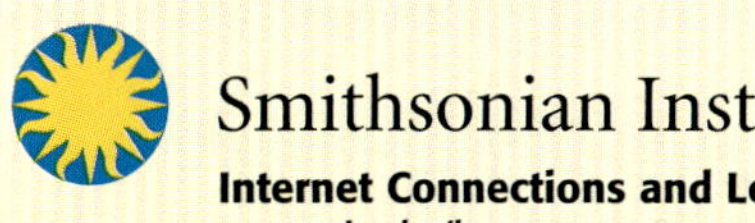

Internet Connections and Lesson 11
www.si.edu/hrw

Hands-On History Activities:

Classroom to Community The **Hands-On History Activities** help students make meaningful connections between events in American history and those in their own hometown. You may wish to use the Chapter 11 Activity, Your Town's Volunteers, to extend the chapter lessons, as alternative assessment, or as a block scheduling option.

Portfolio Projects

The American Nation includes multiple portfolio projects in each Pupil's Edition chapter review, as well as each unit review. Chapter 11 Portfolio Project options on p. 355 include the following:

1. Students will **write a letter**.
2. Students will **write a speech**.
3. Students will **create a poster**.

The American Nation INTERNET RESOURCE DIRECTORY

To access online materials for this chapter, go to go.hrw.com and type in the keywords listed below.

HRW ONLINE RESOURCES
GO TO: go.hrw.com

Online Maps
KEYWORD: SE1 Maps11
- The Schlieffen Plan
- Trench Warfare
- The Convoy System
- World War I Troop Strengths and Casualties

Online Charts
KEYWORD: SE1 Charts11
- The Weapons of World War I
- The Events of World War I

Online Reading Support
KEYWORD: SE1 Strategies11

Online Rubrics
KEYWORD: SE1 Rubrics

CHAPTER ENRICHMENT LINKS
Use these Web links to extend and enrich student learning for Chapter 11.
GO TO: go.hrw.com
KEYWORD: SE1 Ch11

CHAPTER INTERNET ACTIVITIES
GO TO: go.hrw.com
- Pupil's Edition Student Activity
  KEYWORD: SE1 Sarajevo
  (Students examine the history of the city of Sarajevo.)
- Teacher's Edition Student Activity
  KEYWORD: SE1 Somme
  (Students analyze the Battle of the Somme.)
- Teacher's Edition Student Activity
  KEYWORD: SE1 Lusitania
  (Students conduct research on the *Lusitania* controversy.)

ADDITIONAL RESOURCES

Books for Teachers

Herwig, Holger H., ed. *The Outbreak of World War I: Causes and Responsibilities.* Houghton Mifflin, 1997. Presents historians' comments on the outbreak of World War I.

Schneider, Dorothy, and Carl J. Schneider. *Into the Breach: American Women Overseas in World War I.* Viking Penguin, 1991. Tells the story of American women who participated in World War I.

Books for Students

Freidel, Frank. *Over There: The Story of America's First Great Overseas Crusade.* Temple University Press, 1990. Tells the story of U.S. involvement in the war with numerous photographs.

Hoehling, A. A. *The Last Voyage of the* Lusitania. Madison Books, 1996. Recounts one of the events that helped draw the United States into the war.

Primary Sources from the Period

Hemingway, Ernest. *A Farewell to Arms.* Scribner Paperback, 1995. Discusses one man's experiences in the war.

Straubling, Harold Elk. *The Last Magnificent War: Rare Journalistic and Eyewitness Accounts of World War I.* Paragon House, 1989. Presents varied primary sources about the war.

Multimedia Materials

The Great War–1918. Video, 60 min. PBS. Uses soldiers' letters and diaries to discuss U.S. involvement in the war.

Men of Bronze. Video, 58 min. Films Incorporated. Reviews the role of African American soldiers in World War I.

CHAPTER 11

Before You Read

Build on What You Know

Ask students to answer the following questions.

Why might the United States have wanted to remain neutral when war enveloped Europe?

Consider:

- the causes of the war
- the possible human and economic costs of entering a European war

Why might the United States have finally decided to enter the war in Europe?

Consider:

- incidents that might have provoked the United States to declare war
- the desire to protect European allies

---

exploring the time line

AMERICAN EVENTS

PEOPLE IN HISTORY

1916 ■ Jeannette Rankin. As a member of the House of Representatives, Jeannette Rankin worked for national women's suffrage. After she voted against U.S. involvement in World War I, however, she lost a senatorial bid and spent years working for pacifism and the rights of women and children. In 1940 Rankin again won a seat in the House. She soon voted against U.S. involvement in World War II, a stance that cost her the next election. Rankin continued her opposition to war and took an active role in anti–Vietnam War protests.

CRITICAL THINKING Why might Rankin's vote on World War II have caused her to lose her re-election campaign, even though voters knew they had elected a pacifist candidate?

ANSWER: Students might suggest that Rankin's constituents did not foresee the possibility of war when they elected her to Congress. After the Japanese bombed Pearl Harbor, however, voters wanted a representative who supported the war effort.

CHAPTER 11

1914–1920

World War I

Panama Canal brochure

BIRD'S EYE VIEW
OF THE
PANAMA CANAL
AND
MAP OF PANAMA

1914 Science and Technology The Panama Canal opens to traffic.

1914 Daily Life The first national Mother's Day is declared by President Wilson.

World War I tanks

World War I gas mask

1915 Science and Technology Germany becomes the first nation to use poison gas in warfare at the Second Battle of Ypres.

1916 Science and Technology Tanks are used in battle for the first time at the Battle of the Somme.

1914 | **1915** | **1916**

1914 World Events World War I begins.

German troops traveling to war

THE GRANGER COLLECTION, NEW YORK

1915 Business and Finance Driven by high prices and wartime demand, the U.S. wheat harvest tops 1 million bushels for the first time.

1915 The Arts Carl Sandburg's *Chicago Poems* is published.

Jeannette Rankin

1916 Politics Montana representative Jeannette Rankin is the first woman elected to Congress.

1916 Daily Life The Boston Red Sox win their second straight World Series.

Before You Read

Build on What You Know

During the 1800s several empires dominated Europe and much of the world. Nations scrambled to gain control of colonies and their natural resources to fuel the Industrial Revolution. European nations built up strong rivalries, which ultimately helped lead to war. In this chapter you will learn how the United States tried to remain neutral when war swept Europe. Once the United States joined the Allied cause in 1917, the government quickly mobilized the economy and built public support for the war.

Think About Themes

To help students create their Themes Journal entries, provide the following examples of appropriate **agree/disagree** *statements.*

Global Relations

Agree Many of the early presidents followed an isolationist approach to global affairs, placing national self-interest at the top of their agendas.

Disagree Before deciding to join the Patriots in the Revolution, France considered its own rivalry with Great Britain but also the cause of independence in the colonies.

Economic Development

Agree Involvement in an overseas conflict can sometimes stimulate a nation's domestic economy by requiring additional production and spending to supply the country's military.

Disagree British involvement in the French and Indian War weakened the country's economy, leading it to tax the colonies.

Democratic Values

Agree During wartime, citizens should forego their own liberties in consideration of national interests.

Disagree In democratic societies individual liberties should never be sacrificed, not even temporarily.

1917 Business and Finance U.S. income tax revenue exceeds revenue from customs duties for the first time.

1917 Daily Life The Selective Service Act is passed.

1917 Business and Finance U.S. automakers produce 1,745,792 automobiles, more than three times as many as were made in 1914.

The U.S. secretary of war draws numbers for the draft lottery.

The Grand Canyon

1918 World Events U.S. troops join the fighting in Europe.

1919 Daily Life The Grand Canyon National Park is established.

1917 — 1918 — 1919 — 1920

1917 Business and Finance Millionaires in the United States number more than 40,000—up from 4,000 in 1892.

1917 Politics The U.S. Congress declares war on Germany.

The Paris Peace Conference meeting in the Hall of Mirrors at Versailles

1919 World Events World leaders sign the Treaty of Versailles.

1919 Politics The U.S. Senate rejects the Treaty of Versailles.

exploring the time line

internet connect

TOPIC: Battle of the Somme
GO TO: go.hrw.com
KEYWORD: SE1 Somme

Have students access the Internet through the HRW Web site to conduct research on the Battle of the Somme. Then ask students to assume one of the following roles: a British general planning the attack, a German machine gunner defending the trenches, or a British soldier who survived the battle. Have each student write a series of diary entries describing the Battle of the Somme.

Think About Themes

Decide whether you **agree** *or* **disagree** *with the following statements. Note why in your journal.*

Global Relations A country should consider only its own interests in deciding whether to go to war.

Economic Development Fighting in an overseas military conflict can help improve a nation's economy at home.

Democratic Values During wartime, a government has the right to limit the individual liberties of citizens.

327

SECTION 1

After completing Section 1, students should be able to:

OBJECTIVE 1 *Identify the major causes of unrest in Europe.*

OBJECTIVE 2 *Discuss the results of the strategy that was used during the early fighting in the war.*

OBJECTIVE 3 *Explain why the war settled into a stalemate.*

LET'S GET STARTED!

Draw a three-column chart on the chalkboard. Label the first column *Things You Are Positive You Know About World War I*, the second column *Things You Think You Know About World War I*, and the third column *Things You Want to Know About World War I.* As students enter the classroom, tell them to copy the chart and complete it. Have volunteers share their entries. Then tell students that in Section 1 they will learn about the causes and the early events of World War I.

SECTION 1 RESOURCES

PRINT

- Guided Reading Strategy 11.1
- American History Political Cartoon 20: Conflict in the Balkans
- Geography Activity 11: World War I
- Section 1 Review, p. 332
- Daily Quiz 11.1

MULTIMEDIA

- One-Stop Planner, Lesson 11.1
- The American Nation Video Program Segment: Weaponry and Warfare; Teacher's Guide, pp. 99–104
- Holt Researcher: American History CD–ROM

SHELTERED ENGLISH

- Main Idea Activity for Reteaching and Sheltered English 11.1

✔ READING TO UNDERSTAND

To help students master the section objectives, have them answer the **READING CHECKS** and complete **Guided Reading Strategy 11.1** as they read the section.

SECTION 1 World War I Breaks Out

OBJECTIVES

Read to understand:

1. what the major causes of unrest in Europe were
2. what the results of the early fighting in the war were
3. why the war settled into a stalemate

KEY TERMS

militarism
Allied Powers
Central Powers
First Battle of the Marne
no-man's-land
trench warfare
Battle of the Somme

KEY PEOPLE

Franz Ferdinand
Gavrilo Princip
Manfred von Richthofen
Edward Rickenbacker

KEY PLACES

Balkans
Austria-Hungary
Bosnia and Herzegovina
Belgium

EYEWITNESSES TO History

"As I write, Germany is reported to have declared war against Russia and France, and the participation of England on the one side and of Italy on the other seems imminent [close at hand]. Nothing like it has occurred since the great Napoleonic wars, and with modern armaments and larger populations nothing has occurred like it since the world began. . . . All of Europe is to be a battleground. . . . The future looks dark indeed."

—William Howard Taft

World War I artillery

Former president William Howard Taft published "A Message to the People of the United States" in August 1914. He expressed the surprise and fear many Americans felt at the news that Europe was at war. Few Americans had seen the war coming. Europe had appeared peaceful for more than 40 years. However, while the Wilson administration was wrestling with problems created by the Mexican Revolution, tensions in Europe exploded into global war.

The Causes of the War

One longterm cause of the war lay in the growth of nationalism throughout Europe. In the 1860s nationalism united Italians in their fight to free themselves from Austrian rule. Nationalism also helped Otto von Bismarck join the German states into a single nation in the 1870s.

Nationalism and territorial rivalries. Nationalism was particularly strong in the central European region of the Balkans. This region was so unstable that it was called the powder keg of Europe. The Ottoman Empire (Turkey) gained control of the Balkans in the 1400s and ruled the area until the 1800s. By then the region's four main ethnic groups—Albanians, Greeks, Romanians, and Slavs—were each struggling for independence. Greece began a successful revolt in the 1820s, and Romania followed in 1859. Following a war between Russia and the Ottoman Empire in 1878, the Bulgarians, Montenegrins, and Serbs each staked their claims to nationhood. Soon after, Austria-Hungary occupied the small Balkan kingdoms of Bosnia and Herzegovina (often just called Bosnia).

This 1912 British cartoon shows European leaders trying to keep a lid on trouble in the Balkans.

The newly independent Serbia saw Bosnia as part of its rightful territory. Austria-Hungary's 1908 annexation of the territories produced open hostility. Serbia's growing strength threatened Austria-Hungary's control of its territories in the Balkans. This encouraged the Slavs to push for independence. Austro-Hungarian chief of staff Baron Conrad von Hötzendorf foresaw a major conflict:

TEACH OBJECTIVE 1

LEVEL 1: Ask students to identify the causes of unrest in Europe. List students' responses on the chalkboard. *(Students should identify nationalism, militarism, and military alliances.)* Have students define these terms, and write these definitions on the chalkboard as well. *(Students should note that nationalism is loyalty to a nation, even one not in existence; that militarism is the glorification of military strength; and that military alliances are agreements among nations.)* Then ask each student to write a paragraph on the causes of unrest in Europe, incorporating all of the terms in the chalkboard list. Have volunteers read their paragraphs to the class.
Sheltered English

LEVEL 2: Pair students and ask them to complete the Level 1 activity. Then distribute Cartoon 20, Conflict in the Balkans, from **American History Political Cartoons**. Have each pair study the cartoon and answer the questions. To conclude, have each pair create its own political cartoon about the causes of unrest in Europe. Display pairs' cartoons around the classroom.
Cooperative Learning

LEVEL 3: Tell students to imagine that they are political analysts for President Wilson. Have each student write a memo to the president briefing him on the causes of unrest in Europe. *(See the Level 1 lesson for the correct causes.)* Students should conclude their memos by making predictions about the possible consequences of these factors.

> "The unification of the South Slav[s] . . . is one of the powerful national movements which can neither be ignored nor kept down. The question can only be, whether that unification will take place within the boundaries of the Monarchy [the Austro-Hungarian Empire]—that is, at the expense of Serbia's independence—or under Serbia's leadership at the expense of the Monarchy."

Militarism and alliances. Because large European countries frequently overpowered smaller ones, relations between nations were characterized by a strong spirit of **militarism**, or the glorification of military strength. Leaders of the major European powers believed that disputes would ultimately be settled on the battlefield. As a result, they engaged in an arms race in which they tried to develop larger armies and more powerful weapons than their rivals. In this dangerous atmosphere, leaders formed alliances with other nations, each promising to aid the other in case of attack by a third power.

Germany had a longtime ally in Austria. France's 1892 alliance with Russia threatened to surround Germany with enemies. Eventually Italy joined Austria-Hungary and Germany in one alliance, and Great Britain joined France and Russia in another. The alliances avoided war for a time, but created the risk that a minor incident could trigger a major war.

✔ **READING CHECK:** What were the major causes of unrest in Europe?

The Great War Begins

In June 1914 Archduke Franz Ferdinand, the heir to the Austro-Hungarian throne, visited the Bosnian capital, Sarajevo (sahr-uh-YAY-voh). As the archduke rode through the city streets, Serbian nationalist Gavrilo Princip (PREENT-seep) stepped out of the crowd. He fired two shots, killing the archduke and his wife, Sophie.

Austria-Hungary quickly declared war on Serbia. Germany immediately offered its support. Russia, with a large Slav population of its own, was compelled to honor its alliance with Serbia. The alliance system soon turned a local conflict into a global war. The **Allied Powers** of Britain, France, and Russia were pitted against the **Central Powers** of Germany, Austria-Hungary, the Ottoman Empire, and Bulgaria. Italy remained neutral until 1915, when it joined the Allies. Eventually some 30 nations took sides in what became known as the Great War.

Germany's military strategy called for a massive strike against France to defeat it quickly, leaving British forces stranded on the other side of the English Channel. With France and Britain out of

Then and Now

Conflicts in Bosnia

Bosnia and Herzegovina—a nation about the size of West Virginia—has been a place of unrest for many years. After being controlled by various kingdoms for several centuries, Bosnia fought for and gained its independence in about 1200. It remained independent until 1463, when it was conquered by the Ottoman Turks. Bosnia remained under Ottoman rule for the next 400 years. In 1878 Austria-Hungary took control of Bosnia from the Turks.

This man in Gorazde, Bosnia, is gathering supplies dropped from planes.

At the end of World War I, Serbia's ruler was crowned king of the newly created nation of Yugoslavia, which included Bosnia. After World War II, Yugoslavia was reorganized into six republics—Bosnia and Herzegovina, Croatia, Macedonia, Montenegro, Serbia, and Slovenia.

In the late 1980s Yugoslavia's government began to disintegrate. Serbian president Slobodan Milosevic sought to create a Greater Serbia, uniting all Serbs in a single state under his leadership. At that time Bosnia's population of about 4 million included three ethnic groups: Croats, Serbs, and Slavic Muslims. Early in 1992 some 70 percent of the country's voters—including many Bosnian Serbs—voted for independence from the rest of Yugoslavia. That March, Serbian forces began seizing territory in northern and eastern Bosnia. They drove out much of the non-Serbian population. The United States and most of the international community recognized Bosnia's independence in April 1992. On May 22, Bosnia was admitted as a full member of the United Nations. Fighting continued, however, until a 1994 treaty ended the civil war. The United Nations sent in a peacekeeping force to help the country maintain peace.

ACROSS THE CURRICULUM

▶GEOGRAPHY◀

The Short-War Illusion. Historian L. L. Farrar Jr. argued that most European nations chose to enter the war because they saw it as a way to achieve their objectives after diplomacy had failed. Most European leaders believed that the war would be brief. Their military strategies depended on the accuracy of that assumption. Germany, for example, was surrounded by powerful enemies. German military leaders knew that they would have to quickly push through Belgium and conquer France to win the war. Belgian troops and Allied reinforcements soon quashed that plan, however, and the war became a long affair.

CRITICAL THINKING Why might the European nations have been eager to begin any war?

ANSWER: Some students might suggest that European leaders saw war as their only option. Other students might argue that the leaders thought war would boost their national economy and morale.

GRAPH ANSWER
(for p. 330)
about 10,000

TEACH OBJECTIVE 2

ALL LEVELS: Have each student create a rudimentary time line of the early battles of World War I. To help students understand the results of the strategy that was used during the early fighting, copy the graphic organizer to the right on the chalkboard, omitting the italicized answers. Have each student complete it. **Sheltered English**

▶**ASSIGNMENT:** *Ask each student to write two paragraphs on events in Belgium during the early days of World War I. One paragraph should explain the nation's role in foiling Germany's initial strategy and the other should speculate on the course the war might have taken had Belgium crumpled in the face of the German invasion.*

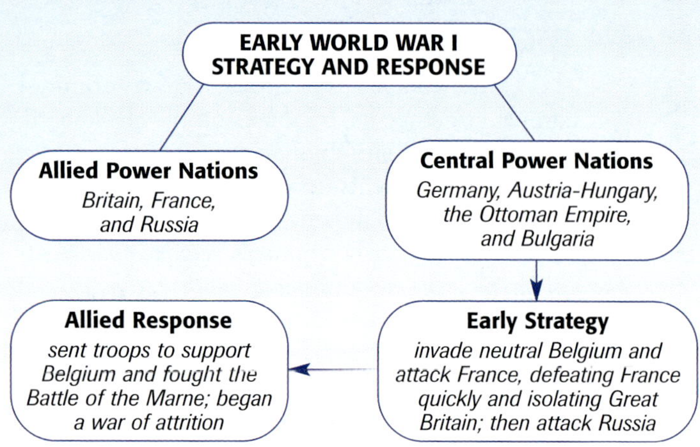

GLOBAL RELATIONS

The Schlieffen Plan. German military officials formulated the Schlieffen Plan between 1891 and 1906 in response to an earlier alliance between France and Russia. The plan relied on the presumed weakness of the Belgian army and the presumed cooperation of Leopold, the Belgian king. Leopold died in 1909, however, after the plan had been formulated but well before the war had begun.

CRITICAL THINKING In addition to the unexpected Belgian resistance, what other factors might have contributed to the failure of the Schlieffen Plan?

ANSWER: Students might suggest that new forms of technology or weaponry—nonexistent at the time of the plan's creation—might have contributed to its failure.

THAT'S INTERESTING!

During the First Battle of the Marne, French officers experienced a shortage of automobiles and train cars. They ordered Paris taxi drivers to transport soldiers to the front. The taxis, along with various other kinds of vehicles, carried thousands of soldiers to the battle.

MAP ANSWER
(for p. 331)
on the eastern front

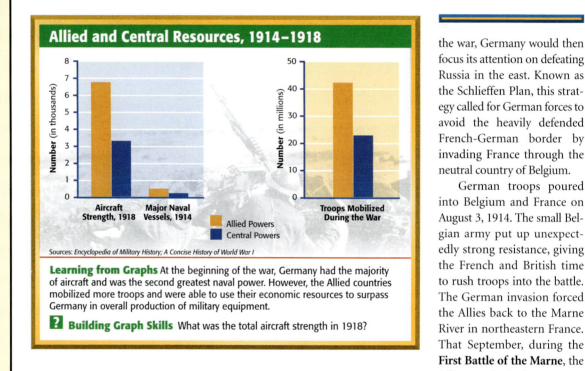

Allied and Central Resources, 1914–1918

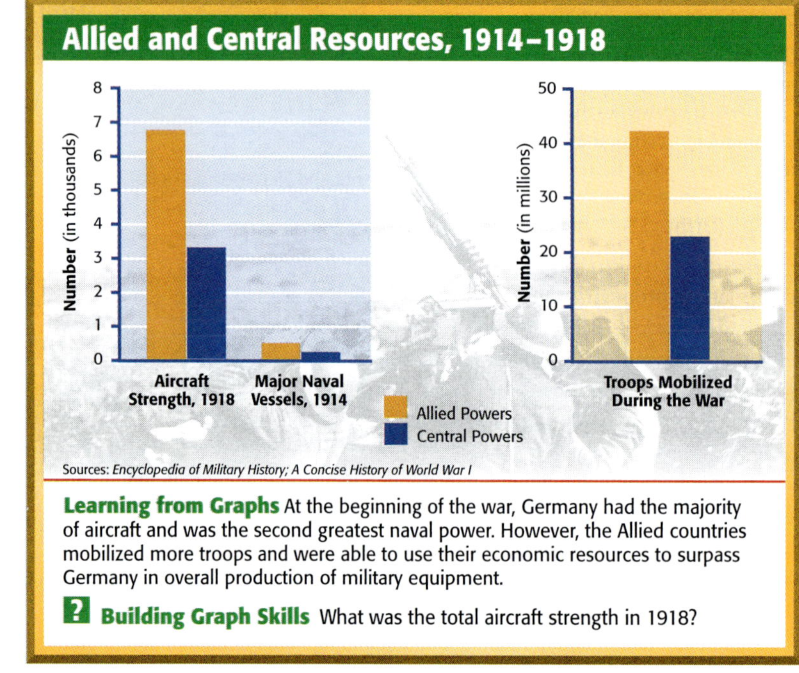

Sources: *Encyclopedia of Military History; A Concise History of World War I*

Learning from Graphs At the beginning of the war, Germany had the majority of aircraft and was the second greatest naval power. However, the Allied countries mobilized more troops and were able to use their economic resources to surpass Germany in overall production of military equipment.

Building Graph Skills What was the total aircraft strength in 1918?

the war, Germany would then focus its attention on defeating Russia in the east. Known as the Schlieffen Plan, this strategy called for German forces to avoid the heavily defended French-German border by invading France through the neutral country of Belgium.

German troops poured into Belgium and France on August 3, 1914. The small Belgian army put up unexpectedly strong resistance, giving the French and British time to rush troops into the battle. The German invasion forced the Allies back to the Marne River in northeastern France. That September, during the **First Battle of the Marne**, the Allies pushed the German lines back some 40 miles. As 1914 drew to a close, leaders of both sides realized that there would be no quick victory.

✔ **READING CHECK:** What were the results of the early fighting in the war?

Read More About It

Free Find:
Trench Warfare
After learning about trench warfare on the Holt Researcher CD–ROM, imagine that you are a soldier fighting on the western front. Write a letter home describing your experiences.

The War Reaches a Stalemate

Leaders had thought that this war would resemble earlier conflicts—with cavalry charges, decisive battles, and a quick victory. German kaiser Wilhelm II told troops they would be home "before the leaves have fallen from the trees." Both sides threw troops and arms into battle, expecting to achieve a clear victory. Instead, each side battered and bloodied the other in a brutal stalemate.

Trench warfare. By early 1915 both armies occupied trenches along a front running for hundreds of miles from the North Sea to the border of Switzerland. Separating the two sides was a thin strip of bombed-out territory—strewn with barbed wire and land mines—called **no-man's-land**. A new type of fighting, known as **trench warfare**, emerged on the western front. Battles began with massive artillery barrages. Then soldiers went "over the top" of the trenches and charged across the no-man's-land toward the enemy trenches. As they ran, thousands of soldiers were cut down by a hail of machine-gun fire.

The war remained locked in a stalemate throughout 1915. Determined to break out, each side prepared massive offensives for 1916. In February 1916 the Germans launched a huge offensive designed to "bleed the French army white" by causing unsustainable casualties. The Germans targeted the fortified French city of Verdun because they knew the French would feel compelled to defend it. The

Soldiers faced horrible conditions in World War I trenches.

TEACH OBJECTIVE 3

LEVEL 1: Write the following terms on the chalkboard: *trench warfare, cavalry charges, artillery barrages, decisive battles.* Have pairs of students identify the terms that did and did not play an important role in the early years of World War I. *(Students' responses might indicate that unlike earlier conflicts, which featured cavalry charges and decisive battles, World War I was characterized by trench warfare and artillery barrages.)* Ask students to write several sentences explaining how trench warfare and artillery barrages led to a stalemate in World War I, and how cavalry charges and decisive battles had prevented stalemates in earlier conflicts.
Sheltered English, Cooperative Learning

LEVEL 2: Tell students to imagine that they are American news reporters stationed in France during the early years of World War I. Have each student write a short article describing and explaining the stalemate in Europe. *(See the Level 1 lesson for the correct factors.)* Ask volunteers to read their articles to the class.

LEVEL 3: Write the following question on the chalkboard: *Why did World War I settle into a stalemate?* Have each student write a short essay in response to the question. *(See the Level 1 lesson for the correct factors.)* Have volunteers read their essays to the class.

battle began with a staggering 21-hour artillery barrage in which more than 1 million shells were fired. Then the 1 million soldiers of the German Fifth Army advanced on some 200,000 French defenders. For months the battle raged back and forth.

In July the Allied Powers launched an offensive near the Somme River in northern France. They had the same goal as the German attack on Verdun—to exhaust the enemy's reserves. In the **Battle of the Somme**, British forces suffered some 60,000 casualties in a single day. This four-month-long battle left more than 1 million dead

World War I, 1914–1917

Learning from Maps The warring powers fought on several battlefronts, with the most intense fighting occurring on the western front.

? MOVEMENT Where did the Central Powers gain the most territory?

The British blockade disrupts German supply lines. As a result, food riots break out in dozens of German cities.

The British withdraw from Gallipoli, ending any hope of sending supplies to Russia.

Allied Powers, 1916
Central Powers, 1916
Neutral countries
Allied forces
Central Powers forces
British naval blockade
Farthest Russian advance (1914)
Farthest advance of Central Powers
Trench line, western front
Battle
Food riots
German submarine activity

ACROSS THE CURRICULUM

ART

Sculpting Faces. Anna Coleman Ladd, a well-known American sculptor, put her skills to use during World War I. Many soldiers incurred disfiguring facial injuries during battle. After plastic surgeons attempted to reshape soldiers' faces, Ladd sculpted "portrait masks" for the men. She took casts of their faces and then made thin copper masks lined with silver and covered with hard enamel paint.

ACTIVITY: Have each student write a poem or short story commenting on the violence of the war and the need for "portrait masks."

The American Nation
VIDEO PROGRAM

Weaponry and Warfare;
Teacher's Guide, pp. 99–104

Search 14847, Play to 20155
Videodisc 2, Side A

Play

Pause

See *Teacher's Guide* for Spanish barcode.

SECTION 1 REVIEW ANSWERS

Define and Identify
For significance, see the following pages:

- militarism, p. 329
- Franz Ferdinand, p. 329

REVIEW

Have students complete the **Section 1 Review** on p. 332.

ASSESS

Have students complete **Daily Quiz 11.1.** As **Alternative Assessment**, you may want to use the unrest memo or the stalemate article in this section's lessons.

RETEACH

Have students complete **Main Idea Activity for Reteaching and Sheltered English 11.1.** Then organize students into triads. Assign one section objective to each member of the triad. Have students create outlines of the material that relates to their assigned objectives. Have students share their outlines within their triads. **Sheltered English, Cooperative Learning**

EXTEND

Ask students to conduct research on the Schlieffen Plan. Students should focus on who devised the plan, the reasoning behind the plan, and when the plan was implemented. Students should also evaluate the success of the plan. Have each student present his or her findings in a detailed report. Students might also include diagrams or illustrations to supplement their reports. **Block Scheduling**

- Gavrilo Princip, p. 329
- Allied Powers, p. 329
- Central Powers, p. 329
- First Battle of the Marne, p. 330
- no-man's-land, p. 330
- trench warfare, p. 330
- Battle of the Somme, p. 331
- Manfred von Richthofen, p. 332
- Edward Rickenbacker, p. 332

Locate

For locations, see the map on p. 331. For importance, see the following pages:

- Balkans, p. 328
- Austria-Hungary, p. 328
- Bosnia and Herzegovina, p. 328
- Belgium, p. 330

1. nationalism, militarism, territorial rivalries, military alliances

2. encouraged the creation of nations based largely on ethnicity and intensified territorial rivalries among different ethnic groups

3. Germany hoped to defeat France quickly using the Schlieffen Plan but failed. The Allied Powers put up strong resistance and rushed troops to the front. Both sides stalemated in trench warfare until 1916, when each prepared massive offensives.

4. Students should mention the horrible conditions in the trenches, the stalemate, and new weapons such as machine guns, tanks, airplanes, submarines, and poison gas.

5. Machine gun attacks rendered cavalry charges useless. Trench-warfare tactics and a reliance on infantry charges also contributed to the stalemate.

Many Allied ships like this one were sunk by torpedoes fired from German submarines.

and wounded. At Verdun, the longest battle of the war, the two sides suffered nearly 1 million more casualties, half of them deaths.

Even for those who avoided death, the trenches were a living nightmare. Rats and lice plagued the soldiers. Rain flooded the trenches, drenching the soldiers in mud. The dead often lay unburied for days. Unsanitary conditions bred disease and sickness that claimed nearly as many lives as the fighting did.

New weapons. Deadly new weapons added to the horror of trench warfare. Machine guns fired hundreds of rounds per minute. Partly to counter the machine gun's deadly impact, the Allies introduced tanks at the Battle of the Somme. One British soldier reported that tanks scared the Germans "out of their wits" and made them "scuttle like frightened rabbits."

Perhaps the most feared new weapon introduced during World War I was poison gas. It could be released as a cloud of mist that silently drifted over the trenches or be launched inside an exploding shell. Either way, soldiers had only seconds to slip on their gas masks or else suffer a slow, suffocating death.

Modern machines such as submarines and airplanes brought terror to the seas and the skies. Submarines slipped silently beneath the waves to sink commercial and military ships with little or no warning. Some airplane pilots engaged enemy planes in aerobatic dogfights. Although these skirmishes did little to influence the course of the war, they made celebrities out of those who survived. Skilled pilots were known as aces. The most successful was the German Baron Manfred von Richthofen, known as the Red Baron. He had a reported 80 kills, or enemy aircraft shot down. The top American ace was Edward Rickenbacker, with 26 kills.

A World War I German airplane

 **READING CHECK:** Why did the war settle into a stalemate?

SECTION 1 REVIEW

Define and explain the significance of the following terms:
militarism
Allied Powers
Central Powers
First Battle of the Marne
no-man's-land
trench warfare
Battle of the Somme

Identify and explain the significance of the following individuals:
Franz Ferdinand
Gavrilo Princip
Manfred von Richthofen
Edward Rickenbacker

Locate and explain the importance of the following places:
Balkans
Austria-Hungary
Bosnia and Herzegovina
Belgium

1. **Using Graphic Organizers** Copy the diagram below. Use it to list the factors that contributed to the outbreak of World War I.

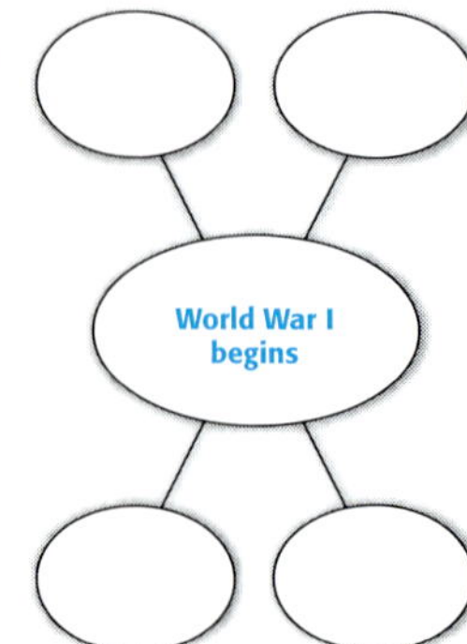

2. **Identifying Cause and Effect** How did nationalism contribute to the unrest in Europe that led to World War I?
3. **Comparing and Contrasting** What battle strategies did each side employ in the war? How effective were these strategies?
4. **Using Historical Imagination** Imagine you are a British reporter at the front during 1916. Write a newspaper article that describes the conditions at the front and encourages the British people to continue fighting.

Critical Thinking

5. What led to the stalemate on the western front?
Consider:
- new weapons used during the war
- the tactics of trench warfare
- the transportation available to the opposing sides

SECTION 2

After completing Section 2, students should be able to:

OBJECTIVE 1 *Relate the challenges the United States faced while trying to remain neutral.*

OBJECTIVE 2 *Identify the events that led to U.S. entry into the war.*

OBJECTIVE 3 *Explain how the United States prepared its military for World War I.*

OBJECTIVE 4 *Describe the types of experiences Americans had while serving in Europe.*

LET'S GET STARTED!

Write the following question on the chalkboard: *If you had been living in the United States when war broke out in Europe, would you have supported U.S. neutrality or would you have wanted the United States to immediately enter the war on the side of the Allies?* As students enter the classroom, have them respond to the question in writing. Have volunteers share their answers with the class. Then tell students that in Section 2 they will learn about the challenges of neutrality and U.S. entry into World War I.

SECTION 2 The United States Goes to War

OBJECTIVES

Read to understand:

1. what challenges the United States faced while trying to remain neutral
2. what events led to U.S. entry into the war
3. how the United States prepared its military for World War I
4. what types of experiences Americans had while serving in Europe

KEY TERMS

Sussex pledge
National Defense Act
Zimmerman Note
Selective Service Act
convoy system

KEY PEOPLE

Robert Lansing
Jeannette Rankin
John J. Pershing

EYEWITNESSES TO History

"In August, 1914, I was a cowboy on a ranch in the interior of British Columbia. . . . An early Saturday morning in August found me jogging slowly along the trail to Dog Creek . . . our post office and trading center. . . . We had heard rumors of a war in Europe. We all talked it over in the evening and decided it was another one of those fights that were always starting in the Balkans. One had just been finished a few months before and we thought it was about time another was underway so we gave the matter no particular thought. But when I got within sight of Dog Creek I knew something was up. The first thing I heard was that . . . the Germans were fighting. . . . Then a big Indian came up to me . . . and told me England's . . . going to war, or had gone. He wasn't certain which, but he was going too. Would I? I laughed at him. 'What do you mean, go to war?' I asked him. I wasn't English; I wasn't Canadian. I was from the good old U. S. A. And from all we could understand the States were neutral. So, I reasoned, I ought to be neutral too."

—Joseph Smith

World War I soldiers carried all the equipment they needed on their backs.

After some thought, Joseph Smith decided to join his Canadian friends and volunteered to fight. Like many people, Smith and his friends first "regarded the whole war . . . as more or less of a lark." Enthusiasm for the glory of war faded quickly when soldiers actually witnessed the horrors of the battlefields.

The National Woman's Peace Party organized a telegram campaign to show Americans' support for peace.

U.S. Neutrality

Most Americans were surprised by the outbreak of war. However, they tended to look on it as a strictly European matter. President Woodrow Wilson received strong support when he announced a policy of neutrality. He urged all Americans to be "neutral in fact as well as in name . . . impartial in thought as well as action." Wilson hoped that the United States would be able to negotiate a settlement to the conflict. He pursued this goal throughout 1915 and 1916, but without success.

The United States remained neutral in action, but few of its citizens were impartial in thought. Some 28 million Americans—nearly 30 percent of the population—were either immigrants or the children of immigrants. Some Americans of Austrian, German, Hungarian, or Turkish background sympathized with the Central Powers. Some Irish Americans hoped the war would help free Ireland from the rule of Great Britain.

Many more Americans, however, backed the Allies. A common language and culture bound many Americans to Great Britain. The British propaganda campaign, which painted the Germans as brutal killers, also increased American support for the Allied cause.

SECTION 2 RESOURCES

PRINT

- Guided Reading Strategy 11.2
- Primary Source Reading 11: A Dark Moment in History
- Graphic Organizer Activity 11: Americans in World War I
- Literature Reading 11: Inside World War I
- Biography Reading 11: Jeannette Rankin
- Section 2 Review, p. 339
- Daily Quiz 11.2

MULTIMEDIA

- One-Stop Planner, Lesson 11.2
- Holt Researcher: American History CD–ROM
- HRW Web site

SHELTERED ENGLISH

- Main Idea Activity for Reteaching and Sheltered English 11.2

✔ READING TO UNDERSTAND

To help students master the section objectives, have them answer the **READING CHECKS** and complete **Guided Reading Strategy 11.2** as they read the section.

TEACH OBJECTIVE 1

LEVEL 1: Conduct a brief discussion on the challenges the United States faced while trying to remain neutral in World War I. *(Students might suggest that Americans found neutrality difficult for a number of reasons—conflicting sympathies and opinions, the British propaganda campaign, the British navy blockade, and German submarine attacks on the* Lusitania *and other civilian ships.)* Then pair students and tell them to imagine that it is 1915. Have each pair develop a short dialogue on the challenges of neutrality. Ask volunteers to perform their dialogues for the class.
Sheltered English, Cooperative Learning

LEVEL 2: Conduct a brief discussion on the challenges the United States faced while trying to remain neutral in World War I. *(See the Level 1 lesson for the correct challenges.)* Then tell students to imagine that they are President Wilson. Have each student write a brief public address on the challenges of neutrality and the need to remain neutral. Ask volunteers to deliver their public addresses to the class. Students may wish to include their addresses in their portfolios.

LEVEL 3: Conduct a brief discussion on the challenges the United States faced while trying to remain neutral in World War I. *(See the Level 1 lesson for the correct challenges.)* Then organize students in the class into two groups—one that

ACROSS THE CURRICULUM

LANGUAGE ARTS

U-Boats. The term *U-boat* is a shortened form of the German word *Unterseeboot*, or submarine. Germany possessed both gas-powered and diesel-powered U-boats. The German U-boats were the first to fire self-propelled torpedoes at enemy ships.

ACTIVITY: Ask students to conduct research on the origins of the word *tank*. Have each student write a paragraph explaining his or her findings.

internetconnect

TOPIC: Lusitania
GO TO: go.hrw.com
KEYWORD: SE1 Lusitania

Have students access the Internet through the HRW Web site to conduct research on the sinking of the *Lusitania*. Then ask each student to create two propaganda posters on the controversy–one from the U.S. or British point of view and one from the German point of view. Have volunteers present their posters to the class. Then conduct a discussion on wartime propaganda products.

The sinking of the **Lusitania**, *shown in this drawing by Charles Dixon, caused strong anti-German feelings in the United States.*

Despite its policy of neutrality, the United States could not remain untouched by the war. When the war began, the British navy blockaded Germany and laid mines in the North Sea. The British even stopped U.S. ships bound for neutral countries and searched their cargoes—including the mail. They were looking for goods that might ultimately be destined for Germany. Wilson protested this violation of U.S. neutrality.

Early in 1915 Germany responded to the blockade by establishing a "war zone" around Britain. Any ships entering this zone—even those from neutral nations—were subject to attack by U-boats, or German submarines. Wilson warned that, in accordance with international laws of neutrality, the United States would hold Germany accountable for any injury to American lives or property on the high seas.

On March 28, 1915, a U-boat sank a British passenger liner in the Irish Sea, killing more than 100 people, including one American. While the White House considered its response, a far more serious incident occurred. On May 7, 1915, a U-boat patrolling off the Irish coast torpedoed another British passenger liner, the *Lusitania*. The dead included 128 Americans. The *New York Times* called the Germans "savages drunk with blood." Outraged Americans agreed. German leaders pointed out that they had placed advertisements in American newspapers warning Americans against sailing into the war zone. They also charged that the *Lusitania* was transporting armaments for Britain—an accusation that later proved true.

Nevertheless, President Wilson protested angrily to the German government. He demanded specific pledges against unrestricted submarine warfare against civilian ships. Secretary of State William Jennings Bryan charged that the president's protest amounted to an ultimatum and resigned. Bryan argued that the United States could not issue ultimatums to other nations and remain neutral.

THROUGH OTHERS' EYES

The Sinking of the *Lusitania*

Germany's Baron von Schwarzenstein offered the following response to the outrage over the sinking of the *Lusitania*.

> **"It was only after England declared the whole North Sea a war zone . . . that Germany with precisely the same right declared the waters around England a war zone and announced her purpose of sinking all hostile commercial vessels found therein. . . . In the case of the *Lusitania* the German Ambassador even further warned Americans through the great American newspapers against taking passage thereon. Does a pirate act thus? Does he take pains to save human lives? . . . Nobody regrets more sincerely than we Germans the hard necessity of sending to their deaths hundreds of men. Yet the sinking was a justifiable act of war. . . . The scene of war is no golf links [course], the ships of belligerent powers no pleasure places. . . . We have sympathy with the victims and their relatives, of course, but did we hear anything about sympathy . . . when England adopted her diabolical [evil] plan of starving a great nation?"**

✔ **READING CHECK:** What challenges did the United States face while trying to remain neutral?

supports neutrality and one that supports entry into the war. Give each group time to prepare supporting arguments for its position. Then conduct a classroom debate on neutrality in World War I. **Cooperative Learning**

▶**ASSIGNMENT:** *Remind students that British and German propaganda had a subtle effect on U.S. neutrality. Have students reread the feature on the* Lusitania *on the previous page. Then ask each student to create two pieces of propaganda on the sinking of the* Lusitania*—one from the British point of view and one from the German point of view. Have students present their propaganda pieces to the class.*

Teacher to Teacher

Janie Maldonado of Austin, Texas, suggested the following activity: Tell students to imagine that they have survived the sinking of either the Lusitania, *the* Sussex, *or the* Arabic. *Have each student describe the experience in a letter to a family member and explain his or her position on U.S. neutrality toward Germany.*

The Road to War

The sinking of the *Lusitania* brought the conflict in Europe closer to home for many Americans. Even so, most people still hoped the United States could stay out of the war. Further challenges to U.S. neutrality, however, were not long in coming.

Wilson's actions criticized. In August 1915 a German submarine sank the *Arabic*, another British liner, killing two Americans. Then, in March 1916, the French passenger vessel *Sussex* was attacked, injuring several Americans. In a sternly worded message to the German government, President Wilson threatened to cut diplomatic ties if Germany did not abandon its unrestricted submarine warfare. The German government responded with the ***Sussex* pledge**, a renewal of an earlier promise not to sink liners without warning or without ensuring the passengers' safety.

Most Americans supported the president's approach. A number of prominent politicians, however, criticized Wilson for not responding more strongly to German aggression. Former president Theodore Roosevelt accused Wilson of "cowardice and weakness."

Others accused Wilson of abandoning neutrality. Former secretary of state William Jennings Bryan argued that Wilson's commercial and trade policies helped the Allies and therefore the United States was no longer impartial in action. As secretary of state, Bryan had discouraged American bankers from making loans to either side, but this policy was soon abandoned. Large American banks lent millions of dollars to Britain and France. Bryan's successor, Robert Lansing, encouraged the trade of war materials with the Allies. By 1916 U.S. arms sales to the Allies had reached some $500 million, about 80 times the amount sold in 1914.

Preparedness and peace. In 1916 President Wilson launched a military "preparedness" program. This program was strongly supported by the banks and war industries that had a large economic interest in an Allied victory. Passed in June 1916, the **National Defense Act** increased the number of soldiers in the regular army from some 90,000 to about 175,000, with an ultimate goal of 223,000. Wilson established the National Guard's size at some 450,000 troops. Two months later, Congress passed another bill appropriating $313 million to build up the navy.

With the presidential election nearing, President Wilson assured Americans that he had not abandoned neutrality. Running on the slogan "He Kept Us Out of War," Wilson narrowly defeated Republican Charles Evans Hughes to win re-election.

Wilson still hoped to negotiate a settlement to the war. In a January 1917 speech, he called for "peace without victory." A lasting peace, he said, had to be one between equals, not between the victor and the defeated. Once again, the warring nations rejected Wilson's effort to mediate.

Diplomatic relations broken. On February 1, 1917, Germany resumed full-scale U-boat warfare. The Germans were gambling that their U-boat fleet could defeat the Allies before the United States joined the war. Wilson followed through on his threat to break off diplomatic relations. He also ordered the arming of American merchant ships sailing into the war zone. Nonetheless, German torpedoes sank five American ships.

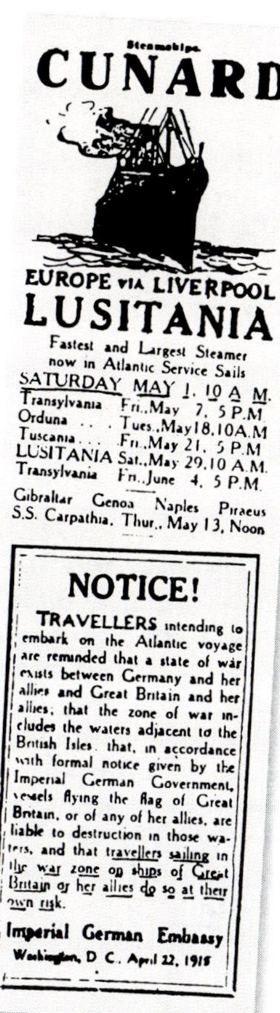

INTERPRETING THE VISUAL RECORD

The *Lusitania*. The German government ran this warning in the announcement of the *Lusitania*'s 1915 voyage. ***Does this notice provide enough warning to Americans traveling on the* Lusitania*? Explain your answer.***

ACROSS THE CURRICULUM

▶GEOGRAPHY◀

The Threat of a North American Invasion.

Many of those who urged the United States to become involved in World War I feared that Germany would defeat the Allies and then invade North America. One pamphlet claimed, "Germany's ambitions for expansion in the New World have shown that we should have to fight Germany later, if not now; and without help, instead of with the help of all other great free peoples."

CRITICAL THINKING How might Americans' fears of a North American invasion have affected German American citizens in the United States?

ANSWER: Some students might suggest that Americans who feared an invasion of North America probably reacted to German American citizens with fear and even hatred.

VISUAL RECORD ANSWER

Answers will vary. Some students might argue that the text in the notice provided travelers with adequate warning. Other students might argue that the advertisement should have included multiple warnings.

TEACH OBJECTIVE 2

ALL LEVELS: To help students identify the events that led to U.S. entry into the war, copy the time line to the right on the chalkboard, omitting the italicized events. Have each student complete it. After students have finished their time lines, conduct a discussion on the events in the time line. Ask students to rank the events in order of importance. Then ask students to name modern-day events that might encourage them to support a war. **Sheltered English**

▶**ASSIGNMENT:** *Have each student write a newspaper headline for each of the events that led to U.S. entry into the war. Students' newspaper headlines should both announce the event and give some indication of its importance.*

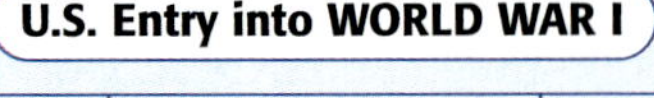

March 1916	February 1917	March 1917	April 1917
Event: *The Germans attack the Sussex.*	**Event:** *Germany resumes full-scale U-boat warfare.*	**Event:** *American newspapers publish the Zimmerman Note.*	**Event:** *The Senate declares war.*
Significance: *President Wilson threatens to cut diplomatic ties; Germany makes the Sussex pledge.*	**Significance:** *Wilson breaks diplomatic ties; orders the arming of American merchant ships.*	**Significance:** *This note proves German hostility.*	**Significance:** *United States joins the war on the Allied side.*

DEMOCRATIC VALUES

Military Service. As hostilities in Europe began to suggest the horrible possibility of a war, many U.S. leaders began thinking about how to prepare the military for a large-scale conflict. Some, such as Theodore Roosevelt and General Leonard Wood, advocated compulsory military training for all American men. Wood argued, "The volunteer system is not dependable because of the uncertainty as to returns, and in any case because of lack of time for training and organization." Others argued against compulsory service. Max Eastman, editor of *The Masses,* wrote: "For my part I do not recognize the right of a government to draft me to a war whose purposes I do not believe in. But to draft me to a war whose purposes it will not so much as communicate to my ear, seems an act of tyranny."

ACTIVITY: Have each student write an editorial either supporting compulsory military service or arguing against it.

VISUAL RECORD ANSWER

Some students might suggest that the German government would not send an official government document through Western Union. Other students might note that the telegram appears to be written in a secret code, suggesting an official origin.

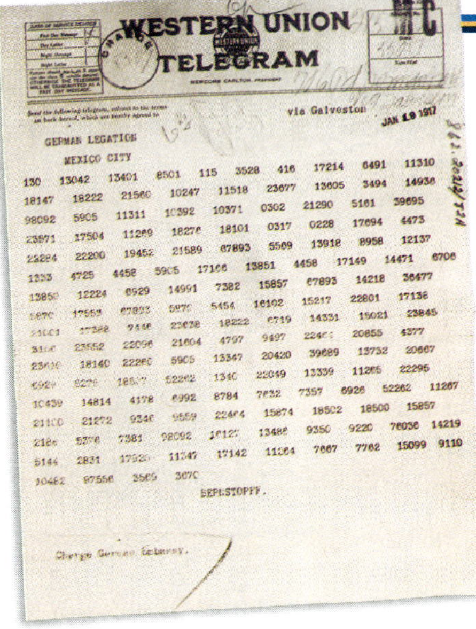

INTERPRETING THE VISUAL RECORD

The Zimmerman Note. This telegram sent to the German minister in Mexico proposed an alliance between Germany and Mexico. ***Does this telegram look like an official document from the German government? Explain your answer.***

On March 1, 1917, American newspapers published an intercepted cable from German foreign secretary Arthur Zimmermann to the German minister in Mexico. Dubbed the **Zimmerman Note**, the cable proposed a Mexican alliance with Germany. The cable offered German support to help Mexico "reconquer the lost territory in New Mexico, Texas, and Arizona."

As the weeks passed, Wilson reluctantly concluded that the United States could no longer stay out of the conflict. On April 2, 1917, the president addressed Congress, asking for a declaration of war.

Congress declares war. A hushed Congress heard Wilson condemn Germany's submarine warfare for its "wanton [vicious] and wholesale destruction." Wilson, however, did not rest his case solely on the evils of U-boat warfare. He summoned Americans to a crusade for a better world.

> **"We are glad . . . to fight thus for the ultimate peace of the world and for the liberation of its peoples, . . . for the rights of nations—great and small—and the privilege of men everywhere to choose their way of life. . . . The world must be made safe for democracy."**

At these words, cheers and applause rang through the Capitol. Later, Wilson told an aide: "My message today was a message of death for our young men. How strange it seems to applaud that."

The Senate declared war on April 4, 1917. The House followed two days later. The vote was not unanimous—six senators and 50 representatives opposed the declaration. Representative Jeannette Rankin of Montana was among the opposition. "I want to stand by my country," she explained, "but I cannot vote for war."

✔ **READING CHECK:** What events led to U.S. entry into the war?

Mobilizing U.S. Military Power

In his war message on April 2, President Wilson pledged all the nation's material resources to the Allied war effort. What the Allies most urgently needed were fresh troops. Few Americans, however, rushed to volunteer for military service.

Recruiting an army. On May 18, 1917, Congress passed the **Selective Service Act**. It required men between the ages of 21 and 30 to register with local draft boards. This was later changed to men between the ages of 18 and 45. By the end of the war, some 24 million men had registered, and 2.8 million of them had been drafted. More than half of the almost 4.8 million Americans who served in the armed forces during World War I were draftees.

Supporters of the draft argued that it would help build a more democratic United States by bringing together soldiers from different backgrounds. In reality, African Americans, American Indians, Mexican Americans, and many foreign-born soldiers faced segregation and often discrimination. Most foreign-born soldiers, for example, were assigned to separate units where they were taught civics

TEACH OBJECTIVE 3

LEVEL 1: Pair students and have each pair write several sentences explaining how the United States prepared its military for the war. *(Pairs' sentences should indicate that Congress passed the Selective Service Act, recruited troops in other ways, and instituted a massive soldier-training program.)* Ask students to share their sentences. Using these responses, compile a comprehensive list on the chalkboard. Then have pairs create recruitment or training posters. Ask volunteers to present their posters to the class and identify the factors that would have made them effective recruitment or training tools. **Sheltered English, Cooperative Learning**

LEVELS 2 AND 3: Tell students to imagine that it is 1917 and that they are new army recruits. Have each student write a series of short journal entries describing the ways in which the United States prepared its military for the war. *(See the Level 1 lesson for the correct methods.)* Have volunteers read their entries to the class. To conclude, ask students to consider how the United States prepared its military for the war. Do students think that those methods were adequate? How else might military officials have recruited and trained troops?

NOTE: For an additional teaching idea, see the Chapter 11 continuum lesson in the **Creative Teaching Strategies** handbook.

and English. Congress did eventually offer citizenship to the some 10,000 American Indians who served during the war.

The more than 370,000 African American recruits experienced particularly harsh discrimination. They were blocked from service in the marines and limited to kitchen duties in the navy. Most African Americans in the army served in all-black support units commanded by white officers. Furthermore, African American draftees who were sent to army training camps in the South often faced harassment from the local population.

Pressure from the National Association for the Advancement of Colored People (NAACP) and other African American organizations convinced the army to open up more opportunities for black soldiers. A school was established to train African American officers, and more African American soldiers were assigned combat duty. However, the army made no effort to integrate black and white soldiers in the same units.

Training the troops. Putting uniforms on young men did not make them soldiers. That required long and hard training, but the United States did not have the facilities to house such a large army. Massive training camps had to be hastily constructed. In the summer of 1917, workers began building barracks to house draftees at 16 separate locations. Completing the task in the planned 60 days seemed impossible. However, by using simple designs, a huge workforce, and mass-production techniques, thousands of buildings were ready by September. There were not enough uniforms and equipment for all the troops yet, but at least they had a place to live while training.

The military hoped to use a similar accelerated process for the troops' training as well. One of the recruits, Private Harry R. Richmond, wrote about his training camp in New Mexico.

> **"The burden of creating an army at short notice, falls most heavily upon the recruit. The rookie is expected to learn now in three weeks, what his fellow soldiers acquired a year ago in three months. We are drilled nearly 7 or 8 hours per day."**

Upon arrival at a training camp, recruits were herded like cattle through a series of medical examinations. Most of their days were spent learning military rules, drilling with their equipment, exercising, and preparing for inspections. "Every man is supposed to be slicked up, shoes shined, clothes clean, and he must be shaved," recalled one recruit. "This is one thing they insist on in the army—everything must be clean."

Soldiers also spent a lot of time learning how to fight the enemy. In addition to many hours on the rifle range, recruits practiced hand-to-hand combat using bayonets. Frank Sweeney wrote that recruits faced dummies "hanging from large cross beams" and were "taught the best method of approach and the

The Doughboy's Pack

BY PAUL BOYER

History is much more than a study of dates, documents, or facts about famous people. Ordinary objects also leave a historical record about an event or an era. For example, common items provided to soldiers during a war tell a story about how that war was fought.

During World War I, U.S. infantry troops carried all their necessary equipment inside a canvas "field kit" strapped to their backs. The around-the-waist design with pockets was adopted during World War I because of automatic weapons. Rifles could now fire as many as five bullets per minute, and a soldier needed easy access to large amounts of ammunition during the heat of battle.

The gas mask filtered out poisonous fumes that could suffocate or blind a soldier. The soldier's steel helmet extended to the top of the ear line to help prevent head wounds. Soldiers also carried a tent, tent poles, a rain poncho, a bayonet, a blanket, a sewing kit, socks, identification tags, a compass, and a flashlight. Sturdy metal containers protected two days' worth of rations–hard biscuits called hardtack and dried meat–from rain, rats, and insects. On a long march, soldiers might have cursed their heavy packs, but they also knew that burden could mean the difference between life and death.

CULTURAL DIVERSITY

African Americans in the War. African American soldiers faced officially sanctioned discrimination. In a 1918 memorandum, Colonel E. D. Anderson suggested that most African American soldiers work solely as laborers, thereby freeing up white soldiers to train for battle. Despite this discrimination many African Americans supported the war effort and welcomed the opportunities for travel, education, and honor that sometimes accompanied the experience. Addie W. Hunton and Kathryn M. Johnson, African American women who accompanied the American Expeditionary Force to France, wrote that some African American soldiers "received the rudiments of an education through direct instruction; a thing that would not have come to them in all the years of a lifetime at home, . . . In addition to this they had an opportunity of making a record for themselves that will be in no wise [ways] hidden from the generations of the future."

ACTIVITY: Tell students to imagine that they are African American soldiers in France. Have each student write a letter to a friend in Alabama describing his or her duties and expressing his or her feelings about World War I.

TEACH OBJECTIVE 4

LEVEL 1: Organize students in the class into two groups, one representing U.S. soldiers or nurses who have recently arrived in Europe and one representing American journalists who have also recently arrived in Europe. Give students time to prepare lists of possible interview questions and answers. Then pair students from the two groups. Ask each pair to conduct an interview on the types of experiences that Americans had while serving in Europe. *(Pairs should discuss John J. Pershing's general military strategy, marching through Paris upon arrival, encountering the battlefields for the first time, and so on.)* Have volunteers perform their interviews for the class. **Sheltered English, Cooperative Learning**

LEVELS 2 AND 3: Tell students to imagine that they are U.S. soldiers or nurses who have recently arrived in Europe with the U.S. Army. Have each student write a letter home describing his or her experiences serving in Europe. *(See the Level 1 lesson for the correct experiences.)* Encourage students to express their emotions upon reaching battlefields and the front lines, with their high casualty rates and trenches. Have volunteers read their letters to the class. Students may wish to include their letters in their portfolios.

CULTURAL DIVERSITY

The Hello Girls. Near the end of World War I the United States decided to send female telephone operators to France to run important military switchboards. Known as Hello Girls, many of the civilian women were stationed in Tours, France, some 200 miles from the front. One Hello Girl remembered her experiences training male operators to work the switchboards on the front lines. "I just reminded them that any soldier could carry a gun, but the safety of a whole division might depend on the switchboard."

CRITICAL THINKING How might the Hello Girls have contributed to Allied successes on the battlefield?

ANSWER: Students might mention that the Hello Girls enabled communication, allowing the Allies to plan more effective strategies.

VISUAL RECORD ANSWER

Answers will vary. Some students might suggest that the ambulances and their drivers look official and competent.

Read More About It

Free Find:
General Pershing
After reading about General John J. Pershing on the **Holt Researcher** CD–ROM, imagine that you are introducing General Pershing at a banquet being held in Pershing's honor. Write a short speech describing his accomplishments.

proper jabs to get him before he gets us." Sweeney noted that "sometimes the men enter into this game so heartily that they break their bayonets." The training left most soldiers in excellent physical health. At the end of his training one soldier felt that "if I am here another year I could outwalk a horse and carry a hundred pounds besides." This strength would be severely tested in France.

✔ **READING CHECK:** How did the United States prepare its military for World War I?

Over There

With mobilization well under way, U.S. troops began sailing to France as part of the American Expeditionary Force (AEF). Under the command of General John J. Pershing, the first U.S. troops reached France in late June 1917.

John J. Pershing

Born in Missouri in 1860, General Pershing was the U.S. Army's most experienced combat officer. He graduated from the U.S. Military Academy at West Point in 1886. Pershing then spent four years fighting with the cavalry against American Indians in the Southwest and in South Dakota. In 1891 Pershing became a military instructor at the University of Nebraska. He later moved on to teach military tactics at the U.S. Military Academy in 1897.

Pershing fought in the Spanish-American War and served a tour of duty in the Philippines from 1899 to 1903. After an assignment as an observer with Japanese forces during the Russo-Japanese War, Pershing was promoted from captain to brigadier general. He returned to the Philippines for a second tour of duty in 1906 before being named commander of the 8th Cavalry Brigade.

Early in 1917 Pershing was ordered to lead the expedition into Mexico that pursued Pancho Villa. Despite the failure to capture Villa, Pershing's appointment to head the AEF came as no surprise. A determined leader, Pershing refused to allow the Allies to dictate how his troops would be used. He insisted that U.S. forces fight as a separate unit, rather than be added to the Allied forces bit by bit.

On July 4, 1917, thousands of "Yanks"—U.S. soldiers—cheered on by huge crowds, marched through Paris, France. They stopped at the tomb of the Marquis de Lafayette, the French hero of the American Revolution. "Lafayette, we are here!" proclaimed one of Pershing's aides. By fighting for France's freedom the United States was repaying the French for their help during the Revolutionary War.

U.S. Army lieutenant Edward F. Graham wrote home about the sense of purpose that he and many other soldiers felt. "The desperate contest between justice and empire . . . is

INTERPRETING THE VISUAL RECORD

Medical care. Many women served as ambulance drivers during World War I. ***Do these ambulances look equipped to provide medical care at the scene of a battle? Explain your answer.***

REVIEW

Have students complete the **Section 2 Review** on p. 339.

ASSESS

Have students complete **Daily Quiz 11.2**. As **Alternative Assessment**, you may want to use the neutrality dialogue or the European experiences interview in this section's lessons.

RETEACH

Have students complete **Main Idea Activity for Reteaching and Sheltered English 11.2**. Then organize students into small groups and assign each group one subsection from Section 2. Have each group create an outline of its assigned subsection. Display the outlines around the classroom and ask students to study them. Have each student use the material on the outlines to write one or two questions about the content of Section 2. Collect students' questions and use them to quiz the class. **Sheltered English, Cooperative Learning**

EXTEND

Have students obtain a copy of the Zimmerman Note and read it in its entirety. Ask each student to write a short essay discussing the document and explaining why it proved so inflammatory to Americans. Alternately, students could rewrite the telegram in modern-day, easy-to-understand language. Have students discuss their work with the class. **Block Scheduling**

now on. You should be proud to have me . . . participate in the struggle as a part of the human wall against a second Dark Ages." As the weeks went by, U.S. troops arrived in France in ever-swelling numbers. Army engineers built docks and railroads and strung up networks of telephone and telegraph lines. The engineers also constructed ammunition depots, camps, hospitals, and storage sheds.

Some 10,000 American women worked in these hospitals. Emily Vuagniaux, an Army Medical Corps nurse, described life in a battlefield hospital.

> **"We . . . have worked . . . sometimes 18 hours straight. I have the operating room and they run four tables day and night and have between 200 and 300 patients right off the field, so you . . . know we are quite close in."**

Thousands more American women went to Europe as volunteers for the Red Cross, the YMCA, and other agencies.

Escorted by U.S. warships, merchant vessels transported troops, supplies, and volunteers through the submarine-infested North Atlantic. This **convoy system** proved quite effective. Of the more than 2 million U.S. soldiers who crossed the Atlantic Ocean, not one died as the result of an enemy attack on the high seas. U.S. warships also patrolled the waters of the western Atlantic, protecting the U.S. coastline. To contain the U-boats, U.S. ships laid some 70,000 mines in a lethal 240-mile necklace across the North Sea from Norway to the Orkney Islands off Britain. This barrier created hazards for German U-boats trying to return to their bases.

World War I soldiers faced both brutal hand-to-hand combat and deadly new weapons.

✔ **READING CHECK:** What types of experiences did Americans have in Europe?

SECTION 2 REVIEW

Define and explain the significance of the following terms:
Sussex pledge
National Defense Act
Zimmerman Note
Selective Service Act
convoy system

Identify and explain the significance of the following individuals:
Robert Lansing
Jeannette Rankin
John J. Pershing

1. **Using Graphic Organizers** Copy the graphic below. Use it to list the steps the U.S. government took to prepare the military for war.

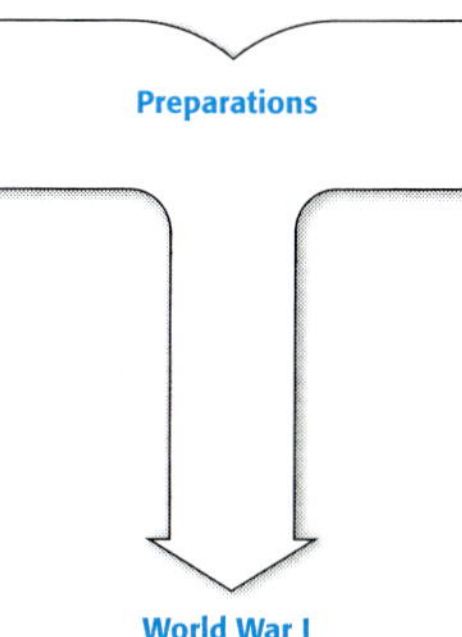

2. **Hypothesizing** How might the United States have responded differently to the events that challenged its neutrality?
3. **Analyzing** Did the draft make the United States more democratic? Explain your answer.
4. **Using Historical Imagination** Imagine that you are a U.S. soldier. Write a letter to President Wilson describing your experiences in Europe.

Critical Thinking

5. Why did the United States declare war on Germany?
Consider:
- the war's economic impact on the United States
- German U-boat attacks on American shipping
- the effect a German victory might have on the United States

SECTION 2 REVIEW ANSWERS

Define and Identify
For significance, see the following pages:
- *Sussex* pledge, p. 335
- Robert Lansing, p. 335
- National Defense Act, p. 335
- Zimmerman Note, p. 336
- Jeannette Rankin, p. 336
- Selective Service Act, p. 336
- John J. Pershing, p. 338
- convoy system, p. 339

1. recruited soldiers, constructed new barracks and training centers, and trained soldiers
2. Answers will vary. Some students might suggest that the United States should have adopted a "turn the other cheek" policy in response to U-boat attacks.
3. yes—brought soldiers of all different classes and races together, provided training opportunities for African Americans, and provided citizenship for some American Indians; no—forced some people to go to war against their will and failed to eradicate discrimination
4. Students' letters will vary. Students should include specific information in their letters to describe their experiences in Europe.
5. Students should mention the war and German U-boat attacks disrupted shipping and commerce and that many Americans were swayed by anti-German propaganda from Great Britain.

SECTION 3

After completing Section 3, students should be able to:

OBJECTIVE 1 *Describe how the U.S. government prepared the nation for war.*

OBJECTIVE 2 *Discuss how organized labor and volunteers contributed to the war effort.*

OBJECTIVE 3 *Explain why African Americans moved to the North.*

OBJECTIVE 4 *Relate how the government created support for, and limited opposition to, the war.*

LET'S GET STARTED!

As students enter the classroom, ask them to list three or four ways in which citizens might support a war effort. Have volunteers share their answers with the class. *(Students might suggest that citizens could fly the country's flag, buy war bonds, or go without certain items in order to save them for soldiers.)* Tell students that in Section 3 they will learn how Americans supported the war effort during World War I.

SECTION 3 RESOURCES

PRINT
- Guided Reading Strategy 11.3
- Section 3 Review, p. 346
- Daily Quiz 11.3

MULTIMEDIA
- One-Stop Planner, Lesson 11.3
- Holt Researcher: American History CD–ROM

SHELTERED ENGLISH
- Main Idea Activity for Reteaching and Sheltered English 11.3

✓ READING TO UNDERSTAND
To help students master the section objectives, have them answer the **READING CHECKS** and complete **Guided Reading Strategy 11.3** as they read the section.

VISUAL RECORD ANSWER
(for p. 341)
Some students might suggest that the happy children and the attractive produce depicted in the poster make a persuasive argument for a victory garden. Other students might suggest that the relatively small amount of produce depicted in the poster reveals the limited supply capacity of such a garden.

The War at Home

OBJECTIVES

Read to understand:
1. how the U.S. government prepared the nation for war
2. how organized labor and volunteers contributed to the war effort
3. why African Americans moved to the North
4. how the government created support for, and limited opposition to, the war

KEY TERMS
- Food Administration
- War Industries Board
- National War Labor Board
- Great Migration
- Committee on Public Information
- Espionage Act
- Sedition Act

KEY PEOPLE
- William McAdoo
- Herbert Hoover
- Bernard Baruch
- Harriot Stanton Blatch
- Juliette Gordon Low

EYEWITNESSES TO History

"Billy, my nephew, is twelve years old. . . . They call the suburb in which Billy lives one hundred per cent patriotic. Everybody is in war work. Even the children under five years have an organization known as the Khaki Babes. . . . Billy's crowd is indefatigable [tireless] in its labors. . . . The boys usher at meetings, assist in parades, deliver bundles and run errands. They are tireless collectors of nutshells, peach pits and tinsel paper. . . . One bit of voluntary war work was carried on through the periods of the gasolineless Sundays when the four boys took positions on Commonwealth Avenue in such a way as to obstruct passing vehicles. If a car did not carry a doctor's or military sign, they threw pebbles and yelled 'O you Slacker!' It was exciting work because guilty drivers put on full speed ahead and Billy admitted that he was almost run over, but he added that the cause was worth it."

—Florence Woolston

THE GRANGER COLLECTION, NEW YORK

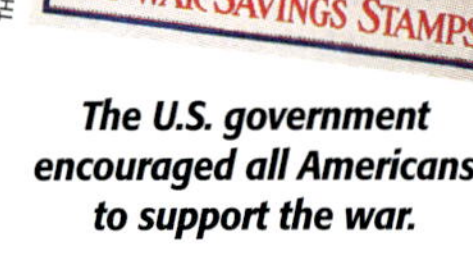

The U.S. government encouraged all Americans to support the war.

Florence Woolston described her nephew's contribution to the war effort in the *New Republic* magazine. The efforts of Billy and millions of other Americans helped win the war.

Mobilizing the Nation

Once the United States entered the war, President Wilson quickly moved to mobilize the nation. The government set up programs to finance the war, conserve scarce resources, and redirect industry and labor toward wartime production. The president also launched a huge propaganda campaign to mobilize support for the war effort. As the government whipped up enthusiasm for the war, however, intolerance of antiwar opinions spread across the land.

Movie stars Douglas Fairbanks, Mary Pickford, and Charlie Chaplin help sell Liberty bonds.

Directing the economy. At the outset of the war, Wilson had noted that "there are no armies in this struggle; there are entire nations armed." Wilson realized that the U.S. economy had to be reorganized. The first step in this process was raising money to pay for the war, which eventually cost the United States about $35 billion, including loans to the Allies.

The government raised money through four issues of Liberty bonds during the war and one of Victory bonds after the end of the fighting. Posters, parades, and rallies promoted each bond issue. William McAdoo was secretary of the treasury and Wilson's son-in-law. He declared that "Every person who refuses to subscribe . . . is a friend of Germany," and "is not entitled to be an American citizen." These promotions were a huge success.

TEACH OBJECTIVE 1

LEVEL 1: Conduct a brief discussion on how the U.S. government prepared the nation for war. *(Students' responses should include that the government established programs to finance the war, to conserve scarce resources, and to redirect industry and labor toward wartime production. President Wilson also launched a propaganda campaign.)* Then pair students and have each pair rank the efforts in order of significance. Ask students to share their rankings. Conduct a classroom debate between students with different rankings.
Sheltered English, Cooperative Learning

LEVEL 2: Conduct a brief discussion on how the U.S. government prepared the nation for war. *(See the Level 1 lesson for the correct steps.)* Then tell students to imagine that they are government information officers. Have each student write a short radio announcement describing the government's efforts. Tell students that they will need to carefully consider the wording of their announcements in order to describe all of the government's efforts in the time allotted. Remind students that their announcements should be both informative and entertaining. Have volunteers deliver their announcements to the class. Students may wish to include the text of their announcements in their portfolios.

The government also sought to raise money by increasing taxes. This proved more difficult than selling bonds. Congress debated a new tax program for months before reaching an agreement in October 1917. The new taxes on business incomes and large personal incomes produced about $10 billion for the war.

Mobilizing the economy for war entailed more than raising money, however. It also involved coordinating the actions of government, business, and industry. This was done through a number of federal war boards. Although the federal government never took complete control of the economy, it exercised sweeping economic power through these various agencies. It set the prices and production levels of commodities and regulated businesses crucial to the war effort.

Conserving resources. Among the most successful of the federal war boards were the **Food Administration** and the Fuel Administration. They were charged with regulating the production and supply of these essential resources. To direct the Food Administration, Wilson chose Herbert Hoover, a prosperous mining engineer who had managed a food-relief campaign for war-stricken Belgium. Hoover saw his task as twofold: to encourage increased agricultural production and to conserve existing food supplies.

To stimulate wartime production, Hoover guaranteed farmers high prices. Farm production soared. For example, farmers increased their production of wheat, harvesting some 921 million bushels in 1919—a dramatic increase over the 1917 figure of some 637 million bushels.

Announcing that "food will win the war," Hoover called on Americans to reduce their food consumption by observing wheatless and meatless days. To supplement their diets, he suggested that they plant "victory gardens" filled with vegetables. The campaign proved very effective—without, as Hoover proudly noted, resorting to forced rationing.

Fuel Administration director Harry Garfield, son of former president James A. Garfield, took a similar course of action, encouraging people to observe heatless Mondays. Garfield was not unwilling to use force, however. When the nation ran short of coal in early 1918, he closed all factories east of the Mississippi River for several days.

INTERPRETING THE VISUAL RECORD

Victory gardens. Many Americans supported the war effort by growing food at home to make more available for troops overseas. ***Does this poster make a persuasive argument for growing a victory garden? Why or why not?***

Organizing industry. Hundreds of other federal boards and agencies were created to regulate industrial production and distribution. Led by William McAdoo, the Railroad Administration reorganized the railroad system by setting limits on transportation rates and workers' wages.

The work of all these boards was coordinated by the government's central war agency, the **War Industries Board** (WIB). Its director, Wall Street investor Bernard Baruch, had overall responsibility for allocating scarce materials, establishing production priorities, and setting prices. Baruch preferred to persuade business leaders to comply with his wishes. However, when steel owners refused to cut prices, the government threatened to take over their foundries and mills.

At first some business leaders were critical of Wilson's economic mobilization programs. They argued that government intervention would permanently damage the U.S. system of free enterprise. When profits soared, however, these business leaders stopped complaining.

✔ **READING CHECK:** How did the U.S. government prepare the nation for war?

GLOBAL RELATIONS

Herbert Hoover in Belgium. Many of Belgium's villages and crops were destroyed during Germany's attack on the country. With their nation on the brink of starvation, Belgian officials asked Britain for help. Through a series of misunderstandings and coincidences, Herbert Hoover, an American engineer working in Britain, suddenly found himself involved in supplying emergency food relief to Belgium. Hoover served on the Commission for Relief in Belgium and began a publicity campaign to urge American organizations to donate food and money. He wrote, "This is not a question of charity or relief to the chronic poor, it is a question of feeding an entire population. . . . There never was a famine emergency so great."

CRITICAL THINKING What role might Hoover's publicity campaign have served in persuading Americans not just to donate but to support U.S. involvement in the war?

ANSWER: Students might suggest that by reminding U.S. citizens of the devastation in Europe, Hoover might have convinced some people that it was necessary for the United States to intervene.

LEVEL 3: Conduct a brief discussion on how the U.S. government prepared the nation for war. *(See the Level 1 lesson for the correct steps.)* Then have students select one particular administration or program involved in the war effort, such as the Food Administration, the War Industries Board, the victory garden program, and so on. Have each student write a few paragraphs describing how the chosen administration or program bolstered the war effort. Alternately, have each student develop an advertising campaign designed to promote his or her chosen agency or program. Ask volunteers to read their paragraphs or present their campaigns to the class.

SPOTLIGHT on Female Workers During the War

Ask students to obtain and read primary sources authored by women who joined the labor force during World War I. [If students have difficulty finding such sources, ask them to reread the quotation from Norma B. Kastl on this page.] Then have students develop their own projects on the topic. Students might write war diaries from the perspective of female workers, design a postage stamp in commemoration of women's efforts, and so on. Ask each student to complete his or her project and present it to the class. **Block Scheduling**

CULTURAL DIVERSITY

The Peace Movement. Not all American women supported the war effort. Women also played leading roles in several pacifist groups. The Women's Peace Party and the Emergency Peace Federation worked together to protest the war and to defend civil liberties such as the right to free speech and free press. The American Union Against Militarism, led in part by Jane Addams, initiated a Bureau of Conscientious Objectors to address the needs of drafted men who opposed the war. Well-known anarchist Emma Goldman helped organize the No-Conscription League, which provided free legal advice to men old enough to be drafted. One of the League's stated beliefs was, "We will fight for what we choose to fight for; we will never fight simply because we are ordered to fight."

CRITICAL THINKING How might war supporters have reacted to peace organizations?

ANSWER: Students might indicate that some supporters simply ignored the organizations. Other students might suggest that war supporters harassed pacifists.

VISUAL RECORD ANSWER

Students might mention injuries from the machines, the heavy material, and the munitions themselves.

INTERPRETING THE VISUAL RECORD

Working women. These women helped the war effort by working in a Detroit munitions factory. ***What dangers do these women face in their workplace?***

Mobilizing Workers

Meeting the demands of the war required a massive, cooperative effort. Millions of people, paid employees and volunteers alike, pitched in as the nation mobilized for the military campaign.

Organized labor. Because of the war, hundreds of thousands of men were drafted into the army and European immigration slowed to a trickle. American industries found themselves desperately short of labor as they geared up for the war effort. Taking advantage of this situation, unionized workers across the country went on strike. They demanded higher wages and other benefits. Nearly 4,500 strikes involving more than 1 million workers erupted in 1917 alone. The tactic worked. Working conditions substantially improved throughout the war.

To ensure that the voice of labor was heard, President Wilson established the **National War Labor Board** (NWLB) in April 1918. Composed of representatives from business and labor, the NWLB arbitrated disputes between workers and employers. The board heard more than 1,200 cases, ruling in favor of labor more often than not. In this climate of official support, union membership grew rapidly. Membership in the American Federation of Labor (AFL) rose from some 2 million in 1916 to roughly 3.2 million by 1919. By the end of the decade, some 15 percent of the nation's nonagricultural workforce was unionized.

The labor shortage strengthened unions and also brought about changes in the workforce. The number of women working outside the home grew by about 6 percent during the war. Many of these women took traditionally male jobs. They worked as automobile mechanics, bricklayers, metalworkers, railroad engineers, or truck drivers. In all, some 1.5 million American women worked in industry during the war. Norma B. Kastl was an interviewer with a women's service bureau during World War I. She explained that many women considered it their patriotic duty to work.

> **"The navy is taking on women as yeomen [clerks] to do shore duty. . . . Every girl that becomes a yeoman can have the satisfaction of knowing that she is releasing, as from prison, some sailor who had been fuming . . . because he had to spend his days in an office instead of on the deck of a destroyer."**

This woman is assembling ammunition for rifles.

Women also helped plan wartime mobilization. Carrie Chapman Catt, a women's suffrage leader, sat on the Women's Committee of the Council of National Defense. This was a civilian agency organized to support the war effort. Harriot Stanton Blatch, the daughter of suffragist Elizabeth Cady Stanton, headed the Food Administration's Speakers' Bureau.

Women's war efforts helped produce one very important political change—the passage of the Nineteenth Amendment. Wilson, who had previously wavered on women's suffrage, threw his support behind the amendment in recognition of women's wartime contributions. "The greatest thing that came out of the war," Catt later noted, "was the emancipation of women, for which no man fought."

TEACH OBJECTIVE 2

ALL LEVELS: To help students understand how organized labor and volunteers contributed to the war effort, copy the graphic organizer to the right on the chalkboard, omitting the italicized answers. Have each student complete it. To conclude, have each student write a short essay assessing the contributions of both organized labor and volunteers to the war effort. **Sheltered English**

▶**ASSIGNMENT:** *Have each student create a collage to represent the actions of organized labor during World War I.*

THE WAR EFFORT

Organized Labor—Contributions and Effects
- *filled posts to replace workers who left to fight in the war*
- *went on strike to demand higher wages and benefits*
- *improved working conditions during the war*

Volunteers—Contributions and Effects
- *conserved energy and recycled essential materials*
- *grew vegetables in victory gardens*
- *purchased liberty bonds*
- *founded support organizations*

Volunteerism. Intense patriotism swept the country, motivating many Americans, from young children to senior citizens, to contribute to the war effort. Americans voluntarily conserved energy, recycled essential materials, and planted victory gardens, all to make more items available for the soldiers overseas. Americans also contributed directly to the war by purchasing Liberty bonds that provided the government with funds to pay for equipment and supplies.

BIOGRAPHY

Juliette Gordon Low

One of the most active American volunteers was Juliette Gordon Low, also known as Daisy. Born in 1860 to a wealthy family in Savannah, Georgia, Juliette Gordon received the finest private-school education. She was a serious student who was particularly gifted in the arts. After completing her education, she traveled extensively. On one trip to England she met wealthy William Low, whom she married in 1886.

The Lows divided their time between homes in the United States and Britain, living the leisurely life of the idle rich. Juliette's life was not a happy one, however. Marital troubles and the challenge of her increasing deafness, caused by two separate ear injuries, led her to suffer from frequent bouts of depression.

After her husband died in 1905, the financially independent widow traveled the world looking for a purpose in her life. She found this purpose in 1911, when she met the founder of the Boy Scouts, British war hero Sir Robert Baden-Powell. Low became actively involved in the Scouts' sister organization, the Girl Guides. She poured her energies into the movement, forming several troops in Britain before bringing the Girl Guides to the United States in 1912.

The organization grew quickly, and by 1915 the American Girl Guides were known as the Girl Scouts of America. Using mostly her own money and refusing to surrender to any obstacle, Low soon spread the Girl Scouts nationwide. The organization grew quickly during the war, and Low encouraged Girl Scouts to throw all their energies into helping the war effort. Many worked directly for the Food Administration. "A girl cannot die for her country, but she can live for it," Low declared. The Girl Scouts' role in the war effort helped boost membership from some 500 girls in 1915 to 50,000 by 1920. By the time of Juliette Low's death in 1927, total membership had reached almost 168,000.

✔ **READING CHECK:** How did organized labor and volunteers contribute to the war effort?

Mobilizing for the War Effort

Wartime mobilization efforts targeted American children and teenagers as well as adults. Young people across the United States volunteered both money and labor to help win the war. Young Americans also contributed money from their own pockets, which they earned working at odd jobs such as painting barns, waiting tables, gathering nuts, and polishing shoes.

These Girl Scouts are collecting peach pits to be used in gas mask filters.

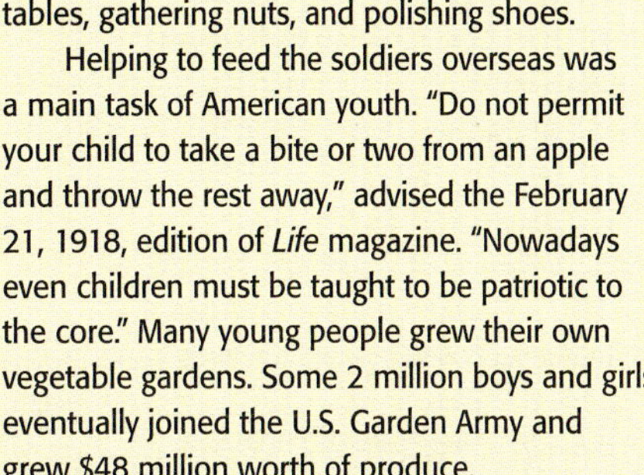

Helping to feed the soldiers overseas was a main task of American youth. "Do not permit your child to take a bite or two from an apple and throw the rest away," advised the February 21, 1918, edition of *Life* magazine. "Nowadays even children must be taught to be patriotic to the core." Many young people grew their own vegetable gardens. Some 2 million boys and girls eventually joined the U.S. Garden Army and grew $48 million worth of produce.

New York passed laws so that 12-year-old children could miss up to seven months of school in order to work on farms. In 1918, boys older than 16 were let out of high schools in the Northwest to help plant the spring wheat crop. They were rewarded with credit for the full school term. Founded in 1917, the U.S. Boy's Working Reserve formed a virtual army of agricultural labor. Some 200,000 young men between the ages of 16 and 20 were recruited to help harvest crops across the United States. In a time of desperate need, American youth performed the work of adults and helped win the war.

ECONOMIC DEVELOPMENT

Children and the War Effort. Under Herbert Hoover's direction, the United States pushed to bring children into the war effort, particularly the food conservation effort. Hoover's officials went door-to-door asking people to sign a pledge to conserve food. Hoover also urged schools to teach food conservation. The Food Administration devised poems, slogans, and songs to interest children in the issue, even reworking popular nursery rhymes. The revised "Little Boy Blue" went as follows:

"Little Boy Blue, come blow your horn!
The cook's using wheat where she ought to use corn!
And terrible famine our country will sweep,
If the cooks and the housewives remain fast asleep!
Go wake them! Go wake them! It's now up to you!
Be a loyal American, Little Boy Blue!"

CRITICAL THINKING Why might the United States have attempted to encourage children to conserve food?

ANSWER: Students might suggest that children probably encouraged their parents to join the effort. Other students might argue that bringing children into the war effort showed the seriousness of the issue.

TEACH OBJECTIVE 3

LEVEL 1: Pair students and have each pair create a cause-and-effect diagram on the migration of African Americans to the North. *(Pairs' diagrams should note that job opportunities, the prospect of higher wages, and recruitment efforts encouraged African Americans to move to the North. Diagrams should note that the move brought better living conditions but also some racial violence.)* To conclude, tell students to imagine that they are African Americans who recently moved from Alabama to Illinois. Have pairs write short poems commenting on the move and on life in the North and in the South. **Sheltered English, Cooperative Learning**

LEVELS 2 AND 3: Tell students to imagine that they are African Americans who have recently moved from Alabama to Illinois. Have each student write an editorial for a southern African American newspaper describing the causes and effects of the migration and offering advice to other African Americans thinking about moving North. *(See the Level 1 lesson for the correct causes and effects.)* Ask volunteers to read their editorials to the class. Students may wish to include their editorials in their portfolios.

ACROSS THE CURRICULUM

▶GEOGRAPHY◀

The Great Migration. African Americans left the South for many reasons. The boll weevil had ruined more than 85 percent of the South's cotton crop by 1922. Floods in the summer of 1915 worsened the situation for African American sharecroppers, most of whom were deeply in debt. An earlier depression had reduced workers' wages. In addition, racism and the fear of lynching led many African Americans to flee to the North. As an editorial in the *Chicago Defender* stated, "To die from the bite of frost is far more glorious than at the hands of a mob."

CRITICAL THINKING Tell students that in recent years many African Americans have moved from the North to the South. Why might this reverse migration be taking place?

ANSWER: Students might suggest that the civil rights movement improved life for African Americans in the South, that job opportunities exist in the South, or that some African Americans might want to escape the harsh northern winters.

SCIENCE & TECHNOLOGY ANSWERS

1. a virus
2. Asia, Africa

Science & Technology

The Influenza Epidemic

In 1918 World War I was raging in Europe, claiming thousands of lives. Meanwhile, a silent killer was sweeping the globe—influenza, commonly known as the flu. Initially, people believed that the illness was nothing serious and that doctors would find a cure. "Everybody had a preconception of what the flu was: it's a miserable cold and, after a few days, you're up and around," explains historian Alfred Crosby. "This was a flu that put people into bed as if they'd been hit with a 2 x 4. That turned into pneumonia, that turned people blue and black and killed them."

Decades of major discoveries and advances had given Americans great faith in science and medicine. However, scientists knew almost nothing about viruses at the time. They thought that a type of bacteria caused the flu. Wild rumors regarding the origin of the pandemic, or worldwide epidemic, spread quickly. One common rumor was that German agents had planted the virus in the United States.

The flu claimed some 12,000 lives in September, but the worst was still to come. In October more than 11,000 people died in the city of Philadelphia, Pennsylvania. Nearly 200,000 died nationwide. Then, like a fire burning itself out, the flu vanished.

The influenza epidemic left almost 600,000 dead in the United States alone, nearly as many Americans as were killed in the Civil War. At least 20 million people died worldwide.

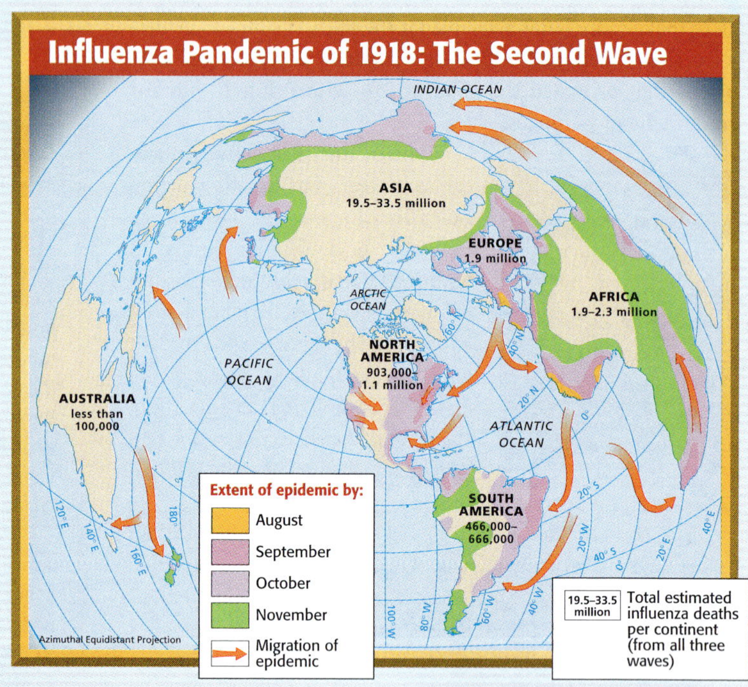

Understanding Science and History

1. What causes influenza?
2. Which continents experienced the greatest number of deaths from influenza?

The Great Trek North

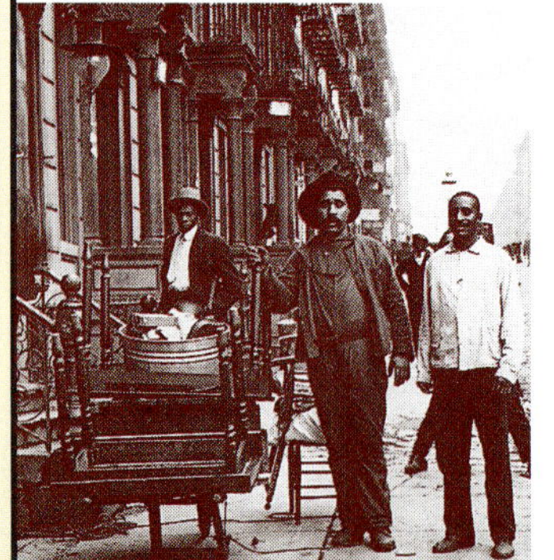
Many African Americans moved to northern cities in search of wartime jobs.

The labor shortage that drew women into the workforce also spurred immigration from Mexico. Some were fleeing the Mexican Revolution. Others were lured by southwestern employers who depended on Mexican labor. Some 150,000 men and women migrated from Mexico to the United States during the war.

Job opportunities and the chance of higher wages brought about one of the most important population shifts in U.S. history. This was the **Great Migration** of African Americans from the South to northern cities between 1915 and 1930. Hundreds of thousands of African Americans moved northward to escape discrimination and difficult living and working conditions. African American newspapers strongly encouraged the migration: "Get out of the South," declared an editorial in the Chicago *Defender*. "The *Defender* says come."

TEACH OBJECTIVE 4

LEVEL 1: Ask students to identify the ways in which the government created support for, and limited opposition to, the war. *(Students' responses should mention that President Wilson created the Committee on Public Information, which issued propaganda. The government also suppressed dissent on war issues.)* Write students' responses on the chalkboard. Then organize students into triads. Have each triad develop at least two statements that might have merited punishment under the Espionage Act or the Sedition Act. *(Example: "The president is sending our young people to fight and die just to protect the rich bankers' overseas investments.")* Have volunteers read their statements to the class. Then conduct a discussion on those statements and wartime security.
Sheltered English, Cooperative Learning

LEVELS 2 AND 3: Ask students to identify the ways in which the government created support for, and limited opposition to, the war. *(See the Level 1 lesson for the correct methods.)* Then tell students to imagine that it is 1917. Have each student write a letter to the editor of a local magazine commenting on the government's efforts to limit opposition to the war. Remind students that they must discuss those efforts and comment on them in their letters. Have volunteers read their letters to the class. Students may wish to include their letters to the editor in their portfolios.

African Americans went to the North with great hope. For many, however, life there proved harsh. Although they typically enjoyed a better standard of living than they had in the South, racial violence remained a serious problem. The most brutal wartime racial incident occurred in East St. Louis, Illinois, on July 2, 1917. White rioters rampaged through African American neighborhoods, leaving at least 39 dead. Shocked and angered, many African Americans asked themselves why they should fight for freedom in Europe when they enjoyed so little of it at home.

✔ **READING CHECK:** Why did African Americans move to the North?

Influencing Attitudes

Whether for religious, political, or personal reasons, many Americans believed that the United States should have stayed out of the war. President Wilson wanted all Americans to support the war effort. Therefore, he established the **Committee on Public Information** (CPI) in the spring of 1917. Headed by George Creel, the CPI led a propaganda campaign to encourage the American people to support the war.

The CPI initially put out fact-based material that was censored to present an upbeat picture of the war. Very quickly, however, the CPI began churning out raw propaganda that pictured the Germans as evil monsters. Hollywood joined in, producing movies such as *The Claws of the Hun,* and *The Kaiser, the Beast of Berlin.* CPI pamphlets warned citizens to be on the lookout for German spies. Dozens of "patriotic organizations" sprang up, with names like the American Protective League and the American Defense Society. These groups spied, tapped telephones, and opened other people's mail in an effort to identify "spies and traitors."

These groups targeted almost anyone who called for peace, questioned the Allies' progress, or criticized the government's policies. They were particularly hard on German Americans, many of whom lost their jobs. Sometimes this anti-German sentiment took absurd turns. German books vanished from library shelves, schools stopped teaching German language courses, and German music disappeared from concert programs. People even renamed German-sounding items: sauerkraut became liberty cabbage, dachshunds became liberty pups, and hamburger became Salisbury steak. Some Americans publicly humiliated people of German heritage by forcing them to kiss the flag, recite the Pledge of Allegiance, or buy war bonds. Sometimes these acts turned violent.

Suppressing Opposition

Despite the hysterical atmosphere, some Americans continued to oppose the war. Quakers and Mennonites, committed by their faith to pacifism—the refusal to use violence to settle disputes—were particularly outspoken. Considered traitors by many Americans, they experienced violence and abuse. Other opponents of the war included Representative Jeannette Rankin, Senator Robert La Follette, and settlement-house leader Jane Addams.

INTERPRETING THE VISUAL RECORD

Propaganda. The U.S. government directed most of its propaganda at Americans, encouraging them to work hard and make sacrifices to help win the war. ***What elements in these posters reflect the behavior they are trying to inspire?***

THE GRANGER COLLECTION, NEW YORK (BOTH)

PEOPLE IN HISTORY

George Creel. During President Wilson's re-election campaign, George Creel—once a muckraking journalist—supported the effort by writing favorable political tracts. President Wilson repaid the favor by appointing Creel to head the Committee on Public Information (CPI). In this role, Creel blanketed the country with pro-war propaganda, distributing some 75 million pamphlets and 14,000 drawings. Creel also encouraged the exportation of films that depicted the "wholesome life of America." He even placed ads in magazines asking people to report anyone who "spreads pessimistic stories, cries for peace, or belittles our efforts to win this war."

ACTIVITY: Have students create pamphlets or drawings that might have been used as pro-war propaganda.

VISUAL RECORD ANSWER

Students might mention the canning jar containing the image of the kaiser with the dagger through it and the flag-waving soldier.

VISUAL RECORD ANSWER

(for p. 346)

Students might suggest that the party focused on uniting workers around the world.

REVIEW

Have students complete the **Section 3 Review** on p. 346.

ASSESS

Have students complete **Daily Quiz 11.3.** As **Alternative Assessment,** you may want to use the African American migration cause-and-effect diagram or the African American migration letter in this section's lessons.

RETEACH

Have students complete **Main Idea Activity for Reteaching and Sheltered English 11.3.** Then write the following names on the chalkboard: *Bernard Baruch, Harriot Stanton Blatch, George Creel, Eugene V. Debs, Herbert Hoover, Juliette Gordon Low, William McAdoo,* and *Jeannette Rankin.* Assign each student two names. Ask students to write sentences identifying and describing the importance of their assigned people. Have volunteers—at least one for each assigned person—read their sentences to the class. **Sheltered English**

EXTEND

Have students conduct research and select examples of paintings, drawings, or sketches that comment on the home front during World War I. Have each student pick one favorite piece and write an analysis of the piece. Remind students to think about how the war might have affected the artist and thus the piece. **Block Scheduling**

SECTION 3 REVIEW ANSWERS

Define and Identify
For significance, see the following pages:

- William McAdoo, p. 340
- Food Administration, p. 341
- Herbert Hoover, p. 341
- War Industries Board, p. 341
- Bernard Baruch, p. 341
- National War Labor Board, p. 342
- Harriot Stanton Blatch, p. 342
- Juliette Gordon Low, p. 343
- Great Migration, p. 344
- Committee on Public Information, p. 345
- Espionage Act, p. 346
- Sedition Act, p. 346

1. raised money for the war effort, regulated the production and supply of essential resources, stimulated production, regulated industrial production

2. Students might argue that the government had to take control of the economy to ensure production of the proper goods or that the government had no right to interfere in the business sector.

3. allowed women, African Americans, and Mexican immigrants to enter the workforce and resulted in gains for workers and unions

4. Students should mention discrimination and violence in the South, the promise of jobs in the North, and racial violence in the North.

5. Students might argue that wartime vulnerabilities require strong action or suggest that the government unfairly restricted and punished war protesters.

INTERPRETING THE VISUAL RECORD

Socialists. Many Socialists questioned the reasons for fighting World War I. ***What does this button suggest about the goals of the Socialist Party?***

The Socialist Party also proclaimed its opposition to the war. To most party members, the warring nations were simply using working people as tools in a capitalist struggle for control of world markets. The Industrial Workers of the World (IWW) had a similar view of the war and led strikes in a number of war-related industries.

To silence opponents of the war, Congress passed the **Espionage Act** in June 1917 and the **Sedition Act** a year later. These measures outlawed acts of treason and made it a crime to "utter, print, write, or publish any disloyal . . . or abusive language" criticizing the government, the flag, or the military. Opposition to the draft, to war-bond drives, or to the arms industry also became a crime.

The CPI rallied support for the war, while the Espionage and Sedition Acts crushed opposition to the war. More than 1,000 people—including some 200 members of the IWW—were convicted of violating these laws. Socialist Party leader Eugene V. Debs was sentenced to 10 years in prison for making a speech against the war.

Many Americans, even some who supported the war, believed that the Espionage and Sedition Acts violated the First Amendment. The Supreme Court, however, disagreed. Justice Oliver Wendell Holmes wrote the opinion in the 1919 landmark case *Schenck* v. *United States.*

> **"The question . . . is whether the words used are used in such circumstances and are of such a nature as to create a clear and present danger. . . . When a nation is at war many things that might be said in time of peace . . . will not be endured [and] no Court could regard them as protected by any constitutional right."**

✔ **READING CHECK:** How did the government try to increase support for, and limit opposition to, the war?

SECTION 3 REVIEW

Define and explain the significance of the following terms:
Food Administration
War Industries Board
National War Labor Board
Great Migration
Committee on Public Information
Espionage Act
Sedition Act

Identify and explain the significance of the following individuals:
William McAdoo
Herbert Hoover
Bernard Baruch
Harriot Stanton Blatch
Juliette Gordon Low

1. **Using Graphic Organizers** Copy the diagram below. Use it to list the steps the U.S. government took to mobilize the economy for war.

2. **Taking a Stand** Do you think the U.S. government was justified in taking control of the economy during the war? Why or why not?
3. **Evaluating** How did wartime labor shortages affect unions and volunteer organizations?
4. **Using Historical Imagination** Imagine that you are an African American who migrated to the North during the war. Write a letter to a northern newspaper that outlines why you moved and what experiences you have had in the North.

Critical Thinking

5. Were the steps the government took to shape and control public opinion during the war appropriate? Explain your answer.
Consider:
   - the constitutional right to free speech
   - the danger of spying and sabotage
   - the need for cooperation on the homefront

After completing Section 4, students should be able to:

OBJECTIVE 1 *List the final events of World War I.*

OBJECTIVE 2 *Identify the goals of President Wilson's Fourteen Points.*

OBJECTIVE 3 *Summarize the terms of the Treaty of Versailles.*

OBJECTIVE 4 *Explain why the U.S. Senate rejected the Treaty of Versailles.*

OBJECTIVE 5 *Discuss the global impact of World War I.*

LET'S GET STARTED!

As students enter the classroom, have them create a list of the causes of World War I. *(Students should include intense nationalism, militarism, and military alliances.)* Then ask students to speculate about the shape and content of the postwar peace agreement, based on these causes. Have students share these speculations with the class. Then tell students that in Section 4 they will learn about the postwar peace agreement.

The War's End and Aftermath

OBJECTIVES

Read to understand:

1. what the final events of World War I were
2. what the goals of President Wilson's Fourteen Points were
3. what the terms of the Treaty of Versailles were
4. why the U.S. Senate rejected the Treaty of Versailles
5. what the global impact of World War I was

KEY TERMS

Bolsheviks
Battle of the Argonne Forest
Fourteen Points
League of Nations
Big Four
reparations
Treaty of Versailles

KEY PEOPLE

David Lloyd George
Georges Clemenceau
Vittorio Orlando
Henry Cabot Lodge

KEY PLACES

Czechoslovakia
Yugoslavia
Estonia
Finland
Latvia
Lithuania
Poland
Saar

EYEWITNESSES TO History

"Along all the roads of France, in all the trenches, in every gunpit you can hear one song being sung. They sing it while they load their guns, they whistle it as they march up the line, they hum it while they munch their bully-beef and hardtack. You hear it on the regimental bands and grinding out from gramophones in hidden dugouts.

Over there. Over there.
Send the word, send the word over there,
That the Yanks are coming—

Men repeat that ragtime promise as tho' it were a prayer. . . . We could have won without the Yanks—we're sure of that. Still, we're glad they're coming and we walk jauntily. We may die before the promise is sufficiently fulfilled to tell. What does that matter? The Yanks are coming. We shall not have died in vain. They will reap the peace for the world which our blood has sown."

—Coningsby Dawson

THE GRANGER COLLECTION, NEW YORK

George M. Cohan's "Over There" celebrated the arrival of U.S. forces in Europe.

Anticipating the arrival of U.S. forces, Coningsby Dawson wrote this letter home from his trench on the western front. His mixed emotions reflected the fact that no victory could erase the horrible costs of World War I. U.S. help was welcomed by the Allied Powers, but it could not undo the damage that had already been done.

The End of the War

The entry of the United States into the war came none too soon for the Allies. In the summer of 1917 the Allies launched an offensive to break the deadlock on the western front. It failed, shattering the Allied troops' already shaky morale. That fall, mutinies broke out in French units all along the front.

Revolution in Russia. More bad news arrived from Russia, which had been hit hard by the war. In March 1917, workers in Petrograd who were unable to buy bread marched out of the factories and protested in the streets. Demanding a change in government and an end to the war, the Russian people overthrew the czar.

Political turmoil continued until November, when the **Bolsheviks**, a group of radical Russian socialists, seized power. The Bolshevik leader, Vladimir Lenin, opposed the war and moved quickly to withdraw Russia from it. The Bolsheviks signed a treaty with the Central Powers in March 1918 that left the Central Powers free to concentrate their forces on the western front.

Germany's last bid for victory. On March 21, 1918, some 1 million German soldiers launched a tremendous offensive against the Allies. The Germans were backed by some 6,000 artillery pieces, including "Big Bertha," heavy guns capable

SECTION 4 RESOURCES

PRINT

- Guided Reading Strategy 11.4
- American History Outline Map 17: World War I in Europe
- Section 4 Review, p. 353
- Daily Quiz 11.4

MULTIMEDIA

- One-Stop Planner, Lesson 11.4
- Holt Researcher: American History CD–ROM

SHELTERED ENGLISH

- Main Idea Activity for Reteaching and Sheltered English 11.4

✔ READING TO UNDERSTAND

To help students master the section objectives, have them answer the **READING CHECKS** and complete **Guided Reading Strategy 11.4** as they read the section.

TEACH OBJECTIVE 1

LEVELS 1 AND 2: Distribute Map 17, World War I in Europe, from the **American History Outline Maps.** Have each student label the locations of the final battles of World War I. *(Students should label Paris, Château-Thierry, Saint-Mihiel, and the Argonne Forest.)* Ask students to annotate their maps with statements explaining the effects of the Bolshevik Revolution and the German mutinies. *(Students' statements should mention that the Russian withdrawal allowed the Central Powers to mass their forces on the western front. The German mutinies weakened the Central Powers.)* Display students' annotated maps and statements around the classroom. **Sheltered English**

LEVEL 3: Tell students to imagine that they are modern-day historians contributing to an encyclopedia on World War I. Have each student write a short entry on the final events of World War I. *(See the Levels 1 and 2 lesson for the correct events.)* Students' entries should mention important people, places, battles, and other events. Students might want to include maps and illustrations to help clarify their entries. Students may wish to include their entries in their portfolios.

ACROSS THE CURRICULUM

▶PSYCHOLOGY◀

The Wounds of War. The intense, bloody fighting of World War I left some soldiers with a nervous disorder called shell shock. The term described a range of symptoms—from headaches to comas to suicidal depression. Shell shock was widespread during the war. One American doctor wrote that "the present war is the first in which . . . the functional nervous diseases [shell shock] have constituted a major medico-military problem. As every nation and race engaged is suffering from the symptoms, it is apparent that new conditions of warfare are chiefly responsible for their prevalence." In many cases, some doctors argued, the symptoms were brought on by horrible experiences that were "beyond [soldiers'] capacity to assimilate."

CRITICAL THINKING What modern-day psychological disorder might be akin to shell shock?

ANSWER: Students might name post-traumatic stress disorder.

STRATEGIES FOR SUCCESS ANSWERS

Practicing the Strategy

1. that trench warfare makes soldiers lose all sense of humanity

2. Students' viewpoints will vary.

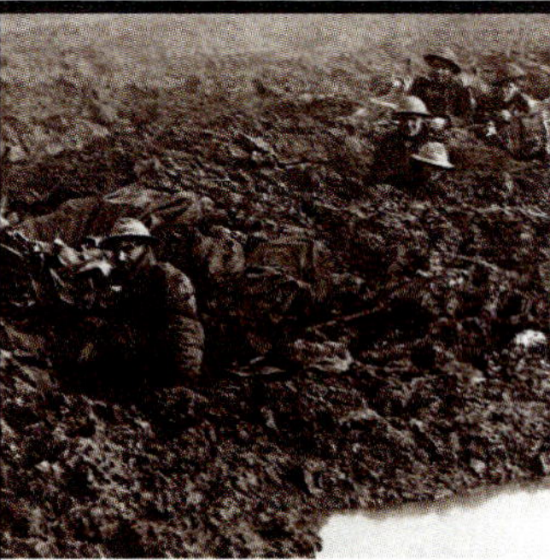

Over time, some trenches became little more than muddy holes.

of firing a 2,100-pound shell almost nine miles. By late May the Germans had pushed the Allies back to the Marne River, just 50 miles from Paris.

In light of the desperate situation, General Pershing agreed to place U.S. troops under the command of Marshal Ferdinand Foch of France. The introduction of U.S. forces made the difference. In a last-ditch defense of Paris, U.S. troops helped the French stop the Germans at Château-Thierry on June 3–4. Nearby, a division of U.S. Marines attacked the Germans and recaptured Belleau Wood and two other villages. After fierce fighting, the German advance was halted. Paris was saved.

On July 15 the Germans threw everything into a final assault around Reims. The Allied lines held, however, and Foch ordered a counterattack three days later. Led by U.S. troops, the charge pushed the Germans back. The tide had turned in favor of the Allies.

Strategies for Success: Interpreting Literature as Historical Evidence

Literature—imaginative or creative writing in all of its various forms—can serve as an extraordinary source of historical knowledge. Poetry and prose contain a wealth of information about the beliefs, customs, ideas, and values that were important to people of different cultures during different historical periods. Because most literature is meant to be subjective, however, it is particularly important to interpret it carefully.

How to Interpret Literature as Historical Evidence

1. **Become familiar with the source.** Before you begin to read a literary work, look over its title, publication information, and table of contents, if it has one. If possible, find out about the personal, social, and historical background of the author.
2. **Read the material carefully.** Read the work carefully and thoroughly. As you do so, take note of any references to real historical settings or events.
3. **Identify the work's themes.** Once you have finished reading the work, identify and think about its central themes. Consider how these themes may reflect the point of view of the author.
4. **Put the information to use.** Compare the themes to information about the historical period that you have gained through other sources. Then determine how the work can help you broaden your understanding of the historical period.

Applying the Strategy

Erich Maria Remarque's novel *All Quiet on the Western Front* portrays fighting in World War I through the eyes of a German soldier. The following excerpt describes an encounter between German and French soldiers.

> **"The moment we are about to retreat three faces rise up from the ground in front of us. Under one of the helmets [I see] a dark pointed beard and two eyes that are fastened on me. I raise my hand, but I cannot throw into those strange eyes; for one mad moment the whole slaughter whirls like a circus round me . . . then the head rises up . . . and my hand-grenade flies through the air and into him.**
>
> **We make for the rear, pull wire cradles into the trench and leave bombs behind us with the strings pulled, which ensures us a fiery retreat. The machine-guns are already firing from the next position.**
>
> **We have become wild beasts. We do not fight, we defend ourselves against annihilation. . . . No longer do we lie helpless, . . . we can destroy and kill, to save ourselves . . . and to be revenged."**

Practicing the Strategy

Use the passage above to answer the following questions.

1. What point is made about trench warfare?
2. How does the passage affect your view of war?

TEACH OBJECTIVE 2

LEVEL 1: Ask students to summarize the main goals of President Wilson's Fourteen Points. *(Students should note that Wilson was concerned with self-determination, territorial disputes, secret diplomacy, the arms race, and trade barriers. He also wanted to establish a League of Nations.)* Then pair students and tell them to imagine that they are President Wilson. Ask each pair to write a short rationale of the Fourteen Points. Have volunteers read their rationales to the class.
Sheltered English, Cooperative Learning

LEVEL 2: Tell students to imagine that they are newspaper reporters. Have each student write a short, informative article explaining the goals of President Wilson's Fourteen Points. *(See the Level 1 lesson for the correct goals.)* Ask volunteers to read their articles to the class. Then ask students why the German government objected to the Fourteen Points. *(Students should indicate that the German government saw the Fourteen Points as evidence of Wilson's interference.)* Conduct a discussion on Wilson's desire to be involved in the postwar peace process.

Allied victory. In the late summer of 1918 Foch seized the initiative and ordered a major offensive along the entire western front. For three months the Allies pushed deep into German-held territory. Americans led the attack that pushed the Germans back at Saint-Mihiel, France, that September. The Americans next drove toward Sedan, a French rail center that the Germans had held since 1914. For more than a month the Americans pushed northward along the Meuse River and through the rugged Argonne Forest, facing artillery and machine-gun fire all the way. The Americans suffered some 120,000 casualties in the **Battle of the Argonne Forest**. By November, however, they had reached and occupied the hills around Sedan.

African American troops played a major role in the Argonne offensive. Members of the 369th Infantry, an African American regiment whose men hailed from New York, so distinguished themselves that the French awarded them the Croix de Guerre (krwah-di-GER), or "Cross of War," a French military honor.

Repeatedly hammered during the Allied offensive, the Central Powers' forces began to disintegrate. Morale in the German military sagged. One soldier expressed his hunger for peace in a letter home.

> **"In what way have we sinned, that we should be treated worse than animals? Hunted from place to place, cold, filthy . . . we are destroyed like vermin. Will they never make peace?"**

The French government rewarded these African American soldiers with the Croix de Guerre (left) for their bravery during the war.

Mutinies broke out in both the German army and navy. German civilians rioted in the streets, demanding food, not war. Realizing that the war was lost, the kaiser fled to the Netherlands in early November. Two days later, Germany's new government agreed to an armistice, or cease-fire. On November 8, 1918, representatives of the German government arrived at the Allied headquarters in Compiègne (kohmp-yehn) to hear the armistice terms. The Allies demanded that the Germans evacuate Alsace-Lorraine, Belgium, France and Luxembourg and surrender an enormous amount of military equipment.

Early on the morning of November 11, the warring parties signed the armistice. At 11 A.M. the cease-fire went into effect. The constant crashing of guns was replaced, according to one American, by a "silence [that] was nearly unbearable." At long last, the war had ended. A peace conference was set for January 1919 in Paris.

✔ **READING CHECK:** What were the final events of World War I?

Americans in Washington, D.C., celebrate the news that the war is over.

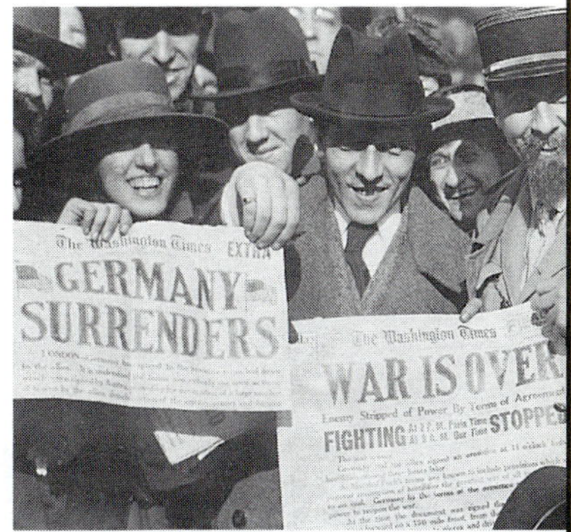

Wilson's Fourteen Points

News of the November 11 armistice set off a joyful celebration in the United States. President Wilson shared the people's great happiness at the Allied victory, but he knew that the difficult task of forging a just peace lay ahead.

HISTORY MAKERS SPEAK

F. A. Voigt in *The Last Magnificent War: Rare Journalistic and Eyewitness Accounts of World War I*

War's End. British soldier F. A. Voigt described the moment of the armistice. While he and his group were in their tents, they heard a strange noise: "There it was again, a low, hollow sound like that of a distant sea. It grew louder and then ceased. Then it became audible once more and grew louder and still louder. Suddenly we realized what it was—it was the sound of cheering. It came nearer and nearer, gathering speed. It flooded the whole town with a great rush, paused a moment, and then burst over our camp." But in the midst of the soldiers' celebrations, they remembered the dead. Voigt wrote that he "saw innumerable rotting dead that lay unburied in all postures on the bare, shell-tossed earth. . . . I knew . . . that the world's misery had been too great ever to be shaken off."

ACTIVITY: Tell students to imagine that they are soldiers on the front who have just learned of the armistice. Have each student write a poem, a short story, or a letter describing his or her emotions.

LEVEL 3: Ask students to reread the excerpt from President Wilson's Fourteen Points on this page. Then organize students into small groups. Have each group write a national Bill of Rights and Responsibilities based on the goals of Wilson's Fourteen Points. *(See the Level 1 lesson for the correct goals.)* Ask volunteers to present their bills to the class. Post these bills around the classroom. **Cooperative Learning**

SPOTLIGHT on the Big Four

Organize students into four groups. Have each group represent one of the Big Four: *Georges Clemenceau, David Lloyd George, Vittorio Orlando,* or *Woodrow Wilson.* Ask each group to prepare for the Allied peace conference, conducting additional research as necessary to learn more about its figure's stance at the meeting. Then act as a moderator and re-enact the peace conference. Finally, ask students to comment on the conference after the re-enactment.
Cooperative Learning, Block Scheduling

ECONOMIC DEVELOPMENT

John Maynard Keynes and Reparations. Shortly after the conference at Versailles, John Maynard Keynes, a British economist, published *The Economic Consequences of the Peace,* a book that condemned reparations. Keynes argued that the reparations were unreasonable, particularly in light of Allied confiscation of German land and Germany's merchant fleet. He also insisted that reparations would destroy the German economy and create future uprisings. In chilling words that foreshadowed the rise of Nazi Germany, Keynes wrote, "Who can say in what direction men will seek at last to escape from their misfortunes?"

CRITICAL THINKING How might the Allied nations have punished Germany without using reparations?

ANSWER: Answers will vary. Some students might suggest that the Allies could have required Germans to work on rebuilding projects in France or Belgium.

MAP ANSWER
(for p. 351)
five

GRAPH ANSWER
(for p. 352)
Russia; Bulgaria

★ HISTORICAL DOCUMENTS ★

PRESIDENT WOODROW WILSON

The Fourteen Points

On January 8, 1918, President Woodrow Wilson presented to Congress his plan for building peace in the postwar world.

The program of the world's peace . . . is our program; and that program, the only possible program, as we see it, is this:
. . . no private international understandings of any kind. . . . Absolute freedom of navigation upon the seas. . . . The removal . . . of all economic barriers and . . . equality of trade conditions among all the nations . . . guarantees . . . that national armaments will be reduced. . . . A free, open-minded, and absolutely impartial adjustment of all colonial claims, . . . the evacuation of all Russian territory. . . . Belgium . . . must be evacuated and restored. . . . All French territory should be freed and the invaded portions restored. . . . A readjustment of the frontiers of Italy . . . along clearly recognizable lines of nationality. . . . The peoples of Austria-Hungary . . . should be accorded the freest opportunity of autonomous development. . . . Rumania, Serbia, and Montenegro should be evacuated, occupied territories restored. . . . The Turkish portions of the present Ottoman Empire should be assured a secure sovereignty, but the other nationalities . . . under Turkish rule should be assured an . . . opportunity of autonomous development. . . . An independent Polish state should be erected. . . . A general association of nations must be formed . . . for the purpose of affording mutual guarantees of political independence and territorial integrity to great and small states alike.

This challenge had long been on Wilson's mind. Late in 1917 he had invited a group of scholars to advise him on peace terms. Drawing from their work, Wilson had developed the **Fourteen Points**, a program for world peace. He presented a summary of his principles and the Allied war aims to Congress on January 8, 1918.

Nine of the points dealt with the issue of self-determination—the right of people to govern themselves—and with the various territorial disputes created by the war. Other points focused on what Wilson considered the causes of modern war: secret diplomacy, the arms race, violations of freedom of the seas, and trade barriers. The final point—the establishment of the **League of Nations**—was the heart of the program. The League would be an international body designed to prevent offensive wars.

Congress and the American public warmly received the Fourteen Points. The reaction of the Allies, however, proved lukewarm. The German government rejected the program, arguing that Wilson was interfering in European affairs.

✔ **READING CHECK:** What were the goals of President Wilson's Fourteen Points?

The Paris Peace Conference

On December 4, 1918, Woodrow Wilson boarded the USS *George Washington* for Europe—becoming the first president to cross the Atlantic while in office. A huge crowd gave Wilson a rousing send-off as the ship steamed out of New York Harbor. His reception at the French port of Brest was no less enthusiastic. Many Europeans welcomed him as a conquering hero.

The peace conference opened on January 18, 1919. It was dominated by the **Big Four**—Wilson, British prime minister David Lloyd George, French premier Georges Clemenceau, and Italian prime minister Vittorio Orlando.

Orlando, Lloyd George, and Clemenceau insisted that Germany bear the financial cost of the war by making huge **reparations**, or payments, to the Allies. They also wanted several secret spoils-of-war treaties honored. Such demands violated many of the principles included in President Wilson's peace plan.

Seated from left to right are Vittorio Orlando, David Lloyd George, Georges Clemenceau, and Woodrow Wilson.

THE GRANGER COLLECTION, NEW YORK

TEACH OBJECTIVES 3 AND 4

ALL LEVELS: To help students understand the terms of the Treaty of Versailles and why the U.S. Senate rejected the treaty, copy the graphic organizer to the right on the chalkboard, omitting the italicized answers. Have each student complete it. To conclude, ask each student to write short press releases summarizing the Treaty of Versailles and announcing the Senate's rejection of the treaty.
Sheltered English

▶**ASSIGNMENT:** *Tell each student to write one or two paragraphs expressing his or her personal opinions of the Treaty of Versailles and the Senate's rejection of the treaty.*

THE TREATY OF VERSAILLES

The Terms of the Treaty
- *divided Germany's colonies and the Ottoman Empire among Allied nations*
- *established a mandate system*
- *created new nations*

The Senate's Objections
- *irreconcilables completely rejected the League of Nations*
- *reservationists objected to Article 10 in the League Covenant, believing that it would force the United States into war in certain circumstances*

After six months of debate, the delegates agreed to a peace treaty. The official signing of the **Treaty of Versailles** took place in the palace of Versailles, just outside Paris, on June 28, 1919. Secretary of State Robert Lansing felt that "the terms of peace appear immeasurably harsh and humiliating."

Germany's colonies and the Ottoman Empire were divided among the Allied nations. At Wilson's insistence, however, the treaty required the new colonial rulers to report on their administration to the League of Nations. The peace treaty created the new nations of Czechoslovakia and Yugoslavia. It also re-established Estonia, Finland, Latvia, Lithuania, and Poland as independent nations. France reclaimed the Alsace-Lorraine region. France also won control of the Saar, an industrial region of Germany rich in coal and iron, for 15 years. Germany was disarmed, forced to admit full responsibility for the war, and charged billions of dollars in reparations.

Harsh as this treatment was, it would have been much worse without Wilson's moderating influence. He strongly opposed some of the Allies' more extreme demands. Above all, the president made sure that the treaty included an agreement creating the League of Nations. He believed this would remedy any injustices the treaty might contain. The agreement required member nations to try to resolve disputes peacefully. If negotiations failed, the nations were to observe a waiting period before going to war. If any member nation failed to follow this procedure, the executive council could apply economic pressure and even recommend the use of force against the offending nation. Article 10, the heart of the agreement, required each member nation to "respect and preserve" the independence and territorial integrity of all other member nations.

Europe and the Middle East After World War I

Learning from Maps Four empires—the Austro-Hungarian, German, Ottoman, and Russian—had collapsed by the end of the First World War.

? LOCATION How many countries were created from or received land that had belonged to Russia before the war?

✔ **READING CHECK:** What were the terms of the Treaty of Versailles?

THAT'S INTERESTING!

Colorado senator Charles S. Thomas rejected President Wilson's ideas about the postwar peace, arguing that people were ruled by self-interest, not morality. "Man is a fighting animal, and life even in the most orderly communities is a continuing contest. . . . Morality, . . . if depended upon as a controlling influence in international affairs, . . . is apt, like a poorly tempered sword, to break in the hands at the moment of its greatest need."

VISUAL RECORD ANSWER

(for p. 353)

Students might suggest a church.

SECTION 4 REVIEW ANSWERS

Define and Identify

For significance, see the following pages:

- Bolsheviks, p. 347
- Battle of the Argonne Forest, p. 349
- Fourteen Points, p. 350
- League of Nations, p. 350
- Big Four, p. 350
- David Lloyd George, p. 350
- Georges Clemenceau, p. 350
- Vittorio Orlando, p. 350
- reparations, p. 350
- Treaty of Versailles, p. 351
- Henry Cabot Lodge, p. 352

Locate

For locations, see the map on p. 351. For importance, see the following page:

- Czechoslovakia, p. 351
- Yugoslavia, p. 351

TEACH OBJECTIVE 5

LEVELS 1 AND 2: Tell students to assume one of the following roles: *an American woman on the home front, a U.S. soldier who fought in France, a German soldier who fought in France,* or *a French civilian.* Have each student develop a detailed monologue about the global impact of World War I. *(Students' monologues should mention the incredible human and economic toll created by the war. Students should also mention the growing chaos in Germany and growing territorial disputes in Europe and the Middle East.)* Ask volunteers to perform their monologues for the class. Students may wish to include the scripts for their monologues in their portfolios. **Sheltered English**

LEVEL 3: Conduct a discussion on the global impact of World War I. *(See the Levels 1 and 2 lesson for the correct impacts.)* Ask students to select, in their opinions, the most devastating human or economic cost of World War I. *(Answers will vary. Students should support their choices.)* Then ask each student to write a proposal outlining a plan for the recovery of Europe. Have volunteers present their plans to the class. Conclude by conducting a discussion on different approaches to recovery.

- Estonia, p. 351
- Finland, p. 351
- Latvia, p. 351
- Lithuania, p. 351
- Poland, p. 351
- Saar, p. 351

1. goal—impartial adjustment of colonial claims; compromise—Allies divided German colonies and Ottoman Empire among themselves; goal—no secret diplomacy; compromise—Allied leaders worked for spoils-of-war treaties; goal—League of Nations; compromise—U.S. Senate refused to ratify treaty

2. launched a massive offensive and pushed German troops out of France, contributing to faltering German morale and incipient riots

3. the creation of new nations, the imposition of reparations, and the destruction of human life and property, among others

4. Students' reasons will vary. Terms: Germany's colonies and the Ottoman Empire divided among Allied nations, established a mandate system that required new colonial rulers to report to the League of Nations; created Czechoslovakia and Yugoslavia, re-established Estonia, Finland, Latvia, Lithuania, and Poland as independent nations; France reclaimed Alsace-Lorraine and won control of Saar for 15 years, and Germany was disarmed, forced to admit full responsibility for the war, and charged reparations.

5. Answers will vary. Students might suggest that Wilson should have compromised on Article 10.

352

This is a printed copy of one of the many speeches that President Wilson gave to win support for the Treaty of Versailles.

The treaty in the Senate. Wilson returned to the United States in July 1919. He immediately began working to win the Senate's approval of the Treaty of Versailles. Wilson expected to receive the votes of most Democratic senators, but he needed support from Republicans to gain the necessary two-thirds majority. Most Republican senators had doubts about the treaty. Fourteen of them—called the irreconcilables—wanted nothing to do with the League of Nations and flatly rejected the treaty. The other 35 Republican senators—the reservationists—said that they could support the treaty if the League Covenant was changed. They particularly objected to Article 10, which seemed to commit the United States to go to war in defense of any League member that came under attack. Wilson's only hope was to gain the support of close to 20 reservationists by compromising on the League. Wilson refused.

Henry Cabot Lodge of Massachusetts, head of the Senate Committee on Foreign Relations and Wilson's longtime enemy, led the reservationists. Lodge kept the treaty stalled in the Foreign Relations Committee through the summer of 1919. Angry and frustrated, on September 4 Wilson began a grueling 9,500-mile speaking tour by train to defend the treaty. The crowds grew more enthusiastic as the tour went on but Lodge remained unmoved. He said, "The only people who have votes on the treaty are here in the Senate."

On the night of September 25, after a speech in Pueblo, Colorado, Wilson complained of a splitting headache. His doctor ordered him back to Washington, D.C. A few days later, Wilson collapsed from a near-fatal stroke. He lived out the rest of his term in seclusion in the White House, cut off from everyone except his wife and his closest aides. Moody, suspicious, and increasingly out of touch with reality, Wilson still refused to compromise.

In November, Lodge presented the treaty, with a list of 14 reservations, to the Senate. On Wilson's orders, all of the Democrats rejected the modified treaty. Without the list of reservations, the treaty met the same fate at the hands of the Republicans. In March 1920 another vote on Lodge's version of the treaty failed. By the time Wilson left office, the League of Nations had been established in Geneva, Switzerland, but without U.S. participation.

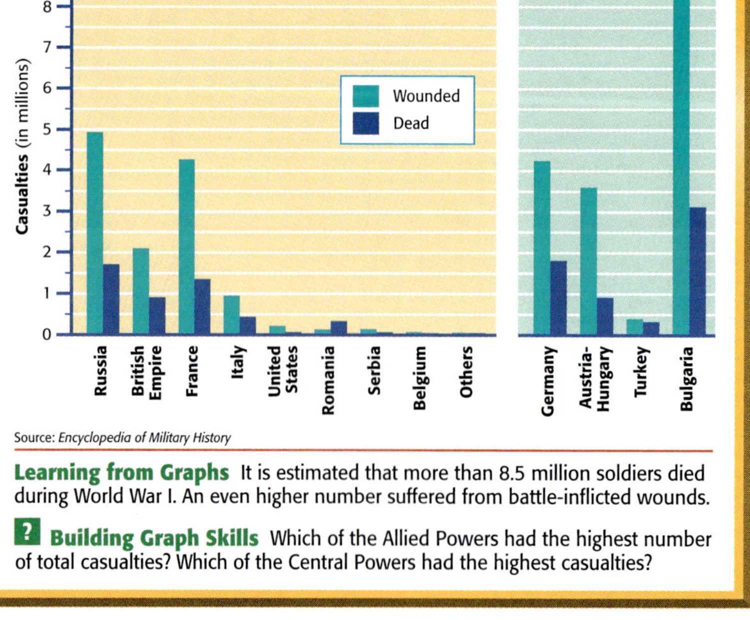

Learning from Graphs It is estimated that more than 8.5 million soldiers died during World War I. An even higher number suffered from battle-inflicted wounds.

Building Graph Skills Which of the Allied Powers had the highest number of total casualties? Which of the Central Powers had the highest casualties?

✔ **READING CHECK:** Why did the U.S. Senate reject the Treaty of Versailles?

REVIEW

Have students complete the **Section 4 Review** on p. 353.

ASSESS

Have students complete **Daily Quiz 11.4.** As **Alternative Assessment**, you may want to use the final events map or the Fourteen Points rationale in this section's lessons.

RETEACH

Have students complete **Main Idea Activity for Reteaching and Sheltered English 11.4.** Then pair students and have each pair devise a crossword puzzle or a hidden-word puzzle utilizing the key terms and key people in Section 4. Have each pair exchange its puzzle with another pair and then solve it.
Sheltered English, Cooperative Learning

EXTEND

Have students conduct research on the Treaty of Versailles and its role in helping to cause World War II. Ask students to discuss their research in a short essay. **Block Scheduling**

The Global Impact of the War

While U.S. leaders debated whether or not to accept the Treaty of Versailles, the Europeans struggled to recover from the war. The war's destruction and human suffering had been almost incomprehensible. In all, more than 8.5 million people had died in battle, and another 21 million were wounded.

The war had left the industry and agriculture of much of continental Europe in ruins. Northern France was completely destroyed. British economist John Maynard Keynes observed the landscape.

> **"For mile after mile nothing was left. No building was habitable and no field fit for the plow. . . . One devastated area was exactly like another—a heap of rubble, a morass [jumble] of shell-holes, and tangle of wire."**

INTERPRETING THE VISUAL RECORD

The cost of war. At the end of the war, many towns and cities, like Houplines, France (above), lay in ruins. ***What might the tall ruins in the middle of the photograph have been?***

Those businesses still operating could not produce enough to meet demand, resulting in rapid inflation. In Germany food shortages were so extreme that it proved almost impossible to keep track of prices.

Throughout Europe, nations competed with one another over territories that they thought the treaty ought to have granted them. Arab nations in the Middle East had sided with the Allies in hopes of winning their independence from the Ottoman Turks. Instead, they found themselves living under French and British authority. Tensions in the region grew after Britain issued the Balfour Declaration in 1917, which declared British support for a Jewish homeland in Palestine.

✔ **READING CHECK:** What was the global impact of World War I?

SECTION  REVIEW

Define and explain the significance of the following terms:
Bolsheviks
Battle of the Argonne Forest
Fourteen Points
League of Nations
Big Four
reparations
Treaty of Versailles

Identify and explain the significance of the following individuals:
David Lloyd George
Georges Clemenceau
Vittorio Orlando
Henry Cabot Lodge

Locate and explain the importance of the following places:
Czechoslovakia
Yugoslavia
Estonia
Finland
Latvia
Lithuania
Poland
Saar

1. **Using Graphic Organizers** Copy the chart below. Use it to list the goals of President Wilson's Fourteen Points and the compromises that Allied demands forced him to make.

Wilson's Goals	Compromises

2. **Synthesizing** How did the Allied Powers finally win the war?
3. **Assessing Consequences** What were some of the effects of the war on Europe and the Middle East?
4. **Using Historical Imagination** Imagine you are a U.S. Senator. Prepare a chart listing the terms of the Treaty of Versailles and your reasons for supporting or opposing each term.

Critical Thinking

5. How might Wilson have won support for the League of Nations?
Consider:
• the concerns of the Republicans who opposed the League
• the mood of the American public at the end of the war
• the possible benefits League membership offered the United States

CHAPTER 11 REVIEW ANSWERS

Creating a Time Line
Each event should have an explanation and the correct date.

Writing a Summary
See the Reading Checks in each section for main ideas.

Identifying People and Ideas
1. the glorification of military strength
2. archduke and heir to Austro-Hungarian throne whose assassination started World War I
3. the countries that fought against the Central Powers
4. Germany's promise not to sink ocean liners without warning
5. groups of warships that accompanied merchant vessels transporting troops and supplies
6. director of the War Industries Board
7. activist and volunteer who helped expand the Girl Scouts
8. the movement of many African Americans from the rural South to the urban North
9. an international organization designed to prevent offensive wars
10. reservationist senator who opposed the Treaty of Versailles

Understanding Main Ideas
1. militarism, nationalism, and military alliances
2. German troops tried to overwhelm France by invading

REVIEW AND ASSESSMENT RESOURCES

PRINT

- Chapter 11 Review, pp. 354–55
- Chapter 11 Tutorial for Students, Parents, Mentors, and Peers
- Chapter 11 Test (Form A or B)
- Portfolio Activities and Alternative Assessment Handbook, Chapter 11

MULTIMEDIA

- Audio Program, Chapter 11 (English and Spanish)
- Chapter 11 Test Generator (on the One-Stop Planner)
- Global Skill Builder CD–ROM
- HRW Web site

SHELTERED ENGLISH

- Spanish Glossary
- Sheltered English Chapter 11 Test

REVIEW

Have students complete the **Chapter 11 Review** on pp. 354–55.

ASSESS

Use one of the chapter tests to assess students' understanding of the content. For **Alternative Assessment**, see the **Portfolio Activities and Alternative Assessment Handbook.**

through Belgium, but Belgian troops delayed them, which gave Britain and France time to send soldiers to meet the offensive.

3. sold weapons to the Allies, offered moral support, and tried to force Germany to restrict submarine warfare

4. filled vacant jobs, served as nurses, and supported the war effort in the United States

5. formed the Committee for Public Information and passed antitreason laws

6. Château-Thierry and the Argonne Forest

Reviewing Themes

1. U-boat attacks and the Zimmerman Note led the United States to declare war. Some students might suggest that continued naval violations made U.S. involvement unavoidable, while other students might suggest that the United States could have worked harder to avoid entering the conflict.

2. The government raised money with war bonds and taxes, conserved resources, stimulated production, and regulated businesses and industries.

3. The government issued sanctions for verbal or written objections to the war; some argued that these efforts violated the First Amendment right to free speech.

Thinking Critically

1. positive–supplied many new soldiers, gave some soldiers new opportunities, and eventually helped some

Review

Creating a Time Line

Copy the time line below onto a sheet of paper. Complete the time line by filling in the events and dates from the chapter that you think were most significant. Pick three events and explain why you think they were significant.

Writing a Summary

Using the Reading Checks as a guide, write an overview of the events in the chapter.

Identifying People and Ideas

Identify the following terms or individuals and explain their significance.

1. militarism
2. Franz Ferdinand
3. Allied Powers
4. *Sussex* pledge
5. convoy system
6. Bernard Baruch
7. Juliette Gordon Low
8. Great Migration
9. League of Nations
10. Henry Cabot Lodge

Understanding Main Ideas

SECTION 1

1. What tensions contributed to the outbreak of war in Europe?
2. What happened during the early weeks of the war?

SECTION 2

3. What contributions did the United States make to the Allied war effort before entering the war?

SECTION 3

4. What role did women play in the war effort?
5. How did the U.S. government ensure the public's cooperation with the war effort?

SECTION 4

6. What were the decisive battles at the end of World War I?

Reviewing Themes

1. **Global Relations** What led to the U.S. declaration of war in 1917? Was U.S. involvement in the conflict unavoidable? Explain your answer.
2. **Economic Development** How was the U.S. economy mobilized for war?
3. **Democratic Values** Did the U.S. government's attempts to rally support for the war interfere with citizens' First Amendment rights? Why or why not?

Thinking Critically

1. **Analyzing** What were the positive and the negative effects of the draft in the United States?
2. **Evaluating** What effect did the wartime labor shortage have on unions, women, African Americans, and Mexican Americans?
3. **Hypothesizing** How might history have been different if President Wilson had been more willing to compromise on the peace treaty?
4. **Recognizing Point of View** How did Germans disagree with Americans about the sinking of the *Lusitania?*
5. **Using Historical Imagination** How might the war have ended differently if the United States had remained neutral?

Writing About History

Writing to Persuade Imagine that you are an African American soldier during the war. Write your commanding officer a letter that tries to convince the army to open up more opportunities for African American soldiers. Use the following graphic to organize your thoughts.

Increased Opportunities for African American Soldiers			
Current Opportunities	Other Possible Opportunities	Benefit for Soldiers	Benefit for Army

RETEACH

Organize students into small groups. Have each group create a short children's book about World War I. Groups' books should be nonfiction and should use images, graphic organizers, and simple explanations to help young readers grasp the content. Encourage students to delegate tasks within their groups, assigning jobs such as researcher, illustrator, and writer. Display students' books in the classroom or in the school library.
Sheltered English, Cooperative Learning

EXTEND

Tell students that the German U-boat, or submarine, played an important role in World War I. Have each student conduct research on U-boats in World War I. Students should select their own topics, such as U-boat construction and strategy, life aboard a U-boat, Allied responses to the U-boat, and so on. Have students create written or oral reports on their topics.
Block Scheduling

Strategies for Success Review the **Strategies for Success** on *Interpreting Literature as Historical Evidence.* Then read the 1918 poem below and answer the questions that follow.

The Ward at Night

The blanket lying dark against the sheet,
The heavy breathing of the sick,
The fevered voices
Telling of the battle
At the front,
Of Home and Mother.

1. What is the setting and subject of the poem?
2. How does it broaden your understanding of the war?

Linking History and Geography

Study the map below. How close did the Germans get to reaching Paris by June 1918?

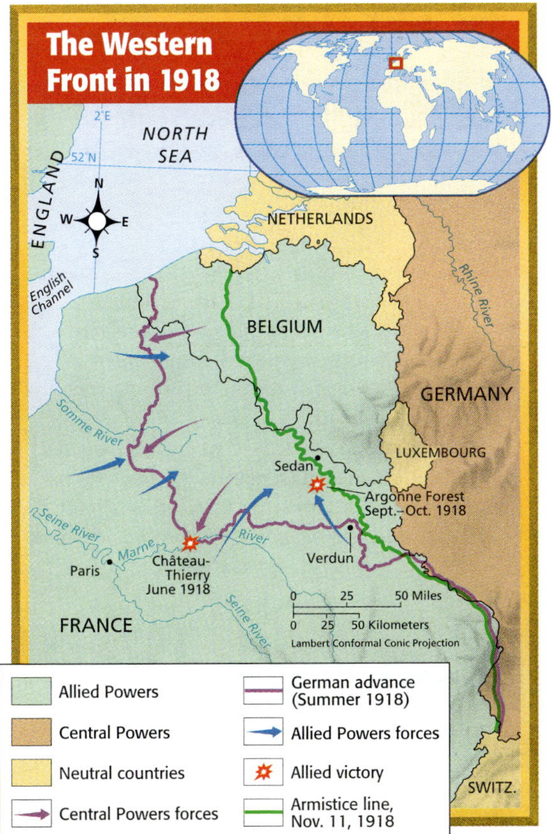

TOPIC: Sarajevo
GO TO: go.hrw.com
KEYWORD: SE1 Sarajevo

Accessing the Internet through the HRW Web site, research the city of Sarajevo. Then write an essay in which you analyze the history of the city and the conflicts that have influenced European society.

Complete one or all of the following projects independently or cooperatively.

1 Global Relations

Imagine that you are the U.S. ambassador to Germany in 1915. ***Write a letter*** to the kaiser protesting German violations of neutral shipping rights.

2 Democratic Values

Imagine that you are a senator committed to U.S. neutrality in World War I. ***Write a speech*** that explains why the United States should remain neutral.

3 Cultural Diversity

Imagine that it is 1915 and you are a recent immigrant to the United States from one of the Allied Powers. ***Create a poster*** encouraging Americans to support U.S. entry into World War I.

THE GRANGER COLLECTION, NEW YORK

World War I recruitment poster

American Indians gain citizenship; negative—forced some people to fight against their will and drafted some people into a conflict they did not support

2. allowed them to move into the workforce and to earn better wages
3. With a compromise, the reservationist senators might have passed the treaty; it might have helped prevent later conflicts.
4. German officials had warned Americans of the dangers involved in travel to Britain. In addition, the *Lusitania* was secretly transporting weapons to aid the Allies. Americans viewed the act as inappropriate action against a neutral country.
5. Some students might argue that the Allied Powers would have eventually defeated the German troops. Other students might argue that the Allies would have lost the war.

Writing About History
Students should note that African American soldiers faced widespread discrimination in the army. They might note that in the absence of discrimination, soldiers might make important military contributions and help the Allies win the war.

Strategies for Success
1. a wartime hospital
2. The poem emphasizes the humanity of the soldiers, who have fought battles but long for home.

Linking History and Geography
approximately 35 miles

REVIEW AND ASSESSMENT RESOURCES

PRINT
- Unit 3 Review, pp. 356–57
- Unit 3 Test (Form A or B)
- Portfolio Activities and Alternative Assessment Handbook, Unit 3

MULTIMEDIA
- Global Skill Builder CD–ROM

SHELTERED ENGLISH
- Spanish Glossary
- Sheltered English Unit 3 Test

To review elements of Unit 3 in a single class period, assign one of the following activities or graphic organizers, omitting the italicized answers, to individuals or groups.

3 Global Relations

AMERICA'S INTERNATIONAL ROLE

Costs
- *heavy economic costs*
- *public opposition from some sectors*
- *conflicts and warfare*

Benefits
- *substantial economic rewards*
- *public support from some sectors*
- *the ability to expand American ideals and culture*

A Selection from Further Reading

The Struggle for Power in the Industrial Workplace. In *A Very Different Age*, Stephen J. Diner discusses the experience of working-class Americans during the early 1900s. In the following excerpt, he explains how industrial laborers competed with their employers for power in the workplace: "A tug-of-war between workers and corporate capitalists shaped America's twentieth-century industrial system. . . . Industrialists . . . installed mass production machinery, broke down complex industrial jobs into shorter and simpler tasks, kept wages as low as possible, and insisted on strict factory discipline. Workers formed unions and went on strike over wages and hours, work rules and control of the shop floor. They changed jobs readily, took days off at will, and slowed the pace of production."

COMPREHENSION According to Diner, how did industrial laborers compete with their employers for power in the workplace?

ANSWER: Students might indicate that workers formed unions, went on strike, changed jobs frequently, took unauthorized days off, and slowed the pace of production.

UNIT 3 Review

BUILDING YOUR PORTFOLIO

Outlined below are four projects. Independently or cooperatively, complete one and use the products to demonstrate your mastery of the historical concepts involved.

1 Constitutional Heritage

During the late 1800s, the transformation of the United States from a rural economy to an industrialized, urban society created numerous social problems. In response, the Progressive Party sought reforms. ***Create a series of Progressive Party campaign posters*** that outline the party's reform goals. Be sure to include the laws, amendments, and government changes the party desires. You may wish to use portfolio materials you designed in the unit chapters to help you.

THE GRANGER COLLECTION, NEW YORK

Progressive Party candidate Theodore Roosevelt

Nurse visiting a tenement house

2 Democratic Values

Historians note that women's suffrage was primarily a middle-class movement and thus did not address many of the concerns of working-class women. ***Create a script for a dialogue*** between a middle-class progressive and a working-class woman on whether the emphasis on women's suffrage best serves the needs of all women. You may wish to use portfolio materials you designed in the unit chapters to help you.

4 Economic Development

Tell students to imagine that it is 1914 and that they are foreign policy advisers to the president. Have each student write a brief describing areas of American colonization, investment, and conflict through World War I. Ask volunteers to read their briefs to the class.

1 Constitutional Heritage

THE PROGRESSIVE PARTY		
Goals	**Actions**	**Successes**
to help immigrants	*established settlement houses and provided kindergartens and schools*	*ran many successful settlement houses and schools*
to reform big business	*pursued court cases regarding labor laws and worked for health and safety standards*	*lost many labor cases but managed to pass certain laws and codes*
to improve cities and city life	*organized urban planning commissions and urged better services and standards*	*managed to provide better city services and facilities*

American troops in France at the close of World War I

3 Global Relations

The Spanish-American War and World War I brought the United States onto the world stage. ***Prepare a speech*** for delivery to Congress outlining some of the costs and benefits of America's international role. You may wish to use portfolio materials you designed in the unit chapters to help you.

4 Economic Development

The expansionist policies of the United States in the late 1800s led to the establishment of U.S. colonies overseas, increased foreign investment, and conflicts with foreign powers. ***Create a world map*** showing areas of U.S. colonization, investment, and conflict through World War I. You may wish to use portfolio materials you designed in the unit chapters to help you.

Banana plantation near the Panama Canal

Further Reading

DeSantis, Vincent P. *The Shaping of Modern America: 1877–1916.* Allyn and Bacon, 1973. A broad survey of reform movements at the turn of the century.

Diner, Steven J. *A Very Different Age: Americans of the Progressive Era.* Hill and Wang, 1998. A cohesive account of the effects of industrialization and reform movements on Americans.

Ettinger, Albert M., and A. Churchill Ettinger. *A Doughboy with the Fighting 69th.* White Mane, 1992. Reminiscence of World War I by a soldier of the 69th Rainbow Division.

Hall, Linda B., and Don M. Coerver. *Revolution on the Border: The United States and Mexico, 1910–1920.* University of New Mexico Press, 1990. Examines the role that trade and investment played in U.S.-Mexico relations.

Liliuokalani. *Hawaii's Story by Hawaii's Queen.* Charles E. Tuttle, 1991. Firsthand account of Hawaii in the 1800s.

Schneider, Dorothy, and Carl J. Schneider. *Into the Breach.* Viking, 1991. Examines the participation of American women in World War I.

Internet Connect and Holt Researcher CD–ROM Review

In assigned groups, develop a multimedia presentation about America between 1897 and 1920. Choose information from the chapter Internet Connect activities and the Holt Researcher CD–ROM that best reflect the major topics of the period. Write an outline and a script for your presentation, which may be shown to the class.

A Selection from Further Reading

American Women and World War I. In *Into the Breach: American Women Overseas in World War One,* Dorothy and Carl J. Schneider examine the roles that American women played in World War I. In the following excerpt, they provide firsthand testimony from two African American women who went overseas to open recreation rooms for black soldiers: "Above all . . . American women went overseas in the 'Great War' to serve. . . . They idealized the 'cause,' and wanted to serve it. . . . Triumphing over the harsh prejudice directed at them, the black women Addie Hunton and Kathryn Johnson wrote: 'We had the greatest opportunity for service that we have ever known; service that was constructive, and prolific with wonderful and satisfying result. For the privilege of serving in this capacity we will always be grateful.'"

COMPREHENSION According to Schneider and Schneider, what motivated American women to go overseas during World War One?

ANSWER: Students might note that a desire to serve the Allied cause motivated American women to go overseas during World War I.

UNIT 4

Prosperity and Crisis

A Turbulent Decade

CHAPTER 12

The end of World War I did not bring calm to the United States. After undergoing a serious recession, the nation experienced protests and strikes. Many people began to fear the possibility of a Bolshevik infiltration and called for sanctions against Communists and other radicals. Over time, however, the Red Scare eased. A series of Republican presidents instituted economic policies that encouraged financial growth.

The Jazz Age

CHAPTER 13

Aided in part by growing prosperity, the 1920s experienced both the creation of a mass culture and a resurgence in all forms of art. Social mores, particularly those concerning women and young people, changed drastically during the decade. These changes worried many Americans. Such worries, in part, led to the rise of new religious movements.

EXAMINING THE VISUAL RECORD

Ask students the questions below. Then use the annotations to expand class discussion.

1 *What might you surmise about the economic class of the people depicted in the painting?*
Some people, such as the middle- and upper-class people shown in the painting, prospered during the economic boom of the 1920s. However, social divisions also deepened during this era, as many people did not share in the wealth created by big business and Wall Street.

2 *What features of this street scene might have represented innovations of the early 1900s?*
Many corporations commissioned architects to design skyscrapers in the 1920s. Theaters were built to show movies, a popular form of entertainment. Also, corporations relied increasingly on advertising and marketing to influence the growing class of consumers with disposable income.

ACTIVITY: Have each student write a poem or a song about urban life during the 1920s. Students might concentrate on the more positive aspects of urban life, such as the excitement and the wide variety of things to do, or students might concentrate on the more negative aspects of urban life, such as crime or poverty.

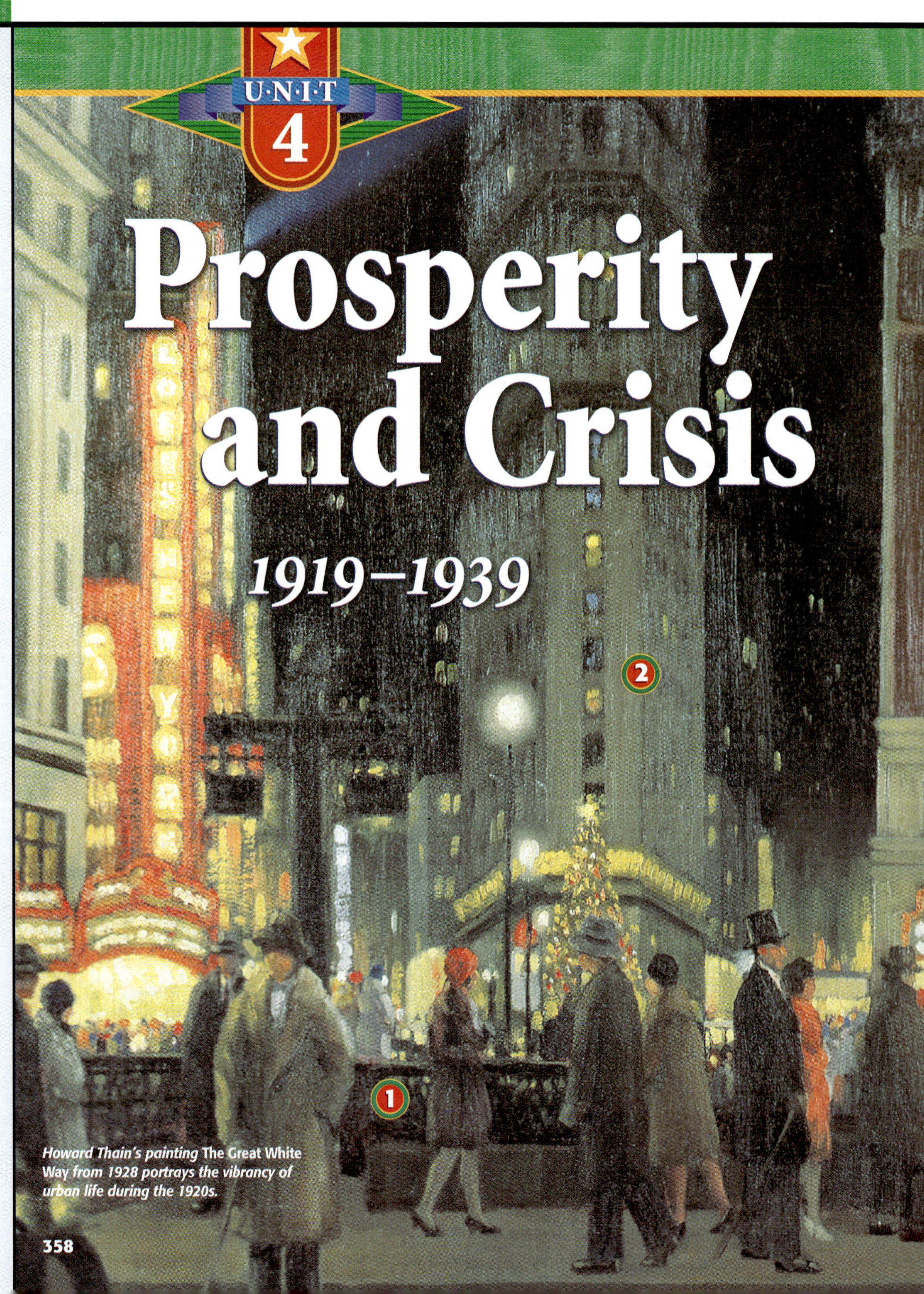

Howard Thain's painting The Great White Way *from 1928 portrays the vibrancy of urban life during the 1920s.*

358

CHAPTER 14 The Great Depression

In 1929 the stock market crashed and the prosperity of the 1920s gave way to the Great Depression of the 1930s. The Great Depression had a number of causes, including the global economic crisis, the national income gap, and consumer debt. It devastated many Americans, who expressed anger at President Hoover's support of "rugged individualism." In 1932 Democrat Franklin D. Roosevelt won the presidency.

CHAPTER 15 The New Deal

After Franklin D. Roosevelt took office, he instituted a New Deal to rescue the economy and assist Americans. President Roosevelt believed that heavy government spending could help the nation recover from the Great Depression. Roosevelt's New Deal programs allocated government funds to create jobs, provide direct relief, and fund small and large-scale public-works projects. Over time, it led many Americans to believe that the federal government had an honor-bound duty to help and assist its citizens.

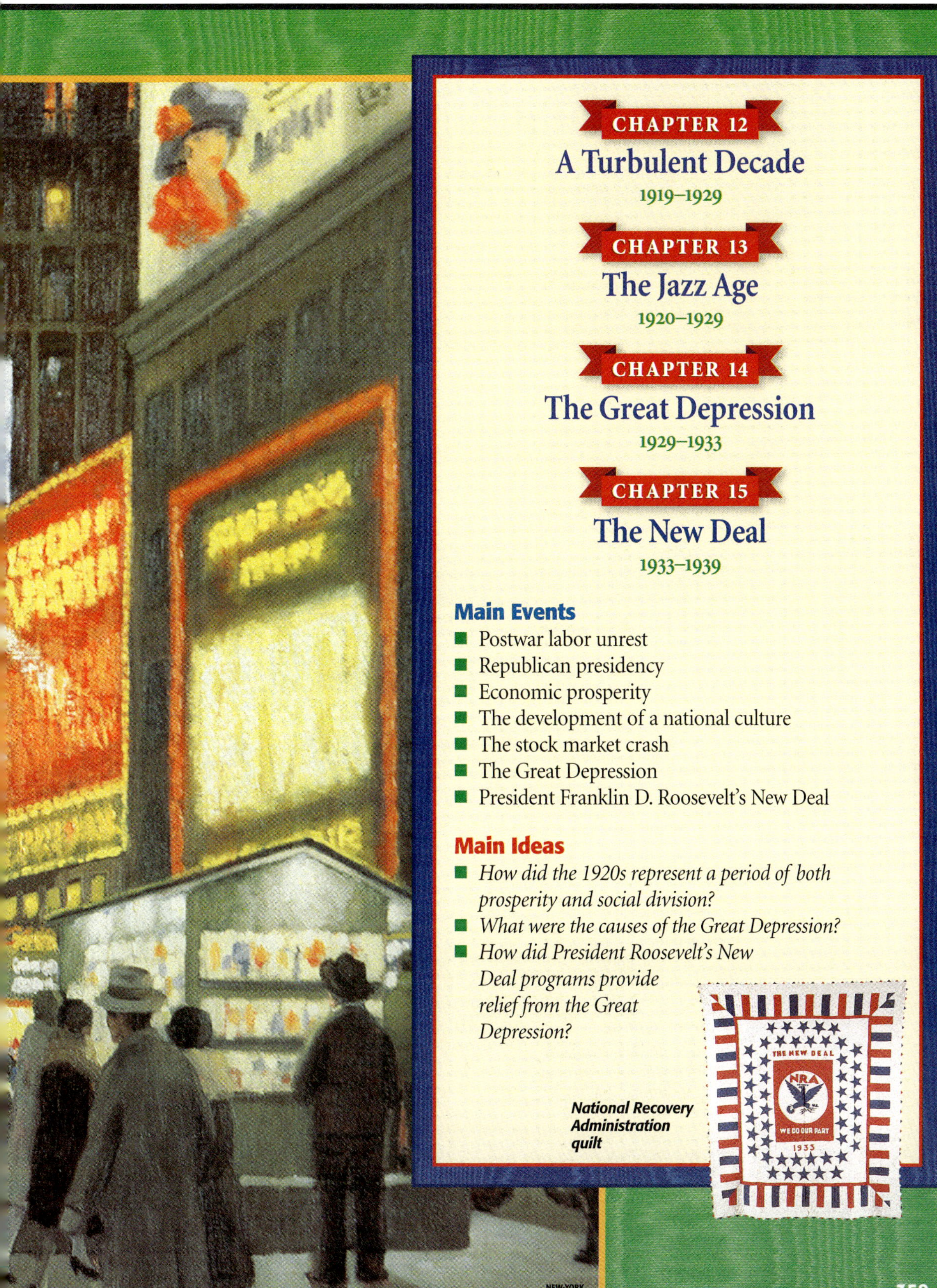

NEW-YORK HISTORICAL SOCIETY

CHAPTER 12
A Turbulent Decade
1919–1929

CHAPTER 13
The Jazz Age
1920–1929

CHAPTER 14
The Great Depression
1929–1933

CHAPTER 15
The New Deal
1933–1939

Main Events

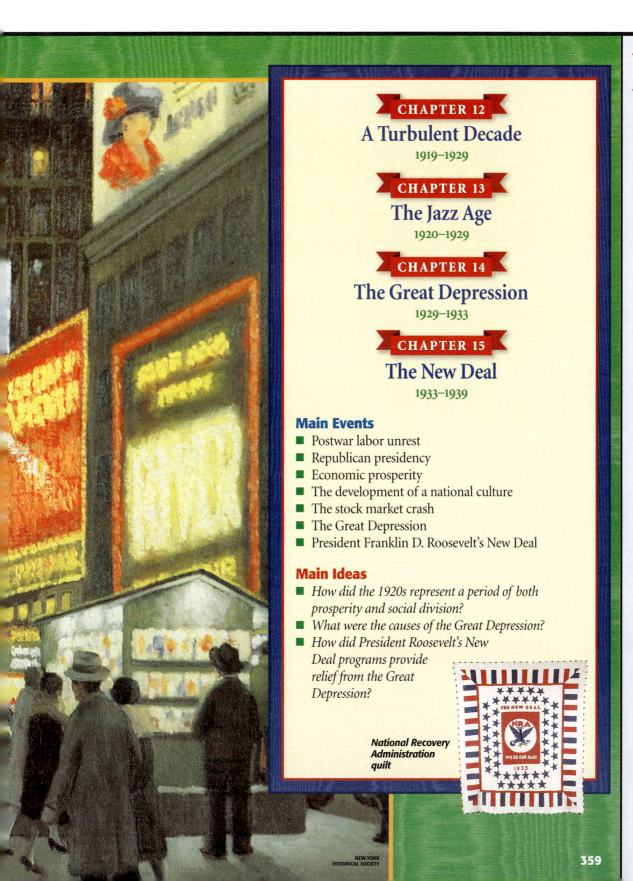

- Postwar labor unrest
- Republican presidency
- Economic prosperity
- The development of a national culture
- The stock market crash
- The Great Depression
- President Franklin D. Roosevelt's New Deal

Main Ideas

- *How did the 1920s represent a period of both prosperity and social division?*
- *What were the causes of the Great Depression?*
- *How did President Roosevelt's New Deal programs provide relief from the Great Depression?*

National Recovery Administration quilt

INTRODUCE UNIT 4

Main Events

List the Main Events on the chalkboard. Ask students to select two and briefly describe what they know about the topics. Have volunteers share their descriptions. Later, when you have finished Unit 4, ask students to return to their original descriptions and revise them using the information they learned in the unit. Students should also create new descriptions for the other Main Events.

Main Ideas

Ask each student to read the Main Ideas and briefly answer the questions in writing. Share the ***Consider*** points with students as necessary. Later, when you have finished Unit 4, ask students to return to their original answers and revise them using the information they learned in the unit.

The Causes of the Great Depression
Consider:

- the long-term economic effects of a disparity in wealth
- the impact of a declining and unstable global trade market

The New Deal Programs
Consider:

- the potential importance of government spending
- the need for a "whole-society" solution

A Turbulent Decade

CHAPTER PLANNING GUIDE

	Section Lesson Objectives	Print Resources	Multimedia Resources	Sheltered English Resources
Section 1 Postwar Troubles, pp. 362–68	1 Discuss some of the economic outcomes of demobilization. 2 Analyze the main causes of the strikes of 1919 and how most Americans reacted to the strikes. 3 Explain what caused the public hysteria of the Red Scare. 4 Recount why the Sacco and Vanzetti trial aroused public interest.	▶ Guided Reading Strategy 12.1 ▶ Graphic Organizer Activity 12: Postwar Conflicts ▶ Literature Reading 12: Justice or Political and Ethnic Bias? ▶ Section 1 Review, p. 368 ▶ Daily Quiz 12.1	▶ One-Stop Planner, Lesson 12.1 ▶ Holt Researcher: American History CD–ROM	▶ Main Idea Activity for Reteaching and Sheltered English 12.1
Section 2 The Republicans in Power, pp. 369–74	1 Describe how Republican policies encouraged economic growth. 2 Evaluate the positive and negative effects of the Harding administration's pro-business policies. 3 Analyze why the movement to pass the Equal Rights Amendment failed. 4 Explain how the Republican Party overcame the political scandals of the Harding administration. 5 Discuss the issues that affected the outcome of the 1928 presidential election.	▶ Guided Reading Strategy 12.2 ▶ Geography Activity 12: The Republican Decade ▶ Primary Source Reading 12: A Scandalous Administration ▶ Section 2 Review, p. 374 ▶ Daily Quiz 12.2	▶ One-Stop Planner, Lesson 12.2 ▶ Holt Researcher: American History CD–ROM	▶ Main Idea Activity for Reteaching and Sheltered English 12.2
Section 3 A Nation Divided, pp. 375–81	1 Explain why many Americans supported the Ku Klux Klan and what factors led to a decline in that support. 2 Identify the actions that African Americans took to combat discrimination and violence. 3 Discuss why many Americans demanded restrictions on immigration. 4 State why Mexican immigration increased during the 1920s. 5 Recount the actions that American Indians took to protect their land.	▶ Guided Reading Strategy 12.3 ▶ Biography Reading 12: A. Philip Randolph ▶ Section 3 Review, p. 381 ▶ Daily Quiz 12.3	▶ One-Stop Planner, Lesson 12.3 ▶ The American Nation Video Program Segment: A Nation of Immigrants; Teacher's Guide, pp. 153–57 ▶ Holt Researcher: American History CD–ROM ▶ HRW Web site	▶ Main Idea Activity for Reteaching and Sheltered English 12.3
Chapter Review and Assessment pp. 382–83		▶ Chapter 12 Review, pp. 382–83 ▶ Chapter 12 Tutorial for Students, Parents, Mentors, and Peers ▶ Chapter 12 Test (Form A or B) ▶ Portfolio Activities and Alternative Assessment Handbook, Chapter 12	▶ Audio Program, Chapter 12 (English and Spanish) ▶ Chapter 12 Test Generator (on the One-Stop Planner) ▶ Global Skill Builder CD–ROM ▶ HRW Web site	▶ Spanish Glossary ▶ Sheltered English Chapter 12 Test

CHAPTER OVERVIEW

The period after World War I was marked by economic troubles and social unrest. The United States experienced a recession and labor strikes as workers protested low wages and poor working conditions. Public opinion turned against a series of strikes in 1919 as fears of a possible Bolshevik revolution overcame many Americans. During the Red Scare, many immigrants suspected of radical political activities were arrested and deported. African Americans also suffered as a resurgent Ku Klux Klan carried out violent acts against African Americans and others in northern as well as southern states.

Politically, the postwar era was marked by Republican rule. The pro-business policies of Warren Harding were popular with many Americans. While business experienced a boom, Republicans and the courts worked to overturn many of the gains made by organized labor during the Progressive Era. Despite the political scandals that occurred during the Harding administration, the Republicans still occupied the White House at the end of the decade.

TIME TAMERS

Block Scheduling

The teacher lesson plans for each section offer a variety of activity choices to help you present the material in a block scheduling format. For further suggestions on block scheduling, see the **Block Scheduling Handbook with Team Teaching Strategies**, pp. 67–72.

Smithsonian Institution®

Internet Connections and Lesson 12
www.si.edu/hrw

Hands-On History Activities:

Classroom to Community The **Hands-On History Activities** help students make meaningful connections between events in American history and those in their own hometown. You may wish to use the Chapter 12 Activity, Labor Unions in Your Region, to extend the chapter lessons, as alternative assessment, or as a block scheduling option.

Portfolio Projects

The American Nation includes multiple portfolio projects in each Pupil's Edition chapter review, as well as each unit review. Chapter 12 Portfolio Project options on p. 383 include the following:

1. Students will **write a news report**.
2. Students will **create an illustrated chart**.
3. Students will **create a flier**.

The American Nation INTERNET RESOURCE DIRECTORY

To access online materials for this chapter, go to **go.hrw.com** and type in the keywords listed below.

HRW ONLINE RESOURCES
GO TO: go.hrw.com

Online Charts
KEYWORD: SE1 Charts12
- The African American Population, 1900–1950

Online Reading Support
KEYWORD: SE1 Strategies12

Online Rubrics
KEYWORD: SE1 Rubrics

CHAPTER ENRICHMENT LINKS
Use these Web links to extend and enrich student learning for Chapter 12.
GO TO: go.hrw.com
KEYWORD: SE1 Ch12

CHAPTER INTERNET ACTIVITIES
GO TO: go.hrw.com
- Pupil's Edition Student Activity
  KEYWORD: SE1 Bolshevik
  (Students conduct research on the Bolshevik Revolution.)
- Teacher's Edition Student Activity
  KEYWORD: SE1 Sacco
  (Students examine the Sacco and Vanzetti case.)
- Teacher's Edition Student Activity
  KEYWORD: SE1 Garvey
  (Students conduct research on Marcus Garvey and W. E. B. Du Bois.)

ADDITIONAL RESOURCES

Books for Teachers

Harrison, Alferdteen, ed. *Black Exodus: The Great Migration from the Great American South.* University Press of Mississippi, 1992. Discusses black migration from the South to the urban North.

Books for Students

Green, Harvey. *The Uncertainty of Everyday Life, 1915–1945.* HarperCollins, 1992. Examines life before, during, and after the 1920s.

Lawler, Mary. *Marcus Garvey.* Holloway, 1990. Presents a biography of the leader of the back-to-Africa movement. Particularly appropriate for students reading below grade level.

Primary Sources from the Period

Cahan, Abraham. *The Rise of David Levinsky.* Harper, 1966. Chronicles a Jewish immigrant's experience in the United States.

Shulman, Alix Kates, ed. *Red Emma Speaks: Selected Writings and Speeches by Emma Goldman.* Random House, 1972. Presents primary sources by Emma Goldman.

Multimedia Materials

The Age of Ballyhoo. Video, 52 min. Republic/SSSS. Discusses the cultural history of the 1920s. Includes newsreels of Sacco and Vanzetti.

The Big Red Scare of 1919–1920, Video, 10 min. Multi-Media Productions/SSSS. Traces the origins of anticommunist and anti-immigrant feelings.

CHAPTER 12

Before You Read

Build on What You Know

Ask students to answer the following questions.

How might demobilization have affected the daily lives of many Americans?

Consider:

- the large numbers of women and African Americans who worked in factories during the war
- the impact of heavy postwar consumer spending

How might oppressed groups have reacted to discrimination or unfair working conditions?

Consider:

- the actions taken by workers in response to bad working conditions
- the organizations created by various minority groups

exploring the time line

AMERICAN EVENTS

internetconnect

TOPIC: Sacco and Vanzetti Case
GO TO: go.hrw.com
KEYWORD: SE1 Sacco

Have students access the Internet through the HRW Web site to conduct research on the Sacco and Vanzetti case. Have each student write a short legal brief summarizing the evidence and supporting the guilt or innocence of the men.

1919–1929 A Turbulent Decade

Harding campaign button

THE GRANGER COLLECTION, NEW YORK

Teapot Dome political cartoon

1919
Daily Life
Looting and mob violence erupt in Boston as the city's police force goes on strike.

1920
Politics
Warren G. Harding is elected president of the United States by the largest popular majority in U.S. history to date.

1921
Business and Finance
An economic recession caused by demobilization leads to 20,000 business failures.

1921
Daily Life
A race riot erupts in Tulsa, Oklahoma, resulting in the deaths of at least 30 people.

1922
Business and Finance
Charles Dawes, head of the Bureau of the Budget, turns the federal government's annual deficit into a surplus.

1922
The Arts
Sinclair Lewis publishes *Babbit,* a novel that criticizes middle-class conservatism and conformity.

1924
Politics
The Teapot Dome scandal is exposed.

1919 · 1921 · 1923

A soldier guards a store during the Boston police strike.

Sinclair Lewis's novel

Before You Read

Build on What You Know

World War I affected the daily lives of many Americans. The government mobilized industry to produce necessary goods for U.S. soldiers and their allies, who finally achieved victory against the Central Powers in 1918. During the war the U.S. government suppressed political protests. In this chapter you will learn about the changes in American life after the war. Although prosperity returned to the United States, economic benefits and political freedom were not enjoyed by everyone.

Think About Themes

To help students create their Themes Journal entries, provide the following examples of appropriate **agree/disagree** *statements.*

Democratic Values

Agree During World War I many Americans tried to suppress the opinions of those who voiced opposition to the war or criticized the government's actions.

Disagree Regardless of the threats to their personal safety, pacifists and socialists expressed their opposition to World War I.

Economic Development

Agree The U.S. government's pro-business policies during the Second Industrial Revolution created inequalities in wealth and led to worker dissatisfaction.

Disagree The implementation of Henry Clay's American System created prosperity in all regions of the country.

Cultural Diversity

Agree Despite fighting in the Civil War, African Americans suffered from discrimination after the war ended.

Disagree Especially since the Civil War, women and minorities have worked to obtain equal rights and to end discrimination.

Ku Klux Klan publication

SHAHN, BEN. BARTOLOMEO VANZETTI AND NICOLA SACCO (1931-1932)

Ben Shahn's painting of Sacco and Vanzetti on trial

1925
Daily Life
The Ku Klux Klan holds a parade in Washington, D.C., with over 40,000 participants.

1925
The Arts
The *Grand Ole Opry* broadcasts its first performance over radio station WSM in Nashville, Tennessee.

1927
Politics
Italian immigrants Nicola Sacco and Bartolomeo Vanzetti are executed after being convicted of murder.

1927
Science and Technology
John Daniel Rust invents the mechanical cotton picker.

1928
World Events
Scottish doctor Alexander Fleming discovers penicillin, the first antibiotic.

1929
Daily Life
Eastman Kodak introduces 16 mm motion picture cameras and projectors for home use.

1929
The Arts
The Museum of Modern Art opens in New York City.

1925 — **1927** — **1929**

1925
Business and Finance
The Pullman Company refuses to recognize the African American union founded by A. Philip Randolph.

1926
Science and Technology
Thomas Hunt Morgan proves a theory of heredity and locates genes in the chromosomes of fruit flies.

1926
Business and Finance
Congress passes the Revenue Act, reducing taxes for the wealthiest Americans.

1929
Science and Technology
Construction of the Empire State Building begins.

Members of A. Philip Randolph's union

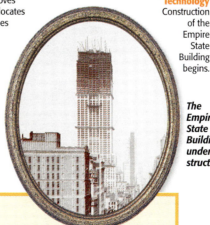

The Empire State Building under construction

exploring the time line

GLOBAL EVENTS

TECHNOLOGY AND SOCIETY

1928 ■ Alexander Fleming Discovers Penicillin. The development of penicillin to treat infections illustrates the importance of scientific cooperation. In 1928 Alexander Fleming accidentally discovered that the penicillin mold inhibited the growth of certain bacteria. As he was untrained in clinical medicine, he published a few papers on his findings and then moved on to other work. In 1938 two other scientists, Ernst Boris Chain and Howard Walter Florey, used Fleming's early research and portions of the penicillin mold from Fleming's lab to produce penicillin in a form that could be used in medicines. In 1945 all three men were awarded the Nobel Prize in physiology.

CRITICAL THINKING How might Fleming's earlier experiments have helped Chain and Florey develop penicillin as a medicine?

ANSWER: Students might suggest that Fleming's reports established that the penicillin mold inhibited some kinds of bacteria and helped the other men narrow and concentrate their experiments.

Think About Themes

Decide whether you **agree** *or* **disagree** *with the following statements. Note why in your journal.*

Democratic Values The fear of radicalism in the United States causes many Americans to sacrifice personal liberties for a sense of security.

Economic Development Government policies that encourage economic growth can also lead to social instability.

Cultural Diversity Restrictions on immigration hurt a country more than they help in the long run.

361

SECTION 1

After completing Section 1, students should be able to:

OBJECTIVE 1 *Discuss some of the economic outcomes of demobilization.*

OBJECTIVE 2 *Analyze the main causes of the strikes of 1919 and how most Americans reacted to the strikes.*

OBJECTIVE 3 *Explain what caused the public hysteria of the Red Scare.*

OBJECTIVE 4 *Recount why the Sacco and Vanzetti trial aroused public interest.*

LET'S GET STARTED!

Have students read the Think About Themes feature on the previous page. Then have students list developments they expect to read about in this chapter, based on the themes themselves. Compile a master list on the chalkboard from the responses of volunteers. Tell students that in Section 1 they will learn about the troubles American society faced after World War I.

SECTION 1 RESOURCES

PRINT
- Guided Reading Strategy 12.1
- Graphic Organizer Activity 12: Postwar Conflicts
- Literature Reading 12: Justice or Political and Ethnic Bias?
- Section 1 Review, p. 368
- Daily Quiz 12.1

MULTIMEDIA
- One-Stop Planner, Lesson 12.1
- Holt Researcher: American History CD–ROM

SHELTERED ENGLISH
- Main Idea Activity for Reteaching and Sheltered English 12.1

✔ READING TO UNDERSTAND
To help students master the section objectives, have them answer the **READING CHECKS** and complete **Guided Reading Strategy 12.1** as they read the section.

Postwar Troubles

OBJECTIVES

Read to understand:
1. what some of the economic outcomes of demobilization were
2. what the main causes of the strikes of 1919 were, and how most Americans reacted to the strikes
3. what caused the public hysteria of the Red Scare
4. why the Sacco and Vanzetti trial aroused public interest

KEY TERMS

demobilization
Seattle general strike
Boston police strike
steel strike of 1919
United Mine Workers strike
Red Scare
Palmer raids

KEY PEOPLE

John L. Lewis
A. Mitchell Palmer
Nicola Sacco
Bartolomeo Vanzetti

“We danced in the streets, embraced old women and pretty girls, swore blood brotherhood with soldiers . . . [and] reeled through the streets.”
—Malcolm Cowley

Malcolm Cowley recalled the spirit of celebration that possessed many Americans after hearing news of the end of World War I. The carefree spirit of celebration was short-lived, however. For many Americans, postwar life did not appear promising.

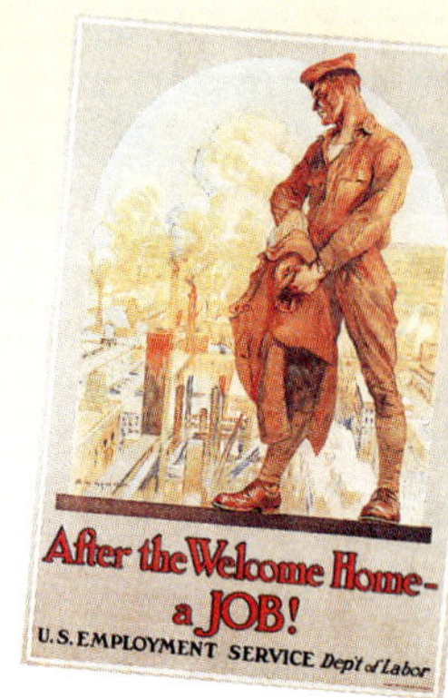

Veteran searching for work

Demobilization

The abrupt ending of World War I caught American industries by surprise. Factories and war-related industries had been operating at full capacity when the demand for military supplies suddenly dried up. The sudden process of **demobilization**, or the transition from wartime to peacetime production levels, caused social and economic strain. The return of some 4 million soldiers to the workforce caused unemployment to rise and wages to fall. Meanwhile, wartime shortages left prices high.

To make room for the returning veterans, women were urged to give up their jobs. “The same patriotism which induced women to enter industry during the war should induce them to vacate their positions,” declared the New York Labor Federation. Many women were forced out of their jobs. As a result, the percentage of women in the workforce in 1920 fell slightly below what it had been in 1910.

Americans who were worried about the impact of demobilization on their jobs also faced a skyrocketing cost of living. With peace at hand, consumers went on a spending spree. They made purchases they had put off during the war. The demand for goods outpaced supply, and prices soared. The cost of goods and services roughly doubled from 1914 to 1920.

Women who worked in factories during World War I were encouraged to give up their jobs to returning veterans.

Soon, however, this trend reversed. Prices fell when a brief but deep recession struck in 1920–21. Demobilization was one of the factors behind the recession. During the war millions of Americans had worked in defense industries. At war's end, however, the government canceled more than $2 billion in military contracts. Factories responded by cutting back production and laying off workers. By 1921 some 5 million workers—nearly 12 percent of the labor force—were unemployed. Even Americans with jobs suffered. “Working conditions . . . seemed harder than ever,” reported one steelworker. “We were only paid forty-two cents an hour, and we worked like a mule.”

The impact of demobilization extended beyond factory life, however. A farm crisis added to the nation's economic problems.

TEACH OBJECTIVE 1

LEVEL 1: To help students understand the costs of demobilization, copy the following graphic organizer on the chalkboard, omitting the italicized answers. Have each student complete it. Conclude by leading a discussion on the economic outcomes of demobilization. **Sheltered English**

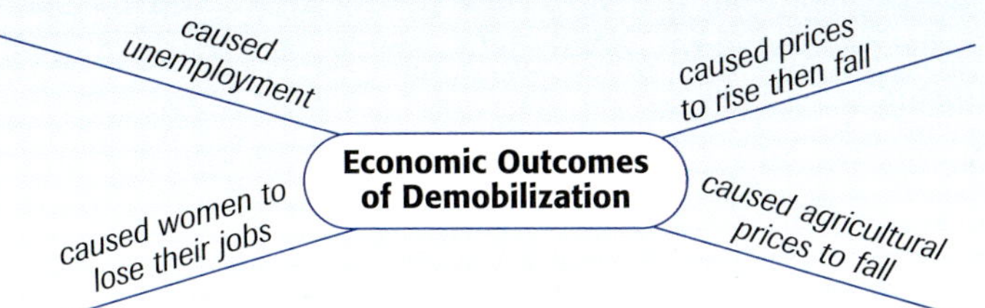

LEVELS 2 AND 3: Tell students to imagine that they are songwriters during the post–World War I era who have been commissioned to write a song called "The Demobilization Blues." Pair students and have each pair write a short song or poem that describes the economic outcomes of demobilization. *(See the graphic organizer for the correct outcomes.)* Ask volunteers to sing or read their songs or poems to the class. Students may wish to include their song or poem in their portfolios. **Cooperative Learning**

Farmers had benefited from wartime markets in Europe. As European farm production revived, however, these markets dried up and farm prices fell. Cotton, for example, fell dramatically from 35 cents per pound in 1919 to 16 cents a year later. Burdened with debt, hundreds of thousands of American farmers lost ownership of their land during the 1920s.

✔ **READING CHECK:** What were some economic outcomes of demobilization?

Labor Strife

Many workers protested in response to the difficulties of demobilization. They demanded higher wages and shorter work hours. When management ignored labor's pleas, many workers went on strike. More than 3,600 work stoppages—involving some 4 million workers—took place in 1919 alone.

The Seattle general strike. The first major strike of 1919 occurred when some 35,000 shipyard workers in Seattle walked off the job. They demanded higher wages and shorter hours. Some 110 local unions joined the workers. The **Seattle general strike** began on February 6 at 10:00 A.M. Some 60,000 workers left their jobs to participate in the strike, which was extremely well organized. "It was," declared one shipyard worker, "the most beautiful thing I [had] ever seen!" The General Strike Committee set up 21 community kitchens to feed strikers. The committee made arrangements for milk delivery to people caring for children.

The strike occurred without a single incident of violence. Nevertheless, city officials and business leaders expressed alarm. Newspapers blamed immigrants for the strike and called the strikers "muddle-headed foreigners." The strikers came under increased public pressure to go back to work. After five days they ended the strike without winning any of their demands.

The strike had been peaceful. However, antilabor forces tried to convince the public that Seattle had been on the brink of a revolution similar to Russia's Bolshevik Revolution. Seattle mayor Ole Hanson told the national press, "Revolution . . . doesn't need violence. The general strike . . . is of itself the weapon of revolution." Many people believed these charges. In the end, the strike helped turn public opinion against organized labor.

The Boston police strike. In September 1919 another strike, the **Boston police strike**, further inflamed antilabor sentiments. The Boston police officers had recently formed a union to seek better pay and working conditions. Officers in other cities had unionized without incident. However, Boston's police commissioner, Edwin Curtis, refused to recognize the union. Instead, he fired 19 officers for engaging in union activities. In response, some 75 percent of the Boston police force went on strike. Public order in the city quickly collapsed. Journalist William Allen White described the first night of the strike:

As the nation's economy suffered after World War I, American farmers experienced a severe crisis. Publications such as this one chronicled farmers' experiences.

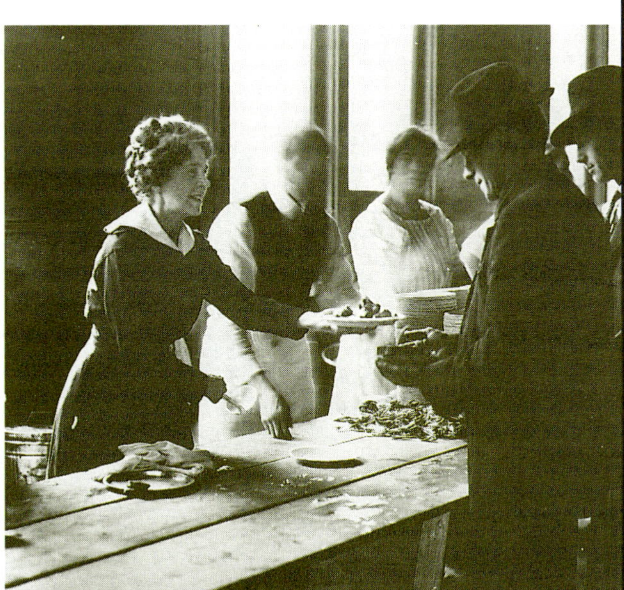

INTERPRETING THE VISUAL RECORD

Seattle general strike. With many of the city services shut down during the Seattle general strike, organizers established community kitchens and provided some limited services. ***What information does this photograph offer about the organization of the strikers?***

ACROSS THE CURRICULUM

▶SOCIOLOGY◀

Unions in the South. Although labor unions were unpopular with business owners and politicians across the nation, they were particularly unpopular in the South. One politician spoke against the "unholy foreign-born, un-American, despotic thing *known as labor unionism."*

CRITICAL THINKING Why might opponents have referred to unions as "unholy" and "foreign-born"?

ANSWER: Answers will vary. Some students might suggest that many people associated unions with immigrants, who often were Catholic or Jewish.

THAT'S INTERESTING!

Some corporations tried to increase employee satisfaction by offering insurance and pension plans.

VISUAL RECORD ANSWER

Students might suggest that the photograph indicates that the strikers were well-organized.

TEACH OBJECTIVE 2

LEVEL 1: Tell students to imagine that it is 1919 and they are newspaper reporters. Pair students and have each pair write headlines reporting the main causes of the strikes of 1919 and the public response to the strikes. *(Pairs should mention the following: causes—inflation, low wages, and long work hours; reactions—violence, work loss, and accusations of radicalism and communism.)* Ask volunteers to present and explain their headlines to the class.

Sheltered English, Cooperative Learning

LEVEL 2: Tell students to imagine that it is 1919 and that they are newspaper reporters who have been assigned to cover the strikes. Have each student choose one of the strikes discussed in the textbook and write a short article analyzing the causes of the strike and public reaction to it. *(See the Level 1 lesson for the correct causes and reactions.)* Have volunteers read their articles to the class. Students may wish to include their articles in their portfolios.

HISTORY MAKERS SPEAK

Emma Goldman in *Red Emma Speaks*

An Anarchist Explains. Emma Goldman wrote many essays expressing her views on life and society. Goldman championed the idea that people should be free to work for the love of the work itself, not simply for wages. A worker should be "one to whom the making of a table, the building of a house, or the tilling of the soil is . . . the result of inspiration, of intense longing, and deep interest in work as a creative force."

CRITICAL THINKING Given Goldman's emphasis on work as a personal creative endeavor, what might she have said about factory work?

ANSWER: Students might suggest that Goldman might have criticized factory work as repetitive and unfulfilling.

VISUAL RECORD ANSWER

Students might note that she is directing traffic.

INTERPRETING THE VISUAL RECORD

Strikes. During the Boston police strike, civilians took over traffic control and other public-safety jobs. ***How does this photograph suggest that this civilian is helping to preserve public safety during the strike?***

During the Pittsburgh steel strike newspapers such as the ***Pittsburgh Chronicle Telegraph*** *urged strikers to go back to work.*

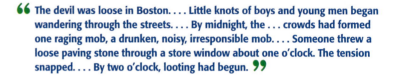

> **"The devil was loose in Boston. . . . Little knots of boys and young men began wandering through the streets. . . . By midnight, the . . . crowds had formed one raging mob, a drunken, noisy, irresponsible mob. . . . Someone threw a loose paving stone through a store window about one o'clock. The tension snapped. . . . By two o'clock, looting had begun."**

After two nights of violence, Governor Calvin Coolidge called in the state militia to restore order. Boston's newspapers denounced the strikers as "agents of Lenin" and the strike as a "Bolshevist nightmare." Public opinion also came out firmly against the strike. Recognizing that their cause was doomed, the police voted unanimously to return to work. Commissioner Curtis, however, refused to reinstate the officers. Instead, he hired a new force made up of unemployed veterans. Union sympathizers protested. Unmoved, Coolidge backed the commissioner. He proclaimed that "there is no right to strike against the public safety by anybody, anywhere, any time."

The steel strike. Two weeks after the Boston strike, some 365,000 steelworkers in western Pennsylvania—many of them immigrants—walked off the job. This action began the **steel strike of 1919**. The strikers were demanding recognition of their union and protesting low wages and long working hours. The massive walkout threatened to shut down the steel industry.

Having fought efforts to unionize steelworkers for years, the major steel companies did everything in their power to break the strike. To divide labor along ethnic lines, they portrayed foreign workers as radicals and called on "loyal" Americans to return to work. The steel companies also brought in thousands of workers—including African Americans and Mexicans—to replace the strikers.

The steel companies also enlisted the aid of police officers to pressure the strikers and even hired armed thugs to intimidate them. Strikers were jailed, beaten, or shot. Faced with such tactics, union leaders called off the strike on January 9, 1920.

The United Mine Workers strike. The last major strike of 1919 erupted in November. Some 400,000 coal miners walked out of the mines in the **United Mine Workers strike**. Miners were protesting the continued enforcement of wartime contracts that kept workers' pay fixed at 1917 rates despite increases in consumer prices. Some members of the United Mine Workers (UMW) demanded a 50 percent pay increase, a five-day workweek, and a six-hour workday.

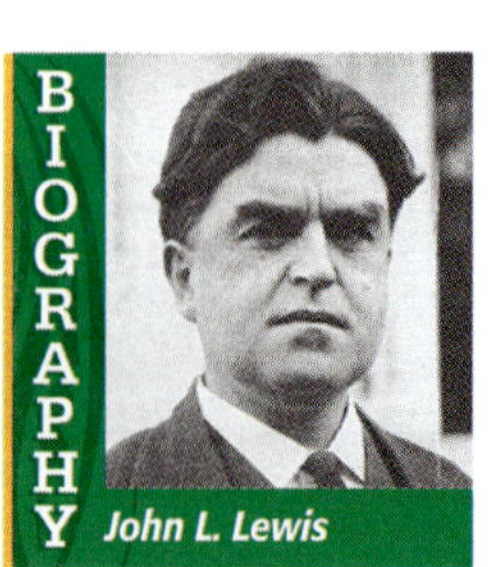

BIOGRAPHY

John L. Lewis

The strike was organized by the newly elected president of the UMW, John L. Lewis. Born in 1880, Lewis was 39 years old and had just gained control of the UMW when the strike was called on November 1, 1919. It was the first strike he organized.

Lewis was well acquainted with the life and concerns of miners and unionists. He was raised in an Iowa mining family. His father spent his days working in the coal pits and his nights organizing miners in the Knights of Labor union. Lewis briefly attended school, then followed in his father's footsteps. He was working in the mines by the age of 15. Lewis soon began to urge fellow workers to demand better and safer working

LEVEL 3: Have each student write a short imaginary dialogue between a striking worker and a member of the public or an official who opposes the strike. The dialogue should include the main reasons for the strike as well as the reaction of the person opposing the strike. *(See the Level 1 lesson for the correct causes and reactions.)* Students may wish to include the script for their dialogues in their portfolios.

TEACH OBJECTIVE 3

LEVEL 1: Have students study the political cartoon on this page. Then lead a discussion about the images depicted in the cartoon. Pair students and have each pair create two political cartoons that depict the causes of the public fears over the Red Scare. *(Pairs' cartoons should somehow reflect the fear of a Bolshevik revolution in the United States, the strikes of 1919, bomb scares in 1919, and the Palmer raids.)* Call on volunteers to display and explain their cartoons to the class. **Sheltered English, Cooperative Learning**

LEVEL 2: Organize students into small groups. Have each group write a short play summarizing the events of the Red Scare and capturing the public fears that resulted from those events. *(See the Level 1 lesson for the correct causes.)* Have volunteers perform their plays for the class. **Cooperative Learning**

conditions. By 1906 he had been elected as a representative to the UMW national convention. In 1911 American Federation of Labor founder Samuel Gompers recruited Lewis to become a field representative who would organize mine workers.

Lewis's experience as a miner and union organizer served him well during the 1919 strike. President Woodrow Wilson condemned the strike, which violated the union's wartime agreement not to strike, as a "grave moral and legal wrong." After Wilson ordered an injunction to halt the strike, Lewis declared the strike over. However, he quietly urged miners not to return to work. The strategy worked. On December 6, President Wilson designed a compromise package in which miners would receive a 14 percent wage increase. Lewis called off the strike, stating, "I will not fight my Government, the greatest government on earth." The UMW victory insured Lewis's position as a national labor leader. Lewis continued to push for miners' concerns until his death in 1969.

As with most of the strikes of 1919, public opinion did not side with labor during the UMW strike. Despite his many patriotic appeals, Lewis was accused of having ties to Bolsheviks in Russia and of urging revolution within the United States.

Read More About It

Free Find:
John L. Lewis

After reading about John L. Lewis on the **Holt Researcher** CD–ROM, write a short essay explaining how his experiences helped him lead the United Mine Workers union.

✔ **READING CHECK:** What were the main causes of the strikes in 1919? How did most Americans react to the strikes?

The Red Scare

The wave of strikes during 1919 struck fear into the hearts of many Americans. The 1919 strikes were prompted primarily by laborers' desires for a fair deal. Many Americans, however, saw the labor unrest as proof of a coming workers' revolution. Fear that a Bolshevik revolution would erupt in the United States reached its height during the **Red Scare**. This was a period of anticommunist hysteria during 1919 and 1920.

The Red Scare in the United States was a response to the 1917 revolution in Russia. This revolution resulted in the establishment of a communist government based on Marxist teachings. Under communism, the Russian government owned and controlled all private property, including every industry and factory. In 1919 Russia's Bolshevik leader Vladimir I. Lenin established an organization called the Communist International. It was designed to encourage a worldwide communist revolution by overthrowing capitalism and free enterprise. The idea that communism might take hold in the United States was frightening to many Americans during 1919.

Marxists in America. Karl Marx's message of an unavoidable working-class revolution has been interpreted in many ways over time. It even won some support in the United States. Labor leader Eugene Debs and others formed the Marxist-inspired Socialist Party in 1901. In contrast to the revolutionary Marxism of the Communist Party, Debs's Socialist Party foresaw a peaceful transition to socialism by democratic means. Debs ran for president five times between 1900 and 1920. His

INTERPRETING THE VISUAL RECORD

Red Scare. This cartoon entitled "Put Them Out & Keep Them Out" appeared in the *Philadelphia Inquirer* in 1919. ***What fears does this cartoon express?***

THE GRANGER COLLECTION, NEW YORK

DEMOCRATIC VALUES

The Aftermath of the Red Scare. As the Red Scare died down in the mid-1920s, the battle against radicalism continued in quieter, but sometimes more widespread ways. Some groups insisted that teachers take loyalty oaths and that textbooks "preach on every page a vivid love of America." In addition, corporations adopted the "American Plan," which was a pledge to maintain open shops. One business owner said, "You can hardly conceive of a more un-American, a more anti-American institution than the closed shop." Some businesses even used union spies and blacklists—lists of people who were union members—to maintain a nonunionized workforce.

ACTIVITY: Have each student choose a short passage from this chapter and rewrite it to represent "a vivid love of America."

VISUAL RECORD ANSWER

Students might suggest that the cartoon expresses fears of Bolshevism and anarchism infiltrating the United States.

LEVEL 3: Organize students into two groups and tell them to imagine that they are modern-day participants in a roundtable discussion entitled Public Fears over the Red Scare of 1919–20. Have one group act as historians and the other group act as facilitators and questioners. Have members of each group prepare notes to assist them in their specific roles, and then conduct the roundtable discussion. *(See the Level 1 lesson for the correct causes.)* To conclude, conduct a discussion on the roundtable gathering and the Red Scare itself. **Cooperative Learning**

TEACH OBJECTIVE 4

LEVEL 1: Pair students and have each pair write a paragraph explaining why the trial of Sacco and Vanzetti aroused public interest. *(Pairs should note that American society was deeply divided over the trial. Some people believed that Sacco and Vanzetti deserved punishment for their views. Others believed that the pair had been condemned to death because they were immigrant radicals and not because of the evidence presented.)* Have volunteers read their paragraphs to the class. **Sheltered English, Cooperative Learning**

DEMOCRATIC VALUES

The Palmer Raids. In the first months of his role as attorney general, A. Mitchell Palmer strongly defended individual rights. After he received a mail bomb, however, he became a leading figure in the war against radicals—a war that many felt abridged individual rights. The Palmer raids began in November 1919 and soon led many Americans to call for the deportation of the supposed radicals. Palmer himself indulged these calls. In December 1919 an army transport ship called the *Buford* ferried some 249 aliens to Finland, where officials loaded them on railroad cars and sent them to the Soviet Union.

CRITICAL THINKING Why might U.S. officials have ordered the supposed radicals to be sent to the Soviet Union?

ANSWER: Students might note that many radicals were suspected of Bolshevism. U.S. officials might have felt that the Soviet Union was an appropriate place for these radicals.

VISUAL RECORD ANSWER

(for p. 368)

Students might note that the signs call for boycotts and strikes and criticize the executioners.

Eugene Debs spread socialist political beliefs during his five bids for the presidency between 1900 and 1920.

Socialist Party platform called for the collective ownership of industry, which was to be achieved by nonviolent means. In the 1912 election Debs received about 900,000 votes.

When the Bolsheviks seized power in Russia in 1917, most American members of the Socialist Party joined Debs in refusing to support the violent overthrow of the government. A smaller number of American radicals did support the Bolsheviks. These Americans openly embraced Marx's revolutionary ideas. Some believed such a revolution should happen in the United States. Many Americans ignored the differences between socialists and communists. After witnessing the massive strikes of 1919, many people believed that all radicals and labor activists were Bolshevik agents who wanted to overthrow the U.S. government. Some Americans believed that communists, or "Reds," were everywhere. Immigrants, particularly those involved in unions, came under great suspicion. Antiradical fears reached such heights that several elected members of the New York State Assembly were expelled because of their membership in the Socialist Party.

RADICALS TRY TO DISRUPT ALL GREAT UNIONS

Efforts to Develop Recent Coal and Steel Strikes Into Real Revolution.

Definite Program to Expand Labor Disturbances for Purpose of Blotting Out Every Semblance of Organized Government—Most Menacing Plot in History of Country—Communist Agitators Infest Every Industrial Locality to Spread Propaganda of Unrest.

OFFICERS ACTIVE IN RUNNING DOWN THE ANARCHISTS

Immigration Station at New York Crowded With Deportation Candidates.

IMPLICATED IN DISPOSAL OF WOOD ALCOHOL BOOZE

THREE KIDS FROM CHICAGO ARRIVE HERE ON BIG HUNT

DAMPER TURNED ON ACTIVITIES OF SPOKANE I. W. W.

Judge Webster Issues Injunction Making It Contempt of Court to Preach or Teach Principles of Communism.

THIS IS NOT EMPTY ORDER

Further, He Declares That Organization Constitutes General Public Nuisance and Menace to This Country.

Attorney General A. Mitchell Palmer waged a public campaign against all perceived radicals.

The Palmer raids.

Many Americans interpreted a rash of bomb scares in 1919 as justification for their antiradical fears. The bomb scares further intensified the hysteria of the Red Scare. In April postal clerks discovered 36 bombs in the mail addressed to prominent citizens, including John D. Rockefeller, Justice Oliver Wendell Holmes of the Supreme Court, and Postmaster General Albert Burleson. Then, less than a month later, several bombings occurred. One bomb damaged the house of Attorney General A. Mitchell Palmer. The bomber, an Italian anarchist, died in the blast.

Newspapers began demanding harsh action against radicals. Hoping to further his presidential ambitions, Attorney General Palmer responded by launching an anticommunist crusade. He created a special government office to gather information on radical activities. Palmer placed J. Edgar Hoover, the future head of the Federal Bureau of Investigation, in charge.

Palmer's most dramatic action was a series of raids to capture alleged radicals. The **Palmer raids** began in November 1919. They peaked on January 2, 1920, when federal officials arrested thousands of suspected radicals in 33 cities nationwide. Although the government claimed that radicals were "armed to the teeth," just three pistols were seized during the raids.

Most of those arrested were poor immigrants who had recently arrived in the country. In most cases, there was no real evidence against them. Nevertheless, hundreds of foreigners suspected of radical activities were deported. Among the deportees was Emma Goldman, a noted feminist, writer, and speaker.

By the summer of 1920 public hysteria over radicalism was dying down. The predictions that a communist revolution was close at hand proved unfounded. Furthermore, many Americans had never supported the witch-hunting tactics employed by the anticommunist crusaders.

✔ **READING CHECK:** What caused the public hysteria of the Red Scare?

LEVELS 2 AND 3: Tell students to imagine that it is 1927 and they are newspaper editors after the execution of Sacco and Vanzetti. Have each student write a short editorial that explains the public interest in the trial of Sacco and Vanzetti. *(See the Level 1 lesson for the correct reasons.)* Based on the evidence presented in this chapter, students should explain to what extent or in what ways, if any, the Sacco and Vanzetti trial should be considered in the context of the Red Scare and hostility toward immigrants.

▶**ASSIGNMENT** *Tell students to read the quotation by John Dos Passos on the following page. Have each student create a collage to illustrate the meaning of his observation in the historical context discussed in this section.*

SPOTLIGHT
on Anarchists in Film

Have each student view a movie that portrays anarchist groups or individuals. Tell students to write a short analysis of the film's depiction of anarchists. **Block Scheduling**

NOTE: For an additional teaching idea, see the Chapter 12 interrupted film lesson in the **Creative Teaching Strategies** handbook.

Strategies for Success Evaluating News Stories

News stories are an extremely important resource for historians. Different types of news media contain an enormous amount of information that historians access regularly to help them create their accounts of the past. News stories, however, possess certain advantages and disadvantages as historical sources.

Although the print media frequently provide news coverage that is thorough and analytically sophisticated, this coverage lacks the sense of immediacy that is conveyed through the broadcast media. In contrast, radio and television reports often sacrifice detail and in-depth analysis of issues to provide news coverage that is as current as possible. In any case, all forms of news media must be examined carefully for fairness and accuracy in their presentation of events.

How to Evaluate a News Story

1. **Become familiar with the source.** First, determine whether the news story is presented through broadcast media or through print media. Then, if possible, find out about the historical background of the story's creator and the story's intended audience.
2. **Assess the story's coverage of events.** As you study the story, determine whether it covers its subject in sufficient depth. Check to see if it includes adequate background information and explores the possible consequences of events.
3. **Assess the fairness and accuracy of the reporting.** Examine the story carefully for fairness and accuracy in its presentation of events. Determine whether the reporting "sticks to the facts," explains any differing points of view in a balanced way, or displays any recognizable biases of its own.
4. **Put the information to use.** If possible, compare the story with other sources that address the same subject. Then use the results of your analysis, along with your knowledge of the historical period, to form generalizations and draw conclusions.

Applying the Strategy

Examine the following excerpt from a news story that appeared in the *Atlanta Constitution* on August 23, 1927.

> **"State Prison, Charlestown, Mass.—Nicola Sacco and Bartolomeo Vanzetti were put to death today.**
>
> **They went to the embrace of the electric chair unswerving in the avowal of their innocence.**
>
> **They paid with their lives for the murder of a paymaster and his guard at South Braintree seven years ago.**
>
> **As the heavy voltage of electricity was shot through their bodies, bayoneted guards surrounded the ancient prison for blocks.**
>
> **In cities on three continents millions awaited word of their death, many of them convinced that the two were executed for their political beliefs, not for the South Braintree murders."**

Practicing the Strategy

Use the excerpt above to answer the following questions.

1. Does this excerpt cover its subject in sufficient depth?
2. Is the reporting in the excerpt fair and accurate? What biases, if any, does it display?
3. How does the excerpt contribute to your understanding of the Red Scare?

Sacco and Vanzetti

Although the Red Scare passed, hostility toward foreigners and radicals persisted. One of the most sensational trials of the 1920s involved two Italian immigrants who were convicted of murder and sentenced to death. Although both were anarchists, they lived fairly quiet lives. Nicola Sacco was a shoemaker, and Bartolomeo Vanzetti peddled fish from a pushcart. Sacco and Vanzetti were charged with the murders of a paymaster and a guard during a 1920 payroll robbery outside a shoe factory near Boston. Upon arrest, the police found the men armed with pistols. After an intense interrogation, the two were charged with murder.

GLOBAL RELATIONS

An Urgent Appeal. People across the United States and in Europe protested the decision in the Sacco and Vanzetti case. Government officials from France, Germany, Great Britain, and Italy sent pleas for a new trial. Anatole France, a well-known French author, published an appeal to the "People of the United States." He wrote, "Save Sacco and Vanzetti. Save them for your honor, for the honor of your children, and for generations unborn."

CRITICAL THINKING Why might France have argued that saving Sacco and Vanzetti would save American honor?

ANSWER: Students might suggest that he meant that U.S. citizens would be dishonored by executing men who had not, in the opinion of many, been given a fair trial.

STRATEGIES FOR SUCCESS ANSWERS

Practicing the Strategy

1. The excerpt contains little background information about the crime or Sacco and Vanzetti's political beliefs.
2. It seems to stick to the facts of the execution, the prisoners' claims of innocence, and the public's opinions.
3. It expresses certain bare facts and also implies that officials expected some violent action during the execution, perhaps by the prisoners' radical supporters.

REVIEW

Have students complete the **Section 1 Review** on p. 368.

ASSESS

Have students complete **Daily Quiz 12.1**. As **Alternative Assessment**, you may want to use the political cartoons or editorial in this section's lessons.

RETEACH

Have students complete **Main Idea Activity for Reteaching and Sheltered English 12.1**. Then organize students into triads. Have each triad create a detailed outline of Section 1. Display triads' outlines around the classroom and ask students to examine them. Have each student note the topics or areas that are still confusing or unclear. Ask volunteers to share their topics or areas and conduct a brief discussion to correct the misunderstandings. **Sheltered English, Cooperative Learning**

EXTEND

Organize the class into small groups. Have groups gather information about the Sacco and Vanzetti trial, the artifacts of the trial, and commentary on the trial during the 1920s. Have each group organize and present a multimedia presentation on the Sacco and Vanzetti case. Students may want to include the scripts of their presentations in their portfolios.
Cooperative Learning, Block Scheduling

SECTION 1 REVIEW ANSWERS

Define and Identify
For significance, see the following pages:

- demobilization, p. 362
- Seattle general strike, p. 363
- Boston police strike, p. 363
- steel strike of 1919, p. 364
- United Mine Workers strike, p. 364
- John L. Lewis, p. 364
- Red Scare, p. 365
- A. Mitchell Palmer, p. 366
- Palmer raids, p. 366
- Nicola Sacco, p. 367
- Bartolomeo Vanzetti, p. 367

1. causes of strikes—high inflation, general economic problems, and demands for higher wages and shorter hours; public reaction—strikers were labeled as Bolsheviks, lost their jobs

2. created unemployment and other economic problems and caused many farmers to lose their farms

3. They were often conducted without valid evidence against the targeted parties.

4. People were already distrustful of immigrants and radicals, and many did not care whether the men were actually guilty. Many others around the world were outraged by the verdict.

5. Many Americans feared that a revolution similar to the 1917 revolution in Russia would occur in the United States.

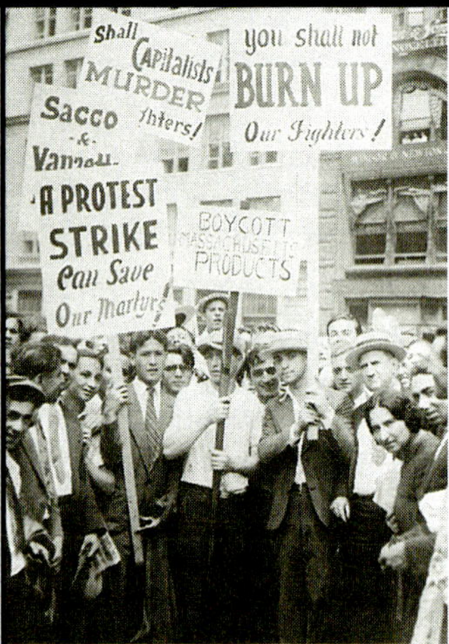

INTERPRETING THE VISUAL RECORD

Sacco and Vanzetti. The trial and execution of Sacco and Vanzetti divided liberals and conservatives during the 1920s. ***How do the picket signs reflect the views of the supporters of Sacco and Vanzetti?***

Sacco and Vanzetti were tried before Judge Webster Thayer, who was known for his strong dislike of radicals. The two immigrants' radical political views and their avoidance of military service in 1917 helped turn the trial against them. Eyewitnesses who could offer alibis for Sacco and Vanzetti were dismissed. The jury returned a guilty verdict. Judge Thayer sentenced the two to death. Judge Thayer ended the trial with a bold statement.

> **"This man [Vanzetti], although he may not actually have committed the crime attributed to him, is nevertheless morally culpable [guilty], because he is an enemy of our existing institutions. . . . The defendant's ideals are cognate [associated] with crime."**

The verdict outraged defenders of civil liberties. They argued that the two men had been convicted not because of the evidence presented but because they were immigrants and radicals. The verdict and subsequent appeals drew worldwide attention. In Paris, New York City, and elsewhere, thousands of people marched in protest. Noted writers and artists rallied to the cause. All pleas for a new trial failed. On August 23, 1927, Sacco and Vanzetti were executed. Many Americans believed that radicals like Sacco and Vanzetti deserved to be punished for their views, while others saw them as heroes. The guilt or innocence of Sacco and Vanzetti served as a subject of heated debate. Some recently discovered evidence indicates that at least one of the men probably was involved in the crime. What remains clear, however, is that antiradical views severely tainted the trial. The case reflected the deep divisions tearing at American society in the postwar era. As American novelist John Dos Passos declared after the execution, "We are two nations."

✔ **READING CHECK:** Why did the trial of Sacco and Vanzetti arouse public interest?

SECTION  REVIEW

Define and explain the significance of the following terms:
demobilization
Seattle general strike
Boston police strike
steel strike of 1919
United Mine Workers strike
Red Scare
Palmer raids

Identify and explain the significance of the following individuals:
John L. Lewis
A. Mitchell Palmer
Nicola Sacco
Bartolomeo Vanzetti

1. **Using Graphic Organizers** Copy the graphic organizer below. Use it to explain the causes of the strikes during 1919 and the public reaction to the strikes.

Causes of 1919 Strikes → Strikes → Public Reaction

2. **Assessing Consequences** How did the process of demobilization alter the lives of many women, factory workers, and farmers?
3. **Evaluating** Why were the tactics of the Palmer raids controversial?
4. **Identifying Cause and Effect** How did the political climate of the Red Scare influence the results of the Sacco and Vanzetti case? What effect did the trial's verdict have on public opinion?

Critical Thinking

5. How did international political events combine with postwar domestic life in the United States to lead to the mounting hysteria associated with the Red Scare?
Consider:
   - the events in Russia between 1917 and 1919
   - the role of socialists and communists in U.S. political life
   - labor unrest of 1919

After completing Section 2, students should be able to:

OBJECTIVE 1 *Describe how Republican policies encouraged economic growth.*

OBJECTIVE 2 *Evaluate the positive and negative effects of the Harding administration's pro-business policies.*

OBJECTIVE 3 *Analyze why the movement to pass the Equal Rights Amendment failed.*

OBJECTIVE 4 *Explain how the Republican Party overcame the political scandals of the Harding administration.*

OBJECTIVE 5 *Discuss the issues that affected the outcome of the 1928 presidential election.*

LET'S GET STARTED!

Write the following question on the chalkboard: *If you had been running for president in 1920, what platform would you have adopted to win?* Have students respond to the question in writing, using the information from Section 1. Tell students that in Section 2 they will learn about Republican policies during the 1920s.

The Republicans in Power

OBJECTIVES

Read to understand:

1. how Republican policies encouraged economic growth
2. what the positive and negative effects of the Harding administration's pro-business policies were
3. why the movement to pass the Equal Rights Amendment failed
4. how the Republican Party overcame the political scandals of the Harding administration
5. what issues affected the outcome of the 1928 presidential election

KEY TERMS

Fordney-McCumber Tariff Act
mergers
American Plan
feminists
Equal Rights Amendment
Teapot Dome scandal

KEY PEOPLE

Warren G. Harding
Andrew Mellon
Charles Dawes
Mary Anderson
Albert Fall
Calvin Coolidge
Alfred E. Smith

"Keep Warren [G. Harding] at home. Don't let him make any speeches. If he goes out on a tour somebody's sure to ask him questions, and Warren's just the sort of . . . fool that will try to answer them."

—Boies Penrose

Harding campaign sign

Pennsylvania Republican political boss Boies (BOYZ) Penrose gave advice to party leaders after the relatively unknown Ohio senator Warren G. Harding was nominated as the Republican presidential candidate for the 1920 election. Penrose and the rest of the Republican Party were confident that their party would win the election. Strikes and the Democrats' preoccupation with the League of Nations had characterized the previous two years. The Republican Party leaders, therefore, believed they had a sure shot at the presidency no matter who ran.

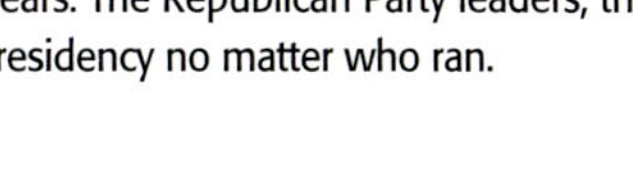

The Election of 1920

Seeking a presidential candidate with broad appeal, Republican Party leaders nominated Warren G. Harding. While many party members thought Senator Harding was friendly and looked presidential, he lacked Woodrow Wilson's intelligence. Confident of their chances to win the election, the Republican leaders did not feel their candidate had to be a political genius.

Harding ran on a pro-business, antilabor platform that promised tax revision, higher tariffs, limits on immigration, and some aid to farmers. What pleased war-weary voters the most, however, was Harding's call for a return to "normalcy." "America's present need is not heroics but healing, not nostrums [false cures] but normalcy, not revolution but restoration," he declared. In contrast, the Democratic candidate, Governor James M. Cox, also from Ohio, bowed to pressure from President Wilson and focused on the League of Nations during his campaign.

The nation's farmers, suffering from falling crop prices, rallied behind Harding. Many middle-class citizens, tired of labor strikes and high taxes, also voted Republican. Harding won the election of 1920 by a greater majority of the popular vote than any previous candidate. He received 16 million votes, more than 60 percent of the popular vote, and 404 electoral votes to Cox's 127. "It wasn't a landslide," suggested Joseph Tumulty. "It was an earthquake."

Harding's Pro-Business Administration

President Harding's administration introduced many policy changes. Harding's primary goal was providing "less government in business and more business in government." His cabinet included such successful business leaders as Secretary of

SECTION 2 RESOURCES

PRINT

- Guided Reading Strategy 12.2
- Geography Activity 12: The Republican Decade
- Primary Source Reading 12: A Scandalous Administration
- Section 2 Review, p. 374
- Daily Quiz 12.2

MULTIMEDIA

- One-Stop Planner, Lesson 12.2
- Holt Researcher: American History CD–ROM

SHELTERED ENGLISH

- Main Idea Activity for Reteaching and Sheltered English 12.2

✓ READING TO UNDERSTAND

To help students master the section objectives, have them answer the **READING CHECKS** and complete **Guided Reading Strategy 12.2** as they read the section.

TEACH OBJECTIVES 1 AND 2

LEVEL 1: Pair students and copy the graphic organizer at right on the chalkboard, omitting the italicized answers. Have each pair complete the graphic organizer. Ask volunteers for their answers. To conclude, lead a discussion on Republican economic policies and the positive and negative consequences of those pro-business policies.
Sheltered English, Cooperative Learning

REPUBLICAN POLICIES TO ENCOURAGE ECONOMIC GROWTH

To reduce debt:
1. *cuts in government spending*
2. *the Fordney-McCumber Tariff*

To promote economic growth:
1. *tax cut for the wealthy*

POSITIVE AND NEGATIVE EFFECTS OF REPUBLICAN POLICIES

Positive effects:
1. *boom in industry*
2. *economic growth*

Negative effects:
1. *mergers*
2. *continuing struggles for workers who did not share in prosperity*
3. *continuing struggles for farmers*
4. *continuing struggles for organized labor as the government and courts tried to roll back labor gains*

HISTORY MAKERS SPEAK

Warren G. Harding in *His Speech of Acceptance Upon his Nomination for the Presidency*

Harding and Industry. Warren G. Harding gave an acceptance speech when he was formally nominated as the Republican candidate for president. Harding called for cooperation between industry and laborers and referred to his prepolitical work experience, saying, "I want the employers in industry to understand the aspirations, the convictions, the yearnings of the millions of American wage-earners, and I want the wage-earners to understand the problems, the anxieties, the obligations of management and capital, and all of them must understand their relationship to the people and their obligation to the republic. . . . I am speaking as one who has counted the contents of the pay envelope from the view-point of the earner as well as the employer."

CRITICAL THINKING Do you think that Harding's policies met his call for workplace cooperation? Why or why not?

ANSWER: Answers will vary. Students might suggest that his policies did little to help workers and offered industrialists more opportunities for higher profits.

Then and Now

The Free Market

The United States has historically operated under a free-market economic system. Consumers and business leaders, not government officials, decide what, how, and for whom goods are produced. However, some political groups such as the Progressive Party have supported the regulation of some business practices.

The Republican administrations of the 1920s created several policies to reduce progressive controls over U.S. business practices. They hoped to encourage an even more open free-market system. "Business should be unhampered and free," President Coolidge argued.

Today the push for a free market has become an international issue. During the 1990s many countries began lowering trade barriers and removing restrictions on free-market practices. Governments have established trade agreements to allow an easier flow of goods between countries. These efforts have expanded the free market and increased economic prosperity. However, many modern Americans, like the progressives before them, are concerned that unregulated businesses fail to benefit everyone. Some companies have used free-trade agreements to get around U.S. labor laws preventing sweatshop labor. These corporations have moved production to underdeveloped countries where they can find workers willing to work long hours for little pay.

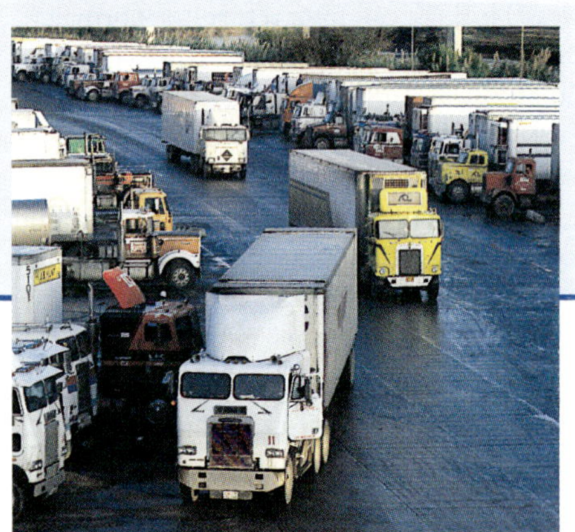

Trucks ship goods from American-owned factories in Mexico.

the Treasury Andrew Mellon and Secretary of Commerce Herbert Hoover. These men believed that government should not interfere with the economy except to aid business.

The administration set two main economic goals: to reduce the national debt and to promote economic growth. Wartime spending had raised the national debt from some $1 billion in 1914 to more than $25 billion in 1919. As head of the Bureau of the Budget, Charles Dawes set out to eliminate debt by slashing spending. In 1922 he succeeded in turning the government's annual budget deficit into a surplus.

The Republican-led Congress further supported businesses by passing the **Fordney-McCumber Tariff Act** in 1922. The law pushed tariff rates on manufactured goods to an all-time high. This helped U.S. manufacturers by enabling them to keep prices high and increase profits.

To achieve the second goal—economic growth—Mellon proposed eliminating the high wartime taxes imposed on the wealthy. If "government takes away an unreasonable share," he argued, "the incentive [encouragement] to work is no longer there and slackening of effort is the result." He claimed that if taxes were lower the rich would have more money to invest and the economy would grow. Mellon argued that the benefits would then trickle down to the middle and lower classes in the form of jobs and higher wages. In accordance with Mellon's proposal, Congress cut taxes for wealthy Americans during the 1920s.

By 1923 Harding's economic policy appeared to be working. The postwar slump was over. Unemployment was low and most sectors of the economy had entered a period of tremendous growth.

✔ **READING CHECK:** How did Republican policies encourage economic growth?

The Effects of Republican Policies

President Harding's pro-business policies significantly affected the economy and the lives of many Americans. The availability of surplus capital from tax cuts caused industry to boom. More than 1,000 **mergers**—the combining of two or more companies—took place in this era of rapid growth. Businesses favored mergers because they brought greater efficiency and higher profits. By 1930 some 200 corporations owned nearly half of the nation's corporate wealth. With its favorable attitude toward business, the federal government encouraged this process of consolidation. The government also made little effort to enforce antitrust laws.

For the most part, workers did not share in the business prosperity of the 1920s. From 1923 to 1929, business profits increased some 60 percent. Over the

LEVELS 2 AND 3: Tell students to imagine that they are producing an educational filmstrip about Republican economic policies during the Harding administration and the positive and negative impact of those policies. *(See the graphic organizer for the correct policies and their effects.)* Then pair students and have each pair create a frame-by-frame presentation of the information it would include in its filmstrip. Have students present their storyboards to the class. **Cooperative Learning**

▶**ASSIGNMENT:** *Distribute Activity 12, The Republican Decade, from **Geography Activities**, and have each student complete it.*

TEACH OBJECTIVE 3

LEVEL 1: Conduct a brief discussion on the Equal Rights Amendment and why the movement to pass the amendment failed. Then pair students and have each pair use the information from the discussion to write a paragraph explaining why the amendment failed. *(Pairs' paragraphs should indicate that political divisions and dissensions caused the amendment to falter. Women who opposed the ERA believed that protective legislation regulating the hours and working conditions of women would be declared illegal if the amendment were passed.)* Have volunteers read their paragraphs to the class. **Sheltered English, Cooperative Learning**

same period, however, workers' incomes grew by about 10 percent. Many workers in so-called sick industries such as the textile industry faced pay cuts and unemployment.

Farmers also struggled. Although the Fordney-McCumber Tariff was intended to help agriculture as well as business, it brought little relief to farmers. The act levied high duties on imported farm products in an effort to boost American crop prices. However, farmers continued to face shrinking markets, low prices, high interest rates, and crushing debt.

Organized labor also suffered during the 1920s. The government and courts sought to roll back the labor gains of the Progressive Era. Federal courts, for example, upheld "yellow-dog contracts," which prevented workers from joining unions. Business leaders promoted a policy known as the **American Plan**, which supported union-free open shops. As a result, union membership shrank from a high of more than 5 million in 1920 to some 3.6 million in 1923.

INTERPRETING THE VISUAL RECORD

Business. Industries like this chemical factory benefited from weakened federal regulations in the 1920s. ***What hazards might this factory pose?***

✔ **READING CHECK:** What were the positive and negative results of Harding's pro-business policies?

New Directions for Women

Working conditions also became a divisive issue among women's rights activists, often called **feminists**. The Nineteenth Amendment had granted women the right to vote. However, it did not revolutionize U.S. politics as many Americans had hoped—or feared. The suffrage issue had unified women with a wide variety of political interests, but after its passage, that unity dissolved.

Many women who had joined the suffrage campaign now moved in different directions. Jane Addams pursued the cause of world peace through the Women's International League for Peace and Freedom. Carrie Chapman Catt and other former suffrage leaders formed the League of Women Voters. Its aim was to inform women about public issues and about candidates for office.

Divisions in the women's movement emerged in the debate over the **Equal Rights Amendment** (ERA). This was a constitutional amendment proposed to Congress in 1923 by Alice Paul of the National Woman's Party. The proposed amendment stated: "Men and women shall have equal rights throughout the United States and every place subject to its jurisdiction."

Equal rights for women seemed a desirable goal. However, Paul's amendment met opposition from many reformers, including women. During the Progressive Era, reformers had battled for legislation regulating the hours and the working conditions of female workers. Mary Anderson, director of the U.S. Women's Bureau, was one of the opponents of the ERA who feared that the amendment would make such legislation unconstitutional:

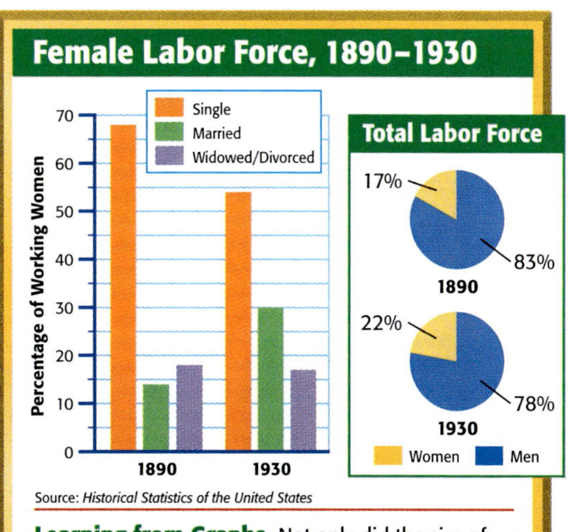

Source: *Historical Statistics of the United States*

Learning from Graphs Not only did the size of the female labor force grow by 1930, its makeup also changed. By 1930 some 30 percent of working women were married, up from just over 10 percent in 1890.

Building Graph Skills Women made up what percentage of the total labor force in 1890? in 1930?

DEMOCRATIC VALUES

Female Voters. Despite the newfound right to vote, guaranteed in the Nineteenth Amendment, many women did not exercise their political liberties during the 1920s. Those who did vote often followed familial preferences in terms of candidates or parties rather than developing their own independent selections. In part to disseminate information to female voters and in part to replace the National Woman Suffrage Association, Carrie Chapman Catt founded the League of Women Voters in 1920.

CRITICAL THINKING Why might many women have chosen to abstain from voting during the 1920s?

ANSWER: Students might suggest that some women did not want the right to vote and so did not exercise it once granted.

VISUAL RECORD ANSWER

Students might identify hazards such as congestion and air pollution.

GRAPH ANSWERS

17 percent in 1890; 22 percent in 1930

LEVELS 2 AND 3: Tell students to imagine that they belong to the editorial board of a women's magazine of the 1920s. As members of the board, they have decided to include articles in their magazine that articulate both positions on the passage of the Equal Rights Amendment (ERA). Tell half of the students in the class to write an editorial supporting the ERA, and have the other half write an editorial opposing the ERA. *(See the Level 1 lesson for the correct reasons.)* Have volunteers read their editorials to the class. To conclude, conduct a brief discussion on why the amendment failed.

TEACH OBJECTIVE 4

LEVEL 1: Pair students and tell them to imagine that they are members of the Republican Party's Platform Committee prior to the party's 1924 convention. Have each pair write an outline for a platform on which Calvin Coolidge will run for election. *(Pairs' platforms should indicate that Coolidge will work to limit the damage from the Harding scandals and will restore the reputation of the presidency. Coolidge will continue to promote pro-business policies.)* Have volunteers read their platforms to the class.

Sheltered English, Cooperative Learning

PEOPLE IN HISTORY

Alice Paul. Alice Paul's determination to ensure equal rights for women put her at the forefront of the women's suffrage movement and for the battle to pass the Equal Rights Amendment. Paul, a New Jersey native, studied at universities in the United States and Great Britain. While in Britain she became involved in the suffrage movement and was arrested three times during protests. After returning to the United States, Paul earned her Ph.D. and continued working for women's suffrage. As head of the National Woman's Party, Paul encouraged her organization to picket the White House and to go on hunger strikes. She was arrested three more times during such activities and was even force-fed while on a hunger strike during her imprisonment. Paul and her followers protested their arrests by claiming that they were political prisoners of their own government.

CRITICAL THINKING Why might Paul have considered herself a political prisoner?

ANSWER: Students might suggest that she felt that she was being held in jail for expressing her beliefs but not for breaking any laws.

Many working-class women saw the Equal Rights Amendment as a middle-class issue that would remove the protective legislation passed during the reform era.

> **"Women who are wage earners, with one job in the factory and another in the home, have little time and energy left to carry on the fight to better their economic status. They need the help of . . . labor laws."**

Supporters of the ERA argued that special legislation for women actually hurt female job seekers, particularly in male-dominated occupations. Employers were discouraged from hiring or promoting women, they claimed, because of legal limitations on the hours women were allowed to work. In the end, the ERA movement failed to win political support.

✔ **READING CHECK:** Why did the movement to pass the Equal Rights Amendment fail?

The Enduring Republican Presidency

The proposal for the Equal Rights Amendment came as President Harding's administration was facing a storm of political scandals. Charges of political wrongdoing by members of the Harding administration began to surface in 1923. They cast a dark shadow over the highest levels of national government.

The Harding scandals. The scandals came to light during the midpoint of Harding's only term in office. A group of Harding's friends known as the Ohio Gang had followed him to Washington, D.C. They were using their connections to the president to enrich themselves at the public's expense.

The first scandal surfaced in the spring of 1923. It was discovered that Charles Forbes, Harding's close friend and director of the Veterans' Bureau, had pocketed millions of dollars through corrupt schemes. Harding was deeply worried by the Forbes scandal and other evidence of wrongdoing in his administration. In June 1923 he confessed to journalist William Allen White, "I have no trouble with my enemies. I can take care of my enemies all right. [It's my] friends . . . that keep me walking the floor nights." Soon after talking to White, Harding set out on an extended tour of the West. On August 2 he died suddenly of an apparent heart attack in San Francisco.

INTERPRETING THE VISUAL RECORD

Teapot Dome scandal. Episodes of corruption like the Teapot Dome scandal threatened the Harding administration's public support. ***How does this cartoon illustrate the danger of the scandal to the Republican administration?***

After Harding's death other scandals were revealed. In 1924 Attorney General Harry Daugherty, who had exposed Forbes's corruption to Harding, came under suspicion himself. The Senate began to investigate Daugherty for his failure to end high-level corruption. The inquiry soon revealed that Daugherty was taking bribes. The attorney general was forced to resign.

The most noted episode of corruption during the Harding administration, the **Teapot Dome scandal**, became news early in 1924. Investigators discovered that in the early months of the Harding administration, Secretary of the Interior Albert Fall had persuaded Secretary of the Navy Edwin Denby to transfer control of naval oil reserves to his department. Fall granted private leases to the oil reserves in Elk

LEVELS 2 AND 3: Tell students to imagine that they are presidential historians who are writing a history of the Coolidge administration. Have each student write a short analysis describing the election of 1924 and explaining how Coolidge successfully overcame the political scandals of the Harding administration to win the election. *(See the Level 1 lesson for the correct details.)* Have students read their analyses to the class.

TEACH OBJECTIVE 5

LEVEL 1: Tell students to imagine that they are political analysts during the 1928 election. Then have each student write a few sentences on the issues that affected the outcome of the 1928 presidential election. *(Students should note that Herbert Hoover had a reputation for administrative skill and efficiency and enjoyed the legacy of prosperity during Republican rule. Al Smith was supported by urban immigrant voters. However, he was a Catholic, opposed prohibition, and had ties to Tammany Hall.)* Have volunteers read their sentences to the class. **Sheltered English**

LEVELS 2 AND 3: Tell students to imagine that it is December 1928 and that they are reporters preparing an election wrap-up. Have each student write a short article describing and assessing the presidential election of 1928. Remind students that their articles should focus on the issues that affected the outcome of the election. *(See the Level 1 lesson for the correct issues.)* Have volunteers read their articles to the class.

Hills, California, and the Teapot Dome reserves in Wyoming. In return, Fall received personal loans, cash, and cattle. Fall was convicted of accepting bribes and jailed.

Coolidge takes charge. After Harding's death, Vice President Calvin Coolidge was sworn in as president. He immediately began working to limit the damage from the Harding scandals and to restore the reputation of the presidency. Coolidge's administration contrasted greatly with the Harding administration. Known as Silent Cal, Coolidge's stern, reserved nature contrasted with Harding's outgoing personality. However, Coolidge continued to promote Harding's popular pro-business policies since the national economy was booming.

Coolidge easily won the Republican presidential nomination in 1924. The Democrats were split over issues such as prohibition. They voted 103 times before finally chosing John W. Davis, a corporate lawyer, as their candidate. Both parties faced strong opposition from the Progressive Party's nominee, Robert La Follette. Backed by angry farmers and workers, the Progressive platform denounced federal policies favoring business and called for increased aid to working people.

Despite rumblings of discontent, Coolidge won by a landslide, receiving 15.7 million votes to Davis's 8.4 million. La Follette received some 4.8 million votes. The Progressive Party faded from the scene when La Follette died soon after the election. Nevertheless, its strong showing in the election made it clear that not all Americans agreed with the Republicans' pro-business policies.

During the 1924 presidential election, Coolidge supporters published songbooks such as this one to build strength for his campaign.

Coolidge's pro-business position. A dedicated conservative, Coolidge was even more pro-business than Harding. "The business of America is business," he declared. Coolidge often invited prominent business leaders for social engagements at the White House. Coolidge favored legislation to aid business. With his support, Congress passed the Revenue Act of 1926, which repealed the gift tax, cut estate taxes in half, and reduced taxes on the wealthy. Coolidge expected these tax cuts would further the economic prosperity of the country.

Coolidge also took a tightfisted approach to government spending. By keeping spending low, Coolidge made possible both a tax cut and further reductions in the national debt. He vetoed spending bills such as a bonus bill designed to aid World War I veterans. He also vetoed the McNary-Haugen Bill, which was designed to boost farm prices by authorizing the government to buy surplus crops and sell them abroad. Coolidge generally opposed laws designed to help farmers or workers. He argued that such legislation limited private initiative and harmed the economy.

The president remained popular throughout his term and almost certainly could have won re-election in 1928. Instead, to almost everyone's surprise, he announced that he would not run. Speaking privately to his staff, Coolidge admitted that he found the work of the presidency burdensome. He looked forward to returning to a life of leisure at his home in Northampton, Massachusetts.

Calvin Coolidge kept his campaign promise to support business. Here he meets with some of the country's most-prominent business leaders.

✔ **READING CHECK:** How did the Republican Party overcome the political scandals of the Harding administration?

THAT'S INTERESTING!

In 1925 Congress passed the Air Mail Act, giving government contracts to commercial air carriers. In the early 1930s a minor scandal resulted from the discovery that government officials had been awarding the contracts to chosen companies without allowing competitive bidding.

VISUAL RECORD ANSWER

(for p. 372)

Students might suggest that the cartoon illustrates that the scandal had potential to "steamroll" the administration.

VISUAL RECORD ANSWER

(p. 374)

Students might note that the table mat, at least, was a highly useful item.

REVIEW

Have students complete the **Section 2 Review** on p. 374.

ASSESS

Have students complete **Daily Quiz 12.2.** As **Alternative Assessment**, you may want to use the Republican policies filmstrip or the party platform in this section's lessons.

RETEACH

Have students complete **Main Idea Activity for Reteaching and Sheltered English 12.2.** Then prepare a set of index cards for each of the Section 1 objectives—each card should include a single key term or key person related to the objective. Organize the class into small groups. Assign one objective to each group, and give each group the prepared cards for its assigned objective. Have the students arrange the cards in an order that will enable them to discuss the objective. Call on each group to answer the question in front of the class, using the index cards as visual prompts to help the rest of the class follow the group's presentation. **Sheltered English, Cooperative Learning**

EXTEND

Tell students to imagine that they are newspaper reporters who are planning to conduct an interview with Alice Paul, Mary Anderson, or Carrie Chapman Catt. Have each student conduct research on one of the women and prepare a transcript of an imaginary interview with her. **Block Scheduling**

SECTION 2 REVIEW ANSWERS

Define and Identify

For significance, see the following pages:

- Warren G. Harding, p. 369
- Andrew Mellon, p. 370
- Charles Dawes, p. 370
- Fordney-McCumber Tariff Act, p. 370
- mergers, p. 370
- American Plan, p. 371
- feminists, p. 371
- Equal Rights Amendment, p. 371
- Mary Anderson, p. 371
- Teapot Dome scandal, p. 372
- Albert Fall, p. 372
- Calvin Coolidge, p. 373
- Alfred E. Smith, p. 374

1. economic factors–prosperity encouraged Republican votes; Smith's weaknesses–his connections to Tammany Hall, his Catholicism, and his anti-prohibition stance; Hoover's strengths–reputation for skill and efficiency and connection to national prosperity

2. Their trickle-down policies enabled wealthy business owners to save money and expand their businesses.

3. wanted to ensure women's equal rights in all areas and to counter employment discrimination; failed due to a lack of unity and cohesion

4. Answers will vary. Students might note pro-business support or general prosperity.

5. Answers will vary. Students might suggest that Coolidge had shown himself to be reserved and frugal and had offered economic prosperity to at least part of the population.

The Election of 1928

In 1928 the Republican Party nominated Secretary of Commerce Herbert Hoover for president. Hoover had a reputation for administrative skill and efficiency. His strongest asset, though, was the nation's apparent prosperity after eight years of Republican rule. He referred to this prosperity in a campaign speech.

> "The poorhouse is vanishing from among us. We have not yet reached the goal, but, given a chance to go forward with the policies of the last eight years, we shall soon . . . be in sight of the day when poverty will be banished from this nation."

After a bitter fight, the Democrats nominated Governor Alfred E. Smith of New York, a moderate progressive. The party's choice signaled a shift in Democratic strategy—a response, in part, to the Progressive Party's strength in the 1924 election. Smith's core support came from urban immigrant voters. By nominating Smith, the Democrats hoped to be seen as "the party of progress and liberal thought," as vice presidential candidate Franklin Roosevelt put it. Many Americans opposed Smith because of his Catholic faith. They feared that a Catholic president might hand control of the United States over to the pope in Rome. Others worried that Smith opposed prohibition and had ties to New York City's Tammany Hall.

Smith's political weaknesses and the country's economic strength carried Hoover to victory. He received 58 percent of the popular vote. Smith lost his own state as well as several southern states that went Republican for the first time since Reconstruction. However, Smith did well in the nation's largest cities. His appeal to these urban voters offered the Democrats hope for the future.

INTERPRETING THE VISUAL RECORD

Herbert Hoover. During the 1928 election, Hoover ran on the same pro-business policies that Presidents Harding and Coolidge had supported. *How do you think these Hoover campaign items appealed to voters?*

✔ **READING CHECK:** What issues affected the outcome of the 1928 election?

SECTION 2 REVIEW

Define and explain the significance of the following terms:

Fordney-McCumber Tariff Act
mergers
American Plan
feminists
Equal Rights Amendment
Teapot Dome scandal

Identify and explain the significance of the following individuals:

Warren G. Harding
Andrew Mellon
Charles Dawes
Mary Anderson
Albert Fall
Calvin Coolidge
Alfred E. Smith

1. **Using Graphic Organizers** Copy the graphic organizer below. Use it to explain how each part of the pyramid helped lead to Herbert Hoover's victory in the 1928 election.

2. **Assessing Consequences** How did Republican pro-business policies encourage economic growth?
3. **Analyzing** Why did the National Woman's Party push for an Equal Rights Amendment? What factors prevented the amendment from gaining support?
4. **Using Historical Imagination** Imagine that you are a political analyst in 1928. What conclusions would you draw as to why the Republican Party was able to maintain control of the presidency?

Critical Thinking

5. Why do you think Calvin Coolidge won the 1924 election despite being vice president in Harding's scandal-ridden administration?
   Consider:
   - what Coolidge achieved in his term as president before the election
   - the differences between Harding and Coolidge
   - the significance of economic prosperity

After completing Section 3, students should be able to:

OBJECTIVE 1 *Explain why many Americans supported the Ku Klux Klan and what factors led to a decline in that support.*

OBJECTIVE 2 *Identify the actions that African Americans took to combat discrimination and violence.*

OBJECTIVE 3 *Discuss why many Americans demanded restrictions on immigration.*

OBJECTIVE 4 *State why Mexican immigration increased during the 1920s.*

OBJECTIVE 5 *Recount the actions that American Indians took to protect their land.*

LET'S GET STARTED!

As students enter the classroom, tell them to cite, in writing, historical reasons for hostility toward migrants and immigrants. Ask volunteers to share their responses. Tell students that in Section 3 they will learn about divisions in American society during the 1920s.

A Nation Divided

OBJECTIVES

Read to understand:

1. why many Americans supported the Ku Klux Klan, and what factors led to a decline in that support
2. what actions African Americans took to combat discrimination and violence
3. why many Americans demanded restrictions on immigration
4. why Mexican immigration increased during the 1920s
5. what actions American Indians took to protect their land

KEY TERMS

Brotherhood of Sleeping Car Porters
Pan-Africanism
black nationalism
Universal Negro Improvement Association
Immigration Act of 1924
Bursum Bill

KEY PEOPLE

William Joseph Simmons
David Stephenson
A. Philip Randolph
Marcus Garvey

EYEWITNESSES TO History

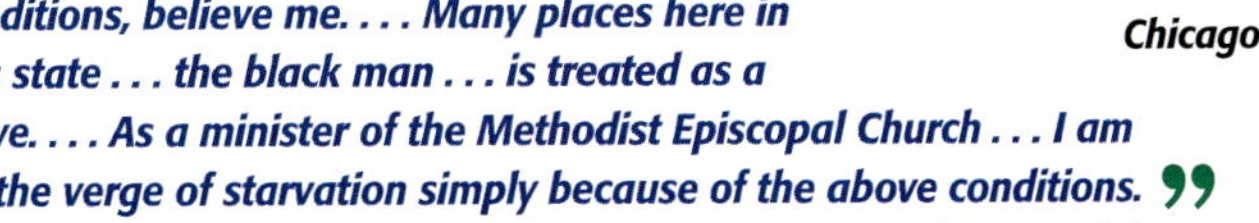

"Doubtless you have learned of the great exodus of our people to the north and west from this and other southern states. I wish to say that we are forced to go when . . . a grown man[']s] wages is only fifty to seventy five cents per day for all grades of work. He is compelled to go where there is better wages and sociable conditions, believe me. . . . Many places here in this state . . . the black man . . . is treated as a slave. . . . As a minister of the Methodist Episcopal Church . . . I am on the verge of starvation simply because of the above conditions."

—Alabama minister

Chicago Defender

…Y'S DISAPPEARANCE BAFFLES THE

Chicago Defender

In the spring of 1917 an African American minister from Alabama wrote this letter to the editors of the Chicago *Defender*. A weekly newspaper, the *Defender* covered the plight of African Americans in the South as well as the North. The *Defender* routinely encouraged African Americans from the South to migrate to northern cities. It contrasted the harsh conditions of the South with tales of freedom and jobs in the North. Although the North was not free of discrimination and racism, thousands of African Americans decided to try to better their lives by leaving the South to settle in northern cities.

African Americans Move North

During the 1920s some 800,000 African Americans joined the hundreds of thousands of African Americans who had moved to the North during World War I. By 1930 the North's African American population had reached almost 2.5 million, more than double its size in 1910. Large African American communities sprang up in Chicago, Detroit, New York City, and other northern cities.

Reasons for the move. African Americans who moved to the North searching for economic opportunities also longed for a new life free from discrimination. A migrant from Georgia who had left domestic work behind for a job in a Chicago box factory exclaimed, "I'll never work in nobody's kitchen but my own any more. No indeed! That's the one thing that makes me stick to this job. You do have some time to call your own."

However, the North was not free of prejudice. African Americans living in the North encountered racial violence and lynch mobs as well as discrimination. As the demand for labor lessened during the recession of the early 1920s, African Americans were often the first to lose their jobs.

Violence erupts. Racial tension mounted with the move of African Americans from southern farms to cities. This tension sometimes erupted in violence. One of the worst incidents occurred in Chicago in July 1919. The trouble began when a

Many African Americans moved to northern cities in search of jobs.

SECTION 3 RESOURCES

PRINT

- Guided Reading Strategy 12.3
- Biography Reading 12: A. Philip Randolph
- Section 3 Review, p. 381
- Daily Quiz 12.3

MULTIMEDIA

- One-Step Planner, Lesson 12.3
- The American Nation Video Program Segment: A Nation of Immigrants; Teacher's Guide, pp. 153–57
- Holt Researcher: American History CD–ROM
- HRW Web Site

SHELTERED ENGLISH

- Main Idea Activity for Reteaching and Sheltered English 12.3

✔ READING TO UNDERSTAND

To help students master the section objectives, have them answer the **READING CHECKS** and complete **Guided Reading Strategy 12.3** as they read the section.

TEACH OBJECTIVE 1

ALL LEVELS: Conduct a brief discussion on why many Americans supported the Ku Klux Klan during the 1920s. To help students understand why the Klan declined, copy the graphic organizer at right on the chalkboard, omitting the italicized answers. Have each student complete it. **Sheltered English**

Rise of the Ku Klux Klan

- *racism toward African Americans in the South*
- *hostility toward African Americans, Catholics, immigrants, Jews, and suspected radicals in the North*
- *rising tensions and suspicions during the Red Scare*

Fall of the Ku Klux Klan

- *decrease in Red Scare tensions*
- *publicity of the Klan's terrorism*
- *corruption and scandals at the Klan's national level*

HISTORY MAKERS SPEAK

William Allen White and Oscar Ameringer in *Redeeming the Time*

Speaking Out Against the Klan. Political activists spoke out against the influence of the Ku Klux Klan. William Allen White wrote a tirade against Klan principles. White called the Klan "a self-constituted body of moral idiots" and "an organization of cowards." Oscar Ameringer mocked the Klan's beliefs by imagining their logical conclusion: "Unless these people are driven out of the country or are shown their proper places, the Reds will raise the . . . flag of socialism over the Capitol . . . (and) the unions wipe out what little business peace is left. . . . Just see what this latest lunacy is doing to your town."

CRITICAL THINKING Why might Ameringer's statement have been effective in revealing the absurdity of Klan beliefs?

ANSWER: Answers will vary. Students might suggest that Ameringer showed the unlikelihood of Klan beliefs and arguments.

MAP ANSWER

California, Illinois, Michigan, New Jersey, Nevada, New York, Ohio, Pennsylvania, and Wisconsin

African American Population Changes, 1920–1930

Learning from Maps The great increase of African Americans in some northern states meant a decline in numbers in some other states.

MOVEMENT In which states did the African American population more than double?

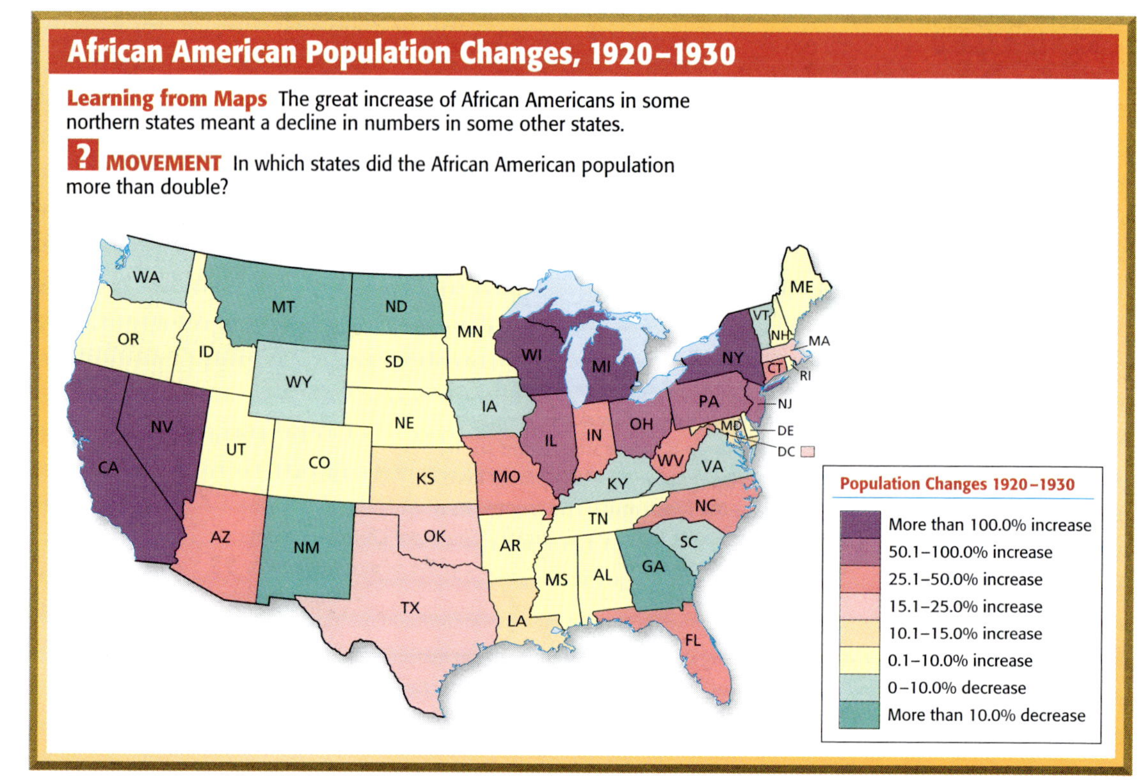

white man threw rocks at an African American teenager swimming in Lake Michigan. The boy drowned. When the police refused to arrest anyone, fights broke out between whites and African Americans on shore and quickly spread to the rest of the city. The rioting continued for more than a week. White gangs prowling the slums were responsible for much of the violence. They attacked African Americans and destroyed property. By the time order was restored, 38 people had been killed and 537 injured.

By late 1919 some 25 race riots had erupted around the country. In June 1921 at least 30 people died during a race riot in Tulsa, Oklahoma. One resident described attacks on the African American section of town, "People were seen to flee from their burning homes, some with babes in their arms." The violence prompted African American soldiers with World War I combat experience to attempt to defend their communities. "The colored troops fought nobly," wrote one African American to a friend in Washington, D.C., after the riots in that city. "We have something to fight for now."

During 1919, race riots erupted around the country. Damage from fires left neighborhoods like this one in Chicago in ruins.

The Return of the Ku Klux Klan

One sign of growing racism was the rebirth of the Ku Klux Klan, which had officially dissolved during Reconstruction. The new Klan was established in 1915 at Stone Mountain, Georgia, by a preacher named William Joseph Simmons. Like the Klan of post–Civil War days, the new Klan carried out kidnappings, beatings, and lynchings to terrorize African Americans in the South. The new Klan also grew

TEACH OBJECTIVE 2

LEVEL 1: Pair students and tell each pair to create three political buttons that describe how the NAACP, A. Philip Randolph, and Marcus Garvey worked to end discrimination or violence against African Americans. *(Pairs' buttons should reflect that the NAACP organized an antilynching campaign, A. Philip Randolph established the Brotherhood of Sleeping Car Porters, and Marcus Garvey supported black nationalism and founded UNIA.)* Have students display their buttons around the classroom and explain them to the class.
Sheltered English, Cooperative Learning

LEVELS 2 AND 3: Organize students into triads. Have each triad create scripts for radio commercials during the 1920s that publicize the campaigns of the NAACP, A. Philip Randolph, and Marcus Garvey to end discrimination against African Americans. *(See the Level 1 lesson for the correct actions.)* Have volunteers perform their radio commercials for the class.
Cooperative Learning

rapidly outside of the South. In northern and midwestern towns and cities, the Klan targeted not only African Americans but also Catholics, immigrants, Jews, and suspected radicals.

The Klan grew slowly at first, but as the Red Scare took hold, membership soared. The group reached its peak in the mid-1920s. At one time it had perhaps as many as 5 million members. The Klan staged mass rallies where white-robed members burned crosses and spoke out against groups and ideas they considered undesirable. It also worked to help candidates win elections in such states as Louisiana, Ohio, Oklahoma, Oregon, and Texas. The group was particularly powerful in Indiana.

The Klan's rapid rise during the early 1920s was followed by an equally speedy fall in the late 1920s. By 1930 the Klan's membership had dropped to some 9,000. The decline in popular support of the Klan resulted from several factors. Particularly significant was a decrease in the hysteria surrounding the Red Scare. With the economy booming and anxiety about radicalism declining, the Klan's message of fear lost its appeal.

Publicity of the Klan's terrorism and violence also led to the shrinking of the organization's ranks. Newspapers nationwide published investigative articles that exposed the violence of local Klan chapters. With the national leadership of the Ku Klux Klan unable to control the actions of its local chapters, many people began to speak out against the group.

Corruption and scandals at the national level of the organization also led to the decline of the Klan. People began to turn away from the Klan when investigations revealed that Klan promoters were getting rich from membership fees and sales of various Klan products. The conviction of Grand Dragon David Stephenson for second-degree murder also hurt the Klan. In the face of scandals, many local chapters broke away from the national organization. Nevertheless, the Klan did not completely die out.

✔ **READING CHECK:** Why did many Americans support the Ku Klux Klan? What factors led to a decline in this support?

INTERPRETING THE VISUAL RECORD
Ku Klux Klan. During the 1920s the Ku Klux Klan held rallies to build support for the organization and to spread its ideas. ***What symbols did the Klan members use in their rallies?***

African Americans Defend Their Rights

Faced with continued violence and discrimination from the Ku Klux Klan and other groups, many African Americans took action to defend their rights. During the 1920s African Americans created several organizations dedicated to the prevention of discrimination and acts of violence.

Antilynching campaign. One early effort to stop the violence committed against African Americans came from the National Association for the Advancement of Colored People (NAACP). The NAACP formed the Antilynching Committee to generate support for antilynching legislation. It also put pressure on law enforcement officials to investigate acts of violence against African Americans. In the articles of its monthly magazine, *The Crisis*, the NAACP publicized lynching

Supporters of the NAACP campaign to end lynchings in the United States wore buttons such as this one to spread their message.

PEOPLE IN HISTORY

Jessie Daniel Ames. In the 1920s and 1930s many white southern women came together to convince southern men to stop participating in and condoning lynchings. Jessie Daniel Ames, a white woman, helped found the Association of Southern Women for the Prevention of Lynching (ASWPL). Besides the usual writing, speaking, and community and church organizing, Ames searched for innovative ways to help people understand the horror of lynching. She sponsored contests for plays that addressed racial violence. She persistently attacked the press for perpetuating notions of female vulnerability and African American inferiority.

CRITICAL THINKING Why might the press have been a useful ally for Ames?

ANSWER: Students might argue that an alliance with the press would lead to sympathetic stories.

VISUAL RECORD ANSWER
Students might identify the cross and the American flag.

Teacher to Teacher

James Pyne of Flossmoor, Illinois, suggested the following activity: Organize students into small groups. Have each group evaluate the effectiveness of campaigns led by W. E. B. Du Bois, A. Philip Randolph, and Marcus Garvey in the 1920s to end violence and discrimination against African Americans. Groups should establish standard criteria for evaluating each campaign. Have each group write a report about its findings and present its report to the class.

TEACH OBJECTIVE 3

LEVEL 1: Pair students and have each pair create a chart to depict why many Americans demanded restrictions on immigration in the 1920s. *(Pairs should note the increase in immigration and the belief that immigrants were political radicals who took jobs from native-born Americans.)* **Sheltered English, Cooperative Learning**

LEVELS 2 AND 3: Tell students to imagine that it is 1922 and that they are recent immigrants. Have each student write a letter to a relative back home describing and explaining the anti-immigrant sentiments of many Americans. *(See the Level 1 lesson for the correct reasons.)* Have volunteers read their letters to the class.

internet connect

TOPIC: Marcus Garvey and W. E. B. Du Bois
GO TO: go.hrw.com
KEYWORD: SE1 Garvey

Have students access the Internet through the HRW Web site to conduct research on Marcus Garvey and W. E. B Du Bois. Then have each student create a graphic organizer that compares and contrasts the thoughts and actions of the two men. Students might make a chart with headings for Garvey and Du Bois, for example, and list specific issues or actions at the side.

A. Philip Randolph established a union for sleeping-car porters and published a journal called* The Messenger *to help African American workers gain better wages and working conditions.

statistics and detailed stories of atrocities. In an article about a 17-year-old African American who was burned to death by a mob in Waco, Texas, W. E. B. Du Bois rallied support for the NAACP cause. He wrote, "This is an account of one lynching. It is horrible, but it is matched in horror by scores of others in the last thirty years. . . . What are we going to do about this record?"

Although the NAACP program generated considerable public support, it achieved limited success. In 1921 Representative L. C. Dyer of Missouri sponsored a federal antilynching law that passed in the House but lost in the Senate. Nevertheless, the NAACP continued to fight for antilynching legislation and an end to discrimination against African Americans.

African American unionization. While some African Americans mobilized to put an end to lynching and racial violence, others attempted to fight discrimination in the workplace. In the early 1900s African American workers were rarely allowed to rise above unskilled, low-paying jobs. African Americans were also barred from joining local labor unions and the American Federation of Labor.

The unions' failure to help African American workers led young black socialist A. Philip Randolph to found the **Brotherhood of Sleeping Car Porters** in 1925. Randolph started the union to better the working conditions of the thousands of African Americans who worked for the Pullman Company. "[The worker's] object is not only to get more wages, better hours of work and improved working conditions," explained Randolph, "but to do his bit in order to raise and progressively improve the standard of Pullman service."

Randolph also sought to end union discrimination against African American workers. The Brotherhood of Sleeping Car Porters provided a union for African Americans. However, Randolph hoped to unite all workers, regardless of color, into a single force opposed to unjust working conditions.

Despite Randolph's efforts, the Pullman Company refused to recognize the Brotherhood of Sleeping Car Porters. The company even began to hire Filipino workers to replace African American porters. Supported by groups such as the NAACP, the union persisted in its efforts to organize. It eventually won recognition by the Pullman Company in the late 1930s.

Marcus Garvey led the black nationalist movement.

Black nationalism. African Americans grew frustrated by the slow pace of change in the unions and the lack of results from NAACP's antilynching legislation. Some African Americans lost hope of ever achieving equality in the United States. They believed that African Americans needed a nation of their own.

The motivation for African Americans to form an independent nation grew out of an existing political movement. The movement known as **Pan-Africanism** aimed to unite people of African descent worldwide. Support for the movement had existed in the United States since the early 1800s. By the 1920s, however, a new leader within the Pan-African movement had emerged. Marcus Garvey, a native of Jamaica, supported the cause of **black nationalism**. This movement aimed to create a new political state for African Americans in Africa.

Marcus Garvey founded the **Universal Negro Improvement Association** (UNIA) in 1914. The UNIA had two main goals. Its members hoped to foster African

TEACH OBJECTIVE 4

LEVEL 1: Tell students to imagine that they are writing a book about Mexican immigration to the United States during the 1920s. Pair students and have each pair write an outline for a chapter that explains why Mexican immigration to the United States increased in the 1920s. *(Pairs should note that limits on immigration during the 1920s did not affect Mexicans. Employers in the Southwest were eager for workers to fill low-wage jobs.)* Have volunteers present their outlines to the class. **Sheltered English, Cooperative Learning**

LEVEL 2: Pair students and have each pair create a collage that illustrates the reasons why Mexican immigration to the United States increased in the 1920s. *(See the Level 1 lesson for the correct reasons.)* Students should write short descriptions of the different elements of their collages. Display pairs' collages around the classroom. **Cooperative Learning**

LEVEL 3: Organize the class into small groups. Have each group write a three-minute play about a Mexican immigrant family in the 1920s. Characters in the play should discuss why Mexican immigration to the United States increased in the 1920s. *(See the Level 1 lesson for reasons.)* Have volunteers perform their plays for the class. **Cooperative Learning**

Americans' economic independence through the establishment of black-owned businesses. They also worked to establish an independent black homeland in Africa. "We shall now organize," Garvey told the delegates to the UNIA's first international convention, "to plant the banner of freedom on the great continent of Africa."

Garvey moved in 1916 to New York, where he continued to organize efforts to form an African American nation. A charismatic speaker, Garvey attracted considerable support from African American communities in the United States. Whereas W. E. B. Du Bois spoke to the well educated, Garvey's speeches and slogans attracted the African American masses. Garvey also organized attention-getting parades. He also urged African Americans to join him in forging a new homeland free from discrimination. Many of his supporters were working-class African Americans living in urban areas.

THROUGH OTHERS' EYES

An African View of the Back-to-Africa Movement

Marcus Garvey's back-to-Africa movement drew many followers both in the United States and in Africa. In 1922 a representative of the king of Abyssinia—present-day Ethiopia—read the following message to a United Negro Improvement Association convention.

> **"Assure them [Garvey's followers] of the cordiality with which I invite them back to the home land, particularly those qualified to help solve our big problems and to develop our vast resources. Teachers, artisans, mechanics, writers, musicians, professional men and women—all who are able to lend a hand in the constructive work which our country so deeply feels, and greatly needs.**
>
> **Here we have abundant room and great opportunities and here destiny is working to elevate and enthrone a race which has suffered slavery, poverty, persecution and martyrdom [death for a cause], but whose expanding soul and growing genius is now the hope of many millions of mankind."**

To encourage economic independence, Garvey founded the Black Star Steamship Company in 1919. He urged African Americans to invest in his company so that they "may exert the same influence on the world as the white man does today." He promised investors huge returns. The company, however, never turned a profit. In 1925 he was jailed for mail fraud in connection with his fund-raising activities. President Coolidge pardoned Garvey in 1927 but ordered him deported.

The black nationalist movement declined after Garvey's imprisonment. Nevertheless, as a newspaper writer said in 1927, "He made black people proud. . . . He taught them that black is beautiful." Other African American leaders such as Du Bois shared Garvey's belief in racial pride and solidarity but opposed his back-to-Africa movement. They insisted that African Americans needed to fight for justice and equality in American society.

✔ **READING CHECK:** What actions did African Americans take to combat discrimination and violence?

Read More About It

Free Find:
Marcus Garvey
After reading about Marcus Garvey and black nationalism on the Holt Researcher CD–ROM, create a script for a scene in a movie about Garvey's back-to-Africa movement.

Immigration Restrictions

The racism and discrimination that led to the resurgence of the Ku Klux Klan in the 1920s also encouraged nativist sentiments. Many Americans feared that the country was being overrun by immigrants. By 1920 nearly 25 percent of the nation's population was foreign born or nonwhite. Furthermore, after a decline during World War I, the number of immigrants was once again rising, increasing from some 140,000 in 1919 to some 805,000 in 1921. This dramatic growth—and the widespread belief that immigrants held radical views and took jobs from native-born Americans—led many citizens to demand federal limits on immigration.

THAT'S INTERESTING!

The first Mexican American U.S. senator took office during the 1920s, despite widespread anti-immigrant tensions. Octaviano Larrazolo was elected to complete the term of a New Mexico senator who had died. Larrazolo was re-elected for a second term in 1929.

***The American Nation* VIDEO PROGRAM**

A Nation of Immigrants; Teacher's Guide, pp. 153–57

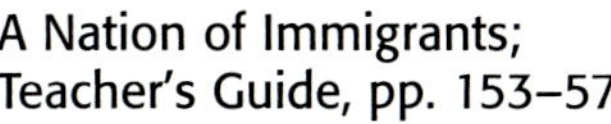

Search 23298, Play to 28272
Videodisc 2, Side B

Play

Pause

See *Teacher's Guide* for Spanish barcode.

VISUAL RECORD ANSWER

(for p. 380)

Students might suggest that the image of an unending line of immigrants in conjunction with the song's title implies that immigration should be limited.

TEACH OBJECTIVE 5

LEVELS 1 AND 2: Pair students and have each pair write a short poem describing the actions that American Indians took in the 1920s to protect their land. *(Pairs should note that American Indians organized to stop the Harding administration's attempt to buy back all tribal land. In 1922, Pueblo tribes organized to fight the Bursum Bill; during their fight the Pueblo appealed to and won the support of many Americans.)* Have volunteers read their poems to the class. Students may wish to include their poems in their portfolios. **Sheltered English, Cooperative Learning**

LEVEL 3: Tell students to imagine that they are American Indian activists who fought government efforts to take Indian lands during the 1920s. Ask each student to write a series of diary entries describing American Indian actions. *(See the Levels 1 and 2 lesson for the correct actions.)* Have volunteers read their diary entries to the class. **Cooperative Learning**

▶**ASSIGNMENT:** *Have each student create a detailed outline of the subsection entitled American Indian Life.*

SECTION 3 REVIEW ANSWERS

Define and Identify
For significance, see the following pages:

- William Joseph Simmons, p. 376
- David Stephenson, p. 377
- A. Philip Randolph, p. 378
- Brotherhood of Sleeping Car Porters, p. 378
- Pan-Africanism, p. 378
- Marcus Garvey, p. 378
- black nationalism, p. 378
- Universal Negro Improvement Association, p. 378
- Immigration Act of 1924, p. 380
- Bursum Bill, p. 381

1. KKK–targeted African Americans as well as other ethnic and religious minority groups; African Americans–encountered discrimination and violence; immigration restriction–enacted because people feared the economic and political effects of immigration

2. The KKK's involvement in terrorism, violence, and scandals caused it to lose popularity.

3. feared economic competition and the introduction of radical political ideas

4. the desire for more workers and the lack of immigration restrictions

5. Answers will vary. Some students might suggest that most groups, such as the organization of the Brotherhood of Sleeping Car Porters, made small gains in defending their rights.

INTERPRETING THE VISUAL RECORD

Anti-immigration. "Ellis Island Blues" was one of the many songs written during the 1920s about immigrants. ***How does the image on the cover of the songbook reflect the ideas behind calls for limits on immigration?***

In 1921 Congress passed a law that limited the number of immigrants from each country allowed into the United States. The law set a quota of 3 percent for each nationality already in the country by 1910, except for Asians, whose immigration was virtually barred. Three years later, the passage of the **Immigration Act of 1924** reduced this quota to 2 percent of the 1890 population figures for each nationality. This change limited southern and eastern European immigration because in 1890 most Americans traced their origins to Great Britain or northern and western Europe. Although the 1924 law did not exclude all Asian immigrants, it set an annual quota of just 100 Japanese immigrants. In 1925 these restrictions reduced the total number of new immigrants from Africa, Asia, Australia, and Europe to some 153,000.

✔ **READING CHECK:** Why did many Americans demand restrictions on immigration?

Mexican American Migration

Mexicans were not affected by the restrictive legislation of the 1920s. With fewer immigrants arriving from Europe and Asia, employers in the Southwest were eager to keep a steady flow of workers to fill low-wage jobs. As a result, during the 1920s some 500,000 immigrants arrived from Mexico, where poverty was widespread, jobs were scarce, and political upheaval from a revolution persisted.

Mexicans who took agricultural jobs in the Southwest worked for low wages and typically lived in ramshackle labor camps. An observer described one camp.

> **"Shelters were made of almost every conceivable thing–burlap, canvas, palm branches. . . . We found one woman carrying water in large milk pails from the irrigation ditch. . . . This is evidently all the water which they have in camp."**

In the 1920s many Mexican immigrants also moved into urban areas. Some were drawn to well-paying factory jobs in cities such as Chicago and Detroit. Most, however, migrated to cities in the Southwest—such as Los Angeles in California and El Paso and San Antonio in Texas. Usually the men came alone. Once established, they sent for their wives and children. Many brought other relatives as well, establishing extended-family networks. These networks helped new arrivals find jobs and housing.

Mexican American Victor Villaseñor wrote about his family's experiences as immigrants in the 1920s. Shown here is the 1929 wedding of his parents.

Economic hardship caused many families to allow their young, unmarried daughters to work outside the home. Many found employment in bakeries, hotels, and laundries. Others worked as maids. Their newfound independence, as one Mexican immigrant woman sadly noted, brought young women "into conflict with their parents. They learn . . . about the outside world, learn how to speak English, and then they become ashamed of their parents who brought them up here." Despite such conflicts, these new immigrants contributed greatly to American life.

✔ **READING CHECK:** Why did Mexican immigration increase during the 1920s?

REVIEW

Have students complete the **Section 3 Review** on p. 381.

ASSESS

Have students complete **Daily Quiz 12.3**. As **Alternative Assessment**, you may want to use the play or the poem in this section's lessons.

RETEACH

Have students complete **Main Idea Activity for Reteaching and Sheltered English 12.3**. Then have each student write a short summary of one of the objectives discussed in this section. Have students read their summaries to the class and ask the class to supply any missing information. **Sheltered English**

EXTEND

Tell students to select a country with heavy immigration to the United States in the late 1800s or early 1900s. Have students conduct research on how the Immigration Act of 1924 affected the flow of immigrants from the selected nation. Have each student describe his or her findings in a short report.

Block Scheduling

American Indian Life

For American Indians the 1920s brought some acknowledgment of the difficulties they faced. The Dawes Act, which attempted to "Americanize" Indians by dividing tribal land into individual plots, had clearly failed. The Board of Indian Commissioners admitted that the act's allotment policies had often been "a short cut to the separation of . . . Indians from their land and cash."

In the 1920s American Indians successfully organized to fight new efforts to take tribal land. American Indian leaders stopped the Harding administration's attempt to buy back all tribal land. Then, in 1922, the various Pueblo tribes of the Southwest organized to fight the **Bursum Bill**, which was designed to legalize non–Indian claims to Pueblo land. The Pueblo appealed to Americans to help defeat the bill.

> "This bill will destroy our common life and will rob us of everything which we hold dear—our lands, our customs, our traditions. Are the American people willing to see this happen?"

Anthropologist James Schultz (left) supported the continuation of American Indian culture in the 1920s.

Many Americans were not. The Pueblo won support from a variety of groups, including the General Federation of Women's Clubs and many anthropologists. As a result, the bill failed to pass.

In 1924 Congress granted citizenship to all American Indians, partly in recognition of those who had fought in World War I. Citizenship, however, did not eliminate the poverty that many American Indians continued to experience.

✔ **READING CHECK:** What actions did American Indians take to protect their land?

SECTION 3 REVIEW

Define and explain the significance of the following terms:
Brotherhood of Sleeping Car Porters
Pan-Africanism
black nationalism
Universal Negro Improvement Association
Immigration Act of 1924
Bursum Bill

Identify and explain the significance of the following individuals:
William Joseph Simmons
David Stephenson
A. Philip Randolph
Marcus Garvey

1. **Using Graphic Organizers** Copy the web below. Use it to explain how each of the listed events reflected the intolerance and discrimination that existed in American society in the 1920s.

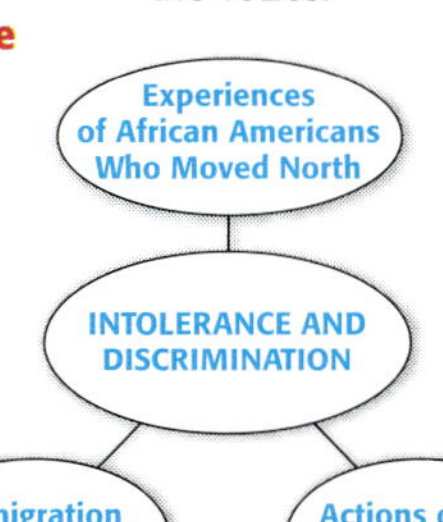

2. **Drawing Conclusions** How did the Ku Klux Klan's policies and actions lead to its rapid decline in popularity during the late 1920s?
3. **Evaluating** Why did many Americans support more restrictive immigration laws in the 1920s?
4. **Analyzing** Why did the immigration of Mexicans to the United States increase during the 1920s?

Critical Thinking

5. In the face of intolerance, discrimination, and violence during the 1920s, many people took action to defend their rights. How successful were they?
   Consider:
   - how African Americans fought against lynching and discrimination
   - how Mexican Americans seeking economic opportunity formed communities
   - how American Indians defended their land

CHAPTER 12 REVIEW ANSWERS

Creating a Time Line

Each event should have an explanation and the correct date.

Writing a Summary

See the Reading Checks in each section for main ideas.

Identifying People and Ideas

1. transition from wartime to peacetime production
2. period of anticommunist hysteria
3. U.S. attorney general who authorized raids on suspected radicals
4. secretary of treasury who proposed cutting taxes on the wealthy to stimulate economic growth
5. proposed amendment to grant men and women equal rights
6. scandal in which some Harding administration officials accepted bribes
7. vice president and president who helped the nation recover from the Harding administration scandals
8. founder of the 1915 Ku Klux Klan
9. leader of the Pan-African movement
10. limited Asian immigration and encouraged western European immigration

Understanding Main Ideas

1. unemployment, falling agriculture prices, and the loss of farms

REVIEW AND ASSESSMENT RESOURCES

PRINT

- Chapter 12 Review, pp. 382–83
- Chapter 12 Tutorial for Students, Parents, Mentors, and Peers
- Chapter 12 Test (Form A or B)
- Portfolio Activities and Alternative Assessment Handbook, Chapter 12

MULTIMEDIA

- Audio Program, Chapter 12 (English and Spanish)
- Chapter 12 Test Generator (on the One-Stop Planner)
- Global Skill Builder CD–ROM
- HRW Web site

SHELTERED ENGLISH

- Spanish Glossary
- Sheltered English Chapter 12 Test

REVIEW

Have students complete the **Chapter 12 Review** on pp. 382–83.

ASSESS

Use one of the chapter tests to assess students' understanding of the content. For **Alternative Assessment**, see the **Portfolio Activities and Alternative Assessment Handbook.**

2. Most strikes were undertaken by workers demanding higher wages and shorter workdays.
3. offered a focus on domestic concerns and a promise of "normalcy"
4. They were the first workers fired when production decreased, and they encountered violence and threats from some white people.
5. Mexican immigration was not restricted and southwestern employers needed many workers

Reviewing Themes

1. The Red Scare made many people afraid to voice their opinions and led officials to ignore personal and legal rights when searching for and arresting suspected radicals.
2. Trickle-down policies enabled wealthy business owners to save money and expand their businesses; laborers did not benefit from these expansions because their pay did not grow along with the owners' profits
3. Immigration increased during the decade, leading to calls for restriction.

Thinking Critically

1. fear and loathing; contributed to an atmosphere of distrust and intolerance
2. The end of the war brought high prices and fewer jobs, which contributed to increased labor agitation. The revolution in Russia contributed to American fears of supposed "radicals."

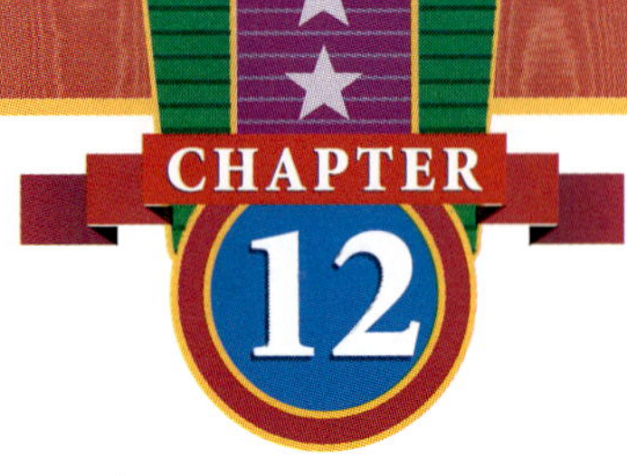

Review

Creating a Time Line

Copy the time line below onto a sheet of paper. Complete the time line by filling in the events and dates from the chapter that you think were most significant. Pick three events and explain why you think they were significant.

Writing a Summary

Using the Reading Checks as a guide, write an overview of the events in the chapter.

Identifying People and Ideas

Identify the following terms or individuals and explain their significance.

1. demobilization
2. Red Scare
3. A. Mitchell Palmer
4. Andrew Mellon
5. Equal Rights Amendment
6. Teapot Dome scandal
7. Calvin Coolidge
8. William Joseph Simmons
9. Marcus Garvey
10. Immigration Act of 1924

Understanding Main Ideas

SECTION 1

1. What impact did demobilization after World War I have on women, factory workers, and farmers?
2. What were some of the causes of the strikes of 1919?

SECTION 2

3. How was Warren G. Harding able to win the election of 1920 by such a large majority?

SECTION 3

4. What types of discrimination did African Americans experience in northern cities?
5. Why did the immigration of Mexicans to the United States increase during the 1920s?

Reviewing Themes

1. **Democratic Values** How did the hysteria of the Red Scare affect the lives of many Americans?
2. **Economic Development** How did the Republicans' pro-business policies affect economic growth?
3. **Cultural Diversity** How did immigration to the United States change in the 1920s?

Thinking Critically

1. **Identifying Cause and Effect** What was the public reaction to the wave of strikes in 1919? How did this reaction relate to the Red Scare?
2. **Synthesizing** How did the ending of World War I and the communist revolution in Russia affect American life in the early 1920s?
3. **Analyzing** How did the Republican Party overcome the scandals of Harding's administration?
4. **Evaluating** How was the new Ku Klux Klan similar to and different from the old Klan?
5. **Assessing Consequences** How did the NAACP, the Brotherhood of Sleeping Car Porters, and black nationalists attempt to better the lives of African Americans? How successful were they?

Writing About History

Writing to Inform Copy the graphic organizer below. Use it to explain the fears and concerns felt by many Americans in 1920 and how the Republicans' pro-business policies proposed to address them. Then explain why Harding's speech on "normalcy" given on May 20, 1920, was a success.

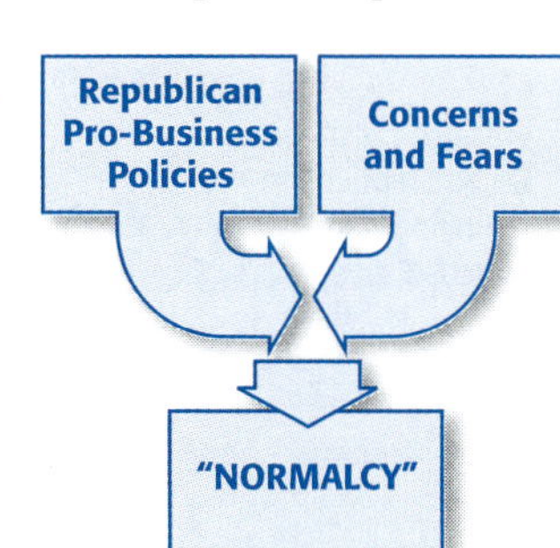

RETEACH

Organize the class into groups of four. Have each group create a crossword puzzle using the key terms and key people from Chapter 12. Have each group exchange its puzzle with another group and then solve them.

Sheltered English, Cooperative Learning

EXTEND

Have each student locate several political cartoons from the 1920s that comment on one of the major events or developments of the decade. Have students write paragraphs explaining and analyzing their cartoons. Students should write one paragraph per cartoon. Ask students to present their cartoons and paragraphs to the class. Students should contextualize each cartoon. **Block Scheduling**

Strategies for Success Review the **Strategies for Success** on *Evaluating News Stories.* Then examine the excerpt below from a news story and answer the questions that follow.

> **"Charlestown State Prison, Mass., Tuesday, August 23—Nicola Sacco and Bartolomeo Vanzetti died in the electric chair early this morning. . . .**
>
> **To the last they protested their innocence, and the efforts of many who believed them guiltless proved futile, although they fought a legal and extra legal battle unprecedented in the history of American jurisprudence [court system]."**

1. Does this excerpt cover its subject in sufficient depth? Does it include adequate background information?
2. Is the reporting in the excerpt fair and accurate? What biases, if any, does it display?
3. How does the excerpt contribute to your understanding of the Sacco and Vanzetti case?

Linking History and Geography

Between 1920 and 1930 some 500,000 Mexicans immigrated to the United States to find work. Study the map below and note which state had the highest percentage of Hispanic residents by 1930.

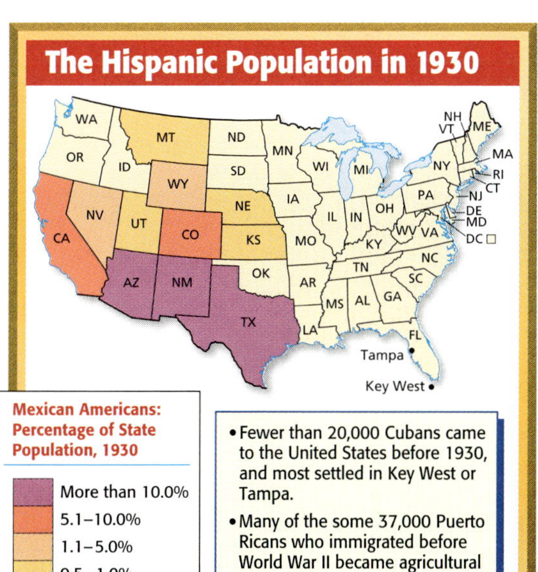

- Fewer than 20,000 Cubans came to the United States before 1930, and most settled in Key West or Tampa.
- Many of the some 37,000 Puerto Ricans who immigrated before World War II became agricultural laborers in Arizona, the Midwest, or the East.

internet connect

TOPIC: Bolshevik Revolution
GO TO: go.hrw.com
KEYWORD: SE1 Bolshevik

Accessing the Internet through the HRW Web site, research the Bolshevik Revolution and create a script for a radio show about the revolution.

BUILDING YOUR PORTFOLIO

Complete one or more of the following projects independently or cooperatively.

1 Constitutional Heritage

Imagine that you are giving a radio broadcast of the news on August 23, 1927—the day that Sacco and Vanzetti were executed. ***Write a news report*** that explains the historical significance of the trial.

2 Democratic Values

Imagine that you are interviewing presidential candidates to write an article for a popular magazine. ***Create an illustrated chart*** to compare and contrast the personalities of Presidents Harding and Coolidge. Then explain how Harding appealed to the voters of 1920 and how Coolidge appealed to voters in 1924.

3 Cultural Diversity

Imagine that you are working with Marcus Garvey's Universal Negro Improvement Association in New York City during the 1920s. Your task is to ***create a flier*** to distribute to African Americans in your city encouraging them to join the UNIA.

3. Coolidge helped overcome the scandals by continuing Harding's plan for normalcy and bringing a calm, reserved demeanor to the presidency.
4. similar—expressed hatred of minority groups, used violence; different—became popular in the Midwest
5. The Brotherhood organized to improve working conditions for African Americans, and the NAACP supported them and also worked to decrease discrimination and violence against African Americans. Black nationalists encouraged African Americans to be proud of their heritage and supported the development of African-American-owned businesses. All three had some success in reducing discrimination.

Writing About History
Students' explanations will vary. Students might cite the following: Republican policies—tax revision, immigration limits, and some farm aid; concerns—economic troubles, political upheavals, and fears about the future.

Strategies for Success
1. The excerpt contains little background information about the details of the crime.
2. The reporting seems mostly accurate; it praises the men for their "unprecedented" legal battle.
3. Some students might suggest that the article contributes little to a deeper understanding of the case.

Linking History and Geography
Texas

The Jazz Age

CHAPTER PLANNING GUIDE

	Section Lesson Objectives	Print Resources	Multimedia Resources	Sheltered English Resources
Section 1 Boom Times, pp. 386–93	1 Evaluate how the economic boom affected consumers and American businesses. 2 Examine how the assembly line spurred the growth of the automobile industry. 3 Describe how Henry Ford changed working conditions during the 1920s. 4 Explain how widespread automobile use affected the daily lives of many Americans. 5 Discuss how American industries encouraged changes in consumer practices.	▶ Guided Reading Strategy 13.1 ▶ Section 1 Review, p. 393 ▶ Daily Quiz 13.1	▶ One-Stop Planner, Lesson 13.1 ▶ The American Nation Video Program Segment: Automobile Assembly Line; Teacher's Guide, pp. 171–72 ▶ Holt Researcher: American History CD–ROM ▶ HRW Web site	▶ Main Idea Activity for Reteaching and Sheltered English 13.1
Section 2 Life in the Twenties, pp. 394–401	1 Analyze the impact prohibition had on crime. 2 Describe the characteristics of the new youth culture. 3 Explain how celebrities and new forms of popular entertainment helped create a mass culture. 4 Examine what the Scopes trial and the religious movements of the 1920s revealed about American society.	▶ Guided Reading Strategy 13.2 ▶ Geography Activity 13: The Prohibition Era ▶ Primary Source Reading 13: Making a Monkey Out of the "Common Man" ▶ Biography Reading 13: Amelia Earhart ▶ Section 2 Review, p. 401 ▶ Daily Quiz 13.2	▶ One-Stop Planner, Lesson 13.2 ▶ The American Nation Video Program Segment: Prohibition; Teacher's Guide, pp. 211–12 ▶ Holt Researcher: American History CD–ROM	▶ Main Idea Activity for Reteaching and Sheltered English 13.2
Section 3 A Creative Era, pp. 402–09	1 Explain how jazz and blues became popular nationwide. 2 Analyze how artists and writers of the Harlem Renaissance used their work to express pride in their cultural heritage. 3 Describe how writers of the Lost Generation portrayed American life. 4 Identify some of the major inspirations behind the new movements in visual arts and architecture.	▶ Guided Reading Strategy 13.3 ▶ Graphic Organizer Activity 13: Artists of the 1920s and 1930s ▶ Literature Reading 13: The Jazz Age ▶ Section 3 Review, p. 409 ▶ Daily Quiz 13.3	▶ One-Stop Planner, Lesson 13.3 ▶ Everyday Life in America Transparency 22: Harlem Renaissance Art, 1920s ▶ American Music Selection 19: "Harmonica Blues" ▶ Holt Researcher: American History CD–ROM	▶ Main Idea Activity for Reteaching and Sheltered English 13.3
Chapter Review and Assessment pp. 410–11		▶ Chapter 13 Review, pp. 410–11 ▶ Chapter 13 Tutorial for Students, Parents, Mentors, and Peers ▶ Chapter 13 Test (Form A or B) ▶ Portfolio Activities and Alternative Assessment Handbook, Chapter 13	▶ Audio Program, Chapter 13 (English and Spanish) ▶ Chapter 13 Test Generator (on the One-Stop Planner) ▶ Global Skill Builder CD–ROM ▶ HRW Web site	▶ Spanish Glossary ▶ Sheltered English Chapter 13 Test

CHAPTER OVERVIEW

The 1920s were marked by economic prosperity, the creation of a mass culture, and artistic achievement. Postwar social and economic troubles gave way to an era in which new consumer goods were available to an increasing number of Americans. American industries helped create a culture of consumption by making products more attractive and creating new marketing practices.

The increasing popularity of media such as the movies and radio contributed to the rise of a mass culture. A new youth culture also emerged. Flappers challenged social conventions regarding dress, behavior, and the role of women in society. Many Americans worried about these rapid social changes. Such concerns, in part, led to the rise of new religious movements. The Scopes trial in 1925 reflected many Americans' unease with new values based on scientific ways of thought.

The era known as the Jazz Age was also important for the emergence of jazz, arguably the preeminent American musical form. African American cultural contributions also included works produced by the artists and writers of the Harlem Renaissance. The literary works of the writers of the Lost Generation also exemplified the spirit of the decade.

TIME TAMERS

Block Scheduling

The teacher lesson plans for each section offer a variety of activity choices to help you present the material in a block scheduling format. For further suggestions on block scheduling, see the **Block Scheduling Handbook with Team Teaching Strategies**, pp. 73–78.

Smithsonian Institution®

Internet Connections and Lesson 13

www.si.edu/hrw

Hands-On History Activities:

Classroom to Community The **Hands-On History Activities** help students make meaningful connections between events in American history and those in their own hometown. You may wish to use the Chapter 13 Activity, Guide to Local Arts and Artists, to extend the chapter lessons, as alternative assessment, or as a block scheduling option.

Portfolio Projects

The American Nation includes multiple portfolio projects in each Pupil's Edition chapter review, as well as each unit review. Chapter 13 Portfolio Project options on p. 411 include the following:

1. Students will **create an advertisement.**
2. Students will **create a poem or painting.**
3. Students will **write a script.**

The American Nation

INTERNET RESOURCE DIRECTORY

To access online materials for this chapter, go to **go.hrw.com** and type in the keywords listed below.

HRW ONLINE RESOURCES

GO TO: go.hrw.com

Online Charts

KEYWORD: SE1 Charts13

- Households with Radios, 1922–1930
- Workforce, 1910, 1920, 1930

Online Reading Support

KEYWORD: SE1 Strategies13

Online Rubrics

KEYWORD: SE1 Rubrics

CHAPTER ENRICHMENT LINKS

Use these Web links to extend and enrich student learning for Chapter 13.

GO TO: go.hrw.com

KEYWORD: SE1 Ch13

CHAPTER INTERNET ACTIVITIES

GO TO: go.hrw.com

- Pupil's Edition Student Activity
  KEYWORD: SE1 Jazz
  (Students conduct research on Duke Ellington and Louis Armstrong.)
- Teacher's Edition Student Activity
  KEYWORD: SE1 Deco
  (Students examine the Art Deco movement.)
- Teacher's Edition Student Activity
  KEYWORD: SE1 Autos
  (Students investigate 1920s automobiles.)

ADDITIONAL

RESOURCES

Books for Teachers

Collier, James L. *The Making of Jazz: A Comprehensive History.* Delta, 1978. Discusses the historical development of jazz.

Smith, Page. *Redeeming the Time, Volume Eight: A People's History of the 1920s and the New Deal.* Viking Penguin, 1991. Provides a picture of American life during the 1920s.

Books for Students

Lewis, David L. *When Harlem Was in Vogue.* Oxford University Press, 1989. Discusses the Harlem Renaissance.

Perrett, Geoffrey. *America in the Twenties: A History.* Simon and Schuster, 1982. Reviews the social history of the 1920s.

Primary Sources from the Period

Fitzgerald, F. Scott. *The Great Gatsby.* Cambridge University Press, 1991. Depicts the shallowness of upper-class life in the United States during the 1920s.

Multimedia Materials

History of the Twentieth Century, 1920–1929. Video, 60 min. ABC Video/SSSS. Provides an overview of prohibition, the activities of Al Capone, and other topics relating to the 1920s.

The Jazz Age, Part 2. Video, 26 min. Covers sports, Lindbergh's flight, Americans in Paris, and the stock-market crash.

CHAPTER 13

Before You Read

Build on What You Know

Ask students to answer the following questions.

How might new products and new forms of entertainment have changed American life during the 1920s?

Consider:

- the advances in science and technology
- the capabilities of postwar American industry

Why might some Americans have found these changes unsettling?

Consider:

- the specific changes that might have affected women, young people, and rural dwellers
- the concerns of religious leaders

exploring the time line

AMERICAN EVENTS

PEOPLE IN HISTORY

1925 ■ Clarence Darrow. By the time Clarence Darrow agreed to defend John Scopes, a Tennessee schoolteacher charged with violating a law that banned the teaching of evolution in the state's public schools, Darrow had already distinguished himself as one of the nation's leading attorneys. He had gained national attention for defending labor leader Eugene Debs against conspiracy charges resulting from the railroad strike of 1894. For the next three decades Darrow served as an attorney in many high-profile cases, including a murder trial in which he introduced psychiatric evidence, a novelty at the time. He also served as a vocal advocate for the civil liberties of individuals and for a variety of reform causes.

CRITICAL THINKING Why might Clarence Darrow have wanted to serve as a defense attorney in the Scopes trial?

ANSWER: Students might suggest that Darrow believed that the Tennessee law banning the teaching of evolution violated a person's right to free speech.

CHAPTER 13

1920–1929

The Jazz Age

Louis Armstrong

Alvin "Shipwreck" Kelly sitting on top of a flagpole

1920
Science and Technology
The first radio broadcasting station, KDKA in Pittsburgh, goes on the air.

1922
The Arts
Jazz trumpeter Louis Armstrong moves to Chicago and joins King Oliver's Creole Jazz Band.

1922
Business and Finance
New York radio station WEAF airs the first paid radio commercials.

1923
World Events
An earthquake in Japan destroys Tokyo, killing some 143,000 people.

1923
The Arts
Cecil B. DeMille's epic silent movie *The Ten Commandments* is released.

1924
Business and Finance
A Hollywood theater hires Alvin "Shipwreck" Kelly to sit on top of a flagpole to generate publicity.

1924
The Arts
George Gershwin "translates" jazz into symphonic form in his musical composition *Rhapsody in Blue.*

1924
Politics
The first radio broadcast of a political convention is conducted from the Republican National Convention in Cleveland.

1920 | 1921 | 1922 | 1923 | 1924

One of the first broadcasters on KDKA

***Scene from the silent film* The Ten Commandments**

Before You Read

Build on What You Know

World War I's sudden conclusion forced many Americans to make major changes in their lives. A postwar economic recession caused many Americans to lose their jobs. Tensions eased, however, with the return of economic prosperity in the mid-1920s. In this chapter you will learn about the impact that postwar industrial products had on American life. You will also learn about the new forms of entertainment—such as radio programs, movies, and jazz music—that were popular with Americans in the 1920s.

384

Think About Themes

To help students create their Themes Journal entries, provide the following examples of appropriate **agree/disagree** *statements.*

Economic Development

Agree The economy of British North America grew stronger as the colonists' demand for consumer goods increased.

Disagree Despite huge sums that the Spanish Empire spent on art, architecture, and the maintenance of colonies, its economic health and international prestige gradually declined.

Technology and Society

Agree The invention of steam-powered riverboats and locomotives helped lead to the expansion of trade across the nation.

Disagree The technological advances of the Second Industrial Revolution did not significantly alter the social status of working-class women.

Cultural Diversity

Agree Attempts by the U.S. government to assimilate the Navajo and other American Indian groups met with failure.

Disagree Irish immigrants created culturally dynamic and politically powerful communities in many U.S. cities during the second half of the 1800s.

exploring the time line

GLOBAL EVENTS

Poster from the Paris Exposition

1925 World Events
The Paris Exposition opens, introducing the "Art Deco" style of industrial design.

1925 The Arts
F. Scott Fitzgerald publishes *The Great Gatsby.*

1925 Politics
Clarence Darrow defends a Tennessee schoolteacher in the Scopes trial.

Babe Ruth

1927 Daily Life
Babe Ruth sets a new baseball record, hitting 60 home runs in a single season.

Automobile advertisement

THE GRANGER COLLECTION, NEW YORK

1929 Business and Finance
American businesses spend more than $3 billion on advertisements in a single year.

internetconnect

TOPIC: Art Deco Style
GO TO: go.hrw.com
KEYWORD: SE1 Deco

Have students access the Internet through the HRW Web site to conduct research on the Art Deco movement during the 1920s. Then have each student design an object in Art Deco style. Ask students to write statements that explain the characteristics of Art Deco style that are represented in their designs.

1925 — 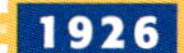 1926 — 1927 — 1928 — 1929

THE METROPOLITAN MUSEUM OF ART, ALFRED STIEGLITZ COLLECTION

Georgia O'Keeffe's Black Iris

1926 The Arts
Georgia O'Keeffe paints *Black Iris.*

1927 Science and Technology
Charles Lindbergh becomes the first pilot to fly solo nonstop from New York to Paris.

1927 Business and Finance
The Ford Motor Company introduces the Model A automobile with a $1.3 million advertising campaign.

1928 Daily Life
Marathon dancers compete for 482 hours in the "Dance Derby of the Century."

Dance marathon contestants

Think About Themes

Decide whether you **agree** *or* **disagree** *with the following statements. Note why in your journal.*

Economic Development Increasing consumer spending will improve a nation's overall economic strength.

Technology and Society New technology transforms the way people interact with each other.

Cultural Diversity The individual cultural traditions of groups of people within a country often conflict with that country's broader, national culture.

385

SECTION 1

After completing Section 1, students should be able to:

OBJECTIVE 1 *Evaluate how the economic boom affected consumers and American businesses.*

OBJECTIVE 2 *Examine how the assembly line spurred the growth of the automobile industry.*

OBJECTIVE 3 *Describe how Henry Ford changed working conditions during the 1920s.*

OBJECTIVE 4 *Explain how widespread automobile use affected the daily lives of many Americans.*

OBJECTIVE 5 *Discuss how American industries encouraged changes in consumer practices.*

LET'S GET STARTED!

Have each student make a list of some major technological innovations developed in his or her lifetime. Students should write a brief explanation of how each item has affected daily life. Call on volunteers to explain their lists to the class. Tell students that in Section 1 they will learn how the technological innovations of the Jazz Age affected Americans' lives.

SECTION 1 RESOURCES

PRINT
- Guided Reading Strategy 13.1
- Section 1 Review, p. 393
- Daily Quiz 13.1

MULTIMEDIA
- One-Stop Planner, Lesson 13.1
- The American Nation Video Program Segment: Automobile Assembly Line; Teacher's Guide, pp. 171–72
- Holt Researcher: American History CD–ROM
- HRW Web site

SHELTERED ENGLISH
- Main Idea Activity for Reteaching and Sheltered English 13.1

✔ READING TO UNDERSTAND

To help students master the section objectives, have them answer the **READING CHECKS** and complete **Guided Reading Strategy 13.1** as they read the section.

SECTION 1

Boom Times

OBJECTIVES

Read to understand:

1. how the economic boom affected consumers and American businesses
2. how the assembly line spurred the growth of the automobile industry
3. how Henry Ford changed working conditions during the 1920s
4. how widespread automobile use affected the daily lives of many Americans
5. how American industries encouraged changes in consumer practices

KEY TERMS

scientific management
Model T
assembly line
auto-touring
installment plan
planned obsolescence

KEY PEOPLE

Frederick W. Taylor
Henry Ford
Alfred P. Sloan

"One hundred thousand people flocked into the showrooms of the Ford Company in Detroit; mounted police were called out to patrol the crowds in Cleveland; in Kansas City so great a mob stormed Convention Hall that platforms had to be built to lift the new car high enough for everyone to see it."

—Charles Merz

A crowd gathers around a 1927 Model A.

In December 1927 the American public clamored to see the Ford Motor Company's new Model A automobile. Ford had kept the new design secret, and public excitement grew in the days before its unveiling. This interest was heightened by a massive advertising campaign that featured a five-day series of full-page newspaper ads costing $1.3 million. The prosperity of the 1920s increased the spending power of many families and allowed them to purchase the wide variety of new products being produced by American industries. These new products transformed Americans' daily lives, changing the way they worked, socialized, and ran their households.

This General Electric advertisement pictures some of the new appliances available in the 1920s.

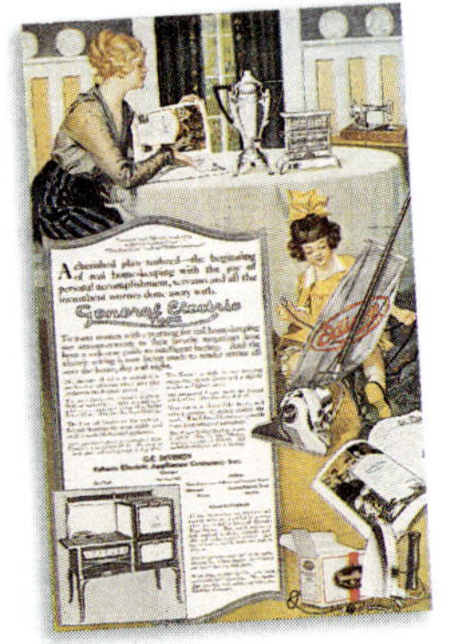

Prosperity and Productivity

After recovering from the turbulent period of demobilization, the U.S. economy soared. The gross national product climbed from $70 billion in 1922 to $100 billion just seven years later. Republican pro-business policies, tax cuts, and confidence among business leaders encouraged investment and led to economic growth. Edward E. Purinton, a business leader during the 1920s, expressed the confidence of the era. "The finest game is business. The rewards are for everybody, and all can win."

The era's business expansion led to wage increases. The average employee's purchasing power increased by 32 percent between 1914 and 1928. With the rise in income, workers became interested in many new products, including electric appliances.

During the 1920s it became common for Americans to have electricity in their homes, particularly in cities. An abundant supply of energy as well as a large network of electrical power plants led to this expansion. Between 1920 and 1929 the annual electrical production rose from more than 56 billion to 117 billion kilowatt-hours. By 1930 more than two thirds of all American homes had electricity. The availability of electricity and the growing purchasing power of consumers provided a market for new products. American industries developed a variety of new electric appliances—such as mixers, food grinders, sewing machines, and washing machines. Radio and phonograph sales boomed.

As American industries attempted to keep pace with the growing demands of consumers, many businesses began experimenting with new ways of increasing the productivity of the nation's factories. One of the new approaches was known as

TEACH OBJECTIVE 1

LEVEL 1: List the following terms and phrases on the chalkboard: *economic prosperity, wage increases, new products, consumer demand, scientific management.* Pair students and have them write a short paragraph using all of the terms listed to analyze how the economic boom of the 1920s affected consumers and American businesses. *(Students' responses might include: Economic prosperity during the 1920s led to wage increases for workers. Workers, with their increased purchasing power, created a market for new products. To keep up with consumer demand, many businesses experimented with scientific management techniques to increase productivity.)*
Sheltered English, Cooperative Learning

LEVELS 2 AND 3: Pair students and have each pair create a collage that depicts the impact of the economic boom of the 1920s on consumers and American businesses. Students should write a short explanation to accompany their collages. *(See the Level 1 lesson for the correct effects.)* Have students display their collages around the classroom. **Cooperative Learning**

scientific management. Frederick W. Taylor, an early supporter of the idea, explained that scientific management was based on the idea that every kind of work could be broken down into a series of smaller tasks. Trained observers conducted "time-and-motion" studies to identify these tasks. They then set rates of production that workers and machines had to meet. Soon "efficiency experts" were applying these methods to many types of business.

✔ **READING CHECK:** How did the economic boom of the 1920s affect American consumers and businesses?

Henry Ford achieved early success with his design for a streamlined racing car. In 1902 the Ford 999 set a world speed record of more than 90 miles per hour.

The Growth of the Automobile Industry

The innovations in productivity proved particularly important to the growing automobile industry of the 1920s. Automobile manufacturers such as Henry Ford could lower the cost of their cars by implementing scientific management practices.

Ford had established an automobile company in 1903 that quickly emerged as the industry leader. By 1908 Ford had developed the **Model T**, a sturdy, low-cost automobile. Ford's Model T was an instant success and sold more than 250,000 a year by 1914. Ford was eager to increase productivity and lower the price of the Model T. Adopting scientific-management techniques used in the slaughterhouses of Chicago, Ford developed a new production method—the **assembly line**—to help factories make goods faster. Workers stood in one place as partially assembled products such as automobiles moved past them on a conveyor belt.

Ford used the assembly line in his Detroit automobile plant. As the conveyor belt advanced at precisely six feet per minute, workers assembled the 5,000 parts of a Model T, or "Tin Lizzie." Machinery did much of the work by producing individual parts and carrying them to workers.

Ford's assembly line cut the engine assembly time for a Model T in half. Other large car manufacturers quickly followed Ford's lead and installed assembly lines. However, few small companies could afford the expense of building or maintaining the new technology. Unable to compete, many were driven out of business.

The assembly line allowed manufacturers to reduce the prices of cars, bringing them within reach of ordinary American families. The price of a Ford automobile dropped from $850 in 1909 to just $290 in 1924. Automobile registrations during the 1920s rose from 8 million to 26 million—an average of one car to every five citizens.

In the 1920s the automobile industry was the nation's biggest business. This new industrial giant consumed huge quantities of glass, rubber, steel, and other materials. By 1929 more than 1 million people labored in the automobile industry or a related business.

✔ **READING CHECK:** How did the development of the assembly line encourage the growth of the automobile industry?

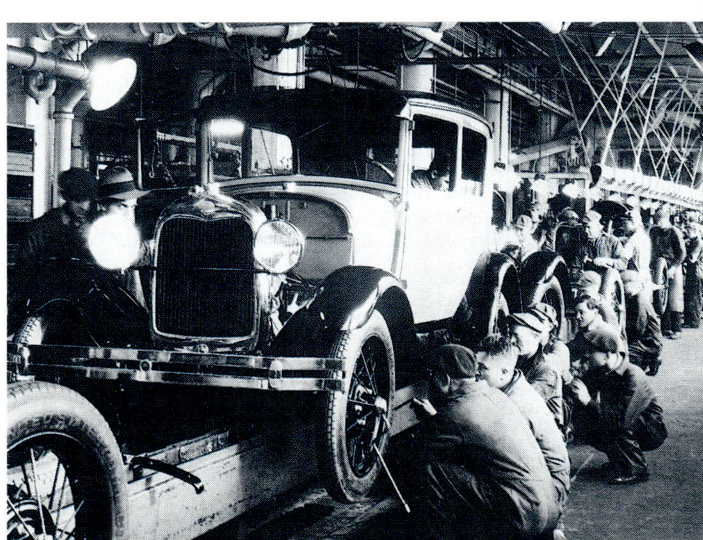

INTERPRETING THE VISUAL RECORD

The assembly line. Henry Ford developed an assembly-line system to manufacture his Model T efficiently. ***How do you think the assembly line might have made work easier for these Ford employees?***

ECONOMIC DEVELOPMENT

The Vertical Integration of the Ford Motor Company. In addition to introducing the assembly line, Henry Ford increased the efficiency of his automobile company through vertical integration. To supply his automobile factories with raw materials, he purchased numerous iron and coal mines, approximately 700,000 acres of timberland, a glassworks, a railroad, and a fleet of ships.

CRITICAL THINKING How might the automobile industry have a ripple effect on a country's economy?

ANSWER: Students might suggest that an increased demand for automobiles could lead to an increased demand for steel.

THAT'S INTERESTING!

Between 1908 and 1927 the Ford Motor Company sold 15.5 million Model T automobiles in the United States, almost 1 million in Canada, and 250,000 in Great Britain. This total represented one half of the world's automobile production.

VISUAL RECORD ANSWER

Students might suggest that workers could remain in one place as the assembly line carried parts to them.

TEACH OBJECTIVE 2

LEVEL 1: Pair students and have each pair draw a graphic organizer to depict how the assembly line spurred the growth of the automobile industry. *(Students might mention that the assembly line cut production time and costs. Manufacturers were able to reduce car prices, which allowed greater numbers of consumers to buy cars.)* Ask volunteers to present their graphic organizers to the class. **Sheltered English, Cooperative Learning**

LEVELS 2 AND 3: Tell students to imagine that they are editors who must write a brief summary for the jacket of a book about the automobile industry. Have each student write a summary to describe how the development of the assembly line spurred the growth of the automobile industry. *(See the Level 1 lesson for the correct effects.)* Have volunteers read their summaries to the class. Students may wish to include their summaries in their portfolios.

TEACH OBJECTIVE 3

LEVEL 1: Pair students and have each pair draw a cartoon to show how Henry Ford changed working conditions during the 1920s. *(Students might indicate that Ford developed the assembly line, which increased productivity but made factory work repetitive. Ford also shortened the workday and raised wages.)* Have volunteers present and explain their cartoons to the class. **Sheltered English, Cooperative Learning**

HISTORY MAKERS SPEAK

Henry Ford in *My Life and Work*

Ford's Assessment of Assembly-Line Work. Henry Ford maintained an unapologetic attitude about the deadening nature of assembly-line work. In an autobiography published in 1922 Ford offered the following assessment of conditions in his factories: "Repetitive labour—the doing of one thing over and over again and always in the same way—is a terrifying prospect to a certain turn of mind. It is terrifying to me. I could not possibly do the same thing day in and day out, but to other minds, perhaps I might say to the majority of minds, repetitive operations hold no terrors. . . . The average worker, I am sorry to say, wants a job in which he does not have to put forth much physical exertion—above all, he wants a job in which he does not have to think."

ACTIVITY: Ask students to write a paragraph in response to Henry Ford's assessment of the "average worker."

SCIENCE & TECHNOLOGY ANSWERS

1. the simple design of its basic components and its high-strength steel chassis
2. The Model T was designed to be easily manufactured on an assembly line.

Science & Technology

The Model T

In addition to revolutionizing manufacturing, Henry Ford made important changes to the design of the automobile. During the early 1900s Ford began experimenting with new designs in an attempt to make cars more affordable.

Ford simplified the automobile's design to create a sturdy car that could be easily manufactured on an assembly line. The Model T contained four basic components: the frame, the front axle, the power plant, and the rear axle. The Model T had a 20-horsepower, four-cylinder engine that was built simply enough that almost anyone could maintain it. Ford's engineers designed a pedal-operated, two-speed transmission that was also easy to operate. To prevent the automobile from getting stuck in the often muddy roads, designers provided the Model T with a high ground clearance. The Model T's high-strength steel chassis, or frame, made it extremely durable.

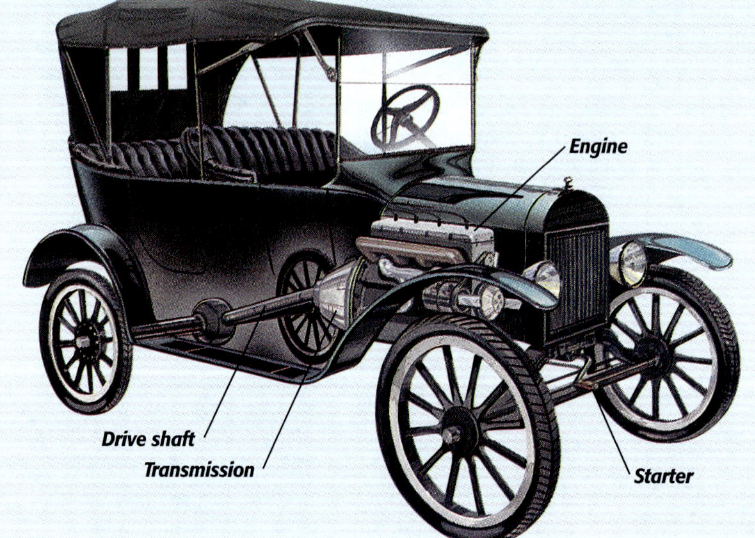

Ford was able to sell the Model T at an affordable price, but his company offered few options. One Ford advertisement read, "We are making 40,000 cylinders, 10,000 engines, 40,000 wheels, 20,000 axles, 10,000 bodies, 10,000 of every part that goes into the car . . . all *exactly alike*." Even color options were limited. "The customer," Ford joked, "can have a Ford any color he wants—so long as it's black."

Understanding Science and History

1. What features made the Model T sturdy and reliable?
2. What impact did the assembly-line system have on the design of the Model T?

At the end of their shift, these assembly-line workers are leaving the Ford factory in Dearborn, Michigan.

Changes in Work

The assembly line transformed the nature of work during the 1920s. Assembly lines increased productivity. However, they made factory work more repetitive and led to increased rates of employee turnover.

Unskilled factory workers had little chance for advancement beyond the assembly line. Upper-level positions for clerical workers, managers, and salespeople increased by 4 million, but these jobs were unavailable to most factory workers. Because most of these jobs required at least a high-school education, few recent immigrants qualified for them. Discriminatory hiring practices also closed most of these jobs to African Americans.

Ford and his workers. Henry Ford revolutionized automobile production by implementing the assembly line in his factories. He won fame for shortening the workday and raising the wages of his employees. Ford also tried to regulate the morality and personal behavior of his workers.

LEVEL 2: Tell students to imagine that they are assembly-line workers during the 1920s. Have each student write several diary entries to describe how working conditions changed during the 1920s. *(See the Level 1 lesson for the correct changes.)* Students should also describe their reaction to the changes.

LEVEL 3: Pair students and have each pair create a pantomime to depict how Ford changed working conditions during the 1920s. *(See the Level 1 lesson for the correct changes.)* Have each pair perform its pantomime for the class.
Cooperative Learning

TEACH OBJECTIVE 4

LEVEL 1: Tell students to imagine that they are newspaper editors during the 1920s. Pair students and have each pair write headlines to describe how the use of the automobile changed the daily lives of many Americans. *(Students might mention that: automobiles linked rural areas to urban areas, contributed to the growth of the suburbs, led to the replacement of horse-drawn vehicles, reduced use of trains and trolley cars for transportation, led to an auto-touring craze, changed family life by creating new social opportunities for teenagers, and reduced people's sense of community.)* Have volunteers read their headlines to the class.
Sheltered English, Cooperative Learning

Henry Ford

Born in 1863 on a farm near Dearborn, Michigan, Ford was well acquainted with hard work. He began work as a machinist at the age of 16. During the 1890s Ford worked as an engineer for the Edison Illuminating Company in Detroit. In his free time he experimented with gasoline engines and automobiles. During the early 1900s he worked closely with talented engineers to design the assembly-line system.

Ford's highly automated system of production limited each worker to one or two specific tasks. The repetitive work was dull, and many workers quit within a few weeks. Concerned about the high turnover of employees, Ford shortened the workday to eight hours and doubled wages to an unheard-of $5 a day.

Workers welcomed these bold steps. However, as the wife of one Ford worker noted, the pay increase did not change working conditions.

> **"The chain system [assembly line] you have is a slave driver! My God! Mr. Ford. My husband has come home & thrown himself down & won't eat his supper—so done out! Can't it be remedied? . . . That $5 a day is a blessing—a bigger one than you know but oh they earn it."**

Ford's influence over his workers' lives extended far beyond their time on the line. The attractive wages paid to workers had strings attached. To earn the full $5 wage, workers were required to meet company standards at work and at home. Ford created a department within his company to analyze workers' home lives and offer plans to remedy any problems that Ford and his researchers believed existed.

Ford hoped to instruct his employees in the values and behaviors that he thought were proper. Ford's personnel department kept a close watch over the private lives of employees. Ford strongly opposed tobacco and alcohol. His workers were warned, "It will cost a man his job to have the odor of beer, wine or liquor on his breath or have any of these intoxicants in his home."

During World War I, Ford stressed the importance of teaching his mostly foreign-born workforce "American values." Ford instructed workers to move out of ethnic neighborhoods. Workers who did not speak English were required to attend the Ford English School, where they were taught the language and lectured on personal hygiene, manners, and proper work habits.

Ford managed his automobile company closely to ensure the efficiency of his workers and assembly-line system. When the company's profits declined in the 1930s, many people questioned his management skills. In 1945 Ford transferred control of his company to his grandson. He died two years later.

✔ **READING CHECK:** How did Henry Ford change working conditions during the 1920s?

The impact of new products. The widespread use of the automobile and new products powered by electricity altered working conditions and decreased the availability of some jobs. Electric appliances made housework easier for those who could afford them. Many people hired fewer domestic servants. In the past, servants had done the laundry and heavy cleaning in most middle- and upper-class homes. With

HOLT RESEARCHER
Read More About It

Free Find: Henry Ford
After reading about Henry Ford on the **Holt Researcher** CD–ROM, create a chart that shows how Ford's business strategies both benefited and created hardships for the average American worker.

INTERPRETING THE VISUAL RECORD

Ford's workers. One of Henry Ford's goals was to instill American values in his workers. ***How does this photograph reflect Ford's goal to Americanize his workers?***

internetconnect

TOPIC: Automobiles in the 1920s
GO TO: go.hrw.com
KEYWORD: SE1 Autos

Have students access the Internet through the HRW Web site to conduct research on the automobiles of the 1920s. Then have each student create an advertisement for a 1920s "dream car." Ask students to design their ads in the style of 1920s advertisements and to include a description of the automobile's appearance and its mechanical characteristics.

The American Nation
VIDEO PROGRAM

Automobile Assembly Line;
Teacher's Guide, pp. 171–72

Search 39871, Play to 40640
Videodisc 2, Side A

Play

Pause

See *Teacher's Guide* for Spanish barcode.

VISUAL RECORD ANSWER

Students might mention the Ford English School sign or the American flags.

LEVEL 2: Tell students to imagine that they are Americans living during the 1920s. Organize the class into triads and have each triad create a three-way conversation about how the use of the automobile has affected the daily lives of Americans. *(See the Level 1 lesson for the correct effects.)* Have each group perform its conversation for the class.
Sheltered English, Cooperative Learning

NOTE: For an additional teaching idea, see the Chapter 13 daily journal writing lesson in the **Creative Teaching Strategies** handbook.

LEVEL 3: Organize students into small groups. Tell students to imagine that they are on the editorial board of a 1920s newspaper. Have each group develop a multipage feature on the effects of automobile use on daily life in the United States. *(See the Level 1 lesson for the correct effects.)* The feature should include articles, cartoons, and interviews. Display the groups' features around the classroom. **Cooperative Learning**

▸ASSIGNMENT *Have each student write a poem about how the use of the automobile affected the daily lives of many Americans.*

HISTORY MAKERS SPEAK

Page Smith in *Redeeming the Time, Volume Eight: A People's History of the 1920s and the New Deal*

The Universal Appeal of the Automobile. Although automobiles were most affordable for middle- and upper-class Americans during the 1920s, members of all income groups made the purchase of a car a high priority. Historian Page Smith has summarized neatly the universal appeal of the automobile for Americans: "[Automobiles] were the nation's most cherished symbol of progress, of prosperity, of 'keeping ahead,' of the promise of American life. Americans schemed and plotted, saved and, if necessary, stole money to buy a car even if they could not afford the gas to run it. Not only did ownership of the most dilapidated car bestow a degree of status, but it meant mobility, the ability to escape, so precious to Americans."

ACTIVITY: Ask students to write several paragraphs about the symbolic value of the automobile in American life today. Ask volunteers to read their paragraphs to the class.

VISUAL RECORD ANSWER

Students might indicate that gasoline and tire-changing services were offered.

INTERPRETING THE VISUAL RECORD

Automobiles. With the growing number of automobiles on the nation's roads, new businesses such as filling stations and drive-in restaurants opened. ***How did this gas station from the 1920s serve the needs of automobile owners?***

the introduction of electrical appliances, however, many middle-class housewives began doing this work themselves. Moreover, the use of the automobile by middle-class families to run errands limited the need for delivery services and led to further unemployment.

A Land of Automobiles

Henry Ford's inexpensive Model T revolutionized the transportation industry. By 1930, cars, trucks, and buses had almost completely replaced horse-drawn vehicles. Trains and trolley cars also lost riders to automobiles.

To accommodate the increased traffic, more than 400,000 miles of new roads were built during the 1920s. A host of new structures—billboards, drive-in restaurants, filling stations, and tourist cabins—appeared along the nation's highways.

The automobile enabled rural residents to have greater contact with their neighbors and more access to shopping and leisure activities. Cars linked rural regions to urban areas. This made it easier for rural residents to relocate to the booming cities and for city-dwellers to visit the country. At the same time, however, the automobile contributed to the depopulation of the nation's inner cities. More accessible than ever, suburbs attracted thousands of middle-class families.

Auto-tourism. Seeking the fresh air of the countryside, millions of Americans participated in a new craze that was sweeping the nation—**auto-touring.** Taking part in this new pastime, Americans used their automobiles for camping and sightseeing vacations. Auto-touring allowed Americans to travel without the restrictions imposed by the schedules and routes of passenger trains. Guidebooks urged Americans to hit the road.

> **"Does father crave to fish for trout and bass and pike and musky? Take him auto-touring. Does sister want to dip in the surf . . . or see the world? Take her automobile vacationing. . . . Does mother sigh for a rest from daily routines? Take her touring. . . . Does baby need fresh mountain air far from flies and heat? Take him auto-camping."**

As thousands of Americans purchased automobiles, traffic jams such as this one near a city park became more common.

THE GRANGER COLLECTION, NEW YORK

Family life. In addition to changing the way Americans traveled on vacation, automobiles transformed family life. The automobile created new social opportunities for teenagers. Sociologists Robert and Helen Lynd took note of this change in *Middletown*, their 1929 book chronicling life in Muncie, Indiana.

> **"The extensive use of this new tool [the automobile] by the young has enormously extended their mobility and the range of alternatives before them; joining a crowd motoring over to a dance . . . twenty miles away may be a matter of a moment's decision, with no one's permission asked."**

Before the use of automobiles became widespread, teenagers spent much of their leisure time at home with their families. "In the nineties [1890s] we were all much more together. People brought chairs . . . and sat

TEACH OBJECTIVE 5

LEVELS 1 AND 2: To help students understand how American industries encouraged the transformation of consumer practices, copy the graphic organizer at right on the chalkboard, omitting the italicized answers. Have each student complete it. Ask volunteers to share their answers with the class. Conclude by leading a discussion with the class about how American industries transformed consumer practices. **Sheltered English**

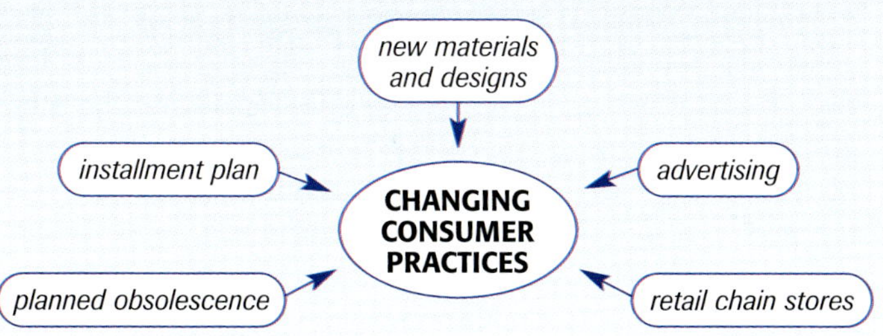

on the lawn evenings," complained one mother. The arrival of the automobile changed the ways that teenagers spent their free time. "What on earth do you want me to do? Just sit around home all evening!" protested one teenage girl when her father expressed his disapproval of her going riding in a car with a young man.

Critics claimed that cars reduced people's sense of community. The Lynds observed that "since the advent of the automobile and the movies" people in Muncie no longer spent "long summer evenings and Sunday afternoons on the porch or in the side yard." Also, by the 1920s cars had begun to cause pollution, traffic jams, and parking problems. Most serious was the rising accident rate.

✔ **READING CHECK:** How did widespread automobile use affect Americans' daily lives?

Strategies for Success — Studying Primary and Secondary Sources

Most of the wide variety of materials used by historians to form their accounts of the past can be classified into two basic categories: primary sources and secondary sources. *Primary sources*—materials made up of firsthand historical information—include artwork, diaries, and legal documents. In contrast, *secondary sources* are descriptions or interpretations of historical events that were written by nonparticipants after the events occurred. *The American Nation* is a secondary source. Primary and secondary sources are both essential tools for historians. Primary sources contain historical information that cannot be found anywhere else. Secondary sources can cover broad historical topics and evaluate the long-term consequences of events.

How to Study a Primary or Secondary Source

1. **Identify the type of source.** First, determine whether the source is a primary source or a secondary source. Then, if possible, find out about the historical background of the source's creator and the intended audience of the source.
2. **Examine the material carefully.** Study the source carefully, taking note of its main ideas and supporting details.
3. **Check for bias.** Check the source for any words, phrases, and ideas that express the point of view of its creator. Make sure to identify any instances in which a one-sided view of a event, person, or topic is presented.
4. **Put the information to use.** If possible, compare the source with other primary or secondary sources that address the same subject. Then use the results of your analysis to form generalizations and draw conclusions.

Applying the Strategy

Study the magazine cover on the right, which was published in the November 1927 issue of the *Ladies' Home Journal.*

Practicing the Strategy

Using the image above, answer the following questions.

1. Is this image a primary source or a secondary source? Explain your answer.
2. Who created the image? Who do you think was the magazine's intended audience?
3. Does the magazine cover express any biases? If so, what are they?
4. How does the source contribute to your understanding of the United States during the 1920s?

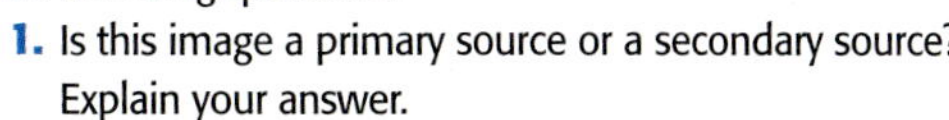

ACROSS THE CURRICULUM

▸SOCIOLOGY◂

Robert Lynd and Helen Lynd's *Middletown.* To write *Middletown,* Robert Lynd and Helen Lynd applied cultural anthropology methods to the examination of a modern U.S. city. This sociological study examined everyday life in Muncie, Indiana, and showed how the consumer culture of the 1920s had influenced the values and behavior of the city's residents. Critic H. L. Mencken called the book "one of the richest and most valuable documents ever concocted by American sociologists." In 1937 Robert and Helen Lynd published *Middletown in Transition,* which described the social effects of the Great Depression on Muncie.

CRITICAL THINKING Why might the Lynds have entitled their book *Middletown*?

ANSWER: Students might suggest that the Lynds wanted to convey that Muncie was a "typical small American city."

STRATEGIES FOR SUCCESS ANSWERS

Practicing the Strategy

1. a primary source—it contains firsthand information
2. *Ladies' Home Journal;* middle-class women
3. middle-class tastes
4. reflects women's styles in hair and clothing during the 1920s

LEVEL 3: Tell students to imagine that they are participants in a panel discussion at a conference on the transformation of consumer practices during the 1920s. Organize the class into two groups. Have one group act as questioners and the other group act as cultural critics. Have both groups prepare for the discussion by taking notes on the techniques and strategies businesses used to change consumer practices. *(See the Levels 1 and 2 lesson for the correct techniques and strategies.)* Then conduct the panel discussion. **Cooperative Learning**

Teacher to Teacher

Paul Horne of Columbia, South Carolina, suggested the following activity: Have each student write a brief essay about an invention or innovation of the 1920s that he or she believes has had the most significant impact on American society. Students should justify their choices in their essays.

ECONOMIC DEVELOPMENT

The General Motors Corporation. Although General Motors Corporation (GM) eventually grew into the largest automobile manufacturer in the world, it began as a risky business venture. Organized in 1908 by William C. Durant, a wealthy carriage maker from Michigan, GM first acquired small car companies that were unable to compete on their own. By the end of 1909 it had acquired more than 20 such enterprises. Over the next decade, GM struggled to finance and coordinate these holdings. The company did not fully succeed until Alfred P. Sloan took control in 1920 and reorganized it into five basic manufacturing divisions: Buick, Cadillac, Chevrolet, Oldsmobile, and Pontiac.

CRITICAL THINKING How might Sloan's action have reflected a marketing strategy that differed from Ford's?

ANSWER: Students might suggest that each division was designed to produce cars in a specific price range.

VISUAL RECORD ANSWER

Students might mention the shining metal and the streamlined shape.

VISUAL RECORD ANSWER

(for p. 393)

Students might suggest soup or other canned goods.

INTERPRETING THE VISUAL RECORD

Design. In the 1920s, manufacturers began to pay attention to the way a product looked. ***What elements of this iron do you think were designed to attract a customer's attention?***

Creating Consumers

Henry Ford manufactured his affordable Model T throughout the 1920s. He made few changes to its design. However, other automobile companies, such as Alfred P. Sloan's General Motors, began designing more expensive cars that emphasized luxury. Sloan explained the effect of car owners buying a second car. They "created the demand, not for basic transportation, but for progress in new cars, for comfort, convenience, power, and style."

Marketing. To allow average consumers to buy his more expensive cars, Sloan offered an **installment plan**. These plans allowed consumers to pay for their cars over time. By 1925, buyers purchased about 75 percent of cars on credit. The practice soon spread to cover the purchase of many other items such as kitchen appliances, pianos, and sewing machines. As one car dealer noted, installment plans were a profitable venture.

> **"To keep America growing we must keep Americans working, and to keep Americans working we must keep them wanting; wanting more than the bare necessities; wanting the luxuries and frills that make life so much more worthwhile, and installment selling makes it easier to keep Americans wanting."**

To make their goods more appealing, industrial designers began to create items that were pleasing to look at as well as functional. Industrial designers used new materials such as stainless steel and plastics to create a wide range of more modern-looking products. They developed streamlining—the shaping of surfaces to reduce wind resistance—for cars, planes, ships, and trains. Designers even applied streamlining to nonmoving objects such as clocks, radios, and appliances.

Manufacturers quickly learned that introducing new models of what was essentially the same product could boost sales. Manufacturers made products specifically designed to go out of style and then replaced them with an up-to-date model. They had discovered what came to be called **planned obsolescence**. Automobile manufacturers were among the first to adopt planned obsolescence. In the early 1920s General Motors introduced to the public the concept of the yearly model change and the trade-in. Thereafter, many families routinely traded in their "old" models and bought new cars every year.

The new consumer practice of purchasing goods on the installment plan only to turn around and purchase the latest style the next season caused problems for many Americans. A Department of Labor study in the 1920s reported that single working women were going into debt buying clothes to keep up with the latest styles.

Advertisements such as this one for mouthwash played on the social fears of many Americans.

Advertising. Advertising became big business in the 1920s, fueling the demand for cars and other consumer goods. Before World War I, money spent on advertising totaled some $500 million yearly. By 1929 the total had soared to more than $3 billion. Ads were everywhere. Commercial messages bombarded potential buyers not only in magazines and newspapers but also on billboards and over the new medium of radio.

REVIEW

Have students complete the **Section 1 Review** on p. 393.

ASSESS

Have students complete **Daily Quiz 13.1**. As **Alternative Assessment**, you may want to use the headlines or three-way conversation from this section's lessons.

RETEACH

Have students complete **Main Idea Activity for Reteaching and Sheltered English 13.1**. Pair students and assign each pair one of the subsections of Section 1. Have each pair write an outline of its subsection as well as four questions and answers that pertain to the subsection. Collect students' questions and use them to quiz the class. **Sheltered English, Cooperative Learning**

EXTEND

Have students conduct research on popular auto-tour destinations during the 1920s. Then have each student write a report about road conditions during the 1920s, roadside accommodations that were available to travelers during the 1920s, and so forth. Have students present their reports to the class.
Block Scheduling

Most advertisements targeted women. They used psychology to play on consumers' hopes and fears. Advertisements for Borden's milk, for example, warned mothers, "Hardly a family—well-to-do and poor alike—escapes the menace of malnutrition. Your own child may fall victim to this . . . evil."

Companies used slogans, jingles, and celebrity testimonials to fix product names in customers' minds. When her husband, Franklin D. Roosevelt, was governor of New York, Eleanor Roosevelt praised Cream of Wheat, a breakfast food that their son John had eaten since infancy. She claimed in advertisements that the cereal "has undoubtedly played its part in building his robust physique."

INTERPRETING THE VISUAL RECORD

Retail. Chain stores like this A&P brought a wide variety of products to American shoppers. ***What products are displayed in this window?***

A growing retail industry. As the number of products increased to meet growing consumer demand, a new type of store spread across the country. The A&P grocery chain grew from some 3,000 stores in 1922 to about 14,000 by 1925. These chain-style grocery stores slowly began to replace the traditional corner markets. New technology allowed stores to stock a wider variety of products. The invention of cellophane—a transparent wrapping material first produced in the United States in 1924—along with quick-freezing techniques preserved fresh foods longer. As a result, food could be shipped over greater distances.

✔ **READING CHECK:** How did American industries encourage the transformation of consumer practices?

SECTION  REVIEW

Define and explain the significance of the following terms:
scientific management
Model T
assembly line
auto-touring
installment plan
planned obsolescence

Identify and explain the significance of the following individuals:
Frederick W. Taylor
Henry Ford
Alfred P. Sloan

1. **Using Graphic Organizers** Copy the following organizational web. Use it to explain how the factors shown below inspired the new consumer demands that emerged during the 1920s.

2. **Identifying Cause and Effect** Why did Henry Ford develop the assembly line? How did it encourage industrial growth?
3. **Taking a Stand** If you had been a factory worker during the 1920s, would you have taken a job with Ford? Why or why not?
4. **Evaluating** How did the widespread use of the automobile affect family life, leisure activities, and working life for some Americans?

Critical Thinking

5. During the 1920s businesses used various tactics to encourage Americans to buy their products. What positive and negative effects did these tactics have?
Consider:
• how installment plans and planned obsolescence altered consumer practices
• what influence advertising had on American consumer habits
• how the growth of the retail industry affected Americans' buying habits

SECTION 1 REVIEW ANSWERS

Define and Identify

For significance, see the following pages:

- scientific management, p. 387
- Frederick W. Taylor, p. 387
- Henry Ford, p. 387
- Model T, p. 387
- assembly line, p. 387
- auto-touring, p. 390
- Alfred P. Sloan, p. 392
- installment plan, p. 392
- planned obsolescence, p. 392

1. economic prosperity–more disposable income; electricity–spur demand for electrical appliances; new products–create and meet new demands; scientific management–raise efficiency and lower prices; advertising–create demand

2. to increase efficiency; cars became more affordable, increasing demand.

3. yes–eight-hour day and $5-a-day wage; no–tedium of assembly-line work and Ford's involvement in his workers' personal lives

4. Family life became less centered on the home. New leisure activities such as auto-touring were created. Middle-class Americans began to commute from the suburbs.

5. Answers will vary. Students might suggest the increased availability and affordability of consumer goods; the creation of monotonous assembly-line jobs; and the encouragement of wasteful consumption habits and personal debt.

SECTION 2

After completing Section 2, students should be able to:

OBJECTIVE 1 *Analyze the impact prohibition had on crime.*

OBJECTIVE 2 *Describe the characteristics of the new youth culture.*

OBJECTIVE 3 *Explain how celebrities and new forms of popular entertainment helped create a mass culture.*

OBJECTIVE 4 *Examine what the Scopes trial and the religious movements of the 1920s revealed about American society.*

LET'S GET STARTED!

Ask students to speculate on how new forms of culture and new trends in society might result in "conflicts between traditional values and modern trends." Call on students to identify such conflicts apparent in American society today. List students' responses on the chalkboard. Tell students that in Section 2 they will learn about changes in American culture during the 1920s that led to conflicts between people who longed for traditional standards and people who embraced modern trends.

SECTION 2 RESOURCES

PRINT

- Guided Reading Strategy 13.2
- Geography Activity 13: The Prohibition Era
- Primary Source Reading 13: Making a Monkey Out of the "Common Man"
- Biography Reading 13: Amelia Earhart
- Section 2 Review, p. 401
- Daily Quiz 13.2

MULTIMEDIA

- One-Stop Planner, Lesson 13.2
- The American Nation Video Program Segment: Prohibition; Teacher's Guide, p. 211–12
- Holt Researcher: American History CD–ROM

SHELTERED ENGLISH

- Main Idea Activity for Reteaching and Sheltered English 13.2

✔ READING TO UNDERSTAND

To help students master the section objectives, have them answer the **READING CHECKS** and complete **Guided Reading Strategy 13.2** as they read the section.

Life in the Twenties

OBJECTIVES

Read to understand:

1. what impact prohibition had on crime
2. what the characteristics of the new youth culture were
3. how celebrities and new forms of popular entertainment helped create a mass culture
4. what the Scopes trial and the religious movements of the 1920s revealed about American society

KEY TERMS

Volstead Act
Untouchables
Twenty-first Amendment
flappers
Fundamentalism
Scopes trial

KEY PEOPLE

Al Capone
Eliot Ness
Cecil B. DeMille
Babe Ruth
Jim Thorpe
Charles Lindbergh
Amelia Earhart
Aimee Semple McPherson
Billy Sunday
Clarence Darrow

"About four or five days after I had gotten the vacuum tube hooked up, I started to hear music coming across the wires. Music! And then, between the music, I could hear somebody talking. . . . 'I am Dr. Conrad. I am experimenting with radio station 8XK.' . . . By January of 1921, I had decided to build my own broadcast station. I built a hundred-watter and then applied for an experimental broadcast license. In March I got a letter saying: 'One of my first official duties as Secretary of Commerce is to award you this license. Aren't you the young fellow I met . . . in Marion, Ohio? . . . What's a fourteen-year-old kid going to do with a broadcast station?' "

—Albert Sindlinger

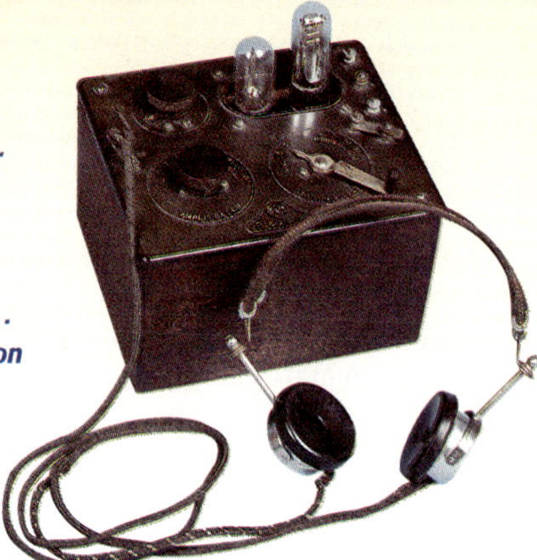

1920s radio receiver

Albert Sindlinger began experimenting with radio broadcasts as a young teenager in the 1920s. The first licensed radio stations were just beginning to broadcast music, news reports, and sports events. Commercial radio linked Americans from coast to coast, leading some to call the decade of the 1920s the gateway to modern America. For the first time, a truly national mass culture took shape in the United States. This emerging mass culture led to conflicts between traditional values and modern trends.

Prohibition

One of the most disruptive issues of the 1920s was the prohibition of the sale and distribution of alcoholic beverages. Progressive reformers seeking to combat crime, family violence, and poverty had long called for a ban on alcohol. During World War I, many reformers had supported prohibition as a wartime measure. They pointed out that drinking reduced the efficiency of soldiers and workers. The Eighteenth Amendment, which prohibited the manufacture, sale, and transportation of alcoholic beverages, was ratified in January 1919. That October, Congress passed the **Volstead Act** to enforce the amendment.

In some regions prohibition was strictly enforced, and alcohol consumption declined. However, in many parts of the country, particularly in the cities, prohibition was extremely unpopular and widely ignored. Americans frequented speakeasies, made their own liquor, and bought bootleg alcohol—or illegal alcohol smuggled in from Canada, Mexico, or the West Indies.

Bootlegging became one of the decade's most profitable businesses. In large cities, criminal gangs controlled liquor sales. Al Capone ruled Chicago's underworld with his small army of mobsters. To gain control over all liquor sales in Chicago, Capone's mob waged a violent war on rival gangs. Chicago's prohibition

TEACH OBJECTIVE 1

LEVEL 1: Tell students that many Americans ignored prohibition and made or sold liquor illegally. Pair students and ask them to list the impact prohibition had on crime. *(Students might suggest that prohibition led to increased crime rates by creating an illegal market for alcohol. People frequented speakeasies, made their own liquor, or bought bootleg alcohol. In large cities, violent criminal gangs controlled this illegal market.)* Have volunteers read their lists to the class. Discuss students' responses as a class.
Sheltered English, Cooperative Learning

LEVELS 2 AND 3: Tell students to imagine that they are members of Congress during the 1920s. They are studying the impact of prohibition on crime in order to prepare a report for a committee meeting. Have each student prepare a brief report about the effects of prohibition on crime. *(See the Level 1 lesson for the correct effects.)* Ask volunteers to read their reports to the class.

gang wars reached a peak on Saint Valentine's Day in 1929. On that day, several members of Capone's gang massacred seven members of the rival O'Banion gang.

Hoping to stem the bootlegging, corruption, and violence, the federal Prohibition Bureau hired a youthful special agent named Eliot Ness. He organized a top squad of young detectives to go after gangsters. Unlike corrupt city police officers who often turned a blind eye to bootlegging, Ness's men strictly enforced prohibition laws. Because of their dedication and honesty, Ness and his detectives were nicknamed the **Untouchables**. Ness put an end to Al Capone's reign over the Chicago underworld in 1931. Ness caught Capone for evading income tax payments. During Capone's 11-year prison sentence he lost his control over organized crime in Chicago.

Al Capone attracted public attention by dressing in expensive clothing and living a lavish lifestyle.

Despite the gang violence that plagued the era, prohibition had some positive consequences. Alcoholism declined and so did the number of alcohol-related deaths. Prohibition's negative results, however, drew more attention. Prohibition led to a widespread breakdown of law and order. It turned millions of otherwise law-abiding Americans into lawbreakers before it was repealed by the ratification of the **Twenty-first Amendment** in 1933.

✔ **READING CHECK:** What impact did prohibition have on crime?

Youth Culture

Many young Americans ignored prohibition laws. Some members of the younger generation of the 1920s openly rejected the values and conventions of previous generations. As a result, a new youth culture began to emerge.

The "new woman." Many challenges to traditional ways were brought on by changes in women's dress and behavior. During the 1920s, magazines, movies, and literature began to discuss the life of the "new woman." This woman was stylish, adventurous, and independent, often with a career of her own.

Reacting against the strict pre–World War I code of behavior, some young women during the 1920s exercised new freedom in how they dressed. They stopped wearing heavy corsets and started wearing shorter skirts and transparent silk hose.

People began to refer to young women who adopted the new style as **flappers**. Flappers enjoyed defying traditional standards of female behavior. Many young women began to wear bobbed, or short, hair, for example. Exploring new realms of independence, young women also drove cars and participated in sports. Although not all women adopted this new lifestyle, the image of the flapper caught the attention of the media.

The new woman sought not only social freedom but also economic independence. Although the proportion of working women remained fairly constant throughout the 1920s, American women worked in a wider variety of occupations. Some drove taxis. Others ran telegraph lines, worked as stenographers, flew airplanes, and hauled freight. Most, however, pursued traditionally female careers such as nursing, teaching, and domestic service.

INTERPRETING THE VISUAL RECORD

Youth culture. This 1920s magazine cover shows some of the characteristics of the new youth culture, such as the woman's bobbed hair and the man's baggy pants. ***What other aspects of life in the 1920s does this magazine cover show?***

THE GRANGER COLLECTION, NEW YORK

THAT'S INTERESTING!

While many Americans simply ignored prohibition, some formed organizations to lobby for its repeal. For example, a group of wealthy industrialists formed the Association Against the Prohibition Amendment (AAPA), which sponsored antiprohibition meetings and supported "wet" political candidates. AAPA members argued that prohibition represented a needless encroachment on individual rights by a federal government that had become too powerful. They also contended that prohibition made the United States look unsophisticated. The AAPA received widespread public support during the early 1930s and played a key role in persuading legislators to vote for the Twenty-first Amendment.

***The American Nation* VIDEO PROGRAM**

Prohibition; Teacher's Guide, pp. 211–12

Search 37756, Play to 38875
Videodisc 2, Side A

Play

Pause

See *Teacher's Guide* for Spanish barcode.

VISUAL RECORD ANSWER

Students might suggest women's independence and changes in women's fashion.

TEACH OBJECTIVE 2

LEVELS 1 AND 2: Tell students to imagine that they have been asked to create a series of trading cards featuring the characteristics of youth culture during the 1920s. Pair students and have them create trading cards depicting the characteristics of the "new woman," college life, and leisure activities. Have students illustrate the front of each card. On the back of each card, students should write a brief summary of the card's subject. *(Students' cards might include: The "new woman" sought social and economic independence. Young women often drove cars, wore bobbed hair and participated in sports. Many held jobs. College life also had its own fashions, including baggy flannel slacks and sport jackets. Leisure activities included dance marathons and novelty events such as flagpole sitting.)* Have students present their trading cards to the class. Conclude by leading a discussion comparing 1920s youth culture with today's youth culture.
Sheltered English, Cooperative Learning

LEVEL 3: Tell students to imagine that they are radio personalities during the 1920s. Pair students and have them write a script for a radio talk show in which they discuss the characteristics of youth culture. *(See the Levels 1 and 2 lesson for the correct characteristics.)* Ask each pair to perform its talk show for the class. **Cooperative Learning**

HISTORY MAKERS SPEAK

George Robinson in *Listening to Radio, 1920–1950*

The "Magical" Effect of Radio. Radio broadcasts made many Americans feel "connected" to people in other parts of the United States in a way they had never experienced. George Robinson, who was a young boy in Mississippi when his family acquired a radio in 1926, later recalled this feeling: "The sounds which came from [the radio] were truly magic to a family in Greenville, Mississippi, who thought that Memphis was somewhere on the other side of the globe. We stared at the thing, and at each other, in wonderment as we realized that the voices were actually coming through the air from KMOX in St. Louis and WLW in Cincinnati and WJR in Detroit. I can't recall what was being broadcast, which is unimportant."

ACTIVITY: Ask students to create a list of other forms of technology that have "connected" Americans during the 1900s. Then call on volunteers for examples and discuss them with the class.

Collegiate clothing, such as school sweaters, and straw hats became fashionable during the 1920s.

College life. In the early part of the century, most Americans' ended their formal education at high school or before. Between 1900 and 1930, however, college enrollment tripled. The greatest jump came during the 1920s. Most of these college students came from middle-and upper-class families.

The growing number of college students influenced popular images of the new youth culture. Advertising, magazines, and movies focused on collegiate fashions and lifestyles. According to a 1923 California university newspaper, "'College style' has a definite meaning. . . . Fall '23 can almost be called the young man's season with the style pace set by the collegian." The "collegiate" look included baggy flannel slacks and sports jackets.

Leisure fun and fads. New leisure activities and a variety of fads spread among American youth during the 1920s. Many young people participated in dance marathons. Couples danced for days, competing for prize money awarded to the last couple to collapse or drop out. To keep their partners awake, couples used smelling salts or ice packs. In 1928, couples danced for almost three weeks—482 hours—in the "Dance Derby of the Century."

Beauty contests were introduced during the 1920s. The hotel operators and merchants of Atlantic City, New Jersey, founded the Miss America beauty pageant in 1921. Contestants were judged primarily on their hair, smile, and appearance in a bathing suit. Despite the emphasis on the competitive display of female beauty, managers of the first beauty contests also stressed traditional morals.

Novelty events such as flagpole sitting attracted media attention and drew crowds of Americans. A flagpole sitter would climb onto a tiny platform atop a flagpole and sit with only stirrups for support. Taking short breaks every hour, flagpole sitters could last for days. Alvin "Shipwreck" Kelly was the most popular flagpole sitter. As the fad caught on, Kelly was routinely hired for publicity stunts by theaters and hotels. He claimed to have sat for a total of 145 days on flagpoles across the United States in 1929.

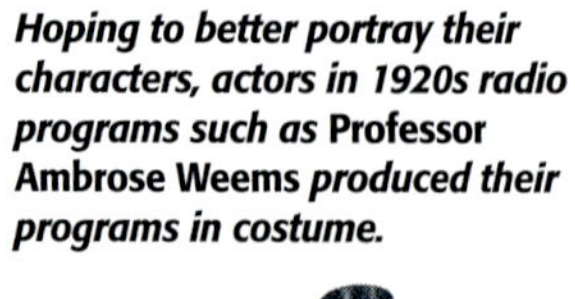

Hoping to better portray their characters, actors in 1920s radio programs such as* Professor Ambrose Weems *produced their programs in costume.

THE GRANGER COLLECTION, NEW YORK

✔ **READING CHECK:** What were the characteristics of the new youth culture that arose in the 1920s?

Mass Entertainment

Leisure activities were not limited to young people. The economic boom of the 1920s meant that many—although not all—Americans had bigger paychecks and more free time than in years past. To help fill their leisure hours, many Americans turned to radio, movies, and professional sports for entertainment.

Radio. Commercial radio stations emerged during the early 1920s and grew in popularity as more Americans purchased radio receivers. The first stations, Detroit's WWJ and Pittsburgh's KDKA, went on the air in 1920. By 1929 more than 800 stations reached over 10 million homes.

The radio programming of the early 1920s was diverse. Early stations broadcast church services, local new reports, music, and sporting

▸ASSIGNMENT *Have each student create a mobile that displays symbols associated with the "new woman" of the 1920s. Students should write an explanation of the symbols they have chosen. Have students display their mobiles around the classroom.*

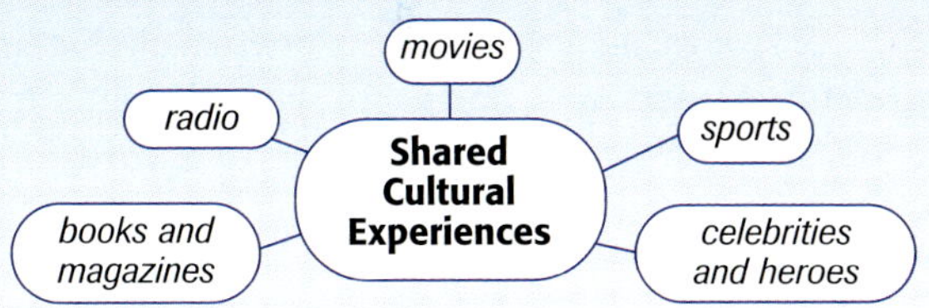

TEACH OBJECTIVE 3

LEVEL 1: To help students understand how celebrities and new forms of popular entertainment helped create a mass culture in the 1920s, copy the graphic organizer at right on the chalkboard, omitting the italicized answers. Have each student complete it. Ask volunteers to share their answers with the class. Conclude by leading a discussion about the mass culture that was created during the 1920s.
Sheltered English

LEVEL 2: Tell students to imagine that they are magazine editors during the 1920s and are responsible for creating a magazine cover on the emergence of a mass culture. Pair students and have them create a magazine cover that shows how celebrities and forms of popular entertainment helped create a mass culture. *(See the Level 1 lesson for the correct ways.)*
Cooperative Learning

events. Two of the biggest radio broadcasts of the early days of radio came in 1921. That year, the Radio Corporation of America broadcast the Dempsey-Carpentier heavyweight title fight, and Westinghouse broadcast the World Series.

Radio stations soon discovered that they could make money by selling advertisement spots to other businesses. Stations provided businesses with the opportunity to sponsor programs. Businesses used these spots to advertise their products. Companies such as the A&P grocery store chain and the maker of Ipana toothpaste sponsored such music programs as the *A&P Gypsies* and the *Ipana Troubadours.*

During the late 1920s networks such as the National Broadcasting Company (NBC) began offering local radio networks packages of programs to broadcast. National radio broadcasts provided Americans with a set of shared cultural experiences. Americans across the country laughed at the same jokes, tapped their feet to the same music, and listened to the same ads. One executive noted that by allowing companies to advertise nationwide, the radio served as "a latchkey to nearly every home in the United States."

Movies. In the 1920s Americans increasingly turned to movies for entertainment. The mass appeal of movie theaters impressed journalist Lloyd Lewis.

> **"In the 'de luxe' [movie] house every man is a king and every woman a queen. Most of these cinema palaces sell all their seats at the same price,—and get it; the rich man stands in line with the poor. . . . In this suave atmosphere, the differences . . . that determine our lives outside are forgotten. All men enter these portals equal, and thus the movies are perhaps a symbol of democracy."**

New advances in the art of moviemaking attracted even larger audiences. Movie director Cecil B. DeMille introduced a new style of filmmaking marked by epic plots and complex characters. DeMille created biblical epics such as *The Ten Commandments* (1923). DeMille also made films that focused on the changing morals of the 1920s, such as *Why Change Your Wife?* (1920) and *Forbidden Fruit* (1921).

Moviegoers were captivated by dramatic performances of famous silent film actors such as Lon Chaney and Charlie Chaplin. Western films enjoyed great success as well. Tom Mix, one of the most popular western film stars, often played the role of a heroic cowboy.

The era of silent films ended abruptly in 1927. That year, Warner Brothers released the first feature-length "talkie," *The Jazz Singer,* starring Al Jolson. The introduction of sound led to the creation of new types of films, such as musicals and newsreels—short films summing up the news of the day. In 1929 some 80 million Americans flocked to the theaters each week.

Censorship

The Roaring Twenties was a time of bathtub gin, gambling, jazz, short skirts, and the first talking movies. Old taboos were challenged one after the other. Alarmed and outraged by what they saw as the breakdown of the nation's moral standards, many community, government, and religious groups took action.

These activists pulled from library and store shelves books and magazines that used foul language, discussed sex frankly, or supported radical political ideas. U.S. Customs officials labeled many foreign books obscene. They even seized some books, including the acclaimed novel *Ulysses* by Irish author James Joyce. Groups like the American Civil Liberties Union opposed these restrictions on literature. They argued that censorship was a violation of the Constitution's First Amendment.

Today the battle between censorship and freedom of speech continues. The National Endowment for the Arts (NEA), for example, has come under attack for funding artists whose works some consider obscene. Although some critics judge the art as unsuitable for public funding, the artists defend their right to freedom of expression. The NEA and other agencies are caught in the middle of the battle.

Is such censorship a violation of free speech or a necessary form of protection? American society and U.S. courts continue to struggle with this question.

Protesting censorship

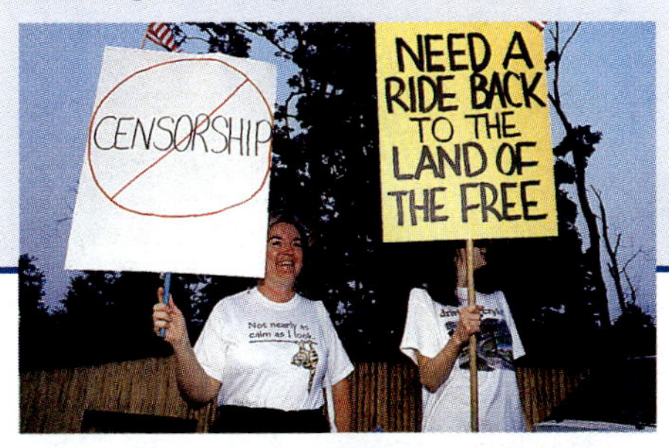

CULTURAL DIVERSITY

Early Radio. Early radio, was noncommercial, and did not attempt to minimize ethnic differences. Some local radio stations aired programs that were specifically designed for ethnic audiences. By 1926, for instance, the city of Chicago had four stations—WGES, WSBC, WEDC, and WCRW—that were devoted to programming for Irish Americans, Italian Americans, Polish Americans, and other ethnic groups.

CRITICAL THINKING What development might have led to a homogenization of radio programming?

ANSWER: Students might suggest that the commercialization of radio led to uniformity in radio programming.

THAT'S INTERESTING!

During his 40-year career, Cecil B. DeMille produced and directed more than 70 movies that grossed a total of about $750 million and were seen by approximately 3 billion people. *The Ten Commandments,* his first biblical epic, was the top-grossing film of the 1920s. A remake of *The Ten Commandments,* which was released in 1956 and was DeMille's final film, was the top-grossing movie of the 1950s.

LEVEL 3: Have each student write a brief essay that analyzes how celebrities and new forms of popular entertainment helped create a mass culture during the 1920s. *(See the Level 1 lesson for the correct ways.)* Have volunteers read their essays to the class.

SPOTLIGHT on 1920s Celebrities

Have each student conduct research on a 1920s celebrity figure from the world of aviation, movies, or sports. Then have students create a postage stamp to commemorate the celebrity. Students should write a brief summary of the celebrity's significance and accomplishments to accompany the postage stamp. Display students' work around the classroom. **Block Scheduling**

SPOTLIGHT on Censorship During the 1920s

Have each student conduct research on a work that was censored during the 1920s. Students should research the issues surrounding the censorship of the work, including the arguments of those who favored censorship and those who opposed censorship. Have students present an oral report about the subject of their research. **Block Scheduling**

ECONOMIC DEVELOPMENT

Money in Professional Sports. In early 1925, Red Grange became the first athlete to appear on the cover of *Time* magazine. He was paid $12,000 for playing in his first professional football game with the Chicago Bears. His immense popularity with the fans soon prompted him to raise his fee to $35,000 per game. In three seasons he earned a total of $1 million—about $1,000 for every minute he was on the field.

CRITICAL THINKING What might have enabled Red Grange to command such a large salary?

ANSWER: Students might suggest that commercial broadcasts of sporting events introduced large amounts of money into professional sports.

VISUAL RECORD ANSWER

Students might mention the plush seats and ornate surroundings.

INTERPRETING THE VISUAL RECORD

The movies. Luxury movie houses such as this theater in New York attracted Americans of all income levels. ***What features does this 1920s theater offer its customers?***

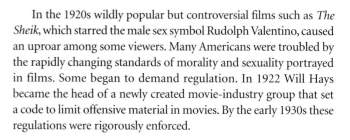

In the 1920s wildly popular but controversial films such as *The Sheik*, which starred the male sex symbol Rudolph Valentino, caused an uproar among some viewers. Many Americans were troubled by the rapidly changing standards of morality and sexuality portrayed in films. Some began to demand regulation. In 1922 Will Hays became the head of a newly created movie-industry group that set a code to limit offensive material in movies. By the early 1930s these regulations were rigorously enforced.

Sports. During the 1920s many Americans turned to sports for entertainment. Professional sports had emerged in the United States during the late 1800s. With the introduction of new technology in the 1920s, however, professional sports became a form of mass entertainment available to almost all Americans.

Professional and college-level football attracted many American fans during the 1920s. Attendance at college football games doubled between 1921 and 1930. College football stars like Red Grange began to join professional football teams. Grange played his first game for the Chicago Bears on Thanksgiving Day 1925. The game attracted 35,000 fans, the largest crowd to attend a professional football game up to that time.

Known as America's national pastime, baseball remained the nation's most popular sport despite charges of corruption. In the 1919 "Black Sox" scandal, "Shoeless" Joe Jackson and seven other Chicago White Sox players were accused of accepting money to lose the 1919 World Series. Order was restored to the game when Judge Kenesaw Mountain Landis was appointed Commissioner of Baseball by team owners. Landis expelled the suspected White Sox players from professional baseball for life. Legendary players such as Babe Ruth, Ty Cobb, and Lou Gehrig had outstanding seasons during the 1920s and attracted new fans. By the end of the 1920s baseball was still by far the nation's most popular sport. Millions of fans tuned in to radio broadcasts and attended games.

The "Black Sox" scandal angered many Americans, but baseball remained a popular attraction.

Books and magazines. For literary entertainment, some Americans turned to new publications. Founded in 1923, the Book-of-the-Month Club enabled publishers to bypass bookstores by selling books directly to consumers.

In the 1920s many Americans read magazines for entertainment. Weekly magazines such as *Collier's* and *The Saturday Evening Post* drew readers with their cartoons, short stories, and many pages of advertising. The husband-and-wife team of DeWitt and Lila Wallace founded *Reader's Digest* in 1921. Designed for busy Americans with less time to read, *Reader's Digest* reprinted articles from other magazines in shortened form. It proved a big success.

Celebrities and Heroes

The mass appeal of movies, radio, and sports generated huge audiences who shared in celebrities' victories and accomplishments. Actors became instantly famous. Young Americans paid special attention to celebrities' personal habits. They often copied the

TEACH OBJECTIVE 4

LEVEL 1: Have students design a "Coming Attractions" poster for a movie about the religious movements of the 1920s and the Scopes trial. Students' posters should reflect the characteristics of American society that the trial and the religious movements revealed. *(Students' posters might include Americans' differing opinions about social change, the influence of movies and radio on religion, or the deep division in American society between traditional religious values and new values based on scientific ways of thought.)*
Sheltered English

LEVEL 2: Tell students to imagine that they are visiting the United States in the 1920s and they attend both a religious revival and the Scopes trial. Have each student write a letter to a friend back home, describing these events and what they reveal about American society in the 1920s. *(See the Level 1 lesson for the correct characteristics.)* Ask volunteers to read their letters to the class.

▸**ASSIGNMENT** *Have students locate and bring to class an artifact that illustrates one form of mass culture during the 1920s. Students might obtain newspaper accounts of sporting events, radio scripts, sheet music, or silent films. Have students prepare an oral report or write a brief essay to explain the artifact.*

---

behavior of stars. In 1928, for example, Greta Garbo wore a slouch hat in the movie *A Woman of Affairs.* The slouch hat instantly became the most popular women's hat style.

Athletes also received celebrity status during the 1920s. One sports favorite was Babe Ruth. Known as the Sultan of Swat, Ruth dominated baseball from 1920 to 1934. During this time he led the New York Yankees to four World Series championships. In 1927 the spindle-legged, pigeon-toed ball player astounded the sports world with a record 60 home runs. Ruth's flashy playing on the field and scandalous life off the field attracted much attention.

Few athletes of the 1920s had more diverse talent than Jim Thorpe. As a student, Thorpe played every intercollegiate sport offered at his school. After leaving school, he began training for the Olympics. At the 1912 games, held in Stockholm, Sweden, Thorpe became the first competitor to win both the pentathlon and the decathlon. Thorpe went on to a career in major-league baseball. He also played professional football for several years.

Probably the biggest celebrity of the 1920s was pilot Charles Lindbergh. Lindbergh was a young, clean-cut pilot from Minnesota who flew airmail cargo planes between St. Louis and Chicago. In May 1927 he took off in a small, single-engine plane. He was aiming to win a $25,000 prize that had been offered to the first pilot to fly nonstop from New York to Paris. Lindbergh overcame bad weather, hunger, and fatigue to fly 33.5 hours alone in his airplane, *Spirit of St. Louis.*

Lindbergh's flight tapped into the American infatuation with contests and media events during the 1920s. It became one of the most talked about exploits of the decade. New Yorkers threw a ticker-tape parade for Lindbergh. President Coolidge received the modest young man at the White House. The next year, Amelia Earhart became the first woman to fly across the Atlantic Ocean.

✔ **READING CHECK:** How did celebrities and new forms of popular entertainment help create a mass culture?

LUCKY LINDY!

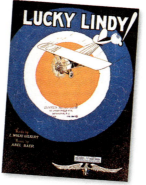

Charles Lindbergh's solo flight across the Atlantic Ocean captured the public's attention. This sheet music celebrates Lindbergh's flight.

Religion in the 1920s

Some Americans found the social changes of the 1920s more troubling than exciting. Many citizens' lives still centered on church, family, and neighborhood, and religion remained a vital part of American culture.

Revivalism. Many Americans were worried about declining moral standards. Religious leaders preached sermons and wrote books denouncing the evils of popular entertainment and alcohol. The popular message of these religious leaders inspired a new era of revivalism.

To compete with Hollywood movies and radio for the public's attention, some religious leaders began using Hollywood-style entertainment to spread their message of morality. Aimee Semple McPherson was one of the most popular revivalists. She combined a strong Christian message with the glamour of Hollywood. From her International

INTERPRETING THE VISUAL RECORD

Religion. Aimee Semple McPherson was a popular revivalist preacher in the 1920s. ***Does this image suggest that McPherson was influenced by the movie industry? Explain.***

PEOPLE IN HISTORY

Amelia Earhart. A Kansas native, Amelia Earhart took an interest in aviation while serving as a military nurse during World War I. She learned to fly while working in a Boston settlement house during the 1920s. In 1928 Earhart was a passenger on a transatlantic flight, which was organized by a New York publisher. It brought her instant fame. Four years later "Lady Lindy" became the first woman to fly solo across the Atlantic Ocean, and in 1935 she completed the first solo flight from Hawaii to California. In 1937, after Purdue University presented her with a new, technologically advanced airplane, Earhart set out with navigator Fred Noonan to fly point-to-point around the world. After completing more than two thirds of the trip, they disappeared over the middle of the Pacific Ocean.

ACTIVITY: Ask students to conduct research on another celebrity from the 1920s. Then have them present brief oral reports on their research to the class.

VISUAL RECORD ANSWER

Students answering "yes" might cite her hair style and pose. Students answering "no" might mention her career choice.

LEVEL 3: Tell students to imagine that they are community leaders during the 1920s who must give a speech in the wake of the Scopes trial. Have each student prepare a brief speech that addresses the trial, and the religious movements of the 1920s, and what they reveal about American society. *(See the Level 1 lesson for the correct characteristics.)* Ask volunteers to deliver their speeches to the class.

SPOTLIGHT on Aimee Semple McPherson

Have each student conduct research on the career of Aimee Semple McPherson. Students' research should focus on her message, reasons for her popularity, and the connection between McPherson and Pentecostalism. Organize students into small groups and have them pool the information they have gathered to prepare a collage. Display students' collages around the classroom.

Cooperative Learning, Block Scheduling

THAT'S INTERESTING!

The Scopes trial was the first jury trial that was brought to the public through live radio broadcasts. Outside the Dayton courthouse where the trial took place, enterprising vendors sold Bibles and toy monkeys as well as hot dogs and lemonade.

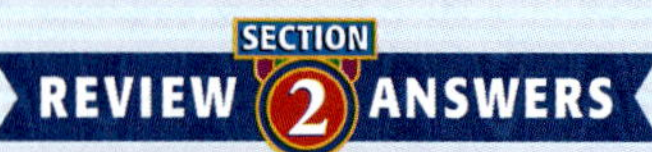

Define and Identify

For significance, see the following pages:

- Volstead Act, p. 394
- Al Capone, p. 394
- Eliot Ness, p. 395
- Untouchables, p. 395
- Twenty-first Amendment, p. 395
- flappers, p. 395
- Cecil B. DeMille, p. 397
- Babe Ruth, p. 398
- Jim Thorpe, p. 399
- Charles Lindbergh, p. 399
- Amelia Earhart, p. 399
- Aimee Semple McPherson, p. 399
- Fundamentalism, p. 400
- Billy Sunday, p. 400
- Clarence Darrow, p. 400
- Scopes trial, p. 400

PENTECOSTALISM

Pentecostalism grew rapidly during the 1920s. The movement, however, had begun decades earlier. Pentecostalism grew out of a series of multidenominational revivals held in the Midwest during the 1890s. Charles F. Parham led the first Pentecostal revival in Topeka, Kansas, in 1901. Parham began the movement because he was convinced that real spirituality lay in experiencing the "baptism of the Holy Spirit." With their emphasis on experiencing the Holy Spirit, Pentecostal worship services were lively and emotional. Services often included faith healing and people speaking in tongues, or unfamiliar languages. Parham and his followers believed that an individual possessed by the Holy Spirit would be able to speak in other languages, and therefore be able to spread the faith.

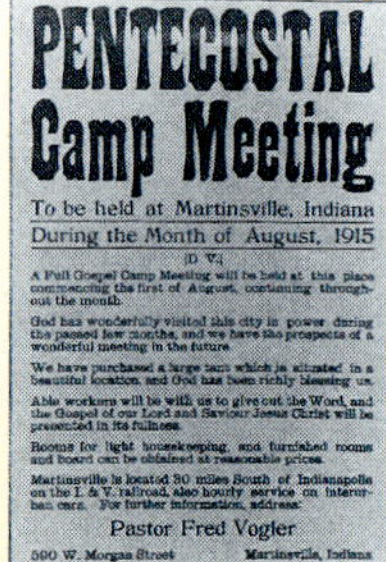
PENTECOSTAL Camp Meeting

To be held at Martinsville, Indiana

During the Month of August, 1915

(D. V.)

A Full Gospel Camp Meeting will be held at this place commencing the first of August, continuing throughout the month.

God has wonderfully visited this city in power during the passed few months, and we have the prospects of a wonderful meeting in the future.

We have purchased a large tent which is situated in a beautiful location and God has been richly blessing us.

Able workers will be with us to give out the Word, and the Gospel of our Lord and Saviour Jesus Christ will be presented in its fullness.

Rooms for light housekeeping, and furnished rooms and board can be obtained at reasonable prices.

Martinsville is located 30 miles South of Indianapolis on the I. & V. railroad, also hourly service on interurban cars. For further information, address:

Pastor Fred Vogler

590 W. Morgan Street Martinsville, Indiana

Revival meetings were popular in the 1920s.

Pentecostalism spread rapidly. The faith's focus on the direct experience of the Holy Spirit rather than on complex religious teachings attracted many Americans, particularly those with little formal education. In addition, the faith's emphasis on missionary work attracted a racially diverse following. In 1906 William Joseph Seymour, an African American preacher, brought the Pentecostal movement to California.

With the spread of Pentecostalism during the 1920s, hundreds of locally independent Pentecostal churches opened. The missionary movement of the Pentecostal faith proved remarkably successful. Today there are some 11.1 million Pentecostals in the United States and several hundred million worldwide.

Church of the Foursquare Gospel, headquartered in the city of Los Angeles, McPherson offered dramatic religious services. The services combined an orchestra, chorus, and elaborate stage sets. Outfitted in her signature white dress, white shoes, and blue cape, McPherson captured the glamour of Hollywood. Her church was closely tied to the rapidly expanding Protestant movement called Pentecostalism.

Fundamentalism. Responding to the rapidly changing society of the 1920s, many Americans turned to a more conservative approach to their religious faith. A Protestant movement called **Fundamentalism** gained popularity during the decade. Followers of fundamentalist views resisted many of the new practices of other Protestant groups. The term *fundamentalist* came from a series of booklets published between 1910 and 1915 called *The Fundamentals.* The booklets argued that traditional Christian doctrine should be accepted without question. Fundamentalists believed that every word of the Bible should be regarded as literally true. They attacked Christian "liberals" who had accepted modern scientific learning, such as the theory of evolution. Fundamentalists claimed that this "modernism" weakened Christianity and contributed to the moral decline of the nation.

Evangelical preachers who spread the Fundamentalist "old-time religion" found an eager audience in rural towns and in urban areas where traditional values remained strong. People were spellbound by preacher Billy Sunday's evangelical showmanship. He attracted people with his rousing attacks on card playing, dancing, and drinking.

The Scopes trial. Fundamentalism went on trial in a famous court case in July 1925. Earlier that year the Tennessee legislature had outlawed the teaching of Charles Darwin's theory of evolution in the state's public schools. To test the law's constitutionality, the American Civil Liberties Union offered to defend any Tennessee schoolteacher who would challenge the statute. John Scopes, a biology teacher from the town of Dayton, accepted the offer. Scopes's chief defense attorney was Clarence Darrow, a famous criminal lawyer from Chicago. The prosecution's star attorney was the elderly William Jennings Bryan. Bryan had been the former three-time Democratic presidential candidate and secretary of state.

The **Scopes trial** exposed a deep division in American society between traditional religious values and new values based on scientific ways of thought. Bryan spoke for many Americans who felt that the theory of evolution contradicted deeply held religious beliefs. Bryan spoke before the trial to an audience of local admirers:

REVIEW

Have students complete the **Section 2 Review** on p. 401.

ASSESS

Have students complete **Daily Quiz 13.2.** As **Alternative Assessment**, you may want to use the radio show script or the trading cards in this section's lessons.

RETEACH

Have students complete **Main Idea Activity for Reteaching and Sheltered English 13.2.** Then prepare several sets of index cards. Write one of this section's key terms or key people on each card. Pair students and distribute a set of cards to each pair. Have each student in the pair take half of the cards. Have each student provide a series of clues about the terms on his or her cards to help his or her partner correctly identify the terms. **Sheltered English, Cooperative Learning**

EXTEND

Using the library and other resources, have students conduct research on the famed exchange between Clarence Darrow and William Jennings Bryan during the Scopes trial. Have students write an essay based on their research in which they explain how Darrow's questioning of Bryan revealed the undercurrent of conflict in American life between traditional religious values and modern trends. **Block Scheduling**

"Our purpose and our only purpose is to vindicate [uphold] the right of parents to guard the religion of their children against efforts made in the name of science to undermine faith in supernatural religion."

Clarence Darrow (left) and William Jennings Bryan (right) represented opposing sides in the Scopes trial.

Clarence Darrow, on the other hand, expressed another widely held view. He attacked the Tennessee law as a threat to free expression. In one courtroom speech, Darrow warned his listeners. "Today it is the public school teachers, tomorrow the private, the next day the preachers and the lecturers, the magazines, the books, the newspapers."

From the beginning, Darrow had little chance of winning the trial. Judge John T. Raulston opened the trial with a prayer and refused to allow testimony from scientific experts. Darrow responded by calling Bryan as an expert witness on the Bible. During his testimony, Bryan affirmed his belief in the literal truth of the Bible. Darrow forced Bryan to reveal inconsistencies in his interpretation of scripture. For example, Darrow asked Bryan if the world was literally created in six days, as stated in the Bible. Bryan responded that a "day" did not necessarily mean 24 hours.

Darrow's defense failed to convince the jury. Scopes was found guilty and fined $100. The verdict seemed a victory for Fundamentalists. However, press accounts of the trial, which often portrayed Bryan and his cause as narrow-minded, lowered some people's opinions of Fundamentalism.

✔ **READING CHECK:** What did the Scopes trial and the religious movements of the 1920s reveal about American society?

SECTION 2 REVIEW

Define and explain the significance of the following terms:
Volstead Act
Untouchables
Twenty-first Amendment
flappers
Fundamentalism
Scopes trial

Identify and explain the significance of the following individuals:
Al Capone
Eliot Ness
Cecil B. DeMille
Babe Ruth
Jim Thorpe
Charles Lindbergh
Amelia Earhart
Aimee Semple McPherson
Billy Sunday
Clarence Darrow

1. **Using Graphic Organizers** Copy the graphic organizer below. Use it to explain how prohibition led to an increase in crime and how the government tried to combat this crime.

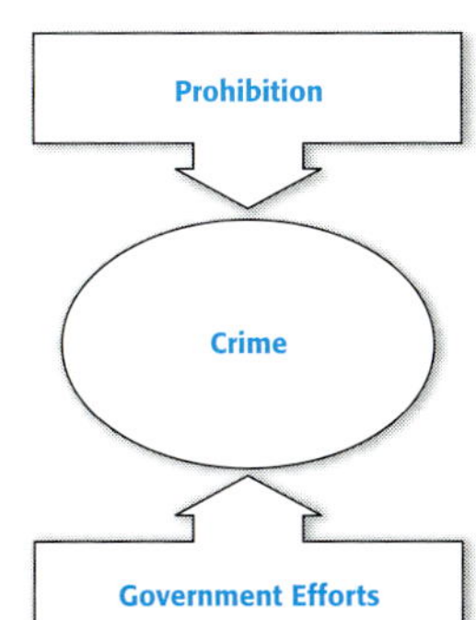

2. **Evaluating** How did the ideals of the "new woman," the lives of college students, and the leisure activities of the 1920s represent a new culture that conflicted with traditional American values?
3. **Assessing Consequences** How did the advances in radio and movies contribute to a growth in popular entertainment and help create a mass culture?
4. **Identifying Values** What values and cultural trends did the heroes and celebrities of the 1920s represent?

Critical Thinking

5. How did the many changes in American society during the 1920s affect the revival of religious activity?
Consider:
- the impact of youth culture and popular entertainment on people's perception of American culture
- the message and activities of Aimee Semple McPherson and Billy Sunday
- what led to the Scopes trial

1. prohibition—turned the sale of illegal liquor into a booming business, and thus led to an increase in crime; government—tried to reduce the growth in crime by strictly enforcing prohibition laws and arresting gangsters such as Al Capone

2. The ideals of the "new woman," collegiate life, and many leisure activities of the 1920s encouraged young people to dress and behave more independently and less conservatively than they had in the past. These ideals thus represented a new culture that differed from traditional American conventions.

3. enabled millions of people across the nation to listen and see the same commercial productions, and thus contributed to the development of a new mass culture.

4. The heroes and celebrities of the 1920s represented an increased emphasis on fame and entertainment; reflected changes in styles of dress, personal appearance, and behavior.

5. Answers will vary, but students might suggest that the youth culture and popular entertainment prompted many Americans to believe that the United States was entering a period of moral decline and thus was in need of religious revitalization; McPherson and Sunday used new methods to encourage religious activism; the Scopes trial revealed a deep division in American society between traditional and modern values.

SECTION 3

OBJECTIVE 4 *Identify some of the major inspirations behind the new movements in visual arts and architecture.*

After completing Section 3, students should be able to:

OBJECTIVE 1 *Explain how jazz and blues became popular nationwide.*

OBJECTIVE 2 *Analyze how artists and writers of the Harlem Renaissance used their work to express pride in their cultural heritage.*

OBJECTIVE 3 *Describe how writers of the Lost Generation portrayed American life.*

LET'S GET STARTED!

Write the term *Harlem Renaissance* on the chalkboard. As students enter the classroom, tell each student to make a list of artists and writers of the Harlem Renaissance. *(Students might name Countee Cullen, Langston Hughes, Rose McClendon, and Paul Robeson, among others.)* Ask volunteers to share their lists with the class. Tell students that in Section 3 they will learn about the Harlem Renaissance and other artistic movements in American society during the 1920s.

SECTION 3 RESOURCES

PRINT

- Guided Reading Strategy 13.3
- Graphic Organizer Activity 13: Artists of the 1920s and 1930s
- Literature Reading 13: The Jazz Age
- Section 3 Review, p. 409
- Daily Quiz 13.3

MULTIMEDIA

- One-Stop Planner, Lesson 13.3
- Everyday Life in America Transparency 22: Harlem Renaissance Art, 1920s
- American Music Selection 19: "Harmonica Blues"
- Holt Researcher: American History CD–ROM

SHELTERED ENGLISH

- Main Idea Activity for Reteaching and Sheltered English 13.3

✔ READING TO UNDERSTAND
To help students master the section objectives, have them answer the **READING CHECKS** and complete **Guided Reading Strategy 13.3** as they read the section.

SECTION 3

A Creative Era

OBJECTIVES

Read to understand:

1. how jazz and blues became popular nationwide
2. how artists and writers of the Harlem Renaissance used their work to express pride in their cultural heritage
3. how writers of the Lost Generation portrayed American life
4. what some of the major inspirations behind new movements in the visual arts and architecture were

KEY TERMS

jazz
blues
Harlem Renaissance
Lost Generation

KEY PEOPLE

Bessie Smith
Louis Armstrong
Bix Beiderbecke
Duke Ellington
Langston Hughes
Paul Robeson
Rose McClendon
James Weldon Johnson
Ernest Hemingway
F. Scott Fitzgerald
Alfred Stieglitz
Diego Rivera

KEY PLACES

Harlem

"When I came back to New York in 1925 the Negro Renaissance was in full swing. Countee Cullen was publishing his early poems, Zora Neale Hurston, Rudolph Fisher, Jean Toomer, and Wallace Thurman were writing, Louis Armstrong was playing, Cora Le Redd was dancing, and the Savoy Ballroom was open with a specially built floor that rocked as the dancers swayed. . . . Art took heart from Harlem creativity. Jazz filled the night air . . . and people came from all around after dark to look upon our city within a city, Black Harlem."

—Langston Hughes

Scene outside the Renaissance Theater in Harlem

An explosion of creativity took place in Harlem, New York, during the 1920s. The 1920s was a period of great creative energy. African American musicians transformed popular music by introducing the nation to jazz. A new generation of writers explored the problems of postwar American life and the experience of being African American. New currents in art and architecture swept the nation.

Music

The 1920s is frequently known as the Jazz Age because **jazz** music first gained a wide following during that era. Jazz originated among African American musicians in the South. As a port city with residents of many different cultural traditions, New Orleans was an early center for the development of jazz. This innovative form of music is a hybrid of various musical styles that existed in New Orleans at the turn of the century. Jazz incorporates West African and Latin American rhythms, elements of African American spirituals, and ragtime as well as European harmonies.

The emergence of jazz. Jazz emerged during the early 1900s in the entertainment district of New Orleans known as Storyville. Big brass bands, which had been popular in New Orleans since the Civil War, began experimenting with the ragtime style of music popularized by Scott Joplin. Brass-band musicians such as Charles "Buddy" Bolden gained a wide audience with their new "ragged" or improvised tunes. Bolden and other early jazz musicians also experimented with another form of African American music known as the **blues**.

The blues grew out of a long history of slave music and religious spirituals. It gained popularity during the early 1900s and greatly influenced jazz. Blues songs featured heartfelt lyrics and altered or slurred notes that echoed the mood of the lyrics. In the early 1920s blues singers such as Mamie Smith, Gertrude "Ma" Rainey, and Bessie Smith brought blues music to a broader audience. Their recordings of songs such as "Crazy Blues," "Down Hearted Blues," and "St. Louis Blues" became classic hits. Bessie Smith's "Down Hearted Blues" sold more than 500,000 copies in 1923.

Singers like Bessie Smith helped popularize the blues.

402

TEACH OBJECTIVE 1

LEVEL 1: Pair students and have them create charts to explain how jazz and blues became popular nationwide. *(Students might mention that both jazz and blues originated in the South but became popular nationwide as musicians moved north. Some white musicians began to play jazz music and jazz clubs opened. Big bands popularized jazz as dance music.)* Have volunteers present their charts to the class. **Sheltered English, Cooperative Learning**

LEVEL 2: Pair students and have each pair write a jazz song that describes how jazz and blues became popular nationwide. *(See the Level 1 lesson for the correct reasons.)* Have volunteers sing or recite their songs to the class. **Cooperative Learning**

LEVEL 3: Have students write an essay discussing how jazz and blues became popular. *(See the Level 1 lesson for the correct reasons.)* Students should also address the question "Why might jazz be considered the ultimate American musical form?" *(Students might suggest that jazz is the ultimate American musical form because it is an indigenous yet hybrid form that draws on influences from around the world.)* Have volunteers read their essays to the class.

As blues music grew in popularity, early jazz musicians from New Orleans such as Louis Armstrong began to adopt some of the unique characteristics of the blues. Jazz musicians re-created the vocal traditions of blues music. They used their instruments to imitate the expressive singing style of blues vocalists.

INTERPRETING THE VISUAL RECORD

Jazz. The members of King Oliver's Creole Jazz Band joined thousands of other African Americans who migrated from the South to northern cities such as Chicago. ***What types of instruments were used to make jazz music?***

Jazz moves north. During the late 1910s thousands of African Americans moved northward. Many of New Orleans's most-noted jazz musicians relocated to cities like Chicago and New York. Pianist and composer Ferdinand "Jelly Roll" Morton helped spread jazz when he moved from New Orleans to Chicago in 1922. Morton formed a band called the Red Hot Peppers and recorded his famous tune—the "Jelly Roll Blues."

Joseph "King" Oliver also moved from New Orleans to Chicago, where he founded the Creole Jazz Band. In 1922 the great jazz trumpeter Louis Armstrong joined Oliver's band in Chicago. Armstrong's brilliant solos were featured in the Creole Jazz Band's Chicago recordings of "Mabel's Dream" and "Froggie Moore." By 1924 Armstrong had begun a renowned solo career. He toured throughout the United States and Europe, performing such classics as "When the Saints Go Marching In," "Savoy Blues," and "Hotter Than That."

The introduction of jazz to the North was met with enthusiasm. One reporter from the *Chicago Defender* was thrilled with the new music. He wrote, "The Fire department is thinking of lining 35th Street with asbestos [fireproof material] to keep those bands from scorching passers-by with their red-hot jazz music."

The popularization of jazz. As jazz grew in popularity, musicians of varying backgrounds began incorporating jazz elements into their music. White musicians—among them the cornetist and pianist Bix Beiderbecke—wove jazz rhythms into their music. George Gershwin's *Rhapsody in Blue,* which premiered in 1924, "translated" jazz into symphonic form. Jazz also influenced classical musicians, including such noted composers as Igor Stravinsky and Aaron Copland.

The development of big-band music in the mid-1920s introduced jazz music to a younger American audience. Big bands popularized jazz as dance music. Big-band jazz swept the nation. Young men and their flapper partners shocked their elders by dancing cheek-to-cheek fox-trots.

Jazz clubs such as Harlem's Cotton Club catered to the growing audience. These clubs brought in the most famous jazz musicians of the era, including Duke Ellington, Ethel Waters, and Cab Calloway. Reflecting the racism of the era, many of these clubs admitted only white customers. This occurred even though the performers frequently were African Americans and the clubs were located in African American neighborhoods.

Jazz music expressed the sadness, pain, and joy of black America. African American poet Langston Hughes noted that jazz proclaimed, "Why should I want to be white? I am a Negro—and beautiful!"

✔ **READING CHECK:** How did jazz and blues become popular nationwide?

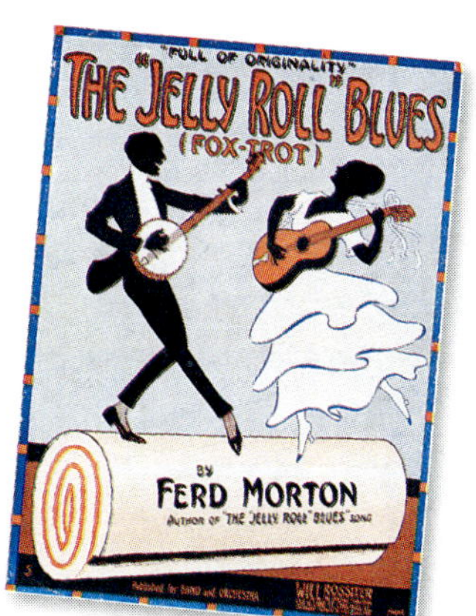

This sheet music reflects the upbeat nature of the 1920s.

PEOPLE IN HISTORY

Louis Armstrong. Louis Armstrong became one of the world's most famous and influential jazz musicians. The son of a domestic servant, he grew up in one of the poorest neighborhoods in New Orleans. As a child, Armstrong earned pennies by singing in street-side barbershop quartets. At age 12 Armstrong was arrested for firing a pistol in public. He was sent to a reform school for African American boys, where he learned to play the trumpet. His immense talent at the instrument was obvious, and soon after his release in 1916 he began to play professionally. By 1918, when he was 18 years old, Armstrong was recognized as the best trumpet player in New Orleans.

CRITICAL THINKING How might Louis Armstrong's life have been different if he had not gone to reform school?"

ANSWER: Students might suggest that Armstrong would have never learned to play the trumpet.

VISUAL RECORD ANSWER

Students' answers might include banjos, clarinets, drums, trombones, trumpets, and pianos.

Multimedia Resources

American Music Selection 19: "Harmonica Blues"

SPOTLIGHT on the Influence of Jazz

Have students conduct research on the popularity of jazz around the world. Each student should focus on a jazz musician or group native to a country other than the United States. Have students obtain recordings of the musician's or group's work and write a brief summary of the musician's or group's lives and the unique characteristics of his or her work. Have students present their summaries and play their recordings for the class. **Block Scheduling**

TEACH OBJECTIVE 2

LEVEL 1: Pair students and ask each pair to read the poems on the following page. Instruct students to use information from the textbook to prepare oral reports on the ways in which Harlem Renaissance artists and writers expressed pride in their cultural heritage. *(Students might answer that performers and playwrights brought new respect to black theater. Writers celebrated their ethnic identity and discussed the struggles faced by many African Americans.)* Have students deliver their reports to the class.
Sheltered English, Cooperative Learning

GEOGRAPHIC DIVERSITY

Harlem. Originally settled by the Dutch, the section of New York City known as Harlem was populated mostly by people of German, Irish, Italian, and Jewish descent during the late 1800s. Shortly after the turn of the century, a national economic depression and overbuilding in the neighborhood prompted some white landlords to begin renting apartments to African American migrants from the South, black West Indians, and black Africans. Despite the protest of white residents—many of whom left the area because of prejudice—black settlement of Harlem continued rapidly. By the time the Harlem Renaissance took place, African Americans had established a variety of social clubs and civic organizations in the neighborhood, including local chapters of the Masons, the Elks, the National Urban League, and the YMCA.

CRITICAL THINKING Why might it be said that Harlem retained its multicultural character despite the departure of white residents?

ANSWER: Students might suggest that the diverse national origins of the new residents created a multicultural neighborhood.

MAP ANSWER
from Fifth Ave. to Eighth Ave. and from 130th St. to 145th St. (about 45 blocks)

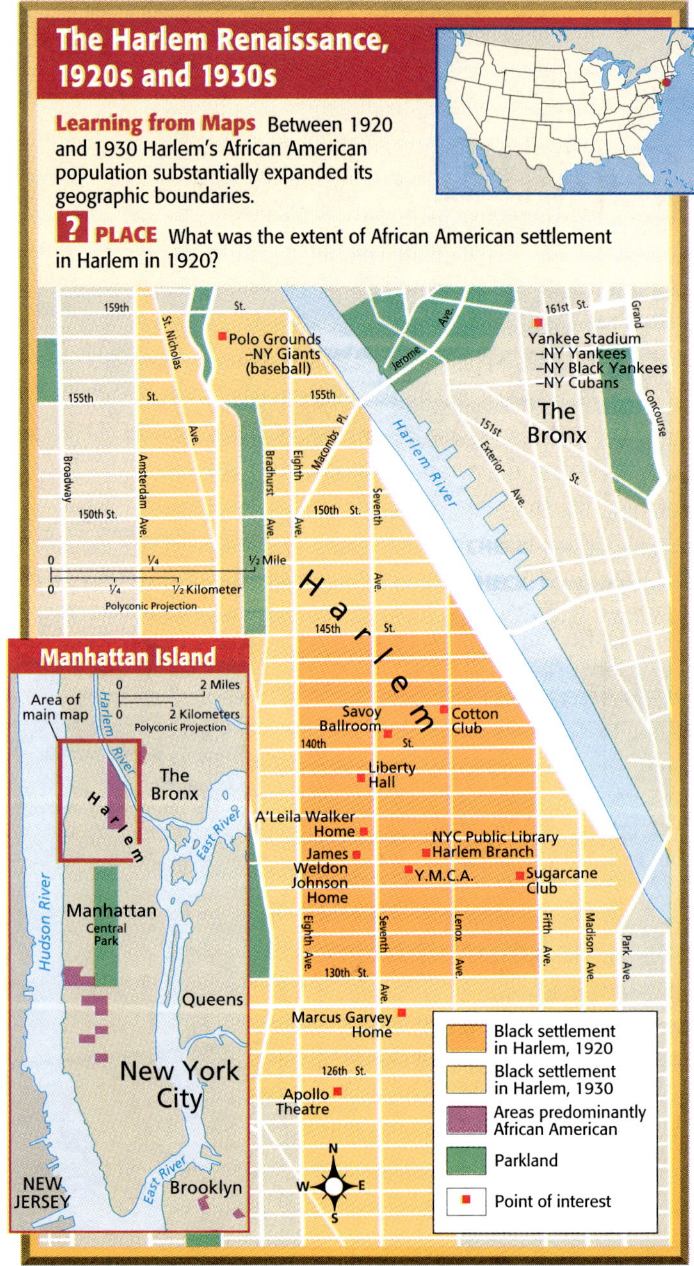

Learning from Maps Between 1920 and 1930 Harlem's African American population substantially expanded its geographic boundaries.

PLACE What was the extent of African American settlement in Harlem in 1920?

The Harlem Renaissance

In the 1920s African Americans expressed a growing pride in their heritage. Nowhere was this pride more evident than in Harlem. This neighborhood in New York City became the cultural center of African American life. So many creative black writers, musicians, and artists lived in Harlem that the flourishing of artistic development in the 1920s is known as the **Harlem Renaissance**.

Theater. During the 1920s African American theater experienced both critical acclaim and increasing popularity. The work of black performers and playwrights brought new respect to black theater. African American theater critic Alain Locke explained, "The black playwright and the black actor will interpret the soul of their people in a way to win the attention and admiration of the world."

The theatrical roles available to African Americans were restricted by the prejudices of the era. Nevertheless, African Americans produced and staged several enormously successful Broadway plays and musicals. One of the most critically successful actors of the 1920s was Paul Robeson, who received praise for his title role in Eugene O'Neill's drama *Emperor Jones*. The grandson of a slave, Robeson turned to acting after graduating from Rutgers University and Columbia University Law School. His performances received high praise. "Robeson . . . is one of the most thoroughly eloquent, impressive and convincing actors that I have looked at and listened to in the past twenty years of theater going," offered one critic. Robeson was also an accomplished singer. He used his powerful baritone voice in such numbers as "Ol' Man River" from the musical *Showboat*. Robeson made history in 1924 as the first African American actor to play a leading role opposite a white actress.

Rose McClendon was another leading African American actor of the 1920s. McClendon first won fame in the 1926 production *Deep River*, a "native opera with jazz." In later years she performed in the Pulitzer Prize–winning tragedy *In Abraham's Bosom* and in the first production of *Porgy*.

LEVEL 2: Ask each student to write a short poem that discusses the ways in which Harlem Renaissance artists and writers expressed pride in their cultural heritage. *(See the Level 1 lesson for the correct ways.)* Have volunteers recite their poems to the class. Students may wish to include their poems in their portfolios.

LEVEL 3: Pair students and have one student in each pair adopt the role of Countee Cullen and the other the role of Langston Hughes. Have each pair write a brief dialogue in which the poets analyze the poems "Yet Do I Marvel" and "I, Too" and discuss how their work expresses their pride in their cultural heritage. *(See the Level 1 lesson for the correct ways .)* Ask volunteers to perform their dialogues for the class. **Cooperative Learning**

▶ASSIGNMENT *Ask students to consult the dictionary and one other source to define the word* renaissance*. Have students write a brief explanation of why this term might have been used to describe the artistic activity that occurred in Harlem during the 1920s and 1930s.*

AMERICAN *Letters*

Harlem Renaissance Writers

During the Harlem Renaissance, African American writers drew upon their personal experiences to create exciting and meaningful works. Poems such as Countee Cullen's "Yet Do I Marvel" and Langston Hughes's "I, Too" expressed the pride many Harlem writers had for their cultural heritage. Although the two poems explore a similar theme, the distinct style of each poem reflects the diversity of Harlem Renaissance literature.

"Yet Do I Marvel"

by Countee Cullen

I doubt not God is good,
well-meaning, kind,
And did He stoop to
quibble could tell why
The little buried mole
continues blind,
Why flesh that mirrors
Him must some day die,
Make plain the reason
tortured Tantalus*
Is baited by the fickle fruit,
declare
If merely brute caprice [whimsy] dooms Sisyphus**
To struggle up a never-ending stair.
Inscrutable [mysterious] His ways are, and immune
To catechism by a mind too strewn
With petty cares to slightly understand
What awful brain compels His awful hand.
Yet do I marvel at this curious thing:
To make a poet black, and bid him sing!

* Tantalus was a character in Greek mythology known for the punishment and torture he suffered in Hades (hell).

** According to Greek mythology, Sisyphus must endlessly push a heavy rock up a steep hill.

Countee Cullen's collection of poems

"I, Too"

by Langston Hughes

I, too, sing America.

I am the darker brother.
They send me to eat in the
kitchen
When company comes,
But I laugh,
And eat well,
And grow strong.

Tomorrow,
I'll be at the table
When company comes.
Nobody'll dare
Say to me,
"Eat in the kitchen,"
Then.

Besides,
They'll see how beautiful I am
And be ashamed—

I, too, am America.

Langston Hughes

UNDERSTANDING LITERATURE

1. What point does Cullen make in his poem?
2. How did Langston Hughes's experience as an African American influence his poem?
3. How does the unique style of language of each poem enhance the poets' message?

PEOPLE IN HISTORY

Langston Hughes. Langston Hughes was one of the most ambitious and talented young poets of the Harlem Renaissance. A descendant of African, American Indian, and French ancestors, Hughes excelled in high school in Cleveland before moving to New York City in 1921 at age 19. That same year, his first published poem appeared in *The Crisis,* the monthly journal of the NAACP. After attending Columbia University, Hughes spent large parts of the next several years working as a steward on ships that traveled to Africa and Europe. In 1925 Hughes won a literary contest sponsored by *Opportunity* magazine. By 1928 he had published two full-length collections of his poetry.

ACTIVITY: Ask students to research an artist or writer of the Harlem Renaissance. Then have students present their research to the class.

AMERICAN LETTERS ANSWERS

1. He is celebrating his identity as a black poet in a world that seems cold and cruel.
2. The poem was influenced by Hughes's experience with racial prejudice and pride in his African American identity.
3. Answers will vary. Students might mention specific words or phrases.

SPOTLIGHT on Paul Robeson

Have each student conduct research on the life and career of Paul Robeson, focusing on his educational background, popularity as an artist in the United States and around the world, and political activities. Have students write brief reports on their findings. Ask volunteers to read their reports to the class. **Block Scheduling**

SPOTLIGHT on Rose McClendon

Pair students and have them conduct research on the life and career of Rose McClendon. Students should focus on her career as an actor, director, and one of the founders of the Negro People's Theater in Harlem. Then have students write transcripts of an interview with McClendon. Ask volunteers to conduct their interviews for the class.
Cooperative Learning, Block Scheduling

CULTURAL DIVERSITY

Sponsorship of African American Writers. Two magazines served as important forums for the Harlem Renaissance writers. *The Crisis,* the NAACP periodical, had a peak monthly circulation of more than 100,000. It published young talents such as Claude McKay and Countee Cullen. *Opportunity,* a magazine founded in 1923 by the National Urban League, sponsored literary contests. Zora Neale Hurston and Langston Hughes were among the winners.

CRITICAL THINKING What might have made *The Crisis* an excellent forum for new writers, other than its wide circulation?

ANSWER: Students might suggest that *The Crisis* was directed to an audience of activists interested in nurturing the talents of African Americans.

Multimedia Resources

Everyday Life in America Transparency 22: Harlem Renaissance Art, 1920s

VISUAL RECORD ANSWER

(for p. 407)

Students might suggest that this soldier did not enjoy the prosperity of the 1920s because he was disillusioned from his war experience.

Literature. African American contributions to literature were central to the Harlem Renaissance. African American novelists and poets produced work marked by bitterness and defiance but also by joy and hope. Writer Nella Larsen described the quest for racial identity in her 1928 novel, *Quicksand.* Also published in 1928, Claude McKay's novel *Home to Harlem* explored the excitement and stresses of life in Harlem for an African American soldier returning from World War I.

Claude McKay and many other writers made Harlem a center of American literature.

Harlem poets celebrated their ethnic identity and acknowledged the struggles faced by many African Americans. McKay expressed his determination to fight racial injustices in his poem "If We Must Die."

> **"If we must die, let it not be like hogs**
> **Hunted and penned in an inglorious spot,**
> **While round us bark the mad and hungry dogs. . . .**
> **What though before us lies the open grave?**
> **Like men we'll face the murderous, cowardly pack,**
> **Pressed to the wall, dying, but fighting back!"**

Langston Hughes was another poet who dealt sensitively with issues of African cultural heritage. Hughes distinguished himself by addressing his poems to African American readers. Hughes focused on the everyday experiences of African Americans, using language and themes familiar to his readers.

BIOGRAPHY
James Weldon Johnson

One of the most active supporters of the Harlem Renaissance was James Weldon Johnson. Born in 1871 in Jacksonville, Florida, Johnson was the son of the first African American woman to teach in Florida's public schools. Johnson excelled as a student and attended Atlanta University. There, he studied the classics and poetry. A man of many talents, Johnson's occupations included educator, lawyer, diplomat to Venezuela and Nicaragua, and official in the National Association for the Advancement of Colored People (NAACP). He was also a writer.

Johnson published a wide variety of works. In 1899 he composed "Lift Ev'ry Voice and Sing" with music by his brother, J. Rosamond Johnson. By the 1920s the song was commonly known as the African American national anthem. Johnson also wrote several novels, including *The Autobiography of an Ex-Colored Man,* published in 1912.

Johnson's main contribution to the Harlem Renaissance was his support of other authors. In 1922 Johnson published *The Book of American Negro Poetry.* Through his work as the executive secretary of the NAACP during the 1920s, Johnson raised money to support African American artists and art programs in Harlem.

Johnson's support of the arts was based on his belief that the artistic advances of the Harlem Renaissance would help further the cause of equal rights. Johnson claimed that the "demonstration of intellectual parity [equality] by the Negro through the production of literature and art" eliminated racial prejudice best. Johnson continued this work until his death on June 26, 1938.

✔ **READING CHECK:** In what ways did the artists and writers of the Harlem Renaissance use their work to express pride in their cultural heritage?

TEACH OBJECTIVE 3

LEVEL 1: To help students understand how writers of the Lost Generation portrayed American life, copy the following graphic organizer on the chalkboard, omitting the italicized answers. Have each student complete it. **Sheltered English**

PORTRAYAL OF AMERICAN LIFE BY LOST GENERATION WRITERS

Ernest Hemingway	F. Scott Fitzgerald	Sinclair Lewis
showed the devastation and uselessness of war	*revealed superficiality of college life and the emptiness associated with the pursuit of status and wealth*	*discussed the emptiness and conformity of middle-class life*

LEVEL 2: Have each student write several proverbs that encapsulate the portrayal of American life by the writers of the Lost Generation. *(See the Level 1 lesson for the correct portrayals.)* Ask volunteers to recite their proverbs to the class.

LEVEL 3: Have each student write a brief summary of the portrayal of American life by writers of the Lost Generation. *(See the Level 1 lesson for the correct portrayals.)* Then have students write a short story that applies one or more of the Lost Generation's portrayals to contemporary life. Ask volunteers to read their stories to the class.

The Lost Generation

The Harlem Renaissance coincided with the rise of a new generation of American writers. Their work reflected their horror at the death and destruction of World War I. Their scorn for middle-class consumerism and the superficiality of the postwar years also showed in their writing. "You are all a lost generation," said poet Gertrude Stein to one such writer, Ernest Hemingway. The label stuck, and the writers of the era became known as the **Lost Generation**.

Stories of disillusionment. Ernest Hemingway spent much of his life in France, Spain, and Cuba. During World War I, he and several other young writers served as ambulance drivers as a way to experience and understand war. Hemingway was seriously wounded while serving on the Italian front. He later expressed his anger at the uselessness of war. His 1929 novel, *A Farewell to Arms,* depicts the devastation of war in its portrayal of a relationship between a wounded soldier and a nurse. In a famous passage the soldier explains what the war means to him.

> **"I was always embarrassed by the words sacred, glorious, and sacrifice and the expression in vain. We had heard them . . . and had read them . . . now for a long time, and I had seen nothing sacred, and the things that were glorious had no glory and the sacrifices were like the stockyards at Chicago if nothing was done with the meat except to bury it."**

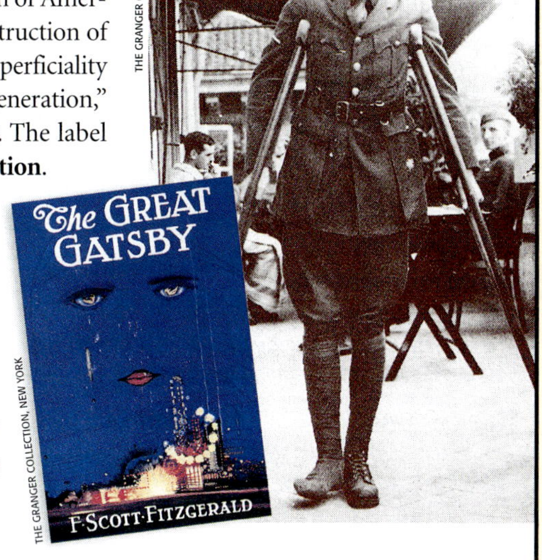

THE GRANGER COLLECTION, NEW YORK

THE GRANGER COLLECTION, NEW YORK

INTERPRETING THE VISUAL RECORD

Memories of war. *The Great Gatsby* tells a story of wealth and power. ***Do you think this soldier enjoyed the prosperity of the 1920s? Explain your answer.***

F. Scott Fitzgerald was another member of the Lost Generation. His novels chronicled the youthful Jazz Age. In *This Side of Paradise* (1920), Fitzgerald wrote about wealthy college students bored by fast living. In *The Great Gatsby* (1925), Fitzgerald portrayed the emptiness of a man's pursuit of money and social status.

Fitzgerald's life was filled with the same tragedies and disillusionment that plagued his characters. Fitzgerald defined the Jazz Age as a time when "a new generation [had] grown up to find . . . all wars fought, all faiths in man shaken." With the extraordinary success of his first novel and his marriage to beautiful Zelda Sayre, Fitzgerald's future appeared bright. Their glamorous lifestyle was cut short, however, by Zelda Fitzgerald's incurable mental illness and Fitzgerald's own alcoholism and declining creativity.

Criticizing the middle class. Sinclair Lewis shared Fitzgerald's skeptical attitude toward American society during the 1920s. However, Lewis focused his criticism on the emptiness and conformity of middle-class life. In *Main Street* (1920), Lewis satirized the close-mindedness of a typical small midwestern town. In his 1922 novel, *Babbitt,* Lewis told the story of a middle-aged realtor and city booster who is dissatisfied with his middle-class life but lacks the courage to change.

The journalist and critic Henry L. Mencken served as a champion of these new writers. In his magazine, *The American Mercury,* Mencken promoted novelists who satirized middle-class Americans, whom he ridiculed as "the booboisie." Mencken made fun of Republican politicians, Fundamentalist Christians, rural southerners, residents of small towns, and many other Americans.

✔ **READING CHECK:** How did the writers of the Lost Generation portray American life?

Read More About It

Free Find:
F. Scott Fitzgerald
After reading about F. Scott Fitzgerald on the **Holt Researcher** CD–ROM, create an outline for a story set in the 1920s about Fitzgerald.

HISTORY MAKERS SPEAK

Malcolm Cowley in *Exile's Return: A Literary Odyssey of the 1920s*

The Lost Generation. In his memoir, writer Malcolm Cowley reflected on the appropriateness of the "Lost Generation" label: "The [lost] generation deserved for a long time the adjective that Gertrude Stein had applied to it. The reasons aren't hard to find. It was lost, first of all, because it was uprooted, schooled away and almost wrenched away from its attachment to any region or tradition. It was lost because its training had prepared it for another world than [that which] existed after the war. . . . It was lost because it accepted no older guides to conduct."

ACTIVITY: Ask students to read a short story by Ernest Hemingway, F. Scott Fitzgerald, or another Lost Generation writer. Then have students write an essay examining the story's major themes.

VISUAL RECORD ANSWER

(for p. 408)

Students might suggest that positive aspects include employment for many different ethnic groups and that negative aspects include the exhausting work.

TEACH OBJECTIVE 4

LEVEL 1: Pair students and have each pair compile a list of the major visual artists and architects of the 1920s and their sources of inspiration. *(Students might indicate that a number of painters and photographers were inspired by urban, industrial settings. Many Mexican muralists were inspired by the nobility of workers and the tyranny of the wealthy. Architects found inspiration in Louis Sullivan's ideas about form and function and in Frank Lloyd Wright's "prairie style.")* Conclude by discussing with students the contributions of these artists and architects.

Sheltered English, Cooperative Learning

LEVELS 2 AND 3: Tell students to imagine that they are participants in a panel discussion entitled Inspiration for the New Movements in Visual Arts and Architecture. Ask volunteers to play the roles of Edward Hopper, Georgia O'Keeffe, Diego Rivera, Charles Sheeler, Alfred Stieglitz, and Frank Lloyd Wright. Ask the other students to act as facilitators and questioners. Have the students who are role-playing the artists prepare for their roles by taking notes on what inspired the artists and architects. Have the other group prepare a list of questions to use during the panel discussion. *(See the Level 1 lesson for the correct sources of inspiration.)* Then conduct the panel discussion.

SECTION 3 REVIEW ANSWERS

Define and Identify

For significance, see the following pages:

- jazz, p. 402
- blues, p. 402
- Bessie Smith, p. 402
- Louis Armstrong p. 403
- Bix Beiderbecke, p. 403
- Duke Ellington, p. 403
- Harlem Renaissance, p. 404
- Paul Robeson, p. 404
- Rose McClendon, p. 404
- Langston Hughes, p. 406
- James Weldon Johnson, p. 406
- Ernest Hemingway, p. 407
- Lost Generation, p. 407
- F. Scott Fitzgerald, p. 407
- Alfred Stieglitz, p. 408
- Diego Rivera, p. 408

Locate

For location, see the map on p. 404. For importance, see the following page:

- Harlem, p. 404

1. influences–West African and Latin American rhythms, African American spirituals, blues, ragtime, European harmonies; expansion–jazz clubs, migration of musicians, big bands

2. by producing works that struggled with issues of ethnic identity and prejudice

3. the futility of World War I and the superficiality of middle- and upper-class life

4. New subjects included urban life, worker's lives, machinery, and functional design.

5. Students should note that writers and artists focused on the effects of urbanization, prejudice, and World War I on U.S. life.

In this 1928 painting,* Manhattan Bridge Loop, *Edward Hopper conveys the isolation and industrialization that many associated with U.S. cities.

The Visual Arts

As the writers of the Lost Generation confronted the boredom and frustration of life after the war, many visual artists concerned themselves with other changes occurring in the United States. Artists of the 1920s addressed the impact of growing cities and the increasing use of machinery on American life.

Painting and photography. Many American painters of the 1920s depicted urban, industrial settings. Edward Hopper's scenes of New York City convey a sense of loneliness and serene stillness. *Early Sunday Morning* (1930) shows a row of darkened stores and a street empty of people. Hopper believed that art should reflect the experiences of modern life. He explained, "The province [role] of art is to react to it [life] and not to shun it." Before she moved to New Mexico, artist Georgia O'Keeffe also depicted city life in her paintings of New York factories and tenements.

Photography came to be widely appreciated as an art form in the 1900s. Alfred Stieglitz (STEEG-luhts) helped popularize photography. In addition to operating an influential New York gallery, Stieglitz photographed people as well as airplanes, skyscrapers, and crowded city streets. Photographer and painter Charles Sheeler won fame for his portraits revealing the beauty of machinery. The Ford Motor Company hired him to photograph its plant near Detroit, Michigan, in 1927.

INTERPRETING THE VISUAL RECORD

Murals. Diego Rivera completed the mural called *Detroit Industry* in 1932, after spending months in the industrial city. Rivera attempted to capture the positive and negative aspects of industrialization. ***How do you think these themes are revealed in this work?***

Murals. Another artistic renaissance of the 1920s took place in Mexico. Mexican muralists emphasized the nobility of ordinary people—peasants and other workers—and the tyranny of the wealthy class. Their favorite medium was the monumental public mural. In the words of artist José Clemente Orozco (oh-ROHS-koh), the public murals "cannot be hidden away for the benefit of a certain privileged few. It is for the people. It is for ALL."

The movement's three major artists—known in Mexico as *los tres grandes,* or "the big three"—were Orozco, David Alfaro Siqueiros (see-KAY-rohs), and Diego Rivera. Each artist visited the United States in the early 1930s to paint murals. Diego Rivera, the most prominent muralist, focused on workers' problems and industrial development in his American murals. In 1932 Rivera painted a mural at the Detroit Institute of Art that featured assembly-line workers in automobile factories.

Rivera and his wife, Frida Kahlo—an accomplished painter—lived and traveled throughout the United States from 1930 to 1933. Some Americans found Rivera's radical politics offensive. In 1933, sponsors of a new Rivera mural commissioned by the Rockefeller Center destroyed the work they had funded. Titled *Man at the Crossroads,* the mural upset the sponsors because it featured an image of the Bolshevik leader Vladimir Lenin. After returning to Mexico, Rivera re-created the mural at the Palace of Fine Arts in Mexico City.

REVIEW

Have students complete the **Section 3 Review** on p. 409.

ASSESS

Have students complete **Daily Quiz 13.3.** As **Alternative Assessment**, you may want to use the short story or the proverbs in this section's lessons.

RETEACH

Have students complete **Main Idea Activity for Reteaching and Sheltered English 13.3.** Then have each student write two or three sentences that summarize the main ideas of each subsection in this section. Have volunteers read their sentences to the class, and have the class supply any information missing from volunteers' sentences. **Sheltered English**

EXTEND

Using the library and other resources, have students locate and read some of the works of one Harlem Renaissance writer mentioned in this section. Have students analyze the works' major themes and report their findings by writing an essay, poem, play, or short story. **Block Scheduling**

Architecture. The spirit of creativity that emerged in the United States in the 1920s also appeared in the era's architecture. Many architects found inspiration in the works of Louis Sullivan and Frank Lloyd Wright. Sullivan's unique buildings were based on a design in which each part of the structure had a functional purpose. Wright studied under Sullivan during the 1890s. By the early 1910s Wright had gained a worldwide reputation for his innovative designs.

Wright developed the "prairie style" of domestic architecture. This new style used rectangular shapes and clean, horizontal lines that echoed the flatness of the prairies. Wright also incorporated Sullivan's idea that every aspect of a house's structure must have a functional purpose.

Many architects of the 1920s were influenced by Sullivan and Wright's thoughts. These architects embraced the idea that a building ought to use the materials and follow the forms most suitable to the building's purpose. The structure that most clearly illustrated this principle was the modern skyscraper. The new type of building was characterized by clean-cut vertical lines, the use of steel, concrete, and glass, and the lack of ornamentation.

New York City experienced a boom in skyscraper construction during the 1920s. Builders began construction of two landmarks—the Chrysler Building and the Empire State Building. Completed in 1930, the Chrysler Building was the tallest building in the world—at 1,048 feet—until the completion of the Empire State Building in 1931. The 102-story Empire State Building cleared 1,250 feet and remained the world's tallest building until 1954.

✔ **READING CHECK:** What were some of the major inspirations for the new movements within the visual arts and architecture?

INTERPRETING THE VISUAL RECORD

The Robie House. Drawing attention to the horizontal lines of his design, Frank Lloyd Wright completed this prairie-style home for Chicago bicycle manufacturer Frederick C. Robie in 1909. ***What aspects of this design help draw out the horizontal lines of this house?***

SECTION 3 REVIEW

Define and explain the significance of the following terms:
jazz
blues
Harlem Renaissance
Lost Generation

Identify and explain the significance of the following individuals:
Bessie Smith
Louis Armstrong
Bix Beiderbecke
Duke Ellington
Langston Hughes
Paul Robeson
Rose McClendon
James Weldon Johnson
Ernest Hemingway
F. Scott Fitzgerald
Alfred Stieglitz
Diego Rivera

Locate and explain the significance of the following place:
Harlem

1. **Using Graphic Organizers** Copy the graphic organizer below. List the original influences of jazz and the blues. Then explain how jazz and the blues expanded nationwide.

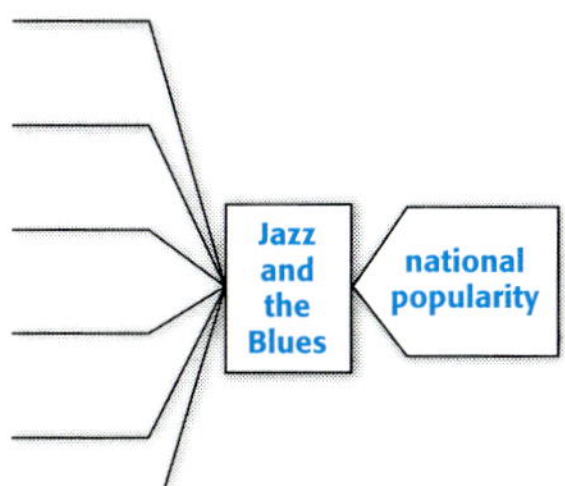

2. **Evaluating** How did the writers of the Harlem Renaissance contribute to American culture?
3. **Recognizing Point of View** What were the major themes expressed in the novels of Lost Generation writers?
4. **Assessing Consequences** How did the growth of U.S. cities and the introduction of new technology influence the visual arts of the 1920s?

Critical Thinking

5. Why might writers and artists of the 1920s be considered social critics?
   Consider:
   - how the African American writers of the Harlem Renaissance wrote about their lives
   - what experiences the writers of the Lost Generation captured in their novels
   - what the visual artists of the 1920s focused on in their works

VISUAL RECORD ANSWER

Students might cite the lighter rows of stone and the various levels.

CHAPTER 13 REVIEW ANSWERS

Creating a Time Line
Each event should have an explanation and the correct date.

Writing a Summary
See the Reading Checks in each section for main ideas.

Identifying People and Ideas
1. inexpensive car designed by Henry Ford
2. production method developed by Ford for the Model T
3. provided for the enforcement of prohibition
4. young women who adopted new styles of dress and behavior
5. first pilot to fly nonstop across the Atlantic Ocean
6. revivalist who combined a Christian message with Hollywood-style entertainment
7. period of great artistic creativity among African Americans
8. supporter of writers and artists during the Harlem Renaissance
9. writers who explored the disillusioning experience of World War I and the superficiality of middle- and upper-class life during the 1920s
10. Mexican muralist whose work focused on industrial development

REVIEW AND ASSESSMENT RESOURCES

PRINT
- Chapter 13 Review, pp. 410–11
- Chapter 13 Tutorial for Students, Parents, Mentors, and Peers
- Chapter 13 Test (Form A or B)
- Portfolio Activities and Alternative Assessment Handbook, Chapter 13

MULTIMEDIA
- Audio Program, Chapter 13 (English and Spanish)
- Chapter 13 Test Generator (on the One-Stop Planner)
- Global Skill Builder CD–ROM
- HRW Web site

SHELTERED ENGLISH
- Spanish Glossary
- Sheltered English Chapter 13 Test

REVIEW
Have students complete the **Chapter 13 Review** on pp. 410–11.

ASSESS
Use one of the chapter tests to assess students' understanding of the content. For **Alternative Assessment**, see the **Portfolio Activities and Alternative Assessment Handbook.**

Understanding Main Ideas
1. by making cars more affordable for consumers and thus encouraging the growth of the automobile industry
2. By dressing and behaving more independently and less strictly than they had in the past, young people rejected traditional American values.
3. by struggling with issues of ethnic identity and racial prejudice and serving as important examples of black artistic achievement
4. the superficiality of middle- and upper-class life during the 1920s

Reviewing Themes
1. Increasing desire for new goods, making them easier to acquire, and designing goods to "go out of style" helped promote consumer demand.
2. They provided millions of Americans with shared cultural experiences.
3. by incorporating elements of African American spirituals, blues, European harmonies, ragtime, and West African and Latin American rhythms

Thinking Critically
1. positive—helped make a wider variety of consumer goods available and affordable for many Americans; negative—increased industrial efficiency, made factory work more tedious, and caused many skilled workers to lose their jobs
2. Answers will vary, but students should note that the expansion of popular entertainment contributed

Chapter 13 Review

Creating a Time Line

Copy the time line below onto a sheet of paper. Complete the time line by filling in the events and dates from the chapter that you think were most significant. Pick three events and explain why you think they were significant.

Writing a Summary

Using the Reading Checks as a guide, write an overview of the events in the chapter.

Identifying People and Ideas

Identify the following terms or individuals and explain their significance.

1. Model T
2. assembly line
3. Volstead Act
4. flappers
5. Charles Lindbergh
6. Aimee Semple McPherson
7. Harlem Renaissance
8. James Weldon Johnson
9. Lost Generation
10. Diego Rivera

Understanding Main Ideas

SECTION 1

1. How did the development of the assembly line encourage the growth of the American automobile industry and affect American life?

SECTION 2

2. In what ways did the activities of many younger Americans during the 1920s represent a rejection of traditional American values?

SECTION 3

3. How did the work of writers and artists of the Harlem Renaissance affect American culture?
4. What aspects of American life did writers of the Lost Generation criticize?

Reviewing Themes

1. **Economic Development** How did advertising, installment buying, and planned obsolescence boost the nation's economy in the 1920s?
2. **Technology and Society** How did the spread of inventions such as radio and movies alter Americans' lives during the 1920s?
3. **Cultural Diversity** How did the influences of jazz reflect the cultural diversity of the United States?

Thinking Critically

1. **Assessing Consequences** How did the rise in productivity during the 1920s have both positive and negative effects for workers and industry?
2. **Evaluating** How did the emergence of popular entertainment contribute to the youth culture of the 1920s?
3. **Comparing and Contrasting** How did the values expressed by leaders of the Fundamentalist and Pentecostal movements of the 1920s differ from the values expressed by the new youth culture?
4. **Recognizing Point of View** How did the visual artists of the 1920s express their views of technology, the plight of workers, and urban life?
5. **Identifying Values** In what ways did African American artists, musicians, and writers of the 1920s express pride in their cultural heritage?

Writing About History

Writing to Describe Write an essay that describes the impact of nationwide broadcasting of radio programs on the lives of Americans. Use the following graphic to organize your thoughts.

RETEACH

Organize the class into three groups and assign each group one of the sections of this chapter. Have each group prepare an outline of its assigned section and either duplicate and distribute it to other members of the class or deliver an oral report to the class. The outline should include the main ideas of the section as well as examples to illustrate each main idea. Call on other class members to comment on the accuracy and thoroughness of each group's outline.

Sheltered English, Cooperative Learning

EXTEND

Direct the attention of students to the characterization of the 1920s as the "gateway to modern America" in this chapter. Based on this chapter and outside research, have each student write an essay on the extent to which that characterization is valid. Students should use one of the major figures, events, or developments associated with the material in the chapter as a case study or representative example to explain their point of view.

Block Scheduling

Strategies for Success Review the **Strategies for Success** on *Studying Primary and Secondary Sources.* Then examine the passage below from *Middletown* and answer the questions that follow.

> **"Advertising has grown rapidly since 1890. . . . Today all sorts of advertising devices are tried: . . . a shoe store conducting a sale offers one dollar each to the first twenty-five women appearing at the store on Monday morning; semi-annual 'dollar days' and 'suburban days' are conducted by the press. . . . The advertising carried in the leading daily paper is six times that in the leading daily of 1890."**

1. Is this passage part of a primary source or a secondary source? Explain your answer.
2. Who do you think was the intended audience of the passage?
3. Do the authors express any biases in the passage?
4. How does the passage contribute to your understanding of the United States during the 1920s?

Linking History and Geography

Examine the map below. Why were there more prohibition arrests made in states bordering Mexico and Canada than in other states?

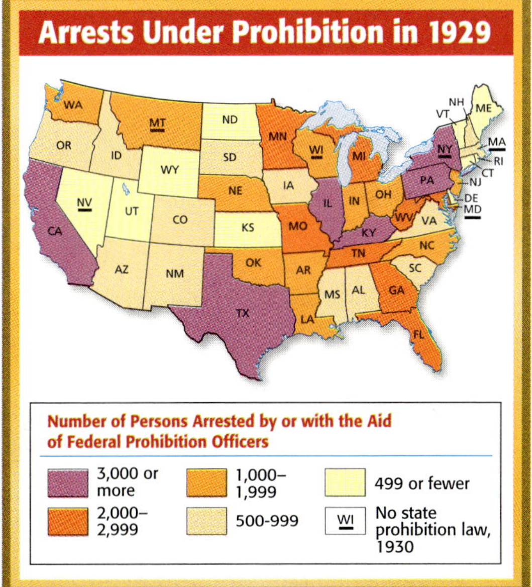

internetconnect

TOPIC: Jazz in the 1920s
GO TO: go.hrw.com
KEYWORD: SE1 Jazz

Accessing the Internet through the HRW Web site, research the lives and accomplishments of jazz artists Duke Ellington and Louis Armstrong. Then create a newspaper page that has interviews with the artists or stories about them.

BUILDING YOUR PORTFOLIO

Complete one or all of the following projects independently or cooperatively.

1 Economic Development

Imagine that you are a prosperous business owner in the 1920s. ***Create an advertisement*** for a new household product aimed at the expanding consumer market.

It hasn't a single belt, fan or drain pipe....
Refrigerator
GENERAL ELECTRIC

2 Cultural Diversity

Imagine that you are a Harlem Renaissance or Lost Generation writer or a mural painter living in the United States during the 1920s. ***Create a poem or painting*** that draws upon your cultural heritage or that reflects 1920s American society.

3 Democratic Values

Imagine that you are a writer for a 1920s radio show. ***Write a script*** for a radio show that addresses the many changes that are taking place in American society.

to new fashion standards, fascination with celebrities, and independent-minded behavior.

3. Religious leaders disparaged the 1920s youth culture and encouraged Americans to devote themselves to traditional values and ways of life.
4. through their paintings, photographs, and murals
5. by producing outstanding works that were distinctively African American

Writing About History

Students' essays will vary but should describe how radio broadcasts provided Americans with new and shared cultural experiences, thus creating a mass culture.

Strategies for Success

1. primary—provides firsthand information
2. students of sociology and other educated readers
3. The passage displays very little bias; some students might suggest that the authors found the amount of advertising in Muncie to be excessive.
4. Answers will vary, but students should note that the passage provides firsthand evidence of the growth and importance of advertising in the United States during the 1920s.

Linking History and Geography

People caught smuggling alcohol from Mexico and Canada would most likely have been arrested in border states.

The Great Depression

CHAPTER PLANNING GUIDE

	Section Lesson Objectives	Print Resources	Multimedia Resources	Sheltered English Resources
Section 1 Prosperity Shattered, pp. 414–19	1 Recount why financial experts issued warnings about business practices during the 1920s. 2 Describe why the stock market crashed in 1929. 3 Explain how the banking crisis and subsequent business failures signaled the beginning of the Great Depression. 4 Identify the main causes of the Great Depression.	▶ Guided Reading Strategy 14.1 ▶ Primary Source Reading 14: A Shattering of Spirit ▶ Section 1 Review, p. 419 ▶ Daily Quiz 14.1	▶ One-Stop Planner, Lesson 14.1 ▶ The American Nation Video Program Segment: The Great Depression; Teacher's Guide, pp. 111–16 ▶ Holt Researcher: American History CD–ROM ▶ HRW Web site	▶ Main Idea Activity for Reteaching and Sheltered English 14.1
Section 2 Hard Times, pp. 420–27	1 Describe how unemployment during the Great Depression affected the lives of American workers. 2 Compare and contrast the hardships that urban and rural residents faced during the depression. 3 Analyze how the Great Depression affected family life and the attitudes of Americans. 4 Explain how popular culture provided an escape from the Great Depression.	▶ Guided Reading Strategy 14.2 ▶ Graphic Organizer Activity 14: Life During the Depression ▶ Literature Reading 14: The Depression Takes Its Toll ▶ Biography Reading 14: Walt Disney ▶ Section 2 Review, p. 427 ▶ Daily Quiz 14.2	▶ One-Stop Planner, Lesson 14.2 ▶ Everyday Life in America Transparency 24: America's Darling: Shirley Temple, 1930s ▶ Holt Researcher: American History CD–ROM	▶ Main Idea Activity for Reteaching and Sheltered English 14.2
Section 3 Hoover's Policies, pp. 428–35	1 Explain why President Hoover opposed government-sponsored direct relief for needy individuals during the Great Depression. 2 Outline the Hoover administration's attempts to solve the economic problems of the depression, and analyze the success of these efforts. 3 Relate how radicals and veterans responded to President Hoover's policies. 4 Analyze why Franklin D. Roosevelt was such a popular candidate in the 1932 election.	▶ Guided Reading Strategy 14.3 ▶ American History Political Cartoon 23: Herbert Hoover and the Depression ▶ Geography Activity 14: Public Unrest During the Depression ▶ Section 3 Review, p. 435 ▶ Daily Quiz 14.3	▶ One-Stop Planner, Lesson 14.3 ▶ Holt Researcher: American History CD–ROM	▶ Main Idea Activity for Reteaching and Sheltered English 14.3
Chapter Review and Assessment pp. 436–37		▶ Chapter 14 Review, pp. 436–37 ▶ Chapter 14 Tutorial for Students, Parents, Mentors, and Peers ▶ Chapter 14 Test (Form A or B) ▶ Portfolio Activities and Alternative Assessment Handbook, Chapter 14	▶ Audio Program, Chapter 14 (English and Spanish) ▶ Chapter 14 Test Generator (on the One-Stop Planner) ▶ Global Skill Builder CD–ROM ▶ HRW Web site	▶ Spanish Glossary ▶ Sheltered English Chapter 14 Test

CHAPTER OVERVIEW

At the end of the decade, the prosperity of the 1920s gave way to the Great Depression. This severe economic downturn had several causes, including a global economic crisis, the national income gap, and consumer debt. The Great Depression significantly affected Americans. Unemployment rose and wages fell. Some families broke apart under the strain.

On the whole, President Herbert Hoover opposed direct government aid to needy individuals, instead supporting a policy of "rugged individualism." Hoover did attempt to stem the depression, however, encouraging voluntarism and supporting the creation of agricultural and financial boards and corporations. Many Americans viewed Hoover's efforts as ineffective and even cruel. Radicals staged protest marches and veterans gathered in Washington, D.C., to demand payment of their pension bonuses. The U.S. Army dispersed these veterans, inspiring angry responses. This situation created a highly unfavorable climate for Hoover and the Republicans in the election of 1932. Democrat Franklin D. Roosevelt won the presidency.

TIME TAMERS

Block Scheduling

The teacher lesson plans for each section offer a variety of activity choices to help you present the material in a block scheduling format. For further suggestions on block scheduling, see the **Block Scheduling Handbook with Team Teaching Strategies**, pp. 79–84.

Hands-On History Activities:

Classroom to Community The **Hands-On History Activities** help students make meaningful connections between events in American history and those in their own hometown. You may wish to use the Chapter 14 Activity, The Economic State of Your State, to extend the chapter lessons, as alternative assessment, or as a block scheduling option.

Portfolio Projects

The American Nation includes multiple portfolio projects in each Pupil's Edition chapter review, as well as each unit review. Chapter 14 Portfolio Project options on p. 437 include the following:

1. Students will **create an editorial cartoon**.
2. Students will **create a series of newspaper headlines**.
3. Students will **create a campaign poster**.

The American Nation
INTERNET RESOURCE DIRECTORY

To access online materials for this chapter, go to **go.hrw.com** and type in the keywords listed below.

HRW ONLINE RESOURCES
GO TO: go.hrw.com

Online Maps
KEYWORD: SE1 Maps14
- Unemployment in Europe, 1932

Online Charts
KEYWORD: SE1 Charts14
- Unemployment, 1929–1941
- Personal Income, 1929–1941

Online Reading Support
KEYWORD: SE1 Strategies14

Online Rubrics
KEYWORD: SE1 Rubrics

CHAPTER ENRICHMENT LINKS
Use these Web links to extend and enrich student learning for Chapter 14.
GO TO: go.hrw.com
KEYWORD: SE1 Ch14

CHAPTER INTERNET ACTIVITIES
GO TO: go.hrw.com
- Pupil's Edition Student Activity
  KEYWORD: SE1 Depression
  (Students conduct research on the Great Depression.)
- Teacher's Edition Student Activity
  KEYWORD: SE1 Hoover
  (Students analyze the history and technology of the Hoover Dam.)
- Teacher's Edition Student Activity
  KEYWORD: SE1 Crash
  (Students examine the causes of the Great Depression.)

ADDITIONAL
RESOURCES

Books for Teachers

Kennedy, David M. *Freedom from Fear: The American People in Depression and War, 1929–1945.* Oxford University Press, 1999. Examines President Hoover's policies.

McElvaine, Robert. *The Great Depression: America, 1929–1941.* Times Books, 1993. Provides an overview of the period; discusses the causes of the depression in detail.

Books for Students

Meltzer, Milton. *Brother, Can You Spare a Dime?* Facts on File, 1990. Details the effects of the Great Depression.

Schraff, Anne E. *The Great Depression and the New Deal.* Watts, 1990. Explores the stock market crash and beyond.

Primary Sources from the Period

Hoover, Herbert C. *Memoirs: The Great Depression.* Macmillan, 1952. Offers President Hoover's defense of his decisions in office.

Terkel, Studs. *Hard Times.* Avon, 1971. Presents oral history accounts from those who lived through the Great Depression; considered a classic in the field.

Multimedia Materials

Great Depression. Video, 28 min. Dallas Community College District. Discusses the Great Depression; includes an interview with well-known historian Studs Terkel.

Great Depression, 1929. Video, 32 min. Guidance Associates. Examines the causes of the crash.

CHAPTER 14

Before You Read

Build on What You Know

Ask students to answer the following questions.

How might enormous debts have led to economic problems in the United States?

Consider:

- the need to make payments on debts and the widespread purchasing repercussions of those payments
- the financial instability of debt

How might the federal government have reversed the country's economic decline?

Consider:

- the limited role of the federal government during the 1920s
- the scope of the government's power

exploring the time line

AMERICAN EVENTS

internetconnect

TOPIC: Hoover Dam
GO TO: go.hrw.com
KEYWORD: SE1 Hoover

Have students access the Internet through the HRW Web site to conduct research on the construction of the Hoover (Boulder) Dam from 1933 to 1935. Then have each student write an essay describing the purpose of the dam, its technology, and the building process.

CHAPTER 14

1929–1933

The Great Depression

STAGE BROADWAY SCREEN

VARIETY 25¢

WALL ST. LAYS AN EGG

Headline describing the stock market crash

1929
Business and Finance
The U.S. stock market crashes.

1929
Science and Technology
The Cascade Tunnel, the longest railroad tunnel in North America, is completed.

1929
Politics
Congress establishes the Federal Farm Board to assist farmers.

1930
Business and Finance
Approximately $180 million of depositors' savings are lost with the financial collapse of one New York City bank.

1930
World Events
France establishes a workers' insurance law.

Bank closing

1929 **1930**

1929
Science and Technology
Harvard physician Samuel Albert Levine establishes a connection between high blood pressure and heart disease.

1929
The Arts
William Faulkner publishes *The Sound and the Fury.*

1930
Daily Life
In New York City more than 6,000 unemployed workers sell apples on the streets to earn money.

1930
World Events
An economic depression hits countries in Europe and South America.

British election poster portraying the effects of the Great Depression

Before You Read

Build on What You Know

The economic boom of the 1920s gave most Americans tremendous faith in the future. For many Americans, prosperity seemed limitless. The economic gains were unevenly distributed, however. The lifestyle of the Jazz Age also led to enormous consumer debt. In this chapter you will learn how debt and many other factors led to the Great Depression. When President Hoover's efforts to revive the economy failed, Americans elected a Democratic president, Franklin D. Roosevelt, in hopes of reversing the country's economic decline.

412

Think About Themes

To help students create their Themes Journal entries, provide the following examples of appropriate **agree/disagree** *statements.*

Economic Development

Agree A stock market crash tends to indicate economic weaknesses.

Disagree The stock market is only one financial indicator among many.

Geographic Diversity

Agree Although financial panics in the late 1800s placed a particularly heavy burden on rural Americans, people in those areas did not flee their homes in enormous numbers.

Disagree Economic stagnation in the South after the Civil War, along with the unfavorable racial climate there, encouraged many African Americans to move to the North.

Cultural Diversity

Agree Even some wealthy people lost huge amounts of money in the financial panics of the late 1800s.

Disagree Economic depressions carry particularly severe consequences for poor people and minority groups.

Boulder Dam on the Colorado River

Members of the Bonus Army

1931 Science and Technology U.S. engineer Henry J. Kaiser designs the Boulder Dam.

1931 Politics President Hoover refuses to support a bill providing direct federal relief for unemployed workers.

1931 Daily Life Cotton prices fall below 6 cents per pound, forcing many tenant farmers from their land.

1931 World Events President Hoover announces a one-year halt on war reparations, hoping to promote European economic recovery.

1932 Business and Finance Industrial output falls to half its 1929 level.

1932 World Events Chile's income from the export of copper and nitrates declines by more than 1.5 billion pesos in less than four years.

1932 Business and Finance Since 1930 more than 5,000 banks have closed.

1932 Daily Life Veterans form the Bonus Army and demonstrate in Washington, D.C., demanding early payments of their pensions.

1932 Politics Congress establishes the Reconstruction Finance Corporation to stabilize the economy by assisting banks and other financial institutions.

1932 Politics Franklin D. Roosevelt is elected president.

1933 The Arts James Hilton publishes *Lost Horizon.*

1933 Daily Life The unemployment rate reaches 24.9 percent of the workforce, as 15 million Americans are out of work.

1931 — 1932 — 1933

James Hilton's novel

Franklin D. Roosevelt campaigning

Think About Themes

Decide whether you **agree** *or* **disagree** *with the following statements. Note why in your journal.*

Economic Development A stock market crash will always result in a severe economic depression.

Geographic Diversity An economic crisis does not affect where people live, since they cannot afford to move.

Cultural Diversity In an economic depression everyone suffers equally, regardless of class, gender, and ethnic background.

exploring the time line

GLOBAL EVENTS

ECONOMIC DEVELOPMENT

1931 ■ A Halt on Reparations. Many European countries incurred heavy debts to the United States during World War I. After the war, many of these countries asked the United States for total debt amnesty, but were refused. As a result, many countries pressed Germany to pay its war reparations, virtually destroying the German economy and slowing economic recovery in Europe. At times, Germany even borrowed money from the United States to pay its debts to other countries, which then used the money to repay their own debts to the United States. Hoping to end this lunacy and encourage economic growth in Europe, Hoover announced a one-year halt on reparations in 1931. The following year, the reparations were abandoned.

CRITICAL THINKING Do you think the United States should have agreed to total debt amnesty? Why or why not?

ANSWER: Some students might suggest that as a wealthy nation, the United States had an obligation to accept debt amnesty. Other students might suggest that Germany had a duty to pay its war reparations.

413

SECTION 1

After completing Section 1, students should be able to:

OBJECTIVE 1 *Recount why financial experts issued warnings about business practices during the 1920s.*

OBJECTIVE 2 *Describe why the stock market crashed in 1929.*

OBJECTIVE 3 *Explain how the banking crisis and subsequent business failures signaled the beginning of the Great Depression.*

OBJECTIVE 4 *Identify the main causes of the Great Depression.*

LET'S GET STARTED!

As students enter the classroom, ask them to write a few sentences about what the causes and effects of a country's economic boom might be. Have volunteers share their responses. *(Students might mention pro-business economic policies, industrial expansion, and the explosion of new products.)* Tell students that in Section 1 they will learn how the prosperity of the 1920s gave way to the Great Depression of the 1930s.

SECTION 1 RESOURCES

PRINT
- Guided Reading Strategy 14.1
- Primary Source Reading 14: A Shattering of Spirit
- Section 1 Review, p. 419
- Daily Quiz 14.1

MULTIMEDIA
- One-Stop Planner, Lesson 14.1
- The American Nation Video Program Segment: The Great Depression; Teacher's Guide, pp. 111–16
- Holt Researcher: American History CD–ROM
- HRW Web site

SHELTERED ENGLISH
- Main Idea Activity for Reteaching and Sheltered English 14.1

✔ READING TO UNDERSTAND
To help students master the section objectives, have them answer the **READING CHECKS** and complete **Guided Reading Strategy 14.1** as they read the section.

Prosperity Shattered

OBJECTIVES

Read to understand:
1. why financial experts issued warnings about business practices during the 1920s
2. why the stock market crashed in 1929
3. how the banking crisis and subsequent business failures signaled the beginning of the Great Depression
4. what the main causes of the Great Depression were

KEY TERMS

bull market
bear market
margin buying
Black Thursday
Black Tuesday
gross national product
Great Depression
Smoot-Hawley Tariff
business cycle

KEY PEOPLE

Herbert Hoover

"'MARKET CRASHES—PANIC HITS NATION!' one headline blared. . . . I couldn't imagine such financial disaster touching my small world; it surely concerned only the rich. But by the first week of November I too knew differently; along with millions of others across the nation, I was with out a job. All that next week I searched for any kind of work that would prevent my leaving school. Again it was, 'We're firing, not hiring.' . . . Finally, on the seventh of November I went to school and cleaned out my locker, knowing it was impossible to stay on. A piercing chill was in the air as I walked back to the rooming house. The hawk had come. I could already feel his wings shadowing me."

—Gordon Parks

Photographer and author Gordon Parks

Gordon Parks was 16 years old when the prosperity of the 1920s came to an abrupt halt. The booming stock market crashed on Thursday, October 24, 1929. In the first few hours of stock trading, share prices fell sharply. At first, investors remained calm. However, as prices continued to fall, panic struck. Frantic orders to sell stock came pouring in. The economic prosperity of the 1920s was over. The worst economic depression in U.S. history had begun. For many Americans, their daily lives became a constant struggle for survival.

Economic Troubles on the Horizon

Although the 1920s appeared to be a decade of unlimited economic prosperity, a few isolated voices warned of problems within the U.S. economy. Some economists identified the nation's agricultural crisis and "sick" industries as problems in need of attention. Yet despite these early warnings of economic troubles, few Americans worried about the nation's economic health in the late 1920s. The country's widespread prosperity led many Americans to believe that the economy would continue to grow in the following decades. President Herbert Hoover expressed this confidence in his speech accepting the Republican nomination in 1928.

> **"We in America today are nearer to the final triumph over poverty than ever before in the history of any land. The poorhouse is vanishing from among us. . . . We shall soon . . . be in sight of the day when poverty will be banished from this nation."**

During the 1928 presidential campaign, Republican Herbert Hoover promised economic prosperity and continued pro-business policies.

Credit. Assured by their faith in the nation's economic prosperity, many Americans purchased new consumer products on credit. By 1929 the total number of purchases made with credit was six times higher than in 1915. Purchases on credit in 1929 reached a total of $7 billion.

The federal government encouraged this borrowing by keeping interest rates low during the late 1920s. The Republican administrations of the time reasoned that

TEACH OBJECTIVE 1

LEVEL 1: Ask students to identify the warnings that financial experts issued during the 1920s. *(Experts warned that the economy was in potential danger and pointed to the farm crisis, "sick" industries, consumers' reliance on credit, and stock speculation as evidence to support their claims.)* Ask students why the public largely ignored such warnings. *(Students should mention that the economy was booming, and the public believed that it would continue to grow.)* Have each student write a paragraph summarizing these warnings and explaining the public's response. **Sheltered English**

LEVELS 2 AND 3: Ask students to identify the warnings that financial experts issued during the 1920s. *(See the Level 1 lesson for the correct warnings.)* Assign each student one of the warnings. Have students create diagrams displaying the economic rationales behind the warnings. *(The farm crisis and "sick" industries pointed to ingrained supply and production problems. Consumers' reliance on credit indicated their financial vulnerability. Stock speculation indicated an overheated market.)* Ask at least four students—one representing each of the specific warnings in the Level 1 lesson—to draw their diagrams on the chalkboard and explain them to the class.

an easy-credit policy would promote business. Easy access to credit enabled consumers to buy goods when they did not actually have the money to pay for them.

Industries' increasing reliance on customers who made purchases with credit generated caution among economic experts. These experts noted that in an economic downturn, such debt could cripple consumers. Consumers, however, ignored these warnings and continued to purchase automobiles, radios, and appliances on credit.

Playing the market. Americans' confidence in the economy of the 1920s was also reflected in the stock market. Investors poured millions of dollars into the market. Stock sales had increased steadily for several years. As demand rose, so did stock prices. Many experts saw no end to the **bull market**—one with an upward trend in stock prices. "There have been bull markets before," observed the *New York Times*, "but the present one surpasses them all." Investors and market analysts claimed that the stock market was in no danger of becoming a **bear market**—one with a downward trend in stock prices.

By the late 1920s, stock speculation—"playing" the market by buying and selling to make a quick profit—was widespread. Although speculation fueled economic growth, it also created problems. Rapid buying and selling inflated the prices of stocks to the point that many stocks were selling for far more than they were actually worth. This speculative buying was fine as long as demand was high, but if investor confidence weakened, prices would tumble.

The situation was made shakier still by **margin buying**—the practice of purchasing stocks with borrowed money. Many speculators put up as little as 10 percent of the price of a stock, borrowing the rest. Buying on margin worked as long as the bull market continued. If prices were to ever fall steeply, however, investors would find themselves deep in debt.

Ticker tape machines like this one were used to get up-to-date stock market prices during the 1920s.

Although consumer confidence in the market remained high throughout the summer of 1929, a few gloomy voices were heard. In early September stock analyst Roger Babson wrote, "Sooner or later a crash is coming, and it may be terrific [immense]." Some shrewd investors began to sell their stocks, but most people ignored the warnings.

✔ **READING CHECK:** Why did financial experts issue warnings about business practices during the 1920s?

The Crash, 1929

Company	High Price Sept. 3, 1929	Low Price Nov. 13, 1929
American Telephone and Telegraph	304	197 1/4
General Electric	396 1/4	168 1/8
General Motors	72 3/4	36
Montgomery Ward	137 7/8	49 1/4
United States Steel	261 3/4	150
Woolworth	100 3/8	52 1/4

Source: *Only Yesterday*

Learning from Charts In the days following the stock market crash on October 29, 1929, stock prices continued to fall. Average stock prices reached their lowest point for the year on November 13, 1929, slightly two months after they had reached the high point for the year on September 3.

Building Chart Skills Which company's stock lost the greatest number of points between September 3 and November 13, 1929?

The Stock Market Crashes

The bubble burst on **Black Thursday**—October 24, 1929. A large number of investors, made nervous by factors such as rising interest rates, suddenly began to sell their shares. The dumping of so much

ECONOMIC DEVELOPMENT

Playing the Market. Many Americans speculated in the stock market because they had heard stories of ordinary citizens earning fortunes. In one popular tale, a peddler turned $4,000 into $250,000. In addition, many people saw the market as a safe way to make money. In an article entitled "Everybody Ought to Be Rich," the *Ladies' Home Journal* assured readers that if they invested just $15 a month in stocks they would earn $80,000 in 20 years.

CRITICAL THINKING What serious financial misconception might some investors have had when they poured money into the stock market after hearing amazing success stories?

ANSWER: Students might mention that some investors entered the stock market assuming that there was little or no risk of financial loss—always a misconception in stock market investments.

THAT'S INTERESTING!

Historians have estimated that just 3 million Americans, or less than 2.5 percent of the nation's population, owned stocks in 1928.

CHART ANSWER
General Electric

TEACH OBJECTIVE 2

ALL LEVELS: Write the following question on the chalkboard: *Once the stock market starts to fall, can anything reverse that decline?* Have students answer the question in writing. Then ask volunteers to share their responses. *(Answers will vary. Some students will suggest that investors themselves might be able to reverse a decline by buying heavily.)* To help students understand why the stock market crashed in 1929, copy the graphic organizer at right on the chalkboard, omitting the italicized answers. Have each student complete it. **Sheltered English**

Factors That Caused the Stock Market Crash

1. *economic factors such as rising interest rates worry investors*
2. *investors sell stocks*
3. *stock prices plunge*
4. *heavy sales continue*

HISTORY MAKERS SPEAK

John Hersch in *Hard Times*

Remembering the Crash. John Hersch, an investment broker, described Black Thursday. "I had about $3,000 in the stock market, which was all the money I had. On Black Friday—Thursday, was it?—that margin account went out of the window. I may have had about $62 left. My wife had a colossal $125 a week job. . . . That night, she came home to our little apartment, and she said, 'Guess what happened today?' I said, 'What?' She said, 'I quit.' I was making about $60 a week and she was making $125. Two-thirds of our income and all of our savings disappeared that day."

CRITICAL THINKING How might the Hersches' financial troubles have affected their later spending? How might such behavior have deepened the Great Depression?

ANSWER: Answers will vary. Students might suggest that the Hersch family probably stopped making all but the most crucial purchases. Taken as a whole, this lack of consumer spending hurt businesses and deepened the depression.

VISUAL RECORD ANSWER

Students might suggest that this man is trying to sell his luxury car for a small amount of cash.

THE GRANGER COLLECTION, NEW YORK

INTERPRETING THE VISUAL RECORD

Stock market crash. The stock market crash of 1929 left many stockholders with huge losses. Some investors who had borrowed money during the prosperous days of the 1920s were unable to pay off their loans. ***How do you think this photograph reflects the transition from a time of prosperity to one of depression for this investor?***

stock on the market jolted investor confidence and caused prices to plunge. Panic gripped Wall Street. A *New York Times* reporter described the crash.

> **"It came with a speed and ferocity [cruelty] that left men dazed. The bottom simply fell out of the market. . . . The streets were crammed with a mixed crowd—agonized little speculators, . . . sold-out traders, . . . inquisitive individuals and tourists seeking . . . a closer view of the national catastrophe. . . . Where was it going to end?"**

Black Thursday was just the beginning of a long downward spiral. Prices dropped still lower the following week, as more investors sold their stocks. On **Black Tuesday**—October 29—prices sank to a shocking new low when panicked investors dumped more than 16 million shares of stock on the market.

As prices fell, brokers contacted customers who owed them money for stocks purchased on margin. The brokers demanded cash to cover their loans. Unable to raise the funds, thousands of people were forced to sell their stocks at huge losses. Many investors were wiped out. By mid-November the average value of leading stocks had been cut in half, and stockholders had lost some $30 billion. By year's end, stock losses exceeded the total cost of U.S. involvement in World War I.

✔ **READING CHECK:** Why did the stock market crash in 1929?

The Depression Begins

In the first months after the stock market crash, business leaders and public officials insisted that the setback was minor and temporary. President Hoover declared, "We have now passed the worst and . . . shall rapidly recover." Yet this optimism could not conceal the grim truth. Within the first months of 1930 it became clear that the nation was slipping into a severe economic depression.

Banking crisis. Just a small percentage of Americans had invested in the stock market in 1929. However, the impact of the crash was soon felt by the entire country. The stock market collapse provoked a major banking crisis. Like many other investors, large banks suffered significant losses. The worst economic crisis for banks came as a result of borrowers defaulting on their loans. Having lost their investments in the stock market, many debt-ridden investors could not repay their loans. Banks were left with depreciating assets and little income. With dwindling cash reserves, some banks were forced to close.

Fear of additional bank failures further aggravated the banking crisis. Customers could lose their entire life savings if their bank closed. Many depositors panicked and tried to withdraw their savings. This caused even more bank failures. Reporting on a banking panic in Akron, Ohio, one newspaper commented, "The bank was failing. Its cash reserve was dropping. Bank depositors waited in dread for a teller to say, 'We cannot give you ten percent of your account. We can't give you anything.'" Between 1930 and 1932, more than 5,000 banks failed. The 1930 collapse of one large New York City bank wiped out some 400,000 depositors.

TEACH OBJECTIVE 3

LEVEL 1: Pair students and write the following phrase on the chalkboard: *The Banking Crisis and Subsequent Business Failures.* Have each pair create a flowchart displaying the effects of bank and business failures and noting how those events signaled the beginning of the Great Depression. *(Pairs' flowcharts should indicate that banks failed due to heavy defaults, margin calls, and depositor withdrawals. Bank failures deprived businesses of necessary resources and customers and forced layoffs and closings.)* Ask volunteers to present their flowcharts to the class. **Sheltered English, Cooperative Learning**

LEVELS 2 AND 3: Conduct a brief discussion on the ways in which the banking crisis and subsequent business failures signaled the beginning of the Great Depression. *(See the Level 1 lesson for the correct details.)* Then organize students into small groups. Have each group create an outline for a skit depicting an event related to a bank or business failure. Skits might show depositors trying to withdraw their savings from an undercapitalized bank, for example. Have each group present its outline to the class. If time allows, ask each group to rehearse and perform its skit for the class. **Cooperative Learning**

Business failures. Many American businesses suffered from the banking crisis. Industries that had already lost money in the stock market crash faced additional hardships with consumers unable or unwilling to buy their products. Debt and the fear of bank failures brought an end to the consumer habit of purchasing new goods on credit. Many companies were forced to trim inventories, scale back production schedules, and lay off employees.

During the early 1930s businesses began to fail at an alarming rate as the economy's downward slide accelerated. More than 26,000 businesses went bankrupt in 1930. Another 28,285 went under the following year. In 1929 the U.S. **gross national product**—the total value of all goods and services produced in a given year—had reached $103 billion. At the height of the depression in 1933 it fell below $56 billion. Factories and mines stood idle. Railroad cars sat silent and empty.

As businesses failed, unemployment reached staggering levels. In 1932, the rate rose to 23.6 percent, up from 3.2 percent three years earlier. The crisis in the banking industry, business failures, and massive unemployment in the early 1930s marked the beginning of the **Great Depression**. This deep economic downturn gripped the United States between 1929 and the beginning of World War II.

Many Americans thought that their bank accounts would be safe during economic hard times.

✔ **READING CHECK:** How did the banking crisis and subsequent business failures signal the beginning of the Great Depression?

What Caused the Great Depression?

The stock market crash of 1929 provoked the banking crisis and business failures that jolted the U.S. economy and destroyed individual fortunes. It alone, however, did not cause the Great Depression. The stock market collapse was a major factor among the depression's many causes.

Global depression. Economic trouble in Europe and other parts of the world was one of the many factors that brought down the U.S. economy. As the economy sank during the early 1930s, many observers, including President Hoover, blamed the U.S. depression on the state of global finances following World War I.

The global economy had suffered enormous setbacks. This was primarily because of the massive war debts built up by European countries. World trade rapidly declined during the late 1920s and early 1930s. The global depression further worsened the economic crisis in the United States. Foreign consumers were unable to purchase American goods. American industries, which relied on sales to consumers abroad, were stuck with large surpluses.

THROUGH OTHERS' EYES

The Global Depression

The impact of the Great Depression was felt in almost every country in the world. In a 1931 radio broadcast by the British Broadcasting Corporation (BBC) on unemployment, British economist John Maynard Keynes described the severe effects of the economic downturn for industrial workers and farmers throughout the world.

> **"The slump in trade and employment and the business losses . . . are as bad as the worst which have ever occurred in the modern history of the world. No country is exempt. The privation [hardship] and—what is sometimes worse—the anxiety which exist today in millions of homes all over the world is extreme. In the three chief industrial countries of the world, Great Britain, Germany, and the United States, I estimate that probably 12 million industrial workers stand idle. But I am not sure that there is not even more human misery today in the great agricultural countries of the world—Canada, Australia, and South America, where millions of small farmers see themselves ruined."**

ECONOMIC DEVELOPMENT

Attitudes Toward the Banking System. In 1929 most of the banks operating in the United States were small, independent institutions that had no outside resources to access in the event of a crisis. Branch banks, or outlying offices of major banks, were rare in this era, although they became common later. Many Americans viewed major banks as the embodiment of "Money Power"—large, menacing banking companies—and feared they would eventually dominate the country's financial system.

CRITICAL THINKING How might the 1920s attitudes of Americans toward banking have contributed to the later banking crisis?

ANSWER: Students might suggest that the fear of "Money Power" led to the creation of small banks with limited capital and resources.

The American Nation **VIDEO PROGRAM**

The Great Depression; Teacher's Guide, pp. 111–16

Search 25392, Play to 31485
Videodisc 2, Side A

Play Pause

See *Teacher's Guide* for Spanish barcode.

TEACH OBJECTIVE 4

LEVELS 1 AND 2: Ask each student to list the main causes of the Great Depression on a sheet of paper. *(Students should list the global economic crisis, the income gap, and consumer debt.)* Have students write a sentence for each factor explaining how it contributed to the depression. *(The global economic crisis deprived the United States of foreign consumers, and the income gap deprived businesses of national consumers. Consumer debt led to individual vulnerability and economic chaos.)* As a class, have students rank these causes from least important to most important. To conclude, describe a normal business cycle and discuss with the class how the Great Depression deviated from that cycle. **Sheltered English**

LEVEL 3: Tell students to imagine that it is 1930 and that they are economists who have been asked to appear on a radio program and explain the causes of the Great Depression to listeners. Have each student write a script for a broadcast discussing those causes and contrasting the depression with a normal business cycle. *(See the Levels 1 and 2 lesson for the correct causes and explanations.)* Have volunteers perform their broadcasts for the class.

▶ASSIGNMENT *Have each student create a diagram representing a typical business cycle. Then ask students to write paragraphs describing how the Great Depression represented a significant deviation from that typical cycle.*

internetconnect

TOPIC: Causes of the Great Depression
GO TO: go.hrw.com
KEYWORD: SE1 Crash

Have students access the Internet through the HRW Web site to conduct research on the causes of the Great Depression. Then have each student create a graphic organizer displaying those causes. Tell students to make sure that their graphic organizers contain a cell or other slot for each of the major causes of the depression.

THAT'S INTERESTING!

In 1929 nearly 80 percent of the nation's families had no savings at all. These families had no financial cushion when the depression hit.

MAP ANSWER

Norway, Denmark, and Germany

VISUAL RECORD ANSWER

(for p. 419)

Students might note the claim that a person who purchases an automobile will provide three months of work to someone.

U.S. policies could have eased the global depression. Instead, the United States contributed to the worldwide economic downturn by slapping high tariffs on imported goods. Even after the crash, Congress continued to pass high tariffs such as the **Smoot-Hawley Tariff** of 1930. It was the highest in U.S. history. The act protected American industries from inexpensive imports. However, it accelerated the global depression by eliminating the American market for foreign manufacturers and industries.

The income gap and consumer debt.

Historians have argued that the unequal distribution of income was another central cause of the Great Depression.

The Beginnings of the Global Depression, 1928–1933

Learning from Maps The worldwide depression created record levels of unemployment.

? PLACE In 1932 which countries had unemployment rates exceeding 30 percent?

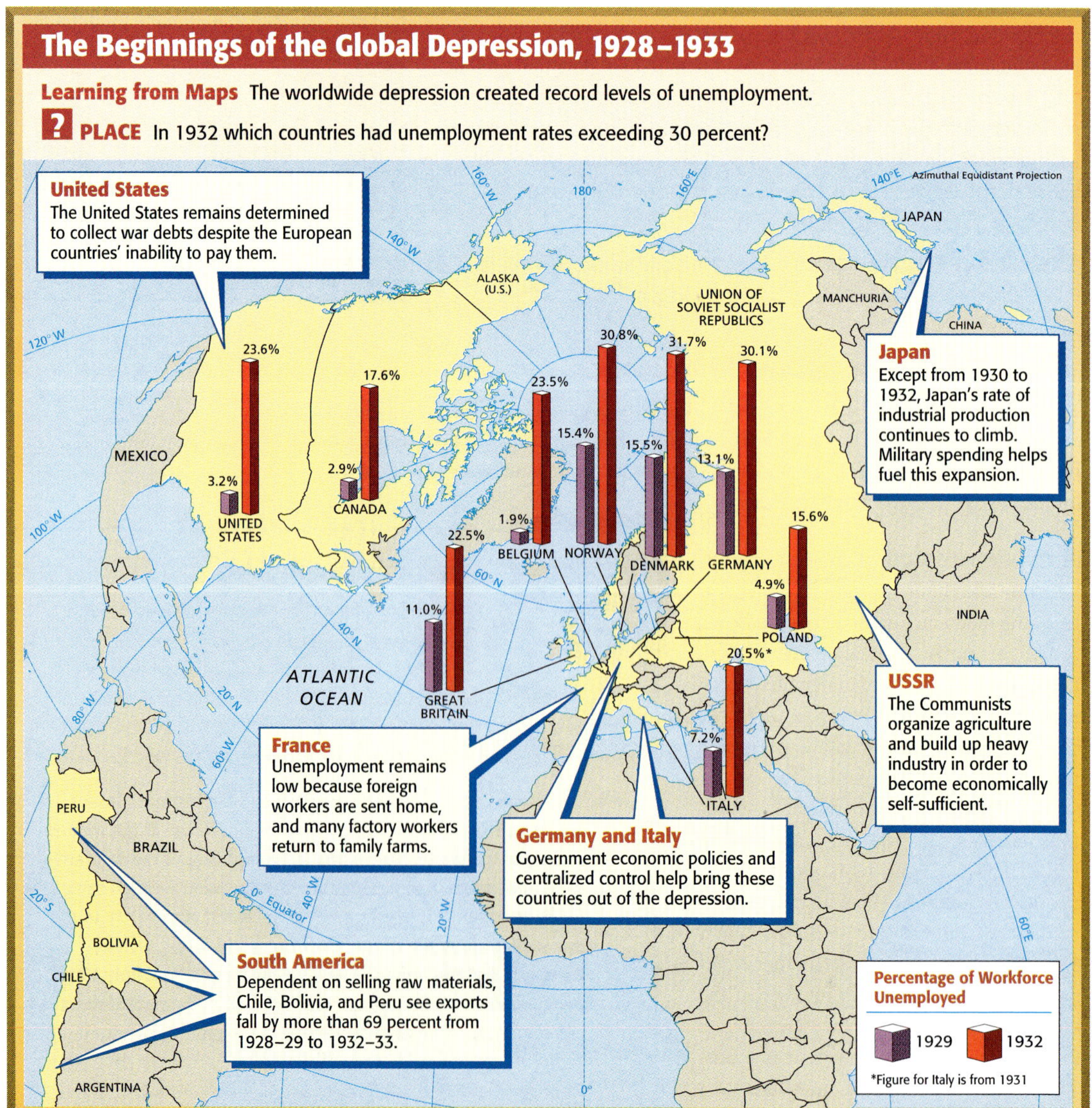

Azimuthal Equidistant Projection
United States
The United States remains determined to collect war debts despite the European countries' inability to pay them.
Japan
Except from 1930 to 1932, Japan's rate of industrial production continues to climb. Military spending helps fuel this expansion.
USSR
The Communists organize agriculture and build up heavy industry in order to become economically self-sufficient.
France
Unemployment remains low because foreign workers are sent home, and many factory workers return to family farms.
Germany and Italy
Government economic policies and centralized control help bring these countries out of the depression.
South America
Dependent on selling raw materials, Chile, Bolivia, and Peru see exports fall by more than 69 percent from 1928–29 to 1932–33.
UNITED STATES
3.2%
23.6%
CANADA
2.9%
17.6%
GREAT BRITAIN
11.0%
22.5%
BELGIUM
1.9%
23.5%
NORWAY
15.4%
30.8%
DENMARK
15.5%
31.7%
GERMANY
13.1%
30.1%
POLAND
4.9%
15.6%
ITALY
7.2%
20.5%*
ALASKA (U.S.)
UNION OF SOVIET SOCIALIST REPUBLICS
MANCHURIA
CHINA
JAPAN
INDIA
MEXICO
ATLANTIC OCEAN
PERU
BRAZIL
BOLIVIA
CHILE
ARGENTINA
Equator
Percentage of Workforce Unemployed
1929
1932
*Figure for Italy is from 1931

REVIEW

Have students complete the **Section 1 Review** on p. 419.

ASSESS

Have students complete **Daily Quiz 14.1**. As **Alternative Assessment**, you may want to use the bank crisis skit outline or the depression broadcast in this section's lessons.

RETEACH

Have students complete **Main Idea Activity for Reteaching and Sheltered English 14.1**. Then organize students into small groups. Have each group create an outline of Section 1. Ask each group to copy its outline on the chalkboard. Conduct a brief discussion on the outlines and the material in the section. **Sheltered English, Cooperative Learning**

EXTEND

Have students conduct introductory research on the workings of the stock market. Then have each student create a mock stock portfolio, starting with a fictional $5,000. Tell students to use the newspaper's financial section to track the performance of their stocks over a specified period of time. After that period, have students write a brief report analyzing the performance of their stocks—gains, losses, and so on. In their reports, students should compare and contrast their stock market experiences with those of Americans in the 1920s. **Block Scheduling**

Between 1923 and 1929 the disposable income of the wealthiest 1 percent of Americans increased by 63 percent. Meanwhile, the income of the poorest 93 percent of Americans decreased by 4 percent. Writer Upton Sinclair noted, "The . . . depression is one of abundance, not of scarcity. . . . The cause of the trouble is that a small class has the wealth, while the rest have the debts." This income gap meant that most people did not have the buying power needed to boost the economy. According to many economists, if workers had received higher wages for their labor and farmers better prices for their crops, the depression would have been less severe. Some even argue that it could have been avoided.

Some Americans bridged the income gap by using credit to purchase goods. The reliance on consumer credit also contributed to economic chaos. Once the economy began to slow and the government raised interest rates, many consumers could not pay their debts. After the crash many businesses stopped extending credit altogether.

The business cycle. Some economists argue that better fiscal planning in the 1920s would not have prevented the onset of the Great Depression. These economists view depressions as an inevitable part of the **business cycle**—the regular ups and downs of business in a free-enterprise economy. According to business-cycle theory, industries increase production and hire more workers during prosperous times, with the result that over time surpluses pile up. Industries then cut back on production and lay off workers, triggering a recession or a depression. According to this theory, however, once the surplus goods are sold, industries again gear up for production and the downturn comes to an end. However, the length and severity of the Great Depression went far beyond the normal rhythms of the business cycle.

✔ **READING CHECK:** What were the main causes of the Great Depression?

When You
BUY an AUTOMOBILE
You GIVE
3 Months' Work
to Someone
Which
Allows
Him to
BUY
OTHER PRODUCTS
BUY A CAR NOW—HELP BRING BACK PROSPERITY

INTERPRETING THE VISUAL RECORD

The depression. Some businesses encouraged Americans to spend money during the depression. They believed that it would lead to more demand for products, more jobs, and eventually an end to the depression. ***How does this automobile advertisement reflect this viewpoint?***

SECTION 1 REVIEW ANSWERS

Define and Identify

For significance, see the following pages:

- Herbert Hoover, p. 414
- bull market, p. 415
- bear market, p. 415
- margin buying, p. 415
- Black Thursday, p. 415
- Black Tuesday, p. 416
- gross national product, p. 417
- Great Depression, p. 417
- Smoot-Hawley Tariff, p. 418
- business cycle, p. 419

1. banking crisis—destroyed personal savings, hurt businesses; business cycles—led to periodic economic downturns; income gap—decreased purchasing power of a large portion of the population; consumer debt—increased instability, deprived debtors of economy-boosting money; global depression—decreased purchasing ability of foreign consumers

2. consumer debt, the overvalued stock market, and the income gap

3. led to financial panic and bankruptcy when investors failed to cover their margins

4. Investors who lost money in the stock market collapse could not repay their loans to banks, many of which then failed. The bank failures hurt businesses and created a financial panic.

5. Consumers and investors relied on credit to make purchases in the belief that the economy would continue to grow. When the economy slowed, many could not pay their debts.

SECTION 1 REVIEW

Define and explain the significance of the following terms:

bull market
bear market
margin buying
Black Thursday
Black Tuesday
gross national product
Great Depression
Smoot-Hawley Tariff
business cycle

Identify and explain the significance of the following individual:

Herbert Hoover

1. Using Graphic Organizers Copy the web below. Use it to explain how each factor contributed to the Great Depression.

2. Using Historical Imagination Imagine that you are an economist during the late 1920s. What problems would you point to in order to warn people of a possible economic downturn?

3. Analyzing How did the practice of buying stocks on margin contribute to the crash?

4. Identifying Cause and Effect How did the stock market crash provoke a banking crisis? How did the banking crisis lead to business failures?

Critical Thinking

5. To what extent did overconfidence contribute to the U.S. economy's slide into depression?

Consider:

- how stockholder overconfidence influenced the stock market crash and banking crisis
- how business overproduction and reliance on consumer credit influenced the rising number of business failures

SECTION 2

After completing Section 2, students should be able to:

OBJECTIVE 1 *Describe how unemployment during the Great Depression affected the lives of American workers.*

OBJECTIVE 2 *Compare and contrast the hardships that urban and rural residents faced during the depression.*

OBJECTIVE 3 *Analyze how the Great Depression affected family life and the attitudes of Americans.*

OBJECTIVE 4 *Explain how popular culture provided an escape from the Great Depression.*

LET'S GET STARTED!

As students enter the classroom, ask them to write down two or three examples of works that depict the Great Depression. *(Students might mention books, movies, songs, and so on.)* Ask volunteers to share their responses. Then conduct a brief discussion about the depression-era hardships depicted by the works mentioned. Tell students that in Section 2 they will learn more about how the Great Depression affected Americans—and how people sought to escape from their troubles.

SECTION 2 RESOURCES

PRINT
- Guided Reading Strategy 14.2
- Graphic Organizer Activity 14: Life During the Depression
- Literature Reading 14: The Depression Takes Its Toll
- Biography Reading 14: Walt Disney
- Section 2 Review, p. 427
- Daily Quiz 14.2

MULTIMEDIA
- One-Stop Planner, Lesson 14.2
- Everyday Life in America Transparency 14: America's Darling: Shirley Temple, 1930s
- Holt Researcher: American History CD–ROM

SHELTERED ENGLISH
- Main Idea Activity for Reteaching and Sheltered English 14.2

✔ READING TO UNDERSTAND

To help students master the section objectives, have them answer the **READING CHECKS** and complete **Guided Reading Strategy 14.2** as they read the section.

Hard Times

OBJECTIVES

Read to understand:

1. how unemployment during the Great Depression affected the lives of American workers
2. what hardships urban and rural residents faced during the depression
3. how the Great Depression affected family life and the attitudes of Americans
4. how popular culture offered an escape from the Great Depression

KEY TERMS

mutualistas
breadlines
shantytowns

KEY PEOPLE

Josefina Fierro de Bright
James Hilton
James T. Farrell
Nathanael West
William Faulkner

EYEWITNESSES TO History

"My father walked the streets everyday. . . . My mother went to work. I even worked, playing the piano for dancing class on Saturday mornings for fifty cents an hour. My mother would find a few pennies and we would go to the greengrocer and wait until he threw out the stuff that was beginning to rot. We would pick out the best rotted potato and greens and carrots that were already soft. Then we would go to the butcher and beg a marrow bone. And then with the few pennies we would buy a box of barley, and we'd have soup to last us for three or four days. I remember she would say to me sometimes, 'You go out and do it. I'm ashamed.'"

—Clara Hancox

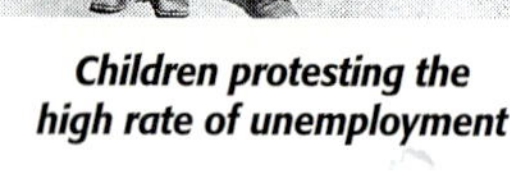

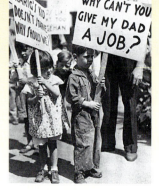

Children protesting the high rate of unemployment

Clara Hancox was 11 years old when the Great Depression began in 1929. She soon became acquainted with the unemployment, poverty, and homelessness that many city-dwellers of the era experienced. Rural Americans also suffered from poverty and despair. Eager to escape the grim reality of the depression, many Americans sought inexpensive forms of popular entertainment, such as movies, radio programs, and popular fiction.

American Workers Face Unemployment

After the stock market crash of 1929 and the subsequent banking crisis, the U.S. economy entered into a serious depression whose effects quickly became visible. Stores closed, factories stood idle, and millions of unemployed workers walked the streets looking for jobs. "These [unemployed] are dead men," wrote one observer, "They are ghosts that walk the streets."

Unemployed workers roamed the streets of U.S. cities searching for work.

Increasing joblessness. In 1929 some 1.5 million Americans were unemployed. By 1933 the figure had risen to some 15 million. In Chicago, approximately 50 percent of the city's workforce was unemployed, while 80 percent of the workers in Toledo, Ohio, were searching for jobs. As poet Langston Hughes observed, it seemed that "everybody in America was looking for work."

Even for those who managed to keep their jobs, wages fell dramatically—in some cases to as low as 10 cents an hour. Factory workers' average annual income fell by nearly one third between 1929 and 1933. Some of the country's largest employers tried to keep as many experienced employees as possible. Rather than laying them off, they reduced the number of hours they worked to keep more people on the payroll. One General Electric employee explained, "They'd just say, 'You come in Monday. Take the rest of the week off.'" This left employees with little income.

TEACH OBJECTIVE 1

LEVEL 1: Pair students and tell them to imagine that it is 1933 and that they are autoworkers who have recently been fired, along with the rest of their coworkers. Have students in each pair develop a dialogue describing the effects of unemployment for themselves and other American workers. *(Pairs should indicate that unemployment rose sharply during the depression and created severe financial and emotional problems for workers.)* Have volunteers perform their dialogues for the class. **Sheltered English, Cooperative Learning**

LEVEL 2: Tell students to imagine that it is 1933 and that they are autoworkers who have recently been fired, along with the rest of their coworkers. Have students write a series of diary entries detailing the effects of unemployment for themselves and others during the Great Depression. *(See the Level 1 lesson for the correct effects.)* In their diary entries, students also might want to discuss the psychological implications of chronic unemployment. Have volunteers read their entries to the class. Students may wish to include their diary entries in their portfolios.

With the drop in wages and employment, the promise of economic prosperity that had attracted waves of immigrants to the United States quickly faded. Immigration to the United States greatly decreased.

The American worker. Workers across the country were hard hit by the depression. African Americans faced particularly difficult times, as economic troubles added to the chronic problem of racial discrimination. When factories laid off employees, African American workers were often the first to go. One study of Chicago unemployment patterns noted that a common opinion of white workers was that African Americans "should not be hired as long as there are white men without work."

Many African American women, who made up the vast majority of domestic servants, lost their jobs. Those domestic servants without regular work often stood on street corners to try to obtain work for the day. Two black women, Ella Baker and Marvel Cooke, witnessed this occurence in New York City and referred to it as the "Bronx Slave Market." They described a typical scene in an investigative article they wrote for *The Crisis.*

> **"Rain or shine, cold or hot, you will find them there—Negro women, old and young—sometimes bedraggled [shabby looking], sometimes neatly dressed . . . waiting expectantly for Bronx housewives to buy their strength and energy."**

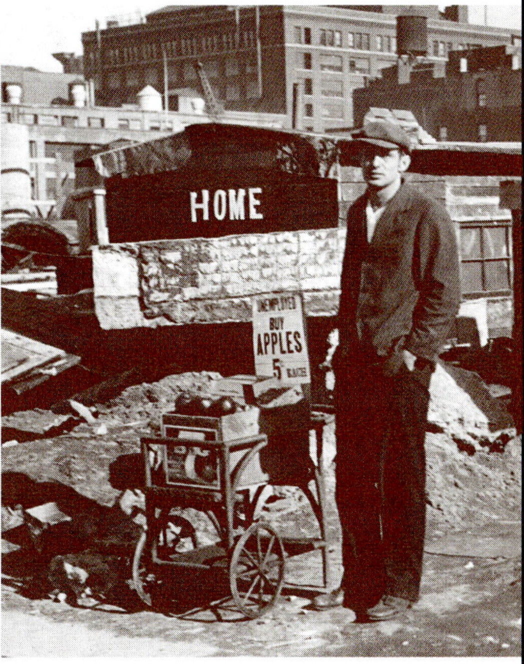

INTERPRETING THE VISUAL RECORD

Poverty. Unemployed workers sold apples for 5 cents apiece to earn money for survival. ***What else do you think unemployed workers such as this young man did to acquire food and shelter?***

Since many employers could hire women more cheaply than men, the percentage of women in the workforce actually increased in the 1930s. Most were employed as office workers or domestic servants. As the percentage of women in the workforce rose overall, however, competition in domestic and agricultural work increased. This caused the percentage of employed African American women to fall.

Trying to maintain a steady source of income and a sense of self-reliance, some unemployed workers took to selling apples on the street. Charging a nickel for each apple, a seller might earn $1.15 on a good day. In the fall of 1930 more than 6,000 unemployed workers sold apples in New York City. President Hoover claimed that "many people have left their jobs for the more profitable one of selling apples." However, during the depression few people had any choice in how or where they worked. Searching for employment, some workers traveled from city to city by hopping freight trains or hitchhiking.

✔ **READING CHECK:** How did unemployment during the Great Depression affect the lives of American workers?

Life in the City

Life in U.S. cities during the Great Depression was difficult. Many city-dwellers faced unemployment and poverty. "We saw the city at its worst. One vivid moment of those dark days we shall never forget," recalled Louise V. Armstrong.

ECONOMIC DEVELOPMENT

Working Women. Female workers came under fire during the depression. One observer argued, "There are approximately 10,000,000 people out of work in the United States today; there are also 10,000,000 or more women, married and single, who are jobholders. Simply fire the women, who shouldn't be working anyway, and hire the men. Presto! No unemployment. No relief rolls. No depression."

ACTIVITY: Tell students to imagine that they are women who teach first grade in New York City during the Great Depression. Have each student write a letter responding to the observer's statement above.

THAT'S INTERESTING!

As the depression deepened, President Hoover became one of the most vilified figures in American life, as the slang of the era revealed. Empty pants pockets became known as Hoover flags and newspapers became known as Hoover blankets.

VISUAL RECORD ANSWER

Students' answers will vary but might include begging for food and building makeshift shelters.

LEVEL 3: Conduct a brief discussion on unemployment during the Great Depression, concentrating on the economic and psychological effects of joblessness. *(See the Level 1 lesson for the correct effects.)* Then tell students to create a fictional depression-era character. This character should be unemployed and struggling to survive. Encourage students to fully detail their characters, creating fictional backgrounds, appearances, and so on. Then tell students to imagine that they are journalists during the Great Depression. Have each student write a profile of his or her fictional character, detailing the effects of unemployment on that figure. Ask volunteers to read their profiles to the class. Students may wish to include their profiles in their portfolios.

Teacher to Teacher

Janie Maldonado of Austin, Texas, suggested the following activity: Organize students into small groups. Have members of each group conduct research on the ways in which charitable organizations in the community assisted the needy during the Great Depression. If possible, have groups obtain a copy of an organization's budget to determine how it allocated its resources. Have each group prepare an oral report to present its findings.

ECONOMIC DEVELOPMENT

Relief Efforts. Although city governments and charities tried to provide assistance to poor people, they simply could not meet the needs of the unemployed. New York City, for example, spent $79 million on relief in 1932—an amount that totaled one month's wages for the city's unemployed. In 1931 Chicago spent $100,000 a day on relief in an effort to replace lost wages that totaled some $2 million per day.

CRITICAL THINKING How might the relatively small aid amounts offered by some cities have affected public opinion toward city and state governments?

ANSWER: Students might suggest that the small amounts of aid probably convinced some people that city and state governments did not care about their problems.

THAT'S INTERESTING!

In 1932 some 250,000 Americans lost their homes because they could not pay their mortgages. In desperation, one New York City couple moved to a cave in Central Park, where they lived for the next year.

VISUAL RECORD ANSWER

Students might mention despair, fatigue, and hopelessness.

INTERPRETING THE VISUAL RECORD

The homeless. During the depression, many city-dwellers lost their homes. ***In your opinion, what emotions does the artist portray in the characters of this depression-era painting?***

"We saw a crowd of some fifty men fighting over a barrel of garbage which had been set outside the back door of a restaurant. American citizens fighting for scraps of food like animals!"

During the early 1930s the federal government did little to assist struggling city-dwellers or their local communities. City governments, religious groups such as the Salvation Army, and charitable organizations including the Red Cross tried to provide direct relief to the needy. Neighbors also helped one another. One woman told a visitor: "My neighbors help me, by bringing me a little to eat, when they knows I ain't got nothing in the house to cook." Mexican American communities formed mutual-aid societies known as ***mutualistas*** to help each other. Some Chinese American communities set out open barrels of rice so that people could draw from them privately, without having to ask for handouts. Harlem residents organized "rent parties." These large social gatherings charged a small admission fee to help pay someone's monthly rent.

Across the country, people engaged in a daily struggle to feed themselves and their children. Poverty-stricken men and women waited in **breadlines** for bowls of soup and pieces of bread given out by charitable organizations. Karl Monroe recalled standing in the breadline on 25th Street in New York City. "To my surprise, I found . . . all types of men—the majority being skilled craftsmen unable to find work." Hunger was so widespread that by 1932 one out of every five children in New York City suffered from malnutrition. When one hungry schoolchild was told to go home for lunch, she replied, "It won't do any good. . . . This is my sister's day to eat." Poor diets caused some Americans to suffer long-term health effects, such as problems with their teeth and eyes.

In addition to hunger, homelessness was a serious urban problem during the depression. Faced with unemployment and falling wages, many urban residents were unable to pay their rent and were evicted from their homes.

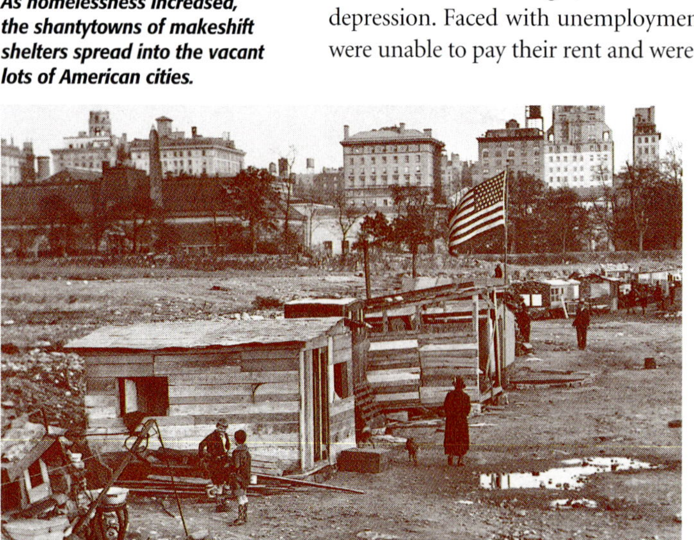

As homelessness increased, the shantytowns of makeshift shelters spread into the vacant lots of American cities.

The homeless often gathered in **shantytowns**—collections of makeshift shelters built out of packing boxes, scrap lumber, corrugated iron, and other thrown-away items. Shantytowns rose up outside most cities. Blaming an unresponsive president for their plight, the homeless mockingly referred to these shantytowns as Hoovervilles.

Life on the Farm

The impact of the depression spread all across the United States. It affected not only city-dwellers but also people living on farms. Increasing poverty during the

TEACH OBJECTIVE 2

ALL LEVELS: Write the following question on the chalkboard: *Would you rather have lived in the city or in the country during the Great Depression?* Have volunteers answer the question. To help students understand how the depression affected both urban and rural residents, copy the Venn diagram at right on the chalkboard, omitting the italicized answers. Have each student complete it.
Sheltered English

The Great Depression in the City and the Country

Urban	Both	Rural
• received some aid from charities *• formed mutual-aid organizations* *• experienced hunger* *• experienced homelessness*	*• experienced poverty* *• experienced diminished expectations*	*• faced lower prices for food products* *• forced to let crops rot and kill animals* *• faced farm foreclosures* *• Mexican aliens and immigrants faced deportation*

depression made it harder and harder for urban residents to purchase farm products. Shrinking demand for farm products caused prices to drop. Farmers found themselves with more goods than they could sell. While people went hungry in the cities, farmers in some areas were forced to let crops rot in the fields and to slaughter excess livestock they could not afford to feed. One newspaper editor, Oscar Ameringer, noted the irony of this situation. "While Oregon sheep raisers fed mutton to the buzzards," Ameringer recalled, "I saw men picking for meat scraps in the garbage cans in the cities of New York and Chicago."

As their incomes fell, many farmers were unable to keep up their mortgage payments. Banks began foreclosing on farms across the country. In some communities, residents banded together to fight the foreclosures. Often when a bank held a foreclosure auction to sell off a family's possessions, neighbors would arrive and bid absurdly low prices, such as 25 cents for a plow. In one example, a farm with an $800 mortgage was sold for $1.90. After the auction the neighbors would then give the goods back to the original owners. This tactic was so successful that several farm states, beginning with Iowa in 1933, passed laws that temporarily banned foreclosure sales.

INTERPRETING THE VISUAL RECORD

Farm life. During the depression, many farm families were evicted from their land. ***What economic circumstances do you believe this African American family experienced during the depression?***

Conditions were particularly bad for tenant farmers in the South, where most rural residents already faced crippling poverty. Cotton prices fell from 16 cents per pound in 1929 to less than 6 cents in 1931. Many tenant farmers—mostly African Americans—were ruined. Some were forced off the land they had lived on all their lives. While farmers in the Midwest faced an overabundance of food, southern cotton farmers faced poverty and devastating harvests because of poor soil. Gracie Turner, a sharecropper's wife, testified to the hardships of a tenant farmer's life in the 1930s.

> **"That's all there is to expect—work hard and go hungry part time. . . . This year's been so hard we had to drop our burial insurance. . . . All it costs is twenty-five cents . . . but they don't come many twenty-five cents in this house."**

Migrant farmworkers in the Southwest, most of them recent immigrants from Mexico, also experienced difficulties. Government officials and many Americans wanted to remove illegal aliens and recent Mexican immigrants from the United States. They believed that this would ease the strain of the depression. To avoid paying the soaring cost of relief efforts for unemployed migrant farmworkers, local authorities provided funds to transport Mexican migrant farmworkers to Mexico. They pressured and even forced the farmworkers to return to their native land. During the 1930s approximately 500,000 people of Mexican descent—some of them U.S. citizens—were pressured into leaving the country. Those who remained often faced discrimination and harsh working conditions.

HISTORY MAKERS SPEAK

Harry Terrell in *Hard Times*

Trouble on the Farm. Harry Terrell, an Iowa resident, described the sense of desperation that a group of farmers felt as they almost lost their farms to foreclosure. "They came very near hanging that judge. Because they caught this judge foreclosing farm mortgages, and they had no other way of stopping it. He had issued the whole bunch of foreclosures on his docket. . . . They took the judge out of his court and took him to the fairgrounds and they had a rope around his neck, and they had the rope over the limb of a tree. They were gonna string him up in the old horse thief fashion. But somebody had sense enough to stop the thing before it got too far."

CRITICAL THINKING What might the farmers' response to the judge have indicated about the severity of the Great Depression?

ANSWER: Students might mention that the farmers' response revealed the incredible financial and personal stresses many people experienced during the depression.

VISUAL RECORD ANSWER

Students might note that the loaded car and the rickety house suggest that the family experienced severe poverty.

TEACH OBJECTIVE 3

LEVEL 1: Tell students to imagine that they are journalists preparing to write a series of articles about the effects of the Great Depression on family life and American attitudes. Have each student write three headlines for the series. *(Students' headlines should note that the depression fractured some families, although it forced others to band together for survival. Divorce rates went up and birthrates went down. Many Americans suffered psychological problems during the era.)* Have volunteers write their headlines on the chalkboard. Discuss these headlines and the topic as a class. Students may wish to include the headlines in their portfolios.
Sheltered English

LEVELS 2 AND 3: Tell students to imagine that they are journalists preparing to write a series of articles about the effects of the Great Depression on family life and American attitudes. Have each student write the first article in the series. *(See the Level 1 lesson for the correct effects.)* Students might choose to focus their articles on a particular family, for example, or to provide a general analysis of the subject. Ask volunteers to read their articles to the class. Students may wish to include their articles in their portfolios.

▶ASSIGNMENT *Have students prepare collages that reflect how the Great Depression affected family life and the attitudes of Americans.*

DEMOCRATIC VALUES

Discrimination Against Mexicans. In May 1935 the governor of Colorado ordered sheriffs in the southern part of the state to prevent workers, almost all of whom were Mexican, from entering Colorado. The following year the governor declared martial law along the border. Officers prevented people from entering the state and took some in Colorado to the New Mexico border. This blockade and resettlement was illegal, but took place nonetheless.

CRITICAL THINKING Why might the governor have wanted to deport Mexican workers from the state?

ANSWER: Students might note that the governor wanted to protect jobs for Americans. Students might also suggest that the governor held anti-Mexican prejudices.

STRATEGIES FOR SUCCESS ANSWERS

(for p. 425)

Practicing the Strategy

1. to transport people's belongings
2. its rusted condition, the goods strapped to the sides; demonstrate the severity of the Great Depression
3. Answers will vary. Some students might suggest that the truck indicates that the depression left many Americans with virtually nothing.

Free Find: Josefina Fierro de Bright
After reading about Josefina Fierro de Bright on the **Holt Researcher** CD–ROM, write a short essay describing how growing up during the Great Depression affected her life.

Josefina Fierro de Bright

Some of the Mexican American families that remained in the United States organized against discrimination in the Southwest. One such activist was Josefina Fierro de Bright, the daughter of migrants who had fled from revolution in Mexico to settle in California. The experience of growing up during the depression in the midst of poverty and ethnic discrimination had a profound effect on her. As with many children of the depression, Fierro's life was unstable. Her family moved often, causing Fierro to change schools eight times. Throughout the hard times, however, her mother always encouraged her to strive for success. "Rely on yourself, be independent," Mrs. Fierro advised. She also emphasized the importance of getting an education.

In 1938, at age 18, Josefina Fierro entered the University of California at Los Angeles. She had planned to study medicine, but activism on behalf of the Mexican American community soon took up most of her time. Aided by her activist husband, Hollywood screenwriter John Bright, she led boycotts of companies that did business in Mexican American communities but did not hire Mexican American workers. Enlisting financial support from a few well-known movie stars, Fierro de Bright also started a radio program for Spanish-speaking audiences.

These activities brought her to the attention of a Mexican American group called El Congreso, which organized Hispanic migrants to resist oppressive conditions. In 1939 El Congreso leaders asked Fierro de Bright to help them establish a branch in Los Angeles. Over the next few years, she worked tirelessly, leading marches and hunger strikes, lobbying for expanded relief programs for Hispanic Americans, and encouraging bilingual education for migrant children. "I used to work so hard it used to kill me," she recalled. Throughout her life she never forgot the lessons her mother taught her during the depression. Those memories spurred her efforts to improve the lives of all working people.

✔ **READING CHECK:** What hardships did urban and rural residents face during the depression?

Photographs such as this one by Dorothea Lange captured the struggles many American families experienced during the depression.

Family Life in the 1930s

The crisis of the Great Depression required that family members pull together to help one another cope with their difficulties. Farmers and city-dwellers alike shared food and money and provided the support and encouragement necessary to get through hard times. In many cases, relatives doubled up in small houses, and young adults moved back in with their parents. Frederick Lewis Allen reported on the changing roles of family members trying to survive the depression. He wrote, "Mrs. Jones, who went daily to her stenographic job, was now the economic mainstay of her family, for Mr. Jones was jobless and was doing the cooking and looking after the children."

Family strains. Economic hardship took its toll on families, and some eventually broke apart under the strain. The marriage rate fell dramatically during the depression. Because many young people put

SPOTLIGHT on Family Life During the Great Depression

Ask students to closely examine the image in the lower left-hand corner of the previous page. Then have each student write a short story about the family pictured in the image. Students should create names, personalities, and situations for the people. Invite volunteers to read part or all of their short stories to the class. **Block Scheduling**

TEACH OBJECTIVE 4

LEVEL 1: Write the following scenario on the chalkboard: *It is 1933. There are no televisions, computers, or video games. What do you do to entertain yourself? You have five cents a week to spend on leisure activities.* Ask students to respond to the scenario in writing. Discuss students' responses. Then conduct a brief discussion on how popular culture provided an escape from the Great Depression. *(Americans went to movies, listened to the radio, and read new forms of popular literature, such as comic books and popular novels. These helped Americans temporarily escape the depression and their troubles.)* After the discussion, ask students to reflect back to their scenario answers. **Sheltered English**

off getting married and starting their own families, birthrates declined, particularly during the early years of the depression. A Chicago schoolteacher looked back on those years.

> **"Do you realize how many people in my generation are not married? . . . It wasn't that we didn't have a chance. I was going with someone when the Depression hit. We probably would have gotten married. . . . Suddenly he was laid off. It hit him like a ton of bricks. And he just disappeared."**

Life was difficult for women during the depression. In the face of economic hardship, the mothers of hard-hit families often played roles of quiet heroism. Such daily challenges as putting food on the table and making clothes and shoes last for one more year brought constant worry. As one woman remarked, "I figured every which way I could to make ends meet . . . but some of [those] ends just wouldn't meet." In rural and small-town households, women revived old crafts such as soap making and bread making.

Strategies for Success: Evaluating Artifacts as Historical Evidence

Artifacts are objects created or shaped by humans. They are a unique type of evidence that historians use to gain a more complete understanding of the past. Much like photographs, artifacts offer valuable clues about the customs, values, and details of daily life in the past that are difficult to find in written sources. Because they were handled by real individuals in history, artifacts also provide a sense of closeness to the past that is usually lacking in other types of evidence.

Artifacts must be analyzed with care. The insights they provide must be considered in the context of knowledge one has gained from other, more traditional sources.

How to Evaluate an Artifact as Historical Evidence

1. **Identify the artifact.** First, identify the artifact and determine its general purpose. Then find out when and where the artifact was created and used and, if possible, who created and used it.
2. **Examine the artifact carefully.** Study the artifact carefully, taking note of its construction and design. If it shows wear, try to determine what this wear says about how the artifact was used.
3. **Put the information to use.** Determine how your analysis of the artifact corresponds to information about the historical period that you have gained through other sources. Then think about how the artifact contributes to your understanding of the historical period.

Applying the Strategy

Examine the photograph below of a truck that was used by migrants during the Great Depression.

Practicing the Strategy

Use the photograph above to answer the following questions.

1. What do you think this truck was used for?
2. What details about the truck do you think are significant? Why?
3. How does the truck contribute to your understanding of the Great Depression?

HISTORY MAKERS SPEAK

Meridel Le Sueur in *For the Record: A Documentary History of America*, Vol. 2

Women in the Depression. Meridel Le Sueur described in an article the effects of the depression. "I've lived in cites for many months broke, without help, too timid to get in bread lines. I've known many women to live like this until they simply faint on the street from privations, without saying a word to anyone. A woman will shut herself up in a room until it is taken away from her, and eat a cracker a day and be as quiet as a mouse so there are no social statistics concerning her. I don't know why it is, but a woman will do this unless she has dependents, will go for weeks, verging on starvation, crawling in some hole, going through the streets ashamed."

CRITICAL THINKING

According to the statement above, how might women have responded to aid offers? Do you think that this response was different from that of men?

ANSWER: Students might suggest that many women refused to take advantage of aid offers. Students might suggest that many men, too, refused to take handouts or charity.

LEVEL 2: Organize students into small groups and tell them to imagine that they are entertainment reporters during the depression. Have each group create an entertainment section for a newspaper. Groups' sections should describe entertainment offerings that were popular during the era, such as movies and radio shows. Ask each group to present its entertainment section to the class, explaining how popular culture provided an escape from the depression. *(See the Level 1 lesson for the correct forms of entertainment and the correct effects.)* Display groups' sections around the classroom. **Cooperative Learning**

LEVEL 3: Conduct a brief discussion on the forms and uses of popular culture during the 1930s. *(See the Level 1 lesson for the correct forms and effects.)* Then organize students into triads and tell them to imagine that they are movie producers during the early years of the Great Depression. Have each triad develop two written movie proposals. Triads' proposals should appeal to Americans who want to escape the depression for a while. Ask each triad to present its proposals to the class, and have students select the most promising movie idea. To extend the lesson, have each triad create storyboards for its favorite proposals. **Cooperative Learning**

CULTURAL DIVERSITY

Gangster Films. Gangster movies, such as the 1930 release *Little Caesar*, were popular with audiences during the early years of the Great Depression. Some historians have argued that people responded positively to these movies because they portrayed acquisitive individuals as selfish, evil, and ultimately self-destructive.

CRITICAL THINKING Ask students to name a popular modern-day film genre. What might the popularity of this genre indicate about the national mood?

ANSWER: Students might name the horror genre and suggest that it reveals Americans' desires to safely experience and express their fears of violence.

Multimedia Resources

Everyday Life in America Transparency 24: America's Darling: Shirley Temple, 1930s

THAT'S INTERESTING!

In 1933 Walt Disney released the cartoon *Three Little Pigs*. A song from the cartoon, "Who's Afraid of the Big Bad Wolf?" became a huge hit, perhaps because it reflected an optimistic response to "the wolf at the door"–the Great Depression itself.

Then and Now

Baseball

In their search for inexpensive entertainment during the Great Depression, many Americans turned to baseball. Made popular by famous players such as Babe Ruth, baseball had become the country's favorite sport by the 1930s. Radio broadcasts of the sport provided cheap entertainment for baseball fans in the depression era. Since fans could listen to the game for free on the radio, baseball teams lost income from ticket sales. Team owners, however, made money from selling broadcasting privileges to radio stations.

Hoping to attract more fans to the ballparks, team owners began to consider new ideas. In 1933, team owners organized the first all-star game. In 1935 Larry MacPhail of the Cincinnati Reds revolutionized the sport by introducing nighttime ball games to professional baseball. Owners also rented out their stadiums to African American baseball teams.

As white team owners maintained a so-called gentleman's agreement not to sign black players, African Americans played in clubs and leagues of their own. The Negro National League and the Negro American League attracted fans with hall-of-fame players like Satchel Paige and William "Judy" Johnson.

Although baseball is now racially integrated, many of the game's 1930s innovations remain. For example, nighttime baseball and all-star games still attract eager fans to the ballpark today.

A nighttime baseball game

Psychological effects. The economic crisis of the 1930s affected the mental health and attitude of many Americans. The term *depression* described the mood of the country as much as it did the economy. More than 20,000 Americans committed suicide in 1932, a 28 percent increase over 1929. For middle-class and wealthy Americans, many of whom had never known poverty, the depression was a cruel blow. Many would never forget the shame they felt at being unemployed, losing their businesses or homes, and being unable to provide for their families. The attitude of an unemployed teacher in New Orleans was typical. "If with all the advantages I've had, I can't make a living, I'm just no good, I guess. I've given up ever amounting to anything. It's no use."

Many men whose lives had been dominated by work did not know what to do without a job. They often spent their days dawdling around the house or roaming the streets. The depression proved equally difficult for working women who lost their jobs, particularly those who were single or whose families depended on two incomes to survive. Many parents who could not support their families were consumed by guilt.

Even after the depression, the memories of those lean years remained vivid. Habits of scrimping and saving and of making every penny count would stay with members of this generation for the rest of their lives. A strong desire for financial stability and material comforts shaped the outlook of many Americans who came of age during the depression.

✔ **READING CHECK:** How did the Great Depression affect family life and the attitudes of Americans?

Popular Culture in the 1930s

As the psychological strain of the Great Depression increased, many Americans looked to popular culture and entertainment for escape. Many people took up inexpensive pastimes, such as reading and playing games at home. Movies and radio were particularly popular.

The sound explosion. With low ticket prices and double features, movie theaters offered inexpensive entertainment. Talking pictures, which had begun to replace silent films in the late 1920s, thrilled audiences. Among the most popular movies of the early 1930s were gangster films that portrayed tough guys fighting their way to the top against all odds. Similarly, strong women such as Bette Davis, Greta Garbo, Mae West, and Marlene Dietrich reinforced the theme of survival in a difficult world.

Movie cartoons also brightened the 1930s, thanks to Walt Disney's Mickey Mouse and Donald Duck. Disney cartoons were often as popular with movie audiences as feature films.

REVIEW

Have students complete the **Section 2 Review** on p. 427.

ASSESS

Have students complete **Daily Quiz 14.2.** As **Alternative Assessment**, you may want to use the unemployment dialogue or the depression entertainment section in this section's lessons.

RETEACH

Have students complete **Main Idea Activity for Reteaching and Sheltered English 14.2.** Then organize students into four groups. Assign each group one objective. Have each group write paragraphs addressing its assigned objective. Ask each group to read its paragraphs to the class.
Sheltered English, Cooperative Learning

EXTEND

Ask students to interview a person who lived through the Great Depression about the era. Alternately, have students read a primary source from an individual who experienced the period. *(You might direct students to Studs Terkel's* Hard Times, *a widely available book.)* Ask each student to prepare a short, casual presentation about his or her interview or primary source, focusing on the person's impressions of the depression. Have students make their presentations to the class. **Block Scheduling**

Radio, which experienced its golden age during the depression, offered free entertainment at home. During the 1930s the number of radios nationwide rose from about 12 million to 28 million. Popular programs allowed listeners to forget the hard times. Heroes such as the Lone Ranger, Little Orphan Annie, and the Shadow always triumphed over evil, offering a hopeful message.

Literature. The public's desire to escape the harsh reality of the depression also gave rise to new forms of popular literature. Inexpensive comic books presented heroes such as Flash Gordon and Tarzan. *Reader's Digest* presented condensed articles from various magazines. Families on a limited budget welcomed this "all-purpose" magazine.

Many of the era's most popular novels offered tales that took readers' minds off their economic worries. In James Hilton's *Lost Horizon* (1933), a weary traveler stumbles upon a peaceful, prosperous utopia hidden in the mountains of Tibet. The idea of discovering a perfect world appealed to many readers.

Not all fiction of the early depression offered an escape. James T. Farrell portrayed the grim life of Chicago's Irish immigrants in his *Studs Lonigan* trilogy (1932–1935), while Nathanael West presented the American dream as a nightmare in *Miss Lonelyhearts* (1933). William Faulkner wrote novels such as *The Sound and the Fury* (1929) and *As I Lay Dying* (1930) that tragically portrayed small-town life in Mississippi.

✔ **READING CHECK:** How did popular culture provide an escape from the depression?

INTERPRETING THE VISUAL RECORD

Entertainment. During the depression, Americans sought affordable ways to escape their troubles, such as books and radio programs. ***What does this image suggest about the importance of radio to this family?***

SECTION  REVIEW

Define and explain the significance of the following terms:
mutualistas
breadlines
shantytowns

Identify and explain the significance of the following individuals:
Josefina Fierro de Bright
James Hilton
James T. Farrell
Nathanael West
William Faulkner

1. **Using Graphic Organizers** Copy the graphic organizer below. Use it to explain how unemployment during the depression had a psychological impact on many Americans and how that psychological impact affected family life.

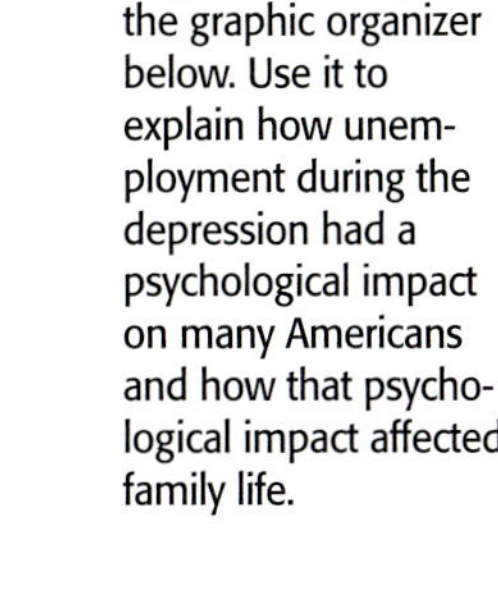

2. **Synthesizing** How did poverty in urban areas create such a drop in agricultural prices that farmers let their crops rot in the field?
3. **Evaluating** How did the hardships of the Great Depression further inflame racial prejudices against African American workers and Mexican migrant farmworkers?
4. **Identifying Values** How did the burdens caused by the Great Depression create new challenges to traditional beliefs in the importance of family?

Critical Thinking

5. In what ways did many Americans take action to better their lives, despite the seemingly overwhelming hardships of the Great Depression?
Consider:
   - how urban residents formed organizations to help their communities
   - how migrant farmworkers took action to defend their rights
   - how popular entertainment helped Americans deal with the depression

VISUAL RECORD ANSWER

Students' answers will vary but might suggest that the radio provided a form of entertainment that the entire family could enjoy together.

SECTION 2 REVIEW ANSWERS

Define and Identify
For significance, see the following pages:

- *mutualistas*, p. 422
- breadlines, p. 422
- shantytowns, p. 422
- Josefina Fierro de Bright, p. 424
- James Hilton, p. 427
- James T. Farrell, p. 427
- Nathanael West, p. 427
- William Faulkner, p. 427

1. Unemployment often led to psychological depression and shame, which placed stress on family relationships. Some families broke up under the pressure.
2. Urban dwellers could not afford to buy farm products, which meant that farmers could not sell their goods.
3. Many white Americans believed that jobs should go to white citizens rather than to African American or Mexican American citizens.
4. Economic stresses led to rising divorce rates and lower birthrates.
5. tried to help neighbors, formed aid organizations, and tried to distract themselves with popular culture

SECTION 3

After completing Section 3, students should be able to:

OBJECTIVE 1 *Explain why President Hoover opposed government-sponsored direct relief for needy individuals during the Great Depression.*

OBJECTIVE 2 *Outline the Hoover administration's attempts to solve the economic problems of the depression, and analyze the success of these efforts.*

OBJECTIVE 3 *Relate how radicals and veterans responded to President Hoover's policies.*

OBJECTIVE 4 *Analyze why Franklin D. Roosevelt was such a popular candidate in the 1932 election.*

LET'S GET STARTED!

As students enter the classroom, distribute Cartoon 23, Herbert Hoover and the Depression, from **American History Political Cartoons**. Ask students to study the cartoon. Discuss the cartoon and accompanying questions with students. Then tell students that in Section 3 they will learn how resentment toward President Hoover and the Republicans affected the 1932 election.

SECTION 3 RESOURCES

PRINT

- Guided Reading Strategy 14.3
- American History Political Cartoon 23: Herbert Hoover and the Depression
- Geography Activity 14: Public Unrest During the Depression
- Section 3 Review, p. 435
- Daily Quiz 14.3

MULTIMEDIA

- One-Stop Planner, Lesson 14.3
- Holt Researcher: American History CD–ROM

SHELTERED ENGLISH

- Main Idea Activity for Reteaching and Sheltered English 14.3

✔ READING TO UNDERSTAND
To help students master the section objectives, have them answer the **READING CHECKS** and complete **Guided Reading Strategy 14.3** as they read the section.

SECTION 3 Hoover's Policies

OBJECTIVES

Read to understand:

1. why President Hoover opposed government-sponsored direct relief for needy individuals during the Great Depression
2. how the Hoover administration attempted to solve the economic problems of the depression, and how successful these efforts were
3. how radicals and veterans responded to Hoover's policies
4. why Franklin D. Roosevelt was such a popular candidate in the 1932 election

KEY TERMS

rugged individualism
Reconstruction Finance Corporation
Bonus Army

KEY PEOPLE

Andrew Mellon
Franklin D. Roosevelt
Eleanor Roosevelt

EYEWITNESSES TO History

"What the country needs is a good big laugh. There seems to be a condition of hysteria. If someone could get off a good joke every ten days I think our troubles would be over."
—Herbert Hoover

Many Americans blamed Hoover for the depression.

Businesses were failing at record levels, and unemployment soared. Yet President Herbert Hoover believed that if only Americans were more optimistic, the troubles of the Great Depression would soon pass. At the beginning of the depression, many Americans had great faith in Herbert Hoover. His skills as a businessman and as an administrator inspired confidence. Under his direction the government did undertake some important measures to fight the depression, but they were not enough to end the crisis.

THE GRANGER COLLECTION, NEW YORK

Soup kitchens fed many hungry people.

Hoover's Philosophy

As the U.S. economy plunged and unemployment spiraled out of control, many Americans looked to President Hoover for leadership and a solution to the crisis. Despite the nation's problems, Hoover remained optimistic. He characterized the depression as "a temporary halt in the prosperity of a great people."

As the depression worsened, the most urgent task facing Hoover was to ease the human suffering. Prior to the crash, most Americans believed that the government should not interfere in the free-enterprise system. Even after the crash, the *New York Times* advised that "the fundamental prescriptions for recovery [are] such homely [simple] things as savings . . . and hopeful waiting for the turn." Hoover agreed that the way to economic recovery was through individual effort and not from government assistance.

Opposing direct relief. As the depression wore on and the crisis worsened, many Americans began to demand that the federal government provide direct relief to the needy. This would include food, clothing, shelter, and money. Writing the president for assistance, one poverty-stricken American complained, "Why are we reduced to poverty and starving and anxiety and Sorrow So quickly under your administration as Chief Executor. Can you not find a quicker way of Executing us than to starve us to death." Despite these pleas, Hoover rejected the idea of direct government aid.

> **"I do not believe that the power and duty of the [federal] Government ought to be extended to the relief of individual suffering. . . . The lesson should be constantly enforced that though the people support the Government the Government should not support the people."**

TEACH OBJECTIVE 1

LEVEL 1: Ask each student to write a few sentences explaining President Hoover's philosophy regarding government-sponsored relief for needy individuals during the Great Depression. *(President Hoover believed that individuals and businesses were responsible for themselves. He thought that government relief would create a bureaucracy.)* Have volunteers share their sentences. Then ask students if they agree or disagree with Hoover's philosophy. Conduct a debate between students with different opinions. **Sheltered English**

LEVEL 2: Tell students to imagine that they are aides to President Hoover. Have each student write a short speech for the president to deliver explaining his opposition to government-sponsored relief programs. *(See the Level 1 lesson for the correct points.)* Ask volunteers to deliver their speeches to the class. To conclude, ask students if they agree or disagree with Hoover's philosophy. Conduct a debate between students with different opinions.

Hoover argued that direct federal relief would create a large bureaucracy. He feared that it would inflate the federal budget and reduce the self-respect of people receiving the aid. Instead, Hoover urged Americans to lift themselves up through hard work and strength of character.

With unemployment rising, some congressmembers responded to demands from constituents for direct relief and assistance. Senators Robert La Follette Jr. and Edward Costigan proposed a bill in 1931 to create a Federal Emergency Relief Board. The board would be authorized to give states $375 million for direct aid to the unemployed. Hoover refused to support the bill. Without the president's support, the proposal fell 14 votes shy of passing in February 1932.

Hoover's firm belief in individualism and the value of character-building experiences kept him from establishing a federal system that would directly aid Americans in need. Referring to Hoover's training as an engineer early in life, Rexford Tugwell remarked, "We all thought he [Hoover] was an engineer, but, in fact, he was a moral philosopher."

Hoover's political beliefs stemmed from his idea of **rugged individualism**. He believed that success comes through individual effort and private enterprise. He also believed that private charities and local communities, not the federal government, could best provide for those in need. "A voluntary deed," claimed Hoover, "is infinitely more precious to our national ideals and spirit than a thousandfold poured from the Treasury."

Encouraging voluntarism.

Hoover was not alone in his beliefs. Millions of Americans agreed that voluntary efforts were preferable to government aid. It soon became clear, however, that voluntary efforts alone could not address the huge scale of the depression. Communities and private charities lacked the resources to cope with the ever-rising tide of human misery. Local governments were forced to stretch already inadequate funds to cover growing numbers of needy families. By 1933, for example, families on public welfare in New York City were paid just $23 a month.

In 1930 Hoover created the President's Committee for Unemployment Relief (PCUR). It was designed to assist state and local relief efforts. He appointed experienced philanthropists and businesspersons to encourage donations to private relief organizations. The most prominent were the Community Chest, the Red Cross, the Salvation Army, and the YMCA. The PCUR collected information about local relief agencies and distributed it to Americans interested in aiding the unemployed.

The committee did little beyond urging Americans to contribute more to charity, however. Provided with little funding, the committee spent just $157,000 on its work during the years of the Hoover administration. The misery of the depression

THE SALVATION ARMY

The Salvation Army was founded in London during the mid-1800s. It was an evangelical organization dedicated to spreading the Protestant Christian faith to nonbelievers. The founders recognized that before a nonbeliever could be convinced of God's love, his or her practical needs for food, shelter, and clothing must be met. Throughout the late 1800s and early 1900s the organization extended its missionary efforts to the United States and throughout the world.

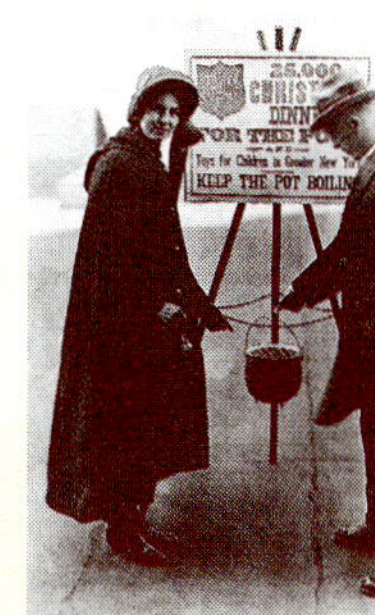

Salvation Army donation site

During the Great Depression divisions of the Salvation Army in the United States worked to provide for the basic needs of the poor. Since President Hoover opposed direct federal aid for the needy, religious institutions became important sources of aid for the unemployed. The Salvation Army was one of the foremost aid providers during the early years of the depression. It organized soup kitchens, shelters for the homeless, and rehabilitation programs for the unemployed.

As resources grew slim for many Americans during the depression, donations to the Salvation Army slowed. The organization faced the challenge of meeting the needs of a greater number of people with dwindling revenue. Some state and local government agencies gave funds directly to aid organizations such as the Salvation Army. These government-provided funds helped organizations provide needed relief to Americans during the Great Depression.

HISTORY MAKERS SPEAK

Herbert Hoover in *For the Record: A Documentary History of America,* Vol. 2

Hoover on Government Action. Herbert Hoover explained his reasons for opposing large-scale government intervention in American life in a 1928 campaign speech. "During the war [World War I] we necessarily turned to the government to solve every difficult economic problem. . . . However justified in time of war if continued in peace time it would destroy not only our American system but with it our progress and freedom as well. . . . We were challenged with a peace-time choice between the American system of rugged individualism and a European philosophy of . . . paternalism and state socialism. The acceptance of these ideas would have meant . . . the undermining of the individual initiative and enterprise through which our people have grown to unparalleled greatness."

ACTIVITY: Tell students to imagine that they heard Hoover deliver the campaign speech excerpted above. Have each student write a letter to the editor expressing his or her opinion of the speech and Hoover's ideas.

LEVEL 3: Tell students to imagine that they are shop clerks who have recently lost their jobs. Tell students that they are struggling to feed three children. Have each student write a letter to the editor criticizing President Hoover's opposition to government-sponsored relief for needy individuals. Students might want to describe their personal situations in their letters. Have volunteers read their letters to the class. Then ask students how Hoover himself might have responded to the arguments contained in the letters. *(See the Level 1 lesson for the correct points.)* Students may wish to include their letters in their portfolios.

▶**ASSIGNMENT** *Tell students that the current debate over federal assistance to needy individuals is a heated one. Have each student find an article on the issue from a reputable newspaper or newsmagazine. Ask each student to write a brief summary of the article. Have volunteers share their summaries with the class, and conduct a discussion on the issues.*

NOTE: For an additional teaching idea, see the Chapter 14 role playing lesson in the **Creative Teaching Strategies** handbook.

PEOPLE IN HISTORY

Andrew Mellon. Born in Pennsylvania in 1855, Andrew Mellon worked in the family bank and became its president in 1902. A renowned financier, Mellon invested in industries as varied as oil, aluminum, and coal, eventually building one of the largest fortunes in America. In 1921 Warren Harding appointed him secretary of the Treasury. Mellon remained popular until the Great Depression, when many Americans blamed him for enacting policies that helped cause the downturn.

CRITICAL THINKING How might Mellon's background have influenced his response to the economic crisis?

ANSWER: Students might suggest that Mellon's personal security led him to favor policies that promoted "rugged individualism."

THAT'S INTERESTING!

Many Americans initially regarded the economic depression as a temporary downturn. In early 1930, editors at the *New York Times* declared that an expedition to the South Pole—not the stock market crash—was the most important story of 1929.

VISUAL RECORD ANSWER

Students' responses might indicate an apparent sense of comfort within the group.

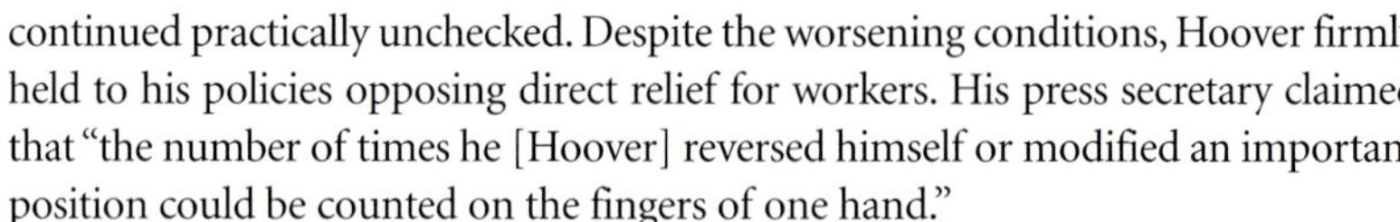

continued practically unchecked. Despite the worsening conditions, Hoover firmly held to his policies opposing direct relief for workers. His press secretary claimed that "the number of times he [Hoover] reversed himself or modified an important position could be counted on the fingers of one hand."

✔ **READING CHECK:** Why did President Hoover oppose government-sponsored direct relief for needy individuals during the Great Depression?

INTERPRETING THE VISUAL RECORD

Hoover. Attempting to find solutions to the economic crisis of the Great Depression, Hoover (left) met regularly with business leaders such as Henry Ford, Thomas Edison, and Harvey Firestone (left to right). ***How does this photograph reflect the close relationship between big business and the White House?***

Boosting the Economy

Critics later charged that President Hoover's relief plans failed because of his refusal to get the government involved. However, Hoover was not totally opposed to government intervention in the economy. Despite its opposition to direct public relief the Hoover administration played a more active role in attempting to shape the economy than any previous administration.

Stimulating the economy. As the nation sank into depression, Hoover's cabinet members proposed a laissez-faire approach to the economy. Secretary of the Treasury Andrew Mellon argued that the government should keep its hands off the economy. He wanted American businesses to deal with the crisis on their own. Aware that this hands-off policy would result in even greater unemployment and suffering, Hoover rejected Mellon's advice. The president believed that something should be done to stimulate the economy.

Within weeks of the stock market crash, Hoover called a White House conference of top business, labor, and political leaders to discuss solutions to the economic crisis. The *New York Times* hailed the meeting as a step in the right direction.

> **"[It is] the largest gathering of noted heads of industrial and other corporations in Washington since the resources of the nation were marshalled for participation in the World War!"**

Hoover urged these leaders to maintain predepression levels of production, employment, and wages voluntarily. Hoover saw this as the first step toward reviving business activity and promoting recovery. The National Business Survey Conference and the U.S. Chamber of Commerce supported the president's plan.

Hoover issued cheerful public statements designed to boost confidence and get the economy going again. His optimism failed to convince many people, however. On March 7, 1930, he declared, "The worst effects of the crash upon unemployment will have passed during the next sixty days." Many citizens grew increasingly doubtful about the administration. "Every time an administration official gives out an optimistic statement about business conditions, the market immediately drops," moaned the head of the Republican National Committee.

At Hoover's request, Congress and state governments funded several public-works programs. By providing contracts for construction and materials, Hoover hoped that these projects would stimulate business and reduce unemployment. One of the largest public-works programs was the construction of the giant Boulder

HOLT RESEARCHER *Read More About It*

Free Find:
Herbert Hoover
After reading about Herbert Hoover on the **Holt Researcher** CD–ROM, outline the policies and programs that Hoover developed to assist the economy during the Great Depression.

TEACH OBJECTIVE 2

ALL LEVELS: Tell students to imagine that they are advisers to President Hoover. Have each student brainstorm and develop two or three measures to foster economic recovery. *(Answers will vary. Some students might suggest direct cash payments to the needy or massive government work programs.)* To help students understand how the Hoover administration attempted to solve the depression—and the success of those efforts—copy the chart at right on the chalkboard, omitting the italicized answers. Have each student complete it. After students have completed their charts, ask them to consider their own plans in light of Hoover's efforts.
Sheltered English

THE HOOVER ADMINISTRATION AND THE GREAT DEPRESSION		
Effort	**Description**	**Effectiveness**
public-works programs	*poured money into public construction projects such as the Boulder Dam*	*failed to affect the entrenched depression*
agricultural efforts	*created the Federal Farm Board; made loans, established cooperatives, and bought surplus goods*	*helped some farmers take advantage of cooperatives and avoid foreclosure, but failed to end the farm crisis*
Reconstruction Finance Corporation (RFC)	*loaned taxpayer money to stabilize industries*	*helped some companies avoid bankruptcy; used money for businesses, not people*

Dam—later renamed the Hoover Dam—on the Colorado River. The federal government also built more than 800 public buildings and assisted states in building approximately 37,000 miles of highway. Overall, Hoover approved some $800 million in funding for public-works projects. Yet this had little impact on the depression.

INTERPRETING THE VISUAL RECORD

Public-works projects. Hoover began large public-works projects such as the construction of the Boulder Dam. ***What benefits of such projects does this mural portray?***

Coping with the farm crisis. Hoover also sought to ease the plight of farmers. In 1929 Congress passed the Agricultural Marketing Act, which established the Federal Farm Board (FFB), and granted it a budget of $500 million. In line with Hoover's notion of rugged individualism, the Federal Farm Board was instructed to find ways to help farmers help themselves. The Federal Farm Board offered loans and also financed the creation of farmers' cooperatives. These organizations reduced farmers' expenses by allowing them to purchase necessary materials—such as equipment, fertilizer, and pesticides—in bulk. The cooperatives were also able to gain higher prices for the farmers' crops. Providing storage facilities allowed cooperatives to store crops until they could be sold during the periods between harvests when market prices were at their highest.

Crop prices continued to fall, however. Hoover instructed the Federal Farm Board to buy up surplus corn, cotton, wheat, and other farm products. Officials believed that a reduction in the volume of crops reaching the market would cause prices to rise. The government could store these goods and then sell them when prices were higher. The scheme did not work. Farmers refused to limit production and reacted to low prices by planting even more crops. In 1931 the Farm Board stopped buying surplus crops, having already spent some $180 million.

Just as he opposed direct relief for jobless factory workers, Hoover resisted giving direct aid to desperate farmers. He did try to aid farmers indirectly, though. He recommended the passage of the Home Loan Bank Act in 1932. The act established the Home Loan Bank Board and provided money to savings banks,

1874–1964
In Office 1929–1933

Herbert Hoover

As a young man Herbert Hoover was shy and awkward but very hardworking. Born into a Quaker family in Iowa, he became an orphan at age nine. Hoover had few friends in college and wandered around with his eyes glued to the ground as if to avoid people. One friend noted that he had an awkward habit of standing "with one foot thrust forward, jingling the keys in his trouser pocket," chuckling sometimes, but rarely laughing out loud. Even as president he remained self-conscious and shy.

After college, Hoover rapidly built a career as a successful mining engineer and business consultant. By the age of 40 he was a millionaire. His role as coordinator of food relief during World War I also won him a reputation as a kind and humanitarian leader. After his presidency he continued to work in public service and wrote many books and articles. "There is little importance to men's lives," he wrote, "except the accomplishments they leave to posterity."

TECHNOLOGY AND SOCIETY

Boulder Dam. The Boulder Dam project served several important purposes. In 1906 the Colorado River had flooded, causing extensive damage. Boulder Dam was designed to regulate the flow of the river and to prevent further floods. The dam also ensured that water would be available to Los Angeles, a rapidly growing city that previously would have been unable to meet its water needs after 1940. Finally, the dam created enough hydroelectric power to supply electricity to the entire Southwest.

CRITICAL THINKING How might Boulder Dam have benefited the long-term economic development of the Southwest?

ANSWER: Students might suggest that the dam controlled the Colorado River, ensured the future growth of Los Angeles, and provided power to businesses and industries in the region.

VISUAL RECORD ANSWER

Students' answers might include providing work for the unemployed.

SPOTLIGHT on Children in the Depression

Tell students to imagine that they were teenagers during the Great Depression. Have each student design or create a personal artifact from the period. Students might draw a visual diary, for example, or design a story quilt about their journey across the United States on the railroads. Ask students to write short statements describing their artifacts. Have volunteers present their artifacts to the class. **Block Scheduling**

SPOTLIGHT on Trickle-Down Economics

Pair students and have them conduct research on trickle-down economics. Have each pair create two diagrams displaying the process—one general diagram and one specific diagram. Suggest that each pair focus on the Reconstruction Finance Corporation for its specific diagram. Have each pair display its diagram around the classroom. Ask students to inspect the diagrams and select the best two. Conduct a discussion on these two diagrams as models of outstanding work. What elements make them clear and helpful?
Cooperative Learning, Block Scheduling

ECONOMIC DEVELOPMENT

The Failure of the RFC. Historians argue that the Reconstruction Finance Corporation (RFC) came too late in the depression to revive the faltering economy. By 1932 public confidence in the economy was very low, and consumers would not spend the little money that they had in a way that would promote recovery. Moreover, the RFC favored large businesses that could repay their loans within six months, a strict requirement that prevented many companies from taking part in the plan. Had the government provided credit to businesses much earlier, the worst of the depression might have been averted.

CRITICAL THINKING What changes might have made the RFC more successful?

ANSWER: Answers will vary. Some students might mention easier repayment terms and wider assistance policies.

VISUAL RECORD ANSWER

(for p. 433)

Students might suggest that they stressed patriotic themes, given the American flags in the photograph.

teen Life

Riding the Rails

The Great Depression transformed everyday life for many teenagers. Thousands of schools were forced to cut their schedules or to close altogether, and many families were evicted from their homes. Many teenagers left their hometowns in search of work, traveling from city to city by hopping railroad freight cars. Some began traveling at the age of 14.

Teens riding the rails

During the early 1930s sociologist Thomas Minehan studied the teenagers who rode the rails. He noted that most traveled in groups for security. "The boys and girls have friends to comfort and care for them," he reported.

Life for these teenagers was hard. One teenager whom Minehan met had lost an eye when a piece of burning coal blew into his face as he rode in an open freight car. In his diary, this teenager described a typical day.

> **"Slept in paper box. Bummed swell breakfast three eggs and four pieces meat. Hit guy in big car in front of garage. Cop told me to scram. Rode freight to Roessville. Small burg, but got dinner. Walked [to] Bronson. . . . Rode to Sidell. . . . Hit homes for meals and turned down. Had to buy supper 20 cents. Raining."**

building and loan associations, and insurance companies for low-interest mortgages.

Hoover believed that the act would reduce foreclosures on homes and farms. This would thus allow more farmers to keep their land. He also believed that the act would encourage home construction. This construction would boost employment and increase the flow of money through the entire economy.

The Reconstruction Finance Corporation. Hoover also tried to stimulate the economy with the **Reconstruction Finance Corporation** (RFC), created by Congress in February 1932. The RFC was authorized to lend up to $2 billion of taxpayer money to stabilize troubled banks, insurance companies, railroad companies, and other financial institutions. By strengthening these key businesses through federal loans, Hoover hoped to reduce business failures and create more jobs. By the end of Hoover's term, RFC loans had helped a number of large corporations avoid collapse. Yet the economy continued to decline, in part because the RFC was not created until the depression was already in full swing. The RFC also provided no direct aid to industries or to small businesses, which continued to fail at an alarming rate.

Critics attacked the RFC's trickle-down approach to economic recovery. "We have the dole [welfare] in America," explained economist Sumner H. Slichter. "But the real recipients . . . are not the men who stand for hours before the Salvation Army soup stations. . . . [They] are the great industries of America." Critics argued that money lent to big business would not filter down quickly enough to help the real victims of the depression—ordinary citizens. As one economist put it, this was like putting fertilizer on the branches of a tree—rather than on its roots—to help it grow. A more effective approach, said critics, would be to funnel money directly to those in need. This would increase consumers' buying power and consequently stimulate business. Newspaper columnist Walter Lippmann expressed the sentiments of most Americans.

> **"It is hard for the country to realize that this era of easy finance is over. . . . In respect to government finance, as in respect to so many other things, Congress and the people of the country have radically to readjust their minds."**

Government activism. Hoover's policies failed to end the Great Depression. However, the RFC and other measures—such as the Home Loan Bank Act and funding for public works—represented a major shift in government policy. The president and Congress accepted the idea that the federal government can and should do something to boost the economy in times of crisis. The government became more active than ever before.

In the early 1930s Secretary of the Treasury Andrew Mellon advised the government to maintain its traditional laissez-faire approach to the economy. He even

TEACH OBJECTIVE 3

LEVEL 1: Pair students and have each pair write topic sentences explaining how both radicals and veterans responded to President Hoover's ineffective policies. *(Radicals staged protests and became involved in at least one legal case; veterans gathered in Washington, D.C., to demand payment of their pension bonuses.)* Then ask pairs to consider these responses, considering the drastic conditions of the Great Depression. Do those responses seem overblown? desperate? possibly treasonous? Conduct a discussion on students' responses and the issue of historical hindsight.
Sheltered English, Cooperative Learning

LEVELS 2 AND 3: Organize students into two large groups, one representing radicals and one representing veterans. Have each student write a short memoir of the Great Depression from his or her assigned perspective. Students' memoirs, written in their notes, should both describe their reactions to Hoover's ineffective policies and explain those reactions in light of the conditions during the depression. *(See the Level 1 lesson for the correct reactions.)* Have volunteers read their memoirs to the class. Students may wish to include their memoirs in their portfolios. **Cooperative Learning**

argued that a short depression would be good for the country because "it will purge the rottenness out of the system." As the depression grew more severe, however, the government took dramatic steps to promote economic recovery. Unfortunately, these measures were not sufficient to halt the downward trend. Americans increasingly blamed their suffering on Herbert Hoover.

✔ **READING CHECK:** How did the Hoover administration attempt to solve the economic problems of the Great Depression? How successful were these attempts?

Rumblings of Discontent

By 1932 President Hoover was perhaps the most hated man in America. His appearance in movie newsreels provoked boos and catcalls from audiences. Yet the president made no attempt to win public support by changing his aloof manner or his stiff, boring speeches. "This is not a showman's job," Hoover remarked. "I will not step out of character."

Radical protests. As public confidence in Hoover eroded, radical political parties grew more vocal. Both the Communist Party and the Socialist Party condemned capitalism, which they believed was to blame for the depression. The two parties helped organize several mass protests in the early 1930s. Socialist leader A. J. Muste gathered the jobless into Unemployed Leagues to demand work. The Communist Party encouraged labor-union activism and led strikes by migrant farmworkers.

The Communist Party also helped expose racial injustice. In 1931 an all-white jury in Scottsboro, Alabama, sentenced to death nine African American youths aged 13 to 21 on a highly questionable rape charge. The Communist Party helped supply legal defense for the defendants and organized mass demonstrations against the verdict. By 1950 all nine had been released from jail.

Many desperate Americans responded to Communist and Socialist calls for direct action. Thousands of unemployed men demanding work participated in a hunger march early in 1932 at the Ford auto plant near Detroit. Four were killed when police opened fire. In Seattle some 5,000 unemployed protesters seized a government building. After two days, local officials finally forced them out.

Some activism was spontaneous, reflecting the desperation of the times. In rural areas people armed with clubs, pitchforks, and shotguns confronted officials trying to foreclose on homes. Hoping that limiting food supplies would push prices up, farmers destroyed crops and blocked roads to prevent food from being shipped to market. "They say blockading the highway's illegal," an Iowa farmer said. "Seems to me there was a Tea Party in Boston that was illegal too."

The Bonus Army. The biggest protest was staged in May 1932 by more than 10,000 World War I veterans and their families. They came to Washington, D.C., to support a veterans' bonus bill then before Congress. The bill would have granted the veterans—many of whom were unemployed—early payment of the pension bonuses

Lawyer Samuel Leibowitz (left) meets with Heywood Patterson, one of the defendants in the Scottsboro case, to prepare for the trial.

INTERPRETING THE VISUAL RECORD

Bonus Army. More than 10,000 veterans marched in Washington, D.C., in May 1932 to petition Congress for payment of pension bonuses earned during World War I. ***What do you think the organizers of the march did to generate support for their cause?***

CONSTITUTIONAL HERITAGE

The Scottsboro Case. The two lawyers who agreed to appear on behalf of the defendants in the Scottsboro case met with the so-called boys for just 30 minutes on the day that their trials began. In the 1932 case *Powell* v. *Alabama*, the Supreme Court ruled that the Scottsboro defendants had been denied the Fourteenth Amendment's right to due process because they had been effectively denied legal counsel. Two justices dissented, arguing that the defendants had received effective assistance.

CRITICAL THINKING Do you agree with the Court's ruling in *Powell* v. *Alabama?* Why or why not?

ANSWER: Answers will vary. Some students might argue that 30 minutes of legal counsel failed to satisfy the terms of the amendment.

THAT'S INTERESTING!

One of General Douglas MacArthur's aides protested the use of troops against the Bonus Army. That aide, Dwight Eisenhower, later became president of the United States.

VISUAL RECORD ANSWER

(for p. 434)

Students might suggest that he relied on his personal popularity and campaign advertising.

TEACH OBJECTIVE 4

LEVEL 1: Conduct a brief discussion on why Franklin D. Roosevelt was such a popular candidate in the 1932 election. *(Roosevelt's optimism contrasted with Hoover's gloom. In addition, Roosevelt had designed imaginative relief programs as governor of New York.)* Then tell students to imagine that they are volunteers on Franklin D. Roosevelt's presidential campaign. Have each student create a poster, flyer, or button promoting Roosevelt's bid for the presidency. Encourage students to include a slogan or statement explaining Roosevelt's superiority over Hoover. Ask volunteers to present their items to the class. **Sheltered English**

LEVELS 2 AND 3: Organize students into two large groups—one representing President Hoover and one representing Franklin D. Roosevelt. Then pair students within the larger groups. Have each pair write a résumé for its assigned presidential candidate. You may want to supply students with real résumés or résumé-writing programs to use as models or templates. Have members of a Hoover pair and members of a Roosevelt pair present their résumés to the class. Then ask students to select a candidate to "hire" for the job of president. Call on volunteers to explain their choices. Regardless of students' choices, tell them that Roosevelt won the election and conduct a brief discussion on his appeal. *(See the Level 1 lesson for the correct points.)* **Cooperative Learning**

SECTION 3 REVIEW ANSWERS

Define and Identify

For significance, see the following pages:

- rugged individualism, p. 429
- Andrew Mellon, p. 430
- Reconstruction Finance Corporation, p. 432
- Bonus Army, p. 434
- Franklin D. Roosevelt, p. 434
- Eleanor Roosevelt, p. 434

1. relief board–deviated from Hoover's belief in individual initiative; president's committee–coordinated voluntary relief efforts; met with business leaders–encouraged voluntary economic planning; public works programs–created jobs rather than provided handouts; Federal Farm Board–assisted farmers with individual initiatives; Reconstruction Finance Corporation–created jobs by helping businesses

2. provided some assistance, but failed to end the economic crisis

3. radical workers–faulted capitalism itself; veterans–demanded war bonuses

4. Neither Hoover nor Roosevelt had a plan for solving the economic crisis, but Roosevelt's optimism contrasted with Hoover's gloom.

5. reflected the belief in a limited role for the federal government; resulted in human suffering and the desire for an expanded federal government

Violence erupts as military and law-enforcement officers attempt to remove the Bonus marchers from their camps.

owed them for their service during the war. This group was soon labeled the **Bonus Army**.

Officials initially allowed the Bonus Army demonstrators to live in empty government buildings and to camp in an open area across the Potomac River. When Congress rejected the bonus bill, most of the demonstrators returned home. Some 2,000 veterans remained, however, defying orders to leave. In a clash with authorities, two veterans and two police officers were killed. The police requested aid, and President Hoover ordered the army to disperse the squatters.

In late July the U.S. Army moved in with machine guns, tanks, and tear gas. One woman recalled her husband's experience that day.

> **"My husband went to Washington. To march with . . . the bonus boys. He was a machine gunner in the war. He'd say them . . . Germans gassed him in Germany. And [then] his own government . . . gassed him and run him off the country up there with a water hose, half drowned him."**

Commanded by General Douglas MacArthur, the troops drove the veterans from the buildings, broke up their encampment, and burned their shacks. Hundreds were injured and three died, including an 11-week-old baby. Many Americans found the government's treatment of the veterans shocking. Across the nation, anger against Hoover grew. As the 1932 presidential election approached, Americans joked bitterly, "In Hoover we trusted and now we are busted."

✔ **READING CHECK:** How did radicals and veterans respond to Hoover's policies?

The Election of 1932

In the summer of 1932 the Republicans reluctantly renominated Herbert Hoover as their presidential candidate for the fall election. With public sentiment running strongly against the Republicans, no other member of the party was eager for the nomination. The Democrats, sensing victory, chose Franklin Delano Roosevelt of New York as their candidate.

INTERPRETING THE VISUAL RECORD

Roosevelt. As the Democratic presidential candidate in 1932, Franklin D. Roosevelt developed a platform based on relief programs he had initiated as governor of New York. ***Based on this photograph, what other campaign strategies do you think Roosevelt used to gain public support?***

The Democratic challenger. Roosevelt—who was often called by his initials, FDR—was a determined and skillful politician. He was born into a wealthy and famous family. Roosevelt's background suggested that he would be more likely to identify with the wealthy than with working-class citizens. He could easily have become a Wall Street stockbroker but chose a career in public service instead.

Roosevelt was greatly influenced by the progressivism of his distant cousin, former president Theodore Roosevelt. His wife, Eleanor Roosevelt—who was Theodore Roosevelt's niece—also proved influential. With her earnest belief in social reform, Mrs. Roosevelt would become one of his most important political assets.

Roosevelt ran as a vice presidential candidate in 1920. His political career, however, appeared to be over after polio left him paralyzed from the waist down in 1921. With the help of his wife, Roosevelt overcame his physical challenges and was elected governor of New York in 1928. As governor he earned high marks for his imaginative relief programs

REVIEW

Have students complete the **Section 3 Review** on p. 435.

ASSESS

Have students complete **Daily Quiz 14.3**. As **Alternative Assessment**, you may want to use the President Hoover speech or the election paraphernalia in this section's lessons.

RETEACH

Have students complete **Main Idea Activity for Reteaching and Sheltered English 14.3**. Then have each student write a summary sentence for each of the subsections in Section 3. Have volunteers read their sentences to the class. **Sheltered English**

EXTEND

Tell students that Franklin D. Roosevelt's wife, Eleanor, was a powerful woman in her own right. Have students conduct research on Eleanor Roosevelt. Then have each student write a biography of Eleanor Roosevelt. Alternately, students might create a multimedia presentation on Eleanor Roosevelt. Encourage students to share some of their more interesting discoveries about this influential first lady. **Block Scheduling**

---

that had instituted unemployment benefits and supported failing industries. In 1932 Roosevelt accepted his party's nomination for president.

> **"Republican leaders not only have failed in material things, they have failed in national vision, because in disaster they have held out no hope. . . . I pledge you, I pledge myself, to a new deal for the American people."**

A change in leadership. The 1932 campaign revolved around the depression. Although Hoover tried to defend his policies, he realized he had little chance of victory. Roosevelt's campaign was short on specifics. Instead, he repeatedly attacked Hoover's record and promised that he would seek a fairer distribution of wealth. He promised to put the U.S. political and economic systems at "the service of the people." Most important, Roosevelt conveyed a genuine spirit of optimism and confidence that contrasted sharply with Hoover's seeming gloom.

On election day Roosevelt and his running mate, John Nance Garner of Texas, carried 42 states. He captured 23 million popular votes and 472 electoral votes to Hoover's 16 million popular votes and 59 electoral votes. The Democrats won decisive majorities in both houses of Congress. As a result, Roosevelt knew that his programs would receive strong congressional support.

In the 1920s most Americans had credited the Republicans with the era's glowing prosperity. In 1932, voters made it clear that the Republicans must take the blame for the depression. Many citizens who voted for Roosevelt were really voting against Herbert Hoover. Other Americans saw in Roosevelt the kind of dynamic personality they believed could lead the country out of its troubles. Roosevelt had promised a "new deal."

FRANKLIN D. ROOSEVELT HOME CLUB

This Roosevelt campaign artifact was used during the 1932 presidential election.

✔ **READING CHECK:** Why was Roosevelt such a popular candidate in the 1932 election?

SECTION 3 REVIEW

Define and explain the significance of the following terms:
rugged individualism
Reconstruction Finance Corporation
Bonus Army

Identify and explain the significance of the following individuals:
Andrew Mellon
Franklin D. Roosevelt
Eleanor Roosevelt

1. **Using Graphic Organizers** Copy the chart below. Use it to explain how each action taken by President Hoover related to his philosophy of rugged individualism.

Hoover's actions	Relationship to rugged individualism
Opposed the creation of the Federal Emergency Relief Board	
Created the President's Committee for Unemployment Relief	
Met with business leaders	
Funded public-works programs	
Established the Federal Farm Board	
Created the Reconstruction Finance Corporation	

2. **Evaluating** How effective were Hoover's programs in easing the effects of the Great Depression?
3. **Recognizing Point of View** Why did World War I veterans and unemployed workers resort to mass protest during the early years of the depression?
4. **Comparing and Contrasting** How did Herbert Hoover's and Franklin Roosevelt's personalities differ? Why was Roosevelt so popular?

Critical Thinking

5. In what ways did Hoover's philosophies reflect the policies of previous presidents? How did they reflect a new era of the presidency?
Consider:
   - how rugged individualism related to the policies of previous presidencies
   - how Hoover's programs corresponded to this philosophy, and how his programs also departed from Republican policies

CHAPTER 14 REVIEW ANSWERS

Creating a Time Line
Each event should have an explanation and the correct date.

Writing a Summary
See the Reading Checks in each section for main ideas.

Identifying People and Ideas
1. practice of purchasing stocks with borrowed money
2. deep economic downturn that lasted from 1929 to the beginning of World War II
3. regular ups and downs of business in a free-enterprise economy
4. mutual-aid societies formed in Mexican American communities
5. Mexican American activist who fought racial discrimination
6. makeshift shelters built by the homeless
7. president who believed in "rugged individualism"
8. Hoover's belief that success comes through individual effort and private enterprise
9. veterans who demanded early payments of pension bonuses
10. Democrat elected president in 1932

Understanding Main Ideas
1. created a heavy surplus and encouraged consumers to use credit to purchase goods
2. After the crash, investors could not repay loans to

REVIEW AND ASSESSMENT RESOURCES

PRINT
- Chapter 14 Review, pp. 436–37
- Chapter 14 Tutorial for Students, Parents, Mentors, and Peers
- Chapter 14 Test (Form A or B)
- Portfolio Activities and Alternative Assessment Handbook, Chapter 14

MULTIMEDIA
- Audio Program, Chapter 14 (English and Spanish)
- Chapter 14 Test Generator (on the One-Stop Planner)
- Global Skill Builder CD-ROM
- HRW Web site

SHELTERED ENGLISH
- Spanish Glossary
- Sheltered English Chapter 14 Test

REVIEW

Have students complete the **Chapter 14 Review** on pp. 436–37.

ASSESS

Use one of the chapter tests to assess students' understanding of the content. For **Alternative Assessment**, see the **Portfolio Activities and Alternative Assessment Handbook**.

banks, many of which failed. Businesses lost customers and saw profits decline.

3. relied on charitable organizations and formed mutual aid societies

4. provided an escape from daily pressures

5. believed that people had the responsibility to help themselves rather than rely on the government

Reviewing Themes

1. The global economic crisis and the national income gap deprived American businesses of foreign and domestic customers. Consumer debt lessened the amount of disposable income and increased financial instability.

2. urban residents—experienced homelessness and hunger; rural residents—experienced the inability to sell their crops and the threat of homelessness

3. Discrimination in the workplace meant that African Americans and Mexican Americans experienced lower wages and higher levels of unemployment.

Thinking Critically

1. the multiple factors of the depression, the farming crisis, and the income gap

2. forced families to work together; caused conflicts and stress that led to rising divorce rates and lower birthrates

Review

Creating a Time Line

Copy the time line below onto a sheet of paper. Complete the time line by filling in the events and dates from the chapter that you think were most significant. Pick three events and explain why you think they were significant.

Writing a Summary

Using the Reading Checks as a guide, write an overview of the events in the chapter.

Identifying People and Ideas

Identify the following terms or individuals and explain their significance.

1. margin buying
2. Great Depression
3. business cycle
4. *mutualistas*
5. Josefina Fierro de Bright
6. shantytowns
7. Herbert Hoover
8. rugged individualism
9. Bonus Army
10. Franklin D. Roosevelt

Understanding Main Ideas

SECTION 1

1. How did the business practices of the 1920s contribute to the stock market crash of 1929?
2. How did the crash lead to the banking crisis and business failures of the early 1930s?

SECTION 2

3. How did urban residents organize to survive the hardships of the depression?
4. How did popular culture provide an escape from the psychological burdens of the depression?

SECTION 3

5. Why did President Hoover oppose direct federal aid for the unemployed?

Reviewing Themes

1. **Economic Development** What were the multiple factors that contributed to the Great Depression?
2. **Geographic Diversity** How did the hardships of the depression differ for rural and urban residents?
3. **Cultural Diversity** How did racial prejudices magnify the effects of the depression for African Americans and Mexican Americans?

Thinking Critically

1. **Distinguishing Fact from Opinion** When President Hoover announced in 1929 that America was "nearer to the final triumph over poverty than ever before," what facts was he overlooking?
2. **Synthesizing** How did the psychological strain of the depression affect family life during the 1930s?
3. **Problem Solving** What type of program would you have developed to ease the burdens of urban residents and farmers during the depression?
4. **Identifying Values** How did Hoover's depression-era programs reflect his belief in rugged individualism and self-reliance?
5. **Evaluating** How was Franklin D. Roosevelt's mood and style during the 1932 presidential election a major change from Hoover?

Writing About History

Writing to Create Write a dialogue between two unemployed factory workers in the 1930s discussing the factors that contributed to their joblessness. Use this organizer to help you.

1. Stock market crash or global depression
2. Bank failures or loss of foreign markets
3. Reduction of purchases on credit
4. Businesses left with surpluses
5. Businesses scale back production
6. Factory workers laid off

RETEACH

Organize students into three groups and assign each group one of the following topics: the causes of the Great Depression, American life during the Great Depression, or the politics of the Great Depression. Have each group develop a visual display covering its assigned topic. Post groups' displays around the classroom. Then assign each group to a topic that it did not work on and have each group study the appropriate display. Have groups write five to ten quiz questions on the material. Use groups' questions to quiz the class.

Sheltered English, Cooperative Learning

EXTEND

Ask students to find examples of depression art, particularly pieces that depict Americans' lives during the economic downturn. Have each student select one piece of art and write an analysis of it. Have volunteers present their pieces to the class and share the information in their analyses.

Block Scheduling

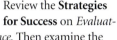

Strategies for Success Review the **Strategies for Success** on *Evaluating Artifacts as Historical Evidence.* Then examine the image below of a radio from the 1930s and answer the questions that follow.

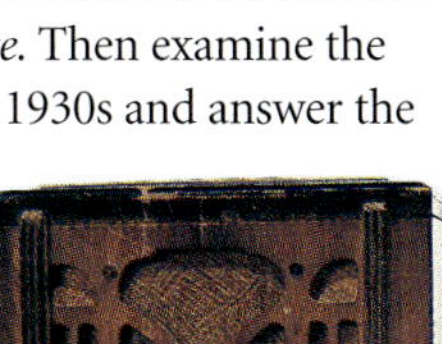

1. What do you think this radio was used for?
2. What details about the radio do you think are significant? Why?
3. Who do you think might have used this radio?
4. How does the radio contribute to your understanding of the Great Depression?

Linking History and Geography

As a departure from President Hoover's policies, President Roosevelt began programs to offer federal unemployment relief. This aid assisted state governments that had established relief programs for the unemployed. Study the map below. Which states had the smallest percentage of people receiving unemployment benefits? Which had the highest?

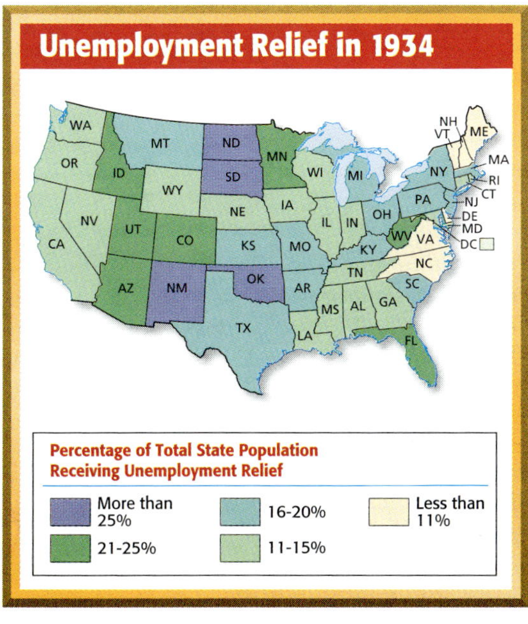

internetconnect

TOPIC: Great Depression
GO TO: go.hrw.com
KEYWORD: SE1 Depression

Accessing the Internet through the HRW Web site, research the Great Depression. Then write three diary entries that describe the daily lives of a civilian working on a public-works project, a middle-class father who has just lost his job, and a teenager who rides the rails as a migrant farmworker.

BUILDING YOUR PORTFOLIO

Complete one or all of the following projects independently or cooperatively.

1 Economic Development

Imagine that you are a political cartoonist in 1929. ***Create an editorial cartoon*** that criticizes the investment practices that led to the stock market crash.

2 Global Relations

Imagine that you are a journalist in the early 1930s at the height of the Great Depression. ***Create a series of newspaper headlines*** that describe the effects of the depression in the United States and around the world. Your headlines might mention stories about individual families, homelessness, food shortages, unemployment, President Hoover's political problems, or international trade issues.

3 Democratic Values

Imagine that you are a campaign worker for Franklin D. Roosevelt. ***Create a campaign poster*** explaining why voters should support your candidate in the 1932 election.

3. Answers will vary. Students might suggest school lunch programs, mortgage payment programs, and rural food purchase programs to feed urban residents.
4. Hoover supported voluntary relief efforts and business aid while he opposed direct relief.
5. Roosevelt's optimism and vitality inspired hope, while Hoover's gloom inspired fear and loathing.

Writing About History

Students' dialogues will vary. Students should note that the stock market crash meant that investors could not repay their debts, which led to decreased consumer purchases and bank failures. Decreased credit purchases and high business surpluses led to overall business instability, leading businesses to increase firings and decrease hirings.

Strategies for Success

1. to listen to music and news broadcasts
2. its size and its design; convey the era of its production
3. the American people
4. suggests the importance of the radio and gives a feel for the "design" of the era

Linking History and Geography

Maine, New Hampshire, Vermont, Delaware, Virginia, and North Carolina; North Dakota, South Dakota, Oklahoma, and New Mexico

The New Deal

CHAPTER PLANNING GUIDE

	Section Lesson Objectives	Print Resources	Multimedia Resources	Sheltered English Resources
Section 1 Restoring Hope, pp. 440–46	1 Describe how the New Deal provided relief for the unemployed. 2 Explain how the New Deal promoted industrial and agricultural recovery. 3 Discuss the New Deal goals for the Tennessee Valley region. 4 Recount how the Roosevelt administration addressed the concerns of African Americans and American Indians.	▶ Guided Reading Strategy 15.1 ▶ Biography Reading 15: Frances Perkins ▶ Geography Activity 15: The Public Works Administration ▶ Section 1 Review, p. 446 ▶ Daily Quiz 15.1	▶ One-Stop Planner, Lesson 15.1 ▶ The American Nation Video Program Segment: Serving the Nation; Teacher's Guide, pp. 117–22 ▶ Holt Researcher: American History CD–ROM	▶ Main Idea Activity for Reteaching and Sheltered English 15.1
Section 2 New Challenges, pp. 447–53	1 Discuss the criticisms aimed at the New Deal. 2 Recount how the Second New Deal enabled President Roosevelt to win re-election easily in 1936. 3 Describe how Roosevelt tried to prevent the Supreme Court from overturning his programs. 4 Analyze how the Second New Deal benefited labor and agriculture. 5 Explain the Roosevelt recession, and describe the effect it had.	▶ Guided Reading Strategy 15.2 ▶ Primary Source Reading 15: "Every Man a King" ▶ American History Political Cartoon 24: FDR and the New Deal ▶ Section 2 Review, p. 453 ▶ Daily Quiz 15.2	▶ One-Stop Planner, Lesson 15.2 ▶ Holt Researcher: American History CD–ROM	▶ Main Idea Activity for Reteaching and Sheltered English 15.2
Section 3 Life in the New Deal Era, pp. 454–58	1 Discuss the effects of the Dust Bowl. 2 Explain how New Deal agencies used photography to promote their goals. 3 Describe how the New Deal improved the lives of ordinary Americans.	▶ Guided Reading Strategy 15.3 ▶ American History Outline Map 18: The Dust Bowl ▶ Section 3 Review, p. 458 ▶ Daily Quiz 15.3	▶ One-Stop Planner, Lesson 15.3 ▶ American Music Selection 21: "Talkin' Dust Bowl" ▶ Holt Researcher: American History CD–ROM ▶ HRW Web site	▶ Main Idea Activity for Reteaching and Sheltered English 15.3
Section 4 The New Deal and the Arts, pp. 459–63	1 Explain how Federal Project Number One aided writers and artists. 2 Identify the common themes that emerged in the novels, films, and plays of the New Deal Era. 3 Describe how music evolved in the 1930s. 4 Discuss the subject matter that influenced American painters in the 1930s.	▶ Guided Reading Strategy 15.4 ▶ Graphic Organizer Activity 15: Social Change in the 1930s ▶ Literature Reading 15: Thoughts of a Young African American ▶ Section 4 Review, p. 463 ▶ Daily Quiz 15.4	▶ One-Stop Planner, Lesson 15.4 ▶ Holt Researcher: American History CD–ROM	▶ Main Idea Activity for Reteaching and Sheltered English 15.4
Chapter Review and Assessment pp. 464–65		▶ Chapter 15 Review, pp. 464–65 ▶ Chapter 15 Tutorial for Students, Parents, Mentors, and Peers ▶ Chapter 15 Test (Form A or B) ▶ Portfolio Activities and Alternative Assessment Handbook, Chapter 15	▶ Audio Program, Chapter 15 (English and Spanish) ▶ Chapter 15 Test Generator (on the One-Stop Planner) ▶ Global Skill Builder CD–ROM ▶ HRW Web site	▶ Spanish Glossary ▶ Sheltered English Chapter 15 Test

CHAPTER OVERVIEW

When Franklin D. Roosevelt took office in 1933, he pledged that the federal government would revive the economy and help Americans deal with the economic difficulties of the Great Depression. Roosevelt's New Deal programs allocated government funds to create jobs and provide direct relief for the unemployed. Some of these programs included small- and large-scale public-works projects. Roosevelt based his efforts to promote economic growth on the theories of economist John Maynard Keynes.

People on the right and left of the political spectrum challenged some of Roosevelt's programs, and the Supreme Court overturned some of Roosevelt's initiatives. Nevertheless, New Deal programs and reforms helped a broad range of families across the country, including farmers and migrant workers suffering through the Dust Bowl, and artists otherwise unable to find work. Many people who previously had been marginalized in American society received federal government aid. The scope and impact of New Deal actions and reforms significantly changed the relationship between the U.S. government and its citizens.

TIME TAMERS

Block Scheduling

The teacher lesson plans for each section offer a variety of activity choices to help you present the material in a block scheduling format. For further suggestions on block scheduling, see the **Block Scheduling Handbook with Team Teaching Strategies**, pp. 85–90.

Internet Connections and Lesson 15
www.si.edu/hrw

Hands-On History Activities:

Classroom to Community The **Hands-On History Activities** help students make meaningful connections between events in American history and those in their own hometown. You may wish to use the Chapter 15 Activity, A Project for Your Town, to extend the chapter lessons, as alternative assessment, or as a block scheduling option.

Portfolio Projects

The American Nation includes multiple portfolio projects in each Pupil's Edition chapter review, as well as each unit review. Chapter 15 Portfolio Project options on p. 465 include the following:

1. Students will **write a proposal.**
2. Students will **write a short, realistic passage.**
3. Students will **hold a debate** or **write a script.**

The American Nation
INTERNET RESOURCE DIRECTORY

To access online materials for this chapter, go to **go.hrw.com** and type in the keywords listed below.

HRW ONLINE RESOURCES
GO TO: go.hrw.com

Online Maps
KEYWORD: SE1 Maps15
- Unemployment Relief

Online Charts
KEYWORD: SE1 Charts15
- Personal Income, 1929–1941
- Unemployment, 1929–1941

Online Reading Support
KEYWORD: SE1 Strategies15

Online Rubrics
KEYWORD: SE1 Rubrics

CHAPTER ENRICHMENT LINKS
Use these Web links to extend and enrich student learning for Chapter 15.
GO TO: go.hrw.com
KEYWORD: SE1 Ch15

CHAPTER INTERNET ACTIVITIES
GO TO: go.hrw.com
- Pupil's Edition Student Activity
  KEYWORD: SE1 WPA
  (Students conduct research on WPA-sponsored murals and posters.)
- Teacher's Edition Student Activity
  KEYWORD: SE1 Hindenburg
  (Students conduct research on the *Hindenburg* disaster.)
- Teacher's Edition Student Activity
  KEYWORD: SE1 Dust
  (Students conduct research on the causes of the Dust Bowl.)

ADDITIONAL
RESOURCES

Books for Teachers

Burg, David F. *The Great Depression: An Eyewitness History.* Facts on File, 1996. Provides an overview with time lines and excerpts from primary sources.

Reiman, Richard A. *The New Deal and American Youth: Ideas and Ideals in a Depression Decade.* University of Georgia Press, 1992. Examines the role of youth in the New Deal.

Books for Students

Freedman, Russell. *Franklin Delano Roosevelt.* Houghton Mifflin, 1992. Presents a biography for young adults. Particularly appropriate for students reading below grade level.

Watkins, T.H. *The Great Depression: America in the 1930s.* Little, Brown and Company, 1993. Provides an overview of the depression and New Deal with accompanying photographs.

Primary Sources from the Period

Agee, James, and Walker Evans. *Let Us Now Praise Famous Men.* Houghton Mifflin, 1941. Provides a written and photographic record of three sharecropper families in Alabama.

Tugwell, Rexford *The Brains Trust.* Viking, 1968. Analyzes New Deal programs.

Multimedia Materials

Franklin D. Roosevelt: The Speeches Collection. Video, 40 min. MPI Home Video/SSSS. Includes a speech to CCC workers and a teacher's guide on Roosevelt.

You May Call Her Madam Secretary. Video, 57 min. Vineyard Video Productions/SSSS. Documents the life of Frances Perkins, the first female cabinet member.

CHAPTER 15

Before You Read

Build on What You Know

Ask students to answer the following questions.

What kinds of problems might occur during a nationwide economic crisis?

Consider:

- what happened during earlier recessions
- how businesses might react during an economic downturn

What might the federal government do to help the nation out of a crisis?

Consider:

- how the government responded during earlier recessions
- how the government might provide money or employment to those out of work

exploring the time line

AMERICAN EVENTS

ECONOMIC DEVELOPMENT

1935 ■ The Social Security Act. Passed in 1935, the Social Security Act ensured an income for several different groups of people, including those who were blind, disabled, elderly, or unemployed. President Franklin D. Roosevelt, however, had wanted the act to include all Americans. He said, "Everybody ought to be in on it—the farmer and his wife and family. . . . I don't see why not. Cradle to the grave—from the cradle to the grave they ought to be in a social insurance system."

CRITICAL THINKING Why might Congress have passed a Social Security Act that did not cover everyone?

ANSWER: Students might suggest that Congress thought that an act covering everyone would be too costly or that Americans would not accept what might be seen as a government handout.

CHAPTER 15

1933–1939
The New Deal

A bank closure

United Automobile Workers union buttons

1933
Business and Finance
A federal bank holiday helps restore public trust in banks.

1934
Daily Life
The board game Monopoly premieres, using themes of the depression.

1935
The Arts
Federal Project Number One seeks to revive the arts in the United States.

1935
Science and Technology
The development of sulfa drugs marks a breakthrough in the treatment of bacterial diseases.

1936
Business and Finance
American industries begin to experience large-scale sit-down strikes.

1933 **1934** **1935** **1936**

1934
Daily Life
Drought hits the Great Plains, marking the beginning of the Dust Bowl.

A dust storm

1935
Politics
Congress passes the Social Security Act.

1936
Daily Life
Life magazine begins publication.

1936
World Events
British king Edward VIII abdicates the throne to marry American divorcée Wallis Simpson.

Social Security poster

Before You Read

Build on What You Know

The prosperous economic times of the 1920s came to a devastating end with the stock market crash in 1929 and the Great Depression that followed. President Hoover's administration dealt cautiously with the economic crisis. American voters elected Franklin D. Roosevelt as president in 1932 in the hope that the federal government would take a more active role in shaping the economy. In this chapter you will learn how Roosevelt's administration dealt with the economic crisis and changed the role of government in American life.

438

Think About Themes

To help students create their Themes Journal entries, provide the following examples of appropriate **agree/disagree** *statements.*

Economic Development

Agree According to the Constitution, one purpose of government is to "promote the general welfare."

Disagree The Constitution does not guarantee the economic well-being of U.S. citizens.

Constitutional Heritage

Agree The Constitution does not explicitly give the federal government authority to regulate markets.

Disagree The government should abide by the spirit of the Constitution, which favors actions that benefit citizens.

Cultural Diversity

Agree Artists rely on sources other than their art to make money.

Disagree During an economic downturn, people will be less likely to contribute to artistic endeavors or spend money on entertainment.

Unemployed Americans

The **Hindenburg** *explosion*

Action Comics' *first issue*

1937
World Events
The German airship *Hindenburg* explodes, killing 36 people.

1937
Politics
President Roosevelt tries to "pack" the Supreme Court.

1937
Business and Finance
A recession sets back recovery from the Great Depression.

1938
Daily Life
Superman makes his debut in *Action Comics*.

1938
Science and Technology
The Biro brothers invent the ballpoint pen.

1939
Business and Finance
More than 17 percent of the American workforce is unemployed.

1939
The Arts
John Steinbeck's *The Grapes of Wrath* is published.

1939
The Arts
Gone With the Wind becomes the most popular film of the 1930s.

Ballpoint pen ad

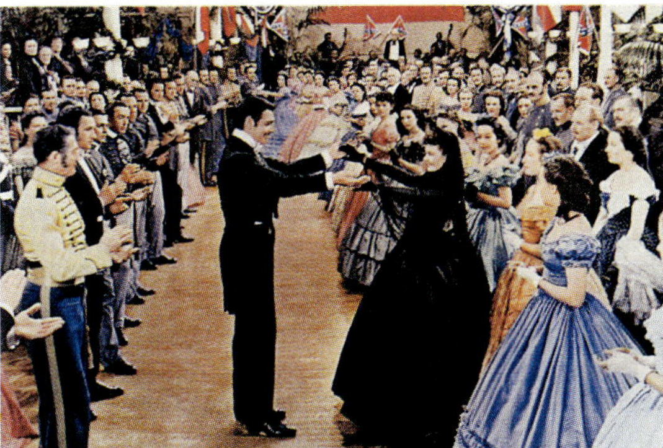

Gone With the Wind

Think About Themes

Decide whether you **agree** *or* **disagree** *with the following statements. Note why in your journal.*

Economic Development The federal government must take responsibility for the well-being of the country's citizens during a crisis.

Constitutional Heritage Government interference in a free-market economy may be unconstitutional.

Cultural Diversity People who work in the arts are never affected by an economic downturn because art is not a business.

exploring the time line

GLOBAL EVENTS

internetconnect

TOPIC: *Hindenburg* Disaster
GO TO: go.hrw.com
KEYWORD: SE1 Hindenburg

Have students access the Internet through the HRW Web site to conduct research on the *Hindenburg* disaster and theories about the disaster's cause. Then ask each student to write an essay that summarizes and analyzes the various theories. Students' essays should conclude with a statement that explains which theory they support and why.

SECTION 1

After completing Section 1, students should be able to:

OBJECTIVE 1 *Describe how the New Deal provided relief for the unemployed.*

OBJECTIVE 2 *Explain how the New Deal promoted industrial and agricultural recovery.*

OBJECTIVE 3 *Discuss the New Deal goals for the Tennessee Valley region.*

OBJECTIVE 4 *Recount how the Roosevelt administration addressed the concerns of African Americans and American Indians.*

LET'S GET STARTED!

Write the following passage from Franklin Roosevelt's inaugural address on the chalkboard: *"Let me assert my firm belief that the only thing we have to fear is fear itself. . . . The people of the United States have not failed."* As students enter the classroom, ask them to respond to the passage in writing. Have volunteers share their responses with the class. Tell students that in Section 1 they will learn about New Deal measures intended to provide relief for the unemployed and promote economic recovery.

SECTION 1 RESOURCES

PRINT

- Guided Reading Strategy 15.1
- Biography Reading 15: Frances Perkins
- Geography Activity 15: The Public Works Administration
- Section 1 Review, p. 446
- Daily Quiz 15.1

MULTIMEDIA

- One-Stop Planner, Lesson 15.1
- The American Nation Video Program Segment: Serving the Nation; Teacher's Guide, pp. 117–22
- Holt Researcher: American History CD–ROM

SHELTERED ENGLISH

- Main Idea Activity for Reteaching and Sheltered English 15.1

✔ READING TO UNDERSTAND

To help students master the section objectives, have them answer the **READING CHECKS** and complete **Guided Reading Strategy 15.1** as they read the section.

Restoring Hope

OBJECTIVES

Read to understand:

1. how the New Deal provided relief for the unemployed
2. how the New Deal promoted industrial and agricultural recovery
3. what the New Deal goals for the Tennessee Valley region were
4. how the Roosevelt administration addressed the concerns of African Americans and American Indians

KEY TERMS

New Deal
bank holiday
Federal Deposit Insurance Corporation
Civilian Conservation Corps
National Industrial Recovery Act
Agricultural Adjustment Administration
Tennessee Valley Authority

KEY PEOPLE

Eleanor Roosevelt
Frances Perkins
Harry L. Hopkins
John Maynard Keynes
Robert C. Weaver
Marian Anderson
John Collier

KEY PLACES

Tennessee River valley

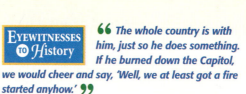

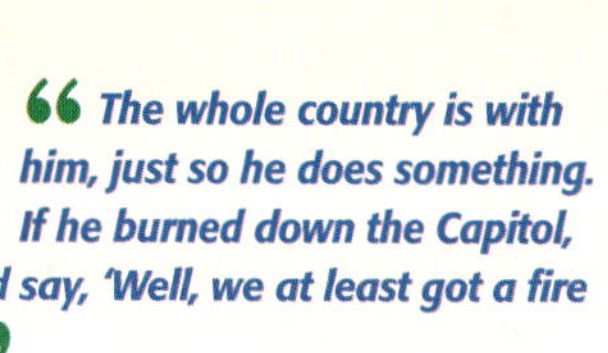

"The whole country is with him, just so he does something. If he burned down the Capitol, we would cheer and say, 'Well, we at least got a fire started anyhow.'"

—Will Rogers

Franklin Roosevelt's (right) enthusiasm encouraged Americans during the Great Depression.

American humorist Will Rogers was not alone in his assessment of Franklin D. Roosevelt. The new president offered the American people much-needed hope. By 1933, Americans had endured three years of economic depression—each year more desperate than the last. On his last day in office, President Herbert Hoover was heard to sigh, "We are at the end of our string. There is nothing more we can do." Roosevelt did not share this despair. The optimistic words of Roosevelt's inaugural address rang out across the land, lifting Americans' spirits and stirring their hopes. Some 500,000 letters supporting the new president poured into the White House soon after his inauguration.

Roosevelt Confronts the Emergency

President Roosevelt did indeed get a fire started. In 1932, while governor of New York, Roosevelt had formed an advisory group known as the Brain Trust. With the help of this group the energetic new president drew up his promised "new deal for the American people," a series of 15 relief and recovery measures. Immediately after taking office on March 5, 1933, Roosevelt called Congress into special session. During the next 100 days Congress approved all 15 measures, which made up the heart of the president's **New Deal** program.

Roosevelt began by focusing on the country's troubled banking system. On March 6 he issued a proclamation closing every bank in the nation for a few days. This so-called **bank holiday** was designed to stop massive withdrawals. On Thursday, March 9, Congress passed the Emergency Banking Act. This act authorized the federal government to examine all banks and allow those that were financially sound to reopen. Roosevelt hoped that the act would restore public confidence in the banking system.

Caught without cash, Americans scrambled to find substitutes during the bank holiday. Many used subway and bus tokens, postage stamps, and IOUs. On Sunday evening, March 12, some 60 million anxious Americans tuned in their radios to hear the president. He explained how the bank holiday would protect their money. In this first of many "fireside chats"—radio broadcasts from the White House—Roosevelt urged Americans to return their money to banks. "I can assure you that it is safer to keep your money in a reopened bank than under the mattress," he advised.

TEACH OBJECTIVE 1

LEVEL 1: Tell students to imagine that it is 1933 and that they are artists who have been hired by the federal government to create informational posters about New Deal programs. Pair students and have each pair create posters describing New Deal unemployment relief programs. *(Students' posters might mention the FERA, which provided direct federal aid; the CWA, which created jobs such as raking leaves and picking up litter; and the CCC, which put young men to work in parks and forests.)* Display students' posters around the classroom. **Sheltered English, Cooperative Learning**

LEVEL 2: Tell students to imagine that it is 1933 and that they work in the White House press office. Pair students and have each pair write a short press release informing the public about one of the federal programs that assists the unemployed. *(See the Level 1 lesson for the correct programs and their provisions.)* Ask volunteers to read their press releases to the class. **Cooperative Learning**

LEVEL 3: Tell students to imagine that they are editing an encyclopedia of the New Deal. Have each student write entries about the New Deal programs that provided unemployment relief. *(See the Level 1 lesson for the correct programs and their provisions.)* Have volunteers read their entries to the class.

Banks began to reopen. By the end of the month more than $1 billion in deposits had flowed into the system. Confidence in banks increased even more when Congress created the **Federal Deposit Insurance Corporation** (FDIC) in June 1933. This organization insured each bank deposit up to $2,500.

In April 1933 Roosevelt urged Congress to create the Home Owners Loan Corporation (HOLC). It was created to assist home owners who could not meet their mortgage payments. Congress passed the measure. By June 1936 the HOLC had saved the homes of some 1 million American families by granting them low-interest, long-term mortgage loans. Roosevelt and his advisers then turned their attention to the plight of the American farmers. He issued an executive order to create the Farm Credit Administration (FCA) in 1933. The FCA provided much needed low-interest, long-term loans to farmers. It allowed many farmers to pay off mortgages and back taxes, buy back lost farms, and purchase seed, fertilizer, and needed equipment.

★ HISTORICAL DOCUMENTS ★

PRESIDENT FRANKLIN D. ROOSEVELT

First Inaugural Address

President Roosevelt set the tone for his administration with his first inaugural address. In it he expressed his confidence in the country's ability to recover from the Great Depression.

"First of all, let me assert my firm belief that the only thing we have to fear is fear itself—nameless, unreasoning, unjustified terror which paralyzes needed efforts to convert retreat into advance. In every dark hour of our national life a leadership of frankness and vigor has met with that understanding and support of the people themselves which is essential to victory. I am convinced that you will again give that support to leadership in these critical days. . . .

The people of the United States have not failed. In their need they have registered a mandate [command] that they want direct, vigorous action. They have asked for discipline and direction under leadership. They have made me the present instrument of their wishes. In the spirit of the gift I take it."

Relief for the Needy

Other measures launched by the Roosevelt administration included large-scale programs of direct relief. The relief was granted to aid the nation's 13 million unemployed workers. In many ways President Roosevelt's direct relief was the type of program that reformers had been trying to get the government to support since the Progressive Era. Aided by First Lady Eleanor Roosevelt and Democratic National Committee member Molly Dewson, the president brought in many veteran reformers to direct his programs, including Frances Perkins as secretary of labor.

In May 1933, at Roosevelt's request, Congress established the Federal Emergency Relief Administration (FERA). It was created to funnel $500 million in relief aid to state and local agencies. One of Roosevelt's most trusted advisers, Harry L. Hopkins, headed the FERA program.

A Washington, D.C., newspaper reported the eagerness of the FERA director to get relief to the needy.

> **"The half-billion dollars for direct relief of States won't last a month if Harry L. Hopkins, the new relief administrator, maintains the pace he set yesterday in disbursing [paying out] more than $5,000,000 during his first two hours in office."**

By 1935 some $3 billion in direct federal aid had been distributed. At one point nearly 8 million American families were receiving public assistance.

INTERPRETING THE VISUAL RECORD

Government spending. Senator Harry Byrd of Virginia questions Harry Hopkins about the effectiveness of government spending. ***What is Hopkins trying to fix by spending money?***

PEOPLE IN HISTORY

Frances Perkins. Before her cabinet appointment as Franklin Roosevelt's secretary of labor, Frances Perkins had been a social worker. She had worked with a variety of progressive reformers and groups, most of whom considered her a dynamic figure. However, some people misunderstood her desire to be taken seriously and called Perkins colorless. This assessment may have arisen from her habit of dressing in a plain black dress and small hat. She said, "Many good and intelligent women do dress in ways that are very attractive and pretty but don't particularly invite confidence in their common sense." Despite some of her conservative ideas, particularly her distrust of labor unions, Perkins was a symbol of the New Deal's liberal policies.

CRITICAL THINKING Why might Perkins have believed that dressing in black would invite confidence in her common sense?

ANSWER: Students might suggest that she might have believed that women who dressed fashionably were perceived as frivolous rather than serious.

VISUAL RECORD ANSWER

Students might suggest that Hopkins was trying to reduce unemployment.

TEACH OBJECTIVE 2

LEVEL 1: Tell students to imagine that it is 1933 and that they are newspaper reporters. Pair students and have each pair write a headline and topic sentences for articles on New Deal programs promoting industrial and agricultural recovery. *(Students' headlines and topic sentences should mention that the NIRA was passed in June 1933 to stimulate business activity and reduce unemployment. The NIRA created the PWA, which initiated public-works projects, and the NRA, which encouraged businesses to draw up codes to regulate hours, prices, production levels, and wages. The Agricultural Adjustment Act, passed in May 1933, created the Agricultural Adjustment Administration, which paid farmers subsidies to reduce their output.)* Ask volunteers to read their headlines and topic sentences to the class. **Sheltered English, Cooperative Learning**

LEVEL 2: Have students write a brief essay about the New Deal programs that promoted agricultural and industrial recovery. Students' essays should describe how each program promoted recovery. *(See the Level 1 lesson for the correct programs and the major provisions of each program.)* Ask volunteers to read their essays to the class.

ACROSS THE CURRICULUM

▶ECONOMICS◀

The National Recovery Administration (NRA). General Hugh S. Johnson, head of the NRA, tried to win support for his agency by associating compliance with the NRA codes with patriotism. When labor leaders, liberals, and progressives complained that the NRA catered to big business, Roosevelt created a review board to investigate complaints. Lawyer Clarence Darrow was appointed to head the inquiry. He soon agreed that the NRA was dominated by monopolies and was not solving any economic problems.

CRITICAL THINKING How might the NRA have boosted public morale?

ANSWER: Students might suggest that the belief that government was taking an active role to solve economic problems boosted morale.

***The American Nation* VIDEO PROGRAM**

Serving the Nation; Teacher's Guide, pp. 117–22

Search 21056, Play to 25391
Videodisc 2, Side A

Play Pause

See *Teacher's Guide* for Spanish barcode.

INTERPRETING THE VISUAL RECORD

The CCC. Americans working for the CCC both earned a living and helped improve the environment. ***What do these workers appear to be doing?***

Most Americans disliked this kind of aid. They wanted jobs, not handouts. Hopkins created the Civil Works Administration (CWA) to address this problem. Most CWA jobs were "make-work" projects such as raking leaves and picking up park litter. From 1933 to 1934, the CWA paid more than $740 million in wages to some 4 million men and women.

To aid the many unemployed young men between the ages of 18 and 25, Congress established the **Civilian Conservation Corps** (CCC) in 1933. Some 250,000 young men left their homes and went to army camps for CCC training. Once trained, they spread out into the nation's parks and forests, where they planted trees, cleared underbrush, created park trails, and developed campgrounds and beaches. They earned $1 a day for their labor. Most of their earnings were sent back home to help their families. During the nearly 10 years of its existence, the CCC employed more than 2.5 million young men. They planted millions of trees, mostly in the South and the Southwest.

✔ **READING CHECK:** How did the New Deal provide relief for the unemployed?

Helping the Nation Recover

In addition to the New Deal relief programs designed to aid needy Americans, President Roosevelt pursued recovery programs to revive the economy. The president saw relief as a short-term remedy. Recovery was his long-term goal.

To stimulate the recovery of businesses and industries, Roosevelt poured money into the economy through federal loans and government spending. This process is sometimes called "priming the pump." Many of the New Deal recovery programs were based on the theories of John Maynard Keynes, a noted British economist. Keynes argued that for a nation to recover fully from a depression, the government had to spend money to encourage investment and consumption.

One of Roosevelt's economic programs was the **National Industrial Recovery Act** (NIRA). Congress passed the NIRA in June 1933 to stimulate industrial and business activity and reduce unemployment. It would do this by stabilizing prices, raising wages, limiting work hours, and providing jobs. To achieve these goals, the NIRA created two new federal agencies—the Public Works Administration (PWA) and the National Recovery Administration (NRA).

Led by Secretary of the Interior Harold Ickes, the PWA worked to create jobs and stimulate business activity. Using federal funds, the PWA contracted with private firms to build roads, public buildings, and other public-works projects. Between 1933 and 1939 the PWA spent more than $4 billion on some 34,000 projects.

The NRA attempted to help the economy recover by encouraging businesses to draw up "codes of fair competition." Under these codes, competing businesses agreed to work together to set hours, prices, production levels, and wages. Businesses were able to do this because the NIRA had suspended antitrust laws. To help protect labor during this period, the NIRA guaranteed workers the "right to organize and bargain collectively through representatives of their own choosing."

HOLT RESEARCHER

Read More About It

Free Find:
John Maynard Keynes

After reading about John Maynard Keynes on the **Holt Researcher** CD–ROM, imagine that you are Keynes. Write a letter to President Roosevelt explaining why you agree or disagree with his New Deal programs.

LEVEL 3: Tell students to imagine that they are representatives of one of the New Deal agencies created to promote industrial or agricultural recovery. Ask each student to write a brief speech about the goals of his or her agency and the steps his or her agency is taking to promote recovery. *(See the Level 1 lesson for the correct programs and the major provisions of each program.)* Ask volunteers to deliver their speeches to the class.

▶**ASSIGNMENT** *Distribute Activity 15, The Public Works Administration, from* ***Geography Activities****, and have each student complete it.*

SPOTLIGHT on the STFU

Have students conduct research on the Southern Tenant Farmers' Union (STFU), focusing on who joined the STFU, the goals of the organization, and its major victories. Then have each student write a short poem about the organization's goals and activities. Ask volunteers to recite their poems to the class. **Block Scheduling**

Led by former army general Hugh S. Johnson, the NRA was initially popular with many people across the country. Parades of workers marched through cities displaying the NRA banner. The banner contained a blue eagle clutching lightning bolts in its claw, with the slogan "We Do Our Part." Johnson compared the NRA to an army.

> "This campaign is a frank dependence on the power and the willingness of the American people to act together as one person in an hour of great danger. . . . The Blue Eagle is a symbol of industrial solidarity and self-government."

The blue eagle of the NRA

Enthusiasm for the NRA soon faded, however. Businesses did not always obey the codes. Workers complained that the codes held their wages down. Consumers complained that the codes pushed prices up. As people lost confidence in the NRA, they joked that it stood for "National Run Around" and "No Recovery Allowed." In 1935 the Supreme Court declared parts of the NIRA and its creation—the NRA—unconstitutional.

Agricultural Recovery

President Roosevelt included farmers in his attempts to encourage economic recovery. As part of his plan Roosevelt called for farmers to cut production. The president believed that such a cut would cause the prices of agricultural goods—and therefore farmers' purchasing power—to rise. Passed by Congress in May 1933, the Agricultural Adjustment Act created the **Agricultural Adjustment Administration** (AAA). The AAA paid farmers to reduce their output of corn, cotton, dairy products, hogs, rice, tobacco, wheat, and other commodities. The money for these subsidies came from taxes levied on food processors, including canners, flour millers, and meat packers.

In one year the plan reduced the cotton crop by more than 3 million bales. This reduction helped to raise cotton prices. Increased income allowed cotton growers and large-scale farmers to spend more cash, thus stimulating overall economic recovery. New Deal supporters pointed to these favorable results as proof of the value of sound federal planning. However, critics pointed out that the taxes on food processors were passed along to consumers in the form of higher prices. They noted that the increase in farmers' incomes came at the expense of consumers.

Critics also claimed that farmers with large landholdings benefited far more from AAA assistance than did small farmers. When large landowners cut production, they forced sharecroppers off their land. They would then keep all of the government payments for themselves. The poorest farmers were forced into even deeper poverty. In response, a group of Arkansas sharecroppers formed the Southern Tenant Farmers' Union (STFU) in 1934. This racially integrated union lobbied the government to halt tenant evictions. They urged the government to force landowners to share federal payments with the farmers who rented land from them.

At meetings like this one, members of the Southern Tenant Farmers' Union worked to win government assistance for some of the poorest farmers in the United States.

DEMOCRATIC VALUES

STFU: Racial Integration and Labor Organizing. When the STFU was created in 1934, African Americans and white people joined the union in segregated local branches. Eventually the groups merged to form a racially integrated union. The STFU helped gather evidence against planters who denied their tenants a share of AAA subsidies. Members also protested discriminatory practices such as the poll tax, demonstrated in favor of labor reforms, and conducted strikes. Planters threatened members with violence. Some members disappeared or were found murdered. The STFU's work eventually led to the creation of the Farm Security Administration.

CRITICAL THINKING Why might a racially integrated union have been effective for sharecroppers?

ANSWER: Students might suggest that if only one group protested, owners could easily undermine the position of the protesters by hiring members of the other group to work the fields.

VISUAL RECORD ANSWER

(for p. 442)

Students might answer that they are clearing away fallen trees.

TEACH OBJECTIVE 3

ALL LEVELS: Tell students that before the New Deal's program in the Tennessee River valley, the region's residents suffered from disease, floods, illiteracy, and poverty. To help students understand the New Deal's goals for the Tennessee River valley, copy the graphic organizer at right on the chalkboard, omitting the italicized answers. Have each student complete the organizer. Ask students why people might have criticized the TVA, despite its efforts to improve the quality of life in the region. *(Students might suggest that the government did not have the constitutional authority to undertake such a project or that private utility companies feared that they would lose money.)* To conclude, lead a class discussion. Ask students to consider whether government or the private sector is responsible for improving the quality of life in impoverished regions. **Sheltered English**

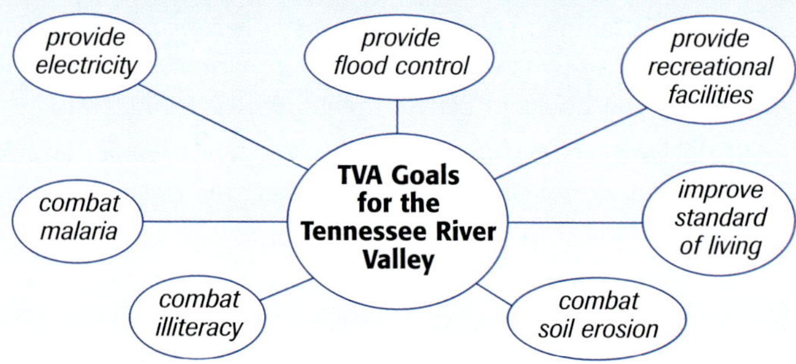

ACROSS THE CURRICULUM

▶GOVERNMENT◀

Antilynching Bill Is Not Passed. For years, activists had been trying to get a federal antilynching bill passed. In 1922 a filibuster by southern congressmembers defeated an antilynching bill. In 1934 Senators Robert Wagner and Edward Costigan introduced an antilynching bill drafted by the NAACP. Despite support from several northern governors, the bill was defeated. Wagner and Costigan reintroduced it in 1935, but southern congressmembers again launched a filibuste. The bill was never brought up for a vote. Supporters abandoned the bill altogether in 1938.

CRITICAL THINKING At what other times might southern senators have claimed that a federal bill violated states' rights?

ANSWER: Students might suggest during the Civil War and Reconstruction.

MAP ANSWER

Alabama, Mississippi, and Tennessee

VISUAL RECORD ANSWER

(for p. 445)

Students might suggest that the painting depicts racial harmony because white people and African Americans are shown enjoying the concert together.

Early in 1936 the Supreme Court struck down the AAA. The Court claimed that the tax on food processors was unconstitutional. Like the ruling against the NIRA and NRA, this decision reflected the Supreme Court's general opposition to New Deal legislation.

✔ **READING CHECK:** How did the New Deal promote industrial and agricultural recovery?

Revitalizing a Region

The largest of the early New Deal programs took place in the Tennessee River valley. This project sought to aid a rural seven-state region that was scarred by deforestation and frequent flooding. Disease, illiteracy, malnutrition, and poverty plagued its 2 million residents. The **Tennessee Valley Authority** (TVA), which was created in May 1933, transformed the economic and social life of the region. Headed by David E. Lilienthal, the TVA built a number of new dams. It also built several power stations that provided electricity, flood control, and recreational facilities for the region. Other TVA projects combated malaria, illiteracy, and soil erosion and tried to improve the region's low standard of living.

Some Americans criticized the TVA, saying it was an example of the government abusing its power. Shareholders in private utility companies feared the TVA projects would cause them to lose money. Although shareholders brought several court cases against the TVA, the Supreme Court refused to strike it down.

✔ **READING CHECK:** What were the New Deal goals for the Tennessee Valley region?

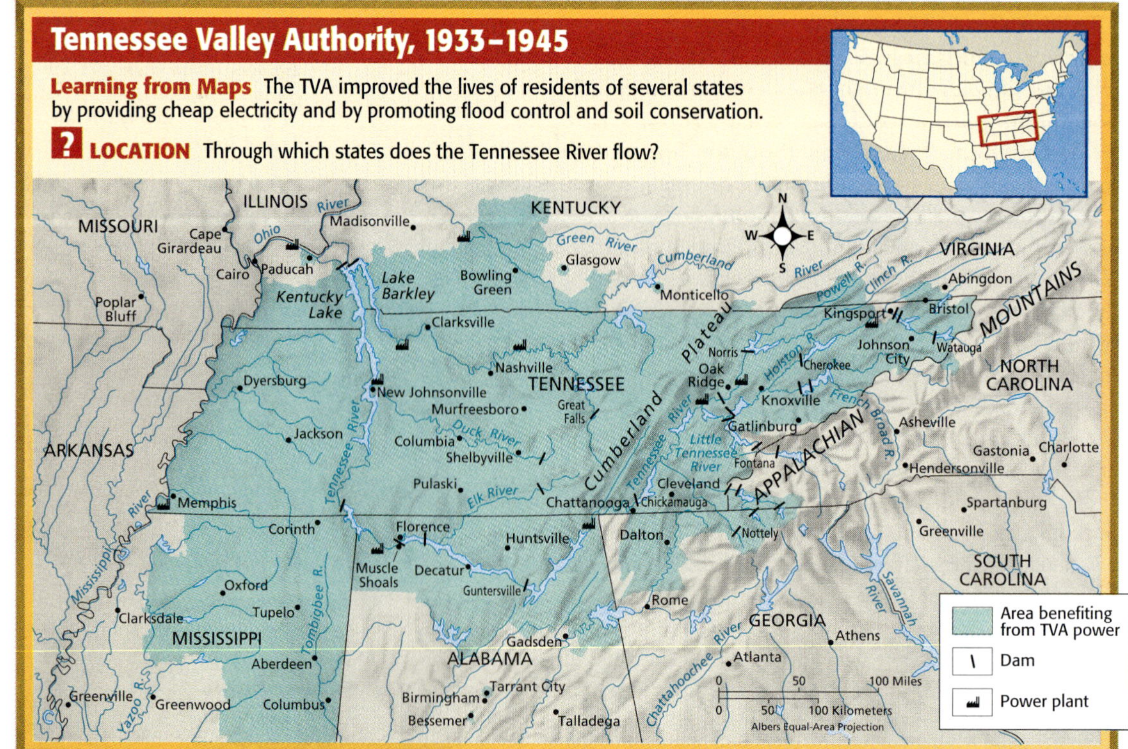

Tennessee Valley Authority, 1933–1945

Learning from Maps The TVA improved the lives of residents of several states by providing cheap electricity and by promoting flood control and soil conservation.

? LOCATION Through which states does the Tennessee River flow?

TEACH OBJECTIVE 4

ALL LEVELS: Pair students and ask each pair to create a chart depicting how the Roosevelt administration addressed the concerns of African Americans and American Indians. *(Pairs' charts should mention the appointment of African Americans to government posts, establishment of the Federal Council on Negro Affairs, and Marian Anderson's concert at the Lincoln Memorial. American Indians concerns were addressed through the appointment of John Collier as commissioner of Indian Affairs and by the passage of the Indian Reorganization Act of 1934.)* Ask volunteers to present their charts to the class. **Sheltered English, Cooperative Learning**

NOTE: For an additional teaching idea, see the Chapter 15 ranking lesson in the **Creative Teaching Strategies** handbook.

Equality Under the New Deal

Although New Deal programs provided aid to people of all races, some programs did discriminate. Some 200,000 young African American men received work and training though the CCC. However, they were strictly segregated from white workers. The TVA employed African American workers. Yet, they were not allowed to live in the model towns built by the organization. NRA codes often set lower wages for African Americans than for whites. This practice led some black leaders to call the NRA the "Negro Run Around" or "Negroes Ruined Again."

This discrimination reflected the social attitudes of many Americans at that time. The depression increased racial tensions in the country, particularly in the South. In 1933 alone, 24 African Americans were lynched. Roosevelt offered little support to legislation to help African Americans, such as a federal antilynching law sponsored by the National Association for the Advancement of Colored People (NAACP). Roosevelt feared a political backlash from southern Democrats.

Fighting discrimination. Despite the lack of progress on civil rights legislation, African Americans did make some advances under the Roosevelt administration. Former NAACP leader Harold Ickes brought in several prominent African Americans to advise the Department of the Interior on racial matters. These advisers included Robert C. Weaver, who held a Ph.D. in economics from Harvard.

Roosevelt named more than 100 African Americans to posts in the federal government during his term. This was more than any other president since Ulysses S. Grant. These appointees included a wide variety of professionals, such as educators, legal scholars, newspaper editors, and social workers. One core group of these African American government officials evolved into the Federal Council on Negro Affairs. The council became known as the Black Cabinet or the Black Brain Trust. According to Weaver, their "common cause was to maximize the participation of blacks in all phases of the New Deal."

INTERPRETING THE VISUAL RECORD

Race relations. This painting shows the enormous crowd that attended Marian Anderson's concert at the Lincoln Memorial. ***Do you think the artist intended to show racial tension or racial harmony in this painting? Explain your answer.***

Many of these appointments came at the request of Eleanor Roosevelt, who was a champion of civil rights. African American leaders noted Mrs. Roosevelt's unusual ability to understand their struggles. "We [white people] are largely to blame" for poverty among the black community, she once said. It was her goal to open greater educational and economic opportunities for African Americans.

In 1939 the Daughters of the American Revolution (DAR) refused to allow Marian Anderson, a world-famous African American singer, to perform at their Washington, D.C., hall. Both Mrs. Roosevelt and Ickes reacted strongly. Roosevelt resigned her longtime membership in the DAR. She argued that "to remain as a member implies approval of that action." Roosevelt and Ickes then arranged for Anderson to give a free concert at the Lincoln Memorial. The concert was a success and attracted an audience of some 75,000 people.

THAT'S INTERESTING!

Many Catholics, Irish Americans, and Jews supported Franklin Roosevelt. His political appointments demonstrated his appreciation of that support. About 11 percent of his appointments were Catholic or Jewish Americans, compared to just 4 percent of Hoover's appointments. FDR also appointed Catholic and Jewish people to about 30 percent of the federal judgeships.

VISUAL RECORD ANSWER

(for p. 446)

Students might answer that her home is made of canvas and tree branches.

SECTION 1 REVIEW ANSWERS

Define and Identify

For significance, see the following pages:

- New Deal, p. 440
- bank holiday, p. 440
- Federal Deposit Insurance Corporation, p. 441
- Eleanor Roosevelt, p. 441
- Frances Perkins, p. 441
- Harry L. Hopkins, p. 441
- Civilian Conservation Corps, p. 442
- John Maynard Keynes, p. 442
- National Industrial Recovery Act, p. 442
- Agricultural Adjustment Administration, p. 443
- Tennessee Valley Authority, p. 444

REVIEW

Have students complete the **Section 1 Review** on p. 446.

ASSESS

Have students complete **Daily Quiz 15.1.** As **Alternative Assessment**, you may want to use the poster or the press release in this section's lessons.

RETEACH

Have students complete **Main Idea Activity for Reteaching and Sheltered English 15.1.** Then organize the class into small groups. Have each group write some questions about New Deal initiatives that can be answered by naming a specific program or person. *(For example, students might ask, "What program insured the savings of bank depositors?" [FDIC])* Collect groups' questions and use them to quiz the class.
Sheltered English, Cooperative Learning

EXTEND

Organize the class into small groups. Assign each group one of the key people for Section 1. Have each group conduct research on its assigned individual. Each group should use the information it gathers to prepare a multimedia presentation on its subject. Have each group give its presentation to the class.
Block Scheduling, Cooperative Learning

- Robert C. Weaver, p. 445
- Marian Anderson, p. 445
- John Collier, p. 446

Locate
For location, see the map on p. 444. For importance, see the following page:

- Tennessee River valley, p. 444

1. banking—examined banks for financial soundness, encouraged people to deposit money, created FDIC; industry—passed NIRA to stabilize prices and contract with business for public projects; agriculture—loans to farmers, passed AAA to limit production and raise prices

2. The CWA and the CCC provided relief to unemployed workers.

3. educated citizens, limited effects of disease, provided electricity and flood control

4. Answers will vary. Students might argue that many African Americans might have criticized FDR's policies for allowing discrimination in government jobs. Others might point out the many appointments of African Americans to government positions. American Indians might agree that the reversal of the Dawes Act helped revive tribal rule.

5. Answers will vary. Students might suggest that Keynes supported government spending to stimulate the economy. The Roosevelt administration used government funds to stimulate agriculture, business, and industry and to provide jobs.

INTERPRETING THE VISUAL RECORD

American Indians. This woman and her child were photographed in 1936 at their home on the Mescalero Apache Reservation. ***What is the woman's home made of?***

Rights of American Indians. The Roosevelt administration also addressed the concerns of American Indians. At the beginning of the New Deal Era, life for many American Indians was bleak. A late-1920s report on American Indian life across the country listed numerous problems facing these communities. Inadequate housing, poor health care, and malnutrition left many of the nation's more than 300,000 American Indians vulnerable to disease. American Indians argued that their culture had been stripped away by measures like the Dawes Act of 1887. The act had ended tribal government and sold off tribal land.

In the 1920s a social worker named John Collier observed the poor living conditions in American Indian communities. Very deeply moved by what he had seen, Collier founded the American Indian Defense Association. The organization fought to protect religious freedom and tribal property. For the next decade Collier championed American Indian reform efforts. Then, in 1933, President Roosevelt appointed Collier as the new commissioner of Indian Affairs. Collier worked to redirect government policy in an attempt to revitalize American Indian life and culture. "Anything less than to let Indian culture live on would be a crime against the earth itself," Collier declared.

Congress put these reforms into law with the passage of the Indian Reorganization Act of 1934. Reversing the Dawes Act policy, the new law tried to revive tribal rule. The bill provided funds to start tribal business ventures and to pay for the college education of young American Indians. It also ordered Congress "to promote the study of Indian civilization and preserve and develop . . . Indian arts, crafts, skills, and traditions."

✔ **READING CHECK:** How did the Roosevelt administration address the concerns of African Americans and American Indians?

SECTION  REVIEW

Define and explain the significance of the following terms:
New Deal
bank holiday
Federal Deposit Insurance Corporation
Civilian Conservation Corps
National Industrial Recovery Act
Agricultural Adjustment Administration
Tennessee Valley Authority

Identify and explain the significance of the following individuals:
Eleanor Roosevelt
Frances Perkins
Harry L. Hopkins
John Maynard Keynes
Robert C. Weaver
Marian Anderson
John Collier

Locate and explain the importance of the following place:
Tennessee River valley

1. **Using Graphic Organizers** Copy the graphic organizer below. Use it to describe the various measures that President Roosevelt took to help banking, industry, and agriculture.

New Deal → Banking; Industry; Agriculture

2. **Analyzing** Which New Deal programs granted direct relief to unemployed workers and created jobs?
3. **Understanding Geography: Human-Environment Interaction** How did the programs of the Tennessee Valley Authority transform the region?
4. **Recognizing Point of View** How might African Americans or American Indians of the 1930s have assessed President Roosevelt's policies? Why?

Critical Thinking

5. How are the economic theories of John Maynard Keynes reflected in the approach taken by the Roosevelt administration toward reviving the economy?
Consider:
- what approach Keynes supported
- what approach the Roosevelt administration took toward the economy

SECTION 2

After completing Section 2, students should be able to:

OBJECTIVE 1 *Discuss the criticisms aimed at the New Deal.*

OBJECTIVE 2 *Recount how the Second New Deal enabled President Roosevelt to win re-election easily in 1936.*

OBJECTIVE 3 *Describe how Roosevelt tried to prevent the Supreme Court from overturning his programs.*

OBJECTIVE 4 *Analyze how the Second New Deal benefited labor and agriculture.*

OBJECTIVE 5 *Explain the Roosevelt recession, and describe the effect it had.*

LET'S GET STARTED!

As students enter the classroom, distribute copies of Cartoon 24, FDR and the New Deal, from **American History Political Cartoons.** Ask students to study the cartoon and complete the questions on the worksheet. Have volunteers share their answers with the class. Tell students that in Section 2 they will learn about the programs of the Second New Deal.

New Challenges

OBJECTIVES

Read to understand:

1. what the criticisms aimed at the New Deal were
2. how the Second New Deal enabled President Roosevelt to win re-election easily in 1936
3. how Roosevelt tried to prevent the Supreme Court from overturning his programs
4. how the Second New Deal benefited labor and agriculture
5. what Roosevelt's recession was, and what effect it had

KEY TERMS

Share-Our-Wealth
Works Progress Administration
National Youth Administration
Social Security Act
Wagner-Connery Act
Congress of Industrial Organizations
sit-down strike

KEY PEOPLE

Francis E. Townsend
Charles E. Coughlin
Huey Long
Mary McLeod Bethune

EYEWITNESSES TO History

> ***"President Roosevelt was elected on November 8, 1932. . . . This is January 1935. We are in our third year of the Roosevelt depression, with the conditions growing worse. . . .***
>
> ***We must become awakened! We must know the truth and speak the truth. There is no use to wait three more years. It is not Roosevelt or ruin; it is Roosevelt's ruin."***
>
> **—Huey Long**

Huey Long

U.S. senator Huey Long of Louisiana was one of several prominent critics who argued that the New Deal was too slow in easing the economic troubles of the nation. Critics like Long increased the administration's determination to enact yet another series of innovative programs that would provide more relief to the nation.

Critics of the New Deal

Criticism of the New Deal came from both conservatives and liberals. Most conservative complaints came from the American Liberty League, an organization made up largely of Republican business interests. Some disenchanted Democrats led by Al Smith also joined. Smith accused New Deal supporters of "irresponsible ravings against millionaires and big business." The league complained that the New Deal measures were destroying both the Constitution and free enterprise.

Among the liberal reformers who opposed the New Deal was Dr. Francis E. Townsend of California. Townsend wanted the government to grant a pension of $200 a month to every American over 60 years old. All recipients were to spend the pensions within 30 days and thus pump money into the economy. Father Charles E. Coughlin, a radio priest from Michigan, urged the government to nationalize all banks and return to the silver standard.

Huey "the Kingfish" Long, a colorful but corrupt U.S. senator from Louisiana, had probably the most radical plan. Like Robin Hood, Long wanted to take from the rich and give to the poor. In 1934 Long proposed a new kind of relief program, which he called **Share-Our-Wealth**. The program would empower the government to seize wealth from the rich through taxes and then provide a guaranteed minimum income and a home to every American family. Long even had a theme song.

> **"Ev'ry man a king, ev'ry man a king,
> For you can be a millionaire,
> There's enough for all people to share.
> When it's sunny June and December too,
> Or in the wintertime or spring:
> There'll be peace without end,
> Ev'ry neighbor a friend,
> With ev'ry man a king."**

Supporters of Huey Long's Share-Our-Wealth program wore badges such as this one.

SECTION 2 RESOURCES

PRINT

- Guided Reading Strategy 15.2
- Primary Source Reading 15: "Every Man a King"
- American History Political Cartoon 24: FDR and the New Deal
- Section 2 Review, p. 453
- Daily Quiz 15.2

MULTIMEDIA

- One-Stop Planner, Lesson 15.2
- Holt Researcher: American History CD–ROM

SHELTERED ENGLISH

- Main Idea Activity for Reteaching and Sheltered English 15.2

✔ READING TO UNDERSTAND

To help students master the section objectives, have them answer the **READING CHECKS** and complete **Guided Reading Strategy 15.2** as they read the section.

TEACH OBJECTIVE 1

ALL LEVELS: Tell students that New Deal measures received criticism from the right and left of the political spectrum. Ask students why criticism of the New Deal may have been so widespread. *(Students might suggest that some people believed that the administration was not doing enough to help poor or older Americans or that business interests felt threatened by government intervention in the economy.)* To help students understand the criticisms aimed at the New Deal, copy the chart at right on the chalkboard, omitting the italicized answers. Have each student complete the organizer. Ask volunteers to share their answers with the class.
Sheltered English

Criticism from the Left	Criticism from the Right
Francis Townsend—wanted the government to grant a pension of $200 a month to Americans over 60 years old *Father Coughlin—wanted the government to nationalize banks and return to the silver standard* *Huey Long—wanted the Share-Our-Wealth program*	*American Liberty League/ Al Smith—claimed New Deal measures were destroying the Constitution and free enterprise; accused New Deal supporters of "irresponsible ravings against millionaires and big business"*

▶**ASSIGNMENT** *Distribute copies of Reading 15, "Every Man a King," from* ***Literature, Primary Source, and Biography Readings****. Have each student read the text and complete the questions and activity accompanying the text.*

PEOPLE IN HISTORY

Huey Long. Louisiana politician Huey Long held populist ideas from the beginning of his career, when he attacked Standard Oil and opposed the Ku Klux Klan. As governor, Long abolished his state's local governments and personally controlled the courts, the militia, police forces, schools, and the tax assessors. He was impeached by the state legislature but not convicted. A supporter of some New Deal programs, Long liked Roosevelt's proposal to regulate public utilities, but worried that "we might as well try to regulate a rattlesnake." He warned that rich people would rather let the nation "go slap down to hell" than give up their economic supremacy. Some 27,000 Share-Our-Wealth clubs had formed across the nation by the time Long was assassinated in 1935.

CRITICAL THINKING Why might Long's Share-Our-Wealth program have been particularly popular during the Great Depression?

ANSWER: Students might suggest that during a time of unemployment and extremely low wages, people would have been more aware of disparities in wealth and been more willing to change them.

1882–1945
In Office 1933–1945

Franklin D. Roosevelt

"Mr. Roosevelt is a unique figure in the modern world: the one statesman . . . who seems able to relax," wrote one journalist about the charming leader. Indeed, President Roosevelt always appeared to be warm, energetic, and easy-going, despite the enormous pressures he faced as president. His optimistic outlook may have helped in his recuperation from polio.

The president always hid his private thoughts behind a dazzling smile. One of his speechwriters noted that one could never tell what was going on in Roosevelt's "heavily forested interior." The president often relied on instinct and idealism in making decisions. Political theories held little value for him. His warm style and caring manner, expressed in his weekly "fireside chats," helped win support for many of his programs. Years after the depression, many Americans would remember Roosevelt almost as a beloved family member.

The Share-Our-Wealth program received a great deal of popular support. Some critics, however, suspected that Long harbored dreams of becoming a dictator. The popular senator threatened to challenge Roosevelt as a third-party candidate in the 1936 election. Both this threat and the Share-Our-Wealth program died when an assassin killed Long in 1935.

✔ **READING CHECK:** What criticisms were aimed at the New Deal?

The Second New Deal

The Democrats gained additional congressional seats in the 1934 elections. The victory, coupled with pressure from liberals, encouraged New Deal planners to initiate more public-works programs, a social-security plan, and wage and hour improvements for laborers. This series of programs eventually came to be called the Second New Deal. Although it continued to promote social relief and economic recovery, the Second New Deal increasingly emphasized long-term reform.

The Works Progress Administration. After the Civil Works Administration (CWA) ended in 1934, President Roosevelt created the **Works Progress Administration** (WPA). Led by Harry Hopkins, this program was designed to help Americans find work. Congress budgeted some $5 billion for the WPA's job-creation programs.

During the next eight years, the WPA employed some 8.5 million people. About 2 million were in the program at any given time. Workers engaged in a variety of tasks. Male blue-collar workers built or rebuilt a total of some 350 airports, more than 100,000 public buildings, some 78,000 bridges, and about 500,000 miles of roads. White-collar workers took on research projects and teaching jobs.

The WPA tried to help struggling young people between the ages of 16 and 25 by establishing the **National Youth Administration** (NYA), a "junior WPA." The NYA provided high-school and college-age Americans with part-time jobs that allowed them to stay in school. Within a year the NYA was providing aid to 500,000 people. Eleanor Roosevelt insisted that Mary McLeod Bethune, an energetic member of the Black Cabinet, be appointed director of the Division of Negro Affairs in the NYA.

Posters like this one (below right) encouraged Americans to support WPA programs, such as the project shown below.

USA
WORK
PROGRAM
WPA
WEAVING
Work Pays America!
PROSPERITY
WORKS PROGRESS ADMINISTRATION
THE GRANGER COLLECTION, NEW YORK

TEACH OBJECTIVE 2

LEVEL 1: Pair students and have each pair compile a list of major initiatives from the Second New Deal and write a paragraph explaining how those initiatives enabled President Roosevelt to win re-election easily in 1936. *(Pairs' lists should include the WPA, the NYA, the Social Security Act, the REA, and the Revenue Act of 1935. Students should explain that these initiatives enabled FDR to gain the support of a broad range of Americans, including African Americans, farmers, labor union members, many Republicans, and unemployed workers.)* Ask volunteers to read their paragraphs to the class.
Sheltered English, Cooperative Learning

LEVEL 2: Tell students to imagine that FDR has just been elected to a second term in office and that they are reporters covering his re-election. Have each student write a headline and a brief newspaper article recounting how the programs of the Second New Deal enabled Roosevelt to win re-election easily. *(See the Level 1 lesson for the correct programs and how those programs contributed to FDR's victory.)* Ask volunteers to read their headlines and articles to the class.

BIOGRAPHY

Mary McLeod Bethune

Mary McLeod Bethune was born in 1875 in Mayesville, South Carolina. Her parents were farmers who had once been slaves. The young girl's chances for an education seemed slim, since the Mayesville school was for whites only. With the aid of a Presbyterian mission school and a series of scholarships, however, she eventually attended the Moody Bible Institute in Chicago.

Bethune initially intended to become a missionary in Africa but soon found her mission to be educating African American children. She once said of her decision: "The drums of Africa still beat in my heart. They will not let me rest while there is a single Negro boy or girl without a chance to prove his [or her] worth." In 1904 she founded a primary school for African American girls in Florida. It eventually evolved into Bethune-Cookman College, a four-year coeducational institution with a mostly African American student body.

Bethune became involved with numerous African American groups, including the NAACP and the Urban League. In 1935 she helped unite all national organizations working on behalf of African American women into the National Council of Negro Women. Through her work with this association, she became close friends with Eleanor Roosevelt. Bethune fought hard, although not always successfully, to rid the NYA of discrimination. Although Bethune left government service after the NYA ended in 1944, she continued to promote civil rights and educational opportunities for young African Americans until her death in 1955.

Free Find: Mary McLeod Bethune
After reading about Mary McLeod Bethune on the Holt Researcher CD–ROM, design a memorial plaque that illustrates her achievements.

Social Security. Another important feature of the Second New Deal was the **Social Security Act**, which Congress passed in August 1935. The act contained three major provisions. First, it provided unemployment insurance to workers who lost their jobs. The funds for this insurance came from a payroll tax on businesses. Second, the act provided pensions to retired workers older than age 65. The money for these pensions came from two sources—a payroll tax on employers and a tax on employees' wages. Third, in a shared federal-state program, the act provided payments to people with disabilities, the elderly, and the wives and children of male workers who had died.

Other programs. In May 1935 Roosevelt created the Rural Electrification Administration (REA) as part of his program to help underprivileged Americans. The REA provided electricity to isolated rural areas. Congress also passed a law giving the government the right to regulate the interstate production, transmission, and sale of gas and electricity. This helped keep utility costs low.

Then and Now

Social Security

Referring to the Social Security Act, Frances Perkins recalled, "Nothing of the sort had ever come before the Congress of the United States." The act altered many Americans' ideas about the government's responsibility to ensure the welfare of citizens. Since its beginning in the 1930s, the program has expanded to cover children, people with disabilities, and many others. Social Security also manages numerous other welfare programs, including subsidized school lunches. Providing monthly pensions to retired people or their widows is the best-known Social Security program. Ida May Fuller of Ludlow, Vermont, was the first person to receive a monthly Social Security pension. Her first check, for $22.54, arrived January 31, 1940.

Over time, the monthly payments have risen along with the cost of living. At the same time, more people are covered by Social Security. Although many people fear that this situation would eventually force the Social Security program into bankruptcy, legislators have long been reluctant to alter the system. Finally, in the late 1990s Congress enacted several measures to reform Social Security and guard it for future generations.

Ida May Fuller holds her first Social Security check.

THEN AND NOW

Food Programs for People in Poverty. The Second New Deal introduced a plan to provide surplus food to people who were eligible for federal work relief. This early food-stamp plan allowed participants to buy orange-colored food stamps. For each dollar of orange stamps purchased, the buyer would be given 50-cents, worth of blue stamps. Orange stamps could be used to buy any kind of food, but blue stamps could be used only for surplus foods. Critics of the program noted that it helped only some people in need and that it required people to purchase the orange stamps in order to receive blue stamps. The program operated until World War II. The Food Stamp Act of 1964 initiated the program in use today. Under this program, financial assets and income determine participants' eligibility.

ACTIVITY: Have students conduct research on depression-era federal assistance programs that have survived in some form to the present day. Ask each student to write paragraphs about the history and goals of a few such programs.

LEVEL 3: Tell students to imagine that it is the day after the 1936 presidential election and that they are radio news analysts. Pair students and have each pair write a brief script for a radio talk show. Scripts should analyze how the programs of the Second New Deal led to FDR's easy re-election. *(See the Level 1 lesson for the correct programs and how those programs contributed to FDR's victory.)* Ask students to conduct their talk show-discussion for the class. **Cooperative Learning**

TEACH OBJECTIVE 3

LEVEL 1: Pair students and ask each pair to write a short paragraph summarizing Roosevelt's plan to prevent the Supreme Court from overturning his New Deal programs and explaining the criticism of his plan. *(Pairs' paragraphs should mention that FDR asked Congress to give him the power to appoint one new justice for each justice over 70 years old. Critics of the "court packing" plan believed that it would tamper with the balance of powers and that Roosevelt was trying to assume dictatorial powers.)* Ask volunteers to read their paragraphs to the class. **Sheltered English, Cooperative Learning**

CONSTITUTIONAL HERITAGE

FDR and the Court Packing Fight. Although Roosevelt's attempt to replace the older Supreme Court justices angered some Americans, others supported his action. Thomas F. Konop, dean of the Notre Dame Law School, said that the Court was "usurping the power of Congress and the President. It . . . has been destroying laws providing for a better life, more liberty and equality, social justice, and the pursuit of happiness of 130,000,000 people." In support of Roosevelt, one senator referred to the millions of people who were hungry and out of work: "They are offered the Constitution. But people can't eat the Constitution."

CRITICAL THINKING What did the senator mean when he said that "people can't eat the Constitution?"

ANSWER: Students might suggest that he meant that the Supreme Court was unduly concerned about the constitutionality of New Deal programs rather than those programs' effect on social welfare.

VISUAL RECORD ANSWER

Answers will vary. Some students might suggest that the number of bottles on the table indicates that the cartoonist was skeptical about the effectiveness of FDR's remedies.

INTERPRETING THE VISUAL RECORD

Dr. New Deal. Treating the United States like a sick patient, Franklin D. Roosevelt tried many cures to get the country healthy again. ***Do you think the cartoonist expected Roosevelt's remedies to work? Explain your answer.***

Roosevelt then targeted the rich. He declared that the existing tax laws had not done enough "to prevent an unjust concentration of wealth and economic power." Congress responded by passing the Revenue Act of 1935. Often referred to as the Wealth Tax Act, the bill sharply raised taxes for the nation's richest people.

The election of 1936. In June 1936 the Democrats nominated Roosevelt for a second term. Labor unions, farmers, those on relief, and even many Republicans also endorsed him. For the first time since Reconstruction, most African Americans in the North supported the Democrats. The Republicans nominated the capable but unexciting governor of Kansas, Alfred M. Landon.

President Roosevelt pledged to continue the New Deal. He won a clear victory, receiving some 28 million popular votes to Landon's 17 million. Roosevelt carried every state but Maine and Vermont—the most lopsided victory in more than a century. The Democrats increased their majorities in both houses of Congress.

✔ **READING CHECK:** How did the Second New Deal enable President Roosevelt to win re-election easily in 1936?

Roosevelt and the Supreme Court

Fresh from his victory, President Roosevelt moved to "reform" the Supreme Court. Roosevelt was angered that the Court had declared several New Deal measures unconstitutional. He labeled the justices "Nine Old Men"—six were 70 or older. He accused them of being stuck in the "horse and buggy" days in their thinking.

In February 1937 Roosevelt asked Congress to grant him the power to appoint one new justice for each of those 70 or older, up to six new justices. Roosevelt's proposal triggered a storm of protests across the nation. Critics—Democrats as well as Republicans—charged that this "court packing" tampered with the balance of powers. Dorothy Thompson, a popular political columnist, considered Roosevelt's scheme a move toward dictatorship.

> "If the American people accept this last audacity [boldness] of the President without letting out a yell to high heaven, they have ceased to be jealous of their liberties and are ripe for ruin. This is the beginning of a pure personal government."

In this cartoon President Roosevelt is shown as a ventriloquist whose dummy refuses to cooperate.

THE GRANGER COLLECTION, NEW YORK

Congress rejected Roosevelt's request. The Supreme Court, however, soon upheld the Social Security Act and the National Labor Relations Act. Some Americans concluded that the justices had become more tolerant of New Deal programs in an attempt to prevent a drastic reform of the Court. During the next four years, several justices died or retired. They were replaced by Roosevelt appointees. By 1945 eight of the nine justices were Roosevelt appointees.

✔ **READING CHECK:** How did Roosevelt try to prevent the Supreme Court from overturning his programs?

LEVELS 2 AND 3: Tell students to imagine that it is February 1937 and that they have just heard about FDR's court packing plan. Have each student write a short letter to a newspaper either supporting or opposing Roosevelt's plan. Tell students to describe the provisions of Roosevelt's plan in their letters and to base their support or opposition on the possible results of the plan. *(See the Level 1 lesson for the provisions of the court packing plan and reasons why people opposed it.)* Have volunteers read their letters to the class.

TEACH OBJECTIVE 4

LEVEL 1: Tell students to imagine that they are artists hired by the WPA to create advertisements for New Deal programs. Pair students and have each pair create three billboards advertising programs of the Second New Deal that benefited labor and agriculture. *(Students' billboards should mention the Wagner-Connery Act, which guaranteed labor's right to organize and bargain collectively; the FSA, which provided low-interest, long-term loans to help tenant farmers and sharecroppers buy land and also established camps providing shelter and medical care for migrant farmworkers; and the AAA of 1938, which authorized subsidies to farmers who practiced soil conservation and crop reduction.)* Display pairs' billboards around the classroom.

Sheltered English, Cooperative Learning

Selected New Deal Programs

Year	First New Deal	Provisions
1933	Emergency Banking Act	Gave administration the right to regulate banks
1933	Farm Credit Administration (FCA)	Refinanced farm mortgages at lower interest and for longer terms
1933	Economy Act	Proposed to balance the budget through savings measures
1933	Civilian Conservation Corps (CCC)	Employed young men on public-works projects
1933	Federal Emergency Relief Administration (FERA)	Provided relief to needy people
1933	Agricultural Adjustment Administration (AAA)	Paid farmers to reduce crops; funded by a tax on food processers; later declared unconstitutional
1933	Tennessee Valley Authority (TVA)	Constructed dams and power plants to improve social and economic welfare in the region
1933	Home Owners Loan Corporation (HOLC)	Loaned money to home owners to refinance mortgages
1933	Emergency Banking Act of 1933	Created FDIC and authorized branch banking
1933	Federal Deposit Insurance Corporation (FDIC)	Initially insured individual bank deposits under $2,500
1933	National Industrial Recovery Act (NIRA)	Established NRA; later declared unconstitutional
1933	National Recovery Administration (NRA)	Regulated industry through fair-trade codes for businesses
1933	Public Works Administration (PWA)	Constructed roads, public buildings, and other projects designed to increase employment and business activity
1933	Civil Works Administration (CWA)	Employed jobless persons to work on federal, state, and local projects
1934	Securities and Exchange Commission (SEC)	Regulated securities market
1934	Federal Housing Administration (FHA)	Insured bank loans for building and repairing homes

Year	Second New Deal	Provisions
1935	Works Progress Administration (WPA)	Employed people to do artistic, public-works, and research projects
1935	Soil Conservation Service (SCS)	Promoted control and prevention of soil erosion
1935	Rural Electrification Administration (REA)	Provided electricity to rural areas lacking public utilities
1935	National Youth Administration (NYA)	Provided job training and work for people age 16–25; provided part-time jobs for needy students
1935	National Labor Relations Act (Wagner-Connery Act)	Recognized rights of labor to organize and bargain collectively; regulated labor practices
1935	Social Security Act	Provided unemployment benefits, pensions for the elderly, and survivor's insurance
1935	Revenue Act of 1935 (Wealth Tax Act)	Increased taxes on the wealthy
1937	Farm Security Administration (FSA)	Provided loans to help tenant farmers buy land
1938	Agricultural Adjustment Act of 1938 (AAA)	Increased government regulation of crop production and increased payments to farmers
1938	Revenue Act of 1938	Reduced taxes on large corporations and increased taxes on smaller businesses
1938	Fair Labor Standards Act (Wages and Hours Law)	Established minimum wage of 40 cents per hour and maximum workweek of 40 hours for businesses in interstate commerce

Source: *Encyclopedia of American History*

Learning from Charts Franklin Roosevelt proposed a wide number of programs to aid in the nation's recovery after he assumed office in 1933. These programs became the first New Deal. Two years later he outlined a broader program of social reform in the Second New Deal.

? Building Chart Skills Which New Deal programs were aimed primarily at helping farmers?

ECONOMIC DEVELOPMENT

Resettlement and Greenbelt Towns. One New Deal program involved resettling poor families in new communities. The government would then build them small homes, give them farm equipment, and train them in farming techniques. The families would repay the government with low-interest mortgages. Rexford Tugwell, a member of FDR's Brain Trust, administered the program. He came under harsh criticism when he failed to keep costs in check. One of Tugwell's plans that was only partially realized was the creation of "greenbelt towns." These were to be planned communities outside of cities, where families would live with the best features of both urban and rural environments. Only a few cities ever established greenbelt towns, and so few people were resettled under the program that it had little impact on the economy.

CRITICAL THINKING How might the creation of greenbelt towns be considered a utopian ideal?

ANSWER: Students might suggest that greenbelt towns seemed to promise a perfect combination of urban and rural living.

CHART ANSWER

AAA, FCA, SCS, FSA, AAA (1938)

LEVELS 2 AND 3: Tell students to imagine that they are historians assessing the effects of the Second New Deal on labor and agriculture. Have each student write a short essay examining how the programs of the Second New Deal affected workers and farmers. *(See the Level 1 lesson for the correct programs and their provisions.)* Ask volunteers to read their essays to the class.

TEACH OBJECTIVE 5

LEVEL 1: Organize students into triads. Have each triad create a cause-and-effect chart explaining the Roosevelt recession and why it occurred. *(Students might cite that an economic recession occurred in response to FDR's reductions on relief programs and public-works projects in response to criticism of excessive spending. Private industry could not employ those dropped from government rolls and the economy took a downturn as factories closed and unemployment rose. In response to the recession, FDR and Congress increased government spending, unemployment declined, and production increased.)* Ask volunteers to present their charts to the class.
Sheltered English, Cooperative Learning

LEVELS 2 AND 3: Pair students and have each pair complete the chart activity from the Level 1 lesson. Then have each pair prepare a brief lecture on the Roosevelt recession, why it occurred, and its effects. *(See the Level 1 lesson for the correct causes and effects.)* Ask volunteers to present their charts and deliver their lectures to the class. **Cooperative Learning**

THAT'S INTERESTING!

Observers remember great excitement among industrial workers in response to the founding of the CIO. The *CIO News* editor wrote, "The workers were waiting for the CIO, pounding on its doors long before the CIO was ready for them." An organizer recalled, "It is difficult to impart on ordinary paper the magic that surrounded the letters *C-I-O* in 1937." A song that soon became popular explained some of the CIO's popularity:

"A union for the masses
To include every craft,
Better wages for each worker,
In CIO there is no class."

VISUAL RECORD ANSWER

Students might suggest that by occupying the plant, the strikers prevented the company from resuming production with replacement workers.

SECTION 2 REVIEW ANSWERS

Define and Identify

For significance, see the following pages:

- Francis E. Townsend, p. 447
- Charles E. Coughlin, p. 447
- Huey Long, p. 447
- Share-Our-Wealth, p. 447
- Works Progress Administration, p. 448
- National Youth Administration, p. 448
- Mary McLeod Bethune, p. 448
- Social Security Act, p. 449
- Wagner-Connery Act, p. 452

Effects of the Second New Deal

Congress assisted the president by passing legislation that would be less likely to be struck down by the courts. In May 1935 the Supreme Court had ruled that the provisions of the National Industrial Recovery Act (NIRA) that protected the rights of labor unions were unconstitutional. Several weeks later, Congress passed the National Labor Relations Act, or **Wagner-Connery Act**. The act guaranteed labor's right to organize unions and to bargain collectively for better wages and working conditions.

INTERPRETING THE VISUAL RECORD

Sit-down strike. These striking autoworkers, using car seats as couches, have settled in for a long fight. The medal shown was given to workers who took part in the strike against General Motors. ***How are these workers affecting their employer?***

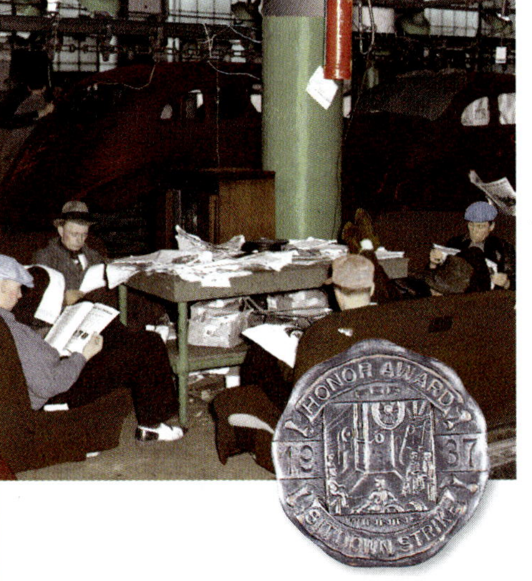

Labor. The American Federation of Labor (AFL) continued its efforts to organize skilled workers. However, the AFL did not move fast enough to please John L. Lewis, the leader of the United Mine Workers union. In 1935 Lewis and several other labor leaders organized what became the **Congress of Industrial Organizations** (CIO). The CIO tried to unite workers in various industries. The new CIO unions included all workers, skilled and unskilled, in a given industry.

The organizing efforts of both the AFL and the CIO resulted in a wave of strikes. One of the most bitter strikes was waged against General Motors (GM) in the winter of 1936–37. Efforts by the United Automobile Workers (UAW) to unionize GM factories faced strong GM opposition. Meanwhile, GM workers were growing increasingly frustrated with factory conditions. On December 31, 1936, this frustration led to a **sit-down strike**. Instead of leaving the automobile plants, workers occupied the factories. They vowed to remain until management met their demands. Finally, after six weeks, General Motors gave in and granted the UAW the right to organize GM workers. Within eight months, the total UAW membership had grown to some 400,000. Owing in part to the Wagner-Connery Act, union membership nationwide shot up from about 4 million in 1936 to some 9 million in 1939.

Farmers. The Second New Deal also brought relief to farmers. After the Supreme Court struck down the Agricultural Adjustment Act in January 1936, Congress created another program to replace it. Like the AAA, the new program sought to keep the prices of agricultural goods high by cutting crop production. To avoid opposition from the Supreme Court, however, Congress linked this crop reduction to a soil conservation plan—a legitimate governmental activity.

The Second New Deal also brought aid to migrant farmworkers, sharecroppers, and tenant farmers. In 1937 Congress created the Farm Security Administration (FSA). It provided low-interest, long-term loans to help tenant farmers and sharecroppers buy land. The FSA also established camps where migrant farmworkers could seek shelter and medical care.

The Roosevelt administration claimed that the soil conservation program did not do enough to promote crop reduction. Congress responded by passing a second Agricultural Adjustment Act in 1938. The law authorized payments to farmers who withdrew land from production and practiced conservation. It also authorized the Department of Agriculture to limit the amount of specific crops that could be brought to market each year. When harvests surpassed these limits, the government

REVIEW

Have students complete the **Section 2 Review** on p. 453.

ASSESS

Have students complete **Daily Quiz 15.2.** As **Alternative Assessment**, you may want to use the radio script or the newspaper article in this section's lessons.

RETEACH

Have students complete **Main Idea Activity for Reteaching and Sheltered English 15.2**. Organize students into small groups. Assign each group a subsection of Section 2. Have each group create a poster summarizing the major points in its subsection. Have volunteers present their posters to the class. Ask the class to supply any information that might be missing from each poster. **Sheltered English, Cooperative Learning**

EXTEND

Have students conduct research on New Deal programs that employed young people and current government programs that employ young people. Students might examine the scale and size of the employment programs or the types of work available. Have each student write an essay comparing a New Deal program and a current program. **Block Scheduling**

stored the surpluses until prices rose. Farmers participating in the program could get government loans based on the value of their stored crops.

✔ **READING CHECK:** How did the Second New Deal benefit labor and agriculture?

This 1936 photograph by Carl Mydans shows the damage caused by soil erosion in Kentucky.

Roosevelt's Recession

In 1936 President Roosevelt began cutting back on New Deal relief and public-works programs. He was reacting to criticism of excessive government spending. Private industry, however, was not yet strong enough to give jobs to those dropped from government rolls because of the cutbacks. The economy soon plunged downward. By the fall of 1937, factories were closing, and unemployment was rising. Republicans called this economic downturn "Roosevelt's recession."

Roosevelt and Congress again increased government lending and spending. By the fall of 1938, unemployment had declined. Industrial production had increased. As the 1938 midterm elections drew near, Roosevelt decided to re-energize the New Deal by opposing conservative Democrats in Congress who did not support the Second New Deal.

Just as his court-packing scheme had backfired, however, so too did his attempt to clean out the Democratic Party. All but one member of Congress opposed by Roosevelt won re-election. Moreover, voters elected additional Democratic critics of New Deal programs. The Republicans gained seven seats in the Senate and 75 in the House. Although the Democrats still maintained majorities in both houses of Congress, their margins were much narrower. Faced with increasing criticism from all sides, Roosevelt decided not to propose any new reforms in 1939.

✔ **READING CHECK:** What was Roosevelt's recession, and what effect did it have?

SECTION 2 REVIEW

Define and explain the significance of the following terms:
Share-Our-Wealth
Works Progress Administration
National Youth Administration
Social Security Act
Wagner-Connery Act
Congress of Industrial Organizations
sit-down strike

Identify and explain the significance of the following individuals:
Francis E. Townsend
Charles E. Coughlin
Huey Long
Mary McLeod Bethune

1. **Using Graphic Organizers** Copy the graphic organizer below. Use it to explain how President Roosevelt won re-election in 1936.

Critics of Roosevelt → Roosevelt's Response → Effect on 1936 Election

2. **Identifying Values** How did criticisms of the New Deal reveal the different views that various leaders held about government?
3. **Taking a Stand** Would you have supported President Roosevelt's plan to add up to six new members to the Supreme Court? Explain your answer.
4. **Evaluating** How did the Wagner-Connery Act benefit labor? How did other Second New Deal programs benefit agriculture?

Critical Thinking

5. How did the Second New Deal differ from the first New Deal?
Consider:
- the major programs of the first New Deal
- the major programs of the Second New Deal
- the effect of the Roosevelt recession

- Congress of Industrial Organizations, p. 452
- sit-down strike, p. 452

1. critics—argued that more government programs were needed to eliminate unemployment and stimulate the economy; Roosevelt's response—initiated more public works and employment programs, signed the Social Security Act, regulated utility companies, and imposed more taxes upon the wealthy; effect—African Americans in the North, farmers, and workers voted for him

2. Conservatives thought that the New Deal intervened too much in business; liberals believed that more government intervention was necessary.

3. Answers will vary. Students might argue that Roosevelt was violating the Constitution by trying to replace justices before they chose to retire. Others might argue that the depression required emergency action by the government.

4. allowed unions to strike for better wages and working conditions; kept food prices high and provided low-interest loans to tenant farmers and sharecroppers

5. Answers will vary. Students might answer that although both New Deals had similar programs, the Second New Deal's programs were more acceptable to the Supreme Court and more successful initially. The Roosevelt recession showed that these programs were necessary.

SECTION 3

After completing Section 3, students should be able to:

OBJECTIVE 1 *Discuss the effects of the Dust Bowl.*

OBJECTIVE 2 *Explain how New Deal agencies used photography to promote their goals.*

OBJECTIVE 3 *Describe how the New Deal improved the lives of ordinary Americans.*

LET'S GET STARTED!

As students enter the classroom, play Selection 21, "Talkin' Dust Bowl," from the **American Music Audio CD Program**. Have students respond to the song in writing. Ask volunteers to share their responses. Tell students that in Section 3 they will learn how the Dust Bowl affected Americans who lived on the Great Plains.

SECTION 3 RESOURCES

PRINT

- Guided Reading Strategy 15.3
- American History Outline Map 18: The Dust Bowl
- Section 3 Review, p. 458
- Daily Quiz 15.3

MULTIMEDIA

- One-Stop Planner, Lesson 15.3
- American Music Selection 21: "Talkin' Dust Bowl"
- Holt Researcher: American History CD–ROM
- HRW Web site

SHELTERED ENGLISH

- Main Idea Activity for Reteaching and Sheltered English 15.3

✔ READING TO UNDERSTAND

To help students master the section objectives, have them answer the **READING CHECKS** and complete **Guided Reading Strategy 15.3** as they read the section.

Multimedia Resources

American Music Selection 21: "Talkin' Dust Bowl"

SECTION 3

Life in the New Deal Era

OBJECTIVES

Read to understand:

1. what the effects of the Dust Bowl were
2. how New Deal agencies used photography to promote their goals
3. how the New Deal improved the lives of ordinary Americans

KEY TERMS

Dust Bowl
Migrant Mother

KEY PEOPLE

Roy E. Stryker
Walker Evans
Gordon Parks
Margaret Bourke-White
Dorothea Lange

"NO JOBS in California. If YOU are looking for work—KEEP OUT!"
—Billboard message

This billboard message appeared on Route 66 just outside Tulsa, Oklahoma, toward the end of the 1930s. The message was clear. The job market for migrant workers on the West Coast was full. The sign was directed at the thousands of migrant farmers who traveled west to California in the mid-1930s. Driven off their land by the forces of nature, they sought a better life elsewhere.

This sign warned unemployed Americans to keep moving.

The Dust Bowl and Migration

The mass migration to California was spurred by a natural disaster. In the mid-1930s a severe drought struck the Great Plains. Winds picked up the topsoil that had loosened and dried, turning a 50-million-acre region into a wasteland.

The Dust Bowl. Throughout the **Dust Bowl**, as the affected region came to be called, clouds of dust darkened the skies at noon and buried fences and farm machinery. Dust crept into houses through tiny cracks. Ships reported great dust clouds hundreds of miles out to sea. One Texas farmer recalled the drought's effects.

> "If the wind blew one way, here came the dark dust from Oklahoma. Another way and it was the gray dust from Kansas. Still another way, the brown dust from Colorado and New Mexico. Little farms were buried. And the towns were blackened."

The devastation in the Dust Bowl is captured in this photograph of a farmer and his children outside their home, which is nearly buried in sand.

To prevent similar natural disasters from occurring in the future, the Department of Agriculture started extensive programs in soil-erosion control. The most dramatic was the planting of some 217 million trees by workers from the Civilian Conservation Corps (CCC). These trees created a windbreak that stretched through the Great Plains from Texas to Canada.

By 1939 the amount of dried-out farmland had decreased dramatically. However, many Dust Bowl farmers had already lost their land. They packed their few belongings into battered old cars or trucks and headed west on Route 66. These migrants saw California and other parts of the West Coast as a Promised Land where they could find work harvesting crops. Since many came from Oklahoma, they were nicknamed "Okies." Once they reached the West Coast they found themselves in fierce competition with other farm laborers looking for work.

TEACH OBJECTIVE 1

LEVEL 1: Tell students that the Dust Bowl was the result of a severe drought that struck the Great Plains. Winds carried away the region's dry and loose topsoil. Pair students and ask each pair to create a cartoon depicting the effects of the Dust Bowl. *(Pairs' cartoons should show that many farmers lost their land, that Dust Bowl farmers migrated west to find work harvesting crops, and that migrants to the West Coast faced stiff competition for jobs.)* Ask volunteers to present their cartoons to the class.
Sheltered English, Cooperative Learning

LEVEL 2: Tell students to imagine that they left their homes during the Dust Bowl to migrate west to California. Ask each student to write a poem about the causes of the Dust Bowl and its effects on farmers' lives. *(See the Level 1 lesson for the correct causes and effects.)* Ask volunteers to recite their poems to the class.

LEVEL 3: Tell students to imagine that they have left their homes during the Dust Bowl and migrated west to California. Have each student write a series of short diary entries about the causes of the Dust Bowl and its effect on his or her life and the lives of other farmers. *(See the Level 1 lesson for the correct causes and effects.)* In their entries, students should reflect on the hardships that they have encountered. Ask volunteers to read their entries to the class.

AMERICAN ARTS

Woody Guthrie and American Folk Music

The popularity of American folk music experienced a revival during the 1930s. Perhaps the most popular folksinger of the era was Woody Guthrie, one of many Americans displaced by the storms of the Dust Bowl. Although he had no formal training in music, he wrote dozens of songs that touched millions of listeners. "I don't know nothing about music. Never could read or write it," Guthrie admitted. Guthrie described the experiences of common people in his music, mostly through ballads. Among his numerous songs was the popular "Talking Dust Bowl."

> "Back in nineteen twenty-seven
> I had a little farm and I called that heaven,
> Well, the price was up and the rain came down
> And I hauled my crops all in to town. . . .
> Rain quit and the wind got high,
> And a black old dust storm filled the sky,
> And I swapped my farm for a Ford machine
> And I poured it full of this gasoline. . . .
> We got out to the West Coast broke,
> So dad gum hungry I thought I'd croak,
> And I bummed up a spud or two,
> And my wife fixed up a 'tater stew."

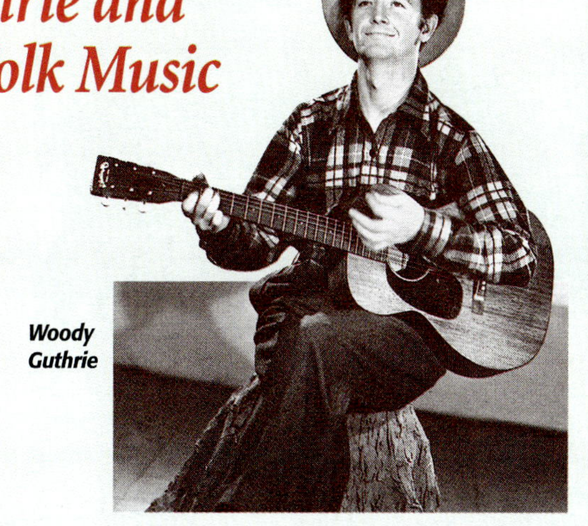

Woody Guthrie

The federal government eventually hired Guthrie to write songs that promoted projects designed to help rural Americans. While touring a federal dam project, he wrote 26 songs in just 26 days. Guthrie's lyrics praised the federal projects, but his songs reflected the sadness of the era. "It's always we ramble, that river and I," he wrote. "Along your green valley I'll work till I die."

Understanding the Arts

1. According to Guthrie's song, how did life change after the Dust Bowl storms?
2. Why might Guthrie's style of music have been popular?

Competition for migrant work. Even before the Dust Bowl refugees started arriving, Mexican Americans had a hard time finding work in the West. Like African Americans, Mexican Americans often found themselves the victims of discrimination in many New Deal programs.

Mexican Americans also faced increased job competition from Filipino laborers. During the 1920s California's Filipino population had grown to more than 30,000. Like Mexican American migrants, most Filipinos worked in agriculture. When the depression hit, both groups faced tough economic times. The Filipino workers, however, fought declining wages by organizing. Throughout the early 1930s the Filipino Labor Union launched a series of strikes to protest wage reductions. In 1936 the American Federation of Labor sponsored the Field Workers Union. The union was a combined organization for Mexican American and Filipino laborers.

internet connect

TOPIC: The Dust Bowl
GO TO: go.hrw.com
KEYWORD: SE1 Dust

Have students access the Internet through the HRW Web site to conduct research on the causes of the Dust Bowl. Ask each student to create a chart summarizing the environmental and economic conditions that forced thousands of people to leave their homes and migrate west.

THAT'S INTERESTING!

The state of California enacted a law making it illegal to bring anyone who was unemployed into the state. One California resident, Fred F. Edwards, was convicted under this law for bringing his unemployed brother-in-law from Texas into the state. The U.S. Supreme Court eventually heard Edwards's case and ruled that California's law was unconstitutional.

AMERICAN ARTS ANSWERS

1. Life was like heaven before the storms. After the storms, people were broke and hungry.
2. Guthrie's songs were simple and focused on problems that were common to millions of people affected by the depression and the Dust Bowl.

TEACH OBJECTIVE 2

LEVEL 1: Ask students why photographs might be a powerful way to convey ideas. *(Students might suggest that photographs provide an objective record of an event or that images of people carry an emotional weight that verbal descriptions might lack.)* Pair students and ask each pair to compile a list of ways that New Deal agencies used photography to promote their goals. *(Pairs' lists should mention that New Deal agencies hoped that opponents of relief programs would change their minds if they saw photographs of suffering Americans, that agencies used photographs in government pamphlets, and that photos were published in magazines to publicize the work of federal agencies.)* Ask volunteers to present their lists to the class.
Sheltered English, Cooperative Learning

LEVELS 2 AND 3: Tell students to imagine that they are advisers to President Roosevelt. Ask each student to write a brief memo to FDR persuading him to approve the use of photography to promote the New Deal's goals. In their memos, students should suggest how New Deal agencies might want to use photography. *(See the Level 1 lesson for the correct uses.)* Ask volunteers to read their memos to the class.

HISTORY MAKERS SPEAK

James Agee in *Let Us Now Praise Famous Men*

Sharecropping in Alabama. In 1936 journalist James Agee and photographer Walker Evans spent eight weeks with three families who were sharecroppers in rural Alabama. Agee and Evans produced a book-length record of their experiences, *Let Us Now Praise Famous Men.* Most of these impoverished farmers received little help from New Deal programs. Agee wrote, "WPA work is available to very few tenants: they are, technically, employed, and thus have no right to it: and if by chance they manage to get it, landlords are more likely than not to intervene. They feel it spoils a tenant to be paid wages, even for a little while. A tenant who so much as tries to get such work is under disapproval."

CRITICAL THINKING Why might owners feel that tenants would be spoiled by wages?

ANSWER: Students might suggest that landlords feared that tenants might abandon sharecropping in favor of wage labor, which would provide a guaranteed income.

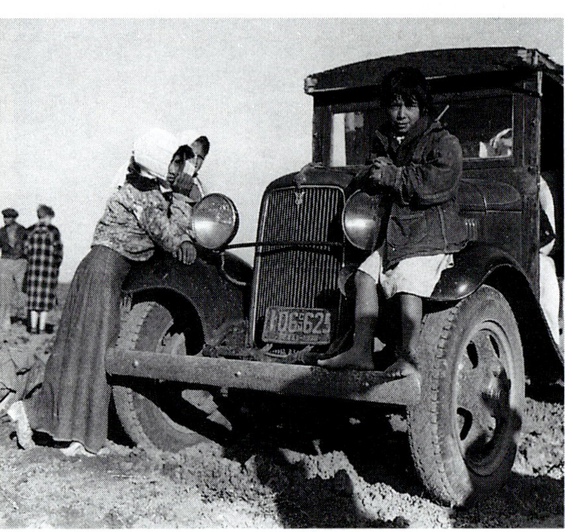

These migrant workers are waiting to start their day picking carrots in Santa Maria, Texas.

The unions were able to slow the fall of wages. Yet, with the arrival of additional migrants from the Dust Bowl, competition for jobs increased. Thus, life for all migrants remained difficult.

✔ **READING CHECK:** What were the effects of the Dust Bowl?

Picturing Life in the Depression

The grim experiences of migrants and others in rural areas of the United States provided powerful subject matter for documentary filmmakers and photographers. These artists created a memorable visual record of the New Deal Era. Their images of the slumped shoulders of unemployed men, the staring faces of hungry children, and the worried expressions of exhausted women convey the human suffering of the era.

Most of these photographers were hired by the federal government. President Roosevelt believed that opponents of federal relief programs might change their minds if they could see the frightful living conditions of city-dwellers and migrant farmworkers. With Roosevelt's encouragement, numerous federal agencies and departments—including the Department of the Interior, the Works Progress Administration (WPA), the Department of Agriculture, and the Farm Security Administration (FSA)—hired photographers to travel across the country and document the lives of ordinary Americans.

No agency used photography more effectively than the FSA, whose staff gathered more than 250,000 images of American life during the depression. Roy E. Stryker, head of the FSA historical section, assembled a team of renowned photographers that included Walker Evans, who depicted life among sharecroppers in rural Alabama. Other photographers included African American Gordon Parks, who later became a filmmaker; international photojournalist Margaret Bourke-White; and Dorothea Lange, probably the best known of the FSA photographers.

HOLT RESEARCHER *Read More About It*

Free Find:
Dorothea Lange
After reading about Dorothea Lange on the **Holt Researcher** CD–ROM, imagine that you are a photographer. Choose a topic for a photographic project and decide what photographs you would take. Write captions that explain the photographs.

Dorothea Lange

Dorothea Lange was one of the most talented photographers of the depression era. Born in 1895 in Hoboken, New Jersey, she decided in her late teens to become a photographer. After studying the craft for several years, she set out to tour the world and record her impressions. Lange was out of money by the time she reached San Francisco, however. She stayed there and opened a portrait studio.

When the depression struck, Lange began taking pictures of the homeless men wandering the streets of San Francisco. Soon the federal government hired her to photograph migrant farmworkers in California. Lange often traveled for weeks at a time, working up to 14 hours a day. Her photographs reveal the migrants' poverty and suffering as well as their great dignity. Lange's most famous photograph, ***Migrant Mother***, is considered a masterpiece. It shows an exhausted single mother whose children survived by eating vegetables they scavenged from California fields. When it

TEACH OBJECTIVE 3

ALL LEVELS: Tell students that the idea that the U.S. government can and should help improve the lives of ordinary Americans originated, in large part, with the New Deal. To help students understand how the New Deal improved the lives of ordinary Americans, copy the graphic organizer at right on the chalkboard, omitting the italicized answers. Have each student complete the organizer. Ask volunteers to share their answers with the class. **Sheltered English**

▶**ASSIGNMENT** *Tell students to imagine that it is 1934 and that they live in a rural area. Their homes do not have electricity or indoor plumbing. Ask each student to write a diary entry describing a typical day in his or her life. Students might include information on when they wake up, and how they get ready for school, prepare dinner, and study.*

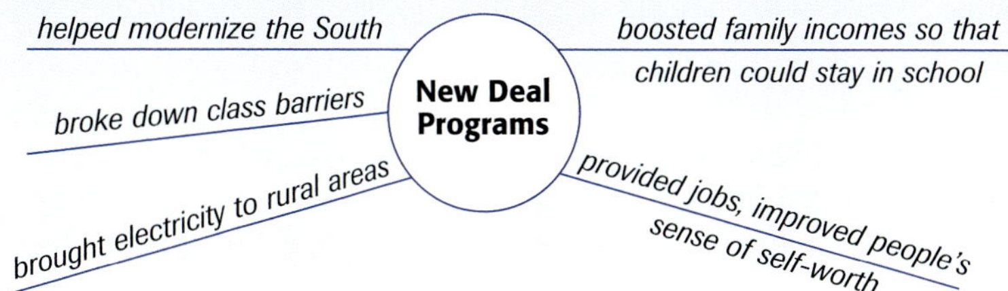

appeared in 1936, *Migrant Mother* inspired Californians to defy the state's powerful growers' associations and insist on decent, government-sponsored housing for seasonal harvesters.

During World War II, Lange continued her documentary work by taking photographs of the many Japanese Americans in California relocation camps. She later produced photo essays for *Life* magazine and traveled the world taking pictures. By the time of her death in 1965, Lange ranked as one of the world's foremost photographers.

Other FSA photographs helped achieve Roosevelt's goal of gaining support for government programs. From 1936 to 1941, FSA photographs were widely published in government pamphlets and in *Time, Life,* and other magazines. The photographs strengthened congressional and public support for federal relief.

✔ **READING CHECK:** How did New Deal agencies use photography to promote their goals?

INTERPRETING THE VISUAL RECORD

Migrant Mother. Photographs like this one by Dorothea Lange capture the suffering of rural Americans. ***What emotions do you think this picture captures?***

Relief for Ordinary Americans

By the late 1930s many families had begun to feel some relief from the depression. Few American families were untouched by the New Deal reforms. This affected many people's views of the role that government should play in providing for people's personal welfare. Many New Deal programs did more than provide additional income. By supplying jobs, the programs improved many Americans' sense of self-worth. Government administrator Louise Armstrong recalled that most people who came to her office preferred jobs to handouts. "I don't want charity," one person told her. "I want work—any kind of work."

Throughout the New Deal, President Roosevelt stressed the importance of providing work that gave meaning to people's lives. "Happiness lies not in the mere possession of money," he once said. "It lies in the joy of achievement, in the thrill of creative effort." This thrill was exemplified in the pride many people took in their government-funded jobs. Some programs also helped break down class barriers. They lifted people's spirits by emphasizing their equality. Said one veteran of the CCC, "They sure made a man out of ya, because you learned that everybody here was equal. There was nobody better than another in the CCC's."

Source: *Historical Statistics of the United States*

Learning from Graphs During the period from the mid-1920s to the mid-1930s, unemployment rose from some of the lowest levels to the highest unemployment rate in U.S. history.

? Building Graph Skills By how much did the unemployment rate change from its lowest to highest point between 1925 and 1939?

THAT'S INTERESTING!

During the Great Depression, thousands of people wrote to Eleanor Roosevelt, telling her of their hardships and suggesting ways that she or the president could help. One pregnant housewife in Troy, New York, begged Mrs. Roosevelt for a small loan: "*Please* Mrs. Roosevelt, I do not want charity, only a chance from someone who will trust me until we can get enough to repay the amount spent for the things I need. As a proof that I am really sincere, I am sending you two of my dearest possessions to keep as security, a ring my husband gave me before we were married, and a ring my mother used to wear."

VISUAL RECORD ANSWER

Answers will vary. Students might suggest despair and apprehension.

GRAPH ANSWER

by 24 percent

VISUAL RECORD ANSWER

(for p. 458)

Students might point out that the poster advertised domestic employment.

REVIEW

Have students complete the **Section 3 Review** on p. 458.

ASSESS

Have students complete **Daily Quiz 15.3.** As **Alternative Assessment**, you may want to use the poem or the cartoon in this section's lessons.

RETEACH

Have students complete **Main Idea Activity for Reteaching and Sheltered English 15.3.** Organize students into small groups. Have each group write a brief summary of the section incorporating all the key terms and key people listed at the beginning of the section. Have volunteers read their summaries to the class. Ask the class to supply any important information or themes that might be missing from each summary. **Sheltered English, Cooperative Learning**

EXTEND

Ask students to conduct research on one of the Farm Security Administration photographers mentioned in the section. Tell each student to write a short biographical capsule for his or her subject, compile examples of the photographer's most famous or compelling images, and explain each image's significance. Have each student present his or her findings to the class in an oral presentation. **Block Scheduling**

SECTION 3 REVIEW ANSWERS

Define and Identify

For significance, see the following pages:

- Dust Bowl, p. 454
- Roy E. Stryker, p. 456
- Walker Evans, p. 456
- Gordon Parks, p. 456
- Margaret Bourke-White, p. 456
- Dorothea Lange, p. 456
- *Migrant Mother*, p. 456

1. causes—drought in the Great Plains made it impossible to grow crops on the dry, dusty land; migration—farmers moved to the Southwest hoping to find work on farms; effects—so many people looked for work in the Southwest that there was fierce competition among farmworkers, and many owners lowered wages

2. Entries will vary. Students should mention fierce competition for jobs.

3. They represented the lives of people who were desperately trying to survive the depression. They showed their suffering and dignity. The photographs persuaded people to take action to end some practices that contributed to hunger and suffering.

4. The programs provided money and food but also allowed people to work for these benefits, thus giving the recipients a sense of meaning and accomplishment.

5. Answers will vary. Students might suggest that the photograph might have forced viewers to acknowledge the desperate situation of migrant families struggling to feed their children.

THE GRANGER COLLECTION, NEW YORK

INTERPRETING THE VISUAL RECORD

Jobs. With the economy struggling, the government stepped in to help Americans find work. ***What types of jobs do you think this poster was advertising?***

Programs sponsored by the National Youth Administration (NYA) helped boost family incomes so that children could stay in school rather than quit to try to find work. Helen Farmer recalled working in an NYA program as a teenager.

> **"I lugged . . . drafts and reams of paper home, night after night. . . . Sometimes I typed all night. . . . This was a good program. It got necessary work done. It gave teenagers a chance to work for pay. . . . It gave my mother relief from my necessary demands for money."**

Few New Deal programs had a greater long-term effect on people's lives than the efforts made to provide electricity to rural areas. Millions of American homes did not have electricity or indoor plumbing in the early 1930s. In 1935 only about 11 percent of American farms had electricity. Within a few years nearly 90 percent did. Improvements in electricity and plumbing made life easier and greatly improved people's health by providing better sanitation and safer water supplies. Furthermore, the availability of electricity and other government services brought modern practices and industry to many parts of the country. The South changed the most. Despite some previous efforts to increase industrialization in the region, the South's economy overall had changed little since Reconstruction. During the New Deal Era the region finally began to diversify its economy and rely less on traditional cash crops like cotton. One southern historian has said, "Electrification must be considered one of the most significant stimulants for modernization of the rural South."

✔ **READING CHECK:** How did the New Deal improve the lives of ordinary Americans?

SECTION 3 REVIEW

Define and explain the significance of the following terms:
Dust Bowl
Migrant Mother

Identify and explain the significance of the following individuals:
Roy E. Stryker
Walker Evans
Gordon Parks
Margaret Bourke-White
Dorothea Lange

1. **Using Graphic Organizers** Copy the following graphic organizer. Use it to explain why farmers migrated from the Dust Bowl region and what effects this migration had.

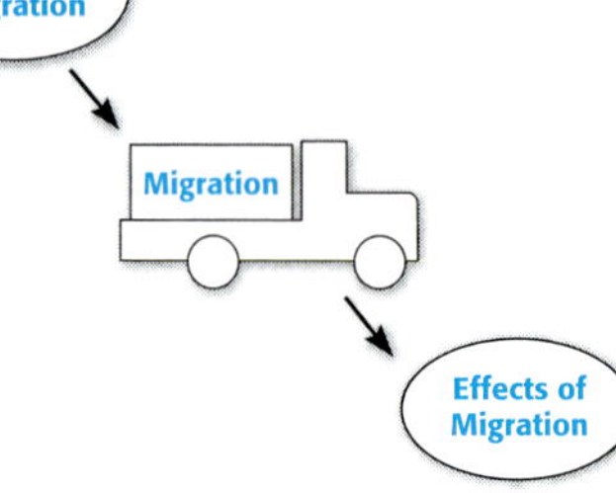

2. **Using Historical Imagination** Imagine you are a farmer from the Great Plains migrating west in 1939. Write a diary entry describing your experiences on the West Coast.
3. **Analyzing** How did photographs of ordinary people affect attitudes toward the New Deal?
4. **Synthesizing** How did the New Deal programs address both the physical and the psychological needs of Americans?

Critical Thinking

5. Why did a photograph like *Migrant Mother* inspire protests against large agricultural growers in California?
Consider:
• the subject of the photograph
• the experiences of migrants in California
• how Californians might have felt upon seeing the image

SECTION 4

After completing Section 4, students should be able to:

OBJECTIVE 1 *Explain how Federal Project Number One aided writers and artists.*

OBJECTIVE 2 *Identify the common themes that emerged in the novels, films, and plays of the New Deal Era.*

OBJECTIVE 3 *Describe how music evolved in the 1930s.*

OBJECTIVE 4 *Discuss the subject matter that influenced American painters in the 1930s.*

LET'S GET STARTED!

Write the following statement on the chalkboard: *The federal government has a responsibility to support the arts and artists.* As students enter the classroom, ask them to respond to the statement in writing and to include specific reasons why government support for the arts is or is not vital to the cultural life of the United States. Have volunteers share their responses. Tell students that in Section 4 they will learn about the arts in the United States during the New Deal Era.

The New Deal and the Arts

OBJECTIVES

Read to understand:

1. how Federal Project Number One aided writers and artists
2. what common themes emerged in the novels, films, and plays of the New Deal Era
3. how music evolved in the 1930s
4. what subject matter influenced American painters in the 1930s

KEY TERMS

Federal Project Number One
The Grapes of Wrath
Gone With the Wind
regionalists
American Gothic

KEY PEOPLE

Zora Neale Hurston
Richard Wright
Frank Capra
Lillian Hellman
Thornton Wilder
Aaron Copland
Thomas A. Dorsey
Mahalia Jackson
Benny Goodman
Jacob Lawrence
Georgia O'Keeffe
Anna "Grandma" Moses

"Two years ago I was living in comfort and apparent security. My husband had a good position in a well-known orchestra, and I was teaching a large and promising class of piano students. When the orchestra disbanded we started on a rapid downhill path. My husband was unable to secure another position. My class gradually dwindled away."

—Ann Rivington

Poster announcing a concert sponsored by the Federal Music Project

Ann Rivington and her husband were among many people trained in the arts who found no job opportunities during the depression. In its attempts to put Americans back to work, the Roosevelt administration did not forget about those who were skilled in the arts.

WPA Programs

All workers struggled with unemployment in depression-era America, including artists. "They've got to eat just like other people," declared Harry Hopkins about the plight of unemployed artists. The Roosevelt administration soon launched a new program to aid writers, musicians, actors, and others. In 1935 the Works Progress Administration (WPA) set aside $300 million to create **Federal Project Number One.** This program sought to encourage pride in American culture by providing work to artists in the fields of writing, theater, music, and visual arts.

The WPA's Federal Writers' Project (FWP) hired some 6,600 unemployed writers to produce a variety of works. The works included state travel guides and histories of various ethnic groups. Others conducted oral history interviews with hundreds of elderly former slaves. Members of the project also studied American folklore and wrote down folktales. These eventually became the basis for the best-selling *Treasury of American Folklore* (1944), one of the more than 1,000 books and pamphlets published by the FWP.

The WPA's Federal Theater Project hired unemployed actors, directors, designers, stagehands, and playwrights to encourage theatrical productions. The project entertained millions of Americans and brought productions to many small towns that had never experienced live theater. The Federal Music Project hired musicians to form orchestras and present some 4,000 musical productions each month to audiences nationwide. The Federal Arts Project hired unemployed artists and designers to produce posters for New Deal programs, teach art in public schools, and paint murals on public buildings.

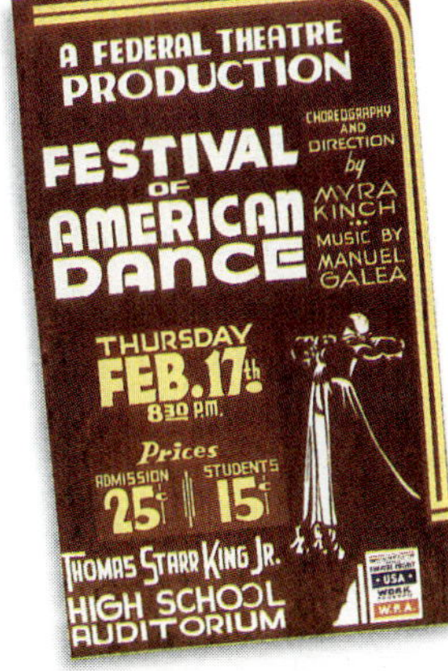

The Federal Theater Project sponsored performances such as this one, providing work for entertainers and amusement for Americans.

✔ **READING CHECK:** How did Federal Project Number One aid writers and artists?

SECTION 4 RESOURCES

PRINT

- Guided Reading Strategy 15.4
- Graphic Organizer Activity 15: Social Change in the 1930s
- Literature Reading 15: Thoughts of a Young African American
- Section 4 Review, p. 463
- Daily Quiz 15.4

MULTIMEDIA

- One-Stop Planner, Lesson 15.4
- Holt Researcher: American History CD–ROM

SHELTERED ENGLISH

- Main Idea Activity for Reteaching and Sheltered English 15.4

✔ READING TO UNDERSTAND

To help students master the section objectives, have them answer the **READING CHECKS** and complete **Guided Reading Strategy 15.4** as they read the section.

TEACH OBJECTIVE 1

ALL LEVELS: Tell students to imagine that they are artists hired through Federal Project Number One to publicize its activities. Pair students and have each pair create a pamphlet explaining how the Project helps unemployed writers and artists. *(Pairs' pamphlets should mention that the Federal Writers' Project hired writers to produce a variety of works, that the Federal Theater Project hired theater artists to produce plays, that the Federal Music Project hired musicians to present musical productions, and that the Federal Arts Project hired artists and designers to paint murals, produce posters, and teach art.)* **Sheltered English, Cooperative Learning**

Teacher to Teacher

Doug Odom of El Dorado, Kansas, suggested the following activity: Organize the class into two groups. Have one group prepare arguments supporting Federal Project Number One, and have the other group prepare arguments opposing Federal Project Number One. When students have finished preparing, conduct a debate.

CULTURAL DIVERSITY

The Federal Theater Project. Because directors in the Federal Theater Project attempted to produce plays with social commentary, the project generated widespread controversy. The project began by producing well-known plays but soon produced plays such as the antifascist *It Can't Happen Here* and *Altars of Steel*, a play that supported southern economic freedom. The project also produced shows that dealt directly with New Deal issues. Historian Lorraine A. Brown argues that Congress ended the project's funding in 1939 because, for Franklin Roosevelt's opponents, the project had come to represent all that was wrong with the New Deal.

CRITICAL THINKING Why might some people have seen the theater project as an example of what was wrong with the New Deal?

ANSWER: Students might suggest that some people believed that spending federal money to produce plays—particularly plays that criticized some U.S. policies—was wasteful.

VISUAL RECORD ANSWER

Students might suggest that the extravagance of the dance number contrasted with the poverty and worries of the audience.

John Steinbeck's **The Grapes of Wrath** *is a gritty tale of life in the United States during the Great Depression.*

Portraying the Depression

The Federal Writers' Project helped launch the careers of numerous successful writers. Many of these writers incorporated themes of the depression into their works.

Novels. John Steinbeck produced a gripping picture of the depression years in ***The Grapes of Wrath*** (1939). The story follows the fortunes of a poor family as they travel from the Dust Bowl region to California.

Other novels described the depression-era experiences of ethnic minorities. Zora Neale Hurston wrote *Their Eyes Were Watching God* (1937). Her novel explores a black woman's search for fulfillment in rural Florida. Richard Wright offered a grim picture of black urban life in *Native Son* (1940). His work chronicles the journey of a young African American man lost in a racist world.

One of the best-selling novels of the decade was Margaret Mitchell's ***Gone With the Wind*** (1936), a sweeping story of the Old South set during the Civil War and Reconstruction. Many depression-era readers could relate to the turmoil faced by the novel's main character, Scarlett O'Hara, who survives war and economic chaos.

Films. Margaret Mitchell's book became the basis of the most popular film of the 1930s. To lift people's spirits, the major studios offered a number of "escapist" films to help viewers forget their troubles. These included the Marx brothers' comedy *Duck Soup* (1933) and Ginger Rogers's upbeat musical *Gold-Diggers of 1933*. This musical contained one of the most optimistic tunes of the decade.

INTERPRETING THE VISUAL RECORD

Film. Films such as the musical *Gold-Diggers of 1933* offered Americans optimism during the depression. ***How do you think this dance number contrasted with the lives of the audience?***

> **"We're in the money,**
> **We're in the money**
> **We've got a lot of what**
> **It takes to get along.**
>
> **We never see a headline**
> **About a breadline**
> **Today."**

Soon some filmmakers began to tackle social issues. Director Frank Capra celebrated simple values and criticized the wealthy and politicians in films like *Mr. Deeds Goes to Town* (1936) and *Mr. Smith Goes to Washington* (1939). By the late 1930s the major studios had recovered sufficiently from the depression to launch several big-budget spectacles. Two such films, the color epic *Gone With the Wind* and the special-effects fantasy *The Wizard of Oz*, were both released in 1939.

Theater. Some films of the 1930s were based on popular plays. On the theatrical stage, plays that dealt with the nation's labor and class struggles drew large audiences. Robert Sherwood's *The Petrified Forest* (1935) attacked the "petrified forest" of ideas destroying the country. Lillian Hellman's *The Little Foxes* (1939) attacked upper-class greed. By the end of the decade, popular plays, like popular films, focused increasingly on traditional American values. Two examples are Thornton Wilder's *Our Town* (1938) and William Saroyan's *The Time of Your Life* (1939).

✔ **READING CHECK:** What common themes emerged in novels, films, and plays of the New Deal Era?

TEACH OBJECTIVE 2

ALL LEVELS: Ask students to identify common themes in present-day books, films, and music. *(Students might suggest teenagers' anxieties about growing up, conspiracy theories, theories of impending disease epidemics, and so on.)* Lead a class discussion about events or situations that might be generating the concerns they have identified. Tell students that common themes appeared in the films, novels, and plays of the New Deal Era. To help students understand these themes, copy the chart at right on the chalkboard, omitting the italicized answers. Have each student complete the organizer. Ask volunteers to share their answers with the class. **Sheltered English**

COMMON THEMES OF NEW DEAL ERA NOVELS, FILMS, AND PLAYS

Novels	*themes of the depression, depression-era experiences of ethnic minorities, economic chaos*
Films	*"escapist" themes, exploration of social issues*
Plays	*labor and class struggles, upper-class greed, traditional American values*

▶**ASSIGNMENT:** *Distribute Literature Reading 15, Thoughts of a Young African American, from **Literature, Primary Source, and Biography Readings**, and have each student complete it.*

AMERICAN *Letters*

Literature of the Great Depression

The late 1930s gave rise to a new era of realism in American literature as prominent authors wrote stories that captured the struggles and mood of the country during the Great Depression. In The Grapes of Wrath, *John Steinbeck portrays the saga of migrants from the Dust Bowl who travel to California in search of work. In* Their Eyes Were Watching God, *Zora Neale Hurston follows the struggle of an African American woman named Janie to find meaning and happiness in her life.*

from *The Grapes of Wrath*
by John Steinbeck

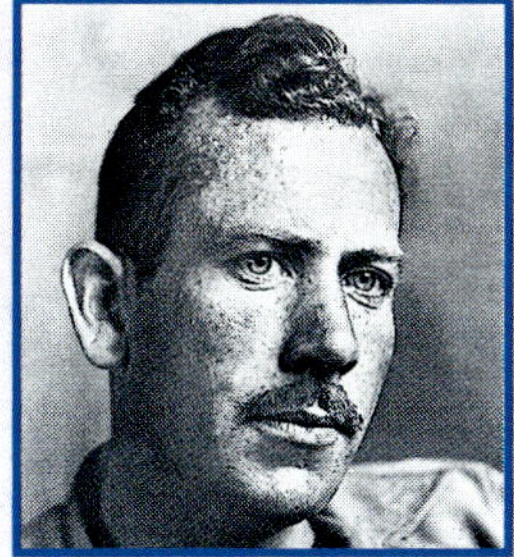
John Steinbeck

Those families who had lived on a little piece of land, who had lived and died on forty acres, had eaten or starved on the produce of forty acres, had now the whole West to rove in. And they scampered about, looking for work; and the highways were streams of people, and the ditch banks were lines of people. . . . The great highways streamed with moving people. . . .

And this was good, for wages went down and prices stayed up. The great owners were glad. . . . And wages went down and prices stayed up. And pretty soon now we'll have serfs again. . . .

And the little farmers . . . lost their farms, and they were taken by the great owners, the banks, and the companies. . . . As time went on, there were fewer farms. The little farmers moved into town for a while and exhausted their credit, exhausted their friends, their relatives. And then they too were on the highways. And the roads were crowded with men ravenous for work, murderous for work.

And the companies, the banks worked at their own doom and they did not know it. The fields were fruitful, and starving men moved on the roads. . . .

The great companies did not know that the line between hunger and anger is a thin line. . . . On the highways the people moved like ants and searched for work, for food. And the anger began to ferment."

from *Their Eyes Were Watching God*
by Zora Neale Hurston

Zora Neale Hurston

Janie saw her life like a great tree in leaf with the things suffered, things enjoyed, things done and undone. Dawn and doom was in the branches. . . .

After awhile she got up from where she was and went over the little garden field entire. She was seeking confirmation of the voice and vision, and everywhere she found and acknowledged answers. . . . Oh to be a pear tree—*any* tree in bloom! With kissing bees singing of the beginning of the world! She was sixteen. She had glossy leaves and bursting buds and she wanted to struggle with life but it seemed to elude her. . . . She searched as much of the world as she could from the top of the front steps and then went on down to the front gate and leaned over to gaze up and down the road. Looking, waiting, breathing short with impatience. Waiting for the world to be made.

UNDERSTANDING LITERATURE

1. What mood do both Steinbeck and Hurston convey?
2. How do both writers use images from nature to describe their characters' feelings?
3. What do both writers reveal about the depression years?

AMERICAN LETTERS ANSWERS

1. Both convey a mood of impatience. The people in their works are waiting for something to change their desperate situations.
2. Steinbeck uses images like "streams" and "ants" to demonstrate the people's ongoing search for food and work. Hurston compares her character Janie to a tree that is struggling to burst into bloom.
3. Both writers reveal both physical and emotional desperation.

STRATEGIES FOR SUCCESS ANSWERS

(for p. 462)

Practicing the Strategy

1. rural America
2. the setting, the subjects' occupation, emotions, and outlook
3. Wood was trying to convey the austere character of rural life in the 1930s. The title attempts to establish a satirical link between medieval Gothic architecture, which was monumental, and rural America.
4. The painting captures the spartan flavor of rural life during the 1930s.

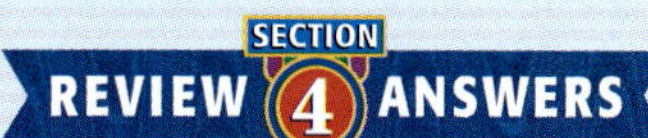

Define and Identify

For significance, see the following pages:

- Federal Project Number One, p. 459

TEACH OBJECTIVE 3

ALL LEVELS: Tell students to imagine that they are music editors working for a record company that is about to release a compilation of 1930s music. Have each student write liner notes for this release to discuss the evolution of musical forms in the 1930s. *(Students' liner notes should mention the use of folk songs and folktales, the popularization of country music, gospel music, jazz, and swing.)* Ask volunteers to read their liner notes to the class. **Sheltered English**

TEACH OBJECTIVE 4

ALL LEVELS: Pair students and have each pair create a chart identifying painters of the New Deal Era and the subject matter that influenced them. *(Pairs' charts should mention Jacob Lawrence, who portrayed the daily lives of African American heroes; Georgia O'Keeffe, who was influenced by the southwestern landscape; the regionalists, including Thomas Hart Benton, John Steuart Curry, and Grant Wood, who were influenced by the rural United States; and Grandma Moses, a folk artist.)* Ask volunteers to present their charts to the class. Then tell each student to use his or her chart to write a paragraph about New Deal–Era painters and the subject matter that influenced them. **Sheltered English, Cooperative Learning**

- *The Grapes of Wrath*, p. 460
- Zora Neale Hurston, p. 460
- Richard Wright, p. 460
- *Gone With the Wind*, p. 460
- Frank Capra, p. 460
- Lillian Hellman, p. 460
- Thornton Wilder, p. 460
- Aaron Copland, p. 462
- Thomas A. Dorsey, p. 462
- Mahalia Jackson, p. 462
- Benny Goodman, p. 463
- Jacob Lawrence, p. 463
- Georgia O'Keeffe, p. 463
- regionalists, p. 463
- *American Gothic*, p. 463
- Anna "Grandma" Moses, p. 463

1. writers–wrote travel guides and ethnic histories, conducted oral history interviews, collected folktales; theater workers–produced entertainment; musicians–formed orchestras and performed; visual artists–produced posters, taught art, and painted murals

2. the desperation of living in poverty and the corruption of many people in power

3. Answers will vary. Students might argue that 1930s music incorporated elements of older musical styles. Others might argue that some 1930s music combined older styles to create completely new styles.

4. Many artists focused on rural people and themes.

5. The project provided jobs, encouraged the production of art, and provided entertainment. Without the project, the New Deal Era would not have produced or encouraged art.

Strategies for Success

Evaluating Art as Historical Evidence

Like photographs and artifacts, visual art can help one understand the past in a number of unique ways. Drawings, engravings, paintings, and sculptures can provide valuable clues about a given historical period. Because visual art often reflects the views of individuals who created it, it is important to interpret it carefully.

How to Evaluate Art as Historical Evidence

1. **Identify the subject.** Look at the work of art as a whole and identify its basic subject. If the work has a title, examine it for clues about the artist's intentions.
2. **Study the details.** Examine the details in the work for information about its subject and the historical context.
3. **Determine the artist's point of view.** Make sure to note if the subject of the work is depicted in a favorable or unfavorable manner. If possible, find out when the work was created and what may have helped to shape the artist's point of view.
4. **Put the information to use.** Compare the results of your analysis with information about the historical period that you have gained through other sources. Then determine how the work contributes to your understanding of the historical period.

Applying the Strategy

Study the reproduction of Grant Wood's painting *American Gothic* to the right.

***Grant Wood's* American Gothic**

Practicing the Strategy

After looking at the reproduction of the painting answer the following questions.

1. What is the subject of this painting?
2. What information is provided by the details in the painting?
3. What message do you think Grant Wood was trying to convey in the painting? Why do you think he titled the painting *American Gothic?*
4. How does the painting contribute to your understanding of the United States during the 1930s?

Music in the New Deal Era

Popular music in the late 1930s increasingly incorporated American traditions and sounds. Some WPA researchers collected and wrote down American folk songs and folktales. Composer Aaron Copland used these as the basis for his most popular compositions, including his 1938 piece, *Billy the Kid.* Meanwhile, country music drew from the traditions of southern folk music to gain a national audience. Broadcast live from Nashville, Tennessee, the *Grand Ole Opry* radio show became a major force in the popularization of country music.

Gospel music, a cross between traditional spirituals and jazz, also gained popularity. African American composer Thomas A. Dorsey wrote songs including "Precious Lord, Take My Hand." Sister Rosetta Tharpe and Mahalia Jackson were two of the most popular gospel singers. Jackson later recalled that some ministers objected to this new style of music.

> **"They didn't like the hand-clapping and the stomping and they said we were bringing jazz into the church and it wasn't dignified. Once at church one of the preachers got up in the pulpit and spoke out against me. I got right up, too. I told him I was born to sing gospel music."**

REVIEW

Have students complete the **Section 4 Review** on p. 463.

ASSESS

Have students complete **Daily Quiz 15.4**. As **Alternative Assessment**, you may want to use the dialogue or the liner notes in this section's lessons.

RETEACH

Have students complete **Main Idea Activity for Reteaching and Sheltered English 15.4**. Organize the class into small groups. Have each group write two or three sentences to identify 10 of the key terms and key people in the section. Collect groups' sentences and use them to conduct a quiz bowl in which each group will work as a team to answer the questions.
Sheltered English, Cooperative Learning

EXTEND

Organize the class into small groups and assign each group one of the following subjects: Frank Capra, Aaron Copland, Benny Goodman, Lillian Hellman, Zora Neale Hurston, Mahalia Jackson, Jacob Lawrence, Grandma Moses, Thornton Wilder, or Richard Wright. Have each group develop a multimedia presentation about its assigned subject complete with musical or visual examples to illustrate its subject's work. Have each group give its multimedia presentation to the class.
Block Scheduling, Cooperative Learning

Jazz continued to rise in popularity, largely through swing, a smooth big-band style popular in dance halls. Swing received its name from Duke Ellington's 1932 hit "It Don't Mean a Thing If It Ain't Got That Swing." White conductor Benny Goodman helped popularize swing with his integrated band.

✔ **READING CHECK:** How did music evolve in the 1930s?

Painters Examine Local Culture

Like their writer and musician peers, American depression-era painters captured a variety of memorable images in their work. Harlem artist Jacob Lawrence portrayed the daily lives of African American heroes, such as Frederick Douglass and Harriet Tubman. New Mexico artist Georgia O'Keeffe painted haunting images of the southwestern desert landscape.

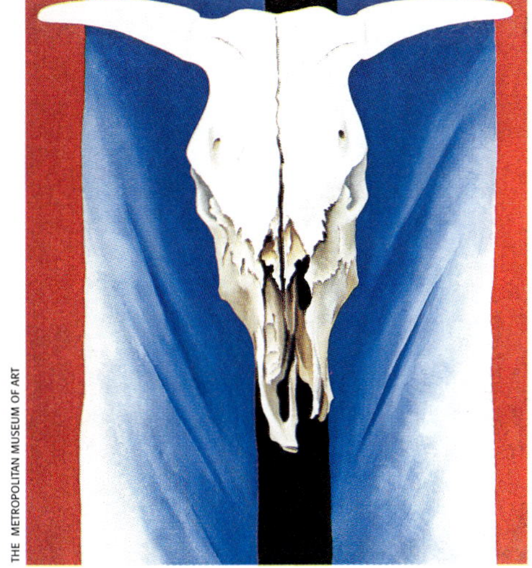

THE METROPOLITAN MUSEUM OF ART

***Georgia O'Keeffe's* Cow's Skull: Red, White, and Blue**

Many artists looked to rural America for their subject matter. A group of midwestern artists known as the **regionalists** stressed local folk themes and customs. The regionalists included Thomas Hart Benton of Missouri, John Steuart Curry of Kansas, and Grant Wood of Iowa. They reminded urban art lovers of America's rural traditions. Wood claimed that his best ideas "came while milking a cow." The most famous of the regionalist paintings is probably Wood's ***American Gothic***.

As interest in regional culture grew, people began to rediscover American folk art, such as handmade quilts and woodcarvings. Some folk artists, including the elderly painter Anna "Grandma" Moses, became well known during this period.

✔ **READING CHECK:** What subject matter influenced American painters in the 1930s?

SECTION 4 REVIEW

Define and explain the significance of the following terms:
Federal Project Number One
The Grapes of Wrath
Gone With the Wind
regionalists
American Gothic

Identify and explain the significance of the following individuals:
Zora Neale Hurston
Richard Wright
Frank Capra
Lillian Hellman
Thornton Wilder
Aaron Copland
Thomas A. Dorsey
Mahalia Jackson
Benny Goodman
Jacob Lawrence
Georgia O'Keeffe
Anna "Grandma" Moses

1. **Using Graphic Organizers** Copy the following chart. Use it to describe the various ways that Federal Project Number One provided work for writers, theater workers, musicians, and visual artists.

	Federal Project Number One
Writers	
Theater Workers	
Musicians	
Visual Artists	

2. **Comparing and Contrasting** What common themes did novels, films, and plays of the 1930s share?
3. **Distinguishing Fact from Opinion** Provide evidence to support or prove wrong the following statement: "Music in the 1930s simply reflected new twists on old themes."
4. **Identifying Values** How did the hard times of the depression influence the subjects that artists painted?

Critical Thinking

5. In what ways did Federal Project Number One save the arts?
Consider:
   - what problems artists were facing before the project
   - how the project promoted the arts
   - what might have happened to the arts without the project

CHAPTER 15 REVIEW ANSWERS

Creating a Time Line
Each event should have an explanation and the correct date.

Writing a Summary
See the Reading Checks in each section for main ideas.

Identifying People and Ideas

1. Roosevelt's program of relief and recovery
2. Roosevelt's secretary of labor
3. bank closure designed to stop massive withdrawals
4. Louisiana senator who advocated taking money from the wealthy and sharing it
5. director of the NYA Division of Negro Affairs
6. provides payments, pensions, and unemployment insurance to retired workers and to the blind, the disabled, and elderly people
7. workers on strike stay at their work stations until management agrees to demands
8. area of Great Plains destroyed by droughts and high winds
9. photographer who took pictures of migrant workers
10. John Steinbeck's novel about an impoverished Oklahoma farm family

REVIEW AND ASSESSMENT RESOURCES

PRINT
- Chapter 15 Review, pp. 464–65
- Chapter 15 Tutorial for Students, Parents, Mentors, and Peers
- Chapter 15 Test (Form A or B)
- Portfolio Activities and Alternative Assessment Handbook, Chapter 15

MULTIMEDIA
- Audio Program, Chapter 15 (English and Spanish)
- Chapter 15 Test Generator (on the One-Stop Planner)
- Global Skill Builder CD–ROM
- HRW Web site

SHELTERED ENGLISH
- Spanish Glossary
- Sheltered English Chapter 15 Test

REVIEW

Have students complete the **Chapter 15 Review** on pp. 464–65.

ASSESS

Use one of the chapter tests to assess students' understanding of the content. For **Alternative Assessment**, see the **Portfolio Activities and Alternative Assessment Handbook.**

Understanding Main Ideas

1. African Americans suffered some discrimination but were also appointed to many government positions. American Indians benefited from reforms allowing them more tribal rights.

2. being against big business, not doing enough to control business, and not providing enough relief

3. get rid of the older justices who consistently opposed the New Deal; most people opposed FDR's efforts

4. documented the hardships and dignity of the people and allowed others to see the need for government action

5. Many chronicled the lives of people struggling to survive, and others criticized wealthy business owners or explored major issues.

Reviewing Themes

1. by providing jobs and wages, allowing businesses to temporarily ignore antitrust laws, initiating large public works projects, and providing subsidies to farmers

2. because they interfered with free enterprise and imposed larger taxes on the wealthy

3. to provide jobs for artists and entertainment for Americans

Thinking Critically

1. Because of calls for social insurance, Congress passed the Social Security Act. They addressed criticisms that the New Deal helped business and industry too much by enacting laws enabling unions to bargain collectively.

Review

Creating a Time Line

Copy the time line below onto a sheet of paper. Complete the time line by filling in the events and dates from the chapter that you think were most significant. Pick three events and explain why you think they were significant.

Writing a Summary

Using the Reading Checks as a guide, write an overview of the events in the chapter.

Identifying People and Ideas

Identify the following terms or individuals and explain their significance.

1. New Deal
2. Frances Perkins
3. bank holiday
4. Huey Long
5. Mary McLeod Bethune
6. Social Security Act
7. sit-down strike
8. Dust Bowl
9. Dorothea Lange
10. *The Grapes of Wrath*

Understanding Main Ideas

SECTION 1

1. How did the New Deal affect African Americans and American Indians?

SECTION 2

2. What were some of the major criticisms of the New Deal?
3. What was President Roosevelt's "court-packing" plan, and how well did it succeed?

SECTION 3

4. What contributions did photographers make to the New Deal?

SECTION 4

5. How did novels, films, and plays of the 1930s reflect themes of the depression years?

Reviewing Themes

1. **Economic Development** How did the Roosevelt administration attempt to promote economic recovery?
2. **Constitutional Heritage** Why might the Supreme Court have declared some New Deal measures unconstitutional?
3. **Cultural Diversity** Why did the government promote the arts in the 1930s?

Thinking Critically

1. **Identifying Cause and Effect** How did criticism of the first New Deal shape the Second New Deal?
2. **Taking a Stand** Do you think that President Roosevelt was justified in trying to "pack" the Supreme Court? Why or why not?
3. **Assessing Consequences** How did Works Progress Administration programs enrich American culture during the 1930s?
4. **Distinguishing Fact from Opinion** Some people consider Franklin D. Roosevelt our greatest president. Use facts from the chapter to evaluate the accuracy of that statement.
5. **Problem Solving** If you had been one of President Roosevelt's advisers, what aspects of the New Deal programs would you have changed?

Writing About History

Writing to Classify Write a brief summary of 10 major New Deal programs and note whether they were designed primarily to help banks, farmers, labor, or business. Use the following graphic to organize your thoughts.

New Deal			
Banks	Farmers	Labor	Business

RETEACH

Organize the class into small groups. Have each group use 25 of the key terms, key people, and key places from this chapter to create a crossword puzzle. Ask groups to trade crossword puzzles and then complete them.
Sheltered English, Cooperative Learning

EXTEND

Ask students to conduct research on historians' and economists' assessment of the effectiveness of New Deal programs in restoring the economic health of the United States. Ask each student to discuss his or her findings in an essay. **Block Scheduling**

Strategies for Success Review the **Strategies for Success** on *Evaluating Art as Historical Evidence.* Then study the following reproduction of Anna "Grandma" Moses's painting *Sugaring Off* and answer the following questions.

GRANDMA MOSES: SUGARING OFF © 1992

1. What is the subject of this painting, and what information is provided by its details?
2. How does the painting contribute to your understanding of regionalism as an artistic movement?

Linking History and Geography

The windstorms of the 1930s picked up dried soil to create "black blizzards" across the country. Study the map below. Which states made up the Dust Bowl? Which other states also experienced severe wind erosion?

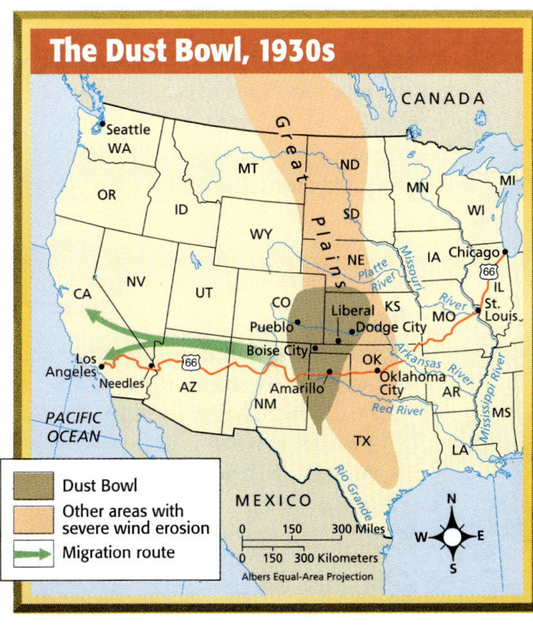

internetconnect

TOPIC: WPA-Sponsored Art
GO TO: go.hrw.com
KEYWORD: SE1 WPA

Accessing the Internet through the HRW Web site, research the WPA-sponsored murals and posters produced during the Great Depression. Then create a poster or mural illustrating a topic of your choice that follows the style of the government-sponsored artwork.

BUILDING YOUR PORTFOLIO

Complete one or all of the following projects independently or cooperatively.

1 Economic Development

Imagine that you are a New Deal legislator. ***Write a proposal*** for a new public-works project. Your proposal should describe what the project is, how workers and businesses will benefit from it, and why your project will be useful to society in terms of relief, recovery, or reform.

Civilian Conservation Corps patch

2 Cultural Diversity

Imagine that you are an author in the 1930s. ***Write a short, realistic passage*** for a novel that describes the Dust Bowl's effects on the main character. You may also wish to add illustrations to your passage.

3 Constitutional Heritage

Hold a debate or ***write a script*** for a debate analyzing the constitutionality of the New Deal programs affecting labor and agriculture.

2. Answers will vary. Students might argue that Roosevelt's actions were unconstitutional. Others might argue that his recovery programs were thwarted by the "Nine Old Men."

3. by providing many national landmarks, public works, and art projects

4. Answers will vary. Students might argue that Roosevelt's success with many New Deal programs make him the best president. Others might argue that Roosevelt's programs often failed, and his court-packing attempt implies that he was moving toward being a dictator.

5. Answers will vary. Students should consider all the possible implications of their desired changes.

Writing About History
Answers will vary. Students might mention: banks–FDIC; farmers–AAA,TVA, FSA; labor–FERA, CCC, NIRA, PWA; business–NIRA, NRA

Strategies for Success
1. activities associated with tapping sap from maple trees; the season, the rural setting, and the equipment used
2. shows a rural, local subject

Linking History and Geography
Colorado, Kansas, Nebraska, New Mexico, Oklahoma, and Texas; Montana, North Dakota, South Dakota, and Wyoming

LET'S GET STARTED!

Pair students and have each pair write a few sentences describing their local environment, classifying it according to the options offered in the map legends. Ask volunteers to read their sentences to the class. Tell students that they will learn more about land use in the United States in the Unit 4 America's Geography. **Cooperative Learning**

TEACH AMERICA'S GEOGRAPHY— LAND USE

Write the following question on the chalkboard: *How did land use change in the United States between 1620 and 1999?* Then pair students and tell them to study the America's Geography feature. Have each pair write a few sentences or paragraphs answering the question on the chalkboard. *(Pairs should note that the amount of grasslands and forests declined, that the area of buffalo range declined, that the number of cattle and hogs and pigs increased, and so on.)* Ask volunteers to read their statements to the class. **Sheltered English, Cooperative Learning**

ACROSS THE CURRICULUM

▶SCIENCE◀

Pesticides. The introduction of pesticides contributed to the agricultural boom of the 1900s. Pesticides are chemicals designed to destroy certain pests, usually insects, that harm or destroy crops. American farmers began to use pesticides in the hopes of realizing larger crop yields. One of the most widely used pesticides was an insecticide called DDT. The letters represent the chemical compound, dichloro-diphenyl-trichloroethane, that make up the insecticide. Over time, scientists discovered that DDT kills beneficial species as well as harmful ones and possibly poses a danger to human food sources. In 1972 the U.S. government banned the widespread use of DDT to prevent health problems.

CRITICAL THINKING How might DDT continue to cause health problems in the United States and around the world?

ANSWER: Students might suggest that many foreign countries do not regulate or ban DDT, giving rise to the possibility of import contamination in the United States.

AMERICA'S GEOGRAPHY ANSWERS

1. forests
2. 2.73 billion bushels
3. corn

AMERICA'S Geography

Land Use

For thousands of years Americans have used the land to grow crops. Many Native American groups cultivated crops on small plots of land long before the arrival of Europeans. In the early days of the Republic, most northern and midwestern farmers grew crops on small plots of land. In the South, agriculture was dominated by large plantations that grew large quantities of tobacco and cotton. By the late 1800s improved farm machinery and fertilizers allowed farmers to grow larger quantities of food on fewer acres of land. Today the amount of land devoted to crops and wild vegetation has dwindled significantly.

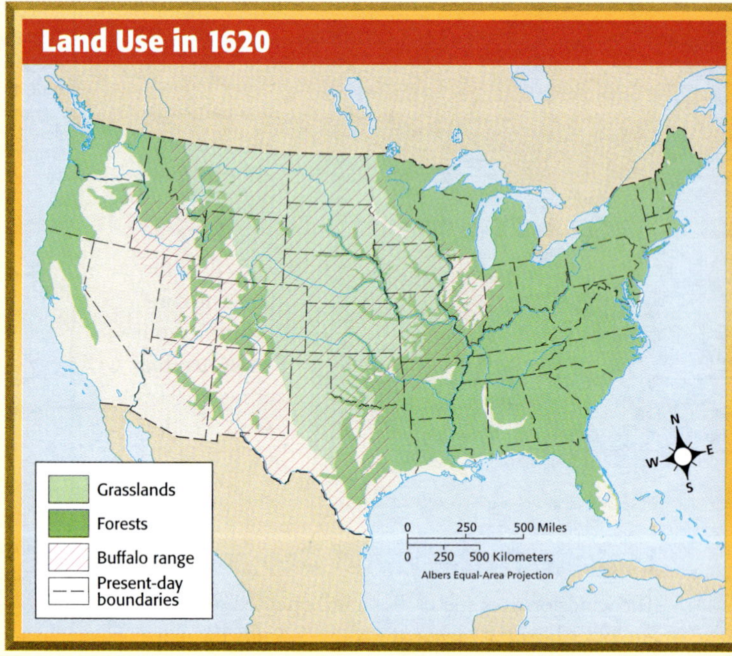

Agricultural Production, 1910–1997

	1910	1997
Corn (in bushels)	2.85 billion	9.37 billion
Wheat (in bushels)	625 million	2.53 billion
Cotton (in bales)	11.61 million	19 million
Tobacco (in pounds)	1.14 billion	1.68 billion
Soybeans (in bushels)	< 50,000	2.73 billion

Sources: *Historical Statistics of the United States; Statistical Abstract of the United States: 1998*

Soybeans. The multipurpose, high-protein soybean became the agricultural wonder of the 1900s. By the 1990s it was one of the most common crops in the United States. Soybeans are used in the processing of cattle feed, fertilizer, insect sprays, and paint, as well as in food products such as soy sauce, soy milk, baby food, processed meats, and tofu.

GEOGRAPHY AND HISTORY Skills

REGION

1. What type of vegetation covered the most land in North America in 1620?
2. How many bushels of soybeans were harvested in 1997?
3. What was the largest crop in the United States in 1997?

SPOTLIGHT on Animals and the Environment

Write the following animals on the chalkboard: *buffalo, cattle,* and *hogs and pigs.* Have each student select one animal group. Then ask students to conduct research on how their chosen group affected land use and the environment in American history. Suggest that students consider such issues as desertification, overgrazing, and so on. Then have students create graphic organizers or other visual presentations to display their research. Have volunteers present their graphic organizers or presentations to the class.

SPOTLIGHT on Local Land Use

Pair students and ask them to conduct research on land use in their local community during the 1800s or 1900s. Remind students to compare and contrast this land use with modern-day land use. Then tell each pair to write a short report describing local land use over time. Have volunteers read their reports to the class. To conclude, conduct a brief discussion on the material presented in the reports.

Cooperative Learning

AMERICA'S Geography

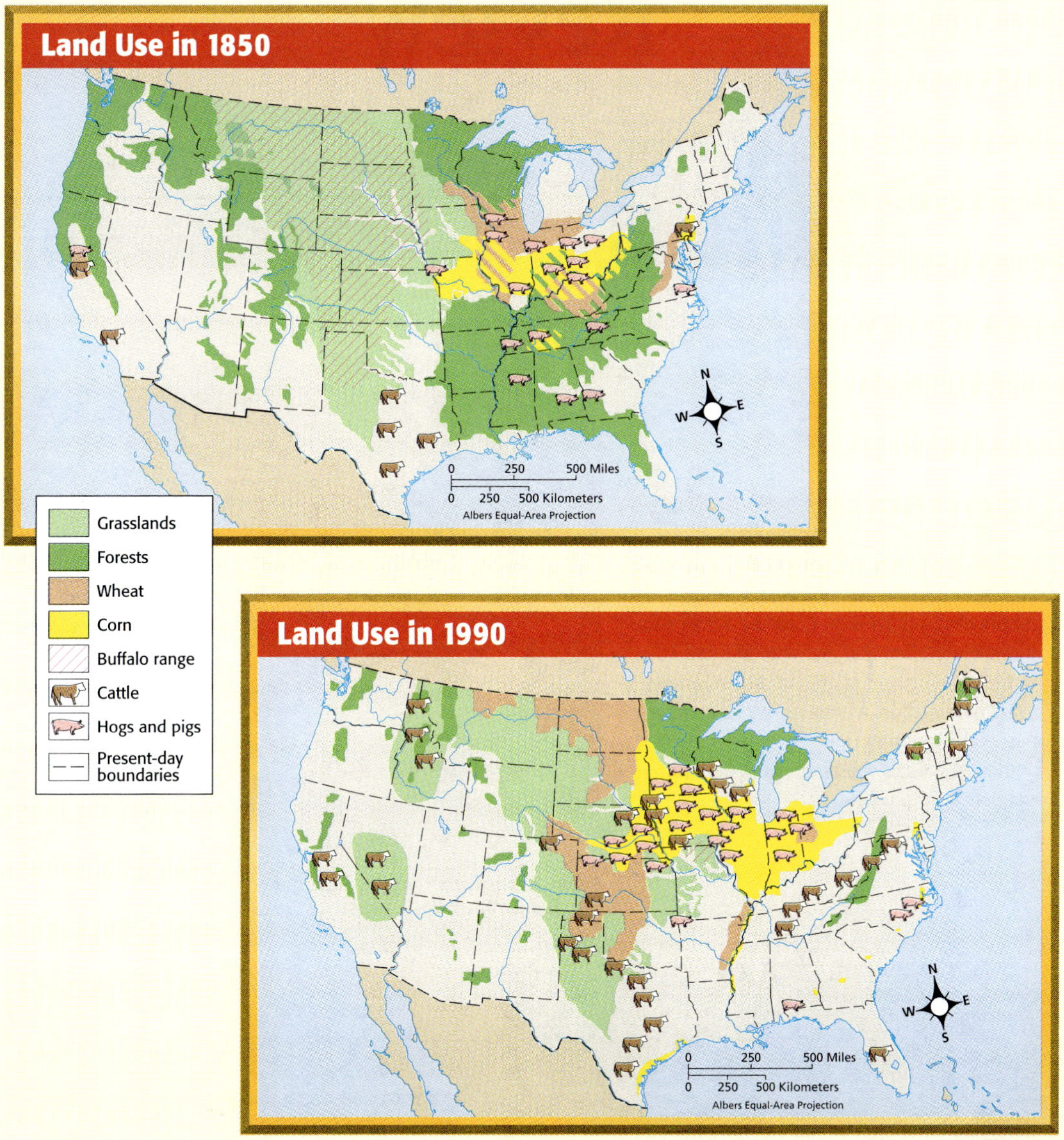

Land Use in 1850

0 250 500 Miles
0 250 500 Kilometers
Albers Equal-Area Projection

Grasslands
Forests
Wheat
Corn
Buffalo range
Cattle
Hogs and pigs
Present-day boundaries

Land Use in 1990

0 250 500 Miles
0 250 500 Kilometers
Albers Equal-Area Projection

Land changes. Agricultural production in the United States had become increasingly diverse by the early 1900s. As the population of buffalo declined in the West, hogs and cattle grew in popularity elsewhere. The biggest change to affect agriculture in the late 1900s was the decline of the small family farm. Although the number of farmers decreased dramatically, the size of farms actually increased as large-scale mechanized farming became the norm.

GEOGRAPHY AND HISTORY Skills

PLACE

1. How did the land used for cattle ranching change between 1850 and 1990?
2. In what ways did grasslands and forests change between 1850 and 1990?

ACROSS THE CURRICULUM

▶GEOGRAPHY◀

Land Use in Iowa. Grasslands covered most of Iowa in 1850. Some 13 years later a young woman who moved there from Norway identified the factors that made it a farmer's paradise. "Our land is beautiful, though there are few trees. . . . We have good spring water near by. Best of all, the land is good meadowland and easily plowed and cultivated."

CRITICAL THINKING Why do you think that the young woman mentioned the lack of trees?

ANSWER: Some students might suggest that she was not used to life on the Great Plains and nostalgic for trees.

THAT'S INTERESTING!

In 1890 the average wage for a farm worker was just 90¢ per day. That amount was only 45¢ higher by 1910. Wages continued to increase slowly until the Great Depression of the 1930s, when wages fell. In 1945, pay averaged $4.35 a day.

AMERICA'S GEOGRAPHY ANSWERS

1. The land used for cattle ranching increased.
2. Both grasslands and forests decreased in size.

467

REVIEW AND ASSESSMENT RESOURCES

PRINT

- Unit 4 Review, pp. 468–69
- Unit 4 Test (Form A or B)
- Portfolio Activities and Alternative Assessment Handbook, Unit 4

MULTIMEDIA

- Global Skill Builder CD–ROM

SHELTERED ENGLISH

- Spanish Glossary
- Sheltered English Unit 4 Test

To review elements of Unit 4 in a single class period, assign one of the following activities or graphic organizers, omitting the italicized answers, to individuals or groups.

2 Cultural Diversity

Tell students to imagine that it is 1925, that they live in Chicago, and that they are either new immigrants or African Americans who have recently migrated from the South. Have each student write a series of diary entries detailing his or her encounters with prejudice and racism and his or her efforts to overcome these factors.

A Selection from Further Reading

The Writers of the Harlem Renaissance. In *This Was Harlem: A Cultural Portrait, 1900-1950*, Jervis Anderson explores the history of New York City's most prominent African American neighborhood. In the following excerpt, he discusses ideas that influenced the writers of the Harlem Renaissance. "To judge from much of their work, [many Harlem Renaissance writers] took the view that the basic truths of the black experience were to be found in the styles and conditions of ordinary life—and that these were as worthy of artistic treatment as were the qualities of middle-class living. . . . Langston Hughes, writing in a 1926 issue of *The Nation*, declared, 'We younger Negro artists who create now intend to express our individual dark-skinned selves without fear or shame. If white people are pleased, we are glad. If they are not, it doesn't matter. We know we are beautiful. And ugly too.'"

COMPREHENSION According to Anderson, what quality characterized the work of many Harlem Renaissance writers?

ANSWER: Students might note that many Harlem Renaissance writers wanted to boldly explore the circumstances of everyday African American life.

UNIT 4 Review

BUILDING YOUR PORTFOLIO

Outlined below are four projects. Independently or cooperatively, complete one and use the products to demonstrate your mastery of the historical concepts involved.

1 Technology and Society

Technological developments in the areas of entertainment and communications helped create a national culture during the 1920s. ***Create a script for a radio program*** that highlights the issues of the era. Programs might include daily news, a jazz presentation, a book review, or an interview with a celebrity. You may wish to use portfolio materials you designed in the unit chapters to help you.

Studio photograph of the St. Louis Cotton Club Jazz Band from 1926

Parade sponsored by Marcus Garvey and the Universal Negro Improvement Association

2 Cultural Diversity

During the late 1910s massive numbers of African Americans and immigrants moved to U.S. cities. Following the wave of newcomers, racial tensions erupted in violence. ***Write a biography*** of an activist, artist, or writer who worked to overcome the racism or prejudices they experienced. You may wish to use portfolio materials you designed in the unit chapters to help you.

3 Global Relations

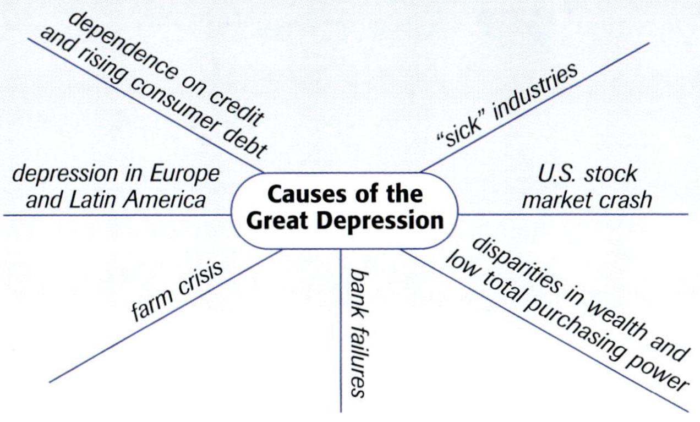

4 Economic Development

NEW DEAL WORK PROGRAMS

Program	Goals/Provisions
Civilian Conservation Corps (CCC)	*public-works projects for young men*
Public Works Administration (PWA)	*set up public-works projects to increase employment and business activity*
Civil Works Administration (CPA)	*provided federal jobs to the unemployed*
Works Progress Administration (WPA)	*employed people to do public works, research, and artistic projects*
National Youth Administration (NYA)	*provided job training and part-time jobs to young people*
Social Security Act	*provided unemployment benefits, pensions for the elderly, and survivor's insurance*

3 Global Relations

Throughout the 1920s and 1930s events around the world affected life in the United States. Economic depressions in Europe and Latin America in the late 1920s contributed to the onset of the Great Depression in the United States. Imagine that it is the early 1930s and that you have a pen pal in a foreign country. ***Draft a letter*** to your pen pal describing what you believe were the causes of the Great Depression and what you have experienced since 1929. You may wish to use portfolio materials you designed in the unit chapters to help you.

New York City soup kitchen

Works Progress Administration project

4 Economic Development

To provide relief from the economic troubles caused by the Great Depression, the federal government worked to implement programs from President Roosevelt's New Deal. ***Create a sketch*** for a mural that depicts some of the programs of the New Deal or the lives of workers in these programs. You may wish to use portfolio materials you designed in the unit chapters to help you.

Further Reading

Anderson, Jervis. *This Was Harlem: A Cultural Portrait, 1900–1950.* Farrar, Straus, and Giroux, 1992. Story of Harlem in the first half of the 1900s.

Garraty, John A. *The Great Depression.* Harcourt Brace Jovanovich, 1986. A thorough account of the causes of the economic depression.

McElvaine, Robert S. *The Great Depression: America, 1929–1941.* Times Books, 1984. Overview of the Great Depression in the United States.

Murray, Robert K. *The Politics of Normalcy.* W. W. Norton, 1973. A history of the policies and presidencies of the Republican administrations of the 1920s.

Parrish, Michael E. *Anxious Decades: America in Prosperity and Depression, 1920–1941.* W. W. Norton, 1992. Broad history of the interwar years.

Terkel, Studs. *Hard Times.* Pantheon Books, 1970. Personal accounts of the effects of the Great Depression on working-class Americans.

HOLT RESEARCHER — *Internet Connect and Holt Researcher CD–ROM Review*

In assigned groups, develop a multimedia presentation about America between 1919 and 1939. Choose information from the chapter Internet Connect activities and from the Holt Researcher CD–ROM that best reflects the major topics of the period. Write an outline and a script for your presentation, which may be shown to the class.

A Selection from Further Reading

The Great Depression, Franklin D. Roosevelt, and the American People. In *The Great Depression: America, 1929-1941*, Robert S. McElvaine provides an informative survey of American society during the Great Depression. In the following excerpt, he discusses the harmonious political relationship that President Franklin Roosevelt shared with many Americans during the Great Depression. "What Franklin D. Roosevelt sought, he said in a 1932 speech, was 'social justice through social action.' The key to understanding FDR's political success is that his positions so often coincided with the values of a people struggling for economic—and in many cases, physical—survival. Roosevelt stated the relationship perfectly in his first inaugural address: 'The people of the United States . . . have made me the present instrument of their wishes.' . . . It was an accurate forecast of the relationship between President and people during the next few years."

COMPREHENSION According to McElvaine, why was Roosevelt so politically successful during the 1930s?

ANSWER: Students might note that Roosevelt viewed himself as an instrument of the people, a stance that made him very popular.

UNIT 5

World Conflicts

CHAPTER 16 The Road to War

After World War I, many nations attempted to work for world peace. These efforts proved fruitless as the global depression led to the rise of dictators in Germany, Italy, Japan, and other countries. During the 1930s, for example, Adolf Hitler came to power in Germany and quickly launched an aggressive expansionist campaign. Other European leaders struggled to control Hitler, finally settling on a policy of appeasement.

CHAPTER 17 Americans in World War II

When Japan bombed Pearl Harbor in December 1941, the United States entered World War II on the Allied side. Americans at home attempted to support the war effort and boost productivity while U.S. soldiers fought in Europe and Japan. In May 1945 the Allies finally conquered Europe. Victory in Japan came in August, when the United States dropped atomic bombs on Nagasaki and Hiroshima.

EXAMINING THE VISUAL RECORD

Ask students the questions below. Then use the annotations to expand class discussion.

1 *Judging from the textual and visual clues in the photograph, what might be the subject of the movie The Ramparts We Watch?*
A "rampart" is a protective barrier or an embankment that is used as a fortification. The presence of the Army and Marine officers and the American flags suggest that the movie might deal with patriotic themes or themes indicating the need to defend the United States.

2 *Why might the armed services have been holding recruitment drives in 1940?*
In September 1939, World War II broke out in Europe. Although the United States was officially neutral at the time the photograph was taken, President Roosevelt and the Congress had increased the defense budget. Despite the United States's neutral status, Roosevelt and Congress sent surplus and outdated military supplies to assist Great Britain in 1940.

ACTIVITY: Tell students to imagine that it is 1942 and that they are Army recruiters. Have each student write a short recruitment speech to deliver at high schools and colleges. Ask volunteers to deliver their speeches.

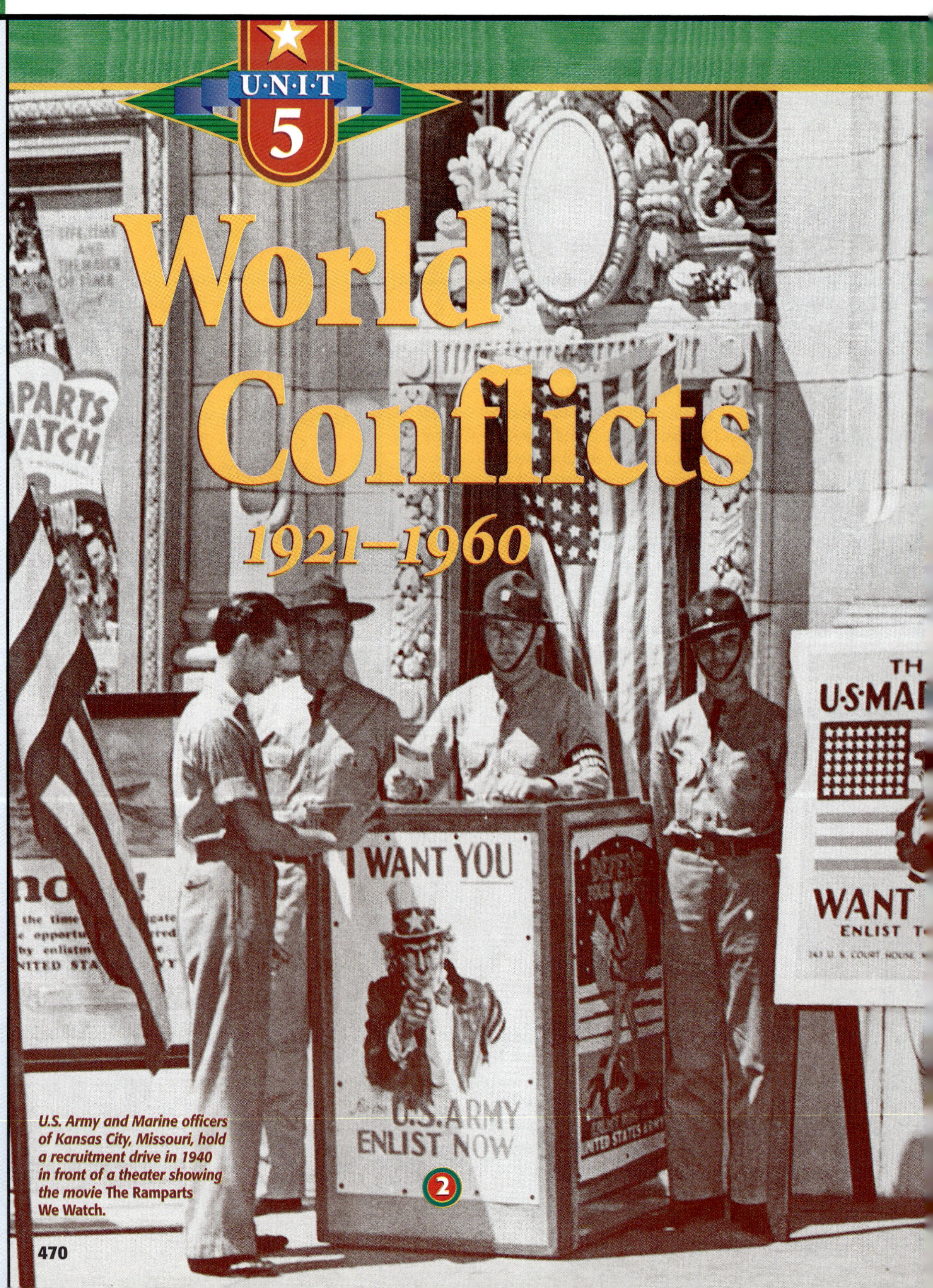

U.S. Army and Marine officers of Kansas City, Missouri, hold a recruitment drive in 1940 in front of a theater showing the movie The Ramparts We Watch.

CHAPTER 18 The Cold War

After the Allies defeated the Axis Powers, many world nations searched for ways to guarantee peace in the future. As the Soviet Union established satellite states throughout Eastern Europe, however, a Cold War between the United States and Soviet Union developed. The Cold War and the massive nuclear arms buildup that accompanied it led to increased fears and tensions at home.

CHAPTER 19 Society After World War II

After World War II ended, the United States feared a depression and labor problems. In part due to the GI Bill, which provided training, schooling, and housing loans to veterans, the depression never materialized. Indeed, the United States entered an era of unprecedented prosperity. In the midst of this material wealth, however, discrimination and segregation existed. To expand their rights, African Americans began the modern civil rights movement.

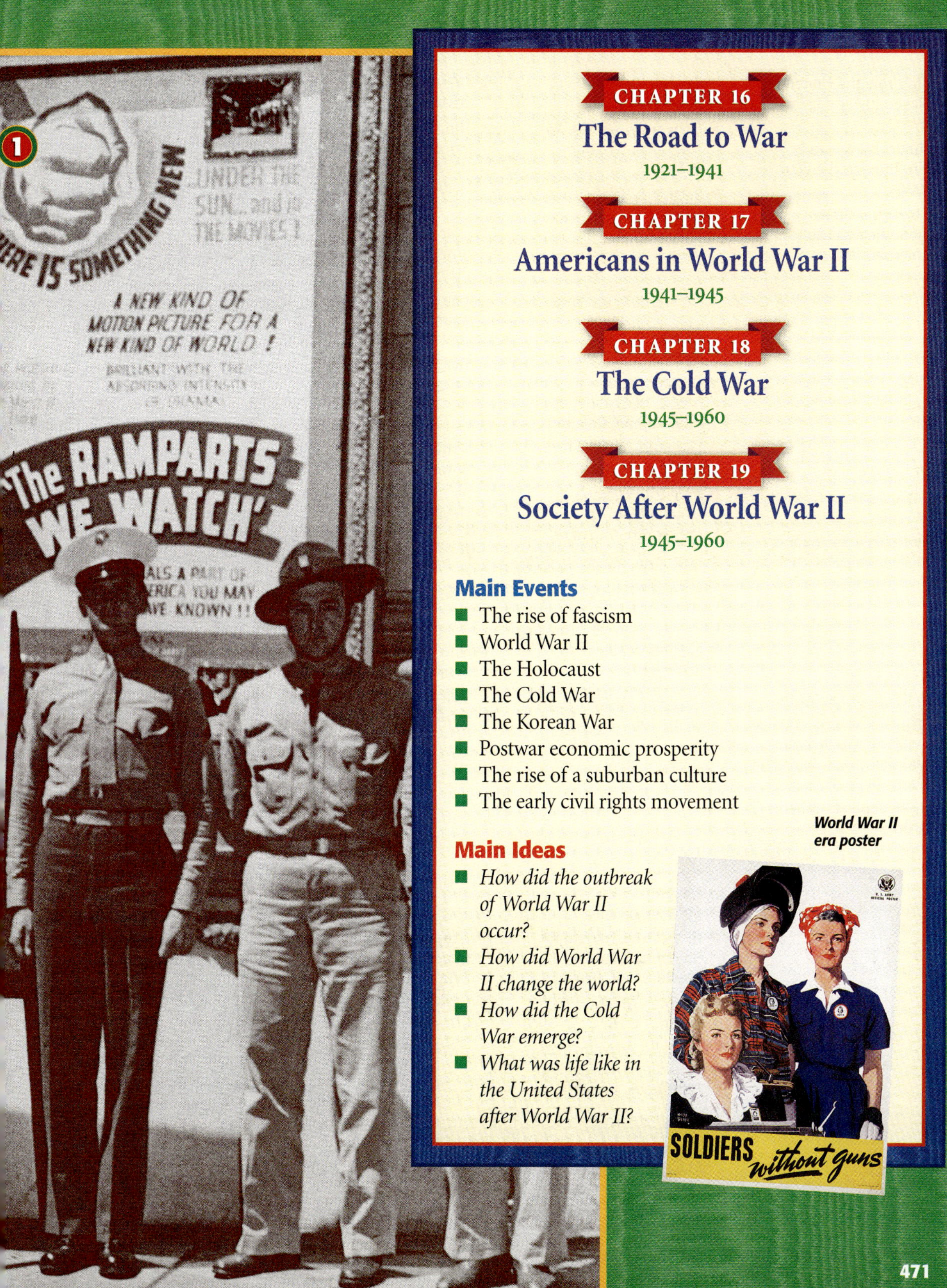

CHAPTER 16
The Road to War
1921–1941

CHAPTER 17
Americans in World War II
1941–1945

CHAPTER 18
The Cold War
1945–1960

CHAPTER 19
Society After World War II
1945–1960

Main Events

- The rise of fascism
- World War II
- The Holocaust
- The Cold War
- The Korean War
- Postwar economic prosperity
- The rise of a suburban culture
- The early civil rights movement

Main Ideas

- *How did the outbreak of World War II occur?*
- *How did World War II change the world?*
- *How did the Cold War emerge?*
- *What was life like in the United States after World War II?*

World War II era poster

INTRODUCE UNIT 5

Main Events

List the Main Events on the chalkboard. Ask students to select two and briefly describe what they know about the topics. Have volunteers share their descriptions. Later, when you have finished Unit 5, ask students to return to their original descriptions and revise them using the information they learned in the unit. Students should also create new descriptions for the other Main Events.

Main Ideas

Ask each student to read the Main Ideas and briefly answer the questions in writing. Share the ***Consider*** points with students as necessary. Later, when you have finished Unit 5, ask students to return to their original answers and revise them using the information they learned in the unit.

The Causes of World War II
Consider:
- the effects of the global depression
- the rise of dictators

The Emergence of the Cold War
Consider:
- the political differences between the United States and the Soviet Union
- the effects of Soviet expansion in Europe

The Road to War

CHAPTER PLANNING GUIDE

	Section Lesson Objectives	Print Resources	Multimedia Resources	Sheltered English Resources
Section 1 The Search for Peace, pp. 474–78	1 Outline the foreign policy the United States followed after World War I. 2 Identify the major postwar peace initiatives. 3 Discuss how war debts and reparations affected European nations after World War I.	▶ Guided Reading Strategy 16.1 ▶ Biography Reading 16: Emily Greene Balch ▶ Primary Source Reading 16: A Diplomatic Failure ▶ Section 1 Review, p. 478 ▶ Daily Quiz 16.1	▶ One-Stop Planner, Lesson 16.1 ▶ Holt Researcher: American History CD–ROM	▶ Main Idea Activity for Reteaching and Sheltered English 16.1
Section 2 Relations with Latin America, pp. 479–83	1 Discuss the role the United States played in Nicaraguan politics. 2 Explain how U.S. relations with Latin America changed in the 1930s. 3 Analyze how the Great Depression affected Latin American countries.	▶ Guided Reading Strategy 16.2 ▶ Geography Activity 16: The Good Neighbor Policy ▶ Section 2 Review, p. 483 ▶ Daily Quiz 16.2	▶ One-Stop Planner, Lesson 16.2 ▶ The American Nation Video Program Segment: U.S. Warships in Havana Harbor; Teacher's Guide, pp. 191–92 ▶ Holt Researcher: American History CD–ROM	▶ Main Idea Activity for Reteaching and Sheltered English 16.2
Section 3 The Rise of Militarism, pp. 484–89	1 Describe how Benito Mussolini created a fascist state in Italy. 2 Explain how Joseph Stalin maintained power in the Soviet Union. 3 Analyze Adolf Hitler's rise to power in Germany. 4 Relate what caused the Spanish Civil War. 5 Discuss what actions Japan's military took during the 1930s.	▶ Guided Reading Strategy 16.3 ▶ Graphic Organizer Activity 16: A Shift in International Relations ▶ Literature Reading 16: Wartime Poet ▶ American History Outline Map 32: East and Southeast Asia ▶ Section 3 Review, p. 489 ▶ Daily Quiz 16.3	▶ One-Stop Planner, Lesson 16.3 ▶ Everyday Life in America Transparency 25: The Rise of the Third Reich ▶ Holt Researcher: American History CD–ROM ▶ HRW Web site	▶ Main Idea Activity for Reteaching and Sheltered English 16.3
Section 4 War Breaks Out, pp. 490–95	1 Explain the international response to fascism. 2 Describe the early events of World War II. 3 Discuss why tension between the United States and Germany increased. 4 Analyze why Japan bombed Pearl Harbor.	▶ Guided Reading Strategy 16.4 ▶ Section 4 Review, p. 495 ▶ Daily Quiz 16.4	▶ One-Stop Planner, Lesson 16.4 ▶ Holt Researcher: American History CD–ROM	▶ Main Idea Activity for Reteaching and Sheltered English 16.4
Chapter Review and Assessment pp. 496–97		▶ Chapter 16 Review, pp. 496–97 ▶ Chapter 16 Tutorial for Students, Parents, Mentors, and Peers ▶ Chapter 16 Test (Form A or B) ▶ Portfolio Activities and Alternative Assessment Handbook, Chapter 16	▶ Audio Program, Chapter 16 (English and Spanish) ▶ Chapter 16 Test Generator (on the One-Stop Planner) ▶ Global Skill Builder CD–ROM ▶ HRW Web site	▶ Spanish Glossary ▶ Sheltered English Chapter 16 Test

CHAPTER OVERVIEW

After World War I the United States followed a foreign policy of partial isolationism in hopes of avoiding involvement in another war. The United States and other nations pursued peace initiatives such as the Kellogg-Briand Pact, which outlawed war. The United States also worked to improve relations with Latin America. President Franklin D. Roosevelt established the Good Neighbor policy and the United States signed treaties giving up its right to intervene in the affairs of various Latin American countries.

The rise of dictatorships with expansionist ambitions in Italy, Germany, and Japan challenged the isolationist stance of the United States. Adolf Hitler's German forces occupied Austria and demanded the Sudetenland in Czechoslovakia. In 1938 European leaders met at the Munich Conference to discuss the situation. The leaders adopted a policy of appeasement to avoid a larger conflict. One year later, however, Germany invaded Poland and World War II began. Although the United States officially maintained a neutral stance toward the belligerents, the Lend-Lease Act appropriated U.S. funds to assist non-Axis countries. After the Japanese attacked Pearl Harbor on December 7, 1941, the United States officially entered the war.

TIME TAMERS

Block Scheduling

The teacher lesson plans for each section offer a variety of activity choices to help you present the material in a block scheduling format. For further suggestions on block scheduling, see the **Block Scheduling Handbook with Team Teaching Strategies**, pp. 91–96.

Internet Connections and Lesson 16
www.si.edu/hrw

Hands-On History Activities:

Classroom to Community The **Hands-On History Activities** help students make meaningful connections between events in American history and those in their own hometown. You may wish to use the Chapter 16 Activity, The Military in Your Community, to extend the chapter lessons, as alternative assessment, or as a block scheduling option.

Portfolio Projects

The American Nation includes multiple portfolio projects in each Pupil's Edition chapter review, as well as each unit review. Chapter 16 Portfolio Project options on p. 497 include the following:

1. Students will **create a chart.**
2. Students will **write a speech.**
3. Students will **create a business plan.**

The American Nation

INTERNET RESOURCE DIRECTORY

To access online materials for this chapter, go to **go.hrw.com** and type in the keywords listed below.

HRW ONLINE RESOURCES
GO TO: go.hrw.com

Online Maps
KEYWORD: SE1 Maps16
- Attack on Pearl Harbor
- Prelude to War: Germany 1939
- Prelude to War: Italy 1939
- Prelude to War: Japan 1939
- European Democracies 1939

Online Charts
KEYWORD: SE1 Charts16
- U.S. Entry into World War II

Online Reading Support
KEYWORD: SE1 Strategies16

Online Rubrics
KEYWORD: SE1 Rubrics

CHAPTER ENRICHMENT LINKS
Use these Web links to extend and enrich student learning for Chapter 16.
GO TO: go.hrw.com
KEYWORD: SE1 Ch16

CHAPTER INTERNET ACTIVITIES
GO TO: go.hrw.com
- Pupil's Edition Student Activity
  KEYWORD: SE1Front
  (Students examine the Spanish Popular Front.)
- Teacher's Edition Student Activity
  KEYWORD: SE1 Tutankhamen
  (Students conduct research on the discovery of King Tutankhamen's tomb.)
- Teacher's Edition Student Activity
  KEYWORD: SE1 Civil
  (Students investigate the involvement of Americans in the Spanish Civil War.)

ADDITIONAL
RESOURCES

Books for Teachers

Divine, Robert. *The Reluctant Belligerent.* Alfred A. Knopf, 1979. Discusses U.S. foreign policy during the 1930s.

Kimball, Warren. *Forged in War.* William Morrow, 1997. Examines the relationship between Franklin D. Roosevelt and Winston Churchill.

Books for Students

Allen, Peter. *The Origins of World War II.* Watts, 1992. Offers an account of the war's origins; includes illustrations.

Overy, Richard. *The Road to War.* Random House, 1990. Provides a highly readable account of the events leading to World War II.

Primary Sources from the Period

Grew, Joseph. *The Turbulent Era.* Houghton Mifflin, 1952. Recounts the memories and thoughts of the U.S. ambassador to Japan during the 1930s through letters and diary entries.

Ickes, Harold. *The Secret Diary of Harold L. Ickes.* Vol. 3, Simon and Schuster, 1954. Chronicles the approach of war.

Multimedia Materials

Roosevelt: Manipulator in Chief. Video, 24 min. Nielsen Ferns International. Assesses Franklin Roosevelt's efforts to prepare the United States to enter World War II.

World at War: A New Germany, 1933–39. Video, 52 min. Thames Television. Examines Hitler's impact on Germany.

Before You Read

Build on What You Know

Ask students to answer the following questions.

Why might World War I have left so many European countries in debt?

Consider:

- the cost of war weapons, machinery, and personnel
- the need to rebuild after the war
- the war's disruption of trade and other sources of revenue

Why might Americans have wanted to focus on matters at home after the war?

Consider:

- the experiences Americans had both in Europe and on the home front during the war
- the desire of the United States to avoid foreign entanglements

exploring the time line

AMERICAN EVENTS

Roosevelt's Third Term. Franklin D. Roosevelt's third term as president was unprecedented but not unconstitutional. George Washington's precedent of a two-term limit had been followed by all other presidents. It was not until 1940 that Roosevelt challenged this pattern. Roosevelt won not only a third term but also a fourth. In 1951 the Twenty-second Amendment officially put a limit on presidential terms.

CRITICAL THINKING Why might Americans have placed an official limit on presidential terms?

ANSWER: Students may suggest that Americans were concerned that allowing presidents to serve an unlimited number of terms would give the executive branch too much power.

CHAPTER 16

1921–1941

The Road to War

Delegates to the Washington Conference

1921
World Events
The Washington Conference begins.

1924
Daily Life
University of Illinois player Red Grange and Notre Dame coach Knute Rockne boost the popularity of football.

Red Grange

1931
Business and Finance
President Herbert Hoover proposes a halt to war-debt and reparations payments.

1921 — 1925 — 1929

1922
Science and Technology
British archaeologist Howard Carter discovers the tomb of Egypt's King Tutankhamen.

Tutankhamen's tomb

1926
Politics
President Coolidge sends U.S. troops to Nicaragua to preserve order and protect American interests after an attempted revolt.

1929
Daily Life
Some 71 percent of American families have incomes below $2,500, considered the minimum for a decent standard of living.

Unemployed man selling apples

Before You Read

Build on What You Know

World War I left Europe in a state of chaos. Germany was required to pay substantial war reparations, and other European countries owed the United States large war debts. In this chapter you will learn how after World War I many Americans hoped to focus on matters at home. However, the Great Depression touched off global economic problems. The rise of dictators in Europe set the stage for another war. Dictators also took power in several Latin American countries. Other Latin American countries tried to reduce U.S. influence in the region.

472

Think About Themes

To help students create their Themes Journal entries, provide the following examples of appropriate **agree**/**disagree** *statements.*

Global Relations

Agree The desire for peace motivated many nations to give up some of their power and join the League of Nations after World War I.

Disagree Prior to World War I, leaders of the major European powers believed that war was a legitimate means to settle political disputes.

Economic Development

Agree The political and economic consequences of the Revolutionary War led to the War of 1812.

Disagree Despite the Civil War's political and economic consequences, the North and South did not fight another war.

Democratic Values

Agree Americans accepted the government's crackdown on suspected communists during the boom years of the 1920s.

Disagree Many Americans demanded a bill of rights even though the U.S. Constitution offered to bring about greater economic stability.

St. Basil's Cathedral in Moscow

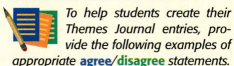

1933
Politics
The United States establishes diplomatic relations with the Soviet Union.

1933
Business and Finance
Following Great Britain's example, the United States goes off the gold standard.

1933
World Events
Adolf Hitler becomes chancellor of Germany.

The Des Moines Register

HUNDREDS UNNERVED BY RADIO SKIT

Headline announcing "The War of the Worlds" broadcast

1938
The Arts
The Mercury Theater radio production of "The War of the Worlds" sets off a national panic.

1941
World Events
Japanese forces attack Pearl Harbor.

1933 — **1937** — **1941**

1932
Daily Life
The average American's weekly wage drops to $17 from $28, its 1929 level.

1932
Business and Finance
American industrial production drops to one third of 1929 levels.

1932
Science and Technology
British physicist John Cockcroft becomes the first to split the atom.

1935
The Arts
Bette Davis wins an Oscar for her role in the film *Dangerous.*

BETTE DAVIS
Dangerous
FRANCHOT TONE

Poster advertising **Dangerous**

1939
World Events
World War II begins when German troops invade Poland.

1939
Science and Technology
Swiss chemist Paul Müller develops the insecticide DDT.

1940
Politics
Franklin D. Roosevelt wins an unprecedented third term as president.

exploring the time line

GLOBAL EVENTS

TOPIC: The Tomb of King Tutankhamen
GO TO: go.hrw.com
KEYWORD: SE1 Tutankhamen

Have students access the Internet through the HRW Web site to conduct research on the discovery of the tomb of Tutankhamen. Then ask each student to create a poster or multimedia presentation that describes the discovery of the tomb and interprets what the artifacts reveal about Tutankhamen's life.

Think About Themes

Decide whether you **agree** *or* **disagree** *with the following statements. Note why in your journal.*

Global Relations Nations should be willing to give up some of their power in order to promote world peace.

Economic Development Wars always have economic and political consequences that inevitably lead to more wars.

Democratic Values Citizens will give up certain liberties if their government provides economic stability.

473

SECTION 1

After completing Section 1, students should be able to:

OBJECTIVE 1 *Outline the foreign policy the United States followed after World War I.*

OBJECTIVE 2 *Identify the major postwar peace initiatives.*

OBJECTIVE 3 *Discuss how war debts and reparations affected European nations after World War I.*

LET'S GET STARTED!

As students enter the classroom, ask them to read the quotation from Senator William E. Borah on this page. Have each student attempt to rewrite the quotation from Borah in his or her own words. *(Borah was expressing his fear that U.S. sovereignty would be undermined if the nation joined the League of Nations.)* Have volunteers share their rewritten quotations with the class. Tell students that in Section 1 they will learn about U.S. foreign policy after World War I.

SECTION 1 RESOURCES

PRINT

- Guided Reading Strategy 16.1
- Biography Reading 16: Emily Greene Balch
- Primary Source Reading 16: A Diplomatic Failure
- Section 1 Review, p. 478
- Daily Quiz 16.1

MULTIMEDIA

- One-Stop Planner, Lesson 16.1
- Holt Researcher: American History CD–ROM

SHELTERED ENGLISH

- Main Idea Activity for Reteaching and Sheltered English 16.1

✔ READING TO UNDERSTAND

To help students master the section objectives, have them answer the **READING CHECKS** and complete **Guided Reading Strategy 16.1** as they read the section.

The Search for Peace

OBJECTIVES

Read to understand:

1. what foreign policy the United States followed after World War I
2. what the major postwar peace initiatives were
3. how war debts and reparations affected European nations after World War I

KEY TERMS

isolationism
disarmament
Washington Conference
Kellogg-Briand Pact

KEY PEOPLE

Emily Greene Balch
Charles Evans Hughes

EYEWITNESSES TO History

"The whole scheme [the League of Nations] has just one ultimate power and that is military force—the same power and the same principle which every despot [dictator] has relied upon in his efforts against the people when the people were seeking greater liberty and greater freedom, the same power which George III and Wilhelm II made the basis of their infamous designs [shameful plans]. . . . Let us leave these things—the lives of our people, the liberty of our whole nation—in the keeping and under the control of those people who have brought this Republic to its present place of prestige and power."

—William E. Borah

Senator William E. Borah

Senator William E. Borah of Idaho argued against membership in the League of Nations shortly after the end of World War I. Like many Americans, Borah feared that involvement in European affairs might draw the United States into another war.

Legacies of World War I

More than 8 million people, including more than 112,000 Americans, died fighting in the Great War. Yet few Americans believed that the war had made the world "safe for democracy." They noted the postwar chaos in government and the founding of a communist government in Russia. The Women's International League for Peace and Freedom summed up the nation's doubts: "War to end war has proved a failure. The war is won, yet nowhere is there peace, security or happiness."

Americans worried about being dragged into another foreign conflict. "We ask only to live our own life in our own way, in friendship and sympathy with all, in alliance with none," declared Senator Hiram W. Johnson in 1922. Such sentiments led the United States to follow a policy of partial **isolationism**, or withdrawal from world affairs, in the 1920s and 1930s.

Isolationists did not want to cut off the United States completely from the affairs of the rest of the world. They merely wanted to avoid what Thomas Jefferson had called "entangling alliances" that could drag the United States into another war. Isolationism led the United States to shun membership in international organizations that were set up after World War I. These included the League of Nations and the Permanent Court of International Justice, or World Court.

The World Court had been created to resolve international disputes. Presidents Coolidge, Hoover, and Roosevelt all proposed that the United States join the organization. Public opinion ran strongly against membership, however. The U.S. Senate set strict terms for

The horrors of World War I led many Americans to oppose war of any kind.

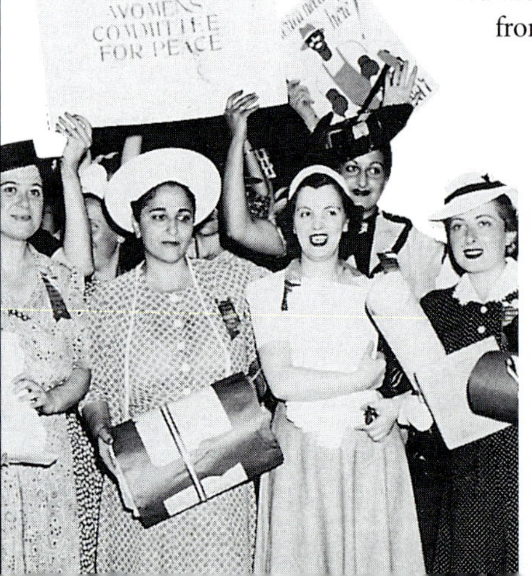

TEACH OBJECTIVE 1

ALL LEVELS: Ask students to identify recent conflicts in which the United States has been involved or has intervened. *(Students might mention U.S. intervention in the Kosovo crisis or U.S. involvement in the Persian Gulf War.)* Ask students why the United States might have involved itself in faraway conflicts that did not directly threaten the security of the United States. *(Students might suggest that the United States intervened to prevent aggressive leaders from expanding their territorial influence.)* To help students understand the post–World War I U.S. foreign policy, copy the graphic organizer at right on the chalkboard, omitting the italicized answers. Have each student complete it. Ask volunteers to share their answers with the class. To conclude, tell students that many Americans were disillusioned by the death, destruction, and political turmoil that resulted from World War I. **Sheltered English**

Americans' Concerns After World War I

Many Americans are worried about entering another foreign conflict.

→

U.S. Foreign Policy After World War I

The United States follows a foreign policy of partial isolationism. The country declines membership in the League of Nations and the World Court.

▶**ASSIGNMENT** *Have each student draw a political cartoon that illustrates U.S. foreign policy after World War I. Display students' cartoons around the classroom.*

---

joining in order to safeguard its right to make treaties. The nations that already belonged to the World Court rejected the Senate's terms, and the matter was dropped.

✔ **READING CHECK:** What foreign policy did the United States follow after World War I?

Promoting Peace

Rather than joining international peacekeeping organizations, the United States used diplomacy to promote world peace. American groups working for peace urged the U.S. government to bring world leaders together to negotiate **disarmament**, or reducing the size of a country's military. Jane Addams, Emily Greene Balch, Jeannette Rankin, and other leaders of the women's movement played important roles in these peace efforts. For their organizing efforts in the United States and abroad, both Addams—in 1931—and Balch—in 1946—received the Nobel Peace Prize.

The Washington Conference. Beginning in November 1921, the United States hosted the **Washington Conference**, an international conference in Washington, D.C., that focused on naval disarmament and Pacific security. The meeting was organized by U.S. secretary of state Charles Evans Hughes.

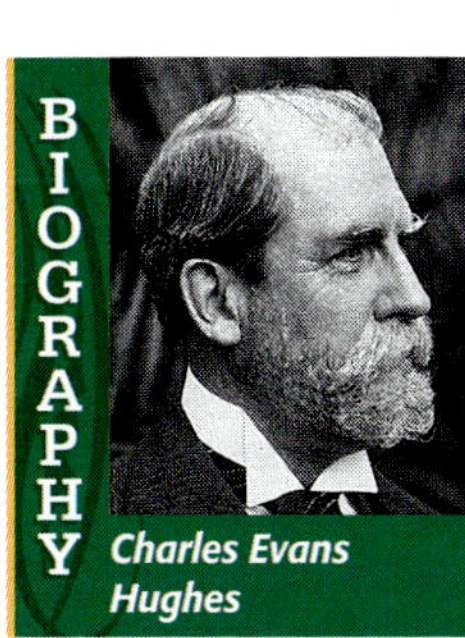

Charles Evans Hughes

Charles Evans Hughes was born in New York in April 1862. He graduated from Brown University in 1881 and received a law degree from Columbia University Law School three years later. After teaching and practicing law for several years, Hughes began his career in public service. Hughes was so busy, it was reported that he grew his beard in 1890 just to save the time it took to get a shave. Hughes served as legal adviser to Progressive Era legislators investigating corruption in the utilities industry. In 1906 he won his first public office when he defeated publishing tycoon William Randolph Hearst to become governor of New York.

Hughes served as a justice on the Supreme Court from 1910 to 1916, when he resigned his position to run for president. Hughes went to bed on election night believing himself the victor. The next morning he awoke to the news that he had lost to Woodrow Wilson by just 23 electoral votes.

After this crushing defeat Hughes turned to the issue of world peace. Putting aside political rivalries, Hughes supported U.S. entry into the League of Nations, the creation of President Wilson. At the end of World War I Hughes envisioned the United States taking an active role in future world affairs.

Then and Now

Peace Movements

The 1920s and 1930s saw a rise in the number of groups working for peace throughout the world. After experiencing the horrors of World War I, many people began to organize in an effort to abolish war. Some American opponents of war belonged to religious groups such as the Mennonites and Quakers. Others were members of political organizations such as the Committee on the Cause and Cure of War. All the groups urged U.S. leaders to reject war as a means of solving conflicts.

Although war has persisted, many groups continue to work to stop the use of violence as a political tool. Some, like the National Campaign for a Peace Tax Fund, have lobbied to allow citizens to redirect the portion of their tax payments that would go into military spending to a special fund to promote international peace. Many peace organizations are affiliated with religious groups, including the Jewish Peace Fellowship, the Muslim Peace Fellowship, and Pax Christi (Peace of Christ) U.S.A. These groups use modern means of communication such as the Internet to spread their message. Many also use film and television to publicize the horrors of war.

These protesters demonstrated in front of the U.S. Capitol in 1991.

PEOPLE IN HISTORY

Emily Greene Balch. Emily Greene Balch became interested in international peace efforts in 1914 when World War I began. She remained active in the peace movement for the rest of her life, helping to found the Women's International League for Peace and Freedom in 1919. She donated most of her Nobel Prize winnings to that organization in 1946. Despite her advocacy of peace, she supported the U.S. entry into World War II as necessary to stop the growth of Nazi Germany.

CRITICAL THINKING How might you reconcile Balch's call for peace with her support for U.S. entry into World War II?

ANSWER: Students might suggest that although Balch believed that wars should be avoided if possible, she believed that some wars must be fought to stop aggression.

THAT'S INTERESTING!

If just 1,711 California voters had cast their ballots for Charles Evans Hughes instead of Woodrow Wilson, Hughes would have won that state's 23 electoral votes and would have been elected president of the United States in 1916.

TEACH OBJECTIVE 2

LEVEL 1: Pair students and have each pair draw cartoons identifying the major peace initiatives after World War I. *(Cartoons should depict the agreements produced by the Washington Conference to limit nations' naval strength [the Five-Power Naval Treaty], guarantee respect for nations' territorial possessions in the Pacific [the Four-Power Treaty], and guarantee China's territorial integrity [the Nine-Power Treaty] and the Kellogg-Briand Pact, which outlawed war.)* Have students present their cartoons to the class.
Sheltered English, Cooperative Learning

LEVELS 2 AND 3: Ask each student to write a brief transcript for an imaginary news conference at which a U.S. diplomat of the 1920s and 1930s answers questions about the major peace initiatives after World War I. *(See the Level 1 lesson for the correct initiatives.)* Students' transcripts should include reporters' questions about the efforts of the United States and the diplomat's responses.

▶ASSIGNMENT *Tell students to imagine that they are Americans living in 1930. Have each student write a letter to his or her congressional representative either supporting or rejecting postwar peace initiatives. Students should give specific reasons why they agree or disagree with these peace efforts.*

ACROSS THE CURRICULUM

▶GEOGRAPHY◀

The Five-Power Treaty. The Five-Power Treaty included a clause prohibiting Great Britain, Japan, and the United States from building new military bases on most of the islands that each nation possessed in the Pacific. This agreement stipulated that the United States could not construct new bases in Guam, Midway, the Philippines, and Wake Islands.

CRITICAL THINKING Why might the United States have been banned from building bases in Guam, Midway, the Philippines, and Wake Islands?

ANSWER: Students might suggest that Japan could have perceived the arming of U.S. possessions in the western Pacific as a threat to its security.

THAT'S INTERESTING!

Because U.S. intelligence experts had broken the Japanese diplomatic code, Charles Evans Hughes knew the level of disarmament that Japanese negotiators would be willing to accept prior to the Washington Conference.

Read More About It

Free Find: Charles Evans Hughes
After reading about Charles Evans Hughes on the Holt Researcher CD–ROM, write a proposal for an arms-reduction conference to be held this year.

“We emerge from the war with a new national consciousness; with a consciousness of power stimulated by extraordinary effort; with a consciousness of the possibility and potency [power] of cooperation. . . . We are unworthy of our victory, if we look forward with timidity. This is the hour and power of light, not of darkness. . . . We have made the world safe for democracy, but democracy is not a phrase or a form, but a life, and what shall that life be? . . . We have fought this War to substitute reason for force. We love our Republic because it represents to us the promise of the rule of reason. . . . If we are to establish peace within our own borders, we must cooperate to destroy the . . . spirit of tyranny wherever we find it.”

In 1930 Charles Evans Hughes was appointed Chief Justice of the United States, a position he held until retiring in 1941. He died seven years later.

As President Harding's secretary of state, Hughes tried to make his goal of a peaceful world a reality at the Washington Conference. Hughes surprised the other delegates at the conference with a bold proposal. He suggested that the major powers destroy 66 large warships. He also called for a 10-year “naval holiday” during which no battleships or battle cruisers would be built.

Hughes proposed that the United States, Great Britain, and Japan destroy or retire some of their warships in order to limit their individual naval strength. Britain and the United States would have equal naval strength. The size of Japan's navy would be limited to 60 percent of that of the British and U.S. navies. Italy and France would both be limited to navies roughly half the size of Japan's. This disarmament plan became known as the Five-Power Naval Treaty. Marveled one observer, “[Secretary Hughes sank more] ships than all the admirals of the world had sunk in a cycle of centuries.”

The Washington Conference produced other important agreements as well. In the Four-Power Treaty, Britain, France, Japan, and the United States pledged to respect one another's territory in the Pacific. The Nine-Power Treaty included the nations that had signed the Five-Power Naval Treaty as well as Belgium, China, the Netherlands, and Portugal. The treaty guaranteed China's territorial integrity and required its signers to uphold the Open Door Policy.

Japan's minister of the navy, Admiral Kato Tomosaburo, explained Japan's support for disarmament.

“Japan is ready for the new order of thought—the spirit of international friendship and cooperation for the greater good of humanity—which the Conference has brought about.”

Carrie Chapman Catt strongly supported the Kellogg-Briand Pact.

For a time the treaties produced at the Washington Conference eased tensions in Asia. Japan began withdrawing from China's Shandong Peninsula, which it had invaded in 1914. Japan also withdrew from the parts of Siberia it had occupied during the Russian Revolution. Japan's 1930 agreement to extend the 10-year ban on warship construction marked the high point of postwar international cooperation efforts.

Unsuccessful efforts. April 6, 1927, marked the 10th anniversary of the U.S. entry into World War I. On that day French foreign minister Aristide Briand

TEACH OBJECTIVE 3

LEVEL 1: Pair students and have each pair create a cause-and-effect chart showing how war debts and reparations affected European nations. *(Pairs' charts should show that Allied nations were in debt to the United States. In order to pay their debt to the United States, the Allies demanded harsh reparations from Germany. Germany was forced to borrow money and to print paper money, causing hyperinflation. This inflation led to a severe economic downturn; financial troubles made Germans increasingly bitter.)* Ask volunteers to present their charts to the class.
Sheltered English, Cooperative Learning

LEVEL 2: Tell students to imagine that they are living in Europe after World War I. Have each student write several diary entries describing the effect of war debts and reparations on European countries. Students should express their opinions and feelings about the situation in their entries. *(See the Level 1 lesson for the correct effects.)* Ask volunteers to read their diary entries to the class.

LEVEL 3: Tell students to imagine that they are newspaper reporters in the late 1920s who have been to Europe and seen firsthand the effects of war debts and reparations on European nations. Have each student write a newspaper editorial summarizing these effects. *(See the Level 1 lesson for the correct effects.)* Ask volunteers to read their editorials to the class.

(ah-ree-steed bree-ahn) proposed that France and the United States enter into an agreement to outlaw war. U.S. secretary of state Frank Kellogg made a counterproposal that the pact include all nations. Eventually, 62 countries signed the **Kellogg-Briand Pact**. The treaty outlawed war "as an instrument of national policy" but allowed countries to go to war in self-defense. The treaty lacked provisions for enforcement, however. One U.S. senator remarked that the treaty was "as effective to keep down war as a carpet would be to smother an earthquake."

The pact's weaknesses became clear in September 1931 when Japan violated the agreement by invading Manchuria, a territory in China. The invasion launched a bloody war between Japan and China. Although many Americans called for an economic boycott of Japan, U.S. leaders refused to support sanctions against the Japanese. The failure of diplomacy to prevent Japanese aggression marked the end of attempts to reach international accords. Preoccupied by the Japanese invasion and the worldwide economic depression, delegates to the 1932 League of Nations World Disarmament Conference went home without agreeing to reduce weapons.

✔ **READING CHECK:** What were the major postwar peace initiatives?

These Japanese troops are celebrating their victory in Manchuria, China.

War Debts and Reparations

The issue of war debts also weakened efforts to maintain peace. In the late 1800s European investors had loaned money to finance U.S. industrial growth. After 1914, however, the United States became a creditor nation. At the start of World War I, U.S. banks lent money to Britain and France so that they could buy armaments from the United States. The U.S. government granted billions more in credit to the Allies. By 1920 the Allies owed more than $10 billion to the United States.

The debtor nations argued that their debts to the United States should be canceled. David Lloyd George, the British prime minister when the United States entered the war, explained their reasoning.

> **"The United States did not from first to last make any sacrifice or contribution remotely comparable to those of her European Associates, in life, limb, money, material or trade, towards the victory which she shared with them."**

U.S. officials rejected appeals from Britain, France, and Italy to cancel their war debts completely. However, the U.S. government did cancel part of the debts. It also reduced the interest rates on the balances. Still, the only way the Allies could pay their war debts to the United States was to collect reparations, or damages, from defeated Germany. In 1921 a reparations commission had set total German reparations at 132 billion gold marks, or $32 billion. The Germans bitterly condemned the reparations as too harsh. Chancellor Joseph Wirth paid part of the reparations by borrowing money from Britain. The German government also printed paper money, resulting in massive inflation and causing the value of the German mark to plunge.

In 1922 writer Ernest Hemingway traveled from Strasburg, France, to Kehl, Germany. He described the extreme difference in prices between France and Germany, an effect of severe inflation in Germany:

British prime minister David Lloyd George urged U.S. leaders to cancel the debts Britain and other European nations owed the United States from World War I.

HISTORY MAKERS SPEAK

Henry Cabot Lodge Jr. in *The Meaning of the Kellogg Treaty*

Criticizing the Kellogg-Briand Pact. Henry Cabot Lodge Jr. criticized the Kellogg-Briand Pact in a 1928 article. Lodge wrote, "The conception of renouncing war by governmental fiat [declaration] seems inherently absurd. The great forces in modern society—and especially American society—are quite independent of the government. We are in great measure our own masters. The banks, the newspapers, the great organizations of business—that whole body of influences which affect our thoughts, our food, our clothes, and our incomes are forging along no matter what Washington says."

CRITICAL THINKING Why might Lodge have believed that the Kellogg-Briand Pact was absurd?

ANSWER: Students might suggest that Lodge believed that governments do not have the power to stop wars from occurring.

VISUAL RECORD ANSWER
(for p. 478)
Students might suggest that German currency had little value.

REVIEW

Have students complete the **Section 1 Review** on p. 478.

ASSESS

Have students complete **Daily Quiz 16.1.** As **Alternative Assessment**, you may want to use the cause-and-effect chart or the diary entries in this section's lessons.

RETEACH

Have students complete **Main Idea Activity for Reteaching and Sheltered English 16.1.** Then organize the class into small groups. Have each group create a list of important results of World War I in the United States and Europe that are discussed in this chapter. Then have groups prepare some illustrations that will help other students study these effects. Display these illustrations around the classroom.
Sheltered English, Cooperative Learning

EXTEND

Have each student interview a local economics expert *(such as an economics professor or a banker)* to learn more about inflation. Then have students interview family members or other community members about their memories of recent periods of inflation. To conclude, have students present the results of their interviews to the class. **Block Scheduling**

SECTION 1 REVIEW ANSWERS

Define and Identify
For significance, see the following pages:

- isolationism, p. 474
- disarmament, p. 475
- Emily Greene Balch, p. 475
- Washington Conference, p. 475
- Charles Evans Hughes, p. 475
- Kellogg-Briand Pact, p. 477

1. Five-Power Naval Treaty—limit size of navies; Four-Power Treaty—respect territories in the Pacific to avoid conflict; Nine-Power Treaty—guarantee China's territorial integrity
2. Nations could not agree on a method of enforcing the pact.
3. Students' memos should discuss the goals of the conference and the nature of the agreements signed there.
4. They created economic crises that led to internal political crises in Germany.
5. Many Americans regretted the cost in lives and money of World War I and believed that the traditional practice of avoiding European conflicts should again be the U.S. foreign policy.

INTERPRETING THE VISUAL RECORD

Inflation. These German children are using bundles of German marks as building blocks. ***What does this photograph suggest about the value of German currency?***

> **"We changed some French money in the railway station at Kehl. For 10 francs I received 670 marks. Ten francs amounted to about 90 cents in Canadian money. That 90 cents lasted Mrs. Hemingway and me for a day of heavy spending and at the end of the day we had 120 marks left! . . . Kehl's best hotel, which is a very well turned-out place, served a five-course table d'hôte meal for 120 marks, which amounts to 15 cents in our money. The same meal could not be duplicated in Strasburg, three miles away, for a dollar."**

With his country near financial collapse, one particularly embittered German World War I veteran sought someone to blame. Adolf Hitler had survived a poison gas attack during the war and remained convinced that politicians, not the German army, were responsible for Germany losing the war. Feeling betrayed, Hitler joined a radical political organization and hatched a plot to overthrow the German government in 1923. The plot failed, and Hitler was sent to jail. There he continued to plan revenge against those whom he believed had betrayed Germany.

In 1924 a plan proposed by Charles Dawes temporarily eased Germany's economic crisis. The Dawes Plan provided loans and gave Germany more time to make its reparations payments. In 1931, as the worldwide depression deepened, President Herbert Hoover declared a year's moratorium, or halt, on reparations and war-debt payments. The moratorium, however, only prolonged the crisis. Most of the war debts remained unpaid. By 1934 Finland was the only debtor nation that could make even a token payment on its debts.

✔ **READING CHECK:** How did war debts and reparations affect European nations?

SECTION 1 REVIEW

Define and explain the significance of the following terms:
isolationism
disarmament
Washington Conference
Kellogg-Briand Pact

Identify and explain the significance of the following individuals:
Emily Greene Balch
Charles Evans Hughes

1. **Using Graphic Organizers** Copy the following graphic organizer. Use it to list the treaties signed at the Washington Conference and their objectives.

2. **Analyzing** Why was the Kellogg-Briand Pact unsuccessful in resolving the conflict in Manchuria?
3. **Recognizing Point of View** Imagine that you are a delegate to the Washington Conference in 1921. Write a memo to your government explaining why you consider the conference a success.
4. **Assessing Consequences** How did war debts and reparations affect Germany and other European countries?

Critical Thinking

5. Why did the United States partially withdraw from world affairs in the 1920s and 1930s?
Consider:
• the costs of World War I
• traditional U.S. foreign policy
• public opinion toward Europe

SECTION 2

After completing Section 2, students should be able to:

OBJECTIVE 1 *Discuss the role the United States played in Nicaraguan politics.*

OBJECTIVE 2 *Explain how U.S. relations with Latin America changed in the 1930s.*

OBJECTIVE 3 *Analyze how the Great Depression affected Latin American countries.*

LET'S GET STARTED!

Write the following terms on the chalkboard: *Monroe Doctrine* and *Roosevelt Corollary.* As students enter the classroom, have them write as much as they can about these two U.S. foreign-policy doctrines. Have volunteers share their responses with the class. *(Students might mention that the Monroe Doctrine stipulated that European intervention in the Western Hemisphere would be considered a threat to U.S. security and that the Americas were off-limits to European expansion. The Roosevelt Corollary extended the Monroe Doctrine to claim a greater U.S. role in maintaining order in Latin America.)* Tell students that in Section 2 they will learn about how U.S. policy toward Latin America changed in the 1920s and 1930s.

Relations with Latin America

OBJECTIVES

Read to understand:

1. what role the United States played in Nicaraguan politics
2. how U.S. relations with Latin America changed in the 1930s
3. how the Great Depression affected Latin American countries

KEY TERMS

Good Neighbor policy
nationalize
caudillos

KEY PEOPLE

Emiliano Chamorro
Henry Stimson
Augusto César Sandino
Adolfo Díaz
Anastasio Somoza
Lázaro Cárdenas
Josephus Daniels

"Ever since the World War we have been manufacturing more goods than we can sell. We are looking for new markets. Latin America and South America afford [provide] these markets. And yet in order to allow a few bankers to exploit [take advantage of] Nicaragua, our oil interests to exploit Mexico, we are willing to ruin the legitimate commercial business of this country. We are willing to let thousands of men remain out of employment who could be working in the manufacturing plants of this country if we by peaceful means sought the friendship and trade of Central and South America."

—Burton K. Wheeler

Senator Burton K. Wheeler

In 1927 Senator Burton K. Wheeler of Montana condemned U.S. policy toward Latin America. For many years the United States had dominated Latin America both economically and militarily. This began to change during the 1930s as the United States tried to build a more equal relationship with its southern neighbors.

Intervention in Nicaragua

The United States played a large role in Nicaraguan politics throughout the 1920s and 1930s. In 1925 General Emiliano Chamorro (chah-MAWR-roh) overthrew the government, sparking a bitter civil war. The United States, however, refused to recognize Chamorro's government. In May 1926 President Coolidge ordered in the U.S. Marine Corps to protect American commercial interests. He also sent Henry Stimson, a longtime public official, to negotiate an end to the civil war. Stimson brought the two sides together, and they negotiated a peace treaty in May 1927. In the treaty, Stimson called for the abolition of Nicaragua's armed forces. U.S. troops would then train a new Nicaraguan National Guard to maintain order after the U.S. withdrawal.

Augusto César Sandino (sahn-DEE-noh), a general who opposed Chamorro, refused to accept Stimson's proposal. During the 1920s Sandino worked as a mechanic for American companies in Honduras and Guatemala. In 1923 he began working for an American-owned oil company in Tampico, Mexico. There Sandino read about Simón Bolívar, the great hero of the Latin American independence struggle.

In 1926, after his return to Nicaragua, Sandino organized a revolt against Chamorro and Chamorro's successor, Adolfo Díaz. He hoped to rid Nicaragua of the Americans, whom he viewed as invaders, and to allow ordinary Nicaraguans to control their country's land and wealth. He planned to help workers and peasants "exploit our own natural resources for the benefit of the Nicaraguan family in general."

Augusto César Sandino led a revolt in Nicaragua.

SECTION 2 RESOURCES

PRINT

- Guided Reading Strategy 16.2
- Geography Activity 16: The Good Neighbor Policy
- Section 2 Review, p. 483
- Daily Quiz 16.2

MULTIMEDIA

- One-Stop Planner, Lesson 16.2
- The American Nation Video Program Segment: U.S. Warships in Havana Harbor; Teacher's Guide, pp. 191–92
- Holt Researcher: American History CD–ROM

SHELTERED ENGLISH

- Main Idea Activity for Reteaching and Sheltered English 16.2

✓ READING TO UNDERSTAND

To help students master the section objectives, have them answer the **READING CHECKS** and complete **Guided Reading Strategy 16.2** as they read the section.

GRAPH ANSWER

(for p. 480)

from 1920 to 1925

TEACH OBJECTIVE 1

LEVEL 1: Pair students and have each pair create an annotated time line chronicling U.S. intervention in Nicaragua during the 1920s and 1930s. *(Time lines should include: 1926—U.S. Marines invade Nicaragua to protect American commercial interests; May 1927—Henry Stimson helps negotiate an end to civil war in Nicaragua; 1927—U.S. troops train the Nicaraguan National Guard; 1926–33—U.S. troops fight against Sandino's forces; 1933—U.S. Marines withdraw from Nicaragua; 1936 and beyond—the U.S. government backs the Somoza regime.)* Have students present their time lines to the class. **Sheltered English, Cooperative Learning**

LEVELS 2 AND 3: Tell students to imagine that they are reporters covering the U.S. role in Nicaraguan politics. It is 1936 and Somoza has just seized political power. Have each student write a newspaper article explaining the role that the United States has played in Nicaraguan politics up to that point. *(See the Level 1 lesson for the correct events related to the U.S. role in Nicaragua.)* Have volunteers read their articles to the class. Students may wish to include their articles in their portfolios.

GLOBAL RELATIONS

The Clark Memorandum. Published in 1930, the Clark Memorandum revealed the changing U.S. attitude toward Latin America. Written in 1928 by State Department official J. Reuben Clark, the memorandum declared that the Monroe Doctrine could not be interpreted to mean that the United States had the right to intervene in the internal affairs of Latin American countries. The Clark Memorandum departed course from the Roosevelt Corollary, which had declared that the Monroe Doctrine included the right of intervention.

CRITICAL THINKING Why did the Clark Memorandum represent a significant change in U.S. foreign policy?

ANSWER: Students might suggest that the memorandum represented a move toward a policy of nonintervention in the affairs of other nations.

The American Nation **VIDEO PROGRAM**

U.S. Warships in Havana Harbor; Teacher's Guide, pp. 191–92

Search 41576, Play to 42493
Videodisc 2, Side A

Play Pause

See *Teacher's Guide* for Spanish barcode.

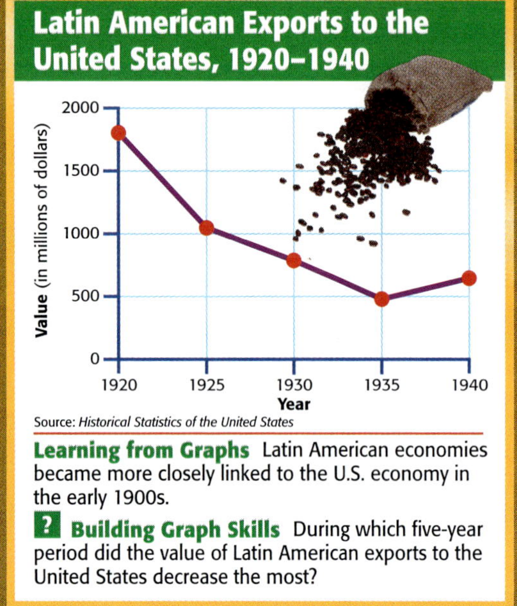

Latin American Exports to the United States, 1920–1940

Source: *Historical Statistics of the United States*

Learning from Graphs Latin American economies became more closely linked to the U.S. economy in the early 1900s.

Building Graph Skills During which five-year period did the value of Latin American exports to the United States decrease the most?

Sandino's forces ranged from as few as 30 to as many as 3,000 soldiers. They proved a tough opponent for the U.S. Marines. The Americans used aerial bombing against Sandino's forces. However, this did not completely destroy the army, which relied on sympathetic farmers to feed and house them.

The marines never defeated Sandino. The war became increasingly costly for the United States, which was in the midst of the Great Depression. In 1933 President Hoover withdrew the last of the U.S. troops. A year later, the commander of the U.S.-trained National Guard, General Anastasio Somoza, ordered Sandino's assassination. With Sandino dead, organized resistance to Somoza and his military evaporated. Somoza forced out the Nicaraguan president in 1936 and took over the presidency the next year. With U.S. backing, Somoza and other members of his family ruled Nicaragua almost without interruption until the Sandinista revolution—named for Sandino—overthrew the dynasty in 1979.

✔ **READING CHECK:** What role did the United States play in Nicaraguan politics?

A Change in Policy

While the United States isolated itself from events in Europe and Asia, Presidents Coolidge, Hoover, and Roosevelt all tried to improve relations with Latin American countries. Before his inauguration, Hoover toured Latin America to promote goodwill, winning many new friends for the United States.

In 1936 Franklin Roosevelt proposed an inter-American Conference for peace in Argentina.

The Good Neighbor. President Franklin D. Roosevelt built upon the goodwill created by previous presidents. In his inaugural speech of 1933 Roosevelt spelled out his policy of mutual respect toward Latin America, which became known as the **Good Neighbor policy**.

> **"In the field of world policy I would dedicate this nation to the policy of the good neighbor—the neighbor who resolutely respects himself and, because he does so, respects the rights of others."**

To back up his words, Roosevelt in 1934 signed a treaty with Cuba that canceled the Platt Amendment. This amendment had given the United States the right to intervene in Cuban affairs. Two years later he gave up the U.S. right to intervene in Panama. Roosevelt also withdrew marines from Haiti, where they had been stationed as an occupying force since 1915.

In economic matters the United States had often behaved more like a landlord than a good neighbor. American investors played a

TEACH OBJECTIVE 2

LEVEL 1: Pair students and ask each pair to write a paragraph describing how U.S. relations with Latin America changed in the 1930s. *(Students should explain that the United States established the Good Neighbor Policy, a policy of mutual respect. As a result, the United States canceled the Platt Amendment, gave up its right to intervene unilaterally in Panama, withdrew marines from Haiti, and did not intervene when the Mexican government decided to nationalize the oil industry.)* Have volunteers read their paragraphs to the class. **Sheltered English, Cooperative Learning**

LEVELS 2 AND 3: Pair students and tell them to imagine that they are news analysts for a radio station in the late 1930s. Have each pair create a transcript of a radio talk show discussion about how U.S. relations with Latin America changed during the1930s. Have one student prepare the reporter's transcript and the other student prepare the transcript for the interviewee. *(See the Level 1 lesson for how U.S. relations with Latin America changed.)* Have students perform their discussions for the class. **Cooperative Learning**

powerful—and sometimes negative—role in Latin America. After World War I, large American companies increased their investments in banana, coffee, and sugar plantations in Central America and the Caribbean. Some countries were run largely to serve the interests of these foreign companies and became known as banana republics.

The United Fruit Company was the largest American company in Latin America. It owned millions of acres in Central America and the Caribbean, and was Guatemala's largest landowner, exporter, and employer. In addition to establishing plantations, United Fruit and other companies built roads and railroads. They also controlled the ports and shipping lines necessary to export their products.

INTERPRETING THE VISUAL RECORD

Latin America. Many foreign companies controlled large plantations in Latin American countries and greatly influenced local governments. ***Do you think this postcard accurately shows what a plantation was like? Explain your answer.***

American companies played a central economic role in Latin America. They also had tremendous political power. The companies made alliances with Latin American landowners and politicians and often played a direct role in governing the countries in which they operated. Many Latin Americans resented the economic and political power of the large American companies. Chilean poet Pablo Neruda (nay-ROO-dah) wrote:

> **"The Fruit Company, Inc.**
> **reserved for itself the most succulent,**
> **the central coast of my own land,**
> **the delicate waist of America.**
> **It rechristened its territories**
> **as the 'Banana Republics.'"**

Relations with Mexico. A serious test of the Good Neighbor policy came in March 1938. Mexico's president, Lázaro Cárdenas (KAHR-day-nahs), began to **nationalize**, or assert government control over, the country's oil industry. Although the Mexican constitution of 1917 proclaimed that Mexico controlled all its underground resources, American and British firms had continued to own and operate oil companies in Mexico. When the foreign companies refused to meet the demands of Mexican oil workers for higher wages and better working conditions, President Cárdenas nationalized the oil fields.

American oil companies hotly criticized Mexico's seizure of their property. They pressed President Roosevelt to intervene. Meanwhile, the U.S. ambassador to Mexico, Josephus Daniels, argued for a

THROUGH OTHERS' EYES

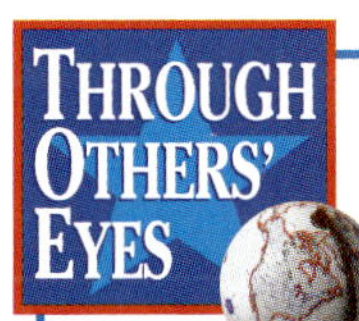

Latin American Views of Foreign Investment

The United States has always had close ties with Latin America. For much of its history the relationship has been marked by U.S. domination of the region, both politically and economically. In 1933 a member of the Honduran congress described the effect foreign investment was having on his country.

> **"The national farmers are condemned to disappear, for the fruit companies are becoming owners of the lands on the coast, including the alternate lots, which they now have almost entirely in their possession, through transfers made by the Hondurans themselves. The villages, the small riverside farms disappear, and the depopulation of the region follows."**

A 1929 report by the Sociedad Económica de Amigos del País described the power of foreign companies in Costa Rica.

> **"It is evident . . . that the fruit company, besides having taken possession of a large portion of the Atlantic Zone, is exercising over it a predominance and control such as not even the government of the republic itself exercises; there it is the company which commands."**

HISTORY MAKERS SPEAK

Franklin D. Roosevelt in *Foreign Affairs*

International Relations. In a 1928 campaign article Franklin Roosevelt expressed his reasons for wanting to improve U.S. foreign relations if elected president: "The outside world views us with less good will today than at any previous period. This is serious unless we take the deliberate position that the people of the United States owe nothing to the rest of mankind and care nothing for the opinion of others so long as our seacoasts are impregnable and our pocketbooks are well filled."

CRITICAL THINKING What might Roosevelt's 1928 statement have revealed about his attitude toward isolationism?

ANSWER: Students might suggest that Roosevelt believed that isolationism would be a selfish policy to pursue.

THAT'S INTERESTING!

In 1934 President Roosevelt became the first president to sail through the Panama Canal and also the first to visit a South American country.

VISUAL RECORD ANSWER

Students might suggest that the postcard inaccurately portrays plantation life because no workers are shown.

TEACH OBJECTIVE 3

ALL LEVELS: Tell students that an economic depression can have social and political effects on a country, as well as economic ones. Ask students to identify the possible social and political effects. *(Students might suggest that depression might affect some sectors of society more than others or that a country's political leaders may be held accountable for an economic downturn.)* To help students understand how the Great Depression affected Latin American countries, copy the following graphic organizer on the chalkboard, omitting the italicized answers. Have each student complete it. Ask volunteers to share their answers with the class. **Sheltered English**

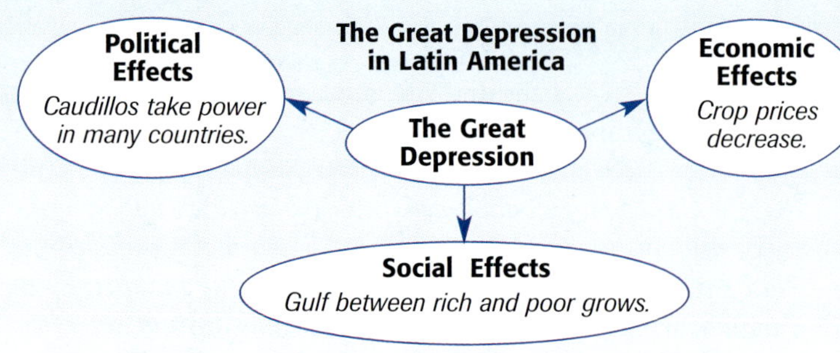

▸ASSIGNMENT *Tell students to imagine that they are editors for an encyclopedia. Have each student write a short entry on the rise of caudillos in Latin American countries during the Great Depression.*

GLOBAL RELATIONS

Relations with Mexico. Officials in the U.S. State Department sent a diplomatic note to the Mexican government demanding immediate payment for the properties seized when the Mexican government nationalized the country's oil fields. To give force to the message, U.S. purchases of Mexican silver were immediately suspended. Ambassador Josephus Daniels, however, advised the Mexican government to ignore the note. With President Franklin Roosevelt's approval, administration officials authorized additional silver purchases from Mexico above the world market price.

CRITICAL THINKING Why might Roosevelt have approved silver purchases from Mexico?

ANSWER: Students might suggest that he wanted to send a clear message to Mexico that conflict over the oil properties would not damage relations between the two nations.

CHANGING WAYS ANSWERS

greatly increased; the United States

VISUAL RECORD ANSWER

(for p. 483)

Students might cite the poor condition of the house and the cattle.

Mexican president Lázaro Cárdenas (center) and his secretary of foreign relations (right) meet with Britain's minister to Mexico (left).

compromise between the Mexican government and the oil companies. He urged the United States to recognize Mexico's right to control its oil resources but added that American companies should be compensated for the property they had lost.

Most of the Mexican people supported Cárdenas's bold action against the oil companies. Many Mexicans worried, however, that the United States might invade their country to restore American oil companies' property rights. President Roosevelt decided to maintain good relations with Mexico. He acknowledged Mexico's right to control its own resources and urged the oil companies to reach an agreement with the Mexican government for fair compensation. Mexico agreed to the compromise and began payments in 1939.

✔ **READING CHECK:** How did U.S. relations with Latin America change during the 1930s?

Changing Ways Investments in Latin America

Understanding Change The economies of the United States and Latin American countries have long been connected. The industrialization of the United States during the late 1800s resulted in a rapid expansion of this connection. Today the United States and the countries of Latin America continue to strengthen the links between their economies. *How has the value of U.S. investments in Latin America changed over time? Has the changing balance of trade between the two regions been more beneficial for the United States or for Latin America?*

	Then	Now
Value of Direct U.S. Investments in Latin America	$3.52 billion	$172.48 billion
Value of U.S. Exports to Latin America	$698 million	$98.67 billion
Value of U.S. Imports from Latin America	$1.12 billion	$94.65 billion

Sources: *Historical Statistics of the United States* and *Statistical Abstract of the United States: 1998.* Data reflect 1929 and 1997.

REVIEW

Have students complete the **Section 2 Review** on p. 483.

ASSESS

Have students complete **Daily Quiz 16.2.** As **Alternative Assessment**, you may want to use the radio talk show or the newspaper article in this section's lessons.

RETEACH

Have students complete **Main Idea Activity for Reteaching and Sheltered English 16.2.** Then organize students into three groups. Have each group create a graphic organizer for one of the objectives in this section. Then have each group exchange its graphic organizer—with answers omitted—with another group and complete the graphic organizer that it receives. **Sheltered English, Cooperative Learning**

EXTEND

Have students conduct research on the history of one of the Latin American countries discussed in this section. Students should focus their research on events that occurred during the 1920s and 1930s. Then have students write a series of diary entries that discuss the economic, social, and political changes that occurred in the country. **Block Scheduling**

The Rise of Dictators

The Wall Street crash of 1929 sent shock waves through Latin America. The worldwide economic depression meant lower prices for bananas, coffee, and other Latin American crops. Farm wages dropped to eight cents a day.

As workers lost their jobs, the gulf between Latin America's small class of wealthy landowners and the large class of poor landless people widened. One U.S. diplomat, Major A. R. Harris, commented on the inequality he saw between the classes in El Salvador in 1931.

> **"The first thing one observes . . . is the number of expensive automobiles on the streets. . . . There seems to be nothing between these high-priced cars and the ox-cart with its barefooted attendant. . . . Roughly 90 percent of the wealth of the country is held by about one-half of one percent of the population."**

In the 1930s **caudillos** (kow-DEE-yohs) took power in many Latin American countries. Caudillos were military leaders who used force to maintain order. During the 1930s caudillos seized power in Cuba, the Dominican Republic, Guatemala, and Honduras. Some U.S. diplomats denounced the bans on opposition parties and restrictions on freedom of speech that the caudillos employed to maintain their power. However, the United States often supported the caudillos, because they created favorable environments for American companies to do business.

INTERPRETING THE VISUAL RECORD

Poverty. The Great Depression devastated many Latin American nations and contributed to the rise of dictators. ***What signs of economic hardship do you see in this picture of a Salvadoran family?***

✔ **READING CHECK:** How did the Great Depression affect Latin American countries?

SECTION 2 REVIEW

Define and explain the significance of the following terms:
Good Neighbor policy
nationalize
caudillos

Identify and explain the significance of the following individuals:
Emiliano Chamorro
Henry Stimson
Augusto César Sandino
Adolfo Díaz
Anastasio Somoza
Lázaro Cárdenas
Josephus Daniels

1. **Using Graphic Organizers** Copy the graphic organizer below. Use it to list the changes that the Good Neighbor policy brought to the U.S. relationship with Latin America.

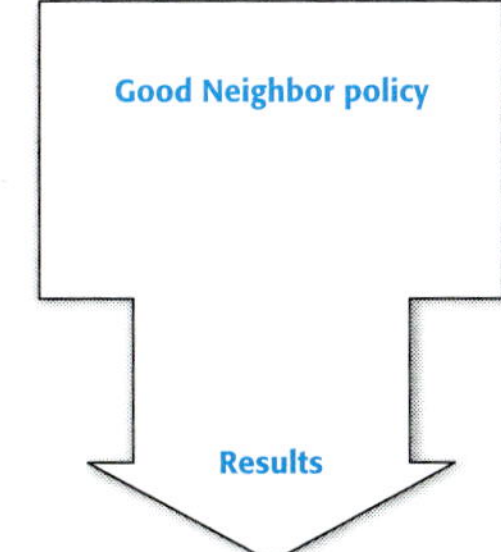

2. **Evaluating** Why did Augusto César Sandino organize a revolt against Adolfo Díaz?
3. **Identifying Cause and Effect** Why did the United States intervene in Nicaraguan politics throughout the 1920s and into the 1930s? What was the effect of this intervention?
4. **Taking a Stand** Imagine that you are Josephus Daniels in 1938. Write a memorandum to President Roosevelt recommending a U.S. response to Mexico after its nationalization of the oil fields.

Critical Thinking

5. Could the United States have prevented the rise of dictators in Latin America?
Consider:
- U.S. policy toward Latin America in the 1920s
- the goals of the Good Neighbor policy
- the effects of the Great Depression on Latin America

SECTION 2 REVIEW ANSWERS

Define and Identify
For significance, see the following pages:
- Emiliano Chamorro, p. 479
- Henry Stimson, p. 479
- Augusto César Sandino, p. 479
- Adolfo Díaz, p. 479
- Anastasio Somoza, p. 480
- Good Neighbor policy, p. 480
- Lázaro Cárdenas, p. 481
- nationalize, p. 481
- Josephus Daniels, p. 482
- caudillos, p. 483

1. The policy limited military intervention but did not end U.S. economic or political domination of much of the region.
2. He wanted to rid Nicaragua of all American influence.
3. The United States intervened to protect American commercial interests; Somoza and his family held control of the country for more than 40 years.
4. Memos should refer to the need to retain Mexico as a friend during an era of growing global tensions.
5. Answers will vary. Students might suggest that the Good Neighbor policy restricted U.S. intervention at a time when Latin American governments were falling to dictators because of the economic crisis. In addition, many American commercial interests supported the dictators.

SECTION 3

After completing Section 3, students should be able to:

OBJECTIVE 1 *Describe how Benito Mussolini created a fascist state in Italy.*

OBJECTIVE 2 *Explain how Joseph Stalin maintained power in the Soviet Union.*

OBJECTIVE 3 *Analyze Adolf Hitler's rise to power in Germany.*

OBJECTIVE 4 *Relate what caused the Spanish Civil War.*

OBJECTIVE 5 *Discuss what actions Japan's military took during the 1930s.*

LET'S GET STARTED!

Write the word *dictator* on the chalkboard and provide a short definition. *(Tell students that a dictator is a ruler who holds absolute power.)* As students enter the classroom, ask them to respond to the term by writing several characteristics that they associate with dictators. Ask volunteers to share their responses. Tell students that in Section 3 they will learn about various dictators and how they came to power in the 1920s and 1930s.

SECTION 3 RESOURCES

PRINT
- Guided Reading Strategy 16.3
- Graphic Organizer Activity 16: A Shift in International Relations
- Literature Reading 16: Wartime Poet
- American History Outline Map 32: East and Southeast Asia
- Section 3 Review, p. 489
- Daily Quiz 16.3

MULTIMEDIA
- One-Stop Planner, Lesson 16.3
- Everyday Life in America Transparency 25: The Rise of the Third Reich
- Holt Researcher: American History CD–ROM
- HRW Web site

SHELTERED ENGLISH
- Main Idea Activity for Reteaching and Sheltered English 16.3

✔ READING TO UNDERSTAND
To help students master the section objectives, have them answer the **READING CHECKS** and complete **Guided Reading Strategy 16.3** as they read the section.

The Rise of Militarism

OBJECTIVES

Read to understand:
1. how Benito Mussolini created a fascist state in Italy
2. how Joseph Stalin maintained power in the Soviet Union
3. how Adolf Hitler rose to power in Germany
4. what caused the Spanish Civil War
5. what actions Japan's military took during the 1930s

KEY TERMS

Fascist Party
Blackshirts
totalitarian state
Nazi Party
Brownshirts
anti-Semitism
Kristallnacht
Spanish Civil War
Popular Front

KEY PEOPLE

Benito Mussolini
Joseph Stalin
Adolf Hitler
Francisco Franco

"The peace, the freedom, and the security of 90 percent of the population of the world is being jeopardized by the remaining 10 percent who are threatening a breakdown of all international order and law. . . . War is a contagion [disease]. . . . It can engulf states and peoples remote from the original scene of hostilities. . . . If civilization is to survive, the principles of [peace] must be restored."

—Franklin D. Roosevelt

President Roosevelt speaks to the American people.

In this 1937 speech, President Franklin D. Roosevelt warned Americans of the growing danger of war. A rise in military activity by a number of nations and leaders made peace seem increasingly fragile.

Mussolini in Italy

Although Italy had been on the winning side when World War I ended, many Italians felt they had not benefited from the Treaty of Versailles. Thousands of Italian veterans were unable to find jobs. Many joined the Italian Communist Party, which urged Italian peasants to take over land and called on workers to seize factories.

To destroy the Communist Party and promote his own rise to power, Benito Mussolini founded the **Fascist Party** in 1921. The Fascists believed that a military-dominated government should control all aspects of society. Beginning in 1921, bloody clashes between Communists and Fascists created a situation bordering on civil war. In October 1922 Mussolini led an army of his followers, whose black uniforms gave them the name **Blackshirts**, in a march on Rome. Supported by nationalists who wanted to strengthen Italy and businesspeople who opposed the Socialists and Communists, the Fascists occupied the city.

The Italian king appointed Mussolini prime minister and granted him dictatorial powers. Mussolini limited freedom of speech, arrested political opponents, and restricted voting rights. Acting on a pledge to make Italy an imperial power, Mussolini sent Italian forces into the African nation of Ethiopia in 1935. The small, poorly equipped Ethiopian army proved no match for Italy's airplanes and machine guns. The U.S. Congress, fearful of being drawn into the conflict, passed a neutrality act banning arms shipments to both sides. The embargo hurt Ethiopia more than it did Italy, which continued to receive weapons from Germany and oil from American companies.

African Americans raised money to send relief and medical aid to the Ethiopians. Thousands of African Americans volunteered to fight in Ethiopia, but pressure from the U.S. government forced Ethiopia to reject the offer. This lack of support convinced other fascist countries, such as Germany, that aggression would go unpunished.

This symbol of the Italian Fascist Party appeared on its membership cards.

✔ READING CHECK: How did Benito Mussolini create a fascist state in Italy?

TEACH OBJECTIVES 1 AND 2

LEVEL 1: On the chalkboard create a two-column chart. In one column write the heading *Mussolini Creates a Fascist State*, and in the other column write *Stalin Maintains Power in the Soviet Union*. Have students suggest events to include under each heading. *(Students might suggest that Mussolini's actions included: leading Fascists in a power struggle against Communists, occupying Rome with the Blackshirts and the support of nationalists and industrialists, being appointed prime minister and given dictatorial powers, limiting freedom of speech and voting rights, and arresting opponents. Students might suggest that Stalin maintained power by seizing private land and collectivizing agriculture, by sending opponents to forced labor camps, by using the police and army to suppress dissent, and by purging the party and army of opposition.)* Conclude by leading a discussion about these two leaders. **Sheltered English**

TEACH OBJECTIVE 1

LEVELS 2 AND 3: Tell students to imagine that they are foreign-exchange students in Italy witnessing Mussolini's rise to power. Have each student write a letter to a family member in the United States. Students' letters should describe the steps that Mussolini is taking to establish a fascist regime in Italy and their response to these actions. *(See the Level 1 lesson for the correct list of events.)* Have volunteers read their letters to the class.

Stalin in the Soviet Union

As Benito Mussolini seized power in Italy, a battle was being waged for power in the Soviet Union—the communist nation formed from Russia and several other surrounding states in 1922. By the early 1920s Vladimir Lenin, the leader of the Bolshevik Revolution, was in poor health. His death in 1924 spurred a struggle for power among Communist Party leaders. Using underhanded tactics and even organizing the assassination of his enemies, Joseph Stalin eventually emerged as the nation's leader.

These workers at the "Lenin's Way Collective Farm" in Russia are sharing a communal lunch.

Driven by ambition, Stalin turned the Soviet Union into a **totalitarian state**—a country where the government has complete control. In 1927 the government began taking control of privately owned lands and reorganizing them into large state-run farms. Farmers who protested this policy were sent to forced labor camps. In all, some 15 million people were sent to Soviet labor camps by 1933. The reorganization policy resulted in decreased food production and widespread famine.

Stalin imposed his will through the Soviet Union's powerful Red Army. Stalin used the army and other police forces to crush all opposition. In the late 1930s, fearing opponents were trying to weaken him, Stalin began a campaign to purge all perceived enemies from the Communist Party and the Red Army. Although the exact figure is not known, some historians estimate that eventually as many as 30 million people may have died as a result of Stalin's policies.

✔ **READING CHECK:** How did Joseph Stalin maintain power in the Soviet Union?

Hitler in Germany

In 1932 Adolf Hitler's National Socialist Party, or **Nazi Party**, won nearly 40 percent of the vote in national elections. Hitler became chancellor of Germany the next year. While in prison, he had written *Mein Kampf (My Struggle)*, which laid out his plans to restore German power. Hitler blamed Jews, Communists, and intellectuals for Germany's decline. Hitler's views won him many supporters, particularly among those ruined by the depression.

The Third Reich. Hitler's government, called the Third Reich (the Third Empire), claimed dictatorial powers. Hitler prohibited Jews and non-Nazis from holding government positions, outlawed strikes, and made military service mandatory. Nazi storm troopers, known as **Brownshirts** because of the color of their uniforms, crushed all political opposition.

Hitler used his tight control over German industry to rearm the country in violation of the Treaty of Versailles. This strengthened the economy and reduced unemployment. Hitler declared:

> **"The buildup of the armed forces is the most important precondition for . . . political power. . . . How is this political power to be used when it is won? . . . Maybe fighting for new export possibilities, maybe . . . conquest of new Lebensraum [space for expansion] in the East."**

The German press often portrayed Adolf Hitler as Germany's savior, as in this image from a 1934 German magazine.

THE GRANGER COLLECTION, NEW YORK

GLOBAL RELATIONS

The United States and the Soviets. Soviet leaders such as Vladimir Lenin and Joseph Stalin believed that the U.S. capitalist economy would eventually fall to a communist revolution. Nonetheless, they admired the technological achievements and efficiency of the U.S. economy. For their part, many American business leaders were eager to work with the Soviets. These attitudes led to growing economic ties between the two nations during the turmoil of Stalin's reign.

CRITICAL THINKING Why might American businesses have wanted to develop ties to the Soviet Union?

ANSWER: Students might suggest that American business leaders viewed the Soviet Union as a large potential market for their products.

THAT'S INTERESTING!

Stalin was born Iosif Dzhugashvili in 1879. He took the name Stalin, which means "steel," in 1912 when he began writing articles for a communist newspaper.

Multimedia Resources

Everyday Life in America Transparency 25: The Rise of the Third Reich

TEACH OBJECTIVE 2

LEVELS 2 AND 3: Ask students to imagine that they are living in the Soviet Union under the Stalin regime. Have each student write a diary entry that discusses steps that Stalin has taken to maintain his power and his or her response to those steps. *(See the Level 1 lesson for the correct steps.)* Ask volunteers to read their diary entries to the class.

TEACH OBJECTIVE 3

ALL LEVELS: Review with students the events in Germany that led to Hitler's imprisonment. *(Tell students that Hitler's belief that politicians were responsible for Germany's defeat in World War I motivated him to attempt to overthrow the government.)* Ask students to recall why Germans were dissatisfied with the government. *(Students might suggest that Germans were bitter about war reparations and suffered from inflation and the falling value of the German mark.)* To help students understand Hitler's rise to power, copy the following graphic organizer on the chalkboard, omitting the italicized answers. Have each student complete it. **Sheltered English**

Hitler's Rise to Power in Germany

Hitler's views win him many supporters.

The Nazi Party wins 40 percent of the vote in national elections.

Hitler is appointed chancellor of Germany.

Hitler claims dictatorial powe[r]. Hitler crushes political opposit[ion].

DEMOCRATIC VALUES

The Refugee Crisis. U.S. immigration laws permitted 23,370 German immigrants to enter the country annually. However, this quota was rarely met during the early and mid-1930s. As early as 1934, German laws kept Jews from leaving the country with any more than the equivalent of $4. Meanwhile, U.S. laws forbade the entry of impoverished immigrants. By the time the war began more emigrants from Germany, most of whom were Jews, arrived in the United States. However, the U.S. government refused to increase the quota for refugees.

CRITICAL THINKING Why did the U.S. government forbid impoverished immigrants from entering the country during the early and mid-1930s?

ANSWER: Students might suggest that the depression led government officials to tighten restrictions and not allow to enter immigrants who might need economic assistance.

VISUAL RECORD ANSWER

Students might suggest that the women wearing civilian clothing do not look like typical soldiers.

THE GRANGER COLLECTION, NEW YORK

The Nazis used posters like this one to appeal to Germans' desire to see their country reclaim its role as a world power.

In March 1936, German troops moved into the Rhineland. Two years later they overran Austria. Hitler then turned toward the Sudetenland (soo-DAYT-uhn-land) region of western Czechoslovakia, where more than 3 million German-speaking people lived. Hitler demanded that Czechoslovakia turn over the region to Germany. Czechoslovakia refused Hitler's demand.

Anti-Semitism. Meanwhile, Hitler's **anti-Semitism**, or hatred of Jews, became official government policy. In 1935 Hitler instituted the Nuremberg Laws, which deprived Jews of their German citizenship and authorized the destruction of Jewish property. Gradually the oppression of Jews increased. On November 9, 1938, Nazi thugs burned down synagogues and destroyed Jewish businesses. Known as ***Kristallnacht***, or "the night of broken glass," the violence provided a chilling preview of the fate that awaited European Jews and others whom Hitler opposed.

Increased oppression caused many Jews to flee the country. Most wealthy or famous Jewish refugees were able to find safe haven abroad. Hundreds of writers, artists, and scientists came to the United States. The vast majority of Jewish refugees, however, had no place to turn. Many countries, including the United States, had strict immigration laws. Despite outrage at events like *Kristallnacht,* most Americans remained unwilling to encourage Jewish immigration.

✔ **READING CHECK:** How did Adolf Hitler rise to power in Germany?

Franco in Spain

Fascism also spread to Spain. In the 1930s Spain experienced bitter political conflicts. In 1931 a constitution that limited the power of the military and the Catholic Church went into effect. It called for reforms including universal suffrage, the nationalization of public utilities, and land for peasants. Conservative military men who felt threatened by the reforms united under the leadership of General Francisco Franco. In July 1936 the Fascist army officers tried to overthrow the government, starting the **Spanish Civil War** between Fascists and Loyalists.

After almost three years of fighting, Franco took over the government with German and Italian military aid. The Soviet Union aided the Loyalists, but President Roosevelt's fears of being drawn into a European war kept the United States from sending direct aid. Some 3,000 individual Americans, however, did join the fight against fascism. Ernest Hemingway covered the Spanish Civil War as a journalist. He expressed his support for the Loyalist cause in the powerful novel *For Whom the Bell Tolls* (1940).

These Americans were part of what was called the **Popular Front**—an international group of organizations united against fascism. Joseph Stalin had coined the term Popular Front in a 1935 speech denouncing fascism. Fearful of Adolf Hitler's military motives, Stalin declared that communism and fascism were incompatible. Although he used many of the same totalitarian tactics as the fascist leaders, Stalin's efforts encouraged many noncommunists to oppose fascism.

INTERPRETING THE VISUAL RECORD

The Spanish Civil War. These Spanish Loyalists are marching from Madrid to fight a rebel army heading toward the city. ***In what ways do these troops appear to differ from a regular army?***

TEACH OBJECTIVE 4

LEVEL 1: Organize students into small groups. Have each group create a cause-and-effect chart explaining the causes of the Spanish Civil War. *(Groups' charts should show that the populist reforms in Spain's new constitution threatened conservative military men. Led by General Franco, Fascist army officers attempted to overthrow the government, thus starting the civil war.)* Have each group present its chart to the class. **Sheltered English, Cooperative Learning**

LEVELS 2 AND 3: Tell students to imagine that it is July 1936 and that they are radio announcers describing the outbreak of the Spanish Civil War. Organize students into small groups. Have each group prepare a radio broadcast describing the events that led to the conflict. *(See the Level 1 lesson for the correct events.)* Have students perform their broadcasts for the class. **Cooperative Learning**

▶**ASSIGNMENT** *Tell students to imagine that they are Americans who have decided to join the fighting in the Spanish Civil War. Have each student write a letter to a friend describing how the fighting started and why he or she has decided to join the Loyalist cause.*

NOTE: For an additional teaching idea, see the Chapter 16 open interviewing lesson in the **Creative Teaching Strategies** handbook.

After the Spanish Civil War, many Loyalists remained bitter over the failure of Western nations to support their cause. In 1940 Julio Alvarez del Vayo, a wartime diplomat for the defeated Spanish republic, charged that this lack of support had cost the Loyalists the war.

> **"My one desire is to show what it would have meant to the Western democracies to have had in Spain a certain ally ready to defend the liberty and dignity of Europe against all attempts at domination and oppression. . . . No, it was not Spanish democracy that failed. It was the other democracies who failed to save democratic Spain, as they will one day learn to their cost."**

✔ **READING CHECK:** What caused the Spanish Civil War?

Residents of Barcelona, Spain, often blocked the streets during the Spanish Civil War.

Strategies for Success — Using Oral Histories

Oral histories—verbal accounts of historical events supplied by people who observed or participated in the events—are useful tools for learning about the past. They provide a uniquely close-up view of how specific people experienced the past. Oral histories also furnish valuable information about the opinions and feelings that people in history had about issues that affected them.

Oral histories are often taken down years or even decades after the events in question. It is therefore important to consider how the passage of time may have affected an interviewee's account of the past.

How to Use Oral Histories

1. **Become familiar with the source.** First, identify the person who was interviewed for the oral history and the general topic that he or she addressed. Then find out when the interview was conducted and, if possible, who conducted it.
2. **Study the account carefully.** Read the oral history thoroughly and carefully, taking note of any words or phrases that signal a statement of opinion.
3. **Assess the reliability of the account.** After you have read the oral history, evaluate its reliability as a piece of historical evidence. Be sure to consider how the interviewee's role in the events described, as well as the passage of time between the events and the interview, may have affected the account.
4. **Put the information to use.** Compare the oral history with other sources that address the same topic. Then use the results of your analysis and your knowledge of the historical period to draw conclusions.

Applying the Strategy

Examine the following excerpt from an oral history from the 1980s provided by Hans Massaquoi, the son of a German mother and a Liberian father who grew up in Germany during the 1930s.

> **"In '32, when I started school, I was six years old. In '33, my first teacher was fired for political reasons. I don't know what her involvements were. Gradually, the old teachers were replaced with younger ones, those with Nazi orientations. Then I began to notice a change in attitude. Teachers would make snide remarks about my race. One teacher would point me out as an example of the non-Aryan race. One time, I must have been ten, a teacher took me aside and said, 'When we're finished with the Jews, you're next.' He still had some inhibitions [reluctance]. He did not make that announcement before the class. (Laughs.) It was a private thing."**

Practicing the Strategy

Use the excerpt above to answer the following questions.

1. What is the general topic of the excerpt?
2. How do you think the passage of time between the events described in the excerpt and the interview affected Massaquoi's account?
3. What is your opinion of the excerpt as a piece of historical evidence?
4. How does the excerpt contribute to your understanding of Nazi Germany during the 1930s?

CULTURAL DIVERSITY

Americans in Spain. The Americans who fought in the Spanish Civil War were a diverse group, hailing from every part of the United States. However, most of them came from urban, industrial areas where they had been exposed to radical political ideas. The Americans, many of whom fought in a group called the Abraham Lincoln Battalion, were not well-trained soldiers. They suffered high casualty rates during the war. About one third of the American volunteers were killed.

CRITICAL THINKING Why might one American battalion have been named after Abraham Lincoln?

ANSWER: Students might suggest that Abraham Lincoln served as a symbol of the struggle for freedom.

STRATEGIES FOR SUCCESS ANSWERS

Practicing the Strategy

1. racial discrimination experienced by a young schoolboy
2. Massaquoi is able to laugh about discrimination he faced. He also knows that his teacher's inhibitions would later change.
3. Answers may vary. Massaquoi was a witness to the events preceding the war.
4. Answers will vary. Students might mention that they have a better understanding of the racial discrimination in Nazi Germany.

TEACH OBJECTIVE 5

LEVEL 1: Distribute Outline Map 32, East and Southeast Asia, from **American History Outline Maps.** Pair students and have each pair use the map on this page to locate Beijing, Manchuria, Nanjing, and northern China on the blank map. Then have students label each of these places on their map with a short description of Japanese military actions at each location. *(Maps should include the following actions: 1931—Japanese troops invade Manchuria; July 1937—Japanese troops clash with Chinese troops near Beijing; Japanese troops occupy northern China and launch bombing raids against Chinese cities; November 1937—Japanese troops assault and occupy Nanjing.)* In addition, tell students that Japan built up its naval forces in violation of Washington Conference pledges. Display students maps around the classroom.
Sheltered English, Cooperative Learning

LEVELS 2 AND 3: Tell students to imagine that they are Chinese diplomats. Have each student write a letter to Franklin D. Roosevelt asking for U.S. assistance against the Japanese military. Students' letters should describe the actions that the Japanese military has taken. *(See the Level 1 lesson for the correct actions.)* Ask volunteers to read their letters to the class.

internet connect

TOPIC: Americans in the Spanish Civil War
GO TO: go.hrw.com
KEYWORD: SE1 Civil

Have students access the Internet through the HRW Web site to conduct research on the involvement of U.S. citizens in the Spanish Civil War. Then have students present their research in the form of an oral history interview in which veterans explain why they fought in the war, describe their involvement in the war, and recount how they were viewed by Americans who did not participate in the war.

THAT'S INTERESTING!

Most Americans showed little interest in the events in Spain. Some two thirds of respondents to a 1937 opinion poll expressed no opinion about the Spanish Civil War.

UNDERSTANDING LITERATURE ANSWERS

1. Mike's lack of regard or respect for military medals reveals his disillusionment with the war.
2. Hemingway urges immediate action.
3. In the first, he expresses little regard for war or honors. In the second, he attaches a higher value to the war and why it is being fought.

Ernest Hemingway and War

Before the United States entered World War I, Ernest Hemingway served with the Italian infantry. He was seriously wounded. Hemingway's novels of the 1920s, including The Sun Also Rises *(1926), reflected many people's disillusionment with war. The story focuses on a group of World War I veterans trying to forget their experiences. In 1940, after working as a correspondent during the Spanish Civil War, Hemingway published* For Whom the Bell Tolls, *which depicted Loyalists battling nobly against Fascists.*

from *The Sun Also Rises*

Ernest Hemingway

"What medals have you got, Mike?"

"I haven't got any medals."

"You must have some."

"I suppose I've the usual medals. But I never sent in for them. One time there was this whopping big dinner . . . and the cards said medals will be worn. So naturally I had no medals, and I stopped at my tailor's . . . and I said to him: 'You've got to fix me up with some medals.' He said: 'What medals, sir?' And I said: 'Oh, any medals. Just give me a few medals.' So he said: 'What medals *have* you, sir?' And I said: 'How should I know?' . . . So he got me some medals, you know, miniature medals, and handed me the box, and I put it in my pocket and forgot it. . . .

Later on in the evening I found the box in my pocket. What's this? I said. Medals? Bloody military medals? So I cut them off their backing–you know, they put them on a strip–and gave them all around. Gave one to each girl. Form of souvenir. . . ."

"Tell the rest, " Brett said.

"Don't you think that was funny?" Mike asked. We were all laughing. "It was. I swear it was. Any rate, my tailor wrote me and wanted the medals back. Sent a man around. Kept on writing for months. Seems some chap had left them to be cleaned. . . ." Mike paused. "Rotten luck for the tailor."

from *For Whom the Bell Tolls*

For Whom the Bell Tolls

Why don't you ever think of how it is to win? You've been on the defensive for so long that you can't think of that. . . . But remember this that as long as we can hold them here we keep the fascists tied up. They can't attack any other country until they finish with us and they can never finish with us. If the French help at all, if only they leave the frontier open and if we get planes from America they can never finish with us. Never, if we get anything at all. These people will fight forever if they're well armed.

No you must not expect victory here, not for several years maybe. This is just a holding attack. . . .

Today is only one day in all the days that will ever be. But what will happen in all the other days that ever come can depend on what you do today.

UNDERSTANDING LITERATURE

1. In the first excerpt, what does Mike's attitude about military medals reflect about his attitude toward his service in World War I?
2. What is the meaning of the last two lines in the excerpt from *For Whom the Bell Tolls?*
3. How do the two excerpts reveal Hemingway's changing views of war?

REVIEW

Have students complete the **Section 3 Review** on p. 489.

ASSESS

Have students complete **Daily Quiz 16.3**. As **Alternative Assessment**, you may want to use the Soviet diary entries, or the map activity in this section's lessons.

RETEACH

Have students complete **Main Idea Activity for Reteaching and Sheltered English 16.3**. Then organize students into five groups and assign each group one of the following countries: Germany, Italy, Japan, Spain, and the Soviet Union. Have each group answer these questions about its country: What actions were taken by the country's leader(s)? What were the leader's policies? How did these policies result in war (if applicable)? Have students discuss their answers with the class.

Sheltered English, Cooperative Learning

EXTEND

Have students conduct research on the Italian invasion of Ethiopia, Ethiopian monarch Haile Selassie's efforts to organize a defense for his country, or the impact of the U.S neutrality act that banned arms shipments to the Italians and Ethiopians. Have each student write a report on his or her findings.

Block Scheduling

Militarists in Japan

As German aggression threatened Europe, Japanese expansion loomed in Asia. In the 1920s, the leaders of Japan's military forces had gained increasing power. These military men wanted to lessen Japan's reliance on foreign imports. They also aimed to reduce the influence of Western countries in Asia and promote Japanese expansion throughout East Asia and the Pacific.

The creation of a Japanese empire would give Japan direct control over territories that produced iron, petroleum, rubber, and timber. Worsening economic conditions in Japan strengthened the popular appeal of the militarists' position. Japan's 1931 invasion of Manchuria signaled its imperialist ambitions. In 1934 and 1935, in violation of their Washington Conference pledges, the Japanese began a rapid naval buildup. Viscount Inoue, a member of the Japanese House of Peers, explained Japan's position on a 1937 visit to London.

> "Not only do we possess no oil supplies but this is true of very many other materials without which today a nation is helpless in wartime. To secure . . . raw materials has become a problem of greatly increased importance. The very life of Japan as a first-class power is dependent on this question."

On July 7, 1937, Japanese and Chinese troops clashed near Beijing. The incident soon developed into a full-scale war. Japan occupied northern China and launched devastating bombing raids against Chinese cities. In November 1937, Japanese troops brutally assaulted and occupied the Chinese city of Nanjing. Although the League of Nations and the United States condemned Japan's actions, they failed to halt Japanese expansion.

✔ **READING CHECK:** What actions did Japan's military take during the 1930s?

Uchida Ryohei was president of the Black Dragon Society, which wanted to drive the Soviet Union out of East Asia.

Read More About It

Free Find:
Military expansion

After learning about German, Italian, and Japanese expansion on the **Holt Researcher** CD–ROM, imagine that you are an adviser to President Roosevelt. Write a memo advising where the greatest chances of war exist.

SECTION 3 REVIEW

Define and explain the significance of the following terms:

Fascist Party
Blackshirts
totalitarian state
Nazi Party
Brownshirts
anti-Semitism
Kristallnacht
Spanish Civil War
Popular Front

Identify and explain the significance of the following individuals:

Benito Mussolini
Joseph Stalin
Adolf Hitler
Francisco Franco

1. **Using Graphic Organizers** Copy the chart below. Use it to describe how aggressive world leaders came to power and what their major policies were.

Leaders	Rise to Power	Policies
Mussolini		
Stalin		
Hitler		
Franco		
Japanese Militarists		

2. **Evaluating** How did dictators in the 1930s use military power against their own people?
3. **Identifying Values** How did the policies of European dictators conflict with democratic ideals?
4. **Using Historical Imagination** Imagine that you are an American supporter of the Popular Front in the 1930s. Write a newspaper article explaining why you are fighting for the Spanish Loyalists.

Critical Thinking

5. Why did other European nations not stop Adolf Hitler's aggressive takeover of additional territory?
   Consider:
   - Hitler's claims on the territory
   - the actions of other nations at the time
   - the amount of international cooperation that existed in the 1930s

REVIEW SECTION 3 ANSWERS

Define and Identify

For significance, see the following pages:

- Benito Mussolini, p. 484
- Fascist Party, p. 484
- Blackshirts, p. 484
- Joseph Stalin, p. 485
- totalitarian state, p. 485
- Adolf Hitler, p. 485
- Nazi Party, p. 485
- Brownshirts, p. 485
- anti-Semitism, p. 486
- *Kristallnacht,* p. 486
- Francisco Franco, p. 486
- Spanish Civil War, p. 486
- Popular Front, p. 486

1. Mussolini—appointed prime minister by Italian king; restrict political rights, make Italy an imperial power; Stalin—used assassination and terror; complete government control of country, including farms; Hitler—voted into power; oppression of political opposition and Jews, conquest of territory; Franco—through civil war; destruction of Loyalist reforms; Japanese militarists—gained power within the government; territorial expansion

2. to suppress dissent and terrorize opponents

3. They restricted or eliminated political and civil rights.

4. Students' articles should mention the fight against fascism.

5. Answers will vary. Students might mention that there was no way to enforce international military cooperation; German-speaking territories were easy for Hitler to claim; many countries did not want to get involved in another country's affairs.

SECTION 4

After completing Section 4, students should be able to:

OBJECTIVE 1 *Explain the international response to fascism.*

OBJECTIVE 2 *Describe the early events of World War II.*

OBJECTIVE 3 *Discuss why tension between the United States and Germany increased.*

OBJECTIVE 4 *Analyze why Japan bombed Pearl Harbor.*

LET'S GET STARTED!

As students enter the classroom, have them study the photograph on this page of the women witnessing the German invasion of the Sudetenland in Czechoslovakia. Have students write a short caption that might have accompanied this photograph. Have volunteers share their captions with the class. Discuss the context of the photograph with students. Then tell students that in Section 4 they will learn about how various countries responded to fascism and the events leading up to World War II.

SECTION 4 RESOURCES

PRINT

- Guided Reading Strategy 16.4
- Section 4 Review, p. 495
- Daily Quiz 16.4

MULTIMEDIA

- One-Stop Planner, Lesson 16.4
- Holt Researcher: American History CD–ROM

SHELTERED ENGLISH

- Main Idea Activity for Reteaching and Sheltered English 16.4

✔ READING TO UNDERSTAND

To help students master the section objectives, have them answer the **READING CHECKS** and complete **Guided Reading Strategy 16.4** as they read the section.

War Breaks Out

OBJECTIVES

Read to understand:

1. what the international response to fascism was
2. what the early events of World War II were
3. why tension between the United States and Germany increased
4. why Japan bombed Pearl Harbor

KEY TERMS

Axis Powers
Munich Conference
appeasement
nonaggression pact
Lend-Lease Act
Blitzkrieg
Maginot Line
Atlantic Charter

KEY PEOPLE

Winston Churchill

KEY PLACES

Munich
Finland
Manchuria
French Indochina

"Ladies and gentlemen, this is the most terrifying thing I have ever witnessed. . . .

A humped shape is rising out of the pit. I can make out a small beam of light against a mirror. What's that? There's a jet of flame springing from that mirror, and it leaps right at the advancing men. It strikes them head on! Good Lord, they're turning into flame!"

—Orson Welles

Orson Welles

Although this report of an attack on the United States by an army of martians was purely fictional, many Americans believed it. On October 30, 1938, the Mercury Theatre on the Air, led by Orson Welles, performed a live radio broadcast of H. G. Wells's science fiction novel *The War of the Worlds.* To enhance the dramatic effect, they staged it as a series of news reports. Many listeners thought the broadcast was real. Throughout the nation, widespread panic ensued, with many people fleeing their homes and preparing to battle the space creatures. The panic reflected very real fears many people had that dangerous invaders were lurking on the horizon.

The Response to Fascism

The spread of fascism in Europe and Asia caused a shake-up in international diplomatic relationships. The most surprising of these realignments was the shift in U.S.-Soviet relations. The Soviets were concerned about curbing the Japanese, who had massed troops in nearby Manchuria. Hoping "to avert the Japanese danger," Soviet foreign-affairs commissar Maksim Litvinov mended diplomatic ties with the United States. In November 1933, after years of hostility between the two countries, the United States formally recognized the Soviet Union.

The fascist powers also formalized their ties. In 1936 the rest of Europe trembled when Germany and Italy formed a military alliance known as the **Axis Powers**. Japan later joined the alliance.

President Roosevelt called for European leaders to meet and resolve their conflicts peacefully. Adolf Hitler and Benito Mussolini joined British prime minister Neville Chamberlain and French premier Édouard Daladier (dah-lahd-yay) in Munich, Germany, in September 1938. The four leaders at the **Munich Conference** signed a pact giving Germany control of the Sudetenland. The European leaders had adopted a policy of **appeasement**, or giving in to demands in an attempt to avoid a larger conflict.

Many politicians underestimated Hitler's expansionist goals. They believed that Hitler sought only to remedy what he considered wrongs created by the Treaty of Versailles. Other politicians, such as

These women salute the German troops occupying the Sudetenland.

TEACH OBJECTIVE 1

ALL LEVELS: Ask students to speculate on how European countries might have responded to fascism, given the horrors of World War I and the U.S. foreign policy of partial isolationism. *(Students might suggest that countries would have been initially reluctant to enter into another conflict.)* To help students understand the international response to fascism, copy the graphic organizer at right on the chalkboard, omitting the italicized answers. Have each student complete it. Ask volunteers to share their answers. Conclude by leading a discussion about the motivation behind various nations' responses to fascism. **Sheltered English**

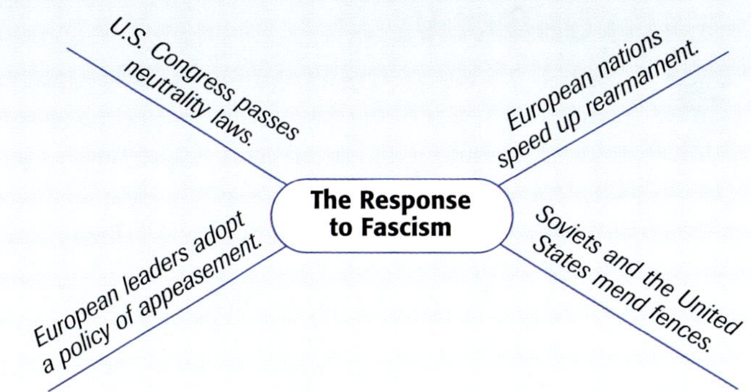

▶**ASSIGNMENT** *Ask students to create a collage to represent the initial international response to fascism. Display students' collages around the classroom.*

Winston Churchill of Great Britain, feared that appeasement would encourage Hitler to seize additional territory. Britain and other nations in Europe sped up their rearmament.

Congress passed a series of neutrality laws between 1935 and 1939 that reflected Americans' desire for peace. The neutrality laws prohibited the shipment of U.S. munitions to warring nations and required warring nations that bought goods from the United States to transport these goods in their own ships. The laws also forbade Americans to travel on the vessels of warring nations.

By 1937 Roosevelt had become convinced that the United States must assist in the quarantine, or isolation, of warring nations. However, most Americans did not yet support this expanded role. In December 1937, Japanese planes attacked the U.S. gunboat *Panay* and three American oil tankers on China's Chang River. Two U.S. citizens were killed, and many others were wounded. Even so, a public-opinion poll revealed that 54 percent of Americans thought the United States should reduce its role in China rather than risk becoming involved in a war.

Chicago Daily Tribune — FINAL

JAPANESE SINK U. S. GUNBOAT

Convicts Defy Governor; Kill Guard

1 DEAD, 18 MISSING, 54 SAVED AS BOMBS WRECK SHIP AIDING NANKING YANKS

Japan's sinking of the U.S. gunboat* Panay *angered many Americans but not enough to push the country into war.

✔ **READING CHECK:** What was the international response to fascism?

War!

American public opinion slowly changed, however, as Germany's aggression continued. In March 1939 Adolf Hitler's armies occupied all of Czechoslovakia. Hitler also proposed to annex the Polish port city of Danzig (DAHNT-sik)—modern-day Gdańsk—but the Poles refused. That same year, Italian troops invaded Albania on April 7.

Fighting begins. Recognizing the growing threat to European security, Britain and France announced that they would go to war if Germany attacked Poland. They called on the Soviet Union to join them in resisting further aggression. Instead, on August 23, 1939, Joseph Stalin—who had been trying to rally the world against fascism—signed a **nonaggression pact** with Hitler. In it Stalin and Hitler agreed not to attack each other. This shocking development came about in part because of a secret clause in the pact in which the two nations agreed to divide Poland between them.

On September 1, 1939, German bombers and armored divisions moved into Poland. Two days later, Britain and France—who became known as the Allied Powers—declared war on Germany. World War II had begun. Meanwhile, Soviet troops invaded Poland from the east, occupied Estonia, Latvia, and Lithuania, and demanded the right to establish military bases in Finland. When Finland refused, the Soviet Union attacked the small nation and soon annexed part of its its territory.

Fortune Magazine's 1939 Survey on War: What Should the U.S. Do?

	Percent
Fight with the Allies now.	2.3%
Fight with the Allies if they are losing.	13.5%
Send supplies to Allies but not to Germany.	20%
Sell supplies to both sides cash and carry.	29%
Give no aid to either side.	25%
Help Germany.	.1%
Do not know and other answers	9%

Percent (0–30)

Source: *Fortune* Due to rounding, numbers may not add up to 100.

Learning from Graphs Most Americans wanted the Allies to win the war, but many were unsure what role the United States should play.

? Building Graph Skills What percentage of Americans wanted the United States to remain totally neutral in the war, either by selling supplies to both sides or by refusing to aid either side?

HISTORY MAKERS SPEAK

Joseph Grew in *Turbulent Era*

Stopping Japanese Aggression. Joseph Grew, U.S. ambassador to Japan, recorded his thoughts about that nation's aggression in a 1937 diary entry. "If our branding of Japan as an aggressor and our appeal to the Nine Power Treaty and the Kellogg-Briand Pact and our support of the League of Nations . . . could serve to stop the fighting in China or limit its sphere or prevent similar aggression in the future, my accord with this step would be complete and wholehearted. But . . . with Manchuria, Ethiopia, and Spain written in big letters across the pages of history, how can we ignore the practical experience of those events and the hopelessness of deterring them *unless we are willing to fight?*"

CRITICAL THINKING What conclusion did Grew draw from the events of the mid-1930s?

ANSWER: Students might suggest that Grew believed that aggression could only be stopped by threats or the use of military force.

GRAPH ANSWER
54 percent

TEACH OBJECTIVE 2

LEVELS 1 AND 2: Organize students into groups and provide each group with a sheet of paper that has the dates *1939* and *1940* written on it. Each group should list and illustrate the events of World War II that took place during those years. *(Groups' illustrations for 1939 should depict France and Britain declaring war on Germany, the signing of the nonaggression pact between the Soviet Union and Germany, and the Soviet invasions of Poland, the Baltic states, and Finland. Groups' illustrations for 1940 should show Roosevelt's efforts to aid Europe with the Lend-Lease Act, the German Blitzkrieg against France and other European nations, the creation of the Vichy government, and Hitler's attack on Britain.)* Ask volunteers to explain their illustrations to the class.
Sheltered English, Cooperative Learning

LEVEL 3: Tell students to imagine that they are U.S. politicians who believe that the United States should enter the war. Have each student write a speech describing the early events of the war and explaining how these events justify U.S. entry into the conflict. *(See the Levels 1 and 2 lesson for the correct events.)* Ask volunteers to deliver their speeches to the class. Students may wish to include their speeches in their portfolios.

PEOPLE IN HISTORY

Charles Lindbergh. The congressional debate over revising the neutrality act that barred the export of military supplies prompted many prominent isolationists to speak out against any revisions. Famous aviator Charles Lindbergh made radio broadcasts calling upon the United States to maintain its isolationist stance. Lindbergh had visited Germany three times during the 1930s and tested new German aircraft, before he spoke out against exporting military supplies. Once the United States joined the fighting, Lindbergh served his country, flying on several combat missions in the Pacific.

CRITICAL THINKING Why might Lindbergh's support for isolationism have hurt his historical reputation?

ANSWER: Students might suggest that critics have linked Lindbergh's isolationist views with support for the Nazis.

MAP ANSWER
bordered Germany on the east

German and Italian Expansion, 1935–1941

Learning from Maps Hitler's and Mussolini's aggressions brought war to most of Europe for the second time in the 1900s.

PLACE Why was Poland a likely target for a German attack?

The U.S. response. President Roosevelt took steps to aid the European countries under siege. Some three weeks after the German invasion of Poland, the president urged Congress to amend the neutrality act that barred the export of military supplies. After a six-week debate, Congress agreed on a compromise. The new law allowed any nation to buy military supplies from the United States but required that the goods be shipped on foreign vessels.

The fighting in Europe was a major issue in the 1940 presidential election. Both candidates—Roosevelt, who sought re-election to a third term, and Republican Wendell Willkie—promised to keep the United States out of the conflict. In a radio talk on September 3, 1939, Roosevelt pledged, "As long as it remains in my power to prevent, there will be no blackout of peace in the United States."

TEACH OBJECTIVE 3

ALL LEVELS: Pair students and have pairs create a list of events that increased tensions between the United States and Germany. *(Lists should include: an increase in U.S. aid to the Allies, German submarine attacks, and Roosevelt's "shoot-on-sight" orders.)* Ask each pair to use its list to create a political cartoon depicting relations between the United States and Germany in 1941. Each cartoon should include a descriptive caption. Display cartoons around the classroom.
Sheltered English, Cooperative Learning

Teacher to Teacher

Karen Hoppes of Lake Oswego, Oregon, suggested the following activity: Tell students to imagine that they are participants in a discussion entitled Will We Go to War with Germany? Organize students into two groups. One group should play the following roles: Emily Greene Balch, Franklin D. Roosevelt, Ernest Hemingway, and Wendell Willkie. Have the other group act as questioners. Have each group prepare by taking notes, and then conduct the discussion.

Roosevelt won his bid for an unprecedented third term. In spite of his public promises, however, he viewed U.S. military involvement in Europe as unavoidable.

Lend-Lease. By the end of 1940 a variety of supplies flowed from the United States to Britain. The British, however, had little cash to pay for needed war materials. Roosevelt proposed that the United States lend or lease arms and other supplies to the Allies. Congress passed the **Lend-Lease Act** in March 1941. It appropriated $7 billion for ships, planes, tanks, and other supplies to non-Axis countries.

While Hitler carried on his **Blitzkrieg** (BLITS-kreeg), or "lightning war," against Poland, the French mobilized. In May 1940, German troops began an attack around the **Maginot Line**, a line of defenses along the French border with Germany. The Germans occupied Belgium, Denmark, northern France, Luxembourg, the Netherlands, and Norway. Hundreds of thousands of British, French and Belgian troops were trapped along the French coast near the town of Dunkirk. Only an evacuation across the English Channel to Britain prevented their capture.

Germany established a puppet government in southern France in the town of Vichy (VI-shee). A secret French organization known as the Resistance continued to oppose the Germans. In London, French general Charles de Gaulle headed a committee called Free France that organized opposition against the Germans.

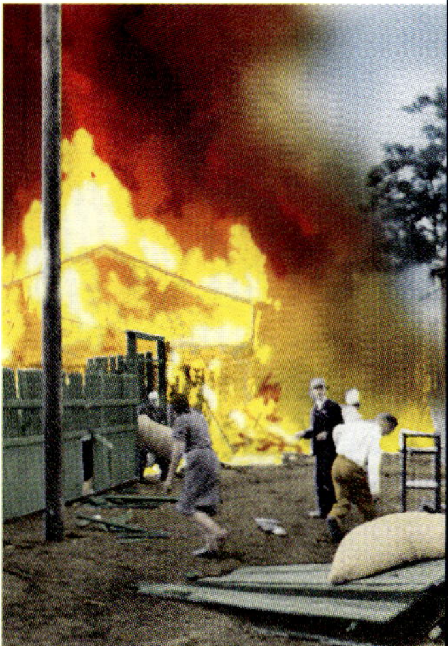

Citizens of Warsaw, Poland, flee before the destructive power of the German Blitzkrieg as fire consumes a working-class neighborhood.

BIOGRAPHY *Winston Churchill*

A new British leader. With the fall of France, Britain stood alone against the Axis Powers. On May 10, 1940, Winston Churchill became prime minister. Born in 1874, Churchill attended the Royal Military College and then served in the British army for several years. Churchill began his political career in 1900 as a member of Parliament. Ten years later, he was appointed to lead the British navy. After receiving widespread criticism for Britain's failure in a World War I campaign, Churchill resigned his position and volunteered to fight on the front lines.

After the war Churchill resumed his rise in British politics. When many other British leaders were pushing for appeasement with Hitler, Churchill warned of the dangers he posed. Once appointed prime minister, Churchill rallied the British.

> **"Hitler knows that he will have to break us in this island or lose the war. . . . Let us therefore brace ourselves to our duties, and so bear ourselves that, if the British Empire and its Commonwealth last for a thousand years, men will still say, 'This was their finest hour.'"**

On June 10, 1940, Italy declared war on France and Britain. In August, Hitler unleashed his bombers against Britain. Although outnumbered, the British Royal Air Force (RAF) flew day and night to combat the German attack.

✔ **READING CHECK:** What were the early events of World War II?

HOLT RESEARCHER — *Read More About It*

Free Find:
Winston Churchill
After reading about Winston Churchill on the **Holt Researcher** CD–ROM, create a sketch of a memorial that will honor Churchill's inspiring leadership during World War II.

Tensions Mount in the Atlantic

As German attacks increased, so did U.S. aid to the Allies. By the spring of 1941, German submarines were turning the North Atlantic into a graveyard of ships. In

TECHNOLOGY AND SOCIETY

The Blitzkrieg. The German method of attack that came to be known as the Blitzkrieg was made possible by technological advances. The development of tanks that could move rapidly, the use of airplanes, bombs, and paratroopers, and coordinated radio communication allowed the German army to make rapid offensive moves that overwhelmed the enemy. The Blitzkrieg was successful in the early years of the war but proved ineffective in later years.

CRITICAL THINKING Why might the Blitzkrieg have become less effective over time?

ANSWER: Students might suggest that the Allies learned ways to defend against the Blitzkrieg, often by using tanks and planes in a similar manner.

THAT'S INTERESTING!

Winston Churchill and Franklin D. Roosevelt met briefly in London in 1918. They began corresponding by letter and telegram in 1939, and by 1945 they had exchanged 1,949 messages.

MAP ANSWER
(for p. 494)

Beijing, Hangzhou, Nanjing, Shanghai, Shenyang, and Tianjin

TEACH OBJECTIVE 4

LEVEL 1: Pair students and have each pair create a graphic organizer showing why the Japanese bombed Pearl Harbor. *(Pairs' organizers should note that Roosevelt froze all Japanese assets in the United States and instituted an embargo on American shipments of gasoline, machine tools, scrap iron, and steel to Japan.)* Have students present and explain their graphic organizers to the class.
Sheltered English, Cooperative Learning

LEVEL 2: Tell students to imagine that they are encyclopedia editors who must write an entry about the motivations behind the Japanese attack at Pearl Harbor. Have each student write an entry about the reasons for Japan's attack. *(See the Level 1 lesson for the correct reasons.)* Have volunteers read their entries to the class.

LEVEL 3: Ask students to imagine that it is December 8, 1941, and that they are advisers to President Roosevelt who have been asked to write a memo analyzing Japan's reasons for bombing Pearl Harbor. Have each student write a short memo analyzing the motivations behind the Japanese attack. *(See Level 1 lesson for the correct reasons.)* Ask volunteers to read their memos to the class.

VISUAL RECORD ANSWER
(for p. 495)
Students might suggest that the damage was extensive.

Define and Identify
For significance, see the following pages:

- Axis Powers, p. 490
- Munich Conference, p. 490
- appeasement, p. 490
- Winston Churchill, p. 491
- nonaggression pact, p. 491
- Lend-Lease Act, p. 493
- Blitzkrieg, p. 493
- Maginot Line, p. 493
- Atlantic Charter, p. 494

Locate
For locations, see the maps on pp. 492 and 494. For importance, see the following pages:

- Munich, p. 490
- Finland, p. 491
- Manchuria, p. 494
- French Indochina, p. 495

1. 2. Germany invades Poland; 3. Germany defeats France; 4. Britain repels Germany's attacks; 5. Japan attacks Pearl Harbor

2. German aggression focused mainly on Europe; Japanese aggression focused on Asia and the Pacific.

3. Students might suggest that war might have come earlier, or that Hitler might have stopped his aggression.

4. to prevent the United States from interfering with its expansion in Asia

Convoys of ships bringing supplies to the Allies were escorted by U.S. warships to protect against attack by German submarines.

September President Roosevelt issued "shoot-on-sight" orders to U.S. warships operating in the North Atlantic.

In August 1941, with the United States moving rapidly toward undeclared war with Germany, Roosevelt and Winston Churchill met secretly off the coast of Newfoundland. The two leaders agreed to follow a series of principles. Known as the **Atlantic Charter**, the agreement pledged that the United States and Britain would not pursue territorial expansion. The two countries affirmed their belief that every nation has the right to choose its own form of government. They also called for freedom of international trade and equal access for all countries to raw materials. Once the war was over, the charter declared, aggressor states should be disarmed, and all nations should work together to rid the world of fear and poverty.

Concern over Adolf Hitler's growing power increased when German troops invaded the Soviet Union in June 1941. Caught off guard by this violation of the German-Soviet nonaggression pact, Soviet troops fared badly in the initial fighting. By the fall of 1941, German troops had advanced deep into Soviet territory.

✔ **READING CHECK:** Why did tensions increase between the United States and Germany?

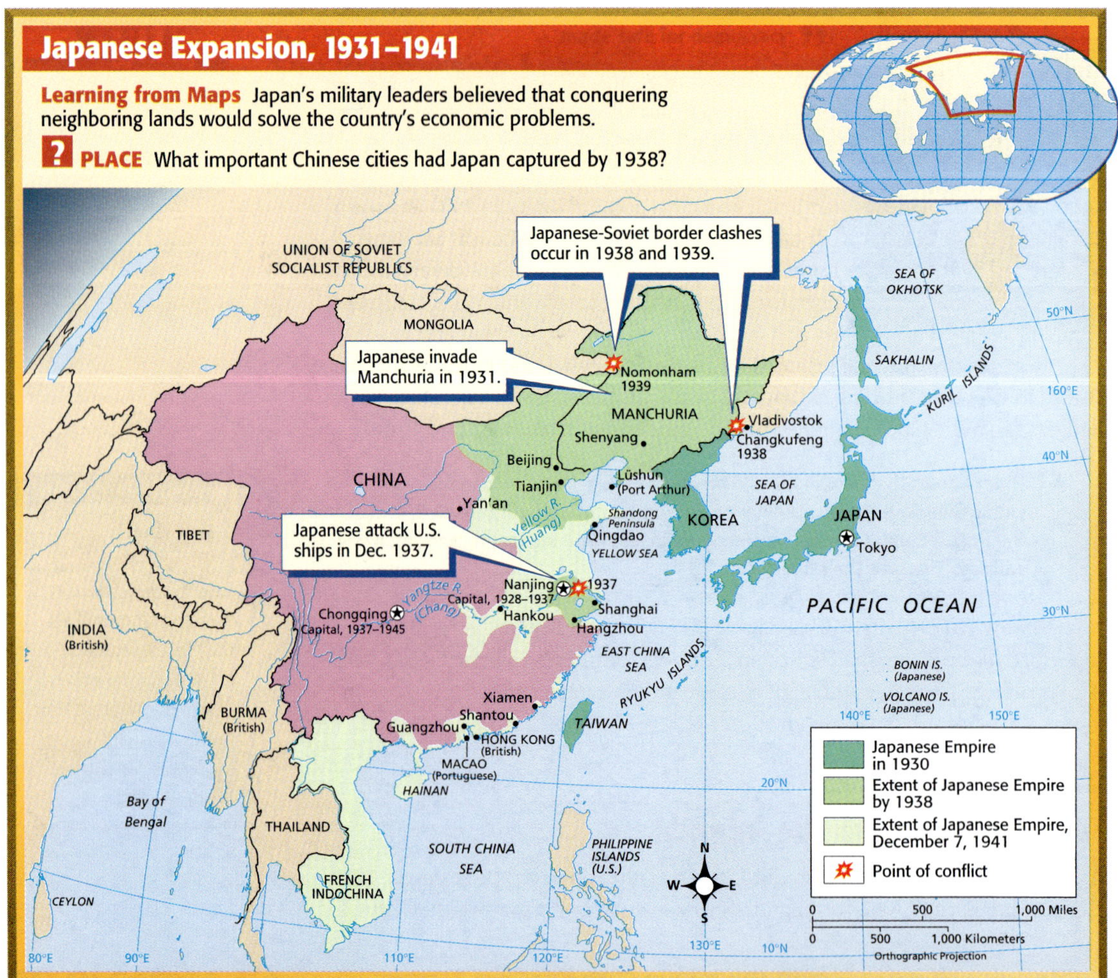

Japanese Expansion, 1931–1941

Learning from Maps Japan's military leaders believed that conquering neighboring lands would solve the country's economic problems.

? PLACE What important Chinese cities had Japan captured by 1938?

REVIEW

Have students complete the **Section 4 Review** on p. 495.

ASSESS

Have students complete **Daily Quiz 16.4**. As **Alternative Assessment**, you may want to use the speech about early events of World War II or the Pearl Harbor graphic organizer.

RETEACH

Have students complete **Main Idea Activity for Reteaching and Sheltered English 16.4**. Then organize students into four groups. Assign each group one of the four objectives and ask each group to create a 10-question quiz about its objective, writing the answers on a separate page. Have groups trade quizzes and try to answer other groups' quizzes. Ask groups to grade each other's quizzes and discuss questions with which other groups had trouble.
Sheltered English, Cooperative Learning

EXTEND

Have students watch the film *Casablanca*. Tell them that this film was made in part to encourage the United States to enter the war. After they watch the film, tell students to imagine that they are Americans seeing the film in 1940. Have each student write a review critiquing the film. **Block Scheduling**

Japan Attacks

As war raged in Europe, Japan continued its expansion in Asia. In July 1941, Japanese troops occupied French Indochina. President Roosevelt immediately froze all Japanese assets in the United States. He also approved an embargo on shipments of gasoline, machine tools, scrap iron, and steel to Japan. Japan responded by freezing all American assets in areas under its control.

As U.S. resistance to Japanese aggression grew stronger, Japan's military leaders secretly planned an attack on the United States. Even as the plan went forward, however, a Japanese peace mission visited Washington, D.C. On November 20, 1941, this mission demanded that the United States unfreeze Japanese assets, supply Japan's gasoline needs, and cease all aid to China. By this time the United States had succeeded in breaking the secret code used to send messages between Tokyo and the Japanese embassy in Washington. The Americans knew that the Japanese planned a strike, but they did not know where.

Shortly before 8:00 A.M. on December 7, 1941, the Japanese launched their attack on the U.S. naval base at Pearl Harbor in the Hawaiian Islands. The core of the U.S. Pacific Fleet was anchored there, and more than 100 U.S. planes lined nearby airfields. Almost 20 U.S. warships and nearly 200 aircraft were destroyed. Among some 2,400 Americans killed were 1,103 sailors entombed on the USS *Arizona* when the battleship sank.

The bombing shocked and united Americans. The next day, a somber President Roosevelt described December 7, 1941, as "a date which will live in infamy." He called on Congress to pass a declaration of war against Japan. Congress quickly approved the call for war.

✔ **READING CHECK:** Why did Japan bomb Pearl Harbor?

THE GRANGER COLLECTION, NEW YORK

INTERPRETING THE VISUAL RECORD

Pearl Harbor. The USS *Shaw* explodes after Japanese planes bombed Pearl Harbor. ***What does this image tell you about the damage done by the Japanese attack?***

SECTION 4 REVIEW

Define and explain the significance of the following terms:

Axis Powers	Lend-Lease Act
Munich Conference	Blitzkrieg
appeasement	Maginot Line
nonaggression pact	Atlantic Charter

Identify and explain the significance of the following individual:
Winston Churchill

Locate and explain the importance of the following places:
Munich
Finland
Manchuria
French Indochina

1. **Using Graphic Organizers** Copy the chart below. Use it to list the early events of World War II.

1. The Munich Conference
2.
3.
4.
5.
6. The United States enters the war.

2. **Comparing and Contrasting** How did German aggression differ from Japanese aggression in the 1930s?
3. **Hypothesizing** How might events in Europe have been different if European leaders had not decided to pursue an appeasement policy toward Hitler?
4. **Recognizing Point of View** Why did Japanese leaders respond to conflicts with the United States by bombing Pearl Harbor?

Critical Thinking

5. Should the United States have entered the war when Britain did?
Consider:
- U.S. foreign policy at the start of the war
- the increased tensions with Germany
- U.S. concerns in the Atlantic

5. Answers will vary. Students might note that U.S. involvement from the beginning might have limited future tensions with Germany and reduced concerns in the Atlantic.

CHAPTER 16 REVIEW ANSWERS

Creating a Time Line
Each event should have an explanation and the correct date.

Writing a Summary
See the Reading Checks in each section for main ideas.

Identifying People and Ideas

1. withdrawal from world affairs that characterized U.S. foreign policy in the 1920s and 1930s
2. U.S. secretary of state who engineered the Washington Conference
3. Nicaraguan general who opposed American forces
4. assert government control over industries
5. Italian Fascist who was appointed prime minister
6. Fascist who came to power in Germany in 1933
7. November 9, 1938, the "night of broken glass," in which Nazis destroyed Jewish businesses and synagogues
8. giving in to demands to avoid a larger conflict
9. 1939 agreement between the Soviet Union and Germany not to attack one another
10. British prime minister of Great Britain who rallied the country for war in 1940

REVIEW AND ASSESSMENT RESOURCES

PRINT

- Chapter 16 Review, pp. 496–97
- Chapter 16 Tutorial for Students, Parents, Mentors, and Peers
- Chapter 16 Test (Form A or B)
- Portfolio Activities and Alternative Assessment Handbook, Chapter 16

MULTIMEDIA

- Audio Program, Chapter 16 (English and Spanish)
- Chapter 16 Test Generator (on the One-Stop Planner)
- Global Skill Builder CD–ROM
- HRW Web site

SHELTERED ENGLISH

- Spanish Glossary
- Sheltered English Chapter 16 Test

REVIEW

Have students complete the **Chapter 16 Review** on pp. 496–97.

ASSESS

Use one of the chapter tests to assess students' understanding of the content. For **Alternative Assessment**, see the **Portfolio Activities and Alternative Assessment Handbook.**

Understanding Main Ideas

1. regret over entering World War I, fear of being dragged into another foreign conflict

2. U.S. government intervened in internal political situations; American businesses were major investors

3. Foreign oil companies refused to raise wages and improve working conditions for Mexican oil workers.

4. through the use of force or through public dissatisfaction over economic issues

5. invaded Manchuria in 1931, initiated a naval buildup, and occupied Nanjing in 1937

6. They hoped it would prevent war; opponents believed that it encouraged Hitler's aggression.

Reviewing Themes

1. by signing treaties limiting naval armaments, by joining the World Court, by signing the Kellogg-Briand Pact

2. led to the rise of leaders who advocated totalitarian governments

3. by limiting free speech and voting, banning strikes, and persecuting religious or ethnic groups

Thinking Critically

1. Answers will vary, but students should note that they offered solutions to economic problems and promised to turn their countries into empires.

CHAPTER 16 Review

Creating a Time Line

Copy the time line below onto a sheet of paper. Complete the time line by filling in the events and dates from the chapter that you think were most significant. Pick three events and explain why you think they were significant.

Writing a Summary

Using the Reading Checks as a guide, write an overview of the events in the chapter.

Identifying People and Ideas

Identify the following terms or individuals and explain their significance.

1. isolationism
2. Charles Evans Hughes
3. Augusto César Sandino
4. nationalize
5. Benito Mussolini
6. Adolf Hitler
7. *Kristallnacht*
8. appeasement
9. nonaggression pact
10. Winston Churchill

Understanding Main Ideas

SECTION 1

1. What factors encouraged the United States to follow a foreign policy of isolationism after World War I?

SECTION 2

2. What economic and political role did the United States play in Latin America?
3. Why did Mexican president Lázaro Cárdenas nationalize his country's oil fields in 1938?

SECTION 3

4. How did dictators come to power in Europe in the 1930s?
5. What aggressive actions did Japan take during the 1930s?

SECTION 4

6. Why did some European leaders favor a policy of appeasement toward Adolf Hitler? Why did others oppose it?

Reviewing Themes

1. **Global Relations** In what ways did countries promote world peace after World War I?
2. **Economic Development** How did economic problems contribute to political unrest after World War I?
3. **Democratic Values** How did the fascist dictatorships in Europe restrict civil liberties?

Thinking Critically

1. **Hypothesizing** Why do you think many people supported Benito Mussolini and Adolf Hitler?
2. **Evaluating** Why did Japan's militarists want to create an empire in East Asia and the Pacific?
3. **Synthesizing** How did the U.S. policy of neutrality change between 1935 and 1941?
4. **Recognizing Point of View** Why did some Germans feel that they were justified in reclaiming territory they had lost in the Treaty of Versailles?
5. **Assessing Consequences** What was the effect of appeasing Adolf Hitler at the Munich Conference?

Writing About History

Writing to Describe

Imagine that you are a Loyalist who fought during the Spanish Civil War. Write a letter to an American friend describing the events during that period. Use the outline at right to organize your thoughts.

I. Franco's Rise
II. Loyalist Views
III. The Spanish Civil War
  A. Foreign Aid
    1. Soviet Union
    2. United States
  B. Outcome
IV. Views of the War

RETEACH

Organize students into six groups and assign each group one of the following countries: Germany, Italy, Japan, Mexico, Nicaragua, or the Soviet Union. Have each group create a graphic organizer that shows the key terms and events of this chapter that relate to its country. Have students present their organizers to the class and discuss their country's place in world events during the 1920s and 1930s.
Sheltered English, Cooperative Learning

EXTEND

Have students conduct research on newspaper or magazine coverage of U.S. foreign relations between 1920 and 1940. Have each student find several different articles that discuss U.S. relations with a particular country. Then ask students to write a report tracing how U.S. relations with this country changed over time. **Block Scheduling**

Strategies for Success Review the **Strategies for Success** on *Using Oral Histories.* Then examine the following excerpt from an interview with Thomas Page, a student at Harvard Law School when global tensions increased in 1941.

> **"A guy named Tom Harris and his wife . . . would observe what people were eating, reading, and the way of advertisements to determine what people really were doing. . . . And I looked at the *New York Times Sunday Magazine*. . . . It was filled with semi-warlike copy and ads. And I thought, my God, this is really an illustration of this guy Harris's theory of mass observation—the country has almost accepted the inevitability of some kind of military action and is all geared up for it mentally."**

How does the excerpt contribute to your understanding of American attitudes in 1941?

Linking History and Geography

Italy invaded Ethiopia in the 1930s. Study the map below. How would control of Ethiopia have helped Italy in its conflict with the Allied Powers?

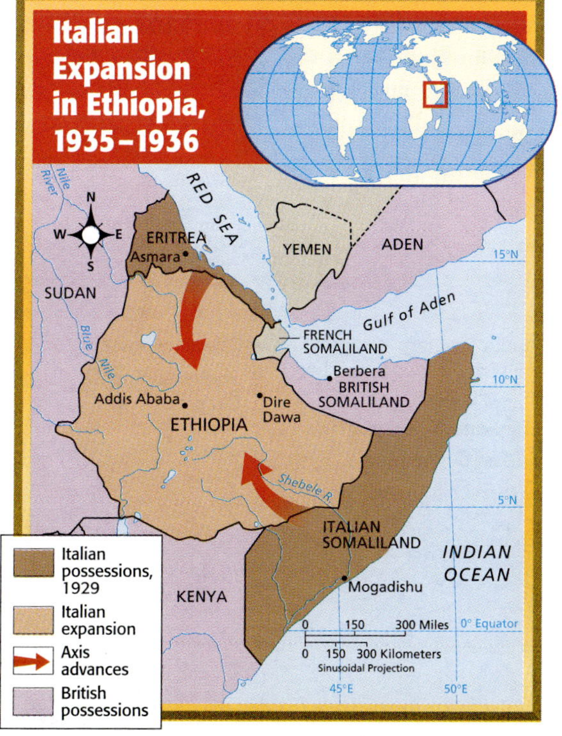

internet connect

TOPIC: The Spanish Civil War
GO TO: go.hrw.com
KEYWORD: SE1 Front

Accessing the Internet through the HRW Web site, research the Spanish Civil War. Then write a series of diary entries from one of the following perspectives: (a) You are Pablo Picasso. Explain why you painted *Guernica.* (b) You are an artist making propaganda posters for the Popular Front. (c) You are a member of the Abraham Lincoln Brigade. Explain why you left America to fight in Spain.

BUILDING YOUR PORTFOLIO

Complete one or all of the following projects independently or cooperatively.

1 Global Relations

Imagine that you are a journalist assigned to evaluate the new political trends of the 1930s. ***Create a chart*** that compares the similarities and differences among fascist dictators around the world.

2 Democratic Values

Imagine that you are a diplomat at the 1938 Munich Conference. ***Write a speech*** aimed at convincing the Allies to abandon their policy of appeasement toward Germany's Adolf Hitler. Your speech should include examples of how Hitler's policies threaten democracy.

THE GRANGER COLLECTION, NEW YORK

3 Economic Development

Imagine that you are an American business leader considering investing in a Latin American country in the 1930s. ***Create a business plan*** that outlines the advantages and disadvantages of such investment for both your company and the Latin American country.

2. to seize resources in Asia and thus reduce Japan's dependence on foreign imports

3. Strict neutralism gave way to the Lend-Lease Act. In 1941 the United States entered the war.

4. They regarded the treaty as unfair.

5. convinced him that other nations would not stop him in his efforts to conquer Europe

Writing About History
Letters will vary but should contrast the views of the Loyalists and the Fascists, the failure of the United States to provide aid, and the war's influence on the growing international crisis.

Strategies for Success
Answers will vary, but students might mention that it reveals American attitudes toward the coming of World War II.

Linking History and Geography
Students might suggest that it would have given Italy better control of the Red Sea and access to the Suez Canal.

Americans in World War II

CHAPTER PLANNING GUIDE

	Section Lesson Objectives	Print Resources	Multimedia Resources	Sheltered English Resources
Section 1 Early Difficulties, pp. 500–06	1 Analyze the strengths and weaknesses of the Allied and Axis Powers in 1941. 2 Outline the steps that the United States took to prepare for war. 3 Identify locations where the Japanese military attacked after Pearl Harbor. 4 Discuss the early turning points of the war in the Pacific. 5 Relate the major battles in Europe and North Africa in 1942.	▶ Guided Reading Strategy 17.1 ▶ Geography Activity 17: Hitler's War Machine ▶ American History Outline Map 20: World War II in the Pacific ▶ American History Outline Map 19: World War II in Europe ▶ Section 1 Review, p. 506 ▶ Daily Quiz 17.1	▶ One-Stop Planner, Lesson 17.1 ▶ Holt Researcher: American History CD–ROM	▶ Main Idea Activity for Reteaching and Sheltered English 17.1
Section 2 The Home Front, pp. 507–13	1 Describe how the U.S. government tried to keep wartime morale high. 2 Describe what life was like in the United States during World War II. 3 Relate how women contributed to the war effort. 4 Analyze what actions the government took to protect the rights of minority groups. 5 Discuss the war's effect on Japanese Americans.	▶ Guided Reading Strategy 17.2 ▶ Primary Source Reading 17: A Mountain Woman's Tale ▶ Graphic Organizer Activity 17: The Effect of War on Life at Home ▶ Section 2 Review, p. 513 ▶ Daily Quiz 17.2	▶ One-Stop Planner, Lesson 17.2 ▶ The American Nation Video Program Segment: Japanese Americans in Relocation Camps; Teacher's Guide, pp. 159–60 ▶ Holt Researcher: American History CD–ROM ▶ HRW Web site	▶ Main Idea Activity for Reteaching and Sheltered English 17.2
Section 3 Victory in Europe, pp. 514–20	1 Identify where the Allied offensive in Europe began. 2 Explain the impact of fighting in the Atlantic and in the air. 3 Relate how the Allies successfully invaded Normandy. 4 Describe the Holocaust. 5 Relate how the Allies finally defeated Germany.	▶ Guided Reading Strategy 17.3 ▶ Section 3 Review, p. 520 ▶ Daily Quiz 17.3	▶ One-Stop Planner, Lesson 17.3 ▶ Linking Geography and History Transparency 18: World War II in Europe, 1942–1945 ▶ Holt Researcher: American History CD–ROM	▶ Main Idea Activity for Reteaching and Sheltered English 17.3
Section 4 Victory in Asia, pp. 521–27	1 Describe the U.S. island-hopping plan. 2 Explain the effect that the battles at Iwo Jima and Okinawa had on the war. 3 Explain why the United States used atomic weapons against Japan. 4 Discuss the costs of the war.	▶ Guided Reading Strategy 17.4 ▶ Biography Reading 17: Enrico Fermi ▶ Literature Reading 17: A City and Its People Destroyed ▶ Section 4 Review, p. 527 ▶ Daily Quiz 17.4	▶ One-Stop Planner, Lesson 17.4 ▶ Holt Researcher: American History CD–ROM	▶ Main Idea Activity for Reteaching and Sheltered English 17.4
Chapter Review and Assessment pp. 528–29		▶ Chapter 17 Review, pp. 528–29 ▶ Chapter 17 Tutorial for Students, Parents, Mentors, and Peers ▶ Chapter 17 Test (Form A or B) ▶ Portfolio Activities and Alternative Assessment Handbook, Chapter 17	▶ Audio Program, Chapter 17 (English and Spanish) ▶ Chapter 17 Test Generator (on the One-Stop Planner) ▶ Global Skill Builder CD–ROM ▶ HRW Web site	▶ Spanish Glossary ▶ Sheltered English Chapter 17 Test

CHAPTER OVERVIEW

Following the attack on Pearl Harbor, the United States joined the Allies in World War II. Although the Axis Powers initially held many advantages, the Allied Powers eventually managed to make important headway in the war.

The U.S. government made many efforts to support the war. The government created new offices and expanded production of war goods, for example. Fearful of treason, the United States interned many Japanese Americans.

Starting in Sicily and southern Italy, the Allies began to invade German-occupied Europe. After this push found success, the Allies moved into Nazi France with the Normandy invasion. Germany surrendered in May 1945. The United States continued to fight in the Pacific, however. After the United States used atomic weapons against Japan, the country surrendered in September 1945. World War II, the most devastating conflict in history, was over.

TIME TAMERS

Block Scheduling

The teacher lesson plans for each section offer a variety of activity choices to help you present the material in a block scheduling format. For further suggestions on block scheduling, see the **Block Scheduling Handbook with Team Teaching Strategies**, pp. 97–102.

Smithsonian Institution®

Internet Connections and Lesson 17

www.si.edu/hrw

Hands-On History Activities:

Classroom to Community the **Hands-On History Activities** help students make meaningful connections between events in American history and those in their own hometown. You may wish to use the Chapter 17 Activity, Your Town During World War II, to extend the chapter lessons, as alternative assessment, or as a block scheduling option.

Portfolio Projects

The American Nation includes multiple portfolio projects in each Pupil's Edition chapter review, as well as each unit review. Chapter 17 Portfolio Project options on p. 529 include the following:

1. Students will **write a letter**.
2. Students will **create a chart**.
3. Students will **create journal entries**.

The American Nation

INTERNET RESOURCE DIRECTORY

To access online materials for this chapter, go to **go.hrw.com** and type in the keywords listed below.

HRW ONLINE RESOURCES

GO TO: go.hrw.com

Online Maps

KEYWORD: SE1 Maps17

- Operation Barbarossa, 1941
- Relocating Japanese Americans
- German Concentration Camps

Online Charts

KEYWORD: SE1 Charts17

- U.S. Entry into World War II
- World War II Alliances
- Japanese American Relocation
- Holocaust Camps

Online Reading Support

KEYWORD: SE1 Strategies17

Online Rubrics

KEYWORD: SE1 Rubrics

CHAPTER ENRICHMENT LINKS

Use these Web links to extend and enrich student learning for Chapter 17.

GO TO: go.hrw.com

KEYWORD: SE1 Ch17

CHAPTER INTERNET ACTIVITIES

GO TO: go.hrw.com

- Pupil's Edition Student Activity
  KEYWORD: SE1 Rockwell
  (Students examine the paintings of Norman Rockwell.)
- Teacher's Edition Student Activity
  KEYWORD: SE1 Musicals
  (Students conduct research on World War II–era musicals.)
- Teacher's Edition Student Activity
  KEYWORD: SE1 Rosie
  (Students analyze the appeal of Rosie the Riveter.)

ADDITIONAL

RESOURCES

Books for Teachers

Bernstein, Alison R. *American Indians and World War II.* University of Oklahoma Press, 1991. Discusses American Indian contributions.

Hilberg, Raul. *Perpetrators, Victims, Bystanders.* HarperCollins, 1993. Investigates the Holocaust's agents, collaborators, and victims. Also discusses the Allies' inaction.

Books for Students

Ambrose, Stephen E. and C. L. Sulzberger. *American Heritage New History of World War II.* Viking Penguin, 1997. Provides an illustrated overview of the war.

Meltzer, Milton. *Never to Forget.* HarperCollins, 1991. Integrates a general account of the Holocaust with comments by firsthand and secondhand observers.

Primary Sources from the Period

Hersey, John. *Hiroshima.* Modern Library, 1946. Describes Hiroshima after the atomic bomb.

Shirer, William L. *Berlin Diary: The Journal of a Foreign Correspondent, 1934–1941.* Alfred A. Knopf, 1941. Records the author's experiences and observations while living in Nazi Germany.

Multimedia Materials

The Holocaust: A Teenager's Experience. Video, 30 min. United Learning/SSSS. Tells the story of Holocaust survivor David Bergman, who was imprisoned in Nazi concentration camps.

The Home Front—1940 to 1945. 3 videos, 180 min. Reader's Digest/SSSS. Documents life on the American home front during World War II.

CHAPTER 17

Before You Read

Build on What You Know

Ask students to answer the following questions.

How might the Allied Powers have battled the Axis Powers in different areas around the world?

Consider:

- the difficulties of fighting wars on multiple fronts
- the factors that would facilitate a multifront war—coordination, cooperation, and so on

How might the Allies have defeated the Axis Powers?

Consider:

- the importance of human and economic resources
- the military importance of new technologies

---

exploring the time line

AMERICAN EVENTS

internet connect

TOPIC: American Musicals
GO TO: go.hrw.com
KEYWORD: SE1 Musicals

Have students access the Internet through the HRW Web site to conduct research on World War II–era musicals, such as *Oklahoma* and *South Pacific.* Have each student design a promotional poster for one particular musical. Students' promotional posters should convey the content and themes of the musicals. After students have finished their posters, display them around the classroom. Ask students to pick their favorite posters, excluding their own. Have each student write a paragraph explaining and justifying his or her choice. Students may wish to include their posters and their paragraphs in their portfolios.

CHAPTER 17

1941–1945

Americans in World War II

Poster advertising **Citizen Kane**

1941
The Arts
Orson Welles's film *Citizen Kane,* inspired by the life of William Randolph Hearst, is released.

1941
Science and Technology
Physicists Glenn Seaborg and Edwin McMillan isolate the element plutonium.

1941
World Events
Japanese planes bomb Pearl Harbor.

A zinc-coated penny

A Glenn Miller album cover

1942
Daily Life
The U.S. Mint begins issuing pennies made of zinc-coated steel to conserve copper for weapons production.

1942
The Arts
Glenn Miller receives the first gold record for having sold more than 1 million copies of his hit song "Chattanooga Choo Choo."

1941 **1942**

1942
Business and Finance
On February 10 the last automobile to be produced in the United States until the end of the war rolls off the Ford assembly line.

1942
World Events
U.S. forces in the Philippines surrender after an extended siege.

A 1942 Packard

U.S. prisoners in the Philippines

Before You Read

Build on What You Know

The economic distress of the Great Depression contributed to the rise of dictatorships in some nations. Military aggression by Germany, Italy, and Japan plunged the world into war. In December 1941 the Japanese bombed Pearl Harbor, bringing the United States into World War II. In this chapter you will learn that the United States and the Allies battled the Axis Powers on land and at sea in Europe, North Africa, and Asia. By August 1945 the Allies had won a difficult war.

Think About Themes

*To help students create their Themes Journal entries, provide the following examples of appropriate **agree**/**disagree** statements.*

Global Relations

Agree The United States supplied crucial weapons and supplies to the Allies during World War I.

Disagree The Union won the Civil War without significant economic assistance from other countries.

Constitutional Heritage

Agree The arrest of Copperheads and other opponents of the Civil War helped restore peace in New York City during the draft riots of 1863.

Disagree American officials unfairly silenced and imprisoned critics of World War I under the Espionage Act of 1917 and the Sedition Act of 1918.

Technology and Society

Agree Given the destructive power of some technologies, governments must consider political and moral issues.

Disagree In some circumstances, such as wartime, deadly technologies must be developed and used without delay in order to secure victory.

Diego Rivera's mural La Gran Tenochtitlán

1943
Science and Technology
Chicago's first subway opens.

1943
Politics
President Roosevelt, British prime minister Winston Churchill, and Soviet premier Joseph Stalin meet at the Tehran Conference.

1944
World Events
On the morning of June 6, some 176,000 Allied troops storm the beaches of Normandy, France.

1944
Business and Finance
The International Bank for Reconstruction, or World Bank, is established in July.

1945
The Arts
Mexican artist Diego Rivera completes his mural *La Gran Tenochtitlán* in Mexico City's National Palace.

1945
World Events
The United States drops atomic bombs on Hiroshima and Nagasaki.

1943 | **1944** | **1945**

1943
The Arts
The musical *Oklahoma!* opens.

1943
World Events
Italy surrenders to the Allies, but German forces occupy the country to prevent the Allies from doing so.

1943
Daily Life
The United States begins rationing shoes, allowing each person three pairs per year.

1944
World Events
Allied forces liberate Paris, France.

1945
Daily Life
In November, rationing of all food items except sugar ends in the United States.

Allied forces arrive in Paris.

World War II ration stamps

Think About Themes

*Decide whether you **agree** or **disagree** with the following statements. Note why in your journal.*

Global Relations Allied nations must pool their economic and military resources in order to win a global war.

Constitutional Heritage A government should be allowed to restrict the rights of citizens during a national emergency.

Technology and Society A government should consider more than just military concerns when developing new defensive technology.

exploring the time line

GLOBAL EVENTS

GLOBAL RELATIONS

1944 ■ The Normandy Invasion. The Normandy invasion was incredibly deadly. The U.S. Navy launched its assault craft 12 miles from the shore. Many of the amphibious craft were sunk on the long journey to land, and many soldiers drowned. Once the troops actually reached land, they faced minefields and machine-gun fire. One general summarized the danger saying, "Two kinds of people are staying on this beach, the dead and those who are going to die—now let's get the hell out of here."

CRITICAL THINKING What might the symbolic importance of the Normandy invasion have been?

ANSWER: Students might suggest that the invasion of German-occupied France demonstrated the Allies' growing strength in the war.

THAT'S INTERESTING!

Hours before the landing on the Normandy beaches, U.S. and British parachutists began to drop into the French countryside. One scholar has called this dangerous mission "a lethal lottery."

SECTION 1

After completing Section 1, students should be able to:

OBJECTIVE 1 *Analyze the strengths and weaknesses of the Allied and Axis Powers in 1941.*

OBJECTIVE 2 *Outline the steps that the United States took to prepare for war.*

OBJECTIVE 3 *Identify locations where the Japanese military attacked after Pearl Harbor.*

OBJECTIVE 4 *Discuss the early turning points of the war in the Pacific.*

OBJECTIVE 5 *Relate the major battles in Europe and North Africa in 1942.*

LET'S GET STARTED!

Write the following term on the chalkboard: *Pearl Harbor.* As students enter the classroom, ask them to write down anything they know about the term. *(Most students will know something about the term from Chapter 16.)* Discuss students' responses. Tell students that in Section 1 they will learn about the war in the Pacific.

SECTION 1 RESOURCES

PRINT

- Guided Reading Strategy 17.1
- Geography Activity 17: Hitler's War Machine
- American History Outline Map 20: World War II in the Pacific
- American History Outline Map 19: World War II in Europe
- Section 1 Review, p. 506
- Daily Quiz 17.1

MULTIMEDIA

- One-Stop Planner, Lesson 17.1
- Holt Researcher: American History CD–ROM

SHELTERED ENGLISH

- Main Idea Activity for Reteaching and Sheltered English 17.1

✔ READING TO UNDERSTAND

To help students master the section objectives, have them answer the **READING CHECKS** and complete **Guided Reading Strategy 17.1** as they read the section.

Early Difficulties

OBJECTIVES

Read to understand:

1. what the strengths and weaknesses of the Allied Powers and Axis Powers were in 1941
2. what steps the United States took to prepare for war
3. where the Japanese military attacked after Pearl Harbor
4. what the early turning points of the war in the Pacific were
5. what the major battles in Europe and North Africa in 1942 were

KEY TERMS

War Production Board
Office of War Mobilization
Selective Training and Service Act
Bataan Death March
Battle of the Coral Sea
Battle of Midway

KEY PEOPLE

Douglas MacArthur
Chester Nimitz
Erwin Rommel
Bernard Montgomery

This medal was made to commemorate the bombing of Pearl Harbor.

"I was sixteen years old, employed . . . at Pearl Harbor Navy Yard. On December 7, 1941, oh, around 8:00 A.M., my grandmother awoke me. She informed me that the Japanese were bombing Pearl Harbor. . . . I was asked . . . to go into the water and get sailors out that had been blown off the ships. Some were unconscious, some were dead. I brought out I don't know how many bodies. . . . I tried to get into the military, but they refused. . . . Finally, I wrote a letter to President Roosevelt. I told him I was angry at the Japanese bombing and had lost some friends. He okayed that I be accepted."

—U.S. sailor

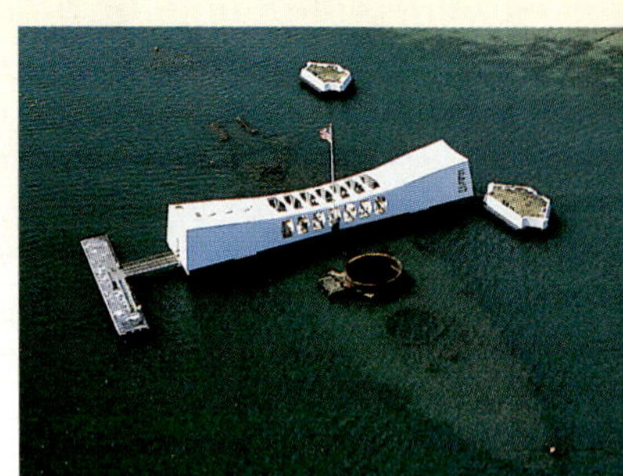

The USS* Arizona *memorial

Like this young sailor, millions of Americans rushed to join the fight after Pearl Harbor. Neutrality was quickly forgotten. Their nation had been attacked. Friends, children, and parents had been killed. Americans were determined to bring an end to the madness of war.

Strengths and Weaknesses

When the United States entered World War II, the Axis Powers had two big advantages. First, Germany and Japan had already secured firm control of the areas they had invaded. As a result, the United States and the Allies faced a long, drawn-out fight on several fronts. Second, Germany and Japan were better prepared for war. In the 1930s both nations had rearmed and built airfields, barracks, and military training centers. By the mid-1930s the Nazis had converted most of the German economy to military production, as had Japan's military-led government.

The Allies did have some advantages, however. The Axis forces were spread over an enormous area stretching from the coast of France to deep into the Soviet Union and from Norway to North Africa. In the Pacific, Japan had occupied a similarly large area. The Germans had not defeated the British or the Soviets and therefore had to maintain troops on two active fronts. The Allies' hopes rested on two factors—the enormous size of the Soviet Union's military and the tremendous production capacity of the United States.

Axis leaders hoped that they could win the conflict before these two factors could combine and overwhelm their smaller but better-prepared forces. The Allies sought to continue to resist long enough to allow the United States to gather its strength.

✔ READING CHECK: What were the strengths and weaknesses of the Allied Powers and Axis Powers in 1941?

TEACH OBJECTIVE 1

ALL LEVELS: To help students understand the strengths and weaknesses of the Allied and Axis Powers in 1941, copy the graphic organizer at right on the chalkboard, omitting the italicized answers. Have each student complete it. **Sheltered English**

▶**ASSIGNMENT** *Have students list the strengths and weaknesses of Allied and Axis Powers. Then ask students to develop three or four ways in which the United States might have countered Axis advantages. Have each student discuss these strategies in a memo to President Roosevelt.*

THE ALLIED AND AXIS POWERS—STRENGTHS AND WEAKNESSES

The Allied Powers
- **advantage:** *the United States had tremendous production capacity*
- **advantage:** *the Soviet Union had vast manpower*
- **advantage:** *Britain and the Soviet Union had not been defeated*
- **disadvantage:** *faced a long, drawn-out fight on several fronts*
- **disadvantage:** *enemy held firm control of conquered areas spread over an enormous area—both in Europe and the Pacific*

The Axis Powers
- **advantage:** *better prepared for war*
- **advantage:** *had firm control over invaded areas*
- **advantage:** *had been rearmed since the 1930s*
- **advantage:** *already had airfields, barracks, and military training centers*
- **advantage:** *economies ready for war*
- **disadvantage:** *had to defend multiple fronts*

Mobilizing for War

After the bombing of Pearl Harbor the United States switched from a peacetime to a wartime economy. Government and private industry cooperated to increase production, and union leaders agreed not to strike during the war.

A production boom. In 1940 government arsenals employed about 22,000 workers who produced ammunition, cannon shells, and rifles. Three years later some 486,000 workers were working in the arsenals. By war's end the United States had built some 300,000 aircraft. Car production was suspended for the duration of the war. Between 1940 and 1945, American factories produced huge numbers of planes, tanks, jeeps, and guns. American shipyards built 88,000 landing craft, 215 submarines, 147 aircraft carriers, 952 other warships, and 5,200 merchant ships.

This massive increase in production created an economic boom that ended the Great Depression. Unemployment dropped from 14.6 percent in 1940 to 1.2 percent in 1944. Earnings nearly doubled between 1939 and 1945. People who had stood in breadlines a decade earlier now brought home fat paychecks. The lure of high-paying jobs in war industries led to vast population shifts. More than 4 million workers left their homes to find work in factories in other states.

Sharecroppers, tenant farmers, and others struggling to make a living on farms flocked to the centers of wartime production. Many went to shipyards on the Gulf and Pacific coasts and factories in the Midwest and West. The West experienced particularly strong growth during the war.

American farms also achieved marvels of productivity. During the war years, farmers produced enough food to supply both the American people and many of the Allied Powers overseas. Although many agricultural workers went off to fight in the war or to work in wartime factories, farm production increased. As part of its lend-lease aid, the United States exported 10 percent of the food it produced, mostly to Great Britain and the Soviet Union.

Government expansion. Mobilizing for war required a greatly expanded federal government. Between 1940 and 1945 the number of federal employees nearly tripled. To fight the Axis Powers, the United States needed to channel all of its resources into producing the maximum amount of military goods. In January 1942 President Roosevelt created the **War Production Board** (WPB) to increase military production. The WPB directed the conversion of existing factories to wartime production and

THROUGH OTHERS' EYES

Japanese View of World War II

Americans were stunned and angered by Japan's sudden attack on Pearl Harbor. The day after the attack, Emperor Hirohito made a speech that was relayed around the world. In this speech he laid out Japan's reasons for declaring war on the United States and Great Britain.

> **"Both America and Britain . . . have aggravated the disturbances in East Asia. . . . These two powers, inducing other countries to follow suit, increased military preparations on all sides of Our Empire. . . . They have obstructed by every means Our peaceful commerce, and finally resorted to a direct severance [cutting off] of economic relations. . . . Patiently have We waited and long have We endured, in hope that Our Government might retrieve the situation in peace. But Our adversaries [enemies], showing not the least spirit of conciliation [peace-making], have unduly [excessively] delayed a settlement. . . . Our Empire for its existence and self defense has no other recourse [choice] but to appeal to arms and to crush every obstacle in its path."**

INTERPRETING THE VISUAL RECORD

Preparing for war. This assembly line at North American Aviation's Inglewood, California, plant turned out B-25 bombers. ***How does this image point to a U.S. advantage in the war?***

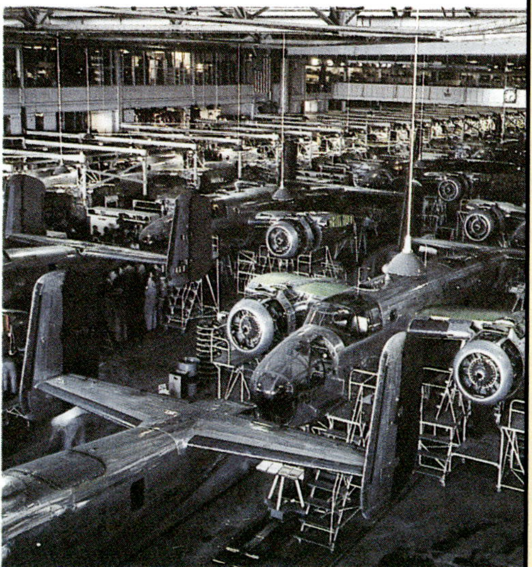

ECONOMIC DEVELOPMENT

No-Strike Agreements. The federal government began to pressure union leaders to avoid strikes well before the United States declared war. In January 1941 President Roosevelt declared that "whatever stands in the way of speed and efficiency in defense preparations must give way to the national need." A short time later his administration established the National Defense Mediation Board to bring union leaders and business managers together to establish a series of wage agreements and a system for arbitrating industrial disputes.

CRITICAL THINKING How might no-strike agreements have affected unions?

ANSWER: Students might suggest that the agreements weakened unions or that they actually strengthened unions by presenting them as intensely patriotic.

VISUAL RECORD ANSWER

Students might suggest that assembly lines increased American productivity.

TEACH OBJECTIVE 2

LEVEL 1: Ask students to outline the steps that the United States took to prepare for war. *(Students should mention the efforts to increase production, expand the government, direct the economy, and raise the army.)* List students' responses on the chalkboard. Then ask each student to consult the chalkboard list to write a paragraph explaining how the United States prepared to fight in World War II.
Sheltered English

LEVEL 2: Pair students and ask students to outline the steps that the United States took to prepare for war. *(See the Level 1 lesson for the correct steps.)* Have each pair select one particular step and create a poster in support of that measure. Students' posters should include catchy phrases and illustrations to attract support for the war. Have each pair write two or three paragraphs explaining its poster.
Sheltered English, Cooperative Learning

LEVEL 3: Tell students to imagine that it is early 1942 and that they are aides to President Roosevelt. Have each student write a brief speech for President Roosevelt to deliver to the nation outlining the steps that the United States has taken to prepare for war. *(See the Level 1 lesson for the correct steps.)* In their speeches students should both describe and justify the steps. Have volunteers deliver their speeches to the class.

ACROSS THE CURRICULUM

▶GOVERNMENT◀

Rationing. The Office of Price Administration (OPA) administered rationing. Local boards of the OPA distributed monthly ration books with an allotted number of coupons for individuals. Shoppers spent red coupons on animal products such as red meat, and green, brown, or blue coupons on processed items such as canned goods. Gasoline was also rationed. Price tags showed cost in both dollars and coupons.

CRITICAL THINKING Why might gasoline have been an important ration item?

ANSWER: Students might suggest that the government needed fuel. In addition, gasoline rationing decreased driving and thus helped conserve rubber.

THAT'S INTERESTING!

Approximately one half of the men who were called up during the first year of the draft were rejected for failing to meet the military's minimum physical standards. These standards included a height of at least five feet, a weight of at least 105 pounds, correctable vision, at least 16 natural teeth, and no flat feet.

GRAPH ANSWER
approximately $250 billion

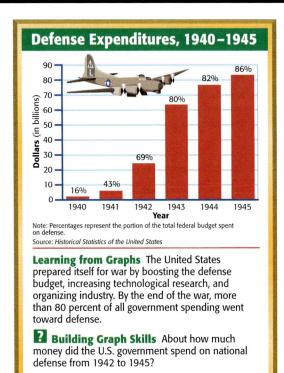

Defense Expenditures, 1940–1945

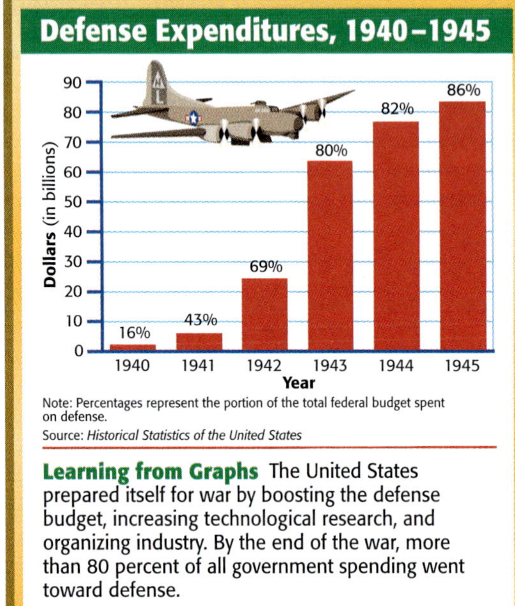

Note: Percentages represent the portion of the total federal budget spent on defense.
Source: *Historical Statistics of the United States*

Learning from Graphs The United States prepared itself for war by boosting the defense budget, increasing technological research, and organizing industry. By the end of the war, more than 80 percent of all government spending went toward defense.

Building Graph Skills About how much money did the U.S. government spend on national defense from 1942 to 1945?

supervised the building of new plants. It assigned raw materials to industry, including scrap iron from factories and recyclable aluminum, paper, tin, and other items from homes. Created on May 27, 1943, the **Office of War Mobilization** (OWM) coordinated all government agencies involved in the war effort. OWM director James F. Byrnes wielded such power that he was often called the assistant president.

The OWM also coordinated the production and distribution of consumer goods. For instance, it diverted nylon to use for making parachutes and even regulated clothing styles to save fabric. Cuffs on men's trousers and pleats in women's skirts were canceled for the duration of the war. Martha Wood of Raleigh, North Carolina, remembers that "rationing was hard to live with, particularly silk stockings. . . . If you had a run in your stocking, you took a needle and thread and worked it back up, because there was no chance of getting any [more]."

Directing the economy. The government also expanded its control over the economy. In order to pay for the war, the government increased by about nine times the number of Americans who had to pay income tax. The new taxes affected most middle- and lower-income groups for the first time. The rest of the money came from borrowing, mainly through war bonds.

The sale of war bonds also helped the government deal with another major concern—keeping inflation down. When incomes remain high but few consumer items are available for people to buy, prices go up and inflation results. Selling war bonds offered a way to channel excess income, thus keeping inflation down.

The government took other anti-inflationary steps as well. One was rationing, which reduced consumer demand by limiting how much people could buy. Rationed items included gasoline, tires, coffee, sugar, meat, butter, and canned goods. The government also tried to keep wages and prices down by freezing wages. After the cost of living rose, the government allowed wages to rise by 15 percent.

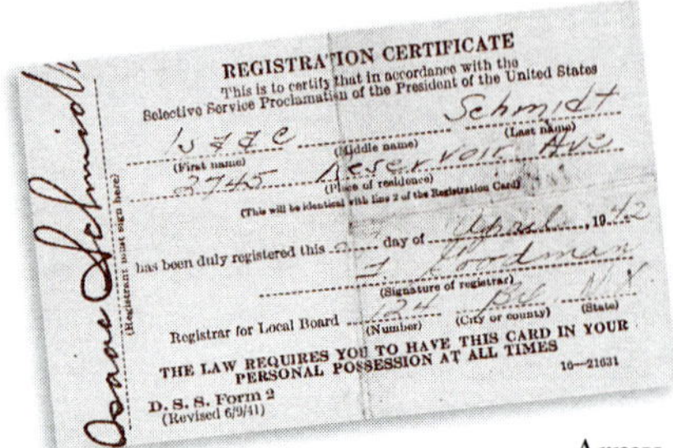

REGISTRATION CERTIFICATE
This is to certify that in accordance with the Selective Service Proclamation of the President of the United States
Schmidt (Last name)
(First name) (Middle name)
(Place of residence)
(This will be identical with line 2 of the Registration Card)
has been duly registered this ___ day of April, 1942
(Signature of registrar)
Registrar for Local Board (Number) (City or county) (State)
THE LAW REQUIRES YOU TO HAVE THIS CARD IN YOUR PERSONAL POSSESSION AT ALL TIMES
10—21631
D. S. S. Form 2
(Revised 6/9/41)
(Registrant must sign here)

Registration certificates like this one proved that a man had made himself available to be drafted.

Raising an army. Along with increased production and expanded government controls, gearing up to fight a war meant recruiting soldiers. In the summer of 1940 the United States called the National Guard to active duty and passed the **Selective Training and Service Act.** This act provided for the first peacetime draft in U.S. history. The law required all men between ages 21 and 35 (later 18 to 45) to register. Local draft boards determined fitness and deferred men for family, religious, or health reasons. At the time of the draft there were just 269,023 soldiers in the U.S. Army, 160,997 in the navy, and 28,345 in the marines. They made up less than 5 percent of the 12 million trained soldiers the military needed to fight the war.

Of the more than 12 million Americans who served during World War II, more than three fourths were draftees and the rest volunteers, including more than 300,000 women. Women enrolled in the Women's Auxiliary Army Corps (WAAC),

TEACH OBJECTIVE 3

ALL LEVELS: Distribute Outline Map 20, World War II in the Pacific, from **American History Outline Maps**. Have each student use information from the textbook to label locations where the Japanese military attacked after Pearl Harbor. *(Students should label Clark Airforce Base in the Philippines, Burma, Borneo, the Netherlands East Indies, Wake Island, and Hong Kong.)* Have students annotate their maps with specific details about each military attack. Students may wish to include their maps in their portfolios.
Sheltered English

TEACH OBJECTIVE 4

LEVEL 1: Ask students to name the early turning points of the war in the Pacific. *(Students should name the Battle of the Coral Sea, the Battle of Midway, and Guadalcanal.)* List students' responses on the chalkboard. Then organize students into triads. Assign each triad one of the battles. Have triads develop an outline for a radio news report relaying the four "Ws" of the battle: What, When, Where, and Why it was significant. *(See pp. 504–05 for specific details about the three battles.)* Ask at least three volunteers—one for each battle—to present their outlines to the class.
Sheltered English, Cooperative Learning

Women Airforce Service Pilots (WASPs), and auxiliary branches of the navy, coast guard, and marines. They worked as nurses, did office work, drove vehicles, and ferried planes in order to free men for active duty. Eunice Hatchitt was a nurse who served in the Philippines at Bataan. She described the terrible conditions and heavy casualties.

> **"Days and nights were an endless nightmare, until it seemed we couldn't stand it any longer. Patients came in by the hundreds, and the doctors and nurses worked continuously under the tents amid the flies and heat and dust. We had from eight to nine hundred victims a day."**

✔ **READING CHECK:** What steps did the United States take to prepare for war?

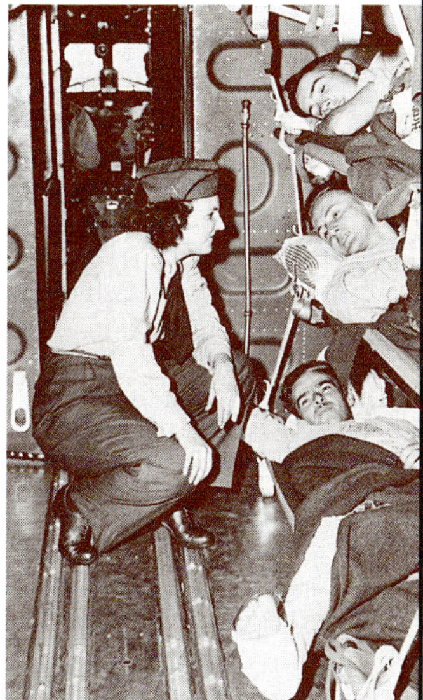

Nurses worked under battlefield conditions to save the lives of wounded soldiers.

War in the Pacific

Japan's assault on Pearl Harbor was just one part of a giant offensive throughout the Pacific region. On December 8, 1941, Japanese planes bombed Clark Air Force Base in the Philippines. Over the following two weeks the Japanese attacked Burma, Borneo, the Netherlands East Indies, Wake Island, and Hong Kong.

On February 27, 1942, in what become known as the Battle of the Java Sea, the Japanese navy crushed a fleet of Australian, British, Dutch, and U.S. warships that had been trying to block a Japanese invasion of Java. The Japanese invaded Java the next day and soon after began their conquest of New Guinea.

BIOGRAPHY *Douglas MacArthur*

Defending the Philippines were more than 30,000 U.S. and 110,000 Filipino troops under the overall command of General Douglas MacArthur. MacArthur was born in 1880, the son of a distinguished general, Arthur MacArthur. He graduated from the U.S. Military Academy at West Point in 1903 with one of the finest academic records in the school's history. MacArthur then served in the Philippines and was later wounded twice in World War I. From 1919 to 1922 he was superintendent of West Point. In 1937 he retired from the U.S. Army and served as a military adviser in the Philippines for several years. President Roosevelt recalled MacArthur to active duty in the summer of 1941. He eventually was given command of all U.S. Army units in the Pacific.

When Japanese bombers attacked Clark Air Force Base they found the U.S. aircraft sitting on the runway. One Japanese pilot recalled, "They squatted there like sitting ducks." The planes that were needed to provide air support for the U.S. fleet in the Philippines were destroyed. Therefore the fleet had to withdraw out of range of the Japanese planes based in Taiwan. With no air or naval opposition, Japanese forces advanced toward Manila. MacArthur recognized that his outnumbered forces would be unable to stop the Japanese advance. He ordered his troops to evacuate the city and retreat to the Bataan Peninsula.

The rapid pace of the evacuation prevented U.S. forces from stockpiling enough supplies, particularly food. The fighting soon settled into a war of attrition. The Japanese kept the pressure on the starving defenders, who were outnumbered, outgunned, and inexperienced. With the situation looking hopeless, MacArthur was ordered to Australia. When he arrived there in March he vowed, "I shall return."

HOLT RESEARCHER *Read More About It*

Free Find:
Douglas MacArthur
After reading about Douglas MacArthur on the **Holt Researcher** CD–ROM, write a short speech to be given at the dedication of a memorial to MacArthur.

GLOBAL RELATIONS

The Fall of Singapore. In February 1942 the British surrendered Singapore to the Japanese. The surrender represented a low point in Britain's Pacific fight. Since December 1941, British, Australian, and Indian troops under British command had conducted a hasty retreat toward Singapore in the face of a swift Japanese assault. By early February 1942 these troops and hundreds of thousands of war refugees were barricaded in the city and in an offshore naval base, which the Japanese attacked in artillery and dive-bomber raids. Japanese forces then captured and cut off Singapore's water supply, threatening a humanitarian disaster in the city. On February 15, 1942, British general Arthur Percival marched toward Japanese lines with a white flag and surrendered, effecting the capitulation of some 80,000 soldiers. One historian has called the incident "the single most catastrophic defeat in British military history."

ACTIVITY: Tell students to imagine that it is February 1942 and that they are editors of a British newspaper. Ask each student to consult a map and write a short editorial discussing the recent fall of Singapore.

LEVEL 2: Ask students to name the early turning points of the war in the Pacific. *(See the Level 1 lesson for the correct battles.)* List students' responses on the chalkboard. Then tell students to imagine that they are radio news announcers. Assign each student one of the battles. Have students develop a short "You Are There" radio presentation about their assigned battles. *(See this two-page spread for specific details about the three battles.)* Have volunteers deliver their radio presentations to the class.

LEVEL 3: Ask students to name the early turning points of the war in the Pacific. *(See the Level 1 lesson for the correct battles.)* List students' responses on the chalkboard. Then organize students into three groups and tell each group to imagine that it is a group of naval officers stationed in the Pacific. Assign each group one of the battles. Have each group write military briefings on its assigned battle. *(See this two-page spread for specific details about the three battles.)* Groups' briefings should review the war in the Pacific up to the time of the battle, identify the battle's location, describe the military action during the battle, note the battle's outcome, and explain how the battle furthered the Allied cause. Have each group present its briefings to the class. **Cooperative Learning**

HISTORY MAKERS SPEAK

Anton Bilek in *"The Good War": An Oral History of World War Two*

The Bataan Death March. The Bataan Death March permanently scarred many of those who lived through it. Anton Bilek, an American survivor, recalled the cruelty of his captors years later: "The Japanese emptied out the hospitals. Anybody that could walk, they forced 'em into line. You found all kinda bodies along the road. Some of 'em bloated, some had just been killed. If you fell out to the side, you were either shot by the guards or you were bayoneted and left there. We lost somewhere between six hundred and seven hundred Americans in the four days of the march. The Filipinos lost close to ten thousand."

CRITICAL THINKING Why might the Japanese have treated the captured soldiers with such extraordinary cruelty?

ANSWER: Some students might suggest that the Japanese soldiers, like soldiers from many nations, regarded their enemies as inhuman.

VISUAL RECORD ANSWER

(for p. 505)

In the photograph, soldiers appear to be bombing a tank or a truck, thus interfering with the enemy's transportation.

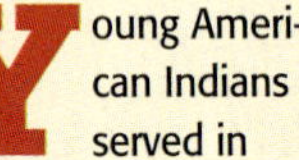

The Navajo Code Talkers

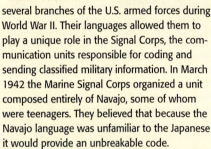

Young American Indians served in several branches of the U.S. armed forces during World War II. Their languages allowed them to play a unique role in the Signal Corps, the communication units responsible for coding and sending classified military information. In March 1942 the Marine Signal Corps organized a unit composed entirely of Navajo, some of whom were teenagers. They believed that because the Navajo language was unfamiliar to the Japanese it would provide an unbreakable code.

The new unit devised and memorized a special Navajo dictionary containing 413 military terms. For example, the Navajo word for "chicken hawk" meant dive-bomber in the code. "Hummingbird" meant fighter plane. "Iron fish" meant submarine. The Navajo Code Talkers first went into action in the fall of 1942 in the Pacific. U.S. field commanders soon reported that the Navajo methods reduced the time needed for decoding and encoding messages by half. As radio operators who tracked Japanese movements, the code talkers often had to work in dangerous conditions behind enemy lines.

By August 1943 nearly 200 Navajo were participating in the Code Talker program, and by the war's end more than 400 had served in the Marine Signal Corps. Their codes completely baffled the Japanese and were never broken.

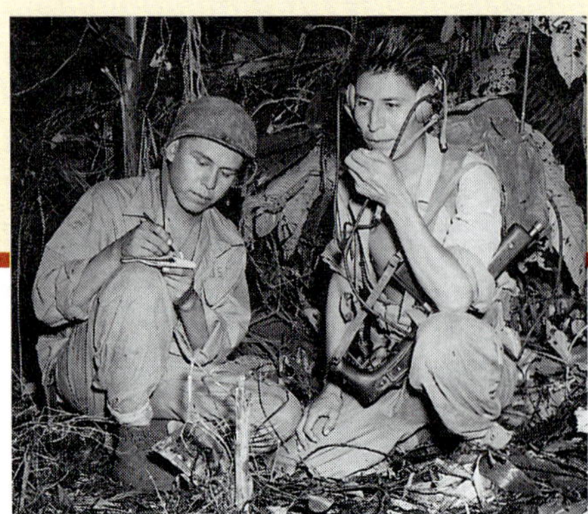

Navajo Code Talkers Henry Bake and George Kirk operate a radio behind enemy lines in the Solomon Islands.

After fighting against overwhelming odds, the hungry, sick, and exhausted survivors who remained on Bataan surrendered in April 1942. Japanese soldiers forced the more than 70,000 survivors to march through the jungle on their way to prison camp. More than 10,000 died on what came to be called the **Bataan Death March**. The Japanese treated U.S. and Filipino soldiers brutally. Some prisoners were prevented from drinking water. Others were beaten or shot. Conditions did not improve when they reached the prison camps. Water was in short supply, and what there was quickly became contaminated. Disease spread quickly through the sick and poorly fed prisoners.

✔ **READING CHECK:** Where did the Japanese military attack after Pearl Harbor?

Halting the Japanese Advance

By the summer of 1942 the Japanese were ready to strike west at India, south at Australia, and east through Hawaii at the Pacific coast of the United States. The commander of the U.S. Pacific Fleet, Admiral Chester Nimitz, did not consider the attack on Pearl Harbor a complete disaster. "It was God's mercy that our fleet was in Pearl Harbor on 7 December 1941," Nimitz said. Much of the sunken battle fleet was salvageable because the ships sat in the shallow waters of the harbor. Furthermore, none of the aircraft carriers had been in port at the time of the attack. The U.S. fleet recovered quickly and was soon fighting again.

The Battle of the Coral Sea. Nimitz was an aggressive commander who preferred to attack, thereby pressuring his opponents into making mistakes. On May 7, 1942, a Japanese force on its way to attack Port Moresby, New Guinea, seized Tulagi (too-LAH-gee) Island, one of the Solomon Islands. Before the Japanese could reach New Guinea, however, a joint British-U.S. naval force intercepted them. Planes from U.S. aircraft carriers damaged one Japanese carrier and destroyed another and several aircraft. The **Battle of the Coral Sea** was an important Allied victory. Although the Allies lost a carrier, the battle stopped the Japanese advance on Australia.

The Battle of Midway. The second major naval battle in the Pacific, the **Battle of Midway**, took place early in June 1942. Seeking to crush the U.S. Pacific Fleet, Japan launched a two-pronged attack. One unit seized two of the Aleutian Islands, near Alaska. They hoped to lure part of the U.S. fleet away from Hawaii. Meanwhile the Japanese carried out their main attack against Midway, two small islands northwest of Hawaii. However, because U.S. experts had broken the Japanese fleet code, the United States had advance warning of the Japanese

TEACH OBJECTIVE 5

LEVEL 1: Distribute Outline Map 19, World War II in Europe, from **American History Outline Maps**. Have each student use information from the textbook to label the map with the major battles in Europe and North Africa in 1942. *(Students should label the Battle of El Alamein and the Battle of Stalingrad.)* Then pair students and have pairs develop four headlines—two for each battle—relating the significance of the conflicts. *(Pairs' headlines should note that both battles broke the Axis momentum and gave the Allies renewed confidence.)* Ask volunteers to read their headlines to the class. **Sheltered English, Cooperative Learning**

LEVELS 2 AND 3: Distribute Outline Map 19, World War II in Europe, from **American History Outline Maps**. Have each student use information from the textbook to label the map with the major battles in Europe and North Africa in 1942. *(See the Level 1 lesson for the correct battles.)* Then tell students to imagine that they are newspaper reporters. Have students write two half-page newspaper articles—one for each battle—relating the significance of the conflicts. *(See the Level 1 lesson for the correct significance.)* Ask volunteers to read their articles to the class. Students may wish to include their articles in their portfolios.

strategy. Nimitz later recalled, "Had we lacked early information of the Japanese movements, . . . the Battle of Midway would have ended differently." Instead, Nimitz was able to assemble U.S. aircraft carriers and destroyers north of Midway to ambush the Japanese attack.

Americans and Japanese clashed June 3–6. U.S. fighters, dive-bombers, and torpedo planes sank four Japanese aircraft carriers and shot down many enemy planes. The U.S. victory proved crucial. Japan lost not only ships and planes but also a number of skilled pilots.

INTERPRETING THE VISUAL RECORD

Midway. The U.S. victory in the Battle of Midway crippled the Japanese navy. ***From the painting, what can you determine about the type of fighting that took place during the Battle of Midway?***

Guadalcanal. After the Battle of Midway, the United States successfully launched its first offensive. In August 1942, American marines waded ashore at Guadalcanal, in the Solomon Islands. For six desperate months, with heavy casualties, they clung to a toehold around the airport.

Major General Alexander A. Vandegrift, commander of the U.S. Marines on Guadalcanal, described the ferocious fighting. "I have never heard or read of this kind of fighting. These people [the Japanese] refuse to surrender. The wounded will wait till men come up to examine them, and blow themselves and the other fellow to death with a hand grenade."

In November the Japanese sent a huge fleet to the Solomons. They hoped to recapture Guadalcanal, but the U.S. fleet defeated the Japanese in a bloody battle. The tide of battle in the Pacific had finally turned in the Allies' favor.

✔ **READING CHECK:** What were the early turning points in the war in the Pacific?

Early Fighting in Europe and the Mediterranean

By the time of the attack on Pearl Harbor, the Axis Powers controlled much of Europe and the lands around the Mediterranean. Bulgaria, Hungary, and Romania had joined the Axis Powers. Yugoslavia and Greece had been occupied, and southern Europe was firmly under Axis control. Throughout most of 1942 the Axis Powers achieved one victory after another.

The Germans and their allies scored victories on many different fronts. German submarines, or U-boats, patrolled the Atlantic Ocean. They sank Allied military and merchant ships and nearly cut off British supply lines. In the first half of 1942, German U-boats sank more than 500 ships off the U.S. East Coast.

North Africa. Italian forces had launched an invasion of North Africa in 1940. When British troops later began to inflict heavy damage on the Italians, Adolf Hitler sent in the German Afrika Korps under commander Erwin Rommel. Known as the Desert Fox, Rommel had advanced as far as El Alamein, Egypt, by July 1942. His troops were ready to take the Suez Canal and the oil fields of the Middle East.

Rommel's skill as a military leader led even Winston Churchill to later admit that "[he was] a great general." However, Rommel suffered from shortages of men and supplies. The British, led by General Bernard Montgomery, turned this shortage to their advantage. In the fall of 1942 Montgomery pushed Rommel's troops steadily westward out of Egypt and into Libya. The British victory in the Battle of El Alamein helped turn the corner for the Allies in North Africa.

INTERPRETING THE VISUAL RECORD

Desert warfare. Effective transportation was vital for troops battling in the wide-open spaces of North Africa. ***What is happening in the photograph?***

PEOPLE IN HISTORY

Chester Nimitz. Despite his many strengths as a military commander, Chester Nimitz was a mild-mannered and modest person. A Texan of German descent, he became a naval officer in 1907 and commanded an experimental submarine during World War I. Noted for his "serene self control, dedication to duty . . . and unswerving loyalty to seniors and subordinates," he rose to the rank of admiral. Within a few days of the attack on Pearl Harbor he was appointed commander of the entire U.S. Pacific Fleet. Nimitz served with distinction in World War II and retired shortly after the conflict ended. Nimitz died in 1966.

ACTIVITY: Ask each student to list schools, libraries, parks, and other public facilities in the community that are named after Americans who participated in World War II. Ask volunteers to share their lists with the class.

VISUAL RECORD ANSWER

Students might suggest that the fighting included heavy artillery shelling.

Define and Identify

For significance, see the following pages:

- War Production Board, p. 501

REVIEW

Have students complete the **Section 1 Review** on p. 506.

ASSESS

Have students complete **Daily Quiz 17.1.** As **Alternative Assessment,** you may want to use the war preparation poster or the Pacific war radio broadcast in this section's lessons.

RETEACH

Have students complete **Main Idea Activity for Reteaching and Sheltered English 17.1.** Then ask each student to outline Section 1. After students have completed their outlines, organize the students into triads. Have members of the triads quiz each other on the material in Section 1. **Sheltered English, Cooperative Learning**

EXTEND

Organize students into four groups, assigning each group one of the following military leaders: Douglas MacArthur, Chester Nimitz, Erwin Rommel, or Bernard Montgomery. Have each group conduct research on its assigned leader. Then ask each group to present oral reports on its leader's activities during World War II. Groups' presentations should include illustrations and graphics. **Cooperative Learning, Block Scheduling**

- Office of War Mobilization, p. 502
- Selective Training and Service Act, p. 502
- Douglas MacArthur, p. 503
- Bataan Death March, p. 504
- Chester Nimitz, p. 504
- Battle of the Coral Sea, p. 504
- Battle of Midway, p. 504
- Erwin Rommel, p. 505
- Bernard Montgomery, p. 505

1. economy—government expanded income tax, sold war bonds, and instituted rationing to finance war effort and control inflation; military strength—government created War Production Board and Office of War Mobilization and passed Selective Service Act to maximize production of military supplies and increase the size of military forces

2. The Axis Powers held firm control of invaded areas and were well prepared for war. The Allied Powers hoped to benefit from the enormous size of the Soviet Union's military and the American production capacity.

3. Japan lost many ships, planes, and pilots and the United States gained valuable experience and new naval confidence

4. Both battles broke Axis momentum and gave Allies a sense of confidence and hope.

5. The United States contributed valuable naval resources salvaged from Pearl Harbor and won crucial victories at the Battle of the Coral Sea, the Battle of Midway, and Guadalcanal.

These soldiers are scrambling across a trench that used to be a city street in Stalingrad.

Stalingrad. In Europe, German troops had penetrated far into the Soviet Union after their initial attack in June 1941. As the Germans advanced, they captured many industrial centers as well as rich grainfields in the Ukraine. By winter German forces were closing in on Moscow. The Germans also laid siege to Leningrad. For months the men, women, and children defending the city endured a nightmare of shell fire and starvation.

In the summer of 1942, German troops that had been pushing toward the oil fields of southern Russia approached the key city of Stalingrad. By the fall of 1942, German troops were fighting for control of the city. A German officer described the fighting.

> **"We have fought during fifteen days for a single house. The 'front' is a corridor between burned-out rooms; it is the thin ceiling between two floors. . . . From story to story, faces black with sweat, we bombard each other with grenades in the middle of explosions, clouds of dust and smoke, heaps of mortar, floods of blood, fragments of furniture and human beings."**

The Soviet forces refused to surrender, however, and eventually surrounded the German soldiers in Stalingrad. Throughout a terrible winter the Germans hung on, forbidden by Hitler to surrender. Trapped in the ruined city with few supplies and little food, the Axis troops finally surrendered in February 1943. After the Battle of Stalingrad, less than one half of the original German force of more than 200,000 remained alive. The Allied victories at El Alamein and Stalingrad broke the momentum of the Axis advance. Said British prime minister Winston Churchill: "Before Alamein we never had a victory. After Alamein we never had a defeat."

✔ **READING CHECK:** What were the major battles in Europe and North Africa in 1942?

SECTION  REVIEW

Define and explain the significance of the following terms:
War Production Board
Office of War Mobilization
Selective Training and Service Act
Bataan Death March
Battle of the Coral Sea
Battle of Midway

Identify and explain the significance of the following individuals:
Douglas MacArthur
Chester Nimitz
Erwin Rommel
Bernard Montgomery

1. **Using Graphic Organizers** Copy the following graphic organizer. Use it to list the actions taken by the government to prepare the economy and the military for war and what each action was intended to do.

	The Economy	Military Strength
Actions Taken		
Goals of Action		

2. **Comparing and Contrasting** What advantages did the Axis Powers have at the beginning of the war? What advantages did the Allies have?
3. **Geographic Diversity: Location** What was the significance of the U.S. victories at the Battles of Midway and Guadalcanal?
4. **Assessing Consequences** Why were the Battles of El Alamein and Stalingrad turning points for the Allies?

Critical Thinking

5. Describe how the United States managed to turn the tide of the war in the Pacific by the end of 1942.
   Consider:
   - the results of the attack on Pearl Harbor
   - where the Japanese attacked after Pearl Harbor
   - Japanese and U.S. strategy at the Battles of the Coral Sea and Midway

After completing Section 2, students should be able to:

OBJECTIVE 1 *Describe how the U.S. government tried to keep wartime morale high.*

OBJECTIVE 2 *Describe what life was like in the United States during World War II.*

OBJECTIVE 3 *Relate how women contributed to the war effort.*

OBJECTIVE 4 *Analyze what actions the government took to protect the rights of minority groups.*

OBJECTIVE 5 *Discuss the war's effect on Japanese Americans.*

LET'S GET STARTED!

As students enter the classroom, ask them to describe, in writing, a popular culture depiction of life on the home front during World War II or an historical artifact relating to life on the home front. Ask volunteers to share their responses. Then tell students that in Section 2 they will learn about life on the home front during World War II.

The Home Front

OBJECTIVES

Read to understand:

1. how the U.S. government tried to keep wartime morale high
2. what life was like in the United States during World War II
3. how women contributed to the war effort
4. what actions the government took to protect the rights of minority groups
5. how Japanese Americans were affected by the war

KEY TERMS

Office of War Information
Rosie the Riveter
Fair Employment Practices Committee
braceros
zoot-suit riots
internment

KEY PEOPLE

A. Philip Randolph
Carlos E. Castañeda
Norman Mineta

EYEWITNESSES TO History

"When my son enlisted in the air force, he went to McDill Field in Florida. So I went there. . . . Then I came back to Westminster . . . [and] found that people who didn't have someone overseas were not too concerned. They were interested in bacon and sugar and gas, which I was not. . . . I did a lot of war work . . . when I was at McDill, I worked in the hospital and at the USO. . . . I started to do some volunteer work in Westminster, like rolling bandages, but I couldn't make it. The people I was doing it with were not in my situation at all. They were more concerned with what they were having to give up than with what was happening in Europe. I had people call me up and ask, 'Do you have coupons? We can get butter tomorrow.' I never stood in a line for a thing. I thought that if the men could do without it, so could I."

—Mary Speir

Americans eagerly planted victory gardens to support the war effort.

Mary Speir of Westminster, Maryland, understood all too well the sacrifices people made to support the war effort. Her husband and son fought in the war, and her son was killed in combat.

Promoting the War

World War II enjoyed broad popular support. Many families proudly displayed window banners with a star. A blue star represented a loved one in the service. A gold star stood for a death in combat.

The U.S. government tried to keep morale high. This was especially important in the early days of the war, when Allied troops faced many setbacks. The government encouraged the media to do their part. Moviemakers, songwriters, and radio-station programmers responded by urging all-out participation in the war effort.

Movie stars advertised war bonds and traveled overseas to entertain the troops. Hundreds of war movies poured out of Hollywood. *So Proudly We Hail*—a story about army nurses in the Philippines—was just one of the patriotic films that built support for the war. Striking a lighter note were comedies like Bob Hope's *Caught in the Draft.* A few films, such as *Wake Island* and *Report from the Aleutians,* offered more realistic views of combat.

Radio stations broadcast both war news and entertainment. Foreign correspondents such as Edward R. Murrow and Eric Sevareid gave on-the-scene accounts of war-ravaged Europe. The government-run **Office of War Information** controlled the flow of war news at home.

Wake Island *and other war movies encouraged Americans to support the war effort.*

SECTION 2 RESOURCES

PRINT

- Guided Reading Strategy 17.2
- Primary Source Reading 17: A Mountain Woman's Tale
- Graphic Organizer Activity 17: The Effect of War on Life at Home
- Section 2 Review, p. 513
- Daily Quiz 17.2

MULTIMEDIA

- One-Stop Planner, Lesson 17.2
- The American Nation Video Program Segment: Japanese Americans in Relocation Camps; Teacher's Guide, pp. 159–60
- Holt Researcher: American History CD–ROM
- HRW Web site

SHELTERED ENGLISH

- Main Idea Activity for Reteaching and Sheltered English 17.2

✔ READING TO UNDERSTAND

To help students master the section objectives, have them answer the **READING CHECKS** and complete **Guided Reading Strategy 17.2** as they read the section.

Teacher to Teacher

Ron Foore of Tulsa, Oklahoma, suggested the following activity: Pair students and have them conduct research on swing dancing in the 1940s and the 1990s. Then tell pairs to choose one of the two decades. Have each pair use its research to develop a short swing dance presentation. Each pair should demonstrate one popular dance and discuss the importance of swing dancing in its chosen decade.

TEACH OBJECTIVE 1

LEVELS 1 AND 2: Conduct a brief discussion on the ways in which the U.S. government tried to keep wartime morale high. *(The government created the Office of War Information. Radio programmers and filmmakers created programs and movies that supported the war effort.)* Then pair students and tell them to imagine that it is 1942. Ask each pair to create two or three slogans in support of the war effort. Provide the following slogans as examples: *Pay Your Taxes, Beat the Axis; Don't Let Them Catch Us with Our Plants Down.* Have each pair write a paragraph explaining how its slogan would benefit wartime morale and the war effort.
Sheltered English, Cooperative Learning

TECHNOLOGY AND SOCIETY

Health Care During the War. Ironically, the war years tended to be healthy ones for Americans on the home front. Although the draft resulted in a temporary shortage of doctors, thousands of new hospitals and health clinics were constructed during the early 1940s. By mid-1940, more doctors and dentists were graduating from medical schools than ever before. The strong economy meant that more Americans could afford their services. The statistical results of the medical-care boom were striking: life expectancy for American civilians increased by three years between 1939 and 1945, while the infant mortality rate dropped by more than one third.

CRITICAL THINKING Why might thousands of new hospitals and health clinics have been constructed in the United States during the early 1940s?

ANSWER: Students might suggest that the nation began to construct sorely needed facilities when the national economy recovered during the early war years.

★ HISTORICAL DOCUMENTS ★

PRESIDENT FRANKLIN D. ROOSEVELT
The Four Freedoms

On January 6, 1941, in his annual message to Congress, President Roosevelt requested support for the Lend-Lease program. In what became known as the Four Freedoms speech, Roosevelt defined the four freedoms that came to represent the ideals Americans were fighting for in the war.

In the future days, which we seek to make secure, we look forward to a world founded upon four essential human freedoms.

The first is freedom of speech and expression everywhere in the world.

The second is freedom of every person to worship God in his own way everywhere in the world.

The third is freedom from want, which, translated into world terms, means economic understandings which will secure to every nation a healthy peacetime life for its inhabitants everywhere in the world.

The fourth is freedom from fear—which, translated into world terms, means a worldwide reduction of armaments to such a point and in such a thorough fashion that no nation will be in a position to commit an act of physical aggression against any neighbor—anywhere in the world.

That is no vision of a distant millennium. It is a definite basis for a kind of world attainable in our own time and generation. That kind of world is the very antithesis [opposite] of the so-called new order of tyranny which the dictators seek to create with the crash of a bomb.

The war also affected popular radio serials. Radio stations abandoned spy and sabotage programs for the duration of the war. Some even banned certain sound effects, such as wailing sirens, to avoid alarming listeners.

✔ **READING CHECK:** How did the U.S. government try to keep wartime morale high?

Life During Wartime

Americans cut back their consumption of both luxuries and necessities to help the war effort. Millions of people grew vegetables and other produce in their backyards. These so-called victory gardens helped make more food available to U.S. and Allied soldiers. Martha Wood recalled that she and her neighbors

> **"[formed] a neighborhood Victory Garden, plowed up the backyards of three houses, and planted beans, corn, tomatoes, okra, squash, and all the things we could use. When the crop came in, . . . [we] used a pressure cooker and canned all day. I was canning until midnight and later, night after night, and I frequently said, 'I wish I had Hitler in that pressure cooker.'"**

AIR RAID PRECAUTIONS HAVE BEEN TAKEN HERE
CD
Signed by
Auxiliary Defense Manual

Civil-defense units helped prepare Americans in case of attack by Axis forces.

After the bombing of Pearl Harbor, U.S. authorities imposed restrictions in case of attack on the mainland. West Coast cities began practicing nighttime blackouts. Authorities feared that brightly lit U.S. cities would make easy targets for Japanese bombers. Civil-defense units searched for signs of enemy aircraft. Across the nation, practice air-raid drills sent Americans scrambling for cover from bombing attacks that never came.

People worked longer hours and made many sacrifices, but daily life in the United States did not change radically during the war. On Broadway stages, musicals such as Irving Berlin's *This Is the Army* (1942) and Leonard Bernstein and Jerome Robbins's *On the Town* (1944) provided laughs and avoided the painful side of wartime. Richard Rodgers and Oscar Hammerstein's production *Oklahoma!* (1943) was the biggest hit during the war. *Oklahoma!* provided Americans with a taste of simpler times.

Wartime music did not have the same innocence of World War I hits such as "Over There." Instead, big hits like "Remember Pearl Harbor" and "Praise the Lord

LEVEL 3: Ask students to identify the ways in which the U.S. government attempted to keep wartime morale high. *(See the Level 1 lesson for the correct methods.)* Then tell students to imagine that they are Hollywood screenwriters. Have each student write a proposal for a movie in support of the war effort and to boost wartime morale. Ask volunteers to share their proposals. Students may wish to include their proposals in their portfolios.

▶**ASSIGNMENT** *Ask students to watch a World War II–era movie that focuses on the home front. Have each student write a brief summary of the movie.*

TEACH OBJECTIVE 2

LEVEL 1: Pair students and tell them to imagine that it is 1942, and that they are U.S. citizens involved in the home front war effort. Have each pair create a dialogue on life in the United States during World War II. *(Pairs might mention victory gardens, long work hours, restrictions, and so on.)* Ask volunteers to perform their dialogues for the class. **Sheltered English, Cooperative Learning**

and Pass the Ammunition!" captured the harsh reality of war. Irving Berlin's song "God Bless America" became a sort of unofficial national anthem. Big-band swing music remained popular, and sentimental songs such as "White Christmas" expressed Americans' longing for a return to peace.

In part as a result of widespread interest in the war, nonfiction became more popular than fiction. The best-selling books of 1941 were William Shirer's *Berlin Diary,* a frightening look inside Nazi Germany, and Joseph Davies's *Mission to Moscow,* a positive portrayal of the Soviet Union. Wartime also brought a change to the publishing industry. Paperback books first appeared in 1939, and wartime rationing helped them quickly surpass hardcover as the format of choice. The lower cost, light weight, and smaller size of paperbacks made them very popular. The military boosted the growth of the paperback format with the Armed Services Editions, which provided paperback books free of charge to U.S. troops. Some 60 million books of all types were distributed during the war.

✔ **READING CHECK:** What was life in the United States like during World War II?

AMERICAN ARTS

Norman Rockwell

Norman Rockwell was born in New York City in 1894. For six decades, until his death in 1978, Rockwell showed the positive side of American life in his illustrations. He once said, "As I grew up . . . I unconsciously decided that, even if it wasn't an ideal world, it should be so, and so I painted the ideal aspects of it." He is best known for the covers he drew for the *Saturday Evening Post.* In 47 years Rockwell drew 322 covers for the *Post,* more than any other artist.

Rockwell lived in Vermont during World War II and often used his neighbors as models for his illustrations. Despite painting just one combat scene during the war, he managed to capture the mood of a nation at war. He did so by reminding people of the reasons behind the war without downplaying the difficulty of the struggle. Rockwell said that he tried to create an image that "makes the reader want to sigh and smile at the same time."

One such picture was his cover for the September 4, 1943, *Saturday Evening Post.* Rockwell painted *Liberty Girl,* to celebrate the Labor Day holiday. The work honored women's contributions to the war effort with its representations of the many different kinds of work that women were performing.

Norman Rockwell's Liberty Girl

Understanding the Arts

1. How many different occupations are represented in this image?
2. How does this image reflect the experiences of Americans on the home front during the war?

HISTORY MAKERS SPEAK

Wendell Willkie in *One World*

A Plea for Postwar Cooperation. In his best-selling book *One World,* Wendell Willkie makes an urgent plea for postwar cooperation. He explains how this cooperation must find its beginnings in the Allied war effort. "As United Nations, we must formulate now the principles which will govern our actions as we move step by step to the freeing of the conquered countries. And we must set up a joint machinery to deal with the multiple problems that will accompany every forward step of our victorious armies. Otherwise we will find ourselves . . . sowing the seeds of future discontents—racial, religious, political—not alone among the peoples that we seek to free, but even among the United Nations themselves."

CRITICAL THINKING What assumption does Willkie make in the passage?

ANSWER: Students might suggest that he assumes that the Allies will win the war.

AMERICAN ARTS ANSWERS

1. farmer, builder, student or teacher, and explorer or surveyor, among others
2. depicts women's many roles

LEVELS 2 AND 3: Tell students to imagine that it is 1942 and that they are U.S. citizens involved in the home front war effort. Have each student write four or five brief diary entries describing life in the United States during World War II. *(See the Level 1 lesson for appropriate elements.)* Ask volunteers to read their diary entries to the class.

TEACH OBJECTIVE 3

ALL LEVELS: To help students understand how women contributed to the war effort, copy the graphic organizer at right on the chalkboard, omitting the italicized answers. Have each student complete it.
Sheltered English

WOMEN AND THE WAR EFFORT

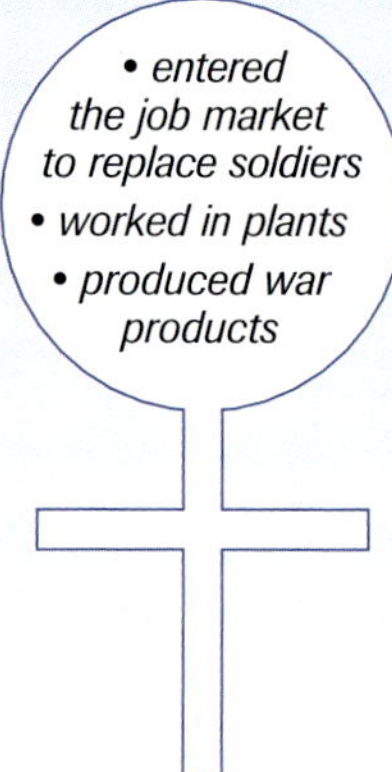

• entered the job market to replace soldiers
• worked in plants
• produced war products

GLOBAL RELATIONS

The Allied Women. Women from other countries, particularly Great Britain and the Soviet Union, also contributed to the Allied war effort. Over the course of the war approximately 70 percent of British women engaged in full-time work. The so-called Land Girls did strenuous farmwork.

ACTIVITY: Tell students to imagine that they are American women working for the war effort. Have each student write a letter to a counterpart in Britain describing her work.

internetconnect

TOPIC: Rosie the Riveter
GO TO: go.hrw.com
KEYWORD: SE1 Rosie

Have students access the Internet through the HRW Web site to conduct research on Rosie the Riveter propaganda during World War II. Then have each student develop a "modern" propaganda character in the style of Rosie the Riveter in order to promote a national goal. Ask students to create a one-page public relations proposal introducing and explaining their propaganda characters. Students should illustrate their proposals.

VISUAL RECORD ANSWER
Students might suggest that they are constructing some kind of aircraft.

We Can Do It!

This image of Rosie the Riveter shows the importance of female workers to the war effort.

Rosie the Riveter

Daily life changed dramatically for some Americans on the home front, particularly for women. During the depression, the government had discouraged women, particularly married women, from working. The government now urged them to enter the job market to replace departing soldiers. One government poster showed a female worker in bandanna and overalls. The caption read: "I'm Proud . . . my husband wants me to do my part." Advertisements and a popular song promoted "**Rosie the Riveter**," the symbol of patriotic female defense workers.

From 1940 to 1944 the number of women in the workforce increased by about 6 million. Women worked in war plants and replaced men in a host of jobs ranging from newspaper reporting to truck driving. Many of these new workers were married women who were taking jobs outside the home for the first time. Many women already in the paid workforce left traditional "women's work" such as domestic service to work in factories.

The participation of women in the war effort gave many of them a new sense of pride and self-worth. One female aircraft worker finally felt a sense of achievement after feeling "average" at other jobs.

> **"Foremen from other departments come to my machine to ask me to do some work for them if I have time because they say I'm the best countersinker in the vast building! At forty-nine I've at last become not better than average, but the best!"**

Female workers continued to be paid less than men for the same work. African American women and women over 40 found few employers willing to hire them. In spite of women's achievements, it was widely assumed—by many women as well as men—that most of the jobs held by women during the war were temporary. A shipyard manager predicted that "these women who are willing . . . to lend a hand with the war will be the . . . office personnel of . . . the future."

✔ **READING CHECK:** How did women contribute to the war effort?

INTERPRETING THE VISUAL RECORD

Female workers. Without the efforts of American women, the United States could not have produced the materials needed to win the war. ***What are these female workers doing?***

Discrimination During the War

Racial tensions did not disappear during wartime. However, the cooperation the war effort required caused the government to try to reduce discrimination in war industries.

Demands for equal treatment. For African Americans, World War II brought both continued discrimination and greater opportunities. Many black workers moved into better-paying industrial jobs and played a key role in the military effort. Almost 1 million African American soldiers served in the armed forces, including several thousand women in the Women's Auxiliary Army Corps. However, African Americans continued to serve in segregated units, and most were kept out of combat. Black soldiers were often assigned to low-level work.

TEACH OBJECTIVE 4

LEVEL 1: Have each student create a graphic organizer displaying the ways in which the government attempted to protect the rights of minorities during World War II. *(The government created the Fair Employment Practices Committee and made attempts to end discrimination in businesses with federal contracts.)* Ask volunteers to copy their graphic organizers on the chalkboard. Then have students consult those organizers to write summary paragraphs explaining how the government attempted to protect minority rights during the war. Students may wish to include their paragraphs in their portfolios. **Sheltered English**

LEVELS 2 AND 3: Pair students and tell one member of each pair to act as a newspaper reporter and the other member to act as a government official. Have members prepare for an interview on governmental actions to protect the rights of minority groups during World War II. Newspaper reporters should develop at least five questions on the subject, while government officials should think of at least five possible questions they may be asked and answers to those questions. Have students conduct their interviews. *(See the Level 1 lesson for the correct government actions.)* Then hold a discussion on the material presented in the interviews. Conclude the lesson by having each student write a brief newspaper article that reflects the interview on governmental actions on behalf of minority groups during World War II. **Cooperative Learning**

The millions of African Americans in the workforce had to struggle to gain acceptance. Many war plants would not hire African Americans or would employ them only as janitors. Despite labor leaders' no-strike pledge, some white workers staged strikes—called hate strikes—designed to keep black workers out of high-paying factory jobs.

In 1941, before the United States entered the war, African American labor leader A. Philip Randolph planned a march on Washington, D.C., to protest discrimination against black workers. Fearing the unrest it might cause, President Roosevelt wanted to prevent the march. Randolph agreed to call off the march after Roosevelt issued an executive order forbidding racial discrimination in defense plants and government offices.

To enforce the order, on June 25, 1941, Roosevelt created the **Fair Employment Practices Committee** (FEPC). The FEPC investigated companies engaged in defense work to make sure that all qualified applicants, regardless of race, were considered for job openings. It was strengthened by a May 27, 1943, executive order requiring nondiscrimination clauses in all war contracts. The FEPC, however, lacked strong enforcement powers and was unable to prevent widespread abuses.

During a rally at Madison Square Garden, A. Philip Randolph fights to save the Fair Employment Practices Committee.

As during World War I, many African Americans moved northward to take advantage of the high wages being offered in war plants. In crowded cities where no new homes were being built, African Americans faced discrimination in housing. Competition for limited housing created tensions that sometimes led to outbursts of violence against African Americans. In Detroit in 1943 a fight between African American and white residents at Belle Isle, a popular Detroit park, spread to other parts of the city. Some 34 people died in several days of rioting before federal troops sent by President Roosevelt restored calm.

The zoot-suit riots. World War II brought both opportunities and problems to Mexican Americans as well. More than 300,000 Mexican Americans served in the military, and 17 earned the Congressional Medal of Honor. The 88th Division, a top combat unit known as the Blue Devils, consisted mostly of Mexican American soldiers.

Mexican Americans also helped meet home-front labor needs. University of Texas history professor Carlos E. Castañeda served as assistant to the chair of the FEPC and worked to improve working conditions for Mexican Americans in Texas. In 1945 the FEPC ordered a major Texas oil company to discontinue hiring and promotion practices that discriminated against Hispanics.

Many Mexican Americans moved from the Southwest to industrial centers in the Midwest and on the West Coast. Under a 1942 agreement between the United States and Mexico, thousands of Mexican farm and railroad workers—known as **braceros**—came north to work in the Southwest during World War II.

These Mexican Americans were arrested during the zoot-suit riots. Many others served heroically during World War II, and 17 won the Congressional Medal of Honor (left).

CULTURAL DIVERSITY

The Tuskegee Airmen. While most African American soldiers served in noncombat positions during the war, others took part in the fighting. The Tuskegee Airmen were an all-black unit of fighter pilots that served with distinction in the air war over Europe. Trained at Tuskegee Army Air Field in Tuskegee, Alabama, the Airmen engaged in their first combat mission in June 1943, when they launched an assault on a small Italian island. During the next two years they played a key role in the Allied air campaign, escorting bombing missions and attacking Axis air fields, supply centers, and communication lines. By the end of the war the Tuskegee Airmen were the only U.S. escort group that had not lost a single bomber to enemy planes.

CRITICAL THINKING How might the service of the Tuskegee Airmen during the war have affected the racial attitudes of some white Americans?

ANSWER: Students may suggest that the Airmen's outstanding performance might have prompted some white Americans to support civil rights.

MAP ANSWER
(for p. 512)
California and Washington

TEACH OBJECTIVE 5

LEVEL 1: Pair students and tell them to imagine that they are Japanese Americans who lived in an internment camp during the war. Have each pair develop a dialogue discussing how the war affected Japanese Americans. *(Pairs should note that the government interned Japanese Americans in some states. Interned Japanese Americans often lost their property. Some Japanese Americans received limited military service opportunities.)* Ask volunteers to perform their dialogues for the class. **Sheltered English, Cooperative Learning**

LEVELS 2 AND 3: Tell students to imagine that they are Japanese Americans who lived in an internment camp during the war. Have each student write a one-page memoir describing how Japanese Americans were affected by the war. *(See the Level 1 lesson for the correct effects.)* Ask volunteers to read their memoirs to the class. Students may wish to include their memoirs in their portfolios.

▶**ASSIGNMENT** *Have each student create an outline of the subsection "Japanese American Relocation." Have students use their outlines to develop three possible essay questions on Japanese American life during the war.*

DEMOCRATIC VALUES

The Injustice of Internment. Many interned Japanese Americans were justifiably angry about the treatment they received. One man registered the following protest. "I was born in Hawaii. I worked most of my life on the west coast. I have never been to Japan. We would have done anything to show our loyalty. . . . That's not democracy. That's not the American way, taking everything away from people. . . . Where are the Germans? Where are the Italians? Do they ask them questions about loyalty?"

CRITICAL THINKING Why might the government have focused suspicion on Japanese Americans?

ANSWER: Some students might point to the existence of anti-Japanese prejudice.

The prejudice and discrimination endured by Hispanics in jobs, housing, and recreational facilities caused bitter resentment. Relations grew particularly hostile in Los Angeles. Mexican American youths had adopted the fad of wearing zoot suits—long, wide-shouldered jackets, trousers pegged at the ankle, and wide-brimmed hats. In June 1943, U.S. sailors roamed the city attacking zoot-suit-clad Mexican American youths in what became known as the **zoot-suit riots**. The government eventually clamped down on the sailors, but not before they had viciously beaten many Mexican Americans.

A citizens' committee later determined that the attacks were motivated by racial prejudice. The committee assigned partial responsibility to the Los Angeles police, who had responded to the riots by arresting Mexican Americans. The committee also blamed biased newspaper reports.

✔**READING CHECK:** What actions did the government take to protect the rights of minority groups?

Japanese American Relocation

In general, World War II did not produce the same level of home-front intolerance as did World War I. One tragic exception was the **internment**, or forced relocation and imprisonment, of Japanese Americans living on the Pacific Coast. U.S. State Department adviser Eugene Rostow called relocation "a tragic and dangerous mistake." In 1941 about 119,000 people of Japanese ancestry lived in California, Oregon, and Washington. About one third of these people—the issei (ee-SAY)—had been born in Japan and were regarded by the U.S. government as aliens ineligible for U.S. citizenship. The rest—the nisei (nee-SAY)—had been born in the United States and thus were U.S. citizens.

No evidence existed of disloyalty on the part of any issei or nisei. Nevertheless, because of strong anti-Japanese feelings among some politicians and residents of western states, the federal government decided to remove people of Japanese descent from the West Coast. In February 1942, Japanese Americans were ordered to detention camps in Wyoming, Utah, and other states. Because Hawaii's Japanese population was too large to relocate, the islands were placed under martial law for the duration of the war.

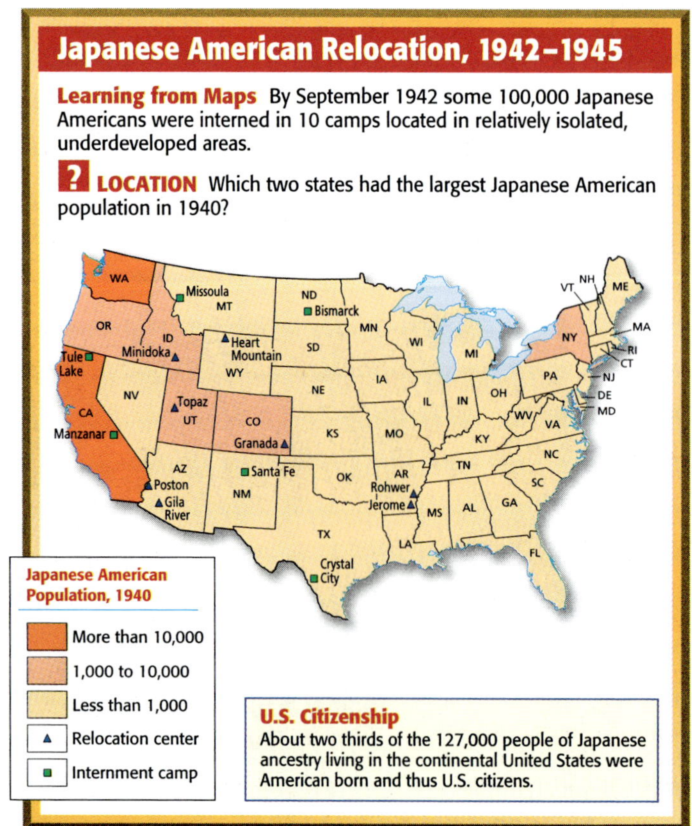

REVIEW

Have students complete the **Section 2 Review** on p. 513.

ASSESS

Have students complete **Daily Quiz 17.2.** As **Alternative Assessment**, you may want to use the minority rights interview or the Japanese American dialogue in this section's lessons.

RETEACH

Have students complete **Main Idea Activity for Reteaching and Sheltered English 17.2.** Then organize students into triads and assign each triad a subsection of Section 2. Ask each triad to develop a poster that summarizes the information in its assigned subsection. Have each triad present its poster to the class. **Sheltered English, Cooperative Learning**

EXTEND

Have students conduct research on the United Service Organization (USO) during World War II. Ask each student to prepare some kind of oral presentation on a specific topic related to the USO. Students might focus on a particular performer, for example, or a particular show or tour. Have students present their work to the class. **Block Scheduling**

Norman Mineta

One imprisoned Japanese American was Norman Mineta, a nisei from San Jose, California. On the day of the Pearl Harbor bombing, the young Mineta fearfully watched his neighbors being taken away for questioning by the FBI. He recalled bitterly that "they had done nothing; the only thing that they had done was to be born of Japanese ancestry."

Just 10 years old when his family was uprooted, Mineta wore his Cub Scout uniform on the train. He hoped that it would show his loyalty to the United States. Mineta's family was interned with some 10,000 others at a camp at Heart Mountain, Wyoming. "These camps were all barbed wire, guard towers, searchlights," recalled Mineta.

After the war Mineta attended college and became an insurance agent. He later went into local politics in San Jose. In 1974 he was elected to the House of Representatives, where he served on several committees. Mineta also introduced legislation seeking reparations for Japanese American internees. He retired in 1995 after 21 years in the House of Representatives.

Read More About It

Free Find:
Norman Mineta
After reading about Norman Mineta on the **Holt Researcher** CD–ROM, create a campaign poster that illustrates Mineta's service during the war.

Patriotism and the desire to disprove accusations of disloyalty inspired many young men in the camps to volunteer for military duty, even though they served in segregated units. One nisei combat team, the 442nd, fought in Europe and became one of the most decorated units in the armed services. Several thousand Japanese Americans also served in the Military Intelligence Service as interpreters and translators in the Pacific. The U.S. Supreme Court upheld internment in 1944, and many Japanese Americans remained imprisoned until 1945.

✔ **READING CHECK:** How were Japanese Americans affected by the war?

SECTION  2 REVIEW

Define and explain the significance of the following terms:
Office of War Information
Rosie the Riveter
Fair Employment Practices Committee
braceros
zoot-suit riots
internment

Identify and explain the significance of the following individuals:
A. Philip Randolph
Carlos E. Castañeda
Norman Mineta

1. **Using Graphic Organizers** Copy the web below. Use it to describe how various groups experienced greater opportunities and/or discrimination as a result of the war.

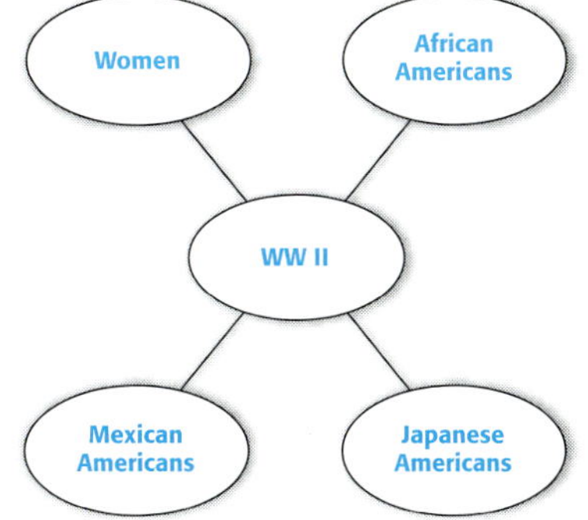

2. **Identifying Cause and Effect** How did the U.S. government seek to keep morale high during World War II? How did most Americans respond to the government's actions?
3. **Using Historical Imagination** Imagine that you are living on the home front during World War II. Write a journal entry describing your daily routine.
4. **Hypothesizing** What long-term effects do you think women's experiences in World War II had on their lives after the war?

Critical Thinking

5. What evidence can you give to support the argument that the war affected virtually all aspects of life on the home front?
   Consider:
   - wartime changes in popular culture
   - wartime changes in daily life
   - the war's effects on job opportunities and racial issues

SECTION 2 REVIEW ANSWERS

Define and Identify
For significance, see the following pages:
- Office of War Information, p. 507
- Rosie the Riveter, p. 510
- A. Philip Randolph, p. 511
- Fair Employment Practices Committee, p. 511
- Carlos E. Castañeda, p. 511
- braceros, p. 511
- zoot-suit riots, p. 512
- internment, p. 512
- Norman Mineta, p. 513

1. The war gave women, African Americans, and Mexican Americans new employment and military service opportunities, although all groups experienced continued job and wage discrimination. African Americans and Mexican Americans also faced new outbursts of harassment and violence. Japanese Americans were interned during the war, although some did receive limited military service opportunities.
2. encouraged the media to endorse the war effort and created the Office of War Information; favorably
3. Entries will vary. Students might describe rationing or working long hours to aid the war effort.
4. Students might suggest that women would continue to broaden their roles outside of the home as a result of their participation in World War II.
5. Students should cite the war's effect on many areas of American life, including employment, popular culture, housing, and so on.

SECTION 3

After completing Section 3, students should be able to:

OBJECTIVE 1 *Identify where the Allied offensive in Europe began.*

OBJECTIVE 2 *Explain the impact of fighting in the Atlantic and in the air.*

OBJECTIVE 3 *Relate how the Allies successfully invaded Normandy.*

OBJECTIVE 4 *Describe the Holocaust.*

OBJECTIVE 5 *Relate how the Allies finally defeated Germany.*

Display Linking Geography and History Transparency 18, World War II in Europe, 1942–1945, from **American History Visual Resources**. As students enter the classroom, tell them to study the map and to imagine that they are planning an invasion of Nazi-occupied France. Have students quickly develop a strategic plan for their invasions. Tell students that in Section 3 they will learn how the Allied Powers defeated the Axis Powers in Europe.

SECTION 3 RESOURCES

PRINT

- Guided Reading Strategy 17.3
- Section 3 Review, p. 520
- Daily Quiz 17.3

MULTIMEDIA

- One-Stop Planner, Lesson 17.3
- Linking Geography and History Transparency 18: World War II in Europe, 1942–1945
- Holt Researcher: American History CD–ROM

SHELTERED ENGLISH

- Main Idea Activity for Reteaching and Sheltered English 17.3

✔ READING TO UNDERSTAND

To help students master the section objectives, have them answer the **READING CHECKS** and complete **Guided Reading Strategy 17.3** as they read the section.

Multimedia Resources

Linking Geography and History Transparency 18: World War II in Europe, 1942–1945

Victory in Europe

OBJECTIVES

Read to understand:

1. where the Allied offensive in Europe began
2. how fighting in the Atlantic and in the air influenced the land war in Europe
3. how the Allies successfully carried out the Normandy invasion
4. how the Holocaust was carried out
5. how the Allies finally defeated Germany

KEY TERMS

Battle of the Atlantic
sonar
D-Day
Holocaust
genocide
Battle of the Bulge
Yalta Conference

KEY PEOPLE

Dwight D. Eisenhower
George S. Patton
Elie Wiesel

KEY PLACES

Vichy France
Tunisia
Sicily
Anzio
Normandy

EYEWITNESSES TO History

"Buck Eversole is a platoon sergeant in an infantry company. His platoon has turned over many times as battle whittles down the old ones and the replacement system brings up the new ones. Only a handful now are veterans. 'It gets so it kinda gets you, seein' these new kids come up,' Buck told me one night. . . . 'Some of them have just got fuzz on their faces, and don't know what it's all about, and they're scared to death. No matter what, some of them are bound to get killed. . . . I know it ain't my fault that they get killed,' Buck finally said. 'And I do the best I can for them, but I've got so I feel like it's me killin' 'em instead of a German. I've got so I feel like a murderer. I hate to look at them when the new ones come in.'"

Ernie Pyle often visited troops at the battlefront.

Reporter Ernie Pyle brought the reality of war home to Americans in numerous news stories such as this interview. Pyle himself was eventually killed while covering the war in the Pacific.

Allied Attacks in the Mediterranean

By late 1942 U.S. supplies and troops began to make a difference in the war. However, it would take another two years of hard fighting to defeat the Axis Powers. Soon after Pearl Harbor, the Allies agreed that they would open a second front against the Axis Powers in order to relieve pressure on the Soviet Union. However, Allied forces were not prepared to launch a direct assault on either German-occupied France or Vichy-controlled southern France. At British prime minister Winston Churchill's urging, they decided to attack first in the Mediterranean region.

Axis surrender in North Africa. After France surrendered in 1940, Germany placed France's colonies in North Africa under the control of Vichy France. The following year British forces turned back the Axis attempt to capture the Suez Canal and drove the German and Italian forces into Libya. In November 1942 the Allies planned Operation Torch, an invasion of the French territory in northwest Africa. General Dwight D. Eisenhower commanded the invasion force of U.S. and British soldiers.

Allied leaders were unsure if the French forces in North Africa would oppose the invasion. Early on the morning of November 8, some 65,000 Allied troops landed at Casablanca in Morocco and Oran and Algiers in Algeria. Nearly twice that number of French forces awaited them. Troops landing at Casablanca faced the greatest difficulties, encountering both heavy surf and French resistance. Allied troops captured Algiers that day and Oran two days later.

TEACH OBJECTIVE 1

LEVEL 1: Pair students and display Linking Geography and History Transparency 18, World War II in Europe, 1942–1945, from **American History Visual Resources**. Ask each pair to identify where the Allied offensive in Europe began. *(Pairs should identify Sicily and southern Europe.)* Then have each pair write a caption for its map explaining why the Allies chose to invade through Sicily and southern Italy. *(The Allies saw Sicily as a launching pad for the invasion of Italy, and Italy as a launching pad for the invasion of Europe.)* Ask each pair to read its caption to the class.
Sheltered English, Cooperative Learning

LEVEL 2: Tell students to imagine that they are military reporters in Washington, D.C. Have each student prepare a broadcast announcement explaining the Allied offensive in Europe with a focus on where it began. *(See the Level 1 lesson for specific details.)* Ask volunteers to read their broadcasts to the class.

LEVEL 3: Tell students to imagine that they are high-level military officials in the days before the Allied invasion of Europe. Have each student prepare a one-page military brief presenting Sicily and Italy as the starting point for the Allied offensive in Europe. Students' briefs should also discuss the advantages and disadvantages of that choice. *(See the Level 1 lesson for specific details.)* Have volunteers read their briefs to the class.

As the soldiers established beachheads in Morocco and Algeria, Allied planes and ships cut Axis supply lines from Italy. Then, during the winter of 1942–43, two Allied land forces—one from the west and the other from the east—began to squeeze the Axis troops into a trap. Several fierce battles took place in Tunisia. Finally, in May 1943, the Axis force of some 250,000 soldiers surrendered.

The invasion of Italy. North Africa offered a gateway to the Italian island of Sicily. Allied leaders decided to invade Sicily next. They sought to clear the Axis forces out of the central Mediterranean and to acquire a launching point for an invasion of the Italian mainland. Battling high winds and rough seas, Allied troops landed in July 1943. They subdued Sicily in a little more than a month. General George S. Patton, who had emerged as a leader during the North Africa campaign, led the U.S. forces.

The Italian king named a new prime minister to replace Benito Mussolini and ordered Mussolini's arrest. Determined not to surrender the Italian peninsula, the Germans took Mussolini to Germany and then set up a base for him in northern Italy. In September the Italian government signed an armistice with the Allies. Soon afterward the Allies invaded southern Italy to attack the Germans. Although the Allies took Naples on October 1, they soon bogged down.

Hoping to outflank the German forces, the Allies landed to the south of Rome at Anzio in January 1944. After the landing, however, the Allies were pinned down for months. U.S. and British forces then began driving slowly north. They were joined by small units of troops from more than 25 countries. After months of bitter mountain warfare, the Germans occupying Italy were finally defeated. Soon afterward Mussolini was captured and shot by Italian rebels. In June 1944 the Allies marched into Rome, making it the first Axis capital to fall.

✔ **READING CHECK:** Where did the Allied offensive in Europe begin?

General Eisenhower led Operation Torch–the Allied invasion of North Africa.

Sea and Air Assaults

During the months of fighting in the Mediterranean region, the Allies waged campaigns on other fronts as well. Although they faced a determined enemy, the Allies eventually overcame all resistance. In the Atlantic, German U-boats continued to take a staggering toll on Allied ships, lives, and supplies. Not until 1943 did this **Battle of the Atlantic** begin to turn in the Allies' favor. An important factor was the refinement of **sonar** equipment, which uses sound waves to detect underwater objects. The Allies also developed fast escort ships for convoys and air-bombed German U-boats and submarine yards. By 1944 the Allies had won the Battle of the Atlantic.

The Allied air campaign also met with success in 1943. The Allies intensified their campaign of strategic bombing aimed at destroying German military production and undermining the morale of the German people. "It was sound strategy to prevent the *Wehrmacht* [German armed forces] from falling back to regroup and be lethal [deadly] again," Lieutenant John Morris explained. "We bombed . . . the railroad marshaling

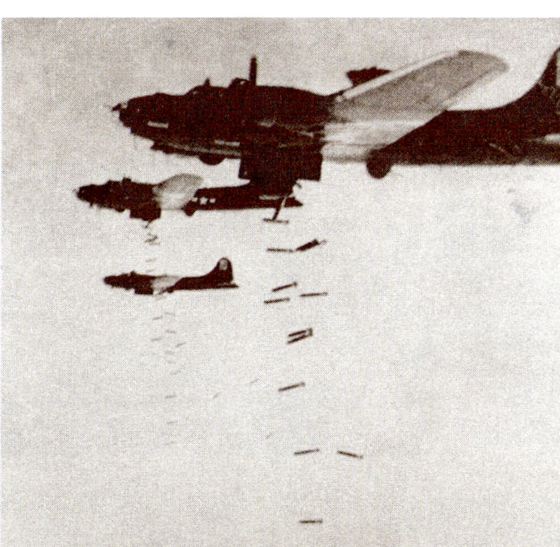

INTERPRETING THE VISUAL RECORD

The air war. Both sides used massive bombing raids to try to destroy their enemy's ability to manufacture war materials. ***What does the photograph suggest about the accuracy of such bombing attacks?***

PEOPLE IN HISTORY

George S. Patton. George S. Patton had a notoriously gruff demeanor and earned the nickname "Old Blood and Guts" for his aggressive tactics and matter-of-fact attitudes toward war. During the invasion of Sicily, Patton's hard-edged personality almost ended his military career. While visiting an army field hospital, he slapped a crying soldier who was suffering from shell shock. News of the incident spread quickly, and Dwight D. Eisenhower reprimanded Patton sharply before deciding not to relieve him of his duties.

ACTIVITY: Ask students to conduct research on an Allied military leader. Then have each student present two-to-four-minute oral reports on his or her chosen leader.

THAT'S INTERESTING!

German attacks trapped Allied forces on the Anzio beach for almost four months. During the siege German propaganda broadcasts attempted to discourage Allied soldiers by calling the area the largest self-supporting prisoner-of-war camp in the world.

VISUAL RECORD ANSWER

Students might suggest that the attacks were scattered and therefore somewhat inaccurate.

TEACH OBJECTIVES 2 AND 3

ALL LEVELS: Display Linking Geography and History Transparency 18, World War II in Europe, 1942–1945, from **American History Visual Resources.** Have students label the location of the Battle of the Atlantic and the site of the Normandy invasion. To help students understand those conflicts, copy the graphic organizer at right on the chalkboard, omitting the italicized answers. Have each student complete it. **Sheltered English**

THE WAR IN EUROPE	
Fighting in the Atlantic	• *Axis attacks took a huge Allied toll* • *with sonar, Allies turned the tide in 1943* • *sea dominance allowed the Allies to protect cargo ships and bomb Axis vessels*
Fighting in the Air	• *as with the Battle of the Atlantic, 1943 was an important year* • *Allies conducted strategic bombing to destroy important German cities*
The Normandy Invasion	• *took place on June 6, 1944* • *Allies needed to invade German-occupied France* • *created a dummy invasion as a decoy* • *stormed the beach with high casualties but ultimate success*

GLOBAL RELATIONS

Operation Fortitude. Code-named Fortitude, the campaign of deception that preceded Operation Overlord was quite elaborate. Months before the invasion at Normandy, U.S. commanders created a "phantom" army, the First U.S. Army Group, which received false radio transmissions at its "base" in southeastern England. Allied planes also dropped tons of bombs on the northeastern coast of France, and on the eve of the invasion thousands of soldiers gathered near a "fleet" of unseaworthy landing craft in British ports across the English Channel from Calais. This dummy invasion force was equipped with cardboard tanks that were made by members of the American and British film industries.

CRITICAL THINKING Why might the northeastern coast of France have seemed like a logical area for the Allies to stage an invasion?

ANSWER: Students might suggest that the northeastern coast of France is near the narrowest part of the English Channel.

VISUAL RECORD ANSWER

Students might mention the open beach and the hills beyond.

yards and road hubs along the *Wehrmacht*'s line of retreat, up and down Germany's eastern border." British Royal Air Force (RAF) planes flew chiefly at night, dropping their bombs in the general area of a given target. U.S. aircraft concentrated on precision bombing in daylight raids. By 1944, bombers had rained hundreds of thousands of tons of explosives on German factories, supply lines, and military centers.

Read More About It

Free Find: D-Day
After learning about the D-Day invasion on the **Holt Researcher** CD–ROM, create a drawing of the invasion site that shows the obstacles the Allied troops faced.

✔ **READING CHECK:** How did the fighting in the Atlantic and in the air influence the land war in Europe?

Operation Overlord

Victory in the Battle of the Atlantic and air assaults on Germany paved the way for Operation Overlord—the long-awaited Allied invasion of German-occupied France. Commanded by General Eisenhower, the invasion had involved years of planning. The Allies put in place a system of dummy installations and false clues to convince the Germans that the invasion would take place near Calais on the English Channel.

Instead, the Allies landed farther south, in Normandy, on **D-Day,** June 6, 1944. Nearly 5,000 troop transports, landing craft, and warships carried some 150,000 U.S., British, and Canadian soldiers across the Channel. Overhead, planes dropped close to 23,000 airborne troops and bombed roads, bridges, and German troop concentrations. Sergeant Ralph G. Martin recalled that "everything was confusion" during the landing and "units were mixed up, many of them leaderless, most of them not being where they were supposed to be." Corporal Samuel Fuller recalled encountering fierce resistance with the U.S. 1st Infantry Division on Omaha Beach.

> **"The only way to get off the beach was to blow a big tank trap that was blocking our way. Finally one of our guys took the trap out. . . . I stood up and tried to run. When you run over unconscious men, or men lying on their bellies, it's tough to keep your balance. You go into the water, but the water is washing bodies in and out. Bodies, heads, flesh, intestines; that's what Omaha Beach was."**

INTERPRETING THE VISUAL RECORD

D-Day. The invasion of France was a risky venture that paid off for the Allies. ***What obstacles face these soldiers who are preparing to land?***

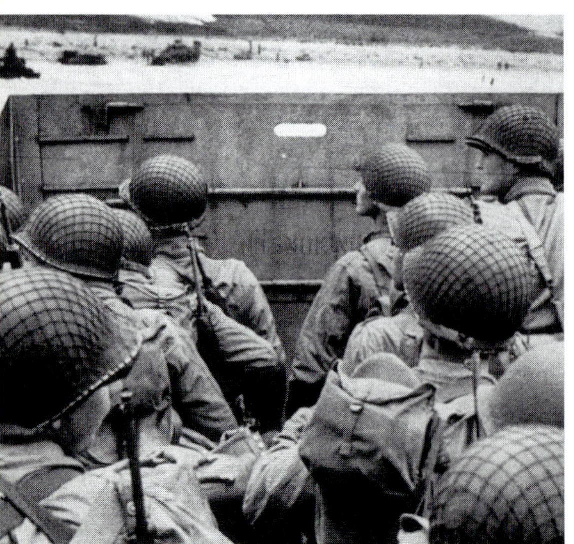

The Germans had fortified the Normandy beaches with concrete bunkers, tank traps, and mines. The beaches resembled a giant fortress, but the Allied campaign of disinformation and distraction had done its job. Adolf Hitler refused to send reinforcements to the area around Normandy. He still believed that the main invasion would occur elsewhere.

Although the Allies met determined opposition, they managed to penetrate 20 miles into France by early July. Aided by the French Resistance, the Allies drove steadily eastward. They liberated Paris on August 25, 1944. By early September more than 2 million Allied troops had landed in western Europe. Another Allied force drove northward through France from the Mediterranean. Meanwhile, Soviet troops pressed Germany from the east.

✔ **READING CHECK:** How did the Allies successfully carry out the Normandy invasion?

TEACH OBJECTIVE 4

LEVEL 1: Pair students and ask each pair to create a flowchart that defines the Holocaust and displays the factors that allowed it to happen. *(Pairs' flowcharts should note that the Holocaust was Nazi Germany's slaughter of European Jews. Factors such as Nazi propaganda, long-standing anti-Semitism, and Allied inaction allowed the Holocaust to happen.)* Have each pair present its flowchart to the class. Then conduct a discussion on the material presented in the flowcharts. **Sheltered English, Cooperative Learning**

LEVEL 2: Organize students into small groups. Ask each group to conduct a discussion in which students define the Holocaust and identify the factors that allowed it to happen. *(See the Level 1 lesson for the correct definition and factors.)* After students have completed their discussions, ask each student to write a one-page essay on the Holocaust. Students may wish to include their essays in their portfolios. **Cooperative Learning**

Strategies for Success: Preparing Questions

Preparing questions is one of the most crucial steps in conducting a successful oral history interview. Most good interview questions are formulated with a specific purpose in mind. At the same time, they are broad enough to allow the subject of the interview to express himself or herself freely. *Who, what, when, where, why,* and *how* are words that often prove particularly useful in creating such questions.

How to Prepare Questions

1. **Do preliminary research.** Gather as much information as you can about the general topic the interview will address and the particular person you will be interviewing.
2. **Decide what you need to know.** Once you have completed your preliminary research, determine what you hope to learn from the interview. Keep in mind what you already know and the types of information that the subject of your interview is likely to possess.
3. **Formulate logical, open-ended questions.** Create questions that address what you hope to learn and that follow one another in a logical fashion. Make sure that the questions are designed to allow your subject to speak freely and that they cannot be answered with a simple "yes" or "no."

Applying the Strategy

Imagine that you have arranged to conduct an oral history interview with a U.S. Army veteran who took part in the D-Day invasion at Normandy on June 6, 1944. Prepare at least six questions that you plan to ask during the interview.

Practicing the Strategy

Answer the following questions.

1. What background information did you use when formulating your questions?
2. What kind of information would you hope to gain from interviewing a veteran of the D-Day invasion at Normandy?
3. What answers do you expect to your questions?

The Holocaust

Not even the savage fighting of D-Day prepared the Allies for the horror of the **Holocaust**, Nazi Germany's systematic slaughter of European Jews. Germany's occupation of France and other countries in western Europe, as well as its attacks on Poland and the Soviet Union, put millions of additional Jews under German rule. In many regions, special squads of German soldiers rounded up Jews and shot them. Elsewhere, Jews were forced into cities and isolated in ghettos. In 1941 the Germans began constructing camps specifically for the purpose of **genocide**—the deliberate annihilation of an entire people. Hitler and senior Nazi officials called this extermination program the "final solution of the Jewish question."

These ovens were used to cremate the bodies of the victims of the Holocaust.

Major death camps included Auschwitz (OWSH-vits), Treblinka, and Majdanek, all in Poland. Jewish men, women, and children were transported to the camps in sealed railroad cars. They were then marched into rooms disguised as shower facilities and gassed. Their bodies were then cremated. All told, some 6 million Jews—two thirds of Europe's Jewish population—perished. The Nazis also killed millions of Gypsies, Poles, the mentally disabled, and religious and political prisoners.

ACROSS THE CURRICULUM

▶LANGUAGE ARTS◀

The Holocaust. The term *Holocaust* derives from the Hebrew word *olah,* which the Greek version of the Hebrew Bible translates as *holokauston.* The original meaning of the word in English was "a sacrifice consumed by fire."

CRITICAL THINKING In what way does the term *Holocaust* describe one aspect of the Nazis' atrocities against Jews and others?

ANSWER: Students should respond that the Nazis cremated many victims of the Holocaust.

STRATEGIES FOR SUCCESS ANSWERS

Applying the Strategy
Students' questions should be clear and address the topic.

Practicing the Strategy

1. Students' answers will vary but should include information from preliminary research, such as the date, size, purpose, and strategy of the invasion.
2. Students' responses might include information about the invasion itself and one soldier's experiences during the attack.
3. Students' responses should indicate that the answer will be reflective of the individual's experiences.

LEVEL 3: Tell students to imagine that they are Holocaust survivors. Have each student write three diary entries from one of the assigned perspectives. One perspective should describe the factors that gave rise to the Holocaust, another should define and describe the Holocaust itself, and another should discuss the lingering psychological effects of the Holocaust. *(See the Level 1 lesson for the correct definition and factors.)* Have volunteers read their diary entries to the class. Students may wish to include their diary entries in their portfolios.

▶**ASSIGNMENT** *Write the following questions on the chalkboard:* How did the Holocaust happen? Could something like the Holocaust happen today? *Have each student write a short essay answering the questions.*

SPOTLIGHT on Holocaust Literature

Have students obtain works by authors who wrote about the Holocaust, such as Elie Wiesel, Anne Frank, or Primo Levi. Ask each student to select and read an entire work or a clearly definable portion of a work, such as a chapter. Then have each student prepare a written book report on the work. In their reports, students should summarize and discuss the work or the subsection. Ask volunteers to discuss their book reports with the class. **Block Scheduling**

HISTORY MAKERS SPEAK

Viktor Frankl in *Never to Forget*

Arriving at Auschwitz. Most of the people arrested and transported to death camps by the Nazis knew the horrible fate that awaited them. Viktor Frankl, a physician from Austria who survived the Holocaust, described his terror upon arriving at Auschwitz. "The train shunted, obviously nearing a main station. Suddenly a cry broke from the ranks of the anxious passengers. 'There is a sign, Auschwitz!' Everyone's heart missed a beat at that moment. Auschwitz—the very name stood for all that was horrible: gas chambers, crematoriums, massacres. . . . There were isolated shouts and whistles of command. We did not know their meaning. My imagination led me to see gallows with people dangling on them. I was horrified."

ACTIVITY: Ask students if they have seen movies, television programs, or museum exhibits about the Holocaust. Call on volunteers to share their experiences. Have students bring in and discuss brochures from museum exhibits or other information about the Holocaust.

VISUAL RECORD ANSWER

Students might mention heavy snow and inferior clearing equipment.

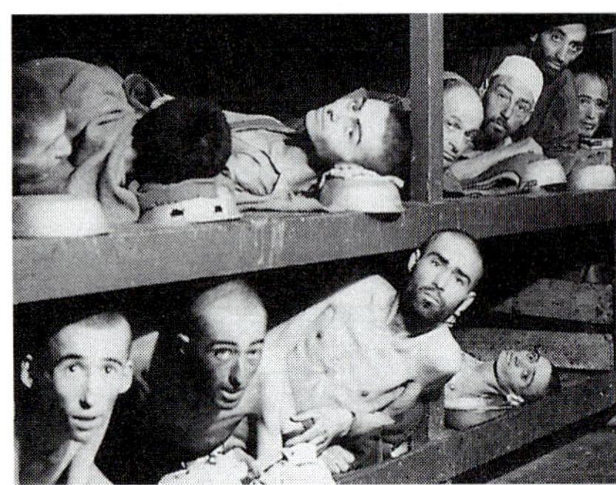

These survivors of the Buchenwald concentration camp were liberated by Allied soldiers in April 1945. Elie Wiesel is on the far right of the top row.

When the Allies liberated the death camps, they found thousands of starving survivors. Romanian-born writer Elie Wiesel was one such survivor. He described the deep psychological scars left on concentration camp survivors.

> **"One day I was able to get up, after gathering all my strength. I wanted to see myself in the mirror hanging on the opposite wall. I had not seen myself since the ghetto. From the depths of the mirror, a corpse gazed back at me. The look in his eyes, as they stared into mine, has never left me."**

To carry out this monstrous genocide, the Nazis took advantage of a long history of anti-Semitism in Europe that stretched back to the Middle Ages. A flood of Nazi propaganda against Jews stirred up this anti-Semitism. Some non-Jews in countries occupied by the Nazis either assisted or failed to prevent the Nazis from sending Jewish citizens off to the death camps. Others worked heroically to save the lives of Jews.

✔ **READING CHECK:** How was the Holocaust carried out?

Defeating Germany

Although Germany's situation was grave, Adolf Hitler refused to give up. In September 1944 the Germans launched their first V-2s, or long-range rockets, at cities in England and Belgium. These bombs could not be shot down easily.

INTERPRETING THE VISUAL RECORD

The Battle of the Bulge. These members of the U.S. 290th Regiment fought in the Ardennes on January 4, 1945. ***What difficulties did these soldiers face?***

The Battle of the Bulge. By September 1944 the Allies had crossed the German border. As they paused to bring in supplies and to regroup, the Germans launched their final counterattack. In heavy snow, they drove against the Allies in the thickly wooded Ardennes region of Belgium and northern France. They pushed westward to create a dangerous bulge in the Allied lines. In the resulting **Battle of the Bulge** some 200,000 Germans attacked an initial U.S. force of about 80,000 troops.

The U.S. 101st Airborne Division defending the Belgian town of Bastogne was completely surrounded. When German officers demanded the 101st's surrender, General Anthony McAuliff offered a one-word reply: "Nuts." Allied generals rushed in reinforcements, and the Allies pushed the Germans back. Francis Tsuzuki, whose Japanese American battalion pursued the Germans, recalled, "the Germans were retreating so fast. At times we were moving . . . more than 100 miles a day." By January 1945 it was clear that the German offensive had failed.

The Yalta Conference. In February 1945 President Franklin D. Roosevelt, Winston Churchill, and Joseph Stalin met at the **Yalta Conference** to plan for the postwar peace. At the conference Stalin pledged to declare war on Japan three months after Germany's surrender. They agreed to divide and occupy Germany after the war and outlined plans for a new international peace organization.

TEACH OBJECTIVE 5

LEVEL 1: Ask each student to create a time line of the events that allowed the Allies to finally defeat Germany. *(Students' time lines should include the following events: September 1944—Battle of the Bulge; February 1945—Yalta Conference; early 1945—Allies bomb Germany; March 1945—Allies invade Germany; April 1945—Hitler commits suicide; May 7, 1945—Germany surrenders.)* Have students annotate their time lines by explaining how each event allowed the Allies to triumph over Germany. Display students' time lines around the classroom. Students may wish to include their time lines in their portfolios. **Sheltered English**

LEVELS 2 AND 3: Ask students to identify the factors that allowed the Allies to finally defeat Germany. *(See the Level 1 lesson for the correct factors.)* Then ask each student to invent a fictional Allied character who would have been involved in the defeat of Germany—a soldier, for example, or a pilot—and either write an eyewitness account or develop a monologue account of the defeat. Have volunteers share their work with the class.

NOTE: For an additional teaching idea, see the Chapter 17 predicting consequences lesson in the **Creative Teaching Strategies** handbook.

HISTORY MAKERS SPEAK

Alex Shulman in *"The Good War": An Oral History of World War Two*

An American Doctor at the Battle of the Bulge. Many of the German soldiers at the Battle of the Bulge were teenagers. Alex Shulman, an American doctor who treated wounded soldiers, remembered one such young man. "This German youngster was brought in. He was fourteen, fifteen. . . . He was a sad, dirty-looking kid, with a terrible gash in his head. . . . I . . . [got] a basin of hot water and some soap and washed his hair. . . . He really started to cry. I said, 'What are you crying about?' He said, 'They told me I'd be killed. And here you are, an American officer, washing my hands and face and my hair.' I reminded him that I was a Jewish doctor, so he would get the full impact of it."

CRITICAL THINKING Why might many of the German soldiers at the Battle of the Bulge have been teenagers?

ANSWER: Students might suggest that high casualty rates forced the German army to induct teenagers.

MAP ANSWER

the coast of France, the border of Belgium and Germany, Berlin, Stalingrad, Anzio, and El Alamein

REVIEW

Have students complete the **Section 3 Review** on p. 520.

ASSESS

Have students complete **Daily Quiz 17.3.** As **Alternative Assessment**, you may want to use the Holocaust flowchart or the final defeat time line in this section's lessons.

RETEACH

Have students complete **Main Idea Activity for Reteaching and Sheltered English 17.3.** Then organize students into small groups and assign each group a subsection of Section 3. Have groups write three to five questions about the material in the assigned subsection. Collect the questions and use them to quiz the class. **Sheltered English, Cooperative Learning**

EXTEND

Ask students to conduct research on the bombing of German cities, including Dresden and Leipzig. Have students focus some of their research on the moral questions and issues raised by those bombings. Then ask each student to list and discuss those questions in a short essay. Have volunteers read their essays to the class. Then conduct a discussion about the issues presented in the essays. **Block Scheduling**

SECTION 3 REVIEW ANSWERS

Define and Identify
For significance, see the following pages:

- Dwight D. Eisenhower, p. 514
- George S. Patton, p. 515
- Battle of the Atlantic, p. 515
- sonar, p. 515
- D-Day, p. 516
- Holocaust, p. 517
- genocide, p. 517
- Elie Wiesel, p. 518
- Battle of the Bulge, p. 518
- Yalta Conference, p. 518

Locate
For locations, see the map on p. 519. For importance, see the following pages:

- Vichy France, p. 514
- Tunisia, p. 515
- Sicily, p. 515
- Anzio, p. 515
- Normandy, p. 516

1. Allies liberate Paris; Soviets continue to push westward; Battle of the Bulge; Allies continue to bomb German cities; Allies occupy Berlin

2. helped the Allies wear down the Axis Powers and eventually close in on Germany from multiple fronts

3. by planning carefully, establishing a campaign of misinformation and distraction, and using overwhelming force during the invasion

4. Students should clearly identify the battle and battle conditions.

5. grew out of earlier anti-Semitism in Europe, Nazi propaganda, and Allied inaction; resulted in the murder of millions of human beings and depleted the continent's Jewish population

These Soviet soldiers celebrate their capture of Berlin by planting the Soviet flag on top of the Reichstag building, or German parliament building.

The urgency of the war effort convinced President Roosevelt to run for an unprecedented fourth term. With Missouri senator Harry S Truman as his running mate, Roosevelt won his party's nomination with little opposition. The Republicans chose Thomas E. Dewey, governor of New York. Dewey lacked the charisma and experience of Roosevelt, however, and was defeated by an electoral vote of 432 to 99.

The race to Berlin. During the early months of 1945, Allied bombers continued to blast German cities, including Leipzig and Berlin. One of the most devastating attacks hit Dresden in February. In one massive two-day attack, Allied bombers caused the worst firestorms of the European war. Total civilian deaths have been estimated at between 30,000 and 60,000.

In March, Allied troops crossed the Rhine River from the west and drove into the heart of Germany. By then, Soviet troops occupied much of eastern Europe. Churchill wanted General Eisenhower to push east as far and as fast as possible. Churchill worried that the Soviets might later lay claim to territories they seized. Eisenhower did not want military strategy to be determined by political considerations and therefore halted the Allied advance at the Elbe River in April.

On April 30, 1945, Hitler committed suicide in his bunker deep under the ruins of Berlin. U.S. sergeant Mack Morriss described the grim mood of the fallen city. "There is a feeling that here has ended not only a city but a nation, that here a titanic force has come to catastrophe." Germany surrendered unconditionally on May 7. The next day, known as V-E (Victory in Europe) Day, marked the formal end of a brutal war that had held Europe in its grip for more than five years.

✔ **READING CHECK:** How did the the Allies finally defeat Germany?

SECTION 3 REVIEW

Define and explain the significance of the following terms:
Battle of the Atlantic
sonar
D-Day
Holocaust
genocide
Battle of the Bulge
Yalta Conference

Identify and explain the significance of the following individuals:
Dwight D. Eisenhower
George S. Patton
Elie Wiesel

Locate and explain the significance of the following places:
Vichy France
Tunisia
Sicily
Anzio
Normandy

1. **Using Graphic Organizers** Copy the chart below. Use it to list the military events that led to Germany's surrender in 1945.

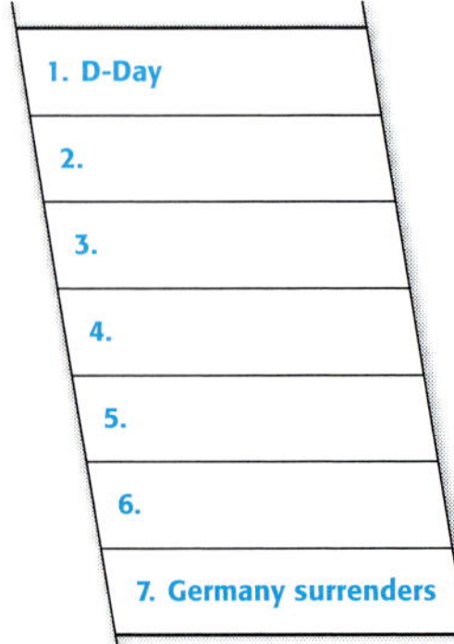

2. **Understanding Geography: Location** How did the campaigns in North Africa, Sicily, in the Atlantic, and in the air help the Allies prepare to defeat Italy and Germany?
3. **Analyzing** How did the Allies achieve victory at Normandy?
4. **Using Historical Imagination** Imagine you are an Allied soldier in the European theater. Write a diary entry that describes the conditions you have experienced in one of the battles mentioned in the text.

Critical Thinking

5. How did the Holocaust occur, and how did it affect Europe?
Consider:
- how the Holocaust developed
- why it was not stopped
- what its effects were

SECTION 4

After completing Section 4, students should be able to:

OBJECTIVE 1 *Describe the U.S. island-hopping plan.*

OBJECTIVE 2 *Explain the effect that the battles at Iwo Jima and Okinawa had on the war.*

OBJECTIVE 3 *Explain why the United States used atomic weapons against Japan.*

OBJECTIVE 4 *Discuss the costs of the war.*

LET'S GET STARTED!

Copy the following statements on the chalkboard: *The Japanese used the strategy of island-hopping in their conquest of the Pacific. The victory at Iwo Jima gave the Japanese a great psychological advantage. The Manhattan Project helped rebuild Japanese cities after the war.* As students enter the classroom, tell them to preview Section 4 by correcting these incorrect statements. *(The Allies used island-hopping; the Allies won the Iwo Jima conflict; the Manhattan Project was established to create and test nuclear bombs.)* Tell students that in Section 4 they will learn how the United States won the war in the Pacific.

Victory in Asia

OBJECTIVES

Read to understand:

1. how the United States carried out its island-hopping plan
2. what effect the battles at Iwo Jima and Okinawa had on the war
3. what led the United States to use atomic weapons against Japan
4. what the human and economic costs of World War II were

KEY TERMS

island-hopping
Battle of Leyte Gulf
Battle of Iwo Jima
kamikaze
Battle of Okinawa
Manhattan Project
Enola Gay

KEY PEOPLE

Harry S Truman

KEY PLACES

Saipan
New Guinea
Hiroshima
Nagasaki

"The Japanese fought by a code they thought was right: bushido. The code of the warrior: no surrender. You don't really comprehend it until you get out there and fight people who are faced with an absolutely hopeless situation and will not give up. If you tried to help one of the Japanese, he'd usually detonate a grenade and kill himself as well as you. To be captured was a disgrace. . . . You developed an attitude of no mercy because they had no mercy on us. It was a no-quarter, savage kind of thing. . . . If you're reduced to savagery by a situation, anything's possible. When [Charles] Lindbergh made a trip to the Philippines, he was horrified at the way American GIs talked about the Japanese. It was so savage. We were savages."

—Eugene B. Sledge

Japanese sword

As U.S. marine Eugene B. Sledge described, the fighting in the Pacific was fierce. The Japanese considered surrender disgraceful and often fought to the death. The U.S. advance across the Pacific was met with ferocious resistance as Japanese defenders dug in, committed to saving their empire or die trying.

Pacific Offensives

In the Pacific the Allies had gone on the offensive by 1943. Their ultimate objective was to come within striking distance of Japan itself.

Island-hopping. Air and sea power were the keys to victory in the Pacific, unlike in Europe where land forces played a much larger role. As early as 1942 the U.S. high command had adopted a strategy of **island-hopping**. This meant that troops would attack and seize only certain strategic Japanese-held islands, rather than trying to recapture all of them. Japanese garrisons located on islands bypassed by the Allies would be cut off from supplies and troop reinforcements. Airstrips built on seized islands would help support the next Allied advance. In the central Pacific, an island-hopping offensive began in November 1943 in the Gilbert Islands. Army troops quickly took Makin Island.

U.S. Marines plunge into the sea during the assault on Tarawa.

Tarawa. The island of Tarawa proved much more difficult to capture than Makin. Because of a coral reef encircling the island, the marines who landed there had to wade in to the beach "in the face of murderous Japanese fire, with no protection," according to Sergeant John Bushemi. Almost 1,000 marines lost their lives and some 2,000 others were wounded before the island was secured. The victory gave the United States control of a vital airstrip and put its forces in position to provide air support for the next landings.

SECTION 4 RESOURCES

PRINT

- Guided Reading Strategy 17.4
- Biography Reading 17: Enrico Fermi
- Literature Reading 17: A City and Its People Destroyed
- Section 4 Review, p. 527
- Daily Quiz 17.4

MULTIMEDIA

- One-Stop Planner, Lesson 17.4
- Holt Researcher: American History CD–ROM

SHELTERED ENGLISH

- Main Idea Activity for Reteaching and Sheltered English 17.4

✔ READING TO UNDERSTAND

To help students master the section objectives, have them answer the **READING CHECKS** and complete **Guided Reading Strategy 17.4** as they read the section.

TEACH OBJECTIVE 1

LEVELS 1 AND 2: Distribute Outline Map 20, World War II in the Pacific, from **American History Outline Maps.** Have each student label the Pacific islands that the United States conquered in the island-hopping offensive. *(Students should label the Gilbert Islands, Makin Island, Tarawa, Saipan, and the Philippines.)* Then ask students to write one or two paragraphs explaining the rationale behind island-hopping. *(The United States used island-hopping to conquer strategically important islands while cutting off other islands. With the conquered islands, the United States hoped to gain important launching pads for an invasion of Japan.)* Display students' maps and rationales around the classroom. **Sheltered English**

LEVEL 3: Tell students to imagine that they are military commanders in the Pacific. Have each student write a one-page military brief explaining and justifying the island-hopping strategy. *(See the Level 1 lesson for the correct details.)* Ask volunteers to read their briefs to the class. Then ask students to consult the map on the following page. Ask students if they can think of any other effective strategy besides island-hopping to conquer the Pacific. Have students share their responses.

GLOBAL RELATIONS

Australia's Contribution to the Allied War Effort. The Australian soldiers who helped recapture the Philippines performed one vital part of their country's overall contribution to the Allied war effort. Australia joined Britain in declaring war against Germany in 1939, and after the fall of the Philippines served as an important base of operations for U.S. forces in the South Pacific. Australian tradition prohibited the drafting of citizens to serve overseas, but the all-volunteer Australian Imperial Force provided the Allies with troops that fought in North Africa, Greece, and the Middle East, as well as the Pacific. Ultimately, more than 550,000 Australian citizens left their homeland to take part in the war; of these, more than 23,000 were killed in action and 8,000 died in Japanese war camps.

ACTIVITY: Tell students to imagine that they are soldiers in the Australian Imperial Force. Then have each student write a short letter home explaining his or her service in the war.

MAP ANSWER ***(for p. 523)***
west

Foxholes like this one on Saipan were often the only protection U.S. soldiers had during battles on the islands in the Pacific. The medal at right celebrates the Allied victory in World War II.

Saipan. The next important series of landings targeted the Marshall Islands, located north of the Gilbert Islands. In the Marshalls, U.S. forces captured several key bases from which they bombed the Truk Islands, where the headquarters of the Japanese fleet was located.

By the summer of 1944, Allied forces had advanced to the Mariana Islands. In June 535 ships carried 127,000 soldiers, two thirds of whom were marines, to the shores of Saipan. Under cover of intense air and naval bombardments from nearby aircraft carriers, landing craft loaded with troops swept in to the beaches. The Japanese gathered the bulk of their remaining fleet and sent it to stop the U.S. offensive.

Japan was already running low on aircraft, and in the battle that followed the United States won a decisive victory. U.S. pilots downed 350 Japanese planes while losing just 30 of their own planes. Running low on fuel and returning to their carriers at night, 80 U.S. pilots had to crash their planes in the ocean. Nearly all the pilots were rescued, and the Japanese aircraft carriers were no longer a threat.

Meanwhile, Saipan's 32,000 Japanese defenders were waging a fierce battle. U.S. forces suffered some 16,000 casualties, including more than 3,400 dead. U.S. troops fighting on Guam experienced equally tough resistance before the island fell in August. These U.S. victories were important because the islands provided airstrips from which U.S. bombers could begin launching missions against the main islands of Japan.

Recapturing the Philippines. Despite these setbacks, Japanese resistance stiffened when the Allies began their New Guinea–Philippines campaign in June 1943. General Douglas MacArthur led U.S. and Australian troops in a series of landings along the north coast of New Guinea. By late July 1944 they had reached the western end of this large island. Allied forces also took smaller islands nearby, such as the Admiralty Islands.

By the fall of 1944 the United States was ready to invade the Philippines. Allied forces poured onto the beaches of the island of Leyte in October. The Japanese navy's counterattack led to the **Battle of Leyte Gulf**—the last, largest, and most decisive naval engagement in the Pacific. The battle was a disaster for the Japanese, who lost four aircraft carriers, three battleships, and several cruisers. From this time on, the Japanese fleet no longer seriously threatened the Allies.

Aided by Filipino guerrillas, Allied troops fanned out over the islands of the Philippines. Overcoming bitter opposition, they entered Manila in February 1945 and subdued most Japanese defense forces within weeks. "I'm a little late," said MacArthur, "but we finally came."

✔ **READING CHECK:** How did the United States carry out its island-hopping plan?

TEACH OBJECTIVE 2

LEVEL 1: Pair students and write the following statements on the chalkboard: *The fighting on Iwo Jima and Okinawa displayed continued Japanese resistance. The two battles proved that the Japanese would not surrender.* Have each pair create a list of points that support the statements. *(Pairs' points should note that the fighting on both islands was incredibly difficult and bloody, although the United States triumphed on both fronts. Pairs should note the existence of kamikaze attacks and high casualty rates.)* Then ask students how Japanese resistance on Iwo Jima and Okinawa affected the Pacific War. *(Students should mention that Japanese resistance forced Truman to decide whether to use atomic weapons.)*
Sheltered English, Cooperative Learning

LEVELS 2 AND 3: Tell students to imagine that they are U.S. soldiers or sailors who are fighting on Iwo Jima or Okinawa. Have each student write a letter home describing the fighting and explaining how that fighting demonstrated continued Japanese resistance. *(See the Level 1 lesson for correct points.)* Have volunteers read their letters to the class. Then ask students how Japanese resistance in Iwo Jima and Okinawa affected the Pacific War. *(See the Level 1 lesson for the correct effect.)* Students may wish to include their letters in their portfolios.

▶ASSIGNMENT *Have students write letters from the perspective of kamikaze pilots preparing for their final flights. Students' letters should be written to close relatives indicating their feelings about this courageous act of loyalty to their country.*

Victory in the Pacific

These Pacific victories gave the United States several strategic bases from which to launch B-29 bombers against the Japanese home islands. U.S. planes bombed most of the country's major cities in an effort to weaken the fighting spirit of the Japanese. The worst raid took place over Tokyo in March 1945 and created huge firestorms that destroyed much of the city. The massive destruction caused Japanese civilian morale to sag, but the country's military leaders refused to surrender.

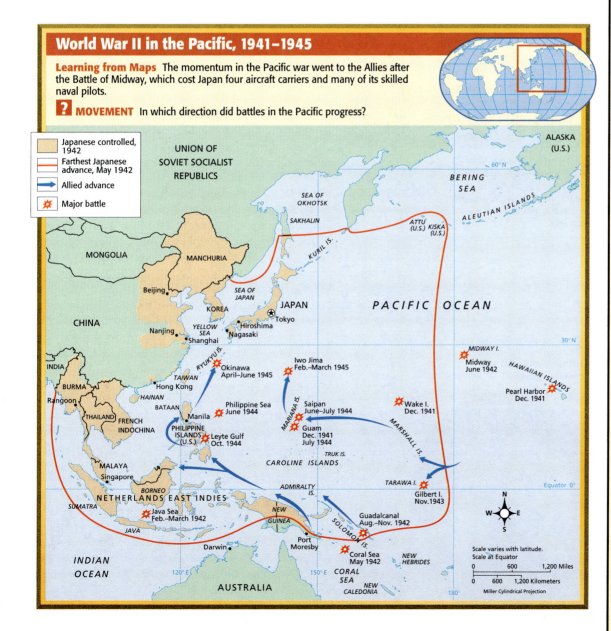

World War II in the Pacific, 1941–1945

Learning from Maps The momentum in the Pacific war went to the Allies after the Battle of Midway, which cost Japan four aircraft carriers and many of its skilled naval pilots.

? MOVEMENT In which direction did battles in the Pacific progress?

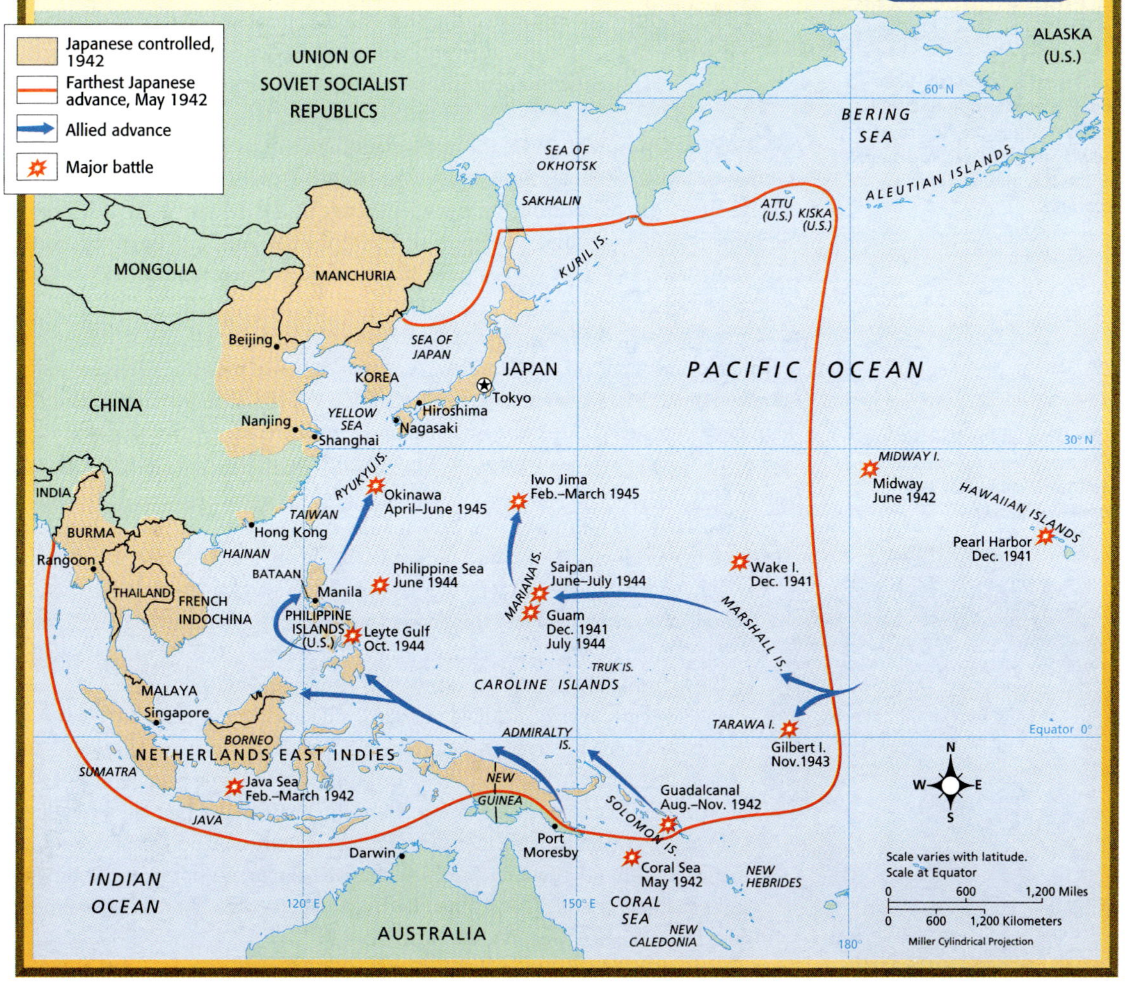

Japanese controlled, 1942
Farthest Japanese advance, May 1942
Allied advance
Major battle

Scale varies with latitude. Scale at Equator
0 600 1,200 Miles
0 600 1,200 Kilometers
Miller Cylindrical Projection

HISTORY MAKERS SPEAK

John Ciardi in *"The Good War": An Oral History of World War Two*

The Bombing of Japan. John Ciardi, a B-29 machine gunner who took part in many of the bombing raids on Japan, reflected on the incredible destruction caused by the raids. "We were in the terrible business of burning out Japanese towns. That meant women and old people, children. . . . I have some of my strike photos at home. Tokyo looked like one leveled bed of ash. The only things standing were some stone buildings. If you looked at the photos carefully, you'd see they were gutted. Some of the people jumped into rivers to get away from these fire storms. They were packed in so tight to get away from the fire, they suffocated. They were so close to one another, they couldn't fall over. It must have been horrible."

CRITICAL THINKING Why might the United States have conducted large-scale bombing raids over Japan during the final year of the war?

ANSWER: Students may respond that the bombing raids were meant to eliminate as much of Japan's infrastructure as possible and to lower civilian morale by killing people and destroying their homes.

TEACH OBJECTIVE 3

LEVEL 1: Conduct a brief discussion on the factors that led the United States to use atomic weapons against Japan. *(Students should mention the enormous costs of an invasion, continued Japanese resistance, and the desire to demonstrate U.S. power to the Soviet Union.)* Then organize the class into two groups. Have students in one group develop headlines for a newspaper that support the use of atomic weapons against Japan. Have the students in the second group develop headlines that oppose the use of atomic weapons against Japan. Have volunteers in each group share their headlines with the class. **Sheltered English, Cooperative Learning**

LEVEL 2: Tell students to imagine that they are high-level military officials who support the use of atomic weapons against Japan. Have each student write a one-page military brief to President Truman explaining the factors that necessitate the use of atomic weapons. *(See the Level 1 lesson for the correct factors.)* Ask volunteers to read their briefs to the class. Students may wish to include their briefs in their portfolios.

▸ASSIGNMENT *Have students look in newspapers, magazines and so on for articles related to the development or use of atomic weapons. Have students bring their articles to class and discuss them.*

TECHNOLOGY AND SOCIETY

Kamikaze Attacks. Kamikaze attacks were an important part of the Japanese military effort during the final months of the war. Introduced in the Battle of Leyte Gulf, they were usually undertaken by young, inexperienced pilots who considered it an honor to die in the line of duty. Before they embarked on their assignments, these pilots performed a solemn ritual that included a final toast to the emperor and the singing of the verse "Let us die close by the side of our sovereign." Approximately 1,300 kamikaze pilots completed their missions, sinking some 30 Allied combat ships and causing some 3,000 deaths.

CRITICAL THINKING Besides the physical and human destruction, how might kamikaze attacks have aided the Japanese war effort?

ANSWER: Students may mention that kamikaze attacks lowered morale on Allied ships.

THAT'S INTERESTING!

The temperature at Ground Zero of the Alamogordo atomic bomb test was 100,000,000 degrees Fahrenheit—approximately 10,000 times hotter than the surface of the sun. All life within a mile of the explosion point was destroyed almost instantly.

Joe Rosenthal's Pulitzer-prize-winning photograph of U.S. soldiers raising the flag over Mount Suribachi was the model for the U.S. Marine Corps Memorial.

Iwo Jima. In February 1945, U.S. Marines attacked Iwo Jima—just 750 miles from Tokyo—and met strong resistance. Despite a U.S. victory being nearly certain, Japanese forces fought as fiercely as ever. The **Battle of Iwo Jima** lasted six weeks. Some 4,000 marines and more than 20,000 Japanese soldiers were killed. Ted Allenby, a marine who took part in the assault on Iwo Jima, described the fighting.

> **"The casualty rate was enormous. It was ghastly. Iwo was a volcanic island with very little concealment. Cover is something you hide behind—a tree, a bush, a rock. Few trees. No grass. It was almost like a piece of the moon that had dropped down to earth."**

U.S. Marines struggled to take Mount Suribachi, which the Japanese held with a strong system of tunnels and bunkers. When the marines finally reached the mountaintop, they planted the U.S. flag in the rocky soil to celebrate their hard-fought victory. Photographer Joe Rosenthal recorded the moment in a picture that would win him a Pulitzer Prize.

Okinawa. On April 1, 1945, the largest landing force in Pacific history invaded Okinawa, about 350 miles from Japan. The Japanese forces chose not to challenge the landing. To avoid putting themselves in range of the massive guns of U.S. battleships and other warships, the Japanese retreated to the southern tip of the island. Five hours after the landing began, the marines had captured one airfield and not a single shot had been fired.

Five days later, the Japanese attacked. Some 700 Japanese planes, including 350 **kamikaze**, or suicide planes (*kamikaze* is a Japanese word meaning "divine wind"), attacked the U.S. beachheads and naval task force. Six U.S. ships were sunk, and 135 kamikaze pilots died. After the war, Admiral Nimitz recalled, "Nothing that happened in the war was a surprise, absolutely nothing except the kamikaze tactics toward the end; we had not visualized these."

U.S. sailors on the USS* Bunker Hill *scramble to escape the explosions caused by two kamikaze attacks.

This **Battle of Okinawa** was perhaps the bloodiest of the Pacific war. The Japanese troops dug in deeply and fought to the death. Japanese troops hid in the caves that dotted the island. The U.S. troops had to attack and subdue each individual cave, often by filling the cave with fire from flamethrowers. The United States suffered 49,200 casualties in the battle. Some 110,070 Japanese died in the fighting, nine times the number of Americans killed.

By early April, an Allied victory in the Pacific was near, but President Roosevelt did not live to see the end of hostilities with Japan. The world was stunned when he died suddenly on April 12. The new president, Harry S Truman, faced a grave decision. Germany's surrender had allowed Allied forces to concentrate their efforts on the war in the Pacific. Despite repeated Allied bombings, however, Japan remained a dangerous opponent, willing to fight to the very end. Truman had to decide whether the United States should use its fearsome new weapon, the atomic bomb.

✔ **READING CHECK:** What effect did Iwo Jima and Okinawa have on the war?

LEVEL 3: Tell students to imagine that they are President Truman preparing to announce the use of atomic weapons against Japan to the American people. Have each student write a speech explaining and justifying the decision. *(See the Level 1 lesson for the correct factors.)* Ask volunteers to deliver their speeches to the class. Students may wish to include their speeches in their portfolios.

▶**ASSIGNMENT** *Have each student list the consequences both of using atomic weapons against Japan and not using atomic weapons. Have students consult their lists and write two or three paragraphs presenting their personal opinions on President Truman's decision to use atomic weapons in the fight against Japan.*

SPOTLIGHT
on J. Robert Oppenheimer

Have students conduct research on the career of physicist J. Robert Oppenheimer. Students may wish to focus either on his scientific research or on the controversy surrounding his political views. Then have each student write a report on his or her findings. **Block Scheduling**

The Atomic Bomb

The new U.S. weapon had been developed by the top-secret **Manhattan Project**, the effort of a group of scientists who had been working on creating an atomic bomb since 1942. The Manhattan Project was aided by many European scientists in its work. In 1933 physicist Albert Einstein moved from Germany to the United States. During the 1930s many European Jewish scientists followed Einstein's example. Enrico Fermi was an Italian physicist who had fled to the United States. He persuaded the world-famous Einstein to warn the U.S. government about research being done by German scientists. In August 1939 Einstein wrote to President Roosevelt. He warned that "a single bomb of this type, carried by boat and exploded in a port, might very well destroy the whole port, together with some of the surrounding territory." He was describing an atomic bomb. The race was on to be the first to build one.

In 1942 General Leslie R. Groves took charge of the Manhattan Project. By year's end, scientists led by Enrico Fermi had created an atomic chain reaction, a major step in the development of a bomb. Huge research centers were established in Los Alamos, New Mexico; Oak Ridge, Tennessee; and Hanford, Washington. At the Los Alamos center, director J. Robert Oppenheimer's team worked on building the first atomic bomb.

The scientists successfully tested their bomb at Alamogordo, New Mexico, on July 16, 1945. The very next day, President Truman met with Allied leaders at Potsdam, south of Berlin. On July 26 the Allies demanded Japan's unconditional surrender. Japan refused. Truman gave the order to use atomic weapons against Japan. As Iwo Jima and Okinawa had shown, the Japanese were still capable of inflicting heavy losses on U.S. forces. An invasion of Japan would be very costly. Estimates ran as high as 1 million U.S. casualties. Japanese losses could be even greater. Using the atomic bomb might end the war quickly and save many lives on both sides. The president may also have wanted to demonstrate the power of this new weapon to the Soviet Union.

At 8:15 A.M. on August 6, the U.S. B-29 bomber ***Enola Gay***, commanded by Colonel Paul Tibbets, dropped an atomic bomb on the city of Hiroshima. A column of fire shot skyward, threatening to bring down the *Enola Gay*. It was followed by an enormous, mushroom-shaped cloud. The city looked like "lava or molasses," tail gunner Robert Caron recalled. As the B-29 passed over the ruined city, co-pilot Robert Lewis wrote in his journal, "My God, what have we done?"

The scene on the ground was even worse than the *Enola Gay*'s crew could imagine. The explosion flattened a huge area of the city and killed an

PRESIDENTIAL

1884–1972
In Office 1945–1953

Harry S Truman

Harry S Truman was born on May 8, 1884, in Missouri. As a boy he developed a strong appetite for reading. "I don't know anybody in the world ever read as much or as consistently as he did," a friend remembered. "He was what you call a 'book worm.'" Truman had no obligation to fight in World War I. Any one of several factors—his poor eyesight, his occupation as a farmer, and his status as his mother's sole support—would have allowed him to avoid service. Instead, saying it was "a job somebody had to do," Truman volunteered and commanded an artillery battery in France.

After the war, Truman returned to Missouri where his habit of studying people helped him begin his political career. "When I was growing up," Truman said, "it occurred to me to watch the people around me to find out what they thought and what pleased them the most."

On July 16, 1945, the first atomic bomb was exploded at Alamogordo, New Mexico.

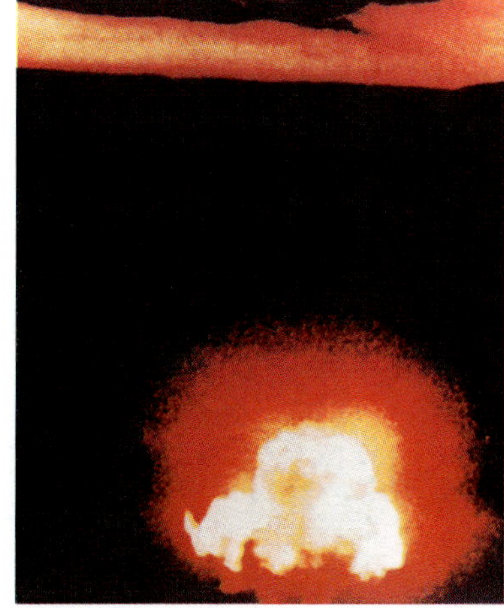

PEOPLE IN HISTORY

J. Robert Oppenheimer. J. Robert Oppenheimer, who is often called the father of the atomic bomb, was a logical but nonetheless controversial pick for director of the Los Alamos Scientific Laboratory. Oppenheimer was a brilliant nuclear physicist. He was also an avowed political activist, however, and some critics claimed that his liberal political views made him a security risk. Convinced that "we were not going to find a better man," Brigadier General Leslie Groves ended the issue by signing a memo taking full responsibility for hiring Oppenheimer.

CRITICAL THINKING Why might some of J. Robert Oppenheimer's critics have claimed that his liberal political views made him a "security risk" for the Manhattan Project?

ANSWER: Students may suggest that some of Oppenheimer's critics feared, groundlessly, that his liberal political views might incline him to share nuclear secrets with the Soviet Union.

GRAPH ANSWER
(for p. 527)
the Soviet Union; China and France

TEACH OBJECTIVE 4

ALL LEVELS: Ask students to select, in their opinions, the most devastating human or economic cost of World War II. *(Answers will vary. Students should support their choices.)* Conduct a brief discussion on students' selections. To help students understand all the human and economic costs of World War II, copy the graphic organizer at right on the chalkboard, omitting the italicized answers. Have each student complete it. **Sheltered English**

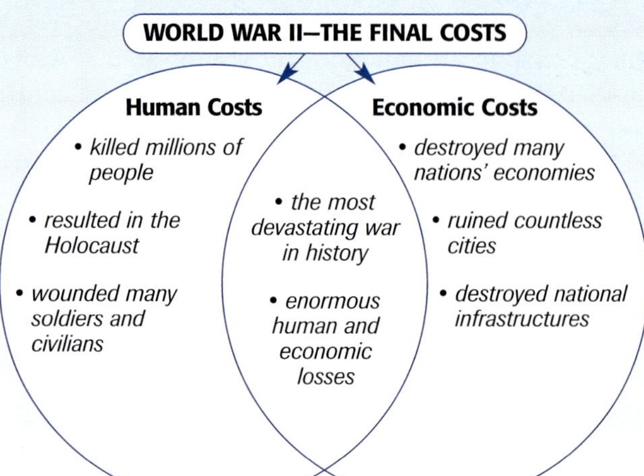

WORLD WAR II—THE FINAL COSTS
Human Costs
• killed millions of people
• resulted in the Holocaust
• wounded many soldiers and civilians
• the most devastating war in history
• enormous human and economic losses
Economic Costs
• destroyed many nations' economies
• ruined countless cities
• destroyed national infrastructures

SECTION 4 REVIEW ANSWERS

Define and Identify
For significance, see the following pages:

- island-hopping, p. 521
- Battle of Leyte Gulf, p. 522
- Battle of Iwo Jima, p. 524
- kamikaze, p. 524
- Battle of Okinawa, p. 524
- Harry S Truman, p. 524
- Manhattan Project, p. 525
- *Enola Gay,* p. 525

Locate
For locations, see the map on p. 523. For importance, see the following pages:

- Saipan, p. 522
- New Guinea, p. 522
- Hiroshima, p. 525
- Nagasaki, p. 526

1. Tarawa—gave the United States control of an important airstrip; Saipan—gave the United States a launching pad for missions against the main islands of Japan; Leyte Gulf—resulted in huge Japanese personnel and supply losses

2. created the strategy of island-hopping

3. Fighting on both islands was extremely slow and deadly, reflecting intense Japanese resistance.

4. millions of deaths and incalculable amounts of property damage for both the Allied and the Axis Powers

5. Answers will vary. Some students might argue that the atomic bomb prevented a costly U.S. invasion of Japan, while others might argue that the bomb was deadly beyond any possible justification.

Great Debates

The Atomic Bomb

President Truman justified his decision to drop atomic bombs on two Japanese cities by noting Japan's refusal to surrender unconditionally. He claimed that the atomic bomb had prevented a costly U.S. invasion of Japan. He also linked the atomic bomb to Pearl Harbor. "The Japanese began the war," said Truman. "They have been repaid manyfold."

Some historians have questioned Truman's explanations. They point out that Tokyo was considering peace negotiations. They note that with the promised Soviet declaration of war by early August, victory would have been possible without either dropping the atomic bomb or launching a U.S. invasion. These scholars argue that Truman dropped the bomb not only to end the war but also to demonstrate the U.S. atomic might and thus strengthen its postwar position.

Other historians point to Japan's wartime atrocities and to the country's bitter-end defense of Okinawa. They note that top military leaders in Tokyo fiercely opposed the peace overtures and favored a desperate defense of the home islands. Although the debate over President Truman's decision continues, all historians agree that it has had long-range consequences that few anticipated at the time.

estimated 100,000 people. Junji Sarashina, a 16-year-old high school junior, later recalled his experiences after the blast.

> **"The entire town of Hiroshima was ablaze. . . . A lot of people were floating in the river; some were swimming, but some of them were dead, drifting with the current downstream. Their skin was red and their clothes were nothing but strips of cloth hanging from them."**

Three days later, the United States dropped a second atomic bomb on Nagasaki. The explosion vaporized people, melted stones, and spontaneously ignited everything combustible within eight tenths of a mile. Japanese estimates put the total number of deaths caused by both bombs at around 200,000.

A day before the bombing of Nagasaki, the Soviet Union had declared war on Japan and begun an invasion of Manchuria. Stunned by the destruction of Hiroshima and Nagasaki, the Japanese soon offered to surrender. Despite their demand for unconditional surrender, the Allies allowed the Japanese emperor to remain on his throne. The formal surrender was signed on September 2, 1945, aboard the USS *Missouri* in Tokyo Bay.

✔ **READING CHECK:** What led the United States to use atomic weapons against Japan?

Nearly every building in the city of Hiroshima was flattened by the atomic bomb. The watch below was found in the rubble, stopped at the exact time of the explosion.

Costs of the War

After years of struggle and sacrifice, World War II had ended in victory for the Allies. The price of this victory was high, however. The toll in lives and property was without precedent. Most disturbing was the knowledge—fully revealed only after Germany's defeat—that Hitler had attempted to exterminate all the Jews of Europe. However, the Allies had achieved their war aims. Germany's Nazi government was destroyed, and Japan's military warlords were overthrown.

World War II was the most devastating war the world has ever known. It resulted in more deaths and destroyed more property than any other war in history. When it finally ended, hundreds of cities lay in ruins. Beautiful churches and palaces were reduced to rubble, and

REVIEW

Have students complete the **Section 4 Review** on p. 527.

ASSESS

Have students complete **Daily Quiz 17.4.** As **Alternative Assessment**, you may want to use the atomic bomb debate or the President Truman speech in this section's lessons.

RETEACH

Have students complete **Main Idea Activity for Reteaching and Sheltered English 17.4.** Then pair students and have each pair create a detailed outline of Section 4. Display students' outlines around the classroom.
Sheltered English, Cooperative Learning

EXTEND

Have each student create a replica or diorama of some aspect of the final war in the Pacific. Students might make a model of the *Enola Gay*, for example, or of the flag-raising on Iwo Jima. Have students write a one-page paper explaining the importance of the event represented by their work. Display students' replicas or dioramas around the classroom.
Block Scheduling

---

priceless works of art had gone up in smoke. Millions of people lacked heat, electricity, running water, adequate food, and the means to travel from one place to another. In some regions, mile upon mile of field and forest had been reduced to utter desolation.

Two examples indicate the extent of property lost in the war. In Düsseldorf, Germany, more than 90 percent of the homes were uninhabitable. The cities of Kiev and Minsk in the Soviet Union had to be completely rebuilt. The war brought untold suffering to civilians. According to one estimate, some 30 million civilians lost their lives from bombing, disease, shelling, or starvation. Millions more suffered from injuries or malnutrition. Millions lost everything they owned. The Soviet Union and China were particularly hard hit. As in World War I, U.S. civilian losses were relatively light. In economic terms, armaments and other military costs probably totaled more than $1 trillion. Along with peace came many uncertainties about the future.

Deaths in World War II

Major Allied Powers — Major Axis Powers

Wartime deaths (in millions): 0–10

Military / Civilian

Soviet Union, China, Great Britain, United States, France, Germany, Japan, Italy

Source: *The Oxford Companion to World War II*

Learning from Graphs Some 50 million people died in World War II. Many were civilians.

? Building Graph Skills Which country suffered the most in total losses? Which countries lost more civilians than military personnel?

✔ **READING CHECK:** What were the human and economic costs of World War II?

SECTION 4 REVIEW

Define and explain the significance of the following terms:
island-hopping
Battle of Leyte Gulf
Battle of Iwo Jima
kamikaze
Battle of Okinawa
Manhattan Project
Enola Gay

Identify and explain the significance of the following person:
Harry S Truman

Locate and explain the significance of the following places:
Saipan
New Guinea
Hiroshima
Nagasaki

1. **Using Graphic Organizers** Copy the following diagram. Use it to explain the significance of the islands that U.S. forces captured after Guadalcanal as they advanced across the Pacific.

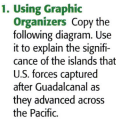

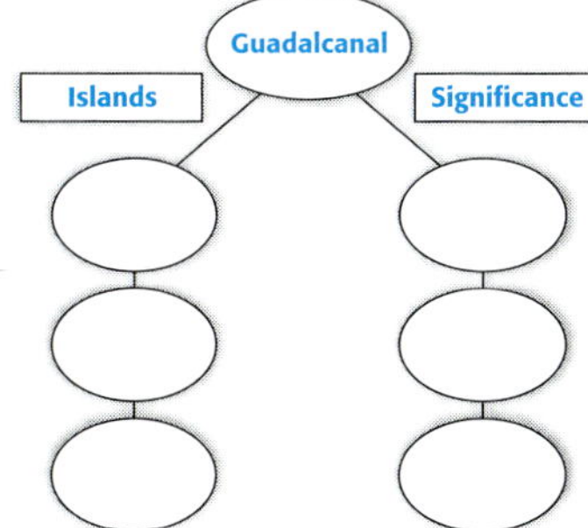

2. **Understanding Geography: Movement** How did U.S. military leaders adapt their strategy to suit the geography of the South Pacific?
3. **Assessing Consequences** How did Iwo Jima and Okinawa affect U.S. fighting in the Pacific?
4. **Synthesizing** Summarize the international consequences of World War II for the Allied Powers and Axis Powers.

Critical Thinking

5. Do you think the United States was justified in using the atomic bomb against Japan? Explain your answer.
Consider:
   - what U.S. leaders knew about the bomb when they used it
   - the casualties in the battles of Iwo Jima and Okinawa
   - the long-term effects of a nuclear blast and the risks of a future nuclear war

CHAPTER 17 REVIEW ANSWERS

Creating a Time Line
Each event should have an explanation and the correct date.

Writing a Summary
See the Reading Checks in each section for main ideas.

Identifying People and Ideas
1. government agency created to help increase military production
2. commander of U.S. Army units in the Pacific
3. naval battle that helped turn the tide in favor of the Allies in the Pacific
4. Mexican laborers who came north to work in the Southwest during the war
5. commander of U.S. Pacific Fleet
6. June 6, 1944; date that Allied troops launched an invasion of German-occupied France
7. the deliberate annihilation of an entire people
8. Romanian-born writer who survived the Holocaust
9. U.S. strategy of attacking and seizing only certain Japanese-held islands in the Pacific
10. Japanese suicide planes

Understanding Main Ideas
1. The Axis Powers held firm control of the areas they had invaded and had better-prepared military forces.

REVIEW AND ASSESSMENT RESOURCES

PRINT

- Chapter 17 Review, pp. 528–29
- Chapter 17 Tutorial for Students, Parents, Mentors, and Peers
- Chapter 17 Test (Form A or B)
- Portfolio Activities and Alternative Assessment Handbook, Chapter 17

MULTIMEDIA

- Audio Program, Chapter 17 (English and Spanish)
- Chapter 17 Test Generator (on the One-Stop Planner)
- Global Skill Builder CD–ROM
- HRW Web site

SHELTERED ENGLISH

- Spanish Glossary
- Sheltered English Chapter 17 Test

REVIEW

Have students complete the **Chapter 17 Review** on pp. 528–29.

ASSESS

Use one of the chapter tests to assess students' understanding of the content. **For Alternative Assessment**, see the **Portfolio Activities and Alternative Assessment Handbook.**

2. created the War Production Board and Office of War Mobilization, passed the Selective Service and Training Act, expanded the income tax, sold war bonds, and instituted rationing during its mobilization effort
3. The war affected all aspects of daily life—the content of popular entertainment, the availability of consumer goods, and the workplace.
4. arrested millions of people and sent them to concentration and death camps
5. El Alamein and Stalingrad, the Axis surrender in North Africa, the Allied invasion of Italy, and the Allied invasion at Normandy on D-Day
6. island-hopping

Reviewing Themes

1. The United States provided the other Allies with military supplies and food during the war, and the Soviet Union provided the Allied war effort with an extraordinarily large number of soldiers. Allied soldiers from different countries also served and fought together in a number of military campaigns.
2. Wartime conditions aggravated anti-Japanese prejudice in the United States, thereby prompting many Americans to question the loyalty of Japanese Americans. In turn, the government interned Japanese Americans living on the West Coast.
3. Massive bombing raids destroyed Germany's ability to manufacture war materials and undermined the morale of the German people.

Review

Creating a Time Line

Copy the time line below onto a sheet of paper. Complete the time line by filling in the events and dates from the chapter that you think were most significant. Pick three events and explain why you think they were significant.

Writing a Summary

Using the Reading Checks as a guide, write an overview of the events in the chapter.

Identifying People and Ideas

Identify the following terms or individuals and explain their significance.

1. War Production Board
2. Douglas MacArthur
3. Battle of Midway
4. braceros
5. Chester Nimitz
6. D-Day
7. genocide
8. Elie Wiesel
9. island-hopping
10. kamikaze

Understanding Main Ideas

SECTION 1

1. What advantages did the Axis Powers have over the Allies at the beginning of the war?
2. What steps did the U.S. government take to mobilize for war?

SECTION 2

3. What was daily life like for Americans during the war?

SECTION 3

4. How did the Nazis carry out the Holocaust?
5. What were the major turning points in the war with Germany?

SECTION 4

6. What was the Allied strategy in the Pacific?

Reviewing Themes

1. **Global Relations** How did the Allies pool their resources to win World War II?
2. **Constitutional Heritage** How did wartime conditions lead to restrictions on the rights of Japanese Americans?
3. **Technology and Society** What role did air power play in the Allied victory during World War II?

Thinking Critically

1. **Evaluating** How did the Japanese miscalculate the U.S. response to the attack on Pearl Harbor?
2. **Analyzing** What actions could the Allies have taken to win the war in Europe sooner?
3. **Taking a Stand** Imagine that you are President Truman. Would you have chosen to drop the atomic bomb or invade Japan? Explain your answer.
4. **Hypothesizing** What might have happened if the D-Day invasion has not succeeded?
5. **Synthesizing** What were the final costs and consequences of World War II?

Writing About History

Writing to Classify Copy the following organizational web. Use it to list the important battles, strategic decisions, and weapons that led to the Allied victory in the Pacific. Then write an encyclopedia entry explaining how the Allies achieved victory.

RETEACH

Assign each student one of the key terms or people from Chapter 17. Tell students to keep their assignments secret. Have each student develop a set of clues about the identify of the assigned term or person. Then ask each student to deliver those clues to the class. Have students compete to guess the identities of the secret terms and people.
Sheltered English

EXTEND

Organize students into seven groups and assign each group a year from 1939 to 1945. Have groups conduct research on events relating to World War II that took place during the assigned year. Ask groups to create an annotated time line of the assigned year. Have each group present its time line to the class. Then display the time lines in chronological order around the classroom. **Block Scheduling, Cooperative Learning**

Strategies for Success Review the **Strategies for Success** on *Preparing Questions.* Then imagine that you have arranged an oral history interview with one of the following people:

a. a U.S. Navy veteran who served as a fighter pilot during the Battle of Midway
b. a Japanese American who was interned during World War II
c. an American woman who worked in a defense factory during the war
d. a scientist who took part in the Manhattan Project

Prepare at least six questions that you plan to ask during the interview.

Linking History and Geography

Allied prisoners on the Bataan Peninsula were forced to march from Mariveles to San Fernando. They were then shipped north by train. Study the map below. About how far did the prisoners have to march to reach San Fernando? About how far did they travel by train?

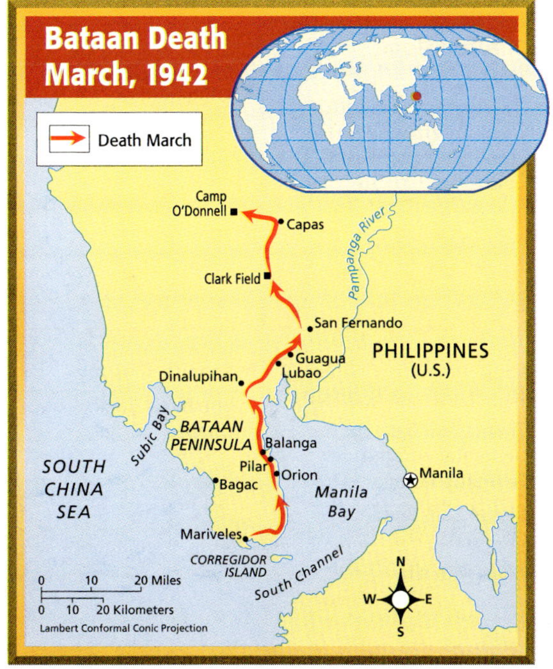

internet connect

TOPIC: Norman Rockwell
GO TO: go.hrw.com
KEYWORD: SE1 Rockwell

Accessing the Internet through the HRW Web site, research the World War II–era paintings of Norman Rockwell. Then write a paper in which you identify what moral values are represented in the Four Freedoms paintings.

BUILDING YOUR PORTFOLIO

Complete one or all of the following projects independently or cooperatively.

1 Global Relations

Imagine that you are a soldier fighting against the Japanese in the Pacific. ***Write a letter*** to your family describing the islands you have been on and the fighting you have seen.

2 Technology and Society

Imagine that you are serving on a government committee examining the effects of technology on the war. ***Create a chart*** that illustrate these effects.

3 Economic Development

Imagine that you are a factory worker during World War II. ***Create a series of journal entries*** expressing your feelings about the economic effect of the war on the home front.

The Sun
NEW YORK
WAR TIME Cook Book
MENUS RECIPES AND CANNING INFORMATION TO HELP MAKE YOUR RATION POINTS GO FURTHER
By EDITH·M·BARBER
FAMED FOOD EDITOR OF THE NEW YORK SUN
25¢

Thinking Critically

1. The Japanese may have miscalculated the forceful response to the Pearl Harbor bombing.

2. Students' responses will vary but might suggest that the Allies could have begun earlier and intensified their bombing missions over Germany.

3. Answers will vary. Students should consider the atomic bomb's destructive potential and the human cost of an invasion.

4. the Allies might not have defeated Hitler in Europe

5. millions of deaths and incalculable amounts of property damage for both sides

Writing About History

battles—Coral Sea, Midway, Guadalcanal, Saipan, Leyte Gulf, Iwo Jima, Okinawa; strategies—surprise interception of Japanese naval forces, island-hopping, use of atomic bomb; weapons—warships, fighter planes, atomic bombs

Strategies for Success

Students' questions should be based on adequate background information, follow one another logically, and allow the interview subject to speak freely.

Linking History and Geography

by foot—about 45 miles; by train—about 25 miles

The Cold War

CHAPTER PLANNING GUIDE

	Section Lesson Objectives	Print Resources	Multimedia Resources	Sheltered English Resources
Section 1 Healing the Wounds of War, pp. 532–37	1 Describe the actions Allied forces took to stabilize Germany and Japan after the war. 2 Discuss how the Allied Powers tried war criminals, and explain why some people were dissatisfied with the trials. 3 Explain why the United Nations was founded, and relate how it was organized. 4 Recount the events that led to the founding of the new country of Israel, and describe how Arab countries responded.	▶ Guided Reading Strategy 18.1 ▶ Geography Activity 18: Postwar Tensions in the Eastern Mediterranean ▶ Biography Reading 18: Ralph Bunche ▶ Section 1 Review, p. 537 ▶ Daily Quiz 18.1	▶ One-Stop Planner, Lesson 18.1 ▶ Holt Researcher: American History CD–ROM ▶ HRW Web site	▶ Main Idea Activity for Reteaching and Sheltered English 18.1
Section 2 The Cold War Begins, pp. 538–43	1 Explain what caused the Cold War, and describe U.S. strategy during the Cold War. 2 Describe how the U.S. government tried to control the development of atomic weapons. 3 Analyze how the Marshall Plan helped block the spread of communism in Europe. 4 Trace how the Western Allies tried to limit Soviet expansion.	▶ Guided Reading Strategy 18.2 ▶ Primary Source Reading 18: New Foreign Policy ▶ Section 2 Review, p. 543 ▶ Daily Quiz 18.2	▶ One-Stop Planner, Lesson 18.2 ▶ Holt Researcher: American History CD–ROM	▶ Main Idea Activity for Reteaching and Sheltered English 18.2
Section 3 The Cold War Turns Hot, pp. 544–50	1 Explain how the Chinese Communists gained control of China. 2 Trace the factors that led to the escalation of the conflict in Korea. 3 Describe the effect the Korean War had on U.S. politics. 4 Discuss the methods that President Eisenhower used to promote U.S. interests abroad.	▶ Guided Reading Strategy 18.3 ▶ American History Political Cartoon 26: Brinksmanship ▶ Section 3 Review, p. 550 ▶ Daily Quiz 18.3	▶ One-Stop Planner, Lesson 18.3 ▶ The American Nation Video Program Segment: MacArthur in Korea; Teacher's Guide, pp. 193–94 ▶ Holt Researcher: American History CD–ROM	▶ Main Idea Activity for Reteaching and Sheltered English 18.3
Section 4 The Cold War at Home, pp. 551–57	1 Discuss the actions the U.S. government took to limit communism at home, and describe how these actions affected Americans' everyday lives. 2 Explain how Senator Joseph McCarthy was able to play upon Americans' fears of communism. 3 Describe how Americans reacted to the prospect of nuclear war.	▶ Guided Reading Strategy 18.4 ▶ Graphic Organizer Activity 18: U.S. Presence in Global Affairs ▶ Literature Reading 18: Innocent Victims ▶ Section 4 Review, p. 557 ▶ Daily Quiz 18.4	▶ One-Stop Planner, Lesson 18.4 ▶ The American Nation Video Program Segment: Bomb Shelters; Teacher's Guide, pp. 175–76 ▶ Holt Researcher: American History CD–ROM	▶ Main Idea Activity for Reteaching and Sheltered English 18.4
Chapter Review and Assessment pp. 558–59		▶ Chapter 18 Review, pp. 558–59 ▶ Chapter 18 Tutorial for Students, Parents, Mentors, and Peers ▶ Chapter 18 Test (Form A or B) ▶ Portfolio Activities and Alternative Assessment Handbook, Chapter 18	▶ Audio Program, Chapter 18 (English and Spanish) ▶ Chapter 18 Test Generator (on the One-Stop Planner) ▶ Global Skill Builder CD–ROM ▶ HRW Web site	▶ Spanish Glossary ▶ Sheltered English Chapter 18 Test

CHAPTER OVERVIEW

The United States and the Soviet Union emerged as the two most powerful countries in the postwar period. These nations had been allies during World War II, united by the common goal of defeating the Axis Powers. However, postwar competition for power and prestige led to increasing tensions. The Americans and Soviets fought the Cold War by competing to expand their political, economic, and military influence around the world. The Western bloc, led by the United States, was organized around a democratic-capitalist political economy and the NATO military alliance. The Eastern bloc, led by the Soviet Union, was organized around a communist political economy and the Warsaw Pact alliance. The Cold War competition extended to Asia, where the United States fought to repel communist North Korean invaders from South Korea.

Domestic politics in the United States was also dominated by Cold War tensions. The country was overtaken by the fear that Communists had infiltrated the U.S. government and American society. Americans were also concerned about the threat of nuclear war, as the United States and Soviet Union engaged in a nuclear arms race. These concerns, in large part, led to the election of Dwight D. Eisenhower as the nation's first Republican president in 20 years.

TIME TAMERS

Block Scheduling

The teacher lesson plans for each section offer a variety of activity choices to help you present the material in a block scheduling format. For further suggestions on block scheduling, see the **Block Scheduling Handbook with Team Teaching Strategies**, pp. 103–08.

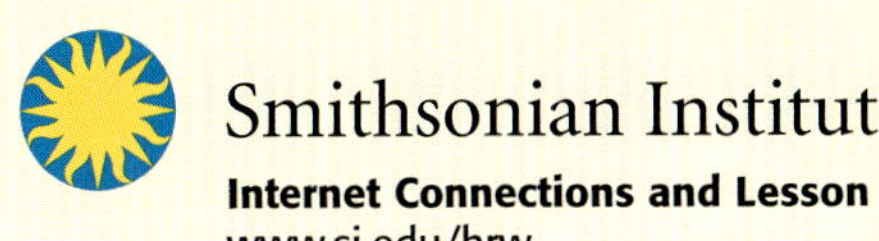

Internet Connections and Lesson 18
www.si.edu/hrw

Hands-On History Activities:

Classroom to Community The **Hands-On History Activities** help students make meaningful connections between events in American history and those in their own hometown. You may wish to use the Chapter 18 Activity, Living with Nuclear Weapons, to extend the chapter lessons, as alternative assessment, or as a block scheduling option.

Portfolio Projects

The American Nation includes multiple portfolio projects in each Pupil's Edition chapter review, as well as each unit review. Chapter 18 Portfolio Project options on p. 559 include the following:

1. Students will **write a memorandum.**
2. Students will **write an article.**
3. Students will **create a flyer.**

The American Nation
INTERNET RESOURCE DIRECTORY

To access online materials for this chapter, go to go.hrw.com and type in the keywords listed below.

HRW ONLINE RESOURCES
GO TO: go.hrw.com

Online Maps
KEYWORD: SE1 Maps18
- The Marshall Plan
- Israel, 1949
- Nuclear Technology

Online Charts
KEYWORD: SE1 Charts18
- UN Decision-Making Bodies

Online Reading Support
KEYWORD: SE1 Strategies18

Online Rubrics
KEYWORD: SE1 Rubrics

CHAPTER ENRICHMENT LINKS
Use these Web links to extend and enrich student learning for Chapter 18.
GO TO: go.hrw.com
KEYWORD: SE1 Ch18

CHAPTER INTERNET ACTIVITIES
GO TO: go.hrw.com
- Pupil's Edition Student Activity
KEYWORD: SE1 United
(Students conduct research on the United Nations.)
- Teacher's Edition Student Activity
KEYWORD: SE1 Sputnik
(Students conduct research on *Sputnik* and the beginnings of the space race.)
- Teacher's Edition Student Activity
KEYWORD: SE1 Israel
(Students explore the founding of Israel.)

ADDITIONAL
RESOURCES

Books for Teachers

Blair, Clay. *The Forgotten War: America in Korea, 1950–1953.* Doubleday, 1989. Chronicles the political and military history of the Korean War.

McCullough, David. *Truman.* Simon & Schuster, 1992. Depicts the political and private lives of Harry S Truman.

Books for Students

Patterson, James T. *Grand Expectations: The United States, 1945–1974.* Oxford University Press, 1996. Provides a detailed history of U.S. affairs in the years following World War II.

Winkler, Allan M. *Life Under a Cloud: American Anxiety About the Atom.* Oxford University Press, 1993. Explores the effects of the nuclear arms race on life in the United States.

Primary Sources from the Period

Bradbury, Ray. *The Martian Chronicles.* Doubleday, 1950. Describes the colonization of Mars by humans while Earth is destroyed by nuclear war.

Miller, Arthur. *The Crucible.* Viking, 1971. Draws parallels between McCarthyism and the Salem witch trials of 1692.

Multimedia Materials

Cold War, Volume 2: The Marshall Plan, 1947–1952 and Berlin, 1948–1949. Video, 93 min. Warner Home Video/CNN Productions. Documents the beginning phases of the Cold War in Europe.

Korea: MacArthur's War with Truman. Video, 40 min. Zenger/SSSS. Uses archival footage, maps, and contemporary images to document the Korean War.

CHAPTER 18

Before You Read

Build on What You Know

Ask students to answer the following questions.

Why might tensions have existed between the United States and the Soviet Union after World War II?

Consider:

- the U.S. military advantage gained from the atomic bomb
- the political tensions that existed before the war

What problems might countries have faced as they rebuilt after the war?

Consider:

- the devastation and loss of life that resulted from the war
- the need to establish new systems of government

exploring the time line

AMERICAN EVENTS

HISTORY MAKERS SPEAK

Richard Nixon in *Homeward Bound*

1959 ■ The "Kitchen Debate." Shortly before Soviet premier Nikita Khrushchev visited the United States in 1959, Vice President Richard Nixon attended the opening of an exhibition of American consumer products in Moscow. Nixon argued that even household items like washing machines showed U.S. superiority: "To us, diversity, the right to choose, . . . is the most important thing. We don't have one decision made at the top by one government official. . . . We have many different manufacturers and many different kinds of washing machines so that the housewives have a choice. . . . Would it not be better to compete in the relative merits of washing machines than in the strength of rockets?"

CRITICAL THINKING What might Nixon's statement reveal about American women's roles during the 1950s?

ANSWER: Students might suggest that many American women performed most of the household chores.

CHAPTER 18

1945–1960

The Cold War

UN medal

THE GRANGER COLLECTION, NEW YORK

Poster of Mao Zedong after the Communist victory

1945
World Events
Delegates from 50 nations meet in San Francisco to create the charter for the United Nations.

1949
World Events
Mao Zedong's Communist forces gain control of most of China.

1951
Daily Life
Americans organize a hero's welcome for General MacArthur upon his return from Korea after being removed by President Truman.

1952
Business and Finance
After 21 months of operation by federal troops, the U.S. government returns the country's railroads to private control.

1945 — 1948 — 1951

1947
Daily Life
Ten people working in the film industry refuse to testify before a House committee and are blacklisted.

Red Channels

A report on Communists in the entertainment industry

1948
Politics
The U.S. Congress passes the European Recovery Act, establishing the Marshall Plan to help stabilize and rebuild Europe.

A cargo of sugar on its way to Europe as part of the Marshall Plan

Before You Read

Build on What You Know

Economic problems during the 1930s contributed to the rise of dictatorships in Germany, Italy, and Japan. Their military expansion and acts of aggression led to World War II. The war destroyed parts of Europe and Asia. In this chapter you will learn that after the war many nations struggled to rebuild their war-torn economies. At the same time, tensions grew between the United States and the Soviet Union.

530

Think About Themes

To help students create their Themes Journal entries, provide the following examples of appropriate **agree/disagree** *statements.*

Global Relations

Agree The rivalry between Russia and Japan during the early 1900s did not affect relationships between the United States and other countries.

Disagree The competitive rivalry between European nations resulted in World War I.

Democratic Values

Agree During the Red Scare in 1919, the U.S. government violated the civil rights of suspected Communists.

Disagree Americans' fears about corruption in city government led to improvements in city election processes, improving civil rights.

Technology and Society

Agree During the early 1800s many authors in the transcendentalist movement expressed their anxiety about machines by retreating from industrial society.

Disagree Much of the literature in the science-fiction genre reflects Americans' fascination with technology and its possibilities.

exploring the time line

GLOBAL EVENTS

Robert Rauschenberg's painting *Bed*

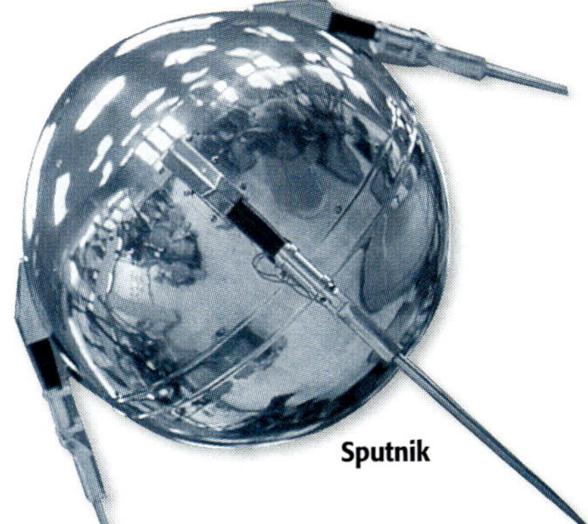

Sputnik

Francis Gary Powers holds a model of his U-2 spy plane.

1953 The Arts Playwright Arthur Miller writes *The Crucible*, in which he compares McCarthyism to the Salem witch trials.

1954

1955 The Arts Robert Rauschenberg's *Bed* makes an important contribution to American art.

1956 World Events Egypt seizes the Suez Canal after the United States withdraws support for an Egyptian dam project on the Nile River.

1957

1957 Science and Technology The Soviet Union launches *Sputnik*, the first artificial satellite, into orbit around Earth.

1958 Science and Technology Congress establishes the National Aeronautics and Space Administration (NASA).

1959 Politics Soviet premier Nikita Khrushchev visits the United States.

1960

1960 World Events The Paris summit between Soviet premier Khrushchev and President Eisenhower is canceled after the Soviets shoot down a U.S. spy plane.

Arthur Miller's The Crucible

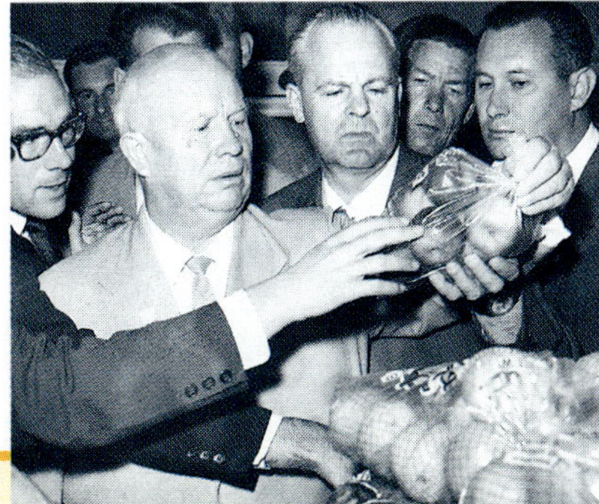

Soviet premier Khrushchev (second from left) visited an American supermarket in 1959.

TOPIC: *Sputnik*: The October Surprise
GO TO: go.hrw.com
KEYWORD: SE1 Sputnik

Have students access the Internet through the HRW Web site to conduct research on the launch of *Sputnik* and the beginnings of the space race. Then ask each student to write a newspaper editorial that discusses the Soviet accomplishment and urges public and government support for the U.S. space program.

Think About Themes

Decide whether you **agree** *or* **disagree** *with the following statements. Note why in your journal.*

Global Relations Rivalry between two powerful nations will rarely affect the relationships between other countries.

Democratic Values The fears of the majority of Americans often limit the rights of groups that hold unpopular views.

Technology and Society The fear of technology affects the behavior of Americans and is often reflected in the literature and arts of the time.

531

SECTION 1

After completing Section 1, students should be able to:

OBJECTIVE 1 *Describe the actions Allied forces took to stabilize Germany and Japan after the war.*

OBJECTIVE 2 *Discuss how the Allied Powers tried war criminals, and explain why some people were dissatisfied with the trials.*

OBJECTIVE 3 *Explain why the United Nations was founded, and relate how it was organized.*

OBJECTIVE 4 *Recount the events that led to the founding of the new country of Israel, and describe how Arab countries responded.*

LET'S GET STARTED!

Write the following question on the chalkboard: *What are the steps that countries devastated by war must take to rebuild?* As students enter the classroom, tell them to answer the question in writing. Ask volunteers to share their responses with the class. Tell students that in Section 1 they will learn about the actions that countries took to rebuild after World War II.

SECTION 1 RESOURCES

PRINT
- Guided Reading Strategy 18.1
- Geography Activity 18: Postwar Tensions in the Eastern Mediterranean
- Biography Reading 18: Ralph Bunche
- Section 1 Review, p. 537
- Daily Quiz 18.1

MULTIMEDIA
- One-Stop Planner, Lesson 18.1
- Holt Researcher: American History CD-ROM
- HRW Web site

SHELTERED ENGLISH
- Main Idea Activity for Reteaching and Sheltered English 18.1

✔ READING TO UNDERSTAND
To help students master the section objectives, have them answer the **READING CHECKS** and complete **Guided Reading Strategy 18.1** as they read the section.

Healing the Wounds of War

OBJECTIVES

Read to understand:
1. what actions Allied forces took to stabilize Germany and Japan after the war
2. how the Allied Powers tried war criminals, and why some people were dissatisfied with the trials
3. why the United Nations was founded, and how it was organized
4. what events led to the founding of the new country of Israel, and how Arab countries responded

KEY TERMS

Potsdam Conference
zaibatsu
Nuremberg Trials
United Nations
Zionism

KEY PEOPLE

Adolf Eichmann
Hideki Tojo
Trygve Lie
Eleanor Roosevelt
David Ben-Gurion
Ralph Bunche

"There are moments when the drama of our times seems to focus on a single scene. The meeting at Potsdam [Germany] is one of those moments. We can hardly take in the sense of what happened until it is spelled out in a picture like this. The picture of three men walking in a graveyard. They are the men who hold in their hands most of the power in the world."

—Anne O'Hare McCormick

President Truman views the destruction in Germany.

Journalist Anne O'Hare McCormick imagined the scene at a conference between Winston Churchill, Joseph Stalin, and Harry S Truman to determine the fate of postwar Germany. The most powerful nations of the world were left with the urgent task of easing the human suffering and political chaos resulting from the war. Many Americans believed that the United States should lead the way. "The war and the victory showed us what we could do in the world," said Melville Grosvenor, a magazine editor. The United States worked with the other Allies to restore peace by occupying Germany and Japan and by creating a new international organization called the United Nations.

Occupation Rule

After the war, Germany and Japan lay in ruins, their wartime governments shattered. German actress Hildegard Knef described a German town "without houses, without windowpanes, without roofs; holes in the asphalt, rubble, rubbish, rats." An American soldier noted that in the area around Tokyo, "there was practically nothing left; the rubble did not even look like much." A Japanese American soldier remarked of the devastation: "Tokyo was all flattened, and people were living in holes with corrugated roofs. They were desperate for food." With the fighting over, Germany and Japan now faced the task of rebuilding their governments, economies, and cities under the watchful eye of the Allies.

The occupation of Germany. To decide how to handle postwar Germany, Allied leaders met in Potsdam, Germany, in July 1945. This **Potsdam Conference** was the first time President Truman had met with Winston Churchill and Joseph Stalin since President Roosevelt's death. Churchill was replaced during the conference by Great Britain's new prime minister, Clement Attlee. The three leaders worked out an agreement over the details of their joint occupation of Germany. The leaders divided Germany into four occupation zones. The British, the French, and the Americans each took control of an area in the western, industrialized part of Germany. The Soviets agreed to control the poorer, more rural eastern part. The four powers also divided Austria into zones and agreed to jointly administer the city of Berlin, within the Soviet-controlled part of Germany.

TEACH OBJECTIVE 1

LEVEL 1: Tell students to imagine that they are advisers to the U.S. government after World War II. Pair students and have them compile lists of actions that the Allies must take to stabilize Germany and Japan. *(Students' lists for Germany should include division of the country into four occupation zones with Allied control, crushing the Nazi Party, re-establishing local governments, and returning refugees to their homes; lists for Japan should include ending militarism, creating a democratic government and constitution, and reforming the economy.)* Have volunteers read their lists to the class.
Sheltered English, Cooperative Learning

LEVELS 2 AND 3: Tell students to imagine that they are advisers to President Truman after World War II. Have each student write a brief memo to the president describing the actions the Allies must take to stabilize Germany and Japan. *(See the Level 1 lesson for the correct actions.)* Ask volunteers to read their memos to the class.

▶**ASSIGNMENT:** *Have each student create an illustrated pamphlet that describes for the American public the actions the Allies must take to stabilize Germany and Japan.*

In order to stabilize Germany, the occupying powers pledged to crush the Nazi Party, re-establish local governments, and rebuild German industry. The Allies also agreed to return German refugees to their homes. The Potsdam Conference attendees recognized that the joint occupation of Germany would require cooperation. However, Soviet occupation of much of Eastern Europe caused tensions among the Allies. Stalin demanded that the other Allies recognize Soviet-backed Poland's claims to German territory it had occupied during the war. They reluctantly agreed but grew increasingly concerned about Soviet expansion in Eastern Europe. Another source of tension was the Soviet Union's demand for immediate reparations from Germany.

Occupied Germany, 1945–1950

Learning from Maps The United States and the Soviet Union occupied the largest portions of Germany.

? PLACE Which country controlled the zone in which Munich was located?

The occupation of Japan.

Postwar Japan also faced huge challenges in its efforts to rebuild. Its economy lay in shambles, and Hiroshima and Nagasaki had been devastated by atomic bombs. The United States occupied defeated Japan from 1945 to 1952.

In addition to helping rebuild the Japanese economy, the United States worked to end Japanese militarism and to establish a democratic government. During the occupation, Emperor Hirohito remained in the imperial palace, but he had no power. Allied Supreme Commander Douglas MacArthur, his staff, and a new Japanese congress ran the country.

Under MacArthur's direction, Japan demobilized several million troops and adopted a new constitution in 1947. The constitution set up a democratic system of government, which gave voting rights to women and granted freedom of religion. The constitution also abolished the Japanese army and navy and prohibited Japan from ever again becoming a military power. Although the constitution was clearly influenced by American ideals, it won wide support from the Japanese people.

The Japanese also made important economic reforms. One program gave land to Japanese farmers. The government allowed labor unions to organize. It also broke up the ***zaibatsu***, huge corporations run by single families that had monopolized the Japanese economy. These political and economic reforms laid the foundation for Japan's tremendous postwar economic recovery.

✔ **READING CHECK:** What actions did the Allied forces take to stabilize Germany and Japan after the war?

Emperor Hirohito unveils Japan's new constitution and announces the abolition of the armed forces.

GLOBAL RELATIONS

The Potsdam Conference. The Potsdam Conference revealed that tensions between the United States and the Soviet Union were on the rise. Scholar David McCullough summed up the atmosphere that surrounded the meeting's end: "The Potsdam Conference should have been a time of celebration . . . marking the start of a new era of good feeling among the Allied powers now that the common foe, the detested Nazi, was destroyed. . . . But it wasn't that way, nor in practicality had there ever been much chance it would be. . . . The first day they met, Stalin had told Truman he wanted to cooperate with the United States in peace as in war, but in peace, he said, that would be more difficult. It was what they all knew, and the underlying tensions felt at the beginning remained to the end."

CRITICAL THINKING Why might it have been easier for the Allies to cooperate during the war than after the war?

ANSWER: Students might suggest that the Allies had the common goal of defeating the Axis Powers during the war but that each country would act in its own self-interest after the war.

MAP ANSWER
the United States

TEACH OBJECTIVE 2

LEVEL 1: Tell students to imagine that they are American journalists who have been sent to postwar Germany and Japan to cover the punishment of war criminals. Have each student write two postcards to a friend or family member back home that discuss how the Allies punished war criminals and describe why some people were dissatisfied with the trials. *(Students should mention the war crimes trials in Germany and Japan, the verdicts in the trials, and that the war crimes were so shocking that many Americans felt that more German and Japanese officials should have been punished.)* Have volunteers read their postcards to the class.

Sheltered English

LEVELS 2 AND 3: Tell students to imagine that they are newspaper editors in the period following World War II. Have each student write an editorial about the punishment of war criminals and some people's dissatisfaction with the trials. *(See the Level 1 lesson for the correct Allied procedures, punishments, and reasons why people were dissatisfied.)* Students may wish to include their editorials in their portfolios.

internetconnect

TOPIC: The Founding of Israel
GO TO: go.hrw.com
KEYWORD: SE1 Israel

Have students access the Internet through the HRW Web site to conduct research on the founding of Israel. Then have each student create an illustrated history that traces the major events leading to the formation of the State of Israel. Ask students to include information about the reasons Israel was founded, to discuss international support for the founding of Israel, to describe the national origins of immigrants to Israel, and to discuss the reactions of Palestinian Arabs.

VISUAL RECORD ANSWER

Students might point to the presence of military police in the courtroom.

INTERPRETING THE VISUAL RECORD

Nuremberg Trials. Allied judges tried German officers in Nuremberg, Germany. The commander of the German air force, Hermann Göring, is shown on the witness stand. ***What characteristics of this courtroom could lead you to assume that this is a military trial?***

The War Crimes Trials

After the war, Allied leaders began to think about how to punish the military leaders who committed or ordered atrocities during the war. At the Potsdam Conference, the Allied leaders agreed that "stern justice shall be meted [given] out to all war criminals, including those who have visited cruelties upon our prisoners." The Allied leaders agreed that convicted German and Japanese war criminals must be punished for waging war and for the mistreatment of prisoners.

Nuremberg Trials. The German war crimes trials were known as the **Nuremberg Trials** because they took place in Nuremberg, Germany, the former rallying place of Adolf Hitler's Nazi Party. The trials began in November 1945. Before an international military court, witnesses gave chilling accounts of Nazi atrocities, including the torture and murder of millions of Jews, Gypsies, and others. Marie Vaillant, a concentration camp survivor, testified.

> **"For months, for years we had one wish only: the wish that some of us would escape alive, in order to tell the world what the Nazi convict prisons were like. . . . There was the systematic . . . urge to use human beings as slaves and to kill them when they could work no more."**

In September 1946 the court made its first rulings. The court had tried a number of Nazi leaders on four charges. They were charged with planning the war, committing war crimes and other crimes against humanity, and conspiring to commit the crimes. Twelve Nazi leaders were sentenced to death. Seven others received jail sentences, and three were acquitted.

In other trials held in the U.S. occupation zone, thousands of former Nazi leaders were tried and jailed, fined, or barred from public office. However, many Nazis, including Adolf Eichmann, the architect of the Jewish extermination program, avoided immediate prosecution by hiding their identities and escaping to Latin America.

Trials in Tokyo. In Tokyo General MacArthur set up the International Military Tribunal for the Far East in early 1946. This court conducted trials against suspected war criminals from the war in the Pacific. The court prosecuted more than 20 leaders of Japan's military. The trials lasted from May 1946 to November 1948. Seven people were sentenced to death, including Hideki Tojo, the premier during the war. Others were sentenced to life in prison.

Shocked by the war crimes, many Americans argued that more German and Japanese officials should have been punished. Nevertheless, the judges followed legal procedures and tried not to act out of anger. The trials set important standards for international law and the conduct of war. The chief lesson was that countries and individuals can be held accountable for their actions during war. Many countries now accept the idea that war crimes cannot be excused on the grounds that those responsible were "just following orders."

✔ **READING CHECK:** How did the Allied Powers put war criminals on trial? Why were some people dissatisfied with the trials?

TEACH OBJECTIVE 3

LEVEL 1: Pair students and have them create a collage that depicts why the United Nations was founded. *(Students should show that the United Nations was founded to promote world peace, human rights, equality between the sexes and between nations, respect for justice and treaty obligations, and social progress and better standards of living.)* Ask students to explain how the United Nations was organized. *(Students should mention that all member nations were included in a General Assembly, and the United States, Great Britain, France, China, the Soviet Union and 10 additional rotating members composed the Security Council.)* Display collages around the classroom. **Sheltered English, Cooperative Learning**

LEVELS 2 AND 3: Tell students to imagine that it is 1945 and that they are U.S. diplomats working to gain Senate approval for U.S. membership in the United Nations. Have each student write a speech describing why the United Nations is being founded and how the United Nations will be organized. *(See the Level 1 lesson for the correct reasons and description.)* Have volunteers deliver their speeches to the class.

The United Nations

During the war, the Allies had met several times to map out strategies to defeat the Axis Powers. Delegates from the United States, Britain, the Soviet Union, and China met in 1944 at Dumbarton Oaks, an estate in Washington, D.C. There they worked out a proposal for a postwar international organization called the **United Nations** (UN).

The founding of the UN. The Allies hoped to use the UN to continue working for world peace. In April 1945, delegates from 50 nations met in San Francisco to draw up the Charter of the United Nations. The charter provided for a General Assembly and a Security Council. The General Assembly includes all member nations. The 15-member Security Council includes 5 permanent members and 10 rotating members. The United States, the Soviet Union, Britain, France, and China are the permanent members. It addresses military and political problems and has the power to veto any action proposed by the General Assembly.

Soon after the creation of the UN Charter, the Senate overwhelmingly approved U.S. membership in the UN. On October 24, 1945, the UN officially came into existence. The UN established its headquarters in New York City. Trygve Lie (TRIG-vuh LEE) of Norway served as the UN's first secretary-general. Former first lady Eleanor Roosevelt served as one of the first U.S. delegates to the UN.

★ HISTORICAL DOCUMENTS ★

The Charter of the United Nations

Foreign ministers from the United States, Britain, and the Soviet Union met in Moscow in October 1943. They established a common goal to form "a general international organization, based on the sovereign equality of all peace-loving states." In a conference held between August and October 1944 in Washington, D.C., the same three countries together with China drew up a tentative charter. After another planning conference in April 1945, the United Nations Charter was adopted by the United States on July 28, 1945.

WE THE PEOPLES OF THE UNITED NATIONS DETERMINED to save succeeding generations from the scourge [destruction] of war, which twice in our lifetime has brought untold sorrow to mankind, and to reaffirm faith in fundamental human rights, in the dignity and worth of the human person, in the equal rights of men and women and of nations large and small, and to establish conditions under which justice and respect for the obligations arising from treaties . . . to promote social progress and better standards of life in larger freedom, AND FOR THESE ENDS to practice tolerance and live together in peace with one another as good neighbors . . . HAVE RESOLVED TO COMBINE OUR EFFORTS TO ACCOMPLISH THESE AIMS.

Accordingly, our respective Governments . . . have agreed to the present Charter of the United Nations and do hereby establish an international organization to be known as the United Nations.

Eleanor Roosevelt's contribution. Born to a distinguished New York City family on October 11, 1884, Eleanor Roosevelt lived a solemn and often lonely childhood. Both of her parents died when she was 10. "It was the grimmest childhood I had ever known. Who did she have? Nobody," sympathized one of Roosevelt's cousins.

BIOGRAPHY Eleanor Roosevelt

At the age of 14, Roosevelt was enrolled in Allenswood, a girl's school outside of London. At the school, Roosevelt found warmth and intellectual encouragement. Describing her years at Allenswood, Roosevelt later explained that "whatever I have become since had its seeds in those three years of contact with a liberal mind and strong personality."

After leaving the boarding school at age 17, Roosevelt returned to New York. She eagerly turned

HOLT RESEARCHER — Read More About It

Free Find: Eleanor Roosevelt

After reading about Eleanor Roosevelt on the **Holt Researcher** CD–ROM, write a short essay explaining how her concern for social issues influenced her political career.

GLOBAL RELATIONS

The United Nations. Two major disputes arose between the United States and the Soviet Union at the Dumbarton Oaks conference. First, the Soviet Union wanted the five permanent members of the UN Security Council to have the power to veto discussion of any issue by the General Assembly. The United States wanted the veto power to cover only proposed actions by the General Assembly. Second, the Soviet Union demanded a vote in the General Assembly for each of its 15 constituent republics. The United States countered that it should receive a vote for each of its 48 states. These issues were eventually resolved at the Yalta Conference, where the Soviet Union yielded to the U.S. version of the Security Council veto. In return, the United States agreed that three Soviet republics—Russia, Byelorussia, and the Ukraine—should receive seats in the General Assembly.

CRITICAL THINKING How might the Security Council's veto power over General Assembly actions be considered undemocratic?

ANSWER: Students might suggest that the fact that a minority vote can override the vote of an overwhelming majority goes against democratic principles.

TEACH OBJECTIVE 4

ALL LEVELS: To help students understand the events that led to the founding of Israel and Arab countries' response to Israel's founding, copy the following graphic organizer on the chalkboard, omitting the italicized answers. Have each student complete the graphic organizer. Ask volunteers to share their answers with the class. Lead the class in a discussion about the issues involved in the Arab-Israeli dispute. **Sheltered English**

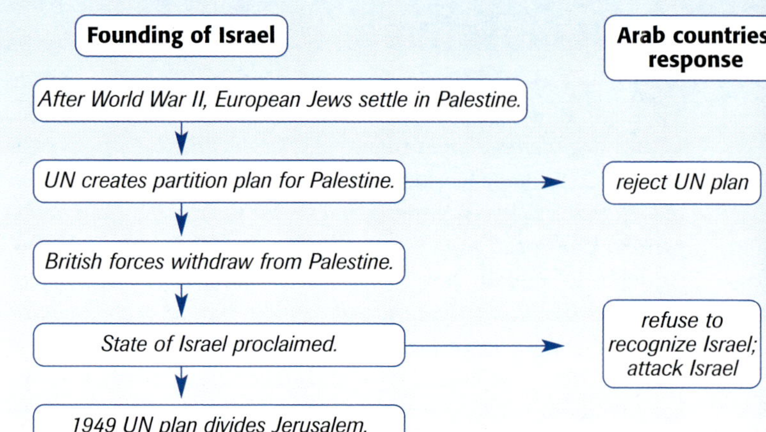

Founding of Israel
Arab countries' response
After World War II, European Jews settle in Palestine.
UN creates partition plan for Palestine.
reject UN plan
British forces withdraw from Palestine.
State of Israel proclaimed.
refuse to recognize Israel; attack Israel
1949 UN plan divides Jerusalem.

THAT'S INTERESTING!

The term *Zionism* is derived from the name of one of the two hills upon which ancient Jerusalem was built. In the Hebrew bible, "Mount Zion" serves as an alternate name for Jerusalem that carries especially strong emotional, religious, and poetic overtones.

SECTION
REVIEW 1 ANSWERS

Define and Identify

For significance, see the following pages:

- Potsdam Conference, p. 532
- *zaibatsu*, p. 533
- Nuremberg Trials, p. 534
- Adolf Eichmann, p. 534
- Hideki Tojo, p. 534
- United Nations, p. 535
- Trygve Lie, p. 535
- Eleanor Roosevelt, p. 535
- Zionism, p. 536
- David Ben-Gurion, p. 536
- Ralph Bunche, p. 537

1. Germany—division into occupation zones, joint administration of Berlin, destruction of Nazi Party, reestablishment of local governments, reconstruction of industry, return of refugees; Japan—occupation by U.S. military, demobilization of Japanese military, establishment of a democratic constitution, encouragement of economic reforms

The Religious Spirit

AMERICAN JUDAISM

Thousands of Jewish refugees and Holocaust survivors from Europe resettled in what would become the nation of Israel. Many others headed for the United States. Between 1935 and 1941 some 150,000 European Jews immigrated to the United States. These new immigrants contributed to the already diverse Jewish American community in the United States.

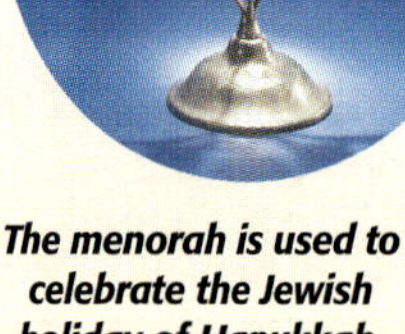

The menorah is used to celebrate the Jewish holiday of Hanukkah.

During the 1950s American Judaism was dominated by three denominations—Orthodox, Conservative, and Reform. Some Jewish immigrants embraced Orthodox Judaism's emphasis on a unity of past and present faith and on the strict observance of religious laws. Conservative and Reform Judaism, however, proved much more popular.

Some immigrants liked the relaxed interpretation of religious observance offered by Reform Judaism. This denomination had been popular in the United States since the late 1800s. It also presented a more Americanized Judaism—holding services in English and establishing a Sunday Sabbath. Reform Judaism also presented the Jewish faith simply as an organized religion. Emphasizing both Jewish religious heritage and Jewish ethnic identity, Conservative Judaism attracted the majority of the Jewish immigrants. All three denominations attempted to spread awareness of anti-Semitism. Orthodox and particularly Conservative Judaism also encouraged Jewish nationalism, primarily in terms of support for the nation of Israel. ■

toward a life of social activism and settlement-house work. By her early twenties, Roosevelt had gained recognition in New York City's growing community of social reformers.

Roosevelt continued her social activism and political work throughout her marriage to her cousin, Franklin D. Roosevelt. Eleanor Roosevelt's political career continued well after her husband's death. In 1945 she was selected to be a U.S. delegate to the United Nations. In this role, Roosevelt was instrumental in creating a declaration of human rights that would provide a universal standard set of inalienable rights. Roosevelt and many other UN delegates realized that building world peace after World War II required cooperation among nations. Roosevelt explained her view.

> **"Security requires both control of the use of force and the elimination of want. No people are secure unless they have the things needed not only to preserve existence, but to make life worth living. . . . All peoples throughout the world must know that there is an organization where their interests can be considered and where justice and security will be sought for all."**

From "En Route to London, January 5, (1946) from *My Day, Volume II: the Post-War Years* by Eleanor Roosevelt, edited by David Emblidge. Copyright © 1990 by Pharos Books. Reprinted by permission of *United Feature Syndicate, Inc.*

Roosevelt remained politically active and worked for human rights until her death in 1962.

Early critics of the UN insisted that it was doomed to fail because it did not have the power to enforce its own decisions. Nevertheless, most Americans were as optimistic as President Truman, who noted in 1945: "This [UN] charter points down the only road to enduring peace. There is no other."

✔ **READING CHECK:** Why was the United Nations founded, and how was it organized?

The Founding of Israel

One of the first major conflicts the United Nations faced concerned Palestine, a small eastern Mediterranean region claimed by both Jews and Arabs. After World War II, many European Jews moved to Palestine—despite Arab protest—rather than return to Europe. Britain, which had ruled Palestine since World War I, could not resolve conflicting claims over the territory. In 1947 Britain turned the issue over to the United Nations. The UN came up with a plan to divide Palestine into two states—one for Jews, the other for Arabs—but Arabs rejected the proposal.

Zionism. The UN plan was a victory for **Zionism**, the movement seeking a Jewish homeland in Palestine. Zionist leader David Ben-Gurion (ben-goohr-YAWN) had supported the idea since the early 1900s. Born in what is now Poland, Ben-Gurion moved to Palestine in 1906. He was expelled in 1915 for Zionist

REVIEW

Have students complete the **Section 1 Review** on p. 537.

ASSESS

Have students complete **Daily Quiz 18.1**. As **Alternative Assessment**, you may want to use the UN collage or the war crimes editorial in this section's lessons.

RETEACH

Have students complete **Main Idea Activity for Reteaching and Sheltered English 18.1**.Then create a five-column chart on the chalkboard entitled *Healing the Wounds of War.* Label the columns Stabilizing Germany, Stabilizing Japan, War Crimes Trials and Responses to Them, Founding the UN, and Founding Israel and the Response of Arab Countries. Then organize students into five groups and assign one column to each group. Have each group present the information from its column to the class.
Sheltered English, Cooperative Learning

EXTEND

Ask each student to conduct research on the founding of the United Nations and the creation of the UN Charter. Students should focus their research on delegates' philosophical differences and important compromises. Have students present their research in the form of a booklet entitled "Creating the United Nations." **Block Scheduling**

activities. Exiled, he went to the United States to raise money and recruit volunteers among the American Jewish community.

When the British forces withdrew from Palestine in 1948, Ben-Gurion and other Jewish leaders promptly proclaimed the new state of Israel. Both the United States and the Soviet Union immediately recognized the new nation.

The Arab-Israeli War. The Arab states, however, reacted violently. They refused to recognize Israel and organized military forces to reclaim the state for Palestine. Armies from the Arab states of Egypt, Iraq, Lebanon, Syria, and Transjordan joined Palestinian forces to attack Israel. Although vastly outnumbered, Israeli forces under Ben-Gurion's overall command captured and held much of Palestine. Israeli soldiers used an impressive arsenal bought in part with millions of dollars that poured in from the American Jewish community.

In an attempt to end the war, the UN sent a mediator, Count Folke Bernadotte of Sweden, to the Middle East. Bernadotte negotiated a shaky cease-fire, but he was assassinated by Israeli extremists. In 1949 a second UN mediator, the U.S. diplomat Ralph Bunche, persuaded both sides to accept an armistice. Bunche won the Nobel Peace Prize in 1950. He was the first African American to receive that honor.

The 1949 agreement gave Israel more territory than the earlier UN partition plan had, but it divided Jerusalem into Arab and Israeli zones. The plan gave Egypt control of the Gaza Strip, and Jordan took over the West Bank of the Jordan River. The Arab countries, however, still refused to recognize the state of Israel. Also left unresolved was the fate of the Palestinian Arabs remaining in Israel.

✔ **READING CHECK:** What events led to the founding of the new country of Israel? How did Arab countries respond?

INTERPRETING THE VISUAL RECORD

Zionism. After World War II thousands of European Jews made their way to British-controlled Palestine. These three Holocaust survivors traveled to Palestine in June 1945. ***What emotions do you think these Jewish settlers felt as they arrived in their new homeland?***

SECTION  REVIEW

Define and explain the significance of the following terms:
Potsdam Conference
zaibatsu
Nuremberg Trials
United Nations
Zionism

Identify and explain the significance of the following individuals:
Adolf Eichmann
Hideki Tojo
Trygve Lie
Eleanor Roosevelt
David Ben-Gurion
Ralph Bunche

1. **Using Graphic Organizers** Copy the graphic organizer below. Use it to compare the ways Allied forces attempted to stabilize Germany and Japan after World War II.

Allied Efforts to Stabilize Germany	Allied Efforts to Stabilize Japan

2. **Taking a Stand** Was justice served in the Nuremberg and Tokyo war crimes trials? Consider both the victims' and the criminals' perspectives.
3. **Hypothesizing** How do you think World War II influenced the purpose of the United Nations? How did this affect its structure?
4. **Analyzing** What events led the UN to try to resolve the conflict over Jewish and Arab claims to Palestine? How successful was this effort?

Critical Thinking

5. How did nations act in a spirit of cooperation after World War II? In what ways did nations compete?
Consider:
   - what actions nations took during the occupation of Germany and Japan
   - what the purpose and goals of the UN were
   - how the conflict in Palestine developed and was resolved

2. Answers will vary. Some students might suggest that a greater number of German and Japanese officials should have been put on trial. Others might suggest that a prolonged period of trials would have been counterproductive to efforts to rebuild Germany and Japan.

3. Answers will vary. Some students might point out that World War II had a direct influence on the basic UN mission and that the membership of the UN Security Council included all the major Allies.

4. Britain could not resolve conflicting claims; Answers will vary. Students might point out that the UN could not prevent Arab states from attacking Israel. Others might point out Ralph Bunche's success in negotiating a cease-fire.

5. cooperation—joint occupation of Germany and establishment of the United Nations; competition—conflict between Arabs and Jews over creation of Israel

VISUAL RECORD ANSWER

Students might mention excitement, joy, and pride.

SECTION 2

After completing Section 2, students should be able to:

OBJECTIVE 1 *Explain what caused the Cold War, and describe U.S. strategy during the Cold War.*

OBJECTIVE 2 *Describe how the U.S. government tried to control the development of atomic weapons.*

OBJECTIVE 3 *Analyze how the Marshall Plan helped block the spread of communism in Europe.*

OBJECTIVE 4 *Trace how the Western Allies tried to limit Soviet expansion.*

LET'S GET STARTED!

Write the following question on the chalkboard: *What do you know about the Cold War?* Tell students to respond to the question in writing. Ask volunteers to share their responses with the class. Tell students that in Section 2 they will learn about the origins of the Cold War.

SECTION 2 RESOURCES

PRINT

- Guided Reading Strategy 18.2
- Primary Source Reading 18: New Foreign Policy
- Section 2 Review, p. 543
- Daily Quiz 18.2

MULTIMEDIA

- One-Stop Planner, Lesson 18.2
- Holt Researcher: American History CD–ROM

SHELTERED ENGLISH

- Main Idea Activity for Reteaching and Sheltered English 18.2

✔ READING TO UNDERSTAND

To help students master the section objectives, have them answer the **READING CHECKS** and complete **Guided Reading Strategy 18.2** as they read the section.

The Cold War Begins

OBJECTIVES

Read to understand:

1. what caused the Cold War, and what the U.S. strategy during the Cold War was
2. how the U.S. government tried to control the development of atomic weapons
3. how the Marshall Plan helped block the spread of communism in Europe
4. how the Western Allies tried to limit Soviet expansion

KEY TERMS

Cold War
satellite nations
containment
Baruch Plan
Atomic Energy Act
Truman Doctrine
Marshall Plan
Berlin Airlift
NATO
Warsaw Pact

KEY PEOPLE

George Kennan
George C. Marshall

KEY PLACES

West Germany
East Germany

"Only two great powers remained in the world, the United States and the Soviet Union. . . . And it was clear that the Soviet Union was aggressive and expanding. For the United States to take steps to strengthen countries threatened with Soviet aggression . . . was to protect not only the security of the United States—it was to protect freedom itself."

—Dean Acheson

This poster reflects the fear of the spread of communism.

One State Department official recalled Secretary of State Dean Acheson's reflections on the developing political standoff between the United States and the Soviet Union after World War II. As the war ended, the wartime alliance between the United States and the Soviet Union collapsed. At odds over competing global objectives and different economic and political systems, the two countries fought for control of Europe and control of atomic weapons.

The Roots of the Cold War

An intense rivalry between the United States and the Soviet Union began after World War II. With once-mighty Germany, Japan, and Great Britain in ruins, only the United States and the Soviet Union were left to struggle for international dominance. Their competition for global power and influence, which came to be known as the **Cold War**, was waged mostly on political and economic fronts rather than on the battlefield. Nonetheless, the threat of all-out war was always present.

The origins of the Cold War lay in economic, political, and philosophical differences between the two nations. Committed to the principles of democratic government, individual freedom, and a capitalist economy, most Americans deeply opposed the Soviet system. Founded on communist theories, the Soviet system had evolved to include a state-run economy, one-party rule, suppression of religion, and the use of force to crush opposition.

Dictator Joseph Stalin ruled the Soviet Union with an iron fist.

Soviet expansionism after World War II fueled American mistrust. During World War II the Soviets had taken over the Baltic states of Estonia, Latvia, and Lithuania. Then they captured large areas of Poland and Romania. By war's end the Soviets also controlled Manchuria. After the war, Soviet leader Joseph Stalin made clear his determination to maintain Soviet influence in Eastern Europe. He claimed the need for a buffer zone of "friendly nations" on the Soviet Union's western border. He installed pro-Soviet governments in Poland and Romania and worked to establish communist rule throughout Eastern Europe. These countries under Soviet control became known as **satellite nations**.

Concerned by Stalin's actions, Britain, France, and the United States strengthened their control of western Germany and revived

TEACH OBJECTIVE 1

LEVEL 1: Organize students into triads and have them create political cartoons with captions to explain the causes of the Cold War and U.S. strategy during the Cold War. *(Students should depict the major economic, political, and philosophical differences between the United States and the Soviet Union and the U.S. strategy of containment.)* Have each group present and explain its cartoons to the class.
Sheltered English, Cooperative Learning

LEVEL 2: Tell students to imagine that they are editing an encyclopedia. Have each student write a brief entry that discusses the causes of the Cold War and the U.S. strategy during the Cold War. *(See the Level 1 lesson for the correct causes and the U.S. strategy.)* Ask volunteers to read their entries to the class.

LEVEL 3: Tell students to imagine that they are history professors who must deliver brief lectures about the Cold War to their classes. Have each student prepare a lecture about the origins of the Cold War and the U.S. strategy during the Cold War. *(See the Level 1 lesson for the correct causes and the U.S. strategy.)* Have volunteers deliver their lectures to the class.

its industries. Winston Churchill, Britain's wartime prime minister, described this expansion of Soviet influence. Churchill declared that a Soviet "Iron Curtain has descended across the Continent," isolating Western Europe from Soviet-dominated Eastern Europe. Churchill called for closer cooperation between Britain and the United States to control Soviet power. At the time, George Kennan, a State Department official and Soviet expert, advised similar action. Kennan suggested a policy of **containment**, or restricting the expansion of Soviet communism. Many Americans applauded this tough stand against communism. Kennan explained his philosophy.

> **"The Soviet pressure against the free institutions of the Western world is something that can be contained by the . . . vigilant [determined] application of counterforce at a series of constantly shifting geographical and political points. . . . The Russians look forward to a duel of infinite duration."**

✔ **READING CHECK:** What caused the Cold War? What was the U.S. strategy during the Cold War?

***George Kennan's article on containment appeared in this issue of* Foreign Affairs.**

THAT'S INTERESTING!

The origins of the term *Cold War* are uncertain. Presidential adviser Bernard Baruch is sometimes credited with having first used it, during a congressional debate in 1947. That same year journalist Walter Lippmann published a study of U.S.-Soviet relations entitled *The Cold War*. Lippmann, however, claimed that the phrase had been used in the late 1930s to describe the tensions between Germany and France. Whatever its origin, the term has entered the world's political vocabulary.

Strategies for Success — Taking Notes

Taking notes—writing down information in a concise and orderly manner—is a basic practice that is particularly important for conducting a successful oral history interview. Taking notes allows you to clarify and organize the content of an interview and provides a valuable key for remembering and working with this content later.

How to Take Notes

1. **Select specific information.** Select specific information to include in your notes, concentrating on the main ideas and any strong opinions that your subject communicates in the interview. Take note of any particularly interesting examples or stories mentioned by your subject.
2. **Paraphrase the information.** Put the information in your own words, rather than trying to copy what your subject says exactly. Feel free to use shorthand terms and symbols, but make sure to write legibly so that you will understand your notes when you review them.
3. **Review the notes thoroughly.** Shortly after the interview has been completed, review your notes and add any important supplementary information that you may remember. If the interview was recorded, listen to the recording and make sure that your notes accurately represent what was said.

Applying the Strategy

Take notes on the following excerpt from an oral history provided by Erhard Dabringhaus, a former U.S. military intelligence officer who took part in the occupation of Germany after World War II. Dabringhaus was interviewed during the early 1980s.

> **"[In] 1948, a new directive came from [intelligence] headquarters. We're no longer interested as we used to be in former German Nazis. We're now interested in what's happening behind the East-West border. Communism becomes our most important interest. We're now looking for communists. We want to know about the newly organized government in France, after the war. How many Communists are in it?"**

Practicing the Strategy

Use the excerpt above to answer the following questions.

1. What is the general topic of the excerpt?
2. What ideas does Dabringhaus communicate in the excerpt?
3. What opinions does Dabringhaus express in the excerpt?

STRATEGIES FOR SUCCESS ANSWERS

Applying the Strategy
Students should concentrate on the change in headquarters's priorities.

Practicing the Strategy

1. anticommunist ideology in the U.S. military after World War II
2. idea that the focus of military intelligence switched from dealing with former Nazis to gathering information about Communists
3. reports the opinion of headquarters that focusing on Communists is more important than focusing on former Nazis

TEACH OBJECTIVE 2

LEVEL 1: Pair students and have each pair create a graphic organizer that summarizes the U.S. government's efforts to control the development of nuclear weapons. *(Students should mention and describe the Baruch Plan and the Atomic Energy Act.)* Have students present their graphic organizers to the class. Students may wish to include their organizers in their portfolios.

Sheltered English, Cooperative Learning

LEVELS 2 AND 3: Have each student create a cause-and-effect chart that describes the efforts of the U.S. government to try to control the development of atomic weapons. *(See the Level 1 lesson for the correct efforts.)* Then instruct students to write essays in which they suggest alternatives that might have prevented the nuclear arms race. Students may wish to include their charts and essays in their portfolios.

▶**ASSIGNMENT** *Have students design a public relations campaign to inform Americans in the mid-1940s about the U.S. government's efforts to control the development of atomic weapons.*

HISTORY MAKERS SPEAK

Robert Frost in *By the Bomb's Early Light*

International Controls and the Atomic Bomb. While many people were hopeful about U.S.-led attempts to place controls on atomic weapons, others—the Soviets in particular—suspected that such plans were designed to maintain a permanent U.S. monopoly on the bomb. In "U.S. 1946 King's X," American poet Robert Frost expressed his doubts about the motivation behind U.S. proposals:

Having invented a new
Holocaust,
And been the first with it to
win a war,
How they make haste to cry
with their fingers crossed,
King's X—no fairs to use it
any more!

CRITICAL THINKING How might the United States have made the nuclear-control agreement more acceptable to the Soviets?

ANSWER: Answers will vary. Students might suggest that the United States could have stopped building and testing nuclear weapons before proposing the agreement.

VISUAL RECORD ANSWER

Students might suggest that the size of the mushroom cloud shows how powerful atomic weapons are.

Deadlock over Atomic Weapons

After World War II the Soviet Union began to develop atomic technology. The United States and the Soviet Union soon became locked in a dispute over the issue. This standoff terrified many Americans, who feared the outbreak of nuclear war. Most people shared lawyer David E. Lilienthal's 1946 opinion that "the awful strength of atomic power . . . directly affects every man, woman, and child in the world."

INTERPRETING THE VISUAL RECORD

Atomic testing. A column of U.S. Army troops observes the testing of an atomic bomb in the Nevada desert in 1951. ***What do you think this photograph reveals about the power of atomic weapons?***

U.S. presidential adviser Bernard Baruch called for the creation of a special international agency with the authority to inspect any country's atomic-energy plants. This proposal, known as the **Baruch Plan**, would impose penalties on countries that did not follow international rules. Until such a plan was in place, Baruch said, the United States would not reveal any atomic-energy secrets or give up its atomic weapons. At the time, U.S. physicists were developing more-powerful nuclear weapons.

Working feverishly on its own bomb, the Soviet Union rejected all inspection and enforcement provisions. With neither country willing to compromise, hopes for international control of atomic energy died. When the Soviet Union tested its first atomic bomb in 1949, the feared nuclear arms race became a reality.

In response to fears of nuclear warfare, Congress passed the **Atomic Energy Act** in August 1946. The act created the civilian-controlled Atomic Energy Commission (AEC) to oversee nuclear weapons research and to promote peacetime uses of atomic energy.

✔ **READING CHECK:** How did the U.S. government try to control the development of atomic weapons?

Containment Around the World

As the Cold War continued, the Truman administration followed a more aggressive policy toward the Soviet Union. The U.S. containment policy was adopted in reaction to certain events in Greece. A civil war had broken out there in 1946. Communist-led rebels fought against the Greek monarchy, which relied on military and financial aid from Britain. In early 1947, however, Britain announced that it could no longer aid Greece. Without aid, Greece's pro-Western government could not defend itself from communist forces.

The Mediterranean. At the same time, the Soviet Union pressured Turkey to give up sole control of the Dardanelles. This narrow strait links the Black Sea and the Mediterranean. President Truman knew that control of this area would give the Soviets a dominant position in the eastern Mediterranean. In a speech to Congress, Truman stated, "It must be the policy of the United States to support free peoples who are resisting attempted subjugation [conquest] by armed minorities or by outside pressures."

TEACH OBJECTIVE 3

LEVELS 1 AND 2: Lead a class discussion about the problems that Europe faced after World War II and why Americans feared that these problems would make European nations more vulnerable to communist influence. *(Students might suggest that people in countries experiencing economic difficulties would be more amenable to communist influence.)* Then ask students to explain how the Marshall Plan helped contain the spread of communism in Europe. *(Students should explain that Marshall Plan aid stabilized European economies and led to European economic recovery.)* To conclude, lead a discussion about why economic welfare might be vital to the existence of democratic political institutions. **Sheltered English**

LEVEL 3: Have each student write an essay analyzing why George Marshall believed that the United States should provide aid to European countries after World War II and how this aid helped contain the spread of communism. *(See the Levels 1 and 2 lesson for the correct reasons.)* Students may wish to include their essays in their portfolios.

His statement became known as the **Truman Doctrine**. It made no mention of the Soviet Union, although clearly Truman had the Soviets in mind. In support of Truman's plan, Congress soon approved $400 million to aid Greece and Turkey.

Europe. After World War II, European economies were in shambles. In 1948 Germany produced just 45 percent of the goods it had produced before the war. The winter of 1946–47 brought the worst blizzards in some 50 years. Some Americans believed that the United States should help Europe. They feared that economic problems would make Western Europe more vulnerable to Communists' influence.

George C. Marshall

Secretary of State George C. Marshall shared this belief. Born in 1880 in Uniontown, Pennsylvania, Marshall was a very shy boy. In his first year at the Virginia Military Institute, he did poorly. Marshall developed his leadership skills and graduated near the top of his class.

Following his graduation in 1901, he pursued a career in the army. During World War I Marshall served under General John J. Pershing and helped develop military strategy. Franklin D. Roosevelt appointed Marshall army chief of staff in 1939.

After the war, Marshall served briefly as a U.S. representative to China before Truman appointed him secretary of state in 1947. Marshall gave a speech at Harvard University on June 5, 1947. He warned that if steps were not taken soon, Europe faced "economic, social, and political" collapse. He called for a major U.S. effort to promote European recovery. Its goal was "to permit the emergence of political and social conditions in which free institutions can exist." Marshall warned that any attempt to block recovery or to take advantage of Europe's difficulties for political ends would face strong U.S. opposition.

In response, Truman asked Congress for $17 billion in economic aid for Europe. Truman's request sparked heated debate. A turning point in the debate came early in 1948, when pro-Soviet Communists overthrew the government of Czechoslovakia. Congress soon funded the European Recovery Program, or **Marshall Plan**, in April 1948. For his efforts, Marshall won the Nobel Peace Prize in 1953.

Marshall resigned as secretary of state in 1949. The following year, Truman appointed him secretary of defense to prepare the U.S. armed forces for possible confrontations with communist forces. After 1951 Marshall became an adviser on defense and military matters. He died in Washington, D.C., in 1959.

✔ **READING CHECK:** How did the Marshall Plan help block the spread of communism?

Then and Now

Extending Economic Aid Abroad

With the Marshall Plan, the United States established a lasting standard. Through financial aid, the United States provided the resources for nations to rebuild industries and economic institutions after a crisis. The Marshall Plan supplied billions of dollars that were used to rebuild European factories, increase agricultural production, and restore roads and bridges. Many Americans believed that the aid would strengthen the postwar U.S. economy, as Europeans would eventually begin to buy American products.

Since the end of World War II, the United States has assisted many nations and maintained a great deal of influence throughout the world by extending economic aid abroad. In recent years, the U.S. government has helped several Latin American countries rebuild after devastating natural disasters. After Hurricane Mitch struck the coasts of Nicaragua and Honduras in 1998, the U.S. Congress passed the Emergency Supplemental Appropriations Bill. It provided some $950 million to aid countries affected by floods and mudslides. The funds were used to establish public health programs, rebuild devastated economies, and create plans for dealing with future disasters. The United States has also assisted Russia and other countries struggling with economic crises. Giving economic aid helps the U.S. economy by strengthening its trading partners worldwide.

Tipper Gore (right) visited Honduras after Hurricane Mitch struck in 1998.

GLOBAL RELATIONS

The Marshall Plan. Although the Marshall Plan was originally intended to provide economic aid to almost all European countries, the Soviet Union refused to participate. At an economic conference held in Paris soon after George Marshall's speech, Soviet foreign minister Vyacheslav Molotov derided the secretary of state's proposal as "nothing but a vicious American scheme for using dollars to buy its way" into European affairs. Ultimately, Soviet pressure prevented Czechoslovakia, Poland, Romania, and other Eastern European nations from taking part in the Marshall Plan.

ACTIVITY: Ask each student to conduct research on the ways that economic aid from the United States has been used in a specific country during the past 20 years. Then have students present short oral reports on their research to the class.

THAT'S INTERESTING!

George C. Marshall was sworn in as chief of staff of the U.S. Army on September 1, 1939—the same day that Germany started World War II by invading Poland. Under his guidance, U.S. forces grew from about 200,000 to 8.5 million soldiers, a feat that prompted Winston Churchill to call Marshall "the true organizer of victory" for the Allies.

TEACH OBJECTIVE 4

ALL LEVELS: Lead a class discussion about why the Western powers might have supported the creation of a West German government. *(Students might suggest that the Western powers wanted to create a cohesive political and economic unit that would ally itself with the Western Allies.)* To help students understand how the Western Allies tried to limit Soviet expansion, copy the following graphic organizer on the chalkboard, omitting the italicized answers. Have each student complete the organizer. Ask volunteers to share their answers with the class. **Sheltered English**

▶**ASSIGNMENT** *Tell students to imagine that they are residents of West Berlin during the Soviet blockade. Have each student write a poem about his or her reaction to the Berlin Airlift, and how the airlift might help contain Soviet expansion.*

THAT'S INTERESTING!

The Soviet blockade of West Berlin stranded approximately 2.5 million people with less than 45 days' worth of food, coal, and other supplies. During the airlift, U.S. and British pilots made more than 270,000 flights into West Berlin, with each plane carrying thousands of pounds of provisions. At peak times, a supply plane landed in the city every four minutes.

MAP ANSWER

Albania, Bulgaria, Czechoslovakia, East Germany, Hungary, Poland, Romania, the Soviet Union

VISUAL RECORD ANSWER

(for p. 543)

Students might mention that the need to guard the shared border signaled a rise in tensions in Berlin.

SECTION 2 REVIEW ANSWERS

Define and Identify

For significance, see the following pages:

- Cold War, p. 538
- satellite nations, p. 538
- George Kennan, p. 539
- containment, p. 539
- Baruch Plan, p. 540
- Atomic Energy Act, p. 540
- Truman Doctrine, p. 541
- George C. Marshall, p. 541
- Marshall Plan, p. 541
- Berlin Airlift, p. 542

The Marshall Plan helped Europe rebuild after World War II.

Crisis in Berlin

The non-Soviet zones of Germany grew stronger as a result of the Marshall Plan. In early June 1948 Britain, France, and the United States announced plans to combine their zones and support the formation of a West German government.

The Berlin Airlift. The Soviet Union opposed this action. On June 24, 1948, the Soviets suddenly blocked all roads, canals, and railways linking Berlin to western Germany. They cut off shipments of food, fuel, and other crucial supplies to the city. The Soviets hoped to drive the Western powers out of Berlin.

Western leaders responded to the Soviet move with the **Berlin Airlift**. Over the next 10 months, U.S. and British planes carried more than 2 million tons of food

REVIEW

Have students complete the **Section 2 Review** on p. 543.

ASSESS

Have students complete **Daily Quiz 18.2**. As **Alternative Assessment**, you may want to use the political cartoon or the lecture in this section's lessons.

RETEACH

Have students complete **Main Idea Activity for Reteaching and Sheltered English 18.2**. Then organize students into four groups and assign each group one of this section's objectives. Ask each group to create a fill-in-the-blank exam by writing a paragraph and leaving blanks for key words and phrases. Make copies of each group's exam and distribute them to other groups. Have students complete the exams.
Sheltered English, Cooperative Learning

EXTEND

Pair students and tell one student in each pair to imagine that he or she is a journalist. Tell the other student to imagine that he or she is a general from the Warsaw Pact or NATO alliance. Have students conduct research on either the NATO or Warsaw Pact alliance. Then have each pair incorporate its findings into a brief interview. Ask students to conduct their interviews for the class. **Cooperative Learning, Block Scheduling**

and supplies to the people of West Berlin. As one Berliner recalled, the airlift became the city's lifeline to the rest of the world.

> **"Early in the morning, when we woke up, the first thing we did was listen to see whether the noise of aircraft engines could be heard. That gave us the certainty that we were not alone, that the whole civilized world took part in the fight for Berlin's freedom."**

The success of the Berlin Airlift proved a huge embarrassment to the Soviet Union. In May 1949 the Soviets lifted the blockade. Soon after, the Federal Republic of Germany, known as West Germany, was founded. In response, the Soviets set up the German Democratic Republic—East Germany—in the Soviet zone. The division of Germany would last for more than 40 years.

The Western alliance. After the Berlin crisis, the United States shifted its attention in Europe from economic recovery to military security. In April 1949 nine Western European nations joined the United States, Canada, and Iceland in a military alliance called the North Atlantic Treaty Organization, or **NATO**. Under the terms of the NATO treaty, each member nation pledged to defend the others in the event of an outside attack.

In 1951 General Dwight D. Eisenhower became the supreme commander of NATO forces. As its contribution to NATO, the United States stationed troops in Europe and gave massive military aid to its European allies. The Soviet Union responded in 1955 by forming its own military alliance with other communist countries in Eastern Europe. This alliance came to be called the **Warsaw Pact**.

✔ **READING CHECK:** How did the Western Allies try to limit Soviet expansion?

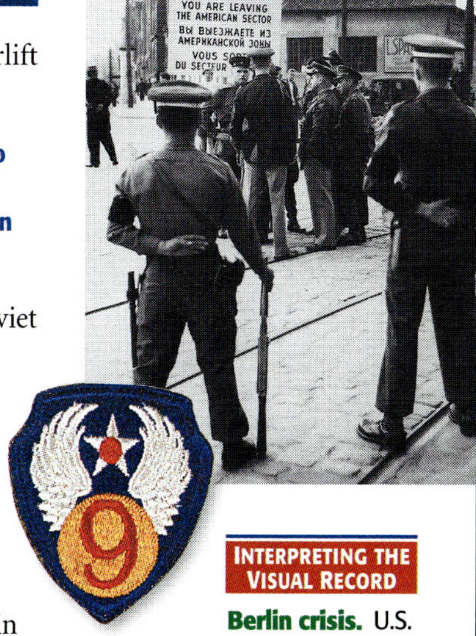

INTERPRETING THE VISUAL RECORD

Berlin crisis. U.S. military police in Berlin face their Soviet counterparts across the dividing line between the Allied and Soviet zones. ***How do the soldiers and the sign in this photograph reflect the growing tension in Berlin?***

SECTION 2 REVIEW

Define and explain the significance of the following terms:
Cold War
satellite nations
containment
Baruch Plan
Atomic Energy Act
Truman Doctrine
Marshall Plan
Berlin Airlift
NATO
Warsaw Pact

Identify and explain the significance of the following individuals:
George Kennan
George C. Marshall

Locate and explain the significance of the following places:
West Germany
East Germany

1. **Using Graphic Organizers** Copy the chart below. Use it to explain how differences between the Soviet Union and the United States led to the Cold War.

Differences in:	Soviet Union	United States
Economic Structure		
Views of Democracy		
Personal Freedom		
Goals for Expansion		

2. **Problem Solving** Imagine that you are working for the U.S. government in 1946. What measures would you propose to help curb the development of atomic weapons?
3. **Hypothesizing** What do you think would have happened if the United States had not implemented the Marshall Plan?
4. **Recognizing Point of View** Why did the Soviet Union view the formation of a West German state and NATO as a threat?

Critical Thinking

5. How was George Kennan's containment policy put into practice?
Consider:
- what the policy of containment was
- how the Marshall Plan fit into the containment strategy
- how NATO and the Berlin Airlift aided the containment strategy

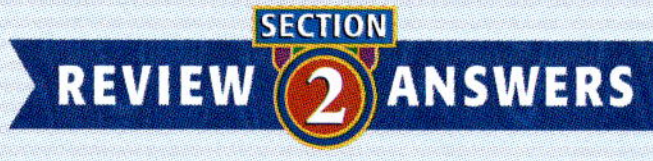

SECTION 2 REVIEW ANSWERS

- NATO, p. 543
- Warsaw Pact, p. 543

Locate
For locations, see the map on p. 542. For importance, see the following page:

- West Germany, p. 543
- East Germany, p. 543

1. economic structure—Soviet Union: communist, state-run economy; United States: capitalist, free-market economy; views of democracy—Soviet Union: one-party rule, suppression of political opposition; United States: democratic government; personal freedom—Soviet Union: suppression of religion and other freedoms; United States: committed to principles of individual freedom; goals for expansion—Soviet Union: establishment of satellite nations in Eastern Europe as "buffer"; United States: exertion of influence in Western Europe

2. Answers will vary. Students might suggest sharing of atomic knowledge between nations or the imposition of penalties.

3. Answers will vary. Students might contend that it would have resulted in political chaos and the expansion of communism in Europe.

4. because they helped revive Germany, helped maintain a strong U.S. political presence in Europe, and posed obstacles to Soviet expansion.

5. through U.S. policies such as the provision of economic aid to Turkey and Greece, the Marshall Plan, the Berlin Airlift, and the formation of NATO

SECTION 3

After completing Section 3, students should be able to:

OBJECTIVE 1 *Explain how the Chinese Communists gained control of China.*

OBJECTIVE 2 *Trace the factors that led to the escalation of the conflict in Korea.*

OBJECTIVE 3 *Describe the effect the Korean War had on U.S. politics.*

OBJECTIVE 4 *Discuss the methods that President Eisenhower used to promote U.S. interests abroad.*

LET'S GET STARTED!

As students enter the classroom, tell them to study the map of North and South Korea in this section and to consider the distance from those countries to the United States. Ask each student to list reasons for and against U.S. involvement in a war in such a distant place. Ask volunteers to share their answers, and compile a list of students' answers on the chalkboard. Tell students that in Section 3 they will learn how Americans fought communism overseas under the leadership of Presidents Truman and Eisenhower.

SECTION 3 RESOURCES

PRINT

- Guided Reading Strategy 18.3
- American History Political Cartoon 26: Brinksmanship
- Section 3 Review, p. 550
- Daily Quiz 18.3

MULTIMEDIA

- One-Stop Planner, Lesson 18.3
- The American Nation Video Program Segment: MacArthur in Korea; Teacher's Guide, pp. 193–94
- Holt Researcher: American History CD–ROM

SHELTERED ENGLISH

- Main Idea Activity for Reteaching and Sheltered English 18.3

✔ READING TO UNDERSTAND

To help students master the section objectives, have them answer the **READING CHECKS** and complete **Guided Reading Strategy 18.3** as they read the section.

VISUAL RECORD ANSWER

(for p. 545)

Students might note the rough terrain and heavy equipment.

The Cold War Turns Hot

OBJECTIVES

Read to understand:

1. how the Chinese Communists gained control of China
2. what factors led to the escalation of the conflict in Korea
3. what effect the Korean War had on U.S. politics
4. what methods President Eisenhower used to promote U.S. interests abroad

KEY TERMS

Korean War
brinkmanship
Central Intelligence Agency
U-2 incident

KEY PEOPLE

Chiang Kai-shek
Mao Zedong
Kim Il Sung
Syngman Rhee
Douglas MacArthur
Dwight D. Eisenhower
Nikita Khrushchev

KEY PLACES

North Korea
South Korea
Inch'ŏn
Seoul

“The responsibility for the failure of our foreign policy in the Far East rests squarely with the White House and the Department of State. . . . Our diplomats and their advisers . . . lost sight of our tremendous stake in a non-Communist China. . . . This House must now assume the responsibility of preventing the onrushing tide of communism from engulfing all of Asia.”

—John F. Kennedy

Chinese Communist troops enter Shanghai

U.S. representative John F. Kennedy of Massachusetts expressed his disappointment that Communists in China had taken over the city of Beijing in 1949. Like most Americans, Kennedy feared that a Communist victory in China would allow communism to spread throughout Asia.

Communist Victory in China

Tensions over the spread of communism came to a head in China. In the early 1900s, revolutionary forces had attempted to overthrow the Qing imperial dynasty. The revolution of 1911 left China an unstable republic. Upset with how the republic was run and inspired by the Bolshevik Revolution, a number of Chinese students established the Chinese Communist Party. By the mid-1920s a civil war had erupted between Nationalist and Communist forces. Led by Chiang Kai-shek, the Kuomintang (KWOH-min-TANG), or Nationalist Party, battled the Chinese Communists. Chiang's war with the Communists kept him from devoting his full attention to Japanese aggression. During World War II, the Communists and the Nationalists cooperated to resist Japanese attacks.

At war's end, however, the conflict resumed. The Communists had prevented the Japanese from controlling all of northwest China. There Communist leader Mao Zedong made reforms that gave land to peasants. This and their fight against the Japanese won additional support for the Communists and increased recruits for their army.

The United States did not want China to become a communist country. During and after World War II, the United States sent economic and military aid, including troops, to China to unite the country under the Nationalists. President Truman sent General George C. Marshall to China in 1945 to arrange a truce between the warring parties, but neither Chiang nor Mao would compromise.

Opposition to Chiang mounted, and Mao's forces gained control of most of the country by 1949. Realizing defeat, Chiang and his army retreated to the island of Taiwan, off the coast of southeast China. The Chinese Communists established the People's Republic of China. The United States rejected this new government, however, and continued to recognize the Nationalists as China's legal government.

✔ READING CHECK: How did the Chinese Communists gain control of China?

TEACH OBJECTIVE 1

ALL LEVELS: To help students understand how Chinese Communists gained control of China, copy the following graphic organizer on the chalkboard, omitting the italicized answers. Have each student complete it. Ask volunteers to share their answers with the class. Then ask students whether the Chinese Communists led a revolution that had popular support. *(Students might suggest that the Communists' resistance against the Japanese, coupled with land reforms, won the Communists' popular support.)* To conclude, lead a class discussion about whether the United States has the right to oppose a revolution that is supported by the majority of a country's residents. **Sheltered English**

CHINESE COMMUNISTS GAIN CONTROL OF CHINA

unstable republic established in 1911
↓
civil war between Nationalist and Communist forces
↓
Nationalists and Communists cooperation to resist Japanese
↓
most of China under Mao's control by 1949; retreat of Chiang's forces to Taiwan
↓
establishment of People's Republic of China

The Korean War Begins

During the 1940s political tensions were also increasing in Korea, a peninsula jutting southward from the northeast corner of China. The Japanese had ruled Korea from 1910 to 1945 but had been driven out by Soviet and U.S. troops at the end of World War II. In 1945 the Allies divided Korea into two zones. Soviet forces occupied the northern zone, and U.S. troops held the southern zone.

A divided Korea. The division was meant to be temporary, but Cold War tensions cemented it. In 1948 North Korea and South Korea set up separate governments. Communist North Korea, led by Kim Il Sung, became known as the Democratic People's Republic of Korea. South Korea, under President Syngman Rhee (SING-muhn REE), called itself the Republic of Korea.

The United States did not want economically unstable South Korea to fall to the Communists. The U.S. government built up the South Korean army. By 1949 both the United States and the Soviet Union had pulled their troops out of Korea. The pullout left the two Korean armies facing each other tensely across the border at the 38th parallel.

After repeated clashes between North Korean and South Korean troops, North Korea invaded South Korea on June 25, 1950. In an emergency session, the UN Security Council called for an immediate cease-fire. At the time the Soviet Union was boycotting the Security Council over its refusal to admit Communist China. Therefore the Soviet delegate was not on hand to veto the UN resolution. On June 27, President Truman pledged U.S. support for South Korea. That same day, the Security Council adopted a U.S.-sponsored resolution branding North Korea an "aggressor" and calling on UN members to come to South Korea's defense. Truman later explained, "I felt certain that if South Korea was allowed to fall, Communist leaders would be emboldened [encouraged] to override nations closer to our own shores."

INTERPRETING THE VISUAL RECORD

The Korean War. Composed primarily of U.S. troops, UN forces scaled Korea's mountainous landscape to advance against Communist forces. Many U.S. soldiers received the Korean service medal shown. ***Based on this photograph, what difficulties do you think U.S. soldiers faced during the conflict?***

Bitter fighting. Truman ordered U.S. forces into action under the command of General Douglas MacArthur. Truman also ordered the U.S. Seventh Fleet to protect Taiwan. Although 15 other UN members contributed monetary and military support, the United States and South Korea played the major role in the **Korean War**. At first the attack by North Korean forces with their Soviet-made weapons was overwhelming. Outgunned and outmanned, the U.S. and South Korean troops fell back. One soldier, Sergeant Raymond Remp, recalled his first encounter with the North Korean army.

> **"Someone fired a green flare, and [the enemy] saw us. . . . They were right on top of us . . . firing down on us. . . . Some colonel—don't know who—said, 'Get out the best way you can.' . . . All day and night we ran like antelopes. We didn't know our officers. They didn't know us. We lost everything we had."**

By September the North Koreans had overrun nearly all of South Korea. The U.S. and South Korean forces were backed into an area around the port city of Pusan.

PEOPLE IN HISTORY

Syngman Rhee and Kim Il Sung. Syngman Rhee was in his seventies when he became president of South Korea. He was a strong anticommunist and advocate of Korean independence, Rhee had spent more than 30 years in the United States as a political exile. Kim Il Sung was in his mid-thirties when he became premier of communist North Korea. As a guerrilla fighter in the 1930s, he had opposed the Japanese occupation of Korea. Kim had received training in the Soviet Union and was the leader of a special Korean unit of the Soviet army in World War II.

CRITICAL THINKING How might the goals of Syngman and Kim have been similar?

ANSWER: Students might suggest that each wanted to lead a reunited Korea.

The American Nation
VIDEO PROGRAM

MacArthur in Korea;
Teacher's Guide, pp. 193–94

Search 46063, Play to 48003
Videodisc 2, Side A

Play Pause

See *Teacher's Guide* for Spanish barcode.

TEACH OBJECTIVE 2

LEVEL 1: Pair students and have them create annotated time lines showing the events leading to the escalation of the conflict in Korea. *(Time lines should include: 1945—Allies divide Korea into two zones; 1948—North and South Korea set up separate governments; 1949—the United States and the Soviet Union pull their troops out of Korea; 1949–50—North and South Korean armies face off at the 38th parallel and engage in repeated clashes; June 1950—North Korea invades South Korea, the UN Security Council brands North Korea an "aggressor," and Truman pledges U.S. support for South Korea.)* To conclude, read to students President Truman's quotation on the previous page and Jou En-lai's quotation on this page. Ask students what these statements reveal about why the United States and China increased their involvement in the Korean conflict. *(Students might suggest that the United States was motivated by a concern about the worldwide spread of communism, while the Chinese were concerned that anticommunist sentiments would lead the United States to invade China.)* **Sheltered English, Cooperative Learning**

HISTORY MAKERS SPEAK

Leonard Korgie in *The Korean War*

China's Entry into the Korean War. China's intervention in the Korean War came as an unpleasant surprise to many U.S. troops. Leonard Korgie was a U.S. Army private in North Korea in late 1950. He recalled the effect that China's entry had on his infantry unit: "We slept soundly that night in a dry, cozy, well-built schoolhouse. Next morning we received hot chow—pancakes and coffee. Heck, North Korea was all right. Things were definitely looking up. . . . [Then,] around 9:00 in the morning, we were ordered to saddle up, we were moving again. This time it would be south! . . . We'd have to move fast or we stood a chance of being cut off. The Chinese were in North Korea in force."

ACTIVITY: Ask students if they agree with President Truman's decision to involve U.S. forces in the Korean War. Then conduct a follow-up discussion.

MAP ANSWER
well into North Korea, north of the 41st parallel

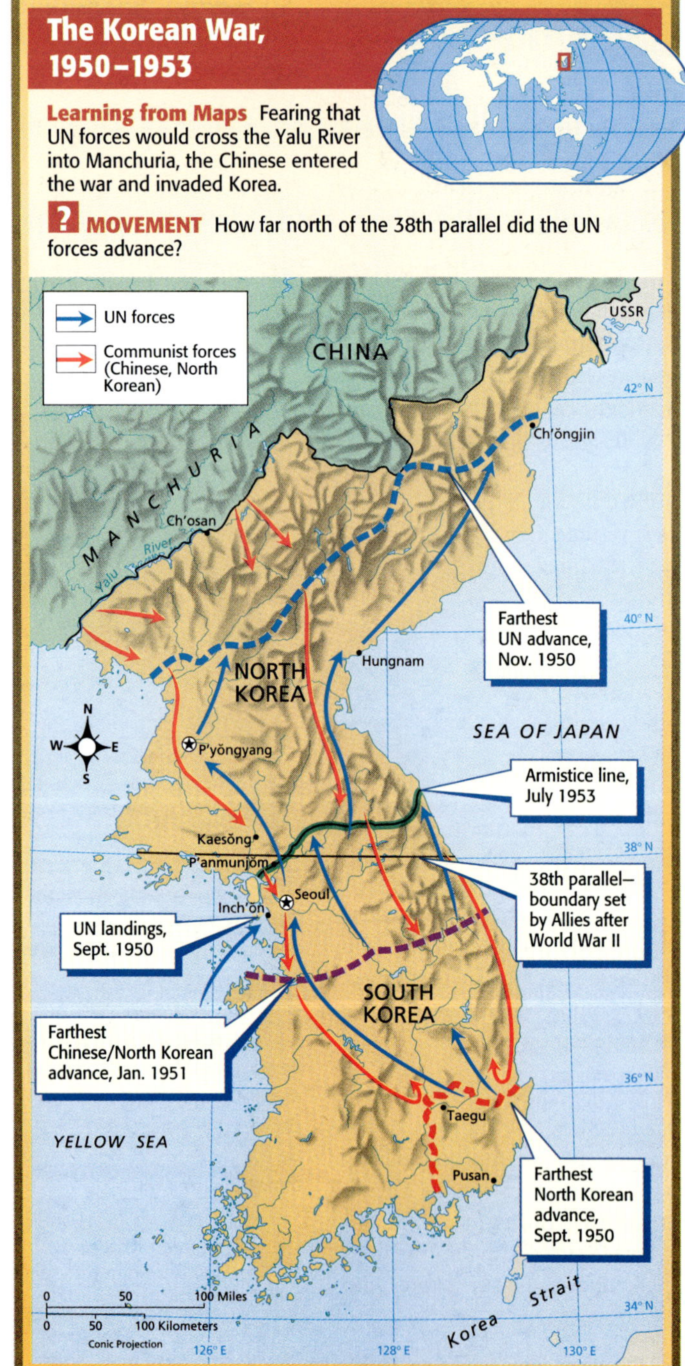

Learning from Maps Fearing that UN forces would cross the Yalu River into Manchuria, the Chinese entered the war and invaded Korea.

MOVEMENT How far north of the 38th parallel did the UN forces advance?

On September 15, 1950, MacArthur launched a powerful counterattack. Coming ashore at Inch'ŏn, MacArthur's forces swept inland and recaptured Seoul (SOHL), South Korea's capital. At the same time, a well-equipped UN army attacked from the south. North Koreans surrendered by the thousands. Others fled north across the 38th parallel with UN forces in hot pursuit. By late October the UN army was approaching the Yalu River, the boundary between North Korea and China.

The tide soon turned again. Late in November, China entered the war on North Korea's side, sending some 300,000 troops across the Yalu. Chinese foreign minister Jou En-lai (JOH EN-LY) explained why China had intervened.

> **"The U.S. imperialists have adopted a hostile attitude towards us . . . while paying lip service to nonaggression and nonintervention. From the information we got, they wanted to calm China first and after occupying North Korea, they will come to attack China."**

Outnumbered and with their troops stretched dangerously thin, the UN forces fell back. After desperate fighting and heavy losses in the winter cold, MacArthur's troops finally established a defensive line near the 38th parallel.

✔ **READING CHECK:** What factors led to the escalation of the conflict in Korea?

Ending the Korean War

With China now involved, General MacArthur called for a major expansion of the war. He proposed to blockade China's coast, bomb the Chinese mainland, and "unleash" Chiang's Nationalist forces to invade mainland China. The plan sparked fierce debate. Supporters said it would bring victory in Korea and overthrow the Chinese Communists. Opponents argued that an attack on China could bring the Soviet Union into the conflict.

LEVELS 2 AND 3: Ask students to recount the events that led to the escalation of the conflict in Korea. *(See the Level 1 lesson for the correct events.)* Tell students to read President Truman's and Jou Enlai's quotations in this section. Have each student write an essay analyzing what these statements reveal about why the United States and China escalated the Korean conflict. *(See the Level 1 lesson for the correct factors.)* Ask volunteers to read their essays to the class.

Teacher to Teacher

Jenifer Rowray of Runnells, Iowa, suggested the following activity: Write the following phrase on the chalkboard: the forgotten war. *Ask students how this phrase describes the Korean War. Write students' responses on the chalkboard and conduct a discussion about the place of the Korean War in American historical memory.*

Conflict between Truman and MacArthur. President Truman strongly opposed MacArthur's plan. He did not want the war in Korea to lead to another world war. MacArthur, however, refused to accept the Korean War as a limited conflict. Publicly criticizing the president, MacArthur appealed to Republican leaders in Congress. He also delivered an ultimatum to the enemy in which he demanded unconditional surrender. The demand upset Truman's plans for peace negotiations. As commander in chief of the military, Truman removed the general from his post in April 1951. Many Americans opposed this move and gave MacArthur a hero's welcome upon his return to the United States. Americans spoke out against Truman's actions, booing the president during his public appearances.

By the summer of 1951 the war had settled into a stalemate. Bitter fighting continued, but little territory changed hands. Combat in Korea's mountainous terrain became frustrating as the American death toll mounted. The conflict became a major issue in the 1952 presidential election.

Read More About It

Free Find:
Douglas MacArthur
After reading about Douglas MacArthur on the **Holt Researcher** CD–ROM, write a short essay that hypothesizes how MacArthur's military experiences could have led him to develop his aggressive strategy for the Korean conflict.

The election of 1952. As 1952 began, President Truman found himself confronted with a series of problems. The Korean War had come to a bloody stalemate, and peace talks were making little progress. With his popularity at an all-time low, Truman decided not to run for re-election. Republicans saw their chance to break the Democrats' 20-year hold on the White House. They chose popular World War II hero General Dwight D. Eisenhower as their presidential candidate. Conservative senator Richard M. Nixon of California served as his running mate.

The Democrats selected Governor Adlai Stevenson of Illinois as their candidate and John Sparkman as his running mate. Stevenson defended Truman's foreign and domestic policies. However, many voters saw him as an intellectual who was out of touch with the common people. Some jokingly referred to Stevenson as an "egghead"—"someone with more brains than hair."

Stevenson also could not match Eisenhower's patriotic appeal. Eisenhower's warmth, vitality, and self-confidence reassured voters that the United States would remain strong throughout the Cold War. His upbeat campaign slogan "I Like Ike" reflected his popularity. Eisenhower promised to resist communism and to end the Korean War. A triumphant Eisenhower received 55 percent of the popular vote and swept the electoral vote 442 to 89.

The war ends. The new president kept his promise to end the war. Eisenhower used military force to get peace negotiations moving. He stepped up bombing raids on North Korea in May 1953 and dropped hints that he would use nuclear weapons, if necessary, to end the conflict.

On July 27, 1953, negotiators agreed to an armistice. Korea was divided into two nations roughly at the 38th parallel—the same dividing line as before the war. Some Americans questioned whether this outcome justified U.S. losses—some 54,000 dead and 103,000 wounded. More than 1.5 million Koreans and Chinese had also died.

✔ **READING CHECK:** What effect did the Korean War have on U.S. politics?

INTERPRETING THE VISUAL RECORD

Eisenhower. Presidential candidate Dwight Eisenhower campaigns in Manhasset, New York, in 1952. ***What signs of Eisenhower's popularity can you see in this picture?***

PEOPLE IN HISTORY

Adlai Stevenson. Adlai Stevenson began a career of public service as a lawyer in Chicago. He became a strong advocate of social institutions such as Hull House and the Immigrants' Protective League. In 1945 Stevenson was part of the U.S. delegation to the San Francisco conference that founded the United Nations. Three years later, he was elected governor of Illinois. He worked to increase state aid to public schools and to improve the care of patients in state mental hospitals. Following a second failed bid for the presidency in 1956, Stevenson served as the chief U.S. ambassador to the United Nations under Presidents Kennedy and Johnson.

CRITICAL THINKING Why might Stevenson's attempts to improve schools and the care of mental patients not have resulted in victory in presidential elections?

ANSWER: Answers will vary. Students might suggest that he did not publicize these efforts or that American voters were more concerned about national defense.

VISUAL RECORD ANSWER

Students might mention the size of the crowd and people's closeness to Eisenhower's car.

TEACH OBJECTIVE 3

LEVEL 1: Lead students in a discussion about the effect the Korean War had on U.S. politics. *(Students should note that MacArthur's removal and the rising number of casualties in Korea made Truman and the Democrats unpopular, while Eisenhower's World War II war record, patriotic appeal, and promise to end the Korean War made him an extremely popular candidate.)* Then pair students and have them create campaign slogans—both for Stevenson and for Eisenhower—that focus on the Korean War. **Sheltered English, Cooperative Learning**

LEVELS 2 AND 3: Tell students to imagine that they are television news commentators on the eve of the 1952 elections. Organize students into triads and have each triad create a script for a television news discussion about the potential effect of the Korean War on U.S. politics. *(See the Level 1 lesson for the correct effect.)* Have each triad conduct its discussion for the class. **Cooperative Learning**

GLOBAL RELATIONS

Nonalignment. Some political leaders resisted pressures to ally with either the Soviet Union or the United States. Jawaharlal Nehru, who served as India's prime minister from 1947 to 1964, decided to distance his country from the Cold War as much as possible. Nehru initiated a foreign policy of nonalignment, or a refusal to take sides with either the United States or the Soviet Union. A growing number of countries, particularly in Asia and Africa, declared their own nonalignment policies during the late 1950s and the 1960s.

CRITICAL THINKING How might a policy of nonalignment have benefited some nations economically during the Cold War?

ANSWER: Students might suggest that it enabled some nations to receive economic aid from both the United States and the Soviet Union during the Cold War.

Dwight D. Eisenhower

1890–1969
In Office 1953–1961

After graduating from the U.S. Military Academy at West Point in the lower half of his class, Dwight D. Eisenhower began his army career slowly. When the United States entered World War I, he hoped to be put in command of a tank battalion. Although he was scheduled to command a tank unit in the spring of 1919, the Germans surrendered before Eisenhower saw any action. Eisenhower went on to graduate from command and general staff school at the top of his class. He rose quickly in rank.

Eisenhower incorporated other people's expertise into the decisions he made. This contributed greatly to his many successes as a World War II general and as president. "No man can be a Napoleon in modern war," the president once said. "I don't believe this government was set up to be operated by anyone acting alone." Discussing the power of the presidency, Eisenhower told friends, "Some people think there is a lot of power and glory attached to the job. On the contrary, the very workings of a democratic system see to it that the job has very little power."

Fighting Communism Abroad

The Eisenhower administration viewed nuclear arms and technology as crucial to ending the expansion of communism. Secretary of State John Foster Dulles called for the liberation of all nations that had fallen under Soviet control since 1945. To fulfill this goal, the United States would have to confront Communist aggression and not back down—even if that meant going all the way to the brink of war. "The ability to get to the verge [brink] without getting into war is the necessary art," Dulles said. This policy of **brinkmanship** rested on the threat of massive retaliation, including the use of nuclear weapons.

Eisenhower proved less confrontational than Dulles's policy might have suggested. Instead, he pursued U.S. goals with more covert, or secret, means and through diplomacy. He used the newly created **Central Intelligence Agency** (CIA) to gather strategic information and forward his Cold War goals.

Covert war and the CIA. Eisenhower tested his covert approach to the Cold War in Iran. Shortly after coming to power in 1951, Iranian premier Mohammad Mosaddeq (MAWS-ad-dek) nationalized British-owned oil fields in Iran. After Eisenhower took office he suspended aid to Iran. Eisenhower also authorized a covert action by the CIA to organize a military coup against the Iranian leader. The plan succeeded. Mosaddeq was arrested and replaced with the young pro-American shah of Iran, Mohammad Reza Pahlavi (RAY-zah pah-HLAHV-ee). Although Eisenhower achieved his goal of removing Mosaddeq, this interference in Iranian affairs provoked anti-American feelings in that country.

In 1954 Eisenhower ordered a covert action in Guatemala. That year the democratically elected Guatemalan president, Jacobo Arbenz Guzmán, took possession of uncultivated sections of Guatemala's largest plantations to redistribute among the rural poor.

Suspecting Arbenz of being sympathetic to communism, Eisenhower called on the CIA to gather a small army to oust him. The CIA-led forces bombed the capital in June 1954 and installed a new pro-U.S. government, which quickly reversed Arbenz's reform program. U.S. intervention in Guatemala stirred up bitter resentment throughout Latin America.

These Iranians are demonstrating to show their support for the return of the shah, Mohammad Reza Pahlavi.

TEACH OBJECTIVE 4

LEVEL 1: Pair students and have them draw political cartoons with written captions about the methods that President Eisenhower used to promote U.S. interests abroad. *(Students should depict Eisenhower using covert means—as he did in Guatemala and Iran—and diplomatic means—as he did when he issued the Eisenhower Doctrine and when he refused to support Hungarian rebels.)* Display students' cartoons around the classroom. **Sheltered English, Cooperative Learning**

LEVEL 2: Tell students to imagine that they are writing books about U.S. foreign policy during the Eisenhower administration. Ask each student to write a detailed outline for a chapter about the various methods that Eisenhower used to promote U.S. interests abroad. *(See the Level 1 lesson for the correct methods.)* Ask volunteers to share their outlines with the class.

LEVEL 3: Have each student write a song about the methods that President Eisenhower used to promote U.S. interests abroad. *(See the Level 1 lesson for the correct methods.)* Ask volunteers to read or perform their songs for the class. Students may wish to include their songs in their portfolios.

▶**ASSIGNMENT** *Distribute Cartoon 26, Brinksmanship, from **American History Political Cartoons**. Have each student study the cartoon and complete the accompanying lessons.*

The Suez crisis. In some cases, Eisenhower used diplomacy rather than covert actions to influence foreign policy. In 1955, after the U.S. government withdrew an offer to finance a large dam in Egypt, Egyptian leader Gamal Abdel Nasser nationalized the Suez Canal. This presented many political problems, including a threat to the Western oil trade. Egypt also refused to allow ships bound for Israel to pass through the canal. Late in October 1956, Israel launched an attack into Egyptian territory toward the Suez Canal. Britain and France seized the Mediterranean end of the waterway a few days later. The Soviet Union threatened war if the three nations did not withdraw from Egypt at once.

Eisenhower supported a UN resolution that called for an immediate cease-fire and the withdrawal of the invading troops. Grudgingly, Britain, France, and Israel withdrew their forces, and the crisis eased. The Soviet Union's support of Egypt during the Suez crisis led to a friendlier relationship between the Soviet Union and Arab nations. Seeking to counter Soviet influence in the Middle East, the president issued the Eisenhower Doctrine in January 1957. Eisenhower offered military aid to any Middle Eastern nation seeking help in resisting communist aggression.

The Nuclear Threat, 1955–1960

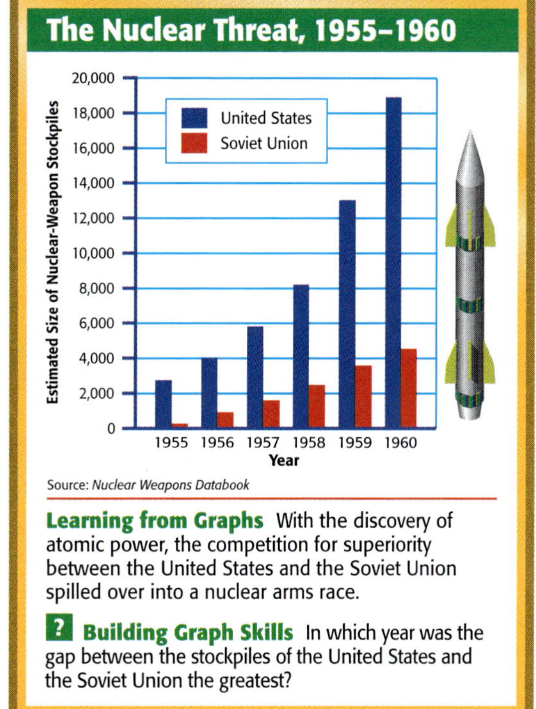

Source: *Nuclear Weapons Databook*

Learning from Graphs With the discovery of atomic power, the competition for superiority between the United States and the Soviet Union spilled over into a nuclear arms race.

? Building Graph Skills In which year was the gap between the stockpiles of the United States and the Soviet Union the greatest?

Uprising in Eastern Europe. While the Suez crisis unfolded, an equally dangerous situation was developing in Eastern Europe. In February 1956 Soviet leader Nikita Khrushchev (KROOSH-chawf) stunned political observers by publicly accusing his predecessor, Joseph Stalin—who had died in 1953—of having committed many ruthless crimes. Observers hoped that this move signaled a new era of reform in the Soviet Union and Eastern Europe. Later in 1956, Polish reformers tested Khrushchev by calling for greater political freedom.

Inspired by Poland's boldness, thousands of Hungarians took to the streets in late October to demand reform. Moderates seized control of the government and called for a Western-style democracy and for Hungary's secession from the Warsaw Pact. Khrushchev responded with swift force. On November 4, heavily armed Soviet troops moved into Budapest, the Hungarian capital, and crushed the revolt within days. A new pro-Soviet government imposed martial law and executed or imprisoned the rebel leaders.

Throughout their struggle, the Hungarian rebels pleaded for help from the West. Eisenhower worried, however, that U.S. intervention in Eastern Europe would lead to all-out nuclear war with the Soviet Union. He condemned the Soviets' actions but refused to aid the rebels. He did help ease immigration laws to allow more Eastern European refugees into the United States, however. As a result, some 40,000 Hungarians fled to the United States after the uprising.

To some observers, Eisenhower's lack of support for the Hungarian uprising indicated a retreat from Dulles's talk of liberating Communist-controlled countries. However, most of the American public supported Eisenhower, whom they reelected by a landslide against Adlai Stevenson in November 1956.

INTERPRETING THE VISUAL RECORD

Hungarian rebels. In October 1956, Hungarians took to the streets to protest Soviet control of their country. ***How does this photograph reflect the Hungarians' desire to be free of Soviet control?***

THAT'S INTERESTING!

Iranian premier Mohammad Mosaddeq was known as an unusual and flamboyant leader. He made public appearances in his pajamas, delivered speeches to Iran's parliament from his bed, and wept in public frequently. Some commentators speculated that his strange behavior was caused by an illness. Others claimed that it was simply a way to gain attention.

GRAPH ANSWER

1960

VISUAL RECORD ANSWER

Students might mention the flag or the people standing on the tank.

SECTION 3 REVIEW ANSWERS

Define and Identify

For significance, see the following pages:

- Chiang Kai-shek, p. 544
- Mao Zedong, p. 544
- Kim Il Sung, p. 545
- Syngman Rhee, p. 545
- Douglas MacArthur, p. 545
- Korean War, p. 545
- Dwight D. Eisenhower, p. 547
- brinkmanship, p. 548
- Central Intelligence Agency, p. 548
- Nikita Khrushchev, p. 549
- U-2 incident, p. 550

REVIEW

Have students complete the **Section 3 Review** on p. 550.

ASSESS

Have students complete **Daily Quiz 18.3.** As **Alternative Assessment**, you may want to use the political cartoon or the television script in this section's lessons.

RETEACH

Have students complete **Main Idea Activity for Reteaching and Sheltered English 18.3.** Then organize students into four groups. Have each group write sentences to identify each of the key terms, key people, and key places for Section 3. Collect groups' sentences and use them to quiz the class.
Sheltered English, Cooperative Learning

EXTEND

Have students conduct further research on the political and constitutional issues involved in the conflict between President Truman and General MacArthur over the escalation of the war in Korea. Have each student write an analytical essay based on his or her research. **Block Scheduling**

Locate
For locations, see the map on p. 546. For importance, see the following pages:

- North Korea, p. 545
- South Korea, p. 545
- Inch'ŏn, p. 546
- Seoul, p. 546

1. China—gave economic and military aid to Nationalists, recognized the Nationalist government in Taiwan; Korea—gave military aid to South Korea, participated in Korean War; Guatemala—sponsored forces that overthrew Guatemala's suspected pro-communist government; Egypt—issued Eisenhower Doctrine

2. detracted from President Truman's popularity and played a major role in the 1952 presidential election

3. Answers will vary. Students might suggest that it would have resulted in the overthrow of China's government, or they might contend that it would have led to a long war between the United States and China.

4. effective—established pro-U.S. governments in Iran and Guatemala, helped end the Korean War and the Suez crisis; new problems—stirred up anti-American feelings in Iran and Latin America, ineffective strategy when Soviets invaded Hungary

5. caused many Americans to worry that communism would continue to spread throughout Asia, and thus encouraged U.S. participation in the Korean War

Soviet leader Nikita Khrushchev (center) studies a chicken for photographers during his goodwill tour of the United States.

A Brief Thaw in the Cold War

Near the end of the decade, the United States and the Soviet Union moved to improve their diplomatic relations. In 1959 Vice President Richard M. Nixon visited the Soviet Union, and Premier Khrushchev then came to the United States. Touring Iowa farms, Pittsburgh steel plants, and Hollywood movie studios, the jovial Khrushchev charmed the American media. He and Eisenhower agreed to meet at a summit conference in Paris the following year to discuss arms reductions.

In May 1960, however, just before the summit was to begin, Khrushchev announced that an American U-2—a high-altitude spy plane—had been shot down over the Soviet Union. At first U.S. officials insisted that it was a weather-research plane that had strayed off course. However, the captured pilot, Francis Gary Powers, admitted he had been on a spying mission.

Khrushchev refused to proceed with the summit unless the United States halted such spying missions and apologized for past flights. Eisenhower promised that the U-2 flights would stop, but he did not apologize. Khrushchev refused to meet with Eisenhower again. The **U-2 incident** caused the brief thaw in the Cold War to come to an abrupt end.

✔ **READING CHECK:** What methods did President Eisenhower use to promote U.S. interests abroad?

SECTION 3 REVIEW

Define and explain the significance of the following terms:
Korean War
brinkmanship
Central Intelligence Agency
U-2 incident

Identify and explain the significance of the following individuals:
Chiang Kai-shek
Mao Zedong
Kim Il Sung
Syngman Rhee
Douglas MacArthur
Dwight D. Eisenhower
Nikita Khrushchev

Locate and explain the significance of the following places:
North Korea
South Korea
Inch'ŏn
Seoul

1. **Using Graphic Organizers** Copy the graphic organizer below. Use it to explain how the United States attempted to slow the spread of communism.

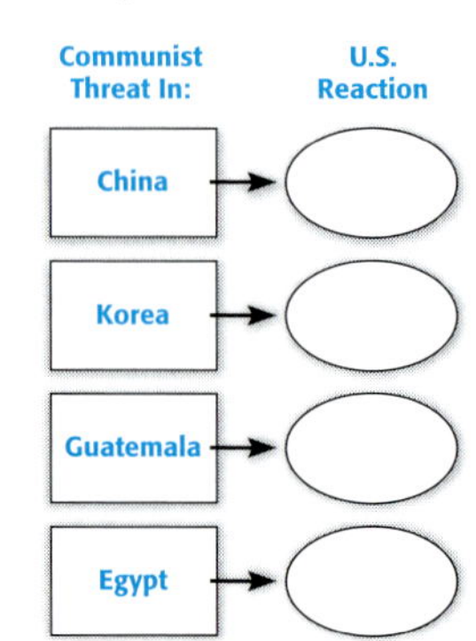

2. **Evaluating** What impact did conflicts in Asia have on politics in the United States?
3. **Hypothesizing** How do you think the Korean War would have proceeded if General MacArthur had been allowed to expand the war into China?
4. **Assessing Consequences** In what ways were President Eisenhower's covert operations and diplomatic strategies effective? What new problems did they present?

Critical Thinking

5. How did the fall of China to the Communists encourage further U.S. military action in Korea?
Consider:
   - how the fall of China to the Communists related to U.S. containment policy
   - how the containment policy influenced U.S. actions in Korea
   - what role Communist China played in the Korean War

After completing Section 4, students should be able to:

OBJECTIVE 1 *Discuss the actions the U.S. government took to limit communism at home, and describe how these actions affected Americans' everyday lives.*

OBJECTIVE 2 *Explain how Senator Joseph McCarthy was able to play upon Americans' fears of communism.*

OBJECTIVE 3 *Describe how Americans reacted to the prospect of nuclear war.*

LET'S GET STARTED!

Write the following scenario on the chalkboard: *Imagine that your school has decided that any student who questions school policy is a negative influence. The principal has decided to question all students suspected of disagreeing with school policy. How would you feel about such a situation? How would this affect school morale?* As students enter the classroom, ask them to respond to the scenario in writing. Ask volunteers to share their responses with the class. Tell students that in Section 4 they will learn about how Cold War fears affected Americans' everyday lives.

The Cold War at Home

OBJECTIVES

Read to understand:

1. what actions the U.S. government took to limit communism at home, and how these actions affected Americans' everyday lives
2. how Senator Joseph McCarthy was able to play upon Americans' fears of communism
3. how Americans reacted to the prospect of nuclear war

KEY TERMS

National Security Council
House Un-American Activities Committee
Hollywood Ten
Internal Security Act
hydrogen bomb
Sputnik
National Aeronautics and Space Administration
National Defense Education Act

KEY PEOPLE

Alger Hiss
Julius Rosenberg
Ethel Rosenberg
Joseph McCarthy
Margaret Chase Smith
Billy Graham

"Beware, commies, spies, traitors, and foreign agents! Captain America, with all loyal, free men behind him, is looking for you."

—Captain America

Captain America *comic book*

The comic book hero Captain America was enormously popular during the 1950s. He reassured Americans that he and other loyal citizens would rid the country of the communist threat within its borders. Concerned about the spread of communism abroad, many Americans also began to worry about Communists infiltrating the U.S. government, the media, and schools. Americans were afraid that leaving Communists unchecked both abroad and within the United States would threaten American values of democracy and freedom. This fear led to a string of public inquiries, loyalty oaths, and trials of suspected Communists and traitors. In addition to communism, Americans also feared nuclear war.

Cold War Fears

The Cold War had a major impact on the United States. As a result of Cold War pressures, the nation streamlined its military to allow for peacetime rearmament. In July 1947 Congress replaced the War Department with the Department of Defense, combining the leadership of the army, navy, and air force under the Joint Chiefs of Staff. In addition, Congress created the **National Security Council** (NSC) to advise the president on strategic matters. Congress also established the CIA to gather strategic military and political information overseas.

Another Red Scare. International Cold War tensions sparked new fears of communism at home. Although President Truman opposed communism abroad, some Republicans accused him of allowing Communists in the U.S. government. Truman responded to the charges by setting up the Loyalty Review Board in 1947 to investigate all federal employees. By the end of 1951, more than 20,000 federal workers had been investigated, some 2,000 had resigned, and more than 300 had been deemed "security risks" and fired.

Meanwhile, Congress cracked down on the Communist Party in the United States. Leading the fight was the **House Un-American Activities Committee** (HUAC), which had originally been established in 1938 to investigate fascist groups in the United States. HUAC questioned the political ties of members of peace organizations, liberal political groups, and labor unions. In 1947 HUAC responded to charges that Hollywood was full of Communists by holding hearings to investigate people in the movie industry. A group of California film directors and writers known as the **Hollywood Ten** went to jail rather than answer HUAC's questions. They were blacklisted—denied work—from the film industry and saw their careers

SECTION 4 RESOURCES

PRINT

- Guided Reading Strategy 18.4
- Graphic Organizer Activity 18: U.S. Presence in Global Affairs
- Literature Reading 18: Innocent Victims
- Section 4 Review, p. 557
- Daily Quiz 18.4

MULTIMEDIA

- One-Stop Planner, Lesson 18.4
- The American Nation Video Program Segment: Bomb Shelters; Teacher's Guide, pp. 175–76
- Holt Researcher: American History CD–ROM

SHELTERED ENGLISH

- Main Idea Activity for Reteaching and Sheltered English 18.4

✓ READING TO UNDERSTAND

To help students master the section objectives, have them answer the **READING CHECKS** and complete **Guided Reading Strategy 18.4** as they read the section.

TEACH OBJECTIVE 1

ALL LEVELS: To help students understand the U.S. government's actions to limit communism and how these actions affected Americans' everyday lives during the Cold War, copy the following graphic organizer on the chalkboard, omitting the italicized answers. Have each student complete the organizer. Ask students to share their answers with the class. Lead the class in a discussion about how the loss of these rights might affect Americans' everyday lives.
Sheltered English

GOVERNMENT ACTIONS TO LIMIT COMMUNISM, AND THE RESULTS

Internal Security Act—required Communist Party members and organizations to register with the federal government and imposed controls on immigrants suspected of being Communist sympathizers

↓

created public hysteria about communist infiltration and led to the infringement of many Americans' civil rights

↑

Loyalty Review Board—investigation of more than 20,000 federal employees, resignation of some 2,000 federal employees, and firing of 300 others

HUAC—investigation of peace organizations, liberal political groups, labor unions, the movie industry, and individuals accused of spying; resulted in blacklisting, hysteria, and scaring people away from unions and progressive groups

THAT'S INTERESTING!

For decades following his release from prison, Alger Hiss continued to assert publicly that he had never served as a Communist spy. In 1992 Russian historian D. A. Volkogonov announced that a search of the former Soviet government's military intelligence archives had revealed nothing to dispute Hiss's claim. Other scholars questioned the comprehensiveness of Volkogonov's investigation, however, and in 1996 the release of secret Soviet cables from World War II provided new evidence that suggested Hiss was indeed guilty. Hiss died that same year.

AMERICAN LETTERS ANSWERS

(for p. 553)

1. suburban life and anxiety about nuclear war
2. by discussing the distance of the travelers from Earth, and the "long and many" days of space travel
3. important but hopelessly doomed in *The Martian Chronicles*; remote and almost unrealistic in "The Martian Way"

VISUAL RECORD ANSWER

Students might point out that the protestors are holding picket signs with the names of the Hollywood Ten.

INTERPRETING THE VISUAL RECORD

The Hollywood Ten. Protesters demonstrate against HUAC's investigation of alleged communist activities of Americans in the film industry. ***How are these activists protesting the actions of HUAC?***

destroyed. Author Bernard De Voto described the fear of blacklisting during this era. He explained that "gossip, rumor, slander, backbiting, malice and drunken invention, . . . when it makes the headlines, shatters the reputations of innocent and harmless people. . . . We are shocked. We are scared."

The hysteria generated by HUAC spread quickly. One group that spoke out against HUAC, the Women's International League for Peace and Freedom, argued in 1949 that the hearings violated democratic rights.

> **"Fully recognizing the danger of fascist and communist totalitarianism, the League believes that such forces can be best opposed by open discussion and by the strengthening of our own democratic procedures, rather than by attempts at direct control."**

Because of the League's support for progressive causes, the Federal Bureau of Investigation (FBI) investigated the national organization and several of its local chapters. The investigation scared many potential members away. HUAC investigations had a similar effect on labor unions and many liberal political groups.

The search for spies. HUAC also investigated individuals accused of spying for the Soviets. In 1948 Whittaker Chambers, a former member of the Communist Party, accused Alger Hiss of being a Communist spy. Chambers told HUAC that Hiss, a New Deal lawyer who had joined the State Department in 1936, had given him secret State Department documents to pass on to the Soviets.

Hiss denied the charges, but persistent questioning by HUAC member Richard M. Nixon, a young Republican member of Congress from California, revealed apparent inconsistencies in Hiss's testimony. When Hiss sued Chambers for slander, Chambers produced microfilmed copies of documents he had kept hidden in a pumpkin at his home. These so-called pumpkin papers revealed evidence that indicated Hiss had lied to HUAC. In 1950 Hiss was convicted of perjury, or lying under oath, and sentenced to five years in prison.

The trial and conviction of Julius and Ethel Rosenberg for spying and giving away U.S. atomic secrets shocked many Americans.

Another notorious spy case also helped fuel domestic fears of communism. In 1951 a U.S. court convicted two Americans, Julius and Ethel Rosenberg, of providing the Soviet Union with atomic-energy secrets during World War II. Defenders of the Rosenbergs claimed that the two were innocent victims of anticommunist hysteria. Despite worldwide protests on their behalf, the Rosenbergs were executed in June 1953.

Other anticommunist measures included the **Internal Security Act**, passed in 1950. The act required Communist Party members and organizations to register with the federal government. It also imposed strict controls on immigrants suspected of being Communist sympathizers. The anticommunist hysteria of these years shattered many lives and careers. Writer Abe Burrows described his experiences after being blacklisted. "My Americanism being under suspicion is very painful to me, not just painful economically but painful as it is to a guy who loves his country."

✔ **READING CHECK:** What actions did the U.S. government take to limit communism at home? How did these actions affect Americans' everyday lives?

SPOTLIGHT on Science-Fiction Movies

Tell students to conduct research on science-fiction movies that explore Cold War themes. Have each student select and watch a science-fiction movie that contains a theme associated with Cold War fears and then write a review of the movie. **Block Scheduling**

▸ASSIGNMENT *Tell students to imagine that they are Americans living during the Cold War. Have each student write a letter to a member of Congress stating his or her opinion about the work of the House Un-American Activities Committee and its effects on Americans' everyday lives.*

SPOTLIGHT on Science-Fiction Literature

Have students consider some of the fears and preoccupations of today that have been examined in science-fiction literature. Ask students to name these fears and preoccupations and to compile a list on the chalkboard. *(Students' suggestions might include artificial intelligence, violent computer games, the Internet, and outbreaks of disease.)* Have each student write a science-fiction short story that addresses one of the fears or preoccupations discussed. Ask volunteers to read their stories to the class. **Block Scheduling**

Science Fiction

During the 1950s, science fiction became popular. Science fiction literature often reflects Americans' fear of or interest in technology, space exploration, and nuclear warfare. Ray Bradbury's novel The Martian Chronicles *(1950) describes the colonization of Mars by Earthlings while Earth is destroyed by nuclear war. Isaac Asimov discusses the adventures and isolation of space travel in his 1952 short story "The Martian Way."*

from *The Martian Chronicles*

by Ray Bradbury

Ray Bradbury's novel

They all came out and looked at the sky that night. They left their suppers or their washing up or their dressing for the show and they came out upon their now-not-quite-as-new porches and watched the green star of Earth there. It was a move without conscious effort; they all did it, to help them understand the news they had heard on the radio a moment before. There was Earth and there the coming war, and there hundreds of thousands of mothers or grandmothers or fathers or brothers or aunts or uncles or cousins. They stood on the porches and tried to believe in the existence of Earth, much as they had once tried to believe in the existence of Mars; it was a problem reversed. To all intents and purposes, Earth was now dead; they had been away from it for three or four years. Space was an anesthetic; seventy million miles of space numbed you, put memory to sleep, depopulated Earth, erased the past, and allowed these people here to go on with their work. But now, tonight, the dead were risen, Earth was reinhabited, memory awoke, a million names were spoken: What was so-and-so doing tonight on Earth? What about this one and that one? The people on the porches glanced sideways at each other's faces.

At nine o'clock Earth seemed to explode, catch fire, and burn.

from "The Martian Way"

by Isaac Asimov

Isaac Asimov's collection of short stories

At first . . . the weeks flew past . . . except for the gnawing feeling that every minute meant an additional number of thousands of miles away from all humanity. That made it worse. . . .

The days were long and many, space was empty. . . .

"Mario?" The voice that broke upon his ear phones was questioning. . . .

"Speaking," he said. . . .

"You know, I've read Earth books—"

"Grounder books, you mean." Rioz yawned.

"—and sometimes I read descriptions of people lying on grass," continued Long. "You know that green stuff like thin, long pieces of paper they have all over the ground down there, and they look up at the blue sky with clouds in it. Did you ever see any films of that?"

"Sure. It didn't attract me. It looked cold."

UNDERSTANDING LITERATURE

1. What aspects of American life in the 1950s does *The Martian Chronicles* address?
2. How does "The Martian Way" describe the isolation of space travel?
3. How important is life on Earth in these two selections?

TECHNOLOGY AND SOCIETY

Science-Fiction Movies. Science-fiction movies reflected popular anxieties about nuclear weapons during the 1950s. In *Them!,* released in 1954, giant mutant ants crawl out of an atomic test site in New Mexico and go on a rampage. One character says that the ants are probably the result of "lingering radiation from the first atomic bomb." *On the Beach,* a 1959 film based on the novel by Nevil Shute, portrays the final days in Australia as people await the arrival of a giant radioactive cloud produced by a nuclear war in the Northern Hemisphere. The final scene shows an empty town square, signifying that the war has left no survivors.

ACTIVITY: Have students create previews for science-fiction movies that reflect current popular anxieties.

VISUAL RECORD ANSWER

(for p. 554)

Students might note that his use of charts seems to suggest a factual basis for his claims.

TEACH OBJECTIVE 2

LEVEL 1: Ask students how Senator Joseph McCarthy was able to play upon Americans' fears of communism. *(Students might explain that McCarthy tapped into fears about communism infiltrating American society and the growing power of the Soviet Union by claiming to have evidence of Communists working in the federal government and using his Senate subcommittee to question the patriotism of hundreds of government workers.)* Pair students and have them create signs to protest McCarthy's tactics. Display protest signs around the classroom. **Sheltered English, Cooperative Learning**

LEVEL 2: Tell students to imagine that they are newspaper editors during the era of McCarthyism. Have each student write an editorial in which he or she describes how Senator Joseph McCarthy was able to play upon Americans' fears of communism. *(See the Level 1 lesson for the correct tactics.)* Students' editorials should also suggest ways that such situations might be prevented in the future and describe how McCarthy's activities led to violations of people's constitutional rights. Students may wish to include their editorials in their portfolios.

DEMOCRATIC VALUES

A Lone Voice. In her Declaration of Conscience, Senator Smith decried the effects of McCarthyism: "Those of us who shout the loudest about Americanism . . . are all too frequently those who . . . ignore some of the basic principles of Americanism–

The right to criticize.
The right to hold unpopular beliefs.
The right to protest.
The right of independent thought. . . .

Freedom of speech . . . has been so abused by some that it is not exercised by others."

CRITICAL THINKING Why might Smith not have mentioned McCarthy's name?

ANSWER: Students might suggest that she did not want to make a personal attack.

***The American Nation* VIDEO PROGRAM**

Bomb Shelters; Teacher's Guide, pp. 175–76

Search 48004, Play to 49285
Videodisc 2, Side A

Play

Pause

See *Teacher's Guide* for Spanish barcode.

McCarthyism

As the Korean conflict escalated during the early 1950s, Americans' fears of communism intensified. This anxiety continued even after the war ended. Many Americans became convinced that spies and Communist sympathizers were everywhere. Joseph McCarthy, a U.S. senator from Wisconsin, helped fuel these suspicions. He argued that "the Communists within our borders have been more responsible for the success of communism abroad than Soviet Russia."

McCarthy's rise. Senator McCarthy came to public attention in 1950 when he claimed to have a list of known Communists who worked at the State Department. Although he never produced the list, dozens of federal employees lost their jobs after being labeled "security risks." McCarthy used his position as chairman of the Senate Permanent Subcommittee on Investigations to wage war against alleged Communist sympathizers in the federal government. With almost no supporting evidence, McCarthy questioned the patriotism—and ruined the reputations—of hundreds of government workers. Frustrated by McCarthy's lack of hard evidence, one journalist claimed, "Joe [McCarthy] couldn't find a Communist in Red Square—he didn't know Karl Marx from Groucho [Marx]." Nevertheless, many Americans, consumed by their fear of communism and the power of the Soviet Union, supported his crusade.

McCarthy's popularity and ruthlessness made many politicians wary of challenging him. One who did, however, was Margaret Chase Smith, a Republican senator from Maine. She stood her ground against McCarthy's crusade.

> **"I think that it is high time that we remembered that the Constitution, as amended, speaks not only of the freedom of speech but also of trial by jury instead of trial by accusation."**

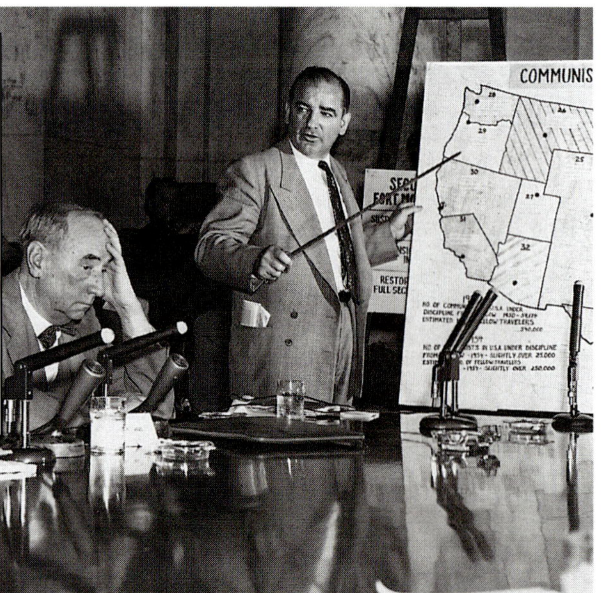

INTERPRETING THE VISUAL RECORD

McCarthyism. Senator McCarthy claimed that communist organizations throughout the United States were plotting to overthrow the government. ***How does McCarthy's style of presentation for this hearing give support to his claims?***

In 1950 Smith and several other senators issued the Declaration of Conscience, which condemned those who had turned the Senate into "a forum of hate and character assassination." The report never mentioned McCarthy by name, but it was clearly directed at him.

McCarthy's downfall. Few others joined in the condemnation, however. Even the president refused to criticize McCarthy. Most of those who did speak out came from the arts or the media. In *The Crucible* (1953), playwright Arthur Miller drew parallels between McCarthyism and the Salem witch trials of 1692. On the television program *See It Now*, newscaster Edward R. Murrow questioned McCarthy's tactics. "We cannot defend freedom abroad," Murrow cautioned, "by deserting it at home." While some viewers praised Murrow, others bombarded him with hate mail.

LEVEL 3: Organize students into small groups and have each group write a skit about how Joseph McCarthy was able to play upon Americans' fears of communism. *(See the Level 1 lesson for the correct tactics.)* Have students perform their skits for the class. **Cooperative Learning**

TEACH OBJECTIVE 3

LEVEL 1: Pair students and have them list ways that Americans reacted to the prospect of nuclear war. *(Students might include turning toward religion, building bomb shelters, conducting air-raid drills, Civil Defense educational campaigns, the organization of SANE, and continued support for the arms race and space exploration.)* Then have each pair create a poster that reflects one of the ways that Americans responded to the prospect of nuclear war.
Sheltered English, Cooperative Learning

LEVEL 2: Have each student create a collage that depicts how Americans reacted to the prospect of nuclear war. *(See the Level 1 lesson for the correct reactions.)* Ask volunteers to present and explain their collages to the class.

In 1954 McCarthy's congressional committee investigated charges that Communists had gained a foothold in the U.S. Army. Each day a vast television audience—sometimes as many as 20 million people—tuned in to the Army-McCarthy hearings. In the circuslike proceedings, McCarthy repeatedly interrupted and ridiculed witnesses. One victim of this treatment complained that McCarthy "acted like the gangster in a B movie rubbing out someone who had got in his way."

Television exposure of McCarthy's bullying tactics contrasted with the calm, dignified behavior of Joseph Welch, the army's chief counsel, and soon turned public opinion against the senator. At one point, Welch criticized McCarthy for his wild charges. "Let us not assassinate this lad further, Senator. You have done enough. Have you no sense of decency, sir, at long last? Have you left no sense of decency?" The audience in the hearing room broke into applause. A few months later, by a vote of 67 to 22, the Senate condemned McCarthy for conduct unbecoming a senator.

✔ **READING CHECK:** How was Senator Joseph McCarthy able to play upon Americans' fears of communism?

Nuclear Anxiety

Increased conflict between the United States and Communists abroad plunged the Soviet Union and the United States into a race to develop ever-more-powerful nuclear weapons. This arms race contributed to Americans' fears of nuclear war. In 1950, U.S. scientists began work on a **hydrogen bomb**, or H-bomb. They claimed it would be 1,000 times more powerful than the atomic bombs dropped on Hiroshima and Nagasaki in World War II. The first U.S. test of a H-bomb in 1952 completely vaporized a small island in the Pacific. Some nine months later, the Soviet Union tested its own H-bomb. J. Robert Oppenheimer, one of the creators of the U.S. atomic bomb, urged caution in the growing arms race.

> **"[The United States and the Soviet Union] are like two scorpions in a bottle, each capable of killing the other but only at the risk of his own life. . . . The atomic clock ticks faster and faster."**

Religion and nuclear war. Anxiety about nuclear war caused many Americans to seek some source of comfort. Many turned to religion. Evangelists such as Billy Graham attracted vast audiences during the 1950s. He warned of the danger of nuclear war and urged Americans to turn to God. Church membership grew rapidly during the era. As a result, investment in the construction of religious institutions rose from $76 million in 1946 to $868 million in 1957.

teen Life

"Duck and Cover"

The fear of nuclear war greatly affected American teenagers' lives during the 1950s. Daily news of the Communists' advances and nuclear tests threw children and teenagers into a quiet panic.

Many schools implemented civil defense plans and conducted "cover drills." Teachers stopped in the middle of normal classroom activities and yelled "drop" or "duck and cover" to simulate what students should do during an attack. Some schools even distributed dog tags and identification necklaces to students to identify them in case of a nuclear blast. Although well-intentioned, these measures increased the youths' fears that nuclear war was soon to come. As an adult, Mary Mackey recalled the terror she experienced during the classroom drills.

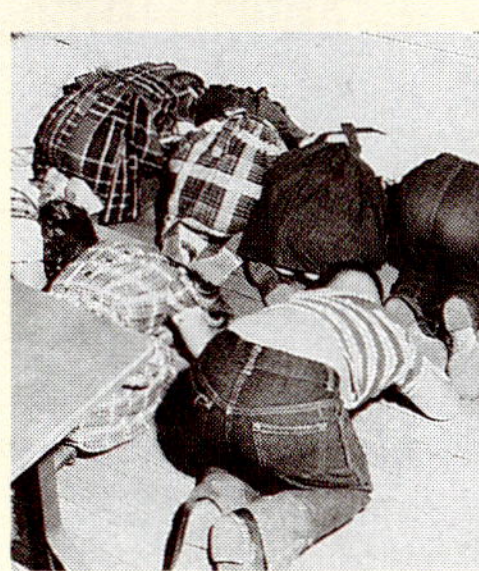

These schoolchildren are performing a duck-and-cover drill.

> **"Obediently we would fold our bodies into that attitude [position] of prayer and supplication [worship] known only to the children of the fifties: legs folded, head between the knees, hands raised to protect the fragile, invisible nerve that floated somewhere in the blackness behind our eyes."**

One author explained the impact of such drills on many adults who grew up during the 1950s. They "never forgot the lesson that their world could someday end in a flash of light and heat while they were crouched helplessly in gyms and basements."

PEOPLE IN HISTORY

Joseph McCarthy. Joseph McCarthy's groundless accusations came as little surprise to those who knew him well. A lawyer and former circuit court judge, he had won Wisconsin's Republican senatorial nomination in 1946 in a primary that featured lies about his opponent's campaign finances. In the general campaign that followed, McCarthy lied about his military record during World War II. He claimed that he had flown some 30 combat missions when he actually had not flown any. He also falsely maintained that he had been wounded in combat during the war. After winning the election, McCarthy gained a reputation in the Senate for rude behavior and heavy drinking. He died of liver failure in 1957, at the age of 48.

CRITICAL THINKING How might political concerns have motivated McCarthy to wage a campaign against alleged Communists in the federal government?

ANSWER: Answers will vary. Students might suggest that McCarthy hoped his anti-communist campaign would bolster his popularity and secure his re-election.

VISUAL RECORD ANSWER
(for p. 556)
Answers will vary. Students should discuss construction methods and location.

LEVEL 3: Tell students to imagine that they are conducting an oral history interview with an American who lived during the 1950s. Pair students and have each pair write a transcript for an interview that focuses on how Americans reacted to the prospect of nuclear war. *(See the Level 1 lesson for the correct reactions.)* Have one student assume the role of interviewer and the other assume the role of interviewee. Have volunteers conduct their interviews for the class. **Cooperative Learning**

NOTE: For an additional teaching idea, see the Chapter 18 quick survey lesson in the **Creative Teaching Strategies** handbook.

SPOTLIGHT on American Life During the Cold War

Ask students to interview Americans who lived during the Cold War. Each student should focus his or her interview on the activities that the interviewee participated in that were related to fears of nuclear war, any personal fears about the Cold War that the interviewee may have had, and the interviewee's reaction to various Cold War–related events. Have volunteers present their transcripts or recorded interviews to the class. **Block Scheduling**

SECTION 4 REVIEW ANSWERS

Define and Identify

For significance, see the following pages:

- National Security Council, p. 551
- House Un-American Activities Committee, p. 551
- Hollywood Ten, p. 551
- Alger Hiss, p. 552
- Julius Rosenberg, p. 552
- Ethel Rosenberg, p. 552
- Internal Security Act, p. 552
- Joseph McCarthy, p. 554
- Margaret Chase Smith, p. 554
- hydrogen bomb, p. 555
- Billy Graham, p. 555
- *Sputnik*, p. 557
- National Aeronautics and Space Administration, p. 557
- National Defense Education Act, p. 557

1. fallout shelters–construction and sale of shelters; religion–increases in church membership and popularity of evangelists; government programs–Federal Civil Defense Administration campaign; space exploration–establishment of NASA

2. generated hysteria, infringed on civil rights, undermined membership of unions and liberal political groups

3. almost none

4. Communists–by the U.S.-Soviet relationship; threat of nuclear war–by the arms race, the hydrogen bomb, and the dangers of nuclear fallout

5. Their tactics violated many of the guarantees of the Bill of Rights.

INTERPRETING THE VISUAL RECORD

Cold War fears. The threat of nuclear war led some Americans to build bomb shelters in their yards. This booklet offered Americans advice on how to survive a nuclear war. ***Do you think this shelter would protect someone during a nuclear war? Explain your answer.***

Americans' religious devotion contrasted sharply with the atheism of the Soviet Union. Reflecting this religious zeal, Congress added the phrase "One Nation Under God" to the Pledge of Allegiance and "In God We Trust" to U.S. coins.

Calming public fears. As concerns about nuclear war grew, the government launched a campaign to calm public fears. The U.S. government issued pamphlets that offered suggestions on how to live through a nuclear attack. Some Americans put these recommendations to use by building backyard bomb shelters. Schoolchildren went through air-raid drills in which they crawled under their desks to protect themselves from radiation.

As Cold War tensions and Americans' fear of a Soviet nuclear attack increased in the 1950s, civil defense hysteria swept the United States. In 1951 the Federal Civil Defense Administration began a campaign to educate the public on what to do in case of a nuclear attack. Pamphlets, films, television shows, magazines, and the "Duck and Cover" program for children all encouraged citizens to protect themselves. For example, the booklet *Survival Under Atomic Attack* reassured fearful Americans.

> **"You can live through an atom bomb raid and you won't have to have a Geiger counter, protective clothing, or special training in order to do it. The secrets of survival are: KNOW THE BOMB'S TRUE DANGERS. KNOW THE STEPS YOU CAN TAKE TO ESCAPE THEM."**

Nuclear fallout. While a nuclear attack remained a grim possibility, radioactive fallout—a by-product of nuclear explosions—already posed a threat. U.S. and Soviet H-bomb tests spewed tons of radioactive material into the atmosphere. In 1954, H-bomb tests in the Pacific Ocean revealed the far-reaching effects of nuclear fallout. The crew of a Japanese fishing boat 85 miles away from the test site developed radiation sickness. People realized that no one would be safe in a nuclear attack. "The alternatives," one civil defense official said, "are to dig, die, or get out." No one wanted to die, and with little warning of incoming missiles, evacuating would not be possible. So some Americans began to dig, constructing backyard fallout shelters.

Pamphlets like the *Family Fallout Shelter* promoted do-it-yourself home shelters. *Life* magazine even presented building a shelter as a father-and-son project. Shelter manufacturers sprang up, selling their concrete-and-steel igloos at county fairs for about $1,500. A typical shelter contained flashlights, a first-aid kit, battery radio, portable toilet, two-week supply of food—mainly canned

REVIEW

Have students complete the **Section 4 Review** on p. 557.

ASSESS

Have students complete **Daily Quiz 18.4.** As **Alternative Assessment**, you may want to use the newspaper editorial or the skit from this section's lessons.

RETEACH

Have students complete **Main Idea Activity for Reteaching and Sheltered English 18.4.** Then organize students into small groups. Assign each group one of two topics: "Fear of Communism" or "Fear of Nuclear War." Have each group create an outline of the events discussed in Section 4 that pertain to its topic. Have volunteers present their outlines to the class. Ask the class to supply any information missing from outlines.

Sheltered English, Cooperative Learning

EXTEND

Have students conduct research on one of the early satellites, such as *Sputnik* or *Explorer I.* Then have each student create a model or a poster of one of these satellites and write a short report containing technical information about the satellite. Have volunteers present their reports to the class.

Block Scheduling

---

meats and vegetables—and water. Some people also purchased guns to prevent anyone from entering their shelter during a raid.

In 1957 Congress held a special hearing on the dangers of radioactive fallout. Defense officials claimed that nuclear testing was perfectly safe. Many scientists disagreed. They argued that radiation released during the tests presented a serious danger to the environment and possibly increased the risk of cancer in human beings. Soon the fear of radiation led to an organized campaign against nuclear testing. In 1957 a group of Americans, including well-known doctor Benjamin Spock, organized the Committee for a Sane Nuclear Policy (SANE). SANE urged the United States to begin negotiations with the Soviet Union to end nuclear tests. Within a year, SANE had grown to more than 25,000 members in some 130 chapters across the country.

Many Americans worried about the possibility of a nuclear attack in the 1950s.

Space programs. The arms race sped on, however, particularly after the Soviet Union launched the satellite ***Sputnik*** into orbit in October 1957. Many Americans worried that this launch proved the United States was falling behind the Soviet Union in technological development. President Eisenhower urged Congress to promote U.S. space technology by establishing the **National Aeronautics and Space Administration** (NASA). In 1958 the government sent the first U.S. satellite, *Explorer I*, into orbit. That same year, Congress approved the **National Defense Education Act**. This act appropriated millions of dollars to improve education in science, mathematics, and foreign languages.

✔ **READING CHECK:** How did Americans react to the prospect of nuclear war?

SECTION  REVIEW

Define and explain the significance of the following terms:
National Security Council
House Un-American Activities Committee
Hollywood Ten
Internal Security Act
hydrogen bomb
Sputnik
National Aeronautics and Space Administration
National Defense Education Act

Identify and explain the significance of the following individuals:
Alger Hiss
Julius Rosenberg
Ethel Rosenberg
Joseph McCarthy
Margaret Chase Smith
Billy Graham

1. **Using Graphic Organizers** Copy the graphic organizer below. Use it to explain how the possibility of nuclear war affected Americans' lives during the 1950s.

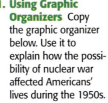

Religion
Government Programs
Fallout Shelters
Space Exploration
NUCLEAR WAR

2. **Evaluating** What effect did HUAC's investigations have on American society?
3. **Distinguishing Fact from Opinion** Joseph McCarthy claimed that Communists inside the United States did more to spread communism around the world than Communists abroad. What evidence did he present to verify this statement?
4. **Synthesizing** How were Americans' fears of Communists and the threat of nuclear war justified?

Critical Thinking

5. In what ways did the efforts of some congressional committees challenge the American values they aimed to protect?
   Consider:
   - what the goals of HUAC and McCarthy's committee were
   - what these two committees did to expose Communists
   - what impact these committees had on the lives of those who were investigated

CHAPTER 18 REVIEW ANSWERS

Creating a Time Line
Each event should have an explanation and the correct date.

Writing a Summary
See the Reading Checks in each section for main ideas.

Identifying People and Ideas

1. war crimes trials that took place in Germany after World War II
2. postwar international organization that was founded to promote world peace
3. former first lady and one of the U.S. representatives to the United Nations
4. State Department official who suggested the containment policy
5. U.S. policy to "support free peoples who are resisting attempted subjugation"
6. economic aid that the United States provided to European countries after World War II
7. leader of Chinese Communists who established the People's Republic of China
8. commander of U.S. forces in the Korean War
9. U.S. senator who made unsubstantiated allegations about Communists in the federal government
10. nuclear weapon that is more powerful than the atomic bombs used in World War II

REVIEW AND ASSESSMENT RESOURCES

PRINT

- Chapter 18 Review, pp. 558–59
- Chapter 18 Tutorial for Students, Parents, Mentors, and Peers
- Chapter 18 Test (Form A or B)
- Portfolio Activities and Alternative Assessment Handbook, Chapter 18

MULTIMEDIA

- Audio Program, Chapter 18 (English and Spanish)
- Chapter 18 Test Generator (on the One-Stop Planner)
- Global Skill Builder CD–ROM
- HRW Web site

SHELTERED ENGLISH

- Spanish Glossary
- Sheltered English Chapter 18 Test

REVIEW

Have students complete the **Chapter 18 Review** on pp. 558–59.

ASSESS

Use one of the chapter tests to assess students' understanding of the content. For **Alternative Assessment**, see the **Portfolio Activities and Alternative Assessment Handbook**.

Understanding Main Ideas

1. resulted in the creation of Israel but failed to prevent the outbreak of the Arab-Israeli war or end that region's tensions
2. the economic, political, and philosophical differences between the United States and the Soviet Union
3. diplomacy and covert operations
4. because many Americans were extremely fearful of communism and the power of the Soviet Union
5. programs that offered suggestions on how to live through a nuclear attack

Reviewing Themes

1. the nations in NATO and the Warsaw Pact, East and West Germany, Greece, Guatemala, Hungary, Iran, North and South Korea, Turkey
2. search for Communists resulted in infringement on civil rights
3. put a new premium on science and math education, contributed to the popularity of science-fiction literature, and led to widespread fears about the possibility of a nuclear attack

Thinking Critically

1. Answers will vary, but students should outline standards for membership and identify committees and mechanisms to enforce the organization's decisions.

Review

Creating a Time Line

Copy the time line below onto a sheet of paper. Complete the time line by filling in the events and dates from the chapter that you think were most significant. Pick three events and explain why you think they were significant.

Writing a Summary

Using the Reading Checks as a guide, write an overview of the events in the chapter.

Identifying People and Ideas

Identify the following terms or individuals and explain their significance.

1. Nuremberg Trials
2. United Nations
3. Eleanor Roosevelt
4. George Kennan
5. Truman Doctrine
6. Marshall Plan
7. Mao Zedong
8. Douglas MacArthur
9. Joseph McCarthy
10. hydrogen bomb

Understanding Main ideas

SECTION 1

1. How successful was the United Nations in stabilizing the conflict between Arabs and Jews in the area of Palestine? Explain your answer.

SECTION 2

2. What were the main causes of the Cold War?

SECTION 3

3. What strategies did President Eisenhower use to slow the spread of communism?

SECTION 4

4. Why was Senator McCarthy able to generate so much attention with his accusations?
5. What types of programs were developed to address concerns about nuclear war in the United States?

Reviewing Themes

1. **Global Relations** What other countries became involved in the conflict between the United States and the Soviet Union?
2. **Democratic Values** How did the U.S. government's response to Cold War tensions lead to limitations on civil liberties?
3. **Technology and Society** How did the development of atomic technology affect education, literature, and other aspects of daily life in the United States?

Thinking Critically

1. **Problem Solving** Imagine that you are establishing an organization to maintain world peace. How would you organize it? Why?
2. **Synthesizing** How did containment influence U.S. foreign policy during the late 1940s and the 1950s?
3. **Evaluating** How did the fall of China to communism in 1949 affect the Korean War in 1950?
4. **Recognizing Point of View** Why did many Palestinians, Iranians, and Guatemalans view the U.S. government with hostility during the 1950s?
5. **Assessing Consequences** How did U.S. efforts to halt communism abroad affect life at home?

Writing About History

Writing to Explain Imagine that it is the mid-1950s and that you are a senator who opposes communism. Using the graphic organizer below, write a speech describing the threat of Communist expansion around the world.

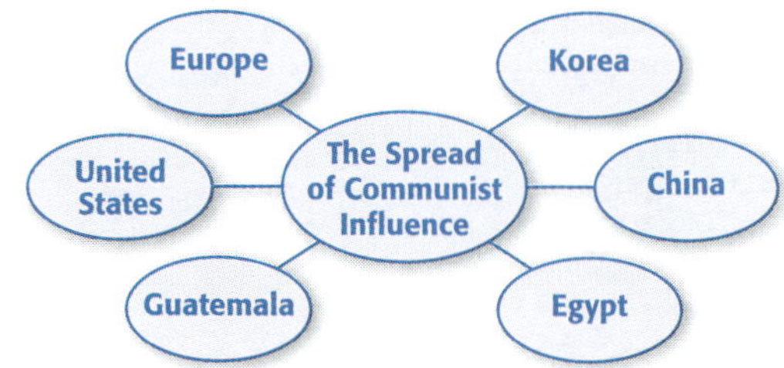

RETEACH

Organize students into small groups and have each group select one key person and one key term from each of the four sections. Then have each group create job descriptions for its key persons and newspaper headlines pertaining to its key terms. Have students read their job descriptions and headlines to the class, and have the class guess what or whom each describes.
Sheltered English, Cooperative Learning

EXTEND

Have students conduct research on recent actions taken by the United Nations. Have them write an essay describing how these actions reflect the initial mission and founding principles of the United Nations. **Block Scheduling**

Strategies for Success Review the **Strategies for Success** on *Taking Notes*. Then take notes on the following excerpt from an oral history provided by Steve McConnell, a U.S. citizen who grew up during the Cold War.

> **"We went through the bomb-shelter era in the late fifties. I remember it as kind of fun. You could go into a shopping center and at the corner of the parking lot was one of these bomb shelters. Gee, that was neat. . . . But there was that sense of nagging that maybe this was more than just fun. Nothing serious was imminent [soon to come] but . . . there was talk.**
>
> **We had drills in school. The alarms would go off and you'd hit the floor and put your back to the windows and cover your head. You were mostly afraid of getting hit by glass. What most of us didn't realize was that that would be the least of our problems. (Laughs.)"**

Linking History and Geography

Alaska and Hawaii both became states in 1959. Study the map below. How might the location of these two areas have lent support for their admission as states?

internet connect

TOPIC: The United Nations
GO TO: go.hrw.com
KEYWORD: SE1 United

Accessing the Internet through the HRW Web site, research the United Nations and then write an essay in which you describe the UN's history, its organizational structure, and its role in world affairs.

Complete one or all of the following projects independently or cooperatively.

1 Global Relations

Imagine that you are a U.S. delegate to the UN conference in San Francisco in 1945. ***Write a memorandum*** to the U.S. Senate detailing world conditions in 1945 that call for the formation of an association of world nations and urging U.S. participation in the association.

2 Democratic Values

Imagine that you are a journalist during the 1950s. ***Write an article*** that explains how the United States justifies its fight against communism abroad while democratic values are being challenged at home.

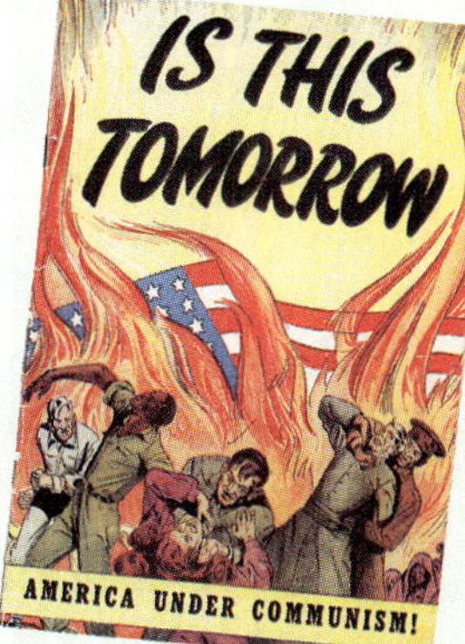

Anticommunist literature

3 Technology and Society

Imagine that you are working for the Federal Civil Defense Administration during the 1950s. ***Create a flyer*** for students that explains the dangers of nuclear war and what they should do in case of an attack.

2. led to the Truman Doctrine, the Marshall Plan, the Berlin Airlift, the formation of NATO, participation in the Korean War, and covert operations in Iran and Guatemala

3. The United States participated in the Korean War because of its fears that communism would continue to spread throughout Asia.

4. Palestinians—U.S. support for Israel; Iranians and Guatemalans—U.S.-sponsored overthrow of their governments

5. resulted in a search for Communists and spies in the United States that infringed on civil rights and created an atmosphere of fear

Writing About History
Europe—establishment of satellite nations in Eastern Europe; Korea—establishment of communist government in North Korea, invasion of South Korea; China—Communists takeover; Egypt—support from the Soviet Union during the Suez crisis; Guatemala—seizure and redistribution of plantation land; United States—fears about communist influence

Strategies for Success
Students' notes will vary but should identify the mixture of humor and anxiety that McConnell expresses.

Linking History and Geography
Alaska—proximity to Soviet Union; Hawaii—closeness to East Asia

LET'S GET STARTED!

Write the following term on the chalkboard: *Cold War*. Have students list everything they know about the term and the topic. *(Students might identify the Cold War as an ideological conflict between the United States and the Soviet Union and mention conflicts such as the Hungary uprising and the Suez Canal conflict.)* Ask volunteers to read their lists to the class. Then tell students that they will learn more about the defenses of the Cold War in the Unit 5 America's Geography.

TEACH AMERICA'S GEOGRAPHY—DEFENSES OF THE COLD WAR

Have each student write a few sentences about the graph and the maps in the America's Geography feature, explaining how the information presented affected Cold War defenses. *(Students should note that the graph on federal spending reveals the high levels of defense spending during the Cold War, that the map on radar systems indicates the high number of squadrons and bombing bases and the global nature of radar systems, and that the map on military bases displays the sheer number of bases and the conflicts of the Cold War.)* **Sheltered English**

ECONOMIC DEVELOPMENT

Cold War Defense. National defense was a top priority in the 1950s. Between 1950 and 1955 the total number of military personnel doubled from some 1.4 million to some 2.9 million. The amount of money spent on defense also increased.

CRITICAL THINKING How might the increase in military personnel have affected the national economy?

ANSWER: Students might suggest that the increase helped fuel economic growth.

THAT'S INTERESTING!

During the Cold War, some Americans suggested that the United States barrage the Soviet people with the products of American capitalism. One Montgomery Ward businessperson wanted to ship mail-order catalogues to the Soviet Union to display the enormous variety and availability of goods in the United States. A sociologist even suggested air-dropping pantyhose on the country.

AMERICA'S GEOGRAPHY ANSWERS

1. Most U.S. radar lines ran through Canada, the closest neighbor to the United States.
2. 36 percent; 48 percent

AMERICA'S Geography

Defenses of the Cold War

During the Cold War the United States invested large sums of money to improve its national defense. This included heavy investment in new types of technology. Initially, most of the funding for the space program was managed by the Department of Defense. Some of the technology developed for these programs changed Americans' daily lives. During the Cold War, for example, scientists began to experiment with new uses for radio waves. They used radio waves in radar systems and satellite technology. These experiments eventually led to the development of such everyday items as the microwave oven and cable television.

Radar Systems and Defenses in North America, 1959–1964

ICBM squadrons
Strategic Air Command bomber bases
Nuclear submarine shipyards
ICBM early warning systems
Ballistic Missile Early Warning System

USSR
ARCTIC OCEAN
Distant Early Warning Line
CANADA
Mid-Canada Line
Pinetree Line
PACIFIC OCEAN
UNITED STATES
ATLANTIC OCEAN
MEXICO
CUBA
0 500 1,000 Miles
0 500 1,000 Kilometers
Azimuthal Equal-Area Projection

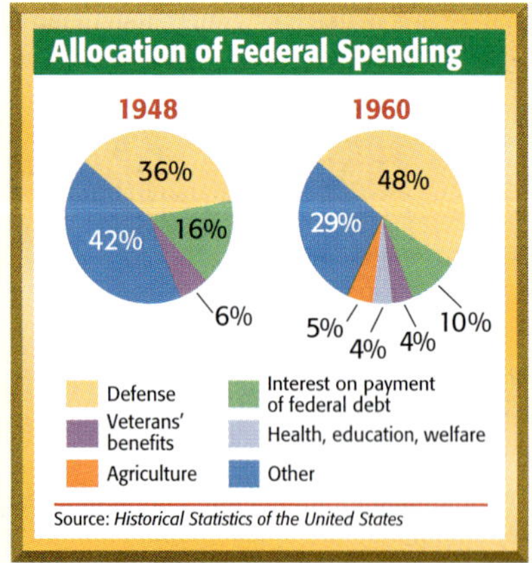

Radar. As the portion of the federal budget for defense increased, the amount of the defense budget for technology also rose. Concern over the Soviet weapons buildup led the United States to create an intricate radar system to detect incoming enemy missiles. At the same time, the United States built up its own supply of intercontinental ballistic missiles (ICBMs).

GEOGRAPHY AND HISTORY Skills

REGION

1. Through which country did most U.S. radar lines run? Why might this be so?
2. What percentage of the federal budget went toward defense in 1948? in 1960?

SPOTLIGHT on Military Bases

Have each student pick a major military base during the 1960s, such as Okinawa in Japan or Holy Loch in the United Kingdom. Ask students to conduct research on their selected military base. Students should investigate the history of the base, its importance during the Cold War, and daily life on the base. Then write the following statement on the chalkboard: *U.S. military bases were crucial components of Cold War defenses.* Have students write essays in response to the question fully discussing their chosen bases in their essays.

SPOTLIGHT on Forms of Technology

Have each student pick one of the forms of military technology listed in the map legend on the previous page, such as ICBM squadrons, nuclear submarines, or various warning systems. Ask students to conduct research on their chosen technology, concentrating on its development, deployment, and significance during the Cold War. Have students summarize the findings of their research in short papers. Ask volunteers to read their papers to the class.

AMERICA'S Geography

Major U.S. Military Bases, c. 1965

United States and allies
Soviet Union and allies
Major U.S. base
Point of conflict
Political status as of 1960

0 1,000 2,000 Miles
0 1,000 2,000 Kilometers
Azimuthal Equidistant Projection

Military bases. During the Cold War the United States increased its commitment to help protect other nations from their enemies. In order to achieve this goal, the U.S. military established a host of new bases throughout the world. Although some conflicts did erupt between the U.S.-backed countries and Soviet-backed countries, most of these skirmishes were short-lived.

GEOGRAPHY AND HISTORY Skills

HUMAN-ENVIRONMENT INTERACTION

1. How many major U.S. military bases existed outside the United States?
2. Where did conflicts erupt during the 1950s?

THEN AND NOW

Dwindling Forces. Since an all-time high in the late 1960s, the size of U.S. armed forces has decreased. By 1993, the number of troops in the army and air force was far less than that of 1955. That same year, the government awarded $138.3 billion in military contracts to businesses.

CRITICAL THINKING How might this trend affect the nation's workforce?

ANSWER: Answers may vary. Students might suggest that military personnel may compete for civilian jobs or private defense contractors may need more employees.

AMERICA'S GEOGRAPHY ANSWERS

1. 25
2. Berlin, Guatemala, Hungary, Iran, Korea, and the Suez Canal

561

Society After World War II

CHAPTER PLANNING GUIDE

	Section Lesson Objectives	Print Resources	Multimedia Resources	Sheltered English Resources
Section 1 The Challenges of Peace, pp. 564–69	**1** Explain how the U.S. economy and American workers fared after World War II. **2** Identify the most important issues of the 1948 election. **3** Describe the major goals of President Truman's Fair Deal, and relate whether they were accomplished.	▶ Guided Reading Strategy 19.1 ▶ Biography Reading 19: Jackie Robinson ▶ Section 1 Review, p. 569 ▶ Daily Quiz 19.1	▶ One-Stop Planner, Lesson 19.1 ▶ Holt Researcher: American History CD–ROM	▶ Main Idea Activity for Reteaching and Sheltered English 19.1
Section 2 The Affluent Society, pp. 570–78	**1** Relate how President Eisenhower tried to manage the nation's problems. **2** Explain how the workforce changed in the 1950s. **3** Describe suburban life during the 1950s. **4** Discuss early television programming. **5** Analyze how the trends in popular culture reflected the larger social changes among teenagers in the 1950s.	▶ Guided Reading Strategy 19.2 ▶ Geography Activity 19: Shifting Populations ▶ Primary Source Reading 19: Rock 'n' Roll Era ▶ Section 2 Review, p. 578 ▶ Daily Quiz 19.2	▶ One-Stop Planner, Lesson 19.2 ▶ Everyday Life in America Transparency 28: Queen of 1950s TV: Lucille Ball ▶ The American Nation Video Program Segment: The Growth of Suburbia; Teacher's Guide, pp. 129–34 ▶ Holt Researcher: American History CD–ROM	▶ Main Idea Activity for Reteaching and Sheltered English 19.2
Section 3 Voices of Dissent, pp. 579–87	**1** Relate how the *Brown* decision affected school segregation and exposed conflict over the segregation issue. **2** Explain how the Montgomery Bus Boycott was a major turning point in the civil rights movement. **3** Identify the challenges that Hispanics, Asian Americans, and American Indians faced in the 1950s. **4** Identify the criticisms that writers and scholars expressed about 1950s society. **5** Describe the problems that the poorest Americans faced in the 1950s.	▶ Guided Reading Strategy 19.3 ▶ Graphic Organizer Activity 19: Voices of Dissent ▶ Literature Reading 19: Lingering Racial Tension ▶ Section 3 Review, p. 587 ▶ Daily Quiz 19.3	▶ One-Stop Planner, Lesson 19.3 ▶ Holt Researcher: American History CD–ROM ▶ HRW Web site	▶ Main Idea Activity for Reteaching and Sheltered English 19.3
Chapter Review and Assessment pp. 588–89		▶ Chapter 19 Review, pp. 588–89 ▶ Chapter 19 Tutorial for Students, Parents, Mentors, and Peers ▶ Chapter 19 Test (Form A or B) ▶ Portfolio Activities and Alternative Assessment Handbook, Chapter 19	▶ Audio Program, Chapter 19 (English and Spanish) ▶ Chapter 19 Test Generator (on the One-Stop Planner) ▶ Global Skill Builder CD–ROM ▶ HRW Web site	▶ Spanish Glossary ▶ Sheltered English Chapter 19 Test

CHAPTER OVERVIEW

When World War II ended, the United States faced multiple challenges created by the process of demobilization. Unemployment and inflation threatened to destroy the nation's hard-won economic equilibrium. A number of government initiatives, however, led the United States into a period of unprecedented prosperity.

The economic boom gave rise to a baby boom and new suburban developments. Suburban culture emphasized consumerism, conformity, and children. Some teenagers rebelled against this culture, idolizing fictional rebels and listening to rock 'n' roll. Television advertisements competed for teenagers' disposable income, as a growing number of Americans bought television sets.

Although many Americans viewed the postwar years as an era of peace and opportunity, others protested the continued presence of discrimination and society's emphasis on conformity. African Americans launched the modern civil rights movement in an attempt to integrate schools and transportation systems. Hispanics also organized to obtain equal rights.

TIME TAMERS

Block Scheduling

The teacher lesson plans for each section offer a variety of activity choices to help you present the material in a block scheduling format. For further suggestions on block scheduling, see the **Block Scheduling Handbook with Team Teaching Strategies**, pp. 109–14.

Smithsonian Institution®
Internet Connections and Lesson 19
www.si.edu/hrw

Hands-On History Activities:

Classroom to Community The **Hands-On History Activities** help students make meaningful connections between events in American history and those in their own hometown. You may wish to use the Chapter 19 Activity, What Things Do You Really Need, to extend the chapter lessons, as alternative assessment, or as a block scheduling option.

Portfolio Projects

The American Nation includes multiple portfolio projects in each Pupil's Edition chapter review, as well as each unit review. Chapter 19 Portfolio Project options on p. 589 include the following:

1. Students will **prepare an illustrated chart.**
2. Students will **develop an illustrated outline.**
3. Students will **write an illustrated report.**

The American Nation
INTERNET RESOURCE DIRECTORY

To access online materials for this chapter, go to **go.hrw.com** and type in the keywords listed below.

HRW ONLINE RESOURCES
GO TO: go.hrw.com

Online Maps
KEYWORD: SE1 Maps19
• Election of 1948

Online Charts
KEYWORD: SE1 Charts19
• Baby Boom
• Civil Rights in the Truman Era
• Homes with Television Sets

Online Reading Support
KEYWORD: SE1 Strategies19

Online Rubrics
KEYWORD: SE1 Rubrics

CHAPTER ENRICHMENT LINKS
Use these Web links to extend and enrich student learning for Chapter 19.
GO TO: go.hrw.com
KEYWORD: SE1 Ch19

CHAPTER INTERNET ACTIVITIES
GO TO: go.hrw.com
• Pupil's Edition Student Activity
KEYWORD: SE1 Culture
(Students analyze popular culture during the 1950s.)
• Teacher's Edition Student Activity
KEYWORD: SE1 Gandhi
(Students conduct research on Mohandas K. Gandhi.)
• Teacher's Edition Student Activity
KEYWORD: SE1 LULAC
(Students analyze the activities of Hispanic activist groups.)

ADDITIONAL
RESOURCES

Books for Teachers

Diggins, John Patrick. *The Proud Decades: America in War and Peace, 1941–1960.* W. W. Norton & Company, 1988. Offers a highly readable overview of the period.

Inglis, Fred. *The Cruel Peace.* Basic Books, 1993. Relates Cold War myths and realities.

Books for Students

Oakley, J. Ronald. *God's Country: America in the Fifties.* Barricade Books, 1990. Examines the decade and offers many entertaining and informative details.

Tames, Richard. *The 1950s: Picture History of the 20th Century.* Watts, 1990. Reviews the major issues and events of the decade. Particularly appropriate for students reading below grade level.

Primary Sources from the Period

Hansberry, Lorraine. *A Raisin in the Sun.* Random House, 1959. Profiles one African American family's search for a place to live.

Salinger, J. D. *The Catcher in the Rye.* Bantam Books, 1951. Tells the story of Holden Caulfield, a troubled teenager.

Multimedia Materials

The Age of Anxiety. Video, 24 min. AIMS Media. Reviews the Eisenhower years.

Postwar Hopes, Cold War Fears. Video, 58 min. PBS. Analyzes the effects of the Cold War on American life during the 1950s.

CHAPTER 19

Before You Read

Build on What You Know

Ask students to answer the following questions.

How might Americans have adjusted to domestic life after the war?

Consider:

- the economic impact of peace—the return of soldiers and the return to a peacetime economy
- the response of labor freed from wartime "no strike" agreements

What kind of tensions might have been apparent by the end of the 1950s?

Consider:

- the experiences and expectations of returning veterans
- the hopes and feelings of Americans who wanted more than simple economic security

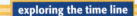

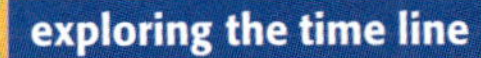

AMERICAN EVENTS

DEMOCRATIC VALUES

1948 ■ Dewey Defeats Truman? As the election of 1948 approached, President Truman found himself in an extremely difficult position. Liberal Democrats had defected to the Progressive Party, and conservative southern Democrats had defected to the States' Rights Party, known as the Dixiecrats. The *Chicago Daily Tribune* was so certain that Truman would lose to Thomas Dewey that it actually printed election-day newspapers with the headline "Dewey Defeats Truman." After being declared the winner, Truman triumphantly displayed a copy of the newspaper. The image became one of the most famous political photographs in U.S. history.

CRITICAL THINKING How might the "Dewey Defeats Truman" incident have affected Americans' opinions of the news media?

ANSWER: Students might suggest that the incident probably made many Americans more skeptical of media pronouncements.

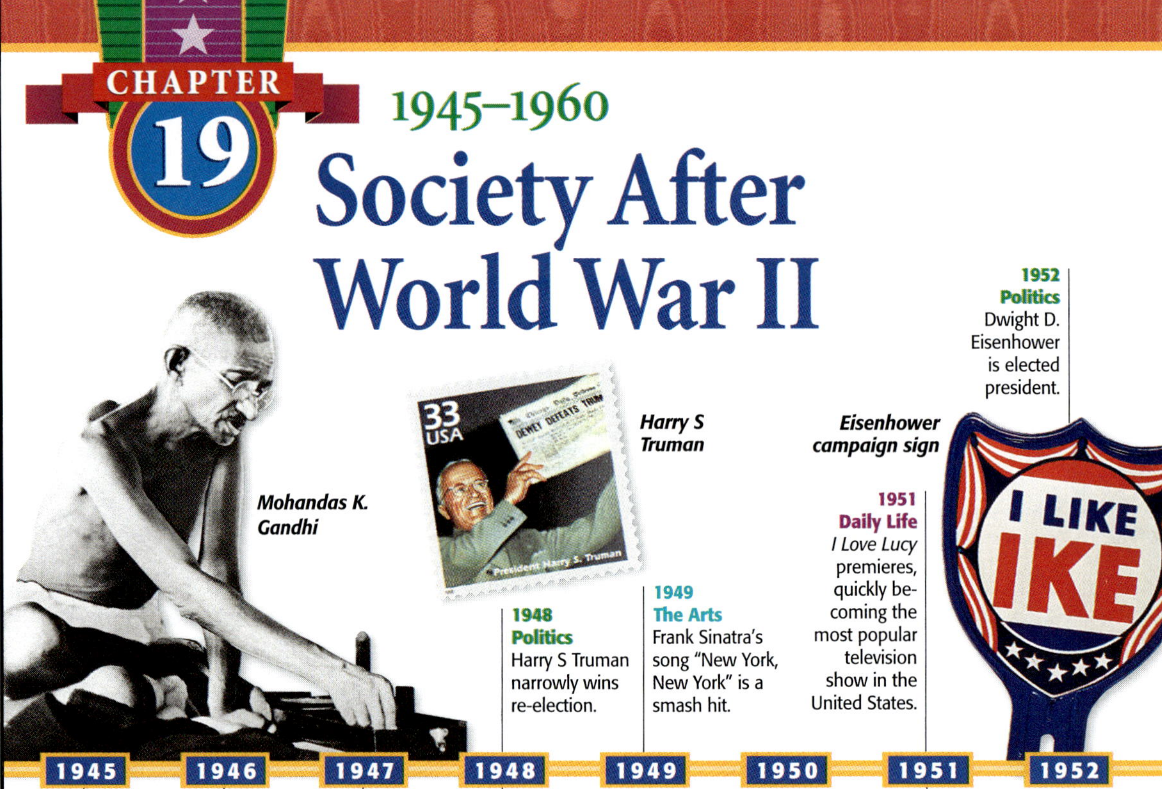

CHAPTER 19 1945–1960 Society After World War II

Mohandas K. Gandhi

Harry S Truman

Eisenhower campaign sign

1945 **The Arts** Mary Chase wins the Pulitzer Prize for her play *Harvey*.

1946 **Daily Life** Dr. Benjamin Spock's *Common Sense Book of Baby and Child Care* becomes the leading guide for parents of the baby boom.

1947 **Daily Life** Jackie Robinson signs on with the Brooklyn Dodgers to become the first African American in major league baseball.

1948 **Politics** Harry S Truman narrowly wins re-election.

1948 **World Events** Mohandas K. Gandhi is assassinated.

1949 **The Arts** Frank Sinatra's song "New York, New York" is a smash hit.

1951 **Daily Life** *I Love Lucy* premieres, quickly becoming the most popular television show in the United States.

1951 **Science and Technology** UNIVAC, the first computer for commercial use, is developed.

1951 **Business and Finance** Some 30 percent of the American workforce is employed in commerce and industry.

1952 **Politics** Dwight D. Eisenhower is elected president.

1945 1946 1947 1948 1949 1950 1951 1952

Jackie Robinson

Before You Read

Build on What You Know

The end of World War II renewed Americans' optimism about the future. Soon, however, the country was caught up in a Cold War with the Soviet Union. President Truman's commitment to contain the spread of communism led to greater U.S. involvement in Korea and a growing suspicion that there were spies at home. The Cold War intensified as President Eisenhower intensified the nuclear arms race. In this chapter you will learn how Americans adjusted to the domestic transition from war to peace.

Think About Themes

To help students create their Themes Journal entries, provide the following examples of appropriate **agree/disagree** *statements.*

Economic Development

Agree Prosperity during the 1920s allowed many people to move to new suburbs.

Disagree The boom during the Second Industrial Revolution led to crowded, dirty cities.

Cultural Diversity

Agree Many people in Nazi Germany went along with Adolf Hitler.

Disagree Abolitionists such as William Lloyd Garrison went against the crowd.

Democratic Values

Agree In the Jim Crow era, African Americans could not end widespread governmental discrimination.

Disagree Women worked to pass the Nineteenth Amendment.

Queen Elizabeth II

Elvis Presley

1953 World Events Queen Elizabeth II is crowned ruler of Great Britain.

1953 Daily Life Maureen "Little Mo" Connolly becomes the first woman to win tennis's Grand Slam.

1954 The Arts Elvis Presley releases his first record.

1954 Politics The Supreme Court outlaws school segregation with its *Brown* v. *Board of Education* ruling.

1955 Science and Technology Jonas Salk announces the development of a successful polio vaccine.

1955 Business and Finance Ray Kroc opens the first McDonald's franchise.

1956 The Arts Cecil B. DeMille remakes his epic film *The Ten Commandments.*

1957 Business and Finance The country's first commercial nuclear power plant begins operation in Pennsylvania.

1957 The Arts Jack Kerouac publishes *On the Road.*

1958 World Events Guinea, the former French-African colony, gains independence.

1959 Politics Alaska and Hawaii become the 49th and 50th states of the Union, respectively.

1960 Science and Technology American scientists launch the first weather satellite.

1960 Daily Life Thirteen former TV-game-show contestants are arrested on perjury charges after investigators discover the show is rigged.

1953 | 1954 | 1955 | 1956 | 1957 | 1958 | 1959 | 1960

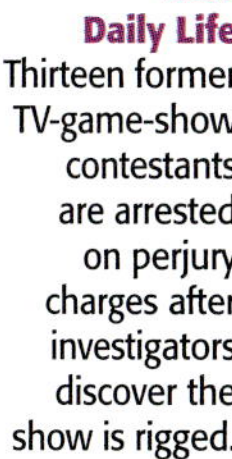

Game-show contestant Charles Van Doren

exploring the time line

GLOBAL EVENTS

internet connect

TOPIC: Mohandas K. Gandhi
GO TO: go.hrw.com
KEYWORD: SE1 Gandhi

Have students access the Internet through the HRW Web site to conduct research on Mohandas K. Gandhi. Then ask each student to create an illustrated biography that describes Gandhi's life, his philosophical outlook, and his influence today. Remind students that they should synthesize and summarize material in their biographies in order to present a full portrait of Gandhi.

Think About Themes

Decide whether you **agree** *or* **disagree** *with the following statements. Note why in your journal.*

Economic Development An economic boom will affect population growth and residential patterns.

Cultural Diversity People generally prefer to "follow the crowd" rather than express their individuality.

Democratic Values Citizens are powerless to change government policies that discriminate against them.

563

SECTION 1

After completing Section 1, students should be able to:

OBJECTIVE 1 *Explain how the U.S. economy and American workers fared after World War II.*

OBJECTIVE 2 *Identify the most important issues of the 1948 election.*

OBJECTIVE 3 *Describe the major goals of President Truman's Fair Deal, and relate whether they were accomplished.*

LET'S GET STARTED!

Write the following questions on the chalkboard: *How might the transition to peace affect a nation's economy after years of war? Why?* As students enter the classroom, ask them to answer the questions in writing. Have volunteers share their responses. *(Students might suggest that the transition to peace could harm a nation's economy by reducing defense spending by the government.)* Tell students that in Section 1 they will learn how the U.S. government attempted to bolster the economy after World War II.

SECTION 1 RESOURCES

PRINT

- Guided Reading Strategy 19.1
- Biography Reading 19: Jackie Robinson
- Section 1 Review, p. 569
- Daily Quiz 19.1

MULTIMEDIA

- One-Stop Planner, Lesson 19.1
- Holt Researcher: American History CD–ROM

SHELTERED ENGLISH

- Main Idea Activity for Reteaching and Sheltered English 19.1

✔ READING TO UNDERSTAND

To help students master the section objectives, have them answer the **READING CHECKS** and complete **Guided Reading Strategy 19.1** as they read the section.

The Challenges of Peace

OBJECTIVES

Read to understand:

1. how the U.S. economy and American workers fared after World War II
2. what the most important issues of the 1948 election were
3. what the major goals of President Truman's Fair Deal were, and whether they were accomplished

KEY TERMS

GI Bill of Rights
Employment Act
Council of Economic Advisers
Taft-Hartley Act
Committee on Civil Rights
Dixiecrats
Fair Deal

KEY PEOPLE

J. Strom Thurmond
Henry Wallace
Thomas Dewey

"When [the war] finally came to a conclusion, I think it set in motion [questions like] 'Here we are now. What are we going to do about life as we try to reestablish it in our community?'"

—Harold Toliver

The Homecoming *by Norman Rockwell*

Reverend Harold Toliver recalled how the end of World War II stirred both hopes and concerns for many Americans. Many New Deal supporters like Toliver looked to President Harry S Truman for guidance. They hoped that he would help the country recover from the war by continuing the reforms begun by President Roosevelt. "Franklin Roosevelt is not dead. His ideals live," declared New York mayor Fiorello La Guardia. President Truman tried to meet these expectations by promoting Roosevelt's ideals with his own reform programs.

The Problems of Demobilization

By mid-1946 more than 9 million men and women had been discharged from the military. The soldiers received a hero's welcome, but their return also sparked concern. How could the economy absorb all these new workers? Many Americans feared that the country would fall into an economic decline similar to the one that had followed World War I.

Postwar measures. Even before the war had ended, Congress began preparing for peace. Preventing an economic depression and helping war-weary veterans make the difficult transition to civilian life were top priorities. Congress passed the Servicemen's Readjustment Act of 1944, more commonly known as the **GI Bill of Rights**. The bill provided pensions and government loans to help veterans start businesses and buy homes or farms. Millions of veterans also received money through the GI Bill to attend college. Between 1944 and 1962 almost 8 million veterans attended college or technical schools on the GI Bill. This led to a dramatic increase in the number of American college graduates. Government worker Nelson Poynter described the impact of the GI Bill.

> **"The GI Bill . . . had more to do with thrusting us into a new era than anything else. Millions of people whose parents or grandparents had never dreamed of going to college saw that they could go. . . . Essentially I think it made us a far more democratic people."**

This recently issued stamp commemorates the passage of the GI Bill in 1944.

To ensure postwar economic growth, Congress passed the **Employment Act** of 1946. The act committed the government to promoting full employment and production. It also established the **Council of Economic Advisers** to confer with the president on economic policy.

SPOTLIGHT on the GI Bill

Ask each student to interview a World War II veteran who received GI Bill benefits. *(If students cannot locate a veteran, ask them to read a primary source on the subject.)* Interviewers should focus on how receiving GI Bill benefits affected the veterans. Then organize students into groups and have each group write a script for a documentary film about the GI Bill.
Cooperative Learning, Block Scheduling

NOTE: For an additional teaching idea, see the Chapter 19 listing and coding lesson in the **Creative Teaching Strategies** handbook.

TEACH OBJECTIVE 1

LEVEL 1: Pair students and tell them to imagine that they are American workers in 1948. Have each pair develop a short dialogue about how the U.S. economy and American workers fared after World War II. *(Students should note that the economy remained fairly strong, despite fears of a depression. Workers suffered many problems, however, including antiunion legislation, high inflation, and job loss.)* Ask volunteers to perform their dialogues for the class.
Sheltered English, Cooperative Learning

Changing Ways: Higher Education

Understanding Change Before the passage of the GI Bill, a college education was often something only the wealthy sought. Since then, obtaining a college education has become much more common. *What differences do you observe between the images of college students in the late 1940s and the late 1990s? What statistics in the chart surprise you the most? Why?*

	Then	Now
Number of Institutions of Higher Education	1,863	3,706
Annual Student Body Enrollment	2,281,000	14,715,000
Annual Number of Bachelor Degrees Conferred	496,874	1,191,000
Student Body (Female / Male)	32% / 68%	54% / 46%

Sources: *Historical Statistics of the United States; Statistical Abstract of the United States: 1998.* Data reflect 1950 and 1995.

THEN

NOW

Despite widespread fears, the postwar depression never came. For example, the government canceled some $23 billion in military contracts. Those plants that had been making tanks and bombers began producing consumer goods instead. Employment levels remained high. Many Americans also began to spend the money they had saved during the war. Furthermore, because agricultural output in foreign countries had been shattered by the war, U.S. food exports increased.

Problems for workers. Not all was rosy on the economic front, however. Government measures encouraged employers to give priority to veterans in hiring. As a result, many workers lost their jobs to returning veterans. Congress abolished the Fair Employment Practices Committee, which had helped protect African Americans from discrimination. The government also retired the character of "Rosie the Riveter." Instead, the government started a campaign to encourage women to quit their jobs and become full-time homemakers. Some women wanted to keep their jobs. This was particularly true for working-class women whose families needed their incomes. "If [women] are capable, I don't see why they should give up their position," said one female steelworker. Despite these sentiments, most women who did not willingly give up their jobs were fired or pressured to quit their jobs after the war.

Another problem that concerned workers was the effect of postwar inflation. The cost of goods soared after most wartime price controls were lifted in 1946. Meat prices zoomed so high that some markets began selling horse meat. Blaming President Truman, angry consumers called him "Horsemeat Harry."

MORE ON THE GRAPH

The Changing Ivy League. The GI Bill profoundly affected the social order at Ivy League universities. In the immediate postwar era, Harvard and other prestigious schools charged $400 per year for tuition. The GI Bill gave veterans up to $500 per year for tuition, making it possible for people some Harvard students disdainfully called "poor boys" to enroll in virtually any school in the country. A *Time* magazine article asked, "Why Go to Podunk College?, When the Government Will Send You to Yale?" Many veterans heeded the implicit advice and enrolled in Ivy League schools. In 1946 alone, Harvard's student population nearly doubled, from 2,750 in February to 5,000 in September.

CRITICAL THINKING Based on the preceding figures, by what percentage did Harvard's enrollment increase in 1946?

ANSWER: Students should indicate that enrollment increased by about 82 percent.

CHANGING WAYS ANSWERS

differences—the 1990s photograph shows a larger, more diverse, and more casually dressed classroom population; statistics—female students now outnumber male students; students' answers will vary.

LEVEL 2: Organize students into small groups and tell them to imagine that they are newsmagazine editors preparing an issue entitled The Postwar Economy. Ask each group to write brief summaries of articles that might appear in the magazine. Remind groups that their articles should describe how the U.S. economy and American workers fared after World War II. *(See the Level 1 lesson for the correct issues.)* After groups have completed their summaries, conduct a discussion on the economy and workers after World War II. **Cooperative Learning**

LEVEL 3: Conduct a brief discussion on how the U.S. economy and American workers fared after World War II. *(See the Level 1 lesson for the correct issues.)* Then have each student write a brief economic analysis of the period from 1945 to 1950. Students should explain why many Americans feared a postwar depression, why that depression failed to materialize, why many workers lost ground after the war, and why the government enacted antilabor policies. Have volunteers read their analyses to the class. Students may wish to include their analyses in their portfolios.

▶**ASSIGNMENT:** *Have each student create a detailed outline of the subsection entitled The Problems of Demobilization. Alternately, have each student interview a person who lived through the demobilization era. Ask students to present the results of their interviews in a short paper.*

ECONOMIC DEVELOPMENT

A Reason to Strike. A month after World War II ended, the *CIO News* reported that between the five-year periods 1935 and 1939 and 1940 and 1944, after-tax profits in the steel industry had risen 113 percent, to more than $1 billion. A University of California study published in 1945 indicated that steelworkers earned just $45.60 per week—totaling far less than the $2,700 per year then needed to achieve a moderate standard of living. Workers in other industries earned even lower weekly wages.

CRITICAL THINKING How might the *CIO News* article, the University of California study, and other similar documents have affected labor?

ANSWER: Students might indicate that the article, the study, and other documents helped give rise to the many strikes launched after World War II.

VISUAL RECORD ANSWER

Students might suggest the importance of worldwide unity of workers.

Labor unrest. As inflation continued to rise, people took matters into their own hands. Freed from their wartime pledges not to strike, millions of workers walked off the job. They fought for wage increases and the preservation of some wartime price controls. In 1946 almost 5 million workers walked the picket lines.

President Truman generally supported labor unions. However, he opposed these strikes because he feared they would disrupt the economy. After some 400,000 coal miners went on strike in the spring of 1946, Truman ordered the army to take control of the mines. The president of the United Mine Workers, John L. Lewis, responded, "You can't dig coal with bayonets." After the courts slapped heavy fines on the union, Lewis ordered the miners back to work. Later, Truman threatened to end a railway strike by drafting the strikers into the army. Truman's threat spurred union leaders to negotiate an end to the strike.

INTERPRETING THE VISUAL RECORD

Labor unions. These workers marched in support of labor unions in 1946. ***What message do you think is conveyed by the signs the marchers are using?***

In 1947 the Republican-controlled Congress passed a bill designed to reduce the strength of organized labor. The bill was known as the **Taft-Hartley Act**. It gave judges the power to end some strikes and outlawed closed-shop agreements. It also restricted unions' political contributions and required union officers to swear that they were not Communists. Truman vetoed the bill, but Congress overrode his veto.

The Taft-Hartley Act stirred angry debate. Conservative supporters of the bill argued that it corrected unfair advantages that had been given to labor by New Deal measures. Pro-labor supporters argued that it was a "slave labor law." Although the act limited the actions unions could take, organized labor continued to make some gains in the postwar years. For example, in 1948 General Motors and the United Automobile Workers (UAW) signed a contract that linked wage increases to increases in the cost of living. Union contracts also began to include such benefits as retirement pensions and health insurance.

✔ **READING CHECK:** How did the U.S. economy and American workers fare after the war?

The 1948 Election

By 1948 high inflation and labor unrest had decreased public support for President Truman. "To err is Truman," people joked. Despite his low standing in the polls, Truman continued to take a strong stand on controversial issues. His position on civil rights in particular became an important issue in the 1948 campaign.

The Committee on Civil Rights. In 1946 civil rights groups urged Truman to take action against the racism that stained American society. They pointed out that most African Americans throughout the nation faced segregation in schools and on buses and discrimination in housing and employment. Furthermore, in some areas African Americans continued to be lynched. Previous efforts to battle these conditions had met a wall of resistance.

TEACH OBJECTIVE 2

ALL LEVELS: Ask students why so many Americans believed that Republican Thomas Dewey would win the presidential election of 1948. *(Students might suggest that Truman's stances on civil rights, labor, and foreign policy alienated many Democrats.)* To help students understand the most important issues of the election, copy the following graphic organizer on the chalkboard, omitting the italicized answers. Have each student complete it. **Sheltered English**

THE 1948 ELECTION

President Truman's Platform
- *supported civil rights in general and issued executive orders banning racial discrimination in the military and in federal hiring*
- *supported the repeal of the Taft-Hartley Act*
- *supported increased federal aid for agriculture, education, and housing*

↓

The Two-Way Split in the Democratic Party
Cause: *southern Democrats' dislike of Truman's stance on civil rights*
Cause: *liberal Democrats' dislike of Truman's stance on labor and foreign policy*
Effects: *split the party and created the possibility of a Republican win*

↓

Election and Results
- *massive campaign effort mounted by Truman*
- *attacked Republicans' conservatism*
- *election won by Truman*

In December 1946 Truman created the **Committee on Civil Rights** to examine the issue. The committee's report, *To Secure These Rights*, appeared in October 1947. The report documented widespread civil rights abuses. These abuses included discrimination against African American veterans and an increase in racial violence. It also called for an end to racial segregation in interstate transportation. Based on the committee's findings, Truman urged Congress to pass an antilynching law and an anti-poll-tax measure. He also worked to end discrimination in federal agencies and the military.

When Congress did not immediately act on the report's recommendations, African American leader A. Philip Randolph threatened to launch a campaign of civil disobedience. In July 1948 Truman issued executive orders banning racial discrimination in the military and in federal hiring. He also took steps to end employment discrimination by companies holding government contracts.

White southern Democrats were outraged both by African American demands for civil rights and by Truman's actions. Senator Olin Johnston of South Carolina warned angrily that the South's electoral votes "won't be for Truman. They'll be for somebody else. He ain't going to be re-elected."

To win the 1948 election, President Truman carried out a "whistle-stop" campaign aboard a train.

Strategies for Success: Conducting an Interview

Oral history interviews are one of the most important methods that historians use to gather information about the past. An effective oral history interview must be accompanied by preliminary research as well as follow-up analysis.

How to Conduct an Interview

1. **Identify and research the topic.** Identify the general topic you wish to investigate and a specific person with firsthand knowledge of the topic. Then gather as much information as you can about the topic and your potential interview subject.
2. **Set up the interview.** Contact your potential interview subject, identify yourself, and clearly state your purpose in requesting an interview. Schedule a convenient time and place for the interview.
3. **Prepare questions.** Prepare questions for the interview that address what you need to know and that follow one another in a logical fashion.
4. **Conduct the interview.** Be an active listener during the interview. Allow your interview subject to respond to your questions freely, but remain in charge of the general direction of the interview. Ask follow-up questions if you need additional information.
5. **Analyze the interview.** Shortly after the interview has been completed, review your notes and listen to a recording of the interview. Summarize the content of the interview and evaluate its reliability as historical evidence. Use the results to form generalizations and draw conclusions about your topic.

Applying the Strategy

Prepare for and conduct an oral history interview with one of the following:

a. a U.S. military veteran who received financial aid for college under the GI Bill
b. a person who voted in the 1948 presidential election
c. a person who was a teenager in the late 1940s

Practicing the Strategy

Answer the following questions.

1. What information about your subject were you able to acquire before the interview?
2. What questions did you prepare for the interview?
3. How did the interview contribute to your understanding of the United States after World War II?

DEMOCRATIC VALUES

President Truman and Civil Rights. President Truman appointed both African American and white citizens to serve on the Committee on Civil Rights. In addition to decrying racial violence, the committee's report called for "the elimination of segregation, based on race, color, creed, or national origin, from American life." Although Truman's later executive orders did not achieve this goal, they did expand opportunities for African Americans.

CRITICAL THINKING How might Truman's executive order on the military have affected recruitment?

ANSWER: Students might suggest that it probably encouraged African American enlistment.

STRATEGIES FOR SUCCESS ANSWERS

Applying the Strategy
Students should research both the topic and the interviewee and prepare questions before conducting the interview.

Practicing the Strategy
1. Answers will vary. Students should have gathered some preliminary information.
2. Answers will vary. Students' questions should be on the topic and open-ended.
3. Answers will vary. Students should have a better understanding of it.

TEACH OBJECTIVE 3

LEVEL 1: Pair students and have them write a series of newspaper headlines on President Truman's Fair Deal—several headlines on the major goals of the policy and several headlines on whether those goals were accomplished. *(Students should note that Truman's Fair Deal promised full employment, a higher minimum wage, a national health insurance program, affordable housing, increased aid to farmers, and expansion of welfare benefits. He did not achieve most of these goals, although Congress did extend Social Security benefits, raise the minimum wage, approve urban renewal programs, and expand water programs.)* Ask volunteers to share their headlines with the class. Post the headlines around the classroom. **Sheltered English, Cooperative Learning**

LEVELS 2 AND 3: Tell students to imagine that it is 1952 and that they are Americans with strong views on President Truman's Fair Deal. Have each student write a letter to the editor of a local newspaper, commenting on the Fair Deal. In their editorials, students should briefly describe the goals of the Fair Deal, note whether President Truman accomplished those goals, and offer their own opinions of the Fair Deal. *(See the Level 1 lesson for the correct goals and achievements.)* Students may wish to include their editorials in their portfolios.

ACROSS THE CURRICULUM

▸GOVERNMENT◂

Henry Wallace and the Progressive Party. As vice president during Franklin D. Roosevelt's third term, Henry Wallace traveled to China, Latin America, and Siberia. His journeys strongly influenced his political views. As the Progressive Party's presidential candidate in 1948, he ran on a platform largely devoted to international issues. Wallace, who had been replaced by Harry S Truman for Roosevelt's fourth term, believed that Truman's firm stand toward the Soviet Union had the potential to result in war. He also feared that it could lead to political persecution. Some commentators called Wallace a "communist dupe" and a "Stalinist stooge." However, his views appealed to many Americans. He won more than 1 million popular votes in the 1948 election.

CRITICAL THINKING Why might Wallace have believed that Truman's approach toward the Soviet Union could result in war?

ANSWER: Students might suggest that Wallace believed that Truman's approach was too confrontational.

MAP ANSWER

the Great Plains, the lower South, and the Northeast

This NAACP button was worn by some Truman supporters who rallied behind the Democratic Party platform committee's proposal of a strong civil rights plank.

The Democratic convention. Southern opposition did not prevent Truman from winning his party's nomination. His support, however, remained weak. Some delegates even wore buttons proclaiming, "We're just mild about Harry," a twist on his campaign slogan "We're just wild about Harry."

The Democratic platform called for the repeal of the Taft-Hartley Act. It also pushed for an increase in federal aid for housing, education, and agriculture; and broader Social Security benefits. The platform committee's proposal of a strong civil rights plank divided the Democratic Party. The all-white southern delegation threatened to walk out of the convention. The National Association for the Advancement of Colored People (NAACP) declared, "LET 'EM WALK."

> **"There is no room . . . for compromise. . . . Those Democrats who say the President's recommendation of such a program is a 'stab in the back' of the South are saying they do not choose to abide by the Constitution. They are also saying . . . that the whole section of our nation believes as they do. . . . We know it is not true!"**

After bitter debate, the delegates adopted the civil rights plank. Southern delegates then stormed out of the convention and formed the States' Rights Party. The party was nicknamed the **Dixiecrats**. The Dixiecrats called for continued racial segregation. The party nominated South Carolina governor J. Strom Thurmond as its presidential candidate.

The Election of 1948

Learning from Maps Truman received slightly less than 50 percent of the popular vote but had a solid majority in the electoral college.

REGION In which areas of the United States was Truman's support weakest?

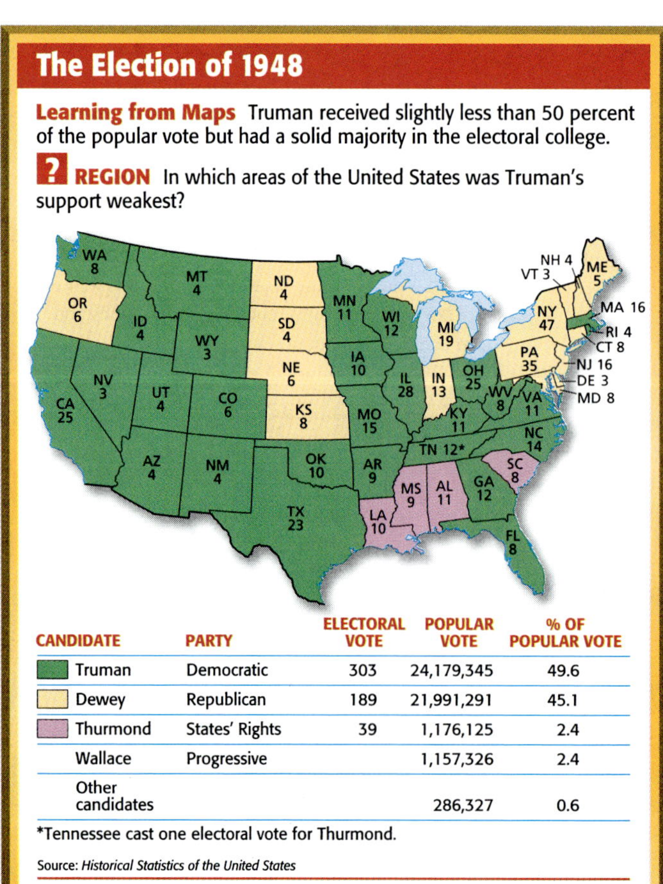

CANDIDATE	PARTY	ELECTORAL VOTE	POPULAR VOTE	% OF POPULAR VOTE
Truman	Democratic	303	24,179,345	49.6
Dewey	Republican	189	21,991,291	45.1
Thurmond	States' Rights	39	1,176,125	2.4
Wallace	Progressive		1,157,326	2.4
Other candidates			286,327	0.6

*Tennessee cast one electoral vote for Thurmond.

Source: *Historical Statistics of the United States*

The gulf widens. A different issue caused another break within the Democratic Party. Troubled by Truman's antilabor actions in 1946, former vice president Henry Wallace and other liberal New Dealers left the Democratic Party to found a new Progressive Party. This group called for an extension of the New Deal. They also called for efforts to improve relations with the Soviet Union.

With the Democratic vote split three ways, the Republicans smelled victory. They nominated Governor Thomas Dewey of New York as their presidential candidate. Earl Warren, the popular governor of California, was nominated as Dewey's running mate. Opinion polls and most newspapers predicted a Dewey victory.

However, the Truman campaign began attacking the conservatism of the Republicans and radicalism of the Progressives. Truman crisscrossed the country by train, criticizing the "do-nothing" Republican-led Congress. Crowds began

REVIEW

Have students complete the **Section 1 Review** on p. 569.

ASSESS

Have students complete **Daily Quiz 19.1**. As **Alternative Assessment**, you may want to use the GI Bill documentary script or the Fair Deal headlines in this section's lessons.

RETEACH

Have students complete **Main Idea Activity for Reteaching and Sheltered English 19.1**. Have students create charts or graphic organizers on one of the following issues: the postwar economy, the presidential election of 1948, or the Fair Deal. After students have finished their charts, organize students into triads and have them discuss the material in Section 1.
Sheltered English, Cooperative Learning

EXTEND

Have students conduct research on both the Wagner-Connery Act and the Taft-Hartley Act. Then have each student compare and contrast the acts in a brief paper. Ask volunteers to read their papers to the class. **Block Scheduling**

---

to chant, "Give 'em hell, Harry." In one of the great upsets of U.S. political history, Truman won the election with 303 electoral votes to Dewey's 189 electoral votes.

✔ **READING CHECK:** What were the most important issues in the 1948 election?

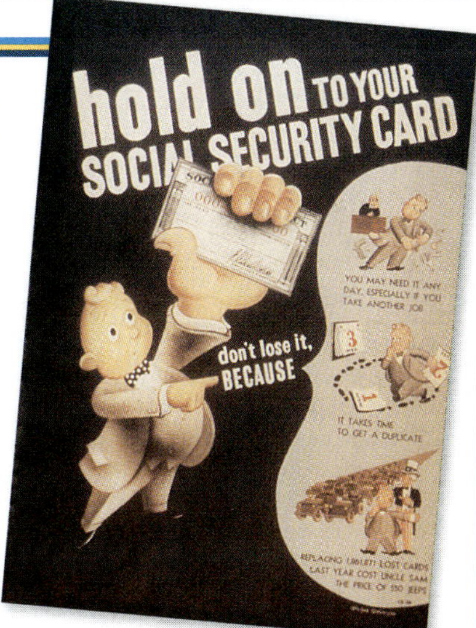

INTERPRETING THE VISUAL RECORD

Social Security. Although Congress expanded Social Security benefits, President Truman had trouble getting other Fair Deal legislation passed. *How does this poster reflect the importance of Social Security?*

The Fair Deal

Encouraged by his victory, President Truman urged Congress to continue Franklin D. Roosevelt's New Deal reforms. Truman proclaimed that "every segment of our population . . . has a right to expect from our government a fair deal." He proposed a series of new reforms called the **Fair Deal**. Truman's Fair Deal promised full employment, a higher minimum wage, a national health insurance program, construction of affordable housing, increased aid to farmers, and the expansion of welfare benefits to more people.

Most Republicans and even some Democrats opposed the president's program. Nevertheless, Truman managed to push through some of his reforms. Between 1949 and 1952 Congress extended Social Security benefits to some 10 million additional people, raised the minimum wage from 40 to 75 cents an hour, and approved programs to demolish or rebuild slums. Congress also expanded federal programs to promote flood control, hydroelectric power, and irrigation.

Overall, though, the Fair Deal had limited success in an increasingly conservative postwar political climate. Americans had become less enthusiastic about reform programs that would further expand the government. Most people, weary of the upheavals of recent years, just wanted peace, stability, and gradual prosperity.

✔ **READING CHECK:** What were the goals of President Truman's Fair Deal? Were these goals accomplished?

SECTION  REVIEW

Define and explain the significance of the following terms:
GI Bill of Rights
Employment Act
Council of Economic Advisers
Taft-Hartley Act
Committee on Civil Rights
Dixiecrats
Fair Deal

Identify and explain the significance of the following individuals:
J. Strom Thurmond
Henry Wallace
Thomas Dewey

1. **Using Graphic Organizers** Copy the chart below. Use it to list the major successes of President Truman's Fair Deal program and changing public opinion of reform.

Successes	Public opinion
1.	1.
2.	2.
3.	3.
4.	4.

2. **Assessing Consequences** How did the end of World War II affect American workers?
3. **Synthesizing** What were the major issues of the 1948 presidential campaign?
4. **Taking a Stand** If you had been a voter in 1948, who would you have chosen for president? Why?

Critical Thinking

5. How did politics in the late 1940s reflect the ways that World War II had changed the United States?
Consider:
• what political steps were taken to ensure economic stability
• what political actions were taken to help veterans
• how political actions reflected desires to expand democracy

---

VISUAL RECORD ANSWER

Students might cite the difficulty of getting a Social Security card replaced.

SECTION 1 REVIEW ANSWERS

Define and Identify
For significance, see the following pages:

• GI Bill of Rights, p. 564
• Employment Act, p. 564
• Council of Economic Advisers, p. 564
• Taft-Hartley Act, p. 566
• Committee on Civil Rights, p. 567
• Dixiecrats, p. 568
• J. Strom Thurmond, p. 568
• Henry Wallace, p. 568
• Thomas Dewey, p. 568
• Fair Deal, p. 569

1. successes—extended Social Security, raised minimum wage, began urban renewal, passed water policies; public opinion—more conservative; less enthusiastic about reform; weary of upheavals; wanted peace, stability, and prosperity

2. forced some workers out of jobs; resulted in high inflation, strikes, and passage of the Taft-Hartley Act

3. civil rights, labor policy and foreign policy

4. Answers will vary. Students should justify their selections.

5. Answers will vary. Students might answer that the politics reflected postwar economic difficulties, such as high inflation and labor unrest. The politics also reflected the rights of veterans and the growing tension over civil rights issues.

SECTION 2

After completing Section 2, students should be able to:

OBJECTIVE 1 *Relate how President Eisenhower tried to manage the nation's problems.*

OBJECTIVE 2 *Explain how the workforce changed in the 1950s.*

OBJECTIVE 3 *Describe suburban life during the 1950s.*

OBJECTIVE 4 *Discuss early television programming.*

OBJECTIVE 5 *Analyze how the trends in popular culture reflected the larger social changes among teenagers in the 1950s.*

LET'S GET STARTED!

As students enter the classroom, display Everyday Life in America Transparency 28, Queen of 1950s TV: Lucille Ball, from **American History Visual Resources.** Distribute the accompanying worksheet and ask students to answer the questions. Have volunteers share their answers. Then tell students that in Section 2 they will learn more about American society and popular culture during the 1950s.

SECTION 2 RESOURCES

PRINT

- Guided Reading Strategy 19.2
- Geography Activity 19: Shifting Populations
- Primary Source Reading 19: Rock 'n' Roll Era
- Section 2 Review, p. 578
- Daily Quiz 19.2

MULTIMEDIA

- One-Stop Planner, Lesson 19.2
- Everyday Life in America Transparency 28: Queen of 1950s TV: Lucille Ball
- The American Nation Video Program Segment: The Growth of Suburbia; Teacher's Guide, pp. 129–34
- Holt Researcher: American History CD–ROM

SHELTERED ENGLISH

- Main Idea Activity for Reteaching and Sheltered English 19.2

✔ READING TO UNDERSTAND

To help students master the section objectives, have them answer the **READING CHECKS** and complete **Guided Reading Strategy 19.2** as they read the section.

The Affluent Society

OBJECTIVES

Read to understand:

1. how President Eisenhower tried to manage the nation's problems
2. how the workforce changed in the 1950s
3. what suburban life was like during the 1950s
4. what early television programming was like
5. how the trends in popular culture reflected the larger social changes among teenagers in the 1950s

KEY TERMS

Modern Republicanism
automation
Highway Act
baby boom
juvenile delinquency
rock 'n' roll

KEY PEOPLE

Oveta Culp Hobby
George Meany
Elvis Presley

"Who decides whether you shall be happy or unhappy? You do! Happiness is achievable and the process for obtaining it is not complicated. Anyone who desires it, who wills it, and who learns and applies the right formula may become a happy person."

—Dr. Norman Vincent Peale

A Practical Guide to Mastering the Problems of Everyday Living — *The Power of Positive Thinking* — Norman Vincent Peale — Author of the great inspirational best seller *A Guide to Confident Living*

Norman Vincent Peale's book

During the 1950s millions of Americans listened to the advice of Dr. Norman Vincent Peale, a dynamic speaker and Protestant minister who wrote the 1952 book *The Power of Positive Thinking.* Peale's claim that all people could achieve success if they had the right attitude represented the optimism of the prosperous decade. In an era dominated by Cold War fears, Peale offered a formula to help people overcome their anxieties.

The Eisenhower Era

President Dwight D. Eisenhower also reflected the optimism of the 1950s. Rejecting the Democrats' New Deal proposals, Americans elected Eisenhower, a Republican, president in 1952. He took office in 1953 determined to boost the economy and reform the federal government. He pledged to cut bureaucracy, to curb what he called the "creeping socialism" of the New Deal, to balance the budget, and to reduce government regulation of the economy.

In his first year as president, Eisenhower eliminated thousands of government jobs and cut billions of dollars from the federal budget. To reduce government influence over the economy, he cut farm subsidies and turned over federally owned coastal lands to states that would allow it to be developed. Nevertheless, Social Security and unemployment benefits were expanded during his administration, and the minimum wage was increased. Eisenhower established the Department of Health, Education, and Welfare, under the supervision of Texan Oveta Culp Hobby. The president also supported the largest increase in educational spending up to that time. This approach to domestic affairs, which Eisenhower described as "conservative when it comes to money and liberal when it comes to human beings," became known as **Modern Republicanism.**

Providing funding for social programs, defense, and other government obligations weakened Eisenhower's pledge to balance the federal budget. Only three of the eight budgets he presided over were balanced. Furthermore, during his years in office the federal debt grew by about 9 percent, to $291 billion.

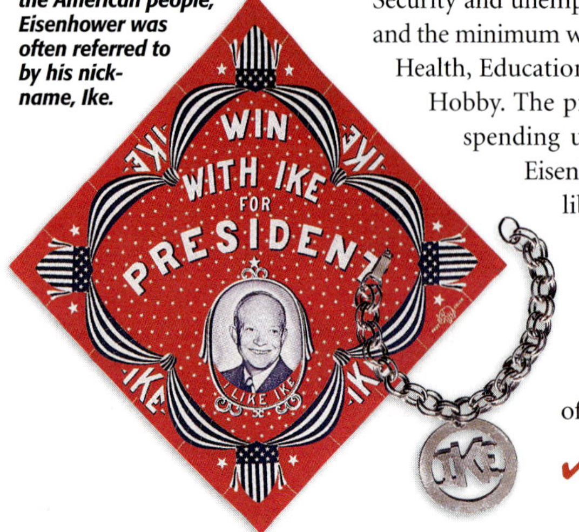

Warmly received by the American people, Eisenhower was often referred to by his nickname, Ike.

✔ **READING CHECK:** How did President Eisenhower try to manage the nation's problems?

TEACH OBJECTIVE 1

LEVEL 1: Pair students and ask them to write paragraphs describing how President Eisenhower tried to manage the nation's problems. *(Students should indicate that Eisenhower followed an approach known as Modern Republicanism. He cut some government programs while protecting and expanding others.)* Have volunteers read their paragraphs to the class. **Sheltered English, Cooperative Learning**

LEVEL 2: Tell students to imagine that they are President Eisenhower and that they have just retired from politics. Ask each student to write a short memoir explaining how Eisenhower attempted to manage the nation's problems. *(See the Level 1 lesson for the correct approaches.)* Have volunteers read their memoirs to the class.

LEVEL 3: Conduct a brief discussion on how President Eisenhower attempted to manage the nation's problems. *(See the Level 1 lesson for the correct approaches.)* Then ask each student to create a detailed graphic organizer that compares and contrasts Eisenhower's approaches with those of previous presidents during the 1900s. Suggest that students consult their textbooks if they do not remember specific details about earlier presidents. Have volunteers present their graphic organizers to the class. Then ask students to "grade" Eisenhower as a president. Conduct a debate between students with different opinions.

The Economy

For many Americans the 1950s was a decade of economic prosperity. One man described the era as an escalator. "You just stood there and you moved up," he said. Unemployment and inflation remained very low. By the mid-1950s more than 60 percent of Americans were earning a middle-class income, which at that time was considered to be $3,000–$10,000 annually. Never before, the popular media declared, had so many people enjoyed such prosperity. "This is a new kind of capitalism," declared the *Reader's Digest*, "capitalism for the many, not for the few."

Changes in the workplace. The economy received a boost from changes in the workforce. Large corporations prospered during the decade. Some 5,000 companies merged to form larger corporations. American factories were changing as well. Throughout the 1950s companies introduced machines that could perform industrial operations faster and more efficiently than human workers. This process of **automation** greatly increased productivity. However, it also reduced the number of manufacturing jobs. Many workers began to fear an automated future, as the song "Automation" noted.

> "I walked, walked, walked into the foreman's office
> To find out what was what.
> I looked him in the eye and said, 'What goes?'
> And this is the answer I got:
> His eyes turned red, then green, then blue
> And it suddenly dawned on me—
> There was a robot sitting in the seat
> Where the foreman used to be."

As the number of blue-collar, or manufacturing, jobs decreased, professional and service jobs increased. Huge new corporations required a multitude of managers and clerical workers, positions referred to as white-collar jobs.

Many of the newly created service jobs were in occupations traditionally filled by women. Those jobs included nursing, teaching, retail sales, and low-level clerical work, sometimes called pink-collar jobs. By 1960, women made up about one third of the total workforce.

The new union style. Changes in the workforce also influenced organized labor. Boosted in part by the merger of the American Federation of Labor (AFL) and the Congress of Industrial Organizations (CIO) in 1955, union membership grew steadily in the 1950s. It peaked at some 18.5 million in 1956.

INTERPRETING THE VISUAL RECORD

Automation. The use of machines allowed workers to make products faster. ***What examples of automation can you identify in this picture?***

PEOPLE IN HISTORY

Oveta Culp Hobby. Before becoming secretary of the Department of Health, Education, and Welfare (HEW), Oveta Culp Hobby played a crucial role in World War II. In 1942 Hobby became the first female colonel in U.S. history when she accepted a position as head of the newly created Women's Army Auxiliary Corps—later known as the Women's Army Corps, or WAC. Hobby believed that women, like men, had a responsibility to help defend their country. She once told WAC recruits, "You have a debt and a date. A debt to democracy, a date with destiny." Hobby eventually commanded more than 100,000 WACs serving all over the globe. She accepted the HEW position in 1953.

CRITICAL THINKING Do you think the federal government should play a role in health and education? Why or why not?

ANSWER: Some students might suggest that the federal government has a special responsibility to protect citizens' health.

VISUAL RECORD ANSWER

Students might mention the assembly line or the lifters suspended fro the ceiling.

Multimedia Resources

Everyday Life in America Transparency 28: Queen of 1950s TV: Lucille Ball

TEACH OBJECTIVE 2

ALL LEVELS: Ask students to share their preconceptions, if any, about the workforce in the 1950s. *(Answers will vary. Some students might suggest that many workers of the era were "men in gray flannel suits.")* Conduct a brief discussion of these preconceptions and stereotypes. To help students understand how the workforce changed in the 1950s, copy the graphic organizer on the chalkboard, omitting the italicized answers. Have each student complete it.
Sheltered English

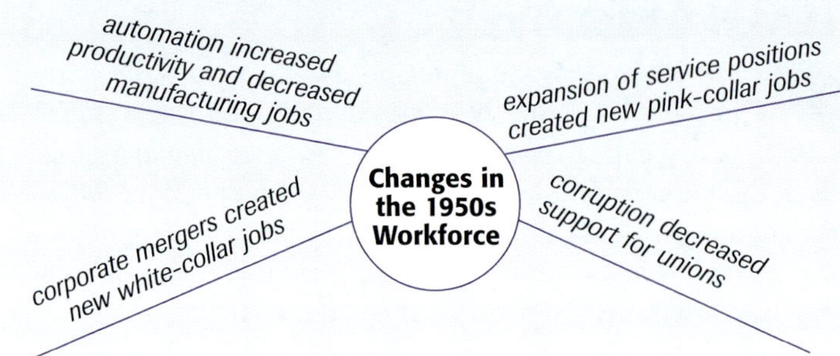

Changes in the 1950s Workforce
automation increased productivity and decreased manufacturing jobs
expansion of service positions created new pink-collar jobs
corporate mergers created new white-collar jobs
corruption decreased support for unions

▶**ASSIGNMENT:** *Write the following terms on the chalkboard:* automation, white collar, pink collar, *and* Landrum-Griffin Act. *Have each student write a sentence defining each term and explaining how it affected the workforce during the 1950s.*

ECONOMIC DEVELOPMENT

Building the Suburbs. Builder William Levitt led the great postwar surge in suburban housing construction. A longtime admirer of Henry Ford, Levitt used mass-production techniques to build communities of small, modestly priced, almost identical single-family homes. In a note to himself for a typical day he wrote, "Eighteen houses completed on the shift from 8 to noon, and 19 more houses finished on the shift from 12:20 to 4:30." By the end of the 1950s other contractors had built similar developments on the outskirts of every major U.S. city.

CRITICAL THINKING How might mass-production techniques have made Levittown homes more affordable?

ANSWER: Students might note that mass-production techniques lowered the cost of Levittown homes by increasing the builder's efficiency.

The American Nation **VIDEO PROGRAM**

The Growth of Suburbia; Teacher's Guide, pp. 129–34

Search 00599, Play to 05932
Videodisc 2, Side B

Play Pause

See *Teacher's Guide* for Spanish barcode.

To help workers improve their economic position, union leaders sought to cooperate with management. George Meany, the AFL–CIO's first president, boasted that he had never led a strike. Meany claimed that he had no interest in reforming society. He stated that his only goal was to ensure "an ever rising standard of living" for his union's members. Many unions fought for and won guaranteed annual wages and cost-of-living adjustments—automatic pay raises linked to the rate of inflation. In return, unions made concessions to management. These included accepting automation plans or changes in work rules or production levels.

Union support weakened in the late 1950s when newspapers reported widespread corruption. They linked many unions to organized crime. As a result of these reports, Congress attempted to crack down on union corruption. In 1959 Congress passed the Landrum-Griffin Act, which banned ex-convicts from holding union offices, required frequent elections of officers, and regulated the investment of union funds. The negative publicity hurt union membership, which steadily declined after 1957.

✔ **READING CHECK:** How did the workforce change in the 1950s?

INTERPRETING THE VISUAL RECORD

Suburbs. The movement of Americans to new suburbs became common in the 1950s. ***How does this staged photograph from the 1950s reflect this trend in American life?***

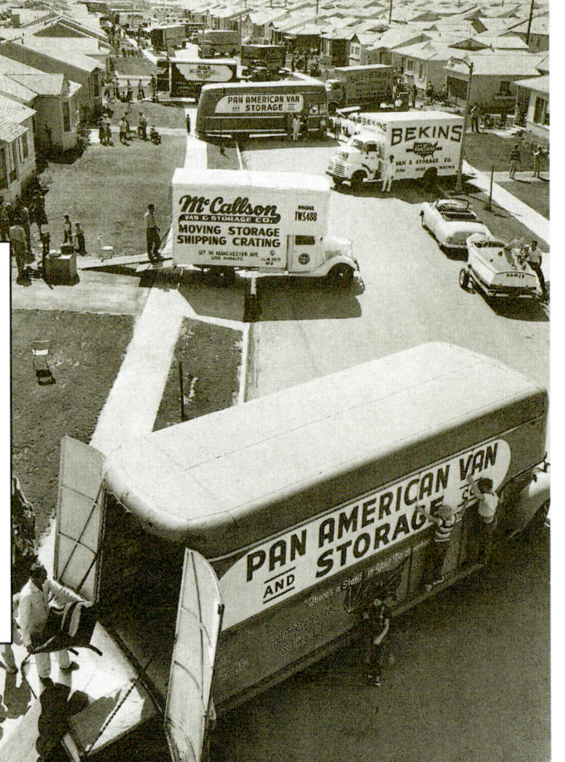

PAN AMERICAN VAN AND STORAGE
BEKINS
McCallson
MOVING STORAGE
SHIPPING CRATING

Suburban Migration

Workforce and income changes also led to increased geographic mobility for Americans. Millions of newly prosperous middle-class workers, particularly young couples, moved to the suburbs surrounding the nation's cities. By 1960 close to 60 million Americans—one third of the total U.S. population—lived in the suburbs.

Many of these suburbs were "planned communities." The entire neighborhoods were built by a single developer to attract new homeowners. To save time and money, developers used the same floorplan to build most houses in the community. As a result, the houses in the neighborhoods looked almost exactly alike. The best known of these suburban developments were the two Levittowns, one in Pennsylvania and one in New York, built by the Levitt Company. These developments expanded so rapidly that they soon grew into small cities. As more companies followed the Levitt Company example, the number of suburbs grew. An average of 1 million new suburban homes were built each year between 1950 and 1960.

The explosion of suburban growth occurred in part because developers were able to keep housing costs low. Growth also occurred because more Americans could afford to purchase homes. Veterans could get low-interest mortgages from such government agencies as the Veterans Administration and the Federal Housing Administration. Private savings and loan associations offered mortgages with relatively easy terms. Suburban growth was also aided by the passage of the **Highway Act** of 1956. This bill greatly expanded the nation's highway system, making it easier for suburban residents to commute to jobs in the cities.

TEACH OBJECTIVE 3

LEVEL 1: Conduct a discussion on suburban life during the 1950s. *(Suburban residents lived in nearly identical communities. Suburban life centered around the family. Consumption and conformity played important roles.)* Then ask students to identify some words that they associate with suburbs. *(Answers will vary. Students might list words such as* boring, pretty, *or* safe.*)* List the most common words on the chalkboard. Have each student use these words in a sentence describing suburban life during the 1950s. To conclude, ask students to express some of their own views on suburban life during the 1950s. Would they have wanted to live in a 1950s suburb? Why or why not? **Sheltered English**

LEVEL 2: Tell students to imagine that they are architects for a suburban-development firm during the 1950s. Have each student design and map a fictional suburb. Remind students to include items such as churches, community centers, and schools. Then ask students to write short reports to accompany their suburb plans. Students' reports should describe suburban life during the 1950s as well as discuss their own fictional suburbs. *(See the Level 1 lesson for the correct description.)* Have volunteers present their suburbs to the class. Students may wish to include their suburban maps and reports in their portfolios.

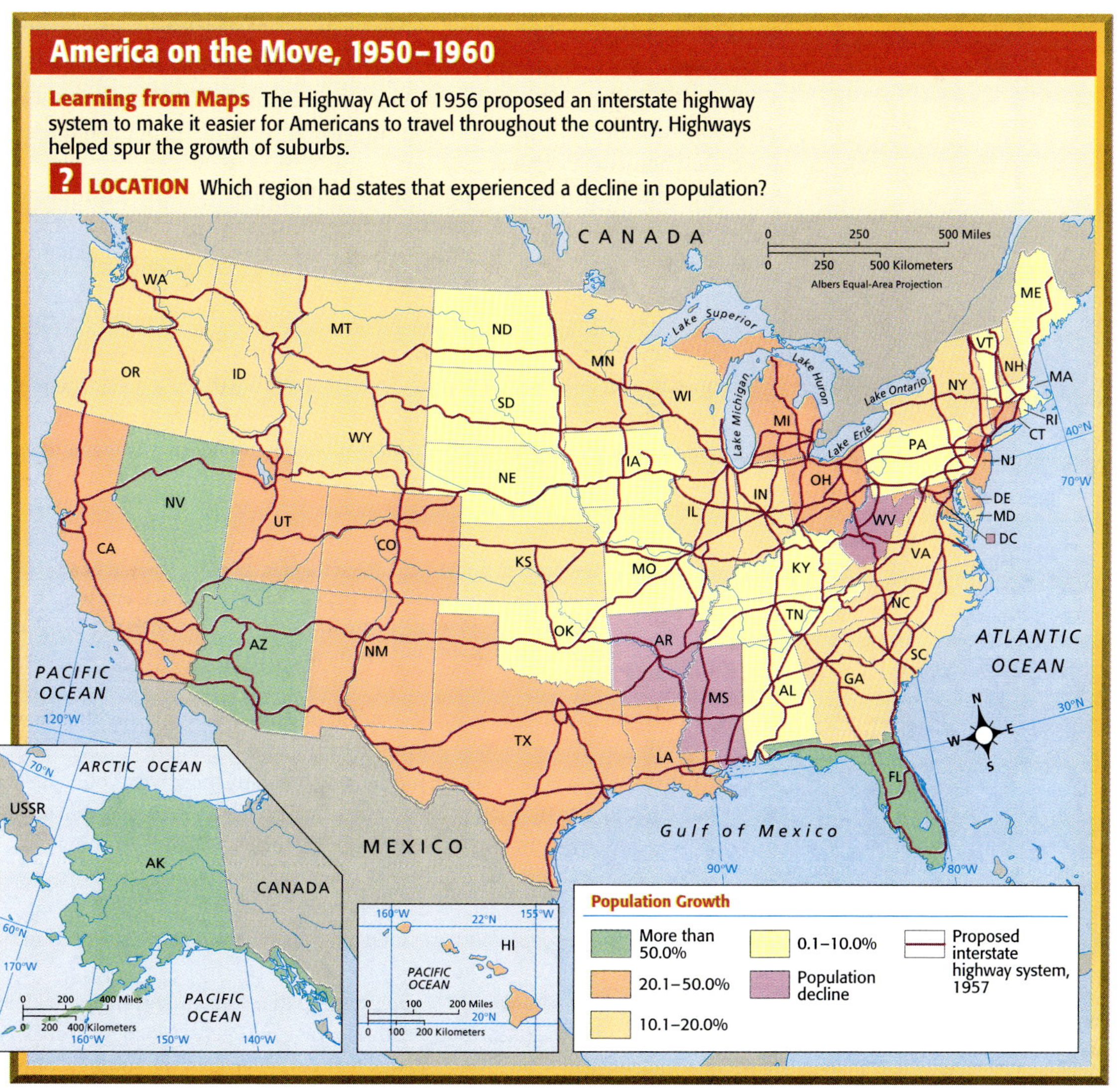

America on the Move, 1950–1960

Learning from Maps The Highway Act of 1956 proposed an interstate highway system to make it easier for Americans to travel throughout the country. Highways helped spur the growth of suburbs.

? LOCATION Which region had states that experienced a decline in population?

Suburban Life

Suburban growth was also spurred by an expanding population. During the Great Depression and World War II, many people had postponed getting married or starting a family. After the war, Americans began to get married at younger ages and in greater numbers than they had for generations. They also began having more children. The soaring birthrate accounted for more than 90 percent of the increase—some 30 million people—in the U.S. population during the 1950s. People began to refer to this increase as the **baby boom**.

Raising the family. Largely because of the baby boom, children became an important focus of suburban life. The baby boom also led to an emphasis on child rearing, focusing on the role of mothers. Many mothers followed the advice of pediatrician Benjamin Spock, who wrote *The Common Sense Book of Baby and Child*

HISTORY MAKERS SPEAK

Harriet Osborn in *The Century*

Children in the Suburbs. Harriet Osborn, who moved into a suburb in 1953, described the role children played in the new communities. "The suburbs was the perfect place to raise children, and children were our primary focus. . . . There was much emphasis placed on babies and bringing them up during their first year of life. We used Dr. Spock's guide religiously, and we would compare notes all the time. . . . There were few worries. We could afford the house, and we could afford to clothe our child, and everybody else clothed their children. It was a good life. It was the American dream. . . ."

ACTIVITY: Tell students that Osborn's husband was a World War II veteran. Ask students to offer reasons why veterans and their families might have viewed suburban life as "the American dream."

VISUAL RECORD ANSWER

(for p. 572)

Students might point out that it shows many people moving into nearly identical homes.

MAP ANSWER

the South

LEVEL 3: Ask a volunteer to read Lewis Mumford's statement on this page to the class. Then ask students to support or challenge Mumford's statement by describing suburban life during the 1950s. *(See the Level 1 lesson for the correct description.)* Note students' responses on the chalkboard. To extend the lesson, ask each student to outline or write a short story set in a suburb.

▶**ASSIGNMENT:** *Have students create cartoons that discuss suburban life during the 1950s. Have students write captions to accompany their cartoons.*

Teacher to Teacher

Karen Hoppes of Lake Oswego, Oregon, suggested the following activity: Organize students into small groups and tell them to imagine that they are members of a think tank in 1958. Have each group conduct research on American suburbs. Suggest that groups examine quality of life, juvenile delinquency, and so on. After groups have completed their research, tell them to prepare for committee meetings. Ask volunteers to conduct their meetings for the class.

CULTURAL DIVERSITY

A Religious Decade. Religion was an important social force during the 1950s. Church membership had grown dramatically. Roman Catholic seminaries, monasteries, and convents had numerous applicants. Even popular culture reflected the decade's interest in religion. A variety of books with religious themes, such as Billy Graham's *Peace with God* and Dale Evans Rogers's *Angel Unaware*, became best-sellers. Westminster Press began publishing its 26-volume *Library of Christian Classics* in the early 1950s. Hollywood made religiously oriented movies, producing *Ben Hur*, *The Robe*, and *The Ten Commandments*.

CRITICAL THINKING What factors might have accounted for the increased interest in religion in the 1950s?

ANSWER: Answers will vary. Students might mention the influence of Cold War fears or the desire to give thanks for peace and prosperity.

VISUAL RECORD ANSWER

Students might suggest that the advertisement portrays the women as thrilled by achieving "white white" laundry.

Care in 1946. Advertisements, popular magazines, and self-help books depicted the ideal wife and mother as a full-time homemaker. They portrayed the homemaker as a woman who devoted all of her energy to making her family happy and buying all the latest household gadgets.

Contrary to these popular images, however, the number of working mothers actually increased during the 1950s. Many families needed two paychecks to achieve a middle-class income. Usually mothers worked part-time and spent the bulk of their income on "extras" for their children, such as music lessons or family vacations.

Some experts argued that working mothers achieved more personal satisfaction than full-time homemakers. *Life* magazine claimed that the homemakers were often "bored stiff." To examine this issue, the popular magazine *Ladies' Home Journal* held a forum in 1956 to ask full-time homemakers about their lives. Rather than reporting boredom, the majority of participants described their lives as a nonstop rush of family activities. One mother said:

> **"At the present time I don't think there is anything I would like to change in the household. We happen to be very close, and we are all happy. I will admit there are times when I am a little overtired . . . but actually it doesn't last too long."**

Some women did say that they felt pressured to make sure that their families fit the ideal image portrayed by popular books and magazines. In other studies, some working mothers, particularly those with young children, said that they felt pressured by other people to live up to this ideal image. Many women considered quitting their jobs and becoming full-time homemakers. "The only person who approved of me in those days was my father," recalled working mother Gail Kaplan. "He had encouraged me to be an accountant and whatever I did was all right with him."

INTERPRETING THE VISUAL RECORD

Consumerism. Advertisements directed at new suburban families maintained the image of women as happy homemakers who spent all of their time doing chores and buying household products. ***How does this advertisement reinforce this image?***

Consumerism and social life. The pressure that Kaplan and many of the forum participants felt to conform to a certain image reflected a broader emphasis on social conformity in the 1950s. This was particularly true in the suburbs. Suburban areas, reported writer Lewis Mumford, "[are] inhabited by people in the same class, the same income, the same age group."

Advertising played a large role in promoting this conformity as it encouraged Americans to enjoy the general prosperity by buying consumer goods. Americans responded by going on a shopping spree, buying as many as nearly 8 million new automobiles and many household gadgets each year. Some suburban families worked hard to "keep up with the Joneses"; that is, to make sure that they had as many modern conveniences as their neighbors.

In addition to buying the same consumer items, suburban families participated in many of the same social activities as their neighbors. These included PTA, scouting, Little League, and religious activities. For uprooted Americans streaming to the suburbs, membership in religious institutions provided not only spiritual guidance but also a sense of belonging. Churches and synagogues often tried to appeal to new members by sponsoring a variety of social and recreational activities.

✔ **READING CHECK:** What was suburban life like during the 1950s?

TEACH OBJECTIVE 4

LEVEL 1: Pair students and ask them to list characteristics of early television programming. *(Pairs should note that major corporations sponsored many early television programs. These programs included dramas, quiz shows, situation comedies, sporting events, and variety shows.)* Have each pair write sentences describing each of the elements on its list. Ask volunteers to share their sentences. To conclude, have students create typical television listings from a newspaper as they might have appeared in the 1950s.
Sheltered English, Cooperative Learning

LEVEL 2: Conduct a brief discussion on early television programming. *(See the Level 1 lesson for the correct description.)* Then tell students to imagine that it is 1957 and they have been asked to rate the quality of television programming. Have each student create a television-viewing log describing all of the programs that he or she watched on a given day, noting which programs they liked best. *(Students should consider what types of programs would have appealed to them and why.)* Ask volunteers to share their viewing logs with the class.

Science & Technology

Jonas Salk's Polio Vaccine

The United States emerged from World War II stronger both economically and militarily. However, many American families lived in fear of a new danger—a deadly polio epidemic that struck the country in the late 1940s. In 1952 alone the disease attacked some 60,000 Americans, many of whom were children. Hospitals were overwhelmed by the number of polio patients.

As the epidemic spread, scientists worked night and day to try to develop a cure or a way to prevent the disease. In 1952 Jonas Salk finally developed a successful vaccine against polio. "If it works," predicted one journalist of the vaccine, "Salk will have scored one of the greatest triumphs in the history of medicine." The vaccine did succeed in ending the epidemic. The number of polio cases continued to drop dramatically after an even better vaccine was developed in 1957.

Dead poliovirus

1 A small amount of dead poliovirus is injected into a healthy person.

2 The dead virus does not cause polio, but tricks cells into creating polio-killing antibodies.

Antibodies

3 Antibodies are released from cells.

4 Antibodies prevent the disease by attaching themselves to, and killing, any new, live polioviruses that invade the body.

Live poliovirus

Understanding Science and History

1. How does the polio vaccine prevent polio?
2. How was the polio epidemic halted?

The Golden Age of Television

One of the most popular family activities was watching television together. Introduced commercially after World War II, television quickly became a favorite form of entertainment. By the end of the 1950s some 46 million households owned at least one television set.

Advertising played a major role in television programming. By reaching viewers daily in their homes, television advertising influenced consumer habits more than any previous medium had ever done. Particularly effective were ads in which television stars promoted their sponsors' products. By 1960, advertisers were spending $1.6 billion annually trying to convince viewers to buy their products. Often one business would sponsor an entire show, such as *General Electric Theatre* and *Kraft Television Theatre*. Their viewers would often connect the program with a company and its products. This advertising monopoly also gave many companies great control over program content.

Viewers could choose from several types of programming. Early television programs included sporting events such as the World Series, situation comedies like *The Honeymooners*, and variety programs like *Your Show of Shows*. Quiz shows like *The $64,000 Question* shared the airwaves with serious dramas like *Playhouse 90*. The most popular

Television became so popular in the 1950s that some companies began to market "TV dinners."

IN THE NEWS

The Continuing Fight Against Polio. Polio still exists in many nations. A World Health Organization (WHO) project to completely eradicate polio by the year 2000 began by targeting specific countries and launching massive inoculation campaigns. The WHO sponsored one such drive in India in 1996. In India the virus strikes about 10,000 children per year, causing widespread physical disabilities. After the WHO shipped the polio vaccine, Indian officials at 500,000 health centers all over the country administered the shots. If children refused to report for the shot, volunteers searched for them, and administered the vaccine. The effort was very successful—in just one day, some 120 million children were vaccinated.

CRITICAL THINKING Why might polio still exist in some countries?

ANSWER: Students might suggest that polio and other diseases tend to linger in nations with limited resources to fight them.

SCIENCE & TECHNOLOGY ANSWERS

1. by tricking cells into creating polio-fighting antibodies
2. Jonas Salk developed a successful vaccine.

LEVEL 3: Conduct a brief discussion on early television programming. *(See the Level 1 lesson for the correct description.)* Then tell students to imagine that it is 1957 and that a major television studio has just announced a contest entitled Create the Show of the Year! Have each student write a proposal for a new television show. Students should also write brief analyses to accompany their proposals. Students' analyses should explain why their proposed shows would be popular in the 1950s national market. Students may wish to include their proposals and analyses in their portfolios.

SPOTLIGHT on the Game Show Scandal

Ask students to conduct research on the game-show scandal of the 1950s. Then tell students to imagine that they are modern-day historians. Have each student write a short article describing and analyzing the scandal, focusing on what it revealed about American culture during the 1950s. Alternately, tell students to imagine that they are Americans who watched game shows regularly and recently learned of the scandal. Have students write letters to the contestants or the networks describing their reactions to the charges of corruption. Ask volunteers to read their articles or letters to the class.

Block Scheduling

TECHNOLOGY AND SOCIETY

Early Television Sets. The television sets of the 1940s were nothing like today's sleek, clearly focused sets. Early sets displayed a fuzzy black-and-white picture. One observer likened the experience to "watching through venetian blinds"! In addition to their technological inferiority, television sets were extremely expensive—about $500 each at a time when many families earned less than $3,000 a year. In the early 1950s, however, the quality improved and the price dropped. By 1960, Americans owned some 45 million television sets.

CRITICAL THINKING Why might some families have spent so much money on television sets during the 1940s?

ANSWER: Students might suggest that these families wanted the latest technology.

VISUAL RECORD ANSWER

Answers will vary. Some students might name Lucille Ball and suggest that her image is familiar from television reruns.

INTERPRETING THE VISUAL RECORD

Television stars. Television stars like the cast of *I Love Lucy* (top) and *The Honeymooners* (bottom) were beloved by their millions of fans. ***Can you name any of the actors in the images above? Why might they look familiar?***

program of the decade was the situation comedy *I Love Lucy,* starring real-life wife and husband Lucille Ball and Desi Arnaz. Thousands of fans tuned in every week to witness Lucy's crazy antics.

Television grew in popularity, but it remained a selective mirror, showing primarily white, middle-class, suburban experiences. Poverty, if shown at all, was treated as a minor problem. Working women, ethnic minorities, and inner-city life rarely appeared. When they were shown, it was usually in a way that reinforced stereotypes. One of the era's most controversial programs was *Amos 'n' Andy,* a comedy about African American urban life. The show was based on a popular radio program that had featured two white men providing the voices of African American characters. When the show moved to television, African American actors took over the roles. Still, for many viewers the characters represented white stereotypes of the African American community. The NAACP launched a protest against the program. Others joined in the protest, and *Amos 'n' Andy* was taken off the air. In 1966 it was banned from being shown in reruns.

Some critics also complained that television advertising reinforced materialism. Game shows in which contestants competed for prizes met with particular criticism. A congressional investigation revealed that some game shows were rigged. Popular contestants such as Columbia University instructor Charles Van Doren were given the answers in advance. Producers hoped to keep popular contestants on the show and thus keep ratings up. Some critics argued that the game-show scandal revealed the dangers of television and its corrupting effect on American values.

✔ **READING CHECK:** What was early television programming like?

Teenagers and Popular Culture

Some parents expressed concern about the impact of popular culture on young people, particularly teenagers. With more free time and spending money than any previous generation of teenagers, American youths of the 1950s sought out new kinds of leisure-time activities. To parents' dismay, these forms of entertainment often seemed to glamorize rebellion against suburban conformity.

Fictional rebels. Many young people found meaning in literature and films that featured discontented rebels. Some identified with Holden Caulfield, the main character of J. D. Salinger's 1951 novel, *The Catcher in the Rye.* Disgusted by the hypocrisy of the adult world, Caulfield declares it "crumby" and "phony." Although the book was very popular with young readers, some adults found its language and content offensive. Some groups demanded that it be banned from school libraries.

Many young people also enjoyed reading satirical comic books or magazines, such as *MAD.* The magazine dedicated itself to making fun of everything associated with "the American way of life." *MAD* soon rivaled *Life* as the most widely read magazine among young people. Many parents worried that reading such magazines would increase **juvenile delinquency**—antisocial behavior by the young.

TEACH OBJECTIVE 5

ALL LEVELS: Ask students to imagine that they have found a time capsule buried by teenagers in the 1950s. A note in the capsule explains that the items included represent trends in 1950s popular culture. As a class, have students brainstorm a list of items that might be in the capsule. Then have students create graphic organizers listing the contents of the capsule and how each item reflects social changes among teenagers in the 1950s. *(Students should note that fictional rebels and satirical magazines and comic books expressed teenagers' confusion and anger. Rock 'n' roll hinted at civil rights challenges to come.)* Have volunteers share their organizers with the class. **Sheltered English**

SPOTLIGHT on Rock Stars of the 1950s

Ask students to select one of the rock 'n' roll stars of the 1950s, such as Chuck Berry, Fats Domino, Buddy Holly, Elvis Presley, Little Richard, or Ritchie Valens. Ask students to conduct research on their chosen star. Then have each student write a short biography of his or her performer, discussing the person's background and music. Ask students to present information about their subject to the class. Then gather students' biographies and compile a rock 'n' roll encyclopedia. **Block Scheduling**

Several of the decade's most popular films showed images of juvenile delinquency and young, angry rebels frustrated with life. Often their anger was directed not at any one particular thing, but at all of society in general. In the 1954 film *The Wild One*, a character asks the motorcycle-gang leader played by Marlon Brando what he is rebelling against. Brando snarls back, "Whadda ya got?"

This image of the rebel with no direction was reinforced in the 1955 movie *Rebel Without a Cause*. The film starred James Dean, Natalie Wood, and Sal Mineo as teenagers confused about the values of their suburban families. Many teenagers could identify with the characters' frustration. One teenager described his feelings when he saw the film. "I walked out of the movie house that day confirmed in my sense of isolation," he said, "but not without taking something precious with me: the feeling that others shared my pain." James Dean became an idol to many young people when the 24-year-old actor died in a car accident following the premiere of the film.

Rock 'n' roll. Teenagers also escaped from the conformity of suburbia through a new type of music called **rock 'n' roll**. This music reworked rhythm and blues, a style popular among African American performers and audiences that combined blues music with more energetic and upbeat rhythms. Rhythm-and-blues music was particularly popular in dance halls. Rock 'n' roll took the music one step further and created a raw sound very different from other popular music of the time. Cleveland disc jockey Alan Freed coined the term "rock 'n' roll" in 1951 when he started a rhythm-and-blues show aimed at young white audiences. Soon the sound caught on among teenagers across the country.

BIOGRAPHY *Elvis Presley*

Elvis Presley emerged as rock's leading talent. Presley was born in 1935 to a poor family in Tupelo, Mississippi. He loved music, particularly gospel. When he was 13 years old, his family moved to Memphis, Tennessee, where he listened to and learned from numerous African American gospel and rhythm-and-blues musicians. After graduating from high school, Presley worked as a truck driver while occasionally singing professionally. In 1954 he made his first major record. By 1955 he was one of the biggest music stars in the country.

Presley once said of his sudden popularity, "I just fell into it, really." Others recognized that this success came from his originality. His record producer noted that Presley sounded like no other singer he had ever heard. He also had a stage presence that electrified audiences. Shy in person, Presley came alive on stage. Journalist Jean Yothers was amazed by her own reaction when she reported on one of Presley's concerts in 1955. "I was awed," she said. "I got a tremendous boot out of this loud, uninhibited music that's sending the country crazy." Presley's many fans were

Teenagers as Consumers

teen Life

Some scholars have argued that the modern teenager was "invented" by advertising agencies in the 1950s. This was the first time that advertisers recognized teenagers as potentially powerful consumers. Many teenagers received allowances from their families or earned money from after-school jobs. Previously, teenagers' earnings usually went to help their families survive. In the 1950s most teenagers were allowed to spend their earnings as they wanted. By 1956 teenagers' earnings represented some $7 billion in purchasing power.

Advertisement from the 1950s

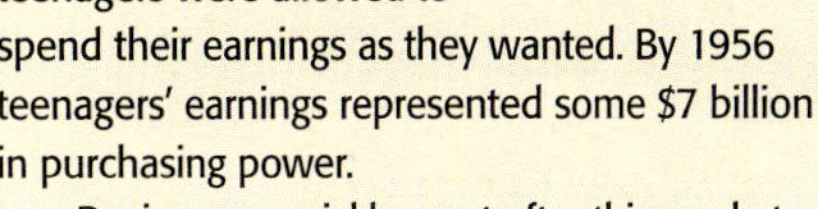

Businesses quickly went after this market, launching dozens of new products geared toward teenage tastes and desires. Advertising also shaped teenagers' desires, presenting ideal images of what a popular teenager should own and wear. If teenagers would buy their products, the advertisers implied, they would enjoy social success.

Read More About It

Free Find: Elvis Presley

After reading about Elvis Presley on the **Holt Researcher** CD–ROM, write a fictional article for a teen music magazine describing how Elvis Presley's early life influenced his music.

THEN AND NOW

American Fads. During the 1950s television advertising and teenagers' disposable incomes fueled many fads and crazes. The Hula Hoop was one of them. Introduced in 1958 by the Wham-O Manufacturing Company, the Hula Hoop became an immediate sensation. Frisbees and Wiffle balls were also popular during the 1950s.

CRITICAL THINKING Ask students to name three current fads. How might fads have changed since the 1950s?

ANSWER: Answers will vary. Students might suggest that current fads can be spread on the Internet, rather than through television advertising.

THAT'S INTERESTING!

Swanson introduced the so-called TV Dinner in 1954. The first TV Dinner offered turkey, dressing, gravy, peas, and whipped sweet potatoes.

REVIEW

Have students complete the **Section 2 Review** on p. 578.

ASSESS

Have students complete **Daily Quiz 19.2.** As **Alternative Assessment**, you may want to use the fictional suburb map or the television-viewing log in this section's lessons.

RETEACH

Have students complete **Main Idea Activity for Reteaching and Sheltered English 19.2.** Then assign each student a subsection of Section 2. Have students write five questions about the material in their assigned subsections. Collect the questions and use them to quiz the entire class. **Sheltered English**

EXTEND

Ask students to interview someone who lived in a suburb in the 1950s. Have students tape or transcribe the interviews. Then ask students to work together to create a collective oral history album of suburban residents of the 1950s. Students might want to illustrate the album with photographs of the people they interviewed. **Block Scheduling, Cooperative Learning**

SECTION 2 REVIEW ANSWERS

Define and Identify

For significance, see the following pages:

- Oveta Culp Hobby, p. 570
- Modern Republicanism, p. 570
- automation, p. 571
- George Meany, p. 572
- Highway Act, p. 572
- baby boom, p. 573
- juvenile delinquency, p. 576
- rock 'n' roll, p. 577
- Elvis Presley, p. 577

1. causes—baby boom, low housing costs, housing loans for veterans, and better highways; effects—emphasis on conformity, consumerism, and children

2. President Eisenhower wanted to control spending while still protecting and even expanding important social programs, an approach called Modern Republicanism.

3. corporations prospered and merged, leading to more white- and pink-collar jobs; increased automation decreased manufacturing jobs; greater union strength led to higher wages

4. conformity, consumerism, and family togetherness; by reading or listening to certain forms of popular culture

5. reflect—showed only a certain portion of society; shape—programs often sponsored by powerful corporations and portrayed certain behaviors and lifestyles as the American "norm"

During the 1950s teenagers listened to rock 'n' roll groups such as the Silhouettes on jukeboxes in local hangouts.

heartbroken when he was forced to take a break from his music career in the late 1950s after being drafted into the army. After completing his service he resumed his successful recording career and starred in 33 films before his death in 1977.

Despite its popularity, many adults disliked rock 'n' roll. They feared that it promoted antisocial behavior in teenagers. Some critics called it immoral. Others simply dismissed it as gibberish. They pointed out that the lyrics of many popular rock songs included made-up words or sounds that did not seem to make any sense. One example was the 1957 hit, "Get a Job," by a group called the Silhouettes.

> **"Sha da da da**
> **Sha da da da da**
> **Bah do**
> **Bah yip yip yip yip yip yip yip yip**
> **Mum mum mum mum mum mum**
> **Get a job."**

Rock 'n' roll also upset many people because it challenged the custom of racial segregation. African American musicians such as Little Richard, Chuck Berry, and Fats Domino, as well as Hispanic performers like Ritchie Valens, profoundly influenced early rock 'n' roll. White rockers such as Presley, Jerry Lee Lewis, and Buddy Holly shared the airwaves, and sometimes the stage, with noted black artists. This breaking down of racial barriers reflected larger social changes on the horizon.

✔ **READING CHECK:** How did the trends in popular culture reflect the larger social changes among teenagers in the 1950s?

SECTION 2 REVIEW

Define and explain the significance of the following terms:
Modern Republicanism
automation
Highway Act
baby boom
juvenile delinquency
rock 'n' roll

Identify and explain the significance of the following individuals:
Oveta Culp Hobby
George Meany
Elvis Presley

1. **Using Graphic Organizers** Copy the chart below. Use it to explain the growth of the suburbs and how that growth affected American middle-class culture.

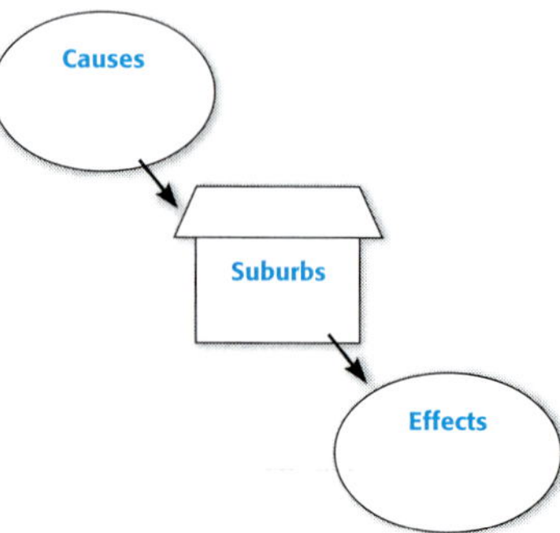

2. **Analyzing** How did President Eisenhower approach the nation's problems?
3. **Identifying Cause and Effect** Why did the workforce change in the 1950s, and how did those changes affect society?
4. **Identifying Values** What social values and patterns of behavior did suburban life encourage? How did teenagers rebel against those values and behaviors?

Critical Thinking

5. How well did television both reflect and shape American society?
Consider
- how television shows portrayed American society
- the role of advertising on television
- how television encouraged certain ideals and consumer habits

SECTION 3

After completing Section 3, students should be able to:

OBJECTIVE 1 *Relate how the* Brown *decision affected school segregation and exposed conflict over the segregation issue.*

OBJECTIVE 2 *Explain how the Montgomery Bus Boycott was a major turning point in the civil rights movement.*

OBJECTIVE 3 *Identify the challenges that Hispanics, Asian Americans, and American Indians faced in the 1950s.*

OBJECTIVE 4 *Identify the criticisms that writers and scholars expressed about 1950s society.*

OBJECTIVE 5 *Describe the problems that the poorest Americans faced in the 1950s.*

LET'S GET STARTED!

As students enter the classroom, ask them to imagine that they are returning war veterans facing discrimination at home. Have them respond to this scenario in writing, and ask volunteers to share their responses. Tell students that in Section 3 they will learn about the civil rights movement in the 1940s and 1950s—and how veterans helped launch that movement.

Voices of Dissent

OBJECTIVES

Read to understand:

1. how the *Brown* decision affected school segregation and exposed conflict over the segregation issue
2. how the Montgomery Bus Boycott was a major turning point in the civil rights movement
3. what challenges Hispanics, Asian Americans, and American Indians faced in the 1950s
4. what criticisms of 1950s society writers and scholars expressed
5. what problems the poorest Americans faced in the 1950s

KEY TERMS

Brown v. *Board of Education*
Little Rock Nine
Montgomery Improvement Association
Civil Rights Act of 1957
League for United Latin American Citizens
beats
urban renewal

KEY PEOPLE

Thurgood Marshall
Orval Faubus
Rosa Parks
Martin Luther King Jr.
Félix Longoria
Ralph Ellison
Jack Kerouac

EYEWITNESSES TO History

"I had grown up in a society where there were very clear lines. The civil rights movement gave me the power to challenge any line that limits me. . . . The movement said that if something puts you down, you have to fight against it."

—Bernice Johnson Reagon

A segregated water fountain

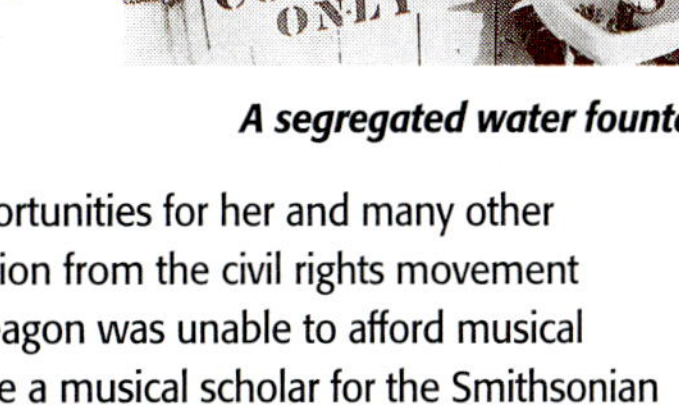

Some people felt held back by society in the 1950s. Bernice Johnson Reagon of Albany, Georgia, recalled how society tried to limit opportunities for her and many other young African Americans. Reagon drew inspiration from the civil rights movement that emerged during the era. A gifted singer, Reagon was unable to afford musical instruments as a child. She later rose to become a musical scholar for the Smithsonian Institution, a college professor, a successful recording artist, and founder of the internationally known singing group Sweet Honey in the Rock.

Brown v. *Board of Education*

The NAACP had long waged a campaign against segregation in educational facilities. The Supreme Court's 1896 decision in *Plessy* v. *Ferguson* had established the legality of "separate but equal" schools. The NAACP had succeeded in opening some all-white universities and graduate schools to African American students. They did this by demonstrating that in most cases separate schools for black students were far inferior to the facilities reserved for white students. However, the Court continued to maintain that segregation in and of itself was legal.

In 1952 a group of legal challenges to segregation in public schools came before the Supreme Court in the form of ***Brown* v. *Board of Education***. The main case involved Linda Brown, an African American student from Topeka, Kansas. Segregation in Topeka's schools prevented her from attending an all-white elementary school a short walk from her home. Instead, she had to travel a long distance and cross dangerous railroad tracks to get to an African American school.

NAACP lawyer Thurgood Marshall argued on Brown's behalf. He introduced data suggesting that segregation psychologically damaged African American students by lowering their self-worth. Marshall's arguments greatly influenced the Court's unanimous ruling, which was issued on May 17, 1954. Written by Chief Justice Earl Warren, the opinion declared racial segregation illegal in public schools.

Many Americans praised the decision as a long-overdue step toward ending segregation entirely. Some African Americans were skeptical that white leaders would really support desegregation. As one NAACP leader warned, history had shown African Americans that there was a "difference between the law in books and the law in action."

SECTION 3 RESOURCES

PRINT

- Guided Reading Strategy 19.3
- Graphic Organizer Activity 19: Voices of Dissent
- Literature Reading 19: LIngering Racial Tension
- Section 3 Review, p. 587
- Daily Quiz 19.3

MULTIMEDIA

- One-Stop Planner, Lesson 19.3
- Holt Researcher: American History CD–ROM
- HRW Web site

SHELTERED ENGLISH

- Main Idea Activity for Reteaching and Sheltered English 19.3

✔ READING TO UNDERSTAND

To help students master the section objectives, have them answer the **READING CHECKS** and complete **Guided Reading Strategy 19.3** as they read the section.

TEACH OBJECTIVE 1

LEVEL 1: Pair students and have each pair define the *Brown* v. *Board of Education* decision in writing. *(Students should indicate that the decision banned racial segregation in public schools.)* Then ask pairs to write a paragraph describing how the decision exposed conflict over the segregation issue. *(Students should note that when the Little Rock Nine attempted to integrate Central High School in Little Rock, Arkansas, they experienced harassment and violence.)* Have volunteers read their paragraphs to the class.
Sheltered English, Cooperative Learning

LEVEL 2: Tell students to imagine that they are newspaper reporters who were present for the announcement of the *Brown* v. *Board of Education* decision and the subsequent desegregation struggle in Little Rock. Have each student write a short memoir describing how the decision affected school segregation and exposed conflict over the segregation issue. *(See the Level 1 lesson for the correct answers.)* Ask volunteers to read their memoirs to the class. Students may wish to include their memoirs in their portfolios.

DEMOCRATIC VALUES

***Sweatt* v. *Painter*.** In February 1946 Heman Marion Sweatt, an African American postal worker, attempted to register at the all-white University of Texas School of Law. The university denied Sweatt's application because state law mandated separate schools for black and white citizens. With the help of Thurgood Marshall and the NAACP, Sweatt filed suit against the university. In June 1950 the Supreme Court ruled in *Sweatt* v. *Painter* that the "separate but equal" law school the state had established for black students was not equal "in educational opportunities" to the University of Texas School of Law. That fall Sweatt became one of 15 African American students to integrate the University of Texas School of Law.

CRITICAL THINKING How might *Sweatt* v. *Painter* have provided a precedent for *Brown* v. *Board of Education*?

ANSWER: Students might suggest that *Sweatt* v. *Painter* established that "separate but equal" facilities did not provide equal educational opportunities.

VISUAL RECORD ANSWER

Students might answer that Eckford appears calm and dignified while the others seem to be an unruly, screaming mob.

Although some states moved quickly to end school segregation, many white southern leaders reacted to the decision with anger and defiance. South Carolina governor James F. Byrnes declared that desegregation "would mark the beginning of the end of civilization in the South as we have known it." Southern resistance caused the Supreme Court to issue a ruling in 1955 instructing federal district courts to end school segregation "with all deliberate speed."

Showdown in Little Rock

Despite the Supreme Court ruling, school desegregation in the South moved slowly. By the end of the 1956–57 school year, the vast majority of southern school systems remained segregated. In Arkansas, however, school desegregation was progressing with relatively little opposition. Two of the three southern school districts that began desegregating in 1954 were in Arkansas. The Little Rock school board was the first in the South to announce that it would comply with the *Brown* decision.

Little Rock's desegregation plan was set to begin in September 1957 with the admission of nine African American students to the all-white Central High School. However, Governor Orval Faubus, about to begin his re-election campaign, spoke out against the desegregation plan. The night before school was to start, he ordered the Arkansas National Guard to surround Central High. He did so, he claimed, to protect the school from attacks by armed protesters. "It will not be possible to restore or to maintain order . . . if forcible integration is carried out tomorrow in the schools of this community," he warned.

INTERPRETING THE VISUAL RECORD

Little Rock. Elizabeth Eckford faces a hostile crowd as she walks by herself to Central High School. ***How does Eckford's expression in this image contrast with those of the people behind her?***

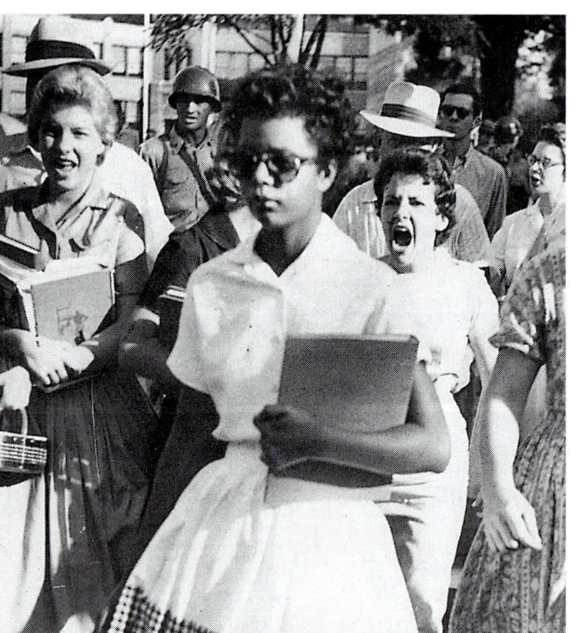

Faubus exaggerated the danger, but his claims spread panic. One of the nine black students, Elizabeth Eckford, did not receive a message that instructed her not to go to school alone. When she attempted to enter the school, a mob of angry protesters and a line of armed National Guardsmen met her. She described the ordeal:

> **"When I got in front of the school . . . I didn't know what to do. . . . Just then the guards let some white students through. . . . I walked up to the guard who had let [them] in. . . . When I tried to squeeze past him, he raised his bayonet, and then the other guard moved in. . . . Somebody [in the crowd] started yelling, *'Lynch her! Lynch her!'*"**

For nearly three weeks, members of the Arkansas National Guard prevented the African American students, now known as the **Little Rock Nine**, from entering the school. Then, under court order, Faubus removed the National Guard. When the nine attempted to enter the school on September 23, the white mob rioted. Angered by the "disgraceful occurrences" at the school, President Eisenhower ordered some 1,000 federal troops to Little Rock. On September 25, 1957, under the protection of the soldiers' fixed bayonets, the Little Rock Nine finally entered Central High.

The Little Rock Nine endured a difficult year that included frequent harassment. One of the group, Minniejean Brown, was suspended for dumping food on

TEACH OBJECTIVE 2

LEVEL 3: Tell students to imagine that they are advisers to President Eisenhower in September 1957. Have each student write a detailed memo describing how the *Brown* decision affected school segregation and exposed conflict over the segregation issue. *(See the Level 1 lesson for the correct answers.)* In their memos, students should recommend a course of action on the Little Rock crisis. Have volunteers share their suggested actions. Then conduct a brief discussion on Eisenhower's response to the Little Rock crisis.

▶**ASSIGNMENT:** *Have each student create an annotated time line of the* Brown v. Board of Education *decision and the Little Rock crisis.*

LEVEL 1: Pair students and tell them to imagine that they participated in the Montgomery Bus Boycott. Have each pair develop a short dialogue discussing the boycott and explaining how it represented a major turning point in the civil rights movement. *(Students should indicate that the boycott struck an important blow against segregation, established Martin Luther King Jr. as a civil rights leader, and lessened the fear of standing up to people in positions of power.)* Ask volunteers to perform their dialogues for the class.
Sheltered English, Cooperative Learning

a white boy who had made a racist comment. In February, when another white student called her a racial and obscene name, Brown responded with much milder insults of her own. For this incident, Brown was permanently expelled from school. After that, white students distributed cards that read, "One Down . . . Eight to Go."

Despite such pressure, the other African American students stayed. In May 1958 Ernest Green became the first African American student ever to graduate from Central High School. "When they called my name . . . nobody clapped," Green recalled of his graduation ceremony. "But I figured they didn't have to . . . because after I got that diploma, that was it. I had accomplished what I came there for."

Governor Faubus continued to look for ways to resist integration. He ordered the shutdown of the Little Rock public school system during the 1958–59 school year. He also helped establish a private school system to serve white students. Most African Americans, including the rest of the Little Rock Nine, as well as poor whites, had no school to attend. In 1959 the school district reopened under court order and slowly began to desegregate.

✔ **READING CHECK:** How did the *Brown* decision affect school segregation and expose conflict over the segregation issue?

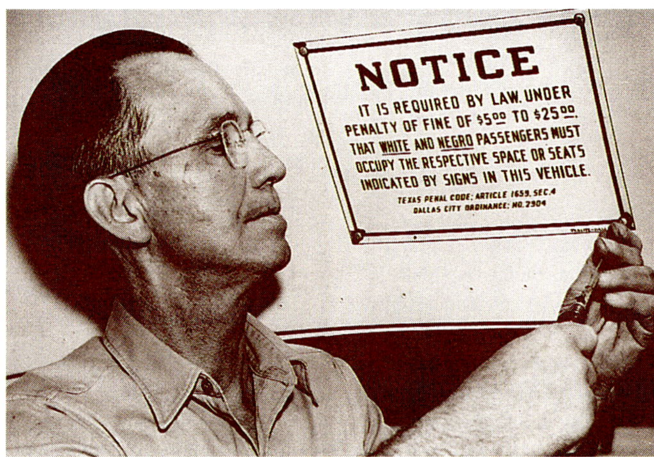

INTERPRETING THE VISUAL RECORD

Segregation. In most southern cities, African Americans had to sit in the back of buses even if seats were available up front. After a court order, this Dallas Transit Company employee is removing a segregation sign. ***How do you think African American bus riders would view the removal of this sign?***

The Montgomery Bus Boycott

In addition to fighting segregation in schools, the NAACP sought to end racial segregation on southern transportation systems. In Montgomery, Alabama, local NAACP leaders planned to challenge the practice of forcing African American citizens to ride in the back of city buses.

BIOGRAPHY *Rosa Parks*

A boycott begins. On December 1, 1955, Rosa Parks, an African American seamstress, provided the NAACP with its opportunity. Parks refused to give up her bus seat to a white passenger and was arrested. Born in 1913 in Tuskegee, Alabama, Parks moved to the Montgomery area at a young age. Her mother was determined that Parks would receive a good education. Montgomery did not have a high school for African American students, so her parents sent her to the laboratory school at Alabama State College. Discrimination prevented her from obtaining a job that matched her education, however. Parks found work as a seamstress. She also became involved in the civil rights movement and held an office in the Montgomery chapter of the NAACP.

In the late 1950s Parks moved to Detroit, where she began working for Representative John Conyers in 1967. She remains committed to civil rights and has won

Read More About It

Free Find: Rosa Parks
After reading about Rosa Parks on the **Holt Researcher** CD–ROM, write a short essay explaining the significance of her contribution to the civil rights movement.

HISTORY MAKERS SPEAK

President Bill Clinton in the *Arkansas Democrat-Gazette*

The Little Rock Anniversary. On September 25, 1997, President Clinton and the Little Rock Nine gathered at Central High to commemorate the 40th anniversary of the school's desegregation. In a speech, Clinton said, "Imagine, all of you, what it would be like to come to school one day and be shoved against lockers, tripped down stairways, taunted day after day by your classmates, to go all through school with no hope of going to a school play or being on a basketball team or learning in simple peace." Clinton urged Americans to continue working for full social integration. ". . . too many Americans of all races have actually begun to give up on the idea of integration and the search for common ground," he said.

ACTIVITY: Ask students to offer suggestions for ways in which people in their school or community might seek the "common ground" of which Clinton spoke. Have students pick the best ideas and implement them.

VISUAL RECORD ANSWER

Students might answer that most African Americans would see it as a positive step.

LEVEL 2: Tell students to imagine that they participated in the Montgomery Bus Boycott. Have each student write a letter to a friend in another state, describing the events of the boycott and explaining how the boycott represented a major turning point in the civil rights movement. *(See the Level 1 lesson for the correct answers.)* Call on volunteers to read their letters to the class. Students may wish to include their letters in their portfolios.

LEVEL 3: Tell students to imagine that they are modern-day historians working on a civil rights encyclopedia. Have each student write a short entry on the Montgomery Bus Boycott. In their entries students should discuss both the boycott and its role as a turning point for the civil rights movement. *(See the Level 1 lesson for the correct answers.)* Have volunteers read their entries to the class. Students may wish to include their entries in their portfolios.

DEMOCRATIC VALUES

The Montgomery Car Pools. Montgomery's African American residents formed car pools to support the bus boycott and provide transportation. Some people donated as much as 20 percent of their weekly salaries to fund the car pools. The NAACP, the United Auto Workers, and sympathetic white residents also lent support. Police officers often stopped the carpoolers for tiny violations. To avoid these encounters, carpool drivers proceeded at very slow speeds and signaled turns far in advance.

ACTIVITY: Tell students to imagine that they live in Montgomery, Alabama, and support the bus boycott. Have each student create a flier supporting the boycott and advertising a car-pool service.

THAT'S INTERESTING!

Throughout the Montgomery Bus Boycott, Martin Luther King Jr. urged his followers to adhere to nonviolence. He said, "We want to love our enemies. . . . We must meet hate with love."

VISUAL RECORD ANSWER

Answers will vary. Some students might suggest that the photograph shows King as charismatic and stylish.

numerous awards, including the Congressional Gold Medal of Honor, the highest honor the United States can award a private citizen.

In the summer of 1955 Parks attended a workshop on social justice that deeply influenced her views. "I found out for the first time . . . that this could be a unified society," she said. "I gained there the strength to persevere in my work for freedom." Her actions in December of that year would put her training to the test. Parks's arrest for refusing to give up her seat led to her conviction for violating the city's segregation laws. In protest, many of Montgomery's 50,000 African Americans organized a boycott against the bus system. The **Montgomery Improvement Association** (MIA), a group of local civil rights leaders, persuaded the community to continue the boycott while the NAACP and Parks appealed her conviction.

The MIA chose as its spokesperson Martin Luther King Jr., a 26-year-old Baptist minister who was new to town. An energetic and moving speaker, King could inspire large audiences. His ability to move people helped hold the African American community together as the bus boycott dragged on for months. White protesters tried every method from intimidation to physical violence to break the boycott. Angry mobs attacked and beat boycotters. The houses of King and other MIA leaders were bombed. Many boycotters—including Rosa Parks—lost their jobs. King, who had studied the nonviolent tactics of Indian nationalist Mohandas K. Gandhi, urged the African American community not to respond to violence with more violence.

INTERPRETING THE VISUAL RECORD

Civil rights. During the Montgomery Bus Boycott Martin Luther King Jr.'s charisma and ability to motivate supporters made him an important leader in the movement. ***How do you think this photograph captures King's personality and role as a leader?***

The boycott succeeds. Finally, the nonviolent protest worked. In November 1956 the Supreme Court declared both the Montgomery and the Alabama segregation laws unconstitutional. By the end of the year, Montgomery had a desegregated bus system, and the civil rights movement had a new leader—Martin Luther King Jr. "We had won self-respect," declared boycott organizer Jo Ann Robinson. "It . . . makes you feel that America is a great country and we're going to do more to make it greater."

The Montgomery victory marked a blow to racial discrimination—and to the fear of standing up to people in positions of power. Cold War hysteria had contributed to this fear of authority. Not surprisingly, Martin Luther King Jr. was accused of being a Communist by opponents of the civil rights movement. Some southern whites, however, accepted that change had to come. As one South Carolina newspaper declared, "Segregation is going—it's all but gone. . . . The South can't reverse the trend."

Congress aided this trend by passing the first new civil rights law since Reconstruction. This **Civil Rights Act of 1957** bill made it a federal crime to prevent qualified persons from voting. It also set up the federal Civil Rights Commission to investigate violations of the law. A follow-up law enacted in 1960 strengthened the courts' power to protect the voting rights of African Americans.

✔ **READING CHECK:** How was the Montgomery Bus Boycott a major turning point in the civil rights movement?

TEACH OBJECTIVE 3

ALL LEVELS: Write the following statement on the chalkboard: *During the 1950s, many white Americans regarded Hispanics, Asian Americans, and American Indians as "the other," which led them to discriminate against these minority groups.* Have students respond to the statement in writing. Ask volunteers to share their responses. *(Answers will vary. Students might discuss the emphasis on conformity during the 1950s or mention the long-term history of discrimination in the United States.)* To help students understand the challenges certain minority groups faced in the 1950s, copy the graphic organizer on the chalkboard, omitting the italicized answers. Have each student complete it. **Sheltered English**

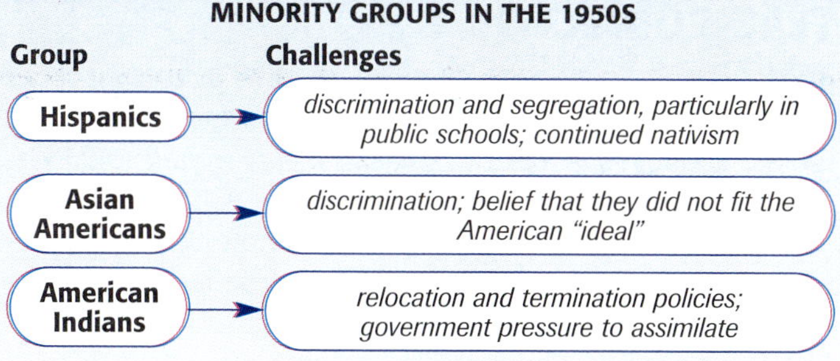
MINORITY GROUPS IN THE 1950S

Group	Challenges
Hispanics	*discrimination and segregation, particularly in public schools; continued nativism*
Asian Americans	*discrimination; belief that they did not fit the American "ideal"*
American Indians	*relocation and termination policies; government pressure to assimilate*

▶ASSIGNMENT: *Have each student create a detailed outline of the subsection entitled Beyond Black and White.*

Beyond Black and White

Segregation and discrimination affected others besides African Americans in the 1950s. Nonwhite Americans throughout the country continued to face prejudice. The experience of fighting for democratic ideals overseas in World War II, however, motivated more people to stand up and defend those ideals at home.

The Hispanic experience. One incident in particular revealed the extent of discrimination endured by Hispanics. Félix Longoria was a Mexican American soldier who was killed during World War II. In 1948 his body was recovered and returned to his hometown, Three Rivers, Texas. The town's only funeral home director refused to handle Longoria's burial because the soldier was Mexican American. When the media publicized this story, many Americans expressed outrage at this treatment of a veteran who had given his life for his country. Senator Lyndon Johnson of Texas stepped in and arranged for Longoria to be buried with full military honors at Arlington National Cemetery near Washington, D.C.

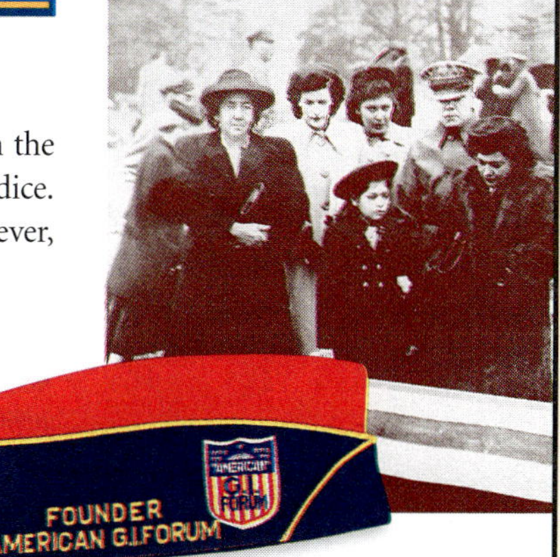

After Félix Longoria was finally buried at Arlington National Cemetery, other Hispanic veterans organized the American GI Forum to fight for other rights.

The Longoria incident led to the formation of the American GI Forum, a group dedicated to protecting the rights of Hispanic veterans. Over time the organization expanded to become a powerful lobbying group on behalf of all Hispanics. The GI Forum received help in its efforts from the **League for United Latin American Citizens** (LULAC). Formed in 1929, LULAC adopted many of the same tactics to fight for Hispanic rights that the NAACP used to champion African American rights.

Like the NAACP, LULAC focused on ending segregation, particularly in schools. In 1945 LULAC won an important case in *Méndez et al.* v. *Westminster School District et al.* In this case a federal judge ruled that the segregation of Mexican American children in a California school district was illegal. An even bigger victory came in 1948 with *Delgado* v. *Bastrop Independent School District.* In the *Delgado* case a judge ruled that the segregation of Mexican American children in a Texas school district was illegal. Soon afterward, state officials ended the segregation of Hispanic children in all Texas public schools.

Asian immigration. Some of the prejudice against Hispanics was the result of continued nativism. Nevertheless, fear of immigration began to ease somewhat after World War II. Asian immigrants in particular experienced the effects of this change. In 1952 Congress repealed the Chinese Exclusion Act to allow more Chinese immigrants into the United States.

Many Asian Americans achieved great success in the United States. However, they still faced constant reminders that they did not fit the profile of an "ideal" American. In 1952, for example, Sing Sheng, a Chinese immigrant and Allied war hero, attempted to buy a house in a San Francisco suburb called Southwood. When the neighborhood's white residents discovered that an Asian family might move in, they began a drive to prevent the Sheng family from buying the house. Noting that his family had fled communism in China, Sheng appealed to the residents of Southwood to practice the values of

Asian immigration to the United States increased after Congress repealed the Chinese Exclusion Act.

DEMOCRATIC VALUES

Discrimination in the Southwest. Through the 1960s, segregation affected Hispanics in many southwestern states. In southern and western Texas towns, for example, there were "Anglo schools" and "Mexican schools" in "white towns" and "little Mexicos." Churches and even cemeteries were also strictly segregated. In Texas legal segregation largely ended in 1969, when the legislature passed five laws banning various forms of segregation and discrimination. Despite the laws, however, segregation continued in a few towns. For example, in Ozona, the bowling alley, the cemeteries, and the swimming pools remained segregated through the early 1970s.

CRITICAL THINKING Why might cemeteries have been segregated in the South and Southwest? What might this segregation reveal about race relations there?

ANSWER: Students might suggest that cemeteries were segregated because churches were segregated. Students might argue that the segregation of cemeteries revealed the deep-seated nature of racial discrimination.

TEACH OBJECTIVE 4

LEVEL 1: Pair students and ask each pair to list some of the criticisms that writers and scholars expressed about 1950s society. *(Students should include conformity, poverty, racism, and a lack of creativity.)* Ask volunteers to share the contents of their lists and then note the most common criticisms on the chalkboard. Then ask pairs to write paragraphs evaluating the validity of the criticisms.
Sheltered English, Cooperative Learning

LEVEL 2: Conduct a brief discussion on the criticisms that writers and scholars expressed about 1950s society. *(See the Level 1 lesson for the correct criticisms.)* Then organize students into small groups and tell them to imagine that they are magazine editors preparing a special insert entitled The 1950s: An Age of Criticism. Have each group plan its insert, identifying potential articles, editorials, interviews, and so on. Then divide the elements among students and have each student create an item for the insert. Tell students to collect their items and compile them into inserts. Students may wish to include their individual items in their portfolios. **Cooperative Learning**

internetconnect

TOPIC: LULAC
GO TO: go.hrw.com
KEYWORD: SE1 LULAC

Have students access the Internet through the HRW Web site to conduct research on the history and political work of the League of United Latin American Citizens (LULAC) and the Mexican American Legal Defense Fund (MALDEF). Then have each student create an annotated and illustrated time line that outlines the activities of both organizations from 1929 to the present.

VISUAL RECORD ANSWER

Students might suggest that people would be more sympathetic toward a young child.

democracy and equality. "Do not make us the victims of a false democracy," he pleaded. Despite this request, the neighborhood association voted overwhelmingly to fight the Shengs. When white residents of other communities heard about the Southwood incident, many sent the Shengs personal letters inviting them to move into their neighborhoods. The Shengs accepted one such offer, settling peacefully in the town of Sonoma, California.

INTERPRETING THE VISUAL RECORD

Protesting. This young American Indian is protesting the government's takeover of reservation land to build a power plant. ***Why might this protester be more effective than others?***

Relocation of American Indians. Many nonwhite families moved into new homes in the postwar era. Unlike other migrants, however, American Indians moved under pressure from the federal government. To promote the assimilation of American Indians into mainstream society, the Eisenhower administration supported the Relocation Act of 1956. The act set up procedures to encourage American Indians to move to urban areas. It even established relocation offices in major cities to assist newcomers. Critics of the legislation feared that it would empty the reservations of future leaders and destroy tribal cultures. Oglala Lakota activist Gerald One Feather recalled the impact of the relocation program.

> **"The relocation program had an impact on our . . . government at Pine Ridge [South Dakota]. Many people who could have provided leadership were lost because they had motivation to go off the reservation to find employment or obtain an education. Relocation drained off a lot of our potential leadership."**

To speed up relocation, the government had adopted a policy of termination in 1953. Termination involved ending the reservation system on a tribe-by-tribe basis. It also cut most federal funding for American Indians. Various tribal groups launched protests and lawsuits against the termination policy. They considered it an attempt to wipe out American Indian communities. By 1958 the Eisenhower administration backed down from this policy.

✔ **READING CHECK:** What challenges did Hispanics, Asian Americans, and American Indians face in the 1950s?

Questioning Conformity

For some writers and scholars, discrimination against nonwhites was a symptom of broader societal trouble. They argued that beneath its surface of conformity, economic prosperity, and peace, the United States faced serious problems that were being ignored. These social critics sought to expose what they called the "crack in the picture window." This meant that the problems grew within a seemingly happy and peaceful society.

Some novelists depicted the experiences of those facing poverty and discrimination. In Ralph Ellison's *Invisible Man* (1952), an African American man searches for his place in a society that is at once both hostile and indifferent to him. Referring to his exclusion from mainstream society, the man states, "I am an invisible man. . . . I am invisible, understand, simply because people refuse to see me."

Ralph Ellison's **Invisible Man** *describes the experiences of an African American man who feels that he is overlooked by mainstream society.*

Several important scholars wrote nonfiction works that reinforced Ellison's message. Harvard economist John Kenneth Galbraith issued a warning to privileged Americans in *The Affluent Society* (1958). He wrote that they were ignoring

LEVEL 3: Conduct a brief discussion on the criticisms that writers and scholars expressed about 1950s society. *(See the Level 1 lesson for the correct criticisms.)* Then tell students to imagine that they are writers or scholars during the decade. Have each student write a short piece of social criticism, either fiction or nonfiction. If necessary, students should provide context for their pieces with brief introductions or conclusions. Ask volunteers to share their pieces with the class. Students may wish to include their pieces in their portfolios.

SPOTLIGHT on 1950s Literature

Have students read an excerpt from a well-known work of literature published during the 1950s, such as *The Catcher in the Rye*, *Invisible Man*, or *On the Road*. Then have each student reflect on the excerpt in writing, explaining how it reveals aspects of American life during the 1950s. Ask students to share their reflections with the class. Then ask each student to select the work of literature that he or she feels best represents his or her vision of the decade. **Block Scheduling**

pressing social issues in their pursuit of material possessions and comfort. Sociologists William Whyte, C. Wright Mills, and David Riesman criticized the new corporate system. Whyte's *The Organization Man* (1956) and Mills's *White Collar* (1951) argued that the pressure to conform in the new corporate order was wiping out workers' independence and individualism. Riesman warned in *The Lonely Crowd* (1950) that the United States faced "a silent revolution against work" because jobs no longer had meaning for people.

The **beats**, a small but influential group of writers and poets, challenged both the literary conventions of the day and the lifestyle of the middle class. Beat writer Allen Ginsberg's poem "Howl," for instance, raged against the threat of nuclear war and the conventions of corporate America. The beats wrote as they lived—on the spur of the moment, without any planning. One of the best-known beat works, Jack Kerouac's 1957 novel, *On the Road*, was written in a continuous three-week-long session at the typewriter. Kerouac celebrated the search for individual identity and the rejection of security and stability. One sentence in the novel captures the beat philosophy. "We gotta go and never stop till we get there."

INTERPRETING THE VISUAL RECORD

The beats. Jack Kerouac was the most famous beat writer. His book *On the Road* inspired ordinary people like these students (above) to join the movement as well. ***How do the styles and activities of the beats differ from those of other teenagers in the 1950s?***

✔ **READING CHECK:** What criticisms of 1950s society did writers and scholars express?

The Nonaffluent Society

Some writers noted that despite the overall strength of the economy many people were left out of the prosperity of the 1950s. A 1957 study found that some 40 million Americans lived below the poverty line of a $3,000 annual income for a family of four.

The rural poor. Rural residents, particularly farmers, represented the poorest segment of the American population. In some areas of the country, including parts of the Appalachian Mountains, many people still had no indoor plumbing or electricity. One study characterized the Appalachians as being filled with "a mood of apathy and despair."

Although farming productivity increased from 1950 to 1960, the income generated from farms actually shrank. As foreign countries recovered from World War II, they imported less food from the United States. The price of agricultural products fell dramatically. Large farms tended to do better than small farms. This was particularly true for those large farms whose owners could afford to invest in new, efficient farm equipment. Increased use of farm technology such as gasoline-powered tractors and other large equipment allowed farm owners to operate with fewer workers. As a result, many of the poorest farm laborers, particularly migrant field hands, found fewer opportunities for employment.

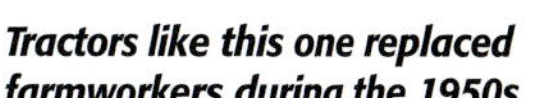

Tractors like this one replaced farmworkers during the 1950s.

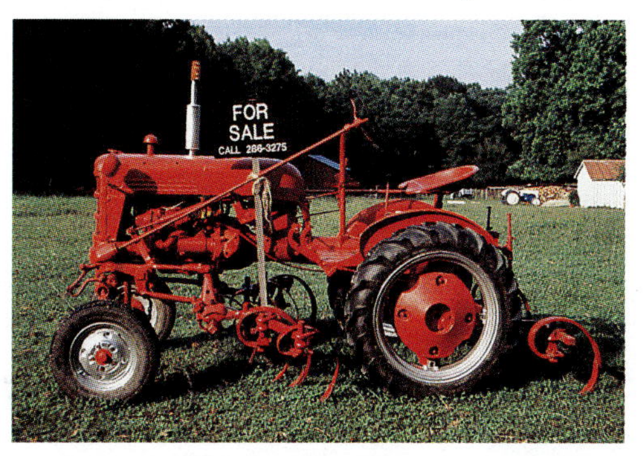

HISTORY MAKERS SPEAK

Jack Trachsel in *The Century*

Businesses and Conformity. During the 1950s large corporations often encouraged conformity in their employees. This affected all aspects of workers' lives, right down to their clothes. Some businesses issued "company neckties." Jack Trachsel, who worked for an Oregon gas company in the late 1950s and early 1960s, remembered, "There was a certain amount of conformity in the atmosphere at the office. Our dress code was pretty rigid, so we were always expected to wear conservative business suits, with conservative ties and white shirts, and polished shoes. Just about everybody in the office had a gray flannel suit—at least the younger crowd. I had two of them. It just didn't do your career any good at all to wear, say, a checkered sport coat."

CRITICAL THINKING Why might companies have encouraged conformity?

ANSWER: Students might suggest that corporations viewed conformity as a way to ensure cooperation and efficiency.

VISUAL RECORD ANSWER

Answers will vary. Students might mention the beats' clothes and hairstyles. In addition, they appear to be performing poetry and music.

TEACH OBJECTIVE 5

LEVELS 1 AND 2: Ask each student to develop a short monologue describing the problems faced by either the rural or urban poor. *(Students' monologues should mention falling farm prices, high cost of farm equipment, fewer farm jobs, increasingly poor urban populations, discrimination, and poor housing, as appropriate.)* Ask volunteers to perform their monologues for the class. To conclude, conduct a discussion about poverty in the United States during the 1930s and 1950s. How might the experience of poverty have differed in those two decades? *(Students might suggest that there was less stigma attached to poverty during the depression, since so many people were affected by it.)* **Sheltered English**

LEVEL 3: Ask students to imagine that they are novelists preparing to write a chapter about poor people in the 1950s. Have each student create a set of research notes to use in his or her later work. Students' research notes should describe the problems that the poorest Americans faced in the 1950s. *(See the Levels 1 and 2 lesson for the correct problems.)* Have students share their notes with the class. To conclude, conduct a discussion about poverty in the United States during the 1930s and 1950s. How might the experience of poverty have differed in those two decades? *(See the Levels 1 and 2 lesson for the correct answer.)*

PEOPLE IN HISTORY

Lawrence Ferlinghetti. Lawrence Ferlinghetti was a leading force in the beat movement. In the early 1950s Ferlinghetti moved to San Francisco and started *City Lights*, a literary magazine. Hoping to support his publication, he opened the City Lights Pocket Book Shop. City Lights soon became a vibrant gathering place for beat writers.

CRITICAL THINKING Why might some literary scholars view Ferlinghetti as a "jack of all trades"?

ANSWER: Students might suggest that some literary scholars call him a "jack of all trades" because of his numerous occupations.

AMERICAN LETTERS ANSWERS

1. white society; African Americans
2. as a time of prosperity overshadowed by the threat of nuclear warfare
3. Both criticize American culture, but Madgett seems more optimistic about the possibility of positive change.

VISUAL RECORD ANSWER

(for p. 587)

Students might answer that the housing project is newer and taller and has a cleaner appearance.

Voices of the Fifties

Many poets captured the spirit of the era in their verse. Beat poet Lawrence Ferlinghetti's "I am Waiting" challenged the confidence of postwar society. African American poet Naomi Long Madgett captured the feelings of many participants in the early civil rights movement in her poem "Midway."

from "I Am Waiting"

by Lawrence Ferlinghetti

Lawrence Ferlinghetti

I am waiting for my number to
be called
and I am waiting for the living
end
and I am waiting
for dad to come home
his pockets full
of irradiated [radioactive] silver
dollars
and I am waiting
for the atomic tests to end
and I am waiting happily
for things to get much worse
before they improve . . .
and I am waiting
for the human crowd
to wander off a cliff somewhere
clutching its atomic umbrella . . .
and I am waiting
for the meek to be blessed
and inherit the earth . . .
and I am waiting for forests and animals
to reclaim the earth as theirs
and I am waiting
for a way to be devised
to destroy all nationalisms
without killing anybody
and I am waiting
for linnets [birds] and planets to fall like rain
and I am waiting for lovers and weepers
to lie down together again
in a new rebirth of wonder.

"Midway"

by Naomi Long Madgett

Naomi Long Madgett

I've come this far to freedom
and I won't turn back.
I'm climbing to the highway
from my old dirt track.
I'm coming and I'm going
And I'm stretching and I'm
growing
And I'll reap what I've been
sowing or my skin's not black.

I've prayed and slaved and waited and I've sung my song.
You've bled me and you've starved me but I've still grown
strong.
You've lashed me and you've treed me
And you've everything but freed me
But in time you'll know you need me and it won't be long.

I've seen the daylight breaking high above the bough.
I've found my destination and I've made my vow;
So whether you abhor me
Or deride me or ignore me,
Mighty mountains loom before me and I won't stop now.

UNDERSTANDING LITERATURE

1. Who is the "you" in Madgett's poem? Other than the poet, who does the "I" in the poem represent?
2. What image does Ferlinghetti present of life in the 1950s?
3. How are Madgett's and Ferlinghetti's views of the 1950s similar? How are they different?

REVIEW

Have students complete the **Section 3 Review** on p. 587.

ASSESS

Have students complete **Daily Quiz 19.3**. As **Alternative Assessment**, you may want to use the social criticism piece or the poverty monologue in this section's lessons.

RETEACH

Have students complete **Main Idea Activity for Reteaching and Sheltered English 19.3**. Then list the major headings of Section 3 on the chalkboard. Tell students to imagine that these headings are newsmagazine headlines. Ask students to fill in the main points of each story. Note students' responses on the chalkboard. **Sheltered English**

EXTEND

Ask students to identify individuals or groups that criticize American society today. Encourage students to identify issues of concern and methods these critics use. Then have students compare the nature of current social criticism with the criticism produced in the 1950s. **Block Scheduling**

Urban communities. Many displaced workers from rural areas flocked to U.S. cities in search of a better life. In the Appalachian area alone, some 1.5 million young people left the mountains for cities. One Cincinnati newspaper referred to the city's Appalachian migrants as "our 50,000 refugees."

Many rural-to-urban migrants experienced little improvement in their economic status. By 1960 more than 20 million city-dwellers were living in poverty. As more and more middle-class white residents moved to the suburbs, poor inner-city communities increasingly consisted of nonwhite residents. In addition to the continuing African American migration to the cities, the Hispanic urban population increased as well. Poverty and discriminatory real estate practices prevented most nonwhite city-dwellers from getting decent housing. They were generally limited to crowded tenements and old housing in the poorest neighborhoods, which were usually segregated by ethnicity.

Despite their poverty, ethnic neighborhoods provided a sense of community for many of those who lived there. Local stores, churches, synagogues, temples, and social clubs gave structure to the lives of new migrants struggling to adjust to city life.

INTERPRETING THE VISUAL RECORD

Urban renewal. High-rise housing projects were supposed to replace poor neighborhoods. ***How does the housing project in the background of this image contrast with the building in front?***

To improve inner-city housing, the federal government proposed **urban renewal** programs. These were created to replace old, run-down inner-city buildings with new ones. Throughout the country, federally financed urban renewal programs bulldozed older neighborhoods to make way for more than 400,000 low-income public housing projects. These new high-rise buildings often had a cold, impersonal atmosphere. Most quickly became run-down themselves and were plagued by problems such as high crime rates.

✔ **READING CHECK:** What problems faced the poorest Americans in the 1950s?

SECTION 3 REVIEW

Define and explain the significance of the following terms:
Brown v. *Board of Education*
Little Rock Nine
Montgomery Improvement Association
Civil Rights Act of 1957
League for United Latin American Citizens
beats
urban renewal

Identify and explain the significance of the following individuals:
Thurgood Marshall
Orval Faubus
Rosa Parks
Martin Luther King Jr.
Félix Longoria
Ralph Ellison
Jack Kerouac

1. **Using Graphic Organizers** Copy the graphic organizer below. Use it to list aspects of rural and urban life in the 1950s, noting shared traits of both.

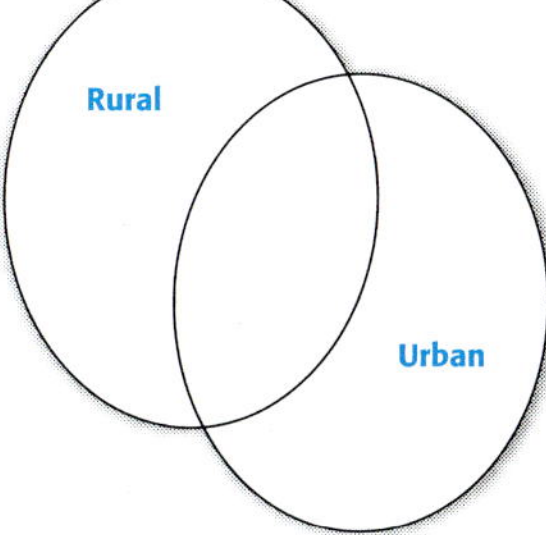

2. **Synthesizing** What effect did the *Brown* decision, the Little Rock crisis, and the Montgomery Bus Boycott have on the civil rights movement?
3. **Analyzing** What did the experiences of Hispanics, Asian Americans, and American Indians reveal about the United States in the 1950s?
4. **Identifying Values** What did writers like John Kenneth Galbraith and the beat poets identify as some of the problems in 1950s society?

Critical Thinking

5. Is it accurate to portray the 1950s as an era of good times for all Americans? Why or why not?
Consider:
- how different people might define "good times"
- what the experiences of minorities and the poor were
- what criticisms were given of society in the 1950s

SECTION 3 REVIEW ANSWERS

Define and Identify
For significance, see the following pages:
- *Brown* v. *Board of Education*, p. 579
- Thurgood Marshall, p. 579
- Orval Faubus, p. 580
- Little Rock Nine, p. 580
- Rosa Parks, p. 581
- Montgomery Improvement Association, p. 582
- Martin Luther King Jr., p. 582
- Civil Rights Act of 1957, p. 582
- Félix Longoria, p. 583
- League for United Latin American Citizens, p. 583
- Ralph Ellison, p. 584
- beats, p. 585
- Jack Kerouac, p. 585
- urban renewal, p. 587

1. rural—falling farm incomes, fewer farm jobs, young people migrate to cities; urban—white, middle class move to suburbs, discrimination, lack of decent housing; shared traits—poverty and struggle
2. *Brown*—banned public school segregation; Little Rock—exposed conflict over segregation; Boycott—King emerges as a leader, desegregates Montgomery buses
3. that many people held prejudices against minorities
4. conformity, poverty, racism, and a lack of creativity
5. Answers will vary. Students might argue that not all citizens shared equally in the good times. Others might suggest that all citizens could fight for their civil rights.

REVIEW AND ASSESSMENT RESOURCES

PRINT
- Chapter 19 Review, pp. 588–89
- Chapter 19 Tutorial for Students, Parents, Mentors, and Peers
- Chapter 19 Test (Form A or B)
- Portfolio Activities and Alternative Assessment Handbook, Chapter 19

MULTIMEDIA
- Audio Program, Chapter 19 (English and Spanish)
- Chapter 19 Test Generator (on the One-Stop Planner)
- Global Skill Builder CD–ROM
- HRW Web site

SHELTERED ENGLISH
- Spanish Glossary
- Sheltered English Chapter 19 Test

REVIEW

Have students complete the **Chapter 19 Review** on pp. 588–89.

ASSESS

Use one of the chapter tests to assess students' understanding of the content. For **Alternative Assessment**, see the **Portfolio Activities and Alternative Assessment Handbook.**

CHAPTER 19 REVIEW ANSWERS

Creating a Time Line
Each event should have an explanation and the correct date.

Writing a Summary
See the Reading Checks in each section for main ideas.

Identifying People and Ideas
1. bill that provided various types of assistance to veterans
2. conservative party of white southern Democrats
3. Truman's reform program
4. the use of machines to perform manufacturing tasks
5. first AFL–CIO president
6. the name given to the rising birthrate in the 1950s
7. rock 'n' roll singer
8. banned segregation in public schools
9. African American seamstress whose arrest led to the Montgomery Bus Boycott
10. group of writers who challenged literary and social conventions

Understanding Main Ideas
1. the GI Bill, the Employment Act of 1946, high consumer spending, farm exports
2. split the Democrats and led to the creation of the States' Rights Party
3. created more white-collar jobs and increased personal incomes for many
4. family-centered, conformist, and consumer-driven

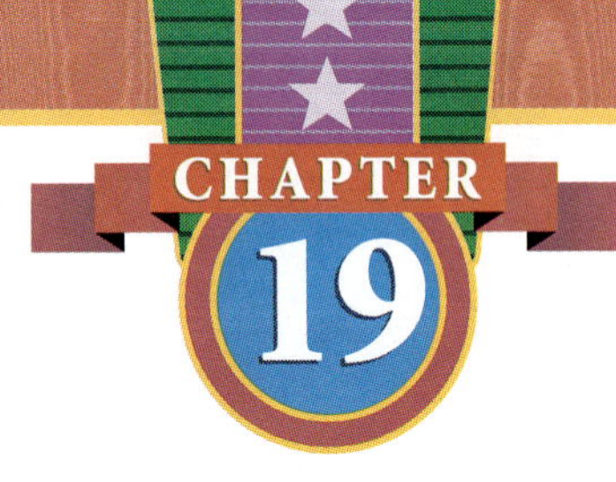

Review

Creating a Time Line

Copy the time line below onto a sheet of paper. Complete the time line by filling in the events and dates from the chapter that you think were most significant. Pick three events and explain why you think they were significant.

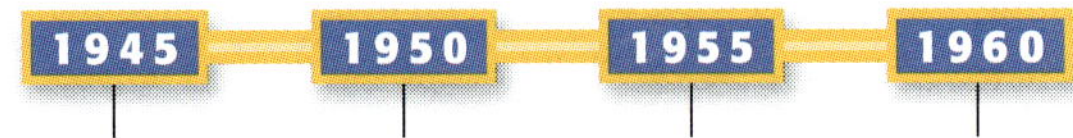

Writing a Summary

Using the Reading Checks as a guide, write an overview of the events in the chapter.

Identifying People and Ideas

Identify the following terms or individuals and explain their significance.

1. GI Bill of Rights
2. Dixiecrats
3. Fair Deal
4. automation
5. George Meany
6. baby boom
7. Elvis Presley
8. *Brown* v. *Board of Education*
9. Rosa Parks
10. beats

Understanding Main Ideas

SECTION 1

1. Why did the feared postwar economic depression never materialize?
2. How did civil rights issues affect the 1948 election?

SECTION 2

3. How did the economic prosperity of the 1950s affect the workforce?
4. What was suburban life like in the 1950s?

SECTION 3

5. What were some of the major successes and setbacks in ending segregation in the 1950s?
6. According to social critics, what were the weaknesses of American society in the 1950s?

Reviewing Themes

1. **Economic Development** How was the increase in population influenced by the economic boom of the 1950s?
2. **Cultural Diversity** How did some Americans rebel against the conformity of the 1950s?
3. **Democratic Values** How did members of minority groups fight discrimination during this decade?

Thinking Critically

1. **Comparing and Contrasting** What was the popular image of a mother's role in society in the 1950s? How did this image conflict with reality?
2. **Assessing Consequences** How did popular entertainment in the 1950s shape the economy?
3. **Identifying Values** What values came into conflict in the 1950s?
4. **Using Historical Imagination** Imagine that you are one of the Little Rock Nine. Are you willing to face constant harassment and threats of violence in order to go to a better school? Explain your answer.
5. **Problem Solving** What do you think was the greatest problem facing American society in the 1950s? If you had been president, what steps would you have taken to combat this problem?

Writing About History

Writing to Describe Write a brief paragraph describing the major concerns of workers in the late 1940s and how the government reacted to union efforts to address these problems. Use the following graphic to organize your thoughts.

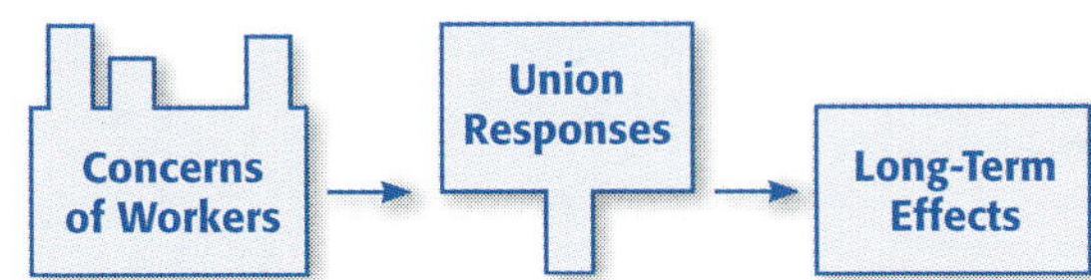

RETEACH

Tell students to imagine that they are planning a museum exhibit on the 1950s. The exhibit will contain a number of different rooms, each of which should focus on a different aspect of the 1950s. Have each student pick and plan a room in the exhibit, using the following topics as a guide: Soldiers Return Home, Labor Issues, The 1948 Election and the Fair Deal, A Booming Economy, The Move to the Suburbs, Popular Culture, The Fight for School Desegregation, The Fight for Transportation Desegregation, and Social Critics. Ask students to present their room plans to the class. **Sheltered English**

EXTEND

Ask students to select and watch a modern-day movie that is set in the 1950s. Then have each student write a movie review that both comments on the movie and discusses its portrayal of the decade. **Block Scheduling**

Strategies for Success Review the **Strategies for Success** on *Conducting an Interview.* Then prepare for and conduct an oral history interview with one of the following:

a. a person who lived in an urban housing project during the 1950s

b. a person who grew up in the suburbs during the 1950s

c. a person who remembers following the Central High crisis or the Montgomery Bus Boycott as they took place

d. a person who listened to rock 'n' roll music during the 1950s

Linking History and Geography

School desegregation proceeded at different rates throughout the country. By 1964 which states were the slowest to achieve desegregation?

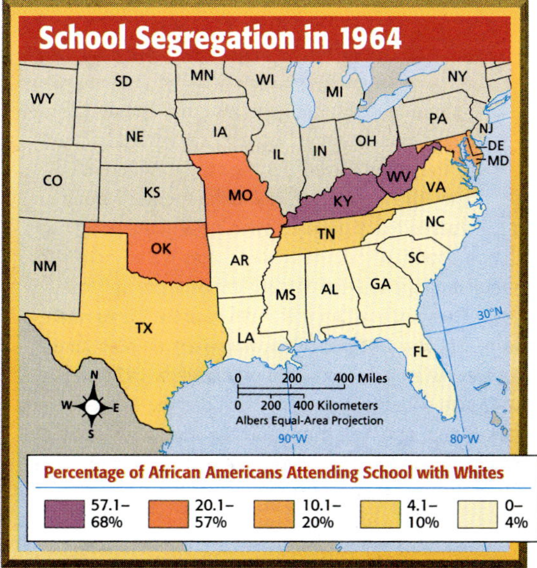

internet connect

TOPIC: Popular Culture in the 1950s
GO TO: go.hrw.com
KEYWORD: SE1 Culture

Accessing the Internet through the HRW Web site, research the popular culture of the 1950s. Then create a poster or multimedia presentation that describes how the popular culture of the 1950s mirrored the social events of that decade.

BUILDING YOUR PORTFOLIO

Complete one or all of the following projects independently or cooperatively.

1 Economic Development

Imagine that you are a staff member of the Department of Labor. ***Prepare an illustrated chart*** that shows how the U.S. government is assisting returning soldiers through various programs designed to help them find civilian jobs, attain college educations, or own their own homes.

2 Democratic Values

Imagine that you are a reporter assigned to cover civil rights issues. ***Develop an illustrated outline*** of the major civil rights events that occurred in the United States between 1945 and 1960.

3 Technology and Society

Imagine that you are the inventor of the electric guitar, an instrument made popular by rock 'n' roll musicians. ***Write an illustrated report*** describing how your invention has affected American culture.

5. successes—*Brown*, integration of Central High School and Montgomery buses; setbacks—violence

6. conformity, racism, poverty, and a lack of creativity

Reviewing Themes

1. encouraged people to have more children.

2. by criticizing it through art or popular culture; by protesting discrimination

3. through the courts, with boycotts, by nonviolent tactics

Thinking Critically

1. as a full-time housewife; many women worked outside the home during the decade

2. Advertising supported the consumer culture.

3. conformity versus individuality; discrimination versus equality

4. Answers will vary. Students should support their position.

5. Answers will vary. Students should identify a problem and explain the steps to combat it.

Writing About History

concerns—automation, high inflation, low wages; responses—strikes and other protests; effects—led to antilabor legislation

Strategies for Success

Students' questions should incorporate earlier research and concentrate on the topic.

Linking History and Geography

Alabama, Arkansas, Florida, Georgia, Louisiana, Mississippi, North Carolina, and South Carolina

REVIEW AND ASSESSMENT RESOURCES

PRINT
- Unit 5 Review, pp. 590–91
- Unit 5 Test (Form A or B)
- Portfolio Activities and Alternative Assessment Handbook, Unit 5

MULTIMEDIA
- Global Skill Builder CD–ROM

SHELTERED ENGLISH
- Spanish Glossary
- Sheltered English Unit 5 Test

To review elements of Unit 5 in a single class period, assign one of the following activities or graphic organizers, omitting the italicized answers, to individuals or groups.

1 Global Relations

Tell students to imagine that it is 1940 and that they are editorial writers. Have each student write an editorial describing the rise of dictators around the world and explaining the actions that the United States should take toward those dictators.

A Selection from Further Reading

The United States and the Holocaust. In *The World Must Know: A History of the Holocaust as Told in the United States Holocaust Memorial Museum*, Michael Berenbaum provides an informative overview of one of history's greatest tragedies. In the following excerpt, he laments the failure of the United States to provide a haven for large numbers of European Jews during the late 1930s. "The United States raised a formidable series of paper walls to keep refugees out. . . . There were financial tests to weed out refugees who were likely to become a public charge. One of the requirements was a certificate of good conduct attesting to the exemplary character of the immigrant. This was supposed to be obtained from one's local police authority, in this case the Gestapo. . . . The United States, a nation of immigrants, was reluctant to become a haven for Jewish refugees. Reflexive nationalism went hand in hand with widespread antisemitism."

COMPREHENSION According to Berenbaum, why did the United States fail to provide a haven for large numbers of European Jews during the late 1930s?

ANSWER: Students might identify factors such as nationalism and anti-Jewish prejudice.

UNIT 5 Review

BUILDING YOUR PORTFOLIO

Outlined below are four projects. Independently or cooperatively, complete one and use the products to demonstrate your mastery of the historical concepts involved.

1 Global Relations

The world experienced severe economic, political, and social unrest in the years leading up to World War II. ***Write a script for a debate*** with representatives from several nations about global relations after World War II. Debates should center around the issue of how the United States should respond in the future to the rise of dictators in other parts of the world. You may wish to use portfolio materials you designed in the unit chapters to help you.

Holocaust survivors being liberated

Civil rights activist protesting

2 Democratic Values

Throughout history various groups of people have been singled out and oppressed because the ruling society deemed them "different" in some way. The rise of fascism and the events of World War II increased many people's awareness of the dangers of such oppression. Within the United States it also increased the resolve of groups like African Americans to see true equality take place within their own country. ***Write and then perform a 15-minute documentary*** on how various groups experienced discrimination between 1921 and 1960. Make sure that the report includes the effects of the discrimination and how the various groups fought against it. You may wish to use portfolio materials you designed in the unit chapters to help you.

3 Technology and Society

EFFECTS OF THE COLD WAR AT HOME

Society
- *The second Red Scare aroused fears of communism at home.*
- *Purchases of home bomb shelters rose.*
- *Liberal groups, labor unions, and artists came under investigation.*

Culture
- *HUAC condemned the movie industry; some careers were destroyed.*
- *Some art, music, and literature reflected fears of nuclear holocaust.*
- *Many artists and writers became very cautious about their self-expression.*

4 Economic Development

Government Involvement in the Economy

Business, Industry, and Labor
- *sets minimum wage*
- *regulates businesses and industry, both large and small*
- *provides aid to ailing industries, farmers, and certain companies*

Banking and Finance
- *allows the Federal Reserve Board to control interest rates*
- *allows the FDIC to guarantee deposits in individual accounts*

Public Health and Welfare
- *dispenses social security, welfare, unemployment benefits*
- *provides emergency and disaster relief*
- *offers Medicare and Medicaid and regulates health care and insurance*

3 Technology and Society

As the Cold War intensified, Americans became increasingly fearful of military conflict and the threat of the deployment of nuclear weapons. ***Create an illustrated cover story for a popular magazine*** that explains how these fears have influenced daily life, literature, popular culture, and the arts. You may wish to use portfolio materials you designed in the unit chapters to help you.

UN troops fighting against Communist forces in Korea

4 Economic Development

After World War II, the U.S. government became increasingly involved in managing and influencing the U.S. economy. ***Create a visual display*** of the different areas of the economy in which the government played a role in the 1950s. Make sure your display shows how each type of government involvement affected the lives of average citizens. You may wish to use portfolio materials you designed in the unit chapters to help you.

Social Security Administration poster

Further Reading

Berenbaum, Michael. *The World Must Know: The History of the Holocaust as Told in the United States Holocaust Memorial Museum.* Little, Brown, 1993. Pictorial and eyewitness history of the Holocaust.

Cohen, Stan. *V for Victory: America's Home Front During World War II.* Motorbooks International, 1991. Overview of the effect of World War II on Americans on the home front.

Cook, Haruko Taya, and Theodore F. Cook. *Japan at War: An Oral History.* New Press, 1992. Accounts of war's effects on the Japanese.

Halberstam, David. *The Fifties.* Villard Books, 1993. A broad account of American life in the 1950s.

King, Martin Luther Jr. *Stride Toward Freedom: The Montgomery Story.* Harper & Row, 1986. Martin Luther King Jr.'s own story of the Montgomery Bus Boycott.

Knox, Donald. *The Korean War: Uncertain Victory.* Harcourt Brace Jovanovich, 1988. Oral history of the war.

Jackson, Kenneth T. *Crabgrass Frontier: The Suburbanization of the United States.* Oxford University Press, 1985. A history of the rise of a suburban culture in the United States.

Internet Connect and Holt Researcher CD–ROM Review

In assigned groups, develop a multimedia presentation about America between 1921 and 1960. Choose information from the chapter Internet Connect activities and from the Holt Researcher CD–ROM that best reflects the major topics of the period. Write an outline and a script for your presentation, which may be shown to the class.

A Selection from Further Reading

Nonviolent Resistance. In *Stride Toward Freedom: The Montgomery Story*, Martin Luther King Jr. presents his account of the Montgomery Bus boycott. In the following excerpt, he discusses the philosophy of nonviolent resistance. "Nonviolent resistance is not a method for cowards; it does resist. . . . It is not a method of stagnant passivity. The phrase 'passive resistance' often gives the false impression that this is a sort of 'do-nothing' method in which the resister quietly and passively accepts evil. But nothing is farther than the truth. For while the nonviolent resister is passive in the sense that he is not physically aggressive toward his opponent, his mind and emotions are always active, constantly seeking to persuade his opponent that he is wrong. The method is passive physically, but strongly active spiritually."

COMPREHENSION According to King, how does a nonviolent resister actively resist injustice?

ANSWER: Students might note that the nonviolent resister behaves in a manner that is intended to persuade the perpetrators of injustice that they are wrong.

UNIT 6

A Changing Home Front

CHAPTER 20 The New Frontier and the Great Society

After winning the presidential election of 1960 in an extremely close contest, John F. Kennedy attempted to manage numerous Cold War conflicts. The popular President Kennedy helped invigorate the nation. In November 1963 an assassin killed Kennedy, ending "Camelot." Lyndon B. Johnson, who succeeded Kennedy, soon launched a War on Poverty and announced social programs called the Great Society.

CHAPTER 21 The Civil Rights Movement

African Americans continued to work for equality during the 1960s, a decade dominated by the civil rights movement. Under the leadership of Martin Luther King Jr. the civil rights movement utilized nonviolent resistance to end segregation and work for equal rights. These efforts led to the passage of major legislation. Other civil rights leaders advocated separatism and violent resistance, however.

EXAMINING THE VISUAL RECORD

Ask students the questions below. Then use the annotations to expand class discussion.

1 ***Where might the protest march be taking place?***
The photograph shows the marchers entering Montgomery, Alabama. Protesters held the march to demonstrate for equal voting rights.

2 ***Who is this man? What might his role in the civil rights movement have been?***
The man in the photograph is Martin Luther King Jr., one of the leaders of the civil rights movement. King led many crucial civil rights efforts, including the Montgomery Bus boycott and the March on Washington. His wife, Coretta, is to the right.

3 ***Why might the mostly African American marchers have included white activists in the front lines of their protest?***
The organizers of the march probably wanted to stress that racial cooperation was possible and productive. White supporters aided the civil rights movement in a number of ways, such as registering voters and marching in protests.

ACTIVITY: Tell students to imagine that they participated in the march. Have each student write a short statement describing and justifying the goals of the march.

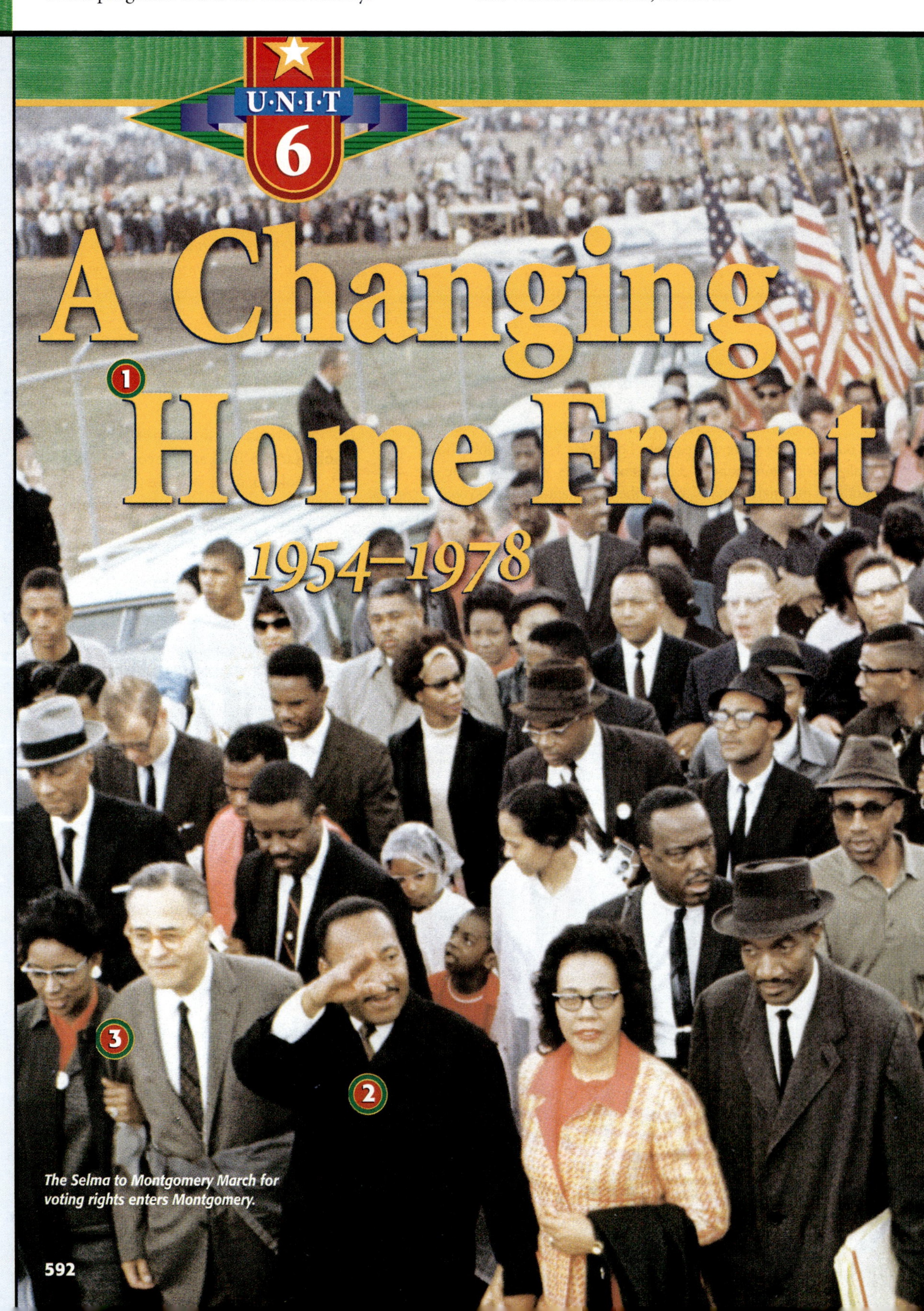

The Selma to Montgomery March for voting rights enters Montgomery.

CHAPTER 22 Struggles for Change

Many minority groups worked for equality during the 1960s and 1970s, including women, American Indians, Hispanics, and disabled Americans. As they pushed for civil rights, many college students pushed for the creation of a new society, one that did not include racism or war. Some even "dropped out" to form a counterculture. Art, religion, and music reflected the upheavals of the time.

CHAPTER 23 War in Vietnam

After winning its independence in 1954, Vietnam broke into two separate nations—communist North Vietnam and anticommunist South Vietnam. The United States, fearful of communism in Southeast Asia, aided the South Vietnamese in their fight against the North Vietnamese and became involved in the Vietnam War. The conflict was long and devastating. The United States agreed to a cease-fire in 1973.

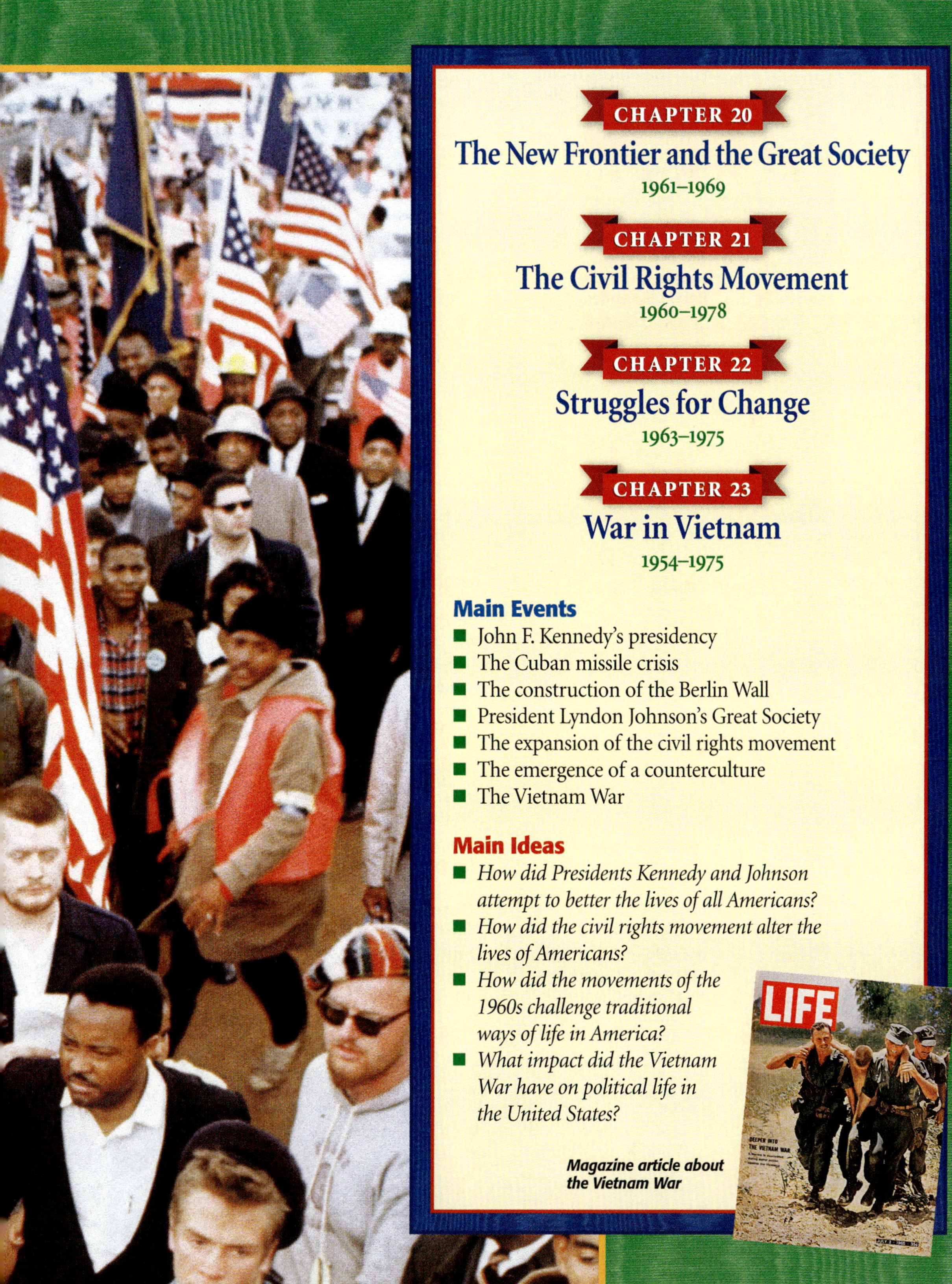

CHAPTER 20
The New Frontier and the Great Society
1961–1969

CHAPTER 21
The Civil Rights Movement
1960–1978

CHAPTER 22
Struggles for Change
1963–1975

CHAPTER 23
War in Vietnam
1954–1975

Main Events
- John F. Kennedy's presidency
- The Cuban missile crisis
- The construction of the Berlin Wall
- President Lyndon Johnson's Great Society
- The expansion of the civil rights movement
- The emergence of a counterculture
- The Vietnam War

Main Ideas
- *How did Presidents Kennedy and Johnson attempt to better the lives of all Americans?*
- *How did the civil rights movement alter the lives of Americans?*
- *How did the movements of the 1960s challenge traditional ways of life in America?*
- *What impact did the Vietnam War have on political life in the United States?*

Magazine article about the Vietnam War

INTRODUCE UNIT 6

Main Events
List the Main Events on the chalkboard. Ask students to select two and briefly describe what they know about the topics. Have volunteers share their descriptions. Later, when you have finished Unit 6, ask students to return to their original descriptions and revise them using the information they learned in the unit. Students should also create new descriptions for the other Main Events.

Main Ideas
Ask each student to read the Main Ideas and briefly answer the questions in writing. Share the ***Consider*** points with students as necessary. Later, when you have finished Unit 6, ask students to return to their original answers and revise them using the information they learned in the unit.

The Civil Rights Movement
Consider:
- the opportunities provided by social and economic integration
- the social impact of a movement that redefined race relations

The Vietnam War
Consider:
- the political effects of a divisive war and conflict
- the political effects of mistrust in the government

The New Frontier and the Great Society

CHAPTER PLANNING GUIDE

	Section Lesson Objectives	Print Resources	Multimedia Resources	Sheltered English Resources
Section 1 Kennedy and the Cold War, pp. 596–602	1 Analyze how television coverage influenced the presidential election of 1960. 2 Summarize how President Kennedy planned to stop the spread of communism. 3 Explain why the Bay of Pigs invasion of Cuba failed. 4 Describe how the Cuban missile crisis almost led to war.	▶ Guided Reading Strategy 20.1 ▶ Geography Activity 20: The Cuban Missile Crisis ▶ Graphic Organizer Activity 20: The Cuban Missile Crisis ▶ Literature Reading 20: A View of Nikita Khrushchev ▶ Primary Source Reading 20: America's Fascination with the "Final Frontier" ▶ Section 1 Review, p. 602 ▶ Daily Quiz 20.1	▶ One-Stop Planner, Lesson 20.1 ▶ American History Simulations CD–ROM: Race to the Moon ▶ Holt Researcher: American History CD–ROM	▶ Main Idea Activity for Reteaching and Sheltered English 20.1
Section 2 The Kennedy White House, pp. 603–09	1 Discuss how President Kennedy's image conflicted with reality. 2 Identify why Kennedy had difficulty getting legislation passed. 3 Explain how the Kennedy administration tried to help poor Americans. 4 Describe how Americans responded to the death of the president.	▶ Guided Reading Strategy 20.2 ▶ Biography Reading 20: Robert F. Kennedy ▶ Section 2 Review, p. 609 ▶ Daily Quiz 20.2	▶ One-Stop Planner, Lesson 20.2 ▶ Holt Researcher: American History CD–ROM ▶ HRW Web site	▶ Main Idea Activity for Reteaching and Sheltered English 20.2
Section 3 Johnson's Great Society, pp. 610–17	1 Explain how President Johnson's War on Poverty affected American communities. 2 Identify the problems that the Great Society programs addressed. 3 Detail how the Warren Court expanded individual liberties. 4 Describe why support for the Great Society programs declined during the late 1960s.	▶ Guided Reading Strategy 20.3 ▶ Section 3 Review, p. 617 ▶ Daily Quiz 20.3	▶ One-Stop Planner, Lesson 20.3 ▶ The American Nation Video Program Segment: VISTA Volunteers; Teacher's Guide, pp. 207–08 ▶ Holt Researcher: American History CD–ROM	▶ Main Idea Activity for Reteaching and Sheltered English 20.3
Chapter Review and Assessment pp. 618–19		▶ Chapter 20 Review, pp. 618–19 ▶ Chapter 20 Tutorial for Students, Parents, Mentors, and Peers ▶ Chapter 20 Test (Form A or B) ▶ Portfolio Activities and Alternative Assessment Handbook, Chapter 20	▶ Audio Program, Chapter 20 (English and Spanish) ▶ Chapter 20 Test Generator (on the One-Stop Planner) ▶ Global Skill Builder CD–ROM ▶ HRW Web site	▶ Spanish Glossary ▶ Sheltered English Chapter 20 Test

CHAPTER OVERVIEW

In an extremely close contest, John F. Kennedy won the presidential election of 1960. Once in office, President Kennedy attempted to halt the advance of communism with an approach called flexible response. Despite his personal popularity, Kennedy found it difficult to pass domestic legislation, although he found some success with antipoverty programs. On November 22, 1963, an assassin killed Kennedy, ending the era of "Camelot."

President Lyndon B. Johnson attempted to comfort the nation in its grief and continue Kennedy's programs. Johnson supported an aggressive War on Poverty and pushed legislators to create his Great Society with a wide variety of programs. Toward the end of the 1960s, however, a number of factors led to the decline of the Great Society.

TIME TAMERS

Block Scheduling

The teacher lesson plans for each section offer a variety of activity choices to help you present the material in a block scheduling format. For further suggestions on block scheduling, see the **Block Scheduling Handbook with Team Teaching Strategies**, pp. 115–20.

Smithsonian Institution®

Internet Connections and Lesson 20
www.si.edu/hrw

Hands-On History Activities:

Classroom to Community The **Hands-On History Activities** help students make meaningful connections between events in American history and those in their own hometown. You may wish to use the Chapter 20 Activity, The Great Society, to extend the chapter lessons, as alternative assessment, or as a block scheduling option.

Portfolio Projects

The American Nation includes multiple portfolio projects in each Pupil's Edition chapter review, as well as each unit review. Chapter 20 Portfolio Project options on p. 619 include the following:

1. Students will **prepare a news bulletin**.
2. Students will **prepare a memorandum**.
3. Students will **prepare an illustrated pamphlet**.

The American Nation
INTERNET RESOURCE DIRECTORY

To access online materials for this chapter, go to **go.hrw.com** and type in the keywords listed below.

HRW ONLINE RESOURCES
GO TO: go.hrw.com

Online Maps
KEYWORD: SE1 Maps20
• NASA

Online Charts
KEYWORD: SE1 Charts20
• Space Race

Online Reading Support
KEYWORD: SE1 Strategies20

Online Rubrics
KEYWORD: SE1 Rubrics

CHAPTER ENRICHMENT LINKS
Use these Web links to extend and enrich student learning for Chapter 20.
GO TO: go.hrw.com
KEYWORD: SE1 Ch20

CHAPTER INTERNET ACTIVITIES
GO TO: go.hrw.com
- Pupil's Edition Student Activity
  KEYWORD: SE1 Corps
  (Students examine the history and present-day role of the Peace Corps.)
- Teacher's Edition Student Activity
  KEYWORD: SE1 Glenn
  (Students conduct research on John Glenn.)
- Teacher's Edition Student Activity
  KEYWORD: SE1 Kennedy
  (Students conduct research on John Kennedy.)

ADDITIONAL
RESOURCES

Books for Teachers

Califano, Joseph A. *The Triumph and Tragedy of Lyndon Johnson: The White House Years.* Simon & Schuster, 1991. Provides a detailed history of Lyndon Johnson's presidency.

Reeves, Richard. *President Kennedy: Profile of Power.* Simon & Schuster, 1993. Provides a detailed history of John F. Kennedy's presidency.

Books for Students

Blum, John M. *Years of Discord: American Politics and Society, 1961–1974.* Norton, 1991. Provides a highly readable overview of American politics during the 1960s.

Thompson, Robert Smith. *The Missiles of October: The Declassified Story of John F. Kennedy and the Cuban Missile Crisis.* Simon & Schuster, 1992. Explains how the United States and the Soviet Union came to the brink of nuclear war in 1962.

Primary Sources from the Period

Carson, Rachel. *Silent Spring.* Houghton Mifflin, 1962. Chronicles the effects of pesticides on the environment and discusses the health risks that such chemicals pose for humans.

Harrington, Michael. *The Other America: Poverty in the United States.* Macmillan, 1962. Examines the plight of Americans who did not share in the prosperity of the 1950s.

Multimedia Materials

From the Bay of Pigs to the Brink. Video, 16 min. Films for the Humanities/Visnews. Documents the circumstances that led to the Cuban missile crisis.

CHAPTER 20

Before You Read

Build on What You Know

Ask students to answer the following questions.

What sorts of programs might Presidents Kennedy and Johnson have implemented to change American life?

Consider:

- social and economic problems during the late 1950s
- the domestic goals of both presidents

How might Kennedy and Johnson have dealt with foreign-policy crises that arose from Cold War tensions?

Consider:

- the seriousness of the communist threat
- the foreign-policy goals of both presidents

exploring the time line

AMERICAN EVENTS

internetconnect

TOPIC: John Glenn
GO TO: go.hrw.com
KEYWORD: SE1 Glenn

Have students access the Internet through the HRW Web site to conduct research on John Glenn. Then ask each student to create a biographical poster or multimedia presentation describing Glenn's career and accomplishments.

CHAPTER 20

1961–1969

The New Frontier and the Great Society

Building the Berlin Wall

Slim Pickens in an advertisement for the movie Dr. Strangelove

1961
World Events
The East German government builds a wall that divides East and West Berlin.

1963
The Arts
Stanley Kubrick's film *Dr. Strangelove,* a black comedy about the Cold War, is released.

1964
Daily Life
An earthquake in Alaska kills 114 people and causes $500 million in damage.

1961 **1962** **1963** **1964**

1961
Politics
President John F. Kennedy gives an inaugural address that calls for Americans to sacrifice in the struggle to defend liberty across the globe.

Kennedy campaign button

Pin honoring John F. Kennedy's military service

1963
Science and Technology
A vaccine against measles becomes available.

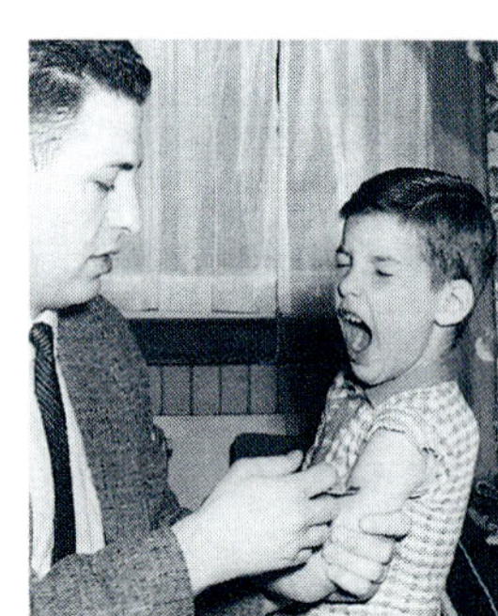

A child receiving a measles vaccine

1964
Politics
Lyndon Johnson is elected president by a landslide.

1964
Science and Technology
The U.S. surgeon general reports that cigarette smoking is the leading cause of lung cancer.

Before You Read

Build on What You Know

During the late 1950s President Eisenhower opposed the expansion of communism. He threatened the use of nuclear weapons and used secret means to keep communism from spreading. At home, Eisenhower shifted domestic policy from the New Deal and Fair Deal to Modern Republicanism. In this chapter you will learn how the Democratic administrations of John F. Kennedy and Lyndon Johnson implemented new policies and programs that changed American life. You will also learn how they dealt with foreign-policy crises caused by Cold War tensions.

594

Think About Themes

To help students create their Themes Journal entries, provide the following examples of appropriate **agree/disagree** *statements.*

Global Relations

Agree The Marshall Plan helped solidify the alliance between the United States and Western European nations during the early stages of the Cold War.

Disagree The payment of reparations heightened political tensions between Germany and other Western European nations during the 1920s and 1930s.

Economic Development

Agree The New Deal included a variety of programs that provided economic assistance to poor Americans during the Great Depression.

Disagree The U.S. government provided relatively little economic aid to formerly enslaved African Americans during Reconstruction.

Democratic Values

Agree Certain circumstances, such as war or national security, require presidents to keep information from the public.

Disagree As national leaders, presidents have the responsibility to share information with the public.

The Apollo I space capsule

India's prime minister, Indira Gandhi

1965 Science and Technology The *Pioneer 6* spacecraft, designed to orbit the Sun, is launched.

1965 Business and Finance France redeems $200 million for U.S. gold, shaking the gold market and prompting President Johnson to ask Americans to take vacations in the United States rather than abroad.

1966 World Events Indira Gandhi becomes prime minister of India.

1967 Science and Technology Three *Apollo I* crewmembers are killed when fire breaks out in the space capsule on the launchpad.

1967 World Events The Six-Day War between Israel and several Arab nations occurs.

1968 Politics Congress rejects Abe Fortas, President Johnson's nominee for Chief Justice of the United States.

1968 World Events North Korea seizes the USS *Pueblo,* a U.S. Navy ship, and releases the crew nearly a year later.

1965 | **1966** | **1967** | **1968**

1965 Politics Congress creates the Department of Housing and Urban Development.

James Hoffa testifying before Congress

1967 Politics The Twenty-fifth Amendment, which details procedures for presidential succession, is ratified.

1967 Business and Finance James Hoffa, president of the Teamsters Union, is jailed for jury tampering.

1968 Business and Finance Corporate profits after taxes exceed $47 billion.

1968 The Arts The musical play *You're a Good Man, Charlie Brown* premieres.

1968 Daily Life Surveys reveal that 86 percent of elementary school teachers are women, while 78 percent of the principals are men.

Think About Themes

Decide whether you **agree** *or* **disagree** *with the following statements. Note why in your journal.*

Global Relations Providing economic assistance to a foreign nation is an effective way to guarantee a political alliance.

Economic Development Governments have a responsibility to provide economic aid to citizens living in poverty.

Democratic Values Under certain circumstances, presidents should conceal facts from the public.

exploring the time line

GLOBAL EVENTS

PEOPLE IN HISTORY

1966 ■ Indira Gandhi. Indira Priyadarshini Gandhi became prime minister of India in 1966. Despite continual challenges Gandhi managed to stay in office. After the 1972 national elections, however, her defeated challenger charged her with election fraud. When the High Court of Allahabad ruled against her, Gandhi declared a state of emergency throughout India and imprisoned her political opponents. When she finally allowed elections to be held again, voters removed her from office. In 1980, however, she was elected prime minister once again. India experienced enormous political conflict during the early part of that decade, with Sikh radicals in the Punjab fighting for an independent state. To quell the effort, Gandhi ordered an attack on the Golden Temple of Amritsar, the Sikhs' holiest shrine. More than 450 Sikhs were killed. Months later, two of Gandhi's Sikh bodyguards killed her in retaliation.

ACTIVITY: Have students conduct research on India's government today and share their findings with the class.

595

SECTION 1

After completing Section 1, students should be able to:

OBJECTIVE 1 *Analyze how television coverage influenced the presidential election of 1960.*

OBJECTIVE 2 *Summarize how President Kennedy planned to stop the spread of communism.*

OBJECTIVE 3 *Explain why the Bay of Pigs invasion of Cuba failed.*

OBJECTIVE 4 *Describe how the Cuban missile crisis almost led to war.*

LET'S GET STARTED!

Write the following question on the chalkboard: *Based on what you have learned about international relations in the 1950s, what do you think international relations in the 1960s were like?* As students enter the classroom, ask them to respond to the question. Have volunteers share their responses. Then tell students that in Section 1 they will learn how President Kennedy struggled to stop the advance of communism.

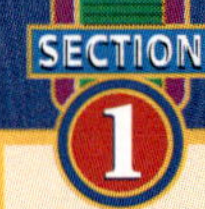

SECTION 1 RESOURCES

PRINT
- Guided Reading Strategy 20.1
- Geography Activity 20: The Cuban Missile Crisis
- Graphic Organizer Activity 20: The Cuban Missile Crisis
- Literature Reading 20: A View of Nikita Khrushchev
- Primary Source Reading 20: America's Fascination With the "Final Frontier"
- Section 1 Review, p. 602
- Daily Quiz 20.1

MULTIMEDIA
- One-Stop Planner, Lesson 20.1
- American History Simulations CD–ROM: Race to the Moon
- Holt Researcher: American History CD–ROM

SHELTERED ENGLISH
- Main Idea Activity for Reteaching and Sheltered English 20.1

✔ READING TO UNDERSTAND

To help students master the section objectives, have them answer the **READING CHECKS** and complete **Guided Reading Strategy 20.1** as they read the section.

Kennedy and the Cold War

OBJECTIVES

Read to understand:
1. how television coverage influenced the presidential election of 1960
2. how President Kennedy planned to stop the spread of communism
3. why the Bay of Pigs invasion of Cuba failed
4. how the Cuban missile crisis almost led to war

KEY TERMS

flexible response
Peace Corps
Alliance for Progress
Berlin Wall
Cuban missile crisis
Limited Nuclear Test Ban Treaty
hot line

KEY PEOPLE

John F. Kennedy
Fidel Castro

KEY PLACES

Bay of Pigs
San Cristóbal

"For six days, time was deformed, everyday life suddenly dwarfed and illuminated, as if by the glare of an explosion that had not yet taken place."

—Todd Gitlin

Todd Gitlin's book about the 1960s

Todd Gitlin reflected on the tense days of October 1962. At that time Gitlin was a student at Harvard University with a strong interest in politics. When President John F. Kennedy appeared on television on October 22 to announce a naval blockade against Cuba, Gitlin and many other Americans feared that a nuclear war between the United States and the Soviet Union might soon occur. He remembered that during the crisis "the country lived out the awe . . . and simmering near-panic always implicit in the thermonuclear age." The incident reflected the crises that President Kennedy faced during his brief presidency.

Fear of communism played a key role in the 1960 presidential election.

The 1960 Campaign

Most Americans were satisfied with President Eisenhower's performance in the White House. However, the passage of the Twenty-second Amendment in 1951 limited a president's tenure in office to two elected terms. This meant that Eisenhower could not run for a third term in 1960.

As expected, the Republicans chose Richard Nixon as their presidential candidate for the upcoming election. His solid performance as Eisenhower's vice president had won him support from many Republican Party members. Trying to appeal to a wide variety of voters, Nixon downplayed his participation in such events as the investigations by the House Un-American Activities Committee.

Senator John F. Kennedy of Massachusetts eventually emerged as the Democratic candidate. His charm, wit, good looks, and record of service during World War II impressed many voters. However, as a Roman Catholic he faced the same religious prejudices that had hurt Al Smith's presidential bid in 1928. Kennedy assured voters that he believed firmly in the separation of church and state. Recalling his brother Joseph, who was killed in combat during World War II, Kennedy told voters, "Nobody asked my brother if he was a Catholic or Protestant before he climbed into an American bomber plane to fly his last mission." Kennedy's reassurances and the Republicans' refusal to exploit the issue convinced many voters that religion need not play a role in their voting decisions.

Nixon chose Henry Cabot Lodge Jr. of Massachusetts as his running mate. Kennedy selected Texas senator Lyndon B. Johnson, who had failed in his own attempt to obtain the Democratic nomination. Kennedy's decision shocked his supporters, many of whom intensely disliked the senator. One aide told Kennedy that choosing Johnson was the "worst mistake" he could possibly make. However,

TEACH OBJECTIVE 1

ALL LEVELS: Ask students how television coverage affects modern elections. *(Students might suggest that television coverage affects voters' perceptions and candidates' positions.)* To help students understand how television coverage affected the election of 1960, copy the following graphic organizer on the chalkboard, omitting the italicized answers. Have each student complete it. After students have finished their graphic organizers, conduct a brief discussion on television and politics. Do students think that television coverage affects politics positively or negatively? Does it help either the voters or the candidates? **Sheltered English**

TELEVISION COVERAGE AND THE ELECTION OF 1960

- **pre-debates**–*Nixon led in the polls*
- **debates**–*showed a vibrant Kennedy and a weary Nixon; radio listeners thought Nixon won and television viewers thought Kennedy won*
- **post debates**–*Kennedy won the election with a narrow victory*

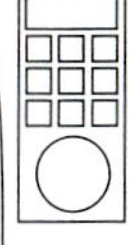

Kennedy had made a strategic choice. Johnson would help the Democrats win votes in Texas and other southern states where Kennedy was not particularly popular. Moreover, Johnson could work closely with Congress—where he was regarded as a master at getting legislation passed—to help the Kennedy administration achieve its goals.

During the campaign, Kennedy told Americans they would have to make sacrifices in the coming years. In a speech to South Dakota farmers, he explained his vision of the future.

> **"I promise you no sure solutions, no easy life. The years ahead for all of us will be as difficult as any in our history. There are new frontiers for America to conquer in education, in science, in national purpose—not frontiers on a map, but frontiers of the mind, the will, the spirit of man."**

Nixon argued that he had the maturity and experience to serve as president. He led in the polls until the first of four televised debates. Public reaction to the debates revealed the growing influence of television on American life. Nixon was weary from nonstop campaigning and was suffering from a painful injury to his knee. The tired candidate stood before the television cameras in a shirt that looked too large and with his makeup smeared by sweat. Kennedy, on the other hand, appeared fit, confident, and relaxed. Many Americans who listened to the first debate on the radio believed that Nixon had won. However, most of those who saw the television broadcast decided that Kennedy would make a better president than Nixon.

Kennedy aide Kenneth O'Donnell later recalled, "After the first debate, the 1960 campaign was an entirely different ball game." Kennedy later recognized the importance of television to his campaign. He confided, "We wouldn't have had a prayer without that gadget." Despite Kennedy's rapidly growing popularity, the election was very close. Kennedy defeated Nixon by fewer than 120,000 popular votes. His electoral victory was more clear cut—303 votes to Nixon's 219. At age 43, John F. Kennedy became the youngest person ever elected to the White House.

✔ **READING CHECK:** How did television coverage influence the 1960 presidential election?

The Election of 1960

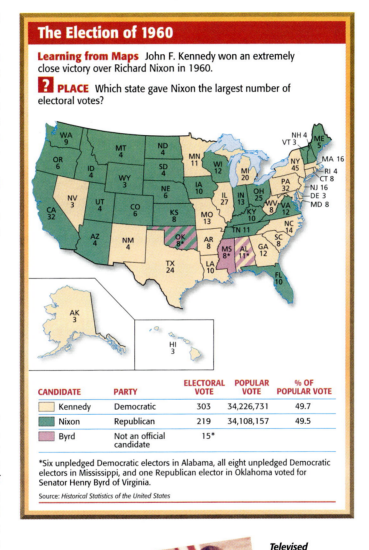

Learning from Maps John F. Kennedy won an extremely close victory over Richard Nixon in 1960.

? PLACE Which state gave Nixon the largest number of electoral votes?

CANDIDATE	PARTY	ELECTORAL VOTE	POPULAR VOTE	% OF POPULAR VOTE
Kennedy	Democratic	303	34,226,731	49.7
Nixon	Republican	219	34,108,157	49.5
Byrd	Not an official candidate	15*		

*Six unpledged Democratic electors in Alabama, all eight unpledged Democratic electors in Mississippi, and one Republican elector in Oklahoma voted for Senator Henry Byrd of Virginia.

Source: *Historical Statistics of the United States*

Televised debates with Richard Nixon helped John Kennedy win the 1960 presidential election.

DEMOCRATIC VALUES

The 1960 Presidential Election. A number of factors contributed to John F. Kennedy's narrow victory in the election of 1960. First, Kennedy spent the majority of his efforts campaigning in industrial states with large numbers of electoral votes, while Nixon exhausted himself by visiting all 50 states. Second, the Nixon campaign received relatively little help from President Dwight D. Eisenhower, who had mixed feelings about his vice president. Finally, Kennedy won the late support of some African American voters in October 1960, when he called Coretta Scott King to comfort her after her husband, Martin Luther King Jr., was imprisoned in Georgia for a traffic violation.

CRITICAL THINKING Which of the three factors stated above do you think most helped Kennedy win the election?

ANSWER: Answers will vary. Students should explain and justify their choices.

MAP ANSWER
California

TEACH OBJECTIVE 2

LEVELS 1 AND 2: Conduct a brief discussion on the ways in which President Kennedy hoped to stop the advance of communism. *(President Kennedy's foreign policy was based on a strategy called flexible response.)* Ask volunteers to offer examples of military and nonmilitary options within the flexible-response policy. *(For military options, students should mention the Bay of Pigs invasion. For nonmilitary options, students should mention the Peace Corps or economic aid programs.)* Then pair students and ask them to create an annotated time line of international events discussed in the section. Ask pairs to label the events as military or nonmilitary and to explain the role of the events in President Kennedy's anticommunism campaign. **Sheltered English, Cooperative Learning**

LEVEL 3: Tell students to imagine that they are President Kennedy. Have each student write a speech explaining how he or she plans to halt the spread of communism. *(See the Level 1 lesson for the correct methods.)* Students may choose to organize their speeches around the "general/specific" rule of speaking and writing—providing a general explanation and then specific examples. Ask volunteers to present their speeches to the class. Students may wish to include their speeches in their portfolios.

ECONOMIC DEVELOPMENT

Defense Spending. During the early 1960s, the U.S. defense budget rose approximately 13 percent, from $47.4 billion in 1961 to $53.6 billion in 1964. Much of the increase went to the construction of nuclear submarines and missiles. The monies also funded an increase in the number of U.S. military personnel—from 2.5 million in 1960 to 2.7 million in 1964.

CRITICAL THINKING How might increased defense spending have affected the national economy?

ANSWER: Students might suggest that the increase probably provided new job opportunities.

VISUAL RECORD ANSWER

Students might answer that the public saw them as powerful, admirable men.

INTERPRETING THE VISUAL RECORD

The Green Berets. Named for the hats they wore (above), the Green Berets had their own theme song. ***What do these images suggest about the popularity of the Green Berets?***

Kennedy's Foreign Policy

In foreign affairs, President Kennedy tended to follow the Cold War policies of his predecessors. He continued the nuclear arms buildup begun by President Eisenhower. However, unlike his predecessors, Kennedy did not want to rely solely on the threat of nuclear weapons to block communist expansion. He preferred to have a number of options in case of international crises. This strategy was called **flexible response**. Kennedy strengthened conventional military forces. He also established special units like the Green Berets to assist countries struggling to fight communism. He took special pride in this special fighting unit and kept one of the berets they wore on his desk in the Oval Office.

Foreign aid. Kennedy also supported nonmilitary options to stop communist expansion. He realized that helping developing countries could strengthen their dependence on the United States and block Soviet influence. To this end, Kennedy introduced a number of aid programs designed to help countries in Africa, Asia, and Latin America. First among these programs was the **Peace Corps**, which sent American volunteers to work for two years in developing countries.

Africa was an area of concern for the Kennedy administration. In 1960, a total of 17 African countries gained their independence from colonial powers. In an effort to support African nationalism, Kennedy called for increased economic aid to the continent. This aid included sending Peace Corps volunteers and food. In addition, the United States nearly doubled the amount of loans offered to African countries during the Kennedy years.

Kennedy also introduced a program to expand economic aid to Latin America. This **Alliance for Progress** offered billions of dollars in aid to participating countries. In exchange for financial assistance, the countries were expected to begin democratic reforms and encourage capitalism. The Alliance proved a disappointment. The rapidly growing population of Latin American countries required far more money than the United States was willing to provide. Moreover, much of the money given to participating countries soon fell into the hands of corrupt politicians. Few Latin American leaders enacted significant reforms. Victor Alba, a Latin American writer, blamed the program's failure on its inability to motivate the poor majority in Latin American countries.

> **"We know who killed the Alliance: the oligarchic governments [governments ruled by a few] of Latin America. . . . We know who supplied the poison: the bureaucrats and technicians. And we know who would have defended it if anyone had bothered to let them know that it existed and needed defenders: the people."**

✔ **READING CHECK:** How did President John F. Kennedy plan to stop the spread of communism?

HOLT RESEARCHER — *Read More About It*

Free Find: Peace Corps

After reading about the Peace Corps on the **Holt Researcher** CD–ROM, create a proposal for a similar program to help people living in the United States.

The Peace Corps offered help to developing nations.

TEACH OBJECTIVE 3

LEVEL 1: Write the following question on the chalkboard: *Why did the Bay of Pigs invasion fail?* Pair students and have each pair list at least three answers to the question. *(Students should note the existence of strong Cuban counterattacks, the absence of a popular revolt, the lack of air strikes, and the lack of naval and air support.)* Ask each pair to use its list to write a paragraph in response to the question. Then conduct a classroom discussion on the various ways President Kennedy might have handled the Cuban situation and the Bay of Pigs invasion.
Sheltered English, Cooperative Learning

LEVEL 2: Tell students to imagine that they are members of the CIA who trained the Bay of Pigs invasion force. Have each student write a letter to a friend stationed in Berlin explaining the causes behind the failed mission and expressing his or her feelings about that failure. *(See the Level 1 lesson for the correct causes.)* Have volunteers read their letters to the class. Students may wish to include their letters in their portfolios.

NOTE: For an additional teaching idea, see the Chapter 20 interpreting cartoons lesson in the **Creative Teaching Strategies** handbook.

Changing Ways The Peace Corps

Understanding Change The Peace Corps has continued to aid countries throughout the world. *How has the number of countries served and number of Peace Corps volunteers changed over the years? How has the type of work performed by Peace Corps workers changed?*

	Then	Now
Number of Volunteers	7,000	6,700
Number of Countries Being Served	44	80

Then

Now

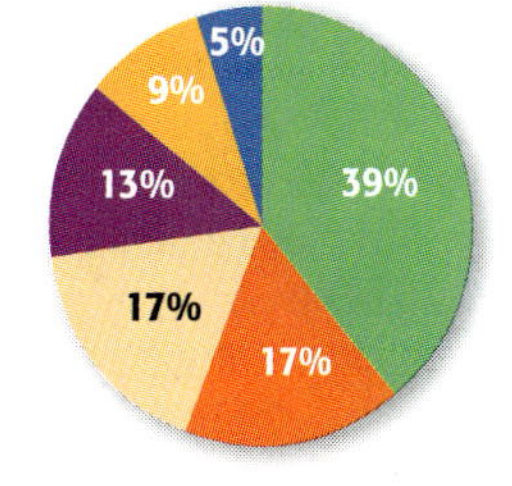

Areas of Service

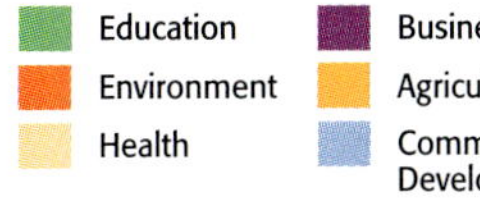

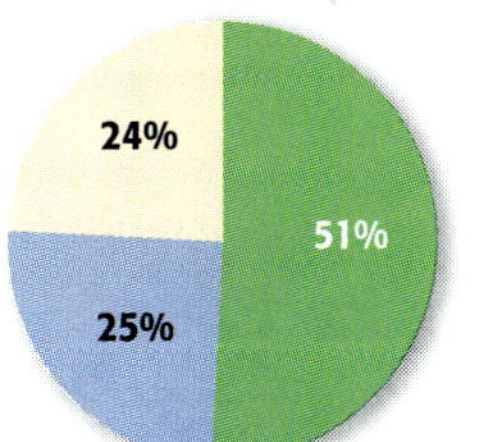

Source: The Peace Corps. Data reflect 1963 and 1999.

The Bay of Pigs. Latin America was a special target for aid from the United States because the Soviet Union had recently gained a foothold in the region. In 1959 Fidel Castro led an uprising that succeeded in overthrowing the Cuban dictator, Fulgencio Batista. Castro quickly established a communist-style dictatorship with ties to the Soviet Union.

Castro boasted that his success was "the reason that President Kennedy can't sleep at night." Indeed, Kennedy was deeply troubled by the fact that a communist government flourished only 90 miles from the United States. He soon learned that during President Eisenhower's administration the Central Intelligence Agency (CIA) had developed a plan for overthrowing Castro. The CIA was training and financing a group of anti-Castro Cuban refugees who were to invade Cuba. After taking office, Kennedy gave his approval for the plan to proceed.

The invasion resulted in disaster. Cuban forces quickly pinned down the nearly 1,500 rebels who came ashore at Cuba's Bay of Pigs on April 17, 1961. The U.S. naval and air support that the rebels expected never materialized. At the last minute, Kennedy decided not to send in air strikes. Equally damaging, the invasion failed to spark a popular uprising among the Cuban people. It took Cuban military forces less than 72 hours to crush the invasion and take prisoner some 1,200 surviving rebels.

One American journalist complained that the Bay of Pigs had made the United States look "like fools to our friends, rascals to our enemies, and incompetents to the rest." The invasion also brought Cuban leaders closer to the Soviets. Kennedy took full responsibility for the incident. After the Bay of Pigs, he resolved to take more control over foreign affairs. He told a close friend, "From now on it's John Kennedy that makes the decisions as to whether or not we're going to do these things."

✔ **READING CHECK:** Why did the Bay of Pigs invasion of Cuba fail?

INTERPRETING THE VISUAL RECORD

The Bay of Pigs. The Bay of Pigs invasion was the cover story of this issue of *Life* magazine. ***How do you think the magazine portrayed the event?***

GEOGRAPHIC DIVERSITY

The Bay of Pigs. The Bay of Pigs was an extremely poor site for an invasion. Sharp coral reefs sank a number of landing craft before they reached the shore. The bay's swampy terrain made it difficult for invading soldiers to find cover from enemy fire. Furthermore, floodlights from a nearby apartment complex illuminated the beach where the rebels landed, ruining their expected nighttime advantage.

ACTIVITY: Tell students to imagine that they are soldiers who participated in the Bay of Pigs invasion. Have each student write a short military report explaining the geographic factors that contributed to the failure of the mission. Students may wish to include their military reports in their portfolios.

CHANGING WAYS ANSWERS

almost doubled; decreased; now includes environmental and business work.

VISUAL RECORD ANSWER

Students might answer that given the cover's portrayal of the soldiers, the magazine probably portrayed the event in a positive light.

LEVEL 3: Tell students to imagine that they are American newspaper reporters in the days following the failed Bay of Pigs invasion. Have each student write an article explaining the failure of the invasion. *(See the Level 1 lesson for the correct causes.)* Then tell students to imagine that they are Americans living in Florida who have just read that article. Have each student write a letter to the editor expressing his or her feelings about the failed invasion. Ask volunteers to read their articles and letters to the class.

▶**ASSIGNMENT** *Have each student create an outline of the subsection entitled The Bay of Pigs.*

SPOTLIGHT on Fidel Castro and Nikita Khrushchev

Tell students that Fidel Castro and Nikita Khrushchev embodied communism to many Americans during the 1960s. Have each student select either Castro or Khrushchev and conduct research on his or her chosen leader. Students should also conduct research on Cuba or the Soviet Union as appropriate. Then tell students to write biographies of their selected figures, emphasizing political beliefs and career. Have volunteers share excerpts from their biographies with the class.

Block Scheduling

HISTORY MAKERS SPEAK

John F. Kennedy in *President Kennedy: Profile of Power*

In June 1961 President Kennedy traveled to West Berlin to see the newly erected Berlin Wall. Shortly after his arrival he delivered a rousing indictment of communism to a crowd of West German citizens. "Freedom has many difficulties and democracy is not perfect, but we have never had to put a wall up to keep our people in. . . . All free men, wherever they may live, are citizens of Berlin, and therefore, as a free man, I take pride in the words 'Ich bin ein Berliner [I am a Berliner].' "

CRITICAL THINKING Some of President Kennedy's advisers disapproved of his speech. Why might they have done so?

ANSWER: Students might suggest that these advisors felt that Kennedy's blunt speech could lead to conflict with the Soviet Union.

Multimedia Resources

American History Simulations CD–ROM: Race to the Moon

SCIENCE & TECHNOLOGY ANSWERS

1. Yuri Gagarin
2. the fuel tanks

Science & Technology

The Space Program

As the United States and the Soviet Union developed missiles to carry nuclear weapons, both nations also sought to use missile technology to begin the exploration of outer space. In 1958, a year after the Soviets successfully launched *Sputnik*, the United States initiated Project Mercury, a program to send a human being into space. However, the United States lost the race to be the first nation to send a human into orbit. On April 12, 1961, Soviet cosmonaut Yuri Gagarin became the first human to circle Earth.

President Kennedy publicly congratulated the Soviets on their achievement. Privately, however, he asked his advisers, "Is there any place where we can catch them [the Soviets]? What can we do? Are we working twenty-four hours a day? Can we go around the moon before them?" Less than a month later, the United States enjoyed its first success when Alan Shepherd completed a suborbital flight. In February 1962 John Glenn left Earth in his Mercury spacecraft *Friendship 7*, lifted into space by an Atlas intercontinental ballistic missile. Glenn spent five hours in space and orbited Earth three times. This event restored American confidence in the space program and set the stage for the race to the Moon. The Apollo program achieved that goal in 1969 using space capsules like the one shown above.

Understanding Science and History

1. Who was the first person to orbit Earth?
2. What takes up the most room in the spacecraft shown?

President Kennedy and Soviet leader Nikita Khrushchev share a light moment during their conference in Vienna.

The Berlin Crisis

The Bay of Pigs convinced Soviet leader Nikita Khrushchev that President Kennedy was weak and could be intimidated. At a summit meeting in June 1961, Khrushchev issued an ultimatum: the West must recognize the sovereignty of communist East Germany and remove all troops from West Berlin. Khrushchev's demands shocked Kennedy. He had no desire to risk war over Berlin, but worried that if he gave in to the Soviets he would lose the confidence of the American people.

In mid-August the East Germans erected a barbed-wire barrier that cut off traffic between East and West Berlin. Kennedy responded by sending additional U.S. troops to the city. For several days U.S. and Soviet soldiers eyed each other nervously across the barbed wire. Tensions gradually eased when it became clear that Khrushchev's real goal had been achieved. The barrier had halted the mass departure of East Germans to the West through Berlin. In time, the East Germans replaced the barbed wire with a wall of gray concrete and watchtowers. The **Berlin Wall** became the most widely recognized symbol of the Cold War.

TEACH OBJECTIVE 4

LEVEL 1: Pair students and have each pair write a series of newspaper headlines on the Cuban missile crisis. Students should explain how the Soviet Union and the United States reached the brink of war, present actual events in the crisis, and discuss Americans' reactions to the crisis. *(Students should note that the two nations nearly went to war when the Soviet Union provided offensive missiles to Cuba and the United States instituted a blockade to prevent those missiles from reaching the island.)* Ask each pair to write topic sentences or introductory sentences for each of its headlines. Have volunteers read their headlines to the class.
Sheltered English, Cooperative Learning

LEVELS 2 AND 3: Have students reread the subsection entitled The Missiles of October. Then ask each student to create a political cartoon commenting on the Cuban missile crisis. Students' cartoons should depict how the United States and the Soviet Union reached the brink of war. *(See the Level 1 lesson for the correct reasons.)* Have students write captions for their cartoons. Display students' cartoons and captions around the classroom.

▶**ASSIGNMENT** *Have each student create a flowchart tracing the relationship between the Bay of Pigs invasion, the building of the Berlin Wall, and the Cuban missile crisis.*

The Missiles of October

Soviet leader Khrushchev's continued testing of the U.S. commitment to containing communism led to the Cold War's greatest crisis. To prevent an invasion, Cuban leader Fidel Castro asked the Soviet Union to provide him with defensive weapons. The Soviets complied and also offered offensive weapons—nuclear missiles that could reach the cities of the eastern United States.

CIA officials monitored the Soviet arms buildup in Cuba throughout the summer of 1962. Photographs taken by a U.S. U-2 spy plane on October 14 revealed the existence of two ballistic-missile launching pads near the Cuban town of San Cristóbal. Additional U-2 flights over the island located more missiles capable of striking targets in the United States within minutes of launching.

On October 22 Kennedy appeared on national television to announce that any armed ships bound for Cuba would be turned back. He also demanded that the Soviets remove the missiles.

The Cuban Missile Crisis, 1962

Learning from Maps The Cuban missile crisis sent shock waves throughout the world. Many people feared the crisis would lead to a nuclear war.

PLACE What U.S. military base was located in Cuba?

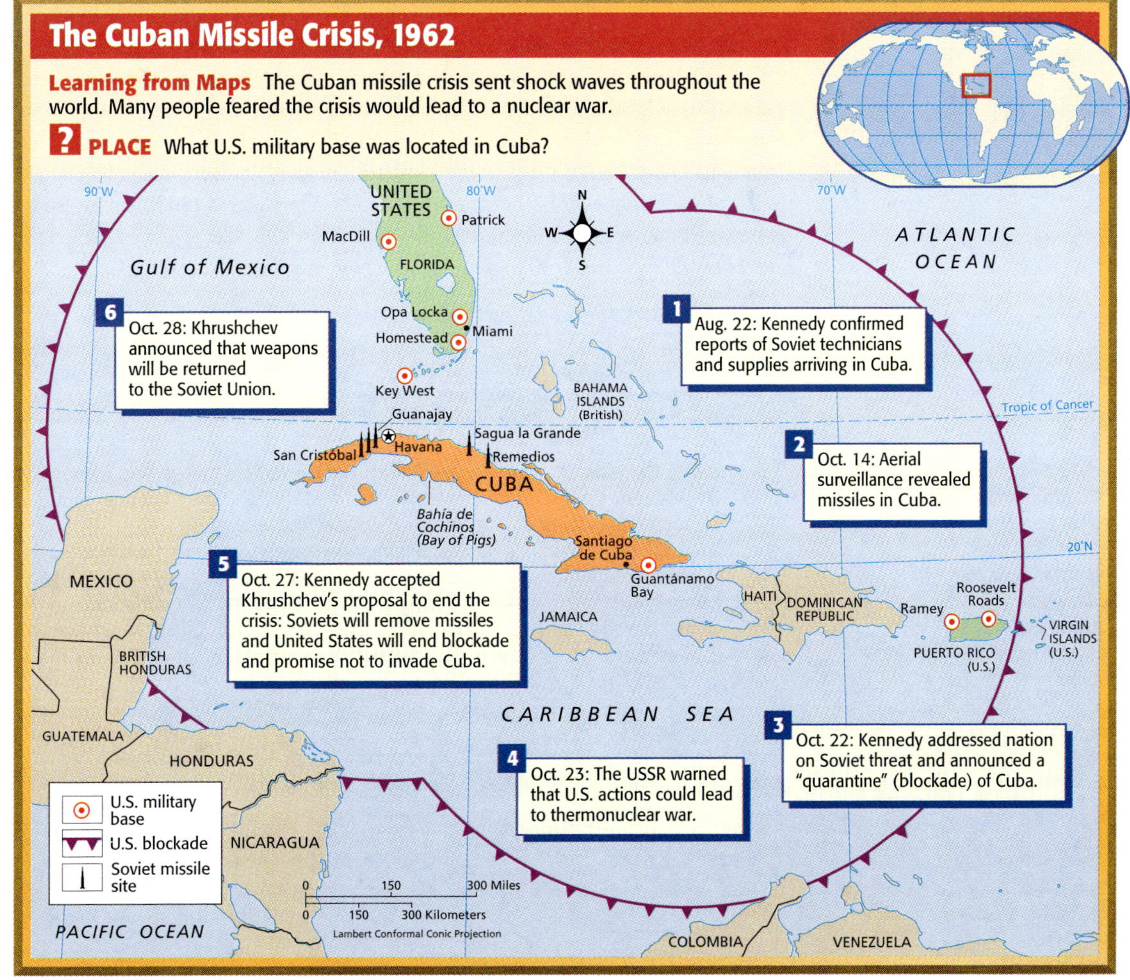

PEOPLE IN HISTORY

Fidel Castro. By the time he displaced Cuban dictator Fulgencio Batista, Fidel Castro had a considerable history as a revolutionary. The son of a prosperous sugarcane farmer, Castro entered law school in 1945 at the University of Havana, where he became deeply involved in politics. After graduating, Castro announced his candidacy for a seat in Cuba's House of Representatives. Batista's cancellation of elections convinced Castro that meaningful change in Cuba required violent rebellion. In late 1953 Castro led a group of like-minded youths in an attack on a government military barracks. Officials arrested him and sentenced him to 15 years in prison. He was released after serving only 11 months, however, and promptly organized another rebel group. This group soon began to wage guerrilla warfare against Batista's government. After years of bloody fighting, the dictator conceded defeat and fled the country.

ACTIVITY: Have students bring to class recent articles about Cuba. Have volunteers share their articles with the class.

MAP ANSWER
Guantánamo Bay

REVIEW

Have students complete the **Section 1 Review** on p. 602.

ASSESS

Have students complete **Daily Quiz 20.1**. As **Alternative Assessment**, you may want to use the Cuban missile crisis headline or the Cuban missile crisis political cartoon in this section's lessons.

RETEACH

Have students complete **Main Idea Activity for Reteaching and Sheltered English 20.1**. Then organize students into groups of four. Assign one section objective to each group member. Direct students to write paragraphs summarizing their assigned objectives. Have students share their paragraphs with the rest of their group. **Sheltered English, Cooperative Learning**

EXTEND

Ask students to conduct research on President Kennedy's Alliance for Progress and to select a country that received aid under the program. Students should also conduct research on the dissemination of aid in the selected country. Ask each student to create a poster presenting information on the Alliance for Progress in the selected country and assessing the success of the program. Conduct a discussion on why the program was more effective in some countries than in others.
Block Scheduling

SECTION 1 REVIEW ANSWERS

Define and Identify
For significance, see the following pages:

- John F. Kennedy, p. 596
- flexible response, p. 598
- Peace Corps, p. 598
- Alliance for Progress, p. 598
- Fidel Castro, p. 599
- Berlin Wall, p. 600
- Cuban missile crisis, p. 602
- Limited Nuclear Test Ban Treaty, p. 602
- hot line, p. 602

Locate
For locations, see the map on p. 601. For importance, see the following pages:

- Bay of Pigs, p. 599
- San Cristóbal, p. 601

1. weapons—nuclear weapons buildup; military forces—strengthened conventional forces, established special military units, such as Green Berets; nonmilitary options—Peace Corps, Alliance for Progress, economic aid

2. Some students might suggest that a president's appearance affects success in office, and that television coverage in the 1960s allowed voters to select the most vital, attractive president.

3. prompted him to continue a nuclear weapons buildup, but also to seek other options

4. Answers will vary; support—the blockade ended the threat of nuclear weapons in Cuba; oppose—the blockade risked the threat of nuclear war

5. led Khrushchev to see Kennedy as weak; led Kennedy to pursue aggressive action against communism in Cuba and Berlin

THROUGH OTHERS' EYES

Soviet View of the Cuban Missile Crisis

During the Cuban missile crisis, the world held its breath for several days as it teetered on the brink of nuclear war. In the end, the Soviets agreed to remove the missiles. Soviet premier Nikita Khrushchev related his memory of the crisis.

> **"It had been, to say the least, an interesting and challenging situation. The two most powerful nations of the world had squared off against each other, each with its finger on the button. You'd have thought that war was inevitable. But both sides showed that if the desire to avoid war is strong enough, even the most pressing dispute can be solved by compromise. . . . I'll always remember the late President Kennedy with deep respect because, in the final analysis, he showed himself to be sober-minded and determined to avoid war."**

Over the next two days, nuclear war loomed over the horizon. In a frenzy of activity, Soviet military advisers armed the missiles in Cuba. U.S. B-52 bombers armed with nuclear weapons prepared for battle. Meanwhile, armed Soviet ships sailed toward the blockade line.

Suddenly, on October 24, Kennedy was informed that most of the Soviet ships had "stopped dead in the water" before reaching the blockade line. The ships then turned and sailed home. "We're eyeball to eyeball," said Secretary of State Dean Rusk, "and I think the other fellow just blinked." On October 28 Khrushchev agreed to dismantle the missile bases in response to Kennedy's promise not to invade Cuba. Kennedy also secretly agreed to remove U.S. missiles from some foreign sites.

The **Cuban missile crisis** marked a historic turning point in U.S.-Soviet relations. Sobered by their brush with nuclear war, Kennedy and Khrushchev sought to ease tensions between their countries. In 1963 the United States, the Soviet Union, and Great Britain signed the **Limited Nuclear Test Ban Treaty** to end the testing of nuclear bombs in the atmosphere and underwater. A **hot line** was also set up between the United States and the Soviet Union. This teletype line enabled the leaders of the two countries to communicate directly during a crisis.

READING CHECK: How did the Cuban missile crisis almost lead to war?

SECTION 1 REVIEW

Define and explain the significance of the following terms:
flexible response
Peace Corps
Alliance for Progress
Berlin Wall
Cuban missile crisis
Limited Nuclear Test Ban Treaty
hot line

Identify and explain the significance of the following individuals:
John F. Kennedy
Fidel Castro

Locate and explain the importance of the following places:
Bay of Pigs
San Cristóbal

1. **Using Graphic Organizers** Copy the following web. Use it to explain the ways in which President Kennedy attempted to stop the advance of communism.

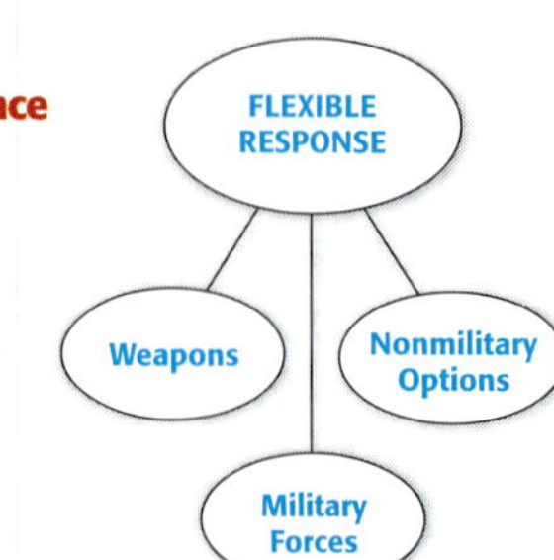

2. **Analyzing** Did television coverage help voters make an informed choice in the 1960 presidential election? Explain your answer.
3. **Assessing Consequences** How did concern over nuclear weapons influence Kennedy's foreign policy?
4. **Taking a Stand** Would you have supported Kennedy's naval blockade of Cuba in 1962? Explain your answer.

Critical Thinking

5. How did the Bay of Pigs incident influence Kennedy's handling of Cold War events?
Consider:
- the outcome of the Bay of Pigs invasion
- Soviet leader Khrushchev's perception of Kennedy's leadership
- Kennedy's foreign-policy decisions after the Bay of Pigs invasion

SECTION 2

After completing Section 2, students should be able to:

OBJECTIVE 1 *Discuss how President Kennedy's image conflicted with reality.*

OBJECTIVE 2 *Identify why Kennedy had difficulty getting legislation passed.*

OBJECTIVE 3 *Explain how the Kennedy administration tried to help poor Americans.*

OBJECTIVE 4 *Describe how Americans responded to the death of the president.*

LET'S GET STARTED!

Create a three-column chart on the chalkboard with the following headings: *What You Definitely Know About President Kennedy and His Administration; What You Probably Know About President Kennedy and His Administration; What You Want to Know About President Kennedy and His Administration.* As students enter the classroom, tell them to copy and complete the chart. Have volunteers share their entries with the class. Tell students that in Section 2 they will learn more about Kennedy myths and realities.

The Kennedy White House

OBJECTIVES

Read to understand:

1. how President Kennedy's image conflicted with reality
2. why Kennedy had difficulty getting legislation passed
3. how the Kennedy administration tried to help poor Americans
4. how Americans responded to the death of the president

KEY TERMS

New Frontier
Area Redevelopment Act
Warren Commission

KEY PEOPLE

Jacqueline Kennedy
Donna Shalala
Robert Kennedy
Michael Harrington
Lee Harvey Oswald

EYEWITNESSES TO History

"[He] had a deep orange-brown suntan of a ski instructor, and when he smiled at the crowd his teeth were amazingly white and clearly visible at a distance of fifty yards."

—Norman Mailer

President Kennedy sails off the coast of Maine.

Author Norman Mailer described presidential candidate John F. Kennedy in 1960. Mailer attended the Democratic National Convention and offered his observations of Kennedy in an article published later that year. Mailer compared Kennedy's arrival at the convention to "the scene where the hero, the matinee movie idol, comes to the palace to claim the princess." Explaining Kennedy's enormous appeal, Mailer argued, "It was a hero America needed . . . because only a hero can capture the secret imagination of a people, and so be good for the vitality of his nation."

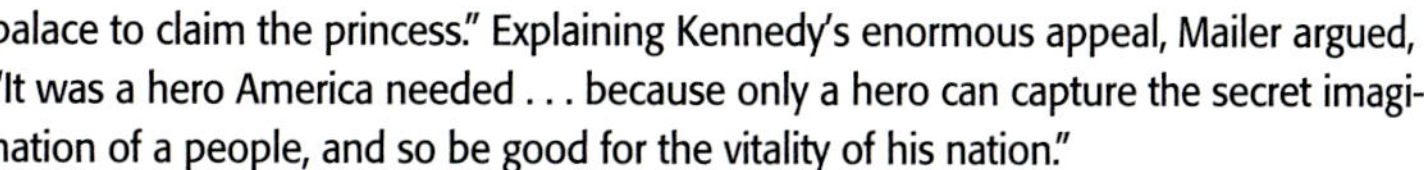

The Kennedy Charisma

Youthful John F. Kennedy offered a marked contrast to the elderly outgoing president, Dwight D. Eisenhower. Kennedy captured the hearts of many Americans in a way that few politicians have. He became so popular that a few months after taking office he had to ask Americans to stop sending congratulatory telegrams to the White House.

Kennedy's appeal stemmed from his cool intellectual personality, athletic appearance, and handsome features. Americans could not doubt that their president had a keen mind. A graduate of Harvard University, he had published two books. His best-selling *Profiles in Courage* won a Pulitzer Prize for biography. Kennedy presented an image of youth and vitality throughout his career in politics. He was frequently photographed engaged in sporting activities such as football, sailing, and swimming.

President Kennedy, his wife, Jacqueline, and their children, John Jr. and Caroline, play with their dogs.

The first family. The president's attractive young wife, Jacqueline "Jackie" Kennedy, contributed to the glamour and mystique that surrounded the Kennedy White House. The first lady quickly rose to the top of polls of women whom Americans most admired. Her popularity spread beyond U.S. borders. When the Kennedys met with Soviet leader Nikita Khrushchev, he said, "I'd like to shake her hand first." The first lady received so much attention on a trip to France that the president called himself "the man who accompanied Jacqueline Kennedy to Paris, and I have enjoyed it."

Jacqueline Kennedy brought an appreciation for the fine arts to the Kennedy administration. She invited prominent artists and

SECTION 2 RESOURCES

PRINT
- Guided Reading Strategy 20.2
- Biography Reading 20: Robert F. Kennedy
- Section 2 Review, p. 609
- Daily Quiz 20.2

MULTIMEDIA
- One-Stop Planner, Lesson 20.2
- Holt Researcher: American History CD–ROM
- HRW Web site

SHELTERED ENGLISH
- Main Idea Activity for Reteaching and Sheltered English 20.2

✓ READING TO UNDERSTAND

To help students master the section objectives, have them answer the **READING CHECKS** and complete **Guided Reading Strategy 20.2** as they read the section.

TEACH OBJECTIVE 1

ALL LEVELS: Tell students that the Kennedy mystique is still a powerful force today, almost 40 years after "Camelot." Call students' attention to the death of John F. Kennedy Jr. and the widespread public mourning that followed the event. Ask students why the public responded so strongly to his death and why national newsmagazines afforded him the title of "America's Prince." *(Some students might suggest that the "Kennedy myth" has led many Americans to view the family as elegant, attractive, and youthful—almost royal.)* To help students understand how President Kennedy's image conflicted with reality, copy the following graphic organizer on the chalkboard, omitting the italicized answers. Have each student complete it. **Sheltered English**

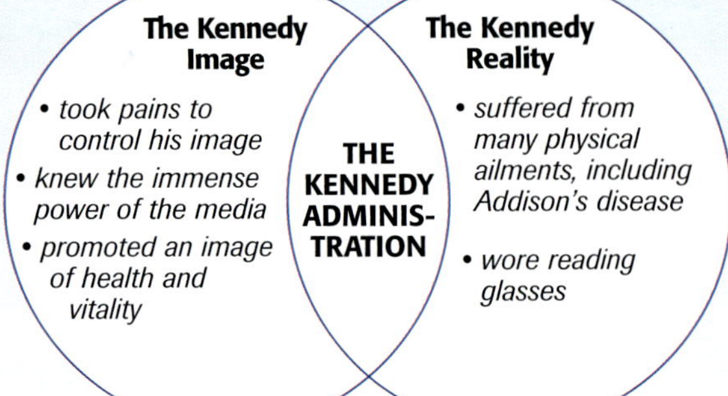
The Kennedy Image
• took pains to control his image
• knew the immense power of the media
• promoted an image of health and vitality
THE KENNEDY ADMINIS-TRATION
The Kennedy Reality
• suffered from many physical ailments, including Addison's disease
• wore reading glasses

PEOPLE IN HISTORY

Jacqueline Kennedy. Jacqueline Kennedy's status as the country's "unofficial Minister of Culture" was partially a result of her privileged upbringing. The daughter of a wealthy stockbroker, she attended exclusive private schools as a child and studied at the Sorbonne in Paris before receiving a degree from George Washington University in Washington, D.C. In 1951 she won a *Vogue* magazine talent contest. The publication offered her a job, but she chose instead to travel in Europe and then work as a society photographer in Washington, D.C.. A short time later she met John F. Kennedy, who was serving as a member of the U.S. House of Representatives. They were married in 1953.

ACTIVITY: Have students compare and contrast Jacqueline Kennedy's role as first lady to the role of another first lady.

THAT'S INTERESTING!

Just before the first televised debate, Richard M. Nixon applied a product called Lazy Shave to hide his five o'clock shadow. The Lazy Shave dulled his complexion, making Nixon look washed-out compared to the vibrant appearance of John F. Kennedy.

PRESIDENTIAL *Lives*

1917–1963

In Office 1961–1963

John F. Kennedy

John F. Kennedy's heroism in World War II enhanced the mystique that surrounded him when he took office. During the war, he served as the commander of a U.S. Navy patrol torpedo boat in the Pacific theater. In the early morning hours of August 2, 1943, Kennedy's boat, the *PT-109,* was rammed by a Japanese destroyer. Two crewmen were killed. The next morning, as the boat slowly sank, Kennedy ordered his men to use a plank as a float and head for a small island about three miles away. Kennedy swam the entire distance, towing a wounded man by clenching the man's life jacket strap in his teeth. The men made it to the island and they were rescued several days later.

Kennedy received some criticism for his role in the affair. Questions were raised as to why the Japanese destroyer had been able to ram the PT boat, a small, fast ship. Nevertheless, he received a medal for his heroic efforts to save his men. A national magazine printed the story of his actions, and the *PT-109* was mentioned frequently during Kennedy's political campaigns. Members of his crew were present during Kennedy's inauguration, and a model of the *PT-109* was displayed in the inaugural parade.

JOHN F. KENNEDY
13c UNITED STATES

musicians to social events. One newspaper referred to her as the "unofficial Minister of Culture." She also organized a major restoration of the White House, declaring, "I want to make the White House the first house in the land." Mrs. Kennedy later hosted a nationally televised tour of the White House.

Americans were also fascinated by the Kennedy children. Caroline, born in 1957, and John Jr., born a few weeks after his father's election to office, were the first young children to live in the White House since Theodore Roosevelt's presidency. One Kennedy aide later recalled that "Caroline Kennedy quickly became a national figure." The public enjoyed seeing photographs of her and her brother playing in the White House. Complaining about the president's popularity, one senator who opposed Kennedy's programs claimed, "The difference is Caroline, and there's nothing we can do about it."

Effects on youth. Although many Americans regarded the Kennedy family as attractive and interesting, young people found Kennedy particularly inspiring. During the presidential campaign, Kennedy's public appearances drew large numbers of young Americans. Many of them responded to Kennedy's call for service and sacrifice. Some of these Americans joined the Peace Corps. One volunteer recalled, "I'd never done anything political, patriotic, or unselfish because nobody ever asked me to. Kennedy asked."

BIOGRAPHY *Donna Shalala*

One of the many Americans motivated to action by Kennedy's vision was Donna Shalala. During the 1990s Shalala served as secretary of health and human services in the administration of President Bill Clinton. In 1961, as a young college graduate, Shalala had responded to Kennedy's call and joined the Peace Corps. She later recalled, "Kennedy was the first president we had voted for. He represented a break with the past." Shalala spent two years in a tiny village called Molasani in Iran, living in a mud hut and teaching English.

Shalala remembered that "everybody laughed" at Kennedy's idea of American volunteers fanning out across the globe, "but it worked." She claimed that her years of Peace Corps service "made me a world citizen. It just changed me at such a young age, giving me confidence in my ability to be dropped down anywhere on earth and be comfortable." Her experience also gave her confidence in young people. She declared, "Having faith in young Americans may be a simple idea, but it works."

HOLT RESEARCHER

Read More About It

Free Find:
Donna Shalala

After reading about Donna Shalala on the **Holt Researcher** CD–ROM, write a resumé for her to use in applying for a cabinet position in a future administration.

TEACH OBJECTIVE 2

LEVEL 1: Pair students and have each pair create a graphic organizer depicting why Kennedy had difficulty getting legislation passed. *(Students should show that a coalition of southern Democrats and conservative Republicans in Congress opposed Kennedy's agenda.)* Then ask students to consider the impact of those difficulties on Kennedy's presidency. Did those difficulties reflect badly on Kennedy's abilities? Did those difficulties adversely affect the nation? How might they have been prevented?
Sheltered English, Cooperative Learning

LEVELS 2 AND 3: Organize students into two large groups. Tell one group to imagine that it represents President Kennedy or his top aides, and the other group to imagine that it represents southern Democrats or conservative Republicans. Have each student write three or four short journal entries in his or her assigned role describing the difficulties President Kennedy had getting legislation passed. *(See the Level 1 lesson for the correct issues.)* Have volunteers from both groups read their journal entries to the class. Then conduct a discussion on how students' different—and opposing—roles affected their reactions, as represented in the journal entries, to the political issues at hand.
Cooperative Learning

Reality. The images of the first family that Americans so admired masked a more complex reality. Well aware of the power of the media, Kennedy took great pains to control his public appearance. He avoided being photographed while wearing his reading glasses, and later during his administration had television lights adjusted to hide a double chin.

Despite his interest in athletic pursuits, President Kennedy was not a healthy man. He struggled with illness throughout his life. His brother Robert once recalled that "at least one half of the days that he spent on this earth were days of intense physical pain." Kennedy suffered from a sometimes fatal condition called Addison's disease. His back had troubled him since childhood, and Kennedy had nearly died in 1954 during an operation on his spine.

✔ **READING CHECK:** How did President Kennedy's image conflict with reality?

★ HISTORICAL DOCUMENTS ★

PRESIDENT JOHN F. KENNEDY

Inaugural Address

John F. Kennedy delivered his inaugural address on January 20, 1961. It was a sunny but bitterly cold day in the nation's capital. The address contained the themes of challenge and sacrifice that had filled his speeches during the presidential campaign. His words that day inspired many Americans. This remains one of the most famous speeches in U.S. history.

In the long history of the world, only a few generations have been granted the role of defending freedom in its hour of maximum danger. I do not shrink from this responsibility—I welcome it. I do not believe that any of us would exchange places with any other people or any other generation. The energy, the faith, the devotion which we bring to this endeavor will light our country and all who serve it—and the glow from that fire can truly light the world.

And so my fellow Americans: ask not what your country can do for you—ask what you can do for your country.

My fellow citizens of the world: ask not what America will do for you, but what together we can do for the freedom of man.

Kennedy's Advisers

President Kennedy hoped to use the government to offer solutions to national and global problems. To advance his programs, Kennedy surrounded himself with others who shared his vision. The average age of his cabinet members was 47, a decade younger than that of President Eisenhower's cabinet. Special Counsel Theodore Sorensen, the speechwriter who composed most of Kennedy's inaugural address, was just 32 years old at the time.

The president wanted only "the brightest and best," and his advisers were well educated. "There's nothing like brains. You can't beat brains," Kennedy claimed. Secretary of Defense Robert McNamara was a graduate of the Harvard Business School. Secretary of State Dean Rusk was a former Rhodes Scholar, and McGeorge Bundy, special assistant for national security affairs, had been a dean at Harvard. However, few of Kennedy's advisers had political experience, and not everyone was impressed by their credentials. Speaker of the House Sam Rayburn told Lyndon Johnson, "You may be right and they may be every bit as intelligent as you say, but I'd feel a whole lot better about them if just one of them had run for sheriff once."

For the position of attorney general, Kennedy selected his younger brother Robert "Bobby" Kennedy. Although Robert Kennedy had graduated from law school, he had never practiced law. Some members of Congress and presidential advisers opposed the president's decision to appoint his brother to high office. Even Robert expressed doubts. Nonetheless, the president told his brother, "I need you. . . . I need someone I know to talk to in this government." Robert proved to be the

President Kennedy and his brother Robert work together in the Oval Office.

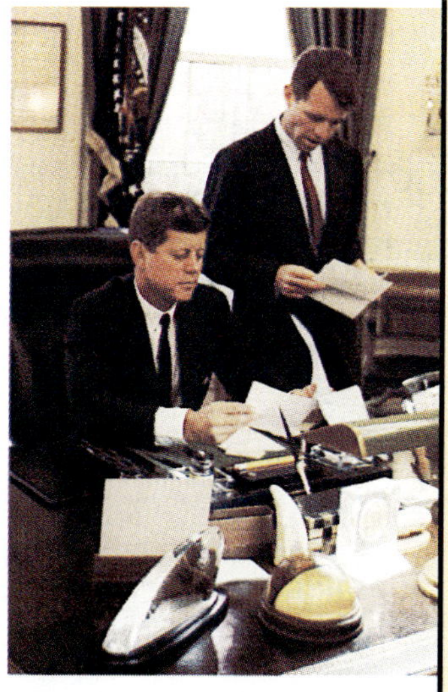

HISTORY MAKERS SPEAK

Jeff Greenfield in *The Century*

President Kennedy and His Cabinet. Jeff Greenfield, a college student during Kennedy's campaign, described the appeal of the candidate and his later cabinet. "So along comes the 1960 campaign, and John Kennedy, the youngest man ever elected. And the idea that this guy, who looked like your cool older brother, might be president of the United States was a really exciting proposition. . . . The idea of a White House run and staffed by younger people suggested that government and politics was not simply the province of people impossibly older than we were. There was the feeling that, well, if they're running the political system, surely we can be somehow involved in it. It gave us a sense that we were entitled to be part of the political process, even as naysayers and protesters. Because, after all, look who was running the country."

CRITICAL THINKING Do you agree with Greenfield's assumption that voters tend to identify more with candidates who share their same chronological age? Explain your answer.

ANSWER: Answers will vary. Some students will suggest that a similar chronological age creates a bond between voters and a candidate.

TEACH OBJECTIVE 3

LEVEL 1: Organize students into triads and have each triad create a poster illustrating how the Kennedy administration tried to help poor Americans. *(Students should indicate that President Kennedy supported the Area Redevelopment Act and other antipoverty programs.)* Ask triads to write paragraphs explaining the rationale of those antipoverty programs. Have volunteers read their paragraphs to the class. Then conduct a brief discussion on how Kennedy might have tried to eradicate poverty in the United States if he had survived the assassination attempt.
Sheltered English, Cooperative Learning

LEVELS 2 AND 3: Ask students to name modern-day government programs designed to alleviate poverty. *(Students might mention foodstamps, Social Security, and so on.)* Tell students to identify President Kennedy's attempts to help poor Americans. *(See the Level 1 lesson for the correct attempts.)* Tell students to imagine that it is 1961 and that Congress is considering the Area Redevelopment Act. Have each student write a letter about the act to his or her congressperson. Students' letters should explain the rationale of the act as well as discuss poverty in general. Have volunteers read their letters to the class. Students may wish to include their letters in their portfolios.

ECONOMIC DEVELOPMENT

Stock Market Decline. On May 28, 1962, the Dow Jones average fell 35 points—the largest drop in a single day since October 1929. It continued to fall. By late June the value of all stocks on the New York Stock Exchange was 27 percent less than it had been in December 1961.

CRITICAL THINKING How might the drop in the stock market have affected congressmembers' feelings toward President Kennedy?

ANSWER: Students might mention that the drop in the stock market might have made Congress wary of Kennedy's economic policies.

THAT'S INTERESTING!

Author David Halberstam called President Kennedy's cabinet "the best and the brightest"—now a well-known name for the group.

internetconnect

TOPIC: John F. Kennedy
GO TO: go.hrw.com
KEYWORD: SE1 Kennedy

Have students access the Internet through the HRW Web site to conduct research on Kennedy. Then have students create scrapbooks of Kennedy's life. Ask students to include information about Kennedy myths and realities.

president's closest adviser. Kennedy also valued advice from a small circle of White House staff members that included Theodore Sorensen, speechwriter Richard Goodwin, and Press Secretary Pierre Salinger. Goodwin later recalled that staff members did not "hesitate to approach Kennedy directly on matters we thought of presidential interest or concern."

The Domestic Frontier

Because John F. Kennedy had spoken of a "new frontier" during the presidential campaign, his agenda became known as the **New Frontier**. Managing the economy was one of Kennedy's first domestic challenges. He wanted to reassure business leaders that his policies would not be disruptive. To do so, he appointed C. Douglas Dillon, a Republican who had served in the Eisenhower administration, as secretary of the treasury. This selection also gave his administration a bipartisan appearance.

INTERPRETING THE VISUAL RECORD

The New Frontier. President Kennedy faced many challenges while trying to create his New Frontier. ***What does the cat in this cartoon represent? What do the cat's many tails represent?***

Economic matters. When he took office, Kennedy faced economic problems that included rising unemployment and inflation. To stimulate economic growth, Kennedy called for an increase in government spending. By the end of 1961, inflation had gone down, but unemployment remained high. Kennedy hoped to keep inflation down and to further the economic recovery by persuading labor and business to agree to informal wage and price controls. Businesses had been granting higher wages to employees and then passing the costs on to consumers in the form of higher prices. Kennedy called on businesses to limit prices in return for workers agreeing to fewer pay raises.

Administration officials worked particularly hard to reach an agreement with the steel industry. They feared that a rise in steel prices would lead manufacturers who used steel to raise the prices of their goods. This could lead to inflation throughout the economy. One adviser told the president that steel was "so large in the manufacturing sector of the economy that it can upset the price applecart all by itself." Thus, Kennedy was furious when Roger Blough, the president of U.S. Steel, announced higher prices. Just two weeks earlier, steelworkers had agreed to accept only small increases in their benefits packages. Kennedy told Blough, "I think you have made a terrible mistake."

The following day Kennedy lashed out at U.S. Steel and five other companies that had announced similar price hikes. The president blamed the crisis on "a tiny handful of steel executives whose pursuit of private power and profit exceeds their sense of public responsibility." He accused the steel executives of showing "utter contempt for the interests of one hundred eighty-five million Americans." Recalling his inaugural theme of sacrifice, Kennedy declared, "Some time ago I asked each American to consider what he would do for this country and I asked the steel companies. In the last twenty-four hours we had their answer."

The Kennedy administration proceeded to wage a nonstop campaign against the steel company executives that included canceling government contracts. Faced with such pressure, steel company executives announced that prices would not increase after all. Although Kennedy received criticism for his heavy-handed tactics, he had scored a significant victory in his efforts to manage the economy.

SPOTLIGHT on *The Other America*

Have students conduct research on poverty in the 1960s and read sections of Michael Harrington's *The Other America.* Then ask each student to select and assume one of the following roles: President Kennedy, a Kennedy administration official, Michael Harrington, a news reporter, and so on. Have students prepare to speak on the issue of poverty in the 1960s in a roundtable discussion. Students should create a list of talking points for the discussion. After students have finished their lists of talking points, act as a moderator and conduct the roundtable discussion. **Block Scheduling**

TEACH OBJECTIVE 4

LEVEL 1: Tell students to imagine that it is November 22, 1963, and that they have just learned that President Kennedy has been assassinated. Ask each student to list at least five words that describe his or her emotions. *(Students might list words such as* shock, fear, vulnerability, anger, *or* sadness.*)* Have volunteers share their chosen words with the class. Then ask students to draw on their lists to write paragraphs describing how Americans responded to the death of the president. *(Most Americans felt shocked, saddened, and outraged. Many felt that they had grown older instantly.)* Have volunteers read their paragraphs to the class. Students may wish to include their paragraphs in their portfolios. **Sheltered English**

Kennedy and Congress. Kennedy was unable to achieve much of his legislative agenda because he received little cooperation from Congress. Although Democrats controlled both houses of Congress, Republicans had gained 21 seats in the House of Representatives and 2 seats in the Senate in the 1960 election. More important, a coalition of southern Democrats and conservative Republicans in Congress opposed Kennedy's agenda and successfully blocked most of the president's domestic programs.

Even before Kennedy took office, his advisers recommended a tax cut as a means of stimulating economic growth. Lower taxes would give consumers more money to spend and in turn would lead business to produce more goods and hire more workers. Kennedy initially rejected the idea. He argued that such a program conflicted with his calls for personal sacrifice on behalf of national good.

A sharp drop in the stock market in May 1962, however, convinced Kennedy to ask Congress to reduce taxes. In his 1963 State of the Union Address, he declared, "I am convinced that the enactment this year of tax reduction and tax reform overshadows all other domestic problems in this Congress." Several members of Congress balked, however, when Kennedy introduced legislation that reduced taxes by some $10 billion. Critics included former president Eisenhower. They charged that without a comparable cut in federal spending, the tax cut "would lead to a vast wasteland of debt and financial chaos." Despite Kennedy's urging, Congress failed to pass the measure in 1963. Other Kennedy initiatives rejected by Congress included legislation to assist older Americans in paying their medical bills and a bill to provide federal aid for education.

✔ **READING CHECK:** Why did Kennedy have difficulty getting legislation passed?

Helping the Disadvantaged

John F. Kennedy ranked high among the wealthiest presidents—in 1962 his personal fortune stood at about $2.5 million. He donated his annual salary of $100,000 to charities. During the presidential campaign, Kennedy was astonished when he saw the living conditions of poor West Virginians. Once he took office he sought ways to help poor Americans improve their standard of living. Kennedy supported passage of the **Area Redevelopment Act** (ARA)—a bill to provide financial assistance to economically distressed regions that former president Eisenhower had previously vetoed. Kennedy signed the ARA into law in May 1961, winning the first legislative victory of his presidency.

The president's interest in poverty was renewed in 1962 when social activist Michael Harrington published *The Other America,* a well-documented study of poverty in the United States. The book shattered the popular notion that all Americans had benefited from the prosperity of the 1950s. Harrington reported that more than 42 million Americans lived on less than $1,000 per year. He challenged the nation's leaders to face the reality of poverty:

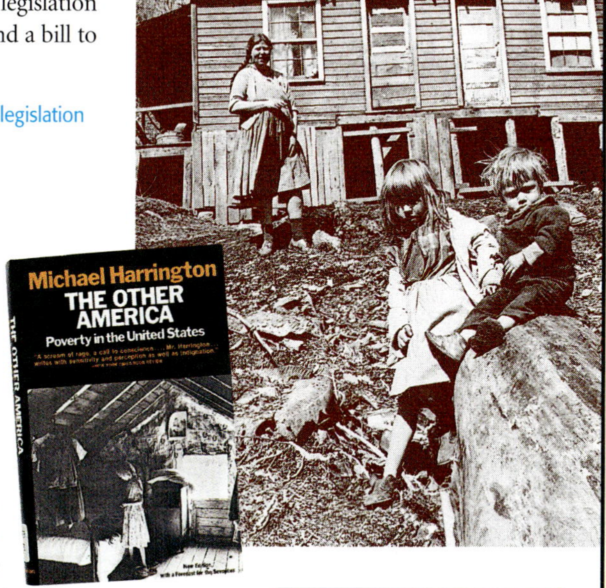

INTERPRETING THE VISUAL RECORD

Poverty. Inspired in part by Michael Harrington's *The Other America,* President Kennedy tried to help the poorest Americans. ***What types of assistance could this family use?***

HISTORY MAKERS SPEAK

Michael Harrington in *The Other America*

The "Culture of Poverty." Michael Harrington's *The Other America* offered a vivid description of poverty in the United States. "Being poor is not one aspect of a person's life in this country; it is his life. Taken as a whole, poverty is a culture. Taken on the family level, it has the same quality. These are people who lack education and skill, who have bad health, poor housing, low levels of aspiration and high levels of mental distress. . . . Each disability is the more intense because it exists within a web of disabilities. And if one problem is solved, and the others are left constant, there is little gain."

CRITICAL THINKING What kinds of antipoverty programs might Harrington have endorsed?

ANSWER: Students might suggest that Harrington might have favored programs that aimed to eliminate all of poverty's symptoms.

VISUAL RECORD ANSWER

(for p. 606)

the steel industry's rising prices; the various steel companies

VISUAL RECORD ANSWER

Students might suggest housing, clothing, and sanitation.

LEVEL 2: Tell students to imagine that they live in a small town that benefited from President Kennedy's antipoverty programs. Tell students to imagine that it is the week after Kennedy's assassination. Have each student write a eulogy for Kennedy. Students' eulogies should describe how the president and his programs affected Americans and how the public responded to his death. *(See the Level 1 lesson for the correct responses.)* Ask volunteers to deliver their eulogies to the class. Students may wish to include their eulogies in their portfolios.

LEVEL 3: Pair students and tell them to imagine that they are artists who have been asked to design a memorial for President John F. Kennedy. Have each pair create a design for a memorial. Students' memorials should be dignified and respectful. Have each pair write a brief artists' statement to accompany its memorial. Artists' statements should describe Americans' feelings toward the president and his death and include the text that will appear on the memorial. *(See the Level 1 lesson for the correct responses.)* If time and resources permit, have students build or sculpt scale models of their proposed memorials.
Cooperative Learning

▶**ASSIGNMENT** *Have students ask people who were teenagers or adults in 1963 about their reactions to President Kennedy's assassination. Ask each student to write two or three paragraphs describing and analyzing these reactions. Conduct a class discussion on students' findings.*

IN THE NEWS

The Kennedy Family.
President Kennedy was not the last member of his immediate family to die tragically. In 1968 an assassin killed his brother Robert. In 1999 President Kennedy's son, John Jr., died with his wife and her sister when his private plane crashed into the Atlantic Ocean. Commentator Garrison Keillor described the impact of his death. "[John F. Kennedy Jr. was] a hero sprung up from tragedy, the son of the murdered President bearing his name whose life was meant in our minds to redeem that evil day in Dallas. I doubt that there were many Americans who didn't want the best for John F. Kennedy Jr. And when his plane was reported missing on Saturday morning, although there was no precedent, no justification, for television to maintain the vigil that it did, there was a rightness about it. He was our boy."

CRITICAL THINKING What might the response to John F. Kennedy Jr.'s death reveal about Americans' long-lingering feelings toward his father, the slain president?

ANSWER: Students might offer that, as Keillor indicates, Americans' strong emotional responses to John F. Kennedy Jr.'s death reveal their warm feelings toward his father and their sadness and anger over his father's death.

> **"[The poor exist] within the most powerful and rich society the world has ever known. Their misery has continued while the majority of the nation talked of itself as being 'affluent [wealthy].' . . . In this way tens of millions of human beings became invisible. They dropped out of sight and out of mind. . . . How long shall we ignore this underdeveloped nation in our midst?"**

Harrington also noted that racism continued to keep many ethnic groups—particularly African Americans—in poverty. He warned that the end of legalized segregation would not change the economic condition of most poor African Americans. "The laws against [discrimination based on] color can be removed," he wrote, "but that will leave the poverty that is the historic consequence of color. As long as this is the case, being born a Negro will continue to be the most profound disability that the United States imposes upon a citizen."

Harrington's work impressed members of the Kennedy administration, including the president himself. He told one adviser, "I want to go beyond the things that have already been accomplished. . . . For example, what about the poverty problem in the United States?" Kennedy's staff began work on the antipoverty programs that the president wanted to present as part of a campaign planned for 1964.

✔ **READING CHECK:** How did the Kennedy administration try to help Americans living in poverty?

CHICAGO DAILY NEWS
RED STREAK
PRESIDENT IS KILLED
Bullet Pierces Head;

Newspapers across the country reported the shocking news of President Kennedy's death.

Tragedy in Dallas

To build support for his 1964 presidential campaign, President Kennedy made a trip to Texas in November 1963. In Dallas on November 22, enthusiastic crowds lined the route of Kennedy's open-car motorcade from the airport. At about 12:30 P.M., as the motorcade moved through the downtown area, shots rang out. Kennedy slumped over, fatally wounded. Within hours, Vice President Lyndon Johnson was sworn in as president. Over the next few days Americans came together to mourn their dead president. Millions watched the funeral on television. Many felt that the death of the youthful, vibrant president had also killed something in them. "We'll never be young again," Kennedy staff member Daniel Patrick Moynihan sadly observed. Donna Shalala later recalled hearing the news while serving in the Peace Corps in Iran.

> **"I remember staying up all night listening to the funeral on the radio. I also recall a beggar walking up to me in the street and I said, 'No, I don't have any money.' He said, 'I don't want any money. I just want to tell you how sorry I am that your young president died.' I remember how difficult it was to sleep and I remember turning cold, which is one of the first signs of shock. . . . His assassination forced us all to grow up."**

Within hours of the shooting, Dallas police arrested Lee Harvey Oswald as a suspect. Two days later, while being moved from one jail to another, Oswald was shot to death by nightclub owner Jack Ruby. This strange turn of events caused many people to question whether Oswald had acted alone in killing the president.

REVIEW

Have students complete the **Section 2 Review** on p. 609.

ASSESS

Have students complete **Daily Quiz 20.2.** As **Alternative Assessment**, you may want to use the image and reality graphic organizer or the President Kennedy eulogy in this section's lessons.

RETEACH

Have students complete **Main Idea Activity for Reteaching and Sheltered English 20.2.** Assign each student one subsection of Section 2. Have students write three or four questions about the material in their assigned subsections. Collect students' questions and use them to quiz the class. **Sheltered English**

EXTEND

Have students conduct research on the Kennedy administration and the myth of "Camelot." Ask each student to create a collage on the subject. Students should include images that represent President Kennedy's domestic and international policies as well as his public image. Have each student write a short paper analyzing the administration and the myth of Camelot to accompany his or her collage. **Block Scheduling**

To end speculation, President Johnson named a commission headed by Chief Justice Earl Warren to investigate the assassination. This **Warren Commission** spent 10 months reviewing the evidence. It concluded that there was no evidence of conspiracy and that both Oswald and Ruby had acted alone. Despite the findings of the Warren Commission, many Americans continued to believe that more than one person was involved in Kennedy's assassination.

After Kennedy's death, his family and friends worked diligently to shape the memory of the fallen president. Jacqueline Kennedy told reporter Theodore White that her husband's life "had more to do with myth, magic, legend, saga, and story than with political theory or political science." She asked White, who was writing a magazine article on the president, to compare his administration to Camelot, King Arthur's medieval court. White agreed, and the image of Camelot became another part of the Kennedy mystique.

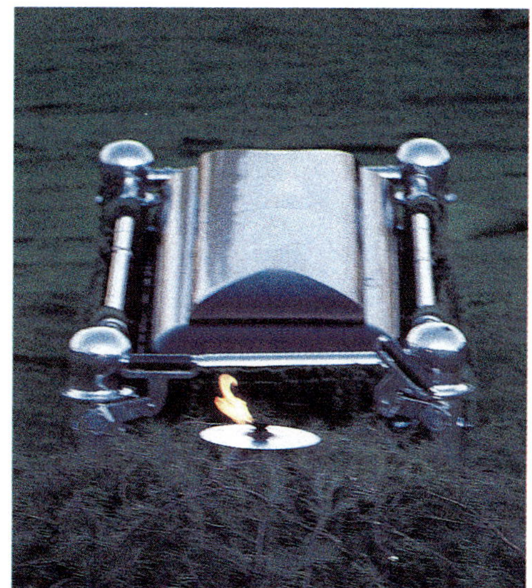

First lighted on November 25, 1963, a flame burns continually at the grave of President John F. Kennedy.

Clark Clifford, an adviser to several presidents, offered a different assessment. He wrote, "In many ways the drama of [Kennedy's] presidency outweighed its achievements." Clifford argued that Kennedy nonetheless had an important influence on American life.

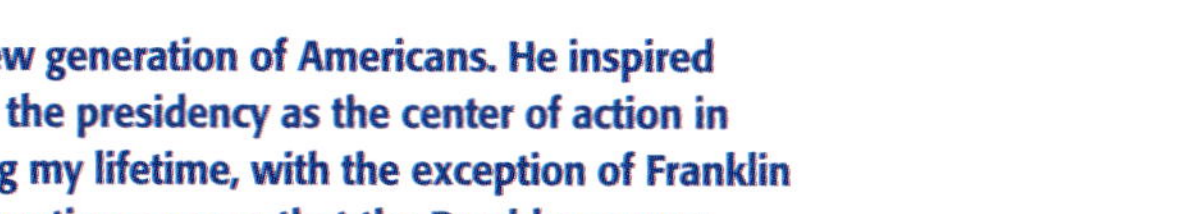

> **"He offered a vast promise to a new generation of Americans. He inspired the nation with a heroic vision of the presidency as the center of action in American life. No President during my lifetime, with the exception of Franklin Roosevelt, matched Kennedy in creating a sense that the Presidency was the center of our national life, the place from which we could solve our most pressing problems."**

✔ **READING CHECK:** How did Americans respond to President Kennedy's death?

SECTION  REVIEW

Define and explain the significance of the following terms:
New Frontier
Area Redevelopment Act
Warren Commission

Identify and explain the significance of the following individuals:
Jacqueline Kennedy
Donna Shalala
Robert Kennedy
Michael Harrington
Lee Harvey Oswald

1. **Using Graphic Organizers** Copy the following chart. Use it to explain President Kennedy's economic policies and how well they succeeded.

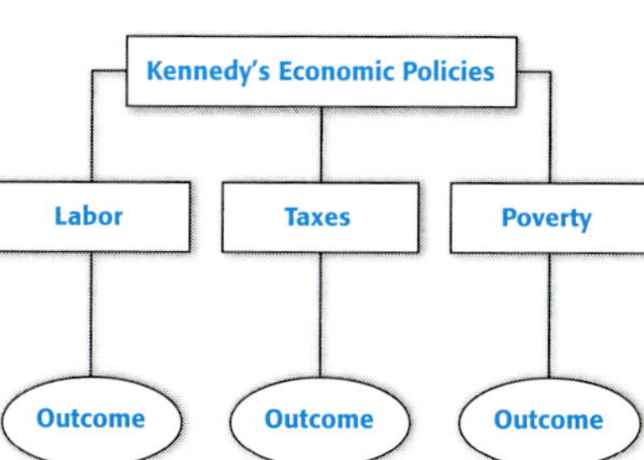

2. **Comparing and Contrasting** How did the reality of the Kennedy administration differ from the popular image?
3. **Analyzing** How did Kennedy try to assist the poor?
4. **Evaluating** Did Kennedy's difficulty in getting legislation passed reduce his effectiveness as a leader? Explain your answer.

Critical Thinking

5. Why might Kennedy's assassination have led many Americans to change their expectations of the nation's future?
Consider:
- the impact of Kennedy's youthful image
- his influence on the nation's young people
- doubts that surrounded his death

SECTION 2 REVIEW ANSWERS

Define and Identify
For significance, see the following pages:

- Jacqueline Kennedy, p. 603
- Donna Shalala, p. 604
- Robert Kennedy, p. 605
- New Frontier, p. 606
- Area Redevelopment Act, p. 607
- Michael Harrington, p. 607
- Lee Harvey Oswald, p. 608
- Warren Commission, p. 609

1. Kennedy wanted to use informal wage and price controls to curb inflation and force steel companies to freeze their prices. He hoped to cut taxes to stimulate economic growth, but Congress rejected the proposal. He wanted to reduce poverty and passed the Area Redevelopment Act.
2. President Kennedy was not as physically healthy as he led people to believe.
3. supported the Area Redevelopment Act
4. effective—the president's ability to inspire Americans and his antipoverty campaign; ineffective—the president's inability to influence Congress
5. His death deeply saddened Americans and made many feel less hopeful about the nation's future.

SECTION 3

After completing Section 3, students should be able to:

OBJECTIVE 1 *Explain how President Johnson's War on Poverty affected American communities.*

OBJECTIVE 2 *Identify the problems that the Great Society programs addressed.*

OBJECTIVE 3 *Detail how the Warren Court expanded individual liberties.*

OBJECTIVE 4 *Describe why support for the Great Society programs declined during the late 1960s.*

LET'S GET STARTED!

As students enter the classroom, ask them to list some of President Kennedy's unfulfilled goals. Then tell them to write a brief paragraph speculating about the ways in which President Johnson might have responded to unfulfilled goals. Have volunteers read their paragraphs to the class. Tell students that in Section 3 they will learn about Johnson's policies, actions, and legacies.

SECTION 3 RESOURCES

PRINT
- Guided Reading Strategy 20.3
- Section 3 Review, p. 617
- Daily Quiz 20.3

MULTIMEDIA
- One-Stop Planner, Lesson 20.3
- The American Nation Video Program Segment: VISTA Volunteers; Teacher's Guide, pp. 207–08
- Holt Researcher: American History CD–ROM

SHELTERED ENGLISH
- Main Idea Activity for Reteaching and Sheltered English 20.3

✔ READING TO UNDERSTAND
To help students master the section objectives, have them answer the **READING CHECKS** and complete **Guided Reading Strategy 20.3** as they read the section.

Johnson's Great Society

OBJECTIVES

Read to understand:
1. how President Johnson's War on Poverty affected American communities
2. what problems the Great Society programs addressed
3. how the Warren Court expanded individual liberties
4. why support for the Great Society programs declined during the late 1960s

KEY TERMS

War on Poverty
Office of Economic Opportunity
Volunteers in Service to America
Great Society
Medicare
Medicaid
Elementary and Secondary Education Act
Corporation for Public Broadcasting

KEY PEOPLE

Lyndon B. Johnson
Barry Goldwater
Robert C. Weaver
Rachel Carson
Earl Warren

EYEWITNESSES TO History

"We have received official confirmation that President Kennedy is dead. I am saddened to have to tell you this grievous news. . . . We have a new President. May God bless our new president and our nation."
—Dean Rusk

Thousands of mourners like these gathered at the funeral of President Kennedy.

Secretary of State Dean Rusk broke the news to his fellow airplane passengers. Earlier that day, Rusk and several other members of President Kennedy's cabinet and staff had boarded an airplane bound for Tokyo to attend an economic conference in Japan. As the plane flew across the Pacific, those on board received garbled teletype messages indicating that something terrible had happened to the president. Secretary Rusk ordered the plane to return to the United States immediately. After Rusk discovered that Kennedy was dead, he shared the news with those on board the flight. His words reflected the anxiety that many Americans felt for the nation and their new president as they faced the tragedy that had unfolded in Dallas that day.

Johnson Takes Over

President Lyndon Johnson was very different from the charismatic and engaging John F. Kennedy. Born in the Hill Country of central Texas, Johnson grew up in a household that had experienced both poverty and relative prosperity. Ambitious and hardworking, Johnson rose rapidly through the Democratic Party ranks. In 1948 he narrowly won a hard-fought race for a seat in the U.S. Senate. After he was re-elected in 1954, Johnson's colleagues made him the Senate majority leader. The position gave him a great deal of influence over legislation. A master of compromise, Johnson always seemed to find the middle course on which most people could agree.

Establishing continuity. Johnson's mastery of the political process, along with years of experience in Washington, enabled him to manage the transition to the presidency with considerable skill and tact. Johnson reassured the nation with promises of continuity between his administration and that of Kennedy. He later recalled, "I felt from the first day in office that I had to carry on for President Kennedy. I considered myself the caretaker of both his people and his policies." Johnson asked Kennedy's cabinet and advisers to continue serving under him. When he spoke to a joint session of Congress on November 27, 1963, Johnson detailed many of Kennedy's achievements. He then declared, "The ideas and ideals which he so nobly represented must and will be translated into effective action." Members of Congress, many of whom had vigorously opposed Kennedy's agenda, applauded enthusiastically to show their support for Johnson.

Lyndon Johnson takes the oath of office. His wife, Lady Bird Johnson, is on the left and Jacqueline Kennedy is on the right.

SPOTLIGHT on the Transition Period

Ask students to identify ways in which President Johnson made the transition into the Oval Office. *(Students should indicate that Johnson comforted the nation in its sorrow and worked to continue President Kennedy's programs.)* Ask students to assess the effectiveness of this transition. *(Most students will indicate that Johnson handled the transition quite well.)* Then ask students to speculate about how Johnson's presidency might have proceeded had he not made an effort to maintain and implement President Kennedy's policies. Tell students to write several scenarios describing the effects and long-term consequences of this course. **Block Scheduling**

TEACH OBJECTIVE 1

LEVEL 1: Pair students and tell them to imagine that they are people living in a community that has been greatly benefited from President Johnson's War on Poverty. Have each pair develop a dialogue discussing certain programs and describing the effects of the programs. *(Students should mention the Office of Economic Opportunity, the Head Start program, and the Volunteers in Service to America program. These initiatives provided antipoverty programs such as job training and preschool education.)* Ask volunteers to perform their dialogues for the class.

Sheltered English, Cooperative Learning

Johnson later claimed, "During my first thirty days in office I believe I averaged no more than three or four hours' sleep a night." He focused his attention on securing passage of Kennedy's tax cut bill and civil rights legislation, both of which had stalled in the Congress. In order to gain support for the tax cut, Johnson had his aides craft a federal budget that held spending to $100 billion. Convinced that the budget offered proof that Johnson intended to curb government spending, Congress approved the tax cut bill in February 1964.

During his first year in office, Johnson kept his pledge to follow in Kennedy's footsteps. However, the ambitious Texan also had plans of his own. "If you look at my record, you would know that I am a Roosevelt New Dealer," he told a former Kennedy aide. "As a matter of fact, John F. Kennedy was a little too conservative to suit my taste."

At his first cabinet meeting in January 1964 he announced, "The day is over when top jobs are reserved for men." Johnson eventually appointed 27 women to upper-level government positions, including consumer activist Betty Furness, economists Alice Rivlin and Penelope Thunberg, and Texas legislator Barbara Jordan. He also appointed Mexican Americans to high positions, assigning Vicente T. Ximenes to chair a presidential committee on Mexican American affairs. Other top appointments went to Héctor P. García, a Texas spokesperson for Mexican American veterans, and to Raúl H. Castro. Castro later became the first Mexican American governor of Arizona.

PRESIDENTIAL *Lives*

1908–1973
In Office 1963–1969

Lyndon B. Johnson

Many observers saw Lyndon Johnson as a stereotypical Texas politician—loud and slightly crude. Johnson loved to shock people with his language, stories, and behavior. He was also a very physical politician. He would shake people's hands until his own bled and slap others on their backs in a friendly gesture. When Johnson visited Thailand in 1961, aides warned him that the Thai people regarded touching someone on the head as offensive. Johnson, however, could not restrain himself. He insisted upon patting the heads of the small children he met.

During his years in the Senate, fellow senators joked that Johnson had two techniques for getting another senator's attention. There was the Half-Johnson—"when he just put a hand on your shoulder"—and the Full-Johnson—"when he put his arm clear around you and thrust his face close to yours." Johnson's techniques got results, however.

Johnson was known as a workaholic who drove himself and his staff to exhaustion to complete multiple tasks. "What's the hurry?" one senator asked another about Johnson's busy schedule. "Rome wasn't built in a day." The other senator replied, "No, but Lyndon Johnson wasn't foreman on that job."

The War on Poverty.

Johnson learned of President Kennedy's antipoverty initiative on November 23, 1963, his first full day in office. Walter Heller, chair of the Council of Economic Advisers, gave Johnson an outline of the plan. Johnson responded, "I'm sympathetic. Go ahead. Give it the highest priority. Push ahead full tilt."

Advisers urged Johnson to implement the antipoverty program slowly, testing its effectiveness in a few cities before expanding its scope. Johnson, however, insisted that the program "be big and bold and hit the nation with real impact." In his first State of the Union Address, delivered on January 8, 1964, the president declared "unconditional war on poverty in America." To launch his **War on Poverty**, Johnson sent to Congress a bill calling for the creation of an **Office of Economic Opportunity** (OEO). With a budget of $1 billion, OEO coordinated a series of new antipoverty programs. These programs included the Job

These children are part of a Head Start program.

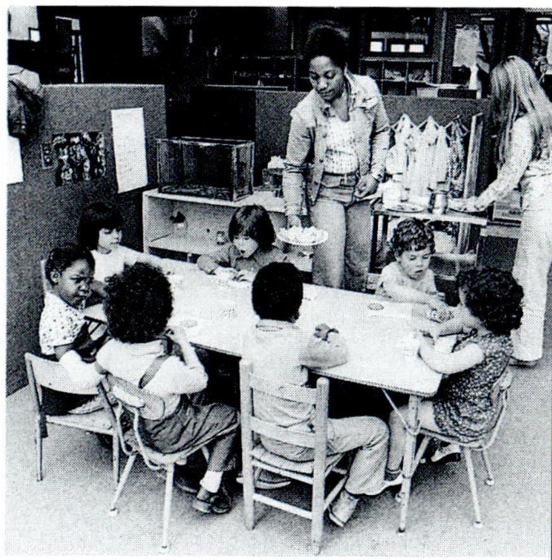

PEOPLE IN HISTORY

Claudia "Lady Bird" Johnson. President Johnson's wife, Claudia "Lady Bird" Johnson, was very different from Jacqueline Kennedy, just as her husband was very different from John F. Kennedy. The daughter of a general store owner, Claudia Alta Taylor grew up in a remote Texas town. She graduated with a degree in journalism from the University of Texas at Austin. In 1934 she met and married Lyndon Johnson, a former schoolteacher. She later used money from her family inheritance to fund his successful campaign for the U.S. House of Representatives. While her husband served in the navy during World War II, Lady Bird Johnson managed his congressional office. In the early 1940s she purchased a debt-ridden radio station in Austin, Texas, and turned it into a broadcasting empire worth millions of dollars. After the war Lady Bird Johnson played an active role in her husband's campaigns. In 1960 she traveled some 35,000 miles and gave many speeches supporting his candidacy for vice president.

CRITICAL THINKING How might Lady Bird Johnson's life belie the myth of the "backseat" political wife?

ANSWER: Students might suggest that Lady Bird Johnson was an educated, successful businessperson.

LEVEL 2: Ask students to describe President Johnson's War on Poverty. *(See the Level 1 lesson for the correct programs.)* Ask students how these programs affected American communities. *(See the Level 1 lesson for the correct effects.)* Then tell each student to invent a fictional community and to create "before" and "after" illustrated and annotated maps displaying the effects of Johnson's policies. In the "before" map, for example, students might draw a dilapidated downtown area. In the "after" map, students might depict a VISTA-refurbished downtown area with a bustling Head Start center. Students may wish to include their maps in their portfolios.

LEVEL 3: Tell students to imagine that they are people who have benefited from President Johnson's War on Poverty. Have each student write a series of journal entries over the course of several years, recording the changes in his or her life due to these programs. *(See the Level 1 lesson for the correct programs and effects.)* Ask volunteers to read portions of their journal entries to the class. Students may wish to include their journal entries in their portfolios.

ECONOMIC DEVELOPMENT

Antipoverty Spending. Federal spending on the poor more than doubled between 1962 and 1968, from almost $12 billion to approximately $27 billion. Government statistics show that an estimated 12 million Americans rose above the official poverty line during this period, reducing the incidence of poverty from 20 percent of the population to 12 percent.

CRITICAL THINKING

Antipoverty programs cost large amounts of money. In theory, how might antipoverty spending actually result in increased government revenues?

ANSWER: Students might mention that antipoverty programs can help people become more prosperous. In general, increasing incomes result in increasing tax revenues.

***The American Nation* VIDEO PROGRAM**

VISTA Volunteers; Teacher's Guide, pp. 207–08

Search 37160, Play to 37755
Videodisc 2, Side B

Play

Pause

See *Teacher's Guide* for Spanish barcode.

teen Life

VISTA Volunteers

John Hough became a VISTA volunteer in 1968. He joined with the support of his parents, who "thought the country could be saved by the determined, idealistic young." Hough was from a small Massachusetts town and had never seen a poverty-stricken inner city. Nevertheless, he still "felt equipped to invade the world of urban poverty, stark and menacing as that world seemed."

VISTA volunteer Rissa Schiff of Brooklyn, New York, plays with Navajo children in Rough Rock, Arizona.

After a six-week training period in Chicago, Hough tutored students in English and mathematics at a school in Detroit, Michigan. Although he was dedicated to his work, Hough soon discovered that the problems he and his students faced were overwhelming. In addition to the constant threat of violence and the presence of drugs, overworked VISTA offices provided little support. Hough left VISTA after one year. In the end, however, he decided that making the effort to help people was in itself of great value.

Corps, a work training program for young people between the ages of 16 and 21; Head Start, a preschool education program for low-income families; and **Volunteers in Service to America** (VISTA), a domestic version of the Peace Corps. Congress passed the antipoverty legislation in late August 1964.

The War on Poverty brought improvements to many communities, including American Indian reservations. It allowed American Indians to establish and operate their own antipoverty programs on the reservations. La Donna Harris, a Comanche involved in OEO programs in Oklahoma, defended the program.

> **"I will stand up and defend OEO as long as I live. Indian leadership developed out of that program. . . . OEO taught us to use our imagination and to look at the future as an exciting adventure. It taught us that there are other ways of doing things."**

✔ **READING CHECK:** How did President Johnson's War on Poverty affect American communities?

Johnson's Vision for America

Whereas President Kennedy had trouble pushing legislation through Congress, President Johnson fulfilled the major legislative goals of his first term within eight months. Comparing the two administrations, Texas journalist Liz Carpenter concluded, "Kennedy inspired. . . . Johnson delivered." Johnson was not content with fulfilling Kennedy's agenda, however. He hoped to be elected president in his own right in 1964 and to advance his own vision for the nation's future. Johnson saw his major task as building a **Great Society**. He shared his vision in a May 1964 speech at the University of Michigan.

> **"The Great Society rests on abundance and liberty for all. It demands an end to poverty and racial injustice. . . . The Great Society is a place where every child can find knowledge to enrich his mind and to enlarge his talents. . . . It is a place where the city of man serves not only the needs of the body and the demands of commerce but the desire for beauty and the hunger for community."**

Johnson campaign item

In short, Johnson wanted the United States to be a place where people would be "more concerned with the quality of their goals than the quantity of their goods."

In order to achieve these lofty goals, Johnson worked hard to ensure victory in the upcoming presidential election. Opinion polls revealed that Americans were impressed with Johnson's achievements. Johnson rode this wave of popularity to easily win the Democratic presidential nomination for the 1964 election. He selected Hubert Humphrey, a liberal senator from Minnesota, as his running mate. The Republicans adopted a platform

TEACH OBJECTIVE 2

LEVEL 1: Organize students into triads. Tell each triad to create a poster depicting problems in American life and advertising Great Society programs designed to alleviate those problems. *(Students should indicate that the Great Society hoped to improve health care, education, housing, American culture, and the environment. Johnson supported Medicare and Medicaid, the Elementary and Secondary Education Act and the Omnibus Housing Act, cultural programs, and environmental protection acts.)* Display the posters around the classroom. **Sheltered English, Cooperative Learning**

LEVEL 2: Tell students to imagine that it is 1965. Have each student write a letter to the editor of a local newspaper describing problems in American life and discussing Great Society efforts to alleviate those problems. *(See the Level 1 lesson for correct problems and Great Society solutions.)* Ask volunteers to read their letters to the class. Students may wish to include their letters in their portfolios.

▶ASSIGNMENT *Have students create collages with a center image representing a problem in American life. The images surrounding the center should represent Great Society solutions to the problem.*

that rejected former president Eisenhower's Modern Republicanism. They chose Senator Barry Goldwater, a conservative from Arizona, as their presidential nominee, with New York representative William E. Miller as his running mate.

In his acceptance speech at the Republican National Convention, Goldwater declared, "Extremism in the defense of liberty is no vice! . . . Moderation in the pursuit of justice is no virtue!" However, many voters regarded Goldwater's brand of conservatism as too extreme. When Goldwater supporters displayed bumper stickers that read "IN YOUR HEART YOU KNOW HE'S RIGHT," Democrats responded with "IN YOUR GUT YOU KNOW HE'S NUTS." The Johnson campaign also produced a commercial that showed a small girl counting to 10 as she pulled petals from a daisy. When she reached "10," an image of an atomic bomb exploding filled the screen. The commercial implied that Goldwater could not be trusted with the nation's nuclear arsenal. The White House was flooded with complaints about the advertisement. It aired only once.

Despite criticism of such campaign tactics, Johnson won the election by a landslide, taking 61 percent of the popular vote and 486 electoral votes to Goldwater's 52. The last president to receive such a mandate was Franklin D. Roosevelt in 1936.

These Lyndon Johnson and Barry Goldwater dolls were made for the 1964 campaign.

Johnson and Congress

At an inaugural ball on the night of January 20, 1965, Lyndon Johnson told partygoers, "Don't stay up late. There's work to be done. We're on our way to the Great Society." Johnson moved quickly to make his vision a reality. While civil rights legislation was a major part of the Great Society legislation, other issues included health care, education, and urban renewal. President Johnson was aided in his efforts by the members of the 89th Congress, which was dominated by Democrats. Many of these Democrats were liberals who supported his call for a Great Society.

The programs. In 1965 Johnson persuaded Congress to establish **Medicare**—a national health insurance program for people over age 65. Congress also authorized funds for states to set up **Medicaid**—a government program that provides free health care to the needy. Johnson traveled to Independence, Missouri, to sign the bill in front of 81-year-old Harry Truman. Truman had first proposed federally funded health insurance in his Fair Deal.

Johnson also urged Congress to take action on funding for education. He gave a moving speech.

> **"My first job after college was a teacher in Cotulla, Texas, in a small Mexican American school. . . . Somehow you never forget what poverty and hatred can do when you see its scars on the hopeful face of a young child. . . . It never even occurred to me in my fondest dreams that I might have the chance to help the sons and daughters of those students and to help people like them all over the country. But now I do have that chance—and I'll let you in on a secret: *I mean to use it.*"**

President Johnson returned to his childhood school and had his first-grade teacher join him as he signed education legislation.

PEOPLE IN HISTORY

Barry Goldwater. Native Arizonan Barry Goldwater went to work in his family's department store chain at the age of 20. During World War II he served in the Army Air Force. After the war, he served as chief of staff of the Arizona Air National Guard, eventually attaining the rank of major general. Goldwater's first experience with politics occurred in 1949, when he successfully ran for a seat on the Phoenix city council. Three years later, in a major political upset, he won the U.S. Senate seat occupied by Majority Leader Ernest MacFarland. In the following years Goldwater established himself as one of the Republican Party's most conservative members. He voted against the censure of Joseph McCarthy and published a widely read book, *The Conscience of a Conservative*, that called for a limited federal government and the elimination of communism. Goldwater became the Republican presidential candidate after winning several key victories in the 1964 primary elections.

ACTIVITY: Have each student select the candidate for whom they might have voted in the 1964 election and write several paragraphs defending his or her choice. Ask volunteers to share their responses. Finally, conduct a mock election.

LEVEL 3: Organize the class into five groups. Assign each group one of the following topics related to Johnson's Great Society: health care, education, housing, culture, or the environment. Have each group develop an outline for a multimedia presentation on its assigned topic. Groups' outlines should include a general summary, possible images, an analysis of Johnson's programs in the given area, and a discussion of the programs' short- and long-term effectiveness. *(See the Level 1 lesson for the correct programs and effects.)* To extend the lesson, have each group create its multimedia presentation.
Cooperative Learning

Teacher to Teacher

Paul Horne, of Columbia, South Carolina, suggested the following activity: Have students choose a problem that President Johnson's Great Society legislation attempted to correct and conduct research on how this legislation affected their city, county, and state. Students should look for specific data such as government grants. Have students report their findings to the class.

HISTORY MAKERS SPEAK

Lyndon B. Johnson in *Remembering America: A Voice from the Sixties*

The Fragile Environment. Like Rachel Carson, President Johnson feared environmental destruction. During a speech to Congress he warned, "The storm of modern change is threatening to blight and diminish in a few decades what has been cherished and protected for generations. . . . Modern technology also has a darker side. Its uncontrolled waste products are menacing the world we live in, our enjoyment and our health. The air we breathe, our water, our soil and wildlife, are being blighted by the poisons and chemicals which are the by-product of technology and industry. The society which receives the benefits of technology must . . . take responsibility for control."

CRITICAL THINKING What might have been some ways for Americans to "take responsibility for control"?

ANSWER: Students might mention industrial controls, pollution controls, or public education.

***President Johnson supported educational television shows like* Sesame Street.**

Congress responded by passing the **Elementary and Secondary Education Act** of 1965, which provided $1.3 billion in aid to schools in poor areas.

Johnson also persuaded Congress to pass the Omnibus Housing Act in 1965. This act authorized billions of dollars to be spent on urban renewal and housing assistance for low-income families. Congress also established the Department of Housing and Urban Development (HUD) to oversee federal housing programs. Robert C. Weaver headed this new department, making him the first African American member of a presidential cabinet. Weaver declared that the new programs had made Americans aware that "our cities are filled with poorly housed, badly educated, underemployed, desperate, unhappy Americans."

Quality of life. Johnson saw the Great Society as a place that fulfilled "the desire for beauty." He supported such programs as the National Endowment for the Arts (NEA) and the National Endowment for the Humanities (NEH), which offered grants and fellowships to artists, writers, and scholars. The Johnson administration also created the **Corporation for Public Broadcasting**, a nonprofit organization dedicated to offering educational television programming.

The president's interest in the quality of life extended to environmental issues. Johnson later recalled, "The cost of our careless technology had caught up with us." Many other Americans also felt a growing concern for the environment.

BIOGRAPHY *Rachel Carson*

Marine biologist Rachel Carson contributed to this environmental movement. Born in Pennsylvania in 1907, Carson later recalled, "I can remember no time when I wasn't interested in the out-of-doors and the whole world of nature." After graduating with honors from Johns Hopkins University in 1929, she taught college and then worked for the U.S. Bureau of Fisheries. She wrote several works on marine science before turning to writing full-time in 1952.

When a friend asked Carson to investigate the impact of the pesticide DDT on birds and other wildlife, she responded with enthusiasm. The resulting book, *Silent Spring,* was published in 1962. Warning Americans that "a grim specter [spirit] has crept upon us almost unnoticed," Carson condemned the uncontrolled use of chemical pesticides, which she called "elixirs [medication] of death." She wrote, "Although today's poisons are more dangerous than any known before, they have amazingly become something to be showered down indiscriminately [carelessly] from the skies [by airplanes]." She continued, "Not only forests and cultivated fields are sprayed, but towns and cities as well." In her book, Carson chronicled the health and safety risks that pesticide use posed for humans. She also presented information regarding the impact of these chemicals on wildlife.

"We should no longer accept the counsel of those who tell us that we must fill our world with poisonous chemicals," Carson argued in the final chapter of *Silent Spring.* "We should look about and see what other course is open to us." In an attempt to protect their industry, pesticide manufacturers attacked Carson and her

HOLT RESEARCHER *Read More About It*

Free Find:
Rachel Carson

After reading about Rachel Carson on the **Holt Researcher** CD–ROM, write a brief description of a book you might write about environmental problems today. Then create a cover for your book that illustrates the issues you would address.

TEACH OBJECTIVE 3

ALL LEVELS: Ask students to identify individual liberties that they exercise every day. *(Students may mention freedom of speech, freedom of association, or freedom of religion.)* Ask students to identify the guarantee of those liberties. *(Students should note that the First Amendment protects those rights. If students do not identify the First Amendment, remind them and have them reread the amendment.)* Tell students that court decisions throughout U.S. history have expanded individual liberties. To help them understand how the Warren court expanded individual liberties, copy the following graphic organizer onto the chalkboard, omitting the italicized answers. Have each student complete it. **Sheltered English**

WARREN COURT DECISIONS

Case	Year	Decision
Baker v. Carr	*1962*	*led to ruling that electoral districts had to have the same number of voters*
Gideon v. Wainright	*1963*	*declared that states had to provide lawyers for impoverished defendants charged with serious crimes*
Escobedo v. Illinois	*1964*	*declared that the accused had the right to have a lawyer present during police investigations*
Miranda v. Arizona	*1966*	*declared that accused persons had to be informed of their rights at the time of arrest*

conclusions. However, her claims prompted President John F. Kennedy to create a panel to study the issue. A final report issued by the panel agreed with Carson's conclusions.

Rachel Carson died in 1964. She did not live to witness the environmental legislation passed during the Johnson years. During his presidency Johnson signed the Water Quality Act of 1965, the Air Quality Act of 1967, the Water Pollution Act of 1968, and several other environmental bills. In addition, Johnson's administration created several new national parks and wilderness areas, making his record on environmental issues one of the most impressive of any U.S. president.

✔ **READING CHECK:** What problems did the Great Society programs address?

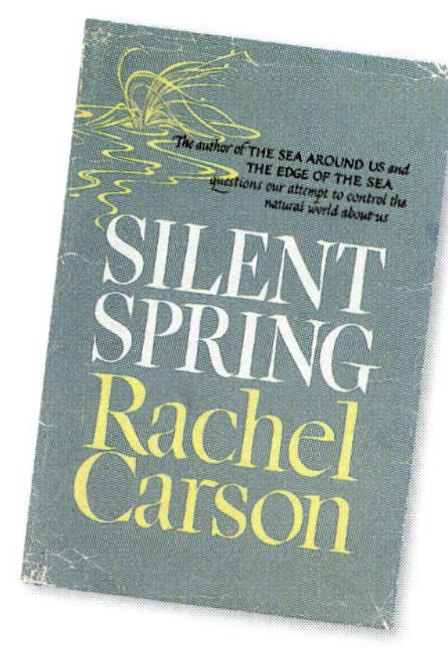

Rachel Carson's* Silent Spring *brought environmental issues to the attention of many Americans.

Strategies for Success — Using the Library

When conducting historical research, one should try to consult as broad an array of sources as possible. Most of the time, these sources are best found in a library. Thus, knowing how to use the library is a crucial skill for students to develop.

Although almost all libraries use the same basic guidelines for organizing their materials, each one has a unique layout, staff, and set of specific holdings. Taking a tour and becoming familiar with one's school or local public library can help make one's subsequent research more efficient and productive.

How to Use the Library

1. **Identify the topic.** First, identify the general topic that you wish to research. Then make a short list of events, issues, or people related to the topic that you can look to for further information if necessary.
2. **Check the reference section.** In the library's reference section, you will find almanacs, atlases, encyclopedias, specialized dictionaries, and indexes to newspaper and magazine articles. Consult each of these sources, when appropriate, to find information about your topic.
3. **Consult the library catalog.** Look in the library's card catalog or electronic catalog to locate books about your topic. Most library catalogs list books by author, title, and subject, and assign each book a call number based on the Library of Congress classification system or the Dewey decimal system. An index of subject headings can usually be found in or near the library catalog.
4. **Look for Internet and multimedia sources.** If possible, use the library's computer system to look for information about your topic on the Internet. Then check for CD–ROMS, videotapes, or other multimedia sources that may aid your research.
5. **Consult a librarian.** Librarians can help you use reference sources and the library catalog and can help direct you to a book's location. They can also suggest additional resources that may aid your research.

Applying the Strategy

Use your school or local public library to conduct research on one of the following topics:

a. the political career of Lyndon B. Johnson
b. a specific government program that was part of President Johnson's War on Poverty, such as the Job Corps, Head Start, or VISTA
c. the 1964 presidential campaign
d. the Housing and Urban Development Act of 1968

Practicing the Strategy

Answer the following questions.

1. What reference sources did you use to find information about your topic?
2. What books about your topic were listed in the library catalog?
3. What other sources, if any, did you find during your research?

CONSTITUTIONAL HERITAGE

The Warren Court. Under the leadership of Chief Justice Earl Warren, the Supreme Court issued a number of controversial rulings. *Engel* v. *Vitale* outlawed the practice of mandatory prayer in public schools. *Griswold* v. *Connecticut* announced the existence of a constitutional right to privacy. *New York Times* v. *Sullivan* concluded that journalistic material about a public figure, even if it contained erroneous statements, could only be considered libelous if it was published as a result of "actual malice."

ACTIVITY: Ask students to share their opinions about the Warren Court's decision in *New York Times* v. *Sullivan.* Conduct a brief discussion about the decision.

STRATEGIES FOR SUCCESS

Practicing the Strategy

1. Answers will vary. Students should have consulted as many sources as necessary in the course of their research.
2. Answers will vary. Students' lists should consist of relevant books.
3. Answers will vary. Students may mention magazine or newspaper articles.

TEACH OBJECTIVE 4

LEVEL 1: Pair students and ask each pair to list reasons why support for the Great Society programs declined during the late 1960s. *(Students should note that the Vietnam War diverted funds and attention, that the fast legislative pace worried legislators, that Republicans gained congressional seats in the 1966 midterm elections, that state and local politicians disliked some programs because they had no control, and that some Americans viewed some programs as worthless.)* Have pairs rank the reasons for the decline in support from most damaging to least damaging. Ask volunteers to share and explain their rankings.
Sheltered English, Cooperative Learning

LEVELS 2 AND 3: Have students complete the Level 1 lesson on an individual basis. Then tell students to imagine that it is 1966 and that they are political cartoonists. Have each student create two political cartoons explaining the declining support for the Great Society programs during the late 1960s. *(See the Level 1 lesson for the correct reasons.)* Ask students to write captions for their cartoons. Have volunteers present their captions and cartoons to the class. Students may wish to include their captions and cartoons in their portfolios.

SECTION 3 REVIEW ANSWERS

Define and Identify
For significance, see the following pages:

- Lyndon B. Johnson, p. 610
- War on Poverty, p. 611
- Office of Economic Opportunity, p. 611
- Volunteers in Service to America, p. 612
- Great Society, p. 612
- Barry Goldwater, p. 613
- Medicare, p. 613
- Medicaid, p. 613
- Elementary and Secondary Education Act, p. 614
- Robert C. Weaver, p. 614
- Corporation for Public Broadcasting, p. 614
- Rachel Carson, p. 614
- Earl Warren, p. 616

1. education–Head Start, Elementary and Secondary Education Act; housing–Omnibus Housing Act, establishment of the Department of Housing and Urban Development; health care–Medicare, Medicaid; environment–Water Quality Act of 1965 and other laws, creation of new national parks and wilderness areas

2. by honoring President Kennedy's legacy and working to fulfill Kennedy's domestic agenda; elected Johnson in 1964

3. defined and extended individual liberties; many approved, others thought Court had overstepped its authority

4. Students might suggest that Johnson give priority to Great Society programs or to the Vietnam War.

The Warren Court Decisions

Like the Johnson administration, the Supreme Court of the 1960s reflected a spirit of activism. Under the leadership of Chief Justice Earl Warren, the Court continued the trend—begun with the 1954 desegregation decision in *Brown* v. *Board of Education*—of defining and extending individual rights. The Court extended equality in the voting booth with the "one person, one vote" principle. In many congressional districts, sparsely populated rural areas were granted the same number of representatives as densely populated urban areas. In the 1962 case *Baker* v. *Carr*, the Court declared that electoral districts must contain approximately the same number of voters in order to ensure fair representation for all Americans.

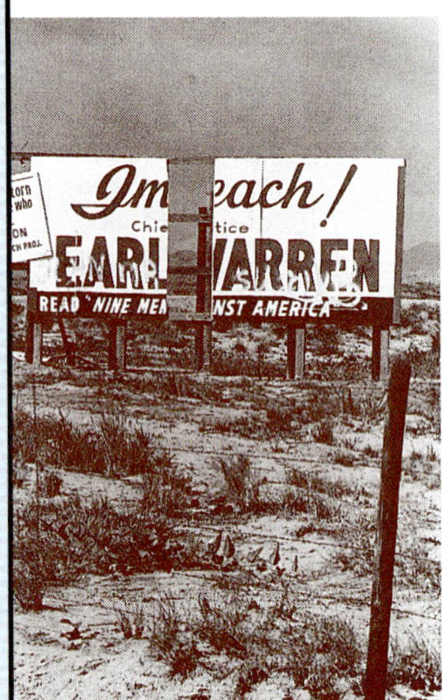

Billboards like this one showed Americans' dissatisfaction with Chief Justice Earl Warren.

The Warren Court also issued a series of decisions protecting the rights of persons accused of crimes. *Gideon* v. *Wainwright* (1963) declared that the states must provide lawyers, at public expense, for poor defendants charged with serious crimes. *Escobedo* v. *Illinois* (1964) granted the accused the right to have a lawyer present during police investigations. *Miranda* v. *Arizona* (1966) said that accused persons must be informed of their rights at the time of their arrest.

Many people saw these decisions as an attempt to ensure that the criminal justice system did not violate individual rights. Others charged that the Court had overstepped its authority by making law rather than interpreting it. One critic claimed, "Earl Warren . . . has defiled [corrupted] our jurisprudence [court system] and made war against the public order." Billboards proclaiming "IMPEACH EARL WARREN!" appeared in some communities.

✔ **READING CHECK:** How did the Warren Court expand individual liberties?

The Decline of the Great Society

Like the other postwar presidents, Lyndon Johnson was committed to fighting the Cold War. Yet unlike Presidents Eisenhower and Kennedy, Johnson was far more interested in domestic policy. Nevertheless, foreign affairs demanded Johnson's attention.

Foreign policy and the Great Society. Johnson quickly became involved in the affairs of the Dominican Republic. In April 1965, factions within the country's military rebelled against the military-led government. The U.S. ambassador believed that the rebels were under communist influence and insisted that Johnson intervene to "prevent another Cuba."

Johnson promptly sent some 22,000 marines to the Dominican Republic. With U.S. support, troops loyal to the military government gained the upper hand, and the situation stabilized. Johnson withdrew the marines in 1966 when relatively free and fair elections put a pro-American government in power.

Many people in Latin America condemned the intervention. Even those who supported Johnson's action did so reluctantly. In the United States, however, the majority of the public backed Johnson and praised his aggressive stand against the threat of communist expansion.

By the spring of 1965 Johnson's focus had shifted to fighting in the southeast Asian country of Vietnam and away from the Great Society. In 1966 the government spent about 18 times more on the Vietnam War than it did on the War on

REVIEW

Have students complete the **Section 3 Review** on p. 617.

ASSESS

Have students complete **Daily Quiz 20.3**. As **Alternative Assessment**, you may want to use the War on Poverty map or the Great Society political cartoon in this section's lessons.

RETEACH

Have students complete **Main Idea Activity for Reteaching and Sheltered English 20.3**. Then ask each student to list the titles of the subsections in Section 3 on a sheet of paper. Have students write summary sentences for each of the subsections. Ask volunteers to read their sentences to the class. Have students choose the best summary sentence for each subsection.
Sheltered English

EXTEND

Tell students that Head Start was a cornerstone program of the War on Poverty. Have students conduct research on Head Start programs in the 1960s and today. Ask each student to write a paper discussing and evaluating the program.
Block Scheduling

Poverty. Civil rights leader Martin Luther King Jr. complained that the Great Society had been "shot down on the battlefields of Vietnam."

Domestic opposition. Growing domestic opposition to the programs of the Great Society also contributed to its decline. Johnson's legislative success record was extraordinary—the 89th Congress passed 181 of the 200 major bills that the president requested in 1965 and 1966. However, many members of Congress urged the president to slow down.

The results of the 1966 midterm elections signaled an additional change in the relations between Congress and the White House. Although Democrats retained their majorities in Congress, Republicans gained 47 House seats and three Senate seats, significantly reducing Johnson's opportunities to press for more legislation.

Problems with specific Great Society programs also raised doubts about the wisdom of Johnson's vision. Many state and local politicians disliked the War on Poverty because they had no control over the selection and funding of community projects. Members of Congress complained that many programs did not merit funding. Representative Frank Bow of Ohio declared, "We cannot have guns and butter," meaning that the Vietnam War should take priority over social programs. Bow ridiculed funding the NEH as wanting "guns with strawberry shortcake covered with whipped cream and cherry on top."

Although support for his programs weakened, Johnson's influence on American life endured long after his presidency ended. The NEH, Head Start, and other Great Society programs continued to bring benefits to Americans in the decades that followed.

✔ **READING CHECK:** Why did support for the Great Society programs decline during the late 1960s?

INTERPRETING THE VISUAL RECORD

The Great Society. Many critics of President Johnson's programs argued that they cost too much. ***Who does this cartoon suggest paid for the Great Society programs?***

SECTION  REVIEW

Define and explain the significance of the following terms:
War on Poverty
Office of Economic Opportunity
Volunteers in Service to America
Great Society
Medicare
Medicaid
Elementary and Secondary Education Act
Corporation for Public Broadcasting

Identify and explain the significance of the following individuals:
Lyndon B. Johnson
Barry Goldwater
Robert C. Weaver
Rachel Carson
Earl Warren

1. **Using Graphic Organizers** Copy the following chart. Use it to explain the effects of the Great Society in education, housing, health care, and the environment.

GREAT SOCIETY	
Education	Housing
Health Care	Environment

2. **Synthesizing** How did President Johnson win the support of the American people during his first year in office? How did Americans show their support?
3. **Hypothesizing** What were the effects of the decisions of the Warren Court, and how did Americans' reactions to them vary?
4. **Problem Solving** What advice would you have given President Johnson regarding the conflict between funding Great Society programs and foreign policy programs?

Critical Thinking

5. Why did Johnson's efforts to help poor Americans generate opposition?
Consider:
   - the specific design of the poverty programs
   - the reaction of local and state politicians
   - concern over government spending during the Vietnam War

VISUAL RECORD ANSWER

the public

5. Some Americans disliked specific antipoverty programs, while others wanted more funding for the Vietnam War.

CHAPTER 20 REVIEW ANSWERS

Creating a Time Line

Each event should have an explanation and the correct date.

Writing a Summary

See the Reading Checks in each section for main ideas.

Identifying People and Ideas

1. Kennedy administration strategy of having a wide range of foreign-policy options
2. program that expanded American economic aid to Latin America
3. leader of an uprising that established a communist dictatorship in Cuba
4. John F. Kennedy's presidential agenda
5. 35th president of the United States, 1961–63
6. investigated the assassination of President Kennedy
7. President Johnson's antipoverty legislation and programs
8. Johnson's social vision
9. 36th president of the United States, 1963–69
10. marine biologist who wrote *Silent Spring*

REVIEW AND ASSESSMENT RESOURCES

PRINT
- Chapter 20 Review, pp. 618–19
- Chapter 20 Tutorial for Students, Parents, Mentors, and Peers
- Chapter 20 Test (Form A or B)
- Portfolio Activities and Alternative Assessment Handbook, Chapter 20

MULTIMEDIA
- Audio Program, Chapter 20 (English and Spanish)
- Chapter 20 Test Generator (on the One-Stop Planner)
- Global Skill Builder CD–ROM
- HRW Web site

SHELTERED ENGLISH
- Spanish Glossary
- Sheltered English Chapter 20 Test

REVIEW

Have students complete the **Chapter 20 Review** on pp. 618–19.

ASSESS

Use one of the chapter tests to assess students' understanding of the content. For **Alternative Assessment**, see the **Portfolio Activities and Alternative Assessment Handbook.**

Understanding Main Ideas

1. helped John F. Kennedy win a close election over Richard Nixon
2. Cuba's promixity to the United States made the prospect of Soviet missiles on the island very threatening.
3. attempted to reduce unemployment, curb inflation, and stimulate economic growth
4. opposition from congressional coalition of southern Democrats and conservative Republicans
5. worked to fulfill Kennedy's domestic agenda
6. Medicare, Medicaid, education efforts, urban renewal and housing programs, support for the arts, environmental legislation

Reviewing Themes

1. continued to build nuclear weapons and oppose communism; expanded conventional weapons options and used economic aid
2. personal concerns, Michael Harrington's book *The Other America*, and the belief that the government had an obligation to help the poor
3. President Kennedy probably knew that his public image augmented his political popularity and authority.

Thinking Critically

1. fear of debt
2. Some students might argue that President Kennedy would have eventually persuaded Congress to cooperate with his legislative agenda or that the political differences were irreconcilable.

CHAPTER 20 Review

Creating a Time Line

Copy the time line below onto a sheet of paper. Complete the time line by filling in the events and dates from the chapter that you think were most significant. Pick three events and explain why you think they were significant.

Writing a Summary

Using the Reading Checks as a guide, write an overview of the events in the chapter.

Identifying People and Ideas

Identify the following terms or individuals and explain their significance.

1. flexible response
2. Alliance for Progress
3. Fidel Castro
4. New Frontier
5. John F. Kennedy
6. Warren Commission
7. War on Poverty
8. Great Society
9. Lyndon B. Johnson
10. Rachel Carson

Understanding Main Ideas

SECTION 1

1. What role did television play in the 1960 presidential election?
2. How did the establishment of a communist government in Cuba lead to increased Cold War tensions?

SECTION 2

3. How did Kennedy attempt to manage the economy?
4. Why did Kennedy fail to gain passage of most of his legislative initiatives?

SECTION 3

5. How did President Johnson establish continuity between his administration and that of John F. Kennedy?
6. What were some of the successes of the Great Society programs?

Reviewing Themes

1. **Global Relations** How did President Kennedy's Cold War foreign policy resemble that of his predecessors? How did it differ?
2. **Economic Development** Why did Presidents Kennedy and Johnson both develop programs to help the poor in America?
3. **Democratic Values** Why did Kennedy work so hard to control his public image?

Thinking Critically

1. **Recognizing Point of View** Why did many members of Congress oppose President Kennedy's tax cut proposal?
2. **Using Historical Imagination** Would Kennedy have been able to fulfill his legislative agenda had he lived? Explain your answer.
3. **Analyzing** What factors contributed to Johnson's landslide victory in the 1964 presidential election?
4. **Evaluating** How did the Warren Court's decisions in *Gideon* v. *Wainwright*, *Escobedo* v. *Illinois*, and *Miranda* v. *Arizona* strengthen individual rights?
5. **Problem Solving** What are the most effective ways for the government to provide assistance to the poor?

Writing about History

Writing to Describe Copy the following chart and use it to write an essay that describes the different goals and achievements of Presidents Kennedy and Johnson.

KENNEDY		JOHNSON	
Goals	Achievements	Goals	Achievements

RETEACH

Organize students into three groups. Assign each group one of the sections in Chapter 20. Have each group work together to develop a lesson plan that covers its assigned section. Then have groups present a brief lesson to the class. Be prepared to round out information gaps or correct misinformation. Encourage students to use visual aids in their lessons. Tell students to take notes on each presentation.
Sheltered English, Cooperative Learning

EXTEND

Have each student list the presidents of the United States from Franklin D. Roosevelt to Lyndon B. Johnson. Have students pick one adjective to describe each president. Caution students to think carefully about their selections. Then ask volunteers to share their adjectives with the class. Conclude by conducting a discussion on the public's perceptions of the presidents of the mid-1900s. **Block Scheduling**

This cartoon shows how President Kennedy's forceful response ended the Cuban missile crisis.

Strategies for Success Review the **Strategies for Success** on *Using the Library.* Then use your school or local public library to conduct research on one of the following topics:

- **a.** the political career of John F. Kennedy
- **b.** the history of the Peace Corps
- **c.** the history of the Berlin Wall
- **d.** the Cuban missile crisis

Linking History and Geography

Study the map below. In what region of the United States were most NASA sites located? How might geographical considerations have influenced the location of the NASA sites?

internetconnect

TOPIC: Peace Corps
GO TO: go.hrw.com
KEYWORD: SE1 Corps

Accessing the Internet through the HRW Web site, research the history, structure, and present-day role of the Peace Corps. Then imagine that you are a Peace Corps recruiter. Write a speech for a rally and present your speech to the class.

BUILDING YOUR PORTFOLIO

Complete one or all of the following activities independently or cooperatively.

1 Global Relations

Imagine that you are a television news reporter. ***Prepare a news bulletin*** summarizing President Kennedy's announcement of the naval blockade of Cuba in 1962.

2 Economic Development

Imagine that you are a presidential aide in the Kennedy White House. ***Prepare a memorandum*** that describes a program designed to assist poor Americans.

3 Democratic Values

Imagine that you are an aide to President Johnson. ***Prepare an illustrated pamphlet*** that describes Great Society programs in the areas of health care, housing, education, and the environment.

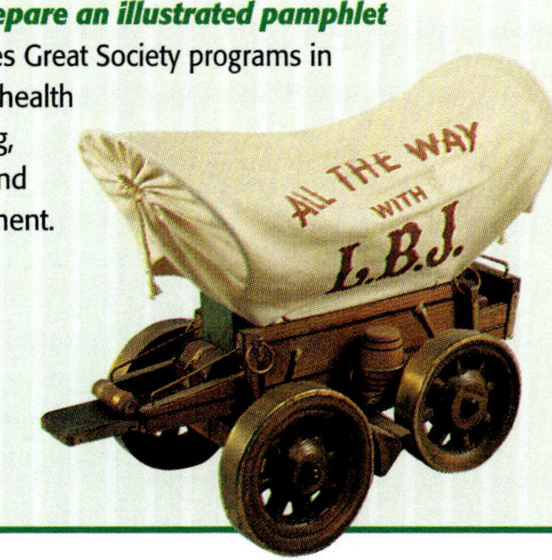

3. the continuity between the Johnson and Kennedy administrations, the rapport between Johnson and Congress, and the campaign against Barry Goldwater's conservatism

4. provided important legal protections to individuals accused of crimes

5. Some students might suggest that government antipoverty programs should provide educational and job training opportunities to aid recipients.

Writing About History
Kennedy: goals—prevention of communist expansion, reduction of unemployment and inflation, stimulation of economic growth, implementation of antipoverty programs; achievements—defense of West Berlin, removal of Soviet missiles from Cuba, passage of Area Redevelopment Act. Johnson: goals—continuation and expansion of Kennedy's domestic agenda, creation of a Great Society; achievements—War on Poverty and Great Society legislation

Strategies for Success
Students' research should be accurate and on topic. Students should consult as many sources as possible in the course of their research.

Linking History and Geography
near Washington, D.C.; available land, size of surrounding populations, proximity to Washington, D.C., and nearby resources

The Civil Rights Movement

CHAPTER PLANNING GUIDE

	Section Lesson Objectives	Print Resources	Multimedia Resources	Sheltered English Resources
Section 1 Freedom Now!, pp. 622–27	1 Explain how civil rights demonstrators used nonviolence to achieve their goals, and note what the effect was. 2 Discuss why civil rights leaders used nonviolent tactics, and explain how protests in Albany, Georgia, and Birmingham, Alabama, differed. 3 Analyze why supporters pushed for a civil rights bill, and discuss what factors influenced the bill's passage.	▶ Guided Reading Strategy 21.1 ▶ Primary Source Reading 21: James Baldwin: Wordsmith and Social Critic ▶ Literature Reading 21: Harper Lee's Masterpiece ▶ Biography Reading 21: Ralph Abernathy ▶ Section 1 Review, p. 627 ▶ Daily Quiz 21.1	▶ One-Stop Planner, Lesson 21.1 ▶ American Music Selection 23: "He's Got the Whole World in His Hands" ▶ Holt Researcher: American History CD–ROM ▶ HRW Web site	▶ Main Idea Activity for Reteaching and Sheltered English 21.1
Section 2 Voting Rights, pp. 628–32	1 Explain why early efforts to register voters in Mississippi failed. 2 Relate why the Freedom Summer project met with limited success. 3 Discuss how the Mississippi Freedom Democratic Party affected relations between civil rights activists and the federal government. 4 Describe how the Selma protest led to the passage of the Voting Rights Act.	▶ Guided Reading Strategy 21.2 ▶ Geography Activity 21: The Civil Rights Movement ▶ Graphic Organizer Activity 21: In the Words of the Leaders ▶ American History Outline Map 21: Desegregation ▶ Section 2 Review, p. 632 ▶ Daily Quiz 21.2	▶ One-Stop Planner, Lesson 21.2 ▶ Holt Researcher: American History CD–ROM	▶ Main Idea Activity for Reteaching and Sheltered English 21.2
Section 3 Challenges for the Movement, pp. 633–38	1 Describe how Malcolm X's message differed from that of the major civil rights organizations during the early 1960s. 2 Explain why nonviolent protest and the goal of racial integration lost support. 3 Discuss how northern racial discrimination and urban riots changed the civil rights movement.	▶ Guided Reading Strategy 21.3 ▶ Section 3 Review, p. 638 ▶ Daily Quiz 21.3	▶ One-Stop Planner, Lesson 21.3 ▶ The American Nation Video Program Segment: Malcolm X; Teacher's Guide, pp. 135–40 ▶ Holt Researcher: American History CD–ROM	▶ Main Idea Activity for Reteaching and Sheltered English 21.3
Section 4 The Movement Continues, pp. 639–43	1 Describe the problems many leading African American organizations encountered in the early 1970s. 2 Explain how the Supreme Court limited the impact of busing and affirmative action programs. 3 Identify the gains African Americans made during the early 1970s.	▶ Guided Reading Strategy 21.4 ▶ Section 4 Review, p. 643 ▶ Daily Quiz 21.4	▶ One-Stop Planner, Lesson 21.4 ▶ Holt Researcher: American History CD–ROM	▶ Main Idea Activity for Reteaching and Sheltered English 21.4
Chapter Review and Assessment pp. 644–45		▶ Chapter 21 Review, pp. 644–45 ▶ Chapter 21 Tutorial for Students, Parents, Mentors, and Peers ▶ Chapter 21 Test (Form A or B) ▶ Portfolio Activities and Alternative Assessment Handbook, Chapter 21	▶ Audio Program, Chapter 21 (English and Spanish) ▶ Chapter 21 Test Generator (on the One-Stop Planner) ▶ Global Skill Builder CD–ROM ▶ HRW Web site	▶ Spanish Glossary ▶ Sheltered English Chapter 21 Test

CHAPTER OVERVIEW

Under the leadership of Martin Luther King Jr. during the early 1960s, the civil rights movement relied on nonviolent resistance to draw attention to the injustice and brutality of racial oppression in the United States. Many civil rights activists concentrated their energies on ending segregation in the South and obtaining voting rights for African Americans. These efforts led to the passage of the Civil Rights Act of 1964 and the Voting Rights Act of 1965.

The full integration of African Americans into the social and economic structures of the United States was not a universal goal of the civil rights movement, however. Malcolm X and other leaders advocated separatism and the use of "any means necessary" to obtain rights for African Americans.

In 1968 King was assassinated, an event that rocked the nation and sparked riots in some cities. However, the civil rights struggle continued during the 1970s.

TIME TAMERS

Block Scheduling

The teacher lesson plans for each section offer a variety of activity choices to help you present the material in a block scheduling format. For further suggestions on block scheduling, see the **Block Scheduling Handbook with Team Teaching Strategies**, pp. 121–26.

Hands-On History Activities:

Classroom to Community The **Hands-On History Activities** help students make meaningful connections between events in American history and those in their own hometown. You may wish to use the Chapter 21 Activity, Voters and Voting Rights in Your Community, to extend the chapter lessons, as alternative assessment, or as a block scheduling option.

Portfolio Projects

The American Nation includes multiple portfolio projects in each Pupil's Edition chapter review, as well as each unit review. Chapter 21 Portfolio Project options on p. 645 include the following:

1. Students will **write a memorandum.**
2. Students will **write a letter.**
3. Students will **create an illustrated time line.**

The American Nation
INTERNET RESOURCE DIRECTORY

To access online materials for this chapter, go to go.hrw.com and type in the keywords listed below.

HRW ONLINE RESOURCES
GO TO: go.hrw.com

Online Maps
KEYWORD: SE1 Maps21
- Black Voter Registration
- School Segregation, 1964
- Urban Unrest

Online Reading Support
KEYWORD: SE1 Strategies21

Online Rubrics
KEYWORD: SE1 Rubrics

CHAPTER ENRICHMENT LINKS
Use these Web links to extend and enrich student learning for Chapter 21.
GO TO: go.hrw.com
KEYWORD: SE1 Ch21

CHAPTER INTERNET ACTIVITIES
GO TO: go.hrw.com
- Pupil's Edition Student Activity
  KEYWORD: SE1 Leaders
  (Students explore the lives of Martin Luther King Jr. and Malcolm X.)
- Teacher's Edition Student Activity
  KEYWORD: SE1 Congo
  (Students explore the independence of the Belgian Congo.)
- Teacher's Edition Student Activity
  KEYWORD: SE1 March
  (Students explore the March on Washington.)

ADDITIONAL
RESOURCES

Books for Teachers

Mills, Nicolaus. *Like a Holy Crusade: Mississippi 1964—The Turning of the Civil Rights Movement in America.* Ivan R. Dee, 1993. Describes the Freedom Summer project.

Powledge, Fred. *Free at Last? The Civil Rights Movement and the People Who Made It.* Little, Brown and Company, 1991. Summarizes key events of the civil rights movement, with interviews.

Books for Students

Ayers, Alex, ed. *The Wisdom of Martin Luther King, Jr.* Meridian, 1993. Provides writings and speeches by and about Martin Luther King Jr. Particularly appropriate for students reading below grade level.

Levine, Ellen. *Freedom's Children: Young Civil Rights Activists Tell Their Own Stories.* Putnam, 1993. Relates the stories of young civil rights workers.

Primary Sources from the Period

Hampton, Henry, Steve Fayer, and Sarah Flynn. *Voices of Freedom: An Oral History of the Civil Rights Movement from the 1950s Through the 1980s.* Bantam, 1990. Offers personal accounts of major events.

X, Malcolm, with Alex Haley. *The Autobiography of Malcolm X.* Ballantine Books, 1973. Tells the life story of Malcolm X.

Multimedia Materials

Eyes on the Prize: America's Civil Rights Years, Vol. 3, Mississippi: Is This America? Video, 120 min. PBS. Chronicles the activities of civil rights workers in Mississippi between 1962 and 1964.

CHAPTER 21

Before You Read

Build on What You Know

Ask students to answer the following questions.

How might some Americans have worked to expand civil rights?

Consider:

- the success of the Montgomery Bus Boycott
- the leadership of Martin Luther King Jr.

How might some people have resisted moves for African American civil rights?

Consider:

- the violence surrounding desegregation efforts in Little Rock
- the actions of state officials who opposed desegregation

exploring the time line

AMERICAN EVENTS

PEOPLE IN HISTORY

1974 ■ Hank Aaron. In 1972 it became clear that Atlanta Braves baseball player Aaron had a chance to break Babe Ruth's home-run record, which had stood since 1935. Aaron soon began receiving racist hate mail. Some writers threatened to hurt him and his family as "punishment" for attempting to break the record of a white man. An Atlanta police officer was assigned to escort Aaron to and from the ballpark. In May 1973 Aaron discussed the hate mail with a journalist and, as a result, began to receive tens of thousands of encouraging letters. The U.S. Postal Service estimated that by the end of the year, Aaron had received 930,000 pieces of mail—more than any other person in the United States, except politicians.

CRITICAL THINKING What might the response to Aaron's pursuit of Ruth's record indicate about the civil rights movement?

ANSWER: Students might suggest that the hate mail indicates that the movement was not entirely successful, but the positive mail might indicate how the civil rights movement had transformed some attitudes.

CHAPTER 21

1960–1978

The Civil Rights Movement

March on Washington for civil rights

Dr. Martin Luther King Jr. receiving the Nobel Peace Prize

1960 — **1962** — **1964** — **1966** — **1968**

1960 World Events
The Belgian Congo becomes an independent nation.

1962 Daily Life
James Meredith integrates the University of Mississippi.

1963 Politics
The March on Washington takes place.

1964 World Events
Martin Luther King Jr. is awarded the Nobel Peace Prize.

1964 The Arts
Jazz pianist Thelonious Monk is featured on the cover of *Time* magazine.

1966 Politics
The Black Panther Party is founded in Oakland, California.

1966 Science and Technology
African American scientist Meredith Gourdine conducts research on the use of low-grade coal to generate electricity.

1968 Science and Technology
Julian Earls heads NASA's Health Physics Section.

1968 Daily Life
Less than 21 percent of African American students in the former Confederate states attend integrated schools.

1968 Politics
The Kerner Commission releases its report on the urban riots that erupted in several major U.S. cities in 1967.

Thelonious Monk

Before You Read

Build on What You Know

The civil rights movement gained momentum from the Supreme Court's 1954 ruling on school desegregation. The success of the Montgomery Bus Boycott showed the effectiveness of peaceful protest in ending racial discrimination. It also transformed Martin Luther King Jr. into a prominent figure in the struggle for civil rights. In this chapter you will learn how some Americans worked to expand civil rights and equality for all Americans. However, many Americans continued to oppose racial equality.

Think About Themes

To help students create their Themes Journal entries, provide the following examples of appropriate **agree/disagree** *statements.*

Democratic Values

Agree Certain methods of social protest, such as boycotts, have been used in many different regions of the country.

Disagree Support for slavery in the antebellum South, rendered certain forms of social protest, such as abolitionist organizations, largely irrelevant.

Constitutional Heritage

Agree The Antifederalists opposed the creation of a strong central government, arguing in part that local officials best knew the needs of local residents.

Disagree The framers believed that a central government was necessary to promote the public good.

Economic Development

Agree Booker T. Washington urged African Americans to concentrate on gaining economic stability and strength within the larger economic system.

Disagree Certain reformers urged minority groups to withdraw from the larger economic system and organize their own economies.

Famine sufferers in Africa

Hank Aaron

1970
The Arts
Charles Gordone wins a Pulitzer Prize for his play *No Place to Be Somebody.*

1970
World Events
The civil war between Nigeria and the breakaway state of Biafra ends.

1972
Politics
Barbara Jordan of Texas is elected to the U.S. House of Representatives.

1974
Daily Life
Baseball player Hank Aaron breaks Babe Ruth's career home-run record.

1974
World Events
Drought in Africa leads to widespread famine.

1976
World Events
Antiapartheid riots erupt in several major cities in South Africa.

1970 | 1972 | 1974 | 1976 | 1978

1970
Daily Life
Cheryl A. Brown of Iowa becomes the first African American contestant in the Miss America Beauty Pageant.

1972
Science and Technology
George Carruthers assists in the development of an ultraviolet camera that is placed on the moon by the *Apollo 16* crew.

1975
Business and Finance
Wally Amos founds Famous Amos Chocolate Chip Cookies, which achieves sales of more than $5 million by 1980.

1978
Politics
The Supreme Court outlaws racial quotas in education in the case *University of California v. Bakke.*

Cheryl Brown

Famous Amos cookies

exploring the time line

GLOBAL EVENTS

internetconnect

TOPIC: The Independence of the Belgian Congo
GO TO: go.hrw.com
KEYWORD: SE1 Congo

Have students access the Internet through the HRW Web site to conduct research on the independence of the Belgian Congo. Then have each student write an essay that discusses the events surrounding the independence of the Congo from Belgian colonial rule and the problems faced by the new government of the Democratic Republic of Congo.

Think About Themes

Decide whether you **agree** *or* **disagree** *with the following statements. Note why in your journal.*

Democratic Values Methods of social protest that prove effective in one part of the country can be used successfully in all regions of the nation.

Constitutional Heritage Local officials should be solely responsible for enforcing the law.

Economic Development Integration within the larger economic system is the best way for minority groups to improve their standard of living.

621

SECTION 1

After completing Section 1, students should be able to:

OBJECTIVE 1 *Explain how civil rights demonstrators used nonviolence to achieve their goals, and note what the effect was.*

OBJECTIVE 2 *Discuss why civil rights leaders used nonviolent tactics, and explain how protests in Albany, Georgia, and Birmingham, Alabama, differed.*

OBJECTIVE 3 *Analyze why supporters pushed for a civil rights bill, and discuss what factors influenced the bill's passage.*

LET'S GET STARTED!

Write the term *nonviolence* on the chalkboard. As students enter the classroom, ask them to write what they know about the term on a sheet of paper. Ask volunteers for their responses, and write the responses on the chalkboard. Tell students that in Section 1 they will learn how activists used nonviolent protest to achieve social change.

SECTION 1 RESOURCES

PRINT

- Guided Reading Strategy 21.1
- Primary Source Reading 21: James Baldwin: Wordsmith and Social Critic
- Literature Reading 21: Harper Lee's Masterpiece
- Biography Reading 21: Ralph Abernathy
- Section 1 Review, p. 627
- Daily Quiz 21.1

MULTIMEDIA

- One-Stop Planner, Lesson 21.1
- American Music Selection 23: "He's Got the Whole World in His Hands"
- Holt Researcher: American History CD–ROM
- HRW Web site

SHELTERED ENGLISH

- Main Idea Activity for Reteaching and Sheltered English 21.1

✔ READING TO UNDERSTAND
To help students master the section objectives, have them answer the **READING CHECKS** and complete **Guided Reading Strategy 21.1** as they read the section.

Freedom Now!

OBJECTIVES

Read to understand:

1. how civil rights demonstrators used nonviolence to achieve their goals, and what the effect was
2. why civil rights leaders used nonviolent tactics, and how protests in Albany, Georgia, and Birmingham, Alabama, differed
3. why supporters pushed for a civil rights bill, and what factors influenced the bill's passage

KEY TERMS

Southern Christian Leadership Conference
nonviolent resistance
sit-ins
Student Nonviolent Coordinating Committee
Congress of Racial Equality
Freedom Riders
Civil Rights Act of 1964

KEY PEOPLE

Martin Luther King Jr.
T. Eugene Connor
Diane Nash
James Meredith
Medgar Evers
Laurie Pritchett

EYEWITNESSES TO History

"What do we do and to whom do we do it against?"
—Joseph McNeil

The lunch counter where McNeil and his friends protested

Joseph McNeil, an African American student at North Carolina Agricultural and Technical College in Greensboro, pondered such questions as he and three friends discussed ways to protest racial segregation. They were impressed by the courage of the African American students who had integrated the schools in Little Rock, Arkansas, in 1957. They "wanted to make a contribution and be a part of something like that," recalled McNeil. On February 1, 1960, the four students went to a nearby dime store and "sat at a lunch counter where blacks never sat before. And people started to look at us." McNeil recalled that "the help, many of whom were black, looked at us in disbelief too. They were concerned about our safety." The management refused to serve them, but the students returned the following day, vowing to continue their protest until they received service. In this way, McNeil and thousands of other young people across the South worked to bring an end to racial segregation.

Nonviolence in Action

Following the success of the Montgomery Bus Boycott, civil rights leaders met in 1957 in Atlanta to discuss future strategy. They expanded the Montgomery Improvement Association (MIA) into the **Southern Christian Leadership Conference** (SCLC), an alliance of church-based African American organizations dedicated to ending discrimination. Martin Luther King Jr. led the new organization. The SCLC pledged to use **nonviolent resistance** in its protests. Nonviolent resistance required that protesters not resort to violence, even when others attacked them. King called it confronting "the forces of hate with the power of love."

Student protests. Many non-SCLC members soon launched nonviolent protests of their own. In 1958, African American protesters in Oklahoma and Kansas conducted protests at segregated lunch counters. At these **sit-ins**, demonstrators protest by sitting down in a location and refusing to leave. By April 1960 some 50,000 students, both African American and white, were involved in sit-in protests. That month, the leaders of these demonstrations founded the **Student Nonviolent Coordinating Committee** (SNCC), a loose association of student activists from throughout the South.

White response to the sit-ins tested the students' commitment to nonviolence. White onlookers taunted the demonstrators and dumped food and drinks on them. When the harassment turned into physical

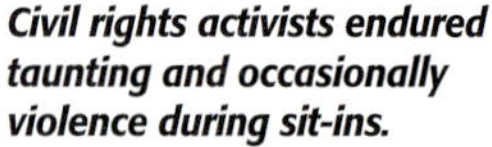
Civil rights activists endured taunting and occasionally violence during sit-ins.

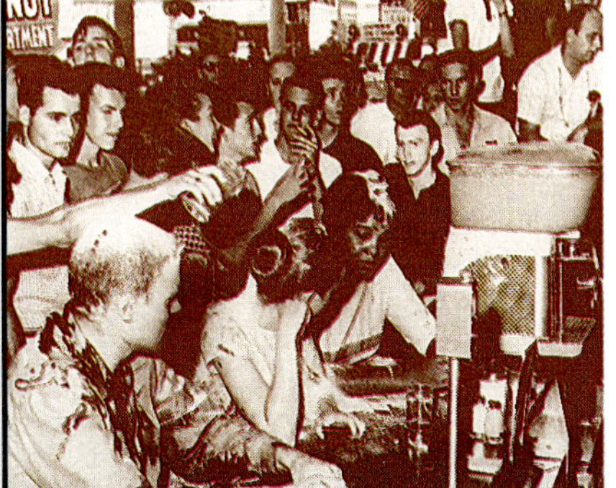

TEACH OBJECTIVE 1

LEVEL 1: Pair students and have each pair create T-shirts to commemorate famous nonviolent protests conducted by civil rights demonstrators. Tell students that the front of each T-shirt should mention the nonviolent action taken. For the back, students should create a slogan to describe the effect of the action. *(Students should note examples of successful nonviolent resistance include sit-ins, which led to the desegregation of lunch counters and restaurants; the march through Birmingham, which led to increased public support for the civil rights movement; the Freedom Rides, which led the Interstate Commerce Commission to strengthen its desegregation regulations; and the Montgomery Bus Boycott, which led to the desegregation of buses in Montgomery, Alabama.)* Have students present their T-shirt designs to the class. **Sheltered English, Cooperative Learning**

LEVELS 2 AND 3: Tell students to imagine that they are television newscasters during the civil rights struggles of the 1960s. Pair students and have each pair prepare an on-location newscast from a civil rights demonstration mentioned in Section 1. Newscasts should describe the nonviolent actions taken by protesters. Newscasts should conclude with a summary of the reasons for the protest and an assessment of the protest's effect. *(See the Level 1 lesson for examples of nonviolent protests and the effects of these protests.)* Have each pair "broadcast" its newscast to the class. **Cooperative Learning**

---

attacks, demonstrators received little assistance from local authorities. When an angry mob beat nonviolent protesters in Nashville, Tennessee, the police ended the confrontation by arresting the protesters. Despite such incidents, the protesters remained committed to nonviolence. The tactic proved effective. Soon many restaurants and other eating establishments across the South had been integrated.

The Freedom Rides. The success of the student sit-ins inspired the **Congress of Racial Equality** (CORE). This northern-based civil rights group hoped to launch new nonviolent protests against racial discrimination. In December 1960 the Supreme Court ruled that segregation in facilities such as bus stations that served interstate travelers was illegal. CORE leaders planned to send an integrated group of **Freedom Riders** on bus trips through the South. They hoped to draw attention to violations of the Supreme Court ruling.

Violence erupted when they crossed the Alabama state line. Outside the town of Anniston, Alabama, a white mob firebombed one of the two buses carrying the activists. They also beat the riders as they tried to escape. The mob then followed the riders to the local hospital to prevent them from receiving medical care.

The Freedom Riders on the other bus were attacked in Birmingham, Alabama. Freedom Rider Walter Bergman, a white man, was beaten so badly that he suffered permanent brain damage. The local police sent no officers to the bus terminal. Birmingham's city commissioner of public safety, T. Eugene "Bull" Connor, blamed the Freedom Riders for the violence. He declared, "I have said for the last 20 years that these out-of-town meddlers were going to cause bloodshed if they kept meddling in the South's business." SNCC leaders moved quickly to find replacement riders for those from CORE.

President John F. Kennedy supported the constitutional rights of the riders to continue their journey. However, he did not want the violence in the South to become an issue in an upcoming meeting with Soviet leader Nikita Khrushchev. Kennedy told his aides to contact civil rights leaders and urge them to end the rides. SNCC refused to comply with the president's request. SNCC leader Diane Nash explained why.

> **"I strongly felt that the future of the movement was going to be cut short if the Freedom Ride had been stopped as a result of violence. The impression would have been given that whenever a movement starts, all you have to do is attack it with massive violence and the blacks will stop."**

SNCC sent the Freedom Riders to Birmingham. There, they were quickly arrested and transported to the state line. The students made their way back to Birmingham. Anxious to prevent further conflict, U.S. Attorney General Robert Kennedy reached an agreement with Alabama's governor, John Patterson. They agreed that the riders would receive protection. The Freedom Riders soon departed from Birmingham. However,

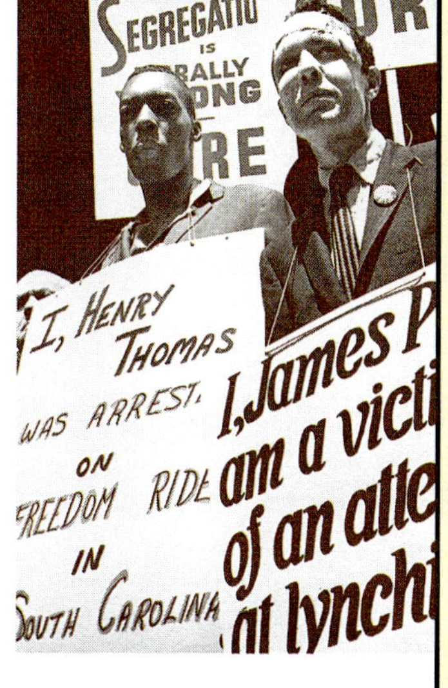

INTERPRETING THE VISUAL RECORD

Violence. Demonstrators like these at a CORE rally often suffered harassment and violence. ***What actions are these two men protesting?***

Freedom Riders regroup outside their bus after it was firebombed in Alabama.

DEMOCRATIC VALUES

Freedom Rides. The Freedom Riders who were arrested in Jackson, Mississippi, were sent to a maximum-security prison. There they tried to keep their spirits up by singing freedom songs. The guards threatened to take their mattresses away if the prisoners kept singing. Freedom Rider Jim Bevel said, "What they're trying to do is take your soul away. It's not the mattress, it's your soul." Another called the guards and said, "Come get my mattress. I'll keep my soul."

CRITICAL THINKING What might Bevel have meant when he said that by taking the mattresses the guards were trying to take the riders' souls?

ANSWER: Students might suggest that Bevel meant that the guards were trying to break the riders' spirits and make them feel demoralized and defeated.

VISUAL RECORD ANSWER

Students might note that the men are protesting a lynching.

TEACH OBJECTIVE 2

LEVEL 1: Pair students and have each pair create two cause-and-effect diagrams to illustrate why civil rights leaders used nonviolent tactics. *(Pairs should mention that nonviolent tactics have the potential to draw attention to a protest by eliciting a violent response from those in power. Nonviolent protest can cause a crisis that forces an otherwise unresponsive opponent to negotiate.)* Have volunteers present and explain their diagrams to the class. Then copy the graphic organizer at right on the chalkboard, omitting the italicized answers. Have students fill in information to compare and contrast the protests in Albany and Birmingham.
Sheltered English, Cooperative Learning

Protest in Albany, Georgia
Protest in Birmingham, Alabama
The police did not resort to violence. The Albany protest was not a success.
Protesters were arrested.
The police attacked protesters. Protesters gained support. The Birmingham protest was a success.

PEOPLE IN HISTORY

James Meredith. James Meredith had served nine years in the air force and nearly completed a degree at the historically black Jackson State College in Jackson, Mississippi, when he decided to apply to the University of Mississippi. Knowing that his application would be rejected, Meredith enlisted the help of civil rights activist Medgar Evers and attorney Thurgood Marshall. Meredith wrote to Marshall, "I am familiar with the probable difficulties involved in such a move as I am undertaking and I am fully prepared to pursue it all the way to a degree from the University of Mississippi." Meredith's subsequent enrollment in the university, with the protection of armed guards, symbolized the commitment of civil rights activists to end segregation.

CRITICAL THINKING What might have convinced Meredith that his application would be rejected?

ANSWER: Students might suggest that Meredith would have known about the tendency of many government officials to disregard federal orders to desegregate.

VISUAL RECORD ANSWER

Students might suggest that James Meredith encountered shock and anger from the white community.

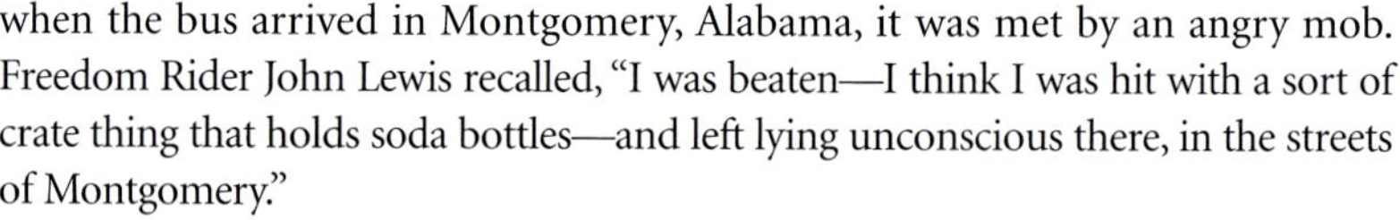

when the bus arrived in Montgomery, Alabama, it was met by an angry mob. Freedom Rider John Lewis recalled, "I was beaten—I think I was hit with a sort of crate thing that holds soda bottles—and left lying unconscious there, in the streets of Montgomery."

President Kennedy finally sent federal marshals to protect the riders. In Jackson, Mississippi, however, state officials arrested the protesters. Hundreds of other activists carried on the protest. In response, Robert Kennedy pressured the Interstate Commerce Commission into strengthening its desegregation regulations. By early 1963 he was able to claim that "in the past year, segregation in interstate commerce has ceased to exist."

✔ **READING CHECK:** How did civil rights demonstrators use nonviolence to achieve their goals? Was it effective?

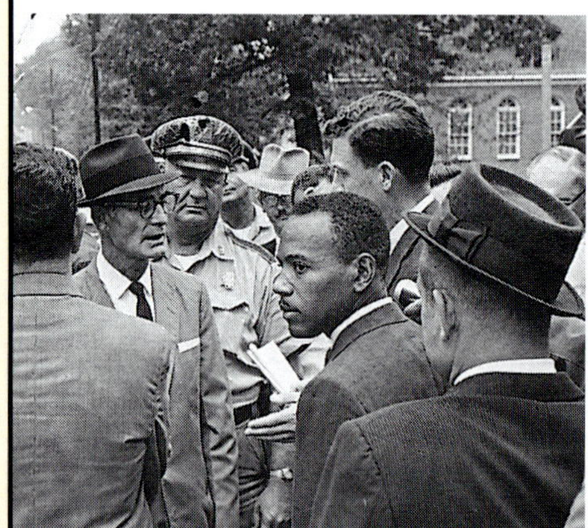

INTERPRETING THE VISUAL RECORD

Integrating universities. The NAACP obtained a court order requiring the University of Mississippi to admit black student James Meredith. ***What type of reaction do you think Meredith encountered?***

Continued Struggles

The Freedom Riders' courage and commitment to nonviolence helped advance their effort to end racial discrimination. However, segregation remained in many areas of southern life, including the South's schools and public facilities.

University of Mississippi. Civil rights activists who worked to open colleges and universities to African American students met with strong opposition. In 1962 the National Association for the Advancement of Colored People (NAACP) obtained a court order. It required the University of Mississippi to admit James Meredith, an African American applicant. Mississippi governor Ross Barnett was defiant. He declared, "No school will be integrated in Mississippi while I am your Governor." Accompanied by two federal officials, Meredith arrived at the campus in September 1962. Barnett personally prevented Meredith from registering.

When word got out on the evening of September 30 that Meredith was on the campus, a riot broke out. President Kennedy ordered army troops to restore order. The outbreak quickly died out, but two people had been killed and 375 injured. Meredith registered the next day and attended classes the rest of the year with the protection of armed guards. He graduated from the university in 1963.

Civil rights activists viewed Meredith's enrollment as a great success. Myrlie Evers recalled, "It was a major breakthrough. It said, indeed, that there is hope, and that we are moving forward and that perhaps the sacrifices that had been made had been worth it." Yet, events elsewhere revealed that the movement for civil rights still faced strong opposition. In 1963 Myrlie Evers's husband, NAACP field secretary Medgar Evers, was killed by a white assassin.

Albany and Birmingham. Nonviolent protests were not always successful. In Albany, Georgia, for example, civil rights organizations held a number of nonviolent protests in 1961. Police Chief Laurie Pritchett was prepared for the demonstrations. He arranged to fill all the jails in the surrounding areas with protesters. Pritchett called his method of law enforcement meeting "nonviolence with nonviolence." He quietly arrested all the protesters.

LEVELS 2 AND 3: Tell students to imagine that they are participants in a roundtable conference entitled The Effectiveness of Nonviolent Protest: Case Studies in Albany, Georgia, and Birmingham, Alabama. Organize the class into two groups. Have one group act as questioners and the other group act as civil rights leaders. Have members of both groups prepare by discussing why civil rights leaders used nonviolent tactics and by contrasting the protests in Albany and Birmingham. *(See the Level 1 lesson for the tactical goals of nonviolent protest and the outcomes of the Albany and Birmingham protests.)* Then conduct the conference. **Cooperative Learning**

TEACH OBJECTIVE 3

LEVEL 1: Tell students to imagine that they are newspaper reporters assigned to cover the passage of the Civil Rights Act of 1964. Pair students and have each pair write headlines explaining why supporters pushed for a civil rights bill and what circumstances were factors in the bill's passage. *(Pairs should mention that supporters believed that federal civil rights legislation—enforced by the federal government—was necessary to give all Americans equal access to educational facilities, public services, and employment. Events in Birmingham, the success of the March on Washington, and the support of Presidents Kennedy and Johnson were factors in the bill's passage.)* **Sheltered English, Cooperative Learning**

Hoping to revive the Albany protests, Martin Luther King Jr. allowed himself to be arrested and jailed. However, Pritchett simply released him. Without a violent incident to draw the attention of the news media, the Albany movement stalled out.

This experience taught SCLC leaders that progress would come only when racists responded to peaceful demonstrations with violence. As the SCLC's Bayard Rustin later noted, "Protest becomes an effective tactic to the degree that it elicits [brings forth] brutality and oppression from the power structure."

After the events in Albany, the SCLC focused its attention on Birmingham. Protesting in Birmingham meant danger and possibly even death. Ralph David Abernathy later explained the civil rights activists' strategy.

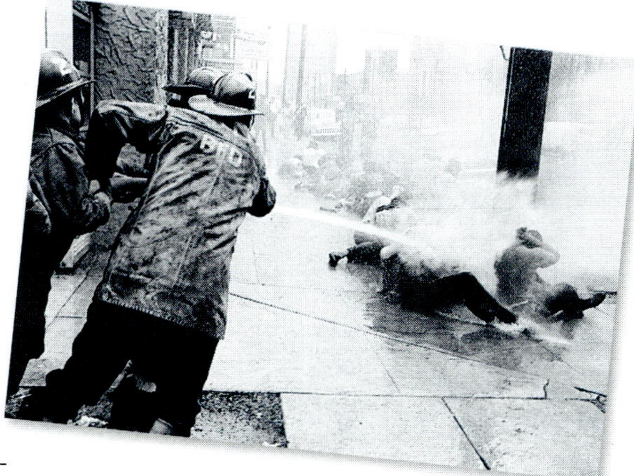

To break up the nonviolent civil rights rally in Birmingham, city firefighters turned their water hoses on protesters.

> **"As for [police chief] Bull Connor and the City of Birmingham, it was true that they constituted the hardest and most mean-spirited establishment in the South. Yet if we beat them on their own home grounds, we might be able to prove to the entire region that it was useless to resist desegregation, that its time had finally come. To win in Birmingham might well be to win in the rest of the nation. So in the long run the gamble [of confronting violence in Birmingham] might actually save time and lives in our struggle for equality."**

In April 1963 the SCLC began a series of boycotts, marches, and sit-ins to protest Birmingham's segregation laws. The protests initially drew hundreds of participants. Many were jailed after violating a judge's order that banned further demonstrations. However, as weeks passed, the number of demonstrators willing to go to jail declined. By the end of April the Birmingham protests seemed likely to end in failure.

To save the Birmingham protest, James Bevel and other SCLC leaders suggested using schoolchildren in the demonstrations. Bevel later recalled, "A boy from high school, he can get the same effect in terms of being in jail, in terms of putting pressure on the city, as his father—and yet there is no economic threat on the family because the father is

★ HISTORICAL DOCUMENTS ★

MARTIN LUTHER KING JR.

Letter from Birmingham Jail

While confined in a Birmingham jail in 1963, Martin Luther King Jr. wrote to a group of clergymen who had urged him to slow down his protests. The letter was widely published by newspapers. It offered an eloquent response to critics who questioned the need for protests against racism.

You may well ask: "Why direct action? Why sit-ins, marches, and so forth? Isn't negotiation a better path?" You are quite right in calling for negotiation. Indeed, this is the very purpose of direct action. Nonviolent direct action seeks to create such a crisis and foster such a tension that a community which has constantly refused to negotiate is forced to confront the issue. . . . I have earnestly opposed violent tension, but there is a type of constructive, nonviolent tension which is necessary for growth. . . .

We know through painful experience that freedom is never voluntarily given by the oppressor; it must be demanded by the oppressed. Frankly, I have yet to engage in a direct-action campaign that was "well timed" in the view of those who have not suffered unduly from the disease of segregation. For years now I have heard the word "Wait!" It rings in the ear of every Negro with piercing familiarity. This "Wait" has almost always meant "Never." We must come to see, with one of our distinguished jurists, that "justice too long delayed is justice denied."

CONSTITUTIONAL HERITAGE

The Governors. Governor George Wallace of Alabama and Governor Ross Barnett of Mississippi became well known for defending segregation. In widely publicized speeches and writings, Wallace and Barnett challenged northern politicians by referring to segregation in northern cities and schools. Barnett argued, "The big difference is that we are honest about segregation in Mississippi and we intend to remain honest, law abiding and segregated." In his 1963 inaugural address in Alabama, Wallace characterized the federal government's actions as "tyranny." Wallace said, "In the name of the greatest people that ever trod the earth, I draw the line in the dust and toss the gauntlet before the feet of tyranny . . . and I say . . . segregation now . . . segregation tomorrow . . . segregation forever."

CRITICAL THINKING Why might Wallace have used the word *tyranny* in his speech?

ANSWER: Students might mention that Wallace's words would have evoked powerful memories of the Civil War and Revolutionary War ideals of freedom from tyranny.

LEVEL 2: Tell students to imagine that they are civil rights workers in 1964. Have each student write a series of journal entries discussing why supporters pushed for a civil rights bill and what factors led to the bill's passage. *(See the Level 1 lesson for why supporters believed that a civil rights bill was necessary and factors leading to the bill's passage.)* Have volunteers read their entries to the class.

LEVEL 3: Tell students to imagine that they are analysts appearing on a weekly television news program shortly after the passage of the Civil Rights Act of 1964. Organize students into triads. Have each triad write a brief dialogue about why supporters pushed for a civil rights bill and what factors led to the bill's passage. *(See the Level 1 lesson for why supporters believed that a civil rights bill was necessary and factors leading to the bill's passage.)* Have volunteers perform their dialogues for the class. **Cooperative Learning**

▶ASSIGNMENT *Have students write a poem or song that explains the need for the Civil Rights Bill of 1964.*

internet**connect**

TOPIC: March on Washington
GO TO: go.hrw.com
KEYWORD: SE1 March

Have students access the Internet through the HRW Web site to conduct research on the March on Washington in August 1963. Then ask students to imagine that they are radio commentators. Have each student write a news broadcast describing the march and some of the speeches, including Martin Luther King Jr.'s "I Have a Dream" speech.

VISUAL RECORD ANSWER

Students might argue that the march leaders managed to meet with the president, demonstrating that civil rights was an important political issue.

Multimedia Resources

American Music Selection 23: "He's Got the Whole World in His Hands"

SECTION 1 REVIEW ANSWERS

Define and Identify

For significance, see the following pages:

- Southern Christian Leadership Conference, p. 622
- Martin Luther King Jr., p. 622
- nonviolent resistance, p. 622
- sit-ins, p. 622
- Student Nonviolent Coordinating Committee, p. 622

INTERPRETING THE VISUAL RECORD

March on Washington. During the 1963 March on Washington, African American leaders met with President John F. Kennedy. ***Based on this photograph, would you conclude that the march leaders were successful in bringing civil rights issues to the forefront of U.S. politics in 1963? Explain your answer.***

still on the job." King was initially reluctant to place young people in danger. In the end, however, he supported Bevel's plan.

On May 2 more than 1,000 youths marched in Birmingham's streets. Police arrested some 600 students that day. When the protests continued the following day, Bull Connor ordered the police to attack the marchers. The police used dogs, fire hoses, and nightsticks against protesters. Public support for the civil rights movement increased when scenes of these attacks appeared in newspapers and on television.

✔ **READING CHECK:** Why did civil rights leaders use nonviolent tactics, and how did the protests in Albany, Georgia, and Birmingham, Alabama, differ?

The Civil Rights Act of 1964

The events in Birmingham forced President Kennedy to take a stand on civil rights. Most of his aides feared such a move would split the Democratic Party and ruin Kennedy's chances for re-election in 1964. Nevertheless, the president moved forward. In the summer of 1963, Kennedy asked Congress "to enact legislation giving all Americans the right to be served in facilities which are open to the public."

The March on Washington. To build public support for the civil rights movement, African American leaders organized a huge march on Washington, D.C. More than 200,000 people gathered together at the Lincoln Memorial on August 28, 1963. Many musicians and speakers from diverse backgrounds celebrated the struggle for civil rights. The director of the march, 74-year-old A. Philip Randolph, opened the ceremonies, testifying to the long struggle for civil rights. Other speakers included SNCC's John Lewis and Rabbi Joachim Prinz of the American Jewish Congress.

BIOGRAPHY

Martin Luther King Jr.

Martin Luther King Jr. gave the final speech. It would mark one of the highlights of his civil rights career. Born on January 15, 1929, in Atlanta, King was the son of a Baptist minister. He received a degree from Morehouse College in 1948. King then attended the integrated Crozer Theological Seminary in Chester, Pennsylvania. There, he excelled in his studies of religion and philosophy. As a seminary student King became familiar with the Social Gospel movement, which encouraged Christians to become involved in social reform. He was also exposed to the thinking of Mohandas K. Gandhi, the nonviolent leader of India's independence movement.

King's love of learning led him to pursue a doctorate at Boston University. There, he met and married Coretta Scott. In 1954 King accepted a position at Dexter Avenue Baptist Church in Montgomery. He soon became involved in the civil rights movement and helped to organize the Montgomery Bus Boycott.

King often faced violence and abuse. In January 1956 his home was bombed, and his wife and young child narrowly escaped injury. His personal courage and commitment to nonviolence soon made him the leading civil rights activist in the eyes of most white Americans.

HOLT RESEARCHER

Read More About It

Free Find:
Martin Luther King Jr.

After reading about Martin Luther King Jr. on the **Holt Researcher** CD–ROM, write a short essay that describes the significance of his "I Have a Dream" speech.

REVIEW

Have students complete the **Section 1 Review** on p. 627.

ASSESS

Have students complete **Daily Quiz 21.1**. As **Alternative Assessment**, you may want to use the T-shirts or the dialogue in this section's lessons.

RETEACH

Have students complete **Main Idea Activity for Reteaching and Sheltered English 21.1**. Have students work in groups, with each student in the group outlining a subsection. Have members of the group exchange outlines and use the outlines to quiz each other. **Sheltered English, Cooperative Learning**

EXTEND

Organize the class into four groups and have each group conduct research on one of the following people: Medgar Evers, Martin Luther King Jr., John Lewis, or James Meredith. After completing the research, members of each group should present an oral report about their subject's activities and contributions to the civil rights movement.
Block Scheduling, Cooperative Learning

King's "I Have a Dream" speech at the March on Washington rally in 1963 has become one of the most famous addresses in American history. King spoke of his vision of what the United States could and should be.

> **"I have a dream that one day this nation will rise up and live out the true meaning of its creed: 'We hold these truths to be self-evident; that all men are created equal. . . . When we let freedom ring, when we let it ring from every village and every hamlet [small town], from every state and every city, we will be able to speed up that day when all of God's children, black men and white men, Jews and Gentiles, Protestants and Catholics, will be able to join hands and sing in the words of the old Negro spiritual, 'Free at last! Free at last! Thank God Almighty, we are free at last!'"**

President Lyndon Johnson signed the Civil Rights Act into law in 1964 in the presence of civil rights leaders including Martin Luther King Jr.

The act passes. The success of the March on Washington raised the hopes of civil rights workers everywhere. However, their joy was short-lived. In September a bomb exploded in a Birmingham church and killed four young African American girls. Then, in November 1963, President Kennedy was assassinated. The future of civil rights legislation, which had stalled in Congress, was unclear.

The new president, Lyndon Johnson, strongly supported passage of a civil rights bill. Several southern members of Congress worked hard to kill the legislation. The House of Representatives approved the bill in February 1964. The Senate debated the measure for 75 days before passing it by a vote of 73 to 27. Johnson signed the bill into law on July 2, 1964, more than a year after Kennedy's speech calling for federal legislation. The **Civil Rights Act of 1964** banned discrimination in employment and in public accommodations. The act gave the Justice Department the power to bring lawsuits to enforce school desegregation.

✔ **READING CHECK:** Why did supporters push for a civil rights bill, and what factors influenced the bill's passage?

SECTION  REVIEW

Define and explain the significance of the following terms:
Southern Christian Leadership Conference
nonviolent resistance
sit-ins
Student Nonviolent Coordinating Committee
Congress of Racial Equality
Freedom Riders
Civil Rights Act of 1964

Identify and explain the significance of the following individuals:
Martin Luther King Jr.
T. Eugene Connor
Diane Nash
James Meredith
Medgar Evers
Laurie Pritchett

1. **Using Graphic Organizers** Copy the chart below. Use it to explain different civil rights initiatives in the early 1960s.

Protest	Goal	Outcome
Student Sit-Ins		
Freedom Rides		
Birmingham Protest		
March on Washington		

2. **Analyzing** Why did Martin Luther King Jr. and other leaders support nonviolence as a strategy for civil rights demonstrations?
3. **Recognizing Point of View** Why was President Kennedy reluctant to use federal authority to resolve conflicts over civil rights in the South?
4. **Comparing and Contrasting** In what ways were Bull Connor and Laurie Pritchett similar? How did they differ in their responses to demonstrators?

Critical Thinking

5. What factors do you think led President Kennedy to introduce civil rights legislation in 1963?
Consider:
- the constitutional issues involved
- King's strategy in Birmingham
- the media's role in Birmingham

- Congress of Racial Equality, p. 623
- Freedom Riders, p. 623
- T. Eugene Connor, p. 623
- Diane Nash, p. 623
- James Meredith, p. 624
- Medgar Evers, p. 624
- Laurie Pritchett, p. 624
- Civil Rights Act of 1964, p. 627

1. sit-ins—to integrate lunch counters, within a year some lunch counters were integrated; Freedom Rides—to integrate facilities serving interstate travelers in the South, eventually the ICC strengthened desegregation regulations; Birmingham protest—to protest segregation, increased support for the civil rights movement; March on Washington—to demonstrate the movement's support, raised spirits of activists

2. The protests contrasted the love and compassion of the protesters with the anger of the social structure they were protesting against.

3. He did not want the country to appear divided when he met with Khrushchev. He also may have worried about damaging his chances of winning the next election.

4. They were similar in their determination to defeat the protesters; however, Connor reacted in anger and Pritchett's reaction was more calculated and effective.

5. Answers will vary. Some students might mention his desire for equality or his desire to bolster the nation's global image.

SECTION 2

After completing Section 2, students should be able to:

OBJECTIVE 1 *Explain why early efforts to register voters in Mississippi failed.*

OBJECTIVE 2 *Relate why the Freedom Summer project met with limited success.*

OBJECTIVE 3 *Discuss how the Mississippi Freedom Democratic Party affected relations between civil rights activists and the federal government.*

OBJECTIVE 4 *Describe how the Selma protest led to the passage of the Voting Rights Act.*

LET'S GET STARTED!

Copy a voter registration card and place it on an overhead transparency. Project the voter registration card for students and ask them to identify the various parts. *(Students might mention the federal congressional district, state district, township, and so on.)* Discuss each political district with students and explain that being registered to vote is a fundamental right for citizens of a democracy. Tell students that in Section 2 they will learn about efforts to register African American voters in the South.

SECTION 2 RESOURCES

PRINT
- Guided Reading Strategy 21.2
- Geography Activity 21: The Civil Rights Movement
- Graphic Organizer Activity 21: In the Words of the Leaders
- American History Outline Map 21: Desegregation
- Section 2 Review, p. 632
- Daily Quiz 21.2

MULTIMEDIA
- One-Stop Planner, Lesson 21.2
- Holt Researcher: American History CD–ROM

SHELTERED ENGLISH
- Main Idea Activity for Reteaching and Sheltered English 21.2

✔ READING TO UNDERSTAND
To help students master the section objectives, have them answer the **READING CHECKS** and complete **Guided Reading Strategy 21.2** as they read the section.

Voting Rights

OBJECTIVES

Read to understand:
1. why early efforts to register voters in Mississippi failed
2. why the Freedom Summer project met with limited success
3. how the Mississippi Freedom Democratic Party affected relations between the civil rights activists and the federal government
4. how the Selma protest led to the passage of the Voting Rights Act

KEY TERMS

Council of Federated Organizations
Freedom Summer
Mississippi Freedom Democratic Party
Voting Rights Act

KEY PEOPLE

Robert Moses
Andrew Goodman
James Chaney
Michael Schwerner
Fannie Lou Hamer

Volunteers help black Mississippians register to vote.

"I just didn't see how the Negroes in Madison County could be so badly off."
—Anne Moody

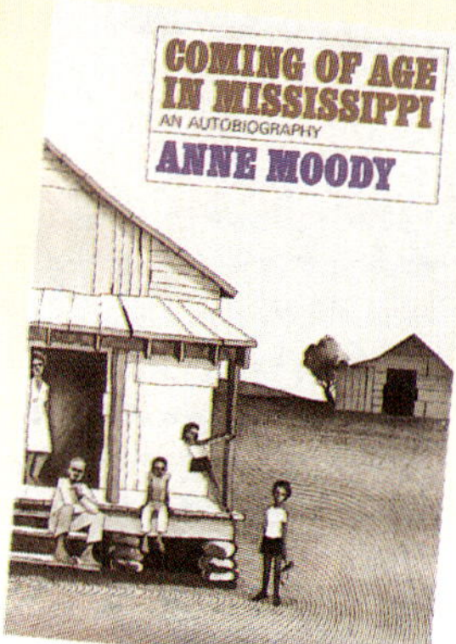

The cover of Anne Moody's autobiography

Anne Moody was a young African American woman who lived in Mississippi during the 1950s. She recalled her reaction to the economic and political status of African American farmers in Madison County, Mississippi. African Americans outnumbered the county's white residents three to one. However, only about 200 of the some 29,000 African Americans in the county were registered to vote. Moody hoped to change that by working in a voter registration drive sponsored by CORE. She quickly learned why life in Madison County was so hard for African Americans. She remembered that after a month, "we had only been able to send a handful of Negroes to the courthouse to attempt to register and those few who went began to get fired from their jobs." Moody also explained that the CORE workers "were constantly being threatened." Moody's experiences revealed the difficulties that civil rights workers faced as they organized voter registration drives in the South.

Registering Voters

While civil rights demonstrators used nonviolent protests to bring an end to racial segregation, other activists focused their attention on voter registration. The Kennedy administration had been troubled by the Freedom Rides and other protests that resulted in violence. However, it supported the voter registration efforts. As Robert Kennedy later recalled, "I felt nobody could really oppose voting. It was not like school desegregation with people saying, 'We don't want our little blond daughter going to school with a Negro.'" However, Kennedy underestimated the extent of opposition to African American suffrage in the South.

Mississippi. Civil rights activists focused their efforts on promoting voter registration in Mississippi, where African Americans were often denied their voting rights. African Americans made up some 40 percent of the state's population, but just 5 percent of eligible black adults were registered to vote. Many counties did not have a single registered African American voter. Literacy tests, which included interpreting portions of the state constitution, were one means used to prevent African Americans from registering.

Mississippi had a history of racial violence—at least 33 lynchings occurred between 1939 and 1950. Still, civil rights organizers believed that it was the best place to carry out their plans. As SNCC organizer John Lewis later argued, "If we can crack Mississippi, we will likely be able to crack the system in the rest of the country."

SNCC's Robert Moses selected McComb, Mississippi, a town of some 12,000 citizens. With just 250 registered African Americans, it would be the site of his first effort

TEACH OBJECTIVES 1 AND 2

ALL LEVELS: To help students understand the failure of early efforts to register voters in Mississippi and the limited success of the Freedom Summer project, copy the graphic organizer at right on the chalkboard, omitting the italicized answers. Pair students and have each pair complete the chart. When students have completed their charts, tell them to imagine that it is the fall of 1964 and that they are SNCC volunteers who have been involved in voter registration drives in Mississippi for the past four years. Ask each student to write a letter to a friend or family member explaining the failure of early efforts to register voters in Mississippi and the limited success of the Freedom Summer project. Ask volunteers to read their letters to the class. **Sheltered English, Cooperative Learning**

Reasons for the Failure of Voter Registration Efforts in Mississippi and the Limited Success of Freedom Summer

Voter Registration in Mississippi	Freedom Summer
1. *murder of Herbert Lee/violence against African Americans* **2.** *violence against SNCC volunteers* **3.** *arrest of student demonstrators in McComb, Mississippi* **4.** *arson at SNCC office*	**1.** *murders of James Chaney, Andrew Goodman, and Michael Schwerner* **2.** *fear of violence against African Americans*

to register black voters. He arrived in July 1961. By mid-August he had helped six African Americans to register to vote. However, this modest success drew the attention of white officials who were determined to stop him. In less than a month's time, Moses was jailed, released, beaten by the sheriff's cousin, and chased by an angry mob.

The violence increased in September. Herbert Lee, a farmer who had driven Moses around the area, was murdered by a member of the Mississippi state legislature. Despite evidence to the contrary, a jury ruled that the killing had been committed in self-defense. Less than two weeks after Lee's death, local high school students held a protest march. Demonstrator Hollis Watkins later recalled the risks associated with civil rights activities.

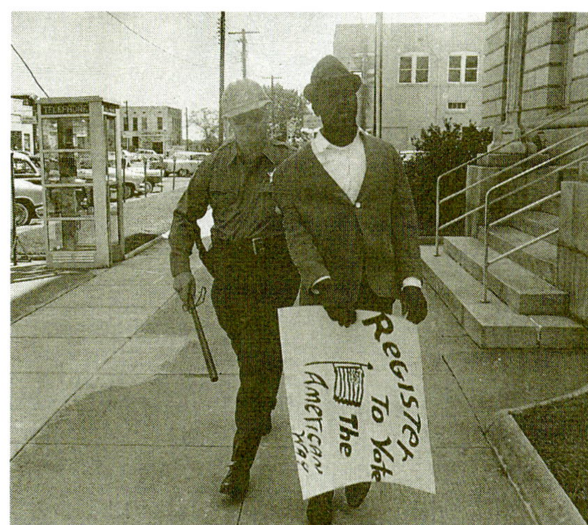

INTERPRETING THE VISUAL RECORD

Voting. Many activists who tried to register African Americans to vote faced harassment. ***How does the message on this activist's sign contrast with the way he is being treated?***

> **"One thing I risked—and did face—was being ostracized [banished] by my family. . . . My relatives would see me walking down the street and then they would pass over on to the other side rather than meet me on the street. Because they was afraid of what white people might do to them because they were my relatives. . . . In addition to that, I put on the line the whole thing of being able to ever get a job in Mississippi. . . . Or whether that mark would go through onto my children and their children—or onto my mother and father."**

Moses and other SNCC workers accompanied the protesters. Police officers arrested the students. Meanwhile, a mob attacked the SNCC workers, who were then also arrested. The voter registration drive in McComb came to an end with fewer than 24 new voters on the rolls.

Renewed efforts. The difficulties facing civil rights workers in McComb did not stop efforts to register African American voters, however. Several civil rights organizations, including SNCC and SCLC, established the **Council of Federated Organizations** (COFO) to coordinate voter registration drives. The Voter Education Project provided money from private foundations to fund registration projects.

The abuse from state and local officials and mob violence continued as activists helped African Americans in Mississippi and other southern states to register to vote. SNCC's Ivanhoe Donaldson recalled, "Fear was always a major reality that you had to live with. . . . Almost every organizer in the Deep South was constantly faced with harassment. They'd been beaten, they'd been shot at." The SNCC office in Greenwood, Mississippi, was burned to the ground. Despite the bloodshed, few officials from the Kennedy administration offered assistance.

The ongoing violence frightened many African Americans. Many refused to attempt to register. A year-long registration drive in Leflore County netted just 50 new voters. Nonetheless, many African Americans in Mississippi still hoped to become voters one day. In 1963 COFO conducted two mock elections in which anyone could vote, even if they were not registered. Some 27,000 African Americans voted in the first mock election, and some 80,000—four times the number of registered black voters in the state—voted in the second election. The "freedom

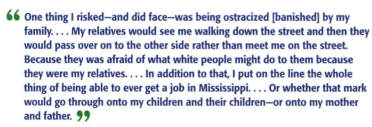

Voter registration was an important weapon in the fight for civil rights.

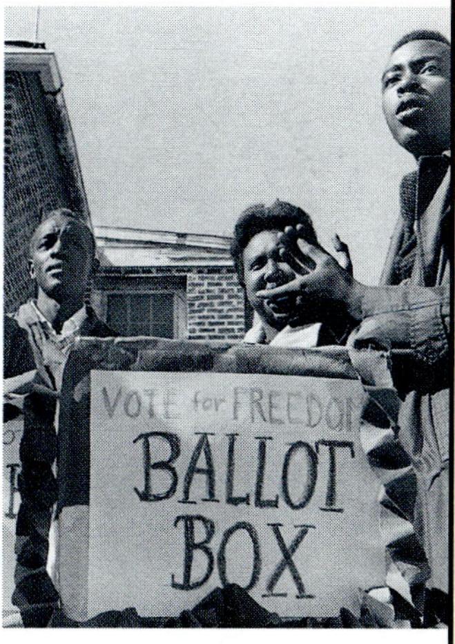

PEOPLE IN HISTORY

Robert Moses. Robert Moses was working at a New York private school when he first heard of the sit-ins in the South. He instantly felt a connection with the demonstrators. Moses went to Mississippi where he became the SNCC field secretary and began a drive to register African American voters. Moses was a good leader for the Mississippi movement, maintaining calm in the face of frightening circumstances. One of the white students working with Moses during Freedom Summer remembered, "Bob Moses stood out for everybody. He was an incredibly strong figure. He was calm. He was effective. What he said made sense, and you wanted to do what he said should be done."

CRITICAL THINKING Why might the Mississippi movement have needed a calm leader?

ANSWER: Students might suggest that because of the constant harassment and danger, the movement needed a leader who would not react in anger or desperation and who could inspire the other workers.

VISUAL RECORD ANSWER

Students might suggest that the activist has gotten in trouble for attempting to exercise his right to free speech and the vote.

ASSIGNMENT *Referring to the recruitment of white volunteers to help register black voters, Robert Moses said, "It changes the whole complexion of what you're doing, so it isn't any longer a question of Negro fighting white. It's a question of rational people fighting against irrational people." Ask students to write a short essay explaining what Moses might have meant. Ask volunteers to read their essays to the class.*

TEACH OBJECTIVE 3

LEVEL 1: Pair students and have each pair write a paragraph based on the following questions: Who helped create the Mississippi Freedom Democratic Party? *(Pairs should note that the Council of Federated Organizations helped to create the MFDP.)* Why was the MFDP created? *(Pairs should indicate that the party was created after Mississippi's 1964 Democratic convention rejected all African American candidates.)* What was the goal of the MFDP delegation to the Democratic National Convention, and what happened to the delegation at the convention? *(Pairs' responses should mention that the MFDP delegates wanted to be recognized instead of the regular state delegation. Instead, the delegates were offered two token seats.)* How did civil rights activists' views of the Democratic Party change after the MFDP's experience at the Democratic National Convention? *(Students should note that activists concluded that the Democratic Party could no longer be trusted to advance their interests.)* Have volunteers read their paragraphs to the class. **Sheltered English, Cooperative Learning**

GEOGRAPHIC DIVERSITY

Freedom Summer and Its Lessons. Many Freedom Summer volunteers wrote about the hard lessons they learned about race, poverty, and the law. Realizing they were in constant danger, the volunteers learned "to live with fear as a condition, like heat or night." For students who had always trusted the police and the government, it was disheartening to learn, as one volunteer put it, that "the instruments of the law and the institutions of the law are your enemy." Aside from their new attention to safety, the volunteers learned about poverty. "I've been to hundreds of houses I could kick down with my feet and a small hammer," wrote one volunteer. Another realized "how much it took to be a Negro in Mississippi twelve months a year for a lifetime."

ACTIVITY: Have students imagine that they are Freedom Summer volunteers risking danger in order to help African Americans register to vote. Have them write diary entries about what they witness or how their work makes them feel.

Freedom Summer Workers

Peter Orris was a white teenager in his freshman year at Harvard University when he decided to volunteer for the Freedom Summer project. He later recalled, "At eighteen years old, to be able to be involved in this kind of a struggle was very important to me."

Orris attended volunteer training sessions in Ohio, where "we playacted situations where angry groups of people, mobs, would be attacking us and how we would handle ourselves in that situation." Orris was assigned to a voter registration drive in Mileston, Mississippi. He recalled, "We were much younger than many of the people we were speaking to, and it was necessary to establish a relationship or an understanding of the respect that we paid to them for their age and their situation." Despite such efforts, African Americans were often reluctant to talk to volunteers. "We knew we were not getting [our message] across, we knew they were just waiting for us to go away because we were a danger to them, and in many ways we were." Orris remembered, "We had much less to risk than they did. This was their lives, their land, their family, and they were going to be here when we were gone."

Freedom Summer volunteers

elections" introduced many African Americans to voting procedures and revealed the deep interest that many unregistered voters had in exercising their rights.

✔ **READING CHECK:** Why did early efforts to register voters in Mississippi fail?

A New Approach

In November 1963, SNCC workers learned that the Voter Education Project was unable to fund voter registration drives in Mississippi. At a meeting later that month, SNCC leaders debated a new strategy. Robert Moses suggested bringing a large number of white volunteers into the voter registration efforts. Moses noted, "It changes the whole complexion of what you're doing, so it isn't any longer Negro fighting white. It's a question of rational people fighting against irrational people." Several SNCC members opposed the new strategy. MacArthur Cotton argued, "We've got too much to lose if . . . [white volunteers] come down here and create a disturbance in two or three months, and they're gone."

Freedom Summer. Despite such objections, SNCC decided to implement Moses's plan, known as **Freedom Summer**, in 1964. That spring, SNCC recruited volunteers on university campuses in the northern states. The volunteers attended training classes in Ohio before heading to Mississippi. Lawyers and health-care professionals also took part in the project, offering legal and medical assistance to the civil rights workers.

Andrew Goodman, a college student from New York, arrived in Mississippi on June 20. The following day Goodman and two CORE workers, James Chaney and Michael Schwerner, disappeared. Their bodies were discovered six weeks later, buried in an earthen dam. The murders of Goodman and Schwerner, both of whom were white, shocked Americans in a way that the murders of African Americans had not. President Johnson ordered the Federal Bureau of Investigation (FBI) to investigate the killings. Stunned volunteers carried on. Fearing that they would also become victims of violence, however, many African Americans refused to register. By the end of the summer, just 1,600 African Americans had been added to the voting rolls.

Despite the limited gains, Freedom Summer changed the lives of many African Americans in Mississippi. Unita Blackwell recalled her experiences with Freedom Summer.

> **"For black people in Mississippi, Freedom Summer was the beginning of a whole new era. People began to feel that they wasn't just helpless anymore, that they had come together. . . . Students came and we wasn't a closed society anymore. They came to talk about that we had a right to register to**

LEVELS 2 AND 3: Tell students to imagine that they are members of the MFDP after the Democratic National Convention in 1964. Have each student write a position paper for the MFDP that outlines why the MFDP was created, and how the MFDP's experience at the national convention changed many civil rights activists' views toward President Johnson and the Democratic Party. *(See the Level 1 lesson for the correct reasons.)* Ask volunteers to read their papers to the class.

TEACH OBJECTIVE 4

LEVEL 1: Tell students to imagine that they were participants in the Selma protest. Have each student write a short memoir about the protest and how those events led to the passage of the Voting Rights Act of 1965. *(Students' memoirs will vary but should note the following: the Selma police's attack on marchers outraged many Americans. Thousands of people went to Montgomery to show support for the marchers. President Johnson was also shocked by the attack and asked Congress to pass a voting rights bill.)* **Sheltered English**

LEVELS 2 AND 3: Tell students to imagine that they are editors who are compiling an encyclopedia of the civil rights movement. Ask each student to write a brief entry on the Selma protest and how it led to the passage of the Voting Rights Act of 1965. *(See the Level 1 lesson for how events during the Selma protest led to the passage of the Voting Rights Act.)* Ask volunteers to read their entries to the class.

---

vote, we had a right to stand up for our rights. . . . I mean, hadn't anybody said that to us, in that open way, like what happened in 1964. ”

✔ **READING CHECK:** Why did the Freedom Summer project meet with limited success?

Political organization. In addition to conducting voter registration drives, COFO leaders worked to place African Americans on Mississippi's delegation to the Democratic National Convention. The convention was to be held in Atlantic City, New Jersey, in August 1964. When a state party convention rejected all African American candidates, COFO helped create the **Mississippi Freedom Democratic Party** (MFDP). The MFDP formed its own delegation. Fannie Lou Hamer, an African American who had lost her job and her house when she registered to vote in 1962, was among the MFDP delegates.

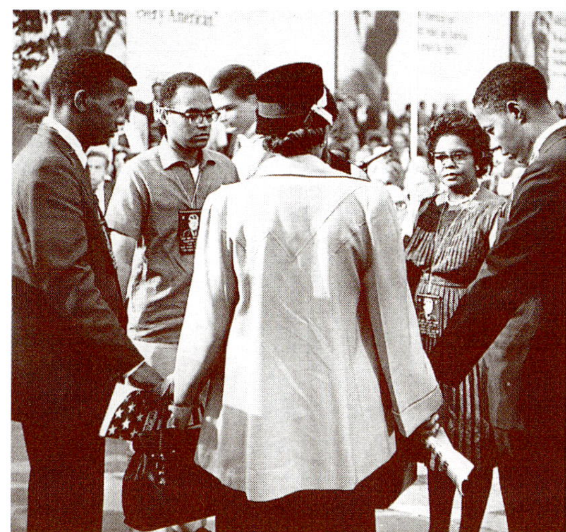

Facing the disappointment of not being recognized by the Democratic National Convention, Mississippi Freedom Democratic Party members join hands in prayer.

The MFDP delegation traveled to Atlantic City. There, they requested that the national convention recognize the MFDP rather than the regular state delegation. The MFDP delegates believed that they should be recognized because so many black Mississippians had been prevented from voting. President Johnson, who wanted the convention to proceed smoothly, worked behind the scenes to grant the MFDP recognition without making it the official delegation. In the end, the MFDP delegates were offered two token seats. The MFDP rejected this compromise as an insult. MFDP delegate Victoria Gray later explained the MFDP decision.

> **“ Those who are unable to understand why we were unable to accept that compromise did not realize that we would have been betraying the many people back there in Mississippi whom we represented. They had not only laid their lives on the line, but many had given their lives in order for this particular event to happen. ”**

Johnson's actions led many activists to conclude that he and the Democratic Party could no longer be trusted to advance their interests.

✔ **READING CHECK:** How did the Mississippi Freedom Democratic Party affect relations between civil rights activists and the federal government?

Selma and the Voting Rights Act

In early 1965, civil rights workers launched a registration drive in Selma, Alabama. Of Selma's 15,000 eligible African Americans, just 383 were registered voters. The activists invited Martin Luther King Jr., who had won the Nobel Peace Prize the previous year, to lead them. The attempts of African Americans to register at election commission offices in the Selma area met with beatings and arrests. Civil rights leaders responded by calling for a protest march from Selma to Montgomery. Governor George Wallace immediately banned the protest.

Despite the governor's opposition, some 600 people began the 50-mile trek on Sunday, March 7. Just outside Selma, police attacked the marchers. An eight-year-old girl taking part in the march recalled that "some of them had clubs, others had

INTERPRETING THE VISUAL RECORD

Selma. This issue of *Life* magazine reached newsstands the week after the civil rights march outside Selma turned violent. ***Based on this cover, what group do you believe the article favored, the civil rights marchers or the Selma police? Explain your answer.***

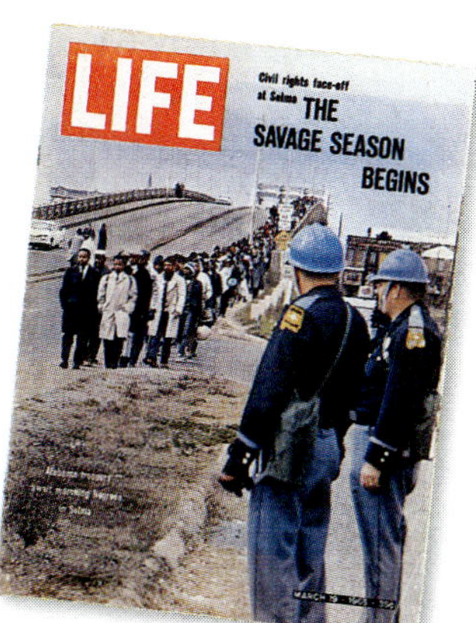

THAT'S INTERESTING!

White SNCC workers in Mississippi were frustrated when African Americans were suspicious of them because they were white. Many African Americans would not answer their doors or would agree with whatever the white worker said. Workers had to beg the potential voters to call them by their first names. One worker said that if he wrote a book about his experiences, he would title it "Don't Call Me Mister."

VISUAL RECORD ANSWER

Students might suggest that the title implies impending violence on the part of the Selma, Alabama, police, thus favoring the marchers.

MAP ANSWER
(for p. 632)
Alabama and Mississippi

REVIEW

Have students complete the **Section 2 Review** on p. 632.

ASSESS

Have students complete **Daily Quiz 21.2.** As **Alternative Assessment**, you may want to use the memoir or the encyclopedia entry in this section's lessons.

RETEACH

Have students complete **Main Idea Activity for Reteaching and Sheltered English 21.2.** Organize students into small groups. Each group should create a poster summarizing the information in a subsection. Have each group present its poster to the class. **Sheltered English, Cooperative Learning**

EXTEND

Provide students with excerpts from the Voting Rights Act of 1965. Pair students and ask each pair to study the excerpts and create a chart that outlines the provisions of the act, the circumstances *(e.g., Jim Crow laws)* that the provision is addressing, and how the provisions are to be implemented. Ask students to present and discuss their work with the class.
Block Scheduling, Cooperative Learning

SECTION 2 REVIEW ANSWERS

Define and Identify
For significance, see the following pages:

- Robert Moses, p. 628
- Council of Federated Organizations, p. 629
- Freedom Summer, p. 630
- Andrew Goodman, p. 630
- James Chaney, p. 630
- Michael Schwerner, p. 630
- Mississippi Freedom Democratic Party, p. 631
- Fannie Lou Hamer, p. 631
- Voting Rights Act, p. 632

1. Freedom Summer—to register African Americans in Mississippi to vote, resulted in deaths but few registrations; MFDP—to give African American voters a voice at the Democratic National Convention, resulted in no official recognition and distrust toward President Johnson; Selma March—to protest attempts to prevent African Americans from registering to vote, resulted in public support of the Voting Rights Act

2. threats, beatings, murder, loss of jobs for African American voters, difficulty gaining people's trust

3. It helped little at first, but the Selma march brought federal protection and the Voting Rights Act.

4. If officials recognized the MFDP at the convention, they risked losing the support of most white Democrats.

5. The initiatives helped some African American Mississipians realize their rights. They also helped civil rights workers realize the depth of racism in the state.

African American Voter Registration, 1960–1992

Learning from Maps After the passage of the 1965 Voting Rights Act, the number of registered African American voters in the South increased dramatically. In Mississippi voter registration increased almost 700 percent.

PLACE Which states experienced the greatest increase in the registration of African American voters?

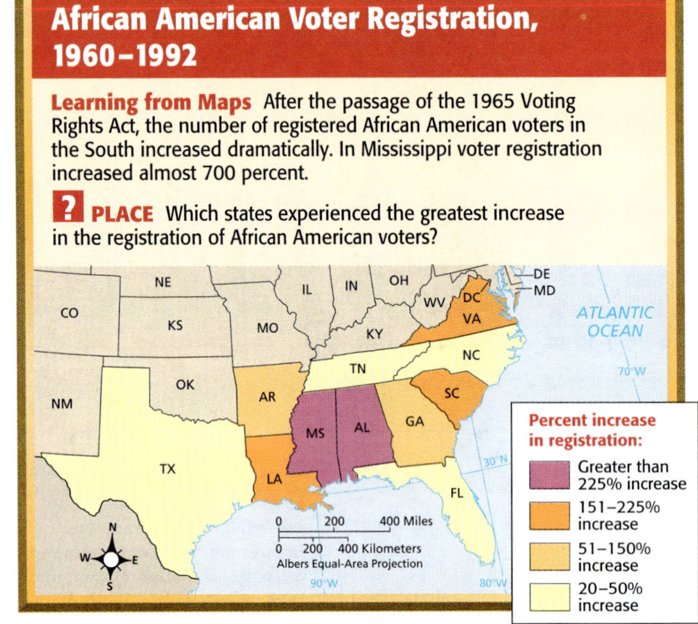

ropes, or whips, which they swung around them like they were driving cattle."

Outraged by the attack, thousands of Americans poured into Montgomery to show support for the marchers. President Johnson was also shocked by Selma's "Bloody Sunday." On March 15, before a joint session of Congress, he asked for speedy passage of a voting rights bill. He also declared that all Americans ought to take up the struggle for civil rights: "All of us . . . must overcome the crippling legacy [history] of bigotry [racism] and injustice. And we *shall* . . . overcome."

About one week later, under the protection of federal marshals and the National Guard, the marchers successfully began their journey again. Five months later, Congress passed the **Voting Rights Act** of 1965, which put the entire registration process under federal control. Within days of the act's passage, federal examiners descended upon the South to sign up new African American voters. By 1968 the number of eligible African Americans who were registered to vote jumped to 57 percent in Alabama. Mississippi experienced the greatest percentage increase, from less than 6 percent in 1964 to some 59 percent in 1968.

✔ **READING CHECK:** How did the Selma protest lead to the passage of the Voting Rights Act?

SECTION 2 REVIEW

Define and explain the significance of the following terms:
Council of Federated Organizations
Freedom Summer
Mississippi Freedom Democratic Party
Voting Rights Act

Identify and explain the significance of the following individuals:
Robert Moses
Andrew Goodman
James Chaney
Michael Schwerner
Fannie Lou Hamer

1. **Using Graphic Organizers** Copy the following chart. Use it to explain the impact of efforts including Freedom Summer, the Mississippi Freedom Democratic Party (MFDP), and the Selma march.

Freedom Summer	MFDP	Selma March
Stated Goal	Stated Goal	Stated Goal
Effect	Effect	Effect

2. **Analyzing** What obstacles did civil rights workers encounter in their attempts to register voters?
3. **Evaluating** How helpful was the federal government to the voter registration drives in Mississippi?
4. **Recognizing Point of View** Why did officials in the Democratic Party regard the MFDP as a potential source of conflict?

Critical Thinking

5. How did voting rights initiatives change the lives of black Mississippians and of civil rights workers?
Consider:
- the violence that people encountered
- the total number of African American voters registered
- the interaction between black Mississippians and civil rights workers

SECTION 3

After completing Section 3, students should be able to:

OBJECTIVE 1 *Describe how Malcolm X's message differed from that of the major civil rights organizations during the early 1960s.*

OBJECTIVE 2 *Explain why nonviolent protest and the goal of racial integration lost support.*

OBJECTIVE 3 *Discuss how northern racial discrimination and urban riots changed the civil rights movement.*

LET'S GET STARTED!

Write the name *Malcolm X* on the chalkboard. As students enter the classroom, tell them to write down what they know about him. Ask volunteers to share their responses, and compile a list of responses on the chalkboard. Tell students that in Section 3 they will learn about alternative means of achieving civil rights that were proposed by civil rights leaders.

Challenges for the Movement

OBJECTIVES

Read to understand:

1. how Malcolm X's message differed from that of the major civil rights organizations during the early 1960s
2. why nonviolent protest and the goal of racial integration lost support
3. how northern racial discrimination and urban riots changed the civil rights movement

KEY TERMS

Nation of Islam
Black Power
Black Panther Party
Kerner Commission
Poor People's Campaign

KEY PEOPLE

James Farmer
Elijah Muhammad
Malcolm X
Stokely Carmichael
Bobby Seale
Huey Newton

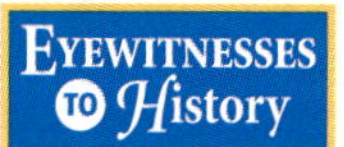

"We wanted control of the communities where we were most numerous, and the institutions therein. At the same time, we felt that we were due, because of taxpaying, free access to and equal treatment in public facilities."

—Huey Newton

A Black Panther pin

Huey Newton recalled his decision to form a new, more confrontational civil rights organization with his friend Bobby Seale. The appearance of this new movement and the prominence of Black Muslim leader Malcolm X signaled a new phase in the struggle for civil rights in the mid-1960s. Many activists were dissatisfied with the direction the civil rights movement had taken and frustrated with the slow pace of change. In reaction, many African American leaders rejected nonviolence as a strategy. Seale and Newton chose the black panther to symbolize their new group. Seale explained, "if you drive a panther into a corner, if he can't go left and he can't go right, then he will tend to come out of that corner to wipe out or stop its aggressor."

New Directions

As the civil rights movement continued, some African Americans questioned the effectiveness of nonviolence and the goals of the movement. In 1962 CORE director James Farmer explained, "We no longer are a tight fellowship of a few dedicated advocates [supporters] of a brilliant new method of social change. We are now a large family spawned [created] by the union of the method-oriented pioneers and the righteously indignant [angry] ends-oriented militants." The "militants" of whom Farmer spoke were people who were attracted to the views of African American organizations such as the Nation of Islam.

Black Muslims. Little is known about Wallace D. Fard, the founder of the **Nation of Islam**. Fard started the group, also known as the Black Muslims, in Detroit, Michigan, in 1930. The organization was based on the Islamic religion founded by the prophet Muhammad. However, the Black Muslims emphasized the supremacy of black people over all other races. By the early 1930s, when Elijah Muhammad became its leader, the Nation of Islam claimed some 8,000 members. Muhammad preached a message of black nationalism. He declared that African Americans should create their own republic within the United States. Many Black Muslims rejected their last names as relics of slavery and used "X" to symbolize lost African names.

Muhammad stressed self-discipline as the way to achieve the dream of a separate African American nation. Black Muslims were not allowed to drink alcohol or smoke

Elijah Muhammad motivated his Black Muslim supporters in this 1961 speech in Washington, D.C. Some Black Muslims wore pins such as this one.

SECTION 3 RESOURCES

PRINT

- Guided Reading Strategy 21.3
- Section 3 Review, p. 638
- Daily Quiz 21.3

MULTIMEDIA

- One-Stop Planner, Lesson 21.3
- The American Nation Video Program Segment: Malcolm X; Teacher's Guide, pp. 135–40
- Holt Researcher: American History CD–ROM

SHELTERED ENGLISH

- Main Idea Activity for Reteaching and Sheltered English 21.3

✔ READING TO UNDERSTAND

To help students master the section objectives, have them answer the **READING CHECKS** and complete **Guided Reading Strategy 21.3** as they read the section.

TEACH OBJECTIVE 1

LEVEL 1: To help students understand how Malcolm X's views differed from those of mainstream civil rights leaders, copy the graphic organizer in the next column on the chalkboard, omitting the italicized answers. Have each student complete the organizer. Ask volunteers to share their answers with the class. Conclude by leading a discussion about the differences of opinion that existed within the civil rights movement about the most effective means of obtaining civil rights for African Americans. **Sheltered English**

LEVELS 2 AND 3: Pair students and tell one student in each pair to imagine that he or she supports the views of mainstream civil rights leaders regarding the strategy for the civil rights movement. Tell the other student to imagine that he or she supports Malcolm X's message. Have students write a brief dialogue discussing their views. *(See the graphic organizer from the Level 1 lesson for major points of difference.)* Ask students to read their dialogues for the class. **Cooperative Learning**

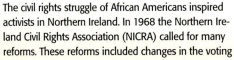

Views of Mainstream Civil Rights Leaders	Views of Malcolm X
Civil rights will be obtained through 1. *nonviolence* and 2. *integration.*	Civil rights will be obtained through 1. *"any means necessary"* and 2. *African American separatism.*

HISTORY MAKERS SPEAK

Ossie Davis in *Voices of Freedom*

Remembering Malcolm X. Many African Americans were uncomfortable with Malcolm X's ideas. Ossie Davis, an African American actor and playwright, described his reaction to Malcolm X. At first, Davis said, "I was amazed at his capacity to communicate and at the naked honesty with which he expressed his feelings about black people, about white people. He scared me. I'm sure he intended to."

CRITICAL THINKING Why might Malcolm X have wanted to alarm his African American listeners?

ANSWER: Students might suggest that he wanted to jar them out of their ways of thinking and make them consider his point of view.

The American Nation **VIDEO PROGRAM**

Malcolm X; Teacher's Guide; pp. 135–40

Search 28273, Play to 35398
Videodisc 2, Side B

Play

Pause

See *Teacher's Guide* for Spanish barcode.

THROUGH OTHERS' EYES

Irish View of the Civil Rights Movement

The civil rights struggle of African Americans inspired activists in Northern Ireland. In 1968 the Northern Ireland Civil Rights Association (NICRA) called for many reforms. These reforms included changes in the voting system. This system discriminated against Catholics. As one Catholic woman later recalled, "Like . . . the blacks [in the United States], we were poor, virtually disenfranchised [deprived of rights], and very angry."

Members of NICRA used many of the tactics that were used in the United States, including nonviolent demonstrations. In August 1968, marchers in Coalisland sang the American civil rights anthem "We Shall Overcome," even though many of them did not know the lyrics. Like the American civil rights demonstrators, the Irish activists experienced violence. At a demonstration in Derry in October 1968, marchers were beaten with clubs and knocked off their feet by water cannons.

and were expected to maintain a strict diet. Muhammad also encouraged self-reliance. During the Great Depression, Black Muslims were not permitted to accept any assistance from the federal government. Black Muslims were also discouraged by their leaders from serving in the U.S. military. As a result, Muhammad and many of his followers were sentenced to prison for draft evasion during World War II.

While in prison, Muhammad realized that African American prisoners were largely ignored by most African American organizations. Muhammad actively recruited convicts, calling on them to change their lives through the strict discipline required by the Nation of Islam. He also brought his message to many lower-income African Americans. These recruitment efforts proved effective. By the early 1960s there were an estimated 100,000 Black Muslims spread throughout the United States.

BIOGRAPHY
Malcolm X

Malcolm X. The growth of the Nation of Islam during the 1950s was in part the work of Malcolm X, a charismatic young minister. Malcolm X was born Malcolm Little in 1925. His father was a Baptist minister and organizer for Marcus Garvey. Malcolm's father was killed in what many people considered a racially motivated murder.

Despite his father's death, Malcolm Little tried to ignore the racism he encountered in his school and community. This changed when Little, who was an excellent student, told his white English teacher that he wanted to become an attorney. The teacher replied that this was an unrealistic goal for an African American. Malcolm X later recalled, "The more I thought afterwards about what he said, the more uneasy it made me. . . . It was then that I began to change—inside." He remembered that he "drew away from white people" after the conversation with his teacher.

Little dropped out of school and drifted into a life of crime. He was eventually sentenced to 10 years in prison. While in prison he embraced the teachings of Elijah Muhammad. Freed in 1952, he changed his name to Malcolm X and soon became a leading minister for the Nation of Islam. A powerful speaker, Malcolm X championed African American separatism and called for freedom to be brought about "by any means necessary." The time for nonviolence had passed, he argued.

"You're getting a new generation that has been growing right now, and they're beginning to think with their own minds and see that you can't negotiate up on freedom nowadays. If something is yours by right, then fight for it or shut up. If you can't fight for it, then forget it."

HOLT RESEARCHER *Read More About It*

Free Find: Malcolm X
After reading about Malcolm X on the **Holt Researcher** CD–ROM, explain how his experiences as a youth influenced his civil rights efforts.

SPOTLIGHT on James Farmer

Have students conduct research on James Farmer. Tell students to focus on Farmer's role in the Congress on Racial Equality (CORE), sit-ins in Chicago, the Freedom Rides, the Nixon administration, and Farmer's life in the 1970s, 1980s, and 1990s. Then ask each student to use this information to create a Coming Attractions poster for a documentary film on Farmer's life. **Block Scheduling**

TEACH OBJECTIVE 2

LEVEL 1: Pair students and tell them to imagine that they are civil rights activists who have grown frustrated with the strategy of nonviolent protest and the goal of racial integration. Have each pair write a letter to Stokely Carmichael explaining its views. *(Pairs should note that activists who had endured violence and jail questioned nonviolence as a strategy. Many African American volunteers on the Freedom Summer project believed that white students were taking over the project. Also, activists were angered that the deaths of white civil rights supporters generated more concern than the deaths of African American activists.)* Have volunteers read their letters to the class. **Sheltered English, Cooperative Learning**

Malcolm X criticized the goals and the strategies of civil rights organizations that worked for racial integration. He argued that "it is not integration that Negroes in America want, it is human dignity." Criticizing Martin Luther King, Malcolm X claimed, "Any Negro who teaches other Negroes to turn the other cheek is disarming that Negro . . . [of] his natural right to defend himself."

Many white Americans found Malcolm X's tone frightening. Malcolm X, however, began undergoing a transformation in his beliefs during the mid-1960s. In 1964 he made a pilgrimage to the Islamic holy city of Mecca. In Mecca he was exposed to more traditional Islamic beliefs. He also gained a greater acceptance of the universal humanity of people of all races. That same year he broke with the Black Muslims. Turning away from separatism, Malcolm X converted to orthodox Islam and began calling for unity among all people. His new outlook was reflected in a 1964 speech. He declared, "We will work with anyone, with any group, no matter what their color is, as long as they are genuinely interested in taking the type of steps necessary to bring an end to the injustices that black people in this country are afflicted by." However, Malcolm X had little time to act on his new ideas. In February 1965 he was gunned down by three Black Muslim assassins.

Martin Luther King Jr. and Malcolm X met only once, at the U.S. Capitol during a Senate filibuster of a civil rights bill in March 1964.

✔ **READING CHECK:** How did Malcolm X's message differ from that of major civil rights organizations during the early 1960s?

The Movement Fractures

Most white Americans perceived the civil rights movement as a unified effort led by Martin Luther King Jr. In fact, the movement was made up of diverse groups united by the common goal of ending racial segregation. By the mid-1960s many conflicts had surfaced among these organizations.

Black Power. Civil rights activists who had endured violence and jailings in their efforts to register voters in Mississippi began to question the strategy of nonviolent protest. CORE's David Dennis summed up the growing frustration with nonviolence in June 1964. Dennis declared, "I'm sick and tired of going to funerals of black men who have been murdered by white men. . . . I've got vengeance in my heart tonight."

Some African American activists also began to question the goal of integration, in part because of their experiences in Mississippi. The presence of white volunteers for the Freedom Summer project had created tensions within SNCC. African American workers believed that white students were taking over the project. "Suddenly, in an instant, in our town are five or six brightly scrubbed white kids from the North," SNCC's Bob Zellner recalled. "Here's Jesse (Negro) laboriously doing the stencil. Sally (white) . . . comes along and says, 'Here, I type 120 words a minute, let me do it.'" These frustrations led many African American activists, particularly those involved with SNCC and CORE, to express a growing interest in black nationalism.

Many African Americans were also angry that the death of white volunteers such as Andrew Goodman and Michael Schwerner generated widespread public

INTERPRETING THE VISUAL RECORD

Black nationalism. Frustrated by their experiences in the civil rights movement, some African Americans began to embrace ideas of black nationalism and oppose the goals of integration. ***How does this button symbolize the new direction and goals of some civil rights activists?***

HISTORY MAKERS SPEAK

Stokely Carmichael in "What We Want"

Carmichael's Definition of Black Power. After Stokely Carmichael's phrase "Black Power" was broadcast all over the nation, people demanded to know what he meant. In the *New York Review of Books*, Carmichael wrote, "Politically, black power means . . . the coming-together of black people to elect representatives and to *force those representatives to speak to their needs.*" Carmichael also argued against integration: "As a goal, [integration] has been based on complete acceptance of the fact that *in order to have* a decent house or education, blacks must move into a white neighborhood or send their children to a white school."

CRITICAL THINKING What might Carmichael have suggested that African Americans do to improve their situation other than integrate?

ANSWER: Students might suggest that Carmichael would have wanted African Americans to attain economic equality and improve their own neighborhoods and schools.

VISUAL RECORD ANSWER

Students might suggest that the clenched fist symbolizes a more aggressive method of achieving equality.

LEVEL 2: Have each student create a collage that expresses the discontent many civil rights activists felt with the strategy of nonviolent protest and the goal of racial integration. *(See the Level 1 lesson for the correct reasons .)* Have students display and explain their collages to the class.

LEVEL 3: Tell students to imagine that they are editors of a major daily newspaper in 1966. Have each student write a one-page editorial that explains why many civil rights activists were frustrated with the strategy of nonviolent protest and the goal of integration. *(See the Level 1 lesson for the correct reasons.)*

▶ASSIGNMENT *Write on the chalkboard the following statement made by Martin Luther King Jr. in reference to the Black Power movement: "If you really have power you don't need a slogan." Ask each student to write one to two paragraphs in agreement or disagreement with King's statement. Students should provide specific reasons for their positions.*

CONSTITUTIONAL HERITAGE

Interracial Marriage. In the midst of the breakup of the civil rights movement, one Virginia couple was becoming a civil rights success story. Mildred Jeter, an African American woman, and Richard Loving, a white man, had been married in Washington, D.C., where interracial marriages were legal. When they returned to their Virginia home, they were charged and indicted for their marriage, which was illegal in Virginia. The couple's sentence was to spend one year in jail or leave the state for 25 years. They chose to move to Washington, D.C., and began a series of appeals of the Virginia court's decision. Their case made it to the Supreme Court as *Loving* v. *Virginia.* In 1967 the Court decided that the ban on interracial marriages violated the Fourteenth Amendment.

ACTIVITY: Have students assume the roles of either the Lovings, representatives of Virginia, or members of the Supreme Court and write a defense of their position.

VISUAL RECORD ANSWER

Students might suggest that the pin represents the Black Panthers' desire for total participation in their movement and attempt to improve African American life.

The deaths of civil rights activists such as Jimmie Lee Jackson, whose 1965 funeral is shown here, led to growing frustration among African American leaders who began to embrace the Black Power movement.

concern. However, African American victims of violence did not receive similar attention. SNCC's Stokely Carmichael noted, "What you want is the nation to be upset when anybody is killed. . . . It's almost like, for this to be recognized, a white person must be killed. Well, what does that say?"

The split in the civil rights movement became public in 1966. That year James Meredith, the first African American to graduate from the University of Mississippi, decided to make a "journey against fear" by marching across Mississippi. After he was shot and wounded on the second day of the march, several civil rights organizations vowed to continue his journey. Determined to turn the march into an expression of black nationalism, Stokely Carmichael convinced the NAACP and the Urban League, two more conservative organizations, to abandon the event.

At a march rally on June 16, Carmichael told the crowd, "This is the 27th time I've been arrested. I ain't gonna be arrested no more." In the days that followed, Carmichael and others asked the crowd, "What do you want?" and received the chanted reply, "Black power!"

King asked Carmichael to stop using the slogan, but Carmichael admitted, "I deliberately decided to raise this issue on the march in order to give it a national forum." The **Black Power** movement called for black separatism. It had many positive aspects, including an emphasis on racial pride and an interest in African culture and heritage. However, many moderate leaders such as King feared that the movement would create hostility toward civil rights among the nation's white population. King confided to one adviser, "If you go around claiming power, the whole society turns on you and crushes you. If you really have power you don't need a slogan."

INTERPRETING THE VISUAL RECORD

Black Panthers. Members of the Black Panther Party drew public attention by carrying guns and supporting the Black Power movement. ***How do you think the message of the pin reflects the values of the Black Panther Party?***

The Black Panthers.

Despite King's misgivings, many African Americans were attracted to Carmichael's Black Power message. Bobby Seale worked with Huey Newton at an antipoverty center in Oakland, California. He later recalled, "Huey and I began to try to figure out how could we organize youthful black folks into some kind of political, electoral *power* movement." The two created a political organization called the **Black Panther Party**. The party platform declared, "Black people will not be free until we are free to determine our own destiny." It called for "land, bread, housing, education, clothing, justice, and peace" for African Americans.

The platform also called for the creation of "black self-defense groups that are dedicated to defending our black community from racist police oppression." Black Panther members often made national headlines. This was particularly true when they appeared in public carrying firearms, which at the time was legal to do in California. A number of highly publicized gun battles with police occurred. Huey Newton was sentenced to prison for murder. Elaine Brown, who joined the organization in 1967, offered one reason why African Americans joined the Black Panthers:

TEACH OBJECTIVE 3

LEVEL 1: Pair students and have each pair create bumper stickers that describe the changing goals of the civil rights movement after it encountered northern racial discrimination and after the urban riots. *(Students' stickers might include that economic power became emphasized. Martin Luther King Jr. believed that the Vietnam War diverted spending from social programs. King planned to lead a Poor People's Campaign to protest what he saw as a misuse of government spending.)* Have each pair present and explain its bumper stickers to the class. **Sheltered English, Cooperative Learning**

LEVEL 2: Tell students to imagine that they are trying to rally support for the changing goals of the civil rights movement in the late 1960s in response to northern racial discrimination and urban riots. Have each student write a short speech advocating these new goals. *(See the Level 1 lesson for the correct goals.)* Have students deliver their speeches to the class.

LEVEL 3: Have each student create a mobile with objects that symbolize the changing goals of the civil rights movement after the urban riots and incidents of northern racial discrimination. *(See the Level 1 lesson for the correct goals.)* Ask each student to display his or her mobile in the classroom and to explain the meaning of each symbol.

"The party reached out mostly to men, to young, black urban men who were on the streets, who knew that there were no options somewhere in their lives. . . . We offered them the opportunity to make their lives meaningful. . . . And a lot of brothers did make their commitment with that conscious understanding that coming away from the gang was something that they were ultimately building for themselves and for the community."

✔ **READING CHECK:** Why did nonviolent protest and the goal of racial integration lose support?

Tragic Events

The Black Power movement was not the only challenge that Martin Luther King Jr. and other civil rights leaders faced during the mid-1960s. Efforts to extend the civil rights struggle beyond desegregation and into areas such as housing and economic justice met a mixed reaction from white Americans. Many white Americans opposed the movement's expanded focus.

Chicago. By 1966 the SCLC was virtually the only major civil rights organization still primarily focused on nonviolent protest. That year King decided to battle racial discrimination in Chicago. In January he and his family moved into a slum apartment. He hoped to draw attention to the housing problems that African Americans faced in the urban North. Throughout that spring, amid periodic journeys to the South, King provided leadership and support for the movement in Chicago.

At a rally on July 10, 1966, King announced his continued determination to end housing discrimination in Chicago. Less than a month later, he was struck in the head by a rock while leading a peaceful march through a Chicago neighborhood. Some 4,000 white people threatened the marchers. The marchers were protected by local police. Next, King announced that he would lead a march in Cicero, Illinois, a town with a history of violence against African Americans. Chicago city leaders pledged to meet King's demands.

King claimed victory in Chicago, but the experience showed that significant obstacles to full equality remained. The fight against racial discrimination in the North did not draw support from white Americans in the way that demonstrations against segregation in the South had a few years earlier.

Urban Unrest, 1965–1968

Learning from Maps Hundreds of race-related riots rocked U.S. cities in the mid-1960s.

REGION Which section of the country experienced the most incidents of urban unrest between 1965 and 1968?

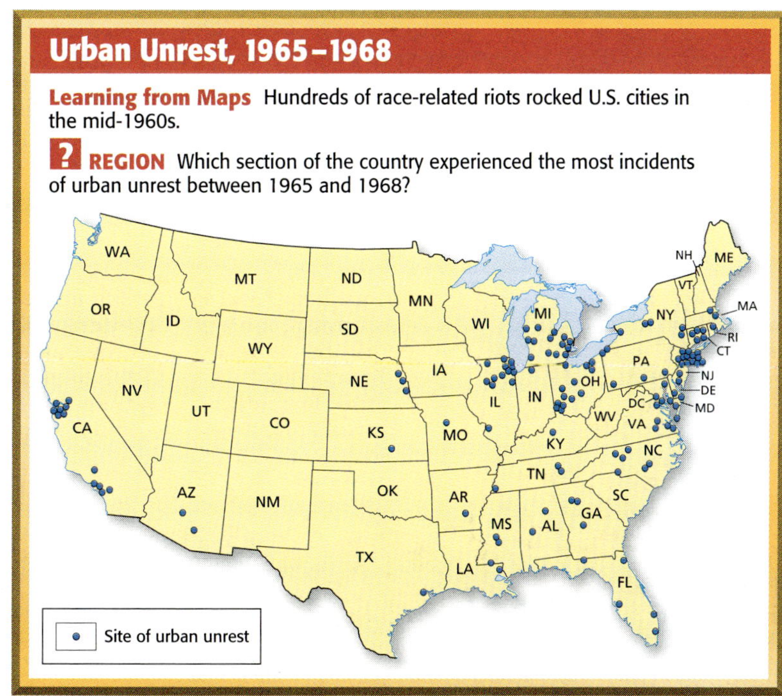

ACROSS THE CURRICULUM

SOCIOLOGY

Homecoming at Howard. In 1966 Robin Gregory—a student at Howard University, a historically black university—ran a unique campaign for homecoming queen. She wore her hair in an Afro, which was a statement of Black Power. Her campaign speeches focused on politics. One student described the presentation of the new queen. "As the stage revolved and turned around toward the audience, the lights began to come up at the same time. Well, before you saw Robin, you saw the way the lights cast a silhouette on the curtains, and you saw the silhouette of her Afro before you saw her. Well, the auditorium exploded. It was a wonderful moment."

CRITICAL THINKING How might Gregory's homecoming victory have been seen as a victory for Black Power?

ANSWER: Students might note Gregory's hair style and political speeches.

MAP ANSWER

the northeastern part of the country

REVIEW

Have students complete the **Section 3 Review** on p. 638.

ASSESS

Have students complete **Daily Quiz 21.3**. As **Alternative Assessment**, you may want to use the speech or the bumper stickers in this section's lessons.

RETEACH

Have students complete **Main Idea Activity for Reteaching and Sheltered English 21.3**. Then pair students and have each pair summarize the subsections in Section 3. Have pairs create at least four questions and answers for each subsection. Collect pairs' questions and use them to quiz the class as a whole. **Sheltered English, Cooperative Learning**

EXTEND

Ask each student to conduct research on and write a report about one of the following: Stokely Carmichael, Elijah Muhammad, Huey Newton, Bobby Seale, or Malcolm X. **Block Scheduling**

SECTION 3 REVIEW ANSWERS

Define and Identify
For significance, see the following pages:

- James Farmer, p. 633
- Nation of Islam, p. 633
- Elijah Muhammad, p. 633
- Malcolm X, p. 634
- Stokely Carmichael, p. 636
- Black Power, p. 636
- Bobby Seale, p. 636
- Huey Newton, p. 636
- Black Panther Party, p. 636
- Kerner Commission, p. 638
- Poor People's Campaign, p. 638

1. 1.–Some activists believed that nonviolent protests were not working or were not working fast enough. 2.–Some began to question the move for integration. 3.–Many were angered when people were outraged over the deaths of white civil rights activists but were not similarly outraged over African Americans' deaths.

2. Malcolm X believed in the possibility of violent action and African American independence within the civil rights movement.

3. discrimination–failed to draw public support in the same levels as southern discrimination; violence–weakened public support for the movement

4. Answers will vary. Students might argue that nonviolent protests continued to show results, even if they were gradual changes.

5. He was troubled by the Black Power movement. He faced the issue of economic empowerment and protested U.S. involvement in Vietnam.

Urban violence. The white backlash against the civil rights movement and the Johnson administration's reluctance to press for further gains were responses to key social issues of the decade. These issues included the Black Power movement and a series of urban uprisings that erupted in the middle of the decade. Despite the successes of the civil rights movement, discrimination still affected the lives of most African Americans. In August 1965 frustration turned to violence. A routine arrest by Los Angeles police in the African American neighborhood of Watts triggered a riot that raged for six days. When the National Guard finally restored order, 34 people had been killed, hundreds injured, and almost 4,000 had been arrested.

Most Americans joined Coretta Scott King in mourning after the assassination of Martin Luther King Jr.

Over the next two years, more than 100 riots broke out in cities across the country. The worst came in Detroit, where 43 people died. A federal report by the **Kerner Commission** charged that white racism was largely responsible for the tensions that led to the riots. "Our nation," the report warned, "is moving toward two societies, one black, one white—separate and unequal."

Seeking to address the frustration of the late 1960s, King began to embrace some of the Black Power movement's ideas, such as the need for African Americans to gain economic power. He also became increasingly upset that funding was being diverted to the war in Vietnam rather than being spent on social programs. In March 1968 King called for a **Poor People's Campaign** that would include a march on Washington, D.C., to protest what he saw as a misuse of government spending.

Before the march, King went to Memphis, Tennessee, to show his support for a sanitation workers' strike. On the evening of April 4, 1968, the man who was the symbol of nonviolence met a violent end when he was shot by a sniper. Within hours of King's death, African American neighborhoods across the country exploded in outrage. A week of rioting left 46 dead and thousands injured.

✔ **READING CHECK:** How did northern racial discrimination and urban riots change the civil rights movement?

SECTION 3 REVIEW

Define and explain the significance of the following terms:
Nation of Islam
Black Power
Black Panther Party
Kerner Commission
Poor People's Campaign

Identify and explain the significance of the following individuals:
James Farmer
Elijah Muhammad
Malcolm X
Stokely Carmichael
Bobby Seale
Huey Newton

1. **Using Graphic Organizers** Copy the following graphic organizer. Use it to explain the factors that led activists to move from nonviolence to Black Power.

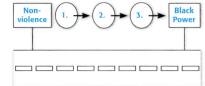

2. **Identifying Values** How did Malcolm X's attitudes differ from other civil rights leaders?
3. **Assessing Consequences** How did northern discrimination and urban violence affect the civil rights movement?
4. **Evaluating** Did nonviolence remain an effective means of bringing about change? Explain.

Critical Thinking

5. What challenges did Martin Luther King Jr. face in the final years of his life?
   Consider:
   - the conflicts within the civil rights movement
   - northern reactions to civil rights demonstrations
   - economic issues for African Americans

SECTION 4

After completing Section 4, students should be able to:

OBJECTIVE 1 *Describe the problems many leading African American organizations encountered in the early 1970s.*

OBJECTIVE 2 *Explain how the Supreme Court limited the impact of busing and affirmative action programs.*

OBJECTIVE 3 *Identify the gains African Americans made during the early 1970s.*

LET'S GET STARTED!

Write the italicized statements below on the chalkboard. As students enter the classroom, tell them to copy the statements into their notebooks and note whether each statement is true or false. Students should correct false statements.

During the late 1960s, civil rights leaders placed new emphasis on increasing the economic power of African Americans. (true)

Civil rights gains during the 1960s resulted almost exclusively from private efforts. (false—through a combination of public and private efforts)

Tell students that in Section 4 they will learn about the civil rights struggle in the 1970s.

SECTION 4

The Movement Continues

OBJECTIVES

Read to understand:

1. what problems many leading African American organizations encountered in the early 1970s
2. how the Supreme Court limited the impact of busing and affirmative action programs
3. what gains African Americans made during the early 1970s

KEY TERMS

busing
affirmative action
University of California v. Bakke
quotas
National Black Political Convention

KEY PEOPLE

Ralph Abernathy
Allan Bakke
Carl Stokes

EYEWITNESSES TO History

Ralph Abernathy

"When I took over from Martin, I did so after the civil rights movement had peaked and the SCLC had already begun to decline in influence. . . . Through our efforts and those of others, legal segregation in most areas of public life had been eliminated. . . . When we tried to change our focus and attack economic injustice, we lost many of our former supporters. . . . After a decade of fighting for racial justice, many people, black and white, were weary of the struggle and were ready to give up, to lay down their swords and shields."

—Ralph Abernathy

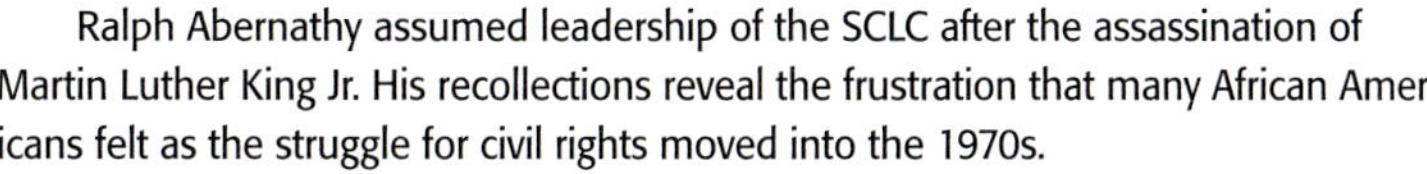

Ralph Abernathy assumed leadership of the SCLC after the assassination of Martin Luther King Jr. His recollections reveal the frustration that many African Americans felt as the struggle for civil rights moved into the 1970s.

A Crisis in Direction

The assassination of Martin Luther King Jr. marked a turning point in the struggle for civil rights. With King's death, the movement lost its most visible figure and the leading supporter of nonviolent protest. At the same time, Black Power groups also began to decline. During the 1970s civil rights leaders addressed new problems trying to improve the lives of African Americans.

SCLC. Determined to continue King's work, SCLC leaders went ahead with the Poor People's Campaign. Ralph Abernathy told the marchers on their way to Capitol Hill, "We have business on the road to freedom. . . . We must prove to white America that you can kill the leader but you cannot kill the dream." Once they had reached Washington, D.C., protesters constructed Resurrection City. They created a settlement of tents and shacks on public land designed to draw attention to poverty. William Rutherford explained, "The technique, the tactic being used, was to gather the poorest of the poor in the nation's capitol in the heart of the wealthiest country in the world . . . [and] take the plea and the complaint of the poor to each of the government agencies."

Resurrection City was a disaster. Constant rain turned the shantytown into a sea of mud. SCLC leaders also had to deal with theft and violence. In June of 1968, police evicted demonstrators from the site and tore down Resurrection City.

The failure of the Poor People's Campaign left many civil rights activists in a state of despair. "It dawned on me that this was the end of an entire period in my life," Michael Harrington recalled. "One of the most marvelous political movements in America in the form which it took under Martin Luther King . . . had come to an end." During the 1970s financial contributions to SCLC shrank. The organization no longer played a leading role in civil rights issues.

This SCLC poster was created to encourage support for the Poor People's Campaign.

SECTION 4 **RESOURCES**

PRINT

- Guided Reading Strategy 21.4
- Section 4 Review, p. 643
- Daily Quiz 21.4

MULTIMEDIA

- One-Stop Planner, Lesson 21.4
- Holt Researcher: American History CD–ROM

SHELTERED ENGLISH

- Main Idea Activity for Reteaching and Sheltered English 21.4

✔ READING TO UNDERSTAND

To help students master the section objectives, have them answer the **READING CHECKS** and complete **Guided Reading Strategy 21.4** as they read the section.

TEACH OBJECTIVE 1

LEVEL 1: Pair students and have each pair create a chart showing the problems faced by civil rights organizations in the 1970s. *(Pairs' answers should include some of the following: the SCLC's new focus on economic justice led to a loss of support for the organization; the SCLC's Resurrection City project was a failure; financial contributions to the SCLC shrank; the FBI investigated black nationalist organizations; internal conflicts plagued many organizations; financial contributions to the SNCC declined; the SNCC disbanded in the early 1970s; the Black Panthers lost influence as many Black Panther leaders were imprisoned or died.)*

Sheltered English, Cooperative Learning

LEVELS 2 AND 3: Tell students to imagine that they must design a Web site about the problems many African American political organizations faced in the early 1970s. Have each student complete a design for a Web site that includes an explanation of how the information is organized as well as suggestions for links. *(See the Level 1 lesson for the correct problems.)* Have volunteers present their designs to the class.

NOTE: For an additional teaching idea, see the Chapter 21 ranking lesson in the **Creative Teaching Strategies** handbook.

CONSTITUTIONAL HERITAGE

The Southern Manifesto. The busing controversy brought the issue of desegregation to the entire nation, but many southern politicians had been working since 1956 to reverse the Supreme Court's *Brown* v. *Board of Education* decision. After the decision, which required schools to desegregate, 96 southern members of Congress signed the Southern Manifesto. Part of it read, "The original Constitution does not mention education. Neither does the 14th Amendment nor any other amendment. . . . This unwarranted exercise of power by the Court . . . is destroying the amicable relations between the white and Negro races. . . . It has planted hatred and suspicion where there had been heretofore friendship and understanding."

CRITICAL THINKING Why might the manifesto have claimed that the races had lived in friendship and understanding prior to *Brown* v. *Board of Education?*

ANSWER: Students might suggest that the absence of civil rights protests prior to the decision was interpreted to be salutary rather than an indicator of oppression.

VISUAL RECORD ANSWER

The cover shows a white child going to an inner-city area, while an African American child is going to a suburban area.

Pictured here leaving a Senate subcommittee hearing, FBI director J. Edgar Hoover organized counterintelligence programs to block the activities of black nationalist and civil rights groups.

Black nationalism. Like the SCLC, organizations that supported black nationalism faced growing problems during this time. These problems included scrutiny by the U.S. government. In 1967 FBI director J. Edgar Hoover launched a program designed to "expose, disrupt, misdirect, discredit, or otherwise neutralize the activities of black nationalist, hate-type organizations and groupings, their leadership, spokesmen, membership, and supporters." Numerous operations were begun against various civil rights organizations.

Many organizations also suffered from internal conflicts. Under Stokely Carmichael's leadership, SNCC began controversial protests against the Vietnam War. Financial contributions to SNCC declined dramatically.

In February 1968, SNCC and Black Panther leaders announced that the two groups planned to unite. However, many SNCC members were reluctant to join a group that openly supported violence. The union lasted only until July. The following month SNCC expelled Stokely Carmichael from the organization. The crises in direction and leadership proved to be too much. SNCC disbanded in the early 1970s. The Black Panthers also lost influence. Many of the group's leaders were imprisoned or dead.

Unlike SNCC and the Black Panthers, the Black Muslims survived the early 1970s, despite losing some support following Malcolm X's departure. Elijah Muhammad continued to lead the Nation of Islam. After Muhammad's death in 1975, his son Wallace took over as leader.

✔ **READING CHECK:** What problems did many leading African American organizations encounter in the early 1970s?

INTERPRETING THE VISUAL RECORD

Busing. Many Americans opposed the integration of public schools by busing children. ***How does this Time magazine cover from 1971 portray the differences in the neighborhoods to which students would be bused?***

Backlash

Civil rights organizations faced growing opposition from white Americans. Some claimed that civil rights reform was depriving them of their own rights. One of the first targets of white anger was court-ordered busing to desegregate the nation's public schools.

Busing. The Supreme Court had banned racial segregation in public schools in the 1954 case *Brown* v. *Board of Education.* However, because residential neighborhoods in most U.S. cities remained segregated, many schools in both the South and the North were also segregated. Some school officials decided to use **busing**, or sending children to schools outside of their neighborhoods, to integrate schools.

In 1971 the Supreme Court approved a busing plan in Charlotte, North Carolina. The plan worked, and Charlotte's schools were quickly desegregated. Polls, however, revealed that white Americans opposed court-ordered busing by a 3-to-1 margin. Many African Americans also had doubts about such plans. Court-ordered busing met with strong opposition in a number of cities, most notably Boston. One angry white Bostonian warned: "You heard of the Hundred Years War? This will be the eternal war. It will be passed down from father to son."

TEACH OBJECTIVE 2

ALL LEVELS: Pair students and have each pair summarize decisions the Supreme Court made in the 1970s that limited the impact of busing and affirmative action. *(Pairs should note that in* Milliken v. Bradley *in 1974, the Court struck down a lower court's order that would have merged inner-city and suburban school districts in Detroit. In* University of California *v.* Bakke *in 1978, the Court ruled that affirmative action plans using quota systems are unconstitutional.)* Then have each student write dissenting opinions in the cases. Have volunteers read their opinions to the class.
Sheltered English, Cooperative Learning

Teacher to Teacher

Andy Turay of Bronx, New York, suggested the following activity: Pair students and have each pair create a chart comparing federal civil rights policy during the Kennedy, Johnson, and Nixon administrations. Then have each pair write two paragraphs that assess the impact of federal policy. Have students present their charts and paragraphs to the class.

By the fall of 1974, violent protests against busing had erupted in Boston. Yet despite the risks, many African American parents believed that busing was necessary to achieve equal education opportunities. One African American woman told her two children that busing would make school difficult.

> **"I'm afraid this isn't going to be an easy year for either of you. You're going to be called a lot of ugly names. You're going to be spat at, maybe pushed around some. But it's not the first time this has happened and it won't be the last. It's something we have to go through—something you have to go through—if this city is ever going to be integrated."**

The busing controversy quieted down after the Supreme Court limited the use of busing as a means to achieve racial integration. In 1974 the Court ruled in *Milliken* v. *Bradley* to end a plan that promoted desegregation in Detroit by merging inner-city school districts with the city's suburban districts. The ruling was a severe blow to activists hoping to continue the process of desegregation in neighborhood schools. Justice Thurgood Marshall dissented from the Court ruling. He declared, "Unless our children begin to learn together, there is little hope that our people will ever learn to live together."

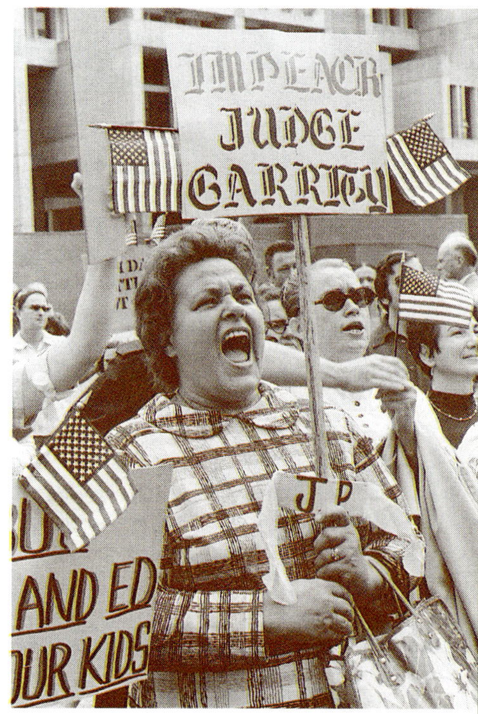

INTERPRETING THE VISUAL RECORD

Reaction to busing. In Boston, the court order to bus students outraged many white residents. ***What clues can you gather from this image of an anti-busing rally in Boston in 1974 that support the argument that the busing issue was an emotional one for many Americans?***

Affirmative action. Civil rights gains during the 1970s resulted from both public and private efforts. In order to uphold federal antidiscrimination laws and to end unfair labor practices, the Civil Rights Division of the Justice Department brought suits against corporations and labor unions. Many schools and businesses instituted **affirmative action** programs to compensate for previous discrimination. These programs gave preference to ethnic minorities and women in admission and hiring.

Many elected politicians did not support affirmative action. The Supreme Court nevertheless upheld the constitutionality of such programs in the 1971 case *Griggs* v. *Duke Power Co.* The Court ruled that tests given by the power company to decide on promotions had the effect of limiting the advancement of its African American workers. In the future, companies would have to explain why such tests were necessary. The case encouraged companies to create affirmative action programs.

Many white critics of affirmative action argued that it led to "reverse discrimination." In 1978 the Supreme Court handed down an important ruling affecting affirmative action. In ***University of California* v. *Bakke***, it ruled that a white man, Allan Bakke, had been unfairly denied admission to medical school on the basis of **quotas**. This system reserved a fixed number of openings for certain groups of people. Although not ruling out all forms of affirmative action, the Court did strike down the quota system in regard to university admissions. Again, Justice Thurgood Marshall dissented from the Court's majority ruling. Marshall explained, "The dream of America as the great melting pot has not been realized for the Negro; because of his skin color he never even made it into the pot."

✔ **READING CHECK:** How did the Supreme Court limit the impact of busing and affirmative action programs?

VISUAL RECORD ANSWER

Students might suggest that the large crowd, patriotic flag symbol, signs calling for impeachment, and the woman's passionate expression show that busing was an emotional issue.

STRATEGIES FOR SUCCESS ANSWERS

(for p. 642)

Practicing the Strategy

1. Answers will vary. Students should include the title and appropriate production information.
2. Answers will vary. Students should provide the main idea of the document as well as supporting evidence.
3. Answers will vary. Students should note the point of view of the document and identify any biases.
4. Answers will vary. Students should note the relation between their topic and the civil rights movement.

TEACH OBJECTIVE 3

ALL LEVELS: To help students understand the gains made by African Americans during the 1970s, copy the graphic organizer at right on the chalkboard, omitting the italicized answers. Have students complete the organizer. Also, have students write an article about African American successes during the 1970s. Ask volunteers to present their articles to the class. **Sheltered English**

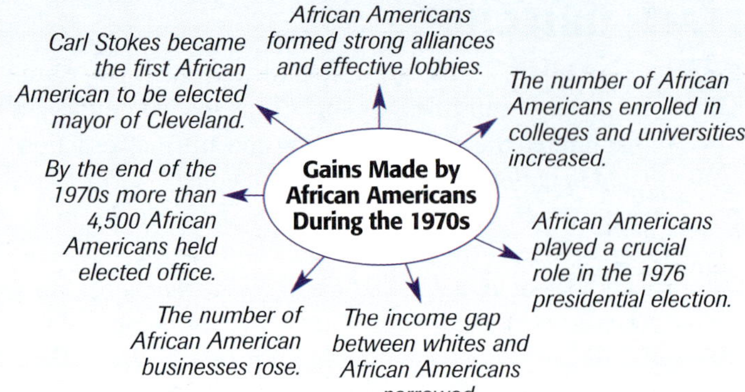

Gains Made by African Americans During the 1970s
Carl Stokes became the first African American to be elected mayor of Cleveland.
African Americans formed strong alliances and effective lobbies.
The number of African Americans enrolled in colleges and universities increased.
African Americans played a crucial role in the 1976 presidential election.
The income gap between whites and African Americans narrowed.
The number of African American businesses rose.
By the end of the 1970s more than 4,500 African Americans held elected office.

SECTION 4 REVIEW ANSWERS

Define and Identify

For significance, see the following pages:

- Ralph Abernathy, p. 639
- busing, p. 640
- affirmative action, p. 641
- *University of California* v. *Bakke*, p. 641
- Allan Bakke, p. 641
- quotas, p. 641
- Carl Stokes, p. 642
- National Black Political Convention, p. 643

1. goals—integrating schools with busing, integrating universities and workplaces with affirmative action; white reactions—angry about busing, some initiated violent protests, some whites challenged affirmative action; outcomes—Supreme Court limited busing and prohibited the use of quotas to achieve racial equality. More African Americans went to college and found better jobs.

2. They suffered from the loss of Martin Luther King Jr. Many white Americans began to work against some gains of the civil rights movement.

3. limited busing—by merging Detroit's school districts; affirmative action—by outlawing the use of quotas

4. Students should support their hypotheses with specific details.

5. Answers will vary. The movement integrated some schools, universities, and workplaces. More African Americans were getting college educations, finding better jobs, voting, and holding elected offices.

Strategies for Success — Using Multimedia Resources

Multimedia resources are sources of information such as television documentaries and CD–ROMS that incorporate words, sounds, and images in a single package. They are among the newest and most interesting research tools available to students. Multimedia resources often include ideas and data on historical topics from a variety of primary and secondary sources. The audiovisual formats they use to present this information can be very interesting.

Multimedia resources must be studied and analyzed carefully. The materials that make up multimedia resources—recordings, photographs, motion pictures, and written documents, for example—are distinct types of historical sources that should always be examined for accuracy and bias. It is also important to evaluate the manner in which a multimedia resource selects, presents, and discusses these materials.

How to Use a Multimedia Resource

1. **Find an appropriate resource.** Use your school or local public library to find a multimedia resource on the topic you wish to research. Once you have located an appropriate resource, take note of its title, publication date, and the people or organization that produced it.
2. **Study the resource carefully.** Study the resource carefully, identifying any main ideas and the specific means it uses to convey information. If you are using a CD–ROM, make sure to explore a variety of the materials it offers.
3. **Evaluate the resource.** Once you have examined the resource thoroughly, identify any factual inaccuracies and assess the manner in which it explains any differing points of view. Then evaluate any general biases that the resource displays in its selection, presentation, and discussion of historical evidence.
4. **Put the information to use.** Compare the resource with other materials that you find while researching your topic. Then use the results of your analysis to form generalizations and draw conclusions.

Applying the Strategy

Use your school or local public library to find a videotape of a film or television documentary about the civil rights movement. Then view the documentary and write a report that summarizes its main ideas and evaluates it.

Practicing the Strategy

Answer the following questions.

1. What is the title of the documentary you found? Who produced it? When was it produced?
2. What main ideas does the documentary convey? What types of evidence does it provide to convey these ideas?
3. How does the documentary handle any differing points of view about the civil rights movement? What biases, if any, does the documentary display?
4. How does the documentary contribute to your understanding of the civil rights movement?

Successes of the Movement

The civil rights movement suffered setbacks during the 1970s. African Americans, however, did make some advances during this period. African Americans scored a major success when Carl Stokes was elected mayor of Cleveland. Stokes was the first African American to be mayor of a major U.S. city. Geraldine Williams, the campaign secretary who helped Stokes win his bid for office, remembered the election.

> **"Definitely there was a connection with the civil rights movement. We got blacks to register, to vote, to take part in government. We convinced them that if you don't speak out and ask for things, you're never going to get them. You can't just sit there. We taught them that their vote does mean something, that it counts."**

REVIEW

Have students complete the **Section 4 Review** on p. 643.

ASSESS

Have students complete **Daily Quiz 21.4.** As **Alternative Assessment**, you may want to use the chart or the dissenting opinions in this section's lessons.

RETEACH

Have students complete **Main Idea Activity for Reteaching and Sheltered English 21.4.** Then ask each student to list the key terms and key people in Section 4. Create a comprehensive list on the chalkboard and have each student use the list to create an annotated time line that includes the events and people discussed in the section. Display students' time lines around the classroom. **Sheltered English**

EXTEND

Ask students to conduct research on an African American mayor of a large city who was elected during the 1970s or 1980s. *(Examples include Tom Bradley, Carl Stokes, and Harold Washington.)* Have each student write a report about the mayor's platform, term of office, whether the mayor received political support from a coalition of white and black Americans, and the mayor's major achievements while in office. **Block Scheduling**

To ensure that African Americans would continue to gain political influence, activists met in Gary, Indiana, in 1972 for the **National Black Political Convention**. Some 2,700 delegates and another 4,000 people attended the convention.

As African American leaders gained political experience, they formed strong alliances and effective lobbies. They also worked hard to get out the African American vote. Although just 58.5 percent of eligible black voters were registered in 1976, African Americans played a crucial role in the presidential election that year. By the end of the 1970s, more than 4,500 African Americans held elected office—three times the number in 1969. The roster of elected black officials in 1978 included 16 members of the House of Representatives.

African Americans also experienced some economic gains during the 1970s. The number of African American-owned businesses rose from 163,073 in 1969 to 231,195 in 1977. However, some 31 percent of African Americans still lived below the poverty line. Nevertheless, in many professions and regions of the nation the income gap between the two groups narrowed. Increased enrollment in colleges and universities ensured that more African Americans would gain better-paying jobs. By 1976 the number of African American college students stood at more than 800,000—four times higher than it had been in 1964.

✔ **READING CHECK:** What gains did African Americans make during the early 1970s?

African American Education, 1960–1975

Percentage of African American Population: 0, 10, 20, 30, 40, 50

1960 1975 Completed High School

1960 1975 Completed College

Sources: *Historical Statistics of the United States; Statistical Abstract of the United States: 1997*

Learning from Graphs As the civil rights movement progressed, the number of African Americans who finished high school and went on to college increased dramatically.

? Building Graph Skills By how much did the percentage of the African American population with a high school diploma increase from 1960 to 1975? By how much did the percentage of those with a college degree increase?

SECTION  REVIEW

Define and explain the significance of the following terms:
busing
affirmative action
University of California v. *Bakke*
quotas
National Black Political Convention

Identify and explain the significance of the following individuals:
Ralph Abernathy
Allan Bakke
Carl Stokes

1. **Using Graphic Organizers** Copy the following flowchart. Use it to explain changing strategies and goals within the post-1968 civil rights movement, white reactions to those goals, and outcomes.

Goals after 1968 → White Reactions → Outcomes

2. **Synthesizing** Why did many African American organizations experience difficulties during the 1970s?
3. **Recognizing Point of View** How and why did the Supreme Court limit busing and affirmative action?
4. **Hypothesizing** How might the civil rights movement have evolved differently in the 1970s if Martin Luther King Jr. had lived?

Critical Thinking

5. How successful was the civil rights movement by the mid-1970s?
Consider:
- the political successes of the movement
- economic and educational advances for African Americans
- civil rights goals left unfinished

GRAPH ANSWER

high school increase: more than doubled; college increase: doubled

CHAPTER 21 REVIEW ANSWERS

Creating a Time Line
Each event should have an explanation and the correct date.

Writing a Summary
See the Reading Checks in each section for main ideas.

Identifying People and Ideas
1. civil rights leader who advocated nonviolent protest
2. people who rode buses through the South to force integration of public facilities on the interstates
3. prohibited discrimination in employment and public facilities
4. summer of 1964, during which civil rights workers tried to register African Americans in Mississippi to vote
5. MFDP delegate who lost her job and house when she registered to vote
6. African American religious sect based on some aspects of Islam
7. African American activist who originated the Black Power movement
8. reported that white racism was causing tensions that led to riots
9. giving preference to ethnic minorities and women in hiring and school admission

REVIEW AND ASSESSMENT RESOURCES

PRINT

- Chapter 21 Review, pp. 644–45
- Chapter 21 Tutorial for Students, Parents, Mentors, and Peers
- Chapter 21 Test (Form A or B)
- Portfolio Activities and Alternative Assessment Handbook, Chapter 21

MULTIMEDIA

- Audio Program, Chapter 21 (English and Spanish)
- Chapter 21 Test Generator (on the One-Stop Planner)
- Global Skill Builder CD–ROM
- HRW Web site

SHELTERED ENGLISH

- Spanish Glossary
- Sheltered English Chapter 21 Test

REVIEW

Have students complete the **Chapter 21 Review** on pp. 644–45.

ASSESS

Use one of the chapter tests to assess students' understanding of the content. For **Alternative Assessment**, see the **Portfolio Activities and Alternative Assessment Handbook.**

10. first African American mayor of a major city (Cleveland)

Understanding Main Ideas

1. It called attention to the need for reforms and to the willingness of many authorities to commit violence against African American protesters.

2. It addressed employment discrimination and segregation of public facilities; gave the Justice Department some jurisdiction over school desegregation.

3. White activists were involved in the drive.

4. It gave the federal government the power to enforce voting rights for African Americans.

5. black separatism; encourage self-reliance

6. Many whites feared that these programs would limit their ability to choose schools and find jobs.

7. More African Americans were going to college, finding better jobs, voting, and holding elected offices.

Reviewing Themes

1. It faced the same threats and violence it had faced in the South, but it also faced a reluctance by the federal government to support civil rights issues in the large northern cities.

2. Many times the police or officials participated in violence against civil rights workers, and often they arrested the demonstrators rather than people who attacked the demonstrators.

Chapter 21 Review

Creating a Time Line

Copy the time line below onto a sheet of paper. Complete the time line by filling in the events and dates from the chapter that you think were most significant. Pick three events and explain why you think they were significant.

Writing a Summary

Using the Reading Checks as a guide, write an overview of the events in the chapter.

Identifying People and Ideas

Identify the following terms or individuals and explain their significance.

1. Martin Luther King Jr.
2. Freedom Riders
3. Civil Rights Act of 1964
4. Freedom Summer
5. Fannie Lou Hamer
6. Nation of Islam
7. Stokely Carmichael
8. Kerner Commission
9. affirmative action
10. Carl Stokes

Understanding Main Ideas

SECTION 1

1. Why was nonviolence effective in the early years of the civil rights movement?
2. In what ways did the Civil Rights Act of 1964 respond to the racial problems in the South?

SECTION 2

3. How did Freedom Summer differ from earlier voter registration drives?
4. Why did the Voting Rights Act mark a major turning point in the civil rights struggle?

SECTION 3

5. What were the goals of the black nationalists?

SECTION 4

6. Why did busing and affirmative action arouse such passionate opposition?
7. What successes could African Americans point to during the early 1970s?

Reviewing Themes

1. **Democratic Values** What difficulties did the SCLC face when it attempted to bring the civil rights struggle to northern cities?
2. **Constitutional Heritage** In what ways did southern officials fail to protect the rights of voter registration workers and other demonstrators?
3. **Economic Development** What type of economic growth did black nationalists favor?

Thinking Critically

1. **Synthesizing** In what circumstances was nonviolent protest most effective? Why?
2. **Assessing Consequences** What effect did Malcolm X have on the civil rights movement?
3. **Recognizing Point of View** Why did SNCC workers such as Stokely Carmichael abandon nonviolent protest?
4. **Using Historical Imagination** How might the civil rights movement have been different if Martin Luther King Jr. and Malcolm X had not been assassinated?
5. **Taking a Stand** Would you have supported the goal of black nationalism at the 1972 National Black Political Convention? Why or why not?

Writing About History

Writing to Explain Copy the following chart and use it to write an essay that explains the benefits and drawbacks of Black Power for the civil rights movement.

Benefits	Drawbacks

RETEACH

Organize students into triads. Have each triad create an annotated time line of important events or developments in the civil rights struggle from the Montgomery Bus Boycott in 1958 through the end of the 1970s. Display students' time lines around the classroom.
Sheltered English, Cooperative Learning

EXTEND

Have each student conduct research on major businesses in the United States owned or controlled by African Americans. Have students represent their findings in a collage.
Block Scheduling

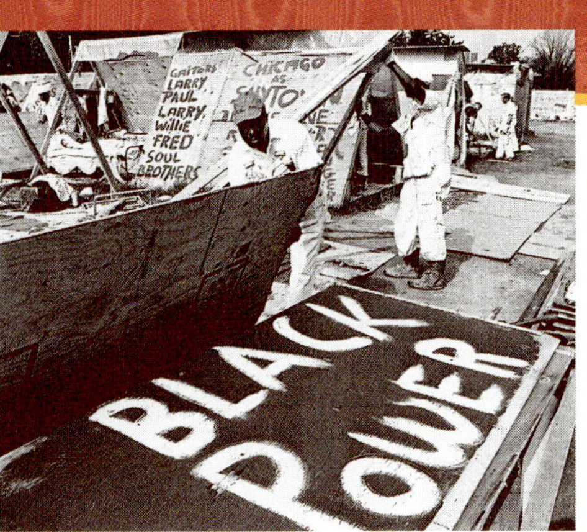

Workers dismantle Resurrection City in 1968 after the failure of the Poor People's Campaign.

Strategies for Success Review the **Strategies for Success** on *Using Multimedia Resources.* Then use your school or local public library to find a CD–ROM about the civil rights movement. Explore the CD–ROM on a computer and write a one-page report that summarizes its main ideas and evaluates the materials it offers.

Linking History and Geography

The Freedom Rides met with violent resistance in the South. Study the map below. Where did the Freedom Rides end for the CORE group and the SNCC group? How far was each group from its intended destination when it was stopped?

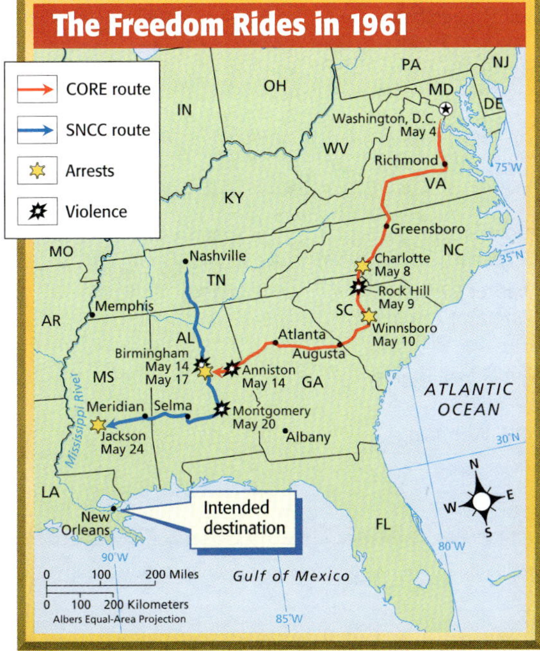

internetconnect

TOPIC: Malcolm X and Martin Luther King Jr.
GO TO: go.hrw.com
KEYWORD: SE1 Leaders

Accessing the Internet through the HRW Web site, research the lives of Martin Luther King Jr. and Malcolm X. Then create an illustrated poster that compares and contrasts the beliefs and goals of these African American leaders.

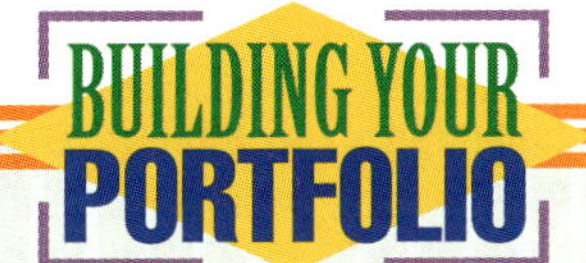

BUILDING YOUR PORTFOLIO

Complete one or all of the following activities independently or cooperatively.

1 Cultural Diversity

Imagine that you are a northern newspaper reporter covering the civil rights movement. ***Write a memorandum*** to your editor explaining why the newspaper should provide coverage of African American civil rights efforts in the South.

2 Democratic Values

Imagine that you are a civil rights activist registering voters during Freedom Summer. ***Write a letter*** to your family explaining the conditions that you face and why you are continuing in your efforts despite the violence.

3 Constitutional Heritage

Imagine that you are a museum curator creating a time line of the civil rights movement from 1965 to 1975. ***Create an illustrated time line*** and write captions for the images you use.

CORE hat

FREEDOM NOW! C·O·R·E· CONGRESS OF RACIAL EQUALITY

3. They favored the growth of African American businesses and political power.

Thinking Critically

1. Integrating public areas, because they interfered with business and because the federal government eventually took steps to protect protesters from violence.
2. encouraged separatism and a break with nonviolent protest; encouraged activists to work for their goals, using any means
3. Some activists believed that nonviolent protests were not working or were not working fast enough. Others questioned the move for integration, partially because they felt that white people were taking over. Many were angered that the deaths of white civil rights activists provoked more outrage that did the deaths of Africans.
4. Students might suggest that the movement would have been more successful.
5. Students should explain their choices.

Writing About History
Answers will vary. Students should clearly identify the reasons for their positions.

Strategies for Success
Summaries should present main ideas and evaluation.

Linking History and Geography
Birmingham, Alabama; Jackson, Mississippi. CORE–300 miles; SNCC–150 miles

Struggles for Change

CHAPTER PLANNING GUIDE

	Section Lesson Objectives	Print Resources	Multimedia Resources	Sheltered English Resources
Section 1 Women's Rights, pp. 648–53	1 Describe what *The Feminine Mystique* revealed about women, and discuss how readers responded to it. 2 Explain how the federal government tried to assist working women in the early 1960s. 3 Relate what tactics the leaders of the women's movement used. 4 Identify the gains and setbacks the women's movement experienced during the 1970s.	▶ Guided Reading Strategy 22.1 ▶ Graphic Organizer Activity 22: Protesting the Status Quo ▶ Section 1 Review, p. 653 ▶ Daily Quiz 22.1	▶ One-Stop Planner, Lesson 22.1 ▶ The American Nation Video Program Segment: The Women's Rights Movement; Teacher's Guide, pp. 209–10 ▶ Holt Researcher: American History CD–ROM	▶ Main Idea Activity for Reteaching and Sheltered English 22.1
Section 2 The Chicano Movement, pp. 654–60	1 Discuss why La Huelga was important to Mexican Americans throughout the country. 2 Explain how conflicts over land rights and education motivated Mexican Americans to protest. 3 Describe how aggressive activists shaped the Chicano movement. 4 Analyze how the Chicano movement changed the lives of Mexican Americans.	▶ Guided Reading Strategy 22.2 ▶ Section 2 Review, p. 660 ▶ Daily Quiz 22.2	▶ One-Stop Planner, Lesson 22.2 ▶ The American Nation Video Program Segment: César Chávez; Teacher's Guide, pp. 167–68 ▶ Holt Researcher: American History CD–ROM	▶ Main Idea Activity for Reteaching and Sheltered English 22.2
Section 3 More Groups Mobilize, pp. 661–65	1 Describe what Red Power movement activists demanded, and discuss how successful they were. 2 Explain how Americans with disabilities gained public support for their causes. 3 Identify the issues activists for senior citizens and children addressed.	▶ Guided Reading Strategy 22.3 ▶ Primary Source Reading 22: American Indian Activism Begins ▶ Biography Reading 22: Marian Wright Edelman ▶ Section 3 Review, p. 665 ▶ Daily Quiz 22.3	▶ One-Stop Planner, Lesson 22.3 ▶ Holt Researcher: American History CD–ROM ▶ HRW Web site	▶ Main Idea Activity for Reteaching and Sheltered English 22.3
Section 4 A Cultural Revolution, pp. 666–71	1 Explain why protests developed on American college campuses. 2 Describe the problems that weakened the counterculture. 3 Explain how doubts about American society led to new movements in religion and the arts. 4 Analyze how musical styles reflected the social changes of the era.	▶ Guided Reading Strategy 22.4 ▶ Literature Reading 22: High Style ▶ Geography Activity 22: The Environment Under Assault ▶ Section 4 Review, p. 671 ▶ Daily Quiz 22.4	▶ One-Stop Planner, Lesson 22.4 ▶ American Music Selection 25: "Blowin' in the Wind" ▶ Holt Researcher: American History CD–ROM	▶ Main Idea Activity for Reteaching and Sheltered English 22.4
Chapter Review and Assessment pp. 672–73		▶ Chapter 22 Review, pp. 672–73 ▶ Chapter 22 Tutorial for Students, Parents, Mentors, and Peers ▶ Chapter 22 Test (Form A or B) ▶ Portfolio Activities and Alternative Assessment Handbook, Chapter 22	▶ Audio Program, Chapter 22 (English and Spanish) ▶ Chapter 22 Test Generator (on the One-Stop Planner) ▶ Global Skill Builder CD–ROM ▶ HRW Web site	▶ Spanish Glossary ▶ Sheltered English Chapter 22 Test

CHAPTER OVERVIEW

Inspired in part by the African American civil rights movement, other groups worked for equality during the 1960s and 1970s. Women tried to expand their social roles and pass a constitutional amendment barring sex discrimination. American Indian activists demanded self-determination, the return of illegally seized land, and economic improvements. Americans with disabilities and advocates for children and senior citizens worked to increase their legal rights, improve health care, and decrease poverty and discrimination.

American society underwent enormous changes from 1963 to 1975. College students and other young people protested what they viewed as civil rights violations, and some "dropped out" to form a counterculture. This counterculture was weakened by drug and alcohol abuse, sexually transmitted diseases, and crime. New movements in art, music, and religion also reflected the upheavals of the time.

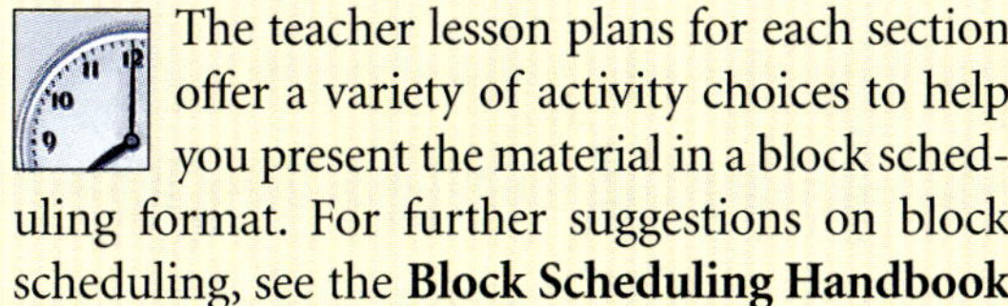

Block Scheduling

The teacher lesson plans for each section offer a variety of activity choices to help you present the material in a block scheduling format. For further suggestions on block scheduling, see the **Block Scheduling Handbook with Team Teaching Strategies**, pp. 127–32.

Smithsonian Institution
Internet Connections and Lesson 22
www.si.edu/hrw

Hands-On History Activities:

Classroom to Community The **Hands-On History Activities** help students make meaningful connections between events in American history and those in their own hometown. You may wish to use the Chapter 22 Activity, Write a Biography, to extend the chapter lessons, as alternative assessment, or as a block scheduling option.

Portfolio Projects

The American Nation includes multiple portfolio projects in each Pupil's Edition chapter review, as well as each unit review. Chapter 22 Portfolio Project options on p. 673 include the following:

1. Students will **create a flier**.
2. Students will **write a brief summary**.
3. Students will **write an illustrated article**.

The American Nation

INTERNET RESOURCE DIRECTORY

To access online materials for this chapter, go to **go.hrw.com** and type in the keywords listed below.

HRW ONLINE RESOURCES
GO TO: go.hrw.com

Online Charts
KEYWORD: SE1 Charts22
- Women in the Professions

Online Reading Support
KEYWORD: SE1 Strategies22

Online Rubrics
KEYWORD: SE1 Rubrics

CHAPTER ENRICHMENT LINKS
Use these Web links to extend and enrich student learning for Chapter 22.
GO TO: go.hrw.com
KEYWORD: SE1 Ch22

CHAPTER INTERNET ACTIVITIES
GO TO: go.hrw.com
- Pupil's Edition Student Activity
  KEYWORD: SE1 Farm
  (Students conduct research on César Chávez and the United Farm Workers.)
- Teacher's Edition Student Activity
  KEYWORD: SE1 Women
  (Students compare and contrast issues from the women's rights movements in 1848 and the 1960s.)
- Teacher's Edition Student Activity
  KEYWORD: SE1 Edelman
  (Students examine the activities of the Children's Defense Fund.)

ADDITIONAL
RESOURCES

Books for Teachers

Rosenberg, Rosalind. *Divided Lives: American Women in the Twentieth Century.* Hill & Wang, 1992. Surveys women's experiences in the 1900s.

Smith, Paul Chaat, and Robert Allen Warrior. *Like a Hurricane: The Indian Movement from Alcatraz to Wounded Knee.* New Press, 1996. Presents an absorbing, readable study of American Indian activism.

Books for Students

Rodriguez, Consuelo. *Cesar Chavez.* Chelsea House, 1991. Presents a biography of the union organizer. Particularly appropriate for students reading below grade level.

Shapiro, Joseph. *No Pity: People with Disabilities Forging a New Civil Rights Movement.* Times Books, 1994. Discusses the formation of the movement and prominent activists.

Primary Sources from the Period

Deloria, Vine Jr. *Custer Died for Your Sins: An Indian Manifesto.* Macmillan, 1969. Explains the sources of American Indian activism.

Friedan, Betty. *The Feminine Mystique.* Dell, 1963. Discusses women's lives in the postwar United States; helped launch the modern feminist movement.

Multimedia Materials

Stop the World, We Want to Get On. Video, 26 min. Bullfrog Films. Studies the disability rights movement.

Women's Rights. Video, 28 min. Altana Films. Includes material from the 1970s.

CHAPTER 22

Before You Read

Build on What You Know

Ask students to answer the following questions.

Why might the African American civil rights movement have inspired other groups to work for civil rights?

Consider:

- the significance of a successful example
- the discrimination that other groups faced

How might women, Mexican Americans, American Indians, and others have begun to demand fair treatment?

Consider:

- the methods used by the African American civil rights movement
- the importance of government action and support

exploring the time line

AMERICAN EVENTS

internet**connect**

TOPIC: Women's Rights Movement
GO TO: go.hrw.com
KEYWORD: SE1 Women

Have students access the Internet through the HRW Web site to conduct research on the history of the women's rights movement. Ask each student to make a graphic organizer comparing and contrasting issues from the women's rights movement in 1848 and in the 1960s. Then ask students to write summary statements about the evolution of the women's rights movement.

CHAPTER 22

1963–1975

Struggles for Change

Valentina Tereshkova

Mexican American migrant workers

1963
Science and Technology
Soviet cosmonaut Valentina V. Tereshkova becomes the first woman in space.

1963
Politics
Congress passes the Equal Pay Act.

1965
Business and Finance
Migrant farmworkers in California begin a strike against grape growers.

1963 **1965** **1967**

The Beatles

1964
The Arts
The Beatles perform on *The Ed Sullivan Show* to a record television audience.

1964
Daily Life
The Ford Motor Company introduces the Mustang, which immediately becomes one of the nation's most popular car models.

1966
Politics
The National Organization for Women (NOW) is founded.

A Ford Mustang

Before You Read

Build on What You Know

The prosperity that followed World War II brought many changes to American society. A youth rebellion began in the 1950s with the beats and rock 'n' roll. African Americans continued to fight for equal rights. In this chapter you will learn how women, Mexican Americans, American Indians, and others began to demand fair treatment. You will also learn that during the 1960s some Americans challenged the beliefs and traditions of older generations. The result was a cultural revolution that eventually affected the entire nation.

646

Think About Themes

To help students create their Themes Journal entries, provide the following examples of appropriate **agree/disagree** *statements.*

Constitutional Heritage

Agree Temperance advocates perceived drinking as a national crisis, although many modern-day historians disagree with that assessment.

Disagree Many groups have attempted to amend the Constitution; some were inspired by a national crisis and some were inspired by a political goal.

Economic Development

Agree As a whole, the prosperous 1920s were not marked by political protest.

Disagree The struggle for African American civil rights intensified during a period of relative economic prosperity.

Cultural Diversity

Agree During the Great Depression, Americans watched motion pictures to forget their problems.

Disagree Harriet Beecher Stowe's novel *Uncle Tom's Cabin* helped galvanize the antislavery movement in the North during the 1850s.

Symbol for the MPAA rating system

1968
The Arts
The Motion Picture Association adopts a film rating system.

1968
Daily Life
Some 100 people protest the Miss America Pageant in Atlantic City, New Jersey.

1968
Politics
The American Indian Movement is organized.

1970
Science and Technology
Marine biologist Sylvia Earle Mead and five other female scientists spend two weeks underwater without surfacing.

The first issue of Ms. magazine

1972
Business and Finance
The first issue of *Ms.* magazine sells 250,000 copies.

1972
Politics
The Equal Rights Amendment is sent to the states for ratification after its approval by Congress.

1974
Daily Life
Engineer Art Fry invents Post-It Notes.

1969 | **1971** | **1973** | **1975**

1969
World Events
Golda Meir becomes the prime minister of Israel.

Golda Meir

1971
Business and Finance
Community organizers in East Los Angeles work with the United Auto Workers to create the East Los Angeles Community Union.

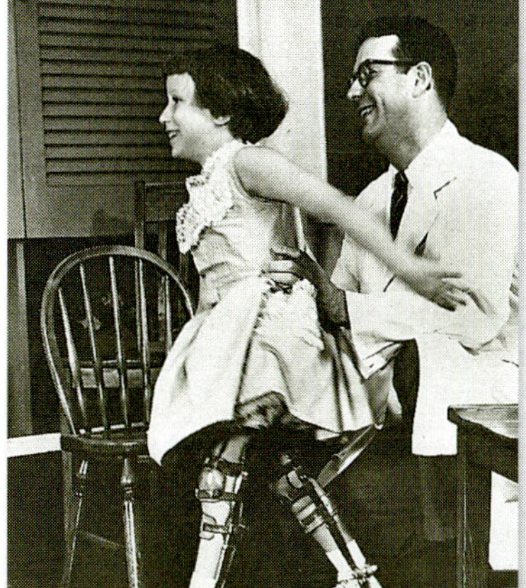

An instructor assists a child learning to walk with leg braces.

1975
Politics
Congress passes the Education for All Handicapped Children Act.

Think About Themes

Decide whether you **agree** *or* **disagree** *with the following statements. Note why in your journal.*

Constitutional Heritage Amending the Constitution is a serious matter that should only be undertaken in the face of a national crisis.

Economic Development A rising standard of living makes young people so satisfied that political protests decrease.

Cultural Diversity Music, fashion, and art are merely for pleasure and entertainment and have little social or political significance.

exploring the time line

GLOBAL EVENTS

1963 ■ Valentina V. Tereshkova. Valentina V. Tereshkova was born in the Soviet Union in 1937, the daughter of a laborer on a collective farm. As an adult, Tereshkova worked in a factory. In her free time she learned to parachute with a local aviation club. This experience eventually led to her selection for the cosmonaut training program. In 1963 she became the first woman in space. However, after her flight she never ventured into space again, but spent much of her time on Communist Party political activities.

ACTIVITY: Tell students to imagine that they are American journalists who have a strong interest in women's achievements and in the space race between the United States and the Soviet Union. Have each student write a short article about Valentina V. Tereshkova's spaceflight and the event's larger significance. Alternately, have each student write several newspaper headlines announcing the flight and its significance.

SECTION 1

After completing Section 1, students should be able to:

OBJECTIVE 1 *Describe what* The Feminine Mystique *revealed about women, and discuss how readers responded to it.*

OBJECTIVE 2 *Explain how the federal government tried to assist working women in the early 1960s.*

OBJECTIVE 3 *Relate what tactics the leaders of the women's movement used.*

OBJECTIVE 4 *Identify the gains and setbacks the women's movement experienced during the 1970s.*

LET'S GET STARTED!

Have students read the quotation by Betty Friedan on this page. Then ask them to respond to the quotation in writing, explaining how the feelings expressed in the quotation might have sparked the modern-day women's movement. Have volunteers share their responses. Then tell students that in Section 1 they will learn about how women pursued equal rights in the 1960s and 1970s.

SECTION 1 RESOURCES

PRINT

- Guided Reading Strategy 22.1
- Graphic Organizer Activity 22: Protesting the Status Quo
- Section 1 Review, p. 653
- Daily Quiz 22.1

MULTIMEDIA

- One-Stop Planner, Lesson 22.1
- The American Nation Video Program Segment: The Women's Rights Movement; Teacher's Guide, pp. 209–10
- Holt Researcher: American History CD–ROM

SHELTERED ENGLISH

- Main Idea Activity for Reteaching and Sheltered English 22.1

✔ READING TO UNDERSTAND

To help students master the section objectives, have them answer the **READING CHECKS** and complete **Guided Reading Strategy 22.1** as they read the section.

GRAPH ANSWER

(for p. 649)

by 6.7 million

Women's Rights

OBJECTIVES

Read to understand:

1. what *The Feminine Mystique* revealed about women, and how readers responded to it
2. how the federal government tried to assist working women in the early 1960s
3. what tactics the leaders of the women's movement used
4. what gains and setbacks the women's movement experienced during the 1970s

KEY TERMS

Equal Pay Act
National Organization for Women
National Women's Political Caucus
Educational Amendments Act

KEY PEOPLE

Betty Friedan
Gloria Steinem
Phyllis Schlafly
Bella Abzug
Shirley Chisholm

"I guess I've been pretty much influenced by the Women's Movement because of the people I work with. . . . A lot of them were in that movement, so I've become more aware of it that way. I've just become much more aware of being a woman and the rights a woman should have. . . . Before, what I knew about the movement was really limited to just what I saw—people in demonstrations and the type of women who were professionals and their side of things."

—Cathy Tuley

In the 1960s and 1970s many American women demanded equal rights.

Cathy Tuley, a hospital clerical worker, discussed her perceptions of the women's movement. Tuley's experiences mirrored those of many other women who entered the workforce during the 1960s and 1970s.

A Revived Women's Movement

One of the lasting effects of the 1960s was a change in the traditional roles of women. After years of inaction, the women's movement experienced a widespread revival, sparked in part by the work of author Betty Friedan.

In 1957 Friedan conducted a survey of women who, like herself, had graduated from Smith College 15 years earlier. She hoped to dispute the popular notion that higher education was harmful to women. To Friedan's surprise, the women who responded to her questionnaire expressed dissatisfaction with their lives. Almost all the women whom Friedan surveyed were full-time homemakers. Many found their lives unfulfilling. In her 1963 book, *The Feminine Mystique*, Friedan concluded that many women felt trapped by the "comfortable concentration camp" of domestic life.

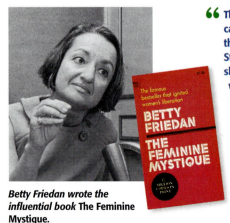

"The problem lay buried, unspoken, for many years in the minds of American women. It was a strange stirring, a sense of dissatisfaction, a yearning that women suffered in the middle of the twentieth century in the United States. Each suburban wife struggled with it alone. As she made the beds, shopped for groceries, matched slipcover material, ate peanut butter sandwiches with her children, chauffeured Cub Scouts and Brownies . . . she was afraid to ask even of herself the silent question—'Is this all?'"

Betty Friedan wrote the influential book **The Feminine Mystique.**

By the end of the decade *The Feminine Mystique* had sold more than 1 million copies. Inspired by its message, many women began to examine their lives. Seeking change, they demanded increased opportunities and fair treatment in the workplace.

✔ READING CHECK: What did *The Feminine Mystique* reveal about women, and how did readers respond to it?

Teacher to Teacher

Jenifer Rowray of Runnells, Iowa, suggested the following activity: Organize students into small groups and have them pick one year between 1963 and 1975. Ask each group to conduct research on events that took place during its chosen year. Tell students to determine the short- and long-term effects of these events. Then have each group prepare a short oral report on the year. To create a living time line, ask students to deliver their reports in chronological order.

TEACH OBJECTIVE 1

ALL LEVELS: Conduct a brief discussion on what *The Feminine Mystique* revealed about women and how readers responded to it. *(Students might answer that many women, particularly homemakers, felt dissatisfied with their lives. Inspired by the book, many women began to demand increased opportunities and fair treatment in the workplace.)* Then pair students and ask each pair to write a paragraph summarizing why many American women were dissatisfied. Have volunteers share their paragraphs with the class.
Sheltered English, Cooperative Learning

Helping Women at Work

Most of the women polled by Betty Friedan were homemakers. However, the number of women in the workplace had grown dramatically in the years before her book was published. The number of working women rose from 25 percent in 1940 to 35 percent in 1960. By 1963 almost 25 million working women made up more than one third of the American labor force. Yet female workers received lower wages than men did. In 1960, for example, women who worked full-time earned 40 percent less than working men. Women typically held service jobs that paid poorly, but in many cases they received lower wages even when they did the same work as men. As one business executive confessed, "We pay [women] less because we can get them for less."

In June 1963 President John F. Kennedy signed the Equal Pay Act, which required that women receive equal pay for equal work.

Kennedy responds. The Kennedy administration hired few women but did not ignore the problems that working women faced. President Kennedy issued an executive order requiring that civil-service hiring occur "solely on the basis of ability to meet the requirements of the position, and without regard to sex." His administration also backed a new law that made it illegal for employers to pay female workers less than male workers for the same job. Congress approved this **Equal Pay Act**, which Kennedy signed in June 1963. The act had a limited impact, however. Its provisions did not cover women in agricultural, professional, or service industries—about two thirds of working women. Nevertheless, the law served as an important first step toward equality in the workplace. In the decade following its passage, 171,000 workers used the law to win $84 million in back pay.

Kennedy also created the President's Commission on the Status of Women (PCSW) and appointed former first lady Eleanor Roosevelt as its chairperson. Kennedy authorized the PCSW to investigate the lives of American women. Completed in October 1963, the commission's report noted that female workers continued to experience discrimination in the workplace despite their increasing numbers. The report set new goals for the treatment of working women and called for "equal opportunity in hiring, training, and promotion."

Title VII. Female workers received additional and unexpected assistance from the federal government in 1964. That year Congress debated legislation intended to protect the civil rights of African Americans. Representative Howard Smith of Virginia proposed adding a clause to the bill that would protect women from discrimination. Smith opposed the civil rights bill and actually hoped that his amendment would weaken its chances of passing.

Occupations of Women, 1960–1970

Number of Women (in millions): 0, 5, 10, 15, 20, 25, 30, 35

1960: Total 22.3 — 11.7; 8.9; 0.4; 1.3
1970: Total 30.3 — 18.4; 11.6; 0.2; 0.06

Manual labor, service
Farming
White collar
Unknown

Source: *Historical Statistics of the United States*

Learning from Graphs The number of working women increased from 1960 to 1970.

? Building Graph Skills By how much did the number of women working in white-collar professions increase?

DEMOCRATIC VALUES

The President's Commission on the Status of Women. President Kennedy gained a significant political advantage when he created the President's Commission on the Status of Women. The creation of the group pleased female voters—citizens who might support Kennedy in future elections. In addition, forming the commission allowed Kennedy to appear to support women's rights without taking a stand on any specific issues. Kennedy's motivations were not purely political, however. He understood that women often experienced discrimination in the workplace. A 1957 study had recommended that the Department of Labor study the underuse of female workers.

CRITICAL THINKING Why might women have been an underused source of labor?

ANSWER: Students might suggest that the limited conception of women's roles barred women from certain occupations.

THAT'S INTERESTING!

Title VII allowed some gender-based hiring. A "bona fide occupational qualification" permitted employers to consider gender when hiring for certain jobs such as modeling men's clothing or playing a woman in a movie.

TEACH OBJECTIVE 2

LEVEL 1: Pair students and ask each pair to list the ways that the federal government tried to assist working women in the early 1960s. *(Pairs should list the Equal Pay Act, the President's Commission on the Status of Women, Title VII, and the Equal Employment Opportunity Commission.)* Then have each pair rank these efforts from most important to least important, writing paragraphs to present and justify its selections. Ask students to share their rankings with the class. Conduct a discussion on their selections. **Sheltered English, Cooperative Learning**

LEVEL 2: Tell students to imagine that it is 1966 and that they are presidential advisers. Have each student write a short memo to the president, describing the government's efforts to assist working women in the early 1960s and suggesting a future course of action. *(See the Level 1 lesson for the correct efforts.)* Have volunteers read their memos to the class.

LEVEL 3: Conduct a brief discussion on the ways that the federal government tried to assist working women in the early 1960s. *(See the Level 1 lesson for the correct efforts.)* Then organize students into two large groups—one that supports further government action on women's rights and one that opposes it. Give students time to prepare their arguments and then conduct a debate on the topic. Remind students that their arguments should be grounded in fact and analysis rather than personal opinion. **Cooperative Learning**

ECONOMIC DEVELOPMENT

Classified Advertisements. In the 1960s many newspapers split their employment advertisements into separate sections for men and women. Women's jobs typically offered low pay and little opportunity for advancement. Women's rights advocates wanted the EEOC to ban the segregational want ads, but the agency refused to force publishers to end the practice. This refusal disillusioned many women and sparked new activism.

CRITICAL THINKING Should the EEOC have forced publishers to ban the segregated classified advertisements?

ANSWER: Answers will vary. Some students might argue that the segregated ads promoted discrimination.

VISUAL RECORD ANSWER

(for p. 651)

Students might note that women of all ages were involved.

The EEOC works to prevent discrimination in employment.

Female members of Congress seized the opportunity. Representative Martha Griffiths of Michigan declared, "A vote against this amendment today by a . . . man is a vote against his wife, or his widow, or his daughter, or his sister." Congress approved the Smith amendment, and the bill passed. As a result, Title VII of the Civil Rights Act of 1964 outlawed sexual discrimination in employment. The act also created the Equal Employment Opportunity Commission (EEOC). This federal agency is charged with ensuring that employers followed the provisions of Title VII.

✔ **READING CHECK:** How did the federal government try to assist working women in the early 1960s?

Heightened Activism

Women quickly discovered that many government officials were more interested in battling racial discrimination than in using civil rights laws to fight gender discrimination. Herman Edelsberg, the director of the EEOC, called the gender-discrimination ban "a fluke." Sonia Pressman, an attorney for the EEOC, later explained why the agency did not respond to women's needs.

> **"We had an agency with a mandate [order] to prohibit sex discrimination . . . in a country that was not conscious of the fact that women were the victims of discrimination. After all, while the creation of the EEOC was in direct response to the movement for black rights in this country, there had been no similar movement immediately prior to 1965 for women's rights."**

NOW. In June 1966 a group of women attending a conference on women's status met in Betty Friedan's hotel room to discuss their frustration with the EEOC. Some wanted to found an organization to lobby on behalf of women's rights. Instead, the group decided to present a resolution to the conference condemning the EEOC. Pauli Murray recalled, "I left Betty Friedan's room that night thoroughly discouraged; it seemed to me that we had fumbled a major opportunity to begin mobilizing [organizing] women nationally to press for their civil rights."

The next day, however, the conference rejected the resolution. During lunch the women decided to form a women's rights group. The **National Organization for Women** (NOW) was the result. NOW claimed some 1,000 members within its first year in existence. The organization pressured elected officials to ensure social and economic equality for women.

Buttons and patches like these served as outward signs of women's determination to win equality with men.

A new generation. Some women rejected NOW's moderate approach to political change. Critic Marlene Dixon maintained that NOW would secure "limited and elitist [exclusive] day-care programs . . . [and] an effective end to job discrimination at least on the elite level." Dixon argued that "these programs give the illusion of success, while in fact assuring the destruction of any hope for women's liberation."

Dixon voiced the opinion of a new generation of female activists. Many of these women had participated in other social movements, such as the struggle for civil rights. Many female activists realized that they faced just as much gender discrimination in these movements as they did in mainstream society. Mary King and Casey Hayden were volunteers for the Student Nonviolent Coordinating

TEACH OBJECTIVE 3

LEVEL 1: Ask students to relate what tactics the leaders of the women's movement used. *(Students should indicate that Betty Friedan and others founded the National Organization for Women (NOW), which pushed for equal rights for women. In addition, other groups encouraged women to run for political office.)* Then pair students and tell them to imagine that it is 1967 and that they are women preparing to form an organization supporting women's rights. Have each pair develop a list of goals and methods for its organization. Ask volunteers to share their lists with the class. Conduct a discussion on the goals and methods.
Sheltered English, Cooperative Learning

LEVELS 2 AND 3: Organize students into triads. Tell them to imagine that it is 1967 and that they are women preparing to form an organization supporting women's rights. Have each triad develop a mission statement that describes the organization and its goals. Have volunteers read their statements to the class. To conclude, conduct a brief discussion on the tactics used by leaders of the women's rights movement. *(See the Level 1 lesson for the correct tactics.)* Post students' mission statements around the classroom. **Cooperative Learning**

▶**ASSIGNMENT:** *Ask each student to write a short poem about the tactics used by the leaders of the women's rights movement.*

Committee (SNCC). In 1964 they noted that SNCC's "assumption of male superiority" was "as widespread and deep rooted and . . . as crippling to . . . women as the assumptions of white supremacy are to the Negro."

During the late 1960s many female social activists began standing up for their own rights. Numerous small women's groups sprang up nationwide. Some held discussion sessions to improve their self-image. Others took direct, and often controversial, action. In 1968, feminists disrupted the Miss America Pageant, charging that beauty contests degraded women.

Gloria Steinem

Journalist Gloria Steinem was one of the women inspired to activism during the late 1960s. Steinem was born on March 25, 1934, in Toledo, Ohio. Her parents divorced in 1946, and Steinem spent most of her teenage years caring for her invalid mother. In 1952 Steinem entered Smith College, where she graduated with honors. "I loved Smith," she recalled. "They gave you three meals a day to eat, and all the books you wanted to read—what more could you want?" Her love of reading and writing led her to become a journalist.

In 1968 Steinem started writing a political column for *New York* magazine. Her work brought her into contact with many activists. Steinem did not initially consider herself a feminist. She later recalled, "Though I was old enough to be part of the *Feminine Mystique* generation, I wasn't living in the suburbs, wondering why I wasn't using my college degree. I'd ended up in the workforce many of these other women were trying to enter."

Steinem's interest in civil rights and political activism eventually led her to consider the status of women in American society. She began writing openly feminist articles that established her as a supporter of the women's movement. In one article Steinem stated that cooperation by radical feminists, middle-class reformers, and poor women could create a powerful movement for women's causes. In 1971 she helped found the **National Women's Political Caucus** to encourage women to run for political office. The next year, she became editor of a new magazine for women entitled *Ms.*

"There is nothing outside of [the movement]," Steinem said. "I once thought I would do this for two or three years and go home to my real life." Steinem remains a leader in the women's movement. She has written several books and helped found numerous organizations for women, including the Coalition of Labor Union Women and Women Against Pornography.

✔ **READING CHECK:** What tactics did the leaders of the women's movement use?

INTERPRETING THE VISUAL RECORD

Women's rights. These women are marching through the streets of Washington, D.C., to demand equal rights. ***Based on this march, how well did the women's movement appeal to women of all ages? Explain your answer.***

PEOPLE IN HISTORY

Angela Davis. While still a high school student, civil and women's rights activist Angela Davis began studying communist philosophy and political theory. She later joined the Communist Party. She was fired from the University of California because of her party membership, which sparked a court challenge that overturned a state law prohibiting colleges from hiring members of the Communist Party. The school reinstated Davis but later refused to renew her teaching contract. Davis remained active in the Communist Party and continued teaching at other colleges in California.

CRITICAL THINKING Do you think that universities should hire or fire professors based on their political beliefs?

ANSWER: Answers will vary. Some students might argue that universities should not take political beliefs into consideration in order to protect academic freedom.

THAT'S INTERESTING!

The first issue of *Ms.*, which appeared in January 1972, was labeled "Spring" because the editors did not know if or when the next edition would be released. The issue sold 300,000 copies in little more than a week and *Ms.* became a monthly magazine.

TEACH OBJECTIVE 4

ALL LEVELS: Ask students to identify common sources of opposition to the women's rights movement in the 1970s. *(Students should identify internal conflict within the movement, debate over the Equal Rights Amendment and* Roe v. Wade, *and opposition from conservative female activists.)* To help students understand the gains and setbacks that the women's movement made during the decade despite this opposition, copy the graphic organizer at right on the chalkboard, omitting the italicized answers. Then have each student complete the organizer. **Sheltered English**

Women's Rights Movement During the 1970s

Gains
- *Educational Amendments Act*
- Roe *v.* Wade
- *Increase in the number of female politicians*

Setbacks
- *ERA*
- *opposition from conservative female activists*

CONSTITUTIONAL HERITAGE

The ERA and Congress. When Congress approved the Equal Rights Amendment in 1972, it included a provision limiting the ratification period to seven years. In 1979 Congress extended the period by an additional three years without the approval of a two-thirds majority. In the 1981 case *Idaho* v. *Freeman,* a federal judge ruled that Congress did not have the power to extend the deadline without the two-thirds majority. The judge also declared that the states that had already approved the amendment could rescind, or withdraw, their approval. The deadline for ratification passed before the U.S. Supreme Court could hear the case.

CRITICAL THINKING Why might Congress have extended the ERA's ratification deadline?

ANSWER: Students might suggest that many congressmembers wanted the ERA to be ratified.

***The American Nation* VIDEO PROGRAM**

The Women's Rights Movement; Teacher's Guide, pp. 209–10

Search 48258, Play to 49209
Videodisc 1, Side B

Play Pause

See *Teacher's Guide* for Spanish barcode.

Then and Now

Women and Sports

Basketball player Chamique Holdsclaw

The women's movement supported increased opportunities for women in all areas of life, including sports. Before 1972 just 1 percent of the money spent on athletic programs at institutions of higher education was spent on women's sports. As a result, only some 16,000 women attending colleges and universities participated in sports programs.

Title IX of the 1972 Educational Amendments Act declared that "no person in the United States shall, on the basis of sex, be excluded from participation in, be denied the benefits of, or be subjected to discrimination under any education program or activity receiving federal financial assistance." The law did not mean that all college sports had to become coeducational. Rather, it required universities to fund women's sports programs fairly. By 1984, spending on women's athletics had improved. That year, women's sports received 16 percent of all athletic funds, and some 150,000 women participated in college sports activities. By the 1990s more than 160,000 women were involved in college athletics. The increase in girls' participation in high school sports programs was even more impressive. The number of female high school athletes rose from 294,105 in 1972 to some 2.5 million in 1997.

The Women's Movement Gains Momentum

The women's movement made significant progress in the 1970s. Leaders worked to shape public policy and to elect more women to public office. Many all-male colleges allowed female students to enroll for the first time. Other universities instituted courses in women's studies. In 1972 Congress passed the **Educational Amendments Act**, which outlawed sexual discrimination in higher education.

Mixed success. In 1973 the Supreme Court handed down a landmark decision affecting women. In the case *Roe* v. *Wade,* the Court overturned a state law limiting women's access to abortion during the first three months of pregnancy. The Court ruled that a woman and her doctor, not the state, should make such decisions. While most feminists hailed *Roe* v. *Wade* as a victory, opponents protested that the ruling violated the right to life of the unborn.

During the 1970s controversy also followed the Equal Rights Amendment (ERA). A proposed constitutional amendment, the ERA sought to bar discrimination on the basis of sex. Activists had first proposed such an amendment during the 1920s, but it did not pass. The ERA received strong support from NOW and other women's groups. Gloria Steinem testified before Congress on behalf of the amendment.

> **"Women suffer second-class treatment from the moment they are born. They are expected to *be* rather than to achieve, to function biologically rather than learn. A brother, whatever his intellect, is more likely to get the family's encouragement and education money, while girls are pressured to conceal ambition and intelligence."**

Congress passed the ERA in 1972, but the amendment required the approval of at least 38 states. Ratification initially seemed certain. However, conservative groups that regarded the ERA as a threat to traditional women's roles launched a campaign to prevent ratification. By the 1982 deadline set by Congress, the ERA was still three states short of ratification. As a result, the amendment failed to become law.

Opposition. The fight over the ERA revealed that many women believed that the women's movement primarily served wealthy white women. Many non-white women and working-class white women felt left out. These women felt that the leaders of NOW and other feminist groups simply did not understand the problems they faced every day. Referring to Gloria Steinem, Cathy Tuley stated, "I feel she's fighting for women like herself, professional women, and that she's not thinking of women in the whole sense, just part of them."

REVIEW

Have students complete the **Section 1 Review** on p. 653.

ASSESS

Have students complete **Daily Quiz 22.1**. As **Alternative Assessment**, you may want to use the government action debate or the women's rights organization mission statement in this section's lessons.

RETEACH

Have students complete **Main Idea Activity for Reteaching and Sheltered English 22.1**. Then organize students into triads. Have each triad create a detailed outline of Section 1. Then ask each triad to exchange its work with another triad. Have triads study each others' outlines and use them to develop and answer between 5 and 10 possible quiz questions.
Sheltered English, Cooperative Learning

EXTEND

Ask students to select a prominent women's rights activist mentioned in Section 1, such as Bella Abzug, Shirley Chisholm, Betty Friedan, or Gloria Steinem. Have students conduct research on their chosen figures. Then tell each student to write a short "Who Am I?" monologue in the role of his or her chosen activist, omitting the person's name. Have volunteers deliver their monologues to the class, and ask students to identify the activist. **Block Scheduling**

The movement also offended many middle-class women. They felt that it minimized the importance of the family and condemned women who chose to be full-time homemakers. These women viewed *Roe* v. *Wade* and the ERA as threats to traditional family life. Critics warned that the ERA would "nullify [cancel] any laws that make any distinction between men and women." Eventually, they argued, men and women would even be forced to share public restrooms! Conservative critic Phyllis Schlafly was pleased when the ERA failed to win ratification. She claimed, "The defeat of the Equal Rights Amendment is the greatest victory for women's rights since the woman's suffrage movement of 1920."

Despite such disagreements over the role of women in American society, women could point to many significant gains by the end of the 1970s. An increasing number of female politicians took office in the U.S. Congress. New York representatives Bella Abzug and Shirley Chisholm received national attention. Abzug became an outspoken supporter of women's issues in Congress. In 1972 Shirley Chisholm—the first African American woman elected to Congress—ran unsuccessfully for the Democratic nomination for president. Although she did not receive the party's nomination, her campaign illustrated how far women had come. Most women still held low-paying jobs, but the number of women holding professional jobs had increased. In 1970 just 5 percent of the nation's lawyers and 25 percent of all accountants were women. Ten years later, 12 percent of lawyers and 33 percent of accountants were women.

Phyllis Schlafly was a vocal opponent of the Equal Rights Amendment.

✔ **READING CHECK:** What gains and setbacks did the women's movement experience during the 1970s?

SECTION  REVIEW

Define and explain the significance of the following terms:
Equal Pay Act
National Organization for Women
National Women's Political Caucus
Educational Amendments Act

Identify and explain the significance of the following individuals:
Betty Friedan
Gloria Steinem
Phyllis Schlafly
Bella Abzug
Shirley Chisholm

1. **Using Graphic Organizers** Copy the graphic organizer below. Use it to explain the development of the women's movement.

2. **Identifying Cause and Effect** What was the source of the frustration that Betty Friedan identified in *The Feminine Mystique?* How did the book affect its readers?
3. **Taking a Stand** Did the federal government provide adequate support to women during the 1960s and 1970s? Explain your answer.
4. **Recognizing Point of View** Why did women such as Phyllis Schlafly celebrate the defeat of the ERA?

Critical Thinking

5. Why were some women critical of NOW and its goals?
Consider:
   - the reforms that NOW hoped to achieve
   - the strategies it used to achieve these reforms
   - the difference in background between NOW members and their critics

SECTION 1 REVIEW ANSWERS

Define and Identify
For significance, see the following pages:
- Betty Friedan, p. 648
- Equal Pay Act, p. 649
- National Organization for Women, p. 650
- Gloria Steinem, p. 651
- National Women's Political Caucus, p. 651
- Educational Amendments Act, p. 652
- Phyllis Schlafly, p. 653
- Bella Abzug, p. 653
- Shirley Chisholm, p. 653

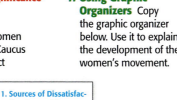

1. dissatisfaction—felt stifled by domestic life and workplace discrimination; responses—Equal Pay Act, presidential commission, Title VII; NOW—pressured elected officials; new generation—direct action; successes—Educational Amendments Act; *Roe* v. *Wade*; and setbacks—ERA
2. limited roles and opportunities available to women; led to increased demands for new opportunities and fair treatment
3. Answers will vary. Some students might note that the government passed the Equal Pay Act and Title VII.
4. Critics believed that the ERA would destroy family life and put an end to all gender distinctions.
5. argued that NOW targeted elite women and offered no assistance to working-class or minority women

SECTION 2

After completing Section 2, students should be able to:

OBJECTIVE 1 *Discuss why La Huelga was important to Mexican Americans throughout the country.*

OBJECTIVE 2 *Explain how conflicts over land rights and education motivated Mexican Americans to protest.*

OBJECTIVE 3 *Describe how aggressive activists shaped the Chicano movement.*

OBJECTIVE 4 *Analyze how the Chicano movement changed the lives of Mexican Americans.*

LET'S GET STARTED!

Write the following terms on the chalkboard: *boycott*, *strike*, and *urban activism*. Ask students to define the terms and to write a brief statement describing how these actions might have been used in a civil rights movement. Have volunteers share their responses. Then tell students that in Section 2 they will learn how the Mexican American civil rights movement and the Chicano movement utilized boycotts, strikes, and urban activism.

SECTION 2 RESOURCES

PRINT
- Guided Reading Strategy 22.2
- Section 2 Review, p. 660
- Daily Quiz 22.2

MULTIMEDIA
- One-Stop Planner, Lesson 22.2
- The American Nation Video Program Segment: César Chávez; Teacher's Guide, pp. 167–68
- Holt Researcher: American History CD–ROM

SHELTERED ENGLISH
- Main Idea Activity for Reteaching and Sheltered English 22.2

✔ READING TO UNDERSTAND

To help students master the section objectives, have them answer the **READING CHECKS** and complete **Guided Reading Strategy 22.2** as they read the section.

SECTION 2 The Chicano Movement

OBJECTIVES

Read to understand:

1. why La Huelga was important to Mexican Americans throughout the country
2. how conflicts over land rights and education motivated Mexican Americans to protest
3. how aggressive activists shaped the Chicano movement
4. how the Chicano movement changed the lives of Mexican Americans

KEY TERMS

La Huelga
United Farm Workers
Alianza Federal de Mercedes
Brown Berets
Crusade for Justice
Mexican American Youth Organization
La Raza Unida Party

KEY PEOPLE

César Chávez
Dolores Huerta
Reies López Tijerina
Rodolfo Gonzales
José Angel Gutiérrez

Read More About It

Free Find:
César Chávez
After reading about César Chávez on the Holt Researcher CD–ROM, write a song that celebrates his work as a labor activist.

EYEWITNESSES TO History

"One night I went to a dance. I didn't know that it was a place with mostly Anglo girls. An Anglo policeman told me to leave the premises. At that point I questioned him, and he arrested me. I asked him why he was arresting me, and he uttered some very racist sentiments. At the station, they let me go. Nevertheless, I spent a very embarrassing and uncomfortable few hours in jail."

—César Caballero

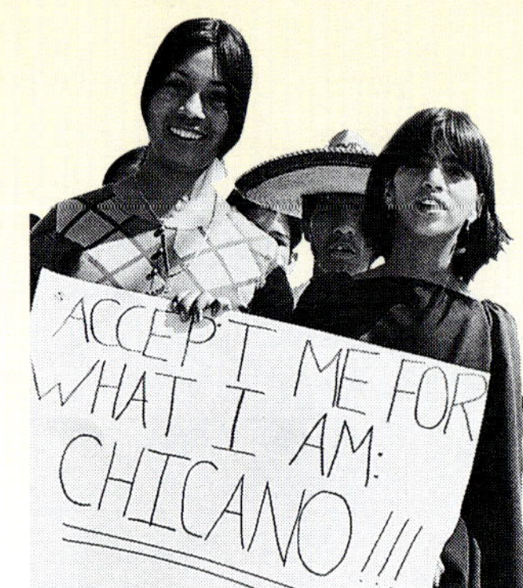

Chicano protesters

César Caballero recalled his years as a high school student in El Paso, Texas, during the early 1960s. Caballero and many other Mexican Americans reacted to the discrimination they experienced by demanding their civil rights and greater opportunities in American life.

Stirrings of Protest

Like the African American civil rights movement and the women's movement, the Mexican American struggle to secure equal rights became a powerful political force during the 1960s. Almost 4 million Mexican Americans lived in the United States in 1960, with more than 3.4 million living in southwestern states. They were among the poorest and least-educated people in the country. Although 80 percent of Mexican Americans lived in cities, it was the actions of California farmworkers that initially inspired many Mexican Americans to activism.

A model for the movement. Migrant agricultural workers, many of them Mexican Americans, received low wages for backbreaking labor. In September 1965 a group of Filipino workers went on strike in Delano, California, in the San Joaquin Valley. They refused to harvest grapes until they received a pay increase. Other migrant workers, including Mexican Americans, soon joined the strike.

When the Filipino workers struck, leaders of a union called the National Farm Workers Association (NFWA) were faced with a dilemma. A few months earlier they had won a labor dispute with rose growers, but this strike promised to be much more difficult to win. Led by César Chávez, NFWA leaders decided to join the strike.

BIOGRAPHY *César Chávez*

Born in Yuma, Arizona, in 1927, César Chávez was the son of Mexican American farmers. After losing their land during the Great Depression, Chávez's family became migrant workers. During his childhood Chávez attended nearly 30 different schools. The Chávez family repeatedly experienced discrimination in their travels searching for work. Looking back on his childhood, Chávez recalled, "There were lots of racist remarks that still hurt my ears when I think of them."

TEACH OBJECTIVE 1

LEVEL 1: Conduct a brief discussion on the importance of La Huelga to Mexican Americans throughout the country. *(Students might mention that it resulted in important advances for workers, elevated César Chávez as a movement leader, and encouraged Mexican Americans to fight discrimination.)* Then tell students to imagine that they are Mexican American farmworkers who participated in the strike. Have each student write a paragraph explaining why the strike was important to him or her. **Sheltered English**

LEVEL 2: Tell students to imagine that they are farmworkers who participated in La Huelga. Have each student write a brief speech explaining why the strike was important to Mexican Americans. *(See the Level 1 lesson for the correct reasons.)* Ask volunteers to deliver their speeches to the class. Students may wish to include the scripts for their speeches in their portfolios.

NOTE: For an additional teaching idea, see the Chapter 22 choosing and acting lesson in the **Creative Teaching Strategies** handbook.

Chávez was strongly influenced by his parents, particularly his mother, who often assisted fellow migrant workers. Chávez remembered, "We were migrants but we were a service center. We did all kinds of work for people." After serving in the navy during World War II, Chávez moved to San Jose, California. He became involved in the Community Service Organization (CSO), where he learned community-organizing techniques. He was influenced by Father Donald McDonnell, a Catholic priest who taught Chávez that labor unions could be a powerful force for social change.

Chávez longed to organize migrant agricultural workers. When this project did not receive support from the CSO, he left the organization. With help from former CSO workers Dolores Huerta and Gil Padilla, Chávez founded the NFWA. At times Chávez received no pay for his efforts. His wife Helen ran the credit union they had created to assist the workers. By 1965 the NFWA claimed some 1,700 members.

Strike and boycott. On September 16, 1965, Mexican Independence Day, Chávez asked a gathering of NFWA members to join the Filipino strikers. Eliseo Medina was then a 19-year-old worker. He later recalled the union meeting.

> **"People started talking about how unfair . . . the growers were . . . and why we needed to fight back. . . . And then, so César gets up, and he's this little guy . . . very soft spoken. I say 'That's César?' You know, I wasn't very impressed . . . but the more he talked, the more I thought that not only could we fight, but we could win."**

After NFWA members voted to strike, Chávez and other leaders collected donations of money and food to support the striking workers. The union also constructed a medical clinic and operated a gas station for its members. As Chávez explained, "We are a union of have-nots. So we must satisfy basic needs before other things."

Chávez realized that a strike alone would not win the union any concessions. He therefore adopted other strategies used in the civil rights movement to gain support. In 1966, to encourage public sympathy for the strike, Chávez conducted a 300-mile march to Sacramento, the capital of California. When Chávez called for a nationwide boycott of grapes, consumers responded enthusiastically. An estimated 17 million Americans refused to buy grapes. The resulting economic pressure forced grape growers to negotiate a settlement.

Known as **La Huelga**, the Delano grape strike lasted until 1970, when the last of the grape growers signed new contracts with the union. During that time the NFWA merged with another union, eventually forming the **United Farm Workers** (UFW). The UFW was not exclusively a Mexican American organization and included many non-Hispanic members. However, its accomplishments and

The Religious Spirit

THE IDEAL OF NONVIOLENCE

Most religions consider life to be sacred and have strict standards against the use of violence. During the early 1900s Mohandas K. Gandhi used the idea of nonviolence taken from Hinduism to oppose British rule in India. Martin Luther King Jr. and other African American civil rights activists followed Gandhi's example. They were also influenced by Christian teachings to use nonviolent tactics in their struggle for equal rights.

Many religions use the dove as a symbol of peace.

César Chávez also believed that nonviolence was the best way to bring about social change. Chávez was a deeply religious man. He once declared, "For me, Christianity happens to be a natural source of faith." He maintained that Jesus Christ "was extremely radical, and he was for social change." Chávez drew strength from his Catholic faith. He also studied Gandhi, whom he called "the most perfect man, not including Christ." Chávez noted, "Gandhi's philosophy of nonviolence, it really forces us to think, really forces us to work hard. But it has power. It attracts the support of the people."

PEOPLE IN HISTORY

Dolores Huerta. Dolores Huerta was born in New Mexico in 1930. During her childhood, her mother moved the family to Stockton, California. Huerta later attended college and tried her hand at several professions, including teaching. She became interested in the plight of farmworkers in the late 1950s. As a union organizer and activist, Huerta was arrested some 20 times. In 1988, during a peaceful protest, a police officer beat her with a club and caused serious injuries.

CRITICAL THINKING What personal sacrifices might Huerta and other Mexican American activists have made in their efforts to achieve social justice?

ANSWER: Students might suggest that Chicano activists endured arrests and injuries.

***The American Nation* VIDEO PROGRAM**

César Chávez; Teacher's Guide, pp. 167–68

Search 38963, Play to 39584
Videodisc 2, Side B

Play Pause

See *Teacher's Guide* for Spanish barcode.

LEVEL 3: Have each student write a brief essay on César Chávez and La Huelga, explaining why both were important to Mexican Americans. *(See the Level 1 lesson for the correct reasons.)* Have volunteers read their essays to the class. Then ask students to identify other past and present civil rights leaders. *(Students might mention Martin Luther King Jr. or Nelson Mandela.)* Conduct a classroom discussion on the role and importance of leaders in civil rights movements.

SPOTLIGHT on Boycotts

Have students conduct research on La Huelga and the grape boycott. Then have each student create a graphic organizer comparing and contrasting La Huelga and the grape boycott with another strike or boycott in American history. Students might focus on the colonial boycott against Great Britain, for example, or a strike in the late 1800s. Ask students to write short essays to accompany their graphic organizers that compare and contrast La Huelga and the grape boycott with another strike or boycott in American history.
Block Scheduling

ECONOMIC DEVELOPMENT

Land Use. One of the first Alianza protests concerned grazing fees on public land in the Kit Carson National Forest. This land had been appropriated from Spanish grants dating back to the 1560s. Many poor Mexican Americans had lived on the lands since before New Mexico became a state. The Forest Service charged local ranchers a fee to pasture their sheep and cattle on forest land. In 1966 the service raised the fees, and many Mexican American ranchers were unable to pay the increase. In response, the *aliancistas* erected a tent city in the forest. The protest ended after a violent encounter with rangers, but in the months that followed, protesters showed their anger by cutting fences and starting fires in the forest.

CRITICAL THINKING Why might the *aliancistas* have become involved in an agricultural issue?

ANSWER: Students might suggest that the *aliancistas* were interested in land use and that grazing rights relate to land ownership rights.

VISUAL RECORD ANSWER

Students might suggest that the workers are picking crops and that the work is labor-intensive.

INTERPRETING THE VISUAL RECORD

The UFW. The UFW fought poor working conditions with boycotts like the one against lettuce growers that the flag above announces. ***What are the workers in this picture doing? Do you think it is hard work? Why?***

Chávez's leadership inspired many Mexican Americans to fight against discrimination in their lives. The union's symbol, a black Aztec eagle, came to represent the Mexican American civil rights movement that developed during the late 1960s. César Chávez led many similar strikes before his death in 1993. His admirers have called him a modern-day saint.

✔ **READING CHECK:** Why was La Huelga important to Mexican Americans throughout the country?

Mexican American Activism

César Chávez became nationally known during the late 1960s. He was respected for his tireless efforts and his commitment to nonviolent protest. Senator Robert Kennedy of New York hailed Chávez as "one of the heroic figures of our time." Other Mexican Americans were also involved with protests during the 1960s. Some of these activists used tactics different from those of Chávez and the UFW.

Land rights. In northern New Mexico, Reies López Tijerina led the **Alianza Federal de Mercedes**, or "Federal Alliance of Land Grants." This organization worked to regain land that had been taken from Mexican Americans—often through fraud or deception—over the years. Tijerina spoke to Mexican American farmers.

> "You have been robbed of your lands by Anglo-Americans with some Spanish-American accomplices. . . . The federal and state governments are not interested in you. Join the Alianza. Together we will get your lands back . . . preferably through court action. If the courts do not respond, then we will have to resort to other methods."

Reies López Tijerina fought to help Mexican Americans regain lands that had been taken from them.

Although New Mexico governor David Cargo showed sympathy for the Alianza cause, many other state officials were determined to stop the *aliancistas*, as Tijerina's followers were known. Several *aliancistas* were arrested for unlawful assembly in June 1967 when they tried to attend a meeting in Coyote, New Mexico. Outraged, other *aliancistas* stormed the courthouse in Tierra Amarilla, New Mexico, in an attempt to free their friends. A gun battle broke out, and two police officers were wounded. Governor Cargo was in Michigan at the time of the courthouse incident. He later recalled being told, "You've got a civil war going on in New Mexico."

The Tierra Amarilla incident marked a turning point in the conflict between the *aliancistas* and their opponents. The group became entangled in lawsuits, and Tijerina eventually spent two years in prison for an assault conviction. Although Tijerina did not achieve any of his goals, he did inspire a generation of young Mexican American activists.

TEACH OBJECTIVE 2

ALL LEVELS: To help students understand how conflicts over land rights and education motivated Mexican Americans to protest, copy the chart at right on the chalkboard, omitting the italicized answers. Have each student complete it. Then pair students and have each pair write either newspaper headlines or newspaper articles describing the attack on the courthouse in Tierra Amarilla, New Mexico, or the school walkouts in East Los Angeles, California. Have volunteers share their work with the class.
Sheltered English, Cooperative Learning

MEXICAN AMERICAN PROTESTS		
Issue	**Conflict**	**Protests**
land rights	*loss of land; theft of land; attempt to regain land*	*Alianza protests*
education	*the poor quality of local schools*	*school walkouts; Brown Beret activism*

Student action. While Tijerina fought his battles in New Mexico, students in California also took to active protest. Many Mexican Americans in East Los Angeles resented the poor quality of the local schools. Some students began planning a mass demonstration. On March 1, 1968, some 300 students at Wilson High School walked out of their classes to protest the cancellation of a school play. The walkout, called a blowout by the students, quickly spread. Within one week some 15,000 students had joined the protest. Police responded by arresting students and, in some cases, beating them.

The walkouts caused a split within the Mexican American community. Some Mexican Americans wanted the students punished, while others supported their efforts. The Educational Issues Coordinating Committee (EICC) tried to use the walkouts to bring about change in the school system. The school reform movement met with opposition in June 1968. That month, 13 people—including many EICC members—were indicted for conspiracy to create riots and disturbing the peace.

Known as the L.A. Thirteen, the individuals indicted included several members of the **Brown Berets**. Inspired by the Black Panthers, the Brown Berets was an activist group formed in 1967 in response to police brutality against Mexican Americans in Los Angeles. Recalling his arrest after being indicted, Carlos Munoz, a Brown Beret leader and L.A. Thirteen member, declared, "They put the cuffs on me. I'll never forget this as long as I live." Charges against Munoz and the other L.A. Thirteen were later dropped.

INTERPRETING THE VISUAL RECORD
The Chicano movement. This Los Angeles mural celebrates the Chicano movement's fight for equal rights. ***What do you think the various elements of the mural represent?***

The East Los Angeles school walkouts brought national attention to Mexican American concerns and drew many students into militant activism. John Ortiz was a college student who took part in the protests. He later recalled, "As the strike intensified and people were getting arrested, the students became politically aware. The events politicized the students. And that's why they walked out of their classes!"

✔ **READING CHECK:** How did conflicts over land rights and education motivate Mexican Americans to protest?

Nationalism and Politics

During the late 1960s some Mexican Americans began embracing a form of cultural nationalism similar to that supported by black nationalists. Calling themselves "Chicanos," these leaders worked to create a national movement by uniting the regional efforts that had already developed in many southwestern states.

IN THE NEWS

Land Rights in New Mexico. The conflict over land ownership in New Mexico continued into the 1990s. The 150th anniversary of the signing of the Treaty of Guadalupe Hidalgo was in February 1998. The treaty had forced Mexico to cede some of its land in the Southwest to the United States. Many holders of Spanish land grants from the 1700s lost their land. In 1998, Mexican American descendants of the original grantees demanded the return of some 1.5 million acres of land controlled by the U.S. Forest Service.

CRITICAL THINKING How might the government resolve conflicts over land claims?

ANSWER: Answers will vary. Some students might argue that the government should honor all previous treaties.

THAT'S INTERESTING!

In 1972 the Brown Berets occupied Santa Catalina, an island off the California coast, for about 24 hours. The Berets hoped that their protest would draw attention to the issue of land rights.

VISUAL RECORD ANSWER

Students might suggest that the fist represents Chicano power and that the eagle symbolizes triumph.

TEACH OBJECTIVE 3

LEVEL 1: Ask students to identify aggressive Chicano activists. *(Students should identify Rodolfo Gonzales and José Angel Gutiérrez.)* Have each student write a paragraph explaining how these activists helped shape the Chicano movement. *(Students should note that Gonzales concentrated on urban residents and promoted Mexican American nationalism. Gutiérrez organized student protests and formed a political party.)* Ask volunteers to read their paragraphs to the class. Students may wish to include their paragraphs in their portfolios.
Sheltered English

LEVELS 2 AND 3: Tell students to imagine that they are aggressive Chicano activists who participated in the Chicano movement. Have each student write a short memoir explaining his or her efforts to shape the movement. *(See the Level 1 lesson for the correct effects.)* Ask volunteers to read their memoirs to the class. Students may wish to include their memoirs in their portfolios.

DEMOCRATIC VALUES

School Walkouts. The Crusade for Justice conducted a number of school walkouts to achieve its goals. One of the most violent walkouts took place in a Denver high school in 1969 after a teacher made racist remarks. The strike lasted for three days. During that period, a riot took place, with heavily armed police officers battling protesters. Many demonstrators, including Rodolfo Gonzales, were arrested and jailed.

CRITICAL THINKING Do you think that school walkouts were an effective protest technique?

ANSWER: Some students might suggest that some observers might have viewed school walkouts as a way for students to skip classes. Other students might suggest that the walkouts drew attention to the protesters' grievances.

MAP ANSWER
in the Southwest

Rodolfo Gonzales testifies before the U.S. Department of Education on discrimination in American schools.

Urban activism. Rodolfo "Corky" Gonzales became one of the leading figures in the Chicano movement. Gonzales looked beyond issues such as farmworkers' rights, land grants, and educational reform. He expressed a vision that appealed to a large number of Mexican Americans, particularly those living in cities.

A former boxer, Gonzales was involved with Democratic Party politics and antipoverty programs in Denver during the late 1950s and early 1960s. Over time Gonzales grew dissatisfied with politics, which he believed did little to help Mexican Americans. He later recalled, "I became disenchanted with the electoral system and disenchanted with the two political parties."

In 1966 Gonzales founded the **Crusade for Justice**, a group that promoted Mexican American nationalism. Operating out of an old church, the group offered legal aid, a theater for promoting cultural awareness, a newspaper, and other community services. It also ran a school. Gonzales praised the Crusade as "the embodiment [representation] of nationalism that now exists here in the Southwest. It has been a dream of the past, but we're now creating a reality out of it."

Gonzales popularized the use of the nationalist term Chicano to refer to Mexican Americans. He also composed an epic poem, *I Am Joaquin,* which served as an anthem for the *movimiento,* or "Chicano movement." In March 1969 Gonzales and the Crusade for Justice sponsored the National Chicano Liberation Youth Conference. Maria Valera attended the conference:

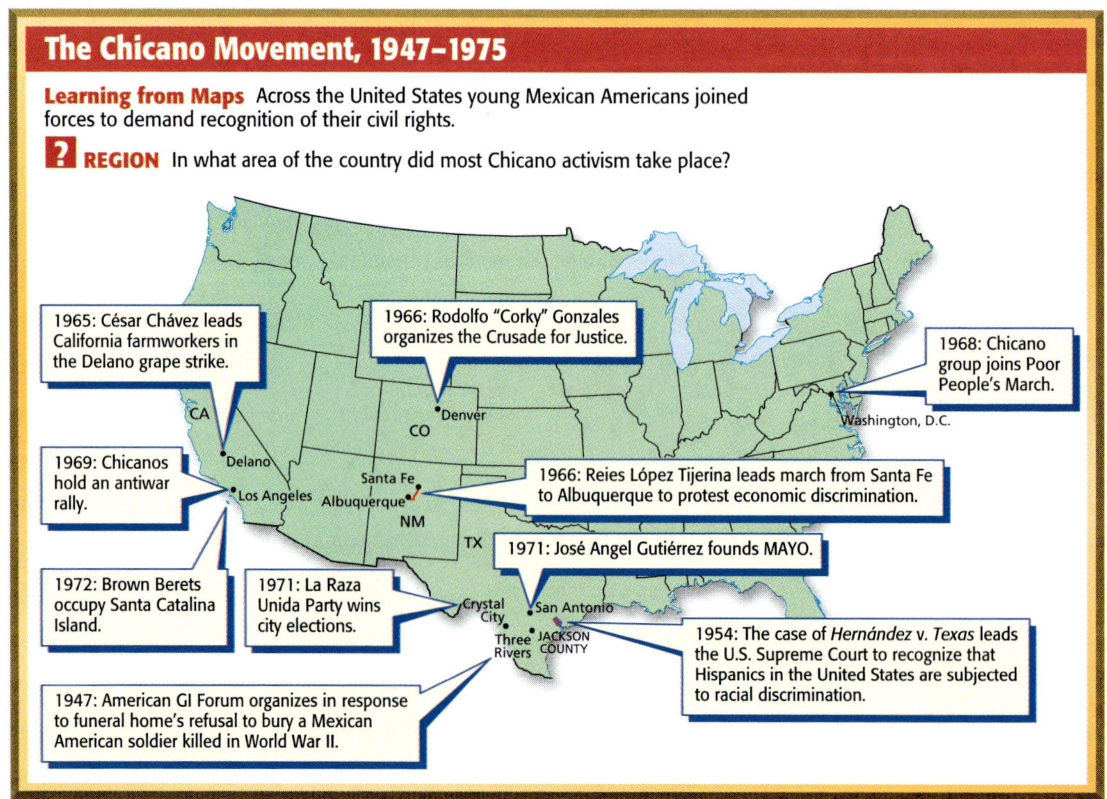

1965: César Chávez leads California farmworkers in the Delano grape strike.
1966: Rodolfo "Corky" Gonzales organizes the Crusade for Justice.
1968: Chicano group joins Poor People's March.
CA
Delano
Denver
CO
Washington, D.C.
1969: Chicanos hold an antiwar rally.
Los Angeles
Santa Fe
Albuquerque
NM
1966: Reies López Tijerina leads march from Santa Fe to Albuquerque to protest economic discrimination.
TX
1971: José Angel Gutiérrez founds MAYO.
1972: Brown Berets occupy Santa Catalina Island.
1971: La Raza Unida Party wins city elections.
Crystal City
San Antonio
Three Rivers
JACKSON COUNTY
1954: The case of Hernández v. Texas leads the U.S. Supreme Court to recognize that Hispanics in the United States are subjected to racial discrimination.
1947: American GI Forum organizes in response to funeral home's refusal to bury a Mexican American soldier killed in World War II.

The Chicano Movement, 1947–1975

Learning from Maps Across the United States young Mexican Americans joined forces to demand recognition of their civil rights.

REGION In what area of the country did most Chicano activism take place?

658

TEACH OBJECTIVE 4

LEVEL 1: Organize the students into small groups. Tell each group to write several sentences explaining how the Chicano movement changed the lives of Mexican Americans. *(Groups should indicate that the movement encouraged universities to establish Chicano Studies programs, helped spark a Chicano Renaissance, and encouraged activists to enter politics.)* As each group reads its sentences, compile a comprehensive list on the chalkboard. When the list is complete, discuss the items with the class. Ask students to analyze each item's short-term and long-term impact on Mexican Americans' lives. **Sheltered English, Cooperative Learning**

LEVELS 2 AND 3: Tell students to imagine that they are Mexican Americans who witnessed key events in the Chicano movement. Have each student write a letter to a friend in Mexico detailing those events and explaining how the Chicano movement changed the lives of Mexican Americans. *(See the Level 1 lesson for the correct changes.)* Letters should describe the activities of both conservative and aggressive groups. Ask volunteers to read their letters to the class.

▶**ASSIGNMENT:** *Have students study the mural in this section. Then ask each student to design a mural celebrating the achievements of the Chicano movement and its effects on Mexican Americans.*

> **"It was in reality a fiesta: days of celebrating what sings in the blood of a people taught to believe that they are ugly, discovering the true beauty in their souls during the years of occupation and intimidation. . . . This affirmation grew into a *grito,* a roar, among the people gathered in the auditorium of the Crusade's Center."**

Conference delegates produced *El Plan Espiritual de Aztlán,* or "The Spiritual Plan of Aztlán," a document calling for Chicano separatism. *El Plan* declared, "We are a bronze people with a bronze culture. Before all the world, before all of North America, before all our brothers in the Bronze Continent, we are a Nation."

The Texas movement. Like their counterparts in California and Colorado, Mexican Americans in Texas also turned to protest during the 1960s. In 1967 a group of students at St. Mary's University in San Antonio formed the **Mexican American Youth Organization** (MAYO). One of MAYO's founders, José Angel Gutiérrez, had been inspired by a 1966 farmworkers' protest march. Gutiérrez recalled, "Mexicans just didn't march in the streets. That was the first demonstration and march that I was involved in."

Under Gutiérrez's leadership, MAYO took radical positions on issues affecting Mexican Americans. Gutiérrez declared, "We have to be revolutionary in our demands and make every sacrifice necessary, even if it means death, to achieve our goals." Moderate opponents of MAYO's radical stance included Henry B. González, the first Mexican American from Texas to be elected to the U.S. Congress. Gutiérrez and MAYO did make some progress in the fight for civil rights in Texas. In 1969 Gutiérrez helped organize a protest in his hometown, Crystal City, Texas. Mexican American students at Crystal City High School were angry about racial discrimination in extracurricular activities such as cheerleading. Gutiérrez and other MAYO leaders staged a student walkout that forced the school board to end the discrimination.

INTERPRETING THE VISUAL RECORD

La Raza. José Gutiérrez (left) and Rodolfo Gonzales (center) appear before the national convention of La Raza Unida in 1972. ***What do you think Gonzales' raised fist symbolizes?***

Political power. Mexican American leaders had begun discussing the possibility of creating a Chicano political party in 1967. After his success with the school protest in Crystal City, Gutiérrez formed **La Raza Unida Party** (LRUP). In elections held in 1970 LRUP gained control of the city council in Crystal City and positions in some other Texas cities. That same year Rodolfo Gonzales organized a Colorado branch of LRUP. The Colorado party could not claim many electoral victories, but it did succeed in drawing attention to Chicano causes in the state. LRUP also expanded into California, where it registered some 10,000 new voters and ran several candidates for state offices. LRUP soon appeared in other states, including Arizona, Nebraska, and New Mexico.

LRUP leaders hoped to transform the party from a collection of regional parties into a strong national organization. However, the 1972 national convention held in El Paso, Texas, revealed a lack of unity among the Chicano activists. Rodolfo Gonzales and José Angel Gutiérrez became locked in a power struggle to control

CULTURAL DIVERSITY

Aztlán. The ancient Aztec identified Aztlán as their homeland. Modern-day scholars do not know whether Aztlán was a real or mythological place. Regardless, the idea of Aztlán united Mexican American activists in their struggle for economic power and civil rights during the 1960s and 1970s. Many of them believed that Aztlán had been located in the American Southwest. The activists worked for the day when the Mexican Americans living there would have political and economic power.

CRITICAL THINKING Why might people be inspired by mythology?

ANSWER: Students might suggest that myths can bring people together by serving as a uniting symbol.

VISUAL RECORD ANSWER

Students might suggest that the raised fist symbolizes strength and struggle.

REVIEW

Have students complete the **Section 2 Review** on p. 660.

ASSESS

Have students complete **Daily Quiz 22.2**. As **Alternative Assessment**, you may want to use the La Huelga script or the activist paragraph in this section's lessons.

RETEACH

Have students complete **Main Idea Activity for Reteaching and Sheltered English 22.2.** Organize students into small groups. Have each group summarize the information in a subsection by designing a poster. Have volunteers present their posters to the class. **Sheltered English, Cooperative Learning**

EXTEND

Ask students to conduct research on a Chicano Renaissance artist. Have each student write a brief biography of the artist, discussing his or her background and work. Ask volunteers to read their biographies to the class. **Block Scheduling**

SECTION 2 REVIEW ANSWERS

Define and Identify

For significance, see the following pages:

- César Chávez, p. 654
- Dolores Huerta, p. 655
- La Huelga, p. 655
- United Farm Workers, p. 655
- Reies López Tijerina, p. 656
- Alianza Federal de Mercedes, p. 656
- Brown Berets, p. 657
- Rodolfo Gonzales, p. 658
- Crusade for Justice, p. 658
- Mexican American Youth Organization, p. 659
- José Angel Gutiérrez, p. 659
- La Raza Unida Party, p. 659

1. Chávez–secure rights for farmworkers; Tijerina–regain lost land in New Mexico; Gonzales–promote nationalism; Gutiérrez–protect and promote civil rights

2. He led a difficult but ultimately successful strike and helped launch the Chicano movement; La Huelga–encouraged Mexican Americans to fight discrimination.

3. *aliancistas*–pursued direct action; farm workers–pursued strikes and boycotts; followed different goals and philosophies

4. frustration with the slow pace of change in the political system

5. Answers will vary. Some students might suggest that fragmentation and internal conflict indicate that the Chicano movement was a group of somewhat related movements.

Members of the United Farm Workers gather at a convention in Fresno, California.

the party. As a result, the party never developed a national presence. LRUP continued to have success in Texas into the late 1970s, but internal conflicts eventually led to its decline.

✔ **READING CHECK:** How did aggressive activists shape the Chicano movement?

The Movement Weakens

The Chicano movement lost some of its political power during the 1970s. The Brown Berets dissolved in 1972, and LRUP's failure to meet its goals ended efforts to create alternative political parties. Some activists later claimed that the ethnic nationalism embraced by many of the movement's members was politically impractical and had caused many moderate Mexican Americans to lose interest.

Despite its shortcomings, the Chicano movement had a positive impact on the lives of many Mexican Americans. During the 1960s and 1970s several universities established Chicano Studies programs. The Chicano movement also inspired Mexican American artists, novelists, and playwrights to create new works. This led one critic to declare a Chicano Renaissance. Some activists entered mainstream politics, inspiring others to maintain their efforts to change American society. One participant, Rosalio Muñoz, later stated that the Chicano movement "helped crystallize for people making a commitment, just like in my own life, a commitment from there to go on."

✔ **READING CHECK:** How did the Chicano movement change the lives of Mexican Americans?

SECTION  REVIEW

Define and explain the significance of the following terms:
La Huelga
United Farm Workers
Alianza Federal de Mercedes
Brown Berets
Crusade for Justice
Mexican American Youth Organization
La Raza Unida Party

Identify and explain the significance of the following individuals:
César Chávez
Dolores Huerta
Reies López Tijerina
Rodolfo Gonzales
José Angel Gutiérrez

1. **Using Graphic Organizers** Copy the chart below. Use it to list the goals of the Mexican American leaders.

Leader	Goals
César Chávez	
Reies López Tijerina	
Rodolfo Gonzales	
José Angel Gutiérrez	

2. **Analyzing** Why did César Chávez and La Huelga become leading symbols of Mexican American activism?
3. **Comparing and Contrasting** What issues motivated Mexican American activists to protest? Why did the various groups use different approaches?
4. **Recognizing Point of View** Why did some activists such as Rodolfo Gonzales and José Angel Gutiérrez turn to aggressive activism during the late 1960s?

Critical Thinking

5. Would it be more accurate to regard the Chicano movement as a group of somewhat related movements?
   Consider:
   - the different goals within the movement
   - the conflicts between movement leaders
   - the movement's effects on Mexican Americans

SECTION 3

After completing Section 3, students should be able to:

OBJECTIVE 1 *Describe what Red Power movement activists demanded, and discuss how successful they were.*

OBJECTIVE 2 *Explain how Americans with disabilities gained public support for their causes.*

OBJECTIVE 3 *Identify the issues activists for senior citizens and children addressed.*

LET'S GET STARTED!

Write the following terms on the chalkboard: *American Indian Movement, American Association of Retired Persons,* and *Children's Defense Fund.* As students enter the classroom, ask them to write a few sentences explaining what these terms have in common. Ask volunteers to share their responses. Then tell students that in Section 3 they will learn about other groups that sought to expand their rights during the 1970s.

SECTION 3 More Groups Mobilize

OBJECTIVES

Read to understand:

1. what Red Power movement activists demanded, and how successful they were
2. how Americans with disabilities gained public support for their causes
3. what issues activists for senior citizens and children addressed

KEY TERMS

American Indian Movement
Rehabilitation Act
Education for All Handicapped Children Act
American Association of Retired Persons
Gray Panthers
Older Americans Act
Children's Defense Fund

KEY PEOPLE

Russell Means
Ed Roberts
Maggie Kuhn
Marian Wright Edelman

"Let me tell you first of all that you can take credit for us being on Alcatraz because you and your government forced our backs against the wall. We're out there to create a starting point for basic changes in Indian-white relations. We reject the alternatives of the federal Indian policy. We reject either extermination of our cultures, which we refuse to have end up on museum walls for the pleasure of non-Indians. We reject the chronic and cyclical [repeating] poverty of reservations and the relocation transfer of that poverty into Red Ghettoes in the cities. We reject these alternatives. . . . We're creating our own alternatives!"

—Shirley Keith

American Indians dance during the Alcatraz occupation.

Shirley Keith explained to a California audience in 1969 why a group of American Indians had occupied Alcatraz Island in San Francisco Bay. American Indians were among the many groups that demanded change in American society during the 1960s and 1970s.

American Indian Activism

Many Americans did not benefit from the nation's widespread prosperity in the 1950s and 1960s. American Indians were particularly affected by poverty. Mary Crow Dog grew up on a Rosebud Sioux reservation in South Dakota. She later recalled, "We had no shoes and went barefoot most of the time. I never had a new dress." In 1960 the average income of American Indian men was less than half that of white men.

Spurred by extreme poverty and inspired by other groups' civil rights gains, American Indians formed the Red Power movement during the 1960s. Participants in the movement called for self-determination, or the right to govern their own communities. They also continued to demand that the U.S. government pay tribes for lands that had been taken from them illegally. Although these issues had long concerned supporters of American Indians' rights, Red Power gained more attention and participation among Indians than any previous movement.

The Alcatraz occupation. In November 1969 a group of Red Power activists called the Indians of All Tribes occupied the abandoned federal prison on Alcatraz Island in San Francisco Bay. The protest received national news coverage. Some 150 American Indians eventually traveled to the island to join the protest. The protesters offered to buy the island from the government with beads and cloth—the same price Dutch colonists had paid for Manhattan Island in 1626. Protest leaders urged other American Indians to support their cause:

In the late 1960s many American Indians protested against discrimination.

SECTION 3 RESOURCES

PRINT

- Guided Reading Strategy 22.3
- Primary Source Reading 22: American Indian Activism Begins
- Biography Reading 22: Marian Wright Edelman
- Section 3 Review, p. 665
- Daily Quiz 22.3

MULTIMEDIA

- One-Stop Planner, Lesson 22.3
- Holt Researcher: American History CD–ROM
- HRW Web site

SHELTERED ENGLISH

- Main Idea Activity for Reteaching and Sheltered English 22.3

✔ READING TO UNDERSTAND

To help students master the section objectives, have them answer the **READING CHECKS** and complete **Guided Reading Strategy 22.3** as they read the section.

TEACH OBJECTIVE 1

LEVEL 1: Pair students and have each pair identify the demands of Red Power activists. *(Pairs should indicate that Red Power activists called for self-determination, repayment for illegally seized land, and a renewal of American Indian culture.)* Then ask pairs to write paragraphs assessing the success of Red Power efforts. *(Paragraphs should indicate that although the Red Power activists attracted public attention, they achieved few of their goals.)* Have volunteers read their paragraphs to the class. **Sheltered English, Cooperative Learning**

LEVELS 2 AND 3: Write the following statement on the chalkboard: *Although Red Power activists succeeded in attracting public attention, they achieved few of their goals.* Have each student write an essay in response to the statement. Have volunteers read their essays to the class.

▶ASSIGNMENT: *Tell students to imagine that it is 1975 and that they are television reporters preparing for an interview with a Red Power activist. Have each student develop several questions to ask the activist. Then ask students to write answers to their questions.*

HISTORY MAKERS SPEAK

Richard Nixon in *Red Power: The American Indians' Fight for Freedom*

President Nixon on American Indian Issues. In a 1970 message to Congress, President Nixon committed his administration to assisting American Indians: "Both as a matter of justice and as a matter of enlightened social policy, we must begin to act on the basis of what the Indians have long been telling us. The time has come to break decisively with the past and to create the conditions for a new era in which the Indian future is determined by Indian acts and Indian decisions."

CRITICAL THINKING What important American Indian activist goal might Nixon have affirmed in his speech when he called for a future "determined by Indian acts and Indian decisions"?

ANSWER: Students might suggest that Nixon affirmed the goal of self-determination.

VISUAL RECORD ANSWER

Students might suggest that changes needed to be made in order for him to have a better future.

INTERPRETING THE VISUAL RECORD

Protest. These American Indians in New Mexico are participating in a civil rights protest. ***What do you think the message of the child's sign is?***

"We are issuing this call in an attempt to unify all our Indian Brothers behind a common cause. . . . If we can gather together as brothers and sisters and come to a common agreement, we feel that we can be much more effective, doing things for ourselves, instead of having someone else do it, telling us what is good for us."

Not all American Indians approved of the Alcatraz occupation. John Knifechief complained that the protesters "have no reason whatsoever to be militant or be demanding of anything. . . . I can't see what these young people are demanding." Interest in the Alcatraz protest gradually declined, and in 1971 federal authorities removed the few remaining protesters from the island.

Wounded Knee. Organized in Minnesota in 1968, the **American Indian Movement** (AIM) became the major force behind the Red Power movement during the 1970s. AIM called for a renewal of American Indian culture and recognition of American Indians' rights. Russell Means, a Sioux who was born on the Pine Ridge Reservation of South Dakota, became a prominent figure in AIM. In 1970 Means and other AIM members occupied the *Mayflower II*—a replica of the Pilgrim ship—during Thanksgiving Day celebrations in Plymouth, Massachusetts. Means justified AIM's aggressive tactics in a 1971 interview. "In all our demonstrations we have yet to hurt anybody or destroy any property," he said. "However, . . . we have found that the only way the white man will listen is by us creating a disturbance in his world."

In 1972, AIM members and other American Indians conducted a protest they called the Trail of Broken Treaties. The group occupied the Bureau of Indian Affairs (BIA) headquarters in Washington, D.C. The following year AIM took its most dramatic action—the seizure of the trading post at Wounded Knee, South Dakota. U.S. cavalry units had killed more than 300 Sioux there in 1890. Means declared that the government had two choices: "Either they attack and wipe us out like they did in 1890, or they negotiate our reasonable demands." AIM wanted the government to initiate hearings on past broken treaties and investigate alleged BIA misconduct.

For 71 days AIM members and U.S. marshals engaged in a grim standoff. Finally, after two AIM activists had been killed and a federal marshal wounded, the government agreed to consider AIM's grievances. The siege came to an end. The following year Means and other AIM leaders were put on trial for the Wounded Knee incident. When defense lawyers presented evidence of government misconduct against AIM, however, the case was dismissed.

HOLT RESEARCHER

Read More About It

Free Find:
Russell Means
After reading about AIM leader Russell Means on the **Holt Researcher** CD–ROM, imagine that you are a writer for a newsmagazine. Write a short profile of Means for an article about AIM.

Gaining ground. AIM's confrontational tactics captured headlines and media attention. Other American Indian leaders worked to renew tribal life through quieter methods, including lawsuits and political lobbying. The Taos Pueblo of New Mexico had struggled for decades to recover 48,000 acres of land that included Blue Lake, which was sacred to them. The tribe rejected a $10 million settlement because they would have had to give up their rights to the land. Their efforts were rewarded in 1970. That year Congress approved legislation returning the land to the Taos Pueblo. American Indians in Maine who claimed that more than half that state had been illegally taken from them also scored a victory. Congress awarded them $81.5 million and the right to buy up to 300,000 acres of land.

TEACH OBJECTIVE 2

LEVEL 1: Ask students to identify the ways in which Americans with disabilities gained public support for their causes. *(Students should indicate that Americans with disabilities appealed for equal access, used the media to attract public attention, and lobbied Congress for various laws.)* Have volunteers list these methods on the chalkboard. Then ask students to write a sentence explaining the rationale and effectiveness of each method. **Sheltered English**

LEVELS 2 AND 3: Conduct a brief discussion on the ways that Americans with disabilities gained public support for their goals. *(See the Level 1 lesson for the correct methods.)* Then have each student write a short essay comparing and contrasting the methods of the disability rights movement with those of the African American or Mexican American civil rights movement. Ask volunteers to read their essays to the class.

▸**ASSIGNMENT:** *Have each student create a detailed outline of the subsection entitled Others Struggle for Their Rights.*

American Indians continued to face many problems. Unemployment rates remained high throughout the 1970s, averaging 40 percent and reaching as high as 90 percent on some reservations. The high school dropout rate among American Indians was the highest in the nation. Nonetheless, the Red Power movement succeeded in drawing public attention to the concerns of American Indians. It also instilled a sense of pride in American Indians nationwide.

✔ **READING CHECK:** What did Red Power movement activists demand, and how successful were they?

Others Struggle for Their Rights

Several other groups of Americans sought recognition and protection of their civil rights during the 1960s and 1970s. Activists fought on behalf of people with disabilities, the elderly, and children during this period.

Disability rights. Many Americans with disabilities wondered why their tax dollars helped pay for the construction of public facilities that they could not easily use. Ed Roberts, a young Californian who had become a quadriplegic after having polio, was among the many Americans with disabilities who wanted to use public facilities. Individuals such as Roberts, who wanted to attend the University of California at Berkeley, insisted that people with disabilities deserved equal access to public facilities. Officials at the university argued that the campus did not have facilities that could accommodate Roberts. Supporters of Roberts used the media to raise public awareness of his cause. The university eventually admitted Roberts and he enrolled in 1962.

Ed Roberts excelled at the university, receiving a master's degree in political science. When other students with disabilities joined him at Berkeley, they formed a support group called the Rolling Quads. In 1969 the group convinced the Berkeley city council to change the design of street curbs so that people in wheelchairs could move easily through the city. Other state and local governments also passed laws requiring wheelchair ramps and special parking spaces at public facilities. Many buildings began to include signs in braille to help the visually impaired.

In 1973 Congress added to these efforts to expand opportunity when it passed the **Rehabilitation Act**. This act forbade discrimination in jobs, education, or housing because of physical disabilities. In 1975 Congress passed the **Education for All Handicapped Children Act**, which required public schools to provide education for children with physical or mental disabilities.

✔ **READING CHECK:** How did Americans with disabilities gain public support for their causes?

Education and Deaf Americans

Thomas Hopkins Gallaudet founded the nation's first school for the deaf in Hartford, Connecticut, in 1817. By 1835 most institutions relied upon a sign language developed by deaf people, which eventually became known as American Sign Language. During the 1880s supporters of "oralism" opposed signing. They claimed that the hard of hearing should be taught to speak English and to read lips. Although most deaf Americans preferred signing, many schools compromised by teaching both signing and oral language. During the 1970s some schools adopted a method of teaching called Total Communication, which combined signed and spoken language.

During the 1980s deaf Americans demanded that society accept them as citizens capable of living their lives without unwanted assistance. A 1988 protest at Gallaudet University, a school for deaf and hard-of-hearing students in Washington, D.C., symbolized this new activism. Gallaudet students responded with anger to the news that the university's new president was not deaf and could not even sign. They demanded a "Deaf President Now." After a week of protests, university officials backed down and announced that I. King Jordan, a university employee, would become Gallaudet's first deaf president.

Students at Gallaudet University protested the appointment of Elisabeth Zinser (left) as president because she was not deaf.

IN THE NEWS

American Indian Poverty. Poverty has remained a persistent problem on many American Indian reservations throughout the 1900s. In 1999 President Clinton visited the Pine Ridge reservation in South Dakota. At the time of his visit, the unemployment rate on the reservation was between 75 and 85 percent—much higher than that during the Great Depression. The reservation, which covers some 3,100 square miles, had just 62 miles of paved road.

CRITICAL THINKING How might geographical location affect poverty on certain American Indian reservations?

ANSWER: Students might note that many reservations are in remote rural areas that have not experienced much economic development.

THAT'S INTERESTING!

In 1995 some 4.4 million Americans between the ages of 6 and 14 had some sort of disability. Some 659,000 had a severe disability.

TEACH OBJECTIVE 3

ALL LEVELS: To help students understand the issues activists for senior citizens and children addressed, copy the graphic organizer at right on the chalkboard, omitting the italicized answers. Have each student complete it. Then ask students to imagine that it is 1975. Have each student write a short letter to the editor of a local newspaper, discussing an issue that either group addressed. Ask volunteers to read their letters to the class. **Sheltered English**

MOTIVATIONS FOR THE SENIOR CITIZENS' AND THE CHILDREN'S RIGHTS MOVEMENTS

	Senior Citizens'	Children's
Issues	*forced retirement, medical care*	*poverty, lack of medical insurance, discrimination*
Groups and Tactics	*American Association of Retired Persons and Gray Panthers; formed organizations and lobbied for improvements*	*Children's Defense Fund; pursued lawsuits and lobbied for improvements*

internet connect

TOPIC: Marian Wright Edelman
GO TO: go.hrw.com
KEYWORD: SE1 Edelman

Have students access the Internet through the HRW Web site to conduct research on Marian Wright Edelman and the Children's Defense Fund (CDF). Then have each student write an essay describing the CDF's mission and its accomplishments. Ask students to end their essays with statements about the status of children in their state.

STRATEGIES FOR SUCCESS

Applying the Strategy
Reports will vary but should clearly summarize the Web site's main ideas and evaluate its content.

Practicing the Strategy
1. Answers will vary but should include the name of the Web site and its authors or producers.
2. Answers will vary but students should summarize the site's main ideas and historical materials it offers.

VISUAL RECORD ANSWER
(for p. 665)
Students might cite affordable housing, clean environment, economic justice, national health system, and peace.

Strategies for Success: Evaluating Web Sites on the Internet

Of all the resources that you can use to conduct historical research, the Internet is one of the largest and most promising. While the Internet is an extremely valuable research tool, it is important that you learn to evaluate the quality of the Web sites you find.

How to Evaluate Web Sites

1. **Determine what topics are covered in the Web site, in how much depth they are covered, and how unique the coverage is.** First you must decide whether a site offers enough of the type of information you are looking for. Would you be better off finding the same information in a reference book? If so, it is probably better to use an already trusted resource. However, the site may contain additional and unique information.
2. **Determine if the information in the Web site is accurate.** The saying that you cannot believe everything you read is more relevant than ever on the Internet, where anyone can be a publisher. Conduct a preliminary review of the site. If there are spelling errors, grammatical errors, or profanity, avoid the site. Compare the information in the site to other reference sources. Examine claims made in the source to see that they are backed up with reasoned arguments and verifiable evidence. Sites full of unsupported claims and undocumented facts should be avoided.
3. **Establish who the author is, and what his or her qualifications are.** You need to determine the credentials of the person or group who created and published a Web page. Look to see if the Web site is published by a reputable firm, institution, or government agency. In the case of individuals, try to find out if the author has credentials in the field or a list of printed publications.
4. **Evaluate how objective the information is.** The objectivity of a site should not be taken for granted. It is important that you identify the purpose of a Web site. Some sites may be made to provide information, to sell things, or to promote a cause. Their facts may be correct, but you should understand the writer's point of view. If the purpose of a Web site is to persuade, then ask yourself what the other side of the issue is.

Applying the Strategy

Use the computer system at your school or local public library to find a Web site on one of the following topics:
a. the history of the American Indian Movement
b. the history of the disability rights movement
c. the history of the Gray Panthers or the American Association of Retired Persons

Then explore the Web site and write a one-page report that summarizes its main ideas and evaluates its content.

Practicing the Strategy

Answer the following questions.
1. What was the name of the Web site you found? Who produced it?
2. What main ideas does the Web site attempt to convey? What historical materials does it offer?

Older Americans organize. During the late 1950s, retired Americans who joined social clubs often discussed political and legal issues affecting older adults. These concerns led to the formation of organizations dedicated to lobbying for the needs of older citizens. Founded in 1958, the **American Association of Retired Persons** (AARP) became the largest such group. AARP sought to eliminate mandatory retirement. The National Council of Senior Citizens (NCSC) represented the interests of lower-income older Americans. In 1965 some 1,400 NCSC members traveled to Washington, D.C., to support Medicare legislation.

Smaller than AARP or NCSC but much more visible to the public eye was a group called the **Gray Panthers**, founded by Maggie Kuhn. She recalled that when she was forced to retire, "I was hurt and then, as time passed, outraged." The Gray Panthers fought for greater rights for older Americans. Kuhn explained the goals of the senior movement when she testified before Congress in 1977:

REVIEW

Have students complete the **Section 3 Review** on p. 665.

ASSESS

Have students complete **Daily Quiz 22.3**. As **Alternative Assessment**, you may want to use the letter to the editor or the Red Power essay in this section's lessons.

RETEACH

Have students complete **Main Idea Activity for Reteaching and Sheltered English 22.3**. Then assign each student a subsection of Section 3. Have students write several quiz questions about the material in their assigned subsections. Then use the questions to quiz the class. **Sheltered English**

EXTEND

Ask students to select one of the following activists: Marian Wright Edelman, Russell Means, Maggie Kuhn, or Ed Roberts. Have each student write a short essay describing and analyzing his or her chosen activist's goals and techniques. Ask volunteers to read their essays to the class. Then have students vote on the most effective leader. **Block Scheduling**

> **"The Gray Panthers are a national coalition of old, young, and middle-aged activists . . . working to eradicate ageism and all forms of age discrimination in our society. We define ageism as the arbitrary [irrational] discrimination against persons and groups on the basis of chronological age."**

The federal government's responses included holding several White House Conferences on Aging. In 1965 Congress passed the **Older Americans Act**, which committed the government to providing the elderly with adequate income and medical care.

Children's issues. Activists also organized for children's rights. In 1967 the Supreme Court ruled in the case *In Re Gault* that minors accused of a crime possessed nearly the same rights as adults. The case sparked interest in children's rights.

People fighting for children's rights pointed to larger problems in American society. The 1970 White House Conference on Children, which was attended by some 3,700 people, issued the Children's Bill of Rights. This document declared that children had the "right to grow in a society which respects the dignity of life and is free of poverty, discrimination, and other forms of degradation." The Children's Bill of Rights also maintained that children had the right to receive an education, "to be healthy," and "to grow up nurtured by affectionate parents."

Founded in 1973, the **Children's Defense Fund** (CDF) quickly became the leading children's rights organization. Director Marian Wright Edelman explained the group's purpose as "identifying, publicizing, and correcting selected serious problems faced by large numbers of American children." The CDF has focused on helping poor and minority children. The group has also sought health insurance for children and federally funded child care.

✔ **READING CHECK:** What issues did activists for senior citizens and children address?

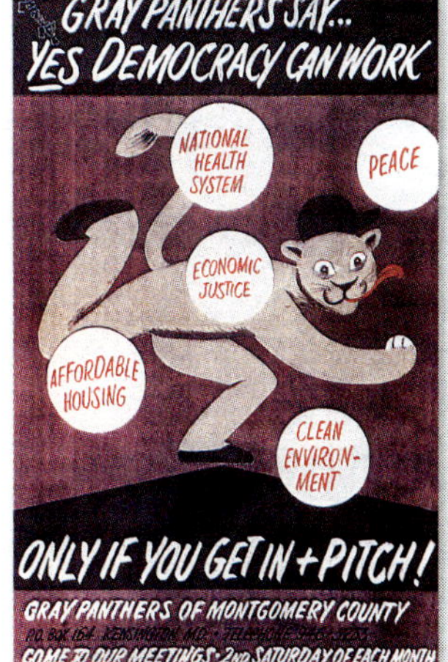

INTERPRETING THE VISUAL RECORD

Senior citizens. The Gray Panthers fought to protect older Americans against discrimination. ***What issues does this poster indicate that the Gray Panthers addressed?***

SECTION 3 REVIEW

Define and explain the significance of the following terms:
American Indian Movement
Rehabilitation Act
Education for All Handicapped Children Act
American Association of Retired Persons
Gray Panthers
Older Americans Act
Children's Defense Fund

Identify and explain the significance of the following individuals:
Russell Means
Ed Roberts
Maggie Kuhn
Marian Wright Edelman

1. **Using Graphic Organizers** Copy the graphic organizer below. Use it to explain the tactics used by activists seeking to expand the rights of the groups listed.

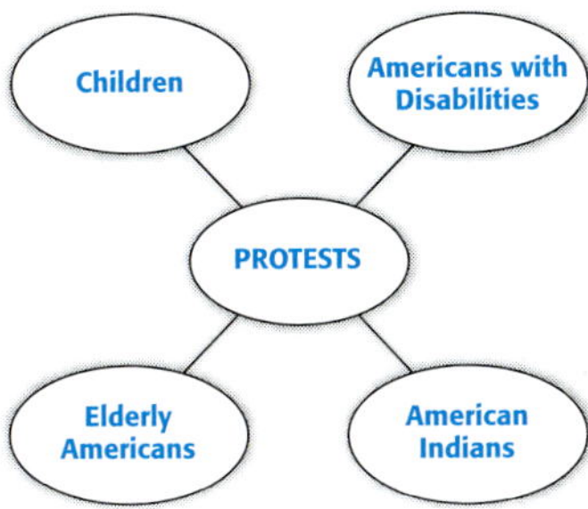

2. **Comparing and Contrasting** How did the demands of American Indians differ from those of other minorities who struggled for their civil rights during this era?
3. **Evaluating** What role did the media play in the disability rights movement?
4. **Problem Solving** What issues would you address if you were organizing a movement for senior citizens? a children's rights organization?

Critical Thinking

5. Did the militant activists involved in the Red Power movement achieve their goals?
Consider:
- the outcome of the Alcatraz occupation
- the response to the occupation at Wounded Knee
- the efforts of other American Indian activists

SECTION 3 REVIEW ANSWERS

Define and Identify
For significance, see the following pages:
- American Indian Movement, p. 662
- Russell Means, p. 662
- Ed Roberts, p. 663
- Rehabilitation Act, p. 663
- Education for All Handicapped Children Act, p. 663
- American Association of Retired Persons, p. 664
- Gray Panthers, p. 664
- Maggie Kuhn, p. 664
- Older Americans Act, p. 665
- Children's Defense Fund, p. 665
- Marian Wright Edelman, p. 665

1. children—established organizations, filed lawsuits, and lobbied for programs; Americans with disabilities—sought media attention and pursued government action; American Indians—staged aggressive protests, filed lawsuits, and lobbied for programs; elderly Americans—formed organizations and lobbied for programs

2. Many American Indians based their demands on treaties.

3. attracted public attention to the movement

4. Answers will vary. Issues addressed should reflect the differing needs of the two groups.

5. Answers will vary. Students might suggest that the militant activists managed to capture public attention but failed to accomplish their goals.

SECTION 4

After completing Section 4, students should be able to:

OBJECTIVE 1 *Explain why protests developed on American college campuses.*

OBJECTIVE 2 *Describe the problems that weakened the counterculture.*

OBJECTIVE 3 *Explain how doubts about American society led to new movements in religion and the arts.*

OBJECTIVE 4 *Analyze how musical styles reflected the social changes of the era.*

LET'S GET STARTED!

As students enter the classroom, play Selection 25, "Blowin' in the Wind," from the **American Music Audio CD Program.** Have students respond to the song in writing. Ask volunteers to share their responses. Then tell students that in Section 4 they will learn more about the counterculture and its music.

SECTION 4 RESOURCES

PRINT
- Guided Reading Strategy 22.4
- Literature Reading 22: High Style
- Geography Activity 22: The Environment Under Assault
- Section 4 Review, p. 671
- Daily Quiz 22.4

MULTIMEDIA
- One-Stop Planner, Lesson 22.4
- American Music Selection 25: "Blowin' in the Wind"
- Holt Researcher: American History CD–ROM

SHELTERED ENGLISH
- Main Idea Activity for Reteaching and Sheltered English 22.4

✓ READING TO UNDERSTAND

To help students master the section objectives, have them answer the **READING CHECKS** and complete **Guided Reading Strategy 22.4** as they read the section.

Multimedia Resources

American Music Selection 25: "Blowin' in the Wind"

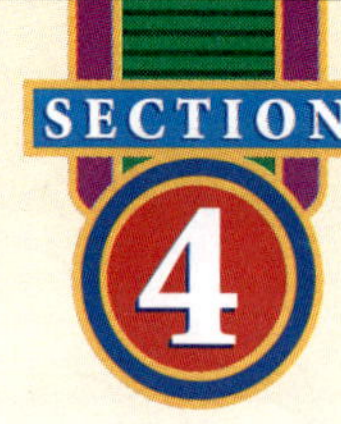

A Cultural Revolution

OBJECTIVES

Read to understand:
1. why protests developed on American college campuses
2. what problems weakened the counterculture
3. how doubts about American society led to new movements in religion and the arts
4. how musical styles reflected the social changes of the era

KEY TERMS

generation gap
counterculture
pop art
British invasion
Woodstock

KEY PEOPLE

Mario Savio
Timothy Leary
Joan Baez
Bob Dylan
James Brown
Aretha Franklin

EYEWITNESSES TO History

"Everything on the tube tearing us apart was almost perfectly balanced by the remarkable unity [we heard] on the radio. It was the only place in the history of the United States where, for a fleeting [brief] moment, we created a world of seemingly genuine racial and sexual equality, embraced by everyone under thirty—and millions more who fell in love with the beat. . . . The composers, performers, managers, and producers . . . filled the airwaves with the most eclectic-electric-wrathful-revolutionary-romantic-soulful-psychedelic music ever played, simultaneously, on every rock-and-roll radio station in the world."

—Charles Kaiser

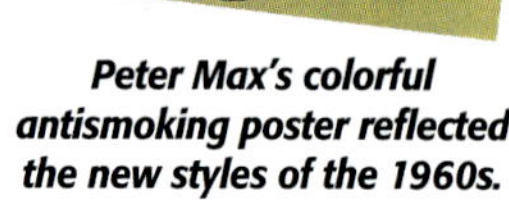

Peter Max's colorful antismoking poster reflected the new styles of the 1960s.

Charles Kaiser was a teenager during the 1960s who later became a writer. He reflected on the contrast between violent events—such as assassinations, riots, and the Vietnam War—that he witnessed on television with the sense of peace of the 1960s youth culture.

The Student Movement

Cold War fears, massive civil rights protests, and the Vietnam War led many young Americans to question the values of American society. They began to blame their parents for creating the problems that the country faced. This **generation gap** between the baby boomers and their elders grew wider as the decade wore on.

The 1960s youth movement began on college campuses among white middle-class students. In 1964 officials at the University of California at Berkeley announced a new policy restricting space available to student groups for organizing and making speeches. To many students, this was a violation of their right to free speech and assembly. Their discontent quickly exploded into protest.

Students demonstrate during the 1960s.

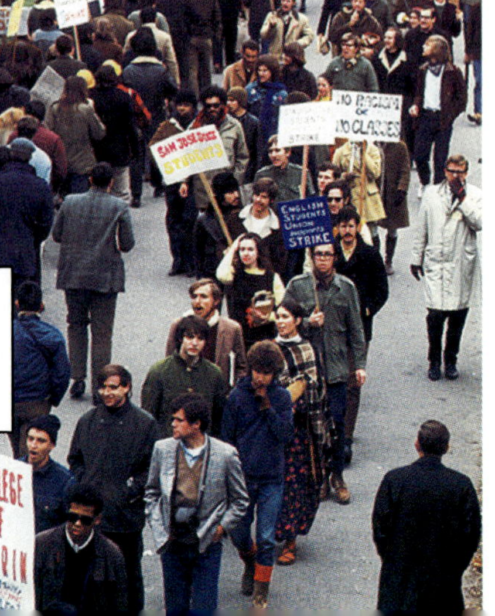

Student activist Mario Savio and others helped organize the protests. Savio compared the university to a machine. He declared, "You've got to indicate to the people who run it, to the people who own it, that unless you're free, the machine will be prevented from working at all." A large number of Berkeley students stopped attending classes. They rallied, held sit-ins, and picketed university administration buildings. Their intention, they declared, was to "Shut This Factory Down." The protests quieted when university officials agreed to many of the students' demands.

In 1965 similar protests took place on college campuses nationwide. One woman who participated in the student movement at Columbia University in New York recalled the mood of the students:

TEACH OBJECTIVE 1

ALL LEVELS: Write the following question on the chalkboard: *How might the existence of a generation gap have created protests on college campuses?* Have students respond to the question in writing. *(Students might suggest that the existence of a generation gap might have led students to rebel against their parents and other authority figures.)* To help students understand why protests developed on American college campuses, copy the graphic organizer at right on the chalkboard, omitting the italicized answers. Have each student complete it. Then, for each cell of the graphic organizer, have students write a sentence that explains why the element sparked protests on campuses. **Sheltered English**

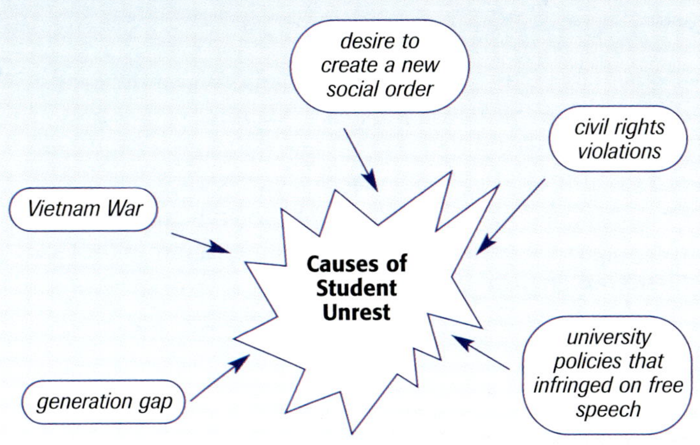

> "There was an incredible exhilaration, that here we were making history, changing the world. . . . Everybody believed that this university would never be the same, that society would be . . . changed, that there'd be a revolution in the United States within five years, and a whole new social order."

✔ **READING CHECK:** Why did protests develop on American college campuses?

The Counterculture

Some Americans hoped to create this "new social order" by rejecting everything connected with mainstream America, which they called the Establishment. Known as hippies, these Americans sought to create a **counterculture**, or alternative lifestyle.

INTERPRETING THE VISUAL RECORD

Hippies. Some young Americans rejected traditional values and customs. Other activist, however, wore traditional clothing such as this African dashiki. ***What evidence can you see that the people in this picture are challenging traditional values?***

An African dashiki

Dropping out. Like the beats before them, hippies rejected the materialism and work ethic of past generations in favor of simplicity and "doing your own thing." Many hippies tried to shock older Americans, whom they dismissed as "squares," with behavior that included public displays of nudity and the use of profanity. Some hippies formed communities in run-down urban neighborhoods, such as the Haight-Ashbury district of San Francisco. Others "dropped out" of society by joining rural communes, where they attempted to live collectively in harmony with nature. Residents of communes typically rejected most modern conveniences, grew their own food, and shared all property. Between 1965 and 1975 some 10,000 such communes were established.

Many hippies searched for new physical experiences by experimenting with harmful mind-altering drugs such as LSD (lysergic acid diethylamide), commonly known as acid. Timothy Leary became the drug's leading supporter. He began using LSD on college students. Leary was fired in 1963 from his job as a Harvard University professor for violating rules governing experiments on human subjects. Leary invited people to "turn on to the scene, tune in to what is happening, and drop out—of high school, college, grad school, junior executive—and follow me, the hard way."

Fashion. Those who followed Leary's advice often adopted a casual and colorful style of dress. Shirts that had been tie-dyed—dipped in colorful dyes while knotted to produce vibrant patterns—grew in popularity. People increasingly wore blue jeans, which traditionally had been considered work clothing. Men began wearing their hair longer, and beards became commonplace. Beads, which on men represented a rejection of the necktie, became a standard accessory. Some African Americans sported Afros, a natural hairstyle that came to symbolize racial pride. Many African Americans adopted the dashiki, an African shirt usually decorated with bright colors.

PEOPLE IN HISTORY

Timothy Leary. Born in 1920, Timothy Leary studied psychotherapy at the University of California at Berkeley. He was a respected scholar before he became well known for his liberal attitudes toward drug use. In the 1960s Leary was convicted of drug possession. He escaped from a California prison in 1970, was recaptured in 1973, and was finally released in 1976. Leary later worked as a lecturer. After his death in 1996, Leary's ashes were shot into space.

ACTIVITY: Tell students to reread the quotation by Timothy Leary on this page. Then have each student write several paragraphs explaining why Leary and his ideas appealed to some Americans during the 1960s.

THAT'S INTERESTING!

During the California Gold Rush, Levi Strauss designed the first blue jeans, which quickly became popular with the working class. Political activists of the 1960s frequently wore blue jeans to capitalize on this heritage.

VISUAL RECORD ANSWER

Students might mention clothing or hairstyles.

TEACH OBJECTIVE 2

LEVEL 1: Conduct a brief discussion on the counterculture. Then ask students to identify the problems that weakened the counterculture. *(Students should identify factors such as drug and alcohol abuse, sexually transmitted diseases, sexual abuse, and crime.)* Have each student write a paragraph on the rise and fall of the counterculture in the 1970s. **Sheltered English**

LEVELS 2 AND 3: Conduct a brief discussion on the counterculture. Then ask students to reread the subsection on the pitfalls of the counterculture. Tell students to imagine that they are anticounterculture leaders in Haight-Ashbury. Have each student develop a leaflet similar to the one mentioned in the subsection. Students' leaflets should identify the problems that weakened the counterculture and urge runaways to return home. *(See the Level 1 lesson for the correct problems.)* Have volunteers discuss their leaflets with the class.

CULTURAL DIVERSITY

Haight-Ashbury. Over time, Haight-Ashbury became so well known that a local bus company operated a tour through the neighborhood called the Hippie Hop. In response to the increased media attention and commercialism, some hippies conducted a Death of Hippie ceremony in October 1967, holding a mock funeral procession.

CRITICAL THINKING Why might tourists have wanted to go on the Hippie Hop tour?

ANSWER: Students might suggest that tourists were intrigued by the hippies and their alternative lifestyle.

THAT'S INTERESTING!

Zen Buddhism teaches that an individual can unite with the universe through contemplation and meditation. The mystical aspects of Zen Buddhism appealed to some young people as an alternative to the materialism of American life.

VISUAL RECORD ANSWER

Answers will vary. Students might suggest that its comic-book appearance makes them think that it is not art.

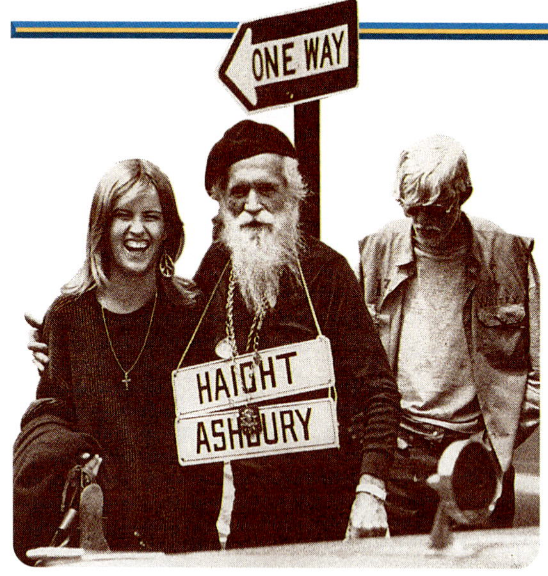

San Francisco's Haight-Ashbury district attracted a wide variety of people.

Pitfalls of the counterculture. For some hippies, the experimentation of the era came at a high price. Reported cases of drug addiction and sexually transmitted diseases increased at an alarming rate. In addition, some women perceived the era's new sexual freedom as yet another way for men to take advantage of women. Feminist Robin Morgan charged that "the so-called Sexual Revolution has . . . reinstituted [recreated] oppression by another name."

Young Americans who moved to Haight-Ashbury in search of cultural freedom found a harsh urban neighborhood troubled by crime. One leaflet handed out during the era declared, "Kids are starving on the Street. Minds and bodies are being maimed as we watch. . . . Are you aware that Haight Street is as bad as the squares say it is?" The counterculture also attracted sinister characters such as Charles Manson, who moved to Haight-Ashbury in 1967. Two years later Manson and a handful of his followers were responsible for a mass murder in California that horrified the nation.

✔ **READING CHECK:** What problems weakened the counterculture?

Changing American Society

The rise of the counterculture reflected the doubts that many citizens—particularly the young—held about the direction of American society. Americans increasingly questioned cultural traditions on a variety of issues from religion to the arts.

INTERPRETING THE VISUAL RECORD

Pop art. Roy Lichtenstein used bright colors and a comic-strip style in his artwork. ***What elements of this painting make you think it is, or is not, art?***

Religion. In a 1957 poll more than 80 percent of Americans claimed that religion could answer all or most of society's problems. By 1969, however, 70 percent said that religion was losing its influence on American life.

Americans did not necessarily lack spiritual faith. However, many Americans lost confidence in the ability of the established churches to provide spiritual direction in the modern world. Some believed that the challenges of the nuclear age had made traditional religious answers irrelevant. Reflecting the search for alternative answers, the number of college courses in religion—and enrollment in them—grew dramatically. Interest in Eastern religions such as Zen Buddhism also rose.

The arts. The questioning of tradition even extended into the art world. Many new visual artists argued that the art world had become a slave to upper-class tastes and customs. They claimed that established artists created works only to please a few cultural critics, not to appeal to the majority of nonartists. These new artists created a style called **pop art**

TEACH OBJECTIVE 3

ALL LEVELS: Write the following statement on the chalkboard: *Both religion and the arts are influenced by doubts about American society, as in the 1960s.* Have each student write a short response to the statement. *(Students should indicate that doubts about American society in the 1960s resulted in expanded interest in Eastern religions and helped give rise to pop art.)* Ask volunteers to read their responses to the class.
Sheltered English

SPOTLIGHT on Pop Art

Have students conduct research on pop art of the 1960s and 1970s. Ask students to bring examples of pop art to class. Display these examples around the classroom and have students study them. Then organize the class into two groups—one that supports pop art and views it as art, and one that opposes pop art and views it as nonart. Give each group time to prepare its arguments and then conduct a debate about the meaning and worth of pop art.
Cooperative Learning, Block Scheduling

because it was intended to appeal to popular tastes. The artists took inspiration from elements of popular culture including advertising, celebrities, comic books, and movies.

Film also underwent a broadening of subject matter as censorship rules were increasingly ignored. Rather than continuing to allow the Catholic Legion of Decency to make recommendations regarding motion pictures, the film industry adopted its own ratings system. The system informed audiences about the content of movies. The ratings system ranged from G, which meant that the film was intended for general audiences, to X, which meant that people under the age of 17 would not be admitted. The rating system was adopted to gain favor with the viewing public, who wanted more information about the content of films. However, some artists argued that the new standards allowed box-office receipts to determine content rather than artistic concerns. Movies rated for adult audiences increasingly drew larger crowds than more family-oriented films.

✔ **READING CHECK:** How did doubts about American society lead to new movements in religion and the arts?

Pop Art

In the early 1960s a number of New York painters and sculptors emerged who wanted to make art more accessible to the general public. They accomplished their goals by using "found objects"—cardboard packaging, cartoon strips, furniture, tin cans, and other everyday articles—as the subjects of their works. The leading supporters of this method, called pop art, included Roy Lichtenstein and Claes Oldenburg. Lichtenstein's huge paintings were done in comic-strip style. Oldenberg used a variety of materials to make giant sculptures of such things as clothespins, hamburgers, and toothpaste tubes.

The best-known pop artist was Andy Warhol. His most notable paintings include depictions of Campbell's soup cans, rows of Coca-Cola bottles, and a brightly colored photograph of Marilyn Monroe reproduced multiple times. Initially, Warhol painted his own works by hand, but he switched to a stencil-printing process called silk screen. Eventually, he simply created designs for his team of assistants to reproduce. Warhol's message—that everything, even art, can be mass-produced—both glorified and mocked American consumerism.

Andy Warhol painted these oversized soup cans in 1962.

Understanding the Arts

1. What did supporters of pop art use as the subjects of their work?
2. What was the goal of pop artists?
3. What do you think Andy Warhol was trying to communicate in the painting shown above?

ACROSS THE CURRICULUM

▶ART◀

Protesting Commercialism. During the 1960s and 1970s some artists worried that works of art had been reduced to mere commodities. These artists attempted to create art that had no monetary value and that would not be bought and sold by collectors. One such artist, Robert Smithson, used a bulldozer to create *Spiral Jetty,* a long spiral of land in the Great Salt Lake.

ACTIVITY: Conduct a brief discussion on noncommercial art. Then have each student design or create a piece of noncommercial art.

AMERICAN ARTS ANSWERS

1. found objects
2. to make art more accessible to the general public
3. Students might suggest that Warhol was trying to convey a sense of beauty or wonder in everyday objects.

TEACH OBJECTIVE 4

LEVEL 1: Pair students and tell them to imagine that they are young people during the 1960s. Direct each pair to create a message for a time capsule that will be opened in 2020. Messages should describe 1960s music and explain how it was influenced by the social changes of the era. *(Pairs should note that the music of the 1960s reflected the era's emphasis on civil rights, diversity, experimentation, and political protest.)* Have volunteers read their messages to the class. Then conduct a discussion comparing and contrasting 1960s music and 1990s music. **Sheltered English, Cooperative Learning**

LEVELS 2 AND 3: Tell students to imagine that they are rock critics at Woodstock. Have each student write a brief review discussing the event, the music, and the performers. Reviews should also discuss how the musical styles reflect the social changes of the era. *(See the Level 1 lesson for the correct answers.)* Have volunteers read their reviews to the class.

▶**ASSIGNMENT:** *Ask each student to write a press release for a rock star of the 1960s or 1970s. The release should contain information about the artist's goals, influence, and music. In their releases, students should explain how the artist's musical style reflects the social changes of the era. Remind students that the purpose of a press release is to advertise the artist while providing information for the fans.*

SECTION 4 REVIEW ANSWERS

Define and Identify

For significance, see the following pages:

- generation gap, p. 666
- Mario Savio, p. 666
- counterculture, p. 667
- Timothy Leary, p. 667
- pop art, p. 668
- British invasion, p. 670
- Joan Baez, p. 670
- Bob Dylan, p. 670
- James Brown, p. 671
- Aretha Franklin, p. 671
- Woodstock, p. 671

1. conflicts–generation gap and social problems such as Cold War fears, civil rights protests, and the Vietnam War; complaints–universities limited free speech and creativity; tactics–launched sit-ins and rallies

2. Answers will vary. Some students might suggest that the counterculture should have emphasized responsibility rather than personal freedom.

3. the influence of the counterculture and internal doubts; led artists to challenge conventions

4. that American culture was in a state of confusion, experimentation, and openness

5. The event proved that a peaceful culture united by music could overcome serious obstacles.

Sounds of the 1960s

Changes in the visual arts were matched by developments in popular music. The social and political movements of the 1960s marched to new forms of music that ranged from rock to folk to soul.

Rock music. A major influence on the youth rebellion of the 1950s, rock 'n' roll continued to reflect social change in the 1960s. Rock 'n' roll branched out into a variety of new forms. The year 1964 marked the musical **British invasion**—the introduction of new British bands to an American audience. Groups such as the Beatles and the Rolling Stones drew on 1950s rock 'n' roll and African American blues, thrilling American teenagers. Jane Berentson was a high school student in 1964. She later recalled of the Beatles, "The girls all decided right away which one they were in love with. And the boys all decided which one they looked like."

The use of electrically amplified instruments such as the electric guitar inspired musicians to try out innovative—and very loud—sounds on their audiences. Seattle native Jimi Hendrix was the master of the electric guitar in the 1960s. This new music served as a soundtrack for the counterculture. As one observer noted, the counterculture "is bright, vivacious [full of life], ecstatic, crowd-loving, joyful—and its music is rock."

Folk's rebirth. During the 1930s artists such as Woody Guthrie had used folk music to point out flaws in American society. By the 1950s this tradition had lost influence. During the 1960s, however, folk music gained popularity once again. Folk artists such as Joan Baez and Bob Dylan wrote lyrics that sent a political message to listeners, such as a 1962 Dylan hit.

> **"How many years can a mountain exist**
> **before it's washed to the sea?**
> **Yes, 'n' How many years can some people exist**
> **before they're allowed to be free?**
> **Yes, 'n' How many times can a man turn his head**
> **pretending he just doesn't see?**
> **The answer, my friend, is blowin' in the wind**
> **The answer is blowin' in the wind."**

The music of the 1960s reflected the many changes that were occurring in American society.

Dylan formed a link between folk and rock music in 1965. That year he appeared on stage with an electric guitar instead of an acoustic guitar, the instrument traditionally used in folk music. Many fans of folk music felt that Dylan had betrayed them. Charles Kaiser attended a 1966 Dylan concert. He noted that the audience "screamed, shouted, walked out . . . even threw things at the stage"—but Dylan had brought folk music firmly into the rock realm.

Motown and soul. Despite rock's roots in African American blues, the British invasion pushed many African American performers off the record charts. Berry Gordy brought African Americans back into the forefront of popular music with Motown Records, his record company based in Detroit. By 1975 Motown was earning over $50 million annually. This made it one of the country's most successful

REVIEW

Have students complete the **Section 4 Review** on p. 671.

ASSESS

Have students complete **Daily Quiz 22.4**. As **Alternative Assessment**, you may want to use the anticounterculture leaflet or the music review in this section's lessons.

RETEACH

Have students complete **Main Idea Activity for Reteaching and Sheltered English 22.4**. Then have each student write a paragraph that summarizes Section 4 and uses all the key terms and key people listed in this section. **Sheltered English**

EXTEND

Organize the class into small groups. Have each group select a musician from the 1960s or 1970s. Ask each group to design a music video for one of the performer's songs. Students should create detailed storyboards that display the sequence and look of their music videos. Have volunteers present their storyboards to the class. **Cooperative Learning, Block Scheduling**

African American–owned businesses. Successful Motown artists included the Supremes and the Temptations.

Perhaps the most dynamic artist of the era was James Brown. Performing a form of rhythm-and-blues music known as soul, Brown captivated audiences with his athletic, emotionally charged shows. Nicknamed the Godfather of Soul, Brown had started performing at the age of 12. He had his first hit record in 1956, with the song "Please Please Please."

Matching Brown in popularity and career length was Aretha Franklin, known as the Queen of Soul. In the late 1960s she scored a string of hits that included "Respect," "Chain of Fools," and "Think."

Woodstock

Rock music was the focal point of the Woodstock Music and Art Fair. The event marked both the height and the beginning of the end for the counterculture movement. In August 1969 some 400,000 young people descended on rural upstate New York for the three-day festival, closing the New York State Thruway in the process. Despite driving rain, knee-deep mud, and severe shortages of food and water, the concert remained a peaceful gathering. Listeners reveled in the music of rock's top performers, including Jimi Hendrix, Joan Baez, and Janis Joplin.

Woodstock was more than just a rock concert. It was the celebration of an era and marked the high point of the counterculture movement. However, the excitement of the Woodstock experience was short-lived. Four months later, the Rolling Stones held a free concert at Altamont Raceway near San Francisco. At the concert a security team made up of members of a motorcycle gang stabbed a young African American to death in full view of the stage. The event raised doubts about the idealistic spirit of the youth movement.

✔ **READING CHECK:** How did musical styles reflect larger changes in society during the 1960s?

INTERPRETING THE VISUAL RECORD

Woodstock. The 1969 Woodstock Music and Art Fair attracted hundreds of thousands of young Americans. ***What do you think the picture on this poster symbolizes?***

SECTION  REVIEW

Define and explain the significance of the following terms:
generation gap
counterculture
pop art
British invasion
Woodstock

Identify and explain the significance of the following individuals:
Mario Savio
Timothy Leary
Joan Baez
Bob Dylan
James Brown
Aretha Franklin

1. **Using Graphic Organizers** Copy the graphic organizer below. Use it to explain how other conflicts in society influenced protests on college campuses.

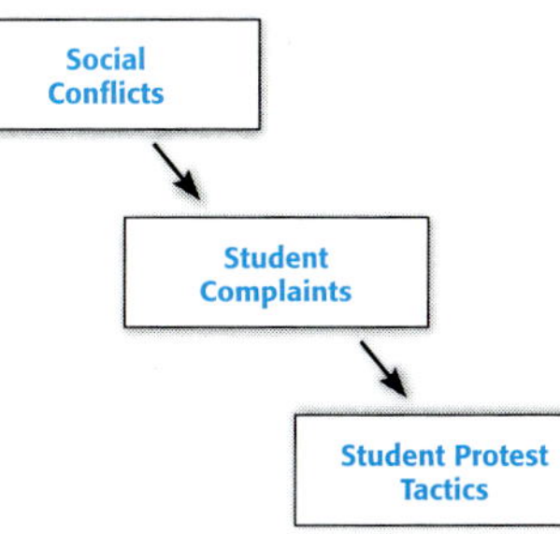

2. **Hypothesizing** How might the counterculture have been more effective in changing American society?
3. **Identifying Values** Why did a growing number of Americans question religion and traditional social values during the 1960s? How did this affect the arts?
4. **Analyzing** What do musical developments reveal about American culture during this period?

Critical Thinking

5. How did Woodstock illustrate the ideals of the counterculture?
   Consider:
   - the beliefs of the counterculture's followers
   - the role of rock music
   - the audience's behavior at Woodstock

VISUAL RECORD ANSWER

Students might suggest that the dove represents peace and love.

CHAPTER 22 REVIEW ANSWERS

Creating a Time Line
Each event should have an explanation and the correct date.

Writing a Summary
See the Reading Checks in each section for main ideas.

Identifying People and Ideas
1. author of *The Feminine Mystique*
2. made it illegal for employers to pay female workers less than male workers who do the same job
3. union organizer who led a boycott and became a symbol for Mexican Americans
4. Mexican American activist group
5. Chicano political party
6. organization that called for a renewal of American Indian culture and the recognition of Indian rights
7. founder of the Gray Panthers
8. rejected the values of mainstream America
9. student activist who helped organize Berkeley protest
10. 1969 concert that celebrated countercultural values

REVIEW AND ASSESSMENT RESOURCES

PRINT
- Chapter 22 Review, pp. 672–73
- Chapter 22 Tutorial for Students, Parents, Mentors, and Peers
- Chapter 22 Test (Form A or B)
- Portfolio Activities and Alternative Assessment Handbook, Chapter 22

MULTIMEDIA
- Audio Program, Chapter 22 (English and Spanish)
- Chapter 22 Test Generator (on the One-Stop Planner)
- Global Skill Builder CD–ROM
- HRW Web site

SHELTERED ENGLISH
- Spanish Glossary
- Sheltered English Chapter 22 Test

REVIEW

Have students complete the **Chapter 22 Review** on pp. 672–73.

ASSESS

Use one of the chapter tests to assess students' understanding of the content. For **Alternative Assessment**, see the **Portfolio Activities and Alternative Assessment Handbook.**

Understanding Main Ideas

1. to pressure elected officials to work for women's equality

2. They believed that it threatened families and all gender distinctions.

3. The strike proved that Mexican Americans could fight discrimination.

4. to protest the poor quality of the schools they attended

5. Students might suggest that AIM gained media attention but achieved few of its goals.

6. Musicians such as Bob Dylan used their lyrics to express political criticism.

Reviewing Themes

1. Answers will vary but should refer to the ERA.

2. They objected to various university policies and social problems. In addition, they had the time and money to pursue protests.

3. art—used to question materialism and capitalism; fashion—used to express rejection of traditional beliefs; music—used to spread certain political messages and offer an innovative sound and a new way of thinking

Review

Creating a Time Line

Copy the time line below onto a sheet of paper. Complete the time line by filling in the events and dates from the chapter that you think were most significant. Pick three events and explain why you think they were significant.

Writing a Summary

Using the Reading Checks as a guide, write an overview of the events in the chapter.

Identifying People and Ideas

Identify the following terms or individuals and explain their significance.

1. Betty Friedan
2. Equal Pay Act
3. César Chávez
4. Brown Berets
5. La Raza Unida Party
6. American Indian Movement
7. Maggie Kuhn
8. counterculture
9. Mario Savio
10. Woodstock

Understanding Main Ideas

SECTION 1

1. Why was the National Organization for Women founded?
2. Why did some women oppose the Equal Rights Amendment?

SECTION 2

3. How did the Delano grape strike come to symbolize the concerns of Mexican Americans throughout the United States?
4. Why did high school students in Los Angeles hold walkouts?

SECTION 3

5. Did the American Indian Movement achieve its goals? Explain your answer.

SECTION 4

6. What was the relationship between music and political protest?

Reviewing Themes

1. **Constitutional Heritage** When should the Constitution be amended? Explain your answer.
2. **Economic Development** Why did middle-class university students turn to political protest?
3. **Cultural Diversity** How did Americans use art, fashion, and music to question American values?

Thinking Critically

1. **Evaluating** What forms of protest proved most effective during the 1960s and 1970s?
2. **Identifying Cause and Effect** In what ways did the African American civil rights movement influence the protest methods of other groups in American society?
3. **Recognizing Point of View** Why might some Americans have been initially resistant to the notion of greater access for people with disabilities?
4. **Using Historical Imagination** Would American life be different today if the Equal Rights Amendment had been ratified? Explain your answer.
5. **Analyzing** What problems did Mexican American activists encounter as they tried to create national organizations?

Writing About History

Writing to Persuade Write a speech intended to persuade an audience to either support or oppose ratification of the Equal Rights Amendment. Use the graphic below to organize your thoughts.

RETEACH

Pair students and assign each pair one of the sections in this chapter. Have each pair create detailed graphic organizers for the material in its assigned section. Ask students to present their graphic organizers to the class. To provide a review tool for students, display the graphic organizers around the classroom. **Sheltered English, Cooperative Learning**

EXTEND

Have students conduct research on a social issue of the late 1990s, such as drug abuse or violence. Ask each student to write a short report discussing experts' analysis of its causes and presenting experts' recommendations for addressing the problem. Then have students compare and contrast their chosen issues with those studied in this chapter. Conduct a discussion on students' responses. **Block Scheduling**

Strategies for Success Review the **Strategies for Success** on *Evaluating Web Sites on the Internet.* Then use the computer system at your school or local public library to find a Web site on one of the following topics:

a. the history of the women's rights movement
b. the history of the United Farm Workers (UFW)
c. the history of rock music

Explore the Web site thoroughly and write a one-page report that evaluates its historical value and identifies any biases of the site.

Linking History and Geography

Study the map below. Use it to analyze the distribution of teenagers throughout the United States in 1970. Which region had the highest population of teenagers? Which region had the lowest? How might these population trends have affected the locations of youth movements?

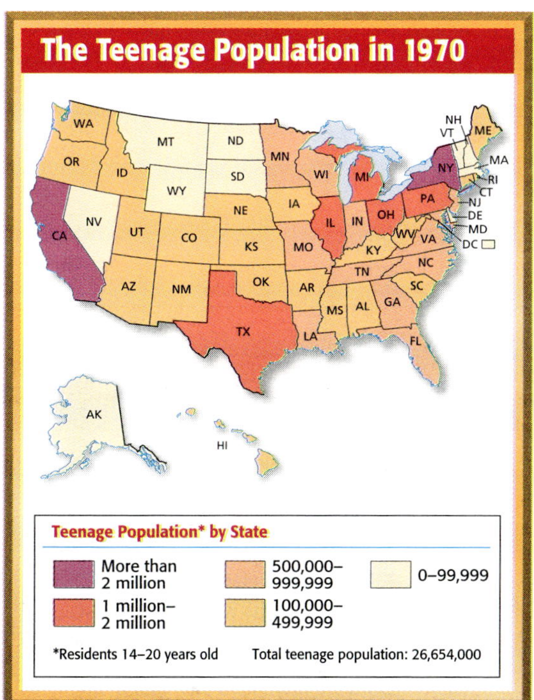

internet connect

TOPIC: César Chávez
GO TO: go.hrw.com
KEYWORD: SE1 Farm

Accessing the Internet through the HRW Web site, research César Chávez and the history of the United Farm Workers. Then create a mural that portrays events from Chávez's life and the struggles of the migrant workers he represented.

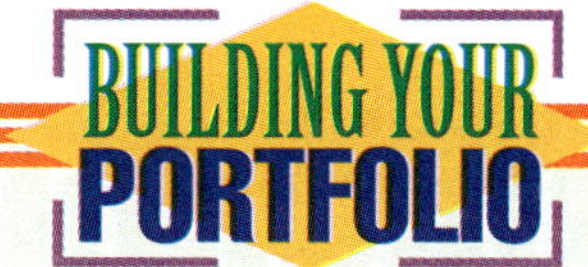

Complete one or all of the following activities independently or cooperatively.

1 Economic Development

Imagine that you are a union organizer working with migrant workers in California. ***Create a flier*** in which you explain why workers should go on strike. Explain how the union will help the striking workers.

2 Democratic Values

Imagine that you are a university professor writing a book on the civil rights movement, and that you have conducted an interview with an AIM member. ***Write a brief summary*** of the interview that explains the attitudes and hopes of the Red Power activist.

3 Cultural Diversity

Imagine that you are a reporter from a national music magazine who is assigned to write an article about the effect of the counterculture on music in the 1960s. ***Write an illustrated article*** that describes the musicians and the styles of music people are listening to.

Thinking Critically

1. Answers will vary. Some students might note that political lobbying proved effective for many groups.
2. inspired the idea of protest in general, contributed the philosophy of nonviolence, and demonstrated the effectiveness of public demonstrations
3. Answers will vary. Students might suggest that some Americans felt that providing greater access was too expensive.
4. Answers will vary. Some students might argue that the ERA would have prevented job discrimination.
5. violent resistance and internal conflicts

Writing About History

support—possibility of better jobs and wages for women and constitutional protection against discrimination; oppose—possibility of negative consequences for families and traditional gender roles

Strategies for Success

Students' reports should clearly summarize the site's ideas and materials.

Linking History and Geography

the Midwest; the northern Great Plains; areas with greater number of teenagers may have had a stronger youth movement

LET'S GET STARTED!

Write the following city on the chalkboard: *Los Angeles.* Have students list all the words that they associate with the city. *(Students might list words such as Hollywood, movies, traffic, and so on.)* Ask volunteers to share their lists with the class. Then tell students that they will learn more about the urban United States, concentrating on Los Angeles as a case study, in the Unit 6 America's Geography.

TEACH AMERICA'S GEOGRAPHY–URBAN AMERICA

Pair students and have them study the America's Geography feature. Then have each pair translate the maps and the graph into written form. *(Pairs should note that the 1920s map shows the importance of electric trolleys and stream trains in the Los Angeles area, that the 1980s map displays the enormous growth of the city and its highway system, and that the graph shows the population boom in the city.)* Ask volunteers to read their summaries to the class. **Sheltered English, Cooperative Learning**

CULTURAL DIVERSITY

Population Distribution. As urban Los Angeles grew, so did the diversity of its population. According to a 1990 census, nonwhite ethnic and racial groups made up more than half of the population. South Central Los Angeles had a primarily African American population while East Los Angeles had a high concentration of Hispanic residents.

CRITICAL THINKING How might residential segregation work against the ideals of a democratic society?

ANSWER: Answers will vary. Some students might suggest that democratic ideals involve social integration.

AMERICA'S GEOGRAPHY ANSWERS

1. steam train
2. approximately 15 miles

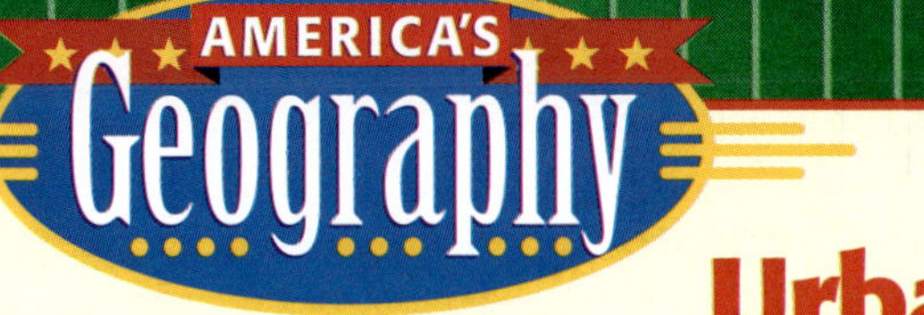

Urban America

As more people moved to the cities and suburbs after World War II, metropolitan areas—large cities or groups of cities and their surrounding areas—were created. The city of Los Angeles is typical of a metroplex. In the 1920s most of the land inside the official city limits was not developed. As the city grew, it engulfed numerous surrounding areas as people increasingly moved outside the city and commuted to work.

Suburban growth. Los Angeles was at the forefront of the creation of the suburban housing system. By the 1920s, as eastern cities grew more crowded, Los Angeles had built the nation's most extensive electric railway-car system to encourage people to live outside the city and commute. City boosters used this system and the area's geography to encourage migration. They noted the sunny climate and pleasant beaches nearby.

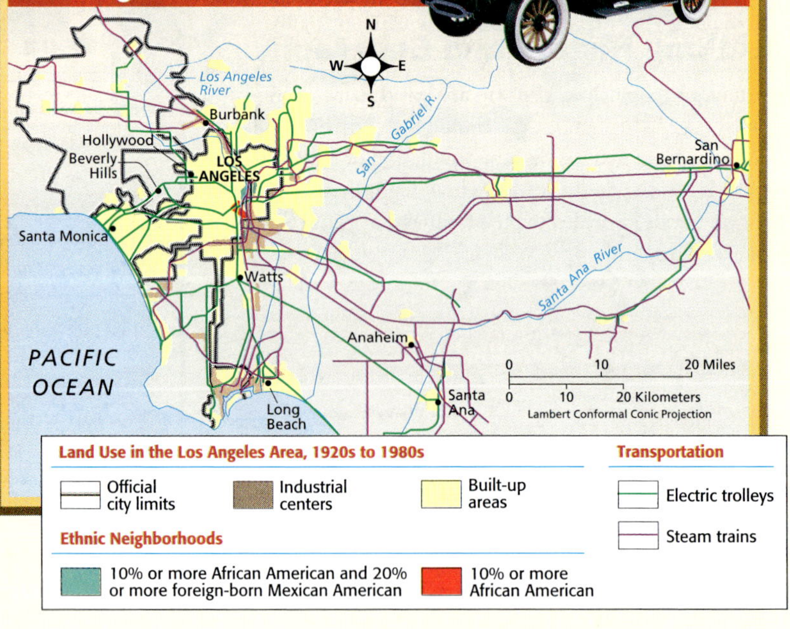

Filming an early Hollywood western

Hollywood. The geography of Los Angeles attracted many early filmmakers because of its dry climate and nearness to many different types of landscape, including the beaches, mountains, and desert.

GEOGRAPHY AND HISTORY Skills

MOVEMENT

1. If you had lived in Anaheim, California, in the 1920s and wanted to commute to downtown Los Angeles, what kind of transportation would you have taken?
2. If you were a Hollywood producer in the 1920s who wanted to film a scene at the beach, how far would you need to travel to reach the ocean?

SPOTLIGHT
on Hollywood and the Movie Industry

Pair students and ask each pair to conduct research on the history of Hollywood, focusing on the role of the movie industry in the city's growth. Have pairs create series of historical maps tracing the growth of Hollywood during the mid- to late 1900s. Ask each pair to write captions for its maps. To conclude, display pairs' maps around the classroom and conduct a brief discussion on Hollywood and the ways in which certain industries expand or diminish growth in certain areas.
Cooperative Learning

SPOTLIGHT
on Public Transportation in Los Angeles

Have students conduct research on the debate over public transportation in Los Angeles, concentrating on subways, buses, and light rail systems. Then write the following question on the chalkboard: *How can Los Angeles ease congestion and provide the best form of public transportation to its citizens?* Conduct a debate on the question. To conclude, ask students to make connections between the issue of public transportation in Los Angeles and that in their own town or city.

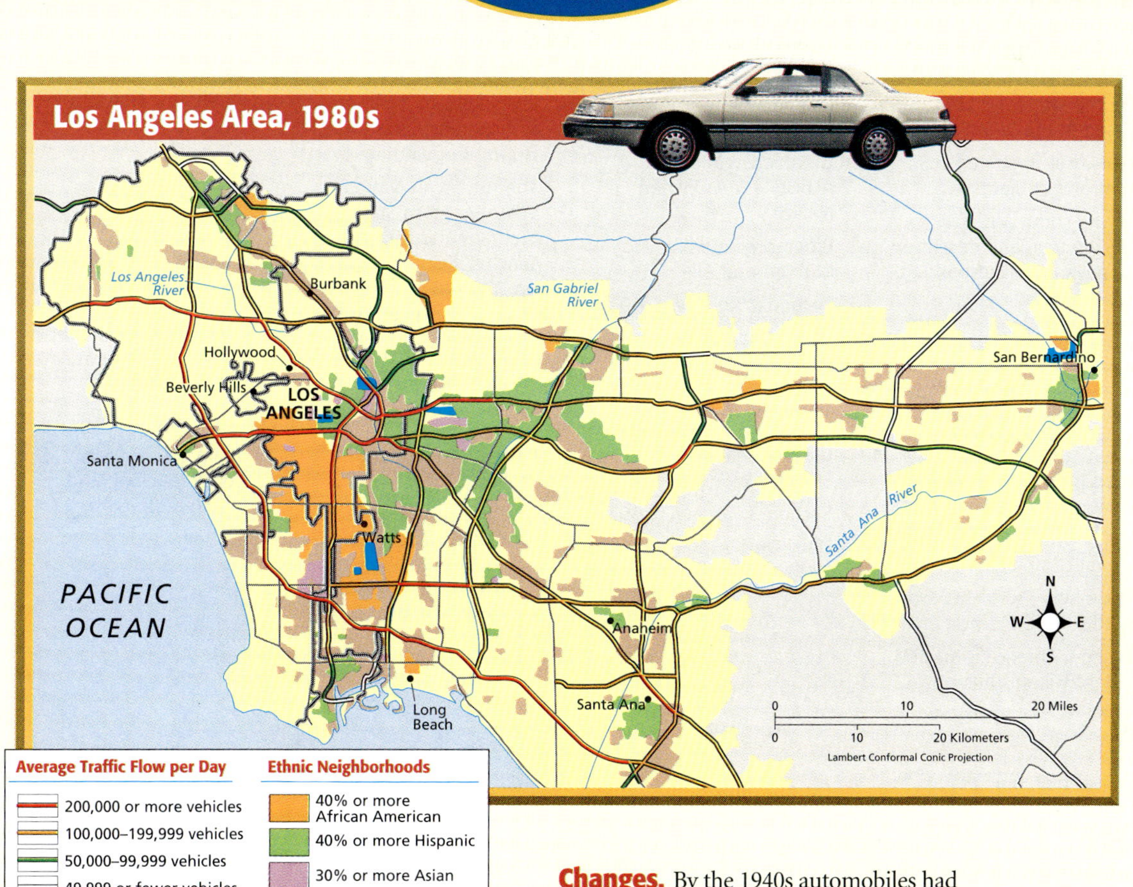

Changes. By the 1940s automobiles had replaced the railway system as the preferred means of transportation in Los Angeles. Wartime employment caused the city to grow rapidly. This growth was encouraged by the creation of a huge new freeway system.

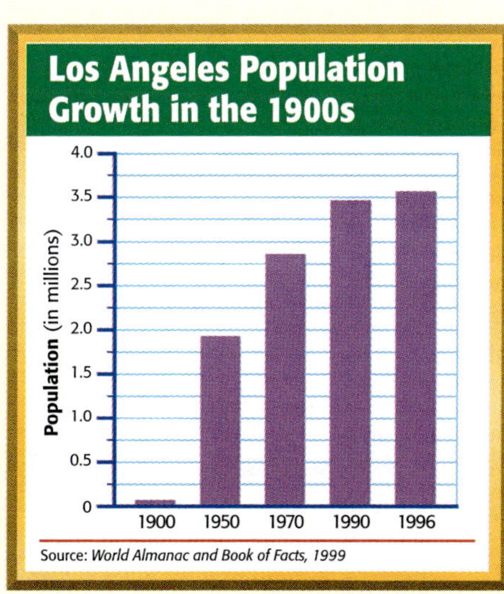

GEOGRAPHY AND HISTORY 

MOVEMENT

1. By how much did the population of Los Angeles increase between 1900 and 1950?
2. How many miles of freeways had an average traffic flow of at least 200,000 vehicles per day?

ACROSS THE CURRICULUM
▶GEOGRAPHY◀

Los Angeles. The city of Los Angeles covers some 464 square miles. Not surprisingly, cars are crucial in this sprawling environment. One commentator, invoking the scholarly practice of studying Italian to read Dante, said that he learned to drive so that he could "read Los Angeles in the original."

ACTIVITY: Ask students to conduct research to identify the 10 largest cities—in terms of square miles—in the United States. Have each student create a visual display presenting the results of his or her research. Ask students to inspect the visual displays. To conclude, conduct a brief discussion on the advantages and disadvantages of so-called "mega cities."

THAT'S INTERESTING!

According to the 1990 census, California had more automobiles than any other state. It also had the highest number of vehicle miles of travel.

AMERICA'S GEOGRAPHY ANSWERS

1. by about 1.75 million people
2. about 115 miles

War in Vietnam

CHAPTER PLANNING GUIDE

	Section Lesson Objectives	Print Resources	Multimedia Resources	Sheltered English Resources
Section 1 Background to Conflict, pp. 678–83	1 Analyze why China and France wanted to control Vietnam. 2 Explain why the United States refused to support Vietnamese independence in the 1940s and 1950s. 3 Discuss why President Kennedy increased U.S. involvement in Vietnam.	▶ Guided Reading Strategy 23.1 ▶ American History Outline Map 22: The Vietnam War ▶ Geography Activity 23: Geography and the Vietnam War ▶ Section 1 Review, p. 683 ▶ Daily Quiz 23.1	▶ One-Stop Planner, Lesson 23.1 ▶ Holt Researcher: American History CD–ROM	▶ Main Idea Activity for Reteaching and Sheltered English 23.1
Section 2 The War Escalates, pp. 684–91	1 Identify the constitutional issue the Tonkin Gulf Resolution raised. 2 Describe the strategies U.S. forces used in the Vietnam War. 3 List factors that frustrated U.S. military efforts in Vietnam. 4 Explain why some Americans opposed the war, and describe how the government responded.	▶ Guided Reading Strategy 23.2 ▶ Literature Reading 23: Jungle Warfare ▶ Graphic Organizer Activity 23: A Divided Nation ▶ Biography Reading 23: Muhammad Ali ▶ Section 2 Review, p. 691 ▶ Daily Quiz 23.2	▶ One-Stop Planner, Lesson 23.2 ▶ Everyday Life in America Transparency 30: Protest During the Vietnam War ▶ The American Nation Video Program Segment: Vietnam and the Media; Teacher's Guide, pp. 141–46 ▶ Holt Researcher: American History CD–ROM	▶ Main Idea Activity for Reteaching and Sheltered English 23.2
Section 3 A Turning Point, pp. 692–97	1 Explain why the Tet Offensive weakened many Americans' confidence in their government. 2 List the key events of the 1968 presidential campaign. 3 Summarize how President Nixon attempted to end the war. 4 Describe how Americans reacted to President Nixon's plan to end the war.	▶ Guided Reading Strategy 23.3 ▶ Section 3 Review, p. 697 ▶ Daily Quiz 23.3	▶ One-Stop Planner, Lesson 23.3 ▶ Holt Researcher: American History CD–ROM	▶ Main Idea Activity for Reteaching and Sheltered English 23.3
Section 4 The War Ends, pp. 698–703	1 Explain why the United States agreed to a cease-fire in January 1973. 2 Describe the war's long-term effects on Vietnam and the Vietnamese people. 3 Evaluate the war's long-term effects on the American people.	▶ Guided Reading Strategy 23.4 ▶ Primary Source Reading 23: The Return of Vietnam Veterans ▶ Section 4 Review, p. 703 ▶ Daily Quiz 23.4	▶ One-Stop Planner, Lesson 23.4 ▶ Holt Researcher: American History CD–ROM ▶ HRW Web site	▶ Main Idea Activity for Reteaching and Sheltered English 23.4
Chapter Review and Assessment pp. 704–05		▶ Chapter 23 Review, pp. 704–05 ▶ Chapter 23 Tutorial for Students, Parents, Mentors, and Peers ▶ Chapter 23 Test (Form A or B) ▶ Portfolio Activities and Alternative Assessment Handbook, Chapter 23	▶ Audio Program, Chapter 23 (English and Spanish) ▶ Chapter 23 Test Generator (on the One-Stop Planner) ▶ Global Skill Builder CD–ROM ▶ HRW Web site	▶ Spanish Glossary ▶ Sheltered English Chapter 23 Test

CHAPTER OVERVIEW

Vietnam has a long history of colonization. China and France both attempted to control the country. China wanted to seize its rich agricultural resources whereas France wanted to dominate its trade and win converts to Christianity. After years of resistance in the mid-1900s, Vietnam won its independence in 1954. The country was soon partitioned into two separate nations, however—communist North Vietnam and anticommunist South Vietnam. Fearful of communism in Southeast Asia, the United States aided the South Vietnamese in their fight against South Vietnamese Communist insurgents and the North Vietnamese. Soon the United States was involved in the Vietnam War.

The war caused horrible devastation in Vietnam and deep political divides in the United States. The antiwar movement in the United States staged many protests. In 1968, after the Tet Offensive, public criticism of the war rose dramatically. Richard Nixon won the presidency in that year with a secret plan to end the conflict. After taking office, however, President Nixon began bombing Cambodia, further inflaming public opinion. The United States finally agreed to a cease-fire in January 1973. The effects of the war linger in both Vietnam and the United States.

TIME TAMERS

Block Scheduling

The teacher lesson plans for each section offer a variety of activity choices to help you present the material in a block scheduling format. For further suggestions on block scheduling, see the **Block Scheduling Handbook with Team Teaching Strategies**, pp. 133–38.

Hands-On History Activities:

Classroom to Community The **Hands-On History Activities** help students make meaningful connections between events in American history and those in their own hometown. You may wish to use the Chapter 23 Activity, The Vietnam Era and the Armed Forces, to extend the chapter lessons, as alternative assessment, or as a block scheduling option.

Portfolio Projects

The American Nation includes multiple portfolio projects in each Pupil's Edition chapter review, as well as each unit review. Chapter 23 Portfolio Project options on p. 705 include the following:

1. Students will **create a visual presentation.**
2. Students will **write a script.**
3. Students will **write a letter to a U.S. veteran.**

The American Nation

INTERNET RESOURCE DIRECTORY

To access online materials for this chapter, go to **go.hrw.com** and type in the keywords listed below.

HRW ONLINE RESOURCES
GO TO: go.hrw.com

Online Maps
KEYWORD: SE1 Maps23
- Landscape of Indochina
- Election of 1968

Online Reading Support
KEYWORD: SE1 Strategies23

Online Rubrics
KEYWORD: SE1 Rubrics

CHAPTER ENRICHMENT LINKS
Use these Web links to extend and enrich student learning for Chapter 23.
GO TO: go.hrw.com
KEYWORD: SE1 Ch23

CHAPTER INTERNET ACTIVITIES
GO TO: go.hrw.com
- Pupil's Edition Student Activity
  KEYWORD: SE1 Vietnam
  (Students examine the history of Vietnam.)
- Teacher's Edition Student Activity
  KEYWORD: SE1 Saigon
  (Students conduct research on the evacuation of Saigon.)
- Teacher's Edition Student Activity
  KEYWORD: SE1 Veterans
  (Students explore the Vietnam Veterans Memorial.)

ADDITIONAL RESOURCES

Books for Teachers

Herring, George C. *America's Longest War: The United States and Vietnam, 1950–1975.* McGraw-Hill, 1996. Chronicles the war over 25 years.

Levy, David W. *The Debate over Vietnam.* Johns Hopkins University Press, 1991. Examines support for and opposition to the war within the United States.

Books for Students

Hoobler, Dorothy, and Thomas Hoobler. *Vietnam: Why We Fought.* Knopf, 1990. Examines the history of Vietnam's foreign relations.

Karnow, Stanley. *Vietnam: A History.* Viking Press, 1983. Surveys Vietnamese history from conflicts with China to the communist victory; considered a classic in the field.

Primary Sources from the Period

Caputo, Philip. *A Rumor of War.* Henry Holt & Company, 1977. Presents the memoirs of a U.S. Marine who served in Vietnam.

The Pentagon Papers. Bantam Books, 1971. Presents a collection of U.S. government documents regarding the war.

Multimedia Materials

Vietnam: A Television History. Video, 120 min. WGBH Boston. Includes documentary footage and interviews.

Vietnam: Lessons of a Lost War. Video, 28 min. NBC. Offers interviews with U.S. military officials.

Vietnam: The War at Home. Video, 100 min. Examines antiwar protests at the University of Wisconsin.

CHAPTER 23

Before You Read

Build on What You Know

Ask students to answer the following questions.

How might the Vietnam War have been similar to the Korean War?

Consider:

- U.S. goals in Korea
- public attitudes toward both wars

Why might the Vietnam War have inspired protests?

Consider:

- the ways in which the United States became involved in the Vietnam War
- the length of the war
- other conflicts in American society during the 1960s

exploring the time line

AMERICAN EVENTS

PEOPLE IN HISTORY

1960 ■ *To Kill a Mockingbird.* Author Harper Lee grew up in the small town of Monroeville, Alabama. Her childhood there inspired the setting and some of the characters of *To Kill A Mockingbird.* Her father, Amasa Lee, was a lawyer and the model for the novel's lawyer and hero Atticus Finch. Harper Lee herself studied to be a lawyer at the University of Alabama and at Oxford University. However, she moved to New York City six months short of a law degree. Lee won a Pulitzer Prize for her novel in 1961. While she continues to do some writing, she has never published another novel.

ACTIVITY: Have students write a brief outline for a novel using their hometown as a model for the setting. In addition to describing their hometown, students should provide a historical context for their novel.

CHAPTER 23

1954–1975

War in Vietnam

Disneyland entrance ticket

An early microchip

1954
Science and Technology
The first nuclear-powered submarine, the *Nautilus*, is launched at Groton, Connecticut.

1955
Daily Life
The Disneyland amusement park opens in Anaheim, California.

1957
Business and Finance
The Treaty of Rome establishes the European Economic Community, removing trade barriers among Belgium, France, Italy, Luxembourg, the Netherlands, and West Germany.

1959
Science and Technology
Working independently, Jack Kilby and Robert Noyce revolutionize electronic technology with the invention of the microchip.

1959
World Events
Cuban dictator Fulgencio Batista is overthrown as rebel leader Fidel Castro seizes power.

1960
The Arts
Alabama writer Harper Lee publishes *To Kill a Mockingbird.*

1960
Science and Technology
The United States launches the world's first communications satellite, *Echo I.*

1963
World Events
Military officers overthrow the South Vietnamese government.

1963
Science and Technology
The Oyster Creek nuclear power plant in New Jersey is the first commercial nuclear reactor.

1963
The Arts
The Beatles have their first hit song, "I Want to Hold Your Hand."

1954 | 1957 | 1960 | 1963

The USS Nautilus

Fulgencio Batista

Before You Read

Build on What You Know

After World War II the United States took a stand opposing the spread of communism anywhere in the world. In the early 1950s U.S. troops fought against communist forces in Korea. In this chapter you will learn how the United States became involved in a similar war in Vietnam, which had won its independence from the French in 1954. Eventually more than 2 million Americans served in the Vietnam War. The conflict, which lasted more than a decade, left deep scars on both Vietnam and the United States.

Think About Themes

To help students create their Themes Journal entries, provide the following examples of appropriate **agree/disagree** *statements.*

Global Relations

Agree U.S. involvement in World War II helped the Allies win the conflict and defeat Nazi Germany, thus saving many lives.

Disagree Every nation has the right to self-determination.

Constitutional Heritage

Agree The framers of the Constitution created a checks-and-balances system to guard against tyranny.

Disagree In the interest of national security, the president often must take action without consulting Congress.

Democratic Values

Agree In a democracy, people have the unlimited right to protest government actions.

Disagree The U.S. government limited civil rights and protests during the Civil War to promote the war effort.

exploring the time line

GLOBAL EVENTS

internetconnect

TOPIC: The Fall of Saigon
GO TO: go.hrw.com
KEYWORD: SE1 Saigon

Have students access the Internet through the HRW Web site to conduct research on the U.S. evacuation of Saigon and the experiences of those who lived through evacuation. Then ask students to assume one of the following roles: a U.S. Marine, a Vietcong soldier, a South Vietnamese civilian, or a Vietnamese citizen who was evacuated out of Saigon. Tell each student to write a diary entry or a series of diary entries from the perspective of his or her chosen role. Have students read their diary entries to the class.

Robert Lowell

The Monterey Pop Festival

The Kent State shooting

1965 The Arts
Poet Robert Lowell speaks out against President Johnson's Vietnam policy at a White House party.

1966

1967 The Arts
The first large rock music gathering, the Monterey Pop Festival, is held in Monterey, California.

1967 Daily Life
Boxer Muhammad Ali is sentenced to five years in prison for refusing to report for military duty.

1968 World Events
Soviet troops invade Czechoslovakia to crush a reform movement.

1969

1970 Daily Life
At an antiwar rally at Kent State University in Ohio, National Guardsmen open fire, killing four people and wounding nine.

1971 World Events
General Idi Amin seizes power in Uganda.

1972

1975 World Events
North Vietnamese forces capture the South Vietnamese capital of Saigon.

1975 Science and Technology
President Gerald Ford signs the Metric Conversion Act to move the United States to the metric system.

1975

Muhammad Ali

Soviet tanks in Prague, Czechoslovakia

Think About Themes

Decide whether you **agree** *or* **disagree** *with the following statements. Note why in your journal.*

Global Relations Under certain circumstances one nation has the right to intervene in the affairs of another.

Constitutional Heritage The system of checks and balances will be damaged if one branch of government becomes too strong.

Democratic Values In a democracy there should be no limits to a person's right to protest government actions.

SECTION 1

After completing Section 1, students should be able to:

OBJECTIVE 1 *Analyze why China and France wanted to control Vietnam.*

OBJECTIVE 2 *Explain why the United States refused to support Vietnamese independence in the 1940s and 1950s.*

OBJECTIVE 3 *Discuss why President Kennedy increased U.S. involvement in Vietnam.*

LET'S GET STARTED!

As students enter the classroom, ask them to list 10 words that they associate with the Vietnam War. Have volunteers share their word lists. *(Students might list words such as violent, unjust, mistake, and so on.)* Tell students that in Section 1 they will learn more about the background of the conflict in Vietnam.

SECTION 1 RESOURCES

PRINT

- Guided Reading Strategy 23.1
- American History Outline Map 22: The Vietnam War
- Geography Activity 23: Geography and the Vietnam War
- Section 1 Review, p. 683
- Daily Quiz 23.1

MULTIMEDIA

- One-Stop Planner, Lesson 23.1
- Holt Researcher: American History CD–ROM

SHELTERED ENGLISH

- Main Idea Activity for Reteaching and Sheltered English 23.1

✔ READING TO UNDERSTAND

To help students master the section objectives, have them answer the **READING CHECKS** and complete **Guided Reading Strategy 23.1** as they read the section.

Background to Conflict

OBJECTIVES

Read to understand:

1. why China and France wanted to control Vietnam
2. why the United States refused to support Vietnamese independence in the 1940s and 1950s
3. why President Kennedy increased U.S. involvement in Vietnam

KEY TERMS

Vietminh
domino theory
Vietcong

KEY PEOPLE

Le Loi
Ho Chi Minh
Ngo Dinh Diem

KEY PLACES

Red River Delta
Mekong Delta
French Indochina
Hanoi
Dien Bien Phu
Saigon

"I want to rail against the wind and the tide, kill the whales in the sea, sweep the whole country to save the people from slavery, and I refuse to be abused."

—Trieu Au

A Vietnamese print showing Trieu Au

Trieu Au's defiant words inspired the Vietnamese people to revolt against China in A.D. 248. Although the rebellion she led was defeated, the cause Trieu Au fought for was not. For centuries invaders desired the fertile river deltas and coastal lowlands of Vietnam. The people of Vietnam were not easily conquered, however. For more than 1,000 years they fought for their freedom and independence.

Vietnam

The easternmost country of Southeast Asia, Vietnam covers about 130,000 square miles of mostly hills and dense forests. It is bordered on the north by China and on the west by Laos and Cambodia. Vietnam's population is centered around the Red River Delta in the far north and the Mekong (MAY-kawng) Delta in the south.

Chinese occupation. The moist, tropical climate of the deltas and coastal lowlands allows Vietnamese farmers to grow at least two crops of rice a year. It was this agricultural abundance that tempted China to invade the Red River Delta about 200 B.C. For more than a thousand years, the Chinese struggled to maintain control over northern and central Vietnam. The Vietnamese resisted and finally won limited independence from China in A.D. 939.

In the 1400s China tried to reassert control over Vietnam. A Vietnamese military leader named Le Loi used guerrilla warfare to defeat the Chinese invaders. Le Loi's rebels worked as peasants by day and took up arms to attack the Chinese by night. By 1428 the rebels had driven the Chinese from the country and won independence for Vietnam. Le Loi became the new emperor.

Vietnam's fertile rice fields produce an abundant food source.

French colonization. Vietnam again lost its independence during a surge of European imperialism in the mid-1800s. This time the invaders were French. Despite the stubborn resistance of the Vietnamese, French military power ultimately won out. In 1883 the Vietnamese were forced to grant France complete control of the country. France later combined Vietnam with Laos and Cambodia to form French Indochina, one of its richest colonial possessions.

✔ READING CHECK: Why did China and France want to control Vietnam?

TEACH OBJECTIVE 1

LEVEL 1: Ask students why China wanted to control Vietnam. *(Students should indicate that China wanted to benefit from Vietnam's agricultural abundance.)* Then ask them why France wanted to control Vietnam. *(Students should indicate that France wanted to gain access to Asian trade and to win converts to Christianity.)* Pair students and have each pair draw a political cartoon commenting on the tug-of-war over Vietnam. Display pairs' cartoons around the classroom.
Sheltered English, Cooperative Learning

LEVEL 2: Distribute Outline Map 22, The Vietnam War, from **American History Outline Maps**. Have each student label Vietnam's major rivers, mountain ranges, highlands, ports, cities, and delta regions. *(See the map on this page for the correct names and locations.)* Then ask students to write accompanying paragraphs explaining why both China and France wanted to control Vietnam. *(See the Level 1 lesson for the correct reasons.)* Display students' maps around the classroom.

Vietnamese Independence

Like the Chinese, the French gained control of the land but not the hearts of the Vietnamese. Nationalist feelings remained strong. Foremost among the nationalists was Nguyen That Thanh (NY-uhn TAHT TAHN). A world wanderer and man of many names, he is best known as Ho Chi Minh (HOH CHEE MIN)—"He Who Enlightens."

During the 1920s and 1930s Ho lived in China and the Soviet Union while working for Vietnamese independence. He became committed to the ideals of communism. In 1940 the Japanese army occupied all of French Indochina, the Philippines, Malaya, and Indonesia. Ho's chance had come.

Ho Chi Minh led the Vietnamese fight for independence.

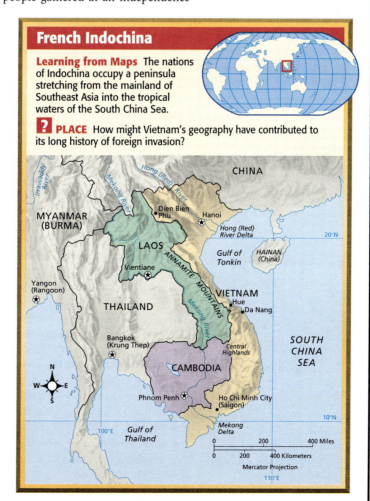

France and the Vietminh go to war. After 30 years away from home, Ho secretly returned to Vietnam in early 1941. He organized a resistance movement called the League for the Independence of Vietnam, or **Vietminh** (vee-ET-MIN). When the Japanese withdrew from Indochina after surrendering to the Allied Powers in August 1945, the Vietminh declared independence. In Hanoi on September 2, 1945, more than 500,000 people gathered at an independence celebration to hear Ho speak. In an effort to gain U.S. support, Ho echoed the language of the U.S. Declaration of Independence in his speech.

U.S. policy toward Vietnam was soon put to the test. By 1946 the French and the Vietnamese were once again locked in battle. President Truman ignored Ho's pleas for assistance and threw U.S. support behind France. Truman viewed France as a vital ally in the struggle against the spread of communism in postwar Europe. He also was unwilling to back the Vietminh because of Ho's Communist Party connections.

Presidential advisers feared that communism would engulf Asia. This fear was reinforced in 1949 when Mao Zedong's Communists took over China—Asia's most populous country and a former U.S. ally. By 1950 the United States was caught up in a bloody ground war, trying to turn back communist North Korea's invasion of South Korea. Meanwhile, Communist-led nationalist revolts rocked Indonesia, the Philippines, and Malaya.

These developments led U.S. policymakers to vow to hold the line against communism in East Asia. Truman's successor, Dwight D. Eisenhower, continued this policy. Eisenhower warned that if

French Indochina

Learning from Maps The nations of Indochina occupy a peninsula stretching from the mainland of Southeast Asia into the tropical waters of the South China Sea.

PLACE How might Vietnam's geography have contributed to its long history of foreign invasion?

CHINA
Hong (Red) River
Irrawaddy River
Mekong River
MYANMAR (BURMA)
Dien Bien Phu
Hanoi
Hong (Red) River Delta
20°N
LAOS
Gulf of Tonkin
HAINAN (China)
Vientiane
ANNAMITE MOUNTAINS
Yangon (Rangoon)
VIETNAM
Hue
Da Nang
THAILAND
Mekong River
Bangkok (Krung Thep)
Central Highlands
SOUTH CHINA SEA
CAMBODIA
N
W
E
S
Phnom Penh
Ho Chi Minh City (Saigon)
10°N
100°E
Gulf of Thailand
Mekong Delta
0 200 400 Miles
0 200 400 Kilometers
Mercator Projection
110°E

ECONOMIC DEVELOPMENT

Southeast Asia. A desire for natural resources was one reason for the long-standing U.S. interest in many Southeast Asian nations. Between the two world wars, the United States imported some 90 percent of its rubber and some 75 percent of its tin from Southeast Asia.

CRITICAL THINKING Why might rubber be a crucial resource in both peacetime and wartime?

ANSWER: Students should note that many peacetime products–such as shoes–and many wartime products–such as tires–are made of rubber.

THAT'S INTERESTING!

During his travels as a young man, Ho Chi Minh stopped in many countries, including the United States. After visiting Boston and San Francisco he worked in Brooklyn, New York. He lived in the United States for about one year.

MAP ANSWER
Vietnam shares a border with China, an enormous and powerful nation.

LEVEL 3: Ask students why both China and France wanted to control Vietnam. *(See the Level 1 lesson for the correct reasons.)* Then have each student write a poem about Vietnam's early history and struggle for independence. Tell students to write their poems from the point of view of the country itself—in other words, from the perspective of Vietnam. Ask volunteers to read their poems to the class. Students may wish to include their poems in their portfolios.

SPOTLIGHT on Dien Bien Phu

Pair students and tell them to conduct research on Dien Bien Phu. Have each pair create a detailed map of the battle that took place at Dien Bien Phu. Each pair should write a short military brief describing the battle to accompany its map. Have volunteers present their maps and briefs to the class.
Cooperative Learning, Block Scheduling

TECHNOLOGY AND SOCIETY

Nuclear Weapons. During the siege at Dien Bien Phu, some U.S. military advisers recommended the use of small nuclear weapons to help the French defeat the Vietminh. President Eisenhower immediately rejected the idea, however, in part because he could not envision the United States using nuclear weapons against an Asian population for the second time in less than a decade.

ACTIVITY: Tell students to imagine that they are presidential advisers. Have each student write a memo to President Eisenhower commenting on the potential use of nuclear weapons at Dien Bien Phu.

THAT'S INTERESTING!

Economic and military aid from the United States increased as the French struggled against the Vietminh. Between 1950 and 1954, U.S. aid to France totaled some $2.6 billion.

VISUAL RECORD ANSWER

Students might suggest that the soldiers appear to be fleeing a bomb or an attack.

THROUGH OTHERS' EYES

Asian View of French Colonization

In the 1880s the Vietnamese were battling against French colonization of their country. Ham Nghi, the 13-year-old emperor of Vietnam, had joined the rebellion against the French. In 1885, while fleeing from French Forces, Ham Nghi issued a royal order to the Vietnamese people. He called upon "the rich to give their wealth, the mighty their strength, and the poor their limbs so that the country might be rescued from the invader." Several years later Phan Chu Trinh, a supporter of Ham Nghi, returned to Vietnam. In an open letter to the French government, Phan Chu attacked France's colonial practices in Vietnam. He criticized France's refusal to grant to the Vietnamese people the same basic human rights it reserved for its citizens.

> **"In your papers, in your books, in your plans, in your private conversations, there is displayed in all its intensity the profound contempt with which you overwhelm us. In your eyes, we are savages, dumb brutes, incapable of distinguishing between good and evil. Some of us, employed by you, still preserve a certain dignity . . . and it is sadness and shame that fills our hearts when we contemplate our humiliation."**

Vietnam fell to communism the rest of Southeast Asia would soon follow. "You have a row of dominoes set up. You knock over the first one, and what will happen to the last one is a certainty that it will go over very quickly." This idea came to be called the **domino theory**. By 1954 the United States was paying much of the cost of France's war effort. Even with massive aid, however, the French suffered defeat after defeat.

Money and military equipment were of limited use against Vietminh guerrilla tactics. The Vietminh chose when and where to attack, struck without warning, and then disappeared into the jungle. In 1946 Ho Chi Minh had expressed to an American journalist his people's determination to succeed. Ho characterized the fight as "a war between an elephant"—the French—"and a tiger"—the Vietnamese.

> **"If the tiger ever stands still, the elephant will crush him with his mighty tusks. But the tiger does not stand still. . . . He will leap upon the back of the elephant, tearing huge chunks from his hide, and then the tiger will leap back into the dark jungle. And slowly the elephant will bleed to death. That will be the war of Indochina."**

INTERPRETING THE VISUAL RECORD

Dien Bien Phu. The Vietminh overwhelmed the French base at Dien Bien Phu. ***What appears to be happening to these soldiers?***

Frustrated, the French tried to lure the Vietminh into a conventional battle at Dien Bien Phu (DYEN BYEN FOO), deep within Vietminh-held northern Vietnam. The plan backfired. Some 13,000 French soldiers soon found themselves encircled by more than 50,000 Vietminh troops. The French commander urged his war-weary soldiers to hold out—offering them the hope of a rescue. "The Americans will not let us down; the free world will not let us down."

Help did not come. Although willing to commit money, Eisenhower was reluctant to become directly involved in another Asian war so soon after the Korean War. The Vietminh defeated the French and on May 7, 1954, forced their surrender.

The Geneva Conference. Just one day after the French surrender at Dien Bien Phu, an international conference to settle the Indochina conflict began in Geneva, Switzerland. There, representatives of the French and the Vietminh attempted to map out Indochina's future. Cambodia, Great Britain, Laos, the People's Republic of China, the Soviet Union, and the United States joined the discussions.

China's communist government had been aiding the Vietminh since 1950 and hoped to limit U.S. influence in the region. The Chinese also wished to prevent the establishment of a strong, unified Vietnam. The Americans, meanwhile, did not want to see Vietnam handed over completely to the Communists.

TEACH OBJECTIVE 2

ALL LEVELS: To help students understand why the United States refused to support Vietnamese independence during the 1940s and 1950s, copy the graphic organizer at right on the chalkboard, omitting the italicized answers. Have each student complete it. To conclude the lesson, have students write short letters explaining the U.S. refusal to support Vietnamese independence. Ask volunteers to read their letters to the class. **Sheltered English**

Why the United States Did Not Support Vietnamese Independence in the 1940s and 1950s
- *valued France as a world ally against communism*
- *disliked Ho Chi Minh's affiliation with the Communist Party*
- *feared the domino effect in Southeast Asia*

▶ASSIGNMENT: *Have each student use the information in his or her completed graphic organizer to write a few sentences agreeing or disagreeing with the U.S. refusal to support Vietnamese independence.*

A cease-fire was agreed to, but no definite political settlement was achieved. Vietnam was temporarily divided at the 17th parallel. Vietminh forces withdrew to the north, where they held undisputed power. South of the line, the French regained control. General elections to reunify the country were scheduled for July 1956. Fearing that the Communists would win a nationwide election, the United States refused to support the agreement.

✔ **READING CHECK:** Why did the United States refuse to support Vietnamese independence in the 1940s and 1950s?

INTERPRETING THE VISUAL RECORD

Victory. Vietminh soldiers march in a parade in Hanoi to celebrate their victory over the French. ***Do these women look like combat troops? Explain your answer.***

The Rule of Ngo Dinh Diem

President Eisenhower hoped that southern Vietnam, at least, might be kept noncommunist. He pinned his hopes on Ngo Dinh Diem (NGOH DIN de-EM), a former government official under the French. U.S. officials hoped that Diem's nationalist beliefs would make him an acceptable leader to the people of South Vietnam.

Diem takes power in the south. Ngo Dinh Diem was strongly anticommunist. He had spent several years in the United States, where his political views attracted powerful backers. In 1955 Diem became president of the newly established Republic of Vietnam, or South Vietnam, in an election that was obviously rigged. In Saigon, for example, Diem received more than 605,000 votes from just 450,000 registered voters. Diem knew that he had no chance of winning a nationwide election against Ho Chi Minh. Therefore, when the July 1956 date set by the Geneva Conference rolled around, Diem refused to call an election in the south.

Diem, a Roman Catholic, was unpopular from the start. The large Buddhist population resented the favoritism he showed toward Catholics. Peasants disliked his land policies, which favored wealthy landholders. Almost everyone objected to power being kept solely in the grip of Diem's family. Above all, people feared his ruthless efforts to root out his political enemies. Diem's hated security forces routinely tortured and imprisoned opponents.

By the late 1950s armed revolution had erupted in the south. In 1959 military assistance began flowing from the north to the Vietminh who had stayed in the south. In 1960 the southern Vietminh formed the National Liberation Front (NLF). The NLF's main goal was the overthrow of Diem's government. Members of this rebel force were called **Vietcong**, for Vietnamese Communists, by their opponents. Not all NLF supporters, however, were Communists.

Many peasants joined the ranks of the NLF. Some did so because of government cruelty. Others joined out of fear of the NLF. Like Diem's forces, the NLF used terrorist tactics, assassinating hundreds of government officials. Soon much of the countryside was under Vietcong control.

This North Vietnamese poster reads "Imperial America is the enemy with whom we cannot live under the same sky."

DEMOCRATIC VALUES

The 1956 Election in Vietnam. As Vietnam's 1956 national election approached, the Communists seemed likely to win because the population in North Vietnam was larger than that in South Vietnam. The U.S. government had been supporting efforts to prevent a communist victory. The Central Intelligence Agency (CIA) had conducted a campaign to destroy communist credibility in the South, distributing leaflets that promised violence if northerners gained control of the country. In addition, the CIA had carried out secret operations in the North. They had destroyed printing presses, put acid in bus oil, and placed explosives in railroad coal.

CRITICAL THINKING Do you think that the United States should have engaged in a campaign to prevent a communist victory?

ANSWER: Answers will vary. Some students might argue that the communist threat justified any action, while others might suggest that many of these methods violated the democratic ideal of a fair election.

VISUAL RECORD ANSWER

Students might answer yes and note the women's clothing and weapons.

TEACH OBJECTIVE 3

LEVEL 1: Pair students and have each pair write a series of newspaper headlines that explain why President Kennedy increased U.S. involvement in Vietnam. *(Pairs' headlines should indicate that President Kennedy subscribed to the domino theory and wanted to bolster the global image of the United States.)* Have volunteers read their headlines to the class. **Sheltered English, Cooperative Learning**

LEVEL 2: Have students complete the Level 1 lesson. Then have each student choose one headline and write a short article to accompany it. Have volunteers read their articles to the class.

LEVEL 3: Organize students into small groups and tell them to imagine that they are foreign-policy advisers to President Kennedy. Have each group develop an oral presentation supporting increased involvement in Vietnam. *(See the Level 1 lesson for the correct motivations.)* Ask volunteers to deliver their presentations to the class. **Cooperative Learning**

PEOPLE IN HISTORY

Ngo Dinh Diem. Ngo Dinh Diem was born in 1901. His ancestors had converted to Christianity during the 1600s. As a child, Diem attended a French Catholic school. He even considered becoming a priest. Diem was a dedicated nationalist who bitterly opposed communism and the Vietminh, who had murdered one of his brothers. During the 1950s Diem spent time in the United States, where he met a number of important politicians, including then Senator John F. Kennedy.

CRITICAL THINKING How might Ngo Dinh Diem have differed from Ho Chi Minh?

ANSWER: Students might suggest that they advocated different means for achieving independence. In addition, Diem followed a religion that many Vietnamese regarded as foreign.

STRATEGIES FOR SUCCESS ANSWERS

Practicing the Strategy

1. Students should list the title of each source and note who produced each source.
2. Students should assess the accuracy of each source and identify possible biases.
3. Students should indicate how they would use each source in a research paper.

Strategies for Success — Determining Good Sources

Interpreting and evaluating historical sources are essential skills for learning about the past. This is particularly true in choosing sources for a research paper or project. To determine whether to use a source, one must assess its reliability and usefulness on a variety of levels. The quality of its reasoning, the accuracy of its information, the biases it displays, and its relevance to the topic at hand are all important factors to consider.

How to Determine a Good Source

1. **Identify the type, title, and creator of the source.** First, identify the type of source you will be evaluating and determine whether its title displays any obvious biases toward its subject. Then, if possible, find out about the historical background of the source's creator and the intended audience of the source.
2. **Examine the source carefully.** Study the source carefully, taking note of its main ideas and supporting details.
3. **Evaluate the source's reasoning.** Once you have examined the source thoroughly, assess the quality of its reasoning. Ask yourself the following questions: Are the arguments in this source logical? Are the cause-and-effect relationships fully proven? Do the conclusions follow from the information provided?
4. **Assess the accuracy and fairness of the source.** As you evaluate the source's reasoning, identify any factual inaccuracies that it contains and assess any biases that it displays in its selection, presentation, and discussion of historical evidence. Make sure to note any instances in which the source presents a one-sided view of a person, event, or topic.
5. **Determine the relevance and usefulness of the source.** After you have evaluated the fundamental soundness of the source, determine the extent to which it relates to the specific topic you are researching. Then decide if and how the source should contribute to your research project and use it accordingly.

Applying the Strategy

After you have read this chapter, use your school or local public library to conduct research on the Vietnam War. Use the following sources:

a. an encyclopedia article
b. two or more books
c. a videotape of a film or television documentary
d. a CD–ROM

Then examine each source and decide if and how you would use it in a research paper that focuses on the early role of the United States in Vietnam.

Practicing the Strategy

Use your sources to answer the following questions.

1. What is the title of each source? Who produced each source, and when?
2. Is the information in each source accurate? What biases does each source display?
3. How would you use each source in a research paper?

U.S. troops arrive in Vietnam.

U.S. involvement deepens. John F. Kennedy, who became president in 1961, fully agreed with the domino theory. He also was eager to improve the U.S. image in the world. This image had been tarnished early in his presidency by the failed Bay of Pigs invasion and the building of the Berlin Wall. Aiding South Vietnam provided the United States with a chance to assert its power.

In December 1960 there were some 900 U.S. military advisers in South Vietnam training Diem's Army of the Republic of Vietnam (ARVN). During the next few years, Kennedy increased that number to more than 16,000. As Vietcong attacks mounted, Kennedy authorized U.S. forces to engage in direct combat. As a result, the number of Americans killed or wounded climbed from 14 in 1961 to nearly 500 in 1963.

Diem's overthrow. Political conflict also increased. South Vietnam's Buddhist leaders had begun to openly oppose Diem's rule. Diem was waging a brutal

REVIEW

Have students complete the **Section 1 Review** on p. 683.

ASSESS

Have students complete **Daily Quiz 23.1**. As **Alternative Assessment**, you may want to use the map activity or the newspaper headlines in this section's lessons.

RETEACH

Have students complete **Main Idea Activity for Reteaching and Sheltered English 23.1**. Then organize students into triads. Ask each member of the triads to select one of the section objectives, avoiding duplication. Direct students to write at least five questions on the material related to their selected objectives. Then have students take turns quizzing each other within their groups. **Sheltered English, Cooperative Learning**

EXTEND

Have students conduct research on Trieu Au, a Vietnamese woman who fought for independence. Have each student write a short report on Trieu Au and her fight. Ask volunteers to read their reports to the class. **Block Scheduling**

---

campaign to control the Buddhists. Hundreds of Buddhists were arrested, and many were killed in the crackdown. In response, several Buddhist monks publicly set themselves on fire. These gruesome protests shocked Americans. U.S. officials in Saigon threatened to withdraw support for Diem unless he ended the campaign.

Henry Cabot Lodge, the U.S. ambassador to South Vietnam, met with Diem in August 1963. Lodge later recalled that Diem "absolutely refused to discuss any of the topics that President Kennedy had instructed me to raise." U.S. leaders began to quietly encourage a group of South Vietnamese army officers plotting Diem's overthrow. In an August 29 cable, Lodge described the situation.

> **"We are launched on a course from which there is no respectable turning back: the overthrow of the Diem government. There is no turning back because U.S. prestige is already publicly committed to this end in large measure, and will become more so as the facts leak out. In a more fundamental sense, there is no turning back because there is no possibility, in my view, that the war can be won under a Diem administration."**

The plotters struck in early November 1963, murdering both Diem and his brother. Diem's assassination upset U.S. advisers, who had been prepared to fly Diem out of the country.

Diem's overthrow did nothing to ease Kennedy's growing concern over U.S. involvement in Vietnam. In an interview shortly before Diem's fall, Kennedy had said of the South Vietnamese: "In the final analysis it is their war. They are the ones who have to win or lose it." It is unknown how Kennedy might have handled the situation. Three weeks after Diem's murder, Kennedy himself was assassinated in Dallas.

Henry Cabot Lodge meets with Ngo Dinh Diem in Saigon.

✔ **READING CHECK:** Why did President Kennedy increase U.S. involvement in Vietnam?

SECTION 1 REVIEW

Define and explain the significance of the following terms:
Vietminh
domino theory
Vietcong

Identify and explain the significance of the following individuals:
Le Loi
Ho Chi Minh
Ngo Dinh Diem

Locate and explain the importance of the following places:
Red River Delta
Mekong Delta
French Indochina
Hanoi
Dien Bien Phu
Saigon

1. **Using Graphic Organizers** Copy the graphic organizer below. Use it to list the steps that led to U.S. troops being sent to Vietnam.

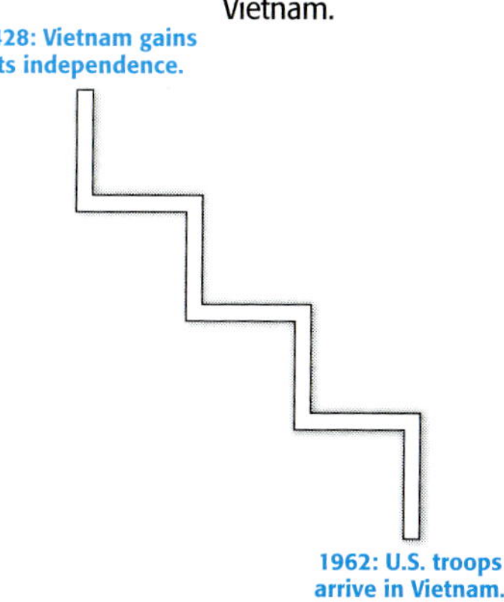
1428: Vietnam gains its independence.
1962: U.S. troops arrive in Vietnam.

2. **Identifying Cause and Effect** Why did President Truman refuse Ho Chi Minh's requests for help against the French?
3. **Understanding Geography: Place** What attracted the Chinese and the French to Vietnam?
4. **Using Historical Imagination** Imagine that you are an adviser to President Eisenhower in 1959. On the basis of what you would know at the time, prepare a statement outlining the benefits and drawbacks of U.S. involvement in Vietnam. Then write a one-paragraph policy recommendation.

Critical Thinking

5. Do you agree with President Kennedy's decision to increase U.S. involvement in Vietnam? Explain your answer.
   Consider:
   - U.S. foreign policy during the early 1960s
   - the goals and actions of the North Vietnamese
   - the strength of the Diem government

SECTION 1 REVIEW ANSWERS

Define and Identify
For significance, see the following pages:
- Le Loi, p. 678
- Ho Chi Minh, p. 679
- Vietminh, p. 679
- domino theory, p. 680
- Ngo Dinh Diem, p. 681
- Vietcong, p. 681

Locate
For locations, see the map on p. 679. For importance, see the following pages:
- Red River Delta, p. 678
- Mekong Delta, p. 678
- French Indochina, p. 678
- Hanoi, p. 679
- Dien Bien Phu, p. 680
- Saigon, p. 681

1. 1883—France gains control of Vietnam; 1945—Vietnam proclaims its independence; 1954—French forces withdraw from Vietnam
2. He wanted to keep France as an ally against the spread of communism and disliked Ho's Communist connections.
3. Chinese—agricultural abundance; French—trade and the possibility of gaining converts to Christianity
4. Policy recommendations will vary but pro and con lists should include: pro—the necessity of opposing communism; con—the possibility of another land war in Asia.
5. Answers will vary. Students should note the Cold War atmosphere, the desire to increase U.S. prestige, the relative success of the North Vietnamese, and the relative unpopularity of Diem in South Vietnam.

SECTION 2

After completing Section 2, students should be able to:

OBJECTIVE 1 *Identify the constitutional issue the Tonkin Gulf Resolution raised.*

OBJECTIVE 2 *Describe the strategies U.S. forces used in the Vietnam War.*

OBJECTIVE 3 *List factors that frustrated U.S. military efforts in Vietnam.*

OBJECTIVE 4 *Explain why some Americans opposed the war, and describe how the government responded.*

LET'S GET STARTED!

As students enter the classroom, display Everyday Life in America Transparency 30, Protest During the Vietnam War, from **American History Visual Resources**. Ask students to complete the accompanying worksheet. Then ask students to share their responses with the class.

SECTION 2 RESOURCES

PRINT

- Guided Reading Strategy 23.2
- Literature Reading 23: Jungle Warfare
- Graphic Organizer Activity 23: A Divided Nation
- Biography Reading 23: Muhammad Ali
- Section 2 Review, p. 691
- Daily Quiz 23.2

MULTIMEDIA

- One-Stop Planner, Lesson 23.2
- Everyday Life in America Transparency 30: Protest During the Vietnam War
- The American Nation Video Program Segment: Vietnam and the Media; Teacher's Guide, pp. 141–46
- Holt Researcher: American History CD–ROM

SHELTERED ENGLISH

- Main Idea Activity for Reteaching and Sheltered English 23.2

✔ READING TO UNDERSTAND

To help students master the section objectives, have them answer the **READING CHECKS** and complete **Guided Reading Strategy 23.2** as they read the section.

The War Escalates

OBJECTIVES

Read to understand:

1. what constitutional issue the Tonkin Gulf Resolution raised
2. what strategies U.S. forces used in the Vietnam War
3. what factors frustrated U.S. military efforts in Vietnam
4. why some Americans opposed the war, and how the government responded

KEY TERMS

Tonkin Gulf Resolution
escalation
Operation Rolling Thunder
Ho Chi Minh Trail
defoliants
search-and-destroy missions
pacification
doves
hawks
Students for a Democratic Society

KEY PEOPLE

Robert S. McNamara
J. William Fulbright

KEY PLACES

South Vietnam
Gulf of Tonkin
North Vietnam
Cambodia
Laos

"Renewed hostile actions against United States ships on the high seas in the Gulf of Tonkin have today required me to order the military forces of the United States to take action in reply. The initial attack on the destroyer Maddox, on August 2, was repeated today by a number of hostile vessels attacking two U.S. destroyers with torpedoes. . . . We believe at least two of the attacking boats were sunk. There were no U.S. losses. . . . But repeated acts of violence against the Armed Forces of the United States must be met not only with alert defense, but with positive reply. That reply is being given as I speak to you tonight. Air action is now in execution against gunboats and certain supporting facilities in North Vietnam which have been used in these hostile operations."

—Lyndon Johnson

The News American

U. S. BOMBERS BLAST N. VIET BASES, 2 PLANES SHOT DOWN

The Gulf of Tonkin incident drew the United States deeper into the Vietnam War.

Near midnight on August 4, 1964, President Lyndon Johnson appeared on national television. His announcement to the American people that night marked a new stage in U.S. involvement in the war in Vietnam.

The Tonkin Gulf Resolution

In 1963 Secretary of Defense Robert S. McNamara had advised President Johnson that he would have to increase the U.S. military commitment to South Vietnam to prevent a Communist victory. Before increasing the U.S. commitment, Johnson needed to get congressional backing. The events in the Gulf of Tonkin gave him the opportunity. Johnson asked Congress to authorize the use of military force "to prevent further aggression." In response, both houses of Congress overwhelmingly passed the **Tonkin Gulf Resolution**. This gave the president authority to take "all necessary measures to repel any armed attack against forces of the United States."

Johnson claimed that the attacks in the Gulf of Tonkin were unprovoked. In reality, however, the U.S. destroyer *Maddox* had been spying in support of South Vietnamese raids against North Vietnam and had fired first. The second attack, moreover, probably never occurred. Some U.S. sailors apparently misinterpreted interference on their radar and sonar as enemy ships and torpedoes. Nonetheless, Johnson and his advisers got what they wanted: authority to expand the war.

Wayne Morse of Oregon was one of just two senators who voted against the Tonkin Gulf Resolution. He warned, "I believe that history will record we have made a great mistake. . . . We are in effect giving the President war-making powers in the absence of a declaration of war." In other words, by passing the resolution, Congress had essentially given up its constitutional power to declare war.

✔ READING CHECK: What constitutional issue did the Tonkin Gulf Resolution raise?

TEACH OBJECTIVE 1

LEVEL 1: Conduct a brief discussion on the constitutional issue raised by the Tonkin Gulf Resolution. *(The Tonkin Gulf Resolution allowed the president to respond to military aggression without further congressional approval.)* Then pair students and ask each pair to write a few sentences or a paragraph summarizing the discussion. Have volunteers read their sentences or paragraphs to the class.
Sheltered English, Cooperative Learning

LEVELS 2 AND 3: Pair students and tell them to imagine that they are members of Congress debating the wisdom of passing the Tonkin Gulf Resolution. Have each pair develop a short dialogue explaining the constitutional issue raised by the Tonkin Gulf Resolution. *(See the Level 1 lesson for the correct issue.)* Ask volunteers to conduct their dialogues for the class.
Cooperative Learning

U.S. Forces in Vietnam

President Johnson soon called for an **escalation**, or buildup, of U.S. military forces in Vietnam. He ordered the Selective Service, the agency charged with carrying out the military draft, to begin calling up young men to serve in the armed forces. In April 1965 the Selective Service notified 13,700 draftees.

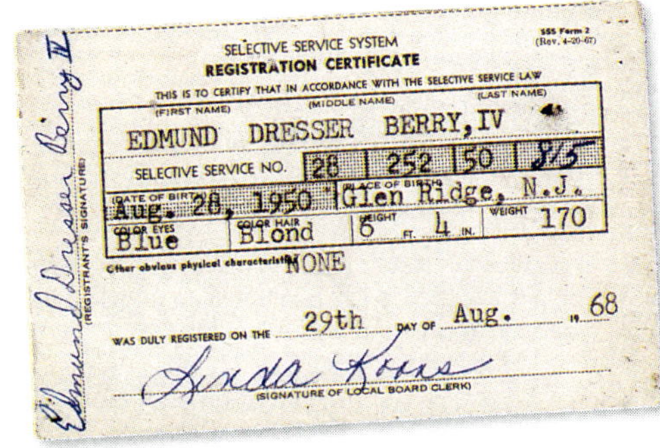

SSS Form 2 (Rev. 4-20-67)
SELECTIVE SERVICE SYSTEM
REGISTRATION CERTIFICATE
THIS IS TO CERTIFY THAT IN ACCORDANCE WITH THE SELECTIVE SERVICE LAW
(FIRST NAME) EDMUND (MIDDLE NAME) DRESSER (LAST NAME) BERRY, IV
SELECTIVE SERVICE NO. 28 | 252 | 50 | 815
(DATE OF BIRTH) Aug. 28, 1950 (PLACE OF BIRTH) Glen Ridge, N.J.
COLOR EYES Blue COLOR HAIR Blond HEIGHT 6 FT. 4 IN. WEIGHT 170
Other obvious physical characteristics NONE
WAS DULY REGISTERED ON THE 29th DAY OF Aug. 19 68
Linda Koons
(SIGNATURE OF LOCAL BOARD CLERK)
Edmund Dresser Berry IV
(REGISTRANT'S SIGNATURE)

During the Vietnam War millions of American men received draft registration certificates like this one.

The troops. During the war more than 2 million Americans served in Vietnam. In the beginning most were professional soldiers who were already enlisted in the armed forces. As the demand for troops grew, however, more and more draftees were shipped to Vietnam. The average U.S. soldier in Vietnam was younger, poorer, and less educated than those who had served in World War II or in the Korean War.

One out of four young men who registered for the draft was excused from service for health reasons. Another 30 percent received non-health-related exemptions or deferments—postponements of service—most often for college enrollment. Mainly because of college deferments, young men from higher-income families were the least likely to be drafted. As a result, poor Americans served in numbers far greater than their proportion in the general population.

African Americans and Hispanics served in combat in very high numbers, particularly during the early years of the war. Many served in the most dangerous ground units. As a result, they experienced very high casualty rates. In 1965, for example, African Americans accounted for almost 24 percent of all battle deaths, even though they made up just 11 percent of the U.S. population.

The most vivid images of the war show soldiers facing the hardships and terrors of battle. Some confronted the enemy in well-defined battles in the highlands. Others cut their way through the jungle, where they heard but seldom saw the enemy. Still others waded through rice paddies and searched rural villages for guerrillas. Most Americans who went to Vietnam, however, served in support positions such as administration, communications, engineering, medical care, and supply and transportation. They were hardly safe, however. Enemy rockets and mortars could—and did—strike anywhere.

Some 10,000 servicewomen filled noncombat positions in Vietnam, mostly as nurses. Although they did not carry guns into battle, they faced the horrors of combat on a daily basis. Edie Meeks described the experience of working as a nurse at a field hospital.

> **"We really saw the worst of it, because the nurses never saw any of the victories. If the Army took a hill, we saw what was left over. I remember one boy who was brought in missing two legs and an arm, and his eyes were bandaged. A general came in later and pinned a Purple Heart on the boy's hospital gown, and the horror of it all was so amazing that it just took my breath away. You thought, was this supposed to be an even trade?"**

Another 20,000 to 45,000 women worked in civilian capacities, many as volunteers for humanitarian organizations such as the Red Cross.

INTERPRETING THE VISUAL RECORD

Nurses. First Lieutenant Elaine Niggemann served at the 24th EVAC Hospital. ***What is the lieutenant doing?***

HISTORY MAKERS SPEAK

Lyndon Johnson in *The Triumph and Tragedy of Lyndon Johnson*

President Johnson on the Draft. The Selective Service System was administered by local draft boards, many of which had only white people as members. In 1966 President Johnson dedicated himself to improving the equality of the draft and diversifying draft boards, saying, "We must continue to ask one form of service—military duty—of our young men. . . . The Nation's requirement that men must serve, however, imposes this obligation: that in this land of equals, men are selected as equals to serve. . . . A just nation must have the fairest system that can be devised for making that selection."

ACTIVITY: Conduct a brief discussion on the draft. Then ask each student to write an editorial commenting on the draft during the Vietnam War.

Multimedia Resources

Everyday Life in America Transparency 30: Protest During the Vietnam War

VISUAL RECORD ANSWER

Students might answer that she is bandaging an injured soldier's foot.

SPOTLIGHT on Soldiers' Lives

Tell students that Vietnam was a grueling environment for U.S. soldiers. Ask students to conduct research on soldiers' experiences in Vietnam. Then tell students to imagine that they are soldiers fighting in Vietnam. Have each student write a series of diary entries about life during the war. Have volunteers read their diary entries to the class.
Block Scheduling

TEACH OBJECTIVE 2

LEVEL 1: Ask students to list the strategies U.S. forces used in the Vietnam War. *(Students should list escalation, the air war, and the ground war.)* Note students' responses on the chalkboard. Then pair students and ask each pair to write sentences describing and analyzing each of the items on the chalkboard list. *(Pairs should note that escalation increased the number of troops in Vietnam, that the air war attempted to secure a quick victory, and that the ground war began when the air war failed.)* Have volunteers read their sentences to the class. **Sheltered English, Cooperative Learning**

TECHNOLOGY AND SOCIETY

The U.S. Air Campaign in Southeast Asia. Between 1962 and 1973, the United States dropped some 8 million tons of bombs on Vietnam, Laos, and Cambodia. More than half of the total tonnage was dropped in South Vietnam. South Vietnam, a U.S. ally, thus became the most bombed country in the history of aerial warfare.

CRITICAL THINKING What might the heavy U.S. aerial bombardment of South Vietnam, presumably an ally, indicate about the nature of the U.S. campaign in Vietnam?

ANSWER: Answers will vary. Some students might suggest that the bombardment of South Vietnam indicated the U.S. military's difficulty in distinguishing between allies and enemies.

MAP ANSWER
The Ho Chi Minh Trail stretched through Laos and Cambodia before veering into South Vietnam.

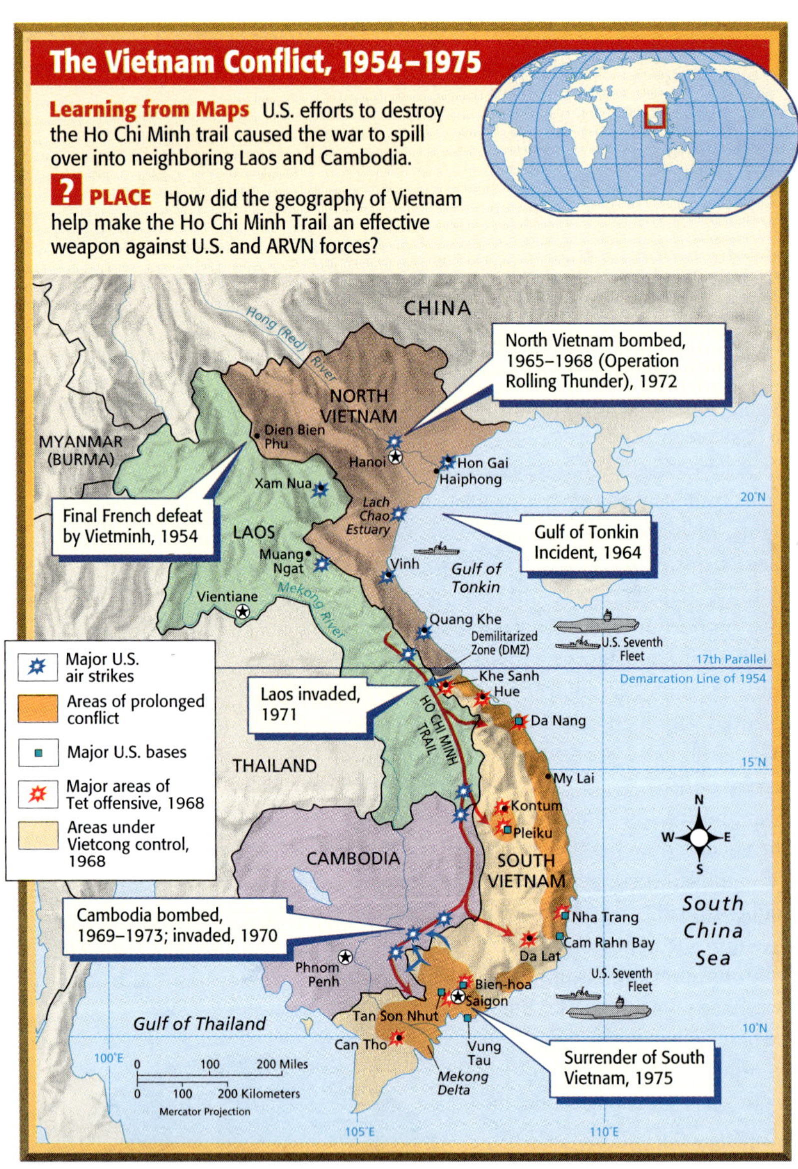

The Vietnam Conflict, 1954–1975

Learning from Maps U.S. efforts to destroy the Ho Chi Minh trail caused the war to spill over into neighboring Laos and Cambodia.

PLACE How did the geography of Vietnam help make the Ho Chi Minh Trail an effective weapon against U.S. and ARVN forces?

The air war. President Johnson hoped that air power could secure a quick victory. In March 1965 he launched **Operation Rolling Thunder**, a bombing campaign against military targets in the North. The goal was to weaken the enemy's will to fight. Johnson also wanted to assure the South Vietnamese of the U.S. commitment to them.

A key target of the bombing was the **Ho Chi Minh Trail**—a network of jungle paths. The North Vietnamese used the Ho Chi Minh Trail to bring weapons and supplies into South Vietnam. Roads and bridges along the trail, parts of which snaked through neighboring Cambodia and Laos, were bombed repeatedly. The Vietcong, however, quickly repaired them or managed without them. They also built many facilities underground to protect against bombing. Some 300,000 people worked full-time to maintain the Ho Chi Minh Trail.

When the bombing did not bring about North Vietnam's collapse, Johnson increased its intensity. By 1967, U.S. aircraft were dropping a daily average of 800 tons of bombs on North Vietnam. Repeated increases in bombing failed to produce the desired results. Frustrated, President Johnson broadened the air war to include strikes against areas of bordering Laos and much of South Vietnam.

U.S. forces used a variety of deadly weapons. Napalm, a jellied gasoline mixture, was used in firebombs. "Cluster bombs" sprayed razor-sharp metal fragments when they exploded. U.S. planes sprayed **defoliants**—chemicals that strip the land of vegetation—over thousands of acres. The goal of the spraying was to expose jungle supply routes and enemy hiding places. They also wanted to destroy the Vietcong food supply. The most widely used of these chemicals was Agent Orange.

The defoliant Agent Orange proved harmful to humans as well as plants.

LEVEL 2: Tell students to imagine that it is 1968 and that they are journalists in Vietnam. Have each student compose a 50-word telegram describing one of the U.S. strategies in the war. *(See the Level 1 lesson for the correct strategies.)* Remind students that they will need to choose their words carefully in order to fully describe the strategy in 50 words or less. Have volunteers read their telegrams to the class. Ask students to select the most concise, descriptive, and effective telegram.

LEVEL 3: Tell students to imagine that it is 1968 and that they are high-level military officials. Have each student write a detailed military brief describing U.S. strategies in Vietnam. *(See the Level 1 lesson for the correct strategies.)* Ask volunteers to read their briefs to the class. Then conduct a classroom discussion on U.S. strategies. Ask students to evaluate both the strategies and their effectiveness. Students may wish to include their military briefs in their portfolios.

The ground war. Physician Ton That Tung recalled that the North Vietnamese clearly understood the goal of the air war. "The Americans thought that the more bombs they dropped, the quicker we would fall to our knees and surrender." Rather than surrender, North Vietnam sent more troops and supplies south.

The bombing led many South Vietnamese to join the Vietcong. Soon the opposition forces included more South Vietnamese than North Vietnamese. The United States countered by launching a ground war. Between 1965 and the end of 1967, the number of U.S. troops in Vietnam grew from about 185,000 to some 486,000.

Sheer numbers were not enough to defeat an enemy who seemed to be everywhere. Aided by regulars of the North Vietnamese Army, the Vietcong struck at U.S. patrols or government-held villages and then melted back into the jungle. Vietnamese peasants who appeared peaceful by day sided with the Vietcong at night. U.S. forces conducted thousands of **search-and-destroy missions** that attempted to drive the Vietcong from their hideouts. Ground patrols first located the enemy and then called in air support to kill them. Once an area was "cleared," the patrols moved on in search of more Vietcong. Snipers and booby traps made these missions extremely dangerous and frustrating. Making matters worse, villages seldom remained cleared of the Vietcong.

To provide security in rural areas, U.S. forces began a program of **pacification**. When security forces were not enough they moved the residents to secure locations and then burned the villages. In such warfare, progress could not be shown on a map. Instead, the daily body count of enemy dead became the sole measure of success—and a questionable measure at that. The U.S. military regularly guessed at or inflated the numbers by counting all Vietnamese dead as the enemy. Said one officer responsible for body-count statistics: "If it's dead and Vietnamese, it's VC [Vietcong]."

INTERPRETING THE VISUAL RECORD

Booby traps. This soldier is exploring a tunnel used by the Vietcong. ***How are this soldier's actions putting him at risk?***

✔ **READING CHECK:** What strategies did U.S. forces use in the Vietnam War?

U.S. morale declines. The first U.S. troops had arrived in Vietnam in a hopeful mood. As marine lieutenant Philip Caputo explained, "When we marched into the rice paddies on that damp March afternoon, we carried, along with our packs and rifles, the implicit [unquestioned] convictions that the Vietcong could be quickly beaten." This optimism began to fade as the hazards of fighting a nearly invisible foe in an alien landscape became apparent. "We kept the packs and rifles," Caputo wrote; "the convictions, we lost."

Equally frustrating was the enemy's will to continue fighting, despite mounting casualties. U.S. war planners believed that superior U.S. technology would win the war. Yet at the end of 1967, victory seemed no closer than in 1963. Ho Chi Minh's earlier warning to the French now seemed applicable to Americans. "You can kill ten of my men for every one I kill of yours, but even at those odds, you will lose and I will win."

✔ **READING CHECK:** What factors frustrated U.S. military efforts in Vietnam?

ACROSS THE CURRICULUM

▶GEOGRAPHY◀

Pacification. Most Vietnamese villagers disliked the pacification program, particularly one early form called the strategic hamlet program. Some villagers were forced to leave their ancestral homelands, which they considered sacred. The villagers resented being moved to new hamlets, or villages, that were often hastily constructed and did not provide protection from the Vietcong. Funds intended for health services and development programs often never reached the villagers, ending up instead in the pockets of corrupt officials. The strategic hamlet program failed so thoroughly that U.S. officials abandoned it.

CRITICAL THINKING Do you think that the strategic hamlet program could have worked under any circumstances?

ANSWER: Answers will vary. Some students might note that, typically, human beings dislike being forced from their homes.

VISUAL RECORD ANSWER

Students might indicate that there is a grenade directly in front of the soldier.

SPOTLIGHT on Opposing Strategies

Pair students and ask one student in each pair to summarize U.S. military strategies and tactics and the other to summarize Vietnamese strategies and tactics. *(Students summarizing U.S. strategies should note intensive bombing, defoliation, pacification of villages, and so on. Students summarizing Vietnamese strategies should note guerrilla warfare, booby traps, and so on.)* Then have pairs compare and contrast these two approaches in a Venn diagram. Ask volunteers to present their summaries and diagrams to the class.

Block Scheduling, Cooperative Learning

TEACH OBJECTIVE 3

LEVEL 1: Pair students and ask each pair to create a bulleted list of the factors that frustrated U.S. military efforts in Vietnam. *(Pairs should note the failure of bombing and technological assaults, guerrilla tactics, and declining morale.)* Have volunteers call out factors as you record them on the chalkboard. Tell students to write in their notes any factors that they missed for future reference.

Sheltered English, Cooperative Learning

AMERICAN LETTERS ANSWERS

1. Ehrhart indicates that the Vietcong dress like civilians and speak the same language as civilians. He also notes that the Vietcong included women and children, not typical enemies.
2. Students might suggest that Trinh Cong Son saw the war as a means of exacting revenge on enemies.
3. Both authors acknowledge the violence of the war, but Trinh Cong Son speaks of directed vengeance while Ehrhart speaks of confused and exhausted retribution.

The American Nation **VIDEO PROGRAM**

Vietnam and the Media; Teacher's Guide, pp. 141–46

Search 13498, Play to 23297
Videodisc 2, Side B

Play Pause

See *Teacher's Guide* for Spanish barcode.

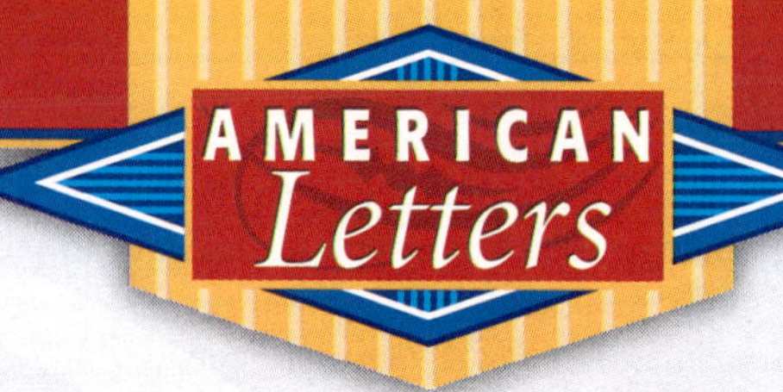

Views of Vietnam

U.S. soldiers and the Vietnamese saw the war from very different perspectives. Some people who were there later expressed their feelings through writing. The following poem by William D. Ehrhart, a marine who served in Vietnam, describes his experiences fighting against the Vietcong guerrillas. Trinh Cong Son, a Vietnamese poet, captured the horror of battle in the poem below.

"Guerrilla War"

by William D. Ehrhart

It's practically impossible
to tell the civilians
from the Vietcong.
Nobody wears uniforms.
They all talk
the same language
(and you couldn't under-
stand them
even if they didn't).
They tape grenades
inside their clothes,
and carry satchel charges
in their market baskets.
Even their women fight;
and young boys,
and girls.
It's practically impossible
to tell civilians
from the Vietcong;
after awhile
you quit trying.

William D. Ehrhart

Trinh Cong Son

[Title Unknown]

by Trinh Cong Son

I saw, I saw, I saw holes and trenches
full of the corpses of my brothers and sisters.
Mothers, clap for joy over war.
Sisters, clap and cheer for peace.
Everyone clap for vengeance.
Everyone clap instead of repentance.

UNDERSTANDING LITERATURE

1. What examples does Ehrhart give of the difficulty identifying the enemy in Vietnam?
2. Do you think Trinh Cong Son believed any good came out of the war?
3. What are the similarities and differences between the two poems?

LEVEL 2: Tell students to imagine that they are U.S. soldiers in the Vietnam War. Have each student write a letter to a friend at home describing the factors that frustrated U.S. military efforts in Vietnam. *(See the Level 1 lesson for the correct factors.)* Ask volunteers to read their letters to the class. Students may wish to include their letters in their portfolios.

LEVEL 3: Have students complete the Level 1 lesson. Ask a volunteer to note the various factors on the chalkboard. Then conduct a discussion on those factors, asking students to rank them from least to most important in terms of the U.S. military effort. Have each student write descriptive paragraphs explaining his or her rankings.

▶**ASSIGNMENT:** *Have students write a military brief providing an analysis of the factors frustrating U.S. military efforts in Vietnam. Students should suggest alternatives to these efforts.*

The Media and the War

By the end of 1967 more than 16,000 Americans had been killed in Vietnam. Thousands more had been injured or disabled. Despite the government's optimistic forecasts, a U.S. victory seemed increasingly distant. The fighting dragged on, frustrating soldiers and citizens alike. In the United States television news programs showed gruesome images of terrified Vietnamese civilians and dead or injured soldiers. Some Americans responded by demanding that the military be allowed to do whatever it took to win. Others wanted the United States to pull out of Vietnam.

The Vietnam War invaded American homes in a way that no previous conflict had. During previous wars the military had imposed tight press restrictions. In this war, reporters, photographers, and TV camera crews accompanied soldiers on patrol and interviewed people throughout South Vietnam. Television beamed footage and reports of the war into people's homes on a nightly basis. As a result, Americans saw images that seemed to contradict the government's reports.

Reporters such as David Halberstam of the *New York Times* and Neil Sheehan of United Press International criticized the government's optimism. As early as 1962 they argued that the war could not be won so long as the United States supported the unpopular and corrupt regime of Ngo Dinh Diem. Journalists also reported on the ineffectiveness of South Vietnam's troops and accused the U.S. government of inflating enemy body counts to give the appearance of progress.

INTERPRETING THE VISUAL RECORD

The media. Television coverage brought the horrors of the Vietnam War into Americans' living rooms. ***What do you think this journalist is doing?***

As the gap between the reports of the U.S. government and what people saw and read grew wider, doubts at home increased. The administration found itself criticized by both **doves**—people who opposed the war—and **hawks**—people who supported the war's goals. Hawks criticized the way the war was being fought. They argued for more U.S. troops and heavier bombing. Air force general Curtis LeMay expressed the frustration of many hawks. "Here we are at the height of our power. The most powerful nation in the world. And yet we're afraid to use that power."

Doves opposed the war for many reasons. Pacifists such as the Reverend Martin Luther King Jr. believed that all war was wrong. Some doves, such as diplomat George Kennan, were convinced that Vietnam was not crucial to national security. Others feared that the United States might resort to using nuclear weapons in Vietnam. Prominent among the war's opponents was respected pediatrician and author Dr. Benjamin Spock. He and others argued that the United States was fighting against the wishes of a majority of Vietnamese.

The Antiwar Movement

A variety of civil rights, pacifist, religious, and student groups shaped the antiwar movement. The pacifist groups included Women Strike for Peace and the National Committee for a Sane Nuclear Policy as well as radical student groups like **Students for a Democratic Society** (SDS). The movement attracted a broad range of people. Doctors, ministers, teachers, and other professionals joined homemakers, retired citizens, and students in protest against the war.

TECHNOLOGY AND SOCIETY

Television and the War. Although television brought the Vietnam War into American living rooms, most viewers were spared the true horror of the war. Television camera crews could not film much of the actual fighting, which occurred at night in distant locales. As a result, most TV news footage of the war did not show scenes of heavy combat. One study concluded that of some 2,300 news broadcasts shown between 1965 and 1970, only 76 broadcasts included scenes of wounded or dead U.S. soldiers. Some historians have concluded that television coverage actually built support for the war during the early years of the conflict because it did not present an accurate picture of events in Vietnam.

CRITICAL THINKING Do you believe that television networks should show graphic film footage during wartime?

ANSWER: Answers will vary. Some students might argue that such footage dangerously limits support for U.S. military efforts.

VISUAL RECORD ANSWER

Students might suggest that the journalist appears to be interviewing a Vietnamese man.

TEACH OBJECTIVE 4

ALL LEVELS: To help students understand who supported and who opposed the war, copy the graphic organizer at right on the chalkboard, omitting the italicized answers. Have each student complete it. Then have students write a few sentences describing the government's response to such opposition. *(Students should note that the U.S. government justified its actions on the grounds of support for an ally.)* Then conduct a brief discussion on the antiwar movement in the 1960s and 1970s. **Sheltered English**

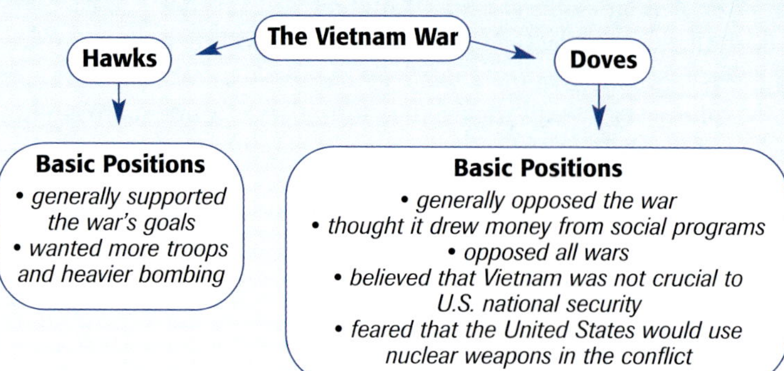

The Vietnam War
Hawks
Doves
Basic Positions
• generally supported the war's goals
• wanted more troops and heavier bombing
Basic Positions
• generally opposed the war
• thought it drew money from social programs
• opposed all wars
• believed that Vietnam was not crucial to U.S. national security
• feared that the United States would use nuclear weapons in the conflict

CULTURAL DIVERSITY

Attitudes Toward the War. The debate over the Vietnam War highlighted racial and gender differences in American society. In a 1966 poll, 65 percent of white men supported the war; 53 percent of African American men did. Among white women, 54 percent approved of the conflict, but just 43 percent of African American women did. A 1970 poll revealed that overall support for the war was diminishing while race and gender differences remained. Some 41 percent of white men and 27 percent of black men supported the war. However, just 30 percent of white women and 19 percent of black women still approved of it.

ACTIVITY: Have each student use the information above to prepare a bar graph demonstrating attitudes toward the war in 1966 and 1970.

VISUAL RECORD ANSWER

(for p. 691)

Students might suggest that the protester is wearing a uniform to show that even military forces opposed the draft.

SECTION 2 REVIEW ANSWERS

Define and Identify

For significance, see the following pages:

- Robert S. McNamara, p. 684
- Tonkin Gulf Resolution, p. 684

★ HISTORICAL DOCUMENTS ★

STUDENTS FOR A DEMOCRATIC SOCIETY

The Port Huron Statement

The Students for a Democratic Society (SDS) national convention met in Port Huron, Michigan, the week of June 11–15, 1962. There the members of the SDS revised a draft paper that was the product of several months of discussion. Known as the Port Huron Statement, the resulting document outlined the organization's goals for change in American society.

We are people of this generation, bred in at least modest comfort, housed now in universities, looking uncomfortably to the world we inherit.

When we were kids the United States was the wealthiest and strongest country in the world: the only one with the atom bomb, the least scarred by modern war, an initiator of the United Nations that we thought would distribute Western influence throughout the world. Freedom and equality for each individual, government of, by, and for the people—these American values we found good, principles by which we could live as men. Many of us began maturing in complacency [self-satisfaction].

As we grew, however, our comfort was penetrated by events too troubling to dismiss. . . .

While two-thirds of mankind suffers undernourishment, our own upper classes revel [celebrate] amidst superfluous abundance. . . . Uncontrolled exploitation [usage] governs the sapping [draining] of the earth's physical resources. . . .

Major social institutions—cultural, educational, rehabilitative, and others—should be generally organized with the well-being and dignity of man as the essential measure of success. . . . As students for a democratic society, we are committed to stimulating this kind of social movement, this kind of vision and program in campus and community across the country. If we appear to seek the unattainable, [as] it has been said, then let it be known that we do so to avoid the unimaginable.

By the end of 1965 the SDS had members on 124 college campuses. Although it was just one of many groups opposing the war, to many Americans the SDS *was* the antiwar movement. At colleges across the United States, the SDS and other student groups and faculty members held antiwar rallies and debates. These groups particularly criticized the involvement of universities in research and development for the military. They also protested the draft, the presence of the Reserve Officers' Training Corps (ROTC) on campus, and the recruitment efforts by the armed services, the Central Intelligence Agency (CIA), and defense contractors.

The SDS organized the first national antiwar demonstration, which was held in Washington, D.C., on April 17, 1965. More than 20,000 people participated. After an afternoon of speeches and singing, the crowd marched to the Capitol and delivered to Congress a petition demanding that lawmakers "act immediately to end the war." Countless demonstrations followed during the next decade. Demonstrators protested U.S. involvement in Southeast Asia with tactics borrowed from the civil rights movement.

Civil rights activists were among the most outspoken critics of the war. In 1967 Martin Luther King Jr. complained that the war was stealing resources from poverty programs.

> **"I watched the [antipoverty] program broken and eviscerated [gutted] as if it were some idle political plaything of a society gone mad on war, and I knew that America would never invest the necessary funds or energies in rehabilitation of its poor so long as Vietnam continued to draw men and skills and money like some demonic, destructive suction tube."**

Many civil rights activists criticized the U.S. government. They said it was sending great numbers of young African Americans off to war yet doing little to end discrimination at home. The Student Nonviolent Coordinating Committee (SNCC) expressed the views of growing numbers of African Americans. SNCC officials noted that "16 percent of the draftees from this country are Negro, called on to stifle [block] the liberation of Vietnam, to preserve a 'democracy' which does not exist

REVIEW

Have students complete the **Section 2 Review** on p. 691.

ASSESS

Have students complete **Daily Quiz 23.2.** As **Alternative Assessment**, you may want to use the U.S. strategy telegram or the Tonkin Gulf dialogue in this section's lessons.

RETEACH

Have students complete **Main Idea Activity for Reteaching and Sheltered English 23.2.** Then organize students into small groups. Assign each group member a subsection of Section 2. Direct students to write a few sentences or paragraphs summarizing their assigned subsections. Have group members circulate their summaries to other group members to read. Then have students take turns quizzing each other within their groups about the information contained in the summaries. **Sheltered English, Cooperative Learning**

EXTEND

Have students locate either a Vietnam War veteran or a former war protester in their community. Ask each student to interview that person and write a short biography. Students' biographies should focus on their subjects' involvement with the Vietnam War but can also include other information. Have volunteers read their biographies to the class. **Block Scheduling**

for them at home." Polls showed that African Americans were much more likely than whites to consider the war a mistake.

Despite their high visibility, antiwar protesters made up a small percentage of the U.S. population. Many Americans opposed the antiwar movement, particularly the extreme groups. Some believed that fighting for one's country was a patriotic duty. Others objected to the antiwar movement's tactics. These people found certain acts of protest—such as burning the American flag, occupying buildings, and burning draft cards—particularly upsetting. Many veterans of past wars were angered by young men who tried to avoid the draft.

Most Americans who disagreed with the antiwar movement expressed their opposition in private. However, some organized rallies in support of the war. Demonstrators at these rallies often carried signs proclaiming "America, Love It or Leave It" or "My Country, Right or Wrong."

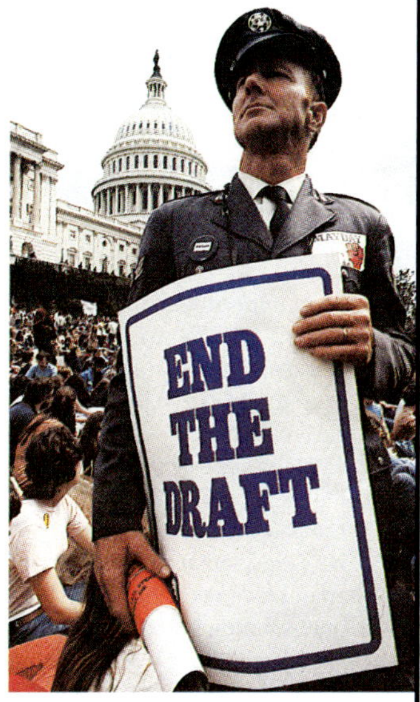

INTERPRETING THE VISUAL RECORD

Protest. This man joined other Americans at a rally in front of the U.S. Capitol Building. ***Why do you think he is wearing a uniform?***

Government in Conflict

President Johnson and his advisers responded to antiwar protesters by insisting that the United States was helping to defend an ally against aggression. If the United States failed to support South Vietnam, asked Secretary of State Dean Rusk, what U.S. ally would ever trust the country again?

The administration also faced criticism in Congress. Doves such as Senator J. William Fulbright of Arkansas, head of the Foreign Relations Committee, sharply criticized the Johnson administration's policies as too extreme. Fulbright held congressional hearings in 1966 to give the war's critics a forum. These televised hearings made the antiwar position more believable to mainstream Americans.

✔ **READING CHECK:** Why did some Americans oppose the war, and how did the government respond?

SECTION  REVIEW

Define and explain the significance of the following terms:

Tonkin Gulf Resolution
escalation
Operation Rolling Thunder
Ho Chi Minh Trail
defoliants
search-and-destroy missions
pacification
doves
hawks
Students for a Democratic Society

Identify and explain the significance of the following individuals:

Robert S. McNamara
J. William Fulbright

Locate and explain the importance of the following places:

South Vietnam
Gulf of Tonkin
North Vietnam
Cambodia
Laos

1. **Using Graphic Organizers** Copy the chart below. Use it to outline U.S. tactics in the air war and on the ground in Vietnam.

Air War	Ground War

2. **Analyzing** Why did some members of Congress believe that the Tonkin Gulf Resolution was unconstitutional?
3. **Understanding Geography: Place** How did Vietnam's geography contribute to the U.S. military's inability to defeat the Vietcong?
4. **Recognizing Point of View** Why did some Americans oppose the war? Why did the government respond the way it did?

Critical Thinking

5. What factor do you think played the biggest role in shaping American views toward the Vietnam War?
Consider:
- television coverage of the war
- economic effects of the war
- social conditions in the United States

- escalation, p. 685
- Operation Rolling Thunder, p. 686
- Ho Chi Minh Trail, p. 686
- defoliants, p. 686
- search-and-destroy missions, p. 687
- pacification, p. 687
- doves, p. 689
- hawks, p. 689
- Students for a Democratic Society, p. 689
- J. William Fulbright, p. 691

Locate

For locations, see the map on p. 686. For importance, see the following pages:

- South Vietnam, p. 684
- Gulf of Tonkin, p. 684
- North Vietnam, p. 684
- Cambodia, p. 686
- Laos, p. 686

1. air war—bombed supply routes and personnel, and dispersed defoliants; ground war—used search-and-destroy missions and pacification

2. because it gave the president war-making powers without a congressional declaration of war

3. Vietnam's mountains and jungles provided hiding places for the Vietcong.

4. believed that the war was immoral, did not serve U.S. security interests, and took resources from domestic programs; government—provided a forum in hopes of defusing criticism

5. Answers will vary. Students should select one factor and support it.

SECTION 3

After completing Section 3, students should be able to:

OBJECTIVE 1 *Explain why the Tet Offensive weakened many Americans' confidence in their government.*

OBJECTIVE 2 *List the key events of the 1968 presidential campaign.*

OBJECTIVE 3 *Summarize how President Nixon attempted to end the war.*

OBJECTIVE 4 *Describe how Americans reacted to President Nixon's plan to end the war.*

LET'S GET STARTED!

As students enter the classroom, ask them to speculate on why the Vietnam War lasted so long despite Americans' expectations of a quick victory. Have students respond in writing. *(Students might note the North Vietnamese guerrilla tactics, the limited support the United States had from the South Vietnamese, or American pride, which prevented withdrawal.)* Ask volunteers to share their responses. Then tell students that in Section 3 they will learn more about the war and related political events in the United States during the late 1960s and early 1970s.

SECTION 3 RESOURCES

PRINT
- Guided Reading Strategy 23.3
- Section 3 Review, p. 697
- Daily Quiz 23.3

MULTIMEDIA
- One-Stop Planner, Lesson 23.3
- Holt Researcher: American History CD–ROM

SHELTERED ENGLISH
- Main Idea Activity for Reteaching and Sheltered English 23.3

✓ READING TO UNDERSTAND
To help students master the section objectives, have them answer the **READING CHECKS** and complete **Guided Reading Strategy 23.3** as they read the section.

A Turning Point

OBJECTIVES

Read to understand:
1. why the Tet Offensive weakened many Americans' confidence in their government
2. what the key events of the 1968 presidential campaign were
3. how President Nixon attempted to end the war
4. how Americans reacted to President Nixon's plan to end the war

KEY TERMS

Tet Offensive
Vietnamization
Kent State shootings
Pentagon Papers

KEY PEOPLE

William Westmoreland
Eugene McCarthy
Robert F. Kennedy
Richard J. Daley
Richard Nixon
Henry Kissinger
Le Duc Tho

EYEWITNESSES TO History

"After a while, survival was the name of the game as you sat there in semidarkness, with the firing going on constantly, like at a rifle range. And the horrible smell. You tasted it as you ate your rations, as if you were eating death. It permeated [seeped into] your clothes, which you couldn't wash because water was very scarce. You couldn't bathe or shave either. My strategy was to keep as many of my marines alive as possible, yet accomplish our mission. You went through the full range of emotions, seeing your buddies being hit, but you couldn't feel sorry for them because you had the others to think about."

—Myron Harrington

U.S. Marines on patrol in Vietnam

Myron Harrington described the fighting through which he led his company of 100 marines. The grim determination Harrington and others felt about the war in Vietnam began to weaken in 1968. That year a massive attack by the Vietcong shattered the illusion that the United States would soon win the war. Soon many Americans were wondering why the country was fighting the war.

These soldiers are taking cover during one of the many battles of the Tet Offensive.

The Tet Offensive

January 30, 1968, marked the start of Tet, the Vietnamese New Year. In past years the holiday had been honored by a lull in fighting. However, late that night, as most South Vietnamese and their U.S. allies slept, Vietcong guerrillas and North Vietnamese troops struck. They crept from their jungle camps and city hideouts to execute a carefully planned strike. Within hours countless villages, more than 100 cities, and 12 U.S. military bases came under attack from nearly 84,000 communist soldiers. Heavy fighting raged in such U.S. strongholds as Saigon and Da Nang. At one point the Vietcong even occupied the courtyard of the U.S. Embassy.

North Vietnam expected the **Tet Offensive** to bring down South Vietnam's government as the people rallied behind their "liberators." North Vietnam's leaders were disappointed, however. When the assault ended, more than a month later, some 40,000 communist soldiers lay dead.

General William Westmoreland, the commander of U.S. forces in Vietnam, described the offensive as a Vietcong defeat. In a military sense, the general had a point. At a cost of 1,100 American and 2,300 ARVN lives, most of the attackers had been repelled. Despite suffering heavy losses, however, the Vietcong remained strong in many places. They had faced overwhelming U.S. firepower and were still standing—more determined than ever to continue fighting.

Tran Do, the deputy commander of communist forces in South Vietnam, had played a major role in the Tet Offensive. He explained the goals and effects of the offensive:

TEACH OBJECTIVE 1

LEVEL 1: Write the following question on the chalkboard: *The Tet Offensive was in fact a military failure for North Vietnamese forces. Why did it weaken many Americans' confidence in their government?* Then pair students and have each pair write a paragraph responding to the question. *(Pairs should note that the Tet Offensive revealed that no part of South Vietnam was secure, exposed how few South Vietnamese supported their own government, and revealed how determined the North Vietnamese were.)* Have volunteers read their paragraphs to the class. **Sheltered English, Cooperative Learning**

LEVELS 2 AND 3: Have students complete the Level 1 activity. Then tell students to imagine that it is February 1968 and that they are watching a television news story on the Tet Offensive. Have each student write a letter to President Johnson explaining why the Tet Offensive has weakened his or her confidence in the U.S. government. Have volunteers read their letters to the class. Students may wish to include their letters in their portfolios.

"In all honesty we didn't achieve our main objective, which was to spur uprisings throughout the south. Still, we inflicted heavy casualties on the Americans and their puppets, and that was a big gain for us. As for making an impact in the United States, it had not been our intention—but it turned out to be a fortunate result."

The political effect of the offensive on the United States was stunning. The Tet Offensive shook U.S. confidence by revealing that no part of South Vietnam was secure—not even downtown Saigon. Respected journalist Walter Cronkite, anchor of the *CBS Evening News*, expressed Americans' bewildered mood: "I thought we were winning the war! What the hell is going on?" To one of his aides, President Johnson groaned, "If I've lost Cronkite I've lost middle America."

After the Tet Offensive, public criticism of the war rose dramatically. Such influential magazines as *Time* and *Newsweek* expressed doubts about the war and began calling for its end. Largely because of the shift in public opinion, Johnson denied General Westmoreland's urgent request for 206,000 more troops. President Johnson granted a small increase in the number of troops but made it clear that he would not increase the number any further.

These soldiers are leading away one of the Vietcong guerrillas who attacked the U.S. Embassy in Saigon during the Tet Offensive.

✔ **READING CHECK:** Why did the Tet Offensive weaken many Americans' confidence in their government?

The Election of 1968

After the Tet Offensive three out of four Americans disapproved of President Johnson's conduct of the war. With the presidential election nearing, Johnson was under attack from all sides.

Democratic challengers. Early in 1968 Senator Eugene McCarthy of Minnesota, a critic of the war, challenged Johnson for the Democratic presidential nomination. In the New Hampshire primary held that March, McCarthy won almost as many votes as Johnson. McCarthy's impressive showing drew another leading critic of the war into the race. Senator Robert F. Kennedy of New York was the brother of the slain President Kennedy and a former U.S. attorney general. His large national following—particularly among African Americans, Hispanics, the poor, and the young—made Robert Kennedy a strong contender for the Democratic nomination.

Shaken by the division within his party, President Johnson made a shocking announcement to the nation on March 31. Physically and emotionally exhausted, Johnson declared that he would not seek re-election. He explained that he wanted to spend his last months in office trying to end the war. Johnson's withdrawal from the race left it wide open. Senators McCarthy and Kennedy and Vice President Hubert Humphrey went head-to-head in several state primaries. Kennedy won most of them, including the crucial California primary in June. To many he seemed destined to receive the Democratic nomination.

Senator Robert Kennedy was so popular that supporters often tore off his cuff links while scrambling to shake his hand.

GEOGRAPHIC DIVERSITY

The Secret Offensive. In order to draw attention away from their preparations for the Tet Offensive, the North Vietnamese created a diversion by attacking a distant U.S. Marine outpost called Khe Sanh. The diversion worked—President Johnson feared that Khe Sanh would become an American Dien Bien Phu. One U.S. commander, however, suspected that the North Vietnamese were coordinating a large-scale offensive. He noticed that his troops were meeting fewer communist soldiers in distant parts of Vietnam, while communist radio communications in the Saigon area were increasing. The U.S. commander requested additional combat battalions for Saigon, which made its later defense easier.

ACTIVITY: Ask students to consider the evidence presented in the annotation above. Then ask each student to write a short military brief evaluating that evidence and either recommending or opposing additional combat battalions for Saigon.

THAT'S INTERESTING!

Eugene McCarthy was particularly popular with young students, many of whom decided to "go clean for Gene" and volunteered to help his presidential campaign.

TEACH OBJECTIVE 2

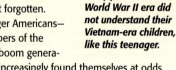

ALL LEVELS: To help students understand the key events of the 1968 presidential campaign, copy the following time line on the chalkboard, omitting the italicized answers. Have each student complete it. Then pair students and have each pair write a newspaper headline and a topic sentence for each event. Ask volunteers to share their headlines and sentences with the class.

Sheltered English, Cooperative Learning

▶ASSIGNMENT *Tell students to imagine that they were delegates at the Democratic National Convention in Chicago. Have each student write a short recollection of the events there.*

March–*Senator Eugene McCarthy wins almost as many votes as President Johnson in the New Hampshire primary.*

March 31–*President Johnson announces his withdrawal from the race.*

June–*Senator Robert F. Kennedy wins the California primary and is assassinated.*

August–*Police violently disperse antiwar protesters at the Democratic convention in Chicago.*

November–*Richard Nixon wins the election.*

1968

HISTORY MAKERS SPEAK

Theodore White in *The Making of the President, 1968*

Conflict in Chicago. Writer Theodore White described the clash between protesters and police in Chicago: "Slam! Like a fist jolting, like a piston exploding from its chamber, comes a hurtling column of police from off Balbo [Avenue] into the intersection, and all things happen too fast: first the charge as the police wedge cleaves through the mob; then screams, whistles, confusion, people running off into Grant Park, across the bridges, into hotel lobbies. And as the scene clears, there are little knots in the open clearing–police clubbing youngsters, police dragging youngsters, police rushing them by the elbows, their heels dragging, to patrol wagons, prodding recalcitrants [resisters] who refuse to enter quietly."

CRITICAL THINKING How might the violence in Chicago have affected voters?

ANSWER: Students might suggest that voters probably linked the violence to the Democrats and consequently considered voting for the Republicans.

The Generation Gap

In the 1960s many young people began to feel that something had gone wrong with the United States. Prosperity had followed World War II, but peace had not. Fascism had been defeated, and the prewar years of depression were all but forgotten. Younger Americans–members of the baby-boom generation–increasingly found themselves at odds with their parents, who had grown up during the Great Depression and World War II. A wide generation gap developed.

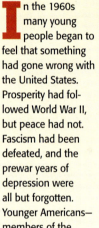

Many parents of the World War II era did not understand their Vietnam-era children, like this teenager.

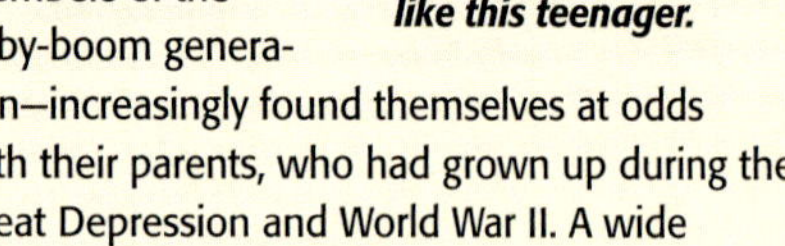

The faith and optimism of American youth were shaken by seemingly senseless violence and death. Many young people demanded change. They accused the previous generation of valuing conformity and material comfort over equality and fairness. Younger Americans also increasingly distrusted their government and questioned the reasons for U.S. involvement in Vietnam. Many older Americans remembered past struggles and urged young people to have faith in their government. This inability to communicate contributed to the violent clash at the Democratic Party's 1968 convention in Chicago.

On the night of his California victory, Kennedy was shot by Sirhan Sirhan, a young Jordanian immigrant. Kennedy died the next day. A nation already in shock over the murder of Martin Luther King Jr. just two months earlier was now faced with yet another assassination.

The convention in Chicago. Society seemed to be spinning out of control. Amid the turmoil, the Democrats met in Chicago to settle on a candidate for the November election. The convention was a cheerless affair. Despite his close identification with the unpopular President Johnson, Vice President Humphrey received the nomination. He chose Senator Edmund Muskie of Maine as his running mate.

The Democrats' difficulties were underscored by the chaos on the streets outside the convention. Some 10,000 antiwar protesters had massed in the city and camped in Grant Park, across from the hotel where many delegates were staying. They held rallies in the sweltering August heat, chanting antiwar slogans and calling police names.

Outraged to see his city overrun by people he viewed as dangerous revolutionaries, Chicago mayor Richard J. Daley ordered helmeted police to clear out the protesters. Attacking on the night of August 28, the police clubbed protesters and used tear gas to disperse the crowd. Hundreds of protesters were injured; hundreds more were hauled to jail. Reporters, passersby, and police were also injured in the struggle.

The Republicans capitalize. The violent spectacle at the Chicago convention raised Republicans' hopes of capturing the White House. The mood was upbeat at the Republican National Convention in Miami Beach, Florida. Richard Nixon dominated the convention. Appealing to the patriotism of mainstream America, Nixon won the nomination easily. He chose Maryland governor Spiro Agnew as his running mate. Promising a "law-and-order" crackdown on urban crime, Nixon sought support from those Americans who neither approved of the disorderly antiwar protests nor wanted a U.S. defeat in Vietnam. Nixon told voters he had a secret plan to end the Vietnam War, although he revealed no details.

As election day neared, Humphrey's campaign picked up steam, boosted somewhat by Johnson's announcement in late October of a bombing halt. Time ran out for the Democrats, however. The election results were close. Of the 73 million votes cast, Richard Nixon received just 510,314 more than Hubert Humphrey. Nixon's margin in the electoral college was much wider. He won 32 states to Humphrey's 13. Former Alabama governor George Wallace campaigned as the candidate of the newly formed American Independent Party. He received some 10 million votes and won five states in the South.

✔ **READING CHECK:** What were the key events of the 1968 presidential campaign?

TEACH OBJECTIVE 3

LEVELS 1 AND 2: Pair students and tell them to imagine that they are Vietnam veterans who have recently returned home. Have each pair develop a short dialogue explaining how President Nixon attempted to end the war. *(Pairs should indicate that President Nixon followed a plan called Vietnamization and ordered the widespread bombing of Cambodia.)* Have volunteers perform their dialogues for the class. **Sheltered English, Cooperative Learning**

LEVEL 3: Tell students to imagine that they are either hawks or doves. Have each student write a short newspaper editorial describing President Nixon's plan to end the war. *(See the Levels 1 and 2 lesson for the correct features.)* Remind students that their editorials should reflect their personal opinions toward that plan as either a hawk or a dove. Ask volunteers to read their editorials to the class. Students may wish to include their editorials in their portfolios.

NOTE: For an additional teaching idea, see the Chapter 23 dialogue debate lesson in the **Creative Teaching Strategies** handbook.

Nixon, Vietnamization, and Cambodia

President Richard Nixon made foreign affairs his top priority. Nixon's key foreign-policy adviser was Henry Kissinger. Born in 1923 in Fürth, Germany, Henry Kissinger fled the country as a teenager with his parents to escape the Nazis. Kissinger arrived in New York City in 1938 and became a U.S. citizen in 1943. That same year, he joined the U.S. Army Counter-Intelligence Corps and served for three years. From 1946 to 1949 Kissinger was a captain in the Military Intelligence Reserve while attending Harvard University, where he graduated with honors. He received his Ph.D. from Harvard in 1954 and joined its faculty as a professor of government.

Henry Kissinger

Kissinger occasionally advised Presidents Eisenhower, Kennedy, and Johnson. He was particularly influential during the Nixon presidency. Kissinger served as national security adviser before becoming secretary of state. In both positions he worked closely with President Nixon to improve relations with communist China and the Soviet Union. Kissinger won the Nobel Peace Prize in 1973 for his role in the negotiations that eventually ended the Vietnam War. He later served as a foreign-affairs adviser to Presidents Ronald Reagan and George Bush.

Kissinger and Nixon devised a plan to fulfill the president's campaign pledge to end the war. Part of this plan was called **Vietnamization**, which involved turning over the fighting to the South Vietnamese while gradually pulling out U.S. troops. This strategy, said Nixon, would bring "peace with honor." At best, Nixon hoped that Vietnamization might produce a stable anticommunist South Vietnam. At worst, it would delay a collapse long enough to spare the United States the humiliation of outright defeat.

Nixon also hoped that Vietnamization would remove a major obstacle that had been blocking a peace agreement with North Vietnam. The North Vietnamese had first warned President Johnson and then Nixon that the United States would have to set a date for troop removals if peace talks were to continue. In August 1969, as U.S. troop withdrawals began, Henry Kissinger met secretly in Paris with longtime revolutionary Le Duc Tho (LAY DUHK TOH) of North Vietnam.

The process of troop withdrawal was slow. When Nixon took office in 1969, U.S. troops in Vietnam numbered about 540,000. At the end of 1972 about 24,200 Americans still remained in Vietnam.

Secretly, Nixon planned to expand the war into neutral Cambodia to cut off the North Vietnamese supply lines along the Ho Chi Minh Trail. Early in 1969 Nixon ordered the widespread bombing of Cambodia. He wanted to show Hanoi that the United States was still willing to use force, and even expand the war, in pursuit of his aim of "peace with honor." Nixon and Kissinger concealed the Cambodian air strikes from the American people, Congress, and key military leaders—even the secretary of the air force.

Read More About It

Free Find:
Henry Kissinger

After reading about Henry Kissinger on the **Holt Researcher** CD–ROM, write an editorial for your local newspaper. Describe Kissinger's accomplishments and explain why you think he helped or hurt the United States.

Soldiers of the 25th Infantry Division withdraw from a Cambodian village as an attack helicopter strikes the village.

PEOPLE IN HISTORY

Henry Kissinger. Henry Kissinger had a strong interest in diplomatic history. This interest led him to consider the effect of nuclear weapons on international negotiations. He concluded that the ability to wage nuclear war did not mean that the United States could abandon traditional diplomatic negotiations. This insight brought Kissinger to the attention of several prominent politicians and led to his role as a presidential adviser.

CRITICAL THINKING Why might presidents and officials have been interested in the question of diplomacy and nuclear weapons?

ANSWER: Students might suggest that presidents and officials did not know how to integrate nuclear weapons with traditional diplomatic approaches.

GRAPH ANSWER

(for p. 696)

between 1965 and 1966

TEACH OBJECTIVE 4

LEVEL 1: Ask students to describe how Americans responded to President Nixon's plan to end the war. *(Students should note that the bombing and invasion of Cambodia provoked outrage in the United States and that Congress repealed the Tonkin Gulf Resolution.)* Then tell students that many doves wore buttons to declare their feelings about the war and other issues. Have each student design a button expressing Americans' reactions to President Nixon's plan to end the war. Students' buttons might express a simple slogan or present a visual image. Have volunteers present their designs to the class. **Sheltered English**

LEVELS 2 AND 3: Pair students and tell one member of each pair to imagine that he or she supports President Nixon's plan to end the war. Tell the other member to imagine that he or she opposes the plan. Have each pair develop a short dialogue expressing its reactions to the plan. *(See the Level 1 lesson for the correct reactions.)* Ask volunteers to present their dialogues to the class. Then have each student write a few paragraphs summarizing the material presented in the dialogues. **Cooperative Learning**

HISTORY MAKERS SPEAK

Richard Nixon in *Grand Expectations*

Bombing Cambodia. President Nixon defended his decision to bomb Cambodia in a nationally televised speech: "If, when the chips are down, the world's most powerful nation, the United States of America, acts like a pitiful, helpless giant, the forces of totalitarianism and anarchy will threaten free nations and institutions around the world. I would rather be a one-term president and do what I believe was right than to be a two-term president at the cost of seeing America become a second-rate power."

CRITICAL THINKING Do you agree with President Nixon's defense of the bombing? Why or why not?

ANSWER: Answers will vary. Some students might argue that the United States had to defend its international prestige and power.

THAT'S INTERESTING!

The parking spaces in which the Kent State victims died remained open to cars until 1999, when the spaces were dedicated as memorials, with markers bearing the students' names.

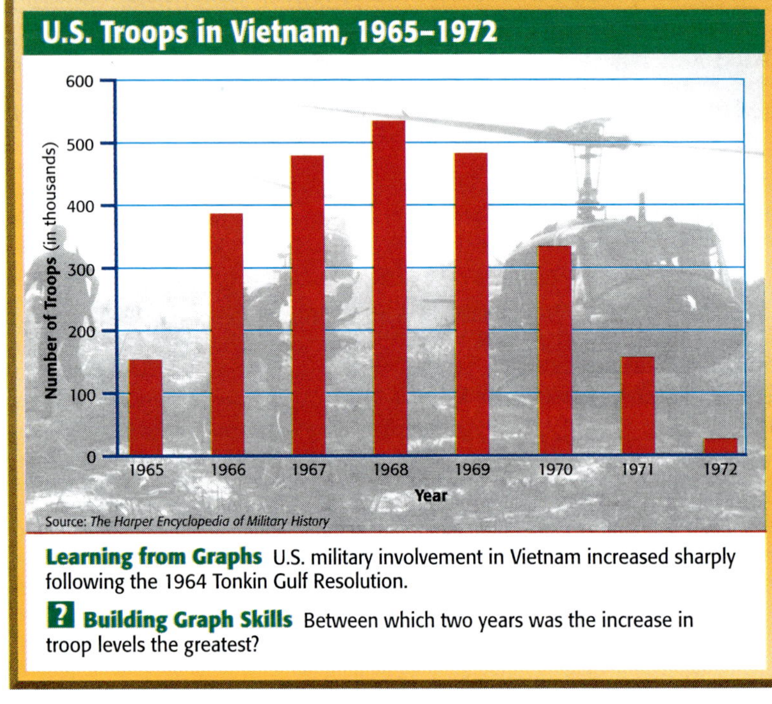

Learning from Graphs U.S. military involvement in Vietnam increased sharply following the 1964 Tonkin Gulf Resolution.

Building Graph Skills Between which two years was the increase in troop levels the greatest?

Because of Cambodia's neutrality, Nixon feared an international uproar over the bombing. When a revolt ousted Cambodia's ruler in March 1970, however, Nixon's strategy changed. Since the new Cambodian government was pro-American, Nixon made his strategy public. He justified the air strikes as defense of a friendly nation. Nixon then sent some 80,000 U.S. and ARVN troops into Cambodia.

This invasion destroyed the delicate balance that had kept Cambodia out of the war. North Vietnamese Army (NVA) troops were forced into the interior of Cambodia, where the bombing destroyed much of the countryside.

✔ **READING CHECK:** How did President Nixon attempt to end the war?

Antiwar Protest Increases

News of the bombing and invasion of Cambodia provoked outrage in the United States, particularly on college campuses. After someone at Kent State University in Ohio set fire to the campus ROTC building, Ohio's governor vowed to "eradicate" the protesters. On May 4, 1970, National Guard troops that had been sent to control demonstrators shot randomly into a large group of students. They killed four and injured nine others. Some of the students were merely walking across campus. The **Kent State shootings** shocked the nation.

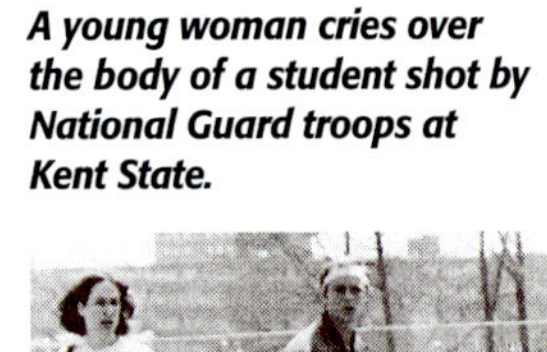

A young woman cries over the body of a student shot by National Guard troops at Kent State.

Just 10 days later, state police in Jackson, Mississippi, fired at protesters in a dormitory at Jackson State College, killing two students and wounding nine others. Enraged, students and faculty on hundreds of college campuses went on strike.

Members of Congress were also upset by the Cambodian invasion. In response, Congress repealed the Tonkin Gulf Resolution in December 1970. Nixon insisted, however, that this action did not affect his authority to carry on the war. Congressional leaders soon developed plans to stop the war by cutting off funding once U.S. troops were withdrawn.

In 1971 another incident boosted the antiwar movement. The *New York Times* began publishing a collection of secret government documents relating to

REVIEW

Have students complete the **Section 3 Review** on p. 697.

ASSESS

Have students complete **Daily Quiz 23.3.** As **Alternative Assessment**, you may want to use the campaign time line or the newspaper editorial in this section's lessons.

RETEACH

Have students complete **Main Idea Activity for Reteaching and Sheltered English 23.3.** Then have each student write a brief summary of one of the subsections in Section 3. Have volunteers read their summaries to the class. Have students vote to choose the best summary of each subsection. **Sheltered English**

EXTEND

Have students conduct research on the bombing campaign in Vietnam. Then have each student write a short analysis of the campaign, explaining why it failed to achieve its objectives. In order to make their analyses, students might compare and contrast the bombing campaign in the Vietnam War with those of previous wars. **Block Scheduling**

the war. Known as the **Pentagon Papers**, these documents revealed that the government had frequently misled the American people about the course of the war. The documents had been leaked to the press by Daniel Ellsberg, a former Department of Defense official. Ellsberg had strongly supported the war until he spent time in Vietnam studying the war's effects. While there, he found that few South Vietnamese supported their government.

"NOW, AS I WAS SAYING, FOUR YEARS AGO"

INTERPRETING THE VISUAL RECORD

Nixon's plan. This 1972 cartoon criticizes President Nixon's efforts to end the war. ***What do you think the cartoonist was suggesting about Nixon's secret plan to end the war?***

The War Continues

As commander in chief, President Nixon not only ordered the invasion of Cambodia but also renewed the bombing of North Vietnam, which President Johnson had stopped. Nixon explained his plan to his chief of staff, H. R. "Bob" Haldeman.

> **"I call it the Madman Theory, Bob. I want the North Vietnamese to believe that I've reached the point where I might do anything to stop the war. We'll just slip the word to them that, 'for God's sake, you know Nixon is obsessed about Communists. We can't restrain him when he's angry—and he has his hand on the nuclear button'—and Ho Chi Minh himself will be in Paris in two days begging for peace."**

Nixon miscalculated the opposition's endurance, however. Rather than ending, the war suddenly grew more fierce. Hoping to reveal the weaknesses of Nixon's Vietnamization strategy, North Vietnam staged a major invasion of South Vietnam in March 1972. NVA troops drove deep into South Vietnam. In response, Nixon ordered heavy bombing of North Vietnam. Despite these steps, the opposition now held more territory in South Vietnam than ever.

✔ **READING CHECK:** How did Americans react to President Nixon's plan to end the war?

SECTION 3 REVIEW

Define and explain the significance of the following terms:
Tet Offensive
Vietnamization
Kent State shootings
Pentagon Papers

Identify and explain the significance of the following individuals:
William Westmoreland
Eugene McCarthy
Robert F. Kennedy
Richard J. Daley
Richard Nixon
Henry Kissinger
Le Duc Tho

1. **Using Graphic Organizers** Copy the chart below. Use it to describe Nixon's efforts to end the war and how well they succeeded.

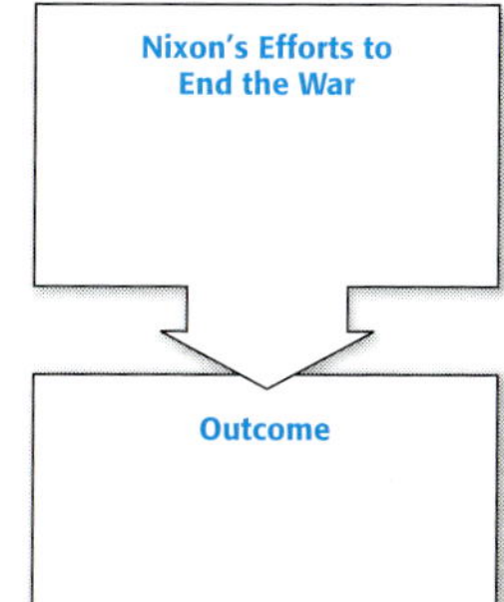

2. **Taking a Stand** Imagine that you are President Lyndon Johnson. Would you run for re-election in 1968? Write a short speech explaining the reasons for your decision.
3. **Analyzing** How did the Tet Offensive cause American dissatisfaction with the war effort?
4. **Identifying Cause and Effect** Which of President Nixon's policies led to renewed antiwar protests?

Critical Thinking

5. In wartime, should the U.S. government make all information about the war available to its citizens?
   Consider:
   - the importance of security to military operations
   - the public's right to know what the government is doing
   - the constitutional protection of free press

VISUAL RECORD ANSWER

Students might suggest that the cartoon indicates that Nixon's plan was going to be ineffective.

SECTION 3 REVIEW ANSWERS

Define and Identify
For significance, see the following pages:

- Tet Offensive, p. 692
- William Westmoreland, p. 692
- Eugene McCarthy, p. 693
- Robert F. Kennedy, p. 693
- Richard J. Daley, p. 694
- Richard Nixon, p. 694
- Henry Kissinger, p. 695
- Vietnamization, p. 695
- Le Duc Tho, p. 695
- Kent State shootings, p. 696
- Pentagon Papers, p. 697

1. efforts—Vietnamization and troop withdrawals backed by continuous bombing; outcome—the bombing widened the war and intensified the fighting

2. Students' speeches will vary. Students might note the existence of strong Democratic contenders.

3. by showing that the United States was not close to winning the war

4. wider bombings and expansion into Cambodia

5. Answers will vary. Some students might argue that without public oversight the government could violate the law.

SECTION 4

After completing Section 4, students should be able to:

OBJECTIVE 1 *Explain why the United States agreed to a cease-fire in January 1973.*

OBJECTIVE 2 *Describe the war's long-term effects on Vietnam and the Vietnamese people.*

OBJECTIVE 3 *Evaluate the war's long-term effects on the American people.*

LET'S GET STARTED!

As students enter the classroom, tell them to reread the quotation by presidential candidate George McGovern on this page and to write a few sentences in response to it. Have volunteers read their responses to the class and conduct a brief discussion on them. Then tell students that in Section 4 they will learn about the end of the Vietnam War and its long-term effects.

SECTION 4 RESOURCES

PRINT
- Guided Reading Strategy 23.4
- Primary Source Reading 23: The Return of Vietnam Veterans
- Section 4 Review, p. 703
- Daily Quiz 23.4

MULTIMEDIA
- One-Stop Planner, Lesson 23.4
- Holt Researcher: American History CD–ROM
- HRW Web site

SHELTERED ENGLISH
- Main Idea Activity for Reteaching and Sheltered English 23.4

✔ READING TO UNDERSTAND
To help students master the section objectives, have them answer the **READING CHECKS** and complete **Guided Reading Strategy 23.4** as they read the section.

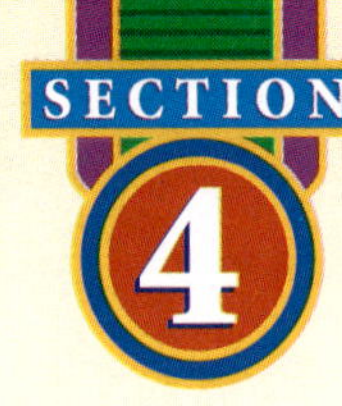

SECTION 4 The War Ends

OBJECTIVES

Read to understand:

1. why the United States agreed to a cease-fire in January 1973
2. what long-term effects the war had on Vietnam and the Vietnamese people
3. what long-term effects the war had on the American people

KEY TERMS

Twenty-sixth Amendment
War Powers Act
Vietnam Veterans Memorial

KEY PEOPLE

George McGovern
George Wallace
Le Ly Hayslip
Maya Ying Lin

EYEWITNESSES TO History

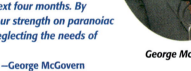

"We have heard many times that Vietnam will no longer be an issue by the time the fall election approaches. . . . For the sake of the thousands of Vietnamese peasants still dying from American bombing raids, the GIs still dying . . . the American POWs rotting in the jails of Hanoi, I sincerely hope it will not be an issue. But Vietnam thinking surely will be an issue, regardless of what happens in Indochina in the next four months. By 'Vietnam thinking' I mean wasting our strength on paranoiac [irrational] defense policies while neglecting the needs of our own people."

—George McGovern

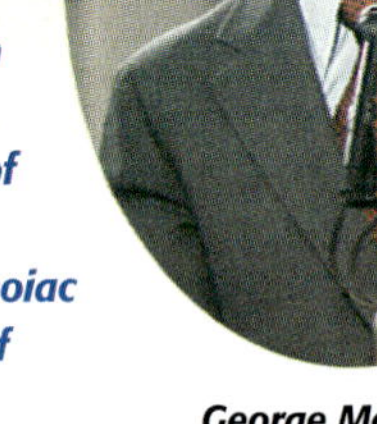

George McGovern

Speaking in July 1972, Senator George McGovern made clear his opposition to the war. He hoped the American people's frustration with Vietnam would carry him into the White House.

Nixon's Re-election

Senator George McGovern of South Dakota campaigned in the 1972 Democratic presidential primaries as an antiwar candidate. An air force pilot in World War II, McGovern had been a history professor before entering politics. His opposition to the war ran deep. In one emotional Senate speech he declared in a trembling voice, "This chamber reeks [smells] of blood." George Wallace opposed McGovern for the Democratic nomination. In May, however, Wallace was shot at a political rally in Maryland. The injury paralyzed him from the waist down, and he withdrew from the race.

After the disastrous 1968 convention, the Democrats adopted new rules to increase the representation of ethnic minorities, women, and young people in party organizations. Passed in 1971, the **Twenty-sixth Amendment** had lowered the voting age from 21 to 18. McGovern drew much of his support from these groups. He easily captured the nomination at the Democratic convention.

An 18-year-old woman registers to vote.

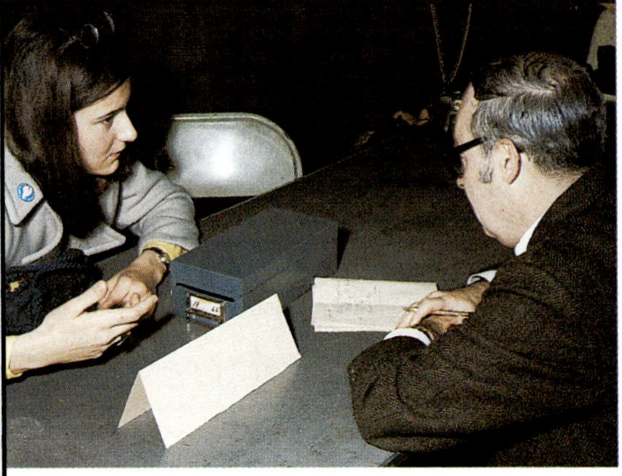

The Republicans renominated Richard Nixon and Spiro Agnew. Nixon again stressed his strong commitment to law and order within the United States and assured voters that the war would soon be over. Indeed, a few weeks before the election, Henry Kissinger announced a breakthrough in the negotiations to end the war. "Peace is at hand," he declared.

Nixon won the election by a landslide—receiving 47 million votes to McGovern's 29 million. In the electoral college, McGovern carried just Massachusetts and the District of Columbia.

TEACH OBJECTIVE 1

ALL LEVELS: To help students understand the key events that led to the 1973 cease-fire, copy the graphic organizer at right on the chalkboard, omitting the italicized answers. Have each student complete it. Then ask students how things might have been different if, for example, the South Vietnamese president had not rejected the first agreement or if President Nixon had not bombed Hanoi and Haiphong. Have each student write a few sentences or paragraphs speculating on the possible outcomes. Ask volunteers to read their sentences or paragraphs to the class.
Sheltered English

STEPS LEADING TO THE 1973 CEASE-FIRE

1. **Henry Kissinger meets with Le Duc Tho.**
2. *South Vietnam's president rejects the agreement and the United States supports him.*
3. *North Vietnam demands reinstatement.*
4. *President Nixon bombs Hanoi and Haiphong.*
5. *Nixon ends the talks, and bombing resumes.*
6. **The parties make minor changes and declare a cease-fire.**

A Cease-Fire at Last

In August 1969 Henry Kissinger and North Vietnam's Le Duc Tho met secretly in Paris to begin negotiations aimed at finding a way to end the war. For nearly three years the two men engaged in a series of difficult peace negotiations. "I don't look back on our meetings with any great joy," Kissinger recalled. "Yet he was a person of substance and discipline who defended the position he represented with dedication."

Finally, in October 1972 North Vietnam offered a peace plan that Kissinger and President Nixon found acceptable. The plan called for a cease-fire, the pullout of all foreign troops from Vietnam, and an end to U.S. military aid. The agreement also planned for the creation of a new government in South Vietnam. This government would include the country's current president, Nguyen Van Thieu, as well as representatives of the National Liberation Front. Thieu, who had not been included in the negotiations, objected to the proposed government. He believed it would reduce his power. Rather than abandon Thieu, the United States rejected the agreement.

When North Vietnam demanded that the agreement be reinstated, Nixon responded by ordering round-the-clock bombing of Hanoi and Haiphong. A furious Nixon declared to the chairman of the Joint Chiefs of Staff: "This is your chance to use military power to win this war, and if you don't, I'll consider you responsible." Some 40,000 tons of bombs rained on the two cities for nearly two weeks, with the barrage only halting for Christmas Day. The intensive bombing did not sway the North Vietnamese, however. At the end of December 1972 Nixon called off the bombing and agreed to resume talks.

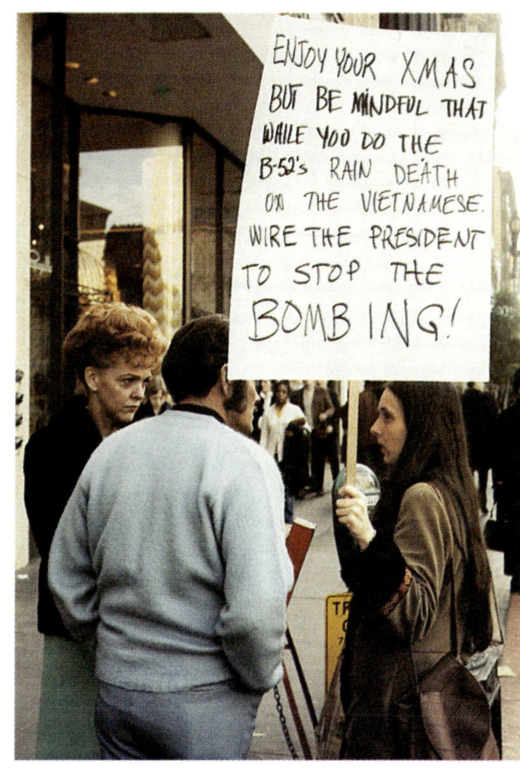

INTERPRETING THE VISUAL RECORD
Protest. This woman is protesting the "Christmas bombing" campaign ordered by President Nixon. ***What does the woman's sign ask Americans to do?***

On January 27, 1973, the negotiators in Paris announced a cease-fire. The plan differed little from the one agreed to in October, but minor changes allowed each side to claim a victory. The United States pledged to withdraw its remaining forces from South Vietnam and to help rebuild Vietnam. The peace settlement also included a prisoner-exchange agreement. It did not, however, address the major issue behind the war—the political future of South Vietnam. While urging Thieu to accept the cease-fire, Nixon secretly pledged that the United States would come to South Vietnam's aid if fighting resumed.

Two years after U.S. forces withdrew, South Vietnam's military government collapsed. In January 1975, North Vietnamese troops overran the northern part of South Vietnam. As South Vietnamese troops retreated in panic, new waves of refugees poured into Saigon.

In early April the noose around Saigon tightened. The U.S. military rushed to evacuate the several thousand Americans still in the city. Some escaped from the U.S. Embassy roof by helicopter as North Vietnamese troops stormed the compound. Some 120,000 Vietnamese who had worked for the U.S. government were flown to the United States. On April 30, 1975, South Vietnam surrendered unconditionally.

DEMOCRATIC VALUES

The Christmas Bombing. The so-called Christmas bombing resulted in a storm of criticism. As a result of the bombing, the United States lost 26 aircraft and 93 airmen. President Nixon's public approval rating dropped to 39 percent, and many members of Congress indicated that they would take action against the president when the next session began.

CRITICAL THINKING Why might the Christmas bombing have received so much criticism?

ANSWER: Students might suggest that it was a brutal attack at a time of year when many Americans want to celebrate peace and goodwill.

THAT'S INTERESTING!

As the peace talks dragged on, U.S. troops in Vietnam became increasingly disillusioned. The desertion rate reached 7 percent, and twice as many soldiers went absent without leave. Some troops even attacked their own officers instead of following orders.

VISUAL RECORD ANSWER

Students might suggest that the sign asks Americans to consider the Vietnamese and the war against them during the Christmas season.

TEACH OBJECTIVE 2

LEVEL 1: Pair students and tell them to imagine that they are Vietnamese citizens who lived through the war. Have each pair create a list of words describing the war's long-term effects. *(Pairs might list words such as death, violence, destruction, and so on.)* Ask volunteers to write their words on the chalkboard. Then have pairs use the words on the chalkboard to write topic sentences describing the effects of the war. *(Pairs' sentences should note that the war resulted in enormous casualties and destroyed the Vietnamese economy.)* Ask volunteers to read their sentences to the class.
Sheltered English, Cooperative Learning

LEVEL 2: Tell students to imagine that they are Vietnamese citizens who lived through the war. Have each student write a poem or a song about the war's long-term effects on Vietnam and the Vietnamese people. *(See the Level 1 lesson for the correct effects.)* Have volunteers read their poems or songs to the class. Students may wish to include their poems or songs in their portfolios.

LEVEL 3: Tell students to imagine that they are reporters leaving Vietnam after the cease-fire. Have each student write a short article on the war's long-term effects on Vietnam and the Vietnamese people. *(See the Level 1 lesson for the correct effects.)* Have volunteers read their articles to the class.

GLOBAL RELATIONS

Cambodia. In April 1975, Cambodian Communists gained control of Phnom Penh, the country's capital. Pol Pot and other Communist leaders soon declared their intention to purify Cambodian society of outside influences. They proclaimed their victory to be the beginning of a new era and designated the year as "Year Zero." Over the next few years, they tortured and murdered their own people. It is estimated that some 2 million Cambodians died under Pol Pot's rule, which ended in 1978 when Vietnam invaded Cambodia.

CRITICAL THINKING What might the events in Cambodia reveal about the legacy of war in Southeast Asia?

ANSWER: Students might suggest that the events reveal that the war disrupted society and made violence a commonplace occurrence.

THAT'S INTERESTING!

The war devastated the Vietnamese economy, leaving the nation one of the poorest in the world. At the war's end, per capita income averaged only $100. By the 1990s, per capita income had reached only $200.

GRAPH ANSWER
1968

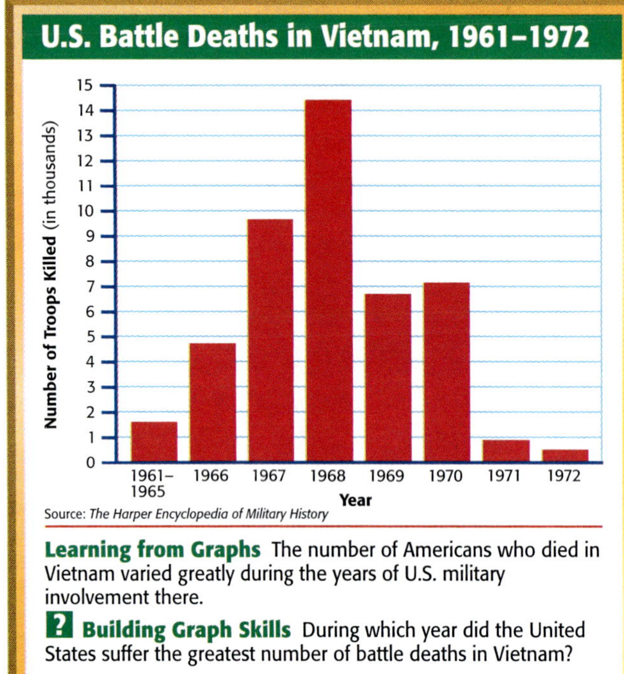

Learning from Graphs The number of Americans who died in Vietnam varied greatly during the years of U.S. military involvement there.

Building Graph Skills During which year did the United States suffer the greatest number of battle deaths in Vietnam?

For Americans the Vietnam War was over. The long, costly effort to prevent the creation of a united, independent Vietnam under Communist rule had failed. The war had spread to Cambodia and Laos, which had been heavily damaged. However, the predicted collapse of all Southeast Asia—the so-called domino theory—never occurred. Quarrels soon broke out between the Communist leaders of Vietnam and those of China and Cambodia. International communism was not as unified a world force as U.S. policy makers had feared.

✔ **READING CHECK:** Why did the United States agree to a cease-fire in January 1973?

Effects of the War

The war devastated the Vietnamese people. According to Saigon government figures, some 185,000 South Vietnamese soldiers died in combat. Estimates put the number of South Vietnamese civilian dead at nearly 500,000. The exact number of Vietcong and North Vietnamese Army war dead is unknown but may have been near 1 million. In addition, approximately 879,000 Vietnamese were orphaned, and 181,000 were disabled. Among the disabled were those exposed to chemicals such as Agent Orange. These people have been plagued by high rates of liver cancer and other illnesses.

Read More About It (Holt Researcher)

Free Find:
Le Ly Hayslip
After reading about Le Ly Hayslip on the Holt Researcher CD–ROM, create a plan for starting your own nonprofit organization. Choose its goals and the methods it will use to achieve them.

BIOGRAPHY

Le Ly Hayslip

Vietnamese refugees. Le Ly Hayslip was one survivor of the Vietnam War. Hayslip was born in a village near Da Nang in 1949. She experienced constant warfare as a child. By the time she was 14, she had been imprisoned by the South Vietnamese government. Suspected of being a revolutionary, Hayslip was tortured and sentenced to death. She escaped, however, and returned home. Surviving as best she could, Hayslip worked in a hospital, as a waitress, and as a black-market vendor.

Hayslip's brothers fought on both sides of the war. In 1970 she married a U.S. civilian worker. Soon they fled to the United States. Although she escaped the fighting, she was unable to escape its effects. Hayslip described watching television coverage of Vietnam with her family.

> **"Where the Munros [Hayslip's in-laws] saw faceless Orientals fleeing burning villages, tied up as prisoners, or as rag dolls in a roadside trench (even innocent villagers were "VC" or "Charlie"), I saw my brother Bon Nghe, who fought twenty-five years for the North; my mother's nephew, who was lieutenant for the South; my sister Lan, who hustled drinks to the Americans in Danang; and**

SPOTLIGHT on MIAs

Remind students that some 2,500 Americans were missing in action at the war's end. Have students conduct research on efforts to honor and commemorate these MIAs. Ask each student to write a short report summarizing his or her research. Have volunteers read their reports to the class. Then conduct a brief discussion on the efforts to honor and commemorate these MIAs. To conclude the lesson, have students create a memorial to the MIAs. **Block Scheduling**

Teacher to Teacher

Andy Turay of The Bronx, New York, suggested the following activity: Ask students to conduct research comparing and contrasting U.S. involvement in Vietnam with Soviet involvement in Afghanistan. Have each student write a short report presenting his or her research.

my sister Hai, who shared sleepless nights with my mother in our family bunker at Ky La. I saw floating on the smoke of battle the soul of my dead brother, Sau Ban, victim of an American land mine, and the spirit of my father, who drank acid to avoid involving me again with the Viet Cong terrorists. I saw in those tiny electronic lines, as I saw in my dreams, the ghosts of a hundred relatives, family friends, and playmates who died fighting for this side or that, or merely to survive. ”

Shortly after arriving in the United States, Hayslip began writing her memoirs. Published in 1989, her highly acclaimed book, *When Heaven and Earth Changed Places,* describes growing up in a constant state of war. In 1987 Hayslip created a charitable organization, the East Meets West Foundation, to provide comfort to all victims of the war. The foundation provides assistance to Vietnamese people trying to rebuild their lives. It also helps U.S. veterans cope with the effects of the war.

Nearly 1.5 million Vietnamese like Hayslip fled Vietnam after the fall of Saigon. Desperate to escape economic and social hardships, many braved the rough South China Sea and Gulf of Thailand in tiny, crowded boats. They were joined by thousands of other refugees from Southeast Asia—such as the Hmong (MUHNG) of Laos—also fleeing grave postwar conditions. More than 730,000 of these refugees have settled in the United States since the war.

✔ **READING CHECK:** What were the long-term effects of the war on Vietnam and the Vietnamese people?

INTERPRETING THE VISUAL RECORD

Destruction. The effects of a B-52 bombing raid are clearly visible in this part of the Vietnamese countryside. ***What long-term effects do you think the bombing might have had?***

Vietnam veterans. More than 2 million Americans were involved in the Vietnam War. More than 58,000 of them died, and more than 300,000 were wounded. About 2,500 were missing in action. Improved emergency medical services saved the lives of many U.S. soldiers who had severe wounds that would have been fatal in previous wars. As a result, there were a large number of paralyzed and otherwise severely disabled Vietnam veterans.

More than 600 Americans were held as prisoners of war (POWs). Some POWs spent more than six years in North Vietnamese jails, where they endured long periods of solitary confinement and torture.

One of the most visible tragedies of the war was the fate of its veterans. No ticker-tape parades celebrated the return of soldiers from the Vietnam conflict. On the contrary, veterans often became targets for the anger, guilt, or shame of fellow citizens frustrated by the war. Many other Americans met the veterans with stony silence.

The public's negative reaction enraged and demoralized many veterans. They had faced a life-and-death struggle, obeying orders that they trusted were in their country's best interests. Vietnam veteran Ron Kovic recalled the pain of this lack of support in his 1976 book, *Born on the Fourth of July:*

Ron Kovic (holding flag) led this 1972 protest against the Vietnam War.

THAT'S INTERESTING!

In the late 1970s the United Nations held a conference to devise ways of assisting the boat people. Several nations, including the United States, agreed to increase the number of refugees they would accept. Despite these actions, some 39,000 Vietnamese lived in refugee camps as late as 1996.

internet connect

TOPIC: Vietnam Veterans Memorial
GO TO: go.hrw.com
KEYWORD: SE1 Veterans

Have students access the Internet through the HRW Web site to conduct research on the Vietnam Veterans Memorial. Then ask each student to create a personal response to the memorial. Students' responses should be in a creative form, such as artwork, fiction, poetry, or songwriting.

VISUAL RECORD ANSWER

Students might note the destruction of the landscape.

TEACH OBJECTIVE 3

LEVEL 1: Write the following headings on the chalkboard: *Vietnam Veterans, Public Policy,* and *Healing the Wounds of the War.* Organize students into three groups and assign each group one of the headings. Have each group create a short lesson plan on the content of its assigned subsection. *(The veterans group should discuss social attitudes and social problems that affected veterans. The public policy group should discuss the War Powers Act and public opinion. The wounds group should discuss the Vietnam Veterans Memorial and other efforts to honor veterans.)* Then have volunteers teach their lessons to the class. Encourage students to take notes on groups' presentations. **Sheltered English, Cooperative Learning**

LEVELS 2 AND 3: Tell students to imagine that they work for a national weekly newsmagazine that will be publishing a feature section called The Legacy of Vietnam in the United States. Have each student write an article on a topic of his or her choice. *(See the Level 1 lesson for the correct effects.)* Encourage students to include images or graphic organizers to complement the information in their articles. Display students' completed articles around the classroom.

▶**ASSIGNMENT:** *Have each student create a detailed outline of the subsection entitled Effects of the War.*

VISUAL RECORD ANSWER

(for p. 703)

Students might suggest that the soldiers experienced a feeling of painful cleansing.

SECTION 4 REVIEW ANSWERS

Define and Identify

For significance, see the following pages:

- George McGovern, p. 698
- George Wallace, p. 698
- Twenty-sixth Amendment, p. 698
- Le Ly Hayslip, p. 700
- War Powers Act, p. 702
- Vietnam Veterans Memorial, p. 702
- Maya Ying Lin, p. 702

1. economic costs—expensive, less money available for domestic programs; lives lost—high casualty and injury rates; other costs—veterans' problems and pubic tensions and divisions

2. Answers will vary. Students should clearly state and support their positions.

3. It led Congress to pass the War Powers Act and attempt to have a greater role in directing U.S. military forces.

4. Students' letters will vary. Some students might call for expanded social services to help veterans with physical and mental illnesses.

5. Answers will vary. Some students will note the enormous human and economic costs of the war. Other students might suggest that the war made the United States more careful about using its military power.

Then and Now

No More Vietnams

During a military crisis in 1990 President George Bush assured the nation, "This will not be another Vietnam." The memories of Vietnam have haunted every U.S. leader who has considered committing U.S. troops to foreign conflicts. To avoid long, drawn-out conflicts, recent presidents have committed U.S. troops only to operations in which the fighting was likely to be over very quickly.

The memory of the Vietnam War has also affected media coverage. To keep the flow of war-zone information from eroding public support, the U.S. military has put tight restrictions on media access to the front lines. It has also closely screened what has been broadcast. The military does not want to expose Americans to the kind of gruesome images and grim statistics that fueled the Vietnam antiwar movement.

The men and women returning from recent armed conflicts have received a very different welcome than their Vietnam-era counterparts. Even many Americans who oppose armed conflicts have emphasized their support for the troops and the sacrifices that they have made.

These high school students are protesting a military operation in the 1990s.

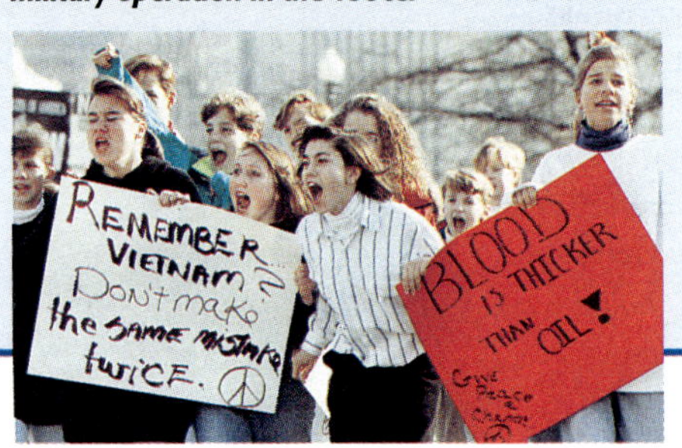

❝ I didn't want to believe it at first—people protesting against us when we were putting our lives on the line for our country. . . . How could they do this to us? Many of us would not be coming back and many others would be wounded or maimed [disabled]. ❞

In their despair, thousands of Vietnam veterans turned to drugs. Many others had trouble finding jobs or adjusting to life as civilians. Some ended up homeless.

Soldiers who were affected by the spraying of defoliants later developed certain forms of cancer at an unusually high rate. Their children had a very high rate of birth defects. Research in the 1970s linked their medical problems to Agent Orange. In 1984 the manufacturers of the chemical created a relief fund for the veterans and their families. In 1991 the government extended permanent disability benefits to these veterans.

Public policy. The war shook Americans' confidence in their government. Many were shocked to discover that their leaders had misled them during the war. The actions of both Presidents Johnson and Nixon raised a crucial constitutional question: under what authority can presidents wage an undeclared war? In 1973, seeking to prevent "another Vietnam," Congress passed the **War Powers Act**. This act reaffirms Congress's constitutional right to declare war by setting a 60-day limit on the presidential commitment of U.S. troops to foreign conflicts.

The Vietnam War also left a dismal economic legacy. The war cost American taxpayers directly more than $150 billion, adding greatly to the national debt and fueling inflation. The war also diverted funding that might have gone to domestic programs, such as those that help the poor.

The Vietnam War taught U.S. policy makers that hostile public opinion and deep national divisions can impose severe restraints on the use of military force. Since Vietnam, leaders have been hesitant to commit U.S. troops in far-off regions without being certain of the consent of the American people and the nation's political allies.

Healing the Wounds of the War

Long after the war's end, Americans continue to seek ways to come to terms with the conflict and its effects. Perhaps the most moving attempt to heal the division caused by the war is the **Vietnam Veterans Memorial** in Washington, D.C., designed by Maya Ying Lin. Lin, a Chinese American, was a young architecture student at Yale University when her design was chosen for the national monument. Of the healing aspects of the memorial, she said, "To overcome grief you have to confront it. An honest memorial makes you accept what happened before you overcome it. I think the memorial makes people accept."

REVIEW

Have students complete the **Section 4 Review** on p. 703.

ASSESS

Have students complete **Daily Quiz 23.4.** As **Alternative Assessment**, you may want to use the graphic organizer activity or the newsmagazine "Legacy of Vietnam" activity in this section's lessons.

RETEACH

Have students complete **Main Idea Activity for Reteaching and Sheltered English 23.4.** Then have each student summarize the entire section in one page or less. Have students trade summaries with a partner and read each other's work, discussing any differences in content or emphasis. **Sheltered English**

EXTEND

Have students conduct research on modern-day Vietnam and the current relationship between the United States and Vietnam. Encourage students to focus their research on a particular topic: growing business contacts, for example, or growing travel contacts. Have each student create an oral presentation on his or her research. Ask volunteers to deliver their presentations to the class. **Block Scheduling**

Inscribed on a huge wall of black granite are the names of the more than 58,000 Americans who died in Vietnam. Lin insisted that the names be listed in chronological order, not in alphabetical order or by rank. She explained that this way "if you were in the war, you could find your time and a few people you knew." Veteran Bruce Weigl attended the dedication ceremony for the memorial on Veterans Day 1982. Weigl later reflected on the reasons he and other veterans attended the ceremony.

> "I think we came, without really knowing it, to make the memorial our wailing wall. We came to find the names of those we lost in the war, as if by tracing the letters cut into the granite we could find what was left of ourselves. . . . No veteran could turn his back on the terrible grace of Maya Lin's wall and the names of the 57,939 who died or disappeared in Vietnam from July 1959 to May 1975."

Hundreds of people, some weeping, visit the memorial daily. Many leave flowers, personal mementos, or written messages. Others simply ponder what the memorial—with its dark silence—has to tell them.

INTERPRETING THE VISUAL RECORD

The wall. Reminders of the war like the Vietnam Veterans Memorial and the hat at left bring back strong emotions. ***How did visiting the memorial affect these soldiers?***

✔ **READING CHECK:** What were the long-term effects of the war on the American people?

SECTION 4 REVIEW

Define and explain the significance of the following terms:
Twenty-sixth Amendment
War Powers Act
Vietnam Veterans Memorial

Identify and explain the significance of the following individuals:
George McGovern
George Wallace
Le Ly Hayslip
Maya Ying Lin

1. **Using Graphic Organizers** Copy the diagram below. Use it to list what you think were the costs of the Vietnam War.

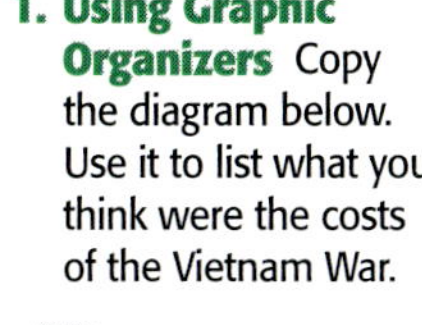

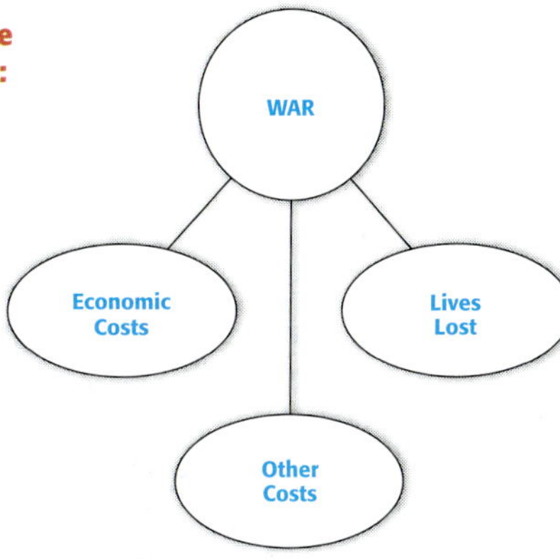

2. **Evaluating** Do you think the terms of the 1973 cease-fire represented a victory or a defeat for the United States? Explain your answer.
3. **Assessing Consequences** What impact did the Vietnam War have on the president's ability to direct U.S. military forces?
4. **Using Historical Imagination** Imagine that you are a veteran of the Vietnam War. Write a letter to the president explaining how you think Vietnam veterans should be honored.

Critical Thinking

5. What long-term effects has the Vietnam War had on the United States?
   Consider:
   - the lives lost on both sides of the war
   - the changes in the way the United States uses its military
   - the increased media attention to government actions

CHAPTER 23 REVIEW ANSWERS

Creating a Time Line
Each event should have an explanation and the correct date.

Writing a Summary
See the Reading Checks in each section for main ideas.

Identifying People and Ideas

1. Communist leader who led the North Vietnamese fight against the South Vietnamese and the United States
2. the theory that if Vietnam fell to communism, its neighbors would soon follow
3. National Liberation Front rebels in South Vietnam
4. gave the president the authority to take action against forces attacking U.S. forces in Vietnam
5. chemicals sprayed in Vietnam to strip the land of vegetation and expose the enemy
6. people who opposed the Vietnam War
7. North Vietnamese surprise attack in 1968 that turned many Americans against the war
8. Nixon's secretary of state
9. Nixon's plan to turn the fighting over to the South Vietnamese while pulling out U.S. troops
10. Vietnamese refugee who wrote *When Heaven and Earth Changed Places*

REVIEW AND ASSESSMENT RESOURCES

PRINT

- Chapter 23 Review, pp. 704–05
- Chapter 23 Tutorial for Students, Parents, Mentors, and Peers
- Chapter 23 Test (Form A or B)
- Portfolio Activities and Alternative Assessment Handbook, Chapter 23

MULTIMEDIA

- Audio Program, Chapter 23 (English and Spanish)
- Chapter 23 Test Generator (on the One-Stop Planner)
- Global Skill Builder CD–ROM
- HRW Web site

SHELTERED ENGLISH

- Spanish Glossary
- Sheltered English Chapter 23 Test

REVIEW

Have students complete the **Chapter 23 Review** on pp. 704–05.

ASSESS

Use one of the chapter tests to assess students' understanding of the content. For **Alternative Assessment**, see the **Portfolio Activities and Alternative Assessment Handbook.**

Understanding Main Ideas

1. to keep France as an ally against communism and to stop the spread of communism in Asia

2. Government officials feared that without increased U.S. involvement the Communists would win the war.

3. Some believed that all war was wrong. Others feared that the United States might use nuclear weapons. Others saw Vietnam as relatively unimportant and thought the war took resources from poverty programs and worked against the wishes of the Vietnamese.

4. It turned American public opinion against the war.

5. resulted in the deaths and injuries of many Americans, caused problems for veterans, cost an enormous amount of money, introduced social divisions, and made many people distrust the government

6. created diplomatic problems between the United States and certain Southeast Asian countries and made U.S. officials more hesitant about committing troops in distant conflicts

Reviewing Themes

1. The United States became involved in the war to stop the advance of communism.

2. Some members of Congress feared that Congress was losing some of its constitutional warmaking authority.

3. by demonstrating that Americans had the freedom to openly criticize their government's actions

Review

Creating a Time Line

Copy the time line below onto a sheet of paper. Complete the time line by filling in the events and dates from the chapter that you think were most significant. Pick three events and explain why you think they were significant.

Writing a Summary

Using the Reading Checks as a guide, write an overview of the events in the chapter.

Identifying People and Ideas

Identify the following terms or individuals and explain their significance.

1. Ho Chi Minh
2. domino theory
3. Vietcong
4. Tonkin Gulf Resolution
5. defoliants
6. doves
7. Tet Offensive
8. Henry Kissinger
9. Vietnamization
10. Le Ly Hayslip

Understanding Main Ideas

SECTION 1

1. What were the main reasons the United States first became involved in Vietnam?

SECTION 2

2. Why did the United States increase its involvement in Vietnam after 1964?
3. What were the main reasons for Americans' opposition to the war?

SECTION 3

4. How did the Tet Offensive change the war?

SECTION 4

5. How has the Vietnam War influenced Americans?
6. What effect did the Vietnam War have on U.S. foreign policy?

Reviewing Themes

1. **Global Relations** How did the U.S. stance on communism lead to involvement in Vietnam?
2. **Constitutional Heritage** During the Vietnam War the president assumed increasing amounts of power. Why did this alarm Congress?
3. **Democratic Values** How did antiwar protests illustrate American democratic values?

Thinking Critically

1. **Problem Solving** Imagine that you are an adviser to President Kennedy. Suggest at least two ways the United States might support South Vietnam without committing U.S. troops to battle.
2. **Evaluating** Do you think President Johnson had good reasons to escalate the U.S. war effort? Explain your answer.
3. **Hypothesizing** Suppose the United States had won a decisive victory in Vietnam. How might life be different in Vietnam? in the United States?
4. **Taking a Stand** Imagine that you are a college student in the 1960s. Would you join the antiwar movement? Explain your answer.
5. **Assessing Consequences** A major goal of U.S. involvement in Vietnam was to stop the spread of communism. What effect did U.S. actions have on the spread of communism?

Writing About History

Writing to Create Imagine that it is 1968 and you have just been drafted. Write a poem or song that expresses your feelings. Use the following graphic to organize your thoughts.

RETEACH

Organize the class into four groups. Assign each group one of the sections of the chapter. Have each group create visual displays to convey the information in its assigned section. Groups might draw graphic organizers, posters, and so on. Have students present their visual displays to the class.
Sheltered English, Cooperative Learning

EXTEND

Organize students into small groups. Have each group prepare a short multimedia presentation about some aspect of the Vietnam War. Encourage students to cover the major events of the war in creative ways: by interviewing veterans about their experiences; by presenting a slide show of images that tell a story by themselves; by playing music of the time period that comments on the war and the feelings of those opposed to it; and so on. Have students deliver their presentations to the class.
Cooperative Learning, Block Scheduling

Strategies for Success Review the **Strategies for Success** on *Determining Good Sources.* Then re-examine each source that you found on the Vietnam War. Decide if and how you would use it in a research paper focusing on the antiwar movement in the United States during the 1960s.

Linking History and Geography

Study the map below, noting the numbers on it. Number your paper one through eight. Then identify each place on the map by selecting a name from the list below. Write the correct name of each place next to its corresponding number on your paper. There are two extra names on the list.

Mekong River	*Hanoi*
Gulf of Tonkin	*China*
South China Sea	*Laos*
Ho Chi Minh City	*Cambodia*
Vietnam	*Soviet Union*

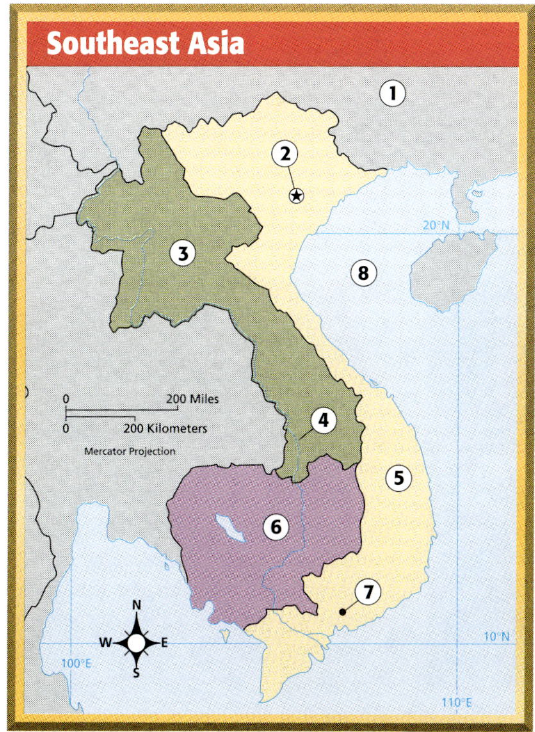

internetconnect

TOPIC: Vietnam
GO TO: go.hrw.com
KEYWORD: SE1 Vietnam

Accessing the Internet through the HRW Web site, research the history of Southeast Asia since the end of the Vietnam War. Then prepare an oral report that outlines the changes in the countries of Southeast Asia since the end of the war.

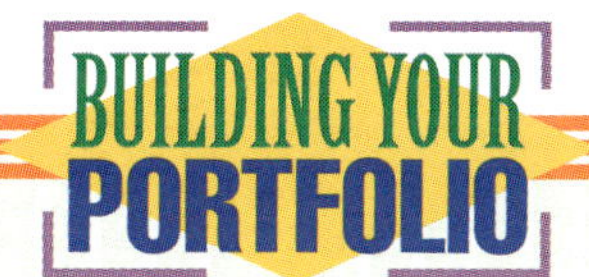

Complete one or all of the following projects independently or cooperatively.

1 Global Relations

Imagine that you are a U.S. delegate to the Geneva conference. ***Create a chart, photo essay, videotape, or other visual presentation*** that shows your proposal for Indochina's future. Then write a short statement indicating how your plan could lessen the risk of U.S. military involvement in Vietnam.

2 Democratic Values

Imagine that you are a reporter covering the civil rights movement. ***Write a script*** for a 15-minute news program that describes the specific concerns of the civil rights leaders about the Vietnam War. Your comments should examine conditions in Vietnam, economic and social factors at home, and U.S. government policies.

3 Cultural Diversity

Imagine that you are a Vietnamese veteran of the Vietnam War. ***Write a letter to a U.S. veteran*** explaining how the Vietnamese people's long history of resisting control by outside powers helped them endure terrible hardships and continue fighting. Describe the similarities and differences between Vietnamese history and U.S. history.

PEACE AT LAST
JAN. 27
1973
VIETNAM CEASEFIRE

Thinking Critically

1. Students' answers will vary. Some students might suggest increased economic or non-personnel military aid.

2. Answers will vary. Some students might argue that Johnson wanted to stop communism, while others might suggest that the escalation harmed both the United States and Vietnam.

3. Answers will vary. Students might incorporate the following points: Vietnam—a more prosperous economy; the United States—more faith in government institutions and a greater willingness to intervene in other nations' affairs.

4. Answers will vary. Students should present reasons for joining or not joining.

5. failed to result in the destruction of communism in Vietnam

Writing About History

Students' poems and songs will vary, but they should include elements such as the Tet Offensive, high casualty rates, and the public's antiwar sentiment

Strategies for Success

Students should clearly indicate if and how they would use each source in a research paper on the antiwar movement.

Linking History and Geography

1–China; 2–Hanoi; 3–Laos; 4–Mekong River; 5–Vietnam; 6–Cambodia; 7–Ho Chi Minh City; 8–Gulf of Tonkin

REVIEW AND ASSESSMENT RESOURCES

PRINT
- Unit 6 Review, pp. 706–07
- Unit 6 Test (Form A or B)
- Portfolio Activities and Alternative Assessment Handbook, Unit 6

MULTIMEDIA
- Global Skill Builder CD–ROM

SHELTERED ENGLISH
- Spanish Glossary
- Sheltered English Unit 6 Test

To review elements of Unit 6 in a single class period, assign one of the following activities or graphic organizers, omitting the italicized answers, to individuals or groups.

2 Democratic Values

Have each student write a brief introduction and a table of contents for a book entitled *Advancements in the U.S. Civil Rights Movement: 1945-1975.* Students' tables of content should include both chapter and section titles.

A Selection from Further Reading

Black Veterans and the Civil Rights Movement. In *Voices of Freedom,* Henry Hampton and Steve Fayer present a far-reaching oral history of the civil rights movement from the 1950s to the 1980s. In the following excerpt, activist Bayard Rustin discusses the origins of the modern civil rights movement. "I think the beginning of this period from 1954 has its roots in the returning soldiers after 1945. There was a great feeling on the part of many of these youngsters that they had been away, that they had fought in the war—they were not getting what they should have. . . . There was a building up of militancy, not so much by going into the streets as by a feeling of 'We are not going to put up with this anymore.' What was lacking was that they did not have the Supreme Court backing them. But when the Supreme Court came out with the Brown [v. Board of Education] decision in '54, things began rapidly to move."

COMPREHENSION According to Rustin, why was the *Brown v. Board of Education* decision so important?

ANSWER: The *Brown* decision represented a fundamental first step toward African American equality. Once the Supreme Court codified that principle, activists began to work in earnest.

Review

BUILDING YOUR PORTFOLIO

Outlined below are four projects. Independently or cooperatively, complete one and use the products to demonstrate your mastery of the historical concepts involved.

1 Economic Development

Presidents Kennedy and Johnson issued a series of reforms designed to transform American society. Many of these programs were designed to improve the economic conditions for poor Americans. Imagine that you are serving as an adviser to President Johnson. ***Create your own proposal*** for a program that addresses an issue facing a group of people that you believe need assistance. You may wish to use portfolio materials you designed in the unit chapters to help you.

Rural poverty in 1965

United Farm Workers marching

2 Democratic Values

For many Americans the greatest strides in civil rights came in the 30 years following World War II. African Americans, Hispanics, Americans with disabilities, women, and other groups made progress in securing rights that had long been guaranteed to others. ***Rehearse and present a 15-minute news program*** to the class discussing the advances made in civil rights. You may wish to use portfolio materials you designed in the unit chapters to help you.

3 Technology and Society

Changes in Daily Life During the 1960s
- *rising political and social activism*
- *continuing population shifts to the suburbs*
- *student rebellions*
- *continuing civil rights struggles*

4 Global Relations

THE VIETNAM WAR

Reasons to Support the War	Reasons to Oppose the War
• *had strong anticommunist sentiments* • *believed winning the war would improve the lives of Vietnamese people* • *felt too much pride to back down* • *believed the United States should police the world to the rise of communism*	• *believed Vietnam was not crucial to U.S. national security* • *believed that the United States should not interfere with Asian affairs* • *argued that the United States was fighting against the wishes of a Vietnamese majority* • *resented resources being funneled toward war rather than domestic improvements*

3 Technology and Society

In the 1960s advances in science and technology, population growth and shifts, and a rising standard of living helped transform the daily lives of Americans. ***Develop a slide show*** that documents some of the changes in everyday life during the 1960s. You may wish to use portfolio materials you designed in the unit chapters to help you.

Cereal advertisement

Anti-Vietnam protest in New York City

4 Global Relations

The U.S. government entered into the conflict between North and South Vietnam to prevent the spread of communism. The U.S. military drafted U.S. citizens to fight in the conflict. ***Create a dialogue*** between a young student about to be drafted and a teacher of government. The dialogue should focus on the importance of the conflict and the responsibilities of both the U.S. government and the student. You may wish to use portfolio materials you designed in the unit chapters to help you.

Further Reading

Evans, Sara M. *Personal Politics.* Knopf, 1979. A discussion of the women's rights movement and its relationship to the civil rights movement.

Hampton, Henry, and Steve Fayer. *Voices of Freedom.* Bantam Books, 1990. Oral history of the civil rights movement.

Howard, Gerald, ed. *The Sixties: Art, Politics, and Media of our Most Explosive Decade.* Paragon House, 1991. A collection of essays from important personalities of the 1960s.

O'Brien, Tim. *The Things They Carried.* Houghton Mifflin, 1990. A war veteran's fictional account of the experiences of soldiers in the Vietnam War.

O'Neil, Doris C., ed. *Life–The '60s.* Little, Brown, 1989. A social history overview of the 1960s.

Thompson, Robert Smith. *The Missiles of October.* Simon & Schuster, 1992. The story of the Cuban missile crisis.

Young, Marilyn B. *The Vietnam Wars, 1945–1990.* HarperCollins, 1991. History of the Vietnam War and its aftermath.

Internet Connect and Holt Researcher CD–ROM *Review*

In assigned groups, develop a multimedia presentation about America between 1960 and 1978. Choose information from the chapter Internet Connect activities and from the Holt Researcher CD–ROM that best reflects the major topics of the period. Write an outline and a script for your presentation, which may be shown to the class.

A Selection from Further Reading

The Experience of War. In *The Things They Carried,* Tim O'Brien provides a fictional account of the experiences of American soldiers in the Vietnam War. In the following excerpt, the novel's narrator explores the thoughts and emotions of the men in his platoon. "They carried all the emotional baggage of men who might die. . . . They carried shameful memories. They carried the common secret of cowardice barely restrained, the instinct to run or freeze or hide, and in many respects this was the heaviest burden of all, for it could never be put down, it required perfect balance and perfect posture. They carried their reputations. They carried the soldier's greatest fear, which was the fear of blushing. Men killed, and died, because they were embarrassed not to. . . [,] to avoid the blush of dishonor. They died so as not to die of embarrassment."

COMPREHENSION According to O'Brien, why did American soldiers in Vietnam take part in the grave risks and responsibilities of war?

ANSWER: Students might indicate that they took part because they did not want to appear weak and unreliable to their fellow soldiers.

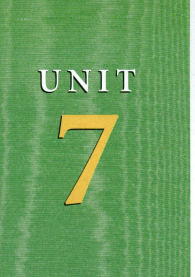

UNIT 7

Modern Times

CHAPTER 24 From Nixon to Carter

When President Richard M. Nixon took office in 1968, the United States was experiencing social and economic turmoil. Nixon worked for an era of détente in foreign relations, establishing a new relationship with China. The Nixon administration faced serious trouble when the Watergate scandal erupted. Nixon resigned from the presidency in August 1974. Gerald Ford succeeded Richard Nixon as president but lost the 1976 election to Jimmy Carter.

CHAPTER 25 The Republican Revolution

With Ronald Reagan's election as president in 1980, many observers hailed the beginning of a "Republican Revolution." President Reagan tried to decrease the size of the federal government, and he reduced taxes and eliminated regulations on certain industries. Reagan pursued a strong anticommunist foreign policy, greatly increasing the defense budget and increasing U.S.

EXAMINING THE VISUAL RECORD

Ask students the questions below. Then use the annotations to expand class discussion.

1 *What might be taking place in the photograph?* The photograph shows a Bicentennial celebration in New York City. During 1976, particularly on the Fourth of July, many cities and states held Bicentennial celebrations. The town of George, Washington, supplied a sixty-square-foot cherry pie for its citizens. In New York City, officials celebrated with an amazing display of fireworks. Some 15 tall ships also sailed up the Hudson River.

2 *Why might organizers of the event have decided to use fireworks to celebrate the occasion?* Fireworks have a long ceremonial history around the world and in the United States. First developed in ancient China, European military officers later used the explosives to announce and herald important military victories. During the 1800s, elements such as magnesium and aluminum began to appear in fireworks, making the displays much brighter.

ACTIVITY: Tell students to imagine that they attended the New York City Bicentennial celebration. Have each student write a short diary entry describing the occasion.

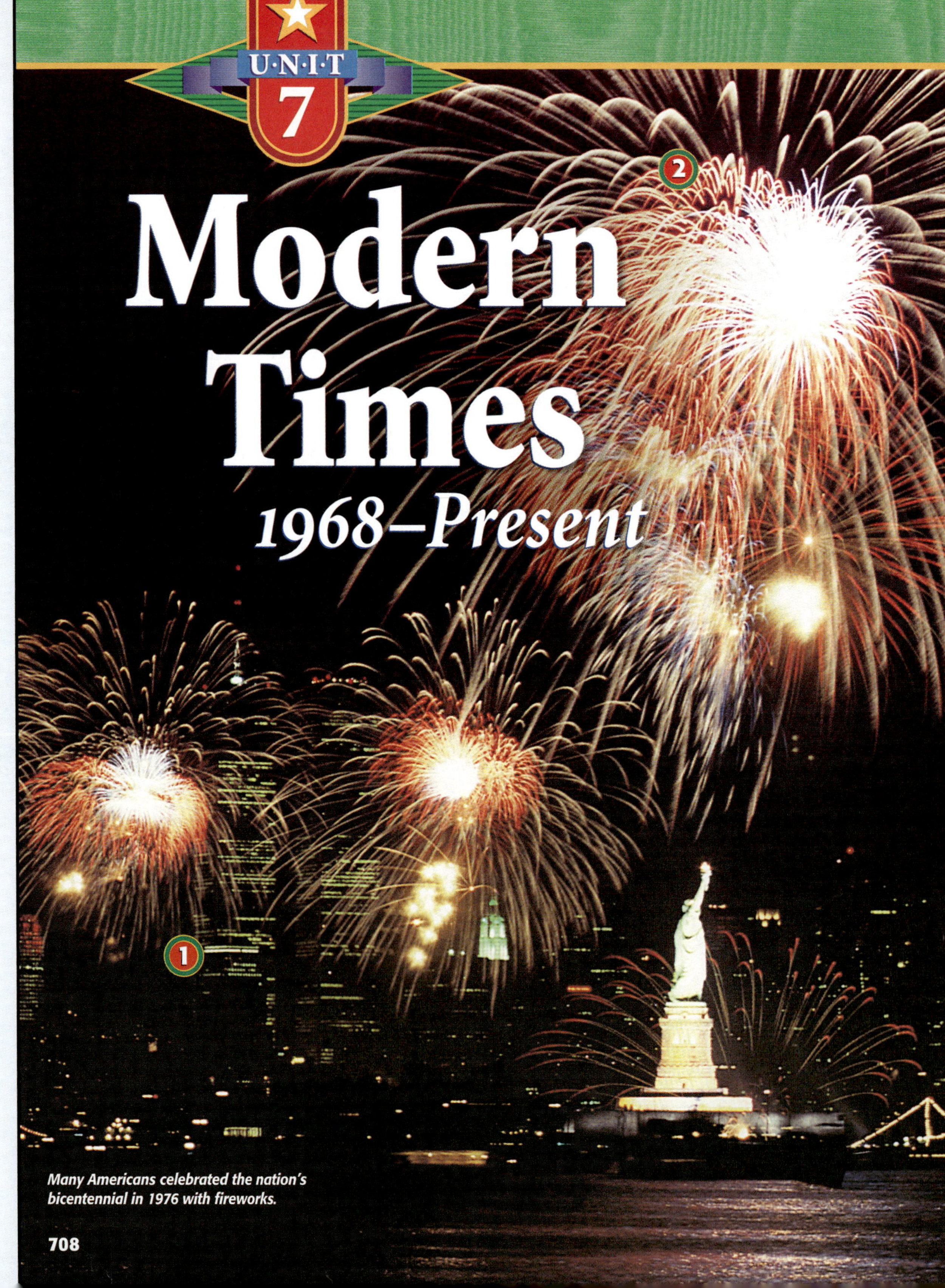

Many Americans celebrated the nation's bicentennial in 1976 with fireworks.

708

involvement in Latin America. During Reagan's last years in office, the Soviet sphere of influence began to dissolve.

Life in the 1990s and Beyond

CHAPTER 26

In 1992 Democrat Bill Clinton won the presidency. In part due to the failure of a national health care plan, the Republicans made stunning gains in House and Senate representation. President Clinton's second term, though marked by domestic prosperity, was dominated by political scandals. Clinton faced many international challenges during his term in office as post-Cold War ethnic tensions flared up in several former Communist countries. The increasing globalization of the economy and the rapid dissemination of information via the Internet also characterized the post-Cold War world.

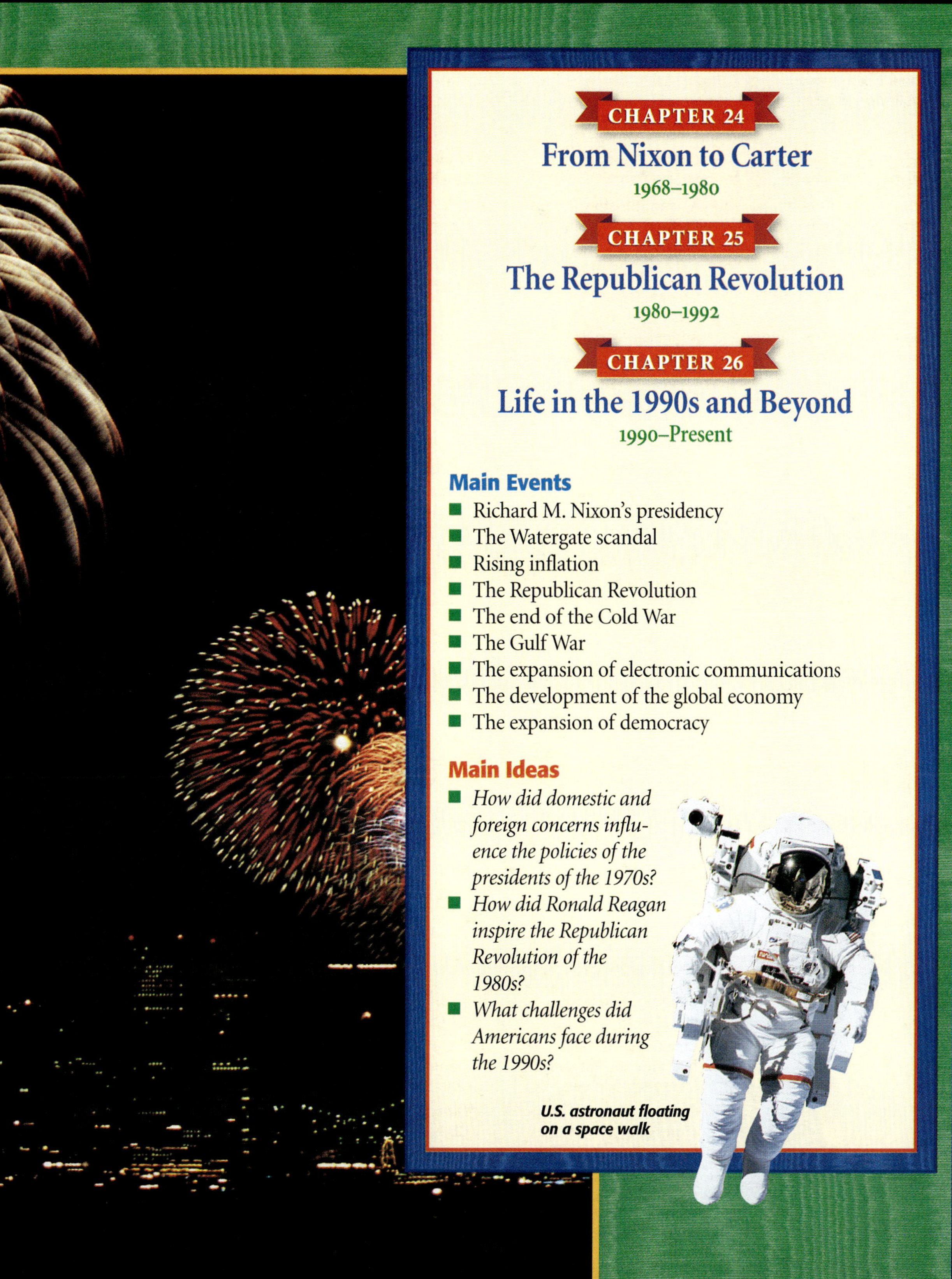

CHAPTER 24

From Nixon to Carter

1968–1980

CHAPTER 25

The Republican Revolution

1980–1992

CHAPTER 26

Life in the 1990s and Beyond

1990–Present

Main Events

- Richard M. Nixon's presidency
- The Watergate scandal
- Rising inflation
- The Republican Revolution
- The end of the Cold War
- The Gulf War
- The expansion of electronic communications
- The development of the global economy
- The expansion of democracy

Main Ideas

- *How did domestic and foreign concerns influence the policies of the presidents of the 1970s?*
- *How did Ronald Reagan inspire the Republican Revolution of the 1980s?*
- *What challenges did Americans face during the 1990s?*

U.S. astronaut floating on a space walk

INTRODUCE UNIT 7

Main Events

List the Main Events on the chalkboard. Ask students to select two and briefly describe what they know about the topics. Have volunteers share their descriptions. Later, when you have finished Unit 7, ask students to return to their original descriptions and revise them using the information they learned in the unit. Students should also create new descriptions for the other Main Events.

Main Ideas

Ask each student to read the Main Ideas and briefly answer the questions in writing. Share the ***Consider*** points with students as necessary. Later, when you have finished Unit 7, ask students to return to their original answers and revise them using the information they learned in the unit.

Policies of the 1970s

Consider:

- the policy implications of forming diplomatic relations with a previously non-recognized nation
- the policy implications of slow economic growth and high inflation

American Challenges

Consider:

- issues such as health care, the environment, and so on
- the opportunities and challenges presented by new forms of technology

From Nixon to Carter

CHAPTER PLANNING GUIDE

	Section Lesson Objectives	Print Resources	Multimedia Resources	Sheltered English Resources
Section 1 The Nixon Years, pp. 712–18	**1** Discuss how President Nixon's domestic policies differed from those of Presidents Johnson and Kennedy. **2** Describe how Nixon responded to economic problems. **3** Identify the causes and effects of the energy crisis. **4** Summarize Americans' efforts to help clean up the environment. **5** Explain how Nixon made foreign-policy decisions.	▶ Guided Reading Strategy 24.1 ▶ Biography Reading 24: Ralph Nader ▶ Literature Reading 24: Nixon's Visit to China ▶ Section 1 Review, p. 718 ▶ Daily Quiz 24.1	▶ One-Stop Planner, Lesson 24.1 ▶ The American Nation Video Program Segment: Nixon in China; Teacher's Guide, pp. 197–98 ▶ Holt Researcher: American History CD–ROM	▶ Main Idea Activity for Reteaching and Sheltered English 24.1
Section 2 From Watergate to Ford, pp. 719–25	**1** Summarize the issues surrounding the Watergate scandal. **2** Discuss the role that the White House tapes played in President Nixon's resignation. **3** Explain why President Ford was unable to achieve his domestic-policy goals. **4** Report on how Ford attempted to continue Nixon's foreign policies.	▶ Guided Reading Strategy 24.2 ▶ American History Political Cartoon 29: Watergate ▶ Primary Source Reading 24: A President Resigns ▶ Graphic Organizer Activity 24: The Nixon Administration ▶ Section 2 Review, p. 725 ▶ Daily Quiz 24.2	▶ One-Stop Planner, Lesson 24.2 ▶ The American Nation Video Program Segment: Richard Nixon Resigns; Teacher's Guide, pp. 215–16 ▶ Holt Researcher: American History CD–ROM ▶ HRW Web site	▶ Main Idea Activity for Reteaching and Sheltered English 24.2
Section 3 Carter: The Outsider as President, pp. 726–31	**1** State why voters thought that Jimmy Carter was a different kind of politician. **2** Explain how President Carter's handling of domestic issues caused some Americans to lose faith in his administration. **3** Contrast Carter's foreign policy with Nixon's and Ford's. **4** Analyze how Carter weakened U.S.-Soviet relations, and relate how he helped achieve peace in the Middle East.	▶ Guided Reading Strategy 24.3 ▶ Geography Activity 24: Southern Africa in the 1970s ▶ Section 3 Review, p. 731 ▶ Daily Quiz 24.3	▶ One-Stop Planner, Lesson 24.3 ▶ Holt Researcher: American History CD–ROM	▶ Main Idea Activity for Reteaching and Sheltered English 24.3
Section 4 Life in the 1970s, pp. 732–37	**1** Describe how the American population and family structure changed during the 1970s. **2** Explain why Americans were said to be self-absorbed. **3** List forms of entertainment that were popular in the 1970s. **4** Analyze how new technologies affected Americans' lives.	▶ Guided Reading Strategy 24.4 ▶ Section 4 Review, p. 737 ▶ Daily Quiz 24.4	▶ One-Stop Planner, Lesson 24.4 ▶ Everyday Life in America Transparency 31: *Star Wars*: Sign of the Seventies ▶ Holt Researcher: American History CD–ROM	▶ Main Idea Activity for Reteaching and Sheltered English 24.4
Chapter Review and Assessment pp. 738–39		▶ Chapter 24 Review, pp. 738–39 ▶ Chapter 24 Tutorial for Students, Parents, Mentors, and Peers ▶ Chapter 24 Test (Form A or B) ▶ Portfolio Activities and Alternative Assessment Handbook, Chapter 24	▶ Audio Program, Chapter 24 (English and Spanish) ▶ Chapter 24 Test Generator (on the One-Stop Planner) ▶ Global Skill Builder CD–ROM ▶ HRW Web site	▶ Spanish Glossary ▶ Sheltered English Chapter 24 Test

CHAPTER OVERVIEW

Richard Nixon was elected to office in 1968 amidst much domestic turmoil. When Nixon took office, the United States was plagued by the dual problems of rising inflation and unemployment. An energy crisis added to the nation's domestic troubles. Despite these problems, Nixon scored a foreign relations triumph when he visited China in 1972. He established improved relations with that nation in order to further divide the communist powers of China and the Soviet Union. However, these accomplishments were overshadowed by the Watergate scandal, which preoccupied the White House and the American public during Nixon's second term. As evidence of his wrongdoing mounted and the likelihood of his impeachment, Nixon resigned in August 1974. He was the first U.S. president to resign.

Gerald Ford succeeded Nixon as president. Ford attempted to continue Nixon's foreign policy and to solve the nation's domestic troubles. Despite his efforts to restore confidence in the presidency, the memory of Watergate loomed in many Americans' minds. Ford lost the 1976 election to Jimmy Carter, a relatively unknown politician from Georgia. Carter worked to restore the nation's confidence in the presidency and to change U.S. relations with the developing world. Carter's crowning achievement as president was the signing of the Camp David Accords between Israel and Egypt.

TIME TAMERS

Block Scheduling

The teacher lesson plans for each section offer a variety of activity choices to help you present the material in a block scheduling format. For further suggestions on block scheduling, see the **Block Scheduling Handbook with Team Teaching Strategies**, pp. 139–44.

Hands-On History Activities:

Classroom to Community The **Hands-On History Activities** help students make meaningful connections between events in American history and those in their own hometown. You may wish to use the Chapter 24 Activity, The Future of Energy, to extend the chapter lessons, as alternative assessment, or as a block scheduling option.

Portfolio Projects

The American Nation includes multiple portfolio projects in each Pupil's Edition chapter review, as well as each unit review. Chapter 24 Portfolio Project options on p. 739 include the following:

1. Students will **write a short article**.
2. Students will **create a flowchart**.
3. Students will **prepare a presentation**.

The American Nation

INTERNET RESOURCE DIRECTORY

To access online materials for this chapter, go to go.hrw.com and type in the keywords listed below.

HRW ONLINE RESOURCES
GO TO: go.hrw.com

Online Charts
KEYWORD: SE1 Charts24
- The Impeachment Process

Online Reading Support
KEYWORD: SE1 Strategies24

Online Rubrics
KEYWORD: SE1 Rubrics

CHAPTER ENRICHMENT LINKS
Use these Web links to extend and enrich student learning for Chapter 24.
GO TO: go.hrw.com
KEYWORD: SE1 Ch24

CHAPTER INTERNET ACTIVITIES
GO TO: go.hrw.com
- Pupil's Edition Student Activity
KEYWORD: SE1 Seventies
(Students explore 1970s fashion.)
- Teacher's Edition Student Activity
KEYWORD: SE1 Nixon
(Students conduct research on Nixon's trip to China.)
- Teacher's Edition Student Activity
KEYWORD: SE1 Watergate
(Students conduct research on the Watergate scandal.)

ADDITIONAL RESOURCES

Books for Teachers

Hoff, Joan. *Nixon Reconsidered.* BasicBooks, 1994. Argues that the Watergate scandal has overshadowed Nixon's achievements in office.

Small, Melvin. *The Presidency of Richard Nixon.* University Press of Kansas, 1999. Provides an overview of the Nixon presidency.

Books for Students

Carroll, Peter. *It Seemed Like Nothing Happened: America in the 1970s.* Rutgers University Press, 1990. Presents a survey of changes in American politics and culture.

Feinberg, Barbara S. *Watergate: Scandal in the White House.* Watts, 1990. Discusses the Watergate scandal. Part of the Twentieth-Century American History series.

Primary Sources from the Period

Ford, Gerald. *A Time to Heal.* Harper & Row, 1979. Presents former president Gerald Ford's memoirs of the presidency.

Woodward, Bob, and Carl Bernstein. *All the President's Men.* Simon & Schuster, 1974. Provides key reporters' account of breaking the Watergate scandal.

Multimedia Materials

The Panama Canal. Video, 11 min. Coronet Films. Includes material on the 1978 treaties.

Watergate: The Secret Story. Video, 90 min. CBS. Offers interviews with key players in the scandal.

CHAPTER 24

Before You Read

Build on What You Know

Ask students to answer the following questions.

Why were many Americans concerned about law and order?

Consider:

- the protests against the Vietnam War
- the increasing militancy of civil rights protesters during the late 1960s

How might a presidential scandal affect the office of the president?

Consider:

- the symbolic importance of the office
- how a scandal might affect Americans' attitudes toward the president

exploring the time line

AMERICAN EVENTS

CONSTITUTIONAL HERITAGE

Cigarette Ads. Broadcasters objected to the law banning cigarette advertisements from radio and television on the grounds that their constitutional rights were being violated. They maintained that if cigarettes were a harmful product, Congress should have banned all advertising, not just radio and television ads. In the case of *Capital Broadcasting Company* v. *U.S.*, however, a federal court ruled that Congress had the power to apply the ban selectively and to single out broadcasters while permitting cigarette advertisements to remain in print media. The federal court ruled that the Constitution did not require Congress to "prohibit all like evils, or none."

CRITICAL THINKING Why might Congress have banned cigarette advertisements from radio and television but not from newspapers or magazines?

ANSWER: Answers will vary. Some students might suggest that Congress believed that young people are more easily influenced by radio and television ads.

CHAPTER 24

1968–1980

From Nixon to Carter

Neil Armstrong walks on the Moon.

1968 **1970** **1972**

1969 Science and Technology Astronaut Neil Armstrong becomes the first person to walk on the Moon.

The cast of All in the Family

1971 The Arts The television situation comedy *All in the Family*, which examines controversial issues such as racial conflict, debuts.

1972 Daily Life A federal law banning cigarette advertisements on radio and television goes into effect.

1972 World Events Chinese leaders welcome Richard Nixon, the first U.S. president to visit China.

President Nixon at the Great Wall of China

1973 Politics Vice President Spiro Agnew resigns from office.

1973 World Events War breaks out in the Middle East when several Arab states attack Israel.

Before You Read

Build on What You Know

Throughout the 1960s the United States increased its involvement in the Vietnam War. As the war escalated, so did criticism of America's role in the conflict. Republican Richard Nixon won the presidential election of 1968 promising to end the war in Vietnam and to restore law and order to society. In this chapter you will learn how scandal ruined Nixon's presidency and how Presidents Gerald Ford and Jimmy Carter struggled to lead the nation. You will also learn how the tensions of the era transformed American culture.

Think About Themes

To help students create their Themes Journal entries, share the following examples of appropriate ***agree/disagree*** *statements.*

Democratic Values

Agree It was necessary to keep the development of the atomic bomb secret from the American public in order to protect the national security of the United States.

Disagree The Pentagon Papers revealed that the U.S. government had frequently misled Americans about U.S. progress in the Vietnam War.

Economic Development

Agree Innovations in technology and production techniques after World War I helped end the economic recession and create prosperity.

Disagree Franklin D. Roosevelt's New Deal helped many Americans who were in a desperate situation during the Great Depression.

Global Relations

Agree Woodrow Wilson's call to make the world save for democracy after World War I was a failure.

Disagree While the United States and European countries tried to avoid involvement in another costly war, Adolf Hitler invaded Austria and the Sudetenland.

Movie poster for Jaws

Protest against Three Mile Island

1975
The Arts
Steven Spielberg's *Jaws* becomes the highest-earning motion picture released to date.

1975
Daily Life
Americans are able to purchase video games that can be played on television sets.

1977
Business and Finance
Steven Jobs and Stephen Wozniak found the Apple Computer company.

1978
Politics
The U.S. Senate ratifies the Panama Canal Treaties by very close votes.

1979
Daily Life
Radiation is released from the Three Mile Island nuclear power plant after a cooling system fails.

1976 | **1978** | **1980**

Bicentennial fireworks in New York City

1976
Daily Life
Americans celebrate the nation's bicentennial, the 200th anniversary of the signing of the Declaration of Independence.

1977
The Arts
The Bee Gees, a disco group, begin their record string of six straight number-one hit singles.

A live recording of the Bee Gees

1979
World Events
Soviet troops invade Afghanistan and install a pro-Soviet government.

1980
Business and Finance
The Rollerblade company begins production of in-line roller skates.

1980
World Events
The United States and 64 other nations boycott the Summer Olympics held in Moscow.

exploring the time line

GLOBAL EVENTS

internetconnect

TOPIC: Nixon and China
GO TO: go.hrw.com
KEYWORD: SE1 Nixon

Have students access the Internet through the HRW Web site to conduct research on President Richard Nixon's trip to China and the establishment of closer ties between the United States and China. Then ask each student to write and illustrate a magazine article that documents the historic trip and discusses its results.

Think About Themes

Decide whether you ***agree*** *or* ***disagree*** *with the following statements. Note why in your journal.*

Democratic Values The president has the right to keep certain information secret from the American public.

Economic Development Government should not intervene during an economic recession because the business cycle will always correct itself.

Global Relations A nation's foreign policy should be based on practical national-security interests, not on moral or ethical ideals.

711

SECTION 1

After completing Section 1, students should be able to:

OBJECTIVE 1 *Discuss how President Nixon's domestic policies differed from those of Presidents Johnson and Kennedy.*

OBJECTIVE 2 *Describe how Nixon responded to economic problems.*

OBJECTIVE 3 *Identify the causes and effects of the energy crisis.*

OBJECTIVE 4 *Summarize Americans' efforts to help clean up the environment.*

OBJECTIVE 5 *Explain how Nixon made foreign-policy decisions.*

LET'S GET STARTED!

As students enter the classroom, tell them to read the quotation from Richard Nixon on this page. Ask each student to summarize the quotation and to briefly explain what Nixon was saying. Ask volunteers to share their summaries with the class. Tell students that in Section 1 they will learn about Richard Nixon's domestic policies and his foreign-policy decisions.

SECTION 1 RESOURCES

PRINT

- Guided Reading Strategy 24.1
- Biography Reading 24: Ralph Nader
- Literature Reading 24: Nixon's Visit to China
- Section 1 Review, p. 718
- Daily Quiz 24.1

MULTIMEDIA

- One-Stop Planner, Lesson 24.1
- The American Nation Video Program Segment: Nixon in China; Teacher's Guide, pp. 197–98
- Holt Researcher: American History CD–ROM

SHELTERED ENGLISH

- Main Idea Activity for Reteaching and Sheltered English 24.1

✔ READING TO UNDERSTAND

To help students master the section objectives, have them answer the **READING CHECKS** and complete **Guided Reading Strategy 24.1** as they read the section.

The Nixon Years

OBJECTIVES

Read to understand:

1. how President Nixon's policies differed from those of Presidents Johnson and Kennedy
2. how President Nixon responded to economic problems
3. what the causes and effects of the energy crisis were
4. what average Americans and the government did to help clean up the environment
5. what beliefs guided Nixon's foreign-policy decisions

KEY TERMS

Silent Majority
Family Assistance Plan
southern strategy
stagflation
Organization of Petroleum Exporting Countries
Environmental Protection Agency
Endangered Species Act
realpolitik
Strategic Arms Limitation Talks
détente

KEY PEOPLE

Warren Burger
Henry Kissinger
Leonid Brezhnev
Salvador Allende
Golda Meir

“As I saw it, America in the 1960s had undergone a misguided crash program aimed at using the power of the presidency and the federal government to right past wrongs by trying to legislate social progress. This was the idea behind Kennedy's New Frontier and Johnson's Great Society. The problems were real and the intention worthy, but the method was foredoomed [bound to fail]. By the end of the decade its costs had become almost prohibitively high in terms of the way it undermined [weakened] fundamental relationships within our federal system, created confusions about our national values, and corroded American belief in ourselves as a people and as a nation.”

—President Richard Nixon

Richard Nixon

After he won the 1968 presidential election, Richard Nixon recalled his attitude toward the policies of Presidents Johnson and Kennedy. Nixon attempted to redefine the relationship between the federal government and the states during the early 1970s. However, he encountered unanticipated domestic and foreign-policy crises.

Courting the Silent Majority

Much of President Nixon's support came from middle-class voters weary of the social unrest of the 1960s. Nixon called these people the **Silent Majority**—“the forgotten Americans, the non-shouters, the non-demonstrators.” He won their votes by pledging to restore law and order and to cut back Democratic programs.

Reforming welfare. Nixon agreed with the criticism that Great Society programs had failed to significantly decrease poverty in the United States. He believed that liberal policies had created a complex, inefficient system that made people dependent on the federal government. The welfare system, which had grown from some 5.9 million recipients in 1960 to some 12.8 million in 1970, came under particular attack. “From the first days of my administration I wanted to get rid of the costly failures of the Great Society,” Nixon later recalled. “Welfare reform was my highest domestic priority.”

Under the existing welfare system, much of the aid for poor families was in the form of services such as Medicaid and nutrition programs. Nixon proposed replacing this system with the **Family Assistance Plan** (FAP), which would guarantee families a minimum income. Under the plan, adults able to work would have to accept job training or work assignments. Supporters of the FAP argued that giving money directly to families would reduce welfare programs and the waste that went with them. Some critics of the plan charged that such direct aid would make poor families even more dependent on the federal government.

TEACH OBJECTIVE 1

ALL LEVELS: Tell students that President Nixon pledged to implement domestic policies that were different from those of Presidents Johnson and Kennedy. Ask students to describe the domestic agendas of Kennedy and Johnson. *(Students should mention civil rights legislation and Great Society programs such as the War on Poverty.)* To help students understand how Nixon's domestic policies differed from those of Presidents Johnson and Kennedy, copy the Venn Diagram at right on the chalkboard, omitting the italicized answers. Have each student complete it. Ask volunteers to share their answers with the class. **Sheltered English**

Kennedy's and Johnson's Policies
- *Great Society programs expanded the welfare system and provided services to poor Americans*
- *proposed and supported civil rights legislation*
- *increased government spending on social programs*

Both
- *believed that some form of government assistance was necessary to combat poverty*

Nixon's Policies
- *wanted to reform welfare system by replacing the government provision of services with the Family Assistance Plan*
- *no new civil rights legislation*
- *pledged to cut back Democratic programs*

The FAP's work requirement also generated intense opposition from welfare-rights supporters. George Wiley, head of the National Welfare Rights Organization, declared, "When Richard Nixon is ready to give up his $200,000 a year salary to scrub floors and empty bedpans in the interest of his family, then we'll take him seriously." The Senate ultimately voted down the FAP.

Chief Justice Warren Burger (center) poses with the other members of the Supreme Court.

Seeking southern support. In addition to trying to reform the welfare system, Nixon planned not to ask for any new civil rights legislation. This decision was part of his **southern strategy**—a plan to woo conservative southern white voters away from the Democratic Party. As part of this approach, Nixon also delayed pressuring southern schools to desegregate. When the Supreme Court ruled in 1971 that busing could be used to integrate schools, Nixon opposed the ruling.

When Chief Justice Earl Warren retired in 1969, Nixon appointed a conservative justice, Warren Burger, to head the Court. The Senate rejected two other Nixon nominees, both from southern states. Nixon used these rejections to win southern support. He complained, "The real reason for their rejection was their legal philosophy . . . and also the accident of their birth, the fact that they were born in the South." The president eventually appointed three conservative justices: Harry Blackmun, Lewis Powell, and William Rehnquist.

✔ **READING CHECK:** How did President Nixon's policies differ from those of Presidents Johnson and Kennedy?

Tackling the Economy

Reversing the liberal policies of the 1960s was not the only challenge President Nixon faced. He also had to manage a faltering economy. The United States had enjoyed an economic boom during the 1960s, but the economy had begun to show signs of trouble by the time Nixon took office. Heavy government spending on social programs and on the Vietnam War had contributed to a recession and growing unemployment. Normally, when unemployment is high, inflation is low. Yet when Nixon took office, both inflation and unemployment rose. This combination of rising unemployment and inflation is called **stagflation**.

PRESIDENTIAL *Lives*

1913–1994
In Office 1969–1974

Richard M. Nixon

Richard Milhous Nixon's hard work and intense ambition helped him rise to the top ranks of the Republican Party. Having grown up in a poor family in California, Nixon was determined to succeed.

One of the most famous examples of Nixon's ability to bounce back from political challenges came during the 1952 presidential election. Nixon, who was Dwight Eisenhower's vice presidential running mate, had been accused of accepting personal gifts from wealthy businessmen. He appeared on national television to deny the charges. In what came to be called the Checkers speech, Nixon admitted to accepting one personal gift. "You know what it was?" the candidate asked. "It was a little cocker spaniel dog . . . black, white, and spotted, and our little girl Tricia, the six-year-old, named it Checkers. . . . And I just want to say this, right now, that regardless of what they say about it, we're going to keep it." The Checkers speech was well received and may have saved Nixon from being dropped from the Republican ticket.

PEOPLE IN HISTORY

Harry Blackmun. Nixon's first appointee to the U.S. Supreme Court, Harry Blackmun, was from Minnesota, as was Chief Justice Warren Burger. At first, Blackmun voted like Burger, so much so that they were dubbed the "Minnesota Twins." However, Blackmun became increasingly liberal, voting in favor of abortion rights, opposing the death penalty, and supporting the expansion of civil liberties.

CRITICAL THINKING What might Blackmun's career reveal about the practice of labeling people as "conservative" or "liberal"?

ANSWER: Students might point out that an individual's views can sometimes change a great deal over time, and that such labels must be applied with caution.

THAT'S INTERESTING!

First Lady Pat Nixon urged her husband to appoint the first woman to the U.S. Supreme Court. Richard Nixon considered nominating Judge Mildred Lillie, but did not because Lillie did not have the support of the American Bar Association, the nation's leading legal organization.

713

TEACH OBJECTIVE 2

LEVEL 1: Ask students to identify the major economic problems that President Nixon faced. *(Students should mention rising unemployment and inflation.)* Then ask students how Nixon dealt with these problems. *(Students should mention that Nixon temporarily froze prices, rents, and wages.)* Pair students and have each pair brainstorm at least two other ways that Nixon might have dealt with stagflation. *(Students might suggest government jobs programs, raising interest rates to curb spending, or ending the Vietnam War.)* Ask volunteers to share their ideas and encourage the class to evaluate and briefly discuss each idea. **Sheltered English, Cooperative Learning**

LEVELS 2 AND 3: Ask students to identify the major economic problems that President Nixon faced and what caused these problems. *(See the level 1 lesson for the correct problems; causes included heavy spending on social programs and the Vietnam War).* Then tell students to imagine that they are President Nixon's press secretary. Have each student write a short press release describing and explaining Nixon's response to stagflation. Ask volunteers to read their press releases to the class.

ECONOMIC DEVELOPMENT

Unemployment. Demographic changes and changing attitudes toward the role of women in American society contributed to the unemployment problem of the 1970s. The baby boom generation was entering the job market, as were an increasing number of women. As a result, some 10.1 million new workers entered the labor force between 1964 and 1970.

ACTIVITY: Have students write a paragraph explaining what changes in the 1960s contributed to the increased number of female workers.

THAT'S INTERESTING!

Nixon administration officials were intent on enforcing the freeze on wages and prices. Treasury agents stopped a Detroit hotel from replacing 10-cent locks on stalls in the men's bathrooms with 25-cent locks.

VISUAL RECORD ANSWER

Students might suggest that the cartoon's title and picture do not show support for Nixon.

MAP ANSWER

Algeria, Iran, Iraq, Kuwait, Libya, Nigeria, Qatar, Saudi Arabia, United Arab Emirates

INTERPRETING THE VISUAL RECORD

Inflation. President Nixon used price and wage freezes to fight inflation. ***Does this cartoon dollar bill support Nixon's actions? Explain your answer.***

In August 1971 Nixon took a drastic step to curb inflation by imposing temporary freezes on prices, rents, and wages. This action surprised many people, since Republicans typically opposed such action. Labor leaders feared that wage freezes would hurt those earning the least. AFL–CIO president George Meany called it "Robin Hood in reverse, because it robs from the poor and gives to the rich." Nixon, however, was bowing to political reality. Democratic Party leaders had started referring to the nation's economic troubles as the result of "Nixonomics." Nixon hoped that taking action on the economy would help him win the upcoming presidential election. The strategy worked. Inflation slowed, and Nixon was re-elected in 1972. However, when he eased controls, inflation shot up again. In 1974 the inflation rate topped 12 percent.

✔ **READING CHECK:** How did President Nixon respond to economic problems?

The Energy Crisis

During the 1970s rising oil costs became a major cause of inflation and consumer worry. Since World War II, the U.S. economy had grown increasingly dependent on foreign oil. By 1973 Americans consumed twice as much oil as they produced.

OPEC Member Nations in the Middle East and North Africa, 1970s

Learning from Maps OPEC produced much of the world's oil supply during the 1970s.

REGION Which countries in the Middle East and North Africa were members of OPEC?

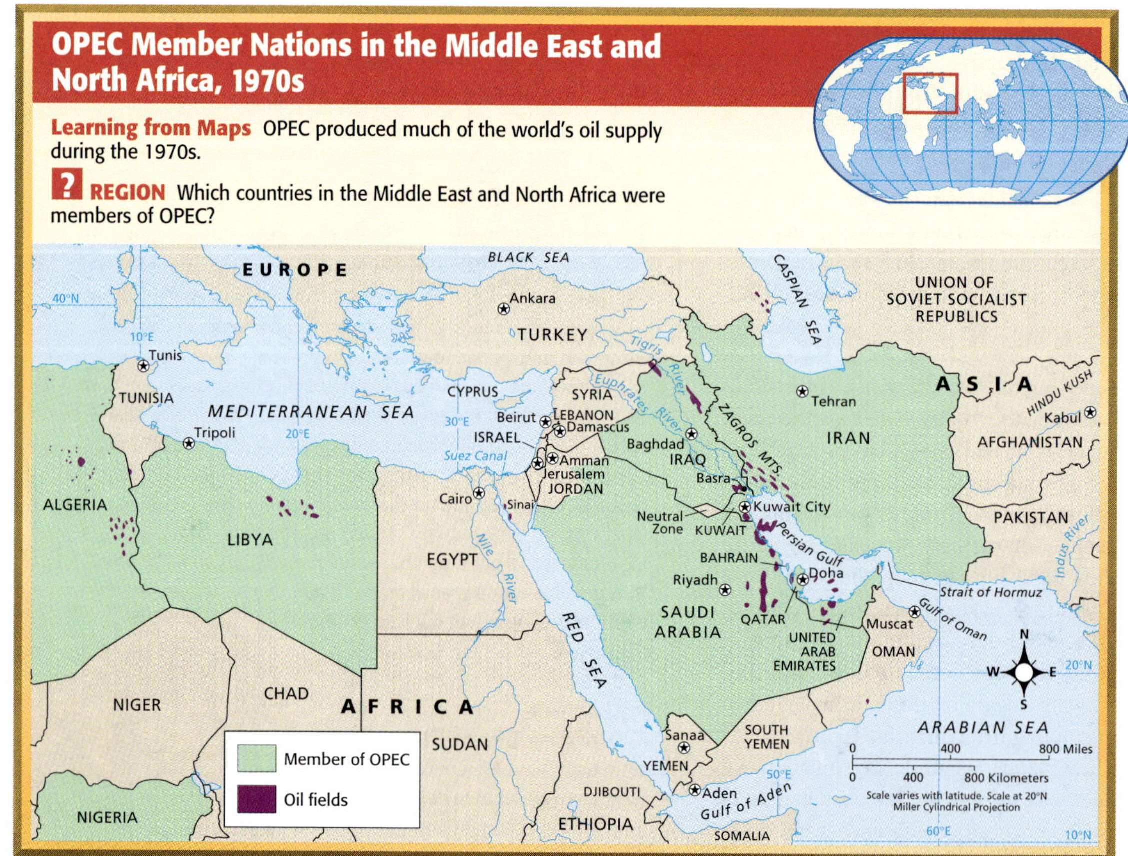

TEACH OBJECTIVE 3

LEVEL 1: Pair students and have each pair create a comic strip that identifies the causes of the energy crisis of 1973–74. *(Comic strips should show U.S. dependence on foreign oil, U.S. support of Israel, the oil embargo, and OPEC price hikes.)* Then ask students how Nixon responded to this crisis. Record responses on the chalkboard and encourage students to copy the information into their notes. *(Students should mention that Nixon called for energy conservation, signed a bill to reduce the speed limit to 55 MPH, approved the construction of an oil pipeline from Alaska, and supported the development of nuclear energy.)* Tell students that U.S. dependence on foreign oil is still a national concern.
Sheltered English, Cooperative Learning

LEVELS 2 AND 3: Have each student create an annotated time line of the events that led to the energy crisis of 1973–74. *(See the Level 1 lesson for the correct causes.)* Then have each student write a few paragraphs identifying and explaining what he or she believes was the primary cause of the crisis. Ask volunteers to share their paragraphs with the class. Students may wish to include their time lines and paragraphs in their portfolios.

Changing Ways Gasoline Consumption

Understanding Change The energy crisis of the 1970s led to increased calls for vehicles that were more fuel-efficient and for an overall decrease in gasoline consumption. *Since then, how much has the average gas mileage per car changed? Given the changes in average gas consumption per car, what might account for the increase in total gasoline consumption?*

Gasoline Consumption

		Then	Now
Total gas consumption		92.3 billion gallons	146.7 billion gallons
Average annual consumption per car		688 gallons	531 gallons
Average gas mileage	cars	13.5 miles per gallon	21.3 miles per gallon
	trucks	5.5 miles per gallon	6.2 miles per gallon

Source: *Statistical Abstract of the United States: 1998.* Data reflect 1970 and 1996.

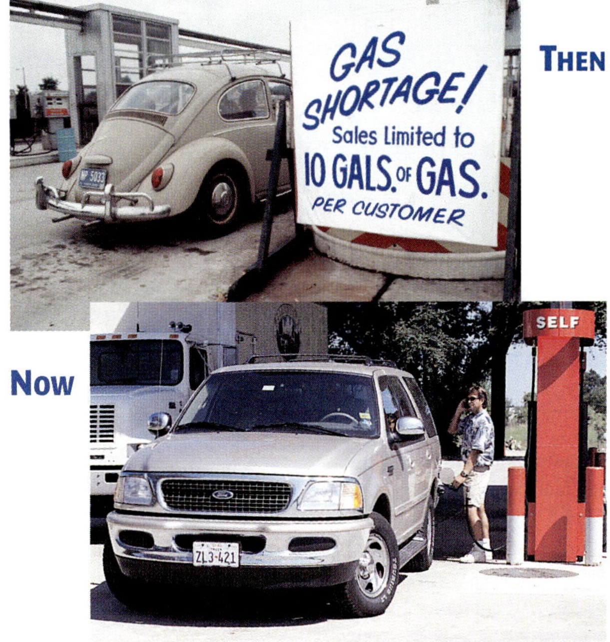

Price hikes. In June 1973 President Nixon warned the nation that the "supply of domestic energy resources available to us is not keeping pace with our ever growing demand." Americans soon learned the costs of this problem. That October several Arab nations cut off oil shipments to the United States as punishment for the U.S. support of Israel in a new Arab-Israeli war. In December the **Organization of Petroleum Exporting Countries** (OPEC)—a group founded in 1960 by five oil-producing countries that wanted to increase oil prices—announced a price hike. A barrel of oil that had sold for about $3.00 in the summer of 1973 cost $11.65 in December 1973, an increase of almost 400 percent.

The oil embargo and price hike triggered an energy crisis in the United States during the winter of 1973–74. The cost of electricity, gasoline, and heating oil soared, causing severe hardship in some parts of the country. One Detroit hospital told its patients to stay in bed to keep warm. "We had so little oil left that we just had to cut back the thermostats," noted one hospital official. "In storage rooms and areas with no patients, it got as low as 40 degrees."

The energy crisis also created a great deal of anxiety. Public-opinion analyst Daniel Yankelovich noted "signs of panic" among Americans who were "growing fearful that the country has run out of energy." Across the nation motorists lined up at gas stations to buy a few extra gallons. Lines in New Jersey sometimes stretched four miles long. The Arab nations lifted their embargo in March 1974, but the price of oil remained high.

Energy policy. In response to the crisis, Nixon announced a program designed to make the United States less dependent on foreign oil. He called for energy

GLOBAL RELATIONS

Oil Imports. The growing domestic demand for oil made the United States increasingly dependent on foreign sources of oil. In 1960 the United States imported 19 percent of its oil; by 1974, that number had risen to 38 percent. Because 77 percent of the world's known oil reserves controlled by noncommunist governments were in the Middle East, Americans were especially dependent on that region's resources. In the mid-1970s as much as half of all imported oil came from Middle Eastern nations.

CRITICAL THINKING What problems might arise when a nation is dependent on resources imported from one region?

ANSWER: Students might suggest that the dependent nation could be affected by economic and political events in that region.

CHANGING WAYS ANSWER

Average gas mileage per car has increased by 7.8 miles per gallon. Students might suggest that the number of vehicles has increased.

TEACH OBJECTIVE 4

LEVEL 1: Tell students to imagine that it is 1974 and that they are organizing a display for Earth Day. Organize students into triads and have each triad prepare a two-panel visual display entitled Protecting Our Environment. The first panel should identify citizen and government initiatives to clean up and protect the environment. *(Students' displays should mention Earth Day activities, the creation of the EPA, and passage of the Clean Air Act, the Water Quality Improvement Act, and the Endangered Species Act.)* The second panel of the display should set goals for the future. Display completed projects around the classroom.
Sheltered English, Cooperative Learning

LEVELS 2 AND 3: Tell students to imagine that they are the officers of an environmentalist group in 1975. Pair students and have each pair prepare an informational brochure for prospective members. The brochure should identify important environmental issues, explain citizen and government initiatives that have cleaned up or protected the environment during the early 1970s, and outline the current goals of the organization. *(See the Level 1 lesson for the correct citizen and government initiatives.)* Display students' completed brochures on the classroom walls. **Cooperative Learning**

ACROSS THE CURRICULUM

▶GOVERNMENT◀

EPA. The EPA was authorized to enforce environmental standards and to assess the environmental impact of all federal projects before they were started. The agency also has to monitor air and water quality and pesticide levels. This broad mandate means that the EPA has to oversee some 200,000 businesses whose activities might pollute the environment. Many of these businesses protest the EPA's standards.

CRITICAL THINKING Why might some businesses object to the EPA's policies?

ANSWER: Students might suggest that businesses do not want to pay to implement the EPA-mandated controls.

VISUAL RECORD ANSWER

Students might suggest that motorists could have formed carpools or found other forms of transportation.

***The American Nation* VIDEO PROGRAM**

Nixon in China; Teacher's Guide, pp. 197–98

Search 45667, Play to 47517
Videodisc 2, Side B

Play

Pause

See *Teacher's Guide* for Spanish barcode.

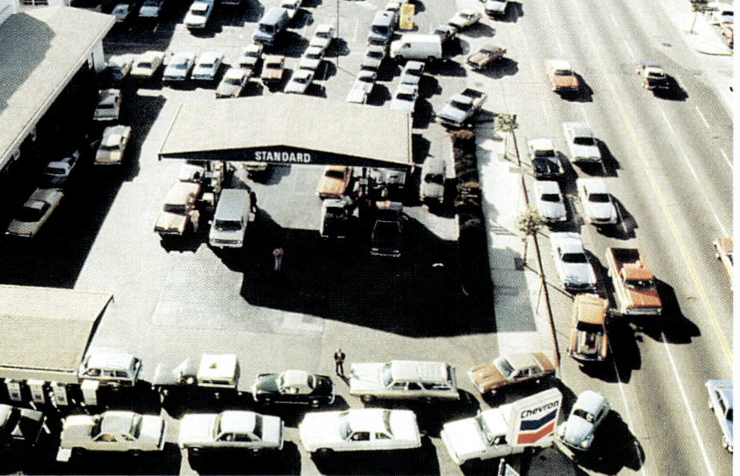

INTERPRETING THE VISUAL RECORD

The energy crisis. Rising prices and fuel shortages made gasoline difficult to find and contributed to many other economic problems. ***How do you think lines such as this one could have been prevented?***

conservation and signed a bill that reduced the highway speed limit to 55 miles per hour, thereby saving some 3.4 billion gallons of gas per year. He also signed a bill authorizing construction of a pipeline to transport oil south from Alaska. Nevertheless, U.S. dependence on foreign oil continued to grow.

The government also supported replacing the use of fossil fuels with nuclear energy. Nuclear power was regarded as a cleaner and more economical source of energy because it did not burn fossil fuels. The Atomic Energy Commission predicted that nuclear power plants would generate half the nation's electrical power by the end of the century. By January 1974 there were 42 nuclear power plants in operation, and more than 160 new plants were under construction or in the planning stages. Yet many critics worried that the risks of a nuclear accident outweighed the benefits of nuclear power.

✔ **READING CHECK:** What were the causes and effects of the energy crisis?

Cleaning up the environment. President Nixon took office at a time when Americans were becoming increasingly worried about the environment. Two events helped raise awareness of environmental issues. The first was a massive oil spill off the coast of Santa Barbara, California, in 1969. The second was the first Earth Day celebration in April 1970. Some 20 million Americans across the nation took part in Earth Day activities. At an event in New York City's Central Park, Episcopal priest Paul Moore spoke to a group of schoolchildren. "Unless we stop stealing, exploiting [taking advantage of] and ruining nature for our own gain, we will lose everything."

In 1970 Congress responded to growing public concern by creating the **Environmental Protection Agency** (EPA), which had power to enforce environmental laws. That same year, Congress passed two laws intended to limit pollution. The Clean Air Act set air-quality standards and tough emissions guidelines for automakers. The Water Quality Improvement Act required oil companies to pay some of the cleanup costs of oil spills. A 1972 act set limits on the discharge of industrial pollutants into water. To protect wildlife in danger of extinction, Congress passed the **Endangered Species Act** in 1973.

✔ **READING CHECK:** What did average Americans and the government do to help clean up the environment?

Earth Day celebrations like this one promote environmental awareness.

Foreign Affairs Under Nixon

Although domestic issues demanded much of President Nixon's attention, his main interest was foreign affairs. Working closely with his national security adviser, Henry Kissinger, Nixon sought to reshape U.S. foreign policy.

TEACH OBJECTIVE 5

LEVELS 1 AND 2: Ask students how Nixon made foreign-policy decisions. *(Students should mention that Nixon and his secretary of state believed in realpolitik—the idea that national interests should take precedence over ideals such as democracy or human rights.)* Organize students into groups of four and have each group evaluate the effectiveness of realpolitik in U.S. relations with China, the Soviet Union, Chile, and the Middle East. Have each group present its evaluations to the class. Encourage students to discuss briefly each group's assessment of Nixon's foreign policy.
Sheltered English, Cooperative Learning

LEVEL 3: Tell students to imagine that they are Henry Kissinger and that they are writing a memoir. Have each student write an excerpt from the memoir describing how Nixon made foreign-policy decisions. Excerpts should also assess the effects of his foreign policy in various parts of the world. *(See the Level 1 lesson for the correct foreign-policy strategy.)* Ask volunteers to share their memoirs with the class. Students may wish to include their memoirs in their portfolios.

▶**ASSIGNMENT:** *Tell students to imagine that they are Chinese reporters covering President Nixon's visit to China. Have them write an article describing his visit including why he came.*

The Nixon-Kissinger approach. Nixon and Kissinger shared a belief in **realpolitik**, or practical politics. This approach argued that national interests, rather than ideals such as democracy and human rights, should guide U.S. foreign policy. Nixon believed that governments allied with the United States should receive U.S. support even if they sometimes violated human rights.

The chief goal of the Nixon-Kissinger foreign policy was to establish a balance of power among the world's five major powers. These powers were China, Japan, the Soviet Union, the United States, and Western Europe. Nixon explained his reasoning in 1972.

> **"The only time in the history of the world that we have had any extended period of peace is when there has been a balance of power. It is when one nation becomes infinitely more powerful in relation to its potential competitors that the danger of war arises."**

INTERPRETING THE VISUAL RECORD

Foreign policy. President Nixon tried to improve relations with China without increasing U.S.-Soviet tensions. ***What does this cartoon suggest about the difficulties Nixon faced?***

The China visit. In keeping with his belief in realpolitik, President Nixon sought to improve relations with the People's Republic of China. By the 1970s China and the Soviet Union had become bitter enemies. Nixon followed the ancient military strategy that "the enemy of my enemy is my friend." He hoped that closer U.S. ties with China would further divide the communist world.

In 1972 Nixon visited China. The two nations agreed to work together to promote peace in the Pacific region and to develop trade relations and cultural and scientific ties. Furthermore, Nixon promised the eventual withdrawal of U.S. forces from Taiwan in order to lessen Chinese support for the North Vietnamese. Although many conservative Americans were stunned by this move, it gave the president leverage to promote a new policy with the Soviet Union.

The Moscow summit. In May 1972, just three months after visiting China, Nixon flew to Moscow for talks with Soviet leader Leonid Brezhnev. The two agreed to promote trade and to cooperate on other issues of mutual concern.

Nixon and Brezhnev also signed a treaty limiting nuclear weapons. This treaty was the product of the **Strategic Arms Limitation Talks** (SALT). It limited the number of intercontinental nuclear missiles—those capable of traveling long distances to other continents—each nation could have. Although the SALT treaty did not end the arms race, it was a small first step toward reducing the nuclear threat. As a result of the arms talks, the United States and the Soviet

THROUGH OTHERS' EYES

Chinese Views of Nixon's Visit

Chinese leaders had their reasons for allowing President Nixon to visit their nation. At a dinner banquet in Nixon's honor, Premier Jou En-lai detailed some of the Chinese government's goals for its meeting with the leader of the United States.

> **"The peoples of our two countries have always been friendly to each other. But owing to reasons known to all, contacts between the two peoples were suspended for over twenty years. . . . At the present time it has become a strong desire of the Chinese and American peoples to promote the normalization of relations between the two countries and work for the relaxation of tension. . . . Differences should not hinder China and the United States from establishing normal state relations on the basis of the Five Principles of mutual respect for sovereignty [political authority] and territorial integrity, mutual nonaggression, noninterference in each other's internal affairs, equality and mutual benefit, and peaceful coexistence."**

GLOBAL RELATIONS

Sino-Soviet Relations. Tensions between the Soviet Union and China increased dramatically during the 1960s. The Soviets claimed that Chinese troops had invaded Soviet territory some 90 times in early 1969. Some Soviet leaders feared a full-scale invasion and at least one high official called for an attack on China's nuclear missile facilities.

ACTIVITY: Have students use the Reference Atlas maps to calculate the distance between the capitals of China and of the former Soviet Union.

VISUAL RECORD ANSWER

Students might point out that the cartoon shows Nixon in a precarious position in his negotiations with the Chinese and Soviets.

Define and Identify

For significance, see the following pages:

- Silent Majority, p. 712
- Family Assistance Plan, p. 712

REVIEW

Have students complete the **Section 1 Review** on p. 718.

ASSESS

Have students complete **Daily Quiz 24.1**. As **Alternative Assessment**, you may want to use the energy crisis comic strips or the realpolitik evaluation activity in this section's lessons.

RETEACH

Have students complete **Main Idea Activity for Reteaching and Sheltered English 24.1**. Then organize students into groups and assign one subsection to each group member. Have each group member summarize his or her assigned subsection. Members should then pass the completed summary to every other group member to read. Finally, have students within their groups take turns quizzing each other about the information in Section 1. **Sheltered English, Cooperative Learning**

EXTEND

Have each student write a position paper responding to the following statement: *As president, Richard Nixon achieved greater success in foreign affairs than he did with domestic programs.* Tell students to justify their responses with facts and examples. Have volunteers read their papers to the class. Encourage the class to discuss the differing opinions. **Block Scheduling**

- southern strategy, p. 713
- Warren Burger, p. 713
- stagflation, p. 713
- Organization of Petroleum Exporting Countries, p. 715
- Environmental Protection Agency, p. 716
- Endangered Species Act, p. 716
- Henry Kissinger, p. 716
- realpolitik, p. 717
- Leonid Brezhnev, p. 717
- Strategic Arms Limitations Talks, p. 717
- détente, p. 718
- Salvador Allende, p. 718
- Golda Meir, p. 718

1. causes–dependence on foreign oil, high energy consumption, conflicts with Arab nations over U.S. support for Israel; responses–55 MPH speed limit, building the Alaska pipeline, more support for nuclear energy

2. Johnson and Kennedy–supported antipoverty programs and civil rights legislation; Nixon–reduced government welfare, offered no new civil rights bills and opposed busing

3. Students might note that it only briefly slowed inflation and did not solve the nation's economic ills.

4. the 1969 oil spill near Santa Barbara and the 1970 Earth Day celebration; created the EPA and passed environmental legislation

5. Some students might note Nixon's achievements in China and the SALT treaty as proof of success, while others might claim that the overthrow of Allende was inappropriate.

Union entered into a period of **détente**—a lessening of military and diplomatic tensions between the countries.

Israeli prime minister Golda Meir

Trouble spots. In general, Nixon and Kissinger ignored countries that were not of direct strategic importance to the United States. One exception was the South American nation of Chile. In 1970 Chile elected Salvador Allende, a Socialist, as president. Fearing that Allende planned to turn Chile into "another Cuba" allied with the Soviet Union, Nixon tried to topple the Allende government. He cut off aid to Chile and provided funds to Allende's opponents in the Chilean military. He also instructed the Central Intelligence Agency (CIA) to disrupt economic and political life in the country. In September 1973 the Chilean army killed Allende and set up a pro-American military dictatorship.

Shortly after the Chilean revolt, conflict erupted in the Middle East. Six years earlier, in 1967, Israel had defeated its Arab neighbors—Egypt, Jordan, and Syria—in the Six-Day War. However, the Arab states continued to harass Israel, and Israel continued to strike back. Israeli prime minister Golda Meir later recalled that "the only time that Arab states were prepared to recognize the existence of . . . Israel was when they attacked it in order to wipe it out."

In October 1973 Egypt and Syria invaded Israel hoping to recover land lost in the Six-Day War. The attack, which came on the Jewish holiday of Yom Kippur, caught the Israelis by surprise. They launched a counterattack, however, that threatened Egypt's capital, Cairo. When the Soviets threatened to intervene by sending troops into the region, President Nixon put all U.S. forces on alert. A major military confrontation seemed possible. Within days, however, the superpowers persuaded the Arabs and Israelis to accept a cease-fire. Détente had survived a critical test, but prospects for a lasting peace in the Middle East remained in doubt.

✔ **READING CHECK:** What belief guided Nixon's foreign-policy decisions?

SECTION 1 REVIEW

Define and explain the significance of the following terms:
Silent Majority
Family Assistance Plan
southern strategy
stagflation
Organization of Petroleum Exporting Countries
Environmental Protection Agency
Endangered Species Act
realpolitik
Strategic Arms Limitation Talks
détente

Identify and explain the significance of the following individuals:
Warren Burger
Henry Kissinger
Leonid Brezhnev
Salvador Allende
Golda Meir

1. **Using Graphic Organizers** Copy the chart below. Use it to explain the causes and effects of the energy crisis.

Causes → Energy Crisis → Effects

2. **Comparing and Contrasting** How did President Nixon's policies differ from those followed by Lyndon Johnson and John F. Kennedy?
3. **Evaluating** Was Nixon's decision to impose wage and price controls an effective way to manage the economy? Explain your answer.
4. **Identifying Values** Why did Americans take an increased interest in the environment during the 1970s? How did government respond?

Critical Thinking

5. Do you agree with President Nixon's belief that realpolitik was an appropriate approach to foreign policy? Why or why not?
Consider:
- the effect of Nixon's visit to China
- the SALT treaty
- events in Chile

SECTION 2

After completing Section 2, students should be able to:

OBJECTIVE 1 *Summarize the issues surrounding the Watergate scandal.*

OBJECTIVE 2 *Discuss the role that the White House tapes played in President Nixon's resignation.*

OBJECTIVE 3 *Explain why President Ford was unable to achieve his domestic-policy goals.*

OBJECTIVE 4 *Report on how Ford attempted to continue Nixon's foreign policies.*

LET'S GET STARTED!

Write the following statement on the chalkboard: *What actions might cause you to question the integrity of an elected official?* As students enter the classroom, tell them to respond to the statement in writing. Tell students that they may use examples of recent controversies surrounding elected officials to support their responses. Ask volunteers to share their responses with the class. Tell students that in Section 2 they will learn how the actions of President Nixon led to his resignation and shook the nation's ideals about integrity in government.

From Watergate to Ford

OBJECTIVES

Read to understand:

1. what the issues surrounding the Watergate scandal were
2. what role the White House tapes played in President Nixon's resignation
3. why President Ford was unable to achieve his domestic-policy goals
4. how Ford attempted to continue Nixon's foreign policies

KEY TERMS

Committee to Re-elect the President
Watergate
Saturday Night Massacre
Whip Inflation Now
Mayaguez

KEY PEOPLE

Bob Woodward
Carl Bernstein
Sam Ervin
James McCord
John Dean
Archibald Cox
Spiro Agnew
Gerald Ford
Barbara Jordan

"Nixon had three goals: to win by the biggest electoral landslide in history; to be remembered as a peacemaker; and to be accepted by the 'Establishment' as an equal. He achieved all these objectives by the end of 1972 and the beginning of 1973. And he lost them all two months later—partly because he turned a dream into an obsession."

—Henry Kissinger

Richard Nixon (left) and Henry Kissinger

Henry Kissinger reflected on the presidency of his former boss years after Richard Nixon left the White House in disgrace. Nixon's personality flaws led him to destroy his presidency. His behavior caused a constitutional crisis that shook the nation and caused many Americans to lose faith in their leaders.

Crisis in the Presidency

During his first term in the White House, President Nixon increasingly behaved as though there should be no limits on his power. He shifted much of the authority of the cabinet, whose appointments required Senate approval, to his personal White House staff. He also hid vital information from Congress and the public.

Dark secrets. In 1971 Nixon ordered his staff to compile an "enemies list" of critics who opposed his policies. After Daniel Ellsberg's leak of the Pentagon Papers, Nixon told aide Charles Colson, "Do whatever has to be done to stop these leaks. . . . I want it done, whatever the cost." The White House organized a secret unit called the plumbers that included former agents of the CIA and Federal Bureau of Investigation (FBI). The group was ordered to stop leaks and to carry out a variety of illegal actions in the name of "national security."

By 1972 these secret activities had grown into a full-scale effort to ensure Nixon's re-election. In June five men were caught breaking into the offices of the Democratic National Committee in the Watergate office and apartment complex in Washington, D.C. They were carrying wiretap equipment and other spying devices. It was soon discovered that these men were being paid with funds from Nixon's campaign organization, the **Committee to Re-elect the President** (CREEP).

The White House denied any link to the break-in, calling it a "third-rate burglary." However, *Washington Post* reporters Bob Woodward and Carl Bernstein kept digging for the truth. A high-level source known as Deep Throat informed them that White House officials and CREEP had hired 50 agents to sabotage the Democrats' chances in the 1972 election.

Bob Woodward (left) and Carl Bernstein investigated the Watergate break-in.

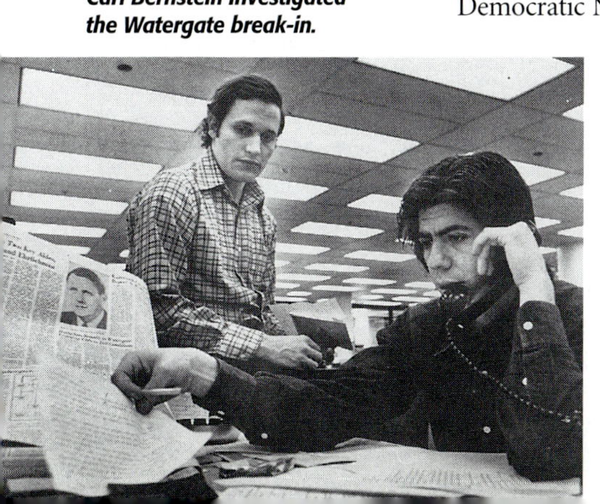

SECTION 2 RESOURCES

PRINT

- Guided Reading Strategy 24.2
- American History Political Cartoon 29: Watergate
- Primary Source Reading 24: A President Resigns
- Graphic Organizer Activity 24: The Nixon Administration
- Section 2 Review, p. 725
- Daily Quiz 24.2

MULTIMEDIA

- One-Stop Planner, Lesson 24.2
- The American Nation Video Program Segment: Richard Nixon Resigns; Teacher's Guide, pp. 215–16
- Holt Researcher: American History CD–ROM
- HRW Web site

SHELTERED ENGLISH

- Main Idea Activity for Reteaching and Sheltered English 24.2

✔ READING TO UNDERSTAND

To help students master the section objectives, have them answer the **READING CHECKS** and complete **Guided Reading Strategy 24.2** as they read the section.

TEACH OBJECTIVE 1

LEVEL 1: Pair students and have each pair list in chronological order the events related to the Watergate scandal. *(Students should mention that Nixon shifted authority from the cabinet to his personal staff, hid information from Congress and the public, ordered his staff to compile an "enemies list" of critics, the Watergate break-in occurred, reporters connected the break-in to CREEP and the White House, the government investigated White House activities and cover-up attempts, witnesses implicated Nixon in the cover-up.)* Ask each pair to read its list to the class. Then ask students to summarize the issues surrounding the Watergate scandal. *(Students should mention that Nixon tried to circumvent the democratic process and constitutional limitations on his power when he broke the law and covered up his activities.)* Tell students that the name "Watergate" has become synonymous with scandal.
Sheltered English, Cooperative Learning

LEVELS 2 AND 3: Tell students to imagine that they are Americans upset by the Watergate scandal. Have each student write a letter to President Nixon that summarizes the issues surrounding the Watergate scandal and describes why Nixon's behavior is of public concern. *(See the Level 1 lesson for the correct issues.)* Ask volunteers to read their letters to the class. Students may wish to include their letters in their portfolios.

internetconnect

TOPIC: The Watergate Scandal
GO TO: go.hrw.com
KEYWORD: SE1 Watergate

Have students access the Internet through the HRW Web site to conduct research on the Watergate scandal. Then have each student create an annotated time line that presents information about the break-in, its investigation, the trials, and Nixon's resignation.

STRATEGIES FOR SUCCESS ANSWERS

Practicing the Strategy

1. evidence that showed that the illegal actions made the difference in Nixon's victory
2. Nixon's popularity with voters, as evidenced by his margin of victory
3. Some students might suggest that Nixon's large margin of victory and the public's initial disinterest in the Watergate investigation supports an alternative hypothesis.

***The American Nation* VIDEO PROGRAM**

Richard Nixon Resigns; Teacher's Guide, pp. 215–16

Search 47518, Play to 49620
Videodisc 2, Side B

Play

Pause

See *Teacher's Guide* for Spanish barcode.

Strategies for Success: Formulating a Hypothesis

To write a successful history research paper, one must first formulate a hypothesis around which to organize the paper. A *hypothesis* is a statement that tries to explain why a situation existed or an event took place. It must be formed from and tested against the historical evidence that one gathers while conducting research. The hypothesis provides a central point for analyzing and discussing this evidence in one's paper.

How to Formulate a Hypothesis

1. **Conduct research.** Identify the topic that you wish to research and develop one or more questions that you hope to answer in your paper. Then conduct research at your school or local public library.
2. **Analyze the evidence.** Study the information in your sources carefully, keeping in mind your questions about the topic. Look for cause-and-effect relationships and long-term developments that emerge from the facts you examine.
3. **Develop an idea that is based on the evidence.** Use your analysis of the evidence to formulate an idea that answers your questions about the topic. Make sure that this idea, or initial *hypothesis*, is supported by specific information in your sources.
4. **Consider other possibilities.** Once you have formed your initial hypothesis, think about other ways to answer your questions about the topic. Then adjust your idea if necessary to include one or more of these different explanations.
5. **State your hypothesis.** After you have settled on a final hypothesis, write it out in a short, declarative statement. This statement should express clearly the central idea that you plan to present in your paper.

Applying the Strategy

Read and evaluate the following hypothesis statement, which tries to explain why Richard Nixon won a landslide victory in the 1972 presidential election.

> Richard Nixon was re-elected to the presidency because of the secret activities and electoral "dirty tricks" of CREEP.

Practicing the Strategy

Answer the following questions.

1. What historical evidence could be used to support the hypothesis presented above?
2. What are some other ways to explain Nixon's landslide victory in 1972? What evidence could be used to support these explanations?
3. In your opinion, what hypothesis best explains Nixon's landslide victory in 1972?

The investigation. Despite the Watergate break-in, Nixon won re-election in 1972 by a landslide. By the spring of 1973 both the executive and the legislative branches of government were investigating the charges of criminal activities and the attempted cover-up. Senator Sam Ervin of North Carolina led the Senate investigation into the scandal known as **Watergate**. One of the witnesses was James McCord, a former CIA agent who had taken part in the Watergate break-in. McCord admitted that top White House officials had helped plan the break-in. He linked the cover-up to "the very highest levels of the White House." McCord's admissions broke the case wide open.

The biggest bombshells were yet to come, however. In May 1973 live television coverage of the Senate hearings began. Across the nation millions of Americans watched as senators grilled witnesses and compiled evidence of official misconduct. Several top White House officials were eventually convicted in criminal trials and sent to jail. However, Nixon's role in Watergate remained unclear. Time and again, Howard Baker of Tennessee, a key member of the Senate committee, asked, "What did the president know and when did he know it?"

SPOTLIGHT on Woodward and Bernstein

Have students find and read Woodward and Bernstein's *Washington Post* articles that exposed the White House/CREEP plot. Have each student write an essay in response to the articles. Encourage students to think about the following questions as they write: How might citizens have reacted to the articles? Were the reporters justified in writing the articles? How might things have been different for the United States if Woodward and Bernstein had not written the articles? Ask volunteers to read their essays to the class.
Block Scheduling

TEACH OBJECTIVE 2

LEVEL 1: Ask students to list the events surrounding the release of the White House tapes and Nixon's resignation. Compile a list of students' responses on the chalkboard. *(Students should mention that Nixon claimed executive privilege, refused to release the tapes, had the special prosecutor fired, released some tapes, was forced by the Supreme Court to turn over all the tapes, and finally resigned. Students should note that the tapes were the key to proving Nixon's involvement in the cover-up.)* Then have each student write a series of newspaper headlines covering the events listed on the chalkboard.
Sheltered English

In June 1973 Nixon's former White House attorney John Dean provided the stunning answer. The president had been directly involved in the cover-up.

✔ **READING CHECK:** What were the issues surrounding the Watergate scandal?

The Nixon Resignation

President Nixon denied John Dean's charges. There seemed to be no way to prove that Dean was telling the truth. Then, in a surprising turn of events, another witness testified that Nixon had secretly tape-recorded his conversations in the White House.

The White House tapes. Investigators believed that the tapes would reveal the truth about Watergate. A battle for control of the tapes followed. The Justice Department's special prosecutor, Archibald Cox, demanded that the president turn over the tapes. Nixon refused. Citing executive privilege, he claimed that releasing the tapes would endanger national security.

In the midst of the controversy over the tapes, in October 1973 Vice President Spiro Agnew was charged with income tax evasion. Agnew pleaded no contest and resigned on October 10 in exchange for reduced punishment. Nixon then nominated Gerald Ford, the Republican leader in the House of Representatives, for vice president.

Archibald Cox (center) is sworn in as special prosecutor.

Shortly before Agnew's resignation, a federal judge ordered Nixon to release the White House tapes. The president refused. On October 20, after Special Prosecutor Cox demanded that he obey the judge's order, Nixon ordered Attorney General Elliot Richardson to fire Cox. Both the attorney general and Deputy Attorney General William Ruckelshaus resigned rather than obey the president. The task of firing Cox fell to Solicitor General Robert Bork, who complied. This series of events, known as the **Saturday Night Massacre**, outraged the public and led to calls to impeach Nixon. In his own defense, Nixon declared, "People have the right to know whether or not their President is a crook. Well, I am not a crook." Partly as a result of these events, in 1978 Congress authorized the appointment of investigators called independent counsels to conduct investigations into high crimes by top government officials.

Final days. Nixon eventually agreed to release some of the White House tapes, but he resisted turning over the entire set. Not until July 1974, when the Supreme Court rejected Nixon's argument of executive privilege, did Nixon abandon his efforts to keep the tapes. About the same time that the Court announced its ruling, the House Judiciary Committee held nationally televised debates on whether to impeach Nixon. Among the members who favored impeachment was Representative Barbara Jordan, a first-term Democrat from Texas.

CONSTITUTIONAL HERITAGE

***United States* v. *Richard M. Nixon*.** In the case of *United States* v. *Richard M. Nixon*, the president's attorneys argued that the courts lacked the authority to tell Nixon what to do with the White House tapes. Nixon's lawyers characterized the struggle for the tapes as a dispute within the executive branch between the president and the special prosecutor. They also claimed that as president, Nixon had certain privileges that protected him from the courts. While agreeing that executive privilege existed, the court ruled that the special prosecutor had established the need for the tapes and that the president had to hand over evidence to be used in criminal proceedings.

CRITICAL THINKING Why might Americans treat presidential claims to executive privilege with skepticism?

ANSWER: Students might point out that for a democracy to function, government must be as open as possible in its affairs.

LEVEL 2: Tell students to imagine that they are reporters and that President Nixon has just resigned. Have each student write a newspaper article summarizing the role that the White House tapes played in Nixon's resignation. *(See the Level 1 activity for the correct role.)* Have volunteers read their articles to the class.

LEVEL 3: Tell students to imagine that they are radio journalists and that President Nixon has just resigned. Pair students and have each pair write a script for a discussion about the role that the White House tapes played in President Nixon's resignation. *(See the Level 1 lesson for the correct role.)* Ask students to conduct their discussion for the class. **Cooperative Learning**

▶ASSIGNMENT *Have each student write a paper analyzing the public's perceptions of government after Watergate. Tell students to trace public sentiment immediately following Watergate through the present. Tell students to pay particular attention to what the Clinton impeachment seemed to indicate about the public's changing attitude toward government officials.*

HISTORY MAKERS SPEAK

Richard Nixon in *Public Papers of the Presidents of the United States*

Nixon's Farewell. Nixon made a farewell speech to the White House staff on the morning of August 9, 1974. "Sure, we have done some things wrong in this Administration, and the top man always takes the responsibility, and I have never ducked it. But I want to say one thing: We can be proud of it—5 1/2 years. No man or no woman came into this Administration and left it with more of this world's goods than when he came in. No man or no woman ever profited at the public expense or the public till. That tells something about you. Mistakes, yes. But for personal gain, never."

CRITICAL THINKING How does Nixon seem to define wrongdoing in this speech?

ANSWER: Students might point out that while Nixon describes wrongdoing as involving personal financial gain at public expense—a definition that excludes his Watergate actions.

VISUAL RECORD ANSWER

Students might suggest that Nixon's expression was inappropriate for the occasion.

Read More About It

Free Find:
Barbara Jordan
After reading about Barbara Jordan on the Holt Researcher CD–ROM, write a script for a short play that illustrates Jordan's accomplishments and the obstacles she overcame.

Barbara Jordan

Barbara Jordan brought a strong sense of moral authority to the Democratic Party. Born in 1936, she grew up in Houston. She excelled in school and eventually received a law degree from Boston University. In 1966 Jordan became the first African American woman elected to the Texas state senate. Her tireless efforts on behalf of social reform won praise from President Lyndon Johnson. He noted, "She proved that black is beautiful before we knew what it meant."

In 1972 Jordan was elected to the U.S. House of Representatives. She soon gained a reputation as a skilled legislator and brilliant public speaker. On July 25, 1974, she explained why she supported impeachment.

> **"'We the people'—it is a very eloquent beginning. But when the Constitution of the United States was completed on the seventeenth of September in 1787, I was not included in that 'We the People.' . . . But through the process of amendment, interpretation and court decision, I have finally been included in 'We the People.' . . . My faith in the Constitution is whole. It is complete. . . . I am not going to sit here and be an idle spectator to the . . . destruction of the Constitution."**

Despite her outstanding record in Congress, Jordan announced in 1977 that she would not run for a fourth term. She accepted a teaching position at the University of Texas at Austin. Jordan became one of the most popular instructors at the university's Lyndon B. Johnson School of Public Affairs. She was inducted into the National Women's Hall of Fame in 1990. Jordan died in 1996.

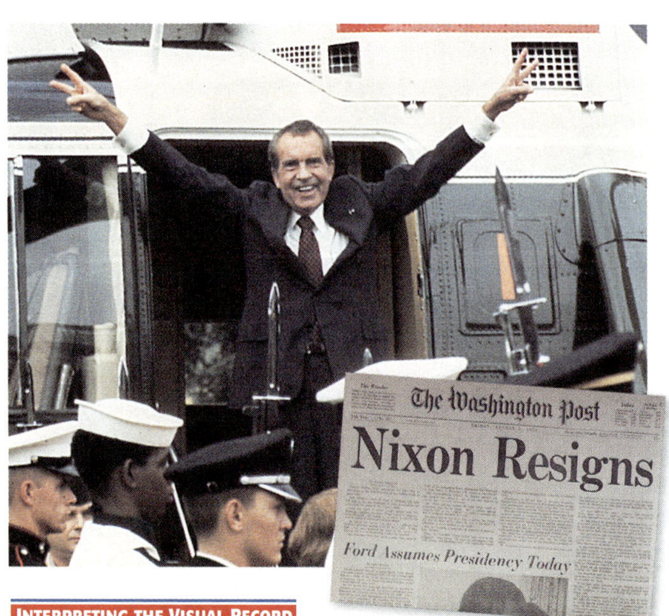

INTERPRETING THE VISUAL RECORD

Nixon. As President Nixon boarded a helicopter to leave the White House, the *Washington Post* announced his resignation. ***Does Nixon's expression seem appropriate for the occasion? Explain your answer.***

With the release of the Nixon tapes, Americans discovered the truth. Nixon had directed the Watergate cover-up and had authorized illegal activities. The House Judiciary Committee recommended that impeachment charges be brought against him. Facing almost certain impeachment by the full House, Nixon finally accepted his fate. On August 8, 1974, he told the nation: "I shall resign the presidency effective at noon tomorrow."

On August 9, 1974, Vice President Gerald Ford was sworn in as the 38th president of the United States. He then nominated Governor Nelson Rockefeller of New York for vice president, and Congress confirmed his choice. For the first time in U.S. history, both the president and vice president held office by appointment, not election.

✔ **READING CHECK:** What role did the White House tapes play in President Nixon's resignation?

TEACH OBJECTIVE 3

ALL LEVELS: To help students understand why President Ford was unable to achieve his domestic-policy goals, copy the following graphic organizer on the chalkboard, omitting the italicized answers. Have each student complete it.

Roadblocks to Ford's Domestic Policy
- *Ford's approval rating drops after he pardons Nixon.*
- *The Democratic majority in Congress blocks presidential legislation, while Ford vetoes Democrats' legislation.*
- *Congress does not approve Ford's budget cuts.*

When students have completed the diagram, organize the class into groups of four. Tell them to imagine that they are advisers to President Ford. Instruct each group to propose at least three suggestions for overcoming these roadblocks. Ask one member of each group to summarize his or her group's ideas for the class. **Sheltered English, Cooperative Learning**

NOTE: For an additional teaching idea, see the Chapter 24 inner-outer circle lesson in the **Creative Teaching Strategies** handbook.

Ford Tries to Reunite the Nation

As leader of the Republicans in the House, Gerald Ford had won the respect of colleagues for his honesty and modesty. "I'm a Ford, not a Lincoln," he once joked. The new president, however, lost much of the nation's goodwill just one month after taking office.

Great Debates: Watergate

On the day he took office, President Ford declared, "Our constitution works. Our great republic is a government of laws and not of men. Here the people rule." After Richard Nixon resigned from office, many journalists and average citizens agreed with Ford's observation that the system had worked. Through the application of the rule of law found in the Constitution, Richard Nixon, the most powerful official in the government, had been forced to resign from office for his misdeeds.

Some observers have not been as optimistic about the effect of Watergate on American political life. They argue that Nixon was only forced from office because he made the error of secretly taping evidence that was used against him. Had the tapes never existed, or been destroyed, he probably would have remained in office. Moreover, these critics point out that congressional reforms intended to prevent future scandals have had little effect. In the years after Watergate, political scandals reaching all the way to the White House continued to trouble the American public.

Pardon and clemency. In September 1974 Ford granted President Nixon a full pardon. He explained that if Nixon were put on trial, "ugly passions would again be aroused. . . . And the credibility [believability] of our free institutions of government would again be challenged at home and abroad." Many people found Ford's explanation unconvincing. They suspected that the pardon had been agreed upon in advance in exchange for Nixon's resignation—a charge that Ford denied. Critics of the pardon argued that the full truth of Watergate would never emerge. They pointed to the double standard that allowed Nixon to go free while his co-conspirators were punished. As a result of the pardon, Ford's popularity fell. His approval rating dropped from 71 percent to 50 percent.

Ford took another controversial step one week later. He offered clemency, or official forgiveness, to Vietnam draft evaders. In exchange, they had to reaffirm their allegiance to the United States and spend up to two years performing public service. Supporters of the Vietnam War believed that the offer was unfair to soldiers who had served their country. Meanwhile, just 19 percent of those eligible responded to the offer. Some war resisters, like Dee Knight, contrasted it with the full pardon that Nixon had been granted.

> "We knew the clemency was proclaimed just to offset [make up for] the Nixon pardon, which was an insult. We weren't criminals, and Nixon was, but Ford proposed to pardon Nixon unconditionally while offering "alternative punishment" to us."

Troubles continue. Ford soon ran into other problems. Although he campaigned tirelessly for Republican candidates in the November 1974 congressional elections, Democrats gained 43 seats in the House and three in the Senate. Ford quickly encountered conflicts with the Democratic majority that controlled Congress. He vetoed a number of social-welfare bills sponsored by Democrats. In all, Ford vetoed 66 bills during his brief term in office, more than any other president had in such a short time.

This political cartoon suggests that Richard Nixon controlled President Ford's policies.

DEMOCRATIC VALUES

Amnesty and Clemency. President Ford did not offer unconditional amnesty to the Vietnam draft evaders. Unconditional amnesty would have meant that they would have been absolved of their offense. Instead, Ford offered the draft evaders clemency, which meant that their crimes would be recognized, but that the punishment would be merciful. Many antiwar activists had hoped that the president would grant the draft evaders amnesty. They called his offer of clemency "shamnesty."

CRITICAL THINKING Why might antiwar activists have been so opposed to the clemency offer?

ANSWER: Some students might suggest that antiwar activists viewed the Vietnam War as an illegitimate undertaking for a democratic nation; therefore, they did not view draft evasion as a crime.

VISUAL RECORD ANSWER

(for p. 724)

Students might suggest that the button was intended to encourage public support for the program.

TEACH OBJECTIVE 4

LEVEL 1: Tell students to imagine that they are editors of a presidential encyclopedia. Pair students and have each pair write a brief entry describing how Ford attempted to continue Nixon's foreign policies. *(Paragraphs should mention that Ford retained Henry Kissinger as secretary of state, tried to maintain U.S. influence in Southeast Asia, supported anticommunist forces in Angola, and tried to continue the policy of détente toward the Soviet Union.)* Ask students to read their paragraphs to the class.
Sheltered English, Cooperative Learning

LEVELS 2 AND 3: Ask each student to write an essay analyzing how Ford tried to continue Nixon's foreign policies. *(See the Level 1 lesson for the correct policy decisions.)* Students may wish to include their essays in their portfolios.

GLOBAL RELATIONS

The *Mayaguez*. Vessels from the United States had been seized by other nations prior to the *Mayaguez* incident. Over a period of 23 years, Ecuador had seized 23 American commercial ships. In those instances, the United States government had chosen to pay fines in exchange for the return of the ships rather than use force.

CRITICAL THINKING What international event might have led Ford and his advisers to decide to use force to recapture the *Mayaguez*?

ANSWER: Students might suggest that after the fall of South Vietnam to communism in April 1975, Ford wanted to show the world that the United States would still respond to threats.

VISUAL RECORD ANSWER
(for p. 725)
Students might note that the cartoon suggests that U.S. involvement in Angola could prove, like Vietnam, to be difficult.

Define and Identify
For significance, see the following pages:

- Committee to Re-elect the President, p. 719
- Bob Woodward, p. 719
- Carl Bernstein, p. 719
- Sam Ervin, p. 720

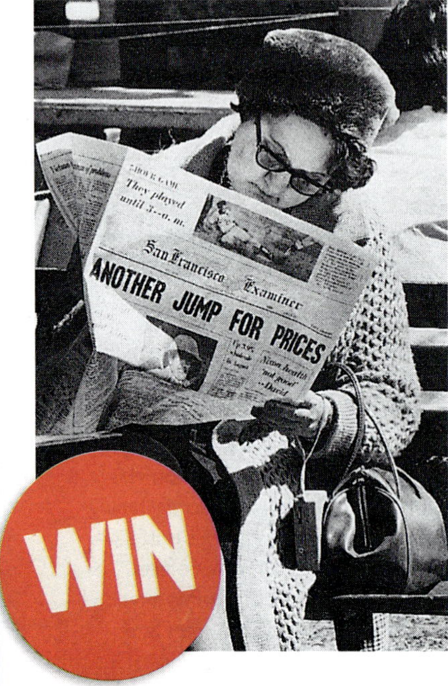

INTERPRETING THE VISUAL RECORD
Inflation. Widespread price increases led President Ford to create his Whip Inflation Now program. ***What do you think the purpose of the button was?***

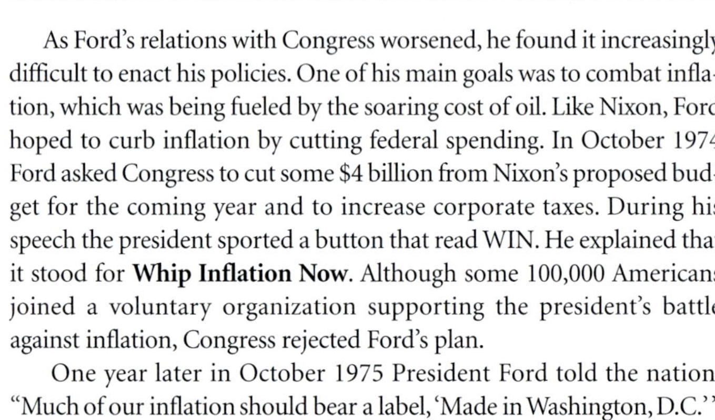

As Ford's relations with Congress worsened, he found it increasingly difficult to enact his policies. One of his main goals was to combat inflation, which was being fueled by the soaring cost of oil. Like Nixon, Ford hoped to curb inflation by cutting federal spending. In October 1974 Ford asked Congress to cut some $4 billion from Nixon's proposed budget for the coming year and to increase corporate taxes. During his speech the president sported a button that read WIN. He explained that it stood for **Whip Inflation Now**. Although some 100,000 Americans joined a voluntary organization supporting the president's battle against inflation, Congress rejected Ford's plan.

One year later in October 1975 President Ford told the nation, "Much of our inflation should bear a label, 'Made in Washington, D.C.'" He recommended a combination of tax cuts and budget cuts. Congress approved the tax cut, but rejected a spending cap. While the White House and Congress battled over economic policy, the nation experienced an economic recession.

✔ **READING CHECK:** Why was President Ford unable to achieve his domestic-policy goals?

Ford's Foreign Policy

In foreign affairs, President Ford continued many of President Nixon's policies. The continuity between the administrations was reflected in Ford's decision to retain Nixon's chief foreign-policy adviser, Henry Kissinger, as secretary of state.

Asia. Ford tried to maintain U.S. influence in Southeast Asia. Toward that end, he requested $722 million in military aid and $20 million in humanitarian aid for Cambodia and South Vietnam. Opposed to additional military ventures in Southeast Asia, Congress rejected any military aid but did approve $300 million in humanitarian assistance. Then, in May 1975, Cambodian Communists seized the ***Mayaguez***, an unarmed U.S. cargo ship. The Ford administration saw the seizure as an opportunity to prove that the president could exercise leadership in a crisis. Henry Kissinger urged, "Let's look ferocious." In response, Ford launched a military action intended to free the vessel and its crew. Forty-one Americans were killed in the effort to release the 39 crew members.

The cargo ship* Mayaguez *was seized by Cambodian Communists in 1975.

The president later claimed that the *Mayaguez* incident "had an electrifying reaction as far as the American people were concerned." Ford's job approval rating climbed 11 points after the rescue attempt. While some applauded the president's action, others criticized it as hasty and ill-timed. It was later discovered that the *Mayaguez* crew had already been released before the U.S. attack began.

REVIEW

Have students complete the **Section 2 Review** on p. 725.

ASSESS

Have students complete **Daily Quiz 24.2.** As **Alternative Assessment**, you may want to use the radio script or letter to the president in this section's lessons.

RETEACH

Have students complete **Main Idea Activity for Reteaching and Sheltered English 24.2.** Then have each student write one or two sentences summarizing the main idea of each subsection in the section. Have volunteers read their sentences to the class. Have the class choose the best summary sentences for each subsection. Compile a list of these sentences on the chalkboard, and tell students to copy them into their notes.
Sheltered English

EXTEND

Have students conduct research on the passage of the 1978 law authorizing the creation of independent counsels and Congress's decision to let the independent counsel statute expire in 1999. Students should focus on the reasons that the law was passed and why Congress decided to let it expire. Have each student present his or her findings in an essay.
Block Scheduling

The Cold War continues. During the mid-1970s Africa became a scene of Cold War conflict. Both Nixon and Ford had largely ignored Africa, but the outbreak of a civil war in Angola attracted U.S. attention. The Soviet Union supported the Popular Front for the Liberation of Angola. The Ford administration secretly provided millions in aid to an opposing group, the National Front. When the Popular Front seized control of Angola, Ford authorized further secret funding. However, Congress learned about the secret payments and ordered the president to halt the operation. Ford complained, "This abdication [giving up] of responsibility by the majority of the Senate will have the greatest consequences for the long-term position of the United States and for international order."

Despite the conflict in Africa, Ford tried to continue the policy of détente toward the Soviet Union. U.S.-Soviet relations grew increasingly strained, however. Former secretary of defense Melvin Laird wrote in 1975, "Clearly, we must shed any lingering illusions we have that détente means the Russians have abandoned their determination to undermine [weaken] Western democracy."

One source of conflict was the Soviet emigration policy, which did not allow Jews and opponents of the government to leave the country. When members of Congress criticized this policy, the Soviets canceled a proposed U.S.-Soviet trade pact. Although Ford successfully negotiated an arms-limitation treaty during a summit meeting in the Soviet Union, the Senate failed to ratify it.

INTERPRETING THE VISUAL RECORD
Angola. President Ford supported the anticommunist National Front in Angola's civil war. ***What does this cartoon suggest about U.S. involvement in the war?***

✔ **READING CHECK:** How did Ford attempt to continue Nixon's foreign policies?

SECTION 2 REVIEW

Define and explain the significance of the following terms:
Committee to Re-elect the President
Watergate
Saturday Night Massacre
Whip Inflation Now
Mayaguez

Identify and explain the significance of the following individuals:
Bob Woodward
Carl Bernstein
Sam Ervin
James McCord
John Dean
Archibald Cox
Spiro Agnew
Gerald Ford
Barbara Jordan

1. **Using Graphic Organizers** Copy the graphic below. Use it to explain the major events of the Watergate scandal.

1. Crime
2. Cover-Up
3. Investigation
4. Nixon's Response
5. The Court Ruling
6. The Resignation

2. **Taking a Stand** Do you agree with the Supreme Court ruling that required President Nixon to turn over the White House tapes? Why or why not?
3. **Analyzing** Did responsibility for the failure to manage the economy lie with President Ford or with Congress? Explain your answer.
4. **Using Historical Imagination** Imagine that you are a State Department official. How would you have advised President Ford to respond to the seizure of the *Mayaguez?*

Critical Thinking

5. How do you rate Gerald Ford's performance as president?
Consider:
- Watergate's effect on public attitudes toward government
- Ford's relations with Congress
- Ford's handling of foreign-policy problems

- Watergate, p. 720
- James McCord, p. 720
- John Dean, p. 721
- Archibald Cox, p. 721
- Spiro Agnew, p. 721
- Gerald Ford, p. 721
- Saturday Night Massacre, p. 721
- Barbara Jordan, p. 721
- Whip Inflation Now, p. 724
- *Mayaguez,* p. 724

1. crime–Watergate break-in, dirty campaign tricks; cover-up–Nixon's denial of involvement; investigation–reporters Woodward and Bernstein, congressional committees; Nixon's response–executive privilege to prevent release of the White House tapes; Court ruling–Nixon could not claim executive privilege; resignation–facing impeachment, Nixon resigned

2. Answers will vary. Some students might agree with the Supreme Court, on the grounds that Nixon invoked executive privilege in an attempt to hide his wrongdoing–not in the interests of national security, as he had claimed.

3. Answers will vary. Some students might note that Congress refused to support Ford's efforts to curb inflation.

4. Answers will vary. Some students might advise the president not to take military action because of its potential cost in human lives.

5. Answers will vary. Students should take into consideration the difficulties Ford faced.

SECTION 3

After completing Section 3, students should be able to:

OBJECTIVE 1 *State why voters thought that Jimmy Carter was a different kind of politician.*

OBJECTIVE 2 *Explain how President Carter's handling of domestic issues caused some Americans to lose faith in his administration.*

OBJECTIVE 3 *Contrast Carter's foreign policy with Nixon's and Ford's.*

OBJECTIVE 4 *Analyze how Carter weakened U.S.-Soviet relations, and relate how he helped achieve peace in the Middle East.*

LET'S GET STARTED!

As students enter the classroom, tell them to note the section's title and think about why a politician might be labeled an outsider. Tell students that many politicians who run for office today depict themselves as outsiders. Ask students to list a few reasons why politicians might believe that the "outsider" label is politically advantageous. Have volunteers share their responses with the class. Tell students that in Section 3 they will learn about the presidency of Jimmy Carter.

SECTION 3 RESOURCES

PRINT
- Guided Reading Strategy 24.3
- Geography Activity 24: Southern Africa in the 1970s
- Section 3 Review, p. 731
- Daily Quiz 24.3

MULTIMEDIA
- One-Stop Planner, Lesson 24.3
- Holt Researcher: American History CD–ROM

SHELTERED ENGLISH
- Main Idea Activity for Reteaching and Sheltered English 24.3

✔ READING TO UNDERSTAND
To help students master the section objectives, have them answer the **READING CHECKS** and complete **Guided Reading Strategy 24.3** as they read the section.

Carter: The Outsider as President

OBJECTIVES

Read to understand:
1. why voters thought that Jimmy Carter was a different kind of politician
2. how President Carter's handling of domestic issues caused some Americans to lose faith in his administration
3. how Carter's foreign policy differed from that of Nixon and Ford
4. how Carter weakened U.S.-Soviet relations, and how he helped achieve peace in the Middle East

KEY TERMS

National Energy Act
Department of Energy
Three Mile Island accident
Panama Canal Treaties
apartheid
Camp David Accords

KEY PEOPLE

Jimmy Carter
Anwar Sadat
Menachem Begin

"Carter has figured out a couple of very important things. What national leaders and other candidates perceive as a political crisis is actually a spiritual crisis, and that more symbolic communication is the best way to reach Americans drifting in an atmosphere saturated with instant communication."

—Richard Reeves

Journalist Richard Reeves evaluated Jimmy Carter, a candidate for the Democratic Party's nomination for president, in a March 1976 magazine article. Frustrated by Watergate, Americans sought a different kind of leader, one who emphasized the values of honesty and openness.

CHALLENGING LEADERSHIP FOR CHALLENGING TIMES
CARTER ★ MONDALE
FOR PRESIDENT ★ FOR VICE PRESIDENT

1976 campaign poster

The Election of 1976

At the 1976 Republican national convention, Gerald Ford narrowly won the party's nomination for president over his more conservative challenger, Ronald Reagan of California. Ford chose conservative senator Bob Dole of Kansas as his running mate.

At the Democratic convention, former Georgia governor Jimmy Carter won his party's nomination. Senator Walter Mondale of Minnesota was his running mate. Little known outside the South, Carter ran as a Washington outsider untouched by Watergate. Central to his campaign was the idea of a new approach to government. Carter promised, "I will never lie to you; I will never mislead you." He noted that he was a born-again Christian whose religious beliefs strongly shaped his politics. During the campaign Carter pledged to make the government decent, honest, and trustworthy. The election was close, however. Carter won by capturing 297 electoral votes to Ford's 240.

On Inauguration Day the new president and his family walked down Pennsylvania Avenue to the White House instead of riding in a limousine. Carter's decision to walk symbolized his desire to keep his administration open to public view. During his presidency, he held several "town meetings" and radio and television call-in sessions to keep in touch with the people.

Jimmy Carter walks to his inauguration with his wife and daughter.

✔ READING CHECK: Why did voters think that Jimmy Carter was a different kind of politician?

Carter's Domestic Agenda

On his first full day in office, President Carter announced an unconditional pardon for most Vietnam-era draft evaders. This pardon went further than the clemency that had been offered by President Ford.

TEACH OBJECTIVE 1

LEVEL 1: Tell students that many Americans became skeptical about politicians' integrity after the Watergate scandal. Ask students why voters thought that Jimmy Carter was a different kind of politician. *(Students should mention that Carter ran as a Washington outsider, held strong religious beliefs, walked to the White House on Inauguration Day instead of riding in a limousine, and held regular "town meeting" and call-in sessions to keep in touch with Americans.)* Ask students whether they would be more or less likely to vote for a candidate on the basis of a label such as "outsider." Discuss students' responses as a class. **Sheltered English**

LEVEL 2: Have students write a short poem about why voters thought that Jimmy Carter was a different kind of politician. *(See the Level 1 answer for the correct reasons.)* Ask volunteers to recite their poems to the class. Students may wish to include their poems in their portfolios.

LEVEL 3: Have each student create a collage that symbolizes why voters thought that Jimmy Carter was a different kind of politician. *(See the Level 1 answer for the correct reasons.)* Ask volunteers to display and explain their collages to the class. Students may wish to include their collages in their portfolios.

Although this gesture helped heal lingering divisions caused by the war, many Americans disagreed with it. Nonetheless, Carter's approval rating rose, reaching 75 percent after his first 100 days in office. Carter's popularity fell, however, when he tried to tackle other problems facing the nation.

Economic policy. One of Carter's first tasks as president was to stimulate the economy, which was just beginning to emerge from a recession. To revive the economy and create jobs, Carter enacted a series of economic measures, including a tax cut. The Carter administration's policies helped reduce unemployment slightly, but they also fueled inflation, which reached 13.3 percent by 1979. To curb inflation, Carter called for voluntary wage and price controls, along with cuts in federal spending. "Hard choices are necessary if we want to avoid consequences that are even worse," he told the nation. Carter's anti-inflation program, however, did not slow inflation and produced more unemployment. By the summer of 1980 the economy was once again in recession. In a report to Congress, Carter admitted, "There are no economic miracles waiting to be performed."

Lower speed limits encouraged Americans to conserve gasoline.

Facing the energy crisis. The high price of oil was a major cause of the nation's economic woes. In April 1977 Carter introduced a complex energy proposal that won approval from the public. However, it did not do well in Congress, where significant changes were made to the bill. By the time the **National Energy Act** passed in 1978, few of Carter's original proposals remained intact.

Congress did create the **Department of Energy** in 1977 to oversee energy issues. Despite the efforts of the White House and Congress, however, world events continued to threaten the nation's energy supply. In January 1979 a revolution in Iran disrupted world oil shipments. A few months later, OPEC raised the price of oil 50 percent, leading to another U.S. energy crisis. As gasoline supplies dwindled, many gas stations closed or reduced their hours. Tempers flared as frustrated drivers had to wait hours to fill their gas tanks. To promote energy conservation, Carter asked Americans to "honor the 55-m.p.h. speed limit, set thermostats no higher than 65 degrees and limit discretionary [nonessential] driving." Some people responded by driving less and by adopting other energy-saving measures such as installing solar heaters in their homes.

In the midst of the energy crisis another event dramatized the energy problems facing the United States. In late March 1979 a nuclear reactor failed at the Three Mile Island power plant in Pennsylvania. The accident nearly caused a catastrophic meltdown—the melting of the reactor's core. Some 100,000 people fled or were evacuated from the area. Despite grave public doubts about nuclear power after the **Three Mile Island accident**, Carter argued that the nation needed nuclear energy. "We cannot simply shut down our nuclear power plants," he declared.

The Energy Crisis: Oil Prices, 1973–1981

Price per Barrel (in dollars): 5, 10, 15, 20, 25, 30, 35

Year: 1973, 1975, 1977, 1979, 1981

Source: *World Energy: The Facts and the Future*

Learning from Graphs Throughout the 1970s the U.S. government struggled to ease the problems caused by skyrocketing oil prices.

? Building Graph Skills During which two-year period did the United States experience its biggest increase in oil prices?

CONSTITUTIONAL HERITAGE

Pardons. The Constitution gives the president the power to grant pardons. The framers of the Constitution regarded the power to grant pardons as a useful tool to end domestic unrest or rebellions. By offering pardons to rebel leaders, the president might effectively end violent conflict. The pardon power often has been used to heal the wounds of war. Pardons were granted to former Confederates after the Civil War, and following World War II President Truman pardoned some 1,500 people who had violated the nation's draft laws.

CRITICAL THINKING Do you agree with President Carter's decision to pardon most Vietnam-era draft evaders?

ANSWER: Answers will vary. Students should take into account Carter's wish to end social conflict over the Vietnam War.

GRAPH ANSWER
between 1977 and 1979

TEACH OBJECTIVE 2

LEVEL 1: Pair students and have each pair create a graphic organizer depicting how President Carter's handling of domestic problems caused some Americans to lose faith in his administration. *(Organizers should mention that Carter's economic policies did not revive the economy, that his energy proposals underwent significant changes in Congress, and that his response to the Three Mile Island accident ignored grave public doubts about nuclear power.)* Ask students to present and explain their graphic organizers to the class.
Sheltered English, Cooperative Learning

LEVEL 2: Tell students to imagine that they are editors who must write a dust jacket summary for a book about the Carter presidency. Have each student write a brief summary describing how President Carter's handling of domestic issues caused some Americans to lose faith in his administration. *(See the Level 1 lesson for the correct issues.)* Students may wish to include their summaries in their portfolios.

LEVEL 3: Tell students to imagine that it is 1979 and that they are political advisers to Carter who have received poll data indicating that some Americans have lost faith in the Carter administration. Have each student write a memo to the president explaining why people have lost faith. *(See the Level 1 lesson for the correct issues.)* Ask volunteers to read their letters to the class.

DEMOCRATIC VALUES

Carter's Popularity. After reaching a high of 75 percent in March 1977, President Carter's job approval ratings slowly sank. They dropped to 28 percent in June 1979 when Americans experienced severe gasoline shortages. By early January 1980, his approval ratings had climbed to 58 percent. By December of that year, however, they had again slipped, falling to 34 percent by the middle of the month.

CRITICAL THINKING Do you believe that job approval ratings accurately reflect a president's job performance?

ANSWER: Some students might note that job approval ratings might reflect positive attitudes among the public toward economic trends or other events that have little to do with the president's performance.

SCIENCE & TECHNOLOGY ANSWERS

1. by using flat black plates that are exposed to the sun and by using special cells that convert solar energy into electricity

2. Water is pumped through solar collectors, where it is heated and then released through the heater.

Science & Technology

Solar Power

The energy crisis of the 1970s prompted Americans to look for new energy sources. Potential energy sources included synthetic fuels, geothermal energy, and even burning garbage. One alternative source that received much attention was solar power. In 1978, supporters of solar energy held Sun Day in order to draw attention to their cause. President Carter also supported the use of solar energy.

Solar energy has several benefits. It is abundant, clean, and renewable. Scientists have estimated that covering 1 percent of the surface of the lower 48 states with solar collectors could supply most of the nation's energy needs. Solar energy can be collected by two different methods. The first method uses flat black plates that are exposed to the sun. The plates grow hot and can then be used to heat air or water. This air or water can heat a house or building. The second method involves using special cells that convert solar energy into electricity. However, the cells are still very expensive. Moreover, both systems require the development of better means of storing energy for those times when clouds block the sun.

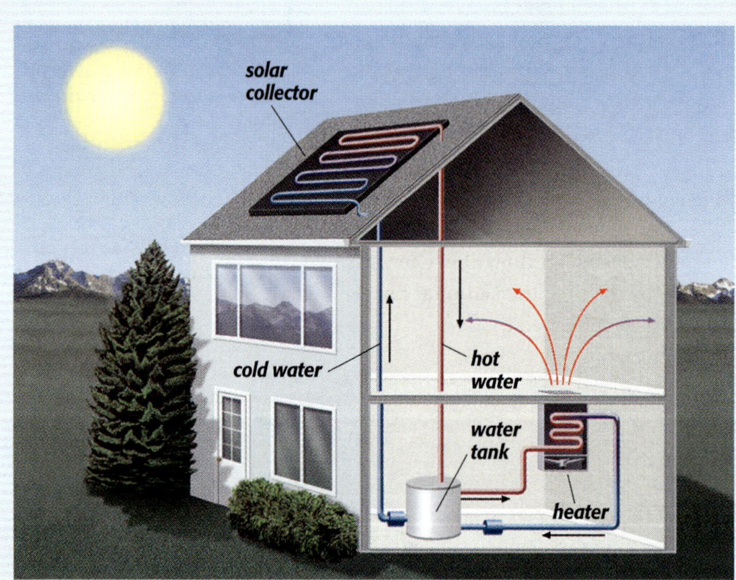

Understanding Science and History

1. What are the two methods by which solar energy can be collected?
2. How does the solar heating system shown at left work?

A loss of faith. While Carter struggled with the nation's problems, Americans lost confidence in his leadership. By March 1979 Carter's job approval rating had dropped considerably. He recognized that his presidency was in trouble. On July 15 he spoke to the nation.

> **"I want to talk to you right now about a fundamental threat to American democracy. . . . In a nation that was once proud of hard work, strong families, close-knit communities, and our faith in God, too many of us now tend to worship self-indulgence [pampering] and consumption."**

Americans responded favorably to Carter's discussion of the nation's spiritual emptiness. However, within days Carter asked some of his cabinet members to resign from office. This gave the American people the impression that the White House lacked leadership and was in disorder.

✔ **READING CHECK:** How did President Carter's handling of domestic issues cause some Americans to lose faith in his administration?

TEACH OBJECTIVE 3

LEVEL 1: In a classroom discussion, ask students how Carter's foreign policy differed from that of Nixon and Ford. *(Students should mention that Carter rejected realpolitik and tried to inject moral principles into foreign policy, particularly in the area of human rights, and that he tried to improve the U.S. image in the developing world, as exemplified by the Panama Canal Treaties.)* Then ask students whether national self-interest or concern for human rights should guide U.S. foreign policy today. Give students a few minutes to think about the question and to jot down some thoughts and ideas. Then call on students to express and justify their opinions. **Sheltered English**

LEVELS 2 AND 3: Organize students into triads. Have each triad write an imaginary dialogue among Presidents Carter, Nixon, and Ford in which they discuss their approaches to foreign policy. *(See the Level 1 lesson for how Carter's approach differed from that of Nixon and Ford.)* Each student should explain his or her president's approach to foreign policy and state why it is the best approach. Ask volunteers to conduct their dialogues for the class. **Cooperative Learning**

▶**ASSIGNMENT:** *Have students conduct research on the status of the Panama Canal today. Students should report their findings in a brief essay.*

A New Foreign Policy

While President Carter was struggling with difficult domestic issues, he was also charting a new course in foreign affairs. Rejecting the realpolitik of the Nixon presidency, Carter tried to inject moral principles into U.S. foreign policy. Carter reflected on past administrations.

> **"We are deeply concerned . . . by the . . . subtle erosion in the focus and morality of our foreign policy. Under the Nixon-Ford administration, there has evolved a kind of secretive 'Lone Ranger' foreign policy—a one-man policy of international adventure. This is not an appropriate policy for America."**

Carter's new approach to foreign policy was most evident in the area of human rights. He particularly supported the universal right to freedom from torture and unlawful detention. Declaring that "our commitment to human rights must be absolute," Carter called for strong diplomatic and economic pressure on countries whose leaders violated human rights. Not surprisingly, many dictatorships that limited the rights of their people strongly opposed Carter's policy. Some U.S. diplomats also had their doubts. They warned that meddling in the domestic affairs of other countries might increase world tensions.

1924–
In Office 1977–1981

Jimmy Carter

Historian John Whiteclay Chambers II has called Jimmy Carter "one of America's greatest ex-presidents." In the years immediately following his presidency, Carter focused on teaching in Atlanta and helping to found the Carter Presidential Center, which includes the Jimmy Carter Museum and Library. During the mid-1980s, however, he committed himself to the humanitarian causes he had championed as president. For example, he lent his support to Habitat for Humanity, a nonprofit organization whose volunteers help build houses for people with low incomes. Carter spent one week each year helping volunteers build houses. In 1991 he announced the creation of The Atlanta Project, which uses corporate contributions and volunteer efforts to aid disadvantaged Atlanta residents.

Carter also became involved in international affairs. He showed special interest in the democratic process, monitoring elections in nations such as Panama and Nicaragua to prevent voter fraud. During the 1990s he acted as an elder statesman for the United States. Carter conducted diplomatic negotiations with governments in Haiti, North Korea, and Somalia. In 1994 he helped bring about a cease-fire in Bosnia that contributed to the peace agreement signed the following year.

The Panama Canal. Carter's position on the Panama Canal added to the controversy over his human rights policy. Carter pushed for Senate ratification of the **Panama Canal Treaties**, which granted control of canal operations to Panama by the year 2000. Critics charged that Carter was giving away the canal. Ronald Reagan condemned the treaties. He charged, "The fatal flaw is the risk they contain for our national security. . . . We're turning one of the world's most important waterways over to a country no one can believe." Gradually, however, public opinion shifted in Carter's favor. After a long and bitter political battle the Senate narrowly ratified the treaties in 1978. In Latin America, where U.S. control of the canal had long been a sore point, the treaties met with general approval.

President Carter's stance on the Panama Canal issue signaled a more flexible approach to relations with

Panamanian students protest U.S. control of the Panama Canal.

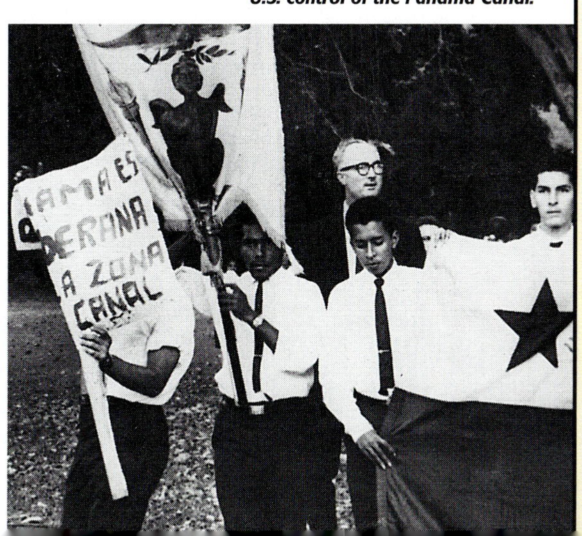

CONSTITUTIONAL HERITAGE

Presidents and Treaties. In 1978, while Congress was not in session, President Carter announced the termination of the Mutual Defense Treaty of 1954 between the United States and Taiwan. Senator Barry Goldwater argued that the president could not terminate a treaty without first obtaining the agreement of the Senate. In the 1979 case of *Goldwater* v. *Carter*, the Supreme Court ruled that the conflict was a political question between two equal branches of government and that the Court did not have the authority to resolve the dispute.

CRITICAL THINKING What do you think was the result of the Court's ruling?

ANSWER: Students might suggest that Carter's termination of the treaty would stand unless Congress found some way to force the president to act otherwise.

TEACH OBJECTIVE 4

ALL LEVELS: Tell students that Jimmy Carter's foreign policies had mixed success. To help students understand how Carter weakened U.S.-Soviet relations and how he helped to achieve peace in the Middle East, copy the graphic organizer at right on the chalkboard, omitting the italicized answers. Have each student complete it. Ask volunteers to share their answers with the class. Then have each student write several paragraphs evaluating President Carter's policies toward the Soviet Union and the Middle East. Tell students to justify their evaluations with facts and examples. Ask volunteers to share their evaluations with the class. **Sheltered English**

Weakened Relations with the Soviet Union	Peace in the Middle East
Event	**Events**
The Soviet Union invades Afghanistan in December 1979.	*In September 1978 Carter hosts meetings between Israel's Menachem Begin and Egypt's Anwar Sadat at Camp David.*
Result	**Result**
President Carter cut grain sales to the Soviets and announced the U.S. boycott of the Moscow Olympics.	*Israel and Egypt sign the Camp David Accords, ending a 30-year state of war between the two countries.*

PEOPLE IN HISTORY

Andrew Young. Jimmy Carter's ambassador to the United Nations, Andrew Young, had a long career in the civil rights movement and in public service. The son of a dentist and schoolteacher, Young graduated from Howard University and the Hartford Theological Seminary and was ordained as a minister. He served as a pastor and then joined the Southern Christian Leadership Conference (SCLC), to which he was appointed executive director in 1964. In 1972 Young became the first African American from Georgia to be elected to the U.S. House of Representatives since the Reconstruction era. As UN ambassador, Young was an outspoken and often controversial figure. He resigned from the UN ambassadorship in 1979 and later served two terms as mayor of Atlanta.

CRITICAL THINKING Why might Jimmy Carter have appointed Andrew Young as UN ambassador?

ANSWER: Students might suggest that the president valued Young's experience with the civil rights movement because of his own interest in human rights.

MAP ANSWER
the Iran hostage crisis and the Soviet invasion of Afghanistan

developing countries. Carter hoped the approach would improve the image of the United States and diminish the appeal of communism.

✔ **READING CHECK:** How did Carter's foreign policy differ from that of Nixon and Ford?

Africa. Carter's approach to foreign policy was evident in his dealings with Africa. The United States and the Soviet Union had been competing for influence among the continent's newly independent states. Carter tried to win friends among African nations by helping them sort out problems in their own way. One Carter official noted, "It is not a sign of weakness to recognize that we alone cannot dictate events elsewhere. It is rather a sign of maturity in a complex world."

Carter's ambassador to the United Nations, former civil rights activist Andrew Young, criticized imperialism in Africa. Young condemned South Africa's policy of **apartheid**, in which the white minority ruled and the black majority had few rights. Young also spoke out in favor of black majority rule in Rhodesia—present-day Zimbabwe. Conservative members of Congress attacked Carter's Africa policy. African leaders such as Kenneth Kaunda, however, asserted that Carter had "brought a breath of fresh air to our troubled world."

Conflicts in the Middle East, 1948–1981

Learning from Maps Growing U.S. dependence on foreign oil required good relations with oil-producing Arab states, a situation complicated by hostility between the Arabs and Israelis.

LOCATION Not all conflicts in the Middle East were between Arabs and Israelis. According to the map, what other conflicts began in 1979?

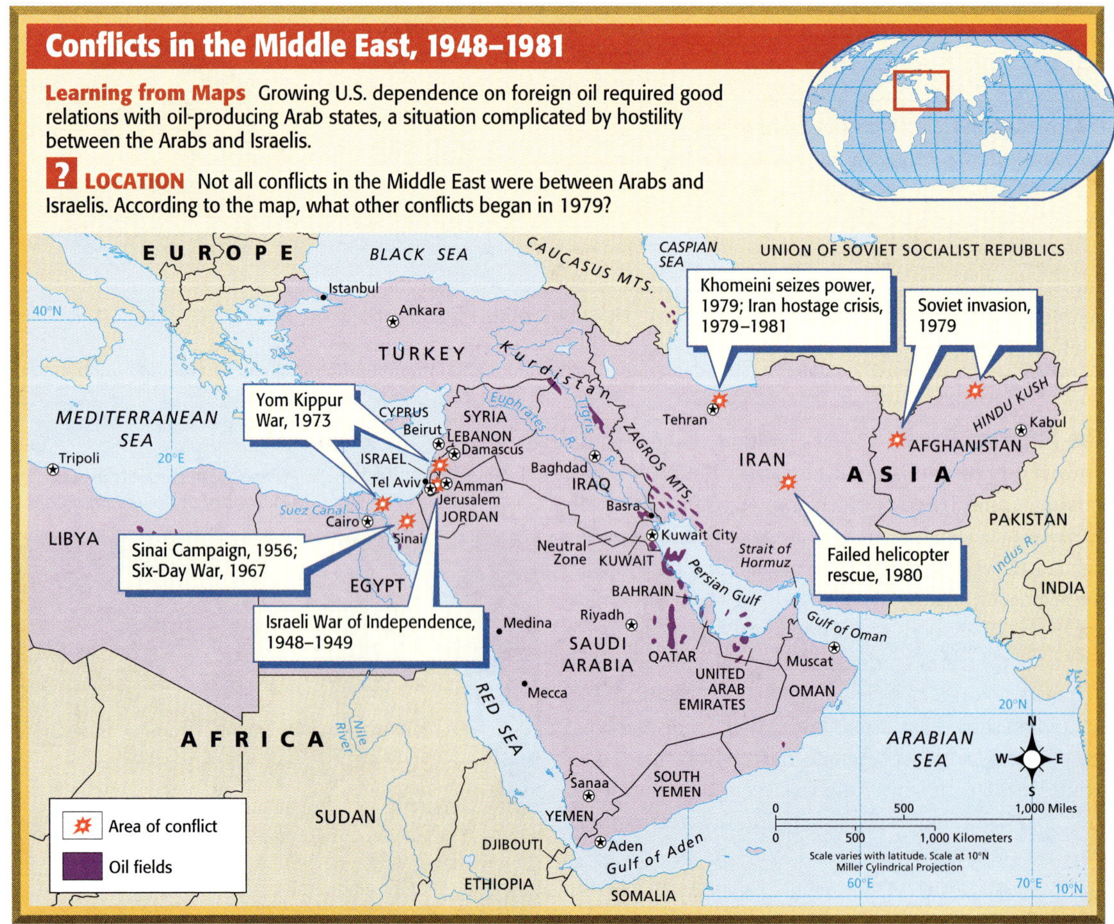

REVIEW

Have students complete the **Section 3 Review** on p. 731.

ASSESS

Have students complete **Daily Quiz 24.3**. As **Alternative Assessment**, you may want to use the Carter domestic-policy graphic organizer or the Carter, Nixon, and Ford dialogue in this section's lessons.

RETEACH

Have students complete **Main Idea Activity for Reteaching and Sheltered English 24.3**. Assign each student one of the objectives in this section. Direct each student to write a question and answer pertaining to his or her assigned objective. Collect the questions and answers and use them to review and quiz the class. **Sheltered English**

EXTEND

Have students conduct research on the transfer of the Panama Canal to Panamanian control that began in 1978. Have each student write a report on the transfer and its effect or potential effect on international relations as well as on shipping and maintenance of the canal. Tell students to conclude their reports by assessing whether the Panama Canal Treaties will benefit or harm the United States's long-term interests. **Block Scheduling**

U.S.-Soviet relations. The decline of détente that had taken place during the Ford administration continued during Carter's presidency. The U.S.-Soviet relationship reached its low point in December 1979. That month Soviet troops invaded the country of Afghanistan to install a pro-Soviet leader. This invasion put Soviet troops within striking distance of major oil routes. Carter warned the Soviets to withdraw from Afghanistan. When they refused, he cut grain sales to the Soviet Union and announced a boycott of the 1980 Summer Olympics in Moscow. Many Americans did not support the decision to boycott the Olympics. Congress also postponed the signing of a key U.S.-Soviet arms-control treaty.

Anwar Sadat (left), President Carter, and Menachem Begin (right) sign the Camp David Accords.

Carter and the Middle East. Not long before the Soviet invasion of Afghanistan, President Carter engineered his chief foreign-policy triumph: a Middle East peace accord. Carter had taken office in 1977 amid fears of another Egyptian-Israeli war. Egyptian president Anwar Sadat and Israeli premier Menachem Begin met for peace talks, but those talks deadlocked.

In September 1978 Carter met with Begin and Sadat at Camp David. After several days of negotiations, the three leaders agreed on a framework for achieving peace in the Middle East. Their agreement became known as the **Camp David Accords**. As a result of their efforts, Sadat and Begin shared the Nobel Peace Prize for 1978. The following year, they signed a formal peace treaty that ended a 30-year state of war between Egypt and Israel. Carter later regarded his work at Camp David as "one of the most gratifying achievements" of his life.

✔ **READING CHECK:** How did Carter weaken relations with the Soviet Union, and how did he help achieve peace in the Middle East?

SECTION  REVIEW

Define and explain the significance of the following terms:
National Energy Act
Department of Energy
Three Mile Island accident
Panama Canal Treaties
apartheid
Camp David Accords

Identify and explain the significance of the following individuals:
Jimmy Carter
Anwar Sadat
Menachem Begin

1. **Using Graphic Organizers** Copy the chart below. Use it to evaluate why Americans lost faith in President Carter's attempts to solve the nation's problems.

Carter's Policies	
Economic	Energy

2. **Identifying Cause and Effect** How did Watergate and Jimmy Carter's image affect the 1976 election?
3. **Taking a Stand** Do you agree with President Carter's decision to make human rights an important issue in U.S. foreign policy? Why or why not?
4. **Analyzing** What were President Carter's contributions to the Middle East peace effort?

Critical Thinking

5. Could President Carter have had more success in improving relations with the Soviet Union? Why or why not?
Consider:
• his commitment to human rights
• the decline of détente during the 1970s
• the invasion of Afghanistan

SECTION 3 REVIEW ANSWERS

Define and Identify

For significance, see the following pages:

- Jimmy Carter, p. 726
- National Energy Act, p. 727
- Department of Energy, p. 727
- Three Mile Island accident, p. 727
- Panama Canal Treaties, p. 729
- apartheid, p. 730
- Anwar Sadat, p. 731
- Menachem Begin, p. 731
- Camp David Accords, p. 731

1. economic—failed to slow inflation; energy—Congress limited his efforts by altering the National Energy Act

2. Voters were disillusioned with the government after Watergate and were attracted to his pledge to make government honest and accountable.

3. Answers will vary. Some students will argue that supporting human rights should be an essential part of U.S. foreign policy.

4. helped Egypt and Israel negotiate a peace settlement

5. Answers will vary. Some students might note that the president's commitment to human rights and opposition to the Afghanistan invasion made better relations impossible.

SECTION 4

After completing Section 4, students should be able to:

OBJECTIVE 1 *Describe how the American population and family structure changed during the 1970s.*

OBJECTIVE 2 *Explain why Americans were said to be self-absorbed.*

OBJECTIVE 3 *List forms of entertainment that were popular in the 1970s.*

OBJECTIVE 4 *Analyze how new technologies affected Americans' lives.*

LET'S GET STARTED!

As students enter the classroom, tell them to compile a list of clothing styles, movies, music, slang words, and other elements of popular culture that they believe originated during the 1970s. Ask students which, if any, of these items are still popular today. Tell students that in Section 4 they will learn about popular culture, family life, population changes, and technological developments during the 1970s.

SECTION 4 RESOURCES

PRINT

- Guided Reading Strategy 24.4
- Section 4 Review, p. 737
- Daily Quiz 24.4

MULTIMEDIA

- One-Stop Planner, Lesson 24.4
- Everyday Life in America Transparency 31: *Star Wars*: Sign of the Seventies
- Holt Researcher: American History CD–ROM

SHELTERED ENGLISH

- Main Idea Activity for Reteaching and Sheltered English 24.4

✔ READING TO UNDERSTAND

To help students master the section objectives, have them answer the **READING CHECKS** and complete **Guided Reading Strategy 24.4** as they read the section.

Life in the 1970s

OBJECTIVES

Read to understand:

1. how the American population and family structure changed during the 1970s
2. why some observers argued that Americans were self-absorbed
3. what forms of entertainment were popular during the 1970s
4. how new technologies affected the lives of many Americans

KEY TERMS

Voting Rights Act of 1975
Bilingual Education Act
Sunbelt
Apollo 11
Skylab
personal computer

KEY PEOPLE

Steven Spielberg
Neil Armstrong
Edwin "Buzz" Aldrin
Steven Jobs
Stephen Wozniak

"Did the way in which Americans commemorated the nation's 200th birthday contribute to the American dream embodied in the Declaration of Independence, the Constitution, and the Bill of Rights? Having witnessed, along with all other Americans, the renewed spirit of dedication, patriotism and friendship that flowed across the land on the Bicentennial weekend, it seems to me that the answer is an unqualified [without reservation] yes. Americans used the Bicentennial to renew their faith in themselves, to gain knowledge and understanding of their neighbors, and to begin again the quest for liberty, justice, and equality for all."

—Edward W. Brooke

This serving dish was decorated to celebrate the bicentennial.

Senator Edward W. Brooke of Massachusetts praised the celebrations that took place throughout the nation on July 4, 1976. For many Americans, the bicentennial celebration provided a welcome break from the anxiety and stress of the decade.

A Changing Population

American society evolved during the 1970s, both across the nation and within the home. Immigration from abroad and migration within the nation's borders changed the makeup and distribution of the population. Americans also experimented with new ways to raise families.

Immigration. During the 1970s the U.S. population was greatly affected by continued immigration, mostly from Asia and Latin America. Most Latin American immigrants came from Mexico, but many others came from the Caribbean. In 1980, for example, nearly 120,000 Cubans fled their communist nation for the United States, settling mainly in the Miami area.

Having opened the way for emigration after President Nixon's visit, China supplied some of the new Asian population in the United States. Many of these Chinese immigrants were highly skilled and well-educated professionals fleeing political persecution. Despite their backgrounds, however, many found that discrimination and their difficulty speaking English prevented them from getting jobs that paid well. The experiences of Wei-Chi Poon, a biology professor from China, and her husband, a skilled architect, were typical. Neither knew any English when they immigrated to the United States. As a result, she had to work in a laundry factory for $1.85 per hour, while he took on two low-paying jobs. "We were so busy working and so tired," she recalled. "We had no time and energy to study English."

Congress passed two new laws designed to aid such immigrants. The **Voting Rights Act of 1975** required states and communities with a large number of

TEACH OBJECTIVE 1

LEVEL 1: Organize students into triads. Have each triad create a collage of images that shows how the American population and family structure changed during the 1970s. *(Collages should depict immigration from Asia and Latin America, people moving to the Sunbelt, the rise in single-person households, the rise in divorce, fewer children per family, and the rise in single-parent households.)* Display students' collages in the classroom.
Sheltered English, Cooperative Learning

LEVELS 2 AND 3: Have each student write a short essay that discusses the changes in the American population and family structure during the 1970s. Essays should compare those trends to current trends in population and family structure. *(See the Level 1 lesson for the correct changes.)* Tell students to evaluate or speculate on whether the trends of the 1970s continue today or whether they have changed. Ask volunteers to read their essays to the class.

non-English-speaking residents to print voting materials in various foreign languages. The **Bilingual Education Act** of 1974 increased funding for public schools to provide instruction to students in their primary languages while they learned English. Some critics opposed bilingual education, which they claimed slowed the adjustment of immigrants to American life. Yet, there was little question that the United States was becoming an increasingly multicultural society. Coping with new immigrants remained an important challenge for the country.

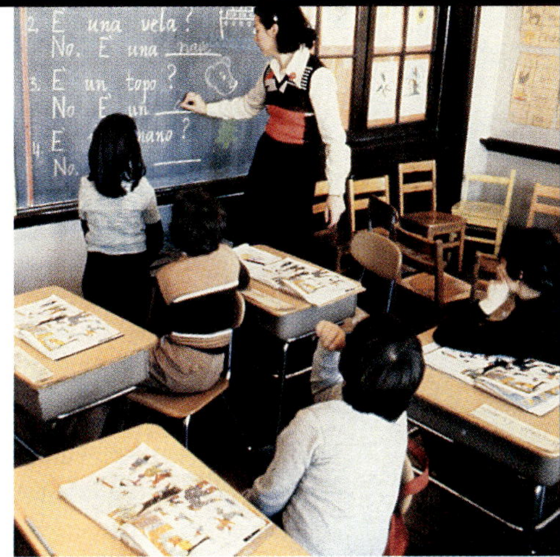

Because of funding for bilingual education, students could receive instruction in their primary language while they learn English.

Rise of the Sunbelt. Americans moved more often in the 1970s than in previous decades. A growing number of Americans migrated from the North and the East, which some people mocked as the Frostbelt. They moved to the **Sunbelt** states of the South and the West. The Sunbelt states became increasingly important in national politics. This was particularly true of California, Florida, and Texas, where migration caused population growth to outpace that of the rest of the nation.

Americans moved to the Sunbelt for a number of reasons. The successes of the civil rights movement of the 1960s made the South a more attractive region in which to live. Some 7 million people moved there between 1970 and 1978. Economic growth spurred by increased defense spending after World War II had created more job opportunities in the region. Some migrants merely sought a warmer climate and a suburban lifestyle. Suburbs were more common and more spacious in the Sunbelt than in the Northeast because of the greater availability of land.

Improved technology also encouraged population growth in the Sunbelt. Air conditioning had become widely available, allowing people to tolerate the region's heat. However, not everyone welcomed this development. One Florida woman complained, "I hate air conditioning; it's a[n] . . . invention of the Yankees. If they don't like it hot, they can move back up North where they belong."

Family life. During the 1970s an increasing number of Americans chose to live alone. By the end of the decade some 22.5 percent of American households included just one person. Men and women waited longer to marry, driving up the average age at marriage. They were also more willing to leave unhappy marriages. This was in part because most states instituted laws that made it easier to obtain a divorce. The divorce rate continued to rise during the 1970s. There were 5.2 divorces per 1,000 Americans in 1980, up from 2.2 in 1960 and 3.5 in 1970. However, the increase in the divorce rate did not mean that Americans rejected the institution of marriage. In fact, remarriage rates also increased during this period.

Attitudes regarding family size also changed. In 1967 some 34 percent of women polled hoped to have four or more children. Four years later, just 15 percent of women polled expressed that desire. Not surprisingly, birthrates dropped sharply, averaging two births per woman. At the peak of the baby boom, the average family had three children. By 1980 that number had dropped to about 1.6 children per family.

By the end of the 1970s the idea of the "average family" had to be revised. Just 15 percent of American families matched the traditional image of a working father and a mother who stayed home to raise the children. During the 1970s the number

INTERPRETING THE VISUAL RECORD

The Sunbelt. Many Americans moved to the Sunbelt states in the 1970s. ***What do most of the people in this photograph have in common?***

GEOGRAPHIC DIVERSITY

The Sunbelt. The Sunbelt states continued their phenomenal growth into the 1980s. California's population—the largest in the nation—grew by some 26 percent during the 1980s. During that same time, Florida's population grew nearly 33 percent, moving it from the seventh-most-populous state to the fourth by 1990. The population of Texas grew by about 19 percent, making it the second-most-populous state.

CRITICAL THINKING How might students determine which state experienced the greatest population increase in actual numbers, rather than percentages?

ANSWER: Students might point out they would need the states' population data.

VISUAL RECORD ANSWER

Students might suggest that most appear to be older and to be wearing hats.

Multimedia Resources

Everyday LIfe in America Transparency 31: *Star Wars*: Sign of the Seventies

TEACH OBJECTIVE 2

ALL LEVELS: Have each student compile a list of American attitudes and trends in the 1970s that might suggest why some observers argued that Americans were self-absorbed. *(Lists should mention the rising divorce rate, self-improvement fads—including new spiritual movements that focused on the self—and the fitness craze).* Call on students to read items from their lists to the class; record these items on the chalkboard. Then ask students to discuss other trends or habits associated with American lifestyles in the 1970s. *(Students might mention the ideal of simple living as well as poor health habits such as alcohol and fast food consumption.)* Ask students what these trends might indicate about society during the 1970s. *(Students might suggest that Americans had little free time or were disenchanted with modern life.)* To conclude, lead a discussion about whether any of 1970s trends, fads, or ideals still exist, and ask students to interpret the meaning of these trends. **Sheltered English**

TEACH OBJECTIVE 3

LEVEL 1: Pair students and have each pair create a poster depicting forms of entertainment that were popular in the 1970s. *(Posters should depict movies, particularly blockbuster movies; and music, particularly big-business rock music, disco, and punk.)* Display students' posters around the classroom. **Sheltered English, Cooperative Learning**

CULTURAL DIVERSITY

New Age Beliefs. During the 1970s many Americans became interested in the various spiritual beliefs known as the New Age movement. Influenced by Asian religions, a desire to improve the self, and health practices such as massage therapy and acupuncture, New Agers held a wide variety of beliefs. Some were interested in health and environmental issues, while others pursued spiritual advancement through practices such as the use of crystals.

CRITICAL THINKING How might changes in U.S. immigration laws have contributed to some New Age practices?

ANSWER: Students might suggest that the increasing number of Asian immigrants contributed to a greater acquaintance with Asian religions.

THAT'S INTERESTING!

In 1965 some 42 percent of American adults smoked. By 1970 that number had dropped to about 37 percent. A decade later it had fallen to some 33 percent. In 1995 just some 25 percent of American adults smoked.

VISUAL RECORD ANSWER

Students might answer that it reflects an emphasis on self.

of households with single women raising children rose to 8 million—an increase of 50 percent from the beginning of the decade. Single men raised children in some 1.5 million households.

✔ **READING CHECK:** How did the American population and family structure change during the 1970s?

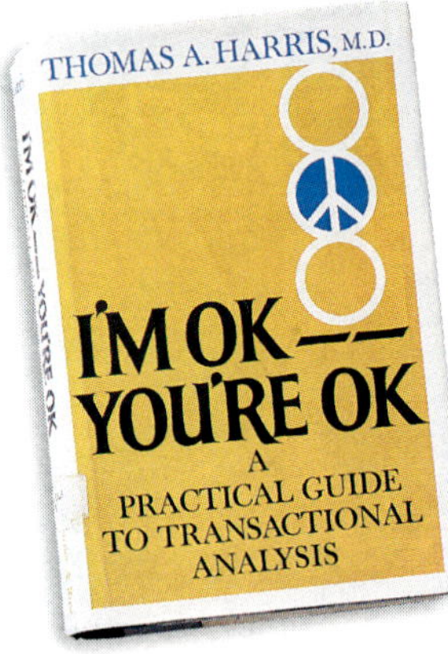

INTERPRETING THE VISUAL RECORD

Changing attitudes. To some observers, Americans seemed increasingly concerned about themselves during the 1970s. ***How does this book cover represent the focus of the 1970s?***

American Attitudes

Some observers cited the rising divorce rate as proof that Americans had become selfish and self-absorbed. Journalist Tom Wolfe agreed, characterizing the 1970s as the "Me Decade." In reality, American attitudes were varied and complex during this period.

Improving the self. One popular response to the political and economic turmoil of the 1970s was the human potential or self-actualization movement. Millions of Americans turned to activities such as yoga in an effort to improve their inner selves. Self-help books such as *Looking Out for Number One* and *I'm OK—You're OK* topped the best-seller lists. Former used-car salesman Werner Erhard made some $9 million per year sponsoring seminars that helped people "get in touch with themselves."

Nontraditional religious groups also enjoyed increased popularity. The Maharishi Mahesh Yogi, teacher of a technique called Transcendental Meditation, claimed some 350,000 followers, including some well-known entertainers. The interest in new spiritual movements also had a dark side. In 1978 some 900 members of the People's Temple religious cult either killed themselves or were murdered. Most of the victims drank poisoned punch at their compound in Jonestown, Guyana. The incident shocked the world and heightened concern about alternative religions.

Some Americans embraced the ideal of simple living. Seeking to escape the tensions of modern life, many moved to rural areas where they could live closer to nature. Others turned to home gardening, an increasingly popular hobby. Writer Tom Bender explained in a 1975 article the reasons for living simply.

> **"We are learning that too much of a good thing is not a good thing, and that we would often be wiser to determine what is enough rather than how much is possible. . . . Our major goal is to be happy with the least . . . services necessary. . . . The fewer our wants, the greater our freedom from having to serve them."**

In the 1970s running became popular among Americans, in part because of Jim Fixx's book.

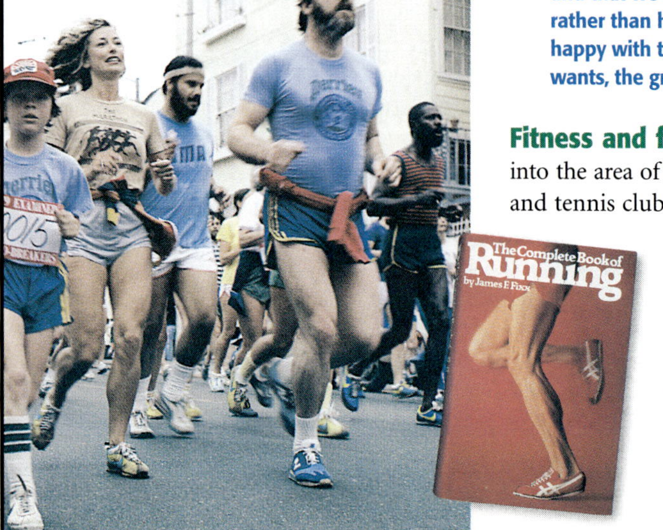

Fitness and food. The interest in self-improvement extended into the area of physical fitness. Americans flocked to health spas and tennis clubs. Sales of running shoes boomed as millions of Americans took up running or jogging to stay fit. Jim Fixx's *The Complete Book of Running* sold some 620,000 copies in 1978. The number of smokers also began to decline.

The interest in fitness may have been sparked by concerns over health habits, particularly alcohol consumption and diet. Liquor consumption rose

LEVELS 2 AND 3: Lead a discussion about the forms of popular entertainment that were popular in the 1970s. *(See the Level 1 lesson for the correct forms.)* Then ask students to explain why movies and disco music grew increasingly popular during the 1970s. *(Students might mention new technologies and the fading of counterculture values.)* Then tell students to imagine that they are high school students in the 1970s. Have each student write a brief personal statement describing whether he or she is a disco fan or a punk fan and why. Ask volunteers to read their statements to the class.

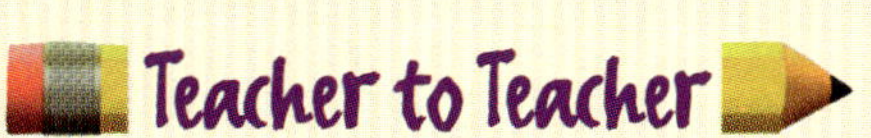

Deanna Spring of Cincinnati, Ohio, suggested the following activity: Organize students into triads. Have each triad identify forms of music that were popular in the 1970s and that are still part of current musical culture. Then have each triad prepare a report that explains how the forms of music that were popular in the 1970s have changed in meaning today.

significantly during the 1970s. The American diet also posed health risks. In 1977 a Senate report on nutrition concluded that an improved diet would reduce deaths from heart disease by 25 percent. The popularity of fast food contributed to Americans' poor eating habits. In 1972 the fast-food chain McDonald's passed the U.S. Army to become the single largest provider of meals in the United States. By 1977 some 35 percent of the money Americans spent on food went to pay for meals prepared outside the home.

✔ **READING CHECK:** Why did some observers argue that Americans were self-absorbed?

Entertainment

During the 1970s Americans spent more money than ever before on music and motion pictures. The entertainment industry underwent significant changes in its attempt to respond to consumer demands.

Movies. The 1970s brought a boom to the motion picture industry, which had grown slowly after the introduction of television. Blockbusters—movies with heavy advance promotion that opened on hundreds or thousands of screens across the country—accounted for much of the increased interest in movies. One of the most popular movies of the decade was *Jaws,* a film directed by 28-year-old Steven Spielberg. It set the standard for blockbusters of the future.

BIOGRAPHY Steven Spielberg

Born in 1947 in Cincinnati, Ohio, Steven Spielberg was a regular television watcher as a child. He later admitted, "I was, and still am, a TV junkie." He was also interested in filmmaking. In 1958 his father loaned him a small movie camera so that he could earn a Boy Scout merit badge in photography. Four years later, the teenager's 40-minute film *Escape to Nowhere* won an amateur film contest.

***Poster advertising* E.T.**

Spielberg remained interested in films while studying at California State University. He dropped out during his junior year in order to direct television programs. His first major motion picture, *Sugarland Express,* received positive reviews but had little success at the box office. His next film, *Jaws,* was based on a novel about a shark that terrorizes a resort town. Released in 1975, *Jaws* became the top-grossing motion picture of all time within just 78 days of its release. Spielberg later explained how he was able to create such a suspenseful movie.

> **"Fear is a very real thing for me. One of the best ways to cope with it is to turn it around and put it out to others. I mean, if you are afraid of the dark, you put the audience in a dark theater. I had a great fear of the ocean."**

Spielberg continued to make movies that the American public enjoyed. His *Close Encounters of the Third Kind* (1977) and *E.T. the Extra-Terrestrial* (1982) portrayed aliens as kind and well intentioned. The 1981 movie *Raiders of the Lost Ark* was influenced by the adventure films that Spielberg had enjoyed as a child. *Jurassic*

HOLT RESEARCHER *Read More About It*

Free Find:
Steven Spielberg
After reading about Steven Spielberg on the Holt Researcher CD–ROM, write a screenplay for a short film about your favorite historical event.

THEN AND NOW

Entertainment. In 1975 Americans spent some $70 billion on recreational and entertainment activities. These expenditures represented 6.9 percent of the total amount of money spent on personal consumption. In 1996 Americans spent some $431 billion on recreation and entertainment. This figure represented 8.3 percent of total personal consumption. Americans spent some $6.3 billion on movies pictures and about $23 billion on books and maps.

ACTIVITY: Have students calculate the total amount of money spent by Americans on personal consumption in 1975 and in 1996. *(1975–$1.0145 trillion; 1996–$5.1928 trillion)*

THAT'S INTERESTING!

As of 1998, Steven Spielberg's films included 6 of the top 25 top-grossing movies of all time, with revenues totaling some $1.7 billion.

TEACH OBJECTIVE 4

ALL LEVELS: To help students understand how technological developments affected the lives of many Americans, copy the chart at right on the chalkboard, omitting the italicized answers. Have each student complete it. **Sheltered English**

▶ASSIGNMENT *Have students choose a technological development from the graphic organizer. Have each student write a brief essay discussing the short- and long-term impact of the 1970s technology and how it has affected Americans' perceptions and attitudes. Tell students to include a few sentences about the ways that technology has affected their lives.*

Technological Development	Short-Term Impact	Long-Term Impact
the space program (Apollo missions and Skylab)	*boosted national pride, improved relations with Soviet Union, changed view of universe*	*development of sophisticated space equipment, advancement of a global point of view*
personal computers	*success of Apple Computer, increased availability of computers*	*revolutionized computer industry, made information revolution and Internet possible*
video games, VCRs, telephone answering machines	*added convenience, changed habits and leisure activities*	*potential negative impact of video games on children's social skills and health*

VISUAL RECORD ANSWER

(for p. 737)

Students should answer Earth.

SECTION 4 REVIEW ANSWERS

Define and Identify

For significance, see the following pages:

- Voting Rights Act of 1975, p. 732
- Bilingual Education Act, p. 733
- Sunbelt, p. 733
- Steven Spielberg, p. 735
- Neil Armstrong, p. 736
- Edwin "Buzz" Aldrin, p. 736
- *Apollo 11*, p. 736
- *Skylab*, p. 737
- Steve Jobs, p. 737
- Stephen Wozniak, p. 737
- personal computer, p. 737

1. more single-person households, increasing divorce rate, declining birthrate, more single-parent households

2. The Sunbelt grew increasingly important in national politics.

3. Answers will vary. Students should discuss the idea of self-improvement versus social improvement, or the ideal of simple living.

4. Answers will vary. Students should consider the impact that personal computers and other technologies introduced in the 1970s have had on the lives of many Americans.

5. Students might suggest that businesses targeted their audiences and shaped their products to appeal to a large number of people.

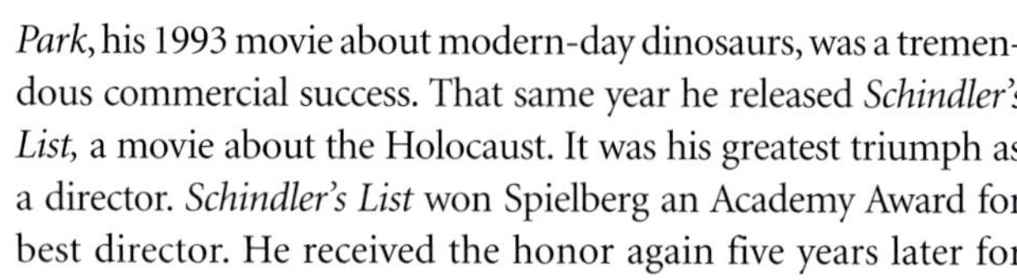

The Disco Generation

teen Life

Many of the discotheques that appeared during the 1970s offered a wild sensory experience. Discos were equipped with fog and bubble machines, strobe lights, and enormous sound systems that pumped out loud dance music. The disco crowd also presented a sight to see, as everyone was well dressed. Blue jeans and sandals were out; fancy dresses, tight pants, jewelry, and blow-dried hair were in. New Yorker Johnny Boy Musto, 18, explained his disco fashion code. "It's very important that you don't wear the same thing for at least four weeks."

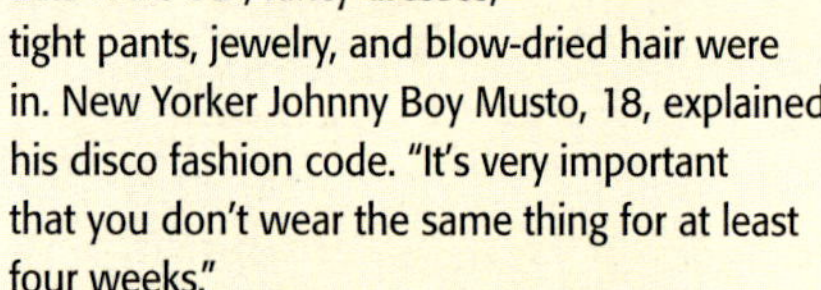

Disco dancers

The young adults who flocked to the clubs offered many reasons for their love of disco. Anibal Campa, a 19-year-old who claimed to go discoing six nights a week, declared, "I'll get tired eventually, but not for another ten to fifteen years. . . . I'd rather disco. If it wasn't for this music, I think I wouldn't want to be in this world." Yolanda Cimino explained, "What I like about dancing here is that you don't have to talk to the guy." A young beautician told a reporter, "I came here to get out of the house. . . . I think kids come here to escape the problems of growing up. When you dance, there's no one to give you a dirty look if you're doing something wrong."

Park, his 1993 movie about modern-day dinosaurs, was a tremendous commercial success. That same year he released *Schindler's List*, a movie about the Holocaust. It was his greatest triumph as a director. *Schindler's List* won Spielberg an Academy Award for best director. He received the honor again five years later for *Saving Private Ryan*, a film about men who fought in World War II. In 1994 he founded the Survivors of Shoah Visual History Foundation, a project that films the testimony of Holocaust survivors.

Music. For some music critics, the beginning of the 1970s represented the end of an era. The most important rock band of the 1960s, the Beatles, officially broke up. During the 1970s rock music changed from being the music of the counterculture to becoming big business. Record company executives and radio stations marketed rock music by packaging it and targeting consumers.

The most popular musical style of the era was a type of dance music known as disco. Discotheques, or clubs where patrons danced to recorded music instead of live bands, had gone out of fashion during the 1960s. Their popularity returned during the 1970s. The clubs featured disc jockeys who operated two turntables, thus ensuring that the beat never stopped and the dancers did not leave the floor. At the height of the disco phenomenon, there were thousands of discotheques in the United States.

Not all Americans enjoyed disco music. Some, tired of the conservative and mindless direction that popular music had taken, latched on to a new sound called punk rock. Artists such as Lou Reed, Patti Smith, and a New York band called the Ramones rejected technical precision in favor of energy and expressive lyrics. Although punk rock received media attention and influenced a new generation of performers, it never matched the commercial success or popularity of disco.

✔ **READING CHECK:** What forms of entertainment were popular during the 1970s?

Technological Advances

Sophisticated technological developments changed the way that Americans viewed the universe. The space program explored the Moon and the planets. Other innovations of the 1970s would eventually change the ways that Americans worked, played, and communicated.

The space program. On July 20, 1969, Americans cheered as astronauts Neil Armstrong and Edwin "Buzz" Aldrin landed their ***Apollo 11*** lunar module on the Moon. Stepping onto the lunar surface, Armstrong declared, "That's one small step

REVIEW

Have students complete the **Section 4 Review** on p. 737.

ASSESS

Have students complete **Daily Quiz 24.4.** As **Alternative Assessment**, you may want to use the collage or the personal statement in this section's lessons.

RETEACH

Have students complete **Main Idea Activity for Reteaching and Sheltered English 24.4.** Then pair students and have each pair summarize Section 4 in one page. Have each pair trade its summary with another pair. Students should read each other's work and discuss any differences in content or emphasis. **Sheltered English, Cooperative Learning**

EXTEND

Have each student select one of the following people: Steven Spielberg, Neil Armstrong, Edwin "Buzz" Aldrin, Steve Jobs, or Stephen Wozniak. Tell each student to write a short biographical profile of his or her chosen individual for inclusion in a book titled *Who's Who of the 1970s.* Students profiles should focus on their subjects' activities and achievements during the 1970s. **Block Scheduling**

for [a] man, one giant leap for mankind." Between 1969 and 1972 the United States sent six more Apollo missions into space. Only *Apollo 13,* which experienced technical problems so severe that the lives of the astronauts were in danger, did not reach the Moon.

Skylab, the first U.S. space station, was placed in orbit in 1973. Over the course of a year, three astronaut teams visited *Skylab*, logging some 171 days aboard the station. In 1975, U.S. astronauts and Soviet cosmonauts met and worked together in space on the Apollo-Soyuz mission. Other notable achievements of the decade included several unmanned flights that explored the planets and the outer solar system.

INTERPRETING THE VISUAL RECORD

Technology. The space program used advanced technology to successfully land astronauts on the Moon. ***Which planet is shown at the top of this photograph?***

Innovations. In 1977 Steven Jobs and Stephen Wozniak, two college dropouts who worked for computer companies, founded Apple Computer company. The two had built a small **personal computer** (PC) in the garage of Jobs's parents' house. Unlike earlier computers, which were very large and very expensive, PC's were affordable and small enough to sit on a desk. In 1977 Jobs and Wozniak introduced the Apple II, a 12-pound computer that revolutionized the computer industry. By 1980 stock in Apple was valued at $1.3 billion, and major corporations such as IBM were preparing to market their own personal computers.

Other technological innovations of the 1970s affected entertainment and communications. In 1975 Atari introduced a video-game system that was played on television sets. Within a year Americans had spent some $250 million on such games. Low-cost videocassette recorders (VCRs) changed television viewing habits. The telephone answering machine also became commonplace after improvements made the devices more affordable.

✔ **READING CHECK:** How did new technologies affect the lives of many Americans?

SECTION 4 REVIEW

Define and explain the significance of the following terms:
Voting Rights Act of 1975
Bilingual Education Act
Sunbelt
Apollo 11
Skylab
personal computer

Identify and explain the significance of the following individuals:
Steven Spielberg
Neil Armstrong
Edwin "Buzz" Aldrin
Steven Jobs
Stephen Wozniak

1. **Using Graphic Organizers** Copy the diagram below. Use it to illustrate changes in American families during the 1970s.

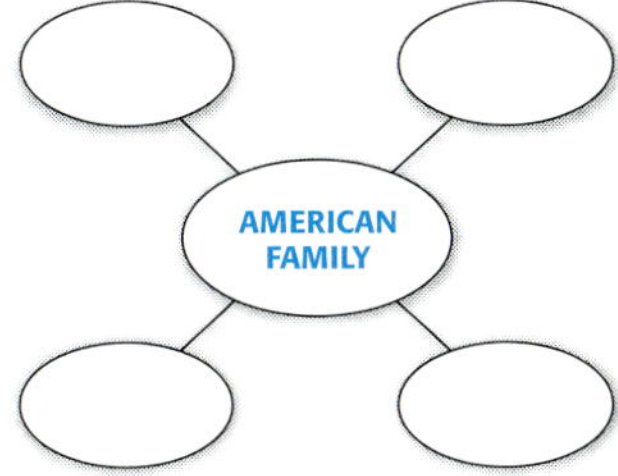

2. **Assessing Consequences** What effects did migration to the Sunbelt have on American life?
3. **Evaluating** Do you agree that Americans were self-absorbed during the 1970s? Why or why not?
4. **Hypothesizing** What would life in the United States today be like without the technological innovations developed in the 1970s?

Critical Thinking

5. How did business considerations shape entertainment in the United States?
Consider:
- the rise of blockbuster movies
- changes in the music industry
- technology in entertainment

CHAPTER 24 REVIEW ANSWERS

Creating a Time Line
Each event should have an explanation and the correct date.

Writing a Summary
See Reading Checks in each section for main ideas.

Identifying People and Ideas
1. Nixon's failed effort to reform the welfare system
2. the combination of rising unemployment and inflation that marked the U.S. economy during the 1970s
3. Nixon's foreign-policy adviser and a supporter of realpolitik
4. the night marking two resignations from the Nixon administration and the firing of the special prosecutor, resulting in the public turning against the president
5. member of Congress from Texas who supported impeachment
6. Democratic president elected as an outsider in 1976
7. Carter's energy package that was substantially changed by Congress
8. South African policy, in which the white minority ruled and the black majority had few rights
9. states in the South and the West that experienced dramatic population growth
10. movie director whose film *Jaws* set a standard for blockbusters

REVIEW AND ASSESSMENT RESOURCES

PRINT
- Chapter 24 Review, pp. 738–39
- Chapter 24 Tutorial for Students, Parents, Mentors, and Peers
- Chapter 24 Test (Form A or B)
- Portfolio Activities and Alternative Assessment Handbook, Chapter 24

MULTIMEDIA
- Audio Program, Chapter 24 (English and Spanish)
- Chapter 24 Test Generator (on the One-Stop Planner)
- Global Skill Builder CD–ROM
- HRW Web site

SHELTERED ENGLISH
- Spanish Glossary
- Sheltered English Chapter 24 Test

REVIEW

Have students complete the **Chapter 24 Review** on pp. 738–39.

ASSESS

Use one of the chapter tests to assess students' understanding of the content. For **Alternative Assessment**, see the **Portfolio Activities and Alternative Assessment Handbook.**

Understanding Main Ideas

1. It led to the oil embargo and rising energy prices.

2. He acted as if there were no limitations on his power, leading him to abuse his powers.

3. because of the Soviet invasion of Afghanistan and the U.S. embargo on grain sales to the Soviets

4. interest in escapist entertainment and the human-potential movement

5. personal computers, videocassette recorders, video games, telephone answering machines

Reviewing Themes

1. Officials claimed that the tapes contained proof of Nixon's efforts to cover up the Watergate scandal.

2. Answers will vary. Some students might suggest that the U.S. government should encourage alternative sources of fuel.

3. Answers will vary. Some students might argue that Carter's support for human rights hurt relations with repressive dictatorships but improved relations with some African nations.

Thinking Critically

1. It emphasized human rights rather than realpolitik. Answers will vary. Students should compare the results of each president's approach.

2. Students should note that without the tapes, it would have been difficult to prove that Nixon had engaged in a cover-up.

CHAPTER 24 Review

Creating a Time Line

Copy the time line below onto a sheet of paper. Complete the time line by filling in the events and dates from the chapter that you think were most significant. Pick three events and explain why you think they were significant.

Writing a Summary

Using the Reading Checks as a guide, write an overview of the events in the chapter.

Identifying People and Ideas

Identify the following terms or individuals and explain their significance.

1. Family Assistance Plan
2. stagflation
3. Henry Kissinger
4. Saturday Night Massacre
5. Barbara Jordan
6. Jimmy Carter
7. National Energy Act
8. apartheid
9. Sunbelt
10. Steven Spielberg

Understanding Main Ideas

SECTION 1

1. How did the 1973 Arab-Israeli war affect life in the United States?

SECTION 2

2. How did President Nixon's management of the presidency contribute to his eventual resignation from office?

SECTION 3

3. Why did U.S.-Soviet relations worsen during President Carter's administration?

SECTION 4

4. What cultural trends indicate that the 1970s were an anxious time for many Americans?
5. What new technologies appeared during the 1970s?

Reviewing Themes

1. **Democratic Values** Why did the Justice Department and Supreme Court demand that Nixon turn over the White House tapes?
2. **Economic Development** Was the U.S. government right to try to end the country's dependence on imported oil in the 1970s? Explain your answer.
3. **Global Relations** Did President Carter's support for human rights serve the international interests of the United States? Explain your answer.

Thinking Critically

1. **Comparing and Contrasting** How did President Carter's foreign-policy approach differ from that of Nixon and Ford? Which do you believe was more effective? Why?
2. **Using Historical Imagination** What might have happened if the Supreme Court had not ordered Nixon to turn over the White House tapes?
3. **Problem Solving** What solutions to the energy crisis would you have recommended?
4. **Identifying Values** Why did Americans become interested in self-improvement during the 1970s?
5. **Hypothesizing** Why did popular music change from the protest songs that had appeared during the 1960s and become more dance-oriented?

Writing About History

Writing to Classify Write an essay that compares Nixon's policy toward Chile, Ford's response to the *Mayaguez* incident, and Carter's position on the Panama Canal Treaties. Use the following graphic to organize your thoughts.

Nixon and Chile	Ford and the *Mayaguez*	Carter and the Panama Canal

RETEACH

Organize the class into four groups and assign each group one of the sections of this chapter. Have each group put together and present a short multimedia presentation that covers the important points of its assigned section. Tell students to be sure to cover all of the sections' objectives in their presentations.
Sheltered English, Cooperative Learning

EXTEND

Have your classes organize a '70s Day celebration. Tell students to work individually, in small groups, or as a class to create an authentic 1970s atmosphere for a day. Help students plan and create costumes, props, food, activities, entertainment, visual displays, and so on. Invite other classes to participate.
Cooperative Learning, Block Scheduling

Strategies for Success Review the **Strategies for Success** on *Formulating a Hypothesis.* The photograph above shows farmers protesting against President Carter. Form a hypothesis that explains why Carter was unpopular with farmers.

Linking History and Geography

Study the map below. Which states had the greatest population growth? Which regions were most affected by population growth and loss?

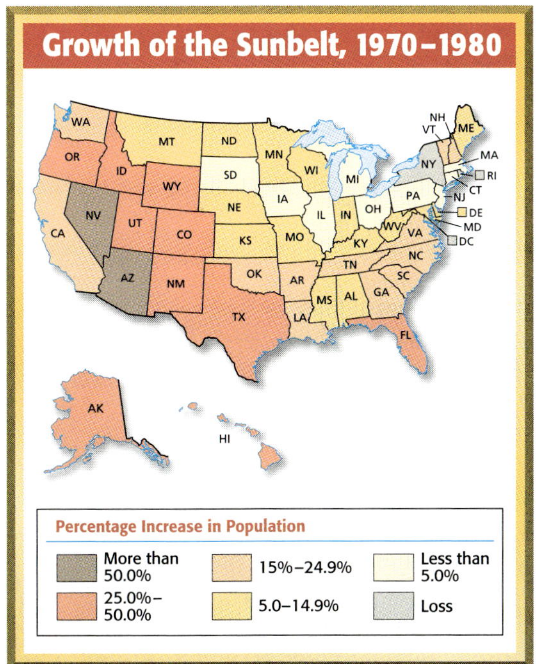

internet connect

TOPIC: 1970s fashion
GO TO: go.hrw.com
KEYWORD: SE1 Seventies

Accessing the Internet through the HRW Web site, research fashion trends and popular culture of the 1970s. Then create an illustrated and annotated scrapbook that could have been written by a high school student in the 1970s.

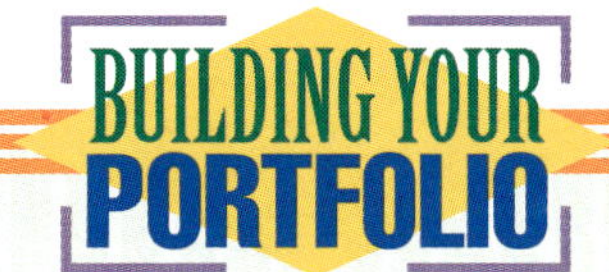

Complete one or all of the following projects individually or cooperatively.

1 Constitutional Heritage

Imagine that you are a Washington, D.C., newspaper reporter covering the Senate investigations into the Watergate affair. ***Write a short article*** outlining the constitutional issues involved in the Watergate break-in, cover-up, and news coverage.

2 Economic Development

Imagine that you are an economist in the 1970s. ***Create a flowchart*** that shows how increases in oil prices overseas affect the cost of consumer goods in the United States.

3 Global Relations

Imagine that you are a foreign-policy expert appearing on a national news program. ***Prepare a presentation*** on 1970s-era détente that explains the concept and discusses its successes and failures.

3. Answers will vary. Some students might mention decreased oil consumption and the development of alternative energy sources.

4. Students might note that the interest in self-improvement arose partly in response to political and economic troubles in the United States.

5. Students might suggest that the counterculture had diminished in social importance.

Writing About History
Essays should compare the motivations of each president and the outcomes of each foreign-policy initiative.

Strategies for Success
Answers will vary. Students might suggest Carter's failure to solve the nation's economic problems.

Linking History and Geography
growth—Nevada and Arizona; regional growth—the Southwest; regional loss—the Northeast

The Republican Revolution

CHAPTER PLANNING GUIDE

	Section Lesson Objectives	Print Resources	Multimedia Resources	Sheltered English Resources
Section 1 Reagan Comes to Power, pp. 742–47	1 Discuss the factors that helped Ronald Reagan win the presidency in 1980. 2 Explain President Reagan's main economic program, and evaluate how successful it was. 3 Describe the significant developments in the Cold War during the early 1980s. 4 Recount how the Reagan administration became involved in events in El Salvador and Nicaragua.	▶ Guided Reading Strategy 25.1 ▶ Literature Reading 25: Corridos: Songs of Exodus ▶ Geography Activity 25: The Arms Race ▶ Primary Source Reading 25: Cutting Government Down to Size ▶ Section 1 Review, p. 747 ▶ Daily Quiz 25.1	▶ One-Stop Planner, Lesson 25.1 ▶ Linking Geography and History Transparency 22: Central America and the Caribbean ▶ Holt Researcher: American History CD–ROM	▶ Main Idea Activity for Reteaching and Sheltered English 25.1
Section 2 Reagan's Second Term, pp. 748–54	1 Analyze how the Republicans won the 1984 election, and discuss how the makeup of the Supreme Court changed in the 1980s. 2 Describe what events began to shake public confidence in the economy. 3 Explain how the Iran-Contra affair developed. 4 Identify the developments that eased tensions between the United States and the Soviet Union in the late 1980s.	▶ Guided Reading Strategy 25.2 ▶ Graphic Organizer Activity 25: Economics in the 1980s ▶ Section 2 Review, p. 754 ▶ Daily Quiz 25.2	▶ One-Stop Planner, Lesson 25.2 ▶ Holt Researcher: American History CD–ROM	▶ Main Idea Activity for Reteaching and Sheltered English 25.2
Section 3 Bush and Life in the 1980s, pp. 755–63	1 Summarize how American society changed in the 1980s. 2 Explain how the Cold War ended. 3 Describe what led to the Persian Gulf War, and analyze how it differed from previous U.S. military conflicts. 4 Discuss the domestic problems the Bush administration faced.	▶ Guided Reading Strategy 25.3 ▶ Biography Reading 25: Sally Ride ▶ Section 3 Review, p. 763 ▶ Daily Quiz 25.3	▶ One-Stop Planner, Lesson 25.3 ▶ Everyday Life in America Transparency 32: The AIDS Quilt Project, 1980s ▶ The American Nation Video Program Segment: U.S. Troops in the Persian Gulf; Teacher's Guide, pp. 199–200 ▶ Holt Researcher: American History CD–ROM ▶ HRW Web site	▶ Main Idea Activity for Reteaching and Sheltered English 25.3
Chapter Review and Assessment pp. 764–65		▶ Chapter 35 Review, pp. 764–65 ▶ Chapter 25 Tutorial for Students, Parents, Mentors, and Peers ▶ Chapter 25 Test (Form A or B) ▶ Portfolio Activities and Alternative Assessment Handbook, Chapter 25	▶ Audio Program, Chapter 25 (English and Spanish) ▶ Chapter 25 Test Generator (on the One-Stop Planner) ▶ Global Skill Builder CD–ROM ▶ HRW Web site	▶ Spanish Glossary ▶ Sheltered English Chapter 25 Test

CHAPTER OVERVIEW

Ronald Reagan's election to the presidency in 1980 was hailed as the beginning of a "Republican Revolution." Reagan cut back the federal government's social programs, eliminated many regulations on industry, and reduced taxes. Reagan's plan for reducing taxes was based on the theory of supply-side economics. The theory held that lowering the highest income tax rates would spur economic growth by creating a pool of capital that would be invested in businesses. Reagan's actions resulted in an economic recovery for all except industrial workers, minorities, and poor Americans.

Reagan's foreign policy was rooted in strident anticommunism. Reagan greatly increased the defense budget and increased U.S. involvement in Latin America. However, Reagan and Soviet leader Mikhail Gorbachev also negotiated a treaty that eliminated medium-range nuclear weapons from Europe. Reagan's aggressive defense spending, in part, is credited with the breakup of the Soviet Union, which could no longer afford to compete in the arms race. Pro-democracy movements in Central and Eastern Europe, as well as Gorbachev's inability to maintain power in the Soviet Union, led to the dissolution of the Soviet Union.

TIME TAMERS

Block Scheduling

The teacher lesson plans for each section offer a variety of activity choices to help you present the material in a block scheduling format. For further suggestions on block scheduling, see the **Block Scheduling Handbook with Team Teaching Strategies**, pp. 145–50.

Hands-On History Activities:

Classroom to Community The **Hands-On History Activities** help students make meaningful connections between events in American history and those in their own hometown. You may wish to use the Chapter 25 Activity, The Americans with Disabilities Act and Your Community, to extend the chapter lessons, as alternative assessment, or as a block scheduling option.

Portfolio Projects

The American Nation includes multiple portfolio projects in each Pupil's Edition chapter review, as well as each unit review. Chapter 25 Portfolio Project options on p. 765 include the following:

1. Students will **create a flowchart.**
2. Students will **write and illustrate a short story.**
3. Students will **prepare a pamphlet.**

The American Nation
INTERNET RESOURCE DIRECTORY

To access online materials for this chapter, go to **go.hrw.com** and type in the keywords listed below.

HRW ONLINE RESOURCES
GO TO: go.hrw.com

Online Maps
KEYWORD: SE1 Maps25
- Breakup of the Soviet Sphere
- Conflicts in the Middle East

Online Charts
KEYWORD: SE1 Charts25
- Living Below the Poverty Level
- U.S. Crime Rate, 1980–1992

Online Reading Support
KEYWORD: SE1 Strategies25

Online Rubrics
KEYWORD: SE1 Rubrics

CHAPTER ENRICHMENT LINKS
Use these Web links to extend and enrich student learning for Chapter 25.
GO TO: go.hrw.com
KEYWORD: SE1 Ch25

CHAPTER INTERNET ACTIVITIES
GO TO: go.hrw.com
- Pupil's Edition Student Activity
  KEYWORD: SE1 Gulf
  (Students examine the Persian Gulf War.)
- Teacher's Edition Student Activity
  KEYWORD: SE1 O'Connor
  (Students conduct research on the life and career of Sandra Day O'Connor.)
- Teacher's Edition Student Activity
  KEYWORD: SE1 CIS
  (Students explore the Commonwealth of Independent States.)

ADDITIONAL
RESOURCES

Books for Teachers

Cannon, Lou. *President Reagan: The Role of a Lifetime.* Simon & Schuster, 1991. Presents a history of the Reagan presidency.

Parmet, Herbert S. *George Bush: The Life of a Lone Star Yankee.* Scribner, 1997. Offers a biography of President Bush.

Books for Students

Blue, Rose, and Corinne J. Naden. *Colin Powell: Straight to the Top.* Millbrook Press, 1997. Provides a brief biography of Colin Powell, ending with the Persian Gulf War. Particularly appropriate for students reading below grade level.

Bratman, Fred. *War in the Persian Gulf.* Millbrook Press, 1991. Chronicles the Persian Gulf War. Particularly appropriate for students reading below grade level.

Primary Sources from the Period

Powell, Colin. *My American Journey.* Random House, 1995. Provides an insider's view of the Persian Gulf War.

Reagan, Ronald. *Ronald Reagan: An American Life.* Simon & Schuster, 1990. Offers an autobiography of the former president.

Multimedia Materials

Major Issues Lectures: Presidential Election 1988. Video, 30 min. John M. Ashbrook School for Public Affairs. Discusses the 1988 election.

Reagan Years: In Pursuit of the American Dream. Video, 75 min. MGM Home Entertainment. Focuses on the president's life story.

CHAPTER 25

Before You Read

Build on What You Know

Ask students to answer the following questions.

Why domestic problems might have hampered Jimmy Carter's presidency?

Consider:

- the energy crisis, inflation, and unemployment
- the public frustration with government after the Watergate scandal

What reforms might Reagan have suggested during his presidential campaign?

Consider:

- the economic problems facing the nation
- the perceptions of U.S. power and prestige abroad

exploring the time line

AMERICAN EVENTS

internetconnect

TOPIC: Sandra Day O'Connor
GO TO: go.hrw.com
KEYWORD: SE1 O'Connor

Have students access the Internet through the HRW Web site to conduct research on the life and career of Sandra Day O'Connor. Then tell each student to imagine that it is 1981 and that he or she is President Ronald Reagan. Have each student write a letter to the U.S. Senate explaining why O'Connor has been nominated and urging the Senate to confirm her nomination.

CHAPTER 25

1980–1992

The Republican Revolution

Ronald and Nancy Reagan

A compact disc

Geraldine Ferraro campaign button

1980
Politics
Ronald Reagan is elected president.

1980
World Events
Labor strikes in Poland threaten Soviet control over the nation.

1981
Politics
Sandra Day O'Connor becomes the first woman to serve on the U.S. Supreme Court.

1982

1983
Science and Technology
CD–ROM technology is introduced.

1983
Business and Finance
Inflation falls to 4 percent, signaling recovery from the economic recession.

1984
Politics
Democratic vice presidential candidate Geraldine Ferraro becomes the first woman to run on a major-party presidential ticket.

1986
Daily Life
Six million Americans form a human chain in Hands Across America, an effort to raise money for the homeless.

1986
Science and Technology
The space shuttle *Challenger* explodes, killing all on board.

A space shuttle being transported by airplane

Before You Read

Build on What You Know

Public frustration with government grew in the 1970s as the Watergate scandal broke, the energy crisis emerged, and the economy continued to weaken. Democrat Jimmy Carter was elected president with a promise to reform government. Numerous obstacles hampered his presidency, however, including a worsening economic situation. In this chapter you will learn how Ronald Reagan was elected president in 1980 and set out to reform the economy and foreign relations.

Think About Themes

To help students create their Themes Journal entries, provide the following examples of appropriate **agree/disagree** *statements.*

Economic Development

Agree Working-class Americans did not benefit from the Republican tax cuts during the 1920s.

Disagree Tax cuts during the Harding and Coolidge administrations helped contribute to U.S. economic prosperity in the 1920s.

Global Relations

Agree The competition among European nations to build more powerful weapons and develop larger armies was a major factor in the outbreak of World War I.

Disagree The development of atomic weapons motivated the United States and the Soviet Union to work to avoid a war.

Technology and Society

Agree The invention of the printing press and its impact on European society occurred independently from modern economic cycles of boom and bust.

Disagree The widespread availability of automobiles and household electricity transformed Americans' lives during the economic boom of the 1920s.

Amy Tan's The Joy Luck Club

The Mall of America

1987 Business and Finance Investors lose almost \$1 trillion when the stock market crashes.

1989 The Arts Amy Tan publishes *The Joy Luck Club.*

1990 Science and Technology The Hubble Space Telescope is launched.

1991 World Events The Persian Gulf War breaks out.

1992 Daily Life The 78-acre Mall of America, the country's largest shopping center, opens in Minnesota.

1988 — **1990** — **1992**

1987 World Events U.S. and Soviet leaders sign the INF Treaty, eliminating medium-range nuclear weapons in Europe.

1988 Politics George Bush is elected president.

1989 World Events The Berlin Wall falls, signaling the end of the Cold War.

George Bush

A piece of the Berlin Wall

exploring the time line

GLOBAL EVENTS

GLOBAL RELATIONS

The INF Treaty. The Intermediate-Range Nuclear Forces (INF) Treaty came about in part because Americans and Europeans protested the buildup of nuclear weapons in Western Europe. After several years of negotiations, the United States and the Soviet Union agreed to eliminate all ground-based missiles with a range of 320–3,400 miles. Some U.S. politicians, including former president Richard Nixon, expressed doubts about the wisdom of the treaty, in part because the Soviets had more intermediate-range missiles. However, the U.S. Senate ratified it with a 93-to-5 vote. The treaty was the first to result in the elimination of nuclear weapons systems. Historians regard the INF Treaty as one of the first signs that the Cold War was coming to an end.

CRITICAL THINKING Why might historians regard the INF Treaty as evidence that U.S.-Soviet relations were improving?

ANSWER: Students might suggest that the ability to reach an agreement to limit nuclear weapons revealed a willingness to cooperate on important issues.

Think About Themes

Decide whether you **agree** *or* **disagree** *with the following statements. Note why in your journal.*

Economic Development Cutting corporate taxes will not boost the economy because it has no effect on ordinary Americans.

Global Relations Building stronger defense systems and weapons will only lead to war, never to peace.

Technology and Society An economic boom will have little effect on how technology shapes society.

741

SECTION 1

After completing Section 1, students should be able to:

OBJECTIVE 1 *Discuss the factors that helped Ronald Reagan win the presidency in 1980.*

OBJECTIVE 2 *Explain President Reagan's main economic program, and evaluate how successful it was.*

OBJECTIVE 3 *Describe the significant developments in the Cold War during the early 1980s.*

OBJECTIVE 4 *Recount how the Reagan administration became involved in events in El Salvador and Nicaragua.*

LET'S GET STARTED!

Write the term *conservative* on the chalkboard. As students enter the classroom, tell them to describe, in writing, what this term means to them in terms of politics. Ask students to explain why measures such as reducing federal regulations and cutting taxes might be considered "conservative." Tell students that in Section 1 they will learn about the conservative policies of Ronald Reagan.

SECTION 1 RESOURCES

PRINT

- Guided Reading Strategy 25.1
- Literature Reading 25: Corridos: Songs of Exodus
- Geography Activity 25: The Arms Race
- Primary Source Reading 25: Cutting Government Down to Size
- Section 1 Review, p. 747
- Daily Quiz 25.1

MULTIMEDIA

- One-Stop Planner, Lesson 25.1
- Linking Geography and History Transparency 22: Central America and the Caribbean
- Holt Researcher: American History CD–ROM

SHELTERED ENGLISH

- Main Idea Activity for Reteaching and Sheltered English 25.1

✓ READING TO UNDERSTAND

To help students master the section objectives, have them answer the **READING CHECKS** and complete **Guided Reading Strategy 25.1** as they read the section.

Reagan Comes to Power

OBJECTIVES

Read to understand:

1. what factors helped Ronald Reagan win the presidency in 1980
2. what President Reagan's main economic program was, and how successful it was
3. what the significant developments in the Cold War during the early 1980s were
4. how the Reagan administration became involved in events in El Salvador and Nicaragua

KEY TERMS

Iran hostage crisis
New Right
Moral Majority
Reaganomics
supply-side economics
Strategic Defense Initiative
Solidarity
Sandinistas
Contras

KEY PEOPLE

Ayatollah Khomeini
Ronald Reagan
Jerry Falwell
Lech Walesa
José Napoleón Duarte

"You always used to think in this country that there would be bad times followed by good times. Now, maybe it's bad times followed by hard times followed by harder times."

—Chicago homemaker

The cheerful smiley face popular in the 1970s seemed out of place by the end of the decade.

This unnamed Chicago homemaker expressed a sentiment that became increasingly common toward the end of the 1970s. Even Jimmy Carter noted that Americans were suffering from a loss of faith in the future. Reporters labeled the condition he described the national "malaise," or illness. The president urged Americans to pull themselves up out of this despair. However, many Americans considered the president to be part of the country's problems.

The Election of 1980

Although Jimmy Carter had chalked up some notable successes as president, by June 1980 just 31 percent of Americans approved of his job performance. Richard Nixon's approval rating had only fallen to 24 percent when he resigned. Many Americans were frustrated with Carter's inability to find solutions to the nation's domestic problems, such as the energy crisis, inflation, and unemployment.

Iran hostage crisis. Of all the difficulties Carter faced, none was more damaging than the **Iran hostage crisis**. Iran had long been regarded as critical to U.S. interests in the Middle East. In the 1950s the United States had helped overthrow Iran's leader and restore Shah Mohammad Reza Pahlavi to power. Although the shah's rule was very harsh, the United States always supported him. In 1979, however, followers of a militant Islamic leader, the Ayatollah Khomeini (eye-uh-TOH-luh koh-MAY-nee), forced the shah to flee the country. The new government was outraged when President Carter allowed the shah into the United States for medical treatment. On November 4, 1979, Iranian militants seized 53 American hostages at the U.S. Embassy in Tehran, Iran's capital. They hoped to force the United States to return the shah to Iran for trial.

The hostage crisis dragged on for months. In April 1980 a rescue mission failed when U.S. military helicopters crashed in the Iranian desert, killing eight Americans. As frustration over the crisis mounted, the American public became angry at Carter. Many felt that his failure to free the hostages signaled America's decline as a world power. Even a former member of Carter's cabinet admitted that "Khomeini would not have touched the Soviet Embassy."

American hostages in Iran

TEACH OBJECTIVE 1

LEVEL 1: Tell students to imagine that they are foreign exchange students living in the United States during 1980. Pair students and have each pair write a letter to a friend or family member back home that analyzes the factors that helped Ronald Reagan win the presidency. *(Students' letters should include the frustration with the Iran hostage crisis, Carter's inability to solve domestic problems, Americans' insecurity about the future, and Reagan's appeal across party lines.)* Have volunteers read their letters to the class.
Sheltered English, Cooperative Learning

LEVEL 2: Tell students to imagine that it is 1980 and that they are television news analysts. Inform students that Ronald Reagan has just been elected president. Have each student write a brief analysis of the factors that helped Reagan win the presidency in 1980. *(See the Level 1 lesson for the correct factors.)* Ask volunteers to read their analyses to the class.

LEVEL 3: Tell students to imagine that it is 1980 and that Ronald Reagan has just been elected president. Pair students and have each pair write a short breakfast-table dialogue discussing the factors that helped Reagan win the election. *(See the Level 1 lesson for the correct factors.)* Ask students to perform their dialogues for the class. **Cooperative Learning**

The campaign. Republican candidate Ronald Reagan echoed these opinions during the 1980 presidential campaign. The former California governor attacked Carter as a weak leader who had presided over a decline in U.S. power. Reagan's promise to "make America strong again" appealed to voters, many of whom crossed party lines to support him. These so-called Reagan Democrats reflected the widespread dissatisfaction with Carter's presidency.

Reagan and his running mate, George Bush of Texas, easily won the election. Reagan captured 489 electoral votes to 49 for Carter and his running mate, Walter Mondale of Minnesota. An independent candidate, John Anderson, failed to capture any electoral votes but did win almost 7 percent of the popular vote. This strong showing further reflected public frustration with the Carter administration. The Democrats' majority in the House declined somewhat, and for the first time since 1952, the Republicans won control of the Senate.

Despite his defeat, Carter continued to negotiate for the release of the hostages. After 444 days in captivity, on January 20, 1981, the hostages were finally freed—just moments after Reagan was sworn in as president.

The Election of 1980

Learning from Maps Ronald Reagan won a substantial victory over incumbent Jimmy Carter in 1980.

? REGION Which state did Reagan lose in the Lower South, and how many electoral votes did it cost him?

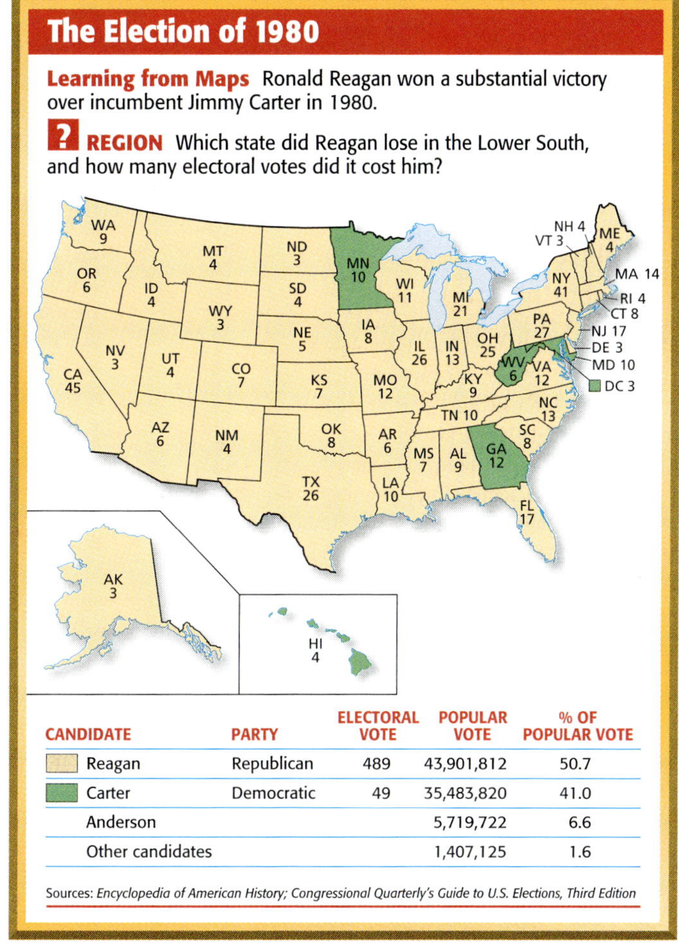

CANDIDATE	PARTY	ELECTORAL VOTE	POPULAR VOTE	% OF POPULAR VOTE
Reagan	Republican	489	43,901,812	50.7
Carter	Democratic	49	35,483,820	41.0
Anderson			5,719,722	6.6
Other candidates			1,407,125	1.6

Sources: *Encyclopedia of American History; Congressional Quarterly's Guide to U.S. Elections, Third Edition*

Role of the New Right. Reagan was a former New Deal Democrat turned conservative Republican. He appealed to a wide range of voters who were unhappy with liberal politics. Reagan's strongest support, however, came from a growing movement of political conservatives known as the **New Right**. At the forefront of the New Right was Reverend Jerry Falwell's **Moral Majority**—a fundamentalist Christian organization founded in 1979.

Reagan and the New Right shared many of the same political goals. Both supported school prayer, a strong defense, and free-market economic policies. Both opposed abortion, the Equal Rights Amendment, gun control, and busing to achieve racial balance in schools.

In addition to helping elect Reagan, members of the New Right were largely responsible for the Republicans gaining control of the Senate in 1980. This powerful political force played a significant role in shaping Republican policy throughout the 1980s.

✔ **READING CHECK:** What factors helped Ronald Reagan win the presidency in 1980?

DEMOCRATIC VALUES

The Anderson Campaign. A long-time Republican, John Anderson ran as an independent candidate in what he called the National Unity Campaign. His running mate was Patrick Lucey, a Democrat who had once been governor of Wisconsin. Anderson opposed income tax cuts for individuals and proposed a 50-cent-per-gallon tax on gasoline. The tax revenues would be used to reduce Social Security taxes. Anderson also wanted to reduce U.S. dependence on foreign oil.

CRITICAL THINKING Why did Anderson, a Republican, choose a Democrat for his running mate?

ANSWER: Students might suggest that he wanted to attract voters from both major parties.

THAT'S INTERESTING!

Ronald Reagan had supported Democrats Franklin D. Roosevelt and Harry Truman, but in the 1952, 1956, and 1960 elections he voted for the Republican candidates. It was not until 1962, however, that Reagan registered as a Republican.

MAP ANSWER
Georgia; 12 votes

TEACH OBJECTIVE 2

ALL LEVELS: Tell students that President Reagan's economic program was considered a radical departure from the programs of previous administrations, since the New Deal. To help students understand President Reagan's economic program and how successful it was, copy the graphic organizer at right on the chalkboard, omitting the italicized answers. Have each student complete the organizer. Ask volunteers to share their answers with the class. **Sheltered English**

REAGAN'S ECONOMIC PROGRAM	
supply-side economics–lowered top income tax rates as a way to increase investment in businesses	*reductions in the size and influence of government–cuts in government regulation of industries and cuts in social programs*
Successes	**Failures**
economic recovery–drop in the inflation rate, increased consumer spending, business recovery, soaring stock market	*some citizens excluded from recovery–cuts in social programs hurt the poorest Americans, high unemployment among African Americans, Hispanics, and factory workers, increased homelessness*

ECONOMIC DEVELOPMENT

Tax Rates. Despite the Reagan tax cuts, the U.S. government receives a higher percentage of its revenues from income tax than most other developed nations. For example, some 36 percent of the government's revenues came from income taxes. Only Canada, with about 39 percent, and Sweden, with about 37 percent, received higher percentages of revenue from income tax. The Netherlands received 20 percent of its revenues from income tax; and France, about 13 percent.

CRITICAL THINKING Do the figures above indicate that people in France pay less in taxes than Americans?

ANSWER: Students might suggest that the French may pay more in other types of taxes.

THAT'S INTERESTING!

The economic recovery that Reagan promised the nation did not occur immediately. In 1982 a severe recession caused the highest U.S. unemployment levels since the Great Depression.

Multimedia Resources

Linking Geography and History Transparency 22: Central America and the Caribbean

A RETURN TO CONSERVATIVE CHURCHES

The New Right benefited from Americans' increased interest in conservative Christian churches after the spiritual experimentation of the 1960s and 1970s. Christian Fundamentalism in particular experienced a surge in followers. The spiritual movement that had become popular in the 1920s continued to grow throughout the 1900s. Many members of the movement found that Fundamentalism's focus on strictly following the Bible gave them clear spiritual direction in a society that seemed to have lost its values.

Led by several prominent and politically active ministers, in the 1980s Fundamentalism became a major force for political and social change in the country. Baptist minister Jerry Falwell started the trend during the country's bicentennial in 1976. Falwell warned that the nation was facing numerous problems because its political leaders and institutions had turned away from the Christian values upon which the country was based. The solution to this problem, he argued, was for conservative Christians to become more involved in politics. As a political movement, Fundamentalism became the driving force behind the antiabortion campaign and efforts to restore prayer in public schools.

The Reverend Jerry Falwell was the head pastor at a Fundamentalist Baptist church.

Reagan's Economic Program

President Reagan entered office with a comprehensive economic program already mapped out. In his inaugural address he explained the plan, which called for less government involvement in the economy.

> **"These United States are confronted with an economic affliction of great proportions. We suffer from the longest and one of the worst sustained inflations in our national history. . . . In this present crisis, government is not the solution to our problem. . . . It is my intention to curb the size and influence of the Federal establishment. . . . In the days ahead I will propose removing the roadblocks that have slowed our economy and reduced productivity. Steps will be taken aimed at restoring the balance between the various levels of government. . . . It is time to reawaken this industrial giant, to get government back within its means, and to lighten our punitive tax burden."**

This plan, called **Reaganomics**, was based on the theory of **supply-side economics**. This "trickle down" theory argued that lowering the top income tax rates would spur economic growth. Supporters of supply-side economics claimed that people would invest their tax savings in businesses, thereby creating jobs, increasing consumer spending, and eventually generating increased tax revenues. Congress responded to Reagan's program by passing a three-year plan to cut federal income taxes by 25 percent.

Congress also supported another part of Reagan's economic plan—drastic cuts in government regulation of industries such as television, trucking, airlines, and banking. The Reagan administration's pro-business, antiregulation stance was evident in the Department of the Interior's handling of public lands. Secretary of the Interior James Watt leased huge areas of the seafloor to private companies searching for off-shore oil and gas. He also leased federal lands to coal companies.

Critics charged that Reagan's tax cuts favored the wealthy and that spending cuts and deregulation weakened programs to protect consumers, the needy, and the environment. They also warned that big tax cuts combined with increased military spending—another important element of Reaganomics—would produce enormous shortages in the federal budget.

By 1983 supply-side economics had begun to turn the economy around. The inflation rate had dropped to a manageable 4 percent. Responding to this development, Americans increased their spending during the mid-1980s. This boosted the economy even further. Businesses revived, the stock market soared, and the future looked bright.

Critics continued to note that not all Americans benefited from the recovery. Deep cuts in federal funding for social programs hurt the poorest citizens. Although

Teacher to Teacher

Denny Shillings of Flossmoor, Illinois, suggested the following activity: Organize students into three groups. Tell one group to imagine that it supports the Reagan economic program and tell the second group to imagine that it is critical of Reaganomics. Tell the third group to act as facilitators and questioners. Have each group prepare notes on who was hurt by and who benefited from Reaganomics. Then conduct a roundtable debate on Reaganomics.

TEACH OBJECTIVE 3

LEVEL 1: Pair students and ask each pair to write several headlines about the significant developments in the Cold War during the early 1980s. *(Pairs' headlines should mention the SDI controversy, the Solidarity movement and the imposition of martial law in Poland, the shooting down of the Korean airliner, the U.S. placement of missiles in Great Britain and Germany, the Soviet departure from arms-control talks, and the Soviet boycott of the 1984 Summer Olympics.)* Ask volunteers to share their headlines with the class.

Sheltered English, Cooperative Learning

employment rose overall, joblessness remained high among African Americans and Hispanics, particularly for unskilled workers living in the inner cities. Unemployment among factory workers in the Midwest, once America's industrial heartland, also remained high.

✔ **READING CHECK:** What was President Reagan's main economic program, and how successful was it?

Reagan and the Cold War

The Reagan administration's emphasis on increased military spending was in part a reflection of Ronald Reagan's strong anticommunist views. He took a hard line against the Soviet Union, even branding it an "evil empire" in one speech. To counter the Soviet threat, Reagan called for new weapons systems and an increased U.S. military presence in such areas as the Indian Ocean and the Persian Gulf.

New weapons. Between 1981 and 1985 the Pentagon's budget grew from some $150 billion to about $250 billion. Much of the money was spent on nuclear weapons. Secretary of State Alexander Haig suggested that "nuclear warning shots" might be useful in a conventional war.

The talk of nuclear war stirred public fears. In town meetings and a few state referendums, voters urged a freeze on the testing and deployment of nuclear weapons. Many Americans marched in rallies to show their support for the proposals.

In response, Reagan proposed the **Strategic Defense Initiative** (SDI), a space-based missile-defense system, in March 1983. SDI quickly stirred controversy. Many critics labeled it "Star Wars" after the popular 1977 movie, saying it was based on untested technological theories and was probably unworkable. They also warned that SDI research would intensify the arms race. President Reagan countered that SDI would be a weapon for peace—one that killed weapons, not people. He explained this in a national address.

> **"I call upon the scientific community in our country, those who gave us nuclear weapons, to turn their great talents now to the cause of mankind and world peace: to give us the means of rendering these nuclear weapons impotent [powerless] and obsolete."**

U.S.-Soviet relations. Even before Reagan took office, U.S.-Soviet relations had cooled because of the Soviet Union's 1979 invasion of Afghanistan. Relations deteriorated further in August 1980, when Polish workers in Gdańsk and Szczecin (SHCHET-sheen) staged a series of massive strikes. They protested high prices and demanded the right to form trade unions free from government or Communist Party control. At first, things went well for the strikers. Faced with the threat of a nationwide general strike, in late August the Polish government legalized independent union activity. Labor activists responded by voting on September 17 to form the independent trade union **Solidarity**. Lech Walesa (vah-LEN-suh), an electrician at a Gdańsk shipyard who had helped launch the initial strikes, became the union's leader.

Holt Researcher — Read More About It

Free Find: Reagan on communism

After reading President Reagan's speech on communism on the **Holt Researcher** CD–ROM, write a letter to a member of Congress explaining why you agree or disagree with Reagan's view of communism.

INTERPRETING THE VISUAL RECORD

SDI. President Reagan's plan for a space-based missile defense system was very controversial. ***Do you think this cartoon supported SDI? Explain your answer.***

HISTORY MAKERS SPEAK

Ronald Reagan in *President Reagan: The Role of a Lifetime*

The "Evil Empire."

Reagan regarded the conflict between the United States and the Soviet Union as a battle between good and evil. His remarks, at a meeting of evangelicals, opposing a possible freeze in the buildup of nuclear weapons are indicative: "So in your discussions of the nuclear freeze proposals, I urge you to beware the temptation of pride—the temptation of blithely declaring yourself above it all and label both sides equally at fault, to ignore the facts of history and the aggressive impulses of an evil empire, to simply call the arms race a giant misunderstanding and thereby remove yourself from the struggle between right and wrong and good and evil."

CRITICAL THINKING Do you think that Reagan actually believed that the Soviet Union was evil?

ANSWER: Answers will vary. Some students might believe that Reagan was sincere, while others might believe that Reagan had found a powerful way to define the Cold War conflict.

VISUAL RECORD ANSWER

Students might point out that the cartoon parodies and therefore opposes SDI.

LEVELS 2 AND 3: Tell students to imagine that they are editors of an encyclopedia of the Cold War. Have each student write an entry on the significant developments in the Cold War during the early 1980s. *(See the Level 1 lesson for the correct developments.)* Ask volunteers to read their entries to the class.

TEACH OBJECTIVE 4

ALL LEVELS: Pair students and have each pair create a graphic organizer depicting how the Reagan administration became involved in events in El Salvador and Nicaragua. *(Organizers should show that Reagan feared that Latin American countries would fall under Soviet influence. In El Salvador, the administration offered aid to the Duarte government, which was fighting rebels in a civil war. In Nicaragua, the administration used the CIA to support Contras in their war with the leftist Sandinista government.)* Have students use their organizers to write an article describing the Reagan administration's actions in Central America. Ask volunteers to read their articles to the class. **Sheltered English, Cooperative Learning**

▶**ASSIGNMENT:** *Tell students to imagine that it is the 1980s and that they are international TV reporters covering Central America. Have each student write a script describing how the Reagan administration became involved in El Salvador and Nicaragua.*

GLOBAL RELATIONS

Aiding the Contras. The term *Contras* comes from the Spanish term *contrarevolucionarios*, which means "counterrevolutionaries" in English. In the late 1970s Argentine government advisers began working with some former members of Nicaraguan dictator Anastasio Somoza's National Guard. These men became the first Contras. The CIA also played an important role in developing the Contras. In 1979 the CIA helped evacuate some Contras from Nicaragua to Miami in a plane disguised with Red Cross symbols. President Reagan approved some $20 million in assistance to the Contras during his first year in office.

CRITICAL THINKING Why might the fact that the United States supported the Contras seem surprising?

ANSWER: Some students might suggest that it is surprising that the United States would support people with antidemocratic views.

VISUAL RECORD ANSWER

Students might suggest that the demonstrators have anticommunist sentiments.

INTERPRETING THE VISUAL RECORD

Solidarity. These Boston residents are demonstrating to show their support for Solidarity. ***What do the people's signs reveal about their motives for demonstrating?***

Then, in December 1981, Poland's Soviet-backed government changed its stand and instituted martial law. Government troops shut down Solidarity centers and arrested union leaders. Expecting resistance, Soviet troops prepared to brutally "restore order." This move was similar to Soviet actions in Hungary in 1956 and in Czechoslovakia in 1968. Reagan warned the Soviets not to invade Poland and called for new trade restrictions against the Soviet Union. Moscow heeded the warning and stayed out of Poland.

Tensions between the United States and the Soviet Union flared again in 1983. On September 1, the Soviets shot down a Korean commercial airliner over Soviet airspace. All 269 passengers, including many Americans, were killed. Despite an international outcry, the Soviets defended their action, claiming the plane had been spying. Later that year, when the United States placed nuclear missiles in Great Britain and Germany, the Soviets walked out of arms-control talks. When the Soviets boycotted the 1984 Summer Olympics in Los Angeles, relations between the two superpowers sank to their lowest point in years.

✔ **READING CHECK:** What were the significant developments in the Cold War during the early 1980s?

Reagan and Latin America

President Reagan feared that the developing nations of Latin America would fall under Soviet influence. To prevent this, Reagan increased U.S. involvement in the region. He focused in particular on the countries of El Salvador and Nicaragua.

The Reagan administration soon found itself pulled into events in El Salvador. In 1979 a group of young military officers had seized power and instituted a brutal government. The army and so-called death squads killed and tortured opposition leaders. Fighting intensified between government forces and rebels who demanded radical reform.

In 1984 José Napoleón Duarte, a moderate, won election by promising reforms and an end to the civil war. Eager to prevent a rebel victory that might allow El Salvador to fall under Soviet influence, the Reagan administration offered Duarte military and economic aid and sent military advisers to train government troops. The civil war raged on, however, until intense international pressure forced both sides to sign a peace treaty in 1992.

PRESIDENTIAL *Lives*

1911–
In Office 1981–1989

Ronald Reagan

Ronald Reagan was nicknamed the Great Communicator because of his speaking abilities. One of Reagan's gifts was a sharp wit. After a debate with Jimmy Carter during the 1980 campaign, a reporter asked if he had been nervous appearing on stage with the president. "No, not at all," Reagan replied. Then, referring to his career in Hollywood, he added, "I've been on the same stage with John Wayne."

Reagan's wit helped reassure the nation after a lone gunman shot him on March 30, 1981. As the wounded president was wheeled into the operating room, he looked around at the surgeons and joked, "Please assure me that you are all Republicans!" While he was recuperating in intensive care, Reagan sent several humorous notes to his staff members. One read, "If I had had this much attention in Hollywood, I'd have stayed there!"

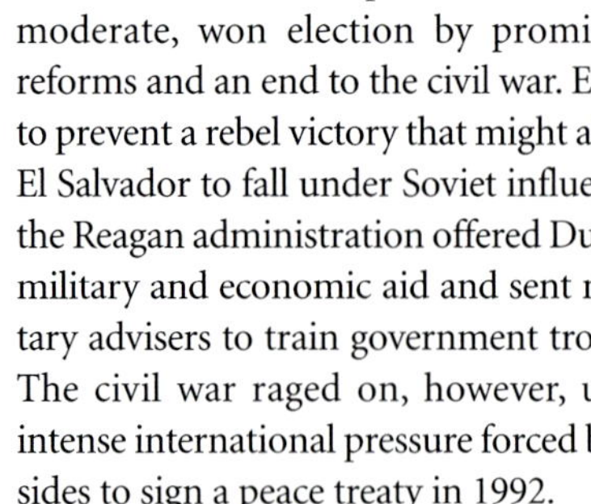

REVIEW

Have students complete the **Section 1 Review** on p. 747.

ASSESS

Have students complete **Daily Quiz 25.1**. As **Alternative Assessment**, you may want to use the headlines or the dialogue in this section's lessons.

RETEACH

Have students complete **Main Idea Activity for Reteaching and Sheltered English 25.1**. Then organize students into small groups. Have each group prepare an outline of one of the subsections of Section 1. Ask each group to present its outline to the class, and ask the class to supply any information missing from groups' outlines.
Sheltered English, Cooperative Learning

EXTEND

Organize the class into four groups. Assign each group one of the following topics: the New Right movement, the Solidarity movement, the Islamic Revolution in Iran, or the Sandinista revolution. Have each group conduct research on its assigned movement, with a focus on the movement's guiding principles, key figures in the movement, and important events in the movement's history. Then have each group create a multimedia presentation on its topic. Have students give their presentations to the class. **Block Scheduling, Cooperative Learning**

Reagan also focused U.S. attention on the political situation in Nicaragua. In 1979, Nicaraguan rebels known as **Sandinistas** had overthrown the dictatorship of Anastasio Somoza. The Somoza family had controlled Nicaragua since the 1930s. Soon after he took office, Reagan cut all U.S. aid to Nicaragua. He argued that the Sandinistas were backed by the Soviet Union. He also charged that the Sandinistas were "exporting revolution" by shipping Cuban and Soviet weapons to the rebels in El Salvador.

The Sandinistas reacted to U.S. pressure by strengthening their ties to the Soviet bloc countries. Reagan then decided to support the Nicaraguan **Contras**, a rebel army recruited, financed, and armed by the CIA. Reagan hoped the revolutionary group would overthrow the Sandinista government. He called the Contras "freedom fighters" and even compared them to the founders of the United States.

These Contra rebels are training for their fight against the Sandinistas.

Many Americans opposed the CIA-sponsored war against the Sandinistas. They feared that it would end up as devastating and as complicated as the Vietnam War had been. Reflecting such concerns, Congress began restricting funds for the Contras late in 1982. However, the nation would soon learn that the White House continued to finance the Contras—despite the congressional ban—using secret funds from wealthy supporters and foreign governments.

✔ **READING CHECK:** How did the Reagan administration become involved in events in El Salvador and Nicaragua?

SECTION 1 REVIEW

Define and explain the significance of the following terms:
Iran hostage crisis
New Right
Moral Majority
Reaganomics
supply-side economics
Strategic Defense Initiative
Solidarity
Sandinistas
Contras

Identify and explain the significance of the following individuals:
Ayatollah Khomeini
Ronald Reagan
Jerry Falwell
Lech Walesa
José Napoleón Duarte

1. **Using Graphic Organizers** Copy the graphic organizer below. Use it to list the factors that led to Ronald Reagan's victory over Jimmy Carter in 1980.

2. **Evaluating** Describe President Reagan's economic program, and evaluate how successful it was.
3. **Synthesizing** Why did Cold War relations sink to a low point in the early 1980s?
4. **Using Historical Imagination** Imagine that you are a citizen of El Salvador or Nicaragua in the early 1980s. Describe the political situation in your country and explain why you think the United States is intervening in your country's affairs.

Critical Thinking

5. How did the Reagan administration's approach to governing differ from that of previous administrations?
Consider:
- Reagan's opinion of the role of government
- the administration's approach to the economy
- the administration's approach to the Cold War

SECTION 1 REVIEW ANSWERS

Define and Identify
For significance, see the following pages:
- Iran hostage crisis, p. 742
- Ayatollah Khomeini, p. 742
- Ronald Reagan, p. 743
- New Right, p. 743
- Jerry Falwell, p. 743
- Moral Majority, p. 743
- Reaganomics, p. 744
- supply-side economics, p. 744
- Strategic Defense Initiative, p. 745
- Solidarity, p. 745
- Lech Walesa, p. 745
- José Napoleón Duarte, p. 746
- Sandinistas, p. 747
- Contras, p. 747

1. frustration with the Iran hostage crisis; Carter's inability to solve domestic problems; Americans' insecurity about the future; Reagan's appeal across party lines
2. tax cuts–spurred economic growth; military spending–created budget deficits; deregulation–promoted business, but hurt consumers and the environment; spending cuts–hurt poor citizens
3. Soviet invasion of Afghanistan, events in Poland, and the shooting down of a Korean plane
4. Students should mention the unstable governments and Americans' fear of communism.
5. Reagan wanted to reduce the size and influence of government; cut taxes for the wealthy and cut government regulations; took an aggressive stance toward the Soviet Union

SECTION 2

After completing Section 2, students should be able to:

OBJECTIVE 1 *Analyze how the Republicans won the 1984 election, and discuss how the makeup of the Supreme Court changed in the 1980s.*

OBJECTIVE 2 *Describe what events began to shake public confidence in the economy.*

OBJECTIVE 3 *Explain how the Iran-Contra affair developed.*

OBJECTIVE 4 *Identify the developments that eased tensions between the United States and the Soviet Union in the late 1980s.*

LET'S GET STARTED!

As students enter the classroom, tell them to read the Reagan campaign poster on this page. Ask students to respond to the poster in writing. Have them identify the ideas that the poster is trying to convey and to characterize its mood. Ask volunteers to share their answers with the class. Tell students that in Section 2 they will learn about how confidence in the economy wavered during Ronald Reagan's second term in office.

SECTION 2 RESOURCES

PRINT

- Guided Reading Strategy 25.2
- Graphic Organizer Activity 25: Economics in the 1980s
- Section 2 Review, p. 754
- Daily Quiz 25.2

MULTIMEDIA

- One-Stop Planner, Lesson 25.2
- Holt Researcher: American History CD–ROM

SHELTERED ENGLISH

- Main Idea Activity for Reteaching and Sheltered English 25.2

✔ READING TO UNDERSTAND

To help students master the section objectives, have them answer the **READING CHECKS** and complete **Guided Reading Strategy 25.2** as they read the section.

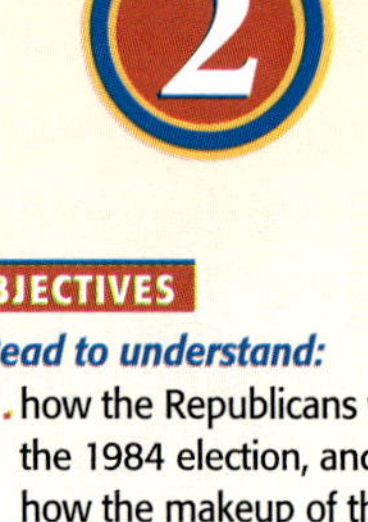

Reagan's Second Term

OBJECTIVES

Read to understand:

1. how the Republicans won the 1984 election, and how the makeup of the Supreme Court changed in the 1980s
2. what events began to shake public confidence in the economy
3. how the Iran-Contra affair developed
4. what developments eased tensions between the United States and the Soviet Union in the late 1980s

KEY TERMS

Gramm-Rudman-Hollings Act
insider trading
S&L crisis
Iran-Contra affair
glasnost
perestroika
Intermediate-Range Nuclear Forces Treaty

KEY PEOPLE

Walter Mondale
Geraldine Ferraro
Sandra Day O'Connor
Oliver North
Mikhail Gorbachev

KEY PLACES

Grenada
Nicaragua

EYEWITNESSES TO History

"It's morning again in America. . . . In a town not too far from where you live, a young family has just moved into a new home. Three years ago, even the smallest house seemed completely out of reach. Right down the street, one of the neighbors has just bought himself a new car with all the options. The factory down the river is working again. Not long ago, people were saying it probably would be closed forever. . . . Life is better. America is back."

—Ronald Reagan campaign ad

Reagan-Bush campaign poster

This advertising campaign promoted the economic achievements of Ronald Reagan's first term in office. By 1984 the economy was booming, consumerism was growing, and the "malaise" of the 1970s was fading. Reagan's supporters asked voters, "Now that our country is turning around, why turn back?"

The Election of 1984

Adding to President Reagan's popularity heading into his 1984 re-election campaign was a small-scale military action in 1983. On the tiny Caribbean island of Grenada, a rebel group overthrew the government and killed the prime minister. Several Caribbean nations requested U.S. intervention. Beginning October 25, 1983, several thousand U.S. Marines and Army Rangers went ashore on Grenada. They unseated the coup leaders and set up a government favorable to the United States. The successful operation boosted Americans' patriotism and confidence in the military.

Soon after the Grenada invasion, Reagan announced that he and Vice President George Bush would seek a second term. Former vice president Walter Mondale won the Democratic nomination. He picked Representative Geraldine Ferraro of New York as his running mate. Ferraro became the first woman to run on a major-party presidential ticket. Some predicted Ferraro's presence would increase support for the Democratic Party among women. Ferraro said:

> **"By choosing an American woman to run for our nation's second-highest office, you send a powerful signal to all Americans. . . . There are no doors we cannot unlock. We will place no limits on achievement. If we can do this, we can do anything."**

Republicans, however, had also been taking steps to expand the role of women in their party. President Reagan had appointed several women to high public offices, including Elizabeth Dole as secretary of transportation and Margaret Heckler as secretary

U.S. forces landed on the island of Grenada in October 1983.

TEACH OBJECTIVE 1

LEVEL 1: Pair students and ask each pair to draw two political cartoons depicting how the Republicans won the 1984 election and how the makeup of the Supreme Court changed in the 1980s. *(Pairs' cartoons should depict the Republicans' efforts to expand the role of women in their party, the appointment of the first woman to the Supreme Court, and the Court's more conservative membership.)* Display pairs' cartoons around the classroom.
Sheltered English, Cooperative Learning

LEVEL 2: Tell students to imagine that they are editors who must write a summary for the dust jacket of a book about the Supreme Court during the 1980s. Have each student write a summary about how the Republicans won the 1984 election and how the makeup of the Supreme Court changed during the 1980s. *(See the Level 1 lesson for the correct changes.)* Ask volunteers to read their dust-jacket summaries to the class.

LEVEL 3: Tell each student to write a short poem about how the Republicans won the 1984 election and how the makeup of the Supreme Court changed during the 1980s. *(See the Level 1 lesson for the correct changes.)* Ask volunteers to recite their poems to the class. Students may wish to include their poems in their portfolios.

of health and human services. He also appointed Jeane Kirkpatrick as head of the U.S. delegation to the United Nations—the first woman to hold the post.

Republicans also sought—and received—the support of women who did not identify with the feminist movement. Female opponents of the Equal Rights Amendment and abortion embraced the Republican Party. As a result, the percentage of female delegates to the Republican National Convention increased from 24 percent in 1980 to 44 percent in 1984.

In the end, Ferraro's presence did not win many votes for the Democrats. On election day, Reagan received 54.5 million popular votes to Mondale's 37.6 million. The Republicans swept the electoral vote 525 to 13.

INTERPRETING THE VISUAL RECORD
1984. Democratic candidates Water Mondale and Geraldine Ferraro received strong support at this 1984 parade in New York. The poster at left shows Ferraro as Liberty. ***What point do you think the poster was making about Ferraro's candidacy?***

The Supreme Court

One issue that arose during the 1984 presidential campaign was the growing conservative emphasis of the Supreme Court. President Reagan vowed to appoint justices who would uphold his conservative agenda. In 1981 Reagan had appointed conservative justice Sandra Day O'Connor, the first woman ever to serve on the Supreme Court.

Sandra Day O'Connor

Sandra Day O'Connor was born in El Paso, Texas, in 1930. She grew up working on her family's cattle ranch. "The whole family had to get out and help on the ranch," she recalled. "We learned to be pretty independent that way." She attended Stanford University and graduated from Stanford Law School in 1952. At Stanford, she met and married fellow law student John O'Connor.

O'Connor began her law career in California but later moved to Arizona. There she served as Arizona's assistant attorney general from 1965 to 1969. From 1974 to 1981 she served in several different judicial positions before being appointed to the Supreme Court. She was once asked whether she would vote differently than a male justice. She answered:

> **"Judges are supposed to be objective; they're supposed to study and look at the law and apply the law to the particular case in an objective way, not from any particular point of view. So does being a woman make a difference in what answer is given? I tend to think that probably at the end of the day, a wise old woman and a wise old man are going to reach the same answer."**

HOLT RESEARCHER *Read More About It*
Free Find:
Sandra Day O'Connor
After reading about Sandra Day O'Connor on the **Holt Researcher** CD–ROM, write a biography about one of your favorite people. Describe the choices he or she made and the obstacles he or she overcame.

CULTURAL DIVERSITY

Professional Women. Sandra Day O'Connor experienced firsthand the problem of gender discrimination. After graduating third in her law school class in 1952—future chief justice William Rehnquist was ranked first—O'Connor could not find a job as an attorney with a private law firm because she was a woman. One law firm offered her a job as a legal secretary. Instead, O'Connor chose to practice law as a county deputy attorney. That position marked the beginning of O'Connor's long career in public service.

CRITICAL THINKING How might women respond to such discrimination today?

ANSWER: Students might mention that the 1964 Civil Rights Act made sex discrimination illegal. Women today also have legal recourse to address discrimination.

THAT'S INTERESTING!

In the 1984 election, Ronald Reagan won the electoral votes of 49 states. Walter Mondale only won the votes of the District of Columbia and Minnesota, his home state.

VISUAL RECORD ANSWER
Students might suggest that the poster is making the point that Ferraro was a standard-bearer for women.

TEACH OBJECTIVE 2

ALL LEVELS: Tell students that developments during President Reagan's second term began to shake the public's confidence in the economy. To help students understand the factors that led to this, copy the graphic organizer at right on the chalkboard, omitting the italicized answers. Have each student complete it. Ask volunteers to share their answers with the class. To conclude, ask students to name some ways in which the nation's economic health is measured. *(Students might mention the Dow Jones average, inflation, unemployment, and so on.)* Tell students that falling public confidence in the economy can exacerbate an economic downturn as consumers reduce spending. **Sheltered English**

Falling Confidence in the Economy

1. *huge federal deficits lead to the passage of the Gramm-Rudman-Hollings Act*
2. *illegal insider trading—the use of personal confidential information for personal gain—is revealed*
3. *stock market crash leads to a sharp drop in stock values*
4. *the S&L crisis forces the federal government to pay billions of dollars to cover losses*

▸ASSIGNMENT *Ask students to write summaries of the following terms: insider trading, stock market crash of 1987, the S&L crisis, the Gramm-Rudman-Hollings Act.*

DEMOCRATIC VALUES

The Bork Nomination. Reagan's nomination of Robert Bork to the Supreme Court led to an unprecedented public debate over the nominee's fitness to serve on the Court. Opponents and supporters mounted public relations campaigns that included radio and television advertisements. Some observers complained that the media coverage was unfair because it favored those who were opposed to Bork's confirmation.

CRITICAL THINKING Should conflicts over appointments to the Supreme Court be waged like other political battles?

ANSWER: Answers will vary. Some students might argue that the Supreme Court should be separate from politics because it is responsible for interpreting the Constitution. Other students might argue that Supreme Court decisions can have a huge impact on U.S. politics and that Court nominations should therefore be debated.

VISUAL RECORD ANSWER

Students might suggest that the cartoonist had a favorable opinion, as indicated by the caption and the pleased look on the statue's face.

GRAPH ANSWERS

about $1.5 trillion; almost $3 trillion

INTERPRETING THE VISUAL RECORD

The Supreme Court. In this 1981 cartoon the spirit of Justice comments on Sandra Day O'Connor's appointment to the Supreme Court. ***What do you think was the cartoonist's opinion of the appointment?***

As a Supreme Court justice, O'Connor has proven to be less conservative than many supporters originally thought she would be. She has often delivered the deciding vote when the Court has been split on certain issues.

When Chief Justice Warren Burger retired in 1986, Reagan elevated Associate Justice William Rehnquist to chief justice. To fill Rehnquist's position, Reagan nominated Antonin Scalia, a conservative. When another justice retired in 1987, Reagan nominated Robert Bork, a federal judge and law professor who held a much narrower interpretation of the Bill of Rights than the Court had upheld in recent years. He believed, for example, that civil rights laws restricted individual freedoms. Bork's views concerned many people, including a number of senators. The Senate rejected Bork's nomination. Reagan's next choice, Douglas Ginsberg, withdrew after press reports emerged that he had smoked marijuana as a law professor. Conservative judge Anthony Kennedy of California eventually won Senate confirmation and joined the Supreme Court.

✔ **READING CHECK:** How did the Republicans win the 1984 election, and how did the makeup of the Supreme Court change in the 1980s?

Concerns over the Economy

The failure of the Bork nomination was one of several signs that the so-called Reagan Revolution might be starting to weaken. Of particular concern was the federal deficit, which had topped $200 billion in 1985. Seeking to balance the budget with forced spending cuts, Congress passed the Balanced Budget and Emergency Control Act in 1985. Called the **Gramm-Rudman-Hollings Act** after its Senate sponsors, the law required automatic across-the-board cuts in government spending when the deficit exceeded a certain amount. Other legislation took aim at specific problems. The Tax Reform Law of 1986, for example, eliminated special tax breaks that certain groups had been receiving.

Total Federal Debt, 1981–1989

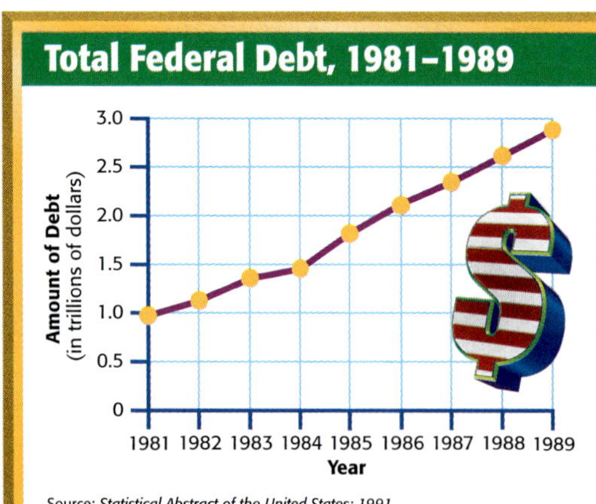

Source: *Statistical Abstract of the United States: 1991*

Learning from Graphs Despite Ronald Reagan's promise to balance the federal budget by 1984, the total federal debt continued to grow dramatically throughout the 1980s.

? Building Graph Skills Approximately how much was the federal debt in 1984? in 1989?

The stock market also showed signs of trouble. President Reagan's tax cuts and business deregulation had stimulated a stock market boom. However, with this boom came a wave of illegal **insider trading**—the use of confidential financial information for personal gain. Stockbroker Chris Burke described the culture of the times.

> **"Wall Street in the 1980s was like nowhere else on this planet. It was a culture of greed and backstabbing and partying. Your best buddy is the one who's gonna stab you in the back tomorrow if it means some more greenbacks in his pocket. It wasn't a good way to live."**

Several large brokerage firms pleaded guilty to illegal activities and faced severe penalties. These scandals eroded investors' trust in stockbrokers.

TEACH OBJECTIVE 3

LEVEL 1: Pair students and have each pair create an annotated time line of the events leading up to the congressional investigation of the Iran-Contra affair. *(Time lines should include the following: Congress cuts off funds to the Contras; the Reagan administration sells arms to Iran to obtain the release of hostages in Lebanon; the administration uses profits from the arms sales to illegally fund the Contras; the illegal arms sales are discovered.)* Ask volunteers to share their time lines with the class. To conclude, lead the class in a discussion about why the Iran-Contra affair was considered a serious crisis in government. **Sheltered English, Cooperative Learning**

LEVELS 2 AND 3: Ask students why the Iran-Contra affair was considered a serious government crisis. *(Students might point out that the Reagan administration circumvented congressional oversight of the government's conduct of foreign policy by using third-party funds to pay for the operation.)* Have each student write a short analytical essay about how the Iran-Contra affair developed and the constitutional implications of the administration's actions. *(See the Level 1 lesson for the correct events.)* Ask volunteers to read their essays to the class.

Then, on October 19, 1987, after several years of a bull market, the stock market crashed. On paper, stock losses totaled almost $1 trillion. The value of Eastman Kodak stock, for example, fell by more than 30 percent. Other major corporations experienced similar sharp drops in their stock values.

In another sign of economic trouble, a crisis hit the nation's savings and loan (S&L) associations and banking industry in the late 1980s and early 1990s. Freed of federal regulation, banks and S&Ls, particularly in the Southwest, had made risky loans to developers to build office towers, shopping malls, and other projects. In the late 1980s the real-estate market collapsed. Hundreds of S&Ls and banks that had loaned money to developers failed. Since the federal government insures S&L and bank depositors, it had to pay billions of dollars to cover these losses, further straining the federal budget. The **S&L crisis** weakened many people's confidence in the health of the economy.

✔ **READING CHECK:** What events began to shake public confidence in the economy?

Dow Dives 508.32 Points In Panic on Wall Street

Billions lost in trading

Navy blasts Iran oil site in retaliation

INTERPRETING THE VISUAL RECORD

Wall Street. The 1987 stock market crash brought back memories of the Great Depression. ***Does this picture of the New York Stock Exchange reflect the headline shown? Explain your answer.***

The Iran-Contra Affair

The Reagan administration also faced continued problems in the Middle East and Latin America. These frustrations led to the most serious crisis to hit the Reagan White House—the **Iran-Contra affair**.

After Congress cut off funds for the Contras' war against Nicaragua's Sandinista government, the Reagan administration sought other sources of funding. At the time, the White House was secretly bargaining with Iran for the release of U.S. hostages held by pro-Iranian groups in Lebanon. As part of the bargain, the administration shipped more than 500 antitank missiles to Iran by way of Israel. Without informing Congress, the administration used the profits from these arms sales to pay for weapons and supplies for the Contras.

When the arms sales became known in 1986, President Reagan appointed a commission to investigate. The commission cleared Reagan of any direct involvement. However, it heavily criticized other White House officials, some of whom resigned. The secret funding of the Contra war soon leaked out as well. It was revealed that Lieutenant Colonel Oliver North, a White House aide, had funneled millions of dollars from the Iranian arms sales to the Contras after Congress had forbidden direct U.S. government aid.

In 1987, House and Senate committees investigated the affair. North admitted that he and his secretary, Fawn Hall, had destroyed key documents. However, North insisted that they had acted out of loyalty and patriotism. North testified: "I am not in the habit of questioning my superiors. . . . I don't believe that what we did even under those circumstances is wrong or illegal."

In its report, the Senate committee denounced North's activities and criticized the loose White House management style that had allowed North to operate as he

HISTORY MAKERS SPEAK

George Shultz in *Reagan: The Man and His Presidency*

The Iran-Contra Affair. Former secretary of state George Shultz reflected on the effect of the Iran-Contra affair on President Reagan. "The revelations weighed on him, and I think the thing that bothered Ronald Reagan more than anything else was that before, he had always felt that if he believed something was in the U.S. interest, he could go to the American people and explain it, and they would support him. He tried to do that in this case, and it was obvious that they didn't support him."

CRITICAL THINKING What might Shultz's remarks reveal about Reagan's attitude toward the Iran-Contra affair?

ANSWER: Students might suggest that Reagan believed he was acting in the nation's best interest.

THAT'S INTERESTING!

In 1980 a total of 11 S&Ls failed. Over the next eight years another 552 S&Ls failed, with 190 failing in 1988 alone.

VISUAL RECORD ANSWER

Answers will vary but students might suggest that the photograph shows panic.

TEACH OBJECTIVE 4

LEVEL 1: Tell students that when Mikhail Gorbachev became leader of the Soviet Union in 1985, he initiated several measures that eased tensions between the United States and the Soviet Union. Ask students to name these measures and other developments that eased Cold War tensions. Compile a list of responses on the chalkboard. *(Students should mention glasnost, perestroika, the INF Treaty, Gorbachev's policy of détente with the United States, and the withdrawal of Soviet troops from Afghanistan.)* Then have each student write a paragraph about the developments that eased tensions between the United States and the Soviet Union in the late 1980s. **Sheltered English**

LEVEL 2: Tell students to imagine that they are writing a book about the easing of Cold War tensions. Have each student prepare a brief summary of a chapter about the developments that eased tensions between the United States and the Soviet Union in the late 1980s. *(See the Level 1 lesson for the correct developments.)* Ask volunteers to share their summaries with the class.

CONSTITUTIONAL HERITAGE

The Power to Make Foreign Policy. An important issue at stake in the Iran-Contra affair was whether Congress and the president should share the power to make U.S. foreign policy. Oliver North and others responsible for diverting funds to the Contras acted in violation of the Boland Amendment, which forbade the U.S. government from providing any military or paramilitary support to the Contras. Moreover, the Constitution gives Congress the exclusive power to appropriate funds to carry out the business of the United States. As historian Theodore Draper put it, the use of foreign or private funds to carry out U.S. foreign-policy goals would put "wealthy donors or foreign countries in a position to conduct, determine, or make American foreign policy."

CRITICAL THINKING Why might the constitutional power to make foreign policy have been given to two branches of government?

ANSWER: Students might suggest that the framers had been guided by the principle of checks and balances.

MAP ANSWER

El Salvador, Grenada, Guatemala, Haiti, and Nicaragua

Oliver North testified before the Senate that he had acted for the good of the country.

did. The chair of the Senate committee, Senator Daniel Inouye (in-oh-e) of Hawaii, countered North's claim that he was just following orders.

> **"[The] colonel was well aware that he was subject to the Uniform Code of Military Justice. . . . And that code makes it abundantly clear that orders of a superior officer must be obeyed by subordinate [lower in rank] members—but it is lawful orders. . . . In fact, it says members of the military have an obligation to disobey unlawful orders."**

In 1988 a court-appointed special prosecutor filed criminal charges against North and against Reagan's national security adviser, Admiral John Poindexter. North was convicted on various charges, including the destruction of government documents and lying to Congress. The conviction was later reversed on a legal technicality.

✔ **READING CHECK:** How did the Iran-Contra affair develop?

Central America and the Caribbean, 1980s

Learning from Maps The United States intervened in Central America and the Caribbean several times during the 1980s.

? PLACE Which Caribbean and Central American nations saw guerrilla activity or civil war during the 1980s?

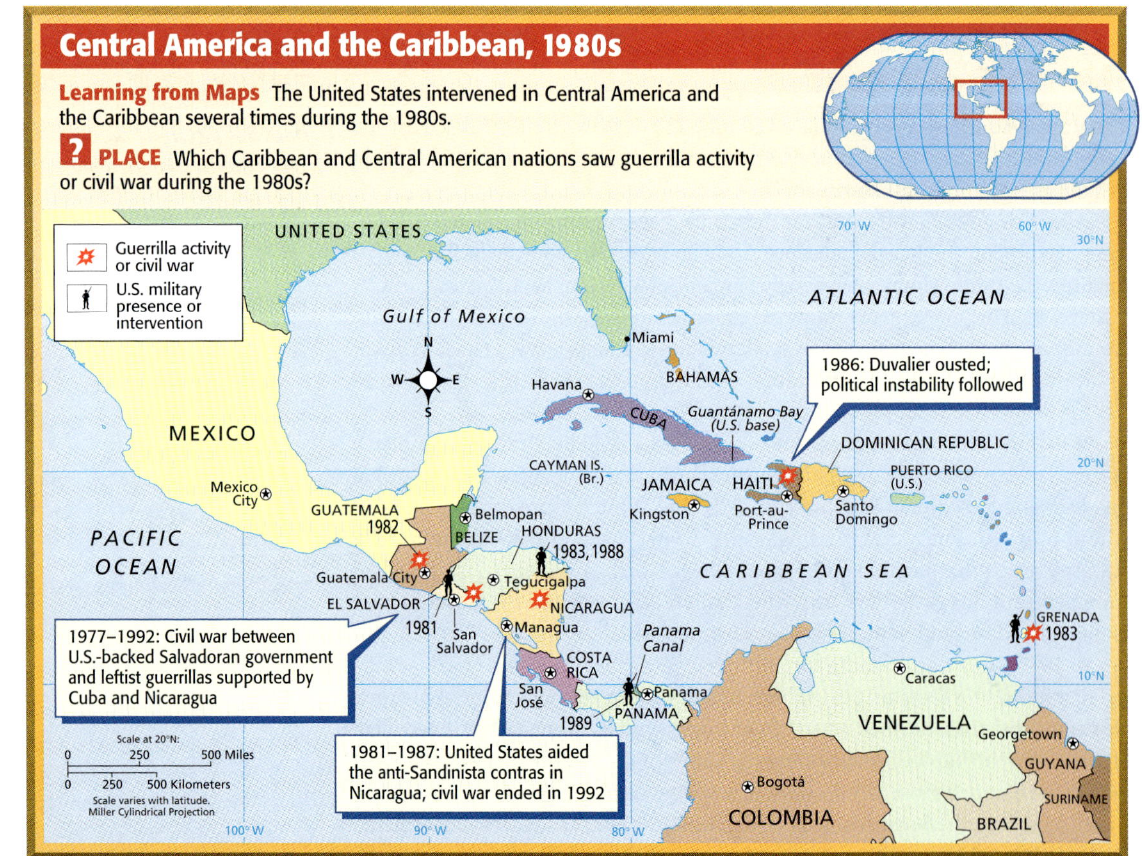

LEVEL 3: Tell students to imagine that they are Mikhail Gorbachev. Have each student write an excerpt from an imaginary memoir in which he or she describes the developments that eased tensions between the United States and the Soviet Union in the late 1980s. *(See the Level 1 lesson for the correct developments.)* Ask volunteers to read their memoirs to the class. Students may wish to include their memoirs in their portfolios.

NOTE: For an additional teaching idea, see the Chapter 25 unfinished story alternatives lesson in the **Creative Teaching Strategies** handbook.

SPOTLIGHT on the INF Treaty

Have students conduct research on the INF Treaty and why it was considered an important measure. Students should focus their research on antinuclear protests in Europe prior to the treaty negotiations, the strategic importance of medium-range missiles, and the provisions of the treaty. Have each student write a report about his or her findings.
Block Scheduling

Strategies for Success: Creating an Outline

Along with formulating a hypothesis, creating an outline is an indispensable part of preparing to write a history research paper. An *outline* is an organizational tool that summarizes the ideas and evidence that one plans to discuss in a speech or piece of writing. By presenting this information concisely and in a logical order, an outline serves as a kind of "road map" that can make the actual process of writing a paper much easier.

How to Create an Outline

1. **Write your thesis statement.** First, formulate the hypothesis that you plan to focus on in your paper and write it out in a short, declarative statement. This thesis statement should make up the first major heading of your outline and be included in your paper's introduction.
2. **Organize your material.** Once you have settled on a thesis statement, organize logically the material that you wish to present in the paper. Determine what information belongs in the introduction, what should make up the body of the paper, and what to put in the conclusion.
3. **Summarize the main ideas.** Identify and briefly summarize the main ideas that you plan to use to support your thesis statement. Each of these main ideas should serve as a major heading in your outline and be labeled with a Roman numeral.
4. **List the supporting details.** As you summarize each main idea, identify the details or facts that support it and list them as subheadings in your outline. Make sure to order the subheadings logically and label them with descending levels of letters and numbers.
5. **Put your outline to use.** When you write your paper, structure it according to your outline. Each major heading, for instance, might form the basis of a topic sentence that begins a paragraph. Corresponding subheadings would then indicate the content of each paragraph. In a more lengthy paper, each subheading might constitute the basis of an entire paragraph.

Applying the Strategy

Read the following thesis statement, which presents a hypothesis about the causes of the Iran-Contra affair and President Reagan's responsibility for the crisis. Then create an outline for the portion of this chapter that discusses the Iran-Contra affair and use it to evaluate the statement.

> A desire to free U.S. hostages held in Lebanon and fight communism in Nicaragua led to the Iran-Contra affair. White House officials sold weapons to Iran and used the profits to supply the Contras. As president of the United States Ronald Reagan was responsible for the actions of people serving in his administration.

Practicing the Strategy

Use your outline to answer the following questions.

1. What main ideas serve as major headings in your outline?
2. What supporting details are listed as subheadings in your outline?
3. How did you order the headings and subheadings in your outline?
4. How does your outline support your thesis statement?

Cold War Tensions Ease

The most significant achievement of President Reagan's second term was a dramatic easing of Cold War hostilities. When Mikhail Gorbachev became leader of the Soviet Union in 1985, a new era of Soviet history began.

By the 1980s the Soviet Union was burdened by a failing economy, a repressive political system, and heavy military costs. Gorbachev's initiatives included his policy of openness, called **glasnost** (GLAZ-nohst), that promised more freedom for the Soviet people. Equally dramatic was **perestroika** (per-uh-STROY-kuh)—Gorbachev's plan to restructure the Soviet economy and government. On the economic front, he called for increased foreign trade and reduced military spending.

THAT'S INTERESTING!

Mikhail Gorbachev was born in 1931 to a poor peasant family in southern Russia. During World War II his village was briefly occupied by German troops. In the summers after the war he worked as a combine harvester operator.

STRATEGIES FOR SUCCESS ANSWERS

Applying the Strategy
Answers will vary but outlines should clearly summarize the main points.

Practicing the Strategy

1. continued problems in the Middle East and Latin America, covert White House operations, Congress investigates White House actions
2. hostage negotiations, funding the Contras, criminal charges filed against White House officials
3. continued problems in the Middle East and Latin America; covert White House operations–hostage negotiations, funding the Contras; Congress investigates White House actions–charges filed against White House officials
4. by listing supporting details and facts

VISUAL RECORD ANSWER
(for p. 754)
Students might point out that the informal setting reflects Reagan's easygoing demeanor.

REVIEW

Have students complete the **Section 2 Review** on p. 754.

ASSESS

Have students complete **Daily Quiz 25.2.** As **Alternative Assessment**, you may want to use the memoir or the time line in this section's lessons.

RETEACH

Have students complete **Main Idea Activity for Reteaching and Sheltered English 25.2.** Organize students into small groups and assign each group a subsection. Have each group prepare a brief summary of the material in its subsection. Ask students to read their summaries to the class.
Sheltered English, Cooperative Learning

EXTEND

Have students conduct research on one of the key people listed in this chapter. Then have each student prepare a short "Who Am I?" monologue in the role of his or her chosen person, omitting the person's name. Have students deliver their monologues to the class, then ask students to identify the person.
Block Scheduling

SECTION 2 REVIEW ANSWERS

Define and Identify
For significance, see the following pages:

- Walter Mondale, p. 748
- Geraldine Ferraro, p. 748
- Sandra Day O'Connor, p. 749
- Gramm-Rudman-Hollings Act, p. 750
- insider trading, p. 750
- S&L crisis, p. 751
- Iran-Contra affair, p. 751
- Oliver North, p. 751
- Mikhail Gorbachev, p. 753
- glasnost, p. 753
- perestroika, p. 753
- Intermediate-Range Nuclear Forces Treaty, p. 754

Locate
For locations, see the map on p. 752. For significance, see the following pages:

- Grenada, p. 748
- Nicaragua, p. 751

1. Republicans—expanded the role of women; Democrats—nominated Geraldine Ferraro
2. made it more conservative and nominated the first female justice
3. Students' letters should detail the events surrounding the scandal and its outcome.
4. Gorbachev's rise to power; the INF Treaty, withdrawal of Soviet troops from Afghanistan
5. because of the growing federal deficit, the stock market crash, and the failure of many S&Ls

INTERPRETING THE VISUAL RECORD

The Reagan style. President Reagan and his wife, Nancy, hosted Mikhail and Raisa Gorbachev at the Reagans' ranch in California. *How does the setting for this photograph reflect Reagan's style?*

The revenues from these changes were to be used to modernize Soviet factories. These reforms marked the first time since the Bolshevik Revolution that a Soviet leader had seemed open to some ideas of capitalist democratic government. These reforms began to dramatically change life in the Soviet Union. Glasnost also encouraged people to criticize the government. Many complained about the economy, which some felt had been weakened by the heightened arms race of the 1980s.

To further his domestic goals and defuse the costly Cold War conflict, Gorbachev pursued détente with the United States. In 1987, after a series of meetings, Gorbachev and President Reagan signed the **Intermediate-Range Nuclear Forces** (INF) **Treaty**. This treaty eliminated all medium-range nuclear weapons from Europe. Gorbachev also agreed to withdraw Soviet troops from Afghanistan. Gorbachev addressed these issues in a speech to the United Nations in 1988.

> "The use or threat of force no longer can or must be an instrument of foreign policy. . . . All of us, and primarily the stronger of us, must exercise self-restraint and totally rule out any outward-oriented use of force."

In May 1988, as the Senate prepared to ratify the INF Treaty, Reagan flew to Moscow. As television cameras whirred, the U.S. president and the Soviet leader embraced like old friends.

✔ **READING CHECK:** What developments eased tensions between the United States and the Soviet Union in the late 1980s?

SECTION 2 REVIEW

Define and explain the significance of the following terms:
Gramm-Rudman-Hollings Act
insider trading
S&L crisis
Iran-Contra affair
glasnost
perestroika
Intermediate-Range Nuclear Forces Treaty

Identify and explain the significance of the following individuals:
Walter Mondale
Geraldine Ferraro
Sandra Day O'Connor
Oliver North
Mikhail Gorbachev

Locate and explain the significance of the following places:
Grenada
Nicaragua

1. **Using Graphic Organizers** Copy the graphic organizer below. Use it to show how each political party tried to appeal to voters in the 1984 presidential election.

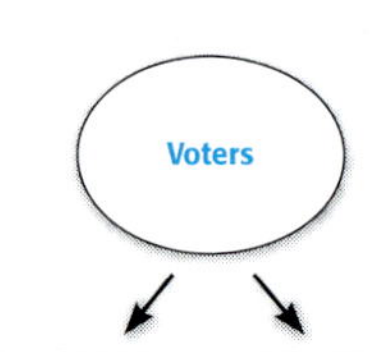

2. **Assessing Consequences** How did President Reagan change the makeup of the Supreme Court?
3. **Using Historical Imagination** Imagine that you are a member of a congressional committee appointed to investigate the Iran-Contra affair. Write a letter to the people you represent that summarizes the results of the investigation.
4. **Identifying Cause and Effect** What led to an easing of U.S.-Soviet tensions in the late 1980s? What were some outcomes of this change?

Critical Thinking

5. Why was public confidence in the economy shaken in the late 1980s?
Consider:
   - the federal deficit
   - the stock market crash
   - the S&L crisis

SECTION 3

After completing Section 3, students should be able to:

OBJECTIVE 1 *Summarize how American society changed in the 1980s.*

OBJECTIVE 2 *Explain how the Cold War ended.*

OBJECTIVE 3 *Describe what led to the Persian Gulf War, and analyze how it differed from previous U.S. military conflicts.*

OBJECTIVE 4 *Discuss the domestic problems the Bush administration faced.*

LET'S GET STARTED!

Write the following statement on the chalkboard: *Presidential popularity usually increases during a war just as it decreases during economic hard times.* As students enter the classroom, have them respond to the statement in writing. Ask students to share their responses with the class. Tell students that in Section 3, they will learn more about the presidency of George Bush, whose term in office could be described by the statement above.

Bush and Life in the 1980s

OBJECTIVES

Read to understand:

1. how American society changed in the 1980s
2. how the Cold War ended
3. what led to the Persian Gulf War, and how it differed from previous U.S. military conflicts
4. what domestic problems the Bush administration faced

KEY TERMS

Challenger
acquired immune deficiency syndrome
Commonwealth of Independent States
Operation Desert Storm
Americans with Disabilities Act
War on Drugs

KEY PEOPLE

Christa McAuliffe
Jesse Jackson
Michael Dukakis
Lloyd Bentsen
George Bush
Dan Quayle
Norman Schwarzkopf
Colin Powell

KEY PLACES

Iraq
Kuwait
Saudi Arabia

"What the president and Mrs. Reagan have done is extraordinary at a time in our history when there was a depressed mood in this country. They came and made it positive. How can you put a value on that? . . . If we have all these negative feelings, I don't think we can function as well as an individual or as a family or as a nation. Didn't it make you feel better? That the nation itself was having a better feeling about itself?"

—Sugar Rautbord

The Yuppie Handbook *reflected the prosperity of the 1980s.*

Sugar Rautbord of Chicago was just one of many Americans who felt the optimism generated by President Reagan in the 1980s. Many people hoped that this feeling would continue even after Reagan left office.

America in the 1980s

Overall, the 1980s were much more positive than the 1970s. Singer Bobby McFerrin summed up the mood of the times with his humorous 1988 tune, "Don't Worry, Be Happy." Other popular singers reflected the spirit of consumerism that characterized the era.

Economics. Most families benefited from the economic boom of the 1980s. Some did extremely well. Many young urban professionals—so-called yuppies—took advantage of the increased number of financial services jobs. The newly wealthy yuppies set many style trends during the decade.

Not all families did well, however, particularly single-parent families. From 1970 to 1991 the number of children living in single-parent households more than doubled. In 1991 some 20 percent of white children, 60 percent of African American children, and 30 percent of Hispanic children lived with one parent, usually their mothers. Most single parents faced serious financial burdens. "Let's see the beginning of the end of this business where if you're born poor, you gotta die in the slums," said Frank Lumpkin, an unemployed steelworker. "All these kids [around here today] can do is sell hubcaps and tires to the junkman. And steal. The answer to crime is full employment. We gotta start figurin' a way to get it. It's no mystery."

Science and technology. During the 1980s Americans spent more and more money on a vast new array of electronic goods. One of the most popular items was the personal computer (PC). The PC explosion began in 1981, when IBM introduced its first model for consumers. By 1984 IBM was selling 3 million PCs per year. Computer experts began to experiment with the possibilities of the new technology. In 1984 Jaron Lanier, a 24-year-old inventor, developed "virtual reality." This system allowed viewers to experience and interact with three-dimensional

SECTION 3 RESOURCES

PRINT

- Guided Reading Strategy 25.3
- Biography Reading 25: Sally Ride
- Section 3 Review, p. 763
- Daily Quiz 25.3

MULTIMEDIA

- One-Stop Planner, Lesson 25.3
- Everyday Life in America Transparency 32: The AIDS Quilt Project, 1980s
- The American Nation Video Program Segment: U.S. Troops in the Persian Gulf; Teacher's Guide, pp. 199–200
- Holt Researcher: American History CD–ROM
- HRW Web site

SHELTERED ENGLISH

- Main Idea Activity for Reteaching and Sheltered English 25.3

✔ READING TO UNDERSTAND

To help students master the section objectives, have them answer the **READING CHECKS** and complete **Guided Reading Strategy 25.3** as they read the section.

TEACH OBJECTIVE 1

LEVEL 1: Tell students that economic growth during the 1980s and the availability of new technology contributed to cultural and social changes in the United States. Pair students and have each pair create a bulleted list of the changes in American society during the 1980s. *(Lists should include the growth of the yuppie lifestyle, a doubling of the number of single-parent households, the PC explosion and rise of technoculture, and the emergence of AIDS.)* Have students share their lists with the class. **Cooperative Learning, Sheltered English**

LEVEL 2: Tell students to imagine that they are sociologists writing a journal article about the 1980s. Have each student write an article about the ways American society changed during the 1980s. *(See the Level 1 lesson for the correct changes.)* Ask volunteers to read their articles to the class.

LEVEL 3: Tell students to imagine that they are cultural historians who must analyze the cultural and social changes that occurred during the 1980s for a television talk show. Pair students and have each pair create a dialogue about how American society changed in the 1980s. *(See the Level 1 lesson for the correct changes.)* Have students perform their dialogues for the class. **Cooperative Learning**

PEOPLE IN HISTORY

Christa McAuliffe. In many ways Christa McAuliffe was an average American. Born in Boston in 1948, she watched with excitement when astronauts from *Apollo 11* walked on the Moon in 1969. The following year she graduated from college and got married. She and her husband had two children. McAuliffe taught history and social sciences in secondary schools while her husband worked on a law degree. When she learned that NASA wanted to send an educator into space, she applied. McAuliffe was chosen from some 11,000 applicants for the position.

CRITICAL THINKING Why would NASA want to send a schoolteacher into space?

ANSWER: Students might suggest that the mission would generate interest in the space program because many Americans could identify with a person who was not a professional scientist.

Multimedia Resources

Everyday Life in America Transparency 32: The AIDS Quilt Project, 1980s

VISUAL RECORD ANSWER

Students might suggest that women, African Americans, and Asian Americans were represented in the crew.

A personal computer from the early 1980s

images created solely through computer technology. Through virtual reality, people could actually experience an imaginary world.

The same year that virtual reality was invented, writer William Gibson published the science-fiction book *Neuromancer*. Gibson warned of a future in which technology takes over the world. He described this new world. "The sky above the port was the color of television, turned to a dead channel." Gibson's work spawned a new generation of computer-oriented science fiction called cyberpunk.

As the cyberpunk writers noted, technology offered hopes as well as challenges. The U.S. space program also experienced these ups and downs. Plagued by rising costs and falling interest in missions, the space program had declined somewhat since the 1970s. To cut costs of future flights, scientists began working on a reusable space shuttle. In 1981 the launch and successful landing of the space shuttle *Columbia* marked a new age in space technology.

Five years later, NASA announced that a civilian would be allowed to travel aboard a space shuttle. Social studies teacher Christa McAuliffe was chosen for a flight aboard the space shuttle ***Challenger***. McAuliffe exhibited an enormous enthusiasm for space exploration.

> **"I remember the excitement in my home when the first satellites were launched. My parents were amazed and I was caught up with their wonder. . . . John Kennedy inspired me with his words about placing a man on the moon. . . . I watched the Space Age being born and I would like to participate."**

In January 1986—about 70 seconds after takeoff—*Challenger* exploded, killing all seven people on board. In part because of McAuliffe's participation, the takeoff was being watched live by a huge television audience. A horrified nation witnessed the worst disaster in NASA's history. Shuttle flights were suspended for two years until corrections could be made to the shuttle systems.

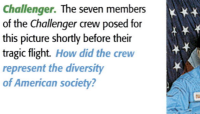

INTERPRETING THE VISUAL RECORD

Challenger. The seven members of the *Challenger* crew posed for this picture shortly before their tragic flight. ***How did the crew represent the diversity of American society?***

TEACH OBJECTIVE 2

LEVEL 1: Tell students that economic problems in the Soviet Union led to the rapid political changes that marked the end of the Cold War. Pair students and have each pair create an annotated time line of the events that led to the Cold War's end. *(Time lines should include the Soviet policy of nonintervention, the free elections in Poland and Hungary, the fall of communist governments in Czechoslovakia and Romania, pro-democracy demonstrations in East Germany, the opening of the Berlin Wall and the reunification of Germany, Gorbachev's loss of power and the dissolution of the Soviet Union.)* Have volunteers share their time lines with the class.

Sheltered English, Cooperative Learning

LEVEL 2: Tell students to imagine that they are citizens of East Germany who are experiencing the rapid political changes of the late 1980s and early 1990s. Have each student write a series of diary entries in which he or she describes the events that are leading to the end of the Cold War. *(See the Level 1 lesson for the correct events.)* Ask volunteers to read their diary entries to the class.

Health. In the 1980s many Americans became concerned by the emergence of a new, deadly disease called **acquired immune deficiency syndrome**, or AIDS. This is the final deadly stage of an illness caused by the human immunodeficiency virus, or HIV. Doctors first reported cases of AIDS in 1981. By the end of the decade, hundreds of thousands of people worldwide had died from the disease.

AIDS left almost no continent untouched. In the African nation of Zambia, President Kenneth Kaunda's son died of AIDS. In 1991 basketball star Earvin "Magic" Johnson of the Los Angeles Lakers announced that he had tested positive for HIV. Other celebrities struck by the disease include movie star Rock Hudson and tennis legend Arthur Ashe.

✔ **READING CHECK:** How did American society change in the 1980s?

These campaign buttons are from the 1988 election.

The 1988 Election

Domestic concerns were among the issues that worried voters as the 1988 presidential election approached. With President Reagan prohibited from running for a third term, the Democrats hoped to regain the White House in 1988. African American leader Jesse Jackson, who had run in 1984, was one of many candidates seeking the Democratic nomination. Jackson hoped to attract a "Rainbow Coalition"—a diverse group of voters representing all races, classes, and creeds. As a candidate in 1984, Jackson had helped generate the largest turnout of African American voters ever for a Democratic primary.

In 1988 Jackson appealed to an even wider range of voters. On "Super Tuesday," the largest single day of primary voting, Jackson won more votes than any other Democratic candidate. Governor Michael Dukakis of Massachusetts won the most delegates, however, and eventually gained the nomination. Dukakis, the son of Greek immigrants, selected Senator Lloyd Bentsen of Texas as his running mate. Vice President George Bush won the Republican presidential nomination and chose Indiana senator Dan Quayle as his running mate.

The 1988 presidential campaign proved to be one of the harshest in recent years. Initially, Bush tried to appeal to voters' sense of optimism by promising "a kinder and gentler nation." By the final weeks of the campaign, however, most of the Republican ads had a negative focus. For instance, one commercial attacked Dukakis's environmental record by showing scenes of Massachusetts's heavily polluted Boston Harbor.

The most controversial Republican advertising campaign, however, was intended to attract voters troubled by the nation's rising crime rate. Crime had increased by more than 12.5 percent between 1984 and 1988. A series of television and print ads portrayed Dukakis as weak on crime by associating him with convicted killer Willie Horton. While out on a weekend pass under a Massachusetts prisoner-release program, Horton had attacked a Maryland couple.

The Democrats were slow to respond to the Republicans' attacks. When they did, their efforts were poorly organized and ineffective. Dukakis tried to convince voters of his skills as a manager, arguing that the election should be about competence. This approach failed. In the November election, Bush won 426 electoral

HISTORY MAKERS SPEAK

Roger Ailes in *Presidential Elections: Strategies and Structures of American Politics*

Negative Campaigning. Roger Ailes, a political adviser to President George Bush, explained why the Bush campaign attacked Michael Dukakis during the presidential race. "You've got to understand that the media has no interest in substance. Print has a little more interest because they have to fill a lot of lines. But electronic media has no interest in substance. There are three ways to get on the air: pictures, attacks, and mistakes, so what you do is spend your time avoiding mistakes, staying on the attack and giving them pictures."

ACTIVITY: Have students discuss negative political advertisements. Then tell students to write a letter to the editor that supports or opposes negative political ads.

LEVEL 3: Have each student create a collage that represents the political events that led to the end of the Cold War. *(See the Level 1 lesson for the correct events.)* Ask volunteers to present and explain their collages to the class.

▶ASSIGNMENT *Have each student write an essay that analyzes the events leading to the end of the Cold War. Students may wish to include their essays in their portfolios.*

SPOTLIGHT on the Reunification of Germany

Have students conduct research on the events leading to the reunification of Germany and the celebrations that took place afterward. Students should focus on political events as well as events that were symbolic of the Cold War's end. Have each student create a multimedia presentation based on his or her research. Then have students give their presentations to the class. **Block Scheduling**

DEMOCRATIC VALUES

The "Velvet Revolution." The "Velvet Revolution" began in Czechoslovakia on November 17, 1989, as protesters began demanding democratic reforms. One of the movement's leaders was playwright Vaclav Havel, who had been jailed in the 1970s and early 1980s for criticizing the government. After a general strike and massive demonstrations, the Czech government gave in to demands for political reforms. Czechoslovakia's first non-communist government since the post–World War II era was formed. The Czechoslovakian parliament elected Havel president. In 1990 more than 96 percent of the population voted during the first free elections held in Czechoslovakia in more than 40 years.

CRITICAL THINKING Why were the events in Czechoslovakia described above referred to as the Velvet Revolution?

ANSWER: Students might suggest that the smoothness of the political transition contributed to the term.

VISUAL RECORD ANSWER

Students might suggest that people would not have been able to climb the Berlin Wall during the Cold War.

votes to Dukakis's 112. The Democrats did increase their majorities in both houses of Congress, however, and kept control of most state legislatures.

The End of the Cold War

President Bush faced a rapidly changing world. Mikhail Gorbachev's reform efforts in the Soviet Union led to the end of the Cold War and the breakup of the Soviet Union. This development was also influenced by frustration over economic turmoil in the Soviet Union. Many scholars argue that President Reagan's plan to increase U.S. defense systems contributed to the instability of the Soviet economy. As the Soviets spent more and more money on defense systems to keep up with the United States, they neglected serious economic issues at home.

The weakening of the Soviet Union was revealed in its reaction to democratic movements that swept Eastern and Central Europe in 1989 and 1990. No longer willing or able to bear the costs of propping up other communist governments, the Soviet Union announced in 1989 that it was adopting a policy of nonintervention in Eastern Europe. The Soviets did nothing when Poland and Hungary held free elections and the communist governments in Czechoslovakia and Romania fell.

The Soviets also did nothing when pro-democracy demonstrations broke out in East Germany in the fall of 1989. Throughout the fall, tens of thousands of East Germans fled to the West through Hungary. Then, in October, demonstrators forced Communist leader Erich Honecker to resign. Hoping to restore calm, the East German government opened the Berlin Wall on November 9 and lifted restrictions on travel to the West. It was too late. The pressure for German reunification—the reuniting of East and West Germany as one nation—was too great. After free elections, the two nations were united as the Federal Republic of Germany on October 3, 1990, without opposition from Gorbachev.

By 1991 Gorbachev had problems of his own in the Soviet Union. Alarmed by the pace of reforms, Communist hard-liners attempted to oust him. Their attempt collapsed quickly, but Gorbachev's days in power were numbered. On December 1 the Ukrainians voted for independence. On December 25 Gorbachev resigned as president of the Soviet Union and turned over control of the armed forces to Boris Yeltsin, the president of Russia. The next day, the presidents of Belarus, Russia, and Ukraine declared that the Soviet Union was "ceasing its existence." They formed a loose confederation

INTERPRETING THE VISUAL RECORD

The Berlin Wall. Protesters climbed the Berlin Wall in 1989. ***How does this scene symbolize the end of the Cold War?***

TEACH OBJECTIVE 3

LEVEL 1: Tell students to imagine that the Persian Gulf War has ended and that they are newspaper reporters who must write a synopsis of the war. Pair students and have each pair prepare an outline of a newspaper article that includes what led to the war as well as an analysis of how the war was different from previous U.S. military conflicts. *(Outlines should mention that Iraq invaded Kuwait and ignored the deadline for withdrawal set by the United Nations; the war was different because it was won with high-tech weapons, featured an unprecedented level of television coverage, and had female troops playing a significant role.)* Have volunteers share their outlines with the class. **Sheltered English, Cooperative Learning**

LEVEL 2: Pair students and tell one student in each pair to imagine that he or she is a newspaper reporter, and tell the second student to imagine that he or she is General Norman Schwarzkopf. Have each pair prepare a transcript of an interview in which General Schwarzkopf explains what led to the Persian Gulf War and analyzes how the war was different from previous U.S. military conflicts. *(See the Level 1 lesson for the correct cause and differences.)* Have students conduct their interviews for the class. **Cooperative Learning**

called the **Commonwealth of Independent States** (CIS). Eventually, the former Soviet republics of Armenia, Azerbaijan, Georgia, Kazakhstan, Kyrgyzstan, Moldova, Tajikistan, Turkmenistan, and Uzbekistan joined the CIS.

In early 1991 President Bush reflected on the promise of a new era free from Cold War pressures. "Now we can see . . . the very real prospect of a new world order," he declared, "a world in which freedom and respect for human rights find a home among all nations."

Communism still posed a threat to freedom, however. Pro-democracy reformers in China met a different fate from those in Europe. In May 1989, students and others took to Beijing's streets to protest Communist Party policies. On June 4 the government sent soldiers and tanks to remove the peaceful protesters gathered in Tiananmen Square. Estimates of the number of protesters killed range from a few hundred to more than a thousand.

✔ **READING CHECK:** How did the Cold War end?

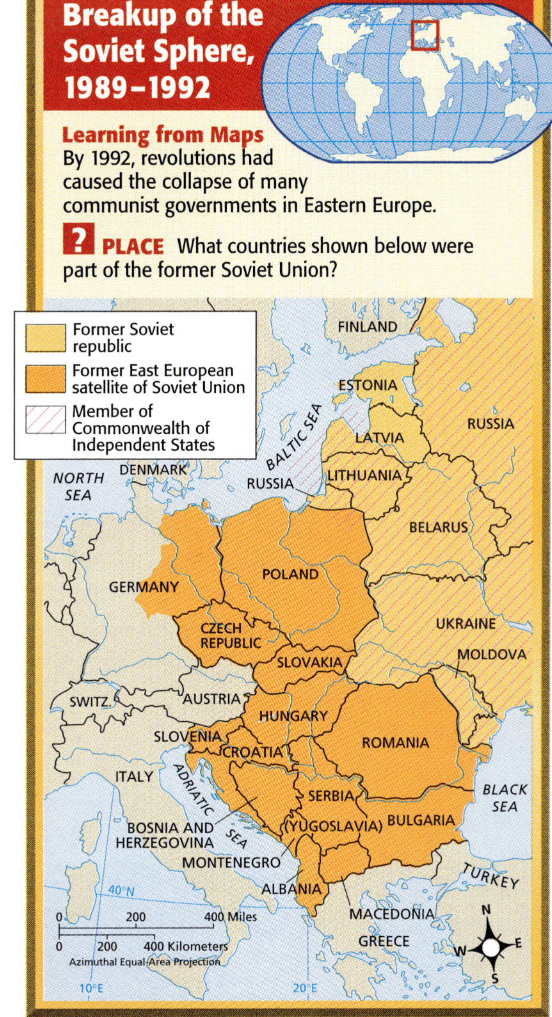

Breakup of the Soviet Sphere, 1989–1992

Learning from Maps By 1992, revolutions had caused the collapse of many communist governments in Eastern Europe.

? PLACE What countries shown below were part of the former Soviet Union?

The Persian Gulf War

With the end of the Cold War, President Bush was determined to reassert the leadership of the United States in world affairs. Before being elected president, Bush had served as U.S. ambassador to the United Nations, representative to China, and director of the CIA. His strong interest in foreign affairs was reflected in his presidency.

Operation Desert Storm. Bush assumed a strong leadership role in August 1990 when Iraq's ruler, Saddam Hussein, invaded neighboring Kuwait, a major oil producer. The United Nations condemned the attack. It also imposed economic sanctions on Iraq and set a deadline for Iraqi withdrawal from Kuwait. As the January 15, 1991, deadline neared, military forces representing the United States, Great Britain, France, Egypt, and Saudi Arabia prepared for war. Some 690,000 troops—including some 540,000 Americans—assembled in Saudi Arabia and on ships in the Persian Gulf. On January 16, bombing attacks began against Iraqi forces and military and industrial targets.

A ground assault began on February 23. Within days, the Iraqis had been driven back, and Kuwait's ruling al-Sabah family returned to power. American casualties included some 150 killed and 450 wounded, while an estimated 100,000 Iraqis died. U.S. air attacks also severely damaged the Iraqi capital, Baghdad, and other cities. Many hailed the success of this offensive, named **Operation Desert Storm**. The commander of U.S. forces, General Norman Schwarzkopf (SHWAWRTS-kawf), received a hero's welcome in New York City. Bush's approval rating soared following the war. The president praised the leadership of Secretary of Defense Richard Cheney and General Colin Powell, chairman of the Joint Chiefs of Staff.

The Persian Gulf War received extensive media coverage.

internetconnect

TOPIC: The Commonwealth of Independent States
GO TO: go.hrw.com
KEYWORD: SE1 CIS

Have students access the Internet through the HRW Web site to conduct research on the collapse of the Soviet Union and the difficulties faced by the new Commonwealth of Independent States (CIS). Then have each student create a graphic organizer with the following categories: **1.** economic challenges; **2.** political/governmental challenges; **3.** effect on crime; and **4.** relations with ethnic minorities.

THAT'S INTERESTING!

President Bush's job approval rating reached nearly 90 percent during the Persian Gulf War. Political analysts note, however, that presidents often receive high approval ratings during times of national crisis, and that such ratings often prove to be short-lived.

MAP ANSWER

Belarus, Estonia, Latvia, Lithuania, Moldova, Russia, and Ukraine

MAP ANSWER
(for p. 760)
Saudi Arabia

LEVEL 3: Organize students into groups of four. Have each group write a skit depicting what led to the Persian Gulf War and how the war was different from previous U.S. military conflicts. *(See the Level 1 lesson for the correct cause and differences.)* Have each group perform its skit for the class.
Cooperative Learning

SPOTLIGHT on Civilian Life During the Persian Gulf War

Have students conduct research on civilian life in Iraq, Israel, or Kuwait during the Persian Gulf War. Students should focus on the dangers and hardships faced by civilians. Have each student write a series of diary entries from the perspective of a civilian in one of the three countries mentioned. Have volunteers read their diary entries to the class. **Block Scheduling**

SPOTLIGHT on Female Soldiers in the Persian Gulf War

Have students conduct research on the various roles played by female soldiers during the Persian Gulf War. Students should attempt to find firsthand accounts from women who served in the U.S. military during the war. Have each student present his or her research in a short report.
Block Scheduling

GLOBAL RELATIONS

Iraq Invades Kuwait. Facing a national debt of $80–100 billion, Iraq claimed that Kuwait was hurting its economy by overproducing oil. This drove down international oil prices. Saddam Hussein began sending Iraqi troops to the Kuwaiti border. The United States and most other nations did not believe, however, that Saddam intended to go to war. They thought he would use the military threat to force Kuwait to negotiate an economic settlement. Saddam interpreted the lack of U.S. concern to mean that the United States would not intervene militarily.

ACTIVITY: Have students write a memo outlining plans for immediate action against Iraq shortly after troops built up along the Kuwaiti border.

The American Nation **VIDEO PROGRAM**

U.S. Troops in the Persian Gulf; Teacher's Guide, pp. 199–200

Search 49621, Play to 51970
Videodisc 2, Side B

Play Pause

See *Teacher's Guide* for Spanish barcode.

HOLT RESEARCHER *Read More About It*

Free Find:
Colin Powell

After reading about Colin Powell on the **Holt Researcher** CD–ROM, create a chart showing reasons why Powell would or would not be a good president.

BIOGRAPHY

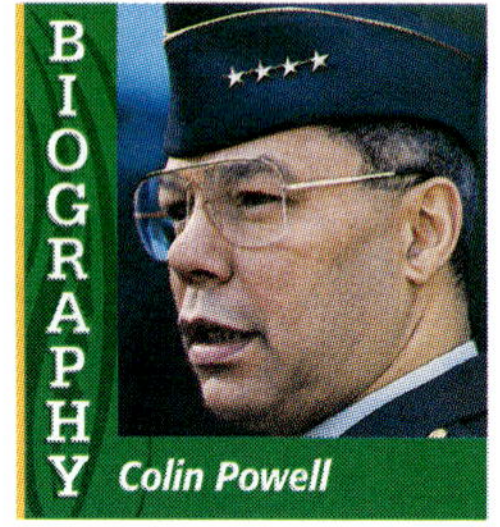

Colin Powell

Colin Powell was born in 1937 to Jamaican immigrants living in New York City. Powell's parents always stressed the importance of education and hard work. While attending City College of New York, Powell joined the Reserve Officers' Training Corps (ROTC). This experience led him to a career in the military. He graduated at the top of his ROTC class in 1958 and immediately received a commission in the United States Army. "The Army was my life," he recalled.

Powell served several tours of duty in Vietnam, where he was wounded twice. During one incident, an injured Powell rescued several comrades from a burning helicopter. After the war, he received an advanced degree from George Washington University and worked in both the Nixon and Carter administrations. During the

The Persian Gulf War, 1991

Learning from Maps After more than a month of bombing, the UN allied forces ended the Gulf War with a short ground offensive.

? MOVEMENT From which country did most of the UN allied troops advance during the ground war?

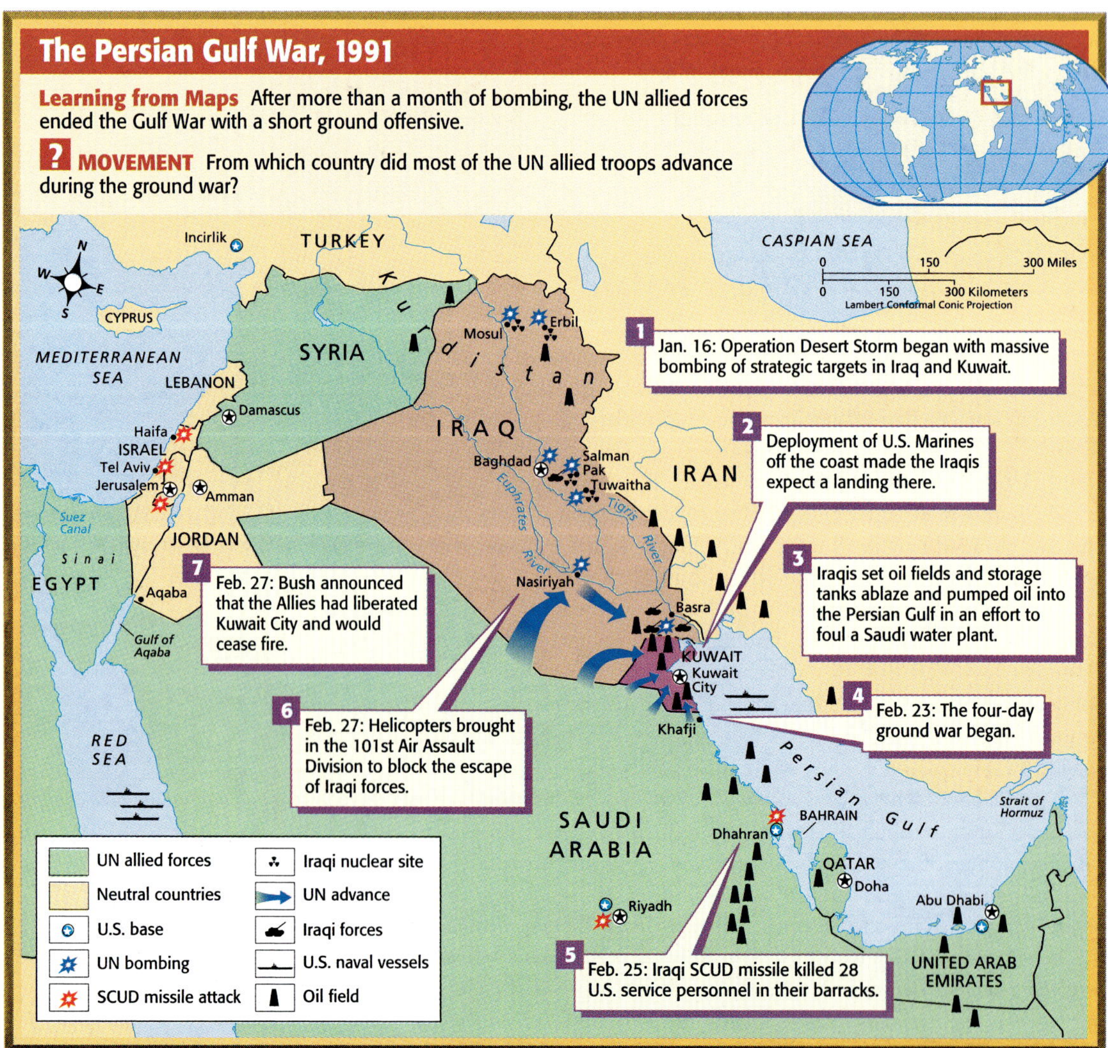

TURKEY
Incirlik
CASPIAN SEA
0 150 300 Miles
0 150 300 Kilometers
Lambert Conformal Conic Projection
CYPRUS
MEDITERRANEAN SEA
SYRIA
LEBANON
Damascus
Kurdistan
Mosul
Erbil
1 Jan. 16: Operation Desert Storm began with massive bombing of strategic targets in Iraq and Kuwait.
IRAQ
Baghdad
Salman Pak
Tuwaitha
IRAN
2 Deployment of U.S. Marines off the coast made the Iraqis expect a landing there.
Haifa
ISRAEL
Tel Aviv
Jerusalem
Amman
Suez Canal
JORDAN
Sinai
EGYPT
Aqaba
Gulf of Aqaba
Euphrates River
Tigris River
Nasiriyah
Basra
3 Iraqis set oil fields and storage tanks ablaze and pumped oil into the Persian Gulf in an effort to foul a Saudi water plant.
7 Feb. 27: Bush announced that the Allies had liberated Kuwait City and would cease fire.
KUWAIT
Kuwait City
Khafji
4 Feb. 23: The four-day ground war began.
6 Feb. 27: Helicopters brought in the 101st Air Assault Division to block the escape of Iraqi forces.
RED SEA
Persian Gulf
Strait of Hormuz
SAUDI ARABIA
Dhahran
BAHRAIN
QATAR
Doha
Riyadh
Abu Dhabi
UNITED ARAB EMIRATES
5 Feb. 25: Iraqi SCUD missile killed 28 U.S. service personnel in their barracks.
UN allied forces
Neutral countries
U.S. base
UN bombing
SCUD missile attack
Iraqi nuclear site
UN advance
Iraqi forces
U.S. naval vessels
Oil field

TEACH OBJECTIVE 4

ALL LEVELS: Tell students that many Americans perceived George Bush as being unconcerned with the nation's domestic problems. To help students understand the domestic problems faced by the Bush administration, copy the graphic organizer at right on the chalkboard, omitting the italicized answers. Have students work in pairs to complete the organizer. Ask volunteers to share their answers with the class. Then ask students why many women might have been angered by the Thomas-Hill hearings. *(Students might suggest that the Senate Judiciary Committee appeared to be insensitive to women or that many women have experienced sexual harassment in the workplace.)* Tell students that the Thomas-Hill hearings publicized the issue of sexual harassment of women in the workplace. **Sheltered English, Cooperative Learning**

DOMESTIC PROBLEMS FACED BY THE BUSH ADMINISTRATION

The Thomas-Hill hearings–law professor Anita Hill alleged that Bush Supreme Court nominee Clarence Thomas sexually harassed her when both of them were working at the EEOC. The bullying tactics used by some members of the Senate Judiciary Committee, which investigated Hill's allegations, outraged many women.	*Economic troubles–the federal deficit surged, partly as a result of the costs of the Persian Gulf War and the S&L bailout. The U.S. trade deficit with Japan persisted, and an economic recession occurred and persisted through the 1992 election year. The number of people living in poverty also grew.*

Persian Gulf War, Powell expressed great faith in the U.S. troops.

> **"I had no doubt that we would be successful. We had the troops, the weapons, and the plan. What I did not know was how long it would take, and how many of our troops would not be coming home."**

In the early 1990s Powell retired from the military. He has continued to serve national and international interests, however. In 1994 he was part of a peacekeeping team that helped lead the transition to democracy in Haiti. In recent years he has focused on increasing volunteerism in the United States. Although many supporters urged Powell to run for president in 1996, he declined.

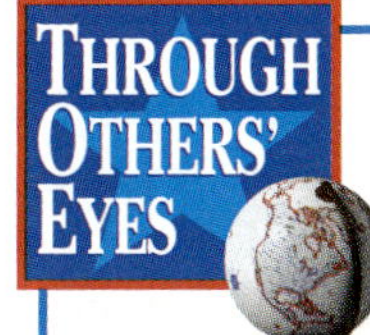

A Palestinian View of the Persian Gulf War

Although the Persian Gulf War was brief, many people were caught in the cross fire, including the residents of Israel. To get revenge against UN forces, Iraq launched a missile attack on Israel. Palestinian philosopher Sari Nusseibeh was living in Israel when the attack came. He recalled his impressions as the war raged.

> **"It was January 29, 13 days since the aerial bombardment in the Gulf War had started. For fully two weeks we had been placed under a total 24-hour curfew, interspersed [interrupted] only by three two-hour intervals in which we were allowed to do our shopping. All of us—my wife, my three children, and myself—had taken to sleeping together on the floor of the sitting-dining area of our apartment. This way we kept each other company through the SCUD [missile] scares (. . . we wondered each time where the rockets would fall, and what deadly poison they might be carrying). . . .**
>
> **For almost two weeks we lived in a state of suspension between TV scenes of missiles hitting Iraqi targets and footage of missiles flying over our heads."**

A unique war. Unlike previous U.S. engagements, the Persian Gulf War was won almost entirely by using high-tech weapons. Television reporters also provided unprecedented coverage of the war, including live coverage of the air assaults. As Americans sat glued to their television sets, news correspondent Bernard Shaw reported the first allied bombings on Iraq. "This is [pause] something is happening outside. . . . The skies over Baghdad have been illuminated. We're seeing bright flashes going off all over the sky."

Military technology quickly became the star of the show as coverage of the war expanded. The technological nature of the war highlighted another unique aspect of Operation Desert Storm—the significant role played by women. More than 35,000 American women served in the Persian Gulf conflict—some 6 percent of all U.S. troops involved. Eleven American female soldiers were killed, and two were taken prisoner. Although the U.S. military banned women from serving as combat pilots, they served in almost every other capacity—including flying support planes and working on missile crews.

The role of women in Desert Storm and the nature of the war caused many people to question the policy of banning women from combat. With technology playing an increasingly significant role in modern warfare, critics charged, physical differences between men and women would become less important than technological skills. Before the war, the number of women in the military had increased dramatically. U.S. Air Force colonel Douglas Kennett commented that his branch of the service "couldn't go to war without women and we couldn't win without them." In August 1991 the Senate removed the ban against women serving as combat pilots, but continued to limit female soldiers' role in ground battles.

This soldier is one of many women who served in the Persian Gulf War.

✔ **READING CHECK:** What led to the Persian Gulf War, and how was it different from previous U.S. military conflicts?

TECHNOLOGY AND SOCIETY

The Missile War. When the Iraqis used SCUD missiles to attack Saudi Arabia and Israel, the United States provided those nations with Patriot air defense missiles. Although there were many technical problems surrounding the use of Patriots to defend against SCUD attacks, the new technology reassured Israelis and contributed to their decision not to declare war on Iraq.

CRITICAL THINKING What might have been the Patriot missiles' most important contribution made during the Gulf War?

ANSWER: Students might indicate that the Patriot missiles provided psychological reassurance if not excellent military performance.

VISUAL RECORD ANSWER

(for p. 762)

Students might suggest that she is wheelchair-bound.

SECTION 3 REVIEW ANSWERS

Define and Identify

For significance, see the following pages:

- Christa McAuliffe, p. 756
- *Challenger,* p. 756
- acquired immune deficiency syndrome, p. 757
- Jesse Jackson, p. 757
- Michael Dukakis, p. 757
- Lloyd Bentsen, p. 757

▸ASSIGNMENT *Tell students to imagine that it is 1991 and that they are women who have been watching the Thomas-Hill hearings. Have each student write a letter to a member of the committee that describes why many women are outraged by committee members' conduct.*

SPOTLIGHT on the Americans with Disabilities Act

Have each student conduct research on the provisions of the Americans with Disabilities Act. Ask students also to find statistics to show how the act has affected the hiring of people with disabilities. Have each student present his or her findings in a short oral report. **Block Scheduling**

SPOTLIGHT on the Trade Deficit

Have each student conduct research on the dollar amount of the current U.S. trade deficit and on the U.S. balance of trade with its major trading partners. Students should find out what types of goods the United States exports to other countries as well as the types of goods the United States imports. Students should also be able to define the term *trade deficit.* Have each student create a poster or a chart to present his or her findings. **Block Scheduling**

- George Bush, p. 757
- Dan Quayle, p. 757
- Commonwealth of Independent States, p. 759
- Operation Desert Storm, p. 759
- Norman Schwarzkopf, p. 759
- Colin Powell, p. 759
- Americans with Disabilities Act, p. 762
- War on Drugs, p. 762

Locate

For locations, see the map on p. 760. For significance, see the following page:

- Iraq, p. 759
- Kuwait, p. 759
- Saudi Arabia, p. 759

1. Poland and Hungary hold free elections; communist governments in Czechoslovakia and Romania fall; East Germans hold pro-democracy demonstrations; Germany reunifies; Ukrainians vote for independence

2. Entries might compare Carter and Reagan, examine the economic boom of the 1980s, or discuss the end of the Cold War.

3. to assert American leadership, protect oil supplies; Bush's approval ratings soared; Iraq was defeated

4. high-tech war, had intensive television coverage, and included female troops

5. Critics charged that Bush neglected domestic problems. Women's response to the Thomas-Hill hearings, the high federal deficit, and the slow economy all weakened Bush's support.

Domestic Concerns

President Bush's successes in foreign affairs won him popularity and international praise, but some critics charged that he was neglecting problems at home. As the 1992 presidential campaign approached, domestic issues—particularly the economy and a growing political controversy—troubled the public and weakened the president's support.

Bush's domestic policies. Although Bush had entered office telling the public, "We don't need radical new directions," he did propose a domestic agenda that differed from that of President Reagan. As he explained:

> **"America is never wholly herself unless she is engaged in high moral principle. We as a people have such a purpose today. It is to make kinder the face of the Nation and gentler the face of the world. My friends, we have work to do. . . . I am speaking of a new engagement in the lives of others, a new activism, hands-on and involved, that gets the job done."**

Promising to be the "education president," he proposed a series of reforms to improve the nation's schools. Meanwhile, First Lady Barbara Bush launched a campaign to stamp out illiteracy. "Everything would be better if people could learn to read, write, and understand," she said. Although Congress rejected many of Bush's proposed education reforms, it did approve increased funding for college loans and the Head Start program.

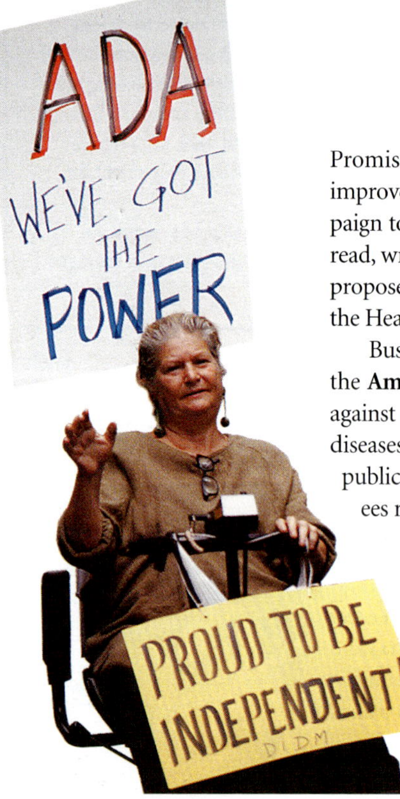

INTERPRETING THE VISUAL RECORD

Americans with disabilities. This woman makes her support of the Americans with Disabilities Act known. ***What obstacle does this woman have to overcome?***

Bush ushered in a new era for citizens with disabilities. In July 1990 he signed the **Americans with Disabilities Act** into law. The act prohibits discrimination against people with physical or mental disabilities—including being afflicted with diseases such as AIDS—in employment, transportation, telephone services, and public buildings. The act also requires that companies with 15 or more employees remove structural barriers from offices.

The president addressed growing concerns over crime and drug use by launching the **War on Drugs**. This initiative provided more money to stop drug smuggling and illegal drug use. As a first step in this attack, Bush ordered the arrest of Panamanian dictator and drug smuggler General Manuel Noriega. In December 1989, U.S. Marines invaded Panama to bring Noriega back to the United States to face drug charges. Guillermo Endara, the democratically elected president, took control of the Panamanian government. In 1992 a Florida court convicted Noriega of drug smuggling and sentenced him to 40 years in prison.

The Thomas-Hill hearings. Bush continued Reagan's efforts to move the Supreme Court in a conservative direction. In 1990 he filled a vacancy on the Court with David Souter, a conservative New Hampshire judge. In 1991 Justice Thurgood Marshall announced his retirement. Bush nominated Clarence Thomas, a conservative African American judge and former head of the federal Equal Employment Opportunity Commission (EEOC), to take his place.

During the confirmation hearings, law professor Anita Hill, a former associate of Thomas' at the EEOC, accused the nominee of sexual harassment. This is the use of unwelcome sexual language or behavior that creates a hostile working

REVIEW

Have students complete the **Section 3 Review** on p. 763.

ASSESS

Have students complete **Daily Quiz 25.3**. As **Alternative Assessment**, you may want to use the interview transcript or the skit in this section's lessons.

RETEACH

Have students complete **Main Idea Activity for Reteaching and Sheltered English 25.3**. Organize students into triads. Have each triad write two or three sentences that identify and explain the significance of six of the key people, places, or terms in Section 3. Collect triads' identifications and use them to quiz the class. **Sheltered English, Cooperative Learning**

EXTEND

Have students conduct research on three of the key people mentioned in this section. Have each student write brief biographical capsules summarizing the pertinent information about each person. **Block Scheduling**

environment. In televised hearings, the Senate Judiciary Committee investigated Hill's charges. The bullying tactics used by some members of the committee in their questioning of Hill outraged many women. After the Senate narrowly approved Thomas's Supreme Court nomination, female activists vowed to show their disapproval in the next election. The hearings stirred debate across the country about sexual harassment.

The economy. Adding to President Bush's concerns was the slowing U.S. economy. The problem only grew worse as the economy weakened. In 1991 the federal deficit surged to some $270 billion and reached $291 billion in 1992. The costs of the Persian Gulf War and the bailout of the S&L and banking industries added to the deficit.

The trade gap persisted as well. Although the trade deficit had declined from its 1990 high of almost $102 billion, in 1991 it still stood at about $66 billion. Japan's massive annual sales of automobiles and electronic goods to American consumers accounted for a large portion of the gap. On a 1992 trade mission to Japan, President Bush and American business leaders tried with little success to persuade the Japanese to increase imports from the United States.

Some Americans favored buying only goods produced in the United States as a way to strengthen the economy and reduce the trade deficit.

Adding to these economic problems, a recession hit late in 1990. As the economy faltered, unemployment rose. States facing budget deficits cut their welfare programs. The number of Americans living below the poverty line grew by more than 2 million in 1990. The recession continued through 1992, hurting President Bush's re-election hopes.

✔ **READING CHECK:** What domestic problems did the Bush administration face?

SECTION 3 REVIEW

Define and explain the significance of the following terms:
Challenger
acquired immune deficiency syndrome
Commonwealth of Independent States
Operation Desert Storm
Americans with Disabilities Act
War on Drugs

Identify and explain the significance of the following individuals:

Christa McAuliffe
Jesse Jackson
Michael Dukakis
Lloyd Bentsen
George Bush
Dan Quayle
Norman Schwarzkopf
Colin Powell

Locate and explain the significance of the following places:

Iraq
Kuwait
Saudi Arabia

1. **Using Graphic Organizers** Copy the graphic organizer below. Use it to describe the events that marked the end of the Cold War.

   1. Soviets adopt non-intervention policy
   2.
   3.
   4.
   5.
   6.
   7. Gorbachev resigns

2. **Using Historical Imagination** Imagine that you are an average American in the 1980s. Write a journal entry describing how the decade is different from the 1970s.
3. **Identifying Cause and Effect** Why did the United States participate in the Persian Gulf War? What were the outcomes of the war?
4. **Synthesizing** In what ways was the Persian Gulf War different from other recent wars in which the United States fought?

Critical Thinking

5. How did domestic issues affect public support for President Bush?
   Consider:
   - Bush's domestic policies and their effects
   - reactions to the Thomas-Hill hearings
   - the state of the economy by the early 1990s

Creating a Time Line
Each event should have an explanation and the correct date.

Writing a Summary
See the Reading Checks in each section for main ideas.

Identifying People and Ideas

1. Incident in which Iranian militants held 53 American hostages for 444 days
2. U.S. president from 1981 to 1989
3. Reagan's vice president who was elected president in 1988
4. theory that lowering top income tax rates will spur economic growth
5. space-based missile-defense system
6. Nicaraguan faction supported by the CIA that opposed the Sandinistas
7. first woman appointed to the U.S. Supreme Court
8. space shuttle that exploded in 1986
9. allied military operation against Iraq in 1991
10. chairman of the Joint Chiefs of Staff who became a hero during the Persian Gulf War

REVIEW AND ASSESSMENT RESOURCES

PRINT
- Chapter 25 Review, pp. 764–65
- Chapter 25 Tutorial for Students, Parents, Mentors, and Peers
- Chapter 25 Test (Form A or B)
- Portfolio Activities and Alternative Assessment Handbook, Chapter 25

MULTIMEDIA
- Audio Program, Chapter 25 (English and Spanish)
- Chapter 25 Test Generator (on the One-Stop Planner)
- Global Skill Builder CD–ROM
- HRW Web site

SHELTERED ENGLISH
- Spanish Glossary
- Sheltered English Chapter 25 Test

REVIEW

Have students complete the **Chapter 25 Review** on pp. 764–65.

ASSESS

Use one of the chapter tests to assess students' understanding of the content. For **Alternative Assessment**, see the **Portfolio Activities and Alternative Assessment Handbook.**

Understanding Main Ideas

1. Reagan promised solutions to problems that Carter seemed unable to solve.
2. increased military spending, a tougher stance toward the Soviet Union
3. rising deficit, 1987 stock market crash, and S&L crisis
4. sale of weapons to Iran, illegal funding of the Contras, Reagan's role in the scandal
5. economic boom, new computer technology, AIDS
6. Iraq's invasion of Kuwait

Reviewing Themes

1. increased the wealth of many Americans but also led to cuts in social programs and decreased government regulation
2. Reagan's hard-line stance led to increased tensions.
3. Personal computers became widely available, and virtual reality was invented.

Thinking Critically

1. the growth of Soviet influence in the region
2. Answers will vary. Some students might advocate more assistance for poor Americans, and others might advocate stricter regulations on the economy.

Review

Creating a Time Line

Copy the time line below onto a sheet of paper. Complete the time line by filling in the events and dates from the chapter that you think were most significant. Pick three events and explain why you think they were significant.

Writing a Summary

Using the Reading Checks as a guide, write an overview of the events in the chapter.

Identifying People and Ideas

Identify the following terms or individuals and explain their significance.

1. Iran hostage crisis
2. Ronald Reagan
3. George Bush
4. supply-side economics
5. Strategic Defense Initiative
6. Contras
7. Sandra Day O'Connor
8. *Challenger*
9. Operation Desert Storm
10. Colin Powell

Understanding Main Ideas

SECTION 1

1. Why did voters choose Ronald Reagan over Jimmy Carter in the 1980 presidential election?
2. How did the Reagan administration fight the Cold War in the early 1980s?

SECTION 2

3. Why did public confidence in the economy begin to weaken in the late 1980s?
4. What were the main issues in the Iran-Contra affair?

SECTION 3

5. What changes occurred in American society in the 1980s?
6. What led to the Persian Gulf War?

Reviewing Themes

1. **Economic Development** What effects did President Reagan's economic policies have on the country?
2. **Global Relations** How did President Reagan's approach to defense change the Cold War?
3. **Technology and Society** How did computer technology change in the 1980s?

Thinking Critically

1. **Identifying Values** What issues were at stake for the United States in El Salvador and Nicaragua?
2. **Problem Solving** How would you have addressed the economic problems of the 1980s?
3. **Comparing and Contrasting** How was the Iran-Contra affair both similar to and different from the Watergate scandal?
4. **Analyzing** How did improved relations affect the United States and the Soviet Union?
5. **Taking a Stand** Was life better for Americans in the 1980s than in the 1970s? Why?

Writing About History

Writing to Explain Write an essay that explains the significance of the passage of the Americans with Disabilities Act. Use the following graphic to organize your thoughts.

Challenges for people with disabilities	Benefits of Americans with Disabilities Act

RETEACH

Organize students into small groups. Have each group use at least 20 of the key people, key places, and key terms in this chapter to create a crossword puzzle with clues. Have students in each group exchange their crossword puzzles with another group and then solve them.

Sheltered English, Cooperative Learning

EXTEND

Have each student conduct research on the so-called Republican Revolution. Why has Ronald Reagan's agenda for the United States been described as revolutionary? What lasting effects has the Republican Revolution had on the U.S. government and U.S. politics? Have each student write an analytical essay presenting his or her research. **Block Scheduling**

Strategies for Success Review the **Strategies for Success** on *Creating an Outline.* Read the following thesis statement, which presents a hypothesis about the effects of President Reagan's economic policies. Then create an outline for a short essay that would focus on and attempt to prove the statement.

> **"Reaganomics affected different Americans differently. While some profited from President Reagan's economic program of tax reductions and relaxed government regulations, others remained unable to find jobs and were hurt by deep cuts in social programs."**

Linking History and Geography

Voter turnout was particularly low in the 1988 presidential election. Only 50 percent of registered voters participated—the lowest turnout since 1924. Study the map below. Which states did Michael Dukakis win?

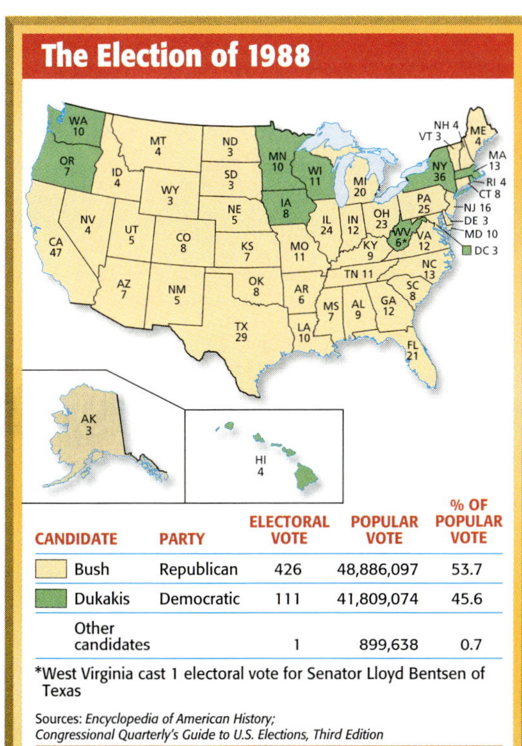

CANDIDATE	PARTY	ELECTORAL VOTE	POPULAR VOTE	% OF POPULAR VOTE
Bush	Republican	426	48,886,097	53.7
Dukakis	Democratic	111	41,809,074	45.6
Other candidates		1	899,638	0.7

*West Virginia cast 1 electoral vote for Senator Lloyd Bentsen of Texas

Sources: *Encyclopedia of American History; Congressional Quarterly's Guide to U.S. Elections, Third Edition*

internetconnect

TOPIC: Persian Gulf War
GO TO: go.hrw.com
KEYWORD: SE1 Gulf

Accessing the Internet through the HRW Web site, research the Persian Gulf War. Then write a journal entry as if you were a U.S. soldier fighting in the Gulf War. Describe your experiences in and thoughts about the war.

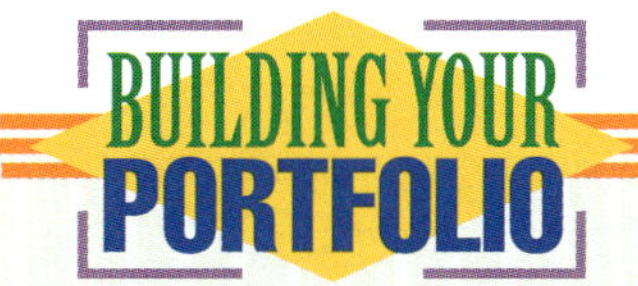

Complete one or all of the following projects independently or cooperatively.

1 Global Relations

Imagine that you are a reporter covering the Iran-Contra affair. ***Create a flowchart*** that traces the transfer of weapons, money, and supplies among the United States, Iran, and the Contras.

2 Technology and Society

Imagine that you are a science fiction writer in the 1980s. ***Write and illustrate a short story*** that reflects your concerns about the future of technology in society.

William Gibson's book *Neuromancer*

3 Economic Development

Imagine that you are one of President Reagan's economic advisers. ***Prepare a pamphlet*** describing Reagan's economic policies and their goals. Include your opinions of the costs and benefits of each policy.

3. Both involved the misuse of government power and money; Nixon was forced out of office, whereas Reagan was never implicated.
4. led to the INF Treaty, which eased tensions regarding nuclear war
5. Answers will vary but many students will point to the economic prosperity and optimism of the 1980s.

Writing About History
challenges—employment discrimination, access to buildings; benefits—banned employment discrimination, made employers remove structural barriers

Strategies for Success
Major headings and subheadings might include Reaganomics; tax cuts—the program, who benefited, who did not; relaxed regulations—increased economic performance, S&L scandal

Linking History and Geography
Dukakis won Hawaii, Iowa, Massachusetts, Minnesota, New York, Oregon, Rhode Island, Washington, West Virginia, and Wisconsin. He also won Washington, D.C.

LET'S GET STARTED!

Ask students to identify recent examples of natural disasters or industrial accidents in their local area or region. Have students share their examples with the class. Then ask students to explain how these disasters or accidents affected the natural environment. Tell students that they will study the *Exxon Valdez* spill, the Yellowstone fires, air pollution, and recycling efforts in the Unit 7 America's Geography.

TEACH AMERICA'S GEOGRAPHY—THE NATURAL ENVIRONMENT

Have students study the America's Geography feature. Then ask each student to write a caption for each of the maps and charts and graphs in the feature. *(Students' captions will vary. Students should accurately and fully represent the information in the given map, chart, or graph in their captions.)* Ask volunteers to read their captions to the class. **Sheltered English**

ACROSS THE CURRICULUM

▶GOVERNMENT◀

The Oil Pollution Act. In response to the *Exxon Valdez* disaster, Congress passed the Oil Pollution Act of 1990. This act enabled various federal agencies to respond more quickly to large oil catastrophes. The act established guidelines for future oil storage, provided for the purchase of damaged land, and set up a trust fund—financed by an oil tax—to aid in future cleanup efforts.

CRITICAL THINKING Why might Congress have failed to consider an oil pollution act prior to 1989?

ANSWER: Answers will vary. Students might suggest that the United States had not expected or conceived of a large oil disaster prior to the *Exxon Valdez* spill.

AMERICA'S GEOGRAPHY ANSWERS

1. the Becharof National Wildlife Refuge, the Chugach National Forest, the Katmai National Park, the Kenai Fjords National Park, and the Kodiak National Wildlife Refuge and Preserve
2. about 475 miles
3. lands in the Chugach National Forest, the Kenai Fjords National Park, the Kenai National Wildlife Refuge, and the Kodiak National Wildlife Refuge

AMERICA'S Geography

The Natural Environment

The increasing population and rapid development of land in the United States has led to increased concerns about the future of the natural environment. In the late 1900s, however, much progress was made toward protecting the environment and decreasing pollution. The creation of national parks and wildlife refuges helps preserve the natural landscape and save endangered animals from possible extinction.

The Alaskan Oil Spill of 1989

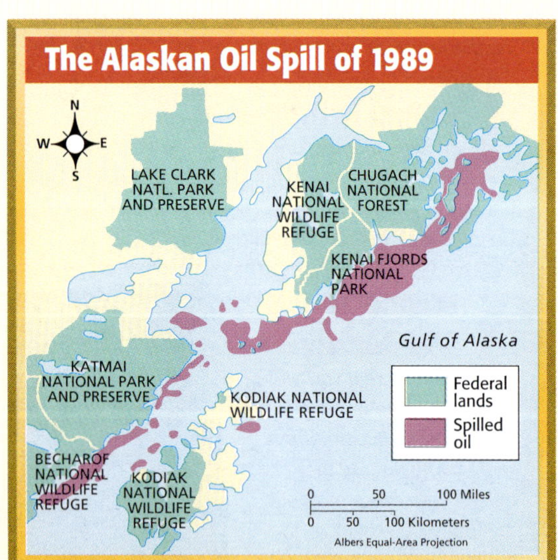

The Alaskan Recovery

Alaskan oil spill. Industrial accidents can have devastating effects on the environment. In 1989 the oil tanker *Exxon Valdez* spilled about 11 million gallons of oil when it ran aground near the Alaskan coastline. The cleanup for the oil spill was long and expensive. To help preserve the coastal areas, the U.S. government purchased some of the affected lands. Ten years later some parts of Alaska still had not fully recovered.

GEOGRAPHY AND HISTORY Skills

HUMAN-ENVIRONMENT INTERACTION

1. Which federal lands were affected by the Alaskan oil spill of 1989?
2. According to the map of the Alaskan oil spill, how many miles did the spilled oil spread?
3. Which lands were purchased by the government after the oil spill?

SPOTLIGHT on the *Exxon Valdez* Spill

Have students conduct research on the *Exxon Valdez* spill. Then tell students to imagine that they are radio reporters at the scene. Have each student write a three-minute broadcast describing the spill and discussing its implications. Remind students that they will need to synthesize and summarize their research in order to present a full broadcast in just three minutes. Ask volunteers to read their broadcasts to the class.

SPOTLIGHT on Air Pollution Control

Pair students and ask them to conduct research on recent efforts to control air pollution. Have each pair develop a visual presentation on these efforts. Pairs' presentations should include both images and text. Tell each pair to set up its presentations around the classroom and ask students to visit their classmates' stations. To conclude, conduct a discussion on air pollution control measures. Ask students to identify the measure that they view as most promising or successful. Ask students to fully justify their answers. **Cooperative Learning**

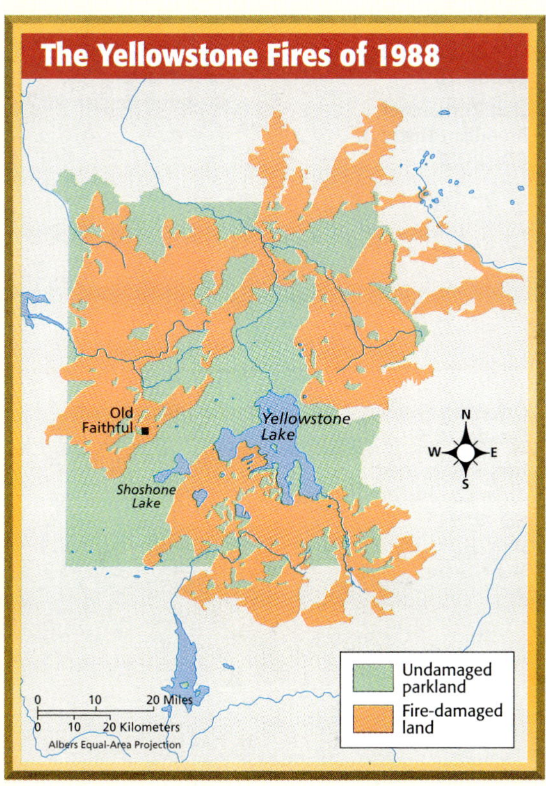

Yellowstone Recovery

Albers Equal-Area Projection 0 10 20 Miles 0 10 20 Kilometers

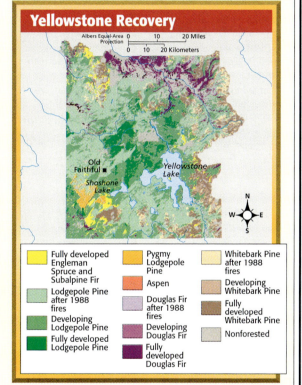

Old Faithful · Yellowstone Lake · Shoshone Lake · N · W · E · S

Fully developed Engleman Spruce and Subalpine Fir · Lodgepole Pine after 1988 fires · Developing Lodgepole Pine · Fully developed Lodgepole Pine · Pygmy Lodgepole Pine · Aspen · Douglas Fir after 1988 fires · Developing Douglas Fir · Fully developed Douglas Fir · Whitebark Pine after 1988 fires · Developing Whitebark Pine · Fully developed Whitebark Pine · Nonforested

Pollution control. Air pollution had become a serious problem by the 1970s. New laws helped decrease air pollutants, particularly lead and carbon dioxide. Americans also fought pollution by recycling more waste items.

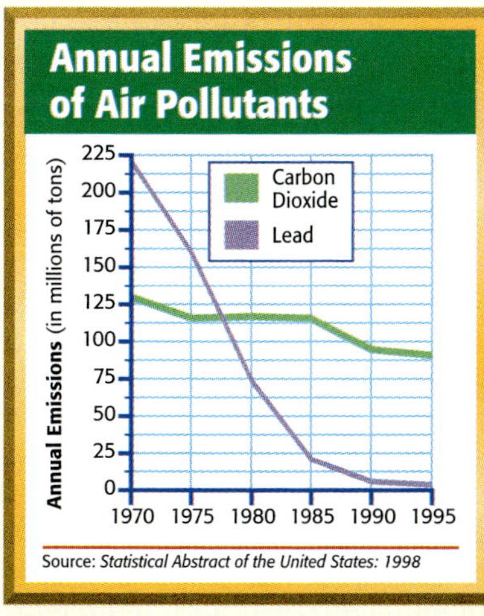

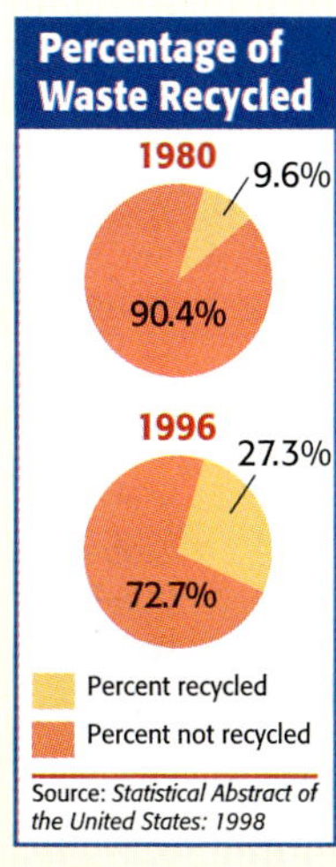

Yellowstone fires. In 1988 a natural disaster struck Yellowstone National Park. Lightning started forest fires that eventually burned some 45 percent of the park. The lands recovered quickly from the fires, however. Within just a few years much of the park had experienced a significant regrowth of its vegetation.

GEOGRAPHY AND HISTORY Skills

Human-Environment Interaction

1. After recovering from the fires of 1988, what plants grew in the areas that had been destroyed by fire?
2. By how much did the level of lead in the air drop between 1970 and 1995?
3. How much did the percentage of waste recycled increase between 1980 and 1996?

ACROSS THE CURRICULUM

▶GOVERNMENT◀

The NEPA. In 1970, in an effort to "establish a national policy for the environment," the United States passed legislation known as the National Environment Policy Act (NEPA). This provided the basis for founding the Environmental Protection Agency and many other federal agencies. These agencies have attempted to protect and enrich the environment. Federal statutes and regulations give these agencies their legal power.

Activity: Have students conduct research on private non-profit organizations that either protect or promote the environment. Have each student prepare a short presentation on his or her chosen organization.

America's Geography Answers

1. Douglas fir, Engleman spruce and subalpine fir, lodgepole pine, and whitebark pine
2. by about 69 millions of tons
3. about 17.7 percent

767

Life in the 1990s and Beyond

CHAPTER PLANNING GUIDE

	Section Lesson Objectives	Print Resources	Multimedia Resources	Sheltered English Resources
Section 1 Clinton's First Term, pp. 770–75	1 Discuss how the 1992 presidential election differed from other recent elections. 2 Explain what led to the Republican comeback in the 1994 congressional elections. 3 Analyze how regional conflicts and terrorism affected the world. 4 Assess how successful the United Nations was in maintaining world peace after the Cold War ended.	▶ Guided Reading Strategy 26.1 ▶ Geography Activity 26: The Republicans Take the House ▶ Section 1 Review, p. 775 ▶ Daily Quiz 26.1	▶ One-Stop Planner, Lesson 26.1 ▶ Holt Researcher: American History CD–ROM	▶ Main Idea Activity for Reteaching and Sheltered English 26.1
Section 2 Clinton's Second Term, pp. 776–81	1 Discuss the issues that affected the 1996 presidential election. 2 Describe the domestic issues that shaped President Clinton's second term. 3 Relate what led to the impeachment of President Clinton, and describe what the outcome was. 4 Analyze why NATO launched air strikes against Yugoslavia in 1999.	▶ Guided Reading Strategy 26.2 ▶ Graphic Organizer Activity 26: The Serbian Conflict ▶ Biography Reading 26: Madeleine Albright ▶ Section 2 Review, p. 781 ▶ Daily Quiz 26.2	▶ One-Stop Planner, Lesson 26.2 ▶ Holt Researcher: American History CD–ROM	▶ Main Idea Activity for Reteaching and Sheltered English 26.2
Section 3 Society in the 1990s, pp. 782–86	1 Discuss the events that shaped the space program in the 1990s. 2 Explain the issues surrounding technology in the 1990s. 3 Analyze how U.S. popular culture affected the rest of the world. 4 Describe how immigration changed in the 1990s. 5 Identify the issues that affected family life in the 1990s.	▶ Guided Reading Strategy 26.3 ▶ Literature Reading 26: Caught Between Two Cultures ▶ Section 3 Review, p. 786 ▶ Daily Quiz 26.3	▶ One-Stop Planner, Lesson 26.3 ▶ Holt Researcher: American History CD–ROM ▶ HRW Web site	▶ Main Idea Activity for Reteaching and Sheltered English 26.3
Section 4 Looking to the Future, pp. 787–91	1 Identify the factors that shaped the global economy. 2 Describe the environmental issues concerning people in the 1990s. 3 Explain why population growth in urban areas and throughout the world caused concern. 4 Analyze the role of the United States in spreading democracy throughout the world.	▶ Guided Reading Strategy 26.4 ▶ Primary Source Reading 26: Antarctica: A New View ▶ Section 4 Review, p. 791 ▶ Daily Quiz 26.4	▶ One-Stop Planner, Lesson 26.4 ▶ Linking Geography and History Transparency 23: The Global Environment ▶ Holt Researcher: American History CD–ROM	▶ Main Idea Activity for Reteaching and Sheltered English 26.4
Chapter Review and Assessment pp. 792–93		▶ Chapter 26 Review, pp. 792–93 ▶ Chapter 26 Tutorial for Students, Parents, Mentors, and Peers ▶ Chapter 26 Test (Form A or B) ▶ Portfolio Activities and Alternative Assessment Handbook, Chapter 26	▶ Audio Program, Chapter 26 (English and Spanish) ▶ Chapter 26 Test Generator (on the One-Stop Planner) ▶ Global Skill Builder CD–ROM ▶ HRW Web site	▶ Spanish Glossary ▶ Sheltered English Chapter 26 Test

CHAPTER OVERVIEW

Bill Clinton was first elected president in 1992, a year in which independent voters expressed their dissatisfaction with both major parties by giving candidate Ross Perot 19 percent of the popular vote. President Clinton's cabinet appointments reflected his commitment to a diverse society. However, his plan to reform the health care system—a cornerstone of his campaign promises—failed to pass Congress. Partly as a result of the failure of his health care plan, the Republicans were able to capture control of the House of Representatives and Senate in 1994. Clinton's second term was marked by domestic prosperity and scandal, as his relationship with a White House intern led to his impeachment by the House of Representatives. The Senate acquitted the president, to most Americans' satisfaction.

During his second term Clinton backed NATO air strikes against Yugoslavia, a move designed to end Serbian aggression against ethnic Albanians in the province of Kosovo. The situation in the Balkans was just one of the outcomes of the end of the Cold War. Ethnic tensions flared up in several formerly communist countries. The increasing globalization of the economy and the rapid dissemination of information via the Internet also characterized the post–Cold War world.

TIME TAMERS

Block Scheduling

The teacher lesson plans for each section offer a variety of activity choices to help you present the material in a block scheduling format. For further suggestions on block scheduling, see the **Block Scheduling Handbook with Team Teaching Strategies**, pp. 151–56.

Smithsonian Institution®

Internet Connections and Lesson 26
www.si.edu/hrw

Hands-On History Activities:

Classroom to Community The **Hands-On History Activities** help students make meaningful connections between events in American history and those in their own hometown. You may wish to use the Chapter 26 Activity, Water—Cool, Clean Water, to extend the chapter lessons, as alternative assessment, or as a block scheduling option.

Portfolio Projects

The American Nation includes multiple portfolio projects in each Pupil's Edition chapter review, as well as each unit review. Chapter 26 Portfolio Project options on p. 793 include the following:

1. Students will **write an outline**.
2. Students will **write a memo**.
3. Students will **prepare a business summary**.

The American Nation
INTERNET RESOURCE DIRECTORY

To access online materials for this chapter, go to **go.hrw.com** and type in the keywords listed below.

HRW ONLINE RESOURCES
GO TO: go.hrw.com

Online Maps
KEYWORD: SE1 Maps26
• Wetlands

Online Charts
KEYWORD: SE1 Charts26
• U.S. Trade Balance

Online Reading Support
KEYWORD: SE1 Strategies26

Online Rubrics
KEYWORD: SE1 Rubrics

CHAPTER ENRICHMENT LINKS
Use these Web links to extend and enrich student learning for Chapter 26.
GO TO: go.hrw.com
KEYWORD: SE1 Ch26

CHAPTER INTERNET ACTIVITIES
GO TO: go.hrw.com

- Pupil's Edition Student Activity
  KEYWORD: SE1 Space
  (Students conduct research on the contemporary U.S. space program.)
- Teacher's Edition Student Activity
  KEYWORD: SE1 NAFTA
  (Students conduct research on NAFTA.)
- Teacher's Edition Student Activity
  KEYWORD: SE1 Internet
  (Students conduct research on the development of the Internet and personal computers.)

ADDITIONAL
RESOURCES

Books for Teachers

Stewart, James. *Blood Sport.* Simon & Schuster, 1996. Chronicles opposition to President Clinton during his first term.

Woodward, Bob. *The Choice.* Simon & Schuster, 1996. Examines Clinton's first term.

Books for Students

Bentley, P. F. *Clinton: Portrait of Victory.* Warner Books, 1993. Presents a pictorial history of the 1992 presidential election.

Epping, Randy C. *A Beginner's Guide to the World Economy.* Random House, 1992. Offers concise explanations of global economic issues.

Primary Sources from the Period

Clinton, Hillary Rodham. *It Takes a Village.* Simon & Schuster, 1996. Presents Hillary Clinton's vision of the future of the United States.

The Starr Report. Public Affairs, 1998. Presents the investigation of the scandal that led to Clinton's impeachment.

Stephanopoulos, George. *All Too Human: A Political Memoir.* Little, Brown, 1999. Gives an insider's view of the Clinton White House.

Multimedia Materials

The Rodney King Case. Video, 116 min. MPI Home Video. Chronicles the court case that sparked the 1992 Los Angeles Riots.

72 Hours to Victory: Behind the Scenes with Bill Clinton. Video, 60 min. ABC News. Features the final three days preceding the 1992 election.

CHAPTER 26

Before You Read

Build on What You Know

Ask students to answer the following questions.

How might economic problems damage a president's political standing?

Consider:

- the importance of the economy in everyday American life
- the president's role in economic matters

How might globalization and new advances in technology change American society?

Consider:

- the effect of new technologies on communications
- the ways that an international market for goods might affect the U.S. economy

---

exploring the time line

AMERICAN EVENTS

DEMOCRATIC VALUES

1995 ■ The Oklahoma City Bombing. Although some early news reports had speculated that the Oklahoma City bombing was the work of foreign terrorists, the terrorist actually responsible for the bombing, Timothy McVeigh, was a U.S. citizen and veteran who had been decorated for his service in the Persian Gulf War. The 27-year-old McVeigh was involved in paramilitary groups that believed the U.S. government had become a threat to Americans' liberty.

CRITICAL THINKING Why might the location of the terrorist attack have left many Americans feeling insecure?

ANSWER: Students might suggest that because Oklahoma City is in the middle of the country, many Americans were concerned that terrorist attacks could occur anywhere in the nation.

1990–Present

Life in the 1990s and Beyond

Los Angeles riots

1990

1991

1991
World Events
The Persian Gulf War ends as a United Nations force pushes Iraqi troops out of Kuwait.

Persian Gulf War veterans

1992

1992
Daily Life
Riots erupt in Los Angeles.

1992
The Arts
Gish Jen publishes her novel *Typical American.*

1993

1993
Science and Technology
Marc Andreesen creates Mosaic, the first browser for the World Wide Web.

1993
Business and Finance
Congress ratifies the North American Free Trade Agreement (NAFTA).

1993
Politics
Bill Clinton is sworn in as the 42nd president of the United States.

President Clinton giving his first inaugural address

1994

1994
World Events
Apartheid ends in South Africa.

1994
Politics
Independent Counsel Kenneth Starr begins investigating alleged wrongdoings by the Clinton administration.

1994
Politics
Republican candidates for Congress present the Contract with America.

Newt Gingrich presents the Contract with America.

Before You Read

Build on What You Know

During the 1980s Republican presidents Ronald Reagan and George Bush won wide support for their efforts to reduce federal regulation. Despite the success of the Persian Gulf War, George Bush's bid for re-election was harmed by an economic recession and an ongoing budget-deficit problem. In this chapter you will learn about Bill Clinton's rise to the presidency. You will also learn how American society changed as a result of increasing globalization, new advances in technology, and the expansion of democracy abroad.

768

Think About Themes

To help students create their Themes Journal entries, provide the following examples of appropriate **agree**/**disagree** *statements.*

Economic Development

Agree Although the Soviet Union was still a military power, its economic troubles led to its political disintegration.

Disagree The United States and its European allies resorted to military means to force Iraq forces to retreat from Kuwait.

Global Relations

Agree The U.S. foreign policy of isolationism allowed the country to avoid geopolitical entanglements during most of the 1800s.

Disagree Despite the wishes of many Americans to maintain U.S. neutrality, the United States was unable to avoid involvement in World Wars I and II.

Technology and Society

Agree The invention of the telephone allowed Americans to communicate with people in distant locations.

Disagree By leading to the creation of many monotonous jobs, the development of the assembly line had a negative impact on many Americans' daily lives.

exploring the time line

GLOBAL EVENTS

internetconnect

TOPIC: The North American Free Trade Agreement
GO TO: go.hrw.com
KEYWORD: SE1 NAFTA

Have students access the Internet through the HRW Web site to conduct research on the North American Free Trade Agreement (NAFTA) and the controversy surrounding the treaty's goals. Then have each student create a chart that lists the key goals of NAFTA and summarizes the pro and con viewpoints regarding each goal.

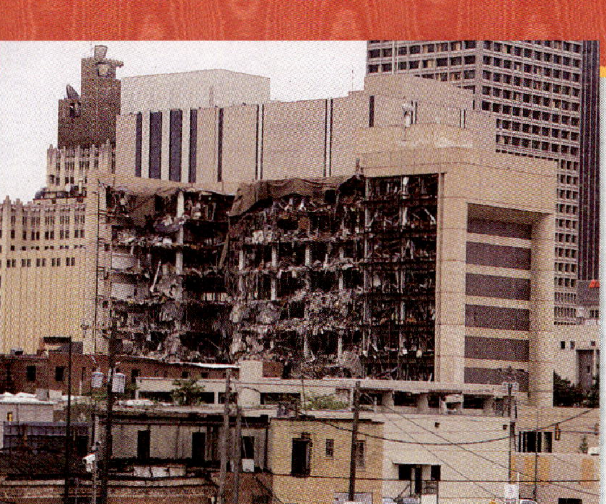

The Murrah Federal Building after a terrorist attack

Poster advertising the musical Rent

John Glenn (waving) and the space shuttle crew

1995
Daily Life
A terrorist truck bomb destroys the Murrah Federal Building in Oklahoma City, killing 168 people.

1995
Daily Life
Louis Farrakhan leads the Million Man March in Washington, D.C.

1996
The Arts
Rent, a Broadway rock musical, wins the Pulitzer Prize for best American drama.

1996
Politics
President Clinton is re-elected as the U.S. economy prospers.

1996
Daily Life
The Summer Olympics in Atlanta are interrupted when a bomb explodes during a concert.

1997
Science and Technology
Scottish scientists successfully clone a mammal, Dolly the sheep, for the first time.

1997
The Arts
The Getty Museum in Los Angeles opens to the public.

1998
Science and Technology
At age 77, John Glenn becomes the oldest person ever to travel in space.

1999
Business and Finance
The Dow Jones industrial average surpasses 10,000 points as the stock market booms in the wake of mergers and record profits.

1999
World Events
NATO launches air attacks on Yugoslavia.

1995 | 1996 | 1997 | 1998 | 1999

African American men participate in the Million Man March.

Dolly, the cloned sheep

Think About Themes

Decide whether you **agree** *or* **disagree** *with the following statements. Note why in your journal.*

Economic Development Economic influence is more important than military strength in determining the political power of nations.

Global Relations Americans' experiences are disconnected from events around the world.

Technology and Society New advances in technology will improve American society by expanding communication and easing the struggles of daily existence.

SECTION 1

After completing Section 1, students should be able to:

OBJECTIVE 1 *Discuss how the 1992 presidential election differed from other recent elections.*

OBJECTIVE 2 *Explain what led to the Republican comeback in the 1994 congressional elections.*

OBJECTIVE 3 *Analyze how regional conflicts and terrorism affected the world.*

OBJECTIVE 4 *Assess how successful the United Nations was in maintaining world peace after the Cold War ended.*

LET'S GET STARTED!

Write the following phrase on the chalkboard: *It's the economy, stupid.* As students enter the classroom, tell them that one of then-candidate Bill Clinton's political strategists coined the phrase during the 1992 presidential election. Tell students to explain in writing what the phrase might mean. Ask volunteers to share their responses with the class. Tell students that in Section 1 they will learn about the role of the economy in the 1992 election and in Clinton's continued political success.

SECTION 1 RESOURCES

PRINT

- Guided Reading Strategy 26.1
- Geography Activity 26: The Republicans Take the House
- Section 1 Review, p. 775
- Daily Quiz 26.1

MULTIMEDIA

- One-Stop Planner, Lesson 26.1
- Holt Researcher: American History CD–ROM

SHELTERED ENGLISH

- Main Idea Activity for Reteaching and Sheltered English 26.1

✔ READING TO UNDERSTAND
To help students master the section objectives, have them answer the **READING CHECKS** and complete **Guided Reading Strategy 26.1** as they read the section.

Clinton's First Term

OBJECTIVES

Read to understand:

1. how the 1992 presidential election differed from other recent elections
2. what led to the Republican comeback in the 1994 congressional elections
3. how regional conflicts and terrorism affected the world
4. how successful the United Nations was in maintaining world peace after the Cold War ended

KEY TERMS

Contract with America
Operation Restore Hope

KEY PEOPLE

Bill Clinton
Hillary Rodham Clinton
Ross Perot
Newt Gingrich
Nelson Mandela
Yasir Arafat
Yitzhak Rabin
Benjamin Netanyahu
Mu'ammar Gadhafi

Hillary Rodham Clinton played an important role in Bill Clinton's campaign.

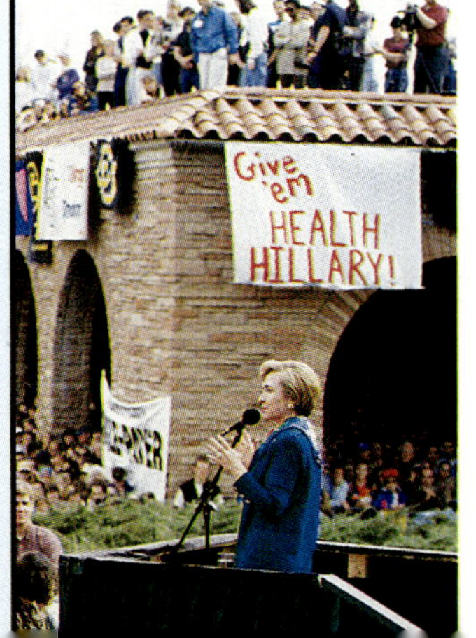

EYEWITNESSES TO History

"Today, a generation raised in the shadows of the Cold War assumes new responsibilities in a world warmed by the sunshine of freedom but threatened still by ancient hatreds and new plagues. . . . Though our challenges are fearsome, so are our strengths. . . . Our democracy must be not only the envy of the world but the engine of our own renewal. There is nothing wrong with America that cannot be cured by what is right with America."

—President Bill Clinton

1992 Democratic Party campaign button

After successfully campaigning on the issue of governmental renewal, Bill Clinton was elected president in November 1992. He continued his message of renewal for the nation in his inaugural address in 1993. With the Cold War over, many Americans optimistically expected solutions to political gridlock, continued violence overseas, and tensions within the United States. This confidence was shaken, however, by new challenges and dangers at home and abroad.

The Election of 1992

Despite the nation's economic woes, President Bush's popularity remained high, particularly after the Persian Gulf War in 1991. One of the few Democrats willing to challenge him in the 1992 election was Governor Bill Clinton of Arkansas.

The Democratic challenger. Bill Clinton was born William Jefferson Blythe in 1946 in Hope, Arkansas, shortly after his father's death. His mother, Virginia, later married Roger Clinton. Bill Clinton's childhood experiences of dealing with poverty and a troubled home life—including an alcoholic adoptive father—shaped his outlook on the world. After meeting President John F. Kennedy as a teenage delegate to Boys' Nation in 1963, Clinton decided on a political career.

While studying law at Yale University he met Hillary Rodham, a fellow law student. Rodham later served as a staff member with the House Judiciary Committee as it considered the impeachment of President Nixon. The couple married in 1975 and settled in Fayetteville, Arkansas. Three years later, Clinton became the nation's youngest governor. As a baby boomer, Clinton reflected many traits of his generation. He opposed the war in Vietnam and for a time tried to avoid being drafted. Influenced by the idealism of the 1960s, he believed strongly in diversity and equality.

As first lady of Arkansas, Hillary Rodham Clinton served on several influential committees, including one that developed a ground-breaking education-reform program. Bill Clinton acknowledged his wife's key role in advising him. During the 1992 campaign he said that voters would be getting "two for the price of one" if he were elected president. Some Americans, however, were uncomfortable with the idea of a president's wife in a policy-making role.

TEACH OBJECTIVE 1

LEVEL 1: Tell students to imagine that they are foreign exchange students living in the United States during the 1992 elections. Have each student write a postcard to a friend or family member back home to describe how the 1992 election has been different from other recent U.S. elections. *(Students should mention high voter turnout, the success of independent candidate Ross Perot, and the record number of female candidates who ran for public office.)* Ask volunteers to read their postcards to the class. **Sheltered English**

LEVEL 2: Tell students to imagine that the 1992 elections have just ended and that they are journalists who must write an article about the elections. Have each student write a short article in which he or she analyzes how the 1992 elections differed from other recent elections. *(See the Level 1 lesson for the correct differences.)* Ask volunteers to share their articles with the class.

The campaign. After years of low voter participation, citizens turned out in large numbers in 1992 to make their voices heard. Candidates used public forums such as television talk shows and radio call-in programs to answer questions directly from the public. A master of this sort of publicity was Ross Perot.

Perot, a billionaire from Texas, ran as an independent candidate for president. Perot promised to reform the federal government by decreasing the influence of political lobbyists and by giving the public a greater voice. He also promised to use his business skills to cut government spending and balance the budget. Perot's message appealed to many voters who were concerned about the economy and the federal deficit.

President Bush said little about the economy in his campaign. He focused largely on the personal character of the candidates. Some people questioned Bill Clinton's integrity. Some of his political enemies in Arkansas referred to him as "Slick Willie," comparing him to old-time con artists selling snake oil as a cure-all. Questions about Clinton's personal conduct in his marriage also emerged.

Comments about Clinton's character had little effect at the polls, however. He and his running mate, Senator Al Gore of Tennessee, won 43 percent of the popular vote and 370 electoral votes. Bush won 38 percent of the popular vote and 168 electoral votes. Although Perot failed to pick up any electoral votes, he captured 19 percent of the popular vote. This was more than any third-party presidential ticket since that of Theodore Roosevelt, the Progressive Party candidate, in 1912.

INTERPRETING THE VISUAL RECORD

The 1992 election. Ross Perot ran a strong third-party campaign for president. ***What type of image does this button suggest?***

Voter frustration. Perot's popularity and the Democratic victory reflected the belief of many voters that politicians were out of touch. Female voters—particularly those outraged by the Clarence Thomas–Anita Hill hearings—were active in the 1992 election. Shortly after the hearings, feminist Eleanor Smeal spoke out. "The Senate did more in one week to underscore the critical need for more women in the Senate than feminists have been able to do in 25 years." Women responded by running for public office in record numbers.

The increase in female candidates led the press to dub 1992 "the year of the woman." Many of these candidates won election. Four prominent female Democrats gained U.S. Senate seats, including Patty Murray of Washington and African American Carol Moseley-Braun of Illinois. California filled both of its Senate seats with women—Barbara Boxer and Dianne Feinstein.

The elections of 1992 brought new female senators to Congress. Pictured (left to right) are Senators Carol Moseley-Braun, Patty Murray, Barbara Boxer, and Barbara Mikulski.

✔ **READING CHECK:** How did the 1992 presidential election differ from other recent elections?

Clinton Takes Office

At President Clinton's inauguration, poet Maya Angelou read a poem of hers that celebrated the diversity of Americans and expressed hope for the future:

DEMOCRATIC VALUES

"Minority" Presidents. Bill Clinton was not the only president to win office without receiving the votes of a majority of the votes cast. Before Clinton, 15 candidates were elected to the presidency with less than 50 percent of the popular vote. Abraham Lincoln, for example, received about 40 percent of the popular vote in 1860. John Quincy Adams, who received only about 31 percent of the popular vote in 1824, actually received fewer popular votes than his chief opponent, Andrew Jackson.

CRITICAL THINKING What problems might a "minority" president face while in office?

ANSWER: Students might point out that a president who does not receive a majority of the popular vote might not have widespread public support for his or her policy initiatives.

THAT'S INTERESTING!

Hillary Rodham Clinton came from a family who supported the Republican Party. During the 1964 presidential election, she was a "Goldwater Girl," a supporter of conservative candidate Barry Goldwater.

VISUAL RECORD ANSWER

Students might answer that it suggests a cowboy.

LEVEL 3: Tell students to imagine that the 1992 elections have just ended and that they are discussing the elections over dinner. Pair students and have each pair write a dinner-table conversation about how the 1992 elections differed from other recent elections. *(See the Level 1 lesson for the correct differences.)* Ask volunteers to perform their conversations for the class. **Cooperative Learning**

TEACH OBJECTIVE 2

LEVEL 1: Tell students that Democrats won a majority in both houses of Congress in 1992, the year Bill Clinton was elected president. Pair students and have each pair compile a list of factors leading to the Republican comeback in the 1994 congressional elections. *(Students should mention the slow economic recovery; the early failures of the Clinton administration, including health care reform and the Whitewater investigation; and Republicans' Contract with America.)* Ask each pair to share its list of factors with the class, then compile a list on the chalkboard. To conclude, lead a class discussion about the role that each factor might have had in the Republicans' success. **Sheltered English, Cooperative Learning**

ECONOMIC DEVELOPMENT

Health Care Costs. The increasing financial burden of health care became an issue of concern for the federal government and state governments in the early 1990s. In 1960 health care had accounted for 5.3 percent of the nation's gross national product (GNP), and the total bill for health care in the United States came to $27.1 billion. By 1990 health care represented 12.2 percent of GNP, and total costs that year came to $666.2 billion.

CRITICAL THINKING Why might health care spending have risen so rapidly?

ANSWER: Students might suggest that the cost of caring for an aging population, inflation, and expensive new technologies led to increased spending.

THAT'S INTERESTING!

The 1994 elections marked the first time since 1952 that Republicans won majorities in both the House of Representatives and the Senate.

1946–
In Office 1993–

Bill Clinton

Bill Clinton's presidency marked many firsts in the White House. He was the first president born in the post–World War II era and the first president from Arkansas. Clinton was also the first president to play the saxophone at his own inaugural celebration.

Clinton's career goal as a youngster was to become a jazz musician. He was heavily influenced by African American jazz artists and early rock 'n' roll stars such as Elvis Presley. He excelled at playing the saxophone and was offered numerous music scholarships to college after he graduated from high school. Although Clinton went on to make a career in politics, he frequently used his musical talents in campaigns. During the 1992 presidential election, he put on a pair of sunglasses and played the saxophone on a popular late-night talk show. Despite his love of music, Clinton believes that he made the right career choice. "I would have been a very good musician," he once noted, "but not a great one."

Read More About It

Free Find: Bill Clinton
After reading about Bill Clinton on the **Holt Researcher** CD–ROM, write a short essay explaining how his values and goals as president may reflect the experiences he had growing up in Arkansas.

"Lift up your eyes upon
This day breaking for you.
Give birth again
To the dream. . . .

Here on the pulse of this new day
You may have the grace to look up
and out
And into your sister's eyes and into
Your brother's face, your country
And say simply
Very simply
With hope
Good morning."

Once in office, Clinton put these ideas into practice by creating a diverse cabinet. His appointees included Mexican American Henry Cisneros as secretary of housing and urban development. He also appointed African Americans Ron Brown and Joycelyn Elders as secretary of commerce and surgeon general, respectively. Other female appointees included Press Secretary Dee Dee Myers, Attorney General Janet Reno, and Secretary of Health and Human Services Donna Shalala. Clinton also nominated Ruth Bader Ginsburg to fill a vacancy on the Supreme Court.

Clinton suffered a series of setbacks early in his presidency. An elaborate plan to reform the nation's health care system, drafted by a task force headed by Hillary Rodham Clinton, died in Congress. Clinton had hoped the reform plan would address voters' concerns about the rising costs of medical care. More Americans were living longer and the baby boom generation was passing middle age. Many Americans feared that they would not be able to afford quality health care in their old age. In addition to being unable to move health care reform forward, the Clintons faced questions of possible past improper financial dealings. Most involved a failed Arkansas real-estate development called Whitewater.

On the economic front, however, President Clinton had some success. In August 1993 Congress narrowly passed a budget act that combined tax increases and spending cuts to reduce the national debt. Over time, the act worked. By 1996 the deficit dropped to about $107 billion, less than half that of 1992. Unemployment dropped to 5.4 percent, the lowest since 1989, and inflation hovered at about 3 percent. As investors gained confidence, the stock market boomed.

A Republican Comeback

The economic recovery did not come fast enough to suit many voters. As the 1994 congressional elections approached, voter frustration with the slow recovery began to build. Encouraged by President Clinton's early setbacks, Republicans geared up for the 1994 midterm election. Many Republican candidates signed the **Contract with America**, which pledged a balanced-budget amendment and other reforms.

LEVELS 2 AND 3: Have each student create a collage representing the factors that led to the Republican comeback in the 1994 congressional elections. *(See the Level 1 lesson for the correct factors.)* Ask volunteers to present and explain their collages to the class. To conclude, lead a class discussion about the role that each factor might have had in the Republicans' success.

TEACH OBJECTIVE 3

LEVEL 1: Tell students to imagine that they are journalists living through the late 1980s and 1990s. Pair students and have each pair write several headlines describing how regional conflicts and terrorism affected the world. *(Headlines should mention conflicts in Eastern Europe, Operation Restore Hope, the Israeli-Palestinian peace accord, U.S. retaliation against Libya and Iraq, and the deaths of Americans in various international and domestic terrorist incidents.)* Ask students to read their headlines to the class.
Sheltered English, Cooperative Learning

LEVELS 2 AND 3: Tell students to imagine that they are journalists who are writing about the effect of regional conflicts and terrorism on the world between 1986 and 1996. Have each student write a magazine article on this topic. *(See the Level 1 lesson for the correct incidents and effects.)* Ask volunteers to read their articles to the class. Students may wish to include their articles in their portfolios.

Voters gave Republicans control of both the House and Senate. Newt Gingrich of Georgia, who became Speaker of the House, commented on the election.

> **"This election was actually about some fairly big ideas: which direction do you want to go in? . . . Those who argued for counterculture values, bigger government, redistributionist economics, and bureaucracies deciding how you should spend your money, were on the losing end in virtually every part of the country."**

✔ **READING CHECK:** What led to the Republican comeback in the 1994 congressional elections?

Foreign and Domestic Dangers

Amid these domestic and political challenges, the Clinton administration confronted a range of global crises. It also wrestled with an increase in terrorism.

Regional conflicts. As the Cold War faded, regional conflicts intensified. The end of Communist rule in Eastern Europe unleashed bitter ethnic and local disputes. Bosnia and Herzegovina, a region that once was part of Yugoslavia, was torn apart by fighting among Serbs, Croatians, and Slovenes.

The 15 newly independent republics of the former Soviet Union experienced conflict as various groups struggled for power and self-rule. Russia and Ukraine argued over control of the Black Sea fleet, while Christians in Armenia battled with Muslims in neighboring Azerbaijan (a-zuhr-by-JAHN).

On a brighter note, a new era dawned in South Africa when decades of apartheid came to an end. In 1994 South Africa held its first elections allowing all races to vote. Black civil rights activist Nelson Mandela, who had spent years as a political prisoner in South Africa, won the presidency. Despite conflict between rival political and ethnic groups, South Africa's future looked hopeful.

Elsewhere in Africa, however, turmoil reigned, worsened by famine and poverty. Civil war raged in Liberia, Mali, Somalia, and Zambia. In December 1992, a UN force, including many Americans, launched **Operation Restore Hope** to provide relief to famine-stricken Somalia. Fighting among rival clans in that country had previously prevented relief workers from getting food and other supplies to starving Somalis. Despite the UN effort, Somalia's suffering continued.

★ HISTORICAL DOCUMENTS ★

Contract with America

Drawn up by members of the Republican Party, the Contract with America offered a list of reforms and 10 pieces of legislation that Republicans promised to propose. Some 300 candidates for public office gathered on the steps of the U.S. Capitol on September 27, 1994, to sign the document. They pledged their support to the positions outlined in the document, stating, "If we break this contract, throw us out."

As Republican members of the House of Representatives and as citizens seeking to join that body we propose not just to change its policies, but even more important, to restore the bonds of trust between the people and their elected representatives. . . .

On the first day of the 104th Congress, the new Republican majority will immediately pass the following major reforms:

First, require all laws that apply to the rest of the country also apply equally to the Congress;

Second, select a major independent auditing firm to conduct a comprehensive audit [complete study] of Congress for waste, fraud, or abuse;

Third, cut the number of House committees, and cut committee staff by one-third;

Fourth, limit the terms of all committee chairs;

Fifth, ban the casting of proxy votes in committee;

Sixth, require committee meetings to be open to the public;

Seventh, require a three-fifths majority vote to pass a tax increase;

Eighth, guarantee honest accounting of our federal budget by implementing [putting into effect] zero baseline budgeting.

PEOPLE IN HISTORY

Nelson Mandela. Nelson Mandela was imprisoned for 27 years because of his political opposition to the apartheid regime in South Africa. Mandela belonged to the then-outlawed African National Congress (ANC), which had been founded in 1912 with the goal of creating a state where all races would share political power. During his early years in prison, Mandela—a lawyer by profession—and fellow political prisoners were forced to do hard labor, including crushing rocks. Mandela was finally released from prison in 1990. Four years later, in the first national elections in which black South Africans were allowed to vote, Mandela was elected president with more than 60 percent of the vote. The ANC won a majority of seats in the national assembly.

CRITICAL THINKING Why might Mandela's long prison term have given him moral authority in the eyes of South Africans?

ANSWER: Students might suggest that Mandela's willingness to suffer for his political beliefs indicated his commitment to those beliefs.

TEACH OBJECTIVE 4

ALL LEVELS: Tell students that when the Cold War ended, many people hoped that the United Nations would be able to maintain world peace. To help students assess the success of the United Nations in maintaining world peace after the Cold War, copy the graphic organizer at right on the chalkboard, omitting the italicized answers. Have each student complete the organizer by describing various UN actions around the world and their results. Ask volunteers to share their answers with the class. To conclude, ask students why UN efforts met with mixed results. *(Students might point out that peacekeepers had difficulty in complicated political situations such as the Somalian civil war and the ethnic fighting in Bosnia.)* Tell students that the end of the Cold War led to the rise of ethnic conflicts that had been previously suppressed by communist governments. **Sheltered English**

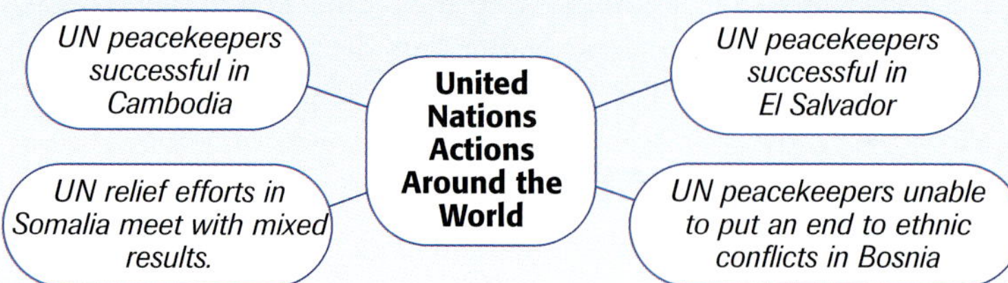

United Nations Actions Around the World
UN peacekeepers successful in Cambodia
UN peacekeepers successful in El Salvador
UN relief efforts in Somalia meet with mixed results.
UN peacekeepers unable to put an end to ethnic conflicts in Bosnia

▶**ASSIGNMENT** *Tell students to imagine that they are editors writing an encyclopedia entry. Have each student write an entry about the success of the United Nations in maintaining world peace after the Cold War.*

GLOBAL RELATIONS

Operation Restore Hope. The fighting in Somalia developed into a full-fledged civil war by 1989. After a 1992 cease-fire failed, the United Nations sent a peacekeeping force into Somalia. In December of that year President Bush announced that the United States would commit some 27,000 soldiers to assist the peacekeepers and to provide humanitarian aid. However, the conflict in Somalia continued, and the UN and U.S. troops were drawn into the conflict. Eighteen U.S. soldiers were killed in October 1993. In response, President Clinton announced that U.S. troops would withdraw from Somalia by March 1994.

CRITICAL THINKING Should the loss of American lives lead to the abandonment of humanitarian efforts?

ANSWER: Answers will vary. Some students might suggest that such efforts may be worth limited casualties.

VISUAL RECORD ANSWER

Students might answer that the memorial reflects grief and sorrow.

VISUAL RECORD ANSWER

(for p. 775)

Students might suggest that the tanks and soldiers provided military protection.

President Clinton looks on as Yitzhak Rabin (left) and Yasir Arafat shake hands to seal their 1993 peace accord.

The Middle East. Instability also threatened many nations in the Middle East. Islamic fundamentalists battled for political power. Hopes for peace between Palestinians and Israelis were renewed in September 1993, when Palestinian leader Yasir Arafat and Israeli prime minister Yitzhak Rabin signed a peace accord. President Clinton oversaw the signing of the agreement at the White House. He described it as a "historic and honorable compromise."

The peace process suffered a setback in 1995, when a young Israeli with extreme nationalist views assassinated Rabin. In 1996 Benjamin Netanyahu was elected prime minister of Israel and pledged to be less willing to compromise in peace negotiations. U.S. Secretary of State Warren Christopher worked hard to bring the two sides together. Yet there were new outbreaks of violence between Israeli soldiers and Palestinians in September 1996. This made it clear that a more peaceful future was far from certain in this troubled region.

Terrorism. Along with the end of the Cold War came an increase in terrorist activity throughout the world. According to one group of experts, the number of terrorist acts rose by 11 percent from 1991 to 1992.

U.S. leaders usually responded quickly to international terrorism linked directly to a particular nation. In 1986 President Reagan had ordered a bombing attack on Libya. Evidence had linked that country's leader, Mu'ammar Gadhafi (guh-DAH-fee), to an attack at a West Berlin nightclub. The attack killed one U.S. soldier and injured many others. In the summer of 1993 Clinton ordered the bombing of the Iraqi intelligence service headquarters. The Federal Bureau of Investigation (FBI) had uncovered an Iraqi plot to assassinate former president George Bush.

Terrorism in the air also took a sad toll. In 1988 a bomb destroyed a Pan American airliner over Lockerbie, Scotland. All 259 aboard were killed, including many Americans. The bomb was traced to two Libyans, but Gadhafi refused to send them to the United States for trial. In 1996 a truck bomb in Saudi Arabia killed 19 U.S. soldiers and wounded 280 others.

INTERPRETING THE VISUAL RECORD

Terrorism at home. Mourners attached mementos to a fence surrounding the destroyed Murrah Federal Building in Oklahoma City. ***How does this memorial reflect many people's emotions after the attack?***

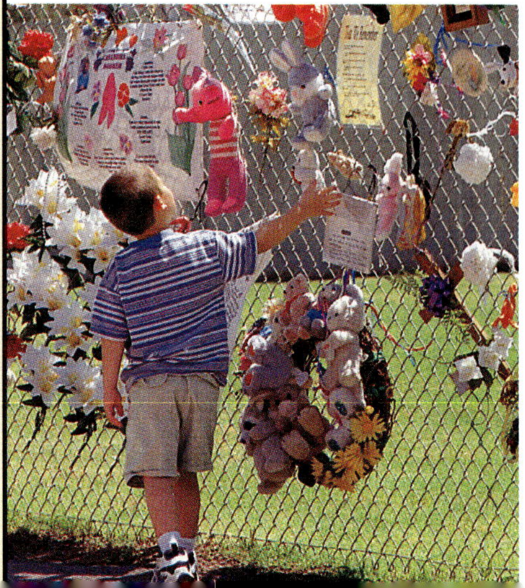

Domestic terrorism proved particularly chilling. On February 26, 1993, a bomb blast rocked the World Trade Center in New York City, killing six people and injuring more than 1,000. The suspects arrested for the bombing had ties to an Egyptian fundamentalist leader who was linked to several other terrorist acts. In April 1995 a truck bomb destroyed a federal building in Oklahoma City, killing 168 people. Two American men with ties to antigovernment militia groups were convicted of the crime. A year later, the FBI arrested the so-called Unabomber, a loner with a grievance against modern technology, who had carried out a series of mail-bombings. Then, during the 1996 Summer Olympics in Atlanta, a bomb killed one person and injured more than 100 others.

✔ **READING CHECK:** How did regional conflicts and terrorism affect the world?

REVIEW

Have students complete the **Section 1 Review** on p. 775.

ASSESS

Have students complete **Daily Quiz 26.1**. As **Alternative Assessment**, you may want to use the postcards or the dinner-table conversation in this section's lessons.

RETEACH

Have students complete **Main Idea Activity for Reteaching and Sheltered English 26.1**. Then pair students and have each pair create flash cards for all of the key terms and key people in this section's lessons. Students should write the name of the key term or key person on one side of the card and a brief description of the term or person on the reverse side of the card. Ask each pair to use the flash cards to quiz each other.
Sheltered English, Cooperative Learning

EXTEND

Ask students to conduct research on one of the following individuals: Yasir Arafat, Ruth Bader Ginsburg, Nelson Mandela, Yitzhak Rabin, or Donna Shalala. Have each student write a biographical report about his or her chosen individual.
Block Scheduling

The Role of the United Nations

With the end of the Cold War, many foreign-policy observers hoped that the United Nations would become the international force for peace that its founders had envisioned. By 1992 there were thousands of UN forces serving on peacekeeping missions in locations throughout the world. In countries such as Cambodia and El Salvador, UN peacekeepers played a successful role.

The United Nations had mixed results, however, in its dealings with complex situations such as in Somalia. In Bosnia and Herzegovina, ethnic fighting among Croatians, Serbs, and Slovenes left some 150,000 people dead or missing by the end of 1993. The United Nations and the North Atlantic Treaty Organization (NATO) sent peacekeeping forces to the area and launched an investigation into war crimes, but the fighting continued.

INTERPRETING THE VISUAL RECORD

United Nations. British troops participating in a UN operation travel past a destroyed mosque in Bosnia. ***What type of protection do you think the UN force provided for the people of Bosnia?***

As the Bosnian Serbs seized land, bombed cities, and killed or expelled Bosnian Muslims, the Clinton administration at first did little. By 1995, however, as the Bosnian Serbs continued their aggression, President Clinton took a stronger stance. The United States and NATO cooperated in bombing Bosnian Serb positions. In November 1995 the United States brought the leaders of the warring groups to Dayton, Ohio, to hammer out a peace accord. The resulting agreement provided for a multiethnic Bosnian federation. It also required war crimes trials and elections, which were held in the fall of 1996. In addition, Clinton sent some 20,000 Americans to Bosnia to help the NATO troops enforce the Dayton accords. Ethnic hatreds in Bosnia ran deep, however, and the fate of the U.S. peace initiative remained uncertain.

✔ **READING CHECK:** How successful was the United Nations in maintaining world peace after the Cold War?

SECTION  1 REVIEW

Define and explain the significance of the following terms:
Contract with America
Operation Restore Hope

Identify and explain the significance of the following individuals:
Bill Clinton
Hillary Rodham Clinton
Ross Perot
Newt Gingrich
Nelson Mandela
Yasir Arafat
Yitzhak Rabin
Benjamin Netanyahu
Mu'ammar Gadhafi

1. **Using Graphic Organizers** Copy the graphic organizer below. Use it to describe the regional conflicts and events that shaped the world in the early 1990s.

2. **Evaluating** How was the 1992 presidential election different from other recent elections?
3. **Synthesizing** How did the Republicans gain control of the House and the Senate just two years after Democrat Bill Clinton was elected president?
4. **Identifying Cause and Effect** What factors led to an increase in regional conflicts and terrorist activity? How did these conflicts affect the United States and the world?

Critical Thinking

5. How did the role of the United Nations in major conflicts reveal the organization's limits?
   Consider:
   - successes of the UN in the 1990s
   - the outcome of the UN missions in Somalia and Bosnia
   - why the UN missions had mixed results

SECTION 1 REVIEW ANSWERS

Define and Identify

For significance, see the following pages:

- Bill Clinton, p. 770
- Hillary Rodham Clinton, p. 770
- Ross Perot, p. 771
- Contract with America, p. 772
- Newt Gingrich, p. 773
- Nelson Mandela, p. 773
- Operation Restore Hope, p. 773
- Yasir Arafat, p. 774
- Yitzhak Rabin, p. 774
- Benjamin Netanyahu, p. 774
- Mu'ammar Gadhafi, p. 774

1. Middle East—violence between Israelis and Palestinians continued; former Soviet Union—conflict between Armenian Christians and Muslims in Azerbaijan, and between Ukraine and Russia over the Black Sea; Africa—civil war in Liberia, Mali, Somalia, and Zambia

2. increased voter turnout; strong independent candidate

3. by capitalizing on voter frustration over economic issues

4. The collapse of the Soviet Union unleashed ethnic and religious tensions in Eastern Europe and the former Soviet Union. The United States became embroiled in conflicts between various ethnic groups. Terrorism led to the deaths of Americans.

5. Although they claimed successes in El Salvador and Cambodia, UN forces could not stop the violence in Somalia and Bosnia.

SECTION 2

After completing Section 2, students should be able to:

OBJECTIVE 1 *Discuss the issues that affected the 1996 presidential election.*

OBJECTIVE 2 *Describe the domestic issues that shaped President Clinton's second term.*

OBJECTIVE 3 *Relate what led to the impeachment of President Clinton, and describe what the outcome was.*

OBJECTIVE 4 *Analyze why NATO launched air strikes against Yugoslavia in 1999.*

LET'S GET STARTED!

Copy the following statement on the chalkboard: *In 1996, Americans cast a vote for divided government—a situation in which one major party controls the White House and the other party controls one or both houses of Congress. Voters have been unable to trust either party enough to give it a clear mandate to run government.* As students enter the classroom, tell them to respond in writing to the statement. Tell students that in Section 2 they will learn about the issues that affected the outcome of the 1996 election and about President Clinton's second term.

SECTION 2 RESOURCES

PRINT
- Guided Reading Strategy 26.2
- Graphic Organizer Activity 26: The Serbian Conflict
- Biography Reading 26: Madeleine Albright
- Section 2 Review, p. 781
- Daily Quiz 26.2

MULTIMEDIA
- One-Stop Planner, Lesson 26.2
- Holt Researcher: American History CD–ROM

SHELTERED ENGLISH
- Main Idea Activity for Reteaching and Sheltered English 26.2

✔ READING TO UNDERSTAND

To help students master the section objectives, have them answer the **READING CHECKS** and complete **Guided Reading Strategy 26.2** as they read the section.

Clinton's Second Term

OBJECTIVES

Read to understand:
1. what issues affected the 1996 presidential election
2. what domestic issues shaped President Clinton's second term
3. what led to the impeachment of President Clinton, and what the outcome was
4. why NATO launched air strikes against Yugoslavia in 1999

KEY TERMS

Reform Party
Los Angeles Riots
Initiative on Race
Kosovo crisis

KEY PEOPLE

Bob Dole
Rodney King
James Byrd Jr.
Kenneth Starr
Slobodan Milosevic
Madeleine Albright

"Let me be the bridge to a time of tranquillity, faith and confidence in action. And to those who say it was never so, that America's not been better, I say you're wrong. And I know because I was there. And I have seen it. And I remember."

—Bob Dole

Bob Dole campaigning in 1996

Campaigning in the months before the presidential election of 1996, Republican Bob Dole of Kansas reminisced about an earlier era of prosperity, morality, and tranquillity in America. Democratic critics viewed the senator's memories as misleading. Nonetheless, Dole attempted to present himself as a mature and dignified candidate in contrast to the emerging accounts of scandals and dishonesty in President Clinton's administration. Many Americans, however, believed that Dole was out of touch with their concerns and problems.

The Election of 1996

Despite Republicans' large gains in the 1994 congressional elections, President Clinton's popularity improved as the economy boomed. Economist David Wyss described the nation's healthy financial conditions.

> **"If you look at the economy during the Clinton administration, you have to say that it's been a success. We have low inflation, full employment, and steady growth. This is really just about the best of all [economic] worlds."**

Americans' approval of the president climbed as the Republican-led Congress failed to enact key measures in the Contract with America. They also tried to cut popular social and environmental programs. When Clinton and Congress battled over a budget bill in 1995, the federal government was briefly shut down. Voters largely blamed the Republicans. Clinton also benefited from divisions among Republicans, who split over such issues as budget cuts, government regulations, social issues, and taxes. These divisions sharpened as the 1996 presidential campaign began. From a large field of Republican candidates, Bob Dole emerged victorious from the primaries and tried to unite his party's competing groups.

The race. Dole was a senator with 34 years of experience as well as a disabled World War II veteran. Yet as a 73-year-old, he would be the oldest person ever elected president if he won. His age concerned voters. Dole also proved to be an ineffective campaigner. "He never . . . offered the sustained and layered argument that precedes the applause line," concluded political analyst Peggy Noonan. "He just declared things—And there'll be no more crime in a Dole Administration—and waited for people to clap as he cleared his throat."

President Clinton won support from organized labor in his 1996 bid for re-election.

TEACH OBJECTIVE 1

LEVEL 1: Tell students that in 1996 voters sent a mixed message to President Clinton and Congress about which issues were important to them. Ask students to identify the issues that affected the 1996 presidential election. *(Students should mention economic prosperity, divisions within the Republican Party, Republicans' failure to enact Contract with America measures and their attempt to cut social and environmental programs, the fact that voters held the Republicans responsible for the government shutdown, Clinton's ability to seize the middle ground, and Dole's lackluster presidential campaign.)* Discuss these issues with students. Then have each student write headlines discussing the issues that affected the 1996 presidential elections. Ask volunteers to read their headlines to the class. **Sheltered English**

LEVELS 2 AND 3: Have each student write a poem about the issues that affected the 1996 presidential election. *(See the Level 1 lesson for the correct issues.)* Ask volunteers to read their poems to the class. To conclude, lead a class discussion about what message voters might have been trying to send the president and Congress.

Meanwhile, Clinton seized the middle ground on many issues. The president echoed the Republicans' call for economic growth, smaller government, anticrime programs, and middle-class tax relief. He urged tougher school discipline and a crackdown on "deadbeat dads" who failed to pay child support. Clinton also echoed the Republican criticism of the nation's welfare system. The president and Republican leaders cooperated to design welfare reforms that would limit benefits, introduce work requirements, and shift programs from federal to state control. Clinton signed a welfare-reform bill in August 1996 that resulted in the most extensive overhaul of the welfare system since the New Deal.

On issues such as environmental protection and gun control, however, Clinton emphasized the differences between himself and his Republican opponent. Another issue dividing the two candidates was tobacco. Clinton called for stricter measures to discourage smoking, particularly among young Americans.

President Clinton celebrates his 1996 re-election.

The result. Clinton's strategy proved successful. He became the first Democrat since Franklin D. Roosevelt to win a second term. He won 50 percent of the popular vote and 379 electoral votes. Dole won 41 percent of the popular vote and 159 electoral votes. Ross Perot won 8.4 percent of the vote as a candidate of the **Reform Party**. The Reform Party promised to change politics in the nation's capital.

Although several members of the Republican "Freshman Class of 1994" failed to win re-election, the party maintained its majorities in Congress. President Clinton's victory marked the first time that a Democrat had been elected president while the Republicans won both the House and the Senate. This event seemed to reveal voters' support for cooperation between the two political parties. As he approached his second term, President Clinton insisted that "the vital American center is alive and well." He pledged to provide health insurance for children and people with disabilities, revise parts of the welfare bill, and connect classrooms to the Internet. Many observers described Clinton's proposals as "small steps" intended to avoid the problems that had doomed some of his first-term goals.

✔ **READING CHECK:** What issues affected the 1996 presidential election?

Domestic Prosperity and Concerns

The continued booming economy helped President Clinton achieve some of his second-term goals. The first step was to maintain the nation's economic health.

The economy. During the 1990s Americans experienced the longest and largest economic boom in U.S. history. While almost everyone benefited from the prosperity, the number of people who were very wealthy grew at an amazing rate. Between 1995 and 1998 some 1 million Americans became new millionaires, raising the total number of American millionaires to approximately 4 million. Between 1998 and 1999 the number of American billionaires grew from 190 to about 250.

INTERPRETING THE VISUAL RECORD

Prosperity. The May 1999 issue of *Money* magazine discussed the booming stock market and rising personal wealth in the United States. ***How does this magazine cover try to attract readers?***

PEOPLE IN HISTORY

Bob Dole. Bob Dole was studying pre-med at the University of Kansas when World War II began. He enlisted in the army and was sent to Italy, where he was wounded by German machine-gun fire. Dole was so badly wounded that he spent more than three years in hospitals. At one point he nearly died. As a result of his injuries, Dole lost the use of his right arm and had to learn to write with his left hand. He decided that his disability would make a medical career difficult, so he switched to the study of law. Dole was elected to the Kansas legislature while still a law student at Washburn University.

CRITICAL THINKING How might Dole's wartime service have served him well in his political career?

ANSWER: Students might point out that Dole could rightfully claim that he had made important sacrifices while serving his country, a fact that appealed to many voters.

VISUAL RECORD ANSWER

Students might point out that the magazine's cover offers to help people get rich.

TEACH OBJECTIVE 2

LEVEL 1: Pair students and have each pair prepare an outline for a report about the domestic issues that shaped President Clinton's second term. *(Outlines should mention the economic boom, which was characterized by a soaring stock market, low unemployment, and low inflation; and race relations, which came to the nation's attention through the Los Angeles Riots, Clinton's Initiative on Race, and the murder of James Byrd Jr.)* Ask volunteers to present their outlines to the class. **Sheltered English, Cooperative Learning**

LEVELS 2 AND 3: Tell students to imagine that they are journalists who work for a newsmagazine and who must produce a lead article and magazine cover for the next issue. Organize the class into small groups. Have each group write an article about the domestic issues that shaped President Clinton's second term and create a magazine cover to accompany the article. *(See the Level 1 lesson for the correct issues.)* Ask students to present their magazine articles and covers to the class.
Cooperative Learning

▶**ASSIGNMENT:** *Have each student select one domestic policy initiative from President Clinton's second term and evaluate its success in a short essay.*

ECONOMIC DEVELOPMENT

Poverty in the 1990s. The percentage of Americans who lived below the poverty line remained fairly constant through the 1990s, despite the decade's prosperity. In 1990 some 13.5 percent of all American families lived in poverty. Six years later, 13.7 percent of American families lived in poverty.

CRITICAL THINKING What do you think the levels of poverty reveal about the economic boom of the 1990s?

ANSWER: Students might point out that the benefits of the boom were not distributed evenly throughout American society.

THAT'S INTERESTING!

When adjusted for inflation, investments in stocks, on average, made no profits for investors during the 1970s. That poor performance turned around during the 1980s, when the total return earned on stocks reached almost 12 percent. From 1990 to 1997 the total return climbed above 13 percent, making stocks a sound investment for many Americans.

CHART ANSWER
Yahoo

Selected Technology Stock Prices, June 1, 1998, to June 1, 1999

Stock	Lowest price per share	Highest price per share
Amazon.com	$13.75	$221.25
Dell	$19.93	$55.00
IBM	$53.00	$123.00
Microsoft	$41.81	$95.62
Yahoo	$25.12	$244.00

Source: New York Stock Exchange

Learning from Charts The boom in computer technology in the 1990s led to enormous investment in technology stocks.

? Building Chart Skills Which stock experienced the greatest increase in price between June 1, 1998, and June 1, 1999?

Much of this new wealth was the result of a booming stock market, which rose higher than ever before. The value of technology stocks in particular soared. Some companies that did not even make a profit in the 1990s still saw the value of their stock rise enormously. Investors looking to the technological future drove up the prices of these stocks. Many people saw the key to financial success as the ability to pick stocks that would quickly rise in value. "It's the first time in the postwar era that so many people seem to be getting so rich with so little relative effort on their part," said economist Robert B. Reich.

The economic boom translated into the lowest unemployment rates in years. Low unemployment usually leads to inflation, which the Federal Reserve then tries to halt by raising interest rates. During the 1990s, however, unemployment, the rate of inflation, and interest rates remained low. This reversal of the stagflation that had crippled the U.S. economy in the 1970s amazed many economists.

Race relations. While trying to support the economic boom, President Clinton also looked for a larger cause to define his second term. He soon focused on race relations in the United States. During the 1990s racial conflicts continued to plague the country. In April 1992 the South Central section of Los Angeles exploded in violence. Four white police officers had been acquitted of beating African American motorist Rodney King. The verdict and the **Los Angeles Riots** disheartened many people who had worked to improve race relations in the city. Even Rodney King appeared on television during the violence, urging people to "try to work it out" peacefully. He asked, "Can we all get along?"

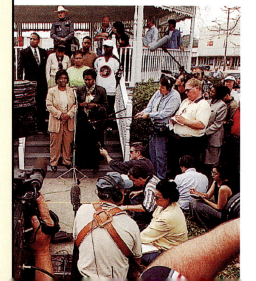

The family of James Byrd Jr. holds a press conference.

In the summer of 1997 Clinton announced the formation of a seven-member advisory committee to help him plan strategies for improving race relations. The president also launched his **Initiative on Race** to encourage people to discuss racial issues and concerns. Critics argued that the program produced little meaningful action.

Meanwhile, racial violence continued. The nation was horrified in June 1998 when white racists in Jasper, Texas, killed James Byrd Jr., an African American. The killers had tied Byrd to a pickup truck and dragged him to death. Some people reacted to this modern-day lynching by calling for tougher federal laws against hate crimes.

✔ **READING CHECK:** What domestic issues shaped President Clinton's second term?

TEACH OBJECTIVE 3

ALL LEVELS: To help students understand what led to President Clinton's impeachment, and what the major outcomes of the trial were, copy the graphic organizer at right on the chalkboard, omitting the italicized answers. Pair students and have each pair complete the organizer. Ask volunteers to share their answers with the class. To conclude, lead a class discussion about why a president might be impeached. *(Students might mention "high crimes and misdemeanors" or suggest that impeachment is a politically driven process.)* Ask students whether the House should have proceeded with impeachment even though a majority of Americans supported the president. **Sheltered English, Cooperative Learning**

What Led to President Clinton's Impeachment

- *Independent Counsel Kenneth Starr expands his investigation to include a civil sexual harassment lawsuit against President Clinton.*
- *Clinton gives a video-taped testimony in the civil trial.*
- *Starr investigates whether Clinton had conducted an improper relationship with a White House intern and lied about it during the civil trial.*
- *The president testifies before a grand jury in the Starr investigation. He acknowledges the affair with the intern but insists he did not commit perjury.*
- *The House Judiciary Committee investigates, disagrees with Clinton, and recommends impeachment.*
- *The House of Representatives votes to impeach the president.*

Senate Trial's Outcome

- *The Senate votes to acquit Clinton.*
- *Many Americans say they distrust the president.*
- *Congress lets the independent counsel law expire.*

Reflecting America in Literature

The national dialogue on race highlighted the growing racial and ethnic diversity of the U.S. population. Many popular writers in the 1990s reflected this diversity in their works. Jimmy Santiago Baca's poem tells the story of a boy growing up in a modern Mexican American community. Gish Jen's novel centers around a Chinese American couple who see the path to success in becoming as "Americanized" as possible.

from "Martín IV"
by Jimmy Santiago Baca

On visiting days with aunts and uncles,
I was shuttled back and forth—
between Chavez bourgeois in the city
and rural Lucero sheepherders,
new cars and gleaming furniture
and leather saddles and burlap sacks,
noon football games and six packs of cokes
and hoes, welfare cards and bottles of goat milk.

I was caught in the middle—
between white skinned, English speaking altar boy
at the communion railing,
and brown skinned, Spanish speaking plains nomadic child
with buffalo heart groaning underworld earth powers. . . .

Caught between Indio-Mejicano rural uncles
who stacked hundred pound sacks of pinto beans
on boxcars all day, . . . and Chavez uncles and aunts
who vacationed and followed the Hollywood model
of My Three Sons* for their own families.

Jimmy Santiago Baca

from *Typical American*
by Gish Jen

Gish Jen's novel

Ralph advocated buying a car.

*"Seems like someone's becoming one-hundred-percent Americanized,"*** Theresa kidded.

"What's so American? We had a car, growing up. Don't you remember?" Ralph argued that in fact this way they could avoid getting too Americanized. *"Everywhere we go, we can keep the children inside. Also they won't catch cold."*

"I thought we agreed the children are going to be American," puzzled Helen.

Ralph furrowed his brow. When Callie turned three they had decided that Mona and Callie would learn English first, and then Chinese. This was what Janis and Old Chao were planning on doing with Alexander; Janis didn't want him to have an accent.

Now Ralph drummed his fingers. He stopped and smiled. *"And what better way to Americanize the children than to buy a car!"*

UNDERSTANDING LITERATURE

1. In Baca's poem, what two different ways of life do the two sides of the speaker's family represent?
2. How do Jen's characters become "Americanized"? What aspects of Chinese culture do they retain?
3. How do you think these works reflect life in the United States in the late 1900s?

* a popular television show of the 1960s
** Italics indicate words spoken in Chinese.

HISTORY MAKERS SPEAK

Bill Clinton in *Public Papers of the Presidents of the United States*

Race in America. President Clinton addressed the troubled state of American race relations in a 1997 speech. "Can we be one America respecting, even celebrating, our differences, but embracing even more what we have in common? . . . Our hearts long to answer yes, but our history reminds us that it will be hard. The ideals that bind us together are as old as our Nation, but so are the forces that pull us apart."

CRITICAL THINKING What ideals and forces might Clinton have been referring to?

ANSWER: Students might suggest that Clinton was referring to the ideals of equality and liberty and the forces of bigotry and racism.

AMERICAN LETTERS ANSWERS

1. an urban life of affluence and a rural life of poverty
2. learning English, buying American products; the Chinese language
3. They reveal the tensions between traditional cultures and the process of Americanization that minority groups face in the United States.

TEACH OBJECTIVE 4

LEVEL 1: Ask students whether they can name the two ethnic groups involved in the Kosovo crisis. *(Students should mention the Serbians and ethnic Albanians.)* Tell students that many ethnic groups inhabit the Balkan region, and that the Balkans have had a troubled history. Explain that Yugoslav president Slobodan Milosevic wanted to drive ethnic Albanians out of Kosovo province, which is part of Serbia. Discuss with students why NATO launched air strikes against Yugoslavia in 1999. *(Students should mention that Serbians were carrying out mass murders and other atrocities against ethnic Albanians in Kosovo, and that NATO air strikes were designed to end the violence.)* Then have each student synthesize information from the class discussion to write two headlines for a newspaper article related to why NATO launched air strikes against Yugoslavia in 1999. Ask volunteers to read their headlines to the class. **Sheltered English**

LEVELS 2 AND 3: Pair students and tell one student to imagine that he or she is Secretary of State Madeleine Albright, and tell the other student to imagine that he or she is a journalist. Have each pair create a transcript for an interview about why NATO launched air strikes against Yugoslavia in 1999. *(See the Level 1 lesson for the correct reasons.)* Ask students to conduct their interviews for the class. **Cooperative Learning**

DEMOCRATIC VALUES

Clinton and the Public. Before and during President Clinton's impeachment and trial, most Americans supported the president. Polls revealed that some 60 percent of Americans believed that Clinton should remain in office even if he had in fact obstructed justice. Nonetheless, a majority of Americans also indicated that they held a negative opinion of Clinton's character and believed that he lacked moral standards.

CRITICAL THINKING Do you think the public's support for Clinton affected the outcome of his Senate trial?

ANSWER: Answers will vary. Some students might note that it was unlikely that senators would remove a president who had such widespread public support.

THAT'S INTERESTING!

No Democrats voted to convict President Clinton on either of the two charges. On the perjury charge, 45 Republicans voted to convict Clinton, and 10 voted to acquit. On the obstruction of justice charge, 50 Republicans voted "guilty," and 5 voted "not guilty."

VISUAL RECORD ANSWER

Students might mention that people are carrying water, clothing, and bedding.

Independent Counsel Kenneth Starr conducted an investigation into Bill Clinton's alleged misconduct.

A Presidential Scandal

Although President Clinton maintained high job-approval ratings in public polls, his second term was marred by scandal. In 1994 a former Arkansas state employee had sued Clinton, claiming that he had sexually harassed her while he was governor of Arkansas. As the civil case proceeded, the woman's lawyers began to investigate other alleged misconduct by Clinton.

During this same time, Independent Counsel Kenneth Starr was investigating Bill and Hillary Clinton's past financial dealings. In January 1998 Starr received permission from a panel of three federal judges to expand his investigation. He included the possibility that Clinton was trying to tamper with witnesses in the civil lawsuit. Although a federal judge later dismissed the civil lawsuit, Clinton's videotaped testimony in the case almost brought down his presidency.

Starr began to investigate whether Clinton had conducted an improper relationship with a young White House intern and lied about it during the civil trial. After the president repeated his testimony to a grand jury, the House Judiciary Committee launched its own investigation. Although Clinton finally acknowledged the affair with the intern and apologized, he insisted he had not committed perjury. The Republican-led Judiciary Committee disagreed and recommended impeachment. On December 20, 1998, the House of Representatives voted to impeach the president.

For just the second time in the nation's history, a U.S. president underwent a trial by the Senate. Some Republicans called for conviction. Most Democrats took the position that Clinton's behavior, while offensive, did not meet the constitutional test of "high crimes and misdemeanors." In public opinion polls, most Americans agreed. In February 1999 the Senate acquitted Clinton of the charges against him.

Although the president and his supporters cheered the victory, the scandal left lingering effects. Many Americans said that they distrusted the president personally. Others worried that the scandal had weakened the office of the president. Critics of Starr's investigation of the Clintons noted that it had cost more than $40 million but had yielded few convictions. A few months after the impeachment trial, Congress let the law providing for independent counsels expire.

✔ **READING CHECK:** What led to the impeachment of President Clinton, and what was the outcome?

INTERPRETING THE VISUAL RECORD

Kosovo crisis. Fleeing violent Serbian attacks, Kosovar Albanian refugees resettled in camps in Albania and Macedonia. ***What do you think these refugees might have carried with them as they fled?***

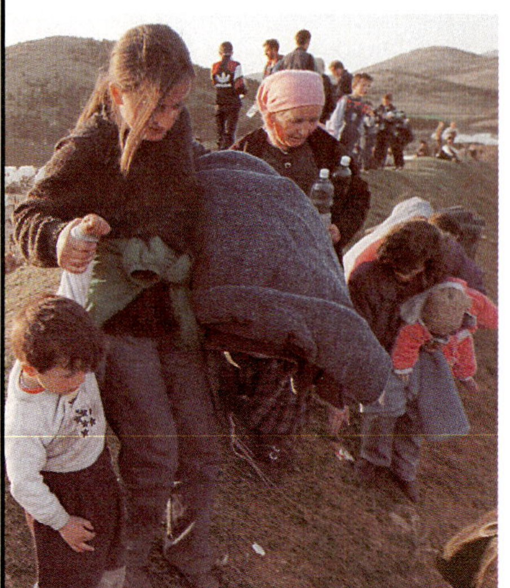

War in Kosovo

As the impeachment trial ended, U.S. officials became concerned about events overseas. The mainly Serbian nation of Yugoslavia, led by President Slobodan Milosevic (sloh-buh-DAHN mi-LOH-suh-vitch), had begun a crackdown on the province of Kosovo. Until 1989, Kosovo, which was home mostly to ethnic Albanians, had been allowed to govern itself. After Milosevic came to power, he ended this self-rule and began moving Serbian settlers into Kosovo. Western nations initially paid little attention to the developing **Kosovo crisis**.

Early in 1999 new reports emerged that the Serbians were carrying out mass murders and other atrocities against ethnic Albanians in Kosovo. In an effort to stop the violence, President Clinton backed a plan for NATO to begin air strikes against Yugoslavia.

REVIEW

Have students complete the **Section 2 Review** on p. 781.

ASSESS

Have students complete **Daily Quiz 26.2**. As **Alternative Assessment**, you may want to use the poem or the interview in this section's lessons.

RETEACH

Have students complete **Main Idea Activity for Reteaching and Sheltered English 26.2**. Organize students into small groups and have each group create an outline of the information in one of Section 2's subsections. Have volunteers present their outlines to the class. **Sheltered English, Cooperative Learning**

EXTEND

Have students conduct research on the process of impeachment and the independent counsel statute. Students should focus their research on the legal basis for impeachment and the independent counsel statute as well as historical information about both. Have each student write one or two paragraphs about each issue. **Block Scheduling**

BIOGRAPHY

Madeleine Albright

U.S. Secretary of State Madeleine Albright played a central role in the Kosovo crisis. Albright was born Madeleine Korbel in Prague, Czechoslovakia, in 1937. The daughter of a Czech diplomat, she had an interest in foreign affairs from a young age. She lived in several countries before her family moved to Colorado. She studied political science at Wellesley College, graduating in 1959, and later received a Ph.D. from Columbia University.

Albright worked for the National Security Council, the White House, the Center for National Policy, and numerous schools and institutes for foreign affairs. In 1993 Clinton appointed her U.S. representative to the United Nations. Four years later, she was sworn in as the first female secretary of state.

Albright took a strong interest in the Kosovo conflict. As a child, her family had fled religious and ethnic oppression from Adolf Hitler's Nazi regime and then from communist forces in Eastern Europe. As secretary of state, she was highly critical of governments that mistreated people because of their religious or ethnic backgrounds. She warned that if NATO delayed in taking action the crisis could get worse, as it had in Bosnia.

After nearly three months, the air strikes paid off. Milosevic agreed to withdraw his troops from Kosovo and to allow NATO forces into the area to enforce a peace agreement. As NATO troops moved in, evidence began to emerge of massive Serbian atrocities against civilians. Some critics were upset that Milosevic, who had been charged with war crimes by an international court, was allowed to stay in power. Secretary Albright noted the lessons of Kosovo.

> **"The crisis in Kosovo should cause a re-examination of . . . the past. As the world has changed, so have the roles of key institutions such as . . . NATO and the United Nations. And so have American interests. In today's world of deadly and mobile dangers, gross violations of human rights are everyone's business."**

✔ **READING CHECK:** Why did NATO launch air strikes against Yugoslavia in 1999?

HOLT RESEARCHER — Read More About It

Free Find:
Madeleine Albright
After reading about Madeleine Albright on the **Holt Researcher** CD–ROM, create a script for a television news show that focuses on Albright's life and work.

SECTION  REVIEW

Define and explain the significance of the following terms:
Reform Party
Los Angeles Riots
Initiative on Race
Kosovo crisis

Identify and explain the significance of the following individuals:
Bob Dole
Rodney King
James Byrd Jr.
Kenneth Starr
Slobodan Milosevic
Madeleine Albright

1. **Using Graphic Organizers** Copy the graphic organizer below. Use it to outline how the candidates in the 1996 presidential election differed on the issues.

Bill Clinton	Bob Dole

2. **Analyzing** What factors caused the economic growth of the 1990s?
3. **Assessing Consequences** What were the major causes of President Clinton's impeachment trial?
4. **Identifying Values** How did the issue of human rights influence NATO's decision to launch air strikes against Yugoslavia?

Critical Thinking

5. Was the Initiative on Race a good solution to the problem of strained race relations?
Consider:
- what events revealed strained race relations
- how talking about the issue might help
- what other approaches might have worked

SECTION 2 REVIEW ANSWERS

Define and Identify
For significance, see the following pages:
- Bob Dole, p. 776
- Reform Party, p. 777
- Rodney King, p. 778
- Los Angeles Riots, p. 778
- Initiative on Race, p. 778
- James Byrd Jr., p. 778
- Kenneth Starr, p. 780
- Slobodan Milosevic, p. 780
- Kosovo crisis, p. 780
- Madeleine Albright, p. 781

1. Clinton—middle ground on economic issues, called for environmental protection and gun control; Dole—failed to present a caring image and to clarify his position on many issues

2. booming stock market, and low unemployment, inflation, and interest rates

3. Starr's investigation expands; Clinton gives testimony in a civil trial; Starr claims Clinton lied about a relationship with an intern; the House investigates and impeaches

4. NATO launched the air strikes to stop the crimes against humanity being committed by Serbians against Albanians in Kosovo.

5. Students might question the effectiveness of the Initiative on Race and offer other solutions more effective than mere discussion of the problem of race relations.

SECTION 3

After completing Section 3, students should be able to:

OBJECTIVE 1 *Discuss the events that shaped the space program in the 1990s.*

OBJECTIVE 2 *Explain the issues surrounding technology in the 1990s.*

OBJECTIVE 3 *Analyze how U.S. popular culture affected the rest of the world.*

OBJECTIVE 4 *Describe how immigration changed in the 1990s.*

OBJECTIVE 5 *Identify the issues that affected family life in the 1990s.*

LET'S GET STARTED!

Write the following names and terms on the chalkboard: *Mir, Dolly, Y2K bug, John Glenn.* Have students write sentences identifying each item. *(Students should identify: the Russian space station, the first successfully cloned mammal, the fear that computer systems would crash on January 1, 2000, and the oldest American to fly in space.)* Ask volunteers to share their responses with the class. Tell students that in Section 3 they will learn more about how Americans reacted to technological developments during the 1990s.

SECTION 3 RESOURCES

PRINT
- Guided Reading Strategy 26.3
- Literature Reading 26: Caught Between Two Cultures
- Section 3 Review, p. 786
- Daily Quiz 26.3

MULTIMEDIA
- One-Stop Planner, Lesson 26.3
- Holt Researcher: American History CD–ROM
- HRW Web site

SHELTERED ENGLISH
- Main Idea Activity for Reteaching and Sheltered English 26.3

✓ READING TO UNDERSTAND
To help students master the section objectives, have them answer the **READING CHECKS** and complete **Guided Reading Strategy 26.3** as they read the section.

Society in the 1990s

OBJECTIVES

Read to understand:
1. what events shaped the space program in the 1990s
2. what issues arose surrounding technology in the 1990s
3. how U.S. popular culture affected the rest of the world
4. how immigration changed in the 1990s
5. what issues affected family life in the 1990s

KEY TERMS

Mir
Internet
World Wide Web
Telecommunications Act
Y2K bug
Immigration Act of 1990
Family and Medical Leave Act

KEY PEOPLE

Shannon Lucid
John Glenn
Bill Gates

"Multiple networks . . . will carry a broad range of services and information technology applications into homes, businesses, schools and hospitals. These networks will form the basis of evolving national and global information infrastructures, in turn creating a seamless web uniting the world in the emergent Information Age. The result will be a new information marketplace, providing opportunities and challenges for individuals, industry and governments."

—Al Gore

A teenager uses the Internet.

In 1994 Vice President Al Gore described the future of information technology and its coming effects on American life. New technologies such as computers, the Internet, and the World Wide Web changed the way Americans communicated, conducted business, and related to the rest of the world.

Technology and Society

Many incredible achievements in science and technology were made during the 1990s. Public fascination with technology encouraged innovation.

Space. After suffering a terrible setback with the space shuttle *Challenger* explosion in 1986, the U.S. space program found renewed energy. With the Cold War over, the National Aeronautics and Space Administration (NASA) focused on commercial and scientific projects more than military efforts. The Hubble space telescope, launched in 1990 and repaired in 1993, transmitted vital information and breathtaking photos from deep space. In 1995 the United States joined with Russia for a project aboard the space station ***Mir***. Astronaut Shannon Lucid broke the U.S. record for the most consecutive days in space. She spent 188 days aboard the *Mir*.

BIOGRAPHY

John Glenn

One U.S. astronaut came out of retirement to break space records during the 1990s. John Glenn had been the first American to orbit Earth. He also became the oldest American to fly in space. Born on July 18, 1921, in Cambridge, Ohio, Glenn enrolled in Muskingum College in 1939 in New Concord, Ohio, his hometown. He studied engineering and began flying at the nearby New Philadelphia airfield. In 1942 he enrolled in the Naval Aviation Cadet Program.

Glenn joined the U.S. Marine Corps in 1943 and flew 59 missions during World War II. During the Korean War he flew 90 more. In 1954 Glenn attended Test Pilot School at the Naval Air Test Center. In 1957, as an

The Sojourner rover explored the surface of Mars.

TEACH OBJECTIVES 1 AND 2

LEVEL 1: Tell students that Americans found renewed interest in space exploration and the space program in the 1990s. Pair students and have each pair draw a cartoon depicting the events that shaped the space program in the 1990s. *(Cartoons should depict the end of the Cold War, photos taken using the Hubble Telescope, the joint U.S.-Russian project aboard the space station* Mir *and Shannon Lucid's 188 days aboard* Mir, *and John Glenn's flight as the oldest American in space.)* Discuss with students some of the issues involving technology in the 1990s. *(Students should mention free-speech rights involving the Internet, the fear that a fully computerized society will make human workers obsolete, the concern that social divisions will deepen because the poor do not have access to computer technology, the Y2K bug, and the ethical issues surrounding the possible cloning of humans.)* Have each pair create a series of bumper stickers that identify the issues surrounding technology in the 1990s. Display students' cartoons and bumper stickers around the classroom.

Sheltered English, Cooperative Learning

NOTE: For an additional teaching idea, see the Chapter 26 open-ended statements lesson in the **Creative Teaching Strategies** handbook.

officer on the project F8U-1 Crusader, Glenn set the transcontinental speed record. He flew from Los Angeles to New York in three hours and 23 minutes. In 1959 he was selected as one of seven astronauts for the Project Mercury space-flight training program. In 1962 Glenn orbited Earth in the space capsule *Friendship 7.*

Glenn retired from the space program in 1964. In 1970 he narrowly lost the Ohio Democratic primary for a U.S. Senate seat. He successfully ran for the U.S. Senate in 1974 and served until 1992. In 1998 Glenn returned to the space program. At age 77 he served as a payload specialist on the space shuttle mission STS-95. NASA scientists studied Glenn's reaction to space travel to learn more about the relationship between the process of aging and the body's ability to adapt to weightlessness.

✔ **READING CHECK:** What events shaped the space program in the 1990s?

The computer age. During the 1990s personal computer (PC) technology evolved rapidly. A leader in the computer revolution was Bill Gates, head of Microsoft Corporation. By the mid-1990s most business offices and public institutions were computerized, and nearly 40 percent of American homes had PCs. Students from grade school to college used computers for many purposes. Computers also proved to be useful to disabled Americans by enhancing communication in a number of ways.

The **Internet**, an enormous computer-based communications and information system, enabled users to communicate worldwide, join discussion groups, and gather information from countless databases. Developed by Swiss scientists in the early 1990s, the **World Wide Web** linked Internet sites offering text, animation, and graphics covering a seemingly endless range of topics. Some observers hoped that this so-called information highway would bring together people from different social classes, cultures, and countries. In this excerpt from his book, *The Road Ahead,* Bill Gates described the potential social impact of the World Wide Web.

> **"The information highway is going to break down boundaries and may promote a world culture, or at least a sharing of cultural activities and values. The highway will also make it easy for patriots, even expatriates, deeply involved in their own ethnic communities to reach out to others with similar interests no matter where they may be located."**

Concerns about technology. Computers did not create utopia, however. The social problems plaguing American society soon appeared in cyberspace as well. In the **Telecommunications Act** of 1996, Congress attempted to regulate indecency on the Internet. A federal court quickly struck down key parts of this law, however, as a violation of the First Amendment right to free speech.

DNA Testing

BY MARY CARROLL JOHANSEN

Modern scientific techniques like DNA testing are enabling scientists and historians to resolve controversial questions that have puzzled people for centuries. For example, in 1802 a journalist published rumors that President Thomas Jefferson had fathered children by his slave Sally Hemings. For years Jefferson's supporters strongly denied it. Recently, scholars such as Joseph Ellis and Annette Gordon-Reed have debated the historical evidence of the Jefferson-Hemings affair without reaching a definitive conclusion. In 1998 the use of DNA analysis brought historians and scientists closer to an answer.

Scientists have found that most of the Y chromosomes in DNA pass intact from father to son, allowing them to trace paternal lineage. Since Jefferson had no sons, scientists compared DNA from male-line descendants of Jefferson's paternal grandfather with DNA from descendants of Eston Hemings, Sally Hemings's youngest son. They found a match. Since the chances of a match were less than one percent, Jefferson very likely was Eston Hemings's father.

DNA has helped settle other historical mysteries. In 1995, scientists announced that Anna Anderson had not been Anastasia, the daughter of murdered czar Nicholas II of Russia, as she had claimed. Pathologists have also used DNA to determine that President Zachary Taylor died of natural causes, not arsenic poisoning as some suspected.

PEOPLE IN HISTORY

Bill Gates. When Bill Gates was 12 years old, he became so interested in computers that he and his friends dug through trash bins at a local computer company to find notes that the company's programmers had discarded. While a senior in high school, Gates was offered a job as a computer programmer. Three years later he cofounded Microsoft. His interest in computers took him far in the business world—Gates became a billionaire at age 31.

CRITICAL THINKING What personal attributes might have contributed to Gates's success?

ANSWER: Students might suggest that Gates's natural aptitude, curiosity, and drive have contributed to his success.

internetconnect

TOPIC: The History of PCs and the Internet
GO TO: go.hrw.com
KEYWORD: SE1 Internet

Have students access the Internet through the HRW Web site to conduct research on the development of the PC and the Internet. Then have each student create a poster or multimedia presentation about the history of the PC and the Internet.

TEACH OBJECTIVES 3 AND 4

LEVELS 2 AND 3: Pair students and tell one student in each pair to imagine that he or she is John Glenn, and tell the other student to imagine that he or she is a journalist assigned to interview Glenn. Have each pair create a transcript of an interview about the events that shaped the space program in the 1990s. *(See the Level 1 lesson for the correct events.)* Ask each pair to conduct its interview for the class. Tell students that many Americans have been concerned about the consequences of technology on society. Have each student write an essay that analyzes the issues surrounding technology in the 1990s. *(See the Level 1 lesson for the correct issues.)* Ask volunteers to read their essays to the class. **Cooperative Learning**

ALL LEVELS: Ask students why the response to the export of U.S. popular culture might not always be positive. *(Students might suggest that people in other countries want to maintain their own cultures and traditions.)* Then discuss where the majority of new and often well-schooled immigrants to the United States are coming from. *(Students should mention Asia, Latin America, and the Caribbean.)* Discuss why these immigrants might be important to the economy. *(Students might answer that many new immigrants tend to be highly skilled and important to high-tech industries.)* Tell students that Congress has hotly debated immigration issues in recent years. **Sheltered English**

CONSTITUTIONAL HERITAGE

The Telecommunications Act. In June 1997 the U.S. Supreme Court ruled that the Communications Decency Act, a section of the Telecommunications Act, was unconstitutional. The Decency Act had made it illegal to display indecent or offensive material to minors over online computer networks. The Court ruled that although the goal of protecting minors was admirable, the law went too far in restricting free expression on the Internet.

ACTIVITY: Have students write a legal brief either supporting or opposing the Supreme Court ruling discussed above.

THAT'S INTERESTING!

A 1998 U.S. government report claimed that a "digital divide" had developed in American society. Wealthier Americans, city-dwellers, and white families were more likely to have access to the Internet in their homes than poor households, rural residents, or minority families.

VISUAL RECORD ANSWER

Students might note that the employees are wearing traditional Islamic clothing.

Worried about computer systems failures, some Americans began to store food and other necessities as the year 2000 approached.

Along with concerns about the kinds of material in cyberspace, some observers worried that a fully computerized society would not need human workers. Such fears were probably exaggerated, though, because new technologies often create new jobs. Just as some people were overcoming their fear that computers would make people obsolete, scientists announced the first successful cloning of a mammal, Dolly the sheep. People debated the widsom of using this technology to eventually clone humans. Other people worried that scientific advances would deepen social divisions as wealthy, well-educated Americans mastered the new technologies, while poorer citizens lagged behind.

As the year 2000 approached, computer programmers revealed another troubling aspect of society's dependence on technology. In order to save space when developing computer programs, some programmers had abbreviated references to years, leaving out the digits 1 and 9. This meant that the computer read the year '90 as 1990. These programs were never updated to recognize the new century. Thus, as the year 2000 approached, programmers warned that many computers would read the year 2000, or '00, as 1900. This error would cause many computer systems to fail. The problem came to be known as the **Y2K bug**. As a result of the Y2K bug, businesses and government agencies spent millions of dollars hiring experts to reprogram their computers before the end of 1999.

✔ **READING CHECK:** What issues arose surrounding technology in the 1990s?

Exporting Mass Culture

The Internet aided in the exportation of American popular culture. By 1990 popular culture had become one of the most profitable U.S. exports, with annual revenues topping $5 billion. The sales of American TV shows in Europe alone totaled some $600 million a year. Similarly, the music industry earned about 70 percent of its revenues from overseas sales. Reported a British economics journal: "America is to entertainment what . . . Saudi Arabia is to oil."

American consumer products, from hamburgers and soda to blue jeans, were also snapped up by people the world over. The overseas division of the McDonald's Corporation, for instance, grew enormously during the 1990s. In 1992 McDonald's opened more restaurants overseas—including one in Beijing, China—than it did in the United States. Of McDonald's $12.4 billion sales in 1995, approximately 60 percent was generated by its some 12,500 restaurants in foreign nations.

Some critics expressed concern that this American popular culture would suffocate other cultures. They also worried that Hollywood movies and television shows gave the world a distorted impression of life in the United States. A Jamaican journalist wrote about the effects of American television on his fellow citizens:

INTERPRETING THE VISUAL RECORD

Exporting mass culture. Many American businesses have spread overseas. ***How do these employees of an American-style fast-food restaurant in Jakarta, Indonesia, maintain their Islamic culture?***

TEACH OBJECTIVE 5

ALL LEVELS: Tell students that many social changes have affected families in the United States during the past two decades. To help students understand the issues that affected family life in the 1990s, copy the graphic organizer at right on the chalkboard, omitting the italicized answers. Have each student complete the organizer. Ask volunteers to share their answers with the class. To conclude, lead a discussion about what the passage of the Family and Medical Leave Act might reveal about the changing priorities of American society. **Sheltered English**

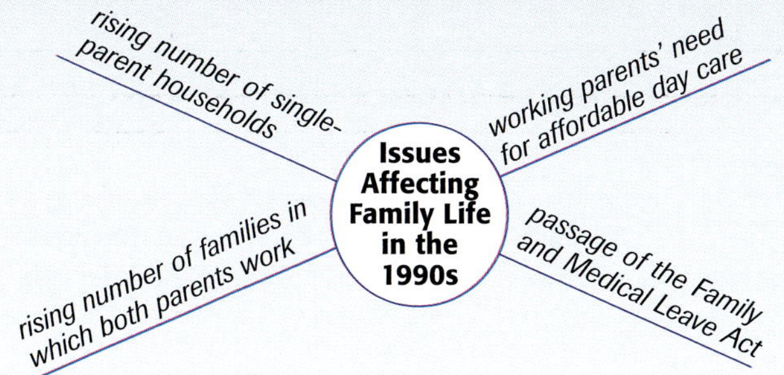

▶**ASSIGNMENT** *Tell students to imagine that it is January 1993 and that they are working parents. Have each student write a letter to his or her congressional representative that describes the issues affecting family life in the 1990s and urges the representative to vote for the Family and Medical Leave Act.*

> **"** Because of what they see on television, everyone in Jamaica thinks . . . that everything in America is wonderful. . . . It makes people think that money and material wealth are the only ways to be rich in this world. **"**

The shared global culture also had advantages, however. Through orbiting communications satellites, television linked the entire world. Events in one nation were instantly transmitted around the globe. Thus, events like natural disasters often quickly produced a global outpouring of sympathy and help.

✔ **READING CHECK:** How did the popular culture of the United States affect the rest of the world?

A New Wave of Immigration

Many people in other countries continued to see the United States as a land of opportunity. The 1990 census revealed that more immigrants had come to the United States in the 1980s than in any decade since 1910. More than 80 percent of these immigrants came from Asia, the Caribbean, and Latin America. By the 1990s many native-born Americans had grown alarmed by the wave of immigrants. Many blamed immigrants for taking jobs from native-born residents.

Supporters of immigration felt differently. They argued that immigrants created new businesses that revitalized urban areas and helped the economy. In addition, supporters of immigration noted that many recent immigrants, most notably those from China, India, Korea, and the Philippines, on average had more schooling than either native-born Americans or European immigrants. Asian immigrants, they pointed out, made up about one third of the engineers in Silicon Valley, California's center of computer technology, located near San Jose.

President George Bush had recognized these benefits when he signed the **Immigration Act of 1990**. The new law changed U.S. immigration policy by increasing the number of immigrants and doubling the number of skilled workers allowed into the United States each year. The act also authorized special visas for overseas investors interested in establishing businesses in economically depressed areas of the country.

Concerned by the growing number of immigrants, in the mid-1990s Congress acted to curb new immigration. In 1996 Congress passed an immigration law that strengthened control of U.S. borders in an effort to halt illegal immigration. The law attempted to keep new immigrants off welfare. For example, sponsors of immigrants were required to have incomes at least 125 percent above the poverty level. It also prevented legal immigrants who were not U.S. citizens from receiving most forms of welfare benefits.

✔ **READING CHECK:** How did immigration change in the 1990s?

GROWING RELIGIOUS DIVERSITY

The Masjid Omar Al-Khattab mosque in Los Angeles

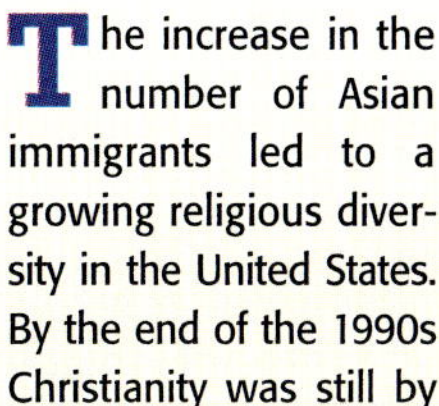

The increase in the number of Asian immigrants led to a growing religious diversity in the United States. By the end of the 1990s Christianity was still by far the most common religion, representing about 84 percent of the U.S. population. However, membership in traditionally Eastern religions such as Buddhism, Hinduism, and Islam was growing. By 1998 Islam, with some 5 to 6 million followers in the United States, was close to overtaking Judaism as the nation's second-most-practiced religion.

As these religions grew in prominence, so did the number of non-Asian converts. By 1998 more than 80,000 American Muslims were of Western European descent. Buddhism also attracted many non-Asian converts. In many places, American Buddhism evolved into a distinct faith. It moved away from Asian Buddhism's traditional focus on the intense spiritual training of monks and nuns. American Buddhism tends to emphasize the personal spiritual growth of lay members. Some followers argue that such an approach is in keeping with the American democratic traditions. "What [American Buddhists] are doing," noted one observer in 1997, "is taking a path of enlightenment in a lay culture without priests and temples and structures, and moving it right into daily practice in everyday life." ■

GLOBAL RELATIONS

American Culture. Some critics have noted that the global market for films has shaped the choices that film production companies make when they invest in a film. Because movies comprehensible only to American audiences have little chance of making profits overseas, many filmmakers choose to de-emphasize dialogue in their films and to make action and adventure movies that people from a wide variety of cultures can enjoy.

CRITICAL THINKING What consequences might filmmakers' choices have for American movie audiences?

ANSWER: Students might suggest that American audiences might have fewer opportunities to see films that have meaningful or complex dialogue.

THAT'S INTERESTING!

In 1996 the United States received more immigrants from Mexico than from any other nation. Some 163,600 Mexicans arrived in the United States that year.

VISUAL RECORD ANSWER

(for p. 786)

Students might note the sign in the background, which points to a child care center.

REVIEW

Have students complete the **Section 3 Review** on p. 786.

ASSESS

Have students complete **Daily Quiz 26.3**. As **Alternative Assessment**, you may want to use the cartoons or the interview in this section's lessons.

RETEACH

Have students complete **Main Idea Activity for Reteaching and Sheltered English 26.3**. Pair students and assign each pair one subsection from Section 3. Have each pair write three questions about the material in its assigned subsection. Collect pairs' questions and use them to quiz the class. **Sheltered English, Cooperative Learning**

EXTEND

Ask each student to conduct research on one of the following people or topics: Shannon Lucid, John Glenn, Bill Gates, *Mir*, or the Y2K bug. Have each student create a collage depicting pertinent facts about his or her chosen subject. Display students' collages around the classroom. **Block Scheduling**

SECTION 3 REVIEW ANSWERS

Define and Identify

For significance, see the following pages:

- *Mir*, p. 782
- Shannon Lucid, p. 782
- John Glenn, p. 782
- Bill Gates, p. 783
- Internet, p. 783
- World Wide Web, p. 783
- Telecommunications Act, p. 783
- Y2K bug, p. 784
- Immigration Act of 1990, p. 785
- Family and Medical Leave Act, p. 786

1. pros—computers and the Internet allow instant access to information, assistance for the disabled, and worldwide communication; cons—indecency not regulated on the Internet, job losses to computers, deepening social divisions, the Y2K bug

2. focus on commercial and scientific projects, joint U.S.-Russian project on the *Mir* space station, John Glenn's successful return to space

3. because of fears that American culture would overwhelm their own

4. Most immigrants came from Asia, the Caribbean, and Latin America; increased quota of immigrants and skilled workers in 1990, immigration restrictions in 1996.

5. The increase in the number of single-parent households made child care an important issue for employers and for working parents trying to balance work and family.

INTERPRETING THE VISUAL RECORD

Children. The number of single-parent households and households with both parents working outside the home is rising. ***What clues in this photograph might lead you to assume that this woman is a working mother?***

Work and Family

Some observers expressed concern about the state of the American family in the 1990s. By 1998 only 26 percent of American households were made up of married couples with children. Most single parents had a difficult time financially. Patricia Mull, a Los Angeles seamstress who stretched her income to send her daughter to private school, described the stress she faced. "I worry about the rent. I worry if I can make the payment in time. I worry if I have enough money left for other things. I worry about money every day, every night."

Many two-parent families shared Mull's concerns as they struggled to balance job and family responsibilities. Nearly 60 percent of married women worked outside the home in 1995, up from about 30 percent in 1960. The increase of single-parent families and families with both parents in the workforce created the need for affordable day care. Employers increasingly realized that family concerns affected their employees' jobs. To help employees balance work and family, a group of businesses in 1992 announced a program to build more day-care and elder-care centers across the country.

The U.S. government also recognized the need to help working families. In February 1993, just two weeks after his inauguration, President Clinton signed into law the **Family and Medical Leave Act**. The legislation requires large companies to provide workers up to 12 weeks of unpaid leave. Workers can use this time for family and medical emergencies without losing their medical insurance or their jobs.

This legislation reflected the significant changes in attitudes toward work and family that have occurred in the United States in the 1990s. As businessperson Florence Skelly noted in 1993, "Rather than trying to climb the economic ladder, people are becoming more concerned with relationships and family and community involvement."

✔ **READING CHECK:** What issues affected family life in the 1990s?

SECTION 3 REVIEW

Define and explain the significance of the following terms:
Mir
Internet
World Wide Web
Telecommunications Act
Y2K bug
Immigration Act of 1990
Family and Medical Leave Act

Identify and explain the significance of the following individuals:
Shannon Lucid
John Glenn
Bill Gates

1. **Using Graphic Organizers** Copy the graphic organizer below. Use it to describe the pros and cons of increasing dependence on technology in the 1990s.

2. **Analyzing** How did the U.S. space program rebound from its setbacks of the 1980s?
3. **Recognizing Point of View** Why might people in other countries oppose the spread of American popular culture?
4. **Comparing and Contrasting** How had immigration changed by the 1990s? How did this affect the 1990 and 1996 immigration bills?

Critical Thinking

5. Why did family issues become a political concern in the 1990s?
Consider:
- the increase in single-parent households
- concerns over child care
- what influenced the passage of the Family and Medical Leave Act

SECTION 4

After completing Section 4, students should be able to:

OBJECTIVE 1 *Identify the factors that shaped the global economy.*

OBJECTIVE 2 *Describe the environmental issues concerning people in the 1990s.*

OBJECTIVE 3 *Explain why population growth in urban areas and throughout the world caused concern.*

OBJECTIVE 4 *Analyze the role of the United States in spreading democracy throughout the world.*

LET'S GET STARTED!

As students enter the classroom, tell them to compile a written list of the major challenges facing the United States and the world today. Ask volunteers to share their lists with the class, and compile a comprehensive list on the chalkboard. Tell students that in Section 4 they will learn about major challenges and developments in the world today.

Looking to the Future

OBJECTIVES

Read to understand:

1. what factors shaped the development of the global economy
2. what environmental issues concerned people in the 1990s
3. why population growth in urban areas and throughout the world caused concern
4. what the role of the United States in spreading democracy throughout the world is

KEY TERMS

European Union
North American Free Trade Agreement
multinational corporations
Chernobyl disaster
recycling

KEY PEOPLE

Indira Gandhi

EYEWITNESSES TO History

" How, then, shall we live? How must we live to preserve free societies and to be worthy of the blood and pain? This is the unfinished business of our century. "

—Michael Novak

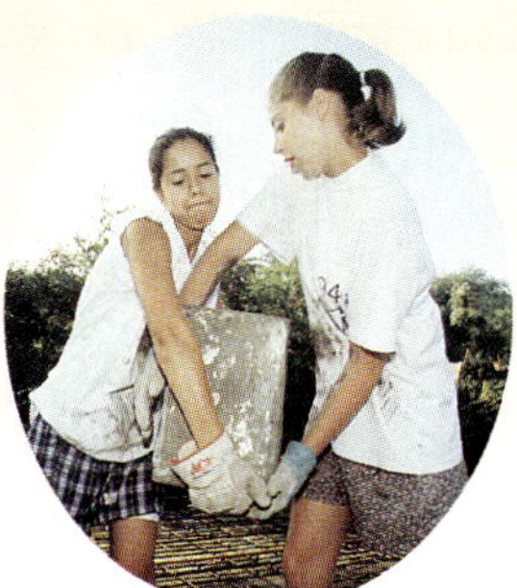

Young Americans perform community service.

In an editorial for the *New York Times,* social critic Michael Novak reflected on the future. At the start of a new millennium, his questions represent a growing reassessment of America's future. What role will Americans play in determining the fate of the world and its inhabitants? What historic trends can we foresee in the future? What challenges do we face in the coming years? While these questions cannot be answered with certainty, we can consider the recent past and offer valuable speculations about the possible future of our country.

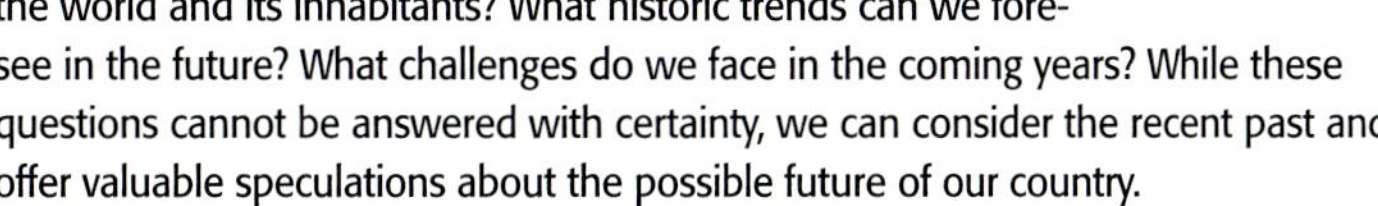

A Global Economy

Billions of dollars' worth of trade links the world's major industrial nations. In the fall of 1992 journalist Bruce W. Nelan predicted the growing importance of global economics.

> **" Just as wars—two World Wars and, equally important, the Cold War—dominated the geopolitical map of the 20th century, economics will rule over the 21st. All the big questions confronting the world in the century ahead are basically economic. "**

International trade. International trading blocs may provide stiff economic competition for the United States in coming years. The **European Union** (EU), a Western European trading bloc, was formed in 1993. The EU is designed to allow capital, goods, and labor to move freely among member nations. The EU also encourages greater cooperation on such matters as crime, culture, education, foreign policy, and health. Some predict that a full political union—the "United States of Europe," which could include as many as 20 member states—will eventually form. If this were to happen, the European Union would be the world's largest trading bloc.

By 1993 concern over such economic competition led to growing support for U.S. ratification of the **North American Free Trade Agreement** (NAFTA). The agreement provides for a lowering of trade barriers among Canada, Mexico, and the United States. Supporters hoped that NAFTA would help the United States compete more effectively in the global economy in the coming years.

The European Union has issued its own currency to aid free trade among European countries.

SECTION 4 RESOURCES

PRINT
- Guided Reading Strategy 26.4
- Primary Source Reading 26: Antarctica: A New View
- Section 4 Review, p. 791
- Daily Quiz 26.4

MULTIMEDIA
- One-Stop Planner, Lesson 26.4
- Linking Geography and History Transparency 23: The Global Environment
- Holt Researcher: American History CD–ROM

SHELTERED ENGLISH
- Main Idea Activity for Reteaching and Sheltered English 26.4

✔ READING TO UNDERSTAND

To help students master the section objectives, have them answer the **READING CHECKS** and complete **Guided Reading Strategy 26.4** as they read the section.

TEACH OBJECTIVE 1

ALL LEVELS: To help students understand what factors have shaped the development of the global economy, copy the graphic organizer at right on the chalkboard, omitting the italicized answers. Have each student complete the organizer. Ask volunteers to share their answers with the class. Then have students write a paragraph analyzing how these factors shape the global economy. **Sheltered English**

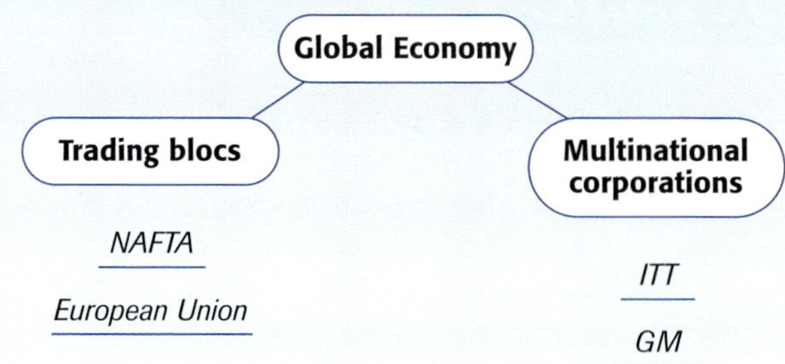

▶**ASSIGNMENT:** *Have students write a brief article on the development of the global economy in the 1990s.*

ACROSS THE CURRICULUM

▶GOVERNMENT◀

NAFTA. Many labor leaders feared that NAFTA would lead to the loss of American jobs. Because labor unions represented a powerful voice within the Democratic Party, many Democrats in Congress refused to support NAFTA. Some of President Clinton's advisers predicted that NAFTA would not pass. Clinton allied with Republicans to secure passage of NAFTA. In order to gain the votes of undecided members, Clinton promised political favors and support for other projects. NAFTA passed in the House by a 234-to-200 vote, and in the Senate by a 61-to-38 vote.

CRITICAL THINKING What political risks might President Clinton have taken in supporting NAFTA?

ANSWER: Students might suggest that he risked losing the support of labor unions and members of his party in Congress.

Multimedia Resources

Linking Geography and History Transparency 23: The Global Environment

VISUAL RECORD ANSWER

Students might answer that the workers are laboring on an assembly line.

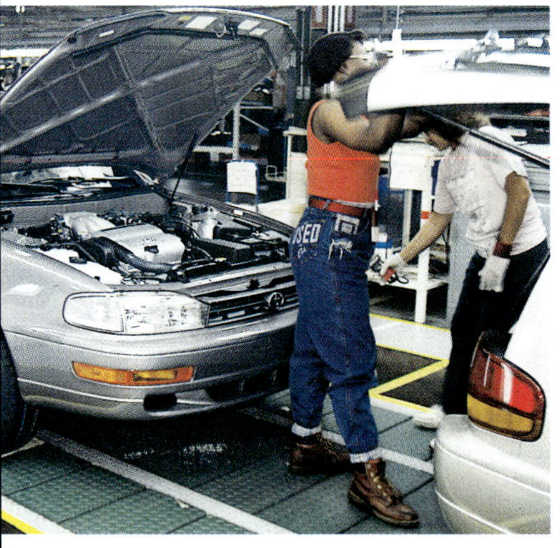

INTERPRETING THE VISUAL RECORD

Global business. Workers assemble Toyota cars in a Kentucky factory. ***What do you think the workers shown are doing?***

Multinational corporations. The global economy is increasingly dominated by **multinational corporations**. These are companies that invest money in a variety of business ventures around the world. Multinational corporations sometimes benefit the United States economically. Leading Japanese corporations, for example, have opened factories in the United States. Such plants boost the U.S. economy, although most of the profits go to the parent corporations in Japan.

Just as foreign companies invest in the United States, many American businesses are expanding their investments in other countries. The New York–based ITT Corporation is one example. ITT began as a communications company known as International Telephone and Telegraph. By the 1990s, however, ITT held major interests worldwide in such diverse businesses as finance, food processing, hotels, insurance, and real estate. Other corporations such as General Motors, IBM, and Texaco, also operate worldwide.

✔ **READING CHECK:** What factors have shaped the development of the global economy?

Energy and the Environment

The future of energy resources and the environment continues to concern many experts. In 1996 the world consumed an amount of energy equivalent to that of about 65 billion barrels of oil. The United States is home to less than 5 percent of the world's population yet accounted for nearly 25 percent of the world's energy consumption that year. Some 38 percent of U.S. energy came from oil, 24 percent from natural gas, and 22 percent from coal. Just 8 percent came from alternative sources such as solar or hydroelectric power and 8 percent from nuclear power.

A 1986 accident at the Chernobyl nuclear power plant in the Soviet Union near Kiev, Ukraine, sent a dangerous radioactive cloud drifting across Europe. The **Chernobyl disaster** released 50 times more radioactive material into the environment than the two atomic bombs dropped on Japan in 1945 combined.

Coming just seven years after the Three Mile Island accident in Pennsylvania, the Chernobyl disaster heightened anxiety over nuclear power. People began calling for increased research on other energy sources. These include solar power, geothermal power (geysers and hot springs), and wind power. They also include biomass (materials such as wood or waste products that can be burned or used to make fuel) and hydrogen. In addition, many utility companies have launched successful energy conservation programs designed to reduce consumer demand and increase the efficiency of energy production.

As scientists search for new ways to meet energy demands many environmentalists focus on protecting the world's remaining forests and wildlife. Population growth, industrialization, and the expansion of commercial agriculture and livestock operations cause forests to disappear at an alarming rate. According to the UN, almost 34 million acres of forests in developing countries were lost each year between 1990 and 1995.

This car uses fuel-cell technology and produces no harmful emissions.

TEACH OBJECTIVE 2

ALL LEVELS: Tell students to imagine that they are editors of an environmental magazine. Organize students into small groups. Have each group prepare a table of contents for a special section on environmental issues concerning people in the 1990s. Each group should also prepare a short summary of each article. *(Students should mention the hazards of nuclear power, the consumption of fossil fuels, the need for alternative energy sources, deforestation and the disappearance of rainforests, the extinction of plants and animals, and the need to protect sensitive natural areas.)* Ask volunteers to present their tables of contents and summaries to the class.
Sheltered English, Cooperative Learning

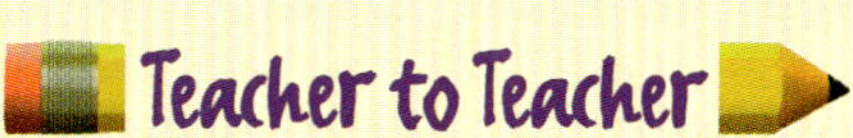

Deanna Spring of Cincinnati, Ohio, suggested the following activity: Pair students and have each pair write a dinner-table conversation about the environmental issues that concerned people in the 1990s. Ask each pair to perform its conversation for the class.

Plant and animal species around the world are in grave danger of extinction because of the pressure generated by the growing population of humans and because of industrialization. Individuals and groups have worked to slow this process and to save endangered species and unique scenic areas. For example, Greenpeace, an international environmental organization, campaigns against whaling, and the U.S. government has acted to protect sensitive natural areas.

The 1994 California Desert Protection Act enlarged the Joshua Tree and Death Valley National Monuments and converted them to national parks. Then, in 1996 President Clinton took steps to protect 1.7 million acres of Utah canyon lands where a Dutch mining company held valuable coal leases. Clinton based his moves on the Antiquities Act—a law President Theodore Roosevelt had used to protect the Grand Canyon from development. The law allowed Clinton to create the Canyons of the Escalante National Monument without congressional approval.

✔ **READING CHECK:** What environmental issues concerned people in the 1990s?

HOLT RESEARCHER *Read More About It*

Free Find:
Hunger in Africa
After studying the digital map on hunger in Africa on the **Holt Researcher** CD–ROM, write a short essay explaining how future environmental problems might worsen conditions in Africa.

Population Growth

As environmental awareness has increased, **recycling**—the collection and processing of waste items for reuse—has gained support. Recycling serves two important purposes. It reuses scarce natural resources. It also reduces the amount of solid waste that must be buried, burned, dumped, or shipped elsewhere. By 1991 some 4,000 curbside recycling programs were under way in the United States, a 250 percent increase from 1989. The United States lags behind other industrialized nations in recycling, however. Japan, for example, recycles 50 percent of its paper and 54 percent of its glass.

Urban areas. The concern over the environment is related to urban growth. One expert estimates that an excess of garbage is risking the health of 40 percent of the urban population in the developing world.

Many cities are instituting innovative waste-management systems. In Cairo, Egypt, several thousand Zabaleens—Christians from southern Egypt—use donkey-drawn carts to collect garbage from the city. They then sort through the garbage and sell the reusable material. Thrown-away food goes to feed pigs. Waste products are used to fertilize crops. Scrap metal, glass, paper, and plastic are recycled. Other cities, such as Ciudad Juárez, Mexico, have developed similar systems. As a result, many urban planners, such as Donella Meadows, are cautiously optimistic about the future. "If humans manage brilliantly starting very soon," she advised in 1993, "it is possible the world might look better than it does now."

INTERPRETING THE VISUAL RECORD
Population growth. The continued growth of urban populations has contributed to environmental problems. ***How does this photograph of Mexico City reflect urban environmental problems?***

The global population. Many of the world's environmental and waste problems have been made worse by a massive increase in population. By 1999 the world's population stood at 6 billion, and it was growing by a rate of nearly three people per second. Population growth is most rapid in poorer countries. Experts predict that India's population will jump from 984 million in 1998 to 1.4 billion by

THAT'S INTERESTING!
Americans concerned with the environment founded the Green Party USA in 1991. Modeled after similar political movements in Europe, the Green Party USA linked environmental issues with a call for social reforms. The party had several successes at the local level in 1992, capturing seats on several city councils. Although the Green Party did not win any seats in the U.S. Congress in the early 1990s, some Green candidates did receive a large number of votes in races for congressional seats.

VISUAL RECORD ANSWER
Students might suggest that the smog in the photograph reflects the air pollution problems faced by many cities.

STRATEGIES FOR SUCCESS ANSWERS
(for p. 790)
Practicing the Strategy
Answers will vary depending upon the student's topic.

TEACH OBJECTIVE 3

ALL LEVELS: Ask students why population growth in urban areas and throughout the world caused concern. *(Students might suggest that high population growth leads to health concerns and worsens other environmental and health problems.)* Tell students that population growth has been more rapid in poorer countries. To conclude, ask students how countries might try to address population growth. *(Students might suggest that birth control programs or the education of women might be critical measures.)* Tell students that the repercussions of population growth in urban areas and across the world will be felt for generations. **Sheltered English**

TEACH OBJECTIVE 4

ALL LEVELS: Ask students how the United States might encourage the spread of democracy around the world. *(Students might suggest that U.S. economic resources and diplomatic efforts will be instrumental.)* Have each student write a proverb or poem about the U.S. role in the spread of democracy around the world. Students may wish to include their proverbs or poems in their portfolios. **Sheltered English**

SECTION 4 REVIEW ANSWERS

Define and Identify

For significance, see the following pages:

- European Union, p. 787
- North American Free Trade Agreement, p. 787
- multinational corporations, p. 788
- Chernobyl disaster, p. 788
- recycling, p. 789
- Indira Gandhi, p. 790

1. international trade–links industrial nations and makes goods, labor, and capital available to many countries; multinational corporations–invest capital to start businesses all across the globe

2. Answers will vary but students might mention increased awareness as a factor in increased interest. Students might mention growing evidence of pollution, concerns about energy, and continued worry over the Chernobyl accident.

3. rapid growth in urban areas and poor countries, leading to more poverty; an increase in environmental problems; and competition for resources

4. Answers will vary but students may say that as an economic and political superpower, the United States can shape the ways in which many countries develop.

5. Increased globalization means that Americans must respond to economic and environmental issues throughout the world and must take responsibility for the development of democracy in emerging nations.

2025. They also predict that Mexico's will rise from 98.6 million to 141.6 million, and Bangladesh's from 127.6 million to 180.7 million.

One key to limiting population growth in developing countries, some argue, is to raise the status of women. Former Indian prime minister Indira Gandhi wrote about this topic in the 1980s.

> **"Men and most women are unaware of the potential ability of women. Their lives are entrapped by pre-conceived notions and attitudes from birth onwards. . . . A lower status for women, or lesser opportunity for women, is a handicap for the growth of mankind as a whole."**

Gandhi believed that when women gain equal rights and opportunities they will no longer be valued primarily for their ability to produce children.

✔ **READING CHECK:** Why did population growth in urban areas and throughout the world cause concern?

Strategies for Success — Writing a Research Paper

Writing a history research paper can be both a challenging and a rewarding experience. Many of the steps that go into preparing for a paper require one to use a variety of important critical thinking skills.

How to Write a Research Paper

1. **Identify the topic, develop questions, conduct research, and evaluate your sources.** First, identify the topic that you wish to research and develop one or more questions that you hope to answer in your paper. Then conduct research at your school or local public library and evaluate the sources that you find.
2. **Formulate a hypothesis.** Analyze the information in your sources and develop a hypothesis that answers your questions about the topic. This hypothesis should serve as the focus of your paper and be presented in a thesis statement in the paper's introduction.
3. **Create an outline.** Organize the ideas and evidence that you plan to discuss in your paper into an outline. This step will make the actual process of writing much easier.
4. **Write a first draft.** Compose a first draft of your paper, using your outline as a guide. It should have an introduction with a clear thesis statement, a body of material that supports the thesis statement, and a conclusion that provides a summary of what has been said.
5. **Review and edit the first draft.** After you have completed a draft of your paper, read it over and make corrections as needed.
6. **Write a final draft.** Once you have settled on a final version of your paper, prepare a neat, clean copy for submission to your teacher or classmates.

Applying the Strategy

Write a five-page research paper on a topic of recent historical importance. You may select your own topic or use one of the following suggestions:

1. global environmental problems during the 1990s
2. the Internet's effect on international commerce
3. relations between the United States and Russia during the late 1990s
4. the 2000 presidential election

Practicing the Strategy

Before writing your paper, answer the following questions.

1. What questions do you hope to answer in your paper?
2. What is your thesis statement?
3. What ideas and evidence will you use in the paper to support your thesis statement?

REVIEW

Have students complete the **Section 4 Review** on p. 791.

ASSESS

Have students complete **Daily Quiz 26.4**. As **Alternative Assessment**, you may want to use the global economy paragraph or the poem or proverb essay in this section's lessons.

RETEACH

Have students complete **Main Idea Activity for Reteaching and Sheltered English 26.4**. Organize the class into small groups. Have each group create a chart to depict the major ideas presented in Section 4. Then have volunteers present their charts to the class. Ask students to supply any information that might be missing from each group's chart.

Sheltered English, Cooperative Learning

EXTEND

Pair students and have each pair conduct research on one of the following topics or people: the Chernobyl disaster, the European Union, Indira Gandhi, NAFTA, or Zabaleens. Have each pair use its research to create a multimedia presentation about its chosen subject.

Cooperative Learning, Block Scheduling

America's Role in a New Era

The end of the Cold War did not bring solutions to all of the world's problems. In many parts of the world, true democracy remains distant. Democratic nations attempt to convince the rest of the world of democracy's appeal by helping solve existing social and economic problems.

The United States is committed to playing a central role in this effort. Some of the earliest English settlers in America believed they were lighting a beacon that would show the way to a new era. After the establishment of a democratic government, the idea of America as a world leader became a reality. However, the nation has not always lived up to these ideals. Many groups have been excluded from the promise of democracy. Over the years, though, the United States has tried to expand democracy, individual freedom, and the privileges and obligations of citizenship to all its citizens.

Global powers may shift, and economies may change, but the appeal of democracy will likely remain. People will continue to strive for individual freedom, self-government, and citizenship in a just nation. This is particularly true for those people living under unjust rulers or in extreme poverty. The vision of democracy and freedom can still inspire acts of great courage and heroism.

The following chapters will examine the key role that the United States has played in global issues such as the environment, human rights, immigration, and world trade. These issues will undoubtedly continue to shape our history in the years to come.

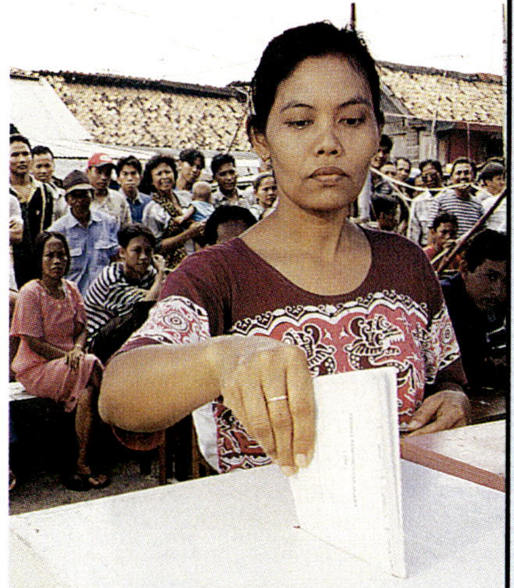

After a considerable struggle, the people of Indonesia gained the right to hold fully democratic elections in 1999.

✔ **READING CHECK:** What is the role of the United States in spreading democracy throughout the world?

SECTION 4 REVIEW

Define and explain the significance of the following terms:
European Union
North American Free Trade Agreement
multinational corporations
Chernobyl disaster
recycling

Identify and explain the significance of the following individual:
Indira Gandhi

1. **Using Graphic Organizers** Copy the graphic organizer below. Use it to describe the factors that supported the development of the global economy.

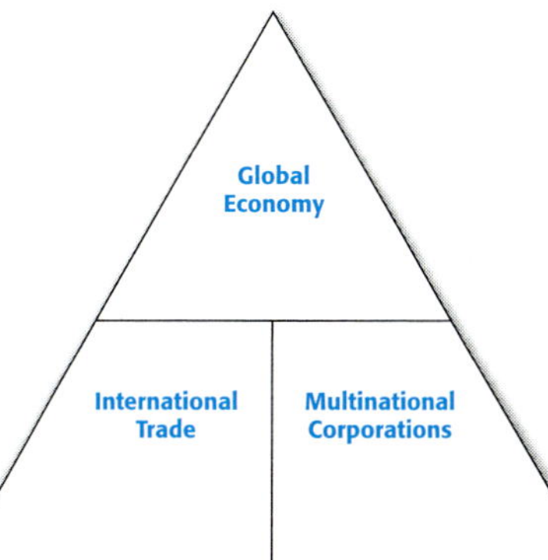

2. **Hypothesizing** Why do you think that many Americans were interested in environmental issues during the 1990s? What issues received public attention?
3. **Assessing Consequences** What are some of the possible consequences of the current trends in population growth?
4. **Evaluating** Does the United States have a responsibility to help spread democracy throughout the world? Explain your answer.

Critical Thinking

5. How might global issues create problems for Americans in the future?
   Consider:
   - the role of American businesses in the global economy
   - future environmental challenges
   - the role of the United States in the spread of democracy

CHAPTER 26 REVIEW ANSWERS

Creating a Time Line

Each event should have an explanation and the correct date.

Writing a Summary

See the Reading Checks in each section for main ideas.

Identifying People and Ideas

1. Democrat elected president in 1992 and 1996
2. 1994 Republican campaign pledge that promised a balanced-budget amendment and other reforms
3. Republican presidential candidate in 1996
4. revealed the persistence of racial tensions in the United States
5. first female secretary of state for the United States
6. astronaut and senator who returned to space in 1998 at age 77
7. computer-based communications and information system
8. computer programming flaw that threatened to cause computer systems to fail on January 1, 2000
9. required large companies to provide workers with time off for family and medical emergencies without losing their insurance or jobs
10. Western European trading bloc

REVIEW AND ASSESSMENT RESOURCES

PRINT
- Chapter 26 Review, pp. 792–93
- Chapter 26 Tutorial for Students, Parents, Mentors, and Peers
- Chapter 26 Test (Form A or B)
- Portfolio Activities and Alternative Assessment Handbook, Chapter 26

MULTIMEDIA
- Audio Program, Chapter 26 (English and Spanish)
- Chapter 26 Test Generator (on the One-Stop Planner)
- Global Skill Builder CD–ROM
- HRW Web site

SHELTERED ENGLISH
- Spanish Glossary
- Sheltered English Chapter 26 Test

REVIEW

Have students complete the **Chapter 26 Review** on pp. 792–93.

ASSESS

Use one of the chapter tests to assess students' understanding of the content. For **Alternative Assessment**, see the **Portfolio Activities and Alternative Assessment Handbook.**

Understanding Main Ideas

1. the participation and election of a record number of women to national political office and the strong showing of independent candidate Ross Perot
2. The United States attempted to bring peace to troubled areas of the world. International and domestic terrorism led to the deaths of hundreds of Americans.
3. Serbians were carrying out mass murders against Albanians in Kosovo.
4. Although it provided new services and access to information, it threatened to deepen social divisions between those with access to technology and those lacking access.
5. through international trade and the growth of multinational corporations
6. energy resources, deforestation, population growth

Reviewing Themes

1. Economic power, like military power, can be used to promote political goals.
2. The exportation of American popular culture creates an impression about American life, leads other countries to fear for the survival of their own cultures, and creates a cultural link between nations.
3. provided new ways to communicate and to send and receive information and new worries about indecency on the Internet, loss of jobs, and the Y2K bug

CHAPTER 26 Review

Creating a Time Line

Copy the time line below onto a sheet of paper. Complete the time line by filling in the events and dates from the chapter that you think were most significant. Pick three events and explain why you think they were significant.

Writing a Summary

Using the Reading Checks as a guide, write an overview of the events in the chapter.

Identifying People and Ideas

Identify the following terms or individuals and explain their significance.

1. Bill Clinton
2. Contract with America
3. Bob Dole
4. Los Angeles Riots
5. Madeleine Albright
6. John Glenn
7. Internet
8. Y2K bug
9. Family and Medical Leave Act
10. European Union

Understanding Main Ideas

SECTION 1

1. What made the elections of 1992 unique?
2. How was the United States affected by conflicts in other countries and by terrorism in the 1990s?

SECTION 2

3. Why did NATO attack Yugoslavia in 1999?

SECTION 3

4. Why was computer technology both helpful and controversial in the 1990s?

SECTION 4

5. How did the global economy develop?
6. What were the important environmental issues of the 1990s?

Reviewing Themes

1. **Economic Development** How has a nation's economic strength become as important as its military power in foreign policy?
2. **Global Relations** How does American culture affect the rest of the world?
3. **Technology and Society** How have new technologies changed American society and the world?

Thinking Critically

1. **Identifying Values** How did the Contract with America reflect the ideals of Republican congressional candidates in 1994?
2. **Problem Solving** What responsible solutions would you suggest to deal with the issues and problems parents faced in the 1990s?
3. **Comparing and Contrasting** How did business leaders in the United States and critics abroad differ in their view of the spread of American popular culture?
4. **Identifying Cause and Effect** How does rapid urban population growth contribute to environmental problems?
5. **Hypothesizing** Describe how the United States can help make the world more democratic in the future.

Writing About History

Writing to Describe Imagine that you are a reporter covering John Glenn's 1998 space shuttle flight. Write a short description of the significance of Glenn's flight. Use this graphic to organize your thoughts.

RETEACH

Organize students into small groups. Have each group use at least 20 of the key terms, key people, and key places in this chapter to create a crossword puzzle with clues. Have each group exchange its crossword puzzle with another group and then solve them. **Sheltered English, Cooperative Learning**

EXTEND

Have each student conduct research on the growth of the world's population during the past 100 years. Students should focus their research on the size of the world's population, changing birthrates, and the projected world population in 2025. Have each student create a chart presenting his or her research. Ask volunteers to present their charts to the class. **Block Scheduling**

Brazilian president Fernando Collor opens the UN Conference on the Environment and Development.

Strategies for Success Review the **Strategies for Success** on *Writing a Research Paper.* Then exchange a first draft of your research paper with that of a classmate and provide editorial suggestions for your classmate's final draft.

Linking History and Geography

Study the map below. What does it reveal about American society in 1990?

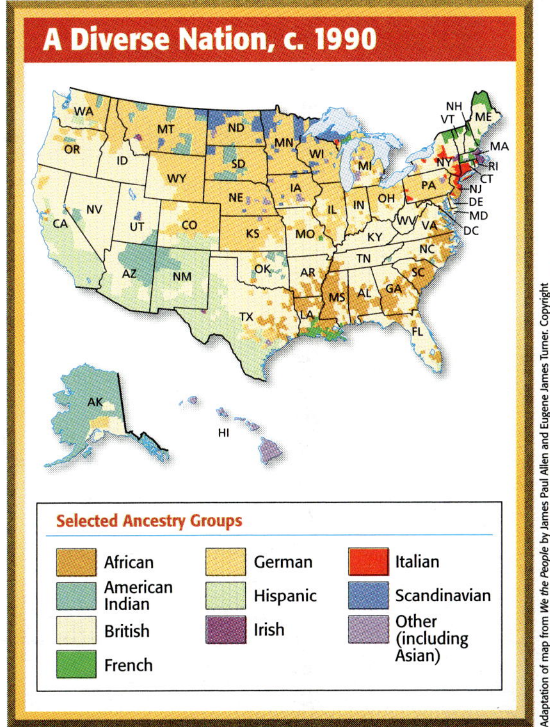

internetconnect

TOPIC: U.S. Space Program
GO TO: go.hrw.com
KEYWORD: SE1 Space

Accessing the Internet through the HRW Web site, research information about the contemporary space program. Then create an annotated and illustrated time line that presents the main events and achievements in space exploration since 1980.

Complete one or all of the following projects independently or cooperatively.

1 Global Relations

Imagine that you are an aide to Secretary of State Madeleine Albright in 1999. ***Write an outline*** for a speech that describes the outcome of NATO's air strikes against Yugoslavia.

2 Technology and Society

Imagine that you are a computer programmer in 1999. ***Write a memo*** to business leaders explaining why the Y2K bug might cause problems with their computers on January 1, 2000.

3 Economic Development

Imagine that you are the chairperson of a multinational corporation. ***Prepare a business summary*** for your stockholders explaining how the development of the global economy has affected your company.

Loading dock for U.S. imports and exports

Thinking Critically

1. Answers will vary. Students might suggest that the candidates wanted to restore trust between voters and elected officials by providing clear campaign promises.
2. Answers will vary. Some students might suggest that companies or the government should subsidize day care.
3. Although the sale of popular culture brings profits to American firms, the spread of American culture to other countries has raised concerns about the survival of other cultural values.
4. Growing populations mean increased waste and more pressure on natural resources.
5. Answers will vary. Some students might argue that the United States should provide additional economic support to nations moving toward democratic governments.

Writing About History
Reports should discuss the *Challenger* explosion, Glenn's first flight in 1962, and the excitement generated by his 1998 trip into space.

Strategies for Success
Students' drafts will vary. Students should provide clear, constructive comments.

Linking History and Geography
American society is composed of people of diverse ancestry.

REVIEW AND ASSESSMENT RESOURCES

PRINT

- Unit 7 Review, pp. 794–95
- Unit 7 Test (Form A or B)
- Portfolio Activities and Alternative Assessment Handbook, Unit 7

MULTIMEDIA

- Global Skill Builder CD–ROM

SHELTERED ENGLISH

- Spanish Glossary
- Sheltered English Unit 7 Test

To review elements of Unit 7 in a single class period, assign one of the following activities or graphic organizers, omitting the italicized answers, to individuals or groups.

2 Economic Development

Have each student create a series of political cartoons that comment on the economic policies of presidents from the 1970s and the 1990s. Ask students to write captions for their cartoons.

A Selection from Further Reading

Richard Nixon's Decision to Resign. In *The Final Days*, Bob Woodward and Carl Bernstein describe the last days of Richard Nixon's presidency. In the following excerpt, they relate an encounter between Nixon and his Secretary of State, Henry Kissinger, on the evening that the President decided to resign from office: "Nixon summoned Kissinger. . . . They sat for a time and reminisced about events, travels, shared decisions. . . . Then Nixon said that he wasn't sure he would be able to resign. Could he be the first President to quit office? Kissinger responded by listing the President's contributions, especially in diplomacy. 'Will history treat me more kindly than my contemporaries?' Nixon asked, tears flooding his eyes. Certainly, definitely, Kissinger said. . . . But he was certain that Nixon would never escape the verdict of Watergate."

COMPREHENSION According to Bernstein and Woodward, what aspect of the resignation did Nixon find particularly troubling?

ANSWER: Students might suggest that Nixon was concerned by the possibility that history would judge him harshly for the Watergate scandal and his decision to resign.

UNIT 7 Review

BUILDING YOUR PORTFOLIO

Outlined below are four projects. Independently or cooperatively, complete one and use the products to demonstrate your mastery of the historical concepts involved.

1 Constitutional Heritage

The Watergate scandal and the Iran-Contra affair challenged the foundation of constitutional government. ***Write an editorial*** that examines the ways in which the Watergate scandal was both similar to and different from the Iran-Contra affair. You may wish to use portfolio materials you designed in the unit chapters to help you.

Nixon aide John Dean testifying before Congress

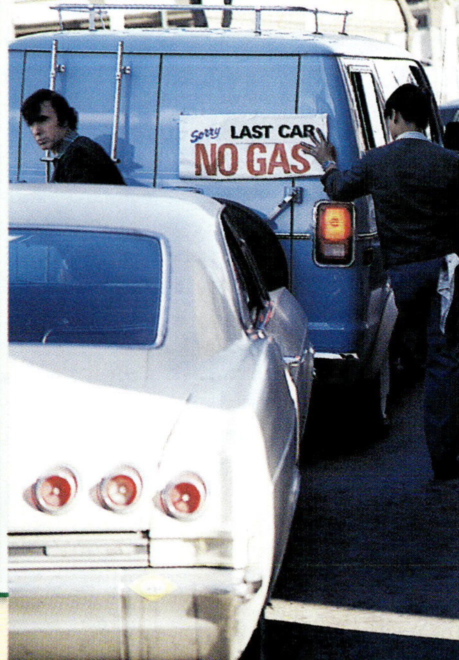

Gas shortages during the energy crisis of 1973

2 Economic Development

Stagflation and the effects of the energy crisis are two of the economic problems Presidents Nixon, Ford, and Carter struggled with in the 1970s. In the 1980s President Reagan attempted to stimulate the economy with conservative reforms. ***Write a press release*** that describes the different ways in which the economic actions taken by these presidents affected poor Americans. Present your report to the class. You may wish to use portfolio materials you designed in the unit chapters to help you.

3 Global Relations

DAILY LIFE	EFFECTS OF COMPUTERS AND THE INTERNET ON AMERICAN SOCIETY	BUSINESS
allows people to communicate with others who share interests around the world		has increased the multinational nature of business
gives anyone with a personal computer access to virtually many different kinds of information		allows individuals and businesses to sell products and services globally through Web sites

4 Technology and Society

The Post-Cold War World

Region	Conflicts
Eastern Europe	• *bitter ethnic and local disputes* • *struggles for power and self-rule* • *border disputes*
Africa	• *civil wars* • *military dictatorships* • *famine and poverty*
Middle East	• *religious struggles for land and political power* • *political assassination* • *terrorism* • *rise of dictatorships* • *control of oil prices*

Destruction of the Berlin Wall

3 Global Relations

During the 1970s and 1980s the United States opened negotiations with China, improved relations with the Soviet Union, and witnessed the end of the Cold War and the breakup of the Soviet Union. Regional and local conflicts emerged, however, as newly formed nations were torn apart by ethnic and religious struggles. ***Conduct a panel discussion*** about the new world order that highlights the sometimes conflicting interests of the world's industrialized nations and developing nations. You may wish to use portfolio materials you designed in the unit chapters to help you.

4 Technology and Society

In the past several decades, new advances in computers have made communications and the transfer of information around the world quicker and easier. These changes have brought Americans into increasing contact with citizens worldwide and have increased the multinational nature of business. ***Prepare an illustrated presentation*** for a conference on the impact of technology on business and daily life in the 1990s and beyond. You may wish to use portfolio materials you designed in the unit chapters to help you.

American fast-food restaurant in Thailand

Further Reading

Edelstein, Andrew J., and Kevin McDoough. *The Seventies: From Hot Pants to Hot Tubs.* E. P. Dutton, 1990. A social history of the 1970s.

Johnson, Haynes. *Sleepwalking Through History: America in the Reagan Years.* Norton, 1991. Overview and critical analysis of the Reagan years.

Lewis, Michael M. *Liar's Poker: Rising Through the Wreckage on Wall Street.* Norton, 1989. An insider account of Wall Street and the savings and loan industry of the 1980s

Maraniss, David. *First in His Class: The Biography of Bill Clinton.* Simon & Schuster, 1996. A thorough and balanced biography of the 42nd president of the United States.

Virga, Vincent. *The Eighties: Images of America.* Edward Burlingame Books, 1992. Photographic essay on life in the United States during the 1980s.

Woodward, Bob, and Carl Bernstein. *The Final Days.* Simon & Schuster, 1976. Chronicle of the last days of Richard Nixon's presidency.

Internet Connect and Holt Researcher CD–ROM Review

In assigned groups, develop a multimedia presentation about America between 1968 and the present. Choose information from the chapter Internet Connect activities and from the Holt Researcher CD–ROM that best reflects the major topics of the period. Write an outline and a script for your presentation, which may be shown to the class.

A Selection from Further Reading

Bill Clinton's Use of Public Opinion Polls. In *First in His Class: A Biography of Bill Clinton*, David Maraniss provides an in-depth account of Bill Clinton's life and career. In the following excerpt, he describes how Clinton used public opinion polls as political tools while serving as the Governor of Arkansas.

"[Clinton used] voter surveys in . . . perpetual fashion, taking poll results to shape the substance and rhetoric of policy debates. The goal was to discover more than whether voters supported or opposed an initiative. Word by word, line by line, phrase by phrase, paragraph by paragraph, rhetorical options would be tested to see which ones were most effective in moving the public a certain direction. It was polling as a form of copy writing, as a way for Clinton to organize his thoughts."

COMPREHENSION According to Maraniss, what role did poll results play in Bill Clinton's political strategy?

ANSWER: Students might indicate that Clinton used poll results to shape both his political positions and the manner in which he discussed these positions.

UNIT 8

America in a Global Context

CHAPTER 27 Imperialism and Independence

Colonial powers had long practiced imperialism, and by the 1880s former colonies like the United States were establishing their own empires. Traditional European imperialism ended with World War II. Newly independent nations had difficulty coping with competing offers of support from the United States and the Soviet Union. They also faced ethnic hostilities and had weak economies.

CHAPTER 28 The Rise of the Global Economy

Free trade promoted the growth of the global economy. The Great Depression slowed this process, but after World War II the United States and other nations crafted agreements that increased international trade. Pacific Rim nations such as China also became more important to the world's economy. The growth of multinational corporations, Internet commerce, and free trade agreements also strengthened the global economy.

EXAMINING THE VISUAL RECORD

Ask students the questions below. Then use the annotations to expand class discussion.

1 *Where was this photograph taken?* This photograph was taken in the payload bay of a space shuttle. The payload bay is 60 feet long and 15 feet in diameter. The shuttle, or orbiter, is 121 feet long and 57 feet high. The wings stretch 78 feet. Flying at 17,500 miles per hour while in orbit, the shuttle circles Earth about every 90 minutes.

2 *What is the astronaut wearing? How does this equipment help the astronaut?* The astronaut is wearing a space suit, which is made of 12 separate layers of protective materials. The suit also provides the astronaut with air to breathe. The suits are equipped with radios so that the astronauts working outside the shuttle can communicate with the astronauts inside the shuttle. When working outside the shuttle, astronauts use the small rockets built into the suits to move around. Space suits allow astronauts to perform a wide variety of tasks.

ACTIVITY: Ask students to imagine that they are astronauts on a shuttle mission. Then have students write a journal entry describing the experience.

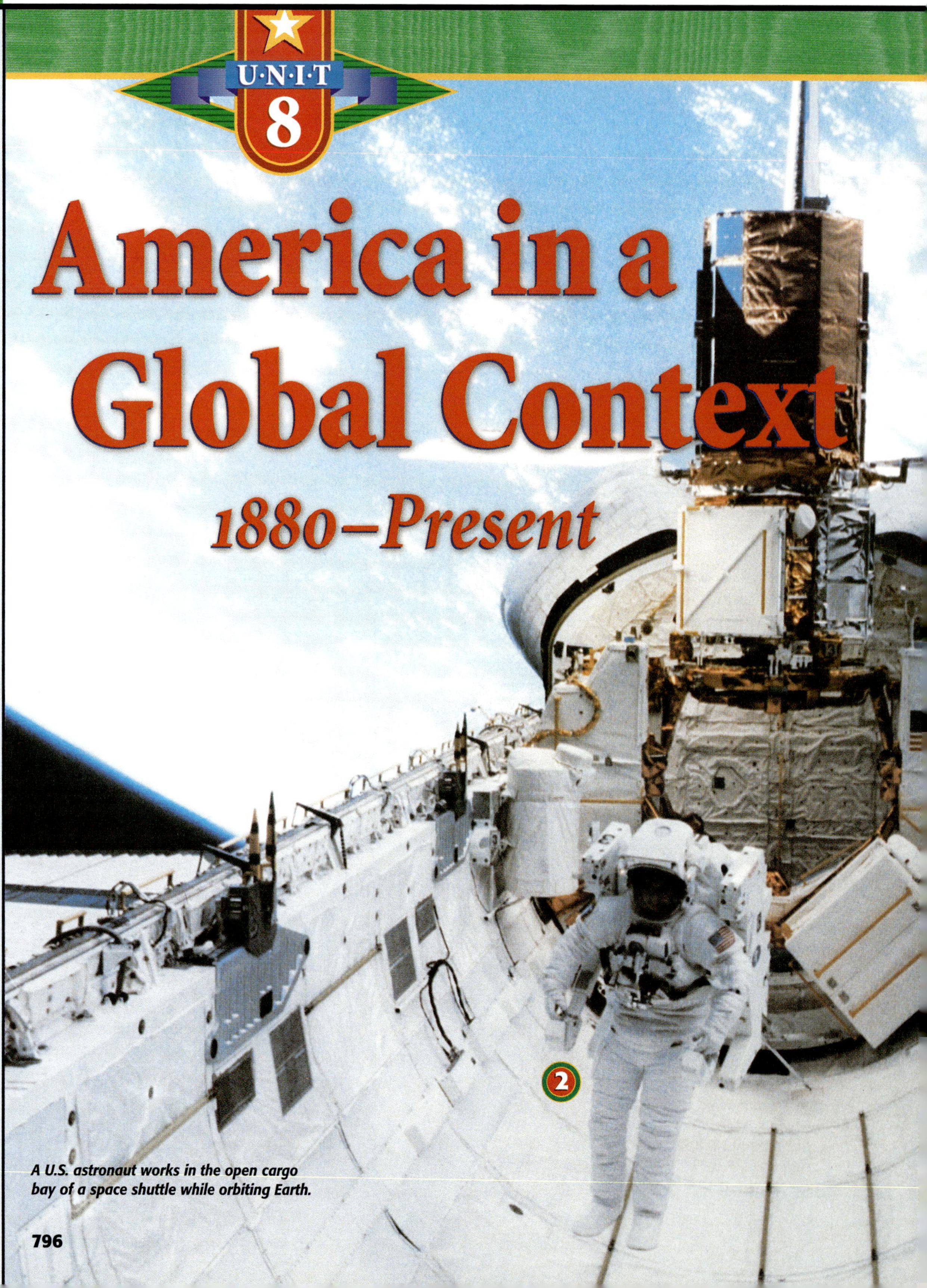

A U.S. astronaut works in the open cargo bay of a space shuttle while orbiting Earth.

796

The Movement of People and Ideas

The worldwide migration of people increased during the late 1800s and early 1900s but slowed during World War I and the Great Depression. However, in the 1930s and after World War II the number of refugees increased dramatically. Aided by technological developments such as the Internet, information also moved globally. Worldwide audiences shared sports, music, and fashion in what became a global culture.

The Struggle for Human Rights

The ideas of Enlightenment philosophy encouraged people worldwide to struggle against repressive governments, slavery, and the oppression of women. In the 1900s gains in the protection of human rights were matched by increased violence during wartime, which led the United Nations to call for protection of human rights. In the postwar era, minorities and women continued to press for their rights.

A New Environmental Awareness

During the 1800s some Americans began to question the idea of nature as something to be tamed. Increased interest in the environment prompted efforts to conserve natural resources and preserve wilderness areas. The Dust Bowl crisis revealed the necessity of environmental management. During the 1900s Americans realized that some environmental problems required international cooperation.

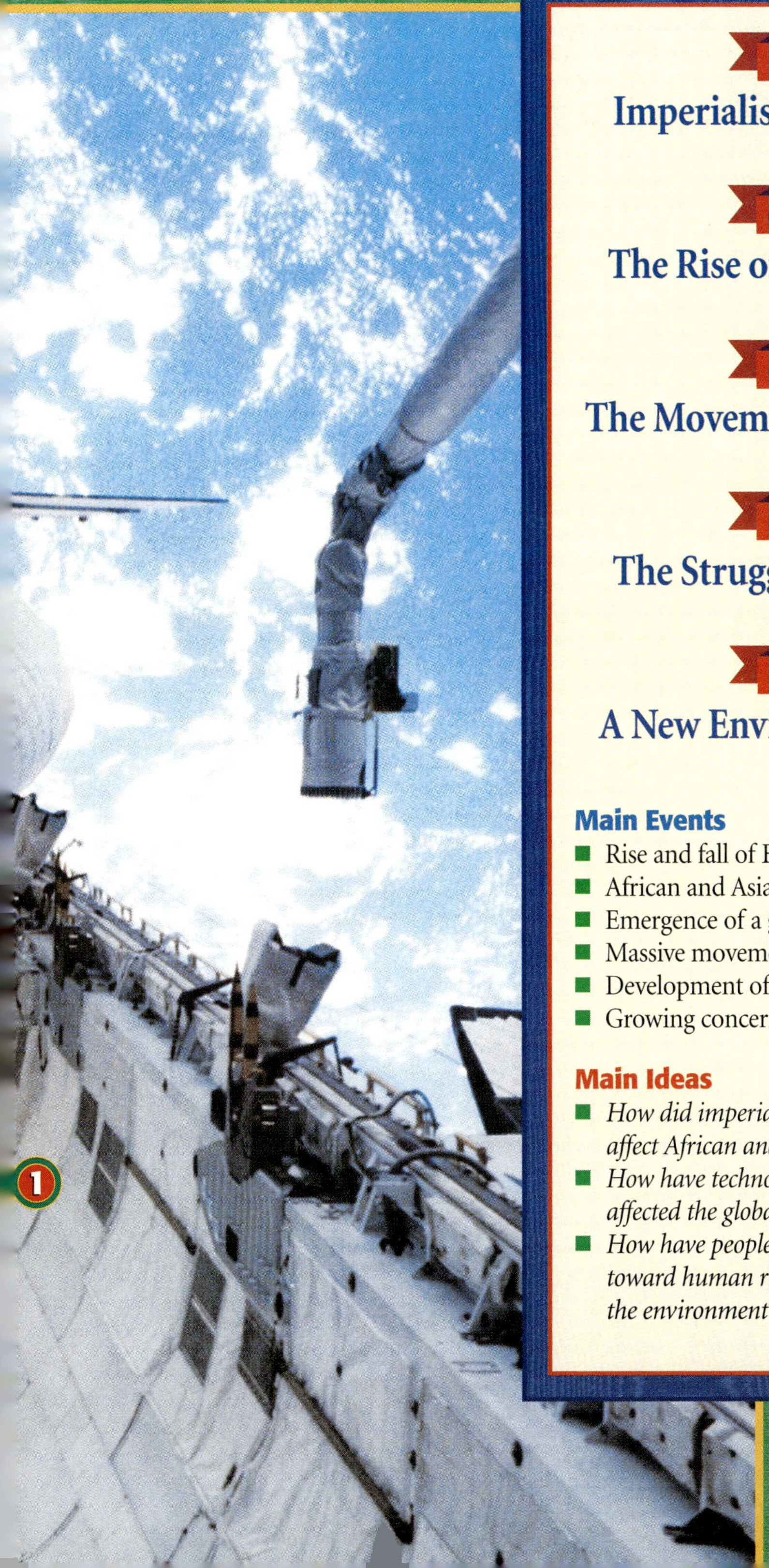

1

CHAPTER 27

Imperialism and Independence

1885–Present

CHAPTER 28

The Rise of the Global Economy

1880–Present

CHAPTER 29

The Movement of People and Ideas

1890–Present

CHAPTER 30

The Struggle for Human Rights

1885–Present

CHAPTER 31

A New Environmental Awareness

1890–Present

Main Events

- Rise and fall of European empires
- African and Asian nations gain independence
- Emergence of a global economy
- Massive movement of immigrants worldwide
- Development of principles of basic human rights
- Growing concern for protecting the environment

Main Ideas

- *How did imperialism and decolonization affect African and Asian nations?*
- *How have technological changes affected the global economy?*
- *How have people's attitudes toward human rights and the environment changed?*

A compass

INTRODUCE UNIT 8

Main Events

List the Main Events on the chalkboard. Ask students to select two and briefly describe what they know about the topics. Have volunteers share their descriptions. Later, when you have finished Unit 8, ask students to return to their original descriptions and revise them using the information they learned in the unit. Students should also create new descriptions for the other Main Events.

Main Ideas

Ask each student to read the Main Ideas and briefly answer the questions in writing. Share the ***Consider*** points with students as necessary. Later, when you have finished Unit 8, ask students to return to their original answers and revise them using the information they learned in the unit.

Imperialism

Consider:

- the events that led to imperialist expansion
- the events that led to the decline of imperialism and the independence of former colonies

Global Trade

Consider:

- why global trade has greatly expanded since the 1800s
- the effect of expanding global trade on politics, cultures, and the environment

Imperialism and Independence

CHAPTER PLANNING GUIDE

	Section Lesson Objectives	Print Resources	Multimedia Resources	Sheltered English Resources
Section 1 **Imperialism to World War I,** **pp. 800–04**	**1** Describe how Americans viewed imperialism. **2** Identify the similarities and differences between U.S. and Russian expansion. **3** Discuss how industrialism affected imperialism. **4** Explain how the various empires governed their colonies.	▶ Guided Reading Strategy 27.1 ▶ Geography Activity 27: Carving Up Africa ▶ Section 1 Review, p. 804 ▶ Daily Quiz 27.1	▶ One-Stop Planner, Lesson 27.1 ▶ Linking Geography and History Transparency 15: The American Empire ▶ Holt Researcher: American History CD–ROM ▶ HRW Web site	▶ Main Idea Activity for Reteaching and Sheltered English 27.1
Section 2 **Imperialism Between the Wars,** **pp. 805–11**	**1** Explain how World War I affected European attitudes about imperialism. **2** Relate how Asian independence movements developed after World War I. **3** Identify why the United States granted independence to the Philippines. **4** Describe how and why Germany, Italy, and Japan created new empires during the 1930s.	▶ Guided Reading Strategy 27.2 ▶ Graphic Organizer Activity 27: Attitudes Toward Imperialism ▶ Literature Reading 27: India under British Rule ▶ Biography Reading 27: Ho Chi Minh ▶ Primary Source Reading 27: A Culmination of Fears ▶ Section 2 Review, p. 811 ▶ Daily Quiz 27.2	▶ One-Stop Planner, Lesson 27.2 ▶ Holt Researcher: American History CD–ROM	▶ Main Idea Activity for Reteaching and Sheltered English 27.2
Section 3 **Decolonization and the Cold War,** **pp. 812–18**	**1** Identify how World War II affected Asian independence efforts. **2** Explain why the United States did not support the Vietnamese independence movement. **3** Relate how and when most African nations gained independence. **4** Describe the major concerns of third-world countries during the Cold War.	▶ Guided Reading Strategy 27.3 ▶ American History Outline Map 31: Africa ▶ Section 3 Review, p. 818 ▶ Daily Quiz 27.3	▶ One-Stop Planner, Lesson 27.3 ▶ Holt Researcher: American History CD–ROM	▶ Main Idea Activity for Reteaching and Sheltered English 27.3
Section 4 **Legacies of Imperialism,** **pp. 819–23**	**1** Explain why domestic conflicts were problems for former colonies. **2** Summarize the economic and political challenges newly independent African nations faced. **3** Describe what problems were faced by nations of the former Soviet sphere.	▶ Guided Reading Strategy 27.4 ▶ Section 4 Review, p. 823 ▶ Daily Quiz 27.4	▶ One-Stop Planner, Lesson 27.4 ▶ Holt Researcher: American History CD–ROM	▶ Main Idea Activity for Reteaching and Sheltered English 27.4
Chapter Review and Assessment **pp. 824–25**		▶ Chapter 27 Review, pp. 824–25 ▶ Chapter 27 Tutorial for Students, Parents, Mentors, and Peers ▶ Chapter 27 Test (Form A or B) ▶ Portfolio Activities and Alternative Assessment Handbook, Chapter 27	▶ Audio Program, Chapter 27 (English and Spanish) ▶ Chapter 27 Test Generator (on the One-Stop Planner) ▶ Global Skill Builder CD–ROM ▶ HRW Web site	▶ Spanish Glossary ▶ Sheltered English Chapter 27 Test

CHAPTER OVERVIEW

The United States became a nation as it rebelled against imperialism. However, by the 1880s the United States, like other nations such as Russia, had become a colonial power. By the end of World War I, changing economic and political circumstances weakened the system of imperialism everywhere. World War II accelerated this trend.

The United States publicly encouraged colonies to seek their independence but decreased its actual support for such movements. The U.S. government worried about the Soviet Union. During the Cold War both the United States and the Soviet Union demanded support from newly independent nations. These countries sought an independent, neutral path and aid from both sides. The legacy of imperialism and insufficient economic resources created terrible problems and led to civil wars and poverty in countries such as Yugoslavia and Russia.

TIME TAMERS

Block Scheduling

The teacher lesson plans for each section offer a variety of activity choices to help you present the material in a block scheduling format. For further suggestions on block scheduling, see the **Block Scheduling Handbook with Team Teaching Strategies**, pp. 157–62.

Internet Connections and Lesson 27
www.si.edu/hrw

Hands-On History Activities:

Classroom to Community The **Hands-On History Activities** help students make meaningful connections between events in American history and those in their own hometown. You may wish to use the Chapter 27 Activity, The Imperialist Model and Your School, to extend the chapter lessons, as alternative assessment, or as a block scheduling option.

Portfolio Projects

The American Nation includes multiple portfolio projects in each Pupil's Edition chapter review, as well as each unit review. Chapter 27 Portfolio Project options on p. 825 include the following:

1. Students will **create a flowchart**.
2. Students will **write a poem**.
3. Students will **write a policy statement**.

The American Nation

INTERNET RESOURCE DIRECTORY

To access online materials for this chapter, go to **go.hrw.com** and type in the keywords listed below.

HRW ONLINE RESOURCES

GO TO: go.hrw.com

Online Maps
KEYWORD: SE1 Maps27
- Prelude to War: Germany 1939
- Prelude to War: Italy 1939
- Prelude to War: Japan 1941

Online Charts
KEYWORD: SE1 Charts27
- WWI Alliances

Online Reading Support
KEYWORD: SE1 Strategies27

Online Rubrics
KEYWORD: SE1 Rubrics

CHAPTER ENRICHMENT LINKS

Use these Web links to extend and enrich student learning for Chapter 27.
GO TO: go.hrw.com
KEYWORD: SE1 Ch27

CHAPTER INTERNET ACTIVITIES

GO TO: go.hrw.com
- Pupil's Edition Student Activity
  KEYWORD: SE1 Philippines
  (Students research the Philippine independence movement.)
- Teacher's Edition Student Activity
  KEYWORD: SE1 Telephone
  (Students explore the history of the telephone.)
- Teacher's Edition Student Activity
  KEYWORD: SE1 Mexican War
  (Students examine the Mexican War.)

ADDITIONAL
RESOURCES

Books for Teachers

Hochschild, Adam. *King Leopold's Ghost.* Houghton Mifflin, 1998. Describes the fight between European imperialist and anti-imperialist forces in colonial Africa.

Musicant, Ivan. *Empire by Default.* Henry Holt and Company, 1998. Documents the Spanish-American War and its consequences for the United States.

Books for Students

De Gramont, Sanche. *The Strong Brown God: The Story of the Niger River.* Houghton Mifflin, 1977. Shows the interaction of European exploration and imperialism in the quest for the source of the Niger River.

Moorhouse, Geoffrey. *India Britannica.* Harper and Row, 1983. Explores the history of the British presence in India.

Primary Sources from the Period

Achebe, Chinua. *Things Fall Apart.* Anchor Books, 1994. Traces the impact of early British colonialism on the Igbo people of present-day Nigeria.

Conrad, Joseph. *Heart of Darkness.* Penguin Books, 1991. Explores the darkness within the human soul as reflected by European imperialism in Africa.

Multimedia Materials

The Africans. Video. 540 min. WETA-TV and BBC-TV. Explores the past, present, and future of Africa, with a focus on the heritage and consequences of imperialism.

Hawaii's Last Queen. Video, 60 min. WGBH Educational Foundation. Recounts the life of Liliuokalani, the last Hawaiian queen.

CHAPTER 27

Before You Read

Build on What You Know

Ask students to answer the following questions.

How might imperialism and anti-imperialism have shaped history during the 1900s?

Consider:

- the economic effect of obtaining raw materials from colonies and returning manufactured products
- the different styles of administering colonies

How might world wars have led to the breakup of global empires?

Consider:

- the difficulty of maintaining global empires in the face of postwar debts
- the spread of strong independence movements throughout the world

exploring the time line

AMERICAN EVENTS

internetconnect

TOPIC: The Telephone
GO TO: go.hrw.com
KEYWORD: SE1 Telephone

Have students access the Internet through the HRW Web site to conduct research on the history of the telephone. Then ask each student to make an illustrated and annotated time line that traces the development of the telephone and its network system from its early days to the present global communications system.

CHAPTER 27

1885–Present

Imperialism and Independence

An advertisement for the SS Titanic's maiden voyage

An early American telephone

1885 **Politics** The Indian National Congress is formed to seek independence for India.

1898 **World Events** The Battle of Omdurman leaves thousands of Africans dead.

1898 **Politics** The United States annexes the Philippines at the end of the Spanish-American War.

1901

1912 **Daily Life** The SS *Titanic* sinks after hitting an iceberg in the North Atlantic.

1914 **World Events** World War I begins.

1915 **Science and Technology** Long-distance telephone service begins between New York and San Francisco.

1917

1917 **Business and Finance** The Trans-Siberian Railroad is completed.

1933

1937 **The Arts** Pablo Picasso paints *Guernica* for the Paris World Exhibition.

1939 **World Events** World War II begins.

***Pablo Picasso's* Guernica**

Before You Read

Build on What You Know

The American colonies were established as part of the British Empire. After the American Revolution the United States became a strong opponent of imperialism. U.S. policy began to change in the late 1800s, however. In this chapter you will learn how imperialism shaped the history of the United States and the world during the 1900s. You will also learn how most global empires broke up after 1945 and how the legacy of imperialism continues to influence world events.

Think About Themes

*To help students create their Themes Journal entries, provide the following examples of appropriate **agree/disagree** statements.*

Democratic Values

Agree U.S. aid through the Marshall Plan encouraged the growth of democracies in Europe.

Disagree The U.S. government helped overthrow a democratically elected leader in Guatemala in 1954.

Economic Development

Agree The British colonies in North America gained economic and political independence.

Disagree In many African nations, imperial powers only wanted to use the country's natural resources.

Global Relations

Agree The conflict in the Balkans in the 1910s led to World War I.

Disagree Switzerland remained neutral during World War I and World War II.

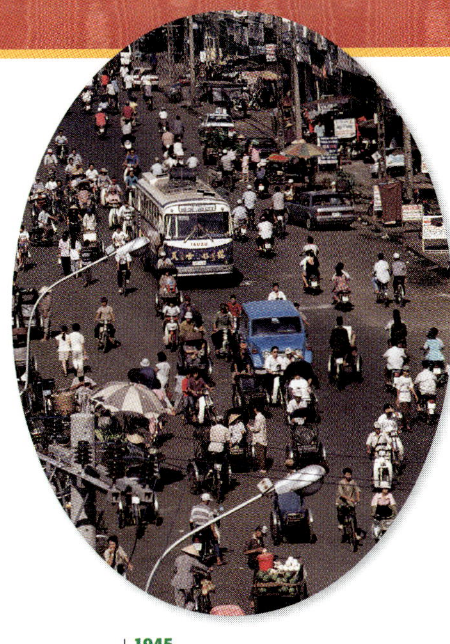

Ho Chi Minh City, Vietnam

Michael Jackson's Thriller won the Grammy Award for Album of the Year.

1945
Politics
Ho Chi Minh declares Vietnam's independence from France.

1963
Politics
African nations form the Organization of African Unity (OAU) in an attempt to prevent territorial conflicts among members.

1963
The Arts
Leonardo da Vinci's painting *Mona Lisa* is displayed in the United States for the first time.

1982
The Arts
Pop singer Michael Jackson's album *Thriller* is an international hit.

1991
World Events
The Soviet Union collapses.

1949 — **1965** — **1981** — **1999**

1969
Science and Technology
U.S. astronaut Neil Armstrong becomes the first person to walk on the Moon.

1983
Daily Life
Millions of people suffer from famine after a two-year drought in Ethiopia.

1998
Business and Finance
The value of the Russian ruble falls to record lows.

U.S. astronauts made a total of six trips to the Moon's surface.

Russian rubles

Think About Themes

Decide whether you ***agree*** *or* ***disagree*** *with the following statements. Note why in your journal.*

Democratic Values Democratic nations can govern an empire and still uphold the principles of democracy.

Economic Development Empires always encourage the economic development of their colonies.

Global Relations Small nations cannot avoid becoming involved in conflicts between major powers.

exploring the time line

GLOBAL EVENTS

GLOBAL RELATIONS

1945 ■ Ho Chi Minh's Declaration of independence. On September 2, 1945, Vietnamese nationalist leader Ho Chi Minh addressed a huge crowd to declare Vietnam's independence from France. An exile who had lived in New York City, London, Paris, and Moscow, Ho had returned to Vietnam to lead the independence movement. Ho organized the Vietminh, or the League for the Independence of Vietnam, which successfully drove the French out of Indochina. Despite being a committed Communist, Ho began his speech with "We hold the truth that all men are created equal, that they are endowed by their Creator with certain unalienable rights, among them life, liberty, and the pursuit of happiness."

CRITICAL THINKING Why do you think Ho Chi Minh paraphrased the U.S. Declaration of Independence in his speech?

ANSWER: Students might suggest that Ho was appealing to the United States to help the newly independent nation.

SECTION 1

After completing Section 1, students should be able to:

OBJECTIVE 1 *Describe how Americans viewed imperialism.*

OBJECTIVE 2 *Identify the similarities and differences between U.S. and Russian expansion.*

OBJECTIVE 3 *Discuss how industrialism affected imperialism.*

OBJECTIVE 4 *Explain how the various empires governed their colonies.*

LET'S GET STARTED!

To begin the class, ask students to write a definition of imperialism using the glossary at the back of their textbooks if necessary. *(Students might define it as the quest for colonial empires.)* Tell students that in Section 1 they will learn about U.S. imperialism up to World War I and Americans' changing attitudes toward it.

SECTION 1 RESOURCES

PRINT

- Guided Reading Strategy 27.1
- Geography Activity 27: Carving Up Africa
- Section 1 Review, p. 804
- Daily Quiz 27.1

MULTIMEDIA

- One-Stop Planner, Lesson 27.1
- Linking Geography and History Transparency 15: The American Empire
- Holt Researcher: American History CD–ROM
- HRW Web site

SHELTERED ENGLISH

- Main Idea Activity for Reteaching and Sheltered English 27.1

✔ READING TO UNDERSTAND

To help students master the section objectives, have them answer the **READING CHECKS** and complete **Guided Reading Strategy 27.1** as they read the section.

Multimedia Resources

Linking Geography and History Transparency 15: The American Empire

Imperialism to World War I

OBJECTIVES

Read to understand:

1. how Americans viewed imperialism
2. what the similarities and differences were between U.S. and Russian expansion
3. how industrialization affected imperialism
4. how the various empires governed their colonies

KEY TERMS

coaling stations
direct rule
indirect rule

KEY PEOPLE

Jules Ferry
William McKinley

“One night late it came to me this way . . . that there was nothing left for us to do but to take them all [the Philippine Islands], and to educate the Filipinos, and uplift and civilize and Christianize them.”

—President William McKinley

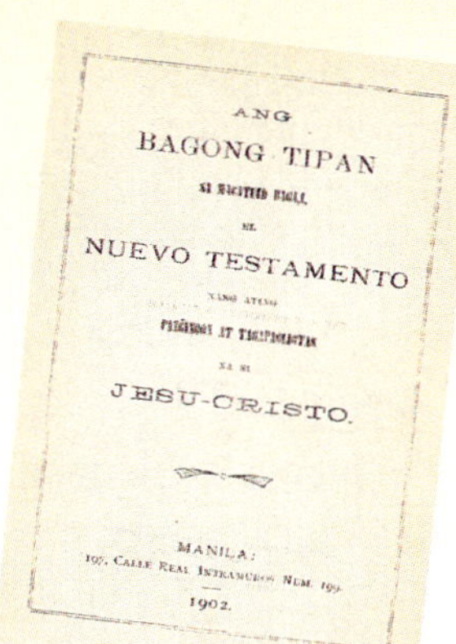

A missionary Bible used in the Philippines

During a meeting with a delegation of Methodist missionaries in 1898, President McKinley explained his position regarding annexation of the Philippines. The president said he had prayed long and hard for guidance. Although well-intentioned, McKinley's statement combined arrogance with ignorance: nearly all the Filipinos were already Christians. As McKinley's words revealed, by the turn of the century many Americans had changed their attitudes toward imperialism.

Free Find: Territorial Expansion, 1820

After studying the map of Territorial Expansion, 1820, on the **Holt Researcher** CD–ROM, create a time line showing the influence of expansion on the United States.

Born of Empire

Americans have never been strangers to imperialism—the quest for colonial empires. In many ways the United States owes its very existence to European imperialism. England founded its North American colonies in an attempt to compete with other European nations for trade and territory. Yet American colonists grew tired of being controlled and taxed by a British government that did not fairly represent them. As a result, the colonies declared their independence from Great Britain. During the American Revolution, a group of Philadelphia women voiced the beliefs of the new nation. They argued that Americans were “born for liberty, disdaining [refusing] to bear the arms of a tyrannical Government.”

During the 30 years following U.S. independence, conflicts between Britain and France regularly interfered with U.S. trade. The United States became involved in hostilities with France in the 1790s and went to war with Britain in 1812. These troubles strengthened Americans' dislike for imperialism. Americans had founded their country on the principle of republicanism—the right of people to rule themselves. Imperialism, which involves one country ruling another, contradicted this principle. In addition, imperialism often interfered with the rights of neutral countries, as the Americans knew firsthand. Even so, Americans did occasionally benefit from the struggles of European empires. For example, one reason the French aided the Patriots in the Revolutionary War was to block the expansion of British imperialism in North America.

During the 1800s the United States expanded west across North America. Settlers streamed into the land gained from the British. Soon they pushed even farther, settling in the Louisiana Territory, Texas, the Southwest, and the Pacific Northwest. Like Europeans, Americans gained some of their new territory through wars—such as the Mexican War of 1840 or the many conflicts with American Indians.

TEACH OBJECTIVE 1

LEVELS 1 AND 2: Pair students and have one student in each pair describe the time frame of and the Americans' opposition to imperialism. Have the other student describe Americans' support of imperialism. *(Students describing opposition might mention that the United States began as a colony and continued to have problems with imperial powers until the War of 1812 and that imperialism contradicted the principle of republicanism. Supporters of imperialism in the 1850s argued that the territories were near the United States and could become states.)* Have students discuss their descriptions. Then have each student write a brief summary of his or her partner's arguments. **Sheltered English, Cooperative Learning**

LEVEL 3: Tell students to imagine that they are living in the United States at the end of the 1800s. Ask them to write an editorial discussing how Americans' views on imperialism have changed. *(See the Levels 1 and 2 lesson for the correct views.)*

Some Americans, including writer Henry David Thoreau, viewed the taking of western territory during the Mexican War as a form of imperialism. Most Americans disagreed, however. While the British, French, and Spanish imperial holdings were far-flung, the new U.S. territories were right next door. Furthermore, the U.S. territories established in the West became states with full representation in the federal government.

In one way, however, U.S. expansion did resemble European imperialism. In both cases the wishes of the original inhabitants of the acquired regions were rarely considered. The Europeans paid little attention to the needs and desires of the native inhabitants living in the colonies they claimed. Similarly, the U.S. government moved American Indians off their original homelands and onto reservations, often using force.

✔ **READING CHECK:** How did many Americans view imperialism during the 1800s?

VALJEAN HESSING, *CHOCTAW REMOVAL* (1966) PHILBROOK MUSEUM OF ART, TULSA

INTERPRETING THE VISUAL RECORD

American Indian removal. In the 1830s the U.S. government forced the Choctaw to move from Mississippi to Indian Territory in present-day Oklahoma. ***What does the painting suggest about the conditions faced by the Choctaw on their journey?***

Russia: Another Land Empire

A process similar to U.S. expansion of the 1800s took place halfway around the world in Russia. For several centuries the Russian Empire moved primarily eastward into central and far eastern Asia. It eventually reached as far as Alaska, which the United States purchased from Russia in 1867.

Russian expansion resembled U.S. expansion in a variety of ways. Like the United States, Russia acquired a large land area through agricultural settlement and conquest. In addition, both Americans and Russians introduced their own economic and political systems to their holdings. Both nations used railway systems to unite their vast territories. Both also developed a sense of manifest destiny, as the Americans termed it, that justified their expansion. Alexis de Tocqueville even believed that Americans and Russians had similar futures. "Their starting-point is different," he wrote. "Yet each of them seems marked out by the will of heaven to sway the destinies of half the globe."

The empires had important differences, however. Russia lacked the massive waves of immigration that helped fuel U.S. expansion. Russian settlers generally occupied and ruled lands in which non-Russian populations remained a majority. In addition, Russian expansion was driven by the need for a warm-water port that would be useable year-round. Most Russian ports froze over during winter, threatening Russia's national security and its international trade. Russian expansion was also blocked by other empires. In 1905 Russia lost a war with Japan over control of lands in northeastern Asia. This defeat was a great blow to Russia's imperial efforts.

✔ **READING CHECK:** What were the similarities and differences between U.S. and Russian expansion?

The Japanese navy battled Russian forces at Port Arthur, in present-day China, during the Russo-Japanese War.

internetconnect

TOPIC: Mexican War
GO TO: go.hrw.com
KEYWORD: SE1 Mexican War

Have students access the Internet through the HRW Web site to conduct research on the reasons for the Mexican War, the division of land after the war, and how the war changed the relations between the United States and Mexico. Then have each student write an editorial discussing the importance of the war for either an American or Mexican newspaper of the time.

THAT'S INTERESTING!

Henry David Thoreau was so angry about U.S. expansion during the Mexican War that he refused to pay his taxes and spent a night in jail. To justify his position he wrote the essay "Civil Disobedience" in 1849. Thoreau's ideas influenced Mohandas K. Gandhi and, through him, Dr. Martin Luther King Jr.

VISUAL RECORD ANSWER

Students might suggest that the Choctaw faced cold and snowy weather.

TEACH OBJECTIVE 2

ALL LEVELS: Pair students and have one student in each pair list the similarities between U.S. and Russian expansion. Have the other student list the differences. *(Similarities might include: acquired land through agricultural settlement; introduced own cultural, economic, and political systems; used railways to unite vast territories; and had sense of manifest destiny. Differences might include: Russia's lack of immigration, and that Russian expansion was driven by the need for a warm-water port and was blocked by other empires.)* Have students use their lists to write a brief essay comparing and contrasting U.S. and Russian expansion prior to World War I. Ask volunteers to read their essays to the class.
Sheltered English, Cooperative Learning

TEACH OBJECTIVE 3

ALL LEVELS: To help students understand how industrialism affected imperialism, copy the graphic organizer on the next page on the chalkboard, omitting the italicized answers. Have each student complete it.
Sheltered English

▶**ASSIGNMENT** *Have students use the graphic organizer to create a political cartoon commenting on industrialization's impact on European imperialism.*

GLOBAL RELATIONS

The Opium War. In the 1780s Great Britain began exporting large amounts of opium to China. The opium was shipped from the British colony of India, where its use was forbidden. By 1830 as many as 4 million Chinese were addicted to the drug. In 1839 the Chinese emperor appointed a special commissioner, Lin Tse-hsu, to eliminate the opium trade. Lin attempted to cut off all British trade. The British navy then attacked China, and the first Opium War began. After about two years, the British were victorious. Among other things, the peace agreement required China to give Britain the island of Hong Kong.

ACTIVITY: Tell students to imagine that they are at the ceremony in 1997 when Hong Kong is returned to China. Have them write a brief speech explaining how Britain gained control of the island.

THAT'S INTERESTING!

German author Karl May became famous in the early 1890s for his stories about American Indians in the West. His work remains widely read in Europe but it is virtually unknown in the United States.

CHANGING WAYS ANSWERS

increased by 47 percent; clothing has changed

This cartoon shows Britain guarding its many colonies from other imperial powers.

Imperialism Renewed

Unlike Russia, most European nations slowed their imperial expansion in the early 1800s. Domestic concerns such as political uprisings and industrialization took up much of their attention. European powers concentrated initially on protecting their foreign economic interests. Britain, for example, established close economic and political ties with many Latin American countries. Although these countries remained independent, such connections gave the British considerable influence in Latin America.

African and Asian colonies. By the mid-1800s, however, the major industrial powers of Europe had begun aggressively seeking colonies in Africa and Asia. The European powers divided Africa among themselves in less than 20 years. In the late 1840s the British government gained firm control of India. France established French Indochina in Southeast Asia in the 1850s. In the 1890s the imperialist powers even divided China into spheres of influence. China remained independent in name, but the authority of the Chinese government was greatly limited.

The United States pursued imperialist goals when it annexed Hawaii, the Philippines, and various other islands in the Pacific and the Caribbean. The United States also held significant economic interests in China, Japan, and Latin America.

Changing Ways — Imperialism Then and Now

Understanding Change In the 1800s and early 1900s European empires grew faster than ever before. Between 1800 and 1914 the European powers added more than 15 million square miles to their territorial holdings. By 1914 only a few major countries, such as China, Persia, and Turkey, had avoided European control. During the 1900s, however, many nations won their independence. *How has the proportion of independent nations in the world changed over time? What differences do you observe between the painting of the British Empire (above) and the independence celebration?*

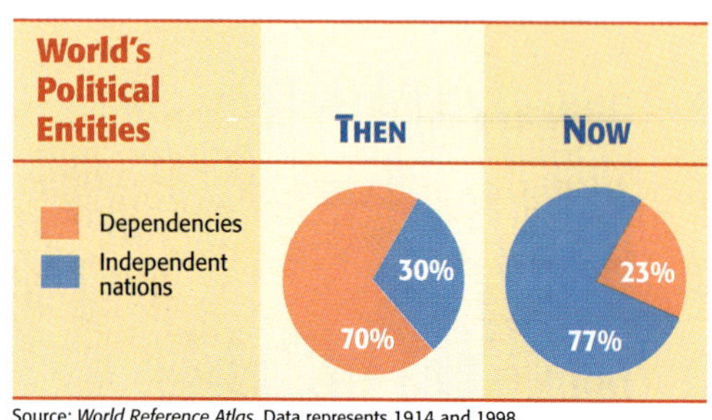

Source: *World Reference Atlas.* Data represents 1914 and 1998.

Modern weaponry eliminated colonial resistance.

Industrialized nations were dependent on foreign countries for raw materials.

How Industrialism Contributed to Imperialism

Imperial powers had to establish numerous coaling stations.

Industrialized nations sought foreign markets.

Steamships extended imperial power on the seas.

TEACH OBJECTIVE 4

ALL LEVELS: Ask students to explain the how the various empires governed their colonies. *(Students might respond that France and the United States used direct rule, in which the colonizing country establishes a new government. Great Britain used indirect rule, in which the colonizing country rules through traditional local leaders.)* Then pair students and tell them to imagine that they are colonial subjects in different empires—one living under direct rule and the other indirect rule. Have each student write a few paragraphs expressing his or her feelings about how his or her country is being governed. Have volunteers read their paragraphs to the class. **Sheltered English, Cooperative Learning**

Industrialization and empire. A variety of motives lay behind the renewed enthusiasm for imperialism. Some people viewed imperialism as a way to spread Christianity. Others claimed that Western culture was superior to other world cultures, and that westerners thus had a duty to spread their culture as far as possible. British poet Rudyard Kipling called this duty the "white man's burden." British imperialist Cecil Rhodes put it bluntly. "We happen to be the best people in the world . . . and the more of the world we inhabit, the better it is for humanity." Even U.S. president Theodore Roosevelt echoed this feeling.

> "Every expansion of a great civilized power means a victory for law, order, and righteousness. This has been the case in every instance of expansion during the present century, whether the expanding power were France or England, Russia or America."

However, many historians believe that industrialization was the primary cause for the renewed interest in imperialism. As countries developed their manufacturing industries, they typically became dependent on foreign countries for raw materials. For example, the imperial powers looked to India and Egypt for cotton and to central Africa and Southeast Asia for rubber. Labor also tended to be cheaper in many Asian and African areas than in Europe. In addition, industrialized nations sought foreign markets to sell their products. China alone had millions of potential consumers of manufactured goods.

Industrialization also helped make the new imperialism possible. Just as railroads had enabled expansion on land, steamships extended imperial power on the seas. Steamships required regular refueling. This meant that imperial powers had to establish numerous **coaling stations**—ports where ships could restock their supplies of coal—to supply their fleets around the world.

Another of industrialization's major contributions to imperialism was modern weaponry like the Maxim machine gun. English writer Hilaire Belloc summed up the importance of such weapons in a famous couplet. "Whatever happens we have got / The Maxim gun and they have not." Modern weapons made it nearly impossible for the inhabitants of the colonized areas to resist Western imperialism. For example, in 1898 a force of Africans armed largely with spears and swords attempted to stop British advances into northeast Africa. The resulting Battle of Omdurman left more than 10,000 Africans dead. Fewer than 50 British soldiers were killed.

✔ **READING CHECK:** How did industrialization affect imperialism?

INTERPRETING THE VISUAL RECORD

Machinery Hall. In 1851 Britain held an international exhibition displaying industrial advances from around the world. ***What types of equipment are on display?***

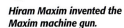

Hiram Maxim invented the Maxim machine gun.

Ruling the Colonies

After taking control of new territories, the imperial powers had to govern them. Two main methods emerged. With **direct rule** the colonizing country established a completely new governmental administration for its colony. Under **indirect rule** the colonizing country ruled through traditional local leaders.

PEOPLE IN HISTORY

Sir George Goldie. As a young man in the 1860s, George Goldie left Britain and moved to West Africa. He soon merged competing British firms trading on the Niger River into one company. In 1886 he obtained a charter for the Royal Niger Company and gained the right to collect taxes and raise troops. British traders also persuaded local chiefs to sign treaties ceding their lands. These treaties violated local land laws, which stated that the land belonged to the clan or tribe as a whole. Blocked from trading on the Niger River, some 1,000 warriors attacked the company's headquarters. Goldie organized his own army and defeated the tribe. In 1899, after further conflict with Africans and the French, Goldie sold the company—and the colony—to Britain.

CRITICAL THINKING Why might Goldie have been able to sell the colony?

ANSWER: Students might answer that he considered the treaties binding.

VISUAL RECORD ANSWER

Students might mention carriages and steam engines.

VISUAL RECORD ANSWER

(for p. 804)

Students might suggest that the French used education.

REVIEW

Have students complete the **Section 1 Review** on p. 804.

ASSESS

Have students complete **Daily Quiz 27.1**. As **Alternative Assessment**, you may want to use the editorial or the political cartoon in this section's lessons.

RETEACH

Have students complete **Main Idea Activity for Reteaching and Sheltered English 27.1**. Then organize students into groups and assign one subsection to each group member. Direct students to write a few paragraphs summarizing their assigned subsection and pass the completed summaries to the other group members to read. Then have students take turns quizzing each other within their groups.
Sheltered English, Cooperative Learning

EXTEND

Have students write short stories set in a European colony in the late 1800s. Tell them to create characters and put them into interesting situations that highlight life in their chosen colony. For example, a character might be a member of the ruling government or of an independence movement. When students have finished writing their stories, ask volunteers to read them to the class. **Block Scheduling**

SECTION 1 REVIEW ANSWERS

Define and Identify
For significance, see the following pages:

- coaling stations, p. 803
- direct rule, p. 803
- indirect rule, p. 803
- Jules Ferry, p. 804
- William McKinley, p. 804

1. similarities–acquired through wars and agricultural settlement; put their own economic, cultural, and political systems in control; used railway systems to unite; differences–Russia lacked large number of settlers, needed a warm-weather port, and was blocked in the east by more powerful countries

2. because the United States had been a colony; by playing one imperial power against another

3. direct–spread language and culture of colonizing country; promoted capitalism and democracy to create stable markets for trade; indirect–tried to allow colonies to keep local cultures intact

4. As imperialist powers became industrialized, they needed raw materials for manufacturing; markets for their products; and coaling stations. Modern weaponry made defeat of non-Western people relatively easy.

5. Some people wanted to introduce Christianity. Others believed that all peoples would benefit from adapting the ways of Western civilization. The need for raw materials and markets and the superiority of industrial technology strengthened imperialism.

INTERPRETING THE VISUAL RECORD

Westernization. Nations such as France wanted to spread their culture to their colonies. ***What does this image reveal about the methods the French used to spread their culture?***

French premier Jules Ferry encouraged rapid colonization in Africa and Asia. He explained France's use of direct rule.

> **"France . . . cannot be merely a free country. . . . She ought to propagate [spread] [her] influence throughout the world and carry everywhere that she can her language, her customs, her flag, her arms, and her genius."**

French colonial subjects who accepted French language and culture could potentially become full French citizens. In French Senegal, for example, thousands of Africans qualified for citizenship.

The United States, on the other hand, used direct rule primarily to promote economic and political changes. Americans wanted to teach U.S. subjects how to run democratic governments and how to establish free-market capitalist economies. U.S. leaders hoped that these measures would create stable markets for U.S. trade. President William McKinley declared, "We want new markets. And as trade follows the flag, it looks very much like we are going to have new markets."

The British eventually adopted indirect rule as a way of managing their territories. British colonial administrators argued that colonial peoples should only gradually adopt Western practices. By using indirect rule, the British tried to leave most aspects of local cultures intact. Regardless of what government the imperialists set up, colonial peoples seldom embraced it. Many years would pass, however, before widespread resistance to colonial rule would be practical.

✔ **READING CHECK:** How did the various empires govern their colonies?

SECTION  REVIEW

Define and explain the significance of the following terms:
coaling stations
direct rule
indirect rule

Identify and explain the significance of the following individuals:
Jules Ferry
William McKinley

1. **Using Graphic Organizers** Copy the graphic organizer below and use it to explain the similarities and differences between U.S. and Russian expansionism.

U.S. and Russian Expansionism	
Similarities	Differences

2. **Recognizing Point of View** Why did many Americans at first oppose imperialism? How did the early United States occasionally benefit from imperialism?
3. **Analyzing** What were the different motivations behind direct and indirect rule?
4. **Identifying Cause and Effect** How did industrialization contribute to imperialism in the late 1800s and early 1900s?

Critical Thinking

5. What conditions made possible the European imperialism of the late 1800s?
Consider:
- the role of religion
- belief in the "white man's burden"
- the ways that industrialization was both a motive and a means for imperialism

After completing Section 2, students should be able to:

OBJECTIVE 1 *Explain how World War I affected European attitudes about imperialism.*

OBJECTIVE 2 *Relate how Asian independence movements developed after World War I.*

OBJECTIVE 3 *Identify why the United States granted independence to the Philippines.*

OBJECTIVE 4 *Describe how and why Germany, Italy, and Japan created new empires during the 1930s.*

LET'S GET STARTED!

To begin the class, have students respond in writing to the following question: *How do you think World War I changed imperialism and attitudes about imperialism?* Tell them to make educated guesses based on what they know of the causes and outcomes of the war. Have volunteers read their paragraphs to the class. Tell students that in Section 2 they will learn about changes in imperialism after World War I.

Imperialism Between the Wars

OBJECTIVES

Read to understand:

1. how World War I affected European attitudes about imperialism
2. how Asian independence movements developed after World War I
3. why the United States granted independence to the Philippines
4. how and why Germany, Italy, and Japan created new empires during the 1930s

KEY TERMS

mandate system
trusteeship
Tydings-McDuffie Act
puppet government

KEY PEOPLE

Mohandas K. Gandhi
Ho Chi Minh
Manuel Quezon
Adolf Hitler

"Peace must be planted upon the tested foundations of political liberty. We have no selfish ends to serve. We desire no conquest, no dominion [power to rule]. . . . We are but one of the champions of the rights of mankind. We shall be satisfied when those rights have been made as secure as the faith and the freedom of nations can make them."

—President Woodrow Wilson

As the United States prepared to enter World War I, President Wilson explained his reasons for committing U.S. forces to the fighting in Europe. The First World War eroded the confidence of the great imperial powers, particularly Britain and France.

I WANT YOU
FOR U.S. ARMY
NEAREST RECRUITING STATION

A U.S. Army World War I recruiting poster

World War I and Imperialism

World War I was only partly caused by imperial rivalries. The war had as much to do with the militarism and nationalism in Europe. Yet the war had a serious impact on European views of imperialism. Before World War I, Europeans had considered themselves more enlightened than most other people in the world. They believed that they had a right and even a duty to rule other cultures. World War I came as a severe shock to Europeans. Never before had a war killed so many people in so little time. If Europe could not even be trusted to manage its own affairs, many asked, how could it hope to manage the affairs of other countries?

President Woodrow Wilson pressed publicly for national self-determination—the right of countries to choose their governments. Wilson wanted to avoid tension with U.S. allies, however. Therefore he insisted on self-determination only for the colonies of defeated Germany, Austria-Hungary, and the Ottoman Empire.

As a result, the new League of Nations established the **mandate system** as a way of overseeing the former German and Ottoman colonies. The mandate system required the Allied nations to ensure the welfare of "peoples not yet able to stand by themselves under the strenuous [difficult] conditions of the modern world." Although the mandate system allowed the victorious imperial powers to expand their territories, it required them to develop the areas under their control. Under the principle of **trusteeship**, mandate governments were required to encourage economic development in their territories. In addition, the governments had to provide educational, medical, and other services needed to modernize the territories. The League of Nations intended the mandate system to be a temporary measure that would lead to full independence for the former colonies. The United States rejected the Treaty of Versailles and thus did not participate in the mandate system.

✔ **READING CHECK:** How did World War I affect European attitudes about imperialism?

This poster shows a British soldier writing a letter home from the trenches.

WHEN THE WAR IS OVER, MOTHER DEAR (1).

SECTION 2 RESOURCES

PRINT

- Guided Reading Strategy 27.2
- Graphic Organizer Activity 27: Attitudes Toward Imperialism
- Literature Reading 27: India under British Rule
- Biography Reading 27: Ho Chi Minh
- Primary Source Reading 27: A Culmination of Fears
- Section 2 Review, p. 811
- Daily Quiz 27.2

MULTIMEDIA

- One-Stop Planner, Lesson 27.2
- Holt Researcher: American History CD–ROM

SHELTERED ENGLISH

- Main Idea Activity for Reteaching and Sheltered English 27.2

✔ READING TO UNDERSTAND

To help students master the section objectives, have them answer the **READING CHECKS** and complete **Guided Reading Strategy 27.2** as they read the section.

TEACH OBJECTIVE 1

LEVEL 1: Write the following phrase on the chalkboard: *Our main purpose for holding colonies is to . . .* Tell students to complete this sentence three times from a European perspective—once to show European attitudes about imperialism before World War I, once to demonstrate their attitudes during the war, and a third time to show how they felt about their colonies after the war. *(Students might respond that the war led Europeans to wonder if they could be trusted to manage the affairs of other countries and led to the creation of mandates and trusteeships.)* Ask volunteers to read their completed statements to the class. **Sheltered English**

LEVELS 2 AND 3: Tell students to imagine that they are living in a European colony before and after World War I. Have each student write a journal entry, dated several months after the end of the war, that describes how European opinions toward imperialism have changed after the war. *(See Level 1 lesson for the correct views.)* Invite volunteers to read their journal entries to the class.

CULTURAL DIVERSITY

Lebanon. After separating its League of Nations mandate into Lebanon and Syria, the French government worried that the Maronite Christian majority in Lebanon might also want independence. The French government then decided to add areas composed of different ethnic and religious groups so that no one group was a majority. For example, France added the predominantly Muslim cities of Beirut and Tripoli. By 1920 Lebanon was composed of Maronites, Greek Orthodox, Sunni Muslims, Shi'ite Muslims, and the Druse. At first, emigration was forbidden so that the artificial balance would not be upset. Since these groups had a long history of conflict, the French could play one against another. The civil wars between Lebanon's ethnic and religious groups in the 1980s and 1990s were in part a result of France's actions.

CRITICAL THINKING How might the League of Nations have prevented France from engaging in such self-interested action?

ANSWER: Students might suggest that the League might have demanded that mandates be given independence in a short time.

VISUAL RECORD ANSWER

Students might answer that they appear to be listening intently.

The Middle East

The mandate system was quickly installed in the Middle East, where the Allies divided the defeated Ottoman Empire into several pieces. France and Britain received the largest Middle Eastern territories. Although they were supposed to be preparing these territories for independence, they concentrated instead on strengthening their influence in the region. France separated its mandate on the eastern shore of the Mediterranean Sea into two parts, Lebanon and Syria. The French established a Christian-controlled government in Lebanon and a Muslim-dominated government in Syria. French leaders hoped that Lebanon would continue to maintain its ties to France even after achieving independence.

INTERPRETING THE VISUAL RECORD

The League of Nations. French prime minister Aristide Briand called for an end to war at this assembly of the League of Nations. ***How do the other delegates appear to be responding to Briand's speech?***

Britain also wanted to preserve its ties to the Middle East. British mandates included Iraq, Palestine, and Transjordan—all strategically important areas. By the 1940s Britain had granted independence to its mandates. The British retained important rights, however, such as access to the region's strategic oil resources and to British-established military bases. As a result, Britain continued to strongly influence affairs in its former mandates.

Not everyone approved of the mandate system. Some critics charged that France and Britain were using the system to disguise a new form of imperialism. Many inhabitants of the mandated territories thought that they should have immediately been granted independence. Defenders of the mandate system argued that the fate of the mandated territories could have been even worse. The oversight of the League of Nations at least ensured their eventual independence.

Independence Movements in Asia

Nationalist leaders in Asia viewed the breakup of the German and Ottoman Empires with great interest. They noted that the arguments used by the Allies to justify this breakup could also be applied to the overseas colonies of Britain and France. If the League of Nations supported self-determination, these nationalists asked, why were some nations allowed to keep their empires?

Mohandas K. Gandhi

British India. One of the strongest protests against imperialism took place in India. During the 1920s and 1930s Mohandas K. Gandhi became the leader, both spiritually and politically, in India's struggle for independence from British rule. Born in 1869, Gandhi traveled to London, England, to study law in 1889. He briefly practiced law in India before moving to South Africa in 1893. While living in South Africa, Gandhi protested the government's treatment of Indian immigrants. He used nonviolent methods to draw attention to discrimination. Gandhi called his approach *satyagraha*, or insistence on truth. This form of protest is also

SPOTLIGHT on the League of Nations

Have students conduct research on the League of Nations. Then tell students to imagine that they are delegates to the inaugural meeting of the League of Nations and that they must give a speech explaining its goals and membership.
Block Scheduling

SPOTLIGHT on the Mandate System

Have each student write a short article about how the mandate system has shaped France's and Great Britain's relationships with the Middle East. Urge students to consider the following questions in their articles: *Has it been effective? Is it morally right? What might be some of the long-term effects of the mandate system?* Ask volunteers to read their articles to the class. Students may wish to include their articles in their portfolios.
Block Scheduling

known as civil disobedience. His efforts led to some reforms in South Africa. After returning to India in 1914, Gandhi started a similar campaign of civil disobedience to protest British rule.

The Indian National Congress had been struggling for India's independence since 1885. The independence movement was not supported by a majority of Indians, most of whom remained unaffected by Western culture in the early 1900s. When Gandhi became active in the movement, he realized that he needed a way to make the struggle for independence meaningful to most Indians.

Mohandas K. Gandhi led many marches protesting British rule in India.

Civil disobedience in India. To achieve his goal of *swaraj*, or self-rule, Gandhi used techniques that many people in India could participate in and understand. For example, he encouraged people to spin and weave their own cloth to protest policies that favored British cotton manufacturers. In 1930 he protested the government monopoly on salt by leading a march to the sea to make his own salt. Despite repeated arrests by the British government, Gandhi remained steadfastly committed to nonviolence. Several times he undertook a "fast unto death" to protest British policies. Such fasts shamed the British as well as Indians who resorted to violence. The common people of India called Gandhi Mahatma, or Great Soul, in recognition of his remarkable leadership and peaceful accomplishments.

During the 1920s and 1930s Indian nationalism became a powerful force that gradually loosened Britain's hold on India. Gandhi did not want India to break apart after British rule ended, however. He believed that the British had begun a positive process of nation-building by bringing together all of India's various states and peoples. He wanted to continue the process of building a united India by creating a new sense of national identity among Indians. At the same time, Gandhi was convinced that Western civilization was doomed. Many Europeans, Gandhi wrote, "appear to be half mad. . . . One has only to be patient and it [European civilization] will be self-destroyed." Because he did not trust the Western nations, Gandhi strongly believed that India had to make its own future.

THROUGH OTHERS' EYES

Resisting British Rule of India

One of the most effective leaders of India's independence movement was Jawaharlal Nehru. During the 1920s and 1930s he was jailed for a total of 10 years for his antigovernment activities. Nehru wrote many letters to his daughter Indira during his time in prison. In this letter he describes independence leader Mohandas K. Gandhi.

> "This voice was somehow different from the others. It was quiet and low, and yet it could be heard above the shouting of the multitude; it was soft and gentle, and yet there seemed to be steel hidden away somewhere in it; it was courteous and full of appeal, and yet there was something grim and frightening in it; every word used was full of meaning and seemed to carry a deadly earnestness [seriousness]. Behind the language of peace and friendship there was power and the quivering shadow of action and a determination not to submit to a wrong. We are familiar with that voice now . . . but it was new to us in February and March 1919; we did not quite know what to make of it, but we were thrilled. This was something very different from our noisy politics of condemnation [criticism] and nothing else, long speeches always ending in the same futile [useless] and ineffective resolutions of protest which nobody took very seriously. This was the politics of action, not of talk."

HISTORY MAKERS SPEAK

Jawaharlal Nehru in *The Age of Empire*

Alternatives to Nonviolence. Although Jawaharlal Nehru would become one of Mohandas K. Gandhi's closest allies in the Indian independence movement, he and many other supporters of independence did not always believe in the strategy of nonviolence. As a young man, Nehru studied in Britain, where he was already thinking about a way toward independence for India. Nehru wrote his father, "Have you heard of Sinn Fein in Ireland? . . . It is a most interesting movement and resembles very closely the so-called Extremist movement in India. Their policy is not to beg favors but to wrest them."

CRITICAL THINKING Why might Gandhi's philosophy of nonviolence have been better suited to the Indian political situation than that of Sinn Fein?

ANSWER: Students might suggest that Gandhi's strategy was more in keeping with Indian traditions and that unlike the Irish, Indians lacked significant access to modern weapons.

TEACH OBJECTIVE 2

ALL LEVELS: To help students understand how Asian independence movements developed after World War I, copy the following graphic organizer on the chalkboard, omitting the italicized answers. Have each student complete it. Pair students and have one student in each pair write a slogan for the independence movement in India after World War I. Have the other devise a slogan for the movement in Indochina. Encourage students to share their slogans with the class. **Sheltered English, Cooperative Learning**

Independence Movements

India	Both	Indochina
• *led by Gandhi* • *turned toward nonviolent protest, or civil disobedience* • *wanted to preserve some of British rulers' influence*	• *strong nationalism* • *convinced that Western civilization was doomed*	• *led by Ho Chi Minh* • *turned toward revolutionary communism* • *wanted to establish completely new social order*

PEOPLE IN HISTORY

Charles Eliot Norton. Like W. E. B. Du Bois, Charles Eliot Norton opposed U.S. imperialism. After graduating from Harvard University in 1846, Norton became a successful merchant. He then spent 20 years studying art and literature in Europe. In 1875 he became Harvard's first professor of fine arts. Norton believed that Americans were sacrificing their ideals in their quest for material wealth and that imperialism was simply an excuse to seek more wealth. When the Spanish-American War broke out, Norton advised his students not to enlist in the U.S. Army. He described the declaration of war as a call to barbarism.

CRITICAL THINKING How does Norton's attack on imperialism differ from Du Bois's criticism?

ANSWER: Students might answer that Du Bois worried about imperialism's effect on native peoples while Norton criticized its effects on Americans.

French Indochina. Opposition to imperialism also increased in France's Asian territories following World War I. At the war's end, Ho Chi Minh, a young Vietnamese nationalist, was living in Paris, France. While Gandhi was turning toward nonviolence, Ho turned toward revolutionary communism. He believed that the relationship between colonies and the colonizer was quite similar to the relationship between workers and the ruling class. He argued that one approach would solve both problems. "Only Socialism and Communism can liberate the oppressed nations and the working people throughout the world from slavery," he wrote. Ho became determined to apply this lesson to his Vietnamese homeland. It would take many years, however, before his efforts achieved meaningful results.

✓ **READING CHECK:** How did Asian independence movements develop after World War I?

The United States and the Philippines

During the postwar era American writers like W. E. B. Du Bois echoed the sentiments of Ho Chi Minh and Mohandas K. Gandhi. Du Bois explained that the imperialist powers took advantage of the "vast sea of human labor" in Africa, China, India, the West Indies, and elsewhere.

> **"[Workers are] paid a wage below the level of decent living; driven, beaten, prisoned and enslaved in all but name; spawning [creating] the world's raw material and luxury—cotton, wool, coffee, tea, cocoa, palm oil, fibers, spices, rubber, silks, lumber, copper, gold, diamonds, leather. . . . All these are gathered up at prices lowest of the low, manufactured, transformed and transported at fabulous gain; and the resultant [resulting] wealth is distributed and displayed and made the basis of world power . . . in London and Paris, Berlin and Rome, New York and Rio de Janeiro."**

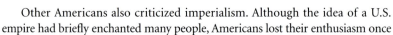

Many European colonies were economically dependent upon a few cash crops, such as coffee, which were grown mainly for export.

Other Americans also criticized imperialism. Although the idea of a U.S. empire had briefly enchanted many people, Americans lost their enthusiasm once they realized the costs of maintaining overseas territories. Many U.S. soldiers had died in a brutal war in the Philippines following its annexation to the United States. Furthermore, although World War I had less of an impact on the United States than on Europe, it heightened Americans' suspicions of imperialism. Soon many Americans began to question U.S. control of the Philippines.

Challenging imperialism. The people of the Philippines sensed American doubts and hoped to use public opinion in the United States to help gain their independence.

▸ASSIGNMENT: *Have students conduct research on Mohandas K. Gandhi's use of nonviolent protest to bring about political change. Have each student relate his or her research in an oral presentation.*

TEACH OBJECTIVE 3

LEVEL 1: Have students list reasons the United States granted independence to the Philippines. *(Lists might include: loss of U.S. soldiers in battles over annexation; expense of maintaining overseas colonies; Americans' heightened suspicions of imperialism; economic competition from the Philippines during the Great Depression; and inconsistencies between democratic ideals and colonial practices.)* Have students give reasons and record them on the chalkboard. Tell students to write down any reasons they missed.
Sheltered English

LEVELS 2 AND 3: Tell students to imagine that it is 1934 and that they are responsible for preparing press releases. Tell them to write a press release explaining why Congress passed the Tydings-McDuffie Act. *(See the Level 1 lesson for correct reasons.)* Have volunteers read their press releases to the class. Then ask students why they think the act called for a 12-year transition period. Students may wish to include their press releases in their portfolios.

Manuel Quezon

Manuel Quezon was a particularly gifted politician. He was born in the Tayabas province of the Philippine island of Luzon in 1878. Quezon had a charismatic personality that helped him gain public recognition. From 1909 to 1916 Quezon served as the Philippine commissioner in the U.S. Congress. In dealings with U.S. leaders, he Americanized his last name to "Casey" and often praised democratic principles.

Quezon's flattery had an underlying purpose. He repeatedly reminded the Americans that they could not be true to their principles if they denied democratic government to Filipinos. In 1923 he joined with other Filipino leaders to send Washington a list of complaints about the U.S. governor-general of the Philippines. Quezon and his comrades criticized the governor-general with language similar to that of the Declaration of Independence.

> **"He has broken asunder [apart] the bonds of harmony that had united Americans and Filipinos. . . .**
>
> **He has sought to establish a colonial despotism [harsh rule] here worse than that which has cursed our country for the last ten generations."**

Quezon made Americans uncomfortable when he pointed out the inconsistencies between democratic principles and U.S. colonial practices.

Granting independence. The Great Depression of the 1930s added economic reasons for Americans to question their imperial connection to the Philippines. The depression drastically reduced demand for American farm products. American farmers called for protection against competition from Philippine sugar and coconut oil. American workers also lobbied to protect their jobs from competition with Filipino immigrants. One way to achieve both goals was to grant the Philippines independence. An independent Philippines would be subject to the same tariffs and immigration limits as any other foreign country.

Traditional anti-imperialism combined with these economic concerns to increase congressional support for Philippine independence. In 1934 Congress passed the **Tydings-McDuffie Act**. This act promised the Philippines independence after a 12-year transition period.

✔ **READING CHECK:** Why did the United States grant independence to the Philippines?

Japanese, Italian, and German Expansion

While Americans were turning away from imperialism in the 1930s, other countries were embracing it. The most aggressive imperial nations were Japan, Italy, and Germany.

The Japanese Empire. Small and resource-poor, Japan looked overseas for raw materials to support its growing population. As early as 1910 Japan had seized control of

INTERPRETING THE VISUAL RECORD

Japanese militarism. Increasing criticism of Japanese imperialism included this 1931 cartoon. ***What does this image suggest about Japan's treatment of international agreements in the early 1900s?***

THE GRANGER COLLECTION, NEW YORK

CONSTITUTIONAL HERITAGE

Developing a Government in the Philippines. As part of the Tydings-McDuffie Act, Filipinos held a constitutional convention in July 1934. The resulting constitution included a clear separation of powers between the executive and legislative branches of government. The constitution also called for a unicameral legislature, restrictions on land ownership, and significant power for the president. Unlike the U.S. president, the Filipino president had the power to veto any revenue items and could assume dictatorial powers during times of declared national emergency. The constitution still had to be approved by the U.S. president.

CRITICAL THINKING Why might the Filipino delegates have created a constitution combining American and Filipino ideas about government?

ANSWER: Students might answer that the constitution had to be approved by the U.S. president, but Filipinos also felt that it should represent their culture and society.

VISUAL RECORD ANSWER

Students might suggest that Japan used military force and ignored various peace agreements.

TEACH OBJECTIVE 4

ALL LEVELS: Organize students into groups of three and assign each student one of the following countries: Germany, Italy, or Japan. Tell students to take notes on how their assigned country created new empires during the 1930s. What regions did they take over? What actions did other nations take in response? *(Students might answer that Japan occupied Manchuria, established a puppet government, and withdrew from the League of Nations after it condemned Japan's action. Italy invaded Ethiopia to gain prestige by acquiring colonies. The world powers condemned Italy's actions but did nothing. Germany annexed Austria, seized the Sudetenland, and dismantled the rest of Czechoslovakia, with little response from the United States or Western Europe.)* When students have finished taking notes, tell them to take turns explaining their findings to the other members of their group. Tell the class that each student should be able to talk for two minutes about any of the three countries if called upon to do so. When groups have finished, call on students to talk about depression-era aggression in each of the three countries.

Sheltered English, Cooperative Learning

DEMOCRATIC VALUES

Japan and Racial Pride. Official government documents released the day Japan attacked Pearl Harbor make clear the unstated goals of Japan's territorial expansion during the 1930s. Japan wanted to create a "new world order" that would "enable all nations and races to assume their proper place in the world." For the Japanese, their proper place was as the leading race of the world. The documents also described a plan to settle Japanese emigrants throughout Asia. These settlers would become leaders of the "new" Asia. However, personal relationships and intermarriage with non-Japanese peoples would be strictly forbidden. Japanese would be the only accepted language, and students would be taught about the superiority of the Japanese race and culture.

CRITICAL THINKING How might other Asian nations have felt about Japan's plan?

ANSWER: Students might answer that other nations may not have agreed with Japan's sense of superiority.

THAT'S INTERESTING!

Adolf Hitler was convinced that Germany had too large a population for its limited area. The only solutions he seriously considered were forced emigration and occupation of neighboring countries.

Korea. During and after World War I, Japan acquired Germany's Pacific possessions. Even so, Japanese leaders believed they needed more land and resources.

This need to expand grew when the Japanese economy began to suffer during the global depression of the 1930s. Japanese leaders responded to the economic problems by increasing military spending. They also looked toward Manchuria, a region in northeastern China. Manchuria had many of the resources that Japan wanted, and the region was only loosely governed by China. In 1931 Japan occupied Manchuria. It set up a **puppet government**—a system in which an imperial power controls a country while pretending that the country is independent. Although Manchuria was officially headed by the Chinese, Japan was in control.

When the League of Nations condemned the Japanese takeover of Manchuria, Japan quit the organization. Japanese leaders did not think the League could stop their imperialist goals. One leading Japanese banker, Hirozo Mori, expressed this confidence. "Expansion towards the continent is the destiny of the Japanese people, decreed by heaven, which neither the world nor we the Japanese ourselves can check [stop] or alter."

Fascism in Germany and Italy. Like Japan, both Italy and Germany suffered severe economic problems during the global depression. Germany was also burdened by the massive war reparations it owed as part of the peace settlement that ended World War I. The economic crisis and the public dissatisfaction that it caused led to increased support for fascist governments in Italy and Germany.

Italy's Fascist dictator, Benito Mussolini, wanted Italy to gain greater prestige by acquiring colonies. He saw that there was no military effort to stop Japan's expansion. In 1935 Italy conquered the African nation of Ethiopia. As with Japan, the other great powers condemned Italy's action but failed to stop its expansion.

German Fascist Adolf Hitler had even bolder plans. "Germany must either be a world power or there will be no Germany," he said. Hitler claimed that Germany needed *Lebensraum*, or living space. Reviving an old German policy called *Drang nach Osten*, or the drive to the East, Hitler described his plan to create a new German civilization in southern Russia and the Ukraine.

The Nazis used large, showy rallies and parades to encourage feelings of national pride and increase support for their policies.

> "The area . . . must be Europeanized! . . . The German agencies and authorities are to have wonderful buildings, the governors' palaces. Around each city, a ring of lovely villages will be placed to within 30 or 40 kilometers. . . . The German cities will be placed, like pearls on a string, and around the cities the German settlements will lie."

Under Hitler's plan, German occupation of the region would be made possible by the extermination or enslavement of the local inhabitants.

Hitler rebuilt Germany's armed forces in defiance of the 1919 Treaty of Versailles. When the great powers did nothing to stop him, he took even bolder measures in the late 1930s. Germany annexed Austria, seized the Sudetenland, and finally dismantled the rest of Czechoslovakia.

REVIEW

Have students complete the **Section 2 Review** on p. 811.

ASSESS

Have students complete **Daily Quiz 27.2.** As **Alternative Assessment**, you may want to use the journal activity or the Philippine independence press release activity in this section's lessons.

RETEACH

Have students complete **Main Idea Activity for Reteaching and Sheltered English 27.2.** Then have students write sentences summarizing the main idea of each subsection in Section 2. Ask students to read their sentences to the class. Have the class choose the best summary sentence for each subsection. Write these sentences on the chalkboard and tell students to copy them into their notes. **Sheltered English**

EXTEND

Have students ask several adults how they feel about the United States or any other country acquiring and governing colonies. Tell them to organize the opinions they gather into a written or oral report. Encourage them to include a simple graphic organizer to show the breakdown of those who favor imperialism and those who disapprove of it. Call on volunteers to summarize their findings and explain why people responded as they did. **Block Scheduling**

Hoping for Peace

The United States and the democratic nations of Western Europe did little to stop the imperialist efforts of Germany, Italy, and Japan in the 1930s. Western leaders hoped to avoid repeating the horrors of World War I in another conflict. Some officials hoped that dictators such as Adolf Hitler and Mussolini would stop on their own rather than risk a war.

Equally important, many western leaders feared the expansion of communism as much as the growth of fascism. The revolutionaries who had created the Soviet Union in 1917 had condemned imperialism along with capitalism. However, Soviet leaders had also expressed a desire to spread communism around the world. Furthermore, the worldwide depression had strengthened communism throughout Europe, as well as in the United States. Neville Chamberlain, the British prime minister, expressed the fears of many democratic officials when he warned of the dangers of overthrowing Hitler. "Who will guarantee that Germany will not become Bolshevistic [communist] afterwards?" he asked.

The governments of Germany and the Soviet Union were opposed to each other. Some democratic leaders hoped that the hostility between Communists and Fascists would prevent either side from gaining too much power or territory. However, Germany and the Soviet Union temporarily settled their differences and signed a nonaggression pact in 1939.

Germany finally went too far when it invaded Poland in 1939. By that time it was almost too late for the United States and the democratic nations of Europe to defeat the imperialist goals of Germany, Italy, and Japan.

INTERPRETING THE VISUAL RECORD

Hitler and Stalin. This 1939 cartoon was a response to the nonaggression pact between Nazi Germany and the Soviet Union. ***What does the cartoon suggest about relations between the two nations?***

✔ **READING CHECK:** How and why did Japan, Italy, and Germany create new empires during the 1930s?

SECTION 2 REVIEW

Define and explain the significance of the following terms:
mandate system
trusteeship
Tydings-McDuffie Act
puppet government

Identify and explain the significance of the following individuals:
Mohandas K. Gandhi
Ho Chi Minh
Manuel Quezon
Adolf Hitler

1. **Using Graphic Organizers** Copy the graphic organizer below and use it to explain depression-era imperialism.

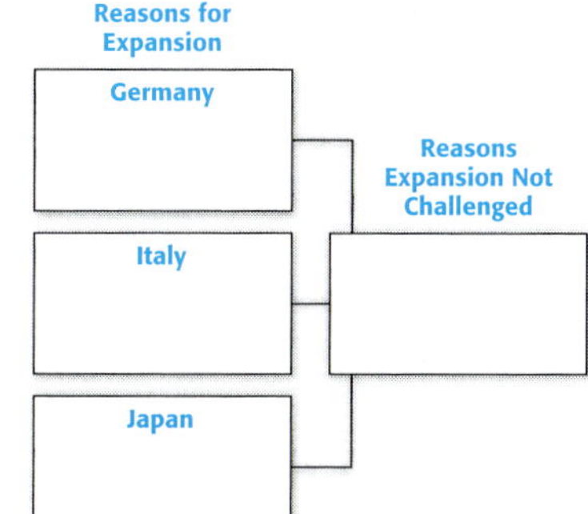

2. **Identifying Cause and Effect** How did World War I influence European beliefs regarding imperialism?
3. **Assessing Consequences** How did World War I affect imperialism in Asia?
4. **Analyzing** Why did the U.S. government decide to grant the Philippines independence?

Critical Thinking

5. Imagine you are a leader of the independence movement in India or in Indochina following World War I. How might you persuade people to join the movement?
Consider:
- European attitudes about imperialism
- the breakup of the German and Ottoman Empires
- problems posed by imperialism

SECTION 2 REVIEW ANSWERS

Define and Identify
For significance, see the following pages:

- mandate system, p. 805
- trusteeship, p. 805
- Mohandas K. Gandhi, p. 806
- Ho Chi Minh, p. 808
- Manuel Quezon, p. 809
- Tydings-McDuffie Act, p. 809
- puppet government, p. 810
- Adolf Hitler, p. 810

1. Germany—need for increased living space; desire to be a world power; Italy—desire for international prestige; Japan—overpopulation, lack of adequate natural resources; not challenged—fear of repeating World War I, fear that communism would spread
2. Europeans began to question their opinions of their own superiority.
3. led to stronger independence movements
4. to protect U.S. jobs and exports; Filipinos also appealed to principles of democracy.
5. Answers will vary but should reflect the fact that many Europeans and Americans began to doubt the worth of imperialism; independence leaders believed that if the mandate system granted independence to German and Ottoman colonies, Allied territories also had the right to independence; and the problems of imperialism included the exploitation of workers and economic dependence on the colonizing country.

SECTION 3

After completing Section 3, students should be able to:

OBJECTIVE 1 *Identify how World War II affected Asian independence efforts.*

OBJECTIVE 2 *Explain why the United States did not support the Vietnamese independence movement.*

OBJECTIVE 3 *Relate how and when most African nations gained independence.*

OBJECTIVE 4 *Describe the major concerns of third-world countries during the Cold War.*

LET'S GET STARTED!

As students enter the classroom, distribute copies of Outline Map 24, The World, from **American History Outline Maps.** Tell students to use the world map in the Reference Section Atlas in their textbooks to label the following countries: Algeria, Cambodia, India, Indonesia, Ivory Coast, Kenya, Laos, Nigeria, Pakistan, and Vietnam. Tell students that this quick geography review will help them as they learn about colonial policies and independence movements in these and other countries in Section 3.

SECTION 3 RESOURCES

PRINT

- Guided Reading Strategy 27.3
- American History Outline Map 31: Africa
- Section 3 Review, p. 818
- Daily Quiz 27.3

MULTIMEDIA

- One-Stop Planner, Lesson 27.3
- Holt Researcher: American History CD–ROM

SHELTERED ENGLISH

- Main Idea Activity for Reteaching and Sheltered English 27.3

✔ READING TO UNDERSTAND

To help students master the section objectives, have them answer the **READING CHECKS** and complete **Guided Reading Strategy 27.3** as they read the section.

Decolonization and the Cold War

OBJECTIVES

Read to understand:

1. how World War II affected Asian independence efforts
2. why the United States did not support the Vietnamese independence movement
3. how and when most African nations gained independence
4. what the major concerns of third-world countries were during the Cold War

KEY TERMS

decolonization
neocolonialism
Bandung Conference
nonaligned movement
third world

KEY PEOPLE

Clement Attlee
Jomo Kenyatta
Jawaharlal Nehru

EYEWITNESSES TO History

"Whether Britain wins or loses, imperialism has to die. It is certainly of no use now to the British people, whatever it may have been in the past."

—Mohandas K. Gandhi

Mohandas K. Gandhi argued for India's independence in the "Quit India" campaign at the end of World War II. Even more than World War I, World War II weakened the European powers and strengthened anticolonial nationalist movements. Shortly after the war, a massive decolonization movement swept the globe.

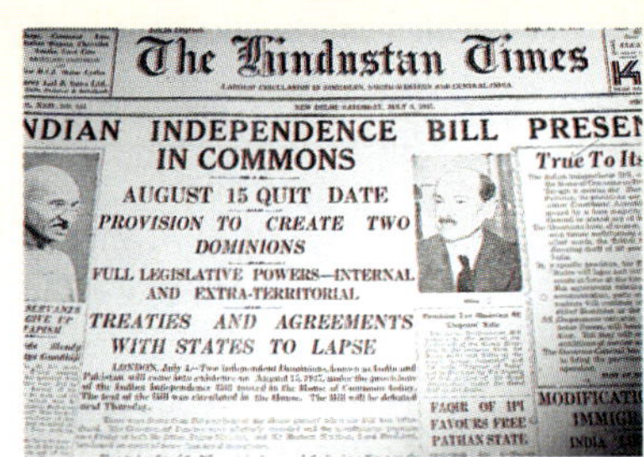

The Hindustan Times

INDIAN INDEPENDENCE BILL PRESENTED IN COMMONS

AUGUST 15 QUIT DATE

PROVISION TO CREATE TWO DOMINIONS

FULL LEGISLATIVE POWERS—INTERNAL AND EXTRA-TERRITORIAL

TREATIES AND AGREEMENTS WITH STATES TO LAPSE

Newspaper headline discussing Indian independence

The Atlantic Charter

The imperialism of Germany, Italy, and Japan led to the global conflict known as World War II. Millions of people lost their lives, and the economies of many nations were devastated. World War II also had a profound effect on imperialism. World War I had shattered Europeans' sense of moral superiority. World War II did the same to Europeans' sense of military superiority. Japan's early victories over U.S. and British forces in the Pacific demonstrated that Asian countries could stand up to Western armies.

The political doctrine of self-determination also had a major effect on the future of imperialism. During World War I President Woodrow Wilson had supported self-determination because he felt it was morally right to do so. In a similar fashion, President Franklin D. Roosevelt insisted that self-determination should be a central objective of World War II. Roosevelt's view was written into the Atlantic Charter of 1941, a proclamation he issued jointly with British prime minister Winston Churchill.

> **"First, [the United States and Britain] seek no aggrandizement [enlargement], territorial or other; Second, they desire to see no territorial changes that do not accord with the freely expressed wishes of the peoples concerned; Third, they respect the right of all peoples to choose the form of government under which they will live; and they wish to see sovereign rights and self-government restored to those who have been forcibly deprived of them."**

The charter also supported international economic cooperation and open trade between all nations after the war. In addition, the charter called for nations to resolve their conflicts peacefully. The Atlantic Charter served as a model for the international resolution that led to the founding of the United Nations.

Winston Churchill was a bold public speaker.

TEACH OBJECTIVE 1

LEVELS 1 AND 2: Organize students into pairs and have them create two time lines showing the events that led to Indian and Indonesian independence. *(Time lines should include: India—Atlantic Charter is signed, Gandhi steps up "Quit India" campaign, Churchill is replaced by Attlee, Britain divides colony into India and Pakistan and grants them independence; Indonesia—Netherlands loses East Indies to Japanese, Japan is defeated, Sukarno declares independence, Netherlands acknowledges it after four years of conflict.)* In a classroom discussion, have students use their time lines to explain how World War II affected Asian independence efforts. *(Students might suggest that the Atlantic Charter inspired independence movements and that the war weakened the imperial nations.)*
Sheltered English, Cooperative Learning

LEVEL 3: Tell students to imagine that they are leaders of an independence movement in India or Indonesia after World War II. Have each student write a policy statement for the movement. Policy statements should explain how World War II affected independence efforts. *(See the Levels 1 and 2 lesson for correct effects.)* Invite volunteers to read their policy statements to the class.

However, Churchill was unwilling to follow the principles outlined in the Atlantic Charter by granting independence to Britain's overseas colonies. "I have not become the King's First Minister," he once said, "in order to preside over the liquidation [breakup] of the British Empire." Churchill did little to change Britain's colonial policies.

Read More About It

Free Find:
Franklin D. Roosevelt
After reading about Franklin D. Roosevelt on the **Holt Researcher** CD–ROM, write a short essay explaining how Roosevelt's experiences as president might have led him to the conclusion that the United States had an international role to play in World War II.

Asian Nationalism After World War II

The Atlantic Charter became a source of inspiration for independence movements around the world. Asian nationalists increased, their calls for **decolonization**—the process of ending colonial rule.

India. In India Mohandas K. Gandhi stepped up his campaign of nonviolent resistance to British rule. British prime minister Winston Churchill tried to crush the movement by having tens of thousands of Indian protesters thrown in jail.

Churchill's actions served as a harsh reminder of the contradiction between the ideals expressed in the Atlantic Charter and the continuing practice of imperialism. A leading newspaper of the Indian nationalist movement questioned the "mysterious silence" of the U.S. government following the British crackdown. Many Americans were also disturbed by their country's failure to criticize British imperialism.

As a result, Americans viewed with interest the events that led to Indian independence. Just as World War II was ending, British voters replaced Churchill with Clement Attlee, the leader of the opposition Labour Party. Attlee and the Labour Party were not completely anti-imperialist. However, the war had left Britain exhausted. The Allies had won, but Britain no longer had the financial resources to support an empire and was weary of governing colonies. The first priority of British voters was to repair their fortunes at home. Had Indian nationalists been less determined, however, even Attlee might have tried to keep India as a British colony.

Eventually Britain agreed to divide the colony into the independent nations of India and Pakistan. Pakistan, the largely Muslim portion of British India, did not want to be part of the new Indian nation, which was predominantly Hindu. In August 1947 Britain turned over power to the Indian and Pakistani governments.

The national flags of Pakistan (top) and India

Indonesia. Led by Achmad Sukarno, the nationalist movement in the Dutch East Indies faced a Dutch government that opposed decolonization. The Dutch had controlled these islands for more than 100 years. The Netherlands then lost control of the East Indies to the Japanese during World War II. After Japan's defeat in 1945, Sukarno declared the colony to be the independent nation of Indonesia.

Although the Netherlands was struggling to recover from World War II, the Dutch fought the Indonesian nationalists fiercely. The Dutch had some victories, but the Indonesian nationalists continued fighting. In 1949, after nearly four years of conflict, the Netherlands finally acknowledged Indonesia's independence. That same year Sukarno became Indonesia's first president.

✔ **READING CHECK:** How did World War II affect Asian independence efforts?

ECONOMIC DEVELOPMENT

Pakistan. While the nations of India and Pakistan were established in August 1947, their borders were not firmly established for many years. Present-day Pakistan includes only the western portion of the lands originally designated as Pakistan. Battles over boundaries resulted in part from Pakistan's poor economic situation after the partition. India had retained the major portion of the British resources. The new Indian border separated Pakistan's jute-growing regions from manufacturing and exporting centers located in northeastern India. India also controlled water access to some of Pakistan. Differences about water management of the rivers that cross both countries were long-standing and prevented Pakistan from gaining some of the British assets it had been promised.

ACTIVITY: Have students use an atlas to draw the borders of Pakistan and India in 1947 and today on a map of South Asia.

THAT'S INTERESTING!

In 1933 Choudhry Rahmat Ali coined the name Pakistan to stand for Muslims living in different regions of India: *P* for Punjab, *A* for Afghan, *K* for Kashmir, *S* for Sind, and *Tan* for Baluchistan.

TEACH OBJECTIVE 2

LEVEL 1: Ask students to list reasons the United States did not support the Vietnamese independence movement. *(Students might note that the United States was reluctant to anger France, wanted French help in fighting communism, and could not support Ho's efforts to establish communism in Vietnam.)* Write these reasons on the chalkboard and encourage students to record them in their notes.
Sheltered English

LEVELS 2 AND 3: Have students complete the Level 1 activity. *(See the Level 1 lesson for the correct reasons.)* Then tell them to write a few sentences evaluating each reason. Also, tell students to write a paragraph stating their opinion about what the United States should have done: support France, support Vietnam, or maintain neutrality. Tell them to explain their opinions in terms of U.S. views on imperialism at the time as well as the U.S. position on the spread of communism.

CULTURAL DIVERSITY

Vo Nguyen Giap and the Influence of French Culture. The career of Vo Nguyen Giap, a nationalist military officer appointed by Ho Chi Minh, demonstrates the impact of imperialist cultures on those who would become their enemies. The son of a peasant who scrimped to afford private school tuition, Giap came to admire greatly French culture. He graduated from a French lycée, or high school, and received a law degree from the University of Hanoi, another French institution. Giap later taught history at a private school. One of his students remembered, "He recounted the battles [of Napoleon] in brilliant detail, as if he were Napoleon himself." In March 1954 Giap's troops surrounded the French army at Dien Bien Phu and forced a surrender. The battle was one of the more decisive defeats of an imperialist power.

CRITICAL THINKING What might French culture and education have meant to an individual of peasant background like Giap?

ANSWER: Students might answer that it liberated him from a limited background and provided a look at a different world.

VISUAL RECORD ANSWER
Students might answer that they felt defeated.

INTERPRETING THE VISUAL RECORD
French defeat. French soldiers in Indochina lowered their national flag after France agreed to withdraw from Vietnam. ***How do you think the French soldiers witnessing this ceremony might have felt?***

Vietnam. France was also unwilling to let go of its colonies. World War II had been particularly humiliating for the French. The Germans had swiftly occupied France after just six weeks of fighting in 1940. Japan then took advantage of France's defeat to capture the French colony of Indochina—which consisted of modern-day Cambodia, Laos, and Vietnam—in Southeast Asia. After the liberation of France in 1945, the government hoped to re-establish French imperial power by reclaiming Indochina.

The Vietnamese had other ideas. Nationalist Ho Chi Minh had led the struggle against French imperialism before the war and against Japanese imperialism during the war. After Japan's defeat, he expected France to recognize Vietnam's independence. Thus when French troops returned to reclaim Indochina, Ho and many others took up arms in resistance.

U.S. leaders were divided about the situation in Vietnam, just as they had long been divided about imperialism. Some U.S. officials sympathized with the desire of the Vietnamese for independence, but the U.S. government hesitated to anger France. The Cold War was just beginning, and the United States wanted French help in fighting the spread of communism worldwide. In addition, Ho proudly proclaimed his plans to bring about a communist revolution in Vietnam. The United States was publicly committed to opposing the spread of communism. Supporting Ho against France was therefore out of the question.

The war in Indochina went poorly for France. Ho's guerrilla forces soon wore the French down. In response, the U.S. government increased its economic and military assistance to the French in Indochina. Despite this aid, in 1954 the French government withdrew from Indochina in defeat.

✔ **READING CHECK:** Why did the United States not support the Vietnamese independence movement?

Independent Africa

Jomo Kenyatta led the Kenyan nationalist movement.

World War II left European empires in Africa in a vulnerable position. Like Asian nationalists, African nationalists recognized the postwar opportunity for independence. Most African nations achieved independence during the late 1950s and early 1960s. The imperial powers, however, did not always let go of their African colonies easily.

Fighting for independence. In the 1940s many Africans in Kenya began to protest British rule. Their greatest complaint was that the British owned most of the land in Kenya, while many Africans had no land and lived in poverty. When British policy remained unchanged, some Kenyans became convinced that violence was necessary to achieve their goals. The leader of the independence movement, Jomo Kenyatta, expressed his beliefs in a 1952 speech about the flag of the Kenya African Union (KAU). African nationalist Karari Njama recalled the speech:

TEACH OBJECTIVE 3

ALL LEVELS: To help students understand how and when most African nations gained independence, copy the following graphic organizer on the chalkboard, omitting the italicized answers. Have each student complete it. **Sheltered English**

ASSIGNMENT: *Have students write a paragraph explaining the challenges newly independent countries faced during the 1960s. Ask volunteers to share their paragraphs with the class.*

African Independence	Date of Independence	How It Achieved Independence
most African nations	*late 1950s to early 1960s*	*took advantage of postwar weakness of imperialist nations*
Kenya	*1963*	*violent uprising*
Algeria	*1962*	*violent uprising*
Belgian Congo	*1960*	*rioting; Belgium left without fighting*

> **"He [Kenyatta] raised the KAU flag to symbolize African Government. . . . He said, 'Black is to show that this is for black people. Red is to show that the blood of an African is the same colour as the blood of a European, and green is to show that when we were given this country by God it was green, fertile and good but now you see the green is below the red and is suppressed.' . . . What he said must mean that our fertile lands (green) could only be regained by the blood (red) of the African (black)."**

Kenyatta helped lead a group of Kenyan rebels known as the Mau Mau. The rebels fought against Britain from 1952 to 1956. Thousands of Africans were killed in the conflict. Kenya finally gained its independence from Britain in 1963. Kenyatta became president in 1964, a position he held until his death in 1978.

In the French African territories, the bloodiest struggle for independence took place in the North African nation of Algeria. About 1 million French colonists lived in Algeria, which France had occupied by force since 1830. In some ways the French considered Algeria a part of France itself. Algerians, however, felt differently. A nationalist revolt in 1954 sparked a brutal war that raged for several years. Both sides committed many atrocities. As casualties mounted, the French began negotiations to end the war. France finally granted Algeria its independence in 1962.

The OAS was a terrorist group that tried to prevent Algeria from gaining independence.

THAT'S INTERESTING!

French World War II hero Charles de Gaulle was one of the leading opponents of Algerian independence in the early 1950s. He argued that any deal with the Algerian nationalists represented a shameful surrender. In 1958 de Gaulle became president of France and assumed emergency powers to protect the French colonists. In 1962, after four years of guerrilla warfare, he agreed to support Algerian independence and announced a settlement plan.

Strategies for Success: Identifying Cause and Effect

Cause-and-effect relationships are crucial to the study of history. Historians ask questions to determine why an event took place and what happened as a result of that event. What was the background, or context, of the event? Who were the people involved in the event? What was the immediate activity that triggered the event?

How to Identify Cause and Effect

1. **Look for clues.** Certain words and phrases are immediate clues to the existence of a cause-and-effect relationship. *Because, led to, provoked,* and *inspired,* for example, often indicate cause. *As a result, originating from, as a consequence, created by,* and *outcome* often indicate effect.
2. **Identify the relationship.** Read carefully to determine the relationship between events. Writers of history do not always state the link between cause and effect. Sometimes the reader has to infer the relationship on his or her own.
3. **Check for complex connections.** Beyond the immediate cause-and-effect relationship, check for other, more complex connections. Note, for example, whether there were additional causes of a given effect, whether a cause had multiple effects, and if the effects themselves caused further events.

Applying the Strategy

The Cold War between the Soviet Union and the United States created a variety of problems for the newly independent nations of Africa and Asia. Using information from Section 3, create a flowchart that traces some of the effects of the Cold War.

Practicing the Strategy

Use the information in Section 3 to answer the following questions.

1. How did World War II affect colonial empires?
2. Why did many newly independent nations in Africa and Asia want to obtain foreign aid?
3. Why was the nonaligned movement formed?

STRATEGIES FOR SUCCESS ANSWERS

Applying the Strategy

Answers will vary, but students' flowcharts should clearly trace some of the effects of the Cold War.

Practicing the Strategy

1. weakened them
2. to help their economies make the transition from a colonial economy to an independent economy
3. to keep countries neutral in the Cold War

Teacher to Teacher

Stephen M. Marlowe of Gastonia, North Carolina, suggested the following activity: Have students compare and contrast several political and economic changes in Africa as the colonial era ended. Students should identify why some changes succeeded and why some failed and report their findings in a paragraph.

TEACH OBJECTIVE 4

LEVEL 1: Have groups of students create collages of images that represent the major concerns and experiences of third-world countries during the Cold War. *(Collages might include images of third-world countries being tied to the economies of former imperial powers; needing foreign aid, development, and modernization; and maintaining neutrality during the Cold War.)* Ask volunteers to share their collages with the class. **Sheltered English, Cooperative Learning**

GLOBAL RELATIONS

The Belgian Congo and the Cold War. Shortly after the Belgian Congo declared its independence in 1960, the province of Katanga and part of the province of Kasai tried to secede. The Belgian government sent troops to the area to protect Belgian citizens and to support the secessionist government in Katanga. Patrice Lumumba, prime minister of the newly independent Congo, asked the United Nations for help restoring order, but the UN troops refused to force the Belgians out. Lumumba then asked for U.S. aid. When the U.S government turned him down, Lumumba appealed to the Soviet Union. He accepted some Soviet airplanes and weapons. In January 1961 Lumumba was assassinated by Katanga province secessionists.

CRITICAL THINKING Why might the United States have been so concerned about Lumumba?

ANSWER: Students might suggest that the Belgian Congo was a nation rich in natural resources and American companies had invested heavily in it.

Civil war in Congo. The Belgian government had no wish to repeat the bloodshed already experienced in Kenya and Algeria. When rioting broke out in 1959 in the Belgian Congo, the Belgians left even before a new government was firmly in place. The Republic of the Congo became independent in 1960. Nationalist leader Patrice Lumumba became the nation's first prime minister, but was assassinated by political enemies after serving only a few months in office. Rival groups quickly began a civil war, which devastated the country.

Soon Congo was also caught up in the Cold War between the United States and the Soviet Union. Each superpower supported the side it hoped would win the civil war. The country renamed itself Zaire in 1971 and became the Democratic Republic of Congo in 1997. Congo's difficult road to independence showed how Cold War rivalries could interfere with nationalist struggles.

✔ **READING CHECK:** How and when did most African nations gain independence?

The Nonaligned Movement

Congo's problems were similar to those faced by many other newly independent countries in the 1950s and 1960s. Decolonization and the Cold War combined to cause many difficulties for such nations.

Cold War politics. Many former colonies had poor economies and remained dependent on their former colonizers. Such links were frustrating for nationalists who had fought for independence. Complicating the situation was the fact that the colonial-era systems remaining in many countries were incompatible with each other. For example, a telephone network in a former British colony might not work well when placing calls to a former French colony. Economic cooperation between former colonies was often complicated by such problems.

These factors combined to make it difficult for many small nations to modernize and industrialize. The leaders of newly independent nations blamed their problems on the old colonial powers. Some accused the former colonial powers of **neocolonialism**—the process of maintaining indirect control over former colonies. To many of these national leaders, aid from the Soviet Union or the United States seemed like a good way to break old colonial ties. Both of the superpowers encouraged this attitude by offering their support. Many nations came to depend upon foreign aid to pursue their modernization and development programs.

However, such foreign aid rarely came without strings attached. The United States saw economic aid as a way to gain allies. The United States was also unwilling to aid communist governments. When faced with the choice between anti-imperialism and anticommunism, the United States consistently chose anticommunism. The U.S. role in the Vietnamese struggle for independence was one example.

Many former colonies in Africa and Asia retained examples of colonial architecture, such as these German-influenced shops.

LEVEL 2: Tell students to imagine that they are representatives of third-world countries to the United Nations during the Cold War. Have them write statements explaining their major concerns to the United Nations on behalf of their countries. *(See the Level 1 lesson for the correct concerns.)* Have volunteers read their statements to the class.

NOTE: For an additional teaching idea, see the Chapter 27 learning stations lesson in the **Creative Teaching Strategies** handbook.

LEVEL 3: Organize students into groups of four and assign each student a third-world country to represent during the Cold War years. Tell each group to brainstorm strategies for resolving some of its major concerns. *(See the Level 1 lesson for the correct concerns.)* Students should create plans to develop and modernize their country while keeping it out of the conflict between the United States and the Soviet Union. When groups have come up with several ideas, call on one member of each group to read them to the class. Encourage the class to discuss the merits of some of the ideas presented.
Cooperative Learning

In addition, accepting assistance from one superpower sometimes led to threats from the other. Small nations in Africa and Asia were often caught in the middle of such Cold War struggles.

The Bandung Conference. In reaction to the Cold War rivalries and as a matter of mutual protection, many leaders of the newly independent nations began to band together in the 1940s and 1950s. One of the key figures in this effort was India's new prime minister, Jawaharlal Nehru. Nehru hoped to extend Mohandas K. Gandhi's doctrine of self-help to other newly independent nations. In 1946 Nehru outlined the reasons for India's policy.

> **"We propose, as far as possible, to keep away from the power politics of groups, aligned against one another, which led in the past to world wars and which may again lead to disasters on an even larger scale. We believe that peace and freedom are indivisible and the denial of freedom anywhere must endanger freedom elsewhere and lead to conflict and war."**

In 1955 Indonesia hosted a meeting in Bandung, a city on the Indonesian island of Java. The **Bandung Conference** reaffirmed Nehru's suggestion that the former colonies should remain neutral in the Cold War. Attending countries produced the Declaration on Promotion of Universal Peace and Co-operation. It stated, "Free from mistrust and fear, and with confidence and goodwill towards each other, nations should practice tolerance and live together in peace with one another."

The conference inspired the establishment of the **nonaligned movement**. The movement's name reflected the member nations' agreement to be neutral toward the two superpowers. Members were encouraged to seek assistance from both sides in the Cold War if necessary. The Bandung Conference also influenced African Americans and minority groups living in some Western nations. American author Richard Wright saw the conference as a historic gathering of oppressed peoples from many different races and cultures. "The underdogs of the human race were meeting. Here were class and racial and religious consciousness on a global scale."

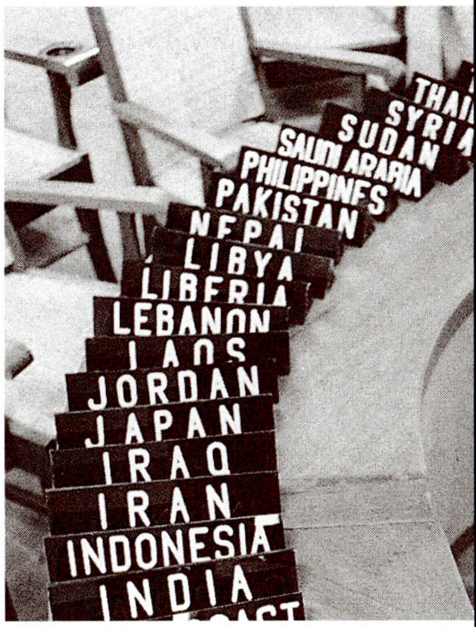

INTERPRETING THE VISUAL RECORD

The Bandung Conference. A total of 29 countries representing more than half the world's population sent delegates to the Bandung Conference in Indonesia. ***What world regions are represented by the nations shown in the photograph?***

The Third World

To the nonaligned movement, the world appeared to be divided into three parts. The first world consisted of the Western capitalist nations. The second world included the Soviet socialist nations. The **third world** made up all the remaining countries, many of which joined the nonaligned movement. Through the nonaligned movement, third-world leaders hoped to keep free of the Cold War struggle and still obtain the resources they needed for development.

A balancing act. As decolonization spread across Asia and Africa, more and more new third-world countries were formed. By the mid-1960s third-world countries made up a majority of members of the United Nations (UN). Although the major industrial powers still controlled the UN Security Council, the General Assembly became an important forum for third-world concerns.

GLOBAL RELATIONS

Bandung Conference. During the Bandung Conference, China and India each saw itself as the legitimate leader of the nonaligned nations. Tensions already existed between the two nations. China had invaded and seized Tibet in 1954, and border incidents between China and India occurred regularly. By 1962 China and India were at war with each other.

ACTIVITY: Have students conduct research on the tensions between China and India in the 1900s. Then have students create a time line of the events.

VISUAL RECORD ANSWER

Students might mention Africa, Asia, and the Middle East.

REVIEW

Have students complete the **Section 3 Review** on p. 818.

ASSESS

Have students complete **Daily Quiz 27.3**. As **Alternative Assessment**, you may want to use the independence movement time lines or the third-world major concerns activity in this section's lessons.

RETEACH

Have students complete **Main Idea Activity for Reteaching and Sheltered English 27.3**. Ask students to identify the key people, places, and terms from the section as you write each of them on the chalkboard. Have each student develop one question and answer for each of the terms. Collect the questions and use them to quiz students on section content. **Sheltered English**

EXTEND

Organize students into groups and have them create and present a television news report about the Bandung Conference. Tell them to use 1950s-style reporting to cover the following topics: the goals of the conference, the attendees, the Declaration on Promotion of Universal Peace and Cooperation, and the impact the conference had on global relations.
Block Scheduling, Cooperative Learning

SECTION 3 REVIEW ANSWERS

Define and Identify
For significance, see the following pages:

- decolonization, p. 813
- Clement Atlee, p. 813
- Jomo Kenyetta, p. 814
- neocolonialism, p. 816
- Jawaharlal Nehru, p. 817
- Bandung Conference, p. 817
- nonaligned movement, p. 817
- third world, p. 817

1. India and Great Britain, India and Pakistan independent in 1947; Indonesia and Netherlands, independent in 1945, Dutch withdraw in 1949; Indochina and France, French withdraw in 1954; Kenya and Great Britain, rebellion 1952–56, independent in 1963; Algeria and France, rebellion begins 1954, independent in 1962; Belgian Congo and Belgium, rebellion in 1959, independent in 1960

2. World War II ended European military superiority and marked the beginning of the dissolution of overseas empires.

3. Answers will vary. Students might mention the vulnerable position of European empires and the strength of independence movements.

4. to avoid being caught in the middle of Cold War struggles

5. Answers will vary. Students might mention that despite anti-imperialist policies, the United States did not support some independence movements if doing so would create conflict with other nations or promote communism.

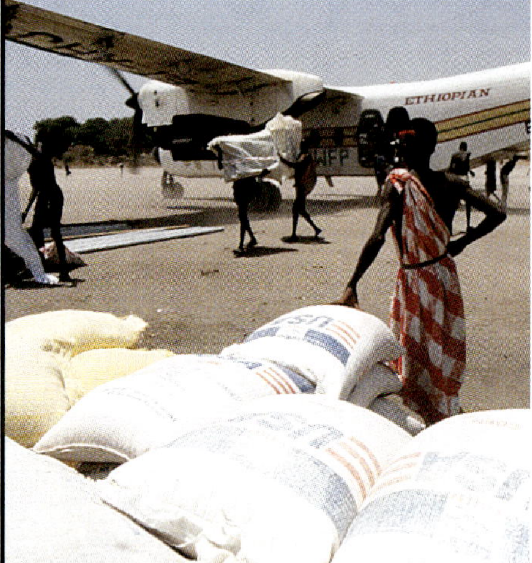

During the Cold War the United States often sent relief aid, such as these grain shipments, to third-world countries in need.

For most U.S. leaders, neutrality in the struggle against worldwide communism was a dangerous idea. John Foster Dulles, U.S. secretary of state under President Dwight D. Eisenhower, even called neutrality "immoral." Eisenhower himself said, "There can be no neutrals when the question is one of moral values or right and wrong."

U.S. relations with many third-world countries became strained over the issue of neutrality. In the United Nations many of the third-world leaders denounced U.S. policies as imperialistic. Even so, they continued to apply for aid from both Western nations and the Soviet Union.

Changing goals. As the nonaligned movement grew larger and more diverse, the policy of neutrality became less important than the goal of development. Soon the movement included some countries that were openly allied with one superpower. Cuba, for example, became a Soviet ally. Pakistan, the Philippines, and several Latin American countries had close ties to the United States.

In addition to the East-West issues of the Cold War, people began to speak of North-South issues. These issues separated the wealthy, industrialized nations of the northern half of the globe from the poorer countries of the southern half. Not all countries fit the profile of these labels. The Southern Hemisphere nation of New Zealand, for example, was wealthy, while North Korea—a nation in the Northern Hemisphere—was poor.

As the colonial empires faded from view, the concerns of former colonies became increasingly important in international affairs. Although none of these countries possessed the power or wealth of the United States or the Soviet Union, their residents made up a majority of the world's people. This gave the third world a significance that not even the superpowers could ignore.

✔ **READING CHECK:** What were the major concerns of third-world nations during the Cold War?

SECTION  REVIEW

Define and explain the significance of the following terms:
decolonization
neocolonialism
Bandung Conference
nonaligned movement
third world

Identify and explain the significance of the following individuals:
Clement Attlee
Jomo Kenyatta
Jawaharlal Nehru

1. **Using Graphic Organizers** Copy the graphic organizer below and use it to identify the results of postwar independence movements in Africa and Asia.

Country and Colonizer	Results of Independence

2. **Identifying Cause and Effect** How did events in World War II contribute to nationalist independence movements in Asia?
3. **Analyzing** Why do you think many African nations gained their independence after World War II?
4. **Evaluating** Why did many third-world nations join the nonaligned movement?

Critical Thinking

5. Why was the United States sometimes reluctant to give support to independence movements and to newly independent countries?
Consider:
- anti-imperialist policies and beliefs
- potential conflicts with other nations
- anticommunist policies and beliefs

After completing Section 4, students should be able to:

OBJECTIVE 1 *Explain why domestic conflicts were problems for former colonies.*

OBJECTIVE 2 *Summarize the economic and political challenges newly independent African nations faced.*

OBJECTIVE 3 *Describe what problems were faced by nations of the former Soviet sphere.*

LET'S GET STARTED!

To begin the class, tell students to list any facts they know about former colonies in Africa or former Soviet nations. If students cannot recall any facts or news stories, tell them to make educated guesses about the problems and progress these nations might have experienced over the last several years or decades. Ask volunteers to share their information with the class. Tell them that in Section 4 they will learn how these countries have fared since declaring independence.

Legacies of Imperialism

OBJECTIVES

Read to understand:

1. why domestic conflicts were problems for former colonies
2. what economic and political challenges newly independent African nations faced
3. what problems were faced by nations of the former Soviet sphere

KEY TERMS

Berlin Conference
Organization of African Unity

KEY PLACES

Kenya
Nigeria
Rwanda

"The government of President Mobutu [in Zaire] has been maintained by a series of military interventions by NATO [the Western military alliance], spearheaded by France, since it was installed."

—Yusufu Bala Usman

President Mobutu Sese Seko

Nigerian political scientist Yusufu Bala Usman protested central Africa's continued dependence on the French in the 1980s. Usman argued that most governments in central Africa "were installed and are maintained by [a] French military presence." This continued many of the problems and injustices of colonial rule. Even after gaining independence, many former Asian and African colonies faced economic, social, and political challenges related to their colonial histories.

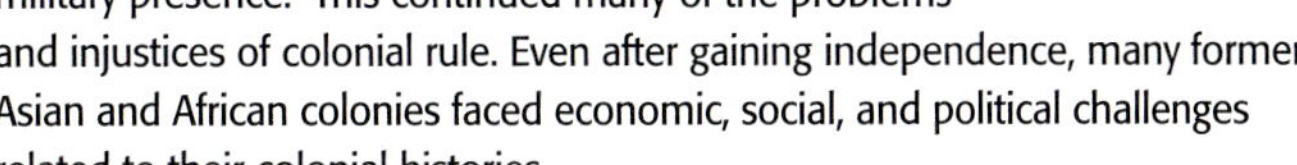

Problems of Independence

The nonaligned movement helped newly independent nations find ways to interact with Europe, the Soviet Union, and the United States. The new nations also faced the difficult tasks of addressing domestic conflicts and establishing political and economic systems.

Apart from small groups of Western-educated nationalists, few people in many of the new nations felt any sense of national identity or loyalty to their governments. Some new nations were made up of many diverse groups of people who had never before been politically unified. This lack of national identity created problems for the countries' new leaders. They often relied on their families and ethnic communities for support. Many leaders also turned to the military to preserve order. As a result, military dictatorships sprang up in many Asian and African nations that gained independence.

National borders were another issue. In many cases, the boundaries established prior to or at independence created terrible conflicts. It was common for different cultural groups to claim the same territory. India and Pakistan, for example, have repeatedly fought over the boundary province of Kashmir. This conflict continued in 1999. India has also suffered from internal conflict between Muslims and Hindus. In the Middle East, violence has raged for decades as Israelis and Arabs have struggled for control over territory considered holy by Christians, Jews, and Muslims.

✔ **READING CHECK:** Why were domestic conflicts problems for former colonies?

Sudan raises its flag and lowers the British flag after gaining independence.

SECTION 4 RESOURCES

PRINT

- Guided Reading Strategy 27.4
- Section 4 Review, p. 823
- Daily Quiz 27.4

MULTIMEDIA

- One-Stop Planner, Lesson 27.4
- Holt Researcher: American History CD–ROM

SHELTERED ENGLISH

- Main Idea Activity for Reteaching and Sheltered English 27.4

✔ **READING TO UNDERSTAND**

To help students master the section objectives, have them answer the **READING CHECKS** and complete **Guided Reading Strategy 27.4** as they read the section.

TEACH OBJECTIVE 1

LEVEL 1: Have students prepare oral presentations explaining why domestic conflicts were problems for former colonies. *(Students should mention that few people felt a sense of national identity, that military dictatorships sprang up, that national borders were in dispute, and that ethnic and religious conflicts erupted.)* **Sheltered English**

LEVELS 2 AND 3: Tell students to imagine that they live in newly independent former colonies. Have them write letters to American pen pals explaining the domestic conflicts their nation is dealing with and how these create problems affecting their daily lives. *(See the Level 1 lesson for the correct conflicts and problems.)* Pair students and have them exchange letters. Ask students to summarize their partners' letters for the class. **Cooperative Learning**

ECONOMIC DEVELOPMENT

Kwame Nkrumah and Ghana. As prime minister and later as president of the new African nation of Ghana, Kwame Nkrumah led efforts to diversify the nation's economy. In the late 1950s Ghana's economy relied almost exclusively on the cocoa crop, but the nation had managed to accumulate some 200 million British pounds in savings. Nkrumah initiated a series of development projects in 1959. The government built a huge dam on the Volta River to produce hydroelectric power. Ghana also became the first West African nation to develop heavy industry, including metallurgy and chemical production. During the 1960s the price for cocoa plummeted, and Ghana's foreign savings were almost completely used up. Nkrumah was forced to abandon his second development plan. In 1966 Nkrumah's regime was overthrown in a military coup.

ACTIVITY: Tell students to imagine that they are Kwame Nkrumah in Ghana in the 1960s. Have them create a pamphlet explaining their development plans.

VISUAL RECORD ANSWER

Students might note that the waterfall is a clearly visible border.

INTERPRETING THE VISUAL RECORD

Drawing borders. Victoria Falls lies along the Zambia-Zimbabwe border. ***Why might a geographic feature such as this waterfall be used to help define an international border?***

Africa: A Case Study

African nations suffered greatly from border disputes, many of which had their origins in the late 1800s. In 1884 the major European powers and the United States held a conference in Berlin, Germany, to decide the future of Africa. Leaders at the **Berlin Conference** arrogantly set policies for the division of Africa into areas of European control. During the establishment of their African colonies, the Europeans ignored features that naturally determined borders, such as landforms or cultural groupings. In some cases, borders lumped together many diverse peoples. Nigeria, for example, was home to more than 250 ethnic groups. In other cases, newly established borders split up ethnic groups. For example, the Somali people found themselves divided among Ethiopia, Kenya, and Somalia.

Striving for unity. By 1963 most of the African nations had gained independence. That year they formed the **Organization of African Unity** (OAU). One of the OAU's main goals was to prevent territorial conflicts among its members. Fearing that redrawing boundaries might spark border disputes, the OAU decided to keep the old colonial boundaries following decolonization. While this decision did limit conflict between African nations, it failed to prevent civil wars within nations.

Ethnic and cultural differences between Sudan's northern and southern regions led to a civil war that continued from independence in 1956 through the 1990s. Civil wars and ethnic conflicts have devastated several other African countries. In Rwanda violence between Hutu and Tutsi factions left an estimated 500,000 people dead in 1994. Millions of Rwandan refugees fled to neighboring countries.

Economic independence. European imperialism left many African nations with limited economies that specialized in producing a few raw materials. Africans thus had little economic diversity to build on. As a result, the countries had difficulty achieving economic self-sufficiency or even creating new international economic ties. Most African nations remained economically dependent on their former colonial rulers. This economic dependence on Europe remains a problem in Africa. During the 1990s just some 5 percent of Africa's total international trade was conducted with other African nations.

Economic independence has been made more difficult by a lack of foreign investment. The small size, political instability, and poverty of many African nations scares away investors. One investment analyst explained the problem.

> **"A lot of African countries, because of their colonial legacy, are so tiny I don't know what they can do. A lot of the products [foreign] companies want to sell, like Coca-Cola [or consumer goods] can't be sold to people without food or running water."**

HOLT RESEARCHER

Read More About It

Free Find: Organization of African Unity

After reading about the Organization of African Unity (OAU) on the **Holt Researcher** CD–ROM, write a short essay describing the goals and work of the organization.

TEACH OBJECTIVE 2

ALL LEVELS: To help students understand the economic and political challenges newly independent African nations faced, copy the following graphic organizer on the chalkboard, omitting the italicized answers. Have each student complete it. **Sheltered English**

Economic Challenges	Political Challenges
• *few raw materials* • *little economic diversity* • *economically dependent on former colonizers* • *lack of foreign investment* • *underdeveloped public services*	• *little education or training for skilled workers or leaders* • *bureaucratic inefficiency* • *political corruption* • *poor economic planning*

▸**ASSIGNMENT:** *Have students use the graphic organizer to write an article for an international newsmagazine entitled* The Legacy of Colonialism in Africa. *Tell students that their articles should include economic and political consequences and mention how some African nations have been working to overcome these problems.*

Managing new governments. In some places European imperialism also failed to prepare Africans for the political challenges they would face following independence. For example, in the former Belgian Congo, Belgians held most government and business jobs during the colonial period. Africans, meanwhile, received little training—not only in government and business but also in services such as education and health care. When the region became independent in 1960, few skilled people remained to manage its affairs effectively. Salim Ahmed Salim, the secretary-general of the OAU, explained that many other African nations faced similar problems. "Colonial education, limited to training very low functionaries [government officials], did not prepare the African for the eventual assumption of leadership and management of the affairs of a modern state."

In many African nations, this lack of political experience has led to problems of bureaucratic inefficiency, political corruption, and poor economic planning. Underdeveloped public services—such as communications and transportation systems—have made trade and investment more difficult.

Not all of Africa's problems can be blamed on its colonial heritage, however. Some parts of Africa have limited natural resources. Droughts and other natural disasters have also contributed to many African nations' lack of prosperity. Nevertheless, historians agree that the legacy of colonialism continues to have a profound effect on the course of events in African nations.

✔ **READING CHECK:** What were the economic and political consequences of colonialism faced by newly independent African nations?

Africa: Imperialism and Independence, 1950–1998

Learning from Maps By 1950 the major imperial powers in Africa were Belgium, Britain, France, and Portugal.

? PLACE Which African country was the first to become independent after 1950?

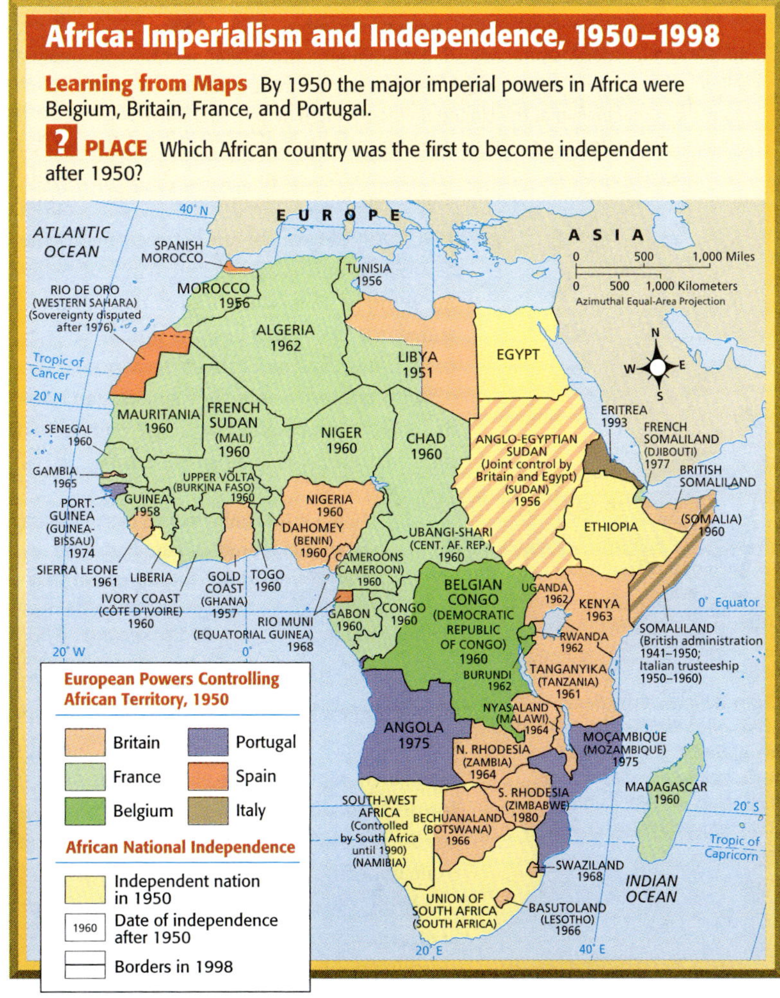

The Soviet Empire Falls

As Africa struggled to shake free of colonial influences in the mid-1980s, the Soviet Union fought to hold together its empire. Sometimes referred to as the Soviet sphere, or bloc, this empire consisted of the Soviet Union's own republics and its satellite nations in

TECHNOLOGY AND SOCIETY

Nuclear Weapons. As the Soviet Union collapsed, it had about 24,500 nuclear warheads located in four former republics. More than 70 percent of Soviet strategic nuclear weapons were located in Russia. Ukraine had the second-largest inventory—about 14 percent—which was a greater arsenal than the combined nuclear forces of Great Britain and France. When the Commonwealth of Independent States demanded that all weapons be moved to Russia for dismantling, the Ukrainian president refused. He worried that Russia would add the weapons to its arsenal instead of disarming them. Ukraine eventually gave up the weapons.

CRITICAL THINKING Why might Ukraine want nuclear weapons?

ANSWER: Students might suggest that possession of such weapons could provide greater political influence.

MAP ANSWER

Libya

TEACH OBJECTIVE 3

LEVEL 1: Have students list the problems faced by nations of the former Soviet sphere. *(Lists might include border disputes, political infighting, underdeveloped economies, ethnic rivalries, limited manufacturing capabilities, breakdown of internal trade network, decreasing value of Russian ruble, and limited foreign investment.)* **Sheltered English**

LEVELS 2 AND 3: Have students complete the Level 1 activity. Then tell them to write paragraphs predicting how the former Soviet sphere might develop economically and politically over the next several decades. Tell students to base their predictions on the progress of the former Soviet nations during their first decade of independence. Call on volunteers to summarize their predictions for the class. Encourage students to respond to each other's ideas.

VISUAL RECORD ANSWER

(for p. 823)

Students might suggest that the destruction reveals that the fighting was severe.

SECTION 4 REVIEW ANSWERS

Define and Identify

For significance, see the following pages:

- Berlin Conference, p. 820
- Organization of African Unity, p. 820

1. problems of independence—lack of national identity, unclear and disputed national boundaries, untrained civil servants, inadequate economic resources, military dictatorships

2. They faced a lack of national identity, ethnic rivalries, and arbitrary international boundaries.

3. Imperialism created limited economies that produced few raw materials. The resulting lack of economic diversity and difficulty of creating economic ties with new countries contributed to dependence on former colonizers.

4. Borders had been determined by colonizers without regard to landforms or cultural groupings. After independence most countries lacked unified populations, and conflicts developed between ethnic groups.

The United States and the Post–Cold War World

As Cold War hostilities began to fade, American commentator Charles Krauthammer wrote, "Nations need enemies. Take away one, and they find another. . . . Countries need mobilizing symbols of 'otherness' to energize the nation and to give it purpose." Krauthammer worried that with the decline of the Soviet Union and the end of the Cold War, the United States would lose its sense of purpose.

Others took a more optimistic view of what the United States might be able to accomplish in the post–Cold War era. The major empires have dissolved, and most nations are now independent. True democracy, however, remains a dream in many parts of the world. Some democratic nations hope to convince the rest of the world of democracy's ability to ease social and economic problems.

Economic and political realities have continued to change during the 1990s. Nevertheless, the appeal of individual freedom, democratic self-government, and opportunity for all remains as strong as ever. Many people believe that the United States should play a central role in helping other countries achieve democracy and freedom.

Eastern Europe. The Soviet sphere began to collapse in the late 1980s. One by one the Eastern European nations broke free of Soviet control. Soon the Soviet republics also declared independence. By 1991 the Soviet Union ceased to exist.

Eastern Europe. The nations created or reshaped by the fall of the Soviet Union found that independence created problems. Many of these challenges are the same ones faced by nations that gained independence earlier in the century. The newly independent nations of Eastern Europe and the former Soviet Union have suffered from border disputes, political infighting, and underdeveloped economies. As in Asia and Africa, ethnic rivalries resurfaced that a strong central authority had previously kept in check.

The former communist-bloc nation of Yugoslavia was devastated by ethnic conflict. Fighting between Croats, Serbs, and Slavic Muslims broke out in the early 1990s. A bitter war began between the former republic of Serbia and the former republic of Bosnia and Herzegovina. Serbian forces carried out ethnic cleansing—the removal of all members of rival ethnic groups from an area. When the war ended in 1995, Serbia began a similar campaign to remove ethnic Albanians from their homes in the Serbian province of Kosovo. Perhaps as many as 200,000 refugees poured over the border between Kosovo and Macedonia during the spring of 1999. Some people feared the conflict would spark another world war. One refugee from Pristina, Kosovo's capital, described her desperate situation.

> **"My place is burning now. I can't go back. . . . I lost my mother and four sisters and a brother. I am here with my father and brother. I can't live without them. I don't know where they are. . . . They [the Serbs] came with masks. . . . They say that, 'This is not your place. This is our place. You must go out.' And we go out."**

This is a piece of the Berlin Wall, which once divided the German city of Berlin. The wall was destroyed by pro-democracy supporters in 1989 as the Communists lost power in East Germany.

The former Soviet Union. Yugoslavia has experienced perhaps the worst of the violence caused by ethnic rivalries, but ethnic tensions have affected the 15 former Soviet republics as well. Russia and Ukraine have argued over control of the former Soviet Black Sea fleet. Russia's Caucasus region remains an area of frequent conflict. Christians in the former Soviet Republic of Armenia have battled Muslims in neighboring Azerbaijan (az-uhr-by-jahn).

Within the Russian Federation itself, ethnic conflict has erupted between the central government and some of its partially self-governing regions with large non-Russian populations. For example, in 1994 fighting broke out in Chechnya between

REVIEW

Have students complete the **Section 4 Review** on p. 823.

ASSESS

Have students complete **Daily Quiz 27.4**. As **Alternative Assessment**, you may want to use the African nations graphic organizer or the former Soviet nations predictions activity in this section's lessons.

RETEACH

Have students complete **Main Idea Activity for Reteaching and Sheltered English 27.4**. Then have each student summarize the entire section in one page. Have students trade summaries with a partner and read each other's work, discussing any differences in content or emphasis.
Sheltered English, Cooperative Learning

EXTEND

Have each student select a nation that was formerly an African or Asian colony or part of the Soviet sphere. Have students use their textbooks, the library, or the Internet to write a short history of that nation since its independence. Tell them to discuss any problems the nation has encountered, the origin of each problem, and how the nation has worked to overcome its problems. Encourage students to include a time line of important events with their reports. **Block Scheduling**

---

the Russian army and Chechen rebels demanding independence. When the war ended in 1996 the central conflict remained unresolved. Chechen separatists believe Chechnya is fully independent but Russia still considers it a Russian republic.

Economic problems have compounded other challenges created by independence. Under Soviet control, each satellite nation and Soviet republic produced the goods that it could manufacture or grow best. Each part of the Soviet Empire relied on the other parts to supply its needs. When the Soviet Union collapsed, however, so too did the trade networks that had kept this system working. Economic hardships increased as the new nations struggled to establish new trade links and manufacturing capabilities. In August 1998 the Russian ruble decreased in value nearly 15 percent in just two days. People lined up outside their banks to withdraw their savings. One Russian woman declared, "I've got no confidence left in the government. I'd like to be able to buy something with my rubles, which have already become worthless."

The economic collapse hit the Russian military particularly hard. Troops went without pay or adequate housing for months. Some observers feared that the once-proud Red Army might stage a rebellion against the country's leaders.

Russia's instability has hurt foreign investment. "The political situation in Russia is chaotic," noted one business expert. "It's just a much riskier environment." Even so, many people in Eastern Europe and the former Soviet Union hope that free-market reforms and democracy will one day bring prosperity.

✔ **READING CHECK:** What problems faced former Soviet bloc nations?

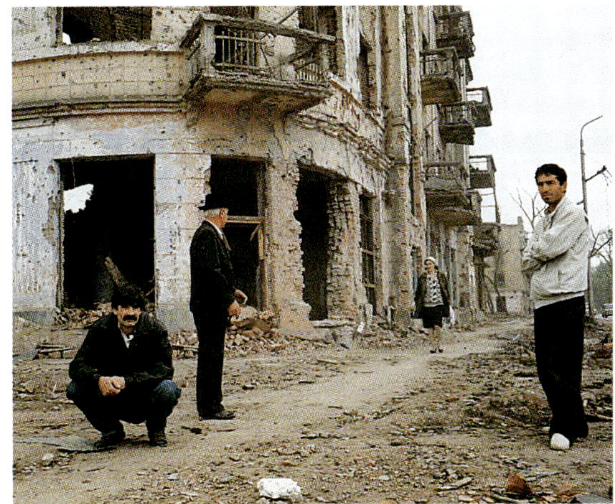

INTERPRETING THE VISUAL RECORD

War. After fleeing their homes during the Russian invasion, these Chechen refugees returned in 1995 to find the city of Grozny in ruins. ***What does this image reveal about the fighting in Chechnya?***

SECTION  REVIEW

Define and explain the significance of the following terms:
Berlin Conference
Organization of African Unity

Locate and explain the importance of the following places:
Kenya
Nigeria
Rwanda

1. **Using Graphic Organizers** Copy the graphic organizer below and use it to describe some of the major challenges faced by nations from the former Soviet sphere and former colonies in Asia and Africa.

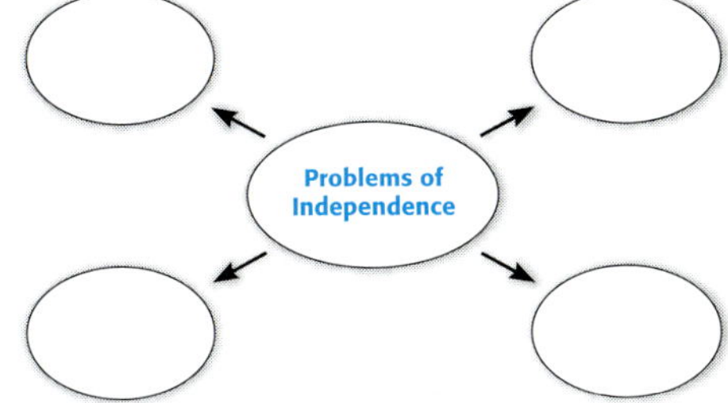

2. **Analyzing** Why might the citizens of newly independent nations have trouble identifying with their new governments?
3. **Assessing Consequences** Why did many African nations experience economic struggles after decolonization?
4. **Identifying Cause and Effect** Why were border disputes a particularly serious problem for newly independent African nations? How did these disputes contribute to ethnic conflict?

Critical Thinking

5. What challenges did countries of the former Soviet sphere face?
Consider:
- conflict among different ethnic groups
- the level of economic ties between parts of the old Soviet Empire
- the need for foreign investment

---

5. Conflict between ethnic groups developed after Soviet control dissolved, specialized economies and trade networks collapsed when the Soviet Union broke apart, and political instability prevented foreign investment, which might have strengthened economies.

CHAPTER 27 REVIEW ANSWERS

Creating A Time Line
Each event should have an explanation and the correct date.

Writing a Summary
See the Reading Checks in each section for main ideas.

Identifying People and Ideas
1. foreign ports where ships could take on coal
2. establishing a completely new government in a colony
3. Indian independence leader known for his nonviolent resistance
4. Philippine independence leader known for charismatic personality and political skills
5. system in which an imperial power controls a country while pretending that the country is independent
6. trying to maintaining indirect control over former colonies
7. Indian prime minister who founded nonaligned movement
8. group of countries whose policy was to avoid alignment with either superpower during the Cold War

REVIEW AND ASSESSMENT RESOURCES

PRINT

- Chapter 27 Review, pp. 824–25
- Chapter 27 Tutorial for Students, Parents, Mentors, and Peers
- Chapter 27 Test (Form A or B)
- Portfolio Activities and Alternative Assessment Handbook, Chapter 27

MULTIMEDIA

- Audio Program, Chapter 27 (English and Spanish)
- Chapter 27 Test Generator (on the One-Stop Planner)
- Global Skill Builder CD–ROM
- HRW Web site

SHELTERED ENGLISH

- Spanish Glossary
- Sheltered English Chapter 27 Test

REVIEW

Have students complete the **Chapter 27 Review** on pp. 824–25.

ASSESS

Use one of the chapter tests to assess students' understanding of the content. For **Alternative Assessment**, see the **Portfolio Activities and Alternative Assessment Handbook.**

9. refers to those countries that were neither first world (capitalist) or second world (communist)

10. meeting of major European powers to decide the future of Africa

Understanding Main Ideas

1. The desire to spread Christianity and Western culture motivated European countries to establish colonies.
2. Industrialization created a need for raw materials, new methods of transportation, and new weapons.
3. The violence caused many Europeans to question their earlier ideas about moral and cultural superiority.
4. Germany, Italy, and Japan
5. marked the beginning of independence movements in Asia
6. European colonizers were weakened by World War II. Native Africans in several colonies began to protest imperial rule.
7. problems both with social structures and with political and economic stability
8. ethnic conflict and economic hardship

Reviewing Themes

1. because the United States was founded on the belief that people had the right to rule themselves
2. Many colonies developed limited economies specializing in producing a few raw materials. These countries found it difficult to become self-sufficient after independence.

Review

Creating a Time Line

Copy the time line below onto a sheet of paper. Complete the time line by filling in the events and dates you think were the most significant. Pick three events and explain why you think they were significant.

Writing a Summary

Using the Reading Checks as a guide, write an overview of the events in the chapter.

Identifying People and Ideas

Identify the following terms or individuals and explain their significance.

1. coaling stations
2. direct rule
3. Mohandas K. Gandhi
4. Manuel Quezon
5. puppet government
6. neocolonialism
7. Jawaharlal Nehru
8. nonaligned movement
9. third world
10. Berlin Conference

Understanding Main Ideas

SECTION 1

1. How did European religious and cultural beliefs affect imperialism during the late 1800s?
2. How did industrialization affect imperialism?

SECTION 2

3. How did World War I affect imperialism?
4. What were the major imperial powers of the 1930s?

SECTION 3

5. How did World War II affect colonialism in Asia?
6. What factors led to the independence of many African colonies?

SECTION 4

7. What are the legacies of imperialism?
8. What challenges have former Soviet-bloc nations faced?

Reviewing Themes

1. **Democratic Values** Why did many Americans oppose imperialism?
2. **Economic Development** How did imperialism affect colonial economies?
3. **Global Relations** What steps did some nations take to avoid becoming involved in the Cold War?

Thinking Critically

1. **Comparing and Contrasting** In what ways did U.S. expansion in the 1800s and early 1900s resemble European expansion? In what ways did it differ?
2. **Hypothesizing** Do you think that wide-scale imperialism would still exist today if World Wars I and II had never happened? Why or why not?
3. **Analyzing** What factors prevented the United States from supporting some countries' bids for independence after World War II?
4. **Identifying Cause and Effect** How did colonization contribute to the many civil wars in newly independent African nations?

Writing About History

Writing to Persuade Imagine that you are the leader of a newly independent nation. Write a speech urging the different factions in the nation to unite peacefully. Explain the benefits of peace. Use the following diagram to organize your thoughts.

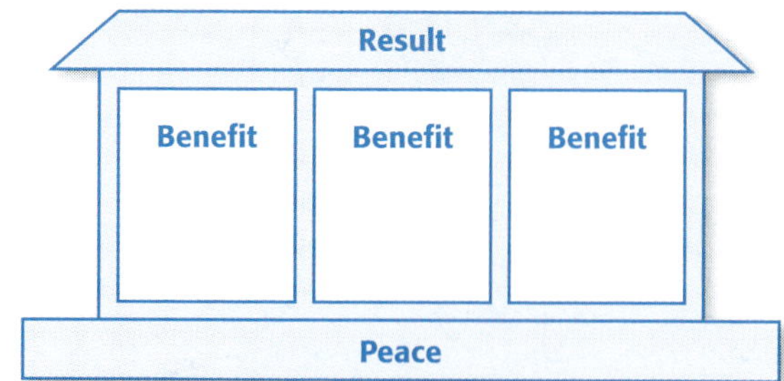

RETEACH

Organize the class into four groups and assign each group one of the sections of this chapter. Have each group create and present a multimedia presentation that covers the important points of its assigned section. Tell students to be sure to cover all the section's objectives in their presentations.
Sheltered English, Cooperative Learning

EXTEND

Have students read the Great Debates feature in Section 4. Then have each student write a newspaper editorial identifying and explaining the role he or she thinks the United States should play in the world in the 2000s and beyond. **Block Scheduling**

Strategies for Success Review the **Strategies for Success** on *Identifying Cause and Effect.* Then read the following excerpt from a speech made by Indonesian nationalist Achmad Sukarno in 1930. Using the information about imperialism from this chapter, examine the causes and effects of the struggle for independence in Indonesia.

> "There is no community of interests between the subject and the object of imperialism. Between the two there is only a contrast of interests and a conflict of needs. All interests of imperialism, social, economic, political, or cultural, are opposed to the interests of the Indonesian people. The imperialists desire the continuation of colonization, the Indonesians desire its abolition. The regulations that came into being under the influence of imperialism are therefore contrary to the interest of the Indonesian people."

Linking History And Geography

After World War II many nations in Southeast Asia gained their independence. Study the map below. During what decade did most of the nations shown become independent?

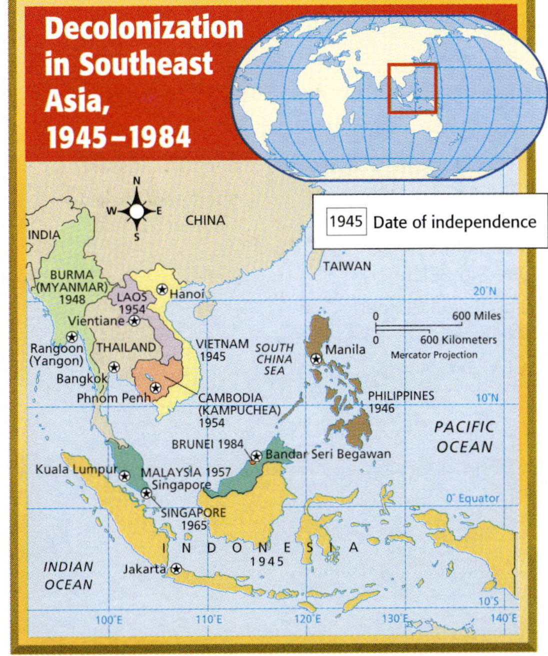

internet connect

TOPIC: Independence and the Philippines
GO TO: go.hrw.com
KEYWORD: SE1 Philippines

Accessing the Internet through the HRW Web site, conduct research on the independence movement in the Philippines. Then write an essay on the process of independence that describes the Tydings-McDuffie Act and the leadership role of Manuel Quezon.

BUILDING YOUR PORTFOLIO

Complete one or all of the following projects independently or cooperatively.

1 Economic Development

Imagine you that are an economist in an independent nation that was a colony for the first half of the 1900s. ***Create a flowchart*** tracing the relationship between your nation's colonial background and current economic status.

2 Democratic Values

Imagine that you are a member of an independence movement in a region under imperial control in the mid-1900s. ***Write a poem*** describing how imperialism has interfered with the rights of your region's inhabitants.

3 Global Relations

Imagine that you are the political leader of a developing country during the Cold War. ***Write a policy statement*** explaining why your government should join the nonaligned movement. Explain why the country should not align with capitalist or communist nations.

The Bandung Conference

3. Some formed the nonaligned movement, while others accepted aid from the United States or the Soviet Union.

Thinking Critically

1. similarities—largely ignored wishes of original inhabitants of conquered lands; differences—allowed territories to become states with equal status

2. Answers will vary. Some students may argue that many nations would still be colonies because European nations would not have been devastated by war. Others may believe that independence movements would have developed despite wars.

3. potential conflicts with other nations, anticommunist policies

4. arbitrary borders drawn by colonizers, dependent economies, lack of leadership training and experience

Writing About History

Students' speeches will vary but might include the problems posed by ethnic conflict and the benefits of unity and diversity.

Strategies for Success

Answers will vary but should discuss the causes and effects of independence in Indonesia.

Linking History and Geography

1940s

The Rise of the Global Economy

CHAPTER PLANNING GUIDE

	Section Lesson Objectives	Print Resources	Multimedia Resources	Sheltered English Resources
Section 1 Industrialization and Global Trade, pp. 828–31	1 Explain why American merchants sought out new foreign markets. 2 Describe how U.S. exports changed in the early 1900s. 3 Summarize how improved communications and transportation affected international trade.	▶ Guided Reading Strategy 28.1 ▶ American History Outline Map 24: The World ▶ Graphic Organizer Activity 28: Building a Global Economy ▶ Section 1 Review, p. 831 ▶ Daily Quiz 28.1	▶ One-Stop Planner, Lesson 28.1 ▶ Holt Researcher: American History CD–ROM ▶ HRW Web site	▶ Main Idea Activity for Reteaching and Sheltered English 28.1
Section 2 The Global Economy Before World War II, pp. 832–38	1 Discuss how the gold standard and free trade helped the global economy grow. 2 Explain why some nations supported protectionism. 3 Describe how World War I affected the role of the United States in the global economy. 4 Relate how the Great Depression affected world trade and finance.	▶ Guided Reading Strategy 28.2 ▶ Literature Reading 28: Visions of a Universal Economy ▶ Section 2 Review, p. 838 ▶ Daily Quiz 28.2	▶ One-Stop Planner, Lesson 28.2 ▶ The American Nation Video Program Segment: The Great Depression; Teacher's Guide, pp. 111–16 ▶ Holt Researcher: American History CD–ROM	▶ Main Idea Activity for Reteaching and Sheltered English 28.2
Section 3 The Era of American Dominance, pp. 839–43	1 Explain how the Bretton Woods system attempted to prevent future economic conflicts. 2 Identify factors that contributed to U.S. economic expansion after World War II. 3 Describe how the economies of West Germany and Japan developed after World War II.	▶ Guided Reading Strategy 28.3 ▶ Geography Activity 28: The Marshall Plan ▶ Section 3 Review, p. 843 ▶ Daily Quiz 28.3	▶ One-Stop Planner, Lesson 28.3 ▶ Holt Researcher: American History CD–ROM	▶ Main Idea Activity for Reteaching and Sheltered English 28.3
Section 4 A New Era in Trade, pp. 844–49	1 Discuss how the U.S. dominance of the global economy came to an end. 2 Relate how the economies of Pacific Rim countries fared during the 1980s and 1990s. 3 Explain how the growth of multinational corporations and the end of the Cold War affected the global economy. 4 Identify what evidence points to a recent movement toward global free trade.	▶ Guided Reading Strategy 28.4 ▶ Primary Source Reading 28: The Plight of Industrial Workers ▶ Biography Reading 28: Rosalynn Carter ▶ American History Political Cartoon 30: Multinational Corporations ▶ Section 4 Review, p. 849 ▶ Daily Quiz 28.4	▶ One-Stop Planner, Lesson 28.4 ▶ Holt Researcher: American History CD–ROM	▶ Main Idea Activity for Reteaching and Sheltered English 28.4
Chapter Review and Assessment pp. 850–51		▶ Chapter 28 Review, pp. 850–51 ▶ Chapter 28 Tutorial for Students, Parents, Mentors, and Peers ▶ Chapter 28 Test (Form A or B) ▶ Portfolio Activities and Alternative Assessment Handbook, Chapter 28	▶ Audio Program, Chapter 28 (English and Spanish) ▶ Chapter 28 Test Generator (on the One-Stop Planner) ▶ Global Skill Builder CD–ROM ▶ HRW Web site	▶ Spanish Glossary ▶ Sheltered English Chapter 28 Test

CHAPTER OVERVIEW

The growth of industry in the United States during the 1800s led American merchants to seek new foreign markets for their goods. Aided by the development of the steamship and the telegraph, Americans increased exports to Asia and Latin America. A global shift from protectionism—the protection of domestic industries through tariffs, to free trade promoted global economic development.

World War I shifted financial power from Europe to the United States. During the Great Depression, however, the United States failed to cooperate with European nations in solving the economic crisis. After World War II, the United States took a leadership role, creating monetary and trade agreements intended to promote world economic growth. Although the dominance of the United States declined as the economies of nations such as those of the Pacific Rim grew stronger, it continued to lead the way in the development of multinational corporations and e-commerce on the Internet.

TIME TAMERS

Block Scheduling

The teacher lesson plans for each section offer a variety of activity choices to help you present the material in a block scheduling format. For further suggestions on block scheduling, see the **Block Scheduling Handbook with Team Teaching Strategies**, pp. 163–68.

Smithsonian Institution

Internet Connections and Lesson 28

www.si.edu/hrw

Hands-On History Activities:

Classroom to Community The **Hands-On History Activities** help students make meaningful connections between events in American history and those in their own hometown. You may wish to use the Chapter 28 Activity, Imports and Exports in Your Community, to extend the chapter lessons, as alternative assessment, or as a block scheduling option.

Portfolio Projects

The American Nation includes multiple portfolio projects in each Pupil's Edition chapter review, as well as each unit review. Chapter 28 Portfolio Project options on p. 851 include the following:

1. Students will **create a chart**.
2. Students will **prepare a speech**.
3. Students will **draft a proposal**.

The American Nation

INTERNET RESOURCE DIRECTORY

To access online materials for this chapter, go to **go.hrw.com** and type in the keywords listed below.

HRW ONLINE RESOURCES

GO TO: go.hrw.com

Online Maps
KEYWORD: SE1 Maps28
- The Marshall Plan
- Breakup of the Soviet Sphere

Online Charts
KEYWORD: SE1 Charts28
- U.S. Foreign Trade, 1865–1915
- U.S. Trade Balance

Online Reading Support
KEYWORD: SE1 Strategies28

Online Rubrics
KEYWORD: SE1 Rubrics

CHAPTER ENRICHMENT LINKS

Use these Web links to extend and enrich student learning for Chapter 28.

GO TO: go.hrw.com
KEYWORD: SE1 Ch28

CHAPTER INTERNET ACTIVITIES

GO TO: go.hrw.com

- Pupil's Edition Student Activity
  KEYWORD: SE1 European Union
  (Students conduct research on the European Union.)
- Teacher's Edition Student Activity
  KEYWORD: SE1 Euro
  (Students learn about the euro.)
- Teacher's Edition Student Activity
  KEYWORD: SE1 Radio
  (Students investigate the development of the radio.)

ADDITIONAL

RESOURCES

Books for Teachers

Friedman, Thomas. *The Lexus and the Olive Tree.* Farrar, Straus, and Giroux, 1999. Emphasizes the positive aspects of globalization.

Greider, William. *One World, Ready or Not.* Simon & Schuster, 1997. Examines the consequences of global capitalism.

Books for Students

Epping, Randy C. *A Beginner's Guide to the World Economy.* Random House, 1992. Offers concise explanations of global economic issues.

Halberstam, David. *The Next Century.* Updated ed. Avon, 1992. Analyzes the global economy as the 21st century approached.

Primary Sources from the Period

Dawes, Charles G. *A Journal of Reparations.* Macmillan, 1939. Presents a memoir by the architect of the reparations negotiations.

Keynes, John Maynard. *The Economic Consequences of the Peace.* Penguin, 1988. Critiques the Treaty of Versailles; originally published in 1919.

Multimedia Materials

The Global Assembly Line. Video, 58 min. New Day Films Library. Examines third-world workers in the global economy.

Pacific Horizons: Economic Change and Challenge. 2 Videos, 28 min. Close-Up Foundation/SSSS. Focuses on the importance of Pacific Rim nations.

Before You Read

Build on What You Know

Ask students to answer the following questions.

Why might merchants seek to create international commercial ties?

Consider:

- the need for new markets
- profits to be made by importing goods for sale in the United States

How might new technologies contribute to global trade?

Consider:

- the ability to travel longer distances
- increasing knowledge of new places and goods

exploring the time line

AMERICAN EVENTS

HISTORY MAKERS SPEAK

Herbert Hoover in *The Annals of America*, Vol. 14

1928 ■ Herbert Hoover. In his presidential bid, self-made millionaire Herbert Hoover advocated limited government involvement in business and the economy. He addressed the issue in a campaign speech: "Even if government conduct of business could give us more efficiency instead of less efficiency, the fundamental objection to it would remain unaltered and unabated [not lessened]. It would destroy political equality. . . . It would stifle initiative and invention. It would undermine the development of leadership. . . . It would extinguish equality and opportunity. It would dry up the spirit of liberty and progress."

CRITICAL THINKING Why do you think many Americans supported Hoover?

ANSWER: Students might answer that during the prosperous 1920s many Americans did not want the government to regulate business.

CHAPTER 28

1880–Present

The Rise of the Global Economy

Guglielmo Marconi and his radio

Hoover campaign advertisement

WHY WE SHOULD VOTE FOR HERBERT HOOVER
TOLD IN TALKING MOTION PICTURES

1880
Science and Technology
Australian merchants ship meat to Great Britain for the first time using refrigerated ships.

1890
Politics
The U.S. Congress passes the McKinley Tariff, raising taxes on imported goods.

1900
Business and Finance
Following Britain's lead, the United States adopts the gold standard.

1901
Science and Technology
Guglielmo Marconi invents the wireless telegraph.

1923
World Events
Skyrocketing inflation of the German mark prevents Germany from repaying World War I debts.

1928
Business and Finance
Republican Herbert Hoover wins the presidential election with a pro-business platform.

1880 | 1905 | 1930

A woman lights her stove with German marks

Before You Read

Build on What You Know

International economic affairs have played a large role in American history. Since Christopher Columbus's initial voyage in search of a shorter trade route to Asia, North America has been involved in global trade. American merchants engaged in overseas trade while part of the British Empire. After independence they established their own commercial ties with other nations. In this chapter you will learn how technology contributed to the rise of the global economy. You will also learn about the changes and challenges caused by the growth of this global economy.

826

Think About Themes

To help students create their Themes Journal entries, provide the following examples of appropriate **agree/disagree** *statements.*

Technology and Society

Agree Countries have developed economic relations in order to obtain new technologies.

Disagree Nuclear technology has not encouraged economic relationships.

Global Relations

Agree During the war of 1812, U.S. trade with European countries suffered.

Disagree Wars can lead to the development of new trade relations and industries that continue to exist in peacetime.

Economic Development

Agree High tariffs during the War of 1812 allowed American manufacturing to prosper.

Disagree In response to the Smoot-Hawley Tariff, some countries limited their imports of U.S. goods.

exploring the time line

Tutankhamen's gold mask

Tokyo stock market

1955

1957
Business and Finance
The European Economic Community (EEC) is formed.

1961
Daily Life
The federal minimum wage rises from $1.00 to $1.15 per hour.

1962
The Arts
American John Steinbeck wins the Nobel Prize in literature.

1970
Science and Technology
The first jumbo jet, the Boeing 747, is put into service.

1977
The Arts
The exhibit "Treasures of Tutankhamen" tours the United States, drawing record crowds.

1977
Daily Life
The first automated teller machine (ATM) network is established.

1980

1983
The Arts
The Metropolitan Opera in New York City celebrates its 100th anniversary.

1993
Business and Finance
The U.S. Congress ratifies NAFTA, a free-trade agreement between Canada, Mexico, and the United States.

1997
World Events
After years of impressive economic growth, the Pacific Rim countries slip into recession.

1999

1999
Business and Finance
Eleven members of the European Union adopt a single currency, the euro.

A Boeing 747

internet connect

TOPIC: The Euro
GO TO: go.hrw.com
KEYWORD: SE1 Euro

Have students access the Internet through the HRW Web site to conduct research on the introduction of the euro and its popularity in different countries. Then ask each student to imagine that he or she is a citizen in one of those countries. Have each student write a newspaper editorial that supports or criticizes the euro.

Think About Themes

Themes Journal

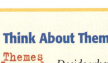

Decide whether you **agree** *or* **disagree** *with the following statements. Note why in your journal.*

Technology and Society Technological advances help shape economic relations between countries.

Global Relations Military conflicts between nations harm global economic development and trade.

Economic Development Limiting the flow of goods imported into a country is good for consumers.

827

SECTION 1

After completing Section 1, students should be able to:

OBJECTIVE 1 *Explain why American merchants sought out new foreign markets.*

OBJECTIVE 2 *Describe how U.S. exports changed in the early 1900s.*

OBJECTIVE 3 *Summarize how improved communications and transportation affected international trade.*

LET'S GET STARTED!

To begin the class, have students read the Alexis de Tocqueville quotation on this page. Then have them write a paragraph stating how de Tocqueville's words, written in 1830, might apply to the world today. Tell them to refer to current technologies that make de Tocqueville's words truer now than they were 170 years ago. Have volunteers summarize their paragraphs for the class. Then tell students that in Section 1 they will learn about how international trade and advances in communications helped create a global economy.

SECTION 1 RESOURCES

PRINT

- Guided Reading Strategy 28.1
- American History Outline Map 24: The World
- Graphic Organizer Activity 28: Building a Global Economy
- Section 1 Review, p. 831
- Daily Quiz 28.1

MULTIMEDIA

- One-Stop Planner, Lesson 28.1
- Holt Researcher: American History CD–ROM
- HRW Web site

SHELTERED ENGLISH

- Main Idea Activity for Reteaching and Sheltered English 28.1

✔ READING TO UNDERSTAND

To help students master the section objectives, have them answer the **READING CHECKS** and complete **Guided Reading Strategy 28.1** as they read the section.

Industrialization and Global Trade

OBJECTIVES

Read to understand:

1. why American merchants sought out new foreign markets
2. how U.S. exports changed in the early 1900s
3. how improved communications and transportation affected international trade

KEY TERMS

staples
perishable goods

KEY PEOPLE

Mark Hanna
Guglielmo Marconi

“At the present time . . . the nations seem to be advancing to unity. Our means of intellectual intercourse [communication] unite the remotest parts of the earth; and men cannot remain strangers to each other, or be ignorant of what is taking place in any corner of the globe.”

—Alexis de Tocqueville

The Paris Exposition of 1889 exhibited new technology.

In 1830 French writer and politician Alexis de Tocqueville predicted that global interaction would bind the many nations of the world together. Events eventually proved de Tocqueville's predictions to be true. Two major developments contributed to the emergence of the global economy during the late 1800s and early 1900s. The first was industrialization, which enabled workers to produce large quantities of goods for export. The second was the introduction of communications and transportation technologies, which brought nations into closer contact with each other. The rapid industrial and technological growth of the United States made it a key player in the developing global economy.

The Rise of American Industry

By 1900 the United States boasted the most powerful industrial economy in the world. American industries produced more than 10 million tons of steel a year, almost as much as Great Britain and Germany combined. American factories and plants rolled out products in record quantities. These products ranged from manufactured goods such as trolley cars to processed agricultural goods such as canned hams.

Industrialization helped bring great prosperity to the United States. It left the U.S. economy vulnerable to cycles of boom and bust, however. The prosperity of boom times could be replaced quickly by an economic recession. In the 1870s and 1890s such economic downturns led to many bankruptcies and layoffs. Part of the problem was that factories and farms equipped with new technology often produced more goods than they could sell. This drove prices down and resulted in business and farm failures.

Many observers believed that the best solution to this problem was to find new markets for American goods. President William McKinley addressed this issue with a gathering of business and civic leaders.

“There is no use in making a product if you cannot find somebody to take it. The maker must find a taker. You will not . . . make a product unless you can find a buyer for that product after you have made it.”

This trade emblem celebrates the industrial advances of the late 1800s.

Near the turn of the century, the most promising place to find the buyers that McKinley spoke of appeared to be overseas. “The time is not

TEACH OBJECTIVE 1

ALL LEVELS: Ask students what two major developments contributed to the emergence of the global economy during the late 1800s and early 1900s. *(Students might answer industrialization and advancements in communications and transportation.)* Then write the following phrase on the chalkboard and have students complete it: *"American merchants began to seek out foreign markets because . . ." (Responses should include that they were producing a surplus of products and needed buyers; that they wished to minimize boom and bust cycles; and that new technologies made it affordable to do business overseas.)* Ask volunteers to read their answers to the class. **Sheltered English**

▶**ASSIGNMENT:** *Have students create an illustrated brochure explaining how industrialization and technological advancements contributed to the emergence of the global economy during the late 1800s and early 1900s.*

far distant," predicted one New York business editor. "When probably all of the principal industries of the Republic will be either compelled [forced] or in a position . . . to seek outlets for their products abroad."

✔ **READING CHECK:** Why did American merchants attempt to seek out new foreign markets?

The Search for Foreign Markets

Since its founding, the United States has maintained close economic ties with European nations. Europeans invested in many emerging American industries, such as railroads. By the late 1800s the European market was increasingly important for U.S. exports as well. In 1900 the value of U.S. exports to Europe exceeded $1 billion for the first time. American exporters also looked for foreign markets in nearby Latin America. The United States had been increasingly involved in Latin American affairs since the announcement of the Monroe Doctrine in 1823. In 1898 U.S. exports to Latin America totaled roughly $90 million. By 1910 that figure had nearly tripled, reaching $263 million.

In addition, American merchants tried to develop new trading partners in Asia. During the mid-1800s the United States had joined major European powers to force China to enter into trade agreements. In the 1850s the United States led the way in opening Japan to foreign commerce. These efforts resulted in increased trade with Asia.

To many Americans, East Asia represented more than a market for exports—it symbolized a new frontier. Some Americans wanted the United States to take over more territory in East Asia in order to provide easier access to foreign markets such as China and Japan. During the debate over U.S. annexation of the Philippines, Senator Mark Hanna of Ohio announced his support of the annexation. "If it is commercialism to want the possession of a strategic point giving the American people an opportunity to maintain a foothold in the markets of . . . [China], for God's sake let us have commercialism."

✔ **READING CHECK:** How did U.S. exports change in the early 1900s?

★ HISTORICAL DOCUMENTS ★

PRESIDENT JAMES MONROE

The Monroe Doctrine

The announcement of the Monroe Doctrine marked an important stage in the growth of the United States as a world economic power. With it, the United States made a declaration to defend not only its own liberty but also the freedom of newly independent Latin American nations. The new policy was created, in part, to protect the countries from economic dominance by European nations. Since its proclamation in 1823, the Monroe Doctrine has contributed to close economic ties between the United States and many Latin American countries.

We . . . declare that we should consider any attempt on their [European power's] part to extend their [political] system to any portion of this hemisphere as dangerous to our peace and safety.

With the existing colonies or dependencies of any European power we have not interfered and shall not interfere. But with the governments who have declared their independence and maintained it, and whose independence we have . . . acknowledged, we could not view any interposition [intervention] for the purpose of oppressing them, or controlling in any other manner their destiny, by any European power in any other light than as the manifestation of an unfriendly disposition toward the United States. . . .

Our policy in regard to Europe . . . remains the same, which is, not to interfere in the internal concerns of any of its powers. . . . But in regard to those continents [of the Western Hemisphere] circumstances are . . . different. It is impossible that the allied powers should extend their political system to any portion of either continent without endangering our peace and happiness. . . . It is equally impossible, therefore, that we should behold such interposition in any form with indifference.

ECONOMIC DEVELOPMENT

American Industrial Growth. Comparing statistics from 1860 and 1900 reveals the phenomenal growth of American industry during the final decades of the 1800s. In 1860 the United States produced about 500,000 barrels of petroleum. By 1900 production had grown to some 46 million barrels, an increase of more than 9,000 percent. In the same four decades, bituminous coal production increased by about 2,400 percent, from 9 million tons annually to some 212 million tons.

CRITICAL THINKING What conclusions might you draw from these statistics?

ANSWER: Students might suggest that the statistics indicate a growing demand for energy resources to fuel industrial growth.

THAT'S INTERESTING!

During the economic crisis of the 1870s, only about 20 percent of American workers held regular full-time jobs. About 40 percent worked for only six or seven months a year. During the 1890s crisis, some 20 percent of American workers were unemployed.

VISUAL RECORD ANSWER

(for p. 830)

Students might suggest that people were not sure that steam power would work.

TEACH OBJECTIVE 2

ALL LEVELS: Distribute copies of Map 24, The World, from **American History Outline Maps**. Have students color in the countries that were affected by changes in U.S. exports during the early 1900s. *(Students should color in China, France, Great Britain, Japan, and the nations of Latin America.)* Then tell students to write a paragraph on the back of the map explaining the results of the merchants' efforts. *(Students might answer that European markets became increasingly important; exports to Latin America tripled; the Japanese market opened; and trade with East Asia grew.)* **Sheltered English**

TEACH OBJECTIVE 3

ALL LEVELS: To help students understand how improved communications and transportation affected international trade, copy the following graphic organizer on the chalkboard, omitting the italicized answers. Have each student complete it. **Sheltered English**

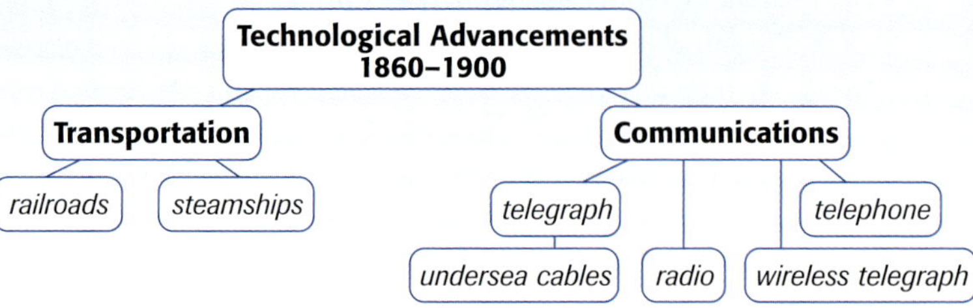

GLOBAL RELATIONS

Trade with Japan. In 1866 the United States exported goods worth about $1 million to Japan. The value of U.S. exports to Japan reached a high point in 1920 at some $378 million. Exports to Japan would not again reach or exceed that amount until 1949. In 1996 the United States exported goods worth some $67 billion to Japan, more than U.S. exports to such countries as Brazil, France, Germany, and Mexico.

CRITICAL THINKING Why might U.S. exports to Japan have declined after 1920?

ANSWER: Students might suggest that the Great Depression and World War II affected trade between the two nations.

 internet**connect**

TOPIC: The Radio
GO TO: go.hrw.com
KEYWORD: SE1 Radio

Have students access the Internet through the HRW Web site to conduct research on the development and use of the radio. Then have each student make a time line that describes the history of the radio. Ask them to include information on improvements in radio technology and the use of radios for communication, entertainment, and public information.

INTERPRETING THE VISUAL RECORD

Sea travel. This iron steamship from the mid-1800s has both a paddle wheel to travel using steam power and sails to make use of wind. ***Why do you think this early steamship had a dual system?***

A Shrinking Planet

Rapid strides in technology helped the United States increase its involvement in world trade. The emergence of a global economy was made possible by new developments in two key areas: transportation and communications.

Faster travel. For most of human history, transportation and communication had been closely linked. Messages typically traveled no faster than the people who carried them. The speed of travel changed very little over the centuries. However, industrialization brought dramatic improvements to transportation and communications during the 1800s.

Railroads greatly increased the speed at which people and goods could travel over land. A railroad journey across Europe or North America took days instead of weeks or even months by horse-drawn carriage. Although railroads cost more to build and operate than the animal-drawn vehicles they replaced, they were more profitable. Between 1860 and 1880, railroad mileage in both Europe and the United States more than tripled. The invention of steamships had a major impact on sea travel. Because they did not depend on unpredictable winds, steamships were quicker and more reliable than sailing vessels. This helped increase business and decrease shipping costs. By the mid-1890s ocean shipping cost half of what it had in the 1870s.

Breakthroughs in communications. The development of the telegraph in the early 1800s made it possible for the first time to send messages almost instantly. By the 1860s an undersea telegraph cable connected Europe and North America. Before long, several cables crossed the ocean floor, and messages could be exchanged between continents in minutes. "At twenty-five cents a word the fourteen Atlantic cables now in operation are fully occupied during the business hours of the day," noted a *New York Times* editorial in 1901. The invention of the telephone in 1876 ultimately provided an even easier means of communication. Telegraphs required skilled operators. In contrast, the telephone was simple to use and allowed people to speak directly to each other. In 1915, telephone lines linked the East and West Coasts. By the late 1920s telephone service across the Atlantic was also available to U.S. residents.

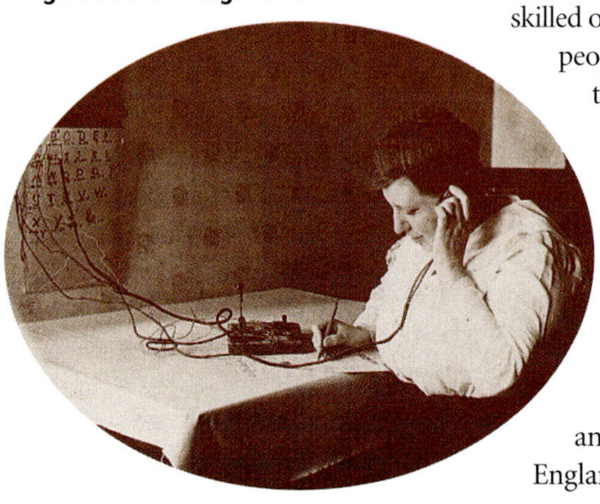

Telegraph and telephone use was limited, however. The cables and wires were expensive to install and could carry only a limited number of messages at a time. Italian scientist Guglielmo Marconi helped solve this problem. He invented a wireless telegraph—an early type of radio—that could send and receive electric signals over long distances. On December 12, 1901, Marconi sat at a tower in St. John's, Newfoundland, and received the Morse code signal for the letter *s* from Cornwall, England. Marconi's achievement astounded one writer:

Using a system called Morse code, telegraph operators translated words into pulses of electricity that could be sent long distances through wires.

REVIEW

Have students complete the **Section 1 Review** on p. 831.

ASSESS

Have students complete **Daily Quiz 28.1**. As **Alternative Assessment**, you may want to use the graphic organizer activity or the brochure in this section's lessons.

RETEACH

Have students complete **Main Idea Activity for Reteaching and Sheltered English 28.1**. Then organize students into triads and assign one Reading Check question to each group member. Direct students to write a paragraph answering their assigned questions and then pass the completed answers to the other group members to read. Finally, have students take turns quizzing each other about the information within their groups. **Sheltered English, Cooperative Learning**

EXTEND

Have students write six entries for an American merchant ship's log during the late 1800s to early 1900s. Entries should reflect changes over a period of years in trading destinations, cargoes carried, technology, speed and frequency of trips, and so on. **Block Scheduling**

> **"** The animating [motivating] spirit of modern invention is to overcome the obstacles of time and space, 'to associate all the races of mankind,' by bringing them nearer together. Commerce, of course, has done more than any other agency to make that association intimate and lasting. . . . Wireless telegraphy will soon prove to be not a mere 'scientific toy' but a system for daily and common use. **"**

The new communications technology had a tremendous impact on daily life. Radio enabled people to learn of events around the world as they happened. It also transformed business practices by allowing companies to advertise their products as never before.

New industrial machinery developed during the late 1800s, such as that produced by the McCormick Harvesting Machine Company, increased the productivity of American farms.

A world of goods. Advances in transportation and communications lowered the cost of many **staples**—goods that are in constant demand and that are often sold in bulk. For example, before the late 1800s American farmers could grow large amounts of wheat but could not afford to ship it to European markets. Railroads and steamships dramatically reduced shipping costs. The telegraph allowed exporters to keep track of grain prices, which can change wildly with news of droughts, wars, and other disasters. Grain dealers could thus find the best markets. As a result, U.S. exports of wheat and flour rose rapidly, from less than $10 million in 1850 to more than $220 million in 1880.

Technological advances also made it possible to trade a wider variety of goods. In the 1870s and 1880s refrigeration was introduced. This technology greatly expanded trade in **perishable goods**—goods that spoil quickly—such as meats, dairy products, and fruits. These changes greatly increased trade in America and expanded exportation of goods abroad.

✔ **READING CHECK:** How did improved communications and transportation affect international trade?

SECTION  REVIEW

Define and explain the significance of the following terms:
staples
perishable goods

Identify and explain the significance of the following individuals:
Mark Hanna
Guglielmo Marconi

1. **Using Graphic Organizers** Copy the graphic organizer below. Use it to explain the effects of industrialization on the U.S. economy in the late 1800s.

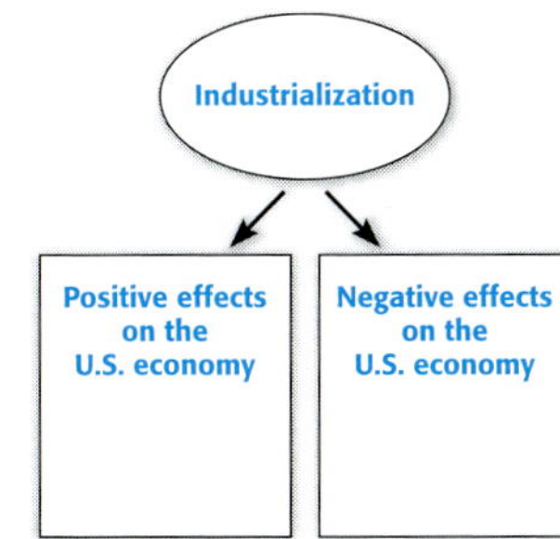

2. **Identifying Cause and Effect** Why did American businesses seek new markets in the early 1900s? Where did they seek these markets?
3. **Evaluating** How have technological innovations influenced global trade?
4. **Hypothesizing** How might the increased involvement of Latin American and Asian countries in the global economy have affected everyday life in those regions?

Critical Thinking

5. How did advances in transportation and communications benefit both merchants and consumers?
Consider:
- what caused prices to change
- how shipping costs were affected
- the availability of goods

SECTION 1 REVIEW ANSWERS

Define and Identify
For significance, see the following pages:
- Mark Hanna, p. 829
- Guglielmo Marconi, p. 830
- staples, p. 831
- perishable goods, p. 831

1. positive—greater variety of manufactured goods, increased farm production; negative—economy tied to business cycle, business and farm failures due to overproduction
2. to sell surplus goods and products; East Asia, Europe, Latin America
3. Advances in communications have allowed greater contact between distant regions and markets, and improvements in transportation have made shipping faster and cheaper.
4. These countries may have shifted from agriculture to industry, and more goods might have become available for purchase.
5. The price of many goods fell as railroads and steamships lowered shipping costs and communications allowed better marketing. A wider variety of goods became available as refrigeration expanded trade in perishable goods.

SECTION 2

After completing Section 2, students should be able to:

OBJECTIVE 1 *Discuss how the gold standard and free trade helped the global economy grow.*

OBJECTIVE 2 *Explain why some nations supported protectionism.*

OBJECTIVE 3 *Describe how World War I affected the role of the United States in the global economy.*

OBJECTIVE 4 *Relate how the Great Depression affected world trade and finance.*

LET'S GET STARTED!

Write the following terms on the chalkboard: *gold standard, free trade, protectionism,* and *devaluation.* To begin the class, have students use each of these words in a sentence, referring to the glossary as necessary. When students have finished writing, have volunteers read one or more of their sentences to the class. Tell students that in Section 2 they will learn about changes in global trade during the early 1900s.

SECTION 2 RESOURCES

PRINT
- Guided Reading Strategy 28.2
- Literature Reading 28: Visions of a Universal Economy
- Section 2 Review, p. 838
- Daily Quiz 28.2

MULTIMEDIA
- One-Stop Planner, Lesson 28.2
- The American Nation Video Program Segment: The Great Depression; Teacher's Guide, pp. 111–16
- Holt Researcher: American History CD–ROM

SHELTERED ENGLISH
- Main Idea Activity for Reteaching and Sheltered English 28.2

✔ READING TO UNDERSTAND
To help students master the section objectives, have them answer the **READING CHECKS** and complete **Guided Reading Strategy 28.2** as they read the section.

The Global Economy Before World War II

OBJECTIVES

Read to understand:
1. how the gold standard and free trade helped the global economy grow
2. why some nations supported protectionism
3. how World War I affected the role of the United States in the global economy
4. how the Great Depression affected global trade and finance

KEY TERMS

Gold Standard Act
free trade
Cobden-Chevalier Treaty
protectionism
McKinley Tariff
Dawes Plan
Young Plan
devaluation

KEY PEOPLE

Robert Peel
John Maynard Keynes
Charles Gates Dawes

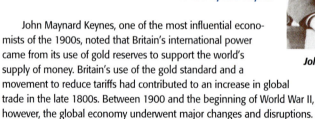

"During the latter half of the nineteenth century the influence of London on credit conditions throughout the world was so predominant [important] that the Bank of England could almost have claimed to be the conductor of the international orchestra."

—John Maynard Keynes

John Maynard Keynes

John Maynard Keynes, one of the most influential economists of the 1900s, noted that Britain's international power came from its use of gold reserves to support the world's supply of money. Britain's use of the gold standard and a movement to reduce tariffs had contributed to an increase in global trade in the late 1800s. Between 1900 and the beginning of World War II, however, the global economy underwent major changes and disruptions.

The Gold Standard

Technological improvements in transportation and communications were only partly responsible for the growth of the global economy in the late 1800s. Economic policies that affected international trade also played a role. One such policy involved the gold standard. Under this monetary system, a nation can exchange its currency for a fixed amount of gold. The gold standard linked the value of a nation's currency with the relatively stable price of gold.

Britain had long used the gold standard. Governments were at times reluctant to tie their currencies to gold, however, because doing so would decrease their control over the value of their currencies. In 1898 British economist David Hume wrote that he believed these fears were groundless. "I should as soon dread, that all our springs and rivers should be exhausted, as that money should abandon a kingdom where there are people and industry." By the end of the 1800s most industrial nations had adopted the gold standard. They were partly influenced by Britain's leading role in the global economy. The discovery of large gold supplies in Australia, Canada, South Africa, and the United States also made the use of the standard more practical. The rising reserves of gold allowed for the printing of additional currency.

The United States officially adopted the gold standard in 1900, when Congress passed the **Gold Standard Act**. The act declared that the gold dollar "shall be the standard unit of value." The value of every U.S. dollar was set to be worth .04837 ounces of pure gold.

As the gold standard became widespread, it brought greater stability to global trade. Merchants doing business in foreign countries did not have to worry about exchange rates. For example, an American selling wheat in Germany could be confident of the worth of the marks paid by the German customer.

During the early 1900s the value of British currency was tied to the value of gold.

TEACH OBJECTIVE 1

LEVEL 1: Ask students to define gold standard and free trade. *(Students might define gold standard as a system by which a nation's currency may be exchanged for gold at a fixed rate, and free trade as international trade not regulated by government.)* Then pair students and have each pair write a paragraph explaining how the gold standard and free trade helped the global economy grow. *(Paragraphs might include that the gold standard gave trade greater stability and free trade brought new and less expensive products to European communities.)* Ask volunteers to read their paragraphs to the class. **Sheltered English, Cooperative Learning**

LEVELS 2 AND 3: Organize students into groups of four and have them imagine that they are representatives of an international trade commission during the 1800s and early 1900s. Tell them that their purpose is to persuade reluctant governments to adopt the gold standard and sign free trade agreements with the United States and its favored trading partners. Have each group either write a persuasive paper or give an oral presentation discussing how the gold standard and free trade helped the global economy grow. **Cooperative Learning**

Free Trade

International commerce was also boosted by the move toward **free trade.** This is trade between nations that is free from government regulation. Until the mid-1800s most nations placed tariffs, or duties, on foreign goods. These tariffs supplied revenues to the governments while protecting domestic producers from foreign competition.

As with the gold standard, Britain led the way in reducing and eliminating tariffs. Sir Robert Peel, the British prime minister during the 1840s, believed that his country's industry was the world's most advanced and did not require protection. He abolished or lowered tariffs on hundreds of items.

Peel also believed that increased free trade might make it easier to sell British goods in foreign markets. If Britain lowered its tariffs, other countries might lower theirs. France and other European countries soon moved toward free trade as well. In 1860 France and Britain signed the **Cobden-Chevalier Treaty,** in which they agreed to remove or reduce tariffs on each other's imports. The treaty included a key provision enabling Britain and France to benefit whenever one of them negotiated tariff reductions with a third country.

Soon a network of treaties—each with similar tariff rules—governed trade among the European nations. This meant that whenever two countries agreed to a tariff reduction, the reduction applied to almost all European countries. As a result, trade among European nations roughly doubled between 1850 and 1870. The expansion of trade resulting from the reduction of tariffs brought new and less expensive products to European communities.

Sir Robert Peel worked to reduce tariffs in Britain, hoping other countries would do likewise.

✔ **READING CHECK:** How did the gold standard and free trade help the global economy grow?

Protectionism

Despite its benefits, free trade still had critics. These opponents wanted **protectionism**—the use of tariffs to protect domestic industrial and agricultural producers. Protectionists argue that free trade exposes domestic companies to unfair foreign competition. When foreign goods cost less than domestic goods, consumers are less likely to buy domestic products. This hurts domestic industries and can lead to layoffs and unemployment.

European concerns. When the global economy sank into a depression in the 1870s, many industrialists blamed free trade practices. They pushed for a return to protectionism. Farmers also increased their demands for protection. Prior to 1870 the distance and expense of overseas shipping had made foreign farm products too expensive to compete with domestic goods. This changed, however, when technological improvements decreased transportation costs and allowed perishable goods to be shipped. Facing increased competition, European farmers wanted protection. Many countries—beginning with Germany in 1879—approved new tariffs. Before long, tariff wars broke out between European nations. Trade between France and Italy

INTERPRETING THE VISUAL RECORD

British industry. British workers and entrepreneurs in industries such as textiles worried that reducing tariffs would hurt them. ***How do you think that greater international competition might hurt these workers?***

ECONOMIC DEVELOPMENT

Tariffs. Nations have long relied on tariffs as a source of revenue. The first U.S. tariff, the Tariff Act of 1789, was intended to generate income for the government. As late as the second half of the 1800s, tariff revenues made up a significant portion of the U.S. government's income. However, the importance of tariffs as a source of revenue declined during the 1900s.

CRITICAL THINKING Why might tariffs no longer be as important as sources of revenue?

ANSWER: Students might mention that the government now relies upon taxes, such as the income tax, for most of its revenue.

THAT'S INTERESTING!

During the 1890s Russia and Germany engaged in a tariff war. German duties on Russian goods were 115 percent higher than those on American goods, and Russian duties on German products were 50 percent higher than those imposed on other countries.

VISUAL RECORD ANSWER

Students might answer that laborers would have to work harder or lose their jobs.

TEACH OBJECTIVE 2

LEVEL 1: Ask a volunteer to define protectionism. *(Students might define protectionism as the use of tariffs to protect domestic industries and agriculture).* Then have each student create a poster that explains why some nations supported protectionism. Posters should include an image and reasons to support protectionism. The target audience is the general public, whose votes and opinions will influence legislators' economic decisions. *(Posters' reasons might include protecting domestic industries and agriculture and therefore jobs.)* Display posters around the classroom. **Sheltered English**

LEVEL 2: Tell students to imagine that it is the late 1800s. Have them write a letter to the editor of a U.S. newspaper supporting protectionism. Students should list why some nations supported protectionism. *(See the Level 1 lesson for the correct reasons.)* Ask volunteers to read their letters to the class. Students may wish to include their letters in their portfolios.

DEMOCRATIC VALUES

The McKinley Tariff. President McKinley and his fellow Republicans crafted a tariff bill that would gain favor with groups throughout American society. To appeal to New England shoe and clothing manufacturers, McKinley allowed cattle hides to enter the country with no tariff. To please western farmers, the bill raised the tariff on farm products such as potatoes and eggs. In an effort to protect the tin found in South Dakota, it placed high duties on imported tin.

CRITICAL THINKING Why might McKinley have made certain that his tariff bill contained provisions regarding different regions of the country?

ANSWER: Students might suggest that he wanted to ensure that Congress would pass the bill.

STRATEGIES FOR SUCCESS

Practicing the Strategy

1. 1860–65
2. 1860, 1920, 1950s to the present
3. the Great Depression

decreased by half between 1887 and 1898. The British Parliament passed a law requiring foreign goods to be labeled to indicate where they were made. Parliament hoped that British consumers would refuse to buy goods that were marked "Made in Germany."

Strategies for Success — Reading Graphs

Graphs are used to organize information in a visual manner. Several types of graphs are particularly useful. A *line graph,* which has both a horizontal and a vertical axis, plots changes in quantities over time. A *bar graph* can also be used to show changes in quantities over time, but is most often used to compare amounts within categories. A *pie chart,* or *circle graph,* displays proportions by dividing a circle into sections, with the whole equaling 100 percent.

How to Read a Graph

1. **Read the title.** Read the title to identify the topic of the graph.
2. **Study the labels.** Read the labels that define each axis, bar, or section of the graph to identify the type of information that each presents.
3. **Analyze the details.** Study the information in the graph. Take note of time intervals, increases or decreases in quantities, and proportions.
4. **Put the data to use.** Use your analysis of the data, along with your knowledge of the historical period, to form generalizations and draw conclusions.

Applying the Strategy

Study the line graph below, which shows the average tariff rates in the United States from 1825 to 1995.

Practicing the Strategy

Use the graph below to answer the following questions.

1. During which 5-year period did the tariff rate increase most rapidly?
2. Identify times in which the tariff rate has been the lowest in the United States.
3. What historic event may have contributed to the highest peaks on the graph after 1905?

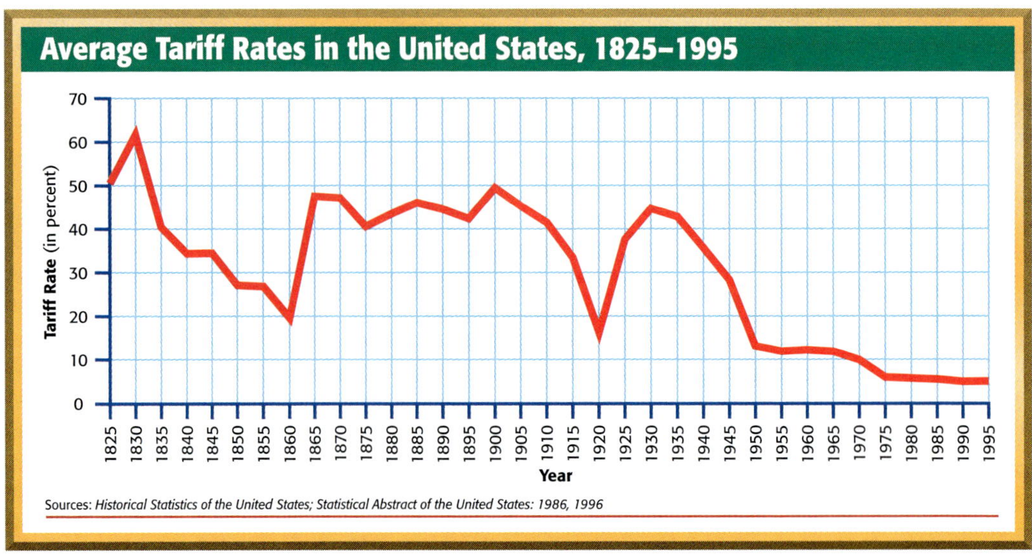

TEACH OBJECTIVE 3

LEVEL 3: Pair students and tell them to imagine that they are lobbyists for two American industries in the late 1800s. One industry supports protectionism while the other demands free trade. Tell students to develop and present opposing persuasive speeches, imagining that the audience is a group of legislators about to vote on new trade policies. *(See the Level 1 lesson for the correct reasons supporting protectionism. Speeches in support of free trade might mention that some companies are strong enough not to need protection and that free trade could lead to overall economic growth.)* Ask volunteers to present their speeches to the class. **Cooperative Learning**

LEVEL 1: Have students make a bulleted list of how World War I affected the role of the United States in the global economy. *(Lists should mention that the United States became a leading financial power and a creditor nation.)* Call on volunteers to read their lists, then record them on the chalkboard for students' reference. **Sheltered English**

U.S. tariffs. Americans had not embraced free trade as enthusiastically as Europeans had. Before the Civil War, however, southern planters who favored free trade had pressured members of Congress to keep tariff rates relatively low. The North's victory in the Civil War enabled the Republican Party to dominate national politics. Northern business leaders who favored protectionist policies gained influence. This change, combined with the economic depressions of the late 1800s, led to a surge of U.S. protectionism.

In 1890 William McKinley, then a U.S. congressmember, sponsored a tariff bill, which Congress passed. This **McKinley Tariff** increased the number of imported goods subject to tariffs and raised tariff rates steeply. Later laws raised tariff rates even higher. When American voters blamed high tariffs for rising living costs, Congress reduced the rates. However, U.S. trade policy remained firmly protectionist.

✔ **READING CHECK:** Why did some nations support protectionism?

After World War I, Allied nations drafted the Treaty of Versailles, which demanded large war reparations from Germany.

World War I and the Peace Settlement

World War I dramatically reshaped the global economy by disrupting the newly developed trade networks. The war cut off trade between warring countries and led to attempts to prevent neutral countries from trading with enemies.

Debt and repayment. A more lasting effect of the war was a shift in the balance of financial power from Britain and other European countries to the United States. From the American Revolution until World War I, the United States was a debtor nation, owing money to other countries. During the 1800s Americans had borrowed money from Europe to finance industrialization and expansion. During World War I, however, the Allied Powers—Britain, France, Italy, and Russia—turned to the United States for goods and for money to finance the war effort. The United States became a creditor nation, lending money to other countries.

After the war, the Allies believed that their debts to the United States should be canceled. However, the U.S. government disagreed. The money loaned to the Allies had come from the American people—partly through the sale of Liberty Bonds. If the debts were canceled, individual Americans would be the ones to suffer.

Repaying the loans, however, was not a simple matter. The Allies—particularly France—could not afford to repay their debts without first receiving the German reparations required by the Treaty of Versailles. Skyrocketing inflation in Germany, however, left it unable to pay. By November 15, 1923, more than 4 trillion German marks were needed to buy a single U.S. dollar. The mark was literally worth less than the paper on which it was printed.

The Dawes and Young Plans. British economist John Maynard Keynes was concerned by the debt situation left by World War I. He wrote:

GLOBAL RELATIONS

U.S. Economic Power. By 1914 American companies had invested some $2.5 billion in foreign enterprises and loaned an additional $1 billion to foreign borrowers. That same year, the United States exported some $1.3 billion in goods. Two years later, while Europe fought World War I, U.S. exports totaled some $5.5 billion. As European businesses sold off their foreign assets to pay for the costs of the war, American firms often stepped in, increasing their total foreign investment.

ACTIVITY: Have students create a chart or graph comparing U.S. loans and exports to Europe before, during, and after World War I.

THAT'S INTERESTING!

War debts to the United States ranged from about $2 million, which Hungary owed, to the $4.6 billion debt of Great Britain.

The American Nation **VIDEO PROGRAM**

The Great Depression; Teacher's Guide, pp. 111–16

Search 25392, Play to 31485
Videodisc 2, Side A

Play

Pause

See *Teacher's Guide* for Spanish barcode.

LEVELS 2 AND 3: Have students complete the Level 1 activity. Then organize students into groups and have them develop short presentations examining how the loans the United States made during the war contributed to its rise as a financial power. *(Students might answer that the loans made the United States a creditor nation and that after the war, U.S. loans to Germany allowed Germany to pay its reparations, which in turn allowed the Allies to pay their war debts to the United States.)* Encourage students to use visual aids in their presentations.

Cooperative Learning

▶ASSIGNMENT *Have students conduct research on how much money the United States currently borrows from other nations. Students should report their findings in a chart or graph.*

ECONOMIC DEVELOPMENT

German Hyperinflation. In 1914 it took 4.2 German marks to purchase one U.S. dollar. By 1918 the dollar was worth 7.43 marks, and by February 1920, the exchange rate was 100 marks to the dollar. In early 1921 the exchange rate stabilized at about 60 marks to the dollar, but over the next two years Germany experienced hyperinflation, and the mark became virtually worthless.

CRITICAL THINKING What effect might hyperinflation have had on German society?

ANSWER: Students might suggest that hyperinflation led to social unrest and to the rise of radical political groups.

THAT'S INTERESTING!

By 1980 the West German government had repaid the $210 million that Germany received under the Dawes Plan, but it did not pay any interest. In 1995 the German government announced that it would pay the $70 million in interest by exchanging Dawes Plan bonds for new German bonds that earned 3 percent interest.

836

"The war has ended with everyone owing everyone else immense sums of money. Germany owes a large sum to the Allies. The Allies owe a large sum . . . to the United States. The holders of war loans in every country are owed a large sum by their . . . states. . . . The whole position is in the highest degree . . . vexatious [distressing]. We shall never be able to move again unless we can be free of these paper shackles [chains]."

The U.S. government took the first step toward correcting the situation when it formed a committee to study the war-debt issue. Chicago banker Charles Gates Dawes was chosen to head the committee.

Charles Gates Dawes

Charles Gates Dawes was born in Marietta, Ohio, in 1865. After attending law school in Cincinnati, he practiced law in Nebraska between 1887 and 1894. In 1897 he became U.S. comptroller of the currency, then returned to private business in 1902. Dawes also served as a brigadier general in World War I, as the first director of the U.S. Bureau of the Budget, and as vice president under Calvin Coolidge. He remained active in the world of finance until his death.

In 1924 Dawes's committee arranged for a $200 million loan to help Germany meet the Allies' reparation demands. Under what became known as the **Dawes Plan**, American bankers provided about $100 million of the loan. Germany's payments thus enabled the Allies to repay their war debts to the United States. The Dawes Plan also rewrote the schedule of reparations. In 1925 Dawes received the Nobel Peace Prize.

The plan operated successfully for several years before being replaced by the **Young Plan**. This plan was named for American businessman Owen D. Young, who hoped to further ease Germany's debt by spreading the payments—totaling about $29 billion, including interest—over 59 years.

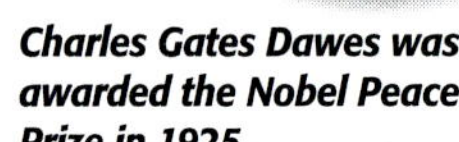
Charles Gates Dawes was awarded the Nobel Peace Prize in 1925.

✔**READING CHECK:** How did World War I affect the role of the United States in the global economy?

The Great Depression

The Young Plan might have solved the financial problems left over from World War I, but it never got the chance. The New York stock market crashed in 1929, followed by similar collapses in other countries. The world economy was devastated. The Young Plan did not survive the global depression. American investment in Germany dried up, and German exports were reduced because of new tariffs. Germany could not make its reparations payments. Consequently, the European Allies could not pay their debts to the United States.

Most people felt the effects of the depression. Factory production fell dramatically, unemployment increased, and basic necessities became unavailable or unaffordable. English author George Orwell observed women "kneeling in the cindery mud [ashes] and the bitter wind searching for tiny chips of coal" in a British mining town:

TEACH OBJECTIVE 4

ALL LEVELS: To help students understand how the Great Depression affected world trade and finance, copy the following graphic organizer on the chalkboard, omitting the italicized answers. Have each student complete it. **Sheltered English**

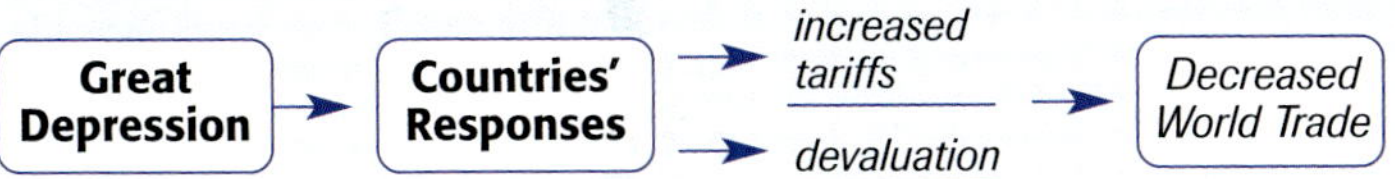

When students have finished the graphic organizer, tell them to write a paragraph suggesting what might have happened if the United States had supported the London Economic Conference. *(Students might suggest that the Great Depression might have ended sooner than it did.)*

NOTE: For an additional teaching idea, see the Chapter 28 decision tree lesson in the **Creative Teaching Strategies** handbook.

> **"In winter they are almost desperate for fuel; it is more important almost than food. Meanwhile, all round, as far as the eye can see are the slag-heaps . . . of collieries [coal mines], and not one of those collieries can sell all the coal it is capable of producing."**

Reaction to the depression. In order to stimulate production and create more jobs during the depression, countries adopted two major economic measures. The first, an increase in tariffs, was intended to provide domestic industries an advantage in the home market. The U.S. Congress, for example, responded to the onset of the depression by passing the Smoot-Hawley Tariff of 1930. The measure raised average tariff rates to their highest levels in U.S. history. It quickly triggered responses by other countries. In France some people compared the U.S. tariff to "a declaration of war, an economic blockade." Even Britain, the traditional champion of free trade, raised its tariffs. By 1931 average tariff rates in 15 European countries had jumped nearly nearly two-thirds higher than in 1927.

The second measure taken by many governments was to make their currencies cheaper in relation to foreign currencies. This currency **devaluation** would make export goods cheaper in outside markets, thus boosting foreign sales. In order to lower the value of their currencies, however, nations had to abandon the gold

THE GRANGER COLLECTION, NEW YORK

During the Great Depression American artists frequently focused on the plight of the homeless.

Major Currency Blocs in the 1930s

Learning from Maps After leaving the gold standard, many nations set the value of their currency according to the value of some of the most dominant currencies in the world. These nations formed currency blocs, which severely restricted trade among different regions.

REGION What were the two main currency blocs in Africa?

NORTH AMERICA
UNITED STATES OF AMERICA
SOUTH AMERICA
GERMANY
GREAT BRITAIN
EUROPE
ASIA
JAPAN
AFRICA
AUSTRALIA
ANTARCTICA
Equator
0 1,500 3,000 Miles
0 1,500 3,000 Kilometers
Scale is accurate only along the Equator.
Robinson Projection

- Gold standard bloc
- Japanese yen bloc
- U.S. dollar bloc
- British sterling bloc
- German mark bloc
- Areas of shifting allegiance due to German-American rivalry

GLOBAL RELATIONS

Hoover Moratorium. When the economic crisis of the 1930s made it impossible for the Allies to repay U.S. war loans and for Germany to pay reparations, President Herbert Hoover called for a one-year moratorium, or a temporary freeze, on Allied war debt payments. Hoover required that the former Allies allow Germany to suspend its reparations payments. Congress approved Hoover's plan in December 1931. However, one year later, when the moratorium ended, almost every single Allied nation defaulted on its loan.

CRITICAL THINKING What might have caused the Allied nations to default on their loans in 1932?

ANSWER: Students might suggest that the depression made it impossible for them to continue making loan payments.

THAT'S INTERESTING!

Finland, which had borrowed $9 million from the United States during World War I, was the only Allied nation to fully pay its war debt.

MAP ANSWER

gold standard and British sterling

REVIEW

Have students complete the **Section 2 Review** on p. 838.

ASSESS

Have students complete **Daily Quiz 28.2.** As **Alternative Assessment**, you may want to use the trade commission persuasive paper or the letters to the editor activity in this section's lessons.

RETEACH

Have students complete **Main Idea Activity for Reteaching and Sheltered English 28.2.** Then have each student write a paragraph that summarizes the main idea of each subsection in Section 2. Call on volunteers to read their paragraphs to the class. Have the class select the best summary for each subsection. **Sheltered English**

EXTEND

Have students make a time line marked in decades from 1890 to 1930. Tell them to write an entry for each decade stating whether they would have supported free trade or protectionism for the United States during that time and why. Allow students to use the library if they need more information to state and justify their opinions. Ask volunteers to read one or more of their entries to the class. **Block Scheduling**

SECTION 2 REVIEW ANSWERS

Define and Identify

For significance, see the following pages:

- Gold Standard Act, p. 832
- free trade, p. 833
- Robert Peel, p. 833
- Cobden-Chevalier Treaty, p. 833
- protectionism, p. 833
- McKinley Tariff, p. 835
- John Maynard Keynes, p. 835
- Charles Dawes, p. 836
- Dawes Plan, p. 836
- Young Plan, p. 836
- devaluation, p. 837

1. gold standard–stabilized exchange rates; free trade–lowered trade barriers and tariffs; Cobden-Chevalier Treaty–reduced trade barriers between Britain and France

2. to attempt to counteract the depression of the 1870s

3. European need for wartime goods and capital allowed the United States to become a financial power and a creditor nation rather than a debtor nation.

4. World trade decreased dramatically. Answers will vary but might include ending the tariff wars and re-establishing the gold standard.

5. The tariff's negative effect on world trade might make repayment of war debts even more difficult, worsen the global depression, and encourage other nations to pass new tariffs.

THROUGH OTHERS' EYES

The London Economic Conference

At the London conference on the world depression in the summer of 1933, many people realized that restoring the global economy would not be simple. American cooperation was seen as essential to solving the international monetary problem. H. D. Davray, a French journalist, explained this perspective in the *British Saturday Review*.

> **"The economic problems submitted to the Conference cannot be solved at all unless . . . currencies are stabilized and a return to the gold standard established. These are from the French point of view indispensable preliminaries, without which any measures of an economic category that may be recommended will be absolutely futile. . . . The actual world situation is on the verge of catastrophe. . . . If the United States want to save themselves from bankruptcy by devaluation which will lighten their debts and increase the value of their stocks, the idea is reasonable. But such a measure must not result in paralyzing and ruining other nations."**

standard. In September 1931 Britain became the first major industrial nation to do so. By April 1933 more than 20 countries, including the United States, had left the gold standard. Without gold as an international standard, currency values rose and fell uncontrollably.

Effects of the depression. While some nations experienced temporary relief as a result of increased tariffs and currency devaluations, the overall impact on global trade was disastrous. Global trade dropped 40 percent between 1927 and 1933. A global trade war loomed. In June 1933 the major industrial powers held a conference in London in an attempt to end the depression. The conference organizers hoped to end the tariff wars, re-establish the gold standard, and promote international cooperation.

Many Americans attributed signs of U.S. economic recovery to the nation's departure from the gold standard. President Franklin D. Roosevelt agreed. He sent a telegram to the London conference stating that "the sound internal economic system of a nation is a greater factor in its well-being than the price of its currency." Without U.S. support, the London conference accomplished little. The depression continued. Most troubling of all, Europe's lingering economic problems contributed to the rise of fascist governments in several countries.

✔ **READING CHECK:** How did the Great Depression affect global trade and finance?

SECTION 2 REVIEW

Define and explain the significance of the following terms:
Gold Standard Act
free trade
Cobden-Chevalier Treaty
protectionism
McKinley Tariff
Dawes Plan
Young Plan
devaluation

Identify and explain the significance of the following individuals:
Robert Peel
John Maynard Keynes
Charles Gates Dawes

1. Using Graphic Organizers Copy the graphic organizer below. Use it to describe the economic policies that led to an expansion of the global economy in the late 1800s.

2. Recognizing Point of View Why did many nations adopt protectionist policies in the late 1800s?

3. Synthesizing How and why did the U.S. position in the global economy change after World War I?

4. Analyzing How did the Great Depression affect global trade? How do you think the trade problems might have been solved?

Critical Thinking

5. Imagine that you are a European leader in 1930. Describe your reaction to the Smoot-Hawley Tariff.

Consider:
- how the tariff affected your country's ability to pay World War I debts
- how the tariff affected the global depression
- how other nations reacted to the tariff

SECTION 3

After completing Section 3, students should be able to:

OBJECTIVE 1 *Explain how the Bretton Woods system attempted to prevent future economic conflicts.*

OBJECTIVE 2 *Identify factors that contributed to U.S. economic expansion after World War II.*

OBJECTIVE 3 *Describe how the economies of West Germany and Japan developed after World War II.*

LET'S GET STARTED!

To begin the class, have students write for five minutes about the U.S. economy after World War II, from the 1950s to the early years of the Cold War. Tell them to write a description of U.S. domestic and foreign economic activity based on their readings in previous chapters. If they cannot remember, tell them to make educated guesses and explain their reasoning. Tell students that in Section 3 they will learn more about American dominance of the global economy following World War II.

SECTION 3 The Era of American Dominance

OBJECTIVES

Read to understand:

1. how the Bretton Woods system attempted to prevent future economic conflicts
2. what factors contributed to U.S. economic expansion after World War II
3. how the economies of West Germany and Japan developed after World War II

KEY TERMS

Bretton Woods system
fixed exchange rates
International Monetary Fund
World Bank
General Agreement on Tariffs and Trade
European Economic Community

KEY PEOPLE

Henry Morgenthau Jr.

EYEWITNESSES TO History

"All of us have seen the great economic tragedy of our time. We saw the world-wide depression of the 1930s. We saw currency disorders develop and spread from land to land, destroying the basis for international trade and . . . investment and even international faith. In their wake, we saw unemployment and wretchedness. . . . We saw bewilderment and bitterness become the breeders of fascism, and, finally, of war."

—Henry Morgenthau Jr.

Post–World War II Soviet Union

U.S. secretary of the treasury Henry Morgenthau Jr. explained the consequences of international monetary and trade policies of the 1930s. Even before World War II ended, political leaders and economic experts from around the world had determined some of the causes of the war. They concluded that the departure from the gold standard, the competitive currency devaluations, and the high tariffs had contributed to the outbreak of the war.

A New Economic Framework

At the end of World War II, the United States took the lead in rebuilding the global economy. This effort required new policies and institutions for international trade. The war-torn economies of Europe and Asia also had to be reconstructed.

U.S. officials and others worked to avoid another war as a result of conflict over currency, debt, and trade by modifying international economic policies. "Commerce is the life blood of a free society," wrote President Franklin D. Roosevelt. "We must see to it that the arteries which carry that blood stream are not clogged again, as they have been in the past, by artificial barriers created through senseless economic rivalries."

In 1944, representatives from several nations met at Bretton Woods, New Hampshire, to limit trade conflicts.

At Roosevelt's urging, economic officials from the United States and 43 other countries met in Bretton Woods, New Hampshire, in July 1944. Their primary goals were to restore the stability of currencies and to prevent tariff increases and trade wars similar to those of the 1930s. The arrangement that emerged became known as the **Bretton Woods system**.

The first element of the system was an agreement between the major economic powers to maintain **fixed exchange rates** between their currencies. They tied the currencies of Britain, France, and the other countries to the value of the U.S. dollar, which became the system's key currency. To increase stability further, the dollar was tied to gold, at a value of $35 per ounce. In effect, this agreement restored the gold standard to the global economy. To help maintain these fixed exchange rates,

SECTION 3 RESOURCES

PRINT

- Guided Reading Strategy 28.3
- Geography Activity 28: The Marshall Plan
- Section 3 Review, p. 843
- Daily Quiz 28.3

MULTIMEDIA

- One-Stop Planner, Lesson 28.3
- Holt Researcher: American History CD–ROM

SHELTERED ENGLISH

- Main Idea Activity for Reteaching and Sheltered English 28.3

✔ READING TO UNDERSTAND

To help students master the section objectives, have them answer the **READING CHECKS** and complete **Guided Reading Strategy 28.3** as they read the section.

TEACH OBJECTIVE 1

LEVEL 1: Tell students to imagine that they are radio news reporters who have been assigned to cover the Bretton Woods conference in July 1944. Have individuals or pairs develop and perform radio reports summarizing how the Bretton Woods system attempted to prevent future economic conflicts. *(Reports should include establishing fixed exchange rates based on the U.S. dollar and gold, creating the IMF and the World Bank, and reducing tariffs through GATT.)* **Sheltered English, Cooperative Learning**

LEVEL 2: Tell students to imagine that they are participants in the Bretton Woods conference and that they must write a summary report of the proceedings to present to their governments. Have them write a concise report describing how the Bretton Woods system attempted to prevent future economic conflicts. *(See the Level 1 lesson for the correct attempts.)* Ask volunteers to read their reports to the class.

LEVEL 3: Have students complete the Level 2 activity. Then tell them to write a paragraph predicting how they think the Bretton Woods system will affect the global economy during the next several decades.

GLOBAL RELATIONS

GATT. GATT was an attempt to prevent trade wars between its member nations. If a trade conflict arose between two nations, they were referred to a neutral panel of trade experts that studied the dispute and made recommendations. Although neither nation had to abide by the ruling of the panel, GATT did provide a mechanism for resolving trade disagreements without resorting to a trade war.

CRITICAL THINKING Why might the panel findings not be binding on the nations that were in conflict?

ANSWER: Students might suggest that nations might have chosen to leave GATT rather than abide by a ruling they did not like.

AMERICAN ARTS ANSWERS

(for p. 841)

1. the participation of everyday Americans
2. His work reflected artistic participation by a wider variety of Americans and thus art styles.

HOLT RESEARCHER — Read More About It

Free Find: IMF
After reading about the International Monetary Fund (IMF) on the **Holt Researcher** CD–ROM, create a visual presentation that shows how the IMF affects the global economy.

the conference created the $8.8 billion **International Monetary Fund** (IMF). The fund provides currency and economic advice to developing countries in economic crisis.

The conference also established the International Bank for Reconstruction and Development, commonly called the **World Bank**. The World Bank was given $10 billion in credit to make loans to boost the economies of the war-damaged countries. Loans from the World Bank were also intended to fund many large-scale infrastructure projects in the less-developed countries of Africa, Asia, and South America. A leading U.S. economist at the conference, Harry White, explained his view of the difference between the IMF and the World Bank.

> "The [International Monetary] Fund is designed chiefly to prevent the disruption of foreign exchange and to strengthen monetary and credit systems and help in the restoration of foreign trade. . . . The Bank is designed chiefly to supply the huge volume of capital to the United Nations . . . that will be needed for reconstruction, for relief, and for economic recovery."

The final part of the Bretton Woods system was the **General Agreement on Tariffs and Trade** (GATT). Although it did not take effect until 1947, the agreement represented a commitment by the member governments to the principle of free trade. Over the next few decades, GATT members succeeded in reducing tariffs on a wide variety of goods to the lowest levels in modern history.

✔ **READING CHECK:** How did the Bretton Woods system attempt to prevent future economic conflicts?

In addition to funding large projects, the World Bank provides small-bussiness loans to people in developing countries.

A New Global Economy

The Bretton Woods system operated in a global economy that differed greatly from the pre–World War II economy. The onset of the Cold War divided the world into two spheres: capitalist nations and communist nations. Economic contact between the two sides effectively ceased for about 25 years. Each side believed that its economic and social system was superior to the other's. In addition, neither side wanted to do anything that might strengthen the other.

Even among the capitalist countries, economic relationships changed. Many of the European nations lay in ruins. The U.S. economy, by contrast, emerged from World War II stronger than ever. Government spending on war supplies had boosted the economy. At the end of the war, Americans produced more than twice as many goods as they had during the worst periods of the Great Depression. In 1944 steel production reached nearly 90 million tons—almost 30 million tons more than prewar production.

Many Americans recognized that government spending on the war effort had helped end the depression. They worried that the economy would enter another recession when the war ended. Surveys at the time revealed that some 70 percent of Americans thought that they would be worse off financially after the war.

TEACH OBJECTIVE 2

LEVELS 1 AND 2: Ask students to list factors that contributed to U.S. economic expansion after World War II. *(Lists might include: government spending on war supplies lifted the U.S. economy out of the Great Depression; consumers had plenty of money to spend; consumer demand was high; factories shifted from war production to civilian consumer goods; government spending remained high during the Cold War; and government social programs created jobs.)* Then have students create an advertisement for any consumer product for sale after the war. Advertisements should appeal to consumers' desire to celebrate the end of war rationing, keep up with their neighbors, or modernize their lives. Display students' advertisements around the classroom. **Sheltered English**

LEVEL 3: Ask students to list factors that contributed to U.S. economic expansion after World War II. *(See the Levels 1 and 2 lesson for the correct factors.)* Then organize students into groups and have them role-play a post–World War II family—two parents and children of various ages. Students should discuss how much better the economy is since the war and what they want to buy for themselves over the next several months—a new house, a car, appliances, or clothing. Have volunteers take turns acting out their discussions for the class. **Cooperative Learning**

Such fears proved groundless. Instead of falling into a recession, the U.S. economy grew dramatically. Between 1945 and 1970 the gross national product (GNP) doubled. One reason for the growth was that American consumers had plenty of money to spend. Most rationing ended shortly after the war, and growing consumer demands kept the economy humming. Factories soon shifted from war production to the production of civilian consumer goods. Business consultant Peter Drucker wrote in 1949 that "the world revolution of our times is 'Made in the USA.'"

The economy also boomed because government spending remained high throughout the Cold War. Military spending kept employment high in defense-related industries. Government social programs established during the 1950s and 1960s also created jobs and enabled people to maintain their purchasing power.

American factories such as this one remained busy and prosperous during the 1950s and 1960s.

✔ **READING CHECK:** What factors contributed to U.S. economic expansion after World War II?

AMERICAN ARTS

The Business of Art

After World War II the arts flourished in the United States. Cultural critics noted a significant change as art became an important part of many Americans' lives for the first time. In 1964 Alvin Toffler wrote *The Culture Consumers.* The title of his book reflected the close relationship between the booming U.S. economy and the renaissance taking place in the arts.

Americans' investment in the arts increased in the postwar years. Toffler argued that the participation of a wider variety of Americans in cultural pursuits such as painting, music, theater, and dance made art more democratic and open. Between 1950 and 1960, spending by private individuals on the arts increased 70 percent, to more than $3 billion. This rate of growth was nearly four times that of the population. Other critics complained that the influence of the masses reduced the quality and value of art. In Toffler's view democracy and culture need not be at odds with each other. He wrote, "Culture is now, for many people, an altogether everyday affair, capable of yielding intense joy, but no longer awesome."

***Jackson Pollock's* Silver over Black, White, Yellow, and Red**

Understanding the Arts

1. What did Alvin Toffler believe caused the increasingly democratic nature of the arts during the 1950s and 1960s?
2. How do you think that Jackson Pollock's unique drip-and-splash paintings reflected the trends in the commercial art world of the mid-1900s?

DEMOCRATIC VALUES

Postwar Economic Fears. At the end of World War II, many American workers received pay cuts or were laid off. In late 1945 take-home pay for some workers decreased as much as 30 percent. At the same time, about 20 percent of working families in U.S. cities received less than $1,500 in cash income per year—the average for full-time employees was $2,190. In response, laborers conducted some 4,750 work stoppages in 1945. The following year there were almost 5,000 stoppages involving 4.6 million workers, or about 1 in every 14 workers.

CRITICAL THINKING What might workers have hoped to achieve with the work stoppages?

ANSWER: Students might mention that workers hoped business owners would pay higher wages rather than lose profits because of the work stoppages.

VISUAL RECORD ANSWER *(for p. 842)*

Students might answer that a productive factory allowed for increased sales.

TEACH OBJECTIVE 3

ALL LEVELS: To help students understand how the economies of West Germany and Japan developed after World War II, copy the following graphic organizer on the chalkboard, omitting the italicized answers. Have each student complete it. **Sheltered English**

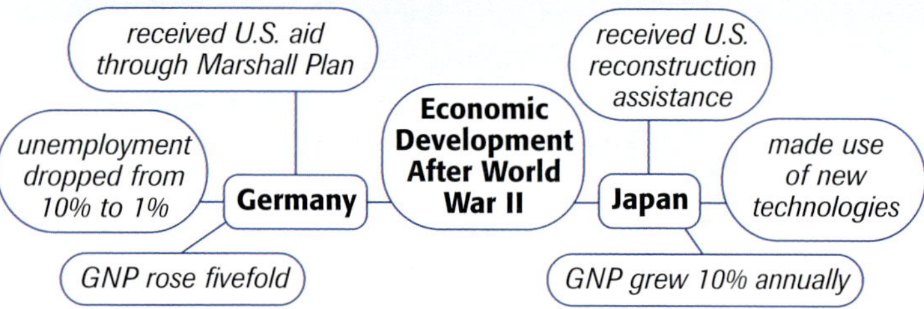

▶**ASSIGNMENT** *Have students use the graphic organizer to help them write a case study of either West Germany's or Japan's postwar economic recovery. Tell students to begin their case studies by briefly describing their chosen country's economy before and during the war.*

SPOTLIGHT on the European Economic Community

Organize students into groups and have them conduct research on the history and accomplishments of the EEC. Tell them to organize their findings into an oral or multimedia presentation. Encourage students to ask questions and take notes on each other's presentations.
Cooperative Learning, Block Scheduling

GLOBAL RELATIONS

European Economic Community. The EEC was not the first post–World War II European cooperation effort. The Organization of European Economic Cooperation was founded in 1948 to coordinate the spending of Marshall Plan funds. In addition, Belgium, the Netherlands, and Luxembourg formed Benelux, a customs organization that ended all tariffs between the three nations. The effort to form a European Defense Community in 1954 failed.

CRITICAL THINKING What might have caused trade organizations to succeed while a defense organization failed?

ANSWER: Students might suggest that trade agreements bring immediate benefits, while a defense agreement might lead a nation into a war it does not wish to fight.

THAT'S INTERESTING!

In 1996 Germany had the fourth-highest gross domestic product in the world. It ranked behind the United States, China, and Japan.

VISUAL RECORD ANSWER

(for p. 843)

Students might mention the huge shipment of manufactured goods.

A poster created by the European Economic Community celebrates the economic cooperation of European nations.

Reconstruction and Growth in Europe

U.S. officials took the initiative in reconstructing Western Europe's war-torn economies. They had two major reasons for doing so. First, if Europe remained weak economically, such weakness might easily spread to the United States. Second, Americans were concerned that a Europe in economic distress might fall prey to communism.

The European Economic Community. The United States created the Marshall Plan as a quick way to help put Western Europe back on its feet. The plan also promoted long-term results. The U.S. aid came mostly in the form of grants that did not have to be repaid but had strings attached. The United States required European nations to work together to coordinate their economic activities. This policy was designed to prevent a return to the competition that preceded World War II.

Europeans responded by forming the Organization for European Economic Cooperation to distribute Marshall Plan aid. Before long, some Europeans were urging economic integration as well as cooperation. In 1951 Belgium, France, Italy, Luxembourg, the Netherlands, and West Germany formed the European Coal and Steel Community (ECSC). This organization enabled coal, iron ore, and steel to be traded freely among its six member nations.

The success of the ECSC inspired a bolder economic step—the formation of the **European Economic Community** (EEC) in 1957. The treaty that created the EEC explained the community's purpose.

> "The EEC aims [to] promote the harmonious growth of economic activity in the Community whole, regular and balanced expansion, augmented [increased] stability, a more rapidly rising standard of living, and closer relations between the participating states."

To achieve these goals, the EEC planned to abolish tariffs and "all barriers to the free movement of persons, services and capital" among members. Commerce among the EEC countries grew rapidly. Trade between France and Germany, for example, grew by about 40 percent from 1958 to 1966. By 1968 all tariffs among the six EEC members had been abolished.

INTERPRETING THE VISUAL RECORD

West Germany. U.S. officials aided West Germany in its industrial recovery after World War II. ***How do you think a productive West German factory might have contributed to a strong economy?***

West Germany. Although all of Western Europe achieved economic recovery in the postwar years, West Germany's recovery was the greatest success story. Immediately after the war, the governments of the victorious powers agreed that Germany should not be allowed to become strong again. During the Cold War, however, the United States came to view West Germany as a needed barrier to the Soviet Union's westward expansion. West Germany was also seen as a key nation in Western Europe's economic revival. As a result, U.S. officials included West Germany in the Marshall Plan and did what they could to foster its economic growth.

With the financial support of the United States, the West German economy soared. Its recovery was

REVIEW

Have students complete the **Section 3 Review** on p. 843.

ASSESS

Have students complete **Daily Quiz 28.3**. As **Alternative Assessment**, you may want to use the Bretton Woods news report or the family role-playing activity in this section's lessons.

RETEACH

Have students complete **Main Idea Activity for Reteaching and Sheltered English 28.3**. Organize students so that a roughly equal number are assigned to each objective in this section. Direct each student to develop a lesson that covers his or her assigned objective. Have students present their lessons to the class and encourage the rest of the class to ask questions and take notes. **Sheltered English**

EXTEND

Organize students into groups and have each group create a two-panel visual display that compares and contrasts the economic systems of capitalism and communism during the Cold War. Displays might include maps, images of leaders, newspaper clippings, graphic organizers that explain the systems, explanatory captions, and so on. Display students' completed projects in the classroom, the school library, or other available space. **Block Scheduling, Cooperative Learning**

---

soon labeled an "economic miracle." Unemployment dropped from more than 10 percent in 1950 to less than 1 percent during most of the 1960s. The country's GNP rose from less than 100 million marks in 1950 to more than 500 million marks in 1968. By the 1960s West Germany had become the economic envy of all of Europe.

Japan

Japan's recovery was more dramatic than West Germany's. Before the war, Japan had never been as economically powerful as Germany, and Japan received no Marshall Plan aid after the war. Moreover, while much of Germany's economic revival resulted from trade with its prosperous European neighbors, Japan's neighbors were generally poor.

Yet Japan did have some advantages. Though not included in the Marshall Plan, Japan received other kinds of U.S. reconstruction and agricultural assistance. More importantly, as in other successful countries, its people were industrious and creative in the adoption and development of new technologies. In the 1970s Japan's economic prosperity surpassed Germany's—as well as that of nearly every other country. Between the late 1940s and the early 1970s, Japan's GNP grew at a rate of more than 10 percent annually. By 1970 Japan had remade itself into an economic powerhouse—the strongest in Asia and one of the strongest in the world. Much of Japan's economic prosperity came from the country's large percentage of exports. Sales of electronics and cars made in Japan have helped preserve the nation's prosperity during the 1970s and 1980s.

INTERPRETING THE VISUAL RECORD

Japanese recovery. New manufactured goods are being unloaded from this Japanese ship docked in Oakland, California. ***How do you think this image reflects the dramatic recovery made by the Japanese economy since World War II?***

✔ **READING CHECK:** How did the economies of West Germany and Japan develop after World War II?

SECTION  REVIEW

Define and explain the significance of the following terms:
Bretton Woods system
fixed exchange rates
International Monetary Fund
World Bank
General Agreement on Tariffs and Trade
European Economic Community

Identify and explain the significance of the following individual:
Henry Morganthau Jr.

1. **Using Graphic Organizers** Copy the graphic organizer below. Use it to explain how postwar efforts such as the Marshall Plan and the Bretton Woods system affected the global economy.

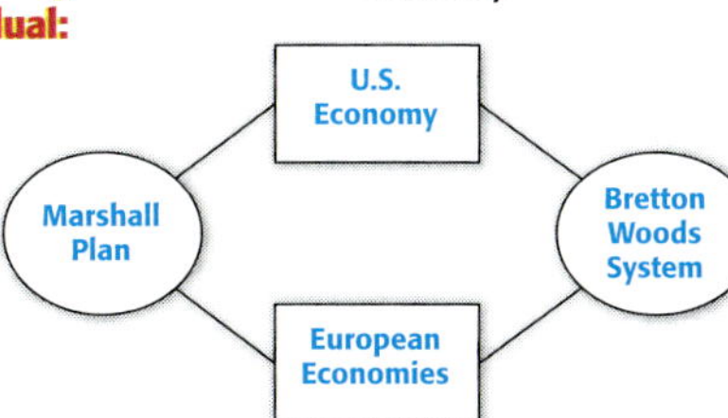

2. **Analyzing** What actions did delegates to the Bretton Woods conference take to promote peace?
3. **Evaluating** What was the state of the U.S. economy after World War II?
4. **Assessing Consequences** How did U.S. aid affect the economies of West Germany and Japan?

Critical Thinking

5. Explain the importance of international commerce to the global economy.
   Consider:
   - what the economic conditions that led to World War II were
   - what the reasons for the establishment of the Bretton Woods system were
   - why the economic recovery of West Germany and Japan was important to the U.S. economy

---

SECTION 3 REVIEW ANSWERS

Define and Identify

For significance, see the following pages:

- Henry Morgenthau Jr., p. 839
- Bretton Woods system, p. 839
- fixed exchange rates, p. 839
- International Monetary Fund, p. 840
- World Bank, p. 840
- General Agreement on Tariffs and Trade, p. 840
- European Economic Community, p. 842

1. Marshall Plan–U.S. economic aid helped European economies recover and stabilized the global economy; Bretton Woods–stabilized European economies and prevented trade rivalries that led to World War II; global economic stability benefited U.S. economy
2. established fixed exchange rates, created International Monetary Fund and World Bank, and initiated GATT
3. dramatic economic growth, partly from increased consumer demand and spending, and continued government spending during the Cold War and on new social programs
4. It helped their economies recover and promoted economic growth.
5. trade barriers and global depression contributed to the outbreak of World War II; Bretton Woods sought to prevent a repeat of high tariffs and fluctuating currencies; U.S. assistance to West Germany and Japan helped stabilize the global economy

SECTION 4

After completing Section 4, students should be able to:

OBJECTIVE 1 *Discuss how the U.S. dominance of the global economy came to an end.*

OBJECTIVE 2 *Relate how the economies of Pacific Rim countries fared during the 1980s and 1990s.*

OBJECTIVE 3 *Explain how the growth of multinational corporations and the end of the Cold War affected the global economy.*

OBJECTIVE 4 *Identify what evidence points to a recent movement toward global free trade.*

LET'S GET STARTED!

To begin the class, tell students to sketch political cartoons that comment on the role of the United States in the global economy after World War II and up to the 1980s. *(Cartoons should indicate strong dominance through currency values being tied to the dollar, loans to other nations, production levels, and so on.)* Tell students that in Section 4 they will learn about the end of the era of U.S. economic dominance and the rise of the Internet and global free trade.

SECTION 4 RESOURCES

PRINT

- Guided Reading Strategy 28.4
- Primary Source Reading 28: The Plight of Industrial Workers
- Biography Reading 28: Rosalynn Carter
- American History Political Cartoon 30: Multinational Corporations
- Section 4 Review, p. 849
- Daily Quiz 28.4

MULTIMEDIA

- One-Stop Planner, Lesson 28.4
- Holt Researcher: American History CD–ROM

SHELTERED ENGLISH

- Main Idea Activity for Reteaching and Sheltered English 28.4

✔ READING TO UNDERSTAND

To help students master the section objectives, have them answer the **READING CHECKS** and complete **Guided Reading Strategy 28.4** as they read the section.

A New Era in Trade

OBJECTIVES

Read to understand:

1. how the U.S. dominance of the global economy came to an end
2. how the economies of Pacific Rim countries fared during the 1980s and 1990s
3. how the growth of multinational corporations and the end of the Cold War affected the global economy
4. what evidence points to a recent movement toward global free trade

KEY TERMS

oil shocks
floating exchange rates
Pacific Rim
e-commerce
euro
World Trade Organization

KEY PEOPLE

Ross Perot

EYEWITNESSES TO History

"Jimmy [Carter] knew well how self-defeating and dangerous [the nation's] dependency on foreign oil was. He decided to go on national television our second week in the White House to explain the seriousness of the problem and the necessity of beginning to conserve energy immediately. The difficulty lay in convincing the public that though the long gas lines of 1973 were gone, the problem had not gone away."

—Rosalynn Carter

Gas lines in the 1970s

Former first lady Rosalynn Carter recalled the early days of President Carter's energy conservation program. In the years following the economic difficulties of the 1970s, the global economy has been dramatically transformed.

The End of Dollar Dominance

Because oil supplies throughout the 1950s and 1960s exceeded demand, oil prices were kept low. Inexpensive oil contributed to the growth of industrial economies after World War II. Oil and the products derived from it could be used to power factories and vehicles, provide light and heat, and manufacture plastics and other products.

The oil crisis. In the early 1970s oil prices rose as demand caught up with supplies. Additional pressure on prices came from the Organization of Petroleum Exporting Countries (OPEC), an alliance of major oil-producing nations. The group included Middle Eastern, Latin American, and African countries. By controlling the production and sale of crude oil, the organization repeatedly raised oil prices during the 1970s. By the early 1980s the price of a barrel of oil stood at more than \$30—up from less than \$3 a barrel prior to 1973. The increase brought greater income to OPEC.

The jump in oil prices sent shock waves throughout the global economy. The **oil shocks**, as the jolts from the price increases were called, tested each country's capacity to adapt. A government official in Japan later recalled, "Both workers and business leaders were very apprehensive [fearful] after 1973. They feared for the survival of their companies, and so everybody worked together."

The breakdown of Bretton Woods. The Bretton Woods system collapsed just before the oil crisis. Moreover, the economic growth of countries like West Germany and Japan eventually began to challenge U.S. supremacy. By 1971 President Richard Nixon had removed the nation from the gold standard. The fixed exchange rates for currencies also collapsed completely and were replaced by a system of

TEACH OBJECTIVE 1

LEVELS 1 AND 2: Have students complete the following sentence: "Events that brought the U.S. dominance of the global economy to an end include. . ." *(Answers should include the oil crisis and the breakdown of the Bretton Woods system.)* Then have students select one of these factors and write a brief news story describing the situation and explaining its impact on the U.S. and global economies. Call on volunteers to read their stories to the class. **Sheltered English**

LEVEL 3: Have students list events that brought the era of U.S. dominance of the global economy to an end. *(See the Levels 1 and 2 lesson for the correct events.)* Then tell them to imagine that they are economic analysts who have been hired in 1993 to write and present a report to President Bill Clinton detailing changes in the U.S. role in the global economy between 1970 and 1992. Have volunteers present their reports to the class.

TEACH OBJECTIVE 2

LEVEL 1: Have students write a series of newspaper headlines on how the economies of the Pacific Rim countries fared during the 1980s and 1990s. *(Headlines might include strong economic growth of the Four Tigers in the late 1980s and early 1990s, capitalist reforms in China, U.S. trade gap with China, economic recession in the late 1990s, shrinking Japanese economy, and optimistic view of recovery by late 1999.)* **Sheltered English**

---

floating exchange rates. Under the new system, the value of each currency varied depending on global demand. For example, if Japanese businesses needed more dollars to pay for imports from the United States, the dollar might rise in value relative to the yen. This was what U.S. policy makers hoped would happen.

Instead, the dollar fell. In the 1980s the United States developed a trade deficit with some countries, particularly Japan. As the United States imported more products than it exported to Japan, the dollar's value fell steadily against the yen. Although the U.S. economy remained the world's largest, the tumble of the dollar marked the end of complete U.S. dominance of the global economy.

✔ **READING CHECK:** How did the U.S. dominance of the global economy come to an end?

INTERPRETING THE VISUAL RECORD

Modernization. Economic prosperity in Asian countries such as Singapore has led to enormous growth and modernization in many of the region's cities. ***How do you think the city skyline pictured here reflects the economic prosperity of Singapore?***

The Pacific Rim

In recent decades, the focus of the world economy has shifted toward the nations of the **Pacific Rim**. These countries include East Asian, Southeast Asian, and Pacific Island nations. In 1997, goods from the Pacific Rim accounted for about 36 percent of all imports to the United States. The region's reputation for producing high-quality and low-priced automobiles, computers, radios, TVs, VCRs, and other goods helped spur demand.

The "Four Tigers" and China. Historically, Japan has been the Pacific Rim's dominant economic power. The nations of the Pacific Rim that experienced the most explosive economic growth in recent years, however, are the so-called Four Tigers—Hong Kong, Singapore, South Korea, and Taiwan. South Korea, for example, had an average annual economic growth rate of nearly 10 percent from 1980 to 1990. In contrast, the U.S. growth rate during the same years averaged less than 4 percent. Other Asian nations, such as Indonesia, Malaysia, and Thailand, also showed impressive ecomonic growth during the 1980s.

In addition, China achieved high economic growth rates during the late 1980s and early 1990s. Although the Chinese government remains communist, it has enacted some freemarket economic reforms. Millions of small private companies have formed in recent years. By spurring rapid growth, such changes have increased incomes in much of China and transformed the country into a major economic power. In part because of this growth, the U.S. trade gap with China between 1995 and 1997 grew by almost $16 billion.

Several factors contributed to the Pacific Rim nations' economic success. Many Asians work long hours, save what they earn, and reinvest the savings. These practices lead to more economic growth. Furthermore, Asian governments have often taken an active role in encouraging economic development. In 1989 several Pacific Rim nations formed a group called the Asia-Pacific Economic Cooperation to promote free trade and cooperation among member nations. Critics of the Asian economies note, however, that the growth has often been based on low wages. Thus, not all of the region's peoples have benefited.

HOLT RESEARCHER *Read More About It*

Free Find: APEC
After reading about the Asia-Pacific Economic Cooperation on the **Holt Researcher** CD–ROM, write a short essay describing the organization and its impact on the economy of Asian countries.

ECONOMIC DEVELOPMENT

Trade Imbalance. The United States experienced a trade imbalance with Japan throughout the late 1990s. In 1997 the United States exported some $66 billion worth of goods to Japan but imported goods from Japan worth about $122 million, resulting in a trade imbalance that favored Japan by some $56 million.

ACTIVITY: Have students conduct research on how U.S. trade balances with Canada and Mexico have changed in the 1990s.

THAT'S INTERESTING!

During the early 1990s some nations experienced negative economic growth. Georgia, a former republic of the Soviet Union, suffered a 16 percent drop in the per capita growth rate of its gross national product in 1994.

VISUAL RECORD ANSWER

Students might answer that the skyscrapers indicate that Singapore's economy is booming.

LEVEL 2: Have students complete the Level 1 activity. Then have them select one headline and write a newspaper story about it. Invite volunteers to read their articles to the class. Students may wish to include their articles in their portfolios.

LEVEL 3: Organize students into groups of four or five and tell them to imagine that they are representatives of Pacific Rim nations attending a conference to discuss ways of ending the economic recession of the late 1990s. Tell them to conduct a discussion in which they outline the problems they are facing and the reasons for these problems. *(See the Level 1 lesson for the correct problems.)* Then have students brainstorm possible solutions based on past experiences and how various countries have recovered from other large-scale recessions around the world. Have one student in each group take notes on the proceedings and present a brief oral report to the rest of the class when the discussions are completed. **Cooperative Learning**

GLOBAL RELATIONS

Asia and Georgia. In the late 1990s American farmers in Georgia felt the effects of the global economy. During the early 1990s Georgia cotton farmers made millions of dollars. When the Asian economic crisis hit, demand for cotton dropped by some 6 percent because Asian nations no longer needed cotton for their industries. To make matters worse, China, which had been the world's largest importer of cotton, banned imports and began exporting cotton to reduce its surplus. As a result, world cotton prices dropped from some 80 cents per pound to about 48 cents per pound. It cost farmers in Georgia 65 cents per pound to grow cotton. As a result, the Asian economic crisis ruined many farmers in the United States.

CRITICAL THINKING How might lowering cotton prices affect Georgia farmers?

ANSWER: Students might mention that lowering prices would not help because production costs remained high.

VISUAL RECORD ANSWER

Students might answer that the workers had jobs.

The Asian financial crisis. Recently, many Asian countries have not been able to sustain their impressive rates of economic growth. During the late 1990s several of the Pacific Rim countries were hit by recession. An agricultural crisis, volatile currency markets, and decreasing export levels contributed to the recession in Asia. Moreover, some Asian banks had made poor investment decisions during the economic boom. In addition, some large companies ran inefficient operations. The Japanese economy—the region's most powerful—continued to shrink throughout 1998. Unemployment reached record highs, and profits for Japanese companies dwindled.

The Japanese government undertook measures such as increased government spending to pull the country out of recession. The government also worked to convince Japanese companies to stop overproducing goods. By the summer of 1999 the outlook for the Pacific Rim countries had turned cautiously optimistic. Japan's economy showed the first signs of growth in two years. Recovery also began in the Philippines, South Korea, and Thailand.

✔ **READING CHECK:** How did the economies of Pacific Rim countries fare during the 1980s and 1990s?

INTERPRETING THE VISUAL RECORD

Multinational corporations. Some foreign-owned multinational corporations have opened manufacturing plants in the United States, such as this Honda factory in Ohio. ***What benefits do you think these workers receive from the growth of multinational corporations?***

Global Businesses

The Pacific Rim's economic growth during the 1980s was partly fueled by Japanese investors seeking lower labor and land costs in other Asian nations. These investment efforts have often been led by multinational corporations. These giant corporations invest money in or own business ventures around the globe.

Multinational corporations. Many American companies have set up operations in foreign nations. Similarly, Japanese automobile companies, such as Honda and Mitsubishi, have opened factories in the United States. The New York–based International Telephone and Telegraph (ITT) owns businesses in countries ranging from Bolivia to France. Other American companies—such as General Motors, International Business Machines (IBM), and Texaco—also operate worldwide. Moreover, European companies have merged recently with American companies to form larger multinational corporations. For example, two giant automobile companies, Daimler-Benz of Germany and Chrysler of the United States, have merged to form a single company. By the 1990s a truly global economy was in place.

It is difficult to determine the economic effects of multinational corporations. In some cases, companies boost employment and development in the countries where they operate. Critics argue, however, that most of the profits return to the country where the corporation is based. Other critics accuse some multinational corporations of underpaying workers and harming the environment.

TEACH OBJECTIVE 3

ALL LEVELS: To help students understand how the growth of multinational corporations and the end of the Cold War affected the global economy, copy the following graphic organizer onto the chalkboard, omitting the italicized answers. Have each student complete it.
Sheltered English

▶ASSIGNMENT *Tell students to use the graphic organizer to help them write a position paper about multinational corporations. Students should decide whether they are in favor of the growth of multinational corporations or wish to limit the spread of such companies.*

EFFECTS ON THE GLOBAL ECONOMY

End of the Cold War

- *established global economy*
- *boosted employment and development in some areas*
- *removed barriers between two spheres (U.S./Soviet)*
- *shifted investment and aid due to breakup of Soviet Union*
- *renewed investment in Eastern Europe*

The end of the Cold War. Following the breakup of the Soviet Union in the early 1990s, multinational corporations began investing in Eastern Europe and the former Soviet republics. Removing the long-standing barriers between the two spheres has taken time, however. Most of the countries of the former communist bloc are just beginning to build close economic ties with the rest of the world.

Not all nations have benefited from the end of the Cold War. Cuba, for example, once received support almost exclusively from the Soviet Union. The island-nation has had to adapt to a sharp decrease in aid and trade. In addition, some African nations fear that they will lose investment dollars from multinational corporations that choose to invest in Eastern Europe instead.

✔ **READING CHECK:** How have the growth of multinational corporations and the end of the Cold War affected the global economy?

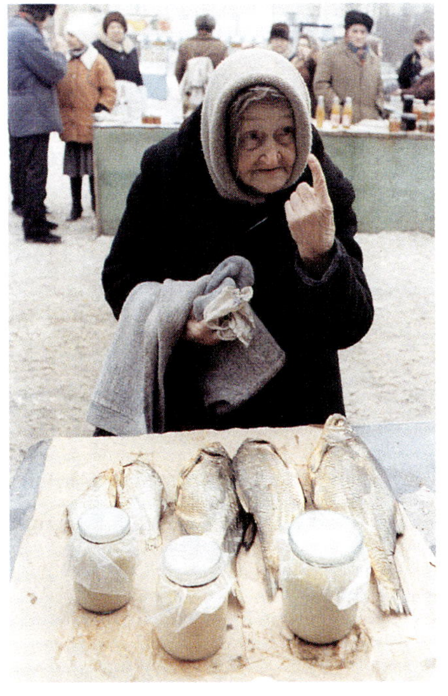

INTERPRETING THE VISUAL RECORD
Moscow. Free trade and economic prosperity have yet to reach many people in the former Soviet Union. This woman is trying to trade a sweater for fish in a Moscow market. ***How do you think this exchange reflects Russia's economic problems during the late 1990s?***

The Internet

Multinational corporations have benefited from improvements in telecommunications. Teleconferencing allows people at multiple locations to hold conferences over the telephone or by computer. The Internet connects many of the world's banks, stock exchanges, government offices, and other institutions. For example, every day banks electronically whisk billions of dollars from New Delhi to New York, while investors in Toronto purchase stock shares being sold in Tokyo.

The Internet has also dramatically changed the way many people buy and sell products. Shopping on the Internet allows consumers to search worldwide for the best deals and for special items. Businesses that use electronic technology to sell their products also enjoy benefits such as reduced overhead costs. Instead of paying stores to stock their products, companies can ship goods directly from their warehouses to consumers. Experts estimate that online sales, also known as **e-commerce**, may reach between $200 billion to $1 trillion in the year 2000.

The United States has taken the lead in establishing Internet businesses. E-commerce, however, has raised challenging questions about trade and taxation. Federal and state governments have found it difficult, if not impossible, to enforce laws regulating trade. For instance, how do federal or state governments collect a tax on the sale of a pair of shoes on a German Web site? Virginia governor Jim Gilmore explained the importance of considering the long term effects of regulations.

> **"The issue we are dealing with is global. . . . We don't want to surrender our position of world leadership in electronic commerce, and we could do that easily if we do something shortsighted."**

Global Trade Agreements

Despite the difficulties experienced by some nations, the postwar era has been the most prosperous time in modern history. Many economists attribute this prosperity to increased free trade around the world, which has made it easier to export

TECHNOLOGY AND SOCIETY

E-commerce. More than 10 million people in the United States and Canada made purchases over the Internet in 1997—double the number in mid-1996. While some 14 million people used the Internet to plan a vacation, about 6.3 million actually purchased tickets or made reservations online. Airline companies receive a great benefit from online sales. It costs an airline $8 to sell a ticket through a travel agent, compared to $1 to sell it via the Internet.

CRITICAL THINKING What benefits might consumers receive from e-commerce?

ANSWER: Students might mention that consumers do not have to leave their homes to shop and can compare prices at various businesses without much effort.

VISUAL RECORD ANSWER
Students might suggest that the former Soviet Union has not established a free market economy.

TEACH OBJECTIVE 4

ALL LEVELS: Have students make a time line identifying evidence for a recent movement toward global free trade. *(Time lines might include 1993—Maastricht Treaty, which created the European Union; January 1994—North American Free Trade Agreement takes effect; 1994—formation of World Trade Organization; January 1999—adoption of the euro; late 1999—talks about free trade between EU and South America; China's campaign for membership in the WTO.)*
Sheltered English

Teacher to Teacher

Jay Harmon of Baton Rouge, Louisiana, suggested the following activity: Ask students to make a list of the origins of any four items of clothing or shoes and of any three of the following: TV, VCR, hair drier, canned goods, computer software, radio, school book bag, or shampoo. Have students match the items to their countries of origin on a copy of a world map.

SECTION 4 REVIEW ANSWERS

Define and Identify
For significance, see the following pages:

- oil shocks, p. 844
- floating exchange rates, p. 845
- Pacific Rim, p. 845
- e-commerce, p. 847
- euro, p. 848
- Ross Perot, p. 848
- World Trade Organization, p. 849

1. oil shocks, floating exchange rates

2. dramatic economic growth in late 1980s and early 1990s, recession in late 1990s, cautious recovery by summer 1999

3. Some have boosted employment and development but others have underpaid workers, harmed the environment, and changed local cultures.

4. Corporations began investing in Eastern Europe and the former Soviet republics; some countries received less aid from the Soviet Union; and some African nations feared that they would receive less European investment.

5. EU—increased free trade among European nations; NAFTA—increased free trade among Canada, United States, and Mexico; WTO—increased free-trade opportunities for countries around the world

and import goods. As a result, more and more countries are trying to arrange or expand free-trade agreements.

The European Union adopted a common currency called the euro in 1999.

Europe. The world's most successful free-trade zone has been in Western Europe. After its formation in 1957, the EEC grew to include 12 of the leading European economies. Tariffs and other barriers to trade continued to fall during the 1970s and 1980s.

In 1993 the EEC nations signed the Maastricht Treaty, which created the European Union (EU). The Union is designed to allow capital, goods, and labor to move freely among member nations. On January 1, 1999, the European Union adopted a single currency called the **euro**. Of the 15 member nations, 11 agreed to share this currency as a way to simplify trade among them.

NAFTA. Other countries have attempted to copy the European Union's success at eliminating trade barriers. Canada and the United States have long been each other's most important trading partner. During the 1980s U.S. and Canadian leaders strengthened the relationship by negotiating a free-trade agreement. Each government approved the pact, despite opposition from both Americans and Canadians who feared increased competition. In the early 1990s Mexico asked to join the group.

The proposed North American Free Trade Agreement (NAFTA) aroused heated debate in all three countries. In the United States, opponents argued that Mexico's low wages and lenient environmental regulation would lure American corporations to move to Mexico. NAFTA critic Ross Perot predicted that if Congress approved NAFTA, Americans would hear a "giant sucking sound" as U.S. jobs were lost to Mexico. Many Americans agreed.

Supporters of NAFTA countered that people were not simply producers; they were also consumers. They pointed out that tariffs and other trade barriers raised prices, thus hurting consumers. Free trade would allow each country to specialize in those goods it produced most efficiently, and nations would be able to trade freely for other goods. They claimed NAFTA would give the citizens of the three countries access to the best possible products at the lowest possible prices. In a narrow vote, Congress agreed. It approved NAFTA in November 1993.

Response to NAFTA—which took effect January 1, 1994—has been generally favorable in all three countries.

Great Debates: The Future of the Global Economy

The prosperity brought about by increased free trade has not been spread evenly throughout the world. Wages remain disturbingly low in many newly industrialized countries. For example, poor residents of Peru have not benefited from the nation's strong economic growth—one of the highest growth rates in the developing world. Even within wealthy countries, pockets of poverty and unemployment remain. The positive impact of the global economy in Africa is even more limited than in Peru. After decades of colonial rule, many African countries have struggled with civil war and other conflicts that have limited foreign investment and economic stability. Attempting to gain a strategic place in the global economy, many Africans have pushed for an increased attempt to achieve peace and political stability. Others have encouraged greater educational opportunities and the further development of information technology.

On the whole, however, the global economy at the end of the 1900s was more unified than ever before. Many people predict that economics will play an even greater international role in the future. Economic historians Richard Nelson and Gavin Wright predicted in 1992 that the importance of the global economy will surpass the importance of national borders and foreign governments.

> **"We believe . . . that the internationalization of trade, business, and technology is here to stay. This means that national borders mean much less than they used to regarding the flow of technology."**

REVIEW

Have students complete the **Section 4 Review** on p. 849.

ASSESS

Have students complete **Daily Quiz 28.4.** As **Alternative Assessment**, you may want to use the presidential economic briefing or the time line activity in this section's lessons.

RETEACH

Have students complete **Main Idea Activity for Reteaching and Sheltered English 28.4.** Then have each student make up a 10-question quiz with answer key for the section. Have students trade quizzes with a partner and answer each other's questions. Tell them to trade back and correct each other's work. **Sheltered English, Cooperative Learning**

EXTEND

Have students conduct research on working conditions and salaries in other parts of the world. Tell them to write a few paragraphs describing life for workers in so-called sweatshops. Then tell students to brainstorm ideas about how they might be able to make a difference as American consumers. *(Students might suggest boycotting goods made in countries that do not enforce a reasonable minimum wage and raising public awareness of human rights violations by writing letters to American newspapers.)* Call on volunteers to summarize their findings for the class. **Block Scheduling**

Mexican trade minister Herminio Blanco reported in 1998 that the agreement has benefited his country.

> "[NAFTA is] a huge success for Mexico. It's been a success from the point of view of foreign direct investment, salaries have increased, . . . and Europe now looks on Mexico as part of North America."

The World Trade Organization. In the background of the debate over NAFTA was another set of trade negotiations involving most of the world's nations. These negotiations, called the Uruguay Round of GATT talks, signaled an effort to boost global free trade during the late 1980s. Among the important issues covered was the trade of agricultural products and of intellectual property, such as movies and computer software.

In 1994 officials from 125 nations signed a 22,000-page agreement. One part of the agreement reorganized GATT as the **World Trade Organization** (WTO). This new name reflected its sponsors' hope that the organization would continue to bring cooperation to world trade issues.

The WTO sponsored a convention in Seattle in December 1999 to begin a new round of talks to reduce trade barriers. The convention drew a wide range of protest over labor and environmental issues that according to many critics the WTO was ignoring. The Seattle convention failed to bring about new trade arrangements, as regional and national conflicts prevented members from reaching agreements on trade regulations. Nevertheless, many nations have continued to press for the expansion of the organization and of free trade, and countries such as China have continued to lobby for membership in the WTO.

✔ **READING CHECK:** What evidence points to a recent movement toward global free trade?

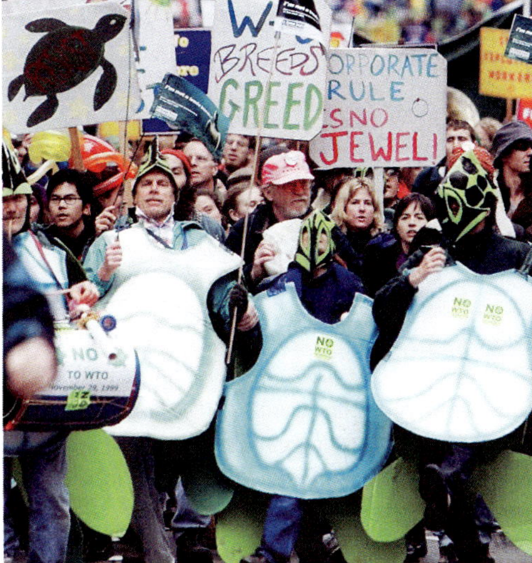

INTERPRETING THE VISUAL RECORD

WTO Environmentalists and labor organizers protested the 1999 WTO talks in Seattle. ***What message do you think these protesters wanted to convey with their costumes?***

SECTION  REVIEW

Define and explain the significance of the following terms:
oil shocks
floating exchange rates
Pacific Rim
e-commerce
euro
World Trade Organization

Identify and explain the significance of the following individual:
Ross Perot

1. **Using Graphic Organizers** Copy the graphic organizer below. Use it to identify the factors that led to the decline of U.S. dominance of the global economy since the 1970s.

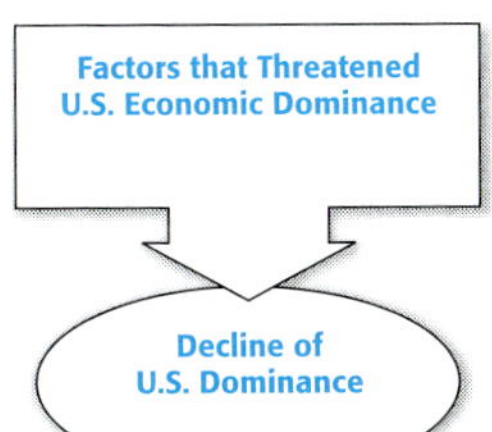

2. **Assessing Consequences** How have the economies of Pacific Rim countries changed in recent decades?
3. **Identifying Cause and Effect** How have multinational corporations changed the global economy?
4. **Evaluating** How has the end of the Cold War affected the global economy?

Critical Thinking

5. How have international organizations and recent trade agreements contributed to global free trade?
Consider:
• how the European Union affects free trade
• what impact NAFTA has had
• how the World Trade Organization has affected free trade

VISUAL RECORD ANSWER

Students might answer that they are protesting environmental policies.

CHAPTER 28 REVIEW ANSWERS

Creating a Time Line
Each event should have an explanation and the correct date.

Writing a Summary
See the Reading Checks in each section for main ideas.

Identifying People and Ideas
1. goods that are in constant demand and are often sold in bulk
2. British prime minister who worked to eliminate tariffs
3. set new schedule for German war reparations payment
4. decrease in the value of one currency in relation to another
5. 1944 plan to stabilize currency and prevent tariff increases and trade wars
6. plan that ties currencies to value of dollar
7. established to provide loans to war-damaged and developing countries
8. nations bordering the Pacific Ocean that form a new center of world economy
9. system that allows the value of each currency to vary
10. designed to bring cooperation to world trade issues

REVIEW AND ASSESSMENT RESOURCES

PRINT
- Chapter 28 Review, pp. 850–51
- Chapter 28 Tutorial for Students, Parents, Mentors, and Peers
- Chapter 28 Test (Form A or B)
- Portfolio Activities and Alternative Assessment Handbook, Chapter 28

MULTIMEDIA
- Audio Program, Chapter 28 (English and Spanish)
- Chapter 28 Test Generator (on the One-Stop Planner)
- Global Skill Builder CD–ROM
- HRW Web site

SHELTERED ENGLISH
- Spanish Glossary
- Sheltered English Chapter 28 Test

REVIEW

Have students complete the **Chapter 28 Review** on pp. 850–51.

ASSESS

Use one of the chapter tests to assess students' understanding of the content. For **Alternative Assessment**, see the **Portfolio Activities and Alternative Assessment Handbook.**

Understanding Main Ideas

1. because overproduction had resulted in a surplus of goods in the United States
2. gold standard stabilized currency values and gave trade greater stability
3. by establishing fixed exchange rates, the IMF, the World Bank, and GATT
4. oil shocks, floating exchange rates, growth of Pacific Rim, spread of multinational corporations, establishment of European Union, development of international trade

Reviewing Themes

1. Faster transportation cut shipping costs, and improved communications increased global communication.
2. massive inflation, worldwide depression, fluctuation in currency values
3. NAFTA opponents felt that it would cost American jobs. Supporters argued that free trade promoted economic specialization and efficiency.

Review

Creating a Time Line

Copy the time line below onto a sheet of paper. Complete the time line by filling in the events and dates from the chapter that you think were most significant. Pick three events and explain why you think they were significant.

Writing a Summary

Using the Reading Checks as a guide, write an overview of the events in the chapter.

Identifying People and Ideas

Identify the following terms or individuals and explain their significance.

1. staples
2. Robert Peel
3. Young Plan
4. devaluation
5. Bretton Woods system
6. fixed exchange rates
7. World Bank
8. Pacific Rim
9. floating exchange rates
10. World Trade Organization

Understanding Main Ideas

SECTION 1

1. Why did Americans look abroad for markets in the late 1800s and early 1900s?

SECTION 2

2. How was the global economy affected by the widespread adoption of the gold standard?

SECTION 3

3. How did the Bretton Woods conference promote economic stability after World War II?

SECTION 4

4. What economic trends and political events have significantly influenced the global economy since the early 1970s?

Reviewing Themes

1. **Technology and Society** How did the invention of steamships and the telegraph contribute to an increase in global trade?
2. **Global Relations** What economic problems did the world experience as a result of World War I?
3. **Economic Development** Why did some people oppose the passage of the North American Free Trade Agreement? Why did others support the agreement?

Thinking Critically

1. **Synthesizing** In what ways did the United States benefit economically from both World War I and World War II?
2. **Assessing Consequences** How did measures such as the Smoot-Hawley Tariff and the British abandonment of the gold standard affect the global economy in the 1930s?
3. **Hypothesizing** What region of the world do you think will experience the greatest economic growth in the next 25 years? Why?
4. **Analyzing** What benefits and problems has the Internet brought to the business world?
5. **Identifying Cause and Effect** How did the collapse of the Soviet Union affect the global economy?

Writing About History

Writing to Persuade Imagine that you are investigating the economic situation after World War I. Write a letter to American bankers explaining why it would be in their interests to make loans to West Germany. Use the following chart to organize your thoughts.

What are the loans for? → How would that help West Germany? → How would the United States benefit?

RETEACH

Organize the class into four groups and assign each group one of the sections of this chapter. Have each group create a large-scale illustrated time line covering the major developments around the world—from the late 1800s to the present—that contributed to the growth of a global economy.
Sheltered English, Cooperative Learning

EXTEND

Have each student write a science-fiction short story set on Earth 200 to 500 years in the future. Tell them to be creative with characters and plot but to make clear in the story's exposition how the global economy has developed since the year 2000 and how the new economic condition affects the daily lives of the characters. **Block Scheduling**

Strategies for Success Review the **Strategies for Success** on *Reading Graphs.* Study the graph below. Then answer the following questions. Which of the two industries do you think will employ more people in the year 2005? Why do you think so?

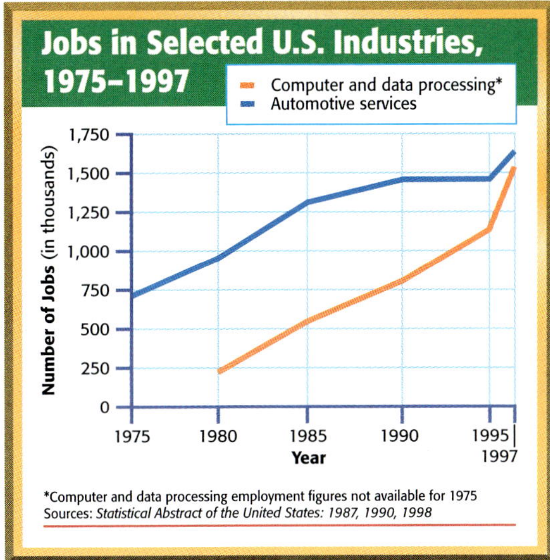

Linking History and Geography

Beginning in the late 1950s European countries began planning the formation of an economic union. Which countries had joined the European Union as of 1999?

internet connect

TOPIC: The European Union
GO TO: go.hrw.com
KEYWORD: SE1 European Union

Accessing the Internet through the HRW Web site, research the European Union. Find information on its history, membership, policies, and accomplishments. Imagine that you represent a small country that may join the European Union. Write a memo to your government summarizing the benefits and problems your country might encounter in the European Union.

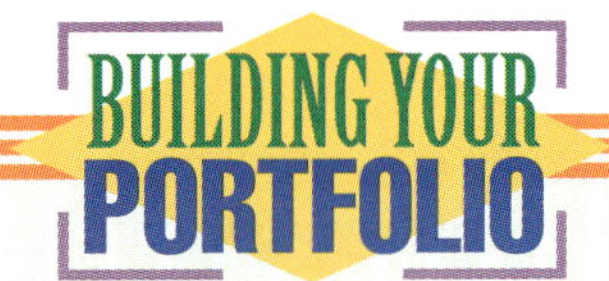

Complete one or all of the following activities independently or cooperatively.

1 Technology and Society

Imagine that you are an economist at the World Bank who is assigned to study how new technology can affect the economies of nations. ***Create a chart*** showing how technological advances in communications have led to the expansion of the global economy.

2 Global Relations

Imagine that you are an administrator at the World Trade Organization (WTO). ***Prepare a speech*** that explains how the WTO will or will not benefit the global economy. To support your claims, include an overview of ways in which international cooperation has or has not helped the global economy during the 1900s.

3 Economic Development

Imagine that you are a policy maker in an industrializing nation trying to decide how to shape your nation's economy. ***Draft a proposal*** explaining how a nation's economic policies can affect its workers, business owners, consumers, and community members.

The euro

Thinking Critically

1. Both wars allowed the United States to become a dominant economic power.
2. led to global economic instability
3. Answers will vary but should consider the growth of the Pacific Rim and the development of new trade agreements.
4. benefits—faster communication, ability to sell products worldwide; problems—enforcing trade regulations and taxation
5. allowed investment in former Soviet sphere

Writing About History

Letters will vary but should indicate the benefits of stable currencies and of maintaining a strong global economy.

Strategies for Success

Answers will vary but students should base their answer on information presented in the chart and the chapter.

Linking History and Geography

Austria, Belgium, Denmark, Finland, France, Germany, Greece, Ireland, Italy, Luxembourg, the Netherlands, Portugal, Spain, Sweden, and the United Kingdom

LET'S GET STARTED!

Write the following quotation from President Clinton on the chalkboard: "*Today, every nation has an important stake in our global economy. The expansion of international markets and the growth of the global economy over the past half century have helped lift millions of people out of poverty and raised living standards for millions more. . . . In a global marketplace, each nation's success depends on every other nation's success.*" To begin the class, ask students to respond to the quotation in writing. Then ask volunteers to share their responses. Tell students that they will learn more about the development of the global economy in the Unit 8 America's Geography.

SPOTLIGHT on U.S. Trading Partners

Ask each student to conduct research on the five nations with whom the United States traded the most in the 1950s and the top five U.S. trading partners today. Students should also conduct research on the types of goods traded. Have each student create a detailed chart to present his or her findings. **Block Scheduling**

HISTORY MAKERS SPEAK

E. J. Hobsbawm in *The Age of Empire*

From Plantation to Dinner Table. In *The Age of Empire,* historian E. J. Hobsbawm describes one effect the creation of a global economy had on consumers living in economically developed countries. "Britons, who had consumed 1.5 lb of tea per head in the 1840s and 3.26 lb in the 1860s, were consuming 5.7 lb in the 1890s. . . . Americans and Germans imported coffee in ever more spectacular quantities, notably from Latin America. . . . The canny Boston businessmen who founded the United Fruit Company in 1885 created private empires in the Caribbean to supply America with the previously insignificant banana. The soap manufacturers, exploiting the market which first demonstrated to the full the capacities of the new advertising industry, looked to the vegetable oils of Africa."

CRITICAL THINKING What might the passage suggest about the types of goods that economically developed countries imported from economically underdeveloped countries?

ANSWER: Students might suggest that developed countries tended to import foodstuffs and raw materials rather than manufactured goods.

AMERICA'S Geography

The Global Economy

As the global economy has grown over the past 150 years, a vast network of transportation and communications systems has been developed to support it. Despite increasing international unity, relationships within the global economy have undergone many changes. For example, the United States once traded almost exclusively with European nations. In recent decades Asian nations have become increasingly important trading partners, and trade with Europe has declined. The growth of the global economy has benefited some nations more than others. Many nations, particularly in Africa and Latin America, have found it difficult to develop their economies.

Exports. Between 1850 and 1920, the total dollar value of exports from the United States grew from some $140 million to more than $8 billion. By 1990 the figure had reached almost $400 billion.

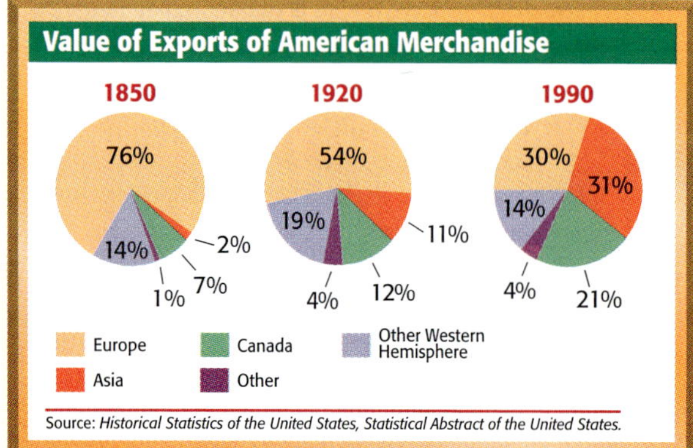

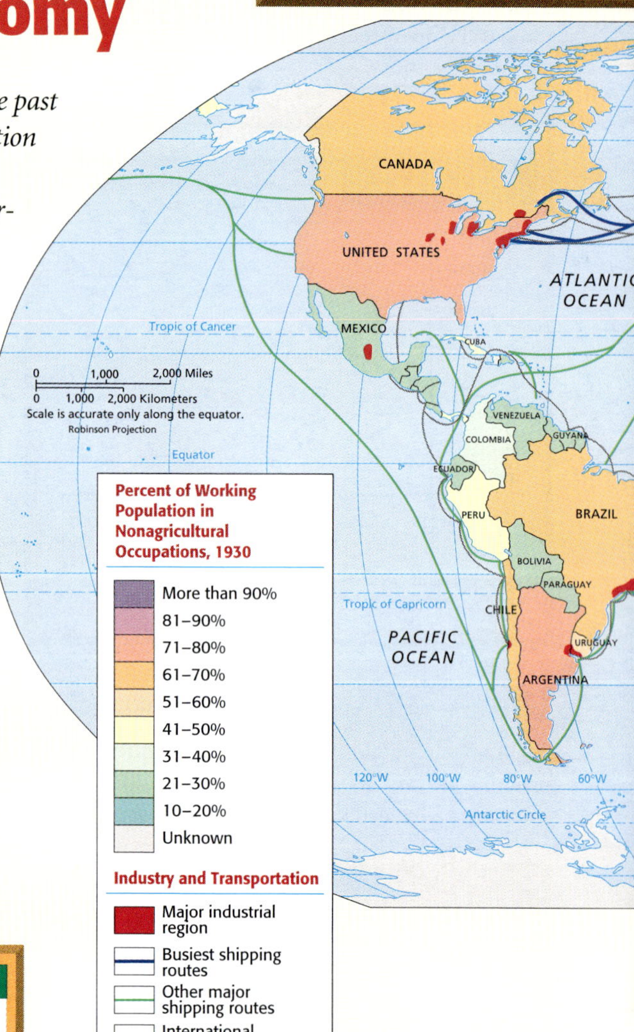

Industrialization. In the late 1800s and early 1900s, a complex communications and transportation network arose to unite the world economically. The industrialized nations of Europe and North America, however, received most of the benefits of this network. Africa, Asia, and parts of Latin America remained primarily agricultural.

TEACH AMERICA'S GEOGRAPHY–GDP AND INFRASTRUCTURE

Pair students and ask each pair to examine the map comparing GDP around the world. Have each pair select one country with a developed economy and one country with a low-income economy and compare their levels of infrastructure—roads, railways, water supply, hospitals, and so on. Ask students to prepare a report presenting their findings and a hypothesis about how a country's infrastructure might relate to its potential for economic growth.

Cooperative Learning, Block Scheduling

SPOTLIGHT on U.S. Exports

Have each student conduct research on the major categories of goods that the United States exports and the percentage of each major category in relation to total U.S. exports. Then have each student create an illustrated pie chart to present his or her findings. **Block Scheduling**

AMERICA'S Geography

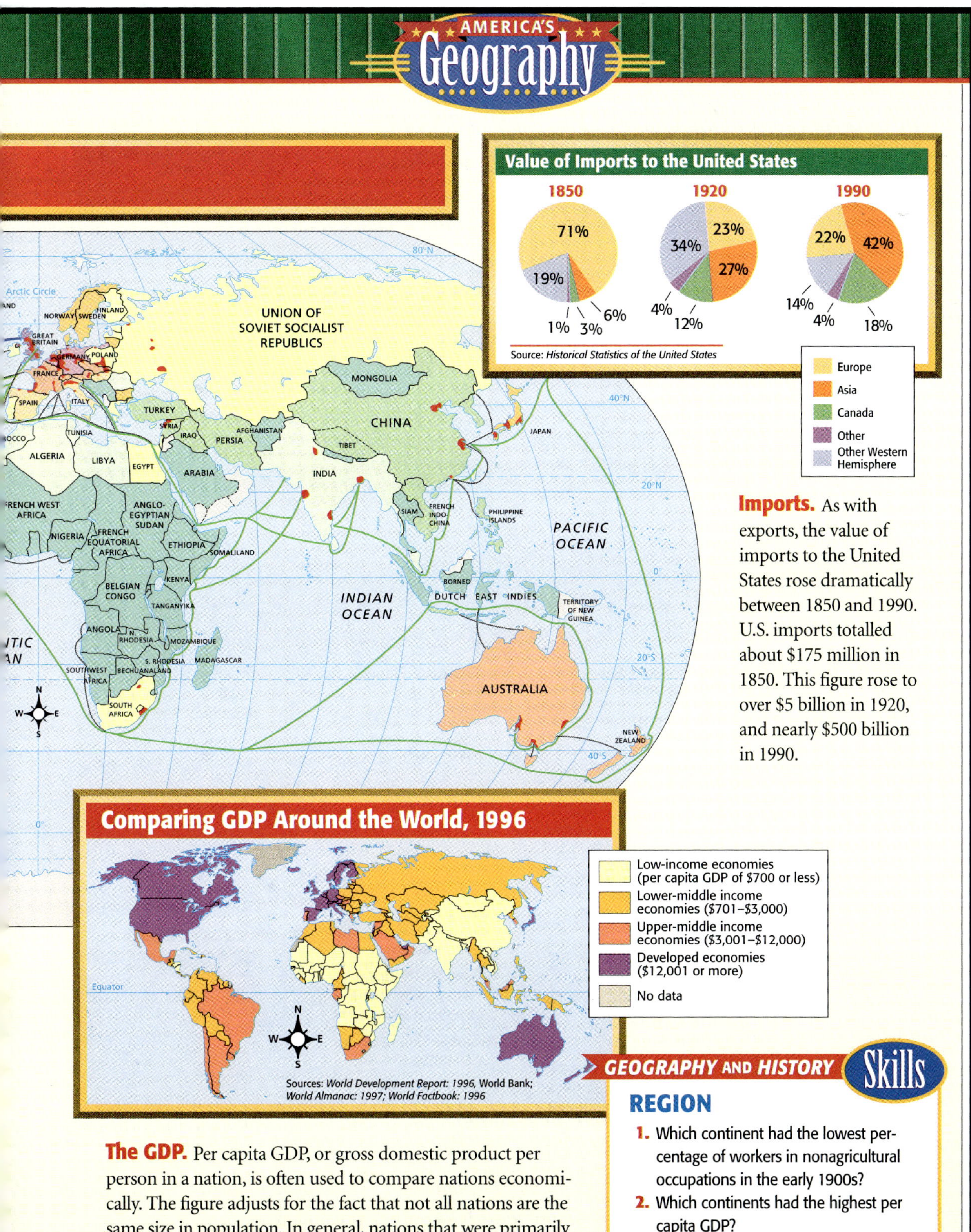

Imports. As with exports, the value of imports to the United States rose dramatically between 1850 and 1990. U.S. imports totalled about $175 million in 1850. This figure rose to over $5 billion in 1920, and nearly $500 billion in 1990.

The GDP. Per capita GDP, or gross domestic product per person in a nation, is often used to compare nations economically. The figure adjusts for the fact that not all nations are the same size in population. In general, nations that were primarily agricultural in 1930 had a low per capita GDP in 1996.

GEOGRAPHY AND HISTORY Skills

REGION

1. Which continent had the lowest percentage of workers in nonagricultural occupations in the early 1900s?
2. Which continents had the highest per capita GDP?

DEMOCRATIC VALUES

Democratic Rights and Economic Security. How does the distribution of a nation's economic resources relate to its form of government? Nobel Prize–winning economist Amartya Sen argues that regardless of a nation's level of economic development, democratic rights can provide the key to preventing economic catastrophes. He observes, "It is not surprising that no famine has ever taken place in the history of the world in a functioning democracy–be it economically rich . . . or relatively poor. . . . Famines have tended to occur in colonial territories governed by rulers from elsewhere (as in British India or in an Ireland administered by alienated English rulers), or in one-party states (as in the Ukraine in the 1930s, or China during 1958–1961, or Cambodia in the 1970s), or in military dictatorships."

CRITICAL THINKING Why might famines have tended to occur under colonial or nondemocratic governments?

ANSWER: Students might suggest that authoritarian governments are not subject to elections and therefore, do not have to curry favor with voters.

AMERICA'S GEOGRAPHY ANSWERS

1. Europe
2. Australia, Europe, and North America

853

The Movement of People and Ideas

CHAPTER PLANNING GUIDE

	Section Lesson Objectives	Print Resources	Multimedia Resources	Sheltered English Resources
Section 1 Patterns of Migration, pp. 856–60	1 Explain why many immigrants chose to leave their homelands. 2 State why the United States was the most likely destination of immigrants. 3 Discuss how migration affected urban and rural populations.	▶ Guided Reading Strategy 29.1 ▶ Geography Activity 29: A Diverse Nation ▶ Primary Source Reading 29: Voices of America's Ethnic Heritage ▶ Section 1 Review, p. 860 ▶ Daily Quiz 29.1	▶ One-Stop Planner, Lesson 29.1 ▶ Linking Geography and History Transparency 11B: Growth of Cities, 1840–1950 ▶ Holt Researcher: American History CD–ROM	▶ Main Idea Activity for Reteaching and Sheltered English 29.1
Section 2 Children of War, pp. 861–66	1 Explain how World War I and the Great Depression affected immigration patterns. 2 State the primary reason for migrating during the 1940s. 3 Identify how immigration in the United States has changed since 1965. 4 Describe what caused people to migrate during the 1980s and 1990s.	▶ Guided Reading Strategy 29.2 ▶ Graphic Organizer Activity 29: Immigration ▶ Literature Reading 29: The Narrative Art of the Storyteller ▶ Section 2 Review, p. 866 ▶ Daily Quiz 29.2	▶ One-Stop Planner, Lesson 29.2 ▶ The American Nation Video Program Segment: A Nation of Immigrants; Teacher's Guide, pp. 153–56 ▶ Holt Researcher: American History CD–ROM ▶ HRW Web site	▶ Main Idea Activity for Reteaching and Sheltered English 29.2
Section 3 The Movement of Information, pp. 867–71	1 Explain how developments in computer technology affected the spread of information. 2 Summarize the challenges and benefits developing nations have faced while trying to improve their communications technology. 3 Discuss privacy concerns that recent technological developments have raised.	▶ Guided Reading Strategy 29.3 ▶ Section 3 Review, p. 871 ▶ Daily Quiz 29.3	▶ One-Stop Planner, Lesson 29.3 ▶ Holt Researcher: American History CD–ROM	▶ Main Idea Activity for Reteaching and Sheltered English 29.3
Section 4 A Global Culture, pp. 872–75	1 Describe how the popularity of sports has grown to include a worldwide audience. 2 Explain how television, the Internet, and movies have contributed to a global culture. 3 Discuss how music and fashion have contributed to a global youth culture.	▶ Guided Reading Strategy 29.4 ▶ Biography Reading 29: Spike Lee ▶ Section 4 Review, p. 875 ▶ Daily Quiz 29.4	▶ One-Stop Planner, Lesson 29.4 ▶ Holt Researcher: American History CD–ROM	▶ Main Idea Activity for Reteaching and Sheltered English 29.4
Chapter Review and Assessment pp. 876–77		▶ Chapter 29 Review, pp. 876–77 ▶ Chapter 29 Tutorial for Students, Parents, Mentors, and Peers ▶ Chapter 29 Test (Form A or B) ▶ Portfolio Activities and Alternative Assessment Handbook, Chapter 29	▶ Audio Program, Chapter 29 (English and Spanish) ▶ Chapter 29 Test Generator (on the One-Stop Planner) ▶ Global Skill Builder CD–ROM ▶ HRW Web site	▶ Spanish Glossary ▶ Sheltered English Chapter 29 Test

CHAPTER OVERVIEW

The 1800s marked a period of migration all around the world as people moved to different countries in search of economic opportunity and personal freedom. Despite the growth of nativist—or anti-immigrant sentiment—in the United States, it was the most popular destination for immigrants. World War I, the Immigration Act of 1924, and the Great Depression slowed immigration to the United States. After World War II migration increased as refugees sought new homes in countries such as Israel. The passage of the Immigration Act of 1965 allowed more immigrants to enter the United States, leading some Americans to question the effect immigrants would have on American life.

The movement of information raised few international concerns, as people benefited from the flow of information on the Internet and cellular communications systems. This technological revolution spurred the development of a global culture that was primarily dominated by American culture.

TIME TAMERS

Block Scheduling

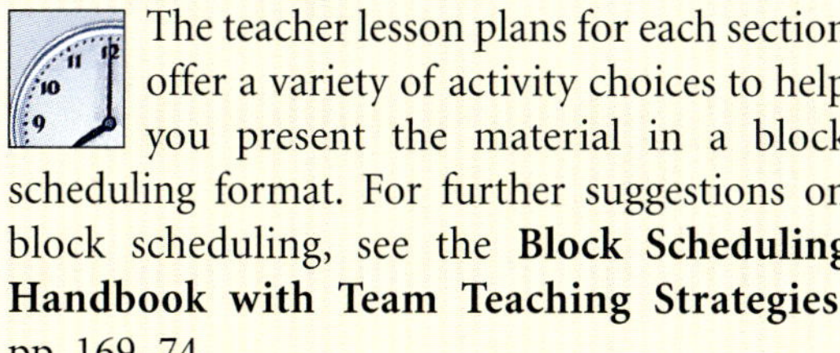

The teacher lesson plans for each section offer a variety of activity choices to help you present the material in a block scheduling format. For further suggestions on block scheduling, see the **Block Scheduling Handbook with Team Teaching Strategies**, pp. 169–74.

Smithsonian Institution®

Internet Connections and Lesson 29

www.si.edu/hrw

Hands-On History Activities:

Classroom to Community The **Hands-On History Activities** help students make meaningful connections between events in American history and those in their own hometown. You may wish to use the Chapter 29 Activity, International Influences in Your Community, to extend the chapter lessons, as alternative assessment, or as a block scheduling option.

Portfolio Projects

The American Nation includes multiple portfolio projects in each Pupil's Edition chapter review, as well as each unit review. Chapter 29 Portfolio Project options on p. 877 include the following:

1. Students will **write a series of journal entries.**
2. Students will **prepare a speech.**
3. Students will **write an opening statement.**

The American Nation
INTERNET RESOURCE DIRECTORY

To access online materials for this chapter, go to go.hrw.com and type in the keywords listed below.

HRW ONLINE RESOURCES
GO TO: go.hrw.com

Online Maps
KEYWORD: SE1 Maps29
- Urban Population, 1940
- U.S. Asian Population, 1980
- U.S. Hispanic Population, 1980

Online Charts
KEYWORD: SE1 Charts29
- U.S. Immigration, 1971–1993

Online Reading Support
KEYWORD: SE1 Strategies29

Online Rubrics
KEYWORD: SE1 Rubrics

CHAPTER ENRICHMENT LINKS
Use these Web links to extend and enrich student learning for Chapter 29.
GO TO: go.hrw.com
KEYWORD: SE1 Ch29

CHAPTER INTERNET ACTIVITIES
GO TO: go.hrw.com
- Pupil's Edition Student Activity
  KEYWORD: SE1 Sports
  (Students research international sports.)
- Teacher's Edition Student Activity
  KEYWORD: SE1 Cubism
  (Students explore the development of cubism.)
- Teacher's Edition Student Activity
  KEYWORD: SE1 Great Migration
  (Students examine the migration of African Americans.)

ADDITIONAL
RESOURCES

Books for Teachers

Barber, Benjamin R. *Jihad vs. McWorld.* Times Books, 1995. Considers forces for and against the development of global culture.

Moschovitis, Christos J. P. *History of the Internet.* ABC-Clio, 1999. Presents a history of technological developments from 1843 to 1999.

Books for Students

Daniels, Roger. *Coming to America.* HarperCollins, 1990. Surveys the history of immigration to the United States.

Santoli, Al. *New Americans: An Oral History.* Viking, 1988. Provides oral histories from recent immigrants to the United States.

Primary Sources from the Period

Gates, Bill. *The Road Ahead.* Viking, 1995. Offers a vision of the technological future from a leading computer expert.

Stoddard, Lathrop. *The Rising Tide of Color Against White World Supremacy.* Revisionist Press, 1984. Presents a nativist work that contributed to anti-immigrant attitudes during the 1920s.

Multimedia Materials

America Becoming. Video, 90 min. WETA. Examines the effect of the Immigration Act of 1965.

The Biggest Jewish City in the World. Video, 60 min. Thames. Describes Jewish immigration to New York City.

CHAPTER 29

Before You Read

Build on What You Know

Ask students to answer the following questions.

Why might the 1800s have been a period of renewed immigration to the United States?

Consider:

- the political freedoms available in the United States
- the development of the U.S. economy during the period

How does technology promote the spread of culture?

Consider:

- recent technological developments in transportation
- recent communications developments

exploring the time line

AMERICAN EVENTS

ACROSS THE CURRICULUM

▶LITERATURE/THEATER◀

West Side Story. The musical *West Side Story* was loosely based on the play *Romeo and Juliet* by William Shakespeare. In *West Side Story* rival gangs in New York City replace Shakespeare's feuding Italian families, the Montagues and the Capulets. Maria, a young Puerto Rican girl whose brother is the leader of a gang called the Sharks, falls in love with Tony. A member of a rival gang, the Jets, Tony is a second-generation Polish American. The movie touches on many issues in American society in the late 1950s and early 1960s, including juvenile delinquency, racial tension, and inner-city problems.

ACTIVITY: Have students write an outline for a musical based on a classic novel or play but revised to reflect contemporary issues.

CHAPTER 29

1890–Present

The Movement of People and Ideas

Olympic flag

Still Life with Violin and Guitar, ***a cubist painting by Juan Gris***

1890

1892 Politics The U.S. Bureau of Immigration opens a receiving station on Ellis Island, New York.

1896 World Events The first modern Olympic Games are held in Athens, Greece.

1900

early 1900s Daily Life U.S. soldiers spread the game of baseball to Latin America.

1908 The Arts Georges Braque helps develop the cubist style.

1910

1912 Business and Finance Germany claims to have 30,000 millionaires.

1920

1930

1930s World Events The rise of fascist governments in Europe spurs massive refugee migrations from the continent.

1932 Daily Life The average weekly wage in the United States drops to $21.75 from $27.10 in 1929.

1939 Business and Finance The U.S. economy begins to grow as a result of European orders for war materials.

1940

Children playing baseball in Havana, Cuba

Before You Read

Build on What You Know

The first people in America arrived thousands of years ago from Asia, migrating across the Beringia land bridge. In the late 1400s a new wave of immigration began—this time from Europe and Africa. Once again in the 1800s immigrants came in large numbers to the Americas. In this chapter you will learn how these immigrants and their descendants contributed to a diverse American culture. You will also learn how recent technological developments have led to the growth of global communication and the spread of American popular culture around the world.

Think About Themes

*To help students create their Themes Journal entries, provide the following examples of appropriate **agree/disagree** statements.*

Cultural Diversity

Agree Immigrants and urban migrants present new perspectives and cultural values.

Disagree Immigrants and rural migrants strive to assimilate into American culture.

Technology and Society

Agree Government funding promotes research and development that private companies cannot afford.

Disagree Government sponsorship stifles free enterprise, the most efficient way to develop technology.

Economic Development

Agree Consumers interested in popular culture will purchase goods from all over the world.

Disagree Globalization allows one nation, the United States, to dominate the global economy as it exports its culture.

U.S. astronaut Alan Shepard

New York Stock Exchange

1955 Business and Finance The Universal Copyright Convention takes effect.

1961 Science and Technology Astronaut Alan Shepard becomes the first American in space.

1962 The Arts *West Side Story* wins an Academy Award for best picture.

1965 Politics The U.S. Congress passes the Immigration Act of 1965, which greatly reduces restrictions on immigration to the United States.

1969 Science and Technology The U.S. Defense Department establishes the forerunner of the contemporary Internet.

1972 Business and Finance The Dow Jones stock index closes above 1,000 for the first time.

1994 World Events Ethnic rivalries trigger a civil war in Rwanda, leading millions of refugees to flee the country.

1996 Science and Technology The Internet links nearly 150 nations worldwide.

1950 | 1960 | 1970 | 1980 | 1990 | 1999

Scene from West Side Story

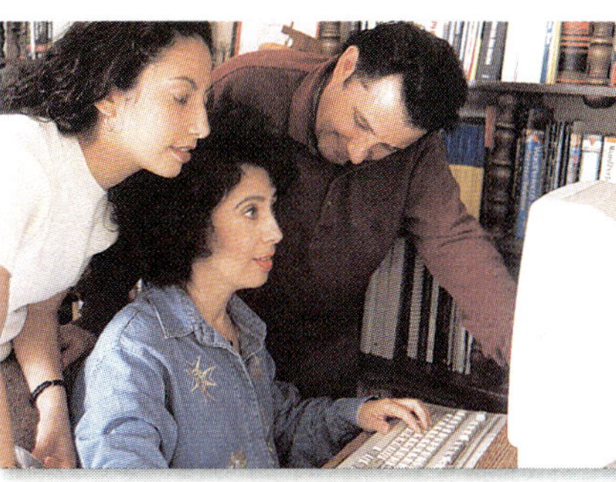

Family using the Internet

exploring the time line

GLOBAL EVENTS

TOPIC: Cubism
GO TO: go.hrw.com
KEYWORD: SE1 Cubism

Have students access the Internet through the HRW Web site to conduct research on cubism, an artistic movement. Then ask students to imagine that they are art critics from the era when cubism began. Have each student write a review of one or more cubist paintings.

Think About Themes

*Decide whether you **agree** or **disagree** with the following statements. Note why in your journal.*

Cultural Diversity Immigration and the movement of people from rural areas to urban areas help to create cultural diversity in a society.

Technology and Society Government investment in technological research and development benefits society.

Economic Development Worldwide interest in sports, movies, and other elements of popular culture benefits the global economy.

SECTION 1

After completing Section 1, students should be able to:

OBJECTIVE 1 *Explain why many immigrants chose to leave their homelands.*

OBJECTIVE 2 *State why the United States was the most likely destination of immigrants.*

OBJECTIVE 3 *Discuss how migration affected urban and rural populations.*

LET'S GET STARTED!

To begin the class, write the following topic on the chalkboard: *Reasons People Move to New Places.* Then have students brainstorm as many reasons as they can and write them down. *(Students should come up with a variety of reasons relating to educational opportunities, employment, family, religion, and so on.)* When students have finished writing, ask volunteers to read some of their reasons to the class. Tell them that many of the reasons they have come up with were valid during the 1800s and early 1900s as well. Finally, tell students that in Section 1 they will learn why people moved from country to country and within the United States during the 1800s and 1900s.

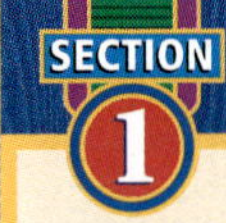

SECTION 1 RESOURCES

PRINT

- Guided Reading Strategy 29.1
- Geography Activity 29: A Diverse Nation
- Primary Source Reading 29: Voices of America's Ethnic Heritage
- Section 1 Review, p. 860
- Daily Quiz 29.1

MULTIMEDIA

- One-Stop Planner, Lesson 29.1
- Linking Geography and History Transparency 11B: Growth of Cities, 1840–1950
- Holt Researcher: American History CD–ROM

SHELTERED ENGLISH

- Main Idea Activity for Reteaching and Sheltered English 29.1

✔ READING TO UNDERSTAND

To help students master the section objectives, have them answer the **READING CHECKS** and complete **Guided Reading Strategy 29.1** as they read the section.

Patterns of Migration

OBJECTIVES

Read to understand:

1. why many immigrants chose to leave their homelands
2. why the United States was the most likely destination of immigrants
3. how migration during the 1800s and early 1900s affected urban and rural populations

KEY TERMS

Ellis Island
Angel Island

"The evolution of America has always involved north and south migration. It was the Europeans who gave it east and west. . . . It's like the bellybutton of the world."

—Luis M. Valdez

Advertisement for travel to the United States

Mexican American playwright Luis M. Valdez spoke about the past and future of immigration in the Americas. "Right at that intersection, four roads meet—the white road, the black road, the yellow road, and the red road. What they represent to me is the promise of America—that four roads will meet and will bear new fruit in this ancient land." During the 1800s and 1900s millions of people emigrated from their birthplaces to other countries. Attracted by industrial jobs, many of these migrants settled in the United States.

People on the Move

The 1800s and early 1900s marked one of the world's great ages of migration. This period of migration affected all the inhabited continents and most countries.

Global Migration. Specific statistics on global migration are difficult to determine because few countries kept good records on who came or left. Estimates suggest, however, that some 60 million people left Europe during the century before World War I. Europeans immigrated to Australia, North America, South America, and to many parts of Africa. Another wave of immigrants left China and Japan for the Americas. Some 12 million Chinese also settled in South and Southeast Asia. From India still more migrants traveled to countries bordering the Indian Ocean. At their height, Indian communities in this region totaled about 3 million people.

The African slave trade continued for centuries before coming to an end in the late 1800s. The slave trade caused the forced movement of millions of Africans to Asia and the Americas. The size of the slave trade to Asia is difficult to calculate because few records exist. Historians estimate that the slave trade transported more than 10 million Africans to the Americas.

Many immigrants carried only a few personal items with them to America.

Why they moved. Immigrants had many different reasons for their decision to travel abroad. One of the most common reasons was economic. Farmers often left home in search of better or less-expensive land. Millions of other immigrants traveled to new countries in search of better jobs and higher wages. Many of these wage-earners did not plan to relocate permanently. They hoped to earn enough money to return to their native countries and live in comfort. Most, however, remained in their new homeland. By the 1930s North Africa's European immigrants had formed an important business class. Similarly, Chinese and Indian immigrants formed a successful merchant class in many Southeast Asian nations.

TEACH OBJECTIVE 1

LEVELS 1 AND 2: Have students look back over their lists of reasons for migration from the Let's Get Started! activity. Tell them to add to it, if necessary, by referring to the subsection "Why They Moved" on the previous page. Then pair students and have them write the text for the book jacket of an autobiography of a late-1800s immigrant to the United States. Students should summarize in a few paragraphs why many immigrants leave their homelands.
Sheltered English, Cooperative Learning

LEVEL 3: Tell students to imagine that they are recent immigrants to the United States during the late 1800s. Have them develop and perform short dramatic monologues in which they explain why they chose to leave their homeland. Students should introduce themselves, identify their countries of origin, explain their reasons for leaving their homelands, and summarize their plans and hopes for the future. Tell students to be creative but to make their characters' stories believable and historically accurate.

NOTE: For an additional teaching idea, see the Chapter 29 range of positions lesson in the **Creative Teaching Strategies** handbook.

Some immigrants sought political freedom. In 1848 a series of radical political revolutions broke out across Europe. Most of these revolutions failed to bring about the desired changes. As a result, many radicals fled their homelands. One of these was Karl Marx, a German radical and co-author of the *Communist Manifesto* (1848), who fled to Great Britain.

Many people left their homes to escape religious persecution. Russian Jews, for instance, had long suffered from discrimination and violence. Thousands seized the opportunity to leave Russia during the 1890s and early 1900s. Some traveled to South America or settled in Canada. The majority, however, immigrated to the United States. Although they often faced anti-Semitism in America, most Jewish immigrants felt that their lives had changed for the better.

✔ **READING CHECK:** Why did many immigrants choose to leave their homelands?

The United States and World Migration

The United States was the single most popular destination for immigrants from around the world. Millions of people entered the United States in the 1800s and early 1900s, mainly from Europe. The United States had large amounts of good farmland as well as many industrial jobs by the late 1800s. The discovery of gold in California and later Alaska drew thousands of immigrants hoping to find their fortunes. U.S. traditions of political and religious freedom also attracted many immigrants. In addition, large numbers of enslaved Africans were brought involuntarily to the United States before the slave trade was banned in 1808. Together all of these immigrants did much of the work that helped shape the United States.

In search of gold, immigrants carried picks and other tools into the mountain ranges of California and Alaska during the 1800s.

A surge in immigration. Immigration to the United States peaked between 1890 and 1914, when some 15 million newcomers landed on U.S. shores. In 1907 alone more than 1.2 million immigrants entered the country. A large amount of money could be made transporting these people. Steamship companies and railroads employed agents throughout Europe to encourage people to move to America. These agents often exaggerated the employment opportunities available in the United States. Steamship lines also charged rock-bottom fares to attract passengers. For many immigrants, however, these low fares meant traveling in steerage—the most crowded and unhealthy accommodations of the ships. An Italian immigrant reflected on his voyage to America.

> **"How can a steerage passenger remember that he is a human being when he must first pick the worms from his food . . . and eat in his stuffy, stinking bunk, or in the hot . . . atmosphere of a compartment where 150 men sleep?"**

Many of these immigrants welcomed their first sight of America. Immigrants entering New York arrived at **Ellis Island**, an immigration station in New York Harbor that opened in 1892. Immigrants were subjected to physical examination and questioned about their background before they were allowed to enter the United States.

GEOGRAPHIC DIVERSITY

American Jews. The first Jews to settle in the American colonies lived in port cities along the Atlantic coast. German Jews arriving in the 1800s settled in urban areas along trade routes across the United States. Jewish immigrants from eastern Europe in the late 1800s and early 1900s tended to settle in large urban areas such as Boston and New York in the East and Chicago in the Midwest.

CRITICAL THINKING Why might Jewish immigrants and other newcomers settle in large urban areas?

ANSWER: Answers will vary but might include the greater economic opportunity to be found in cities and a desire to live in neighborhoods with fellow immigrants.

THAT'S INTERESTING!

The U.S. government began gathering information on immigration in 1819, when a new law required ship captains to compile passenger lists containing information regarding the nationality, occupation, sex, and age of passengers.

TEACH OBJECTIVE 2

ALL LEVELS: To help students understand why the United States was the most likely destination of immigrants, copy the graphic organizer to the right on the chalkboard, omitting the italicized answers. Have each student complete it. **Sheltered English**

▶ASSIGNMENT *Tell students to use the graphic organizer to help them create an advertisement for an American steamship company. The goal of the advertisement is to attract European passengers by painting a glowing picture of the opportunities to be found in the United States. Students may wish to include the advertisement in their portfolios.*

IMMIGRATION—1800s AND EARLY 1900s

Why People Came to the United States
- *involuntarily as slaves*
- *in search of economic opportunity: land, jobs, freedom*
- *to escape religious persecution*
- *in search of wealth in the gold rush*

DEMOCRATIC VALUES

Ellis Island. Immigrants arriving at Ellis Island received a medical examination, had their documents checked, and were briefly questioned. Most were then allowed to enter the United States. However, a small number were detained for further physical or mental examinations. Although most immigrants were eventually released, a few were deported. In 1905 about 1 percent of those who arrived at Ellis Island were barred from entering the United States.

CRITICAL THINKING Should the U.S. government deny entry to people with physical and mental problems?

ANSWER: Answers will vary. Some students might suggest that the U.S. government should restrict immigrants who need special medical care or who might become burdens on U.S. taxpayers.

STRATEGIES FOR SUCCESS ANSWERS

Practicing the Strategy

1. special-purpose map
2. the West End and Beacon Hill
3. Irish
4. east-central Boston
5. the Charles River

Strategies for Success — Reading Maps

A map represents a geographic area and is drawn to scale. Maps often serve as effective tools for conveying historical information. Types of maps include physical maps, political maps, and special-purpose maps. A *physical map* illustrates the natural landscape of a specific area. A *political map* illustrates political units such as capitals, cities, nations, states, territories, and military alliances. A *special-purpose* map presents a specific type of information, such as the route of an explorer, the outcome of an election, the economic activity of a region, or the course of a military battle.

While maps vary in design depending on their purposes, many maps share one or more common features. The *legend,* or *key*, explains any special symbols, colors, or shadings used on a map. The *directional indicator* marks the four cardinal points: *N* for north, *S* for south, *E* for east, and *W* for west. The *scale*, which is usually labeled in both miles and kilometers, relates distances on a map to actual distances on Earth's surface. *Grid lines* provide a frame of reference for a map in terms of *latitude*—number of degrees north or south of the equator—and *longitude*—number of degrees east or west of the prime meridian. Finally, a *locator map* may be used to place a map's area of focus in context by showing it in relation to a larger geographic area.

How to Read a Map

1. **Determine the focus of the map.** Read the map's title and labels to determine its subject and the geographic area it covers.
2. **Study the legend.** Read the legend and become familiar with any special symbols, colors, or shading used on the map.
3. **Check directions and distances.** Consult the directional indicator and the scale to determine the map's directions and distances.
4. **Check the geographic context.** Refer to the map's grid lines or locator map to determine its larger geographic context.
5. **Analyze the information.** Examine the map's features and details, referring to the legend when necessary. If it is a special-purpose map, study all of the specific information being presented.
6. **Put the data to use.** Use your analysis of the data, along with your knowledge of the historical period, to form generalizations and draw conclusions.

Applying the Strategy

Study the map accompanying this feature, which shows the neighborhoods of the city of Boston, Massachusetts, in 1850.

Practicing the Strategy

Using the map below, answer the following questions.

1. What type of map is this?
2. Which areas of Boston had the greatest concentration of African American population in 1850?
3. Did Boston have more primarily African American neighborhoods or more primarily Irish neighborhoods?
4. Which parts of Boston appear to have had the lowest concentration Irish residents in 1850?
5. What body of water borders Boston to the north and west?

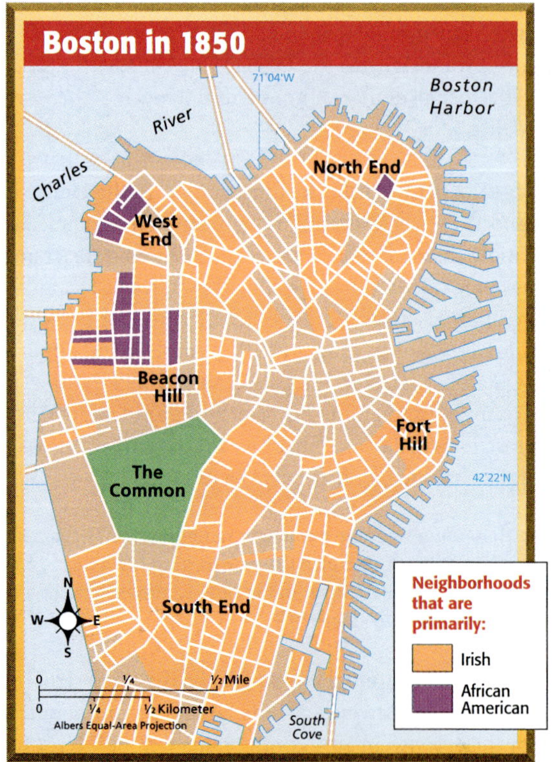

TEACH OBJECTIVE 3

LEVEL 1: Organize students into triads and tell them to work together to list ways that migration affected rural and urban populations. *(Students might answer that urban populations experienced a huge increase that contributed to a rise in nativism, and that rural populations declined significantly.)* Ask one student from each triad to read his or her group's responses to the class.
Sheltered English, Cooperative Learning

LEVELS 2 AND 3: Tell students to imagine that they are farmers during the late 1800s who are concerned about the number of rural families moving to cities and the potential shortage of agricultural workers. Have each student write and present a speech to a group of fellow farmers urging them to stay on their farms. In their speeches, students should acknowledge reasons others might have for moving to cities, but should counter each with reasons to stay in the country. *(Students might suggest cleaner air, necessity of food production, simpler way of life, and so on.)* Students may wish to include their speeches in their portfolios.

Nativist response. Many native-born Americans opposed the latest wave of immigrants. Much of this opposition was based on prejudice. The majority of immigrants to the United States from 1890 to 1914 came from eastern and southern Europe. They included Hungarians, Italians, Poles, Russian Jews, and Slovaks. These individuals often spoke different languages and practiced different religions than earlier immigrants to the United States. Some nativists complained that these cultural differences would prevent the new immigrants from becoming good citizens.

Other nativists opposed immigration for economic reasons. One critic noted that many new immigrants were willing to work for low wages. He claimed their numbers hurt "the standard of living of hundreds of thousands of [native] workers —workers, too, who are also citizens, fathers, husbands."

Pressured by nativists, congress passed the Chinese Exclusion Act in 1882. This law blocked Chinese immigration and forced thousands of Chinese to leave the United States. The time period covered by the law was later extended. It became very difficult for Chinese immigrants to gain permission to enter the United States at all. Between 1910 and 1940, Chinese arrivals were detained at **Angel Island**, a West Coast version of Ellis Island located in San Francisco. There, authorities investigated the arrivals' claims that they were legal immigrants. One Chinese immigrant described his struggles in a poem on his cell wall at Angel Island.

> **"The day I am rid of this prison and attain success,**
> **I must remember that this prison once existed. . . .**
> **All my compatriots [fellow citizens] please be mindful.**
> **Once you have some small gains, return home [to China] early."**

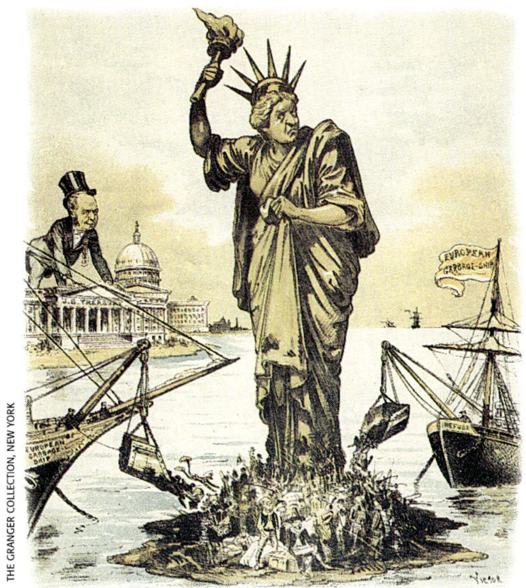

THE GRANGER COLLECTION, NEW YORK

INTERPRETING THE VISUAL RECORD

The nativist response. Many native-born Americans opposed the rising number of immigrants. ***How does this cartoon reflect this nativist opposition to immigration?***

Emigration from the United States. Some Americans emigrated to other countries in search of new opportunities. Gold rushes in Australia and Canada attracted thousands of Americans. American farmers also were attracted to Canada. Between 1900 and 1920, nearly 300,000 Americans moved north of the border to establish homesteads in Alberta, Manitoba, and Saskatchewan.

Christian missionaries left the United States to spread their faith rather than to gain land or wealth. Many missionaries and church groups focused their attention on China and the Philippines. "We are not merely teachers," wrote one young missionary to her parents back in Massachusetts. "We are social assets and emissaries [ambassadors] of good will." Because they promoted U.S. interests, however, the missionaries were not always welcome.

✔ **READING CHECK:** Why was the United States the most likely destination of immigrants?

Some Americans left the United States to establish missions in countries such as the Philippines.

HISTORY MAKERS SPEAK

Henry Ward Beecher in *Closing the Gate*

Chinese Exclusion. Reverend Henry Ward Beecher offered one reason for Americans to oppose passage of the Chinese Exclusion Act. "In a score of years we shall have no race that will be willing to do what we call the menial work. . . . More and more the other races are going up from the bottom and leaving the underwork of society to the poor of other and less ambitious peoples; and here is a race offered to us that by reason of their training, by the habits of a thousand years, are adapted to do that work."

CRITICAL THINKING Why might Beecher have favored continued Chinese immigration?

ANSWER: Students might mention that he wanted the Chinese to perform labor that other people refused to do.

VISUAL RECORD ANSWER

Students might answer that the immigrants are represented as trash being dumped on American soil.

Multimedia Resources

Linking Geography and History Transparency 11B: Growth of Cities, 1840–1950

REVIEW

Have students complete the **Section 1 Review** on p. 860.

ASSESS

Have students complete **Daily Quiz 29.1**. As **Alternative Assessment**, you may want to use the graphic organizer and advertisement activity or the farmer's speech assignment in this section's lessons.

RETEACH

Have students complete **Main Idea Activity for Reteaching and Sheltered English 29.1**. Then organize students into groups of four and tell them to imagine that they are writers for a national newsmagazine publishing a special issue about U.S. immigration and migration. Each group will create a version of the issue. Students should combine articles, images, graphic organizers, and other information to summarize global migration trends of the time period, reasons for immigration to the United States, and migration patterns within the United States. **Sheltered English, Cooperative Learning**

EXTEND

Have students conduct research on immigrants' emotions, experiences, and impressions at Ellis or Angel Island. Tell them to use images, personal accounts, and statistics to put together a posterboard-size visual display that portrays the Ellis or Angel Island experience. **Block Scheduling**

SECTION 1 REVIEW ANSWERS

Define and Identify

For significance, see the following pages:

- Ellis Island, p. 857
- Angel Island, p. 859

1. nation to nation—to find better jobs and higher wages, to gain greater personal freedom; rural to urban—to find better jobs and higher wages

2. Millions of Europeans and Asians settled in the United States; cities grew as people moved from rural areas to find jobs.

3. Answers will vary. Students may suggest searching for a higher quality of life, joining relatives, or escaping persecution.

4. Cities grew as people left rural areas in search of jobs.

5. Answers will vary but should mention that immigrants diversified American culture. Nativists feared the loss of jobs and the impact of different cultures and religions. At times nativists' arguments led to restrictions on immigration.

INTERPRETING THE VISUAL RECORD

Cities. The arrival of immigrants and rural migrants during the early 1900s led to overcrowding in many U.S. cities. ***What problems do you think overcrowding caused?***

From Country to City

The 1800s and early 1900s also marked a huge migration from rural areas to cities. This migration was closely tied to the Industrial Revolution. The location of factories in urban areas lured thousands of migrants to cities.

In Britain, for example, the populations of Birmingham and Manchester more than tripled between 1800 and 1850. As the century progressed, these and other British cities played an increasing role in the industrial economy. In 1881 one member of Parliament wrote, "Our towns are the backbone of the nation. They give it strength, cohesion [unity], vitality."

Urban growth followed industrial development throughout Europe and the United States. The population of New York City, for instance, grew from 2 million to nearly 3.5 million between 1880 and 1900. During the same period, Chicago's population grew from some 500,000 to more than 1.5 million. Denver, St. Paul, and Minneapolis also tripled in population. In the Midwest and New England, farming areas lost thousands of residents to big cities. Many who witnessed this movement to the cities believed that urban growth was unavoidable. Newspaper editor Horace Greeley had once noted, "We cannot all live in cities, yet nearly all seem determined to do so." The 1920 census seemed to confirm Greeley's observation. For the first time in U.S. history, more than half the population lived in cities.

✔ **READING CHECK:** How did migration during the 1800s and early 1900s affect urban and rural populations?

SECTION 1 REVIEW

Define and explain the significance of the following terms:
Ellis Island
Angel Island

1. **Using Graphic Organizers** Copy the graphic organizer below. Use it to compare the reasons people immigrated to a new country to the reasons people moved from rural to urban areas.

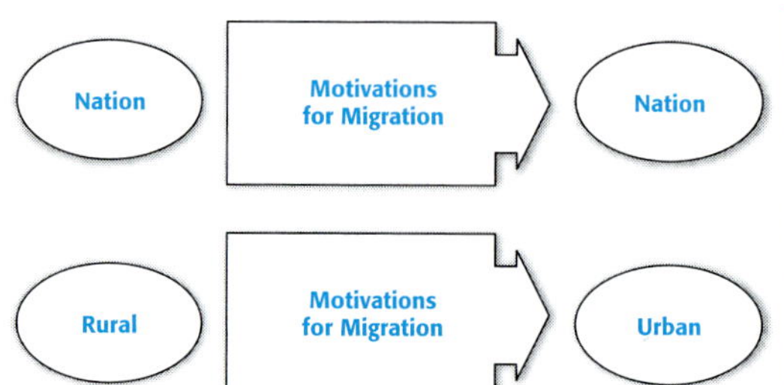

2. **Assessing Consequences** What was the impact of global migration during the 1800s and early 1900s?
3. **Using Historical Imagination** Imagine that you are an immigrant during the late 1800s. What reasons might you have for wanting to leave your homeland?
4. **Identifying Cause and Effect** How did the population movements before World War I affect cities and rural areas?

Critical Thinking

5. How did immigration change the United States during the 1800s and early 1900s?
Consider:
   - why immigrants chose to come to the United States
   - what the impact of immigration on American culture was
   - how nativists reacted to immigrants

After completing Section 2, students should be able to:

OBJECTIVE 1 *Explain how World War I and the Great Depression affected immigration patterns.*

OBJECTIVE 2 *State the primary reason for migrating during the 1940s.*

OBJECTIVE 3 *Identify how immigration in the United States has changed since 1965.*

OBJECTIVE 4 *Describe what caused people to migrate during the 1980s and 1990s.*

LET'S GET STARTED!

As students enter the classroom, ask them if they are, or know, recent immigrants. Have them write a paragraph explaining the challenges recent immigrants face in a new country. If students do not know any recent immigrants, tell them to make educated guesses. Tell students that in Section 2 they will learn about migration patterns between World War I and the 1990s.

Children of War

OBJECTIVES

Read to understand:

1. how World War I and the Great Depression affected immigration patterns
2. what the primary reason for migrating during the 1940s was
3. how immigration to the United States has changed since 1965
4. what caused people to migrate during the 1980s and 1990s

KEY TERMS

refugees
Displaced Persons Act
Immigration Act of 1965
asylum

KEY PEOPLE

Bette Bao Lord

KEY PLACES

Bosnia
Somalia
Rwanda

"The Wheelbarrow of life is too heavy for my shoulders. . . . Take me where you are . . . otherwise I shall perish."

—Anonymous Polish woman

World War II immigrants

A Polish woman wrote her husband in the late 1800s, pleading to join him in the United States. Running the farm without her husband's help was extremely difficult. Many southern and eastern European immigrants during this era were men who left their families at home and tried to earn money abroad. During the 1900s economic motivations were the driving force behind immigration. Other migrants were displaced by war and natural disasters. By the 1990s tens of millions of people lived outside their homelands.

World War I and Its Aftermath

The outbreak of World War I caused immigration to drop. Some nations restricted emigration to make sure that young men would remain to serve in the military. Ocean travel also became more dangerous during wartime. After World War I ended in 1918, global migration rates climbed again. Immigration to the United States, however, did not reach former levels. Nativists persuaded Congress to pass the Immigration Act of 1924. This act sharply reduced the number of immigrants allowed into the country.

The global economic depression of the 1930s further slowed international migration. Few jobs were available anywhere. Countries that had once welcomed immigrants now closed their borders to keep job-seekers from entering. The U.S. government even deported some 500,000 people of Mexican descent to reduce job competition.

As immigration declined in the 1930s, the number of **refugees**—people forced to flee their homes because of political persecution, war, or natural disasters—rose dramatically. For example, many German Jews, particularly those with education or job skills, left Germany during the 1930s to escape Nazi persecution. Scientist Albert Einstein, winner of the 1921 Nobel Prize for physics, was one of the most prominent Jewish refugees to resettle in the United States. A large number of Jews, however, were unable to leave Germany. The global depression and anti-Semitism made most countries reluctant to accept Jewish refugees.

Asia also experienced a refugee crisis in the 1930s. A Chinese civil war combined with the Japanese invasion of northern China to drive some 95 million Chinese from their homes.

✔ **READING CHECK:** How did World War I and the Great Depression affect immigration patterns?

SECTION 2 RESOURCES

PRINT

- Guided Reading Strategy 29.2
- Graphic Organizer Activity 29: Immigration
- Literature Reading 29: The Narrative Art of the Storyteller
- Section 2 Review, p. 866
- Daily Quiz 29.2

MULTIMEDIA

- One-Stop Planner, Lesson 29.2
- The American Nation Video Program Segment: A Nation of Immigrants; Teacher's Guide, pp. 153–56
- Holt Researcher: American History CD–ROM
- HRW Web site

SHELTERED ENGLISH

- Main Idea Activity for Reteaching and Sheltered English 29.2

✔ **READING TO UNDERSTAND**

To help students master the section objectives, have them answer the **READING CHECKS** and complete **Guided Reading Strategy 29.2** as they read the section.

TEACH OBJECTIVE 1

ALL LEVELS: Organize students into groups of four and tell them to imagine that they are migration experts developing a report about global migration patterns between 1910 and 1940. Tell them to put together a brief presentation about how World War I and the Great Depression affected migration patterns. *(Reports should show that World War I and the Great Depression caused a drop in immigration but a dramatic increase in the number of refugees.)* Encourage students to create visual aids, such as graphic organizers, to help them in their presentations. Students may wish to include their reports in their portfolios.
Sheltered English, Cooperative Learning

Teacher to Teacher

Karen Hoppes of Lake Oswego, Oregon, suggested the following activity: Ask students to draw a predictive concept tree using these components—cause, effect, possible problems, and possible solutions. After drawing the concept tree, have students write a generalization about the movement of people after World War I.

internetconnect

TOPIC: Great Migration
GO TO: go.hrw.com
KEYWORD: SE1 Great Migration

Have students access the Internet through the HRW Web site to conduct research on the Great Migration. Have each student imagine that he or she is an African American teenager who traveled as part of the Great Migration. Ask students to write three journal entries that describe why they left home, an event during their journey, and what they found when they reached their destination.

THAT'S INTERESTING!

The Displaced Persons Act maintained quotas for European refugees. However, nations were allowed to exceed their quota by borrowing admission slots from future years. In four years, Latvia, which had an annual quota of 286 people, borrowed its permitted number of entries through the year 2274.

The American Nation VIDEO PROGRAM

A Nation of Immigrants; Teacher's Guide, pp. 153–56

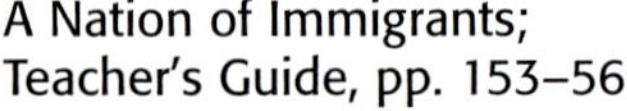

Search 23298, Play to 28272
Videodisc 2, Side B

Play Pause

See *Teacher's Guide* for Spanish barcode.

Then and Now

Migration and Disease

When people move from place to place, they carry microbes. Sometimes these microbes introduce disease that are new to the traveler's destination. As a result, throughout history the arrival of explorers, merchants, settlers, and soldiers has often resulted in epidemics. European colonists brought measles, smallpox, and other diseases to the Americas in the 1500s and 1600s. These sicknesses devastated American Indian populations.

Epidemics continue to spread through migration and global travel. For example, AIDS—acquired immune deficiency syndrome—is widely believed to have originated in Africa. Modern forms of transportation, such as cars and airplanes, helped spread AIDS swiftly around the world. The Centers for Disease Control (CDC) estimated in 1999 that 13.9 million people had died worldwide from AIDS since the epidemic began. The CDC also estimated that some 33 million people are infected with the human immunodeficiency virus (HIV) that causes AIDS. The vast majority—more than 95 percent—of AIDS deaths and HIV infections have occurred in the developing world.

AIDS researcher

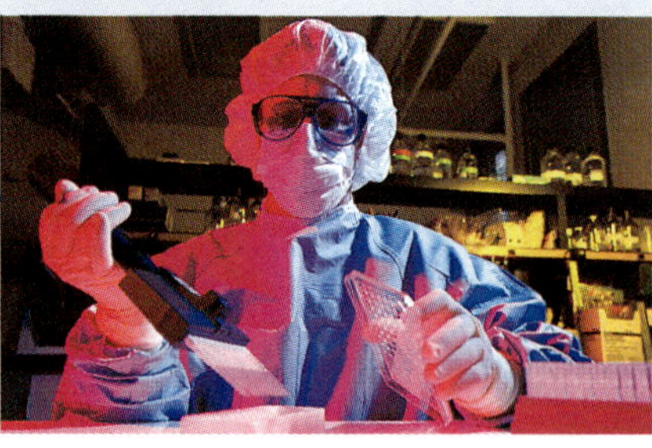

Postwar Migrations

The end of World War II brought a surge in refugee migration. Congress responded by passing the **Displaced Persons Act** of 1948. The act enabled some 400,000 European refugees to enter the United States. Many of these immigrants were Jewish survivors of Nazi concentration camps.

Decolonization also led to widespread movements of refugees. As European powers withdrew from Africa and Asia, civil wars and border conflicts broke out in many former colonies. For example, when the British pulled out of India, they divided the region into two nations—India and Pakistan. India was populated mostly by Hindus, while Pakistan was primarily Muslim. The British hoped that this division would prevent religious conflict. However, when independence was declared, thousands of Hindus and Muslims found themselves living on the wrong side of the border. Many people fled their homes in search of safety in the neighboring country.

Palestine also experienced violence in the 1940s as Zionists eager to establish a Jewish state fought British rule. These activists had sympathy from many nations concerned for the plight of Jews displaced by the Holocaust. In 1947 the United Nations voted to divide Palestine in two, creating one Jewish state and one Arab state. Jews from around the world settled in the Jewish state, Israel.

Many Palestinians bitterly opposed the creation of Israel. In 1948 Arab armies attacked the new nation. Israel defeated the Arabs and actually enlarged its borders. Hundreds of thousands of Palestinians found themselves homeless and in poverty. An estimated 1 million Palestinian refugees fled to Jordan, Lebanon, and other nearby countries. The 1967 Arab-Israeli War created even more refugees, as Palestinians fled from the territory that Israel occupied. The refugee issue has remained a source of conflict between Israel and surrounding countries.

✔ **READING CHECK:** What was the primary reason for migrating during the 1940s?

Immigration to the United States Since 1965

The U.S. Congress encouraged more immigration by passing the **Immigration Act of 1965**. This act greatly eased the quota restrictions that had limited immigration from many countries. It also increased the total number of immigrants allowed to come to the United States each year. The act led to a jump in the number of immigrants from Asia and Latin America. For example, Asian immigrants made up less than 7 percent of the total immigrants to the United States between 1951 and 1965. By 1978 that figure had reached to 28 percent. At the same time, the number of European immigrants to the United States decreased.

TEACH OBJECTIVE 2

LEVEL 1: In a classroom discussion, ask students to identify the primary reason for migration during the 1940s. *(Students should mention that after World War II refugees fled various types of political unrest, including decolonization and the creation of Israel.)* Then tell students to imagine that they are refugees after World War II who have relocated to the United States. Have them write and perform short oral histories from the point of view of their chosen character. In their monologues students should explain why they left their homeland, their feelings about the situation, and their thoughts about the future. **Sheltered English**

LEVEL 2: Tell students to imagine that they are refugees living in the United States many years after they fled their homelands following World War II. Tell them that a publishing company is putting together a collection of memoirs from World War II survivors. Have each student write a memoir from the point of view of a character of his or her choice, for inclusion in the book. The memoirs should include reasons the character migrated. *(See the Level 1 lesson for the correct reason.)*

LEVEL 3: Have each student write a short story about a young person whose family is forced to flee its homeland in Europe or the Middle East during the 1940s. Invite volunteers to read all or part of their stories to the class. Students may wish to include their stories in their portfolios.

The Global Refugee Problem, 1976–1997

Learning from Maps In some places, such as Rwanda and Bosnia, the forcing out of ethnic groups was one of the primary goals of war rather than an unintended result.

REGION Which region shown on the map had the largest number of refugees?

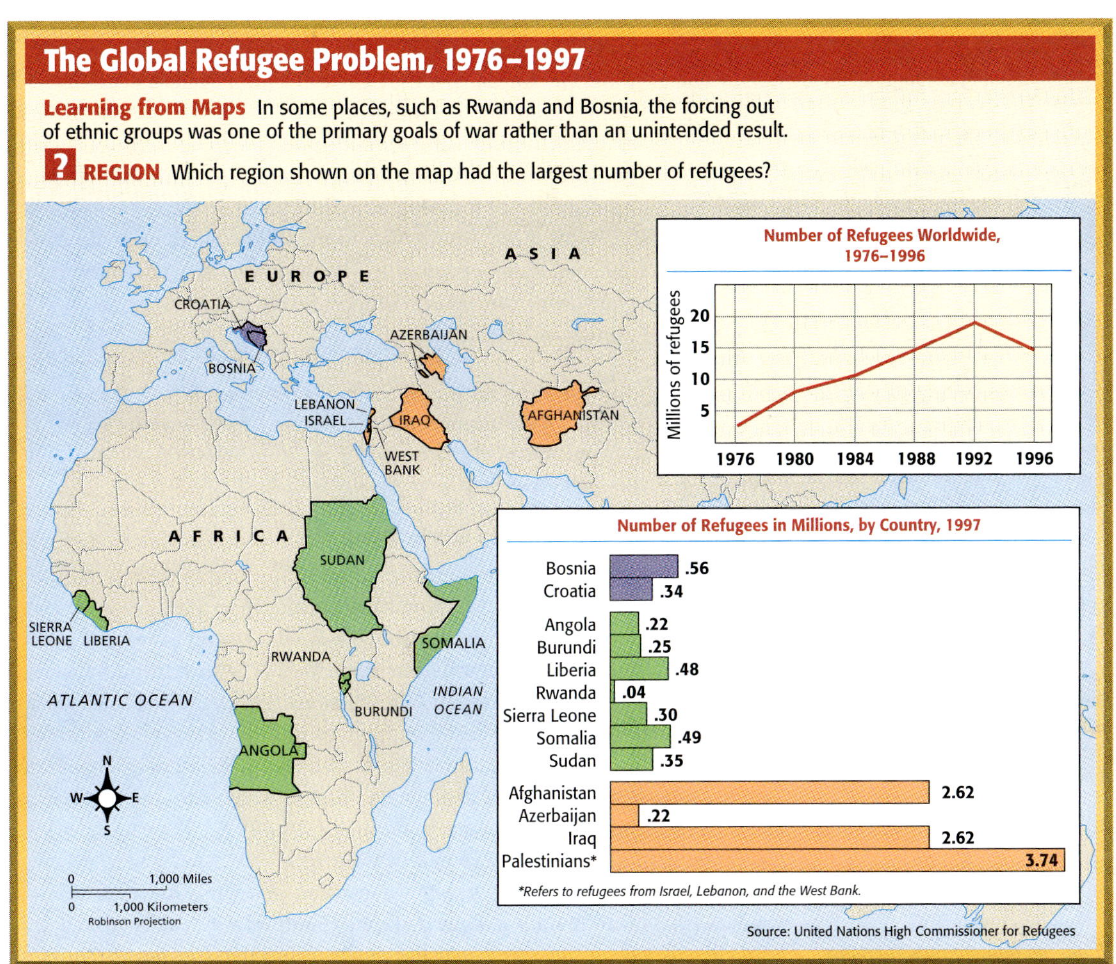

Motivations. Since the 1960s, many of the Asian and Latin American immigrants to the United States have been refugees. As communist North Vietnam took over South Vietnam in 1975, hundreds of thousands of Vietnamese fled their country in crowded boats. Other refugees fled fighting in Cambodia and Laos. The U.S. government, which had supported South Vietnam's war against the Communists, created programs to allow these refugees to settle in the United States.

Thousands of refugees have also fled violent or oppressive governments in Latin American nations such as Cuba and El Salvador. U.S. reactions to these refugees have been complicated. Cuba is a prime example. For years the official U.S. policy was to accept Cuban refugees from Fidel Castro's communist state. This changed in 1994, however, when Castro threatened to flood southern Florida with thousands of refugees who wanted to escape Cuba's

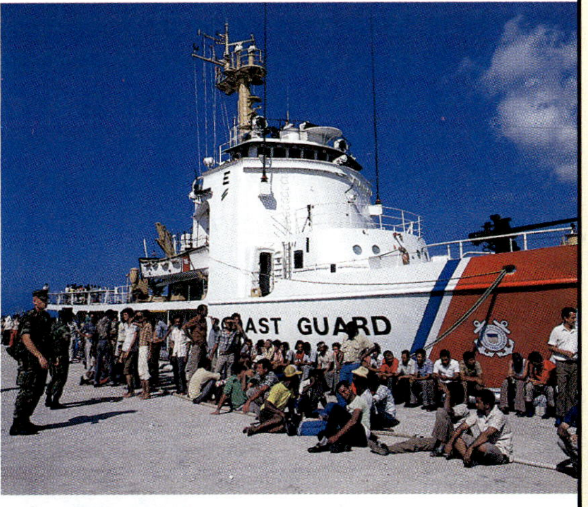

Many Cuban refugees immigrated to southern Florida after 1994.

HISTORY MAKERS SPEAK

Lyndon Johnson in *Public Papers of the Presidents of the United States*

Immigration Act of 1965. President Johnson explained the Immigration Act when he signed it into law in 1965. "This bill says simply that from this day forth those wishing to immigrate to America shall be admitted on the basis of their skills and their close relationship to those already here. . . . Those who can contribute most to this country—to its growth, to its strength, to its spirit—will be the first that are admitted to this land."

CRITICAL THINKING Why might the Immigration Act of 1965 have favored the admission of skilled workers and relatives?

ANSWER: Students might answer that these immigrants would most likely be able to support themselves.

THAT'S INTERESTING!

Of the estimated 5 million illegal immigrants living in the United States in 1996, some 2.7 million—more than 50 percent—came from Mexico.

MAP ANSWER
the Middle East

TEACH OBJECTIVE 3

ALL LEVELS: To help students identify how immigration to the United States has changed since 1965, copy the graphic organizer to the right on the chalkboard, omitting the italicized answers. Have each student complete it. When students have finished filling in the graphic organizer, tell them to write a paragraph summarizing the shift in the countries of origin of immigrants to the United States between 1965 and the present. *(Students should note the shift from primarily European refugees to more Asians and Latin Americans.)*
Sheltered English

IMMIGRATION TO THE UNITED STATES SINCE 1965

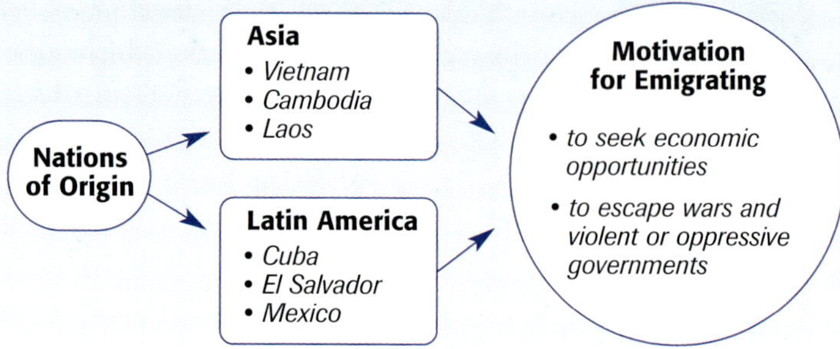

▶**ASSIGNMENT** *Have students conduct research on current immigration issues between Cuba and the United States. Then have them write a newspaper article explaining one issue.*

IN THE NEWS

Cuban Refugees. On Thanksgiving Day 1999 five-year-old Elian Gonzalez was rescued from the Atlantic Ocean off the coast of Florida. His mother and several other Cubans died in their attempt to reach the United States by boat. U.S. authorities released the boy to relatives in Miami. However, his father in communist Cuba wanted his son returned to live with him. Cuban leader Fidel Castro also demanded the boy's return, citing U.S.-Cuban immigration agreements. Immigrants who reach land in the United States are allowed to stay. Those who are picked up at sea, as Gonzalez was, are returned to Cuba. The case sparked an international debate on whether the boy's interests would be best served by returning him to communist Cuba.

CRITICAL THINKING What problems might the U.S.-Cuban immigration policy cause?

ANSWER: Students might mention that refugees might risk everything to reach land, while law enforcement officials might go to unreasonable lengths to prevent them from doing so.

In some states that border Mexico, greater efforts have been made to halt the continued illegal immigration of Latin Americans to the United States.

poverty. Florida governor Lawton Chiles declared that "Florida cannot stand another influx [crowd]." The U.S. Coast Guard began stopping the refugees at sea and sending them to camps outside the United States. Eventually, however, the U.S. government decided to resettle most of the refugees in the United States.

Most recent immigrants to the United States have come seeking economic opportunities. For example, many Mexican immigrants work for wages to support family members back home. One immigrant explained why.

> **"There are people who come from Tijuana [a city of Mexico near San Diego, California] who work for six, seven, or eight dollars an hour for work that is worth more than 18 or 20 dollars an hour. They come to work like that because they [still] earn more than they can earn in Tijuana."**

The future of U.S. immigration. The 1990 census revealed that more immigrants had come to the United States in the 1980s than in any other decade since the 1910s. The Immigration Act of 1990 further loosened immigration restrictions. The act raised immigration quotas and significantly increased the number of skilled workers allowed into the United States each year. President George Bush noted when signing the bill that "immigration is not just a link to America's past, it is also a bridge to America's future." This record pace has continued throughout the 1990s. The vast majority of these immigrants came from Asia and Latin America.

Many Americans still struggle with the question of whether to welcome immigrants. Critics of immigration argue that immigrants take jobs away from native-born citizens. Part of the controversy has resulted from the large number of illegal immigrants. The majority of illegal aliens cross the long border between Mexico and the United States. To address this problem Congress passed a bill in 1996 that strengthened the Border Patrol. It also increased the penalties for smuggling illegal aliens into the country.

Supporters of immigration argue that immigrants create new businesses that help revitalize urban areas. Supporters also suggest that immigrants help the U.S. balance of trade by starting their own export companies and help local companies become more competitive globally. In addition, supporters note that many recent immigrants from China, India, and Korea are well-educated workers. These immigrants contribute to the high-tech industries in the United Sates.

HOLT RESEARCHER — *Read More About It*

Free Find: Immigration Act of 1990
After reading about the Immigration Act of 1990 on the **Holt Researcher** CD–ROM, create a visual presentation about recent changes in immigration to the United States.

BIOGRAPHY
Bette Bao Lord

Chinese American author Bette Bao Lord urged native-born and immigrant Americans to celebrate each other's cultures.

> **"I do not believe that the loss of one's native culture is the price one must pay for becoming an American. On the contrary, I feel doubly blessed. I can choose from two rich cultures those parts that suit my mood or the occasion best."**

TEACH OBJECTIVE 4

LEVEL 1: Pair students and have one student in each pair research what caused people to migrate from Europe after the Cold War. Have the other student examine what caused people to migrate from the developing world. *(Students should mention breakup of the Soviet Union, warfare and political upheaval, economic problems, ethnic conflicts, and drought and famine.)* Have each student develop a lesson about his or her topic and teach it to the other student in the pair. Encourage students to take notes on each other's lessons. **Sheltered English, Cooperative Learning**

LEVELS 2 AND 3: Have students make a list of reasons people migrated during the 1980s and 1990s. *(See the Level 1 lesson for the correct causes.)* Then have them write a letter to the editor of a current American newspaper expressing an opinion about immigration. Tell them to state how they feel about immigration—whether it should be allowed to increase, be decreased, or stay the same—and to explain why they feel as they do. Call on volunteers to read their letters to the class. Students may wish to include their letters in their portfolios.

Bette Bao Lord was born in Shanghai in 1938 and came to the United States with her family in 1946. Her father was a Chinese official who decided to stay in the United States after Communists took control of China. However, the family was not able to bring the youngest daughter to America until 1962. Lord wrote her first novel, *Eighth Moon,* about her sister's experiences. She visited China in 1973 with her husband, Winston Lord, a U.S. government official. While there she wrote her next novel, *Spring Moon,* about her reunion with relatives. A graduate of Tufts University and the Fletcher School of Law and Diplomacy, Lord resides in the United States. She continues to write and to comment on Asian American issues.

Neither supporters nor opponents of immigration held a strong majority at the end of the 1990s. A 1999 Gallup poll indicated that 51 percent of Americans supported keeping immigration at its current level or increasing it. The same poll reported that 44 percent of Americans wanted to lower immigration levels.

✔ **READING CHECK:** How has immigration to the United States changed since 1965?

Global Immigration in the 1990s

Political changes led to immigration controversies around the world in the 1990s. These controversies brought changes to immigration patterns.

Europe after the Cold War. Since the breakup of the Soviet bloc, large numbers of immigrants from Eastern Europe have moved west to find jobs or avoid ethnic conflicts. In the early 1990s more than 1 million refugees fled to Germany. Germany had a policy of allowing **asylum**, or a place of protection, to all "persons persecuted on political grounds." Germans, however, were struggling with high unemployment and other economic problems brought about by the reunification of East Germany and West Germany. Resentment against immigrants sometimes sparked violence, including riots in August 1992.

INTERPRETING THE VISUAL RECORD

Kosovo. Violence in Kosovo has led to increasing migration of ethnic Albanians and Serbians seeking refuge from the conflict. ***What problems do you think this type of mass migration might cause?***

Many residents of the former Soviet Union have chosen to move south rather than west. The former Soviet republics in Central Asia, for example, have many historical cultural ties to Iran, Turkey, and other Middle Eastern countries. More than 1 million Jews have immigrated to Israel in recent years from the former Soviet Union. Many of these immigrants have sought to escape discrimination.

In the former Yugoslavia, the civil war caused by the fall of communism left thousands homeless. Many people had no choice but to seek refuge in other countries. In the spring of 1999, ethnic conflict in the province of Kosovo forced hundreds of thousands of ethnic Albanians to flee to neighboring countries. More than 500,000 people from nearby Bosnia and Croatia already had been displaced.

Migration in the developing world. In recent years, the world's largest migrations have taken place within and among developing countries. These migrations have taken place for a variety of reasons. Economics plays a key role. People frequently move from poor rural areas to big cities in search of work. The UN Population Fund reported in 1993 that some 20 to 30 million people in developing

GLOBAL RELATIONS

Continued Immigration. Of the some 916,000 immigrants who entered the United States in 1996, almost 148,000 came from Europe, including the republics of the former Soviet Union. About 308,000 came from Asia, 62,000 from South America, and 53,000 from Africa. The greatest number of immigrants—about 341,000 people—came from nations in North America, in particular Mexico and islands in the Caribbean.

CRITICAL THINKING Why might the largest number of immigrants to the United States come from other North American countries?

ANSWER: Students might mention that the proximity of those nations to the United States makes it possible for a larger number of people to migrate.

THAT'S INTERESTING!

Some 2 million illegal immigrants—or 40 percent of the total number of illegal immigrants residing in the United States in 1996—lived in California.

VISUAL RECORD ANSWER

Students might cite an inadequate supply of provisions and housing.

REVIEW

Have students complete the **Section 2 Review** on p. 866.

ASSESS

Have students complete **Daily Quiz 29.2**. As **Alternative Assessment**, you may want to use the global migration report or the oral histories activity in this section's lessons.

RETEACH

Have students complete **Main Idea Activity for Reteaching and Sheltered English 29.2**. Then have each student create a crossword puzzle that makes use of the section objectives as well as the key terms, people, and places. Have students trade their crosswords with a partner and solve each other's puzzles.
Sheltered English, Cooperative Learning

EXTEND

Organize students into pairs or triads and have them create a large time line, marked in decades from the 1900s to the 1990s. Tell them to make a small and simple graphic organizer that illustrates trends in global migration for each significant time period (for example, World War I, the Great Depression, World War II, the 1950s to the 1970s, and the 1980s to the 1990s) and attach it at the appropriate decade(s) on the time line. Display students' completed time lines in the classroom.
Cooperative Learning, Block Scheduling

SECTION 2 REVIEW ANSWERS

Define and Identify
For significance, see the following pages:

- refugees, p. 861
- Displaced Persons Act, p. 862
- Immigration Act of 1965, p. 862
- Bette Bao Lord, p. 864
- asylum, p. 865

Locate
For locations, see the map on p. 863. For importance, see the following pages:

- Bosnia, p. 865
- Somalia, p. 866
- Rwanda, p. 866

1. end of World War I, political persecution, war, and natural disasters

2. Migration slowed as a result of World War I and the Great Depression; an increasing number of people became refugees after World War II.

3. Loosened immigration restrictions in 1965 and 1990 significantly increased the number of immigrants from Asia and Latin America. Some came as refugees; others sought economic opportunity.

4. Answers will vary, but students should address fears of increased economic strain as well as the desire to provide opportunities for more people.

5. Many people migrated from the former Soviet sphere to find jobs or avoid ethnic conflicts. War and ethnic conflict caused people to migrate from developing countries. The UN worked to resettle refugees; U.S. immigration policy changed to allow more immigrants.

countries move from rural to urban areas each year. Often these migrants find only poverty. Large shantytowns surround many cities, such as São Paulo in Brazil, Jakarta in Indonesia, and Calcutta in India.

In other cases, rural residents have fled their homes to escape drought and famine. This has been the case in some parts of Africa, including Somalia, during the 1990s. When civil war made the situation worse, UN forces launched Operation Restore Hope to ensure that food and other necessities reached the starving Somali people.

Warfare in the developing world continues to create masses of refugees. The Persian Gulf War drew attention to the plight of Kurds, an ethnic group living along the borders of Armenia, Iran, Iraq, Syria, and Turkey. After Kurds in Iraq unsuccessfully rebelled against the Iraqi government, some 2 million of them tried to enter Iran and Turkey. This migration created political tension, particularly in Turkey.

Fleeing civil war in Rwanda, refugees crowd together in a camp in neighboring Tanzania.

The arrival of refugees can create large problems for host countries. Following the 1994 civil war in Rwanda between Hutus and Tutsis, thousands of Hutus fled to refugee camps in Zaire—now called the Democratic Republic of Congo. Tutsi rebels in Congo have attacked these camps. Hutu soldiers have used the camps as bases for attacks on Rwanda and Burundi. The government of Zaire and many international aid officials argued that the very existence of the camps inside Zaire fostered conflict.

The United Nations High Commissioner for Refugees (UNHCR) is the primary agency offering legal protection to refugees. The organization also works to resettle refugees or help them go back to their country of origin.

✔ **READING CHECK:** What caused people to migrate during the 1980s and 1990s?

SECTION 2 REVIEW

Define and explain the significance of the following terms:
refugees
Displaced Persons Act
Immigration Act of 1965
asylum

Identify and explain the significance of the following individual:
Bette Bao Lord

Locate and explain the importance of the following places:
Bosnia
Somalia
Rwanda

1. **Using Graphic Organizers** Copy the graphic organizer below. Use it to explain why many people migrated between 1900 and 1945.

2. **Synthesizing** What roles did World War I, the Great Depression, and World War II play in the migration of people?
3. **Comparing and Contrasting** How did immigration to the United States change between 1945 and 2000?
4. **Recognizing Point of View** Why might some people oppose and others support increased immigration?

Critical Thinking

5. What factors affected migration around the globe during the 1980s and 1990s?
Consider:
- what the impact of the end of the Cold War was
- how warfare in various regions of the world affected migration
- how UN programs and U.S. immigration policies affected migration

After completing Section 3, students should be able to:

OBJECTIVE 1 *Explain how developments in computer technology affected the spread of information.*

OBJECTIVE 2 *Summarize the challenges and benefits developing nations have faced while trying to improve their communications technology.*

OBJECTIVE 3 *Discuss privacy concerns that recent technological developments have raised.*

LET'S GET STARTED!

To begin the class, have students write down as many ways as they can think of to receive or convey information. *(Students might mention books, e-mail, the Internet, letters, newspapers, radio, telephones, and television.)* Call on students to share their lists with the class. Tell them to think about how each of these affects the flow of ideas and information around the world. Then tell students that in Section 3 they will learn more about the impact of recent technologies on global communication.

The Movement of Information

OBJECTIVES

Read to understand:

1. how developments in computer technology affected the spread of information
2. what challenges and benefits developing nations have faced while trying to improve their communications technology
3. what privacy concerns recent technological developments have raised

KEY TERMS

Information Revolution
minicomputers
modems
e-mail
barcodes

KEY PEOPLE

Al Gore

"Your car breaks down. Your refrigerator breaks down. As you use more technology, you rely on it . . . but you have to realize that things can cause disruptions."

—Jenny Haynes

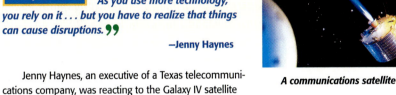

A communications satellite

Jenny Haynes, an executive of a Texas telecommunications company, was reacting to the Galaxy IV satellite malfunction on May 19,1998. Some 90 percent of the 45 million pagers in the United States stopped working. Among other problems, the malfunction silenced pagers used to notify hospitals that an organ has become available for transplant. Doctors rely on immediate communication for patients in critical condition. Numerous other everyday activities were affected by the satellite glitch. Many credit cards would not work. Some radio and television broadcasts went out. Modern society had become dependent on rapid communications. Throughout most of history ideas have moved only as quickly as the people who held them. During the 1900s new technological developments have allowed ideas and information to spread around the world more and more rapidly.

The growing availability of computers has led to an increasing exchange of information.

The Information Revolution

Travelers and migrants have long carried knowledge from one region to another. During the 1930s and 1940s, for example, Jewish scientists fleeing Nazi Germany helped develop the U.S. atomic bomb. Today much of the global exchange of information takes place using computers. Computers allow people to quickly access huge amounts of data. For example, the U.S. Patent and Trademark Office has an online database containing the text of every U.S. patent filed since 1976. Medline, the National Library of Medicine's service, indexes some 7,300 references a week. Computers and new information technologies have made the widespread transfer of information possible. This transfer has become known as the **Information Revolution**.

The Internet. One of computer technology's most useful advances has been the development of computer networks. These networks allow multiple computers in distant locations to share access to files and programs. The largest of these computer networks is the Internet, which linked millions of computers in nearly 150 countries in 1999.

The development of the Internet began in the 1960s during the Cold War. The U.S. Department of Defense wanted a system that would allow research facilities at universities and private laboratories to communicate with each other. In 1969 the Defense Department linked together the computer systems of four universities. The creators designed the network so that it could expand easily, and

SECTION 3 RESOURCES

PRINT

- Guided Reading Strategy 29.3
- Section 3 Review, p. 871
- Daily Quiz 29.3

MULTIMEDIA

- One-Stop Planner, Lesson 29.3
- Holt Researcher: American History CD–ROM

SHELTERED ENGLISH

- Main Idea Activity for Reteaching and Sheltered English 29.3

✔ READING TO UNDERSTAND

To help students master the section objectives, have them answer the **READING CHECKS** and complete **Guided Reading Strategy 29.3** as they read the section.

TEACH OBJECTIVE 1

LEVELS 1 AND 2: Ask students to list advancements in computer technology that have improved global communications during the last three decades. *(Students might mention the development of computer networks, the Internet, minicomputers, modems, e-mail, and the World Wide Web.)* Then have each student write a few paragraphs about how one or more of these advancements has affected the spread of information. Call on volunteers to read their paragraphs to the class. **Sheltered English**

LEVEL 3: Have each student create an informational booklet about the Internet for students about two years younger than themselves. Each booklet should tell students about the history of the Internet, how it can be used to gather or spread information, and the various means of accessing or making use of the Internet. Students might also include warnings about the dangers people might encounter when using the Internet.

PEOPLE IN HISTORY

Andrew S. Grove. In 1997 *Time* magazine chose Andrew S. Grove, Intel founder and executive, as its Person of the Year because of his role in the development of the microchip. Born Andras Gróf in Budapest, Hungary, in 1936, Grove nearly died at age four from scarlet fever. In 1944 he and his mother went into hiding when the Nazis occupied Budapest. Twelve years later, when Soviet troops entered Budapest to put down a revolution, Grove fled to Austria. He then moved to New York City, where he moved in with relatives.

ACTIVITY: Have students write brief reports on how the development of the microchip and the personal computer have helped recent immigrants to the United States keep in touch with relatives in their homelands.

THAT'S INTERESTING!

Some 82 percent of teenagers surveyed in a 1999 poll used the Internet for e-mail or to surf the World Wide Web.

SCIENCE & TECHNOLOGY ANSWERS

1. hardware and software
2. Answers will vary. Students might suggest that the system controls action much like the human brain controls action.

Science & Technology

How Personal Computers Work

The word *computer* can apply to any tool used to make calculations. Today, however, most people use the term to refer to electronic computers. Modern computers have many uses because they can store and access huge amounts of information and quickly perform complex calculations.

Computers function through the interaction of their physical parts, called *hardware*, and their programs, called *software*. Computer programs are sets of instructions that tell the computer how to process data. Key pieces of hardware include the central processing unit (CPU), random access memory (RAM), and one or more bulk data storage devices called drives. Most personal computers also have a video screen that displays information to the user. Software includes the computer's operating system and various programs that perform special functions, such as e-mail or word processing.

The operating system acts like the computer's "brain." When a computer user requests a program, the operating system pulls that program from the appropriate drive. The program data is placed in RAM, where it can be accessed more quickly. The CPU carries out the calculations and instructions needed for the program to work. The operating system manages all of these interactions and assigns computer resources to various tasks.

Engineers and computer programmers are constantly working to improve hardware and software. Each advance causes other changes. For example, the creation of faster CPUs contributed to the development of bigger and more complex programs. As a result computer designs tend to change rapidly.

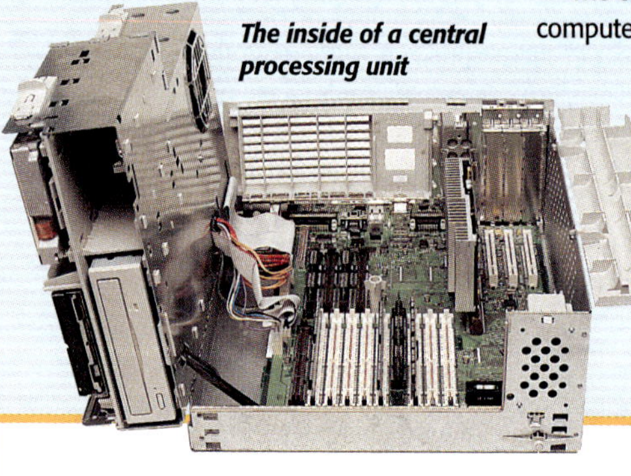

The inside of a central processing unit

Understanding Science and History

1. What two elements of a computer work together so it can function?
2. Why do you think some people refer to the operating system as the computer's brain?

more research institutions were quickly added. As more universities joined the network, it was eventually opened up to the public. Soon other networks were also being created for a variety of uses.

At the same time that access to computer networks was growing, advances in technology were making computers themselves smaller, cheaper, and easier to use. These **minicomputers**, or personal computers, became increasingly popular and encouraged the expansion of networks. The development of **modems**, devices that allow computers to send data over telephone lines, enabled networks to use the public phone system. This made network access easier and less expensive. The Internet was beginning to take shape.

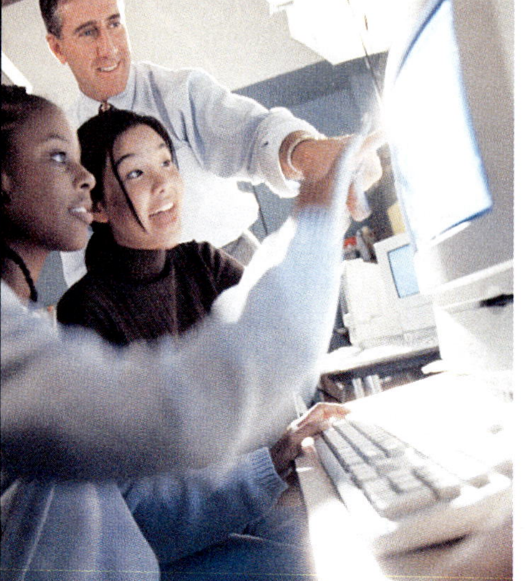

Electronic communication and the Internet have been used in many schools, universities, and research centers.

Communicating online. One of the most important features of the Internet is electronic mail, commonly called **e-mail**. By 1982 the Usenet network enabled computer users to send e-mail to each other across the world. Worldwide electronic bulletin boards, called newsgroups, were created to discuss specific topics. In addition, e-mail has begun changing the way that companies operate. Andrew S. Grove, an executive of Intel Corporation, stated that e-mail promotes a more democratic business model:

TEACH OBJECTIVE 2

ALL LEVELS: To help students understand the challenges and benefits developing nations have faced while trying to improve their communications technology, copy the following graphic organizer on the chalkboard, omitting the italicized answers. Have each student complete it. When students have finished filling in the graphic organizer, ask them to predict which country besides the United States will most likely see the fastest technological growth during the next decade. *(Students might say Japan or China; ask them to justify their responses.)* Then ask them which is likely to have the slowest technological growth. *(Most will probably say Russia.)*
Sheltered English

DEVELOPING NATIONS AND COMMUNICATIONS TECHNOLOGY

Challenges	Benefits
• *cost of communications systems*	• *Cellular phone networks can improve phone service in developing nations.*
• *inadequate supplies of computers or phone lines*	• *E-mail could be less expensive than post office or fax machines.*
	• *Internet databases could improve education resources.*
	• *Two-way television could allow doctors to help patients in isolated areas.*

"Companies that use e-mail are much faster, much less hierarchical [structured]. From the moment you do it yourself, you're available to anybody and everybody. The elimination of the screening process in my e-mail . . . tends to lead to a . . . more democratic way of operating—whether it's inside a corporation, inside a country, or across countries."

In the early 1990s the development of the World Wide Web, commonly called the Web, led to a dramatic increase in Internet use. The Web is a network of Internet sites that use hypertext markup language (HTML) to link to one another. By using a program called a Web browser, computer users can navigate quickly through the huge amount of information available on Web sites around the world. The Web also allows users to incorporate multimedia—animation, music, and video—into Internet documents. The Web has grown dramatically, from an estimated 25,000 Web sites in 1995 to more than 4 million sites in 1998.

✔ **READING CHECK:** How have developments in computer technology affected the spread of information around the world?

Read More About It

Free Find:
International Telecommunication Union
After reading about the International Telecommunication Union (ITU) on the **Holt Researcher** CD–ROM, write a short essay explaining how this organization has contributed to the spread of ideas around the world.

Communications Technology

Governments around the globe have recognized the importance of promoting the development of technology in their countries. Technological innovations often encourage economic growth by improving citizens' access to goods and services.

Technology in the United States. The U.S. government has made significant financial and technological contributions to the development of the Internet. As part of this investment, the government established the National Science Foundation Network (NSFnet) in the late 1980s. The NSFnet used the latest technology to link a small number of supercomputer centers across the United States. The NSFnet served as the core network, or backbone, of the Internet. In 1995, however, the National Science Foundation, which had been managing the NSFnet, turned over the network to the private sector.

In 1993 President Clinton created the U.S. Advisory Council on the National Information Infrastructure (NII), headed by Vice President Al Gore. The vice president argued that the expansion of the communications network could create an "Information Superhighway" that would benefit all Americans. As Gore described it, this Information Superhighway would change users' lives.

"[It would be] a seamless web of communications networks, computers, databases, and consumer electronics that will put vast amounts of information at users' fingertips. . . . The NII can transform the lives of the American people . . . giving all Americans a fair opportunity to go as far as their talents and ambitions will take them."

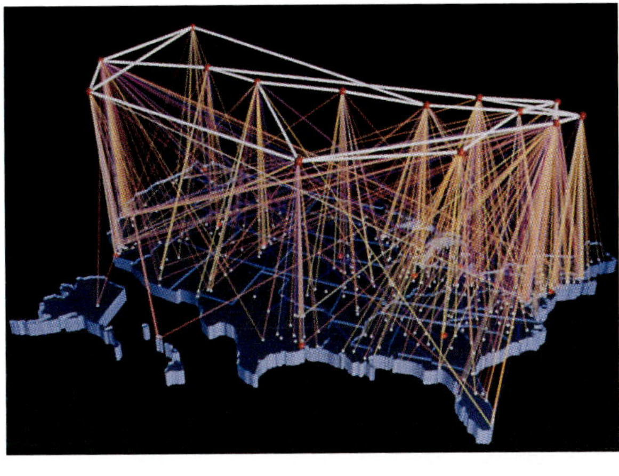

INTERPRETING THE VISUAL RECORD

The NSFnet. This portrayal of the NSFnet uses purple lines to indicate a free flow of data and white lines to show a heavy backup caused by 100 billion bytes of moving data. ***What relationship might exist between data backups and population density?***

TECHNOLOGY AND SOCIETY

Web Politics. During the 2000 presidential campaign, candidates used the Internet to gain political support. In his effort to win the Iowa straw poll in 1999, Republican Steve Forbes had his supporters send e-mails to all their friends and relatives in Iowa, urging them to vote for Forbes. Some 250 people responded to the e-mail requests. They made up 5 percent of those who voted for Forbes and helped him take second place in the straw poll. Other presidential hopefuls, including Bill Bradley, George W. Bush, and Al Gore, used Web sites to attract and inform voters.

CRITICAL THINKING How might the Internet be a useful campaign tool?

ANSWER: Students might mention that large numbers of Americans use the Internet and that information can be made widely available at a low cost on a Web site.

VISUAL RECORD ANSWER

Students might suggest that information lines would bunch at heavy population centers.

▸**ASSIGNMENT** *Tell students to use the graphic organizer on the previous page to write a short science-fiction story in which they describe the world and its technological developments in communications 50 or 100 years from now.*

TEACH OBJECTIVE 3

LEVELS 1 AND 2: In a classroom discussion, ask students if they have any concerns about violations of privacy from new technological developments. *(Students might mention the possibility of e-mail being read, the possibility of recording information on car crashes, and abuse of personal information such as credit reports, job applications, and rental agreements.)* Tell them to select one of these and to create a flyer or poster that warns others of the possibility of this type of violation of privacy. **Sheltered English**

LEVEL 3: Organize students into groups of four or five and tell them to imagine that they are the founders of a group whose goal is to help protect people from possible violations of privacy through new technologies. Tell them to write a mission statement and to list their concerns in order of priority. Then have them write up an action list that states how they intend to act on each concern. *(See the Levels 1 and 2 lesson for the correct concerns.)* **Cooperative Learning**

ECONOMIC DEVELOPMENT

Selling Cell Phones. Polls revealed in 1999 that American teenagers regarded a cellular phone as the most important item a teen could have. Some 16 percent of the teenagers surveyed already owned a cellular phone. In order to take advantage of the teen market, communications companies directed their advertising at parents. Companies wanted to convince parents that cellular phones would benefit them as well as their children.

CRITICAL THINKING How might companies use teenagers' interest to market cellular phones to parents?

ANSWER: Students might mention that advertisements could show parents that they could easily contact their children.

THAT'S INTERESTING!

The popularity of cellular phones led some people to wonder if they posed any health risks. As of 1999, researchers had found no clear evidence that the microwave radio emissions from cellular phones cause brain cancer.

VISUAL RECORD ANSWER

Students might answer that the technology exists side-by-side with traditional structures.

Technology in developing nations. Although the Internet is a worldwide network, nations vary widely in terms of their Internet use. Internet access is limited in many parts of Africa, southern Asia, and South America. In some cases government-owned telephone monopolies have been slow to adjust to the new technology. In Argentina, for example, telephone users in 1999 were still charged by the minute for local phone calls. Because high speed Internet connections can cost 50 times as much as in the United States, few people can afford to stay online long enough for regular Internet use. In India the growth of e-commerce has been slowed by government regulations that make it more difficult to buy goods online.

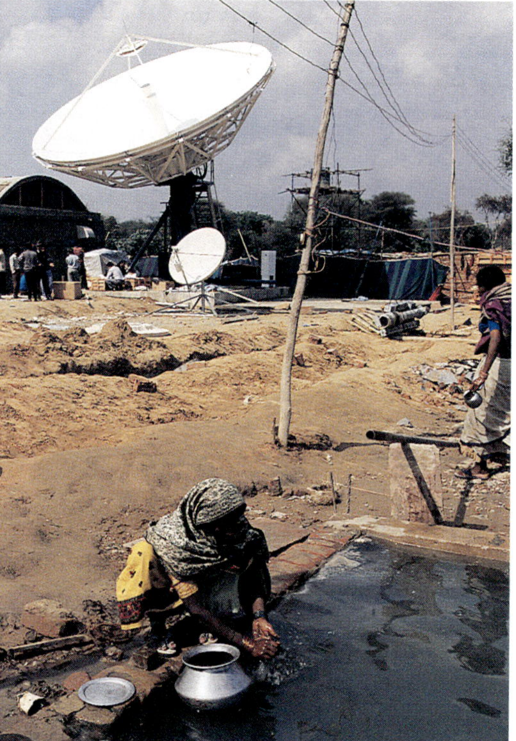

INTERPRETING THE VISUAL RECORD

Information technology. Within the past few decades, efforts have been made to introduce the latest communications technology to the developing world. ***How has the new technology affected the physical landscape of New Delhi, India?***

In many nations there are not enough computers or phone lines to allow widespread Internet access. In 1995 the vice president of South Africa claimed that "over half the human race has never dialed a phone." One 1999 study estimated that the entire continent of Africa had only about 1.2 million Internet users. Although there have been efforts to expand telephone service in Africa and Latin America, the cost in many countries remains high, while the quality of the phone connections is often too poor for Internet requirements. Another limitation is that the majority of Web sites are in English, which is not the primary language in most developing nations.

In spite of these challenges, global Internet use is growing rapidly. Spanish is quickly becoming the second most popular language on the Internet. The number of Internet users in India is increasing dramatically. Some governments are investing heavily in new communications systems to replace outdated equipment. For example, the Chinese government plans to add some 80 million phone lines and thousands of miles of fiber-optic cable to upgrade its telecommunications network.

The potential advantages of improving communications technology in developing nations are great. Cellular phone networks can provide improved phone service in many developing nations at a lower cost than would expansion of existing copper-wire networks. In Africa sending documents by e-mail is often much less expensive than using the postal service or fax machines. Access to Internet databases can provide valuable educational resources to university students and professors. Innovations such as two-way television even allow doctors to assist with the treatment of patients in isolated areas.

✔ **READING CHECK:** What challenges and benefits have developing nations faced while trying to improve their communications technology?

Information Technology and Privacy

Although new technology benefits society, the creation of electronic information systems has also contributed to growing concerns about privacy. Many Americans worry that electronic data storage and communication will make information about their private lives easily available to others. In some cases, these fears are

REVIEW

Have students complete the **Section 3 Review** on p. 871.

ASSESS

Have students complete **Daily Quiz 29.3**. As **Alternative Assessment**, you may want to use the Internet informational booklet activity or the government contributions graphic organizer in this section's lessons.

RETEACH

Have students complete **Main Idea Activity for Reteaching and Sheltered English 29.3**. Then organize students into triads. Have each student write five quiz questions on one of the objectives from this section. Have students trade quizzes and answer each other's questions. Encourage them to help each other understand any information pertaining to questions their group members miss.
Sheltered English, Cooperative Learning

EXTEND

Organize students into triads and have each group create a three-panel visual display that shows the evolution of communications technology during the 1900s. Display students' completed displays in the classroom or the school library.
Block Scheduling, Cooperative Learning

justified. Today, some companies monitor their employees' use of e-mail messages, raising new issues of privacy. One e-mail administrator in California supported the privacy of electronic communications by saying: "You don't read other people's mail, just as you don't listen to their phone conversations."

In some cases, technological innovations provide unexpected opportunities to monitor activities. In 1999 General Motors began installing black boxes in some of its automobiles. Similar to equipment used on airplanes, these devices collect data when a car crashes. The device records information such as the speed of the car, whether the driver was wearing a seat belt, and whether the driver used the brakes just before a crash. Some people are concerned that the information might be used against them in lawsuits.

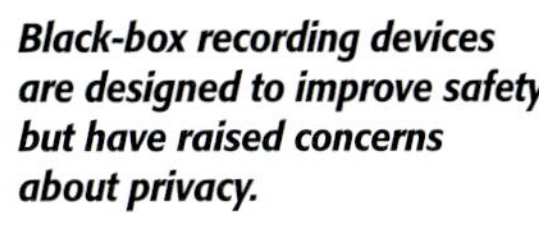

Black-box recording devices are designed to improve safety but have raised concerns about privacy.

As more and more information is cataloged and made available, a growing number of people are becoming concerned with the possible abuse of knowledge. Some libraries use electronic **barcodes** to keep track of their collections. This data could also be used to provide a record of a borrower's reading habits. E-mail has raised other privacy concerns because it can be captured at any of the computer systems it passes through. Web sites store information about their visitors that can help speed future commercial transactions but could also be used in ways that invade privacy. Credit reports, job applications, and rental agreements result in the collection of personal information that can also be entered into a computer and analyzed in any number of ways. For those who are concerned about keeping records confidential, the Information Revolution poses new challenges.

✔ **READING CHECK:** What are some of the privacy concerns that recent technological developments have raised?

SECTION 3 REVIEW

Define and explain the significance of the following terms:
Information Revolution
minicomputers
modems
e-mail
barcodes

Identify and explain the significance of the following individual:
Al Gore

1. **Using Graphic Organizers** Copy the graphic organizer below. Use it to show the applications of recent advances in communications.

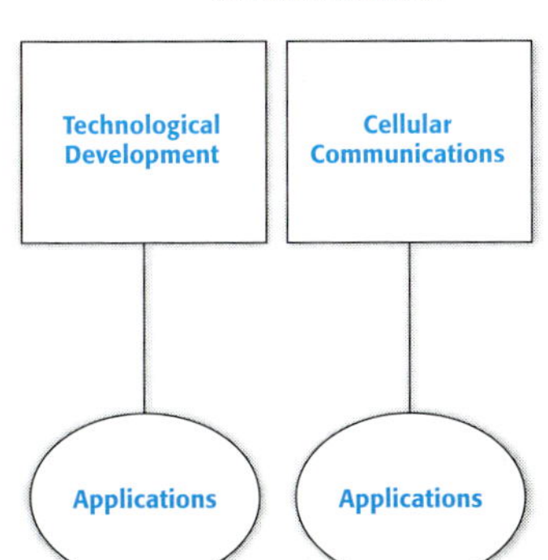

2. **Assessing Consequences** How did technology influence the spread of information during the late 1900s?
3. **Evaluating** What challenges face developing nations attempting to acquire new communications technologies?
4. **Recognizing Point of View** Why do some people fear that the growth of electronic communication will threaten privacy? How are their concerns justified?

Critical Thinking

5. How has the Information Revolution changed life in the United States and the developing world?
Consider:
   - how the ways that business is conducted and services are provided have changed
   - what new opportunities have come about for developing countries
   - what privacy issues have been raised as a result of recent technologies

SECTION 3 REVIEW ANSWERS

Define and Identify
For significance, see the following pages:
- Information Revolution, p. 867
- minicomputers, p. 868
- modems, p. 868
- e-mail, p. 868
- Al Gore, p. 869
- barcodes, p. 871

1. The Internet has led to e-mail and the World Wide Web; cellular telephones allow people to make telephone calls from nearly any location.
2. Developments in communications, such as advances in computers and satellite technology, allowed information to spread quickly.
3. cost, government regulations, and availability
4. Electronic communication enables access to confidential information. Examples include monitoring library use through barcodes or private e-mail communications.
5. Businesses can communicate more quickly across distances and can also sell goods and services worldwide through the Internet. Developing nations can access up-to-date information. New technologies make people's private information more accessible.

SECTION 4

After completing Section 4, students should be able to:

OBJECTIVE 1 *Describe how the popularity of sports has grown to include a worldwide audience.*

OBJECTIVE 2 *Explain how television, the Internet, and movies have contributed to a global culture.*

OBJECTIVE 3 *Discuss how music and fashion have contributed to a global youth culture.*

LET'S GET STARTED!

As students enter the classroom, tell them to think about how their tastes in music, sports, movies, television, food, and fashions might have been influenced by people in other countries. Have them make a list of all the things in their lives that they can think of that come from other countries. *(Lists might include video games, cartoons, soccer, music, fashion, and so on.)* Call on students to share their lists with the class. Then tell them that in Section 4 they will learn about the growth of a global culture through sports, the media, and the Internet.

SECTION 4 RESOURCES

PRINT
- Guided Reading Strategy 29.4
- Biography Reading 29: Spike Lee
- Section 4 Review, p. 875
- Daily Quiz 29.4

MULTIMEDIA
- One-Stop Planner, Lesson 29.4
- Holt Researcher: American History CD–ROM

SHELTERED ENGLISH
- Main Idea Activity for Reteaching and Sheltered English 29.4

✔ READING TO UNDERSTAND

To help students master the section objectives, have them answer the **READING CHECKS** and complete **Guided Reading Strategy 29.4** as they read the section.

A Global Culture

OBJECTIVES

Read to understand:

1. how the popularity of sports has grown to include a global audience
2. how television, the Internet, and movies have contributed to a global culture
3. how music and fashion contributed to a global youth culture

KEY TERMS

Olympic Games
cultural diffusion

KEY PEOPLE

Baron Pierre de Coubertin

EYEWITNESSES TO History

“I went out to talk to Nomo [a native of Japan] and I started speaking Spanish. I caught myself and just started laughing. He looked at me and started laughing. And then he just said, ‘Bueno’ [okay].”

—Dave Wallace

Hideo Nomo

Los Angeles Dodgers pitching coach Dave Wallace recalled a humorous situation on the pitching mound in 1996 that reflects the growing internationalization of sports. Like a growing number of baseball teams, the Dodgers boasted a culturally diverse pitching staff for their 1996 season: Hideo Nomo of Japan, one pitcher from South Korea, two pitchers from Mexico, and two more from the Dominican Republic. When people around the globe mingle, they not only share technical knowledge and expertise but also exchange ways of having fun. As people moved from country to country during the 1900s, their interactions created the beginnings of a global culture.

World Sports

International sporting events have a long history. The first recorded **Olympic Games** took place in 776 B.C. as part of a religious festival in ancient Greece. The games were officially ended in A.D. 393. In 1894 Baron Pierre de Coubertin, a French educator, proposed reviving the competitions. Two years later, the first modern Olympic Games were held in Athens, Greece. Initially a contest held during the summer for male athletes, the Olympics expanded to include women in 1912 and winter events in 1924. Countries not only competed in the games but also competed to be the host of the Olympics. Over the years the Olympic Games have been held in Europe, North America, Asia, and Australia.

During the 1900s advances in communications and transportation contributed to the growing popularity of sports. Athletic teams travel around the world to participate in competitions. Many individual athletes also play for teams outside their own countries. The widespread enthusiasm for athletic competition has enabled many sports to gain a global following.

In many cases, sports have been introduced to new countries by soldiers stationed far from home. Baseball was carried overseas by U.S. soldiers to Asia, Central America, and the Caribbean. Some players from these regions—including former Pittsburgh Pirates Hall of Famer Roberto Clemente, a Puerto Rican, and Chicago Cubs outfielder Sammy Sosa, from the Dominican Republic—have become major league stars. Japan has its own professional baseball league, which has attracted hundreds of foreign players since the 1950s. In 1996 Oakland Athletics manager Sandy Alderson predicted that baseball's popularity would continue to grow outside the United States:

British soldiers introduced cricket to British colonies such as India.

TEACH OBJECTIVE 1

ALL LEVELS: Organize students into groups of five and have each group create a children's nonfiction book about how the popularity of sports has grown to include a worldwide audience. Tell them to develop one page about each of the major sports or events mentioned in the section—the Olympics, baseball, basketball, football, and soccer—and its growing international popularity. *(Students might mention that advances in communications and transportation and traveling armies as well as soldiers stationed abroad helped spread sports.)* Tell students to use language for young children. Display students' completed books in the classroom or the school library. **Sheltered English, Cooperative Learning**

TEACH OBJECTIVE 2

ALL LEVELS: Ask students if they have seen or experienced some form of entertainment imported from another country. *(Students might mention Japanese cartoons or video games as well as foreign musical groups; some might mention British television shows, Latin American newscasts, or Canadian sporting events.)* Tell students to write a paragraph explaining how television, movies, and the Internet have helped create a global culture. *(Paragraphs should mention cultural items imported to the United States as well as those exported.)* **Sheltered English**

> **"We're just in the early stages of the internationalization of the game. And I think the game will change significantly as we get players from eastern Europe, Russia, China. I think eventually we'll end up with [major league baseball] teams [located] outside North America."**

Basketball and football are other American sports with international appeal. Europe has many professional basketball teams as well as an American-style football league. Europe also had women's professional basketball long before the creation in 1997 of the WNBA—the U.S. women's professional basketball league. As a result, many American women have pursued pro careers in Europe. "It's not NBA money," said basketball player Vicki Hall, referring to her European salary. "But I could make more than a decent living there [in Europe]."

While Americans exported baseball and basketball, they imported soccer. Called football in most of the world, the game is played all over the globe. Much of soccer's popularity stems from its simplicity. Requiring only a ball and an open patch of ground, the game is easily playable under many conditions. Although millions of American girls and boys play in youth soccer leagues, professional soccer has been slow to attract a following in the United States. The sport received a boost when the United States hosted the 1994 Men's World Cup championship. An estimated 2 billion people worldwide watched the televised event. The 1999 Women's World Cup championship received even greater publicity in the United States. The U.S. women's thrilling victory over the Chinese team in the finals was watched by more than 40 million U.S. viewers. President Clinton, who attended the match, called it "the biggest sporting event of the last decade. . . . It will have a very far-reaching impact, not only for the United States, but for the world."

INTERPRETING THE VISUAL RECORD

Women's soccer. American fans enthusiastically responded to the U.S. victory in the Women's World Cup championship. ***How do you think the U.S. women's victory might affect the popularity of soccer in the United States?***

✔ **READING CHECK:** How has the popularity of sports grown to include a worldwide audience?

World Television and Movies

News and entertainment broadcast on television and carried over the Internet have also contributed to the global exchange of culture. Cable News Network (CNN) International broadcasts news programs around the world. All major U.S. news networks run Web sites, making breaking news accessible from virtually anywhere.

Foreign films and television have also become very popular in the United States. Australian, British, and Canadian films often have an advantage over other foreign films in the U.S. market because they are made in English. However, foreign-language films that use subtitles—such as the French film *Cyrano de Bergerac*—have also been successful in the United States. Some foreign-born actors have become Hollywood stars. These include action stars such as Austrian-born Arnold Schwarzenegger and Belgian Jean Claude Van Damme.

Nevertheless, the United States dominates the world market in films and television. Products of American popular culture are the nation's second-largest export. As of 1999, U.S. companies had produced all 40 of the world's top

This advertisement for the Elvis Presley film **Jailhouse Rock** *was published in Japanese.*

HISTORY MAKERS SPEAK

Miklos Vamos in *Jihad vs. McWorld*

Global Culture. Miklos Vamos, a journalist from Hungary, explained the problems that former communist nations faced in preserving their cultures. "Hungarians, Czechoslovaks and Bulgarians try to imitate everything that is American—and I mean *everything*. . . . The state-run financing system of culture doesn't exist any longer, but neither does any network of foundations and other private funds that can be used, as in the West, to support the arts. East European films and literature cannot compete with their American counterparts. If we keep going on like this, our small countries will gradually lose their national cultures."

CRITICAL THINKING How might the collapse of communism have affected artists in Eastern Europe?

ANSWER: Students might answer that they lost state funding.

VISUAL RECORD ANSWER

Students might suggest that the women's victory inspired many young athletes to participate in sports.

TEACH OBJECTIVE 3

ALL LEVELS: To help students understand how music and fashion have contributed to a global youth culture, copy the following graphic organizer on the chalkboard, omitting the italicized answers. Have each student complete it. **Sheltered English**

▶ASSIGNMENT *Tell students to use the graphic organizer to write an article for a popular teen magazine about how the youth of the world participate in and contribute to a global youth culture. Students should include specific examples of cultural exchanges and explain how the exchanges take place.*

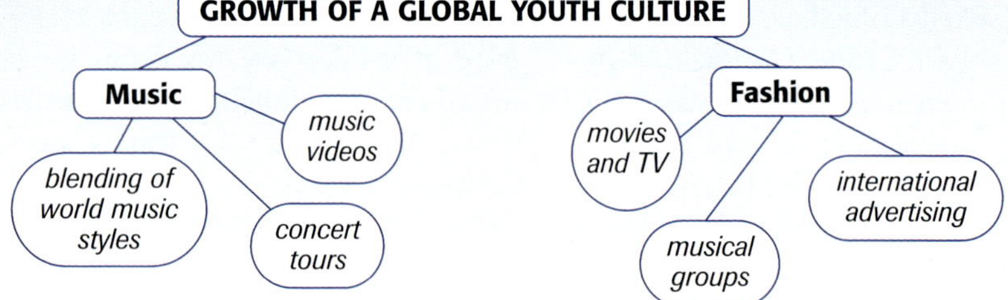

VISUAL RECORD ANSWER

Students might suggest that technology allows for greater access to different forms of entertainment.

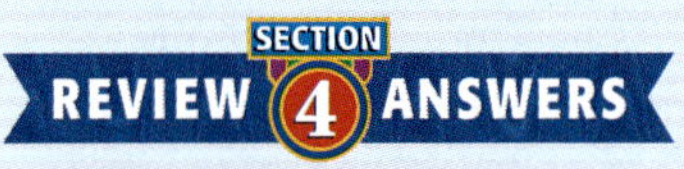

Define and Identify

For significance, see the following pages:

- Olympic Games, p. 872
- Baron Pierre de Coubertin, p. 872
- cultural diffusion, p. 874

1. Answers will vary but should identify relevant examples of the global popularity of various media.

2. Answers will vary but students may suggest that the global popularity of sports has led to an increase in the number of foreign players in U.S. professional sports.

3. The world's economy grows through international trade as people from around the world want to adopt or purchase elements of other cultures for their own use.

4. Statements will vary but should address concerns about cultural diffusion and describe the economic impact of imported movies and television shows on the domestic entertainment industry.

5. A global youth culture has been created from exposure to movies, television, music, and fashion, which have been exported largely from the United States.

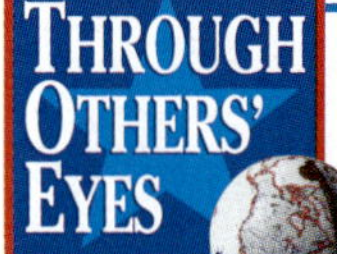

American Culture Abroad

"This is the '90s," declared Disney's top executive, Michael Eisner, "the decade we reinvent the Disney experience not just in California, but worldwide." However, not everyone welcomed Eisner's vision. When Euro Disney opened outside Paris in April 1992, critics called it a "cultural Chernobyl." "It took a money-hungry little mouse to trigger a debate on issues that we have been evading [avoiding]," noted Jean-Marie Rouart in the Paris newspaper *Le Figaro.* "Should we allow culture to be ruled by profitability?"

Such concerns have long been present in France. In 1982, a decade before Euro Disney opened, France's minister of culture, Jack Lang, warned the world about what he called American cultural imperialism. "Certain great nations who taught us about freedom and called on people to rise up against oppression, yet who today . . . have no other morality than that of profit, . . . seek to impose a uniform culture on the whole world."

money-earning films overseas. For example, the movie *Titantic* was a huge hit in China as well as in the United States. During the 1980s the television drama *Dallas* seemed to represent American life to people all over the world. Some Americans worry that the worst television programs receive the widest distribution. For example, American soap operas are wildly popular in Egypt, India, and other developing countries. Foreign critics worry about how American movies and television will affect their cultures. In 1994 France's minister of culture, Jacques Toubon, called U.S. domination of the market a "pure monopoly in the worst sense."

✔ **READING CHECK:** How have television, the Internet, and movies contributed to a global culture?

World Youth

The international links formed by the entertainment industry have contributed to **cultural diffusion**, the process of spreading cultural practices or beliefs. Young people around the world often look to mass media for ideas about music and dress.

World music. This Kaiapo Indian in Altamira, Brazil, listens to a cassette-playing boom box. ***How might technology expose people to different forms of entertainment?***

Music. Although rock 'n' roll music originated in the United States, it quickly gained international popularity. More recent musical styles such as hip-hop have a growing international fan base as well. By the late 1980s the growth of cable television allowed music videos to become an important marketing tool for the music industry. This phenomenon is not limited to English-speaking fans or musicians. MTV Asia, which is broadcast across the continent, focuses on bands from India and other Asian countries. MTV Europe broadcasts in English, but most of its programming features European musicians. The network reaches some 60 million homes in Europe. Some 88 million viewers in the former Soviet Union receive the network for an hour each week.

Music videos and concert tours provide musicians with worldwide popularity. At any given time, U2 of Ireland might be performing in the United States, India's Ravi Shankar in Rio de Janeiro, Cuban-born Gloria Estefan in Rome, and Britain's Rolling Stones in Tokyo. Fans who are unable to get to a concert can find the latest CDs in stores from Mexico City to Hong Kong. Moreover, various musical styles—from jazz to electronic music—have incorporated sounds and rhythms from around the world. A representative for the world music band Ancient Future described the growth of world music on the band's Web page:

REVIEW

Have students complete the **Section 4 Review** on p. 875.

ASSESS

Have students complete **Daily Quiz 29.4**. As **Alternative Assessment**, you may want to use the children's book activity or the global culture paragraphs in this section's lessons.

RETEACH

Have students complete **Main Idea Activity for Reteaching and Sheltered English 29.4**. Then have each student create a detailed outline of the section. Tell students to be sure to cover all of the section's objectives as well as the main idea of each subsection in their outlines. **Sheltered English**

EXTEND

Organize students into groups of four or five and tell them to imagine that they are a group of social scientists several hundred years in the future. Tell them that they are compiling a report about the cultural changes around the world during the last part of the 1900s. Tell students to create a short multimedia presentation about how sports, the entertainment industry, and the Internet contributed to the creation of a global culture. **Block Scheduling, Cooperative Learning**

> “Of course, musicians have been exchanging knowledge across national boundaries as long as there has been contact between cultures. . . . What is new is the conscious decision on the part of some artists to make cross-cultural music in an effort to show how people from different cultures can grow by learning from each other. As this planet becomes more aware of itself as a whole, a growing number of musicians are now experimenting with new combinations of world music styles.”

Fashion. Movies and television also provide teens with inspiration in the world of fashion. When American director Spike Lee's film *Malcolm X* was released in Japan in 1993, many people there became interested in Malcolm X's life and beliefs. They also began to wear the same "X"-labeled baseball caps, T-shirts, and jackets that many American youths wore when the film opened in the United States.

Japanese teens have also adopted a range of American casual styles, which they call *Amekaji.* National Football League (NFL) hats are common among Japanese teens, as are black leather jackets and university athletic warm-up suits. One Japanese advertising executive said, "Sharing in America can release Japanese teenagers from the restraints they live with every day. Through fashion, they can capture a bit of the life-style they can never hope to live."

The export of many kinds of entertainment has provided more cultural connections. Music, sports, movies, and television all allow people in different areas of the world to develop and to share common interests. Furthermore, technology has increased the speed and ease with which ideas have spread around the world.

American-style clothing such as these cowboy boots is popular with many Japanese teens.

✔ **READING CHECK:** How have music and fashion contributed to a global youth culture?

SECTION 4 REVIEW

Define and explain the significance of the following terms:
Olympic Games
cultural diffusion

Identify and explain the significance of the following individual:
Baron Pierre de Coubertin

1. **Using Graphic Organizers** Copy the graphic organizer below. Use it to explain how particular sports, movies, television shows, music, and fashion trends have gained world-wide popularity in recent decades.

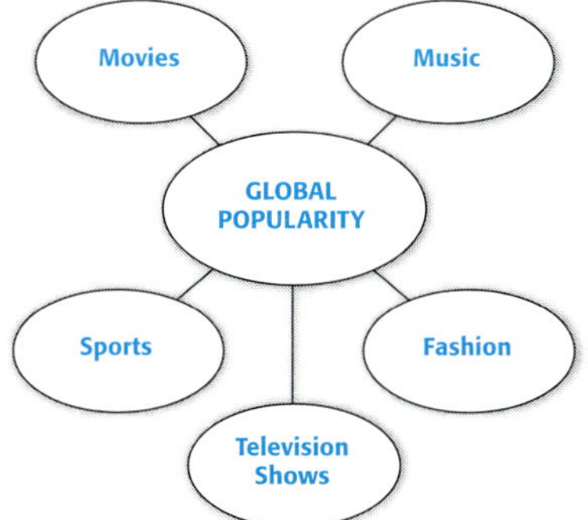

2. **Evaluating** How do you think the global popularity of sports has affected professional sports in the United States?
3. **Analyzing** How do you think the creation of a global culture through sports, movies, television, and music influences the development of the world's economy?
4. **Using Historical Imagination** Imagine that you are the minister of culture in another country. Write a statement explaining your country's official policy on imported movies, television programs, music, and fashion. Explain why you have adopted the policy.

Critical Thinking

5. How has the movement of ideas and people contributed to the development of a global youth culture?
Consider:
   - how have media such as movies and television contributed to the global youth culture
   - the influence of music and music videos
   - how fashion has been a part of the growing global youth culture

CHAPTER 29 REVIEW ANSWERS

Creating a Time Line
Each event should have an explanation and the correct date.

Writing a Summary
See the Reading Checks in each section for main ideas.

Identifying People and Ideas
1. immigration station in New York Harbor
2. point of entry for immigrants who arrived on the West Coast
3. legislation that eased quota system based on country of origin
4. place of protection
5. Chinese American novelist who advocates acceptance of immigrants
6. widespread transfer of information made possible by computers and other new technologies
7. electronic mail
8. vice president who led the U.S. Advisory Council on the National Information Infrastructure
9. international sporting event
10. spread of cultural beliefs and practices

Understanding Main Ideas
1. During the 1800s and early 1900s, immigration to the United States surged and large numbers of Americans migrated from rural areas to cities.

REVIEW AND ASSESSMENT RESOURCES

PRINT

- Chapter 29 Review, pp. 876–77
- Chapter 29 Tutorial for Students, Parents, Mentors, and Peers
- Chapter 29 Test (Form A or B)
- Portfolio Activities and Alternative Assessment Handbook, Chapter 29

MULTIMEDIA

- Audio Program, Chapter 29 (English and Spanish)
- Chapter 29 Test Generator (on the One-Stop Planner)
- Global Skill Builder CD–ROM
- HRW Web site

SHELTERED ENGLISH

- Spanish Glossary
- Sheltered English Chapter 29 Test

REVIEW

Have students complete the **Chapter 29 Review** on pp. 876–77.

ASSESS

Use one of the chapter tests to assess students' understanding of the content. For **Alternative Assessment**, see the **Portfolio Activities and Alternative Assessment Handbook.**

2. The Great Depression and World War II slowed immigration, but the number of refugees rose dramatically. The end of World War II also brought a surge in refugee migration.

3. Answers will vary. Students might suggest that new technologies are allowing businesses to communicate more quickly across distances and that developing nations are able to update their communications.

4. by providing easier and faster access to a wider variety of information

Reviewing Themes

1. Immigration restrictions in 1924 sharply reduced the number of immigrants. The Displaced Persons Act of 1948 increased the number of European immigrants, particularly Jews. Loosened restrictions in 1965 and 1990 allowed immigrants from more diverse ethnic backgrounds—particularly from Asia and Latin America—to settle in the United States.

2. The Department of Defense linked together computer systems at four universities. Later, as more universities joined the network, it was opened up to the public.

3. As people are exposed to global cultural goods, they want more of them, which leads to increased international trade.

Review

Creating a Time Line

Copy the time line below onto a sheet of paper. Complete the time line by filling in the events and dates from the chapter that you think were most significant. Pick three events and explain why you think they were significant.

Writing a Summary

Using the Reading Checks as a guide, write an overview of the events in the chapter.

Identifying People and Ideas

Identify the following terms or individuals and explain their significance.

1. Ellis Island
2. Angel Island
3. Immigration Act of 1965
4. asylum
5. Bette Bao Lord
6. Information Revolution
7. e-mail
8. Al Gore
9. Olympic Games
10. cultural diffusion

Understanding Main Ideas

SECTION 1

1. What patterns of migration marked the late 1800s and early 1900s?

SECTION 2

2. What economic and political forces affected migration in the 1930s and 1940s?

SECTION 3

3. How are new communications technologies transforming businesses and politics?

SECTION 4

4. In what ways do various types of media encourage the spread of ideas about different cultures?

Reviewing Themes

1. **Cultural Diversity** What effect did the U.S. immigration policies of the 1900s have on the cultural makeup of the nation's population?
2. **Technology and Society** How has the U.S. government contributed to the development of the Internet?
3. **Economic Development** How has an increasingly global culture led to increased international trade of various goods such as movies?

Thinking Critically

1. **Recognizing Point of View** What were some of the arguments made by people wanting to limit immigration to the United States?
2. **Hypothesizing** Do you think the migration patterns of the 1980s and 1990s will continue over the next 25 years? Why or why not?
3. **Evaluating** How has the growth of the Internet affected Americans' daily lives?
4. **Analyzing** In what ways has a global youth culture emerged in the 1990s?
5. **Synthesizing** In what ways can the movement of people influence the movement of ideas?

Writing About History

Writing to Create Imagine that you are a foreign teenager. Write a letter to a friend explaining how your life is influenced by American culture. Use specific examples. Use the graphic organizer below to organize your thoughts.

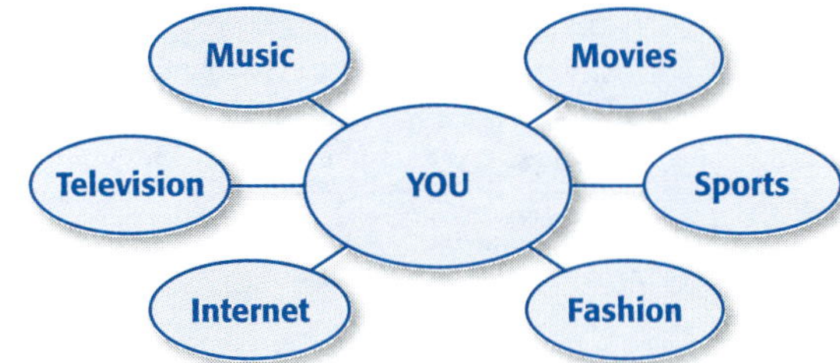

RETEACH

Organize the class into four groups and assign each group one of the following topics: patterns of migration during the 1800s and early 1900s; patterns of migration from World War I to the late 1990s; new technological developments in the field of communications; and the growth of a global culture. Tell each group to prepare a short television documentary about its topic. Supply students with video cameras and other appropriate equipment if possible.
Sheltered English, Cooperative Learning

EXTEND

Tell students to imagine that it is 70 years in the future and that they are grandparents telling their grandchildren about their childhoods. Have students take turns presenting brief dramatic monologues in which they tell their audience about their favorite sports, television shows, clothes, and music, as well as how they used the Internet. Tell students to emphasize the emergence of a global culture and to state how they felt about it.
Block Scheduling

Review the **Strategies for Success** on *Reading Maps.* Examine the map on page 863, then answer the questions below.

1. What is the focus of the map?
2. Why do you think the countries depicted were selected for this map?

Linking History and Geography

The State of Israel has been settled by Jewish immigrants from around the world. Conflict between Israel and its Arab neighbors has in turn led to mass migration in the region. What are some of the political changes shown on the map that might have encouraged migration?

internet connect

TOPIC: International Sports
GO TO: go.hrw.com
KEYWORD: SE1 Sports

Accessing the Internet through the HRW Web site, research information about sports that are played internationally. Then make a poster or multimedia presentation about one sport. Include information about its history, how it spread, its players and teams, and its fans.

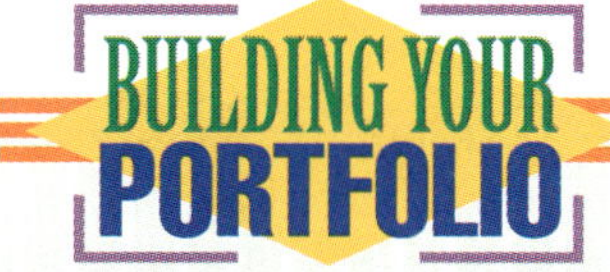

Complete one or all of the following projects independently or cooperatively.

1 Cultural Diversity

Imagine that you are a refugee fleeing from a war in your home country. ***Write a series of journal entries*** describing your feelings about the conflict from which you are escaping, the problems you encounter as a refugee in a new land, and your plans for the future.

2 Economic Development

Imagine that you are the director of a private agency that assists immigrant business-people. ***Prepare a speech*** on how immigrant-owned businesses are helping to boost the economy.

3 Technology and Society

Imagine that you are an attorney representing a client involved in a lawsuit about a company reading an employee's e-mail. ***Write an opening statement*** for the trial arguing why the information in e-mail should or should not be used in the case.

Thinking Critically

1. Some people believed that the different cultures and religions immigrants brought with them prevented a unified American culture; others argued that immigrants took jobs away from native-born Americans.
2. Answers will vary but should reflect current immigration trends and attitudes toward immigration.
3. Americans' have gained access to more information and a wider range of opportunities but have also opened themselves up to potential privacy violations.
4. Answers will vary but should use specific examples from music, music videos, clothing, and so on.
5. Answers should discuss the fact that people bring their ideas with them when they relocate. Examples may include the German scientists who worked in the United States and the Soviet Union after World War II.

Writing About History

Students' letters will vary but should identify specific examples from American movies, sports, fashion, the Internet, television, and music.

Strategies for Success

1. refugees
2. because of their sizable refugee problems

Linking History and Geography

creation of Jewish state, Israeli occupation, return of Israeli-occupied territories

The Struggle for Human Rights

CHAPTER PLANNING GUIDE

	Section Lesson Objectives	Print Resources	Multimedia Resources	Sheltered English Resources
Section 1 Human Rights Before World War I, pp. 880–84	1 State how the modern concept of human rights developed. 2 Identify ways the movement to abolish slavery was an international effort. 3 Discuss how the women's movement developed, and identify its primary goal. 4 Describe the human rights issues American progressives addressed.	▶ Guided Reading Strategy 30.1 ▶ American History Outline Map 24: The World ▶ Geography Activity 30: A Woman's Right to Vote ▶ Biography Reading 30: Lucretia Mott ▶ Section 1 Review, p. 884 ▶ Daily Quiz 30.1	▶ One-Stop Planner, Lesson 30.1 ▶ Holt Researcher: American History CD–ROM	▶ Main Idea Activity for Reteaching and Sheltered English 30.1
Section 2 The Cruelties of War, pp. 885–90	1 Explain how World War I changed Europeans' ideas about warfare. 2 Discuss how fascism and militarism endangered human rights in the 1930s. 3 Describe how human rights were violated during World War II. 4 List steps the world community took to protect human rights after World War II.	▶ Guided Reading Strategy 30.2 ▶ Primary Source Reading 30: The International Bill of Human Rights ▶ Section 2 Review, p. 890 ▶ Daily Quiz 30.2	▶ One-Stop Planner, Lesson 30.2 ▶ Everyday Life in America Transparency 23: The 1936 Olympic Games ▶ Holt Researcher: American History CD–ROM ▶ HRW Web site	▶ Main Idea Activity for Reteaching and Sheltered English 30.2
Section 3 Striving for Equality, pp. 891–94	1 Explain how the movement for racial equality progressed after World War II. 2 Summarize how efforts to protect human rights fared in the 1960s and early 1970s. 3 Describe what President Carter did to encourage human rights.	▶ Guided Reading Strategy 30.3 ▶ Literature Reading 30: A World of Infinite Possibilities ▶ Section 3 Review, p. 894 ▶ Daily Quiz 30.3	▶ One-Stop Planner, Lesson 30.3 ▶ Holt Researcher: American History CD–ROM	▶ Main Idea Activity for Reteaching and Sheltered English 30.3
Section 4 The Continuing Struggle, pp. 895–99	1 Identify what political events during the late 1980s and early 1990s led to advances in human rights. 2 Describe some characteristics of the worldwide women's movement. 3 Discuss what global challenges remain to human rights.	▶ Guided Reading Strategy 30.4 ▶ Graphic Organizer Activity 30: Human Rights Leaders ▶ Section 4 Review, p. 899 ▶ Daily Quiz 30.4	▶ One-Stop Planner, Lesson 30.4 ▶ The American Nation Video Program Segment: The Women's Rights Movement; Teacher's Guide, pp. 209–10 ▶ Holt Researcher: American History CD–ROM	▶ Main Idea Activity for Reteaching and Sheltered English 30.4
Chapter Review and Assessment pp. 900–01		▶ Chapter 30 Review, pp. 900–01 ▶ Chapter 30 Tutorial for Students, Parents, Mentors, and Peers ▶ Chapter 30 Test (Form A or B) ▶ Portfolio Activities and Alternative Assessment Handbook, Chapter 30	▶ Audio Program, Chapter 30 (English and Spanish) ▶ Chapter 30 Test Generator (on the One-Stop Planner) ▶ Global Skill Builder CD–ROM ▶ HRW Web site	▶ Spanish Glossary ▶ Sheltered English Chapter 30 Test

CHAPTER OVERVIEW

In the 1600s, enlightenment philosophers developed a theory of human rights that found expression in revolutions in the United States and France. New ideas about human rights led to protests against slavery throughout the world. Women involved in the abolition movement pressed for recognition of their rights. In their struggle for the suffrage, women drew attention to other human rights violations, such as child labor. However, during this same era war became far more deadly, causing greater numbers of deaths of soldiers and civilians.

The devastation of World War II led the newly created United Nations to press for recognition of human rights, including racial equality, throughout the world. Activists in the United States and South Africa pressed for an end to racial segregation. The United Nations also addressed rights violations brought on by the Cold War. The end of the Cold War and continuing efforts by women to improve their status are evidence of the ongoing struggle for human rights.

TIME TAMERS

Block Scheduling

The teacher lesson plans for each section offer a variety of activity choices to help you present the material in a block scheduling format. For further suggestions on block scheduling, see the **Block Scheduling Handbook with Team Teaching Strategies**, pp. 175–80.

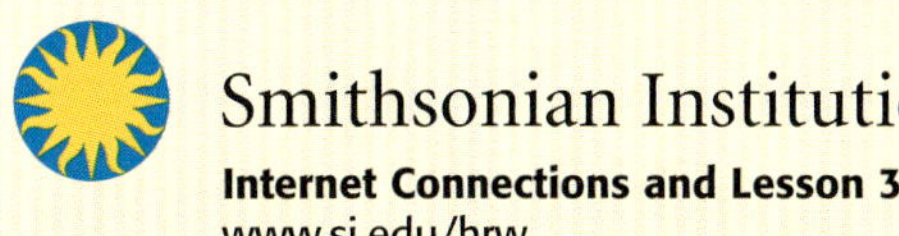

Smithsonian Institution®

Internet Connections and Lesson 30
www.si.edu/hrw

Hands-On History Activities:

Classroom to Community The **Hands-On History Activities** help students make meaningful connections between events in American history and those in their own hometown. You may wish to use the Chapter 30 Activity, Publicize Human Rights Issues, to extend the chapter lessons, as alternative assessment, or as a block scheduling option.

Portfolio Projects

The American Nation includes multiple portfolio projects in each Pupil's Edition chapter review, as well as each unit review. Chapter 30 Portfolio Project options on p. 901 include the following:

1. Students will **construct a time line**.
2. Students will **write a letter**.
3. Students will **write a petition**.

The American Nation
INTERNET RESOURCE DIRECTORY

To access online materials for this chapter, go to go.hrw.com and type in the keywords listed below.

HRW ONLINE RESOURCES
GO TO: go.hrw.com

Online Maps
KEYWORD: SE1 Maps30
- Civil Rights in the Truman Era
- Conflicts in the Middle East

Online Charts
KEYWORD: SE1 Charts30
- Reform and Society
- Social Reform

Online Reading Support
KEYWORD: SE1 Strategies30

Online Rubrics
KEYWORD: SE1 Rubrics

CHAPTER ENRICHMENT LINKS
Use these Web links to extend and enrich student learning for Chapter 30.
GO TO: go.hrw.com
KEYWORD: SE1 Ch30

CHAPTER INTERNET ACTIVITIES
GO TO: go.hrw.com
- Pupil's Edition Student Activity
KEYWORD: SE1 Rights
(Students examine the lives of women's rights activists.)
- Teacher's Edition Student Activity
KEYWORD: SE1 Mandela
(Students research the life of Nelson Mandela.)
- Teacher's Edition Student Activity
KEYWORD: SE1 Anne Frank
(Students learn about Anne Frank.)

ADDITIONAL
RESOURCES

Books for Teachers

Bovard, Marguerite. *Women Reshaping Human Rights.* Scholarly Resources, 1996. Discusses achievements of female activists.

Robertson, A. H., and J. G. Merrills. *Human Rights in the World.* St. Martin's Press, 1996. Provides an overview of human rights with some material on the post–Cold War era.

Books for Students

Carter, Jimmy. *Talking Peace.* Dutton Children's Books, 1993. Presents a discussion on peace by former president Carter. Particularly appropriate for students reading below grade level.

Magill, Frank, ed. *Great Events from History II: Human Rights Series.* Salem Press, 1992. Offers a collection of brief articles on significant human rights events.

Primary Sources from the Period

Lawson, Edward. *Encyclopedia of Human Rights.* Taylor & Francis, 1991. Provides important human rights documents.

Mandela, Nelson. *Long Walk to Freedom.* Little, Brown, 1994. Presents the autobiography of the South African leader.

Multimedia Materials

Islam and Feminism. Video, 25 min. First Run/Icarus Films. Studies Pakistani women's struggle for human rights.

Out of the Silence: Fighting for Human Rights. Video, 55 min. Olin Video. Assesses the impact of the Universal Declaration of Human Rights.

Before You Read

Build on What You Know

Ask students to answer the following questions.

How might religious values contribute to the idea of human rights?

Consider:

- the belief that life is sacred
- the emphasis on moral behavior found in most religions

Why might the United States be a leader in the human rights struggle?

Consider:

- the values outlined in the Declaration of Independence and the Constitution
- the commitment to democratic principles during the Cold War

exploring the time line

AMERICAN EVENTS

PEOPLE IN HISTORY

Jesse Owens. Born in 1913 to a family of Alabama sharecroppers, James Cleveland Owens was called Jesse after a schoolteacher misunderstood him when he called himself J. C. Because of a disagreement with U.S. athletic officials after his Olympic victory, Owens was banned from participating in amateur athletic contests. He campaigned for the Republican Party during the late 1930s and remained a Republican throughout his life. Owens had little interest in the civil rights movement, and some activists accused him of accepting the secondary status of African Americans in the United States. During the 1970s he received numerous awards, including the Presidential Medal of Freedom, for serving as an inspiration to all Americans.

ACTIVITY: Have students debate whether modern sports figures should serve as role models for Americans.

CHAPTER 30

1885–Present

The Struggle for Human Rights

A suffragist parade

Mosquitoes carry the malaria virus.

1885 | **1910** | **1935**

1888
World Events
Brazil becomes the last nation to officially outlaw slavery.

1903
Politics
Emmeline Pankhurst forms the Women's Social and Political Union in Great Britain.

1906
Science and Technology
Germany launches its first U-boats, changing naval warfare.

1920
Politics
The Nineteenth Amendment is ratified, giving U.S. women the right to vote.

1920
Science and Technology
Czech playwright Karel Capek introduces the term *robot* in his play *R.U.R.,* which criticizes the effect of technology on human society.

1934
Science and Technology
An effective malaria treatment is developed.

1936
Daily Life
African American athlete Jesse Owens wins four gold medals at the Olympic Games in Berlin, Germany.

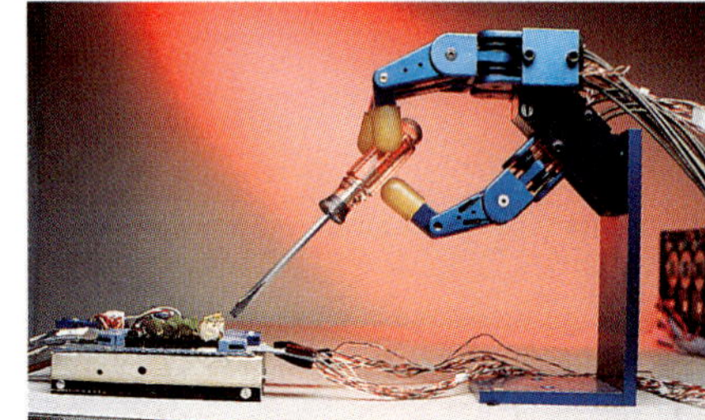

A modern robot assembling electronics

Before You Read

Build on What You Know

Many of the world's religions have long promoted the value of human life. The modern concept of human rights, however, grew out of ideas that date back only to the 1600s and 1700s. In this chapter you will learn how the modern concept of human rights developed and how protection and support for human rights has expanded during the 1900s. You will also learn how the United States has been a leader in this process, improving its own human rights record and often encouraging other countries to do the same.

Think About Themes

To help students create their Themes Journal entries, provide the following examples of appropriate **agree/disagree** *statements.*

Democratic Values

Agree The United States, which is committed to democracy, is a leading nation in the struggle for human rights.

Disagree The United States still faces problems with the treatment of women and minorities.

Global Relations

Agree Organizations can use the media to draw international attention to human rights violations.

Disagree Nations willing to violate the rights of citizens are likely to ignore international criticism.

Cultural Diversity

Agree All cultures agree on basic human rights such as liberty and freedom from violence.

Disagree Different cultures' attitudes toward human rights must be respected.

Amnesty International protesters

South Africans vote in their nation's first open elections

1948 World Events The United Nations (UN) adopts the Universal Declaration of Human Rights.

1960

1961 World Events The human rights organization Amnesty International is founded in London, England.

1964 The Arts Singer and actor Harry Belafonte sponsors a delegation of the Student Nonviolent Coordinating Committee on a tour of Africa.

1971 The Arts *Fiddler on the Roof* becomes the longest-running Broadway musical to date.

1976 The Arts Alex Haley publishes the best-seller *Roots.*

1985

1985 Business and Finance The World Bank organizes famine relief for the Sudan.

1990 World Events South African civil rights activist Nelson Mandela is released from prison.

1994 Politics South Africa holds its first national election in which all South Africans can vote.

1999

1999 Daily Life The U.S. women's soccer team wins the World Cup.

The seal of the United Nations

The television miniseries Roots showed millions of Americans the hardships of slavery.

Think About Themes

Decide whether you **agree** *or* **disagree** *with the following statements. Note why in your journal.*

Democratic Values A democratic form of government is better able to protect human rights than other forms of government.

Global Relations Nations and international organizations can influence human rights in other countries.

Cultural Diversity Human rights is a universal concept, with little difference from culture to culture.

exploring the time line

internet connect

TOPIC: Nelson Mandela
GO TO: go.hrw.com
KEYWORD: SE1 Mandela

Have students access the Internet through the HRW Web site to conduct research on Nelson Mandela. Then ask students to make a graphic organizer that analyzes the importance of Mandela as a revolutionary, prisoner, world leader, and private person.

SECTION 1

After completing Section 1, students should be able to:

OBJECTIVE 1 *State how the modern concept of human rights developed.*

OBJECTIVE 2 *Identify ways the movement to abolish slavery was an international effort.*

OBJECTIVE 3 *Discuss how the women's movement developed, and identify its primary goal.*

OBJECTIVE 4 *Describe the human rights issues American progressives addressed.*

LET'S GET STARTED!

To begin the class, tell students to write the definition of human rights. *(Definitions should include basic rights and freedoms to which all people are entitled.)* Then have them free-write for five minutes on the topic of human rights. They may write about human rights in history, in the present, in their own lives, and so on. Call on volunteers to summarize what they wrote. Then tell students that in Section 1 they will learn about the concept of human rights and how it applied to the abolition movement and the women's movement.

SECTION 1 RESOURCES

PRINT

- Guided Reading Strategy 30.1
- American History Outline Map 24: The World
- Geography Activity 30: A Woman's Right to Vote
- Biography Reading 30: Lucretia Mott
- Section 1 Review, p. 884
- Daily Quiz 30.1

MULTIMEDIA

- One-Stop Planner, Lesson 30.1
- Holt Researcher: American History CD–ROM

SHELTERED ENGLISH

- Main Idea Activity for Reteaching and Sheltered English 30.1

✔ READING TO UNDERSTAND

To help students master the section objectives, have them answer the **READING CHECKS** and complete **Guided Reading Strategy 30.1** as they read the section.

Human Rights Before World War I

OBJECTIVES

Read to understand:

1. how the modern concept of human rights developed
2. in what ways the movement to abolish slavery was an international effort
3. how the women's movement developed, and what its primary goal was
4. what human rights issues American progressives addressed

KEY TERMS

natural rights
Glorious Revolution
Declaration of the Rights of Man and Citizen
Women's Social and Political Union

KEY PEOPLE

John Locke
William Wilberforce
Emmeline Pankhurst

"It has already been 10 years since June 4th, but the government ignores this incident. As the living, we feel we have to stand up."

—You Weijie

You Weijie offered this reflection on the massacre in China's Tiananmen Square that took place in 1989. Weijie's husband was one of hundreds of people shot and killed while demonstrating for democratic reforms. Hundreds of other demonstrators were wounded and thousands jailed. World outrage at the massacre reflected a widely shared concept of human rights that has developed over the last several centuries.

Tiananmen Square "Goddess of Democracy" statue

Origins of the Concept of Human Rights

The modern concept of human rights is a fairly recent innovation. In ancient and medieval times, certain individuals had rights because of their positions in society. For example, some Greeks had special rights as citizens of Athens that their slaves did not possess. During the Middle Ages feudal lords had unique rights as nobles, while peasants had few rights at all.

In Europe this view of individual rights began to change in the 1600s during a period known as the Enlightenment. Some Enlightenment philosophers argued that all people have basic rights simply because they are human beings. One of the most influential Enlightenment philosophers was John Locke of England. Locke lived during the mid- to late 1600s, when the English Parliament challenged the absolute power of the king. Siding with Parliament, Locke argued that individuals held certain **natural rights** that governments could not violate. He claimed that governments existed to protect these individual rights. Locke believed that the most important natural rights were the rights to life, liberty, and property.

In what became known as the **Glorious Revolution**, Parliament broke the absolute power of the monarchy in 1688. As a result, the English people came to expect the natural rights described by Locke. The natural-rights philosophy also spread to the English colonies in North America. By the mid-1700s many American colonists believed that their natural rights were being violated by the English government. In 1776, colonial leaders presented the Declaration of Independence, which outlined British abuses. The Declaration, which states that "all men are created equal," is considered to be one of history's most important human rights documents.

English philosopher John Locke helped develop the theory of natural rights.

The Declaration of Independence and the American victory in the Revolutionary War inspired democratic activists in other countries. In 1789 the people of France revolted against the monarchy. France's newly formed National Assembly issued the **Declaration of the Rights of Man and Citizen**. Like the Declaration of Independence, the French document identified certain basic human rights:

TEACH OBJECTIVE 1

ALL LEVELS: To help students understand how the modern concept of human rights developed, copy the following graphic organizer on the chalkboard, omitting the italicized answers. Have each student complete it. **Sheltered English**

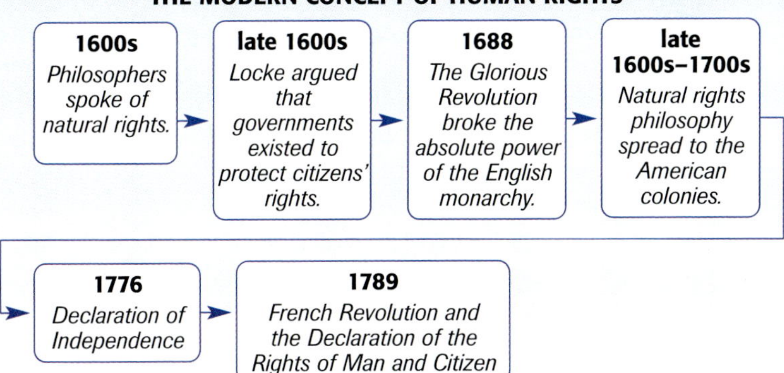

> **"The aim of all political association is the conservation of the natural and inalienable [unchangeable] rights of man. These rights are: liberty, property, security and resistance to oppression."**

Equality, while not listed as a right in itself, was implied by the declaration's claim that all men were "equal in rights."

✔ **READING CHECK:** How did the modern concept of human rights develop?

The Antislavery Movement

Many signers of the Declaration of Independence—including Thomas Jefferson—were also slaveholders. Critics have noted that the right to liberty that these founding fathers proclaimed for "all men" was something they denied their slaves. The international slave trade was a subject of heated debate at the Constitutional Convention. Congress eventually banned the Atlantic slave trade in 1808. The institution of slavery continued, however.

Abolition movements in other countries. Criticism of the slave trade was not limited to the United States. In 1807, British abolitionists persuaded Parliament to outlaw the slave trade. The British government began pressuring other European powers to do the same. At an 1815 meeting, Britain persuaded the other major European powers to condemn the slave trade. British abolitionists, led by William Wilberforce, were not satisfied. They demanded that Britain outlaw slavery completely. Largely as a result of efforts by Wilberforce and others, Parliament voted in 1833 to ban the practice of slavery within the British Empire.

Once the British had put a stop to slavery in their own territories, they tried to end it elsewhere. As British warships patrolled the Atlantic and Indian Oceans during the mid- and late 1800s, they seized slave ships and released the slaves. Sometimes these efforts ended in tragedy when ship captains threw slaves overboard in order to prevent their vessels from being seized. Nevertheless, the British patrols did help limit the international slave trade.

Abolitionist efforts also made progress outside of Britain. Most of Spain's Latin American colonies banned slavery when they won their independence during the 1810s and 1820s. Meanwhile, in Russia reformers called for an end to serfdom. Under this feudal system, peasants called serfs were required to work the land they lived on for the benefit of the landowner. Czar Alexander II freed the Russian serfs in 1861.

The British navy tried to capture slave ships such as this one off the coast of Africa.

Emancipation in the United States. American abolitionists took heart from these foreign efforts to expand human freedom. Abolitionist leaders, including Frederick Douglass and William Lloyd Garrison, pressed for an end to slavery in the United States. The political power of southern slaveholders blocked these abolitionist efforts, however.

CONSTITUTIONAL HERITAGE

Banning the Slave Trade. The U.S. Constitution prohibited Congress from banning the Atlantic slave trade before 1808. As that year approached, antislavery advocates pressed for passage of such a ban. After extended debate, Congress passed the Prohibition of the Slave Trade Act. Historians estimate, however, that as many as 50,000 slaves were brought into the United States illegally between 1808 and 1861.

CRITICAL THINKING Why might Congress ban the slave trade but not slavery?

ANSWER: Students might suggest that while southerners dependent on slavery would never agree to ban the institution, they might believe that the United States had enough slaves to justify ending the Atlantic slave trade.

THAT'S INTERESTING!

Despite its emphasis on human rights, the French Revolution was a violent affair. At least some 15,000 people were executed, many of them on the guillotine, during a phase of the Revolution known appropriately as the Terror.

TEACH OBJECTIVE 2

ALL LEVELS: Distribute copies of Map 24, The World, from **American History Outline Maps.** Have students shade in the regions where antislavery movements arose during the 1800s. *(Students should shade in the United States, Great Britain and its territories, Latin America, and Russia.)* Then tell them to use the map to write an article about international antislavery movements for an American abolitionist newspaper in the 1850s. *(Articles should discuss the international nature of the movement and Britain's role.)*

Sheltered English

TEACH OBJECTIVE 3

LEVEL 1: Ask students how the women's movement developed and what its primary goal was. *(Students might mention that the abolitionist movement made women aware of their lack of rights and helped them develop organizational and educational methods and that its goal was women's right to vote.)* Pair students and have each pair brainstorm slogans for the U.S. women's rights movement of the late 1800s. Tell them to select their favorite slogan and share it with the class.

Sheltered English, Cooperative Learning

▶**ASSIGNMENT** *Have students write a short biographical profile about one of the human rights leaders mentioned in this section.*

ECONOMIC DEVELOPMENT

Russian Serfs. Russian serfdom had its origins in feudal laws that prohibited peasants from moving away from the land on which they lived. These laws ensured that large landowners had a ready supply of labor. By 1861 some 23 million people, or 40 percent of the Russian population, were serfs. Czar Alexander II freed the serfs because he believed that Russia was a backward country that had to modernize to avoid falling even further behind its European neighbors.

CRITICAL THINKING Why might serfdom prevent a country from modernizing?

ANSWER: Students might suggest that wealthy landowners had no reason to invest money in industry or other modernizing ventures when they had a guaranteed labor supply.

THAT'S INTERESTING!

Mississippi became the final state to ratify the Thirteenth Amendment in March 1995. The state legislature voted to approve the measure some 130 years after the amendment had become part of the Constitution.

VISUAL RECORD ANSWER

Students might suggest that slaves should be freed.

INTERPRETING THE VISUAL RECORD

Abolition. Antislavery activists produced items like this British medallion and this banner for William Lloyd Garrison's abolitionist newspaper, *The Liberator*. ***What are the messages of these items?***

During the 1850s abolitionists helped establish the Republican Party, which challenged the expansion of slavery. Reformers applauded Republican Abraham Lincoln's victory in the 1860 presidential election, but the South responded by seceding. The nation was soon plunged into a bloody Civil War between the North and the South. The North's victory was followed shortly by the passage of the Thirteenth Amendment, which abolished slavery in the United States. Although reformers generally were shocked by the violence of the war, they hoped that the end of slavery in the United States was worth the cost in human life.

✔ **READING CHECK:** In what ways was the movement to abolish slavery an international effort?

The Struggle for Women's Rights

Many abolitionists were women. As these women argued for the rights of African Americans, they realized that their own rights were being denied. American abolitionist Angelina Grimké explained in 1836 that "the investigation of the rights of the slave has led me to a better understanding of my own." Elizabeth Cady Stanton and Lucretia Mott came to a similar realization when they were denied the chance to speak at an antislavery convention in London because of their gender.

The American women's movement. Through their reform efforts, female abolitionists met other women with similar views. Together they learned organizational and educational methods that helped their cause. At the 1848 Seneca Falls Convention women's rights activists adopted the Declaration of Sentiments. This document detailed the injustices that they believed had been committed against women.

Throughout the late 1800s and early 1900s reformers in the United States pushed for a constitutional amendment guaranteeing women the right to vote. Success finally came when the Nineteenth Amendment was ratified in 1920.

Read More About It

Free Find: Declaration of Sentiments

After reading about the Declaration of Sentiments on the **Holt Researcher** CD–ROM, imagine that you are a reporter at the Seneca Falls Convention and write a short article on what the signers of the declaration hoped to achieve.

BIOGRAPHY *Emmeline Pankhurst*

The British women's movement. British women also campaigned for the right to vote. One of their key leaders was Emmeline Pankhurst. Born in 1858, Emmeline Goulden devoted her life to winning the vote for British women. In 1879 she married Richard Pankhurst, author of the first women's suffrage bill in Britain. She founded the Women's Franchise League in 1889. In 1894 this organization won the right for married women to vote in local elections.

In 1903 Pankhurst founded a new women's rights organization, the **Women's Social and Political Union** (WSPU). In 1906 Pankhurst became the WSPU director. Disappointed by the British government's refusal to allow women to vote in national elections, Pankhurst recommended more aggressive tactics. To get greater publicity and public support, Pankhurst encouraged members of the WSPU to attack public property with the goal of getting arrested:

LEVELS 2 AND 3: Have students write a brief essay on the development of the women's movement and its primary goal. *(See the Level 1 lesson for the correct steps and goals.)* Tell students to include a comparison of the women's suffrage movements in the United States and Britain. Call on volunteers to read their essays to the class.

TEACH OBJECTIVE 4

LEVELS 1 AND 2: Pair students and have each pair create posters depicting the human rights issues American progressives addressed. *(Posters might mention industrialization, urban growth, and child labor.)* Tell students to draw an eye-catching image and to include a memorable slogan on their posters. Display students' posters around the classroom. **Sheltered English, Cooperative Learning**

LEVEL 3: Pair students and tell each pair to imagine that they are American progressive reformers. One member of each pair should be a reformer concerned about industrialization and urban growth and the other member a reformer concerned about child labor. Each student should share information about its reforms with his or her partner. Then call on one student from each pair to summarize the discussion for the class. **Cooperative Learning**

> **"There is something that Governments care for far more than human life, and that is the security of property. So it is through property that we shall strike the enemy."**

Once arrested, the protesters often went on hunger strikes. To prevent the women from dying while they were in prison, the government required that they be fed against their will.

The WSPU's struggle took years. Although British women over the age of 30 gained the right to vote in 1918, it was not until 1928 that all adult women were granted suffrage.

✔ **READING CHECK:** How did the women's movement develop? What was its primary goal?

Strategies for Success — Reading Charts

Charts are used to organize and present information visually. They can categorize and display data in a variety of ways, depending on the subject matter. A time line is a chart that lists events from a particular historical period in chronological order. Other types of charts include flowcharts, organizational charts, and tables. A *flowchart* displays a sequence of related events or the steps in a process. Cause-and-effect relationships are often shown by flowcharts. An *organizational chart* displays the structure of an organization and the function, ranking, and relationships among its internal parts. A *table* is a chart that presents data in rows and columns that are easy to understand and compare.

How to Read a Chart

1. **Read the title.** Read the title to identify the topic of the chart.
2. **Study the major components.** Read the chart's headings and labels to identify the categories it uses and the type of data it provides for each category.
3. **Analyze the details.** Read the chart's data carefully and systematically. When studying dates, take note of time intervals. When studying numerical information, take note of increases or decreases in amounts. Finally, when studying textual information, take note of special terms and definitions.
4. **Put the data to use.** Use your analysis of the data, along with your knowledge of the historical period, to form generalizations and draw conclusions.

Applying the Strategy

Study the following flowchart, which illustrates the evolution of the modern concept of human rights.

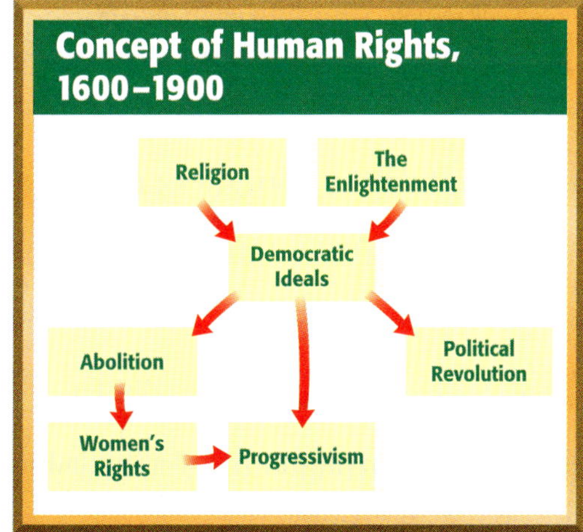

Practicing the Strategy

Use the flowchart above to answer the following questions.

1. What information does this chart provide?
2. What movements were influenced by the development of democratic ideals?
3. What are the two most immediate influences on progressivism shown on the chart?

HISTORY MAKERS SPEAK

Elizabeth Cady Stanton in *Feminist Quotations*

Opposition to the Women's Movement. In an 1876 letter Elizabeth Cady Stanton noted the opposition facing female reformers. "Our demands at the first seemed so rational that I thought the mere statement of woman's wrongs would bring immediate redress [relief]. I thought an appeal to the reason and conscience of men against the unjust and unequal laws for women . . . must settle the question. But I soon found, while no attempt was made to answer our arguments, that an opposition, bitter, malignant, and persevering, rooted in custom and privilege, grew stronger with every new demand made."

ACTIVITY: Have students list the "woman's wrongs" to which Stanton referred, and explain why these wrongs needed to be corrected.

STRATEGIES FOR SUCCESS

Practicing the Strategy

1. the development of the concept of human rights
2. abolition, women's rights, progressivism, and political revolution
3. democratic ideals and women's rights

REVIEW

Have students complete the **Section 1 Review** on p. 884.

ASSESS

Have students complete **Daily Quiz 30.1**. As **Alternative Assessment**, you may want to use the antislavery article or the women's movement essay activity in this section's lessons.

RETEACH

Have students complete **Main Idea Activity for Reteaching and Sheltered English 30.1**. Then have students use each of the key terms from the section in a sentence, write one or two sentences about each of the key people, and write a few paragraphs summarizing the content of Section 1. **Sheltered English**

EXTEND

Have students conduct research on John Locke's ideas and their influence on documents such as the Declaration of Independence. Tell students to make a list of ideas from the Declaration of Independence and the U.S. Constitution that may have been inspired by John Locke's writings. **Block Scheduling**

SECTION 1 REVIEW ANSWERS

Define and Identify

For significance, see the following pages:

- John Locke, p. 880
- natural rights, p. 880
- Glorious Revolution, p. 880
- Declaration of the Rights of Man and Citizen, p. 880
- William Wilberforce, p. 881
- Emmeline Pankhurst, p. 882
- Women's Social and Political Union, p. 882

1. Britain led abolition efforts, outlawing slavery in 1833, and pressured other countries to do the same; Latin American nations responded by outlawing slavery in the 1810s and 1820s, the United States did so in 1865, and Russia ended serfdom in 1861.

2. Enlightenment philosophers–John Locke in particular– argued that individuals held rights that should be protected by government; the Declaration of Independence and the Declaration of the Rights of Man and Citizen identified basic human rights in the 1700s.

3. Many women began to seek equality for themselves after being denied full participation in the abolitionist movement; they focused on gaining the vote.

4. by working for the protection of individual rights and the right of children not to work

5. Locke believed that individuals had natural rights, including the rights to life, liberty, and property and that governments should protect these rights.

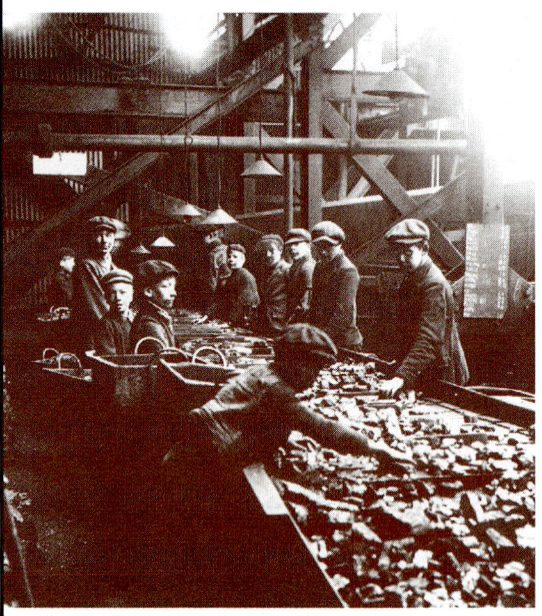

INTERPRETING THE VISUAL RECORD

Child labor. These boys are picking out rubble from piles of coal before it is shipped. ***What type of work conditions does this photograph reveal?***

Progressivism and Human Rights

Many of the American suffragists concerned about human rights during the late 1800s and early 1900s also became active in the progressive movement. The progressives were concerned with problems caused by industrialization and urban growth. These problems included corrupt city and state governments, corporate monopolies, and the wasteful use of natural resources. Many reformers linked the goals of women's suffrage with the goals of the progressive movement. These reformers believed that women voters would support many of the changes that progressives wanted. Such changes included election reform and antitrust laws.

Progressives also tried to limit the use of child labor. During the Industrial Revolution large numbers of boys and girls were employed in mills, mines, and other industrial workplaces. These child workers cost less to employ than adults. Progressives argued that children should not have to work long hours under such harsh conditions.

British reformer had tried with limited success to restrict child labor in the 1830s and 1840s. American progressives also faced opposition when they passed a number of laws in the early 1900s to limit child labor. Critics of these laws argued that children had the right to work as they pleased. Progressives countered that children did not work in coal mines out of free choice but out of economic necessity. They said that child-labor laws actually increased the freedom of children by allowing them the right *not* to work.

✔ **READING CHECK:** What human rights issues did American progressives address?

SECTION  REVIEW

Define and explain the significance of the following terms:
natural rights
Glorious Revolution
Declaration of the Rights of Man and Citizen
Women's Social and Political Union

Identify and explain the significance of the following individuals:
John Locke
William Wilberforce
Emmeline Pankhurst

1. **Using Graphic Organizers** Copy the web below. Use it to explain the relationship between the antislavery movement in Great Britain and reform movements in other countries.

BRITISH ABOLITION
U.S. Abolition
Latin American Abolition
Russian Serfs Freed

2. **Identifying Cause and Effect** How did the modern concept of human rights develop?
3. **Identifying Values** What sparked the rise of the women's movement in the 1800s? What was the main goal of the movement?
4. **Assessing Consequences** How did the progressive movement contribute to the expansion of human rights?

Critical Thinking

5. How did the Declaration of Independence and the Declaration of the Rights of Man and Citizen reflect John Locke's ideas about the purpose of government?
Consider:
- what John Locke's ideas about natural rights were
- why the belief in individual rights was included
- what basic human rights were identified

SECTION 2

After completing Section 2, students should be able to:

OBJECTIVE 1 *Explain how World War I changed Europeans' ideas about warfare.*

OBJECTIVE 2 *Discuss how fascism and militarism endangered human rights in the 1930s.*

OBJECTIVE 3 *Describe how human rights were violated during World War II.*

OBJECTIVE 4 *List steps the world community took to protect human rights after World War II.*

LET'S GET STARTED!

Write the following terms on the chalkboard: *human rights, civil rights, suffrage, abolition, war,* and *atrocities.* As students enter the classroom, tell them to think of words that they associate with each term. Have them write down as many words as they can for each. Students should notice how the last two terms carry connotations that are opposite of the other terms listed. Tell students that in Section 2 they will learn about how the two world wars brought about great violations of human rights.

The Cruelties of War

OBJECTIVES

Read to understand:

1. how World War I changed Europeans' ideas about warfare
2. how fascism and militarism endangered human rights in the 1930s
3. how human rights were violated during World War II
4. what steps the world community took to protect human rights after World War II

KEY TERMS

Red Cross
Geneva Convention
Universal Declaration of Human Rights

KEY PEOPLE

Florence Nightingale
Jesse Owens

"Now I know something of the horrors of war. . . . Imagine 1,000 badly wounded per diem [each day]. The surgeons are beginning to get sleep, because after working night and day they realize we may be at this for some months. . . . Oh, if you could see our wards, tents, huts, crammed with terrible wounds."

—John M. S. Walker

A German artillery crew wearing gas masks

In a 1916 diary entry, Reverend John M. S. Walker described the horrors of World War I and his experiences during the Battle of the Somme. By the end of the four-month battle, the Allies had advanced a total of five miles. The death toll was massive. Together the two sides lost more than 1 million soldiers in the battle. The massive destruction and death caused by World War I led to efforts to restrict the use of certain weapons and tactics of war. The war also inspired efforts to increase global support for human rights and to prevent future wars.

The Horrors of War

In 1863 a group of private Swiss citizens created an organization called the **Red Cross** to care for wounded soldiers from all nations. The earlier efforts of individuals such as English nurse Florence Nightingale had helped raise public awareness of the need for better medical care for military personnel. Twelve western nations took a larger step toward making war more humane by agreeing to the **Geneva Convention** in 1864. The Convention required participants to care for captured enemy soldiers during wartime as well as for their own sick and wounded.

A new kind of war. The Geneva Convention was just one of many political and social reforms that took place in Europe during the mid- to late 1800s. By the early 1900s many Europeans believed that they had achieved a level of civilization unmatched in human history. One reason for this belief was that Europe had not experienced a major war for nearly a century.

World War I shattered Europeans' illusions about civilized warfare. The use in battle of modern artillery and machine guns caused tremendous casualties. Military commanders were slow to adjust to these new weapons. They also continued to use outdated tactics such as cavalry attacks and infantry charges. In the Battle of the Somme, for example, thousands died in only minutes of fighting. Poison gas, a horribly painful weapon, was also introduced. Those that gas did not kill often suffered permanent lung damage. Unlike guns, gas could not be accurately aimed. The wind blew it across the battlefield, killing friend and foe alike.

World War I also brought the first significant use of submarines. Prior to the war, naval blockades had been relatively nonviolent. Vessels were seized but few were destroyed and few passengers were harmed. Submarine warfare changed these

Florence Nightingale founded the first school for training nurses.

SECTION 2 RESOURCES

PRINT

- Guided Reading Strategy 30.2
- Primary Source Reading 30: The International Bill of Human Rights
- Section 2 Review, p. 890
- Daily Quiz 30.2

MULTIMEDIA

- One-Stop Planner, Lesson 30.2
- Everyday Life in America Transparency 23: The 1936 Olympic Games
- Holt Researcher: American History CD–ROM
- HRW Web site

SHELTERED ENGLISH

- Main Idea Activity for Reteaching and Sheltered English 30.2

✔ READING TO UNDERSTAND

To help students master the section objectives, have them answer the **READING CHECKS** and complete **Guided Reading Strategy 30.2** as they read the section.

TEACH OBJECTIVE 1

LEVELS 1 AND 2: Tell students to list ways in which World War I changed Europeans' ideas about warfare. *(Students might mention that Europeans no longer believed that warfare could be civilized; that modern weapons brought about many more casualties; that submarines sank ships and offered no chance for surrender or mercy; and that Turkey's government slaughtered Armenians and put them in prison camps.)* Then pair students and have each pair select one of these items to use as a topic for an encyclopedia entry. Have each pair write a few paragraphs about its topic. Students may wish to include their entries in their portfolios.
Sheltered English, Cooperative Learning

LEVEL 3: Tell students to imagine that they are Europeans shortly after World War I. Have each student write a few pages describing how his or her ideas of warfare have changed. Students should also write about how they think such warfare might be minimized or even avoided in the future.

▶ASSIGNMENT *Have students find out how many people, both soldiers and civilians, were wounded or killed during World War I. Tell them to use the information they find to create a graphic organizer that shows casualties by country and that distinguishes between deaths and injuries and between military and civilian casualties.*

DEMOCRATIC VALUES

Turkey and the Kurds. During the 1990s the Turkish government was involved in conflicts with the Kurds, an ethnic minority. Some 12 million Kurds live in Turkey. The government denied official approval of Kurdish cultural practices and the Kurdish language. It also banned public performances of Kurdish music. The Kurds fought a guerrilla war against the Turkish government. By 1999 many observers hoped that the conflict would end, as some Kurdish leaders had indicated a willingness to end the 15-year-long war that had resulted in some 35,000 deaths.

CRITICAL THINKING Why might the Turkish government ban broadcasts of Kurdish music?

ANSWER: Students might mention that banning broadcasts was another way of oppressing the ethnic minority.

VISUAL RECORD ANSWER

Students might answer that because submarines travel beneath the water's surface, other vessels cannot see them and therefore are unable to defend themselves from attack.

INTERPRETING THE VISUAL RECORD

Submarine warfare. Submarine crews concentrated on surprising and sinking enemy merchant ships. ***Why might the use of submarines in war be considered inhumane?***

tactics. Submarine attacks took their targets by surprise and often sank ships without regard for the safety of crew or civilian passengers. Germany used submarines extensively, and many charges of brutality were aimed at the German government. The Germans responded that by blockading German ports, the British were killing children, the elderly, and the sick. Preventing the supply of food and medicine, the Germans argued, was worse than submarine warfare.

Turkey. Not all human rights violations took place on battlefields or the high seas. The rulers of Ottoman Turkey used the war as an opportunity to crush a discontented Armenian minority. The Turks massacred hundreds of thousands of Armenians and forcibly deported hundreds of thousands more. One observer described how Armenians were "brutally dragged out of their native land, torn from their homes and families, . . . [and] penned up in the open like cattle." In one Turkish prison camp, this observer continued, "mounds are seen containing 200 or 300 corpses buried in the ground . . . women, children, and old people."

Few outsiders knew of these events, and little was done. The Allies were already at war with Turkey. With so many Allied soldiers dying in battle elsewhere, the atrocities against the Armenians attracted little attention.

✔ **READING CHECK:** How did World War I change Europeans' ideas about warfare?

Peacemaking and Human Rights

World War I revealed that modern warfare, which targeted civilians and soldiers alike, was a major threat to human rights. The horrors of the conflict spurred efforts to safeguard human rights by preventing future wars. The most important of these efforts was the establishment of the League of Nations in 1919. This international body was created to settle disputes between countries. In 1922 the United States, which was not a League member, hosted the Washington Conference. At this meeting the great powers agreed to reduce the size of their navies.

Private efforts. Not all efforts to promote peace were led by governments. Peace activists in the United States and elsewhere formed organizations devoted to studying the causes and the prevention of war. For example, Quakers founded the American Friends Service Committee (AFSC) in 1917. The organization's intent was to provide "a conscientious service of love for humanity in wartime." It hosted gatherings of pacifist groups in Berlin, Geneva, Moscow, and Paris.

The AFSC also provided humanitarian aid to Germany and Poland following World War I. In Germany the AFSC organized a relief effort that, with the help of many German volunteers, fed more than 1 million children daily during 1921 and 1922. The AFSC's 1928 Annual Report described the challenges it faced:

The American Friends Service Committee promotes peace and provided humanitarian aid.

TEACH OBJECTIVE 2

ALL LEVELS: To help students understand how fascism and militarism endangered human rights in the 1930s, copy the following graphic organizer on the chalkboard, omitting the italicized answers. Have each student complete it. When students have finished, tell them to write a newspaper headline for each of the bulleted items in the right-hand column. **Sheltered English**

	HUMAN RIGHTS VIOLATIONS
Fascism in Europe	• *held that needs of society were more important than individuals' rights* • *promoted violent racism*
Militarism in Japan	• *promoted aggressive expansion and oppression of conquered peoples* • *inflicted mass atrocities on Chinese*

"Feeding the hungry and clothing the naked is spectacular and inspiring work. . . . [But] it is a much harder task to prevent war, to encourage nations to settle their differences by arbitration [negotiation], to develop a new type of patriotism."

The issue of equality. Little progress was made on the human rights issue of racial equality following World War I. Japan, a member of the victorious Allied Powers, asked that a statement supporting racial equality be included in the League of Nations Covenant. The Japanese and other Asian peoples had long been treated as racial inferiors by Europeans and Americans. The Japanese wanted such views to be condemned by world powers.

The other victors refused. President Woodrow Wilson knew that adding a section on racial equality would increase the U.S. Senate's opposition to the League of Nations. Western states such as California had long opposed immigration from Asia. In addition, many white southerners were prejudiced against African Americans and therefore took racial inequality for granted. The British government faced similar political problems and likewise declined the Japanese request. Consequently, the League's commitment to human rights was tarnished.

The Threat of Fascism

During the 1920s many human rights supporters believed they were regaining some of the ground lost during World War I. The existence of the League of Nations seemed to hold promise for a lasting peace. The events of the 1930s ended this optimism. The Great Depression aided the rise of fascist governments in Germany and Spain and strengthened the existing fascist government of Italy.

Fascism and inequality. During the 1800s and early 1900s, the trend among most countries—particularly in Europe and the Americas—had been toward greater individual rights and freedom. The rise of fascism reversed this trend. Fascism was based on the idea that the needs of society were more important than the rights of individuals. Individuals had no rights, only responsibilities to the state. Italian dictator Benito Mussolini argued that each citizen was individually insignificant but that when united they were powerful.

Fascists also argued that some ethnic and racial groups were superior to others. German Fascists, also called Nazis, were the most racist of all. Adolf Hitler and other Nazis gave countless speeches praising the supposed virtues of the "Aryan race" and expressing their distaste for other races and peoples. Hitler's racist philosophy also led to violent anti-Semitism—prejudice against Jews. Hitler and the Nazis blamed many of Germany's problems on Jews. The Nazis stripped German Jews of their citizenship, burned synagogues, and destroyed Jewish-owned businesses.

INTERPRETING THE VISUAL RECORD

Nazi propaganda. The caption on this Nazi poster reads, "One People, one Empire, one Leader!" ***How does this poster reveal fascist attitudes about individual freedom?***

Ein Volk, ein Reich, ein Führer!

HISTORY MAKERS SPEAK

William Eves in *Quakers in Action*

Quaker Relief Efforts. William Eves, who headed a Quaker relief mission in Germany during the 1920s, explained the goal of the Quaker program. "We hoped that our work of extending aid to those in need might result in breaking down to some extent the feeling of hatred which had been engendered [caused] by the war. . . . A bridge of friendship is being built which will span difficulties. Our work is no longer an experiment. It is proving its success and is producing results."

CRITICAL THINKING How might aid programs prevent conflicts between nations?

ANSWER: Students might mention that aid might help a nation avoid internal conflicts or wars with other nations over resources.

THAT'S INTERESTING!

Historians are still not sure how many Armenians were massacred during World War I. Estimates range from 600,000 to about 2 million.

VISUAL RECORD ANSWER

Students might suggest that fascism values the group over individual freedoms.

TEACH OBJECTIVE 3

ALL LEVELS: Ask students to list ways in which human rights were violated during World War II. *(Students might mention some 40 million dead, aerial bombardment used against civilians, atomic bombs, Japan's forced removal of Korean men, and the Holocaust.)* Organize students into five groups and assign each group one of the atrocities listed. Tell them to imagine that they have been asked to create a visual display for a local museum staging an exhibit of past atrocities in hopes of preventing such atrocities in the future. Allow students to display their museum exhibits in the classroom or school library. **Sheltered English, Cooperative Learning**

Teacher to Teacher

Gennie Westbrook of Port Lavaca, Texas, suggested the following activity: Have students conduct research on how the events on the chapter time line, such as the launch of U-boats, Karel Capek's play, and the development of an effective malaria treatment, relate to human rights. Then have them write a brief essay presenting their research.

PEOPLE IN HISTORY

Elie Wiesel. Elie Wiesel was born in Transylvania in 1928. During World War II he was sent to a concentration camp with his family. Elie survived but most of his family did not. After the war Wiesel went to France, where he became a journalist. Initially he did not write about his wartime experiences, but in 1958 he published *Night,* his memoir of the Holocaust. Thereafter Wiesel devoted himself to making the world remember the Holocaust and to advancing the cause of human rights. He has received the U.S. Congressional Gold Medal of Achievement as well as the Nobel Peace Prize.

CRITICAL THINKING Why might Wiesel have taken a vow of silence regarding his concentration-camp experience?

ANSWER: Students might suggest that Wiesel wanted to reflect upon the experience and find the right words to describe what he and his family suffered.

AMERICAN LETTERS ANSWERS

1. She writes that he cannot believe that war has begun.
2. They shaped the themes he explores in his writing.
3. They both mention the military's role in violating human rights.

The Pain of War

Numerous wars marked the 1900s. Some, such as World Wars I and II, have affected Americans as well as many people around the world. All wars are significant, however, to those who experience them personally. Chilean writer Isabel Allende and Romanian-born concentration-camp survivor Elie Wiesel are two authors who came to the United States and who have experienced the horrors of war.

from *House of the Spirits*

by Isabel Allende

Isabel Allende

Then came the roar of the airplanes, and the bombing began. Jaime threw himself to the floor with everyone else, unable to believe what he was seeing; until the day before, he had been convinced that nothing like this would ever happen in his country and that even the military respected the law. . . . Jaime crawled among the broken furniture and bits of plaster that were falling around him like a deadly rain, attempting to help the wounded, but he could only offer words of comfort and close the eyes of the dead. In a sudden pause in the shooting, the President gathered the survivors and told them to leave because he did not want any martyrs [sufferers] or needless sacrifice; everyone had a family, and important tasks lay ahead. "I'm going to call a truce so you can leave," he added. But no one moved. Though a few of them were trembling, all were in apparent possession of their dignity. The bombing was brief, but it left the palace in ruins. By two o'clock in the afternoon the fire had consumed the old drawing rooms that had been used since colonial times, and only a handful of men were left around the President. Soldiers entered the building and took what was left of the first floor. Above the din was heard the hysterical voice of an officer ordering them to surrender and come down single file with their hands on their heads. The president shook each of them by the hand. "I'll go last," he said. They never again saw him alive.

from *Night*

by Elie Wiesel

Elie Wiesel

In front of us flames. In the air that smell of burning flesh. It must have been about midnight. We had arrived—at Birkenau, reception center for Auschwitz.

The cherished objects we had brought with us thus far were left behind in the train, and with them, at last, our illusions.

Every two yards or so an SS man held his Tommy gun* trained on us. Hand in hand we followed the crowd.

An SS noncommissioned officer came to meet us, a truncheon [club] in his hand. He gave the order:

"Men to the left! Women to the right!"

Eight words spoken quietly, indifferently, without emotion. Eight short, simple words. Yet that was the moment when I parted from my mother. I had not time to think, but already I felt the pressure of my father's hand: we were alone.

*machine gun

UNDERSTANDING LITERATURE

1. How does Allende describe Jaime's reaction to the outbreak of war?
2. How do you think Wiesel's experiences as a concentration-camp survivor influenced his writing?
3. What do you think these excerpts say about the ways in which warfare violates human rights?

TEACH OBJECTIVE 4

LEVEL 1: Organize students into triads and have each group list the steps the world community took to protect human rights after World War II. *(Students should mention the creation of the United Nations, the Nuremberg Trials, and the Universal Declaration of Human Rights.)* Then have groups draft a bill of rights to protect human rights today. Students should model their draft on the Universal Declaration of Human Rights and focus on human rights issues of current concern. Encourage groups to be realistic in choosing rights that most nations are likely to accept. Have one student from each triad read his or her bill of rights to the class. Students may wish to include their bill of rights in their portfolios. **Sheltered English, Cooperative Learning**

LEVELS 2 AND 3: Have students write a few paragraphs evaluating the long-term effectiveness of the steps the world community took to protect human rights after World War II. *(See the Level 1 lesson for the correct steps.)* Tell them to cite examples of the successes and failures of these efforts. Provide old newsmagazines for students' use. Call on volunteers to summarize their evaluations for the class.

NOTE: For an additional teaching idea, see the Chapter 30 music, poetry, and law lesson in the **Creative Teaching Strategies** handbook.

The late 1930s. Sometimes Hitler's boasting merely made him look foolish. When Germany hosted the 1936 summer Olympic Games, he predicted that Germany's "Aryan" athletes would defeat all others. Much to Hitler's disappointment, African American Jesse Owens dominated the track-and-field competition, winning four gold medals. Even as spectators loudly applauded Owens's amazing performance, Hitler fumed. "The Americans ought to be ashamed of themselves for letting their medals be won by Negroes," he said privately. "I myself would never shake hands with one of them."

The brutality of the 1930s was not limited to Europe. Japan's government was not fascist, but it was militaristic and violent. Japan invaded China during the 1930s and inflicted mass atrocities on the Chinese. Japan's 1937 assault on Nanjing was particularly brutal. For weeks Japanese soldiers engaged in a campaign of terror against civilians. Millions were left homeless, and tens of thousands were killed. One observer said that people in the streets "were hunted like rabbits. Everyone seen to move was shot."

Jesse Owens became a national celebrity after his record-setting track and field performance in the 1936 Summer Olympics.

✔ **READING CHECK:** How did fascism and militarism endanger human rights in the 1930s?

World War II. When the troubles of the 1930s erupted into full-scale war, the atrocities of World War I were repeated on an even larger scale. The fighting in Europe and Asia left more than 40 million dead. More than any previous war, World War II placed civilians at the center of the fighting. Both sides used aerial bombardment to attack the enemy's major cities. The Germans bombed London for almost a year from 1940 to 1941. Later in the war, the Allies firebombed the German town of Dresden as well as Tokyo, Japan. Finally, the United States dropped atomic bombs on the Japanese cities of Hiroshima and Nagasaki. Unavoidably, and in some cases deliberately, most of the casualties in the bombing attacks against cities were civilians.

Some atrocities took place far from the battlefield. Japan, for example, forcibly removed thousands of Korean men from their homeland to work in Japanese war industries and to fight in the war. The most appalling wartime atrocity was the systematic killing of European Jews by the Nazis. Known as the Holocaust, this attempted genocide resulted in the murder of some 6 million Jews and millions of others.

✔ **READING CHECK:** How were human rights violated during World War II?

The United Nations

With war raging and human rights in serious danger, President Franklin D. Roosevelt helped initiate what he termed a "declaration by United Nations." The declaration was issued at the start of 1942 by the United States and 25 other nations fighting against Germany and Japan. It pledged the signing nations to

> **"defend life, liberty, independence, and religious freedom, and to preserve human rights and justice in their own lands as well as in other lands."**

Allied soldiers were shocked by the atrocities committed in the Nazi concentration camps and by the weakened condition of the survivors.

---

internet connect

TOPIC: Anne Frank
GO TO: go.hrw.com
KEYWORD: SE1 Anne Frank

Have students access the Internet through the HRW Web site to conduct research on the experiences of Anne Frank and her family during the Holocaust. Then ask students to imagine that they resisted the Nazis and helped the Franks hide. Have each student write a series of journal entries about his or her reasons for helping the Franks, fears about being caught, and thoughts on the betrayal and capture of the Franks.

THAT'S INTERESTING!

In 1944 and 1945 Japan launched about 9,300 high-altitude balloons that had been assembled by schoolchildren. The balloons carried bombs designed to start fires. The Japanese hoped that the bombs would start massive fires in the western United States. Some balloons did reach the United States, causing minor fires and six deaths.

Multimedia Resources

Everyday Life in America Transparency 23: The 1936 Olympic Games

REVIEW

Have students complete the **Section 2 Review** on p. 890.

ASSESS

Have students complete **Daily Quiz 30.2.** As **Alternative Assessment,** you may want to use the encyclopedia entry or the bill of rights activity in this section's lessons.

RETEACH

Have students complete **Main Idea Activity for Reteaching and Sheltered English 30.2.** Then pair students and have each pair make a set of flashcards for the section's key terms and people, as well as questions and answers dealing with the section's main ideas. Tell students to use the section reviews as models when making their flashcards. When students have made about 15 cards, have partners take turns quizzing each other on the information. **Sheltered English, Cooperative Learning**

EXTEND

Organize students into groups of four or five. Have each group create an oral or multimedia presentation about how the period between 1910 and 1950 represented great challenges to human rights and great advancements in the acceptance of human rights. **Block Scheduling, Cooperative Learning**

SECTION 2 REVIEW ANSWERS

Define and Identify

For significance, see the following pages:

- Red Cross, p. 885
- Florence Nightingale, p. 885
- Geneva Convention, p. 885
- Jesse Owens, p. 889
- Universal Declaration of Human Rights, p. 890

1. WWI—tremendous casualties, use of poison gas and submarines, Turkish massacre of Armenians; WWII—aerial bombardment of civilians, atomic bombs, forced removal of Korean men, the Holocaust

2. World War I destroyed many Europeans' illusions about civilized warfare.

3. fascism—took away individual rights, fostered violent racism; militarism—used violence to subdue others

4. Students' brochures will vary but should discuss humanitarian aid and pacifism.

5. Students should note that World War II atrocities included civilians as war victims, the Holocaust, and the Japanese relocation of Koreans; to protect human rights, U.S. president Roosevelt initiated a "declaration by United Nations;" and the United Nations adopted the Universal Declaration of Human Rights.

First Lady Eleanor Roosevelt was a strong supporter of human rights. Here she poses with a copy of the UN declaration.

After the war ended, the international community took further steps to safeguard human rights. In the Nuremberg Trials, Nazi leaders were convicted of genocide as well as a host of other "crimes against humanity." The message was clear: certain human rights must be respected regardless of a person's nationality or ethnic background. This concern with human rights was also an essential part of the United Nations's mission. The UN charter resolved to promote "universal respect for . . . human rights and fundamental freedoms for all without distinction as to race, sex, language or religion."

Unsatisfied with the charter, some UN member nations called for the inclusion of a bill of rights. President Harry S Truman agreed, noting that without freedom, "we cannot have permanent peace and security." On December 10, 1948, the UN General Assembly adopted the **Universal Declaration of Human Rights**. The document listed a series of rights held by "all human beings."

However, the United Nations had no way to enforce the Declaration of Human Rights. Indeed, many countries insisted that any efforts at enforcement would violate another UN principle—the guarantee of national sovereignty. This apparent contradiction would remain an issue for years to come.

✔ **READING CHECK:** What steps did the world community take to protect human rights after World War II?

SECTION 2 REVIEW

Define and explain the significance of the following terms:
Red Cross
Geneva Convention
Universal Declaration of Human Rights

Identify and explain the significance of the following individuals:
Florence Nightingale
Jesse Owens

1. **Using Graphic Organizers** Copy the graphic organizer below. Use it to compare the human rights violations that took place during World War I and World War II.

Human Rights Violations	
WWI	WWII

2. **Identifying Cause and Effect** How did World War I affect the way Europeans viewed modern warfare?
3. **Synthesizing** How did fascism in Europe and militarism in Japan affect human rights in the years between World War I and World War II?
4. **Using Historical Imagination** Imagine that you are a member of a private peace organization during the 1920s. Write a brochure explaining how individuals might promote international peace.

Critical Thinking

5. How did World War II affect the course of human rights protection?
   Consider:
   - what atrocities were committed during World War II
   - how the United States worked to protect human rights
   - what measures the United Nations took to protect human rights

SECTION 3

After completing Section 3, students should be able to:

OBJECTIVE 1 *Explain how the movement for racial equality progressed after World War II.*

OBJECTIVE 2 *Summarize how efforts to protect human rights fared in the 1960s and early 1970s.*

OBJECTIVE 3 *Describe what President Carter did to encourage human rights.*

LET'S GET STARTED!

To begin the class, tell students to write down five things they know about the civil rights movement and efforts to enforce human rights globally during the 1960s and early 1970s, along with five questions they have about these efforts. Tell the class to keep their questions in mind as they read Section 3 and learn about human rights movements in the 1960s and early 1970s.

Striving for Equality

OBJECTIVES

Read to understand:

1. how the movement for racial equality progressed after World War II
2. how efforts to protect human rights fared in the 1960s and early 1970s
3. what President Carter did to encourage human rights

KEY TERMS

Covenant on Civil and Political Rights
Covenant on Economic, Social, and Cultural Rights

KEY PEOPLE

Nelson Mandela
Patricia Derian

EYEWITNESSES TO History

"If you will protest courageously and yet with dignity and Christian love, in the history books that are written in future generations, historians will have to pause and say 'there lived a great people—a black people—who injected new meaning and dignity into the veins of civilization.'"

—Martin Luther King Jr.

Rosa Parks helped begin the Montgomery Bus Boycott.

The Reverend Martin Luther King Jr. addressed several thousand African Americans on the first night of the Montgomery Bus Boycott in 1955. The boycott lasted 13 months and sparked a powerful movement for racial equality in the United States. The American civil rights movement was part of a broader international movement toward improving human rights in the years after World War II. The dismantling of the system of racial segregation in the United States as well as decolonization in Asia and Africa represented progress toward racial equality.

The Fight for Racial Equality

The wave of decolonization that swept across Asia and Africa after World War II represented a major advance for human rights. Western imperialism had supported the legal and social superiority of European colonists over groups such as Asians and Africans. Decolonization helped challenge these biased policies.

Martin Luther King Jr. and his wife Coretta met with Indian prime minister Jawaharlal Nehru in 1959.

The American civil rights movement. Americans had long prided themselves on being more enlightened in terms of human rights than people in most other countries. However, critics accused the United States of the second-class treatment of African Americans and other ethnic minority groups. As European nations granted independence to their colonies in the 1950s and 1960s, Americans found themselves lagging behind Europe on the issue of racial equality.

Many of the leaders of the American civil rights movement took inspiration from the methods used by anticolonial leaders. Franklin McCain was one of the students who participated in the lunch-counter sit-in in Greensboro, North Carolina. He later recalled, "The individual who had probably the most influence on us was Gandhi, more than any single individual." Martin Luther King Jr. traveled to India to see the results of Gandhi's nonviolent protests and to meet many of his followers. After King returned to the United States he told civil rights activists that they were taking "honored places in the worldwide struggle for freedom." Many young African Americans

SECTION 3 RESOURCES

PRINT

- Guided Reading Strategy 30.3
- Literature Reading 30: A World of Infinite Possibilities
- Section 3 Review, p. 894
- Daily Quiz 30.3

MULTIMEDIA

- One-Stop Planner, Lesson 30.3
- Holt Researcher: American History CD–ROM

SHELTERED ENGLISH

- Main Idea Activity for Reteaching and Sheltered English 30.3

✔ READING TO UNDERSTAND

To help students master the section objectives, have them answer the READING CHECKS and complete **Guided Reading Strategy 30.3** as they read the section.

TEACH OBJECTIVE 1

ALL LEVELS: Organize students into triads and have them create a scrapbook on the movement for racial equality after World War II. *(Students might mention that decolonization and African independence movements inspired many African Americans; that South Africa tightened its policy of apartheid; and that the United Nations established a convention on eliminating racial discrimination.)* Encourage students to include written information, images, and objects to explain the movement's progress during this period. Have volunteers show their triads' scrapbooks to the class and explain why they chose certain items.
Sheltered English, Cooperative Learning

TEACH OBJECTIVE 2

LEVELS 1 AND 2: Ask students how efforts to protect human rights fared in the 1960s and early 1970s. *(Students might mention that the United Nations passed two human rights covenants that proved unenforceable and that communist countries and many right-wing governments frequently violated their citizens' human rights.)* Then pair students and have each pair brainstorm ways that the United Nations might try to enforce the provisions of these covenants. *(Students might suggest economic sanctions, military force, and so on.)* **Sheltered English, Cooperative Learning**

PEOPLE IN HISTORY

Nelson Mandela. In 1944 Nelson Mandela helped establish the African National Congress. The organization wanted to overthrow the white government, which denied black Africans their rights. Initially committed to nonviolent protest, Mandela decided in the 1960s that black Africans had to use force to achieve their goals. Arrested in 1962, he remained in prison until 1990. After his release and the dismantling of apartheid, Mandela and South African president F. W. de Klerk shared the Nobel Peace Prize. Mandela was elected president in 1994.

CRITICAL THINKING Under what circumstances might protesters turn to violence?

ANSWER: Students might answer that violence might be used in self-defense or when nonviolent efforts prove ineffective.

THAT'S INTERESTING!

The International Convention on the Elimination of All Forms of Racial Discrimination was the first UN human rights declaration that also created an oversight committee. The committee was formed to investigate alleged violations of the convention and to settle disputes.

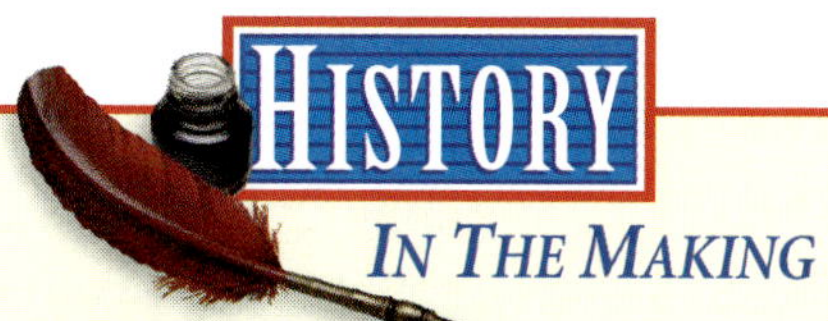

HISTORY IN THE MAKING

Songs of Freedom

BY DR. STERLING STUCKEY

The struggle for racial equality in the 1950s and 1960s was based on an African American culture of great spiritual depth that rose out of the experience of slavery in the South. Southern black musical traditions, in particular, helped fuel the civil rights movement in its drive to end racial discrimination and violence against blacks.

Wyatt Tee Walker, an aide to Martin Luther King Jr., summed up the impact of music on the movement. He stated that "there was no movement in the South that was not a great singing movement." During the Montgomery Bus Boycott, for example, Georgia Black of the Holt Street Baptist Church—where the boycott officially began—sang slave songs to inspire blacks to continue to oppose segregated seating on buses.

> **"We got to hold up the**
> **Bloodstained banner**
> **One Day I'm gonna get old**
> **And Can't fight anymore**
> **But I'm gonna**
> **Fight anyhow**
> **We got to hold it up**
> **Until we die."**

Singing provided a source of inspiration and strength to the movement, particularly during periods of hardship. When Freedom Riders were arrested and jailed in Jackson, Mississippi, many of them sang as a way of keeping up their spirits. Prison officials demanded that they stop, but despite threats the activists continued to sing.

were also inspired by independence movements in Africa. In 1964, for example, African American singer and actor Harry Belafonte sponsored a delegation of Student Nonviolent Coordinating Committee (SNCC) members on a tour of Africa. Most of the participants found the experience electrifying. "I saw black men flying the airplanes, driving buses, sitting behind big desks in the bank and just doing everything that I was used to seeing white people do," one SNCC worker later remembered.

Apartheid. Even as the United States began to change its racially biased laws, South Africa was reinforcing apartheid—its rigid system of segregation. Influenced in part by the American civil rights movement, black South Africans had intensified their demands for greater political and social equality. The white minority that ruled South Africa under apartheid opposed these demands.

Black South Africans protested the policy of apartheid, as did some white South Africans. Many black protesters died, and others were driven into exile. Still others were arrested and sentenced to long prison terms. In 1962 Nelson Mandela was jailed for protesting apartheid. Mandela led the African National Congress, the major black nationalist organization in South Africa. At his trial in 1963, Mandela explained some of the grievances held by black South Africans.

> **"South Africa is the richest country in Africa, and could be one of the richest in the world. But it is a land of extremes and remarkable contrasts. The Whites enjoy what may well be the highest standard of living in the world, whilst Africans live in poverty and misery. . . . The lack of human dignity experienced by Africans is the direct result of the policy of White supremacy."**

Many nations also objected to apartheid. In 1973 the UN General Assembly passed the Convention on the Suppression of Apartheid. Eventually the European Community and the United States imposed economic sanctions on South Africa.

UN efforts to end discrimination. The United Nations took other steps to combat racial discrimination throughout the world. In 1965 the United Nations had established the International Convention on the Elimination of All Forms of Racial Discrimination. Under the terms of this agreement, the signing nations agreed to make it illegal to spread ideas that advocated any form of racial superiority or hatred. The agreement also called on the signers to outlaw all organizations engaging in such activities. By 1998 the Convention had been ratified by 150 nations.

✔ **READING CHECK:** How did the movement for racial equality progress after World War II?

LEVEL 3: Tell students to imagine that they are U.S. representatives to the United Nations during the early 1970s. Have them write a brief report for the president and Congress about international efforts to protect human rights in the 1960s and early 1970s. *(See the Levels 1 and 2 lesson for the correct results.)*

TEACH OBJECTIVE 3

ALL LEVELS: To help students understand what President Carter did to encourage human rights, copy the following graphic organizer on the chalkboard, omitting the italicized answers. Have each student complete it. Then ask students if they think the United States should make human rights requirements of nations that receive financial aid. *(Students' answers will vary.)* **Sheltered English**

Carter and Human Rights

- *placed human rights at top of U.S. diplomatic agenda*
- *appointed Patricia Derian as assistant secretary of state for human rights and humanitarian affairs*
- *Carter administration tried to link human rights to economic aid*
- *refused to allow fear of communism to guide foreign policy*
- *pledged to stop ignoring human rights abuses of certain governments*

▶ASSIGNMENT *Have students use the information in the graphic organizer to help them write a brief evaluation of the effectiveness and appropriateness of Carter's human rights policies and actions. Students may wish to include their evaluations in their portfolios.*

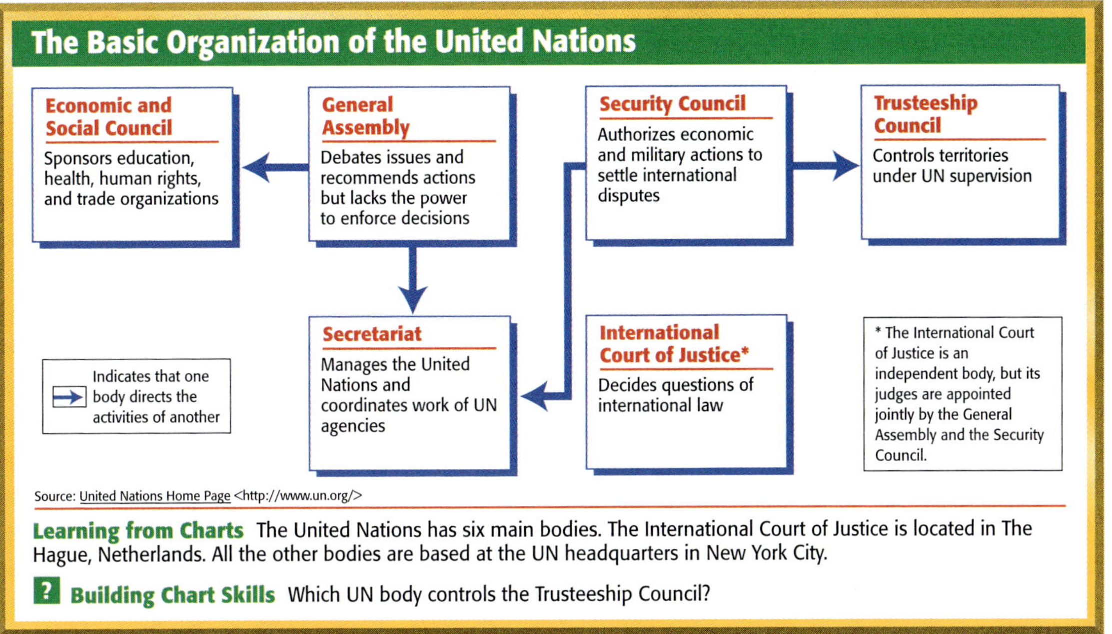

The Basic Organization of the United Nations
Economic and Social Council
Sponsors education, health, human rights, and trade organizations
General Assembly
Debates issues and recommends actions but lacks the power to enforce decisions
Security Council
Authorizes economic and military actions to settle international disputes
Trusteeship Council
Controls territories under UN supervision
Indicates that one body directs the activities of another
Secretariat
Manages the United Nations and coordinates work of UN agencies
International Court of Justice*
Decides questions of international law
* The International Court of Justice is an independent body, but its judges are appointed jointly by the General Assembly and the Security Council.
Source: United Nations Home Page <http://www.un.org/>

Learning from Charts The United Nations has six main bodies. The International Court of Justice is located in The Hague, Netherlands. All the other bodies are based at the UN headquarters in New York City.

Building Chart Skills Which UN body controls the Trusteeship Council?

Human Rights and the Cold War

The United Nations also addressed broader human rights issues during the Cold War. In 1966 the UN General Assembly approved two covenants on human rights. The first was the **Covenant on Civil and Political Rights**. The nations signing this covenant pledged not to interfere with individual liberties. The second agreement was the **Covenant on Economic, Social, and Cultural Rights**. The provisions of the second covenant were different from the first. The agreement required governments not only to refrain from certain actions but also to take positive steps toward improving protections for human rights. These included providing jobs, increasing educational opportunities, and improving health care.

The absence of any enforcement agency, however, made the covenants little more than promises, and many nations disregarded them. For example, the Soviet Union often sent political protesters to "internal exile" in Siberia. China, too, was frequently criticized for its treatment of political radicals.

Communist countries were not the only ones in which human rights were threatened. Many right-wing governments—some of which were supported by the U.S. government in its eagerness to fight communism worldwide—had little tolerance for political dissent. This was particularly true in Central and South America. For example, dictator Augusto Pinochet seized control of Chile in 1973. His military government was frequently criticized by human rights organizations for its use of torture and for repressing political opposition.

U.S. ambassador Andrew Young worked to promote human rights issues in third-world nations.

✔ **READING CHECK:** How did international efforts to protect human rights fare in the 1960s and early 1970s?

IN THE NEWS

Augusto Pinochet. In 1998 a Spanish prosecutor charged Chilean dictator Augusto Pinochet with crimes, including torturing political opponents, during his rule in Chile. The British government arrested Pinochet—who was in London at the time—and debated sending him to Spain to stand trial. Pinochet's attorneys maintained that Britain had no right to detain him. The court ruled, however, that Britain could keep him under house arrest and then send him to Spain to stand trial. In January 2000 a British court determined that the 84-year-old Pinochet was medically unfit to stand trial. Human rights activists protested the decision.

CRITICAL THINKING Was Britain, which had not charged Pinochet with a crime, justified in arresting him?

ANSWER: Students might suggest that Britain was complying with international agreements regarding human rights.

THAT'S INTERESTING!

The human rights organization Amnesty International reported human rights violations in 141 countries in 1997.

CHART ANSWER
the Security Council

REVIEW

Have students complete the **Section 3 Review** on p. 894.

ASSESS

Have students complete **Daily Quiz 30.3.** As **Alternative Assessment,** you may want to use the civil rights scrapbook activity or the evaluation of Carter's human rights policies in this section's lessons.

RETEACH

Have students complete **Main Idea Activity for Reteaching and Sheltered English 30.3.** Then organize students into triads. Assign each of the section's objectives to one member of each group. Tell each student to create a set of notes that covers the information pertaining to his or her assigned objective. Then have students trade and copy each other's notes, asking questions of their partners when necessary.
Sheltered English, Cooperative Learning

EXTEND

Have students write a poem or song about the worldwide struggle for human rights. They may write about a specific event or they might write an inspirational piece meant to encourage global respect for human rights. Invite volunteers to read their poems or songs to the class. **Block Scheduling**

SECTION 3 REVIEW ANSWERS

Define and Identify

For significance, see the following pages:

- Nelson Mandela, p. 892
- Covenant on Civil and Political Rights, p. 893
- Covenant on Economic, Social, and Cultural Rights, p. 893
- Patricia Derian, p. 894

1. communist countries–violated human rights of political dissidents; UN activities–Covenant on Civil and Political Rights, Covenant on Economic, Social, and Cultural Rights; military governments–repressed political opposition through torture and other means; President Carter's policies–tried to link economic aid to human rights

2. decolonization, African independence movements, and two UN conventions

3. reinforced power of white minority over black South Africans and represented a step backward

4. Carter linked U.S. economic aid to human rights records.

5. American civil rights leaders were inspired by Gandhi's use of nonviolent protest; African independence efforts inspired civil rights leaders in the United States; the American civil rights movement inspired black South Africans to fight for greater political and social equality.

INTERPRETING THE VISUAL RECORD

Promoting peace. In 1978 President Carter (center) brought Anwar Sadat of Egypt (left) and Menachem Begin of Israel (right) together to sign the first treaty between Israel and an Arab nation. ***How does this photograph suggest the foreign leaders felt about the peace accord?***

Carter and Human Rights

When Jimmy Carter took office as president in 1977, he resolved to make human rights a major priority of U.S. foreign policy. Carter later described the public mood.

> **"Human rights had become the central theme of our foreign policy in the minds of the press and public. It seemed that a spark had been ignited."**

President Carter argued that the United States had allowed its fear of communism to govern its foreign-policy decisions for too long. He pledged to stop ignoring the human rights abuses of certain governments simply because those governments were anticommunist.

Carter appointed Patricia Derian as the assistant secretary of state for human rights and humanitarian affairs. Derian, a former civil rights worker, challenged those who supported "moderately repressive" regimes. She demanded to know what moderately repressive meant: "That you only torture half of the people?"

Carter's administration tried to link human rights reforms to U.S. economic aid. When the U.S. government sent offers of aid to Argentina, Brazil, El Salvador, Guatemala, and Uruguay, it included critiques of the human rights records of those countries' governments. Carter's policy sent the message that the United States placed human rights at the top of its diplomatic agenda. Some nations tried to satisfy U.S. human rights requirements. Many nations, however, refused U.S. aid and criticized Carter for interfering in their internal affairs.

✔ **READING CHECK:** What did President Carter do to encourage human rights?

SECTION 3 REVIEW

Define and explain the significance of the following terms:
Covenant on Civil and Political Rights
Covenant on Economic, Social, and Cultural Rights

Identify and explain the significance of the following individuals:
Nelson Mandela
Patricia Derian

1. Using Graphic Organizers Copy the web below. Use it to explain the status of human rights during the Cold War.

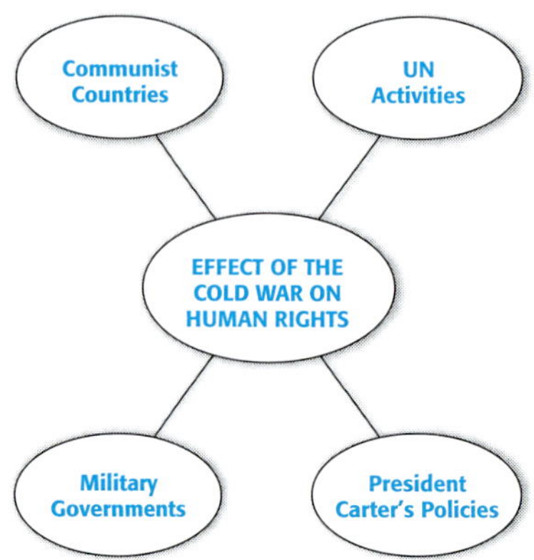

2. Evaluating What events advanced the struggle for racial equality following World War II?

3. Identifying Cause and Effect How did the establishment of apartheid in South Africa affect the struggle for racial equality?

4. Identifying Values How did President Carter's foreign policy address the issue of human rights?

Critical Thinking

5. What connection did the American civil rights movement have to the struggles for human rights in other areas of the world?

Consider:
- what influence human rights activists such as Mohandas K. Gandhi had in the United States and abroad
- how African independence influenced African American civil rights activists
- how the American civil rights movement influenced African civil rights efforts.

SECTION 4

After completing Section 4, students should be able to:

OBJECTIVE 1 *Identify what political events during the late 1980s and early 1990s led to advances in human rights.*

OBJECTIVE 2 *Describe some characteristics of the worldwide women's movement.*

OBJECTIVE 3 *Discuss what global challenges remain to human rights.*

LET'S GET STARTED!

To begin the class, have students write a personal statement on human rights. Tell them to write several sentences stating their beliefs about human rights and setting a personal action plan for furthering those beliefs. Invite volunteers to read their statements to the class. Then tell students that in Section 4 they will learn about advances in and challenges to human rights in the 1980s and 1990s.

The Continuing Struggle

OBJECTIVES

Read to understand:

1. what political events in the late 1980s and early 1990s led to advances in human rights
2. what some characteristics of the worldwide women's movement were
3. what global challenges remain to human rights

KEY TERMS

Taliban

KEY PEOPLE

Jehan Sadat
Benazir Bhutto
Aung San Suu Kyi

"In my country, many grave crimes are committed. . . . I am convinced that they can be alleviated [corrected], not by continuation and intensification of repressions [crackdowns], but only through a moral upsurge, through people's turning to simple and true values shared by mankind, through bringing the people of the world closer together."

—Andrei Sakharov

Soviet dissident Andrei Sakharov

Andrei Sakharov peacefully protested the social and political policies of the Soviet government. Although he was the scientist responsible for developing the hydrogen bomb in his country, Sakharov became an outspoken supporter of peace and human rights. Like other political protesters, Sakharov was placed in "internal exile" in Siberia to quiet his criticism of the government. In 1975 he received the Nobel Peace Prize, but the Soviet government prevented him from attending the ceremony.

The End of the Cold War

During the late 1980s and early 1990s major changes took place in the Soviet Union. Just as the breakup of the European empires in Asia and Africa had boosted human rights, so did the collapse of the Soviet sphere. The region's new governments did not always protect human rights—particularly when ethnic tensions led to violence, as in Yugoslavia. In general, however, the new governments were an improvement over what they replaced. Countries such as Lithuania and the Czech Republic peacefully established new governments and held free elections. Communist institutions crumbled and democratic elections gave people a chance to choose their own leaders.

Nelson Mandela helped lead the struggle to end apartheid in South Africa.

Recent improvements in human rights cannot all be directly linked to the end of the Cold War. In South Africa, for example, apartheid began to crumble in the late 1980s. In 1990 President F. W. de Klerk legalized the African National Congress and other opposition groups. That same year, Nelson Mandela and others who had been imprisoned for protesting apartheid were released from prison. As a result, the European Community

SECTION 4 RESOURCES

PRINT

- Guided Reading Strategy 30.4
- Graphic Organizer Activity 30: Human Rights Leaders
- Section 4 Review, p. 899
- Daily Quiz 30.4

MULTIMEDIA

- One-Stop Planner, Lesson 30.4
- The American Nation Video Program Segment: The Women's Rights Movement; Teacher's Guide, pp. 209–10
- Holt Researcher: American History CD–ROM

SHELTERED ENGLISH

- Main Idea Activity for Reteaching and Sheltered English 30.4

✔ READING TO UNDERSTAND

To help students master the section objectives, have them answer the READING CHECKS and complete **Guided Reading Strategy 30.4** as they read the section.

TEACH OBJECTIVE 1

LEVEL 1: In a classroom discussion, ask students to list major events during the late 1980s and early 1990s that led to advances in human rights. *(Students might mention the collapse of the Soviet sphere and the end of apartheid in South Africa.)* Pair students and have each pair create a model or mock-up of a monument commemorating one or both of these events and expressing hope for the future of human rights in the world. **Sheltered English, Cooperative Learning**

LEVELS 2 AND 3: Organize students into six groups. Assign half the groups to cover the collapse of the Soviet sphere and the other half of the groups the end of apartheid in South Africa. Have each group develop a short article for an American newsmagazine. Students should summarize the event, what it means for the future of human rights in the world, and what people might expect to see result from it. Tell students to include some pictures and a graphic organizer or a time line if appropriate. Encourage students to read other groups' articles when they have finished their assignment. Students may wish to include the articles in their portfolios. **Cooperative Learning**

CULTURAL DIVERSITY

The Taliban. Women in Afghanistan experienced severe restrictions on their freedom when the Taliban took power. Most women were not allowed to leave their homes without a male escort. They could not visit a male physician, which meant that some women unnecessarily suffered from treatable diseases. Women were also forbidden to work, leaving many widows without a source of income. Violations of the law could result in beatings or even execution.

ACTIVITY: Have students conduct research on efforts led by American women to help women in Afghanistan regain some freedom. Have students use their information to write an action memo, detailing actions Americans can take to support freedom for women in Afghanistan.

THAT'S INTERESTING!

Women control 45 percent of the earned income in Tanzania, the highest percentage in the world. The United States, where women control some 35 percent of the earned income, is ranked 31st among nations.

VISUAL RECORD ANSWER

Students might suggest clothing fashions and hairstyles.

and the United States gradually lifted their sanctions against South Africa. In 1994 the nation held its first elections in which black South Africans were free to vote, and Mandela was elected president.

✔ **READING CHECK:** What political events in the late 1980s and early 1990s led to advances in human rights?

Women's Rights in the Modern Era

Women played an important part in the global campaign for human rights in the 1900s. Participating in civil rights movements made many women aware of the need to fight for their own rights.

INTERPRETING THE VISUAL RECORD

A blend of cultures. Although many women in the Middle East today wear traditional clothing, others have adopted Western styles. ***What distinguishes Western customs from traditional customs in this picture?***

Women in the Muslim world. The lack of equality for women was a global issue. In parts of Southwest Asia and North Africa, for example, some governments sought to restrict women's activities. Muslim men sometimes cited the Qur'an, the holy book of Islam, as justification for their actions. Some prominent women, however, denied that Islam required such restrictions on women. Jehan Sadat, the wife of Egyptian president Anwar Sadat, addressed the subject.

> **"Nothing in our religion supported the total subservience [servitude] of women. In no place in the Qur'an is it written that women must remain at home and do no work in public. No. The Qur'an treats men and women equally, in life and in death."**

Some Middle Eastern activists called for women's rights comparable to those in the West. Others, however, rejected Western notions of women's legal and social rights. Instead, these activists used Islamic principles to guide their ideas about women's rights. In theory Muslim women had long possessed certain rights that Western women had only recently gained. These included the right to initiate legal action and the right to own property.

Some Muslim governments, however, took a different view of Muslim religious law. The most extreme example occurred in Afghanistan. In 1996 the **Taliban**—a fundamentalist Islamic military and political group—took over most of the country. The Taliban enforced a strict Islamic code of law. Under this code women were required to cover themselves completely—including their faces—when in public. The government also closed schools for girls and prohibited women from working.

Women in the United States. In Western countries women had become increasingly visible in public life throughout the 1900s. The number of women in the U.S. workforce grew steadily. The problem of sexual discrimination in the workplace, particularly in the form of unequal pay, helped fuel the women's movement of the 1970s. Women's demands included equal pay for equal work, better access to male-dominated career fields, and fair treatment in the workplace. By the

TEACH OBJECTIVE 2

ALL LEVELS: To help students understand some characteristics of the worldwide women's movement, copy the following graphic organizer on the chalkboard, omitting the italicized answers. Have each student complete it. **Sheltered English**

▶ASSIGNMENT *Have students select one of the female political leaders mentioned on this page and write a biographical profile of her.*

CHARACTERISTICS OF THE WOMEN'S MOVEMENT

Muslim World
- *Some women called for women's rights comparable to those in the West.*
- *Some wanted rights in accordance with Islamic principles.*
- *Afghanistan's Taliban government completely oppressed women.*

United States
- *The number of women in the workforce grew steadily.*
- *Women demanded equal pay for equal work, better access to male-dominated fields, and fair treatment.*
- *The ERA failed to pass.*
- *More women gained positions of authority.*

Female Political Leaders
- *Women led several countries, including Great Britain, India, Ireland, Latvia, Nicaragua, Pakistan, the Philippines, and Sri Lanka.*

end of the 1970s nearly all legal barriers to gender equality in the United States had been eliminated. However, the proposed Equal Rights Amendment (ERA) to the Constitution fell short of the 38-state approval required for ratification in 1982.

Despite the defeat of the ERA, in the 1980s and 1990s it became increasingly common to see women in positions of authority. Sandra Day O'Connor and Ruth Bader Ginsberg were appointed as Supreme Court justices. Sally Ride became the first female astronaut, and Eileen Collins served as the first female commander of the space shuttle. Women also played important roles in the armed forces during the Persian Gulf War. In addition to these prominent roles, many other women worked as community leaders. Nonetheless, professional women continued to struggle to break through the so-called glass ceiling that held them back from upper-management positions. In 1998 women still earned generally just 76 cents for every dollar earned by a man.

THROUGH OTHERS' EYES

Human Rights or Cultural Imperialism?

Some people in non-Western nations object to what they perceive as a Western emphasis on individual rights. Many claim that their definition of rights is based on a different set of cultural values that place more emphasis on communities than on individuals. They claim that Western nations are practicing a form of cultural imperialism by trying to impose their sense of human rights on other peoples. "Human rights in Iran are based on Islamic values," said Iran's foreign minister in 1994. "We will not accept the values of foreign countries imposed on us under the cover of human rights."

Even some westerners are critical of Western nations' attempts to influence human rights policies elsewhere. In the British newspaper *The Guardian,* John Gray of Oxford University expressed such criticism.

> **"For the most part, Western thought and policy remain based on the premise [theory] that Western ideals and practices have universal authority. . . . The American presumption [belief] is that any regime [government] that does not conform to Western . . . conceptions of human rights is tyrannical and illegitimate. . . . It should surely be possible for policy to be guided by the ideal of harmonious coexistence among different cultures. . . . We need to have the confidence that our way of life is worth living without seeing it as obligatory [required] for the entire human species."**

Female political leaders. At a time when few American women held the highest elective offices, several countries chose female leaders. Indira Gandhi became prime minister of India following an impressive performance as the nation's minister of information and broadcasting. In 1979 Margaret Thatcher became prime minister of Great Britain and held that office longer than anyone else in the 1900s. In the Philippines, Corazon Aquino became president in 1986. Benazir Bhutto, elected prime minister of Pakistan in 1988, became the first female leader of an Islamic nation. In the 1990s women were also elected to head the governments of Ireland, Nicaragua, and Sri Lanka. In June 1999 Vaira Vike-Freiberga of Latvia became the first woman to be elected president of a country in Eastern Europe.

✔ **READING CHECK:** What were some characteristics of the worldwide women's movement?

Private Human Rights Efforts

Currently many private citizens and organizations work to protect human rights around the world. The Red Cross has provided assistance to victims of war and natural disasters for more than a century. Amnesty International investigates the status of human rights in every country of the world. The organization's annual reports detail human rights abuses and encourage the international community to take action.

INTERPRETING THE VISUAL RECORD

Human rights watchdog. In 1997 Amnesty International received the Nobel Peace Prize for its efforts on behalf of human rights. ***What do you think the barbed wire wrapped around the candle in the logo is supposed to represent?***

THAT'S INTERESTING!

A 1995 United Nations report provided information on the number of women serving in national legislatures. In Finland, women held 39 percent of the seats in the legislature, the highest percentage in the world. Women held about 10 percent of the seats in the U.S. Congress. In Congo, Ethiopia, Morocco, South Korea, Togo, and Yemen women held just 1 percent of the seats in the national legislatures.

The American Nation **VIDEO PROGRAM**

The Women's Rights Movement; Teacher's Guide, pp. 209–10

Search 48258, Play to 49209
Videodisc 1, Side B

Play Pause

See *Teacher's Guide* for Spanish barcode.

VISUAL RECORD ANSWER

Students might suggest that the barbed wire signifies threats to hope.

SPOTLIGHT on Human Rights Organizations

Organize students into small groups and have each group conduct research on international human rights organizations such as Amnesty International and the Red Cross. Then have each group use these organizations as models to draft a charter for a new international human rights organization for teenagers. The charter should include a mission statement, a list of goals, and a preliminary action plan.

Block Scheduling, Cooperative Learning

TEACH OBJECTIVE 3

ALL LEVELS: Tell students to list global challenges that remain to human rights. *(Lists might include people working under conditions of slavery; violence against civilians by paramilitary groups, rebel movements, and terrorists; and communist governments jailing and killing dissenters.)* Have students create a poster to raise awareness of one or more of these problems. Then have students write a paragraph offering recommendations on how to address some of these challenges.

Sheltered English

CHART ANSWER

the Democratic Republic of Congo and Libya; Afghanistan, Burundi, Colombia, Iran, Iraq, Sri Lanka, and Yugoslavia

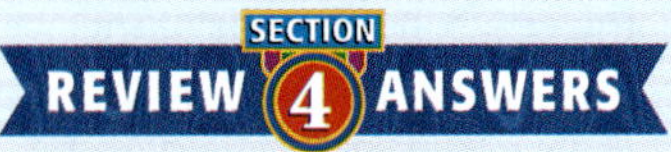

Define and Identify

For significance, see the following pages:

- Jehan Sadat, p. 896
- Taliban, p. 896
- Benazir Bhutto, p. 897
- Aung San Suu Kyi, p. 898

1. Answers will vary depending on the countries selected.

2. Answers will vary but should mention that in general the end of the Cold War and the collapse of the Soviet sphere led to improvements in human rights and allowed for more democratic elections but that in certain countries new governments did not protect human rights.

3. Students might mention that as many women fought for rights in the West, others struggled to reconcile their religion with their rights.

4. Answers will vary but should reflect an understanding of human rights issues and of national sovereignty.

5. Answers will vary, but students should note U.S. leadership in protesting human rights violations, the positive and negative effects of the end of the Cold War, and the current challenges to human rights.

Aung San Suu Kyi

Many individuals also fight against oppression in their homelands. One such activist was Aung San Suu Kyi (awng sahn soo chee). Born in 1945, Suu Kyi was the daughter of a hero of the 1940s Burmese independence movement against British rule. Although Suu Kyi lived most of her adult life in the West, she returned to Burma in 1988. That year a military government seized control of the nation. Suu Kyi helped form a pro-democracy opposition movement. The military government responded in 1989 by placing her under house arrest. Nonetheless, Suu Kyi remained committed to the cause. Her vision of the ideal government was similar to that of many other political reformers throughout the world.

> **"To provide the people with . . . peace and security, rulers must observe . . . the concepts of truth, righteousness, and loving kindness. It is government based on these very qualities that the people of Burma are seeking in their struggle for democracy."**

For her efforts, Suu Kyi was awarded the Nobel Peace Prize in 1991. Still under house arrest, she was unable to attend the awards ceremony. Suu Kyi was finally released in July 1995. She remains an influential critic of Burma's military government.

Human Rights Abuses Around the World in 1999

Amnesty International—a London-based organization that publicizes cases of political repression, torture, and the imprisonment of people for their political beliefs—reported that the following abuses took place in 1999.

Africa In Burundi hundreds of civilians were killed by the military and by armed opposition groups. In the Democratic Republic of Congo dozens of people were executed by the Military Order Court after unfair trials. In Ethiopia some 54,000 Eritreans were expelled from the country.

Asia In Afghanistan thousands of civilians were threatened with violence by both pro- and anti-Taliban military forces. In China the government arrested and tortured members of Falun Gong, a meditation group. In East Timor militia groups forced thousands of independence activists to flee the country. In Sri Lanka the military and its rebel opposition both attacked civilian targets, killing dozens of people.

Europe In Belarus the government arrested peaceful political protesters. In the Kosovo province of Yugoslavia thousands of ethnic Albanians and Serbs were forced out of their homes by ethnic violence. In Northern Ireland a human rights lawyer was murdered.

Latin America In Colombia hundreds of civilians were killed by paramilitary units and armed opposition groups because of their political beliefs. In Venezuela hundreds of Colombian refugees were forced to return to dangerous conditions at home. In Argentina a judge investigating human rights abuses under military rule faced death threats against himself and his family.

Middle East In Iran security forces attacked student demonstrators who criticized government policies. In Iraq security forces regularly arrested, tortured, and executed opponents of the government. In Libya political opponents were imprisoned without trial.

Learning from Charts Many countries targeted human rights supporters for persecution. "Human rights defenders often became the first victims of governments trying to build a good human rights image abroad and fearful of the damage human rights activists can do to that image," said an Amnesty International spokesperson.

? Building Chart Skills What countries were accused of holding unfair trials of opposition members or protesters? In which countries did armed forces attack civilians?

REVIEW

Have students complete the **Section 4 Review** on p. 899.

ASSESS

Have students complete **Daily Quiz 30.4.** As **Alternative Assessment**, you may want to use the newsmagazine article activity or the charter activity in this section's lessons.

RETEACH

Have students complete **Main Idea Activity for Reteaching and Sheltered English 30.4.** Then have each student summarize the material in the section in about five paragraphs. Tell students to be sure to cover all of the section's objectives as well as the main idea of each subsection. **Sheltered English**

EXTEND

Have the class stage a human rights rally. The rally may focus on human rights issues in the United States, such as the struggle for equality between races and genders, or it might address one or more international violations of human rights. Encourage students to present short speeches, make posters and signs, conduct interviews and panel discussions, or otherwise creatively convey their message. If possible, invite other social studies classes to act as audience members.

Block Scheduling, Cooperative Learning

Remaining Challenges

Although every nation in the world has officially banned slavery, not all countries enforce these laws effectively. It is estimated that millions of people—particularly women and children—labor under conditions of slavery in nations such as Mauritania, Nepal, Pakistan, and Sudan.

Civilians in many nations face violence at the hands of paramilitary groups or rebel movements. In Columbia paramilitary groups have carried out kidnappings and mass killings. Observers estimate that some 100,000 Algerians have been killed since 1992 during a conflict between Islamic rebels and government forces. In East Timor, armed militia groups terrorized citizens who voted for independence from Indonesia in a 1999 referendum. UN observers accused the Indonesian military of aiding these militia groups. Western leaders also criticized Russia's invasion of the breakaway republic of Chechnya in late 1999 which caused many civilian casualties. Russia had already fought one war against Chechen separatists from 1994 to 1996. In addition to such domestic conflicts, international terrorism threatens the safety of civilians around the world.

Many governments greatly limit political freedom. The communist governments of China and Cuba routinely arrest political dissidents and prevent free speech. In June 1999 Chinese authorities banned demonstrations observing the 10-year anniversary of the Tiananmen Square Massacre of pro-democracy students.

Changing the human rights practices of other nations is difficult. Many countries regard these issues as domestic matters and are angered by foreign interference. Creating and enforcing effective international agreements on human rights thus remains a challenge for the future.

✔ **READING CHECK:** What global challenges remain to human rights?

Chinese dissident Li Lu spoke out in the United States and Europe against China's communist government.

SECTION 4 REVIEW

Define and explain the significance of the following term:
Taliban

Identify and explain the significance of the following individuals:
Jehan Sadat
Benazir Bhutto
Aung San Suu Kyi

1. **Using Graphic Organizers** Copy the graphic organizer below. Use it to explain some of the current challenges to human rights.

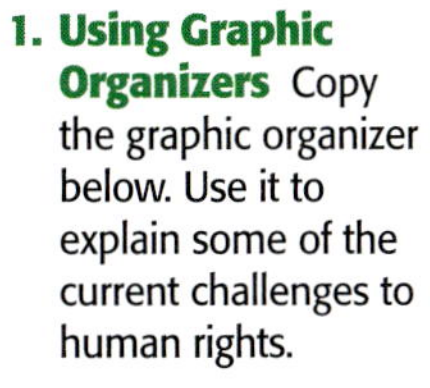

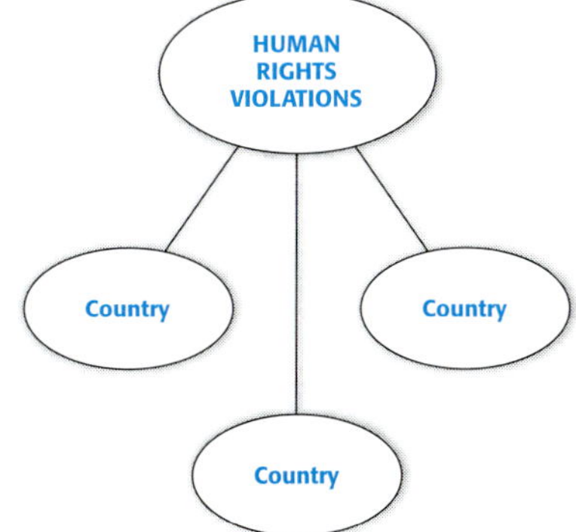

2. **Identifying Cause and Effect** What effects did the end of the Cold War have on human rights?
3. **Identifying Values** What were some of the characteristics of the women's rights movement in the modern era?
4. **Taking a Stand** To what extent do you think the United States should interfere when another nation takes actions that many Americans consider to be human rights violations?

Critical Thinking

5. Do you believe the status of human rights will improve or worsen during the next decade? Explain your answer.
Consider:
   - the role the United States has played in protesting human rights abuses
   - how events in the 1980s and 1990s affected human rights
   - what challenges to human rights persist

CHAPTER 30 REVIEW ANSWERS

Creating a Time Line
Each event should have an explanation and the correct date.

Writing a Summary
See the Reading Checks in each section for main ideas.

Identifying People and Ideas
1. English philosopher who argued that governments exist to protect the rights of the governed
2. abolitionist who worked to end slavery in the British Empire
3. British women's rights organization founded by Emmeline Pankhurst
4. international humanitarian organization
5. 1864 agreement in which 12 western nations pledged to care for captured enemy soldiers during wartime
6. leader of African National Congress who became president of South Africa in 1994
7. UN agreement that countries would not take actions limiting individual liberties
8. assistant secretary of state for human rights and humanitarian affairs under President Carter
9. fundamentalist Islamic military and political group in Afghanistan
10. prime minister of Pakistan and the first female leader of an Islamic nation

REVIEW AND ASSESSMENT RESOURCES

PRINT

- Chapter 30 Review, pp. 900–01
- Chapter 30 Tutorial for Students, Parents, Mentors, and Peers
- Chapter 30 Test (Form A or B)
- Portfolio Activities and Alternative Assessment Handbook, Chapter 30

MULTIMEDIA

- Audio Program, Chapter 30 (English and Spanish)
- Chapter 30 Test Generator (on the One-Stop Planner)
- Global Skill Builder CD–ROM
- HRW Web site

SHELTERED ENGLISH

- Spanish Glossary
- Sheltered English Chapter 30 Test

REVIEW

Have students complete the **Chapter 30 Review** on pp. 900–01.

ASSESS

Use one of the chapter tests to assess students' understanding of the content. For **Alternative Assessment**, see the **Portfolio Activities and Alternative Assessment Handbook.**

Understanding Main Ideas

1. It began with the Enlightenment during the 1600s; Locke argued individuals held rights that should be protected by government; the Declaration of Independence and Declaration of the Rights of Man and Citizen identified basic human rights.

2. British abolitionists' efforts to end slavery throughout the British Empire inspired newly independent Latin American nations to outlaw slavery, and helped Russia end serfdom.

3. Answers will vary but should include high casualty rates for troops and civilians, use of modern weaponry, the Holocaust, and the forced removal or massacre of other groups.

4. He linked U.S. economic aid to human rights records.

5. the Universal Declaration of Human Rights, the Convention on the Elimination of All Forms of Racial Discrimination, the Convention on the Suppression of Apartheid, and the Covenant on Economic, Social, and Cultural Rights

6. The end of the Cold War led to the collapse of the Soviet sphere, which allowed for more democratically elected governments.

Reviewing Themes

1. Answers will vary but should discuss efforts in Burma and in South Africa.

2. Nations have used economic measures such as embargoes, tariffs, and aid to encourage other nations to respect human rights.

Review

Creating a Time Line

Copy the time line below onto a sheet of paper. Complete the time line by filling in the events and dates from the chapter that you think were most significant. Pick three events and explain why you think they were significant.

Writing a Summary

Using the Reading Checks as a guide, write an overview of the events in the chapter.

Identifying People and Ideas

Identify the following terms or individuals and explain their significance.

1. John Locke
2. William Wilberforce
3. Women's Social and Political Union
4. Red Cross
5. Geneva Convention
6. Nelson Mandela
7. Covenant on Civil and Political Rights
8. Patricia Derian
9. Taliban
10. Benazir Bhutto

Understanding Main Ideas

SECTION 1

1. How did the modern concept of human rights develop?
2. How was abolition a global movement?

SECTION 2

3. What human rights violations occurred during World Wars I and II?

SECTION 3

4. How did President Carter address human rights?
5. What UN agreements promoted human rights issues?

SECTION 4

6. How did the end of the Cold War advance human rights?

Reviewing Themes

1. **Democratic Values** How have activists in Africa and Asia linked democracy to their struggle for human rights?
2. **Global Relations** How have nations used economic means to encourage other nations to respect human rights? Give examples.
3. **Cultural Diversity** How have definitions of human rights differed over time and from culture to culture? Give specific examples.

Thinking Critically

1. **Evaluating** How did progressivism further the cause of human rights in the United States?
2. **Comparing and Contrasting** How were efforts to protect human rights after World War I and World War II similar? How were they different?
3. **Analyzing** What effects did apartheid in South Africa have on human rights in that country?
4. **Synthesizing** How was decolonization in Africa and Asia related to the American civil rights movement?
5. **Taking a Stand** How do you think the United States should respond to human rights violations by other major powers such as China?

Writing About History

Writing to Express a Viewpoint In the style of the U.S. Declaration of Independence or France's Declaration of the Rights of Man and Citizen, write a statement expressing your view of human rights. Be sure to list the rights that you believe are most important. Use the graphic organizer below to help you organize your thoughts.

What rights do all humans have? → 

→ How do you propose to protect those rights?

RETEACH

Organize students into four groups. Assign each group one of the following topics: human rights before 1910, human rights from 1911 to 1945, human rights from 1945 to 1979, or human rights from 1980 to the present. Tell each group to prepare a triptych, or a three-panel visual display, about its topic. Encourage them to include images, graphic organizers, newspaper and magazine clippings, narrative captions, samples of buttons or bumper stickers, and other items to convey the necessary information. Display students' triptychs in the classroom or school library. **Sheltered English, Cooperative Learning**

EXTEND

Invite a person from your community who has left his or her country due to harsh conditions and violations of human rights to speak to the class. Before the speaker arrives, have each student write down three questions to ask about the person's country of origin, past life, reasons for leaving, and hopes for the future. **Block Scheduling**

Strategies for Success Review the **Strategies for Success** on *Reading Charts.* Then study the organizational chart in Section 3 titled "The Basic Organization of the United Nations" and answer the following questions.

1. How many main bodies work together to form the United Nations?
2. Which UN body directs the activities of the Economic and Social Council?
3. Which UN body receives direction from both the General Assembly and the Security Council?

Linking History and Geography

Study the map of South America below. Note that many countries in South America changed from military-controlled governments to democratic forms of government during the 1980s. Which South American nations established civilian governments after 1985? How many South American nations had changed from military-controlled to democratic governments before 1975?

internetconnect

TOPIC: Women's Rights Activists
GO TO: go.hrw.com
KEYWORD: SE1 Rights

Accessing the Internet through the HRW Web site, research the lives and accomplishments of Susan B. Anthony, Elizabeth Cady Stanton, Sojourner Truth, Lucy Stone, and Lucretia Mott. Then create a political "talk show" in which you assume the identities of the women and debate the issues of their time.

BUILDING YOUR PORTFOLIO

Complete one or all of the following projects independently or cooperatively.

1 Global Relations

Imagine that you are a reporter researching efforts of the United Nations to protect human rights worldwide over the past few decades. ***Construct a time line*** tracing these efforts and write two or three sentences about each entry.

2 Democratic Values

Imagine that you are a black African in South Africa who has just voted in a national election for the first time. ***Write a letter*** to a friend describing the experience and explaining how it fits into the historical struggle for civil rights worldwide.

3 Cultural Diversity

Imagine that you are a refugee fleeing violent conflict in Rwanda or Kosovo or that you are fleeing a repressive government. ***Write a petition*** to the United Nations describing human rights abuses in your homeland, the way your culture views human rights, and what role you think the United Nations should play in your home country.

3. Answers will vary but may reflect the different definitions of human rights that women living in the United States and in the Muslim world have.

Thinking Critically

1. expanded voting rights, passed child labor laws
2. similar—spurred international and private efforts to protect human rights; different—trials to punish human rights violators were held after World War II and more efforts were made to promote racial equality
3. established white authority over black majority
4. Leaders of the decolonization movement, such as Gandhi, inspired activists and leaders in the U.S. civil rights movement.
5. Answers will vary but should reflect an understanding of human rights issues.

Writing About History
Statements will vary but should reflect both the style of the documents mentioned and an understanding of human rights issues.

Strategies for Success

1. six
2. the General Assembly
3. the Secretariat

Linking History and Geography
Chile, Paraguay, and Suriname; two

A New Environmental Awareness

CHAPTER PLANNING GUIDE

	Section Lesson Objectives	Print Resources	Multimedia Resources	Sheltered English Resources
Section 1 Subduing the Wilderness, pp. 904–07	**1** Describe what attitudes colonists and early Americans had toward the wilderness. **2** Explain what new views of the wilderness emerged in the United States during the 1800s. **3** Discuss how the science of ecology developed, and identify what it studies.	▶ Guided Reading Strategy 31.1 ▶ Primary Source Reading 31: Humankind's Impact on Nature ▶ Section 1 Review, p. 907 ▶ Daily Quiz 31.1	▶ One-Stop Planner, Lesson 31.1 ▶ Holt Researcher: American History CD–ROM	▶ Main Idea Activity for Reteaching and Sheltered English 31.1
Section 2 Expanding Horizons, pp. 908–12	**1** Identify the steps progressive conservationists took to protect the environment. **2** Discuss how preservationists' view of the environment differed from that of conservationists. **3** Explain how the Dust Bowl led to changes in U.S. environmental policy.	▶ Guided Reading Strategy 31.2 ▶ Graphic Organizer Activity 31: A Changing View ▶ Literature Reading 31: Recognizing Beauty in Nature ▶ Biography Reading 31: John Muir ▶ Section 2 Review, p. 912 ▶ Daily Quiz 31.2	▶ One-Stop Planner, Lesson 31.2 ▶ American Music Selection 21, "Talkin' Dust Bowl" ▶ Holt Researcher: American History CD–ROM	▶ Main Idea Activity for Reteaching and Sheltered English 31.2
Section 3 Environmentalism Goes Global, pp. 913–16	**1** Explain why many people considered nuclear-weapons tests to be dangerous. **2** Discuss how the threat of nuclear weapons encouraged international cooperation. **3** Describe how activists in Europe and the United States used political measures to draw attention to environmental problems.	▶ Guided Reading Strategy 31.3 ▶ Section 3 Review, p. 916 ▶ Daily Quiz 31.3	▶ One-Stop Planner, Lesson 31.3 ▶ Holt Researcher: American History CD–ROM	▶ Main Idea Activity for Reteaching and Sheltered English 31.3
Section 4 A Small Planet, pp. 917–23	**1** Identify recent global environmental problems nations have faced. **2** Discuss how deforestation and biodiversity are related. **3** Explain concerns that have arisen over population growth. **4** Describe how governments and environmentalists have tried to solve current environmental problems.	▶ Guided Reading Strategy 31.4 ▶ Geography Activity 31: Great Lakes Pollution ▶ Section 4 Review, p. 923 ▶ Daily Quiz 31.4	▶ One-Stop Planner, Lesson 31.4 ▶ Holt Researcher: American History CD–ROM ▶ HRW Web site	▶ Main Idea Activity for Reteaching and Sheltered English 31.4
Chapter Review and Assessment pp. 924–25		▶ Chapter 31 Review, pp. 924–25 ▶ Chapter 31 Tutorial for Students, Parents, Mentors, and Peers ▶ Chapter 31 Test (Form A or B) ▶ Portfolio Activities and Alternative Assessment Handbook, Chapter 31	▶ Audio Program, Chapter 31 (English and Spanish) ▶ Chapter 31 Test Generator (on the One-Stop Planner) ▶ Global Skill Builder CD–ROM ▶ HRW Web site	▶ Spanish Glossary ▶ Sheltered English Chapter 31 Test

CHAPTER OVERVIEW

During the colonial era, settlers sought to tame the North American wilderness and to use it to fulfill their needs. During the 1800s, however, the expansion of the U.S. population had brought about dramatic environmental changes, including the near extinction of the buffalo. In the mid-1800s observers such as Henry David Thoreau began urging Americans to revere nature. The development of the science of ecology also sparked an interest in environmental issues in the United States.

The environmental movement was not unified. Conservationists called for the wise, managed use of natural resources. Preservationists such as Aldo Leopold wanted to leave wilderness areas untouched and thus unexploited. During the 1930s topsoil erosion transformed parts of the Great Plains into a Dust Bowl. This environmental crisis reinforced the need for a national environmental policy. Concerns over environmental problems—including nuclear fallout, population growth, and global warming—prompted international efforts to protect the environment in the post–World War II era.

TIME TAMERS

Block Scheduling

The teacher lesson plans for each section offer a variety of activity choices to help you present the material in a block scheduling format. For further suggestions on block scheduling, see the **Block Scheduling Handbook with Team Teaching Strategies**, pp. 181–86.

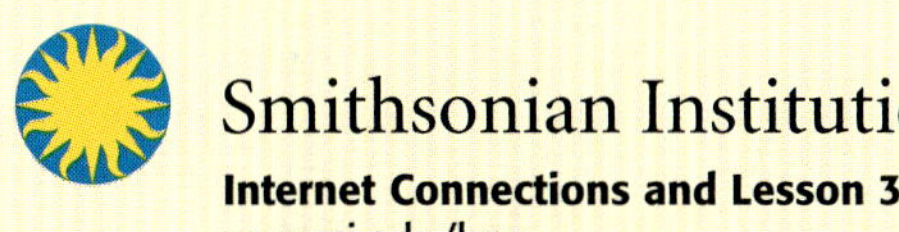

Smithsonian Institution®

Internet Connections and Lesson 31
www.si.edu/hrw

Hands-On History Activities:

Classroom to Community The **Hands-On History Activities** help students make meaningful connections between events in American history and those in their own hometown. You may wish to use the Chapter 31 Activity, Make a Change for the Environment, to extend the chapter lessons, as alternative assessment, or as a block scheduling option.

Portfolio Projects

The American Nation includes multiple portfolio projects in each Pupil's Edition chapter review, as well as each unit review. Chapter 31 Portfolio Project options on p. 925 include the following:

1. Students will **create a pamphlet**.
2. Students will **make a poster**.
3. Students will **write a script**.

The American Nation

INTERNET RESOURCE DIRECTORY

To access online materials for this chapter, go to **go.hrw.com** and type in the keywords listed below.

HRW ONLINE RESOURCES

GO TO: go.hrw.com

Online Maps

KEYWORD: SE1 Maps31

- National Parks
- Nuclear Technology

Online Reading Support

KEYWORD: SE1 Strategies31

Online Rubrics

KEYWORD: SE1 Rubrics

CHAPTER ENRICHMENT LINKS

Use these Web links to extend and enrich student learning for Chapter 31.

GO TO: go.hrw.com
KEYWORD: SE1 Ch31

CHAPTER INTERNET ACTIVITIES

GO TO: go.hrw.com

- Pupil's Edition Student Activity
  KEYWORD: SE1 Rain Forest
  (Students explore the rain forest and biodiversity.)
- Teacher's Edition Student Activity
  KEYWORD: SE1 Oil Spill
  (Students conduct research on the *Exxon Valdez* oil spill.)
- Teacher's Edition Student Activity
  KEYWORD: SE1 Recycling
  (Students learn about recycling.)

ADDITIONAL

RESOURCES

Books for Teachers

Newton, David E. *Global Warming: A Reference Handbook.* ABC-Clio, 1993. Offers a guide to the science and controversy concerning global warming.

West, Elliott. *The Contested Plains.* University Press of Kansas, 1998. Details the environmental changes on the Great Plains.

Books for Students

Edmonds, Alex. *The Greenhouse Effect (Closer Look At).* Copper Beech Books, 1997. Discusses the science behind the theory of global warming. Particularly appropriate for students reading below grade level.

Kellert, Stephen R. *Encyclopedia of the Environment.* Simon & Schuster, 1997. Provides detailed coverage of environmental issues.

Primary Sources from the Period

Leopold, Aldo. *A Sand County Almanac.* Oxford University Press, 1949. Presents the thoughts of a leading preservationist on the value of wilderness.

Thoreau, Henry David. *Walden.* Houghton Mifflin, 1995. Offers an annotated edition of the 1854 classic.

Multimedia Materials

Global Warming. Video, 12 min. Rangeley Productions. Examines issues surrounding global warming.

Rain Forests: Proving Their Worth. Video, 30 min. Video Project Media for a Safe and Sustainable World. Studies the importance of the rain forests to humans and the ecosystem.

CHAPTER 31

Before You Read

Build on What You Know

Ask students to answer the following questions.

How might the first English settlers have reacted to their new lands?

Consider:

- the apparent natural abundance they saw
- the importance of agriculture to the survival of early settlers

Why might American attitudes toward nature have changed over time?

Consider:

- the growing urban population
- the effect of technologies such as the automobile

exploring the time line

AMERICAN EVENTS

internetconnect

TOPIC: The *Exxon Valdez* Oil Spill
GO TO: go.hrw.com
KEYWORD: SE1 Oil Spill

Have students conduct research on the *Exxon Valdez* oil spill. Then have each student create a graphic organizer that includes the following categories: the oil spill, cleanup efforts, harm to the ecosystem, recovery of the ecosystem, and the status of lawsuits.

CHAPTER 31

1890–Present

A New Environmental Awareness

Yosemite National Park

1890
Daily Life
Yosemite National Park is established.

1917
Science and Technology
A 100-inch reflecting telescope is built at Mount Wilson, California.

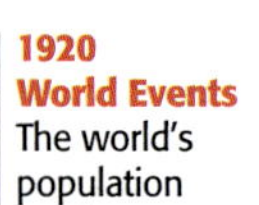

1920
World Events
The world's population reaches 1.8 billion.

A canister of DDT

1944
Science and Technology
The insecticide DDT is used to prevent a typhus epidemic by killing disease-carrying lice.

1890 | **1905** | **1920** | **1935**

1890
Daily Life
According to the 1890 U.S. Census, the frontier no longer exists in the United States.

1900
Politics
The Canadian Forestry Association is founded.

1918
The Arts
Spanish artist Joan Miró first exhibits his work.

***Joan Miró's* The Farm**

Before You Read

Build on What You Know

Americans' ideas about the environment grew out of a European agricultural tradition that arrived with the first English settlers. This tradition taught that nature existed to serve human needs. This idea dominated American attitudes about nature for decades. In this chapter you will learn how Americans altered the environment and how an environmental awareness developed in the United States. You will also learn how factors such as nuclear power and deforestation have encouraged international efforts to protect the environment.

902

Think About Themes

*To help students create their Themes Journal entries, provide the following examples of appropriate **agree**/**disagree** statements.*

Technology and Society

Agree Solar power has decreased the need for fossil fuels.

Disagree Increased industrialization has contributed to air pollution.

Global Relations

Agree Environmental pollution can cross borders and is therefore an international problem.

Disagree Nations have no right to impose environmental policies on other nations.

Economic Development

Agree Economic development is necessary to improve the standard of living.

Disagree Some nations cannot afford to implement environmental regulations.

An oil rig on the North Sea

Crowded city street in Tokyo, Japan

1945 Science and Technology The first atomic bomb is detonated in New Mexico.

1950

1962 Daily Life Rachel Carson's environmental book *Silent Spring* is published.

1964 Business and Finance Great Britain grants the first licenses to drill for oil and gas in the North Sea.

1965

1970 Daily Life The first Earth Day is celebrated on April 22.

1973 Politics The Endangered Species Act establishes regulations to protect plants and animals threatened with extinction.

1980

1986 World Events The Chernobyl nuclear accident occurs in the Ukraine.

1989 Business and Finance The *Exxon Valdez* spills oil along the Alaska coast.

1993 Science and Technology The Convention on Biological Diversity takes effect with the goal of preserving the diversity of plants and animals worldwide.

1999 World Events The United Nations announces that the world's population has reached 6 billion.

1999

A pin celebrating Earth Day 2000

An oil-covered sea otter

Think About Themes

*Decide whether you **agree** or **disagree** with the following statements. Note why in your journal.*

Technology and Society Technological changes usually have a positive effect on the global environment.

Global Relations Successful protection of the environment depends on cooperation among nations.

Economic Development Nations must balance environmental protection with economic development.

exploring the time line

GEOGRAPHIC DIVERSITY

1999 ■ Six Billion People. It took just 12 years—from 1987 to 1999—for the world's population to climb from 5 billion to 6 billion. Statisticians noted in 1999 that birthrates remained high because so many women were of childbearing age. Longer lifespans also contributed to the size of the global population. Some 100,000 people were more than 100 years old in 1999, a number that was forecast to increase by six times in the following 50 years.

CRITICAL THINKING What problems might population growth cause?

ANSWER: Students might suggest shortages of resources such as food, drinking water, and energy.

903

SECTION 1

After completing Section 1, students should be able to:

OBJECTIVE 1 *Describe what attitudes colonists and early Americans had toward the wilderness.*

OBJECTIVE 2 *Explain what new views of the wilderness emerged in the United States during the 1800s.*

OBJECTIVE 3 *Discuss how the science of ecology developed, and identify what it studies.*

LET'S GET STARTED!

To begin the class, have students look at the chapter opener time line. Then have them write a paragraph about how the events on the time line indicate changing attitudes about the environment during the last 100 years, in the United States and around the world. Then tell students that in Section 1 they will learn about the ways that Americans viewed the environment during the 1600s through the late 1800s.

SECTION 1 RESOURCES

PRINT

- Guided Reading Strategy 31.1
- Primary Source Reading 31: Humankind's Impact on Nature
- Section 1 Review, p. 907
- Daily Quiz 31.1

MULTIMEDIA

- One-Stop Planner, Lesson 31.1
- Holt Researcher: American History CD–ROM

SHELTERED ENGLISH

- Main Idea Activity for Reteaching and Sheltered English 31.1

✔ READING TO UNDERSTAND

To help students master the section objectives, have them answer the **READING CHECKS** and complete **Guided Reading Strategy 31.1** as they read the section.

Subduing the Wilderness

OBJECTIVES

Read to understand:

1. what attitudes colonists and early Americans had toward the wilderness
2. what new views of the wilderness emerged in the United States during the 1800s
3. how the science of ecology developed, and what it studies

KEY TERMS

ecology
ecosystem

KEY PEOPLE

Ralph Waldo Emerson
Henry David Thoreau
Frederick Jackson Turner
Charles Darwin
Ernst Haeckel
Henry C. Cowles

“The whole earth is the Lord's Garden and He hath given it to the sons of men, with a general Condition: 'Increase and multiply, replenish [make full] the earth and subdue it' [Genesis 1:28].”

—John Winthrop

Puritan minister John Winthrop explained in 1629 why the Puritans should go “into . . . the wilderness” rather than “suffer a whole Continent . . . to lie waste without any improvement.” European settlers such as Winthrop brought to the Americas their Christian belief that humans should establish control over nature. For much of the early history of the United States, Americans sought to tame the wilderness.

THE GRANGER COLLECTION, NEW YORK

European colonists meeting American Indians

The American Wilderness

English settlers first arrived in Virginia and New England in the early 1600s. Most believed that God had given them the Americas to use as they saw fit. They happily accepted the biblical command to rule over the land and “every living thing that moveth upon the earth.” For these settlers the wilderness was something to be feared and conquered, not cherished and preserved. From the beginning they set out to change the “remote, rocky, barren, bushy, wild-woody wilderness” into “a second England for fertilness,” as Massachusetts colonist Edward Johnson approvingly noted in 1653.

European settlers wanted to clear and cultivate the American wilderness.

European settlement. The colonists' approach to nature grew out of a long tradition of land use. Like their ancestors in Europe, they were farmers. To them, farming meant clearing the land of trees, plowing it, and planting crops. Unlike the American Indians they encountered, the colonists had metal tools and domesticated animals. This allowed them to cultivate greater areas of land. However, transforming the natural environment often destroyed the habitats of many species. Most farmers probably did not think about the environmental consequences of their methods. Many probably believed that they had little choice in the methods they used. They needed the land.

TEACH OBJECTIVE 1

ALL LEVELS: Ask students to summarize how colonists and early Americans felt about the wilderness. *(Students might answer that they regarded it as something to be feared and conquered.)* Then organize students into triads and have each group create a brochure to attract settlers to the frontier during the 1700s. Encourage students to include pictures, maps, and text to convey the message that the wilderness is there to be conquered and tamed. Display students' completed brochures around the classroom.
Sheltered English, Cooperative Learning

TEACH OBJECTIVE 2

ALL LEVELS: Pair students and have each pair choose one of the quotations by individuals in the subsection "The Beginnings of Dissent." Then tell students to discuss the quotation with their partners, interpreting its meaning and deciding whether they agree or disagree with the sentiment expressed. *(Answers will vary, but students might mention that transcendentalists wanted individuals to regain close touch with the natural world while others, like historian Frederick Jackson Turner, valued the wilderness for more than its beauty.)* Call on one student from each pair to summarize their discussion for the class. Encourage the class to comment on each other's conclusions. **Sheltered English, Cooperative Learning**

Expansion. As the European population grew in North America, settlement spread inland from the coast. New technologies increased people's ability to modify the landscape. Better roads made travel faster and cheaper. The invention of steamboats and the construction of canals eventually provided better access to the country's interior. Construction of railroads brought much of the country within easy reach of cities and their markets. This spurred further settlement.

The railroad boom's most dramatic effect on the environment was the destruction of the buffalo herds of the Great Plains. As late as the mid-1800s, the grasses of the Plains supported millions of buffalo. The buffalo, in turn, supported a thriving Plains Indian culture. Like many American Indian groups, the Plains Indians attempted to live in harmony with nature. They only killed the buffalo they could use. The completion of the first railroad lines across the Plains in the late 1800s brought great change to the region. Farmers began to fence and plow the grasslands. Hunters slaughtered thousands of buffalo daily. In little more than a generation, the buffalo were nearly extinct.

✔ **READING CHECK:** What were the attitudes of colonists and early Americans toward the wilderness?

The Beginnings of Dissent

Some citizens objected to the subduing of America's vast wilderness. In the mid-1800s Ralph Waldo Emerson, Henry David Thoreau, and other transcendentalists called for the return to a simple life. The transcendentalists were intellectuals who believed that simple living would enable individuals to regain close touch with the natural world. They believed that this contact with nature would heal the human spirit. "In the woods," wrote Emerson, "we return to reason and faith." Voicing a similar view, Thoreau declared, "In Wildness is the preservation of the World."

Transcendentalists and others urged that some wild lands be set aside before the wilderness disappeared entirely. As early as 1857 New York writer Samuel Hammond called for the creation of a nature reserve 100 miles in diameter in New York's Adirondack Mountains.

> **"I would make it a forest forever. It should be a misdemeanor to chop down a tree, and a felony to clear an acre within its boundaries. The old woods should stand here always as God made them, growing on until the earthworm ate away their roots, and the strong winds hurled them to the ground, and new woods should be permitted to supply the place of the old so long as the earth remained."**

The Religious Spirit

FAITH AND THE WILDERNESS

As people began to domesticate animals and plants thousands of years ago, they were in effect developing a new concept of the wilderness. This early idea of wilderness simply applied to whatever plants and animals that were not under human control. During the Middle Ages the teaching of Christianity in Europe further influenced this concept. During the 1300s, the theologian John Wycliffe used the word *wilderness* to describe the environment where some important events of the Bible took place. Wycliffe's English translation of the Latin Bible referred to the dry and unlivable desert lands of the Middle East as a wilderness. This view of the environment contributed to the Christian conception of the wilderness as a place of hardship.

King James Bible

European colonists brought this Christian view of the environment with them to the Americas. They believed God had commanded humans to transform the wilderness into civilized order. Puritans and other settlers were influenced by the first book of the Bible. Genesis 1:28 states, "Be fruitful, and multiply, and replenish the earth, and subdue it: and have dominion [command] over the fish of the sea, and over the fowl of the air, and over every living thing that moveth upon the earth." For many years, Christian beliefs continued to shape Americans' interaction with their environment. Senator Lewis Cass argued, "There can be no doubt that the Creator intended the earth should be reclaimed from a state of nature and cultivated."

THAT'S INTERESTING!

By studying environmental factors such as rainfall and the availability of grass, historians estimate that some 28 million bison might have lived on the Great Plains before the arrival of the horse.

HISTORY MAKERS SPEAK

Henry David Thoreau in *Walden*

The Value of Nature. Thoreau explained the benefit that nature brought to him. "I went to the woods because I wished to live deliberately, to front only the essential facts of life, and see if I could not learn what it had to teach, and not, when I came to die, discover that I had not lived."

CRITICAL THINKING What might Thoreau have been hoping to learn from nature?

ANSWER: Students might answer that he hoped to discover the meaning of human existence.

TEACH OBJECTIVE 3

ALL LEVELS: To help students understand how the science of ecology developed and what it studies, copy the following graphic organizer on the chalkboard, omitting the italicized answers. Have each student complete the graphic organizer. **Sheltered English**

▶ASSIGNMENT *Have students write a paragraph about how Darwin's theory of evolution affects people's modern-day environmental attitudes and ideas.*

Darwin publishes theory of evolution based on process of natural selection.

↓

Haeckel develops science of ecology based on Darwin's theories.

→ **ECOLOGY, the study of**

the interrelationship of plants and animals with each other and with their environment

ecosystems

PEOPLE IN HISTORY

Frederick Jackson Turner. Frederick Jackson Turner was born in a small frontier town in Wisconsin in 1861. He later studied history at the University of Wisconsin and at Johns Hopkins University in Maryland. Turner never completed writing a book, but his essays were published in several collections, one of which won the Pulitzer Prize in 1932.

CRITICAL THINKING How might Turner's early life have shaped his ideas concerning U.S. history?

ANSWER: Students might suggest that being born in a frontier town made Turner interested in the importance of the frontier.

THAT'S INTERESTING!

The word *ecology* is derived from two Greek words, *oikos*, which means "household," and *logy*, which means "the study of."

VISUAL RECORD ANSWER

Students might answer that they are studying its size.

Read More About It

Free Find: Henry David Thoreau

After reading about Henry David Thoreau on the Holt Researcher CD–ROM, write a short play or story about Thoreau's life, explaining why he believed that it is important to preserve the wilderness.

Others, such as historian Frederick Jackson Turner, valued the wilderness and the frontier for more than its beauty. In an influential 1893 paper, Turner argued that the frontier had helped form the American character.

> **"The frontier is the line of most rapid and effective Americanization. The wilderness masters the colonist. . . . In short, at the frontier the environment is at first too strong for the man. He must accept the conditions which it furnishes, or perish. . . . Thus the advance of the frontier has meant a steady movement away from the influence of Europe, a steady growth of independence on American lines."**

Turner went on to argue that "the most important effect of the frontier has been in the promotion of democracy." Not all historians agree with Turner's view that the frontier created a new identity for western settlers. Some historians have noted that life in many frontier communities, such as mining camps, strongly resembled life in eastern factories and did not necessarily foster individualism and independence. Still, this belief in the connection between democracy and the frontier led some Americans to support efforts to protect the wilderness.

✔ **READING CHECK:** What new views of the wilderness emerged in America during the 1800s?

The Birth of Ecology

During the mid- to late 1800s developments in the natural sciences also increased public interest in the environment. In 1859 British scientist Charles Darwin published *On the Origin of Species by Means of Natural Selection.* Darwin's theory of natural selection stated that the plants and animals that were best adapted to their environment were the ones most likely to survive and reproduce. This meant that species needed to adjust to new environmental conditions in order to survive. Darwin argued that natural selection led to evolution—the change and development of organisms over time.

INTERPRETING THE VISUAL RECORD

Ecology. Ecologists took measurements of this juniper tree in the 1920s. It proved to be nearly 6,000 years old. ***What aspect of the tree are the scientists studying in this picture?***

A new science. This theory of evolution brought new attention to the environment. Inspired by Darwin's work, in the 1860s German biologist Ernst Haeckel developed a new science named **ecology**. Ecology is the study of the interrelationship of plants and animals with each other and with their environment. Haeckel argued that ecology was a logical outgrowth of the study of evolution and the process of natural selection. Ecologists attempt to identify how environmental changes might affect the survival of a species.

European botanists were the first to practice ecology. Their studies emphasized the relationship of plants to the environment.

REVIEW

Have students complete the **Section 1 Review** on p. 907.

ASSESS

Have students complete **Daily Quiz 31.1**. As **Alternative Assessment**, you may want to use the brochure or the evolution paragraph activity in this section's lessons.

RETEACH

Have students complete **Main Idea Activity for Reteaching and Sheltered English 31.1**. Then pair students and have them make flashcards for each of the key terms and key people in the section. Have pairs write one paragraph summarizing the content of each subsection. Finally, have the students in each pair review the information together and quiz each other on the information they recorded.
Sheltered English, Cooperative Learning

EXTEND

Organize students into triads and have them conduct research on the science of ecology as it developed during the late 1800s and early 1900s. Tell each triad to create a poster-size flowchart showing how the study of ecology came about and how it developed in its early years. Tell students to use arrows to indicate which scientists' ideas influenced other scientists' studies and theories. **Block Scheduling, Cooperative Learning**

For example, Eugenius Warming, a Danish professor, showed how environmental factors such as heat and humidity affect plant growth.

Ecology in the United States. The new science soon spread to the United States. In 1864 geographer George Perkins Marsh wrote *Man and Nature,* one of the first great American works on environmental issues. Marsh studied the ways in which human beings altered their immediate environments and how this affected nature. By the 1890s ecologists such as Henry C. Cowles were considering a new way of studying nature. They developed the idea of an **ecosystem**—the varied webs of interaction between living things and their environment. Another scientist, Frederic Clements, published the first American book on the subject. His *Research Methods in Ecology* theorized that climate was the most important factor in determining the survival of competing species.

In the early 1900s scientists became increasingly interested in the study of ecosystems. American ecologist Victor Shelford described this interaction.

> **"Ecology is the science of communities. A study of the relations of a single species to the environment conceived without reference to communities . . . is not properly included in the field of ecology."**

Ecologists' focus on ecosystems led to a concern for conservation of habitats. In 1916 Shelford became the first president of the Ecological Society of America. Members of this organization thought that the science of ecology would provide a foundation for managing the country's natural resources. In keeping with the progressive spirit of the time, they believed that the study of ecology could provide the knowledge necessary to protect the environment.

✔ **READING CHECK:** How did the science of ecology develop, and what does it study?

Ecologists often drew detailed pictures of wildlife they encountered, such as these pitcher plants.

SECTION 1 REVIEW

Define and explain the significance of the following terms:
ecology
ecosystem

Identify and explain the significance of the following individuals:
Ralph Waldo Emerson
Henry David Thoreau
Frederick Jackson Turner
Charles Darwin
Ernst Haeckel
Henry C. Cowles

1. **Using Graphic Organizers** Copy the web below. Use it to list some of the different influences on Americans' attitudes toward the environment during the 1600s, 1700s, and 1800s.

2. **Identifying Values** How did the religious beliefs of some European colonists affect the way they viewed the environment?
3. **Taking a Stand** Imagine that you are a transcendentalist. Write a paragraph explaining why you think the wilderness should be preserved.
4. **Analyzing** How did Charles Darwin's ideas influence the creation of the science of ecology?

Critical Thinking

5. How does the science of ecology expand our knowledge of the environment?
Consider:
- what ecologists study about the environment
- how ecosystems change over time
- how people and nature interact

SECTION 1 REVIEW ANSWERS

Define and Identify
For significance, see the following pages:
- Ralph Waldo Emerson, p. 905
- Henry David Thoreau, p. 905
- Frederick Jackson Turner, p. 906
- Charles Darwin, p. 906
- Ernst Haeckel, p. 906
- ecology, p. 906
- Henry C. Cowles, p. 907
- ecosystem, p. 907

1. religious beliefs, European tradition of land use, transcendentalism, Darwinism, and ecology

2. Many European colonists held the Christian belief that humans should establish control over nature.

3. Answers will vary but should reflect the transcendentalist belief that the environment was a source of reason, faith, and healing for the human spirit.

4. They brought new attention to the study of the environment and inspired Haeckel to develop the science of ecology.

5. Answers will vary but might include that the study of ecology helps to explain how natural selection, changes in ecosystems, and the interaction of organisms affect the environment.

SECTION 2

After completing Section 2, students should be able to:

OBJECTIVE 1 *Identify the steps progressive conservationists took to protect the environment.*

OBJECTIVE 2 *Discuss how preservationists' view of the environment differed from that of conservationists.*

OBJECTIVE 3 *Explain how the Dust Bowl led to changes in U.S. environmental policy.*

LET'S GET STARTED!

As students enter the classroom, play Selection 21, "Talkin' Dust Bowl," from the **American Music Audio CD Program.** Explain to students that the Dust Bowl was a dry, wind-eroded area stretching from Texas to Nebraska that could not be farmed. Then have students respond in writing to this song, focusing on its environmental implications. When students have finished, tell them that in Section 2 they will learn about growing movements for conservation and preservation of the environment during the early decades of the 1900s and how the Dust Bowl disaster led to changes in U.S. environmental policy.

SECTION 2 RESOURCES

PRINT

- Guided Reading Strategy 31.2
- Graphic Organizer Activity 31: A Changing View
- Literature Reading 31: Recognizing Beauty in Nature
- Biography Reading 31: John Muir
- Section 2 Review, p. 912
- Daily Quiz 31.2

MULTIMEDIA

- One-Stop Planner, Lesson 31.2
- American Music Selection 21, "Talkin' Dust Bowl"
- Holt Researcher: American History CD–ROM

SHELTERED ENGLISH

- Main Idea Activity for Reteaching and Sheltered English 31.2

✔ READING TO UNDERSTAND

To help students master the section objectives, have them answer the **READING CHECKS** and complete **Guided Reading Strategy 31.2** as they read the section.

Expanding Horizons

OBJECTIVES

Read to understand:

1. what steps progressive conservationists took to protect the environment
2. how preservationists' view of the environment differed from that of conservationists
3. how the Dust Bowl led to changes in U.S. environmental policy

KEY TERMS

conservation
National Monuments Act
preservation

KEY PEOPLE

John Muir
Aldo Leopold

"It is true that trees are for human use. But there are aesthetic [artistic] uses as well as commercial uses—uses for the spiritual wealth of all, as well as for the material wealth of some."

—Joseph Le Conte

Joseph Le Conte's argument in a 1902 *Sierra Club Bulletin* highlighted the different opinions held by conservationists and preservationists in the early 1900s. The Progressive Era brought new importance to environmental issues in the United States. However, this period also brought debate between conservationists and preservationists about the proper use of the nation's resources.

California redwoods

Conservation and Progressivism

At first, few Americans were familiar with the work of ecologists. This changed, however, when the progressive movement called attention to environmental issues in the early 1900s. Progressives believed that the government should actively tackle economic and political issues. These issues included control of the country's natural resources.

Conservation. Most progressives believed that the nation's natural resources ought to be used, but used wisely. For example, most progressives were unhappy that large areas of forests were being cut down with no concern beyond short-term profits. Many progressives worried that such practices would destroy U.S. forests completely. They proposed an environmental policy of conserving natural resources for future generations, which became known as **conservation.**

Conservation became a national priority when Theodore Roosevelt became president in 1901. As a ranch owner in the Dakota Territory, Roosevelt had observed the need for conservation firsthand. He knew that unlimited use of ranges and forests, however profitable in the short run, could cause long-term environmental damage. He believed that people should always consider the effects of their actions on the environment.

> **"Conservation means development as much as it does protection. I recognize the right and duty of this generation to develop and use the natural resources of our land; but I do not recognize the right to waste them, or to rob, by wasteful use, the generations that come after us."**

THE GRANGER COLLECTION, NEW YORK

As head of the U.S. Forest Service, Gifford Pinchot called for practical forest management.

Roosevelt's chief lieutenant in the conservation effort was Gifford Pinchot, the head of the U.S. Forest Service. Pinchot sought to expand the federal government's

TEACH OBJECTIVE 1

LEVEL 1: Tell students to list the steps that progressive conservationists took to protect the environment. *(Lists might include creating national forests, supporting the Newlands Reclamation Act and the National Monuments Act, charging fees for grazing on public lands, and supporting international movements to establish conservation commissions.)* Then tell students to write a paragraph identifying which of these steps they believe has had the greatest impact in the United States and why. **Sheltered English**

LEVELS 2 AND 3: Tell students to list the steps progressive conservationists took to protect the environment. *(See the Level 1 lesson for the correct steps.)* Then organize the class into groups of four or five and tell them to imagine that they are progressive activists during the early 1900s. Have each group write a mission statement and a list of specific goals for promoting conservation at the national level. Call on one student from each group to read his or her group's list to the class. **Cooperative Learning**

▶ASSIGNMENT *Have students identify 5 of the 16 national monuments created by the National Monuments Act. Students may need to use the library for their research.*

control of the nation's forests. His goals included enlarging "forest reserves," later called national forests. Pinchot also used a system of fees to regulate the use of forest resources. Pinchot believed that forests were economically valuable resources and that conserving them was common sense. "Forestry is the art of using a forest without destroying it," he once declared.

Conservationist legislation. President Roosevelt and other progressives took additional steps to conserve resources. In 1902 Congress passed the Newlands Reclamation Act. This law promoted irrigation projects in the West's arid regions. The **National Monuments Act** of 1906 allowed the president to declare certain areas of federal lands to be protected historic or scientific monuments. Roosevelt used this act to create 16 national monuments, some of which later became national parks. He also issued numerous executive orders establishing dozens of wildlife refuges across the country. However, some landowners believed that Roosevelt's conservation programs went too far by disregarding their property rights.

Roosevelt also began charging fees for grazing on public lands to address the problem of overgrazing. This system discouraged the overgrazing that had already laid waste to much of the western range.

Conservation issues were not confined to the United States. A number of Canadian officials were strongly influenced by the view of the American progressives that natural resources should be used wisely. The Canadian Forestry Association was founded in 1900. This organization promoted government control of forest areas and called for fire prevention, additional forest reserves, and better education for foresters. In 1909, representatives from Canada, Mexico, Newfoundland, and the United States met to identify common environmental problems and to establish national conservation commissions. Only Canada was successful in establishing a permanent commission, however. In Great Britain a private environmental group called the Society for the Promotion of Nature Reserves was founded in 1912. The British government did not establish the Nature Conservancy, which acquires nature reserves, until after World War II.

✔ **READING CHECK:** What steps did progressive conservationists take to protect the environment?

Forest Conservation in Germany

Carl Schurz was born in Germany and lived there as a young man before immigrating to the United States in 1852. After serving as U.S. secretary of the interior from 1877 to 1881, Schurz became concerned that the United States was not properly managing and protecting its natural resources. In 1889 he spoke to the Forestry Association about the conservation practices used in his native Germany.

> **"Let me say to you that the laws of nature are the same everywhere. Whoever violates them anywhere must always pay the penalty. . . . But when I . . . asked Congress for rational [sensible] forestry legislation, you should have witnessed the sneers at the outlandish [ridiculous] notions of this 'foreigner' in the Interior Department; notions that, as was said, might do for a picayunish [small] German principality. . . . By the way, some of the gentlemen who sneered so greatly might learn some lessons from those picayunish German principalities, which would do them much good. I recently revisited my native land and saw again some of the forests I had known in my younger days—forests which in the meantime had yielded to their owners or to the government large revenues from the timber cut, but were now nevertheless as stately as they had been before, because the cutting had been done upon rational principles and the forests had been steadily improved by scientific cultivation. . . . Instead of sneering, our supercilious [arrogant] scoffers [doubters] would do better for themselves as well as for the country if they devoted their time a little more to studying and learning the valuable lessons with which the experience of other countries abound."**

HOLT RESEARCHER *Read More About It*

Free Find:
National Parks
After learning about national parks on the Holt Researcher CD–ROM, write a short essay describing the parks' locations and the benefits of maintaining the parks.

THEN AND NOW

Irrigation. In 1900, Americans used some 40 billion gallons of water per day, about half of which was used to irrigate crops. During the 1930s, when well pumps and electricity became widely available, farmers turned increasingly to groundwater—water located under the ground instead of on the surface—for irrigation. By 1990, Americans were using almost 400 billion gallons of water per day, of which 74 billion gallons was groundwater. The amount of water used daily for irrigation came to 137 billion gallons in 1990 and was expected to reach more than 150 billion gallons per day by 2000.

CRITICAL THINKING What problems might arise from increased water consumption?

ANSWER: Students might suggest that because fresh water is a limited natural resource, the water supply might dry up.

Multimedia Resources

American Music Selection 21, "Talkin' Dust Bowl"

TEACH OBJECTIVE 2

ALL LEVELS: To help students understand how preservationists' view of the environment differed from that of conservationists, copy the following graphic organizer on the chalkboard, omitting the italicized answers. Have each student complete the Venn diagram. When students have finished, tell them to write a paragraph stating which of these philosophies they more agree with and why. Call on volunteers to read their paragraphs to the class. Encourage students to discuss each other's responses. **Sheltered English**

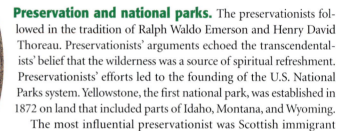

CONSERVATIONISTS	Both	PRESERVATIONISTS
• *believed natural resources ought to be used, but used wisely* • *sought to expand national control of forests and monuments* • *limited use of some resources and tried to minimize wastefulness*	• *outraged by wasteful use of resources* • *argued some land should be kept untouched* • *agreed that some development would have to be allowed in the West*	• *believed wild areas should be left untouched* • *found wilderness a source of spiritual refreshment* • *established U.S. system of national parks* • *applied principles of ecology to wildlife management* • *stressed importance of balanced environment*

PEOPLE IN HISTORY

John Muir. Born in Scotland in 1838, John Muir and his family immigrated to the United States in 1849. An avid reader and inventor—one of his inventions earned him admission to the University of Wisconsin—Muir was also fascinated by nature. He took long walks to study the environment, once walking from Indiana to Florida. Muir was also interested in geology. He determined that the Yosemite Valley in California had been formed by glaciers, a controversial theory that later proved to be correct. Muir later traveled to Alaska, where he discovered a glacier. He died in 1914.

CRITICAL THINKING Why might Muir have become an advocate of preservation?

ANSWER: Students might suggest that his travels led him to appreciate nature.

THAT'S INTERESTING!

Aldo Leopold, an advocate of wilderness preservation, played a key role in the 1924 creation of the nation's first designated wilderness area, the Gila Wilderness Area in New Mexico.

VISUAL RECORD ANSWER

Students might mention that Muir might have influenced Roosevelt.

Preservationists

President Theodore Roosevelt was not surprised that his efforts on behalf of conservation provoked opposition among landowners and people who profited from the old system. He was more surprised at the objections raised by those who believed that conservation did not go far enough. These people favored **preservation**—the practice of leaving wild areas untouched and thus unexploited. Conservationists, on the other hand, argued for the wise, managed use of resources.

INTERPRETING THE VISUAL RECORD

A wilderness trip. In 1903 President Theodore Roosevelt accompanied preservationist John Muir on a camping trip in the Yosemite region. ***How might this trip have influenced Roosevelt to set aside more public land?***

Preservation and national parks. The preservationists followed in the tradition of Ralph Waldo Emerson and Henry David Thoreau. Preservationists' arguments echoed the transcendentalists' belief that the wilderness was a source of spiritual refreshment. Preservationists' efforts led to the founding of the U.S. National Parks system. Yellowstone, the first national park, was established in 1872 on land that included parts of Idaho, Montana, and Wyoming.

The most influential preservationist was Scottish immigrant John Muir. After living in the Midwest for nearly 20 years, Muir decided to see more of the American landscape. He left Indiana in 1867 and walked all the way to the Gulf of Mexico. Muir eventually settled in California, where he worked to preserve the western wilderness. He led the effort to create the Yosemite National Park in California from 1880 to 1890. In 1892 Muir and other preservationists founded the Sierra Club, an organization dedicated to preserving the natural environment. Muir later influenced President Roosevelt to set aside some 148 million acres of additional forest reserves. In 1908 the government established the Muir Woods National Monument in northern California in his honor.

Muir wrote passionately about his deep appreciation for unspoiled nature. He published numerous articles and books, including *Our National Parks* and *The Yosemite.* In his writing Muir described preserving the environment as a way of preserving human well-being. At a time when industrialization was intensifying the pace of life, Muir called on Americans to catch their breath and enjoy the gifts of nature.

> **"Thousands of tired, nerve-shaken, over-civilized people are beginning to find out that going to the mountains is going home; that wildness is a necessity; and that mountain parks and reservations are useful not only as fountains of timber and irrigating rivers, but as fountains of life."**

BIOGRAPHY *Aldo Leopold*

Wildlife management. Another influential preservationist, Aldo Leopold, was one of the first to apply the principles of ecology to wildlife management. After graduating from Yale University in 1909, Leopold joined the Forest Service. He soon became the nation's leading expert on wild game. In 1933 Leopold joined the faculty of the University of Wisconsin. Two years later he and other preservationists founded the Wilderness Society.

TEACH OBJECTIVE 3

ALL LEVELS: Tell students to write a headline and topic sentence for a newspaper article reporting on how the Dust Bowl led to changes in U.S. environmental policy. *(Headlines and sentences might mention that New Deal legislation limited grazing on drought-sensitive grassland, called for the planting of rows of trees as windbreaks, and encouraged the responsible use of natural resources.)* To conclude, ask students what other programs following the Dust Bowl disaster encouraged responsible use of natural resources. *(Students might identify the Civilian Conservation Corps, the Tennessee Valley Authority, and the Grand Coulee Dam.)* **Sheltered English**

Teacher to Teacher

Stephen Marlowe of Gastonia, North Carolina, suggested the following activity: Have students research the history of an environmental project completed between 1890 and 1939. Students should focus on a local or state project if possible and identify why the project was started and who implemented it. Students should present their research in the form of a visitors' brochure.

Leopold began his career as a firm believer in game management. For instance, he supported killing wolves to protect deer populations. He eventually changed his views on wildlife conservation, however. After a research trip to Germany, Leopold became a preservationist. Many conservationists considered German practices to be a model of sound forest management. In Germany both forests and deer herds had been carefully managed since the 1400s. German forestry officials had come to recognize the importance of ecological principles in forest management. In 1914 they started programs to restore mixed forests and wildlife. At the same time, however, German foresters continued to manage the forest for high timber yields and to use supplemental feeding to support large deer herds.

The results of those practices disturbed Leopold. He argued that the Germans' techniques interfered with natural forces and drove out many native species of plants and animals. Leopold wrote about the importance of a balanced environment.

> **"We Americans, in most states at least, have not yet experienced a bearless, wolfless, eagleless, catless woods. We yearn for more deer and more pines, and we shall probably get them. But do we realize that to get them, as the Germans have, at the expense of their wild environment and their wild enemies, is to get very little indeed?"**

Preservationists and conservationists did agree that some land should be left untouched. Many preservationists also conceded that some development would have to be allowed in the West.

✓ **READING CHECK:** How did preservationists' view of the environment differ from that of conservationists?

INTERPRETING THE VISUAL RECORD

A mighty forest. Early visitors to the redwood forests of the West Coast were amazed by the scale and beauty of the trees. ***Did the painter provide a sense of the size of the trees?***

The Dust Bowl Era

From the 1800s through the early 1900s most environmental debates focused on the West. By the 1930s, however, many Americans were beginning to understand that the abuse of natural resources resulted in problems for the entire nation.

By the early 1900s the center of American agriculture had shifted to the Great Plains. Yet, some observers questioned whether the Plains were really suited to large-scale farming. They noted that erosion increased and that creeks grew muddy as more and more acres were plowed. Terrible dust storms followed weeks of little rain.

Much of the grass that had once covered the Great Plains—and held the topsoil in place—was gone. What had not been plowed under to plant crops had been destroyed by overgrazing. Mourning the loss, one Texas sheepherder declared that grass "saves us all. . . . Grass is what holds the earth together." As farming and herding increased, the loss of grass and topsoil created a host of environmental problems on the Plains. The 1934 *Yearbook of Agriculture* listed the damage: 100 million acres of cropland had lost most or all of their topsoil. An additional 125 million

GEOGRAPHIC DIVERSITY

Dust Storms. The dust storms on the Great Plains affected the entire nation. In 1934 a storm gathered some 350 million tons of dirt from Montana and Wyoming and swept it eastward, dropping some 12 million tons on Chicago. Ships 300 miles at sea in the Atlantic Ocean had dust on their decks from that storm. However, the people on the southern plains experienced the greatest hardship. For example, residents of Amarillo, Texas, experienced total blackouts seven times during the winter of 1937 when huge dust storms obscured the sun, sometimes for an entire day.

CRITICAL THINKING What problems might dust storms cause?

ANSWER: Students might mention crop failures, difficulty in traveling, and health problems associated with breathing dust.

VISUAL RECORD ANSWER

Students might suggest that the horse at the bottom of the trees provides a sense of scale.

VISUAL RECORD ANSWER

(for p. 912)

Students might suggest that it would have severely limited agricultural production.

REVIEW

Have students complete the **Section 2 Review** on p. 912.

ASSESS

Have students complete **Daily Quiz 31.2**. As **Alternative Assessment**, you may want to use the conservation and preservation graphic organizer or the Dust Bowl headlines activity in this section's lessons.

RETEACH

Have students complete **Main Idea Activity for Reteaching and Sheltered English 31.2**. Then organize students into groups of four and assign each group member one of the four section objectives. Tell students to write all the information important to their assigned objective on an index card. Have students exchange index cards within their groups and copy the information on each others' cards onto cards of their own. After exchanging cards two more times, each student should have four complete cards to study.
Sheltered English, Cooperative Learning

EXTEND

Have students conduct research on current or recent events that indicate a continuing controversy between conservationists and preservationists. Tell students to present a brief oral report summarizing their findings and expressing an opinion on the subject. **Block Scheduling**

SECTION 2 REVIEW ANSWERS

Define and Identify
For significance, see the following pages:

- conservation, p. 908
- National Monuments Act, p. 909
- preservation, p. 910
- John Muir, p. 910
- Aldo Leopold, p. 910

1. conservation—tried to promote wise use of resources, preservation—tried to preserve natural resources; resulting changes—more government involvement in environmental issues, federally sponsored conservation programs, some areas preserved

2. both agreed that some land should be left untouched; preservationists—wanted to prohibit all use of wilderness areas; conservationists—believed the environment should be used wisely rather than exploited

3. passed legislation to limit grazing, encouraged development of windbreaks, developed flood-control projects, and planted trees

4. showed him that predators play an important role in game management and wilderness development and motivated him to support preservation over conservation

5. Removing grass and overgrazing livestock caused erosion. The combination of drought and the loss of topsoil caused dust storms and prevented further agricultural use of the land.

INTERPRETING THE VISUAL RECORD

The Dust Bowl. A huge dust storm approaches Springfield, Colorado, in 1937. The sky turned black for half an hour. ***What effect do you think this environmental disaster might have had on agricultural production in the late 1930s?***

acres were rapidly losing topsoil. These statistics were driven home by the huge dust storms that plagued the Great Plains. Many people fled the Dust Bowl during the 1930s. Some left behind houses buried to the windowsills in drifts of grit.

As Congress considered what to do, a monstrous storm carried dust from the Great Plains all the way to Washington, D.C. While testifying before a Senate committee, the head of the Soil Conservation Service pointed out the window at the wind-borne soil. He commented, "There, gentlemen, goes part of Oklahoma now."

Unable to ignore the environmental catastrophe on the Great Plains, Congress passed legislation to encourage soil conservation. The legislation formed part of President Franklin D. Roosevelt's New Deal. It included measures to limit grazing on drought-sensitive grasslands and to plant rows of trees as windbreaks.

Other New Deal programs encouraged the responsible use of natural resources. The Civilian Conservation Corps (CCC), for example, sent thousands of young men into the national forests. CCC workers attempted to prevent fires and planted tree seedlings. The Tennessee Valley Authority (TVA) combined flood control with electrification projects. The Grand Coulee Dam on the Columbia River provided irrigation as well as hydroelectric power. These New Deal programs emphasized the wise use of resources, as Theodore Roosevelt's programs had. The New Deal programs also reflected a growing understanding of the national significance of environmental problems.

✔ **READING CHECK:** How did the Dust Bowl lead to changes in U.S. environmental policy?

SECTION  REVIEW

Define and explain the significance of the following terms:
conservation
National Monuments Act
preservation

Identify and explain the significance of the following individuals:
John Muir
Aldo Leopold

1. **Using Graphic Organizers** Copy the flowchart below. Use it to explain how environmental movements led to changes in environmental policy during the Progressive Era.

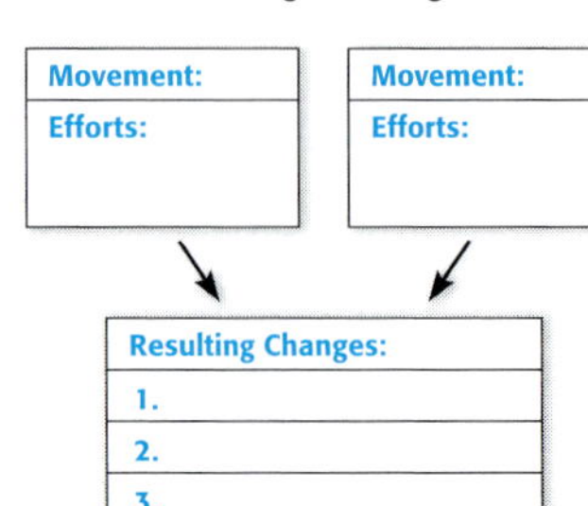

2. **Comparing and Contrasting** How did preservationists and conservationists agree and differ in their views on the environment?
3. **Analyzing** How did the government respond to the problems of the Dust Bowl?
4. **Identifying Cause and Effect** How did Aldo Leopold's trip to Germany influence his views on wildlife conservation?

Critical Thinking

5. How did agricultural techniques contribute to the Dust Bowl disaster?
Consider:
   - the effects of removing grass in order to plant crops
   - the effects of grazing livestock
   - how loss of topsoil affected the environment

SECTION 3

After completing Section 3, students should be able to:

OBJECTIVE 1 *Explain why many people considered nuclear-weapons tests to be dangerous.*

OBJECTIVE 2 *Discuss how the threat of nuclear weapons encouraged international cooperation.*

OBJECTIVE 3 *Describe how activists in Europe and the United States used political measures to draw attention to environmental problems.*

LET'S GET STARTED!

To begin the class, tell students to preview Section 3 and write down five questions they have about the upcoming section. Then tell students to keep these questions in mind as they learn about global environmentalism from the 1940s to the 1970s in Section 3.

SECTION 3 Environmentalism Goes Global

OBJECTIVES

Read to understand:

1. why many people considered nuclear-weapons tests to be dangerous
2. how the threat of nuclear weapons encouraged international cooperation
3. how activists in Europe and the United States used political measures to draw attention to environmental problems

KEY TERMS

nuclear fallout
food chain
unilateral disarmament
Antarctic Treaty
Nuclear Nonproliferation Treaty
Green parties

KEY PEOPLE

Petra Kelly
Barry Commoner

EYEWITNESSES TO History

"'Security policy' has led us into the most dire [terrible] insecurity the world has ever faced. The politics of nuclear confrontation imposes a brand of insanity upon us which runs, 'In order to defend freedom, we must be prepared to destroy life itself.' . . . Every day the United States and the Soviet Union add new weapons of mass destruction to arsenals which already have the equivalent of three tons of TNT in store for every man, woman, and child in the world."

—Petra Kelly

Petra Kelly

German environmentalist Petra Kelly described the environmental dangers of nuclear weapons developed during the Cold War. In the decades after World War II, nuclear technology posed new threats to the global environment. Increased awareness of these threats sparked worldwide efforts to change public policy.

The Nuclear Age

Ecological problems during the 1930s revealed to Americans the importance of caring for their environment. Events during and following World War II, however, quickly proved that environmental issues crossed political borders.

Nuclear testing. For almost two decades after 1945, countries with nuclear weapons tested their bombs in aboveground explosions. The United States and the Soviet Union were particularly active in nuclear testing. These tests created **nuclear fallout**, or airborne radioactive particles, which the wind blew thousands of miles. Eventually, scientific instruments detected radioactivity in nearly every area of the planet.

No one knew exactly how nuclear fallout would affect humans. However, the radiation sickness suffered by survivors of the Hiroshima and Nagasaki bombings frightened people around the world. In addition, radiation began to appear in the **food chain**. This is a sequence in which each animal feeds on the plant or animal below it in the chain. Radioactive particles in the atmosphere were often deposited in the soil. Once in the ground, the particles were absorbed by crops. The radioactive particles then accumulated in the bodies of people who ate contaminated foods.

Scientists debated the effects of fallout. Some pointed out that humans have always been exposed to naturally occurring radiation. Others responded that humans had never before faced such high levels of exposure. Some scientists predicted a rise in the occurrence of cancer, particularly in children.

✔ **READING CHECK:** Why did many people consider nuclear-weapons tests to be dangerous?

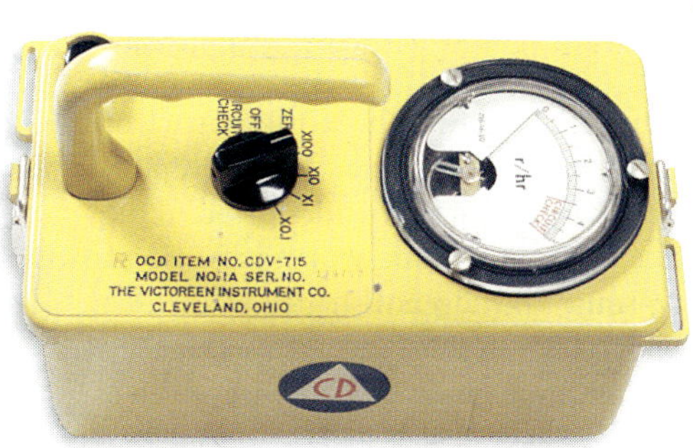

Geiger counters such as this 1962 model were used to measure radiation levels in the environment.

SECTION 3 RESOURCES

PRINT
- Guided Reading Strategy 31.3
- Section 3 Review, p. 916
- Daily Quiz 31.3

MULTIMEDIA
- One-Stop Planner, Lesson 31.3
- Holt Researcher: American History CD–ROM

SHELTERED ENGLISH
- Main Idea Activity for Reteaching and Sheltered English 31.3

✔ **READING TO UNDERSTAND**

To help students master the section objectives, have them answer the **READING CHECKS** and complete **Guided Reading Strategy 31.3** as they read the section.

TEACH OBJECTIVE 1

ALL LEVELS: Tell students to create a comic strip that explains why many people considered nuclear-weapons tests to be dangerous. *(Comic strips should show a nuclear test, the spread of radioactive particles, and the effects of radioactivity on plants, animals, and people.)* Display students' completed comic strips around the classroom. **Sheltered English**

TEACH OBJECTIVE 2

ALL LEVELS: Organize students into groups of five or six. Tell students to imagine that it is 1970. Have each group prepare and present a short television news report about how the threat of nuclear weapons has encouraged international cooperation. Reports should focus on international events and agreements of the 1960s. *(Students should mention the creation of SANE and the CND as well as agreements to limit the development and use of atomic weapons. These agreements included the Antarctic Treaty and the Nuclear Nonproliferation Treaty.)* Tell students to assign roles, such as news anchor, reporter, interviewee, and camera person, to group members. Provide a video camera and props if possible. Students may wish to include their reports in their portfolios.
Sheltered English, Cooperative Learning

IN THE NEWS

Nuclear Testing. In 1999 the U.S. Senate refused to ratify the Comprehensive Test Ban Treaty, which called for a ban on the testing of nuclear devices. Although 153 nations had signed the treaty and President Bill Clinton supported it, many senators argued that a test ban would compromise U.S. national security. They maintained that the treaty did not contain adequate provisions to prevent nations from violating its terms. International reaction to the Senate's decision was largely negative. Many observers feared that the U.S. refusal to ratify the treaty would lead other nations, such as China and Russia, to reject it.

ACTIVITY Tell students to imagine that they are U.S. senators who voted on the Comprehensive Test Ban Treaty. Have them write letters explaining how they voted to their constituents.

VISUAL RECORD ANSWER

Students might answer that her sign suggests that bomb shelters could not protect against nuclear war or radioactive fallout.

INTERPRETING THE VISUAL RECORD

Nuclear protest. Antinuclear activist Susan Ginzberg brought her infant son to a 1961 protest. ***What is the significance of the message on Ginzberg's sign?***

International reactions. The threat of nuclear fallout sparked an international outcry against nuclear testing. People quickly realized that ending nuclear testing would require international cooperation. Activists in the United States formed the National Committee for a Sane Nuclear Policy (SANE) in 1957. SANE called for an end to testing and to the nuclear arms race. In Britain the Campaign for Nuclear Disarmament (CND) supported **unilateral disarmament**, or a one-sided ban on such weapons. The CND wanted Britain to completely eliminate its nuclear weapons despite their existence in the United States and the Soviet Union.

Both the United States and the Soviet Union worked toward eliminating aboveground testing. As President John F. Kennedy pointed out in a speech in 1963, "We all inhabit this planet. We all breathe the same air." Later that year, Britain, the Soviet Union, and the United States agreed to the Limited Nuclear Test Ban Treaty. The discovery of new ways to conduct underground nuclear-weapons tests greatly contributed to the success of the treaty. Underground testing satisfied those who believed that continued testing was necessary to protect national security, as well as those who wanted to end nuclear fallout.

International leaders also signed agreements to limit the development and use of atomic weapons. The **Antarctic Treaty** of 1959 established Antarctica as a nuclear-free zone. In 1968 Britain, the Soviet Union, the United States, and 59 other nations signed the **Nuclear Nonproliferation Treaty**. This agreement attempted to keep nuclear weapons technology from spreading to more countries. By 1997 more than 180 nations had ratified the treaty. Despite these agreements, however, 20 countries were believed to be capable of building nuclear weapons by the end of the 1990s.

✔ **READING CHECK:** How did the threat of nuclear weapons encourage international cooperation?

The Use of Pesticides

Nuclear weapons and fallout were not the only new threats to the environment. Pesticide use increased dramatically following the development of new chemicals during World War II. The most popular of the new chemicals was DDT. This pesticide first proved its value in 1944 in Naples, Italy. DDT prevented an epidemic of typhus by killing the lice that spread the disease.

DDT and other chemicals were soon used widely by farmers to protect their crops from harmful insects and weeds. At first these products led to tremendous gains for agriculture. However, over time it was discovered that some insects developed a resistance to the new pesticides. This meant that the application of greater doses was necessary to control pests.

By the 1960s some scientists had begun to worry about the impact of increased pesticide use on the environment. Rachel Carson's *Silent Spring*, published in 1962, alerted many people to the dangers that pesticides posed to the environment. Carson warned that pesticides threatened more than just insects. "These insecticides are not selective poisons. They do not single out the one species of which we desire to be rid," she wrote. "Each of them is used for the simple reason that it is a deadly poison. It therefore poisons all life with which it comes in contact."

Read More About It

Free Find:
Rachel Carson
After reading about Rachel Carson on the **Holt Researcher** CD–ROM, write a short essay discussing the impact of her book *Silent Spring* and what experiences led her to write the book.

TEACH OBJECTIVE 3

ALL LEVELS: To help students understand how activists in Europe and the United States used political measures to draw attention to environmental problems, copy the following graphic organizer on the chalkboard, omitting the italicized answers. Have each student complete it. **Sheltered English**

▶ASSIGNMENT *Tell students to write an article entitled Germany's Green Party for a newsletter for an American environmental action group. Tell students to use the graphic organizer to help them write a few paragraphs about the history and successes of Germany's Die Grünen Party.*

ENVIRONMENTAL ACTIVISM

Europe
- *environmental issues linked to politics by Green parties*
- *Greens organized protests.*
- *Greens reminded individuals of their responsibility to change environmental policy.*

United States
- *environmental issues sometimes politicized by major parties*
- *Environmental protests lead to new legislation.*
- *New environmental legislation included Clean Air Act, Federal Water Pollution Control Act, Safe Drinking Water Act, and Endangered Species Act.*

growing realization that environmental problems are global and interrelated

Politics and the Environment

Concerns about pesticides and nuclear fallout prompted a new kind of political activism. People began to pressure governments around the world to take the environment into account when making policy decisions.

Green parties. In the United States, environmental issues became political issues only when they were adopted by a major party. In other nations, **Green parties** established a more direct link between these issues and politics. Green parties were so named because their platforms emphasize ecological concerns. Although the parties remain small, the Greens have successfully drawn attention to environmental issues in Britain, France, Germany, and other Western European countries.

The German Green Party, Die Grünen, has been one of Europe's most successful. Die Grünen developed out of a series of antinuclear protest movements in the 1950s. In the 1960s its activities centered around student protests against U.S. involvement in Vietnam. During the 1970s a new wave of protests expressed opposition to nuclear power. Thousands of people from France, Germany, and Switzerland protested against a planned nuclear power station at Wyhl, in southern Germany.

As these protesters began to address other environmental issues in the late 1970s, they came together to form Die Grünen. The new party based its platform on the "recognition that in a limited world growth cannot be unlimited." Party members demanded "a policy of active partnership with nature and with the human race." Ecology, explained party activist Manon Maren-Grisebach, would provide the "scientific . . . basis for action." She argued that ecology is important to human existence.

> **"But ecology is demanding. At the risk of our own destruction, we cannot ignore its insights; we are not free to act at will because we are forced to obey laws which reach beyond our [selves] and deal with our very existence."**

The party also reminded individuals of their responsibility to change environmental policy. In 1982 Petra Kelly, who was then the head of Die Grünen, asserted that "change . . . has to come from the bottom, not the top." Germany's Green Party has continued to grow and succeed in the 1990s. In 1998 it won almost 7 percent of the vote in national elections. For the first time the Greens became part of the governing coalition, joining Gerhard Schroeder's Social Democrats.

Teen Environmentalists Make a Difference

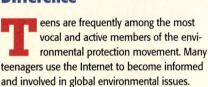

Teens are frequently among the most vocal and active members of the environmental protection movement. Many teenagers use the Internet to become informed and involved in global environmental issues.

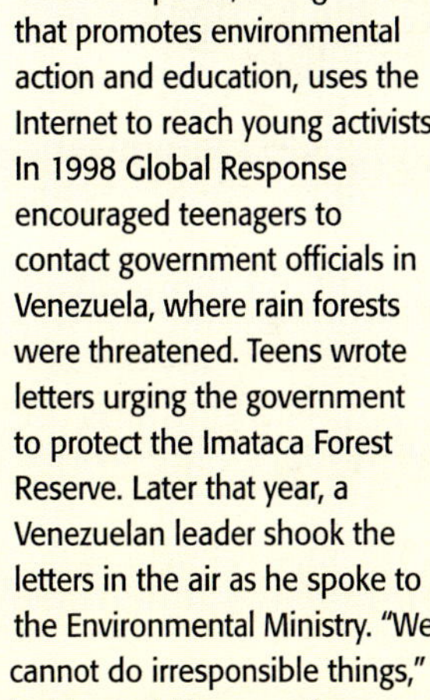
Volunteers help clean a Texas beach.

Global Response, an organization that promotes environmental action and education, uses the Internet to reach young activists. In 1998 Global Response encouraged teenagers to contact government officials in Venezuela, where rain forests were threatened. Teens wrote letters urging the government to protect the Imataca Forest Reserve. Later that year, a Venezuelan leader shook the letters in the air as he spoke to the Environmental Ministry. "We cannot do irresponsible things," he shouted, "because the eyes of the world are watching us. . . . Here I have . . . letters from all over the world. . . . *The letters from children are the ones that impress me the most.*"

Other teens have been inspired to bring knowledge about global environmental problems to their local communities. Xiomara Cornejo was president of an environmental club at her high school in California. She decided to get her club involved in an effort to prevent logging on Maya Indian lands in Belize. Club members made posters and hung them around the school. They visited classrooms to speak about the problems and organized a drive for signatures. They gathered more than 3,680 signatures to protest logging on Maya lands. In response to protests, the government of Belize promised to consider the concerns of the Maya people.

PEOPLE IN HISTORY

Petra Kelly. Petra Kelly was born in West Germany in 1947 but grew up in the United States. Like many activists of her generation, Kelly protested against the Vietnam War. She later returned to Germany and in 1980 helped establish the German Green Party. Kelly, who served in the German parliament from 1983 to 1990, argued that Greens had a responsibility to draw public attention to social and ecological issues. She also maintained that Greens should not enter into compromises with other parties in order to achieve power. Conflicts within the German Green Party made Kelly increasingly dissatisfied. She had largely abandoned the party by 1990.

CRITICAL THINKING Should parties compromise on issues in order to gain power? Explain your answer.

ANSWER: Answers will vary. Students might suggest that some compromise is necessary in democratic governments.

REVIEW

Have students complete the **Section 3 Review** on p. 916.

ASSESS

Have students complete **Daily Quiz 31.3**. As **Alternative Assessment**, you may want to use the comic strip activity or the television news special report in this section's lessons.

RETEACH

Have students complete **Main Idea Activity for Reteaching and Sheltered English 31.3**. Then organize students into triads and assign a subsection to each group member. Tell them to prepare short lessons that cover the information contained in their assigned subsections. Have students take turns presenting their lessons to their groups, and tell them to take notes on each other's lessons. **Sheltered English, Cooperative Learning**

EXTEND

Organize students into triads and have them research the impact of the fear of nuclear war on Americans' daily lives during the 1950s and 1960s. Tell them to use this information to create a three-panel visual display. Images might include instructional material to educate children on how to react to a nuclear attack, advertisements for bomb shelters, pictures of protesters, examples of antinuclear slogans or bumper stickers, and so on. **Block Scheduling, Cooperative Learning**

VISUAL RECORD ANSWER

Students might respond that the test allows for detection of pollutants.

SECTION 3 REVIEW ANSWERS

Define and Identify

For significance, see the following pages:

- nuclear fallout, p. 913
- food chain, p. 913
- unilateral disarmament, p. 914
- Antarctic Treaty, p. 914
- Nuclear Nonproliferation Treaty, p. 914
- Green parties, p. 915
- Petra Kelly, p. 915
- Barry Commoner, p. 916

1. Nuclear-weapons tests released radioactive fallout into the atmosphere. The resulting environmental concerns spurred people to call for unilateral disarmament and to support arms limitations agreements.

2. Activists formed SANE and the CND. International leaders signed treaties to limit the development and use of nuclear weapons, including the Antarctic Treaty and the Nuclear Nonproliferation Treaty.

3. They relied on protests and strikes and formed Green parties.

4. Answers will vary but should reflect an understanding of Green parties and environmental politics in the United States.

5. Answers will vary but should indicate an understanding of unilateral disarmament.

INTERPRETING THE VISUAL RECORD

Pollution. Within the past few decades efforts have been made to reduce pollutants in water supplies in the United States. ***How do you think activities such as this test at the National Water Quality Laboratory might help to prevent contaminated water?***

Environmental activism in the United States. The idea of an organized Green party has failed to win much support in the United States. However, environmental protests did produce new legislation. In 1970 Congress passed the Clean Air Act, which was designed to reduce air pollution. This included the smog—air polluted by chemical fumes, car exhaust, and smoke—plaguing most large cities. The Federal Water Pollution Control Act of 1972 addressed the problem of contaminated water. The Safe Drinking Water Act of 1974 was also aimed at preventing the contamination of water supplies. The Endangered Species Act of 1973 required the government to take action to safeguard animal species threatened with extinction.

The legislation of the early 1970s applied only to the United States. However, it reflected a growing realization that environmental problems were interrelated. More and more people came to appreciate the four laws of ecology that environmentalist Barry Commoner proposed in his 1971 book, *The Closing Circle.*

> "Everything is connected to everything else.
> Everything must go somewhere.
> Nature knows best.
> There is no such thing as a free lunch."

READING CHECK: How did activists in Europe and the United States use political measures to draw attention to environmental problems?

SECTION 3 REVIEW

Define and explain the significance of the following terms:
nuclear fallout
food chain
unilateral disarmament
Antarctic Treaty
Nuclear Nonproliferation Treaty
Green parties

Identify and explain the significance of the following individuals:
Petra Kelly
Barry Commoner

1. **Using Graphic Organizers** Copy the web below. Use it to explain the effect of nuclear-weapons tests on the environment and people's responses to these tests.

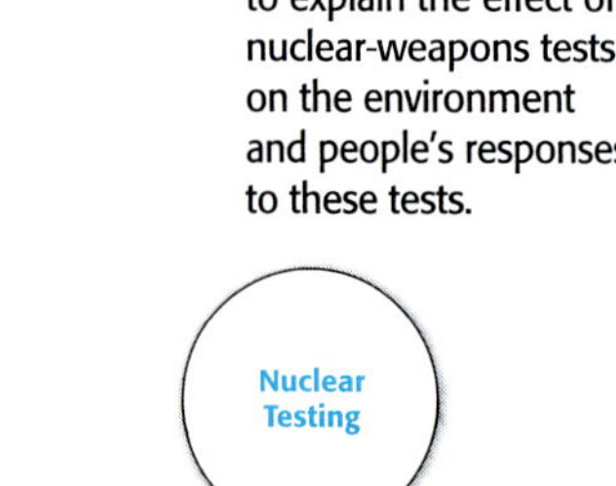

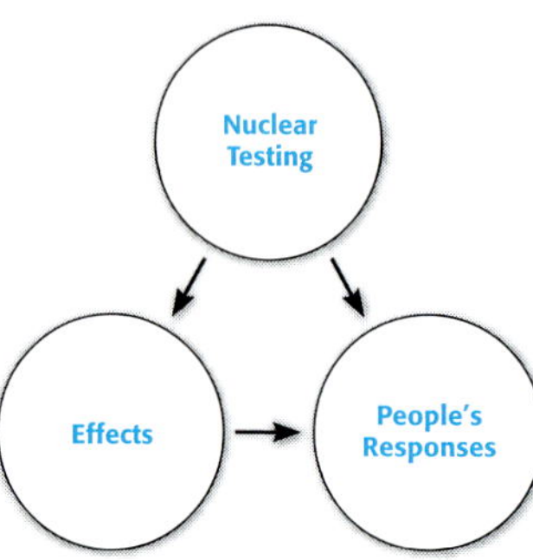

2. **Evaluating** What international efforts were made to limit the threat of nuclear war?
3. **Analyzing** What methods did activists in Europe use to call attention to environmental problems?
4. **Hypothesizing** How might voters respond to the development of a Green party in the United States?

Critical Thinking

5. Imagine that you are a British member of the Campaign for Nuclear Disarmament and must make an argument for or against the adoption of a policy of unilateral disarmament. What reasons would you give to support your argument?
   Consider:
   - what the possibility of nuclear war is
   - what effect fallout from testing nuclear weapons might have
   - the impact of the nuclear arms race between the United States and the Soviet Union

After completing Section 4, students should be able to:

OBJECTIVE 1 *Identify recent global environmental problems nations have faced.*

OBJECTIVE 2 *Discuss how deforestation and biodiversity are related.*

OBJECTIVE 3 *Explain concerns that have arisen over population growth.*

OBJECTIVE 4 *Describe how governments and environmentalists have tried to solve current environmental problems.*

LET'S GET STARTED!

Write the following environmental issues on the chalkboard: *nuclear-weapons proliferation, global warming, pollution of air and water, deforestation, endangered species, depletion of nonrenewable natural resources,* and *overpopulation.* Tell students to rank these issues in order of importance and to write a paragraph justifying their rankings. Then tell students that in Section 4 they will learn about efforts to solve global environmental problems from the 1970s to the present.

A Small Planet

OBJECTIVES

Read to understand:

1. what recent global environmental problems nations have faced
2. how deforestation and biodiversity are related
3. what concerns have arisen over population growth
4. how governments and environmentalists have tried to solve current environmental problems

KEY TERMS

global warming
ozone layer
ultraviolet solar radiation
chlorofluorocarbons
acid rain
biodiversity
Convention on Biological Diversity

KEY PEOPLE

Chico Mendes

KEY PLACES

Antarctica
Chernobyl

"If the present growth trends in world population, industrialization, pollution, food production, and resource depletion continue unchanged, the limits to growth on this planet will be reached sometime within the next one hundred years. The most probable result will be a rather sudden and uncontrollable decline in both population and industrial capacity."

—The Club of Rome

In 1972 an international group of scientists and business leaders known as The Club of Rome published a report called *The Limits to Growth.* This report projected trends in such critical areas as population growth, food production, and pollution. The report predicted a global crisis if current trends in these areas continued. Many business and political leaders, particularly in the United States, criticized The Club of Rome for being too pessimistic.

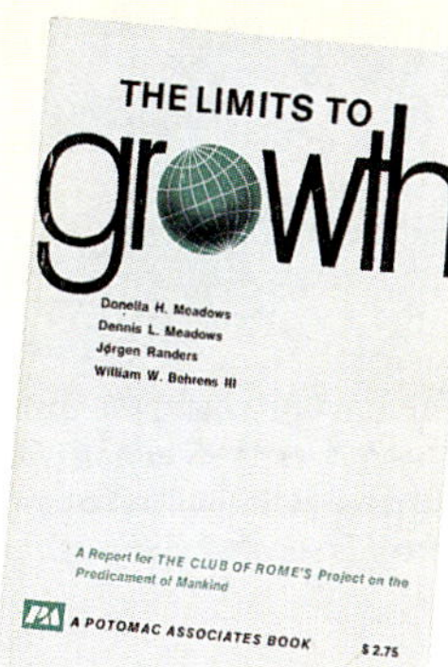

The Limits to Growth

Environmental Pollution

Pollution is one typical result of industrial growth around the world. Many environmentalists and some scientists have connected this pollution to the process of **global warming**—the increase in the temperature of Earth's atmosphere.

The global warming debate. Recently, scientists have measured an increase in the global temperature since preindustrial times. Many scientists argue that the burning of fossil fuels and the destruction of forests have polluted the atmosphere with excess levels of carbon dioxide and other gases. These so-called greenhouse gases trap the solar radiation that reaches Earth's surface, thereby increasing the temperature. This phenomenon is called the greenhouse effect. Some researchers fear that over time the greenhouse effect could raise Earth's temperature enough to kill off agricultural crops in some regions. The greenhouse effect could also cause the melting of the polar ice caps, raising ocean levels and flooding coastal areas.

However, many scientists disagree about the potential threat of global warming. Some argue that we know too little about how Earth's ecosystems work to predict how fast or high temperatures will rise due to atmospheric pollution. Others claim that the world is heating up as part of a natural pattern of rising and falling temperatures that has occurred throughout Earth's history.

In spite of the scientific debate, political leaders have taken actions to reduce the risks of global warming. In December 1997 the United States and 37 other countries signed an agreement to reduce the production of greenhouse gases by 2012. This has sparked debate in the United States, where some legislators argue that the regulations are unfairly limiting the freedom of business and industry.

SECTION 4 RESOURCES

PRINT

- Guided Reading Strategy 31.4
- Geography Activity 31: Great Lakes Pollution
- Section 4 Review, p. 923
- Daily Quiz 31.4

MULTIMEDIA

- One-Stop Planner, Lesson 31.4
- Holt Researcher: American History CD–ROM
- HRW Web site

SHELTERED ENGLISH

- Main Idea Activity for Reteaching and Sheltered English 31.4

✔ READING TO UNDERSTAND

To help students master the section objectives, have them answer the **READING CHECKS** and complete **Guided Reading Strategy 31.4** as they read the section.

TEACH OBJECTIVE 1

LEVEL 1: Pair students and have each pair make a list of recent global environmental problems nations have faced. *(Students might mention global warming, thinning of the ozone layer, acid rain, and environmental disasters.)* Have one student from each pair read his or her list to the class. **Sheltered English, Cooperative Learning**

LEVEL 2: Organize students into groups and assign each group one of the following environmental problems: global warming, thinning of the ozone layer, acid rain, or environmental disasters. Have each group prepare and present a multimedia presentation about its topic. Tell students to include information about what it is and why it presents a problem. Encourage audience members to ask questions and to take notes on each other's presentations. **Cooperative Learning**

GLOBAL RELATIONS

Deforestation. In 1999 the United Nations began working with North Korea to solve problems caused by deforestation. North Koreans use wood for cooking and heating and sell lumber to China. The loss of the forests has led to increased erosion and flooding. In 1995 North Korea suffered major floods that wiped out many crops. Between 2 and 3 million people died in the resulting famine, which lasted from 1995 to 1998. In response, the North Korean government accepted assistance from the UN Development Programme in order to plant millions of trees and other vegetation.

CRITICAL THINKING What other measures might North Korea undertake to protect its environment?

ANSWER: Students might suggest that North Korea should develop and use alternate fuel sources.

THAT'S INTERESTING!

Despite growing concerns over global warming, the emission of greenhouse gases in the United States increased by some 10 percent between 1990 and 1997.

VISUAL RECORD ANSWER

Students might answer that acid rain appears to be killing the trees.

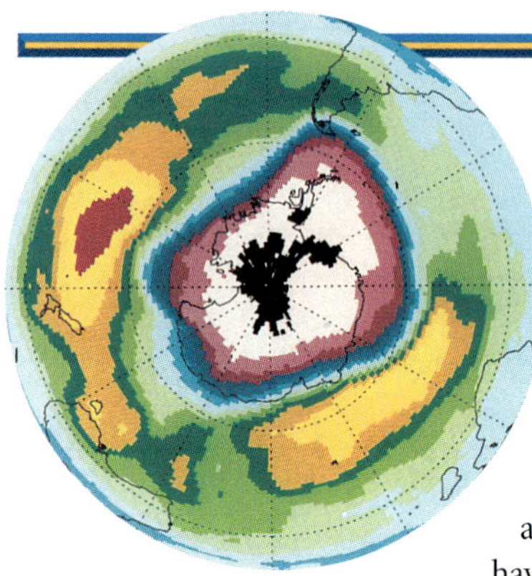

This image shows the ozone layer over the Southern Hemisphere in 1994. The ozone hole is located in the center.

The ozone layer and acid rain. Another environmental danger that some scientists point to is the thinning of the **ozone layer**. This thin layer of ozone molecules, some 10 to 30 miles above Earth's surface, protects the planet from **ultraviolet solar radiation**, or UV rays. Ultraviolet solar radiation can cause skin cancer, damage marine life, and harm crops. To date, the greatest area of ozone thinning has been above Antarctica. Much of the damage to the ozone layer has been caused by chemicals called **chlorofluorocarbons** (CFCs). CFCs are combinations of carbon, chlorine, and fluorine. They are used mainly in the manufacture of aerosol sprays, air-conditioner and refrigerator coolants, and plastics. Industrialized nations have emitted CFCs into the atmosphere for decades.

A third hazard of atmospheric pollution is **acid rain**. Factories and automobiles emit sulfur dioxide and nitrogen oxide into the atmosphere. These pollutants combine with the moisture in the atmosphere and later fall as acid rain. The rain often falls far from the original source of pollution. Acid rain gradually kills trees and makes lakes unsafe for fish. In the 1980s and the 1990s many regions suffered the effects of acid rain. Southern China, the Appalachian Mountains in eastern North America, lakes in northern Canada, and mountains in Central Europe were all damaged by acid rain.

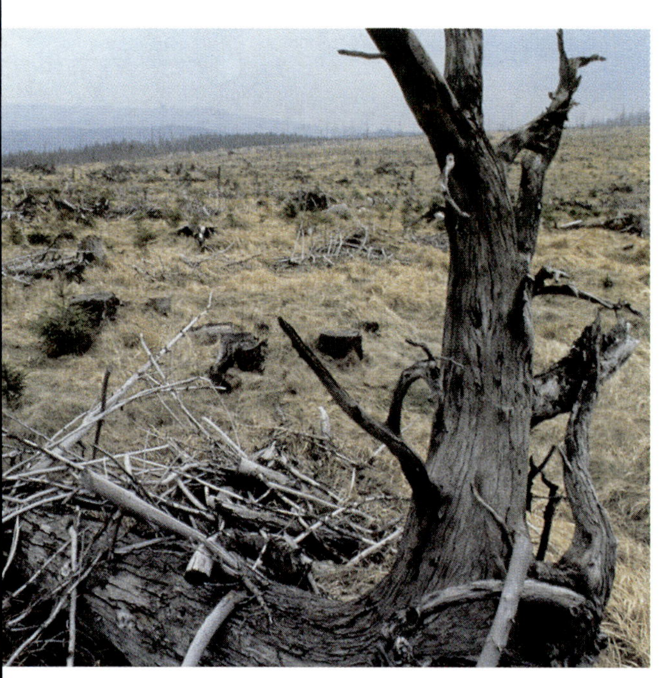

INTERPRETING THE VISUAL RECORD

Acid rain. This European park has received large amounts of acid rain. ***What effect does the acid rain appear to have had on the park's trees?***

Acid rain has become a source of conflict between the United States and Canada. Industrial smoke from factories in Michigan is believed to contribute to acid rain in Canada. When the United States weakened its environmental standards during the 1980s, Canadians protested that this action unfairly affected their environment. As a result, Canada has become one of the leaders in trying to improve global awareness about acid rain.

Environmental disasters. Industrial accidents are another source of global pollution. Although such accidents are onetime events, major disasters can cause long-term damage to the environment. For example, oil spills kill countless fish and waterfowl and cost millions of dollars to clean up. The 1989 *Exxon Valdez* oil spill along the coast of Alaska was one of the worst in recent U.S. history. Such environmental disasters have encouraged activists and politicians to call for stricter regulations on the shipping of oil.

Nuclear accidents pose another serious threat to the environment. In 1986 a failure occurred at the Chernobyl nuclear power plant near Kiev, Ukraine. The resulting accident sent a cloud of radioactivity drifting across Europe and made the surrounding land unsafe for human and animal life. The Chernobyl disaster pumped approximately 30 to 40 times more radioactive materials into the environment than the bombs that were dropped on Hiroshima and Nagasaki during World War II. While Chernobyl led many nations to evaluate their safety procedures

LEVEL 3: To help students understand recent global environmental problems nations have faced, have them write a letter to a public official such as a state representative or senator. Letters should urge the official to support funding for continued research into environmental problems. Tell students to explain in their letters why such research is necessary. Encourage students to mail their letters to the official(s) they have chosen. Students may wish to include copies of their letters in their portfolios.

TEACH OBJECTIVE 2

LEVEL 1: In a classroom discussion, ask students to define deforestation and biodiversity. *(Students should define deforestation as the destruction of forests and biodiversity as the wide variety of Earth's animal and plant species.)* Then pair students. Have each pair create storyboards for a television public service announcement to educate people about how deforestation and biodiversity are related. Explain to students that storyboards map out the action and the dialogue of a film, and that they resemble a comic book. Display students' completed storyboards around the classroom.
Sheltered English, Cooperative Learning

for nuclear power, such accidents still remain a danger. In 1999, workers at a nuclear power plant in Tokaimura, Japan, ignored safety regulations and caused the worst nuclear power disaster in Japanese history.

✔ **READING CHECK:** What recent global environmental problems have nations faced?

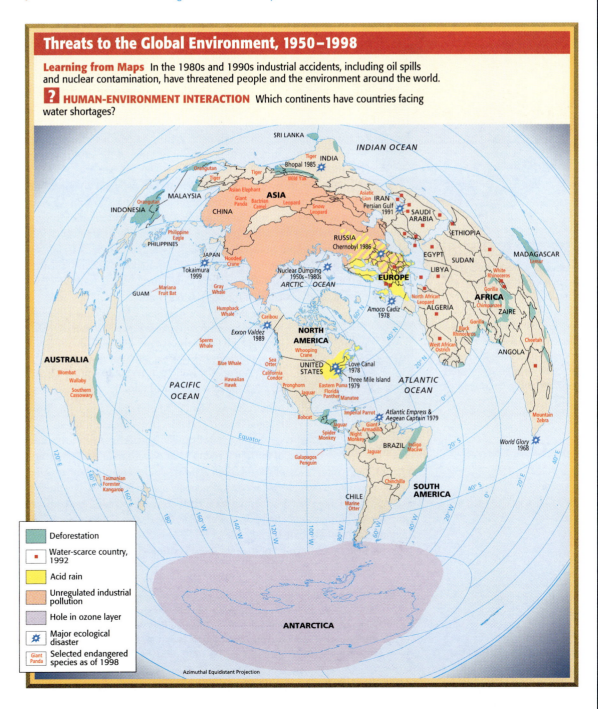

Threats to the Global Environment, 1950–1998

Learning from Maps In the 1980s and 1990s industrial accidents, including oil spills and nuclear contamination, have threatened people and the environment around the world.

? HUMAN-ENVIRONMENT INTERACTION Which continents have countries facing water shortages?

Deforestation
Water-scarce country, 1992
Acid rain
Unregulated industrial pollution
Hole in ozone layer
Major ecological disaster
Selected endangered species as of 1998

Azimuthal Equidistant Projection

ECONOMIC DEVELOPMENT

Global Warming. Americans who argued that greenhouse gas emissions do not cause global warming pointed out the economic consequences of adhering to the December 1997 agreement to reduce such emissions. One petroleum industry spokesman argued that the average American family would pay an additional $2,000 each year for energy resources and that some 2 million industrial jobs would be lost in the United States.

CRITICAL THINKING How might the statistics cited be biased?

ANSWER: Students might suggest that representatives from the petroleum industry might offer worst-case scenarios in order to turn public opinion against the 1997 agreement.

MAP ANSWER
Africa, Asia, and Europe

LEVELS 2 AND 3: Pair students and tell each pair to brainstorm ways of slowing deforestation and of maintaining biodiversity in developing countries. How might the people who depend on the land and resources of the rain forests be persuaded to preserve the forests? *(Students might suggest offering financial aid to compensate them for lost income; imposing international sanctions on countries that irresponsibly destroy their forests; educating residents of the rain forests in ways to optimize existing land use and minimize the need to clear new land; and so on.)* Call on one student from each pair to report the ideas to the class. Encourage the class to comment on and discuss each others' ideas. **Cooperative Learning**

NOTE: For an additional teaching idea, see the Chapter 31 structured discussion lesson in the **Creative Teaching Strategies** handbook.

IN THE NEWS

Acid Rain. A 1999 study revealed that lakes in many parts of North America remained highly acidic despite reductions in sulfur dioxide emissions. Some scientists argued that calcium and magnesium—substances that counter acidity—had been leached out of soils in those heavily polluted lakes. Thus, although the lakes were no longer being intensely polluted, the acid they already contained could not be countered. Some scientists predicted that it might be decades or even centuries before those lakes return to normal.

CRITICAL THINKING How might scientists work to rehabilitate the acidic lakes?

ANSWER: Students might note that they could study ways to increase calcium and magnesium levels in acidic lakes.

THAT'S INTERESTING!

The *Exxon Valdez* oil spill killed an estimated 5,000 sea otters, 300 seals, 22 killer whales, and some 250,000 birds.

VISUAL RECORD ANSWER

Students might suggest that preserving rare species allows for a more diverse ecosystem.

Deforestation

Forests play an important role in the global ecosystem. They help prevent soil erosion and flooding. Because trees absorb carbon dioxide from the air, the loss of forests also contributes to global warming. Tropical rain forests are also home to about half of Earth's species, many of which may not yet have been discovered by scientists. This makes rain forests vital to maintaining **biodiversity**—the wide variety of Earth's animal and plant species.

Population growth and the expansion of agriculture and industry are major causes of deforestation—the destruction of forests. The rate of rain forest destruction in 1999 was some 214,000 acres—approximately the area of New York City—per day. Some researchers estimate that this rate of deforestation will result in the extinction of 25 percent or more of the world's species in the next 50 years.

INTERPRETING THE VISUAL RECORD

Biodiversity. Rain forests contain many species of insects and plants that are adapted to live under special conditions found nowhere else in the world. Some species have been found only in a single group of trees. ***What might be the value of preserving rare species found in the rain forest?***

The debate over the loss of the rain forests is not a simple one. Much of the world's current deforestation is taking place within developing nations in Africa, Asia, and South America. In poor nations, the land and resources of the rain forests often are viewed by the public as sources of jobs and income. Some people in developing nations argue that it is unfair for the industrialized world to expect poorer nations to make economic sacrifices to preserve the rain forests. Others in the developing world, however, have actively protested the destruction of the region's rain forests.

BIOGRAPHY

Chico Mendes

In the 1980s a Brazilian named Chico Mendes organized a campaign against ranchers' efforts to create grazing land by destroying the Amazonian rain forest. Born Francisco Alves Mendes Filho in 1944, Mendes grew up with a deep appreciation of nature. "I became an ecologist long before I had ever heard the word," he once recalled. Mendes's family made its living from tapping the sap of rubber trees in the rain forest.

In the 1960s Brazilian leaders ordered the burning of the rain forest to make way for industrialization and large-scale agriculture. To oppose this destruction, Mendes organized other workers who also used the rain forest in environmentally responsible ways. The protesters used nonviolent methods of resistance, such as human blockades, to stop heavy equipment. Through these methods, the protesters were able to focus worldwide attention on the plight of the rain forest.

Nevertheless, the burning of the rain forest continued. In 1988 Mendes spoke out against this devastation.

> **"In the last half century Amazônia has never seen so many fires as in 1988. They are burning everything. Our airports were closed one week in 1987 because of the smoke. This year they were closed one month for the same reason. . . . Amazônia is nothing but smoke. How it hurts!"**

✔ **READING CHECK:** How are deforestation and biodiversity related?

TEACH OBJECTIVE 3

ALL LEVELS: To help students identify concerns that have arisen over population growth, copy the following graphic organizer on the chalkboard, omitting the italicized answers. Have each student complete the graphic organizer. **Sheltered English**

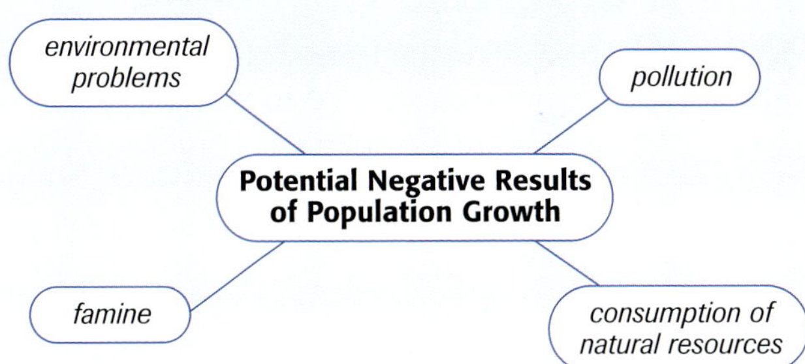

ASSIGNMENT: *Tell students to imagine that they work for an organization called the World Population Council. Have them prepare a brochure suggesting some solutions to the problems caused by increased population.*

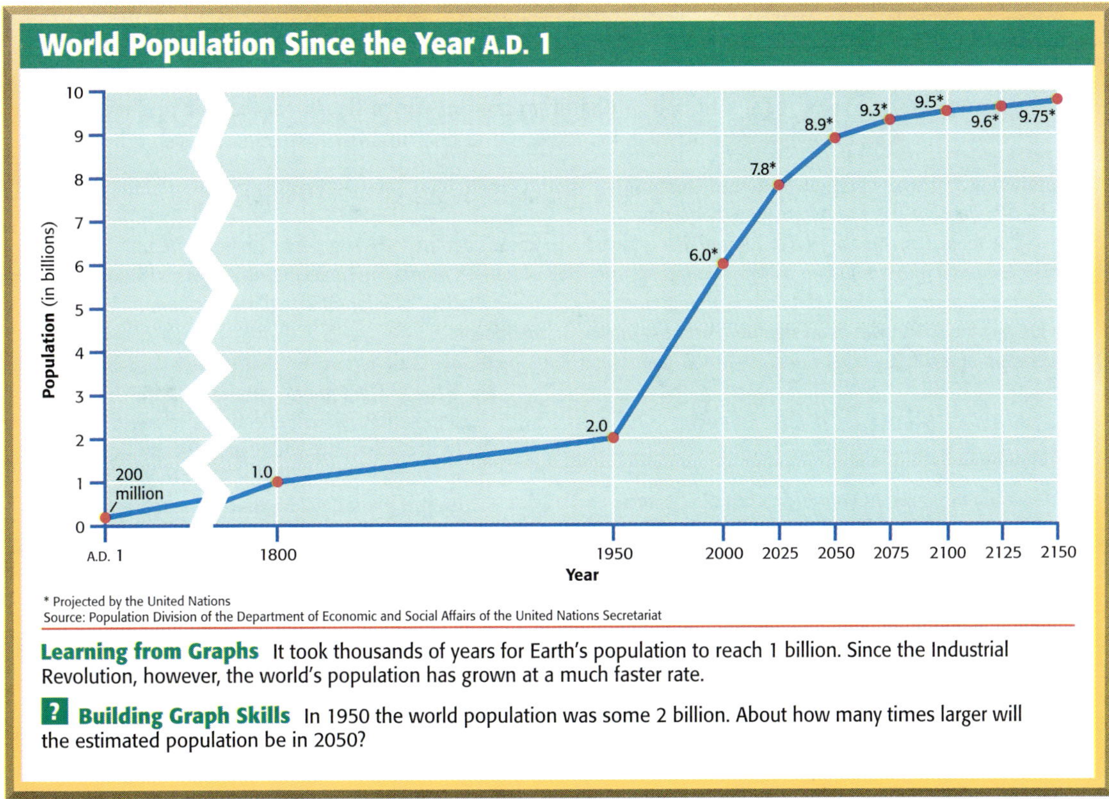

* Projected by the United Nations
Source: Population Division of the Department of Economic and Social Affairs of the United Nations Secretariat

Learning from Graphs It took thousands of years for Earth's population to reach 1 billion. Since the Industrial Revolution, however, the world's population has grown at a much faster rate.

? Building Graph Skills In 1950 the world population was some 2 billion. About how many times larger will the estimated population be in 2050?

The Population Explosion

Many of the world's most difficult problems, such as pollution and famine, have been made worse by a massive increase in population. In 1999 the world's population reached 6 billion, double its size in 1960. Most of this growth has been concentrated in the developing world. Experts predict that India's population will jump from 984 million in 1998 to 1.4 billion by 2025. By 2050 Africa is expected to account for about 17 percent of the world's population, compared to 9 percent in 1950.

Obviously, population growth will not slow until families have fewer children. However, some researchers charge that blaming the world's environmental problems on population growth in the developing world is unfair. They note that poor nations use relatively little of the world's resources. Brazilian historian Fatima Vianna Mello argues that the developed world should begin to limit its consumption of the world's resources before it calls for limits on population growth in the developing world. Other researchers warn that population growth in the developing world will cause shortages of food and limited resources, such as land and water.

On October 12, 1999, UN secretary general Kofi Annan traveled to Bosnia to meet the baby designated as the world's 6-billionth person.

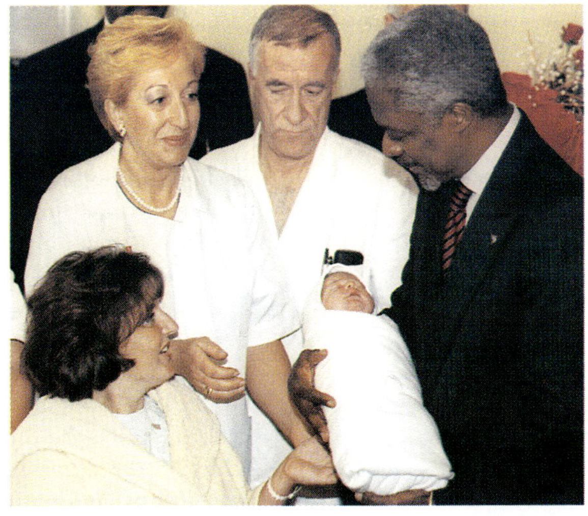

internetconnect

TOPIC: Recycling
GO TO: go.hrw.com
KEYWORD: SE1 Recycle

Have students access the Internet through the HRW Web site to conduct research on recycling. Then ask each student to create a poster explaining the importance of recycling and describing ways people can participate in recycling.

GRAPH ANSWER

4.5

STRATEGIES FOR SUCCESS

(for p. 922)

Practicing the Strategy

1. Answers will vary, but students might mention the use of "if" and the phrase "most probable result."
2. Answers will vary but should mention specific words and phrases.

VISUAL RECORD ANSWER

(for p. 923)

Students might mention newspapers.

TEACH OBJECTIVE 4

LEVEL 1: Have students create a bulleted list of the ways that governments and environmentalists have tried to solve current environmental problems. *(Lists might include recycling, international treaties, and membership in private organizations and lobbying groups.)* **Sheltered English**

LEVELS 2 AND 3: Have students complete the Level 1 lesson. Then pair students and have each pair brainstorm ways that it can help solve current environmental problems. *(Students might suggest that they could start or join clubs, write letters, initiate petitions, recycle and encourage others to do the same, go into careers in environmental science to research new solutions, volunteer to campaign for candidates who support pro-environment policies, and so on.)* Call on one student from each pair to share his or her pair's ideas with the class. **Cooperative Learning**

▶**ASSIGNMENT** *Have students create a collage of images and words that highlight current global environmental problems and efforts to solve them. Display students' completed collages around the classroom.*

SECTION 4 REVIEW ANSWERS

Define and Identify
For significance, see the following pages:

- global warming, p. 917
- ozone layer, p. 918
- ultraviolet solar radiation, p. 918
- chlorofluorocarbons, p. 918
- acid rain, p. 918
- biodiversity, p. 920
- Chico Mendes, p. 920
- Convention on Biological Diversity, p. 923

Locate
For locations, see the map on p. 919. For importance, see the following pages:

- Antarctica, p. 918
- Chernobyl, p. 918

1. Forests are important to ecosystems because they help prevent soil erosion and flooding, absorb carbon dioxide, and help maintain biodiversity.

2. because population growth may cause shortages of food and limited resources

3. destruction of rain forests, loss of species, global warming, thinning of ozone layer, acid rain, population explosion

4. Answers will vary, but students may suggest legislation, international agreements, and recycling.

5. Answers will vary but should reflect an understanding of past international environmental efforts that might be adapted or improved upon to meet future environmental challenges.

Strategies for Success: Distinguishing Fact from Opinion

Most historical sources contain a mixture of facts and opinions. A *fact* is a piece of information that can be proved or verified. An *opinion* is a statement that is based on the beliefs or judgment of an individual or group. The ability to distinguish between fact and opinion is essential for judging the soundness of an argument or the reliability of a historical account.

How to Distinguish Fact from Opinion

1. **Identify the facts.** As you study a historical source, determine whether the information it presents could be checked for accuracy in an encyclopedia, almanac, or some other historical reference work. If so, the information is probably factual; if not, it possibly contains an opinion.
2. **Identify the opinions.** When you encounter material that does not seem wholly factual, look for (1) phrases indicating a belief or conviction, such as *I think* or *in their view,* (2) comparative words like *greater, better, more,* or *less,* (3) words that imply a judgment or evaluation, such as *useful, unfortunate,* or *admirable.* Such language usually indicates a statement of opinion.

Applying the Strategy

Reconsider the following quotation from The Club of Rome's report *The Limits to Growth.* As you study the quotation, look for signs that it is a statement of opinion.

> **"If the present growth trends in world population, industrialization, pollution, food production, and resource depletion continue unchanged, the limits to growth on this planet will be reached sometime within the next one hundred years. The most probable result will be a rather sudden and uncontrollable decline in both population and industrial capacity."**

Practicing the Strategy

Use the quotation to answer the following questions.

1. What are indications that the statement is an opinion rather than a fact?
2. How does the section text use facts and opinions to explain the different views surrounding this statement?

These shortages can lead to conflict. In Bangladesh, for example, rapid population growth has contributed to a scarcity of land. As a result, millions of Bangladeshis have emigrated to India, sparking ethnic conflict.

✔ **READING CHECK:** What concerns have arisen over rapid population growth?

The World Responds

Environmentalists and governments are working to address today's environmental challenges. These efforts often involve international cooperation.

Recycling. As environmental awareness grows, recycling—the collection and processing of used items for reuse—has been winning support. Recycling serves two important purposes. It reuses scarce natural resources and reduces the amount of solid waste. This waste must either be burned in incinerators, buried in overflowing landfills, dumped into the sea, or shipped to disposal facilities in poorer nations. In 1994 the United States recycled an estimated 23 percent of its solid waste. By 1997 Japanese citizens recycled 54 percent of the nation's newspaper and more than 67 percent of its glass bottles.

REVIEW

Have students complete the **Section 4 Review** on p. 923.

ASSESS

Have students complete **Daily Quiz 31.4**. As **Alternative Assessment**, you may want to use the graphic organizer or the problem-solving activity in this section's lessons.

RETEACH

Have students complete **Main Idea Activity for Reteaching and Sheltered English 31.4**. Then organize students into five groups and assign one of the following topics to each group: alternative energy sources, deforestation, water and air pollution, overpopulation, or efforts to solve environmental problems. Have each group prepare and present an oral presentation on its topic. Tell students to take notes on each other's presentations. **Sheltered English, Cooperative Learning**

EXTEND

Tell students to imagine that they work for a toy company that has decided to create a line of toys promoting environmental awareness. Organize the class into groups of four. Have students work together to design a simple toy that teaches children about current environmental issues.
Block Scheduling, Cooperative Learning

Global approaches. The year 1992 marked the 20th anniversary of the first United Nations conference on the environment. That year the United Nations sponsored the Conference on Environment and Development—dubbed the Earth Summit—in Rio de Janeiro, Brazil. Attracting delegations from 178 nations and about 1,200 private environmental organizations, the conference yielded some significant compromises. One was a treaty, the **Convention on Biological Diversity**, that went into effect on December 29, 1993. The treaty committed the 168 nations signing it to the protection of biodiversity.

A rise in environmental awareness has also been evident in the growth of private organizations and lobbying groups. Greenpeace, an international environmental organization, has successfully campaigned against whaling. Other groups, such as the international Worldwatch Institute, have tried to work together to promote international cooperation and concern about the environment. As the Worldwatch Institute noted in 1992, "In an environmentally interdependent world, no country can separate its fate from that of the world as a whole."

Protecting the environment is only one of the many challenges facing the United States at the dawn of a new century. As has been true throughout our history, America's response to these challenges will be determined by new generations' willingness to tackle tough problems. In this book you have learned of our nation's history up to the present. The next chapters in this still-unfolding story are yours to write.

✓ **READING CHECK:** How have governments and environmentalists tried to solve current environmental problems?

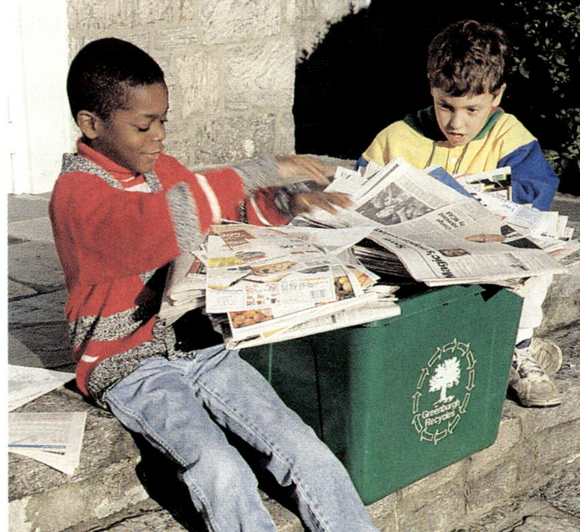

INTERPRETING THE VISUAL RECORD

Recycling. Many U.S. cities have established recycling programs for certain materials. ***What are these children recycling?***

SECTION  REVIEW

Define and explain the significance of the following terms:
global warming
ozone layer
ultraviolet solar radiation
chlorofluorocarbons
acid rain
biodiversity
Convention on Biological Diversity

Identify and explain the significance of the following individual:
Chico Mendes

Locate and explain the importance of the following places:
Chernobyl
Antarctica

1. **Using Graphic Organizers** Copy the graphic organizer below. Use it to explain the importance of forests to the ecosystem.

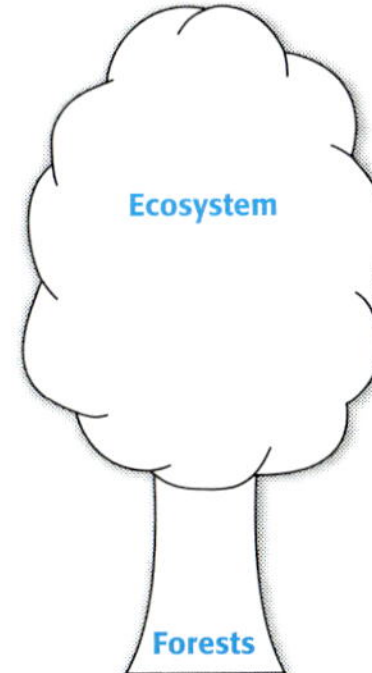

2. **Assessing Consequences** Why is population growth an environmental concern?
3. **Analyzing** What environmental problems plagued the world in the 1990s?
4. **Problem Solving** What measures do you think the U.S. government and your local community could take to solve the problem of the rapid depletion of natural resources?

Critical Thinking

5. What efforts do you think the international community could take to maintain a healthy global environment in the coming years?
Consider:
- what efforts might be taken to protect the oceans
- what might be done to protect the atmosphere
- how the international community could help protect biodiversity

---

CHAPTER 31 REVIEW ANSWERS

Creating a Time Line
Each event should have an explanation and the correct date.

Writing a Summary
See the Reading Checks in each section for main ideas.

Identifying People and Ideas
1. science that focuses on relationships between species and the environment
2. the varied webs of interaction between living things and their environment
3. idea that environment should be used, but used wisely
4. influential preservationist who helped create Yosemite National Park and helped found the Sierra Club
5. radioactive debris produced by nuclear reactions
6. elimination of nuclear weapons by one country
7. political parties whose platforms emphasize ecological concerns
8. the increase in temperature of Earth's atmosphere
9. the wide variety of Earth's animal and plant species
10. Brazilian activist who worked to save rain forests

Understanding Main Ideas
1. In the colonial period, most people wanted to conquer the wilderness; by the 1900s some Americans wanted to protect and preserve it.

CHAPTER 31

REVIEW AND ASSESSMENT RESOURCES

PRINT

- Chapter 31 Review, pp. 924–25
- Chapter 31 Tutorial for Students, Parents, Mentors, and Peers
- Chapter 31 Test (Form A or B)
- Portfolio Activities and Alternative Assessment Handbook, Chapter 31

MULTIMEDIA

- Audio Program, Chapter 31 (English and Spanish)
- Chapter 31 Test Generator (on the One-Stop Planner)
- Global Skill Builder CD–ROM
- HRW Web site

SHELTERED ENGLISH

- Spanish Glossary
- Sheltered English Chapter 31 Test

REVIEW

Have students complete the **Chapter 31 Review** on pp. 924–25.

ASSESS

Use one of the chapter tests to assess students' understanding of the content. For **Alternative Assessment**, see the **Portfolio Activities and Alternative Assessment Handbook.**

2. Conservationists supported the wise use of the environment, while preservationists want to keep some wilderness areas untouched.

3. People called for unilateral disarmament and the elimination of aboveground testing. They also supported arms limitation agreements.

4. Answers will vary but may include global warming, ozone depletion, acid rain, industrial accidents, deforestation, and population growth.

5. international agreements, recycling, population control, industrial controls

Reviewing Themes

1. Answers will vary but may note that some technological developments have harmed the environment by increasing pollution and destroying natural resources while others have helped the environment.

2. by entering into international agreements such as the Convention on Biological Diversity

3. need for economic development often overrides concern for environment

Thinking Critically

1. Darwin's work brought new attention to the study of the environment and inspired Ernst Haeckel to develop the science of ecology.

2. encouraged Americans to think about the ways in which they used the environment and the role government should play in protecting the environment

Review

Creating a Time Line

Copy the time line below onto a sheet of paper. Complete the time line by filling in the events and dates from the chapter that you think were most significant. Pick three events and explain why you think they were significant.

Writing a Summary

Using the Reading Checks as a guide, write an overview of the events in the chapter.

Identifying People and Ideas

Identify the following terms or individuals and explain their significance.

1. ecology
2. ecosystem
3. conservation
4. John Muir
5. nuclear fallout
6. unilateral disarmament
7. Green parties
8. global warming
9. biodiversity
10. Chico Mendes

Understanding Main Ideas

SECTION 1

1. How did American attitudes toward the wilderness change between the colonial period and the 1900s?

SECTION 2

2. How did preservationists' views of the environment differ from those held by conservationists?

SECTION 3

3. What was the international response to nuclear-weapons testing?

SECTION 4

4. What are some of the major global environmental issues being debated today?
5. What solutions were proposed to deal with major environmental problems of the 1990s?

Reviewing Themes

1. **Technology and Society** How have technological developments affected the environment?
2. **Global Relations** How have nations tried to work together to solve environmental problems?
3. **Economic Development** How does the need for economic development sometimes influence a country's policy on the environment?

Thinking Critically

1. **Identifying Cause and Effect** How did Darwin's theory of evolution influence the science of ecology?
2. **Evaluating** What effect did progressives have on Americans' views of the environment?
3. **Comparing and Contrasting** How does the link between environmental protest and politics differ in the United States compared to Europe?
4. **Assessing Consequences** What are the problems associated with deforestation?
5. **Hypothesizing** How do you think population growth will affect environmental problems during the next 100 years?

Writing About History

Writing to Persuade Imagine that you are working for the U.S. Forest Service during the early 1900s. Write a government report directed to President Theodore Roosevelt and Gifford Pinchot explaining why it is important to create national parks. Use the graphic organizer below to help organize your thoughts.

National Parks	
Benefits	**Costs**

RETEACH

Organize the class into four groups and assign each group one of the following topics: attitudes toward the environment during the 1600s, 1700s, and early 1800s; changing attitudes toward the environment during the 1800s; global environmentalism from the 1940s to the 1960s; or environmentalism from the 1970s to the present. Tell each group to create a display for a children's science education center that covers its assigned topic. Encourage students to make their displays visually stimulating, easy to understand, and interactive so as to appeal to young children. **Sheltered English, Cooperative Learning**

EXTEND

Invite two people from your community—one who is an active preservationist favoring strong government intervention in environmental issues, and one who is opposed to excessive government environmental regulations—to speak to your classes. Have each speaker present his or her point of view and reasoning, and then encourage students to ask questions. To conclude, have each student write a few paragraphs expressing an opinion about the level of government involvement they feel is necessary to protect the environment. **Block Scheduling**

Strategies for Success Review the **Strategies for Success** on *Distinguishing Fact from Opinion.* Next, study the remarks by conservationist Carl Schurz and preservationist Aldo Leopold in the text and feature in Section 2. Then answer the following questions.

1. What do Schurz and Leopold say about German forest management?
2. What parts of their statements appear to be based on facts?
3. What parts of their statements appear to be based on opinion?
4. How does the text explain the different views of conservationists and preservationists?

Linking History and Geography

Deforestation was a major environmental concern of the late 1900s. Study the map below and identify where African rain forests have been destroyed. Which parts of Africa have suffered the greatest degree of rain forest destruction?

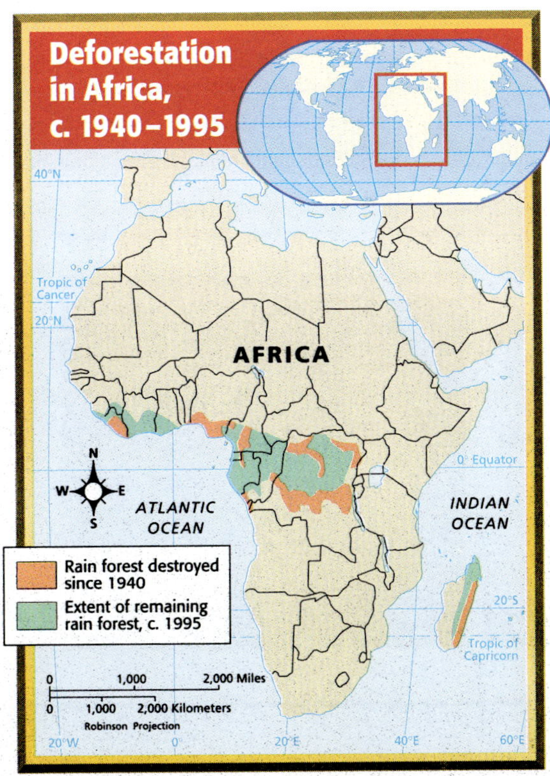

internetconnect

TOPIC: The Rain Forest
GO TO: go.hrw.com
KEYWORD: SE1 Rain Forest

Accessing the Internet through the HRW Web site, research rain forests in different areas of the world. Then make a poster or multimedia presentation that explains the importance of the rain forest ecosystem, describes their current destruction, and tells what students can do to help solve the problem.

BUILDING YOUR PORTFOLIO

Complete one or all of the following projects independently or cooperatively.

1 Technology and Society

Imagine that you belong to an environmental organization during the 1950s or 1960s. ***Create a pamphlet*** explaining how technology developed for the Cold War is affecting the environment. Your pamphlet should urge people to take action that will prevent Cold War rivalries from causing further environmental damage.

2 Global Relations

Imagine that you are a U.S. government official preparing to meet with environmental groups. ***Make a poster*** showing your government's involvement in international efforts to protect the environment during the 1980s and 1990s.

3 Economic Development

Imagine that you work for an advertising agency that specializes in environmental topics. ***Write a script*** for a commercial urging people to follow ecological practices and explaining why such practices will benefit the economy in the long run.

3. In Europe environmental protestors organized political parties with pro-environment platforms; in the United States—environmental protests sometimes led to congressional legislation
4. soil erosion, flooding, global warming, and decreased biodiversity
5. Answers will vary, but students may suggest shortages of food and of renewable resources, as well as ethnic conflict.

Writing About History
Students' reports will vary but should include benefits and costs.

Strategies for Success
1. Schurz—forest management has positive effects; Leopold—forest management has negative effects
2. Answers will vary but students should support their answers with specific words or phrases from the remarks.
3. Answers will vary, but students may suggest that the authors' view of the effect of forest management is based on opinion.
4. by presenting both views

Linking History and Geography
sub-Saharan Africa

REVIEW AND ASSESSMENT RESOURCES

PRINT
- Unit 8 Review, pp. 926–27
- Unit 8 Test (Form A or B)
- Portfolio Activities and Alternative Assessment Handbook, Unit 8

MULTIMEDIA
- Global Skill Builder CD–ROM

SHELTERED ENGLISH
- Spanish Glossary
- Sheltered English Unit 8 Test

To review elements of Unit 8 in a single class period, assign one of the following activities or graphic organizers, omitting the italicized answers, to individuals or groups.

1 Technology and Society

Have each student create a collage to represent the effects of technology on society during the past 100 years. Students may wish to focus on the effects of technology during World War I, World War II, and the Cold War, or on the ways in which technology has led to the creation of a global economy.

A Selection from Further Reading

Imperialism. In *Uncertain Dimensions*, Raymond Betts offers an introduction to imperialism in the 1900s. In the following excerpt, he describes how modern technology introduced by colonial powers affected less-industrialized societies. "There were good works, even major works, to be seen and praised. Health institutes were established, educational systems developed, roads and railroads laid out nearly everywhere. The technology of empire was a very serious business and quite a disturbing one culturally. It played a special part in the maintenance of the *pax colonia* [colonial peace], because it shook the traditional base on which that *pax* was based. Indigenous people were uprooted to work in mines or on roadbed construction or as stevedores in the ports. Local customs and family traditions were questioned and denied by a wage economy, new work habits, and the mobility that bicycle, bus, and train provided."

COMPREHENSION According to Betts, what effect did the "technology of empire" have on colonized people?

ANSWER: Students might answer that they were forced to move and perform new types of work and that their customs and traditions were damaged by a new economic system.

Review

BUILDING YOUR PORTFOLIO

Outlined below are four projects. Independently or cooperatively, complete one and use the products to demonstrate your mastery of the historical concepts involved.

1 Technology and Society

War almost always has profound effects on the economy, the peoples, and the natural environment of a society. ***Create a script*** for a one-act play showing the various effects of the technology used in wars such as World War I, World War II, and the Cold War. Each scene of the play should focus on a different effect or group of people. You may wish to use portfolio materials you designed in the unit chapters to help you.

U.S. fighter planes

2 Economic Development

Nearly every global event can be linked in some way to economics. ***Write a report and create a visual display*** to be presented by the World Bank on how nations around the world today might improve their economies. Your report should take into account the different economic needs of different nations. You may wish to use portfolio materials you designed in the unit chapters to help you.

Currency from around the world

2 Economic Development

ARGUMENTS FOR AND AGAINST FREE TRADE

Pros	Cons
• *Exports help a country increase its wealth.* • *Consumers benefit from cheaper goods.* • *Expansion of trade between nations leads to greater economic and political cooperation between nations.* • *Free trade allows countries to specialize in goods that they can produce more efficiently.*	• *Domestic producers and industries suffer from increased competition, leading to layoffs and unemployment.* • *Free trade leads to lower wages for workers, as companies tend to move factories to countries where labor costs are lower.* • *Free trade can lead to environmental problems if manufacturers move production to countries where environmental protection is weak or nonexistent.*

4 Democratic Values

THREATS TO INDIVIDUAL RIGHTS DURING THE 1900s

1. *denial of equal rights to women*
2. *child labor*
3. *tactics of modern warfare*
4. *colonialism*
5. *fascism and militarism*
6. *racial oppression*
7. *internal political repression*

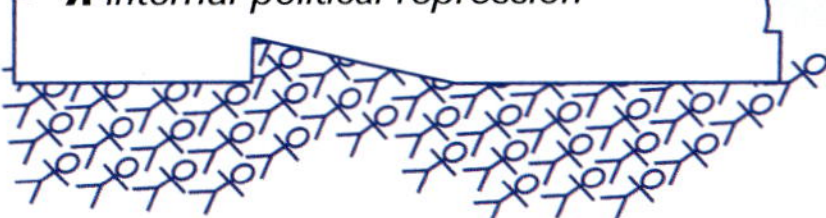

UN Insignia

3 Global Relations

The 1900s have been marked by numerous international efforts to cooperate on such matters as the global economy, human rights, and the environment. ***Write a script and conduct a talk show*** with guests from several nations evaluating the effectiveness of various efforts at international cooperation. The show might also address how to ensure the success of future efforts. You may wish to use portfolio materials you designed in the unit chapters to help you.

A pro-democracy protest

4 Democratic Values

Although individual rights have generally expanded over the past several centuries, even in the 1900s some groups found their rights limited. ***Create a museum exhibition*** showing how individual rights have been threatened in different parts of the world during the 1900s. Your display should also include examples of improvements in the realm of individual rights. You may wish to use portfolio materials you designed in the unit chapters to help you.

Further Reading

Betts, Raymond F. *Uncertain Dimensions: Western Overseas Empires in the Twentieth Century.* University of Minnesota Press, 1985. Thematic analysis of imperialism from World War I through decolonization.

Cameron, Rondo. *A Concise Economic History of the World.* Oxford, 1993. Overview of international economic history from ancient times to the present.

Drinan, Robert F. *Cry of the Oppressed: The History and Hope of the Human Rights Revolution.* Harper & Row, 1987. Overview of efforts to protect human rights since 1945.

Maltby, Richard. *Passing Parade: A History of Popular Culture in the Twentieth Century.* Oxford, 1989. Pictorial history of popular culture in a global context.

Sassen, Saskia. *The Global City: New York, London, Tokyo.* Princeton University Press, 1991. A look at how the global economy has transformed urban areas.

Worster, Donald. *Nature's Economy.* Cambridge, 1994. A history of ecological ideas.

Internet Connect and Holt Researcher CD–ROM Review

In assigned groups, develop a multimedia presentation about America between 1880 and the present. Choose information from the chapter Internet Connect activities and from the Holt Researcher CD–ROM that best reflects the major topics of the period. Write an outline and a script for your presentations, which may be shown to the class.

A Selection from Further Reading

Environmental Awareness. In *Nature's Economy*, Donald Worster presents a history of the study of ecology from the 1700s to the present. In the following excerpt, Worster discusses how Americans have viewed nature. "We have made distinctions in our national reaction to wildlife, chosen favorites as well as singled out enemies. Here as in other matters, the Anglo-American mind has exhibited a peculiarly intense moralism that, in this case, assigns every species to an absolute ethical category: good or bad. A few wild animals, songbirds chiefly, have been pronounced good; everything else is of use only for target practice. . . . Essentially these are the animals with teeth and claws: the carnivores, including wolves, pumas, bears—and latest in line, coyotes. From the time the Puritans of New England first put a bounty on their heads, the carnivores were most often viewed as . . . foes who deserved nothing less than total extermination."

COMPREHENSION According to Worster, what has influenced how Americans have viewed wildlife?

ANSWER: Students might answer that intense moralism has led Americans to view wildlife in absolute terms.

928

Reference

929

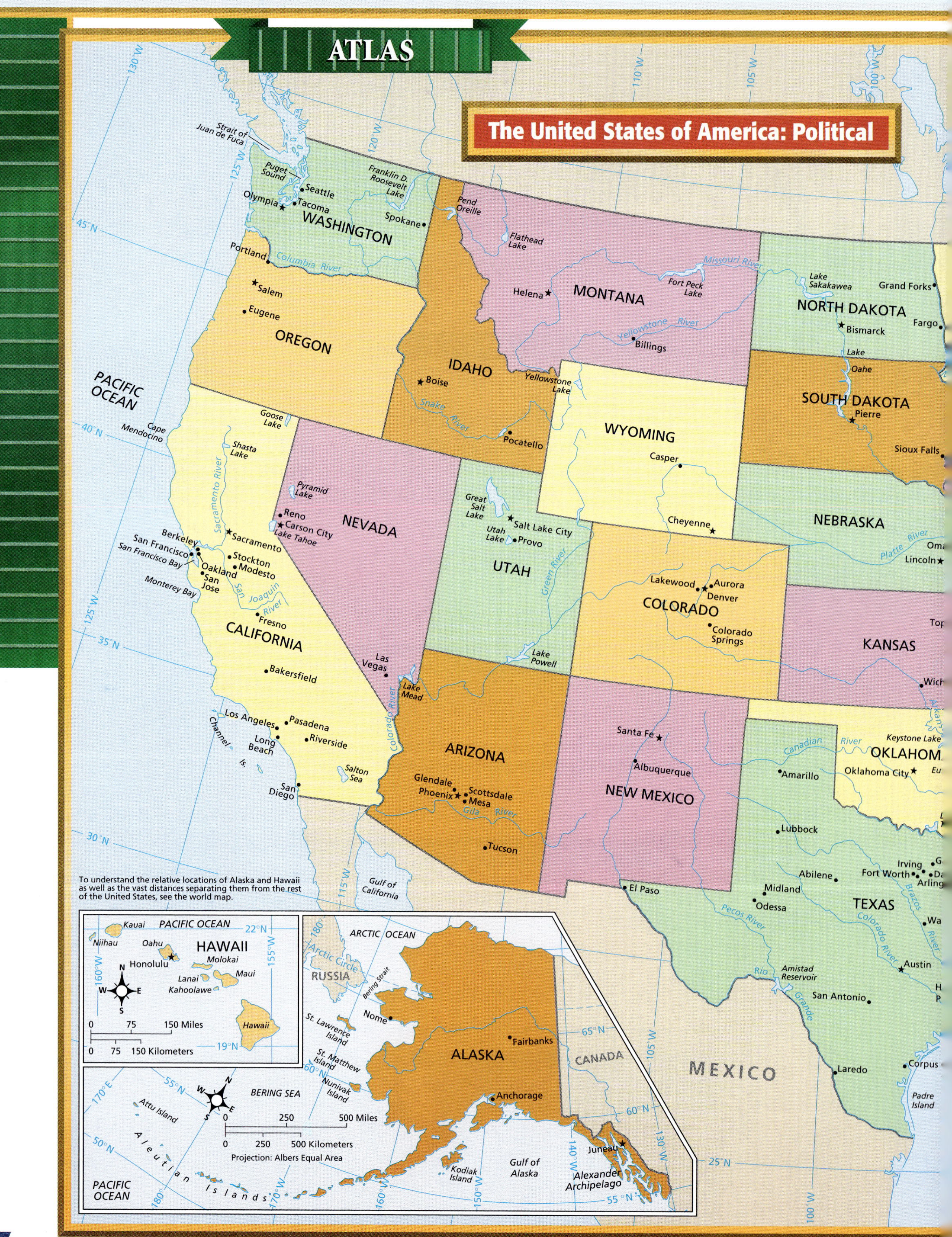
ATLAS
The United States of America: Political
PACIFIC OCEAN
Strait of Juan de Fuca
Puget Sound
Seattle
Olympia
Tacoma
WASHINGTON
Franklin D. Roosevelt Lake
Spokane
Portland
Columbia River
Salem
Eugene
OREGON
Pend Oreille
Flathead Lake
Helena
MONTANA
Missouri River
Fort Peck Lake
Yellowstone River
Billings
IDAHO
Boise
Snake River
Pocatello
Yellowstone Lake
WYOMING
Casper
Cheyenne
Lake Sakakawea
Grand Forks
NORTH DAKOTA
Bismarck
Fargo
Lake Oahe
SOUTH DAKOTA
Pierre
Sioux Falls
NEBRASKA
Platte River
Lincoln
Cape Mendocino
Goose Lake
Shasta Lake
Sacramento River
Pyramid Lake
Reno
Carson City
Lake Tahoe
NEVADA
Great Salt Lake
Salt Lake City
Utah Lake
Provo
UTAH
Green River
Berkeley
San Francisco
San Francisco Bay
Oakland
San Jose
Monterey Bay
Sacramento
Stockton
Modesto
San Joaquin River
Fresno
CALIFORNIA
Bakersfield
Las Vegas
Lake Mead
Lake Powell
Lakewood
Aurora
Denver
COLORADO
Colorado Springs
KANSAS
Los Angeles
Pasadena
Long Beach
Riverside
Channel Is.
Salton Sea
San Diego
Colorado River
ARIZONA
Glendale
Phoenix
Scottsdale
Mesa
Gila River
Tucson
Santa Fe
Albuquerque
NEW MEXICO
El Paso
Canadian River
Keystone Lake
OKLAHOMA
Oklahoma City
Amarillo
Lubbock
Abilene
Irving
Fort Worth
Midland
Odessa
TEXAS
Pecos River
Colorado River
Brazos River
Austin
Amistad Reservoir
Rio Grande
San Antonio
Laredo
Corpus
Padre Island
MEXICO
Gulf of California
To understand the relative locations of Alaska and Hawaii as well as the vast distances separating them from the rest of the United States, see the world map.
Kauai
PACIFIC OCEAN
Niihau
Oahu
HAWAII
Honolulu
Molokai
Lanai
Maui
Kahoolawe
Hawaii
0 75 150 Miles
0 75 150 Kilometers
ARCTIC OCEAN
Arctic Circle
RUSSIA
Bering Strait
Nome
St. Lawrence Island
St. Matthew Island
Nunivak Island
Fairbanks
ALASKA
CANADA
BERING SEA
Anchorage
Attu Island
Aleutian Islands
0 250 500 Miles
0 250 500 Kilometers
Projection: Albers Equal Area
Kodiak Island
Gulf of Alaska
Juneau
Alexander Archipelago
PACIFIC OCEAN
130° W
125° W
120° W
115° W
110° W
105° W
100° W
45° N
40° N
35° N
30° N
25° N
22° N
19° N
160° W
155° W
180°
170° E
170° W
150° W
140° W
55° N
50° N
60° N
65° N

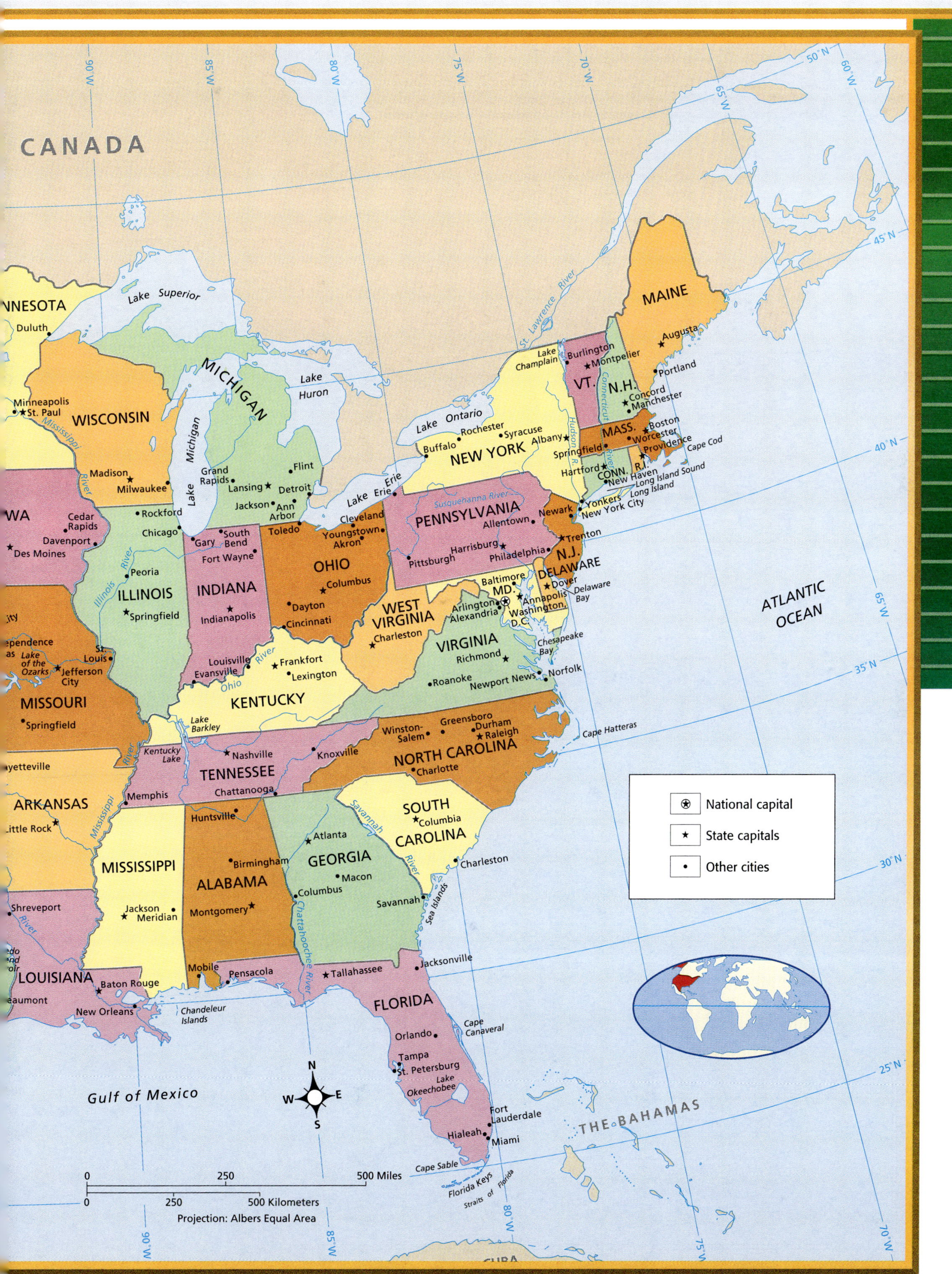
CANADA
Lake Superior
Lake Huron
Lake Michigan
Lake Ontario
Lake Erie
Lake Champlain
St. Lawrence River
MINNESOTA
Duluth
Minneapolis
St. Paul
WISCONSIN
Madison
Milwaukee
MICHIGAN
Grand Rapids
Lansing
Flint
Detroit
Jackson
Ann Arbor
IOWA
Cedar Rapids
Davenport
Des Moines
ILLINOIS
Rockford
Chicago
Peoria
Springfield
Illinois River
Mississippi River
INDIANA
Gary
South Bend
Fort Wayne
Indianapolis
Evansville
OHIO
Toledo
Cleveland
Youngstown
Akron
Columbus
Dayton
Cincinnati
Ohio River
PENNSYLVANIA
Susquehanna River
Pittsburgh
Harrisburg
Allentown
Philadelphia
NEW YORK
Buffalo
Rochester
Syracuse
Albany
Hudson R.
New York City
Yonkers
Long Island
Long Island Sound
VT.
Burlington
Montpelier
N.H.
Concord
Manchester
Connecticut River
MAINE
Augusta
Portland
MASS.
Boston
Worcester
Springfield
Cape Cod
R.I.
Providence
CONN.
Hartford
New Haven
N.J.
Newark
Trenton
DELAWARE
Dover
Delaware Bay
MD.
Baltimore
Annapolis
Washington, D.C.
Arlington
Alexandria
Chesapeake Bay
WEST VIRGINIA
Charleston
VIRGINIA
Richmond
Roanoke
Newport News
Norfolk
KENTUCKY
Louisville
Frankfort
Lexington
Lake Barkley
Kentucky Lake
MISSOURI
Independence
Lake of the Ozarks
Jefferson City
St. Louis
Springfield
TENNESSEE
Nashville
Knoxville
Chattanooga
Memphis
NORTH CAROLINA
Winston-Salem
Greensboro
Durham
Raleigh
Charlotte
Cape Hatteras
SOUTH CAROLINA
Columbia
Charleston
Savannah River
ARKANSAS
Fayetteville
Little Rock
MISSISSIPPI
Jackson
Meridian
ALABAMA
Huntsville
Birmingham
Montgomery
Mobile
GEORGIA
Atlanta
Macon
Columbus
Savannah
Sea Islands
Chattahoochee River
LOUISIANA
Shreveport
Baton Rouge
New Orleans
Beaumont
Red River
Chandeleur Islands
FLORIDA
Pensacola
Tallahassee
Jacksonville
Orlando
Cape Canaveral
Tampa
St. Petersburg
Lake Okeechobee
Fort Lauderdale
Hialeah
Miami
Cape Sable
Florida Keys
Straits of Florida
THE BAHAMAS
CUBA
Gulf of Mexico
ATLANTIC OCEAN
N
S
E
W
National capital
State capitals
Other cities
0
250
500 Miles
0
250
500 Kilometers
Projection: Albers Equal Area
50°N
45°N
40°N
35°N
30°N
25°N
90°W
85°W
80°W
75°W
70°W
65°W
60°W

The United States of America: Physical
To understand the relative locations of Alaska and Hawaii, as well as the vast distances separating them from the rest of the United States, see the world map.
PACIFIC OCEAN
Strait of Juan de Fuca
Puget Sound
Mount Rainier (14,410 ft. 4392 m)
Franklin D. Roosevelt Lake
Pend Oreille
Clark Fork
Flathead River
Flathead Lake
LEWIS RANGE
Milk River
Missouri River
Fort Peck Lake
Lake Sakakawea
Lake Oahe
James River
Red River
CASCADE RANGE
COAST RANGES
Columbia River
Willamette River
BITTERROOT RANGE
Salmon River
SALMON RIVER MTS.
SAWTOOTH MTS.
COLUMBIA PLATEAU
Snake River
ROCKY MOUNTAINS
Yellowstone Lake
Yellowstone River
GRAND TETONS
CONTINENTAL DIVIDE
WIND RIVER RANGE
Gannett Peak (13,804 ft. 4207 m)
BIGHORN MTS.
Bighorn River
Powder River
BLACK HILLS
Cheyenne River
White River
Niobrara River
North Platte River
Platte River
South Platte River
Republican River
Smoky Hill River
GREAT INTERIOR PLAINS
Klamath River
Goose Lake
Cape Mendocino
Shasta Lake
Sacramento River
CENTRAL VALLEY
SIERRA NEVADA
Pyramid Lake
Lake Tahoe
GREAT BASIN
Great Salt Lake
Utah Lake
WASATCH RANGE
UINTA MTS.
Green River
Colorado River
FRONT RANGE
Mount Elbert (14,433 ft. 4400 m)
Pikes Peak (14,110 ft. 4301 m)
San Francisco Bay
Monterey Bay
San Joaquin River
Mount Whitney (14,494 ft. 4419 m)
DEATH VALLEY
COLORADO PLATEAU
Lake Powell
San Juan River
SAN LUIS VALLEY
SANGRE DE CRISTO MTS.
GRAND CANYON
Lake Mead
PAINTED DESERT
MOJAVE DESERT
Channel Islands
Salton Sea
IMPERIAL VALLEY
Gila River
SONORA DESERT
Gulf of California
Canadian River
Keystone Lake
Arkansas River
Pecos River
Rio Grande
Amistad Reservoir
Brazos River
Colorado River
Nueces River
Falcon Lake
Padre Island
MEXICO
Kauai
Niihau
Oahu
PACIFIC OCEAN
Molokai
Maui
Lanai
Kahoolawe
Mauna Kea (13,796 ft. 4206 m)
Hawaii
0 75 150 Miles
0 75 150 Kilometers
ARCTIC OCEAN
Arctic Circle
RUSSIA
Bering Strait
BROOKS RANGE
Yukon River
Tanana River
St. Lawrence Island
St. Matthew Island
Nunivak Island
Kuskokwim River
ALASKA RANGE
Mount McKinley (20,320 ft. 6194 m)
CANADA
BERING SEA
0 250 500 Miles
0 250 500 Kilometers
Projection: Albers Equal Area
Attu Island
Aleutian Islands
Kodiak Island
Gulf of Alaska
Alexander Archipelago
PACIFIC OCEAN

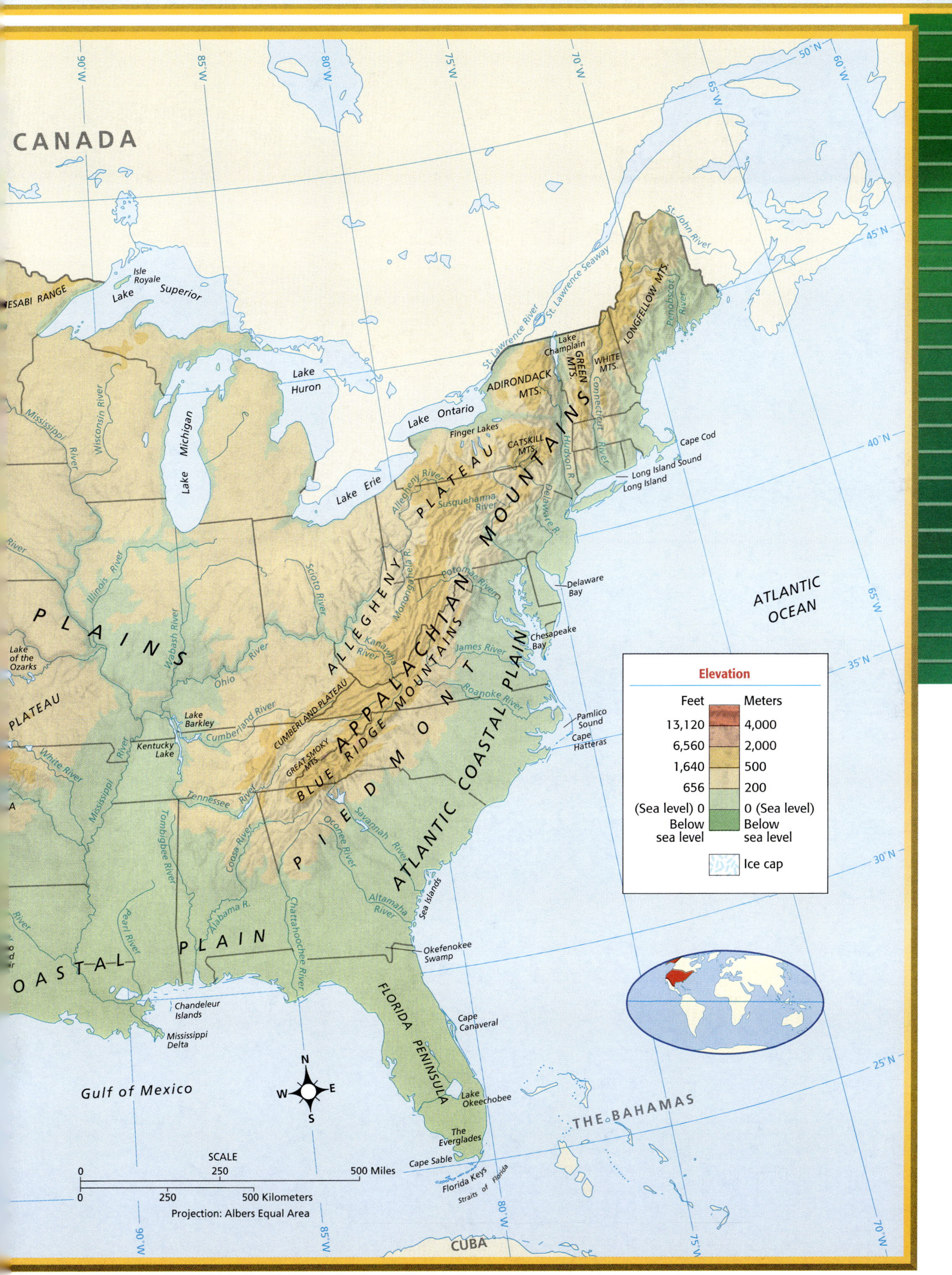
CANADA
Lake Superior
Isle Royale
MESABI RANGE
Lake Huron
Lake Michigan
Lake Ontario
Lake Erie
St. Lawrence River
St. Lawrence Seaway
St. John River
Lake Champlain
ADIRONDACK MTS.
GREEN MTS.
WHITE MTS.
LONGFELLOW MTS.
Penobscot River
Connecticut River
Hudson R.
Finger Lakes
CATSKILL MTS.
Cape Cod
Long Island Sound
Long Island
Delaware R.
Delaware Bay
Susquehanna River
Allegheny River
Monongahela R.
Potomac River
Chesapeake Bay
James River
Roanoke River
Pamlico Sound
Cape Hatteras
ATLANTIC OCEAN
ALLEGHENY PLATEAU
APPALACHIAN MOUNTAINS
BLUE RIDGE MOUNTAINS
CUMBERLAND PLATEAU
GREAT SMOKY MTS.
PIEDMONT
ATLANTIC COASTAL PLAIN
Kanawha River
Scioto River
Ohio River
Wabash River
Illinois River
Wisconsin River
Mississippi River
PLAINS
PLATEAU
Lake of the Ozarks
White River
Lake Barkley
Kentucky Lake
Cumberland River
Tennessee River
Tombigbee River
Pearl River
Coosa River
Alabama R.
Chattahoochee River
Oconee River
Savannah River
Altamaha River
Sea Islands
Okefenokee Swamp
COASTAL PLAIN
Chandeleur Islands
Mississippi Delta
Gulf of Mexico
FLORIDA PENINSULA
Cape Canaveral
Lake Okeechobee
The Everglades
Cape Sable
Florida Keys
Straits of Florida
THE BAHAMAS
CUBA
Elevation
Feet
Meters
13,120
4,000
6,560
2,000
1,640
500
656
200
(Sea level) 0
0 (Sea level)
Below sea level
Below sea level
Ice cap
SCALE
0
250
500 Miles
0
250
500 Kilometers
Projection: Albers Equal Area
N
S
E
W
90°W
85°W
80°W
75°W
70°W
65°W
60°W
50°N
45°N
40°N
35°N
30°N
25°N

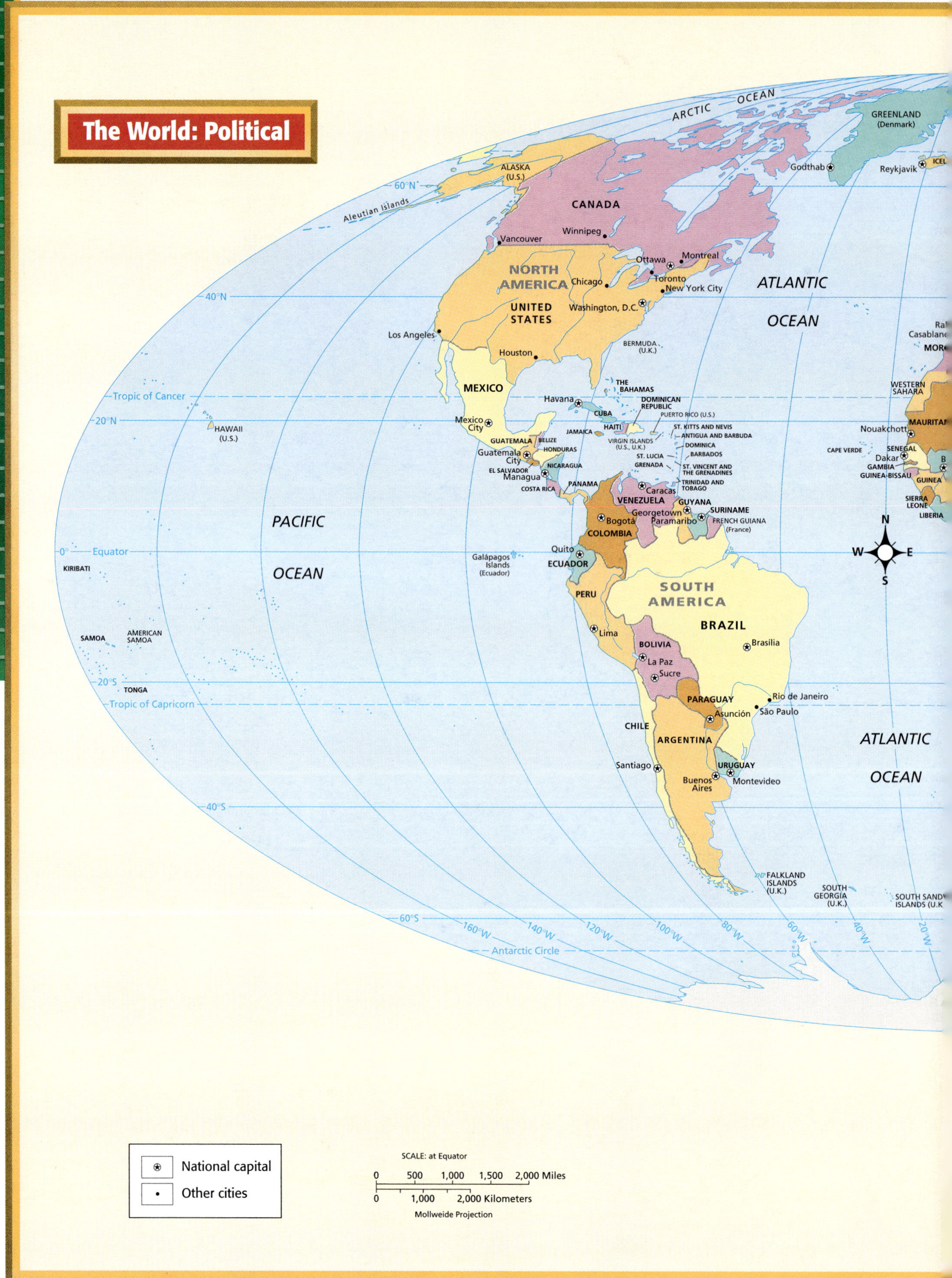
The World: Political
ARCTIC OCEAN
GREENLAND (Denmark)
Godthab
Reykjavik
ALASKA (U.S.)
60°N
Aleutian Islands
CANADA
Winnipeg
Vancouver
Ottawa
Montreal
Toronto
New York City
NORTH AMERICA
Chicago
UNITED STATES
Washington, D.C.
Los Angeles
Houston
BERMUDA (U.K.)
ATLANTIC OCEAN
Casablanca
WESTERN SAHARA
MAURITANIA
Nouakchott
CAPE VERDE
SENEGAL
Dakar
GAMBIA
GUINEA-BISSAU
GUINEA
SIERRA LEONE
LIBERIA
40°N
MEXICO
Tropic of Cancer
THE BAHAMAS
Havana
CUBA
DOMINICAN REPUBLIC
PUERTO RICO (U.S.)
20°N
HAWAII (U.S.)
Mexico City
JAMAICA
HAITI
VIRGIN ISLANDS (U.S., U.K.)
ST. KITTS AND NEVIS
ANTIGUA AND BARBUDA
DOMINICA
BARBADOS
ST. LUCIA
GRENADA
ST. VINCENT AND THE GRENADINES
TRINIDAD AND TOBAGO
GUATEMALA
BELIZE
HONDURAS
Guatemala City
EL SALVADOR
Managua
NICARAGUA
COSTA RICA
PANAMA
Caracas
VENEZUELA
GUYANA
Georgetown
SURINAME
Paramaribo
FRENCH GUIANA (France)
Bogotá
COLOMBIA
PACIFIC OCEAN
0° Equator
KIRIBATI
Galápagos Islands (Ecuador)
Quito
ECUADOR
N
W
E
S
SOUTH AMERICA
PERU
BRAZIL
Lima
Brasília
SAMOA
AMERICAN SAMOA
BOLIVIA
La Paz
Sucre
20°S
TONGA
Tropic of Capricorn
PARAGUAY
Asunción
Rio de Janeiro
São Paulo
CHILE
ARGENTINA
Santiago
URUGUAY
Buenos Aires
Montevideo
40°S
FALKLAND ISLANDS (U.K.)
SOUTH GEORGIA (U.K.)
60°S
160°W
140°W
120°W
100°W
80°W
60°W
40°W
20°W
Antarctic Circle
National capital
Other cities
SCALE: at Equator
0 500 1,000 1,500 2,000 Miles
0 1,000 2,000 Kilometers
Mollweide Projection

	COUNTRY	CAPITAL
1	Czech Republic	Prague
2	Slovakia	Bratislava
3	Slovenia	Ljubljana
4	Croatia	Zagreb
5	Bosnia and Herzegovina	Sarajevo
6	Macedonia	Skopje
7	Yugoslavia (Serbia and Montenegro)	Belgrade
8	Lithuania	Vilnius
9	Latvia	Riga
10	Estonia	Tallinn

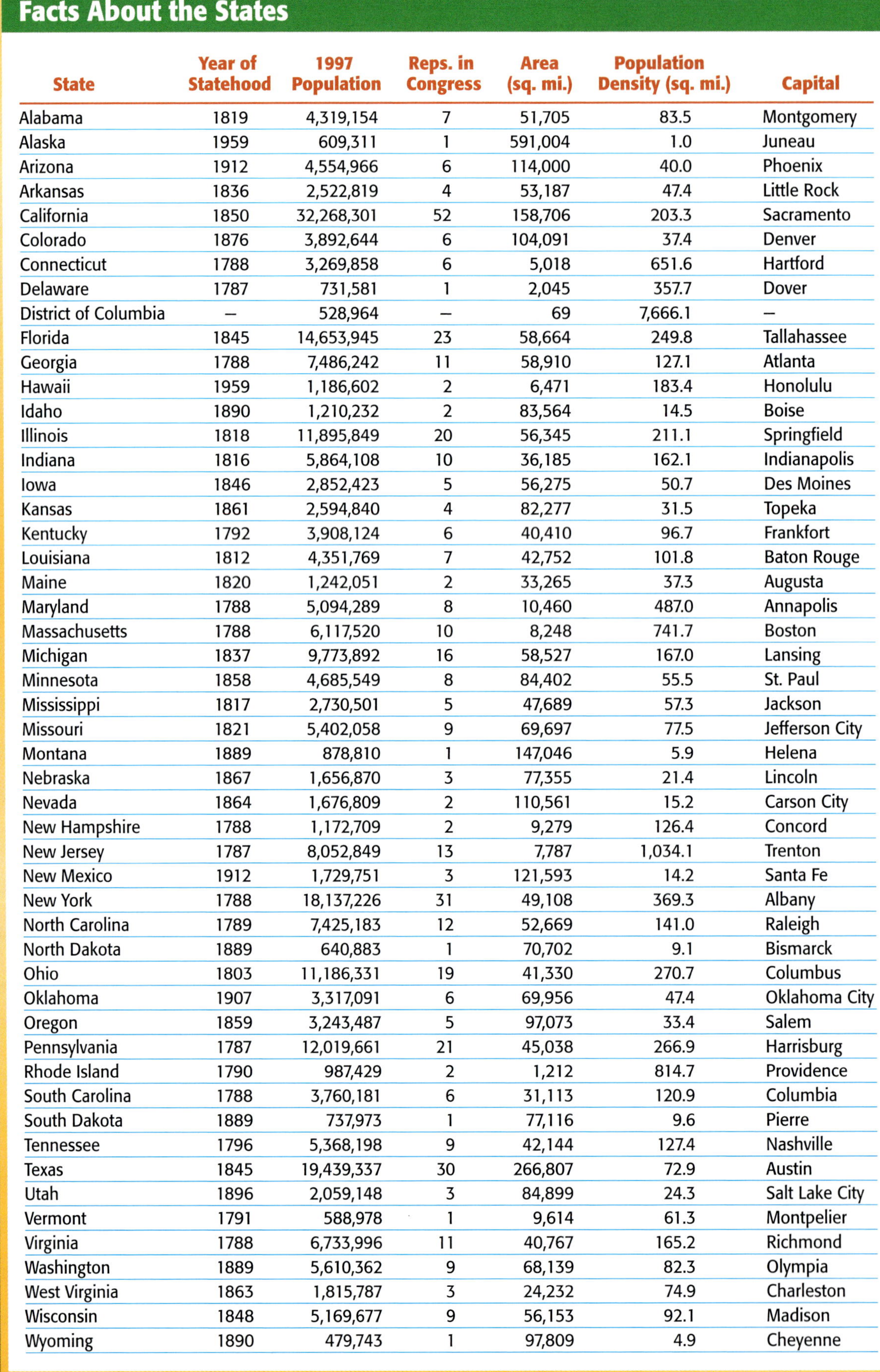

Facts About the States

State	Year of Statehood	1997 Population	Reps. in Congress	Area (sq. mi.)	Population Density (sq. mi.)	Capital
Alabama	1819	4,319,154	7	51,705	83.5	Montgomery
Alaska	1959	609,311	1	591,004	1.0	Juneau
Arizona	1912	4,554,966	6	114,000	40.0	Phoenix
Arkansas	1836	2,522,819	4	53,187	47.4	Little Rock
California	1850	32,268,301	52	158,706	203.3	Sacramento
Colorado	1876	3,892,644	6	104,091	37.4	Denver
Connecticut	1788	3,269,858	6	5,018	651.6	Hartford
Delaware	1787	731,581	1	2,045	357.7	Dover
District of Columbia	–	528,964	–	69	7,666.1	–
Florida	1845	14,653,945	23	58,664	249.8	Tallahassee
Georgia	1788	7,486,242	11	58,910	127.1	Atlanta
Hawaii	1959	1,186,602	2	6,471	183.4	Honolulu
Idaho	1890	1,210,232	2	83,564	14.5	Boise
Illinois	1818	11,895,849	20	56,345	211.1	Springfield
Indiana	1816	5,864,108	10	36,185	162.1	Indianapolis
Iowa	1846	2,852,423	5	56,275	50.7	Des Moines
Kansas	1861	2,594,840	4	82,277	31.5	Topeka
Kentucky	1792	3,908,124	6	40,410	96.7	Frankfort
Louisiana	1812	4,351,769	7	42,752	101.8	Baton Rouge
Maine	1820	1,242,051	2	33,265	37.3	Augusta
Maryland	1788	5,094,289	8	10,460	487.0	Annapolis
Massachusetts	1788	6,117,520	10	8,248	741.7	Boston
Michigan	1837	9,773,892	16	58,527	167.0	Lansing
Minnesota	1858	4,685,549	8	84,402	55.5	St. Paul
Mississippi	1817	2,730,501	5	47,689	57.3	Jackson
Missouri	1821	5,402,058	9	69,697	77.5	Jefferson City
Montana	1889	878,810	1	147,046	5.9	Helena
Nebraska	1867	1,656,870	3	77,355	21.4	Lincoln
Nevada	1864	1,676,809	2	110,561	15.2	Carson City
New Hampshire	1788	1,172,709	2	9,279	126.4	Concord
New Jersey	1787	8,052,849	13	7,787	1,034.1	Trenton
New Mexico	1912	1,729,751	3	121,593	14.2	Santa Fe
New York	1788	18,137,226	31	49,108	369.3	Albany
North Carolina	1789	7,425,183	12	52,669	141.0	Raleigh
North Dakota	1889	640,883	1	70,702	9.1	Bismarck
Ohio	1803	11,186,331	19	41,330	270.7	Columbus
Oklahoma	1907	3,317,091	6	69,956	47.4	Oklahoma City
Oregon	1859	3,243,487	5	97,073	33.4	Salem
Pennsylvania	1787	12,019,661	21	45,038	266.9	Harrisburg
Rhode Island	1790	987,429	2	1,212	814.7	Providence
South Carolina	1788	3,760,181	6	31,113	120.9	Columbia
South Dakota	1889	737,973	1	77,116	9.6	Pierre
Tennessee	1796	5,368,198	9	42,144	127.4	Nashville
Texas	1845	19,439,337	30	266,807	72.9	Austin
Utah	1896	2,059,148	3	84,899	24.3	Salt Lake City
Vermont	1791	588,978	1	9,614	61.3	Montpelier
Virginia	1788	6,733,996	11	40,767	165.2	Richmond
Washington	1889	5,610,362	9	68,139	82.3	Olympia
West Virginia	1863	1,815,787	3	24,232	74.9	Charleston
Wisconsin	1848	5,169,677	9	56,153	92.1	Madison
Wyoming	1890	479,743	1	97,809	4.9	Cheyenne

PRESIDENTS OF THE UNITED STATES

PRESIDENTS OF THE UNITED STATES

The Official Portraits

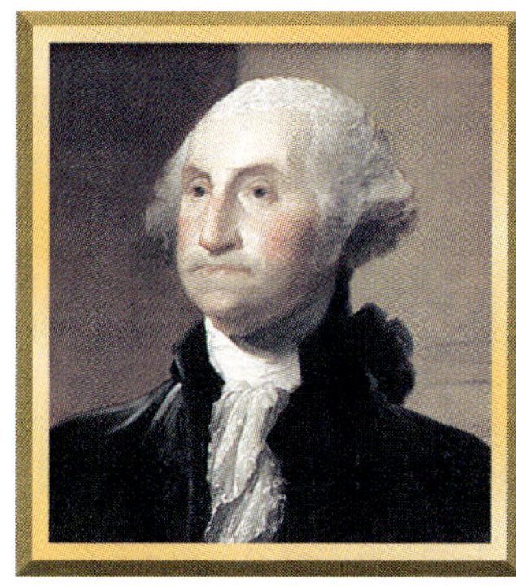

1 George Washington

Born: 1732 **Died:** 1799
Years in Office: 1789–97
Political Party: None
Home State: Virginia
Vice President: John Adams

2 John Adams

Born: 1735 **Died:** 1826
Years in Office: 1797–1801
Political Party: Federalist
Home State: Massachusetts
Vice President: Thomas Jefferson

3 Thomas Jefferson

Born: 1743 **Died:** 1826
Years in Office: 1801–09
Political Party: Republican*
Home State: Virginia
Vice Presidents: Aaron Burr, George Clinton

4 James Madison

Born: 1751 **Died:** 1836
Years in Office: 1809–17
Political Party: Republican
Home State: Virginia
Vice Presidents: George Clinton, Elbridge Gerry

5 James Monroe

Born: 1758 **Died:** 1831
Years in Office: 1817–25
Political Party: Republican
Home State: Virginia
Vice President: Daniel D. Tompkins

6 John Quincy Adams

Born: 1767 **Died:** 1848
Years in Office: 1825–29
Political Party: Republican
Home State: Massachusetts
Vice President: John C. Calhoun

7 Andrew Jackson

Born: 1767 **Died:** 1845
Years in Office: 1829–37
Political Party: Democratic
Home State: Tennessee
Vice Presidents: John C. Calhoun, Martin Van Buren

8 Martin Van Buren

Born: 1782 **Died:** 1862
Years in Office: 1837–41
Political Party: Democratic
Home State: New York
Vice President: Richard M. Johnson

* The Republican Party of the third through sixth presidents is not the Republican Party of Abraham Lincoln, which was founded in 1854.

PRESIDENTS OF THE UNITED STATES

9 William Henry Harrison

Born: 1773 **Died:** 1841
Years in Office: 1841
Political Party: Whig
Home State: Ohio
Vice President: John Tyler

10 John Tyler

Born: 1790 **Died:** 1862
Years in Office: 1841–45
Political Party: Whig
Home State: Virginia
Vice President: None

11 James K. Polk

Born: 1795 **Died:** 1849
Years in Office: 1845–49
Political Party: Democratic
Home State: Tennessee
Vice President: George M. Dallas

12 Zachary Taylor

Born: 1784 **Died:** 1850
Years in Office: 1849–50
Political Party: Whig
Home State: Louisiana
Vice President: Millard Fillmore

13 Millard Fillmore

Born: 1800 **Died:** 1874
Years in Office: 1850–53
Political Party: Whig
Home State: New York
Vice President: None

14 Franklin Pierce

Born: 1804 **Died:** 1869
Years in Office: 1853–57
Political Party: Democratic
Home State: New Hampshire
Vice President: William R. King

15 James Buchanan

Born: 1791 **Died:** 1868
Years in Office: 1857–61
Political Party: Democratic
Home State: Pennsylvania
Vice President: John C. Breckinridge

16 Abraham Lincoln

Born: 1809 **Died:** 1865
Years in Office: 1861–65
Political Party: Republican
Home State: Illinois
Vice President: Hannibal Hamlin, Andrew Johnson

17 Andrew Johnson

Born: 1808 **Died:** 1875
Years in Office: 1865-69
Political Party: Republican
Home State: Tennessee
Vice President: None

PRESIDENTS OF THE UNITED STATES

18 Ulysses S. Grant

Born: 1822 **Died:** 1885
Years in Office: 1869–77
Political Party: Republican
Home State: Illinois
Vice President: Schuyler Colfax, Henry Wilson

19 Rutherford B. Hayes

Born: 1822 **Died:** 1893
Years in Office: 1877–81
Political Party: Republican
Home State: Ohio
Vice President: William A. Wheeler

20 James A. Garfield

Born: 1831 **Died:** 1881
Years in Office: 1881
Political Party: Republican
Home State: Ohio
Vice President: Chester A. Arthur

21 Chester A. Arthur

Born: 1829 **Died:** 1886
Years in Office: 1881–85
Political Party: Republican
Home State: New York
Vice President: None

22 Grover Cleveland

Born: 1837 **Died:** 1908
Years in Office: 1885–89
Political Party: Democratic
Home State: New York
Vice President: Thomas A. Hendricks

23 Benjamin Harrison

Born: 1833 **Died:** 1901
Years in Office: 1889–93
Political Party: Republican
Home State: Indiana
Vice President: Levi P. Morton

24 Grover Cleveland

Born: 1837 **Died:** 1908
Years in Office: 1893–97
Political Party: Democratic
Home State: New York
Vice President: Adlai E. Stevenson

25 William McKinley

Born: 1843 **Died:** 1901
Years in Office: 1897–1901
Political Party: Republican
Home State: Ohio
Vice President: Garret A. Hobart, Theodore Roosevelt

26 Theodore Roosevelt

Born: 1858 **Died:** 1919
Years in Office: 1901-09
Political Party: Republican
Home State: New York
Vice President: Charles W. Fairbanks

PRESIDENTS OF THE UNITED STATES

27 William Howard Taft

Born: 1857 **Died:** 1930
Years in Office: 1909–13
Political Party: Republican
Home State: Ohio
Vice President: James S. Sherman

28 Woodrow Wilson

Born: 1856 **Died:** 1924
Years in Office: 1913–21
Political Party: Democratic
Home State: New Jersey
Vice President: Thomas R. Marshall

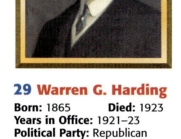

29 Warren G. Harding

Born: 1865 **Died:** 1923
Years in Office: 1921–23
Political Party: Republican
Home State: Ohio
Vice President: Calvin Coolidge

30 Calvin Coolidge

Born: 1872 **Died:** 1933
Years in Office: 1923–29
Political Party: Republican
Home State: Massachusetts
Vice President: Charles G. Dawes

31 Herbert Hoover

Born: 1874 **Died:** 1964
Years in Office: 1929–33
Political Party: Republican
Home State: California
Vice President: Charles Curtis

32 Franklin D. Roosevelt

Born: 1882 **Died:** 1945
Years in Office: 1933–45
Political Party: Democratic
Home State: New York
Vice President: John Nance Garner, Henry Wallace, Harry S Truman

33 Harry S Truman

Born: 1884 **Died:** 1972
Years in Office: 1945–53
Political Party: Democratic
Home State: Missouri
Vice President: Alben W. Barkley

34 Dwight D. Eisenhower

Born: 1890 **Died:** 1969
Years in Office: 1953–61
Political Party: Republican
Home State: Kansas
Vice President: Richard M. Nixon

35 John F. Kennedy

Born: 1917 **Died:** 1963
Years in Office: 1961–63
Political Party: Democratic
Home State: Massachusetts
Vice President: Lyndon B. Johnson

PRESIDENTS OF THE UNITED STATES

36 Lyndon B. Johnson

Born: 1908 **Died:** 1973
Years in Office: 1963–69
Political Party: Democratic
Home State: Texas
Vice President: Hubert H. Humphrey

37 Richard M. Nixon

Born: 1913 **Died:** 1994
Years in Office: 1969–74
Political Party: Republican
Home State: California
Vice President: Spiro T. Agnew, Gerald R. Ford

38 Gerald R. Ford

Born: 1913
Years in Office: 1974–77
Political Party: Republican
Home State: Michigan
Vice President: Nelson A. Rockefeller

39 Jimmy Carter

Born: 1924
Years in Office: 1977–81
Political Party: Democratic
Home State: Georgia
Vice President: Walter F. Mondale

40 Ronald Reagan

Born: 1911
Years in Office: 1981–89
Political Party: Republican
Home State: California
Vice President: George Bush

41 George Bush

Born: 1924
Years in Office: 1989–93
Political Party: Republican
Home State: Texas
Vice President: Dan Quayle

42 Bill Clinton

Born: 1946
Years in Office: 1993–
Political Party: Democratic
Home State: Arkansas
Vice President: Al Gore Jr.

LEADING SUPREME COURT CASES

1 *Marbury* v. *Madison*

1 Cranch (5 U.S.) 137 (1803)

What was this case about?

The story. The Federalist Party had been defeated in the election of 1800. However, President-elect Thomas Jefferson was not scheduled to take office until March 4, 1801. In the meantime, the outgoing president, John Adams, chose a number of Federalist supporters as justices of the peace in the District of Columbia. These justices received their appointments in the final hours of the Adams administration. However, they were unable to take office until their commissions were delivered. After the new president took over, he found that the previous secretary of state, John Marshall, had not had time to deliver all of the commissions. Jefferson immediately ordered his new secretary of state, James Madison, not to deliver the remaining commissions.

As one of the people whose commission was not delivered, William Marbury sued Madison. Marbury took advantage of a law passed by Congress that allowed him to make this kind of complaint directly to the Supreme Court. He asked the Court to order Madison to deliver the commission even though this request meant disobeying the president. Marbury probably expected the Court to do as he asked because John Marshall had been appointed Chief Justice of the United States.

The question. As Chief Justice Marshall saw it, the question before the Court had three parts. First, did Marbury have a right to receive the commission? Second, if he did have a right to the commission, was the government required to ensure that he received the commission? Finally, if the government was required to do so, would it have to order Madison to deliver Marbury's commission, as Marbury requested?

The issues. Chief Justice Marshall wanted the Court to be able to decide if laws passed by Congress were constitutional. Whether the Court had this power of judicial review—the power to decide if laws made by Congress are allowed by the Constitution—had not yet been decided. Marshall posed the question before the Court in three parts in order to discuss judicial review.

How was the case decided?

In 1803 the Court ruled against ordering Madison to deliver Marbury's commission.

What did the Court say about governmental powers?

The Court's reasoning passed through three stages:

Step 1. Pointing to a federal law that outlined the appointment process for District of Columbia justices of the peace, the Court said that Marbury had a right to the commission.

Step 2. The Court said that when government officials hurt people by neglecting legal duties, our laws require a remedy.

Step 3. Marbury had asked that the Supreme Court order Madison to deliver the commission. Here Chief Justice Marshall did something surprising. He declared that a court could issue such an order, but that the Supreme Court was not the right court to issue it.

Marbury had taken advantage of a federal law that allowed complaints such as his to be taken straight to the Supreme Court. However, Chief Justice Marshall declared this law unconstitutional. The Constitution mentions several kinds of cases that can be brought straight to the Supreme Court. All other kinds of cases must go through lower courts first. The chief justice explained that Marbury's lawsuit was one of the kinds of cases that must go through lower courts first. It did not matter that Congress had passed a law saying something different, because the Constitution is a higher law.

Marshall's cleverly written opinion excused the Supreme Court from hearing lawsuits such as the Marbury case before lower courts had heard them. Marshall accomplished this by claiming for the Court an even greater power—the power of judicial review.

What implications did this case have for the future?

If the Supreme Court did not have judicial review, Congress would decide for itself on the constitutionality of the laws it passed. Marshall's opinion in *Marbury* v. *Madison* removed that power from Congress. By deciding on the constitutionality of the other two branches' actions, the Supreme Court is the nation's final authority on the meaning of the Constitution.

2 *Martin* v. *Hunter's Lessee*

1 Wheaton (14 U.S.) 304 (1816)

What was this case about?

The story. In 1777, during the Revolutionary War, Virginia passed a law declaring that land owned by people who were still loyal to Great Britain no longer belonged to them. One person affected by this law was

Thomas Lord Fairfax. When he died in England in 1782, his Virginia lands passed to his American relative, Thomas Martin. However, Virginia gave Fairfax's land to David Hunter.

Thomas Martin considered himself the true owner of the land. Hunter disagreed and rented it to someone else. The renter (called the "lessee") tried to have Martin evicted. Virginia's highest court ruled that Hunter owned the land.

Martin appealed his case to the U.S. Supreme Court. He reminded the Court of the treaties between the United States and Britain. These treaties promised to protect the rights of British subjects who had owned property in America before the Revolution. Because of these treaties, he said, Virginia's 1777 law was not valid. The Supreme Court agreed. It sent the case back to the Virginia court with orders to change its decision.

However, the Virginia court denied that the Supreme Court had the authority to tell a state court what to do. Therefore, Martin asked the Supreme Court to reverse the Virginia court's judgment.

The question. In cases that involve the federal Constitution, laws, and treaties, does the Constitution give federal courts the power to reverse state court judgments?

The issues. In *Marbury* v. *Madison* the Supreme Court asserted the power of judicial review, but that did not settle the issue of how far the power of judicial review extends. In *Marbury* v. *Madison* one of the other branches of the federal government had been overruled, but in this case Martin was asking the Supreme Court to overrule one of the branches of a state government.

How was the case decided?

In 1816, in an opinion written by Justice Joseph Story, the Supreme Court did what Martin asked. It reversed the judgment of the Virginia court.

What did the Court say about governmental powers?

Justice Story thought that the Constitution gave the Supreme Court the power to reverse state courts in cases involving the federal Constitution, laws, and treaties. To explain his decision, he first tried to show why various objections to his view were mistaken. One such objection was that the Constitution does not affect state governments, but rather the people living in those states. Justice Story pointed out that the Constitution is "crowded" with conditions that affect the state governments. Another objection was that federal judges might abuse the power they had to decide the meaning of the federal Constitution, laws, and treaties. Justice Story explained that the power of final decision has to be put somewhere and that it was placed with the Supreme Court.

Finally, Justice Story asserted the need for uniformity. If federal judges were not allowed to reverse state court judgments, then state courts all over the country might interpret the federal Constitution, laws, and treaties in different ways.

What implications did this case have for the future?

Under the Constitution, power is divided between two levels: state and national. U.S. history is full of various kinds of conflicts between the states and the national government. Usually, as in *Martin* v. *Hunter's Lessee,* the national government has won these conflicts. Thus, there has been a slow drift of power from the states to the national government. Justice Story, however, did not claim that federal courts could overrule state courts in all cases. He said only that they could overrule state courts in cases involving the U.S. Constitution, laws, and treaties.

3 *McCulloch* v. *Maryland*

4 Wheaton (17 U.S.) 316 (1819)

What was this case about?

The story. In 1791 Congress passed a law that set up the Bank of the United States. An attempt to renew the Bank's charter in 1811 failed. A number of states took advantage of this situation to charter their own banks.

After the War of 1812, the federal government needed money to pay for the war. Instead of being able to borrow money from one central bank, it had to deal with many state banks. Thus, Congress set up the Second Bank of the United States in 1816. The states generally opposed the National Bank, and several states passed laws that hindered it. For instance, they taxed branches of the Bank within their borders. When the Maryland branch of the Bank refused to pay the tax, Maryland sued the bank's cashier, James McCulloch. In 1919 the legal battle reached the Supreme Court.

The question. As Chief Justice John Marshall saw it, the question before the Court had two parts. Does the Constitution give Congress the power to establish a national bank? If so, does the Constitution allow a state to tax that bank?

The issues. The question of whether Congress had the power to establish a bank was not new. In 1791, after Congress had passed the bill that established the First Bank of the United States, President George Washington had asked his cabinet for advice. He noted

943

that although Article I, Section 8, of the Constitution lists the powers of Congress, it does not mention the power to charter a bank. Yet the article does state that in addition to the listed powers, Congress may also make all laws that are "necessary and proper" for carrying out the listed powers.

Alexander Hamilton and Thomas Jefferson presented Washington with sharply opposing views. Hamilton considered the power to charter a bank constitutional because it had "a natural relation" to the powers of collecting taxes and regulating trade. By contrast, Jefferson said that while the power to charter a bank may be "convenient" for carrying out this power, it was not "necessary," and thus was unconstitutional. Finding Hamilton's argument more convincing, Washington signed the bill. Maryland, however, wanted the Supreme Court to interpret the Constitution as Jefferson had done.

How was the case decided?

Led by Chief Justice Marshall, the Supreme Court ruled that the Constitution allowed Congress to establish the National Bank. The Court also asserted that the Constitution did not allow a state to tax the Bank.

What did the Court say about governmental powers?

Jefferson's argument against the First Bank of the United States had rested on a strict interpretation of the word "necessary" in the necessary and proper clause. The state of Maryland used the same argument. In deciding the first question, Marshall said that Maryland's interpretation of the Constitution was not broad enough. He explained that when the Constitution says that certain means are "necessary" to an end, it usually does not mean that the end cannot be achieved without them. Rather, it means that they are "calculated to produce" the end. The power to charter a bank is calculated to help carry out the other constitutional powers, so the Constitution permits it.

The second question before the Court was whether the Constitution allows a state to tax the National Bank. If the states could tax one of the federal government's activities, they could tax any of them. Marshall said that because "the power to tax involves the power to destroy," this could not be permitted. The supremacy clause in Article VI states that the Constitution and laws of the federal government come before state constitutions and laws.

What implications did this case have for the future?

As new cases arise, members of the Supreme Court try to settle them by using principles that have been established in earlier cases. This case involves the principles of implied powers and national supremacy. Some powers given to the federal government by the Constitution are listed. These are called enumerated powers. Others, called implied powers, are understood as given because they are needed to help carry out the enumerated powers. The federal government has only those powers that are enumerated and implied in the Constitution. However, when the federal government is using powers that do belong to it, the states must give way.

4 *Scott* v. *Sandford*

19 Howard (60 U.S.) 393 (1857)

What was this case about?

The story. In 1833 a slave named Dred Scott was purchased by John Emerson, an army doctor. As the army transferred Emerson from post to post, Scott went with him. First they went to Illinois; later they moved to Wisconsin Territory. When Emerson was transferred yet again, he sent Scott to Missouri, a slave state, to live with his wife, Eliza Irene Sanford Emerson. She inherited Scott when her husband died in 1843.

At this time, slavery was illegal in Illinois and in Wisconsin Territory. Scott believed that because he had lived on free soil for five years, he should be free.

In 1846 Emerson moved to New England and left Scott with sons of Scott's original owner. One son opposed the spread of slavery. He helped Scott file a lawsuit. In 1850 a Missouri court declared Scott free.

In 1852 the Missouri Supreme Court reversed the lower court's ruling. In 1854, however, Scott's original lawsuit was revived by lawyers who wanted the issue of slavery in the territories to be resolved. Scott's case worked its way to the Supreme Court.

The question. As Chief Justice Roger B. Taney saw it, the case raised two questions. First, does the Constitution give an African American the right to file a suit in federal court? Second, does the Constitution allow Congress to pass a law that frees slaves who are brought into a free territory?

The issues. If African Americans were U.S. citizens, then they must have all of the rights of other citizens, including the right to sue in a federal court. Therefore, the first question before the court involved the Constitution's definition of a citizen.

The second question before the Court involved the kinds of limits the Constitution puts on laws about property. If slaves were property, then Congress faced the same limits when it made a law about slavery as when it made a law about property.

How was the case decided?

The Court ruled that the Constitution denied African Americans the right to sue in federal court and denied Congress the power to make a law abolishing or prohibiting slavery in the territories.

What did the Court say about constitutional rights?

The first theme of the Court's opinion was the relationship between race and citizenship. The opinion reflected the prejudices of the day. Taney said that African Americans had "none of the rights and privileges" of citizens. This statement was particularly startling because it applied to free African Americans as well as to slaves. Taney ignored the important fact that many states considered free African Americans to be state citizens. In addition, Article III, Section 2, of the Constitution gives the federal courts jurisdiction over various kinds of suits involving state citizens.

The other theme of the Court's opinion concerned slavery. The Fifth Amendment states that no one may be "deprived of life, liberty, or property, without due process of law." First, the chief justice reasoned that because slaves are "property," they could not be taken away without due process of law. Second, he reasoned that a law taking away citizens' property just because they entered a free territory cheated them of their due process of law. In addition, Taney ruled that the Missouri Compromise was unconstitutional.

What implications did this case have for the future?

By the time the Court made its decision, the Kansas-Nebraska Act had already canceled the Missouri Compromise's ban on slavery in certain federal territories. Therefore, it might seem that the Court's judgment did not matter. However, the Kansas-Nebraska Act was unpopular with people who opposed the spread of slavery. Many of them would have liked to have seen a return to something like the Missouri Compromise. The decision made such a return impossible and worsened the controversy over slavery in the territories.

Furthermore, this case established that merely freeing slaves was not enough to guarantee their U.S. citizenship. Not until 1868, when the Fourteenth Amendment was passed, did the Constitution guarantee that African Americans were U.S. citizens.

5 *Lochner* v. *New York*

198 U.S. 45 (1905)

What was this case about?

The story. In 1895 the New York legislature passed a law regulating the number of hours that bakery employees could be required or allowed to work. This law was necessary to prevent workers from having to agree to work long hours out of fear of losing their jobs. The legislature claimed that workers should not be allowed to work long hours because of potential harm to their health.

Joseph Lochner, a bakery owner convicted of violating the law, appealed. He said that the law was unconstitutional because it took away his liberty to make a contract. Lochner said that liberty of contract is promised by a clause in the Fourteenth Amendment that says that no state may "deprive any person of life, liberty, or property, without due process of law."

The question. Do limits on the number of hours an employee may work violate the Fourteenth Amendment?

The issues. State governments have a general power—called the police power—to make regulations that support the safety, health, morals, and general welfare of their citizens. The basic issue in this case is whether the Constitution can limit state governments' police power in some cases.

Various amendments set limits on the power of state governments, but the most general is the due process clause of the Fourteenth Amendment. To apply this clause to the New York bakery law, the Supreme Court had to decide what freedoms are meant by the word *liberty* and what is promised by the guarantee of due process of law.

How was the case decided?

The Court ruled that the law limiting the hours of labor in bakeries was unconstitutional.

What did the Court say about governmental powers?

Justice Rufus Wheeler Peckham argued that the New York legislature's interference with liberty of contract was improper. Peckham did not mean that the Constitution forbids all interference with liberty of contract. In fact, he stressed that the Court had approved a similar Utah law that said that no one could work more than eight hours a day in an underground mine except in cases of emergency. Such uses of the police power, he said, were "fair, reasonable, and appropriate." They regulate liberty without taking it away. By contrast, he argued, the New York law had nothing to do with safety, morals, or general welfare and was not necessary to protect health.

What implications did this case have for the future?

Even though the Court tries to rely on the same principles over and over, sometimes its members change

945

their minds about controversial issues. Four justices dissented, or disagreed with the *Lochner* ruling. As the membership of the Supreme Court has changed, so have the attitudes of the justices. In 1937 the Court began to reverse the precedent it had set in *Lochner*.

6 *Plessy* v. *Ferguson*
163 U.S. 537 (1896)
Brown v. *Board of Education*
347 U.S. 483 (1954)

What were these cases about?

The stories. These two cases illustrate a major change in the legality of racial segregation. *Plessy* v. *Ferguson* began with an 1890 Louisiana law that required all railway companies to provide "equal but separate" accommodations for white and African American passengers. A group of people who thought the law was unfair recruited Homer Plessy to get arrested in order to test the law. Plessy entered a train and took an empty seat in an all-white area. When he refused to move to an all-black section, he was arrested and jailed. In his defense, he said that the 1890 law was unconstitutional. The case eventually worked its way up to the Supreme Court.

More than 50 years later, an African American man named Oliver Brown and his family moved into a white neighborhood in Topeka, Kansas. The Browns assumed that their daughter Linda would attend the neighborhood school. Instead, the Board of Education ordered her to attend a distant all-black school that was supposedly "separate but equal." Charging that school segregation violated the Fourteenth Amendment to the Constitution, Mr. Brown sued the Board.

The question. The question raised by the Court was the same in both cases. Do racially segregated facilities violate the equal protection clause of the Fourteenth Amendment?

The issues. The state of Louisiana argued that separate railway carriages could be equal. For instance, they could be equally clean and equally safe. The state of Kansas said much the same thing, claiming that its all-black and all-white schools were equal in such features as teachers' skills and buildings' quality.

In the days of racial segregation, the claim that segregated facilities were equal in tangible, or measurable, features was almost always a terrible lie. The issue facing the Court, however, went deeper. Even if things were made equal in racially segregated facilities, was there something fundamentally unequal about segregation?

How were the cases decided?

In *Plessy* v. *Ferguson,* the Court ruled that the Fourteenth Amendment's equal protection clause allows racial segregation. In *Brown* v. *Board of Education,* however, the Court unanimously ruled that the clause does not allow racial segregation.

What did the Court say about constitutional rights?

Justice Henry Billings Brown wrote the Court's opinion in *Plessy.* He admitted that the purpose of the Fourteenth Amendment was "to enforce the absolute equality of the two races before the law." However, he said that this statement meant political equality, not social equality. Brown declared that there was no truth to the argument that separate facilities implied that African Americans were inferior.

In *Brown* the Court's opinion was written by Chief Justice Earl Warren. He said that separation of black schoolchildren from white schoolchildren of the same age and ability "generates a feeling of inferiority . . . that may affect their hearts and minds in a way unlikely ever to be undone." He said that when racial segregation is required by law, the harm is even greater. It makes no difference that "the physical facilities and other 'tangible' factors may be equal."

What implications did these cases have for the future?

In *Brown* v. *Board of Education,* the Court did not say that the "separate but equal" doctrine was completely invalid. It ruled that the doctrine had no place in public education. This statement, although limited, influenced future cases that eventually abolished all segregation. Taken together, *Plessy* and *Brown* show that interpretation of the Constitution's legal principles may change as society changes.

7 *Gideon* v. *Wainwright*
372 U.S. 335 (1963)

What was this case about?

The story. Clarence Earl Gideon was accused of breaking and entering a Florida poolroom. When Gideon's case came to trial, he could not afford a lawyer, so he asked that the court pay for one. The judge refused, the case proceeded, and Gideon was found guilty. While in prison, Gideon appealed to the U.S. Supreme Court. He claimed that by refusing to appoint him a lawyer, Florida had violated rights promised him by the Sixth and Fourteenth Amendments.

The question. Do the Sixth and the Fourteenth Amendments require that a poor person accused of a crime have access to an attorney free of charge?

The issues. The Sixth Amendment ensures certain rights to people accused of crimes. For example, "The accused shall enjoy the right . . . to have the Assistance of Counsel [a lawyer] for his defense." By itself, this amendment requires that poor people be provided with free lawyers in federal trials. Yet Gideon had been accused of breaking state laws and was tried in a state court. Still, the Fourteenth Amendment ensures that states cannot deprive people of life, liberty, or property without due process of law. Jailed, Gideon had been deprived of liberty. Had this liberty been taken away without due process of law?

How was the case decided?

In a unanimous opinion written by Justice Hugo Black, the Court ruled in Gideon's favor.

What did the Court say about constitutional rights?

Members of the Court based their decision on two different views of the Fourteenth Amendment. One is the incorporation view, which holds that the purpose of the due process clause is to incorporate most of the Bill of Rights into state court procedures. The second is the fundamental liberties view, which holds that "due process of law" means "whatever is necessary for justice." What is necessary for justice may not include every assurance in the Bill of Rights, but it may include assurances that go beyond anything in the Bill of Rights. In *Gideon* v. *Wainwright* the justices came to the same conclusion by different means.

Justice Black had to tailor the Court's decision to accommodate both the incorporation view and the fundamental liberties view. The opinion was a compromise. It said that the Sixth Amendment's assurance of the "assistance of counsel" is necessary for a fair trial in any court, but it did not say that due process covers every other assurance in the first eight amendments.

What implications did this case have for the future?

Gideon v. *Wainwright* was one of several Supreme Court cases guaranteeing government payment to lawyers defending poor people accused of crimes. The Criminal Justice Act of 1964, signed into law the year after the *Gideon* decision, provided the funding.

8 *Miranda* v. *Arizona*

384 U.S. 436 (1966)

What was this case about?

The story. On March 13, 1963, a woman was kidnapped near Phoenix. Ernesto Miranda was arrested for the crime, and the victim identified him in a police lineup. Two officers then questioned him. Although at first Miranda denied the crime, after a short time he wrote out and signed a confession.

At the trial the officers testified that they had warned Miranda that anything he might say could be used against him in court and that Miranda had understood. The officers also said that he had confessed without any threats or force. They admitted, however, that they had not told Miranda about his right to silence or legal assistance. Miranda was found guilty. Eventually, he appealed to the U.S. Supreme Court.

The question. Is it a violation of the Fifth, Sixth, or Fourteenth Amendment to use a confession to convict someone who has not been informed of the constitutional rights to silence and legal assistance?

The issues. The Fifth Amendment ensures a person the right to remain silent: "No person . . . shall be compelled [forced] in any criminal case to be a witness against himself." Without such a right, innocent people could be tortured into confessing to a crime they did not commit. The Sixth Amendment ensures the assistance of a lawyer to defendants in criminal trials in federal courts. The Fourteenth Amendment does the same for defendants in state courts.

One issue is the point at which Fifth and Sixth Amendment rights begin. Do they begin only at the trial? Or do these rights begin earlier?

A deeper issue concerns the meaning of being forced to be a witness against oneself. Perhaps keeping a person ignorant of his or her rights is a kind of force. If so, then it violates the Fifth Amendment.

How was the case decided?

By a 5-to-4 majority, the Supreme Court ruled that taking Miranda's confession without informing him of his rights to silence and legal assistance had violated his constitutional rights.

What did the Court say about constitutional rights?

The Court ruled that the Fifth and Sixth Amendment rights exist as soon as a person is in custody. The Court also ruled that failing to inform the accused of his or her rights is a violation of the right not to testify against oneself.

Today if prisoners are not informed of their rights, judges may rule that what the accused tells the police cannot be used as evidence in court. Furthermore, the court must disregard any evidence that is based on what the accused said.

What implications did this case have for the future?

The *Miranda* ruling has been controversial because it deals with the delicate balance between protecting the

947

accused and protecting society. A hotly debated aspect of the decision has been the ruling that confessions given by accused people who have not been informed of their rights may not be used as evidence. The Court did this to prevent innocent people from being found guilty. Some people argue, however, that it prevents the guilty from being convicted.

9 *Roe* v. *Wade*

410 U.S. 113 (1973)

What was this case about?

The story. In 1970 Norma McCorvey, an unmarried pregnant woman living in Texas, sought to obtain a legal abortion in a medical facility. Because of Texas's antiabortion statute, no licensed physician would agree to perform the procedure. McCorvey was financially unable to travel to another state with a less-restrictive abortion law. She faced either continuing an unwanted pregnancy or having the procedure performed in a nonmedical facility, which she believed would endanger her life.

McCorvey claimed that the Texas antiabortion law was unconstitutional because it interfered with her right of personal privacy that is protected by the Ninth and Fourteenth Amendments. She took legal action, naming the Dallas County district attorney, Henry Wade, in her lawsuit. Throughout the case, McCorvey used the pseudonym Jane Roe.

The question. Is it a violation of a person's right to privacy for a state to prevent a woman from terminating a pregnancy through an abortion?

The issues. The Fourteenth Amendment states that "no state shall make or enforce any law which shall abridge [diminish] the privileges . . . of citizens of the United States . . . nor deny to any person . . . the equal protection of the laws." The Ninth Amendment states that "the enumeration [naming] in the Constitution of certain rights shall not be construed [interpreted] to deny or disparage [reduce] others retained by the people." Do these amendments include and protect a woman's right to a legal abortion?

How was the case decided?

In an opinion written by Justice Harry Blackmun, the Court ruled that the Fourteenth Amendment's due process guarantee of personal liberty ensures the right to personal privacy. This guarantee protects a woman's decision about abortion and assures that a state's laws do not abridge this right. The vote was seven to two.

What did the Court say about constitutional rights?

In ruling that a state cannot prevent a woman from terminating a pregnancy during the first three months, the Court relied on the citizens' right to privacy. Justice Blackmun stated in his opinion that "[t]his right of privacy, whether it be founded in the Fourteenth Amendment's concept of personal liberty and restrictions upon state action, as we feel it is, or . . . in the Ninth Amendment's reservation of rights to the people, is broad enough to encompass [include] a woman's decision whether or not to terminate her pregnancy." In its ruling, however, the Court recognized the right of a state to regulate abortions as a pregnancy progressed. During the first three months of a pregnancy, a woman has a virtually unrestricted right to an abortion.

During the second trimester, a state can regulate abortions to protect a woman's health. Only in the final three months of a pregnancy can a state forbid an abortion, unless the procedure is necessary to protect a woman's life.

The ruling also said that a state cannot adopt a theory of when life begins. This prevents a state from giving a fetus the same rights as a newborn.

What implications did this case have for the future?

Since the 1973 ruling, related cases have been decided that some people claim weaken the legislative impact of *Roe* v. *Wade*. In *Harris* v. *McRae* (1980), the Court upheld a law that blocked the use of federal funds to pay for abortions for women on welfare. Critics of the ruling claimed that women who could not afford the procedure would, like Jane Roe, be faced with either continuing an unwanted pregnancy or resorting to dangerous measures to terminate it. The ruling in *Webster* v. *Reproductive Health Services* (1989) added more restrictions to the availability of abortions.

10 *Regents of the University of California* v. *Bakke*

438 U.S. 265 (1978)

What was this case about?

The story. A white man named Allan Bakke twice applied to the medical school at the University of California, Davis, during the years in which the medical school operated two different admissions programs. After the Civil Rights Act of 1964, schools and other institutions were under pressure to provide special admissions programs for minority students. There were, however, no specific guidelines on how to accomplish this.

At the University of California, Davis, medical school 84 of the 100 places in the incoming class were filled from the regular program. The remaining 16 spots were set aside for a special program that used a quota system. The regular program was for students of all races, as long as they met admission requirements, including a minimum grade point average. Only members of racial minorities could apply through the special program, and their grades did not have to meet the minimum.

Bakke applied through the regular program and was turned down. He thought he had been treated unfairly because in both years, students had been admitted through the special program whose grades and test scores were much lower than his. He sued the state university system. Bakke said the special program, established to fulfill the racial quota, violated his Fourteenth Amendment right to equal protection of the law.

The California Supreme Court made two rulings. One said that Davis's admission system was illegal and ordered Bakke admitted. The other ordered that in the future, admissions decisions must not take race into consideration. The California university system appealed to the U.S. Supreme Court.

The questions. First, does the use of a racial quota in admissions violate the Fourteenth Amendment's equal protection clause? Second, does this clause require that race be completely ignored in admissions?

The issues. Historically, most racial discrimination in our country has hurt members of racial minorities. Bakke complained of reverse discrimination, a type of discrimination that supposedly hurt members of the racial majority in order to help members of racial minorities.

The Fourteenth Amendment was primarily written because African Americans who had recently been freed from slavery needed protection from discrimination by the white majority. This fact suggests that the equal protection clause protects racial minorities more than the racial majority. On the other hand, what the amendment actually says is that no state may deny to any person the equal protection of the laws. This fact suggests that the equal protection clause gives the same protection to people of all races. The intent of the amendment seems to have been to protect minorities, but its wording does not specify this intent.

How was the case decided?

The U.S. Supreme Court agreed that racial quotas in admissions was unconstitutional and ordered that Bakke be admitted. It rejected the idea that an admissions system may never pay any attention to race.

What did the Court say about constitutional rights?

Justice Lewis Powell wrote the Court's opinion. He said that the equal protection clause does not completely prohibit states from taking race into account when they are making laws and official policies. However, it does make the consideration of race "suspect," or suspicious. When such a law or policy is challenged in court, judges must apply a two-part test. First, are the purposes of the law or policy legitimate? Second, is the consideration given to race necessary to achieve these purposes? California told the Court that its racial quota had four purposes.

Purpose 1. To correct the shortage of racial minorities in medical schools and among doctors. Justice Powell said that this purpose was not acceptable. "Preferring members of any one group for no reason other than race or ethnic origin is discrimination for its own sake."

Purpose 2. To counteract the effects of racial discrimination in society. Justice Powell said that this was an acceptable purpose. He approved of helping people who belong to groups that have been hurt by past discrimination. However, he said that helping them by hurting others is right only when it makes up for hurts caused by those other people. There was no evidence that Bakke had ever discriminated against people of racial minorities.

Purpose 3: To increase the number of doctors who will be willing to practice medicine in communities where there are not enough doctors. This purpose was also acceptable. However, California had not shown that racial quotas were needed to accomplish this purpose.

Purpose 4. To improve education by making the student body more diverse. This purpose, too, was acceptable. However, Justice Powell pointed out that racial diversity is only one aspect of overall diversity and that racial quotas are not the only way to increase racial diversity.

What implications did this case have for the future?

This decision revealed that the members of the Court disagreed sharply about reverse discrimination. Furthermore, Powell stressed that the Court's decision concerned only reverse racial discrimination. He warned that reverse sexual discrimination may or may not have to be treated the same way as reverse racial discrimination. In the 1982 case *Mississippi University for Women* v. *Hogan,* however, the Court ruled that it was unconstitutional for a state-run school of nursing to refuse admission to men.

949

GLOSSARY

GLOSSARY

This glossary contains terms you need to understand as you study American history. After each key term there is a brief definition or explanation of the meaning of the term as it is used in *The American Nation*. The page number refers to the page on which the term is introduced in the textbook.

Phonetic Respelling and Pronunciation Guide

Many of the key terms in this textbook have been respelled to help you pronounce them. The letter combinations used in the respellings throughout the narrative are explained in the following phonetic respelling and pronunciation guide. The guide is adapted from *Merriam-Webster's Collegiate Dictionary, Merriam-Webster's Geographical Dictionary,* and *Merriam-Webster's Biographical Dictionary.*

MARK	AS IN	RESPELLING	EXAMPLE
a	alphabet	a	*AL-fuh-bet
ā	Asia	ay	AY-zhuh
ä	cart, top	ah	KAHRT, TAHP
e	let, ten	e	LET, TEN
ē	even, leaf	ee	EE-vuhn, LEEF
i	it, tip, British	i	IT, TIP, BRIT-ish
ī	site, buy, Ohio	y	SYT, BY, oh-HY-oh
	iris	eye	EYE-ris
k	card	k	KAHRD
ō	over, rainbow	oh	OH-vuhr, RAYN-boh
ü	book, wood	ooh	BOOHK, WOOHD
ȯ	all, orchid	aw	AWL, AWR-kid
ȯi	foil, coin	oy	FOYL, KOYN
aü	out	ow	OWT
ə	cup, butter	uh	KUHP, BUHT-uhr
ü	rule, food	oo	ROOL, FOOD
yü	few	yoo	FYOO
zh	vision	zh	VIZH-uhn

*A syllable printed in small capital letters receives heavier emphasis than the other syllable(s) in a word.

A

acid rain Rainfall containing chemicals such as nitrogen oxide and sulfur dioxide that gradually kills trees and lake-dwelling fish; caused by atmospheric pollution. **918**

acquired immune deficiency syndrome (AIDS) Often-fatal disease that forces the body's immune system to shut down, making it easier for a person to contract other fatal illnesses. **757**

Adamson Act (1916) Federal law reducing the workday for railroad workers from 10 to 8 hours with no cut in pay. **289**

affirmative action Practice by some government agencies, businesses, and schools of giving preference to ethnic minorities and women in admissions and hiring. **641**

Agricultural Adjustment Administration (AAA) Federal agency created by the Agricultural Adjustment Act in 1933 to reduce farmers' output and increase crop prices. **443**

Agricultural Revolution Ancient shift from hunting and gathering to the domestication of plants. **4**

Alianza Federal de Mercedes Federal Alliance of Land Grants; group led by Reies López Tijerina to try to regain land taken from Mexican Americans. **656**

Alliance for Progress President John F. Kennedy's program of economic aid to Latin America; designed to encourage democratic reforms and to promote capitalism. **598**

Allied Powers World War I alliance that included Britain, France, Russia, and later the United States, and that fought against the Central Powers. **329**; World War II alliance between Britain and France, and later the United States and other countries, that fought against the Axis Powers. **491**

American Association of Retired Persons (AARP) Largest lobbying group on behalf of senior citizens; founded in 1958. **664**

American Federation of Labor (AFL) Union founded in 1886 by Samuel Gompers for skilled workers. **186**

American Gothic One of the most famous regionalist paintings, by Grant Wood. **463**

American Indian Movement (AIM) Organization formed in 1968 to fight for the rights of American Indians. **662**

American Plan Policy promoted by business leaders during the 1920s that called for open shops. **371**

Americans with Disabilities Act (ADA) (1990) Law that prohibits discrimination against people with disabilities in employment, transportation, telephone services, and public buildings. **762**

American System Plan developed by Henry Clay for raising tariffs to pay for internal improvements such as roads and canals. **21**

amnesty An official pardon issued by the government. **103**

GLOSSARY

Anaconda Plan Union plan during the Civil War for a naval blockade of the South; compared to an Anaconda snake. **75**
anarchists People who oppose all forms of government. **185**
Angel Island Immigrant receiving station for Asian immigrants opened in 1910 in San Francisco, California. **859**
Antarctic Treaty (1959) International treaty establishing Antarctica as a nuclear-free zone. **914**
anti-Semitism Hatred of Jews. **486**
apartheid South African political system in which the white minority ruled and the black majority had few rights. **730**
Apollo 11 U.S. space mission that resulted in the first man on the Moon on July 20, 1969. **736**
appeasement Giving in to an aggressor to avoid conflict. **490**
arbitration Process by which two opposing sides allow a third party to settle a dispute. **276**
Area Redevelopment Act (ARA) Law passed in 1961 that provided financial assistance to economically distressed regions. **607**
Articles of Confederation (1777) Document that created an association of states while guaranteeing each state its "sovereignty, freedom, and independence." **13**
assembly line Production system created by Henry Ford to make goods faster by moving parts on a conveyer belt past workers. **387**
asylum Policy of nations offering a place of protection to anyone being persecuted for political reasons. **865**
Atlantic Charter (1941) Pledge signed by U.S. president Franklin D. Roosevelt and British prime minister Winston Churchill not to acquire new territory as a result of World War II and to work for peace after the war. **494**
Atomic Energy Act (1946) Federal law that created the Atomic Energy Commission to oversee nuclear weapons research and to promote peacetime uses of atomic energy. **540**
automation Use of machines to replace humans in production. **571**
auto-touring Craze that encouraged Americans to take long sightseeing trips in their automobiles. **390**
Axis Powers Military alliance formed by Italy and Germany in 1936; later joined by Japan. **490**
Aztec Mexica; warrior empire that dominated what is now Mexico during the Middle Ages. **5**

B

baby boom Soaring birthrate in the United States following World War II. **573**
Ballinger-Pinchot affair Incident in which President William Howard Taft fired Gifford Pinchot as head of the U.S. Forestry Service for criticizing Secretary of the Interior Richard Ballinger's sale of Alaskan land; weakened support for Taft. **283**
Bandung Conference (1955) Meeting of third-world nations in Indonesia that inspired the nonaligned movement. **817**
bank holiday (1933) New Deal proclamation that temporarily closed every U.S. bank to stop massive withdrawals. **440**
barbed wire Inexpensive fencing material invented by Joseph Glidden in 1874. **153**
barcodes Series of vertical bars of varying widths printed on products; used to track inventory. **871**
Baruch Plan (1946) Bernard Baruch's proposal to create an international agency that would impose penalties on countries that violated international controls on nuclear weapons. **540**
Bataan Death March (1942) Brutal forced march of American and Filipino prisoners during World War II up the Bataan Peninsula; more than 10,000 died. **504**
Battle of Antietam (1862) Union victory in Maryland during the Civil War; marked the bloodiest single-day battle in U.S. military history. **86**
Battle of Gettysburg (1863) Union victory at Gettysburg, Pennsylvania, during the Civil War that turned the tide against the Confederates; more than 40,000 soldiers died. **90**
Battle of Iwo Jima (1945) Six-week struggle for control of a key Pacific island that resulted in an Allied victory. **524**
Battle of Leyte Gulf (1944) Last, largest, and most decisive naval engagement in the Pacific during World War II; afterward, the Japanese fleet no longer seriously threatened the Allies. **522**
Battle of Midway (1942) World War II battle in which the Allied forces crippled Japan's navy. **504**
Battle of Okinawa (1945) Bloody battle in the Pacific during World War II; resulted in an Allied victory. **524**
Battle of Shiloh (1862) Civil War battle; resulted in greater Union control over the Mississippi River valley. **82**
Battle of the Argonne Forest (1918) Successful Allied effort to push back German troops from a rail center in Sedan, France. **349**
Battle of the Atlantic World War II naval campaign fought between German U-boats and Allied naval and air forces. **515**
Battle of the Bulge (1944) World War II battle in which the Allies defeated the final German offensive. **518**
Battle of the Coral Sea (1942) World War II battle in which the Allies stopped the Japanese advance to New Guinea. **504**
Battle of the Little Bighorn (1876) Battle between U.S. soldiers, led by George Armstrong Custer, and Sioux warriors; worst U.S. Army defeat in the West. **137**
Battle of the Somme (1916) World War I battle in which the British lost some 60,000 troops in a single day. **331**
Battle of Yorktown (1781) Last major battle of the Revolutionary War; site of British general Charles Cornwallis's surrender to the Patriots in Virginia. **12**
bear market Downward trend in stock prices. **415**
beats Small but influential group of writers who challenged literary conventions and the lifestyle of the middle-class in the 1950s. **585**
benevolent societies Organizations that helped immigrants in cases of sickness, unemployment, and death. **195**
Berlin Airlift (1948–49) Operation in which British and U.S. planes carried food and supplies to West Berlin, which had been cut off by a Soviet blockade. **542**
Berlin Conference (1884) Conference held by Western imperial powers in Berlin, Germany, to set policies for the division of Africa into areas of European control. **820**
Berlin Wall Barrier built between East and West Berlin; widely recognized symbol of the Cold War. **600**
Bessemer process Efficient method of making steel; developed by British inventor Henry Bessemer and American inventor William Kelly in the 1850s. **164**
Big Four Collective name given to U.S. president Woodrow Wilson, British prime minister David Lloyd George, French premier Georges Clemenceau, and Italian prime minister Vittorio Orlando during the 1919 peace conference at Versailles. **350**
Bilingual Education Act (1974) Law that encouraged public schools to provide instruction to students in their primary language while they learned English. **733**
Bill of Rights First 10 amendments to the U.S. Constitution; ratified in 1791. **14**
biodiversity The variety of Earth's animal and plant species. **920**
Black Codes Laws passed in the southern states during Reconstruction that greatly limited the freedom of former slaves. **105**
black nationalism Movement to create a new political state for African Americans in Africa. **378**
Black Panther Party Political organization formed in the 1960s that called for empowerment and defense for African Americans. **636**
Black Power Black separatist movement founded due to frustration with the slow pace of the civil rights movement. **636**
Blackshirts Followers of Benito Mussolini who gained power in Italy in the early 1920s. **484**
Black Thursday October 24, 1929; the day investors caused a panic on Wall Street by selling their stocks. **415**
Black Tuesday October 29, 1929; day the stock market crashed; contributed to the Great Depression. **416**
Bland-Allison Act (1878) Federal law that required the government to buy and mint silver each month. **235**
Blitzkrieg "Lightning war"; type of fast-moving warfare used by German forces in 1939. **493**
blues Music that grew out of slave music and religious spirituals; featured heartfelt lyrics and altered or slurred notes that echoed the mood of the lyrics. **402**

951

GLOSSARY

Bolsheviks–containment

Bolsheviks Group of radical Russian socialists who seized power in 1917 following the overthrow of the czar. **347**

bonanza farm Large-scale farm usually owned by a large company and run like a factory. **145**

Bonus Army Group of World War I veterans who marched on Washington, D.C., in 1932 to demand the immediate payment of their pension bonuses. **434**

Boston Massacre (1770) Incident in which British soldiers fired into a group of colonists gathered in front of a customs house, killing several people. **10**

Boston police strike (1919) Failed police strike that led to public disorder and the firing of all striking officers. **363**

Boston Tea Party (1773) Protest against the Tea Act in which a group of colonists boarded British tea ships and dumped 342 chests of tea into Boston Harbor. **11**

Boxer Rebellion (1900) Revolt in which Chinese nationalists known as Boxers attacked foreigners in order to end foreign involvement in China's affairs; put down by an international force after two months. **302**

braceros Mexican farm and railroad workers who came to the United States during World War II. **511**

breadlines Lines formed by people waiting for free food, such as those that occurred during the Great Depression. **422**

Bretton Woods system Framework for international economic relations established in 1944 by the United States and 43 other countries. **839**

brinkmanship Policy in the 1950s that called for threatening all-out war in order to confront Communist aggression. **548**

British invasion Introduction of new British bands to Americans in the 1960s. **670**

Brotherhood of Sleeping Car Porters Union founded by A. Philip Randolph in 1925 to help African Americans who worked for the Pullman Company. **378**

Brown Berets Activist group formed in 1967 in response to police treatment of Mexican Americans. **657**

Brownshirts Nazi storm troopers. **485**

Brown v. Board of Education (1954) Supreme Court case that declared segregated public schools unconstitutional. **579**

bull market Upward trend in stock prices. **415**

Bureau of Indian Affairs Government agency responsible for managing American Indian issues. **134**

Bursum Bill Bill proposed in 1922 to legalize non-American Indian claims to Pueblo lands in the Southwest; failed to pass. **381**

business cycle Regular ups and downs of business in a free-enterprise economy. **419**

busing Sending children to schools outside of their neighborhoods, usually to promote integration. **640**

C

Camp David Accords (1978) Peace agreement between Israel and Egypt, negotiated by President Jimmy Carter. **731**

carpetbaggers Northern Republicans who moved to the South during Reconstruction. **116**

caudillos Latin American military leaders during the 1930s who used force to maintain order. **483**

Central Intelligence Agency (CIA) Federal agency created in the late 1940s to conduct covert operations. **548**

Central Powers World War I alliance that included Austria-Hungary, Germany, the Ottoman Empire, and Bulgaria. **329**

Challenger U.S. space shuttle that exploded in 1986 after takeoff, killing all seven crew members. **756**

Chernobyl disaster (1986) Nuclear accident near Kiev, Ukraine, that released massive amounts of radiation into the air. **788**

Children's Defense Fund (CDF) Children's rights organization founded in 1973. **665**

Chinese Exclusion Act (1882) Law that denied U.S. citizenship to people born in China and prohibited Chinese immigration of laborers. **197**

chlorofluorocarbons (CFCs) Chemicals created by a combination of carbon, chlorine, and fluorine that damage the ozone layer; used mainly in the manufacture of aerosol sprays, coolants, and plastics. **918**

City Beautiful movement Movement that stressed the importance of including public parks and attractive boulevards in the designs of cities. **208**

Civilian Conservation Corps (CCC) New Deal agency established in 1933; employed young men on conservation projects. **442**

Civil Rights Act of 1866 First U.S. civil rights law; declared everyone born in the United States a citizen with full civil rights. **110**

Civil Rights Act of 1875 Law that prohibited businesses that served the public from discriminating against African Americans. **118**

Civil Rights Act of 1957 Law that made it a federal crime to prevent qualified persons from voting. **582**

Civil Rights Act of 1964 Law banning racial discrimination in the use of public facilities and in employment practices. **627**

Clayton Antitrust Act (1914) Law that clarified and strengthened the Sherman Antitrust Act by clearly defining what a monopoly or trust was. **288**

closed shop Workplace in which all the employees must belong to a union. **255**

coaling stations Ports where steamships could restock their supplies of coal. **803**

Cobden-Chevalier Treaty (1860) Treaty in which France and Great Britain agreed to remove or reduce tariffs on each others' goods; included a provision allowing France and Britain to benefit whenever one of them gained tariff reductions from a third country. **833**

Cold War (1945–91) Long power struggle between the United States and the Soviet Union; waged mostly on economic and political fronts, rather than on the battlefield. **538**

Committee on Civil Rights Committee appointed by President Harry S Truman in 1946 to examine racial issues. **567**

Committee on Public Information (CPI) Agency created in 1917 to increase public support for World War I. **345**

Committee to Re-elect the President (CREEP) Organization that ran President Richard Nixon's 1972 re-election campaign; used "dirty tricks" to undermine the Democrats. **719**

Commonwealth of Independent States (CIS) An alliance formed by many of the former Soviet republics in December 1991. **759**

communism Political theory that proposes that all people should collectively own property and the means of production and that individual ownership should not be allowed. **174**

Compromise of 1850 Agreement proposed by Henry Clay; allowed California to enter the Union as a free state and divided the rest of the Mexican Cession into two territories where slavery would be decided by popular sovereignty; also settled land claims between Texas and New Mexico, abolished the slave trade in the District of Columbia, and toughened fugitive slave laws. **31**

Compromise of 1877 Agreement to settle the disputed presidential election of 1876; Democrats agreed to accept Republican Rutherford B. Hayes as president in return for the removal of federal troops from the South. **119**

compulsory education laws Laws requiring parents to send their children to school. **205**

Comstock Lode One of the world's richest silver mines, discovered in Nevada in the mid-1800s. **155**

Confederate States of America The Confederacy; nation formed by seceding southern states in 1861. **33**

Congress of Industrial Organizations (CIO) Labor group formed in 1935 that organized all workers in a particular industry into one union. **452**

Congress of Racial Equality (CORE) Northern-based civil rights group that organized nonviolent protests. **623**

conscription Compulsory draft into military service. **80**

conservation Environmental policy of conserving natural resources for future generations. **908**

conspicuous consumption Spending money just to display one's wealth. **200**

Constitutional Convention (1787) Meeting in Philadelphia at which state delegates wrote the U.S. Constitution. **13**

containment U.S. foreign policy during the Cold War that sought to prevent the expansion of Soviet communism. **539**

Contract with America 1994 Republican reform plan. **772**

Contras Anti-Sandinista rebel army in Nicaragua that was supported by the Reagan administration. **747**

Convention on Biological Diversity (1993) International treaty signed by 168 nations promising to protect biodiversity. **923**

convoy system Use of armed vessels to escort unarmed merchant vessels transporting troops, supplies, or volunteers through the North Atlantic during World War I. **339**

cooperatives Groups that pool members' resources to sell products directly to markets and to buy goods at wholesale prices. **232**

Copperheads Northern Democrats who sympathized with the South during the Civil War. **81**

corporation Company that sells shares of ownership called stock to investors in order to raise money. **174**

Corporation for Public Broadcasting Nonprofit organization created during the Johnson administration; offers educational television programming. **614**

cotton gin Device developed by Eli Whitney in 1793 to separate short-staple cotton seeds from the bolls. **24**

Council of Economic Advisers Federal agency created by the Employment Act of 1946 to counsel the president on economic policy. **564**

Council of Federated Organizations (COFO) Group created by several civil rights organizations to coordinate voter registration drives in the 1960s. **629**

counterculture Alternative lifestyle; for example, the culture of the hippies in the 1960s. **667**

Covenant on Civil and Political Rights (1966) UN General Assembly agreement on human rights that prohibited signing governments from interfering with individual liberties. **893**

Covenant on Economic, Social, and Cultural Rights (1966) UN General Assembly agreement requiring signing nations to improve human rights by providing jobs, educational opportunities, and health care. **893**

Crittenden Compromise (1860) Senator John Crittenden's plan to resolve conflict between North and South by extending the Missouri Compromise line westward through the remaining territories; rejected by President Lincoln. **68**

crop-lien system Arrangement in which sharecroppers promised their crops to merchants in exchange for supplies on credit. **120**

Crusade for Justice Group founded in 1966 by Rodolfo "Corky" Gonzales to promote Mexican American nationalism. **658**

Crusades (1096–1221) Series of five wars fought between Christians and Muslims for control of Palestine. **6**

Cuban missile crisis (1962) Standoff between the United States and the Soviet Union in which the Soviets agreed to remove missiles from Cuba if the United States promised not to invade the island; followed by an easing of Cold War tensions. **602**

cultural diffusion The process of spreading cultural practices or beliefs. **874**

D

Dawes General Allotment Act (1887) Legislation that required that American Indian lands be surveyed and Indian families be given allotments of 160 acres, with the remaining land sold; resulted in the loss of two thirds of American Indian land. **140**

Dawes Plan (1924) Plan that reduced Germany's reparations, loaned Germany some $200 million, and set up a new schedule of German war-debt repayments. **836**

D-Day (1944) June 6; World War II Allied invasion of France. **516**

Declaration of Independence (1776) Statement of the Second Continental Congress that officially declared the new United States of America to be independent of Great Britain. **12**

Declaration of the Rights of Man and Citizen (1789) Proclamation of France's Second Assembly that identified certain basic human rights, including liberty, property, security, and resistance to oppression. **880**

decolonization The process of ending colonial rule. **813**

defoliants Chemicals that strip land of vegetation. **686**

demobilization Transition from wartime to peacetime production and employment levels. **362**

Department of Energy Executive department created in 1977 to oversee energy issues. **727**

détente Period in the 1970s when tensions between the United States and the Soviet Union lessened. **718**

devaluation Reduction in the value of a currency to make it cheaper than other currencies. **837**

direct primary Nominating election in which voters choose the candidates who later run in a general election. **270**

direct rule Governing method in which a colonizing nation establishes a completely new administration to rule a colony. **803**

disarmament Reduction of the size of a country's military. **475**

Displaced Persons Act (1948) Federal law that enabled 400,000 European refugees to enter the United States following World War II. **862**

Dixiecrats States' Rights Party; formed in 1946 by southern Democrats who were dissatisfied with President Harry S Truman's support for civil rights issues. **568**

dollar diplomacy President William Howard Taft's policy of influencing Latin American affairs through economic influence rather than military force. **316**

domino theory Cold War–era belief that if one nation in Southeast Asia fell to communism, the rest of Southeast Asia would also fall. **680**

doves Americans who opposed the Vietnam War. **689**

***Dred Scott* decision** (1857) Supreme Court ruling that African Americans were not U.S. citizens, that the Missouri Compromise's restriction on slavery was unconstitutional, and that Congress did not have the right to ban slavery in any federal territory. **33**

Dust Bowl Name given to parts of the Great Plains in the 1930s after a severe drought struck the region. **454**

E

ecology Study of the interrelationship of plants and animals with each other and their environment. **906**

e-commerce Sales of goods and services over the Internet. **847**

ecosystem Biological system formed by the interaction of living things and their environment. **907**

Educational Amendments Act (1972) Federal law prohibiting sexual discrimination in higher education. **652**

Education for All Handicapped Children Act (1975) Federal law requiring public schools to provide education for children with physical and mental disabilities. **663**

Eighteenth Amendment (1919) Constitutional amendment that barred the manufacture, sale, and distribution of alcoholic beverages in the United States; repealed in 1933. **261**

Elementary and Secondary Education Act (1965) Federal law that provided $1.3 billion to aid schools in poor areas. **614**

Elkins Act (1903) Federal law that prohibited shippers from accepting rebates. **277**

Ellis Island Immigrant receiving station established in New York Harbor in 1892. **857**

e-mail Electronic mail; messages transmitted electronically by computers. **868**

Emancipation Proclamation (1863) Order announced by President Abraham Lincoln in 1862 that freed the slaves in areas rebelling against the Union; took effect January 1, 1863. **86**

Employment Act (1946) Law that established the Council of Economic Advisers and pledged that the government would promote full employment and production. **564**

Endangered Species Act (1973) Law to protect wildlife in danger of extinction. **716**

Enforcement Acts (1870–71) Three acts passed by Congress allowing the government to use military force to stop violence against southern African Americans. **117**

Enola Gay U.S. B-29 bomber that dropped the first atomic bomb on Hiroshima, Japan, on August 6, 1945. **525**

GLOSSARY

Environmental Protection Agency–graft

Environmental Protection Agency (EPA) Federal agency established in 1970 to enforce environmental laws. **716**

Equal Pay Act (1963) Federal law that made it illegal for employers to pay female workers less than male workers for the same job. **649**

Equal Rights Amendment (ERA) Proposed constitutional amendment that would guarantee women's rights by outlawing discrimination based on gender. **371**

escalation President Lyndon B. Johnson's policy of building up U.S. military forces in the Vietnam War. **685**

Espionage Act (1917) Federal law that outlawed acts of treason during World War I. **346**

Euro Single currency adopted by the European Union in 1999 to simplify trade between member nations. **848**

European Economic Community Economic union formed in 1957 to promote trade and cooperation among European member nations. **842**

European Union (EU) Western European trading bloc formed in 1993. **787**

Exodusters Southern African Americans who settled western lands in the late 1800s. **144**

F

Fair Deal Series of reform programs proposed by President Harry S Truman after the 1948 election; achieved mixed results. **569**

Fair Employment Practices Committee (FEPC) Group created in 1941 to prevent discrimination in war industries and government jobs. **511**

Family and Medical Leave Act (1993) Federal law requiring large companies to provide workers up to 12 weeks of unpaid leave for family and medical emergencies without losing their medical insurance or jobs. **786**

Family Assistance Plan (FAP) President Richard M. Nixon's proposed replacement for the welfare system; would guarantee families a minimum income; voted down by the Senate. **712**

Fascist Party Political party founded in Italy in the 1920s; followers believed a military-dominated government should control all aspects of society. **484**

Federal Deposit Insurance Corporation (FDIC) New Deal agency created in 1933 to insure bank savings deposits. **441**

federalism Division of power between a strong central government and state governments. **13**

Federal Project Number One New Deal program that encouraged pride in American culture by employing artists and writers. **459**

Federal Reserve Act (1913) Act that created a national banking system to help the government control the economy. **288**

Federal Trade Commission (FTC) Commission established in 1914 to investigate corporations and to try to keep them from conducting unfair trade practices. **289**

feminists Women's rights activists. **371**

feudalism System in the Middle Ages in which nobles pledged loyalty and military aid to rulers in return for land and protection. **5**

Fifteenth Amendment (1870) Constitutional amendment that gave African American men the right to vote. **114**

54th Massachusetts Infantry African American Union regiment that helped capture Fort Wagner in South Carolina during the Civil War. **87**

First Battle of Bull Run (1861) Battle of Manassas; first major battle of the Civil War; resulted in a Confederate victory. **73**

First Battle of the Marne (1914) World War I battle in which the Allies stopped a German advance near the Marne River. **330**

fixed exchange rates Economic system in which the value of other currencies were tied to the value of the U.S. dollar, which was fixed at a set value of gold. **839**

flappers Young women in the 1920s who challenged social traditions with their dress and behavior. **395**

flexible response Strategy adopted by the Kennedy administration of keeping a range of options open for dealing with international crises. **598**

floating exchange rates System in which the value of currencies varies depending upon their global demand. **845**

Food Administration World War I agency headed by Herbert Hoover; encouraged increased agricultural production and the conservation of existing food supplies. **341**

food chain Sequence in which each animal feeds on the plants or animal before it. **913**

Foraker Act (1900) U.S. law establishing that Puerto Rico's governor and upper house be appointed by the United States and lower house be elected by Puerto Ricans. **312**

Fordney-McCumber Tariff Act (1922) Federal law that raised tariff rates on manufactured goods and levied high duties on imported agricultural goods. **370**

Fourteen Points (1918) President Woodrow Wilson's plan for organizing post–World War I Europe and for avoiding future wars. **350**

Fourteenth Amendment (1868) Constitutional amendment giving full rights of citizenship to all people born or naturalized in the United States, except for American Indians. **110**

Freedmen's Bureau Agency established by Congress in 1865 to help southerners left homeless and hungry by the Civil War. **109**

freedom of contract Freedom of workers to negotiate the terms of their employment. **255**

Freedom Riders Group of civil rights workers who took bus trips through southern states in 1961 to protest illegal bus segregation. **623**

Freedom Summer Campaign to register African American voters in Mississippi during the summer of 1964. **630**

free enterprise Belief that the economy will prosper if businesses are left free from government regulation and allowed to compete in a free market. **173**

free trade International trade free from government regulation. **833**

Fundamentalism Protestant religious movement that teaches that that the Bible is literally true. **400**

G

General Agreement on Tariffs and Trade A commitment to the principles of free trade made by the member nations of the Bretton Woods conference. **840**

generation gap Difference in years, attitudes, and cultural beliefs between generations; applied to baby boomers and their elders during the 1960s. **666**

Geneva Convention (1864) Agreement among 12 nations for care for sick and wounded enemy soldiers as well as their own. **885**

genocide Deliberate annihilation of an entire people. **517**

Gettysburg Address (1863) Speech given by President Abraham Lincoln to dedicate a cemetery at the Gettysburg, Virginia, battlefield; a classic statement of democratic ideals. **91**

GI Bill of Rights (1944) Servicemen's Readjustment Act; law that established pensions and government loans to veterans for education, businesses, or to buy houses or farms. **564**

Gilded Age Name applied by Mark Twain and Charles Dudley Warner to late 1800s America to describe the corruption and greed that lurked below the surface of society. **227**

glasnost Soviet policy established in the 1980s that promoted political openness and freedom of expression. **753**

global warming Gradual increase in the temperature of Earth's atmosphere. **917**

Glorious Revolution (1688) A revolt in England in which Parliament broke the absolute power of the monarchy. **880**

gold standard Type of monetary system in which money is worth a specific amount in gold. **234**

Gold Standard Act (1900) Federal law declaring the U.S. dollar to be worth a fixed amount of gold. **832**

Gone With the Wind (1936) The best-selling novel of the 1930s, by Margaret Mitchell; made into one of the most popular films of all time in 1939. **460**

Good Neighbor policy President Franklin D. Roosevelt's foreign policy of promoting better relations with Latin America through mutual respect. **480**

graduated income tax System in which the rate of taxation varies according to income. **232**

graft Acquisition of money or political power through illegal or dishonest methods. **221**

Gramm-Rudman-Hollings Act (1985) Law that required the government to cut spending when the deficit grows above a certain level. **750**

Grapes of Wrath, The (1939) John Steinbeck's classic novel about Dust Bowl migrants who move to California during the Great Depression. **460**

Gray Panthers Activist group for senior citizens' rights; founded by Maggie Kuhn in 1970. **664**

Great Depression Serious global economic decline that began with the crash of the U.S. stock market in 1929. **417**

Great Migration Mass migration of African Americans to the northern United States during and after World War I. **344**

Great Society President Lyndon B. Johnson's program to improve American society. **612**

Great Upheaval (1886) Year of intense worker strikes and violent labor confrontations in the United States. **185**

Green parties Political parties whose platforms emphasize environmental concerns. **915**

gross national product Total value of all goods and services produced by a country in a given year. **417**

H

habeas corpus Constitutional protection against unlawful imprisonment. **81**

hard-rock mining Mining technique that involves sinking deep mine shafts to get at ore in veins of rock. **159**

Harlem Renaissance Period of great African American artistic accomplishment that began in the 1920s in the Harlem neighborhood of New York City. **404**

hawks Americans who supported the Vietnam War. **689**

Hay–Bunau-Varilla Treaty (1903) Agreement that gave the United States sovereignty over a 10-mile-wide canal zone across the Isthmus of Panama. **313**

Haymarket Riot (1886) Incident in which a bomb exploded during a labor protest held in Haymarket Square in Chicago, killing several police officers. **185**

Hepburn Act (1906) Law that authorized the Interstate Commerce Commission to set railroad rates and to regulate other companies engaged in interstate commerce. **277**

Highway Act (1956) Law that provided money to create a national highway system. **572**

Ho Chi Minh Trail Network of jungle paths from North Vietnam through Laos and Cambodia and into South Vietnam; served as the major supply route of the Vietcong. **686**

Hollywood Ten Group of film directors and writers who went to jail rather than answer questions from the House Un-American Activities Committee. **551**

Holocaust Nazi Germany's slaughter of European Jews. **517**

Homestead Act (1862) Law that encouraged settlement in the West by giving government-owned land to small farmers. **142**

horizontal integration Ownership of several companies that make the same product. **177**

hot line Teletype connection between the United States and the Soviet Union that allowed leaders to communicate directly. **602**

House Un-American Activities Committee (HUAC) Congressional committee originally created in 1938 to investigate fascists; became known for investigating U.S. citizens accused of communist ties in the late 1940s. **551**

hydraulic mining Mining technique that uses water pressure to remove gravel and dirt, exposing the minerals underneath. **159**

hydrogen bomb H-bomb; a type of nuclear bomb. **555**

I

Immigration Act of 1924 Federal law reducing the annual immigration quota for each nationality to 2 percent of the 1890 census figures. **380**

Immigration Act of 1965 Federal law that eased the quota restrictions on immigrations from many nations and increased the total number of immigrants allowed into the United States. **862**

Immigration Act of 1990 Federal law that increased the number of immigrants allowed into the United States each year. **785**

Immigration Restriction League Organization formed in 1894 that sought to impose a literacy test on all U.S. immigrants. **197**

imperialism Quest for colonial empires. **298**

Inca South American civilization that controlled the Andes. **5**

indirect rule Governing method in which a colonizing country rules a colony through the use of traditional local leaders. **803**

Industrial Workers of the World (IWW) Union formed in 1905 that opposed capitalism. **256**

Information Revolution Widespread transfer of information made possible by the development of computers and new communications technologies. **867**

initiative Policy allowing voters to introduce new legislation. **271**

Initiative on Race Initiative launched by President Bill Clinton in 1997 to encourage discussion of racial issues and concerns. **778**

insider trading Use of confidential financial information by stockbrokers for personal gain. **750**

installment plan A way of purchasing goods in which the consumer pays for goods in small increments over time. **392**

Intermediate-Range Nuclear Forces Treaty (INF) (1985) Treaty signed by President Ronald Reagan and Soviet leader Mikhail Gorbachev; eliminated all medium-range nuclear weapons from Europe. **754**

Internal Security Act (1950) Law that required suspected communist groups to register with the government and imposed controls on immigrants suspected of being communist sympathizers. **552**

International Ladies' Garment Workers Union (ILGWU) Influential union established in New York City in 1900 to organize workers in sewing shops. **256**

International Monetary Fund (IMF) Fund of $8.8 billion established at the Bretton Woods conference to help maintain fixed exchange rates. **840**

Internet Worldwide system of computer networks. **783**

internment Forced relocation and imprisonment of people. **512**

Interstate Commerce Act (1887) Law that regulated railroad shipping between states. **232**

Intolerable Acts (1774) Coercive Acts; four laws passed by Parliament to punish colonists for the Boston Tea Party and to tighten government control of the colonies. **11**

Iran-Contra affair Name given to the 1980s scandal in which the Reagan administration secretly sold weapons to Iran in exchange for the release of American hostages in Lebanon and then used the profits from the sale to fund the Contras in Nicaragua. **751**

Iran hostage crisis (1979–81) Situation in which 53 Americans were taken hostage from the U.S. Embassy in Tehran, Iran. **742**

island-hopping U.S. World War II strategy of conquering only the Pacific islands that were important to the Allied advance toward Japan. **521**

isolationism National policy of avoiding involvement in the affairs of other nations. **474**

J

jazz Music combining a variety of musical styles; originated with African American musicians in New Orleans and gained national popularity in the 1920s. **402**

Jim Crow laws Laws that enforced segregation in the South. **122**

Jones Act of 1916 U.S. law that gave Filipinos the right to elect both houses of their legislature. **311**

juvenile delinquency Antisocial behavior by young people. **576**

K

kamikaze Japanese suicide planes during World War II. **524**

Kansas-Nebraska Act (1854) Law that created the territories of Kansas and Nebraska and allowed voters there to choose whether to allow slavery. **32**

Keating-Owen Child Labor Act (1916) Law that outlawed the interstate sale of products produced by child labor; declared unconstitutional by the Supreme Court in 1918. **290**

GLOSSARY

Kellog-Briand Pact–Monroe Doctrine

Kellogg-Briand Pact (1928) Pact signed by the United States and 14 other nations that outlawed war, except for self-defense. **477**
Kent State shootings (1970) Incident in which National Guard troops fired at a group of students during an antiwar protest at Kent State University in Ohio, killing four people. **696**
Kerner Commission Federal commission that investigated the 1960s riots and blamed them on white racism. **638**
kickbacks Payments of part of the earnings from a job. **221**
Knights of Labor One of the first national labor unions in the United States, organized in 1869; after 1879 it included workers of different races, genders, and skills. **184**
Korean War (1950–53) UN-led effort to repel a North Korean invasion of South Korea; resulted in the establishment of a border between the two countries at about the 39th parallel. **545**
Kosovo crisis Result of a violent campaign launched by Serbian forces against Albanians in Kosovo; stopped by UN bombing strikes in 1999. **780**
Kristallnacht (1938) "Night of Broken Glass"; November 9; night when Nazis destroyed many Jewish buildings. **486**
Ku Klux Klan Secret society created by former Confederates in 1866 that used terror and violence to keep African Americans from obtaining their civil rights. **116**

L

La Huelga (1965–70) Successful strike by migrant farmworkers in California against grape growers; led by César Chávez. **655**
laissez-faire capitalism Theory that opposes government regulation of economic matters. **173**
La Raza Unida Party (LRUP) Mexican American political party formed by José Angel Gutiérrez in the late 1960s. **659**
League for United Latin American Citizens (LULAC) Group formed in 1929 to lobby for Hispanic concerns and issues. **583**
League of Nations International body of nations formed in 1919 to prevent wars. **350**
Lend-Lease Act (1941) Law that allowed the United States to offer weapons and other war supplies to the Allied Powers to fight against the Axis Powers in World War II. **493**
Limited Nuclear Test Ban Treaty (1963) Agreement signed by U.S. president John F. Kennedy and Soviet leader Nikita Khrushchev; ended above-ground testing of new nuclear weapons. **602**
literacy tests Tests used to prevent people who could not read from voting. **121**
Little Rock Nine Nine African American students who first integrated Central High School in Little Rock, Arkansas, in 1957. **580**
long drives Long overland treks on which cowboys herded cattle from ranches to rail lines. **150**
Los Angeles Riots (1992) Riots that erupted after four white police officers were acquitted of using excessive force against an African American motorist. **778**
Lost Generation A group of writers whose works reflected the horrors of the death and destruction of World War I and criticized consumerism and superficiality in postwar society. **407**
Louisiana Purchase (1803) U.S. purchase of French land between the Mississippi River and the Rocky Mountains. **15**

M

Maginot Line Line of defenses built by France along its border with Germany after World War I. **493**
mandate system Provision established by the League of Nations that allowed Allied countries temporarily to occupy former German and Ottoman colonies after World War I. **805**
Manhattan Project Secret U.S. project begun in 1942 to develop an atomic bomb. **525**
manifest destiny Belief of many Americans in the mid-1800s that God intended the United States to expand westward. **28**
Mann-Elkins Act (1910) Federal law that extended the regulatory powers of the Interstate Commerce Commission to telephone and telegraph companies. **282**
margin buying Purchasing stock with borrowed money. **415**
Marshall Plan European Recovery Program; U.S. program of giving money to European countries to help them rebuild their economies after World War II. **541**
Massacre at Wounded Knee (1890) U.S. Army's killing of approximately 300 Sioux at Wounded Knee Creek in South Dakota; ended U.S.–American Indian wars on the Great Plains. **138**
mass transit Public transportation systems, such as commuter trains and subways. **198**
Maya Mesoamerican civilization that rose to prominence about A.D. 300. **5**
Mayaguez Unarmed U.S. cargo ship seized by Cambodian Communists in 1975; 41 Americans died in the effort to save the 39 crew members. **724**
McClure's Magazine Progressive magazine that explored corruption in politics and business. **249**
McKinley Tariff (1890) Tariff sponsored by President William McKinley that greatly increased tariff rates as well as the number of imported goods subject to tariffs. **835**
Meat Inspection Act (1906) Federal law that required government inspection of meat shipped across state lines. **278**
Medicaid Federal program created in 1965 to provide free health care to the needy. **613**
Medicare Federal health insurance program for people over the age of 65; created in 1965. **613**
mergers The combining of two or more companies to achieve greater efficiency and higher profits. **370**
Mexican American Youth Organization (MAYO) Mexican American activist group formed in 1967 by college students in San Antonio, Texas. **659**
Mexican Cession Land that Mexico gave to the United States after the Mexican War through the Treaty of Guadalupe Hidalgo; includes present-day California, Nevada, and Utah, as well as parts of Arizona, Colorado, New Mexico, Texas, and Wyoming. **29**
Mexican Revolution Struggle to end dictatorship that led to years of instability in Mexico in the early 1900s. **318**
Mexican War of 1846 (1846–47) Conflict between Mexico and the United States that ended with the United States gaining control over most Mexican territory in the Southwest. **29**
Middle Ages Period of European history that lasted from about A.D. 500 to 1500. **5**
Middle Passage Voyage that brought enslaved Africans across the Atlantic Ocean to North America and the West Indies. **8**
Migrant Mother Dorothea Lange's most famous photograph from the Great Depression, showing an exhausted mother and her children; led to increased support for migrant workers in California. **456**
militarism Glorification of military strength. **329**
minicomputers Personal computers introduced in the late 1970s that are smaller, cheaper, and easier to use than mainframe computers. **868**
Mir Russian space station; site of joint U.S.-Soviet space projects in the 1990s. **782**
Mississippi Freedom Democratic Party (MFDP) Group that sent its own delegates to the Democratic National Convention in 1964 to protest discrimination against black voters in Mississippi. **631**
Missouri Compromise (1820) Agreement proposed by Henry Clay that allowed Missouri to enter the Union as a slave state, Maine to enter as a free state, and banned slavery in the Louisiana Purchase north of the 36°30' line. **22**
Model T Popular low-cost automobile developed by Henry Ford in 1908. **387**
modems Devices that allow computers to send data over telephone lines. **868**
Modern Republicanism Name given to President Dwight D. Eisenhower's attempt to balance liberal domestic reforms with conservative spending during the 1950s. **570**
monopoly Exclusive economic control of an industry. **175**
Monroe Doctrine (1823) President James Monroe's statement that the United States would not interfere in European colonies in Latin America but would consider any new attempt to colonize in the Western Hemisphere an act of hostility. **21**

Montgomery Improvement Association (MIA) Organization formed by African Americans in Montgomery, Alabama, in 1956 to strengthen the bus boycott and to coordinate protest efforts of African Americans; led by Martin Luther King Jr. **582**
Moral Majority Conservative religious political organization; founded in 1979. **743**
Morrill Act (1862) Federal law that gave land to western states to build agricultural and engineering colleges. **142**
muckrakers Investigative journalists who wrote about corruption in business and politics, hoping to bring about reform. **249**
mugwumps "Big chiefs"; referred to Republican reformers who supported Democrat Grover Cleveland in the presidential election of 1884. **229**
Muller* v. *Oregon (1908) Supreme Court case that upheld protective legislation for workers in Oregon. **255**
multinational corporations Companies that invest money in a variety of international business ventures. **788**
Munich Conference (1938) Meeting between British, French, German, and Italian leaders in which Germany was given control of the Sudetenland in exchange for German leader Adolf Hitler's promise to make no more claims on European territory. **490**
mutualistas Mutual-aid societies formed by Mexican American communities to help local residents. **422**

N

National Aeronautics and Space Administration (NASA) Agency established by Congress in 1958 to promote space technology. **557**
National American Woman Suffrage Association (NAWSA) Group formed in 1890 to win the vote for women. **291**
National Association for the Advancement of Colored People (NAACP) Group founded by W. E. B. Du Bois and others in 1909 to end racial discrimination. **263**
National Black Political Convention (1972) Meeting of civil rights activists to ensure that African Americans would continue to gain political influence. **643**
National Defense Act (1916) Military preparedness program established prior to U.S. entry into World War I that increased the size of the National Guard and the regular U.S. army. **335**
National Defense Education Act (1958) Federal law that appropriated money to improve education in science, math, and foreign languages. **557**
National Energy Act (1978) Law passed to ease the energy crisis. **727**
National Grange National Grange of the Patrons of Husbandry; organization founded by Oliver Hudson Kelley in 1867; addressed economic and political issues concerning farmers. **232**
National Industrial Recovery Act (NIRA) (1933) Federal law designed to encourage economic growth by suspending antitrust laws and eliminating unfair competition between employers; declared unconstitutional in 1935. **442**
nationalism National pride or loyalty. **21**
nationalize To assert government control over a business. **481**
National Monuments Act (1906) Federal law that allows the president to declare certain areas of federal lands to be protected historical or scientific monuments. **909**
National Organization for Women (NOW) Women's rights group; formed in 1966 to pressure elected officials to ensure social and political equality for women. **650**
National Security Council (NSC) Organization created in 1947 by Congress to advise the president on strategic matters. **551**
National Urban League Group founded in 1910 to fight for racial equality. **263**
National War Labor Board (NWLB) Agency created during World War I to settle disputes between workers and employers. **342**
National Women's Political Caucus Group founded by Gloria Steinem and others in 1971 to encourage women to run for political office. **651**
National Youth Administration (NYA) New Deal agency that provided part-time jobs to people between the ages of 16 and 25. **448**
Nation of Islam Black Muslims; black nationalist religious group founded by Wallace D. Fard in 1930. **633**
nativism Favoring native-born Americans over foreign-born. **24**
NATO North Atlantic Treaty Organization; alliance formed in 1949 by the United States, Western European nations, and other countries to help defend each other in case of attack. **543**
natural rights Fundamental individual human rights, such as the rights to life, liberty, and freedom of property. **880**
Nazi Party National Socialist Party; political group led by Adolf Hitler that rose to power in Germany in the 1930s. **485**
neocolonialism Process of maintaining indirect economic and political control over former colonies. **816**
New Deal President Franklin D. Roosevelt's programs for helping the U.S. economy during the Great Depression. **440**
New Freedom President Woodrow Wilson's progressive reform program; proposed during the 1912 presidential election. **285**
New Frontier President John F. Kennedy's domestic agenda. **606**
new immigrants Immigrants who came to the United States between the 1880s and 1910s, mostly from southern and eastern Europe. **192**
New Right Various conservative voters' groups that grew in strength in the 1980s. **743**
Nineteenth Amendment (1920) Constitutional amendment that granted women the right to vote. **293**
no-man's-land Strip of bombed-out territory that separated the trenches of opposing armies along the Western Front during World War I. **330**
nonaggression pact (1939) Agreement between German leader Adolf Hitler and Soviet leader Joseph Stalin not to attack one another and to divide Poland. **491**
nonaligned movement Movement begun by former colonies proclaiming neutrality toward the superpowers during the Cold War. **817**
nonviolent resistance Protest strategy that calls for peaceful demonstrations and the rejection of violence. **622**
North American Free Trade Agreement (NAFTA) (1993) Trade agreement among the United States, Canada, and Mexico. **787**
nouveau riche "Newly rich"; new class of American city-dwellers that arose in the late 1800s; most made their fortunes from business during the Second Industrial Revolution. **200**
nuclear fallout Airborne radioactive particles created by nuclear explosions. **913**
Nuclear Nonproliferation Treaty (1968) Agreement initially signed by the United States and 61 other nations to keep nuclear weapons technology from spreading to more countries. **914**
Nuremberg Trials War crimes trials of high-ranking Nazi officials held by an international military tribunal in Nuremberg, Germany; began in 1945. **534**

O

Office of Economic Opportunity (OEO) Government agency formed in 1964 to coordinate antipoverty programs. **611**
Office of War Information U.S. agency that controlled the flow of war news at home during World War II. **507**
Office of War Mobilization (OWM) Federal agency that coordinated all government agencies involved in the war effort during World War II. **502**
oil shocks Jolts to the world economy caused by sharp increases in oil prices during the 1970s. **844**
Older Americans Act (1965) Law committing the government to provide the elderly with adequate income and medical care. **665**
old immigrants Immigrants who came to the United States before the 1880s, mostly Protestants from northwestern Europe. **192**
Olympic Games International sporting event based on athletic competitions held in ancient Greece; first modern Olympics held in 1896; now divided into summer and winter competitions. **872**
Open Door Policy (1899) Declaration made by Secretary of State John Hay that all nations should have equal access to trade and investment in China. **302**
open range Public land used by cattle ranchers. **152**
open shop Nonunion workplace. **256**

Operation Desert Storm–recycling

Operation Desert Storm (1991) UN invasion led by the United States to make Iraq withdraw from Kuwait. **759**

Operation Restore Hope (1992) UN attempt to ensure that relief efforts reached famine-stricken Somalia. **773**

Operation Rolling Thunder U.S. bombing campaign during the Vietnam War. **686**

Organization of African Unity (OAU) Group of African nations; formed in 1963 to prevent territorial conflicts among its members following African independence. **820**

Organization of Petroleum Exporting Countries (OPEC) Alliance formed in 1960 by major oil-producing nations to maintain high prices by controlling the production and sale of oil. **715**

ozone layer Layer of molecules some 10 to 30 miles above Earth's surface that protects the planet from ultraviolet radiation. **918**

P

pacification U.S. and South Vietnamese policy of moving villagers to refugee camps and then burning their villages. **687**

Pacific Railway Act (1862) Law that provided land grants to railroad companies to help them build a rail line linking the East and West Coasts. **142**

Pacific Rim East Asian, South Asian, and Pacific Island nations. **845**

Paleo-Indians The first Americans; crossed from Asia into North America sometime between 12,000 and 40,000 years ago. **4**

Palmer raids (1919–20) Raids ordered by U.S. attorney general A. Mitchell Palmer on suspected radical organizations. **366**

Pan-Africanism Movement to unite people of African descent worldwide. **378**

Panama Canal Treaties Agreements by U.S. and Panamanian leaders in the 1970s to transfer control of the Panama Canal to Panama by the year 2000. **729**

Panic of 1873 U.S. economic depression that distracted the Republicans from Reconstruction efforts. **117**

patent Exclusive right to manufacture or sell an invention. **165**

***patio* process** Mining technique developed in Mexico and South America during the 1700s that used mercury to extract silver from ore; used in the western United States. **156**

Payne-Aldrich Tariff (1909) High-tariff measure signed by President William Howard Taft; angered progressives. **283**

Peace Corps Program begun by President John F. Kennedy to send volunteers to work in developing nations for two years. **598**

Pendleton Civil Service Act (1883) Act that established the Civil Service Commission to administer competitive examinations to people seeking government jobs. **229**

Pentagon Papers Secret government documents published in 1971; revealed that the U.S. government had misled Americans about the Vietnam War. **697**

perestroika Soviet policy established in the 1980s that initiated political and economic reforms. **753**

perishable goods Goods that spoil quickly. **831**

personal computer (PC) Small computer for individual use. **737**

Philippine Government Act (1902) Organic Act; federal law that established a governor and a two-house legislature for the Philippines, with the governor and members of the legislature's upper house appointed by the United States. **311**

Pickett's Charge (1863) Failed Confederate attack during the Battle of Gettysburg. **91**

Pilgrims First English settlers in Massachusetts; left England because of religious conflicts. **8**

planned obsolescence Practice of manufacturing products that are designed to go out of style. **392**

Platt Amendment (1902) Amendment to the Cuban constitution; limited Cuba's right to make treaties and authorized the United States to intervene in Cuban affairs as it saw necessary. **312**

Plessy* v. *Ferguson (1896) Supreme Court ruling that established the "separate-but-equal" doctrine for public facilities. **122**

political bosses Leaders of political machines. **218**

political machines Well-organized political parties that dominated local and state governments in the late 1800s. **218**

poll taxes Taxes that a person had to pay in order to vote. **121**

Poor People's Campaign Martin Luther King Jr.'s movement to protest the perceived misuse of government spending away from antipoverty programs. **638**

pop art Movement that challenged the values of traditional art by taking inspiration from popular culture. **668**

Popular Front International coalition united against fascism; term coined by Soviet leader Joseph Stalin in a 1935 speech. **486**

popular sovereignty Practice of allowing voters in a territory to decide whether to permit slavery there. **31**

Populist Party People's Party; national political party formed in 1892 that supported a graduated income tax, bank regulation, government ownership of some companies, restrictions on immigration, shorter workdays, and voting reform. **235**

Potsdam Conference (1945) Meeting of U.S. president Harry S Truman, British prime minister Winston Churchill, and Soviet leader Joseph Stalin after Germany's surrender in World War II; resulted in the division of Germany into four zones of occupation. **532**

preservation Practice of leaving wild areas intact and untouched by development. **910**

Proclamation of 1763 British ban on colonial settlement west of the Appalachian Mountains. **10**

Progressive Party Bull Moose Party; reform party that ran Theodore Roosevelt for president in 1912. **285**

progressivism Reform movement of the early 1900s concerned with curing problems of urbanization and industrialization. **246**

prohibition Complete ban on the manufacture, sale, and distribution of alcohol. **260**

protectionism The use of tariffs to protect domestic agricultural and industrial producers. **833**

protectorate Country dependent on another for protection. **312**

puppet government System in which an imperial power controls a country while pretending that the country is independent. **810**

Pure Food and Drug Act (1906) Law that prohibited the manufacture, sale, or transportation of food and patented medicine containing harmful ingredients; also required food and medicine containers to carry ingredient labels. **278**

Puritans People who wanted to purify the Anglican Church. **8**

Q

quotas System of reserving a fixed number of openings in schools or jobs for certain groups of people. **641**

R

ragtime Style of music created in the 1890s by African American pianists who played a driving rhythm with one hand and an improvised melody with the other. **210**

railhead Town located along a railroad; long cattle drives usually ended there. **150**

Reaganomics President Ronald Reagan's economic program; based on large tax cuts to encourage business investment. **744**

realpolitik "Practical politics"; President Richard M. Nixon's policy that national interests rather than moral principles should be the guiding force in U.S. foreign policy. **717**

recall Procedure enabling voters to remove an official from office by calling for a special election. **271**

reclamation Process of making damaged land productive. **281**

Reconstruction (1865–77) Period following the Civil War during which the U.S. government worked to rebuild the former Confederate states and reunite the nation. **103**

Reconstruction Acts (1867) Laws that divided the former Confederate states, except Tennessee, into military zones and required them to draft new constitutions upholding the Fourteenth Amendment. **112**

Reconstruction Finance Corporation (RFC) Agency created in 1932 to stimulate the economy by lending money to railroads, insurance companies, and banks and other financial institutions. **432**

recycling Collection and processing of waste items for reuse. **789**

Red Cross Organization formed by private Swiss citizens in 1863 to care for wounded soldiers of all nations; present-day efforts aid victims of natural disasters. **885**

Redeemers Democratic supporters of white-controlled governments in the South during the 1870s. **118**

Red Scare Period of anticommunist hysteria; swept the United States after World War I. **365**

referendum Procedure allowing citizens to force the legislature to place a recently passed law on the ballot for public approval. **271**

Reform Party Political party created in the 1990s promising to reform national politics. **777**

refugees People forced to flee their homes because of political persecution, wars, or natural disasters. **861**

regionalists Midwestern artists popular in the 1930s who emphasized local folk themes and customs in their work. **463**

Rehabilitation Act (1973) Federal law forbidding discrimination in education, jobs, or housing because of physical disabilities. **663**

Renaissance Rebirth of European learning and artistic creativity that began in the late Middle Ages. **6**

reparations Payments for damages and expenses in war. **350**

Republican Party Political party formed in 1854 by antislavery Whigs and Democrats, along with some Free-Soilers. **32**

rock 'n' roll Popular music introduced in the 1950s; influenced by African American rhythm and blues. **577**

Roosevelt Corollary (1904) President Theodore Roosevelt's addition to the Monroe Doctrine; stated that the United States would police affairs in the Western Hemisphere to keep Europeans from intervening in the region. **315**

Rosie the Riveter Symbol of patriotic female defense workers during World War II. **510**

Rough Riders U.S. cavalry unit in the Spanish-American War led by Theodore Roosevelt. **308**

rugged individualism Belief that success comes through individual effort and private enterprise. **429**

Russo-Japanese War (1904–05) War between Russia and Japan; peace negotiated by President Theodore Roosevelt. **304**

S

Sand Creek Massacre (1864) Attack by U.S. Army troops in which some 200 peaceful Cheyenne were killed in Colorado. **135**

Sandinistas Revolutionary political party in Nicaragua that overthrew a pro-U.S. dictator in 1979. **747**

S&L crisis Economic collapse in the savings and loan and banking industries caused by risky loans in the 1980s. **751**

satellite nations Countries controlled by the Soviet Union. **538**

Saturday Night Massacre Name given to the series of events in 1973 that included the firing of a special prosecutor investigating Watergate and the resignations of the U.S. attorney general and his next in command for refusing to fire the prosecutor. **721**

scalawags "Scoundrels"; name that former Confederates gave to southern Republicans during Reconstruction. **116**

scientific management Theory promoted by Frederick W. Taylor; held that every kind of work could be broken into a series of smaller tasks and that rates of production could be set for each individual task. **387**

Scopes trial (1925) Trial of John Scopes, a high school science teacher who was prosecuted for teaching evolution. **400**

search-and-destroy missions U.S. strategy in Vietnam in which ground patrols searched for hidden enemy camps and supplies and destroyed them with massive firepower and air raids. **687**

Seattle general strike (1919) Large-scale strike that opponents blamed on Bolsheviks and foreigners; weakened support for organized labor. **363**

Second Great Awakening Evangelical religious movement that spread through the United States beginning in the early 1800s. **25**

Sedition Act (1918) Federal law enacted during World War I that made written criticism of the government a crime. **346**

segregation Separation of people by category, usually race. **122**

Selective Service Act (1917) Law that initially required men between the ages of 21 and 30 to register for the draft. **336**

Selective Training and Service Act (1940) Law providing for the first peacetime draft in U.S. history. **502**

Seneca Falls Convention (1848) First national women's rights convention; site where the Declaration of Sentiments was written. **27**

settlement houses Community-service centers that were founded in the late 1800s to offer educational opportunities, skills training, and cultural events to impoverished neighborhoods. **203**

Seventeenth Amendment (1913) Constitutional amendment that gives voters the power to directly elect U.S. senators. **271**

shantytowns Collections of makeshift shelters built by homeless people. **422**

sharecropping System used on southern farms after the Civil War in which farmers worked land owned by someone else in return for supplies and a small share of the crops. **120**

Share-Our-Wealth Radical relief program proposed by Senator Huey Long in the 1930s; sought to empower the government to seize wealth from the rich through taxes and to provide a guaranteed minimum income and home to every American family. **447**

Sherman Antitrust Act (1890) Law prohibiting monopolies and trusts that restrained trade. **181**

Sherman Silver Purchase Act (1890) Federal law that required the government to buy and mint silver each month. **235**

Siege of Vicksburg (1863) Union army's blockade of Vicksburg, Mississippi, that led the city to surrender during the Civil War. **92**

Silent Majority Middle-class voters weary of the social upheaval of the 1960s; sought after by Richard Nixon during his presidential campaigns. **712**

sit-down strike Method used by striking workers of preventing owners from replacing them by refusing to leave the factories. **452**

sit-ins Demonstrations in which protesters sit down in a location and refuse to leave. **622**

Sixteenth Amendment (1913) Constitutional amendment that permitted Congress to levy income taxes. **283**

Skylab First U.S. space station; placed in orbit in 1973. **737**

skyscrapers Large, multistory buildings. **198**

Smoot-Hawley Tariff (1930) High-tariff law that contributed to a global economic downturn in the 1930s. **418**

social Darwinism Theory adapted by philosopher Herbert Spencer from Charles Darwin's theory of evolution; argued that society progresses through competition, with the fittest rising to positions of wealth and power. **174**

Social Gospel Movement begun by Protestant ministers in the late 1800s; applied Christian principles to social problems. **204**

socialism Economic system in which the government or the workers own most of the factories, utilities, and transportation and communications systems. **255**

Social Security Act (1935) Law that provides retirement pensions, unemployment insurance, and payments to people with disabilities and to widows and children of male workers who have died. **449**

Society of American Indians Organization formed in 1911 by middle-class American Indians to address Indian problems. **264**

sod houses Buildings made from chunks cut from heavy topsoil that were stacked like bricks. **145**

Solidarity Polish independent trade union and social movement that was formed in 1980. **745**

sonar Equipment that uses sound waves to detect underwater objects. **515**

Southern Christian Leadership Conference (SCLC) Alliance of church-based African American organizations formed in 1957 and dedicated to ending discrimination. **622**

southern strategy President Richard M. Nixon's attempt to woo conservative white voters from the Democratic Party by promising not to support new civil rights legislation. **713**

Spanish-American War (1898) War declared by the United States on Spain to help Cuba overthrow Spanish rule. **307**

Spanish Civil War Struggle between Fascists and Loyalists in Spain that started in 1936. **486**

spheres of influence Regions where a particular country has exclusive rights over mines, railroads, and trade. **302**

959

GLOSSARY

Sputnik–Universal Negro Improvement Association

Sputnik The world's first artificial satellite; launched by the Soviet Union in 1957. **557**

Square Deal Theodore Roosevelt's 1904 presidential campaign slogan pledging to balance the interests of business, consumers, and labor. **276**

stagflation Economic condition characterized by rising inflation and unemployment. **713**

Stalwarts Republicans in the late 1800s who opposed reform. **227**

Stamp Act (1765) Law passed by Parliament that placed a tax on printed matter. **10**

staples Goods that are in constant demand and that are often sold in bulk. **831**

steel strike of 1919 Strike that failed when steel company officials used rumors, threats, and even violence against strikers. **364**

steerage Poor accommodations in a ship's lower levels; many immigrants to the United States traveled in this space. **193**

Strategic Arms Limitation Talks (SALT) (1972) Talks between U.S. president Richard M. Nixon and Soviet leader Leonid Brezhnev that led to a treaty limiting the number of ICBM missiles each country could have. **717**

Strategic Defense Initiative (SDI) Plan for a defense system in space to protect the United States from Soviet missiles; never actually implemented. **745**

strike Refusal of workers to perform their job until employers meet union demands. **24**

Student Nonviolent Coordinating Committee (SNCC) Student organization formed in 1960 to coordinate civil rights demonstrations and to provide training for protesters. **622**

Students for a Democratic Society (SDS) Student group that actively protested the Vietnam War. **689**

subsidy Government payment made to farmers. **300**

suburbs Residential neighborhoods on the outskirts of a city. **199**

Sunbelt States in the South and the West that attracted many new residents and businesses in the 1970s. **733**

supply-side economics Economic theory stating that tax cuts would lead to increased economic activity and tax revenues, and therefore to a balanced budget. **744**

***Sussex* pledge** (1916) Promise issued by German officials during World War I not to sink merchant vessels without warning or without assuring the passengers' safety. **335**

T

Taft-Hartley Act (1947) Law that gave judges the power to end some strikes, outlawed closed-shop agreements, restricted unions' political contributions, and required union leaders to swear they were not Communists. **566**

Taliban Fundamentalist Islamic military and political group that took over most of Afghanistan in 1996. **896**

Teapot Dome scandal Scandal during President Warren Harding's administration; involved Secretary of the Interior Albert Fall's leasing of oil reserves in return for personal gifts and loans. **372**

Telecommunications Act (1996) Law that attempted to regulate indecency on the Internet; parts of it were later struck down by a federal court. **783**

telegraph Machine patented by Samuel Morse in 1837; sent messages over long distances by using electric current to transmit a system of dots and dashes over wire. **168**

Teller Amendment (1898) Resolution stating that the United States did not intend to take over and annex Cuba. **307**

tenements Poorly built apartment buildings that housed many impoverished city-dwellers in the late 1800s and early 1900s. **202**

Tennessee Valley Authority (TVA) New Deal program established in 1933; built dams and power stations to provide hydroelectric power and flood control to the Tennessee River valley. **444**

Tet Offensive (1968) Attack by North Vietnamese and Vietcong troops against South Vietnam during the Vietnam War; came during Tet, the Vietnamese New Year; demonstrated that the North Vietnamese were still militarily strong. **692**

Texas longhorn Hardy breed of cattle created by interbreeding English and Spanish cattle. **149**

Texas Revolution (1835–36) Revolt against Mexico by American settlers and Tejanos in Texas. **28**

third world The developing nations of Africa, Asia, and Latin America. **817**

Thirteenth Amendment (1865) Constitutional amendment that abolished slavery. **105**

Three Mile Island accident (1979) Incident in which a nuclear reactor in Pennsylvania nearly had a catastrophic meltdown. **727**

Tonkin Gulf Resolution (1964) Congressional measure that gave President Lyndon B. Johnson the authority to wage war in Vietnam. **684**

totalitarian state Political system in which the government controls every aspect of citizens' lives. **485**

total war Strategy of fighting in which an army destroys its opponent's ability to fight by attacking civilian and economic, as well as military, targets. **94**

Trail of Tears (1838–39) An 800-mile forced march the Cherokee made from their homeland in the Southeast to Indian Territory in present-day Oklahoma; resulted in the deaths of almost one quarter of the tribe's members. **23**

transcontinental railroad Railroad that crossed the continental United States; completed in 1869. **166**

Treaty of Versailles (1919) Treaty ending World War I that required Germany to pay huge war reparations and that established the League of Nations. **351**

trench warfare World War I military strategy of defending a position by fighting from the protection of deep ditches. **330**

Triangle Shirtwaist Fire (1911) Incident that resulted in the deaths of some 140 garment workers; led to increased safety regulations for businesses. **254**

Truman Doctrine (1947) President Harry S Truman's policy stating that the United States would help any country fighting against communism. **541**

trunk lines Major railroads connected to outlying areas by feeder or branch lines. **166**

trust Arrangement grouping several companies under a single board of directors to eliminate competition and to regulate production. **175**

trusteeship Provision established by the League of Nations that required Allied nations to develop and modernize the former German and Ottoman colonies. **805**

Twenty-first Amendment (1933) Constitutional amendment that ended prohibition by repealing the Eighteenth Amendment. **395**

Twenty-sixth Amendment (1971) Constitutional amendment that lowered the federal voting age from 21 to 18. **698**

Tydings–McDuffie Act (1934) Federal law that granted independence to the Philippines after a 12-year transition period. **809**

U

ultraviolet solar radiation Solar rays that can cause skin cancer, damage marine life, and harm plant life. **918**

Underground Railroad Network of abolitionists who helped slaves escape to the North and Canada. **25**

unilateral disarmament A one-sided ban on nuclear weapons despite their existence in other countries. **914**

United Farm Workers (UFW) Group formed in the 1960s to improve working conditions for migrant farmworkers. **655**

United Mine Workers strike (1919) Strike for pay increases and better working hours that further weakened public support for unions; first UMW strike led by John L. Lewis. **364**

United Nations (UN) International organization chartered in 1945; created to settle problems between nations. **535**

Universal Declaration of Human Rights (1948) UN document listing a series of basic rights held by all human beings. **890**

Universal Negro Improvement Association (UNIA) Association founded by Marcus Garvey in 1914 to foster African American economic independence and establish an independent black homeland in Africa. **378**

University of California* v. *Bakke (1978) Supreme Court decision that established that while some forms of affirmative action were legal, quota systems were not. **641**

Untouchables Nickname given to a group of detectives led by Eliot Ness who targeted gangsters during Prohibition. **395**

urban renewal Program launched by the federal government in the 1950s to replace old, run-down inner-city buildings. **587**

U.S. Department of Agriculture Executive department created in 1862 to help farmers. **145**

U.S. Sanitary Commission Federal agency headed in part by Dr. Elizabeth Blackwell; battled disease and infection among Union soldiers during the Civil War. **79**

USS *Maine* U.S. battleship that exploded in Havana Harbor in 1898; although cause was never determined, the incident was a catalyst for the Spanish-American War. **307**

U-2 incident Incident in which U.S. pilot Francis Gary Powers was captured while spying on the Soviet Union; damaged relations between the United States and the Soviet Union. **550**

V

vaudeville "Light play"; type of variety show featuring a wide selection of short performances. **210**

vertical integration Ownership of businesses involved in each step of a manufacturing process. **176**

Vietcong National Liberation Front; communist guerrilla force that began fighting against Ngo Dinh Diem's government in South Vietnam in the 1950s. **681**

Vietminh League for the Independence of Vietnam; group of Vietnamese nationalists organized in the 1940s by Ho Chi Minh to drive the Japanese out of Vietnam. **679**

Vietnamization Policy followed by the Nixon administration of gradually turning over all the fighting in the Vietnam War to the South Vietnamese Army. **695**

Vietnam Veterans Memorial Memorial dedicated in Washington, D.C., in 1982 to honor those people who died in or are missing from the Vietnam War. **702**

Volstead Act (1919) Federal law that enforced the Eighteenth Amendment (prohibition). **394**

Volunteers in Service to America (VISTA) Domestic version of the Peace Corps; established in 1964. **612**

Voting Rights Act (1965) Law that put voter registration under federal government control. **632**

Voting Rights Act of 1975 Federal law requiring states and communities with large non-English speaking populations to print voting materials in various foreign languages. **732**

W

Wagner-Connery Act (1935) National Labor Relations Act; law that guaranteed labor's right to organize unions and to bargain for better wages and working conditions. **452**

War Industries Board (WIB) Agency led by Bernard Baruch during World War I; allocated scarce goods, established production priorities, and set prices on goods. **341**

war of attrition Union general Grant's Civil War strategy of fighting until the South ran out of men, supplies, and will. **92**

War on Drugs President George Bush's organized effort to end drug smuggling and illegal drug use. **762**

War on Poverty President Lyndon B. Johnson's programs to help poor Americans; announced in 1964. **611**

War Powers Act (1973) Legislation that reaffirmed Congress's constitutional power to declare war; set a 60-day limit on the president's authority to commit U.S. troops to serve in a foreign conflict. **702**

War Production Board (WPB) World War II agency that was in charge of converting factories to war production. **501**

Warren Commission Special group led by Chief Justice Earl Warren to investigate the assassination of President John F. Kennedy. **609**

Warsaw Pact Military alliance formed in 1955 by the Soviet Union and other Eastern European communist countries. **543**

Washington Conference (1921) International conference held in Washington, D.C., that focused on naval disarmament and security in the Pacific. **475**

Watergate Scandal in which President Richard M. Nixon authorized the cover-up of a break-in at the Democratic National Committee headquarters; led to Nixon's resignation in 1974. **720**

Whip Inflation Now (WIN) President Gerald Ford's slogan to garner support for his anti-inflation program. **724**

Wisconsin Idea Robert M. La Follette's reform program for Wisconsin in the early 1900s; became a model for other state governments. **274**

Women's Christian Temperance Union (WCTU) Reform organization that led the fight against alcohol in the late 1800s. **261**

Women's Social and Political Union (WSPU) British women's suffrage organization led by Emmeline Pankhurst; its aggressive tactics helped win British women the right to vote. **882**

Woodstock (1969) Rock concert near Woodstock, New York, that marked the highpoint of the counterculture era. **671**

Works Progress Administration (WPA) New Deal agency created in 1934 to put American men and women to work. **448**

World Bank Institution created at the Bretton Woods conference to make loans to boost the economies of war-damaged countries and developing nations in Africa, Asia, and South America. **840**

World Trade Organization Union of 125 nations formed in 1994 to foster free trade and cooperation on world trade issues. **849**

World Wide Web System developed by Swiss scientists in the early 1980s that links Internet sites. **783**

Y

Yalta Conference (1945) Meeting of U.S. president Franklin D. Roosevelt, British prime minister Winston Churchill, and Soviet leader Joseph Stalin to plan for the postwar world. **518**

yellow journalism Style of sensational reporting used by newspapers to attract readers. **207**

Young Plan Plan that spread Germany's war debt repayments over a 59-year period; replaced the Dawes Plan. **836**

Y2K bug Widespread computer progamming problem created by date abbreviations that threatened to shut down computer systems on January 1, 2000. **784**

Z

zaibatsu Huge corporations run by single families that monopolized the Japanese economy before World War II. **533**

Zimmerman Note Cable sent to Mexico by Germany's foreign secretary during World War I; proposed an alliance between the two countries. **336**

Zionism Movement pushing for the formation of a Jewish homeland in Palestine. **536**

zoot-suit riots (1943) Series of attacks by U.S. sailors against Mexican Americans in Los Angeles. **512**

INDEX

A

B

Berry–censorship

C

G

J

M

N

O

Pacific–public space

P

R

Roosevelt–slavery

S

T

U

INDEX

For permission to reprint copyrighted material, grateful acknowledgment is made to the following sources:

Beacon Press, Boston: From *Man's Search for Meaning* by Viktor E. Frankl. Copyright © 1959, 1962, 1984, 1992 by Viktor E. Frankl.

Donadio & Olson, Inc.: From *The Good War: An Oral History of World War Two* by Studs Terkel. Copyright © 1984 by Studs Terkel.

Greenwood Publishing Group, Inc., Westport, CT: Quote by George Robinson from *Listening to Radio, 1920–1950* by Ray Barfield. Copyright © 1996 by Ray Barfield.

Harcourt, Inc.: Quote by Leonard Korgie from *The Korean War: Pusan to Chosin, An Oral History* by Donald Knox. Copyright © 1985 by Donald Knox.

Henry Holt and Company, LLC: From "U.S. 1946 King's X" from *Complete Poems of Robert Frost, 1949.* Copyright © 1949 by Robert Frost.

Houghton Mifflin Company: From *Turbulent Era: A Diplomatic Record of Forty Years, 1904–1945* by Joseph C. Grew, edited by Walter Johnson. Copyright 1952 by Joseph C. Grew; copyright renewed © 1980 by Elizabeth Lyon, Anita J. English, and Lilla Levitt. All rights reserved.

ACKNOWLEDGMENTS

For permission to reprint copyrighted material, grateful acknowledgment is made to the following sources:

ABCNEWS.com: From "Leaving Home: Stunned, Angry Kosovar Refugees Tell Their Stories" by Mike Porath from ABCNewsWorld.com, April 8, 1999. Copyright © 1999 by ABC News Internet Ventures. Available at http://more.abcnews.go.com/sections/world/DailyNews/kosovo990407_porath.html.

Víctor Alba: From *Alliance Without Allies: The Mythology of Progress in Latin America* by Víctor Alba. Copyright © 1965 by Víctor Alba.

Ancient Future: From "World Fusion Music" by Matthew Montfort from *Ancient Future,* October 18, 1999. Copyright © 1998, 1999 by Matthew Montfort. Available at http://www.ancient-future.com/links/.

Associated Press: Quotes by pitching coach Dave Wallace and general manager Sandy Alderson from "Cubans, Japanese May Be Ripple of Baseball's Next Foreign Wave," July 13, 1999. Available at http://cgi.nando.net/newsroom/ap/bbo/1996/mlb/mlb/feat/archive/032596/mlb18700.html. Copyright © 1996 by Associated Press.

Bantam Books, a division of Random House, Inc.: From *Voices of Freedom* by Henry Hampton and Steve Fayer. Copyright © 1990 by Blackside, Inc.

Bethune-Cookman College Archives: Quote by Mary McLeod Bethune.

Robert Bly: From "The United Fruit Co." by Pablo Neruda from *Neruda and Vallejo: Selected Poems,* chosen and translated by Robert Bly. Copyright © 1971 by Beacon Press. Published by Beacon Press, 1974.

Peter N. Carroll: Quote by a Chicago housewife from "The Loss of Connection" from *It Seemed Like Nothing Happened: America in the 1970s* by Peter N. Carroll. Copyright © 1982 by Peter Carroll.

Sheyann Webb Christburg: Quote by eight-year-old Sheyann Webb from "The Turbulent Sixties" from *The Enduring Vision: A History of the American People* by Paul S. Boyer et al.

The Christian Science Monitor: Quotes by analyst Bill Moses and professor Debora Spar from "Developing Nations Win More Investment" by David Rohde from *The Christian Science Monitor,* August 31, 1994. Copyright © 1994 by The Christian Science Publishing Society.

Don Congdon Associates, Inc.: From "The Watchers" from *Weird Tales* by Ray Bradbury. Copyright © 1945 by Street & Smith Publications; copyright renewed © 1972 by Ray Bradbury.

Crisis Publishing Co., Inc.: From "The Bronx Slave Market" by Ella Baker and Marvel Cooke from *The Crisis,* vol. 42, November 1935. Copyright 1935 by Crisis Publishing Co., Inc.

The Dallas Morning News: Quote by Jenny Haynes from "Up to 90% of pagers in U.S. crash: Wayward satellite's full impact unknown" by Jennifer Files and Joy Dickinson from *The Dallas Morning News,* May 20, 1998 from *Electric Library Business Edition,* November 24, 1999. Copyright © 1998 by The Dallas Morning News. Available at http://library_j&dtype=0~0&dinst=0.

Donadio & Olson, Inc.: Quotes by Ted Allenby, Erhaud Dabringhaus, Steve McConnell, and Hans Massaquoi from *The Good War: An Oral History of World War Two* by Studs Terkel. Copyright © 1984 by Studs Terkel.

Doubleday, a division of Random House, Inc.: From "The Martian Way" from *The Martian Way and Other Stories* by Isaac Asimov. Copyright © 1955 by Isaac Asimov. From *Child of War, Woman of Peace* by Le Ly Hayslip. Copyright © 1993 by Doubleday. From *The Century* by Peter Jennings and Todd Brewster. Copyright © 1998 by ABC Television Network Group, a division of Capitol Cities, Inc. From *The Blue Eagle from Egg to Earth* by Hugh S. Johnson. Copyright 1935 by Hugh S. Johnson. From "Can Wars Be Just?" by Sari Nusseibeh from *But Was It Just?: Reflections on the Morality of the Persian Gulf War* by Jean Bethke Elshtain et al., translated by Peter Heinegg, edited by David E. Decosse. Copyright © 1992 by Jean Bethke Elshtain, Stanley Hauerwas, Sari Nusseibeh, and George Weigel.

Dutton, a division of Penguin Putnam Inc.: From *Movin' On Up* by Mahalia Jackson and Evan McLeod Wylie. Copyright © 1966 by Mahalia Jackson and Evan McLeod Wylie.

The Economist Newspaper Group, Inc.: Quote by Iran's foreign minister from "Iran: Walk in Fear" from *The Economist,* vol. 332, no. 7873, July 23, 1994. Copyright © 1994 by The Economist Newspaper Group, Inc.

W. D. Ehrhart: "Guerrilla War" from *Beautiful Wreckage: New & Selected Poems* by W. D. Ehrhart. Copyright © 1980 by W. D. Ehrhart. Published by Adastra Press, 1999.

Facts On File, Inc.: From "Carla Martinelli" from *Ellis Island Interviews: In Their Own Words* by Peter Morton Coan. Copyright © 1997 by Peter Morton Coan.

Farrar, Straus and Giroux, LLC: From *No Downlink: A Dramatic Narrative about the Challenger Accident and Our Time* by Claus Jensen, translated by Barbara Haveland. Translation copyright © 1996 by Barbara Haveland.

The Gale Group: Adaptation of map "A Diverse Nation, c. 1990," from *We the People* by James Paul Allen and Eugene James Turner. Copyright © 1988 by Macmillan Publishing Company.

GRM Associates, Inc., Agents for the Estate of Ida M. Cullen: From "Yet Do I Marvel" from *Color* by Countee Cullen. Copyright 1925 by Harper & Brothers; copyright renewed 1953 by Ida M. Cullen.

Grove/Atlantic, Inc.: From *1968 in America: Music, Politics, Chaos, Counterculture, and the Shaping of a Generation* by Charles Kaiser. Copyright © 1988 by Charles Kaiser.

The Guardian: From "The Hubris Is Staggering" by John Gray from *The Guardian,* April 8, 1994. Copyright © 1994 by John Gray.

Hikaru Hayashi: Quote by Hikaru Hayashi from "American Casual Seizes Japan" by Barry Hillenbrand from *Time,* November 13, 1989.

Heinemann Educational Books, Ltd.: From "The Rivonia Trial" from *No Easy Walk to Freedom* by Nelson Mandela. Copyright © 1965 by Nelson Mandela.

James A. Henretta: Quote by a Chicago schoolteacher from "Family Values" and quote by a coal miner's daughter from "Herbert Hoover and the Great Depression" from *America's History* by James A. Henretta et al. Copyright © 1987 by The Dorsey Press.

Hill and Wang, a division of Farrar, Straus and Giroux, LLC.: From *Night* by Elie Wiesel, translated by Stella Rodway. Copyright © 1960 by MacGibbon & Kee; copyright renewed © 1988 by The Collins Publishing Group.

Roy Hoopes Publishing: From *Americans Remember the Home Front: An Oral Narrative of the World War II Years in America* by Roy Hoopes. Copyright © 1977, 1992 by Roy Hoopes.

Houghton Mifflin Company: From *Typical American* by Gish Jen. Copyright © 1991 by Gish Jen. All rights reserved.

Howe Brothers Publishers: Excerpt by Gerald One Feather from *Indian Self-Rule: First-Hand Accounts of Indian-White Relations from Roosevelt to Reagan,* edited by Kenneth R. Philp. Published by Howe Brothers Publishers, 1986.

Independent Woman: From a quote by female aircraft worker from "Comments on 'Womanpower 4F'" from *Independent Woman,* November 1943; and quote by a shipyard manager from "Anchors Aweigh!" by Beatrice Oppenheim from *Independent Woman,* March 1943. Published by the Washington National Federation of Business and Professional Women's Clubs, Inc.

Charles H. Kerr & Company, Chicago: From "The March of the Mill Children" from *The Autobiography of Mother Jones,* edited by Mary Field Parton. Copyright 1925, © 1972 by Charles H. Kerr & Company.

Alfred A. Knopf, Inc., a division of Random House, Inc.: From "The Terror" from *The House of the Spirits* by Isabel Allende, translated by Magda Bogin. Translation copyright © 1985 by Alfred A. Knopf, Inc. "I, Too" from *Collected Poems* by Langston Hughes. Copyright © 1994 by the Estate of Langston Hughes.

Kodansha International Ltd.: From *War Wasted Asia: Letters, 1945–46,* edited by Otis Cary. Copyright © 1975 by Kodansha International Ltd. All rights reserved.

Maya Ying Lin: Quote about the Vietnam Veterans Memorial.

Bette Bao Lord: From "Walking in Lucky Shoes" by Bette Bao Lord from *Newsweek,* July 6, 1992. Copyright © 1992 by Bette Bao Lord.

Ludlow Music, Inc.: From lyrics from "Talking Dust Bowl." Words and music composed by Woody Guthrie. TRO—© Copyright 1960, copyright renewed © 1963 by Ludlow Music, Inc., New York, NY.

Macmillan Ltd.: From "Economy (1931)" from *The Collected Writings of John Maynard Keynes: Volume IX, Essays in Persuasion.* Originally published as "The Problem of Unemployment-II" in the *Listener,* January 4, 1931.

Naomi Long Madgett: "Midway" from *Star by Star* by Naomi Long Madgett. Copyright © 1965 by Naomi Long Madgett. Published by Harlo Press in 1965, Evenill in 1970, and Lotus in 1972.

The McGraw-Hill Companies: From *Over There: The Story of America's First Great Overseas Crusade* by Frank Freidel. Copyright © 1990 by McGraw-Hill, Inc. All rights reserved. From *America Inside Out* by David Schoenbrun. Copyright © 1994 by McGraw-Hill Companies, Inc.

Monthly Review Foundation: From "Karari's Hill" from *Mau Mau from Within* by Donald L. Barnett and Karari Njama. Copyright © 1966 by Donald L. Barnett.

William Morrow & Company, Inc.: Quote by Donna Shalala from *What You Can Do for Your Country: An Oral History of the Peace Corps* by Karen Schwarz. Copyright © 1991 by William Morrow & Company, Inc.

Patricia Mull: Quote by Patricia Mull from "What $152 a Week Buys" by Nancy Gibbs from *Time,* September 10, 1990. Copyright © 1990 by Patricia Mull.

Multimedia Product Development, Chicago, IL, agent for Jeane Westin: From "Erma's Story" from *Making Do: How Women Survived the '30s* by Jeane Westin. Copyright © 1976 by Jeane Westin. All rights reserved.

NAACP: From advertisement "Let 'Em Walk" by the NAACP.

National Audubon Society: Excerpt by Aldo Leopold from "Naturschutz in Germany" from *Bird-Lore,* vol. 38, no. 2, March—April 1936.

Jawaharlal Nehru Memorial Fund on behalf of Sonia Gandhi: From "India Follows Gandhi" from *Glimpses of World History* by Jawaharlal Nehru. Copyright 1942 by Jawaharlal Nehru.

New Directions Publishing Corporation: From "Martín IV" *from Martín and Meditations on the South Valley* by Jimmy Santiago Baca. Copyright © 1987 by Jimmy Santiago Baca. From "I Am Waiting" from *A Coney Island of the Mind* by Lawrence Ferlinghetti. Copyright © 1958 by Lawrence Ferlinghetti.

New Internationalist: Quote by Salim Ahmed Salim from "Africa: The Continent that Lost Its Way" by Victoria Brittain from *New Statesman and Society* from *The New Internationalist.* Copyright © 1994 by New Internationalist.

The New Republic: From "The De Luxe Picture Palace" by Lloyd Lewis from *The New Republic,* vol. 58, March 27, 1929. Copyright 1929 by The New Republic.

The New York Times Company: From "The Most Religious Century" (Op-Ed) by Michael Novak from *The New York Times,* May 24, 1998. Copyright © 1998 by The New York Times Company. From "Son Picks Up Nobel Prize for a Detained Burmese Dissenter" by John Tagliabue from *The New York Times,* December 11, 1991. Copyright © 1991 by The New York Times Company.

Newsweek, Inc.: Quote by Hugh Austin from "Business and Finance" from *Newsweek,* November 19, 1973. Copyright © 1973 by Newsweek, Inc. All rights reserved. From "Nursing the Dying" by Edie Meeks from *Newsweek,* March 8, 1999, p. 61. Copyright © 1999 by Newsweek, Inc. All rights reserved.

W. W. Norton & Company, Inc.: From *Sleepwalking Through History: America in the Reagan Years* by Haynes Johnson. Copyright © 1991 by Haynes Johnson.

Harold Ober Associates Incorporated: From "...I Could Not Eat the Poems I Wrote" by Langston Hughes. Copyright © 1963 by Langston Hughes. Published by Freedomways.

Pathfinder Press: From "OAAU Founding Rally" and from "Short Statements: Fight or Forget It" from *By Any Means Necessary: Speeches, Interviews, and a Letter by Malcolm X.* Copyright © 1970 by Betty Shabazz and Pathfinder Press.

Publishers Weekly: From interview with Gloria Steinem from *Publishers Weekly,* August 12, 1983. Copyright © 1983 by R. R. Bowker Company.

G. P. Putnam's Sons, a division of Penguin Putnam Inc. From "Their Finest Hour," a speech delivered to the House of Commons, June 18, 1940, by Winston Churchill from *Blood, Sweat, and Tears* by The Right Honorable Winston S. Churchill. Copyright 1941 by Winston S. Churchill. From "The Yom Kippur War" from *My Life* by Golda Meir. Copyright © 1975 by Golda Meir.

Random House, Inc.: From "On the Pulse of Morning" from *On the Pulse of Morning* by Maya Angelou. Copyright © 1993 by Maya Angelou.

The Reader's Digest Association, Inc.: From "The Spread of Grass-Roots Capitalism" by Edward Maher from *Reader's Digest,* June 1955. Copyright © 1955 by The Reader's Digest Association, Inc.

Estate of Erich Maria Remarque: From *All Quiet on the Western Front* by Erich Maria Remarque. Copyright 1929, 1930 by Little, Brown and Company; copyright renewed © 1957, 1958 by Erich Maria Remarque. All rights reserved. "Im Westen Nichts Neues" copyright 1928 by Ullstein A. G.; copyright renewed © 1956 by Erich Maria Remarque.

Republican National Committee: From "Morning in America" advertisement for Ronald Reagan 1984 presidential campaign.

Roosevelt University, Labor Education Division: From "Automation" by Joe Glazer from *Songs of Work and Freedom,* edited by Edith Fowke and Joe Glazer. Published by Roosevelt University, Labor Education Division, 1960.

Saturday Review Publications, Ltd.: From "The World Conference: A French Point of View" by H. D. Davray from *The Saturday Review,* vol. 155, June 24, 1933. Copyright © 1933 by Saturday Review Publications, Ltd.

Scribner, a division of Simon & Schuster, Inc.: From "The Black Worker" from *Black Reconstruction in America, 1860–1880* by W. E. B. Du Bois. Copyright 1935, © 1962 by W. E. Burghardt Du Bois. From *For Whom the Bell Tolls* by Ernest Hemingway. Copyright 1940 by Ernest Hemingway; copyright renewed © 1968 by Mary Hemingway. From *The Sun Also Rises* by Ernest Hemingway. Copyright 1926 by Charles Scribner's Sons; copyright renewed 1954 by Ernest Hemingway. From "We Lived on Relief" by Ann Rivington from *Scribner's Magazine,* vol. 95, 1934, pp. 282–5. Copyright 1934 and renewed © 1962 by Charles Scribner's Sons. From *By-line: Ernest Hemingway,* edited by William White. Copyright © 1967 by William White.

Scripps Howard Foundation: From *Ernie's War: The Best of Ernie Pyle's World War II Dispatches,* edited by David Nichols. Copyright © 1986 by Simon and Schuster.

SIGI Productions, Inc.: Quotes by Arthur Komori and Francis Tsuzuki from *"I Can Never Forget": Men of the 100th/442nd* by Thelma Chang. Copyright © 1991 by SIGI Productions, Inc.

Simon & Schuster, Inc.: From "Special Problems of the Depression" from *Interpretations, 1931-1932* by Walter Lippmann. Copyright © 1932 by Walter Lippmann. From *Nobody Speaks for Me! Self -Portraits of American Working-Class Women* by Nancy Seifer. Copyright © 1976 by Nancy Seifer. From *A Woman of Egypt* by Jehan Sadat. Copyright © 1987 by Simon & Schuster, Inc.

Small Planet Communications, Inc.: From "Expansion in the Pacific" from *An On-Line History of the United States: The Age of Imperialism,* on-line, September 22, 1999. Copyright © 1996 by Small Planet Communications, Inc. Available at http://www.smplanet.com/imperialism/hawaii.html.

Special Rider Music: From lyrics from "Blowin' in the Wind" by Bob Dylan. Copyright © 1962 by Warner Bros. Music; copyright renewed © 1990 by Special Rider Music. All rights reserved.

Gloria Steinem: Quotes by Gloria Steinem about the women's movement.

Time Inc.: From "The Century Ahead: How The World Will Look in 50 Years" by Bruce W. Nelan from *Time,* October 15, 1992. Copyright © 1992 by Time Inc. From "The Men Who Fought" from *Time,* vol. 143, no. 23, June 6, 1994. Copyright © 1994 by Time Inc.

Sheila Tobias: Quote by Sonia Pressman Fuentes from *Faces of Feminism: An Activist's Reflections on the Women's Movement* by Sheila Tobias. Copyright © 1997 by Westview Press, a division of HarperCollins Publishers, Inc.

Margaret Truman and SCG, Inc., 381 Park Ave., So., NYC, NY 10016: From *Memoirs by Harry S. Truman: Years of Trial and Hope.* Copyright © 1956 by Time Inc. Published by Doubleday and Company.

The University of North Carolina Press: From "Tore Up and a-Movin'" from *These Are Our Lives* by the Federal Writers' Project. Copyright © 1939 by The University of North Carolina Press.

University of Washington Press: From *Island: Poetry and History of Chinese Immigrants on Angel Island, 1910–1940* by Him Mark Lai, Genny Lim, and Judy Young. Copyright © 1991 by University of Washington Press.

Luis Valdez, Founder & Artistic Director, El Teatro Campesino: From "Perspectives on 'Borders'" by Luis M. Valdez from a 1986 Public Humanities Lecture sponsored by the California Council for the Humanities.

Viking Penguin, a division of Penguin Putnam Inc.: Poem "I saw, I saw, I saw holes and trenches" by Trinh Cong Son from *Vietnam: A History* by Stanley Karnow. Copyright © 1983 by WGBH Educational Foundation and Stanley Karnow.

Warner Books, Inc.: From *The Memoirs of Richard Nixon* by Richard Nixon. Copyright © 1978 by Richard Nixon. Published by Grosset & Dunlap.

Warner Bros. Publications U.S., Inc., Miami, Fl, 33014: From lyrics from "Get a Job" by Earl Beal, Richard Lewis, Raymond Edwards, and William Horton. Copyright © 1957 and renewed © 1985 by Windswept Pacific Entertainment Co. d/b/a Longitude Music Co. All rights reserved. From lyrics from "We're In the Money" by Harry Warren and Al Dubin. Copyright 1933 by Remick Music, Inc.

Wieser & Wieser, Inc., Literary Agency: From *Japan's War: The Great Pacific Conflict, 1853 to 1952* by Edwin P. Hoyt. Copyright © 1986 by Edwin P. Hoyt.

Women's International League for Peace and Freedom: From "Freedom of Thought and Speech" statement at the Annual Meeting of the Women's International League for Peace and Freedom, 1949.

The Heirs to the Estate of Martin Luther King, Jr., c/o Writers House, Inc. as agent for the proprietor: From "I Have a Dream" and "Letter from Birmingham Jail" from *Why We Can't Wait* by Martin Luther King, Jr. Copyright © 1963 by Martin Luther King, Jr.; copyright renewed © 1991 by Coretta Scott King. From "Sermon Against the War in Vietnam" by Martin Luther King, Jr. Copyright © 1967 by Martin Luther King, Jr.; copyright renewed © 1995 by The Estate of Martin Luther King, Jr.

SOURCES CITED:

From *And the Walls Came Tumbling Down* by Ralph David Abernathy. Published by HarperCollins Publishers, Inc., New York, 1989.

Quote by an African American woman from *The American Slave: Georgia Narratives,* Part 1, vol. 12, edited by George P. Rawick. Published by Greenwood Publishing Group.

Excerpt about the Bay of Pigs from *The New York Times.*

From "The Stock Market Crash" by Elliott V. Bell from *The New York Times,* October 24, 1929.

From *Sharing Smaller Pies* by Tom Bender. First published in *Rain,* Portland, OR, 1975.

Quote by Jane Berentson from interview with Charles Kaiser, July 7, 1986, from *1968 in America: Music, Politics, Chaos, Counterculture, and the Shaping of a Generation* by Charles Kaiser. Published by Weidenfeld & Nicolson, New York, 1988.

Quote by Herminio Blanco from "Mexico Faces Challenges Despite 5 Years Free Trade" (Reuters), December 3, 1998, CNN interactive, CNN.com. Available at http://search.cnn.com:80/query.html?col=cnni&qp=&qc=&pw=460&ws=0&la=&fs=&qt=NAFTA&qm=0&ql=&.

Quotes from a Boxer handbill and from a British officer from "Missionary Martyrs of the Boxer Rebellion," from *Christian History Magazine,* issue 52, vol. XV, no. 4.

Quote by D. Clayton Brown of Texas Christian University, from *Encyclopedia of Southern Culture, vol. 1, Agriculture–Environment,* edited by Charles Reagan Wilson et al. Published by the University of North Carolina Press, Chapel Hill, NC, 1989.

Quote by Cesar Caballero from "Chuppies" from *New Americans: An Oral History: Immigrants and Refugees in the U.S. Today* by Al Santoli. Published by Viking Press, New York, 1988.

From "The First Tanks in Action, 15 September 1916" by Bert Chaney from *People at War, 1914-1918* by Michael Moynihan. Published by David and Charles, 1973.

From *Cesar Chavez: Autobiography of La Causa* by Jacques E. Levy. Published by W. W. Norton & Company, Inc., New York, 1975.

Quote by Eleanor Roosevelt's cousin, Corinne, from "Biographical Sketch" by William H. Chafe from *Without Precedent: The Life and Career of Eleanor Roosevelt,* edited by Joan Hoff-Wilson and Marjorie Lightman. Published by Indiana University Press, Bloomington, IN, 1984.

Quote by Dr. Alfred Crosby from *The American Experience: Influenza 1918,* on-line, June 28, 1991. Available at http://www.pbs.org/wgbh/pages/amex/influenza/filmmore/transcript/.

Quote by Jorge Diaz from *Shadowed Lives: Undocumented Immigrants in American Society* by Leo R. Chavez. Published by Harcourt, Inc., Orlando, FL, 1992.

Quote by Tran Do from *Vietnam: A History* by Stanley Karnow. Published by Penguin Books, New York, 1983.

From "Driving Cattle from Texas to Iowa, 1866" by George Crawford Duffield from *Annals of Iowa,* vol. XIV, 1924.

Quote by Helen Farmer from *The Great Depression: America in the 1930s* by T. H. Watkins. Published by Little, Brown and Company, New York, 1993.

Quote by Captain José Fernandez, translated by Valeska Bari from *The Course Of Empire: First Hand Accounts of California in the Days of the Gold Rush of '49,* compiled by Valeska Bari. Published by Coward-McCann, Inc., New York, 1931.

Ellen Levine Literary Agency: From "Goodbye to Our Boy" by Garrison Keillor from *Time,* August 2, 1999, p.1. Copyright © 1999 by Garrison Keillor.

The Nation: From "U.S. Cultural Invasion: Hungary for American Pop" by Miklos Vamos from *The Nation,* March 25, 1991. Copyright © 1991 by The Nation.

Sierra Club Books: From *Nature's Economy: The Roots of Ecology* by Donald Worster. Copyright © 1977 by Donald Worster.

University of Minnesota Press: From *Uncertain Dimensions: Western Overseas Empires in the Twentieth Century* by Raymond F. Betts. Copyright © 1985 by the University of Minnesota.

Sources Cited:

Quote by Roger Ailes from "Ailes: What He Wants Next: Bush Adman Aims Attack at Madison Ave." by Steven W. Colford from *Advertising Age,* November 14, 1988, p. 67. Published by Crain Communications, Inc., New York, 1988.

Quotes by Oscar Ameringer, Len De Caux, CIO organizer Sidney Lens, William Allen White, and from a union song from *Redeeming the Time: A People's History of the 1920s and the New Deal* by Page Smith. Published by Penguin Books, New York, 1991.

Quotes by Lisa Anderson, Sally Belfrage, and Marshall Ganz from *Like a Holy Crusade: Mississippi 1964—The Turning of the Civil Rights Movement in America* by Nicolaus Mills. Published by Ivan R. Dee, Inc., Chicago, IL, 1992.

ACKNOWLEDGMENTS

Quote by a Florida woman from *Searching for the Sunbelt: Historical Perspectives on a Region,* edited by Raymond A. Mohl. Published by The University of Tennessee Press, Knoxville, TN, 1990.

Quote by Mary Margaret Funk from "Buddhism in America" by Jeanne McDowell and Richard N. Ostling from *Time,* on-line, October 13, 1997, vol. 150, New York, 1997.

Quote by Indira Gandhi from "The India of My Dreams" from *My Truth* by Indira Gandhi, presented by Emmanuel Pouchpadass. First published in English in 1981 by Vision Books Pvt. Ltd., New Delhi, in collaboration with Editions Stock, Paris.

From *The Road Ahead* by Bill Gates with Nathan Myhrvold and Peter Rinearson. Published by Penguin Books, New York, 1996.

Quote by a German officer describing the fighting at Stalingrad, 1942, from *The Century* by Peter Jennings and Todd Brewster. Published by Doubleday, a division of Bantam Doubleday Dell Publishing Group, Inc., New York, 1998.

Quote by Jim Gilmore, Governor of Virginia, from "A Taxing Conundrum" by Curt Anderson. Published by The Associated Press, June 21, 1999.

Quote about Lyndon B. Johnson from *With No Apologies: The Personal and Political Memoirs of United States Senator Barry Goldwater* by Barry Goldwater. Published by Greenwillow Books, a division of William Morrow & Company, New York, 1996.

Quotes by José Angel Gutiérrez from interview by Hector Galán, December 12, 1994. Transcripts from National Latino Communications Center, Los Angeles, CA, and Galán Productions, Rodulfo Acuña, Austin, TX.

Quote by Colonel Jacobo Arbenz Guzmán from *Modern Latin America,* Second Edition, by Thomas E. Skidmore and Peter H. Smith. Published by Oxford University Press, Inc., New York, 1984, 1989.

Quote by Clara Hancox from *The Century* by Peter Jennings and Todd Brewster. Published by Doubleday, a division of Random House, Inc., New York, 1998.

From a quote by Myron Harrington from *Vietnam: A History* by Stanley Karnow. Published by Penguin Books, New York, 1983.

From *Everyday Life in Early America* by David Freeman Hawke. Published by HarperCollins Publishers, Inc., New York, 1988.

From memo from Heller to President John F. Kennedy, August 2, 1961, Steel file, Sorensen Papers, John F. Kennedy Library.

From *A Farewell to Arms* by Ernest Hemingway. Published by Charles Scribner's Sons, New York, 1929.

From *Their Eyes Were Watching God* by Zora Neale Hurston. Published by Harper & Row Publishers, New York, 1937.

Quotes by Bernice Johnson and Charles Houston from *Eyes on the Prize* by Juan Williams. Published by Penguin Books, New York, 1988.

From *Great Expectations: America and the Baby Boom Generation* by Landon Y. Jones. Published by Coward, McCann & Geoghegan, New York, 1980.

From "Before the Colors Fade: Last of the Rough Riders" by V. C. Jones from *American Heritage Magazine,* August 1969.

From *Red Power: The American Indians' Fight for Freedom* by Alvin M. Josephy, Jr. Published by McGraw-Hill, New York, 1971.

Quote by Shirley Keith in concert, "Benefit for Alcatraz," at Stanford, CA, December 18, 1969. Recording at Pacifica Radio Archives, North Hollywood, CA .

From *Petra Kelly: Fighting for Hope,* translated by Marianne Howarth. Published by South End Press, Boston, MA, 1984. First published in German under the title *Um Hoffnung Kämpfen* by Lamuv Verlag, Martinstrasse 7, 5303 Bornheim-Merten, 1983.

Quote by Martin Luther King, Jr. regarding the year-long bus boycott, Montgomery, AL, 1956.

Quote by Mary Mackey from *Great Expectations: America and the Baby Boom Generation* by Landon Y. Jones. Published by Coward, McCann & Geoghegan, New York, 1980.

From *The Presidential Papers* by Norman Mailer. Published by G. P. Putnam's Sons, New York, 1963.

From *Steven Spielberg: A Biography* by Joseph McBride. Published by Simon & Schuster, New York, 1997.

From a quote by Anne O'Hare McCormick from *Truman* by David McCullough. Published by Simon & Schuster, New York, 1992.

From "Still 'A Little Left of Center'" by Anne O'Hare McCormick from *The New York Times,* June 21, 1936.

Quote by Robert McElvaine from *The Great Depression: America in the 1930s* by T. H. Watkins. Published by Little, Brown and Company, New York, 1993.

Quotes by Eliseo Medina from interview by Sylvia Morales, November 18, 1995. Transcripts from National Latino Communications Center, Los Angeles, CA, and Galán Productions, Austin, TX.

Quotes by Thomas Minehan and by an anonymous teenager from *The Great Depression: America in the 1930s* by T. H. Watkins. Published by Little, Brown and Company, New York, 1993.

Quote by Martha Ann Morrison Minto from "Female Pioneering in Oregon, 1844" from a Manuscript Diary, Bancroft Library, University of California, Berkeley, CA.

Quotes by J. García Monge and M. A. Zumbado R. from Sociedad Económica de Amigos del País, *Estudio relativo a los Contratos Bananeros celebrados entre el Gobierno de Costa Rica y Mr. M. M. Marsh y la United Fruit Company,* San Jose, CA, 1929.

Quotes by Bob Moses, MacArthur Cotton, and Mendy Samstein from Notes on Mississippi Staff Meeting, November 1963, State Historical Society of Wisconsin: Howard Zinn Papers.

Quotes by New Yorker Johnny Boy Musto, Anibal Campa, and a 21-year-old beautician from "Get Up and Boogie" by Maureen Orth et al. from *Newsweek,* November 8, 1976. Published by Newsweek, Inc., New York, 1976.

Quote by John Ortiz from *Social Protest in an Urban Barrio: A Study of the Chicano Movement, 1966–1974* by Marguerite V. Marin. Published by University Press of America, Lanham, MD, 1991.

Quote by a Panhandle county sheriff from "Race, Labor, and the Frontier" from *Anglos and Mexicans in the Making of Texas, 1836–1986* by David Montejano. Published by the University of Texas Press, Austin, TX, 1987.

From "...The hawk had come" by Gordon Parks from *Brother Can You Spare a Dime? The Great Depression, 1929–1933* by Milton Meltzer. Published by Alfred A. Knopf, Inc., New York, 1969.

Quote by Ed Paulsen from *Hard Times: An Oral History of the Great Depression* by Studs Terkel. Published by Avon Books, a division of the Hearst Corporation, New York, 1970.

Quote by a Polish coal miner from *Workers' World* by John Bodnar. Published by Workers' World, Baltimore, MD, 1982.

Quote by Sugar Rautbord from *The Great Divide* by Studs Terkel. Published by Pantheon Books, New York, 1988.

Quote by Robert Reich from "They're Rich (and You're Not)" by Adam Bryant from *Newsweek,* July 5, 1999. Published by Newsweek, Inc., New York, 1999.

From a quote by Deputy Reyes to the Honduran Congress from *Boletín Legislativo* (Legislative Record), series iv, no. 31, January 23, 1933.

Quote by William Rutherford from a telephone conversation between Rutherford and Levison, June 2, 1968, from the FBI Levison File, Library and Archive, Martin Luther King, Jr., Center for Nonviolent Social Change, Atlanta, GA.

From *My Country and the World* by Andrei Sakharov, translated by Guy V. Daniels. Published by Alfred A. Knopf, Inc., New York, 1975.

Quote by Harley Shaiken from "Big Brown's Union Blues" by Daniel Pedersen from *Newsweek,* August 18, 1997. Published by Newsweek, Inc., New York, 1997.

Quotes by Donna Shalala from "Shalala Remembers Kennedy's Call to Peace; Cabinet Secretary Comes to Austin for Peace Corps Reunion" by Ben Wear from *Austin American-Statesman,* August 4, 1995.

Quote by Alana Shoars from "Do Employees Have a Right to Electronic Privacy?" by Glenn Rifkin from *The New York Times,* December 8, 1991.

Quote by Albert Sindlinger from "Tinkering with the Wireless: Can Anyone Hear Me West of Steubenville?" from *The Century* by Peter Jennings and Todd Brewster. Published by Doubleday, a division of Random House, Inc., New York, 1998.

From a quote by a Slav immigrant from "Relief and Revolution" by Charles R. Walker from *The Forum,* 73, August 1932, Washington, D.C.

From *The Grapes of Wrath* by John Steinbeck. Published by the Viking Press, New York, 1939.

Quote by Elisha Stockwell from *The Boys' War: Confederate and Union Soldiers Talk About the Civil War* by Jim Murphy. Published by Clarion Books, a Houghton Mifflin Company imprint, New York, 1990.

Quotes by Reverend Harold Toliver and Nelson Poynter from *Americans Remember the Home Front: An Oral Narrative of the World War II Years in America* by Roy Hoopes. Published by Berkley Books, New York, 1992.

Quote by Mrs. Townsend from "Young Mother" from *Ladies' Home Journal,* 1956.

Quote by Ton That Tung from *Vietnam: A History* by Stanley Karnow. Published by Penguin Books, New York, 1983.

Quote by Maria Valera about the National Chicano Liberation Youth Conference, 1969, from *Youth, Identity, Power: The Chicano Movement* by Carlos Muñoz. Published by Verso, London, England, 1989.

Quote by an anonymous Venezuelan government official from "ECA Letters 'Shake' for Venezuelan Forest" from *Eco-Club Action Newsletter,* July, 1999. Published by Global Response—Environmental Action and Education Network, Boulder, CO, 1999.

Quote by Reverend John M. S. Walker from *People at War: 1914–1918,* edited by Michael Moynihan. Published by David & Charles, Ltd., Newton Abbot, England, 1973.

Quote by Bruce Weigl from *The Vietnam Wars: 1945–1990* by Marilyn B. Young. Published by HarperCollins Publishers, New York, 1991.

Quote by You Weijie from "Little Protest Seen in Beijing" by John Leicester. Published by The Associated Press, New York, 1999.

Quote by David Wyss from "Ace in the Hole" by John Cassidy from *The New Yorker,* June 10, 1996.

Photo Credits

Abreviations used: (t) top, (c) center, (b) bottom, (l) left, (r) right, (bckgd) background), (bdr) border

FRONT COVER, title page: Rohan/Tony Stone Images; (bkgd), CORBIS/Bill Ross.

TABLE OF CONTENTS AND FRONT MATTER: Page iii, courtesy Paul Boyer; courtesy Dr. Sterling Stuckey; courtesy Ronald Foore; courtesy Nan Woodruff; courtesy Yasuhide Kawashima; courtesy Alfred Young; courtesy Lucinda Lucero Sachs; v, Rick Vargas / Smithsonian Institution / PRC Archive; vi (t), Museum of the City of New York, Gift of Mary and Charles Odgen; (bl), The Granger Collection, New York; (br), Smithsonian Institution, neg no. 91-6501 / PRC Archive; vii, Library of Congress; viii (t), The Granger Collection, New York; (b), Frank Driggs Collection; ix, Corbis-Bettmann; x (l), HRW Photo by Sam Dudgeon; (r), Sylvia Johnson/Woodfin Camp & Associates, Inc.; xi (t), David Hume Kennerly / Corbis Sygma; (b), Richard B. Levine; xii (t), Selwyn Tait / Liaison Agency; (b), George Hall/Check Six; xiii (t), NASA; (b), Printed by permission of the Norman Rockwell Family Trust ©1943 / Photo courtesy of the Curtis Publishing Company, xiv (both), U.S. Postal Service / Harcourt Inc.; xv (t), Library of Congress / PRC Archive; (b), Bob Daemmrich Photo, Inc.; xvi, HRW Photo by Victoria Smith; xviii through xx (all flags), Image Copyright © 1997 PhotoDisc, Inc.; xviii (l), Courtesy of the Museum of the American Numismatic Association; (r), Cook Collection, Valentine Museum, Richmond, Virginia / PRC Archive; xix, NASA; xx, Photo by Byron, The Byron Collection, Museum of the City of New York / PRC Archive; xxi (t), Library of Congress; (b), Richard B. Levine.

UNIT 1: Page 0-1, Kirby Collection of Historical Paintings, Lafayette College, Easton, Pennsylvania / courtesy PRC; 1, Colorado Historical Society.

CHAPTER 1: Page 2 (tl), Grant Heilman Photography; 2 (tr), AKG Photo; 2 (b), Ancient Art & Architecture Collection Ltd.; 3 (tl), Corbis-Bettmann; 3 (tr), Library of Congress/ PRC Archive; 3 (b), CORBIS/ Gianni Dagli Orti; 4, North Wind Picture Archives; 5 (t), ©Robert Frerck/Woodfin Camp & Associates, Inc.; 5 (b), AKG Photo, London; 6, Library of Congress; 7, ©Marilyn "Angel" Wynn, Sun Valley, Idaho; 8 (t), The Granger Collection, New York; 8 (b), SuperStock; 9, The Granger Collection, New York; 10 (b), Courtesy the Bostonian Society, The Old State House; 10 (t), Peter Newark's American Pictures; 11, Library of Congress; 13 (t), Rare Books and Manuscripts Division, The Astor, Lenox and Tilden Foundations, The New York Public Library; 13 (b), Peter Newark's American Pictures; 14, Tom Pantages; 15 (t), The Granger Collection, New York; 15 (b), Peter Newark's Western Americana; 16, Archive Photos; 21, The Granger Collection, New York; 22 (t), Archive Photos; 22 (b), The Granger Collection, New York; 23, Woolaroc Museum, Bartlesville, Oklahoma; 24, Slater Mill Historic Site/ PRC Archive; 25 (t), Collection of the New-York Historical Society/ PRC Archive; 25 (b), Courtesy of the Illinois State Historical Society/ PRC Archive; 26 (b), The Metropolitan Museum of Art, Gift of I.N. Phelps Stokes, Edward S. Hawes, Alice Mary Hawes, Marion Augusta Hawes, 1937. [37.14.22]; 26 (t), Library of Congress / PRC Archive; 27, The Granger Collection, New York; 28 (t), Carl Socolon/The Landis Valley Museum/ PRC Archive; 28 (b), *Fall of the Alamo* by Robert Onderdonk, Courtesy of Friends of the Governor's Mansion, Austin, Texas/ PRC Archive; 29 (t), Texas State Library and Archives Commission; 29 (b), Courtesy of the California History Room, California State Library, Sacramento, California; 31 (t), Rare Books and Manuscripts Division, The New York Public Library, Astor, Lenox and Tilden Foundations/ PRC Archive; 31 (b), The Granger Collection, New York; 32, The Granger Collection, New York; 33, Library of Congress / PRC Archive; 35, Colonial Williamsburg Foundation.

CONSTITUTION HANDBOOK: Page 36, Library of Congress; 37, Independence National Historical Park Collection; 38 (t), The Granger Collection, New York; 38 (c), U.S. Postal Service/ Harcourt, Inc.; 38 (b), U.S. Postal Service/ Harcourt Inc.; 39 (t), Independence National Historical Park Collection; 39 (b), David Young-Wolff/PhotoEdit; 40, Nebraska State Historical Society; 42 (t), The Granger Collection, New York; 42 (b), Corbis-Bettmann; 43 (t), National Archives 43 (b), Independence National Historical Park Collection; 48, Independence National Historical Park Collection; 51, Collection, The Supreme Court Historical Society; 55 (t), Joe Marquette/AP/Wide World Photos; 55 (b), Jeffrey Brown/Liaison Agency; 56, Bob Daemmrich Photo, Inc.; 58, Library of Congress; 60 (t), HRW Photo by Sam Dudgeon; 60 (b), Underwood & Underwood/ Corbis-Bettmann; 61, Sophia Smith Collection, Smith College; 62, R. Foulds / Washington Stock Photo; 63, AP / Wide World Photos, Inc.; 64, Jeff Greenberg/PhotoEdit; 65 (t), The Granger Collection, New York; 65 (cr), Chicago Historical Society, #X.1354; 65 (cl), HRW Photo by Sam Dudgeon; 65 (b), Tom Pantages.

CHAPTER 2: 66 (tr), George Eastman House/ PRC Archive; 66 (tl), Library of Congress/ PRC Archive; 66 (bl), The Granger Collection, New York; 67 (tr), Courtesy of the Museum of the American Numismatic Association; Page 66 (bc), Library of Congress/photo by Ken Cobb; 66 (br), Corbis-Bettmann; 67 (tl), Tom Lovell / National Geographic Image Collection; 68 (t), Chicago Historical Society/PRC Archive; 67 (b), The Museum of the Confederacy, Richmond, Virginia/ PRC Archive; 68 (b), Frank & Marie-Therese Wood Print Collections, Alexandria, VA; 69 (t), Library of Congress; 69 (b), U.S. Postal Service / Harcourt Inc.; 70, PRC Archive; 71, The Museum of the Confederacy Richmond, Virginia/ PRC Archive; 72, Museum of the Confederacy, Richmond, VA. Photo by Katherine Wetzel/PRC Archive; 73, From The Civil War: Forward to Richmond. Photograph by Al Freni, © 1983 Time-Life Books, Inc. Courtesy, Troiani Collection; 74, The Granger Collection, New York; 75 (tl), © Collection of Kean Wilcox All rights reserved./PRC Archive; 75 (tr), Private Collection/ PRC Archive; 75 (b), Library of Congress/ PRC Archive; 76 (t), Library of Congress; 76 (br), Library of Congress; 76 (bl), The Museum of the Confederacy Richmond, Virginia. Photography by Katherine Wetzel; 77, Library of Congress / PRC Archive; 78 (t), National Portrait Gallery, Smithsonian Institution, Washington DC/Art Resource, NY; 78 (b), Courtesy Mulberry Plantation, Camden, SC/Photo by Alt Lee, Columbia, SC/PRC Archive; 79, Smithsonian Institution, neg. #84-9312/ PRC Archive; ; 80 (t), Chicago Historical Society / PRC Archive; 80 (b), Museum of the Confederacy, Richmond, VA from *Echoes of Glory, Arms, and Equipment of the Confederacy* © 1991, Time-Life Books, Inc. Photo High Impact/Larry Sherer; 81, The Granger Collection, New York; 82 (t), Collection of Michael J. McAfee/ PRC Archive; 82 (b), Cincinnati Museum Center/PRC Archive; 83, Chicago Historical Society/PRC Archive; 85 (t), ©The Bucks Historical Society 1999; 85 (b), Library of Congress; 86, Corbis-Bettmann; 87, Library Company of Philadelphia/ PRC Archive; 88, West Point Museum Collections, United States Military Academy/ PRC Archive; 89, Anne S. Brown Military Collection, Brown University/PRC Archive; 90 (t), PRC Archive; 90 (b), State Museum of Pennsylvania; 92 (t), Laurie Platt Winfrey/Woodfin Camp & Associates,Inc.; 92 (b), Library of Congress; 93, Atlanta History Center; 94, Library of Congress; 95, Tom Lovell / National Geographic Image Collection (detail); 97, Rick Vargas/ Smithsonian Institution/ PRC Archive.

CHAPTER 3: Page 100 (tl), Corbis-Bettmann; 100 (tr), The Granger Collection, New York; 100 (b), Jubilee Singers, Courtesy of Fisk University Library Special Collections; 101 (tl), Atlanta History Center; 101 (tr), The Western Reserve Historical Society, Cleveland, Ohio/ PRC Archive;\; 101 (b), National Archives of New Zealand; 102 (t), Hulton Getty @ Liaison Agency; 102 (b), Library of Congress; 103, Bob Daemmrich Photography; 104, Library of Congress; 105, Miriam and Ira D. Wallach Division of Art, Prints and Photographs, The New York Public Library. Astor, Lenox and Tilden Foundations/ PRC Archive; 106, The Western Reserve Historical Society, Cleveland, Ohio; 107 (t), National Archives (NARA)/ PRC Archive; 107 (b), Corbis-Bettmann; 108, Library of Congress; 109 (t), Library of Congress/ PRC Archive; 109 (b), The Granger Collection, New York; 110 (b), Library of Congress; 111 (b), Louisiana Collection, Howard Tilton Memorial Library, New Orleans, LA 70118; 111 (t), U.S. Postal Service/ Harcourt Inc.; 112 (b), The Granger Collection, New York; 112 (t), The Granger Collection, New York; 113 (b), Frank and Marie-Therese Wood Print Collections, Alexandria, VA / PRC Archive; 113 (t), U.S. Postal Service / Harcourt Inc.; 114 (t), Library of Congress; 115 (t), North Wind Picture Archives; 115 (b), Cook Collection, Valentine Museum, Richmond, Virginia/ PRC Archive; 116 (tl), Library of Congress/ PRC Archive; 116 (tr), Collection of Nancy Gewirz, Antique Textile Resource/ PRC Archive; 116 (b), Tennessee State Museum Collection/ Photo by June Dorman; 118 (b), Frank & Marie-Therese Wood Print Collections, Alexandria, VA / PRC Archive; 120 (t), The Metropolitan Museum of Art , Morris K. Jesup Fund, 1940. (40.40). All rights reserved, The Metropolitan Museum of Art; 120 (b), Cook Collection, Valentine Museum, Richmond, Virginia/ PRC Archive; 121 (b), The Granger Collection, New York; 121 (tl), Brown Brothers/ PRC ; 121 (tr), © Joe Sohm / The Image Works; 122 (t), The Granger Collection, New York; 122 (b), South Carolina Historical Society/ PRC Archive; 123 (l), The Western Reserve Historical Society, Cleveland, Ohio/ PRC Archive; 123 (r), Ohio Historical Society; 124 (b), Schomburg Center for Research in Black Culture, New York Public Library/PRC Archive; 124 (t), PRC Archive; 125, Corbis-Bettmann; 127, Illinois State Historical Library/PRC Archive; 128, Peter Newark's American Pictures; 129 (t), Private Collection / PRC Archive; 129 (b), Peter Newark's American Pictures.

UNIT 2: Page 130, Peter Newark's American Pictures; 131, National Park Service Collection / Gift of Angelo Forgione, c. 1991.

CHAPTER 4: 132 (tl), Courtesy Wells Fargo Bank/ PRC Archive; 132 (tc), Historic Seward House/ PRC Archive; 132 (tr), FORBES Magazine Collection, New York/The Bridgeman Art Library, New York/London; 132 (t), Keystone-Mast Collection, #ACT 24040, UCR/ California Museum of Photography, University of California, Riverside; Page 132 (b), *The Luck of Roaring Camp* by Bret Harte, 1876. Trustees of the Boston Public Library/ PRC Archive; 133 (tl), Nawrocki Stock Photo; 133 (tr), Library of Congress/ PRC Archive; 133 (b), Corbis-Bettmann; 134 (t), Arizona Historical Society; 134 (b), The Granger Collection, New York; 135 (b), National Museum of American Art, Smithsonian Institution, Washington DC/Art Resource, NY; 136 (t), Courtesy of Colorado Historical Society/PRC Archive; 136 (b), Photo by Blair Clark, courtesy Museum of New Mexico, Neg. no. 155365; 137 (b), COURTESY OF THE SOUTHWEST MUSEUM, LOS ANGELES; 137 (t), Denver Public Library, Western History Department/ PRC Archive; 138, The Field Museum of Natural History, #A111822c, Chicago; 139, National Anthropological Archives, Smithsonian Institution, Washington, D.C.; 140 (t), Helen Hunt Jackson. *A Century of Dishonor*, 1881. Trustees of the Boston Public Library/ PRC Archive; 140 (b), The Granger Collection, New York; 141 (both), National Anthropological Archives, Smithsonian Institution, Washington, DC/ PRC Archive; 142 (t), California Historical Society/ Ticor Title Insurance/ PRC Archive; 142 (b), Collection of the New-York Historical Society/ PRC Archive; 143 (tr), Peter Newark's Western Americana; 143 (tl), Kansas Collection/ University of Kansas Libraries/ PRC Archive; 143 (b), PRC Archive; 144 (t), Denver Public Library Western History Collection; 144 (b), Courtesy of the California History Room, California State Library, Sacramento, California; 145 (t), Batavia Depot Museum, Batavia, Illinois/Courtesy, Chicago Historical Society/PRC; 145 (b), Colorado Historical Society/ PRC Archive; 146 (r), California Historical Society/PRC Archive; 146 (l), State Historical Society of Wisconsin/ PRC Archive; 147 (t), Solomon D. Butcher Collection, Nebraska State Historical Society/ PRC Archive; 147 (b), The Kansas State Historical Society, Topeka, Kansas; 148 (b), *My Antonia* by Willa Cather, Trustees of the Boston Public Library/ PRC Archive; 148 (t), Photography Collection, Miriam and Ira D. Wallach Division of Art, Prints and Photographs, The New York Public Library, Astor, Lenox and Tilden Foundations/ PRC Archive; 149 (t), The Kansas State Historical Society, Topeka, Kansas/PRC Archive; 149 (b), © Laurence Parent; 150 (t), Peter Newark's Western Americana; 150 (b), Charles M. Russell "Jerked Down" 1907 oil on canvas #0137.2246. From the Collection of Gilcrease Museum, Tulsa/PRC; 151 (t), The Granger Collection, New York; 151 (b), The Museum of Fine Arts, Houston, The Hogg Brothers Collection, Gift of Miss Ima Hogg; 152, © John Eastcott/Yva Momatiuk/The Image Works; 153, Peter Newark's Western Americana; 154, The Granger Collection, New York; 155 (t), Oakland Museum History Department; 155 (b), Haynes Foundation Collection. Montana Historical Society; 156, The Granger Collection, New York; 157, Colorado Historical Society/ PRC Archive; 158, Montana Historical Society, Helena/ PRC Archive; 159, Colorado Historical Society/PRC Archive; 161, Kansas State Historical Society, Topeka, Kansas/ PRC Archive.

CHAPTER 5: Page 162 (tl), Chicago Historical Society; 162 (tc), Property of AT&T Archives. Printed with permission of AT&T.; Page 162 (tr), Private Collection/PRC Archive; 162 (bl), Library of Congress/PRC Archive; 162 (br), Los Angeles County Museum of Art, Acquisition made possible through Museum Trustees: Robert O. Anderson, R. Stanton Avery, B. Gerald Cantor, Edward W. Carter, Justin Dart, Charles E. Ducommun, Mrs. F. Daniel Frost, Julian Ganz, Jr., Dr. Armand Hammer, Hart Lenart, Dr. Franklin D. Murphy, Mrs. Joan Palevsky, Richard E. Sherwood, Maynard J. Toll and Hal B. Wallis/ PRC Archive. 163 (br), PRC Archive; 163 (tr), Carnegie Library of Pittsburgh; 163 (bl), Corbis-Bettmann; 163 (tl), Ann Ronan / Image Select, Inc.; 164 (t), Property of AT&T Archives. Reprinted with permission of AT&T / PRC Archive; 164 (b), The Metropolitan Museum of Art, Purchase, Lyman G. Bloomingdale Gift, 1901. (01.7.1) Photograph © 1983 The Metropolitan Museum of Art. All rights reserved, The Metropolitan Museum of Art; 165, Collection of the Drake Well Museum; 166 (l), Union Pacific Railroad Museum / PRC Archive; 166 (r), Chicago Historical Society/PRC Archive; 167, Library of Congress / PRC Archive; 168 (t), National Air & Space Museum, Smithsonian Institution, Washington, D.C., neg. no. A26767B-2 / PRC Archive; 168 (bl), National Museum of American History, Smithsonian Institution, neg no. 91-6501 / PRC Archive; 168 (br), Smithsonian Institution / Charles Phillips / PRC Archive; 169 (tl), The Granger Collection, New York; 169 (tr), David Young-Wolff/Photo Edit; 169 (b), The Granger Collection, New York; 169 (c), The Granger Collection, New York; 171 (b), The Granger Collection, New York; 170, Division of Political History, Smithsonian Institution,

Quotes by Jim Bevel, Ossie Davis, and Paula Giddings from *Voices of Freedom: An Oral History of the Civil Rights Movement from the 1950s Through the 1980s* by Henry Hampton, Steve Fayer, with Sarah Flynn. Published by Bantam Books, New York, 1990.

From *A Very Different Age: Americans of the Progressive Era* by Steven J. Diner. Published by Hill and Wang, a division of Farrar, Straus and Giroux, LLC, New York, 1998.

Quote by Miss Egan ("Hello Girls") from *American Women in World War I: They Also Served* by Lettie Gavin. Published by University Press of Colorado, Niwot, CO, 1997.

Quotes by Jeff Greenfield, Harriet Osborn, and Jack Trachsel from *The Century* by Peter Jennings and Todd Brewster. Published by Doubleday, a division of Random House, Inc., New York, 1998.

From "Women on the Breadlines" by Meridel Le Sueur, *New Masses 7*, January 1932.

From "The Meaning of the Kellogg Treaty" by Henry Cabot Lodge, Jr., from *Harper's Magazine*, New York, December 1928.

From *Three Years in Mississippi* by James H. Meredith. Published by Indiana University Press, Bloomington, IN, 1966.

Quote by George Washington Plunkitt from *Plunkitt of Tammany Hall* by William L. Riordon. Published by E. P. Dutton, New York, 1963.

Washington, D.C./ PRC Archive; 171 (t), National Portrait Gallery, Smithsonian Institution, Art Resource, NY ; 172, Harcourt, Inc.; 173 (t), Collection of Dennis Kurlander; 173 (b), Frank & Marie-Therese Wood Print Collections (The Picture Bank); 174, Portrait of Charles Darwin, 1840 by George Richmond. Downe House, Downe, Kent, UK/The Bridgeman Art Library; 175 (t), Culver Pictures, Inc.; 175 (b), National Portrait Gallery, Smithsonian Institution, Washington D.C./ Art Resource, NY ; 176, Carnegie Library, Pittsburgh; 177, Archive Photos; 178, The Granger Collection, New York; 179 (t), Illinois Historical Society; 179 (b), Picture Research Consultants & Archives; 180 (b), Chicago Historical Society, Neg no. IChi 01622 / PRC Archive; 180 (t), Sears Roebuck and Company; 181 (t), Culver Pictures, Inc.; 181 (b), PRC Archive; 182, PRC Archive; 183, Corbis-Bettmann; 184 (b), The Granger Collection, New York; 184 (t), Corbis-Bettmann; 185, Corbis-Bettmann; 186, Corbis-Bettmann; 187, The Granger Collection, New York; 189, Chicago Historical Society.

CHAPTER 6: Page 190 (tl), Library of Congress; 190 (tr), The New York World, 1883; 190 (bl), Library of Congress/PRC Archive; 190 (br), New-York Hisorical Society/PRC Archive; 191 (tl), PRC Archive; 191 (tr), The Rockefeller University Archives; 191 (b), Collection of Sandy Marrone; 192 (b), Courtesy George Eastman House; 192 (t), Chermayeff and Geismar, Inc./MetaForm, Inc.; 193, Library of Congress; 194 (b), The California Department of Parks and Recreation; 194 (tl), Brown Brothers; 194 (tr), Uniphoto Picture Agency; 195 (b), "Children's Playground on Ellis Island (Roof Garden)," c. 1890. Photographed by Augustus Sherman, The Jacob A. Riis Collection #476, Museum of the City of New York; 195 (t), St. Cosman and St. Damian, patron saints of doctors, Cretan icon, 17th century (panel), Mark Gallery, London, Bridgeman Art Library, New York/London ; 196 (t), Courtesy George Eastman House; 196 (b), Culver Pictures, Inc.; 197, Strong Museum; 198 (t), Detroit Publishing Company Collection, Library of Congress; 198 (b), Courtesy George Eastman House; 199, Photo by Byron, The Byron Collection, Museum of the City of New York / PRC Archive; 200 (t), Culver Pictures, Inc.; 200 (bl), Museum of the City of New York, Gift of Mary and Charles Odgen.; 200 (br), Courtesy of the Oakland Museum of California. Courtesy PRC ; 201, *At the Ball* by Stewart, Julius Leblanc (1855-1919), Whitford & Hughes, London, UK / Bridgeman Art Library, London/New York; 202 (t), Corbis-Bettmann; 202 (b), Courtesy the Museum of the City of New York / PRC Archive; 203 (br), University of Illinois at Chicago. The University Library Jane Addams Memorial Collection; 203 (bl), The Newberry Library; 203 (t), Brown Brothers; 204, Caroline Bartlett Crane Collection, Archives and Regional History Collections, Western Michigan University; 205 (t), Curt Teich Postcard Archives, Lake County (IL) Museum; 205 (b), State Historical Society of North Dakota; 206, Library of Congress/ PRC Archive; 207 (t), New York World / PRC Archive; 207 (b), New York Journal, Jan 5, 1896; 208 (t), Brooklyn Historical Society / PRC Archive; 208 (b), The Granger Collection, New York; 209 (tl), Cincinnati Museum Center; 209 (tr), Division of Political History, Smithsonian Institution, Washington, D.C. / PRC Archive; 209 (b), Corbis-Bettmann; 210 (t), The Granger Collection, New York; 210 (b), The Harvard Theatre Collection, The Houghton Library; Fredric Woodbridge Wilson, Curator; 211 (l), Library of Congress / PRC Archive; 213, CALIFORNIA MUSEUM OF PHOTOGRAPHY, Keystone-Mast Collection, University of California, Riverside, negative 55458 /PRC Archive; 211 (r), Division of American Political History,Smithsonian Institution / PRC Archive.

CHAPTER 7: Page 216 (tl), Courtesy of the Museum of the American Numismatic Association; 216 (tr), *Young Mother Sewing* by Mary Cassat, Musee d'Orsay, Paris, France / Bridgeman Art Library, London / New York; 216 (bl), The Granger Collection, New York; 216 (br), Corbis-Bettmann; 217 (tl), Replica Courtesy Deere & Company / PRC Archive; 217 (tc), Brown Brothers; 217 (tr), Courtesy George Eastman House / PRC Archive; 217 (bl), National Museum of American History / Smithsonian Institution, Washington, D.C.; 217 (br), The WILL K. KELLOGG signature logo is a trademark of Kellogg Company. All rights reserved. Used with permission; 218 (t), Corbis-Bettmann; 219 (t), Collection of Janice L. and David J. Frent/ PRC Archive; 218 (b), City Archives of Philadelphia; 219 (b), From Political History of Jackson County; Kansas City: Marshall & Morrison, 1902; KC27, N4, Western Historical Manuscript Collection-Kansas City; 220, Library of Congress / PRC Archive; 221, New-York Historical Society; 222, Library of Congress / PRC Archive; 223, Library of Congress / PRC Archive; 224 (t), The Granger Collection, New York; 224 (b), Timothy Hughes Rare Newspapers / PRC; 225 (tl), Museum of American Political Life, Sally Anderson-Bruce /PRC Archive; 225 (tr), Collection of Janice L. and David J. Frent/ PRC Archive; 225 (b), The Granger Collection, New York; 226 (l), University of California at Berkeley, Bancroft Library; 226 (r), The Newberry Library; 227 (t), The Newberry Library; 227 (b), National Postal Museum, Smithsonian Institution; 228 (b), The Granger Collection, New York; 228 (t), Paul Conklin/Photo Edit; 229 (b), Collection of Janice L. and David J. Frent / PRC Archive; 229 (t), United States Postal Service / Harcourt Inc.; 231 (t), Kansas State Historical Society / PRC Archive; 231 (b), Randy Leffingwell; 232, The Granger Collection, New York; 233, The Granger Collection, New York; 234 (t), The Burns Archive; 234 (bl), State Historical Society of Wisconsin / PRC Archive; 234 (br), Grant Heilman Photography; 235 (tr), Courtesy of the Museum of the American Numismatic Association ; 235 (tl), Courtesy of the Museum of the American Numismatic Association; 235 (b), Nebraska Historical Society / PRC Archive; 236 (t), Corbis-Bettmann; 236 (b), Library of Congress / PRC Archive; 237, United States Postal Service / Harcourt Inc.; 239, Elias Carr Papers, East Carolina Manuscript Collection, J.Y. Joyner Library, East Carolina University, Greenville, NC. Photo by Dewane Frutiger / PRC Archive; 240 (t), Corbis-Bettmann; 240 (b), Sally Fox Collection / PRC Archive; 241 (t), The Granger Collection, New York; 241 (b), The Granger Collection, New York/Courtesy of PRC.

UNIT 3: Page 242-243, Gift of Dwight Franklin, Museum of the City of New York; 243, Collection of David J. and Janice L. Frent / PRC Archive.

CHAPTER 8: Page 244 (tl), Archive Photos; 244 (tr), Brown Brothers; 244 (b), Edison National Historic Site, National Park Service/ U.S. Department of the Interior; 245 (tl), Courtesy of the Whitney Museum of American Art / Photo by Pency Rainfold; 245 (tr), Detroit Publishing Company Photograph Collection, Library of Congress; 245 (c), The George Meany Memorial Archives; 245 (bl), Corbis-Bettmann; 245 (br), Corbis-Bettmann; 246, The Newberry Library; 247 (t), Image Copyright © 1998 PhotoDisc, Inc.; 247 (b), Corbis-Bettmann; 248 (t), Brown Brothers; 248 (b), The Granger Collection, New York; 249 (l), Corbis-Bettmann; 249 (r), Culver Pictures, Inc.; 250 (t), Library of Congress / PRC Archive; 250 (b), George Eastman House; 251 (t), The Newberry Library; 251 (c), The Newberry Library; 251 (b), Special Collections Department, Van Pelt Library, University of Pennsylvania, Philadelphia, PA; 252 (t), The George Meany Memorial Archives / PRC Archive; 252 (b), Culver Pictures; 253 (t), Library of Congress / PRC Archive; 253 (b), The George Meany Memorial Archives; 254 (t), The Granger Collection, New York; 254 (b), UPI/Corbis-Bettmann; 255 (t), Archive Photos; 255 (b), HRW Photo by Victoria Smith; 256 (t), ILGWU Archives, Labor-Management Documentation Center/ PRC Archive; 256 (b), The Granger Collection, New York; 257, Corbis-Bettmann; 258 (t), Library of Congress / PRC Archive; 258 (b), Brown Brothers; 259 (t), Daniel H. Burnham in a flowered tie, signed. Photograph © 1996, The Art Institute of Chicago.; 259 (b), View of the City from Jackson Park to Grant Park, plate 49 from Plan of Chicago, 1907, 104x477 cm delineated by Jules Guerin, watercolor and pencil on paper, 1907, on permanent loan to the Art Institute of Chicago from the City of Chicago, 2.148.1966, detail. Photograph © 1996, The Art Institute of Chicago. All rights reserved.; 260 (t), Uniphoto; 261 (c), HRW Photo Research Library; 260 (b), Culver Pictures; 261 (t), John Hay Library, Brown University / PRC Library; 261 (b), Corbis-Bettmann; 262 (t), Library of Congress; 262 (b), The Newberry Library; 263, The Newberry Library; 264, Corbis-Bettmann; 265, Courtesy Chermayeff and Geismar, Inc./MetaForm, Inc. / PRC Archive; 267 (l), The Granger Collection, New York; 267 (r), Sophia Smith Collection, Smith College.

CHAPTER 9:; Page 268 (tl), Archives Division - Texas State Library / PRC Archive; 268 (tr), Corbis-Bettmann; 268 (bl), Courtesy of the Rosenberg Library, Galveston, Texas; 268 (br), PRC Archive 269 (t), The Granger Collection, New York; 269 (bl), Collection of Janice L. and David J. Frent/PRC Archive;; 269 (br), Library of Congress; 270 (t), Brown Brothers; 270 (b), The Granger Collection, New York; 271, The Granger Collection, New York; 272 (t), Library Legacy Foundation, Toledo-Lucas County Public Library; 272 (b), Library Legacy Foundation, Toledo-Lucas County Public Library; 273, The Granger Collection, New York; 274, Library of Congress; 275 (t), Collection of Janice L. and David J. Frent/ PRC Archive; 275 (b), Collection of Janice L. and David J. Frent/ PRC Archive; 276 (t), United States Postal Service / Harcourt Inc.; 276 (c), Sagamore Hill National Historic Site / PRC Archive; 276 (b), George Meany Memorial Archives; 277, Library of Congress / PRC Archive; 278 (t), Culver Pictures; 278 (b), Chicago Historical Society, neg # ICHI1978.154.4 / PRC Archive; 279 (l), Newberry Library/ PRC Archive; 279 (r), © Laurie Platt Winfrey / Woodfin Camp & Associates, Inc.; 280, National Museum of American Art, Smithsonian Institution, lent by the U.S. Department of the Interior/ Art Resource, NY; 281, Andre Jenny/New England Stock Photos; 282 (t), Theodore Roosevelt Collection, Harvard College Library/ PRC Archive; 282 (b), Library of Congress; 284 (t), The Houghton Library, Theodore Roosevelt Collection, Harvard University; 284 (b), The Granger Collection, New York; 285, Theodore Roosevelt Collection, Harvard College Library; 286, Corbis-Bettmann; 287 (t), National Archives/ PRC Archive; 287 (b), Corbis-Bettmann; 288 (b), Stock Montage, Inc.; 288 (t), United States Postal Service / Harcourt Inc.; 289 (t), Picture Research Consultants Archive; 289 (b), Archives of Labor and Urban Affairs , Wayne State University/ PRC Archive; 290, "Nude Descending a Staircase," ©1997 Artists Rights Society (ARS), New York/ADAGP, Paris/Estate of Marcel Duchamp/Bridgeman Art Library, New York/London; 291 (t), Culver Pictures; 291 (b), Corbis-Bettmann; 292 (l), PRC Archive; 292 (r), Library of Congress / PRC Archive; 295 (t), Corbis-Bettmann 295 (b), Collection of Janice L. and David J. Frent/ PRC Archive.

CHAPTER 10: Page 296 (tl), ©Topham/The Image Works; 296 (tr), The Granger Collection, New York; 296 (bl), FPG International Corp.; 296 (br), Knudsens Fotosenter, Oslo; 297 (tl), Photo Deutsches Museum, Munich; 297 (tr), Library of Congress / PRC Archive; 297 (b), Special Collections, Milton S. Eisenhower Library, The Johns Hopkins Library, courtesy PRC; 298 (t), The Granger Collection, New York; 298 (b), Courtesy of the U. S. Naval Academy Museum / PRC Archive; 299, By permission of Houghton Library, Harvard University / PRC Archive; 300 (t), © Hawaiian Legacy Archive / Pacific Stock; 300 (b), Culver Pictures; 301 (b), Hawaiian Legacy Archive / Pacific Stock; 301 (t), Hawaii State Archives; 302 (t), Dawson Gallery, courtesy PRC; 302 (b), Trustees of the British Museum; 303, Library of Congress; 304, The Mariners Museum, Newport News, VA; 305 (t), The Granger Collection, New York; 305 (b), Brown Brothers; 306 (b), Nawrocki Stock Photo; 306 (t), Hulton Getty / Liaison Agency ; 307 (t), Woodfin Camp & Associates, Inc.; 307 (b), Library of Congress; 308 (t), Courtesy LIFE Magazine, © Time, Inc. Watercolor by C.J. Post, photo by Herb Orth.; 308 (b), National Archive / PRC Archive; 309, The Granger Collection, New York; 310, Corbis; 311, Corbis-Bettmann; 312 (b), Underwood & Underwood/Corbis-Bettmann ; 314, The Granger Collection, New York; 316, Corbis-Bettmann; 317 (t), Corbis/Bettmann-UPI; 317 (b), The Granger Collection, New York; 318 (t), Corbis/Bettmann-UPI; 318 (bl), Latin Focus © All rights reserved.; 318 (br), Keith Dannemiller/ SABA; 319 (t), Library of Congress/ PRC Archive; 319 (b), UPI/Corbis-Bettmann ; 320, Corbis-Bettmann; 321, The Granger Collection, New York; 323, Library of Congress.

CHAPTER 11: Page 326 (tl), PRC Archive; 326 (tc), Collection of Colonel Stuart S. Corning. © Rob Huntley/ Lightstream/Courtesy of PRC Archive; 326 (tr), Corbis- Bettmann; 326 (bl), The Granger Collection, New York; 326 (br), UPI/Corbis-Bettmann; 327 (tl), HRW Photo by Sam Dudgeon; 327 (tr), Willard Clay/FPG International Corp.; 327 (b), The Trustees of the Imperial War Museum, London; 328 (t), Culver Pictures, Inc.; 328 (b), Nawrocki Stock Photo; 329, Andrew Reid /Liaison Agency; 330, Trustees of the Imperial War Museum, London; 330 (t), National Archives (NARA); 332 (t), Trustees of The Imperial War Museum, London; 332 (b), Dale Hrabak/National Air and Space Museum, Smithsonian Institution, Washington, DC, photo no. 80-2086; 333 (t), HRW Photo; 333 (b), UPI/Bettman Newsphotos; 334, Woodfin Camp & Associates, Inc.; 335, Stock Montage, Inc.; 336, National Archives; 338 (t), The Granger Collection, New York; 338 (b), Archive Photos; 339, Archive Photos; 340 (t), The Granger Collection, New York; 340 (b), UPI/Corbis-Bettmann Newsphotos; 341, Hoover Presidential Library/ PRC Archive; 342 (t), Corbis-Bettmann; 342 (b), Culver Pictures, Inc.; 343 (l), PRC Archive; 343 (r), The Bettmann Archive; 344, Brown Brothers; 345 (t), The Granger Collection, New York; 345 (b), The Granger Collection, New York; 346, HRW Photo by Lance Schriner; 347, The Granger Collection, New York; 348, The Trustees of the Imperial War Museum, London; 349 (tr), Archive Photos; 349 (tl), ©Dorling Kindersley Ltd./Courtesy of Spink & Son Ltd., London; 349 (b), UPI/Corbis-Bettmann; 350, The Granger Collection, New York; 352, Property HRW Photo Research Library; 353, Culver Pictures, Inc.; 355, The Granger Collection, New York; 356 (t), The Granger Collection, New York; 356 (b), PRC Archive; 357 (t), Snark International / Art Resource, NY 357 (b), Curt Teich Postcard Archives, Lake County Museum, Illinois;.

UNIT 4: Page 358-359, New-York Historical Society; 359, Christie's Images.

CHAPTER 12: Page 360 (tl), Collection of Janice L. and David J. Frent/ PRC Archive; 360 (tr), The Granger Collection, 360 (bl), Corbis-Bettmann; 360 (br), *Babbit* by Sinclaire Lewis; Newberry Library; New York; 361 (tl), Private Collection / PRC Archive; 361 (tr), Shahn, Ben. *Bartolomeo Vanzetti and Nicola Sacco* from the Sacco-Vanzetti series of twenty-three paintings (1931-32). Tempera on paper over composition board 10 1/2 x 14 1/2" (26.7 x 36.8 cm). The Museum of Modern Art, New York. Gift of Abby Aldrich Rockefeller, Photograph ©1997 The Museum of Modern Art, New York. ©1997 Estate of Ben Shahn/Licensed by VAGA, New York, NY; 361 (bl), Chicago Historical Society, ICHI-22640; 361 (br), Brown Brothers; 362 (t), Library of Congress / PRC Archive; 362 (b), Courtesy George Eastman House; 363 (t), Leslie's Illustrated Newspaper September 20, 1920/ PRC Archive; 363 (b), Museum of History and Industry, Seattle, WA; 364 (t), UPI/Bettmann-Corbis; 364 (bl), Archives of Labor and Urban Affairs, Wayne State University; 364 (br), AP / Wide World Photos; 365, The Granger Collection, New York; 366 (t), Collection of Janice L. and David J. Frent/PRC Archive; 366 (c), Brown Brothers; 366 (b), *The Anaconda Standard*, Jan. 4, 1920; 368, AP / Wide World Photos, Inc.; 369, Collection of Janice L. and David J. Frent/ PRC Archive; 370, Bob Daemmrich Photo, Inc.; 371, The Hagley Museum and Library; 372 (t), Courtesy George Eastman House; 372 (b), The Granger Collection, New York; 373 (t), Collection of Janice L. and David J. Frent/ PRC Archive; 373 (br), Coolidge Collection at Forbes Library; 373 (bl), Museum of American Political Life, University of Hartford, Photo by Steven Laschever; 374 (r), Collection of Janice L. and David J. Frent/PRC Archive; 374 (l), Collection of Janice L. and David J. Frent/ PRC Archive; 375 (t), The Chicago *Defender*, April 7, 1917; 375 (b), Courtesy George Eastman House; 376, Brown Brothers; 377 (t), Archive Photos; 377 (b), Collection of Janice L. and David J. Frent/ PRC Archive; 378 (tl), Chicago Historical Society, Photo # IChi-12255; 378 (tr), "The Messenger" magazine Sep 1926 (Vol VIII, no. 9); Newberry Library; 378 (b), James Van Der Zee photo; 380 (t), Frank Driggs Collection; 380 (b), "Juan Salvador and Lupe's Wedding, 1929", from *Rain of Gold* by Victor Villasenor is reprinted with permission of the publisher (Arte Publico Press, University of Houston, 1991); 381, Underwood Photo Archives; 383, Collection of Janice L. and David J. Frent/ PRC Archive.

CHAPTER 13: Page 384 (tl), Archive Photos; 384 (tr), Brown Brothers; 384 (bl), Library of American Broadcasting/University of Maryland; 384 (br), The Kobal Collection; 385 (bl), The Metropolitan Museum of Art, Alfred Stieglitz Collection, 1969. (69.278.1) Photograph by Malcolm Varon. All rights reserved, The Metropolitan Museum of Art; 385 (tc), Culver Pictures; 385 (br), Brown Brothers; 385 (tl), Gift of John P. Axelrod. courtesy Museum of Fine Arts, Boston. Courtesy PRC; 385 (tr), The Granger Collection, New York; 386 (t), Corbis-Bettmann; 386 (b), PRC Archive; 387 (t), Archive Photos; 387 (b), From the Collections of Henry Ford Museum and Greenfield Village; 388, From the Collections of Henry Ford Museum and Greenfield Village; 389 (both), From the Collections of Henry Ford Museum and Greenfield Village, courtesy PRC; 390 (t), Brown Brothers; 390 (b), The Granger Collection, New York; 391, November 1927 "Ladies Home Journal," The Newberry Library; 392 (t), Christie's Images; 392 (b), Duke University Archives / PRC Archive; 393, Brown Brothers; 394 (t), Private Collection / PRC Archive; 395 (t), Chicago Historical Society, Photo no. IChi 14414; 395 (b), The Granger Collection, New York; 396 (tl), CIRCA / PRC Archive; 396 (tr), CIRCA / PRC Archive; 396 (b), The Granger Collection, New York; 397, Robin Nelson/Black Star; 398 (t), Henry Groskinsky; 398 (c), *The Denver Times*, September 29, 1920; 398 (b), National Baseball Hall of Fame; 399 (t), PRC Archive; 399 (b), Corbis-Bettmann; 400, Flower Pentecostal Heritage Center; 401, Brown Brothers; 402 (both), Frank Driggs Collection; 403 (t), Frank Driggs Collection; 403 (b), Historic New Orleans Collection; 405 (r), Archive Photos; 405 (l), *Color* by Countee Cullen, poetry 1926 reprint of author's first (1925) book, Harper and Brothers, NY; 406 (t), Courtesy of the Yale Collection of American Literature, Beinecke Rare Book and Manuscript Library, Yale University; 406 (b), Library of Congress / PRC Archive; 407 (l), The Granger Collection, New York; 407 (r), The Granger Collection, New York; 408 (t), © Addison Gallery of American Art, Phillips Academy, Andover, Massachusettes. All Rights Reserved; 408 (b), The Detroit Institute of Arts; 408, Farrell Grehan/ESTO Photographics, Inc.; 411, Culver Pictures.

CHAPTER 14: Page 412 (tl), Culver Pictures, Inc.; 412 (tr), UPI/Bettmann-Corbis; 412 (b), Private Collection / Bridgeman Art Library; 413 (tl), Culver Pictures, Inc.; 413 (tr), AP / Wide World Photos, Inc. ; 413 (bl), Franklin D. Roosevelt Library; 413 (br), Lost Horizon by James Hilton, Newberry Library; PRC Archive; 414 (t), © 1945 Gordon Parks; 414 (b), Collection of Janice L. and David J. Frent/ PRC Archive; 415 (t), Archive Photos; 415 (b), © Corbis Images; 416, The Granger Collection, New York; 417, John T. McCutcheon, courtesy Tribune Media Services; 419, PRC Archive; 420 (t), Minnesota Historical Society; 420 (b), Milton (Pete) Brooks/*The Detroit News*; 421, Culver Pictures; 422 (t), National Museum of American Art, Smithsonian Institution, Washington, DC / Art Resource, NY; 422 (b), Corbis-Bettmann; 423, National Archives / PRC Archive; 424 (b), Library of Congress; 424 (t), Courtesy of Bert Corona and Mario T. Garcia; 425, Cindy Lewis Photography; 426, National Museum of American Art, Washington, DC/Art Resource, NY; 427 (r), Corbis-Bettmann; 427 (l), *Lost Horizon* by James Hilton, Newberry Library; PRC Archive; 428 (t), Corbis-Bettmann; 428 (b), The Granger Collection, New York; 429, The Salvation Army National Archives; 430, Herbert Hoover Presidential Library; 431 (t), Department of the Interior, National Park Service, 1937. National Museum of American Art, Washington, DC; Art Resource, NY; 431 (b), U.S. Postal Service / Harcourt Inc.; 432, CORBIS-Bettmann; 433 (t), The Bettmann Archive; 433 (b), Culver Pictures, Inc.; 434 (t), Culver Pictures; 434 (b), Corbis- Bettmann; 435, Franklin D. Roosevelt Library; 437 (l), Smithsonian Institution; 437 (r), Culver Pictures, Inc.

CHAPTER 15: Page 438 (tl), Corbis-Bettmann; 438 (tr), HRW Photo by Sam Dudgeon; 438 (bl), AP/Wide World Photos, Inc.; 438 (br), Library of Congress/Courtesy of PRC; 439 (tl), National Archives, courtesy PRC; 439 (tc), The Michael Barson Collection/ Past Perfect/PRC Archive; 439 (tr), Margaret Bourke-White/Life Magazine © 1937 Time Inc.; 439 (bl), From *The Incredible Ball Point Pen* by Stuart Schneider and Henry Gostony, Schiffer Publishing Ltd., Atglen, PA; 439 (br), Shooting Star International; 440, Franklin D. Roosevelt Library; 441, Franklin D. Roosevelt Library; 442, National Archives; 443 (t), Culver Pictures, Inc.; 443 (b), Louise Boyle/Southern Historical Collection, University of North Carolina at Chapel Hil.; 445, United States Department of the Interior/ PRC Archive; 446, Library of Congress/ PRC Archive; 447 (t), Brown Brothers; 447 (b), Louisiana State University Special Collections, courtesy PRC; ; 448 (t), U.S. Postal Service/Harcourt Inc.; 448 (bl), Franklin D. Roosevelt Library; 448 (br), The Granger Collection, New York; 449 (l), Franklin D. Roosevelt Library; 449 (r), Social Security Administration, Courtesy PRC; 450 (t), Stock Montage, Inc.; 450 (b), The Granger Collection, New York; 452 (l), Library of Congress/ PRC Archive; 452 (r), Archives of Labor and Urban Affairs, Wayne State University; 453, Library of Congress; 454 (t), John E. Allen, Inc./Franklin D. Roosevelt Presidential Library; 454 (b), Library of Congress; 455, Frank Driggs Collection/ Corbis-Bettmann/ PRC Archive; 456 (t), Library of Congress; 456 (b), The Granger Collection, New York; 457 (both) Library of Congress; 458, The Granger Collection, New York; 459 (both), National Archives; 460 (t), The Granger Collection, New York. From THE GRAPES OF WRATH by John Steinbeck. Copyright 1939 renewed © 1967 by John Steinbeck. Used by permission of Viking Penguin, a division of Penguin Putnam, Inc.; 460 (b), Photofest; 461 (l), Corbis/Bettmann-UPI; 461 (r), The Beinecke Rare Book and Manuscript Library, Yale University; 462, Grant Wood, American, 1891-1942, American Gothic, oil on beaverboard, 1930, 74.3 x 62.4 cm. Friends of American Art Collection, All rights reserved by the Art Institute of Chicago and VAGA, New York, NY; 463, © 1999 The Georgia O'Keefe Foundation/ Artists Rights Society (ARS), New York. The Metropolitan Museum of Art, Alfred Stieglitz Collection, 1952. (52.203) Photograph © 1994 The Metropolitan Museum of Art. All rights reserved, The Metropolitan Museum of Art; 465 (l), Grandma Moses: "Sugaring Off" © 1992 Grandma Moses Properties Co., New York; ; 465 (r), Collection of David J. & Janice L. Frent/ PRC Archive; 468 (t), Missouri Historical Society; 469 (t), The Granger Collection, New York; 469 (b), Corbis-Bettmann.

UNIT 5: Page 470-471, Corbis/Bettmann-UPI; 471, Library of Congress.

CHAPTER 16: Page 472 (tl), Brown Brothers; 472 (tr), AP/Wide World Photos 472 (bl), Erich Lessing/Art Resource; 472 (br), FPG International Corp.; 473 (tl), Steve Vidler/Nawrocki Stock Photo; 473 (tr), *The Des Moines Register*, October 31, 1938; 473 (b), Hershenson-Allen Archives/ PRC Archive; 474 (t), Corbis-Bettmann/UPI; 474 (b), Stock Montage, Inc.; 475 (l), Corbis-Bettmann; 475 (r), Jean Louis Atlan / Corbis Sygma; 476, National Portrait Gallery, Washington, D.C./ Art Resource, NY; 477 (t), Nawrocki Stock Photo; 477 (b), Corbis/Bettmann; 478, AKG London; 479 (t), Corbis/Bettmann-UPI; 479 (b), UPI/Corbis-Bettmann ; 480 (t), HRW Photo by Sam Dudgeon; 480 (b), Franklin D. Roosevelt Library;; 481, Curt Teich Postcard Archives; 482 (t), Everett/ CSU Archives; 482 (c), Curt Teich Postcard Archives/ Lake County, IL Museum; 482 (b), Rob Schoenboum/Black Star; 483, Library of Congress; 484 (t), UPI/Corbis-Bettmann; 484 (b), Poseidon Pictures; 485 (t), UPI/Bettmann; 485 (b), The Granger Collection, New York; 486 (t), The Granger Collection, New York; 486 (b), Corbis-Bettmann; 487, Brown Brothers; 487, Library of Congress; 488 (l), Brown Brothers; 488 (r), Ernest Hemingway, *For Whom the Bell Tolls* © 1940, Charles Scribner's Sons, Macmillan Publishing Company, PRC Archive; 490 (t), CBS Radio / PRC Archive; 490 (b), UPI/Corbis-Bettmann; 491 (t), *Chicago Daily Tribune*, Dec 1937; 491 (b), Courtesy of "Fortune" magazine, from the General Libraries, University of Texas at Austin. HRW Photo by Sam Dudgeon; 493 (t), CORBIS/Bettmann; 493 (b), LIFE Magazine © 1940; 494, Archive Photos; 495, The Granger Collection, New York; 497, The Granger Collection, New York.

CHAPTER 17: Page 498 (tl), Private Collection/ PRC Archive; 498 (tc), Courtesy of the Museum of the American Numismatic Association; 498 (tr), Private Collection/ PRC Archive; 498 (bl), Cindy Lewis Photography; 498 (br), Nawrocki Stock Photo499 (tl), Chicago Historical Society; 499 (tr), Schalwijk / Art Resource, NY; 499 (bl), FSA/OWI Collection, Library of Congress; 499 (br), HRW Photo by Sam Dudgeon, stamps courtesy Kristen Darby; 500 (t), Dana Edmunds / Pacific Stock; 500 (b), Courtesy of Joseph Rygiel / PRC Archive; 501, FSA-OWI Collection, Library of Congress; 502 (b), Corbis-Bettmann; 503 (t), U.S. Government Photo; 503 (b), National Archives/ PRC Archive; 504, United States Marine Corps; 505 (t), Division of Political History, Smithsonian Institution, Washington, D.C.; 505 (b), Trustees of the Imperial War Museum; 506, Ria-Novosti/Sovfoto; 507 (t), National Archives/ PRC Archive; 507 (b), Hershenson-Allen Archives/ PRC Archive; 508 (r), Collection of Chester Scott/ PRC Archive; 508 (l), PRC Archive; 509, Printed by permission of the Norman Rockwell Family Trust ©1943 / Photo courtesy of the Curtis Publishing Company; 510 (t), National Archives/ PRC Archive; 510 (b), FSA-OWI Collection, Library of Congress; 511 (t), UPI/Corbis-Bettmann; 511 (bl), FSA-OWI Collection, Library of Congress; 511 (br), National Archives/ PRC Archive; 513, AP / Wide World Photos; 514, National Archives/ PRC Archive; 515 (t), Library of Congress/PRC Archive; 515 (b), 390th Bomb Group Collection, courtesy PRC; 516, Corbis; 517, National Archives (NARA); 518 (t), AP / Wide World Photos; 518 (b), National Archives; 520, Yevgeni Khaldei - Sovfoto / Eastfoto; 521 (t), Christie's Images; 521 (b), United States Marine Corps Museum/ PRC Archive; 522 (l), National Archives/PRC Archive; 522 (r), Photri; 524 (t), Press Association Limited / PRC Archive; 524 (b), National Archives; 525 (t), United States Postal Service / Harcourt Inc.; 525 (b), Corbis; 526 (l), U.S. Air Force/ PRC Archive; 526 (r), Philip Jones-Griffiths/Magnum Photos, Inc.; 529, Private Collection/ PRC Archive.

CHAPTER 18: Page 530 (tl), Collection of Col. Stuart S. Corning, Jr. Courtesy PRC Archive; 530 (tr), The Granger Collection, New York; 530 (bl), Collection of Michael Barson/Past Perfect/ PRC Archive; 530 (br), Woodfin Camp & Associates, Inc.; 531 (tl), RAUSCHENBERG, Robert. *Bed.* (1955) Combine painting: oil and pencil on pillow, quilt, and sheet on wood supports, 6' 3 3/4" x 31 1/2" x 8" (191.1 x 80 x 20.3 cm). The Museum of Modern Art, New York. Gift of Leo Castelli in honor of Alfred H. Barr, Jr. Photograph © 1999 The Museum of Modern Art, New York.; 531 (tc), Sovfoto/Eastfoto; 531 (tr), UPI/ Corbis-Bettmann; 531 (bl), *The Crucible* by Arthur Miller, courtesy

From letter by pregnant housewife to Eleanor Roosevelt, January 2, 1935, from *Down and Out in the Great Depression: Letters from the "Forgotten Man,"* edited by Robert S. McElvaine. Published by University of North Carolina Press, Chapel Hill, NC, 1983.

From *Development as Freedom* by Amartya Sen. Published by Alfred A. Knopf, Inc., a division of Random House, Inc., New York, 1999.

From *Combed Out* by F. A. Voigt. Published by Dial Press, New York, 1929.

Quotes by volunteers from *Letters from Mississippi*, edited by Elizabeth Sutherland. Published by McGraw-Hill, Inc., New York, 1965.

ACKNOWLEDGMENTS

The Viking Press, New York City; 531 (br), AP/Wide World Photos, Inc.; 532, U.S. Army Photo/Harry S. Truman Presidential Library; 533, UPI/Corbis-Bettmann; 534, Corbis-Bettmann; 535, Franklin D. Roosevelt Library; 536, The Jewish Museum, NY / Art Resource, NY; 537, National Archives/PRC Archive; 538 (t), Archive Photos; 538 (b), National Portrait Gallery, Smithsonian Institution, Washington, DC, Gift of TIME Magazine/ Courtesy PRC; 539, "Foreign Affairs," July 1947; 540, National Archives/ PRC Archive; 541 (l), The National Portrait Gallery, Smithsonian Institution, Washington, D.C. / Art Resource, NY; 541 (r), Vimonen / Corbis-Sygma; 542, Courtesy of the German Marshall Fund of the United States; 543 (l), Fortier Collection, Cowles Archive; courtesy PRC; 543 (r), FPG International; 544, Corbis/Bettmann-UPI; 545 (l), PRC Archive; 545 (r), Photri; 547, Corbis-Bettmann; 548 (t), U.S. Postal Service/Harcourt Inc.; 548 (b), AP/Wide World Photos; 549, AP/Wide World Photos; 550, © Jerry Cook; 551, The Michael Barson Collection / Past Perfect/ PRC Archive; 552 (t), Photofest; 552 (b), Archive Photos; 553 (l), The Michael Barson Collection / Past Perfect/ PRC Archive; 553 (r), *The Martian Way* by Isaac Asimov, 1955, Signet Books, courtesy PRC; 554, UPI/Corbis-Bettmann; 555, Archive Photos; 556 (t), Loomis Dean / Time-Life Picture Agency © Time, Inc.; 556 (b), The Michael Barson Collection/Past Perfect/ PRC Archive; 557, The Michael Barson Collection / Past Perfect; courtesy PRC Archive; 559, The Michael Barson Collection / Past Perfect. Courtesy PRC Archive.
CHAPTER 19: Page 562 (tl), Archive Photos; 562 (tc), U.S. Postal Service; 562 (tr), Corbis-Bettmann; 562 (b), CORBIS/Bettmann; 563 (tl), CORBIS/ Bettmann; 563 (tc), Corbis-Bettmann; 563 (b), CORBIS/Bettmann; 564 (tr, Library of Congress; 564 (bl, U.S. Postal Service; 565 (t), Lambert/Archive Photos; 565 (b), © 1994 Tom & Dee Ann McCarthy/ The Stock Market; 566, Corbis-Bettmann; 567 (l), Collection of Janice L. and David J. Frent/ PRC Archive; 567 (r), Harry S Truman Library; 568, Collection of David J. and Janice L. Frent / PRC Archive; 569, National Archives (NARA); 570 (t), *The Power of Positive Thinking* ©1952, 1978 by Prentice-Hall, Inc. Courtesy Norman Vincent Peale Center for Christian Living. HRW Photo by Sam Dudgeon; 570 (bl), Collection of Janice L. and David J. Frent / PRC Archive; 570 (br), HRW Photo by Sam Dudgeon; 571, Ewing Galloway; 572, J.R. Eyerman/LIFE Magazine, © Time, Inc.; 574, Corbis-Bettmann; 575 (r), Picture Research Consultants & Archives; 575 (l), Campbell Soup Company; 576 (t), AP /Wide World Photos, Inc.; 576 (b), By permission of *TV Guide*, courtesy Lenore's TV Guides. HRW Photo by Sam Dudgeon; 577 (t), Library of Congress/ PRC Archive; 577 (b), The Michael Barson Collection/Past Perfect / PRC Archive; 578 (l), SuperStock / PRC; 579, Corbis-Bettmann; 580, UPI/Corbis-Bettmann; 581 (t), UPI/Corbis-Bettmann; 581 (b), AP/ Wide World Photos, Inc.; 582, Charles Moore / Black Star; 583 (tr), Dr. Hector P. Garcia Papers, Special Collections & Archives, Texas A&M University, Corpus Christi Bell Library; 583 (tl), Dr. Hector P. Garcia Papers, Special Collections and Archives, Texas A&M University-Corpus Christi Bell Library; 583 (b), Francis L.K. Hsu and Family from his 1971 book, *The Challenge of the American Family: The Chinese in the United States*; 584 (t), AP /Wide World Photos, Inc.; 584 (b), *Invisible Man* by Ralph Ellison, Vintage Books, a division of Random House, Inc.; 585 (tl), Facsimile edition of Jack Kerouac's *On The Road* ©1957 published by the First Edition Library, Shelton, CT, by arrangement with Viking Penguin, Inc.; 585 (tr), CORBIS/Bettmann; 585 (b), © Joe Sohm/Chromosohm/Stock Connection; 586 (l), Harry Red / Time Magazine; 586 (r), Courtesy Naomi Long Madgett; 587, Courtesy of the Ford Foundation; 589 (t), *The Common Sense Book of Baby and Child Care* by Dr. Benjamin Spock, published by Duell, Sloan and Pearce, NY, © 1957; 589 (b), Christie's Images; 590 (r), U.S. Army Photograph; 590 (l), Moorland-Spingarn Research Center, Howard University, courtesy PRC; 591 (t), Photri, Inc.; 591 (b), National Archives (NARA).
UNIT 6: Page 592-593, © 1976 Matt Herron/Take Stock; 593, Bill Eppridge / Life Magazine © Time, Inc.
CHAPTER 20: Page 594 (tl), Topham Picture Service, 594 (tr), AP / Wide World Photos; 594 (bl), HRW Photo by Sam Dudgeon ; 594 (bc), Sally Andersen-Bruce, Museum of American Political Life; 594 (br), UPI/Corbis-Bettmann; 595 (t), Corbis-Bettmann; 595 (c), UPI/Corbis-Bettmann; 595 (b), UPI/Corbis-Bettmann; 596 (t), Bantam Doubleday Dell Publishing Group, Inc.; 596 (b), Collection of Janice L. and David J. Frent / PRC Archive; 597 (l), Corbis-Bettmann; 597 (r), Corbis-Bettmann; 598 (tl), West Point Museum, U.S. Military Academy, West Point, NY. Photo by Josh Nefsky; 598 (tr), Collection of Sandy Marrone / PRC Archive; 598 (b), Collection of Janice L. and David J. Frent/ Colorfax/ PRC Archive; 599 (b), Sanford Kossin/ LIFE Magazine © Time, Inc.; 599 (tl), Paul Conklin / Peace Corps Photograph; 599 (tr), Michael Dwyer/ Stock, Boston; 600, UPI/Corbis-Bettmann; 603 (t), John F. Kennedy Library; 603 (b), John F. Kennedy Presidential Library; ; 604 (l), United States Postal Service / Harcourt Inc.; 604 (r), AP / Wide World Photos; 605, Arthur Rickerby / Black Star; 606, Sarge O'Neill/John F. Kennedy Library; 607 (l), *The Other America: Poverty in the United States* by Michael Harrington © 1962, eleventh printing 1970, Macmillan Publishing Company; 607 (r), AP / Wide World Photos, Inc.; 608, Chicago Daily News; 609, Library of Congress / Stanley Tretick / Look Collection/ PRC Archive; 610 (t), Archive Photos; 610 (b), AP / Wide World Photos, Inc.; 611 (b), Elizabeth Hamlin / Stock Boston; 611 (t), United States Postal Service / Harcourt Inc.; 612 (t), Paul Conklin; 612 (b), Collection of Janice L. and David J. Frent/ PRC Archive; 613 (t), Michelle Bridwell / Frontera Fotos; 613 (b), Lyndon Baines Johnson Library; 614 (t), Children's Television Workshop; 614 (b), Alfred Eisenstadt/ LIFE Magazine Time, Inc.; 615, SILENT SPRING courtesy Houghton Mifflin Company; 616, Paul Conklin; 617, Lyndon B. Johnson Presidential Library, reprinted through the courtesy of Edward Germano and the *Brockton Enterprise*; 619 (t), Les Immel / *Peoria Journal Star*; 619 (b), Collection of Janice L. and David J. Frent/ PRC Archive.
CHAPTER 21: Page 620 (tl), UPI/Bettmann-Corbis; 620 (tr), Corbis/Bettmann; 620 (b), © 1964 Time Inc. Reprinted by Permission; 621 (tl), courtesy CARE, from PRC; 621 (tr), Corbis-Bettmann; 621 (bl), AP/Wide World Photos; 621 (br), Courtesy Famous Amos Cookies, Keebler Company; 622 (t), Smithsonian Institution / photo courtesy of Salamander Books. Ltd.; 622 (b), AP / Wide World Photos, Inc.; 623 (t), UPI/Corbis-Bettmann; 623 (b), UPI/Bettmann-Corbis; 624, AP / Wide World Photos, Inc.; 625, Charles Moore/ Black Star ; 626 (tl), LOOK/ Trestick in the John F. Kennedy Library; 626 (tr), PRC Archive; 626 (b), Francis Miller / LIFE Magazine ©Time, Inc.; 627, Cecil Stoughton / Lyndon Baines Johnson Presidential Library ; 628 (t), PRC Archive; 628 (b), Charles Moore / Black Star; 629 (t), © Danny Lyon / Magnum Photos ; 629 (b), © 1978 Matt Herron / Take Stock; 630, Matt Herron / TAKE STOCK; 631 (t), Corbis-Bettmann ; 631 (b), LIFE Magazine March 19, 1965 © Time, Inc.; 633 (t), Collection of Janice L. and David J. Frent/PRC Archive; 633 (bl), Corbis/Bettmann-UPI; 633 (br), Collection of Janice L. and David J. Frent/ PRC Archive; 634, UPI/Bettmann-Corbis; 635 (t), AP / Wide World Photos, Inc. ; 635 (b), Collection of Janice L. and David J. Frent/ PRC Archive; 636 (t), UPI/Corbis-Bettmann; 636 (bl), Dominique Berretty / Black Star; 636 (br), HRW Photo by Sam Dudgeon; 638, AP / Wide World Photos, Inc.; 639 (t), UPI/ Corbis-Bettmann; 639 (b), Collection of Janice L. and David J. Frent/ PRC Archive; 640 (t), UPI/Corbis-Bettmann; 640 (b), ©1971 Time, Inc. Reprinted by Permission.; 641, Stock, Boston ; 643, Robin Nelson / Black Star; 645 (t), AP/Wide World Photos, Inc.; 645 (b), Collection of Janice L. and David J. Frent / PRC Archive.
CHAPTER 22: Page 646 (tl), SOVFOTO/EASTFOTO; 646 (tr), © 1973 Bob Fitch / Take Stock; 646 (bl), Corbis-Bettmann; 646 (br), © 1988 Cindy Lewis. All Rights Reserved; 647 (b), Corbis-Bettmann/UPI; 647 (tr), Courtesy of Lang Communications/ PRC Archive; 647 (bl), © 1969 Time, Inc. Reprinted by permission; 647 (tl), Motion Picture Corporation; 648 (t), PRC Archive; 648 (bl), UPI / Corbis- Bettmann; 648 (br), Collection of Bettye Lane/ PRC Archive; 649 (t), UPI/Corbis-Bettmann; 649 (b), Ewing Galloway; 650 (t), US Equal Employment Opportunity Commission; 650 (bl), Al Freni / LIFE Magazine © Time, Inc. ; 650 (br), PRC Archive; 651 (t), Tim Boxer / Archive Photos; 651 (b), Sylvia Johnson/Woodfin Camp & Associates, Inc.; 652, Bob Rosato / Sports Illustrated © Time Inc. ; 653, Corbis-Bettmann; 654 (t), © 1978 George Ballis/TAKE STOCK; 654 (b), Archive Photos; 655, Jack Weinhold, courtesy PRC; 656 (t), Collection of Janice L. and David J. Frent / PRC Archive; 656 (c), Archive Photos; 656 (b), © 1976 George Ballis / Take Stock; 657, Woodfin Camp & Associates, Inc.; 658, Maria Varela / Take Stock; 659, AP /Wide World Photos, Inc.; 660, Carlos Chavez/AP/Wide World Photos; 661 (t), Ralph Crane / LIFE Magazine © Time, Inc.; 661 (b), Collection of David J. and Janice L. Frent/ PRC Archive; 662, Paul Fusco / Magnum Photos, Inc.; 663, Corbis-Bettmann/UPI; 665, PRC Archive; 666 (t), The American Cancer Society; courtesy PRC; 666 (b), Fred Kaplan/Black Star/PNI; 667 (t), Henry Diltz / Corbis; 667 (b), HRW Photo by Chris Casselli; 668 (t), UPI/Corbis-Bettmann; 668 (b), Corbis-Bettmann; 669, © 1999 The Andy Warhol Foundation for the Visual Arts / ARS, New York, Corbis-Bettmann; 670 (t), Archive Photos; 670 (c), Archive Photos; 670 (b), Archive Photos; 671, Library of Congress; 673, Gene Anthony / Black Star.
CHAPTER 23: Page 676 (tl), © Disney Enterprises, Inc.; 676 (tr), Courtesy Texas Instruments, Inc.; 676 (bl), National Archives / PRC Archive; 676 (br), AP / Wide World Photos, Inc.; 677 (tl), AP / Wide World Photos; 677 (tc), Bruce McBroom/Motion Picture & Television Photo Archive; 677 (tr), © Life Magazine 1970 © Time, Inc. / PRC Archive; 677 (bl), AP / Wide World Photos; 677 (br), AP / Wide World Photos, Inc.; 678 (t), Maurice Durand Collection of Vietnamese Art, Yale University; 678 (b), Erica Lansner / Black Star; 678, Archive Photos; 680, Archive Photos; 681 (t), © Roger Viollet / The Liaison Agency; 681 (b), Lee Lockwood, courtesy PRC Archive; 682, AP / Wide World Photos, Inc.; 683, Larry Burrows / LIFE Magazine © Time, Inc.; 684, ; 685 (t), PRC Archive; 685 (b), National Archives ; 686, Collection of Janice L and David J. Frent/PRC Archive; 687, Robert Ellison / Black Star; 688 (l), Courtesy William Ehrhart; 688 (r), Ho Thanh Duc / Vietnam Art Gallery / Kicon; 689, CBS News; 691, Shelly Rusten / Black Star; 692 (t), Larry Burrows / LIFE Magazine ©Time Inc. ; 692 (b), John Olson, U.S. Army / PRC Archive; 693 (tl), Corbis-Bettmann; 693 (b), Steve Schapiro / Black Star; 693 (tl), HRW Photo by Sam Dudgeon; 694, CORBIS/Henry Diltz; 695 (b), © Larry Burrows Collection; 695 (t), AP / Wide World Photos; 696 (b), John Filo; 696 (t), National Archives (NARA); 697, © 1972 by Herblock in The Washington Post; 698 (t), Dennis Brack / Black Star; 698 (b), Black Star; 699, Roger Lubin / Jeroboam; 700, Courtesy Le Ly Hayslip / PRC Archive; 701 (t), Charles Bonnay / Black Star; 701 (b), Eddie Adams / Time Magazine © 1972 Time, Inc.; 702, AP / Wide World Photos, Inc.; 703 (l), PRC Archive; 703 (r), Christopher Morris / Black Star; 705, Collection of Janice L. and David J. Frent/PRC Archive; 706 (t), AP / Wide World Photos, Inc.; 706 (b), © Hap Stewart / Jeroboam; 707 (l), PRC Archive; 707 (r), Hulton Getty / Liaison Agency.
UNIT 7: Page 708-709, Ralph Krubner / H. Armstrong Roberts; 709, NASA.
CHAPTER 24: Page 710 (bl), © CBS, Inc. 1991/The Kobal Collection; 710 (t), NASA; 710 (br), AP / Wide World Photos, Inc.; 711 (bl), R. Krubner / H. Armstrong Roberts; 711 (tl), Hershenson-Allen Archives / PRC Archive; 711 (tr), Martin A. Levick; 711 (br), PGD/Polygram Records. Photo by PRC Archive; 712, Erich Hartmann/ Magnum Photos; 713 (t), Collection of David J. and Janice L. Frent / PRC Archive; 713 (b), Archive Photos; 714, Archive Photos; 715 (t), Corbis; 715 (b), Bob Daemmrich Photo, Inc.; 716 (t), UPI / Bettmann; 716 (b), Jason Laure / Woodfin Camp & Assoc., Inc.; 717, © R.R. Lurie; 718, UPI/Corbis-Bettmann; 719 (t), Corbis/Bettmann-UPI; 719 (b), UPI /Corbis- Bettmann Newsphotos; 721, Corbis- Bettmann; 722 (bl), Corbis-Bettmann; 722 (br), Photri; 722 (t), Bob Daemmrich Photo, Inc.; 723, Joseph A. Smith as printed in Newsweek, September 23, 1974. Collection of the Artist; 724 (tl), Corbis-Bettmann; 724 (tr), Rose Skytta / Jeroboam; 724 (b), UPI/Corbis- Bettmann ; 725, courtesy PRC Archive; 726 (t), Collection of Janice L. and David J. Frent/ PRC Archive; 726 (b), Wally McNamee / Woodfin Camp & Associates, Inc.; 727, Bob Daemmrich Photo, Inc.; 729 (b), UPI/Corbis-Bettmann; 729 (t), Collection of Janice L. and David J. Frent/ PRC Archive; 731, D.B. Owen / Black Star; 732, Gerald R. Ford Presidential Library; 733 (t), Bohdan Hrynewych / Stock, Boston; 733 (b), Mike Yamashita / Woodfin Camp & Associates, Inc.; 734 (t), *I'm O.K.—You're O.K.* by Thomas Harris. Courtesy Harper and Row Publishers, ©1967; 734 (bl), Kent Reno/Jeroboam; 734 (br), *The Complete Book of Running* by Jim Fixx, © 1977 by Random House, New York; 735 (l), © 1982 Universal City Studios, Inc. All rights reserved / The Kobal Collection; 735 (r), Collection of Hershenson-Allen Archives / PRC Archive; 736, CORBIS/James L. Amos; 737, NASA; 739 (l), Corbis- Bettmann; 739 (r), © Newsweek July 30, 1973.
CHAPTER 25: Page 740 (tl), Lester Sloan/ Woodfin Camp & Associates, Inc.; 740 (tc), PRC Archive; 740 (tr), HRW Photo by Sam Dudgeon; 740 (br), NASA; 741 (tl), *The Joy Luck Club* by Amy Tan, © 1989, published by G.P. Putnam's Sons; 741 (br), Courtesy of The Patton Museum of Cavalry & Armor, Fort Knox, KY.; 741 (tr), © Mall of America; 741 (bl), George Bush Presidential Library; 742 (t), Image Copyright © 1998 PhotoDisc, Inc.; 742 (b), UPI / Corbis-Bettman; 744, Wally McNamee / Woodfin Camp & Assoc., Inc.; 745, Ben Sargent; 746 (t), Mike Cullen / The Picture Cube; 746 (b), Richard B. Levine; 747, AP / Wide World Photos, Inc.; 748 (t), Collection of Janice L. and David J. Frent / PRC Archive; 748 (b), Lochon / Liaison Agency; 749 (c), Collection of Janice L. and David J. Frent/PRC Archive; 749 (t), UPI / Corbis-Bettmann; 749 (b), Collection, the Supreme Court of the United States, courtesy the Supreme Court Historical Society; 750 (t), © 1981 by Herblock in The Washington Post.; 751 (b), Ed Carlin / The Picture Cube; 751 (t), Alex Quesada / Woodfin Camp & Associates, Inc.; 752, Corbis-Bettmann; 754, Reuters / Corbis-Bettmann; 755, *The Yuppie Handbook* © Marissa Piesman, Marilee Hartley and Ultra Communications, Inc. A Long Shadow book, published by Pocket Books, a division of Simon & Schuster, Inc., New York. HRW Photo by Sam Dudgeon; 756 (t), Division of Political History, Smithsonian Institution, Washington, D.C.; 756 (b), NASA; 757 (t), HRW Photo by Sam Dudgeon; 757 (br), Bob Daemmrich Photo; 757 (bl), HRW photo by Sam Dudgeon; 758, Woodfin Camp & Associates, Inc.; 759, © 1991 Time Inc. ; 760, AP / Wide World Photos, Inc.; 761, Bill Gentile/SIPA Press Photos/Woodfin Camp & Associates, Inc.; 762, Richard B. Levine; 763, Michael J. Okonlewski / Liaison Agency; 765, *Neuromancer* by William Gibson © 1984, Ace Science Books, Berkeley Group. Courtesy PRC.
CHAPTER 26: Page 768 ; (t), Tannenbaum/Corbis Sygma; 768 (bl), AP/ Wide World Photos, Inc. ; 768 (bc), Ron Edmonds/AP /Wide World Photos; 768 (br), John Harrington/Black Star769 (bl), Tannenbaum /Corbis Sygma; 769 (tl), Bob Daemmrich Photo, Inc.; 769 (tc), courtesy RENT; 769 (tr), David Hume Kennerly / Corbis Sygma; 769 (br), Matthew Polak / Corbis Sygma; 770 (t), Collection of Janice L. and David J. Frent/PRC Archive; 770 (b), Eric Lars Bakke / Black Star; 771 (t), Collection of Janice L. and David J. Frent / PRC Archive; 771 (b), Mike Theiler / Corbis-Bettmann; 772, Bob Daemmrich Photo, Inc.; 774 (t), The White House; 774 (b), Gail Oskin, AP / Wide World Photos; 775, Corinne Dufka, Corbis-Bettmann; 776 (t), Corbis / Bettmann; 776 (b), Collection of Janice L. and David J. Frent / PRC Archive; 777 (t), Cynthia Johnson/Liaision Agency; 777 (b), © Money Magazine, May 1999; 778 (b), Ente Beaumont/Corbis Sygma; 778 (t), Image Copyright © 1998 PhotoDisc, Inc.; 779 (l), © 1998 David Huang; 779 (r), *Typical American* by Gish Jen © 1991 Houghton Mifflin, Boston; 780 (t), Haviv / SABA Press Photos; 780 (b), Bill Greene / Boston Globe; courtesy PRC; 781, Timothy Greenfield-Sanders / Outline; courtesy PRC; 782 (t), Bob Daemmrich Photo, Inc.; 782 (bl), NASA; 782 (br), William Coupon's Gallery of Politicians, Liaison Agency; 784 (t), Lara Jo Regan / Liaison Agency; 784 (b), AP / Wide World Photos, Inc.; 785, Michael Newman/PhotoEdit; 786, Jonathan Nourok / PhotoEdit; 787 (t), Robert Baker/ Habitat for Humanity; 787 (bl), © European Communities; 787 (br), © European Communities; 788 (t), Renato Rotolo/Liaison Agency; 788 (b), Robert Trippett/ SIPA Press Photos; 789, Uniphoto; 791, Paula Bronstein / Liaison Agency; 793 (t), Corbis-Bettmann; 793 (b), Uniphoto; 794 (t), Gjon Mili / LIFE Magazine, © Time, Inc.; 794 (b), © Bruce Kliewe / Jeroboam; 795 (t), Guans/SIPA Press/Woodfin Camp & Associates, Inc.; 795 (b), Lisa Quinones / Black Star.
UNIT 8: Page 796-797, NASA/Photri-Microstock; 797, HRW Photo by Michael Lyon.
CHAPTER 27: Page 798 (tl), Denis Cochrane Collection/E.T. Archive; 798 (b), Giraudon / Art Resource, NY. By permission of Artists Rights Society (ARS), NY; 799 (tr), Sam Dudgeon/HRW Photo; 799 (tc), Courtesy Sony/Epic Records; 799 (tl), Andrew Holbrooke / The Stock Market; 799 (b), NASA; 800, American Bible Society; 801 (t), Valjean Hessing, *Choctaw Removal*, 1966. Philbrook Museum of Art, Tulsa, Oklahoma; 801 (b), AKG London; 802 (t), Corbis-Bettmann; 802 (bl), Mary Evans Picture Library; 802 (br), Ginsan/SIPA Press; 803 (t), Guildhall Library, Corporation of London, UK / Bridgeman Art Library, London/New York; 803 (b), Tom Pantages; 804, The Granger Collection; 805 (t), The Granger Collection, New York; 805 (b), Nawrocki Stock Photo; 806 (t), Mary Evans Picture Library; 806 (b), ©Hulton Getty/Liaison Agency; 808, SuperStock; 809 (l), FPG; 809 (r), The Granger Collection, New York; 810 (b), Nawrocki Stock Photo; 811, Stock Montage, Inc.; 812 (t), Amrit P. Singh; 812 (b), Corbis Images; 813 (t), © 1998 Stockbyte; 813 (b), ©Hulton Getty/Liaison Agency; 814 (t), Howard Sochurek/LIFE Magazine ©Time Inc. ; 814 (b), John Moss / Black Star; 815, E.T. Archive; 816, Robert Harding Picture Library; 817, Howard Sochurek/LIFE Magazine ©Time Inc.; 818, Jon Jones/Sygma; 819 (t), SIPA Press; 819 (b), AP / Wide World Photos, Inc.; 820, Milton & Joan Mann / Cameramann International; 822, CORBIS/Dave Bartruff; 823, Ahmet Sel / SIPA Press Photos.
CHAPTER 28: Page 826 (tl), The Granger Collection, New York; 826 (tr), Herbert Hoover Presidential Library / Corbis; 826 (b), UPI/Corbis-Bettmann Newsphotos; 827 (tl), AKG Photo, London; 827 (tr), Stuart Isett/Sygma; 827 (b), George Hall/Check Six; 828 (t), Art Resource, NY; 828 (b), Trade Union Congress, London, UK / Bridgeman Art Library, London/New York; 830 (t), The Granger Collection, New York; 830 (b), Culver Pictures, Inc.; 831, Corbis-Bettmann; 832 (t), Hulton-Deutsch Collection/CORBIS; 832 (b), HRW Photo by Sam Dudgeon; 833 (t), AKG Photo, London; 833 (b), The Granger Collection, New York; 835, AKG Photo, London; 836 (t), Brown Brothers; 836 (b), AP / Wide World Photos, Inc.; 837, The Granger Collection, New York; 839 (t), AKG London; 839 (b), Brown Brothers; 840, Sean Sprague/Panos Pictures; 841 (t), Ewing Galloway; 841 (b), Musee National d'Art Moderne, Paris, France/ Giraudon/Art Resource, NY / © 1999 Pollock-Krasner Foundation / Artists Rights Society (ARS) New York; 842 (b), Hulton Getty Picture Library/Liaison Agency; 842 (t), George C. Marshall Foundation in Lexington, VA; 843, Frank Wing / Stock, Boston; 844, Tony Korody / Corbis - Sygma; 845, David Stoecklin / The Stock Market; 846, Erich Hartmann / Magnum Photos; 847, Reuters / Corbis-Bettmann; 848, European Monetary Institution, 1997/HRW Photo Library; 848, European Monetary Institution, 1997/HRW Photo Library; 849, AP/Wide World Photos, Inc.
CHAPTER 29: Page 854 (tl), Paul J. Sutton/Duomo; 854 (b), Alex Garcia/Latin Focus; 854 (tr), Bridgeman Art Library, London/New York; ARS; 855 (tr), Superstock; 855 (br), Superstock; 855 (bl), The Kobal Collection; 855 (tl), Photri; 856 (bl), Karen Yamauchi, Chermayeff & Geismar Inc./MetaForm Inc. ; 856 (t), Photography by Karen Yamauchi for Chermayeff & Geismar Inc./Metaform Inc.; 856 (br), Karen Yamauchi, Chermayeff & Geismar Inc./MetaForm Inc. ; 857 (t), Photodisc ©1999; 857 (b), Superstock; 859 (t), The Granger Collection, New York; 859 (b), Brown Brothers; 861, Superstock; 862, Eric Sander/Liaison Agency; 863, Olivier Rebbot / Woodfin Camp & Associates, Inc.; 864 (t), Alon Reinenger / Contact Press Images; 864 (b), Dennis Cox/ChinaStock; 865, Reuters/Arben Celi/Archive Photos; 866, Liz Gilbert / Corbis- Sygma; 867 (t), Photri; 867 (b), Sam Dudgeon/HRW Photo; 868 (b), Superstock; 868 (t), Sam Dudgeon/HRW Photo; 869, NCSA / UIUC (University of Illinois Carbondale); 870, Dilip Mehta / Contact Press Images; 871, George Hall/Check Six; 872 (b), Image Copyright ©1999 PhotoDisc, Inc. ; 872 (t), Allsport; 873 (t), Chris Trotman/Duomo; 873 (b), Elvis Presley Enterprises, Inc. ; 874, Reuters/Corbis-Bettmann; 875, Corbis; 877, Photography by Karen Yamauchi for Chermayeff & Geismar Inc./Metaform Inc.
CHAPTER 30: Page 878 (tr), Sinclair Stammers/Science Photo Library/Photo Researchers, Inc.; 878 (b), John Madere '92/The Stock Market; 878 (bl), The Granger Collection, New York; 879 (tr), Raymond Preston / SIPA Press Photos; 879 (br), Shooting Star International; 879 (bl), Wally McNamee/Sygma; 879 (tl), Sion Touhig/Sygma; 880 (t), Stuart Franklin / Corbis-Sygma; 880 (b), AKG London; 881, E.T. Archive; 882 (tr), Courtesy of the Massachusettes Historical Society; 882 (tl), Photographs and Prints Division, Schomburg Center for Research in Black Culture, Astor, Lenox and Tilden Foundations, The New York Public Library; 882 (b), Hulton Getty Picture Library/Liaison Agency; 884, Hulton Getty Picture Library/Liaison Agency; 885 (t), Hulton Getty Picture Library/Liaison Agency; 885 (b), *Florence Nightingale*, Private Collection / Bridgeman Art Library, London / New York; 886 (b), HRW Photo by Sam Dudgeon; 886 (t), Erich Lessing/Art Resource, NY; 887, A.K.G., Berlin/SuperStock; 888 (r), UPI/Corbis-Bettmann; 888 (l), David Toerge 1998/Black Star; 889 (t), Brown Brothers; 889 (b), Corbis/Bettmann-UPI; 890, Franklin D. Roosevelt Library; 891 (t), UPI/Corbis-Bettmann; 891 (b), UPI/Corbis-Bettmann; 893, Bernard Gotfryd/Woodfin Camp & Associates, Inc.; 894, UPI/Corbis-Bettmann; 895 (b), Selwyn Tait / Liaison Agency; 895 (t), Novosti/Sygma; 896, Robert Azzi / Woodfin Camp & Associates, Inc. ; 897, Amnesty International; 898, Robin Moyer / Liaison Agency; 899, R. Ellis/Sygma; 901, Amnesty International.
CHAPTER 31: Page 902 (tl), Superstock; 902 (tr), Corbis; 902 (b), Private Collection/Superstock; 903 (tl), Toby Adamson/ Environmental Images; 903 (tr), Uniphoto; 903 (bl), HRW Photo by Sam Dudgeon; 903 (br), Henk Merjenburgh/Environmental Images; 904 (t), The Granger Collection, New York; 904 (b), I.N. Phelps Stokes Collection, Miriam and Ira D. Wallach Division of Art, Prints and Photographs; 905, American Bible Society; 906, UPI / Bettmann; 907, HRW Photo by Sam Dudgeon; 908 (t), Gary Braasch/Tony Stone Images; 908 (b), The Granger Collection, New York; 910 (t), Corbis; 910 (b), Aldo Leopold Foundation, Inc.; 911, Art Resource, NY; 912, AP/Wide World Photos; 913 (t), Jordi Cami/Environmental Images; 913 (b), HRW Photo by Sam Dudgeon; 914, The Bettmann Archive; 915, Uniphoto; 916, Donald Emmerich/National Archives (NARA); 917, *The Limits to Growth* by Donella Meadows, Dennis Meadows, Jorgen Randers and William Behrens III. A Potomac Associates Book, published by Universe Books, New York, 1972. HRW Photo by Victoria Smith; 918 (t), NASA; 918 (b), C.T.K. / Gamma Liaison; 920 (b), Pilly Cowell/Environmental Images; 920 (t), Simon D. Pollard/Photo Researchers; 921, Sava Radovanovic/AP/Wide World Photos; 923, Ken Lax/Photo Researchers,Inc.; 926 (t), Photri; 926 (b), HRW Photo by Sam Dudgeon ; 927 (t), Collection of Col. Stuart S. Corning, Jr. Courtesy PRC Archive; 927 (b), Baldev/Corbis - Sygma.
REFERENCE SECTION: Page 928, CORBIS/Bill Ross; 929, HRW Photo by Sam Dudgeon; 937-941, White House Collection, copyright White House Historical Association; 941 (b), The White House.

Illustrations

Abbreviations used: (t) top, (c) center, (b) bottom, (l) left, (r) right
All maps created by MapQuest.com, Inc. All other illustrations, unless noted below, created by Holt, Rinehart and Winston.
TABLE OF CONTENTS: Page xiv(br), Craig Attebery/Jeff Lavaty Artist Agent
UNIT 1: Page 41 (b), Saul Rosenbaum/Deborah Wolfe Ltd.; 65 (l), DECODE, Inc.; 88 (bl), Craig Attebery/Jeff Lavaty Artist Agent; 99 (bl), 121 (tr), DECODE, Inc.
UNIT 2: Page 169 (tl), DECODE, Inc.; 170 (b), Uhl Studio Inc.; 194 (t), 214 (cl, cr), 215 (bl), 234 (bl), DECODE, Inc.
UNIT 3: Page 314 (b), Uhl Studio Inc.; 318 (bl), 324 (bl), DECODE, Inc.
UNIT 4: Page 371 (br), DECODE, Inc.; 388 (tl), Craig Attebery/Jeff Lavaty Artist Agent; 466 (bl), DECODE, Inc.
UNIT 5: 482 (bl), DECODE, Inc.; 502 (tl), Leslie Kell; 549 (tr), Saul Rosenbaum/Deborah Wolfe Ltd.; 560 (bl), 565 (tl), DECODE, Inc.; 575 (t), Christy Krames
UNIT 6: 599, DECODE, Inc.; 600, Craig Attebery/Jeff Lavaty Artist Agent; 675 (bl), DECODE, Inc.
UNIT 7: 715 (tl), DECODE, Inc.; 727 (br), Saul Rosenbaum/Deborah Wolfe Ltd.; 728, Uhl Studio Inc.; 750 (bl), Saul Rosenbaum/Deborah Wolfe Ltd.; 767 (bl, bc), DECODE, Inc.
UNIT 8: 802 (bl), 852 (bl), 853 (tr), 883 (br), DECODE, Inc.